Linux: The Complete Reference
Book 2: Advanced Linux

1999   Edited By: John Purcell jvpurcel@oakland.edu

7th edition.

Contents

Part I

"The Linux Network Administrator's Guide 1.0" by Olaf Kirch

Contents

Net-Admin Guide

Preface

With the Internet much of a buzzword recently, and otherwise serious people joyriding along the "Informational Super-highway," computer networking seems to be moving toward the status of TV sets and microwave ovens. The Internet is recently getting an unusually high media coverage, and social science majors are descending on Usenet newsgroups to conduct researches on the "Internet Culture." Carrier companies are working to introduce new transmission techniques like ATM that offer many times the bandwidth the average network link of today has.

Of course, networking has been around for a long time. Connecting computers to form local area networks has been common practice even at small installations, and so have been long-haul links using public telephone lines. A rapidly growing conglomerate of world-wide networks has, however, made joining the global village a viable option even for small non-profit organizations of private computer users. Setting up an Internet host with mail and news capabilities offering dial-up access has become affordable, and the advent of ISDN will doubtlessly accelerate this trend.

Talking of computer networks quite frequently means talking about UNIX. Of course, UNIX is neither the only operating system with network capabilities, nor will it remain a front-runner forever, but it has been in the networking business for a long time, and will surely continue to do so for some time to come.

What makes it particularly interesting to private users is that there has been much activity to bring free UNIXoid operating systems to the PC, being 386BSD, FreeBSD — and Linux. However, Linux is *not* UNIX. That is a registered trademark of whoever currently holds the rights to it (Univel, while I'm typing this), while Linux is an operating system that strives to offer all functionality the POSIX standards require for UNIX-like operating systems, but is a complete reimplementation.

The Linux kernel was written largely by Linus Torvalds, who started it as a project to get to know the Intel i386, and to "make MINIX better." MINIX was then another popular PC operating system offering vital ingredients of UNIX functionality, and was written by Prof. Andrew S. Tanenbaum.

Linux is covered by the GNU General Public License (GPL), which allows free distribution of the code (please read the GPL in appendix C for a definition of what "free software" means). Outgrowing its child's diseases, and drawing from a large and ever-growing base of free application programs, it is quickly becoming the oprating system of choice for many PC owners. The kernel and C library have become that good that most standard software may be compiled with no more effort than is required on any other mainstream UNIXish system, and a broad assortment of packaged Linux distributions allows you to almost drop it onto your hard disk and start playing.

Documentation on Linux

One of the complaints that are frequently levelled at Linux (and free software in general) is the sorry state or complete lack of documentation. In the early days it was not unusual for a package to come with a handful of *README*s and installation notes. They gave the moderately experienced UNIX wizard enough information to successfully install and run it, but left the average newbie out in the cold. Back in late 1992, Lars Wirzenius and Michael K. Johnson suggested to form the Linux Documentation Project, or LDP, which aims at providing a coherent set of manuals. Stopping short of answering questions like "How?", or "Why?", or "What's the meaning of life, universe, and all the rest?", these manuals attempt to cover most aspects of running and using a Linux system users without requiring a prior degree in UNIX.

Among the achievements of the LDP are the *Installation and Getting Started Guide*, written by Matt Welsh, the *Kernel Hacker's Guide* by Michael K. Johnson, and the manpage project coordinated by Rik Faith, which so far supplied a set of roughly 450 manual pages for most system and C library calls. The *System Administrators' Guide*, written by Lars Wirzenius, is still at the Alpha stage. A User's Guide is being prepared.

This book, the *Linux Network Administrators' Guide*, is part of the LDP series, too. As such, it may be copied and distributed freely under the LDP copying license which is reproduced on the second page.

However, the LDP books are not the only source of information on Linux. At the moment, there are more than a dozen HOWTOs that are posted to **comp.os.linux.announce** regularly and archived at various FTP sites. HOWTOs are short documents of a few pages that give you a brief introduction into topics such as Ethernet support under Linux, or the configuration of Usenet news software, and answer frequently asked questions. They usually provide the most accurate and up-to-date information avaliable on the topic. A list of available HOWTOs is produced in the "Annotated Bibliography" toward the end of this book.

About This Book

When I joined the Linux Documentation Project in 1992, I wrote two small chapters on UUCP and *smail*, which I meant to contribute to the System Administrator's Guide. Development of TCP/IP networking was just beginning, and when those "small chapters" started to grow, I wondered aloud if it wouldn't be nice to have a Networking Guide. "Great", everyone said, "I'd say, go for it!" So I went for it, and wrote a first version of the Networking Guide, which I released in September 1993.

The new Networking Guide you are reading right now is a complete rewrite that features several new applications that have become available to Linux users since the first release.

The book is organized roughly in the sequence of steps you have to take to configure your system for networking. It starts by discussing basic concepts of networks, and TCP/IP-based networks in particular. We then slowly work our way up from configuring TCP/IP at the device level to the setup of common applications such as *rlogin* and friends, the Network File System, and the Network Information System. This is followed by a chapter on how to set up your machine as a UUCP node. The remainder of the book is dedicated to two major applications that run on top of both TCP/IP and UUCP: electronic mail and news.

The email part features an introduction of the more intimate parts of mail transport and routing, and the myriads of addressing schemes you may be confronted with. It describes the configuration and management of *smail*, a mail transport agent commonly used on smaller mail hubs, and *sendmail*, which is for people who have to do more complicated routing, or have to handle a large volume of mail. The *sendmail* chapter has been written and contributed by Vince Skahan.

The news part attempts to give you an overview of how Usenet news works, covers C news, the most widely used news transport software at the moment, and the use of NNTP to provide newsreading access to a local network. The book closes with a short chapter on the care and feeding of the most popular newsreaders on Linux.

The Official Printed Version

In autumn 1993, Andy Oram, who has been around the LDP mailing list from almost the very beginning, asked me about publishing my book at O'Reilly and Associates. I was excited about this; I had never imagined my book being that successful. We finally agreed that O'Reilly would produce an enhanced Official Printed Version of the Networking Guide with me, while I retained the original copyright so that the source of the book could be freely distributed.[1] This means that you can choose freely: you can get the LATEXsource distributed on the network (or the preformatted DVI or PostScript versions, for that matter), and print it out. Or you can purchase the official printed version from O'Reilly, which will be available some time later this year.

---

[1] The copyright notice is reproduced on the page immediately following the title page.

Then, why would you want to pay money for something you can get for free? Is Tim O'Reilly out of his mind for publishing something everyone can print and even sell herself?[2] Or is there any difference between these versions?

The answers are "it depends," "no, definitely not," and "yes and no." O'Reilly and Associates do take a risk in publishing the Networking Guide, but I hope it will finally pay off for them. If it does, I believe this project can serve as an example how the free software world and companies can cooperate to produce something both benefit from. In my view, the great service O'Reilly is doing to the Linux community (apart from the book being readily available in your local bookstore) is that it may help Linux being recognized as something to be taken seriously: a viable and useful alternative to commercial PC UNIX operating systems.

So what about the differences between the printed version and the online one? Andy Oram has made great efforts at transforming my early ramblings into something actually worth printing. (He has also been reviewing the other books put out by the Linux Documentation Project, trying to contribute whatever professional skills he can to the Linux community.)

Since Andy started reviewing the Networking Guide and editing the copies I sent him, the book has improved vastly over what it was half a year ago. It would be nowhere close to where it is now without his contributions. All his edits have been fed back into online version, as will any changes that will be made to the Networking Guide during the copy-editing phase at O'Reilly. So there will be no difference in content. Still, the O'Reilly version *will* be different: On one hand, people at O'Reilly are putting a lot of work into the look and feel, producing a much more pleasant layout than you could ever get out of standard LaTeX. On the other hand, it will feature a couple of enhancements like an improved index, and better and more figures.

More Information

If you follow the instructions in this book, and something does not work nevertheless, please be patient. Some of your problems may be due to stupid mistakes on my part, but may also be caused by changes in the networking software. Therefore, you should probably ask on **comp.os.linux.help** first. There's a good chance that you are not alone with your problems, so that a fix or at least a proposed workaround is likely to be known. If you have the opportunity, you should also try to get the latest kernel and network release from one of the Linux FTP sites, or a BBS near you. Many problems are caused by software from different stages of development, which fail to work together properly. After all, Linux is "work in progress".

Another good place to inform yourself about current development is the Networking HOWTO. It is maintained by Terry Dawson[3]. It is posted to **comp.os.linux.announce** once a month, and contains the most up-to-date information. The current version can also be obtained (among others) from **tsx-11.mit.edu**, in */pub/linux/doc*. For problems you can't solve in any other way, you may also contact the author of this book at the address given in the preface. However, please, refrain from asking developers for help. They are already devoting a major part of their spare time to Linux anyway, and occasionally even have a life beyond the net : -)

On the Authors

Olaf has been a UNIX user and part-time administrator for a couple of years while he was studying mathematics. At the moment, he's working as a UNIX programmer and is writing a book. One of his favorite sports is doing things with *sed* that other people would reach for their *perl* interpreter for. He has about as much fun with this as with mountain hiking with a backpack and a tent.

Vince Skahan has been administering large numbers of UNIX systems since 1987 and currently runs sendmail+IDA on approximately 300 UNIX workstations for over 2000 users. He admits to losing considerable sleep from editing quite a few *sendmail.cf* files 'the hard way' before discovering sendmail+IDA in 1990. He also admits to anxiously awaiting the delivery of the first perl-based version of sendmail for even more obscure fun[4]...

Olaf can be reached at the following address:

Olaf Kirch
Kattreinstr. 38

---

[2]Note that while you are allowed to print out the online version, you may *not* run the O'Reilly book through a photocopier, and much less sell any of those (hypothetical) copies.

[3]Terry Dawson can be reached at **terryd@extro.ucc.su.oz.au**.

[4]Don't you think we could do it with *sed*, Vince?

64295 Darmstadt
Germany

okir@monad.swb.de

Vince can be reached at:

Vince Skahan
vince@victrola.wa.com

We are open to your questions, comments, postcards, etc. However, we ask you *not* to telephone us unless it's really important.

Thanks

Olaf says: This book owes very much to the numerous people who took the time to proofread it and helped iron out many mistakes, both technical and grammatical (never knew that there's such a thing as a dangling participle). The most vigorous among them was Andy Oram at O'Reilly and Associates.

I am greatly indebted to Andres Sepúlveda, Wolfgang Michaelis, Michael K. Johnson, and all developers who spared the time to check the information provided in the Networking Guide. I also wish to thank all those who read the first version of the Networking Guide and sent me corrections and suggestions. You can find hopefully complete list of contributors in the file *Thanks* in the online distribution. Finally, this book would not have been possible without the support of Holger Grothe, who provided me with the critical Internet connectivity.

I would also like to thank the following groups and companies who printed the first edition of the Networking Guide and have donated money either to me, or to the Linux Documentation Project as a whole.

- Linux Support Team, Erlangen, Germany

- S.u.S.E. GmbH, Fuerth, Germany

- Linux System Labs, Inc., United States

Vince says: Thanks go to Neil Rickert and Paul Pomes for lots of help over the years regarding the care and feeding of sendmail+IDA and to Rich Braun for doing the initial port of sendmail+IDA to Linux. The biggest thanks by far go to my wife Susan for all the support on this and other projects.

Typographical Conventions

In writing this book, a number of typographical conventions were employed to mark shell commands, variable arguments, etc. They are explained below.

Bold Font	Used to mark hostnames and mail addresses, as well as new concepts and warnings.
Italics Font	Used to mark file names, UNIX commands, and keywords in configuration files. Also used for *emphasis* in text.
`Typewriter Font`	Used to represent screen interaction, such as user interaction when running a program. Also used for code examples, whether it is a configuration file, a shell script, or something else.
`Typewriter Slanted Font`	Used to mark meta-variables in the text, especially in representations of the command line. For example,

```
$ ls -l foo
```

	where `foo` would "stand for" a filename, such as */tmp*.
Key	Represents a key to press. You will often see it in this form:

Press return to continue.

◇	A diamond in the margin, like a black diamond on a ski hill, marks "danger" or "caution." Read paragraphs marked this way carefully.
$ and #	When preceding a shell command to be typed, these denote the shell prompt. The '$' symbol is used when the command may be executed as a normal user; '#' means that the command requires super user privilieges.

The Linux Documentation Project

The Linux Documentation Project, or LDP, is a loose team of writers, proofreaders, and editors who are working together to provide complete documentation for the Linux operating system. The overall coordinator of the project is Matt Welsh, who is heavily aided by Lars Wirzenius and Michael K. Johnson.

This manual is one in a set of several being distributed by the LDP, including a Linux Users' Guide, System Administrators' Guide, Network Administrators' Guide, and Kernel Hackers' Guide.   These manuals are all available in LaTeX source format, `.dvi` format, and postscript output by anonymous FTP from `nic.funet.fi`, in the directory `/pub/OS/Linux/doc/doc-project`, and from `tsx-11.mit.edu`, in the directory `/pub/linux/docs/guides`.

We encourage anyone with a penchant for writing or editing to join us in improving Linux documentation. If you have Internet e-mail access, you can join the DOC channel of the `Linux-Activists` mailing list by sending mail to

```
linux-activists-request@niksula.hut.fi
```

with the line

```
X-Mn-Admin:   join DOC
```

in the header or as the first line of the message body. An empty mail without the additional header line will make the mail-server return a help message. To leave the channel, send a message to the same address, including the line

```
X-Mn-Admin:   leave DOC
```

Filesystem Standards

Throughout the past, one of the problems that afflicted Linux distributions as well as separate packages was that there was no single accepted file system layout. This resulted in incompatibilities between different packages, and confronted users and administrators alike with the task to locate various files and programs.

To improve this situation, in August 1993, several people formed the Linux File System Standard Group, or FSSTND Group for short, coordinated by Daniel Quinlan. After six months of discussion, the group presented a draft that presents a coherent file sytem structure and defines the location of most essential programs and configuration files.

This standard is supposed to be implemented by most major Linux distributions and packages. Throughout this book, we will therefore assume that any files discussed reside in the location specified by the standard; only where there is a long tradition that conflicts with this specification will alternative locations be mentioned.

The Linux File System Standard can be obtained from all major Linux FTP sites and their mirrors; for instance, you can find it on **sunsite.unc.edu** below */pub/linux/docs*. Daniel Quinlan, the coordinator of the FSSTND group can be reached at **quinlan@bucknell.edu**.

Net-Admin Guide

Chapter 1

Introduction to Networking

1.1 History

The idea of networking is probably as old as telecommunications itself. Consider people living in the stone age, where drums may have been used to transmit messages between individuals. Suppose caveman A wants to invite caveman B for a game of hurling rocks at each other, but they live too far apart for B to hear A banging his drum. So what are A's options? He could 1) walk over to B's place, 2) get a bigger drum, or 3) ask C, who lives halfway between them, to forward the message. The last is called networking.

Of course, we have come a long way from the primitive pursuits and devices of our forebears. Nowadays, we have computers talk to each other over vast assemblages of wires, fiber optics, microwaves, and the like, to make an appointment for saturday's soccer match.[1] In the following, we will deal with the means and ways by which this is accomplished, but leave out the wires, as well as the soccer part.

We will describe two types of networks in this guide: those based on UUCP, and those based on TCP/IP. These are protocol suites and software packages that supply means to transport data between two computers. In this chapter, we will look at both types of networks, and discuss their underlying principles.

We define a network as a collection of *hosts* that are able to communicate with each other, often by relying on the services of a number of dedicated hosts that relay data between the participants. Hosts are very often computers, but need not be; one can also think of X-terminals or intelligent printers as hosts. Small agglomerations of hosts are also called *sites*.

Communication is impossible without some sort of language or code. In computer networks, these languages are collectively referred to as *protocols*. However, you shouldn't think of written protocols here, but rather of the highly formalized code of behavior observed when heads of state meet, for instance. In a very similar fashion, the protocols used in computer networks are nothing but very strict rules for the exchange of messages between two or more hosts.

1.2 UUCP Networks

UUCP is an abbreviation for Unix-to-Unix Copy. It started out as a package of programs to transfer files over serial lines, schedule those transfers, and initiate execution of programs on remote sites. It has undergone major changes since its first implementation in the late seventies, but is still rather spartan in the services it offers. Its main application is still in wide-area networks based on dial-up telephone links.

UUCP was first developed by Bell Laboratories in 1977 for communication between their Unix-development sites. In mid-1978, this network already connected over 80 sites. It was running email as an application, as well as remote printing. However, the system's central use was in distributing new software and bugfixes.[2] Today, UUCP is not confined to the UNIX environment anymore. There are both free and commercial ports available for a variety of platforms, including AmigaOS, DOS, Atari's TOS, etc.

---

[1]The original spirit of which (see above) still shows on some occasions in Europe.
[2]Not that the times had changed that much...

One of the main disadvantages of UUCP networks is their low bandwidth. On one hand, telephone equipment places a tight limit on the maximum transfer rate. On the other hand, UUCP links are rarely permanent connections; instead, hosts rather dial up each other at regular intervals. Hence, most of the time it takes a mail message to travel a UUCP network it sits idly on some host's disk, awaiting the next time a connection is established.

Despite these limitations, there are still many UUCP networks operating all over the world, run mainly by hobbyists, which offer private users network access at reasonable prices. The main reason for the popularity of UUCP is that it is dirt cheap compared to having your computer connected to The Big Internet Cable. To make your computer a UUCP node, all you need is a modem, a working UUCP implementation, and another UUCP node that is willing to feed you mail and news.

1.2.1   How to Use UUCP

The idea behind UUCP is rather simple: as its name indicates, it basically copies files from one host to another, but it also allows certain actions to be performed on the remote host.

Suppose your machine is allowed to access a hypothetical host named **swim**, and have it execute the *lpr* print command for you. Then you could type the following on your command line to have this book printed on **swim**:[3]

```
$ uux -r swim!lpr !netguide.dvi
```

This makes *uux*, a command from the UUCP suite, schedule a *job* for **swim**. This job consists of the input file, *net-guide.dvi*, and the request to feed this file to *lpr*. The -r flag tells *uux* not to call the remote system immediately, but to rather store the job away until a connection is established at a later occasion. This is called *spooling*.

Another property of UUCP is that it allows to forward jobs and files through several hosts, provided they cooperate. Assume that **swim** from the above examples has a UUCP link with **groucho**, which maintains a large archive of UNIX applications. To download the file *tripwire-1.0.tar.gz* to your site, you might issue

```
$ uucp -mr swim!groucho!~/security/tripwire-1.0.tar.gz trip.tgz
```

The job created will request **swim** to fetch the file from **groucho**, and send it to your site, where UUCP will store it in *trip.tgz* and notify you via mail of the file's arrival. This will be done in three steps. First, your site sends the job to **swim**. When **swim** establishes contact with **groucho** the next time, it downloads the file. The final step is the actual transfer from **swim** to your host.

The most important services provided by UUCP networks these days are electronic mail and news. We will come back to these later, so we will give only a brief introduction here.

Electronic mail – email for short – allows you to exchange messages with users on remote hosts without actually having to know how to access these hosts. The task of directing a message from your site to the destination site is performed entirely by the mail handling system. In a UUCP environment, mail is usually transported by executing the *rmail* command on a neighboring host, passing it the recipient address and the mail message. *rmail* will then forward the message to another host, and so on, until it reaches the destination host. We will look at this in detail in chapter 13.

News may best be described as sort of a distributed bulletin board system. Most often, this term refers to Usenet News, which is by far the most widely known news exchange network with an estimated number of 120,000 participating sites. The origins of Usenet date back to 1979, when, after the release of UUCP with the new Unix V7, three graduate students had the idea of a general information exchange within the Unix community. They put together some scripts, which became the first netnews system. In 1980, this network connected **duke**, **unc**, and **phs**, at two Universities in North Carolina. Out of this, Usenet eventually grew. Although it originated as a UUCP-based network, it is no longer confined to one single type of network.

---

[3]When using *bash*, the GNU Bourne Again Shell, you might have to escape the exclamation mark, because it uses it as its history character.

The basic unit of information is the article, which may be posted to a hierarchy of newsgroups dedicated to specific topics. Most sites receive only a selection of all newsgroups, which carry an average of 60MB worth of articles a day.

In the UUCP world, news is generally sent across a UUCP link by collecting all articles from the groups requested, and packing them up in a number of *batches*. These are sent to the receiving site, where they are fed to the *rnews* command for unpacking and further processing.

Finally, UUCP is also the medium of choice for many dial-up archive sites which offer public access. You can usually access them by dialing them up with UUCP, logging in as a guest user, and download files from a publicly accessible archive area. These guest accounts often have a login name and password of **uucp/nuucp** or something similar.

1.3 TCP/IP Networks

Although UUCP may be a reasonable choice for low-cost dial-up network links, there are many situations in which its store-and-forward technique proves too inflexible, for example in Local Area Networks (LANs). These are usually made up of a small number of machines located in the same building, or even on the same floor, that are interconnected to provide a homogeneous working environment. Typically, you would want to share files between these hosts, or run distributed applications on different machines.

These tasks require a completely different approach to networking. Instead of forwarding entire files along with a job description, all data is broken up in smaller chunks (packets), which are forwarded immediately to the destination host, where they are reassembled. This type of network is called a *packet-switched* network. Among other things, this allows to run interactive applications over the network. The cost of this is, of course, a greatly increased complexity in software.

The solution that UNIX system — and many non-UNIX sites — have adopted is known as TCP/IP. In this section, we will have a look at its underlying concepts.

1.3.1   Introduction to TCP/IP-Networks

TCP/IP traces its origins to a research project funded by the United States DARPA (Defense Advanced Research Projects Agency) in 1969. This was an experimental network, the ARPANET, which was converted into an operational one in 1975, after it had proven to be a success.

In 1983, the new protocol suite TCP/IP was adopted as a standard, and all hosts on the network were required to use it. When ARPANET finally grew into the Internet (with ARPANET itself passing out of existence in 1990), the use of TCP/IP had spread to networks beyond the Internet itself. Most notable are UNIX local area networks, but in the advent of fast digital telephone equipment, such as ISDN, it also has a promising future as a transport for dial-up networks.

For something concrete to look at as we discuss TCP/IP throughout the following sections, we will consider Groucho Marx University (GMU), situated somewhere in Fredland, as an example. Most departments run their own local area networks, while some share one, and others run several of them. They are all interconnected, and are hooked to the Internet through a single high-speed link.

Suppose your Linux box is connected to a LAN of UNIX hosts at the Mathematics Department, and its name is **erdos**. To access a host at the Physics Department, say **quark**, you enter the following command:

```
$ rlogin quark.physics
Welcome to the Physics Department at GMU
(ttyq2) login:
```

At the prompt, you enter your login name, say **andres**, and your password. You are then given a shell on **quark**, to which you can type as if you were sitting at the system's console. After you exit the shell, you are returned to your own machine's prompt. You have just used one of the instantaneous, interactive applications that TCP/IP provides: remote login.

While being logged into **quark**, you might also want to run an X11-based application, like a function plotting program, or a PostScript previewer. To tell this application that you want to have its windows displayed on your host's screen, you have to set the *DISPLAY* environment variable:

```
$ export DISPLAY=erdos.maths:0.0
```

If you now start your application, it will contact your X server instead of **quark**'s, and display all its windows on your screen. Of course, this requires that you have X11 runnning on **erdos**. The point here is that TCP/IP allows **quark** and **erdos** to send X11 packets back and forth to give you the illusion that you're on a single system. The network is almost transparent here.

Another very important application in TCP/IP networks is NFS, which stands for *Network File System*. It is another form of making the network transparent, because it basically allows you to mount directory hierarchies from other hosts, so that they appear like local file systems. For example, all users' home directories can be on a central server machine, from which all other hosts on the LAN mount the directory. The effect of this is that users can log into any machine, and find themselves in the same home directory. Similarly, it is possible to install applications that require large amounts of disk space (such as TeX) on only one machine, and export these directories to other machines. We will come back to NFS in chapter 11.

Of course, these are only examples of what you can do over TCP/IP networks. The possibilities are almost limitless.

We will now have a closer look at the way TCP/IP works. You will need this to understand how and why you have to configure your machine. We will start by examining the hardware, and slowly work our way up.

1.3.2   Ethernets

The type of hardware most widely used throughout LANs is what is commonly known as *Ethernet*. It consists of a single cable with hosts being attached to it through connectors, taps or transceivers. Simple Ethernets are quite inexpensive to install, which, together with a net transfer rate of 10 Megabits per second accounts for much of its popularity.

Ethernets come in three flavors, called *thick* and *thin*, respectively, and *twisted pair*. Thin and thick Ethernet each use a coaxial cable, differing in width and the way you may attach a host to this cable. Thin Ethernet uses a T-shaped "BNC" connector, which you insert into the cable, and twist onto a plug on the back of your computer. Thick Ethernet requires that you drill a small hole into the cable, and attach a transceiver using a "vampire tap". One or more hosts can then be connected to the transceiver. Thin and thick Ethernet cable may run for a maximum of 200 and 500 meters, respectively, and are therefore also called 10base-2 and 10base-5. Twisted pair uses a cable made of two copper wires which is also found in ordinary telephone installations, but usually requires additional hardware. It is also known as 10base-T.

Although adding a host to a thick Ethernet is a little hairy, it does not bring down the network. To add a host to a thinnet installation, you have to disrupt network service for at least a few minutes because you have to cut the cable to insert the connector.

Most people prefer thin Ethernet, because it is very cheap: PC cards come for as little as US$ 50, and cable is in the range of a few cent per meter. However, for large-scale installations, thick Ethernet is more appropriate. For example, the Ethernet at GMU's Mathematics Department uses thick Ethernet, so traffic will not be disrupted each time a host is added to the network.

One of the drawbacks of Ethernet technology is its limited cable length, which precludes any use of it other than for LANs. However, several Ethernet segments may be linked to each other using repeaters, bridges or routers. Repeaters simply copy the signals between two or more segments, so that all segments together will act as if it was one Ethernet. timing requirements, there may not be more than four repeaters any two hosts on the network. Bridges and Routers are more sophisticated. They analyze incoming data and forward it only when the recipient host is not on the local Ethernet.

Ethernet works like a bus system, where a host may send packets (or *frames*) of up to 1500 bytes to another host on the same Ethernet. A host is addressed by a six-byte address hardcoded into the firmware of its Ethernet board. These addresses are usually written as a sequence of two-digit hex numbers separated by colons, as in **aa:bb:cc:dd:ee:ff**.

A frame sent by one station is seen by all attached stations, but only the destination host actually picks it up and processes it. If two stations try to send at the same time, a *collision* occurs, which is resolved by the two stations aborting the send, and reattempting it a few moments later.

1.3.3 Other Types of Hardware

In larger installations, such as Groucho Marx University, Ethernet is usually not the only type of equipment used. At Groucho Marx University, each department's LAN is linked to the campus backbone, which is a fiber optics cable running FDDI (*Fiber Distributed Data Interface*). FDDI uses an entirely different approach to transmitting data, which basically involves sending around a number of *tokens*, with a station only being allowed to send a frame if it captures a token. The main advantage of FDDI is a speed of up to 100 Mbps, and a maximum cable length of up to 200 km.

For long-distance network links, a different type of equipment is frequently used, which is based on a standard named X.25. Many so-called Public Data Networks, like Tymnet in the U.S., or Datex-P in Germany, offer this service. X.25 requires special hardware, namely a Packet Assembler/Disassembler or *PAD*. X.25 defines a set of networking protocols of its own right, but is nevertheless frequently used to connect networks running TCP/IP and other protocols. Since IP packets cannot simply be mapped onto X.25 (and vice versa), they are simply encapsulated in X.25 packets and sent over the network.

Frequently, radio amateurs use their equipment to network their computers; this is called *packet radio* or *ham radio*. The protocol used by ham radios is called AX.25, which was derived from X.25.

Other techniques involve using slow but cheap serial lines for dial-up access. These require yet another protocol for transmission of packets, such as SLIP or PPP, which will be described below.

1.3.4 The Internet Protocol

Of course, you wouldn't want your networking to be limited to one Ethernet. Ideally, you would want to be able to use a network regardless of what hardware it runs on and how many subunits it is made up of. For example, in larger installations such as Groucho Marx University, you usually have a number of separate Ethernets that have to be connected in some way. At GMU, the maths department runs two Ethernets: one network of fast machines for professors and graduates, and another one with slow machines for students. Both are linked to the FDDI campus backbone.

This connection is handled by a dedicated host, a so-called *gateway*, which handles incoming and outgoing packets by copying them between the two Ethernets and the fiber optics cable. For example, if you are at the Maths Department, and want to access **quark** on the Physics Deparment's LAN from your Linux box, the networking software cannot send packets to **quark** directly, because it is not on the same Ethernet. Therefore, it has to rely on the gateway to act as a forwarder. The gateway (name it **sophus**) then forwards these packets to its peer gateway **niels** at the Physics Department, using the backbone, with **niels** delivering it to the destination machine. Data flow between **erdos** and **quark** is shown in figure 1.1 (With apologies to Guy L. Steele).

This scheme of directing data to a remote host is called *routing*, and packets are often referred to as *datagrams* in this context. To facilitate things, datagram exchange is governed by a single protocol that is independent of the hardware used: IP, or *Internet Protocol*. In chapter 2, we will cover IP and the issues of routing in greater detail.

The main benefit of IP is that it turns physically dissimilar networks into one apparently homogeneous network. This is called internetworking, and the resulting "meta-network" is called an *internet*. Note the subtle difference between *an* internet and *the* Internet here. The latter is the official name of one particular global internet.

Of course, IP also requires a hardware-independent addressing scheme. This is achieved by assigning each host a unique 32-bit number, called the *IP address*. An IP address is usually written as four decimal numbers, one for each 8-bit portion, separated by dots. For example, **quark** might have an IP address of **0x954C0C04**, which would be written as **149.76.12.4**. This format is also called *dotted quad* notation.

You will notice that we now have three different types of addresses: first there is the host's name, like **quark**, then there are IP addresses, and finally, there are hardware addresses, like the 6-byte Ethernet address. All these somehow have to match, so that when you type *rlogin quark*, the networking software can be given **quark**'s IP address; and when IP

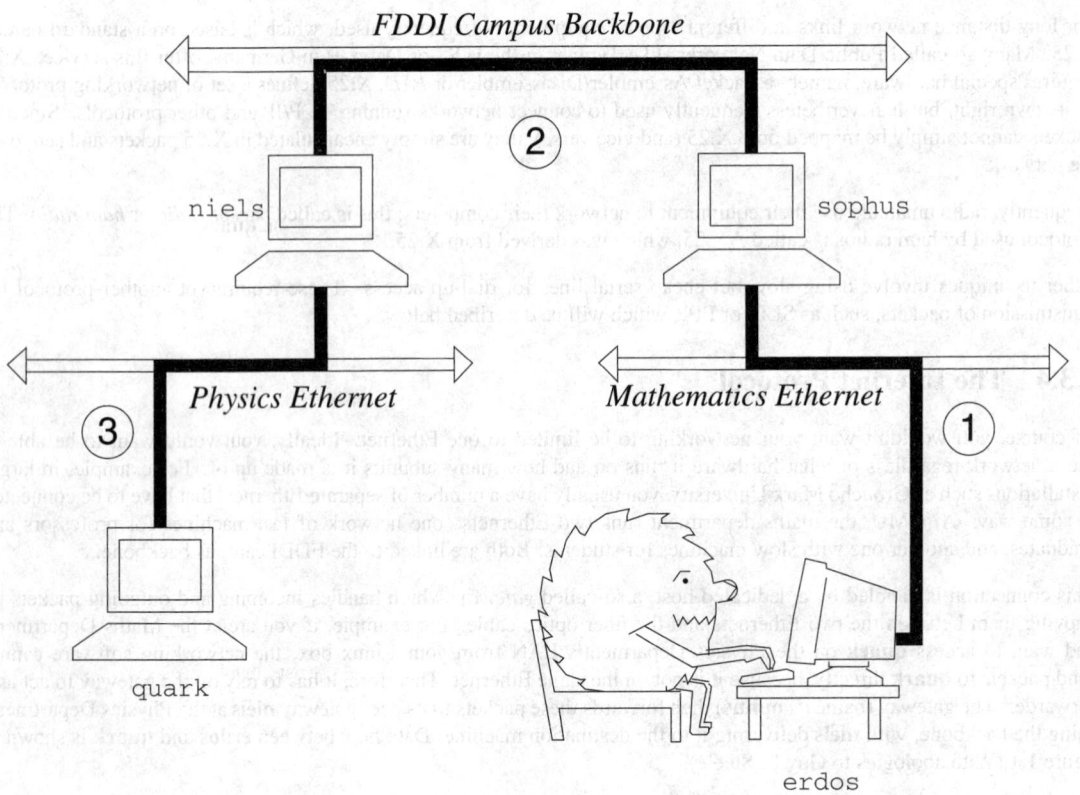

Figure 1.1: The three steps of sending a datagram from **erdos** to **quark**.

delivers any data to the Physics Department's Ethernet, it somehow has to find out what Ethernet address corresponds to the IP address. Which is rather confusing.

We will not go into this here, and deal with it in chapter 2 instead. For now, it's enough to remember that these steps of finding addresses are called *hostname resolution*, for mapping host names onto IP addresses, and *address resolution*, for mapping the latter to hardware addresses.

1.3.5   IP over Serial Lines

On serial lines, a "de facto" standard known as SLIP or *Serial Line IP* is frequently used. A modification of SLIP is known as CSLIP, or *compressed SLIP*, and performs compression of IP headers to make better use of the relatively low bandwidth provided by serial links.[4] A different serial protocol is PPP, or *Point-to-Point Protocol*. PPP has many more features than SLIP, including a link negotiation phase. Its main advantage over SLIP is, however, that it isn't limited to transporting IP datagrams, but that it was designed to allow for any type of datagrams to be transmitted.

1.3.6   The Transmission Control Protocol

Now, of course, sending datagrams from one host to another is not the whole story. If you log into **quark**, you want to have a reliable connection between your *rlogin* process on **erdos** and the shell process on **quark**. Thus, the information sent to and fro must be split up into packets by the sender, and reassembled into a character stream by the receiver. Trivial as it seems, this involves a number of hairy tasks.

A very important thing to know about IP is that, by intent, it is not reliable. Assume that ten people on your Ethernet started downloading the latest release of XFree86 from GMU's FTP server. The amount of traffic generated by this might be too much for the gateway to handle, because it's too slow, and it's tight on memory. Now if you happen to send a packet to **quark**, **sophus** might just be out of buffer space for a moment and therefore unable to forward it. IP solves this problem by simply discarding it. The packet is irrevocably lost. It is therefore the responsibility of the communicating hosts to check the integrity and completeness of the data, and retransmit it in case of an error.

This is performed by yet another protocol, TCP, or *Transmission Control Protocol*, which builds a reliable service on top of IP. The essential property of TCP is that it uses IP to give you the illusion of a simple connection between the two processes on your host and the remote machine, so that you don't have to care about how and along which route your data actually travels. A TCP connection works essentially like a two-way pipe that both processes may write to and read from. Think of it as a telephone conversation.

TCP identifies the end points of such a connection by the IP addresses of the two hosts involved, and the number of a so-called *port* on each host. Ports may be viewed as attachment points for network connections. If we are to strain the telephone example a little more, one might compare IP addresses to area codes (numbers map to cities), and port numbers to local codes (numbers map to individual people's telephones).

In the *rlogin* example, the client application (*rlogin*) opens a port on **erdos**, and connects to port 513 on **quark**, which the *rlogind* server is known to listen to. This establishes a TCP connection. Using this connection, *rlogind* performs the authorization procedure, and then spawns the shell. The shell's standard input and output are redirected to the TCP connection, so that anything you type to *rlogin* on your machine will be passed through the TCP stream and be given to the shell as standard input.

1.3.7   The User Datagram Protocol

Of course, TCP isn't the only user protocol in TCP/IP networking. Although suitable for applications like *rlogin*, the overhead involved is prohibitve for applications like NFS. Instead, it uses a sibling protocol of TCP called UDP, or *User Datagram Protocol*. Just like TCP, UDP also allows an application to contact a service on a certain port on the remote machine, but it doesn't establish a connection for this. Instead, you may use it to send single packets to the destination service – hence its name.

---

[4]SLIP is described in RFC 1055. The header compression CSLIP is based in is described in RFC 1144.

Assume you have mounted the TEX directory hierarchy from the department's central NFS server, *galois*, and you want to view a document describing how to use LATEX. You start your editor, who first reads in the entire file. However, it would take too long to establish a TCP connection with *galois*, send the file, and release it again. Instead, a request is made to *galois*, who sends the file in a couple of UDP packets, which is much faster. However, UDP was not made to deal with packet loss or corruption. It is up to the application – NFS in this case – to take care of this.

1.3.8   More on Ports

Ports may be viewed as attachment points for network connections. If an application wants to offer a certain service, it attaches itself to a port and waits for clients (this is also called *listening* on the port). A client that wants to use this service allocates a port on its local host, and connects to the server's port on the remote host.

An important property of ports is that once a connection has been established between the client and the server, another copy of the server may attach to the server port and listen for more clients. This permits, for instance, several concurrent remote logins to the same host, all using the same port 513. TCP is able to tell these connections from each other, because they all come from different ports or hosts. For example, if you twice log into **quark** from **erdos**, then the first *rlogin* client will use the local port 1023, and the second one will use port 1022. Both however, will connect to the same port 513 on **quark**.

This example shows the use of ports as rendezvous points, where a client contacts a specific port to obtain a specific service. In order for a client to know the proper port number, an agreement has to be reached between the administrators of both systems on the assignment of these numbers. For services that are widely used, such as *rlogin*, these numbers have to be administered centrally. This is done by the IETF (or *Internet Engineering Task Force*), which regularly releases an RFC titled *Assigned Numbers*. It describes, among other things, the port numbers assigned to *well-known services*. Linux uses a file mapping service names to numbers, called */etc/services*. It is described in section 9.3.

It is worth noting that although both TCP and UDP connections rely on ports, these numbers do not conflict. This means that TCP port 513, for example, is different from UDP port 513. In fact, these ports serve as access points for two different services, namely *rlogin* (TCP) and *rwho* (UDP).

1.3.9   The Socket Library

In UNIX operating systems, the software performing all the tasks and protocols described above is usually part of the kernel, and so it is in Linux. The programming interface most common in the UNIX world is the *Berkeley Socket Library*. Its name derives from a popular analogy that views ports as sockets, and connecting to a port as plugging in. It provides the (*bind(2)*) call to specifiy a remote host, a transport protocol, and a service which a program can connect or listen to (using *connect(2)*, *listen(2)*, and *accept(2)*). The socket library is however somewhat more general, in that it provides not only a class of TCP/IP-based sockets (the *AF_INET* sockets), but also a class that handles connections local to the machine (the *AF_UNIX* class). Some implementations can also handle other classes as well, like the XNS (*Xerox Networking System*) protocol, or X.25.

In Linux, the socket library is part of the standard *libc* C library. Currently, it only supports *AF_INET* and *AF_UNIX* sockets, but efforts are made to incorporate support for Novell's networking protocols, so that eventually one or more socket classes for these would be added.

1.4   Linux Networking

Being the result of a concerted effort of programmers around the world, Linux wouldn't have been possible without the global network. So it's not surprising that already in early stages of development, several people started to work on providing it with network capabilities. A UUCP implementation was running on Linux almost from the very beginning, and work on TCP/IP-based networking started around autumn 1992, when Ross Biro and others created what now has become known as Net-1.

After Ross quit active development in May 1993, Fred van Kempen began to work on a new implementation, rewriting major parts of the code. This ongoing effort is known as Net-2. A first public release, Net-2d, was made in Summer 1992 (as part of the 0.99.10 kernel), and has since been maintained and expanded by several people, most notably Alan Cox, as Net-2Debugged. After heavy debugging and numerous improvements to the code, he changed its name to Net-3 after Linux 1.0 was released. This is the version of the networking code currently included in the official kernel releases.

Net-3 offers device drivers for a wide variety of Ethernet boards, as well as SLIP (for sending network traffic over serial lines), and PLIP (for parallel lines). With Net-3, Linux has a TCP/IP implementation that behaves very well in a local area network environment, showing uptimes that beat some of the commercial PC Unices. Development currently moves toward the necessary stability to reliably run it on Internet hosts.

Beside these facilities, there are several projects going on that will enhance the versatility of Linux. A driver for PPP (the point-to-point protocol, another way to send network traffic over serial lines), is at Beta stage currently, and an AX.25 driver for ham radio is at Alpha stage. Alan Cox has also implemented a driver for Novell's IPX protocol, but the effort for a complete networking suite compatible with Novell's has been put on hold for the moment, because of Novell's unwillingness to provide the necessary documentation. Another very promising undertaking is *samba*, a free NetBIOS server for Unices, written by Andrew Tridgell.[5]

1.4.1 Different Streaks of Development

In the meanwhile, Fred continued development, going on to Net-2e, which features a much revised design of the networking layer. At the time of writing, Net-2e is still Beta software. Most notable about Net-2e is the incorporation of DDI, the *Device Driver Interface*. DDI offers a uniform access and configuration method to all networking devices and protocols.

Yet another implemtation of TCP/IP networking comes from Matthias Urlichs, who wrote an ISDN driver for Linux and FreeBSD. For this, he integrated some of the BSD networking code in the Linux kernel.

For the foreseeable future, however, Net-3 seems to be here to stay. Alan currently works on an implementation of the AX.25 protocol used by ham radio amateurs. Doubtlessly, the yet to be developed "module" code for the kernel will also bring new impulses to the networking code. Modules allow you to add drivers to the kernel at run time.

Although these different network implementations all strive to provide the same service, there are major differences between them at the kernel and device level. Therefore, you will not be able to configure a system running a Net-2e kernel with utilities from Net-2d or Net-3, and vice versa. This only applies to commands that deal with kernel internals rather closely; applications and common networking commands such as *rlogin* or *telnet* run on either of them.

Nevertheless, all these different network version should not worry you. Unless you are participating in active development, you will not have to worry about which version of the TCP/IP code you run. The official kernel releases will always be accompanied by a set of networking tools that are compatible with the networking code present in the kernel.

1.4.2 Where to Get the Code

The latest version of the Linux network code can be obtained by anonymous FTP from various sites. The official FTP site for Net-3 is **sunacm.swan.ac.uk**, mirrored by **sunsite.unc.edu** below *system/Network/sunacm*. The latest Net-2e patch kit and binaries are available from **ftp.aris.com**. Matthias Urlichs' BSD-derived networking code can be gotten from **ftp.ira.uka.de** in */pub/system/linux/netbsd*.

The latest kernels can be found on **nic.funet.fi** in */pub/OS/Linux/PEOPLE/Linus*; **sunsite** and **tsx-11.mit.edu** mirror this directory.

---

[5]NetBIOS is the protocol on which applications like *lanmanager* and Windows for Workgroups are based.

1.5   Maintaining Your System

Throughout this book, we will mainly deal with installation and configuration issues. Administration is, however, much more than that — after setting up a service, you have to keep it running, too. For most of them, only little attendance will be necessary, while some, like mail and news, require that you perform routine tasks to keep your system up-to-date. We will discuss these tasks in later chapters.

The absolute minimum in maintenance is to check system and per-application log files regularly for error conditions and unusual events. Commonly, you will want to do this by writing a couple of administrative shell scripts and run them from *cron* periodically. The source distribution of some major applications, like *smail* or C News, contain such scripts. You only have to tailor them to suit your needs and preferences.

The output from any of your *cron* jobs should be mailed to an administrative account. By default, many applications will send error reports, usage statistics, or logfile summaries to the **root** account. This only makes sense if you log in as **root** frequently; a much better idea is to forward **root**'s mail to your personal account setting up a mail alias as described in chapter 14.

However carefully you have configured your site, Murphy's law guarantees that some problem *will* surface eventually. Therefore, maintaining a system also means being available for complaints. Usually, people expect that the system administrator can at least be reached via email as **root**, but there are also other addresses that are commonly used to reach the person responsible for a specific aspect of maintenance. For instance, complaints about a malfunctioning mail configuration will usually be addressed **postmaster**; and problems with the news system may be reported to **newsmaster** or **usenet**. Mail to **hostmaster** should be redirected to the person in charge of the host's basic network services, and the DNS name service if you run a name server.

1.5.1   System Security

Another very important aspect of system administration in a network environment is protecting your system and users from intruders. Carelessly managed systems offer malicious people many targets: attacks range from password guessing to Ethernet snooping, and the damage caused may range from faked mail messages to data loss or violation of your users' privacy. We will mention some particular problems when discussing the context they may occur in, and some common defenses against them.

This section will discuss a few examples and basic techniques in dealing with system security. Of course, the topics covered can not treat all security issues you may be faced with exhaustively; they merely serve to illustrate the problems that may arise. Therefore, reading a good book on security is an absolute must, especially in a networked system. Simon Garfinkel's "Practical UNIX Security" (see [Spaf93]) is highly recommendable.

System security starts with good system administration. This includes checking the ownership and permissions of all vital files and directories, monitoring use of privileged accounts, etc. The COPS program, for instance, will check your file system and common configuration files for unusual permissions or other anomalies. It is also wise to use a password suite that enforces certain rules on the users' passwords that make them hard to guess. The shadow password suite, for instance, requires a password to have at least five letters, and contain both upper and lower case numbers and digits.

When making a service accessible to the network, make sure to give it "least privilege," meaning that you don't permit it to do things that aren't required for it to work as designed. For example, you should make programs setuid to **root** or some other privileged account only when they really need this. Also, if you want to use a service for only a very limited application, don't hesitate to configure it as restrictively as your special application allows. For instance, if you want to allow diskless hosts to boot from your machine, you must provide the TFTP (trivial file transfer service) so that they can download basic configuration files from the */boot* directory. However, when used unrestricted, TFTP allows any user anywhere in the world to download any world-readable file from your system. If this is not what you want, why not restrict TFTP service to the */boot* directory?[6]

Along the same line of thought, you might want to restrict certain services to users from certain hosts, say from your local network. In chapter 9, we introduce *tcpd* which does this for a variety of network applications.

---

[6]We will come back to this in chapter 9.

Another important point is to avoid "dangerous" software. Of course, any software you use can be dangerous, because software may have bugs that clever people might exploit to gain access to your system. Things like these happen, and there's no complete protection against this. This problem affects free software and commercial products alike.[7] However, programs that require special privilege are inherently more dangerous than others, because any loophole can have drastic consequences.[8] If you install a setuid program for network purposes be doubly careful that you don't miss anything from the documentation, so that you don't create a security breach by accident.

You can never rule out that your precautions might fail, regardless how careful you have been. You should therefore make sure you detect intruders early. Checking the system log files is a good starting point, but the intruder is probably as clever, and will delete any obvious traces he or she left. However, there are tools like *tripwire*[9] that allow you to check vital system files to see if their contents or permissions have been changed. *tripwire* computes various strong checksums over these files and stores them in a database. During subsequent runs, the checksums are re-computed and compared to the stored ones to detect any modifications.

1.6 Outlook on the Following Chapters

The next few chapters will deal with configuring Linux for TCP/IP networking, and with running some major applications. Before getting our hands dirty with file editing and the like, we will examine IP a little closer in chapter 2. If you already know about the way IP routing works, and how address resolution is performed, you might want to skip this chapter.

Chapter 3 deals with the very basic configuration issues, such as building a kernel and setting up your Ethernet board. The configuration of your serial ports is covered in a separate chapter, because the discussion does not apply to TCP/IP networking only, but is also relevant for UUCP.

Chapter 5 helps you to set up your machine for TCP/IP networking. It contains installation hints for standalone hosts with only loopback enabled, and hosts connected to an Ethernet. It will also introduce you to a few useful tools you can use to test and debug your setup. The next chapter discusses how to configure hostname resolution, and explains how to set up a name server.

This is followed by two chapters featuring the configuration and use of SLIP and PPP, respectively. Chapter 7 explains how to establish SLIP connections, and gives a detailed reference of *dip*, a tool that allows you to automate most of the necessary steps. Chapter 8 covers PPP and *pppd*, the PPP daemon you need for this.

Chapter 9 gives a short introduction to setting up some of the most important network applications, such as *rlogin*, *rcp*, etc, in chapter 9. This also covers how services are managed by the *inetd* super, and how you may restrict certain security-relevant services to a set of trusted hosts.

The next two chapters discuss NIS, the Network Information System, and NFS, the Network File System. NIS is a useful tool to distribute administative information such as user passwords in a local area network. NFS allows you to share file systems between several hosts in your network.

Chapter 12 gives you an extensive introduction to the administration of Taylor UUCP, a free implementation of the UUCP suite.

The remainder of the book is taken up by a detailed tour of electronic mail and Usenet News. Chapter 13 introduces you to the central concepts of electronic mail, like what a mail address looks like, and how the mail handling system manages to get your message to the recipient.

Chapters 14 and 15 each cover the setup of *smail* and *sendmail*, two mail transport agents you can use for Linux. This book explains both of them, because *smail* is easier to install for the beginner, while *sendmail* is more flexible.

---

[7] There have been commercial Unices you have to pay lots of money for that came with a setuid-**root** shell script which allowed users to gain **root** privilege using a simple standard trick.

[8] In 1988, the RTM worm brought much of the Internet to a grinding halt, partly by exploiting a gaping hole in some *sendmail* programs. This hole has long been fixed since.

[9] Written by Gene Kim and Gene Spafford.

Chapters 1.3 and 17 explain the way news are managed in Usenet, and how you install and use C news, a popular software package for managing Usenet news. Chapter 18 briefly covers how to set up an NNTP daemon to provide news reading access for your local network. Chapter 19 finally shows you how to configure and maintain various newsreaders.

Chapter 2

Issues of TCP/IP Networking

We will now turn to the details you'll come in touch with when connecting your Linux machine to a TCP/IP network including dealing with IP addresses, host names, and sometimes routing issues. This chapter gives you the background you need in order to understand what your setup requires, while the next chapters will cover the tools to deal with these.

2.1 Networking Interfaces

To hide the diversity of equipment that may be used in a networking environment, TCP/IP defines an abstract *interface* through which the hardware is accessed. This interface offers a set of operations which is the same for all types of hardware and basically deals with sending and receiving packets.

For each periphereal device you want to use for networking, a corresponding interface has to be present in the kernel. For example, Ethernet interfaces in Linux are called *eth0* and *eth1*, and SLIP interfaces come as *sl0*, *sl1*, etc. These interface names are used for configuration purposes when you want to name a particular physical device to the kernel. They have no meaning beyond that.

To be useable for TCP/IP networking, an interface must be assigned an IP address which serves as its identifcation when communicating with the rest of the world. This address is different from the interface name mentioned above; if you compare an interface to door, then the address is like the name-plate pinned on it.

Of course, there are other device parameters that may be set; one of these is the maximum size of datagrams that can be processed by that particular piece of hardware, also called *Maximum Transfer Unit*, or MTU. Other attributes will be introduced later.

2.2 IP Addresses

As mentioned in the previous chapter, the addresses understood by the IP networking protocol are 32-bit numbers. Every machine must be assigned a number unique to the networking environment. If you are running a local network that does not have TCP/IP traffic with other networks, you may assign these numbers according to your personal preferences. However, for sites on the Internet, numbers are assigned by a central authority, the Network Information Center, or NIC.[1]

For easier reading, IP addresses are split up into four 8 bit numbers called *octets*. For example, **quark.physics.groucho.edu** has an IP address of **0x954C0C04**, which is written as **149.76.12.4**. This format is often referred to as the *dotted quad notation*.

Another reason for this notation is that IP addresses are split into a *network* number, which is contained in the leading octets, and a *host* number, which is the remainder. When applying to the NIC for IP addresses, you are not assigned an address for each single host you plan to use. Instead, you are given a network number, and are allowed to assign all valid IP addresses within this range to hosts on your network according to your preferences.

---

[1]Frequently, IP addresses will be assigned to you by the provider you buy your IP connectivity from. However, you may also apply to NIC directly for an IP address for your network by sending a mail to **hostmaster@internic.net**.

Depending on the size of the network, the host part may need to be smaller or larger. To accomodate different needs, there are several classes of networks, defining different splits of IP addresses.

Class A   Class A comprises networks **1.0.0.0** through **127.0.0.0**. The network number is contained in the first octet. This provides for a 24 bit host part, allowing roughly 1.6 million hosts.

Class B   Class B contains networks **128.0.0.0** through **191.255.0.0**; the network number is in the first two octets. This allows for 16320 nets with 65024 hosts each.

Class C   Class C networks range from **192.0.0.0** through **223.255.255.0**, with the network number being contained in the first three octets. This allows for nearly 2 million networks with up to 254 hosts.

Classes D, E, and F   Addresses falling into the range of **224.0.0.0** through **254.0.0.0** are either experimental, or are reserved for future use and don't specify any network.

If we go back to the example in the previous chapter, we find that **149.76.12.4**, the address of **quark**, refers to host **12.4** on the class B network **149.76.0.0**.

You may have noticed that in the above list not all possible values were allowed for each octet in the host part. This is because host numbers with octets all **0** or all **255** are reserved for special purposes. An address where all host part bits are zero refers to the network, and one where all bits of the host part are 1 is called a broadcast address. This refers to all hosts on the specified network simultaneously. Thus, **149.76.255.255** is not a valid host address, but refers to all hosts on network **149.76.0.0**.

There are also two network addresses that are reserved, **0.0.0.0** and **127.0.0.0**. The first is called the *default route*, the latter the *loopback address*. The default route has something to do with the way IP routes datagrams, which will be dealt with below.

Network **127.0.0.0** is reserved for IP traffic local to your host. Usually, address **127.0.0.1** will be assigned to a special interface on your host, the so-called *loopback interface*, which acts like a closed circuit. Any IP packet handed to it from TCP or UDP will be returned to them as if it had just arrived from some network. This allows you to develop and test networking software without ever using a "real" network. Another useful application is when you want to use networking software on a standalone host. This may not be as uncommon as it sounds; for instance, many UUCP sites don't have IP connectivity at all, but still want to run the INN news system nevertheless. For proper operation on Linux, INN requires the loopback interface.

2.3   Address Resolution

Now that you've seen how IP addresses are made up, you may be wondering how they are used on an Ethernet to address different hosts. After all, the Ethernet protocol identifies hosts by a six-octet number that has absolutely nothing in common with an IP address, doesn't it?

Right. That's why a mechanism is needed to map IP addresses onto Ethernet addresses. This is the so-called *Address Resolution Protocol*, or ARP. In fact, ARP is not confined to Ethernets at all, but is used on other types networks such as ham radio as well. The idea underlying ARP is exactly what most people do when they have to find Mr. X. Ample in a throng of 150 people: they go round, calling out his name, confident that he will respond if he's there.

When ARP wants to find out the Ethernet address corresponding to a given IP address, it uses a feature of Ethernet known as "broadcasting," where a datagram is addressed to all stations on the network simultaneously. The broadcast datagram sent by ARP contains a query for the IP address. Each receiving host compares this to its own IP address, and if it matches, returns an ARP reply to the inquiring host. The inquiring host can now extract the sender's Ethernet address from the reply.

Of course you might wonder how a host may know on which of the zillions of Ethernets throughout the world it is to find the desired host, and why this should even be an Ethernet. These questions all involve what is called routing, namely finding out the physical location of a host in a network. This will be the topic of the following section.

For a moment, let's talk about ARP a little longer. Once a host has discovered an Ethernet address, it stores it in its ARP cache, so that it doesn't have to query for it the next time it wants to send a datagram to the host in question. However, it is unwise to keep this information forever; for instance, the remote host's Ethernet card may be replaced because of technical problems, so the ARP entry becomes invalid. To force another query for the IP address, entries in the ARP cache are therefore discarded after some time.

Sometimes, it is also necessary to find out the IP address associated with a given Ethernet address. This happens when a diskless machine wants to boot from a server on the network, which is quite a common situation on local area networks. A diskless client, however, has virtually no information about itself – except for its Ethernet address! So what it basically does is broadcast a message containing a plea for boot servers to tell it its IP address. There's another protocol for this, named *Reverse Address Resolution Protocol*, or RARP. Along with the BOOTP protocol, it serves to define a procedure for bootstrapping diskless clients over the network.

2.4 IP Routing

2.4.1 IP Networks

◇ When you write a letter to someone, you usually put a complete address on the envelope, specifying the country, state, zip code, etc. After you put it into the letter box, the postal service will deliver it to its destination: it will be sent to the country indicated, whose national service will dispatch it to the proper state and region, etc. The advantage of this hierarchical scheme is rather obvious: Wherever you post the letter, the local postmaster will know roughly the direction to forward the letter to, but doesn't have to care which way the letter will travel by within the destination country.

IP networks are structured in a similar way. The whole Internet consists of a number of proper networks, called *autonomous systems*. Each such system performs any routing between its member hosts internally, so that the task of delivering a datagram is reduced to finding a path to the destination host's network. This means, as soon as the datagram is handed to *any* host that is on that particular network, further processing is done exclusively by the network itself.

2.4.2 Subnetworks

This structure is reflected by splitting IP addresses into a host and network part, as explained above. By default, the destination network is derived from the network part of the IP address. Thus, hosts with identical IP network numbers should be found within the same network, and vice versa.[2]

It makes sense to offer a similar scheme *inside* the network, too, since it may consist of a collection of hundreds of smaller networks itself, with the smallest units being physical networks like Ethernets. Therefore, IP allows you to subdivide an IP network into several *subnets*.

A subnet takes over responsibility for delivering datagrams to a certain range of IP addresses from the IP network it is part of. As with classes A, B, or C, it is identified by the network part of the IP addresses. However, the network part is now extended to include some bits from the host part. The number of bits that are interpreted as the subnet number is given by the so-called *subnet mask*, or *netmask*. This is a 32 bit number, too, which specifies the bit mask for the network part of the IP address.

The campus network of Groucho Marx University is an example of such a network. It has a class B network number of **149.76.0.0**, and its netmask is therefore **255.255.0.0**.

Internally, GMU's campus network consists of several smaller networks, such as the LANs of various departments. So the range of IP addresses is broken up into 254 subnets, **149.76.1.0** through **149.76.254.0**. For example, the Department of Theoretical Physics has been assigned **149.76.12.0**. The campus backbone is a network by its own right, and is given **149.76.1.0**. These subnets share the same IP network number, while the third octet is used to distinguish between them. Thus they will use a subnet mask of **255.255.255.0**.

---

[2]Autonomous systems are slightly more general, however. They may comprise more than one IP network.

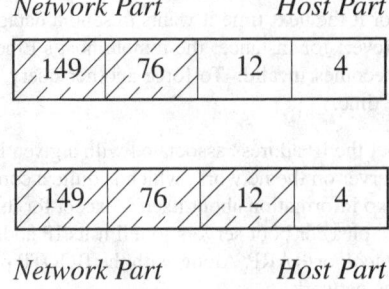

Figure 2.1: Subnetting a class B network

Figure 2.1 shows how **149.76.12.4**, the address of **quark**, is interpreted differently when the address is taken as an ordinary class B network, and when used with subnetting.

It is worth noting that subnetting (as the technique of generating subnets is called) is only an *internal division* of the network. Subnets are generated by the network owner (or the administrators). Frequently, subnets are created to reflect existing boundaries, be they physical (between two Ethernets), administrative (between two departments), or geographical, and authority over these subnets is delegated to some contact person. However, this structure affects only the network's internal behavior, and is completely invisible to the outside world.

2.4.3   Gateways

Subnetting is not only an organizational benefit, it is frequently a natural consequence of hardware boundaries. The viewpoint of a host on a given physical network, such as an Ethernet, is a very limited one: the only hosts it is able to talk to directly are those of the network it is on. All other hosts can be accessed only through so-called *gateways*. A gateway is a host that is connected to two or more physical networks simultaneously and is configured to switch packets between them.

For IP to be able to easily recognize if a host is on a local physical network, different physical networks have to belong to different IP networks. For example the network number **149.76.4.0** is reserved for hosts on the mathematics LAN. When sending a datagram to **quark**, the network software on **erdos** immediately sees from the IP address, **149.76.12.4**, that the destination host is on a different physical network, and therefore can be reached only through a gateway (**sophus** by default).

sophus itself is connected to two distinct subnets: the Mathematics Department, and the campus backbone. It accesses each through a different interface, *eth0* and *fddi0*, respectively. Now, what IP address do we assign it? Should we give it one on subnet **149.76.1.0**, or on **149.76.4.0**?

The answer is: both. When talking to a host on the Maths LAN, **sophus** should use an IP address of **149.76.4.1**, and when talking to a host on the backbone, it should use **149.76.1.4**.

Thus, a gateway is assigned one IP address per network it is on. These addresses — along with the corresponding netmask — are tied to the interface the subnet is accessed through. Thus, the mapping of interfaces and addresses for **sophus** would look like this:

iface	address	netmask
eth0	**149.76.4.1**	**255.255.255.0**
fddi0	**149.76.1.4**	**255.255.255.0**
lo	**127.0.0.1**	**255.0.0.0**

The last entry describes the loopback interface *lo*, which was introduced above.

Figure 2.2 shows a part of the network topology at Groucho Marx University (GMU). Hosts that are on two subnets at the same time are shown with both addresses.

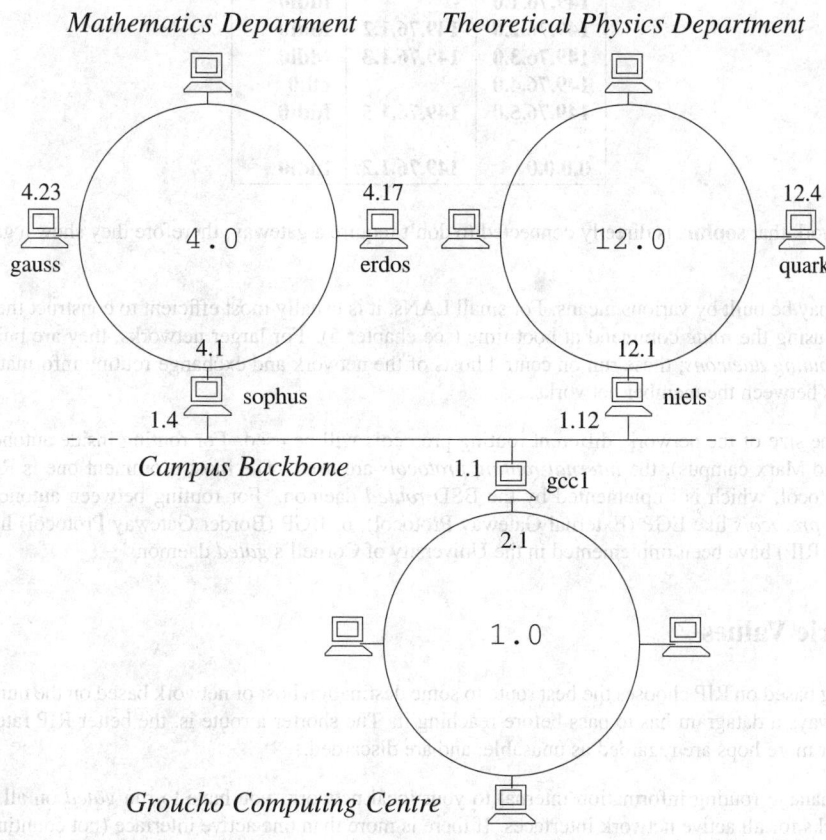

Figure 2.2: A part of the net topology at Groucho Marx Univ.

Generally, you can ignore the subtle difference between attaching an address to a host or its interface. For hosts that are on one network only, like **erdos**, you would generally refer of the host as having this-and-that IP address although strictly speaking, it's the Ethernet interface that has this IP address. However, this distinction is only really important when you refer to a gateway.

2.4.4 The Routing Table

We are now focusing our attention on how IP chooses a gateway to use when delivering a datagram to a remote network.

We have seen before that **erdos**, when given a datagram for **quark**, checks the destination address and finds it is not on the local network. It therefore sends it to the default gateway, **sophus**, which is now basically faced with the same task. **sophus** recognizes that **quark** is not on any of the networks it is connected to directly, so it has to find yet another gateway to forward it through. The correct choice would be *niels*, the gateway to the Physics Department. **sophus** therefore needs some information to associate a destination network with a suitable gateway.

The routing information IP uses for this is basically a table linking networks to gateways that reach them. A catch-all entry (the *default route*) must generally be supplied, too; this is the gateway associated with network **0.0.0.0**. All packets to an unknown network are sent through the default route. On **sophus**, this table might look like this:

Network	Gateway	Interface
149.76.1.0	-	**fddi0**
149.76.2.0	**149.76.1.2**	**fddi0**
149.76.3.0	**149.76.1.3**	**fddi0**
149.76.4.0	-	**eth0**
149.76.5.0	**149.76.1.5**	**fddi0**
...	...	...
0.0.0.0	**149.76.1.2**	**fddi0**

Routes to a network that **sophus** is directly connected to don't require a gateway; therefore they show a gateway entry of "-".

Routing tables may be built by various means. For small LANs, it is usually most efficient to construct them by hand and feed them to IP using the *route* command at boot time (see chapter 5). For larger networks, they are built and adjusted at run-time by *routing daemons*; these run on central hosts of the network and exchange routing information to compute "optimal" routes between the member networks.

Depending on the size of the network, different routing protocols will be used. For routing inside autonomous systems (such as Groucho Marx campus), the *internal routing protocols* are used. The most prominent one is RIP, the Routing Information Protocol, which is implemented by the BSD *routed* daemon. For routing between autonomous systems, *external routing protocols* like EGP (External Gateway Protocol), or BGP (Border Gateway Protocol) have to be used; these (as well as RIP) have been implemented in the University of Cornell's *gated* daemon.[3]

2.4.5   Metric Values

Dynamic routing based on RIP chooses the best route to some destination host or network based on the number of "hops", that is, the gateways a datagram has to pass before reaching it. The shorter a route is, the better RIP rates it. Very long routes with 16 or more hops are regarded as unusable, and are discarded.

To use RIP to manage routing information internal to your local network, you have to run *gated* on all hosts. At boot time, *gated* checks for all active network interfaces. If there is more than one active interface (not counting the loopback interface), it assumes the host is switching packets between several networks, and will actively exchange and broadcast routing information. Otherwise, it will only passively receive any RIP updates and update the local routing table.

When broadcasting the information from the local routing table, *gated* computes the length of the route from the so-called *metric value* associated with the routing table entry. This metric value is set by the system administrator when configuring the route and should reflect the actual cost of using this route. Therefore, the metric of a route to a subnet the host is directly connected to should always be zero, while a route going through two gateways should have a metric of two. However, note that you don't have to bother about metrics when you don't use *RIP* or *gated*.

2.5   The Internet Control Message Protocol

IP has a companion protocol that we haven't talked about yet. This is the *Internet Control Message Protocol* (ICMP) and is used by the kernel networking code to communicate error messages and the like to other hosts. For instance, assume that you are on **erdos** again and want to *telnet* to port 12345 on **quark**, but there's no process listening on that port. When the first TCP packet for this port arrives on **quark**, the networking layer will recognize this and immediately return an ICMP message to **erdos** stating "Port Unreachable".

---

[3] *routed* is considered broken by many people. Since *gated* supports RIP as well, it is better to use that instead.

There are quite a number of messages ICMP understands, many of which deal with error conditions. However, there is one very interesting message called the Redirect message. It is generated by the routing module when it detects that another host is using it as a gateway, although there is a much shorter route. For example, after booting the routing table of **sophus** may be incomplete, containing the routes to the Mathematics network, to the FDDI backbone, and the default route pointing at the Groucho Computing Center's gateway (**gcc1**). Therefore, any packets for **quark** would be sent to **gcc1** rather than to **niels**, the gateway to the Physics Department. When receiving such a datagram, **gcc1** will notice that this is a poor choice of route, and will forward the packet to **niels**, at the same time returning an ICMP Redirect message to **sophus** telling it of the superior route.

Now, this seems a very clever way to avoid having to set up any but the most basic routes manually. However be warned that relying on dynamic routing schemes, be it RIP or ICMP Redirect messages, is not always a good idea. ICMP Redirect and RIP offer you little or no choice in verifying that some routing information is indeed authentic. This allows malicious good-for-nothings to disrupt your entire network traffic, or do even worse things. For this reason, there are some versions of the Linux networking code that treat Redirect messages that affect network routes, as if they were only Redirects for host routes.

2.6 The Domain Name System

2.6.1 Hostname Resolution

◇ As described above, addressing in TCP/IP networking revolves around 32 bit numbers. However, you will have a hard time remembering more than a few of these. Therefore, hosts are generally known by "ordinary" names such as **gauss** or **strange**. It is then the application's duty to find the IP address corresponding to this name. This process is called *host name resolution*.

An application that wants to find the IP address of a given host name does not have to provide its own routines for looking up a hosts and IP adresses. Instead, it relies on number of library functions that do this transparently, called *gethostbyname(3)* and *gethostbyaddr(3)*. Traditionally, these and a number of related procedures were grouped in a separate library called the resolver library; on Linux, these are part of the standard *libc*. Colloquially, this collection of functions are therefore referred to as "the resolver".

Now, on a small network like an Ethernet, or even a cluster of them, it is not very difficult to maintain tables mapping host names to addresses. This information is usually kept in a file named */etc/hosts*. When adding or removing hosts, or reassigning addresses, all you have to do is update the *hosts* on all hosts. Quite obviously, this will become burdensome with networks than comprise more than a handful of machines.

One solution to this problem is NIS, the *Network Information System* developed by Sun Microsystems, colloquially called YP, or *Yellow Pages*. NIS stores the *hosts* file (and other information) in a database on a master host, from which clients may retrieve it as needed. Still, this approach is only suitable for medium-sized networks such as LANs, because it involves maintaining the entire *hosts* database centrally, and distributing it to all servers.

On the Internet, address information was initially stored in a single *HOSTS.TXT* database, too. This file was maintained at the Network Information Center, or NIC, and had to be downloaded and installed by all participating sites. When the network grew, several problems with this scheme arose. Beside the administrative overhead involved in installing *HOSTS.TXT* regularly, the load on the servers that distributed it became too high. Even more severe was the problem that all names had to be registered with the NIC, which had to make sure that no name was issued twice.

This is why, in 1984, a new name resolution scheme has been adopted, the *Domain Name System*. DNS was designed by Paul Mockapetris, and addresses both problems simultaneously.

2.6.2 Enter DNS

DNS organizes host names in a hierarchy of domains. A domain is a collection of sites that are related in some sense — be it because they form a proper network (e.g. all machines on a campus, or all hosts on BITNET), because they all belong to a certain organization (like the U.S. government), or because they're simply geographically close. For instance, universities are grouped in the **edu** domain, with each University or College using a separate *subdomain* below which their hosts are subsumed. Groucho Marx University might be given the **groucho.edu** domain, with the LAN of the Mathematics Department being assigned **maths.groucho.edu**. Hosts on the departmental network would have this domain name tacked onto their host name; so **erdos** would be known as **erdos.maths.groucho.edu**. This is called the *fully qualified domain name*, or FQDN, which uniquely identifies this host world-wide.

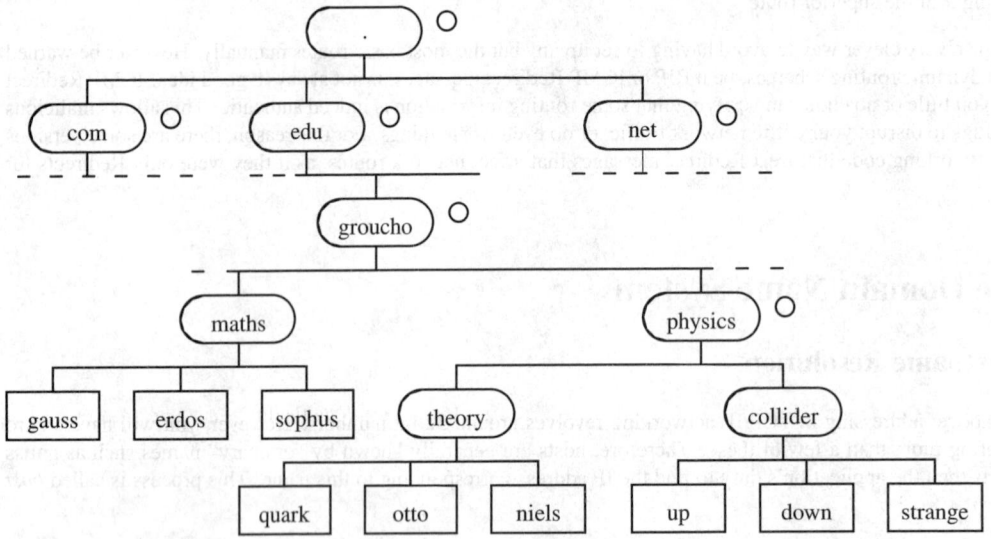

Figure 2.3: A part of the domain name space

Figure 2.3 shows a section of the name space. The entry at the root of this tree, which is denoted by a single dot, is quite appropriately called the *root domain*, and encompasses all other domains. To indicate that a host name is a fully qualified domain name, rather than a name relative to some (implicit) local domain, it is sometimes written with a trailing dot. This signifies that the name's last component is the root domain.

Depending on its location in the name hierarchy, a domain may be called top-level, second-level, or third-level. More levels of subdivision occur, but are rare. These are a couple of top-level domains you may see frequently:

edu	(Mostly US) educational institutions like universities, etc.
com	Commercial organizations, companies.
org	Non-commercial organizations. Often private UUCP networks are in this domain.
net	Gateways and other administrative host on a network.
mil	US military institutions.
gov	US government institutions.
uucp	Officially, all site names formerly used as UUCP names without domain, have been moved to this domain.

Technically, the first four of these belong to the US part of the Internet, but you may also see non-US sites in these domains. This is especially true of the **net** domain. However, **mil** and **gov** are used exclusively in the US.

Outside the US, each country generally uses a top-level domain of its own named after the two-letter country code defined in ISO-3166. Finland, for instance, uses the **fi** domain, **fr** is used by France, **de** by Germany, or **au** by Australia etc.

Below this top-level domain, each country's NIC is free to organize host names in whatever way they want. Australia, for example, has second-level domain similar to the international top-level domains, named **com.au**, **edu.au**, and so on. Others, like Germany, don't use this extra level, but rather have slightly longish names that refer directly to the organizations running a particular domain. For example, it's not uncommon to see host names like **ftp.informatik.uni-erlangen.de**. Chalk that up to German efficiency.

Of course, these national domains do not imply that a host below that domain is actually located in that country; it only signals that the host has been registered with that country's NIC. A Swedish manufacturer might have a branch in Australia, and still have all its hosts registered with the **se** top-level domain.

Now, organizing the name space in a hierarchy of domain names nicely solves the problem of name uniqueness; with DNS, a host name has to be unique only within its domain to give it a name different from all other hosts world-wide. Furthermore, fully qualified names are quite easy to remember. Taken by themselves, these are already very good resaons to split up a large domain into several subdomains.

But DNS does even more for you than than this: it allows you to delegate authority over a subdomain to its administrators. For example, the maintainers at the Groucho Computing Center might create a subdomain for each department; we already encountered the **maths** and **physics** subdomains above. When they find the network at the Physics Department too large and chaotic to manage from outside (after all, physicists are known to be an unruly bunch of people), they may simply pass control over the **physics.groucho.edu** domain to the administrators of this network. These are then free to use whatever host names they like, and assign them IP addresses from their network in whatever fashion the like, without outside interference.

To this end, the name space is split up into *zones*, each rooted at a domain. Note the subtle difference between a zone and a domain: the *domain* **groucho.edu** encompasses all hosts at the Groucho Marx University, while the *zone* **groucho.edu** includes only the hosts that are managed by the Computing Center directly, for example those at the Mathematics Department. The hosts at the Physics Department belong to a different zone, namely **physics.groucho.edu**. In figure 2.3, the start of a zone is marked by a small circle to the right of the domain name.

2.6.3   Name Lookups with DNS

At first glance, all this domain and zone fuss seems to make name resolution an awfully complicated business. After all, if no central authority controls what names are assigned to which hosts, then how is a humble application supposed to know?!

Now comes the really ingenuous part about DNS. If you want to find out the IP address of **erdos**, then, DNS says, go ask the people that manage it, and they will tell you.

In fact, DNS is a giant distributed database. It is implemented by means of so-called name servers that supply information on a given domain or set of domains. For each zone, there are at least two, at most a few, name servers that hold all authoritative information on hosts in that zone. To obtain the IP address of **erdos**, all you have to do is contact the name server for the **groucho.edu** zone, which will then return the desired data.

Easier said than done, you might think. So how do I know how to reach the name server at Groucho Marx University? In case your computer isn't equipped with an address-resolving oracle, DNS provides for this, too. When your application wants to look up information on **erdos**, it contacts a local name server, which conducts a so-called iterative query for it. It starts off by sending a query to a name server for the root domain, asking for the address of **erdos.maths.groucho.edu**. The root name server recognizes that this name does not belong to its zone of authority, but rather to one below the **edu** domain. Thus, it tells you to contact an **edu** zone name server for more information, and encloses a list of all **edu** name servers along with their addresses. Your local name server will then go on and query one of those, for instance **a.isi.edu**. In a manner similar to the root name server, **a.isi.edu** knows that the **groucho.edu** people run a zone of their own, and point you to their servers. The local name server will then present its query for **erdos** to one of these, which will finally recognize the name as belonging to its zone, and return the corresponding IP address.

Now, this looks like a lot of traffic being generated for looking up a measly IP address, but it's really only miniscule compared to the amount of data that would have to be transferred if we were still stuck with *HOSTS.TXT*. But there's still room for improvement with this scheme.

To improve response time during future queries, the name server will store the information obtained in its local *cache*. So the next time anyone on your local network wants to look up the address of a host in the **groucho.edu** domain, your name server will not have to go through the whole process again, but will rather go to the **groucho.edu** name server directly.[4]

Of course, the name server will not keep this information forever, but rather discard it after some period. This expiry interval is called the *time to live*, or TTL. Each datum in the DNS database is assigned such a TTL by administrators of the responsible zone.

2.6.4   Domain Name Servers

Name servers that hold all information on hosts within a zone are called *authoritative* for this zone, and are sometimes referred to as *master name servers*. Any query for a host within this zone will finally wind down at one of these master name servers.

To provide a coherent picture of a zone, its master servers must be fairly well synchronized. This is achieved by making one of them the *primary* server, which loads its zone information from data files, and making the others *secondary* servers who transfer the zone data from the primary server at regular intervals.

One reason to have several name servers is to distribute work load, another is redundance. When one name server machine fails in a benign way, like crashing or losing its network connection, all queries will fall back to the other servers. Of course, this scheme doesn't protect you from server malfunctions that produce wrong replies to all DNS requests, e.g. from software bugs in the server program itself.

Of course, you can also think of running a name server that is not authoritative for any domain.[5] This type of server is useful nevertheless, as it is still able to conduct DNS queries for the applications running on the local network, and cache the information. It is therefore called a *caching-only* server.

2.6.5   The DNS Database

We have seen above that DNS does not only deal with IP addresses of hosts, but also exchanges information on name servers. There are in fact a whole bunch of different types of entries the DNS database may have.

A single piece of information from the DNS database is called a *resource record*, or RR for short. Each record has a type associated with it, describing the sort of data it represents, and a class specifying the type of network it applies to. The latter accomodates the needs of different addressing schemes, like IP addresses (the IN class), or addresses of Hesiod networks (used at MIT), and a few more. The prototypical resource record type is the A record which associates a fully qualified domain name with an IP address.

Of course, a host may have more than one name. However, one of these names must be identified as the official, or *canonical host name*, while the others are simply aliases referring to the former. The difference is that the canonical host name is the one with an A record associated, while the others only have a record of type CNAME which points to the canonical host name.

We will not go through all record types here, but save them for a later chapter, but rather give you a brief example here. Figure 2.4 shows a part of the domain database that is loaded into the name servers for the **physics.groucho.edu** zone.

Apart from A and CNAME records, you can see a special record at the top of the file, stretching several lines. This is the SOA resource record, signalling the *Start of Authority*, which holds general information on the zone the server is authoritative for. This comprises, for instance, the default time-to-live for all records.

Note that all names in the sample file that do not end with a dot should be interpreted relative to the **groucho.edu** domain. The special name "@" used in the SOA record refers to the domain name by itself.

We have seen above that the name servers for the **groucho.edu** domain somehow have to know about the **physics** zone so that they can point queries to their name servers. This is usually achieved by a pair of records: the NS record that

---

[4]If it didn't, then DNS would be about as bad as any other method, because each query would involve the root name servers.

[5]Well, almost. A name server at least has to provide name service for **localhost** and reverse lookups of **127.0.0.1**.

```
;
; Authoritative Information on physics.groucho.edu
@                       IN      SOA         {
                        niels.physics.groucho.edu.
                        hostmaster.niels.physics.groucho.edu.
                        1034                    ; serial no
                        360000                  ; refresh
                        3600                    ; retry
                        3600000                 ; expire
                        3600                    ; default ttl
                        }
;
; Name servers
                        IN      NS          niels
                        IN      NS          gauss.maths.groucho.edu.
gauss.maths.groucho.edu. IN     A           149.76.4.23
;
; Theoretical Physics (subnet 12)
niels                   IN      A           149.76.12.1
                        IN      A           149.76.1.12
nameserver              IN      CNAME       niels
otto                    IN      A           149.76.12.2
quark                   IN      A           149.76.12.4
down                    IN      A           149.76.12.5
strange                 IN      A           149.76.12.6
...
; Collider Lab. (subnet 14)
boson                   IN      A           149.76.14.1
muon                    IN      A           149.76.14.7
bogon                   IN      A           149.76.14.12
```

Figure 2.4: An excerpt from the *named.hosts* file for the Physics Department.

gives the server's FQDN, and an A record associating an address with that name. Since these records are what holds
the name space together, they are frequently called the *glue records*. They are the only instances of records where a
parent zone actually holds information on hosts in the subordinate zone. The glue records pointing to the name servers
for **physics.groucho.edu** are shown in figure 2.5.

```
;
; Zone data for the groucho.edu zone.
@                     IN      SOA           {
                      vax12.gcc.groucho.edu.
                      hostmaster.vax12.gcc.groucho.edu.
                      233             ; serial no
                      360000          ; refresh
                      3600            ; retry
                      3600000         ; expire
                      3600            ; default ttl
                      }
....
;
; Glue records for the physics.groucho.edu zone
physics               IN      NS            niels.physics.groucho.edu.
                      IN      NS            gauss.maths.groucho.edu.
niels.physics         IN      A             149.76.12.1
gauss.maths           IN      A             149.76.4.23
...
```

Figure 2.5: An excerpt from the *named.hosts* file for GMU.

2.6.6   Reverse Lookups

Beside looking up the IP address belonging to a host, it is sometimes desirable to find out the canonical host name
corresponding to an address. This is called *reverse mapping* and is used by several network services to verify a client's
identity. When using a single *hosts* file, reverse lookups simply involve searching the file for a host that owns the
IP address in question. With DNS, an exhaustive search of the name space is out of the question, of course. Instead,
a special domain, **in-addr.arpa**, has been created which contains the IP addresses of all hosts in a reverted dotted-quad
notation. For instance, an IP address of **149.76.12.4** corresponds to the name **4.12.76.149.in-addr.arpa**. The resource
record type linking these names to their canonical host names is PTR.

Creating a zone of authority usually means that its administrators are given full control over how they assign addresses to
names. Since they usually have one or more IP networks or subnets at their hands, there's a one-to-many mapping between
DNS zones and IP networks. The Physics Department, for instance, comprises the subnets **149.76.8.0**, **149.76.12.0**, and
149.76.14.0.

As a consequence, new zones in the **in-addr.arpa** domain have to be created along with the **physics** zone and delegated to the network administrators at the department: **8.76.149.in-addr.arpa**, **12.76.149.in-addr.arpa**, and **14.76.149.in-
addr.arpa**. Otherwise, installing a new host at the Collider Lab would require them to contact their parent domain to
have the new address entered into their **in-addr.arpa** zone file.

The zone database for subnet 12 is shown in figure 2.6. The corresponding glue records in the database of their parent
zone is shown in figure 2.7.

One important consequence of this is that zones can only be created as supersets of IP networks, and, even more severe, that these network's netmasks have to be on byte boundaries. All subnets at Groucho Marx University have a
netmask of **255.255.255.0**, whence an **in-addr.arpa** zone could be created for each subnet. However, if the netmask was
255.255.255.128 instead, creating zones for the subnet **149.76.12.128** would be impossible, because there's no way to

```
;
; the 12.76.149.in-addr.arpa domain.
@               IN      SOA     {
                        niels.physics.groucho.edu.
                        hostmaster.niels.physics.groucho.edu.
                        233 360000 3600 3600000 3600
                    }
2               IN      PTR         otto.physics.groucho.edu.
4               IN      PTR         quark.physics.groucho.edu.
5               IN      PTR         down.physics.groucho.edu.
6               IN      PTR         strange.physics.groucho.edu.
```

Figure 2.6: An excerpt from the *named.rev* file for subnet 12.

```
;
; the 76.149.in-addr.arpa domain.
@                   IN      SOA         {
                        vax12.gcc.groucho.edu.
                        hostmaster.vax12.gcc.groucho.edu.
                        233 360000 3600 3600000 3600
                    }
...
; subnet 4: Mathematics Dept.
1.4             IN      PTR         sophus.maths.groucho.edu.
17.4            IN      PTR         erdos.maths.groucho.edu.
23.4            IN      PTR         gauss.maths.groucho.edu.
...
; subnet 12: Physics Dept, separate zone
12              IN      NS          niels.physics.groucho.edu.
                IN      NS          gauss.maths.groucho.edu.
niels.physics.groucho.edu. IN  A 149.76.12.1
gauss.maths.groucho.edu. IN  A   149.76.4.23
...
```

Figure 2.7: An excerpt from the *named.rev* file for network **149.76**.

tell DNS that the **12.76.149.in-addr.arpa** domain has been split in two zones of authority, with host names ranging from **1** through **127**, and **128** through **255**, respectively.

Chapter 3

Configuring the Networking Hardware

3.1   Devices, Drivers, and all that

Up to now, we've been talking quite a bit about network interfaces and general TCP/IP issues, but didn't really cover exactly *what* happens when "the networking code" in the kernel accesses a piece of hardware. For this, we have to talk a little about the concept of interfaces and drivers.

First, of course, there's the hardware itself, for example an Ethernet board: this is a slice of Epoxy, cluttered with lots of tiny chips with silly numbers on them, sitting in a slot of your PC. This is what we generally call a device.

For you to be able to use the Ethernet board, special functions have to be present in your Linux kernel that understand the particular way this device is accessed. These are the so-called device drivers. For example, Linux has device drivers for several brands of Ethernet boards that are very similar in function. They are known as the "Becker Series Drivers", named after their author, Donald Becker. A different example is the D-Link driver that handles a D-Link pocket adaptor attached to a parallel port.

But, what do we mean when we say a driver "handles" a device? Let's go back to that Ethernet board we examined above. The driver has to be able to communicate with the peripheral's on-board logic somehow: it has to send commands and data to the board, while the board should deliver any data received to the driver.

In PCs, this communication takes place through an area of I/O memory that is mapped to on-board registers and the like. All commands and data the kernel sends to the board have to go through these registers. I/O memory is generally described by giving its starting or *base address*. Typical base addresses for Ethernet boards are 0x300, or 0x360.

Usually, you don't have to worry about any hardware issues such as the base address, because the kernel makes an attempt at boot time to detect a board's location. This is called autoprobing, which means that the kernel reads several memory locations and compares the data read with what it should see if a certain Ethernet board was installed. However, there may be Ethernet boards it cannot detect automatically; this is sometimes the case with cheap Ethernet cards that are not-quite clones of standard boards from other manufacturers. Also, the kernel will attempt to detect only one Ethernet device when booting. If you're using more than one board, you have to tell the kernel about this board explicitly.

Another such parameter that you might have to tell the kernel about is the interrupt request channel. Hardware components usually interrupt the kernel when they need care taken of them, e.g. when data has arrived, or a special condition occurs. In a PC, interrupts may occur on one of 15 interrupt channels numbered 0, 1, and 3 through 15. The interrupt number assigned to a hardware component is called its *interrupt request number*, or IRQ.[1]

As described in chapter 2, the kernel accesses a device through a so-called interface. Interfaces offer an abstract set of functions that is the same across all types of hardware, such as sending or receiving a datagram.

Interfaces are identified by means of names. These are names defined internally in the kernel, and are not device files in the */dev* directory. Typical names are *eth0*, *eth1*, etc, for Ethernet interfaces. The assignment of interfaces to devices usually depends on the order in which devices are configured; for instance the first Ethernet board installed will become

---

[1] IRQs 2 and 9 are the same because the PC has two cascaded interrupt processors with eight IRQs each; the secondary processor is connected to IRQ 2 of the primary one.

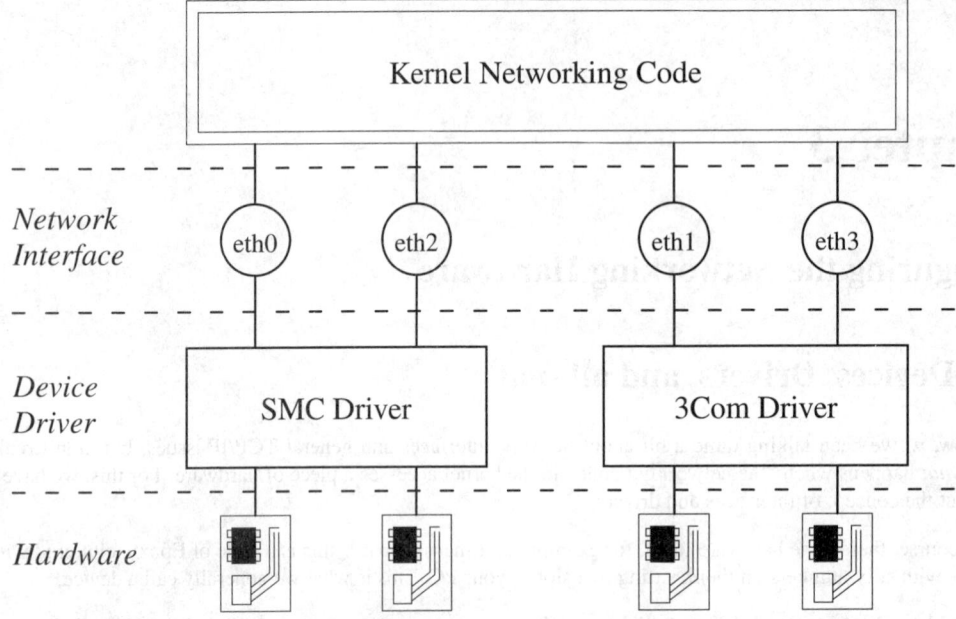

Figure 3.1: The relationship between drivers, interfaces, and the hardware.

eth0, the next will be *eth1*, and so on. One exception from this rule are SLIP interfaces, which are assigned dynamically; that is, whenever a SLIP connection is established, an interface is assigned to the serial port.

The picture given in figure 3.1 tries to show the relationship between the hardware, device drivers and interfaces.

When booting, the kernel displays what devices it detects, and what interfaces it installs. The following is an excerpt of a typical boot screen:

```
        .
        .
This processor honours the WP bit even when in supervisor mode. Good.
Floppy drive(s): fd0 is 1.44M
Swansea University Computer Society NET3.010
IP Protocols: ICMP, UDP, TCP
PPP: version 0.2.1 (4 channels) OPTIMIZE_FLAGS
TCP compression code copyright 1989 Regents of the University of California
PPP line discipline registered.
SLIP: version 0.7.5 (4 channels)
CSLIP: code copyright 1989 Regents of the University of California
dl0: D-Link DE-600 pocket adapter, Ethernet Address: 00:80:C8:71:76:95
Checking 386/387 coupling... Ok, fpu using exception 16 error reporting.
Linux version 1.1.11 (okir@monad) #3 Sat May 7 14:57:18 MET DST 1994
```

This shows that the kernel has been compiled with TCP/IP enabled, and drivers for SLIP, CSLIP, and PPP included. The third line from below says that a D-Link pocket adaptor was detected, and installed as interface *dl0*. If you have a different type of Ethernet card, the kernel will usually print a line starting with *eth0*, followed by the type of card detected. If you have an Ethernet card installed but don't see any such message, this means that the kernel is unable to detect your board properly. This is dealt with in a later section.

3.2   Kernel Configuration

Most Linux distributions come along with boot disks that work for all common types of PC hardware. This means that the kernel on those disks has all sorts of drivers configured in that you will never need, but which waste precious system memory because parts of the kernel cannot be swapped out. Therefore, you will generally roll your own kernel, including only those drivers you actually need or want.

When running a Linux system, you should be familiar with building a kernel. The basics of this are explained in Matt Welsh's "Installation and Getting Started" Guide, which is also part of the Linux Documentation Project's series. In this section, we will therefore discuss only those configuration options that affect networking.

When running `make config`, you will first be asked general configurations, for instance whether you want kernel math emulation or not, etc. One of these asks you whether you want TCP/IP networking support. You must answer this with `y` to get a kernel capable of networking.

3.2.1   Kernel Options in Linux 1.0 and Higher

After the general option part is complete, the configuration will go on to ask you for various features such as SCSI drivers, etc. The subsequent list questions deal with networking support. The exact set of configuration options is in constant flux because of the ongoing development. A typical list of options offered by most kernel versions around 1.0 and 1.1 looks like this (comments are given in italics):

```
*
* Network device support
*
Network device support? (CONFIG_ETHERCARDS) [y]
```

Despite the macro name displayed in brackets, you must answer this question with `y` if you want to use *any* type of networking devices, regardless of whether this is Ethernet, SLIP, or PPP. When answering this question with `y`, support for Ethernet-type devices is enabled automatically. Support for other types of network drivers must be enabled separately:

```
SLIP (serial line) support? (CONFIG_SLIP) [y]
 SLIP compressed headers (SL_COMPRESSED) [y]
PPP (point-to-point) support (CONFIG_PPP) [y]
PLIP (parallel port) support (CONFIG_PLIP) [n]
```

These questions concern the various link layer protocols supported by Linux. SLIP allows you to transport IP datagrams across serial lines. The compressed header option provides support for CSLIP, a technique that compresses TCP/IP headers to as little as three bytes. Note that this kernel option does not turn on CSLIP automatically, it merely provides the necessary kernel functions for it.

PPP is another protocol to send network traffic across serial lines. It is much more flexible than SLIP, and is not limited to IP, but will also support IPX once it is implemented. As PPP support has been completed only lately, this option may not be present in your kernel.

PLIP provides for a way to send IP datagrams across a parallel port connection. It is mostly used to communicate with PCs running DOS.

The following questions deal with Ethernet boards from various vendors. As more drivers are being developed, you are likely to see questions added to this section. If you want to build a kernel you can use on a number of different machines, you can enable more than one driver.

```
NE2000/NE1000 support (CONFIG_NE2000) [y]
WD80*3 support (CONFIG_WD80x3) [n]
SMC Ultra support (CONFIG_ULTRA) [n]
3c501 support (CONFIG_EL1) [n]
```

Net-Admin Guide

```
3c503 support (CONFIG_EL2) [n]
3c509/3c579 support (CONFIG_EL3) [n]
HP PCLAN support (CONFIG_HPLAN) [n]
AT1500 and NE2100 (LANCE and PCnet-ISA) support (CONFIG_LANCE) [n]
AT1700 support (CONFIG_AT1700) [n]
DEPCA support (CONFIG_DEPCA) [n]
D-Link DE600 pocket adaptor support (CONFIG_DE600) [y]
AT-LAN-TEC/RealTek pocket adaptor support (CONFIG_ATP) [n]
*
* CD-ROM drivers
*
...
```

Finally, in the filesystem section, the configuration script will ask you whether you want support for NFS, the networking filesystem. NFS lets you export filesystems to several hosts, which makes the files appear as if they were on an ordinary hard disk attached to the host.

```
NFS filesystem support (CONFIG_NFS_FS) [y]
```

3.2.2   Kernel Options in Linux 1.1.14 and Higher

Starting with Linux 1.1.14, which added alpha support for IPX, the configuration procedure changed slightly. The general options section now asks whether you want networking support in general. It is immediately followed by a couple of question on miscellaneous networking options.

```
*
* Networking options
*
TCP/IP networking (CONFIG_INET) [y]
```

To use TCP/IP networking, you must answer this question with y. If you answer with n, however, you will still be able to compile the kernel with IPX support.

```
IP forwarding/gatewaying (CONFIG_IP_FORWARD) [n]
```

You have to enable this option if your system acts as a gateway between two Ethernets, or between and Ethernet and a SLIP link, etc. Although it doesn't hurt to enable this by default, you may want to disable this to configure a host as a so-called firewall. Firewalls are hosts that are connected to two or more networks, but don't route traffic between them. They are commonly used to provide users from a company network with Internet access at a minimal risk to the internal network. Users will be allowed to log into the firewall and use Internet services, but the company's machines will be protected from outside attacks because any incoming connections can't cross the firewall.

```
*
* (it is safe to leave these untouched)
*
PC/TCP compatibility mode (CONFIG_INET_PCTCP) [n]
```

This option works around an incompatibility with some versions of PC/TCP, a commercial TCP/IP implementation for DOS-based PCs. If you enable this option, you will still be able to communicate with normal UNIX machines, but performance may be hurt over slow links.

```
Reverse ARP (CONFIG_INET_RARP) [n]
```

This function enables RARP, the Reverse Address Resolution Protocol. RARP is used by diskless clients and X terminals to inquire their IP address when booting. You should enable RARP only when you plan to serve this sort of clients. The latest package of network utilities (*net-0.32d*) contains a small utility named *rarp* that allows you to add systems to the RARP cache.

> Assume subnets are local (CONFIG_INET_SNARL) [y]

When sending data over TCP, the kernel has to break up the stream into several packets before giving it to IP. For hosts that can be reached over a local network such as an Ethernet, larger packets will be used than for hosts where data has to go through long-distance links.[2] If you don't enable *SNARL*, the kernel will assume only those networks are local that it actually has an interface to. However, if you look at the class B network at Groucho Marx University, the whole class B network is local, but most hosts interface to only one or two subnets. If you enable *SNARL*, the kernel will assume *all* subnets are local and use large packets when talking to all hosts on campus.

If you do want to use smaller packet sizes for data sent to specific hosts (because, for instance, the data goes through a SLIP link), you can do so using the *mtu* option of *route*, which is briefly discussed at the end of this chapter.

> Disable NAGLE algorithm (normally enabled) (CONFIG_TCP_NAGLE_OFF) [n]

Nagle's rule is a heuristic to avoid sending particularly small IP packets, also called tinygrams. Tinygrams are usually created by interactive networking tools that transmit single keystrokes, such as *telnet* or *rsh*. Tinygrams can become particularly wasteful on low-bandwidth links like SLIP. The Nagle algorithm attempts to avoid them by holding back transmission of TCP data briefly under some circumstances. You might only want to disable Nalge's algorithm if you have severe problems with packets getting dropped.

> The IPX protocol (CONFIG_IPX) [n]

This enables support for IPX, the transport protocol used by Novell Networking. It is still under development, and isn't really useful yet. One benefit of this will be that you can exchange data with IPX-based DOS utilities one day, and route traffic between your Novell-based networks through a PPP link. Support for the high-level protocols of Novell networking is however not in sight, as the specifications for these are available only at horrendous cost and under a non-disclosure agreement.

Starting in the 1.1.16 kernel, Linux supports another driver type, the dummy driver. The following question appears toward the start of the device driver section.

> Dummy net driver support (CONFIG_DUMMY) [y]

The dummy driver doesn't really do much, but is quite useful on standalone or SLIP hosts. It is basically a masqueraded loopback interface. The reason to have this sort of interface is that on hosts that do SLIP but have no Ethernet, you want to have an interface that bears your IP address all the time. This is discussed in a little more detail in section 5.7.7 in chapter 5.

3.3   A Tour of Linux Network Devices

The Linux kernel supports a number of hardware drivers for various types of equipment. This section gives a short overview of the driver families available, and the interface names used for them.

There are a number of standard names for interfaces in Linux, which are listed below. Most drivers support more than one interface, in which case the interfaces are numbered, as in *eth0*, *eth1*, etc.

---

[2]This is to avoid fragmentation by links that have a very small maximum packet size.

lo   The local loopback interface. It is used for testing purposes, as well as a couple of network applica-
                tions. It works like a closed circuit in that any datagram written to it will be immediately returned
                to the host's networking layer. There's always one loopback device present in the kernel, and there's
                little sense in having fewer or more.

ethn   The *n*-th Ethernet card. This is the generic interface name for most Ethernet boards.

dln   These interfaces access a D-Link DE-600 pocket adapter, another Ethernet device. It is a little special
                in that the DE-600 is driven through a parallel port.

sln   The *n*-th SLIP interface. SLIP interfaces are associated with serial lines in the order in which they
                are allocated for SLIP; i.e., the first serial line being configured for SLIP becomes *sl0*, etc. The kernel
                supports up to four SLIP interfaces.

pppn   The *n*-th PPP interface. Just like SLIP interfaces, a PPP interface is associated with a serial line once
                it is converted to PPP mode. At the moment, up to four interfaces are supported.

plipn   The *n*-th PLIP interface. PLIP transports IP datagrams over parallel lines. Up to three PLIP interfaces
                are supported. They are allocated by the PLIP driver at system boot time, and are mapped onto
                parallel ports.

For other interface drivers that may be added in the future, like ISDN, or AX.25, other names will be introduced. Drivers
for IPX (Novell's networking protocol), and AX.25 (used by ham radio amateurs) are under development, but are at alpha
stage still.

During the following sections, we will discuss the details of using the drivers described above.

3.4   Ethernet Installation

The current Linux network code supports various brands of Ethernet cards. Most drivers were written by Donald Becker
(**becker@cesdis.gsfc.nasa.gov**), who authored a family of drivers for cards based on the National Semiconductor 8390
chip; these have become known as the Becker Series Drivers. There are also drivers for a couple of products from
D-Link, among them the D-Link pocket adaptor that allows you to access an Ethernet through a parallel port. The
driver for this was written by Bjørn Ekwall (**bj0rn@blox.se**). The DEPCA driver was written by David C. Davies
(**davies@wanton.lkg.dec.com**).

3.4.1   Ethernet Cabling

If you're installing an Ethernet for the first time in your life, a few words about the cabling may be in order here. Ethernet
is very picky about proper cabling. The cable must be terminated on both ends with a 50 Ohm resistor, and you must not
have any branches (i.e. three cables connected in a star-shape). If you are using a thin coax cable with T-shaped BNC
junctions, these junctions must be twisted on the board's connector directly; you should not insert a cable segment.

If you connect to a thicknet installation, you have to attach your host through a transceiver (sometimes called Ethernet
Attachment Unit). You can plug the transceiver into the 15-pin AUI port on your board directly, but may also use a
shielded cable.

3.4.2   Supported Boards

A complete list of supported boards is available in the Ethernet HOWTOs posted monthly to **comp.os.linux.announce**
by Paul Gortmaker.[3]

Here's a list of the more widely-known boards supported by Linux. The actual list in the HOWTO is about three times
longer. However, even if you find your board in this list, check the HOWTO first; there are sometimes important details

---
[3]Paul can be reached at **gpg109@rsphysse.anu.edu.au**.

about operating these cards. A case in point is the case of some DMA-based Ethernet boards that use the same DMA channel as the Adaptec 1542 SCSI controller by default. Unless you move either of them to a different DMA channel, you will wind up with the Ethernet board writing packet data to arbitrary locations on your hard disk.

3Com EtherLink	Both 3c503 and 3c503/16 are supported, as are 3c507 and 3c509. The 3c501 is supported, too, but is too slow to be worth buying.
Novell Eagle	NE1000 and NE2000, and a variety of clones. NE1500 and NE2100 are supported, too.
Western Digital/SMC	WD8003 and WD8013 (same as SMC Elite and SMC Elite Plus) are supported, and also the newer SMC Elite 16 Ultra.
Hewlett Packard	HP 27252, HP 27247B, and HP J2405A.
D-Link	DE-600 pocket adaptor, DE-100, DE-200, and DE-220-T. There's also a patch kit for the DE-650-T, which is a PCMCIA card.[4]
DEC	DE200 (32K/64K), DE202, DE100, and DEPCA rev E.
Allied Teliesis	AT1500 and AT1700.

To use one of these cards with Linux, you may use a precompiled kernel from one of the major Linux distributions. These generally have drivers for all of them built in. In the long term, however, it's better to roll your own kernel and compile in only those drivers you actually need.

3.4.3 Ethernet Autoprobing

At boot time, the Ethernet code will try to locate your board and determine its type. Cards are probed for at the following addresses and in the following order:

Board	Addresses probed for
WD/SMC	0x300, 0x280, 0x380, 0x240
SMC 16 Ultra	0x300, 0x280
3c501	0x280
3c503	0x300, 0x310, 0x330, 0x350, 0x250, 0x280, 0x2a0, 0x2e0
NEx000	0x300, 0x280, 0x320, 0x340, 0x360
HP	0x300, 0x320, 0x340, 0x280, 0x2C0, 0x200, 0x240
DEPCA	0x300, 0x320, 0x340, 0x360

There are two limitations to the autoprobing code. For one, it may not recognize all boards properly. This is especially true for some of the cheaper clones of common boards, but also for some WD80x3 boards. The second problem is that the kernel will not auto-probe for more than one board at the moment. This is a feature, because it is assumed you want to have control about which board is assigned which interface.

If you are using more than one board, or if the autoprobe should fail to detect your board, you have to tell the kernel explicitly about the card's base address and name.

In Net-3, you have can use two different schemes to accomplish this. One way is to change or add information in the *drivers/net/Space.c* file in the kernel source code that contains all information about drivers. This is recommended only if you are familiar with the networking code. A much better way is to provide the kernel with this information at boot time. If you use *lilo* to boot your system, you can pass parameters to the kernel by specifying them through the *append* option in *lilo.conf*. To inform the kernel about an Ethernet device, you can pass the following parameter:

```
ether=irq,base_addr,param1,param2,name
```

---

[4]It can be gotten – along with other Laptop-related stuff – from **tsx-11.mit.edu** in *packages/laptops*.

The first four parameters are numerical, while the last is the device name. All numerical values are optional; if they are omitted or set to zero, the kernel will try to detect the value by probing for it, or use a default value.

The first parameter sets the IRQ assigned to the device. By default, the kernel will try to auto-detect the device's IRQ channel. The 3c503 driver has a special feature that selects a free IRQ from the list 5, 9, 3, 4, and configures the board to use this line.

The *base_addr* parameter gives the I/O base address of the board; a value of zero tells the kernel to probe the addresses listed above.

The remaining two parameters may be used differently by different drivers. For shared-memory boards such as the WD80x3, they specify start and end addresses of the shared memory area. Other cards commonly use *param1* to set the level of debugging information that is being displayed. Values of 1 through 7 denote increasing levels of verbosity, while 8 turns them off altogether; 0 denotes the default. The 3c503 driver uses *param2* to select the internal transceiver (default) or an external transceiver (a value of 1). The former uses the board's BNC connector; the latter uses its AUI port.

If you have two Ethernet boards, you can have Linux autodetect one board, and pass the second board's parameters with *lilo*. However, you must make sure the driver doesn't accidentally find the second board first, else the other one won't be registered at all. You do this by passing *lilo* a `reserve` option, which explicitly tells the kernel to avoid probing the I/O space taken up by the second board.

For instance, to make Linux install a second Ethernet board at 0x300 as *eth1*, you would pass the following parameters to the kernel:

```
reserve=0x300,32 ether=0,0x300,eth1
```

The *reserve* option makes sure no driver accesses the board's I/O space when probing for some device. You may also use the kernel parameters to override autoprobing for *eth0*:

```
reserve=0x340,32 ether=0,0x340,eth0
```

To turn off autoprobing altogether, you can specify a *base_addr* argument of -1:

```
ether=0,-1,eth0
```

3.5 The PLIP Driver

PLIP stands for *Parallel Line IP* and is a cheap way to network when you want to connect only two machines. It uses a parallel port and a special cable, achieving speeds of 10kBps to 20kBps.

PLIP was originally developed by Crynwr, Inc. Its design is rather ingenuous (or, if you prefer, hackish): for a long time, the parallel ports on PCs used to be only uni-directional printer ports; that is, the eight data lines could only be used to send from the PC to the peripheral device, but not the other way round. PLIP works around this by using the port's five status line for input, which limits it to transferring all data as nibbles (half bytes) only. This mode of operation is called mode zero PLIP. Today, these uni-directional ports don't seem to be used much anymore. Therefore, there is also a PLIP extension called mode 1 that uses the full 8 bit interface.

Currently, Linux only supports mode 0. Unlike earlier versions of the PLIP code, it now attempts to be compatible with the PLIP implementations from Crynwr, as well as the PLIP driver in NCSA *telnet*.[5] To connect two machines using PLIP, you need a special cable sold at some shops as "Null Printer" or "Turbo Laplink" cable. You can, however, make one yourself fairly easily. Appendix A shows you how.

---

[5]NCSA *telnet* is a popular program for DOS that runs TCP/IP over Ethernet or PLIP, and supports *telnet* and FTP.

The PLIP driver for Linux is the work of almost countless persons. It is currently maintained by Niibe Yutaka. If compiled into the kernel, it sets up a network interface for each of the possible printer ports, with *plip0* corresponding to parallel port *lp0*, *plip1* corresponding to *lp1*, etc. The mapping of interface to ports is currently this:

Interface	I/O Port	IRQ
plip0	0x3BC	7
plip1	0x378	7
plip2	0x278	5

If you have configured your printer port in a different way, you have to change these values in *drivers/net/Space.c* in the Linux kernel source, and build a new kernel.

This mapping does not mean, however, that you cannot use these parallel ports as usual. They are accessed by the PLIP driver only when the corresponding interface is configured *up*.

3.6 The SLIP and PPP Drivers

SLIP (Serial Line IP), and PPP (Point-to-Point Protocol) are a widely used protocol for sending IP packets over a serial link. A number of institutions offer dialup SLIP and PPP access to machines that are on the Internet, thus providing IP connectivity to private persons (something that's otherwise hardly affordable).

To run SLIP or PPP, no hardware modifications are necessary; you can use any serial port. Since serial port configuration is not specific to TCP/IP networking, a separate chapter has been devoted to this. Please refer to chapter 4 for more information.

Net-Admin Guide

Chapter 4

Setting up the Serial Hardware

There are rumors that there are some people out there in netland who only own one PC and don't have the money to spend on a T1 Internet link. To get their daily dose of news and mail nevertheless, they are said to rely on SLIP links, UUCP networks, and bulletin board systems (BBS's) that utilize public telephone networks.

This chapter is intended to help all those people who rely on modems to maintain their link. However, there are many details that this chapter cannot go into, for instance how to configure your modem for dialin. All these topics will be covered in the upcoming Serial HOWTO by Greg Hankins,[1] to be posted to **comp.os.linux.announce** on a regular basis.

4.1   Communication Software for Modem Links

There are a number of communication packages available for Linux. Many of them are *terminal programs* which allow a user to dial into another computer as if she was sitting in front of a simple terminal. The traditional terminal program for Unices is *kermit*. It is, however, somewhat Spartan. There are more comfortable programs available that support a dictionary of telephone numers, script languages for calling and logging into remote computer systems, etc. One of them is *minicom*, which is close to some terminal programs former DOS users might be accustomed to. There are also X-based communications packages, e.g. *seyon*.

Also, a number of Linux-based BBS packages are available for people that want to run a bulletin board system. Some of these packages can be found at **sunsite.unc.edu** in */pub/Linux/system/Network*.

Apart from terminal programs, there is also software that uses a serial link non-interactively to transport data to or from your computer. The advantage of this technique is that it takes much less time to download a few dozen kilobytes automatically, than it might take you to read your mail on-line in some mailbox and browse a bulletin board for interesting articles. On the other hand, this requires more disk storage because of the loads of useless information you usually get.

The epitome of this sort of communications software is UUCP. It is a program suite that copies files from one host to another, executes programs on a remote host, etc. It is frequently used to transport mail or news in private networks. Ian Taylor's UUCP package, which also runs under Linux, is described in the following chapter. Other non-interactive communication software is, for example, used throughout Fidonet. Ports of Fidonet applications like *ifmail* are also available.

SLIP, the serial line Internet protocol, is somewhat inbetween, allowing both interactive and non-interactive use. Many people use SLIP to dial up their campus network or some other sort of public SLIP server to run FTP sessions, etc. SLIP may however also be used over permanent or semi-permanent connections for LAN-to-LAN coupling, although this is really only interesting with ISDN.

---

[1] To be reached at **gregh@cc.gatech.edu**.

4.2   Introduction to Serial Devices

The devices a UNIX kernel provides for accessing serial devices are typically called *ttys*. This is an abbreviation for *Teletype*™, which used to be one of the major manufacturers of terminals in the early days of Unix. The term is used nowadays for any character-based data terminal. Throughout this chapter, we will use the term exclusively to refer to kernel devices.

Linux distinguishes three classes of ttys: (virtual) consoles, pseudo-terminals (similar to a two-way pipe, used by application such as X11), and serial devices. The latter are also counted as ttys, because they permit interactive sessions over a serial connection; be it from a hard-wired terminal or a remote computer over a telephone line.

Ttys have a number of configurable parameters which can be set using the *ioctl(2)* system call. Many of them apply only to serial devices, since they need a great deal more flexibility to handle varying types of connections.

Among the most prominent line parameters are the line speed and parity. But there are also flags for the conversion between upper and lower case characters, of carriage return into line feed, etc. The tty driver may also support various *line disciplines* which make the device driver behave completely different. For example, the SLIP driver for Linux is implemented by means of a special line discipline.

There is a bit of ambiguity about how to measure a line's speed. The correct the term is *Bit rate*, which is related to the line's transfer speed measured in bits per second (or bps for short). Sometimes, you hear people refer to it as the *Baud rate*, which is not quite correct. These two terms are, however, not interchangeable. The Baud rate refers to a physical characteristic of some serial device, namely the clock rate at which pulses are transmitted. The bit rate rather denotes a current state of an existing serial connection between two points, namely the average number of bits transferred per second. It is important to know that these two values are usually different, as most devices encode more than one bit per electrical pulse.

4.3   Accessing Serial Devices

Like all devices in a UNIX system, serial ports are accessed through device special files, located in the */dev* directory. There are two varieties of device files related to serial drivers, and for each port, there is one device file from each of them. Depending on the file it is accessed by, the device will behave differently.

The first variety is used whenever the port is used for dialing in; it has a major number of 4, and the files are named *ttyS0*, *ttyS1*, etc. The second variety is used when dialing out through a port; the files are called *cua0*, etc, and have a major number of 5.

Minor numbers are identical for both types. If you have your modem on one of the ports *COM1* through *COM4*, its minor number will be the *COM* port number plus 63. If your setup is different from that, for example when using a board supporting multiple serial lines, please refer to the Serial Howto.

Assume your modem is on *COM2*. Thus its minor number will be 65, and its major number will be 5 for dialing out. There should be a device *cua1* which has these numbers. List the serial ttys in the */dev* directory. Columns 5 and 6 should show major and minor numbers, respectively:

```
$ ls -l /dev/cua*
crw-rw-rw-   1 root      root       5,   64 Nov 30 19:31 /dev/cua0
crw-rw-rw-   1 root      root       5,   65 Nov 30 22:08 /dev/cua1
crw-rw-rw-   1 root      root       5,   66 Oct 28 11:56 /dev/cua2
crw-rw-rw-   1 root      root       5,   67 Mar 19  1992 /dev/cua3
```

If there is no such device, you will have to create one: become super-user and type

```
# mknod -m 666 /dev/cua1 c 5 65
# chown root.root /dev/cua1
```

Some people suggest making */dev/modem* a symbolic link to your modem device, so that casual users don't have to remember the somewhat unintuitive *cual*. However, you cannot use *modem* in one program, and the real device file name in another. This is because these programs use so-called *lock files* to signal that the device is used. By convention, the lock file name for *cual*, for instance, is *LCK..cual*. Using different device files for the same port means that programs will fail to recognize each other's lock files, and will both use the device at the same time. As a result, both applications will not work at all.

4.4 Serial Hardware

Linux currently supports a wide variety of serial boards which use the RS-232 standard. RS-232 is currently the most common standard for serial communnications in the PC world. It uses a number of circuits for transmitting single bits as well as for synchronization. Additional lines may be used for signaling the presence of a carrier (used by modems), and handshake.

Although hardware handshake is optional, it is very useful. It allows either of the two stations to signal whether it is ready to receive more data, or if the other station should pause until the receiver is done processing the incoming data. The lines used for this are called "Clear to Send" (CTS) and "Ready to Send" (RTS), respectively, which accounts for the colloquial name of hardware handshake, namely "RTS/CTS".

In PCs, the RS-232 interface is usually driven by a UART chip derived from the National Semiconductor 16450 chip, or a newer version thereof, the NSC 16550A[2]. Some brands (most notably internal modems equipped with the Rockwell chipset) also use completely different chips that have been programmed to behave as if they were 16550's.

The main difference between 16450's and 16550's that the latter have a FIFO buffer of 16 Bytes, while the former only have a 1-Byte buffer. This makes 16450's suitable for speeds up to 9600 Baud, while higher speeds require a 16550-compatible chip. Besides these chips, Linux also supports the 8250 chip, which was the original UART for the PC-AT.

In the default configuration, the kernel checks the four standard serial ports *COM1* through *COM4*. These will be assigned device minor numbers 64 through 67, as described above.

If you want to configure your serial ports properly, you should install Ted Tso's *setserial* command along with the *rc.serial* script. This script should be invoked from */etc/rc* at system boot time. It uses *setserial* to configure the kernel serial devices. A typical *rc.serial* script looks like this:

```
# /etc/rc.serial - serial line configuration script.
#
# Do wild interrupt detection
/sbin/setserial -W /dev/cua*

# Configure serial devices
/sbin/setserial /dev/cua0 auto_irq skip_test autoconfig
/sbin/setserial /dev/cua1 auto_irq skip_test autoconfig
/sbin/setserial /dev/cua2 auto_irq skip_test autoconfig
/sbin/setserial /dev/cua3 auto_irq skip_test autoconfig

# Display serial device configuration
/sbin/setserial -bg /dev/cua*
```

Please refer to the documentation that comes along with *setserial* for an explanation of the parameters.

If your serial card is not detected, or the *setserial -bg* command shows an incorrect setting, you will have to force the configuration by explicitly supplying the correct values. Users with internal modems equipped with the Rockwell chipset are reported to experience this problem. If, for example, the UART chip is reported to be a NSC 16450, while in fact it is NSC 16550-compatible, you have to change the configuration command for the offending port to

---

[2]There was also a NSC 16550, but it's FIFO never really worked.

```
/sbin/setserial /dev/cua1 auto_irq skip_test autoconfig uart 16550
```

Similar options exist to force *COM* port, base address, and IRQ setting. Please refer to the *setserial(8)* manual page.

If your modem supports hardware handshake, you should make sure to enable it. Surprising as it is, most communication programs do not attempt to enable this by default; you have to set it manually instead. This is best performed in the *rc.serial* script, using the *stty* command:

```
$ stty crtscts < /dev/cua1
```

To check if hardware handshake is in effect, use

```
$ stty -a < /dev/cua1
```

This gives you the status of all flags for that device; a flag shown with a preceding minus as in -crtscts means that the flag has been turned off.

Chapter 5

Configuring TCP/IP Networking

In this chapter, we will go through all the steps necessary to setting up TCP/IP networking on your machine. Starting with the assignment of IP addresses, we will slowly work our way through the configuration of TCP/IP network interfaces, and introduce a few tools that come quite handy when hunting down problems with your network installation.

Most of the tasks covered in this chapter you will generally have to do only once. Afterwards, you have to touch most configuration files only when adding a new system to your network, or when you reconfigure your system entirely. Some of the commands used to configure TCP/IP, however, have to be executed each time the system is booted. This is usually done by invoking them from the system /etc/rc scripts.

Commonly, the network-specific part of this procedure is contained in a script called rc.net or rc.inet. Sometimes, you will also see two scripts named rc.inet1 and rc.inet2, where the former initializes the kernel part of networking, while the latter starts basic networking services and applications. Throughout the following, I will adhere to the latter concept.

Below, I will discuss the actions performed by rc.inet1, while applications will be covered in later chapters. After finishing this chapter, you should have established a sequence of commands that properly configure TCP/IP networking on your computer. You should then replace any sample commands in rc.inet1 with your commands, make sure rc.inet1 is executed at startup time, and reboot your machine. The networking rc scripts that come along with your favorite Linux distribution should give you a good example.

5.1   Setting up the *proc* Filesystem

Some of the configuration tools of the Net-2 release rely on the *proc* filesystem for communicating with the kernel. This is an interface that permits access to kernel run-time information through a filesystem-like mechanism. When mounted, you can list its files like any other filesystem, or display their contents. Typical items include the *loadavg* file that contains the system load average, or *meminfo*, which shows current core memory and swap usage.

To this, the networking code adds the *net* directory. It contains a number of files that show things like the kernel ARP tables, the state of TCP connections, and the routing tables. Most network administration tools get their information from these files.

The *proc* filesystem (or *procfs* as it is also known) is usually mounted on /proc at system boot time. The best method is to add the following line to /etc/fstab:

```
# procfs mont point:
none /proc proc defaults
```

and execute "mount /proc" from your /etc/rc script.

The *procfs* is nowadays configured into most kernels by default. If the *procfs* is not in your kernel, you will get a message like "mount: fs type procfs not supported by kernel". You will then have to recompile the kernel and answer "yes" when asked for *procfs* support.

5.2   Installing the Binaries

If you are using one of the pre-packaged Linux distributions, it will most probably contain the major networking applications and utilities along with a coherent set of sample files. The only case where you might have to obtain and install new
utilities is when you install a new kernel release. As they occasionally involve changes in the kernel networking layer,
you will need to update the basic configuration tools. This at least involves recompiling, but sometimes you may also be
required to obtain the latest set of binaries. These are usually distributed along with the kernel, packaged in an archive
called *net-XXX.tar.gz*, where *XXX* is the version number. The release matching Linux 1.0 is 0.32b, the latest kernel as of
this writing (1.1.12 and later) require 0.32d.

If you want to compile and install the standard TCP/IP network applications yourself, you can obtain the sources from
most Linux FTP servers. These are more or less heavily patched versions of programs from Net-BSD or other sources.
Other applications, such as *Xmosaic*, *xarchie*, or Gopher and IRC clients must be obtained separately. Most of them
compile out of the box if you follow the instructions.

The official FTP site for Net-3 is **sunacm.swan.ac.uk**, mirrored by **sunsite.unc.edu** below *system/Network/sunacm*. The
latest Net-2e patch kit and binaries are available from **ftp.aris.com**. Matthias Urlichs' BSD-derived networking code can
be gotten from **ftp.ira.uka.de** in */pub/system/linux/netbsd*.

5.3   Another Example

For the remainder of this book, let me introduce a new example that is less complex than Groucho Marx University, and
may be closer to the tasks you will actually encounter. Consider the Virtual Brewery, a small company that brews, as
the name indicates, virtual beer. To manage their business more efficiently, the virtual brewers want to network their
computers, which all happen to be PCs running a bright and shiny Linux 1.0.

On the same floor, just across the hall, there's the Virtual Winery, who work closely with the brewery. They run an
Ethernet of their own. Quite naturally, the two companies want to link their networks once they are operational. As a first
step, they want to set up a gateway host that forwards datagrams between the two subnets. Later, they also want to have
a UUCP link to the outside world, through which they exchange mail and news. In the long run, the also want to set up a
SLIP connection to connect to the Internet occasionally.

5.4   Setting the Hostname

Most, if not all, network applications rely on the local host's name having been set to some reasonable value. This is
usually done during the boot procedure by executing the *hostname* command. To set the hostname to *name*, it is invoked
as

```
# hostname name
```

It is common practice to use the unqualified hostname without any domain name for this. For instance, hosts at the Virtual
Brewery might be called **vale.vbrew.com**, **vlager.vbrew.com**, etc. These are their official, fully qualified domain names.
Their local hostnames would be only the first component of the name, such as **vale**. However, as the local hostname is
frequently used to look up the host's IP address, you have to make sure that the resolver library is able to look up the
host's IP address. This usually means that you have to enter the name in */etc/hosts* (see below).

Some people suggest to use the *domainname* command to set the kernel's idea of a domain name to the remaining part of
the FQDN. In this way you could combine the output from *hostname* and *domainname* to get the FQDN again. However,
this is at best only half correct. *domainname* is generally used to set the host's NIS domain, which may be entirely
different from the DNS domain your host belongs to. NIS is covered in chapter 10.

5.5   Assigning IP Addresses

If you configure the networking software on your host for standalone operation (for instance, to be able to run the INN netnews software), you can safely skip this section, because you will need an IP address just for the loopback interface, which is always **127.0.0.1**.

Things are a little more complicated with real networks like Ethernets. If you want to connect your host to an existing network, you have to ask its administrators to give you an IP address on this network. When setting up the network all by yourself, you have to assign IP addresses yourself as described below.

Hosts within a local network should usually share addresses from the same logical IP network. Hence you have to assign an IP network address. If you have several physical networks, you either have to assign them different network numbers, or use subnetting to split your IP address range into several subnetworks.

If your network is not connected to the Internet, you are free to choose any (legal) network address. You only have to make sure to choose one from classes A, B, or C, else things will most likely not work properly. However, if you intend to get on the Internet in the near future, you should obtain an official IP address *now*. The best way to proceed is to ask your network service provider to help you. If you want to obtain a network number just in case you might get on the Internet someday, request a Network Address Application Form from **hostmaster@internic.net**.

To operate several Ethernets (or other networks, once a driver is available), you have to split your network into subnets. Note that subnetting is required only if you have more than one *broadcast network*; point-to-point links don't count. For instance, if you have one Ethernet, and one or more SLIP links to the outside world, you don't need to subnet your network. The reason for this will be explained in chapter 7.

As an example, the brewery's network manager applies to the NIC for a class B network number, and is given **191.72.0.0**. To accomodate the two Ethernets, she decides to use eight bits of the host part as additional subnet bits. This leaves another eight bits for the host part, allowing for 254 hosts on each of the subnets. She then assigns subnet number 1 to the brewery, and gives the winery number 2. Their respective network addresses are thus **191.72.1.0** and **191.72.2.0**. The subnet mask is **255.255.255.0**.

vlager, which is the gateway between the two networks, is assigned a host number of 1 on both of them, which gives it the IP addresses **191.72.1.1** and **191.72.2.1**, respectively. Figure 5.1 shows the two subnets, and the gateway.

Note that in this example I am using a class B network to keep things simple; a class C network would be more realistic. With the new networking code, subnetting is not limited to byte boundaries, so even a class C network may be split into several subnets. For instance, you could use 2 bits of the host part for the netmask, giving you four possible subnets with 64 hosts on each.[1]

5.6   Writing *hosts* and *networks* Files

After you have subnetted your network, you should prepare for some simple sort of hostname resolution using the */etc/hosts* file. If you are not going to use DNS or NIS for address resolution, you have to put all hosts in the *hosts* file.

Even if you want to run DNS or NIS during normal operation, you want to have some subset of all hostnames in */etc/hosts* nevertheless. For one, you want to have some sort of name resolution even when no network interfaces are running, for example during boot time. This is not only a matter of convenience, but also allows you to use symbolic hostnames in your *rc.inet* scripts. Thus, when changing IP addresses, you only have to copy an updated *hosts* file to all machines and reboot, rather than having to edit a large number of *rc* files separately. Usually, you will put all local hostnames and addresses in *hosts*, adding those of any gateways and NIS servers if used.[2]

---

[1]The last number on each subnet is reserved as the broadcast address, so it's in fact 63 hosts per subnet.

[2]You will need the address of any NIS servers only if you use Peter Eriksson's NYS. Other NIS implementations locate their servers at run-time only by using *ypbind*.

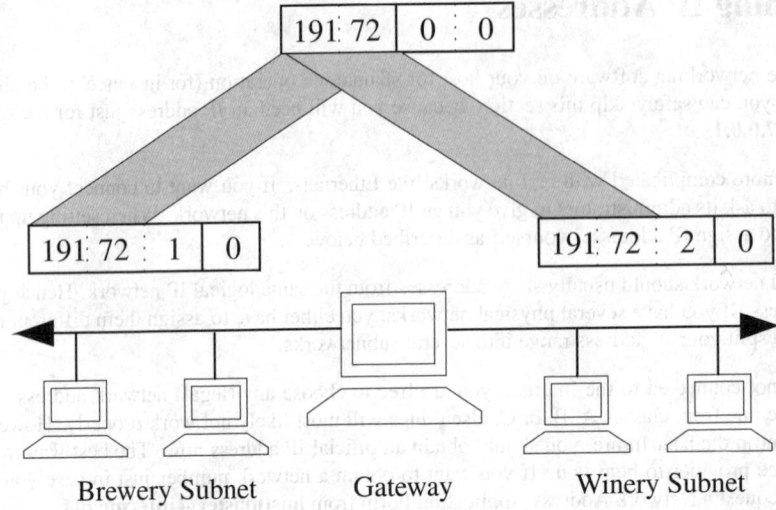

Figure 5.1: Virtual Brewery and Virtual Winery – the two subnets.

Also, during intial testing, you should make sure your resolver only uses information from the *hosts* file. Your DNS or NIS software may come with sample files that may produce strange results when being used. To make all applications use */etc/hosts* exclusively when looking up the IP address of a host, you have to edit the */etc/host.conf* file. Comment out any lines that begin with the keyword *order* by preceding them with a hash sign, and insert the line

```
order hosts
```

The configuration of the resolver library will be covered in detail in chapter 6.

The *hosts* file contains one entry per line, consisting of an IP address, a hostname, and an optional list of aliases for the hostname. The fields are separated by spaces or tabs, and the address field must begin in column one. Anything following a hash sign (*#*) is regarded as a comment and is ignored.

Hostnames can be either fully qualified, or relative to the local domain. For **vale**, you would usually enter the the fully qualified name, **vale.vbrew.com**, and **vale** by itself in the *hosts* file, so that it is known by both its official name and the shorter local name.

This is an example how a *hosts* file at the Virtual Brewery might look. Two special names are included, **vlager-if1** and **vlager-if2** that give the addresses for both interfaces used on **vlager**.

```
#
# Hosts file for Virtual Brewery/Virtual Winery
#
# IP          local         fully qualified domain name
#
127.0.0.1     localhost
#
191.72.1.1    vlager        vlager.vbrew.com
191.72.1.1    vlager-if1
191.72.1.2    vstout        vstout.vbrew.com
191.72.1.3    vale          vale.vbrew.com
#
```

```
191.72.2.1        vlager-if2
191.72.2.2        vbeaujolais     vbeaujolais.vbrew.com
191.72.2.3        vbardolino      vbardolino.vbrew.com
191.72.2.4        vchianti        vchianti.vbrew.com
```

Just as with a host's IP address, you sometimes would like to use a symbolic name for network numbers, too. Therefore, the *hosts* file has a companion called */etc/networks* that maps network names to network numbers and vice versa. At the Virtual Brewery, we might install a *networks* file like this:[3]

```
# /etc/networks for the Virtual Brewery
brew-net     191.72.1.0
wine-net     191.72.2.0
```

5.7 Interface Configuration for IP

After setting up your hardware as explained in the previous chapter, you have to make these devices known to the kernel networking software. A couple of commands are used to configure the network interfaces, and initialize the routing table. These tasks are usually performed from the *rc.inet1* script each time the system is booted. The basic tools for this are called *ifconfig* (where "if" stands for interface), and *route*.

ifconfig is used to make an interface accessible to the kernel networking layer. This involves the assignment of an IP address and other parameters, and activating the interface, also known as "taking up." Being active here means that the kernel will send and receive IP datagrams through the interface. The simplest way to invoking it is

> ifconfig *interface ip-address*

which assigns *ip-address* to *interface* and activates it. All other parameters are set to default values. For instance, the default subnet mask is derived from the network class of the IP address, such as **255.255.0.0** for a class B address. *ifconfig* is described in detail at the end of this chapter.

route allows you to add or remove routes from the kernel routing table. It can be invoked as

> route [add|del] *target*

where the add and del arguments determine whether to add or delete the route to *target*.

5.7.1 The Loopback Interface

The very first interface to be activated is the loopback interface:

```
# ifconfig lo 127.0.0.1
```

Occasionally, you will also see the dummy hostname **localhost** being used instead of the IP address. *ifconfig* will look up the name in the *hosts* file where an entry should declare it as the hostname for **127.0.0.1**:

```
# Sample /etc/hosts entry for localhost
localhost     127.0.0.1
```

To view the configuration of an interface, you invoke *ifconfig* giving it the interface name as argument:

---

[3]Note that names in *networks* must not collide with hostnames from the *hosts* file, else some programs may produce strange results.

```
$ ifconfig lo
lo            Link encap Local Loopback
              inet addr 127.0.0.1  Bcast [NONE SET]  Mask 255.0.0.0
              UP BROADCAST LOOPBACK RUNNING  MTU 2000  Metric 1
              RX packets 0 errors 0 dropped 0 overrun 0
              TX packets 0 errors 0 dropped 0 overrun 0
```

As you can see, the loopback interface has been assigned a netmask of **255.0.0.0**, since **127.0.0.1** is a class A address. As you can see, the interface doesn't have a broadcast address set, which isn't normally very useful for the loopback anyway. However, if you run the *rwhod* daemon on your host, you may have to set the loopback device's broadcast address in order for *rwho* to function properly. Setting the broadcast is explained in section "All about *ifconfig*" below.

Now, you can almost start playing with your mini-"network." What is still missing is an entry in the routing table that tells IP that it may use this interface as route to destination **127.0.0.1**. This is accomplished by typing

```
# route add 127.0.0.1
```

Again, you can use **localhost** instead of the IP address.

Next, you should check that everything works fine, for example by using *ping*. *ping* is the networking equivalent of a sonar device[4] and is used to verify that a given address is actually reachable, and to measure the delay that occurs when sending a datagram to it and back again. The time required for this is often referred to as the round-trip time.

```
# ping localhost
PING localhost (127.0.0.1): 56 data bytes
64 bytes from 127.0.0.1: icmp_seq=0 ttl=32 time=1 ms
64 bytes from 127.0.0.1: icmp_seq=1 ttl=32 time=0 ms
64 bytes from 127.0.0.1: icmp_seq=2 ttl=32 time=0 ms
^C
--- localhost ping statistics ---
3 packets transmitted, 3 packets received, 0% packet loss
round-trip min/avg/max = 0/0/1 ms
```

When invoking *ping* as shown here, it will go on emitting packets forever unless interrupted by the user. The ^C above marks the place where we pressed Ctrl-C.

The above example shows that packets for **127.0.0.1** are properly delivered and a reply is returned to *ping* almost instantaneously. This shows you have succeeded in setting up your first network interface.

If the output you get from *ping* does not resemble that shown above, you are in trouble. Check any error if they indicate some file hasn't been installed properly. Check that the *ifconfig* and *route* binaries you use are compatible with the kernel release you run, and, above all, that the kernel has been compiled with networking enabled (you see this from the presence of the */proc/net* directory). If you get an error message saying "Network unreachable," then you probably have got the *route* command wrong. Make sure you use the same address as you gave to *ifconfig*.

The steps described above are enough to use networking applications on a standalone host. After adding the above lines to *rc.inet1* and making sure both *rc.inet* scripts are executed from */etc/rc*, you may reboot your machine and try out various applications. For instance, "*telnet localhost*" should establish a *telnet* connection to your host, giving you a login prompt.

However, the loopback interface is useful not only as an example in networking books, or as a testbed during development, but is actually used by some applications during normal operation.[5] Therefore, you always have to configure it, regardless of whether your machine is attached to a network or not.

---

[4] Anyone remember Pink Floyd's "Echoes"?

[5] For instance, all applications based on RPC use the loopback interface to register themselves with the *portmapper* daemon at startup.

5.7.2 Ethernet Interfaces

Configuring an Ethernet interface goes pretty much the same as with the loopback interface, it just requires a few more parameters when you are using subnetting.

At the Virtual Brewery, we have subnetted the IP network, which was originally a class B network, into class C subnetworks. To make the interface recognize this, the *ifconfig* incantation would look like this:

```
# ifconfig eth0 vstout netmask 255.255.255.0
```

This assigns the *eth0* interface the IP address of **vstout** (**191.72.1.2**). If we had omitted the netmask, *ifconfig* would have deduced the the netmask from the IP network class, which would have resulted in a netmask of **255.255.0.0**. Now a quick check shows:

```
# ifconfig eth0
eth0      Link encap 10Mps Ethernet  HWaddr  00:00:C0:90:B3:42
          inet addr 191.72.1.2 Bcast 191.72.1.255 Mask 255.255.255.0
          UP BROADCAST RUNNING  MTU 1500  Metric 1
          RX packets 0 errors 0 dropped 0 overrun 0
          TX packets 0 errors 0 dropped 0 overrun 0
```

You can see that *ifconfig* automatically set the broadcast address (the Bcast field above) to the usual value, which is the hosts network number with the host bits all set. Also, the message transfer unit (the maximum size of Ethernet frames the kernel will generate for this interface) has been set to the maximum value of 1500 bytes. All these values can be overidden with special options that will be described later.

Quite similar to the loopback case, you now have to install a routing entry that informs the kernel about the network that can be reached through *eth0*. For the Virtual Brewery, you would invoke *route* as

```
# route add -net 191.72.1.0
```

At first, this looks a little like magic, because it's not really clear how *route* detects which interface to route through. However, the trick is rather simple: the kernel checks all interfaces that have been configured so far and compares the destination address (**191.72.1.0** in this case) to the network part of the interface address (that is, the bitwise and of the interface address and the netmask). The only interface that matches is *eth0*.

Now, what's that -net option for? This is used because *route* can handle both routes to networks and routes to single hosts (as you have seen above with **localhost**). When being given an address in dotted quad notation, it attempts to guess whether it is a network or a hostname by looking at the host part bits. If the address' host part is zero, *route* assumes it denotes a network, otherwise it takes it as a host address. Therefore, *route* would think that **191.72.1.0** is a host address rather than a network number, because it cannot know that we use subnetting. We therefore have to tell it explicitly that it denotes a network, giving it the -net flag.

Of course, the above *route* command is a little tedious to type, and it's prone to spelling mistakes. A more convenient approach is to use the network names we have defined in */etc/networks* above. This makes the command much more readable; even the -net flag can now be omitted, because *route* now knows that **191.72.1.0** denotes a network.

```
# route add brew-net
```

Now that you've finished the basic configuration steps, we want to make sure your Ethernet interface is indeed running happily. Choose a host from your Ethernet, for instance **vlager**, and type

```
# ping vlager
PING vlager: 64 byte packets
64 bytes from 191.72.1.1: icmp_seq=0. time=11. ms
64 bytes from 191.72.1.1: icmp_seq=1. time=7. ms
```

```
64 bytes from 191.72.1.1: icmp_seq=2. time=12. ms
64 bytes from 191.72.1.1: icmp_seq=3. time=3. ms
^C

----vstout.vbrew.com PING Statistics----
4 packets transmitted, 4 packets received, 0% packet loss
round-trip (ms)  min/avg/max = 3/8/12
```

If you don't see any output similar to this, then something is broken, obviously. If you encounter unusual packet loss rates, this hints at a hardware problem, like bad or missing terminators, etc. If you don't receive any packets at all, you should check the interface configuration with *netstat*. The packet statistics displayed by *ifconfig* should tell you whether any packets have been sent out on the interface at all. If you have access to the remote host, too, you should go over to that machine and check the interface statistics, too. In this way, you can determine exactly where the packets got dropped. In addition, you should display the routing information with *route* to see if both hosts have the correct routing entry. *route* prints out the complete kernel routing table when invoked without any arguments (the -n option only makes it print addresses as dotted quad instead of using the hostname):

```
# route -n
Kernel routing table
Destination      Gateway        Genmask          Flags Metric Re-
f Use    Iface
127.0.0.1        *              255.255.255.255 UH     1     0       112 lo
191.72.1.0       *              255.255.255.0   U      1     0        10 eth0
```

The detailed meaning of these fields is explained below in section 5.9. The Flag column contains a list of flags set for each interface. U is always set for active interfaces, and H says the destination address denotes a host. If the H flag is set for a route that you meant to be a network route, then you have to specify the -net option with the *route* command. To check whether a route you have entered is used at all, check if the Use field in the second to last column increases between two invocations of *ping*.

5.7.3   Routing through a Gateway

In the previous section, I covered only the case of setting up a host on a single Ethernet. Quite frequently, however, one encounters networks connected to one another by gateways. These gateways may simply link two or more Ethernets, but may provide a link to the outside world, the Internet, as well. In order to use the service of a gateway, you have to provide additional routing information to the networking layer.

For instance, the Ethernets of the Virtual Brewery and the Virtual Winery are linked through such a gateway, namely the host **vlager**. Assuming that **vlager** has already been configured, we only have to add another entry to **vstout**'s routing table that tells the kernel it can reach all hosts on the Winery's network through **vlager**. The appropriate incantation of *route* is shown below; the gw keyword tells it that the next argument denotes a gateway.

```
# route add wine-net gw vlager
```

Of course, any host on the Winery network you wish to talk to must have a corresponding routing entry for the Brewery's network, otherwise you would only be able to send data from **vstout** to **vbardolino**, but any response returned by the latter would go into the great bit bucket.

This example describes only a gateway that switches packets between two isolated Ethernets. Now assume that **vlager** also has a connection to the Internet (say, through an additional SLIP link). Then we would want datagrams to *any* destination network other than the Brewery to be handed to **vlager**. This can be accomplished by making it the default gateway for **vstout**:

```
# route add default gw vlager
```

The network name **default** is a shorthand for **0.0.0.0**, which denotes the default route. You do not have to add this name to */etc/networks*, because it is built into *route*.

When you see high packet loss rates when *ping*ing a host behind one or more gateways, this may hint at a very congested network. Packet loss is not so much due to technical deficiencies as due to temporary excess loads on forwarding hosts, which makes them delay or even drop incoming datagrams.

5.7.4   Configuring a Gateway

Configuring a machine to switch packets between two Ethernets is pretty straightforward. Assume we're back at **vlager**, which is equipped with two Ethernet boards, each being connected to one of the two networks. All you have to do is configure both interfaces separately, giving them their respective IP address, and that's it.

It is quite useful to add information on the two interfaces to the *hosts* file in the way shown below, so we have handy names for them, too:

```
191.72.1.1        vlager        vlager.vbrew.com
191.72.1.1        vlager-if1
191.72.2.1        vlager-if2
```

The sequence of commands to set up the two interfaces is then:

```
# ifconfig eth0 vlager-if1
# ifconfig eth1 vlager-if2
# route add brew-net
# route add wine-net
```

5.7.5   The PLIP Interface

When using a PLIP link to connect two machines, things are a little different from what you have to do when using an Ethernet. The former are so-called *point-to-point* links, because they involve ony two hosts ("points"), as opposed to broadcast networks.

As an example, we consider the laptop computer of some employee at the Virtual Brewery that is connected to **vlager** via PLIP. The laptop itself is called **vlite**, and has only one parallel port. At boot time, this port will be registered as *plip1*. To activate the link, you have to configure the *plip1* interface using the following commands:[6]

```
# ifconfig plip1 vlite pointopoint vlager
# route add default gw vlager
```

The first command configures the interface, telling the kernel that this is a point-to-point link, with the remote side having the address of **vlager**. The second installs the default route, using **vlager** as gateway. On **vlager**, a similar *ifconfig* command is necessary to activate the link (a *route* invocation is not needed):

```
# ifconfig plip1 vlager pointopoint vlite
```

The interesting point is that the *plip1* interface on **vlager** does not have to have a separate IP address, but may also be given the address **191.72.1.1**.[7]

Now, we have configured routing from the laptop to the Brewery's network; what's still missing is a way to route from any of the Brewery's hosts to **vlite**. One particularly cumbersome way is to add a specific route to every host's routing table that names **vlager** as a gateway to **vlite**:

---

[6]Note that `pointopoint` is not a typo. It's really spelt like this.

[7]Just as a matter of caution, you should however configure a PLIP or SLIP link only after you have completely set up the routing table entries for your Ethernets. With some older kernels, your network route might otherwise end up pointing at the point-to-point link.

```
# route add vlite gw vlager
```

A much better option when faced with temporary routes is to use dynamic routing. One way to do so is to use *gated*, a routing daemon, which you would have to install on each host in the network in order to distribute routing information dynamically. The easiest way, however, is to use *proxy* ARP. With proxy ARP, **vlager** will respond to any ARP query for **vlite** by sending its own Ethernet address. The effect of this is that all packets for **vlite** will wind up at **vlager**, which then forwards them to the laptop. We will come back to proxy ARP in section 5.10 below.

Future Net-3 releases will contain a tool called *plipconfig* which will allow you to set the IRQ of the printer port to use. Later, this may even be replaced by a more general *ifconfig* command.

5.7.6   The SLIP and PPP Interface

Although SLIP and PPP links are only simple point-to-point links like PLIP connections, there is much more to be said about them. Usually, establishing a SLIP connection involves dialing up a remote site through your modem, and setting the serial line to SLIP mode. PPP is used in a similar fashion. The tools required for setting up a SLIP or PPP link will be described in chapters 7 and 8.

5.7.7   The Dummy Interface

The dummy interface is really a little exotic, but rather useful nevertheless. Its main benefit is with standalone hosts, and machines whose only IP network connection is a dial-up link. In fact, the latter are standalone hosts most of the time, too.

The dilemma with standalone hosts is that they only have a single network device active, the loopback device, which is usually assigned the address **127.0.0.1**. On some occasions, however, you need to send data to the 'official' IP address of the local host. For instance, consider the laptop **vlite**, that has been disconnected from any network for the duration of this example. An application on **vlite** may now want to send some data to another application on the same host. Looking up **vlite** in */etc/hosts* yields an IP address of **191.72.1.65**, so the application tries to send to this address. As the loopback interface is currently the only active interface on the machine, the kernel has no idea that this address actually refers to itself! As a consequence, the kernel discards the datagram, and returns an error to the application.

This is where the dummy device steps in. It solves the dilemma by simply serving as the alter ego of the loopback interface. In the case of **vlite**, you would simply give it the address **191.72.1.65** and add a host route pointing to it. Every datagram for **191.72.1.65** would then be delivered locally. The proper invocation is:

```
# ifconfig dummy vlite
# route add vlite
```

5.8   All About *ifconfig*

There are a lot more parameters to *ifconfig* than we have described above. Its normal invocation is this:

```
ifconfig interface [[-net|-host] address [parameters]]
```

interface is the interface name, and *address* is the IP address to be assigned to the interface. This may either be an IP address in dotted quad notation, or a name *ifconfig* will look up in */etc/hosts* and */etc/networks*. The -net and -host options force *ifconfig* to treat the address as network number or host address, respectively.

If *ifconfig* is invoked with only the interface name, it displays that interface's configuration. When invoked without any parameters, it displays all interfaces you configured so far; an option of -a forces it to show the inactive ones as well. A sample invocation for the Ethernet interface *eth0* may look like this:

```
# ifconfig eth0
eth0      Link encap 10Mbps Ethernet  HWaddr 00:00:C0:90:B3:42
          inet addr 191.72.1.2 Bcast 191.72.1.255 Mask 255.255.255.0
          UP BROADCAST RUNNING  MTU 1500  Metric 0
          RX packets 3136 errors 217 dropped 7 overrun 26
          TX packets 1752 errors 25 dropped 0 overrun 0
```

The MTU and Metric fields show the current MTU and metric value for that interface. The metric value is traditionally used by some operating systems to compute the cost of a route. Linux doesn't use this value yet, but defines it for compatibility nevertheless.

The RX and TX lines show how many packets have been received or transmitted error free, how many errors occurred, how many packets were dropped, probably because of low memory, and how many were lost because of an overrun. Receiver overruns usually happen when packets come in faster than the kernel can service the last interrupt. The flag values printed by *ifconfig* correspond more or less to the names of its command line options; they will be explained below.

The following is a list of parameters recognized by *ifconfig* with the corresponding flag names are given in brackets. Options that simply turn on a feature also allow it to be turned off again by preceding the option name by a dash (-).

up   This marks an interface "up", i.e. accessible to the IP layer. This option is implied when an *address* is given on the command line. It may also be used to re-eenable an interface that has been taken down temporarily using the down option.

              (This option corresponds to the flags UP RUNNING.)

down   This marks an interface "down", i.e. inaccessible to the IP layer. This effectively disables any IP traffic through the interface. Note that this does not delete all routing entries that use this interface automatically. If you take the interface down permanently, you should to delete these routing entries and supply alternative routes if possible.

netmask *mask*   This assigns a subnet mask to be used by the interface. It may be given as either a 32-bit hexadecimal number preceded by 0x, or as a dotted quad of decimal numbers.

pointopoint *address*   This option is used for point-to-point IP links that involve only two hosts. This option is needed to configure, for example, SLIP or PLIP interfaces.

              (If a point-to-point address has been set, *ifconfig* displays the POINTOPOINT flag.)

broadcast *address*   The broadcast address is usually made up from the network number by setting all bits of the host part. Some IP implementations use a different scheme; this option is there to adapt to these strange environments.

              (If a broadcast address has been set, *ifconfig* displays the BROADCAST flag.)

metric *number*   This option may be used to assign a metric value to the routing table entry created for the interface. This metric is used by the Routing Information Protocol (RIP) to build routing tables for the network.[8] The default metric used by *ifconfig* is a value of zero. If you don't run a RIP daemon, you don't need this option at all; if you do, you will rarely need to change the metric value.

mtu *bytes*   This sets the Maximum Transmission Unit, which is the maximum number of octets the interface is able to handle in one transaction. For Ethernets, the MTU defaults to 1500; for SLIP interfaces, this is 296.

arp   This is an option specific to broadcast networks such as Ethernets or packet radio. It enables the use of ARP, the Address Resolution Protocol, to detect the physical addresses of hosts attached to the network. For broadcast networks, is on by default.

---

[8] RIP chooses the optimal route to a given host based on the "length" of the path. It is computed by summing up the individual metric values of each host-to-host link. By default, a hop has length 1, but this may be any positive integer less than 16. (A route length of 16 is equal to infinity. Such routes are considered unusable.) The metric parameter sets this hop cost, which is then broadcast by the routing daemon.

(If ARP is disabled, *ifconfig* displays the flag NOARP.)

-arp	Disables the use of ARP on this interface.
promisc	Puts the interface in promiscuous mode. On a broadcast network, this makes the interface receive all packets, regardless of whether they were destined for another host or not. This allows an analysis of network traffic using packet filters and such, also called *Ethernet snooping*. Usually, this is a good technique of hunting down network problems that are otherwise hard to come by.

On the other hand, this allows attackers to skim the traffic of your network for passwords and do other nasty things. One protection against this type of attack is not to let anyone just plug in their computers in your Ethernet. Another option is to use secure authentication protocols, such as Kerberos, or the SRA login suite.[9]

(This option corresponds to the flag PROMISC.)

-promisc	Turns off promiscuous mode.
allmulti	Multicast addresses are some sort of broadcast to a group of hosts who don't necessarily have to be on the same subnet. Multicast addresses are not yet supported by the kernel.

(This option corresponds to the flag ALLMULTI.)

-allmulti	Turns off multicast addresses.

5.9   Checking with *netstat*

Next, I will turn to a useful tool for checking your network configuration and activity. It is called *netstat* and is, in fact, rather a collection of several tools lumped together. We will discuss each of its functions in the following sections.

5.9.1   Displaying the Routing Table

When invoking *netstat* with the -r flag, it displays the kernel routing table in the way we've been doing this with *route* above. On **vstout**, it produces:

```
# netstat -nr
Kernel routing table
Destination     Gateway          Genmask          Flags Metric Re-
f Use    Iface
127.0.0.1       *                255.255.255.255  UH    1      0        50 lo
191.72.1.0      *                255.255.255.0    U     1      0       478 eth0
191.72.2.0      191.72.1.1       255.255.255.0    UGN   1      0       250 eth0
```

The -n option makes *netstat* print addresses as dotted quad IP numbers rather than the symbolic host and network names. This is especially useful when you want to avoid address lookups over the network (e.g. to a DNS or NIS server).

The second column of *netstat*'s output shows the gateway the routing entry points to. If no gateway is used, an asterisk is printed instead. Column three shows the "generality" of the route. When given an IP address to find a suitable route for, the kernel goes through all routing table entries, taking the bitwise AND of the address and the genmask before comparing it to the target of the route.

The fourth column displays various flags that describe the route:

G	The route uses a gateway.
U	The interface to be used is up.

---

[9]SRA can be obtained from **ftp.tamu.edu** in */pub/sec/TAMU*.

H	Only a single host can be reached through the route. For example, this is the case for the loopback entry **127.0.0.1**.
D	This is set if the table entry has been generated by an ICMP redirect message (see section 2.5).
M	This is set if the table entry was modified by an ICMP redirect message.

The Ref column of _netstat_'s output shows the number of references to this route, that is, how many other routes (e.g. through gateways) rely on the presence of this route. The last two columns show the number of times the routing entry has been used, and the interface that datagrams are passed to for delivery.

5.9.2 Displaying Interface Statistics

When invoked with the -i flag, _netstat_ will display statistics for the network interfaces currently configured. If, in addition, the -a option is given, it will print _all_ interfaces present in the kernel, not only those that have been configured currently. On **vstaout**, the output from _netstat_ will look like this:

```
$ netstat -i
Kernel Interface table
Iface   MTU Met   RX-OK RX-ERR RX-DRP RX-OVR   TX-OK TX-ERR TX-DRP TX-
OVR Flags
lo        0   0    3185      0      0      0    3185      0      0
    0 BLRU
eth0   1500   0  972633     17     20    120  628711    217      0
    0 BRU
```

The MTU and Met fields show the current MTU and metric value for that interface. The RX and TX columns show how many packets have been received or transmitted error free (RX-OK/TX-OK), damaged (RX-ERR/TX-ERR), how many were dropped (RX-DRP/TX-DRP), and how many were lost because of an overrun (RX-OVR/TX-OVR).

The last column shows the flags that have been set for this interface. These are one-character versions of the long flag names the are printed when you display the interface configuration with _ifconfig_.

B	A broadcast address has been set.
L	This interface is a loopback device.
M	All packets are received (promiscuous mode).
N	Trailers are avoided.
O	ARP is turned off for this interface.
P	This is a point-to-point connection.
R	Interface is running.
U	Interface is up.

5.9.3 Displaying Connections

netstat supports a set of options to display active or passive sockets. The options -t, -u, -w, and -x show active TCP, UDP, RAW, or UNIX socket connections. If you provide the -a flag in addition, sockets that are waiting for a connection (i.e. listening) are displayed as well. This will give you a list of all servers that are currently running on your system.

Invoking _netstat -ta_ on **vlager** produces

```
$ netstat -ta
Active Internet connections
Proto Recv-Q Send-Q Local Address    Foreign Address   (State)
tcp        0      0 *:domain         *:*               LISTEN
tcp        0      0 *:time           *:*               LISTEN
```

```
tcp     0     0 *:smtp              *:*                LISTEN
tcp     0     0 vlager:smtp         vstout:1040        ESTABLISHED
tcp     0     0 *:telnet            *:*                LISTEN
tcp     0     0 localhost:1046      vbardolino:telnet  ESTABLISHED
tcp     0     0 *:chargen           *:*                LISTEN
tcp     0     0 *:daytime           *:*                LISTEN
tcp     0     0 *:discard           *:*                LISTEN
tcp     0     0 *:echo              *:*                LISTEN
tcp     0     0 *:shell             *:*                LISTEN
tcp     0     0 *:login             *:*                LISTEN
```

This shows most servers simply waiting for an incoming connection. However, the fourth line shows an incoming SMTP connection from **vstout**, and the sixth line tells you there is an outgoing *telnet* connection to **vbardolino**.[10]

Using the −a flag all by itself will display all sockets from all families.

5.10   Checking the ARP Tables

On some occasions, it is useful to view or even alter the contents of the kernel's ARP tables, for example when you suspect a duplicate Internet address is the cause for some intermittent network problem. The *arp* tool was made for things like these. Its command line options are

```
arp [-v] [-t hwtype] -a [hostname]
arp [-v] [-t hwtype] -s hostname hwaddr
arp [-v] -d hostname [hostname...]
```

All *hostname* arguments may be either symbolic host names or IP addresses in dotted quad notation.

The first invocation displays the ARP entry for the IP address or host specified, or all hosts known if no *hostname* is given. For example, invoking *arp* on **vlager** may yield

```
# arp -a
IP address      HW type            HW address
191.72.1.3      10Mbps Ethernet    00:00:C0:5A:42:C1
191.72.1.2      10Mbps Ethernet    00:00:C0:90:B3:42
191.72.2.4      10Mbps Ethernet    00:00:C0:04:69:AA
```

which shows the Ethernet addresses of **vlager**, **vstout** and **vale**.

Using the −t option you can limit the display to the hardware type specified. This may be *ether*, *ax25*, or *pronet*, standing for 10Mbps Ethernet, AMPR AX.25, and IEEE 802.5 token ring equipment, respectively.

The −s option is used to permanently add *hostname*'s Ethernet address to the ARP tables. The *hwaddr* argument specifies the hardware address, which is by default expected to be an Ethernet address, specified as six hexadecimal bytes separated by colons. You may also set the hardware address for other types of hardware, too, using the −t option.

One problem which may require you to manually add an IP address to the ARP table is when for some reasons ARP queries for the remote host fail, for instance when its ARP driver is buggy or there is another host in the network that erroneously identifies itself with that host's IP address. Hard-wiring IP addresses in the ARP table is also a (very drastic) measure to protect yourself from hosts on your Ethernet that pose as someone else.

---

[10]You can tell whether a connection is outgoing or not from the port numbers involved. The port number shown for the *calling* host will always be a simple integer, while on the host being called, a well-known service port will be in use, for which *netstat* uses the symbolic name found in */etc/services*.

Invoking *arp* using the -d switch deletes all ARP entries relating to the given host. This may be used to force the interface to re-attempt to obtain the Ethernet address for the IP address in question. This is useful when a misconfigured system has broadcast wrong ARP information (of course, you have to reconfigure the broken host before).

The -s option may also be used to implement *proxy* ARP. This is a special technique where a host, say **gate**, acts as a gateway to another host named **fnord**, by pretending that both addresses refer to the same host, namely **gate**. It does so by publishing an ARP entry for **fnord** that points to its own Ethernet interface. Now when a host sends out an ARP query for **fnord**, **gate** will return a reply containing its own Ethernet address. The querying host will then send all datagrams to **gate**, which dutyfully forwards them to **fnord**.

These contortions may be necessary, for instance, when you want to access **fnord** from a DOS machine with a broken TCP implementation that doesn't understand routing too well. When you use proxy ARP, it will appear to the DOS machine as if **fnord** was on the local subnet, so it doesn't have to know about how to route through a gateway.

Another very useful application of proxy ARP is when one of your hosts acts as a gateway to some other host only temporarily, for instance through a dial-up link. In a previous example, we already encountered the laptop **vlite** which was connected to **vlager** through a PLIP link only from time to time. Of course, this will work only if the address of the host you want to provide proxy ARP for is on the same IP subnet as your gateway. For instance, **vstout** could proxy ARP for any host on the Brewery subnet (**191.72.1.0**), but never for a host on the Winery subnet (**191.72.2.0**).

The proper invocation to provide proxy ARP for **fnord** is given below; of course, the Ethernet address given must be that of **gate**.

```
# arp -s fnord 00:00:c0:a1:42:e0 pub
```

The proxy ARP entry may be removed again by invoking:

```
# arp -d fnord
```

5.11 The Future

Linux networking is still evolving. Major changes at the kernel layer will bring a very flexible configuration scheme that will allow you to configure the network devices at run time. For instance, the *ifconfig* command will take arguments that set the IRQ line and DMA channel.

Another change to come soon is the additional mtu flag to the *route* command which will set the Maximum Transmission Unit for a particular route. This route-specific MTU overrides the MTU specified for the interface. You will typically use this option for routes through a gateway, where the link between the gateway and the destination host requires a very low MTU. For instance, assume host **wanderer** is connected to **vlager** through a SLIP link. When sending data from **vstout** to **wanderer**, the networking layer on **wanderer** would would use packets of up to 1500 bytes, because packets are sent across the Ethernet. The SLIP link, on the other hand, is operated with an MTU of 296, so the network layer on **vlager** would have to break up the IP packets into smaller fragments that fit into 296 bytes. If instead, you would have configured the route on **vstout** to use a MTU of 296 right from the start, this relatively expensive fragmentation could be avoided:

```
# route add wanderer gw vlager mtu 296
```

Note that the mtu option also allows you to selectively undo the effects of the 'Subnets Are Local' Policy (SNARL). This policy is a kernel configuration option and is described in chapter 3.

Chapter 6

Name Service and Resolver Configuraton

As discussed in chapter 2, TCP/IP networking may rely on different schemes to convert names into addresses. The simplest way, which takes no advantage of the way the name space has been split up into zones is a host table stored in */etc/hosts*. This is useful only for small LANs that are run by one single administrator, and otherwise have no IP traffic with the outside world. The format of the *hosts* file has already been described in chapter 5.

Alternatively, you may use BIND – the Berkeley Internet Name Domain Service – for resolving host names to IP addresses. Configuring BIND may be a real chore, but once you've done it, changes in the network topology are easily made. On Linux, as on many other UNIXish systems, name service is provided through a program called *named*. At startup, it loads a set of master files into its cache, and waits for queries from remote or local user processes. There are different ways to set up BIND, and not all require you to run a name server on every host.

This chapter can do little more but give a rough sketch of how to operate a name server. If you plan to use BIND in an enviroment with more than just a small LAN and probably an Internet uplink, you should get a good book on BIND, for instance Cricket Liu's "DNS and BIND" (see [AlbitzLiu92]). For current information, you may also want to check the release notes contained in the BIND sources. There's also a newsgroup for DNS questions called **comp.protocols.tcp-ip.domains**.

6.1 The Resolver Library

When talking of "the resolver", we do not mean any special application, but rather refer to the *resolver library*, a collection of functions that can be found in the standard C library. The central routines are *gethostbyname(2)* and *gethostbyaddr(2)* which look up all IP addresses belonging to a host, and vice versa. They may be configured to simply look up the information in *hosts*, query a number of name servers, or use the *hosts* database of NIS (Network Information Service). Other applications, like *smail*, may include different drivers for any of these, and need special care.

6.1.1 The *host.conf* File

The central file that controls your resolver setup is *host.conf*. It resides in */etc* and tells the resolver which services to use, and in what order.

Options in *host.conf* must occur on separate lines. Fields may be separated by white space (spaces or tabs). A hash sign (#) introduces a comment that extends to the next newline.

The following options are available:

order   This determines the order in which the resolving services are tried. Valid options are *bind* for querying the name server, *hosts* for lookups in */etc/hosts*, and *nis* for NIS lookups. Any or all of them may be specified. The order in which they appear on the line detemines the order in which the respective services are tried.

multi   Takes *on* or *off* as options. This detemines if a host in */etc/hosts* is allowed to have several IP addresses, which is usually referred to as being "multi-homed". This flag has no effect on DNS or NIS queries.

nospoof   As explained in the previous chapter, DNS allows you to find the hostname belonging to an IP address by using the **in-addr.arpa** domain. Attempts by name servers to supply a false hostname are called "*spoofing*". To guard against this, the resolver may be configured to check if the original IP address is in fact associated with the hostname obtained. If not, the name is rejected and an error returned. This behavior is turned on by setting *nospoof on*.

alert   This option takes *on* or *off* as arguments. If it is turned on, any spoof attempts (see above) will cause the resolver to log a message to the *syslog* facility.

trim   This option takes a domain name as an argument, which will be removed from hostnames before lookup. This is useful for *hosts* entries, where you might only want to specify hostnames without local domain. A lookup of a host with the local domain name appended will have this removed, thus allowing the lookup in */etc/hosts* to succeed.

                 trim options accumulate, making it possible to consider your host as being local to several domains.

A sample file for **vlager** is shown below:

```
# /etc/host.conf
# We have named running, but no NIS (yet)
order    bind hosts
# Allow multiple addrs
multi    on
# Guard against spoof attempts
nospoof on
# Trim local domain (not really necessary).
trim     vbrew.com.
```

6.1.2 Resolver Environment Variables

The settings from *host.conf* may be overridden using a number of environment variables. These are

RESOLV_HOST_CONF This specifies a file to be read instead of */etc/host.conf*.

RESOLV_SERV_ORDER Overrides the *order* option given in *host.conf*. Services are given as *hosts*, *bind*, and *nis*, separated by a space, comma, colon, or semicolon.

RESOLV_SPOOF_CHECK Determines the measures taken against spoofing. It is completely disabled by *off*. The values *warn* and *warn off* enable spoof checking, but turn logging on and off, respectively. A value of * turns on spoof checks, but leaves the logging facility as defined in *host.conf*.

RESOLV_MULTI A value of *on* or *off* may be used to override the *multi* options from tt host.conf.

RESOLV_OVERRIDE_TRIM_DOMAINS This environment specifies a list of trim domains which override those given in *host.conf*.

RESOLV_ADD_TRIM_DOMAINS This environment specifies a list of trim domains which are added to those given in *host.conf*.

6.1.3 Configuring Name Server Lookups — *resolv.conf*

When configuring the resolver library to use the BIND name service for host lookups, you also have to tell it which name servers to use. There is a separate file for this, called *resolv.conf*. If this file does not exist or is empty, the resolver assumes the name server is on your local host.

If you run a name server on your local host, you have to set it up separately, as will be explained in the following section. If your are on a local network and have the opportunity to use an existing nameserver, this should always be preferred.

The most important option in *resolv.conf* is *nameserver*, which gives the IP address of a name server to use. If you specifiy several name servers by giving the *nameserver* option several times, they are tried in the order given. You should therefore put the most reliable server first. Currently, up to three name servers are supported.

If no *nameserver* option is given, the resolver attempts to connect to the name server on the local host.

Two other options, *domain* and *search* deal with default domains that are tacked onto a hostname if BIND fails to resolve it with the first query. The *search* option specifies a list of domain names to be tried. The list items are separated by spaces or tabs.

If no *search* option is given, a default search list is constructed from the local domain name by using the domain name itself, plus all parent domains up to the root. The local domain name may be given using the *domain* statement; if none is given, the resolver obtains it through the *getdomainname(2)* system call.

If this sounds confusing to you, consider this sample *resolv.conf* file for the Virtual Brewery:

```
# /etc/resolv.conf
# Our domain
domain          vbrew.com
#
# We use vlager as central nameserver:
nameserver      191.72.1.1
```

When resolving the name **vale**, the resolver would look up **vale**, and failing this, **vale.vbrew.com**, and **vale.com**.

6.1.4   Resolver Robustness

If you are running a LAN inside a larger network, you definitely should use central name servers if they are available. The advantage of this is that these will develop rich caches, since all queries are forwarded to them. This scheme, however has a drawback: when a fire recently destroyed the backbone cable at our university, no more work was possible on our department's LAN, because the resolver couldn't reach any of the name servers anymore. There was no logging in on X terminals anymore, no printing, etc.

Although it is not very common for campus backbones to go down in flames, one might want to take precautions against cases like these.

One option is to set up a local name server that resolves hostnames from your local domain, and forwards all queries for other hostnames to the main servers. Of course, this is applicable only if you are running your own domain.

Alternatively, you can maintain a backup host table for your domain or LAN in */etc/hosts*. In */etc/host.conf* you would then include *"order bind hosts"* to make the resolver fall back to the hosts file if the central name server is down.

6.2   Running *named*

The program that provides domain name service on most UNIX machines is usually called *named* (pronounced *name-dee*). This is a server program originally developed for BSD providing name service to clients, and possibly to other name servers. The version currently used on most Linux installations seems to be BIND-4.8.3. The new version, BIND-4.9.3, is being Beta-tested at the moment, and should be available on Linux soon.

This section requires some understanding of the way the Domain Name System works. If the following discussion is all Greek to you, you may want to re-read chapter 2, which has some more information on the basics of DNS.

named is usually started at system boot time, and runs until the machine goes down again. It takes its information from a configuration file called */etc/named.boot*, and various files that contain data mapping domain names to addresses and the like. The latter are called *zone files*. The formats and semantics of these files will be explained in the following section.

To run *named*, simply enter

```
# /usr/sbin/named
```

at the prompt. *named* will come up, read the *named.boot* file and any zone files specified therein. It writes its process id to */var/run/named.pid* in ASCII, downloads any zone files from primary servers, if necessary, and starts listening on port 53 for DNS queries.[1]

6.2.1   The *named.boot* File

The *named.boot* file is generally very small and contains little else but pointers to master files containing zone information, and pointers to other name servers. Comments in the boot file start with a semicolon and extend to the next newline. Before we discuss the format of *named.boot* in more detail, we will take a look at the sample file for **vlager** given in figure 6.1.[2]

```
;
; /etc/named.boot file for vlager.vbrew.com
;
directory        /var/named
;
;                domain                          file
;---------------------------------------------------------
cache            .                               named.ca
primary          vbrew.com                       named.hosts
primary          0.0.127.in-addr.arpa            named.local
primary          72.191.in-addr.arpa             named.rev
```

Figure 6.1: The *named.boot* file for *vlager*.

The *cache* and *primary* commands shown in this example load information into *named*. This information is taken from the master files specified in the second argument. They contain textual representations of DNS resource records, which we will look at below.

In this example, we configured *named* as the primary name server for three domains, as indicated by the *primary* statements at the end of the file. The first of these lines, for instance, instructs *named* to act as a primary server for **vbrew.com**, taking the zone data from the file *named.hosts*. The *directory* keyword tells it that all zone files are located in */var/named*.

The *cache* entry is very special and should be present on virtually all machines running a name server. Its function is two-fold: it instructs *named* to enable its cache, and to load the *root name server hints* from the cache file specified (*named.ca* in our example). We will come back to the name server hints below.

Here's a list of the most important options you can use in *named.boot*:

directory   This specifies a directory in which zone files reside. Names of files may be given relative to this
                     directory. Several directories may be specified by repeatedly using *directory*. According to the Linux
                     filesystem standard, this should be */var/named*.

---

[1]There are various *named* binaries floating around Linux FTP sites, each configured a little differently. Some have their pid file in */etc*, some store it in */tmp* or */var/tmp*.

[2]Note that the domain names in this example are given *without* trailing dot. Earlier versions of *named* seem to treat trailing dots in *named.boot* as an error, and silently discards the line. BIND-4.9.3 is said to fix this.

primary   This takes a `domain name` and a `file name` as an argument, declaring the local server authoritative for the named domain. As a primary server, *named* loads the zone information from the given master file.

Generally, there will always be at least one *primary* entry in every boot file, namely for reverse mapping of network **127.0.0.0**, which is the local loopback network.

secondary   This statement takes a `domain name`, an `address list`, and a `file name` as an argument. It declares the local server a secondary master server for the domain specified.

A secondary server holds authoritative data on the domain, too, but it doesn't gather it from files, but tries to download it from the primary server. The IP address of at least one primary server must thus be given to *named* in the address list. The local server will contact each of them in turn until it successfully transfers the zone database, which is then stored in the backup file given as the third argument. If none of the primary servers responds, the zone data is retrieved from the backup file instead.

named will then attempt to refresh the zone data at regular intervals. This is explained below along in connection with the SOA resource record type.

cache   This takes a `domain` and a `file name` as arguments. This file contains the root server hints, that is a list of records pointing to the root name servers. Only NS and A records will be recognized. The `domain` argument is generally the root domain name ".".

This information is absolutely crucial to *named*: if the *cache* statement does not occur in the boot file, *named* will not develop a local cache at all. This will severely degrade performance and increase network load if the next server queried is not on the local net. Moreover, *named* will not be able to reach any root name servers, and thus it won't resolve any addresses except those it is authoritative for. An exception from this rule is when using forwarding servers (cf. the *forwarders* option below).

forwarders This statement takes an `address list` as an argument. The IP addresses in this list specify a list of name servers that *named* may query if it fails to resolve a query from its local cache. They are tried in order until one of them responds to the query.

slave   This statement makes the name server a *slave* server. That is, it will never perform recursive queries itself, but only forwards them to servers specified with the *forwarders* statement.

There are two options which we will not describe here, being *sortlist* and *domain*. Additionally, there are two directives that may be used inside the zone database files. These are *$INCLUDE* and *$ORIGIN*. Since they are rarely needed, we will not describe them here, either.

6.2.2   The DNS Database Files

Master files included by *named*, like *named.hosts*, always have a domain associated with them, which is called the *origin*. This is the domain name specified with the *cache* and *primary* commands. Within a master file, you are allowed to specify domain and host names relative to this domain. A name given in a configuration file is considered *absolute* if it ends in a single dot, otherwise it is considered relative to the origin. The origin all by itself may be referred to using "@".

All data contained in a master file is split up in *resource records*, or RRs for short. They make up the smallest unit of information available through DNS. Each resource record has a type. A records, for instance, map a hostname to an IP address, and a CNAME record associates an alias for a host with its official hostname. As an example, take a look at figure 6.3 on page 80, which shows the *named.hosts* master file for the virtual brewery.

Resource record representations in master files share a common format, which is

        `[domain] [ttl] [class] type rdata`

Fields are separated by spaces or tabs. An entry may be continued across several lines if an opening brace occurs before the first newline, and the last field is followed by a closing brace. Anything between a semicolon and a newline is ignored.

domain   This is the domain name to which the entry applies. If no domain name is given, the RR is assumed to apply to the domain of the previous RR.

ttl   In order to force resolvers to discard information after a certain time, each RR is associated a "*time to live*", or *ttl* for short. The *ttl* field specifies the time in seconds the information is valid after it has been retrieved from the server. It is a decimal number with at most eight digits.

If no *ttl* value is given, it defaults to the value of the *minimum* field of the preceding SOA record.

class   This is an address class, like IN for IP addresses, or HS for objects in the Hesiod class. For TCP/IP networking, you have to make this IN.

If no *class* field is given, the class of the preceding RR is assumed.

type   This describes the type of the RR. The most common types are A, SOA, PTR, and NS. The following sections describe the various types of RR's.

rdata   This holds the data associated with the RR. The format of this field depends on the type of the RR. Below, it will be described for each RR separately.

The following is an incomplete list of RRs to be used in DNS master files. There are a couple more of them, which we will not explain. They are experimental, and of little use generally.

SOA   This describes a zone of authority (SOA means "Start of Authority"). It signals that the records following the SOA RR contain authoritative information for the domain. Every master file included by a *primary* statement must contain an SOA record for this zone. The resource data contains the following fields:

    origin   This is the canonical hostname of the primary name server for this domain. It is usually given as an absolute name.

    contact   This is the email address of the person responsible for maintaining the domain, with the '@' character replaced by a dot. For instance, if the responsible person at the Virtual Brewery is **janet**, then this field would contain *janet.vbrew.com*.

    serial   This is the version number of the zone file, expressed as a single decimal number. Whenever data is changed in the zone file, this number should be incremented.

         The serial number is used by secondary name servers to recognize when zone information has changed. To stay up to date, secondary servers request the primary server's SOA record at certain intervals, and compare the serial number to that of the cached SOA record. If the number has changed, the secondary servers transfers the whole zone database from the primary server.

    refresh   This specifies the interval in seconds that the secondary servers should wait between checking the SOA record of the primary server. Again, this is a decimal number with at most eight digits.

         Generally, the network topology doesn't change too often, so that this number should specify an interval of roughly a day for larger networks, and even more for smaller ones.

    retry   This number determines the intervals at which a secondary server should retry contacting the primary server if a request or a zone refresh fails. It must not be too low, or else a temporary failure of the server or a network problem may cause the secondary server to waste network resources. One hour, or perhaps one half hour, might be a good choice.

    expire   This specifies the time in seconds after which the server should finally discard all zone data if it hasn't been able to contact the primary server. It should normally be very large. Craig Hunt ([Hunt92]) recommends 42 days.

    minimum   This is the default ttl value for resource records that do not explicitly specify one. This requires other name servers to discard the RR after a certain amount of time.

It has however nothing to do with the time after which a secondary server tries to update the zone information.

minimum should be a large value, especially for LANs where the network topology almost never changes. A value of around a week or a month is probably a good choice. In the case that single RRs may change more frequently, you can still assign them different ttl's.

A   This associates an IP address with a hostname. The resource data field contains the address in dotted quad notation.

For each host, there must be only one A record. The hostname used in this A record is considered the official or *canonical* hostname. All other hostnames are aliases and must be mapped onto the canonical hostname using a CNAME record.

NS   This points to a master name server of a subordinate zone. For an explanation why one has to have NS records, see section 2.6. The resource data field contains the hostname of the name server. To resolve the hostname, an additional A record is needed, the so-called *glue record* which gives the name server's IP address.

CNAME   This associates an alias for a host with its *canonical hostname*. The canonical hostname is the one the master file provides an A record for; aliases are simply linked to that name by a CNAME record, but don't have any other records of their own.

PTR   This type of record is used to associate names in the **in-addr.arpa** domain with hostnames. This is used for reverse mapping of IP addresses to hostnames. The hostname given must be the canonical hostname.

MX   This RR announces a *mail exchanger* for a domain. The reasons to have mail exchangers are discussed in section 13.4.1 in chapter 13. The syntax of an MX record is

```
[domain] [ttl] [class] MX preference host
```

host names the mail exchanger for *domain*. Every mail exchanger has an integer *preference* associated with it. A mail transport agent who desires to deliver mail to *domain* will try all hosts who have an MX record for this domain until it succeeds. The one with the lowest preference value is tried first, then the others in order of increasing preference value.

HINFO   This record provides information on the system's hardware and software. Its syntax is

```
[domain] [ttl] [class] HINFO hardware software
```

The *hardware* field identifies the hardware used by this host. There are special conventions to specify this. A list of valid names is given in the "Assigned Numbers" (RFC 1340). If the field contains any blanks, it must be enclosed in double quotes. The *software* field names the operating system software used by the system. Again, a valid name from the "Assigned Numbers" RFC should be chosen.

6.2.3   Writing the Master Files

Figures 6.2, 6.3, 6.4, and 6.5 give sample files for a name server at the brewery, located on *vlager*. Owing to the nature of the network discussed (a single LAN), the example is pretty straightforward. If your requirements are more complex, and you can't get *named* going, get "DNS and BIND" by Cricket Liu and Paul Albitz ([AlbitzLiu92]).

The *named.ca* cache file shown in figure 6.2 shows sample hint records for a root name server. A typical cache file usually describes about a dozen name servers, or so. You can obtain the current list of name servers for the root domain using the *nslookup* tool described toward the end of this chapter.[3]

---

[3] Note that you can't query your name server for the root servers if you don't have any root server hints installed: Catch 22! To escape this dilemma, you can either make *nslookup* use a different name server, or you can use the sample file in figure 6.2 as a starting point, and then obtain the full list of valid servers.

```
;
; /var/named/named.ca             Cache file for the brewery.
;                     We're not on the Internet, so we don't need
;                     any root servers. To activate these
;                     records, remove the semicolons.
;
; .                99999999   IN    NS  NS.NIC.DDN.MIL
; NS.NIC.DDN.MIL   99999999   IN    A   26.3.0.103
; .                99999999   IN    NS  NS.NASA.GOV
; NS.NASA.GOV      99999999   IN    A   128.102.16.10
```

Figure 6.2: The *named.ca* file.

```
;
; /var/named/named.hosts         Local hosts at the brewery
;                     Origin is vbrew.com
;
@              IN   SOA   vlager.vbrew.com. (
                          janet.vbrew.com.
                          16          ; serial
                          86400       ; refresh: once per day
                          3600        ; retry:    one hour
                          3600000     ; expire:   42 days
                          604800      ; minimum: 1 week
                          )
               IN   NS    vlager.vbrew.com.
;
; local mail is distributed on vlager
               IN   MX    10 vlager
;
; loopback address
localhost.     IN   A     127.0.0.1
; brewery Ethernet
vlager         IN   A     191.72.1.1
vlager-if1     IN   CNAME vlager
; vlager is also news server
news           IN   CNAME vlager
vstout         IN   A     191.72.1.2
vale           IN   A     191.72.1.3
; winery Ethernet
vlager-if2     IN   A     191.72.2.1
vbardolino     IN   A     191.72.2.2
vchianti       IN   A     191.72.2.3
vbeaujolais    IN   A     191.72.2.4
```

Figure 6.3: The *named.hosts* file.

```
;
; /var/named/named.local           Reverse mapping of 127.0.0
;                                   Origin is 0.0.127.in-addr.arpa.
;
@               IN  SOA  vlager.vbrew.com. (
                         joe.vbrew.com.
                         1            ; serial
                         360000       ; refresh: 100 hrs
                         3600         ; retry:   one hour
                         3600000      ; expire:  42 days
                         360000       ; minimum: 100 hrs
                         )
                IN  NS   vlager.vbrew.com.
1               IN  PTR  localhost.
```

Figure 6.4: The *named.local* file.

```
;
; /var/named/named.rev            Reverse mapping of our IP addresses
;                                  Origin is 72.191.in-addr.arpa.
;
@               IN  SOA  vlager.vbrew.com. (
                         joe.vbrew.com.
                         16           ; serial
                         86400        ; refresh: once per day
                         3600         ; retry:   one hour
                         3600000      ; expire:  42 days
                         604800       ; minimum: 1 week
                         )
                IN  NS   vlager.vbrew.com.
; brewery
1.1             IN  PTR  vlager.vbrew.com.
2.1             IN  PTR  vstout.vbrew.com.
3.1             IN  PTR  vale.vbrew.com.
; winery
1.2             IN  PTR  vlager-if1.vbrew.com.
2.2             IN  PTR  vbardolino.vbrew.com.
3.2             IN  PTR  vchianti.vbrew.com.
4.2             IN  PTR  vbeaujolais.vbrew.com.
```

Figure 6.5: The *named.rev* file.

6.2.4   Verifying the Name Server Setup

There's a fine tool for checking the operation of your name server setup. It is called *nslookup*, and may be used both interactively and from the command line. In the latter case, you simply invoke it as

```
nslookup hostname
```

and it will query the name server specified in *resolv.conf* for `hostname`. (If this file names more than one server, *nslookup* will choose one at random).

The interactive mode, however, is much more exciting. Besides looking up individual hosts, you may query for any type of DNS record, and transfer the entire zone information for a domain.

When invoked without argument, *nslookup* will display the name server it uses, and enter interactive mode. At the '>' prompt, you may type any domain name it should query for. By default, it asks for class A records, those containing the IP address relating to the domain name.

You may change this type by issuing "`set type=`*type*", where *type* is one of the resource record names described above in section 6.2, or ANY.

For example, you might have the following dialogue with it:

```
$ nslookup
Default Name Server:  rs10.hrz.th-darmstadt.de
Address:  130.83.56.60

> sunsite.unc.edu
Name Server:  rs10.hrz.th-darmstadt.de
Address:  130.83.56.60

Non-authoritative answer:
Name:     sunsite.unc.edu
Address:  152.2.22.81
```

If you try to query for a name that has no IP address associated, but other records were found in the DNS database, *nslookup* will come back with an error message saying "`No type A records found`". However, you can make it query for records other than type A by issuing the "`set type`" command. For example, to get the SOA record of **unc.edu**, you would issue:

```
> unc.edu
*** No address (A) records available for unc.edu
Name Server:  rs10.hrz.th-darmstadt.de
Address:  130.83.56.60

> set type=SOA
> unc.edu
Name Server:  rs10.hrz.th-darmstadt.de
Address:  130.83.56.60

Non-authoritative answer:
unc.edu
        origin = ns.unc.edu
        mail addr = shava.ns.unc.edu
        serial = 930408
        refresh = 28800 (8 hours)
        retry   = 3600 (1 hour)
```

```
        expire   = 1209600 (14 days)
        minimum ttl = 86400 (1 day)

Authoritative answers can be found from:
UNC.EDU nameserver = SAMBA.ACS.UNC.EDU
SAMBA.ACS.UNC.EDU        internet address = 128.109.157.30
```

In a similar fashion you can query for MX records, etc. Using a type of ANY returns all resource records associated with a given name.

```
> set type=MX
> unc.edu
Non-authoritative answer:
unc.edu preference = 10, mail exchanger = lambada.oit.unc.edu
lambada.oit.unc.edu      internet address = 152.2.22.80

Authoritative answers can be found from:
UNC.EDU nameserver = SAMBA.ACS.UNC.EDU
SAMBA.ACS.UNC.EDU        internet address = 128.109.157.30
```

A practical application of *nslookup* beside debugging is to obtain the current list of root name servers for the *named.ca* file. You can do this by querying for all type NS records associated with the root domain:

```
> set typ=NS
> .
Name Server:  fb0430.mathematik.th-darmstadt.de
Address:  130.83.2.30

Non-authoritative answer:
(root)    nameserver = NS.INTERNIC.NET
(root)    nameserver = AOS.ARL.ARMY.MIL
(root)    nameserver = C.NYSER.NET
(root)    nameserver = TERP.UMD.EDU
(root)    nameserver = NS.NASA.GOV
(root)    nameserver = NIC.NORDU.NET
(root)    nameserver = NS.NIC.DDN.MIL

Authoritative answers can be found from:
(root)    nameserver = NS.INTERNIC.NET
(root)    nameserver = AOS.ARL.ARMY.MIL
(root)    nameserver = C.NYSER.NET
(root)    nameserver = TERP.UMD.EDU
(root)    nameserver = NS.NASA.GOV
(root)    nameserver = NIC.NORDU.NET
(root)    nameserver = NS.NIC.DDN.MIL
NS.INTERNIC.NET internet address = 198.41.0.4
AOS.ARL.ARMY.MIL        internet address = 128.63.4.82
AOS.ARL.ARMY.MIL        internet address = 192.5.25.82
AOS.ARL.ARMY.MIL        internet address = 26.3.0.29
C.NYSER.NET     internet address = 192.33.4.12
TERP.UMD.EDU    internet address = 128.8.10.90
NS.NASA.GOV     internet address = 128.102.16.10
NS.NASA.GOV     internet address = 192.52.195.10
NS.NASA.GOV     internet address = 45.13.10.121
NIC.NORDU.NET   internet address = 192.36.148.17
```

```
NS.NIC.DDN.MIL   internet address = 192.112.36.4
```

The complete set of commands available with *nslookup* may be obtained by the `help` command from within *nslookup*.

6.2.5   Other Useful Tools

There are a few tools that can help you with your tasks as a BIND administrator. I will briefly describe two of them here. Please refer to the documentation that comes with these tools for information on how to use them.

hostcvt is a tool that helps you with your initial BIND configuration by converting your */etc/hosts* file into master files for *named*. It generates both the forward (A) and reverse mapping (PTR) entries, and takes care of aliases and the like. Of course, it won't do the whole job for you, as you may still want to tune the timeout values in the SOA record, for instance, or add MX records and the like. Still, it may help you save a few aspirins. *hostcvt* is part of the BIND source, but can also be found as a standalone package on a few Linux FTP servers.

After setting up your name server, you may want to test your configuration. The ideal (and, to my knowledge) only tool for this is *dnswalk*, a *perl*-based package that walks your DNS database, looking for common mistakes and verifying that the information is consistent. *dnswalk* has been released on **comp.sources.misc** recently, and should be available on all FTP sites that archive this group (**ftp.uu.net** should be a safe bet if you don't know of any such site near you).

Chapter 7

Serial Line IP

The serial line protocols, SLIP and PPP, provide the Internet connectivity for the poor. Apart from a modem and a serial board equipped with a FIFO buffer, no hardware is needed. Using it is not much more complicated than a mailbox, and an increasing number of private organizations offer dial-up IP at an affordable cost to everyone.

There are both SLIP and PPP drivers available for Linux. SLIP has been there for quite a while, and works fairly reliable. A PPP driver has been developed recently by Michael Callahan and Al Longyear. It will be described in the next chapter.

7.1 General Requirements

To use SLIP or PPP, you have to configure some basic networking features as described in the previous chapters, of course. At the least, you have to set up the loopback interface, and provide for name resolution. When connecting to the Internet, you will of course want to use DNS. The simplest option is to put the address of some name server into your *resolv.conf* file; this server will be queried as soon as the SLIP link is activated. The closer this name server is to the point where you dial in, the better.

However, this solution is not optimal, because all name lookups will still go through your SLIP/PPP link. If you worry about the bandwidth this consumes, you can also set up a *caching-only* name server. It doesn't really serve a domain, but only acts as a relay for all DNS queries produced on your host. The advantage of this scheme is that it builds up a cache, so that most queries have to be sent over the serial line only once. A *named.boot* file for a caching-only server looks like this:

```
; named.boot file for caching-only server
directory                          /var/named

primary      0.0.127.in-addr.arpa   db.127.0.0 ; loopback net
cache        .                      db.cache   ; root servers
```

In addition to this *name.boot* file, you also have to set up the *db.cache* file with a valid list of root name servers. This is described toward the end of the Resolver Configuration chapter.

7.2 SLIP Operation

Dial-up IP servers frequently offer SLIP service through special user accounts. After logging into such an account, you are not dropped into the common shell; instead a program or shell script is executed that enables the server's SLIP driver for the serial line and configures the appropriate network interface. Then you have to do the same at your end of the link.

On some operating systems, the SLIP driver is a user-space program; under Linux, it is part of the kernel, which makes it a lot faster. This requires, however, that the serial line be converted to SLIP mode explicitly. This is done by means of a special tty line discipline, SLIPDISC. While the tty is in normal line discipline (DISC0), it will exchange data only with user processes, using the normal *read(2)* and *write(2)* calls, and the SLIP driver is unable to write to or read from the tty. In SLIPDISC, the roles are reversed: now any user-space processes are blocked from writing to or reading from the tty, while all data coming in on the serial port will be passed directly to the SLIP driver.

The SLIP driver itself understands a number of variations on the SLIP protocol. Apart from ordinary SLIP, it also understands CSLIP, which performs the so-called Van Jacobson header compression on outgoing IP packets.[1] This improves throughput for interactive sessions noticeably. Additionally, there are six-bit versions for each of these protocols.

A simple way to convert a serial line to SLIP mode is by using the *slattach* tool. Assume you have your modem on */dev/cua3*, and have logged into the SLIP server successfully. You will then execute:

```
# slattach /dev/cua3 &
```

This will switch the line discipline of *cua3* to SLIPDISC, and attach it to one of the SLIP network interfaces. If this is your first active SLIP link, the line will be attached to *sl0*; the second would be attached to *sl1*, and so on. The current kernels support up to eight simultaneous SLIP links.

The default encapsulation chosen by *slattach* is CSLIP. You may choose any other mode using the -p switch. To use normal SLIP (no compression), you would use

```
# slattach -p slip /dev/cua3 &
```

Other modes are cslip, slip6, cslip6 (for the six-bit version of SLIP), and adaptive for adaptive SLIP. The latter leaves it to the kernel to find out which type of SLIP encapsulation the remote end uses.

Note that you must use the same encapsulation as your peer does. For example, if **cowslip** uses CSLIP, you have to do so, too. The symptoms of a mismatch will be that a *ping* to the remote host will not receive any packets back. If the other host *ping*s you, you may also see messages like "Can't build ICMP header" on your console. One way to avoid these difficulties is to use adaptive SLIP.

In fact, *slattach* does not only allow you to enable SLIP, but other protocols that use the serial line as well, like PPP or KISS (another protocol used by ham radio people). For details, please refer to the *slattach(8)* manual page.

After turning over the line to the SLIP driver, you have to configure the network interface. Again, we do this using the standard *ifconfig* and *route* commands. Assume that from **vlager**, we have dialed up a server named **cowslip**. You would then execute

```
# ifconfig sl0 vlager pointopoint cowslip
# route add cowslip
# route add default gw cowslip
```

The first command configures the interface as a point-to-point link to **cowslip**, while the second and third add the route to **cowslip** and the default route using **cowslip** as a gateway.

When taking down the SLIP link, you first have to remove all routes through **cowslip** using *route* with the del option, take the interface down, and send *slattach* the hangup signal. Afterwards you have to hang up the modem using your terminal program again:

```
# route del default
# route del cowslip
# ifconfig sl0 down
# kill -HUP 516
```

---

[1] Van Jacobson header compression is described in RFC 1441.

7.3 Using *dip*

Now, that was rather simple. Nevertheless, you might want to automate the above steps so that you only have to invoke a simple command that performs all steps shown above. This is what *dip* is for.[2] The current release as of this writing is version 3.3.7. It has been patched very heavily by a number of people, so that you can't speak of *the dip* program anymore. These different strains of development will hopefully be merged in a future release.

dip provides an interpreter for a simple scripting language that can handle the modem for you, convert the line to SLIP mode, and configure the interfaces. This is rather primitive and restrictive, but sufficient for most cases. A new release of *dip* may feature a more versatile language one day.

To be able to configure the SLIP interface, *dip* requires root privilege. It would now be tempting to make *dip* setuid to **root**, so that all users can dial up some SLIP server without having to give them root access. This is very dangerous, because setting up bogus interfaces and default routes with *dip* may disrupt routing on your network badly. Even worse, this will give your users the power to connect to *any* SLIP server, and launch dangerous attacks on your network. So if you want to allow your users to fire up a SLIP connection, write small wrapper programs for each prospective SLIP server, and have these wrappers invoke *dip* with the specific script that establishes the connection. These programs can then safely be made setuid **root**.[3]

7.3.1 A Sample Script

A sample script is produced in figure 7.1. It can be used to connect to **cowslip** by invoking *dip* with the script name as argument:

```
# dip cowslip.dip
DIP: Dialup IP Protocol Driver version 3.3.7 (12/13/93)
Written by Fred N. van Kempen, MicroWalt Corporation.

connected to cowslip.moo.com with addr 193.174.7.129
#
```

After connecting to **cowslip** and enabling SLIP, *dip* will detach from the terminal and go to the background. You can then start using the normal networking services on the SLIP link. To terminate the connection, simply invoke **dip** with the -k option. This sends a hangup signal to *dip* process, using the process id *dip* records in */etc/dip.pid*:[4]

```
# kill -k
```

In *dip*'s scripting language, keywords prefixed with a dollar symbol denote variable names. *dip* has a predefined set of variables which will be listed below. *$remote* and *$local*, for instance, contain the hostnames of the local and remote host involved in the SLIP link.

The first two statements in the sample script are *get* commands, which is *dip*'s way to set a variable. Here, the local and remote hostname are set to **vlager** and **cowslip**, respectively.

The next five statements set up the terminal line and the modem. The *reset* sends a reset string to the modem; for Hayes-compatible modems, this is the *ATZ* command. The next statement flushes out the modem response, so that the login chat in the next few lines will work properly. This chat is pretty straight-forward: it simply dials 41988, the phone number of **cowslip**, and logs into the account *Svlager* using the password *hey-jude*. The *wait* command makes *dip* wait for the string given as its first argument; the number given as second argument make the wait time out after that many seconds if no such string is received. The *if* commands interspersed in the login procedure check that no error has occurred while executing the command.

---

[2]*dip* means *Dialup IP*. It was written by Fred van Kempen.

[3]*diplogin* can (and must) be run setuid, too. See the section at the end of this chapter.

[4]See the newsgroup **alt.tla** for more palindromic fun with three-letter acronyms.

Net-Admin Guide

```
# Sample dip script for dialing up cowslip

# Set local and remote name and address
get $local vlager
get $remote cowslip

port cua3                       # choose a serial port
speed 38400                     # set speed to max
modem HAYES                     # set modem type
reset                           # reset modem and tty
flush                           # flush out modem response

# Prepare for dialing.
send ATQ0V1E1X1\r
wait OK 2
if $errlvl != 0 goto error
dial 41988
if $errlvl != 0 goto error
wait CONNECT 60
if $errlvl != 0 goto error

# Okay, we're connected now
sleep 3
send \r\n\r\n
wait ogin: 10
if $errlvl != 0 goto error
send Svlager\n
wait ssword: 5
if $errlvl != 0 goto error
send hey-jude\n
wait running 30
if $errlvl != 0 goto error

# We have logged in, and the remote side is firing up SLIP.
print Connected to $remote with address $rmtip
default                         # Make this link our default route
mode SLIP                       # We go to SLIP mode, too
# fall through in case of error

error:
print SLIP to $remote failed.
```

Figure 7.1: A sample *dip* script

The final commands executed after logging in are *default*, which makes the SLIP link the default route to all hosts, and *mode*, which enables SLIP mode on the line and configures the interface and routing table for you.

7.3.2 A *dip* Reference

Although widely used, *dip* hasn't been very well documented yet. In this section, we will therefore give a reference for most of *dip*'s commands. You can get an overview of all commands it provides by invoking *dip* in test mode, and entering the *help* command. To find out about the syntax of a command, you may enter it without any arguments; of course this does not work with commands that take no arguments.

```
$ dip -t
DIP: Dialup IP Protocol Driver version 3.3.7 (12/13/93)
Written by Fred N. van Kempen, MicroWalt Corporation.

DIP> help
DIP knows about the following commands:

databits   default   dial     echo    flush
get        goto      help     if      init
mode       modem     parity   print   port
reset      send      sleep    speed   stopbits
term       wait

DIP> echo
Usage: echo on|off
DIP> _
```

Throughout the following, examples that display the DIP> prompt show how to enter a command in test mode, and what output it produces. Examples lacking this prompt should be taken as script excerpts.

7.3.2.1 The Modem Commands

There is a number of commands *dip* provides to configure your serial line and modem. Some of these are obvious, such as *port*, which selects a serial port, and *speed*, *databits*, *stopbits*, and *parity*, which set the common line parameters.

The *modem* command selects a modem type. Currently, the only type supported is *HAYES* (capitalization required). You have to provide *dip* with a modem type, else it will refuse to execute the *dial* and *reset* commands. The *reset* command sends a reset string to the modem; the string used depends on the modem type selected. For Hayes-compatible modems, this is *ATZ*.

The *flush* code can be used to flush out all responses the modem has sent so far. Otherwise a chat script following the *reset* might be confused, because it reads the *OK* responses from earlier commands.

The *init* command selects an initialization string to be passed to the modem before dialling. The default for Hayes modems is "*ATE0 Q0 V1 X1*", which turns on echoing of commands and long result codes, and selects blind dialing (no checking of dial tone).

The *dial* command finally sends the initialization string to the modem and dials up the remote system. The default dial command for Hayes modems is *ATD*.

7.3.2.2 *echo* and *term*

The *echo* command serves as a debugging aid, in that using *echo on* makes *dip* echo to the console everything sends to the serial device. This can be turned off again by calling *echo off*.

dip also allows you to leave script mode temporarily and enter terminal mode. In this mode, you can use *dip* just like any ordinary terminal program, writing to the serial line and reading from it. To leave this mode, enter Ctrl-] .

7.3.2.3 The *get* Command

The *get* command is *dip*'s way of setting a variable. The simplest form is to set a variable to a constant, as used throughout the above example. You may, however, also prompt the user for input by specifying the keyword *ask* instead of a value:

```
DIP> get $local ask
Enter the value for $local: _
```

A third method is to try to obtain the value from the remote host. Bizarre as it seems first, this is very useful in some cases: Some SLIP servers will not allow you to use your own IP address on the SLIP link, but will rather assign you one from a pool of addresses whenever you dial in, printing some message that informs you about the address you have been assigned. If the message looks something like this "`Your address:  193.174.7.202`", then the following piece of *dip* code would let you pick up the address:

```
... login chat ....
wait address: 10
get $locip remote
```

7.3.2.4 The *print* Command

This is the command to echo text to the console *dip* was started from. Any of *dip*'s variables may be used in print commands, such as

```
DIP> print Using port $port at speed $speed
Using port cua3 at speed 38400
```

7.3.2.5 Variable Names

dip only understands a predefined set of variables. A variable name always begins with a dollar symbol and must be written in lower-case letters.

The *$local* and *$locip* variables contain the local host's name and IP address. Setting the hostname makes *dip* store the canonical hostname in *$local*, at the same time assigning *$locip* the corresponding IP address. The analogous thing happens when setting the *$locip*.

The *$remote* and *$rmtip* variables do the same for the remote host's name and address. *$mtu* contains the MTU value for the connection.

These five variables are the only ones that may be assigned values directly using the *get* command. A host of other variables can only be set through corresponding commands, but may be used *print* statements; these are *$modem*, *$port*, and *$speed*.

$errlvl is the variable through which you can access the result of the last command executed. An error level of 0 indicates success, while a non-zero value denotes an error.

7.3.2.6 The *if* and *goto* Commands

The *if* command is rather a conditional branch than what one usually calls an if. Its syntax is

```
if var op number goto label
```

where the expression must be a simple comparison between one of the variables *$errlvl*, *$locip*, and *$rmtip*. The second operand must be an integer number; the operator *op* may be one of ==, ! =, <, >, <=, and >=.

The *goto* command makes the execution of the script continue at the line following that bearing the label. A label must occur as the very first token on the line, and must be followed immediately by a colon.

7.3.2.7 *send, wait* and *sleep*

These commands help implement simple chat scripts in *dip*. *send* outputs its arguments to the serial line. It does not support variables, but understands all C-style backslash character sequences such as \n and \b. The tilde character (~) is used as an abbreviation for carriage return/newline.

wait takes a word as an argument, and scans all input on the serial line until it recognizes this word. The word itself may not contain any blanks. Optionally, you may give *wait* a timeout value as second argument; if the expected word is not received within that many seconds, the command will return with an *$errlvl* value of one.

The *sleep* statement may be used to wait for a certain amount of time, for instance to patiently wait for any login sequence to complete. Again, the interval is specified in seconds.

7.3.2.8 *mode* and *default*

These commands are used to flip the serial line to SLIP mode and configure the interface.

The *mode* command is the last command executed by *dip* before gong into daemon mode. Unless an error occurs, the command does not return.

mode takes a protocol name as argument. *dip* currently recognizes *SLIP* and *CSLIP* as valid names. The current version of *dip* does not understand adaptive SLIP, however.

After enabling SLIP mode on the serial line, *dip* executes *ifconfig* to configure the interface as a point-to-point link, and invokes *route* to set the route to the remote host.

If, in addition, the script executes the *default* command before *mode*, *dip* will also make the default route point to the SLIP link.

7.4   Running in Server Mode

Setting up your SLIP client was the hard part. Doing the opposite, namely configuring your host to act as a SLIP server, is much easier.

One way to do this is to to use *dip* in server mode, which can be achieved by invoking it as *diplogin*. Its main configuration file is */etc/diphosts*, which associates login names with the address this host is assigned. Alternatively, you can also use *sliplogin*, a BSD-derived tool that features a more flexible configuration scheme that lets you execute shell scripts whenever a host connects and disconnects. It is currently at Beta.

Both programs require that you set up one login account per SLIP client. For instance, assume you provide SLIP service to Arthur Dent at **dent.beta.com**, you might create an account named **dent** by adding the following line to your *passwd* file:

```
dent:*:501:60:Arthur Dent's SLIP account:/tmp:/usr/sbin/diplogin
```

Afterwards, you would set **dent**'s password using the *passwd* utility.

Now, when **dent** logs in, *dip* will start up as a server. To find out if he is indeed permitted to use SLIP, it will look up the user name in */etc/diphosts*. This file details the access rights and connection parameter for each SLIP user. A sample entry for **dent** could look like this:

```
dent::dent.beta.com:Arthur Dent:SLIP,296
```

The first of the colon-separated fields is the name the user must log in as. The second field may contain an additional password (see below). The third is the hostname or IP address of the calling host. Next comes an informational field without any special meaning (yet). The last field describes the connection parameters. This is a comma-separated list specifying the protocol (currently one of *SLIP* or *CSLIP*), followed by the MTU.

Net-Admin Guide

When **dent** logs in, *diplogin* extracts the information on him from the *diphosts* file, and, if the second field is not empty, prompts for an "external security password". The string entered by the user is compared to the (unencrypted) password from *diphosts*. If they do not match, the login attempt is rejected.

Otherwise, *diplogin* proceeds by flipping the serial line to CSLIP or SLIP mode, and sets up the interface and route. This connection remains established until the user disconnects and the modem drops the line. *diplogin* will then return the line to normal line discipline, and exit.

diplogin requires super-user privilege. If you don't have *dip* running setuid **root**, you should make *diplogin* a separate copy of *dip* instead of a simple link. *diplogin* can then safely be made setuid, without affecting the status of *dip* itself.

Chapter 8

The Point-to-Point Protocol

8.1   Untangling the P's

Just like SLIP, PPP is a protocol to send datagrams across a serial connection, but addresses a couple of deficiencies of the former. It lets the communicating sides negotiate options such as the IP address and the maximum datagram size at startup time, and provides for client authorization. For each of these capabilities, PPP has a separate protocol. Below, we will briefly cover these basic building blocks of PPP. This discussion is far from complete; if you want to know more about PPP, you are urged to read its specification in RFC 1548, as well as the dozen or so companion RFCs.[1]

At the very bottom of PPP is the *High-Level Data Link Control* Protocol, abbreviated HDLC,[2] which defines the boundaries around the individual PPP frames, and provides a 16 bit checksum. As opposed to the more primitive SLIP encapsulation, a PPP frame is capable of holding packets from other protocols than IP, such as Novell's IPX, or Appletalk. PPP achieves this by adding a protocol field to the basic HDLC frame that identifies the type of packet is carried by the frame.

LCP, the Link Control Protocol, is used on top of HDLC to negotiate options pertaining to the data link, such as the Maximum Receive Unit (MRU) that states the maximum datagram size one side of the link agrees to receive.

An important step at the configuration stage of a PPP link is client authorization. Although it is not mandatory, it is really a must for dial-up lines. Usually, the called host (the server) asks the client to authorize itself by proving it knows some secret key. If the caller fails to produce the correct secret, the connection is terminated. With PPP, authorization works both ways; that is, the caller may also ask the server to authenticate itself. These authentication procedures are totally independent of each other. There are two protocols for different types of authorization, which we will discuss further below. They are named Password Authentication Protocol, or PAP, and Challenge Handshake Authentication Protocol, or CHAP.

Each network protocol that is routed across the data link, like IP, AppleTalk, etc, is configured dynamically using a corresponding Network Control Protocol (NCP). For instance, to send IP datagrams across the link, both PPPs must first negotiate which IP address each of them uses. The control protocol used for this is IPCP, the Internet Protocol Control Protocol.

Beside sending standard IP datagrams across the link, PPP also supports Van Jacobson header compression of IP datagrams. This is a technique to shrink the headers of TCP packets to as little as three bytes. It is also used in CSLIP, and is more colloquially referred to as VJ header compression. The use of compression may be negotiated at startup time through IPCP as well.

8.2   PPP on Linux

On Linux, PPP functionality is split up in two parts, a low-level HDLC driver located in the kernel, and the user space *pppd* daemon that handles the various control protocols. The current release of PPP for Linux is *linux-ppp-1.0.0*, and contains the kernel PPP module, *pppd*, and a program named *chat* used to dial up the remote system.

---

[1] The relevant RFCs are listed in the Annoted Bibiliography at the end of this book.
[2] In fact, HDLC is a much more general protocol devised by the International Standards Organization (ISO).

The PPP kernel driver was written by Michael Callahan. *pppd* was derived from a free PPP implementation for Sun and 386BSD machines, which was written by Drew Perkins and others, and is maintained by Paul Mackerras. It was ported to Linux by Al Longyear.[3] *chat* was written by Karl Fox.[4]

Just like SLIP, PPP is implemented by means of a special line discipline. To use some serial line as a PPP link, you first establish the connection over your modem as usual, and subsequently convert the line to PPP mode. In this mode, all incoming data is passed to the PPP driver, which checks the incoming HDLC frames for validity (each HDLC frame carries a 16 bit checksum), and unwraps and dispatches them. Currently, it is able to handle IP datagrams, optionally using Van Jacobson header compression. As soon as Linux supports IPX, the PPP driver will be extended to handle IPX packets, too.

The kernel driver is aided by *pppd*, the PPP daemon, which performs the entire initialization and authentication phase that is necessary before actual network traffic can be sent across the link. *pppd*'s behavior may be fine-tuned using a number of options. As PPP is rather complex, it is impossible to explain all of them in a single chapter. This book therefore cannot cover all aspects of *pppd*, but only give you an introduction. For more information, refer to the manual pages and *README*s in the *pppd* source distribution, which should help you sort out most questions this chapter fails to discuss. If your problems persist even after reading all documentation, you should turn to the newsgroup **comp.protocols.ppp** for help, which is the place where you will reach most of the people involved in the development of *pppd*.

8.3   Running *pppd*

When you want to connect to the Internet through a PPP link, you have to set up basic networking capabilities such as the loopback device, and the resolver. Both have been covered in the previous chapters. There are some things to be said about using DNS over a serial link; please refer to the SLIP chapter for a discussion of this.

As an introductory example of how to establish a PPP connection with *pppd*, assume you are at **vlager** again. You have already dialed up the PPP server, **c3po**, and logged into the **ppp** account. **c3po** has already fired up its PPP driver. After exiting the communications program you used for dialing, you execute the following command:

```
# pppd /dev/cua3 38400 crtscts defaultroute
```

This will flip the serial line *cua3* to PPP mode and establish an IP link to **c3po**. The transfer speed used on the serial port will be 38400bps. The *crtscts* option turns on hardware handshake on the port, which is an absolute must at speeds above 9600 bps.

The first thing *pppd* does after starting up is to negotiate several link characteristics with the remote end, using LCP. Usually, the default set of options *pppd* tries to negotiate will work, so we won't go into this here. We will return to LCP in more detail in some later section.

For the time being, we also assume that **c3po** doesn't require any authentication from us, so that the configuration phase is completed successfully.

pppd will then negotiate the IP parameters with its peer using IPCP, the IP control protocol. Since we didn't specify any particular IP address to *pppd* above, it will try to use the address obtained by having the resolver look up the local hostname. Both will then announce their address to each other.

Usually, there's nothing wrong with these defaults. Even if your machine is on an Ethernet, you can use the same IP address for both the Ethernet and the PPP interface. Nevertheless, *pppd* allows you to use a different address, or even to ask your peer to use some specific address. These options are discussed in a later section.

After going through the IPCP setup phase, *pppd* will prepare your host's networking layer to use the PPP link. It first configures the PPP network interface as a point-to-point link, using *ppp0* for the first PPP link that is active, *ppp1* for

---

[3]Both authors have said they will be very busy for some time to come. If you have any questions on PPP in general, you'd best ask the people on the NET channel of the Linux activists mailing list.

[4]**karl@morningstar.com**.

the second, and so on. Next, it will set up a routing table entry that points to the host at the other end of the link. In the example shown above, *pppd* will make the default network route point to **c3po**, because we gave it the *defaultroute* option.[5] This causes all datagrams to hosts not on your local network to be sent to **c3po**. There are a number of different routing schemes *pppd* supports, which we will cover in detail later in this chapter.

8.4 Using Options Files

Before *pppd* parses its command line arguments, it scans several files for default options. These files may contain any valid command line arguments, spread out across an arbitrary number of lines. comments are introduced by has signs.

The first options file is */etc/ppp/options*, which is always scanned when *pppd* starts up. Using it to set some global defaults is a good idea, because it allows you to keep your users from doing several things that may compromise security. For instance, to make *pppd* require some kind of authentication (either PAP or CHAP) from the peer, you would add the `auth` option to this file. This option cannot be overridden by the user, so that it becomes impossible to establish a PPP connection with any system that is not in our authentication databases.

The other option file, which is read after */etc/ppp/options*, is *.ppprc* in the user's home directory. It allows each user to specify her own set of default options.

A sample */etc/ppp/options* file might look like this:

```
# Global options for pppd running on vlager.vbrew.com
auth                    # require authentication
usehostname             # use local hostname for CHAP
lock                    # use UUCP-style device locking
domain vbrew.com        # our domain name
```

The first two of these options apply to authentication and will be explained below. The `lock` keyword makes *pppd* comply to the standard UUCP method of device locking. With this convention, each process that accesses a serial device, say */dev/cua3*, creates a lock file named *LCK..cua3* in the UUCP spool directory to signal that the device is in use. This is necessary to prevent any other programs such as *minicom* or *uucico* to open the serial device while used by PPP.

The reason to provide these options in the global configuration file is that options such as those shown above cannot be overridden, and so provide for a reasonable level of security. Note however, that some options can be overridden later; one such an example is the *connect* string.

8.5 Dialing out with *chat*

One of the things that may have struck you as inconvenient in the above example is that you had to establish the connection manually before you could fire up *pppd*. Unlike *dip*, *pppd* does not have its own scripting language for dialing the remote system and logging in, but rather relies on some external program or shell script to do this. The command to be executed can be given to *pppd* with the *connect* command line option. *pppd* will redirect the command's standard input and output to the serial line. One useful program for this is *expect*, written by Don Libes. It has a very powerful language based on Tcl, and was designed exactly for this sort of application.

The *pppd* package comes along with a similar program called *chat*, which lets you specify a UUCP-style chat script. Basically, a chat script consists of an alternating sequence of strings that we expect to receive from the remote system, and the answers we are to send. We will call the expect and send strings, respectively. This is a typical excerpt from a chat script;

```
ogin: b1ff ssword: s3kr3t
```

---

[5]The default network route is only installed if none is present yet.

This tells *chat* to wait for the remote system to send the login prompt, and return the login name **b1ff**. We only wait for `ogin:` so that it doesn't matter if the login prompt starts with an uppercase or lowercase l, or if it arrives garbled. The following string is an expect-string again that makes *chat* wait for the password prompt, and send our password in response.

This is basically all that chat scripts are about. A complete script to dial up a PPP server would, of course, also have to include the appropriate modem commands. Assume your modem understands the Hayes command set, and the server's telephone number was 318714. The complete *chat* invocation to establish a connection with **c3po** would then be

```
$ chat -v '' ATZ OK ATDT318714 CONNECT '' ogin: ppp word: GaGariN
```

By definition, the first string must be an expect string, but as the modem won't say anything before we have kicked it, we make *chat* skip the first expect by specifying an empty string. We go on and send `ATZ`, the reset command for Hayes-compatible modems, and wait for its response (`OK`). The next string sends the dial command along with the phone number to *chat*, and expects the `CONNECT` message in response. This is followed by an empty string again, because we don't want to send anything now, but rather wait for the login prompt. The remainder of the chat script works exactly as described above.

The `-v` option makes *chat* log all activities to the *syslog* daemon's *local2* facility.[6]

Specifying the chat script on the command line bears a certain risk, because users can view a process' command line with the *ps* command. You can avoid this by putting the chat script in a file, say *dial-c3po*. You make *chat* read the script from the file instead of the command line by giving it the `-f` option, followed by the file name. The complete *pppd* incantation would now look like this:

```
# pppd connect "chat -f dial-c3po" /dev/cua3 38400 -detach \
        crtscts modem defaultroute
```

Beside the *connect* option that specifies the dial-up script, we have added two more options to the command line: *-detach*, which tells *pppd* not to detach from the console and become a background process. The *modem* keyword makes it perform some modem-specific actions on the serial device, like hanging up the line before and after the call. If you don't use this keyword, *pppd* will not monitor the port's DCD line, and will therefore not detect if the remote end hangs up unexpectedly.

The examples shown above were rather simple; *chat* allows for much more complex chat scripts. One very useful feature is the ability to specify strings on which to abort the chat with an error. Typical abort strings are messages like `BUSY`, or `NO CARRIER`, that your modem usually generates when the called number is busy, or doesn't pick up the phone. To make *chat* recognize these immediately, rather than timing out, you can specify them at the beginning of the script using the `ABORT` keyword:

```
$ chat -v ABORT BUSY ABORT 'NO CARRIER' '' ATZ OK ...
```

In a similar fashion, you may change the timeout value for parts of the chat scripts by inserting `TIMEOUT` options. For details, please check the *chat(8)* manual page.

Sometimes, you'd also want to have some sort of conditional execution of parts of the chat script. For instance, when you don't receive the remote end's login prompt, you might want to send a BREAK, or a carriage return. You can achieve this by appending a sub-script to an expect string. It consists of a sequence of send- and expect-strings, just like the overall script itself, which are separated by hyphens. The sub-script is executed whenever the expected string they are appended to is not received in time. In the example above, we would modify the chat script as follows:

```
ogin:-BREAK-ogin: ppp ssword: GaGariN
```

---

[6]If you edit *syslog.conf* to redirect these log messages to a file, make sure this file isn't world readable, as *chat* also logs the entire chat script by default – including passwords and all.

Now, when *chat* doesn't see the remote system send the login prompt, the sub-script is executed by first sending a BREAK, and then waiting for the login prompt again. If the prompt now appears, the script continues as usual, otherwise it will terminate with an error.

8.6 Debugging Your PPP Setup

By default, *pppd* will log any warnings and error messages to *syslog*'s *daemon* facility. You have to add an entry to *syslog.conf* that redirects this to a file, or even the console, otherwise *syslog* simply discards these messages. The following entry sends all messages to */var/log/ppp-log*:

```
daemon.*                    /var/log/ppp-log
```

If your PPP setup doesn't work at once, looking into this log file should give you a first hint of what goes wrong. If this doesn't help, you can also turn on extra debugging output using the debug option. This makes *pppd* log the contents of all control packets sent or received to *syslog*. All messages will go to the *daemon* facility.

Finally, the most drastic feature is to enable kernel-level debugging by invoking *pppd* with the *kdebug* option. It is followed by a numeric argument that is the bitwise OR of the following values: 1 for general debug messages, 2 for printing the contents of all incoming HDLC frames, and 4 to make the driver print all outgoing HDLC frames. To capture kernel debugging messages, you must either run a *syslogd* daemon that reads the */proc/kmsg* file, or the *klogd* daemon. Either of them directs kernel debugging to *syslog*'s *kernel* facility.

8.7 IP Configuration Options

IPCP is used to negotiate a couple of IP parameters at link configuration time. Usually, each peer may send an IPCP Configuration Request packet, indicating which values it wants to change from the defaults, and to what value. Upon receipt, the remote end inspects each option in turn, and either acknowledges or rejects it.

pppd gives you a lot of control about which IPCP options it will try to negotiate. You can tune this through various command line options we will discuss below.

8.7.1 Choosing IP Addresses

In the example above, we had *pppd* dial up **c3po** and establish an IP link. No provisions were taken to choose a particular IP address on either end of the link. Instead, we picked **vlager**'s address as the local IP address, and let **c3po** provide its own. Sometimes, however, it is useful to have control over what address is used on one or the other end of the link. *pppd* supports several variations of this.

To ask for particular addresses, you generally provide *pppd* with the following option:

```
local_addr:remote_addr
```

where `local_addr` and `remote_addr` may be specified either in dotted quad notation, or as hostnames.[7] This makes *pppd* attempt to use the first address as its own IP address, and the second as the peer's. If the peer rejects either of them during IPCP negotiation, no IP link will be established.[8]

If you want to set only the local address, but accept any address the peer uses, you simply leave out the `remote_addr` part. For instance, to make **vlager** use the IP address **130.83.4.27** instead of its own, you would give it `130.83.4.27:`

---

[7]Using hostnames in this option has consequences on CHAP authentication. Please refer to the section on CHAP below.

[8]You can allow the peer PPP to override your ideas of IP addresses by giving *pppd* the `ipcp-accept-local` and `ipcp-accept-remote` options. Please refer to the manual page for details.

on the command line. Similarly, to set the remote address only, you would leave the *local_addr* field blank. By default, *pppd* will then use the address associated with your hostname.

Some PPP servers that handle a lot of client sites assign addresses dynamically: addresses are assigned to systems only when calling in, and are claimed after they have logged off again. When dialing up such a server, you must make sure that *pppd* doesn't request any particular IP address from the server, but rather accept the address the server asks you to use. This means that you mustn't specify a *local_addr* argument. In addition, you have to use the noipdefault option, which makes *pppd* wait for the peer to provide the IP address instead of using the local host's address.

8.7.2   Routing Through a PPP Link

After setting up the network interface, *pppd* will usually set up a host route to its peer only. If the remote host is on a LAN, you certainly want to be able to connect to hosts "behind" your peer as well; that is, a network route must be set up.

We have already seen above that *pppd* can be asked to set the default route using the defaultroute option. This option is very useful if the PPP server you dialed up will act as your Internet gateway.

The reverse case, where your system acts as a gateway for a single host, is also relatively easy to accomplish. For example, take some employee at the Virtual Brewery whose home machine is called **loner**. When connecting to **vlager** through PPP, he uses an address on the Brewery's subnet. At **vlager**, we can now give *pppd* the proxyarp option, which will install a proxy ARP entry for **loner**. This will automatically make **loner** accessible from all hosts at the Brewery and the Winery.

However, things aren't always as easy as that, for instance when linking two local area networks. This usually requires adding a specific network route, because these networks may have their own default routes. Besides, having both peers use the PPP link as the default route would generate a loop, where packets to unknown destinations would ping-pong between the peers until their time-to-live expired.

As an example, suppose the Virtual Brewery opens a branch in some other city. The subsidiary runs an Ethernet of their own using the IP network number **191.72.3.0**, which is subnet 3 of the Brewery's class B network. They want to connect to the Brewery's main Ethernet via PPP to update customer databases, etc. Again, **vlager** acts as the gateway; its peer is called **sub-etha** and has an IP address of **191.72.3.1**..

When **sub-etha** connects to **vlager**, it will make the default route point to **vlager** as usual. On **vlager**, however, we will have to install a network route for subnet 3 that goes through **sub-etha**. For this, we use a feature of *pppd* not discussed so far – the *ip-up* command. This is a shell script or program located in */etc/ppp* that is executed after the PPP interface has been configured. When present, it is invoked with the following parameters:

```
ip-up iface device speed local_addr remote_addr
```

where *iface* names the network interface used, *device* is the pathname of the serial device file used (*/dev/tty* if stdin/stdout are used), and *speed* is the device's speed. *local_addr* and *remote_addr* give the IP addresses used at both ends of the link in dotted quad notation. In our case, the *ip-up* script may contain the following code fragment:

```
#!/bin/sh
case $5 in
191.72.3.1)                   # this is sub-etha
        route add -net 191.72.3.0 gw 191.72.3.1;;
...
esac
exit 0
```

In a similar fashion, */etc/ppp/ip-down* is used to undo all actions of *ip-up* after the PPP link has been taken down again.

However, the routing scheme is not yet complete. We have set up routing table entries on both PPP hosts, but so far, all other hosts on both networks don't know anything about the PPP link. This is not a big problem if all hosts at the subsidiary have their default route pointing at **sub-etha**, and all Brewery hosts route to **vlager** by default. If this is not the case, your only option will usually be to use a routing daemon like *gated*. After creating the network route on **vlager**, the routing daemon would broadcast the new route to all hosts on the attached subnets.

8.8 Link Control Options

Above, we already encountered LCP, the Link Control Protocol, which is used to negotiate link characteristics, and to test the link.

The two most important options that may be negotiated by LCP are the maximum receive unit, and the Asynchronous Control Character Map. There are a number of other LCP configuration options, but they are far too specialized to discuss here. Please refer to RFC 1548 for a description of those.

The Asynchronous Control Character Map, colloquially called the async map, is used on asynchronous links such as telephone lines to identify control characters that must be escaped (replaced by a specific two-character sequence). For instance, you may want to avoid the XON and XOFF characters used for software handshake, because some misconfigured modem might choke upon receipt of an XOFF. Other candidates include Ctrl-] (the *telnet* escape character). PPP allows you to escape any of the characters with ASCII codes 0 through 31 by specifying them in the async map.

The async map is a bitmap 32 bits wide, with the least significant bit corresponding to the ASCII NUL character, and the most significant bit corrsponding to ASCII 31. If a bit is set, it signals that the corresponding character must be escaped before sending it across the link. Initially, the async map is set to *0xffffffff*, that is, all control characters will be esaped.

To tell your peer that it doesn't have to escape all control characters but only a few of them, you can specify a new asyncmap to *pppd* using the asyncmap option. For instance, if only ^S and ^Q (ASCII 17 and 19, commonly used for XON and XOFF) must be escaped, use the following option:

```
asyncmap 0x000A0000
```

The Maximum Receive Unit, or MRU, signals to the peer the maximum size of HDLC frames we want to receive. Although this may remind you of the MTU value (Maximum Transfer Unit), these two have little in common. The MTU is a parameter of the kernel networking device, and describes the maximum frame size the interface is able to handle. The MRU is more of an advice to the remote end not to generate any frames larger than the MRU; the interface must nevertheless be able to receive frames of up to 1500 bytes.

Choosing an MRU is therefore not so much a question of what the link is capable of transferring, but of what gives you the best throughput. If you intend to run interactive applications over the link, setting the MRU to values as low as 296 is a good idea, so that an occasional larger packet (say, from an FTP session) doesn't make your cursor "jump". To tell *pppd* to request an MRU of 296, you would give it the option mru 296. Small MRUs, however, only make sense if you don't have VJ header compression disabled (it is enabled by default).

pppd understands also a couple of LCP options that configure the overall behavior of the negotiation process, such as the maximum number of configuration requests that may be exchanged before the link is terminated. Unless you kow exactly what you are doing, you should leave these alone.

Finally, there are two options that apply to LCP echo messages. PPP defines two messages, Echo Request and Echo Response. *pppd* uses this feature to check if a link is still operating. You can enable this by using the lcp-echo-interval option together with a time in seconds. If no frames are received from the remote host within this interval, *pppd* generates an Echo Request, and expects the peer to return an Echo Response. If the peer does not produce a response, the link is terminated after a certain number of requests sent. This number can be set using the lcp-echo-failure option. By default, this feature is disabled altogether.

8.9 General Security Considerations

A misconfigured PPP daemon can be a devastating security breach. It can be as bad as letting anyone plug in their machine into your Ethernet (and that is very bad). In this section, we will discuss a few measures that should make your PPP configuration safe.

One problem with *pppd* is that to configure the network device and the routing table, it requires **root** privilege. You will usually solve this by running it setuid **root**. However, *pppd* allows users to set various security-relevant options. To protect against any attacks a user may launch by manipulating these options, it is suggested you set a couple of default values in the global */etc/ppp/options* file, like those shown in the sample file in section 8.4. Some of them, such as the authentication options, cannot be overridden by the user, and so provide a reasonable protection against manipulations.

Of course, you have to protect yourself from the systems you speak PPP with, too. To fend off hosts posing as someone else, you should always some sort of authentication from your peer. Additionally, you should not allow foreign hosts to use any IP address they choose, but restrict them to at least a few. The following section will deal with these topics.

8.10 Authentication with PPP

8.10.1 CHAP versus PAP

With PPP, each system may require its peer to authenticate itself using one of two authentication protocols. These are the Password Authentication Protocol (PAP), and the Challenge Handshake Authentication Protocol (CHAP). When a connection is established, each end can request the other to authenticate itself, regardless of whether it is the caller or the callee. Below I will loosely talk of 'client' and 'server' when I want to distinguish between the authenticating system and the authenticator. A PPP daemon can ask its peer for authentication by sending yet another LCP configuration request identifying the desired authentication protocol.

PAP works basically the same way as the normal login procedure. The client authenticates itself by sending a user name and an (optionally encrypted) password to the server, which the server compares to its secrets database. This technique is vulnerable to eavesdroppers who may try to obtain the password by listening in on the serial line, and to repeated trial and error attacks.

CHAP does not have these deficiencies. With CHAP, the authenticator (i.e. the server) sends a randomly generated "challenge" string to the client, along with its hostname. The client uses the hostname to look up the appropriate secret, combines it with the challenge, and encrypts the string using a one-way hashing function. The result is returned to the server along with the client's hostname. The server now performs the same computation, and acknowledges the client if it arrives at the same result.

Another feature of CHAP is that it doesn't only require the client to authenticate itself at startup time, but sends challenges at regular intervals to make sure the client hasn't been replaced by an intruder, for instance by just switching phone lines.

pppd keeps the secret keys for CHAP and PAP in two separate files, called */etc/ppp/chap-secrets* and *pap-secrets*, respectively. By entering a remote host in one or the other file, you have a fine control over whether CHAP or PAP is used to authenticate ourselves with our peer, and vice versa.

By default, *pppd* doesn't require authentication from the remote, but will agree to authenticate itself when requested by the remote. As CHAP is so much stronger than PAP, *pppd* tries to use the former whenever possible. If the peer does not support it, or if *pppd* can't find a CHAP secret for the remote system in its *chap-secrets* file, it reverts to PAP. If it doesn't have a PAP secret for its peer either, it will refuse to authenticate altogether. As a consequence, the connection is closed down.

This behavior can be modified in several ways. For instance, when given the `auth` keyword, *pppd* will require the peer to authenticate itself. *pppd* will agree to use either CHAP or PAP for this, as long as it has a secret for the peer in its CHAP or PAP database, respectively. There are other options to turn a particular authentication protocol on or off, but I won't describe them here. Please refer to the *pppd(8)* manual page for details.

If all systems you talk PPP with agree to authenticate themselves with you, you should put the `auth` option in the global */etc/ppp/options* file and define passwords for each system in the *chap-secrets* file. If a system doesn't support CHAP, add an entry for it to the *pap-secrets* file. In this way, you can make sure no unauthenticated system connects to your host.

The next two sections discuss the two PPP secrets files, *pap-secrets* and *chap-secrets*. They are located in */etc/ppp* and contain triples of clients, servers and passwords, optionally followed by a list of IP addresses. The interpretation of the client and server fields is different for CHAP and PAP, and also depends on whether we authenticate ourselves with the peer, or whether we require the server to authenticate itself with us.

8.10.2 The CHAP Secrets File

When it has to authenticate itself with some server using CHAP, *pppd* searches the *pap-secrets* file for an entry with the client field equal to the local hostname, and the server field equal to the remote hostname sent in the CHAP Challenge. When requiring the peer to authenticate itself, the roles are simply reversed: *pppd* will then look for an entry with the client field equal to the remote hostname (sent in the client's CHAP Response), and the server field equal to the local hostname.

The following is a sample *chap-secrets* file for **vlager**:[9]

```
# CHAP secrets for vlager.vbrew.com
#
# client          server          secret                 addrs
#-----------------------------------------------------------------------
vlager.vbrew.com  c3po.lucas.com  "Use The Source Luke"  vlager.vbrew.com
c3po.lucas.com    vlager.vbrew.com  "riverrun, pasteve"  c3po.lucas.com
*                 vlager.vbrew.com  "VeryStupidPassword"  pub.vbrew.com
```

When establishing a PPP connection with **c3po**, **c3po** asks **vlager** to authenticate itself using CHAP by sending a CHAP challenge. *pppd* then scans *chap-secrets* for an entry with the client field equal to **vlager.vbrew.com** and the server field equal to **c3po.lucas.com**,[10] and finds the first line shown above. It then produces the CHAP Response from the challenge string and the secret (`Use The Source Luke`), and sends it off to **c3po**.

At the same time, *pppd* composes a CHAP challenge for **c3po**, containing a unique challenge string, and its fully qualified hostname **vlager.vbrew.com**. **c3po** constructs a CHAP Response in the manner we just discussed, and returns it to **vlager**. *pppd* now extracts the client hostname (**c3po.vbrew.com**) from the Response, and searches the *chap-secrets* file for a line matching **c3po** as a client, and **vlager** as the server. The second line does this, so *pppd* combines the CHAP challenge and the secret `riverrun, pasteve`, encrypts them, and compares the result to **c3po**'s CHAP respnose.

The optional fourth field lists the IP addresses that are acceptable for the clients named in the first field. The addresses may be given in dotted quad notation or as hostnames that are looked up with the resolver. For instance, if **c3po** requests to use an IP address during IPCP negotiation that is not in this list, the request will be rejected, and IPCP will be shut down. In the sample file shown above, **c3po** is therefore limited to using its own IP address. If the address field is empty, any addresses will be allowed; a value of - prevents the use of IP with that client altogether.

The third line of the sample *chap-secrets* file allows any host to establish a PPP link with **vlager** because a client or server field of * matches any hostname. The only requirement is that it knows the secret, and uses the address of **pub.vbrew.com**. Entries with wildcard hostnames may appear anywhere in the secrets file, since *pppd* will always use the most specific entry that applies to a server/client pair.

There are some words to be said about the way *pppd* arrives at the hostnames it looks up in the secrets file. As explained before, the remote hostname is always provided by the peer in the CHAP Challenge or Response packet. The local hostname will be derived by calling the *gethostname(2)* function by default. If you have set the system name to your unqualified hostname, such you have to provide *pppd* with the domain name in addition using the `domain` option:

---

[9] The double quotes are not part of the password, they merely serve to protect the white space within the password.

[10] This hostname is taken from the CHAP challenge.

```
# pppd ...domain vbrew.com
```

This will append the Brewery's domain name to **vlager** for all authentication-related activities. Other options that modify
progpppd's idea of the local hostname are usehostname and name. When you give the local IP address on the
command line using "`local`: varremote", and `local` is a name instead of a dotted quad, *pppd* will use this as the local
hostname. For details, please refer to the *pppd(8)* manual page.

8.10.3 The PAP Secrets File

The PAP secrets file is very similar to that used by CHAP. The first two fields always contain a user name and a server
name; the third holds the PAP secret. When the remote sends an authenticate request, *pppd* uses the entry that has a server
field equal to the local hostname, and a user field equal to the user name sent in the request. When authenticating itself
with the peer, *pppd* picks the secret to be sent from the line with the user field equal to the local user name, and the server
field equal to the remote hostname.

A sample PAP secrets file might look like this:

```
# /etc/ppp/pap-secrets
#
# user            server          secret          addrs
vlager-pap        c3po            cresspahl       vlager.vbrew.com
c3po              vlager          DonaldGNUth     c3po.lucas.com
```

The first line is used to authenticate ourselves when talking to **c3po**. The second line describes how a user named **c3po**
has to authenticate itself with us.

The name **vlager-pap** in column one is the user name we send to **c3po**. By default, *pppd* will pick the local hostname as
the user name, but you can also specify a different name by giving the user option, followed by that name.

When picking an entry from the *pap-secrets* file for authentication with the peer, *pppd* has to know the remote host's
name. As it has no way of finding that out, you have to specify it on the command line using the remotename keyword,
followed by the peer's hostname. For instance, to use the above entry for authentication with **c3po**, we have to add the
following option to *pppd*'s command line:

```
\#{} pppd ... remotename c3po user vlager-pap
```

In the fourth field (and all fields following), you may specify what IP addresses are allowed for that particular host, just
as in the CHAP secrets file. The peer may then only request addresses from that list. In the sample file, we require **c3po**
to use its real IP address.

Note that PAP is a rather weak authentication method, and it is suggested you use CHAP instead whenever possible.
We will therefore not cover PAP in greater detail here; if you are interested in using PAP, you will find some more PAP
features in the *pppd(8)* manual page.

8.11   Configuring a PPP Server

Running *pppd* as a server is just a matter of adding the appropriate options to the command line. Ideally, you would
create a special account, say **ppp**, and give it a script or program as login shell that invokes *pppd* with these options. For
instance, you would add the following line to */etc/passwd*:

```
ppp:*:500:200:Public PPP Account:/tmp:/etc/ppp/ppplogin
```

Of course, you may want to use different uids and gids than those shown above. You would also have to set the password for the above account using the *passwd* command.

The *ppplogin* script might then look like this:

```
#!/bin/sh
# ppplogin - script to fire up pppd on login
mesg n
stty -echo
exec pppd -detach silent modem crtscts
```

The *mesg* command disables other users to write to the tty using, for instance, the *write* command. The *stty* command turns off character echoing. The is necessary, because otherwise everything the peer sends would be echoed back to it. The most important *pppd* option given above is -detach, because it prevents *pppd* drom detaching from the controlling tty. If we didn't specify this option, it would go to the background, making the shell script exit. This would in turn would cause the serial line to be hung up and the connection to be dropped. The *silent* option causes *pppd* to wait until it receives a packet from the calling system before it starts sending. This prevents transmit timeouts to occur when the calling system is slow in firing up its PPP client. The modem makes *pppd* watch the DTR line to see if the peer has dropped the connection, and crtscts turns on hardware handshake.

Beside these options, you might want to force some sort of authentication, for example by specifying auth on *pppd*'s command line, or in the global options file. The manual page also discusses more specific options for turning individual authentication protocols on and off.

Net-Admin Guide

Chapter 9

Various Network Applications

After successfully setting up IP and the resolver, you have to turn to the services you want to provide over the network. This chapter covers the configuration of a few simple network applications, including the *inetd* server, and the programs from the *rlogin* family. The Remote Procedure Call interface that services like the Network File System (NFS) and the Network Information System (NIS) are based upon will be dealt with briefly, too. The configuration of NFS and NIS, however, takes up more room, will be described in separate chapters. This applies to electronic mail and netnews as well.

Of course, we can't cover all network applications in this book. If you want to install one that's not discussed here, like *talk*, *gopher*, or *Xmosaic* please refer to its manual pages for details.

9.1   The *inetd* Super-Server

Frequently, services are performed by so-called *daemons*. A daemon is a program that opens a certain port, and waits for incoming connections. If one occurs, it creates a child process which accepts the connection, while the parent continues to listen for further requests. This concept has the drawback that for every service offered, a daemon has to run that listens on the port for a connection to occur, which generally means a waste of system resources like swap space.

Thus, almost all UNIX installations run a "super-server" that creates sockets for a number of services, and listens on all of them simultaneously using the *select(2)* system call. When a remote host requests one of the services, the super-server notices this and spawns the server specified for this port.

The super-server commonly used is *inetd*, the Internet Daemon. It is started at system boot time, and takes the list of services it is to manage from a startup file named */etc/inetd.conf*. In addition to those servers invoked, there are a number of trivial services which are performed by *inetd* itself called *internal services*. They include *chargen* which simply generates a string of characters, and *daytime* which returns the system's idea of the time of day.

An entry in this file consists of a single line made up of the following fields:

```
service type protocol wait user server cmdline
```

The meaning of each field is as follows:

service   gives the service name. The service name has to be translated to a port number by looking it up in the */etc/services* file. This file will be described in section 9.3 below.

type   specifies a socket type, either *stream* (for connection-oriented protocols) or *dgram* (for datagram protocols). TCP-based services should therefore always use *stream*, while UDP-based services should always use *dgram*.

protocol   names the transport protocol used by the service. This must be a valid protocol name found in the *protocols* file, also explained below.

wait   This option applies only to *dgram* sockets. It may be either *wait* or *nowait*. If *wait* is specified, *inetd* will only execute one server for the specified port at any time. Otherwise, it will immediately continue to listen on the port after executing the server.

This is useful for "single-threaded" servers that read all incoming datagrams until no more arrive, and then exit. Most RPC servers are of this type and should therefore specify *wait*. The opposite type, "multi-threaded" servers, allow an unlimited number of instances to run concurrently; this is only rarely used. These servers should specify *nowait*.

stream sockets should always use *nowait*.

`user`   This is the login id of the user the process is executed under. This will frequently be the **root** user, but some services may use different accounts. It is a very good idea to apply the principle of least privilege here, which states that you shouldn't run a command under a privileged account if the program doesn't require this for proper functioning. For example, the NNTP news server will run as **news**, while services that may pose a security risk (such as *tftp* or *finger*) are often run as **nobody**.

`server`   gives the full path name of the server program to be executed. Internal services are marked by the keyword *internal*.

`cmdline`   This is the command line to be passed to the server. This includes argument 0, that is the command name. Usually, this will be the program name of the server, unless the program behaves differently when invoked by a different name.

This field is empty for internal services.

```
#
# inetd services
ftp        stream tcp nowait root   /usr/sbin/ftpd      in.ftpd -l
telnet     stream tcp nowait root   /usr/sbin/telnetd in.telnetd -
b/etc/issue
#finger    stream tcp nowait bin    /usr/sbin/fingerd in.fingerd
#tftp      dgram  udp wait   nobody /usr/sbin/tftpd   in.tftpd
#tftp      dgram  udp wait   nobody /usr/sbin/tftpd   in.tftpd /boot/diskless
login      stream tcp nowait root   /usr/sbin/rlogind in.rlogind
shell      stream tcp nowait root   /usr/sbin/rshd    in.rshd
exec       stream tcp nowait root   /usr/sbin/rexecd  in.rexecd
#
#          inetd internal services
#
daytime    stream tcp nowait root internal
daytime    dgram  udp nowait root internal
time       stream tcp nowait root internal
time       dgram  udp nowait root internal
echo       stream tcp nowait root internal
echo       dgram  udp nowait root internal
discard    stream tcp nowait root internal
discard    dgram  udp nowait root internal
chargen    stream tcp nowait root internal
chargen    dgram  udp nowait root internal
```

Figure 9.1: A sample */etc/inetd.conf* file.

A sample *inetd.conf* file is shown in figure 9.1. The *finger* service commented out, so that it is not available. This is often done for security reasons, because may be used by attackers to obtain names of users on your system.

The *tftp* is shown commented out as well. *tftp* implements the *Primitive File Transfer Protocol* that allows to transfer any world-readable files from your system without password checking etc. This is especially harmful with the */etc/passwd* file, even more so when you don't use shadow password.

TFTP is commonly used by diskless clients and X terminals to download their code from a boot server. If you need to run *tftpd* for this reason, make sure to limit its scope to those directories clients will retrieve files from by adding those directory names to *tftpd*'s command line. This is shown in the second *tftp* line in the example.

9.2 The *tcpd* access control facility

Since opening a computer to network access involves many security risks, applications are designed to guard against several types of attacks. Some of these, however, may be flawed (most drastically demonstrated by the RTM Internet worm), or do not distinguish between secure hosts from which requests for a particular service will be accepted, and insecure hosts whose requests should be rejected. We already briefly discussed the *finger* and *tftp* services above. Thus, one would want to limit access to these services to "trusted hosts" only, which is impossible with the usual setup, where *inetd* either provides this service to all clients, or not at all.

A useful tool for this is *tcpd*,[1] a so-called daemon wrapper. For TCP services you want to monitor or protect, it is invoked instead of the server program. *tcpd* logs the request to the *syslog* daemon, ckecks if the remote host is allowed to use that service, and only if this succeeds will it executes the real server program. Note that this does not work with UDP-based services.

For example, to wrap the *finger* daemon, you have to change the corresponding line in *inetd.conf* to

```
# wrap finger daemon
finger   stream  tcp    nowait  root    /usr/sbin/tcpd   in.fingerd
```

Without adding any access control, this will appear to the client just as a usual *finger* setup, except that any requests are logged to *syslog*'s *auth* facility.

Access control is implemented by means of two files called */etc/hosts.allow* and */etc/hosts.deny*. They contain entries allowing and denying access, respectively, to certain services and hosts. When *tcpd* handles a request for a service such as *finger* from a client host named **biff.foobar.com**, it scans *hosts.allow* and *hosts.deny* (in this order) for an entry matching both the service and client host. If a matching entry is found in *hosts.allow*, access is granted, regardless of any entry in *hosts.deny*. If a match is found in *hosts.deny*, the request is rejected by closing down the connection. If no match is found at all, the request is accepted.

Entries in the access files look like this:

```
servicelist:  hostlist [:shellcmd]
```

`servicelist` is a list of service names from */etc/services*, or the keyword *ALL*. To match all services except *finger* and *tftp*, use "*ALL EXCEPT finger, tftp*".

`hostlist` is a list of host names or IP addresses, or the keywords *ALL*, *LOCAL*, or *UNKNOWN*. *ALL* matches any host, while *LOCAL* matches host names not containing a dot.[2] *UNKNOWN* matches any hosts whose name or address lookup failed. A name starting with a dot matches all hosts whose domain is equal to this name. For example, **.foobar.com** matches **biff.foobar.com**. There are also provisions for IP network addresses and subnet numbers. Please refer to the *hosts_access(5)* manual page for details.

To deny access to the *finger* and *tftp* services to all but the local hosts, put the following in */etc/hosts.deny*, and leave */etc/hosts.allow* empty:

```
in.tftpd, in.fingerd:  ALL EXCEPT LOCAL, .your.domain
```

The optional `shellcmd` field may contain a shell command to be invoked when the entry is matched. This is useful to set up traps that may expose potential attackers:

---

[1] Written by Wietse Venema, **wietse@wzv.win.tue.nl**.
[2] Usually only local host names obtained from lookups in */etc/hosts* contain no dots.

```
in.ftpd: ALL EXCEPT LOCAL, .vbrew.com : \
     echo "request from %d@%h" >> /var/log/finger.log; \
     if [ %h != "vlager.vbrew.com" ]; then \
          finger -l @%h >> /var/log/finger.log \
     fi
```

The *%h* and *%d* arguments are expanded by *tcpd* to the client host name and service name, respectively. Please refer to the *hosts_access(5)* manual page for details.

9.3 The *services* and *protocols* Files

The port numbers on which certain "standard" services are offered are defined in the "Assigned Numbers" RFC. To enable server and client programs to convert service names to these numbers, at least a part of the list is kept on each host; it is stored in a file called */etc/services*. An entry is made up like this:

```
service port/protocol [aliases]
```

Here, `service` specifies the service name, `port` defines the port the service is offered on, and `protocol` defines which transport protocol is used. Commonly, this is either *udp* or *tcp*. It is possible for a service to be offered for more than one protocol, as well as offering different services on the same port, as long as the protocols are different. The `aliases` field allows to specify alternative names for the same service.

Usually, you don't have to change the services file that comes along with the network software on your Linux system. Nevertheless, we give a small excerpt from that file below.

```
# The services file:
#
# well-known services
echo           7/tcp                      # Echo
echo           7/udp                      #
discard        9/tcp    sink null         # Discard
discard        9/udp    sink null         #
daytime       13/tcp                      # Daytime
daytime       13/udp                      #
chargen       19/tcp    ttytst source     # Character Generator
chargen       19/udp    ttytst source     #
ftp-data      20/tcp                      # File Transfer Protocol (Data)
ftp           21/tcp                      # File Transfer Protocol (Control)
telnet        23/tcp                      # Virtual Terminal Protocol
smtp          25/tcp                      # Simple Mail Transfer Protocol
nntp         119/tcp    readnews          # Network News Transfer Protocol
#
# UNIX services
exec         512/tcp                      # BSD rexecd
biff         512/udp    comsat            # mail notification
login        513/tcp                      # remote login
who          513/udp    whod              # remote who and uptime
shell        514/tcp    cmd               # remote command, no passwd used
syslog       514/udp                      # remote system logging
printer      515/tcp    spooler           # remote print spooling
route        520/udp    router routed     # routing information protocol
```

Note that, for example, the *echo* service is offered on port 7 for both TCP and UDP, and that port 512 is used for two different services, namely the COMSAT daemon (which notifies users of newly arrived mail, see *xbiff(1x)*), over UDP, and for remote execution (*rexec(1)*), using TCP.

Similar to the services file, the networking library needs a way to translate protocol names — for example, those used in the services file — to protocol numbers understood by the IP layer on other hosts. This is done by looking up the name in the */etc/protocols* file. It contains one entry per line, each containing a protocol name, and the associated number. Having to touch this file is even more unlikely than having to meddle with */etc/services*. A sample file is given below:

```
#
# Internet (IP) protocols
#
ip      0       IP              # internet protocol, pseudo protocol number
icmp    1       ICMP            # internet control message protocol
igmp    2       IGMP            # internet group multicast protocol
tcp     6       TCP             # transmission control protocol
udp     17      UDP             # user datagram protocol
raw     255     RAW             # RAW IP interface
```

9.4   Remote Procedure Call

A very general mechanism for client-server applications is provided by RPC, the *Remote Procedure Call* package. RPC was developed by Sun Micrsystems, and is a collection of tools and library functions. Important applications built on top of RPC are NFS, the Network Filesystem, and NIS, the Network Information System, both of which will be introduced in later chapters.

An RPC server consists of a collection of procedures that client may call by sending an RPC request to the server, along with the procedure parameters. The server will invoke the indicated procedure on behalf of the client, handing back the return value, if there is any. In order to be machine-independent, all data exchanged between client and server is converted to a so-called *External Data Representation* format (XDR) by the sender, and converted back to the machine-local representation by the receiver.

Sometimes, improvements to an RPC application introduce incompatible changes in the procedure call interface. Of course, simply changing the server would crash all application that still expect the original behavior. Therefore, RPC programs have version numbers assigned to them, usually starting with 1, and with each new version of the RPC interface this counter will be bumped. Often, a server may offer several versions simultaneously; clients then indicate by the version number in their requests which implementation of the service they want to use.

The network communication between RPC servers and clients is somewhat peculiar. An RPC server offers one or more collections of procedures; each set is being called a *program*, and is uniquely identified by a *program number*. A list mapping service names to program numbers is usually kept in */etc/rpc*, an excerpt of which is reproduced below in figure 9.2.

In TCP/IP networks, the authors of RPC were faced with the problem of mapping program numbers to generic network services. They chose to have each server provide both a TCP and a UDP port for each program and each version. Generally, RPC applications will use UDP when sending data, and only fall back to TCP when the data to be transferred doesn't fit into a single UDP datagram.

Of course, client programs have to have a way to find out which port a program number maps to. Using a configuration file for this would be too unflexible; since RPC applications don't use reserved ports, there's no guarantee that a port originally meant to be used by our database application hasn't been taken by some other process. Therefore, RPC applications pick any port they can get, and register it with the so-called *portmapper daemon*. The latter acts as a service broker for all RPC servers running on its machine: a client that wishes to contact a service with a given program number will first query the portmapper on the server's host which returns the TCP and UDP port numbers the service can be reached at.

```
#
# /etc/rpc - miscellaenous RPC-based services
#
portmapper       100000    portmap sunrpc
rstatd           100001    rstat rstat_svc rup perfmeter
rusersd          100002    rusers
nfs              100003    nfsprog
ypserv           100004    ypprog
mountd           100005    mount showmount
ypbind           100007
walld            100008    rwall shutdown
yppasswdd        100009    yppasswd
bootparam        100026
ypupdated        100028    ypupdate
```

Figure 9.2: A sample /etc/rpc file.

This method has the particular drawback that it introduces a single point of failure, much like the *inetd* daemon does for the standard Berkeley services. However, this case is even a little worse, because when the portmapper dies, all RPC port information is lost; this usually means you have to restart all RPC servers manually, or reboot the entire machine.

On Linux, the portmapper is called *rpc.portmap* and resides in */usr/sbin*. Other than making sure it is started form *rc.inet2*, the portmapper doesn't require any configuration work.

9.5   Configuring the *r* Commands

There are a number of commands for executing commands on remote hosts. These are *rlogin*, *rsh*, *rcp* and *rcmd*. They all spawn a shell on the remote host and allow the user to execute commands. Of course, the client needs to have an account on the host where the commmand is to be executed. Thus all these commands perform an authorization procedure. Usually, the client will tell the user's login name to the server, which in turn requests a password that is validated in the usual way.

Sometimes, however, it is desirable to relax authorization checks for certain users. For instance, if you frequently have to log into other machines on your LAN, you might want to be admitted without having to type your password every time.

Disabling authorization is advisable only on a small number of hosts whose password databases are synchronized, or for a small number of privileged users who need to access many machines for administrative reasons. Whenever you want to allow people to log into your host without having to specify a login id or password, make sure that you don't accidentally grant access to anybody else.

There are two ways to disable authorization checks for the *r* commands. One is for the super user to allow certain or all users on certain or all hosts (the latter definitely being a bad idea) to log in without being asked for a password. This access is controlled by a file called */etc/hosts.equiv*. It contains a list of host and user names that are considered equivalent to users on the local host. An alternative option is for a user to grant other users on certain hosts access to her account. These may be listed in the file *.rhosts* in the user's home directory. For security reasons, this file must be owned by the user or the super user, and must not be a symbolic link, otherwise it will be ignored.[3]

When a client requests an *r* service, her host and user name are searched in the */etc/hosts.equiv* file, and then in the *.rhosts* file of the user she wants to log in as. As am example, assume **janet** is working on **gauss** and tries to log into **joe**'s account on **euler**. Throughout the following, we will refer to Janet as the *client* user, and to Joe as the *local* user. Now, when Janet types

---

[3] In an NFS environment, you may need to give it a protection of 444, because the super user is often very restricted in accessing files on disks mounted via NFS.

```
$ rlogin -l joe euler
```

on **gauss**, the server will first check *hosts.equiv*[4] if Janet should be granted free access, and if this fails, it will try to look her up in *.rhosts* in **joe**'s home directory.

The *hosts.equiv* file on **euler** looks like this:

```
gauss
euler
-public
quark.physics.groucho.edu      andres
```

An entry consists of a host name, optionally followed by a user name. If a host name appears all by itself, all users from that host will be admitted to their local accounts without any checks. In the above example, Janet would be allowed to log into her account **janet** when coming from **gauss**, and the same applies to any other user except **root**. However, if Janet wants to log in as **joe**, she will be prompted for a password as usual.

If a host name is followed by a user name, as in the last line of the above sample file, this user is given password-free access to *all* accounts except the **root** account.

The host name may also be preceded by a minus sign, as in the entry "**-public**". This requires authorization for all accounts on **public**, regardless of what rights individual users grant in their *.rhosts* file.

The format of the *.rhosts* file is identical to that of *hosts.equiv*, but its meaning is a little different. Consider Joe's *.rhosts* file on **euler**:

```
chomp.cs.groucho.edu
gauss         janet
```

The first entry grants **joe** free acess when logging in from **chomp.cs.groucho.edu**, but does not affect the rights of any other account on **euler** or **chomp**. The second entry is a slight variation of this, in that it grants **janet** free access to Joe's account when logging in from **gauss**.

Note that the client's host name is obtained by reverse mapping the caller's address to a name, so that this feature will fail with hosts unknown to the resolver. The client's host name is considered to match the name in the hosts files in one of the following cases:

- The client's canonical host name (not an alias) literally matches the host name in the file.
- If the client's host name is a fully qualified domain name (such as returned by the resolver when you have DNS running), and it doesn't literally match the host name in the hosts file, it is compared to that host name expanded with the local domain name.

---

[4]Note that the *hosts.equiv* file is *not* searched when someone attempts to log in as **root**.

Chapter 10

The Network Information System

When you are running a local area network, your overall goal is usually to provide an environment to your users that makes the network transparent. An important stepping stone to this end is to keep vital data such as user account information synchronized between all hosts. We have seen before that for host name resolution, a powerful and sophisticated service exists, being DNS. For others tasks, there is no such specialized service. Moreover, if you manage only a small LAN with no Internet connectivity, setting up DNS may not seem worth the trouble for many administrators.

This is why Sun developed NIS, the *Network Information System*. NIS provides generic database access facilities that can be used to distribute information such as that contained in the *passwd* and *groups* files to all hosts on your network. This makes the network appear just as a single system, with the same accounts on all hosts. In a similar fashion, you can use NIS to distribute the hostname information form */etc/hosts* to all machines on the network.

NIS is based on RPC, and comprises a server, a client-side library, and several administrative tools. Originally, NIS was called *Yellow Pages*, or YP, which is still widely used to informally refer this service. On the other hand, Yellow Pages is a trademark of British Telecom, which required Sun to drop that name. As things go, some names stick with people, and so YP lives on as a prefix to the names of most NIS-related commands such as *ypserv*, *ypbind*, etc.

Today, NIS is available for virtually all Unices, and there are even free implementations of it. One is from the BSD Net-2 release, and has been derived from a public domain reference implementation donated by Sun. The library client code from this release has been in the GNU *libc* for a long time, while the administrative programs have only recently been ported to Linux by Swen Thümmler.[1] An NIS server is missing from the reference implementation. Tobias Reber has written another NIS package including all tools and a server; it is called *yps*.[2]

Currently, a complete rewrite of the NIS code called NYS is being done by Peter Eriksson,[3] which supports both plain NIS and Sun's much revised NIS+. NYS not only provides a set of NIS tools and a server, but also adds a whole new set of library functions which will most probably make it into the standard *libc* eventually. This includes a new configuration scheme for hostname resolution that replaces the current scheme using *host.conf*. The features of these functions will be discussed below.

This chapter will focus on NYS rather than the other two packages, to which I will refer as the "traditional" NIS code. If you do want to run any of these packages, the instructions in this chapter may or may not be enough. To obtain additional information, please get a standard book on NIS, such as Hal Stern's *NFS and NIS* (see [Stern92]).

For the time being, NYS is still under development, and therefore standard Linux utilities such as the network programs or the *login* program are not yet aware of the NYS configuration scheme. Until NYS is merged into the mainstream *libc* you therefore have to recompile all these binaries if you want to make them use NYS. In any of these applications' *Makefiles*, specify *-lnsl* as the last option before *libc* to the linker. This links in the relevant functions from *libnsl*, the NYS library, instead of the standard C library.

---

[1]To be reached at **swen@uni-paderborn.de**. The NIS clients are available as `yp-linux.tar.gz` from **sunsite.unc.edu** in *system/Network*.

[2]The current version (as of this writing) is `yps-0.21` and can be obtained from **ftp.lysator.liu.se** in the */pub/NYS* directory.

[3]To be reached at **pen@lysator.liu.se**.

10.1   Getting Acquainted with NIS

NIS keeps database information is in so-called *maps* containing key-value pairs. Maps are stored on a central host running the NIS server, from which clients may retrieve the information through various RPC calls. Quite frequently, maps are stored in DBM files.[4]

The maps themselves are usually generated from master text files such as */etc/hosts* or */etc/passwd*. For some files, several maps are created, one for each search key type. For instance, you may search the *hosts* file for a host name as well as for an IP address. Accordingly, two NIS maps are derived from it, called *hosts.byname* and *hosts.byaddr*, respectively. Table 10.1 lists common maps and the files they are generated form.

Master File	Map(s)	
/etc/hosts	*hosts.byname*	*hosts.byaddr*
/etc/networks	*networks.byname*	*networks.byaddr*
/etc/passwd	*passwd.byname*	*passwd.byuid*
/etc/group	*group.byname*	*group.bygid*
/etc/services	*services.byname*	*services.bynumber*
/etc/rpc	*rpc.byname*	*rpc.bynumber*
/etc/protocols	*protocols.byname*	*protocols.bynumber*
/usr/lib/aliases	*mail.aliases*	

Table 10.1: Some standard NIS maps and the corresponding files.

There are other files and maps you may find support for in some NIS package or other. These may contain information for applications not discussed in this book, such as the *bootparams* map that may used by some BOOTP servers, or which currently don't have any function in Linux (like the *ethers.byname* and *ethers.byaddr* maps).

For some maps, people commonly use *nicknames*, which are shorter and therefore easier to type. To obtain a full list of nicknames understood by your NIS tools, run the following command:

```
$ ypcat -x
NIS map nickname translation table:
        "passwd" -> "passwd.byname"
        "group" -> "group.byname"
        "networks" -> "networks.byaddr"
        "hosts" -> "hosts.byname"
        "protocols" -> "protocols.bynumber"
        "services" -> "services.byname"
        "aliases" -> "mail.aliases"
        "ethers" -> "ethers.byname"
        "rpc" -> "rpc.bynumber"
        "netmasks" -> "netmasks.byaddr"
        "publickey" -> "publickey.byname"
        "netid" -> "netid.byname"
        "passwd.adjunct" -> "passwd.adjunct.byname"
        "group.adjunct" -> "group.adjunct.byname"
        "timezone" -> "timezone.byname"
```

The NIS server is traditionally called *ypserv*. For an average network, a single server usually suffices; large networks may choose to run several of these on different machines and different segments of the network to relieve the load on the

---

[4]DBM is a simple database management library that uses hashing techniques to speed up search operations. There's a free DBM implementation from the GNU project called *gdbm*, which is part of most Linux distributions.

server machines and routers. These servers are synchronized by making one of them the *master server*, and the others *slave servers*. Maps will be created only on the master server's host. From there, they are distributed to all slaves.

You will have noticed that we have been talking about "networks" very vaguely all the time; of course there's a distinctive concept in NIS that refers to such a network, that is the collection of all hosts that share part of their system configuration data through NIS: the *NIS domain*. Unfortunately, NIS domains have absolutely nothing in common with the domains we encountered in DNS. To avoid any ambiguity throughout this chapter, I will therefore always specify which type of domain I mean.

NIS domains have a purely administrative function only. They are mostly invisible to users, except for the sharing of passwords between all machines in the domain. Therefore, the name given to a NIS domain is relevant only to the administrators. Usually, any name will do, as long as it is different from any other NIS domain name on your local network. For instance, the administrator at the Virtual Brewery may choose to create two NIS domains, one for the Brewery itself, and one for the Winery, which she names **brewery** and **winery**, respectively. Another quite common scheme is to simply use the DNS domain name for NIS as well. To set and display the NIS domain name of your host, you can use the *domainname* command. When invoked without any argument, it prints the current NIS domain name; to set the domain name, you must become super user and type:

```
# domainname brewery
```

NIS domains determine which NIS server an application will query. For instance, the *login* program on a host at the Winery should, of course, only query the Winery's NIS server (or one of them, if there were several) for a user's password information; while an application on a Brewery host should stick with the Brewery's server.

One mystery now remains to be solved, namely how a client finds out which server to connect to. The simplest approach would be to have a configuration file that names the host on which to find the server. However, this approach is rather inflexible, because it doesn't allow clients to use different servers (from the same domain, of course), depending on their availability. Therefore, traditional NIS implementations rely on a special daemon called *ypbind* to detect a suitable NIS server in their NIS domain. Before being able to perform any NIS queries, any application first finds out from *ypbind* which server to use.

ypbind probes for servers by broadcasting to the local IP network; the first to respond is assumed to be the potentially fastest one and will be used in all subsequent NIS queries. After a certain interval has elapsed, or if the server becomes unavailable, *ypbind* will probe for active servers again.

Now, the arguable point about dynamic binding is that you rarely need it, and that it introduces a security problem: *ypbind* blindly believes whoever answers, which could be a humble NIS server as well as a malicious intruder. Needless to say this becomes especially troublesome if you manage your password databases over NIS. To guard against this, NYS does *not* use *ypbind* by default, but rather picks up the server host name from a configuration file.

10.2 NIS versus NIS+

NIS and NIS+ share little more than their name and a common goal. NIS+ is structured in an entirely different way. Instead of a flat name space with disjoint NIS domains, it uses a hierarchical name space similar to that of DNS. Instead of maps, so called *tables* are used that are made up of rows and columns, where each row represents an object in the NIS+ database, while the columns cover those properties of the objects that NIS+ knows and cares about. Each table for a given NIS+ domain comprises those of its parent domains. In addition, an entry in a table may contain a link to another table. These features make it possible to structure information in many ways.

Traditional NIS has an RPC version number of 2, while NIS+ is version 3.

NIS+ does not seem to be very widely used yet, and I don't really know that much about it. (Well, almost nothing). For this reason, we will not deal with it here. If you are interested in learning more about it, please refer to Sun's NIS+ administration manual ([NISPlus]).

10.3   The Client Side of NIS

If you are familiar with writing or porting network applications, you will notice that most NIS maps listed above correspond to library functions in the C library. For instance, to obtain *passwd* information, you generally use the *getpwnam(3)* and *getpwuid(3)* functions which return the account information associated with the given user name or numerical user id, repsectively. Under normal circumstances, these functions will perform the requested lookup on the standard file, such as */etc/passwd*.

A NIS-aware implementation of these functions, however, will modify this behavior, and place an RPC call to have the NIS server look up the user name or id. This happens completely transparent to the application. The function may either "append" the NIS map to or "replace" the original file with it. Of course, this does not refer to a real modification of the file, it only means that it *appears* to the application as if the file had been replaced or appended to.

For traditional NIS implementations, there used to be certain conventions as to which maps replaced, and which were appended to the original information. Some, like the *passwd* maps, required kludgy modifications of the *passwd* file which, when done wrong, would open up security holes. To avoid these pitfalls, NYS uses a general configuration scheme that determines whether a particular set of client functions uses the original files, NIS, or NIS+, and in which order. It will be described in a later section of this chapter.

10.4   Running a NIS Server

After so much theoretical techno-babble, it's time to get our hands dirty with actual configuration work. In this section, we will cover the configuration of a NIS server. If there's already a NIS server running on your network, you won't have to set up your own server; in this case, you may safely skip this section.

◇   Note that if you are just going to experiment with the server, make sure you don't set it up for a NIS domain
      name that is already in use on your network. This may disrupt the entire network service and make a lot of
      people very unhappy, and very angry.

There are currently two NIS servers freely available for Linux, one contained in Tobias Reber's *yps* package, and the other in Peter Eriksson's *ypserv* package. It shouldn't matter which one you run, regardless of whether you use NYS or the standard NIS client code that is in *libc* currently. At the time of this writing, the code for the handling of NIS slave servers seems to be more complete in *yps*. So if you have to deal with slave servers, *yps* might be a better choice.

After installing the server program (*ypserv*) in */usr/sbin*, you should create the directory that is going to hold the map files your server is to distribute. When setting up a NIS domain for the **brewery** domain, the maps would go to */var/yp/brewery*. The server determines if it is serving a particular NIS domain by checking if the map directory is present. If you are disabling service for some NIS domain, make sure to remove the directory as well.

Maps are usually stored in DBM files to speed up lookups. They are created from the master files using a program called *makedbm* (for Tobias' server) or *dbmload* (for Peter's server). These may not be interchangeable. Transforming a master file into a form parseable by *dbmload* usually requires some *awk* or *sed* magic, which tend to be a little tedious to type and hard to remember. Therefore, Peter Eriksson's *ypserv* package contains a Makefile (called *ypMakefile*) that does all these jobs for you. You should install it as *Makefile* in your map directory, and edit it to reflect the maps you want to distribute. Towards the top of the file, you find the *all* target that lists the services *ypserv* is to offer. By default, the line looks something like this:

```
all: ethers hosts networks protocols rpc services passwd group netid
```

If you don't want to produce the *ethers.byname* and *ethers.byaddr* maps, for example, simply remove the *ethers* prerequisite from this rule. To test your setup, it may suffice to start with just one or two maps, like the *services.** maps.

After editing the *Makefile*, while in the map directory, type "make". This will automatically generate and install the maps. You have to make sure to update the maps whenever you change the master files, otherwise the changes will remain invisible to the network.

The next section explains how to configure the NIS client code. If your setup doesn't work, you should try to find out whether any requests arrive at your server or not. If you specify the -D command line flag to the NYS server, it prints debugging messages to the console about all incoming NIS queries, and the results returned. These should give you a hint as to where the problem lies. Tobias' server has no such option.

10.5   Setting up a NIS Client with NYS

Throughout the remainder of this chapter, we will cover the configuration of a NIS client.

Your first step should be to tell NYS which server to use for NIS service, setting it in the */etc/yp.conf* configuration file. A very simple sample file for a host on the Winery's network may look like this:

```
# yp.conf - YP configuration for NYS library.
#
domainname winery
server vbardolino
```

The first statement tells all NIS clients that they belong to the **winery** NIS domain. If you omit this line, NYS will use the domain name you assigned your system through the *domainname* command. The *server* statement names the NIS server to use. Of course, the IP address corresponding to **vbardolino** must be set in the *hosts* file; alternatively, you may use the IP address itself with the *server* statement.

In the form shown above, the *server* command tells NYS to use the named server whatever the current NIS domain may be. If, however, you are moving your machine between different NIS domains frequently, you may want to keep information for several domains in the *yp.conf* file. You can have information on the servers for various NIS domains in *yp.conf* by adding the NIS domain name to the *server* statement. For instance, you might change the above sample file for a laptop to look like this:

```
# yp.conf - YP configuration for NYS library.
#
server vbardolino winery
server vstout      brewery
```

This allows you to bring up the laptop in any of the two domains by simply setting the desired NIS domain at boot time through the *domainname* command.

After creating this basic configuration file and making sure it is world-readable, you should run your first test to check if you can connect to your server. Make sure to choose any map your server distributes, like *hosts.byname*, and try to retrieve it by using the *ypcat* utility. *ypcat*, like all other administrative NIS tools, should live in */usr/sbin*.

```
# ypcat hosts.byname
191.72.2.2      vbeaujolais    vbeaujolais.linus.lxnet.org
191.72.2.3      vbardolino     vbardolino.linus.lxnet.org
191.72.1.1      vlager         vlager.linus.lxnet.org
191.72.2.1      vlager         vlager.linus.lxnet.org
191.72.1.2      vstout         vstout.linus.lxnet.org
191.72.1.3      vale           vale.linus.lxnet.org
191.72.2.4      vchianti       vchianti.linus.lxnet.org
```

The output you get should look somthing like that shown above. If you get an error message instead that says "Can't bind to server which serves domain" or something similar, then either the NIS domain name you've set doesn't have a matching server defined in *yp.conf*, or the server is unreachable for some reason. In the latter case, make sure that a *ping* to the host yields a positive result, and that it is indeed running a NIS server. You can verify the latter by using *rpcinfo*, which should produce the following output:

```
    # rpcinfo -u serverhost ypserv
    program 100004 version 2 ready and waiting
```

10.6 Choosing the Right Maps

Having made sure you can reach the NIS server, you have to decide which configuration files to replace or augment with NIS maps. Commonly, you will want use NIS maps for the host and password lookup functions. The former is especially useful if you do not run BIND. The latter permits all users to log into their account from any system in the NIS domain; this usually requires sharing a central */home* directory between all hosts via NFS. It is explained detail in section 10.7 below. Other maps, like *services.byname*, aren't such a dramatic gain, but save you some editing work if you install any network applications that use a service name that's not in the standard *services* file.

Generally, you want to have some freedom of choice when a lookup function uses the local files, and when it queries the NIS server. NYS allows you to configure the order in which a function accesses these services. This is controlled through the */etc/nsswitch.conf* file, which stands for *Name Service Switch* but of course isn't limited to the name service. For any of the data lookup functions supported by NYS, it contains a line naming the services to use.

The right order of services depends on the type of data. It is unlikely that the *services.byname* map will contain entries differing from those in the local *services* file; it may only contain more. So a good choice may be to query the local files first, and check NIS only if the service name wasn't found. Hostname information, on the other hand, may change very frequently, so that DNS or the NIS server should always have the most accurate account, while the local *hosts* file is only kept as a backup if DNS and NIS should fail. In this case, you would want to check the local file last.

The example below shows how to configure *gethostbyname(2)*, *gethostbyaddr(2)*, and *getservbyname(2)* functions as described above. They will try the listed services in turn; if a lookup succeeds, the result is returned, otherwise the next service is tried.

```
    # small sample /etc/nsswitch.conf
    #
    hosts:      nis dns files
    services:   files nis
```

The complete list of services that may be used with an entry in the *nsswitch.conf* file is shown below. The actual maps, files, servers and objects being queried depend on the entry name.

nisplus or *nis+*   Use the NIS+ server for this domain. The location of the server is obtained from the */etc/nis.conf* file.

nis   Use the current NIS server of this domain. The location of the server queried is configured in the *yp.conf* file as shown in the previous section. For the *hosts* entry, the maps *hosts.byname* and *hosts.byaddr* are queried.

dns   Use the DNS name server. This service type is only useful with the *hosts* entry. The name servers queried are still determined by the standard *resolv.conf* file.

files   Use the local file, such as the */etc/hosts* file for the *hosts* entry.

dbm   Look up the information from DBM files located in */var/dbm*. The name used for the file is that of the corresponding NIS map.

Currently, NYS supports the following *nsswitch.conf* entries: *hosts*, *networks*, *passwd*, *group*, *shadow*, *gshadow*, *services*, *protocols*, *rpc*, and *ethers*. More entries are likely to be added.

Figure 10.1 shows a more complete example which introduces another feature of *nsswitch.conf*: the *[NOT-FOUND=return]* keyword in the *hosts* entry tells NYS to return if the desired item couldn't be found in the NIS or DNS database. That is, NYS will continue and search the local files *only* if calls to the NIS and DNS servers failed for some other reason. The local files will then only be used at boot time and as a backup when the NIS server is down.

```
# /etc/nsswitch.conf
#
hosts:          nis dns [NOTFOUND=return] files
networks:       nis [NOTFOUND=return] files

services:       files nis
protocols:      files nis
rpc:            files nis
```

Figure 10.1: Sample *nsswitch.conf* file.

10.7 Using the *passwd* and *group* Maps

One of the major applications of NIS is in synchronizing user and account information on all hosts in a NIS domain. To this end, you usually keep only a small local */etc/passwd* file, to which the site-wide information from the NIS maps is appended. However, simply enabling NIS lookups for this service in *nsswitch.conf* is not nearly enough.

When relying on the password information distributed by NIS, you first have to make sure that the numeric user id's of any users you have in your local *passwd* file match the NIS server's idea of user id's. You will want this for other purposes as well, like mounting NFS volumes from other hosts in your network.

If any of the numeric ids in */etc/passwd* or */etc/group* deviate from those in the maps, you have to adjust file ownerships for all files that belong to that user. First you should change all uids and gids in *passwd* and *group* to the new values; then find all files that belong to the users just changed, and finally change their ownership. Assume **news** used to have a user id of 9, and **okir** had a user id of 103, which were changed to some other value; you could then issue the following commands:

```
# find / -uid   9 -print >/tmp/uid.9
# find / -uid 103 -print >/tmp/uid.103
# cat /tmp/uid.9   | xargs chown news
# cat /tmp/uid.103 | xargs chown okir
```

It is important that you execute these commands with the *new passwd* file installed, and that you collect all file names before you change the ownership of any of them. To update the group ownerships of files, you will use a similar command.

Having done this, the numerical uid's and gid's on your system will agree with those on all other hosts in your NIS domain. The next step will be to add configuration lines to *nsswitch.conf* that enables NIS lookups for user and group information:

```
# /etc/nsswitch.conf - passwd and group treatment
passwd: nis files
group:  nis files
```

This makes the *login* command and all its friends first query the NIS maps when a user tries to log in, and if this lookup fails, fall back to the local files. Usually, you will remove almost all users from your local files, and only leave entries for **root** and generic accounts like **mail** in it. This is because some vital system tasks may require to map uids to user names or vice versa. For example, administrative *cron* jobs may execute the *su* command to temporarily become **news**, or the UUCP subsystem may mail a status report. If **news** and **uucp** don't have entries in the local *passwd* file, these jobs will fail miserably during a NIS brownout.

There are two big caveats in order here: on one hand, the setup as described up to here only works for login suites that don't use shadow password, like those included in the *util-linux* package. The intricacies of using shadow passwords with NIS will be covered below. On the other hand, the login commands are not the only ones that access the *passwd* file – look at the *ls* command which most people use almost constantly. Whenever doing a long listing, *ls* will display the symbolic names for user and group owners of a file; that is, for each uid and gid it encounters, it will have to query the NIS server once. This will slow things down rather badly if your local network is clogged, or, even worse, when the NIS server is not on the same physical network, so that datagrams have to pass through a router.

Still, this is not the whole story yet. Imagine what happens if a user wants to change her password. Usually, she will invoke *passwd*, which reads the new password and updates the local *passwd* file. This is impossible with NIS, since that file isn't available locally anymore, but having users log into the NIS server whenever they want to change their password is not an option either. Therefore, NIS provides a drop-in replacement for *passwd* called *yppasswd*, which does the analoguous thing in the presence of NIS. To change the password on the server host, it contacts the *yppasswdd* daemon on that host via RPC, and provides it with the updated password information. Usually, you install *yppasswd* over the normal program by doing something like this:

```
# cd /bin
# mv passwd passwd.old
# ln yppasswd passwd
```

At the same time you have to install *rpc.yppasswdd* on the server and start it from *rc.inet2*. This will effectively hide any of the contortions of NIS from your users.

10.8   Using NIS with Shadow Support

There is no NIS support yet for sites that use the shadow login suite. John F. Haugh, the author of the shadow suite, recently released a version of the shadow library functions covered by the GNU Library GPL to **comp.sources.misc**. It already has some support for NIS, but it isn't complete, and the files haven't been added to the standard C library yet. On the other hand, publishing the information from */etc/shadow* via NIS kind of defeats the purpose of the shadow suite.

Although the NYS password lookup functions don't use a *shadow.byname* map or anything likewise, NYS supports using a local */etc/shadow* file transparently. When the NYS implementation of *getpwnam* is called to look up information related to a given login name, the facilities specified by the *passwd* entry in *nsswitch.conf* are queried. The *nis* service will simply look up the name in the *passwd.byname* map on the NIS server. The *files* service, however, will check if */etc/shadow* is present, and if so, try to open it. If none is present, or if the user doesn't have **root** privilege, if reverts to the traditional behavior of looking up the user information in */etc/passwd* only. However, if the *shadow* file exists and can be opened, NYS will extract the user password from *shadow*. The *getpwuid* function is implemented accordingly. In this fashion, binaries compiled with NYS will deal with a local the shadow suite installation transparently.

10.9   Using the Traditional NIS Code

If you are using the client code that is in the standard *libc* currently, configuring a NIS client is a little different. On one hand, it uses a *ypbind* daemon to broadcast for active servers rather than gathering this information from a configuration file. You therefore have to make sure to start *ypbind* at boot time. It must be invoked after the NIS domain has been set and the RPC portmapper has been started. Invoking *ypcat* to test the server should then work as shown above.

Recently, there have been numerous bug reports that NIS fails with an error message saying "`clntudp_create:`
`RPC: portmapper failure - RPC: unable to receive`". These are due to an incompatible change in the way *ypbind* communicates the binding information to the library functions. Obtaining the latest sources for the NIS utilities and recompiling them should cure this problem.[5]

Also, the way traditional NIS decides if and how to merge NIS information with that from the local files deviates from that used by NYS. For instance, to use the NIS password maps, you have to include the following line somewhere in your */etc/passwd* map:

---

[5]The source for *yp-linux* can be gotten from **ftp.uni-paderborn.de** in directory */pub/Linux/LOCAL*.

```
+:*:0:0:::
```

This marks the place where the password lookup functions "insert" the NIS maps. Inserting a similar line (minus the last two colons) into *etc/group* does the same for the *group.** maps. To use the *hosts.** maps distributed by NIS, change the *order* line in the *host.conf* file. For instance, if you want to use NIS, DNS, and the */etc/hosts* file (in that order), you need to change the line to

```
order yp bind hosts
```

The traditional NIS implementation does not support any other maps at the moment.

Net-Admin Guide

Chapter 11

The Network File System

NFS, the network filesystem, is probably the most prominent network services using RPC. It allows to access files on remote hosts in exactly the same way as a user would access any local files. This is made possible by a mixture of kernel functionality on the client side (that uses the remote file system) and an NFS server on the server side (that provides the file data). This file access is completely transparent to the client, and works across a variety of server and host architectures.

NFS offers a number of advantages:

- Data accessed by all users can be kept on a central host, with clients mounting this directory at boot time. For example, you can keep all user accounts on one host, and have all hosts on your network mount /home from that host. If installed alongside with NIS, users can then log into any system, and still work on one set of files.

- Data consuming large amounts of disk space may be kept on a single host. For example, all files and programs relating to LaTeX and METAFONT could be kept and maintained in one place.

- Administrative data may be kept on a single host. No need to use *rcp* anymore to install the same stupid file on 20 different machines.

Linux NFS is largely the work of Rick Sladkey,[1] who wrote the NFS kernel code and large parts of the NFS server. The latter is derived from the *unfsd* user-space NFS server originally written by Mark Shand, and the *hnfs* Harris NFS server written by Donald Becker.

Let's have a look now at how NFS works: A client may request to mount a directory from a remote host on a local directory just the same way it can mount a physical device. However, the syntax used to specify the remote directory is different. For example, to mount /home from host **vlager** to /users on **vale**, the administrator would issue the following command on **vale**:[2]

```
# mount -t nfs vlager:/home /users
```

mount will then try to connect to the *mountd* mount daemon on **vlager** via RPC. The server will check if **vale** is permitted to mount the directory in question, and if so, return it a file handle. This file handle will be used in all subsequent requests to files below /users.

When someone accesses a file over NFS, the kernel places an RPC call to *nfsd* (the NFS daemon) on the server machine. This call takes the file handle, the name of the file to be accessed, and the user's user and group id as parameters. These are used in determining access rights to the specified file. In order to prevent unauthorized users from reading or modifying files, user and group ids must be the same on both hosts.

On most UNIX implementations, the NFS functionality of both client and server are implemented as kernel-level daemons that are started from user space at system boot. These are the NFS daemon (*nfsd*) on the server host, and the *Block I/O Daemon* (*biod*) running on the client host. To improve throughput, *biod* performs asynchronous I/O using read-ahead and write-behind; also, several *nfsd* daemons are usually run concurrently.

---

[1]Rick can be reached at **jrs@world.std.com**.
[2]Note that you can omit the -t nfs argument, because *mount* sees from the colon that this specifies an NFS volume.

The NFS implementation of Linux is a little different in that the client code is tightly integrated in the virtual file system (VFS) layer of the kernel and doesn't require additional control through *biod*. On the other hand, the server code runs entirely in user space, so that running several copies of the server at the same time is almost impossible because of the synchronization issues this would involve. Linux NFS currently also lacks read-ahead and write-behind, but Rick Sladkey plans to add this someday.[3]

The biggest problem with the Linux NFS code is that the Linux kernel as of version 1.0 is not able to allocate memory in chunks bigger than 4K; as a consequence, the networking code cannot handle datagrams bigger than roughly 3500 bytes after subtracting header sizes etc. This means that transfers to and from NFS daemons running on systems that use large UDP datagrams by default (e.g. 8K on SunOS) need to be downsized artificially. This hurts performance badly under some circumstances.[4] This limit is gone in late Linux-1.1 kernels, and the client code has been modified to take advantage of this.

11.1   Preparing NFS

Before you can use NFS, be it as server or client, you must make sure your kernel has NFS support compiled in. Newer kernels have a simple interface on the proc filesystem for this, the */proc/filesystems* file, which you can display using *cat*:

```
$ cat /proc/filesystems
minix
ext2
msdos
nodev proc
nodev nfs
```

If *nfs* is missing from this list, then you have to compile your own kernel with NFS enabled. Configuring the kernel network options is explained in section "Kernel Configuration" in chapter 3.

For older kernels prior to Linux 1.1, the easiest way to find out whether your kernel has NFS support enabled is to actually try to mount an NFS file system. For this, you could create a directory below */tmp*, and try to mount a local directory on it:

```
# mkdir /tmp/test
# mount localhost:/etc /tmp/test
```

If this mount attempt fails with an error message saying "fs type nfs no supported by kernel", you must make a new kernel with NFS enabled. Any other error messages are completely harmless, as you haven't configured the NFS daemons on your host yet.

11.2   Mounting an NFS Volume

NFS volumes[5] are mounted very much the way usual file systems are mounted. You invoke *mount* using the following syntax:

```
# mount -t nfs nfs_volume local_dir options
```

---

[3]The problem with write-behind is that the kernel buffer cache is indexed by device/inode pairs, and therefore can't be used for NFS-mounted file systems.

[4]As explained to me by Alan Cox: The NFS specification requires the server to flush each write to disk before it returns an acknowledgement. As BSD kernels are only capable of page-sized writes (4K), writing a 4 chunks of 1K each to a BSD-based NFS server results in 4 write operations of 4K each.

[5]One doesn't say file system, because these are not proper file systems.

nfs_volume is given as *remote_host:remote_dir*. Since this notation is unique to NFS file systems, you can leave out the -t nfs option.

There are a number of additional options that you may specify to *mount* upon mounting an NFS volume. These may either be given following the -o switch on the command line, or in the options field of the */etc/fstab* entry for the volume. In both cases, multiple options are separated from each other by commas. Options specified on the command line always override those given in the *fstab* file.

A sample entry in */etc/fstab* might be

```
# volume                mount point       type   options
news:/usr/spool/news    /usr/spool/news   nfs    timeo=14,intr
```

This volume may then be mounted using

```
# mount news:/usr/spool/news
```

In the absence of a *fstab* entry, NFS *mount* invocations look a lot uglier. For instance, suppose you mount your users' home directories from a machine named **moonshot**, which uses a default block size of 4K for read/write operations. You might decrease block size to 2K to suit Linux' datagram size limit by issuing

```
# mount moonshot:/home /home -o rsize=2048,wsize=2048
```

The list of all valid options is described in its entirety in the *nfs(5)* manual page that comes with Rick Sladkey's NFS-aware *mount* tool which can be found in Rik Faith's *util-linux* package). The following is an incomplete list of those you would probably want to use:

rsize=n and *wsize=n* These specify the datagram size used by the NFS clients on read and write requests, respectively. They currently default to 1024 bytes, due to the limit on UDP datagram size described above.

timeo=n This sets the time (in tenths of a second) the NFS client will wait for a request to complete. The default values is 0.7 seconds.

hard Explicitly mark this volume as hard-mounted. This is on by default.

soft Soft-mount the driver (as opposed to hard-mount).

intr Allow signals to interrupt an NFS call. Useful for aborting when the server doesn't respond.

Except for *rsize* and *wsize*, all of these options apply to the client's behavior if the server should become inaccessible temporarily. They play together in the following way: whenever the client sends a request to the NFS server, it expects the operation to have finished after a given interval (specified in the *timeout* option). If no confirmation is received within this time, a so-called *minor timeout* occurs, and the operation is retried with the timeout interval doubled. After reaching a maximum timeout of 60 seconds, a *major timeout* occurs.

By default, a major timeout will cause the client to print a message to the console and start all over again, this time with an initial timeout interval twice that of the previous cascade. Potentially, this may go on forever. Volumes that stubbornly retry an operation until the server becomes available again are called *hard-mounted*. The opposite variety, *soft-mounted* volumes gerenates an I/O error for the calling process whenever a major timeout occurs. Because of the write-behind introduced by the buffer cache, this error condition is not propagated to the process itself before it calls the *write(2)* function the next time, so a program can never be sure that a write operation to a soft-mounted volume has succeded at all.

Whether you hard- or soft-mount a volume is not simply a question of taste, but also has to do with what sort of information you want to access from this volume. For example, if you mount your X programs by NFS, you certainly would not want your X session to go berserk just because someone brought the network to a grinding halt by firing up seven copies of *xv* at the same time, or by pulling the Ethernet plug for a moment. By hard-mounting these, you make sure that your computer will wait until it is able to re-establish contact with your NFS-server. On the other hand, non-critical data such as NFS-mounted news partititons or FTP archives may as well be soft-mounted, so it doesn't hang your session in case the remote machine should be temporarily unreachable, or down. If your network connection to the server is flakey or goes through a loaded router, you may either increase the initial timeout using the *timeo* option, or hard-mount the volumes, but allow for signals interrupting the NFS call so that you may still abort any hanging file access.

Usually, the *mountd* daemon will in some way or other keep track of which directories have been mounted by what hosts. This information can be displayed using the *showmount* program, which is also included in the NFS server package. The Linux *mountd*, however, does not do this yet.

11.3   The NFS Daemons

If you want to provide NFS service to other hosts, you have to run the *nfsd* and *mountd* daemons on your machine. As RPC-based programs, they are not managed by *inetd*, but are started up at boot time, and register themselves with the portmapper. Therefore, you have to make sure to start them only after *rpc.portmap* is running. Usually, you include the following two lines in your *rc.inet2* script:

```
if [ -x /usr/sbin/rpc.mountd ]; then
        /usr/sbin/rpc.mountd; echo -n " mountd"
fi
if [ -x /usr/sbin/rpc.nfsd ]; then
        /usr/sbin/rpc.nfsd; echo -n " nfsd"
fi
```

The ownership information of files a NFS daemon provides to its clients usually contains only numerical user and group id's. If both client and server associate the same user and group names with these numerical id's, they are said to share the same uid/gid space. For example, this is the case when you use NIS to distribute the *passwd* information to all hosts on your LAN.

On some occasions, however, they do not match. Rather updating the uid's and gid's of the client to match those of the server, you can use the *ugidd* mapping daemon to work around this. Using the *map_daemon* option explained below, you can tell *nfsd* to map the server's uid/gid space to the client's uid/gid space with the aid of the *ugidd* on the client.

ugidd is an RPC-based server, and is started from *rc.inet2* just like *nfsd* and *mountd*.

```
if [ -x /usr/sbin/rpc.ugidd ]; then
        /usr/sbin/rpc.ugidd; echo -n " ugidd"
fi
```

11.4   The *exports* File

While the above options applied to the client's NFS configuration, there is a different set of options on the server side that configure its per-client behavior. These options must be set in the */etc/exports* file.

By default, *mountd* will not allow anyone to mount directories from the local host, which is a rather sensible attitude. To permit one or more hosts to NFS-mount a directory, it must *exported*, that is, must be specified in the *exports* file. A sample file may look like this:

```
# exports file for vlager
/home           vale(rw) vstout(rw) vlight(rw)
/usr/X386       vale(ro) vstout(ro) vlight(ro)
/usr/TeX        vale(ro) vstout(ro) vlight(ro)
/               vale(rw,no_root_squash)
/home/ftp       (ro)
```

Each line defines a directory, and the hosts allowed to mount it. A host name is usually a fully qualified domain name, but may additionally contain the * and ? wildcard, which act the way they do with the Bourne shell. For instance, **lab*.foo.com** matches **lab01.foo.com** as well as **laber.foo.com**. If no host name is given, as with the */home/ftp* directory in the example above, any host is allowed to mount this directory.

When checking a client host against the *exports* file, *mountd* will look up the client's hostname using the *gethostbyaddr(2)* call. With DNS, this call returns the client's canonical hostname, so you must make sure not to use aliases in *exports*. Without using DNS, the returned name is the first hostname found in the *hosts* file that matches the client's address.

The host name is followed by an optional, comma-separated list of flags, enclosed in brackets. These flags may take the following values:

insecure	Permit non-authenticated access from this machine.
unix-rpc	Require UNIX-domain RPC authentication from this machine. This simply requires that requests originate from a reserved internet port (i.e. the port number has to be less than 1024). This option is on by default.
secure-rpc	Require secure RPC authentication from this machine. This has not been implemented yet. See Sun's documentation on Secure RPC.
kerberos	Require Kerberos authentication on accesses from this machine. This has not been implemented yet. See the MIT documentation on the Kerberos authentication system.
root_squash	This is a security feature that denies the super user on the specified hosts any special access rights by mapping requests from uid 0 on the client to uid 65534 (-2) on the server. This uid should be associated with the user **nobody**.
no_root_squash	Don't map requests from uid 0. This option is on by default.
ro	Mount file hierarchy read-only. This option is on by default.
rw	Mount file hierarchy read-write.
link_relative	Convert absolute symbolic links (where the link contents start with a slash) into relative links by prepending the necessary number of ../'s to get from the directory containing the link to the root on the server. This option only makes sense when a host's entire file system is mounted, else some of the links might point to nowhere, or even worse, files they were never meant to point to.
	This option is on by default.
link_absolute	Leave all symbolic link as they are (the normal behavior for Sun-supplied NFS servers).
map_identity	The *map_identity* option tells the server to assume that the client uses the same uid's and gid's as the server. This option is on by default.
map_daemon	This option tells the NFS server to assume that client and server do not share the same uid/gid space. *nfsd* will then build a list mapping id's between client and server by querying the client's *ugidd* daemon.

An error parsing the *exports* file is reported to *syslogd*'s *daemon* facility at level *notice* whenever *nfsd* or *mountd* is started up.

Note that host names are obtained from the client's IP address by reverse mapping, so you have to have the resolver configured properly. If you use BIND and are very security-conscious, you should enable spoof checking in your *host.conf* file.

11.5 The Linux Automounter

Sometimes, it is wasteful to mount all NFS volumes users might possibly want to access; either because of the sheer number of volumes to be mounted, or because of the time this would take at startup. A viable alternative to this is a so-called *automounter*. This is a daemon that automatically and transparently mounts any NFS volume as needed, and unmounts them after they have not been used for some time. One of the clever things about an automounter is that it is able to mount a certain volume from alternative places. For instance, you may keep copies of your X programs and support files on two or three hosts, and have all other hosts mount them via NFS. Using an automounter, you may specify all three of them to be mounted on */usr/X386*; the automounter will then try to mount any of these until one of the mount attempts succeeds.

The automounter commonly used with Linux is called *amd*. It was originally written by Jan-Simon Pendry and has been ported to Linux by Rick Sladkey. The current version is *amd-5.3*.

Explaining *amd* is beyond the scope of this chapter; for a good manual please refer to the sources; they contain a texinfo file with very detailed information.

Chapter 12

Managing Taylor UUCP

12.1   History

UUCP was designed in the late seventies by Mike Lesk at AT&T Bell Laboratories to provide a simple dial-up network over public telephone lines. Since most people that want to have email and Usenet News on their home machine still communicate through modems, UUCP has remained very popular. Although there are many implementations running on a wide variety of hardware platforms and operating systems, they are compatible to a high degree.

However, as with most software that has somehow become "standard" over the years, there is no UUCP which one would call *the* UUCP. It has undergone a steady process of evolution since the first version which was implemented in 1976. Currently, there are two major species which differ mainly in their support of hardware and their configuration. Of these, various implementations exist, each varying slightly from its siblings.

One species is the so-called "Version 2 UUCP", which dates back to a 1977 implementation by Mike Lesk, David A. Novitz, and Greg Chesson. Although it is fairly old, it is still in frequent use. Recent implementations of Version 2 provide much of the comfort of the newer UUCP species.

The second species was developed in 1983, and is commonly referred to as BNU (Basic Networking Utilities), HoneyDanBer UUCP, or HDB for short. The name is derived from the authors' names, P. Honeyman, D. A. Novitz, and B. E. Redman. HDB was conceived to eliminate some of Version 2 UUCP's deficiencies. For example, new transfer protocols were added, and the spool directory was split so that now there is one directory for each site you have UUCP traffic with.

The implementation of UUCP currently distributed with Linux is Taylor UUCP 1.04,[1] which is the version this chapter is based upon. Taylor UUCP Version 1.04 was released in February 1993. Apart from traditional configuration files, Taylor UUCP may also be compiled to understand the new-style – a.k.a. "Taylor" – configuration files.

Version 1.05 has been released recently, and will soon make its way into most distributions. The differences between these versions mostly affect features you will never use, so you should be able to configure Taylor UUCP 1.05 using the information form this book.

As included in most Linux distributions, Taylor UUCP is usually compiled for BNU compatibility, or the Taylor configuration scheme, or both. As the latter is much more flexible, and probably easier to understand than the often rather obscure BNU configuration files, I will describe the Taylor scheme below.

The purpose of this chapter is not to give you an exhaustive description of what the command line options for the UUCP commands are and what they do, but to give you an introduction on how to set up a working UUCP node. The first section gives a hopefully gentle introduction about how UUCP implements remote execution and file transfers. If you are not entirely new to UUCP, you might want to skip this and move on to section 12.3, which explains the various files used to set up UUCP.

We will however assume that you are familiar with the user programs of the UUCP suite. These are *uucp* and *uux*. For a description, please refer to the on-line manual pages.

---

[1] Written and copyrighted by Ian Taylor, 1993.

Besides the publicly accessible programs, *uux* and *uucp*, the UUCP suite contains a number of commands used for administrative purposes only. They are used to monitor UUCP traffic across your node, remove old log files, or compile statistics. None of these will be described here, because they're peripheral to the main tasks of UUCP. Besides, they're well documented and fairly easy to understand. However, there is a third category, which comprises the actual UUCP "work horses". They are called *uucico* (where cico stands for copy-in copy-out), and *uuxqt*, which executes jobs sent from remote systems.

12.1.1   More Information on UUCP

Those who don't find everything they need in this chapter should read the documentation that comes along with the package. This is a set of texinfo files that describe the setup using the Taylor configuration scheme. Texinfo can be converted to DVI and to GNU info files using *tex* and *makeinfo*, respectively.

If you want to use BNU or even (shudder!) Version 2 configuration files, there is a very good book, "Managing UUCP and Usenet" ([OReilly89]). I find it very useful. Another good source for information about UUCP on Linux is Vince Skahan's UUCP-HOWTO, which is posted regularly to **comp.os.linux.announce**.

There's also a newsgroup for the discussion of UUCP, called **comp.mail.uucp**. If you have questions specific to Taylor UUCP, you may be better off asking them there, rather than on the **comp.os.linux** groups.

12.2   Introduction

12.2.1   Layout of UUCP Transfers and Remote Execution

Vital to the understanding of UUCP is the concept of *jobs*. Every transfer a user initiates with *uucp* or *uux* is called a job. It is made up of a *command* to be executed on a remote system, and a collection of *files* to be transferred between sites. One of these parts may be missing.

As an example, assume you issued the following command on your host, which makes UUCP copy the file *netguide.ps* to host **pablo**, and makes it execute the *lpr* command to print the file.

```
$ uux -r pablo!lpr !netguide.ps
```

UUCP does not generally call the remote system immediately to execute a job (else you could make do with *kermit*). Instead, it temporarily stores the job description away. This is called *spooling*. The directory tree under which jobs are stored is therefore called the *spool directory* and is generally located in */var/spool/uucp*. In our example, the job description would contain information about the remote command to be executed (*lpr*), the user who requested the execution, and a couple of other items. In addition to the job description, UUCP has to store the input file, *netguide.ps*.

The exact location and naming of spool files may vary, depending on some compile-time options. HDB-compatible UUCP's generally store spool files in a directory named */var/spool/uucp/*`site`, where `site` is the name of the remote site. When compiled for Taylor configuration, UUCP will create subdirectories below the site-specific spool directory for different types of spool files.

At regular intervals, UUCP dials up the remote system. When a connection to the remote machine is established, UUCP transfers the files describing the job, plus any input files. The incoming jobs will not be executed immediately, but only after the connection terminates. This is done by *uuxqt*, which also takes care of forwarding any jobs if they are designated for another site.

To distinguish between important and less important jobs, UUCP associates a *grade* with each job. This is a single letter, ranging from 0 through 9, A though Z, and a through z, in decreasing precedence. Mail is customarily spooled with grade B or C, while news is spooled with grade N. Jobs with higher grade are transferred earlier. Grades may be assigned using the -g flag when invoking *uucp* or *uux*.

You can also disallow the transfer of jobs below a given grade at certain times. This is also called the *maximum spool grade* allowed during a conversation and defaults to z. Note the terminological ambiguity here: a file is transferred only if it is *equal or above* the maximum spool grade.

12.2.2 The Inner Workings of *uucico*

◇ To understand why *uucico* needs to know certain things, a quick description of how it actually connects to a remote system might be in order here.

When you execute *uucico -s* `system` from the command line, it first has to connect physically. The actions taken depend on the type of connection to open – e.g. when using telephone line, it has to find a modem, and dial out. Over TCP, it has to call *gethostbyname(3)* to convert the name to a network address, find out which port to open, and bind the address to the corresponding socket.

After this connection has been established, an authorization procedure has to be passed. It generally consists of the remote system asking for a login name, and possibly a password. This is commonly called the *login chat*. The authorization procedure is performed either by the usual *getty/login* suite, or – on TCP sockets – by *uucico* itself. If authorization succeeds, the remote end fires up *uucico*. The local copy of *uucico* which initiated the connection is referred to as *master*, the remote copy as *slave*.

Next follows the *handshake phase*: the master now sends its hostname, plus several flags. The slave checks this hostname for permission to log in, send and receive files, etc. The flags describe (among other things) the maximum grade of spool files to transfer. If enabled, a conversation count, or *call sequence number* check takes place here. With this feature, both sites maintain a count of successful connections, which are compared. If they do not match, the handshake fails. This is useful to protect yourself against impostors.

Finally, the two *uucico*'s try to agree on a common *transfer protocol*. This protocol governs the way data is transferred, checked for consistency, and retransmitted in case of an error. There is a need for different protocols because of the differing types of connections supported. For example, telephone lines require a "safe" protocol which is pessimistic about errors, while TCP transmission is inherently reliable and can use a more efficient protocol that foregoes most extra error checking.

After the handshake is complete, the actual transmission phase begins. Both ends turn on the selected protocol driver. The drivers possibly perform a protocol-specific initialization sequence.

First, the master sends all files queued for the remote system whose spool grade is high enough. When it has finished, it informs the slave that it is done, and that the slave may now hang up. The slave now can either agree to hang up, or take over the conversation. This is a change of roles: now the remote system becomes master, and the local one becomes slave. The new master now sends its files. When done, both *uucico*'s exchange termination messages, and close the connection.

We will not go into this in greater detail: please refer to either the sources or any good book on UUCP for this. There is also a really antique article floating around the net, written by David A. Novitz, which gives a detailed description of the UUCP protocol. The Taylor UUCP FAQ also disucsses some details of the way UUCP is implemented. It is posted to **comp.mail.uucp** regularly.

12.2.3 *uucico* Command Line Options

This section describes the most important command line options for *uucico*. For a complete list, please refer to the *uucico(1)* manual page.

-s `system`	Call the named `system` unless prohibited by call time restrictions.
-S `system`	Call the named `system` unconditionally.
-r1	Start *uucico* in master mode. This is the default when -s or -S is given. All by itself, the -r1 option causes *uucico* to try to call all systems in *sys*, unless prohibited by call or retry time restrictions.

-r0   Start *uucico* in slave mode. This is the default when no -s or -S is given. In slave mode, either
                standard input/output are assumed to be connected to a serial port, or the TCP port specified by the
                -p option is used.

-x *type*, -X *type*   Turn on debugging of the specified type. Several types may be given as a comma-separated list.
                The following types are valid: *abnormal, chat, handshake, uucp-proto, proto, port, config, spooldir,*
                execute, incoming, outgoing. Using *all* turns on all options. For compatibility with other UUCP
                implementations, a number may be specified instead, which turns on debugging for the first *n* items
                from the above list.

                Debugging messages will be logged to the file *Debug* below */var/spool/uucp*.

12.3   UUCP Configuration Files

In contrast to simpler file transfer programs, UUCP was designed to be able to handle all transfers automatically. Once
it is set up properly, interference by the administrator should not be necessary on a day-to-day basis. The information
required for this is is kept in a couple of *configuration files* that reside in the directory */usr/lib/uucp*. Most of these files
are used only when dialing out.

12.3.1   A Gentle Introduction to Taylor UUCP

To say that UUCP configuration is hard would be an understatement. It is really a hairy subject, and the sometimes terse
format of the configuration files doesn't make things easier (although the Talyor format is almost easy reading compared
to the older formats in HDB or Version 2).

To give you a feel how all these files interact, we will introduce you to the most important ones, and have a look at sample
entries of these files. We won't explain everything in detail now; a more accurate account is given in separate sections
below. If you want to set up your machine for UUCP, you had best start with some sample files, and adapt them gradually.
You can pick either those shown below, or those included in your favorite Linux distribution.

All files described in this section are kept in */usr/lib/uucp* or a subdirectory thereof. Some Linux distributions contain
UUCP binaries that have support for both HDB and Taylor configuration enabled, and use different subdirectories for
each configuration file set. There will usually be a *README* file in */usr/lib/uucp*.

For UUCP to work properly, these files must be owned by the **uucp** user. Some of them contain passwords and telephone
numbers, and therefore should have permissions of 600.[2]

The central UUCP configuration file is */usr/lib/uucp/config*, and is used to set general parameters. The most important
of them (and for now, the only one), is your host's UUCP name. At the Virtual Brewery, they use **vstout** as their UUCP
gateway:

```
        # /usr/lib/uucp/config - UUCP main configuration file
        hostname        vstout
```

The next important configuration file is the *sys* file. It contains all system-specific information of sites you are linked to.
This includes the site's name, and information on the link itself, such as the telephone number when using a modem link.
A typical entry for a modem-connected site called **pablo** would be

```
        # /usr/lib/uucp/sys - name UUCP neighbors
        # system: pablo
        system          pablo
        time            Any
```

---

[2]Note that although most UUCP commands must be setuid to **uucp**, you must make sure the *uuchk* program is *not*. Otherwise, users
will be able to display passwords even though they have mode 600.

```
phone            123-456
port             serial1
speed            38400
chat             ogin: vstout ssword: lorca
```

The *port* names a port to be used, and *time* specifies the times at which it may be called. *chat* describes the login chat scripts – the sequence of strings that must be exchanged between to allow *uucico* to log into **pablo**. We will get back to chat scripts later. The *port* command does not name a device special file such as */dev/cua1*, but rather names an entry in the *port* file. You can assign these names as you like as long as they refer to a valid entry in *port*.

The *port* file holds information specific to the link itself. For modem links, it describes the device special file to be used, the range of speeds supported, and the type of dialing equipment connected to the port. The entry below describes */dev/cua1* (a.k.a. COM 2), to which a NakWell modem is connected that is capable of running at speeds up to 38400bps. The entry's name way chosen to match the port name given in the *sys* file.

```
# /usr/lib/uucp/port - UUCP ports
# /dev/cua1 (COM2)
port             serial1
type             modem
device           /dev/cua1
speed            38400
dialer           nakwell
```

The information pertaining to the dialers itself is kept in yet another file, called – you guessed it: *dial*. For each dialer type, it basically contains the sequence of commands to be issued to dial up a remote site, given the telephone number. Again, this is specified as a chat script. For example, the entry for the above NakWell might look like this:

```
# /usr/lib/uucp/dial - per-dialer information
# NakWell modems
dialer           nakwell
chat             "" ATZ OK ATDT\T CONNECT
```

The line starting with *chat* specifies the modem chat, which is the sequence of commands sent to and received from the modem to initialize it and make it dial the desired number. The "\T" sequence will be replaced with the phone number by *uucico*.

To give you a rough idea how *uucico* deals with these configuration files, assume you issued the command

```
$ uucico -s pablo
```

on the command line. The first thing *uucico* does is look up **pablo** in the *sys* file. From the *sys* file entry for **pablo** it sees that it should use the *serial1* port to establish the connection. The *port* file tells it that this is a modem port, and that it has a NakWell modem attached.

uucico now searches *dial* for the entry describing the NakWell modem, and having found one, opens the serial port */dev/cua1* and executes the dialer chat. That is, it sends "ATZ", waits for the "OK" response, etc. When encountering the string "\T", it substitutes the phone number (123–456) extracted from the *sys* file.

After the modem returns CONNECT, the connection has been established, and the modem chat is complete. *uucico* now returns to the *sys* file and executes the login chat. In our example, it would wait for the "login:" prompt, then send its user name (neruda), wait for the "password:" prompt, and send its password, "lorca".

After completing authorization, the remote end is assumed to fire up its own *uucico*. The two will then enter the handshake phase described in the previous section.

The way the configuration files depend on each other is also shown in figure 12.1.

Net-Admin Guide

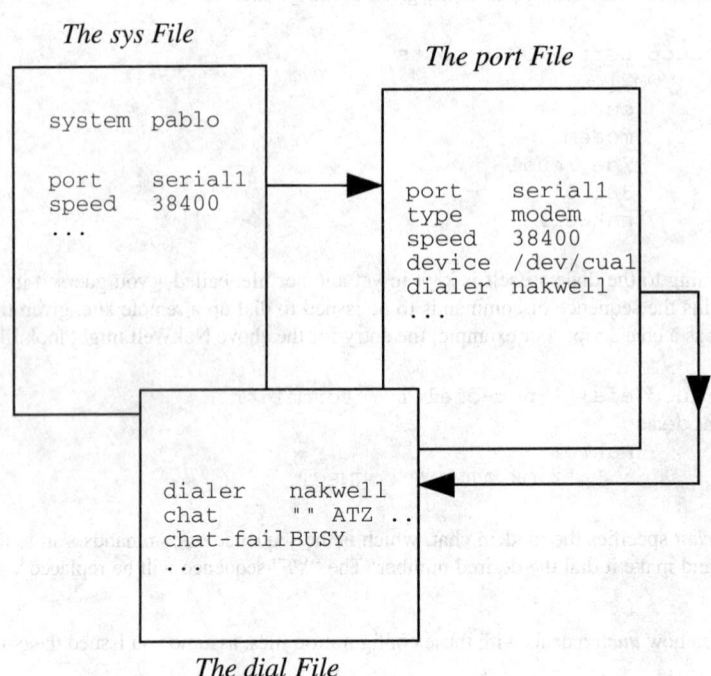

The sys File

```
system  pablo

port    serial1
speed   38400
...
```

The port File

```
port    serial1
type    modem
speed   38400
device  /dev/cua1
dialer  nakwell
...
```

The dial File

```
dialer   nakwell
chat     "" ATZ ..
chat-fail BUSY
...
```

Figure 12.1: Interaction of Taylor UUCP Configuration Files.

12.3.2 What UUCP Needs to Know

Before you start writing the UUCP configuration files, you have to gather some information it needs to know.

First, you will have to figure out what serial device your modem is attached to. Usually, the (DOS) ports COM1 through COM4 map to the device special files */dev/cua0* through */dev/cua3*. Most distributions, such as Slackware, create a link */dev/modem* as a link to the appropriate *cua** device file, and configure *kermit, seyon*, etc, to use this generic file. In this case, you should either use */dev/modem* in your UUCP configuration, too.

The reason for this is that all dial-out programs use so-called *lock files* to signal when a serial port is in use. The names of these lock files are a concatenation of the string *LCK..* and the device file name, for instance *LCK..cual*. If programs use different names for the same device, they will fail to recognize each other's lock files. As a consequence, they will disrupt each other's session when started at the same time. This is not an unlikely event when you schedule your UUCP calls using a *crontab* entry.

For details of setting up your serial ports, please refer to chapter 4.

Next, you must find out at what speed your modem and Linux will communicate. You will have to set this to the maximum effective transfer rate you expect to get. The effective transfer rate may be much higher than the raw physical transfer rate your modem is capable of. For instance, many modems send and receive data at 2400bps (bits per second). Using compression protocols such as V.42bis, the actual transfer rate may climb up to 9600bps.

Of course, if UUCP is to do anything, you will need the phone number of a system to call. Also, you will need a valid login id and possibly a password for the remote machine.[3]

You will also have to know *exactly* how to log into the system. E.g., do you have to press the BREAK key before the login prompt appears? Does it display `login:` or `user:`? This is necessary for composing the *chat script*, which is a recipe telling *uucico* how to log in. If you don't know, or if the usual chat script fails, try to call the system with a terminal program like *kermit* or *minicom*, and write down exactly what you have to do.

12.3.3 Site Naming

As with TCP/IP-based networking, your host has to have a name for UUCP networking. As long as you simply want to use UUCP for file transfers to or from sites you dial up directly, or on a local network, this name does not have to meet any standards.[4]

However, if you use UUCP for a mail or news link, you should think about having the name registered with the UUCP Mapping project. The UUCP Mapping Project is described in chapter 13. Even if you participate in a domain, you might consider having an official UUCP name for your site.

Frequently, people choose their UUCP name to match the first component of their fully qualified domain name. Suppose your site's domain address is **swim.twobirds.com**, then your UUCP host name would be **swim**. Think of UUCP sites as knowing each other on a first-name basis. Of course, you can also use a UUCP name completely unrelated to your fully qualified domain name.

However, make sure not to use the unqualified site name in mail addresses unless you have registered it as your official UUCP name.[5] At the very best, mail to an unregistered UUCP host will vanish in some big black bit bucket. If you use a name already held by some other site, this mail will be routed to that site, and cause its postmaster no end of headaches.

By default, the UUCP suite uses the name set by *hostname* as the site's UUCP name. This name is commonly set in the */etc/rc.local* script. If your UUCP name is different from what you set your host name to, you have to use the *hostname* option in the *config* file to tell *uucico* about your UUCP name. This is described below.

---

[3]If you're just going to try out UUCP, get the number of an archive site near you. Write down the login and password – they're public to make anonymous downloads possible. In most cases, they're something like **uucp/uucp** or **nuucp/uucp**.

[4]The only limitation is that it shouldn't be longer than 7 characters, so as to not confuse hosts with filesystems that impose a narrow limit on file names.

[5]The UUCP Mapping Project registers all UUCP hostnames world-wide and makes sure they are unique. To register your UUCP name, ask the maintainers of the site that handles your mail; they will be able to help you with it.

12.3.4   Taylor Configuration Files

We now return to the configuration files. Taylor UUCP gets its information from the following files:

config   This is the main configuration file. You can define your site's UUCP name here.

sys   This file describes all sites known to you. For each site, it specifies its name, at what times to call it, which number to dial (if any), what type of device to use, and how to log on.

port   Contains entries describing each port available, together with the line speed supported and the dialer to be used.

dial   Describes dialers used to establish a telephone connection.

dialcode   Contains expansions for symbolic dialcodes.

call   Contains the login name and password to be used when calling a system. Rarely used.

passwd   Contains login names and passwords systems may use when logging in. This file is used only when *uucico* does its own password checking.

Taylor configuration files are generally made up of lines containing keyword-value pairs. A hash sign introduces a comment that entends to the end of the line. To use a hash sign by itself, you may escape it with a backslash.

There are quite a number of options you can tune with these configuration files. We can't go into all parameters here, but will only cover the most important ones. They you should be able to configure a modem-based UUCP link. Additional sections will describe the modifications necessary if you want to use UUCP over TCP/IP or over a direct serial line. A complete reference is given in the Texinfo documents that accompany the Taylor UUCP sources.

When you think you have configured your UUCP system completely, you can check your configuration using the *uuchk* tool (located in */usr/lib/uucp*). *uuchk* reads your configuration files, and prints out a detailed report of the configuration values used for each system.

12.3.5   General Configuration Options – the *config* File

You won't generally use this file to describe much beside your UUCP hostname. By default, UUCP will use the name you set with the *hostname* command, but it is generally a good idea to set the UUCP name explicitly. A sample file is shown below:

```
    # /usr/lib/uucp/config - UUCP main configuration file
    hostname        vstout
```

Of course, there are a number of miscellaneous parameters that may be set here, too, such as the name of the spool directory, or access rights for anonymous UUCP. The latter will be described in a later section.

12.3.6   How to Tell UUCP about other Systems – the *sys* File

The *sys* file describes the systems your machine knows about. An entry is introduced by the *system* keyword; the subsequent lines up to the next *system* directive detail the parameters specific to that site. Commonly, a system entry will define parameters such as the telephone number and the login chat.

Parameters before the very first *system* line set default values used for all systems. Usually, you will set protocol paramters and the like in the defaults section.

Below, the most prominent fields are discussed in some detail.

12.3.6.1   System Name

The *system* command names the remote system. You must specify the correct name of the remote system, not an alias you invented, because *uucico* will check it against what the remote system says it is called when you log on.[6]

Each system name may appear more only once. If you want to use several sets of configurations for the same system (such as different telephone numbers *uucico* should try in turn), you can specify *alternates*. Alternates are described below.

12.3.6.2   Telephone Number

If the remote system is to be reached over a telephone line, the *phone* field specifies the number the modem should dial. It may contain several tokens interpreted by *uucico*'s dialing procedure. An equal sign means to wait for a secondary dial tone, and a dash generates a one-second pause. For instance, some telephone installations will choke when you don't pause between dialing the prefix code and telephone number.

[Don't know the proper English term for this – you know, something like a company's private internal installation where you have to dial a 0 or 9 to get a line to the outside.]

Any embedded alphabetic string may be used to hide site-dependent information like area codes. Any such string is translated to a dialcode using the *dialcode* file. Suppose you have the following *dialcode* file:

```
# /usr/lib/uucp/dialcode - dialcode translation
Bogoham          024881
Coxton           035119
```

With these translations, you can use a phone number such as *Bogoham7732* in the *sys* file, which makes things probably a little more legible.

12.3.6.3   Port and Speed

The *port* and *speed* options are used to select the device used for calling the remote system, and the maximum speed to which the device should be set.[7] A *system* entry may use either option alone, or both options in conjunction. When looking up a suitable device in the *port* file, only those ports are selected that have a matching port name and/or speed range.

Generally, using the *speed* option should suffice. If you have only one serial device defined in *port*, *uucico* will always pick the right one, anyway, so you only have to give it the desired speed. If you have several modems attached to your systems, you still often don't want to name a particular port, because if *uucico* finds that there are several matches, it tries each device in turn until it finds an unused one.

12.3.6.4   The Login Chat

Above, we already encountered the login chat script, which tells *uucico* how to log into the remote system. It consists of a list of tokens, specifying strings expected and sent by the local *uucico* process. The intention is to make *uucico* wait until the remote machine sends a login prompt, then return the login name, wait for the remote system to send the password prompt, and send the password. Expect and send strings are given in alternation. *uucico* automatically appends a carriage return character ($\backslash r$) to any send string. Thus, a simple chat script would look like

```
ogin: vstout ssword: catch22
```

You will notice that the expect fields don't contain the whole prompts. This is to make sure that the login succeeds even if the remote system broadcasts Login: instead of login:.

---

[6]Older Version 2 UUCP's don't broadcast their name when being called; however, newer implementations often do, and so does Taylor UUCP.

[7]The Baud rate of the tty must be at least as high as the maximum transfer speed.

uucico also allows for some sort of conditional execution, for example in the case that the remote machine's *getty* needs to be reset before sending a prompt. For this, you can attach a sub-chat to an expect string, offset by a dash. The sub-chat is executed only if the main expect fails, i.e. a timeout occurs. One way to use this feature is to send a BREAK if the remote site doesn't display a login prompt. The following example gives an allround chat script that should also work in case you have to hit return before the login appears. `" "` tells UUCP to not wait for anything and continue with the next send string immediately.

```
    " " \n\r\d\r\n\c ogin:-BREAK-ogin: vstout ssword: catch22
```

There are a couple of special strings and escape characters which may occur in the chat script. The following is an incomplete list of characters legal in expect strings:

`" "`	The empty string. It tells *uucico* not to wait for anything, but proceed with the next send string immediately.
`\t`	Tab character.
`\r`	Carriage return character.
`\s`	Space character. You need this to embed spaces in a chat string.
`\n`	Newline character.
`\\`	Backslash character.

On send strings, the following escape characters and strings are legal in addition to the above:

EOT	End of transmission character (^D).
BREAK	Break character.
`\c`	Suppress sending of carriage return at end of string.
`\d`	Delay sending for 1 second.
`\E`	Enable echo checking. This requires *uucico* to wait for the echo of everything it writes to be read back from the device before it can continue with the chat. It is primarily useful when used in modem chats (which we will encounter below). Echo checking is off by default.
`\e`	Disable echo checking.
`\K`	Same as *BREAK*.
`\p`	Pause for fraction of a second.

12.3.6.5 Alternates

Sometimes it is desirable to have multiple entries for a single system, for instance if the system can be reached on different modem lines. With Taylor UUCP, you can do this by defining a so-called *alternate*.

An alternate entry retains all settings from the main system entry, and and specifies only those values that should be overridden in the default system entry, or added to it. An alternate is offset from the system entry by a line containing the keyword *alternate*.

To use two phone numbers for **pablo**, you would modify its *sys* entry in the following way:

```
    system          pablo
    phone           123-456
    ... entries as above ...
    alternate
    phone           123-455
```

When calling **pablo**, *uucico* will now first dial 123-456, and if this fails, try the alternate. The alternate entry retains all settings from the main system entry, and overrides only the telephone number.

12.3.6.6 Restricting Call Times

Taylor UUCP provides a number of ways you may restrict the times when calls can be placed to a remote system. You might do this either because of limitations the remote host places on its services during business hours, or simply to avoid times with high call rates. Note that it is always possible to override call time restrictions by giving *uucico* the -S or -f option.

By default, Taylor UUCP will disallow connections at any time, so you *have* to use some sort of time specification in the *sys* file. If you don't care about call time restrictions, you can specify the *time* option with a value of *Any* in your *sys* file.

The simplest way to restrict call time is the *time* entry, which is followed by a string made up of a day and a time subfield. Day may be any of *Mo, Tu, We, Th, Fr, Sa, Su* combined, or *Any, Never,* or *Wk* for weekdays. The time consists of two 24-hour clock values, separated by a dash. They specify the range during which calls may be placed. The combination of these tokens is written without white space in between. Any number of day and time specifications may be grouped together with commas. For example,

```
        time                    MoWe0300-0730,Fr1805-2000
```

allows calls on Monday and Wednesdays from 3 a.m. to 7.30, and on Fridays between 18.05 and 20.00. When a time field spans midnight, say *Mo1830-0600*, it actually means Monday, between midnight and 6 a.m., and between 6.30 p.m. and midnight.

The special time strings *Any* and *Never* mean what they say: Calls may be placed at any or no time, respectively.

The *time* command takes an optional second argument that describes a retry time in minutes. When an attempt to establish a connection fails, *uucico* will not allow another attempt to dial up the remote host within a certain interval. By default, *uucico* uses an exponential backoff scheme, where the retry interval increases with each repeated failure. For instance, when you specify a retry time of 5 minutes, *uucico* will refuse to call the remote system within 5 minutes after the last failure.

The *timegrade* command allows you to attach a maximum spool grade to a schedule. For instance, assume you have the following *timegrade* commands in a *system* entry:

```
        timegrade               N Wk1900-0700,SaSu
        timegrade               C Any
```

This allows jobs with a spoolgrade of C or higher (usually, mail is queued with grade B or C) to be transferred whenever a call is established, while news (usually queued with grade N) will be transferred only during the night and at weekends.

Just like *time*, the *timegrade* command takes a retry interval in minutes as an optional third argument.

However, a caveat about spool grades is in order here: First, the *timegrade* option applies only to what *your* systems sends; the remote system may still transfer anything it likes. You can use the *call-timegrade* option to explicitly request it to send only jobs above some given spool grade; but there's no guarantee it will obey this request.[8]

Similarly, the *timegrade* field is not checked when a remote system calls in, so any jobs queued for the calling system will be sent. However, the remote system can explicitly request your *uucico* to restrict itself to a certain spool grade.

12.3.7   What Devices there are – the *port* File

The *port* file tells *uucico* about the available ports. These may be modem ports, but other types such as direct serial lines and TCP sockets are supported as well.

---

[8]If the remote system runs Talyor UUCP, it will obey.

Like the *sys* file, *port* consists of separate entries starting with the keyword *port*, followed by the port name. This name may be used by in the *sys* file's *port* statement. The name need not be unique; if there are several ports with the same name, *uucico* will try each in turn until it finds one that is not currently being used.

The *port* command should be immediately followed by the *type* statement that describes what type of port is described. Valid types are *modem*, *direct* for direct connections, and *tcp* for TCP sockets. If the *port* command is missing, the port type defaults to modem.

In this section, we will cover only modem ports; TCP ports and direct lines are discussed in a later section.

For modem and direct ports, you have to specify the device for calling out using the *device* directive. Usually, this is the name of a device special file in the */dev* directory, like */dev/cua1*.[9]

In the case of a modem device, the port entry also determines what type of modem is connected to the port. Different types of modems have to be configured differently. Even modems that claim to be Hayes-compatible needn't be really compatible with each other. Therefore, you have to tell *uucico* how to initialize the modem and how to make it dial the desired number. Taylor UUCP keeps the descriptions of all dialers in a file named *dial*. To use any of these, you have to specify the dialer's name using the *dialer* command.

Sometimes, you will want to use a modem in different ways, depending on which system you call. For instance, some older modems don't understand when a high-speed modem attempts to connect at 14400bps; they simply drop the line instead of negotiating a connect at, say, 9600bps. When you know site **drop** uses such a dumb modem, you have to set up your modem differently when calling them. For this, you need an additional port entry in the *port* file that specifies a different dialer. Now you can give the new port a different name, such as *serial1-slow*, and use the *port* directive in **drop** system entry in *sys*.

A better way is to distinguish the ports by the speeds they support. For instance, the two port entries for the above situation may look like this:

```
# NakWell modem; connect at high speed
port        serial1          # port name
type        modem            # modem port
device      /dev/cua1        # this is COM2
speed       38400            # supported speed
dialer      nakwell          # normal dialer

# NakWell modem; connect at low speed
port        serial1          # port name
type        modem            # modem port
device      /dev/cua1        # this is COM2
speed       9600             # supported speed
dialer      nakwell-slow     # don't attempt fast connect
```

The system entry for site **drop** would now give *serial1* as port name, but request to use it at 9600bps only. *uucico* will then automatically use the second port entry. All remaining sites that have a speed of 38400bps in the system entry will be called using the first port entry.

12.3.8   How to Dial a Number – the *dial* File

The *dial* file describes the way various dialers are used. Traditionally, UUCP talks of dialers rather than modems, because in earlier times, it was usual practice to have one (expensive) automatic dialing device serve a whole bank of modems. Today, most modems have dialing support builtin, so this distinction gets a little blurred.

Nevertheless, different dialers or modems may require a different configuration. You can describe each of them in the *dial* file. Entries in *dial* start with the *dialer* command that gives the dialer's name.

---

[9]Some people use the *ttyS** devices instead, which are intended for dial-in only.

The most important entry beside this is the modem chat, specified by the *chat* command. Similar to the login chat, it consists of a sequence of strings *uucico* sends to the dialer and the responses it expects in return. It is commonly used to reset the modem to some known state, and dial the number. The following sample dialer entry shows a typical modem chat for a Hayes-compatible modem:

```
# NakWell modem; connect at high speed
dialer        nakwell      # dialer name
chat          "" ATZ OK\r ATH1E0Q0 OK\r ATDT\T CONNECT
chat-fail     BUSY
chat-fail     ERROR
chat-fail     NO\sCARRIER
dtr-toggle    true
```

The modem chat begins with `" "`, the empty expect string. *uucico* will therefore send the first command (ATZ) right away. ATZ is the Hayes command to reset the modem. It then waits until the modem has sent OK, and sends the next command which turns off local echo, and the like. After the modem returns OK again, *uucico* sends the dialing command (ATDT). The escape sequence \T in this string is replaced with the phone number taken from the system entry *sys* file. *uucico* then waits for the modem to return the string CONNECT, which signals that a connection with the remote modem has been established successfully.

Often, the modem fails to connect to the remote system, for instance if the other system is talking to someone else and the line is busy. In this case, the modem will return some error message indicating the reason. Modem chats are not capable to detect such messages; *uucico* will continue to wait for the expected string until it times out. The UUCP log file will therefore only show a bland "timed out in chat script" instead of the true reason.

However, Taylor UUCP allows you to tell *uucico* about these error messages using the *chat-fail* command as shown above. When *uucico* detects a chat-fail string while executing the modem chat, it aborts the call, and logs the error message in the UUCP log file.

The last command in the example shown above tells UUCP to toggle the DTR line before starting the modem chat. Most modems can be configured to go on-hook when detecting a change on the DTR line, and enter command mode.[10]

12.3.9 UUCP Over TCP

Absurd as it may sound at the first moment, using UUCP to transfer data over TCP not that bad an idea, especially when transferring large amount of data such as Usenet news. On TCP-based links, news is generally exchanged using the NNTP protocol, where articles are requested and sent individually, without compression or any other optimization. Although adequate for large sites with several concurrent newsfeeds, this technique is very unfavorable for small sites that receive their news over a slow connection such as ISDN. These sites will usually want to combine the qualities of TCP with the advantages of sending news in large batches, which can be compressed and thus transferred with very low overhead. A standard way to transfer these batches is to use UUCP over TCP.

In *sys*, you would specify a system to be called via TCP in the following way:

```
system        gmu
address       news.groucho.edu
time          Any
port          tcp-conn
chat          ogin: vstout word: clouseau
```

The *address* command gives the IP address of the host, or its fully qualified domain name. The corresponding *port* entry would read:

---

[10]You can also configure some modems to reset themselves when detecting a transition on DTR. Some of them, however, don't seem to like this, and occasionally get hung.

```
port        tcp-conn
type        tcp
service     540
```

The entry states that a TCP connection should be used when a *sys* entry references *tcp-conn*, and that *uucico* should attempt to connect to the TCP network port 540 on the remote host. This is the default port number of the UUCP service. Instead of the port number, you may also give a symbolic port name to the *service* command. The port number corresponding to this name will be looked up in */etc/services*. The common name for the UUCP service is *uucpd*.

12.3.10   Using a Direct Connection

Assume you use a direct line connecting your system **vstout** to **tiny**. Very much like in the modem case, you have to write a system entry in the *sys* file. The *port* command identifies the serial port *tiny* is hooked up to.

```
system      tiny
time        Any
port        direct1
speed       38400
chat        ogin: cathcart word: catch22
```

In the *port* file, you have to describe the serial port for the direct connection. A *dialer* entry is not needed, because there's no need for dialing.

```
port        direct1
type        direct
speed       38400
```

12.4   The Do's and Dont's of UUCP – Tuning Permissions

12.4.1   Command Execution

UUCP's task is to copy files from one system to another, and to request execution of certain commands on remote hosts. Of course, you as an administrator would want to control what rights you grant other systems – allowing them to execute any command on your system is definitely not a good idea.

By default, the only commands Taylor UUCP allows other systems to execute on your machine are *rmail* and *rnews*, which are commonly used to to exchange email and Usent news over UUCP. The default search path used by *uuxqt* is a compile-time option, but should usually contain */bin*, */usr/bin*, and */usr/local/bin*. To change the set of commands for a particular system, you can use the *commands* keyword in the *sys* file. Similarly, the search path can be changed with the *command-path* statement. For instance, you may want to allow system **pablo** to execute the *rsmtp* command in addition to *rmail* and *rnews*:[11]

```
system      pablo
...
commands    rmail rnews rsmtp
```

12.4.2   File Transfers

Taylor UUCP also allows you to fine-tune file transfers in great detail. At one extreme, you can disable transfers to and from a particular system. Just set *request* to *no*, and the remote system will not be able either to retrieve files from your

---

[11]*rsmtp* is used to deliver mail with batched SMTP. This is described in the mail chapters.

system or send it any files. Similarly, you can prohibit your users from transferring files to or from a system by setting *transfer* to *no*. By default, users on both the local and the remote system are allowed to up- and download files.

In addition, you can configure the directories to and from which files may be copied. Usually, you will want to restrict access from remote systems to a single directory hierarchy, but still allow your users to send files from their home directory. Commonly, remote users will be allowed to receive files only from the public UUCP directory, */var/spool/uucppublic*. This is the traditional place to make files publicly available; very much like FTP servers on the Internet. It is commonly referred to using the tilde character.

Therefore, Taylor UUCP provides four different commands to configure the directories for sending and receiving files. They are *local-send*, which specifies the list of directories a user may ask UUCP to send files from; *local-receive*, which gives the the list of directories a user may ask to receive files to; and *remote-send* and *remote-receive*, which do the analogous for requests from a foreign system. Consider the following example:

```
system          pablo
...
local-send      /home ~
local-receive   /home ~/receive
remote-send     ~ !~/incoming !~/receive
remote-receive  ~/incoming
```

The *local-send* command allows users on your host to send any files below */home* and from the public UUCP directory to **pablo**. The *local-receive* command allows them to receive files either to the world-writable *receive* directory in the *uucppublic*, or any world-writable directory below */home*. The *remote-send* directive allows **pablo** to request files from */var/spool/uucppublic*, except for files below the *incoming* and *receive* directories. This is signaled to *uucico* by preceding the directory names with exclamation marks. Finally, the last line allows **pablo** to upload any files to **incoming**.

One of the biggest problems with file transfers using UUCP is that will only receive files to directories that are world-writable. This may tempt some users to set up traps for other users, etc. However, there's no way escaping this problem except disabling UUCP file transfers altogether.

12.4.3 Forwarding

UUCP provides a mechanism to have other systems execute file transfers on your behalf. For instance, this allows you to make **seci** retrieve a file from **uchile** for you, and send it to your system. The following command would achieve this:

```
$ uucp -r seci!uchile!~/find-ls.gz ~/uchile.files.gz
```

This technique of passing a job through several systems is called *forwarding*. In the above example, the reason to use forwarding may be that **seci** has UUCP access to **uchile**, but your host doesn't. However, if you run a UUCP system, you would want to limit the forwarding service to a few hosts you trust not to run up a horrendous phone bill by making you download the latest X11R6 source release for them.

By default, Taylor UUCP disallows forwarding altogether. To enable forwarding for a particular system, you can use the *forward* command. This command specifies a list of sites the system may request you to forward jobs to and from. For instance, the UUCP administrator of **seci** would have to add the following lines to the *sys* file to allow **pablo** to request files from **uchile**:

```
###################
# pablo
system          pablo
...
forward         uchile
###################
# uchile
system          uchile
```

```
        ...
        forward-to        pablo
```

The *forward-to* entry for **uchile** is necessary so that any files returned by it are actually passed on to **pablo**. Otherwise UUCP would drop them. This entry uses a variation of the *forward* command that permits **uchile** only to send files to **pablo** through **seci**; not the other way round.

To permit forwarding to any system, use the special keyword *ANY* (capital letters required).

12.5   Setting up your System for Dialing in

If you want to set up your site for dialing in, you have to permit logins on your serial port, and customize some system files to provide UUCP accounts. This will be the topic of the current section.

12.5.1   Setting up *getty*

If you want to use a serial line as a dialin port, you have to enable a *getty* process on this port. However, some *getty* implementations aren't really suitable for this, because you usually want to use a serial port for dialing in and out. You therefore have to make sure to use a *getty* that is able to share the line with other programs like *uucico*, or *minicom*. One program that does this is *uugetty* from the *getty_ps* package. Most Linux distributions have it; check for *uugetty* in your */sbin* directory. Another program I am aware of is Gert Doering's *mgetty*, which also supports reception of facsimiles. You can also obtain the latest versions of these from **sunsite.unc.edu** as either binary or source.

Explaining the differences in the way *uugetty* and *mgetty* handle logins is beyond the scope of this little section; for more information, please refer to the Serial HOWTO by Grag Hankins, as well as the documentation that comes along with *getty_ps* and *mgetty*.

12.5.2   Providing UUCP Accounts

Next, you have to set up user accounts that let remote sites log into your system and establish a UUCP connection. Generally, you will provide a separate login name to each system that polls you. When setting up an account for system **pablo**, you would probably give it **Upablo** as the user name.

For systems that dial in through the serial port, you usually have to add these accounts to the system password file, */etc/passwd*. A good practice is to put all UUCP logins in a special group such as **uuguest**. The account's home directory should be set to the public spool directory */var/spool/uucppublic*; its login shell must be *uucico*.

If you have the shadow password suite installed, you can do this with the *useradd* command:

```
# useradd -d /var/spool/uucppublic -G uuguest -s /us-
r/lib/uucp/uucico Upablo
```

If you don't use the shadow password suite, you probably have to edit */etc/passwd* by hand, adding a line like that shown below, where 5000 and 150 are the numerical uid and gid assigned to user **Upablo** and group **uuguest**, respectively.

```
Upablo:x:5000:150:UUCP Account:/var/spool/uucppublic:/usr/lib/uucp/uucico
```

After installing the account, you have to activate it by setting its password with the *passwd* command.

To serve UUCP systems that connect to your site over TCP, you have to set up *inetd* to handle incoming connections on the *uucp* port. You do this by adding the following line to */etc/inetd.conf*:[12]

---

[12]Note that usually, *tcpd* has mode 700, so that you must invoke it as user **root**, not **uucp** as you would usually do.

```
uucp    stream  tcp   nowait  root  /usr/sbin/tcpd  /usr/lib/uucp/uucico -l
```

The -l option makes *uucico* perform its own login authorization. It will prompt for a login name and a password just like
the standard *login* program, but will rely on its private password database instead of */etc/passwd*. This private password
file is named */usr/lib/uucp/passwd* and contains pairs of login names and passwords:

```
Upablo  IslaNegra
Ulorca  co'rdoba
```

Of course, this file must be owned by **uucp** and have permissions of 600.

If this database sounds like such a good idea you would like to use on normal serial logins, too, you will be disappointed
to hear that this isn't possible at the moment without major contortions. First off, you need Taylor UUCP 1.05 for this,
because it allows *getty* to pass the login name of the calling user to *uucico* using the -u option.[13] Then, you have to trick
the *getty* you are using into invoking *uucico* instead of the usual */bin/login*. With *getty_ps*, you can do this by setting the
LOGIN option in the configuration file. However, this disables interactive logins altogether. *mgetty*, on the other hand,
has a nice feature that allows you to invoke different login commands based on the name the user provided. For instance,
you can tell *mgetty* to use *uucico* for all users that provide a login name beginning with a capital U, but let everyone else
be handled by the standard *login* command.

To protect your UUCP users from callers giving a false system name and snarfing all their mail, you should add *called-
login* commands to each system entry in the *sys* file. This is described in section 12.5.3 above.

12.5.3   Protecting Yourself Against Swindlers

One of the biggest problems about UUCP is that the calling system can lie about its name; it announces its name to the
called system after logging in, but the server doesn't have a way to check this. Thus, an attacker could log into his or her
own UUCP account, pretend to be someone else, and pick up that other site's mail. This is particularly troublesome if
you offer login via anonymous UUCP, where the password is made public.

Unless you know you can trust all sites that call your system to be honest, you *must* guard against this sort of impostors.
The cure against this disease is to require each system to use a particular login name by specifying a *called-login* in *sys*.
A sample system entry may look like this:

```
system          pablo
... usual options ...
called-login    Upablo
```

The upshot of this is that whenever a system logs in and pretends it is **pablo**, *uucico* will check whether it has logged in
as **Upablo**. If it hasn't, the calling system will be turned down, and the connection is dropped. You should make it a habit
to add the *called-login* command to every system entry you add to your *sys* file. It is important that you do this for *all*
sytems, regardless of whether they will ever call your site or not. For those sites that never call you, you should probably
set *called-login* to some totally bogus user name, such as **neverlogsin**.

12.5.4   Be Paranoid – Call Sequence Checks

Another way to fend off and detect impostors is to use call sequence checks. Call sequence checks help you protect
against intruders that somehow managed to find out the password you log into your UUCP system with.

When using call sequence checks, both machines keep track of the number of connections established so far. It is
incremented with each connection. After logging in, the caller sends its call sequence number, and the callee checks it
against its own number. If they don't match, the connection attempt will be rejected. If the initial number is chosen at
random, attackers will have a hard time guessing the correct call sequence number.

---

[13]The -u option is present in 1.04, too, but is only a no-op.

But call sequence checks do more for you than this: even if some very clever person should detect your call sequence number as well as your password, you will find this out. When the attacker call your UUCP feed and steals your mail, this will increase the feeds call sequence number by one. The next time *you* call your feed and try to log in, the remote *uucico* will refuse you, because the numbers don't match anymore!

If you have enabled call sequence checks, you should check your log files regularly for error messages that hint at possible attacks. If your system rejects the call sequence number the calling system offers it, *uucico* will put a message into the log file saying something like "Out of sequence call rejected". If your system is rejected by its feed because the sequence numbers are out of sync, it will put a message in the log file saying "Handshake failed (RBADSEQ)".

To enable call sequence checks, you have to add following command to the system entry:

```
# enable call sequence checks
sequence            true
```

Beside this, you have to create the file containing the sequence number itself. Taylor UUCP keeps the sequence number is in a file called *.Sequence* in the remote site's spool directory. It *must* be owned by **uucp**, and must be mode 600 (i.e. readable and writeable only by **uucp**). It is best to initialize this file with an arbitrary, agreed-upon start value. Otherwise, an attacker might manage to guess the number by trying out all values smaller than, say, 60.

```
# cd /var/spool/uucp/pablo
# echo 94316 > .Sequence
# chmod 600 .Sequence
# chown uucp.uucp .Sequence
```

Of course, the remote site has to enable call sequence checks as well, and start by using exactly the same sequence number as you.

12.5.5 Anonymous UUCP

If you want to provide anonymous UUCP access to your system, you first have to set up a special account for it as described above. A common practive is to give it a login name and a password of **uucp**.

In addition, you have to set a few of the security options for unknown systems. For instance, you may want to prohibit them from executing any commands on your system. However, you cannot set these parameters in a *sys* file entry, because the *system* command requires the system's name, which you don't have. Taylor UUCP solves this dilemma through the *unknown* command. *unknown* can be used in the *config* file to specify any command that can usually appear in a system entry:

```
unknown       remote-receive ~/incoming
unknown       remote-send ~/pub
unknown       max-remote-debug none
unknown       command-path /usr/lib/uucp/anon-bin
unknown       commands rmail
```

This will restrict unknown systems to downloading files from below the *pub* directory and uploading files to the *incoming* directory below */var/spool/uucppublic*. The next line will make *uucico* ignore any requests from the remote system to turn on debugging locally. The last two lines permit unknown systems to execute *rmail*; but the command path specified makes *uucico* look for the *rmail* command in a private directory named *anon-bin* only. This allows you to provide some special *rmail* that, for instance, forwards all mail to the super-user for examination. This allows anonymous users to reach the maintainer of the system, but prevents them at the same time from injecting any mail to other sites.

To enable anonymous UUCP, you must specify at least one *unknown* statement in *config*. Otherwise *uucico* will reject any unknown systems.

12.6 UUCP Low-Level Protocols

To negotiate session control and file transfers with the remote end, *uucico* uses a set of standardized messages. This is often referred to as the high-level protocol. During the initialization phase and the hangup phase these are simply sent across as strings. However, during the real transfer phase, an additional low-level protocol is employed which is mostly transparent to the higher levels. This is to make error checks possible when using unreliable lines, for instance.

12.6.1 Protocol Overview

As UUCP is used over different types of connections, such as serial lines or TCP, or even X.25, specific low-level protocols are needed. In addition, several implementations of UUCP have introduced different protocols that do roughly the same thing.

Protocols can be divided into two categories: streaming and packet-oriented protocols. Protocols of the latter variety transfer a file as a whole, possibly computing a checksum over it. This is nearly free of any overhead, but requires a reliable connection, because any error will cause the whole file to be retransmitted. These protocols are commonly used over TCP connections, but are not suitable for use over telephone lines. Although modern modems do quite a good job at error correction, they are not perfect, nor is there any error detection between your computer and the modem.

On the other hand, packet protocols split up the file into several chunks of equal size. Each packet is sent and received separately, a checksum is computed, and an acknowledgement is returned to the sender. To make this more efficient, sliding-window protocols were invented, which allow for a limited number (a window) of outstanding acknoledgements at any time. This greatly reduces the amount of time *uucico* has to wait during a transmission. Still, the relatively large overhead compared to a streaming protocol make packet protocls inefficient for use over TCP.

The width of the data path also makes a difference. Sometimes, sending eight-bit characters over a serial connection is impossible, for instance if the connection goes through a stupid terminal server. In this case, characters with the eighth bit set have to be quoted on transmission. When you transmit eight-bit characters over a seven-bit connection, they have to be Under worst-case assumptions, this doubles the amount of data to be transmitted, although compression done by the hardware may compensate for this. Lines that can transmit arbitrary eight-bit characters are usually called eight-bit clean. This is the case for all TCP connections, as well as for most modem connections.

The following protocols are available with Taylor UUCP 1.04:

g	This is the most common protocol and should be understood by virtually all *uucico*'s. It does thorough error checking and is therefore well-suited for noisy telephone links. *g* requires an eight-bit clean connection. It is a packet-oriented protocol which uses a sliding-window technique.
i	This is a bidirectional packet protocol which can send and receive files at the same time. It requires a full-duplex connection and an eight-bit clean data path. It is currently understood only by Taylor UUCP.
t	This is a protocol intended for use over a TCP connection, or other truly error-free networks. It uses packets of 1024 bytes and requires an eight-bit clean connection.
e	This should basically do the same as *t*. The main difference is that *e* is a streaming protocol.
f	This is intended for use with reliable X.25 connections. It is a streaming protocol and expects a seven-bit data path. Eight-bit characters are quoted, which can make it very inefficient.
G	This is the System V Release 4 version of the *g* protocol. It is also understood by some other versions of UUCP.
a	This protocol is similiar to ZMODEM. It requires an eight bit connection, but quotes certain control characters like XON and XOFF.

Net-Admin Guide

12.6.2   Tuning the Transmission Protocol

All protocols allow for some variation in packet sizes, timeouts, and the like. Usually, the defaults provided work well under standard circumstances, but may not be optimal for your situation. The *g* protocol, for instance, uses window sizes from 1 to 7, and packet sizes in powers of 2 ranging from 64 through 4096.[14] If your telephone line is usually so noisy that it drops more than 5 percent all packets, you should probably lower the packet size and shrink the window. On the other hand, on very good telephone lines the protocol overhead of sending ACKs for every 128 bytes may prove wasteful, so that you might increase the packet size to 512 or even 1024.

Taylor UUCP provides a meachanism to suit your needs by tuning these parameters with the *protocol-parameter* command in the *sys* file. For instance, to set the *g* protocol's packet size to 512 when talking to **pablo**, you have to add:

```
system          pablo
...
protocol-parameter g  packet-size  512
```

The tunable parameters and their names vary from protocol to protocol. For a complete list of them please refer to the documentation enclosed in the Taylor UUCP source.

12.6.3   Selecting Specific Protocols

Not every implementation of *uucico* speaks and understand each protocol, so during the initial handshake phase, both processes have to agree on a common protocol. The master *uucico* offers the slave a list of supported protocols by sending P*protlist*, from which the slave may pick one.

Based on the type of port used (modem, TCP, or direct), *uucico* will compose a default list of protocols. For modem and direct connections, this list usually comprises *i*, *a*, *g*, *G*, and *j*. For TCP connections, the list is *t*, *e*, *i*, *a*, *g*, *G*, *j*, and *f*. You can override this default list with the *protocols* command, which may be specified in a system entry as well as a port entry. For instance, you might edit the *port* file entry for your modem port like this:

```
port          serial1
...
protocols     igG
```

This will require any incoming or outgoing connection through this port to use *i*, *g*, or *G*. If the remote system does not support any of these, the conversation will fail.

12.7   Troubleshooting

This section describes what may go wrong with your UUCP connection, and makes suggestions where to look for the error. However, the questions were compiled off the top of my head. There's much more that can go wrong.

In any case, enable debugging with -x all, and take a look at the output in *Debug* in the spool directory. It should help you to quickly recognize where the problem lies. Also, I have always found it helpful to turn on my modem's speaker when it didn't connect. With Hayes-compatible modems, this is accomplished by adding "ATL1M1 OK" to the modem chat in the *dial* file.

The first check always should be whether all file permissions are set correctly. *uucico* should be setuid **uucp**, and all files in */usr/lib/uucp*, */var/spool/uucp* and */var/spool/uucppublic* should be owned by **uucp**. There are also some hidden files[15] in the spool directory which must be owned by **uucp** as well.

---

[14]Most binaries included in Linux distributions default to a window size of 7 and 128 byte packets.

[15]That is, files whose name begins with a dot. Such files aren't normally displayed by the *ls* command.

uucico **keeps saying "Wrong time to call":** This probably means that in the system entry in *sys*, you didn't specify a *time* command that details when the remote system may be called, or you gave one which actually forbids calling at the current time. If no call schedule is given, *uucico* assumes that the system may never be called.

uucico **complains that the site is already locked:** This means that *uucico* detected a lock file for the remote system in */var/spool/uucp*. The lock file may be from an earlier call to the system that crashed, or was killed. However, it's also likely that there's another *uucico* process sitting around that is trying to dial the remote system and got stuck in a chat script, etc. If this *uucico* process doesn't succeed in connecting to the remote system, kill it with a hangup signal, and remove any lock files it left lying around.

I can connect to the remote site, but the chat script fails: Look at the text you receive from the remote site. If it's garbled, this might be a speed-related problem. Otherwise, confirm if it really agrees with what your chat script expects. Remember, the chat script starts with an expect string. If you receive the login prompt, then send your name, but never get the password prompt, insert some delays before sending it, or even in-between the letters. You might be too fast for your modem.

My modem does not dial: If your modem doesn't indicate that the DTR line has been raised when *uucico* calls out, you possibly haven't given the right device to *uucico*. If your modem recognizes DTR, check with a terminal program that you can write to it. If this works, turn on echoing with \E at the start of the modem chat. If it doesn't echo your commands during the modem chat, check if your line speed is too high or low for your modem. If you see the echo, check if you have disabled modem responses, or set them to number codes. Verify that the chat script itself is correct. Remember that you have to write two backslashes to send one to the modem.

My modem tries to dial, but doesn't get out: Insert a delay into the phone number. This is especially useful when dialing out from a company's internal telephone net. For people in Europe, who usually dial pulse-tone, try touch-tone. In some countries, postal services have been upgrading their nets recently. Touch-tone sometimes helps.

I log file says I have extremely high packet loss rates: This looks like a speed problem. Maybe the link between computer and modem is too slow (remember to adapt it to the highest effective rate possible)? Or is it your hardware that is too slow to service interrupts in time? With a NSC 16550A chipset on your serial port, 38kbps are said to work reasonably well; however, without FIFOs (like 16450 chips), 9600 bps is the limit. Also, you should make sure hardware handshake is enabled on the serial line.

Another likely cause is that hardware handshake isn't enabled on the port. Taylor UUCP 1.04 has no provisions for turning on RTS/CTS handshake. You have to enable this explicitly from *rc.serial* using the following command:

```
$ stty crtscts < /dev/cua3
```

I can log in, but handshake fails: Well, there can be a number of problems. The output in the log file should tell you a lot. Look at what protocols the remote site offers (It sends a string `Pprotlist` during the handshake). Maybe they don't have any in common (did you select any protocols in *sys* or *port*?).

If the remote system sends `RLCK`, there is a stale lockfile for you on the remote system. If it's not because you're already connected to the remote system on a different line, ask to have it removed.

If it sends `RBADSEQ`, the other site has conversation count checks enabled for you, but numbers didn't match. If it sends `RLOGIN`, you were not permitted to login under this id.

12.8 Log Files

When compiling the UUCP suite to use Taylor-style logging, you have only three global log files, all of which reside in the spool directory. The main log file is named *Log* and contains all information about connections established and files transferred. A typical excerpt looks like this (after a little reformatting to make it fit the page):

```
uucico pablo - (1994-05-28 17:15:01.66 539) Calling sys-
tem pablo (port cua3)
```

```
uucico pablo - (1994-05-28 17:15:39.25 539) Login successful
uucico pablo - (1994-05-28 17:15:39.90 539) Handshake successful
                 (protocol 'g' packet size 1024 window 7)
uucico pablo postmaster (1994-05-28 17:15:43.65 539) Receiving D.pabloB04aj
uucico pablo postmaster (1994-05-28 17:15:46.51 539) Receiving X.pabloX04ai
uucico pablo postmaster (1994-05-28 17:15:48.91 539) Receiving D.pabloB04at
uucico pablo postmaster (1994-05-28 17:15:51.52 539) Receiving X.pabloX04as
uucico pablo postmaster (1994-05-28 17:15:54.01 539) Receiving D.pabloB04c2
uucico pablo postmaster (1994-05-28 17:15:57.17 539) Receiving X.pabloX04c1
uucico pablo - (1994-05-28 17:15:59.05 539) Protocol 'g' packets: sent 15,
                 resent 0, received 32
uucico pablo - (1994-05-28 17:16:02.50 539) Call complete (26 seconds)
uuxqt pablo postmaster (1994-05-28 17:16:11.41 546) Executing X.pabloX04ai
                 (rmail okir)
uuxqt pablo postmaster (1994-05-28 17:16:13.30 546) Executing X.pabloX04as
                 (rmail okir)
uuxqt pablo postmaster (1994-05-28 17:16:13.51 546) Executing X.pabloX04c1
                 (rmail okir)
```

The next important log file is *Stats*, which lists file transfer statistics. The section of *Stats* corresponding to the above transfer looks like this:

```
postmaster pablo (1994-05-28 17:15:44.78)
                 received 1714 bytes in 1.802 seconds (951 bytes/sec)
postmaster pablo (1994-05-28 17:15:46.66)
                 received 57 bytes in 0.634 seconds (89 bytes/sec)
postmaster pablo (1994-05-28 17:15:49.91)
                 received 1898 bytes in 1.599 seconds (1186 bytes/sec)
postmaster pablo (1994-05-28 17:15:51.67)
                 received 65 bytes in 0.555 seconds (117 bytes/sec)
postmaster pablo (1994-05-28 17:15:55.71)
                 received 3217 bytes in 2.254 seconds (1427 bytes/sec)
postmaster pablo (1994-05-28 17:15:57.31)
                 received 65 bytes in 0.590 seconds (110 bytes/sec)
```

Again, the lines have been split to make it fit the page.

The third file if *Debug*. This is the place where debugging information is written. If you use debugging, you should make sure that this file has a protection mode of 600. Depending on the debug mode you selected, it may contain the login and password you use to connect to the remote system.

Some UUCP binaries included in Linux distributions have been compiled to use HDB-style logging. HDB UUCP uses a whole bunch of log files stored below */var/spool/uucp/.Log*. This directory contains three more directories, named *uucico*, *uuxqt*, and *uux*. They contain the logging output generated by each of the corresponding commands, sorted into different files for each site. Thus, output from *uucico* when calling site **pablo** will go into *.Log/uucico/pablo*, while the subsequent *uuxqt* run will write to *.Log/uuxqt/pablo*. The lines written to the various lofiles are however the same as with Taylor logging.

When you enable debugging output with HDB-style logging compiled in, it will go to the *.Admin* directory below */var/spool/uucp*. During outgoing calls, debugging information will be sent to *.Admin/audit.local*, while the output from *uucico* when someone calls in will go to *.Admin/audit*.

Chapter 13

Electronic Mail

One of the most prominent uses of networking since the first networks were devised, has been eletronic mail. It started as a simple service that copied a file from one machine to another, and appended it to the recipient's *mailbox* file. Basically, this is still what email is all about, although an ever growing net with its complex routing requirements and its ever increasing load of messages has made a more elaborate scheme necessary.

Various standards of mail exchange have been devised. Sites on the Internet adhere to one laid out in RFC 822, augmented by some RFCs that describe a machine-independent way of transferring special characters, and the like. Much thought has also been given recently to "multi-media mail", which deals with including pictures and sound in mail messages. Another standard, X.400, has been defined by CCITT.

Quite a number of mail transport programs have been implemented for UNIX systems. One of the best-known is the University of Berkeley's *sendmail*, which is used on a number of platforms. The original author was Eric Allman, who is now actively working on the *sendmail* team again. There are two Linux ports of *sendmail-5.56c* available, one of which will be described in chapter 15. The *sendmail* version currently being developed is 8.6.5.

The mail agent most commonly used with Linux is *smail-3.1.28*, written and copyrighted by Curt Landon Noll and Ronald S. Karr. This is the one included in most Linux distributions. In the following, we will refer to it simply as *smail*, although there are other versions of it which are entirely different, and which we don't describe here.

Compared to *sendmail*, *smail* is rather young. When handling mail for a small site without complicated routing requirements, their capabilities are pretty close. For large sites, however, *sendmail* always wins, because its configuration scheme is much more flexible.

Both *smail* and *sendmail* support a set of configuration files that have to be customized. Apart from the information that is required to make the mail subsystem run (such as the local hostname), there are many more parameters that may be tuned. *sendmail*'s main configuration file is very hard to understand at first. It looks as if your cat had taken a nap on your keyboard with the shift key pressed. *smail* configuration files are more structured and easier to understand than *sendmail*'s, but don't give the user as much power in tuning the mailer's behavior. However, for small UUCP or Internet sites the work required in setting up any of them is roughly the same.

In this chapter, we will deal with what email is and what issues you as an administrator will have to deal with. Chapters 14 and 15 will give instructions on setting up *smail* and *sendmail* for the first time. The information provided there should suffice to get smaller sites operational, but there are many more options, and you can spend many happy hours in front of your computer configuring the fanciest features.

Toward the end of the current chapter we will briefly cover setting up *elm*, a very common mail user agent on many UNIXish systems, including Linux.

For more information about issues specific to electronic mail on Linux, please refer to the Electronic Mail HOWTO by Vince Skahan, which is posted to **comp.os.linux.announce** regularly. The source distributions of *elm*, *smail* and *sendmail* also contain very extensive documentation that should answer most of your questions on setting them up. If you are looking for information on email in general, there's a number of RFCs that deal with this topic. They are listed in the bibliography at the end of the book.

13.1   What is a Mail Message?

A Mail message generally consists of a message body, which is the text the sender wrote, and special data specifying recipients, transport medium, etc., very much like what you see when you look at a letter's envelope.

This administrative data falls into two categories; in the first category is any data that is specific to the transport medium, like the address of sender and recipient. It is therefore called *the envelope*. It may be transformed by the transport software as the message is passed along.

The second variety is any data necessary for handling the mail message, which is not particular to any transport mechanism, such as the message's subject line, a list of all recipients, and the date the message was sent. In many networks, it has become standard to prepend this data to the mail message, forming the so-called *mail header*. It is offset from the *mail body* by an empty line.[1]

Most mail transport software in the UNIX world uses a header format outlined in a RFC 822. Its original purpose was to specify a standard for use on the ARPANET, but since it was designed to be independent from any environment, it has been easily adapted to other networks, including many UUCP-based networks.

RFC 822 however is only the greatest common denominator. More recent standards have been conceived to cope with growing needs as, for example, data encryption, international character set support, and multi-media mail extensions (MIME).

In all these standards, the header consists of several lines, separated by newline characters. A line is made up of a field name, beginning in column one, and the field itself, offset by a colon and white space. The format and semantics of each field vary depending on the field name. A header field may be continued across a newline, if the next line begins with a TAB. Fields can appear in any order.

A typical mail header may look like this:

```
From brewhq.swb.de!ora.com!andyo Wed Apr 13 00:17:03 1994
Return-Path: <brewhq.swb.de!ora.com!andyo>
Received: from brewhq.swb.de by monad.swb.de with uucp
        (Smail3.1.28.1 #6) id m0pqqlT-00023aB; Wed, 13 Apr 94 00:17 MET DST
Received: from ora.com (ruby.ora.com) by brewhq.swb.de with smtp
        (Smail3.1.28.1 #28.6) id <m0pqoQr-0008qhC>; Tue, 12 Apr 94 21:47 MEST
Received: by ruby.ora.com (8.6.8/8.6.4) id RAA26438; Tue, 12 Apr 94 15:56 -
0400
Date: Tue, 12 Apr 1994 15:56:49 -0400
Message-Id: <199404121956.PAA07787@ruby>
From: andyo@ora.com (Andy Oram)
To: okir@monad.swb.de
Subject: Re: Your RPC section
```

Usually, all necessary header fields are generated by the mailer interface you use, like *elm*, *pine*, *mush*, or *mailx*. Some however are optional, and may be added by the user. *elm*, for example, allows you to edit part of the message header. Others are added by the mail transport software. A list of common header fields and their meaning are given below:

From:	This contains the sender's email address, and possibly the "real name". A complete zoo of formats is used here.
To:	This is the recipient's email address.
Subject:	Describes the content of the mail in a few words. At least that's what it *should* do.
Date:	The date the mail was sent.

---

[1] It is customary to append a *signature* or *.sig* to a mail message, usually containing information on the author, along with a joke or a motto. It is offset from the mail message by a line containing "- ".

`Reply-To:`   Specifies the address the sender wants the recipient's reply directed to. This may be useful if you have several accounts, but want to receive the bulk of mail only on the one you use most frequently. This field is optional.

`Organization:`   The organization that owns the machine from which the mail originates. If your machine is owned by you privately, either leave this out, or insert "private" or some complete nonsense. This field is optional.

`Message-ID:`   A string generated by mail transport on the originating system. It is unique to this message.

`Received:`   Every site that processes your mail (including the machines of sender and recipient) inserts such a field into the header, giving its site name, a message id, time and date it received the message, which site it is from, and which transport software was used. This is so that you can trace which route the message took, and can complain to the person responsible if something went wrong.

`X-`*anything:*   No mail-related programs should complain about any header which starts with `X-`. It is used to implement additional features that have not yet made it into an RFC, or never will. This is used by the Linux Activists mailing list, for example, where the channel is selected by the `X-Mn-Key:` header field.

The one exception to this structure is the very first line. It starts with the keyword `From` which is followed by a blank instead of a colon. To distinguish it from the ordinary `From:` field, it is frequently referred to as `From_`. It contains the route the message has taken in UUCP bang-path style (explained below), time and date when it was received by the last machine having processed it, and an optional part specifying which host it was received from. Since this field is regenerated by every system that processes the message, it is somtimes subsumed under the envelope data.

The `From_` field is there for backward compatibilty with some older mailers, but is not used very much anymore, except by mail user interfaces that rely on it to mark the beginning of a message in the user's mailbox. To avoid potential trouble with lines in the message body that begin with "From ", too, it has become standard procedure to escape any such occurence by preceding it with ">".

13.2   How is Mail Delivered?

Generally, you will compose mail using a mailer interface like *mail* or *mailx*; or more sophisticated ones like *elm*, *mush*, or *pine*. These programs are called *mail user agents*, or MUA's for short. If you send a mail message, the interface program will in most cases hand it to another program for delivery. This is called the *mail transport agent*, or MTA. On some systems, there are different mail transport agents for local and remote delivery; on others, there is only one. The command for remote delivery is usually called *rmail*, the other is called *lmail* (if it exists).

Local delivery of mail is, of course, more than just appending the incoming message to the recipient's mailxbox. Usually, the local MTA will understand aliasing (setting up local recipient addresses pointing to other addresses), and forwarding (redirecting a user's mail to some other destination). Also, messages that cannot be delivered must usually be *bounced*, that is, returned to the sender along with some error message.

For remote delivery, the transport software used depends on the nature of the link. If the mail must be delivered over a network using TCP/IP, SMTP is commonly used. SMTP stands for Simple Mail Transfer Protocol, and is defined in RFC 788 and RFC 821. SMTP usually connects to the recipient's machine directly, negotiating the message transfer with the remote side's SMTP daemon.

In UUCP networks, mail will usually not be delivered directly, but rather be forwarded to the destination host by a number of intermediate systems. To send a message over a UUCP link, the sending MTA will usually execute *rmail* on the forwarding system using *uux*, and feed it the message on standard input.

Since this is done for each message separately, it may produce a considerable work load on a major mail hub, as well as clutter the UUCP spool queues with hundreds of small files taking up an unproportional amount of disk space.[2] Some

---

[2]This is because disk space is usually allocated in blocks of 1024 Bytes. So even a message of at most 400 Bytes will eat a full KB.

MTAs therefore allow you to collect several messages for a remote system in a single batch file. The batch file contains the SMTP commands that the local host would normally issue if a direct SMTP connection was used. This is called BSMTP, or *batched* SMTP. The batch is then fed to the *rsmtp* or *bsmtp* program on the remote system, which will process the input as if a normal SMTP connection had occurred.

13.3 Email Addresses

For electronic mail, an address is made up of at least the name of a machine handling the person's mail, and a user identification recognized by this system. This may be the recipient's login name, but may also be anything else. Other mail addressing schemes, like X.400, use a more general set of "attributes" which are used to look up the recipient's host in an X.500 directory server.

The way a machine name is interpreted, i.e. at which site your message will finally wind up, and how to combine this name with the recipient's user name greatly depends on the network you are on.

Internet sites adhere to the RFC 822 standard, which requires a notation of **user@host.domain**, where **host.domain** is the host's fully qualified domain name. The middle thing is called an "at" sign. Because this notation does not involve a route to the destination host but gives the (unique) hostname instead, this is called an *absolute* address.

In the original UUCP environment, the prevalent form was **path!host!user**, where **path** described a sequence of hosts the message had to travel before reaching the destination **host**. This construct is called the *bang path* notation, because an exclamation mark is loosely called a "bang". Today, many UUCP-based networks have adopted RFC 822, and will understand this type of address.

Now, these two types of addressing don't mix too well. Assume an address of **hostA!user@hostB**. It is not clear whether the '@' sign takes precedence over the path, or vice versa: do we have to send the message to **hostB**, which mails it to **hostA!user**, or should it be sent to **hostA**, which fowards it to **user@hostB**?

Addresses that mix different types of address operators are called *hybrid addresses*. Most notorious is the above example. It is usually resolved by giving the '@' sign precedence over the path. In the above example, this means sending the message to **hostB** first.

However, there is a way to specify routes in RFC 822-conformant ways: **<@hostA,@hostB:user@hostC>** denotes the address of **user** on **hostC**, where **hostC** is to be reached through **hostA** and **hostB** (in that order). This type of address is freqeuently called a *route-addr address*.

Then, there is the '%' address operator: **user%hostB@hostA** will first be sent to **hostA**, which expands the rightmost (in this case, only) percent sign to an '@' sign. The address is now **user@hostB**, and the mailer will happily forward your message to **hostB** which delivers it to **user**. This type of address is sometimes referred to as "Ye Olde ARPANET Kludge", and its use is discouraged. Nevertheless, many mail transport agents generate this type of address.

Other networks have still different means of addressing. DECnet-based networks, for example, use two colons as an address separator, yielding an address of host::user.[3] Lastly, the X.400 standard uses an entirely different scheme, by describing a recipient by a set of attribute-value pairs, like country and organization.

On FidoNet, each user is identified by a code like **2:320/204.9**, consisting of four numbers denoting zone (2 is for Europe), net (320 being Paris and Banlieue), node (the local hub), and point (the individual user's PC). Fidonet addresses can be mapped to RFC 822; the above would be written as **Thomas.Quinot@p9.f204.n320.z2.fidonet.org**. Now didn't I say domain names are easy to remember?

There are some implications to using these different types of addressing which will be described throughout the following sections. In a RFC 822 environment, however, you will rarely use anything else than absolute addresses like user@host.domain.

---

[3]When trying to reach a DECnet address from an RFC 822 environment, you may use **"host::user"@relay**, where *relay* is the name of a known Internet-DECnet relay.

13.4 How does Mail Routing Work?

The process of directing a message to the recipient's host is called *routing*. Apart from finding a path from the sending site to the destination, it involves error checking as well as speed and cost optimization.

There is a big difference between the way a UUCP site handles routing, and the way an Internet site does. On the Internet, the main job of directing data to the recipient host (once it is known by it's IP address) is done by the IP networking layer, while in the UUCP zone, the route has to be supplied by the user, or generated by the mail transfer agent.

13.4.1 Mail Routing on the Internet

On the Internet, it depends entirely on the destination host whether any specific mail routing is performed at all. The default is to deliver the message to the destination host directly by looking up its IP address, and leave the actual routing of the data to the IP transport layer.

Most sites will usually want to direct all inbound mail to a highly available mail server that is capable of handling all this traffic, and have it distribute this mail locally. To announce this service, the site publishes a so-called MX record for their local domain in the DNS database. MX stands for *Mail Exchanger* and basically states that the server host is willing to act as a mail forwarder for all machines in this domain. MX records may also be used to handle traffic for hosts that are not connected to the Internet themselves, like UUCP networks, or company networks with hosts carrying confidential information.

MX records also have a *preference* associated with them. This is a positive integer. If several mail exchangers exist for one host, the mail transport agent will try to transfer the message to the exchanger with the lowest preference value, and only if this fails will it try a host with a higher value. If the local host is itself a mail exchanger for the destination address, it must not forward messages to any MX hosts with a higher preference than its own; this is a safe way of avoiding mail loops.

Suppose that an organization, say Foobar Inc., want all their mail handled by their machine called **mailhub**. They will then have an MX record like this in the DNS database:

```
foobar.com        IN   MX     5    mailhub.foobar.com
```

This announces **mailhub.foobar.com** as a mail exchanger for **foobar.com** with a preference value of 5. A host that wishes to deliver a message to **joe@greenhouse.foobar.com** will check DNS for **foobar.com**, and finds the MX record pointing at **mailhub**. If there's no MX with a preference smaller than 5, the message will be delivered to **mailhub**, which then dispatches it to **greenhouse**.

The above is really only a sketch of how MX records work. For more information on the mail routing on the Internet, please refer to RFC 974.

13.4.2 Mail Routing in the UUCP World

Mail routing on UUCP networks is much more complicated than on the Internet, because the transport software does not perform any routing itself. In earlier times, all mail had to be addressed using bang paths. Bang paths specified a list of hosts through which to forward the message, separated by exclamation marks, and followed by the user's name. To address a letter to Janet User on a machine named **moria**, you would have used the path **eek!swim!moria!janet**. Whis would have sent the mail from your host to **eek**, from there on to **swim** and finally to **moria**.

The obvious drawback of this technique is that it requires you to remember much about the network topology, fast links, etc. Much worse than that, changes in the network topology — like links being deleted or hosts being removed — may cause messages to fail simply because you weren't aware of the change. And finally, in case you move to a different place, you will most likely have to update all these routes.

One thing, however, that made the use of source routing necessary was the presence of ambiguous hostnames: For instance, assume there are two sites named **moria**, one in the U.S., and one in France. Which site now does **moria!janet** refer to? This can be made clear by specifying what path to reach **moria** through.

The first step in disambiguating hostnames was the founding of *The UUCP Mapping Project*. It is located at Rutgers University, and registers all official UUCP hostnames, along with information on their UUCP neighbors and their geographic location, making sure no hostname is used twice. The information gathered by the Mapping Project is published as the *Usenet Maps*, which are distributed regularly through Usenet.[4] A typical system entry in a Map (after removing the comments) looks like this.

```
moria
        bert(DAILY/2),
        swim(WEEKLY)
```

This entry says that **moria** has a link to **bert**, which it calls twice a day, and **swim**, which it calls weekly. We will come back to the Map file format in more detail below.

Using the connectivity information provided in the maps, you can automatically generate the full paths from your host to any destination site. This information is usually stored in the *paths* file, also called *pathalias database* sometimes. Assume the Maps state that you can reach **bert** through **ernie**, then a pathalias entry for **moria** generated from the Map snippet above may look like this:

```
moria            ernie!bert!moria!%s
```

If you now give a destination address of **janet@moria.uucp**, your MTA will pick the route shown above, and send the message to **ernie** with an envelope address of **bert!moria!janet**.

Building a *paths* file from the full Usenet maps is however not a very good idea. The information provided in them is usually rather distorted, and occasionally out of date. Therefore, only a number of major hosts use the complete UUCP world maps to build their *paths* file. Most sites only maintain routing information for sites in their neighborhood, and send any mail to sites they don't find in their databases to a smarter host with more complete routing information. This scheme is called *smart-host routing*. Hosts that have only one UUCP mail link (so-called *leaf sites*) don't do any routing of their own; they rely entirely on their smart-host.

13.4.3   Mixing UUCP and RFC 822

The best cure against the problems of mail routing in UUCP networks so far is the adoption of the domain name system in UUCP networks. Of course, you can't query a name server over UUCP. Nevertheless, many UUCP sites have formed small domains that coordinate their routing internally. In the Maps, these domains announce one or two host as their mail gateways, so that there doesn't have to be a map entry for each host in the domain. The gateways handle all mail that flows into and out of the domain. The routing scheme inside the domain is completely invisible to the outside world.

This works very well with the smart-host routing scheme described above. Global routing information is maintained by the gateways only; minor hosts within a domain will get along with only a small hand-written *paths* file that lists the routes inside their domain, and the route to the mail hub. Even the mail gateways do not have to have routing information for every single UUCP host in the world anymore. Beside the complete routing information for the domain they serve, they only need to have routes to entire domains in their databases now. For instance, the pathalias entry shown below will route all mail for sites in the **sub.org** domain to **smurf**:

```
.sub.org          swim!smurf!%s
```

Any mail addressed to **claire@jones.sub.org** will be sent to **swim** with an envelope address of **smurf!jones!claire**.

---

[4]Maps for sites registered with The UUCP Mapping Project are distributed through the newsgroup **comp.mail.maps**; other organizations may publish separate maps for their network.

The hierarchical organization of the domain name space allows mail servers to mix more specific routes with less specific ones. For instance, a system in France may have specific routes for subdomains of **fr**, but route any mail for hosts in the **us** domain toward some system in the U.S. In this way, domain-based routing (as this technique is called) greatly reduces the size of routing datbases as well as te administrative overhead needed.

The main benefit of using domain names in a UUCP environment, however, is that compliance with RFC 822 permits easy gatewaying between UUCP networks and the Internet. Many UUCP domains nowadays have a link with an Internet gateway that acts as their smart-host. Sending messages across the Internet is faster, and routing information is much more reliable because Internet hosts can use DNS instead of the Usenet Maps.

In order to be reachable from the Internet, UUCP-based domains usually have their Internet gateway announce an MX record for them (MX records were described above). For instance, assume that **moria** belongs to the **orcnet.org** domain. **gcc2.groucho.edu** acts as their Internet gateway. **moria** would therefore use **gcc2** as its smart-host, so that all mail for foreign domains is delivered across the Internet. On the other hand, **gcc2** would announce an MX record for **orcnet.org**, and deliver all incoming mail for **orcnet** sites to **moria**.

The only remaining problem is that the UUCP transport programs can't deal with fully qualified domain names. Most UUCP suites were designed to cope with site names of up to eight characters, some even less, and using non-alphanumeric characters such as dots is completely out of the question for most.

Therefore, some mapping between RFC 822 names and UUCP hostnames is needed. The way this mapping is done is completely implementation-dependent. One common way of mapping FQDNs to UUCP names is to use the pathalias file for this:

```
moria.orcnet.org  ernie!bert!moria!%s
```

This will produce a pure UUCP-style bang path from an address that specifies a fully qualified domain name. Some mailers provide a special files for this; *sendmail*, for instance, uses the *uucpxtable* for this.

The reverse transformation (colloquially called domainizing) is sometimes required when sending mail from a UUCP network to the Internet. As long as the mail sender uses the fully qualified domain name in the destination address, this problem can be avoided by not removing the domain name from the envelope address when forwarding the message to the smart-host. However, there are still some UUCP sites that are not part of any domain. They are usually domainized by appending the pseudo-domain **uucp**.

13.5 Pathalias and Map File Format

The pathalias database provides the main routing information in UUCP-based networks. A typical entry looks like this (site name and path are separated by TABs):

```
moria.orcnet.org  ernie!bert!moria!%s
moria             ernie!bert!moria!%s
```

This makes any message to **moria** be delivered via **ernie** and **bert**. Both **moria**'s fully qualified name and its UUCP name have to be given if the mailer does not have a separate way to map between these name spaces.

If you want to direct all messages to hosts inside some domain to its mail relay, you may also specify a path in the pathalias database, giving the domain name as target, preceded by a dot. For example, if all hosts in the **sub.org** may be reached through **swim!smurf**, the pathalias entry might look like this:

```
.sub.org       swim!smurf!%s
```

Writing a pathalias file is acceptable only when you are running a site that does not have to do much routing. If you have to do routing for a large number of hosts, a better way is to use the *pathalias* command to create the file from map files. Maps can be maintained much easier, because you may simply add or remove a system by editing the system's map entry, and re-create the map file. Although the maps published by the Usenet Mapping Project aren't used for routing very much anymore, smaller UUCP networks may provide routing information in their own set of maps.

A map file mainly consists of a list of sites, listing the sites each system polls or is polled by. The system name begins in column one, and is followed by a comma-separated list of links. The list may be continued across newlines if the next line begins with a tab. Each link consists of the name of the site, followed by a cost given in brackets. The cost is an arithmetic expression, made up of numbers and symbolic costs. Lines beginning with a hash sign are ignored.

As an example, consider **moria**, which polls **swim.twobirds.com** twice a day, and **bert.sesame.com** once per week. Moreover, the link to **bert** only uses a slow 2400bps modem. **moria**'s would publish the following maps entry:

```
moria.orcnet.org
        bert.sesame.com(DAILY/2),
        swim.twobirds.com(WEEKLY+LOW)

moria.orcnet.org = moria
```

The last line would make it known under its UUCP name, too. Note that it must be *DAILY/2*, because calling twice a day actually halves the cost for this link.

Using the information from such map files, *pathalias* is able to calculate optimal routes to any destination site listed in the paths file, and produce a pathalias database from this which can then be used for routing to these sites.

pathalias provides a couple of other features like site-hiding (i.e. making sites accessible only through a gateway) etc. See the manual page for *pathalias* for details, as well as a complete list of link costs.

Comments in the map file generally contain additional information on the sites described in it. There is a rigid format in which to specify this, so that it can be retrieved from the maps. For instance, a program called *uuwho* uses a database created from the map files to display this information in a nicely formatted way.

When you register your site with an organization that distributes map files to its members, you generally have to fill out such a map entry.

Below is a sample map entry (in fact, it's the one for my site):

```
#N      monad, monad.swb.de, monad.swb.sub.org
#S      AT 486DX50; Linux 0.99
#O      private
#C      Olaf Kirch
#E      okir@monad.swb.de
#P      Kattreinstr. 38, D-64295 Darmstadt, FRG
#L      49 52 03 N / 08 38 40 E
#U      brewhq
#W      okir@monad.swb.de (Olaf Kirch); Sun Jul 25 16:59:32 MET DST 1993
#
monad   brewhq(DAILY/2)
# Domains
monad = monad.swb.de
monad = monad.swb.sub.org
```

The white space after the first two characters is a TAB. The meaning of most of the fields is pretty obvious; you will receive a detailed description from whichever domain you register with. The *L* field is the most fun to find out: it gives your geographical position in latitude/longitude and is used to draw the postscript maps that show all sites for each country, as well as world-wide.[5]

---

[5]They are posted regularly in **news.lists.ps-maps**. Beware. They're HUGE.

13.6 Configuring *elm*

elm stands for "electronic mail" and is one of the more reasonably named UNIX tools. It provides a full-screen interface with a good help feature. We won't discuss here how to use *elm*, but only dwell on its configuration options.

Theoretically, you can run *elm* unconfigured, and everything works well — if you are lucky. But there are a few options that must be set, although only required on occasions.

When it starts, *elm* reads a set of configuration variables from the *elm.rc* file in */usr/lib/elm*. Then, it will attempt to read the file *.elm/elmrc* in your home directory. You don't usually write this file yourself. It is created when you choose "save options" from *elm*'s options menu.

The set of options for the private *elmrc* file is also available in the global *elm.rc* file. Most settings in your private *elmrc* file override those of the global file.

13.6.1 Global *elm* Options

In the global *elm.rc* file, you must set the options that pertain to your host's name. For example, at the Virtual Brewery, the file for **vlager** would contain the following:

```
#
# The local hostname
hostname = vlager
#
# Domain name
hostdomain = .vbrew.com
#
# Fully qualified domain name
hostfullname = vlager.vbrew.com
```

These options set *elm*'s idea of the local hostname. Although this information is rarely used, you should set these options nevertheless. Note that these options only take effect when giving them in the global configuration file; when found in your private *elmrc*, they will be ignored.

13.6.2 National Character Sets

Recently, there have been proposals to amend the RFC 822 standard to support various types of messages, such as plain text, binary data, Postscript files, etc. The set of standards and RFCs covering these aspects are commonly referred to as MIME, or Multipurpose Internet Mail Extensions. Among other things, this also lets the recipient know if a character set other than standard ASCII has been used when writing the message, for example using French accents, or German umlauts. This is supported by *elm* to some extent.

The character set used by Linux internally to represent characters is usually referred to as ISO-8859-1, which is the name of the standard it conforms to. It is also known as Latin-1. Any message using characters from this character set should have the following line in its header:

```
Content-Type:  text/plain; charset=iso-8859-1
```

The receiving system should recognize this field and take appropriate measures when displaying the message. The default for *text/plain* messages is a *charset* value of *us-ascii*.

To be able to display messages with character sets other than ASCII, *elm* must know how to print these characters. By default, when *elm* receives a message with a *charset* field other than *us-ascii* (or a content type other than *text/plain*, for that matter), it tries to display the message using a command called *metamail*. Messages that require *metamail* to be displayed are shown with an 'M' in the very first column in the overview screen.

Since Linux' native character set is ISO-8859-1, calling *metamail* is not necessary to display messages using this character set. If *elm* is told that the display understands ISO-8859-1, it will not use *metamail* but will display the message directly instead. This can be done by setting the following option in the global *elm.rc*:

```
displaycharset = iso-8859-1
```

Note that you should set this options even when you are never going to send or receive any messages that actually contain characters other than ASCII. This is because people who do send such messages usually configure their mailer to put the proper Content-Type: field into the mail header by default, whether or not they are sending ASCII-only messages.

However, setting this option in *elm.rc* is not enough. The problem is that when displaying the message with its builtin pager, *elm* calls a library function for each character to determine whether it is printable or not. By default, this function will only recognize ASCII characters as printable, and display all other characters as "^?". You may overcome this by setting the environment variable *LC_CTYPE* to *ISO-8859-1*, which tells the library to accept Latin-1 characters as printable. Support for this and other features is available since *libc-4.5.8*.

When sending messages that contain special characters from ISO-8859-1, you should make sure to set two more variables in the *elm.rc* file:

```
charset = iso-8859-1
textencoding = 8bit
```

This makes *elm* report the character set as ISO-8859-1 in the mail header, and send it as an 8 bit value (the default is to strip all characters to 7 bit).

Of course, any of these options can also be set in the private *elmrc* file instead of the global one.

Chapter 14

Getting *smail* Up and Running

This chapter will give you a quick introduction to setting up *smail*, and an overview of the functionality it provides. Although *smail* is largely compatible with *sendmail* in its behaviour, their configuration files are completely different.

The main configuration file is the */usr/lib/smail/config*. You always have to edit this file to reflect values specific to your site. If you are only a UUCP leaf site, you will have relatively little else to do, ever. Other files that configure routing and transport options may also be used; they will be dealt with briefly, too.

By default, *smail* processes and delivers all incoming mail immediately. If you have relatively high traffic, you may instead have *smail* collect all messages in the so-called *queue*, and process it at regular intervals only.

When handling mail within a TCP/IP network, *smail* is frequently run in daemon mode: at system boot time, it is invoked from *rc.inet2*, and puts itself in the background where it waits for incoming TCP connections on the SMTP port (usually port 25). This is very beneficial whenever you expect to have a significant amount of traffic, because *smail* isn't started up separately for every incoming connection. The alternative would be to have *inetd* manage the SMTP port, and have it spawn *smail* whenever there is a connection on this port.

smail has a lot a flags that control it behavior; describing them in detail here wouldn't make help you much. Fortunately, *smail* supports a number of standard modes of operation that are enabled when you invoke it by a special command name, like *rmail*, or *smtpd*. Usually, these aliases are symbolic links to the *smail* binary itself. We will encounter most of them when discussing the various features of *smail*.

There are two links to *smail* you should have under all circumstances; namely */usr/bin/rmail* and */usr/sbin/sendmail*.[1] When you compose and send a mail message with a user agent like *elm*, the message will be piped into *rmail* for delivery, with the recipient list given to it on the command line. The same happens with mail coming in via UUCP. Some versions of *elm*, however, invoke */usr/sbin/sendmail* instead of *rmail*, so you need both of them. For example, if you keep *smail* in */usr/local/bin*, type the following at the shell prompt:

```
# ln -s /usr/local/bin/smail /usr/bin/rmail
# ln -s /usr/local/bin/smail /usr/sbin/sendmail
```

If you want to dig further into the details of configuring *smail*, please refer to the manual pages *smail(1)* and *smail(5)*. If it isn't included in your favorite Linux distribution, you can get it from the source to *smail*.

14.1   UUCP Setup

To use *smail* in a UUCP-only environment, the basic installation is rather simple. First, you must make sure you have the two symbolic links to *rmail* and *sendmail* mentioned above. If you expect to receive SMTP batches from other sites, you also have to make *rsmtp* a link to *smail*.

In Vince Skahan's *smail* distribution, you will find a sample configuration file. It is named *config.sample* and resides in */usr/lib/smail*. You have to copy it to *config* and edit it to reflect values specific to your site.

---

[1]This is the new standard location of *sendmail* according to the Linux File System Standard. Another common location is */usr/lib*.

Assume your site is named *swim.twobirds.com*, and is registered in the UUCP maps as *swim*. Your smarthost is *ulysses*. Then your *config* file should look like this:

```
#
# Our domain names
visible_domain=two.birds:uucp
#
# Our name on outgoing mails
visible_name=swim.twobirds.com
#
# Use this as uucp-name as well
uucp_name=swim.twobirds.com
#
# Our smarthost
smart_host=ulysses
```

The first statement tells *smail* about the domains your site belongs to. Insert their names here, separated by colons. If your site name is registered in the UUCP maps, you should also add *uucp*. When being handed a mail message, *smail* determines your host's name using the *hostname(2)* system call, and checks the recipient's address against this hostname, tacking on all names from this list in turn. If the address matches any of these names, or the unqualified hostname, the recipient is considered local, and *smail* attempts to deliver the message to a user or alias on the local host. Otherwise, the recipient is considered remote, and delivery to the destination host is attempted.

visible_name should contain a single, fully qualified domain name of your site that you want to use on outgoing mails. This name is used when generating the sender's address on all outgoing mail. You must make sure to use a name that *smail* recognizes as referring to the local host (i.e. the hostname with one of the domains listed in the *visible_domain* attribute). Otherwise, replies to your mails will bounce off your site.

The last statement sets the path used for smart-host routing (described in section 13.4). With this sample setup, *smail* will forward any mail for remote addresses to the smart host. The path specified in the *smart_path* attribute will be used as a route to the smart host. Since messages will be delivered via UUCP, the attribute must specify a system known to your UUCP software. Please refer to chapter 12 on making a site known to UUCP.

There's one option used in the above file that we haven't explained yet; this is *uucp_name*. The reason to use the option is this: By default, *smail* uses the value returned by *hostname(2)* for UUCP-specific things such as the return path given in the *From_* header line. If your hostname is *not* registered with the UUCP mapping project, you should tell *smail* to use your fully qualified domain name instead.[2] This can be done by adding the *uucp_name* option to the *config* file.

There is another file in */usr/lib/smail*, called *paths.sample*. It is an example of what a *paths* file might look like. However, you will not need one unless you have mail links to more than one site. If you do, however, you will have to write one yourself, or generate one from the Usenet maps. The *paths* file will be described later in this chapter.

14.2   Setup for a LAN

If you are running a site with two or more hosts connected by a LAN, you will have to designate one host that handles your UUCP connection with the outside world. Between the hosts on your LAN, you will most probably want to exchange mail with SMTP over TCP/IP. Assume we're back at the Virtual Brewery again, and **vstout** is set up as the UUCP gateway.

In a networked environment, it is best to keep all user mailboxes on a single file system, which is NFS-mounted on all other hosts. This allows users to move from machine to machine, without having to move their mail around (or even worse, check some three or four machines for newly-arrived mail each morning). Therefore, you also want to make

---

[2]The reason is this: Assume your hostname is *monad*, but is not registered in the maps. However, there is a site in the maps called *monad*, so every mail to *monad!root*, even sent from a direct UUCP neighbor of yours, will wind up on the other *monad*. This is a nuisance for everybody.

sender addresses independent from the machine the mail was written on. It is common practice to use the domain name all by itself in the sender address, instead of a hostname. Janet User, for example, would specify **janet@vbrew.com** instead of **janet@vale.vbrew.com**. We will explain below how to make the server recognize the domain name as a valid name for your site.

A different way of keeping all mailboxes on a central host is to use POP or IMAP. POP stands for *Post Office Protocol* and lets users access their mailboxes over a simple TCP/IP conection. IMAP, the *Interactive Mail Access Protocol*, is similar to POP, but more general. Both clients and servers for IMAP and POP have been ported to Linux, and are available from **sunsite.unc.edu** below */pub/Linux/system/Network*.

14.2.1   Writing the Configuration Files

The configuration for the Brewery works as follows: all hosts except the mail server **vstout** itself route all outgoing mail to the server, using smart host routing. **vstout** itself sends all outgoing mail to the real smart host that routes all of the Brewery's mail; this host is called **moria**.

The standard *config* file for all hosts other than **vstout** looks like this:

```
#
# Our domain:
visible_domain=vbrew.com
#
# What we name ourselves
visible_name=vbrew.com
#
# Smart-host routing: via SMTP to vstout
smart_path=vstout
smart_transport=smtp
```

This is very similar to what we used for a UUCP-only site. The main difference is that the transport used to send mail to the smart host is, of course, SMTP. The *visible_domain* attribute makes *smail* use the domain name instead of the local hostname on all outgoing mail.

On the UUCP mail gateway **vstout**, the *config* file looks a little different:

```
#
# Our hostnames:
hostnames=vbrew.com:vstout.vbrew.com:vstout
#
# What we name ourselves
visible_name=vbrew.com
#
# in the uucp world, we're known as vbrew.com
uucp_name=vbrew.com
#
# Smart transport: via uucp to moria
smart_path=moria
smart_transport=uux
#
# we're authoritative for our domain
auth_domains=vbrew.com
```

This *config* file uses a different scheme to tell *smail* what the local host is called. Instead of giving it a list of domains and letting it find the hostname with a system call, it specifies a list explicitly. The above list contains both the fully qualified and the unqualified hostname, and the domain name all by itself. This makes *smail* recognize **janet@vbrew.com** as a local address, and deliver the message to **janet**.

The *auth_domains* variable names the domains for which **vstout** is considered to be authoritative. That is, if *smail* receives any mail addressed to *host*.**vbrew.com** where *host* does not name an existing local machine, it rejects the message and returns it to the sender. If this entry isn't present, any such message will be sent to the smart-host, who will return it to **vstout**, and so on until it is discarded for exceeding the maximum hop count.

14.2.2 Running *smail*

First, you have to decide whether to run *smail* as a separate daemon, or whether to have *inetd* manage the SMTP port and invoke *smail* only whenever an SMTP connection is requested from some client. Usually, you will prefer daemon operation on the mail server, because this loads the machine far less than spawning *smail* over and over again for each single connection. As the mail server also delivers most incoming mail directly to the users, you will choose *inetd* operation on most other hosts.

Whatever mode of operation you choose for each individual host, you have to make sure you have the following entry in your */etc/services* file:

```
smtp                    25/tcp              # Simple Mail Transfer Protocol
```

This defines the TCP port number that *smail* should use for SMTP conversations. 25 is the standard defined by the Assigned Numbers RFC.

When run in daemon mode, *smail* will put itself in the background, and wait for a connection to occur on the SMTP port. When a connection occurs, it forks and conducts an SMTP conversation with the peer process. The *smail* daemon is usually started by invoking it from the *rc.inet2* script using the following command:

```
/usr/local/bin/smail -bd -q15m
```

The -bd flag turns on daemon mode, and -q15m makes it process whatever messages have accumulated in the message queue every 15 minutes.

If you want to use *inetd* instead, your */etc/inetd.conf* file should contain a line like this:

```
smtp    stream tcp nowait root  /usr/sbin/smtpd smtpd
```

smtpd should be a symbolic link to the *smail* binary. Remember you have to make *inetd* re-read *inetd.conf* by sending it a *HUP* signal after making these changes.

Daemon mode and *inetd* mode are mutually exclusive. If you run *smail* in deamon mode, you should make sure to comment out any line in *inetd.conf* for the *smtp* service. Equivalently, when having *inetd* manage *smail*, make sure that *rc.inet2* does not start the *smail* daemon.

14.3 If You Don't Get Through...

If something goes wrong with your installation, there are a number of features that may help you to find what's at the root of the problem. The first place to check are *smail*'s log files. They are kept in */var/spool/smail/log*, and are named *logfile* and *paniclog*, respectively. The former lists all transactions, while the latter is only for error messages related to configuration errors and the like.

A typical entry in *logfile* looks like this:

```
04/24/94 07:12:04: [m0puwU8-00023UB] received
             from: root
          program: sendmail
             size: 1468 bytes
```

```
04/24/94 07:12:04: [m0puwU8-00023UB] delivered
             via: vstout.vbrew.com
              to: root@vstout.vbrew.com
         orig-to: root@vstout.vbrew.com
          router: smart_host
       transport: smtp
```

This shows that a message from **root** to **root@vstout.vbrew.com** has been properly delivered to host **vstout** over SMTP.

Messages *smail* could not deliver generate a similar entry in the log file, but with an error message instead of the de-livered part:

```
04/24/94 07:12:04: [m0puwU8-00023UB] received
            from: root
         program: sendmail
            size: 1468 bytes
04/24/94 07:12:04: [m0puwU8-00023UB] root@vstout.vbrew.com ... deferred
     (ERR_148) transport smtp: connect: Connection refused
```

The above error is typical for a situation in which *smail* properly recognizes that the message should be delivered to **vstout** but was not able to connect to the SMTP service on **vstout**. If this happens, you either have a configuration problem, or TCP support is missing from your *smail* binaries.

This problem is not as uncommon as one might think. There have been precompiled *smail* binaries around, even in some Linux distributions, without support for TCP/IP networking. If this is the case for you, you have to compile *smail* yourself. Having installed *smail*, you can check if it has TCP networking support by telnetting to the SMTP port on your machine. A successful connect to the SMTP server is shown below (your input is marked *like this*):

```
$ telnet localhost smtp
Trying 127.0.0.1...
Connected to localhost.
Escape character is '^]'.
220 monad.swb.de Smail3.1.28.1 #6 ready at Sun, 23 Jan 94 19:26 MET
QUIT
221 monad.swb.de closing connection
```

If this test doesn't produce the SMTP banner (the line starting with the 220 code), first make sure that your configuration is *really* correct before you go through compiling *smail* yourself, which is described below.

If you encounter a problem with *smail* that you are unable to locate from the error message *smail* generates, you may want to turn on debugging messages. You can do this using the -d flag, optionally followed by a number specifying the level of verbosity (you may not have any space between the flag and the numerical argument). *smail* will then print a report of its operation to the screen, which may give you more hints about what is going wrong.

[Don't know,...Maybe people don't find this funny:] If nothing else helps, you may want to invoke *smail* in Rogue mode by giving the -bR option on the command line. The manpage says on this option: "Enter the hostile domain of giant mail messages, and RFC standard scrolls. Attempt to make it down to protocol level 26 and back." Although this option won't solve your problems, it may provide you some comfort and consolation.[3]

14.3.1 Compiling *smail*

If you know for sure that *smail* is lacking TCP network support, you have to get the source. It is probably included in your distribution, if you got it via CD-ROM, otherwise you may get it from the net via FTP.[4]

---

[3]Don't use this if you're in a really bad mood.

[4]If you bought this with a Linux distribution from a vendor, you are entitled to the source code "for a nominal shipping charge", according to *smail*'s copying conditions.

When compiling *smail*, you had best start with the set of configuration files from Vince Skahan's *newspak* distribution. To compile in the TCP networking driver, you have to set the *DRIVER_CONFIGURATION* macro in the *conf/EDITME* file to either *bsd-network* or *arpa-network*. The former is suitable for LAN installations, but the Internet requires *arpa-network*. The difference between these two is that the latter has a special driver for BIND service that is able to recognize MX records, which the former doesn't.

14.4   Mail Delivery Modes

As noted above, *smail* is able to deliver messages immediately, or queue them for later processing. If you choose to queue messages, *smail* will store away all mail in the *messages* directory below */var/spool/smail*. It will not process them until explicitly told so (this is also called "running the queue").

You can select one of three delivery modes by setting the *delivery_mode* attribute in the *config* file to either of *foreground*, *background*, or *queued*. These select delivery in the foreground (immediate processing of incoming messages), in the background, (message is delivered by a child of the receiving process, with the parent process exiting immediately after forking), and queued. Incoming mail will always be queued regardless of this option if the boolean variable *queue_only* is set in the *config* file.

If you turn on queuing, you have to make sure the queues are checked regularly; probably every 10 or 15 minutes. If you run *smail* in daemon mode, you have to add the option -q10m on the command line to process the queue every 10 minutes. Alternatively, you can invoke *runq* from *cron* at these intervals. *runq* should be a link to *smail*.

You can display the current mail queue by invoking *smail* with the -bp option. Equivalently, you can make *mailq* a link to *smail*, and invoke *mailq*:

```
$ mailq -v
m0pvB1r-00023UB From: root  (in /var/spool/smail/input)
                Date: Sun, 24 Apr 94 07:12 MET DST
                Args: -oem -oMP sendmail root@vstout.vbrew.com
Log of transactions:
  Xdefer: <root@vstout.vbrew.com> reason: (ERR_148) transport smtp:
  connect: Connection refused
```

This shows a single message sitting in the message queue. The transaction log (which is only displayed if you give *mailq* the -v option) may give an additional reason why it is still waiting for delivery. If no attempt has been made yet to deliver the message, no transaction log will be displayed.

Even when you don't use queuing, *smail* will occasionally put messages into the queue when it finds immediate delivery fails for a transient reason. For SMTP connections, this may be an unreachable host; but messages may also be deferred when the file system is found to be full. You should therefore put in a queue run every hour or so (using *runq*), else any deferred message will stick around the queue forever.

14.5   Miscellaneous *config* Options

There are quite a number of options you may set in the *config* file, which, although useful, are not essential to running *smail*, and which we will not discuss here. Instead, we will only mention a few that you might find a reason to use:

error_copy_postmaster   If this boolean variable is set, any error will generate a message to the postmaster. Usually, this is only done for errors that are due to a faulty configuration. The variable can be turned on by putting it in the *config* file, preceded by a plus (+).

max_hop_count   If the hop count for a message (i.e. the number of hosts already traversed) equals or exceeds this number, attempts at remote delivery will result in an error message being returned to the sender. This is used to prevent messages from looping forever. The hop count is generally computed from the number of *Received:* fields in the mail header, but may also be set manually using the -h option on the command line.

This variable defaults to 20.

postmaster   The postmaster's address. If the address **Postmaster** cannot be resolved to a valid local address, then this is used as the last resort. The default is **root**.

14.6   Message Routing and Delivery

smail splits up mail delivery into three different tasks, the router, director, and transport module.

The router module resolves all remote addresses, determining to which host the message should be sent to next, and which transport must be used. Depending on the nature of the link, different transports such as UUCP or SMTP may be used.

Local addresses are given to the director task which resolves any forwarding or aliasing. For example, the address might be an alias or a mailing list, or the user might want to forward her mail to another address. If the resulting address is remote, it is handed to the router module for additional routing, otherwise it is assigned a transport for local delivery. By far the most common case will be delivery to a mailbox, but messages may also be piped into a command, or appended to some arbitrary file.

The transport module, finally, is responsible for whatever method of delivery has been chosen. It tries to deliver the message, and in case of failure either generates a bounce message, or defers it for a later retry.

With *smail*, you have much freedom in configuring these tasks. For each of them, a number of drivers are available, from which you can choose those you need. You describe them to *smail* in a couple of files, namely *routers*, *directors*, and *transports*, located in */usr/lib/smail*. If these files do not exist, reasonable defaults are assumed that should be suitable for many sites that either use SMTP or UUCP for transport. If you want to change *smail*'s routing policy, or modify a transport, you should get the sample files from the *smail* source distribution,[5] copy the sample files to */usr/lib/smail*, and modify them according to your needs. Sample configuration files are also given in Appendix B.

14.7   Routing Messages

When given a message, *smail* first checks if the destination is the local host, or a remote site. If the target host address is one of the local hostnames configured in *config*, the message is handed to the director module. Otherwise, *smail* hands the destination address to a number of router drivers to find out which host to forward a message to. They can be described in the *routers* file; if this file does not exist, a set of default routers are used.

The destination host is passed to all routers in turn, and the one finding the most specific route is selected. Consider a message addressed to **joe@foo.bar.com**. Then, one router might know a default route for all hosts in the **bar.com** domain, while another one has information for **foo.bar.com** itself. Since the latter is more specific, it is chosen over the former. If there are two routers that provide a "best match", the one coming first in the *routers* file is chosen.

This router now specifies the transport to be used, for instance UUCP, and generates a new destination address. The new address is passed to the transport along with the host to forward the message to. In the above example, *smail* might find out that **foo.bar.com** is to be reached via UUCP using the path **ernie!bert**. It will then generate a new target of **bert!foo.bar.com!user**, and have the UUCP transport use this as the envelope address to be passed to **ernie**.

When using the default setup, the following routers are available:

---

[5]The default configuration files can be found in *samples/generic* below the source directory.

- If the destination host address can be resolved using the *gethostbyname(3)* or *gethostbyaddr(3)* library call, the message will be delivered via SMTP. The only exception is if the address is found to refer to the local host, it is handed to the director module, too.

  smail also recognizes IP addresses written as dotted quad as a legal hostname, as long as they can be resolved through a *gethostbyaddr(3)* call. For example, **scrooge@[149.76.12.4]** would be a valid although highly unusual mail address for **scrooge** on **quark.physics.groucho.edu**.

  If your machine is on the Internet, these routers are not what you are looking for, because they do not support MX records. See below for what to do in this case.

- If */usr/lib/smail/paths*, the pathalias database, exists, *smail* will try to look up the target host (minus any trailing **.uucp**) in this file. Mail to an address matched by this router will be delivered using UUCP, using the path found in the database.

- The host address (minus any trailing **.uucp**) will be compared to the output of the *uuname* command to check if the target host is in fact a UUCP neighbor. If this is the case, the message will be delivered using the UUCP transport.

- If the address has not been matched by any of the above routers, it will be delivered to the smart host. The path to the smart host as well as the transport to be used are set in the *config* file.

These defaults work for many simple setups, but fail if routing requirements get a little more complicated. If you are faced with any of the problems discussed below, you will have to install your own *routers* file to override the defaults. A sample *routers* file you might start with is given in appendix B. Some Linux distributions also come with a set of configuration files that are tailored to work around these difficulties.

Probably the worst problems arise when your host lives in a dual universe with both dialup IP and UUCP links. You will then have hostnames in your *hosts* file that you only talk occasionally to through your SLIP link, so *smail* will attempt to deliver any mail for these hosts via SMTP. This is usually not what you want, because even if the SLIP link is activated regularly, SMTP is much slower than sending the mail over UUCP. With the default setup, there's no way escaping *smail*.

You can avoid this problem by having *smail* check the *paths* file before querying the resolver, and put all hosts you want to force UUCP delivery to into the *paths* file. If you don't want to send any messages over SMTP *ever*, you can also comment out the resolver-based routers altogether.

Another problem is that the default setup doesn't provide for true Internet mail routing, because the resolver-based router does not evaluate MX records. To enable full support for Internet mail routing, comment out this router, and uncomment the one that used BIND instead. There are, however, *smail* binaries included in some Linux distributions that don't have BIND support compiled in. If you enable BIND, but get a message in the *paniclog* file saying "`router inet_hosts: driver bind not found`", then you have to get the sources and recompile *smail* (see section 14.2 above).

Finally, it is not generally a good idea to use the *uuname* driver. For one, it will generate a configuration error when you don't have UUCP installed, because no *uuname* command will be found. The second is when you have more sites listed in your UUCP *Systems* file than you actually have mail links with. These may be sites you only exchange news with, or sites you occasionally download files from via anonymous UUCP, but have no traffic with otherwise.

To work around the first problem, you can substitute a shell script for *uuname* which does a simple *exit 0*. The more general solution is, however, to edit the *routers* file and remove this driver altogether.

14.7.1   The *paths* database

smail expects to find the pathalias database in the *paths* file below */usr/lib/smail*. This file is optional, so if you don't want to perform any pathalias routing at all, simply remove any existing *paths* file.

paths must be a sorted ASCII file that contains entries which map destination site names to UUCP bang paths. The file has to be sorted because *smail* uses a binary search for looking up a site. Comments are not allowed in this file, and the site name must be separated from the path using a TAB. Pathalias databases are discussed in somewhat greater detail in chapter 13.

If you generate this file by hand, you should make sure to include all legal names for a site. For example, if a site is known by both a plain UUCP name and a fully qualified domain name, you have to add an entry for each of them. The file can be sorted by piping it through the *sort(1)* command.

If your site is only a leaf site, however, then no *paths* file should be necessary at all: just set up the smart host attributes in your *config* file, and leave all routing to your mail feed.

14.8 Delivering Messages to Local Addresses

Most commonly, a local address is just a user's login name, in which case the message is delivered to her mailbox, */var/spool/mail/*`user`. Other cases include aliases and mailing list names, and mail forwarding by the user. In these cases, the local address expands to a new list of addresses, which may be either local or remote.

Apart from these "normal" addresses, *smail* can handle other types of local message destinations, like file names, and pipe commands. These are not addresses in their own right, so you can't send mail to, say, **/etc/passwd@vbrew.com**; they are only valid if they have been taken from forwarding or alias files.

A *file name* is anything that begins with a slash (/) or a tilde (~). The latter refers to the user's home directory, and is possible only if the filename was taken from a *.forward* file or a forwarding entry in the mailbox (see below). When delivering to a file, *smail* appends the messages to the file, creating it if necessary.

A *pipe command* may be any UNIX command preceded by the pipe symbol (|). This causes *smail* to hand the command to the shell along with its arguments, but without the leading ' | '. The message itself is fed to this command on standard input.

For example, to gate a mailing list into a local newsgroup, you might use a shell script named *gateit*, and set up a local alias which delivers all messages from this mailing list to the script using *"|gateit"*.

If the invocation contains white space, it has to be enclosed in double quotes. Due to the security issues involved, care is taken not to execute the command if the address has been obtained in a somewhat dubious way (for example, if the alias file from which the address was taken was writable by everyone).

14.8.1 Local Users

The most common case for a local address is to denote a user's mailbox. This mailbox is located in */var/spool/mail* and has the name of the user. It is owned by her, with a group of **mail**, and has mode 660. If it does not exist, it is created by *smail*.

Note that although */var/spool/mail* is currently the standard place to put the mailbox files, some mail software may have different paths compiled in, for example */usr/spool/mail*. If delivery to users on your machine fails consistently, you should try if it helps to make this a symbolic link to */var/spool/mail*.

There are two addresses *smail* requires to exist: **MAILER-DAEMON** and **Postmaster**. When generating a bounce message for an undeliverable mail, a carbon copy is sent to the **postmaster** account for examination (in case this might be due to a configuration problem). The **MAILER-DAEMON** is used as the sender's address on the bounce message.

If these addresses do not name valid accounts on your system, *smail* implicitly maps **MAILER-DAEMON** to **postmaser**, and **postmaster** to **root**, respectively. You should usually override this by aliasing the **postmaster** account to whoever is responsible for maintaining the mail software.

14.8.2 Forwarding

A user may redirect her mail by having it forwarded to an alternative address using one of two methods supported by *smail*. One option is to put

```
Forward to recipient,...
```

in the first line of her mailbox file. This will send all incoming mail to the specified list of recipients. Alternatively, she might create a *.forward* file in her home directory, which contains the comma-separated list of recipients. With this variety of forwarding, all lines of the file are read and interpreted.

Note that any type of address may be used. Thus, a practical example of a *.forward* file for vacations might be

```
janet, "|vacation"
```

The first address delivers the incoming message to **janet**'s mailbox nevertheless, while the *vacation* command returns a short notification to the sender.

14.8.3   Alias Files

smail is able to handle alias files compatible with those known by Berkeley's *sendmail*. Entries in the alias file may have the form

  `alias:` *recipients*

`recipients` is a comma-separated list of addresses that will be substituted for the alias. The recipient list may be continued across newlines if the next line begins with a TAB.

There is a special feature that allows *smail* to handle mailing lists from the alias file: if you specify "`:include:`*filename*" as recipient, *smail* will read the file specified, and substitute its contents as a list of recipients.

The main aliases file is */usr/lib/aliases*. If you choose to make this file world-writable, *smail* wil not deliver any messages to shell commands given in this file. A sample file is shown below:

```
# vbrew.com /usr/lib/aliases file
hostmaster: janet
postmaster: janet
usenet: phil
# The development mailing list.
development: joe, sue, mark, biff
          /var/mail/log/development
owner-development: joe
# Announcements of general interest are mailed to all
# of the staff
announce: :include: /usr/lib/smail/staff,
          /var/mail/log/announce
owner-announce: root
# gate the foobar mailing list to a local newsgroup
ppp-list: "|/usr/local/lib/gateit local.lists.ppp"
```

If an error occurs while delivering to an address generated from the *aliases* file, *smail* will attempt to send a copy of the error message to the "alias owner". For example, if delivery to **biff** fails when delivering a message to the **development** mailing list, a copy of the error message will be mailed to the sender, as well as to **postmaster** and **owner-development**. If the owner address does not exist, no additional error message will be generated.

When delivering to files or when invoking programs given in the *aliases* file, *smail* will become the **nobody** user to avoid any security hassles. Especially when delivering to files, this can be a real nuisance. In the file given above, for instance, the log files must be owned and writable by **nobody**, or delivery to them will fail.

14.8.4 Mailing Lists

Instead of using the *aliases* file, mailing lists may also be managed by means of files in the */usr/lib/smail/lists* directory. A mailing list named *nag-bugs* is described by the file *lists/nag-bugs*, which should contain the members' addresses, separated by commas. The list may be given on multiple lines, with comments being introduced by a hash sign.

For each mailing list, a user (or alias) named **owner-**`listname` should exist; any errors occurring when resolving an address are reported to this user. This address is also used as the sender's address on all outgoing messages in the `Sender:` header field.

14.9 UUCP-based Transports

There are a number of transports compiled into *smail* that utilize the UUCP suite. In a UUCP environment, messages are usually passed on by invoking *rmail* on the next host, giving it the message on standard input and the envelope address on the command line. On your host, *rmail* should be a link to the *smail* command.

When handing a message to the UUCP transport, *smail* converts the target address to a UUCP bang path. For example, **user@host** will be transformed to **host!user**. Any occurrence of the '**%**' address operator is preserved, so **user%host@gateway** will become **gateway!user%host**. However, *smail* will never generate such addresses itself.

Alternatively, *smail* can send and receive BSMTP batches via UUCP. With BSMTP, one or more messages are wrapped up in a single batch that contains the commands the local mailer would issue if a real SMTP connection had be established. BSMTP is frequently used in store-and-forward (e.g. UUCP-based) networks to save disk space. The sample *transports* file in appendix B contains a transport dubbed *bsmtp* that generates partial BSMTP batches in a queue directory. They must be combined into the final batches later, using a shell script that adds the appropriate *HELO* and *QUIT* command.

To enable the *bsmtp* transport for specific UUCP links you have to use so-called *method* files (please refer to the *smail(5)* manual page for details). If you have only one UUCP link, and use the smart host router, you enable sending SMTP batches by setting the *smart_transport* configuration variable to *bsmtp* instead of *uux*.

To receive SMTP batches over UUCP, you must make sure that you have the unbatching command the remote site sends its batches to. If the remote site uses *smail*, too, you need to make *rsmtp* a link to *smail*. If the remote site runs *sendmail*, you should additionally install a shell script named */usr/bin/bsmtp* that does a simple "*exec rsmtp*" (a symbolic link won't work).

14.10 SMTP-based Transports

smail currently supports an SMTP driver to deliver mail over TCP connections.[6] It is capable of delivering a message to any number of addresses on one single host, with the hostname being specified as either a fully qualified domain name that can be resolved by the networking software, or in dotted quad notation enclosed in square brackets. Generally, addresses resolved by any of the BIND, *gethostbyname(3)*, or *gethostbyaddr(3)* router drivers will be delivered to the SMTP transport.

The SMTP driver will attempt to connect to the remote host immediately through the *smtp* port as listed in */etc/services*. If it cannot be reached, or the connection times out, delivery will be reattempted at a later time.

Delivery on the Internet requires that routes to the destination host be specified in the *route-addr* format described in chapter 13, rather than as a bang path.[7] *smail* will therefore transform **user%host@gateway**, where **gateway** is reached via **host1!host2!host3**, into the source-route address **<@host2,@host3:user%host@gateway>** which will be sent as the

---

[6]The authors call this support "simple". For a future version of *smail*, they advertise a complete backend which will handle this more efficiently.

[7]However, the use of routes in the Internet is discouraged altogether. Fully qualified domain names should be used instead.

message's envelope address to **host1**. To enable these transformation (along with the built-in BIND driver), you have to edit the entry for the *smtp* driver in the *transports* file. A sample *transports* file is given in Appendix B.

14.11   Hostname Qualification

Sometimes it is desirable to catch unqualified hostnames (i.e. those that don't have a domain name) specified in sender or recipient addresses, for example when gatewaying between two networks, where one requires fully qualified domain names. On an Internet-UUCP relay, unqualifed hostnames should be mapped to the **uucp** domain by default. Other address modifications than these are questionable.

The */usr/lib/smail/qualify* file tells *smail* which domain names to tack onto which hostnames. Entries in the *qualify* file consists of a hostname beginning in column one, followed by domain name. Lines containing a hash sign as its first non-white character are considered comments. Entries are searched in the order they appear in.

If no *qualify* file exists, no hostname qualification is performed at all.

A special hostname of * matches any hostnames, thus enabling you to map all hosts not mentioned before into a default domain. It should be used only as the last entry.

At the Virtual Brewery, all hosts have been set up to use fully qualified domain names in the sender's addresses. Unqualified recipient addresses are considered to be in the **uucp** domain, so only a single entry in the *qualify* file is needed.

```
#  /usr/lib/smail/qualify, last changed Feb 12, 1994 by janet
#
*               uucp
```

Chapter 15

Sendmail+IDA

15.1 Introduction to Sendmail+IDA

It's been said that you aren't a *real* Unix system administrator until you've edited a *sendmail.cf* file. It's also been said that you're crazy if you've attempted to do so twice : -)

Sendmail is an incredibly powerful program. It's also incredibly difficult to learn and understand for most people. Any program whose definitive reference (*Sendmail*, published by O'Reilly and Associates) is 792 pages long quite justifiably scares most people off.

Sendmail+IDA is different. It removes the need to edit the always cryptic *sendmail.cf* file and allows the administrator to define the site-specific routing and addressing configuration through relatively easy to understand support files called *tables*. Switching to sendmail+IDA can save you many hours of work and stress.

Compared to the other major mail transport agents, there is probably nothing that can't be done faster and simpler with sendmail+IDA. Typical things that are needed to run a normal UUCP or Internet site become simple to accomplish. Configurations that normally are extremely difficult are simple to create and maintain.

At this writing, the current version of *sendmail5.67b+IDA1.5* is available via anonymous FTP from **vixen.cso.uiuc.edu**. It compiles without any patching required under Linux.

All the configuration files required to get sendmail+IDA sources to compile, install, and run under Linux are included in *newspak-2.2.tar.gz* which is available via anonymous FTP on **sunsite.unc.edu** in the directory */pub/Linux/system/Mail*.

15.2 Configuration Files — Overview

Traditional sendmail is set up through a system configuration file (typically */etc/sendmail.cf* or */usr/lib/sendmail.cf*), that is not anything close to any language you've seen before. Editing the *sendmail.cf* file to provide customized behavior can be a humbling experience.

Sendmail+IDA makes such pain essentially a thing of the past by having all configuration options table-driven with rather easy to understand syntax. These options are configured by running *m4* (a macro processor) or *dbm* (a database processor) on a number of data files via Makefiles supplied with the sources.

The *sendmail.cf* file defines only the default behavior of the system. Virtually all special customization is done through a number of optional tables rather than by directly editing the *sendmail.cf* file. A list of all *sendmail* tables is given in figure 15.1.

mailertable	defines special behavior for remote hosts or domains.
uucpxtable	forces UUCP delivery of mail to hosts that are in DNS format.
pathtable	defines UUCP bang-paths to remote hosts or domains.
uucprelays	short-circuits the pathalias path to well-known remote hosts.
genericfrom	converts internal addresses into generic ones visible to the outside world.
xaliases	converts generic addresses to/from valid internal ones.
decnetxtable	converts RFC-822 addresses to DECnet-style addresses.

Figure 15.1: *sendmail* Support Files.

15.3   The *sendmail.cf* File

The *sendmail.cf* file for sendmail+IDA is not edited directly, but is generated from an *m4* configuration file provided by the local system administrator. In the following, we will refer to it as *sendmail.m4*.

This file contains a few definitions and otherwise merely points to the tables where the real work gets done. In general, it is only necessary to specify:

- the pathnames and filenames used on the local system.
- the name(s) the site is known by for e-mail purposes.
- which default mailer (and perhaps smart relay host) is desired.

There are a large variety of parameters that can be defined to establish the behavior of the local site or to override compiled-in configuration items. These configuration options are identified in the file *ida/cf/OPTIONS* in the source directory.

A *sendmail.m4* file for a minimal configuration (UUCP or SMTP with all non-local mail being relayed to a directly connected smart-host) can be as short as 10 or 15 lines excluding comments.

15.3.1   An Example *sendmail.m4* File

A *sendmail.m4* file for **vstout** at the Virtual Brewery is shown below. **vstout** uses SMTP to talk to all hosts on the Brewery's LAN, and sends all mail for other destinations to **moria**, its Internet relay host, via UUCP.

15.3.2   Typically Used *sendmail.m4* Parameters

A few or the items in the *sendmail.m4* file are required all the time; others can be ignored if you can get away with defaults. The following sections describe each of the items in the example *sendmail.m4* file in more detail.

15.3.2.1   Items that Define Paths

```
dnl #define(LIBDIR,/usr/local/lib/mail)dnl  # where all support files go
```

LIBDIR defines the directory where sendmail+IDA expects to find configuration files, the various dbm tables, and special local definitions. In a typical binary distribution, this is compiled into the sendmail binary and does not need to be explicitly set in the sendmail.m4 file.

The above example has a leading *dnl* which means that this line is essentially a comment for information only.

To change the location of the support files to a different location, remove the leading *dnl* from the above line, set the path to the desired location, and rebuild and reinstall the *sendmail.cf* file.

```
dnl #---------------- SAMPLE SENDMAIL.M4 FILE ----------------
dnl # (the string 'dnl' is the m4 equivalent of commenting out a line)
dnl # you generally don't want to override LIBDIR from the compiled in paths
dnl #define(LIBDIR,/usr/local/lib/mail)dnl     # where all support files go
define(LOCAL_MAILER_DEF, mailers.linux)dnl     # mailer for local delivery
define(POSTMASTERBOUNCE)dnl                    # postmaster gets bounces
define(PSEUDODOMAINS, BITNET UUCP)dnl          # don't try DNS on these
dnl #---------------------------------------------------------------
dnl #
define(PSEUDONYMS, vstout.vbrew.com  vstout.UUCP vbrew.com)
dnl                                            # names we're known by
define(DEFAULT_HOST, vstout.vbrew.com)dnl      # our primary 'name' for mail
define(UUCPNAME, vstout)dnl                    # our uucp name
dnl #
dnl #---------------------------------------------------------------
dnl #
define(UUCPNODES, |uuname|sort|uniq)dnl        # our uucp neighbors
define(BANGIMPLIESUUCP)dnl                     # make certain that uucp
define(BANGONLYUUCP)dnl                        #  mail is treated correctly
define(RELAY_HOST, moria)dnl                   # our smart relay host
define(RELAY_MAILER, UUCP-A)dnl                # we reach moria via uucp
dnl #
dnl #----------------------------------------------------------------------
dnl #
dnl # the various dbm lookup tables
dnl #
define(ALIASES, LIBDIR/aliases)dnl             # system aliases
define(DOMAINTABLE, LIBDIR/domaintable)dnl     # domainize hosts
define(PATHTABLE, LIBDIR/pathtable)dnl         # paths database
define(GENERICFROM, LIBDIR/generics)dnl        # generic from addresses
define(MAILERTABLE, LIBDIR/mailertable)dnl     # mailers per host or domain
define(UUCPXTABLE, LIBDIR/uucpxtable)dnl       # paths to hosts we feed
define(UUCPRELAYS, LIBDIR/uucprelays)dnl       # short-circuit paths
dnl #
dnl #----------------------------------------------------------------------
dnl #
dnl # include the 'real' code that makes it all work
dnl # (provided with the source code)
dnl #
include(Sendmail.mc)dnl                              # REQUIRED ENTRY !!!
dnl #
dnl #----------- END OF SAMPLE SENDMAIL.M4 FILE -------
```

Figure 15.2: A sample *sendmail.m4* file for **vstout**.

15.3.2.2   Defining the Local Mailer

```
define(LOCAL_MAILER_DEF, mailers.linux)dnl  # mailer for local delivery
```

Most operating systems provide a program to handle local delivery of mail. Typical programs for many of the major variants of Unix are already built into the sendmail binary.

In Linux, it is necessary to explicitly define the appropriate local mailer since a local delivery program is not necessarily present in the distribution you've installed. This is done by specifying *LOCAL_MAILER_DEF* in the *sendmail.m4* file.

For example, to have the commonly used *deliver* program[1] provide this service, you would set *LOCAL_MAILER_DEF* to *mailers.linux*.

The following file should then be installed as *mailers.linux* in the directory pointed to by *LIBDIR*. It explicitly defines the *deliver* program in the internal *Mlocal* mailer with the proper parameters to result in *sendmail* correctly delivering mail targeted for the local system. Unless you are a sendmail expert, you probably do not want to alter the following example.

```
# -- /usr/local/lib/mail/mailers.linux --
#    (local mailers for use on Linux )
Mlocal, P=/usr/bin/deliver, F=SlsmFDMP, S=10, R=25/10, A=deliver $u
Mprog,  P=/bin/sh,          F=lsDFMeuP,  S=10, R=10, A=sh -c $u
```

There is a also built-in default for *deliver* in the *Sendmail.mc* file that gets included into the *sendmail.cf* file. To specify it, you would not use the mailers.linux file and would instead define the following in your *sendmail.m4* file:

```
dnl --- (in sendmail.m4) ---
define(LOCAL_MAILER_DEF, DELIVER)dnl       # mailer for local delivery
```

Unfortunately, *Sendmail.mc* assumes deliver is installed in */bin*, which is not the case with Slackware1.1.1 (which installs it in */usr/bin*). In that case you'd need to either fake it with a link or rebuild deliver from sources so that it resides in */bin*.

15.3.2.3   Dealing with Bounced Mail

```
define(POSTMASTERBOUNCE)dnl                     # postmaster gets bounces
```

Many sites find that it is important to ensure that mail is sent and received with close to a 100% success rate. While examining *syslogd(8)* logs is helpful, the local mail administrator generally needs to see the headers on bounced mail in order to determine if the mail was undeliverable because of user error or a configuration error on one of the systems involved.

Defining *POSTMASTERBOUNCE* results in a copy of each bounced message being set to the person defined as **Postmaster** for the system.

Unfortunately, setting this parameter also results in the *text* of the message being sent to the Postmaster, which potentially has related privacy concerns for people using mail on the system.

Site postmasters should in general attempt to discipline themselves (or do so via technical means through shell scripts that delete the text of the bounce messages they receive) from reading mail not addressed to them.

15.3.2.4   Domain Name Service Related Items

```
define(PSEUDODOMAINS, BITNET UUCP)dnl       # don't try DNS on these
```

There are several well known networks that are commonly referenced in mail addresses for historical reasons but that are not valid for DNS purposes. Defining *PSEUDODOMAINS* prevents needless DNS lookup attempts that will always fail.

---

[1]*deliver* was written by Chip Salzenberg (**chip%tct@ateng.com**). It is part of several Linux distributions and can be found in the usual anonymous FTP archives such as **ftp.uu.net**.

15.3.2.5 Defining Names the Local System is Known by

```
define(PSEUDONYMS, vstout.vbrew.com  vstout.UUCP vbrew.com)
dnl                                               # names we're known by
define(DEFAULT_HOST, vstout.vbrew.com)dnl    # our primary 'name' for mail
```

Frequently, systems wish to hide their true identity, serve as mail gateways, or receive and process mail addressed to 'old' names by which they used to be known.

PSEUDONYMS specifies the list of all hostnames for which the local system will accept mail.

DEFAULT_HOST specifies the hostname that will appear in messages originating on the local host. It is important that this parameter be set to a valid value or all return mail will be undeliverable.

15.3.2.6 UUCP-Related Items

```
define(UUCPNAME, vstout)dnl                  # our uucp name
define(UUCPNODES, |uuname|sort|uniq)dnl      # our uucp neighbors
define(BANGIMPLIESUUCP)dnl                   # make certain that uucp
define(BANGONLYUUCP)dnl                      #  mail is treated correctly
```

Frequently, systems are known by one name for DNS purposes and another for UUCP purposes. *UUCPNAME* permits you to define a different hostname that appears in the headers of outgoing UUCP mail.

UUCPNODES defines the commands that return a list of hostnames for the systems we are connected directly to via UUCP connections.

BANGIMPLIESUUCP and *BANGONLYUUCP* ensure that mail addressed with UUCP 'bang' syntax is treated according to UUCP behavior rather than the more current Domain Name Service behavior used today on Internet.

15.3.2.7 Relay Systems and Mailers

```
define(RELAY_HOST, moria)dnl                 # our smart relay host
define(RELAY_MAILER, UUCP-A)dnl              # we reach moria via UUCP
```

Many system administrators do not want to be bothered with the work needed to ensure that their system is able to reach all the networks (and therefore systems) on all networks worldwide. Instead of doing so, they would rather relay all outgoing mail to another system that is known to be indeed "smart".

RELAY_HOST defines the UUCP hostname of such a smart neighboring system.

RELAY_MAILER defines the mailer used to relay the messages there.

It is important to note that setting these parameters results in your outgoing mail being forwarded to this remote system, which will affect the load of their system. Be certain to get explicit agreement from the remote Postmaster before you configure your system to use another system as a general purpose relay host.

15.3.2.8 The Various Configuration Tables

```
define(ALIASES, LIBDIR/aliases)dnl           # system aliases
define(DOMAINTABLE, LIBDIR/domaintable)dnl   # domainize hosts
define(PATHTABLE, LIBDIR/pathtable)dnl       # paths database
define(GENERICFROM, LIBDIR/generics)dnl      # generic from addresses
define(MAILERTABLE, LIBDIR/mailertable)dnl   # mailers per host or domain
define(UUCPXTABLE, LIBDIR/uucpxtable)dnl     # paths to hosts we feed
define(UUCPRELAYS, LIBDIR/uucprelays)dnl     # short-circuit paths
```

With these macros, you can change the location where sendmail+IDA looks for the various dbm tables that define the system's "real" behavior. It is generally wise to leave them in *LIBDIR*.

15.3.2.9   The Master *Sendmail.mc* File

```
include(Sendmail.mc)dnl                          # REQUIRED ENTRY !!!
```

The authors of sendmail+IDA provide the *Sendmail.mc* file which contains the true "guts" of what becomes the send-mail.cf file. Periodically, new versions are released to fix bugs or add functionality without requiring a full release and recompilation of sendmail from sources.

It is important *not* to edit this file.

15.3.2.10   So Which Entries are Really Required?

When not using any of the optional dbm tables, sendmail+IDA delivers mail via the *DEFAULT_MAILER* (and possibly *RELAY_HOST* and *RELAY_MAILER*) defined in the *sendmail.m4* file used to generate *sendmail.cf*. It is easily possible to override this behavior through entries in the *domaintable* or *uucpxtable*.

A generic site that is on Internet and speaks Domain Name Service, or one that is UUCP-only and forwards all mail via UUCP through a smart *RELAY_HOST*, probably does not need any specific table entries at all.

Virtually all systems should set the *DEFAULT_HOST* and *PSEUDONYMS* macros, which define the canonical site name and aliases it is known by, and *DEFAULT_MAILER*. If all you have is a relay host and relay mailer, you don't need to set these defaults since it works automagically.

UUCP hosts will probably also need to set *UUCPNAME* to their official UUCP name. They will also probably set *RELAY_MAILER*, and *RELAY_HOST* which enable smart-host routing through a mail relay. The mail transport to be used is defined in *RELAY_MAILER* and should usually be *UUCP-A* for UUCP sites.

If your site is SMTP-only and talks 'Domain Name Service', you would change the *DEFAULT_MAILER* to *TCP-A* and probably delete the *RELAY_MAILER* and *RELAY_HOST* lines.

15.4   A Tour of Sendmail+IDA Tables

Sendmail+IDA provides a number of tables that allow you to override the default behavior of sendmail (specified in the *sendmail.m4* file) and define special behavior for unique situations, remote systems, and networks. These tables are post-processed with *dbm* using the Makefile provided with the distribution.

Most sites will need few, if any, of these tables. If your site does not require these tables, the easiest thing is probably to make them zero length files (with the *touch* command) and use the default Makefile in *LIBDIR* rather than editing the Makefile itself.

15.4.1   *mailertable*

The *mailertable* defines special treatment for specific hosts or domains based on the remote host or network name. It is frequently used on Internet sites to select an intermediate mail relay host or gateway to reach a remote network through, and to specify a particular protocol (UUCP or SMTP) to be used. UUCP sites will generally not need to use this file.

Order is important. Sendmail reads the file top-down and processes the message according to the first rule it matches. So it is generally wise to place the most explicit rules at the top of the file and the more generic rules below.

Suppose you want to forward all mail for the Computer Science department at Groucho Marx University via UUCP to a relay host **ada**. To do so, you would have a *mailertable* entry that looked like the following:

```
# (in mailertable)
#
# forward all mail for the domain .cs.groucho.edu via UUCP to ada
UUCP-A,ada          .cs.groucho.edu
```

Suppose you want all mail to the larger **groucho.edu** domain to go to a different relayhost **bighub** for address resolution and delivery. The expanded mailertable entries would look quite similar.

```
# (in mailertable)
#
# forward all mail for the domain cs.groucho.edu via UUCP to ada
UUCP-A,ada          .cs.groucho.edu
#
# forward all mail for the domain groucho.edu via UUCP to bighub
UUCP-A,bighub       .groucho.edu
```

As mentioned above, order is important. Reversing the order of the two rules shown above will result in all mail to **.cs.groucho.edu** going through the more generic **bighub** path instead of the explicit **ada** path that is really desired.

```
# (in mailertable)
#
# forward all mail for the domain .groucho.edu via UUCP to bighub
UUCP-A,bighub       .groucho.edu
#
# (it is impossible to reach the next line because
#    the rule above will be matched first)
UUCP-A,ada          .cs.groucho.edu
#
```

In the mailertable examples above, the *UUCP-A* mailer makes *sendmail* use UUCP delivery with domainized headers.

The comma between the mailer and remote system tells it to forward the message to **ada** for address resolution and delivery.

Mailertable entries are of the format:

> *mailer delimiter relayhost*   *host_or_domain*

There are a number of possible mailers. The differences are generally in how they treat addresses. Typical mailers are *TCP-A* (TCP/IP with Internet-style addresses), *TCP-U* (TCP/IP with UUCP-style addresses), and *UUCP-A* (UUCP with Internet-style addresses).

The character that separates the mailer from the host portion on the left-hand-side of a mailertable line defines how the address is modified by the mailertable. The important thing to realize is that this only rewrites the envelope (to get the mail into the remote system). Rewriting anything other than the envelope is generally frowned upon due to the high probability of breaking the mail configuration.

!	An exclamation point strips off the recipient hostname before forwarding to the mailer. This can be used when you want to wish to essentially force mail into a misconfigured remote site.
,	A comma does not change the address in any way. The message is merely forwarded via the specified mailer to the specified relay host.
:	A colon removes the recipient hostname only if there are intermediate hosts between you and the destination. Thus, **foo!bar!joe** will have **foo** removed, while **xyzzy!janet** will remain unchanged.

15.4.2 *uucpxtable*

Usually, mail to hosts with fully-qualified domain names is delivered via Internet style (SMTP) delivery using Domain Name Service (DNS), or via the relay host. The *uucpxtable* forces delivery via UUCP routing by converting the domainized name into a UUCP-style un-domainized remote hostname.

It is frequently used when you're a mail forwarder for a site or domain or when you wish to send mail via a direct and reliable UUCP link rather than potentially multiple hops through the default mailer and any intermediate systems and networks.

UUCP sites that talk to UUCP neighbors who use domainized mail headers would use this file to force delivery of the mail through the direct UUCP point-to-point link between the two systems rather than using the less direct route through the *RELAY_MAILER* and *RELAY_HOST* or through the *DEFAULT_MAILER*.

Internet sites who do not talk UUCP probably would not use the *uucpxtable*.

Suppose you provide mail forwarding service to a system called **sesame.com** in DNS and **sesame** in the UUCP maps. You would need the following *uucpxtable* entry to force mail for their host to go through your direct UUCP connection.

```
#=============== /usr/local/lib/mail/uucpxtable ============
# Mail sent to joe@sesame.com is rewritten to sesame!joe and
# therefore delivered via UUCP
#
sesame      sesame.com
#
#----------------------------------------------------------
```

15.4.3 *pathtable*

The *pathtable* is used to define explicit routing to remote hosts or networks. The *pathtable* file should be in pathalias-style syntax, sorted alphabetically. The two fields on each line must be separated by a real TAB, else *dbm* might complain.

Most systems will not need any *pathtable* entries.

```
#================ /usr/local/lib/mail/pathtable =================
#
# this is a pathalias-style paths file to let you kick mail to
# UUCP neighbors to the direct UUCP path so you don't have to
# go the long way through your smart host that takes other traffic
#
# you want real tabs on each line or m4 might complain
#
# route mail through one or more intermediate sites to a remote
# system using UUCP-style addressing.
#
sesame!ernie!%s            ernie
#
# forwarding to a system that is a UUCP neighbor of a reachable
# internet site.
#
swim!%s@gcc.groucho.edu    swim
#
# The following sends all mail for two networks through different
# gateways (see the leading '.' ?).
# In this example, "uugate" and "byte" are specific systems that serve
# as mail gateways to the .UUCP and .BITNET pseudo-domains respectively
#
%s@uugate.groucho.edu          .UUCP
byte!%s@mail.shift.com         .BITNET
#
#==================== end of pathtable =======================
```

15.4.4 *domaintable*

The *domaintable* is generally used to force certain behavior after a DNS lookup has occurred. It permits the administrator to make shorthand names available for commonly referenced systems or domains by replacing the shorthand name with the proper one automatically. It can also be used to replace incorrect host or domain names with the "correct" information.

Most sites will not need any *domaintable* entries.

The following example shows how to replace an incorrect address people are attempting to mail to with the correct address:

```
#============= /usr/local/lib/mail/domaintable =================
#
#
brokenhost.correct.domain          brokenhost.wrong.domain
#
#
#=================== end of domaintable ========================
```

15.4.5 *aliases*

Aliases permit a number of things to happen:

- They provide a shorthand or well-known name for mail to be addressed to in order to go to one or more persons.
- They invoke a program with the mail message as the input to the program.
- They send mail to a file.

All systems require aliases for **Postmaster** and **MAILER-DAEMON** to be RFC-compliant.

Always be extremely aware of security when defining aliases that invoke programs or write to programs since sendmail generally runs setuid-root.

Changes to the *aliases* file do not take effect until the command

```
# /usr/lib/sendmail -bi
```

is executed to build the required dbm tables. This can also be done by executing the *newaliases* command, usually from cron.

Details concerning mail aliases may be found in the *aliases(5)* manual page.

```
#-------------------- /usr/local/lib/mail/aliases -------------------
#
# demonstrate commonly seen types of aliases
#
usenet:         janet                  # alias for a person
admin:          joe,janet              # alias for several people
newspak-users:  :include:/usr/lib/lists/newspak
                                       # read recipients from a file
changefeed:     |/usr/local/lib/gup    # alias that invokes a program
complaints:     /var/log/complaints    # alias that writes mail to a file
#
# The following two aliases must be present to be RFC-compliant.
# It is important to have them resolve to 'a person' who read-
s mail routinely.
```

```
#
postmaster:      root                        # required entry
MAILER-DAEMON:  postmaster                    # required entry
#
#-------------------------------------------------------------------
```

15.4.6   Rarely Used Tables

The following tables are available, but rather infrequently used. Consult with the documentation that comes with the sendmail+IDA sources for details.

uucprelays   The *uucprelays* file is used to "short-circuit" the UUCP path to especially well known sites rather than using a multi-hop or unreliable path generated by processing the UUCP maps with *pathalias*.

genericfrom and *xaliases*   The *genericfrom* file hides local usernames and addresses from the outside world by automatically converting local usernames to generic sender addresses that do not match internal usernames.

The associated *xalparse* utility automates the generation of the genericfrom and aliases file so that both incoming and outgoing username translations occur from a master xaliases file.

decnetxtable   The *decnetxtable* rewrites domainized addresses into decnet-style addresses much like the domaintable can be used to rewrite undomainized addresses into domainized SMTP-style addresses.

15.5   Installing *sendmail*

In this section, we'll take a look at how to install a typical binary distribution of sendmail+IDA, and walk through what needs to be done to make it localized and functional.

The current binary distribution of sendmail+IDA for Linux can be gotten from **sunsite.unc.edu** in */pub/Linux/system/Mail*. Even if you have an earlier version of *sendmail* I strongly recommend you go to the *sendmail5.67b+IDA1.5* version since all required Linux-specific patches are now in the vanilla sources and several significant security holes have been plugged that were in versions prior to about December 1, 1993.

If you are building *sendmail* from the sources, you should follow the instructions in the *README*s included in the source distribution. The current sendmail+IDA source is available from **vixen.cso.uiuc.edu**. To build sendmail+IDA on Linux, you also need the Linux-specific configuration files from *newspak-2.2.tar.gz*, which is available on **sunsite.unc.edu** in the */pub/Linux/system/Mail* directory.

If you have previously installed *smail* or another mail delivery agent, you'll probably want to remove (or rename) all the files from smail to be safe.

15.5.1   Extracting the binary distribution

First, you have to unpack the archive file in some safe location:

```
$ gunzip -c sendmail5.65b+IDA1.5+mailx5.3b.tgz | tar xvf -
```

If you have a "modern" *tar*, for example from a recent Slackware Distribution, you can probably just do a `tar -zxvf` `filename.tgz` and get the same results.

Unpacking the archive creates a directory named *sendmail5.65b+IDA1.5+mailx5.3b*. In this directory, you find a complete installation of sendmail+IDA plus a binary of the *mailx* user agent. All file paths below this directory reflect the location where the files should be installed, so it's safe to work up a *tar* command to move 'em over:

```
# cd sendmail5.65b+IDA1.5+mailx5.3b
# tar cf - . | (cd /; tar xvvpoof -)
```

15.5.2   Building *sendmail.cf*

To build a *sendmail.cf* file customized for your site, you have to write a *sendmail.m4* file, and process it with *m4*. In */usr/local/lib/mail/CF*, you find a sample file called *sample.m4*. Copy it to `yourhostname`.m4, and edit it to reflect the situation of your site.

The sample file is set up for a UUCP-only site that has domainized headers and talks to a smart host. Sites like this only need to edit a few items.

In the current section, I will only give a short overview of the macros you have to change. For a complete description of what they do, please refer to the earlier discussion of the *sendmail.m4*.

LOCAL_MAILER_DEF   Define define the file that defines the mailers for local mail delivery. See section "Defining the Local Mailer" above for what goes in here.

PSEUDONYMS   Define all the names your local host is known by.

DEFAULT_HOST   Put in your fully qualified domain name. This name will appear as your hostname in all outgoing mail.

UUCPNAME   Put in your unqualified hostnmae.

RELAY_HOST and *RELAY_MAILER*   If you talk UUCP to a smart-host, set *RELAY_HOST* to the UUCP name of your 'smart relay' uucp neighbor. Use the UUCP-A mailer if you want domainized headers.

DEFAULT_MAILER   If you are on Internet and talk DNS, you should set this to *TCP-A*. This tells sendmail to use the *TCP-A* mailer, which delivers mail via SMTP using normal RFC style addressing for the envelope. Internet sites probably do not need to define *RELAY_HOST* or *RELAY_MAILER*.

To create the *sendmail.cf* file, execute the command

```
# make yourhostname.cf
```

This processes the `yourhostname`.m4 file and creates `yourhostname`.cf from it.

Next, you should test whether the configuration file you've created does what you expect it to do. This is explained in the following two sections.

Once you're happy with its behavior, copy it into place with the command:

```
# cp yourhostname.cf /etc/sendmail.cf
```

At this point, your sendmail system is ready for action. Put the following line in the appropriate startup file (generally */etc/rc.inet2*). You can also execute it by hand to have the process start up now.

```
# /usr/lib/sendmail -bd -q1h
```

15.5.3   Testing the *sendmail.cf* file

To put sendmail into 'test' mode, you invoke it with the `-bt` flag. The default configuration file is the sendmail.cf file that is installed on the system. You can test an alternate file by using the `-Cfilename` option.

In the following examples, we test *vstout.cf*, the configuration file generated from the *vstout.m4* file shown in figure 15.2.

```
# /usr/lib/sendmail -bt -Cvstout.cf
ADDRESS TEST MODE
Enter <ruleset> <address>
[Note: No initial ruleset 3 call]
>
```

The following tests ensure that *sendmail* is able to deliver all mail to users on your system. In all cases the result of the test should be the same and point to the local system name with the *LOCAL* mailer.

First test how a mail to a local user would be delivered.

```
# /usr/lib/sendmail -bt -Cvstout.cf
ADDRESS TEST MODE
Enter <ruleset> <address>
[Note: No initial ruleset 3 call]
> 3,0 me
rewrite: ruleset  3    input: me
rewrite: ruleset  7    input: me
rewrite: ruleset  9    input: me
rewrite: ruleset  9 returns: < me >
rewrite: ruleset  7 returns: < > , me
rewrite: ruleset  3 returns: < > , me
rewrite: ruleset  0    input: < > , me
rewrite: ruleset  8    input: < > , me
rewrite: ruleset 20    input: < > , me
rewrite: ruleset 20 returns: < > , @ vstout . vbrew . com , me
rewrite: ruleset  8 returns: < > , @ vstout . vbrew . com , me
rewrite: ruleset 26    input: < > , @ vstout . vbrew . com , me
rewrite: ruleset 26 returns: $# LOCAL $@ vstout . vbrew . com $: me
rewrite: ruleset  0 returns: $# LOCAL $@ vstout . vbrew . com $: me
```

The output shows how *sendmail* processes the address internally. It is handed to various rulesets which analyze it, invoke other rulesets in turn, and break it up into its components.

In our example, we passed the address **me** to rulesets 3 and 0 (this is the meaning of the 3 , 0 entered before the address). The last line shows the parsed address as returned by ruleset 0, containing the mailer the message would be delivered by, and the host and user name given to the mailer.

Next, test mail to a user on your system with UUCP syntax.

```
# /usr/lib/sendmail -bt -Cvstout.cf
ADDRESS TEST MODE
Enter <ruleset> <address>
[Note: No initial ruleset 3 call]
> 3,0 vstout!me
rewrite: ruleset  3    input: vstout ! me
[...]
rewrite: ruleset  0 returns: $# LOCAL $@ vstout . vbrew . com $: me
>
```

Next, test mail addressed to a user on your system with Internet syntax to your fully qualified hostname.

```
# /usr/lib/sendmail -bt -Cvstout.cf
ADDRESS TEST MODE
Enter <ruleset> <address>
[Note: No initial ruleset 3 call]
> 3,0 me@vstout.vbrew.com
rewrite: ruleset  3    input: me @ vstout . vbrew . com
```

```
[...]
rewrite: ruleset   0 returns: $# LOCAL $@ vstout . vbrew . com $: me
>
```

You should repeat the above two tests with each of the names you specified in the *PSEUDONYMS* and *DEFAULT_NAME* parameters in your *sendmail.m4* file.

Lastly, test that you can mail to your relay host.

```
# /usr/lib/sendmail -bt -Cvstout.cf
ADDRESS TEST MODE
Enter <ruleset> <address>
[Note: No initial ruleset 3 call]
> 3,0 fred@moria.com
rewrite: ruleset  3    input: fred @ moria . com
rewrite: ruleset  7    input: fred @ moria . com
rewrite: ruleset  9    input: fred @ moria . com
rewrite: ruleset  9 returns: < fred > @ moria . com
rewrite: ruleset  7 returns: < @ moria . com > , fred
rewrite: ruleset  3 returns: < @ moria . com > , fred
rewrite: ruleset  0    input: < @ moria . com > , fred
rewrite: ruleset  8    input: < @ moria . com > , fred
rewrite: ruleset  8 returns: < @ moria . com > , fred
rewrite: ruleset 29    input: < @ moria . com > , fred
rewrite: ruleset 29 returns: < @ moria . com > , fred
rewrite: ruleset 26    input: < @ moria . com > , fred
rewrite: ruleset 25    input: < @ moria . com > , fred
rewrite: ruleset 25 returns: < @ moria . com > , fred
rewrite: ruleset  4    input: < @ moria . com > , fred
rewrite: ruleset  4 returns: fred @ moria . com
rewrite: ruleset 26 returns: < @ moria . com > , fred
rewrite: ruleset  0 returns: $# UUCP-A $@ moria $: < @ moria . com > , fred
>
```

15.5.4   Putting it all together - Integration Testing *sendmail.cf* and the tables

At this point, you've verified that mail will have the desired default behavior and that you'll be able to both send and received validly addressed mail. To complete the installation, it may be necessary to create the appropriate dbm tables to get the desired final results.

After creating the table(s) that are required for your site, you must process them through *dbm* by typing *make* in the directory containing the tables.

If you are UUCP-only, you do *not* need to create any of the tables mentioned in the *README.linux* file. You'll just have to touch the files so that the Makefile works.

If you're UUCP-only and you talk to sites in addition to your smart-host, you'll need to add *uucpxtable* entries for each (or mail to them will also go through the smart host) and run *dbm* against the revised *uucpxtable*.

First, you need to make certain that mail through your *RELAY_HOST* is sent to them via the *RELAY_MAILER*.

```
# /usr/lib/sendmail -bt -Cvstout.cf
```

```
ADDRESS TEST MODE
Enter <ruleset> <address>
[Note: No initial ruleset 3 call]
> 3,0 fred@sesame.com
rewrite: ruleset  3   input: fred @ sesame . com
rewrite: ruleset  7   input: fred @ sesame . com
rewrite: ruleset  9   input: fred @ sesame . com
rewrite: ruleset  9 returns: < fred > @ sesame . com
rewrite: ruleset  7 returns: < @ sesame . com > , fred
rewrite: ruleset  3 returns: < @ sesame . com > , fred
rewrite: ruleset  0   input: < @ sesame . com > , fred
rewrite: ruleset  8   input: < @ sesame . com > , fred
rewrite: ruleset  8 returns: < @ sesame . com > , fred
rewrite: ruleset 29   input: < @ sesame . com > , fred
rewrite: ruleset 29 returns: < @ sesame . com > , fred
rewrite: ruleset 26   input: < @ sesame . com > , fred
rewrite: ruleset 25   input: < @ sesame . com > , fred
rewrite: ruleset 25 returns: < @ sesame . com > , fred
rewrite: ruleset  4   input: < @ sesame . com > , fred
rewrite: ruleset  4 returns: fred @ sesame . com
rewrite: ruleset 26 returns: < @ sesame . com > , fred
rewrite: ruleset  0 returns: $# UUCP-A $@ moria $: < @ s-
esame . com > , fred
>
```

If you have UUCP neighbors other than your *RELAY_HOST*, you need to ensure that mail to them has the proper behavior. Mail addressed with UUCP-style syntax to a host you talk UUCP with should go directly to them (unless you explicitly prevent it with a *domaintable* entry). Assume host **swim** is a direct UUCP neighbor of yours. Then feeding **swim!fred** to *sendmail* should produce the following result:

```
# /usr/lib/sendmail -bt -Cvstout.cf
ADDRESS TEST MODE
Enter <ruleset> <address>
[Note: No initial ruleset 3 call]
> 3,0 swim!fred
rewrite: ruleset  3   input: swim ! fred
[...lines omitted...]
rewrite: ruleset  0 returns: $# UUCP $@ swim $: < > , fred
>
```

If you have *uucpxtable* entries to force UUCP delivery to certain UUCP neighbors who send their mail with Internet style domainized headers, that also needs to be tested.

```
# /usr/lib/sendmail -bt -Cvstout.cf
ADDRESS TEST MODE
Enter <ruleset> <address>
[Note: No initial ruleset 3 call]
> 3,0 dude@swim.2birds.com
rewrite: ruleset  3   input: dude @ swim . 2birds . com
[...lines omitted...]
rewrite: ruleset  0 returns: $# UUCP $@ swim . 2birds $: < > , dude
>
```

15.6 Administrivia and Stupid Mail Tricks

Now that we've discussed the theory of configuring, installing, and testing a sendmail+IDA system, lets take a few moments to look into things that *do* happen routinely in the life of a mail administrator.

Remote systems sometimes break. Modems or phone lines fail, DNS definitions are set incorrectly due to human error. Networks go down unexpectedly. In such cases, mail administrators need to know how to react quickly, effectively, and *safely* to keep mail flowing through alternate routes until the remote systems or service providers can restore normal services.

The rest of this chapter is intended to provide you with the solutions to the most frequently encountered "electronic mail emergencies".

15.6.1 Forwarding Mail to a Relay Host

To forward mail for a particular host or domain to a designated relay system, you generally use the *mailertable*.

For example, to forward mail for **backwood.org** to their UUCP gateway system **backdoor**, you'd put the following entry into *mailertable*:

```
UUCP-A,backdoor    backwood.org
```

15.6.2 Forcing Mail into Misconfigured Remote Sites

Frequently, Internet hosts will have trouble getting mail into misconfigured remote sites. There are several variants of this problem, but the general symptom is that mail is bounced by the remote system or never gets there at all.

These problems can put the local system administrator in a bad position because your users generally don't care that you don't personally administer every system worldwide (or know how to get the remote administrator to fix the problem). They just know that their mail didn't get through to the desired recipient on the other end and that you're a likely person to complain to.

A remote site's configuration is their problem, not yours. In all cases, be certain to *not* break your site in order to communicate with a misconfigured remote site. If you can't get in touch with the Postmaster at the remote site to get them to fix their configuration in a timely manner, you have two options.

- It is generally possible to force mail into the remote system successfully, although since the remote system is misconfigured, replies on the remote end might not work...but then that's the remote administrator's problem.

  You can fix the bad headers in the envelope on your outgoing messages only by using a *domaintable* entry for their host/domain that results in the invalid information being corrected in mail originating from your site:

  ```
  braindead.correct.domain.com        braindead.wrong.domain.com
  ```

- Frequently, misconfigured sites 'bounce' mail back to the sending system and effectively say "that mail isn't for this site" because they do not have their *PSEUDONYMNS* or equivalent set properly in their configuration. It is possible to totally strip off all hostname and domain information from the envelope of messages going from your site to them.

  The *!* in the following *mailertable* delivers mail to their remote site making it appear to their *sendmail* as if it had originated locally on their system. Note that this changes only the envelope address, so the proper return address will still show up in the message.

  ```
  TCP!braindead.correct.domain.com    braindead.wrong.domain.com
  ```

Regardless, even if you get mail into their system, there is no guarantee that they can reply to your message (they're broken, remember...) but then their users are yelling at their administrators rather than your users yelling at you.

15.6.3   Forcing Mail to be Transferred via UUCP

In an ideal world (from the Internet perspective), all hosts have records in the Domain Name Service (DNS) and will send mail with fully qualified domain names.

If you happen to talk via UUCP to such a site, you can force mail to go through the point-to-point UUCP connection rather than through your default mailer by essentially "undomainizing" their hostname through the *uucpxtable*.

To force UUCP delivery to **sesame.com**, you would put the following in your *uucpxtable*:

```
# un-domainize sesame.com to force UUCP delivery
sesame      sesame.com
```

The result is that sendmail will then determine (via *UUCPNODES* in the *sendmail.m4* file) that you are directly connected to the remote system and will queue the mail for delivery with UUCP.

15.6.4   Preventing Mail from Being Delivered via UUCP

The opposite condition also occurs. Frequently, systems may have a number of direct UUCP connections that are used infrequently or that are not as reliable and always available as the default mailer or relay host.

For example, in the Seattle area there are a number of systems that exchange the various Linux distributions via anony-mous UUCP when the distributions are released. These systems talk UUCP only when necessary, so it is generally faster and more reliable to send mail through multiple very reliable hops and common (and always available) relay hosts.

It is easily possible to prevent UUCP delivery of mail to a host that you are directly connected to. If the remote system has a fully-qualified domain name, you can add an entry like this to the *domaintable*:

```
# prevent mail delivery via UUCP to a neighbor
snorkel.com       snorkel
```

This will replace any occurence of the UUCP name with the FQDN, and thus prevent a match by the *UUCPNODES* line in the *sendmail.m4* file. The result is generally that mail will go via the *RELAY_MAILER* and *RELAY_HOST* (or *DEFAULT_MAILER*).

15.6.5   Running the Sendmail Queue on Demand

To process queued messages immediately, merely type '/usr/lib/runq'. This invokes sendmail with the appropriate options to cause sendmail to run through the queue of pending jobs immediately rather than waiting for the next scheduled run.

15.6.6   Reporting Mail Statistics

Many site administrators (and the persons they work for) are interested in the volume of mail passing to, from, and through the local site. There are a number of ways to quantify mail traffic.

- Sendmail comes with a utility called *mailstats* that reads a file called */usr/local/lib/mail/sendmail.st* and reports the number of messages and number of bytes transferred by each of the mailers used in the *sendmail.cf* file. This file must be created by the local administrator manually for sendmail logging to occur. The running totals are cleared by removing and recreating the *sendmail.st* file. One way is to do the following:

  ```
  # cp /dev/null /usr/lib/local/mail/sendmail.st
  ```

- Probably the best way to do quality reporting regarding who uses mail and how much volume passes to, from, and through the local system is to turn on mail debugging with *syslogd(8)*. Generally, this means running the */etc/syslogd* daemon from your system startup file (which you should be doing anyway), and adding a line to */etc/syslog.conf(5)* that looks something like the following:

```
mail.debug                                    /var/log/syslog.mail
```

If you use *mail.debug* and get any medium to high mail volume, the syslog output can get quite large. Output files from *syslogd* generally need to be rotated or purged on a routine basis from *crond(8)*.

There are a number of commonly available utilities that can summarize the output of mail logging from syslogd. One of the more well known utilities is *syslog-stat.pl*, a *perl* script that is distributed with the sendmail+IDA sources.

15.7 Mixing and Matching Binary Distributions

There is no true standard configuration of electronic mail transport and delivery agents and there is no "one true directory structure."

Accordingly, it is necessary to ensure that all the various pieces of the system (USENET news, mail, TCP/IP) agree on the location of the local mail delivery program (*lmail*, *deliver*, etc.), remote mail delivery program (*rmail*), and the mail transport program (*sendmail* or *smail*). Such assumptions are not generally documented, although use of the *strings* command can help determine what files and directories are expected. The following are some problems we've seen in the past with some of the commonly available Linux binary distributions and sources.

- Some versions of the NET-2 distribution of TCP/IP have services defined for a program called *umail* rather than *sendmail*.

- There are various ports of *elm* and *mailx* that look for a delivery agent of */usr/bin/smail* rather than sendmail.

- Sendmail+IDA has a built-in local mailer for *deliver*, but expects it to be located in */bin* rather than the more typical Linux location of */usr/bin*.

Rather than go through the trouble of building all the mail clients from sources, we generally fake it with the appropriate soft links...

15.8 Where to Get More Information

There are many places you can look for more information on *sendmail*. For a list, see the Linux MAIL Howto posted regularly to **comp.answers**. It is also available for anonymous FTP on **rtfm.mit.edu**. However, the definitive place is in the sendmail+IDA sources. Look in the directory *ida/cf* below the source directory for the files *DBM-GUIDE*, *OPTIONS*, and *Sendmail.mc*.

15.7 Mixing and Matching Binary Distributions

15.8 Where To Get More Information

Chapter 16

Netnews

16.1 Usenet History

The idea of network news was born in 1979 when two graduate students, Tom Truscott and Jim Ellis, thought of using UUCP to connect machines for the purpose of information exchange among UNIX users. They set up a small network of three machines in North Carolina.

Initially, traffic was handled by a number of shell scripts (later rewritten in C), but they were never released to the public. They were quickly replaced by "A" news, the first public release of news software.

"A" news was not designed to handle more than a few articles per group and day. When the volume continued to grow, it was rewritten by Mark Horton and Matt Glickman, who called it the "B" release (a.k.a. Bnews). The first public release of Bnews was version 2.1 in 1982. It was expanded continuously, with several new features being added. Its current version is Bnews 2.11. It is slowly becoming obsolete, with its last official maintainer having switched to INN.

Another rewrite was done and released in 1987 by Geoff Collyer and Henry Spencer; this is release "C", or C News. In the time following there have been a number of patches to C News, the most prominent being the C News Performance Release. On sites that carry a large number of groups, the overhead involved in frequently invoking *relaynews*, which is responsible for dispatching incoming articles to other hosts, is significant. The Performance Release adds an option to *relaynews* that allows to run it in *daemon mode*, in which the program puts itself in the background.

The Performance Release is the C News version currently included in most Linux releases.

All news releases up to "C" are primarily targeted for UUCP networks, although they may be used in other environments as well. Efficient news transfer over networks like TCP/IP, DECNet, or related requires a new scheme. This was the reason why, in 1986, the "Network News Transfer Protocol", NNTP, was introduced. It is based on network connections, and specifies a number of commands to interactively transfer and retrieve articles.

There are a number of NNTP-based applications available from the Net. One of them is the *nntpd* package by Brian Barber and Phil Lapsley, which you can use, among other things, to provides newsreading service to a number of hosts inside a local network. *nntpd* was designed to complement news packages such as Bnews or C News to give them NNTP features.

A different NNTP package is INN, or Internet News. It is not merely a front end, but a news system by its own right. It comprises a sophisticated news relay daemon that is capable of maintaining several concurrent NNTP links efficiently, and is therefore the news server of choice for many Internet sites.

16.2 What *is* Usenet, Anyway?

One of the most astounding facts about Usenet is that it isn't part of any organization, or has any sort of centralized network management authority. In fact, it's part of Usenet lore that except for a technical description, you cannot define *what* it is, you can only say what it isn't. If you have Brendan Kehoe's excellent "Zen and the Art of the Internet" (available online or through Prentice-Hall, see [Kehoe92]) at hand, you will find an amusing list of Usenet's non-properties.

At the risk of sounding stupid, one might define Usenet as a collaboration of separate sites who exchange Usenet news. To be a Usenet site, all you have to do is find another site Usenet site, and strike an agreement with its owners and maintainers to exchange news with you. Providing another site with news is also called *feeding* it, whence another common axiom of Usenet philosophy originates: "Get a feed and you're on it."

The basic unit of Usenet news is the article. This is a message a user writes and "posts" to the net. In order to enable news sytems to deal with it, it is prepended with administrative information, the so-called article header. It is very similar to the mail header format laid down in the Internet mail standard RFC 822, in that it consists of several lines of text, each beginning with a field name terminated by a colon, which is followed by the field's value.[1]

Articles are submitted to one or more *newsgroups*. One may consider a newsgroup a forum for articles relating to a common topic. All newsgroups are organized in a hierarchy, with each group's name indicating its place in the hierarchy. This often makes it easy to see what a group is all about. For example, anybody can see from the newsgroup name that **comp.os.linux.announce** is used for announcements concerning a computer operating system named Linux.

These articles are then exchanged between all Usenet sites that are willing to carry news from this group. When two sites agree to exchange news, they are free to exchange whatever newsgroups they like to, and may even add their own local news hierarchies. For example, **groucho.edu** might have a news link to **barnyard.edu**, which is a major news feed, and several links to minor sites which it feeds news. Now, Barnyard College might receive all Usenet groups, while GMU only wants to carry a few major hierarchies like **sci**, **comp**, **rec**, etc. Some of the downstream sites, say a UUCP site called **brewhq**, will want to carry even fewer groups, because they don't have the network or hardware resources. On the other hand, **brewhq** might want to receive newsgroups from the **fj** hierarchy, which GMU doesn't carry. It therefore maintains another link with **gargleblaster.com**, who carry all **fj** groups, and feed them to **brewhq**. The news flow is shown in figure 16.1.

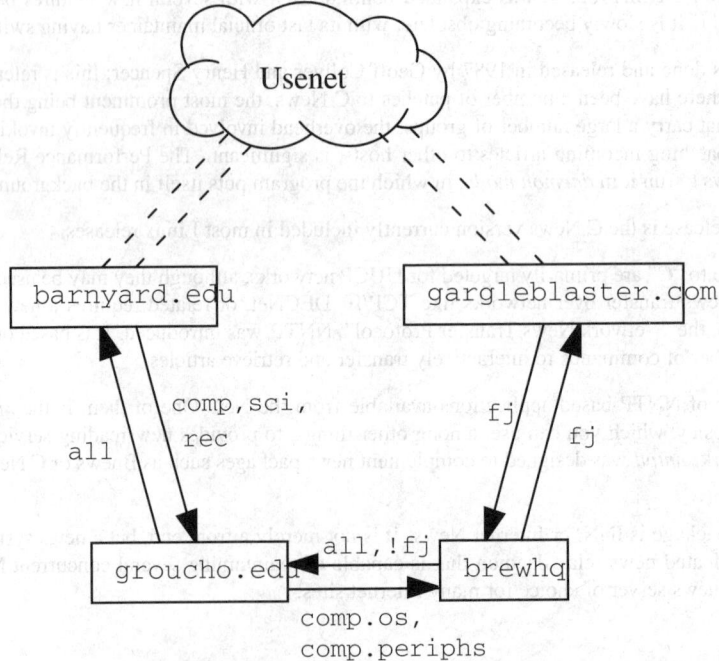

Figure 16.1: Usenet news flow through Groucho Marx University.

The labels on the arrows originating from **brewhq** may require some explanation, though. By default, it wants all locally

---

[1]The format of Usenet news messages is specified in RFC 1036, "Standard for interchange of USENET messages".

generated news to be sent to **groucho.edu**. However, as **groucho.edu** does not carry the **fj** groups, there's no pointing in sending it any messages from those groups. Therefore, the feed from **brewhq** to GMU is labelled **all,!fj**, meaning that all groups except those below **fj** are sent to it.

16.3 How Does Usenet Handle News?

Today, Usenet has grown to enormous proportions. Sites that carry the whole of netnews usually transfer something like a paltry sixty megabytes a day.[2] Of course this requires much more than pushing around files. So let's take a look at the way most UNIX systems handle Usenet news.

News is distributed through the net by various transports. The historical medium used to be UUCP, but today the main traffic is carried by Internet sites. The routing algorithm used is called *flooding*: Each site maintains a number of links (*news feeds*) to other sites. Any article generated or received by the local news system is forwarded to them, unless it has already been seen at that site, in which case it is discarded. A site may find out about all other sites the article has already traversed by looking at the `Path:` header field. This header contains a list of all systems the article has been forwarded by in bang path notation.

To distinguish articles and recognize duplicates, Usenet articles have to carry a message id (specified in the `Message-Id:` header field), which combines the posting site's name and a serial number into "`<serial@site>`". For each article processed, the news system logs this id into a *history* file against which all newly arrived articles are checked.

The flow between any two sites may be limited by two criteria: for one, an article is assigned a distribution (in the `Distribution:` header field) which may be used to confine it to a certain group of sites. On the other hand, the newsgroups exchanged may be limited by both the sending or receiving system. The set of newsgroups and distributions allowed for transmission to a site are usually kept in the *sys* file.

The sheer number of articles usually requires that improvements be made to the above scheme. On UUCP networks, the natural thing to do is to collect articles over a period of time, and combine them into a single file, which is compressed and sent to the remote site. This is called *batching*.[3]

An alternative technique is the *ihave/sendme* protocol that prevents duplicate articles from being transferred in the first place, thus saving net bandwidth. Instead of putting all articles in batch files and sending them along, only the message ids of articles are combined into a giant "ihave" message and sent to the remote site. It reads this message, compares it to its history file, and returns the list of articles it wants in a "sendme" message. Only these articles are then sent.

Of course, ihave/sendme only makes sense if it involves two big sites that receive news from several independent feeds each, and who poll each other often enough for an efficient flow of news.

Sites that are on the Internet generally rely on TCP/IP-based software that uses the Network News Transfer Protocol, NNTP.[4] It transfers news between feeds and provides Usenet access to single users on remote hosts.

NNTP knows three different ways to transfer news. One is a real-time version of ihave/sendme, also referred to as *pushing* news. The second technique is called *pulling* news, in which the client requests a list of articles in a given newsgroup or hierarchy that have arrived at the server's site after a specified date, and chooses those it cannot find in its history file. The third mode is for interactive newsreading, and allows you or your newsreader to retrieve articles from specified newgroups, as well as post articles with incomplete header information.

At each site, news are kept in a directory hierarchy below */var/spool/news*, each article in a separate file, and each newsgroup in a separate directory. The directory name is made up of the newsgroup name, with the components being the path components. Thus, **comp.os.linux.misc** articles are kept in */var/spool/news/comp/os/linux/misc*. The articles in a newsgroup are assigned numbers in the order they arrive. This number serves as the file's name. The range of numbers

---

[2] Wait a moment: 60 Megs at 9600 bps, that's 60 million by 1200, that is... mutter, mutter,... Hey! That's 34 hours!

[3] The golden rule of netnews, according to Geoff Collyer: "Thou shalt batch thine articles."

[4] Described in RFC 977.

of articles currently online is kept in a file called *active*, which at the same time serves as a list of newsgroups known at your site.

Since disk space is a finite resource,[5] one has to start throwing away articles after some time. This is called *expiring*. Usually, articles from certain groups and hierarchies are expired at a fixed number of days after they arrive. This may be overridden by the poster by specifying a date of expiration in the Expires: field of the article header.

Chapter 17

C News

One of the most popular software packages for Netnews is C News. It was designed for sites that carry news over UUCP links. This chapter will discuss the central concepts of C News, and the basic installation and maintenance tasks.

C News stores its configuration files in */usr/lib/news*, and most of its binaries in the */usr/lib/news/bin* directory. Articles are kept below */var/spool/news*. You should make sure virtually all files in these directories are owned by user **news**, group **news**. Most problems arise from files being inaccessible to C News. Make it a rule for you to become user **news** using *su* before you touch anything in there. The only exceptions is *setnewsids*, which is used to set the real user id of some news programs. It must be owned by **root** and must have the setuid bit set.

In the following, we describe all C News configuration files in detail, and show you what you have to do to keep your site running.

17.1 Delivering News

Articles may be fed to C News in several ways. When a local user posts an article, the newsreader usually hands it to the *inews* command, which completes the header information. News from remote sites, be it a single article or a whole batch, is given to the *rnews* command, which stores it in the */var/spool/newsin.coming* directory, from where it will be picked up at a later time by *newsrun*. With any of these two techniques, however, the article will eventually be handed to the *relaynews* command.

For each article, the *relaynews* command first checks if the article has already been seen at the local site by looking up the message id in the *history* file. Duplicate articles will be dropped. Then, *relaynews* looks at the Newsgroups: header line to find out if the local site requests articles from any of these groups. If it does, and the newsgroup is listed in the *active* file, *relaynews* tries to store the article in the corresponding directory in the news spool area. If this directory does not exist, it is created. The article's message id will then be logged to the *history* file. Otherwise, *relaynews* drops the article.

If *relaynews* fails to store an incoming article because a group it has been posted to is not listed in your *active* file, the article will be moved to the **junk** group.[1] *relaynews* will also check for stale or misdated articles and reject them. Incoming batches that fail for any other reason are moved to */var/spool/news/in.coming/bad*, and an error message is logged.

After this, the article will be relayed to all other sites that request news from these groups, using the transport specified for each particular site. To make sure it isn't sent to a site that already has seen it, each destination site is checked against the article's Path: header field, which contains the list of sites the article has traversed so far, written in bang path style. Only if the destination site's name does not appear in this list will the article be sent to it.

C News is commonly used to relay news between UUCP sites, altough it is also possible to use it in a NNTP environment. To deliver news to a remote UUCP site — either single articles or whole batches — *uux* is used to execute the *rnews*

---

[1]There may be a difference between the groups that exist at your site, and those that your site is willing to receive. For example, the subscription list may specify **comp.all**, which means all newsgroups below the **comp** hierarchy, but at your site, only a number of **comp** groups are listed in *active*. articles posted to those groups will be moved to **junk**.

command on the remote site, and feed the article or batch to it on standard input.

When batching is enabled for a given site, C News does not send any incoming article immediately, but appends its path name to a file, usually *out.going/site/togo*. Periodically, a batcher program is executed from a crontab entry,[2] which puts the articles in one or more files, optionally compresses them, and sends them to *rnews* at the remote site.

Figure 17.1 shows the news flow through *relaynews*. Articles may be relayed to the local site (denoted by *ME*), to some site named **ponderosa** via email, and a site named **moria**, for which batching is enabled.

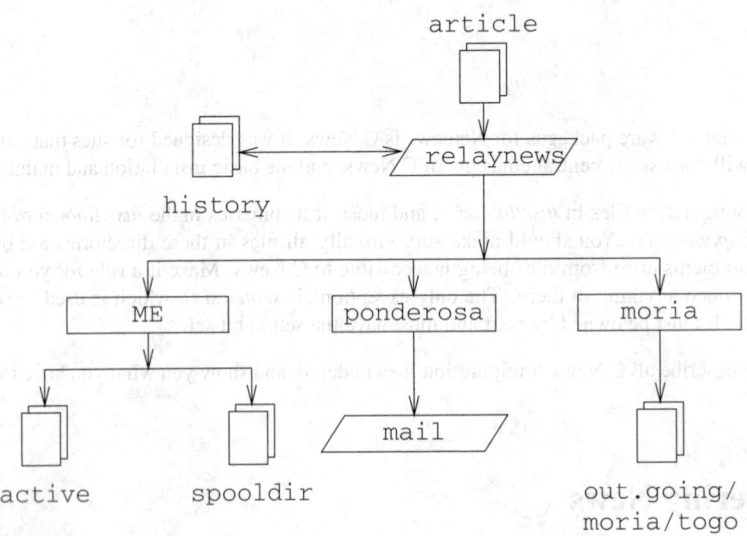

Figure 17.1: News flow through *relaynews*.

17.2   Installation

To install C News, untar the files into their proper places if you haven't done so yet, and edit the configuration files listed below. They are all located in */usr/lib/news*. Their formats will be described in the following sections.

sys
:   You probably have to modify the *ME* line that describes your system, although using *all/all* is always a safe bet. You also have to add a line for each site you feed news to.

    If you are a leaf site, you only need a line that sends all locally generated articles to your feed. Assume your feed is **moria**, then your *sys* file should look like this:

    ```
    ME:all/all::
    moria/moria.orcnet.org:all/all,!local:f:
    ```

organization
:   Your organization's name. For example, "Virtual Brewery, Inc.". On your home machine, enter "private site", or anything else you like. Most people will not call your site properly configured if you haven't customized this file.

newsgroups

mailname
:   Your site's mail name, e.g. **vbrew.com**.

whoami
:   Your site's name for news purposes. Quite often, the UUCP site name is used, for example **vbrew**.

---

[2]Note that this should be the crontab of **news**, in order not to mangle file permissions.

explist   You should probably edit this file to reflect your preferred expiry times for some special newsgroups. Disk space may play an important role in it.

To create an initial hierarchy of newsgroups, obtain an *active* and a *newsgroups* file from the site that feeds you, and install them in */usr/lib/news*, making sure they are owned by news and have a mode of 644. Remove all **to.*** groups from the active file, and add **to.***mysite* and **to.***feedsite*, as well as **junk** and **control**. The **to.*** groups are normally used for exchanging ihave/sendme messages, but you should create them regardless of whether you plan to use ihave/sendme or not. Next, replace all article numbers in the second and third field of *active* using the following command:

```
# cp active active.old
# sed 's/ [0-9]* [0-9]* / 0000000000 00001 /' active.old > active
# rm active.old
```

The second command is an invocation of *sed(1)*, one of my favorite UNIX commands. This invocation replaces two strings of digits with a string of zeroes and the string `000001`, respectively.

Finally, create the news spool directory and the subdirectories used for incoming and outgoing news:

```
# cd /var/spool
# mkdir news news/in.coming news/out.going
# chown -R news.news news
# chmod -R 755 news
```

If you're using a later release of C News, you may also have to create the *out.master* directory in the news spool directory.

If you're using newsreaders from a different distribution than the C News you have running, you may find that some expect the news spool on */usr/spool/news* rather than in */var/spool/news*. If your newsreader doesn't seem to find any articles, create a symbolic from */usr/spool/news* to */var/spool/news*.

Now, you are ready to receive news. Note that you don't have to create any directories other than those shown above, because each time C News receives an article from a group for which there's no spool directory yet, it will create it.

In particular, this happens to *all* groups an article has been crossposted to. So, after a while, you will find your news spool cluttered with directories for newsgroups you have never subscribed to, like **alt.lang.teco**. You may prevent this by either removing all unwanted groups from *active*, or by regularly running a shell script which removes all empty directories below */var/spool/news* (except *out.going* and *in.coming*, of course).

C News needs a user to send error messages and status reports to. By default, this is **usenet**. If you use the default, you have to set up an alias for it which forwards all of its mail to one or more responsible persons. (Chapters 14 and 15 explain how to do so for *smail* and *sendmail*). You may also override this behavior by setting the environment variable *NEWSMASTER* to the appropriate name. You have to do so in **news**' crontab file, as well as every time you invoke an administrative tool manually, so installing an alias is probably easier.

While you're hacking */etc/passwd*, make sure that every user has her real name in the *pw_gecos* field of the password file (this is the fourth field). It is a question of Usenet netiquette that the sender's real name appears in the `From:` field of the article. Of course, you will want to do so anyway when you use mail.

17.3   The sys file

The *sys* file, located in */usr/lib/news*, controls which hierarchies you receive and forward to other sites. Although there are maintenance tools named *addfeed* and *delfeed*, I think it's better to maintain this file by hand.

The *sys* file contains entries for each site you forward news to, as well as a description of the groups you will accept. An entry looks like

```
    site[/exclusions]:grouplist[/distlist][:flags[:cmds]]
```

Entries may be continued across newlines using a backslash (\). A hash sign (#) denotes a comment.

site   This is the name of the site the entry applies to. One usually chooses the site's UUCP name for this. There has to be an entry for your site in the *sys* file, too, else you will not receive any articles yourself.

The special site name *ME* denotes your site. The *ME* entry defines all groups you are willing to store locally. Articles that aren't matched by the *ME* line will go to the **junk** group.

Since C News checks *site* against the site names in the *Path:* header field, you have to make sure they really match. Some sites use their fully qualified domain name in this field, or an alias like **news.***site.domain*. To prevent any articles from being returned to these sites, you have to add these to the exclusion list, separated by commas.

For the entry applying to site **moria**, for instance, the site field would contain **moria/moria.orcnet.org**.

grouplist   This is a comma-separated subscription list of groups and hierarchies for that particular site. A hierarchy may be specified by giving the hierarchy's prefix (such as **comp.os** for all groups whose name starts with this prefix), optionally followed by the keyword **all** (e.g. **comp.os.all**).

A hierarchy or group is excluded from forwarding by preceding it with an exclamation mark. If a newsgroup is checked against the list, the longest match applies. For example, if *grouplist* contains

```
        !comp,comp.os.linux,comp.folklore.computers
```

no groups from the **comp** hierarchy except **comp.folklore.computers** and all groups below **comp.os.linux** will be fed to that site.

If the site requests to be forwarded all news you receive yourself, enter *all* as *grouplist*.

distlist   is offset from the *grouplist* by a slash, and contains a list of distributions to be forwarded. Again, you may exclude certain distributions by preceding them with an exclamation mark. All distributions are denoted by *all*. Omitting *distlist* implies a list of *all*.

For example, you may use a distribution list of *all,!local* to prevent news for local use only from being sent to remote sites.

There are usually at least two distributions: *world*, which is often the default distribution used when none is specified by the user, and *local*. There may be other distributions that apply to a certain region, state, country, etc. Finally, there are two distributions used by C News only; these are *sendme* and *ihave*, and are used for the sendme/ihave protocol.

The use of distributions is a subject of debate. For one, some newsreaders create bogus distributions by simply using the top level hierarchy, for example **comp** when posting to **comp.os.linux**. Distributions that apply to regions are often questionable, too, because news may travel outside of your region when sent across the Internet.[3] Distributions applying to an organization, however, are very meaningful, for example to prevent confidential information from leaving the company network. This purpose, however, is generally served better by creating a separate newsgroup or hierarchy.

flags   This describes certain parameters for the feed. It may be empty, or a combination of the following:

F   This flag enables batching.

f   This is almost identical to the *F* flag, but allows C News to calculate the size of outgoing batches more precisely.

I   This flag makes C News produce an article list suitable for use by ihave/sendme. Additional modifications to the *sys* and the *batchparms* file are required to enable ihave/sendme.

---

[3]It is not uncommon for an article posted in, say Hamburg, to go to Frankfurt via **reston.ans.net** in the Netherlands, or even via some site in the U.S.

n	This creates batch files for active NNTP transfer clients like *nntpxmit* (see chapter 18). The batch files contain the article's filename along with its message id.
L	This tells C News to transmit only articles posted at your site. This flag may be followed by a decimal number *n*, which makes C News only transfer articles posted within *n* hops from your site. C News determines the number of hops from the Path: field.
u	This tells C News to batch only articles from unmoderated groups.
m	This tells C News to batch only articles from moderated groups.

You may use at most one of *F*, *f*, *I*, or *n*.

cmds	This field contains a command to be executed for each article, unless batching is enabled. The article will be fed to the command on standard input. This should only be used for very small feeds; otherwise the load on both systems will be too high.

The default command is

```
uux - -r -z system!rnews
```

which invokes *rnews* on the remote system, feeding it the article on standard input.

The default search path for commands given in this field is */bin:/usr/bin:/usr/lib/news/bin/batch*. The latter directory contains a number of shell scripts whose name starts with *via*; they are briefly described later in this chapter.

If batching is enabled using either of the *F* or *f*, *I* or *n* flags, C News expects to find a file name in this field rather than a command. If the file name does not begin with a slash (*/*), it is assumed to be relative to */var/spool/news/out.going*. If the field is empty, it defaults to *system*/togo.

When setting up C News, you will most probably have to write your own *sys* file. To help you with it, we give a sample file for **vbrew.com** below, from which you might copy what you need.

```
# We take whatever they give us.
ME:all/all::

# We send everything we receive to moria, except for local and
# brewery-related articles. We use batching.
moria/moria.orcnet.org:all,!to,to.moria/all,!local,!brewery:f:

# We mail comp.risks to jack@ponderosa.uucp
ponderosa:comp.risks/all::rmail jack@ponderosa.uucp

# swim gets a minor feed
swim/swim.twobirds.com:comp.os.linux,rec.humor.oracle/all,!local:f:

# Log mail map articles for later processing
usenet-maps:comp.mail.maps/all:F:/var/spool/uumaps/work/batch
```

17.4   The *active* file

The *active* file is located in */usr/lib/news* and lists all groups known at your site, and the articles currently online. You will rarely have to touch it, but we explain it nevertheless for sake of completeness. Entries take the following form:

```
newsgroup high low perm
```

newsgroup is, of course, the group's name. *low* and *high* are the lowest and highest numbers of articles currently available. If none are available at the moment, *low* is equal to *high*+1.

At least, that's what the *low* field is meant to do. However, for efficiency reasons, C News doesn't update this field. This wouldn't be such a big loss if there weren't some newsreaders that depend on it. For instance, *trn* checks this field to see if it can purge any articles from its thread database. To update the *low* field, you therefore have to run the *updatemin* command regularly (or, in earlier version of C News, the *upact* script).

perm is a parameter detailing the access users are granted to the group. It takes one of the following values:

y	Users are allowed to post to this group.
n	Users are not allowed to post to this group. However, the group may still be read.
x	This group has been disabled locally. This happens sometimes when news admininistrators (or their superiors) take offense to articles posted to certain groups.
	Articles received for this group are not stored locally, although they are forwarded to the sites that request them.
m	This denotes a moderated group. When a user tries to post to this group, an intelligent newsreader will notify her of this, and send the article to the moderator instead. The moderator's address is taken from the *moderators* file in */usr/lib/news*.
=*real-group*	This marks *newsgroup* as being a local alias for another group, namely *real-group*. All articles posted to *newsgroup* will be redirected to it.

In C News, you will generally not have to access this file directly. Groups may be added or deleted locally using *addgroup* and *delgroup* (see below in section 17.10). When groups are added or deleted for the whole of Usenet, this is usually done by sending a *newgroup* or *rmgroup* control message, respectively. *Never send such a message yourself!* For instructions on how to create a newsgroup, read the monthly postings in **news.announce.newusers**.

A file closely related to *active* is *active.times*. Whenever a group is created, C News logs a message to this file, containing the name of the group created, the date of creation, whether it was done by a *newgroup* control message or locally, and who did it. This is for the convenience of newsreaders who may notify the user of any recently created groups. It is also used by the *NEWGROUPS* command of NNTP.

17.5   Article Batching

Newsbatches follow a particular format which is the same for Bnews, C News, and INN. Each article is preceded by a line like this:

```
#! rnews count
```

where *count* is the number of bytes in the article. When batch compression is used, the resulting file is compressed as a whole, and preceded by another line, indicated by the message to be used for unpacking. The standard compression tool is **compress**, which is marked by

```
#! cunbatch
```

Sometimes, when having to send batches via mail software that removes the eighth bit from all data, a compressed batch may be protected using what is called c7-encoding; these batches will be marked by *c7unbatch*.

When a batch is fed to *rnews* on the remote site, it checks for these markers and processes the batch appropriately. Some sites also use other compression tools, like *gzip*, and precede their gzipped files with *zunbatch* instead. C News does not recognize non-standard headers like these; you have to modify the source to support them.

In C News, article batching is performed by */usr/lib/news/bin/batch/sendbatches*, which takes a list of articles from the *site*/*togo* file, and puts them into several newsbatches. It should be executed once per hour or even more frequently, depending on the volume of traffic.

Its operation is controlled by the *batchparms* file in */usr/lib/news*. This file describes the maximum batch size allowed for each site, the batching and optional compression program to be used, and the transport for delivering it to the remote site. You may specify batching parameters on a per-site basis, as well as a set of default parameters for sites not explicitly mentioned.

To perform batching for a specific site, you invoke it as

```
# su news -c "/usr/lib/news/bin/batch/sendbatches site"
```

When invoked without arguments, *sendbatches* handles all batch queues. The interpretation of "all" depends on the presence of a default entry in *batchparms*. If one is found, all directories in */var/spool/news/out.going* are checked, otherwise, it cycles through all entries in *batchparms*. Note that *sendbatches*, when scanning the *out.going* directory, takes only those directories that contain no dot or at sign (@) as site names.

When installing C News, you will most likely find a *batchparms* file in your distribution which contains a reasonable default entry, so there's a good chance that you wouldn't have to touch the file. Just in case, we describe its format nevertheless. Each line consists of six fields, separated by spaces or tabs:

```
site size max batcher muncher transport
```

The meaning of these fields is as follows:

site is the name of the site the entry applies to. The *togo* file for this site must reside in *out.going/togo* below the news spool. A site name of */default/* denotes the default entry.

size is the maximum size of article batches created (before compression). For single articles larger than this, C News makes an exception and puts them in a single batch by themselves.

max is the maximum number of batches created and scheduled for transfer before batching stalls for this particular site. This is useful in case the remote site should be down for a long time, because it prevents C News from cluttering your UUCP spool directories with zillions of newsbatches.

C News determines the number of queued batches using the *queuelen* script in */usr/lib/news/bin*. Vince Skahan's *newspak* release should contain a script for BNU-compatible UUCPs. If you use a different flavor of spool directories, for example, Taylor UUCP, you might have to write your own.[4]

The *batcher* field contains the command used for producing a batch from the list of articles in the *togo* file. For regular feeds, this is usually *batcher*. For other purposes, alternative batchers may be provided. For instance, the ihave/sendme protocol requires the article list to be turned into ihave or sendme control messages, which are posted to the newsgroup **to.*site***. This is performed by *batchih* and *batchsm*.

The *muncher* field specifies the command used for compression. Usually, this is **compcun**, a script that produces a compressed batch.[5] Alternatively, you might provide a muncher that uses *gzip*, say *gzipcun* (to be clear: you have to write it yourself). You have to make sure that *uncompress* on the remote site is patched to recognize files compressed with *gzip*.

If the remote site does not have an *uncompress* command, you may specify *nocomp* which does not do any compression.

The last field, *transport*, describes the transport to be used. A number of standard commands for different transports are available whose names begin with *via*. *sendbatches* passes them the destination site name on the command line. If

---

[4]If you don't care about the number of spool files (because you're the only person using your computer, and you don't write articles by the megabyte), you may replace the script's contents by a simple *exit 0* statement.

[5]As shipped with C News, **compcun** uses **compress** with the 12 bit option, since this is the least common denominator for most sites. You may produce a copy of it, say **compcun16**, where you use 16 bit compression. The improvement is not too impressive, though.

the *batchparms* entry was not */default/*, it derives the site name from the `site` field by stripping of anything after and including the first dot or slash. If entry was */default/*, the directory names in *out.going* are used.

There are two commands that use *uux* to execute *rnews* on the remote system; *viauux* and *viauuxz*. The latter sets the `-z` flag for (older versions of) *uux* to keep it from returning success messages for each article delivered. Another command, *viamail*, sends article batches to the user **rnews** on the remote system via mail. Of course, this requires that the remote system somehow feeds all mail for **rnews** to their local news system. For a complete list of these transports, refer to the *newsbatch(8)* manual page.

All commands from the last three fields must be located in either of *out.going/*`site` or */usr/lib/news/bin/batch*. Most of them are scripts, so that you may easily tailor new tools for your personal needs. They are invoked as a pipe. The list of articles is fed to the batcher on standard input, which produces the batch on standard output. This is piped into the muncher, and so on.

A sample file is given below.

```
# batchparms file for the brewery
# site          | size   |max    |batcher   |muncher    |transport
#-------------+--------+-------+---------+-----------+-----------
/default/       100000  22      batcher   compcun    viauux
swim            10000   10      batcher   nocomp     viauux
```

17.6   Expiring News

In Bnews, expiring used to be performed by a program called *expire*, which took a list of newsgroups as arguments, along with a time specification after which articles had to be expired. To have different hierarchies expired at different times, you had to write a script that invoked *expire* for each of them separately. C News offers a more convenient solution to this: in a file called *explist*, you may specify newsgroups and expiration intervals. A command called *doexpire* is usually run once a day from *cron*, and processes all groups according to this list.

Occasionally, you may want to retain articles from certain groups even after they have been expired; for example, you might want to keep programs posted to **comp.sources.unix**. This is called *archiving*. *explist* permits you to mark groups for archiving.

An entry in *explist* looks like this:

```
grouplist perm times archive
```

`grouplist` is a comma-separated list of newsgroups to which the entry applies. Hierarchies may be specified by giving the group name prefix, optionally appended with *all*. For example, for an entry applying to all groups below **comp.os**, you might either enter **comp.os** or **comp.os.all** in `grouplist`.

When expiring news from a group, the name is checked against all entries in *explist* in the order given. The first matching entry applies. For example, to throw away the majority of **comp** after four days, except for **comp.os.linux.announce** which you want to keep for a week, you simply have an entry for the latter, which specifies a seven-day expiration period, followed by that for **comp**, which specifies four days.

The `perm` field details if the entry applies to moderated, unmoderated, or any groups. It may take the values *m*, *u*, or *x*, which denote moderated, unmoderated, or any type.

The third field, `times`, usually contains only a single number. This is the number of days after which articles will be expired if they haven't been assigned an artificial expiration date in an `Expires:` field in the article header. Note that this is the number of days counting from its *arrival* at your site, not the date of posting.

The `times` field may, however, be more complex than that. It may be a combination of up to three numbers, separated from one another by a dash. The first denotes the number of days that have to pass before the article is considered a candidate for expiration. It is rarely useful to use a value other than zero. The second field is the above-mentioned default number of days after which it will be expired. The third is the number of days after which an article will be expired unconditionally, regardless of whether it has an `Expires`: field or not. If only the middle number is given, the other two take default values. These may be specified using the special entry */bounds/*, which is described below.

The fourth field, `archive`, denotes whether the newsgroup is to be archived, and where. If no archiving is intended, a dash should be used. Otherwise, you either use a full path name (pointing to a directory), or an at sign (@). The at sign denotes the default archive directory which must then be given to *doexpire* by using the `-a` flag on the command line. An archive directory should be owned by **news**. When *doexpire* archives an article from, say **comp.sources.unix**, it stores it in the directory **comp/sources/unix** below the archive directory, creating it if not existent. The archive directory itself, however, will not be created.

There are two special entries in your *explist* file that *doexpire* relies on. Instead of a list of newsgroups, they have the keywords */bounds/* and */expired/*. The */bounds/* entry contains the default values for the three values of the `times` field described above.

The */expired/* field determines how long C News will hold on to lines in the *history* file. This is needed because C News will not remove a line from the history file once the corresponding article(s) have been expired, but will hold on to it in case a duplicate should arrive after this date. If you are fed by only one site, you can keep this value small. Otherwise, a couple of weeks is advisable on UUCP networks, depending on the delays you experience with articles from these sites.

A sample *explist* file with rather tight expiry intervals is reproduced below:

```
# keep history lines for two weeks. Nobody gets more than three months
/expired/                          x       14        -
/bounds/                           x       0-1-90    -

# groups we want to keep longer than the rest
comp.os.linux.announce             m       10        -
comp.os.linux                      x       5         -
alt.folklore.computers             u       10        -
rec.humor.oracle                   m       10        -
soc.feminism                       m       10        -

# Archive *.sources groups
comp.sources,alt.sources           x       5         @

# defaults for tech groups
comp,sci                           x       7         -

# enough for a long weekend
misc,talk                          x       4         -

# throw away junk quickly
junk                               x       1         -

# control messages are of scant interest, too
control                            x       1         -

# catch-all entry for the rest of it
all                                x       2         -
```

With expiring in C News, there are a number of potential troubles looming. One is that your newsreader might rely on the third field of the active file, which contains the number of the lowest article on-line. When expiring articles, C News does not update this field. If you need (or want) to have this field represent the real situation, you need to run a program called *updatemiin* after each run of *doexpire*.[6]

Second, C News does not expire by scanning the newsgroup's directory, but simply checks the *history* file if the article is due for expiration.[7] If your history file somehow gets out of sync, articles may be around on your disk forever, because C News has literally forgotten them.[8] You can repair this using the *addmissing* script in */usr/lib/news/bin/maint*, which will add missing articles to the *history* file, or *mkhistory*, which re-builds the entire file from scratch. Don't forget to become **news** before invoking it, else you will wind up with a *history* file unreadable by C News.

17.7   Miscellaneous Files

There are a number of files that control C News' behavior, but are not essential to its functioning. All of them reside in */usr/lib/news*. We will describe them briefly.

newsgroups   This is a companion file of *active* which contains a list of newsgroup names, along with a one-line description of its main topic. This file is automatically updated when C News receives a *checknews* control message (see section 17.8).

localgroups   If you have a number of local groups that you don't want C News to complain about every time you receive a *checknews* message, put their names and descriptions in this file, just like they would appear in *newsgroups*.

mailpaths   This file contains the moderator's address for each moderated group. Each line contains the group name, followed by the moderator's email address (offset by a tab).

Two special entries are provided as default. These are *backbone* and *internet*. Both provide — in bang-path notation — the path to the nearest backbone site, and the site that understands RFC 822-style addresses (**user@host**). The default entries are

```
internet      backbone
```

You will not have to change the *internet* entry if you have *smail* or *sendmail* installed, because they understand RFC 822-addressing.

The *backbone* entry is used whenever a user posts to a moderated group whose moderator is not listed explicitly. If the newsgroup's name is **alt.sewer**, and the *backbone* entry contains **path!%s**, C News will mail the article to **path!alt-sewer**, hoping that the backbone machine is able to forward the article. To find out which path to use, ask the news admins at the site that feeds you. As a last resort, you can also use **uunet.uu.net!%s**.

distributions   This file is not really a C News file, but it is used by some newsreaders, and *nntpd*. It contains the list of distributions recognized by your site, and a description of its (intended) effect. For example, Virtual Brewery has the following file:

```
world         everywhere in the world
local         Only local to this site
nl            Netherlands only
mugnet        MUGNET only
fr            France only
de            Germany only
brewery        Virtual Brewery only
```

log   This file contains a log of all C News activities. It is culled regularly by running *newsdaily*; copies of the old logfiles are kept in *log.o*, *log.oo*, etc.

---

[6]In older versions of C News, this was done by a script called *upact*.
[7]The article's date of arrival is kept in the middle field of the history line, given in seconds since January 1, 1970.
[8]I don't know *why* this happens, but for me, it does from time to time.

Net-Admin Guide

errlog   This is a log of all error messages created by C News. These do not include articles junked due to wrong group, etc. This file is mailed to the newsmaster (**usenet** by default) automatically by *newsdaily* if it is found to be non-empty.

errlog is cleared by *newsdaily*. Old copies are kept in *errlog.o* and companions.

batchlog   This logs all runs of *sendbatches*. It is usually of scant interest only. It is also attended by *newsdaily*.

watchtime   This is an empty file created each time *newswatch* is run.

17.8   Control Messages

The Usenet news protocol knows a special category of articles which evoke certain responses or actions by the news system. These are called *control* messages. They are recognized by the presence of a `Control:` field in the article header, which contains the name of the control operation to be performed. There are several types of them, all of which are handled by shell scripts located in */usr/lib/news/ctl*.

Most of these will perform their action automatically at the time the article is processed by C News, without notifying the newsmaster. By default, only *checkgroups* messages will be handed to the newsmaster,[9] but you may change this by editing the scripts.

17.8.1   The *cancel* Message

The most widely known message is *cancel*, with which a user may cancel an article sent by her earlier. This effectively removes the article from the spool directories, if it exists. The *cancel* message is forwarded to all sites that receive news from the groups affected, regardless of whether the article has been seen already or not. This is to take into account the possibility that the original article has been delayed over the cancellation message. Some news systems allow users to cancel other person's messages; this is of course a definite no-no.

17.8.2   *newgroup* and *rmgroup*

Two messages dealing with creation or removal of newsgroups are the *newgroup* and *rmgroup* message. Newsgroups below the "usual" hierarchies may be created only after a discussion and voting has been held among Usenet readers. The rules applying to the **alt** hierarchy allow for something close to anarchy. For more information, see the regular postings in **news.announce.newusers** and **news.announce.newgroups**. Never send a *newgroup* or *rmgroup* message yourself unless you definitely know that you are allowed to.

17.8.3   The *checkgroups* Message

checkgroups messages are sent by news administrators to make all sites within a network synchronize their *active* files with the realities of Usenet. For example, commercial Internet service providers might send out such a message to their customers' sites. Once a month, the "official" *checkgroups* message for the major hierarchies is posted to **comp.announce.newgroups** by its moderator. However, it is posted as an ordinary article, not as a control message. To perform the *checkgroups* operation, save this article to a file, say */tmp/check*, remove everything up to the beginning of the control message itself, and feed it to the *checkgroups* script using the following command:

```
# su news -c "/usr/lib/news/bin/ctl/checkgroups" < /tmp/check
```

This will update your *newsgroups* file, adding the groups listed in *localgroups*. The old *newsgroups* file will be moved to *newsgroups.bac*. Note that posting the message locally will rarely work, because *inews* refuses to accept that large an article.

---

[9]There's a funny typo in RFC 1036 (p.12): "Implementors and administrators may choose to allow control messages to be carried out automatically, or to queue them for annual processing."

If C News finds mismatches between the *checkgroups* list and the *active* file, it will produce a list of commands that
would bring your site up to date, and mail it to the news administrator. The output typically looks like this:

```
From news Sun Jan 30 16:18:11 1994
Date: Sun, 30 Jan 94 16:18 MET
From: news (News Subsystem)
To: usenet
Subject: Problems with your active file

The following newsgroups are not valid and should be removed.
        alt.ascii-art
        bionet.molbio.gene-org
        comp.windows.x.intrisics
        de.answers

You can do this by executing the commands:
        /usr/lib/news/bin/maint/delgroup alt.ascii-art
        /usr/lib/news/bin/maint/delgroup bionet.molbio.gene-org
        /usr/lib/news/bin/maint/delgroup comp.windows.x.intrisics
        /usr/lib/news/bin/maint/delgroup de.answers

The following newsgroups were missing.
        comp.binaries.cbm
        comp.databases.rdb
        comp.os.geos
        comp.os.qnx
        comp.unix.user-friendly
        misc.legal.moderated
        news.newsites
        soc.culture.scientists
        talk.politics.crypto
        talk.politics.tibet
```

When you receive a message like this from your news system, don't believe it blindly. Depending on who sent the
checkgroups message, it may lack a few groups or even entire hierarchies; so you should be careful about removing any
groups. If you find groups are listed as missing that you want to carry at your site, you have to add them using the
addgroup script. Save the list of missing groups to a file and feed it to the following little script:

```
#!/bin/sh
cd /usr/lib/news

while read group; do
    if grep -si "^$group[[:space:]].*moderated" newsgroup; then
        mod=m
    else
        mod=y
    fi
    /usr/lib/news/bin/maint/addgroup $group $mod
done
```

17.8.4 *sendsys, version,* **and** *senduuname*

Finally, there are three messages that may be used to find out about the network's topology. These are *sendsys, version,*
and *senduuname.* They cause C News to return to the sender the *sys* file, a software version string, and the output of

uuname(1), respectively. C News is very laconic about *version* messages; it returns a simple, unadorned "C".

Again, you should *never* issue such a message, unless you have made sure that it cannot leave a your (regional) network. Replies to *sendsys* messages can quickly bring down a UUCP network.[10]

17.9   C News in an NFS Environment

A simple way to distribute news within a local network is to keep all news on a central host, and export the relevant directories via NFS, so that newsreaders may scan the articles directly. The advantage of this method over NNTP is that the overhead involved in retrieving and threading articles is significantly lower. NNTP, on the other hand, wins in a heterogeneous network where equipment varies widely among hosts, or where users don't have equivalent accounts on the server machine.

When using NFS, articles posted on a local host have to be forwarded to the central machine, because accessing administrative files might otherwise expose the system to race-conditions that leave the files inconsistent. Also, you might want to protect your news spool area by exporting it read-only, which requires forwarding to the central machine, too.

C News handles this transparently. When you post an article, your newsreader usually invokes *inews* to inject the article into the news system. This command runs a number of checks on the article, completes the header, and checks the file *server* in */usr/lib/news*. If this file exists and contains a hostname different from the local host's name, *inews* is invoked on that server host via *rsh*. Since the *inews* script uses a number of binary commands and support files from C News, you have to either have C News installed locally, or mount the news software from the server.

For the *rsh* invocation to work properly, each user must have an equivalent account on the server system, i.e. one to which she can log in without being asked for a password.

Make sure that the hostname given in *server* literally matches the output of the *hostname(1)* command on the server machine, else C News will loop forever when trying to deliver the article.

17.10   Maintenance Tools and Tasks

Despite the complexity of C News, a news administrator's life can be fairly easy, because C News provides you with a wide variety of maintenance tools. Some of these are intended to be run regularly from *cron*, like *newsdaily*. Using these scripts reduces daily care and feeding requirements of your C News installation greatly.

Unless stated otherwise, these commands are located in */usr/lib/news/bin/maint*. Note that you must become user **news** before invoking these commands. Running them as super-user may render these files inaccessible to C News.

newsdaily   The name already says it: runs this once a day. It is an important script that helps you keep log files small, retaining copies of each from the last three runs. It also tries to sense any anomalies, like stale batches in the incoming and outgoing directories, postings to unkown or moderated newsgroups, etc. Resulting error messages will be mailed to the newsmaster.

newswatch   This is a script that should be run regularly to look for anomalies in the news system, once an hour or so. It is intended to detect problems that will have immediate effect on the operability of your news system and mail a trouble report to the newsmaster. Things checked include stale lock files that don't get removed, unattended input batches, and disk space shortage.

addgroup   Adds a group to your site locally. The proper invocation is

```
addgroup groupname y|n|m|=realgroup
```

---

[10]I wouldn't try this on the Internet, either.

The second argument has the same meaning as the flag in the *active* file, meaning that anyone may post to the group (*y*), that no-one may post (*n*), that it is moderated (*m*), or that it is an alias for another group (=*realgroup*).

You might also want to use *addgroup* when the first articles in a newly created group arrive earlier than the *newgroup* control message that is intended to create it.

delgroup Allows you to delete a group locally. Invoke it as

```
delgroup groupname
```

You still have to delete the articles that remain in the newsgroup's spool directory. Alternatively, you might leave it to the natural course of events (a.k.a. *expire*) to make them go away.

addmissing Adds missing articles to the *history* file. Run this script when there are articles that seem to hang around forever.[11]

newsboot This script should be run at system boot time. It removes any lock files left over when news processes were killed at shutdown, and closes and executes any batches left over from NNTP connections that were terminated when shutting down the system.

newsrunning This resides in */usr/lib/news/bin/input*, and may be used to disable unbatching of incoming news, for instance during work hours. You may turn off unbatching by invoking

```
/usr/lib/news/bin/input/newsrunning off
```

It is turned on by using *on* instead of *off*.

---

[11]Ever wondered how to get rid of that "Help! I can't get X11 to work with 0.97.2!!!" article?

Chapter 18

A Description of NNTP

18.1   Introduction

Due to the different network transport used, NNTP provides for a vastly different approach to news exchange from C news. NNTP stands for "Network News Transfer Protocol", and is not a particular software package, but an Internet Standard.[1] It is based on a stream-oriented connection – usually over TCP – between a client anywhere in the network, and a server on a host that keeps netnews on disk storage. The stream connection allows the client and server to interactively negotiate article transfer with nearly no turnaround delay, thus keeping the number of duplicate articles low. Together with the Internet's high transfer rates, this adds up to a news transport that surpasses the original UUCP networks by far. While some years ago it was not uncommon for an article to take two weeks or more before it arrived in the last corner of Usenet, this is now often less than two days; on the Internet itself, it is even within the range of minutes.

Various commands allow clients to retrieve, send and post articles. The difference between sending and posting is that the latter may involve articles with incomplete header information.[2] Article retrieval may be used by news transfer clients as well as newsreaders. This makes NNTP an excellent tool for providing news access to many clients on a local network without going through the contortions that are necessary when using NFS.

NNTP also provides for an active and a passive way of news transfer, colloquially called "pushing" and "pulling". Pushing is basically the same as the C news ihave/sendme protocol. The client offers an article to the server through the "*IHAVE <varmsgid>*" command, and the server returns a response code that indicates whether it already has the article, or if it wants it. If so, the client sends the article, terminated by a single dot on a separate line.

Pushing news has the single disadvantage that it places a heavy load on the server system, since it has to search its history database for every single article.

The opposite technique is pulling news, in which the client requests a list of all (available) articles from a group that have arrived after a specified date. This query is performed by the *NEWNEWS* command. From the returned list of message ids, the client selects those articles it does not yet have, using the *ARTICLE* command for each of them in turn.

The problem with pulling news is that it needs tight control by the server over which groups and distributions it allows a client to request. For example, it has to make sure that no confidential material from newsgroups local to the site are sent to unauthorized clients.

There are also a number of convenience commands for newsreaders that permit them to retrieve the article header and body separately, or even single header lines from a range of articles. This lets you keep all news on a central host, with all users on the (presumably local) network using NNTP-based client programs for reading and posting. This is an alternative to exporting the news directories via NFS which is described in chapter 17.

An overall problem of NNTP is that it allows the knowledgeable to insert articles into the news stream with false sender specification. This is called *news faking*.[3] An extension to NNTP allows to require a user authentication for certain

---

[1] Formally specified in RFC 977.

[2] When posting an article over NNTP, the server always adds at least one header field, which is `Nntp-Posting-Host:`. It contains the client's host name.

[3] The same problem exists with SMTP, the Simple Mail Transfer Protocol.

commands.

There are a number of NNTP packages available. One of the more widely known is the NNTP daemon, also known as the *reference implementation*. Originally, it was written by Stan Barber and Phil Lapsley to illustrate the details of RFC 977. Its most recent version is *nntpd-1.5.11*, which will be described below. You may either get the sources and compile it yourself, or use the *nntpd* from Fred van Kempen's *net-std* binary package. No ready-to-go binaries of *nntpd* are provided, because of various site-specific values that must be compiled in.

The *nntpd* package consists of a server and two clients for pulling and pushing news, respectively, as well as an *inews* replacement. They live in a Bnews environment, but with a little tweaking, they will be happy with C news, too. However if you plan to use NNTP for more than offering newsreaders access to your news server, the reference implementation is not really an option. We will therefore discuss only the NNTP daemon contained in the *nntpd* package, and leave out the client programs.

There is also a package called "InterNet News", or INN for short, that was written by Rich Salz. It provides both NNTP and UUCP-based news transport, and is more suitable for large news hubs. When it comes to news transport over NNTP, it is definitely better than *nntpd*. INN is currently at version *inn-1.4sec*. There is a kit for building INN on a Linux machine from Arjan de Vet; it is available from **sunsite.unc.edu** in the *system/Mail* directory. If you want to set up INN, please refer to the documentation that comes along with the source, as well as the INN FAQ posted regularly to **news.software.b**.

18.2   Installing the NNTP server

The NNTP server is called *nntpd*, and may be compiled in two ways, depending on the expected load on the news system. There are no compiled versions available, because of some site-specific defaults that are hard-coded into the executable. All configuration is done through macro definines in *common/conf.h*.

nntpd may be configured as either a standalone server that is started at system boot time from *rc.inet2*, or a daemon managed by *inetd*. In the latter case you have to have the following entry in */etc/inetd.conf*:

```
    nntp    stream  tcp nowait      news    /usr/etc/in.nntpd   nntpd
```

If you configure *nntpd* as standalone, make sure that any such line in *inetd.conf* is commented out. In either case, you have to make sure there's the following line in */etc/services*:

```
    nntp    119/tcp   readnews untp   # Network News Transfer Protocol
```

To temporarily store any incoming articles, etc, *nntpd* also needs a *.tmp* directory in your news spool. You should create it using

```
    # mkdir /var/spool/news/.tmp
    # chown news.news /var/spool/news/.tmp
```

18.3   Restricting NNTP Access

Access to NNTP resources is governed by the file *nntp_access* in */usr/lib/news*. Lines in the file describe the access rights granted to foreign hosts. Each line has the following format:

```
    site  read|xfer|both|no post|no [!exceptgroups]
```

If a client connects to the NNTP port, *nntpd* attempts to obtain the host's fully qualified domain name from its IP address by reverse lookup. The client's hostname and IP address are checked against the `site` field of each entry in the order in which they appear in the file. Matches may be either partial or exact. If an entry matches exactly, it applies; if the match is partial, it only applies if there is no other match following which is at least as good. *site* may be specified in one of the following ways:

hostname	This is a fully qualified domain name of a host. If this matches the client's canonical hostname literally, the entry applies, and all following entries are ignored.
IP address	This is an IP address in dotted quad notation. If the client's IP address matches this, the entry applies, and all following entries are ignored.
domain name	This is a domain name, specified as ******.domain*. If the client's hostname matches the domain name, the entry matches.
network name	This is the name of a network as specified in */etc/networks*. If the network number of the client's IP address matches the network number associated with the network name, the entry matches.
default	The *default* matches any client.

Entries with a more general site specification should be specified earlier, because any matches by these will be overridden by later, more exact matches.

The second and third field describe the access rights granted to the client. The second details the permissions to retrieve news by pulling (*read*), and transmit news by pushing (*xfer*). A value of *both* enables both, *no* denies access altogether. The third field grants the client the right to post articles, that is, deliver articles with incomplete header information which is completed by the news software. If the second field contains *no*, the third field is ignored.

The fourth field is optional, and contains a comma-separated list of groups the client is denied access to.

A sample *nntp_access* file is shown below:

```
#
# by default, anyone may transfer news, but not read or post
default                 xfer            no
#
# public.vbrew.com offers public access via modem, we allow
# them to read and post to any but the local.* groups
public.vbrew.com        read            post    !local
#
# all other hosts at the brewery may read and post
*.vbrew.com             read            post
```

18.4 NNTP Authorization

When capitalizing the access tokens like *xfer* or *read* in the *nntp_acces* file, *nntpd* requires the authorization from the client for the respective operations. For instance, when specifying a permission of *Xfer* or *XFER*, *nntpd* will not let the client transfer articles to your site unless it passes authorization.

The authorization procedure is implemented by means of a new NNTP command named *AUTHINFO*. Using this command, the client transmits a user name and a password to the NNTP server. *nntpd* will validate them by checking them against the */etc/passwd* database, and verify that the user belongs to the **nntp** group.

The current implementation of NNTP authorization is only experimental, and has therefore not been implemented very portably. The result of this is that it works only with plain-style password databases; shadow passwords will not be recognized.

18.5   *nntpd* Interaction with C News

When receiving an article, *nntpd* has to deliver it to the news subsystem. Depending on whether it was received as a result of an *IHAVE* or *POST* command, the article is handed to *rnews* or *inews*, respectively. Instead of invoking *rnews*, you may also configure it (at compile time) to batch the incoming articles and move the resulting batches to */var/spool/news/in.coming*, where they are left for *relaynews* to pick them up at the next queue run.

To be able to properly perform the ihave/sendme protocol, *nntpd* has to be able to access the *history* file. At compile time, you therefore have to make sure the path is set correctly. You should also make sure that C news and *nntpd* agree on the format of your history file. C news uses *dbm* hashing functions to access it; however, there are quite a number of different and slightly incompatible implementations of the *dbm* library. If C news has been linked with the a different *dbm* library than you have in your standard *libc*, you have to link *nntpd* with this library, too.

A typical symptom of *nntpd* and C news disagreeing on the database format are error messages in the system log that *nntpd* could not open it properly, or duplicate articles received via NNTP. A good test is to pick an article from your spool area, telnet to the *nntp* port, and offer it to *nntpd* as shown in the example below (your input is marked `like this`). Of course, you have to replace `<msg@id>` with the message-ID of the article you want to feed to *nntpd* again.

```
$ telnet localhost nntp
Trying 127.0.0.1...
Connected to loalhost
Escape characters is '^]'.
201 vstout NNTP[auth] server version 1.5.11t (16 November 1991) ready
at Sun Feb 6 16:02:32 1194 (no posting)
IHAVE <msg@id>
435 Got it.
QUIT
```

This conversation shows the proper reaction of *nntpd*; the message "`Got it`" tells you that it already has this article. If you get a message of "`335 Ok`" instead, the lookup in the history file failed for some reason. Terminate the conversation by typing Ctrl-D. You can check what has gone wrong by checking the system log; *nntpd* logs all kinds of messages to the *daemon* facility of *syslog*. An incompatible *dbm* library usually manifests itself in a message complaining that *dbminit* failed.

Chapter 19

Newsreader Configuration

Newsreaders are intended to offer the user functionality that allows her to access the functions of the news system easily, like posting articles, or skimming the contents of a newsgroup in a comfortable way. The quality of this interface is subject of endless flame wars.

There are a couple of newsreaders available which have been ported to Linux. Below I will describe the basic setup for the three most popular ones, namely *tin*, *trn*, and *nn*.

One of the most effective newsreaders is

```
$ find /var/spool/news -name '[0-9]*' -exec cat {} \; | more
```

This is the way UNIX die-hards read their news.

The majority of newsreaders, however, are much more sophisticated. They usually offer a full-screen interface with separate levels for displaying all groups the user has subscribed to, for displaying an overview of all articles in one group, and for individual articles.

At the newsgroup level, most newsreaders display a list of articles, showing their subject line, and the author. In big groups, it is impossible for the user to keep track of articles relating to each other, although it is possible to identify responses to earlier articles.

A response usually repeats the original article's subject, prepending it with "Re: ". Additionally, the message id of the article it is a direct follow-up to may be given in the References: header line. Sorting articles by these two criteria generates small clusters (in fact, trees) of articles, which are called *threads*. One of the tasks in writing a newsreader is devising an efficient scheme of threading, because the time required for this is proportional to the square of the number of articles.

Here, we will not dig any further into how the user interfaces are built. All newsreaders currently available for Linux have a good help function, so you ought to get along.

In the following, we will only deal with administrative tasks. Most of these relate to the creation of threads databases and accounting.

19.1   *tin* Configuration

The most versatile newsreader with respect to threading is *tin*. It was written by Iain Lea and is loosely modeled on an older newsreader named *tass*.[1] It does its threading when the user enters the newsgroup, and it is pretty fast at this unless you're doing this via NNTP.

---

[1] Written by Rich Skrenta.

On an 486DX50, it takes roughly 30 seconds to thread 1000 articles when reading directly from disk. Over NNTP to a loaded news server, this would be somewhere above 5 minutes.[2] You may improve this by regularly updating your index file with the -u option, or by invoking *tin* with the -U option.

Usually, *tin* dumps its threading databases in the user's home directory below *.tin/index*. This may however be costly in terms of resources, so that you should want to keep a single copy of them in a central location. This may be achieved by making *tin* setuid to **news**, for example, or some entirely unprivileged account.[3] *tin* will then keep all thread databases below */var/spool/news/.index*. For any file access or shell escape, it will reset its effective uid to the real uid of the user who invoked it.[4]

A better solution is to install the *tind* indexing daemon that runs as a daemon and regularly updates the index files. This daemon is however not included in any release of Linux, so you would have to compile it yourself. If you are running a LAN with a central news server, you may even run *tind* on the server and have all clients retrieve the index files via NNTP. This, of course, requires an extension to NNTP. Patches for *nntpd* that implement this extension are included in the *tin* source.

The version of *tin* included in some Linux distributions has no NNTP support compiled in, but most do have it now. When invoked as *rtin* or with the -r option, *tin* tries to connect to the NNTP server specified in the file */etc/nntpserver* or in the NNTPSERVER environment variable. The *nntpserver* file simply contains the server's name on a single line.

19.2   *trn* Configuration

trn is the successor to an older newsreader, too, namely *rn* (which means *read news*). The "t" in its name stands for "threaded". It was written by Wayne Davidson.

Unlike *tin*, *trn* has no provision for generating its threading database at run-time. Instead, it uses those prepared by a program called *mthreads* that has to be invoked regularly from *cron* to update the index files.

Not running *mthreads*, however, doesn't mean you cannot access new articles, it only means you will have all those "Novell buys out Linux!!" articles scattered across your article selection menu, instead of a single thread you may easily skip.

To turn on threading for particular newsgroups, *mthreads* is invoked with the list of newsgroups on the command line. The list is made up in exactly the same fashion as the one in the *sys* file:

```
mthreads comp,rec,!rec.games.go
```

will enable threading for all of **comp** and **rec**, except for **rec.games.go** (people who play Go don't need fancy threads). After that, you simply invoke it without any option at all to make it thread any newly arrived articles. Threading of all groups found in your *active* file can be turned on by invoking *mthreads* with a group list of **all**.

If you're receiving news during the night, you will customarily run *mthreads* once in the morning, but you can also to do so more frequently if needed. Sites that have very heavy traffic may want to run *mthreads* in daemon mode. When it is started at boot time using the -d option, it puts itself in the background, and wakes up every 10 minutes to check if there are any newly-arrived articles, and threads them. To run *mthreads* in daemon mode, put the following line in your *rc.news* script:

```
/usr/local/bin/rn/mthreads -deav
```

---

[2]Things improve drastically if the NNTP server does the threading itself, and lets the client retrieve the threads databases; INN-1.4 does this, for instance.

[3]However, do *not* use **nobody** for this. As a rule, no files or commands whatsoever should be associated with this user.

[4]This is the reason why you will get ugly error messages when invoking it as super user. But then, you shouldn't work as **root**, anyway.

The -a option makes *mthread* automatically turn on threading for new groups as they are created; -v enables verbose log messages to *mthreads'* log file, *mt.log* in the directory where you have *trn* installed.

Old articles no longer available must be removed from the index files regularly. By default, only articles whose number is below the low water mark will be removed.[5] Articles above this number who have been expired nevertheless (because the oldest article has been assigned an long expiry date by an Expires: header field) may be removed by giving *mthreads* the -e option to force an "enhanced" expiry run. When *mthreads* is running in daemon mode, the -e option makes it put in such an enhanced expiry run once a day, shortly after midnight.

19.3 *nn* Configuration

nn, written by Kim F. Storm, claims to be a newsreader whose ultimate goal is not to read news. It's name stands for "No News", and its motto is "No news is good news. *nn* is better."

To achieve this ambitious goal, *nn* comes along with a large assortment of maintenance tools that not only allow generation of threads, but also extensive checks on the consistency of these databases, accounting, gathering of usage statistics, and access restrictions. There is also an administration program called *nnadmin*, which allows you to perform these tasks interactively. It is very intuitive, hence we will not dwell on these aspects, and only deal with the generation of the index files.

The *nn* threads database manager is called *nnmaster*. It is usually run as a daemon, started from the *rc.news* or *rc.inet2* script. It is invoked as

```
/usr/local/lib/nn/nnmaster -l -r -C
```

This enables threading for all newsgroups present in your *active* file.

Equivalently, you may invoke *nnmaster* periodically from *cron*, giving it a list of groups to act upon. This list is very similar to the subscription list in the *sys* file, except that it uses blanks instead of commas. Instead of the fake group name **all**, an empty argument of " " should be used to denote all groups. A sample invocation is

```
# /usr/local/lib/nn/nnmaster !rec.games.go rec comp
```

Note that the order is significant here: The leftmost group specification that matches always wins. Thus, if we had put *!rec.games.go* after *rec*, all articles from this group had been threaded nevertheless.

nn offers several methods to remove expired articles from its databases. The first is to update the database by scanning the news group directories and discarding the entries whose corresponding article is no longer available. This is the default operation obtained by invoking *nnmaster* with the -E option. It is reasonably fast unless you're doing this via NNTP.

Method 2 behaves exactly like a default expiry run of *mthreads*, in that it only removes those entries that refer to articles whose number is below the low water mark in the *active* file. It may be enabled using the -e option.

Finally, a third strategy is to discard the entire database and recollect all articles. This may be done by giving -E3 to *nnmaster*.

The list of groups to be expired is given by the -F option in the same fashion as above. However, if you have *nnmaster* running as daemon, you must kill it (using -k) before expiry can take place, and to re-start it with the original options afterwards. Thus the proper command to run expire on all groups using method 1 is:

```
# nnmaster -kF ""
# nnmaster -lrC
```

---

[5]Note that C news doesn't update this low water mark automatically; you have to run *updatemin* to do so. Please refer to chapter 17.

There are many more flags that may be used to fine-tune the behavior of *nn*. If you are concerned about removing bad articles or digestifying article digests, read the *nnmaster* manual page.

nnmaster relies on a file named *GROUPS*, which is located in */usr/local/lib/nn*. If it does not exist initially, it is created. For each newsgroup, it contains a line that begins with the group's name, optionally followed by a time stamp, and flags. You may edit these flags to enable certain behavior for the group in question, but you may not change the order in which the groups appear.[6] The flags allowed and their effects are detailed in the *nnmaster* manual page, too.

---

[6]This is because their order has to agree with that of the entries in the (binary) *MASTER* file.

Appendix A

A Null Printer Cable for PLIP

To make a Null Printer Cable for use with a PLIP connection, you need two 25-pin connectors (called DB-25) and some 11-conductor cable. The cable must be at most 15 meters long.

If you look at the connector, you should be able to read tiny numbers at the base of each pin, from 1 for the pin top left (if you hold the broader side up) to 25 for the pin bottom right. For the Null Printer cable, you have to connect the following pins of both connectors with each other:

```
D0        2—15   ERROR
D1        3—13   SLCT
D2        4—12   PAPOUT
D3        5—10   ACK
D4        6—11   BUSY
GROUND   25—25   GROUND
ERROR    15— 2   D0
SLCT     13— 3   D1
PAPOUT   12— 4   D2
ACK      10— 5   D3
BUSY     11— 6   D4
```

All remaining pins remain unconnected. If the cable is shielded, the shield should be connected to the DB-25's metallic shell on one end only.

Appendix B

Sample *smail* Configuration Files

This section shows sample configuration files for a UUCP leaf site on a local area network. They are based on the sample files included in the source distribution of *smail-3.1.28*. Although I make a feeble attempt to explain how these files work, you are advised to read the very fine *smail(8)* manual page, which discusses these files in great length. Once you've understood the basic idea behind *smail* configuration, it's worthwhile reading. It's easy!

The first file shown is the *routers* file, which describes a set of routers to *smail*. When *smail* has to deliver a message to a given address, it hands the address to all routers in turn, until one of them matches it. Matching here means that the router finds the destination host in its database, be it the *paths* file, */etc/hosts*, or whatever routing mechanism the router interfaces to.

Entries in *smail* configuration files always begin with a unique name identifying the router, transport, or director. They are followed by a list of attributes that define its behavior. This list consists of a set of global attributes, such as the *driver* used, and private attributes that are only understood by that particular driver. Attributes are separated by commas, while the sets of global and private attributes are separated from each other using a semicolon.

To make these fine distinctions clear, assume you want to maintain two separate pathalias files; one containing the routing information for your domain, and a second one containing global routing information, probably genpratzed from the UUCP maps. With *smail*, you can now specify two routers in the *routers* file, both of which use the *pathalias* driver. This driver looks up hostnames in a pathalias database. It expects to be given the name of the file in a private attribute:

```
#
# pathalias database for intra-domain routing
domain_paths:
        driver=pathalias,          # look up host in a paths file
        transport=uux;             # if matched, deliver over UUCP

        file=paths/domain,         # file is /usr/lib/smail/paths/domain
        proto=lsearch,             # file is unsorted (linear search)
        optional,                  # ignore if the file does not exist
        required=vbrew.com,        # look up only *.vbrew.com hosts

#
# pathalias database for routing to hosts outside our domain
world_paths:
        driver=pathalias,          # look up host in a paths file
        transport=uux;             # if matched, deliver over UUCP

        file=paths/world,          # file is /usr/lib/smail/paths/world
        proto=bsearch,             # file is sorted with sort(1)
        optional,                  # ignore if the file does not exist
        -required,                 # no required domains
        domain=uucp,               # strip ending ".uucp" before searching
```

The second global attribute given in each of the two *routers* entries above defines the transport that should be used when the router matches the address. In our case, the message will be delivered using the *uux* transport. Transports are defined in the *transports* file, which is exlained below.

You can fine-tune by which transport a message will be delivered if you specify a mathod file instead of the *transports* attribute. Method files provide a mapping from target hostnames to transports. We won't deal with them here.

The following *routers* file defines routers for a local area network that query the resolver library. On an Internet host, however, you would want to use a router that handles MX records. You should therefore uncomment the alternative *inet_bind* router that uses *smail*'s builtin BIND driver.

In an environment that mixes UUCP and TCP/IP, you may encounterthe problem that you have hosts in your */etc/hosts* file that you have only occasional SLIP or PPP contact with. Usually, you would still want to send any mail for them over UUCP. To prevent the *inet_hosts* driver from matching these hosts, you have to put them into the *paths/force* file. This is another pathalias-style database, and is consulted before *smail* queries the resolver.

```
# A sample /usr/lib/smail/routers file
#
# force - force UUCP delivery to certain hosts, even when
#        they are in our /etc/hosts
force:
        driver=pathalias,            # look up host in a paths file
        transport=uux;               # if matched, deliver over UUCP

        file=paths/force,            # file is /usr/lib/smail/paths/force
        optional,                    # ignore if the file does not exist
        proto=lsearch,               # file is unsorted (linear search)
        -required,                   # no required domains
        domain=uucp,                 # strip ending ".uucp" before searching

# inet_addrs - match domain literals containing literal
#        IP addresses, such as in janet@[191.72.2.1]
inet_addrs:
        driver=gethostbyaddr,        # driver to match IP domain literals
        transport=smtp;              # deliver using SMTP over TCP/IP

        fail_if_error,               # fail if address is malformed
        check_for_local,             # deliver directly if host is ourself

# inet_hosts - match hostnames with gethostbyname(3N)
#        Comment this out if you wish to use the BIND version instead.
inet_hosts:
        driver=gethostbyname,        # match hosts with the library function
        transport=smtp;              # use default SMTP

        -required,                   # no required domains
        -domain,                     # no defined domain suffixes
        -only_local_domain,          # don't restrict to defined domains

# inet_hosts - alternate version using BIND to access the DNS
#inet_hosts:
#       driver=bind,                 # use built-in BIND driver
#       transport=smtp;              # use TCP/IP SMTP for delivery
#
#       defnames,                    # use standard domain searching
```

```
#         defer_no_connect,           # try again if the nameserver is down
#         -local_mx_okay,             # fail (don't pass through) an MX
#                                     # to the local host


#
# pathalias database for intra-domain routing
domain_paths:
        driver=pathalias,            # look up host in a paths file
        transport=uux;               # if matched, deliver over UUCP

        file=paths/domain,           # file is /usr/lib/smail/paths/domain
        proto=lsearch,               # file is unsorted (linear search)
        optional,                    # ignore if the file does not exist
        required=vbrew.com,          # look up only *.vbrew.com hosts

#
# pathalias database for routing to hosts outside our domain
world_paths:
        driver=pathalias,            # look up host in a paths file
        transport=uux;               # if matched, deliver over UUCP

        file=paths/world,            # file is /usr/lib/smail/paths/world
        proto=bsearch,               # file is sorted with sort(1)
        optional,                    # ignore if the file does not exist
        -required,                   # no required domains
        domain=uucp,                 # strip ending ".uucp" before searching


# smart_host - a partically specified smarthost director
#       If the smart_path attribute is not defined in
#       /usr/lib/smail/config, this router is ignored.
#       The transport attribute is overridden by the global
#       smart_transport variable
smart_host:
        driver=smarthost,            # special-case driver
        transport=uux;               # by default deliver over UUCP

        -path,                       # use smart_path config file variable
```

The handling of mail for local addresses is configured in the *directors* file. It is made up just like the *routers* file, with a list of entries that define a director each. Directors do *not* deliver a message, they merely perform all the redirection that is possible, for instance through aliases, mail forwarding, and the like.

When delivering mail to a local address, such as **janet**, *smail* passes the usr name to all directors in turn. If a director matches, it either specifies a transport the message should be delivered by (for instance, to the user's mailbox file), or generates a new address (for instance, after evaluating an alias).

Because of the security issues involved, directors usually do a lot of checking of whether the files they use may be compromised or not. Addresses obtained in a somewhat dubious way (for instance from a world-writable *aliases* file) are flagged as unsecure. Some transport drivers will turn down such addresses, for instance the transport that delivers a message to a file.

Apart from this, *smail* also *associates a user* with each address. Any write or read operations are performed as the user. For delivery to, say **janet**'s mailbox, the address is of course associated with **janet**. Other addresses, such as those obtained from the *aliases* file, have other users associated from them, for instance, the **nobody** user.

For details of these features, please refer to the *smail(8)* manpage.

```
# A sample /usr/lib/smail/directors file

# aliasinclude - expand ":include:filename" addresses produced
#         by alias files
aliasinclude:
        driver=aliasinclude,        # use this special-case driver
        nobody;                     # access file as nobody user if unsecure

        copysecure,                 # get permissions from alias director
        copyowners,                 # get owners from alias director

# forwardinclude - expand ":include:filename" addrs produced
#         by forward files
forwardinclude:
        driver=forwardinclude,      # use this special-case driver
        nobody;                     # access file as nobody user if unsecure

        checkpath,                  # check path accessibility
        copysecure,                 # get perms from forwarding director
        copyowners,                 # get owners from forwarding director

# aliases - search for alias expansions stored in a database
aliases:
        driver=aliasfile,           # general-purpose aliasing director
        -nobody,                    # all addresses are associated
                                    # with nobody by default anyway
        sender_okay,                # don't remove sender from expansions
        owner=owner-$user;          # problems go to an owner address

        file=/usr/lib/aliases,      # default: sendmail compatible
        modemask=002,               # should not be globally writable
        optional,                   # ignore if file does not exist
        proto=lsearch,              # unsorted ASCII file

# dotforward - expand .forward files in user home directories
dotforward:
        driver=forwardfile,         # general-purpose forwarding director
        owner=real-$user,           # problems go to the user's mailbox
        nobody,                     # use nobody user, if unsecure
        sender_okay;                # sender never removed from expansion

        file=~/.forward,            # .forward file in home directories
        checkowner,                 # the user can own this file
        owners=root,                # or root can own the file
        modemask=002,               # it should not be globally writable
        caution=0-10:uucp:daemon,   # don't run things as root or daemons
        # be extra careful of remotely accessible home directories
        unsecure="~ftp:~uucp:~nuucp:/tmp:/usr/tmp",

# forwardto - expand a "Forward to " line at the top of
#         the user's mailbox file
forwardto:
        driver=forwardfile,
```

```
        owner=Postmaster,          # errors go to Postmaster
        nobody,                    # use nobody user, if unsecure
        sender_okay;               # don't remove sender from expansion

        file=/var/spool/mail/${lc:user}, # location of user's mailbox
        forwardto,                 # enable "Forward to " check
        checkowner,                # the user can own this file
        owners=root,               # or root can own the file
        modemask=0002,             # under System V, group mail can write
        caution=0-10:uucp:daemon,  # don't run things as root or daemons

# user - match users on the local host with delivery to their mailboxes
user:   driver=user;               # driver to match usernames

        transport=local,           # local transport goes to mailboxes

# real_user - match usernames when prefixed with the string "real-"
real_user:
        driver=user;               # driver to match usernames

        transport=local,           # local transport goes to mailboxes
        prefix="real-",            # for example, match real-root

# lists - expand mailing lists stored below /usr/lib/smail/lists
lists:  driver=forwardfile,
        caution,                   # flag all addresses with caution
        nobody,                    # and then associate the nobody user
        sender_okay,               # do NOT remove the sender
        owner=owner-$user;         # the list owner

        # map the name of the mailing list to lower case
        file=lists/${lc:user},
```

After successfully routing or directing a message, *smail* hands the message to the transport specified by the router or director that matched the address. These transports are defined in the *transports* file. Again, a transport is defined by a set of global and private options.

The most important option defined by each entry is driver that handles the transport, for instance the *pipe* driver, which invokes the command specified in the *cmd* attribute. Apart from this, there are a number of global attributes a transport may use, that perform various transformations on the message header, and possibly message body. The *return_path* attribute, for instance, makes the transport insert a *return_path* field in the message header The *unix_from_hack* attribute makes it precede every occurrence of the word From at the beginning of a line with a > sign.

```
# A sample /usr/lib/smail/transports file

# local - deliver mail to local users
local:  driver=appendfile,         # append message to a file
        return_path,               # include a Return-Path: field
        from,                      # supply a From_ envelope line
        unix_from_hack,            # insert > before From in body
        local;                     # use local forms for delivery

        file=/var/spool/mail/${lc:user}, # location of mailbox files
        group=mail,                # group to own file for System V
```

```
        mode=0660,                   # group mail can access
        suffix="\n",                 # append an extra newline

# pipe - deliver mail to shell commands
pipe:   driver=pipe,                 # pipe message to another program
        return_path,                 # include a Return-Path: field
        from,                        # supply a From_ envelope line
        unix_from_hack,              # insert > before From in body
        local;                       # use local forms for delivery

        cmd="/bin/sh -c $user",      # send address to the Bourne Shell
        parent_env,                  # environment info from parent addr
        pipe_as_user,                # use user-id associated with address
        ignore_status,               # ignore a non-zero exit status
        ignore_write_errors,         # ignore write errors, i.e., broken pipe
        umask=0022,                  # umask for child process
        -log_output,                 # do not log stdout/stderr


# file - deliver mail to files
file:   driver=appendfile,
        return_path,                 # include a Return-Path: field
        from,                        # supply a From_ envelope line
        unix_from_hack,              # insert > before From in body
        local;                       # use local forms for delivery

        file=$user,                  # file is taken from address
        append_as_user,              # use user-id associated with address
        expand_user,                 # expand ~ and $ within address
        suffix="\n",                 # append an extra newline
        mode=0600,                   # set permissions to 600

# uux - deliver to the rmail program on a remote UUCP site
uux:    driver=pipe,
        uucp,                        # use UUCP-style addressing forms
        from,                        # supply a From_ envelope line
        max_addrs=5,                 # at most 5 addresses per invocation
        max_chars=200;               # at most 200 chars of addresses

        cmd="/usr/bin/uux - -r -a$sender -g$grade $host!rmail $(($user)$)",
        pipe_as_sender,              # have uucp logs contain caller
        log_output,                  # save error output for bounce messages
#       defer_child_errors,          # retry if uux returns an error

# demand - deliver to a remote rmail program, polling immediately
demand: driver=pipe,
        uucp,                        # use UUCP-style addressing forms
        from,                        # supply a From_ envelope line
        max_addrs=5,                 # at most 5 addresses per invocation
        max_chars=200;               # at most 200 chars of addresses

        cmd="/usr/bin/uux - -a$sender -g$grade $host!rmail $(($user)$)",
        pipe_as_sender,              # have uucp logs contain caller
        log_output,                  # save error output for bounce messages
#       defer_child_errors,          # retry if uux returns an error
```

```
# hbsmtp - half-baked BSMTP. The output files must
#         be processed regularly and sent out via UUCP.
hbsmtp: driver=appendfile,
        inet,                       # use RFC 822-addressing
        hbsmtp,                     # batched SMTP w/o HELO and QUIT
        -max_addrs, -max_chars;     # no limit on number of addresses

        file="/var/spool/smail/hbsmtp/$host",
        user=root,                  # file is owned by root
        mode=0600,                  # only read-/writeable by root.

# smtp - deliver using SMTP over TCP/IP
smtp:   driver=tcpsmtp,
        inet,
        -max_addrs, -max_chars;     # no limit on number of addresses

        short_timeout=5m,           # timeout for short operations
        long_timeout=2h,            # timeout for longer SMTP operations
        service=smtp,               # connect to this service port
# For internet use: uncomment the below 4 lines
#       use_bind,                   # resolve MX and multiple A records
#       defnames,                   # use standard domain searching
#       defer_no_connect,           # try again if the nameserver is down
#       -local_mx_okay,             # fail an MX to the local host
```

Appendix C

The GNU General Public License

Printed below is the GNU General Public License (the *GPL* or *copyleft*), under which Linux is licensed. It is reproduced here to clear up some of the confusion about Linux's copyright status—Linux is *not* shareware, and it is *not* in the public domain. The bulk of the Linux kernel is copyright ©1993 by Linus Torvalds, and other software and parts of the kernel are copyrighted by their authors. Thus, Linux *is* copyrighted, however, you may redistribute it under the terms of the GPL printed below.

GNU GENERAL PUBLIC LICENSE
Version 2, June 1991

Copyright (C) 1989, 1991 Free Software Foundation, Inc. 675 Mass Ave, Cambridge, MA 02139, USA Everyone is permitted to copy and distribute verbatim copies of this license document, but changing it is not allowed.

C.1 Preamble

The licenses for most software are designed to take away your freedom to share and change it. By contrast, the GNU General Public License is intended to guarantee your freedom to share and change free software–to make sure the software is free for all its users. This General Public License applies to most of the Free Software Foundation's software and to any other program whose authors commit to using it. (Some other Free Software Foundation software is covered by the GNU Library General Public License instead.) You can apply it to your programs, too.

When we speak of free software, we are referring to freedom, not price. Our General Public Licenses are designed to make sure that you have the freedom to distribute copies of free software (and charge for this service if you wish), that you receive source code or can get it if you want it, that you can change the software or use pieces of it in new free programs; and that you know you can do these things.

To protect your rights, we need to make restrictions that forbid anyone to deny you these rights or to ask you to surrender the rights. These restrictions translate to certain responsibilities for you if you distribute copies of the software, or if you modify it.

For example, if you distribute copies of such a program, whether gratis or for a fee, you must give the recipients all the rights that you have. You must make sure that they, too, receive or can get the source code. And you must show them these terms so they know their rights.

We protect your rights with two steps: (1) copyright the software, and (2) offer you this license which gives you legal permission to copy, distribute and/or modify the software.

Also, for each author's protection and ours, we want to make certain that everyone understands that there is no warranty for this free software. If the software is modified by someone else and passed on, we want its recipients to know that what they have is not the original, so that any problems introduced by others will not reflect on the original authors' reputations.

Finally, any free program is threatened constantly by software patents. We wish to avoid the danger that redistributors of a free program will individually obtain patent licenses, in effect making the program proprietary. To prevent this, we

227

have made it clear that any patent must be licensed for everyone's free use or not licensed at all.

The precise terms and conditions for copying, distribution and modification follow.

C.2   Terms and Conditions for Copying, Distribution, and Modification

0. This License applies to any program or other work which contains a notice placed by the copyright holder saying it may be distributed under the terms of this General Public License. The "Program", below, refers to any such program or work, and a "work based on the Program" means either the Program or any derivative work under copyright law: that is to say, a work containing the Program or a portion of it, either verbatim or with modifications and/or translated into another language. (Hereinafter, translation is included without limitation in the term "modification".) Each licensee is addressed as "you".

    Activities other than copying, distribution and modification are not covered by this License; they are outside its scope. The act of running the Program is not restricted, and the output from the Program is covered only if its contents constitute a work based on the Program (independent of having been made by running the Program). Whether that is true depends on what the Program does.

1. You may copy and distribute verbatim copies of the Program's source code as you receive it, in any medium, provided that you conspicuously and appropriately publish on each copy an appropriate copyright notice and disclaimer of warranty; keep intact all the notices that refer to this License and to the absence of any warranty; and give any other recipients of the Program a copy of this License along with the Program.

    You may charge a fee for the physical act of transferring a copy, and you may at your option offer warranty protection in exchange for a fee.

2. You may modify your copy or copies of the Program or any portion of it, thus forming a work based on the Program, and copy and distribute such modifications or work under the terms of Section 1 above, provided that you also meet all of these conditions:

    a. You must cause the modified files to carry prominent notices stating that you changed the files and the date of any change.

    b. You must cause any work that you distribute or publish, that in whole or in part contains or is derived from the Program or any part thereof, to be licensed as a whole at no charge to all third parties under the terms of this License.

    c. If the modified program normally reads commands interactively when run, you must cause it, when started running for such interactive use in the most ordinary way, to print or display an announcement including an appropriate copyright notice and a notice that there is no warranty (or else, saying that you provide a warranty) and that users may redistribute the program under these conditions, and telling the user how to view a copy of this License. (Exception: if the Program itself is interactive but does not normally print such an announcement, your work based on the Program is not required to print an announcement.)

    These requirements apply to the modified work as a whole. If identifiable sections of that work are not derived from the Program, and can be reasonably considered independent and separate works in themselves, then this License, and its terms, do not apply to those sections when you distribute them as separate works. But when you distribute the same sections as part of a whole which is a work based on the Program, the distribution of the whole must be on the terms of this License, whose permissions for other licensees extend to the entire whole, and thus to each and every part regardless of who wrote it.

    Thus, it is not the intent of this section to claim rights or contest your rights to work written entirely by you; rather, the intent is to exercise the right to control the distribution of derivative or collective works based on the Program.

    In addition, mere aggregation of another work not based on the Program with the Program (or with a work based on the Program) on a volume of a storage or distribution medium does not bring the other work under the scope of this License.

3. You may copy and distribute the Program (or a work based on it, under Section 2) in object code or executable form under the terms of Sections 1 and 2 above provided that you also do one of the following:

a. Accompany it with the complete corresponding machine-readable source code, which must be distributed under the terms of Sections 1 and 2 above on a medium customarily used for software interchange; or,

b. Accompany it with a written offer, valid for at least three years, to give any third party, for a charge no more than your cost of physically performing source distribution, a complete machine-readable copy of the corresponding source code, to be distributed under the terms of Sections 1 and 2 above on a medium customarily used for software interchange; or,

c. Accompany it with the information you received as to the offer to distribute corresponding source code. (This alternative is allowed only for noncommercial distribution and only if you received the program in object code or executable form with such an offer, in accord with Subsection b above.)

The source code for a work means the preferred form of the work for making modifications to it. For an executable work, complete source code means all the source code for all modules it contains, plus any associated interface definition files, plus the scripts used to control compilation and installation of the executable. However, as a special exception, the source code distributed need not include anything that is normally distributed (in either source or binary form) with the major components (compiler, kernel, and so on) of the operating system on which the executable runs, unless that component itself accompanies the executable.

If distribution of executable or object code is made by offering access to copy from a designated place, then offering equivalent access to copy the source code from the same place counts as distribution of the source code, even though third parties are not compelled to copy the source along with the object code.

4. You may not copy, modify, sublicense, or distribute the Program except as expressly provided under this License. Any attempt otherwise to copy, modify, sublicense or distribute the Program is void, and will automatically terminate your rights under this License. However, parties who have received copies, or rights, from you under this License will not have their licenses terminated so long as such parties remain in full compliance.

5. You are not required to accept this License, since you have not signed it. However, nothing else grants you permission to modify or distribute the Program or its derivative works. These actions are prohibited by law if you do not accept this License. Therefore, by modifying or distributing the Program (or any work based on the Program), you indicate your acceptance of this License to do so, and all its terms and conditions for copying, distributing or modifying the Program or works based on it.

6. Each time you redistribute the Program (or any work based on the Program), the recipient automatically receives a license from the original licensor to copy, distribute or modify the Program subject to these terms and conditions. You may not impose any further restrictions on the recipients' exercise of the rights granted herein. You are not responsible for enforcing compliance by third parties to this License.

7. If, as a consequence of a court judgment or allegation of patent infringement or for any other reason (not limited to patent issues), conditions are imposed on you (whether by court order, agreement or otherwise) that contradict the conditions of this License, they do not excuse you from the conditions of this License. If you cannot distribute so as to satisfy simultaneously your obligations under this License and any other pertinent obligations, then as a consequence you may not distribute the Program at all. For example, if a patent license would not permit royalty-free redistribution of the Program by all those who receive copies directly or indirectly through you, then the only way you could satisfy both it and this License would be to refrain entirely from distribution of the Program.

If any portion of this section is held invalid or unenforceable under any particular circumstance, the balance of the section is intended to apply and the section as a whole is intended to apply in other circumstances.

It is not the purpose of this section to induce you to infringe any patents or other property right claims or to contest validity of any such claims; this section has the sole purpose of protecting the integrity of the free software distribution system, which is implemented by public license practices. Many people have made generous contributions to the wide range of software distributed through that system in reliance on consistent application of that system; it is up to the author/donor to decide if he or she is willing to distribute software through any other system and a licensee cannot impose that choice.

This section is intended to make thoroughly clear what is believed to be a consequence of the rest of this License.

8. If the distribution and/or use of the Program is restricted in certain countries either by patents or by copyrighted interfaces, the original copyright holder who places the Program under this License may add an explicit geographical distribution limitation excluding those countries, so that distribution is permitted only in or among countries not thus excluded. In such case, this License incorporates the limitation as if written in the body of this License.

9. The Free Software Foundation may publish revised and/or new versions of the General Public License from time to time. Such new versions will be similar in spirit to the present version, but may differ in detail to address new problems or concerns.

   Each version is given a distinguishing version number. If the Program specifies a version number of this License which applies to it and "any later version", you have the option of following the terms and conditions either of that version or of any later version published by the Free Software Foundation. If the Program does not specify a version number of this License, you may choose any version ever published by the Free Software Foundation.

10. If you wish to incorporate parts of the Program into other free programs whose distribution conditions are different, write to the author to ask for permission. For software which is copyrighted by the Free Software Foundation, write to the Free Software Foundation; we sometimes make exceptions for this. Our decision will be guided by the two goals of preserving the free status of all derivatives of our free software and of promoting the sharing and reuse of software generally.

NO WARRANTY

11. BECAUSE THE PROGRAM IS LICENSED FREE OF CHARGE, THERE IS NO WARRANTY FOR THE PRO-GRAM, TO THE EXTENT PERMITTED BY APPLICABLE LAW. EXCEPT WHEN OTHERWISE STATED IN WRITING THE COPYRIGHT HOLDERS AND/OR OTHER PARTIES PROVIDE THE PROGRAM "AS IS" WITHOUT WARRANTY OF ANY KIND, EITHER EXPRESSED OR IMPLIED, INCLUDING, BUT NOT LIMITED TO, THE IMPLIED WARRANTIES OF MERCHANTABILITY AND FITNESS FOR A PARTICU-LAR PURPOSE. THE ENTIRE RISK AS TO THE QUALITY AND PERFORMANCE OF THE PROGRAM IS WITH YOU. SHOULD THE PROGRAM PROVE DEFECTIVE, YOU ASSUME THE COST OF ALL NECES-SARY SERVICING, REPAIR OR CORRECTION.

12. IN NO EVENT UNLESS REQUIRED BY APPLICABLE LAW OR AGREED TO IN WRITING WILL ANY COPYRIGHT HOLDER, OR ANY OTHER PARTY WHO MAY MODIFY AND/OR REDISTRIBUTE THE PROGRAM AS PERMITTED ABOVE, BE LIABLE TO YOU FOR DAMAGES, INCLUDING ANY GENER-AL, SPECIAL, INCIDENTAL OR CONSEQUENTIAL DAMAGES ARISING OUT OF THE USE OR INABIL-ITY TO USE THE PROGRAM (INCLUDING BUT NOT LIMITED TO LOSS OF DATA OR DATA BEING RENDERED INACCURATE OR LOSSES SUSTAINED BY YOU OR THIRD PARTIES OR A FAILURE OF THE PROGRAM TO OPERATE WITH ANY OTHER PROGRAMS), EVEN IF SUCH HOLDER OR OTHER PARTY HAS BEEN ADVISED OF THE POSSIBILITY OF SUCH DAMAGES.

END OF TERMS AND CONDITIONS

C.3   Appendix: How to Apply These Terms to Your New Programs

If you develop a new program, and you want it to be of the greatest possible use to the public, the best way to achieve this is to make it free software which everyone can redistribute and change under these terms.

To do so, attach the following notices to the program. It is safest to attach them to the start of each source file to most effectively convey the exclusion of warranty; and each file should have at least the "copyright" line and a pointer to where the full notice is found.

   ⟨one line to give the program's name and a brief idea of what it does.⟩ Copyright ©19yy ⟨name of author⟩

   This program is free software; you can redistribute it and/or modify it under the terms of the GNU General Public License as published by the Free Software Foundation; either version 2 of the License, or (at your option) any later version.

   This program is distributed in the hope that it will be useful, but WITHOUT ANY WARRANTY; without even the implied warranty of MERCHANTABILITY or FITNESS FOR A PARTICULAR PURPOSE. See the GNU General Public License for more details.

   You should have received a copy of the GNU General Public License along with this program; if not, write to the Free Software Foundation, Inc., 675 Mass Ave, Cambridge, MA 02139, USA.

Also add information on how to contact you by electronic and paper mail.

If the program is interactive, make it output a short notice like this when it starts in an interactive mode:

```
Gnomovision version 69, Copyright (C) 19yy name of author Gnomovision
comes with ABSOLUTELY NO WARRANTY; for details type 'show w'.  This
is free software, and you are welcome to redistribute it under certain
conditions; type 'show c' for details.
```

The hypothetical commands 'show w' and 'show c' should show the appropriate parts of the General Public License. Of course, the commands you use may be called something other than 'show w' and 'show c'; they could even be mouse-clicks or menu items–whatever suits your program.

You should also get your employer (if you work as a programmer) or your school, if any, to sign a "copyright disclaimer" for the program, if necessary. Here is a sample; alter the names:

Yoyodyne, Inc., hereby disclaims all copyright interest in the program 'Gnomovision' (which makes passes at compilers) written by James Hacker.

⟨*signature of Ty Coon*⟩, 1 April 1989 Ty Coon, President of Vice

This General Public License does not permit incorporating your program into proprietary programs. If your program is a subroutine library, you may consider it more useful to permit linking proprietary applications with the library. If this is what you want to do, use the GNU Library General Public License instead of this License.

Glossary

[Meta: This could use more entries, and a little polishing. Feel free to make suggestions.]

An enormous difficulty in networking is to remember what all the abbreviations and terms one encounters really mean. Here's a list of those used frequently throughout the guide, along with a short explanation.

ACU	Automatic Call Unit. A modem.[1]
ARP	Address Resolution Protocol. Used to map IP addresses to Ethernet addresses.
ARPA	Advanced Research Project Agency, later DARPA. Founder of the Internet.
ARPANET	The ancestor of today's Internet; an experimental network funded by the U.S. Defense Advanced Research Project Agency (DARPA).
Assigned Numbers	The title of an *RFC* published regularly that lists the publicly allocated numbers used for various things in TCP/IP networking. For example, it contains the list of all port numbers of well-known services like *rlogin*, *telnet*, etc. The most recent release of this document is RFC 1340.
bang path	In UUCP networks, a special notation for the path from one UUCP site to another. The name derives from the use of exclamation marks ('bangs') to separate the host names. Example: **foo!bar!ernie!bert** denotes a path to host **bert**, travelling (in this order) **foo**, **bar**, and **ernie**.
BBS	Bulletin Board System. A dial-up mailbox system.
BGP	Border Gateway Protocol. A protocol for exchanging routing information between autonomous systems.
BIND	The Berkeley Internet Name Domain server. An implementation of a DNS server.
BNU	Basic Networking Utilities. This is the most common UUCP variety at the moment. It is also known as HoneyDanBer UUCP. This name is derived from the authors' names: P. Honeyman, D.A. Novitz, and B.E. Redman.
broadcast network	A network that allows one station to address a datagram to all other stations on the network simultaneously.
BSD	Berkeley Software Distribution. A UNIX flavor.
canonical hostname	A host's primary name within the Domain Name System. This is the host's only name that has an A record associated with it, and which is returned when performing a reverse lookup.
CCITT	Comiteé Consultatif International de Télégraphique et Téléphonique. An International organization of telephone services, etc.
CSLIP	Compressed Serial Line IP. A protocol for exchanging IP packets over a serial line, using header compression of most TCP/IP datagrams.
DNS	Domain name system. This is a distributed database used on the Internet for mapping of host names to IP addresses.
EGP	External Gateway Protocol. A protocol for exchanging routing information between autonomous systems.
Ethernet	In colloquial terms, the name of a sort of network equipment. Technically, Ethernet is part of a set of standards set forth by the IEEE. The Ethernet hardware uses a single piece of cable, frequently coax cable, to connect a number of hosts, and allows transfer rates of up to 10Mbps. The Ethernet protocol

---

[1] Alternatively: A teenager with a telephone.

defines the manner in which hosts may communicate over this cable.[2]

FQDN	Fully Qualified Domain Name. A hostname with a domain name tacked onto it, so that it is a valid index into the Domain Name database.
FTP	File Transfer Protocol. The protocol one of the best-known file transfer service is based on and named after.
FYI	"For Your Information." Series of documents with informal information on Internet topics.
GMU	Groucho Marx University. Fictitious University used as an example throughout this book.
GNU	GNU's not Unix – this recursive acronym is the name of a project by the Free Software Association to provide a coherent set of UNIX-tools that may be used and copied free of charge. All GNU software is covered by a special Copyright notice, also called the GNU General Public License (GPL), or Copyleft. The GPL is reproduced in section C.
HoneyDanBer	The name of a UUCP variety. See also BNU.
host	Generally, a network node: something that is able to receive and transmit network messages. This will usually be a computer, but you can also think of X-Terminals, or smart printers.
ICMP	Internet Control Message Protocol. A networking protocol used by IP to return error information to the sending host, etc.
IEEE	Institute of Electrical and Eletronics Engineers. Another standards organization. From a UNIX user's point of view, their most important achievement are probably the POSIX standards which define aspects of a UNIX systems, ranging from system call interfaces and semantics to administration tools.
	Apart from this, the IEEE developed the specifications for Ethernet, Token Ring, and Token Bus networks. A widely-used standard for binary representation of real numbers is also due to the IEEE.
IETF	Internet Engineering Task Force.
internet	A computer network formed of a collection of individual smaller networks.
Internet	A particular world-wide internet.
IP	Internet Protocol. A networking protocol.
ISO	International Standards Organization.
ISDN	Integrated Services Digital Network. New telecommunications technology using digital instead of analogue circuitry.
LAN	Local Area Network. A small computer network.
MX	Mail Exchanger. A DNS resource record type used for marking a host as mail gateway for a domain.
network, packet-switched	A variety of networks that provide instantaneous forwarding of data by all data up in small packets, which are tramsported to their destination individually. Packet-switched networks rely on permanent or semi-permanent connections.
network, store-and-forward	They are pretty much the opposite of packet-switched networks. These networks transfer data as entire files, and don't use permanent connections. Instead, hosts conect to each other at certain intervals only, and transfer all data at once. This requires that data be stored intermediately until a connection is established.
NFS	Network File System. A standard networking protocol and software suite for accessing data on remote disks transparently.
NIS	Network Information System. An RPC-based application that allows to share configuration files such as the password file between several hosts. See also the entry under YP.
NNTP	Network News Transfer Protocol. Used to transfer news over TCP network connections.

---

[2] As an aside, the Ethernet *protocol* commonly used by TCP/IP is *not* exactly the same as IEEE 802.3. Ethernet frames have a type field where IEEE 802.3 frames have a length field.

octet	On the Internet, the technical term referring to a quantity of eight bits. It is used rather than *byte*, because there are machines on the Internet that have byte sizes other than eight bits.
OSI	Open Systems Interconnection. An ISO standard on network software.
path	Often used in UUCP networks as a synonym for *route*. Also see *bang path*.
PLIP	Parallel Line IP. A protocol for exchanging IP packets over a parallel line such as a printer port.
port, TCP or UDP	Ports are TCP's and UDP's abstraction of a service endpoint. Before a process can provide or access some networking service, it must claim (bind) a port. Together with the hosts' IP addresses, ports uniquely identify the two peers of a TCP connection.
portmapper	The portmapper is the mediator between the program numbers used by RPC as an identification of individual RPC servers, and the TCP and UDP port numbers those services are listening to.
PPP	The point-to-point protocol. PPP is a flexible and fast link-layer protocol to send various network protocols such as IP or IPX across a point-to-point connection. Apart from being used on serial (modem) links, PPP can also be employed as the link-level protocol on top of ISDN.
RARP	Reverse Address Resolution Protocol. It permits hosts to find out their IP address at boot time.
resolver	This is a library responsible for mapping hostnames to IP addresses and vice versa.
resource record	This is the basic unit of information in the DNS database, commonly abbreviated as RR. Each record has a certain type and class associated with it, for instance a record mapping a host name to an IP address has a type of A (for address), and a class of IN (for the Internet Protocol).
reverse lookup	The act of looking up a host's name based on a given IP address. Within DNS, this is done by looking up the host's IP address in the **in-addr.arpa** domain.
RFC	Request For Comments. Series of documents describing Internet standards.
RIP	Routing Information Protocol. This is a routing protocol used dynamically adjust routes inside a (small) network.
route	The sequence of hosts a piece of information has to travel from the originating host to the destination host. Finding an appropriate route is also called *routing*.
routing daemon	In larger networks, network topology changes are hard to adapt to manually, so facilities are used to distribute current routing information to the network's member hosts. This is called dynamic routing; the routing information is exchanged by *routing daemons* running on central hosts in the network. The protocols they employ are called *routing protocols*.
RPC	Remote Procedure Call. Protocol for executing procdures inside a process on a remote host.
RR	Short for *resource record*.
RS-232	This is a very common standard for serial interfaces.
RTS/CTS	A colloquial name for the hardware handshake performed by two devices communicating over RS-232. The name derives from the two cicuits involved, RTS ("Ready To Send"), and CTS ("Clear To Send").
RTM Internet Worm	A Virus-like program that used several flaws in VMS and BSD 4.3 Unix to spread through the Internet. Several "mistakes" in the program caused it to multiply without bound, and so effectively bringing down large parts of the Internet. RTM are the author's initials (Robert T. Morris), which he left in the program.
site	An agglomeration of hosts which, to the outside, behave almost like a single network node. For example, when speaking from an Internet point of view, one would call a Groucho Marx University a site, regardless of the complexity of its interior network.
SLIP	Serial Line IP. This is a protocol for exchanging IP packets over a serial line, see also CSLIP.
SMTP	Simple Mail Transfer Protocol. Used for mail transport over TCP connections, but also for mail batches transported over UUCP links (batched SMTP).
SOA	Start of Authority. A DNS resource record type.

System V	A UNIX flavor.
TCP	Transmission Control Protocol. A networking protocol.
TCP/IP	Sloppy description of the Internet protocol suite as a whole.
UDP	User Datagram Protocol. A networking protocol.
UUCP	Unix to Unix Copy. A suite of network transport commands for dial-up networks.
Version 2 UUCP	An aging UUCP variety.
virtual beer	Every Linuxer's favorite drink. The first mention of virtual beer I remember was in the release note of the Linux 0.98.X kernel, where Linus listed the "Oxford Beer Trolls" in his credits section for sending along some virtual beer.
well-known services	This term is frequently used to refer to common networking services such as *telnet* and *rlogin*. In a more technical sense, it describes all services that have been assigned an official port number in the "Assigned Numbers" RFC.
YP	Yellow Pages. An older name for NIS which is no longer used, because Yellow Pages is a trademark of British Telecom. Nevertheless, most NIS utilities have retained names with a prefix of *yp*.

Annotated Bibliography

Books

The following is a list of books you might want to read to if you want to know more about some of the topics covered in the Networking Guide. It is not very complete or systematic, I just happen to have read them and find them quite useful. Any additions to, and enhancement of this list are welcome.

General Books on the Internet

[Kehoe92]   Brendan P. Kehoe: *Zen and the Art of the Internet*. .

"Zen" was one of, if not *the* first Internet Guide, introducing the novice user to the various trades, services and the folklore of the Internet. Being a 100-page tome, it covered topics ranging from email to Usenet news to the Internet Worm. It is available via anonymous FTP from many FTP servers, and may be freely distributed and printed. A printed copy is also available from Prentice-Hall.

Administration Issues

[Hunt92]   Craig Hunt: *TCP/IP Network Administration*. O'Reilly and Associates, 1992. ISBN 0-937175-82-X.

If the Linux Network Administrators' Guide is not enough for you, get this book. It deals with everything from obtaining an IP address to troubleshooting your network to security issues.

Its focus is on setting up TCP/IP, that is, interface configuration, the setup of routing, and name resolution. It includes a detailed description of the facilities offered by the routing daemons routed and gated, which supply dynamic routing.

It also describes the configuration of application programs and network daemons, such as inetd, the r commands, NIS, and NFS.

The appendix has a detailed reference of gated, and named, and a description of Berkeley's sendmail configuration.

[Stern92]   Hal Stern: *Managing NIS and NFS*. O'Reilly and Associates, 1992. ISBN 0-937175-75-7.

This is a companion book to Craig Hunt's "TCP/IP Network Administration" book. It covers the use of NIS, the Network Information System, and NFS, the Network File System, in extenso, including the configuration of an automounter, and PC/NFS.

[OReilly89]   Tim O'Reilly and Grace Todino: *Managing UUCP and Usenet, 10th ed*. O'Reilly and Associates, 1992. ISBN 0-93717593-5.

This is the standard book on UUCP networking. It covers Version 2 UUCP as well as BNU. It helps you to set up your UUCP node from the start, giving practical tips and solutions for many problems, like testing the connection, or writing good chat scripts. It also deals with more exotic topics, like how to set up a travelling UUCP node, or the subtleties present in different flavors of UUCP.

The second part of the book deals with Usenet and netnews software. It explains the configuration of both Bnews (version 2.11) and C news, and introduces you to netnews maintenance tasks.

[Spaf93]   Gene Spafford and Simson Garfinkel: *Practical UNIX Security*. O'Reilly and Associates, 1992. ISBN 0-937175-72-2.

This is a must-have for everyone who manages a system with network access, and for others as well. The book discusses all issues relevant to computer security, ranging the basic security features UNIX offers physical security. Although you should strive to secure all parts of your system, the discussion of networks and security is the most interesting part of the book in our context. Apart from basic security policies that concern the Berkeley services (*telnet*, *rlogin*, etc), NFS and NIS, it also deals with enhanced security features like MIT's Kerberos, Sun's Secure RPC, and the use of firewalls to shield your network from attacks from the Internet.

[AlbitzLiu92]   Paul Albitz and Cricket Liu: *DNS and BIND*. O'Reilly and Associates, 1992. ISBN 1-56592-010-4.

This book is useful for all those that have to manage DNS name service. It explains all features of DNS in great detail and give examples that make even those BIND options plausible that appear outright weird at first sight. I found it fun to read, and really learned a lot from it.

[NISPlus]   Rick Ramsey: *All about Administering NIS+*. Prentice-Hall, 1993. ISBN 0-13-068800-2.

The Background

The following is a list of books that might be of interest to people who want to know more about *how* TCP/IP and its applications work, but don't want to read RFCs.

[Stevens90]   Richard W. Stevens: *UNIX Network Programming*. Prentice-Hall International, 1990. ISBN 0-13-949876-X.

This is probably *the* most widely used book on TCP/IP network programming, which, at the same time, tells you a lot about the nuts and bolts of the Internet Protocols.[3]

---

[3]Note that Stevens has just written a new TCP/IP, called *TCP/IP Illustrated, Volume 1, The Protocols*, published by Addison Wesley. I didn't have the time to look at it, though.

[Tanen89]	Andrew S. Tanenbaum: *Computer Networks*. Prentice-Hall International, 1989. ISBN 0-13-166836-6[4].

This book gives you a very good insight into general networking issues. Using the OSI Reference Model, it explains the design issues of each layer, and the algorithms that may be used to achieve these. At each layer, the implementations of several networks, among them the ARPAnet, are compared to each other.

The only drawback this book has is the abundance of abbreviations, which sometimes makes it hard to follow what the author says. But this is probably inherent to networking.

[Comer88]	Douglas R. Comer: *Internetworking with TCP/IP: Principles, Protocols, and Architecture.* Prentice-Hall International, 1988.

HOWTOs

The following is an excerpt of the HOWTO-INDEX, version 2.0 (17 March 1994), written by Matt Welsh.

What are Linux HOWTOs?

Linux HOWTOs are short online documents which describe in detail a certain aspect of configuring or using the Linux system. For example, there is the Installation HOWTO, which gives instructions on installing Linux, and the Mail HOWTO, which describes how to set up and configure mail under Linux. Other examples include the NET-2-HOWTO (previously the NET-2-FAQ) and the Printing HOWTO.

Information in HOWTOs is generally more detailed and in-depth than what can be squeezed into the Linux FAQ. For this reason, the Linux FAQ is being rewritten. A large amount of the information contained therein will be relegated to various HOWTO documents. The FAQ will be a shorter list of frequently asked questions about Linux, covering small specific topics. Most of the "useful" information in the FAQ will now be covered in the HOWTOs.

HOWTOs are comprehensive documents—much like an FAQ but generally not in question-and-answer format. However, many HOWTOs contain an FAQ section at the end. For example, the NET-2-FAQ has been renamed to the NET-2-HOWTO, because it wasn't in question-and-answer format. However, you will see the NET-2-HOWTO named as the NET-2-FAQ in many places. The two docs are one and the same.

Where to get Linux HOWTOs

HOWTOs can be retrieved via anonymous FTP from the following sites:

- *sunsite.unc.edu:/pub/Linux/docs/HOWTO*
- *tsx-11.mit.edu:/pub/linux/docs/HOWTO*

as well as the many mirror sites, which are listed in the Linux META-FAQ (see below).

The Index, printed below, lists the currently available HOWTOs.

HOWTOs are also posted regularly to the newsgroups **comp.os.linux** and **comp.os.linux.announce**. In addition, a number of the HOWTOs will be crossposted to **news.answers**. Therefore, you can find the Linux HOWTOs on the **news.answers** archive site **rtfm.mit.edu**.

---

[4]The ISBN under which it is available in North America might be different.

HOWTO Index

The following Linux HOWTOs are currently available.

- Linux Busmouse HOWTO, by **mike@starbug.apana.org.au** (Mike Battersby). Information on bus mouse compatibility with Linux.
- Linux CDROM HOWTO, by **tranter@software.mitel.com** (Jeff Tranter). Information on CD-ROM drive compatibility for Linux.
- Linux DOSEMU HOWTO, by **deisher@enws125.EAS.ASU.EDU** (Michael E. Deisher). HOWTO about the Linux MS-DOS Emulator, DOSEMU.
- Linux Distribution HOWTO, by **mdw@sunsite.unc.edu** (Matt Welsh). A list of mail order distributions and other commercial services.
- Linux Ethernet HOWTO, by Paul Gortmaker **gpg109@rsphysse.anu.edu.au**. Information on Ethernet hardware compatibility for Linux.
- Linux Ftape HOWTO, by **ftape@mic.dth.dk** (Linux ftape-HOWTO maintainer). Information on ftape drive compatibility with Linux.
- Linux HOWTO Index, by **mdw@sunsite.unc.edu** (Matt Welsh). Index of HOWTO documents about Linux.
- Linux Hardware Compatibility HOWTO, by **erc@apple.com** (Ed Carp). A near-extensive list of hardware known to work with Linux.
- Linux Installation HOWTO, by **mdw@sunsite.unc.edu** (Matt Welsh). How to obtain and install the Linux software.
- Linux JE-HOWTO, by Yasuhiro Yamazaki **hiro@rainbow.physics.utoronto.ca**. Information on JE, a set of Japanese language extensions for Linux.
- Linux Keystroke HOWTO, by Zenon Fortuna (**zenon@netcom.com**). HOWTO bind macro actions to keystrokes under Linux.
- Linux MGR HOWTO, by **broman@Np.nosc.mil** (Vincent Broman). Information on the MGR graphics interface for Linux.
- Linux Electronic Mail HOWTO, by **vince@victrola.wa.com** (Vince Skahan). Information on Linux-based mail servers and clients.
- Linux NET-2 HOWTO, by **terryd@extro.ucc.su.oz.au** (Terry Dawson). HOWTO configure TCP/IP networking, SLIP, PLIP, and PPP under Linux.
- Linux News HOWTO, by **vince@victrola.wa.com** (Vince Skahan). Information on USENET news server and client software for Linux.
- Linux PCI-HOWTO, by Michael Will **michaelw@desaster.student.uni-tuebingen.de**. Information on PCI-architecture compatibility with Linux.
- Linux Printing HOWTO, by **gtaylor@cs.tufts.edu** (Grant Taylor). HOWTO on printing software for Linux.
- Linux SCSI HOWTO, by Drew Eckhardt **drew@kinglear.cs.Colorado.EDU**. Information on SCSI driver compatibility with Linux.
- Linux Serial HOWTO, by **gregh@cc.gatech.edu** (Greg Hankins). Information on use of serial devices and communications software.
- Linux Sound HOWTO, by **tranter@software.mitel.com** (Jeff Tranter). Sound hardware and software for the Linux operating system.
- Linux Term HOWTO, by Bill Reynolds **bill@goshawk.lanl.gov**. HOWTO use the 'term' communications package on Linux systems.
- Linux Tips HOWTO, by Vince Reed **reedv@rpi.edu**. HOWTO on miscellaneous tips and tricks for Linux.
- Linux UUCP HOWTO, by **vince@victrola.wa.com** (Vince Skahan). Information on UUCP software for Linux.
- Linux XFree86 HOWTO, by **geyer@polyhymnia.iwr.uni-heidelberg.de** (Helmut Geyer). HOWTO on installation of XFree86 (X11R5) for Linux.

Miscellaneous and Legalese

RFCs

The following is a list of RFCs mentioned throughout this book. All RFCs are available via anonymous FTP from **nic.ddn.mil**, **ftp.uu.net**. To obtain an RFC via email, send a message to **service@nic.ddn.mil**, putting the request `send RFC-number.TXT` in the subject header line.

1340   Assigned Numbers, *Postel, J.*, and *Reynolds, J.* The Assigned Numbers RFC defines the meaning of numbers used in various protocols, such as the port numbers standard TCP and UDP servers are known to listen on, and the protocol numbers used in the IP datagram header.

1144   Compressing TCP/IP headers for low-speed serial links, *Jacobson, V.* This document describes the algorithm used to compress TCP/IP headers in CSLIP and PPP. Very worthwhile reading!

1033   Domain Administrators Operations Guide, *Lottor, M.* Together with its companion RFCs, RFC 1034 and RFC 1035, this is the definitive source on DNS, the Domain Name System.

1034   Domain Names - Concepts and Facilities, *Mockapetris, P.V.* A companion to RFC 1033.

1035   Domain names - Implementation and Specification, *Mockapetris, P.V.* A companion to RFC 1033.

974   Mail Routing and the Domain System, *Partridge, C.* This RFC describes mail routing on the Internet. Read this for the full story about MX records...

977   Network News Transfer Protocol, *Kantor, B.*, and *Lapsley, P.* The definition of NNTP, the common news transport used on the Internet.

1094   NFS: Network File System Protocol specification, *Nowicki, B.* The formal specification of the NFS and mount protocols (version 2).

1055   Nonstandard for Transmission of IP Datagrams over Serial Lines: SLIP, *Romkey, J.L.* Describes SLIP, the Serial Line Internet Protocol.

1057   RPC: Remote Procedure Call Protocol Specification: Version 2, *Sun Microsystems, Inc*

1058   Routing Information Protocol, *Hedrick, C.L.* Describes RIP, which is used to exchange dynamic routing information within LANs and MANs.

821   Simple Mail Transfer Protocol, *Postel, J.B.* Defines SMTP, the mail transport protocol over TCP/IP.

1036   Standard for the Interchange of USENET messages, *Adams, R.*, and *Horton, M.R.* This RFC describes the format of Usenet News messages, and how they are exchanged on the Internet as well as on UUCP networks. A revision of this RFC is expected to be released sometime soon.

822   Standard for the Format of ARPA Internet text messages, *Crocker, D.* This is the definitive source of wisdom regarding, well, RFC-conformant mail. Everyone knows it, few have really read it.

968   Twas the Night Before Start-up, *Cerf, V.* Who says the heroes of networking remain unsung?

Part II

"The Linux System Administrators' Guide" by Lars Wirzenius

Date: 1999/02/08 17:38:10 Version 0.6.1 An introduction to system administration of a Linux system for novices.

Dedication This place is dedicated to a future dedication.

Source and pre-formatted versions available The source code and and other machine readable formats of this book can be found on the Internet via anonymous FTP at the Linux Documentation Project home page http://sunsite.unc.edu/LDP/, or at the home page of this book at http://www.iki.fi/liw/linux/sag/. Available are at least PostScript and TeX .DVI formats.

SysAdmin Guide

1 Introduction

> In the beginning, the file was without form, and void; and emptiness was upon the face of the bits. And the Fingers of the Author moved upon the face of the keyboard. And the Author said, Let there be words, and there were words.

This manual, the Linux System Administrators' Guide, describes the system administration aspects of using Linux. It is intended for people who know next to nothing about system administration (as in "what is it?"), but who have already mastered at least the basics of normal usage. This manual also doesn't tell you how to install Linux; that is described in the Installation and Getting Started document. See below for more information about Linux manuals.

System administration is all the things that one has to do to keep a computer system in a useable shape. It includes things like backing up files (and restoring them if necessary), installing new programs, creating accounts for users (and deleting them when no longer needed), making certain that the filesystem is not corrupted, and so on. If a computer were, say, a house, system administration would be called maintenance, and would include cleaning, fixing broken windows, and other such things. System administration is not called maintenance, because that would be too simple. [5]

The structure of this manual is such that many of the chapters should be usable independently, so that if you need information about, say, backups, you can read just that chapter. This hopefully makes the book easier to use as a reference manual, and makes it possible to read just a small part when needed, instead of having to read everything. However, this manual is first and foremost a tutorial, and a reference manual only as a lucky coincidence.

This manual is not intended to be used completely by itself. Plenty of the rest of the Linux documentation is also important for system administrators. After all, a system administrator is just a user with special privileges and duties. A very important resource are the manual pages, which should always be consulted when a command is not familiar.

While this manual is targeted at Linux, a general principle has been that it should be useful with other UNIX based operating systems as well. Unfortunately, since there is so much variance between different versions of UNIX in general,

---

[5]There are some people who do call it that, but that's just because they have never read this manual, poor things.

and in system administration in particular, there is little hope to cover all variants. Even covering all possibilities for Linux is difficult, due to the nature of its development.

There is no one official Linux distribution, so different people have different setups, and many people have a setup they have built up themselves. This book is not targeted at any one distribution, even though I use the Debian GNU/Linux system almost exclusively. When possible, I have tried to point out differences, and explain several alternatives.

I have tried to describe how things work, rather than just listing "five easy steps" for each task. This means that there is much information here that is not necessary for everyone, but those parts are marked as such and can be skipped if you use a preconfigured system. Reading everything will, naturally, increase your understanding of the system and should make using and administering it more pleasant.

Like all other Linux related development, the work was done on a volunteer basis: I did it because I thought it might be fun and because I felt it should be done. However, like all volunteer work, there is a limit to how much effort I have been able to spend, and also on how much knowledge and experience I have. This means that the manual is not necessarily as good as it would be if a wizard had been paid handsomely to write it and had spent a few years to perfect it. I think, of course, that it is pretty nice, but be warned.

One particular point where I have cut corners is that I have not covered very thoroughly many things that are already well documented in other freely available manuals. This applies especially to program specific documentation, such as all the details of using mkfs}. I only describe the purpose of the program, and as much of its usage as is necessary for the purposes of this manual. For further information, I refer the gentle reader to these other manuals. Usually, all of the referred to documentation is part of the full Linux documentation set.

While I have tried to make this manual as good as possible, I would really like to hear from you if you have any ideas on how to make it better. Bad language, factual errors, ideas for new areas to cover, rewritten sections, information about how various UNIX versions do things, I am interested in all of it. My contact information is available via the World Wide Web at http://www.iki.fi/liw/mail-to-lasu.html.

Many people have helped me with this book, directly or indirectly. I would like to especially thank Matt Welsh for inspiration and LDP leadership, Andy Oram for getting me to work again with much-valued feedback, Olaf Kirch for showing me that it can be done, and Adam Richter at Yggdrasil and others for showing me that other people can find it interesting as well.

Stephen Tweedie, H.˜Peter Anvin, R\'emy Card, Theodore Ts'o, and Stephen Tweedie have let me borrow their work (and thus make the book look thicker and much more impressive): a comparison between the xia and ext2 filesystems, the device list and a description of the ext2 filesystem. These aren't part of the book any more. I am most grateful for this, and very apologetic for the earlier versions that sometimes lacked proper attribution.

In addition, I would like to thank Mark Komarinski for sending his material in 1993 and the many system administration columns in Linux Journal. They are quite informative and inspirational.

Many useful comments have been sent by a large number of people. My miniature black hole of an archive doesn't let me find all their names, but some of them are, in alphabetical order: Paul Caprioli, Ales Cepek, Marie-France Declerfayt, Dave Dobson, Olaf Flebbe, Helmut Geyer, Larry Greenfield and his father, Stephen Harris, Jyrki Havia, Jim Haynes, York Lam, Timothy Andrew Lister, Jim Lynch, Michael J. Micek, Jacob Navia, Dan Poirier, Daniel Quinlan, Jouni K Seppänen, Philippe Steindl, G.B.\ Stotte. My apologies to anyone I have forgotten.

META need to add typographical conventsions and LDP blurb here.

1.1   The Linux Documentation Project

The Linux Documentation Project, or LDP, is a loose team of writers, proofreaders, and editors who are working together to provide complete documentation for the Linux operating system. The overall coordinator of the project is Greg Hankins.This manual is one in a set of several being distributed by the LDP, including a Linux Users' Guide, System Administrators' Guide, Network Administrators' Guide, and Kernel Hackers' Guide. These manuals are all available in source format, .dvi format, and postscript output by anonymous FTP from sunsite.unc.edu, in the directory /pub/Linux/docs/LDP.We encourage anyone with a penchant for writing or editing to join us in improving Linux documentation. If you have Internet e-mail access, you can contact Greg Hankins at gregh@sunsite.unc.edu.

2   Overview of a Linux System

God looked over everything he had made, and saw that it was very good.

(Genesis 1:31)

This chapter gives an overview of a Linux system. First, the major services provided by the operating system are described. Then, the programs that implement these services are described with a considerable lack of detail. The purpose of this chapter is to give an understanding of the system as a whole, so that each part is described in detail elsewhere.

2.1   Various parts of an operating system

A UNIX operating system consists of a kernel and some system programs. There are also some application programs} for doing work. The kernel is the heart of the operating system. [6]

It keeps track of files on the disk, starts programs and runs them concurrently, assigns memory and other resources to various processes, receives packets from and sends packets to the network, and so on. The kernel does very little by itself, but it provides tools with which all services can be built. It also prevents anyone from accessing the hardware directly, forcing everyone to use the tools it provides. This way the kernel provides some protection for users from each other. The tools provided by the kernel are used via system calls; see manual page section 2 for more information on these. The system programs use the tools provided by the kernel to implement the various services required from an operating system. System programs, and all other programs, run 'on top of the kernel', in what is called the user mode. The difference between system and application programs is one of intent: applications are intended for getting useful things done (or for playing, if it happens to be a game), whereas system programs are needed to get the system working. A word processor is an application; telnet is a system program. The difference is often somewhat blurry, however, and is important only to compulsive categorizers.An operating system can also contain compilers and their corresponding libraries (GCC and the C library in particular under Linux), although not all programming languages need be part of the operating system. Documentation, and sometimes even games, can also be part of it. Traditionally, the operating system has been defined by the contents of the installation tape or disks; with Linux it is not as clear since it is spread all over the FTP sites of the world.

2.2   Important parts of the kernel

The Linux kernel consists of several important parts: process management, memory management, hardware device drivers, filesystem drivers, network management, and various other bits and pieces. Figure 2.2 shows some of them. Probably the most important parts of the kernel (nothing else works without them) are memory management and process management. Memory management takes care of assigning memory areas and swap space areas to processes, parts of the kernel, and for the buffer cache. Process management creates processes, and implements multitasking by switching the active process on the processor.At the lowest level, the kernel contains a hardware device driver for each kind of hardware it supports. Since the world is full of different kinds of hardware, the number of hardware device drivers is large. There are often many otherwise similar pieces of hardware that differ in how they are controlled by software. The similarities make it possible to have general classes of drivers that support similar operations; each member of the class has the same interface to the rest of the kernel but differs in what it needs to do to implement them. For example, all disk drivers look alike to the rest of the kernel, i.e., they all have operations like 'initialize the drive', 'read sector N', and 'write sector N'.Some software services provided by the kernel itself have similar properties, and can therefore be abstracted into classes. For example, the various network protocols have been abstracted into one programming interface, the BSD socket library. Another example is the virtual filesystem (VFS) layer that abstracts the filesystem operations away from their implementation. Each filesystem type provides an implementation of each filesystem operation. When some entity tries to use a filesystem, the request goes via the VFS, which routes the request to the proper filesystem driver.

---

[6]In fact, it is often mistakenly considered to be the operating system itself, but it is not. An operating system provides many more services than a plain kernel.

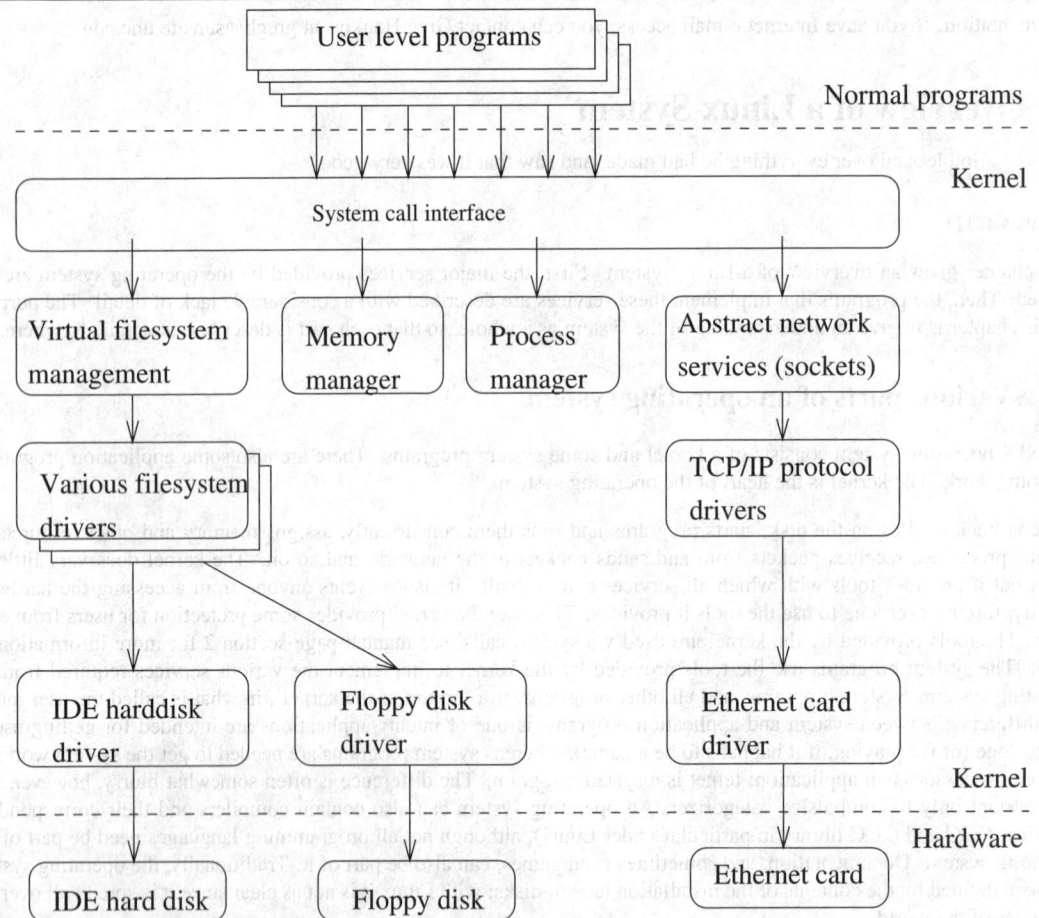

Figure 1: Some of the more important parts of the Linux kernel

2.3 Major services in a UNIX system

This section describes some of the more important UNIX services, but without much detail. They are described more thoroughly in later chapters.

2.3.1 init

The single most important service in a UNIX system is provided by init. init is started as the first process of every UNIX system, as the last thing the kernel does when it boots. When init starts, it continues the boot process by doing various startup chores (checking and mounting filesystems, starting daemons, etc).The exact list of things that init does depends on which flavor it is; there are several to choose from. init usually provides the concept of single user mode, in which no one can log in and root uses a shell at the console; the usual mode is called multiuser mode. Some flavors generalize this as run levels; single and multiuser modes are considered to be two run levels, and there can be additional ones as well, for example, to run X on the console.In normal operation, init makes sure getty is working (to allow users to log in), and to adopt orphan processes (processes whose parent has died; in UNIX all processes must be in a single tree, so orphans must be adopted).When the system is shut down, it is init that is in charge of killing all other processes, unmounting all filesystems and stopping the processor, along with anything else it has been configured to do.

2.3.2 Logins from terminals

Logins from terminals (via serial lines) and the console (when not running X) are provided by the getty program. init starts a separate instance of getty for each terminal for which logins are to be allowed. getty reads the username and runs the login program, which reads the password. If the username and password are correct, login runs the shell. When the shell terminates, i.e., the user logs out, or when login terminated because the username and password didn't match, init notices this and starts a new instance of getty. The kernel has no notion of logins, this is all handled by the system programs.

2.3.3 Syslog

The kernel and many system programs produce error, warning, and other messages. It is often important that these messages can be viewed later, even much later, so they should be written to a file. The program doing this is syslog. It can be configured to sort the messages to different files according to writer or degree of importance. For example, kernel messages are often directed to a separate file from the others, since kernel messages are often more important and need to be read regularly to spot problems.

2.3.4 Periodic command execution: cron and at

Both users and system administrators often need to run commands periodically. For example, the system administrator might want to run a command to clean the directories with temporary files (/tmp and /var/tmp) from old files, to keep the disks from filling up, since not all programs clean up after themselves correctly.The cron service is set up to do this. Each user has a crontab file, where he lists the commands he wants to execute and the times they should be executed. The cron daemon takes care of starting the commands when specified.The at service is similar to cron, but it is once only: the command is executed at the given time, but it is not repeated.

2.3.5 Graphical user interface

UNIX and Linux don't incorporate the user interface into the kernel; instead, they let it be implemented by user level programs. This applies for both text mode and graphical environments.This arrangement makes the system more flexible, but has the disadvantage that it is simple to implement a different user interface for each program, making the system harder to learn.The graphical environment primarily used with Linux is called the X Window System (X for short). X also does not implement a user interface; it only implements a window system, i.e., tools with which a graphical user interface can be implemented. The three most popular user interface styles implemented over X are Athena, Motif, and Open Look.

2.3.6 Networking

Networking is the act of connecting two or more computers so that they can communicate with each other. The actual methods of connecting and communicating are slightly complicated, but the end result is very useful.UNIX operating systems have many networking features. Most basic services (filesystems, printing, backups, etc) can be done over the network. This can make system administration easier, since it allows centralized administration, while still reaping in the benefits of microcomputing and distributed computing, such as lower costs and better fault tolerance.However, this book merely glances at networking; see the Linux Network Administrators' Guide for more information, including a basic description of how networks operate.

2.3.7 Network logins

Network logins work a little differently than normal logins. There is a separate physical serial line for each terminal via which it is possible to log in. For each person logging in via the network, there is a separate virtual network connection, and there can be any number of these. [7]

It is therefore not possible to run a separate getty for each possible virtual connection. There are also several different ways to log in via a network, telnet and rlogin being the major ones in TCP/IP networks.Network logins have, instead of a herd of gettys, a single daemon per way of logging in (telnet and rlogin have separate daemons) that listens for all

---

[7]Well, at least there can be many. Network bandwidth still being a scarce resource, there is still some practical upper limit to the number of concurrent logins via one network connection.

SysAdmin Guide

incoming login attempts. When it notices one, it starts a new instance of itself to handle that single attempt; the original instance continues to listen for other attempts. The new instance works similarly to getty.

2.3.8 Network file systems

One of the more useful things that can be done with networking services is sharing files via a network file system. The one usually used is called the Network File System, or NFS, developed by Sun.With a network file system any file operations done by a program on one machine are sent over the network to another computer. This fools the program to think that all the files on the other computer are actually on the computer the program is running on. This makes information sharing extremely simple, since it requires no modifications to programs.

2.3.9 Mail

Electronic mail is usually the most important method for communicating via computer. An electronic letter is stored in a file using a special format, and special mail programs are used to send and read the letters.Each user has an incoming mailbox (a file in the special format), where all new mail is stored. When someone sends mail, the mail program locates the receiver's mailbox and appends the letter to the mailbox file. If the receiver's mailbox is in another machine, the letter is sent to the other machine, which delivers it to the mailbox as it best sees fit.The mail system consists of many programs. The delivery of mail to local or remote mailboxes is done by one program (the mail transfer agent or MTA, e.g., sendmail or smail), while the programs users use are many and varied (mail user agent or MUA, e.g., pine or elm). The mailboxes are usually stored in /var/spool/mail.

2.3.10 Printing

Only one person can use a printer at one time, but it is uneconomical not to share printers between users. The printer is therefore managed by software that implements a print queue: all print jobs are put into a queue and whenever the printer is done with one job, the next one is sent to it automatically. This relieves the users from organizing the print queue and fighting over control of the printer. [8]

The print queue software also spools the printouts on disk, i.e., the text is kept in a file while the job is in the queue. This allows an application program to spit out the print jobs quickly to the print queue software; the application does not have to wait until the job is actually printed to continue. This is really convenient, since it allows one to print out one version, and not have to wait for it to be printed before one can make a completely revised new version.

2.3.11 The filesystem layout

The filesystem is divided into many parts; usually along the lines of a root filesystem with /bin, /lib, /etc, /dev, and a few others; a /usr filesystem with programs and unchanging data; a /var filesystem with changing data (such as log files); and a /home filesystem for everyone's personal files. Depending on the hardware configuration and the decisions of the system administrator, the division can be different; it can even be all in one filesystem. describes the filesystem layout in some detail; the Linux Filesystem Standard covers it in somewhat more detail.

Overview of the Directory Tree

> Two days later, there was Pooh, sitting on his branch, dangling his legs, and there, beside him, were four
> pots of honey...

(A.A.\ Milne) This chapter describes the important parts of a standard Linux directory tree, based on the FSSTND filesystem standard. It outlines the normal way of breaking the directory tree into separate filesystems with different purposes and gives the motivation behind this particular split. Some alternative ways of splitting are also described.

---

[8]Instead, they form a new queue at the printer, waiting for their printouts, since no one ever seems to be able to get the queue software to know exactly when anyone's printout is really finished. This is a great boost to intra-office social relations.

2.4   Background

This chapter is loosely based on the Linux filesystem standard, FSSTND, version 1.2 (see the bibliography), which attempts to set a standard for how the directory tree in a Linux system is organized. Such a standard has the advantage that it will be easier to write or port software for Linux, and to administer Linux machines, since everything will be in their usual places. There is no authority behind the standard that forces anyone to comply with it, but it has got the support of most, if not all, Linux distributions. It is not a good idea to break with the FSSTND without very compelling reasons. The FSSTND attempts to follow Unix tradition and current trends, making Linux systems familiar to those with experience with other Unix systems, and vice versa.This chapter is not as detailed as the FSSTND. A system administrator should also read the FSSTND for a complete understanding.This chapter does not explain all files in detail. The intention is not to describe every file, but to give an overview of the system from a filesystem point of view. Further information on each file is available elsewhere in this manual or the manual pages.The full directory tree is intended to be breakable into smaller parts, each on its own disk or partition, to accomodate to disk size limits and to ease backup and other system administration. The major parts are the root, /usr, /var, and /home filesystems (see Figure 2.4). Each part has a different purpose. The directory tree has been designed so that it works well in a network of Linux machines which may share some parts of the filesystems over a read-only device (e.g., a CD-ROM), or over the network with NFS. The roles of the different parts of the directory tree are described below.

The root filesystem is specific for each machine (it is generally stored on a local disk, although it could be a ramdisk or network drive as well) and contains the files that are necessary for booting the system up, and to bring it up to such a state that the other filesystems may be mounted. The contents of the root filesystem will therefore be sufficient for the single user state. It will also contain tools for fixing a broken system, and for recovering lost files from backups. The /usr filesystem contains all commands, libraries, manual pages, and other unchanging files needed during normal operation. No files in /usr should be specific for any given machine, nor should they be modified during normal use. This allows the files to be shared over the network, which can be cost-effective since it saves disk space (there can easily be hundreds of megabytes in /usr), and can make administration easier (only the master /usr needs to be changed when updating an application, not each machine separately). Even if the filesystem is on a local disk, it could be mounted read-only, to lessen the chance of filesystem corruption during a crash.The /var filesystem contains files that change, such as spool directories (for mail, news, printers, etc), log files, formatted manual pages, and temporary files. Traditionally everything in /var has been somewhere below /usr, but that made it impossible to mount /usr read-only. The /home filesystem contains the users' home directories, i.e., all the real data on the system. Separating home directories to their own directory tree or filesystem makes backups easier; the other parts often do not have to be backed up, or at least not as often (they seldom change). A big /home might have to be broken on several filesystems, which requires adding an extra naming level below /home, e.g., /home/students and /home/staff. Although the different parts have been called filesystems above, there is no requirement that they actually be on separate filesystems. They could easily be kept in a single one if the system is a small single-user system and the user wants to keep things simple. The directory tree might also be divided into filesystems differently, depending on how large the disks are, and how space is allocated for various purposes. The important part, though, is that all the standard names work; even if, say, /var and /usr are actually on the same partition, the names

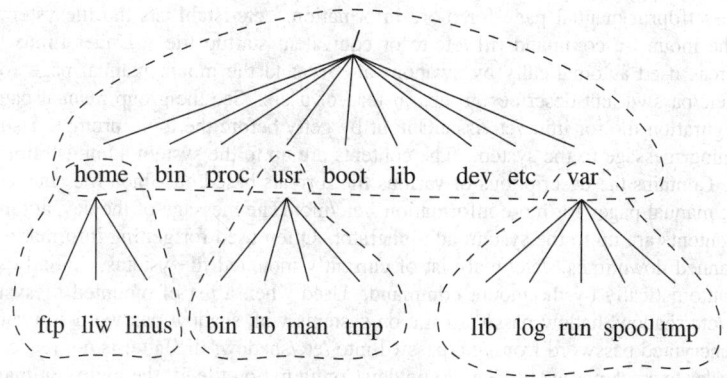

Figure 2: Parts of a Unix directory tree. Dashed lines indicate partition limits.

/usr/lib/libc.a and /var/log/messages must work, for example by moving files below /var into /usr/var, and making /var a symlink to /usr/var.The Unix filesystem structure groups files according to purpose, i.e., all commands are in one place, all data files in another, documentation in a third, and so on. An alternative would be to group files files according to the program they belong to, i.e., all Emacs files would be in one directory, all TeX in another, and so on. The problem with the latter approach is that it makes it difficult to share files (the program directory often contains both static and shareable and changing and non-shareable files), and sometimes to even find the files (e.g., manual pages in a huge number of places, and making the manual page programs find all of them is a maintenance nightmare).

2.5   The root filesystem

The root filesystem should generally be small, since it contains very critical files and a small, infrequently modified filesystem has a better chance of not getting corrupted. A corrupted root filesystem will generally mean that the system becomes unbootable except with special measures (e.g., from a floppy), so you don't want to risk it.The root directory generally doesn't contain any files, except perhaps the standard boot image for the system, usually called /vmlinuz. All other files are in subdirectories in the root filesystems:

/binCommands needed during bootup that might be used by normal users (probably after bootup)./sbinLike /bin, but the commands are not intended for normal users, although they may use them if necessary and allowed./etcConfiguration files specific to the machine./rootThe home directory for user \texttt{root}./libShared libraries needed by the programs on the root filesystem./lib/modulesLoadable kernel modules, especially those that are needed to boot the system when recovering from disasters (e.g., network and filesystem drivers)./devDevice files./tmpTemporary files. Programs running after bootup should use /var/tmp, not /tmp, since the former is probably on a disk with more space./bootFiles used by the bootstrap loader, e.g., LILO. Kernel images are often kept here instead of in the root directory. If there are many kernel images, the directory can easily grow rather big, and it might be better to keep it in a separate filesystem. Another reason would be to make sure the kernel images are within the first 1024 cylinders of an IDE disk./mntMount point for temporary mounts by the system administrator. Programs aren't supposed to mount on /mnt automatically. /mnt might be divided into subdirectories (e.g., /mnt/dosa might be the floppy drive using an MS-DOS filesystem, and /mnt/exta might be the same with an ext2 filesystem)./proc, /usr, /var, /homeMount points for the other filesystems.

2.6   The /etc directory

The /etc directory contains a lot of files. Some of them are described below. For others, you should determine which program they belong to and read the manual page for that program. Many networking configuration files are in /etc as well, and are described in the Networking Administrators' Guide.

/etc/rc or /etc/rc.d or /etc/rc?.dScripts or directories of scripts to run at startup or when changing the run level. See the chapter on init for further information. /etc/passwdThe user database, with fields giving the username, real name, home directory, encrypted password, and other information about each user. The format is documented in the \man{passwd} manual page. /etc/fdprmFloppy disk parameter table. Describes what different floppy disk formats look like. Used by setfdprm. See the setfdprm manual page for more information. /etc/fstabLists the filesystems mounted automatically at startup by the mount -a command (in /etc/rc or equivalent startup file). Under Linux, also contains information about swap areas used automatically by swapon -a. See and the mount manual page for more information. /etc/groupSimilar to /etc/passwd, but describes groups instead of users. See the group manual page for more information. /etc/inittabConfiguration file for init. /etc/issueOutput by getty before the login prompt. Usually contains a short description or welcoming message to the system. The contents are up to the system administrator. /etc/magicThe configuration file for file. Contains the descriptions of various file formats based on which file guesses the type of the file. See the magic and file manual pages for more information. /etc/motdThe message of the day, automatically output after a successful login. Contents are up to the system administrator. Often used for getting information to every user, such as warnings about planned downtimes. /etc/mtabList of currently mounted filesystems. Initially set up by the bootup scripts, and updated automatically by the mount command. Used when a list of mounted filesystems is needed, e.g., by the df command. /etc/shadowShadow password file on systems with shadow password software installed. Shadow passwords move the encrypted password from /etc/passwd into /etc/shadow; the latter is not readable by anyone except root. This makes it harder to crack passwords. /etc/login.defsConfiguration file for the login command. /etc/printcapLike /etc/termcap, but intended for printers. Different syntax. /etc/profile, /etc/csh.login, /etc/csh.cshrcFiles executed at login or startup time by the Bourne or C shells. These allow the system administrator to set global defaults for all users. See the manual pages for the respective shells. /etc/securettyIdentifies secure terminals, i.e., the terminals from which root is allowed to log in. Typically only the virtual consoles are listed, so that it becomes impossible (or at least harder) to gain superuser privileges by breaking into a system over a modem or a network. /etc/shellsLists trusted shells. The chsh command allows users to change their login shell only to shells listed in this file. ftpd, the server process that provides FTP services for a machine, will check that the user's shell is listed in /etc/shells and will not let people log in unles the shell is listed there. /etc/termcapThe terminal capability database. Describes by what "escape sequences" various terminals can be controlled. Programs are written so that instead of directly outputting an escape sequence that only works on a particular brand of terminal, they look up the correct sequence to do whatever it is they want to do in /etc/termcap. As a result most programs work with most kinds of terminals. See the termcap, curs_termcap, and terminfo manual pages for more information.

2.7   The /dev directory

The /dev directory contains the special device files for all the devices. The device files are named using special conventions; these are described in the Device list (see XXX). The device files are created during installation, and later with the /dev/MAKEDEV script. The /dev/MAKEDEV.local is a script written by the system administrator that creates local-only device files or links (i.e., those that are not part of the standard MAKEDEV, such as device files for some non-standard device driver).

2.8   The /usr filesystem

The /usr filesystem is often large, since all programs are installed there. All files in /usr usually come from a Linux distribution; locally installed programs and other stuff goes below /usr/local. This makes it possible to update the system from a new version of the distribution, or even a completely new distribution, without having to install all programs again. Some of the subdirectories of /usr are listed below (some of the less important directories have been dropped; see the FSSTND for more information).

/usr/X11R6The X Window System, all files. To simplify the development and installation of X, the X files have not been integrated into the rest of the system. There is a directory tree below /usr/X11R6 similar to that below /usr itself. /usr/X386Similar to /usr/X11R6, but for X11 Release 5. /usr/binAlmost all user commands. Some commands are in /bin or in /usr/local/bin. /usr/sbinSystem administration commands that are not needed on the root filesystem, e.g., most server programs. /usr/man, /usr/info, /usr/docManual pages, GNU Info documents, and miscellaneous other documentation files, respectively. /usr/includeHeader files for the C programming language. This should actually be below /usr/lib for consistency, but the tradition is overwhelmingly in support for this name. /usr/libUnchanging data files for programs and subsystems, including some site-wide configuration files. The name lib comes from library; originally libraries of programming subroutines were stored in /usr/lib. /usr/localThe place for locally installed software and other files.

2.9   The /var filesystem

The /var contains data that is changed when the system is running normally. It is specific for each system, i.e., not shared over the network with other computers.

/var/catmanA cache for man pages that are formatted on demand. The source for manual pages is usually stored in /usr/man/man*; some manual pages might come with a pre-formatted version, which is stored in /usr/man/cat*. Other manual pages need to be formatted when they are first viewed; the formatted version is then stored in /var/man so that the next person to view the same page won't have to wait for it to be formatted. (/var/catman is often cleaned in the same way temporary directories are cleaned.)/var/libFiles that change while the system is running normally./var/localVariable data for programs that are installed in /usr/local (i.e., programs that have been installed by the system administrator). Note that even locally installed programs should use the other /var directories if they are appropriate, e.g., /var/lock./var/lockLock files. Many programs follow a convention to create a lock file in /var/lock to indicate that they are using a particular device or file. Other programs will notice the lock file and won't attempt to use the device or file./var/logLog files from various programs, especially login (/var/log/wtmp, which logs all logins and logouts into the system) and syslog (/var/log/messages, where all kernel and system program message are usually stored). Files in /var/log can often grow indefinitely, and may require cleaning at regular intervals./var/runFiles that contain information about the system that is valid until the system is next booted. For example, /var/run/utmp contains information about people currently logged in./var/spoolDirectories for mail, news, printer queues, and other queued work. Each different spool has its own subdirectory below /var/spool, e.g., the mailboxes of the users are in /var/spool/mail./var/tmpTemporary files that are large or that need to exist for a longer time than what is allowed for /tmp. (Although the system administrator might not allow very old files in /var/tmp either.)

2.10 The /proc filesystem

The /proc filesystem contains a illusionary filesystem. It does not exist on a disk. Instead, the kernel creates it in memory. It is used to provide information about the system (originally about processes, hence the name). Some of the more important files and directories are explained below. The /proc filesystem is described in more detail in the proc manual page.

/proc/1A directory with information about process number 1. Each process has a directory below /proc with the name being its process identification number. /proc/cpuinfoInformation about the processor, such as its type, make, model, and perfomance. /proc/devicesList of device drivers configured into the currently running kernel. /proc/dmaShows which DMA channels are being used at the moment. /proc/filesystemsFilesystems configured into the kernel. /proc/interruptsShows which interrupts are in use, and how many of each there have been. /proc/ioportsWhich I/O ports are in use at the moment. /proc/kcoreAn image of the physical memory of the system. This is exactly the same size as your physical memory, but does not really take up that much memory; it is generated on the fly as programs access it. (Remember: unless you copy it elsewhere, nothing under /proc takes up any disk space at all.) /proc/kmsgMessages output by the kernel. These are also routed to syslog. /proc/ksymsSymbol table for the kernel. /proc/loadavgThe 'load average' of the system; three meaningless indicators of how much work the system has to do at the moment. /proc/meminfoInformation about memory usage, both physical and swap. /proc/modulesWhich kernel modules are loaded at the moment. /proc/netStatus information about network protocols. /proc/selfA symbolic link to the process directory of the program that is looking at /proc. When two processes look at /proc, they get different links. This is mainly a convenience to make it easier for programs to get at their process directory. /proc/statVarious statistics about the system, such as the number of page faults since the system was booted. /proc/uptimeThe time the system has been up. /proc/versionThe kernel version. Note that while the above files tend to be easily readable text files, they can sometimes be formatted in a way that is not easily digestable. There are many commands that do little more than read the above files and format them for easier understanding. For example, the free program reads /proc/meminfo and converts the amounts given in bytes to kilobytes (and adds a little more information, as well).

3   Using Disks and Other Storage Media

On a clear disk you can seek forever.

When you install or upgrade your system, you need to do a fair amount of work on your disks. You have to make filesystems on your disks so that files can be stored on them and reserve space for the different parts of your system.

This chapter explains all these initial activities. Usually, once you get your system set up, you won't have to go through the work again, except for using floppies. You'll need to come back to this chapter if you add a new disk or want to fine-tune your disk usage. The basic tasks in administering disks are:

Format your disk. This does various things to prepare it for use, such as checking for bad sectors. (Formatting is nowadays not necessary for most hard disks.) Partition a hard disk, if you want to use it for several activities that aren't supposed to interfere with one another. One reason for partitioning is to store different operating systems on the same disk. Another reason is to keep user files separate from system files, which simplifies back-ups and helps protect the system files from corruption. Make a filesystem (of a suitable type) on each disk or partition. The disk means nothing to Linux until you make a filesystem; then files can be created and accessed on it. Mount different filesystems to form a single tree structure, either automatically, or manually as needed. (Manually mounted filesystems usually need to be unmounted manually as well.)

contains information about virtual memory and disk caching, of which you also need to be aware when using disks.

3.1 Two kinds of devices

UNIX, and therefore Linux, recognizes two different kinds of device: random-access block devices (such as disks), and character devices (such as tapes and serial lines), some of which may be serial, and some random-access. Each supported device is represented in the filesystem as a device file. When you read or write a device file, the data comes from or goes to the device it represents. This way no special programs (and no special application programming methodology, such as catching interrupts or polling a serial port) are necessary to access devices; for example, to send a file to the printer, one could just say

```
$ cat filename > /dev/lp1
$
```

and the contents of the file are printed (the file must, of course, be in a form that the printer understands). However, since it is not a good idea to have several people cat their files to the printer at the same time, one usually uses a special program to send the files to be printed (usually lpr). This program makes sure that only one file is being printed at a time, and will automatically send files to the printer as soon as it finishes with the previous file. Something similar is needed for most devices. In fact, one seldom needs to worry about device files at all.Since devices show up as files in the filesystem (in the /dev directory), it is easy to see just what device files exist, using ls or another suitable command. In the output of ls -l, the first column contains the type of the file and its permissions. For example, inspecting a serial device gives on my system

```
$ ls -l /dev/cua0
crw-rw-rw- 1 root uucp 5, 64 Nov 30 1993 /dev/cua0
$
```

The first character in the first column, i.e., 'c' in crw-rw-rw- above, tells an informed user the type of the file, in this case a character device. For ordinary files, the first character is '-', for directories it is 'd', and for block devices 'b'; see the ls man page for further information.Note that usually all device files exist even though the device itself might be not be installed. So just because you have a file /dev/sda, it doesn't mean that you really do have an SCSI hard disk. Having all the device files makes the installation programs simpler, and makes it easier to add new hardware (there is no need to find out the correct parameters for and create the device files for the new device).

3.2 Hard disks

This subsection introduces terminology related to hard disks. If you already know the terms and concepts, you can skip this subsection.See Figure 3.2 for a schematic picture of the important parts in a hard disk. A hard disk consists of one or more circular platters, [9]

of which either or both surfaces are coated with a magnetic substance used for recording the data. For each surface, there is a read-write head that examines or alters the recorded data. The platters rotate on a common axis; a typical rotation speed is 3600 rotations per minute, although high-performance hard disks have higher speeds. The heads move along the radius of the platters; this movement combined with the rotation of the platters allows the head to access all parts of the surfaces.The processor (CPU) and the actual disk communicate through a disk controller. This relieves the rest of the computer from knowing how to use the drive, since the controllers for different types of disks can be made to use the same interface towards the rest of the computer. Therefore, the computer can say just "hey disk, gimme what I want", instead of a long and complex series of electric signals to move the head to the proper location and waiting for the correct position to come under the head and doing all the other unpleasant stuff necessary. (In reality, the interface to the controller is still complex, but much less so than it would otherwise be.) The controller can also do some other stuff, such as caching, or automatic bad sector replacement.The above is usually all one needs to understand about the hardware. There is also a bunch of other stuff, such as the motor that rotates the platters and moves the heads, and the electronics that control the operation of the mechanical parts, but that is mostly not relevant for understanding the working principle of a hard disk.The surfaces are usually divided into concentric rings, called tracks, and these in turn are divided into sectors. This division is used to specify locations on the hard disk and to allocate disk space to files. To find a given place on the hard

---

[9]The platters are made of a hard substance, e.g., aluminium, which gives the hard disk its name.

disk, one might say "surface 3, track 5, sector 7". Usually the number of sectors is the same for all tracks, but some hard disks put more sectors in outer tracks (all sectors are of the same physical size, so more of them fit in the longer outer tracks). Typically, a sector will hold 512 bytes of data. The disk itself can't handle smaller amounts of data than one sector. Each surface is divided into tracks (and sectors) in the same way. This means that when the head for one surface is on a track, the heads for the other surfaces are also on the corresponding tracks. All the corresponding tracks taken together are called a cylinder. It takes time to move the heads from one track (cylinder) to another, so by placing the data that is often accessed together (say, a file) so that it is within one cylinder, it is not necessary to move the heads to read all of it. This improves performance. It is not always possible to place files like this; files that are stored in several places on the disk are called fragmented.The number of surfaces (or heads, which is the same thing), cylinders, and sectors vary a lot; the specification of the number of each is called the geometry of a hard disk. The geometry is usually stored in a special, battery-powered memory location called the CMOS RAM, from where the operating system can fetch it during bootup or driver initialization.Unfortunately, the BIOS [10]

has a design limitation, which makes it impossible to specify a track number that is larger than 1024 in the CMOS RAM, which is too little for a large hard disk. To overcome this, the hard disk controller lies about the geometry, and translates the addresses given by the computer into something that fits reality. For example, a hard disk might have 8 heads, 2048 tracks, and 35 sectors per track. [11]

Its controller could lie to the computer and claim that it has 16 heads, 1024 tracks, and 35 sectors per track, thus not exceeding the limit on tracks, and translates the address that the computer gives it by halving the head number, and doubling the track number. The math can be more complicated in reality, because the numbers are not as nice as here (but again, the details are not relevant for understanding the principle). This translation distorts the operating system's view of how the disk is organized, thus making it impractical to use the all-data-on-one-cylinder trick to boost performance.The translation is only a problem for IDE disks. SCSI disks use a sequential sector number (i.e., the controller translates a sequential sector number to a head, cylinder, and sector triplet), and a completely different method for the CPU to talk with the controller, so they are insulated from the problem. Note, however, that the computer might not know the real geometry of an SCSI disk either.Since Linux often will not know the real geometry of a disk, its filesystems don't even try to keep files within a single cylinder. Instead, it tries to assign sequentially numbered sectors to files, which almost always gives similar performance. The issue is further complicated by on-controller caches, and automatic prefetches done by the controller.Each hard disk is represented by a separate device file. There can (usually) be only two or four IDE hard disks. These are known as /dev/hda, /dev/hdb, /dev/hdc, and /dev/hdd, respectively. SCSI hard disks are known as /dev/sda, /dev/sdb, and so on. Similar naming conventions exist for other hard disk types; see XXX (device list) for more information. Note that the device files for the hard disks give access to the entire disk, with no regard to partitions (which will be discussed below), and it's easy to mess up the partitions or the data in them if you aren't careful. The disks' device files are usually used only to get access to the master boot record (which will also be discussed below).

3.3 Floppies

A floppy disk consists of a flexible membrane covered on one or both sides with similar magnetic substance as a hard disk. The floppy disk itself doesn't have a read-write head, that is included in the drive. A floppy corresponds to one platter in a hard disk, but is removable and one drive can be used to access different floppies, whereas the hard disk is one indivisible unit.Like a hard disk, a floppy is divided into tracks and sectors (and the two corresponding tracks on either side of a floppy form a cylinder), but there are many fewer of them than on a hard disk.A floppy drive can usually use several different types of disks; for example, a 3.5 inch drive can use both 720 kB and 1.44 MB disks. Since the drive has to operate a bit differently and the operating system must know how big the disk is, there are many device files for floppy drives, one per combination of drive and disk type. Therefore, /dev/fd0H1440 is the first floppy drive (fd0), which must be a 3.5 inch drive, using a 3.5 inch, high density disk (H) of size 1440 kB (1440), i.e., a normal 3.5 inch HD floppy. For more information on the naming conventions for the floppy devices, see XXX (device list).The names for floppy drives are complex, however, and Linux therefore has a special floppy device type that automatically detects the type of the disk in the drive. It works by trying to read the first sector of a newly inserted floppy using different floppy types until it finds the correct one. This naturally requires that the floppy is formatted first. The automatic devices are called /dev/fd0, /dev/fd1, and so on.The parameters the automatic device uses to access a disk can also be set using the program \cmd{setfdprm}. This can be useful if you need to use disks that do not follow any usual floppy sizes, e.g., if they have

---

[10]The BIOS is some built-in software stored on ROM chips. It takes care, among other things, of the initial stages of booting.

[11]The numbers are completely imaginary.

an unusual number of sectors, or if the autodetecting for some reason fails and the proper device file is missing.Linux can handle many nonstandard floppy disk formats in addition to all the standard ones. Some of these require using special formatting programs. We'll skip these disk types for now, but in the mean time you can examine the /etc/fdprm file. It specifies the settings that setfdprm recognizes.The operating system must know when a disk has been changed in a floppy drive, for example, in order to avoid using cached data from the previous disk. Unfortunately, the signal line that is used for this is sometimes broken, and worse, this won't always be noticeable when using the drive from within MS-DOS. If you are experiencing weird problems using floppies, this might be the reason. The only way to correct it is to repair the floppy drive.

3.4   CD-ROM's

A CD-ROM drive uses an optically read, plastic coated disk. The information is recorded on the surface of the disk [12]

in small 'holes' aligned along a spiral from the center to the edge. The drive directs a laser beam along the spiral to read the disk. When the laser hits a hole, the laser is reflected in one way; when it hits smooth surface, it is reflected in another way. This makes it easy to code bits, and therefore information. The rest is easy, mere mechanics.CD-ROM drives are slow compared to hard disks. Whereas a typical hard disk will have an average seek time less than 15 milliseconds, a fast CD-ROM drive can use tenths of a second for seeks. The actual data transfer rate is fairly high at hundreds of kilobytes per second. The slowness means that CD-ROM drives are not as pleasant to use instead of hard disks (some Linux distributions provide 'live' filesystems on CD-ROM's, making it unnecessary to copy the files to the hard disk, making installation easier and saving a lot of hard disk space), although it is still possible. For installing new software, CD-ROM's are very good, since it maximum speed is not essential during installation.There are several ways to arrange data on a CD-ROM. The most popular one is specified by the international standard ISO 9660. This standard specifies a very minimal filesystem, which is even more crude than the one MS-DOS uses. On the other hand, it is so minimal that every operating system should be able to map it to its native system.For normal UNIX use, the ISO 9660 filesystem is not usable, so an extension to the standard has been developed, called the Rock Ridge extension. Rock Ridge allows longer filenames, symbolic links, and a lot of other goodies, making a CD-ROM look more or less like any contemporary UNIX filesystem. Even better, a Rock Ridge filesystem is still a valid ISO 9660 filesystem, making it usable by non-UNIX systems as well. Linux supports both ISO 9660 and the Rock Ridge extensions; the extensions are recognized and used automatically.The filesystem is only half the battle, however. Most CD-ROM's contain data that requires a special program to access, and most of these programs do not run under Linux (except, possibly, under dosemu, the Linux MS-DOS emulator).A CD-ROM drive is accessed via the corresponding device file. There are several ways to connect a CD-ROM drive to the computer: via SCSI, via a sound card, or via EIDE. The hardware hacking needed to do this is outside the scope of this book, but the type of connection decides the device file. See XXX (device-list) for enlightment.

3.5   Tapes

A tape drive uses a tape, similar [13]

to cassettes used for music. A tape is serial in nature, which means that in order to get to any given part of it, you first have to go through all the parts in between. A disk can be accessed randomly, i.e., you can jump directly to any place on the disk. The serial access of tapes makes them slow.On the other hand, tapes are relatively cheap to make, since they do not need to be fast. They can also easily be made quite long, and can therefore contain a large amount of data. This makes tapes very suitable for things like archiving and backups, which do not require large speeds, but benefit from low costs and large storage capacities.

3.6   Formatting

Formatting is the process of writing marks on the magnetic media that are used to mark tracks and sectors. Before a disk is formatted, its magnetic surface is a complete mess of magnetic signals. When it is formatted, some order is brought into the chaos by essentially drawing lines where the tracks go, and where they are divided into sectors. The actual details are not quite exactly like this, but that is irrelevant. What is important is that a disk cannot be used unless it has been

---

[12]That is, the surface inside the disk, on the metal disk inside the plastic coating.
[13]But completely different, of course.

formatted.The terminology is a bit confusing here: in MS-DOS, the word formatting is used to cover also the process of creating a filesystem (which will be discussed below). There, the two processes are often combined, especially for floppies. When the distinction needs to be made, the real formatting is called low-level formatting, while making the filesystem is called high-level formatting. In UNIX circles, the two are called formatting and making a filesystem, so that's what is used in this book as well.For IDE and some SCSI disks the formatting is actually done at the factory and doesn't need to be repeated; hence most people rarely need to worry about it. In fact, formatting a hard disk can cause it to work less well, for example because a disk might need to be formatted in some very special way to allow automatic bad sector replacement to work.Disks that need to be or can be formatted often require a special program anyway, because the interface to the formatting logic inside the drive is different from drive to drive. The formatting program is often either on the controller BIOS, or is supplied as an MS-DOS program; neither of these can easily be used from within Linux.During formatting one might encounter bad spots on the disk, called bad blocks or bad sectors. These are sometimes handled by the drive itself, but even then, if more of them develop, something needs to be done to avoid using those parts of the disk. The logic to do this is built into the filesystem; how to add the information into the filesystem is described below. Alternatively, one might create a small partition that covers just the bad part of the disk; this approach might be a good idea if the bad spot is very large, since filesystems can sometimes have trouble with very large bad areas.Floppies are formatted with fdformat. The floppy device file to use is given as the parameter. For example, the following command would format a high density, 3.5 inch floppy in the first floppy drive:

```
$ fdformat /dev/fd0H1440
Double-sided, 80 tracks, 18 sec/track.  Total capacity 1440 kB.
Formatting ...  done
Verifying ...  done
$
```

Note that if you want to use an autodetecting device (e.g., /dev/fd0), you must set the parameters of the device with setfdprm first. To achieve the same effect as above, one would have to do the following:

```
$ setfdprm /dev/fd0 1440/1440
$ fdformat /dev/fd0
Double-sided, 80 tracks, 18 sec/track.  Total capacity 1440 kB.
Formatting ...  done
Verifying ...  done
$
```

It is usually more convenient to choose the correct device file that matches the type of the floppy. Note that it is unwise to format floppies to contain more information than what they are designed for.fdformat will also validate the floppy, i.e., check it for bad blocks. It will try a bad block several times (you can usually hear this, the drive noise changes dramatically). If the floppy is only marginally bad (due to dirt on the read/write head, some errors are false signals), fdformat won't complain, but a real error will abort the validation process. The kernel will print log messages for each I/O error it finds; these will go to the console or, if syslog is being used, to the file /usr/log/messages. fdformat itself won't tell where the error is (one usually doesn't care, floppies are cheap enough that a bad one is automatically thrown away).

```
$ fdformat /dev/fd0H1440
Double-sided, 80 tracks, 18 sec/track.  Total capacity 1440 kB.
Formatting ...  done
Verifying ...  read:  Unknown error
$
```

The badblocks command can be used to search any disk or partition for bad blocks (including a floppy). It does not format the disk, so it can be used to check even existing filesystems. The example below checks a 3.5 inch floppy with two bad blocks.

```
$ badblocks /dev/fd0H1440 1440
718
```

```
719
$
```

badblocks outputs the block numbers of the bad blocks it finds. Most filesystems can avoid such bad blocks. They maintain a list of known bad blocks, which is initialized when the filesystem is made, and can be modified later. The initial search for bad blocks can be done by the mkfs command (which initializes the filesystem), but later checks should be done with badblocks and the new blocks should be added with fsck. We'll describe \cmd{mkfs} and fsck later.Many modern disks automatically notice bad blocks, and attempt to fix them by using a special, reserved good block instead. This is invisible to the operating system. This feature should be documented in the disk's manual, if you're curious if it is happening. Even such disks can fail, if the number of bad blocks grows too large, although chances are that by then the disk will be so rotten as to be unusable.

3.7   Partitions

A hard disk can be divided into several partitions. Each partition functions as if it were a separate hard disk. The idea is that if you have one hard disk, and want to have, say, two operating systems on it, you can divide the disk into two partitions. Each operating system uses its partition as it wishes and doesn't touch the other one's. This way the two operating systems can co-exist peacefully on the same hard disk. Without partitions one would have to buy a hard disk for each operating system.Floppies are not partitioned. There is no technical reason against this, but since they're so small, partitions would be useful only very rarely. CD-ROM's are usually also not partitioned, since it's easier to use them as one big disk, and there is seldom a need to have several operating systems on one.

3.7.1   The MBR, boot sectors and partition table

The information about how a hard disk has been partitioned is stored in its first sector (that is, the first sector of the first track on the first disk surface). The first sector is the master boot record (MBR) of the disk; this is the sector that the BIOS reads in and starts when the machine is first booted. The master boot record contains a small program that reads the partition table, checks which partition is active (that is, marked bootable), and reads the first sector of that partition, the partition's boot sector (the MBR is also a boot sector, but it has a special status and therefore a special name). This boot sector contains another small program that reads the first part of the operating system stored on that partition (assuming it is bootable), and then starts it.The partitioning scheme is not built into the hardware, or even into the BIOS. It is only a convention that many operating systems follow. Not all operating systems do follow it, but they are the exceptions. Some operating systems support partitions, but they occupy one partition on the hard disk, and use their internal partitioning method within that partition. The latter type exists peacefully with other operating systems (including Linux), and does not require any special measures, but an operating system that doesn't support partitions cannot co-exist on the same disk with any other operating system.As a safety precaution, it is a good idea to write down the partition table on a piece of paper, so that if it ever corrupts you don't have to lose all your files. (A bad partition table can be fixed with fdisk). The relevant information is given by the fdisk -l command:

```
$ fdisk -l /dev/hda

Disk /dev/hda:  15 heads, 57 sectors, 790 cylinders
Units = cylinders of 855 * 512 bytes

Device Boot Begin Start End Blocks Id System
/dev/hda1 1 1 24 10231+ 82 Linux swap
/dev/hda2 25 25 48 10260 83 Linux native
/dev/hda3 49 49 408 153900 83 Linux native
/dev/hda4 409 409 790 163305 5 Extended
/dev/hda5 409 409 744 143611+ 83 Linux native
/dev/hda6 745 745 790 19636+ 83 Linux native
$
```

3.7.2   Extended and logical partitions

The original partitioning scheme for PC hard disks allowed only four partitions. This quickly turned out to be too little in real life, partly because some people want more than four operating systems (Linux, MS-DOS, OS/2, Minix, FreeBSD, NetBSD, or Windows/NT, to name a few), but primarily because sometimes it is a good idea to have several partitions for one operating system. For example, swap space is usually best put in its own partition for Linux instead of in the main Linux partition for reasons of speed (see below).To overcome this design problem, extended partitions were invented. This trick allows partitioning a primary partition into sub-partitions. The primary partition thus subdivided is the extended partition; the subpartitions are logical partitions. They behave like primary [14]

partitions, but are created differently. There is no speed difference between them.The partition structure of a hard disk might look like that in Figure 3.7.2. The disk is divided into three primary partitions, the second of which is divided into two logical partitions. Part of the disk is not partitioned at all. The disk as a whole and each primary partition has a boot sector.

3.7.3   Partition types

The partition tables (the one in the MBR, and the ones for extended partitions) contain one byte per partition that identifies the type of that partition. This attempts to identify the operating system that uses the partition, or what it uses it for. The purpose is to make it possible to avoid having two operating systems accidentally using the same partition. However, in reality, operating systems do not really care about the partition type byte; e.g., Linux doesn't care at all what it is. Worse, some of them use it incorrectly; e.g., at least some versions of DR-DOS ignore the most significant bit of the byte, while others don't.There is no standardization agency to specify what each byte value means, but some commonly accepted ones are included in in . The same list is available in the Linux fdisk program.

3.7.4   Partitioning a hard disk

There are many programs for creating and removing partitions. Most operating systems have their own, and it can be a good idea to use each operating system's own, just in case it does something unusual that the others can't. Many of the programs are called fdisk, including the Linux one, or variations thereof. Details on using the Linux fdisk are given on its man page. The cfdisk command is similar to fdisk, but has a nicer (full screen) user interface.When using IDE disks, the boot partition (the partition with the bootable kernel image files) must be completely within the first 1024 cylinders. This is because the disk is used via the BIOS during boot (before the system goes into protected mode), and BIOS can't handle more than 1024 cylinders. It is sometimes possible to use a boot partition that is only partly within the first 1024 cylinders. This works as long as all the files that are read with the BIOS are within the first 1024 cylinders. Since this is difficult to arrange, it is a very bad idea to do it; you never know when a kernel update or disk defragmentation will result in an unbootable system. Therefore, make sure your boot partition is completely within the first 1024 cylinders.Some newer versions of the BIOS and IDE disks can, in fact, handle disks with more than 1024 cylinders. If you have such a system, you can forget about the problem; if you aren't quite sure of it, put it within the first 1024 cylinders.Each partition should have an even number of sectors, since the Linux filesystems use a 1 kilobyte block size, i.e., two sectors. An odd number of sectors will result in the last sector being unused. This won't result in any problems, but it is ugly, and some versions of fdisk will warn about it.Changing a partition's size usually requires first backing up everything you want to save from that partition (preferably the whole disk, just in case), deleting the partition, creating new partition, then restoring everything to the new partition. If the partition is growing, you may need to adjust the sizes (and backup and restore) of the adjoining partitions as well.Since changing partition sizes is painful, it is preferable to get the partitions right the first time, or have an effective and easy to use backup system. If you're installing from a media that does not require much human intervention (say, from CD-ROM, as opposed to floppies), it is often easy to play with different configuration at first. Since you don't already have data to back up, it is not so painful to modify partition sizes several times.There is a program for MS-DOS, called fips, which resizes an MS-DOS partition without requiring the backup and restore, but for other filesystems it is still necessary.

3.7.5   Device files and partitions

Each partition and extended partition has its own device file. The naming convention for these files is that a partition's number is appended after the name of the whole disk, with the convention that 1-4 are primary partitions (regardless of

---

[14]Illogical?

how many primary partitions there are) and 5-8 are logical partitions (regardless of within which primary partition they reside). For example, /dev/hda1 is the first primary partition on the first IDE hard disk, and /dev/sdb7 is the third extended partition on the second SCSI hard disk. The device list in XXX (device list) gives more information.

3.8 Filesystems

3.8.1 What are filesystems?

A filesystem is the methods and data structures that an operating system uses to keep track of files on a disk or partition; that is, the way the files are organized on the disk. The word is also used to refer to a partition or disk that is used to store the files or the type of the filesystem. Thus, one might say "I have two filesystems" meaning one has two partitions on which one stores files, or that one is using the "extended filesystem", meaning the type of the filesystem.The difference between a disk or partition and the filesystem it contains is important. A few programs (including, reasonably enough, programs that create filesystems) operate directly on the raw sectors of a disk or partition; if there is an existing file system there it will be destroyed or seriously corrupted. Most programs operate on a filesystem, and therefore won't work on a partition that doesn't contain one (or that contains one of the wrong type).Before a partition or disk can be used as a filesystem, it needs to be initialized, and the bookkeeping data structures need to be written to the disk. This process is called making a filesystem.Most UNIX filesystem types have a similar general structure, although the exact details vary quite a bit. The central concepts are superblock, inode, data block, directory block, and indirection block. The superblock contains information about the filesystem as a whole, such as its size (the exact information here depends on the filesystem). An inode contains all information about a file, except its name. The name is stored in the directory, together with the number of the inode. A directory entry consists of a filename and the number of the inode which represents the file. The inode contains the numbers of several data blocks, which are used to store the data in the file. There is space only for a few data block numbers in the inode, however, and if more are needed, more space for pointers to the data blocks is allocated dynamically. These dynamically allocated blocks are indirect blocks; the name indicates that in order to find the data block, one has to find its number in the indirect block first.UNIX filesystems usually allow one to create a hole in a file (this is done with lseek; check the manual page), which means that the filesystem just pretends that at a particular place in the file there is just zero bytes, but no actual disk sectors are reserved for that place in the file (this means that the file will use a bit less disk space). This happens especially often for small binaries, Linux shared libraries, some databases, and a few other special cases. (Holes are implemented by storing a special value as the address of the data block in the indirect block or inode. This special address means that no data block is allocated for that part of the file, ergo, there is a hole in the file.)Holes are moderately useful. On the author's system, a simple measurement showed a potential for about 4 MB of savings through holes of about 200 MB total used disk space. That system, however, contains relatively few programs and no database files.

3.8.2 Filesystems galore

Linux supports several types of filesystems. As of this writing the most important ones are:

minix The oldest, presumed to be the most reliable, but quite limited in features (some time stamps are missing, at most 30 character filenames) and restricted in capabilities (at most 64 MB per filesystem). xia A modified version of the minix filesystem that lifts the limits on the filenames and filesystem sizes, but does not otherwise introduce new features. It is not very popular, but is reported to work very well. ext2 The most featureful of the native Linux filesystems, currently also the most popular one. It is designed to be easily upwards compatible, so that new versions of the filesystem code do not require re-making the existing filesystems. ext An older version of ext2 that wasn't upwards compatible. It is hardly ever used in new installations any more, and most people have converted to ext2.

In addition, support for several foreign filesystem exists, to make it easier to exchange files with other operating systems. These foreign filesystems work just like native ones, except that they may be lacking in some usual UNIX features, or have curious limitations, or other oddities.

msdos Compatibility with MS-DOS (and OS/2 and Windows NT) FAT filesystems. usmdos Extends the msdos filesystem driver under Linux to get long filenames, owners, permissions, links, and device files. This allows a normal msdos filesystem to be used as if it were a Linux one, thus removing the need for a separate partition for Linux. iso9660 The standard CD-ROM filesystem; the popular Rock Ridge extension to the CD-ROM standard that allows longer file names is supported automatically. nfs A networked filesystem that allows sharing a filesystem between many computers to allow easy access to the files from all of them. hpfs The OS/2 filesystem. sysv SystemV/386, Coherent, and Xenix filesystems.

The choice of filesystem to use depends on the situation. If compatibility or other reasons make one of the non-native filesystems necessary, then that one must be used. If one can choose freely, then it is probably wisest to use ext2, since it has all the features but does not suffer from lack of performance.There is also the proc filesystem, usually accessible as the /proc directory, which is not really a filesystem at all, even though it looks like one. The proc filesystem makes it easy to access certain kernel data structures, such as the process list (hence the name). It makes these data structures look like a filesystem, and that filesystem can be manipulated with all the usual file tools. For example, to get a listing of all processes one might use the command

```
$ ls -l /proc
total 0
dr-xr-xr-x 4 root root 0 Jan 31 20:37 1
dr-xr-xr-x 4 liw users 0 Jan 31 20:37 63
dr-xr-xr-x 4 liw users 0 Jan 31 20:37 94
dr-xr-xr-x 4 liw users 0 Jan 31 20:37 95
dr-xr-xr-x 4 root users 0 Jan 31 20:37 98
dr-xr-xr-x 4 liw users 0 Jan 31 20:37 99
-r-r-r- 1 root root 0 Jan 31 20:37 devices
-r-r-r- 1 root root 0 Jan 31 20:37 dma
-r-r-r- 1 root root 0 Jan 31 20:37 filesystems
-r-r-r- 1 root root 0 Jan 31 20:37 interrupts
-r------ 1 root root 8654848 Jan 31 20:37 kcore
-r-r-r- 1 root root 0 Jan 31 11:50 kmsg
-r-r-r- 1 root root 0 Jan 31 20:37 ksyms
-r-r-r- 1 root root 0 Jan 31 11:51 loadavg
-r-r-r- 1 root root 0 Jan 31 20:37 meminfo
-r-r-r- 1 root root 0 Jan 31 20:37 modules
dr-xr-xr-x 2 root root 0 Jan 31 20:37 net
dr-xr-xr-x 4 root root 0 Jan 31 20:37 self
-r-r-r- 1 root root 0 Jan 31 20:37 stat
-r-r-r- 1 root root 0 Jan 31 20:37 uptime
-r-r-r- 1 root root 0 Jan 31 20:37 version
$
```

(There will be a few extra files that don't correspond to processes, though. The above example has been shortened.)Note that even though it is called a filesystem, no part of the proc filesystem touches any disk. It exists only in the kernel's imagination. Whenever anyone tries to look at any part of the proc filesystem, the kernel makes it look as if the part existed somewhere, even though it doesn't. So, even though there is a multi-megabyte /proc/kcore file, it doesn't take any disk space.

3.8.3 Which filesystem should be used?

There is usually little point in using many different filesystems. Currently, ext2fs is the most popular one, and it is probably the wisest choice. Depending on the overhead for bookkeeping structures, speed, (perceived) reliability, compatibility, and various other reasons, it may be advisable to use another file system. This needs to be decided on a case-by-case basis.

3.8.4 Creating a filesystem

Filesystems are created, i.e., initialized, with the mkfs command. There is actually a separate program for each filesystem type. mkfs is just a front end that runs the appropriate program depending on the desired filesystem type. The type is selected with the -t fstype option.The programs called by mkfs have slightly different command line interfaces. The common and most important options are summarized below; see the manual pages for more.

-t fstype Select the type of the filesystem. -c Search for bad blocks and initialize the bad block list accordingly. -l filename Read the initial bad block list from the name file.

To create an ext2 filesystem on a floppy, one would give the following commands:

```
$ fdformat -n /dev/fd0H1440
Double-sided, 80 tracks, 18 sec/track.  Total capacity 1440 kB.
Formatting ...  done
$ badblocks /dev/fd0H1440 1440 $>$ bad-blocks
$ mkfs -t ext2 -l bad-blocks /dev/fd0H1440
mke2fs 0.5a, 5-Apr-94 for EXT2 FS 0.5, 94/03/10
360 inodes, 1440 blocks
72 blocks (5.00%) reserved for the super user
First data block=1
Block size=1024 (log=0)
Fragment size=1024 (log=0)
1 block group
8192 blocks per group, 8192 fragments per group
360 inodes per group

Writing inode tables:  done
Writing superblocks and filesystem accounting information:  done
$
```

First, the floppy was formatted (the -n option prevents validation, i.e., bad block checking). Then bad blocks were searched with badblocks, with the output redirected to a file, bad-blocks. Finally, the filesystem was created, with the bad block list initialized by whatever badblocks found.The -c option could have been used with mkfs instead of badblocks and a separate file. The example below does that.

```
$ mkfs -t ext2 -c /dev/fd0H1440
mke2fs 0.5a, 5-Apr-94 for EXT2 FS 0.5, 94/03/10
360 inodes, 1440 blocks
72 blocks (5.00%) reserved for the super user
First data block=1
Block size=1024 (log=0)
Fragment size=1024 (log=0)
1 block group
8192 blocks per group, 8192 fragments per group
360 inodes per group

Checking for bad blocks (read-only test):  done
Writing inode tables:  done
Writing superblocks and filesystem accounting information:  done
$
```

The -c option is more convenient than a separate use of badblocks, but badblocks is necessary for checking after the filesystem has been created.The process to prepare filesystems on hard disks or partitions is the same as for floppies, except that the formatting isn't needed.

3.8.5 Mounting and unmounting

Before one can use a filesystem, it has to be mounted. The operating system then does various bookkeeping things to make sure that everything works. Since all files in UNIX are in a single directory tree, the mount operation will make it look like the contents of the new filesystem are the contents of an existing subdirectory in some already mounted filesystem.For example, Figure 3.8.5 shows three separate filesystems, each with their own root directory. When the last two filesystems are mounted below /home and /usr, respectively, on the first filesystem, we can get a single directory tree, as in Figure 3.8.5 . The mounts could be done as in the following example:

```
$ mount /dev/hda2 /home
$ mount /dev/hda3 /usr
$
```

The mount command takes two arguments. The first one is the device file corresponding to the disk or partition containing the filesystem. The second one is the directory below which it will be mounted. After these commands the contents of the two filesystems look just like the contents of the /home and /usr directories, respectively. One would then say that "/dev/hda2 is mounted on /home", and similarly for /usr. To look at either filesystem, one would look at the contents of the directory on which it has been mounted, just as if it were any other directory. Note the difference between the device file, /dev/hda2, and the mounted-on directory, /home. The device file gives access to the raw contents of the disk, the mounted-on directory gives access to the files on the disk. The mounted-on directory is called the mount point.Linux supports many filesystem types. mount tries to guess the type of the filesystem. You can also use the -t fstype option to specify the type directly; this is sometimes necessary, since the heuristics mount uses do not always work. For example, to mount an MS-DOS floppy, you could use the following command:

```
$ mount -t msdos /dev/fd0 /floppy
$
```

The mounted-on directory need not be empty, although it must exist. Any files in it, however, will be inaccessible by name while the filesystem is mounted. (Any files that have already been opened will still be accessible. Files that have hard links from other directories can be accessed using those names.) There is no harm done with this, and it can even be useful. For instance, some people like to have /tmp and /var/tmp synonymous, and make /tmp be a symbolic link to /var/tmp. When the system is booted, before the /var filesystem is mounted, a /var/tmp directory residing on the root filesystem is used instead. When /var is mounted, it will make the /var/tmp directory on the root filesystem inaccessible. If /var/tmp didn't exist on the root filesystem, it would be impossible to use temporary files before mounting /var.If you don't intend to write anything to the filesystem, use the -r switch for mount to do a readonly mount. This will make the kernel stop any attempts at writing to the filesystem, and will also stop the kernel from updating file access times in the inodes. Read-only mounts are necessary for unwritable media, e.g., CD-ROM's.The alert reader has already noticed a slight logistical problem. How is the first filesystem (called the root filesystem, because it contains the root directory) mounted, since it obviously can't be mounted on another filesystem? Well, the answer is that it is done by magic. [15]

The root filesystem is magically mounted at boot time, and one can rely on it to always be mounted. If the root filesystem can't be mounted, the system does not boot. The name of the filesystem that is magically mounted as root is either compiled into the kernel, or set using LILO or rdev.The root filesystem is usually first mounted readonly. The startup scripts will then run fsck to verify its validity, and if there are no problems, they will re-mount it so that writes will also be allowed. fsck must not be run on a mounted filesystem, since any changes to the filesystem while fsck is running will cause trouble. Since the root filesystem is mounted readonly while it is being checked, fsck can fix any problems without worry, since the remount operation will flush any metadata that the filesystem keeps in memory.On many systems there are other filesystems that should also be mounted automatically at boot time. These are specified in the /etc/fstab file; see the fstab man page for details on the format. The details of exactly when the extra filesystems are mounted depend on many factors, and can be configured by each administrator if need be; see .When a filesystem no longer needs to be mounted, it can be unmounted with umount. [16]

umount takes one argument: either the device file or the mount point. For example, to unmount the directories of the previous example, one could use the commands

```
$ umount /dev/hda2
$ umount /usr
$
```

[15]For more information, see the kernel source or the Kernel Hackers' Guide.

[16]It should of course be unmount, but the n mysteriously disappeared in the 70's, and hasn't been seen since. Please return it to Bell Labs, NJ, if you find it.

See the man page for further instructions on how to use the command. It is imperative that you always unmount a mounted floppy. Don't just pop the floppy out of the drive! Because of disk caching, the data is not necessarily written to the floppy until you unmount it, so removing the floppy from the drive too early might cause the contents to become garbled. If you only read from the floppy, this is not very likely, but if you write, even accidentally, the result may be catastrophic.Mounting and unmounting requires super user privileges, i.e., only root can do it. The reason for this is that if any user can mount a floppy on any directory, then it is rather easy to create a floppy with, say, a Trojan horse disguised as /bin/sh, or any other often used program. However, it is often necessary to allow users to use floppies, and there are several ways to do this:

Give the users the root password. This is obviously bad security, but is the easiest solution. It works well if there is no need for security anyway, which is the case on many non-networked, personal systems.Use a program such as sudo to allow users to use mount. This is still bad security, but doesn't directly give super user privileges to everyone. [17] Make the users use mtools, a package for manipulating MS-DOS filesystems, without mounting them. This works well if MS-DOS floppies are all that is needed, but is rather awkward otherwise. List the floppy devices and their allowable mount points together with the suitable options in /etc/fstab.

The last alternative can be implemented by adding a line like the following to the \fn{/etc/fstab} file:

```
/dev/fd0 /floppy msdos user,noauto 0 0
```

The columns are: device file to mount, directory to mount on, filesystem type, options, backup frequency (used by dump), and fsck pass number (to specify the order in which filesystems should be checked upon boot; 0 means no check).The noauto option stops this mount to be done automatically when the system is started (i.e., it stops mount -a from mounting it). The user option allows any user to mount the filesystem, and, because of security reasons, disallows execution of programs (normal or setuid) and interpretation of device files from the mounted filesystem. After this, any user can mount a floppy with an msdos filesystem with the following command:

```
$ mount /floppy
$
```

The floppy can (and needs to, of course) be unmounted with the corresponding \cmd{umount} command.If you want to provide access to several types of floppies, you need to give several mount points. The settings can be different for each mount point. For example, to give access to both MS-DOS and ext2 floppies, you could have the following to lines in /etc/fstab:

```
/dev/fd0 /dosfloppy msdos user,noauto 0 0
/dev/fd0 /ext2floppy ext2 user,noauto 0 0
```

For MS-DOS filesystems (not just floppies), you probably want to restrict access to it by using the uid, gid, and umask filesystem options, described in detail on the mount manual page. If you aren't careful, mounting an MS-DOS filesystem gives everyone at least read access to the files in it, which is not a good idea.

3.8.6 Checking filesystem integrity with fsck

Filesystems are complex creatures, and as such, they tend to be somewhat error-prone. A filesystem's correctness and validity can be checked using the fsck command. It can be instructed to repair any minor problems it finds, and to alert the user if there any unrepairable problems. Fortunately, the code to implement filesystems is debugged quite effectively, so there are seldom any problems at all, and they are usually caused by power failures, failing hardware, or operator errors; for example, by not shutting down the system properly.Most systems are setup to run fsck automatically at boot time, so that any errors are detected (and hopefully corrected) before the system is used. Use of a corrupted filesystem tends to make things worse: if the data structures are messed up, using the filesystem will probably mess them up even more, resulting in more data loss. However, fsck can take a while to run on big filesystems, and since errors almost never occur if the system has been shut down properly, a couple of tricks are used to avoid doing the checks in such cases. The first is that if the file /etc/fastboot exists, no checks are made. The second is that the ext2 filesystem has a special

---

[17]It requires several seconds of hard thinking on the users' behalf.

marker in its superblock that tells whether the filesystem was unmounted properly after the previous mount. This allows e2fsck (the version of fsck for the ext2 filesystem) to avoid checking the filesystem if the flag indicates that the unmount was done (the assumption being that a proper unmount indicates no problems). Whether the /etc/fastboot trick works on your system depends on your startup scripts, but the ext2 trick works every time you use e2fsck. It has to be explicitly bypassed with an option to e2fsck to be avoided. (See the e2fsck man page for details on how.)The automatic checking only works for the filesystems that are mounted automatically at boot time. Use fsck manually to check other filesystems, e.g., floppies.If fsck finds unrepairable problems, you need either in-depth knowlege of how filesystems work in general, and the type of the corrupt filesystem in particular, or good backups. The latter is easy (although sometimes tedious) to arrange, the former can sometimes be arranged via a friend, the Linux newsgroups and mailing lists, or some other source of support, if you don't have the know-how yourself. I'd like to tell you more about it, but my lack of education and experience in this regard hinders me. The debugfs program by Theodore T'so should be useful.fsck must only be run on unmounted filesystems, never on mounted filesystems (with the exception of the read-only root during startup). This is because it accesses the raw disk, and can therefore modify the filesystem without the operating system realizing it. There will be trouble, if the operating system is confused.

3.8.7 Checking for disk errors with badblocks

It can be a good idea to periodically check for bad blocks. This is done with the badblocks command. It outputs a list of the numbers of all bad blocks it can find. This list can be fed to fsck to be recorded in the filesystem data structures so that the operating system won't try to use the bad blocks for storing data. The following example will show how this could be done.

```
$ badblocks /dev/fd0H1440 1440 > bad-blocks
$ fsck -t ext2 -l bad-blocks /dev/fd0H1440
Parallelizing fsck version 0.5a (5-Apr-94)
e2fsck 0.5a, 5-Apr-94 for EXT2 FS 0.5, 94/03/10
Pass 1:  Checking inodes, blocks, and sizes
Pass 2:  Checking directory structure
Pass 3:  Checking directory connectivity
Pass 4:  Check reference counts.
Pass 5:  Checking group summary information.

/dev/fd0H1440:  ***** FILE SYSTEM WAS MODIFIED *****
/dev/fd0H1440:  11/360 files, 63/1440 blocks
$
```

If badblocks reports a block that was already used, e2fsck will try to move the block to another place. If the block was really bad, not just marginal, the contents of the file may be corrupted.

3.8.8 Fighting fragmentation

When a file is written to disk, it can't always be written in consecutive blocks. A file that is not stored in consecutive blocks is fragmented. It takes longer to read a fragmented file, since the disk's read-write head will have to move more. It is desireable to avoid fragmentation, although it is less of a problem in a system with a good buffer cache with read-ahead.The ext2 filesystem attempts to keep fragmentation at a minimum, by keeping all blocks in a file close together, even if they can't be stored in consecutive sectors. Ext2 effectively always allocates the free block that is nearest to other blocks in a file. For ext2, it is therefore seldom necessary to worry about fragmentation. There is a program for defragmenting an ext2 filesystem, see XXX (ext2-defrag) in the bibliography.There are many MS-DOS defragmentation programs that move blocks around in the filesystem to remove fragmentation. For other filesystems, defragmentation must be done by backing up the filesystem, re-creating it, and restoring the files from backups. Backing up a filesystem before defragmening is a good idea for all filesystems, since many things can go wrong during the defragmentation.

3.8.9 Other tools for all filesystems

Some other tools are also useful for managing filesystems. df shows the free disk space on one or more filesystems; du shows how much disk space a directory and all its files contain. These can be used to hunt down disk space wasters.sync forces all unwritten blocks in the buffer cache (see) to be written to disk. It is seldom necessary to do this by hand; the daemon process update does this automatically. It can be useful in catastrophies, for example if update or its helper process bdflush dies, or if you must turn off power now and can't wait for update to run.

3.8.10 Other tools for the ext2 filesystem

In addition to the filesystem creator (mke2fs) and checker (e2fsck) accessible directly or via the filesystem type independent front ends, the ext2 filesystem has some additional tools that can be useful.tune2fs adjusts filesystem parameters. Some of the more interesting parameters are:

A maximal mount count. e2fsck enforces a check when filesystem has been mounted too many times, even if the clean flag is set. For a system that is used for developing or testing the system, it might be a good idea to reduce this limit. A maximal time between checks. e2fsck can also enforce a maximal time between two checks, even if the clean flag is set, and the filesystem hasn't been mounted very often. This can be disabled, however. Number of blocks reserved for root. Ext2 reserves some blocks for root so that if the filesystem fills up, it is still possible to do system administration without having to delete anything. The reserved amount is by default 5 percent, which on most disks isn't enough to be wasteful. However, for floppies there is no point in reserving any blocks.

See the tune2fs manual page for more information.dumpe2fs shows information about an ext2 filesystem, mostly from the superblock. Figure 3.8.10 shows a sample output. Some of the information in the output is technical and requires understanding of how the filesystem works (see appendix XXX ext2fspaper), but much of it is readily understandable even for layadmins. debugfs is a filesystem debugger. It allows direct access to the filesystem data structures stored on disk and can thus be used to repair a disk that is so broken that fsck can't fix it automatically. It has also been known to be used to recover deleted files. However, debugfs very much requires that you understand what you're doing; a failure to understand can destroy all your data.dump and restore can be used to back up an ext2 filesystem. They are ext2 specific versions of the traditional UNIX backup tools. See for more information on backups.

3.9 Disks without filesystems

Not all disks or partitions are used as filesystems. A swap partition, for example, will not have a filesystem on it. Many floppies are used in a tape-drive emulating fashion, so that a tar or other file is written directly on the raw disk, without a filesystem. Linux boot floppies don't contain a filesystem, only the raw kernel.Avoiding a filesystem has the advantage of making more of the disk usable, since a filesystem always has some bookkeeping overhead. It also makes the disks more easily compatible with other systems: for example, the tar file format is the same on all systems, while filesystems are different on most systems. You will quickly get used to disks without filesystems if you need them. Bootable Linux floppies also do not necessarily have a filesystem, although that is also possible.One reason to use raw disks is to make image copies of them. For instance, if the disk contains a partially damaged filesystem, it is a good idea to make an exact copy of it before trying to fix it, since then you can start again if your fixing breaks things even more. One way to do this is to use dd:

```
$ dd if=/dev/fd0H1440 of=floppy-image
2880+0 records in
2880+0 records out
$ dd if=floppy-image of=/dev/fd0H1440
2880+0 records in
2880+0 records out
$
```

The first dd makes an exact image of the floppy to the file floppy-image, the second one writes the image to the floppy. (The user has presumably switched the floppy before the second command. Otherwise the command pair is of doubtful usefulness.)

3.10 Allocating disk space

3.10.1 Partitioning schemes

It is not easy to partition a disk in the best possible way. Worse, there is no universally correct way to do it; there are too many factors involved.The traditional way is to have a (relatively) small root filesystem, which contains /bin, /etc, /dev, /lib, /tmp, and other stuff that is needed to get the system up and running. This way, the root filesystem (in its own partition or on its own disk) is all that is needed to bring up the system. The reasoning is that if the root filesystem is small and is not heavily used, it is less likely to become corrupt when the system crashes, and you will therefore find it easier to fix any problems caused by the crash. Then you create separate partitions or use separate disks for the directory tree below /usr, the users' home directories (often under /home), and the swap space. Separating the home directories (with the users' files) in their own partition makes backups easier, since it is usually not necessary to backup programs (which reside below /usr). In a networked environment it is also possible to share /usr among several machines (e.g., by using NFS), thereby reducing the total disk space required by several tens or hundreds of megabytes times the number of machines.The problem with having many partitions is that it splits the total amount of free disk space into many small pieces. Nowadays, when disks and (hopefully) operating systems are more reliable, many people prefer to have just one partition that holds all their files. On the other hand, it can be less painful to back up (and restore) a small partition.For a small hard disk (assuming you don't do kernel development), the best way to go is probably to have just one partition. For large hard disks, it is probably better to have a few large partitions, just in case something does go wrong. (Note that 'small' and 'large' are used in a relative sense here; your needs for disk space decide what the threshold is.)If you have several disks, you might wish to have the root filesystem (including /usr) on one, and the users' home directories on another.It is a good idea to be prepared to experiment a bit with different partitioning schemes (over time, not just while first installing the system). This is a bit of work, since it essentially requires you to install the system from scratch several times, but it is the only way to be sure you do it right.

3.10.2 Space requirements

The Linux distribution you install will give some indication of how much disk space you need for various configurations. Programs installed separately may also do the same. This will help you plan your disk space usage, but you should prepare for the future and reserve some extra space for things you will notice later that you need.The amount you need for user files depends on what your users wish to do. Most people seem to need as much space for their files as possible, but the amount they will live happily with varies a lot. Some people do only light text processing and will survive nicely with a few megabytes, others do heavy image processing and will need gigabytes.By the way, when comparing file sizes given in kilobytes or megabytes and disk space given in megabytes, it can be important to know that the two units can be different. Some disk manufacturers like to pretend that a kilobyte is 1000 bytes and a megabyte is 1000 kilobytes, while all the rest of the computing world uses 1024 for both factors. Therefore, my 345 MB hard disk was really a 330 MB hard disk. [18] Swap space allocation is discussed in .

3.10.3 Examples of hard disk allocation

I used to have a 109 MB hard disk. Now I am using a 330 MB hard disk. I'll explain how and why I partitioned these disks.The 109 MB disk I partitioned in a lot of ways, when my needs and the operating systems I used changed; I'll explain two typical scenarios. First, I used to run MS-DOS together with Linux. For that, I needed about 20 MB of hard disk, or just enough to have MS-DOS, a C compiler, an editor, a few other utilities, the program I was working on, and enough free disk space to not feel claustrophobic. For Linux, I had a 10 MB swap partition, and the rest, or 79 MB, was a single partition with all the files I had under Linux. I experimented with having separate root, /usr, and /home partitions, but there was never enough free disk space in one piece to do much interesting.When I didn't need MS-DOS anymore, I repartitioned the disk so that I had a 12 MB swap partition, and again had the rest as a single filesystem.The 330 MB disk is partitioned into several partitions, like this:

5 MBroot filesystem 10 MBswap partition180 MB\fn{/usr} filesystem120 MB\fn{/home} filesystem 15 MBscratch partition

The scratch partition is for playing around with things that require their own partition, e.g., trying different Linux distributions, or comparing speeds of filesystems. When not needed for anything else, it is used as swap space (I like to have a

---

[18]Sic transit discus mundi.

lot of open windows).

3.10.4   Adding more disk space for Linux

Adding more disk space for Linux is easy, at least after the hardware has been properly installed (the hardware installation is outside the scope of this book). You format it if necessary, then create the partitions and filesystem as described above, and add the proper lines to /etc/fstab so that it is mounted automatically.

3.10.5   Tips for saving disk space

The best tip for saving disk space is to avoid installing unnecessary programs. Most Linux distributions have an option to install only part of the packages they contain, and by analyzing your needs you might notice that you don't need most of them. This will help save a lot of disk space, since many programs are quite large. Even if you do need a particular package or program, you might not need all of it. For example, some on-line documentation might be unnecessary, as might some of the Elisp files for GNU Emacs, some of the fonts for X11, or some of the libraries for programming.If you cannot uninstall packages, you might look into compression. Compression programs such as gzip or zip will compress (and uncompress) individual files or groups of files. The gzexe system will compress and uncompress programs invisibly to the user (unused programs are compressed, then uncompressed as they are used). The experimental DouBle system will compress all files in a filesystem, invisibly to the programs that use them. (If you are familiar with products such as Stacker for MS-DOS, the principle is the same.) Memory Management

> Minnet, jag har tappat mitt minne, är jag svensk eller finne, kommer inte ihåg...

(Bosse Österberg) This section describes the Linux memory management features, i.e., virtual memory and the disk buffer cache. The purpose and workings and the things the system administrator needs to take into consideration are described.

3.11   What is virtual memory?

Linux supports virtual memory, that is, using a disk as an extension of RAM so that the effective size of usable memory grows correspondingly. The kernel will write the contents of a currently unused block of memory to the hard disk so that the memory can be used for another purpose. When the original contents are needed again, they are read back into memory. This is all made completely transparent to the user; programs running under Linux only see the larger amount of memory available and don't notice that parts of them reside on the disk from time to time. Of course, reading and writing the hard disk is slower (on the order of a thousand times slower) than using real memory, so the programs don't run as fast. The part of the hard disk that is used as virtual memory is called the swap space.Linux can use either a normal file in the filesystem or a separate partition for swap space. A swap partition is faster, but it is easier to change the size of a swap file (there's no need to repartition the whole hard disk, and possibly install everything from scratch). When you know how much swap space you need, you should go for a swap partition, but if you are uncertain, you can use a swap file first, use the system for a while so that you can get a feel for how much swap you need, and then make a swap partition when you're confident about its size.You should also know that Linux allows one to use several swap partitions and/or swap files at the same time. This means that if you only occasionally need an unusual amount of swap space, you can set up an extra swap file at such times, instead of keeping the whole amount allocated all the time.A note on operating system terminology: computer science usually distinguishes between swapping (writing the whole process out to swap space) and paging (writing only fixed size parts, usually a few kilobytes, at a time). Paging is usually more efficient, and that's what Linux does, but traditional Linux terminology talks about swapping anyway. [19]

3.12   Creating a swap space

A swap file is an ordinary file; it is in no way special to the kernel. The only thing that matters to the kernel is that it has no holes, and that it is prepared for use with mkswap. It must reside on a local disk, however; it can't reside in a filesystem that has been mounted over NFS due to implementation reasons.The bit about holes is important. The swap file reserves the disk space so that the kernel can quickly swap out a page without having to go through all the things that are necessary when allocating a disk sector to a file. The kernel merely uses any sectors that have already been allocated

---

[19] Thus quite needlessly annoying a number of computer scientists something horrible.

to the file. Because a hole in a file means that there are no disk sectors allocated (for that place in the file), it is not good for the kernel to try to use them.One good way to create the swap file without holes is through the following command:

```
$ dd if=/dev/zero of=/extra-swap bs=1024 count=1024
1024+0 records in
1024+0 records out
$
```

where /extra-swap is the name of the swap file and the size of is given after the count=. It is best for the size to be a multiple of 4, because the kernel writes out memory pages, which are 4 kilobytes in size. If the size is not a multiple of 4, the last couple of kilobytes may be unused.A swap partition is also not special in any way. You create it just like any other partition; the only difference is that it is used as a raw partition, that is, it will not contain any filesystem at all. It is a good idea to mark swap partitions as type 82 (Linux swap); this will the make partition listings clearer, even though it is not strictly necessary to the kernel.After you have created a swap file or a swap partition, you need to write a signature to its beginning; this contains some administrative information and is used by the kernel. The command to do this is \cmd{mkswap}, used like this:

```
$ mkswap /extra-swap 1024
Setting up swapspace, size = 1044480 bytes
$
```

Note that the swap space is still not in use yet: it exists, but the kernel does not use it to provide virtual memory.You should be very careful when using mkswap, since it does not check that the file or partition isn't used for anything else. You can easily overwrite important files and partitions with mkswap! Fortunately, you should only need to use mkswap when you install your system.The Linux memory manager limits the size of each swap space to about 127 MB (for various technical reasons, the actual limit is (4096-10) * 8 * 4096 = 133890048$ bytes, or 127.6875 megabytes). You can, however, use up to 16 swap spaces simultaneously, for a total of almost 2 GB. [20]

3.13 Using a swap space

An initialized swap space is taken into use with swapon. This command tells the kernel that the swap space can be used. The path to the swap space is given as the argument, so to start swapping on a temporary swap file one might use the following command.

```
$ swapon /extra-swap
$
```

Swap spaces can be used automatically by listing them in the /etc/fstab file.

```
/dev/hda8 none swap sw 0 0
/swapfile none swap sw 0 0
```

The startup scripts will run the command swapon -a, which will start swapping on all the swap spaces listed in /etc/fstab. Therefore, the swapon command is usually used only when extra swap is needed.You can monitor the use of swap spaces with free. It will tell the total amount of swap space used.

```
$ free
total used free shared buffers
Mem: 15152 14896 256 12404 2528
-/+ buffers: 12368 2784
Swap: 32452 6684 25768
$
```

---

[20]A gigabyte here, a gigabyte there, pretty soon we start talking about real memory.

The first line of output (Mem:) shows the physical memory. The total column does not show the physical memory used by the kernel, which is usually about a megabyte. The used column shows the amount of memory used (the second line does not count buffers). The free column shows completely unused memory. The shared column shows the amount of memory shared by several processes; the more, the merrier. The buffers column shows the current size of the disk buffer cache.That last line (Swap:) shows similar information for the swap spaces. If this line is all zeroes, your swap space is not activated.The same information is available via top, or using the proc filesystem in file /proc/meminfo. It is currently difficult to get information on the use of a specific swap space.A swap space can be removed from use with swapoff. It is usually not necessary to do it, except for temporary swap spaces. Any pages in use in the swap space are swapped in first; if there is not sufficient physical memory to hold them, they will then be swapped out (to some other swap space). If there is not enough virtual memory to hold all of the pages Linux will start to thrash; after a long while it should recover, but meanwhile the system is unusable. You should check (e.g., with free) that there is enough free memory before removing a swap space from use.All the swap spaces that are used automatically with swapon -a can be removed from use with swapoff -a; it looks at the file /etc/fstab to find what to remove. Any manually used swap spaces will remain in use.Sometimes a lot of swap space can be in use even though there is a lot of free physical memory. This can happen for instance if at one point there is need to swap, but later a big process that occupied much of the physical memory terminates and frees the memory. The swapped-out data is not automatically swapped in until it is needed, so the physical memory may remain free for a long time. There is no need to worry about this, but it can be comforting to know what is happening.

3.14   Sharing swap spaces with other operating systems

Virtual memory is built into many operating systems. Since they each need it only when they are running, i.e., never at the same time, the swap spaces of all but the currently running one are being wasted. It would be more efficient for them to share a single swap space. This is possible, but can require a bit of hacking. The Tips-HOWTO contains some advice on how to implement this.

3.15   Allocating swap space

Some people will tell you that you should allocate twice as much swap space as you have physical memory, but this is a bogus rule. Here's how to do it properly:

Estimate your total memory needs. This is the largest amount of memory you'll probably need at a time, that is the sum of the memory requirements of all the programs you want to run at the same time. This can be done by running at the same time all the programs you are likely to ever be running at the same time. For instance, if you want to run X, you should allocate about 8 MB for it, gcc wants several megabytes (some files need an unusually large amount, up to tens of megabytes, but usually about four should do), and so on. The kernel will use about a megabyte by itself, and the usual shells and other small utilities perhaps a few hundred kilobytes (say a megabyte together). There is no need to try to be exact, rough estimates are fine, but you might want to be on the pessimistic side.Remember that if there are going to be several people using the system at the same time, they are all going to consume memory. However, if two people run the same program at the same time, the total memory consumption is usually not double, since code pages and shared libraries exist only once.The free and ps commands are useful for estimating the memory needs.

Add some security to the estimate in step 1. This is because estimates of program sizes will probably be wrong, because you'll probably forget some programs you want to run, and to make certain that you have some extra space just in case. A couple of megabytes should be fine. (It is better to allocate too much than too little swap space, but there's no need to over-do it and allocate the whole disk, since unused swap space is wasted space; see later about adding more swap.) Also, since it is nicer to deal with even numbers, you can round the value up to the next full megabyte.Based on the computations above, you know how much memory you'll be needing in total. So, in order to allocate swap space, you just need to subtract the size of your physical memory from the total memory needed, and you know how much swap space you need. (On some versions of UNIX, you need to allocate space for an image of the physical memory as well, so the amount computed in step 2 is what you need and you shouldn't do the subtraction.)If your calculated swap space is very much larger than your physical memory (more than a couple times larger), you should probably invest in more physical memory, otherwise performance will be too low.

It's a good idea to have at least some swap space, even if your calculations indicate that you need none. Linux uses swap space somewhat aggressively, so that as much physical memory as possible can be kept free. Linux will swap out memory pages that have not been used, even if the memory is not yet needed for anything. This avoids waiting for swapping when it is needed: the swapping can be done earlier, when the disk is otherwise idle.Swap space can be divided among several disks. This can sometimes improve performance, depending on the relative speeds of the disks and the access patterns of the disks. You might want to experiment with a few schemes, but be aware that doing the experiments properly is quite difficult. You should not believe claims that any one scheme is superior to any other, since it won't always be true.

3.16   The buffer cache

Reading from a disk [21]

is very slow compared to accessing (real) memory. In addition, it is common to read the same part of a disk several times during relatively short periods of time. For example, one might first read an e-mail message, then read the letter into an editor when replying to it, then make the mail program read it again when copying it to a folder. Or, consider how often the command ls might be run on a system with many users. By reading the information from disk only once and then keeping it in memory until no longer needed, one can speed up all but the first read. This is called disk buffering, and the memory used for the purpose is called the buffer cache.Since memory is, unfortunately, a finite, nay, scarce resource, the buffer cache usually cannot be big enough (it can't hold all the data one ever wants to use). When the cache fills up, the data that has been unused for the longest time is discarded and the memory thus freed is used for the new data.Disk buffering works for writes as well. On the one hand, data that is written is often soon read again (e.g., a source code file is saved to a file, then read by the compiler), so putting data that is written in the cache is a good idea. On the other hand, by only putting the data into the cache, not writing it to disk at once, the program that writes runs quicker. The writes can then be done in the background, without slowing down the other programs.Most operating systems have buffer caches (although they might be called something else), but not all of them work according to the above principles. Some are write-through: the data is written to disk at once (it is kept in the cache as well, of course). The cache is called write-back if the writes are done at a later time. Write-back is more efficient than write-through, but also a bit more prone to errors: if the machine crashes, or the power is cut at a bad moment, or the floppy is removed from the disk drive before the data in the cache waiting to be written gets written, the changes in the cache are usually lost. This might even mean that the filesystem (if there is one) is not in full working order, perhaps because the unwritten data held important changes to the bookkeeping information.Because of this, you should never turn off the power without using a proper shutdown procedure (see), or remove a floppy from the disk drive until it has been unmounted (if it was mounted) or after whatever program is using it has signaled that it is finished and the floppy drive light doesn't shine anymore. The sync command flushes the buffer, i.e., forces all unwritten data to be written to disk, and can be used when one wants to be sure that everything is safely written. In traditional UNIX systems, there is a program called update running in the background which does a sync every 30 seconds, so it is usually not necessary to use sync. Linux has an additional daemon, bdflush, which does a more imperfect sync more frequently to avoid the sudden freeze due to heavy disk I/O that sync sometimes causes.Under Linux, bdflush is started by update. There is usually no reason to worry about it, but if bdflush happens to die for some reason, the kernel will warn about this, and you should start it by hand (/sbin/update).The cache does not actually buffer files, but blocks, which are the smallest units of disk I/O (under Linux, they are usually 1 kB). This way, also directories, super blocks, other filesystem bookkeeping data, and non-filesystem disks are cached.The effectiveness of a cache is primarily decided by its size. A small cache is next to useless: it will hold so little data that all cached data is flushed from the cache before it is reused. The critical size depends on how much data is read and written, and how often the same data is accessed. The only way to know is to experiment.If the cache is of a fixed size, it is not very good to have it too big, either, because that might make the free memory too small and cause swapping (which is also slow). To make the most efficient use of real memory, Linux automatically uses all free RAM for buffer cache, but also automatically makes the cache smaller when programs need more memory.Under Linux, you do not need to do anything to make use of the cache, it happens completely automatically. Except for following the proper procedures for shutdown and removing floppies, you do not need to worry about it. Boots And Shutdowns Start me up Ah... you've got to... you've got to Never, never never stop Start it up Ah... start it up, never, never, never You make a grown man cry, you make a grown man cry (Rolling Stones) This section explains what goes on when a Linux system is brought up and taken down, and how it should be done properly. If proper procedures are not followed, files might be corrupted or lost.

---

[21]Except a RAM disk, for obvious reasons.

3.17   An overview of boots and shutdowns

The act of turning on a computer system and causing its operating system to be loaded [22]

is called booting. The name comes from an image of the computer pulling itself up from its bootstraps, but the act itself slightly more realistic.During bootstrapping, the computer first loads a small piece of code called the bootstrap loader, which in turn loads and starts the operating system. The bootstrap loader is usually stored in a fixed location on a hard disk or a floppy. The reason for this two step process is that the operating system is big and complicated, but the first piece of code that the computer loads must be very small (a few hundred bytes), to avoid making the firmware unnecessarily complicated.Different computers do the bootstrapping differently. For PC's, the computer (its BIOS) reads in the first sector (called the boot sector) of a floppy or hard disk. The bootstrap loader is contained within this sector. It loads the operating system from elsewhere on the disk (or from some other place).After Linux has been loaded, it initializes the hardware and device drivers, and then runs init. init starts other processes to allow users to log in, and do things. The details of this part will be discussed below.In order to shut down a Linux system, first all processes are told to terminate (this makes them close any files and do other necessary things to keep things tidy), then filesystems and swap areas are unmounted, and finally a message is printed to the console that the power can be turned off. If the proper procedure is not followed, terrible things can and will happen; most importantly, the filesystem buffer cache might not be flushed, which means that all data in it is lost and the filesystem on disk is inconsistent, and therefore possibly unusable.

3.18   The boot process in closer look

You can boot Linux either from a floppy or from the hard disk. The installation section in the Installation and Getting Started guide (XXX citation) tells you how to install Linux so you can boot it the way you want to.When a PC is booted, the BIOS will do various tests to check that everything looks all right, [23]

and will then start the actual booting. It will choose a disk drive (typically the first floppy drive, if there is a floppy inserted, otherwise the first hard disk, if one is installed in the computer; the order might be configurable, however) and will then read its very first sector. This is called the boot sector; for a hard disk, it is also called the master boot record, since a hard disk can contain several partitions, each with their own boot sectors.The boot sector contains a small program (small enough to fit into one sector) whose responsibility is to read the actual operating system from the disk and start it. When booting Linux from a floppy disk, the boot sector contains code that just reads the first few hundred blocks (depending on the actual kernel size, of course) to a predetermined place in memory. On a Linux boot floppy, there is no filesystem, the kernel is just stored in consecutive sectors, since this simplifies the boot process. It is possible, however, to boot from a floppy with a filesystem, by using LILO, the LInux LOader.When booting from the hard disk, the code in the master boot record will examine the partition table (also in the master boot record), identify the active partition (the partition that is marked to be bootable), read the boot sector from that partition, and then start the code in that boot sector. The code in the partition's boot sector does what a floppy disk's boot sector does: it will read in the kernel from the partition and start it. The details vary, however, since it is generally not useful to have a separate partition for just the kernel image, so the code in the partition's boot sector can't just read the disk in sequential order, it has to find the sectors wherever the filesystem has put them. There are several ways around this problem, but the most common way is to use LILO. (The details about how to do this are irrelevant for this discussion, however; see the LILO documentation for more information; it is most thorough.)When booting with LILO, it will normally go right ahead and read in and boot the default kernel. It is also possible to configure LILO to be able to boot one of several kernels, or even other operating systems than Linux, and it is possible for the user to choose which kernel or operating system is to be booted at boot time. LILO can be configured so that if one holds down the alt, shift, or ctrl key at boot time (when LILO is loaded), LILO will ask what is to be booted and not boot the default right away. Alternatively, LILO can be configured so that it will always ask, with an optional timeout that will cause the default kernel to be booted.With LILO, it is also possible to give a kernel command line argument, after the name of the kernel or operating system.Booting from floppy and from hard disk have both their advantages, but generally booting from the hard disk is nicer, since it avoids the hassle of playing around with floppies. It is also faster. However, it can be more troublesome to install the system to boot from the hard disk, so many people will first boot from floppy, then, when the system is otherwise installed and working well, will install LILO and

---

[22]On early computers, it wasn't enough to merely turn on the computer, you had to manually load the operating system as well. These new-fangled thing-a-ma-jigs do it all by themselves.

[23]This is called the power on self test, or POST for short.

start booting from the hard disk.After the Linux kernel has been read into the memory, by whatever means, and is started for real, roughly the following things happen:

The Linux kernel is installed compressed, so it will first uncompress itself. The beginning of the kernel image contains a small program that does this. If you have a super-VGA card that Linux recognizes and that has some special text modes (such as 100 columns by 40 rows), Linux asks you which mode you want to use. During the kernel compilation, it is possible to preset a video mode, so that this is never asked. This can also be done with LILO or rdev. After this, the kernel checks what other hardware there is (hard disks, floppies, network adapters, etc), and configures some of its device drivers appropriately; while it does this, it outputs messages about its findings. For example, when I boot, I it looks like this:

```
LILO boot:
Loading linux.
Console:  colour EGA+ 80x25, 8 virtual consoles
Serial driver version 3.94 with no serial options enabled
tty00 at 0x03f8 (irq = 4) is a 16450
tty01 at 0x02f8 (irq = 3) is a 16450
lp_init:  lp1 exists (0), using polling driver
Memory:  7332k/8192k available (300k kernel code, 384k reserved, 176k
data)
Floppy drive(s):  fd0 is 1.44M, fd1 is 1.2M
Loopback device init
Warning WD8013 board not found at i/o = 280.
Math coprocessor using irq13 error reporting.
Partition check:
hda:  hda1 hda2 hda3
VFS: Mounted root (ext filesystem).
Linux version 0.99.pl9-1 (root@haven) 05/01/93 14:12:20
```

The exact texts are different on different systems, depending on the hardware, the version of Linux being used, and how it has been configured. Then the kernel will try to mount the root filesystem. The place is configurable at compilation time, or any time with rdev or LILO. The filesystem type is detected automatically. If the mounting of the root filesystem fails, for example because you didn't remember to include the corresponding filesystem driver in the kernel, the kernel panics and halts the system (there isn't much it can do, anyway). The root filesystem is usually mounted read-only (this can be set in the same way as the place). This makes it possible to check the filesystem while it is mounted; it is not a good idea to check a filesystem that is mounted read-write. After this, the kernel starts the program init (located in /sbin/init) in the background (this will always become process number 1). init does various startup chores. The exact things it does depends on how it is configured; see for more information (not yet written). It will at least start some essential background daemons. init then switches to multi-user mode, and starts a getty for virtual consoles and serial lines. getty is the program which lets people log in via virtual consoles and serial terminals. init may also start some other programs, depending on how it is configured. After this, the boot is complete, and the system is up and running normally.

3.19   More about shutdowns

It is important to follow the correct procedures when you shut down a Linux system. If you fail do so, your filesystems probably will become trashed and the files probably will become scrambled. This is because Linux has a disk cache that won't write things to disk at once, but only at intervals. This greatly improves performance but also means that if you just turn off the power at a whim the cache may hold a lot of data and that what is on the disk may not be a fully working filesystem (because only some things have been written to the disk).Another reason against just flipping the power switch is that in a multi-tasking system there can be lots of things going on in the background, and shutting the power can be quite disastrous. By using the proper shutdown sequence, you ensure that all background processes can save their data.The command for properly shutting down a Linux system is shutdown. It is usually used in one of two ways.If you are running a system where you are the only user, the usual way of using shutdown is to quit all running programs, log out on all virtual consoles, log in as root on one of them (or stay logged in as root if you already are, but you should change to root's home directory or the root directory, to avoid problems with unmounting), then give the command shutdown -h now (substitute now with a plus sign and a number in minutes if you want a delay, though you usually don't on a single user system).Alternatively, if your system has many users, use the command shutdown -h +time message, where time is the time in minutes until the system is halted, and message is a short explanation of why the system is shutting down.

```
# shutdown -h +10 'We will install a new disk.  System should
> be back on-line in three hours.'
#
```

This will warn everybody that the system will shut down in ten minutes, and that they'd better get lost or lose data. The warning is printed to every terminal on which someone is logged in, including all xterms:

```
Broadcast message from root (ttyp0) Wed Aug 2 01:03:25 1995...

We will install a new disk.  System should
be back on-line in three hours.
The system is going DOWN for system halt in 10 minutes !!
```

The warning is automatically repeated a few times before the boot, with shorter and shorter intervals as the time runs out.When the real shutting down starts after any delays, all filesystems (except the root one) are unmounted, user processes (if anybody is still logged in) are killed, daemons are shut down, all filesystem are unmounted, and generally everything settles down. When that is done, init prints out a message that you can power down the machine. Then, and only then, should you move your fingers towards the power switch.Sometimes, although rarely on any good system, it is impossible to shut down properly. For instance, if the kernel panics and crashes and burns and generally misbehaves, it might be completely impossible to give any new commands, hence shutting down properly is somewhat difficult, and just about everything you can do is hope that nothing has been too severely damaged and turn off the power. If the troubles are a bit less severe (say, somebody hit your keyboard with an axe), and the kernel and the update program still run normally, it is probably a good idea to wait a couple of minutes to give update a chance to flush the buffer cache, and only cut the power after that.Some people like to shut down using the command sync [24]

three times, waiting for the disk I/O to stop, then turn off the power. If there are no running programs, this is about equivalent to using shutdown. However, it does not unmount any filesystems and this can lead to problems with the ext2fs "clean filesystem" flag. The triple-sync method is not recommended.(In case you're wondering: the reason for three syncs is that in the early days of UNIX, when the commands were typed separately, that usually gave sufficient time for most disk I/O to be finished.)

3.20   Rebooting

Rebooting means booting the system again. This can be accomplished by first shutting it down completely, turning power off, and then turning it back on. A simpler way is to ask shutdown to reboot the system, instead of merely halting it. This is accomplished by using the -r option to shutdown, for example, by giving the command shutdown -r now.Most Linux systems run shutdown -r now when ctrl-alt-del is pressed on the keyboard. This reboots the system. The action on ctrl-alt-del is configurable, however, and it might be better to allow for some delay before the reboot on a multiuser machine. Systems that are physically accessible to anyone might even be configured to do nothing when ctrl-alt-del is pressed.

3.21   Single user mode

The shutdown command can also be used to bring the system down to single user mode, in which no one can log in, but root can use the console. This is useful for system administration tasks that can't be done while the system is running normally.

---

[24]sync flushes the buffer cache.

SysAdmin Guide

3.22 Emergency boot floppies

It is not always possible to boot a computer from the hard disk. For example, if you make a mistake in configuring LILO, you might make your system unbootable. For these situations, you need an alternative way of booting that will always work (as long as the hardware works). For typical PC's, this means booting from the floppy drive.Most Linux distributions allow one to create an emergency boot floppy during installation. It is a good idea to do this. However, some such boot disks contain only the kernel, and assume you will be using the programs on the distribution's installation disks to fix whatever problem you have. Sometimes those programs aren't enough; for example, you might have to restore some files from backups made with software not on the installation disks.Thus, it might be necessary to create a custom root floppy as well. The Bootdisk HOWTO by Graham Chapman (XXX citation) contains instructions for doing this. You must, of course, remember to keep your emergency boot and root floppies up to date.You can't use the floppy drive you use to mount the root floppy for anything else. This can be inconvenient if you only have one floppy drive. However, if you have enough memory, you can configure your boot floppy to load the root disk to a ramdisk (the boot floppy's kernel needs to be specially configured for this). Once the root floppy has been loaded into the ramdisk, the floppy drive is free to mount other disks. init

> Uuno on numero yksi

(Slogan for a series of Finnish movies.)

This chapter describes the init process, which is the first user level process started by the kernel. init has many important duties, such as starting getty (so that users can log in), implementing run levels, and taking care of orphaned processes. This chapter explains how init is configured and how you can make use of the different run levels.

3.23 init comes first

init is one of those programs that are absolutely essential to the operation of a Linux system, but that you still can mostly ignore. A good Linux distribution will come with a configuration for init that will work for most systems, and on these systems there is nothing you need to do about init. Usually, you only need to worry about init if you hook up serial terminals, dial-in (not dial-out) modems, or if you want to change the default run level.When the kernel has started itself (has been loaded into memory, has started running, and has initialized all device drivers and data structures and such), it finishes its own part of the boot process by starting a user level program, init. Thus, init is always the first process (its process number is always 1).The kernel looks for init in a few locations that have been historically used for it, but the proper location for it (on a Linux system) is /sbin/init. If the kernel can't find init, it tries to run /bin/sh, and if that also fails, the startup of the system fails.When init starts, it finishes the boot process by doing a number of administrative tasks, such as checking filesystems, cleaning up /tmp, starting various services, and starting a getty for each terminal and virtual console where users should be able to log in (see).After the system is properly up, init restarts getty for each terminal after a user has logged out (so that the next user can log in). init also adopts orphan processes: when a process starts a child process and dies before its child, the child immediately becomes a child of init. This is important for various technical reasons, but it is good to know it, since it makes it easier to understand process lists and process tree graphs. [25]

There are a few variants of init available. Most Linux distributions use sysvinit (written by Miquel van Smoorenburg), which is based on the System V init design. The BSD versions of Unix have a different init. The primary difference is run levels: System V has them, BSD does not (at least traditionally). This difference is not essential. We'll look at sysvinit only.

3.24 Configuring init to start getty: the /etc/inittab file

When it starts up, init reads the /etc/inittab configuration file. While the system is running, it will re-read it, if sent the HUP signal; [26]

---

[25]init itself is not allowed to die. You can't kill init even with SIGKILL.

[26]Using the command kill -HUP 1 as root, for example

this feature makes it unnecessary to boot the system to make changes to the init configuration take effect. The /etc/inittab file is a bit complicated. We'll start with the simple case of configuring getty lines. Lines in /etc/inittab consist of four colon-delimited fields:

```
id:runlevels:action:process
```

The fields are described below. In addition, /etc/inittab can contain empty lines, and lines that begin with a number sign ('#'); these are both ignored.

id This identifies the line in the file. For getty lines, it specifies the terminal it runs on (the characters after /dev/tty in the device file name). For other lines, it doesn't matter (except for length restrictions), but it should be unique. runlevels The run levels the line should be considered for. The run levels are given as single digits, without delimiters. (Run levels are described in the next section.) action What action should be taken by the line, e.g., respawn to run the command in the next field again, when it exits, or once to run it just once. process The command to run.

To start a getty on the first virtual terminal (/dev/tty1 }), in all the normal multi-user run levels (2-5), one would write the following line:

```
1:2345:respawn:/sbin/getty 9600 tty1
```

The first field says that this is the line for /dev/tty1. The second field says that it applies to run levels 2, 3, 4, and 5. The third field means that the command should be run again, after it exits (so that one can log in, log out, and then log in again). The last field is the command that runs getty on the first virtual terminal. [27] If you wanted to add terminals or dial-in modem lines to a system, you'd add more lines to /etc/inittab, one for each terminal or dial-in line. For more details, see the manual pages init, inittab, and getty. If a command fails when it starts, and init is configured to restart it, it will use a lot of system resources: init starts it, it fails, init starts it, it fails, init starts it, it fails, and so on, ad infinitum. To prevent this, init will keep track of how often it restarts a command, and if the frequency grows to high, it will delay for five minutes before restarting again.

3.25   Run levels

A run level is a state of init and the whole system that defines what system services are operating. Run levels are identified by numbers, see . There is no consensus of how to use the user defined run levels (2 through 5). Some system administrators use run levels to define which subsystems are working, e.g., whether X is running, whether the network is operational, and so on. Others have all subsystems always running or start and stop them individually, without changing run levels, since run levels are too coarse for controlling their systems. You need to decide for yourself, but it might be easiest to follow the way your Linux distribution does things. Run levels are configured in /etc/inittab by lines like the following:

```
12:2:wait:/etc/init.d/rc 2
```

The first field is an arbitrary label, the second one means that this applies for run level 2. The third field means that init should run the command in the fourth field once, when the run level is entered, and that init should wait for it to complete. The /etc/init.d/rc command runs whatever commands are necessary to start and stop services to enter run level 2. The command in the fourth field does all the hard work of setting up a run level. It starts services that aren't already running, and stops services that shouldn't be running in the new run level any more. Exactly what the command is, and how run levels are configured, depends on the Linux distribution. When init starts, it looks for a line in /etc/inittab that specifies the default run level:

```
id:2:initdefault:
```

You can ask init to go to a non-default run level at startup by giving the kernel a command line argument of single or emergency. Kernel command line arguments can be given via LILO, for example. This allows you to choose the single user mode (run level 1). While the system is running, the telinit command can change the run level. When the run level is changed, init runs the relevant command from /etc/inittab.

---

[27]Different versions of getty are run differently. Consult your manual page, and make sure it is the correct manual page.

3.26   Special configuration in /etc/inittab

The /etc/inittab has some special features that allow init to react to special circumstances. These special features are marked by special keywords in the third field. Some examples:

powerwait Allows init to shut the system down, when the power fails. This assumes the use of a UPS, and software that watches the UPS and informs init that the power is off. ctrlaltdel Allows init to reboot the system, when the user presses ctrl-alt-del on the console keyboard. Note that the system administrator can configure the reaction to ctrl-alt-del to be something else instead, e.g., to be ignored, if the system is in a public location. (Or to start nethack.) sysinit Command to be run when the system is booted. This command usually cleans up /tmp, for example.

The list above is not exhaustive. See your inittab manual page for all possibilities, and for details on how to use the above ones.

3.27   Booting in single user mode

An important run level is single user mode (run level 1), in which only the system administrator is using the machine and as few system services, including logins, as possible are running. Single user mode is necessary for a few administrative tasks, [28]

such as running fsck on a /usr partition, since this requires that the partition be unmounted, and that can't happen, unless just about all system services are killed.A running system can be taken to single user mode by using telinit to request run level 1. At bootup, it can be entered by giving the word single or emergency on the kernel command line: the kernel gives the command line to init as well, and init understands from that word that it shouldn't use the default run level. (The kernel command line is entered in a way that depends on how you boot the system.)Booting into single user mode is sometimes necessary so that one can run fsck by hand, before anything mounts or otherwise touches a broken /usr partition (any activity on a broken filesystem is likely to break it more, so fsck should be run as soon as possible).The bootup scripts init runs will automatically enter single user mode, if the automatic fsck at bootup fails. This is an attempt to prevent the system from using a filesystem that is so broken that fsck can't fix it automatically. Such breakage is relatively rare, and usually involves a broken hard disk or an experimental kernel release, but it's good to be prepared.As a security measure, a properly configured system will ask for the root password before starting the shell in single user mode. Otherwise, it would be simple to just enter a suitable line to LILO to get in as root. (This will break if /etc/passwd has been broken by filesystem problems, of course, and in that case you'd better have a boot floppy handy.) Logging In And Out

> I don't care to belong to a club that accepts people like me as a member.

(Groucho Marx) This section describes what happens when a user logs in or out. The various interactions of background processes, log files, configuration files, and so on are described in some detail.

3.28   Logins via terminals

Figure 3.28 shows how logins happen via terminals. First, init makes sure there is a getty program for the terminal connection (or console). getty listens at the terminal and waits for the user to notify that he is ready to login in (this usually means that the user must type something). When it notices a user, getty outputs a welcome message (stored in /etc/issue), and prompts for the username, and finally runs the login program. login gets the username as a parameter, and prompts the user for the password. If these match, login starts the shell configured for the user; else it just exits and terminates the process (perhaps after giving the user another chance at entering the username and password). init notices that the process terminated, and starts a new getty for the terminal.

Note that the only new process is the one created by init (using the fork system call); getty and login only replace the program running in the process (using the exec system call). A separate program, for noticing the user, is needed for serial lines, since it can be (and traditionally was) complicated to notice when a terminal becomes active. getty also adapts to the speed and other settings of the connection, which is important especially for dial-in connections, where

---

[28]It probably shouldn't be used for playing nethack.

these parameters may change from call to call. There are several versions of getty and init in use, all with their good and bad points. It is a good idea to learn about the versions on your system, and also about the other versions (you could use the Linux Software Map to search them). If you don't have dial-in's, you probably don't have to worry about getty, but init is still important.

3.29   Logins via the network

Two computers in the same network are usually linked via a single physical cable. When they communicate over the network, the programs in each computer that take part in the communication are linked via a virtual connection, a sort of imaginary cable. As far as the programs at either end of the virtual connection are concerned, they have a monopoly on their own cable. However, since the cable is not real, only imaginary, the operating systems of both computers can have several virtual connections share the same physical cable. This way, using just a single cable, several programs can communicate without having to know of or care about the other communications. It is even possible to have several computers use the same cable; the virtual connections exist between two computers, and the other computers ignore those connections that they don't take part in. That's a complicated and over-abstracted description of the reality. It might, however, be good enough to understand the important reason why network logins are somewhat different from normal logins. The virtual connections are established when there are two programs on different computers that wish to communicate. Since it is in principle possible to login from any computer in a network to any other computer, there is a huge number of potential virtual communications. Because of this, it is not practical to start a getty for each potential login. There is a single process inetd (corresponding to getty) that handles all network logins. When it notices an incoming network login (i.e., it notices that it gets a new virtual connection to some other computer), it starts a new process to handle that single login. The original process remains and continues to listen for new logins. To make things a bit more complicated, there is more than one communication protocol for network logins. The two most important ones are telnet and rlogin. In addition to logins, there are many other virtual connections that may be made (for FTP, Gopher, HTTP, and other network services). It would be ineffective to have a separate process listening for a particular type of connection, so instead there is only one listener that can recognize the type of the connection and can start the correct type of program to provide the service. This single listener is called \cmd{inetd}; see the Linux Network Administrators' Guide for more information.

3.30   What login does

The login program takes care of authenticating the user (making sure that the username and password match), and of setting up an initial environment for the user by setting permissions for the serial line and starting the shell. Part of the initial setup is outputting the contents of the file /etc/motd (short for message of the day) and checking for electronic mail. These can be disabled by creating a file called .hushlogin in the user's home directory. If the file /etc/nologin exists, logins are disabled. That file is typically created by shutdown and relatives. login checks for this file, and will refuse to accept a login if it exists. If it does exist, login outputs its contents to the terminal before it quits. login logs all failed login attempts in a system log file (via syslog). It also logs all logins by root. Both of these can be useful when tracking down intruders. Currently logged in people are listed in /var/run/utmp. This file is valid only until the system is next rebooted or shut down; it is cleared when the system is booted. It lists each user and the terminal (or network connection) he is using, along with some other useful information. The who, w, and other similar commands look in utmp to see who are logged in. All successful logins are recorded into /var/log/wtmp. This file will grow without limit, so it must be cleaned regularly, for example by having a weekly cron job to clear it. [29]

The last command browses wtmp. Both utmp and wtmp are in a binary format (see the utmp manual page); it is unfortunately not convenient to examine them without special programs.

3.31   X and xdm

XXX X implements logins via xdm; also: xterm -ls

---

[29]Good Linux distributions do this out of the box.

3.32 Access control

The user database is traditionally contained in the /etc/passwd file. Some systems use shadow passwords, and have moved the passwords to /etc/shadow. Sites with many computers that share the accounts use NIS or some other method to store the user database; they might also automatically copy the database from one central location to all other computers. The user database contains not only the passwords, but also some additional information about the users, such as their real names, home directories, and login shells. This other information needs to be public, so that anyone can read it. Therefore the password is stored encrypted. This does have the drawback that anyone with access to the encrypted password can use various cryptographical methods to guess it, without trying to actually log into the computer. Shadow passwords try to avoid this by moving the password into another file, which only root can read (the password is still stored encrypted). However, installing shadow passwords later onto a system that did not support them can be difficult. With or without passwords, it is important to make sure that all passwords in a system are good, i.e., not easily guessable. The crack program can be used to crack passwords; any password it can find is by definition not a good one. While crack can be run by intruders, it can also be run by the system adminstrator to avoid bad passwords. Good passwords can also be enforced by the passwd program; this is in fact more effective in CPU cycles, since cracking passwords requires quite a lot of computation. The user group database is kept in /etc/group; for systems with shadow passwords, there can be a /etc/shadow.group. root usually can't login via most terminals or the network, only via terminals listed in the /etc/securetty file. This makes it necessary to get physical access to one of these terminals. It is, however, possible to log in via any terminal as any other user, and use the su command to become root.

3.33 Shell startup

When an interactive login shell starts, it automatically executes one or more pre-defined files. Different shells execute different files; see the documentation of each shell for further information. Most shells first run some global file, for example, the Bourne shell (/bin/sh) and its derivatives execute /etc/profile; in addition, they execute .profile in the user's home directory. /etc/profile allows the system administrator to have set up a common user environment, especially by setting the PATH to include local command directories in addition to the normal ones. On the other hand, .profile allows the user to customize the environment to his own tastes by overriding, if necessary, the default environment.

4 Managing user accounts

> The similarities of sysadmins and drug dealers: both measure stuff in K's, and both have users.

(Old, tired computer joke.)

This chapter explains how to create new user accounts, how to modify the properties of those accounts, and how to remove the accounts. Different Linux systems have different tools for doing this.

4.1 What's an account?

When a computer is used by many people it is usually necessary to differentiate between the users, for example, so that their private files can be kept private. This is important even if the computer can only be used by a single person at a time, as with most microcomputers. [30]

Thus, each user is given a unique username, and that name is used to log in. There's more to a user than just a name, however. An account is all the files, resources, and information belonging to one user. The term hints at banks, and in a commercial system each account usually has some money attached to it, and that money vanishes at different speeds depending on how much the user stresses the system. For example, disk space might have a price per megabyte and day, and processing time might have a price per second.

---

[30]It might be quite embarrassing if my sister could read my love letters.

4.2 Creating a user

The Linux kernel itself treats users are mere numbers. Each user is identified by a unique integer, the user id or uid, because numbers are faster and easier for a computer to process than textual names. A separate database outside the kernel assigns a textual name, the username, to each user id. The database contains additional information as well. To create a user, you need to add information about the user to the user database, and create a home directory for him. It may also be necessary to educate the user, and set up a suitable initial environment for him. Most Linux distributions come with a program for creating accounts. There are several such programs available. Two command line alternatives are adduser and useradd; there may be a GUI tool as well. Whatever the program, the result is that there is little if any manual work to be done. Even if the details are many and intricate, these programs make everything seem trivial. However, describes how to do it by hand.

4.2.1 /etc/passwd and other informative files

The basic user database in a Unix system is the text file, /etc/passwd (called the password file), which lists all valid usernames and their associated information. The file has one line per username, and is divided into seven colon-delimited fields:

Username.Password, in an encrypted form.Numeric user id.Numeric group id.Full name or other description of account.Home directory.Login shell (program to run at login).

The format is explained in more detail on the passwd manual page. Any user on the system may read the password file, so that they can, for example, learn the name of another user. This means that the password (the second field) is also available to everyone. The password file encrypts the password, so in theory there is no problem. However, the encryption is breakable, especially if the password is weak (e.g., it is short or it can be found in a dictionary). Therefore it is not a good idea to have the password in the password file. Many Linux systems have shadow passwords. This is an alternative way of storing the password: the encrypted password is stored in a separate file, /etc/shadow, which only root can read. The /etc/passwd file only contains a special marker in the second field. Any program that needs to verify a user is setuid, and can therefore access the shadow password file. Normal programs, which only use the other fields in the password file, can't get at the password. [31]

4.2.2 Picking numeric user and group ids

On most systems it doesn't matter what the numeric user and group ids are, but if you use the Network filesystem (NFS), you need to have the same uid and gid on all systems. This is because NFS also identifies users with the numeric uids. If you aren't using NFS, you can let your account creation tool pick them automatically. If you are using NFS, you'll have to be invent a mechanism for synchronizing account information. One alternative is to the NIS system (see XXX network-admin-guide). However, you should try to avoid re-using numeric uid's (and textual usernames), because the new owner of the uid (or username) may get access to the old owner's files (or mail, or whatever).

4.2.3 Initial environment: /etc/skel

When the home directory for a new user is created, it is initialized with files from the /etc/skel directory. The system administrator can create files in /etc/skel that will provide a nice default environment for users. For example, he might create a /etc/skel/.profile that sets the EDITOR environment variable to some editor that is friendly towards new users. However, it is usually best to try to keep /etc/skel as small as possible, since it will be next to impossible to update existing users' files. For example, if the name of the friendly editor changes, all existing users would have to edit their .profile. The system administrator could try to do it automatically, with a script, but that is almost certain going to break someone's file. Whenever possible, it is better to put global configuration into global files, such as /etc/profile. This way it is possible to update it without breaking users' own setups.

4.2.4 Creating a user by hand

To create a new account manually, follow these steps:

---

[31] Yes, this means that the password file has all the information about a user except his password. The wonder of development.

Edit /etc/passwd with vipw and add a new line for the new account. Be careful with the syntax. Do not edit directly with an editor! vipw locks the file, so that other commands won't try to update it at the same time. You should make the password field be '*', so that it is impossible to log in. Similarly, edit /etc/group with vigr, if you need to create a new group as well. Create the home directory of the user with mkdir. Copy the files from /etc/skel to the new home directory. Fix ownerships and permissions with chown and chmod. The -R option is most useful. The correct permissions vary a little from one site to another, but usually the following commands do the right thing:

```
cd /home/newusername
chown -R username.group .
chmod -R go=u,go-w .
chmod go= .
```

Set the password with passwd.

After you set the password in the last step, the account will work. You shouldn't set it until everything else has been done, otherwise the user may inadvertently log in while you're still copying the files. It is sometimes necessary to create dummy accounts [32]

that are not used by people. For example, to set up an anonymous FTP server (so that anyone can download files from it, without having to get an account first), you need to create an account called ftp. In such cases, it is usually not necessary to set the password (last step above). Indeed, it is better not to, so that no-one can use the account, unless they first become root, since root can become any user.

4.3 Changing user properties

There are a few commands for changing various properties of an account (i.e., the relevant field in /etc/passwd):

chfn Change the full name field. chsh Change the login shell. passwdChange the password.

The super-user may use these commands to change the properties of any account. Normal users can only change the properties of their own account. It may sometimes be necessary to disable these commands (with chmod) for normal users, for example in an environment with many novice users. Other tasks need to be done by hand. For example, to change the username, you need to edit /etc/passwd directly (with vipw, remember). Likewise, to add or remove the user to more groups, you need to edit /etc/group (with vigr). Such tasks tend to be rare, however, and should be done with caution: for example, if you change the username, e-mail will no longer reach the user, unless you also create a mail alias. [33]

4.4 Removing a user

To remove a user, you first remove all his files, mailboxes, mail aliases, print jobs, cron and at jobs, and all other references to the user. Then you remove the relevant lines from /etc/passwd and /etc/group (remember to remove the username from all groups it's been added to). It may be a good idea to first disable the account (see below), before you start removing stuff, to prevent the user from using the account while it is being removed. Remember that users may have files outside their home directory. The find command can find them:

```
find / -user username
```

However, note that the above command will take a long time, if you have large disks. If you mount network disks, you need to be careful so that you won't trash the network or the server. Some Linux distributions come with special commands to do this; look for deluser or userdel. However, it is easy to do it by hand as well, and the commands might not do everything.

---

[32]Surreal users?

[33]The user's name might change due to marriage, for example, and he might want to have his username reflect his new name.}

4.5   Disabling a user temporarily

It is sometimes necessary to temporarily disable an account, without removing it. For example, the user might not have paid his fees, or the system administrator may suspect that a cracker has got the password of that account. The best way to disable an account is to change its shell into a special program that just prints a message. This way, whoever tries to log into the account, will fail, and will know why. The message can tell the user to contact the system administrator so that any problems may be dealt with. It would also be possible to change the username or password to something else, but then the user won't know what is going on. Confused users mean more work. [34]

A simple way to create the special programs is to write 'tail scripts':

```
#!/usr/bin/tail +2
This account has been closed due to a security breach.
Please call 555-1234 and wait for the men in black to arrive.
```

The first two characters ('#!') tell the kernel that the rest of the line is a command that needs to be run to interpret this file. The tail command in this case outputs everything except the first line to the standard output. If user billg is suspected of a security breach, the system administrator would do something like this:

```
# chsh -s /usr/local/lib/no-login/security billg
# su - tester
This account has been closed due to a security breach.
Please call 555-1234 and wait for the men in black to arrive.
#
```

The purpose of the su is to test that the change worked, of course. Tail scripts should be kept in a separate directory, so that their names don't interfere with normal user commands.

Backups Hardware is indeterministically reliable. Software is deterministically unreliable. People are indeterministically unreliable. Nature is deterministically reliable. This chapter explains about why, how, and when to make backups, and how to restore things from backups.

4.6   On the importance of being backed up

Your data is valuable. It will cost you time and effort re-create it, and that costs money or at least personal grief and tears; sometimes it can't even be re-created, e.g., if it is the results of some experiments. Since it is an investment, you should protect it and take steps to avoid losing it. There are basically four reasons why you might lose data: hardware failures, software bugs, human action, or natural disasters. [35]

Although modern hardware tends to be quite reliable, it can still break seemingly spontaneously. The most critical piece of hardware for storing data is the hard disk, which relies on tiny magnetic fields remaining intact in a world filled with electromagnetic noise. Modern software doesn't even tend to be reliable; a rock solid program is an exception, not a rule. Humans are quite unreliable, they will either make a mistake, or they will be malicious and destroy data on purpose. Nature might not be evil, but it can wreak havoc even when being good. All in all, it is a small miracle that anything works at all. Backups are a way to protect the investment in data. By having several copies of the data, it does not matter as much if one is destroyed (the cost is only that of the restoration of the lost data from the backup). It is important to do backups properly. Like everything else that is related to the physical world, backups will fail sooner or later. Part of doing backups well is to make sure they work; you don't want to notice that your backups didn't work. [36]

Adding insult to injury, you might have a bad crash just as you're making the backup; if you have only one backup medium, it might destroyed as well, leaving you with the smoking ashes of hard work. [37]

---

[34] But they can be so fun, if you're a BOFH.

[35] The fifth reason is "something else".

[36] Don't laugh. This has happened to several people.

[37] Been there, done that...

Or you might notice, when trying to restore, that you forgot to back up something important, like the user database on a 15000 user site. Best of all, all your backups might be working perfectly, but the last known tape drive reading the kind of tapes you used was the one that now has a bucketful of water in it. When it comes to backups, paranoia is in the job description.

4.7 Selecting the backup medium

The most important decision regarding backups is the choice of backup medium. You need to consider cost, reliability, speed, availability, and usability. Cost is important, since you should preferably have several times more backup storage than what you need for the data. A cheap medium is usually a must. Reliability is extremely important, since a broken backup can make a grown man cry. A backup medium must be able to hold data without corruption for years. The way you use the medium affects it reliability as a backup medium. A hard disk is typically very reliable, but as a backup medium it is not very reliable, if it is in the same computer as the disk you are backing up. Speed is usually not very important, if backups can be done without interaction. It doesn't matter if a backup takes two hours, as long as it needs no supervision. On the other hand, if the backup can't be done when the computer would otherwise be idle, then speed is an issue. Availability is obviously necessary, since you can't use a backup medium if it doesn't exist. Less obvious is the need for the medium to be available even in the future, and on computers other than your own. Otherwise you may not be able to restore your backups after a disaster. Usability is a large factor in how often backups are made. The easier it is to make backups, the better. A backup medium mustn't be hard or boring to use. The typical alternatives are floppies and tapes. Floppies are very cheap, fairly reliable, not very fast, very available, but not very usable for large amounts of data. Tapes are cheap to somewhat expensive, fairly reliable, fairly fast, quite available, and, depending on the size of the tape, quite comfortable. There are other alternatives. They are usually not very good on availability, but if that is not a problem, they can be better in other ways. For example, magneto-optical disks can have good sides of both floppies (they're random access, making restoration of a single file quick) and tapes (contain a lot of data).

4.8 Selecting the backup tool

There are many tools that can be used to make backups. The traditional UNIX tools used for backups are tar, cpio, and dump. In addition, there are large number of third party packages (both freeware and commercial) that can be used. The choice of backup medium can affect the choice of tool. tar and cpio are similar, and mostly equivalent from a backup point of view. Both are capable of storing files on tapes, and retrieving files from them. Both are capable of using almost any media, since the kernel device drivers take care of the low level device handling and the devices all tend to look alike to user level programs. Some UNIX versions of tar and cpio may have problems with unusual files (symbolic links, device files, files with very long pathnames, and so on), but the Linux versions should handle all files correctly. dump is different in that it reads the filesystem directly and not via the filesystem. It is also written specifically for backups; tar and cpio are really for archiving files, although they work for backups as well. Reading the filesystem directly has some advantages. It makes it possible to back files up without affecting their time stamps; for tar and cpio, you would have to mount the filesystem read-only first. Directly reading the filesystem is also more effective, if everything needs to be backed up, since it can be done with much less disk head movement. The major disadvantage is that it makes the backup program specific to one filesystem type; the Linux dump program understands the ext2 filesystem only. dump also directly supports backup levels (which we'll be discussing below); with tar and cpio this has to be implemented with other tools. A comparison of the third party backup tools is beyond the scope of this book. The Linux Software Map lists many of the freeware ones.

4.9 Simple backups

A simple backup scheme is to back up everything once, then back up everything that has been modified since the previous backup. The first backup is called a full backup, the subsequent ones are incremental backups. A full backup is often more laborius than incremental ones, since there is more data to write to the tape and a full backup might not fit onto one tape (or floppy). Restoring from incremental backups can be many times more work than from a full one. Restoration can be optimized so that you always back up everything since the previous full backup; this way, backups are a bit more work, but there should never be a need to restore more than a full backup and an incremental backup. If you want to make backups every day and have six tapes, you could use tape~1 for the first full backup (say, on a Friday), and tapes 2 to 5 for the incremental backups (Monday through Thursday). Then you make a new full backup on tape 6 (second Friday), and start doing incremental ones with tapes 2 to 5 again. You don't want to overwrite tape 1 until you've got a new full backup, lest something happens while you're making the full backup. After you've made a full backup to tape 6, you want to keep tape 1 somewhere else, so that when your other backup tapes are destroyed in the fire, you still have at least something left. When you need to make the next full backup, you fetch tape 1 and leave tape 6 in its place. If you have more than six tapes, you can use the extra ones for full backups. Each time you make a full backup, you use the oldest tape. This way you can have full backups from several previous weeks, which is good if you want to find an old, now deleted file, or an old version of a file.

4.9.1 Making backups with tar

A full backup can easily be made with tar:

```
# tar -create -file /dev/ftape /usr/src
tar:  Removing leading / from absolute path names in the archive
#
```

The example above uses the GNU version of tar and its long option names. The traditional version of tar only understands single character options. The GNU version can also handle backups that don't fit on one tape or floppy, and also very long paths; not all traditional versions can do these things. (Linux only uses GNU tar.) If your backup doesn't fit on one tape, you need to use the –multi-volume (-M) option:

```
# tar -cMf /dev/fd0H1440 /usr/src
tar:  Removing leading / from absolute path names in the archive
Prepare volume \#2 for /dev/fd0H1440 and hit return:
#
```

Note that you should format the floppies before you begin the backup, or else use another window or virtual terminal and do it when tar asks for a new floppy. After you've made a backup, you should check that it is OK, using the –compare (-d) option:

```
# tar -compare -verbose -f /dev/ftape
usr/src/
usr/src/linux
usr/src/linux-1.2.10-includes/
....
#
```

Failing to check a backup means that you will not notice that your backups aren't working until after you've lost the original data. An incremental backup can be done with tar using the –newer (-N) option:

```
# tar -create -newer '8 Sep 1995' -file /dev/ftape /usr/src -verbose
tar:  Removing leading / from absolute path names in the archive
usr/src/
usr/src/linux-1.2.10-includes/
usr/src/linux-1.2.10-includes/include/
usr/src/linux-1.2.10-includes/include/linux/
usr/src/linux-1.2.10-includes/include/linux/modules/
usr/src/linux-1.2.10-includes/include/asm-generic/
usr/src/linux-1.2.10-includes/include/asm-i386/
usr/src/linux-1.2.10-includes/include/asm-mips/
usr/src/linux-1.2.10-includes/include/asm-alpha/
usr/src/linux-1.2.10-includes/include/asm-m68k/
usr/src/linux-1.2.10-includes/include/asm-sparc/
usr/src/patch-1.2.11.gz
#
```

Unfortunately, tar can't notice when a file's inode information has changed, for example, that it's permission bits have been changed, or when its name has been changed. This can be worked around using find and comparing current filesystem state with lists of files that have been previously backed up. Scripts and programs for doing this can be found on Linux ftp sites.

4.9.2 Restoring files with tar

The –extract (-x) option for tar extracts files:

```
# tar -extract -same-permissions -verbose -file /dev/fd0H1440
usr/src/
usr/src/linux
usr/src/linux-1.2.10-includes/
usr/src/linux-1.2.10-includes/include/
usr/src/linux-1.2.10-includes/include/linux/
usr/src/linux-1.2.10-includes/include/linux/hdreg.h
usr/src/linux-1.2.10-includes/include/linux/kernel.h
...
#
```

You also extract only specific files or directories (which includes all their files and subdirectories) by naming on the command line:

```
# tar xpvf /dev/fd0H1440 usr/src/linux-1.2.10-includes/include/linux/hdreg.h
usr/src/linux-1.2.10-includes/include/linux/hdreg.h
#
```

Use the –list (-t) option, if you just want to see what files are on a backup volume:

```
# tar -list -file /dev/fd0H1440
usr/src/
usr/src/linux
usr/src/linux-1.2.10-includes/
usr/src/linux-1.2.10-includes/include/
usr/src/linux-1.2.10-includes/include/linux/
usr/src/linux-1.2.10-includes/include/linux/hdreg.h
usr/src/linux-1.2.10-includes/include/linux/kernel.h
...
#
```

Note that tar always reads the backup volume sequentially, so for large volumes it is rather slow. It is not possible, however, to use random access database techniques when using a tape drive or some other sequential medium. tar doesn't handle deleted files properly. If you need to restore a filesystem from a full and an incremental backup, and you have deleted a file between the two backups, it will exist again after you have done the restore. This can be a big problem, if the file has sensitive data that should no longer be available.

4.10   Multilevel backups

The simple backup method outlined in the previous section is often quite adequate for personal use or small sites. For more heavy duty use, multilevel backups are more appropriate. The simple method has two backup levels: full and incremental backups. This can be generalized to any number of levels. A full backup would be level 0, and the different levels of incremental backups levels 1, 2, 3, etc. At each incremental backup level you back up everything that has changed since the previous backup at the same or a previous level. The purpose for doing this is that it allows a longer backup history cheaply. In the example in the previous section, the backup history went back to the previous full backup. This could be extended by having more tapes, but only a week per new tape, which might be too expensive. A longer backup history is useful, since deleted or corrupted files are often not noticed for a long time. Even a version of a file that is not very up to date is better than no file at all. With multiple levels the backup history can be extended more cheaply. For example, if we buy ten tapes, we could use tapes 1 and 2 for monthly backups (first Friday each month), tapes 3 to 6 for weekly backups (other Fridays; note that there can be five Fridays in one month, so we need four more tapes), and tapes 7 to 10 for daily backups (Monday to Thursday). With only four more tapes, we've been able to extend the backup history from two weeks (after all daily tapes have been used) to two months. It is true that we can't restore every version of each file during those two months, but what we can restore is often good enough. Figure 4.10 shows which backup level is used each day, and which backups can be restored from at the end of the month. Backup levels can also be used to keep filesystem restoration time to a minimum. If you have many incremental backups with monotonously growing level numbers, you need to restore all of them if you need to rebuild the whole filesystem. Instead you can use level numbers that aren't monotonous, and keep down the number of backups to restore. To minimize the number of tapes needed to restore, you could use a smaller level for each incremental tape. However, then the time to make the backups increases (each backup copies everything since the previous full backup). A better scheme is suggested by the dump manual page and described by the table XX (efficient-backup-levels). Use the following succession of backup levels: 3, 2, 5, 4, 7, 6, 9, 8, 9, etc. This keeps both the backup and restore times low. The most you have to backup is two day's worth of work. The number of tapes for a restore depends on how long you keep between full backups, but it is less than in the simple schemes. A fancy scheme can reduce the amount of labor needed, but it does mean there are more things to keep track of. You must decide if it is worth it. dump has built-in support for backup levels. For tar and cpio it must be implemented with shell scripts.

4.11 What to back up

You want to back up as much as possible. The major exception is software that can be easily reinstalled, [38]

but even they may have configuration files that it is important to back up, lest you need to do all the work to configure them all over again. Another major exception is the /proc filesystem; since that only contains data that the kernel always generates automatically, it is never a good idea to back it up. Expecially the /proc/kcore file is unnecessary, since it is just an image of your current physical memory; it's pretty large as well. Gray areas include the news spool, log files, and many other things in /var. You must decide what you consider important. The obvious things to back up are user files (/home) and system configuration files (/etc, but possibly other things scattered all over the filesystem).

4.12 Compressed backups

Backups take a lot of space, which can cost quite a lot of money. To reduce the space needed, the backups can be compressed. There are several ways of doing this. Some programs have support for for compression built in; for example, the –gzip (-z) option for GNU tar pipes the whole backup through the gzip compression program, before writing it to the backup medium. Unfortunately, compressed backups can cause trouble. Due to the nature of how compression works, if a single bit is wrong, all the rest of the compressed data will be unusable. Some backup programs have some built in error correction, but no method can handle a large number of errors. This means that if the backup is compressed the way GNU tar does it, with the whole output compressed as a unit, a single error makes all the rest of the backup lost. Backups must be reliable, and this method of compression is not a good idea. An alternative way is to compress each file separately. This still means that the one file is lost, but all other files are unharmed. The lost file would have been corrupted anyway, so this situation is not much worse than not using compression at all. The afio program (a variant of cpio) can do this. Compression takes some time, which may make the backup program unable to write data fast enough for a tape drive. [39]

This can be avoided by buffering the output (either internally, if the backup program if smart enough, or by using another program), but even that might not work well enough. This should only be a problem on slow computers.

5 Keeping Time

Time is an illusion. Lunchtime double so.

---

[38] You get to decide what's easy. Some people consider installing from dozens of floppies easy.

[39] If a tape drive doesn't data fast enough, it has to stop; this makes backups even slower, and can be bad for the tape and the drive.

(Douglas Adams.)

This chapter explains how a Linux system keeps time, and what you need to do to avoid causing trouble. Usually, you don't need to do anything about time, but it is good to understand it.

5.1   Time zones

Time measurement is based on mostly regular natural phenomena, such as alternating light and dark periods caused by the rotation of the planet. The total time taken by two successive periods is constant, but the lengths of the light and dark period vary. One simple constant is noon. Noon is the time of the day when the Sun is at its highest position. Since the Earth is round, [40]

noon happens at different times in different places. This leads to the concept of local time. Humans measure time in many units, most of which are tied to natural phenomena like noon. As long as you stay in the same place, it doesn't matter that local times differ. As soon as you need to communicate with distant places, you'll notice the need for a common time. In modern times, most of the places in the world communicate with most other places in the world, so a global standard for measuring time has been defined. This time is called universal time (UT or UTC, formerly known as Greenwich Mean Time or GMT, since it used to be local time in Greenwich, England). When people with different local times need to communicate, they can express times in universal time, so that there is no confusion about when things should happen. Each local time is called a time zone. While geography would allow all places that have noon at the same time have the same time zone, politics makes it difficult. For various reasons, many countries use daylight savings time, that is, they move their clocks to have more natural light while they work, and then move the clocks back during winter. Other countries do not do this. Those that do, do not agree when the clocks should be moved, and they change the rules from year to year. This makes time zone conversions definitely non-trivial. Time zones are best named by the location or by telling the difference between local and universal time. In the US and some other countries, the local time zones have a name and a three letter abbreviation. The abbreviations are not unique, however, and should not be used unless the country is also named. It is better to talk about the local time in, say, Helsinki, than about East European time, since not all countries in Eastern Europe follow the same rules. Linux has a time zone package that knows about all existing time zones, and that can easily be updated when the rules change. All the system administrator needs to do is to select the appropriate time zone. Also, each user can set his own time zone; this is important since many people work with computers in different countries over the Internet. When the rules for daylight savings time change in your local time zone, make sure you'll upgrade at least that part of your Linux system. Other than setting the system time zone and upgrading the time zone data files, there is little need to bother about time.

5.2   The hardware and software clocks

A personal computer has a battery driven hardware clock. The battery ensures that the clock will work even if the rest of the computer is without electricity. The hardware clock can be set from the BIOS setup screen or from whatever operating system is running. The Linux kernel keeps track of time independently from the hardware clock. During the boot, Linux sets its own clock to the same time as the hardware clock. After this, both clocks run independently. Linux maintains its own clock because looking at the hardware is slow and complicated. The kernel clock always shows universal time. This way, the kernel does not need to know about time zones at all. The simplicity results in higher reliability and makes it easier to update the time zone information. Each process handles time zone conversions itself (using standard tools that are part of the time zone package). The hardware clock can be in local time or in universal time. It is usually better to have it in universal time, because then you don't need to change the hardware clock when daylight savings time begins or ends (UTC does not have DST). Unfortunately, some PC operating systems, including MS-DOS, Windows, and OS/2, assume the hardware clock shows local time. Linux can handle either, but if the hardware clock shows local time, then it must be modified when daylight savings time begins or ends (otherwise it wouldn't show local time).

5.3   Showing and setting time

In the Debian system, the system time zone is determined by the symbolic link /etc/localtime. This link points at a time zone data file that describes the local time zone. The time zone data files are stored in /usr/lib/zoneinfo. Other Linux

---

[40] According to recent research.

distributions may do this differently. A user can change his private time zone by setting the TZ environment variable. If it is unset, the system time zone is assumed. The syntax of the TZ variable is described in the tzset manual page. The date command shows the current date and time. [41]

For example:

```
$ date
Sun Jul 14 21:53:41 EET DST 1996
$
```

That time is Sunday, 14th of July, 1996, at about ten before ten at the evening, in the time zone called "EET DST" (which might be East European Daylight Savings Time). date can also show the univeral time:

```
$ date -u
Sun Jul 14 18:53:42 UTC 1996
Sun Jul 14 18:53:42 UTC 1996
$
```

date is also used to set the kernel's software clock:

```
# date 07142157
Sun Jul 14 21:57:00 EET DST 1996
# date
Sun Jul 14 21:57:02 EET DST 1996
#
```

See the date manual page for more details; the syntax is a bit arcane. Only root can set the time. While each user can have his own time zone, the clock is the same for everyone. date only shows or sets the software clock. The clock commands syncronizes the hardware and software clocks. It is used when the system boots, to read the hardware clock and set the software clock. If you need to set both clocks, you first set the software clock with date, and then the hardware clock with clock -w. The -u option to clock tells it that the hardware clock is in universal time. You must use the -u option correctly. If you don't, your computer will be quite confused about what the time is. The clocks should be changed with care. Many parts of a Unix system require the clocks to work correctly. For example, the cron daemon runs commands periodically. If you change the clock, it can be confused of whether it needs to run the commands or not. On one early Unix system, someone set the clock twenty years into the future, and cron wanted to run all the periodic commands for twenty years all at once. Current versions of cron can handle this correctly, but you should still be careful. Big jumps or backward jumps are more dangeours than smaller or forward ones.

5.4   When the clock is wrong

The Linux software clock is not always accurate. It is kept running by a periodic timer interrupt generated by PC hardware. If the system has too many processes running, it may take too long to service the timer interrupt, and the software clock starts slipping behind. The hardware clock runs independently and is usually more accurate. If you boot your computer often (as is the case for most systems that aren't servers), it will usually keep fairly accurate time. If you need to adjust the hardware clock, it is usually simplest to reboot, go into the BIOS setup screen, and do it from there. This avoids all trouble that changing system time might cause. If doing it via BIOS is not an option, set the new time with date and clock (in that order), but be prepared to reboot, if some part of the system starts acting funny. A networked computer (even if just over the modem) can check its own clock automatically, by comparing it to some other computer's time. If the other computer is known to keep very accurate time, then both computers will keep accurate time. This can be done by using the rdate and netdate commands. Both check the time of a remote computer (netdate can handle several remote computers), and set the local computer's time to that. By running one these commands regularly, your computer will keep as accurate time as the remote computer. XXX say something intelligent about NTP Glossary (DRAFT)

---

[41] Beware of the time command, which does not show the current time.

The Librarian of the Unseen University had unilaterally decided to aid comprehension by producing an Orang-utan/Human Dictionary. He'd been working on it for three months. It wasn't easy. He'd got as far as 'Oook.'

(Terry Pratchett, "Men At Arms") This is a short list of word definitions for concepts relating to Linux and system administration. ambition The act of writing funny sentences in the hope of getting them into the Linux cookie file. application program Software that does something useful. The results of using an application program is what the computer was bought for. See also system program, operating system. daemon A process lurking in the background, usually unnoticed, until something triggers it into action. For example, the \cmd{update} daemon wakes up every thirty seconds or so to flush the buffer cache, and the \cmd{sendmail} daemon awakes whenever someone sends mail. file system The methods and data structures that an operating system uses to keep track of files on a disk or partition; the way the files are organized on the disk. Also used about a partition or disk that is used to store the files or the type of the filesystem. glossary A list of words and explanations of what they do. Not to be confused with a dictionary, which is also a list of words and explanations. kernel Part of an operating system that implements the interaction with hardware and the sharing of resources. See also system program. operating system Software that shares a computer system's resources (processor, memory, disk space, network bandwidth, and so on) between users and the application programs they run. Controls access to the system to provide security. See also kernel, system program, application program. system call The services provided by the kernel to application programs, and the way in which they are invoked. See section 2 of the manual pages. system program Programs that implement high level functionality of an operating system, i.e., things that aren't directly dependent on the hardware. May sometimes require special privileges to run (e.g., for delivering electronic mail), but often just commonly thought of as part of the system (e.g., a compiler). See also application program, kernel, operating system.

From above

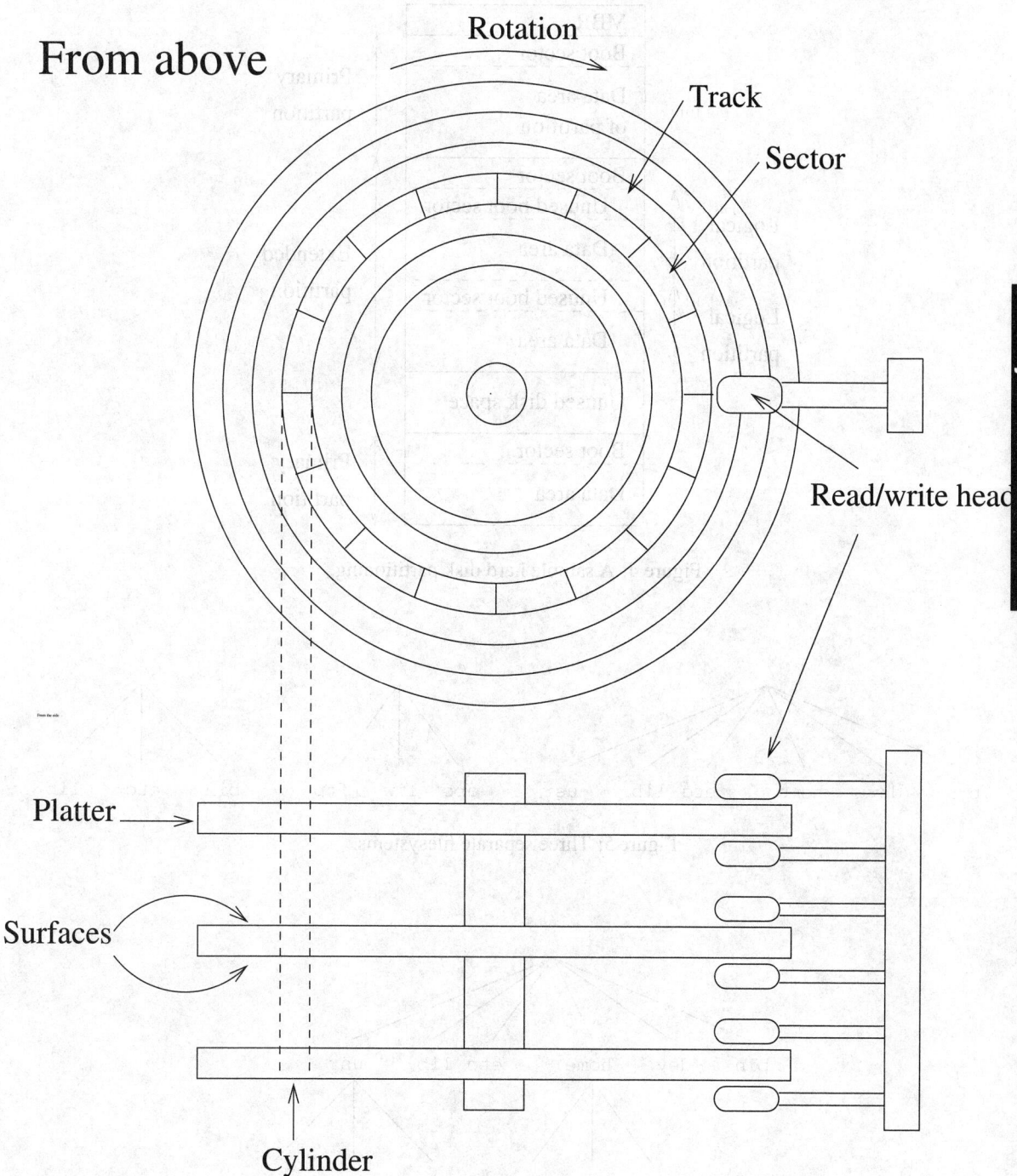

Figure 3: A schematic picture of a hard disk.

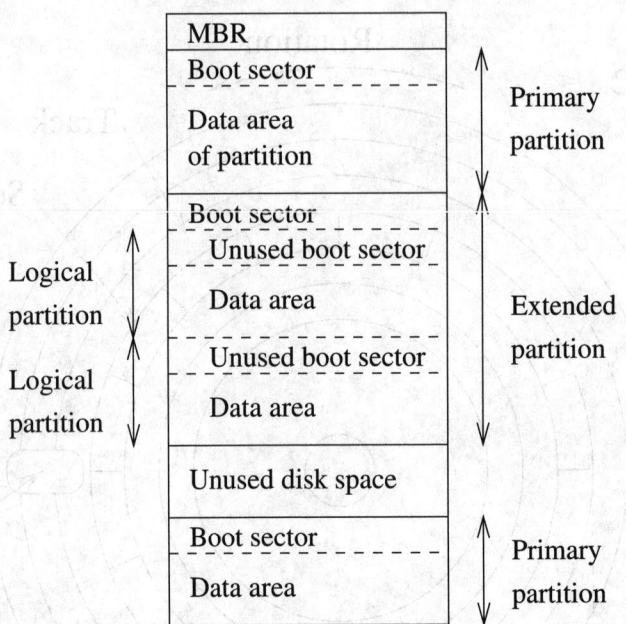

Figure 4: A sample hard disk partitioning.

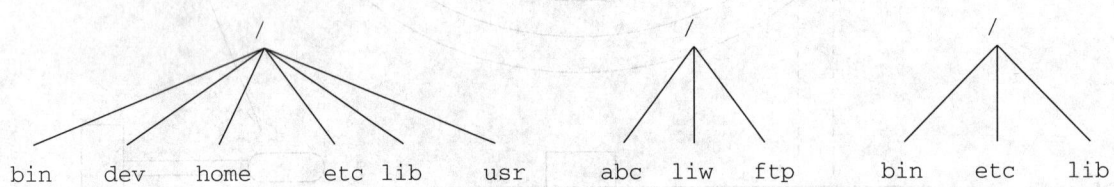

Figure 5: Three separate filesystems.

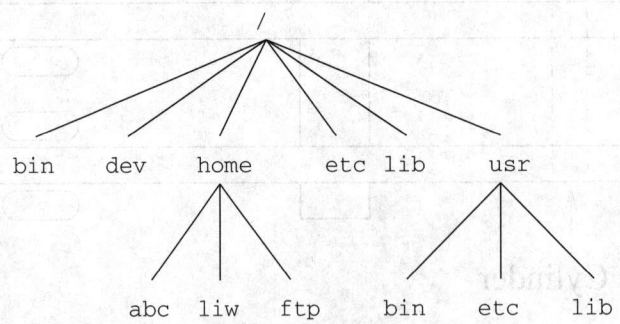

Figure 6: /home and /usr have been mounted.

```
dumpe2fs 0.5b, 11-Mar-95 for EXT2 FS 0.5a, 94/10/23
Filesystem magic number:    0xEF53
Filesystem state:           clean
Errors behavior:            Continue
Inode count:                360
Block count:                1440
Reserved block count:       72
Free blocks:                1133
Free inodes:                326
First block:                1
Block size:                 1024
Fragment size:              1024
Blocks per group:           8192
Fragments per group:        8192
Inodes per group:           360
Last mount time:            Tue Aug  8 01:52:52 1995
Last write time:            Tue Aug  8 01:53:28 1995
Mount count:                3
Maximum mount count:        20
Last checked:               Tue Aug  8 01:06:31 1995
Check interval:             0
Reserved blocks uid:        0 (user root)
Reserved blocks gid:        0 (group root)

Group 0:
  Block bitmap at 3, Inode bitmap at 4, Inode table at 5
  1133 free blocks, 326 free inodes, 2 directories
  Free blocks: 307-1439
  Free inodes: 35-360
```

Figure 7: Sample output from dumpe2fs

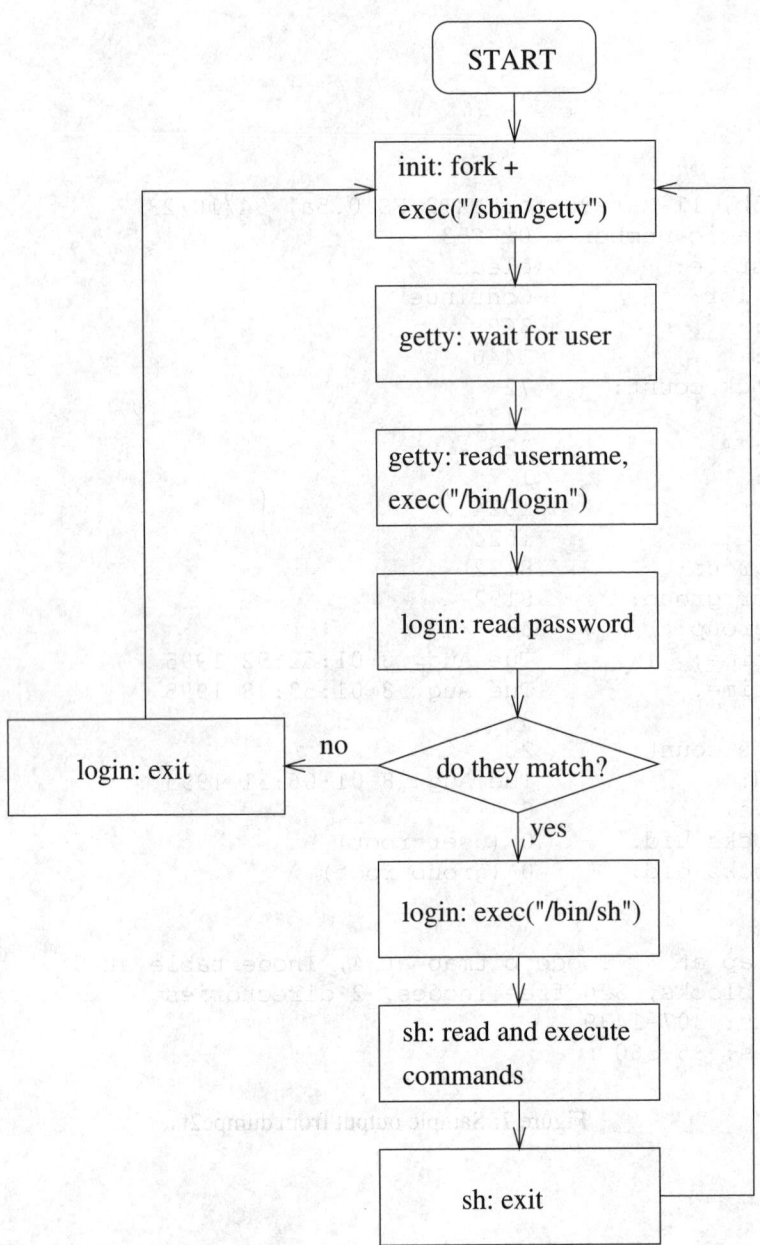

Figure 8: Logins via terminals: the interaction of init, getty, login, and the shell.

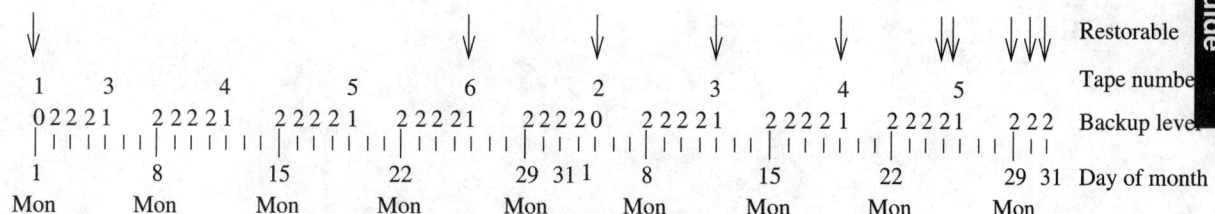

Figure 9: A sample multilevel backup schedule.

## Part III

"Brief Introduction to Alpha Systems and Processors" Neal Crook

Digital Equipment (Editor: *David Mosberger* <mailto:davidm@azstarnet.com>)
V0.11, 6 June 1997
This document is a brief overview of existing Alpha CPUs, chipsets and systems. It has something of a hardware bias, reflecting my own area of expertese. Although I am an employee of Digital Equipment Corporation, this is not an official statement by Digital and any opinions expressed are mine and not Digital's.

Contents

HOWTO

1   What is Alpha

"Alpha" is the name given to Digital's 64-bit RISC architecture. The Alpha project in Digital began in mid-1989, with the goal of providing a high-performance migration path for VAX customers. This was not the first RISC architecture to be produced by Digital, but it was the first to reach the market. When Digital announced Alpha, in March 1992, it made the decision to enter the merchant semicondutor market by selling Alpha microprocessors.

Alpha is also sometimes referred to as Alpha AXP, for obscure and arcane reasons that aren't worth persuing. Suffice it to say that they are one and the same.

2   What is Digital Semiconductor

Digital Semiconductor <http://www.digital.com/info/semiconductor/> (DS) is the business unit within Digital Equipment Corporation (Digital - we don't like the name DEC) that sells semiconductors on the merchant market. Digital's products include CPUs, support chipsets, PCI-PCI bridges and PCI peripheral chips for comms and multimedia.

3 Alpha CPUs

There are currently 2 generations of CPU core that implement the Alpha architecture:

- EV4
- EV5

Opinions differ as to what "EV" stands for (Editor's note: the true answer is of course "Electro Vlassic" 12 ([1])), but the number represents the first generation of Digital's CMOS technology that the core was implemented in. So, the EV4 was originally implemented in CMOS4. As time goes by, a CPU tends to get a mid-life performance kick by being optically shrunk into the next generation of CMOS process. EV45, then, is the EV4 core implemented in CMOS5 process. There is a big difference between shrinking a design into a particular technology and implementing it from scratch in that technology (but I don't want to go into that now). There are a few other wildcards in here: there is also a CMOS4S (optical shrink in CMOS4) and a CMOS5L.

True technophiles will be interested to know that CMOS4 is a 0.75 micron process, CMOS5 is a 0.5 micron process and CMOS6 is a 0.35 micron process.

To map these CPU cores to *chips* we get:

21064-150,166
> EV4 (originally), EV4S (now)

21064-200
> EV4S

21064A-233,275,300
> EV45

21066
> LCA4S (EV4 core, with EV4 FPU)

21066A-233
> LCA45 (EV4 core, but with EV45 FPU)

21164-233,300,333
> EV5

21164A-417
> EV56

21264
> *EV6* <http://www.mdronline.com/report/articles/21264/21264.html>

The EV4 core is a dual-issue (it can issue 2 instructions per CPU clock) superpipelined core with integer unit, floating point unit and branch prediction. It is fully bypassed and has 64-bit internal data paths and tightly coupled 8Kbyte caches, one each for Instruction and Data. The caches are write-through (they never get dirty).

The EV45 core has a couple of tweaks to the EV4 core: it has a slightly improved floating point unit, and 16KB caches, one each for Instruction and Data (it also has cache parity). (Editor's note: Neal Crook indicated in a separate mail that the changes to the floating point unit (FPU) improve the performance of the divider. The EV4 FPU divider takes 34 cycles for a single-precision divide and 63 cycles for a double-precision divide (non data-dependent). In constrast, the EV45 divider takes typically 19 cycles (34 cycles max) for single-precision and typically 29 cycles (63 cycles max) for a double-precision division (data-dependent).)

The EV5 core is a quad-issue core, also superpipelined, fully bypassed etc etc. It has tightly-coupled 8Kbyte caches, one each for I and D. These caches are write-through. It also has a tightly-coupled 96Kbyte on-chip second-level cache (the Scache) which is 3-way set associative and write-back (it can be dirty). The EV4->EV5 performance increase is better than just the increase achieved by clock speed improvements. As well as the bigger caches and quad issue, there are microarchitectural improvements to reduce producer/consumer latencies in some paths.

The EV56 core is fundamentally the same microarchitecture as the EV5, but it adds some new instructions for 8 and 16-bit loads and stores (see Section 8 (Bytes and all that stuff)). These are primarily intended for use by device drivers. The EV56 core is implemented in CMOS6, which is a 2.0V process.

The 21064 was anounced in March 1992. It uses the EV4 core, with a 128-bit bus interface. The bus interface supports the 'easy' connection of an external second-level cache, with a block size of 256-bits (2 data beats on the bus). The Bcache timing is completely software configurable. The 21064 can also be configured to use a 64-bit external bus, (but I'm not sure if any shipping system uses this mode). The 21064 does not impose any policy on the Bcache, but it is usually configured as a write-back cache. The 21064 does contain hooks to allow external hardware to maintain cache coherence with the Bcache and internal caches, but this is hairy.

The 21066 uses the EV4 core and integrates a memory controller and PCI host bridge. To save pins, the memory controller has a 64-bit data bus (but the internal caches have a block size of 256 bits, just like the 21064, therefore a block fill takes 4 beats on the bus). The memory controller supports an external Bcache and external DRAMs. The timing of the Bcache and DRAMs is completely software configurable, and can be controlled to the resolution of the CPU clock period. Having a 4-beat process to fill a cache block isn't as bad as it sounds because the DRAM access is done in page mode. Unfortunately, the memory controller doesn't support any of the new esoteric DRAMs (SDRAM, EDO or BEDO) or synchronous cache RAMs. The PCI bus interface is fully rev2.0 compliant and runs at upto 33MHz.

The 21164 has a 128-bit data bus and supports split reads, with upto 2 reads outstanding at any time (this allows 100% data bus utilisation under best-case dream-on conditions, i.e., you can theoretically transfer 128-bits of data on every bus clock). The 21164 supports easy connection of an external 3-rd level cache (Bcache) and has all the hooks to allow external systems to maintain full cache coherence with all caches. Therefore, symmetric multiprocessor designs are 'easy'.

The 21164A was announced in October, 1995. It uses the EV56 core. It is nominally pin-compatible with the 21164, but requires split power rails; all of the power pins that were +3.3V power on the 21164 have now been split into two groups; one group provided 2.0V power to the CPU core, the other group supplies 3.3V to the I/O cells. Unlike older implementations, the 21164 pins are not 5V-tolerant. The end result of this change is that 21164 systems are, in general, not upgradeable to the 21164A (though note that it would be relatively straightforward to design a 21164A system that could also accommodate a 21164). The 21164A also has a couple of new pins to support the new 8 and 16-bit loads and stores. It also improves the 21164 support for using synchronus SRAMs to implement the external Bcache.

4   21064 performance vs 21066 performance

The 21064 and the 21066 have the same (EV4) CPU core. If the same program is run on a 21064 and a 21066, at the same CPU speed, then the difference in performance comes only as a result of system Bcache/memory bandwidth. Any code thread that has a high hit-rate on the *internal* caches will perform the same. There are 2 big performance killers:

1. Code that is write-intensive. Even though the 21064 and the 21066 have write buffers to swallow some of the delays, code that is write-intensive will be throttled by write bandwidth at the system bus. This arises because the on-chip caches are write-through.

2. Code that wants to treat floats as integers. The Alpha architecture does not allow register-register transfers from integer registers to floating point registers. Such a conversion has to be done via memory (And therefore, because the on-chip caches are write-through, via the Bcache). (Editor's note: it seems that both the EV4 and EV45 can perform the conversion through the primary data cache (Dcache), provided that the memory is cached already. In such a case, the store in the conversion sequence will update the Dcache and the subsequent load is, under certain circumstances, able to read the updated d-cache value, thus avoiding a costly roundtrip to the Bcache. In particular, it seems best to execute the stq/ldt or stt/ldq instructions back-to-back, which is somewhat counter-intuitive.)

If you make the same comparison between a 21064A and a 21066A, there is an additional factor due to the different Icache and Dcache sizes between the two chips.

Now, the 21164 solves both these problems: it achieve *much* higher system bus bandwidths (despite having the same number of signal pins - yes, I *know* it's got about twice as many pins as a 21064, but all those extra ones are power and ground! (yes, really!!)) and it has write-back caches. The only remaining problem is the answer to the question "how much does it cost?"

5   A Few Notes On Clocking

All of the current Alpha CPUs use high-speed clocks, because their microarchitectures have been designed as so-called short-tick designs. None of the sytem busses have to run at horrendous speeds as a result though:

- on the 21066(A), 21064(A), 21164 the off-chip cache (Bcache) timing is completely programmable, to the resolution of the CPU clock. For example, on a 275MHz CPU, the Bcache read access time can be controller with a resolution of 3.6ns
- on the 21066(A), the DRAM timing is completely programmable, to the resolution of the CPU clock (*not* the PCI clock, the CPU clock).
- on the 21064(A), 21164(A), the system bus frequency is a sub-multiple of the CPU clock frequency. Most of the 21064 motherboards use a 33MHz system bus clock.
- Systems that use the 21066 can run the PCI at any frequency relative to the CPU. Generally, the PCI runs at 33MHz.
- Systems that use the APECs chipset (see Section 6 ()) always have their CPU system bus equal to their PCI bus frequency. This means that both busses tends to run at either 25MHz or 33MHz (since these are the frequencies that scale up to match the CPU frequencies). On APECs systems, the DRAM controller timings are software programmable in terms of the CPU system bus frequency

Aside: someone suggested that they were getting bad performance on a 21066 because the 21066 memory controller was only running at 33MHz. Actually, it's the superfast 21064A systems that have memory controllers that 'only' run at 33MHz.

6   The chip-sets

DS sells two CPU support chipsets. The 2107x chipset (aka APECS) is a 21064(A) support chiset. The 2117x chipset (aka ALCOR) is a 21164 support chipset. There will also be 2117xA chipset (aka ALCOR 2) as a 21164A support chipset.

Both chipsets provide memory controllers and PCI host bridges for their CPU. APECS provides a 32-bit PCI host bridge, ALCOR provides a 64-bit PCI host bridge which (in accordance with the requirements of the PCI spec) can support both 32-bit and 64-bit PCI devices.

APECS consists of 6, 208-pin chips (4, 32-bit data slices (DECADE), 1 system controller (COMANCHE), 1 PCI controller (EPIC)). It provides a DRAM controller (128-bit memory bus) and a PCI interface. It also does all the work to maintain memory coherence when a PCI device DMAs into (or out of) memory.

ALCOR consists of 5 chips (4, 64-bit data slices (Data Switch, DSW) - 208-pin PQFP and 1 control (Control, I/O Address, CIA) - a 383 pin plastic PGA). It provides a DRAM controller (256-bit memory bus) and a PCI interface. It also does all the work required to support an external Bcache and to maintain memory coherence when a PCI device DMAs into (or out of) memory.

There is no support chipset for the 21066, since the memory controller and PCI host bridge functionality are integrated onto the chip.

7   The Systems

The applications engineering group in DS produces example designs using the CPUs and support chipsets. These are typically PC-AT size motherboards, with all the functionality that you'd typically find on a high-end Pentium motherboard.

Originally, these example designs were intended to be used as starting points for third-parties to produce motherboard designs from. These first-generation designs were called Evaluation Boards (EBs). As the amount of engineering required to build a motherboard has increased (due to higher-speed clocks and the need to meet RF emission and susceptibility regulations) the emphasis has shifted towards providing motherboards that are suitable for volume manufacture.

Digital's system groups have produced several generations of machines using Alpha processors. Some of these systems use support logic that is designed by the systems groups, and some use commodity chipsets from DS. In some cases, systems use a combination of both.

Various third-parties build systems using Alpha processors. Some of these companies design systems from scratch, and others use DS support chipsets, clone/modify DS example designs or simply package systems using build and tested boards from DS.

The EB64: Obsolete design using 21064 with memory controller implemented using programmable logic. I/O provided by using programmable logic to interface a 486<->ISA bridge chip. On-board Ethernet, SuperI/O (2S, 1P, FD), Ethernet and ISA. PC-AT size. Runs from standard PC power supply.

The EB64+: Uses 21064 or 21064A and APECs. Has ISA and PCI expansion (3 ISA, 2 PCI, one pair are on a shared slot). Supports 36-bit DRAM SIMs. ISA bus generated by Intel SaturnI/O PCI-ISA bridge. On-board SCSI (NCR 810 on PCI) Ethernet (Digital 21040), KBD, MOUSE (PS2 style), SuperI/O (2S, 1P, FD), RTC/NVRAM. Boot ROM is EPROM. PC-AT size. Runs from standard PC power supply.

The EB66: Uses 21066 or 21066A. I/O sub-system is identical to EB64+. Baby PC-AT size. Runs from standard PC power supply. The EB66 schematic was published as a marketing poster advertising the 21066 as "the first microprocessor in the world with embedded PCI" (for trivia fans: there are actually 2 versions of this poster - I drew the circuits and wrote the spiel for the first version, and some Americans mauled the spiel for the second version)

The EB164: Uses 21164 and ALCOR. Has ISA and PCI expansion (3 ISA slots, 2 64-bit PCI slots (one is shared with an ISA slot) and 2 32-bit PCI slots. Uses plus-in Bcache SIMMs. I/O sub-system provides SuperI/O (2S, 1P, FD), KBD, MOUSE (PS2 style), RTC/NVRAM. Boot ROM is Flash. PC-AT-sized motherboard. Requires power supply with 3.3V output.

The AlphaPC64 (aka Cabriolet): derived from EB64+ but now baby-AT with Flash boot ROM, no on-board SCSI or Ethernet. 3 ISA slots, 4 PCI slots (one pair are on a shared slot), uses plug-in Bcache SIMMs. Requires power supply with 3.3V output.

The AXPpci33 (aka NoName), is based on the EB66. This design is produced by Digital's Technical OEM (TOEM) group. It uses the 21066 processor running at 166MHz or 233MHz. It is a baby-AT size, and runs from a standard PC power supply. It has 5 ISA slots and 3 PCI slots (one pair are a shared slot). There are 2 versions, with either PS/2 or large DIN connectors for the keyboard.

Other 21066-based motherboards: most if not all other 21066-based motherboards on the market are also based on EB66 - there's really not many system options when designing a 21066 system, because all the control is done on-chip.

Multia (aka the Universal Desktop Box): This is a very compact pedestal desktop system based on the 21066. It includes 2 PCMCIA sockets, 21030 (TGA) graphics, 21040 Ethernet and NCR 810 SCSI disk along with floppy, 2 serial ports and a parallel port. It has limited expansion capability (one PCI slot) due to its compact size. (There is some restriction on when you can use the PCI slot, can't remember what) (Note that 21066A-based and Pentium-based Multia's are also available).

DEC PC 150 AXP (aka Jensen): This is a very old Digital system - one of the first-generation Alpha systems. It is only mentioned here because a number of these systems seem to be available on the second-hand market. The Jensen is a floor-standing tower system which used a 150MHz 21064 (later versions used faster CPUs but I'm not sure what speeds). It used programmable logic to interface a 486 EISA I/O bridge to the CPU.

Other 21064(A) systems: There are 3 or 4 motherboard designs around (I'm not including Digital *systems* here) and all the ones I know of are derived from the EB64+ design. These include:

- EB64+ (some vendors package the board and sell it unmodified); AT form-factor.

- Aspen Systems motherboard: EB64+ derivative; baby-AT form-factor.
- Aspen Systems server board: many PCI slots (includes PCI bridge).
- AlphaPC64 (aka Cabriolet), baby AT form-factor.

Other 21164(A) systems: The only one I'm aware of that isn't simply an EB164 clone is a system made by DeskStation. That system is implemented using a memory and I/O controller proprietary to Desk Station. I don't know what their attitude towards Linux is.

8   Bytes and all that stuff

When the Alpha architecture was introduced, it was unique amongst RISC architectures for eschewing 8-bit and 16-bit loads and stores. It supported 32-bit and 64-bit loads and stores (longword and quadword, in Digital's nomenclature). The co-architects (Dick Sites, Rich Witek) justified this decision by citing the advantages:

1. Byte support in the cache and memory sub-system tends to slow down accesses for 32-bit and 64-bit quantities.
2. Byte support makes it hard to build high-speed error-correction circuitry into the cache/memory sub-system.

Alpha compensates by providing powerful instructions for manipulating bytes and byte groups within 64-bit registers. Standard benchmarks for string operations (e.g., some of the Byte benchmarks) show that Alpha performs very well on byte manipulation.

The absence of byte loads and stores impacts some software semaphores and impacts the design of I/O sub-systems. Digital's solution to the I/O problem is to use some low-order address lines to specify the data size during I/O transfers, and to decode these as byte enables. This so-called Sparse Addressing wastes address space and has the consequence that I/O space is non-contiguous (more on the intricacies of Sparse Addressing when I get around to writing it). Note that I/O space, in this context, refers to all system resources present on the PCI and therefore includes both PCI memory space and PCI I/O space.

With the 21164A introduction, the Alpha archtecture was ECO'd to include byte addressing. Executing these new instructions on an earlier CPU will cause an OPCDEC PALcode exception, so that the PALcode will handle the access. This will have a performance impact. The ramifications of this are that use of these new instructions (IMO) should be restricted to device drivers rather than applications code.

These new byte load and stores mean that future support chipsets will be able to support contiguous I/O space.

9   PALcode and all that stuff

This is a placeholder for a section explaining PALcode. I will write it if there is sufficient interest.

10   Porting

The ability of any Alpha-based machine to run Linux is really only limited by your ability to get information on the gory details of its innards. Since there are Linux ports for the E66, EB64+ and EB164 boards, all systems based on the 21066, 21064/APECS or 21164/ALCOR should run Linux with little or no modification. The major thing that is different between any of these motherboards is the way that they route interrupts. There are three sources of interrupts:

- on-board devices
- PCI devices
- ISA devices

All the systems use an Intel System I/O bridge (SIO) to act as a bridge between PCI and ISA (the main I/O bus is PCI, the ISA bus is a secondary bus used to support slow-speed and 'legacy' I/O devices). The SIO contains the traditional pair of daisy-chained 8259s.

Some systems (e.g., the Noname) route all of their interrupts through the SIO and thence to the CPU. Some systems have a separate interrupt controller and route all PCI interrupts plus the SIO interrupt (8259 output) through that, and all ISA interrupts through the SIO.

Other differences between the systems include:

- how many slots they have
- what on-board PCI devices they have
- whether they have Flash or EPROM

11 More Information

All of the DS evaluation boards and motherboard designs are license-free and the whole documentation kit for a design costs about \\$50. That includes all the schematics, programmable parts sources, data sheets for CPU and support chipset. The doc kits are available from Digital Semiconductor distributors. I'm not suggesting that many people will want to rush out and buy this, but I do want to point out that the information is available.

Hope that was helpful. Comments/updates/suggestions for expansion to *Neal Crook* `<mailto:neal.crook@reo.mts.digital.com>`.

12 References

[1] `<http://www.research.digital.com/wrl/publications/abstracts/TN-13.html>` Bill Hamburgen, Jeff Mogul, Brian Reid, Alan Eustace, Richard Swan, Mary Jo Doherty, and Joel Bartlett. *Characterization of Organic Illumination Systems*. DEC WRL, Technical Note 13, April 1989.

HOWTO

Part IV

"Assembly HOWTO" François-René Rideau

rideau@ens.fr
v0.4l, 16 November 1997
This is the Linux Assembly HOWTO. This document describes how to program in assembly using *FREE* programming tools, focusing on development for or from the Linux Operating System on i386 platforms. Included material may or may not be applicable to other hardware and/or software platforms. Contributions about these would be gladly accepted. *keywords*: assembly, assembler, free, macroprocessor, preprocessor, asm, inline asm, 32-bit, x86, i386, gas, as86, nasm

Contents

HOWTO

1   INTRODUCTION

1.1   Legal Blurp

Copyright © 1996,1997 by François-René Rideau. This document may be distributed under the terms set forth in the LDP license at <http://sunsite.unc.edu/LDP/COPYRIGHT.html>.

1.2   IMPORTANT NOTE

This is expectedly the last release I'll make of this document. There's one candidate new maintainer, but until he really takes the HOWTO over, I'll accept feedback.

You are especially invited to ask questions, to answer to questions, to correct given answers, to add new FAQ answers, to give pointers to other software, to point the current maintainer to bugs or deficiencies in the pages. If you're motivated, you could even *TAKE OVER THE MAINTENANCE OF THE FAQ*. In one word, contribute!

To contribute, please contact whoever appears to maintain the Assembly-HOWTO. Current maintainers are *François-René Rideau* <mailto:rideau@clipper.ens.fr> and now *Paul Anderson* <mailto:paul@geeky1. ebtech.net>.

1.3   Foreword

This document aims at answering frequently asked questions of people who program or want to program 32-bit x86 assembly using *free* assemblers, particularly under the Linux operating system. It may also point to other documents about non-free, non-x86, or non-32-bit assemblers, though such is not its primary goal.

Because the main interest of assembly programming is to build to write the guts of operating systems, interpreters, compilers, and games, where a C compiler fails to provide the needed expressivity (performance is more and more seldom an issue), we stress on development of such software.

1.3.1   How to use this document

This document contains answers to some frequently asked questions. At many places, Universal Resource Locators (URL) are given for some software or documentation repository. Please see that the most useful repositories are mirrored, and that by accessing a nearer mirror site, you relieve the whole Internet from unneeded network traffic, while saving your own precious time. Particularly, there are large repositories all over the world, that mirror other popular repositories. You should learn and note what are those places near you (networkwise). Sometimes, the list of mirrors is listed in a file, or in a login message. Please heed the advice. Else, you should ask archie about the software you're looking for...

The most recent version for this documents sits in

<http://www.eleves.ens.fr:8080/home/rideau/Assembly-HOWTO> or <http://www.eleves. ens.fr:8080/home/rideau/Assembly-HOWTO.sgml>

but what's in Linux HOWTO repositories *should* be fairly up to date, too (I can't know):

<ftp://sunsite.unc.edu/pub/Linux/docs/HOWTO/> (?)

A french translation of this HOWTO can be found around

<ftp://ftp.ibp.fr/pub/linux/french/HOWTO/>

1.3.2 Other related documents

- If you don't know what *free* software is, please do read *carefully* the GNU General Public License, which is used in a lot of free software, and is a model for most of their licenses. It generally comes in a file named COPYING, with a library version in a file named COPYING.LIB. Litterature from the FSF (free software foundation) might help you, too.

- Particularly, the interesting kind of free software comes with sources that you can consult and correct, or sometimes even borrow from. Read your particular license carefully, and do comply to it.

- There is a FAQ for comp.lang.asm.x86 that answers generic questions about x86 assembly programming, and questions about some commercial assemblers in a 16-bit DOS environment. Some of it apply to free 32-bit asm programming, so you may want to read this FAQ...

  <http://www2.dgsys.com/raymoon/faq/asmfaq.zip>

- FAQs and docs exist about programming on your favorite platform, whichever it is, that you should consult for platform-specific issues not directly related to programming in assembler.

1.4 History

Each version includes a few fixes and minor corrections, which needs not be repeatedly mentionned every time.

Version 0.1 23 Apr 1996

Francois-Rene "Faré" Rideau <rideau@ens.fr> creates and publishes the first mini-HOWTO, because "I'm sick of answering ever the same questions on comp.lang.asm.x86"

Version 0.2 4 May 1996

*

Version 0.3c 15 Jun 1996

*

Version 0.3f 17 Oct 1996

found -fasm option to enable GCC inline assembler w/o -O optimizations

Version 0.3g 2 Nov 1996

Created the History. Added pointers in cross-compiling section. Added section about I/O programming under Linux (particularly video).

Version 0.3h 6 Nov 1996

more about cross-compiling – See on sunsite: devel/msdos/

Version 0.3i 16 Nov 1996

NASM is getting pretty slick

Version 0.3j 24 Nov 1996

point to french translated version

Version 0.3k 19 Dec 1996

What? I had forgotten to point to terse???

Version 0.3l 11 Jan 1997

*

Version 0.4pre1 13 Jan 1997

text mini-HOWTO transformed into a full linuxdoc-sgml HOWTO, to see what the SGML tools are like.

Version 0.4 20 Jan 1997

first release of the HOWTO as such.

Version 0.4a 20 Jan 1997

CREDITS section added

HOWTO

Version 0.4b 3 Feb 1997

NASM moved: now is before AS86

Version 0.4c 9 Feb 1997

Added section "DO YOU NEED ASSEMBLY?"

Version 0.4d 28 Feb 1997

Vapor announce of a new Assembly-HOWTO maintainer.

Version 0.4e 13 Mar 1997

Release for DrLinux

Version 0.4f 20 Mar 1997

*

Version 0.4g 30 Mar 1997

*

Version 0.4h 19 Jun 1997

still more on "how not to use assembly"; updates on NASM, GAS.

Version 0.4i 17 July 1997

info on 16-bit mode access from Linux.

Version 0.4j 7 September 1997

*

Version 0.4k 19 October 1997

*

Version 0.4l 16 November 1997

release for LSL 6th edition.

This is yet another last-release-by-Faré-before-new-maintainer-takes-over (?)

1.5 Credits

I would like to thanks the following persons, by order of appearance:

- *Linus Torvalds* <mailto:buried.alive@in.mail> for Linux
- *Bruce Evans* <mailto:bde@zeta.org.au> for bcc from which as86 is extracted
- *Simon Tatham* <mailto:anakin@poboxes.com> and *Julian Hall* <mailto:jules@earthcorp.com> for NASM
- *Jim Neil* <mailto:jim-neil@digital.net> for Terse
- *Tim Bynum* <mailto:linux-howto@sunsite.unc.edu> for maintaining HOWTOs
- *Raymond Moon* <mailto:raymoon@moonware.dgsys.com> for his FAQ
- *Eric Dumas* <mailto:dumas@excalibur.ibp.fr> for his translation of the mini-HOWTO into french (sad thing for the original author to be french and write in english)
- *Paul Anderson* <mailto:paul@geeky1.ebtech.net> and *Rahim Azizarab* <mailto:rahim@megsinet.net> for helping me, if not for taking over the HOWTO.
- All the people who have contributed ideas, remarks, and moral support.

2 DO YOU NEED ASSEMBLY?

Well, I wouldn't want to interfere with what you're doing, but here are a few advice from hard-earned experience.

2.1 Pros and Cons

2.1.1 The advantages of Assembly

Assembly can express very low-level things:

- you can access machine-dependent registers and I/O.
- you can control the exact behavior of code in critical sections that might involve hardware or I/O lock-ups
- you can break the conventions of your usual compiler, which might allow some optimizations (like temporarily breaking rules about GC, threading, etc.).
- get access to unusual programming modes of your processor (e.g. 16 bit code for startup or BIOS interface on Intel PCs)
- you can build interfaces between code fragments using incompatible conventions (e.g. produced by different compilers, or separated by a low-level interface).
- you can produce reasonably fast code for tight loops to cope with a bad non-optimizing compiler (but then, there are free optimizing compilers available!)
- you can produce hand-optimized code that's perfectly tuned for your particular hardware setup, though not to anyone else's.
- you can write some code for your new language's optimizing compiler (that's something few will ever do, and even they, not often).

2.1.2 The disadvantages of Assembly

Assembly is a very low-level language (the lowest above hand-coding the binary instruction patterns). This means

- it's long and tedious to write initially,
- it's very bug-prone,
- your bugs will be very difficult to chase,
- it's very difficult to understand and modify, i.e. to maintain.
- the result is very non-portable to other architectures, existing or future,
- your code will be optimized only for a certain implementation of a same architecture: for instance, among Intel-compatible platforms, each CPU design and variation (bus width, relative speed and size of CPU/caches/RAM/Bus/disks presence of FPU, MMX extensions, etc) implies potentially completely different optimization techniques. CPU designs already include Intel 386, 486, Pentium, PPro, Pentium II; Cyrix 5x86, 6x86; AMD K5, K6. New designs keep appearing, so don't expect either this listing or your code to be up-to-date.
- your code might also be unportable accross different OS platforms on the same architecture, by lack of proper tools. (well, GAS seems to work on all platforms; NASM seems to work or be workable on all intel platforms).
- you spend more time on a few details, and can't focus on small and large algorithmic design, that are known to bring the largest part of the speed up. [e.g. you might spend some time building very fast list/array manipulation primitives in assembly; only a hash table would have sped up your program much more; or, in another context, a binary tree; or some high-level structure distributed over a cluster of CPUs]
- a small change in algorithmic design might completely invalidate all your existing assembly code. So that either you're ready (and able) to rewrite it all, or you're tied to a particular algorithmic design;
- On code that ain't too far from what's in standard benchmarks, commercial optimizing compilers outperform hand-coded assembly (well, that's less true on the x86 architecture than on RISC architectures, and perhaps less true for widely available/free compilers; anyway, for typical C code, GCC is fairly good);
- And in any case, as says moderator John Levine on comp.compilers, "compilers make it a lot easier to use complex data structures, and compilers don't get bored halfway through and generate reliably pretty good code." They will also *correctly* propagate code transformations throughout the whole (huge) program when optimizing code between procedures and module boundaries.

HOWTO

2.1.3 Assessment

All in all, you might find that though using assembly is sometimes needed, and might even be useful in a few cases where it is not, you'll want to:

- minimize the use of assembly code,
- encapsulate this code in well-defined interfaces
- have your assembly code automatically generated from patterns expressed in a higher-level language than assembly (e.g. GCC inline-assembly macros).
- have automatic tools translate these programs into assembly code
- have this code be optimized if possible
- All of the above, i.e. write (an extension to) an optimizing compiler back-end.

Even in cases when Assembly is needed (e.g. OS development), you'll find that not so much of it is, and that the above principles hold.

See the sources for the Linux kernel about it: as little assembly as needed, resulting in a fast, reliable, portable, maintainable OS. Even a successful game like DOOM was almost massively written in C, with a tiny part only being written in assembly for speed up.

2.2 How to NOT use Assembly

2.2.1 General procedure to achieve efficient code

As says Charles Fiterman on comp.compilers about human vs computer-generated assembly code,

"The human should always win and here is why.

- First the human writes the whole thing in a high level language.
- Second he profiles it to find the hot spots where it spends its time.
- Third he has the compiler produce assembly for those small sections of code.
- Fourth he hand tunes them looking for tiny improvements over the machine generated code.

The human wins because he can use the machine."

2.2.2 Languages with optimizing compilers

Languages like ObjectiveCAML, SML, CommonLISP, Scheme, ADA, Pascal, C, C++, among others, all have free optimizing compilers that'll optimize the bulk of your programs, and often do better than hand-coded assembly even for tight loops, while allowing you to focus on higher-level details, and without forbidding you to grab a few percent of extra performance in the above-mentionned way, once you've reached a stable design. Of course, there are also commercial optimizing compilers for most of these languages, too!

Some languages have compilers that produce C code, which can be further optimized by a C compiler. LISP, Scheme, Perl, and many other are suches. Speed is fairly good.

2.2.3 General procedure to speed your code up

As for speeding code up, you should do it only for parts of a program that a profiling tool has consistently identified as being a performance bottleneck.

Hence, if you identify some code portion as being too slow, you should

- first try to use a better algorithm;

- then try to compile it rather than interpret it;
- then try to enable and tweak optimization from your compiler;
- then give the compiler hints about how to optimize (typing information in LISP; register usage with GCC; lots of options in most compilers, etc).
- then possibly fallback to assembly programming

Finally, before you end up writing assembly, you should inspect generated code, to check that the problem really is with bad code generation, as this might really not be the case: compiler-generated code might be better than what you'd have written, particularly on modern multi-pipelined architectures! Slow parts of a program might be intrinsically so. Biggest problems on modern architectures with fast processors are due to delays from memory access, cache-misses, TLB-misses, and page-faults; register optimization becomes useless, and you'll more profitably re-think data structures and threading to achieve better locality in memory access. Perhaps a completely different approach to the problem might help, then.

2.2.4 Inspecting compiler-generated code

There are many reasons to inspect compiler-generated assembly code. Here are what you'll do with such code:

- check whether generated code can be obviously enhanced with hand-coded assembly (or by tweaking compiler switches)
- when that's the case, start from generated code and modify it instead of starting from scratch
- more generally, use generated code as stubs to modify, which at least gets right the way your assembly routines interface to the external world
- track down bugs in your compiler (hopefully rarer)

The standard way to have assembly code be generated is to invoke your compiler with the -S flag. This works with most Unix compilers, including the GNU C Compiler (GCC), but YMMV. As for GCC, it will produce more understandable assembly code with the -fverbose-asm command-line option. Of course, if you want to get good assembly code, don't forget your usual optimization options and hints!

3 ASSEMBLERS

3.1 GCC Inline Assembly

The well-known GNU C/C++ Compiler (GCC), an optimizing 32-bit compiler at the heart of the GNU project, supports the x86 architecture quite well, and includes the ability to insert assembly code in C programs, in such a way that register allocation can be either specified or left to GCC. GCC works on most available platforms, notably Linux, *BSD, VSTa, OS/2, *DOS, Win*, etc.

3.1.1 Where to find GCC

The original GCC site is the GNU FTP site `<ftp://prep.ai.mit.edu/pub/gnu/>` together with all the released application software from the GNU project. Linux-configured and precompiled versions can be found in `<ftp://sunsite.unc.edu/pub/Linux/GCC/>` There exists a lot of FTP mirrors of both sites. everywhere around the world, as well as CD-ROM copies.

GCC development has split in two branches recently. See more about the experimental version, egcs, at `<http://www.cygnus.com/egcs/>`

Sources adapted to your favorite OS, and binaries precompiled for it, should be found at your usual FTP sites.

For most popular DOS port of GCC is named DJGPP, and can be found in directories of such name in FTP sites. See:

`<http://www.delorie.com/djgpp/>`

HOWTO

There is also a port of GCC to OS/2 named EMX, that also works under DOS, and includes lots of unix-emulation library routines. See around:

`<http://www.leo.org/pub/comp/os/os2/gnu/emx+gcc/>`

`<http://warp.eecs.berkeley.edu/os2/software/shareware/emx.html>`

`<ftp://ftp-os2.cdrom.com/pub/os2/emx09c/>`

3.1.2 Where to find docs for GCC Inline Asm

The documentation of GCC includes documentation files in texinfo format. You can compile them with tex and print then result, or convert them to .info, and browse them with emacs, or convert them to .html, or nearly whatever you like. convert (with the right tools) to whatever you like, or just read as is. The .info files are generally found on any good installation for GCC.

The right section to look for is: `C Extensions::Extended Asm::`

Section `Invoking GCC::Submodel Options::i386 Options::` might help too. Particularly, it gives the i386 specific constraint names for registers: abcdSDB correspond to `%eax`, `%ebx`, `%ecx`, `%edx`, `%esi`, `%edi`, `%ebp` respectively (no letter for `%esp`).

The DJGPP Games resource (not only for game hackers) has this page specifically about assembly:

`<http://www.rt66.com/brennan/djgpp/djgpp_asm.html>`

Finally, there is a web page called, "DJGPP Quick ASM Programming Guide", that covers URLs to FAQs, AT&T x86 ASM Syntax, Some inline ASM information, and converting .obj/.lib files:

`<http://remus.rutgers.edu/avly/djasm.html>`

GCC depends on GAS for assembling, and follow its syntax (see below); do mind that inline asm needs percent characters to be quoted so they be passed to GAS. See the section about GAS below.

Find *lots* of useful examples in the `linux/include/asm-i386/` subdirectory of the sources for the Linux kernel.

3.1.3 Invoking GCC to have it properly inline assembly code ?

Be sure to invoke GCC with the -O flag (or -O2, -O3, etc), to enable optimizations and inline assembly. If you don't, your code may compile, but not run properly!!! Actually (kudos to Tim Potter, timbo@moshpit.air.net.au), it is enough to use the -fasm flag (and perhaps -finline-functions) which is part of all the features enabled by -O. So if you have problems with buggy optimizations in your particular implementation/version of GCC, you can still use inline asm. Similarly, use -fno-asm to disable inline assembly (why would you?).

More generally, good compile flags for GCC on the x86 platform are

```
gcc -O2 -fomit-frame-pointer -m386 -Wall
```

-O2 is the good optimization level. Optimizing besides it yields code that is a lot larger, but only a bit faster; such overoptimizationn might be useful for tight loops only (if any), which you may be doing in assembly anyway; if you need that, do it just for the few routines that need it.

-fomit-frame-pointer allows generated code to skip the stupid frame pointer maintenance, which makes code smaller and faster, and frees a register for further optimizations. It precludes the easy use of debugging tools (gdb), but when you use these, you just don't care about size and speed anymore anyway.

-m386 yields more compact code, without any measurable slowdown, (note that small code also means less disk I/O and faster execution) but perhaps on the above-mentioned tight loops; you might appreciate -mpentium for special pentium-optimizing GCC targetting a specifically pentium platform.

`-Wall` enables all warnings and helps you catch obvious stupid errors.

To optimize even more, option `-mregparm=2` and/or corresponding function attribute might help, but might pose lots of problems when linking to foreign code...

Note that you can add make these flags the default by editing file `/usr/lib/gcc-lib/i486-linux/2.7.2.2/specs` or wherever that is on your system (better not add -Wall there, though).

3.2 GAS

GAS is the GNU Assembler, that GCC relies upon.

3.2.1 Where to find it

Find it at the same place where you found GCC, in a package named binutils.

3.2.2 What is this AT&T syntax

Because GAS was invented to support a 32-bit unix compiler, it uses standard "AT&T" syntax, which resembles a lot the syntax for standard m68k assemblers, and is standard in the UNIX world. This syntax is no worse, no better than the "Intel" syntax. It's just different. When you get used to it, you find it much more regular than the Intel syntax, though a bit boring.

Here are the major caveats about GAS syntax:

- Register names are prefixed with `%`, so that registers are `%eax`, `%dl` and suches instead of just `eax`, `dl`, etc. This makes it possible to include external C symbols directly in assembly source, without any risk of confusion, or any need for ugly underscore prefixes.

- The order of operands is source(s) first, and destination last, as opposed to the intel convention of destination first and sources last. Hence, what in intel syntax is `mov ax,dx` (move contents of register `dx` into register `ax`) will be in att syntax `mov %dx, %ax`.

- The operand length is specified as a suffix to the instruction name. The suffix is `b` for (8-bit) byte, `w` for (16-bit) word, and `l` for (32-bit) long. For instance, the correct syntax for the above instruction would have been `movw %dx,%ax`. However, gas does not require strict att syntax was, so the suffix is optional when length can be guessed from register operands, and else defaults to 32-bit (with a warning).

- Immediate operands are marked with a `$` prefix, as in `addl $5,%eax` (add immediate long value 5 to register `%eax`).

- No prefix to an operand indicates it is a memory-address; hence `movl $foo,%eax` puts the *address* of variable `foo` in register `%eax`, but `movl foo,%eax` puts the contents of variable `foo` in register `%eax`.

- Indexing or indirection is done by enclosing the index register or indirection memory cell address in parentheses, as in `testb $0x80,17(%ebp)` (test the high bit of the byte value at offset 17 from the cell pointed to by `%ebp`).

A program exists to help you convert programs from TASM syntax to AT&T syntax. See

`<ftp://x2ftp.oulu.fi/pub/msdos/programming/convert/ta2asv08.zip>`

GAS has comprehensive documentation in TeXinfo format, which comes at least with the source distribution. Browse extracted .info pages with Emacs or whatever. There used to be a file named gas.doc or as.doc around the GAS source package, but it was merged into the TeXinfo docs. Of course, in case of doubt, the ultimate documentation is the sources themselves! A section that will particularly interest you is `Machine Dependencies::i386-Dependent::`

Again, the sources for Linux (the OS kernel), come in as good examples; see under linux/arch/i386, the following files: `kernel/*.S, boot/compressed/*.S, mathemu/*.S`

If you are writing kind of a language, a thread package, etc you might as well see how other languages (OCaml, gforth, etc), or thread packages (QuickThreads, MIT pthreads, LinuxThreads, etc), or whatever, do it.

Finally, just compiling a C program to assembly might show you the syntax for the kind of instructions you want. See section 2 (Do you need Assembly?) above.

3.2.3 Limited 16-bit mode

GAS is a 32-bit assembler, meant to support a 32-bit compiler. It currently has only limited support for 16-bit mode, which consists in prepending the 32-bit prefixes to instructions, so you write 32-bit code that runs in 16-bit mode on a 32 bit CPU. In both modes, it supports 16-bit register usage, but what is unsupported is 16-bit addressing. Use the directive `.code16` and `.code32` to switch between modes. Note that an inline assembly statement `asm(".code16\n")` will allow GCC to produce 32-bit code that'll run in real mode!

I've been told that most code needed to fully support 16-bit mode programming was added to GAS by Bryan Ford (please confirm?), but at least, it doesn't show up in any of the distribution I tried, up to binutils-2.8.1.x ... more info on this subject would be welcome.

A cheap solution is to define macros (see below) that somehow produce the binary encoding (with `.byte`) for just the 16-bit mode instructions you need (almost nothing if you use code16 as above, and can safely assume the code will run on a 32-bit capable x86 CPU). To find the proper encoding, you can get inspiration from the sources of 16-bit capable assemblers for the encoding.

3.3 GASP

GASP is the GAS Preprocessor. It adds macros and some nice syntax to GAS.

3.3.1 Where to find GASP

GASP comes together with GAS in the GNU binutils archive.

3.3.2 How it works

It works as a filter, much like cpp and the like. I have no idea on details, but it comes with its own texinfo documentation, so just browse them (in .info), print them, grok them. GAS with GASP looks like a regular macro-assembler to me.

3.4 NASM

The Netwide Assembler project is producing yet another assembler, written in C, that should be modular enough to eventually support all known syntaxes and object formats.

3.4.1 Where to find NASM

`<http://www.cryogen.com/Nasm>`

Binary release on your usual sunsite mirror in `devel/lang/asm/` Should also be available as .rpm or .deb in your usual RedHat/Debian distributions' contrib.

3.4.2 What it does

At the time this HOWTO is written, the current NASM version is 0.96.

The syntax is Intel-style. Some macroprocessing support is integrated.

Supported object file formats are `bin`, `aout`, `coff`, `elf`, `as86`, (DOS) `obj`, `win32`, (their own format) `rdf`.

NASM can be used as a backend for the free LCC compiler (support files included).

Surely NASM evolves too fast for this HOWTO to be kept up to date. Unless you're using BCC as a 16-bit compiler (which is out of scope of this 32-bit HOWTO), you should use NASM instead of say AS86 or MASM, because it is actively supported online, and runs on all platforms.

Note: NASM also comes with a disassembler, NDISASM.

Its hand-written parser makes it much faster than GAS, though of course, it doesn't support three bazillion different architectures. For the x86 target, it should be the assembler of choice...

3.5 AS86

AS86 is a 80x86 assembler, both 16-bit and 32-bit, part of Bruce Evans' C Compiler (BCC). It has mostly Intel-syntax, though it differs slightly as for addressing modes.

3.5.1 Where to get AS86

A completely outdated version of AS86 is distributed by HJLu just to compile the Linux kernel, in a package named bin86 (current version 0.4), available in any Linux GCC repository. But I advise no one to use it for anything else but compiling Linux. This version supports only a hacked minix object file format, which is not supported by the GNU binutils or anything, and it has a few bugs in 32-bit mode, so you really should better keep it only for compiling Linux.

The most recent versions by Bruce Evans (bde@zeta.org.au) are published together with the FreeBSD distribution. Well, they were: I could not find the sources from distribution 2.1 on :(Hence, I put the sources at my place:

`<http:///www.eleves.ens.fr:8080/home/rideau/files/bcc-95.3.12.src.tgz>`

The Linux/8086 (aka ELKS) project is somehow maintaining bcc (though I don't think they included the 32-bit patches). See around `<http://www.linux.org.uk/Linux8086.html>` `<ftp://linux.mit.edu/>`.

Among other things, these more recent versions, unlike HJLu's, supports Linux GNU a.out format, so you can link you code to Linux programs, and/or use the usual tools from the GNU binutil package to manipulate your data. This version can co-exist without any harm with the previous one (see according question below).

BCC from 12 march 1995 and earlier version has a misfeature that makes all segment pushing/popping 16-bit, which is quite annoying when programming in 32-bit mode. A patch is published in the Tunes project `<http://www.eleves.ens.fr:8080/home/rideau/Tunes/>`subpage `files/tgz/tunes.0.0.0.25.src.tgz` in unpacked subdirectory `LLL/i386/` The patch should also be in available directly from `<http://www.eleves.ens.fr:8080/home/rideau/files/as86.bcc.patch.gz>` Bruce Evans accepted this patch, so if there is a more recent version of bcc somewhere someday, the patch should have been included...

3.5.2 How to invoke the assembler?

Here's the GNU Makefile entry for using bcc to transform `.s` asm into both GNU a.out `.o` object and `.l` listing:

```
%.o %.l:        %.s
        bcc -3 -G -c -A-d -A-l -A$*.l -o $*.o $<
```

Remove the `%.l`, `-A-l`, and `-A$*.l`, if you don't want any listing. If you want something else than GNU a.out, you can see the docs of bcc about the other supported formats, and/or use the objcopy utility from the GNU binutils package.

3.5.3 Where to find docs

The docs are what is included in the bcc package. Man pages are also available somewhere on the FreeBSD site. When in doubt, the sources themselves are often a good docs: it's not very well commented, but the programming style is straightforward. You might try to see how as86 is used in Tunes 0.0.0.25...

3.5.4 What if I can't compile Linux anymore with this new version ?

Linus is buried alive in mail, and my patch for compiling Linux with a Linux a.out as86 didn't make it to him (!). Now, this shouldn't matter: just keep your as86 from the bin86 package in /usr/bin, and let bcc install the good as86 as /usr/local/libexec/i386/bcc/as where it should be. You never need explicitly call this "good" as86, because bcc does

HOWTO

everything right, including conversion to Linux a.out, when invoked with the right options; so assemble files exclusively with bcc as a frontend, not directly with as86.

3.6 OTHER ASSEMBLERS

These are other, non-regular, options, in case the previous didn't satisfy you (why?), that I don't recommend in the usual (?) case, but that could prove quite useful if the assembler must be integrated in the software you're designing (i.e. an OS or development environment).

3.6.1 Win32Forth assembler

Win32Forth is a *free* 32-bit ANS FORTH system that successfully runs under Win32s, Win95, Win/NT. It includes a free 32-bit assembler (either prefix or postfix syntax) integrated into the FORTH language. Macro processing is done with the full power of the reflective language FORTH; however, the only supported input and output contexts is Win32For itself (no dumping of .obj file – you could add that yourself, of course). Find it at `<ftp://ftp.forth.org/pub/Forth/win32for/>`

3.6.2 Terse

Terse is a programming tool that provides *THE* most compact assembler syntax for the x86 family! See `<http://www.terse.com>`. It is said that there was a free clone somewhere, that was abandonned after worthless pretenses that the syntax would be owned by the original author, and that I invite you to take over, in case the syntax interests you.

3.6.3 Non-free and/or Non-32bit x86 assemblers.

You may find more about them, together with the basics of x86 assembly programming, in Raymond Moon's FAQ for comp.lang.asm.x86 `<http://www2.dgsys.com/raymoon/faq/asmfaq.zip>`

Note that all DOS-based assemblers should work inside the Linux DOS Emulator, as well as other similar emulators, so that if you already own one, you can still use it inside a real OS. Recent DOS-based assemblers also support COFF and/or other object file formats that are supported by the GNU BFD library, so that you can use them together with your free 32-bit tools, perhaps using GNU objcopy (part of the binutils) as a conversion filter.

4 METAPROGRAMMING/MACROPROCESSING

Assembly programming is a bore, but for critical parts of programs.

You should use the appropriate tool for the right task, so don't choose assembly when it's not fit; C, OCAML, perl, Scheme, might be a better choice for most of your programming.

However, there are cases when these tools do not give a fine enough control on the machine, and assembly is useful or needed. In those case, you'll appreciate a system of macroprocessing and metaprogramming that'll allow recurring patterns to be factored each into a one indefinitely reusable definition, which allows safer programming, automatic propagation of pattern modification, etc. A "plain" assembler is often not enough, even when one is doing only small routines to link with C.

4.1 What's integrated into the above

Yes I know this section does not contain much useful up-to-date information. Feel free to contribute what you discover the hard way...

4.1.1 GCC

GCC allows (and requires) you to specify register constraints in your "inline assembly" code, so the optimizer always know about it; thus, inline assembly code is really made of patterns, not forcibly exact code.

Then, you can make put your assembly into CPP macros, and inline C functions, so anyone can use it in as any C function/macro. Inline functions resemble macros very much, but are sometimes cleaner to use. Beware that in all those cases, code will be duplicated, so only local labels (of 1 : style) should be defined in that asm code. However, a macro would allow the name for a non local defined label to be passed as a parameter (or else, you should use additional meta-programming methods). Also, note that propagating inline asm code will spread potential bugs in them, so watch out doubly for register constraints in such inline asm code.

Lastly, the C language itself may be considered as a good abstraction to assembly programming, which relieves you from most of the trouble of assembling.

Beware that some optimizations that involve passing arguments to functions through registers may make those functions unsuitable to be called from external (and particularly hand-written assembly) routines in the standard way; the "asmlinkage" attribute may prevent a routine to be concerned by such optimization flag; see the linux kernel sources for examples.

4.1.2 GAS

GAS has some macro capability included, as detailed in the texinfo docs. Moreover, while GCC recognizes .s files as raw assembly to send to GAS, it also recognizes .S files as files to pipe through CPP before to feed them to GAS. Again and again, see Linux sources for examples.

4.1.3 GASP

It adds all the usual macroassembly tricks to GAS. See its texinfo docs.

4.1.4 NASM

NASM has some macro support, too. See according docs. If you have some bright idea, you might wanna contact the authors, as they are actively developing it. Meanwhile, see about external filters below.

4.1.5 AS86

It has some simple macro support, but I couldn't find docs. Now the sources are very straightforward, so if you're interested, you should understand them easily. If you need more than the basics, you should use an external filter (see below).

4.1.6 OTHER ASSEMBLERS

- Win32FORTH: CODE and END-CODE are normal that do not switch from interpretation mode to compilation mode, so you have access to the full power of FORTH while assembling.
- TUNES: it doesn't work yet, but the Scheme language is a real high-level language that allows arbitrary meta-programming.

4.2 External Filters

Whatever is the macro support from your assembler, or whatever language you use (even C !), if the language is not expressive enough to you, you can have files passed through an external filter with a Makefile rule like that:

```
%.s:     %.S other_dependencies
         $(FILTER) $(FILTER_OPTIONS) < $< > $@
```

4.2.1 CPP

CPP is truely not very expressive, but it's enough for easy things, it's standard, and called transparently by GCC.

As an example of its limitations, you can't declare objects so that destructors are automatically called at the end of the declaring block; you don't have diversions or scoping, etc.

CPP comes with any C compiler. If you could make it without one, don't bother fetching CPP (though I wonder how you could).

4.2.2 M4

M4 gives you the full power of macroprocessing, with a Turing equivalent language, recursion, regular expressions, etc. You can do with it everything that CPP cannot.

See macro4th/This4th from `<ftp://ftp.forth.org/pub/Forth/>` in Reviewed/ ANS/ (?), or the Tunes 0.0.0.25 sources as examples of advanced macroprogramming using m4.

However, its disfunctional quoting and unquoting semantics force you to use explicit continuation-passing tail-recursive macro style if you want to do *advanced* macro programming (which is remindful of TeX – BTW, has anyone tried to use TeX as a macroprocessor for anything else than typesetting ?). This is NOT worse than CPP that does not allow quoting and recursion anyway.

The right version of m4 to get is GNU m4 1.4 (or later if exists), which has the most features and the least bugs or limitations of all. m4 is designed to be slow for anything but the simplest uses, which might still be ok for most assembly programming (you're not writing million-lines assembly programs, are you?).

4.2.3 Macroprocessing with yer own filter

You can write your own simple macro-expansion filter with the usual tools: perl, awk, sed, etc. That's quick to do, and you control everything. But of course, any power in macroprocessing must be earned the hard way.

4.2.4 Metaprogramming

Instead of using an external filter that expands macros, one way to do things is to write programs that write part or all of other programs.

For instance, you could use a program outputing source code

- to generate sine/cosine/whatever lookup tables,
- to extract a source-form representation of a binary file,
- to compile your bitmaps into fast display routines,
- to extract documentation, initialization/finalization code, description tables, as well as normal code from the same source files,
- to have customized assembly code, generated from a perl/shell/scheme script that does arbitrary processing,
- to propagate data defined at one point only into several cross-referencing tables and code chunks.
- etc.

Think about it!

Backends from existing compilers   Compilers like SML/NJ, Objective CAML, MIT-Scheme, etc, do have their own generic assembler backend, which you might or not want to use, if you intend to generate code semi-automatically from the according languages.

The New-Jersey Machine-Code Toolkit   There is a project, using the programming language Icon, to build a basis for producing assembly-manipulating code. See around `<http://www.cs.virginia.edu/nr/toolkit/>`

Tunes   The Tunes OS project is developping its own assembler as an extension to the Scheme language, as part of its development process. It doesn't run at all yet, though help is welcome.

The assembler manipulates symbolic syntax trees, so it could equally serve as the basis for a assembly syntax translator, a disassembler, a common assembler/compiler back-end, etc. Also, the full power of a real language, Scheme, make it unchallenged as for macroprocessing/metaprograming.

`<http://www.eleves.ens.fr:8080/home/rideau/Tunes/>`

5   CALLING CONVENTIONS

5.1   Linux

5.1.1   Linking to GCC

That's the preferred way. Check GCC docs and examples from Linux kernel .S files that go through gas (not those that go through as86).

32-bit arguments are pushed down stack in reverse syntactic order (hence accessed/popped in the right order), above the 32-bit near return address. %ebp, %esi, %edi, %ebx are callee-saved, other registers are caller-saved; %eax is to hold the result, or %edx:%eax for 64-bit results.

FP stack: I'm not sure, but I think it's result in st(0), whole stack caller-saved.

Note that GCC has options to modify the calling conventions by reserving registers, having arguments in registers, not assuming the FPU, etc. Check the i386 .info pages.

Beware that you must then declare the cdecl attribute for a function that will follow standard GCC calling conventions (I don't know what it does with modified calling conventions). See in the GCC info pages the section: C Extensions::Extended Asm::

5.1.2   ELF vs a.out problems

Some C compilers prepend an underscore before every symbol, while others do not.

Particularly, Linux a.out GCC does such prepending, while Linux ELF GCC does not.

If you need cope with both behaviors at once, see how existing packages do. For instance, get an old Linux source tree, the Elk, qthreads, or OCAML...

You can also override the implicit C->asm renaming by inserting statements like

```
      void foo asm("bar") (void);
```

to be sure that the C function foo will be called really bar in assembly.

Note that the utility objcopy, from the binutils package, should allow you to transform your a.out objects into ELF objects, and perhaps the contrary too, in some cases. More generally, it will do lots of file format conversions.

5.1.3   Direct Linux syscalls

This is specifically *NOT* recommended, because the conventions change from time to time or from kernel flavor to kernel flavor (cf L4Linux), plus it's not portable, it's a burden to write, it's redundant with the libc effort, AND it precludes fixes and extensions that are made to the libc, like, for instance the zlibc package, that does on-the-fly transparent decompression of gzip-compressed files. The standard, recommended way to call Linux system services is, and will stay, to go through the libc.

Shared objects should keep your stuff small. And if you really want smaller binaries, do use #! stuff, with the interpreter having all the overhead you want to keep out of your binaries.

Now, if for some reason, you don't want to link to the libc, go get the libc and understand how it works! After all, you're pretending to replace it, ain't you?

You might also take a look at how my *eforth 1.0c* `<ftp://ftp.forth.org/pub/Forth/Linux/linux-eforth-1.0c.tgz>` does it.

The sources for Linux come in handy, too, particularly the asm/unistd.h header file, that describes how to do system calls...

Basically, you issue an `int $0x80`, with the __NR_syscallname number (from `asm/unistd.h`) in `%eax`, and parameters (up to five) in `%ebx, %ecx, %edx, %esi, %edi` respectively. Result is returned in `%eax`, with a negative result being an error whose opposite is what libc would put in errno. The user-stack is not touched, so you needn't have a valid one when doing a syscall.

5.1.4 I/O under Linux

If you want to do direct I/O under Linux, either it's something very simple that needn't OS arbitration, and you should see the `IO-Port-Programming` mini-HOWTO; or it needs a kernel device driver, and you should try to learn more about kernel hacking, device driver development, kernel modules, etc, for which there are other excellent HOWTOs and documents from the LDP.

Particularly, if what you want is Graphics programming, then do join the GGI project: `<http://synergy.caltech.edu/ggi/>` `<http://sunserver1.rz.uni-duesseldorf.de/becka/doc/scrdrv.html>`

Anyway, in all these cases, you'll be better off using GCC inline assembly with the macros from linux/asm/*.h than writing full assembly source files.

5.1.5 Accessing 16-bit drivers from Linux/i386

Such thing is theoretically possible (proof: see how DOSEMU can selectively grant hardware port access to programs),and I've heard rumors that someone somewhere did actually do it (in the PCI driver? Some VESA access stuff? ISA PnP? dunno). If you have some more precise information on that, you'll be most welcome. Anyway, good places to look for more information are the Linux kernel sources, DOSEMU sources (and other programs in the *DOSEMU repository* `<ftp://tsx-11.mit.edu/pub/linux/ALPHA/dosemu/>`), and sources for various low-level programs under Linux... (perhaps GGI if it supports VESA).

Basically, you must either use 16-bit protected mode or vm86 mode.

The first is simpler to setup, but only works with well-behaved code that won't do any kind of segment arithmetics or absolute segment addressing (particularly addressing segment 0), unless by chance it happens that all segments used can be setup in advance in the LDT.

The later allows for more "compatibility" with vanilla 16-bit environments, but requires more complicated handling.

In both cases, before you can jump to 16-bit code, you must

- mmap any absolute address used in the 16-bit code (such as ROM, video buffers, DMA targets, and memory-mapped I/O) from /dev/mem to your process' address space,
- setup the LDT and/or vm86 mode monitor.
- grab proper I/O permissions from the kernel (see the above section)

Again, carefully read the source for the stuff contributed to the DOSEMU repository above, particularly these mini-emulators for running ELKS and/or simple .COM programs under Linux/i386.

5.2 DOS

Most DOS extenders come with some interface to DOS services. Read their docs about that, but often, they just simulate `int $0x21` and such, so you do "as if" you were in real mode (I doubt they have more than stubs and extend things to work with 32-bit operands; they most likely will just reflect the interrupt into the real-mode or vm86 handler).

Docs about DPMI and such (and much more) can be found on `<ftp://x2ftp.oulu.fi/pub/msdos/programming/>`

DJGPP comes with its own (limited) glibc derivative/subset/replacement, too.

It is possible to cross-compile from Linux to DOS, see the devel/msdos/ directory of your local FTP mirror for sunsite.unc.edu Also see the MOSS dos-extender from the Flux project in utah.

Other documents and FAQs are more DOS-centered. We do not recommend DOS development.

5.3 Winblows and suches

Hey, this document covers only free software. Ring me when Winblows becomes free, or when there are free dev tools for it!

Well, after all there is: *Cygnus Solutions* `<http://www.cygnus.com>` has developped the cygwin32.dll library, for GNU programs to run on MacroShit platforms. Thus, you can use GCC, GAS, all the GNU tools, and many other Unix applications. Have a look around their homepage. I (Faré) don'ţ intend to expand on Losedoze programming, but I'm sure you can find lots of documents about it everywhere...

5.4 Yer very own OS

Control being what attract many programmers to assembly, want of OS development is often what leads to or stems from assembly hacking. Note that any system that allows self-development could be qualified an "OS" even though it might run "on top" of an underlying system that multitasking or I/O (much like Linux over Mach or OpenGenera over Unix), etc. Hence, for easier debugging purpose, you might like to develop your "OS" first as a process running on top of Linux (despite the slowness), then use the *Flux OS kit* `<http://ww.cs.utah.edu/projects/flux/>` (which grants use of Linux and BSD drivers in yer own OS) to make it standalone. When your OS is stable, it's still time to write your own hardware drivers if you really love that.

This HOWTO will not itself cover topics such as Boot loader code & getting into 32-bit mode, Handling Interrupts, The basics about intel "protected mode" or "V86/R86" braindeadness, defining your object format and calling conventions. The main place where to find reliable information about that all is source code of existing OSes and bootloaders. Lots of pointers lie in the following WWW page: `<http://www.eleves.ens.fr:8080/home/rideau/Tunes/Review/OSes.html>`

6 TODO & POINTERS

- fill incomplete sections
- add more pointers to software and docs
- add simple examples from real life to illustrate the syntax, power, and limitations of each proposed solution.
- ask people to help with this HOWTO
- find someone who has got some time to takeover the maintenance
- perhaps give a few words for assembly on other platforms?
- A few pointers (in addition to those already in the rest of the HOWTO)
    - *pentium manuals* `<http://www.intel.com/design/pentium/manuals/>`
    - *cpu bugs in the x86 family* `<http://www.xs4all.nl/feldmann>`

- *hornet.eng.ufl.edu for assembly coders* `<http://www.eng.ufl.edu/ftp>`
- *ftp.luth.se* `<ftp://ftp.luth.se/pub/msdos/demos/code/>`
- *PM FAQ* `<ftp://zfja-gate.fuw.edu.pl/cpu/protect.mod>`
- *80x86 Assembly Page* `<http://www.fys.ruu.nl/faber/Amain.html>`
- *Courseware* `<http://www.cit.ac.nz/smac/csware.htm>`
- *game programming* `<http://www.ee.ucl.ac.uk/phart/gameprog.html>`
- *experiments with asm-only linux programming* `<http://bewoner.dma.be/JanW>`

- And of course, do use your usual Internet Search Tools to look for more information, and tell me anything interesting you find!

Authors' .sig:

```
--     ,                                        ,      _ v   ^ --
-- Fare -- rideau@clipper.ens.fr -- Francois-Rene Rideau -- +)ang-Vu Ban --
--                                    ,                        / .        --
Join the TUNES project for a computing system based on computing freedom !
               TUNES is a Useful, Not Expedient System
WWW page at URL: http://www.eleves.ens.fr:8080/home/rideau/Tunes/
```

## Part V

"Linux Benchmarking HOWTO" by André D. Balsa

andrewbalsa@usa.net <mailto:andrewbalsa@usa.net>
v0.12, 15 August 1997

The Linux Benchmarking HOWTO discusses some issues associated with the benchmarking of Linux systems and presents a basic benchmarking toolkit, as well as an associated form, which enable one to produce significant benchmarking information in a couple of hours. Perhaps it will also help diminish the amount of useless articles in comp.os.linux.hardware...

Contents

HOWTO

1   Introduction

"What we cannot speak about we must pass over in silence."

    Ludwig Wittgenstein (1889-1951), Austrian philosopher

Benchmarking means **measuring** the speed with which a computer system will execute a computing task, in a way that will allow comparison between different hard/software combinations. It **does not** involve user-friendliness, aesthetic or ergonomic considerations or any other subjective judgment.

Benchmarking is a tedious, repetitive task, and takes attention to details. Very often the results are not what one would expect, and subject to interpretation (which actually may be the most important part of a benchmarking procedure).

Finally, benchmarking deals with facts and figures, not opinion or approximation.

1.1   Why is benchmarking so important ?

Apart from the reasons pointed out in the BogoMips Mini-HOWTO (section 7, paragraph 2), one occasionally is confronted with a limited budget and/or minimum performance requirements while putting together a Linux box. In other words, when confronted with the following questions:

- How do I maximize performance within a given budget ?
- How do I minimize costs for a required minimum performance level ?
- How do I obtain the best performance/cost ratio (within a given budget or given performance requirements)?

one will have to examine, compare and/or produce benchmarks. Minimizing costs with no performance requirements usually involves putting together a machine with leftover parts (that old 386SX-16 box lying around in the garage will do fine) and does not require benchmarks, and maximizing performance with no cost ceiling is not a realistic situation (unless one is willing to put a Cray box in his/her living room - the leather-covered power supplies around it look nice, don't they ?).

Benchmarking per se is senseless, a waste of time and money; it is only meaningful as part of a decision process, i.e. if one has to make a choice between two or more alternatives.

Usually another parameter in the decision process is **cost**, but it could be availability, service, reliability, strategic considerations or any other rational, measurable characteristic of a computer system. When comparing the performance of different Linux kernel versions, for example, **stability** is almost always more important than speed.

1.2 Invalid benchmarking considerations

Very often read in newsgroups and mailing lists, unfortunately:

1. Reputation of manufacturer (unmeasurable and meaningless).

2. Market share of manufacturer (meaningless and irrelevant).

3. Irrational parameters (for example, superstition or prejudice: would you buy a processor labeled 131313ZAP and painted pink ?)

4. Perceived value (meaningless, unmeasurable and irrational).

5. Amount of marketing hype: this one is the worst, I guess. I personally am fed up with the "XXX inside" or "kkkkkws compatible" logos (now the "aaaaaPowered" has joined the band - what next ?). IMHO, the billions of dollars spent on such campaigns would be better used by research teams on the design of new, faster, (cheaper :-) bug-free processors. No amount of marketing hype will remove a floating-point bug in the FPU of the brand-new processor you just plugged in your motherboard, but an exchange against a redesigned processor will.

6. "You get what you pay for" opinions are just that: opinions. Give me the facts, please.

2 Benchmarking procedures and interpretation of results

A few semi-obvious recommendations:

1. First and foremost, **identify your benchmarking goals**. What is it you are exactly trying to benchmark ? In what way will the benchmarking process help later in your decision making ? How much time and resources are you willing to put into your benchmarking effort ?

2. **Use standard tools**. Use a current, stable kernel version, standard, current gcc and libc and a standard benchmark. In short, use the LBT (see below).

3. Give a **complete description** of your setup (see the LBT report form below).

4. Try to **isolate a single variable**. Comparative benchmarking is more informative than "absolute" benchmarking. **I cannot stress this enough.**

5. **Verify your results**. Run your benchmarks a few times and verify the variations in your results, if any. Unexplained variations will invalidate your results.

6. If you think your benchmarking effort produced meaningful information, **share it** with the Linux community in a **precise** and **concise** way.

7. Please **forget about BogoMips**. I promise myself I shall someday implement a very fast ASIC with the BogoMips loop wired in. Then we shall see what we shall see !

2.1 Understanding benchmarking choices

2.1.1 Synthetic vs. applications benchmarks

Before spending any amount of time on benchmarking chores, a basic choice must be made between "synthetic" benchmarks and "applications" benchmarks.

Synthetic benchmarks are specifically designed to measure the performance of individual components of a computer system, usually by exercising the chosen component to its maximum capacity. An example of a well-known synthetic benchmark is the **Whetstone** suite, originally programmed in 1972 by Harold Curnow in FORTRAN (or was that ALGOL ?) and still in widespread use nowadays. The Whestone suite will measure the floating-point performance of a CPU.

The main critic that can be made to synthetic benchmarks is that they do not represent a computer system's performance in real-life situations. Take for example the Whetstone suite: the main loop is very short and will easily fit in the primary cache of a CPU, keeping the FPU pipeline constantly filled and so exercising the FPU to its maximum speed. We cannot

HOWTO

really criticize the Whetstone suite if we remember it was programmed 25 years ago (its design dates even earlier than that !), but we must make sure we interpret its results with care, when it comes to benchmarking modern microprocessors.

Another very important point to note about synthetic benchmarks is that, ideally, they should tell us something about a **specific** aspect of the system being tested, independently of all other aspects: a synthetic benchmark for Ethernet card I/O throughput should result in the same or similar figures whether it is run on a 386SX-16 with 4 MBytes of RAM or a Pentium 200 MMX with 64 MBytes of RAM. Otherwise, the test will be measuring the overall performance of the CPU/Motherboard/Bus/Ethernet card/Memory subsystem/DMA combination: not very useful since the variation in CPU will cause a greater impact than the change in Ethernet network card (this of course assumes we are using the same kernel/driver combination, which could cause an even greater variation)!

Finally, a very common mistake is to average various synthetic benchmarks and claim that such an average is a good representation of real-life performance for any given system.

Here is a comment on FPU benchmarks quoted with permission from the Cyrix Corp. Web site:

> *"A Floating Point Unit (FPU) accelerates software designed to use floating point mathematics : typically CAD programs, spreadsheets, 3D games and design applications. However, today's most popular PC applications make use of both floating point and integer instructions. As a result, Cyrix chose to emphasize "parallelism" in the design of the 6x86 processor to speed up software that intermixes these two instruction types.*
>
> *The x86 floating point exception model allows integer instructions to issue and complete while a floating point instruction is executing. In contrast, a second floating point instruction cannot begin execution while a previous floating point instruction is executing. To remove the performance limitation created by the floating point exception model, the 6x86 can speculatively issue up to four floating point instructions to the on-chip FPU while continuing to issue and execute integer instructions. As an example, in a code sequence of two floating point instructions (FLTs) followed by six integer instructions (INTs) followed by two FLTs, the 6x86 processor can issue all ten instructions to the appropriate execution units prior to completion of the first FLT. If none of the instructions fault (the typical case), execution continues with both the integer and floating point units completing instructions in parallel. If one of the FLTs faults (the atypical case), the speculative execution capability of the 6x86 allows the processor state to be restored in such a way that it is compatible with the x86 floating point exception model.*
>
> *Examination of benchmark tests reveals that synthetic floating point benchmarks use a pure floating point-only code stream not found in real-world applications. This type of benchmark does not take advantage of the speculative execution capability of the 6x86 processor. Cyrix believes that non-synthetic benchmarks based on real-world applications better reflect the actual performance users will achieve. Real-world applications contain intermixed integer and floating point instructions and therefore benefit from the 6x86 speculative execution capability."*

So, the recent trend in benchmarking is to choose common applications and use them to test the performance of complete computer systems. For example, **SPEC**, the non-profit corporation that designed the well-known SPECINT and SPECFP synthetic benchmark suites, has launched a project for a new applications benchmark suite. But then again, it is very unlikely that such commercial benchmarks will ever include any Linux code.

Summarizing, synthetic benchmarks are valid as long as you understand their purposes and limitations. Applications benchmarks will better reflect a computer system's performance, but none are available for Linux.

2.1.2   High-level vs. low-level benchmarks

Low-level benchmarks will directly measure the performance of the hardware: CPU clock, DRAM and cache SRAM cycle times, hard disk average access time, latency, track-to-track stepping time, etc... This can be useful in case you bought a system and are wondering what components it was built with, but a better way to check these figures would be to open the case, list whatever part numbers you can find and somehow obtain the data sheet for each part (usually on the Web).

Another use for low-level benchmarks is to check that a kernel driver was correctly configured for a specific piece of hardware: if you have the data sheet for the component, you can compare the results of the low-level benchmarks to the theoretical, printed specs.

High-level benchmarks are more concerned with the performance of the hardware/driver/OS combination for a specific aspect of a microcomputer system, for example file I/O performance, or even for a specific hardware/driver/OS/application performance, e.g. an Apache benchmark on different microcomputer systems.

Of course, all low-level benchmarks are synthetic. High-level benchmarks may be synthetic or applications benchmarks.

2.2 Standard benchmarks available for Linux

IMHO a simple test that anyone can do while upgrading any component in his/her Linux box is to launch a kernel compile before and after the hard/software upgrade and compare compilation times. If all other conditions are kept equal then the test is valid as a measure of compilation performance and one can be confident to say that:

> "Changing A to B led to an improvement of x % in the compile time of the Linux kernel under such and such conditions".

No more, no less !

Since kernel compilation is a very usual task under Linux, and since it exercises most functions that get exercised by normal benchmarks (except floating-point performance), it constitutes a rather good **individual** test. In most cases, however, results from such a test cannot be reproduced by other Linux users because of variations in hard/software configurations and so this kind of test cannot be used as a "yardstick" to compare dissimilar systems (unless we all agree on a standard kernel to compile - see below).

Unfortunately, there are no Linux-specific benchmarking tools, except perhaps the Byte Linux Benchmarks which are a slightly modified version of the Byte Unix Benchmarks dating back from May 1991 (Linux mods by Jon Tombs, original authors Ben Smith, Rick Grehan and Tom Yager).

There is a central *Web site* for the Byte Linux Benchmarks.

An improved, updated version of the Byte Unix Benchmarks was put together by David C. Niemi. It is called UnixBench 4.01 to avoid confusion with earlier versions. Here is what David wrote about his mods:

> *"The original and slightly modified BYTE Unix benchmarks are broken in quite a number of ways which make them an unusually unreliable indicator of system performance. I intentionally made my "index" values look a lot different to avoid confusion with the old benchmarks."*

David has setup a majordomo mailing list for discussion of benchmarking on Linux and competing OSs. Join with "subscribe bench" sent in the body of a message to *majordomo@wauug.erols.com* <mailto:majordomo@wauug. erols.com>. The Washington Area Unix User Group is also in the process of setting up a *Web site* for Linux benchmarks.

Also recently, Uwe F. Mayer, *mayer@math.vanderbilt.edu* <mailto:mayer@math.vanderbilt.edu>ported the BYTE Bytemark suite to Linux. This is a modern suite carefully put together by Rick Grehan at BYTE Magazine to test the CPU, FPU and memory system performance of modern microcomputer systems (these are strictly processor-performance oriented benchmarks, no I/O or system performance is taken into account).

Uwe has also put together a *Web site* with a database of test results for his version of the Linux BYTEmark benchmarks.

While searching for synthetic benchmarks for Linux, you will notice that sunsite.unc.edu carries few benchmarking tools. To test the relative speed of X servers and graphics cards, the xbench-0.2 suite by Claus Gittinger is available from sunsite.unc.edu, ftp.x.org and other sites. Xfree86.org refuses (wisely) to carry or recommend any benchmarks.

The *XFree86-benchmarks Survey* is a Web site with a database of x-bench results.

HOWTO

For pure disk I/O throughput, the hdparm program (included with most distributions, otherwise available from sunsite.unc.edu) will measure transfer rates if called with the -t and -T switches.

There are many other tools freely available on the Internet to test various performance aspects of your Linux box.

2.3 Links and references

The comp.benchmarks.faq by Dave Sill is the standard reference for benchmarking. It is not Linux specific, but recommended reading for anybody serious about benchmarking. It is available from a number of FTP and web sites and lists **56 different benchmarks**, with links to FTP or Web sites that carry them. Some of the benchmarks listed are commercial (SPEC for example), though.

I will not go through each one of the benchmarks mentionned in the comp.benchmarks.faq, but there is at least one low-level suite which I would like to comment on: the *lmbench suite*, by Larry McVoy. Quoting David C. Niemi:

> *"Linus and David Miller use this a lot because it does some useful low-level measurements and can also measure network throughput and latency if you have 2 boxes to test with. But it does not attempt to come up with anything like an overall "figure of merit"..."*

A rather complete *FTP site* for **freely** available benchmarks was put together by Alfred Aburto. The Whetstone suite used in the LBT can be found at this site.

There is a **multipart FAQ by Eugene Miya** that gets posted regularly to comp.benchmarks; it is an excellent reference.

3 The Linux Benchmarking Toolkit (LBT)

I will propose a basic benchmarking toolkit for Linux. This is a preliminary version of a comprehensive Linux Benchmarking Toolkit, to be expanded and improved. Take it for what it's worth, i.e. as a proposal. If you don't think it is a valid test suite, feel free to email me your critics and I will be glad to make the changes and improve it if I can. Before getting into an argument, however, read this HOWTO and the mentionned references: informed criticism is welcomed, empty criticism is not.

3.1 Rationale

This is just common sense:

1. It should not take a whole day to run. When it comes to comparative benchmarking (various runs), nobody wants to spend days trying to figure out the fastest setup for a given system. Ideally, the entire benchmark set should take about 15 minutes to complete on an average machine.

2. All source code for the software used must be freely available on the Net, for obvious reasons.

3. Benchmarks should provide simple figures reflecting the measured performance.

4. There should be a mix of synthetic benchmarks and application benchmarks (with separate results, of course).

5. Each **synthetic** benchmarks should exercise a particular subsystem to its maximum capacity.

6. Results of **synthetic** benchmarks should **not** be averaged into a single figure of merit (that defeats the whole idea behind synthetic benchmarks, with considerable loss of information).

7. Applications benchmarks should consist of commonly executed tasks on Linux systems.

3.2 Benchmark selection

I have selected five different benchmark suites, trying as much as possible to avoid overlap in the tests:

1. Kernel 2.0.0 (default configuration) compilation using gcc.

2. Whetstone version 10/03/97 (latest version by Roy Longbottom).
3. xbench-0.2 (with fast execution parameters).
4. UnixBench benchmarks version 4.01 (partial results).
5. BYTE Magazine's BYTEmark benchmarks beta release 2 (partial results).

For tests 4 and 5, "(partial results)" means that not all results produced by these benchmarks are considered.

3.3 Test duration

1. Kernel 2.0.0 compilation: 5 - 30 minutes, depending on the **real** performance of your system.
2. Whetstone: 100 seconds.
3. Xbench-0.2: < 1 hour.
4. UnixBench benchmarks version 4.01: approx. 15 minutes.
5. BYTE Magazine's BYTEmark benchmarks: approx. 10 minutes.

3.4 Comments

3.4.1 Kernel 2.0.0 compilation:

- **What:** it is the only application benchmark in the LBT.
- The code is widely available (i.e. I finally found some use for my old Linux CD-ROMs).
- Most linuxers recompile the kernel quite often, so it is a significant measure of overall performance.
- The kernel is large and gcc uses a large chunk of memory: attenuates L2 cache size bias with small tests.
- It does frequent I/O to disk.
- Test procedure: get a pristine 2.0.0 source, compile with default options (make config, press Enter repeatedly). The reported time should be the time spent on compilation i.e. after you type make zImage, **not** including make dep, make clean. Note that the default target architecture for the kernel is the i386, so if compiled on another architecture, gcc too should be set to cross-compile, with i386 as the target architecture.
- **Results:** compilation time in minutes and seconds (please don't report fractions of seconds).

3.4.2 Whetstone:

- **What:** measures pure floating point performance with a short, tight loop. The source (in C) is quite readable and it is very easy to see which floating-point operations are involved.
- Shortest test in the LBT :-).
- It's an "Old Classic" test: comparable figures are available, its flaws and shortcomings are well known.
- Test procedure: the newest C source should be obtained from Aburto's site. Compile and run in double precision mode. Specify gcc and -O2 as precompiler and precompiler options, and define POSIX 1 to specify machine type.
- **Results:** a floating-point performance figure in MWIPS.

3.4.3 Xbench-0.2:

- **What:** measures X server performance.
- The xStones measure provided by xbench is a weighted average of several tests indexed to an old Sun station with a single-bit-depth display. Hmmm... it is questionable as a test of modern X servers, but it's still the best tool I have found.
- Test procedure: compile with -O2. We specify a few options for a shorter run: `./xbench -timegoal 3 > results/name_of_your_linux_box.out`. To get the xStones rating, we must run an awk script; the simplest way is to type `make summary.ms`. Check the summary.ms file: the xStone rating for your system is in the last column of the line with your machine name specified during the test.
- **Results:** an X performance figure in xStones.
- Note: this test, as it stands, is outdated. It should be re-coded.

HOWTO

3.4.4 UnixBench version 4.01:

- **What:** measures overall Unix performance. This test will exercice the file I/O and kernel multitasking performance.

- I have discarded all arithmetic test results, keeping only the system-related test results.

- Test procedure: make with -O2. Execute with `./Run -1` (run each test once). You will find the results in the ./results/report file. Calculate the geometric mean of the EXECL THROUGHPUT, FILECOPY 1, 2, 3, PIPE THROUGHPUT, PIPE-BASED CONTEXT SWITCHING, PROCESS CREATION, SHELL SCRIPTS and SYSTEM CALL OVERHEAD indexes.

- **Results:** a system index.

3.4.5 BYTE Magazine's BYTEmark benchmarks:

- **What:** provides a good measure of CPU performance. Here is an excerpt from the documentation: *"These benchmarks are meant to expose the theoretical upper limit of the CPU, FPU, and memory architecture of a system. They cannot measure video, disk, or network throughput (those are the domains of a different set of benchmarks). You should, therefore, use the results of these tests as part, not all, of any evaluation of a system."*

- I have discarded the FPU test results since the Whetstone test is just as representative of FPU performance.

- I have split the integer tests in two groups: those more representative of memory-cache-CPU performance and the CPU integer tests.

- Test procedure: make with -O2. Run the test with `./nbench > myresults.dat` or similar. Then, from myresults.dat, calculate geometric mean of STRING SORT, ASSIGNMENT and BITFIELD test indexes; this is the **memory index**; calculate the geometric mean of NUMERIC SORT, IDEA, HUFFMAN and FP EMULATION test indexes; this is the **integer index**.

- **Results:** a memory index and an integer index calculated as explained above.

3.5 Possible improvements

The ideal benchmark suite would run in a few minutes, with synthetic benchmarks testing every subsystem separately and applications benchmarks providing results for different applications. It would also automatically generate a complete report and eventually email the report to a central database on the Web.

We are not really interested in portability here, but it should at least run on all recent ($> 2.0.0$) versions and flavours (i386, Alpha, Sparc...) of Linux.

If anybody has any idea about benchmarking network performance in a simple, easy and reliable way, with a short (less than 30 minutes to setup and run) test, please contact me.

3.6 LBT Report Form

Besides the tests, the benchmarking procedure would not be complete without a form describing the setup, so here it is (following the guidelines from comp.benchmarks.faq):

```
LINUX BENCHMARKING TOOLKIT REPORT FORM
```

```
CPU
==
Vendor:
Model:
Core clock:
Motherboard vendor:
Mbd. model:
Mbd. chipset:
```

```
Bus type:
Bus clock:
Cache total:
Cache type/speed:
SMP (number of processors):
```

```
RAM
====
Total:
Type:
Speed:
```

```
Disk
====
Vendor:
Model:
Size:
Interface:
Driver/Settings:
```

```
Video board
===========
Vendor:
Model:
Bus:
Video RAM type:
Video RAM total:
X server vendor:
X server version:
X server chipset choice:
Resolution/vert. refresh rate:
Color depth:
```

```
Kernel
=====
Version:
Swap size:
```

```
gcc
===
Version:
Options:
libc version:
```

```
Test notes
==========
```

```
RESULTS
========
Linux kernel 2.0.0 Compilation Time: (minutes and seconds)
```

```
Whetstones: results are in MWIPS.
Xbench: results are in xstones.
Unixbench Benchmarks 4.01 system INDEX:
BYTEmark integer INDEX:
BYTEmark memory INDEX:
```

```
Comments*
=========
```
* This field is included for possible interpretations of the results, and as such, it is optional. It could be the most significant part of your report, though, specially if you are doing comparative benchmarking.

3.7 Network performance tests

Testing network performance is a challenging task since it involves at least two machines, a server and a client machine, hence twice the time to setup and many more variables to control, etc... On an ethernet network, I guess your best bet would be the ttcp package. (to be expanded)

3.8 SMP tests

SMP tests are another challenge, and any benchmark specifically designed for SMP testing will have a hard time proving itself valid in real-life settings, since algorithms that can take advantage of SMP are hard to come by. It seems later versions of the Linux kernel ($> 2.1.30$ or around that) will do "fine-grained" multiprocessing, but I have no more information than that for the moment.

According to David Niemi, " ... *shell8* [part of the Unixbench 4.01 benchmaks]*does a good job at comparing similar hardware/OS in SMP and UP modes."*

4   Example run and results

The LBT was run on my home machine, a Pentium-class Linux box that I put together myself and that I used to write this HOWTO. Here is the LBT Report Form for this system:

```
LINUX BENCHMARKING TOOLKIT REPORT FORM

CPU

==

Vendor: Cyrix/IBM

Model: 6x86L P166+

Core clock: 133 MHz

Motherboard vendor: Elite Computer Systems (ECS)

Mbd. model: P5VX-Be

Mbd. chipset: Intel VX

Bus type: PCI
```

Bus clock: 33 MHz

Cache total: 256 KB

Cache type/speed: Pipeline burst 6 ns

SMP (number of processors): 1

RAM

====

Total: 32 MB

Type: EDO SIMMs

Speed: 60 ns

Disk

====

Vendor: IBM

Model: IBM-DAQA-33240

Size: 3.2 GB

Interface: EIDE

Driver/Settings: Bus Master DMA mode 2

Video board

===========

Vendor: Generic S3

Model: Trio64-V2

Bus: PCI

Video RAM type: EDO DRAM

Video RAM total: 2 MB

X server vendor: XFree86

X server version: 3.3

X server chipset choice: S3 accelerated

Resolution/vert. refresh rate: 1152x864 @ 70 Hz

Color depth: 16 bits

Kernel

=====

Version: 2.0.29

Swap size: 64 MB

gcc

===

Version: 2.7.2.1

Options: -O2

libc version: 5.4.23

Test notes

==========

Very light load. The above tests were run with some of the special
Cyrix/IBM 6x86 features enabled with the setx86 program: fast ADS,
fast IORT, Enable DTE, fast LOOP, fast Lin. VidMem.

RESULTS

========

Linux kernel 2.0.0 Compilation Time: 7m12s

Whetstones: 38.169 MWIPS.

Xbench: 97243 xStones.

BYTE Unix Benchmarks 4.01 system INDEX: 58.43

BYTEmark integer INDEX: 1.50

BYTEmark memory INDEX: 2.50

Comments

=========

This is a very stable system with homogeneous performance, ideal
for home use and/or Linux development. I will report results
with a 6x86MX processor as soon as I can get my hands on one!

5 Pitfalls and caveats of benchmarking

After putting together this HOWTO I began to understand why the words "pitfalls" and "caveats" are so often associated with benchmarking...

5.1 Comparing apples and oranges

Or should I say Apples and PCs ? This is so obvious and such an old dispute that I won't go into any details. I doubt the time it takes to load Word on a Mac compared to an average Pentium is a real measure of anything. Likewise booting Linux and Windows NT, etc... Try as much as possible to compare identical machines with a single modification.

5.2 Incomplete information

A single example will illustrate this very common mistake. One often reads in comp.os.linux.hardware the following or similar statement: "I just plugged in processor XYZ running at nnn MHz and now compiling the linux kernel only takes i minutes" (adjust XYZ, nnn and i as required). This is irritating, because no other information is given, i.e. we don't even know the amount of RAM, size of swap, other tasks running simultaneously, kernel version, modules selected, hard disk type, gcc version, etc... I recommend you use the LBT Report Form, which at least provides a standard information framework.

5.3 Proprietary hardware/software

A well-known processor manufacturer once published results of benchmarks produced by a special, customized version of gcc. Ethical considerations apart, those results were meaningless, since 100% of the Linux community would go on using the standard version of gcc. The same goes for proprietary hardware. Benchmarking is much more useful when it deals with off-the-shelf hardware and free (in the GNU/GPL sense) software.

5.4 Relevance

We are talking Linux, right ? So we should forget about benchmarks produced on other operating systems (this is a special case of the "Comparing apples and oranges" pitfall above). Also, if one is going to benchmark Web server performance, **do not** quote FPU performance and other irrelevant information. In such cases, less is more. Also, you do **not** need to mention the age of your cat, your mood while benchmarking, etc..

6 FAQ

Q1.

Is there any single figure of merit for Linux systems ?

A:

No, thankfully nobody has yet come up with a Lhinuxstone (tm) measurement. And if there was one, it would not make much sense: Linux systems are used for many different tasks, from heavily loaded Web servers to graphics workstations for individual use. No single figure of merit can describe the performance of a Linux system under such different situations.

Q2.

Then, how about a dozen figures summarizing the performance of diverse Linux systems ?

A:

That would be the ideal situation. I would like to see that come true. Anybody volunteers for a **Linux Benchmarking Project** ? With a Web site and an on-line, complete, well-designed reports database ?

Q3.

... BogoMips ... ?

A:

BogoMips has nothing to do with the performance of your system. Check the BogoMips Mini-HOWTO.

Q4.

What is the "best" benchmark for Linux ?

A:

It all depends on which performance aspect of a Linux system one wants to measure. There are different benchmarks to measure the network (Ethernet sustained transfer rates), file server (NFS), disk I/O, FPU, integer, graphics, 3D, processor-memory bandwidth, CAD performance, transaction time, SQL performance, Web server performance, real-time performance, CD-ROM performance, Quake performance (!), etc ... AFAIK no bechmark suite exists for Linux that supports all these tests.

Q5.

What is the fastest processor under Linux ?

A:

Fastest at what task ? If one is heavily number-crunching oriented, a very high clock rate Alpha (600 MHz and going) should be faster than anything else, since Alphas have been designed for that kind of performance. If, on the other hand, one wants to put together a very fast news server, it is probable that the choice of a fast hard disk subsystem and lots of RAM will result in higher performance improvements than a change of processor, for the same amount of $.

Q6.

Let me rephrase the last question, then: is there a processor that is fastest for general purpose applications ?

A:

This is a tricky question but it takes a very simple answer: **NO**. One can always design a faster system even for general purpose applications, independent of the processor. Usually, all other things being equal, higher clock rates will result in higher performance systems (and more headaches too). Taking out an old 100 MHz Pentium from an (usually not) upgradable motherboard, and plugging in the 200 MHz version, one should feel the extra "hummph". Of course, with only 16 MBytes of RAM, the same investment would have been more wisely spent on extra SIMMs...

Q7.

So clock rates influence the performance of a system ?

A:

For most tasks except for NOP empty loops (BTW these get removed by modern optimizing compilers), an increase in clock rate will not give you a linear increase in performance. Very small processor intensive programs that will fit entirely in the primary cache inside the processor (the L1 cache, usually 8 or 16 K) will have a performance increase equivalent to the clock rate increase, but most "true" programs are much larger than that, have loops that do not fit in the L1 cache, share the L2 (external) cache with other processes, depend on external components and will give much smaller performance increases. This is because the L1 cache runs at the same clock rate as the processor, whereas most L2 caches and all other subsystems (DRAM, for example) will run asynchronously at lower clock rates.

Q8.

OK, then, one last question on that matter: which is the processor with the best price/performance ratio for general purpose Linux use ?

A:

Defining "general purpose Linux use" in not an easy thing ! For any particular application, there is always a processor with THE BEST price/performance ratio at any given time, but it changes rather frequently as manufacturers release new processors, so answering Processor XYZ running at n MHz would be a snapshot answer. However, the price of the processor is insignificant when compared to the price of the whole system one will be putting together. So, really, the question should be how can one maximize the price/performance ratio for a given system ? And the answer to that question depends heavily on the minimum performance requirements and/or maximum cost established for the configuration being considered. Sometimes, off-the-shelf hardware will not meet minimum performance requirements and expensive RISC systems will be the only alternative. For home use, I recommend a balanced, homogeneous system for overall performance (now go figure what I mean by balanced and homogeneous :-); the choice of a processor is an important decision , but no more than choosing hard disk type and capacity, amount of RAM, video card, etc...

Q9.

What is a "significant" increase in performance ?

A:

I would say that anything under 1% is not significant (could be described as "marginal"). We, humans, will hardly perceive the difference between two systems with a 5 % difference in response time. Of course some hard-core benchmarkers are not humans and will tell you that, when comparing systems with 65.9 and 66.5 performance indexes, the later is "definitely faster".

Q10.

How do I obtain "significant" increases in performance at the lowest cost ?

A:

Since most source code is available for Linux, careful examination and algorithmic redesign of key subroutines could yield order-of-magnitude increases in performance in some cases. If one is dealing with a commercial project and does not wish to delve deeply in C source code a **Linux consultant should be called in**. See the Consultants-HOWTO.

7 Copyright, acknowledgments and miscellaneous

7.1 How this document was produced

The first step was reading section 4 "Writing and submitting a HOWTO" of the HOWTO Index by Tim Bynum.

I knew absolutely nothing about SGML or LaTeX, but was tempted to use an automated documentation generation package after reading the various comments about SGML-Tools. However, inserting tags manually in a document reminds me of the days I hand-assembled a 512 byte monitor program for a now defunct 8-bit microprocessor, so I got hold of the LyX sources, compiled it, and used its LinuxDoc mode. Highly recommended combination: **LyX and SGML-Tools**.

7.2 Copyright

The Linux Benchmarking HOWTO is copyright (C) 1997 by André D. Balsa. Linux HOWTO documents may be reproduced and distributed in whole or in part, in any medium physical or electronic, as long as this copyright notice is retained on all copies. Commercial redistribution is allowed and encouraged; however, the author would like to be notified of any such distributions.

All translations, derivative works, or aggregate works incorporating any Linux HOWTO documents must be covered under this copyright notice. That is, you may not produce a derivative work from a HOWTO and impose additional restrictions on its distribution. Exceptions to these rules may be granted under certain conditions; please contact the Linux HOWTO coordinator at the address given below.

In short, we wish to promote dissemination of this information through as many channels as possible. However, we do wish to retain copyright on the HOWTO documents, and would like to be notified of any plans to redistribute the HOWTOs.

If you have questions, please contact Tim Bynum, the Linux HOWTO coordinator, at linux-howto@sunsite.unc.edu via email.

7.3 New versions of this document

New versions of the Linux Benchmarking-HOWTO will be placed on sunsite.unc.edu and mirror sites. There are other formats, such as a Postscript and dvi version in the other-formats directory. The Linux Benchmarking-HOWTO is

HOWTO

also available for WWW clients such as Grail, a Web browser written in Python. It will also be posted regularly to comp.os.linux.answers.

7.4 Feedback

Suggestions, corrections, additions wanted. Contributors wanted and acknowledged. Flames not wanted.

I can always be reached at andrewbalsa@usa.net.

7.5 Acknowledgments

David Niemi, the author of the Unixbench suite, has proved to be an endless source of information and (valid) criticism.

I also want to thank Greg Hankins one of the main contributors to the SGML-tools package, Linus Torvalds and the entire Linux community. This HOWTO is my way of giving back.

7.6 Disclaimer

Your mileage may, and will, vary. Be aware that benchmarking is a touchy subject and a great time-and-energy consuming activity.

7.7 Trademarks

Pentium and Windows NT are trademarks of Intel and Microsoft Corporations respectively.

BYTE and BYTEmark are trademarks of McGraw-Hill, Inc.

Cyrix and 6x86 are trademarks of Cyrix Corporation.

Linux is not a trademark, hopefully never will be.

Part VI

"Beowulf HOWTO " Jacek Radajewski and Douglas Eadline

v1.1.1, 22 November 1998
This document introduces the Beowulf Supercomputer architecture and provides background information on parallel programming, including links to other more specific documents, and web pages.

Contents

HOWTO

1   Preamble

1.1   Disclaimer

We will not accept any responsibility for any incorrect information within this document, nor for any damage it might cause when applied.

1.2   Copyright

Copyright © 1997 - 1998 Jacek Radajewski and Douglas Eadline. Permission to distribute and modify this document is granted under the GNU General Public Licence.

1.3   About this HOWTO

Jacek Radajewski started work on this document in November 1997 and was soon joined by Douglas Eadline. Over a few months the Beowulf HOWTO grew into a large document, and in August 1998 it was split into three documents: Beowulf HOWTO, Beowulf Architecture Design HOWTO, and the Beowulf Installation and Administration HOWTO. Version 1.0.0 of the Beowulf HOWTO was released to the Linux Documentation Project on 11 November 1998. We hope that this is only the beginning of what will become a complete Beowulf Documentation Project.

1.4   About the authors

- Jacek Radajewski works as a Network Manager, and is studying for an honors degree in computer science at the University of Southern Queensland, Australia. Jacek's first contact with Linux was in 1995 and it was love at first sight. Jacek built his first Beowulf cluster in May 1997 and has been playing with the technology ever since, always trying to find new and better ways of setting things up. You can contact Jacek by sending e-mail to *jacek@usq.edu.au*

- Douglas Eadline, Ph.D. is President and Principal Scientist at Paralogic, Inc., Bethlehem, PA, USA. Trained as Physical/Analytical Chemist, he has been involved with computers since 1978 when he built his first single board computer for use with chemical instrumentation. Dr. Eadline's interests now include Linux, Beowulf clusters, and parallel algorithms. Dr. Eadline can be contacted by sending email to *deadline@plogic.com*

1.5   Acknowledgements

The writing of the Beowulf HOWTO was a long proces and is finally complete, thanks to many individuals. I would like to thank the following people for their help and contribution to this HOWTO.

- Becky for her love, support, and understanding.
- Tom Sterling, Don Becker, and other people at NASA who started the Beowulf project.

- Thanh Tran-Cong and the Faculty of Engineering and Surveying for making the *topcat* Beowulf machine available for experiments.
- My supervisor Christopher Vance for many great ideas.
- My friend Russell Waldron for great programming ideas, his general interest in the project, and support.
- My friend David Smith for proof reading this document.
- Many other people on the Beowulf mailing list who provided me with feedback and ideas.
- All the people who are responsible for the Linux operating system and all the other free software packages used on *topcat* and other Beowulf machines.

2 Introduction

As the performance of commodity computer and network hardware increase, and their prices decrease, it becomes more and more practical to build parallel computational systems from off-the-shelf components, rather than buying CPU time on very expensive Supercomputers. In fact, the price per performance ratio of a Beowulf type machine is between three to ten times better than that for traditional supercomputers. Beowulf architecture scales well, it is easy to construct and you only pay for the hardware as most of the software is free.

2.1 Who should read this HOWTO ?

This HOWTO is designed for a person with at least some exposure to the Linux operating system. Knowledge of Beowulf technology or understanding of more complex operating system and networking concepts is not essential, but some exposure to parallel computing would be advantageous (after all you must have some reason to read this document). This HOWTO will not answer all possible questions you might have about Beowulf, but hopefully will give you ideas and guide you in the right direction. The purpose of this HOWTO is to provide background information, links and references to more advanced documents.

2.2 What is a Beowulf ?

Famed was this Beowulf: far flew the boast of him, son of Scyld, in the Scandian lands. So becomes it a youth to quit him well with his father's friends, by fee and gift, that to aid him, aged, in after days, come warriors willing, should war draw nigh, liegemen loyal: by lauded deeds shall an earl have honor in every clan. Beowulf is the earliest surviving epic poem written in English. It is a story about a hero of great strength and courage who defeted a monster called Grendel. See 5.7 (History) to find out more about the Beowulf hero.

There are probably as many Beowulf definitions as there are people who build or use Beowulf Supercomputer facilities. Some claim that one can call their system Beowulf only if it is built in the same way as the NASA's original machine. Others go to the other extreme and call Beowulf any system of workstations running parallel code. My definition of Beowulf fits somewhere between the two views described above, and is based on many postings to the Beowulf mailing list:

Beowulf is a multi computer architecture which can be used for parallel computations. It is a system which usually consists of one server node, and one or more client nodes connected together via Ethernet or some other network. It is a system built using commodity hardware components, like any PC capable of running Linux, standard Ethernet adapters, and switches. It does not contain any custom hardware components and is trivially reproducible. Beowulf also uses commodity software like the Linux operating system, Parallel Virtual Machine (PVM) and Message Passing Interface (MPI). The server node controls the whole cluster and serves files to the client nodes. It is also the cluster's console and gateway to the outside world. Large Beowulf machines might have more than one server node, and possibly other nodes dedicated to particular tasks, for example consoles or monitoring stations. In most cases client nodes in a Beowulf system are dumb, the dumber the better. Nodes are configured and controlled by the server node, and do only what they are told to do. In a disk-less client configuration, client nodes don't even know their IP address or name until the server tells them what it is. One of the main differences between Beowulf and a Cluster of Workstations (COW) is the fact that Beowulf behaves more like a single machine rather than many workstations. In most cases client nodes do not have keyboards or monitors, and are accessed only via remote login or possibly serial terminal. Beowulf nodes can be thought of as a

CPU + memory package which can be plugged in to the cluster, just like a CPU or memory module can be plugged into a motherboard.

Beowulf is not a special software package, new network topology or the latest kernel hack. Beowulf is a technology of clustering Linux computers to form a parallel, virtual supercomputer. Although there are many software packages such as kernel modifications, PVM and MPI libraries, and configuration tools which make the Beowulf architecture faster, easier to configure, and much more usable, one can build a Beowulf class machine using standard Linux distribution without any additional software. If you have two networked Linux computers which share at least the /home file system via NFS, and trust each other to execute remote shells (rsh), then it could be argued that you have a simple, two node Beowulf machine.

2.3   Classification

Beowulf systems have been constructed from a variety of parts. For the sake of performance some non-commodity components (i.e. produced by a single manufacturer) have been employed. In order to account for the different types of systems and to make discussions about machines a bit easier, we propose the following simple classification scheme:

CLASS I BEOWULF:

This class of machines built entirely from commodity "off-the-shelf" parts. We shall use the "Computer Shopper" certification test to define commodity "off-the-shelf" parts. (Computer Shopper is a 1 inch thick monthly magazine/catalog of PC systems and components.) The test is as follows:

A CLASS I Beowulf is a machine that can be assembled from parts found in at least 3 nationally/globally circulated advertising catalogs.

The advantages of a CLASS I system are:

- hardware is available form multiple sources (low prices, easy maintenance)

- no reliance on a single hardware vendor

- driver support from Linux commodity

- usually based on standards (SCSI, Ethernet, etc.)

The disadvantages of a CLASS I system are:

- best performance may require CLASS II hardware

CLASS II BEOWULF

A CLASS II Beowulf is simply any machine that does not pass the Computer Shopper certification test. This is not a bad thing. Indeed, it is merely a classification of the machine.

The advantages of a CLASS II system are:

- Performance can be quite good!

The disadvantages of a CLASS II system are:

- driver support may vary

- reliance on single hardware vendor

- may be more expensive than CLASS I systems.

One CLASS is not necessarily better than the other. It all depends on your needs and budget. This classification system is only intended to make discussions about Beowulf systems a bit more succinct. The "System Design" section may help determine what kind of system is best suited for your needs.

3   Architecture Overview

3.1   What does it look like ?

I think that the best way of describing the Beowulf supercomputer architecture is to use an example which is very similar to the actual Beowulf, but familiar to most system administrators. The example that is closest to a Beowulf machine is a Unix computer laboratory with a server and a number of clients. To be more specific I'll use the DEC Alpha undergraduate computer laboratory at the Faculty of Sciences, USQ as the example. The server computer is called *beldin* and the client machines are called *scilab01*, *scilab02*, *scilab03*, up to *scilab20*. All clients have a local copy of the Digital Unix 4.0 operating system installed, but get the user file space (/home) and /usr/local from the server via NFS (Network File System). Each client has an entry for the server and all the other clients in its /etc/hosts.equiv file, so all clients can execute a remote shell (rsh) to all others. The server machine is a NIS server for the whole laboratory, so account information is the same across all the machines. A person can sit at the *scilab02* console, login, and have the same environment as if he logged onto the server or *scilab15*. The reason all the clients have the same look and feel is that the operating system is installed and configured in the same way on all machines, and both the user's /home and /usr/local areas are physically on the server and accessed by the clients via NFS. For more information on NIS and NFS please read the *NIS* and *NFS* HOWTOs.

3.2   How to utilise the other nodes ?

Now that we have some idea about the system architecture, let us take a look at how we can utilise the available CPU cycles of the machines in the computer laboratory. Any person can logon to any of the machines, and run a program in their home directory, but they can also spawn the same job on a different machine simply by executing remote shell. For example, assume that we want to calculate the sum of the square roots of all integers between 1 and 10 inclusive. We write a simple program called sigmasqrt (please see 6.2 (source code)) which does exactly that. To calculate the sum of the square roots of numbers from 1 to 10 we execute :

```
[jacek@beldin sigmasqrt]$ time ./sigmasqrt 1 10
22.468278

real    0m0.029s
user    0m0.001s
sys     0m0.024s
```

The time command allows us to check the wall-clock (the elapsed time) of running this job. As we can see, this example took only a small fraction of a second (0.029 sec) to execute, but what if I want to add the square root of integers from 1 to 1 000 000 000 ? Let us try this, and again calculate the wall-clock time.

```
[jacek@beldin sigmasqrt]$ time ./sigmasqrt 1 1000000000
21081851083600.559000

real    16m45.937s
user    16m43.527s
sys     0m0.108s
```

This time, the execution time of the program is considerably longer. The obvious question to ask is what can we do to speed up the execution time of the job? How can we change the way the job is running to minimize the wall-clock time of running this job? The obvious answer is to split the job into a number of sub-jobs and to run these sub-jobs in parallel on all computers. We could split one big addition task into 20 parts, calculating one range of square roots and adding them on each node. When all nodes finish the calculation and return their results, the 20 numbers could be added together to obtain the final solution. Before we run this job we will make a named pipe which will be used by all processes to write their results.

```
[jacek@beldin sigmasqrt]$ mkfifo output
```

```
[jacek@beldin sigmasqrt]$ ./prun.sh & time cat output | ./sum
[1] 5085
21081851083600.941000
[1]+  Done                    ./prun.sh

real    0m58.539s
user    0m0.061s
sys     0m0.206s
```

This time we get about 58.5 seconds. This is the time from starting the job until all the nodes have finished their computations and written their results into the pipe. The time does not include the final addition of the twenty numbers, but this time is a very small fraction of a second and can be ignored. We can see that there is a significant improvement in running this job in parallel. In fact the parallel job ran about 17 times faster, which is very reasonable for a 20 fold increase in the number of CPUs. The purpose of the above example is to illustrate the simplest method of parallelising concurrent code. In practice such simple examples are rare and different techniques (PVM and PMI APIs) are used to achieve the parallelism.

3.3 How does Beowulf differ from a COW ?

The computer laboratory described above is a perfect example of a Cluster of Workstations (COW). So what is so special about Beowulf, and how is it different from a COW? The truth is that there is not much difference, but Beowulf does have few unique characteristics. First of all, in most cases client nodes in a Beowulf cluster do not have keyboards, mice, video cards nor monitors. All access to the client nodes is done via remote connections from the server node, dedicated console node, or a serial console. Because there is no need for client nodes to access machines outside the cluster, nor for machines outside the cluster to access client nodes directly, it is a common practice for the client nodes to use private IP addresses like the 10.0.0.0/8 or 192.168.0.0/16 address ranges (RFC 1918 *http://www.alternic.net/rfcs/1900/rfc1918.txt.html*). Usually the only machine that is also connected to the outside world using a second network card is the server node. The most common ways of using the system is to access the server's console directly, or either telnet or remote login to the server node from personal workstation. Once on the server node, users can edit and compile their code, and also spawn jobs on all nodes in the cluster. In most cases COWs are used for parallel computations at night, and over weekends when people do not actually use the workstations for every day work, thus utilising idle CPU cycles. Beowulf on the other hand is a machine usually dedicated to parallel computing, and optimised for this purpose. Beowulf also gives better price/performance ratio as it is built from off-the-shelf components and runs mainly free software. Beowulf has also more single system image features which help the users to see the Beowulf cluster as a single computing workstation.

4 System Design

Before you purchase any hardware, it may be a good idea to consider the design of your system. There are basically two hardware issues involved with design of a Beowulf system: the type of nodes or computers you are going to use; and way you connect the computer nodes. There is one software issue that may effect your hardware decisions; the communication library or API. A more detailed discussion of hardware and communication software is provided later in this document.

While the number of choices is not large, there are some important design decisions that must be made when constructing a Beowulf systems. Because the science (or art) of "parallel computing" has many different interpretations, an introduction is provided below. If you do not like to read background material, you may skip this section, but it is advised that you read section 4.4 (Suitability) before you make you final hardware decisions.

4.1 A brief background on parallel computing.

This section provides background on parallel computing concepts. It is NOT an exhaustive or complete description of parallel computing science and technology. It is a brief description of the issues that may be important to a Beowulf designer and user.

As you design and build your Beowulf, many of these issues described below will become important in your decision process. Due to its component nature, a Beowulf Supercomputer requires that we consider many factors carefully because they are now under our control. In general, it is not all that difficult to understand the issues involved with parallel computing. Indeed, once the issues are understood, your expectations will be more realistic and success will be more likely. Unlike the "sequential world" where processor speed is considered the single most important factor, processor speed in the "parallel world" is just one of several factors that will determine overall system performance and efficiency.

4.2 The methods of parallel computing

Parallel computing can take many forms. From a user's perspective, it is important to consider the advantages and disadvantages of each methodology. The following section attempts to provide some perspective on the methods of parallel computing and indicate where the Beowulf machine falls on this continuum.

4.2.1 Why more than one CPU?

Answering this question is important. Using 8 CPUs to run your word processor sounds a little like "over-kill" – and it is. What about a web server, a database, a rendering program, or a project scheduler? Maybe extra CPUs would help. What about a complex simulation, a fluid dynamics code, or a data mining application. Extra CPUs definitely help in these situations. Indeed, multiple CPUs are being used to solve more and more problems.

The next question usually is: "Why do I need two or four CPUs, I will just wait for the 986 turbo-hyper chip." There are several reasons:

1. Due to the use of multi-tasking Operating Systems, it is possible to do several things at once. This is a natural "parallelism" that is easily exploited by more than one low cost CPU.

2. Processor speeds have been doubling every 18 months, but what about RAM speeds or hard disk speeds? Unfortunately, these speeds are not increasing as fast as the CPU speeds. Keep in mind most applications require "out of cache memory access" and hard disk access. Doing things in parallel is one way to get around some of these limitations.

3. Predictions indicate that processor speeds will not continue to double every 18 months after the year 2005. There are some very serious obstacles to overcome in order to maintain this trend.

4. Depending on the application, parallel computing can speed things up by any where from 2 to 500 times faster (in some cases even faster). Such performance is not available using a single processor. Even supercomputers that at one time used very fast custom processors are now built from multiple "commodity- off-the-shelf" CPUs.

If you need speed - either due to a compute bound problem and/or an I/O bound problem, parallel is worth considering. Because parallel computing is implemented in a variety of ways, solving your problem in parallel will require some very important decisions to be made. These decisions may dramatically effect portability, performance, and cost of your application.

Before we get technical, let's look take a look at a real "parallel computing problem" using an example with which we are familiar - waiting in long lines at a store.

4.2.2 The Parallel Computing Store

Consider a big store with 8 cash registers grouped together in the front of the store. Assume each cash register/cashier is a CPU and each customer is a computer program. The size of the computer program (amount of work) is the size of each customer's order. The following analogies can be used to illustrate parallel computing concepts.

Single-tasking Operating System One cash register open (is in use) and must process each customer one at a time.

Computer Example: MS DOS

Multi-tasking Operating System: One cash register open, but now we process only a part of each order at a time, move to the next person and process some of their order. Everyone "seems" to be moving through the line together, but if no one else is in the line, you will get through the line faster.

Computer Example: UNIX, NT using a single CPU

Multitasking Operating Systems with Multiple CPUs: Now we open several cash registers in the store. Each order can be processed by a separate cash register and the line can move much faster. This is called SMP - Symmetric Multi-processing. Although there are extra cash registers open, you will still never get through the line any faster than just you and a single cash register.

Computer Example: UNIX and NT with multiple CPUs

Threads on a Multitasking Operating Systems extra CPUs If you "break-up" the items in your order, you might be able to move through the line faster by using several cash registers at one time. First, we must assume you have a large amount of goods, because the time you invest "breaking up your order" must be regained by using multiple cash registers. In theory, you should be able to move through the line "n" times faster than before*; where "n" is the number of cash registers. When the cashiers need to get sub- totals, they can exchange information quickly by looking and talking to all the other "local" cash registers. They can even snoop around the other cash registers to find information they need to work faster. There is a limit, however, as to how many cash registers the store can effectively locate in any one place.

Amdals law will also limit the application speed-up to the slowest sequential portion of the program.

Computer Example: UNIX or NT with extra CPU on the same motherboard running multi-threaded programs.

Sending Messages on Multitasking Operating Systems with extra CPUs: In order to improve performance, the store adds 8 cash registers at the back of the store. Because the new cash registers are far away from the front cash registers, the cashiers must call on the phone to send their sub-totals to the front of the store. This distance adds extra overhead (time) to communication between cashiers, but if communication is minimized, it is not a problem. If you have a really big order, one that requires all the cash registers, then as before your speed can be improved by using all cash registers at the same time, the extra overhead must be considered. In some cases, the store may have single cash registers (or islands of cash registers) located all over the store - each cash register (or island) must communicate by phone. Since all the cashiers working the cash registers can talk to each other by phone, it does not matter too much where they are.

Computer Example: One or several copies of UNIX or NT with extra CPUs on the same or different motherboard communicating through messages.

The above scenarios, although not exact, are a good representation of constraints placed on parallel systems. Unlike a single CPU (or cash register) communication is an issue.

4.3   Architectures for parallel computing

The common methods and architectures of parallel computing are presented below. While this description is by no means exhaustive, it is enough to understand the basic issues involved with Beowulf design.

4.3.1   Hardware Architectures

There are basically two ways parallel computer hardware is put together:

1. Local memory machines that communicate by messages (Beowulf Clusters)
2. Shared memory machines that communicate through memory (SMP machines)

A typical Beowulf is a collection of single CPU machines connected using fast Ethernet and is, therefore, a local memory machine. A 4 way SMP box is a shared memory machine and can be used for parallel computing - parallel applications communicate using shared memory. Just as in the computer store analogy, local memory machines (individual cash registers) can be scaled up to large numbers of CPUs, while the number of CPUs shared memory machines (the number of cash registers you can place in one spot) can have is limited due to memory contention.

It is possible, however, to connect many shared memory machines to create a "hybrid" shared memory machine. These hybrid machines "look" like a single large SMP machine to the user and are often called NUMA (non uniform memory access) machines because the global memory seen by the programmer and shared by all the CPUs can have different latencies. At some level, however, a NUMA machine must "pass messages" between local shared memory pools.

It is also possible to connect SMP machines as local memory compute nodes. Typical CLASS I motherboards have either 2 or 4 CPUs and are often used as a means to reduce the overall system cost. The Linux internal scheduler determines how these CPUs get shared. The user cannot (at this point) assign a specific task to a specific SMP processor. The user can however, start two independent processes or a threaded processes and expect to see a performance increase over a single CPU system.

4.3.2 Software API Architectures

There basically two ways to "express" concurrency in a program:

1. Using Messages sent between processors
2. Using operating system Threads

Other methods do exist, but these are the two most widely used. It is important to remember that the expression of concurrency is not necessary controlled by the underlying hardware. Both Messages and Threads can be implemented on SMP, NUMA-SMP, and clusters - although as explained below efficiently and portability are important issues.

Messages Historically, messages passing technology reflected the design of early local memory parallel computers. Messages require copying data while Threads use data in place. The latency and speed at which messages can be copied are the limiting factor with message passing models. A Message is quite simple: some data and a destination processor. Common message passing APIs are *PVM* or *MPI*. Message passing can be efficiently implemented using Threads and Messages work well both on SMP machine and between clusters of machines. The advantage to using messages on an SMP machine, as opposed to Threads, is that if you decided to use clusters in the future it is easy to add machines or scale your application.

Threads Operating system Threads were developed because shared memory SMP (symmetrical multiprocessing) designs allowed very fast shared memory communication and synchronization between concurrent parts of a program. Threads work well on SMP systems because communication is through shared memory. For this reason the user must isolate local data from global data, otherwise programs will not work properly. In contrast to messages, a large amount of copying can be eliminated with threads because the data is shared between processes (threads). Linux supports POSIX threads. The problem with threads is that it is difficult to extend them beyond one SMP machine and because data is shared between CPUs, cache coherence issues can contribute to overhead. Extending threads beyond the SMP boundary efficiently requires NUMA technology which is expensive and not natively supported by Linux. Implementing threads on top of messages has been done ((*http://syntron.com/ptools/ptools_pg.htm*)), but Threads are often inefficient when implemented using messages.

The following can be stated about performance:

	SMP machine performance	cluster of machines performance	scalability
messages	good	best	best
threads	best	poor*	poor*

* requires expensive NUMA technology.

4.3.3 Application Architecture

In order to run an application in parallel on multiple CPUs, it must be explicitly broken in to concurrent parts. A standard single CPU application will run no faster than a single CPU application on multiple processors. There are some tools and compilers that can break up programs, but parallelizing codes is not a "plug and play" operation. Depending on the application, parallelizing code can be easy, extremely difficult, or in some cases impossible due to algorithm dependencies.

Before the software issues can be addressed the concept of Suitability needs to be introduced.

4.4   Suitability

Most questions about parallel computing have the same answer:

"It all depends upon the application."

Before we jump into the issues, there is one very important distinction that needs to be made - the difference between CONCURRENT and PARALLEL. For the sake of this discussion we will define these two concepts as follows:

CONCURRENT parts of a program are those that can be computed independently.

PARALLEL parts of a program are those CONCURRENT parts that are executed on separate processing elements at the same time.

The distinction is very important, because CONCURRENCY is a property of the program and efficient PARALLELISM is a property of the machine. Ideally, PARALLEL execution should result in faster performance. The limiting factor in parallel performance is the communication speed and latency between compute nodes. (Latency also exists with threaded SMP applications due to cache coherency.) Many of the common parallel benchmarks are highly parallel and communication and latency are not the bottle neck. This type of problem can be called "obviously parallel". Other applications are not so simple and executing CONCURRENT parts of the program in PARALLEL may actually cause the program to run slower, thus offsetting any performance gains in other CONCURRENT parts of the program. In simple terms, the cost of communication time must pay for the savings in computation time, otherwise the PARALLEL execution of the CONCURRENT part is inefficient.

The task of the programmer is to determining what CONCURRENT parts of the program SHOULD be executed in PARALLEL and what parts SHOULD NOT. The answer to this will determine the EFFICIENCY of application. The following graph summarizes the situation for the programmer:

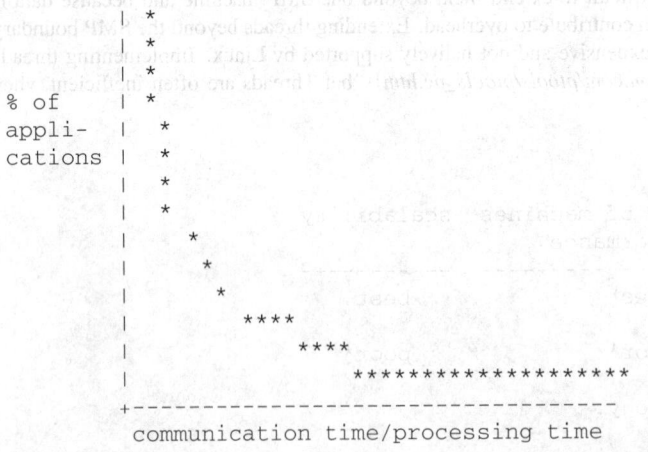

```
            |  *
            |   *
            |   *
% of        |   *
appli-      |   *
cations     |    *
            |    *
            |     *
            |      *
            |       *
            |        ****
            |          ****
            |           ******************
            +-----------------------------------
              communication time/processing time
```

In a perfect parallel computer, the ratio of communication/processing would be equal and anything that is CONCURRENT could be implemented in PARALLEL. Unfortunately, Real parallel computers, including shared memory machines, are subject to the effects described in this graph. When designing a Beowulf, the user may want to keep this graph in mind because parallel efficiency depends upon ratio of communication time and processing time for A SPECIFIC PARALLEL COMPUTER. Applications may be portable between parallel computers, but there is no guarantee they will be efficient on a different platform.

IN GENERAL, THERE IS NO SUCH THING AS A PORTABLE AND EFFICIENT PARALLEL PROGRAM

There is yet another consequence to the above graph. Since efficiency depends upon the comm./process. ratio, just changing one component of the ratio does not necessary mean a specific application will perform faster. A change in processor speed, while keeping the communication speed that same may have non- intuitive effects on your program. For example, doubling or tripling the CPU speed, while keeping the communication speed the same, may now make some previously efficient PARALLEL portions of your program, more efficient if they were executed SEQUENTIALLY. That is, it may now be faster to run the previously PARALLEL parts as SEQUENTIAL. Furthermore, running inefficient parts in parallel will actually keep your application from reaching its maximum speed. Thus, by adding faster processor, you may actually slowed down your application (you are keeping the new CPU from running at its maximum speed for that application)

UPGRADING TO A FASTER CPU MAY ACTUALLY SLOW DOWN YOUR APPLICATION

So, in conclusion, to know whether or not you can use a parallel hardware environment, you need to have some insight into the suitability of a particular machine to your application. You need to look at a lot of issues including CPU speeds, compiler, message passing API, network, etc. Please note, just profiling an application, does not give the whole story. You may identify a computationally heavy portion of your program, but you do not know the communication cost for this portion. It may be that for a given system, the communication cost as do not make parallelizing this code efficient.

A final note about a common misconception. It is often stated that "a program is PARALLELIZED", but in reality only the CONCURRENT parts of the program have been located. For all the reasons given above, the program is not PARALLELIZED. Efficient PARALLELIZATION is a property of the machine.

4.5 Writing and porting parallel software

Once you decide that you need parallel computing and would like to design and build a Beowulf, a few moments considering your application with respect to the previous discussion may be a good idea.

In general there are two things you can do:

1. Go ahead and construct a CLASS I Beowulf and then "fit" your application to it. Or run existing parallel applications that you know work on your Beowulf (but beware of the portability and efficiently issues mentioned above)

2. Look at the applications you need to run on your Beowulf and make some estimations as to the type of hardware and software you need.

In either case, at some point you will need to look at the efficiency issues. In general, there are three things you need to do:

1. Determine concurrent parts of your program
2. Estimate parallel efficiently
3. Describing the concurrent parts of your program

Let's look at these one at a time.

4.5.1 Determine concurrent parts of your program

This step is often considered "parallelizing your program". Parallelization decisions will be made in step 2. In this step, you need to determine data dependencies.

>From a practical standpoint, applications may exhibit two types of concurrency: compute (number crunching) and I/O (database). Although in many cases compute and I/O concurrency are orthogonal, there are application that require both.

HOWTO

There are tools available that can perform concurrency analysis on existing applications. Most of these tools are designed for FORTRAN. There are two reasons FORTRAN is used: historically most number crunching applications were written in FORTRAN and it is easier to analyze. If no tools are available, then this step can be some what difficult for existing applications.

4.5.2 Estimate parallel efficiency

Without the help of tools, this step may require trial and error tests or just a plain old educated guess. If you have a specific application in mind, try to determine if it is CPU limited (compute bound) or hard disk limited (I/O bound). The requirements of your Beowulf may be quite different depending upon your needs. For example, a compute bound problem may need a few very fast CPUs and high speed low latency network, while an I/O bound problem may work better with more slower CPUs and fast Ethernet.

This recommendation often comes as a surprise to most people because, the standard assumption is that faster processor are always better. While this is true if your have an unlimited budget, real systems may have cost constraints that should be maximized. For I/O bound problems, there is a little known rule (called the Eadline-Dedkov Law) that is quite helpful:

For two given parallel computers with the same cumulative CPU performance index, the one which has slower processors (and a probably correspondingly slower interprocessor communication network) will have better performance for I/O-dominant applications.

While the proof of this rule is beyond the scope of this document, you find it interesting to download the paper *Performance Considerations for I/O-Dominant Applications on Parallel Computers* (Postscript format 109K) (ftp://www.plogic.com/pub/papers/exs-pap6.ps)

Once you have determined what type of concurrency you have in your application, you will need to estimate how efficient it will be in parallel. See Section 4 (Software) for a description of Software tools.

In the absence of tools, you may try to guess your way through this step. If a compute bound loop measured in minutes and the data can be transferred in seconds, then it might be a good candidate for parallelization. But remember, if you take a 16 minute loop and break it into 32 parts, and your data transfers require several seconds per part, then things are going to get tight. You will reach a point of diminishing returns.

4.5.3 Describing the concurrent parts of your program

There are several ways to describe concurrent parts of your program:

1. Explicit parallel execution
2. Implicit parallel execution

The major difference between the two is that explicit parallelism is determined by the user where implicit parallelism is determined by the compiler.

Explicit Methods   These are basically method where the user must modify source code specifically for a parallel computer. The user must either add messages using *PVM* or *MPI* or add threads using POSIX threads. (Keep in mind however, threads can not move between SMP motherboards).

Explicit methods tend to be the most difficult to implement and debug. Users typically embed explicit function calls in standard FORTRAN 77 or C/C++ source code. The MPI library has added some functions to make some standard parallel methods easier to implement (i.e. scatter/gather functions). In addition, it is also possible to use standard libraries that have been written for parallel computers. Keep in mind, however, the portability vs. efficiently trade-off)

For historical reasons, most number crunching codes are written in FORTRAN. For this reasons, FORTRAN has the largest amount of support (tools, libraries, etc.) for parallel computing. Many programmers now use C or re- write existing FORTRAN applications in C with the notion the C will allow faster execution. While this may be true as C is the closest thing to a universal machine code, it has some major drawbacks. The use of pointers in C makes determining data dependencies extremely difficult. Automatic analysis of pointers is extremely difficult. If you have an existing FORTRAN program and think that you might want to parallelize it in the future - DO NOT CONVERT IT TO C!

Implicit Methods Implicit methods are those where the user gives up some (or all) of the parallelization decisions to the compiler. Examples are FORTRAN 90, High Performance FORTRAN (HPF), Bulk Synchronous Parallel (BSP), and a whole collection of other methods that are under development.

Implicit methods require the user to provide some information about the concurrent nature of their application, but the compiler will then make many decisions about how to execute this concurrency in parallel. These methods provide some level of portability and efficiency, but there is still no "best way" to describe a concurrent problem for a parallel computer.

5 Beowulf Resources

5.1 Starting Points

- Beowulf mailing list. To subscribe send mail to *beowulf-request@cesdis.gsfc.nasa.gov* with the word *subscribe* in the message body.

- Beowulf Homepage *http://www.beowulf.org*

- Extreme Linux *http://www.extremelinux.org*

- Extreme Linux Software from Red Hat *http://www.redhat.com/extreme*

5.2 Documentation

- The latest version of the Beowulf HOWTO *http://www.sci.usq.edu.au/staff/jacek/beowulf.*

- Building a Beowulf System *http://www.cacr.caltech.edu/beowulf/tutorial/building.html*

- Jacek's Beowulf Links *http://www.sci.usq.edu.au/staff/jacek/beowulf.*

- Beowulf Installation and Administration HOWTO (DRAFT) *http://www.sci.usq.edu.au/staff/jacek/beowulf.*

- Linux Parallel Processing HOWTO *http://yara.ecn.purdue.edu/~pplinux/PPHOWTO/pphowto.html*

5.3 Papers

- Chance Reschke, Thomas Sterling, Daniel Ridge, Daniel Savarese, Donald Becker, and Phillip Merkey *A Design Study of Alternative Network Topologies for the Beowulf Parallel Workstation.* Proceedings Fifth IEEE International Symposium on High Performance Distributed Computing, 1996. *http://www.beowulf.org/papers/HPDC96/hpdc96.html*

- Daniel Ridge, Donald Becker, Phillip Merkey, Thomas Sterling Becker, and Phillip Merkey. *Harnessing the Power of Parallelism in a Pile-of-PCs.* Proceedings, IEEE Aerospace, 1997. *http://www.beowulf.org/papers/AA97/aa97.ps*

- Thomas Sterling, Donald J. Becker, Daniel Savarese, Michael R. Berry, and Chance Res. *Achieving a Balanced Low-Cost Architecture for Mass Storage Management through Multiple Fast Ethernet Channels on the Beowulf Parallel Workstation.* Proceedings, International Parallel Processing Symposium, 1996. *http://www.beowulf.org/papers/IPPS96/ipps96.html*

- Donald J. Becker, Thomas Sterling, Daniel Savarese, Bruce Fryxell, Kevin Olson. *Communication Overhead for Space Science Applications on the Beowulf Parallel Workstation.* Proceedings,High Performance and Distributed Computing, 1995. *http://www.beowulf.org/papers/HPDC95/hpdc95.html*

- Donald J. Becker, Thomas Sterling, Daniel Savarese, John E. Dorband, Udaya A. Ranawak, Charles V. Packer. *BEOWULF: A PARALLEL WORKSTATION FOR SCIENTIFIC COMPUTATION.* Proceedings, International Conference on Parallel Processing, 95. *http://www.beowulf.org/papers/ICPP95/icpp95.html*

- Papers at the Beowulf site *http://www.beowulf.org/papers/papers.html*

5.4 Software

- PVM - Parallel Virtual Machine *http://www.epm.ornl.gov/pvm/pvm_home.html*
- LAM/MPI (Local Area Multicomputer / Message Passing Interface *http://www.mpi.nd.edu/lam*
- BERT77 - FORTRAN conversion tool *http://www.plogic.com/bert.html*
- Beowulf software from Beowulf Project Page *http://beowulf.gsfc.nasa.gov/software/software.html*
- Jacek's Beowulf-utils *ftp://ftp.sci.usq.edu.au/pub/jacek/beowulf-utils*
- bWatch - cluster monitoring tool *http://www.sci.usq.edu.au/staff/jacek/bWatch*

5.5 Beowulf Machines

- Avalon consists of 140 Alpha processors, 36 GB of RAM, and is probably the fastest Beowulf machine, cruising at 47.7 Gflops and ranking 114th on the Top 500 list. *http://swift.lanl.gov/avalon/*
- Megalon-A Massively PArallel CompuTer Resource (MPACTR) consists of 14, quad CPU Pentium Pro 200 nodes, and 14 GB of RAM. *http://megalon.ca.sandia.gov/description.html*
- theHIVE - Highly-parallel Integrated Virtual Environment is another fast Beowulf Supercomputer. theHIVE is a 64 node, 128 CPU machine with the total of 4 GB RAM. *http://newton.gsfc.nasa.gov/thehive/*
- Topcat is a much smaller machine and consists of 16 CPUs and 1.2 GB RAM. *http://www.sci.usq.edu.au/staff/jacek/topcat*
- MAGI cluster - this is a very interesting site with many good links. *http://noel.feld.cvut.cz/magi/*

5.6 Other Interesting Sites

- SMP Linux *http://www.linux.org.uk/SMP/title.html*
- Paralogic - Buy a Beowulf *http://www.plogic.com*

5.7 History

- Legends - Beowulf *http://legends.dm.net/beowulf/index.html*
- The Adventures of Beowulf *http://www.lnstar.com/literature/beowulf/beowulf.html*

6 Source code

6.1 sum.c

```
/* Jacek Radajewski jacek@usq.edu.au */
/* 21/08/1998 */

#include <stdio.h>
#include <math.h>

int main (void) {

    double result = 0.0;
    double number = 0.0;
    char string[80];

    while (scanf("%s", string) != EOF) {
```

```
    number = atof(string);
    result = result + number;
  }

  printf("%lf\n", result);

  return 0;

}
```

6.2   sigmasqrt.c

```
/* Jacek Radajewski jacek@usq.edu.au */
/* 21/08/1998 */

#include <stdio.h>
#include <math.h>

int main (int argc, char** argv) {

  long number1, number2, counter;
  double result;

  if (argc < 3) {
    printf ("usage : %s number1 number2\n",argv[0]);
    exit(1);
  } else {
    number1 = atol (argv[1]);
    number2 = atol (argv[2]);
    result = 0.0;
  }

  for (counter = number1; counter <= number2; counter++) {
    result = result + sqrt((double)counter);
  }

  printf("%lf\n", result);

  return 0;

}
```

6.3   prun.sh

```
#!/bin/bash
# Jacek Radajewski jacek@usq.edu.au
# 21/08/1998

export SIGMASQRT=/home/staff/jacek/beowulf/HOWTO/example1/sigmasqrt

# $OUTPUT must be a named pipe
# mkfifo output

export OUTPUT=/home/staff/jacek/beowulf/HOWTO/example1/output
```

```
rsh scilab01 $SIGMASQRT          1  50000000 > $OUTPUT < /dev/null&
rsh scilab02 $SIGMASQRT   50000001 100000000 > $OUTPUT < /dev/null&
rsh scilab03 $SIGMASQRT  100000001 150000000 > $OUTPUT < /dev/null&
rsh scilab04 $SIGMASQRT  150000001 200000000 > $OUTPUT < /dev/null&
rsh scilab05 $SIGMASQRT  200000001 250000000 > $OUTPUT < /dev/null&
rsh scilab06 $SIGMASQRT  250000001 300000000 > $OUTPUT < /dev/null&
rsh scilab07 $SIGMASQRT  300000001 350000000 > $OUTPUT < /dev/null&
rsh scilab08 $SIGMASQRT  350000001 400000000 > $OUTPUT < /dev/null&
rsh scilab09 $SIGMASQRT  400000001 450000000 > $OUTPUT < /dev/null&
rsh scilab10 $SIGMASQRT  450000001 500000000 > $OUTPUT < /dev/null&
rsh scilab11 $SIGMASQRT  500000001 550000000 > $OUTPUT < /dev/null&
rsh scilab12 $SIGMASQRT  550000001 600000000 > $OUTPUT < /dev/null&
rsh scilab13 $SIGMASQRT  600000001 650000000 > $OUTPUT < /dev/null&
rsh scilab14 $SIGMASQRT  650000001 700000000 > $OUTPUT < /dev/null&
rsh scilab15 $SIGMASQRT  700000001 750000000 > $OUTPUT < /dev/null&
rsh scilab16 $SIGMASQRT  750000001 800000000 > $OUTPUT < /dev/null&
rsh scilab17 $SIGMASQRT  800000001 850000000 > $OUTPUT < /dev/null&
rsh scilab18 $SIGMASQRT  850000001 900000000 > $OUTPUT < /dev/null&
rsh scilab19 $SIGMASQRT  900000001 950000000 > $OUTPUT < /dev/null&
rsh scilab20 $SIGMASQRT  950000001 1000000000 > $OUTPUT < /dev/null&
```

## Part VII

"The Linux BootPrompt-HowTo" by Paul Gortmaker.

v1.14, 1 February 1998
This is the BootPrompt-Howto, which is a compilation of all the possible boot time arguments that can be passed to the Linux kernel at boot time. This includes all kernel and device parameters. A discussion of how the kernel sorts boot time arguments, along with an overview of some of the popular software used to boot Linux kernels is also included.

Contents

354

1 Introduction

The kernel has a limited capability to accept information at boot in the form of a 'command line', similar to an argument list you would give to a program. In general this is used to supply the kernel with information about hardware parameters that the kernel would not be able to determine on its own, or to avoid/override the values that the kernel would otherwise detect.

However, if you just copy a kernel image directly to a floppy, (e.g. `cp zImage /dev/fd0`) then you are not given a chance to specify any arguments to that kernel. So most Linux users will use software like *LILO* or *loadlin* that takes care of handing these arguments to the kernel, and then booting it.

IMPORTANT NOTE TO MODULE USERS: Boot Prompt arguments typically only apply to hardware drivers that are compiled directly into the kernel. They have *no effect* on drivers that are loaded as modules. Most distributions use modules. If you are unsure, then look at `man depmod` and `man modprobe` along with the contents of `/etc/conf.modules`.

This present revision covers kernels up to and including v2.0.33. Some features that are unique to development/testing kernels up to v2.1.84 are also documented.

The BootPrompt-Howto is by:

   Paul Gortmaker, `gpg109@rsphy1.anu.edu.au`

[Please note that boot prompt arguments that are specific to the non-i386 ports and devices (esp. Atari/Amiga) are not currently documented.]

1.1   Disclaimer and Copyright

This document is *not* gospel. However, it is probably the most up to date info that you will be able to find. Nobody is responsible for what happens to your hardware but yourself. If your hardware goes up in smoke (...nearly impossible!) I take no responsibility. ie. THE AUTHOR IS NOT RESPONSIBLE FOR ANY DAMAGES INCURRED DUE TO ACTIONS TAKEN BASED ON THE INFORMATION INCLUDED IN THIS DOCUMENT.

This document is Copyright (C) 1995-1998 by Paul Gortmaker.

This document may be copied according to the conditions of the GNU General Public License, version 2, included herein by reference. See the file `linux/COPYING` that comes with the Linux kernel for full details.

If you are intending to incorporate this document into a published work, please contact me, and I will make an effort to ensure that you have the most up to date information available. In the past, out of date versions of the Linux howto documents have been published, which caused the developers undue grief from being plagued with questions that were already answered in the up to date versions.

1.2   Related Documentation

The most up-to-date documentation will always be the kernel source itself. Hold on! Don't get scared. You don't need to know any programming to read the comments in the source files. For example, if you were looking for what arguments could be passed to the AHA1542 SCSI driver, then you would go to the `linux/drivers/scsi` directory, and look at the file `aha1542.c` – and within the first 100 lines, you would find a plain english description of the boot time arguments that the 1542 driver accepts.

The next best thing will be any documentation files that are distributed with the kernel itself. There are now quite a few of these, and most of them can be found in the directory `linux/Documentation` and subdirectories from there. The `linux` directory is usually found in `/usr/src/`. Sometimes there will be `README.foo` files that can be found in the related driver directory (e.g. `linux/drivers/XXX/`, where XXX will be `scsi`, `char`, or `net`).

If you have figured out what boot-args you intend to use, and now want to know how to get that information to the kernel, then look at the documentation that comes with the software that you use to boot the kernel (e.g. LILO or loadlin). A brief overview is given below, but it is no substitute for the documentation that comes with the booting software.

1.3 The Linux Newsgroups

If you have questions about passing boot arguments to the kernel, please READ this document first. If this and the related documentation mentioned above does not answer your question(s) then you can try the Linux newsgroups. Of course you should try reading the group before blindly posting your question, as somebody else may have already asked it, or it may even be a Frequently Asked Question (a FAQ). A quick browse of the linux FAQ before posting is a *good* idea. You should be able to find the FAQ somewhere close to where you found this document.

General questions on how to configure your system should be directed to the comp.os.linux.setup newsgroup. We ask that you *please* respect this general guideline for content, and don't cross-post your request to other groups.

1.4 New Versions of this Document

New versions of this document can be retrieved via anonymous FTP from the site sunsite.unc.edu, in the directory `/pub/Linux/docs/HOWTO/`. Note that *SunSITE* is usually heavily loaded, and you are better advised to get the document from one of the Linux ftp mirror sites. Updates will be made as new information and/or drivers becomes available. If this copy that you are presently reading is more than a few months old, then you should probably check to see if a newer copy exists.

This document was produced by using a modified SGML system that was specifically set up for the Linux Howto project, and there are various output formats available, including, postscript, dvi, ascii, html, and soon TeXinfo. I would recommend viewing it in the html (via a WWW browser) or the Postscript/dvi format. Both of these contain cross-references that are lost in the ascii translation.

If you want to get the official copy off sunsite, here is URL.

BootPrompt-HOWTO <http://sunsite.unc.edu/mdw/HOWTO/BootPrompt-HOWTO.html>

2 Overview of Boot Prompt Arguments

This section gives some examples of software that can be used to pass kernel boot-time arguments to the kernel itself. It also gives you an idea of how the arguments are processed, what limitations there are on the boot args, and how they filter down to each appropriate device that they are intended for.

It is *important* to note that spaces should *not* be used in a boot argument, but only between separate arguments. A list of values that are for a single argument are to be separated with a comma between the values, and again without any spaces. See the following examples below.

```
ether=9,0x300,0xd0000,0xd4000,eth0  root=/dev/hda1          *RIGHT*
ether = 9, 0x300, 0xd0000, 0xd4000, eth0  root = /dev/hda1   *WRONG*
```

2.1 LILO (LInux LOader)

The LILO program (LInux LOader) written by Werner Almesberger is the most commonly used. It has the ability to boot various kernels, and stores the configuration information in a plain text file. Most distributions ship with LILO as the default boot-loader. LILO can boot DOS, OS/2, Linux, FreeBSD, etc. without any difficulties, and is quite flexible.

A typical configuration will have LILO stop and print `LILO:` shortly after you turn on your computer. It will then wait for a few seconds for any optional input from the user, and failing that it will then boot the default system. Typical system labels that people use in the LILO configuration files are `linux` and `backup` and `msdos`. If you want to type in a boot argument, you type it in here, after typing in the system label that you want LILO to boot from, as shown in the example below.

```
LILO: linux root=/dev/hda1
```

LILO comes with excellent documentation, and for the purposes of boot args discussed here, the LILO `append=` command is of significant importance when one wants to add a boot time argument as a permanent addition to the LILO config file. You simply add something like `append = "foo=bar"` to the `/etc/lilo.conf` file. It can either be added at the top of the config file, making it apply to all sections, or to a single system section by adding it inside an `image=` section. Please see the LILO documentation for a more complete description.

2.2 LoadLin

The other commonly used Linux loader is 'LoadLin' which is a DOS program that has the capability to launch a Linux kernel from the DOS prompt (with boot-args) assuming that certain resources are available. This is good for people that use DOS and want to launch into Linux from DOS.

It is also very useful if you have certain hardware which relies on the supplied DOS driver to put the hardware into a known state. A common example is 'SoundBlaster Compatible' sound cards that require the DOS driver to set a few proprietary registers to put the card into a SB compatible mode. Booting DOS with the supplied driver, and then loading Linux from the DOS prompt with `LOADLIN.EXE` avoids the reset of the card that happens if one rebooted instead. Thus the card is left in a SB compatible mode and hence is useable under Linux.

There are also other programs that can be used to boot Linux. For a complete list, please look at the programs available on your local Linux ftp mirror, under `system/Linux-boot/`.

2.3 The "rdev" utility

There are a few of the kernel boot parameters that have their default values stored in various bytes in the kernel image itself. There is a utility called `rdev` that is installed on most systems that knows where these values are, and how to change them. It can also change things that have no kernel boot argument equivalent, such as the default video mode used.

The rdev utility is usually also aliased to swapdev, ramsize, vidmode and rootflags. These are the five things that rdev can change, those being the root device, the swap device, the RAM disk parameters, the default video mode, and the readonly/readwrite setting of root device.

More information on `rdev` can be found by typing `rdev -h` or by reading the supplied man page (`man rdev`).

2.4 How the Kernel Sorts the Arguments

Most of the boot args take the form of:

```
name[=value_1][,value_2]...[,value_11]
```

where 'name' is a unique keyword that is used to identify what part of the kernel the associated values (if any) are to be given to. Multiple boot args are just a space separated list of the above format. Note the limit of 11 is real, as the present code only handles 11 comma separated parameters per keyword. (However, you can re-use the same keyword with up to an additional 11 parameters in unusually complicated situations, assuming the setup function supports it.) Also note that the kernel splits the list into a maximum of ten integer arguments, and a following string, so you can't really supply 11 integers unless you convert the 11th arg from a string to an int in the driver itself.

Most of the sorting goes on in `linux/init/main.c`. First, the kernel checks to see if the argument is any of the special arguments 'root=', 'ro', 'rw', or 'debug'. The meaning of these special arguments is described further on in the document.

Then it walks a list of setup functions (contained in the `bootsetups` array) to see if the specified argument string (such as 'foo') has been associated with a setup function (`foo_setup()`) for a particular device or part of the kernel. If you passed the kernel the line `foo=3,4,5,6,bar` then the kernel would search the `bootsetups` array to see if 'foo' was registered. If it was, then it would call the setup function associated with 'foo' (`foo_setup()`) and hand it the integer arguments 3, 4, 5 and 6 as given on the kernel command line, and also hand it the string argument `bar`.

2.5 Setting Environment Variables.

Anything of the form 'foo=bar' that is not accepted as a setup function as described above is then interpreted as an environment variable to be set. A (useless?) example would be to use 'TERM=vt100' as a boot argument.

2.6 Passing Arguments to the 'init' program

Any remaining arguments that were not picked up by the kernel and were not interpreted as environment variables are then passed onto process one, which is usually the `init` program. The most common argument that is passed to the `init` process is the word *single* which instructs `init` to boot the computer in single user mode, and not launch all the usual daemons. Check the manual page for the version of `init` installed on your system to see what arguments it accepts.

3 General Non-Device Specific Boot Args

These are the boot arguments that are not related to any specific device or peripheral. They are instead related to certain internal kernel parameters, such as memory handling, ramdisk handling, root file system handling and others.

3.1 Root Filesystem options

The following options all pertain to how the kernel selects and handles the root filesystem.

3.1.1 The 'root=' Argument

This argument tells the kernel what device is to be used as the root filesystem while booting. The default of this setting is the value of the root device of the system that the kernel was built on. For example, if the kernel in question was built on a system that used '/dev/hda1' as the root partition, then the default root device would be '/dev/hda1'. To override this default value, and select the second floppy drive as the root device, one would use 'root=/dev/fd1'.

Valid root devices are any of the following devices:

(1) /dev/hdaN to /dev/hddN, which is partition N on ST-506 compatible disk 'a to d'.

(2) /dev/sdaN to /dev/sdeN, which is partition N on SCSI compatible disk 'a to e'.

(3) /dev/xdaN to /dev/xdbN, which is partition N on XT compatible disk 'a to b'.

(4) /dev/fdN, which is floppy disk drive number N. Having N=0 would be the DOS 'A:' drive, and N=1 would be 'B:'.

(5) /dev/nfs, which is not really a device, but rather a flag to tell the kernel to get the root fs via the network.

The more awkward and less portable numeric specification of the above possible disk devices in major/minor format is also accepted. (e.g. /dev/sda3 is major 8, minor 3, so you could use `root=0x803` as an alternative.)

This is one of the few kernel boot arguments that has its default stored in the kernel image, and which can thus be altered with the `rdev` utility.

3.1.2 The 'ro' Argument

When the kernel boots, it needs a root filesystem to read basic things off of. This is the root filesystem that is mounted at boot. However, if the root filesystem is mounted with write access, you can not reliably check the filesystem integrity with half-written files in progress. The 'ro' option tells the kernel to mount the root filesystem as 'readonly' so that any filesystem consistency check programs (fsck) can safely assume that there are no half-written files in progress while performing the check. No programs or processes can write to files on the filesystem in question until it is 'remounted' as read/write capable.

This is one of the few kernel boot arguments that has its default stored in the kernel image, and which can thus be altered with the `rdev` utility.

3.1.3   The 'rw' Argument

This is the exact opposite of the above, in that it tells the kernel to mount the root filesystem as read/write. The default is to mount the root filesystem as read/write anyway. Do not run any 'fsck' type programs on a filesystem that is mounted read/write.

The same value stored in the image file mentioned above is also used for this parameter, accessible via `rdev`.

3.2   Options Relating to RAM Disk Management

The following options all relate to how the kernel handles the RAM disk device, which is usually used for bootstrapping machines during the install phase, or for machines with modular drivers that need to be installed to access the root filesystem.

3.2.1   The 'ramdisk_start=' Argument

To allow a kernel image to reside on a floppy disk along with a compressed ramdisk image, the 'ramdisk_start=<offset>' command was added. The kernel can't be included into the compressed ramdisk filesystem image, because it needs to be stored starting at block zero so that the BIOS can load the bootsector and then the kernel can bootstrap itself to get going.

Note: If you are using an uncompressed ramdisk image, then the kernel can be a part of the filesystem image that is being loaded into the ramdisk, and the floppy can be booted with LILO, or the two can be separate as is done for the compressed images.

If you are using a two-disk boot/root setup (kernel on disk 1, ramdisk image on disk 2) then the ramdisk would start at block zero, and an offset of zero would be used. Since this is the default value, you would not need to actually use the command at all.

3.2.2   The 'load_ramdisk=' Argument

This parameter tells the kernel whether it is to try to load a ramdisk image or not. Specifying 'load_ramdisk=1' will tell the kernel to load a floppy into the ramdisk. The default value is zero, meaning that the kernel should not try to load a ramdisk.

Please see the file `linux/Documentation/ramdisk.txt` for a complete description of the new boot time arguments, and how to use them. A description of how this parameter can be set and stored in the kernel image via 'rdev' is also described.

3.2.3   The 'prompt_ramdisk=' Argument

This parameter tells the kernel whether or not to give you a prompt asking you to insert the floppy containing the ramdisk image. In a single floppy configuration the ramdisk image is on the same floppy as the kernel that just finished loading/booting and so a prompt is not needed. In this case one can use 'prompt_ramdisk=0'. In a two floppy configuration, you will need the chance to switch disks, and thus 'prompt_ramdisk=1' can be used. Since this is the default value, it doesn't really need to be specified. ((Historical note: Sneaky people used to use the 'vga=ask' LILO option to temporarily pause the boot process and allow a chance to switch from boot to root floppy.)

Please see the file `linux/Documentation/ramdisk.txt` for a complete description of the new boot time arguments, and how to use them. A description of how this parameter can be set and stored in the kernel image via 'rdev' is also described.

3.2.4 The 'ramdisk_size=' Argument

While it is true that the ramdisk grows dynamically as required, there is an upper bound on its size so that it doesn't consume all available RAM and leave you in a mess. The default is 4096 (i.e. 4MB) which should be large enough for most needs. You can override the default to a bigger or smaller size with this boot argument.

Please see the file `linux/Documentation/ramdisk.txt` for a complete description of the new boot time arguments, and how to use them. A description of how this parameter can be set and stored in the kernel image via 'rdev' is also described.

3.2.5 The 'ramdisk=' Argument (obsolete)

(NOTE: This argument is obsolete, and should not be used except on kernels v1.3.47 and older. The commands that should be used for the ramdisk device are documented above.)

This specifies the size in kB of the RAM disk device. For example, if one wished to have a root filesystem on a 1.44MB floppy loaded into the RAM disk device, they would use:

```
ramdisk=1440
```

This is one of the few kernel boot arguments that has its default stored in the kernel image, and which can thus be altered with the `rdev` utility.

3.2.6 The 'noinitrd' (initial RAM disk) Argument

The v2.x and newer kernels have a feature where the root filesystem is initially a RAM disk, and the kernel executes `/linuxrc` on that RAM image. This feature is typically used to allow loading of modules needed to mount the real root filesystem (e.g. load the SCSI driver modules stored in the RAM disk image, and then mount the real root filesystem on a SCSI disk.)

The actual 'noinitrd' argument determines what happens to the initrd data after the kernel has booted. When specified, instead of converting it to a RAM disk, it is accessible via `/dev/initrd`, which can be read once before the RAM is released back to the system. For full details on using the initial RAM disk, please consult `linux/Documentation/initrd.txt`. In addition, the most recent versions of `LILO` and `LOADLIN` should have additional useful information.

3.3 Boot Arguments Related to Memory Handling

The following arguments alter how linux detects or handles the physical and virtual memory of your system.

3.3.1 The 'mem=' Argument

This argument has two purposes: The original purpose was to specify the amount of installed memory (or a value less than that if you wanted to limit the amount of memory available to linux). The second (and hardly used) purpose is to specify `mem=nopentium` which tells the linux kernel to not use the 4MB page table performance feature.

The original BIOS call defined in the PC specification that returns the amount of installed memory was only designed to be able to report up to 64MB. (Yes, another lack of foresight, just like the 1024 cylinder disks... sigh.) Linux uses this BIOS call at boot to determine how much memory is installed. If you have more than 64MB of RAM installed, you can use this boot argument to tell Linux how much memory you have. Here is a quote from Linus on usage of the `mem=` parameter.

"The kernel will accept any 'mem=xx' parameter you give it, and if it turns out that you lied to it, it will crash horribly sooner or later. The parameter indicates the highest addressable RAM address, so 'mem=0x1000000' means you have 16MB of memory, for example. For a 96MB machine this would be 'mem=0x6000000'.

NOTE NOTE NOTE: some machines might use the top of memory for BIOS cacheing or whatever, so you might not actually have up to the full 96MB addressable. The reverse is also true: some chipsets will map the physical memory that is covered by the BIOS area into the area just past the top of memory, so the top-of-mem might actually be 96MB + 384kB for example. If you tell linux that it has more memory than it actually does have, bad things will happen: maybe not at once, but surely eventually."

Note that the argument does not have to be in hex, and the suffixes 'k' and 'M' (case insensitive) can be used to specify kilobytes and Megabytes, respectively. (A 'k' will cause a 10 bit shift on your value, and a 'M' will cause a 20 bit shift.) The above warning still holds, in that a 96MB machine may work with `mem=97920k` but fail with either `mem=98304k` or `mem=96M`.

3.3.2 The 'swap=' Argument

This allows the user to tune some of the virtual memory (VM) parameters that are related to swapping to disk. It accepts the following eight parameters:

```
MAX_PAGE_AGE
PAGE_ADVANCE
PAGE_DECLINE
PAGE_INITIAL_AGE
AGE_CLUSTER_FRACT
AGE_CLUSTER_MIN
PAGEOUT_WEIGHT
BUFFEROUT_WEIGHT
```

Interested hackers are advised to have a read of `linux/mm/swap.c` and also make note of the goodies in `/proc/sys/vm`.

3.3.3 The 'buff=' Argument

Similar to the 'swap=' argument, this allows the user to tune some of the parameters related to buffer memory management. It accepts the following six parameters:

```
MAX_BUFF_AGE
BUFF_ADVANCE
BUFF_DECLINE
BUFF_INITIAL_AGE
BUFFEROUT_WEIGHT
BUFFERMEM_GRACE
```

Interested hackers are advised to have a read of `linux/mm/swap.c` and also make note of the goodies in `/proc/sys/vm`.

3.4 Boot Arguments for NFS Root Filesystem

Linux supports systems such as diskless workstations via having their root filesystem as NFS (Network FileSystem). These arguments are used to tell the diskless workstation which machine it is to get its system from. Also note that the argument `root=/dev/nfs` is required. Detailed information on using an NFS root fs is in the file `linux/Documentation/nfsroot.txt`. You should read that file, as the following is only a quick summary taken directly from that file.

3.4.1 The 'nfsroot=' Argument

This argument tells the kernel which machine, what directory and what NFS options to use for the root filesystem. The form of the argument is as follows:

```
nfsroot=[<server-ip>:]<root-dir>[,<nfs-options>]
```

If the nfsroot parameter is not given on the command line, the default '/tftpboot/%s' will be used. The other options are as follows:

<server-ip> – Specifies the IP address of the NFS server. If this field is not given, the default address as determined by the nfsaddrs variable (see below) is used. One use of this parameter is for example to allow using different servers for RARP and NFS. Usually you can leave this blank.

<root-dir> – Name of the directory on the server to mount as root. If there is a '%s' token in the string, the token will be replaced by the ASCII-representation of the client's IP address.

<nfs-options> – Standard NFS options. All options are separated by commas. If the options field is not given, the following defaults will be used:

```
port             = as given by server portmap daemon
rsize            = 1024
wsize            = 1024
timeo            = 7
retrans          = 3
acregmin         = 3
acregmax         = 60
acdirmin         = 30
acdirmax         = 60
flags            = hard, nointr, noposix, cto, ac
```

3.4.2   The 'nfsaddrs=' Argument

This boot argument sets up the various network interface addresses that are required to communicate over the network. If this argument is not given, then the kernel tries to use RARP and/or BOOTP to figure out these parameters. The form is as follows:

```
nfsaddrs=<my-ip>:<serv-ip>:<gw-ip>:<netmask>:<name>:<dev>:<auto>
```

<my-ip> – IP address of the client. If empty, the address will either be determined by RARP or BOOTP. What protocol is used de- pends on what has been enabled during kernel configuration and on the <auto> parameter. If this parameter is not empty, neither RARP nor BOOTP will be used.

<serv-ip> – IP address of the NFS server. If RARP is used to determine the client address and this parameter is NOT empty only replies from the specified server are accepted. To use different RARP and NFS server, specify your RARP server here (or leave it blank), and specify your NFS server in the nfsroot parameter (see above). If this entry is blank the address of the server is used which answered the RARP or BOOTP request.

<gw-ip> – IP address of a gateway if the server in on a different subnet. If this entry is empty no gateway is used and the server is assumed to be on the local network, unless a value has been received by BOOTP.

<netmask> – Netmask for local network interface. If this is empty, the netmask is derived from the client IP address, unless a value has been received by BOOTP.

<name> – Name of the client. If empty, the client IP address is used in ASCII-notation, or the value received by BOOTP.

<dev> – Name of network device to use. If this is empty, all devices are used for RARP requests, and the first one found for BOOTP. For NFS the device is used on which either RARP or BOOTP replies have been received. If you only have one device you can safely leave this blank.

<auto> – Method to use for autoconfiguration. If this is either 'rarp' or 'bootp' the specified protocol is being used. If the value is 'both' or empty, both protocols are used so far as they have been enabled during kernel configuration Using

'none' means no autoconfiguration. In this case you have to specify all necessary values in the fields before.

The <auto> parameter can appear alone as the value to the nfsaddrs parameter (without all the ':' characters before) in which case autoconfiguration is used. However, the 'none' value is not available in that case.

3.5 Other Misc. Kernel Boot Arguments

These various boot arguments let the user tune certain internal kernel parameters.

3.5.1 The 'debug' Argument

The kernel communicates important (and not-so important) messages to the operator via the `printk()` function. If the message is considered important, the `printk()` function will put a copy on the present console as well as handing it off to the `klogd()` facility so that it gets logged to disk. The reason for printing important messages to the console as well as logging them to disk is because under unfortunate circumstances (e.g. a disk failure) the message won't make it to disk and will be lost.

The threshold for what is and what isn't considered important is set by the `console_loglevel` variable. The default is to log anything more important than DEBUG (level 7) to the console. (These levels are defined in the include file `kernel.h`) Specifying debug as a boot argument will set the console loglevel to 10, so that *all* kernel messages appear on the console.

The console loglevel can usually also be set at run time via an option to the `klogd()` program. Check the man page for the version installed on your system to see how to do this.

3.5.2 The 'init=' Argument

The kernel defaults to starting the 'init' program at boot, which then takes care of setting up the computer for users via launching getty programs, running 'rc' scripts and the like. The kernel first looks for `/sbin/init`, then `/etc/init` (depreciated), and as a last resort, it will try to use `/bin/sh` (possibly on `/etc/rc`). If for example, your init program got corrupted and thus stopped you from being able to boot, you could simply use the boot prompt `init=/bin/sh` which would drop you directly into a shell at boot, allowing you to replace the corrupted program.

3.5.3 The 'no387' Argument

Some i387 coprocessor chips have bugs that show up when used in 32 bit protected mode. For example, some of the early ULSI-387 chips would cause solid lockups while performing floating point calculations, apparently due to a bug in the FRSAV/FRRESTOR instructions. Using the 'no387' boot argument causes Linux to ignore the math coprocessor even if you have one. Of course you must then have your kernel compiled with math emulation support! This may also be useful if you have one of those *really* old 386 machines that could use an 80287 FPU, as linux can't use an 80287.

3.5.4 The 'no-hlt' Argument

The i386 (and successors thereof) family of CPUs have a 'hlt' instruction which tells the CPU that nothing is going to happen until an external device (keyboard, modem, disk, etc.) calls upon the CPU to do a task. This allows the CPU to enter a 'low-power' mode where it sits like a zombie until an external device wakes it up (usually via an interrupt). Some of the early i486DX-100 chips had a problem with the 'hlt' instruction, in that they couldn't reliably return to operating mode after this instruction was used. Using the 'no-hlt' instruction tells Linux to just run an infinite loop when there is nothing else to do, and to *not* halt your CPU when there is no activity. This allows people with these broken chips to use Linux, although they would be well advised to seek a replacement through a warranty where possible.

3.5.5 The 'no-scroll' Argument

Using this argument at boot disables scrolling features that make it difficult to use Braille terminals.

3.5.6 The 'panic=' Argument

In the unlikely event of a kernel panic (i.e. an internal error that has been detected by the kernel, and which the kernel decides is serious enough to moan loudly and then halt everything), the default behaviour is to just sit there until someone comes along and notices the panic message on the screen and reboots the machine. However if a machine is running unattended in an isolated location it may be desirable for it to automatically reset itself so that the machine comes back on line. For example, using `panic=30` at boot would cause the kernel to try and reboot itself 30 seconds after the kernel panic happened. A value of zero gives the default behaviour, which is to wait forever.

Note that this timeout value can also be read and set via the `/proc/sys/kernel/panic` sysctl interface.

3.5.7 The 'profile=' Argument

Kernel developers can enable an option that allows them to profile how and where the kernel is spending its CPU cycles in an effort to maximize efficiency and performance. This option lets you set the profile shift count at boot. Typically it is set to two. You can also compile your kernel with profiling enabled by default. In either case, you need a tool such as `readprofile.c` that can make use of the `/proc/profile` output.

3.5.8 The 'reboot=' Argument

This option controls the type of reboot that Linux will do when it resets the computer (typically via `/sbin/init` handling a Control-Alt-Delete). The default as of late v2.0 kernels is to do a 'cold' reboot (i.e. full reset, BIOS does memory check, etc.) instead of a 'warm' reboot (i.e. no full reset, no memory check). It was changed to be cold by default since that tends to work on cheap/broken hardware that fails to reboot when a warm reboot is requested. To get the old behaviour (i.e. warm reboots) use `reboot=w` or in fact any word that starts with w will work.

Why would you bother? Some disk controllers with cache memory on board can sense a warm reboot, and flush any cached data to disk. Upon a cold boot, the card may be reset and the write-back data in your cache card's memory is lost. Others have reported systems that take a long time to go through the memory check, and/or SCSI BIOSes that take longer to initialize on a cold boot as a good reason to use warm reboots.

3.5.9 The 'reserve=' Argument

This is used to *protect* I/O port regions from probes. The form of the command is:

```
reserve=iobase,extent[,iobase,extent]...
```

In some machines it may be necessary to prevent device drivers from checking for devices (auto-probing) in a specific region. This may be because of poorly designed hardware that causes the boot to *freeze* (such as some ethercards), hardware that is mistakenly identified, hardware whose state is changed by an earlier probe, or merely hardware you don't want the kernel to initialize.

The `reserve` boot-time argument addresses this problem by specifying an I/O port region that shouldn't be probed. That region is reserved in the kernel's port registration table as if a device has already been found in that region (with the name `reserved`). Note that this mechanism shouldn't be necessary on most machines. Only when there is a problem or special case would it be necessary to use this.

The I/O ports in the specified region are protected against device probes that do a `check_region()` prior to probing blindly into a region of I/O space. This was put in to be used when some driver was hanging on a NE2000, or misidentifying some other device as its own. A correct device driver shouldn't probe a reserved region, unless another boot argument explicitly specifies that it do so. This implies that `reserve` will most often be used with some other boot argument. Hence if you specify a `reserve` region to protect a specific device, you must generally specify an explicit probe for that device. Most drivers ignore the port registration table if they are given an explicit address.

For example, the boot line

```
reserve=0x300,32  blah=0x300
```

keeps all device drivers except the driver for 'blah' from probing `0x300-0x31f`.

As usual with boot-time specifiers there is an 11 parameter limit, thus you can only specify 5 reserved regions per `reserve` keyword. Multiple `reserve` specifiers will work if you have an unusually complicated request.

3.5.10 The 'vga=' Argument

Note that this is not really a boot argument. It is an option that is interpreted by LILO and not by the kernel like all the other boot arguments are. However its use has become so common that it deserves a mention here. It can also be set via using `rdev -v` or equivalently `vidmode` on the vmlinuz file. This allows the setup code to use the video BIOS to change the default display mode before actually booting the Linux kernel. Typical modes are 80x50, 132x44 and so on. The best way to use this option is to start with `vga=ask` which will prompt you with a list of various modes that you can use with your video adapter before booting the kernel. Once you have the number from the above list that you want to use, you can later put it in place of the 'ask'. For more information, please see the file `linux/Documentation/svga.txt` that comes with all recent kernel versions.

Note that newer kernels (v2.1 and up) have the setup code that changes the video mode as an option, listed as *Video mode selection support* so you need to enable this option if you want to use this feature.

4   Boot Arguments for SCSI Peripherals.

This section contains the descriptions of the boot args that are used for passing information about the installed SCSI host adapters, and SCSI devices.

4.1   Arguments for Mid-level Drivers

The mid level drivers handle things like disks, CD-ROMs and tapes without getting into host adapter specifics.

4.1.1   Maximum Probed LUNs ('max_scsi_luns=')

Each SCSI device can have a number of 'sub-devices' contained within itself. The most common example is one of the new SCSI CD-ROMs that handle more than one disk at a time. Each CD is addressed as a 'Logical Unit Number' (LUN) of that particular device. But most devices, such as hard disks, tape drives and such are only one device, and will be assigned to LUN zero.

The problem arises with single LUN devices with bad firmware. Some poorly designed SCSI devices (old and unfortunately new) can not handle being probed for LUNs not equal to zero. They will respond by locking up, and possibly taking the whole SCSI bus down with them.

Newer kernels have the configuration option that allows you to set the maximum number of probed LUNs. The default is to only probe LUN zero, to avoid the problem described above.

To specify the number of probed LUNs at boot, one enters 'max_scsi_luns=n' as a boot arg, where n is a number between one and eight. To avoid problems as described above, one would use n=1 to avoid upsetting such broken devices

4.1.2   Parameters for the SCSI Tape Driver ('st=')

Some boot time configuration of the SCSI tape driver can be achieved by using the following:

```
st=buf_size[,write_threshold[,max_bufs]]
```

The first two numbers are specified in units of kB. The default `buf_size` is 32kB, and the maximum size that can be specified is a ridiculous 16384kB. The `write_threshold` is the value at which the buffer is committed to tape, with a default value of 30kB. The maximum number of buffers varies with the number of drives detected, and has a default of two. An example usage would be:

```
st=32,30,2
```

Full details can be found in the README.st file that is in the scsi directory of the kernel source tree.

4.2 Arguments for SCSI Host Adapters

General notation for this section:

iobase – the first I/O port that the SCSI host occupies. These are specified in hexidecimal notation, and usually lie in the range from 0x200 to 0x3ff.

irq – the hardware interrupt that the card is configured to use. Valid values will be dependent on the card in question, but will usually be 5, 7, 9, 10, 11, 12, and 15. The other values are usually used for common peripherals like IDE hard disks, floppies, serial ports, etc.

dma – the DMA (Direct Memory Access) channel that the card uses. Typically only applies to bus-mastering cards. PCI and VLB cards are native bus-masters, and do not require and ISA DMA channel.

scsi-id – the ID that the host adapter uses to identify itself on the SCSI bus. Only some host adapters allow you to change this value, as most have it permanently specified internally. The usual default value is seven, but the Seagate and Future Domain TMC-950 boards use six.

parity – whether the SCSI host adapter expects the attached devices to supply a parity value with all information exchanges. Specifying a one indicates parity checking is enabled, and a zero disables parity checking. Again, not all adapters will support selection of parity behaviour as a boot argument.

4.2.1 Adaptec aha151x, aha152x, aic6260, aic6360, SB16-SCSI ('aha152x=')

The aha numbers refer to cards and the aic numbers refer to the actual SCSI chip on these type of cards, including the Soundblaster-16 SCSI.

The probe code for these SCSI hosts looks for an installed BIOS, and if none is present, the probe will not find your card. Then you will have to use a boot argument of the form:

```
aha152x=iobase[,irq[,scsi-id[,reconnect[,parity]]]]
```

Note that if the driver was compiled with debugging enabled, a sixth value can be specified to set the debug level.

All the parameters are as described at the top of this section, and the reconnect value will allow device disconnect/reconnect if a non-zero value is used. An example usage is as follows:

```
aha152x=0x340,11,7,1
```

Note that the parameters must be specified in order, meaning that if you want to specify a parity setting, then you will have to specify an iobase, irq, scsi-id and reconnect value as well.

4.2.2 Adaptec aha154x ('aha1542=')

These are the aha154x series cards. The aha1542 series cards have an i82077 floppy controller onboard, while the aha1540 series cards do not. These are busmastering cards, and have parameters to set the "fairness" that is used to share the bus with other devices. The boot argument looks like the following.

```
aha1542=iobase[,buson,busoff[,dmaspeed]]
```

Valid `iobase` values are usually one of: `0x130, 0x134, 0x230, 0x234, 0x330, 0x334`. Clone cards may permit other values.

The `buson, busoff` values refer to the number of microseconds that the card dominates the ISA bus. The defaults are 11us on, and 4us off, so that other cards (such as an ISA LANCE Ethernet card) have a chance to get access to the ISA bus.

The `dmaspeed` value refers to the rate (in MB/s) at which the DMA (Direct Memory Access) transfers proceed at. The default is 5MB/s. Newer revision cards allow you to select this value as part of the soft-configuration, older cards use jumpers. You can use values up to 10MB/s assuming that your motherboard is capable of handling it. Experiment with caution if using values over 5MB/s.

4.2.3   Adaptec aha274x, aha284x, aic7xxx ('aic7xxx=')

These boards can accept an argument of the form:

```
aic7xxx=extended,no_reset
```

The `extended` value, if non-zero, indicates that extended translation for large disks is enabled. The `no_reset` value, if non-zero, tells the driver not to reset the SCSI bus when setting up the host adaptor at boot.

4.2.4   AdvanSys SCSI Host Adaptors ('advansys=')

The AdvanSys driver can accept up to four i/o addresses that will be probed for an AdvanSys SCSI card. Note that these values (if used) do not effect EISA or PCI probing in any way. They are only used for probing ISA and VLB cards. In addition, if the driver has been compiled with debugging enabled, the level of debugging output can be set by adding an `0xdeb[0-f]` parameter. The `0-f` allows setting the level of the debugging messages to any of 16 levels of verbosity.

4.2.5   Always IN2000 Host Adaptor ('in2000=')

Unlike other SCSI host boot arguments, the IN2000 driver uses ASCII string prefixes for most of its integer arguments. Here is a list of the supported arguments:

ioport:addr – Where addr is IO address of a (usually ROM-less) card.

noreset – No optional args. Prevents SCSI bus reset at boot time.

nosync:x – x is a bitmask where the 1st 7 bits correspond with the 7 possible SCSI devices (bit 0 for device #0, etc). Set a bit to PREVENT sync negotiation on that device. The driver default is sync DISABLED on all devices.

period:ns – ns is the minimum # of nanoseconds in a SCSI data transfer period. Default is 500; acceptable values are 250 to 1000.

disconnect:x – x = 0 to never allow disconnects, 2 to always allow them. x = 1 does 'adaptive' disconnects, which is the default and generally the best choice.

debug:x If 'DEBUGGING_ON' is defined, x is a bitmask that causes various types of debug output to printed - see the DB_xxx defines in in2000.h

proc:x – If 'PROC_INTERFACE' is defined, x is a bitmask that determines how the /proc interface works and what it does - see the PR_xxx defines in in2000.h

Some example usages are listed below:

```
in2000=ioport:0x220,noreset
in2000=period:250,disconnect:2,nosync:0x03
in2000=debug:0x1e
in2000=proc:3
```

4.2.6 AMD AM53C974 based hardware ('AM53C974=')

Unlike other drivers, this one does not use boot parameters to communicate i/o, IRQ or DMA channels. (Since the AM53C974 is a PCI device, there shouldn't be a need to do so.) Instead, the parameters are used to communicate the transfer modes and rates that are to be used between the host and the target device. This is best described with an example:

```
AM53C974=7,2,8,15
```

This would be interpreted as follows: 'For communication between the controller with SCSI-ID 7 and the device with SCSI-ID 2, a transfer rate of 8MHz in synchronous mode with max. 15 bytes offset should be negotiated.' More details can be found in the file linux/drivers/scsi/README.AM53C974

4.2.7 BusLogic SCSI Hosts with v1.2 kernels ('buslogic=')

In older kernels, the buslogic driver accepts only one parameter, that being the I/O base. It expects that to be one of the following valid values: 0x130, 0x134, 0x230, 0x234, 0x330, 0x334.

4.2.8 BusLogic SCSI Hosts with v2.x kernels ('BusLogic=')

With v2.x kernels, the BusLogic driver accepts many parameters. (Note the case in the above; upper case B and L!!!). The following detailed description is taken directly from Leonard N. Zubkoff's driver as included in the v2.0 kernel.

For the BusLogic driver, a Kernel command line entry comprises the driver identifier "BusLogic=" optionally followed by a comma-separated sequence of integers and then optionally followed by a comma-separated sequence of strings. Each command line entry applies to one BusLogic Host Adapter. Multiple command line entries may be used in systems which contain multiple BusLogic Host Adapters.

The first integer specified is the I/O Address at which the Host Adapter is located. If unspecified, it defaults to 0 which means to apply this entry to the first BusLogic Host Adapter found during the default probe sequence. If any I/O Address parameters are provided on the command line, then the default probe sequence is omitted.

The second integer specified is the Tagged Queue Depth to use for Target Devices that support Tagged Queuing. The Queue Depth is the number of SCSI commands that are allowed to be concurrently presented for execution. If unspecified, it defaults to 0 which means to use a value determined automatically based on the Host Adapter's Total Queue Depth and the number, type, speed, and capabilities of the detected Target Devices. For Host Adapters that require ISA Bounce Buffers, the Tagged Queue Depth is automatically set to BusLogic_TaggedQueueDepth_BB to avoid excessive preallocation of DMA Bounce Buffer memory. Target Devices that do not support Tagged Queuing use a Queue Depth of BusLogic_UntaggedQueueDepth.

The third integer specified is the Bus Settle Time in seconds. This is the amount of time to wait between a Host Adapter Hard Reset which initiates a SCSI Bus Reset and issuing any SCSI Commands. If unspecified, it defaults to 0 which means to use the value of BusLogic_DefaultBusSettleTime.

The fourth integer specified is the Local Options. If unspecified, it defaults to 0. Note that Local Options are only applied to a specific Host Adapter.

The fifth integer specified is the Global Options. If unspecified, it defaults to 0. Note that Global Options are applied across all Host Adapters.

The string options are used to provide control over Tagged Queuing, Error Recovery, and Host Adapter Probing.

The Tagged Queuing specification begins with "TQ:" and allows for explicitly specifying whether Tagged Queuing is permitted on Target Devices that support it. The following specification options are available:

TQ:Default – Tagged Queuing will be permitted based on the firmware version of the BusLogic Host Adapter and based on whether the Tagged Queue Depth value allows queuing multiple commands.

TQ:Enable – Tagged Queuing will be enabled for all Target Devices on this Host Adapter overriding any limitation that would otherwise be imposed based on the Host Adapter firmware version.

TQ:Disable – Tagged Queuing will be disabled for all Target Devices on this Host Adapter.

TQ:<Per-Target-Spec> – Tagged Queuing will be controlled individually for each Target Device. <Per-Target-Spec> is a sequence of "Y", "N", and "X" characters. "Y" enabled Tagged Queuing, "N" disables Tagged Queuing, and "X" accepts the default based on the firmware version. The first character refers to Target Device 0, the second to Target Device 1, and so on; if the sequence of "Y", "N", and "X" characters does not cover all the Target Devices, unspecified characters are assumed to be "X".

Note that explicitly requesting Tagged Queuing may lead to problems; this facility is provided primarily to allow disabling Tagged Queuing on Target Devices that do not implement it correctly.

The Error Recovery Strategy specification begins with "ER:" and allows for explicitly specifying the Error Recovery action to be performed when ResetCommand is called due to a SCSI Command failing to complete successfully. The following specification options are available:

ER:Default – Error Recovery will select between the Hard Reset and Bus Device Reset options based on the recommendation of the SCSI Subsystem.

ER:HardReset – Error Recovery will initiate a Host Adapter Hard Reset which also causes a SCSI Bus Reset.

ER:BusDeviceReset – Error Recovery will send a Bus Device Reset message to the individual Target Device causing the error. If Error Recovery is again initiated for this Target Device and no SCSI Command to this Target Device has completed successfully since the Bus Device Reset message was sent, then a Hard Reset will be attempted.

ER:None – Error Recovery will be suppressed. This option should only be selected if a SCSI Bus Reset or Bus Device Reset will cause the Target Device to fail completely and unrecoverably.

ER:<Per-Target-Spec> – Error Recovery will be controlled individually for each Target Device. <Per-Target-Spec> is a sequence of "D", "H", "B", and "N" characters. "D" selects Default, "H" selects Hard Reset, "B" selects Bus Device Reset, and "N" selects None. The first character refers to Target Device 0, the second to Target Device 1, and so on; if the sequence of "D", "H", "B", and "N" characters does not cover all the possible Target Devices, unspecified characters are assumed to be "D".

The Host Adapter Probing specification comprises the following strings:

NoProbe – No probing of any kind is to be performed, and hence no BusLogic Host Adapters will be detected.

NoProbeISA – No probing of the standard ISA I/O Addresses will be done, and hence only PCI Host Adapters will be detected.

NoSortPCI – PCI Host Adapters will be enumerated in the order provided by the PCI BIOS, ignoring any setting of the AutoSCSI "Use Bus And Device # For PCI Scanning Seq." option.

4.2.9 EATA SCSI Cards ('eata=')

As of late v2.0 kernels, the EATA drivers will accept a boot argument to specify the i/o base(s) to be probed. It is of the form:

```
eata=iobase1[,iobase2][,iobase3]...[,iobaseN]
```

The driver will probe the addresses in the order that they are listed.

4.2.10 Future Domain TMC-8xx, TMC-950 ('tmc8xx=')

The probe code for these SCSI hosts looks for an installed BIOS, and if none is present, the probe will not find your card. Or, if the signature string of your BIOS is not recognized then it will also not be found. In either case, you will then have to use a boot argument of the form:

```
tmc8xx=mem_base,irq
```

The `mem_base` value is the value of the memory mapped I/O region that the card uses. This will usually be one of the following values: `0xc8000, 0xca000, 0xcc000, 0xce000, 0xdc000, 0xde000`.

4.2.11 Future Domain TMC-16xx, TMC-3260, AHA-2920 ('fdomain=')

The driver detects these cards according to a list of known BIOS ROM signatures. For a full list of known BIOS revisions, please see `linux/drivers/scsi/fdomain.c` as it has a lot of information at the top of that file. If your BIOS is not known to the driver, you can use an override of the form:

```
fdomain=iobase,irq[,scsi_id]
```

4.2.12 IOMEGA Parallel Port / ZIP drive ('ppa=')

This driver is for the IOMEGA Parallel Port SCSI adapter which is embedded into the IOMEGA ZIP drives. It may also work with the original IOMEGA PPA3 device. The boot argument for this driver is of the form:

```
ppa=iobase,speed_high,speed_low,nybble
```

with all but iobase being optionally specified values. If you wish to alter any of the three optional parameters, you are advised to read `linux/drivers/scsi/README.ppa` for details of what they control.

4.2.13 NCR5380 based controllers ('ncr5380=')

Depending on your board, the 5380 can be either i/o mapped or memory mapped. (An address below 0x400 usually implies i/o mapping, but PCI and EISA hardware use i/o addresses above 0x3ff.) In either case, you specify the address, the IRQ value and the DMA channel value. An example for an i/o mapped card would be: `ncr5380=0x350,5,3`. If the card doesn't use interrupts, then an IRQ value of 255 (`0xff`) will disable interrupts. An IRQ value of 254 means to autoprobe. More details can be found in the file `linux/drivers/scsi/README.g_NCR5380`

4.2.14 NCR53c400 based controllers ('ncr53c400=')

The generic 53c400 support is done with the same driver as the generic 5380 support mentioned above. The boot argument is identical to the above with the exception that no DMA channel is used by the 53c400.

4.2.15 NCR53c406a based controllers ('ncr53c406a=')

This driver uses a boot argument of the form:

```
ncr53c406a=PORTBASE,IRQ,FASTPIO
```

where the IRQ and FASTPIO parameters are optional. An interrupt value of zero disables the use of interrupts. Using a value of one for the FASTPIO parameter enables the use of `insl` and `outsl` instructions instead of the single-byte `inb` and `outb` instructions. The driver can also use DMA as a compile-time option.

4.2.16 Pro Audio Spectrum ('pas16=')

The PAS16 uses a NCR5380 SCSI chip, and newer models support jumper-less configuration. The boot argument is of the form:

```
pas16=iobase,irq
```

The only difference is that you can specify an IRQ value of 255, which will tell the driver to work without using interrupts, albeit at a performance loss. The `iobase` is usually `0x388`.

4.2.17 Seagate ST-0x ('st0x=')

The probe code for these SCSI hosts looks for an installed BIOS, and if none is present, the probe will not find your card. Or, if the signature string of your BIOS is not recognized then it will also not be found. In either case, you will then have to use a boot argument of the form:

```
st0x=mem_base,irq
```

The `mem_base` value is the value of the memory mapped I/O region that the card uses. This will usually be one of the following values: `0xc8000`, `0xca000`, `0xcc000`, `0xce000`, `0xdc000`, `0xde000`.

4.2.18 Trantor T128 ('t128=')

These cards are also based on the NCR5380 chip, and accept the following options:

```
t128=mem_base,irq
```

The valid values for `mem_base` are as follows: `0xcc000`, `0xc8000`, `0xdc000`, `0xd8000`.

4.2.19 Ultrastor SCSI cards ('u14-34f=')

Note that there appears to be two independent drivers for this card, namely `CONFIG_SCSI_U14_34F` that uses `u14-34f.c` and `CONFIG_SCSI_ULTRASTOR` that uses `ultrastor.c`. It is the u14-34f one that (as of late v2.0 kernels) accepts a boot argument of the form:

```
u14-34f=iobase1[,iobase2][,iobase3]...[,iobaseN]
```

The driver will probe the addresses in the order that they are listed.

4.2.20 Western Digital WD7000 cards ('wd7000=')

The driver probe for the wd7000 looks for a known BIOS ROM string and knows about a few standard configuration settings. If it doesn't come up with the correct values for your card, or you have an unrecognized BIOS version, you can use a boot argument of the form:

```
wd7000=irq,dma,iobase
```

4.3 SCSI Host Adapters that don't Accept Boot Args

At present, the following SCSI cards do not make use of any boot-time parameters. In some cases, you can *hard-wire* values by directly editing the driver itself, if required.

```
Adaptec aha1740 (EISA probing),
NCR53c7xx,8xx (PCI, both drivers)
Qlogic Fast (0x230, 0x330)
Qlogic ISP (PCI)
```

5   Hard Disks

This section lists all the boot args associated with standard MFM/RLL, ST-506, XT, and IDE disk drive devices. Note that both the IDE and the generic ST-506 HD driver both accept the 'hd=' option.

5.1   IDE Disk/CD-ROM Driver Parameters

The IDE driver accepts a number of parameters, which range from disk geometry specifications, to support for advanced or broken controller chips. The following is a summary of all the possible boot arguments. For full details, you *really* should consult the file ide.txt in the linux/Documentation directory, from which this summary was extracted.

```
"hdx=" is recognized for all "x" from "a" to "h", such as "hdc".
"idex=" is recognized for all "x" from "0" to "3", such as "ide1".

"hdx=noprobe"         : drive may be present, but do not probe for it
"hdx=none"            : drive is NOT present, ignore cmos and do not probe
"hdx=nowerr"          : ignore the WRERR_STAT bit on this drive
"hdx=cdrom"           : drive is present, and is a cdrom drive
"hdx=cyl,head,sect"   : disk drive is present, with specified geometry
"hdx=autotune"        : driver will attempt to tune interface speed
                              to the fastest PIO mode supported,
                              if possible for this drive only.
                              Not fully supported by all chipset types,
                              and quite likely to cause trouble with
                              older/odd IDE drives.

"idex=noprobe"        : do not attempt to access/use this interface
"idex=base"           : probe for an interface at the addr specified,
                              where "base" is usually 0x1f0 or 0x170
                              and "ctl" is assumed to be "base"+0x206
"idex=base,ctl"       : specify both base and ctl
"idex=base,ctl,irq"   : specify base, ctl, and irq number
"idex=autotune"       : driver will attempt to tune interface speed
                              to the fastest PIO mode supported,
                              for all drives on this interface.
                              Not fully supported by all chipset types,
                              and quite likely to cause trouble with
                              older/odd IDE drives.
"idex=noautotune"     : driver will NOT attempt to tune interface speed
                              This is the default for most chipsets,
                              except the cmd640.
"idex=serialize"      : do not overlap operations on idex and ide(x^1)
```

The following are valid ONLY on ide0, and the defaults for the base,ctl ports must not be altered.

```
"ide0=dtc2278"      : probe/support DTC2278 interface
"ide0=ht6560b"      : probe/support HT6560B interface
"ide0=cmd640_vlb"   : *REQUIRED* for VLB cards with the CMD640 chip
                      (not for PCI -- automatically detected)
"ide0=qd6580"       : probe/support qd6580 interface
"ide0=ali14xx"      : probe/support ali14xx chipsets (ALI M1439/M1445)
"ide0=umc8672"      : probe/support umc8672 chipsets
```

Everything else is rejected with a "BAD OPTION" message.

5.2 Standard ST-506 Disk Driver Options ('hd=')

The standard disk driver can accept geometry arguments for the disks similar to the IDE driver. Note however that it only expects three values (C/H/S) – any more or any less and it will silently ignore you. Also, it only accepts 'hd=' as an argument, i.e. 'hda=', 'hdb=' and so on are not valid here. The format is as follows:

```
hd=cyls,heads,sects
```

If there are two disks installed, the above is repeated with the geometry parameters of the second disk.

5.3 XT Disk Driver Options ('xd=')

If you are unfortunate enough to be using one of these old 8 bit cards that move data at a whopping 125kB/s then here is the scoop. The probe code for these cards looks for an installed BIOS, and if none is present, the probe will not find your card. Or, if the signature string of your BIOS is not recognized then it will also not be found. In either case, you will then have to use a boot argument of the form:

```
xd=type,irq,iobase,dma_chan
```

The type value specifies the particular manufacturer of the card, and are as follows: 0=generic; 1=DTC; 2,3,4=Western Digital, 5,6,7=Seagate; 8=OMTI. The only difference between multiple types from the same manufacturer is the BIOS string used for detection, which is not used if the type is specified.

The xd_setup() function does no checking on the values, and assumes that you entered all four values. Don't disappoint it. Here is an example usage for a WD1002 controller with the BIOS disabled/removed, using the 'default' XT controller parameters:

```
xd=2,5,0x320,3
```

6 CD-ROMs (Non-SCSI/ATAPI/IDE)

This section lists all the possible boot args pertaining to CD-ROM devices. Note that this does not include SCSI or IDE/ATAPI CD-ROMs. See the appropriate section(s) for those types of CD-ROMs.

Note that most of these CD-ROMs have documentation files that you *should* read, and they are all in one handy place:
linux/Documentation/cdrom.

6.1 The Aztech Interface ('aztcd=')

The syntax for this type of card is:

```
aztcd=iobase[,magic_number]
```

If you set the `magic_number` to `0x79` then the driver will try and run anyway in the event of an unknown firmware version. All other values are ignored.

6.2 The CDU-31A and CDU-33A Sony Interface ('cdu31a=')

This CD-ROM interface is found on some of the Pro Audio Spectrum sound cards, and other Sony supplied interface cards. The syntax is as follows:

```
cdu31a=iobase,[irq[,is_pas_card]]
```

Specifying an IRQ value of zero tells the driver that hardware interrupts aren't supported (as on some PAS cards). If your card supports interrupts, you should use them as it cuts down on the CPU usage of the driver.

The 'is_pas_card' should be entered as 'PAS' if using a Pro Audio Spectrum card, and otherwise it should not be specified at all.

6.3 The CDU-535 Sony Interface ('sonycd535=')

The syntax for this CD-ROM interface is:

```
sonycd535=iobase[,irq]
```

A zero can be used for the I/O base as a 'placeholder' if one wishes to specify an IRQ value.

6.4 The GoldStar Interface ('gscd=')

The syntax for this CD-ROM interface is:

```
gscd=iobase
```

6.5 The ISP16 Interface ('isp16=')

The syntax for this CD-ROM interface is:

```
isp16=[port[,irq[,dma]]][[,]drive_type]
```

Using a zero for `irq` or `dma` means that they are not used. The allowable values for `drive_type` are `noisp16`, `Sanyo`, `Panasonic`, `Sony`, and `Mitsumi`. Using `noisp16` disables the driver altogether.

6.6 The Mitsumi Standard Interface ('mcd=')

The syntax for this CD-ROM interface is:

```
mcd=iobase,[irq[,wait_value]]
```

The `wait_value` is used as an internal timeout value for people who are having problems with their drive, and may or may not be implemented depending on a compile time `DEFINE`.

6.7 The Mitsumi XA/MultiSession Interface ('mcdx=')

At present this 'experimental' driver has a setup function, but no parameters are implemented yet (as of 1.3.15). This is for the same hardware as above, but the driver has extended features.

6.8 The Optics Storage Interface ('optcd=')

The syntax for this type of card is:

```
optcd=iobase
```

6.9 The Phillips CM206 Interface ('cm206=')

The syntax for this type of card is:

```
cm206=[iobase][,irq]
```

The driver assumes numbers between 3 and 11 are IRQ values, and numbers between `0x300` and `0x370` are I/O ports, so you can specify one, or both numbers, in any order. It also accepts 'cm206=auto' to enable autoprobing.

6.10 The Sanyo Interface ('sjcd=')

The syntax for this type of card is:

```
sjcd=iobase[,irq[,dma_channel]]
```

6.11 The SoundBlaster Pro Interface ('sbpcd=')

The syntax for this type of card is:

```
sbpcd=iobase,type
```

where `type` is one of the following (case sensitive) strings: 'SoundBlaster', 'LaserMate', or 'SPEA'. The I/O base is that of the CD-ROM interface, and *not* that of the sound portion of the card.

7 Other Hardware Devices

Any other devices that didn't fit into any of the above categories got lumped together here.

7.1 Ethernet Devices ('ether=')

Different drivers make use of different parameters, but they all at least share having an IRQ, an I/O port base value, and a name. In its most generic form, it looks something like this:

```
ether=irq,iobase[,param_1[,param_2,...param_8]]],name
```

The first non-numeric argument is taken as the name. The param_n values (if applicable) usually have different meanings for each different card/driver. Typical param_n values are used to specify things like shared memory address, interface selection, DMA channel and the like.

The most common use of this parameter is to force probing for a second ethercard, as the default is to only probe for one. This can be accomplished with a simple:

```
ether=0,0,eth1
```

Note that the values of zero for the IRQ and I/O base in the above example tell the driver(s) to autoprobe.

IMPORTANT NOTE TO MODULE USERS: The above will *not* force a probe for a second card if you are using the driver(s) as run time loadable modules (instead of having them complied into the kernel). Most Linux distributions use a bare bones kernel combined with a large selection of modular drivers. The ether= only applies to drivers compiled directly into the kernel.

The Ethernet-HowTo has complete and extensive documentation on using multiple cards and on the card/driver specific implementation of the param_n values where used. Interested readers should refer to the section in that document on their particular card for more complete information. *Ethernet-HowTo* <http://sunsite.unc.edu/mdw/HOWTO/ Ethernet-HOWTO.html>

7.2 The Floppy Disk Driver ('floppy=')

There are many floppy driver options, and they are all listed in README.fd in linux/drivers/block. This information is taken directly from that file.

floppy=mask,allowed_drive_mask

Sets the bitmask of allowed drives to mask. By default, only units 0 and 1 of each floppy controller are allowed. This is done because certain non-standard hardware (ASUS PCI motherboards) mess up the keyboard when accessing units 2 or 3. This option is somewhat obsoleted by the cmos option.

floppy=all_drives

Sets the bitmask of allowed drives to all drives. Use this if you have more than two drives connected to a floppy controller.

floppy=asus_pci

Sets the bitmask to allow only units 0 and 1. (The default)

floppy=daring

Tells the floppy driver that you have a well behaved floppy controller. This allows more efficient and smoother operation, but may fail on certain controllers. This may speed up certain operations.

floppy=0,daring

Tells the floppy driver that your floppy controller should be used with caution.

floppy=one_fdc

Tells the floppy driver that you have only floppy controller (default)

floppy=two_fdc *or* floppy=address,two_fdc

Tells the floppy driver that you have two floppy controllers. The second floppy controller is assumed to be at address. If address is not given, 0x370 is assumed.

floppy=thinkpad

Tells the floppy driver that you have a Thinkpad. Thinkpads use an inverted convention for the disk change line.

floppy=0,thinkpad

Tells the floppy driver that you don't have a Thinkpad.

floppy=drive,type,cmos

Sets the cmos type of `drive` to `type`. Additionally, this drive is allowed in the bitmask. This is useful if you have more than two floppy drives (only two can be described in the physical cmos), or if your BIOS uses non-standard CMOS types. Setting the CMOS to 0 for the first two drives (default) makes the floppy driver read the physical cmos for those drives.

floppy=unexpected_interrupts

Print a warning message when an unexpected interrupt is received (default behaviour)

floppy=no_unexpected_interrupts *or* floppy=L40SX

Don't print a message when an unexpected interrupt is received. This is needed on IBM L40SX laptops in certain video modes. (There seems to be an interaction between video and floppy. The unexpected interrupts only affect performance, and can safely be ignored.)

7.3   The Sound Driver ('sound=')

The sound driver can also accept boot args to override the compiled in values. This is not recommended, as it is rather complex. It is (was?) described in the `Readme.Linux` file, in `linux/drivers/sound`. It accepts a boot arg of the form:

```
sound=device1[,device2[,device3...[,device11]]]
```

where each `deviceN` value is of the following format `0xTaaaId` and the bytes are used as follows:

T - device type: 1=FM, 2=SB, 3=PAS, 4=GUS, 5=MPU401, 6=SB16, 7=SB16-MPU401

aaa - I/O address in hex.

I - interrupt line in hex (i.e 10=a, 11=b, ...)

d - DMA channel.

As you can see it gets pretty messy, and you are better off to compile in your own personal values as recommended. Using a boot arg of 'sound=0' will disable the sound driver entirely.

7.4   The Bus Mouse Driver ('bmouse=')

The busmouse driver only accepts one parameter, that being the hardware IRQ value to be used.

7.5   The MS Bus Mouse Driver ('msmouse=')

The MS mouse driver only accepts one parameter, that being the hardware IRQ value to be used.

7.6   The Printer Driver ('lp=')

As of kernels newer than 1.3.75, you can tell the printer driver what ports to use and what ports *not* to use. The latter comes in handy if you don't want the printer driver to claim all available parallel ports, so that other drivers (e.g. PLIP, PPA) can use them instead.

The format of the argument is multiple i/o, IRQ pairs. For example, `lp=0x3bc,0,0x378,7` would use the port at 0x3bc in IRQ-less (polling) mode, and use IRQ 7 for the port at 0x378. The port at 0x278 (if any) would not be probed, since autoprobing only takes place in the absence of a 'lp=' argument. To disable the printer driver entirely, one can use `lp=0`.

7.7   The ICN ISDN driver ('icn=')

This ISDN driver expects a boot argument of the form:

```
icn=iobase,membase,icn_id1,icn_id2
```

where `iobase` is the i/o port address of the card, `membase` is the shared memory base address of the card, and the two `icn_id` are unique ASCII string identifiers.

7.8   The PCBIT ISDN driver ('pcbit=')

This boot argument takes integer pair arguments of the form:

```
pcbit=membase1,irq1[,membase2,irq2]
```

where `membaseN` is the shared memory base of the N'th card, and `irqN` is the interrupt setting of the N'th card. The default is IRQ 5 and membase 0xD0000.

7.9   The Teles ISDN driver ('teles=')

This ISDN driver expects a boot argument of the form:

```
teles=iobase,irq,membase,protocol,teles_id
```

where `iobase` is the i/o port address of the card, `membase` is the shared memory base address of the card, `irq` is the interrupt channel the card uses, and `teles_id` is the unique ASCII string identifier.

7.10   The DigiBoard Driver ('digi=')

The DigiBoard driver accepts a string of six comma separated identifiers or integers. The 6 values in order are:

```
Enable/Disable this card
Type of card: PC/Xi(0), PC/Xe(1), PC/Xeve(2), PC/Xem(3)
Enable/Disable alternate pin arrangement
Number of ports on this card
I/O Port where card is configured (in HEX if using string identifiers)
Base of memory window (in HEX if using string identifiers)
```

An example of a correct boot prompt argument (in both identifier and integer form) is:

```
digi=E,PC/Xi,D,16,200,D0000
digi=1,0,0,16,512,851968
```

Note that the driver defaults to an i/o of $0x200$ and a shared memory base of $0xD0000$ in the absence of a `digi=` boot argument. There is no autoprobing performed. More details can be found in the file `linux/Documentation/digiboard.txt`.

7.11   The RISCom/8 Multiport Serial Driver ('riscom8=')

Up to four boards can be supported by supplying four unique i/o port values for each individual board installed. Other details can be found in the file `linux/Documentation/riscom8.txt`.

7.12   The Baycom Serial/Parallel Radio Modem ('baycom=')

The format of the boot argument for these devices is:

```
baycom=modem,io,irq,options[,modem,io,irq,options]
```

Using modem=1 means you have the ser12 device, modem=2 means you have the par96 device. Using options=0 means use hardware DCD, and options=1 means use software DCD. The `io` and `irq` are the i/o port base and interrupt settings as usual. There is more details in the file `README.baycom` which is currently in the `/linux/drivers/char/` directory.

8   Closing

If you have found any glaring typos, or outdated info in this document, please let me know. It is easy to overlook stuff.

Thanks,

Paul Gortmaker, `gpg109@rsphy1.anu.edu.au`

HOWTO

Part VIII

"The Linux Bootdisk HOWTO" Tom Fawcett

`fawcett@croftj.net`

v3.3, November 1998
This document describes how to design and build your own boot/root diskettes for Linux. These disks could be used as rescue disks or to test new system components. If you haven't read the Linux FAQ and related documents, such as the Linux Installation HOWTO and the Linux Install Guide, you should not be trying to build boot diskettes. If you just want a rescue disk to have for emergencies, see Appendix 11.1 (Pre-made bootdisks).

Contents

HOWTO

1 Preface.

Note: This document may be outdated. If the date on the title page is more than six months ago, please check the Linux Documentation Project homepage <http://sunsite.unc.edu/LDP/HOWTO/Bootdisk-HOWTO.html> to see if a more recent version exists.

Although this document should be legible in its text form, it looks *much* better in Postscript (.ps) or HTML because of the typographical notation used. We encourage you to select one of these forms. The Info version, as of this writing, ends up so damaged as to be unusable.

1.1 Version notes.

Graham Chapman (grahamc@zeta.org.au) wrote the original Bootdisk-HOWTO and he supported it through version 3.1. Tom Fawcett (fawcett@croftj.net) added a lot of material for kernel 2.0, and he is the document's maintainer as of version 3.2. Much of Chapman's original content remains.

This document is intended for **Linux kernel 2.0 and later**. If you have an older kernel (1.2.xx or before), please consult previous versions of the Bootdisk-HOWTO archived on *Graham Chapman's homepage* <http://www.zeta.org.au/~grahamc/linux.html>.

This information is intended for Linux on the **Intel** platform. Much of this information may be applicable to Linux on other processors, but we have no first-hand experience or information about this. If anyone has experience with bootdisks on other platforms, please contact us.

1.2 Feedback and credits.

We welcome any feedback, good or bad, on the content of this document. We have done our best to ensure that the instructions and information herein are accurate and reliable. Please let us know if you find errors or omissions.

We thank the many people who assisted with corrections and suggestions. Their contributions have made it far better than we could ever have done alone.

Send comments, corrections and questions to the author at the email address above. I don't mind trying to answer questions, but please read section 3.10 (Troubleshooting) first.

1.3 Distribution policy.

Copyright © 1995,1996,1997,1998 by Tom Fawcett and Graham Chapman. This document may be distributed under the terms set forth in the Linux Documentation Project License at `<http://sunsite.unc.edu/LDP/COPYRIGHT.html>`. Please contact the authors if you are unable to get the license.

This is free documentation. It is distributed in the hope that it will be useful, but **without any warranty**; without even the implied warranty of **merchantability** or **fitness for a particular purpose**.

2 Introduction.

Linux boot disks are useful in a number of situations, such as:

- Testing a new kernel.

- Recovering from a disk failure – anything from a lost boot sector to a disk head crash.

- Fixing a disabled system. A minor mistake as root can leave your system unusable, and you may have to boot from diskette to fix it.

- Upgrading critical system files, such as `libc.so`.

There are several ways of obtaining boot disks:

- Use one from a distribution such as Slackware. This will at least allow you to boot.

- Use a rescue package to set up disks designed to be used as rescue disks.

- Learn what is required for each of the types of disk to operate, then build your own.

Some people choose the last option so they can do it themselves. That way, if something breaks, they can work out what to do to fix it. Plus it's a great way to learn about how a Linux system works.

This document assumes some basic familiarity with Linux system administration concepts. For example, you should know about directories, filesystems and floppy diskettes. You should know how to use `mount` and `df`. You should know what `/etc/passwd` and `fstab` files are for and what they look like. You should know that most of the commands in this HOWTO should be run as root.

Constructing your own bootdisk from scratch can be complicated. If you haven't read the Linux FAQ and related documents, such as the Linux Installation HOWTO and the Linux Install Guide, you should not be trying to build boot diskettes. If you just need a working bootdisk for emergencies, it is *much* easier to download a prefabricated one. See Appendix 11.1 (Pre-made bootdisks), below, for where to find these.

3 Bootdisks and the boot process.

A bootdisk is basically a miniature, self-contained Linux system on a floppy diskette. It must perform many of the same functions that a complete full-size Linux system performs. Before trying to build one you should understand the basic Linux boot process. We present the basics here, which are sufficient for understanding the rest of this document. Many details and alternative options have been omitted.

3.1   The boot process.

All PC systems start the boot process by executing code in ROM (specifically, the BIOS) to load the sector from sector 0, cylinder 0 of the boot drive. The boot drive is usually the first floppy drive (designated A: in DOS and /dev/fd0 in Linux). The BIOS then tries to execute this sector. On most bootable disks, sector 0, cylinder 0 contains either:

- code from a boot loader such as LILO, which locates the kernel, loads it and executes it to start the boot proper.

- the start of an operating system kernel, such as Linux.

If a Linux kernel has been raw-copied to a diskette, the first sector of the disk will be the first sector of the Linux kernel itself. This first sector will continue the boot process by loading the rest of the kernel from the boot device.

Once the kernel is completely loaded, it goes through some basic device initialization. It then tries to load and mount a **root filesystem** from some device. A root filesystem is simply a filesystem that is mounted as "/". The kernel has to be told where to look for the root filesystem; if it cannot find a loadable image there, it halts.

In some boot situations – often when booting from a diskette – the root filesystem is loaded into a **ramdisk**, which is RAM accessed by the system as if it were a disk. There are two reasons why the system loads to ramdisk. First, RAM is several orders of magnitude faster than a floppy disk, so system operation is fast; and second, the kernel can load a **compressed filesystem** from the floppy and uncompress it onto the ramdisk, allowing many more files to be squeezed onto the diskette.

Once the root filesystem is loaded and mounted, you see a message like:

```
VFS: Mounted root (ext2 filesystem) readonly.
```

At this point the system finds the init program on the root filesystem (in /bin or /sbin) and executes it. init reads its configuration file /etc/inittab, looks for a line designated sysinit, and executes the named script . The sysinit script is usually something like /etc/rc or /etc/init.d/boot. This script is a set of shell commands that set up basic system services, such as:

- Running fsck on all the disks,
- Loading necessary kernel modules,
- Starting swapping,
- Initializing the network,
- Mounting disks mentioned in fstab.

This script often invokes various other scripts to do modular initialization. For example, in the common SysVinit structure, the directory /etc/rc.d/ contains a complex structure of subdirectories whose files specify how to enable and shut down most system services. However, on a bootdisk the sysinit script is often very simple.

When the sysinit script finishes control returns to init, which then enters the *default runlevel*, specified in inittab with the initdefault keyword. The runlevel line usually specifies a program like getty, which is responsible for handling commununications through the console and ttys. It is the getty program which prints the familiar "login:" prompt. The getty program in turn invokes the login program to handle login validation and to set up user sessions.

3.2   Disk types.

Having reviewed the basic boot process, we can now define various kinds of disks involved. We classify disks into four types. The discussion here and throughout this document uses the term "disk" to refer to floppy diskettes unless otherwise specified, though most of the discussion could apply equally well to hard disks.

A disk containing a kernel which can be booted. The disk can be used to boot the kernel, which then may load a root file system on another disk. The kernel on a bootdisk usually must be told where to find its root filesystem.

Often a bootdisk loads a root filesystem from another diskette, but it is possible for a bootdisk to be set up to load a hard disk's root filesystem instead. This is commonly done when testing a new kernel. (in fact, "`make zdisk`" will create such a bootdisk automatically from the kernel source code).

root

A disk with a filesystem containing files required to run a Linux system. Such a disk does not necessarily contain either a kernel or a boot loader.

A root disk can be used to run the system independently of any other disks, once the kernel has been booted. Usually the root disk is automatically copied to a ramdisk. This makes root disk accesses much faster, and frees up the disk drive for a utility disk.

boot/root

A disk which contains both the kernel and a root filesystem. In other words, it contains everything necessary to boot and run a Linux system without a hard disk. The advantage of this type of disk is that is it compact – everything required is on a single disk. However, the gradually increasing size of everything means that it is increasingly difficult to fit everything on a single diskette, even with compression.

utility

A disk which contains a filesystem, but is not intended to be mounted as a root file system. It is an additional data disk. You would use this type of disk to carry additional utilities where you have too much to fit on your root disk.

In general, when we talk about "building a bootdisk" we mean creating both the boot (kernel) and root (files) portions. They may be either together (a single boot/root disk) or separate (boot + root disks). The most flexible approach for rescue diskettes is probably to use separate boot and root diskettes, and one or more utility diskettes to handle the overflow.

4 Building a root filesystem.

Creating the root filesystem involves selecting files necessary for the system to run. In this section we describe how to build a *compressed root filesystem*. A less common option is to build an uncompressed filesystem on a diskette that is directly mounted as root; this alternative is described in section 8.2 (Non-ramdisk Root Filesystem).

4.1 Overview.

A root filesystem must contain everything needed to support a full Linux system. To be able to do this, the disk must include the minimum requirements for a Linux system:

- The basic file system structure,
- Minimum set of directories: `/dev`, `/proc`, `/bin`, `/etc`, `/lib`, `/usr`, `/tmp`,
- Basic set of utilities: `sh`, `ls`, `cp`, `mv`, etc.,
- Minimum set of config files: `rc`, `inittab`, `fstab`, etc.,
- Devices: `/dev/hd*`, `/dev/tty*`, `/dev/fd0`, etc.,
- Runtime library to provide basic functions used by utilities.

Of course, any system only becomes useful when you can run something on it, and a root diskette usually only becomes useful when you can do something like:

- Check a file system on another drive, for example to check your root file system on your hard drive, you need to be able to boot Linux from another drive, as you can with a root diskette system. Then you can run `fsck` on your original root drive while it is not mounted.

- Restore all or part of your original root drive from backup using archive and compression utilities such as `cpio`, `tar`, `gzip` and `ftape`.

We will describe how to build a *compressed* filesystem, so called because it is compressed on disk and, when booted, is uncompressed onto a ramdisk. With a compressed filesystem you can fit many files (approximately six megabytes) onto a standard 1440K diskette. Because the filesystem is much larger than a diskette, it cannot be built on the diskette. We have to build it elsewhere, compress it, then copy it to the diskette.

4.2 Creating the filesystem.

In order to build such a root filesystem, you need a spare device that is large enough to hold all the files before compression. You will need a device capable of holding about four megabytes. There are several choices:

- Use a **ramdisk** (DEVICE = /dev/ram0). In this case, memory is used to simulate a disk drive. The ramdisk must be large enough to hold a filesystem of the appropriate size. If you use LILO, check your configuration file (/etc/lilo.conf) for a line like:

        RAMDISK_SIZE = nnn

    which determines how much RAM will be allocated. The default is 4096K, which should be sufficient. You should probably not try to use such a ramdisk on a machine with less than 8MB of RAM.

    Check to make sure you have a device like /dev/ram0, /dev/ram or /dev/ramdisk. If not, create /dev/ram0 with mknod (major number 1, minor 0).

- If you have an unused hard disk partition that is large enough (several megabytes), this is a good solution.

- Use a **loopback device**, which allows a disk file to be treated as a device. Using a loopback device you can create a three megabyte file on your hard disk and build the filesystem on it.

    In order to use loopback devices you need specially modified mount and unmount programs. You can find these in the directory:

    <ftp://ftp.win.tue.nl:/pub/linux/util/mount/>

    If you do not have a loop device (/dev/loop0, /dev/loop1, etc.) on your system, you will have to create one with "mknod /dev/loop0 b 7 0". One you've installed these special mount and umount binaries, create a temporary file on a hard disk with enough capacity (eg, /tmp/fsfile). You can use a command like

        dd if=/dev/zero of=/tmp/fsfile bs=1k count=nnn

    to create an *nnn*-block file.

    Use the file name in place of DEVICE below. When you issue a mount command you must include the option "-o loop" to tell mount to use a loopback device. For example:

        mount -o loop -t ext2 /tmp/fsfile /mnt

    will mount /tmp/fsfile (via a loopback device) at the mount point /mnt. A df will confirm this.

After you've chosen one of these options, prepare the DEVICE with:

        dd if=/dev/zero of=DEVICE bs=1k count=3000

This command zeroes out the device. This step is important because the filesystem on the device will be compressed later, so all unused portions should be filled with zeroes to achieve maximum compression.

Next, create the filesystem. The Linux kernel recognizes two file system types for root disks to be automatically copied to ramdisk. These are minix and ext2, of which ext2 is the preferred file system. If using ext2, you may find it useful to use the -i option to specify more inodes than the default; -i 2000 is suggested so that you don't run out of inodes. Alternatively, you can save on inodes by removing lots of unnecessary /dev files. mke2fs will by default create 360 inodes on a 1.44Mb diskette. I find that 120 inodes is ample on my current rescue root diskette, but if you include all the devices in the /dev directory then you will easily exceed 360. Using a compressed root filesystem allows a larger filesystem, and hence more inodes by default, but you may still need to either reduce the number of files or increase the number of inodes.

So the command you use will look like:

```
mke2fs -m 0 -i 2000 DEVICE
```

(If you're using a loopback device, the disk file you're using should be supplied in place of this DEVICE. In this case, `mke2fs` will ask if you really want to do this; say yes.)

The `mke2fs` command will automatically detect the space available and configure itself accordingly. The `-m 0` parameter prevents it from reserving space for root, and hence provides more usable space on the disk.

Next, mount the device:

```
mount -t ext2 DEVICE /mnt
```

(You must create a mount point `/mnt` if it does not already exist.) In the remaining sections, all destination directory names are assumed to be relative to `/mnt`.

4.3   Populating the filesystem.

Here is a reasonable minimum set of directories for your root filesystem:

- `/dev` – Devices, required to perform I/O
- `/proc` – Directory stub required by the proc filesystem
- `/etc` – System configuration files
- `/sbin` – Critical system binaries
- `/bin` – Basic binaries considered part of the system
- `/lib` – Shared libraries to provide run-time support
- `/mnt` – A mount point for maintenance on other disks
- `/usr` – Additional utilities and applications

(The directory structure presented here is for root diskette use only. Real Linux systems have a more complex and disciplined set of policies, called the File System Standard, for determining where files should go.)

Three of these directories will be empty on the root filesystem, so they only need to be created with `mkdir`. The `/proc` directory is basically a stub under which the proc filesystem is placed. The directories `/mnt` and `/usr` are only mount points for use after the boot/root system is running. Hence again, these directories only need to be created.

The remaining four directories are described in the following sections.

4.3.1   /dev

A `/dev` directory containing a special file for all devices to be used by the system is mandatory for any Linux system. The directory itself is a normal directory, and can be created with `mkdir` in the normal way. The device special files, however, must be created in a special way, using the `mknod` command.

There is a shortcut, though – copy your existing `/dev` directory contents, and delete the ones you don't want. The only requirement is that you copy the device special files using `-R` option. This will copy the directory without attempting to copy the contents of the files. *Be sure to use an upper case R.* If you use the lower case switch `-r`, you will probably end up copying the entire contents of all of your hard disks – or at least as much of them as will fit on a diskette! Therefore, take care, and use the command:

```
cp -dpR /dev /mnt
```

assuming that the diskette is mounted at `/mnt`. The `dp` switches ensure that symbolic links are copied as links, rather than using the target file, and that the original file attributes are preserved, thus preserving ownership information.

Alternatively, you can use the cpio program with the -p option, because cpio handles device special files correctly, and will not try to copy the contents. For example, the commands:

```
cd /dev
find . -print | cpio -pmd /mnt/dev
```

will copy all device special files from /dev to /mnt/dev. In fact it will copy all files in the directory tree starting at /dev, and will create any required subdirectories in the target directory tree.

If you want to do it the hard way, use ls -l to display the major and minor device numbers for the devices you want, and create them on the diskette using mknod.

However the devices are copied, it is worth checking that any special devices you need have been placed on the rescue diskette. For example, ftape uses tape devices, so you will need to copy all of these if you intend to access your floppy tape drive from the bootdisk.

Note that one inode is required for each device special file, and inodes can at times be a scarce resource, especially on diskette filesystems. It therefore makes sense to remove any device special files that you don't need from the diskette /dev directory. Many devices are obviously unnecessary on specific systems. For example, if you do not have SCSI disks you can safely remove all the device files starting with sd. Similarly, if you don't intend to use your serial port then all device files starting with cua can go.

Be sure to include the following files from this directory: console, kmem, mem, null, ram, tty1.

4.3.2 /etc

This directory must contain a number of configuration files. On most systems, these can be divided into three groups:

1. Required at all times, *e.g.* rc, fstab, passwd.

2. May be required, but no-one is too sure.

3. Junk that crept in.

Files which are not essential can be identified with the command:

```
ls -ltru
```

This lists files in reverse order of date last accessed, so if any files are not being accessed, they can be omitted from a root diskette.

On my root diskettes, I have the number of config files down to 15. This reduces my work to dealing with three sets of files:

1. The ones I must configure for a boot/root system:

   (a) rc.d/* – system startup and run level change scripts

   (b) fstab – list of file systems to be mounted

   (c) inittab – parameters for the init process, the first process started at boot time.

2. The ones I should tidy up for a boot/root system:

   (a) passwd – list of users, home directories, etc.

   (b) group – user groups.

   (c) shadow – passwords of users. You may not have this.

If security is important, `passwd` and `shadow` should be pruned to avoid copying user passwords off the system, and so that when you boot from diskette, unwanted logins are rejected. However, there is a reason *not* to prune `passwd` and `group`. `tar` (and probably other archivers) stores user and group names with files. If you restore files to your hard disk from tape, the files will be restored with their original names. If these names do not exist in `passwd`/`group` when they are restored, the UIDs/GIDs will not be correct.

Be sure that `passwd` contains at least `root`. If you intend other users to login, be sure their home directories and shells exist.

3. The rest. They work at the moment, so I leave them alone.

Out of this, I only really have to configure two files, and what they should contain is surprisingly small.

- `rc` should contain:

  ```
  #!/bin/sh
  /bin/mount -av
  /bin/hostname Kangaroo
  ```

Be sure the directories are right. You don't really need to run `hostname` – it just looks nicer if you do.

- `fstab` should contain at least:

  ```
  /dev/ram0      /                  ext2    defaults
  /dev/fd0       /                  ext2    defaults
  /proc          /proc              proc    defaults
  ```

You can copy entries from your existing `fstab`, but you should not automatically mount any of your hard disk partitions; use the `noauto` keyword with them. Your hard disk may be damaged or dead when the bootdisk is used.

Your `inittab` should be changed so that its `sysinit` line runs `rc` or whatever basic boot script will be used. Also, if you want to ensure that users on serial ports cannot login, comment out all the entries for `getty` which include a `ttys` or `ttyS` device at the end of the line. Leave in the `tty` ports so that you can login at the console.

A minimal `inittab` file looks like this:

```
id:2:initdefault:
si::sysinit:/etc/rc
1:2345:respawn:/sbin/getty 9600 tty1
2:23:respawn:/sbin/getty 9600 tty2
```

The `inittab` file defines what the system will run in various states including startup, move to multi-user mode, etc. A point to be careful of here is to carefully check that the commands entered in `inittab` refer to programs which are present and to the correct directory. If you place your command files on your rescue disk using Section 13 (Sample root-disk directory listings) as a guide, and then copy your `inittab` to your rescue disk without checking it, the probability of failure will be quite high because half of the `inittab` entries will refer to missing programs or to the wrong directory.

Note that some programs cannot be moved elsewhere because other programs have hardcoded their locations. For example on my system, `/etc/shutdown` has hardcoded in it `/etc/reboot`. If I move `reboot` to `/bin/reboot`, and then issue a `shutdown` command, it will fail because it cannot find the `reboot` file.

For the rest, just copy all the text files in your `/etc` directory, plus all the executables in your `/etc` directory that you cannot be sure you do not need. As a guide, consult the sample listing in Section 13 (Sample rootdisk directory listings). Probably it will suffice to copy only those files, but systems differ a great deal, so you cannot be sure that the same set of files on your system is equivalent to the files in the list. The only sure method is to start with `inittab` and work out what is required.

Most systems now use an `/etc/rc.d/` directory containing shell scripts for different run levels. The minimum is a single `rc` script, but it may be simpler just to copy `inittab` and the `/etc/rc.d` directory from your existing system, and prune the shell scripts in the `rc.d` directory to remove processing not relevent to a diskette system environment.

4.3.3 /bin and /sbin

The /bin directory is a convenient place for extra utilities you need to perform basic operations, utilities such as ls, mv, cat and dd. See Appendix 13 (Sample rootdisk directory listings) for an example list of files that go in a /bin and /sbin directories. It does not include any of the utilities required to restore from backup, such as cpio, tar and gzip. That is because I place these on a separate utility diskette, to save space on the boot/root diskette. Once the boot/root diskette is booted, it is copied to the ramdisk leaving the diskette drive free to mount another diskette, the utility diskette. I usually mount this as /usr.

Creation of a utility diskette is described below in the section Section 8.3 (Building a utility disk). It is probably desirable to maintain a copy of the same version of backup utilities used to write the backups so you don't waste time trying to install versions that cannot read your backup tapes.

Make sure you include the following programs: init, getty or equivalent, login, mount, some shell capable of running your rc scripts, a link from sh to the shell.

4.3.4 /lib

In /lib you place necessary shared libraries and loaders. If the necessary libraries are not found in your /lib directory then the system will be unable to boot. If you're lucky you may see an error message telling you why.

Nearly every program requires at least the libc library, libc.so.N, where N is the current version number. Check your /lib directory. libc.so.5 is usually a symlink to a filename with a complete version number:

```
% ls -l /lib/libc.so*
lrwxrwxrwx  1 root root      14 Nov  1 20:34 /lib/libc.so.5 -
> libc.so.5.4.33*
-rwxr-xr-x  1 root root  573176 Jun 12 02:05 /lib/libc.so.5.4.33*
```

In this case, you want libc.so.5.4.33. To find other libraries you should go through all the binaries you plan to include and check their dependencies with the ldd command. For example:

```
% ldd /sbin/mke2fs
        libext2fs.so.2 => /lib/libext2fs.so.2
        libcom_err.so.2 => /lib/libcom_err.so.2
        libuuid.so.1 => /lib/libuuid.so.1
        libc.so.5 => /lib/libc.so.5
```

Each file on the right-hand side is required. Keep in mind that the libraries listed may be symbolic links.

In /lib you must also include a loader for the libraries. The loader will be either ld.so (for a.out libraries) or ld-linux.so (for ELF libraries). If you're not sure which you need, run the file command on the library. For example:

```
% file /lib/libc.so.5.4.33 /lib/libc.so.4.7.2
        /lib/libc.so.4.7.2: Linux/i386 demand-paged executable (QMAG-
IC), stripped
        /lib/libc.so.5.4.33: ELF 32-bit LSB shared object, Intel 386, ver-
sion 1, stripped
```

The QMAGIC indicates that 4.7.2 is for a.out libraries, and ELF indicates that 5.4.33 is for ELF.

Copy the specific loader(s) you need to the root filesystem you're building. Libraries and loaders should be checked *carefully* against the included binaries. If the kernel cannot load a necessary library, the kernel will usually hang with no error message.

4.4 Providing for PAM and NSS.

Your system may require dynamically loaded libraries that are not visible to `ldd`.

4.4.1 PAM (Pluggable Authentication Modules).

If your system uses PAM (Pluggable Authentication Modules), you must make some provision for it on your bootdisk or you will not be able to login. PAM, briefly, is a sophisticated modular method for authenticating users and controlling their access to services. An easy way to determine if your system uses PAM is to check your hard disks's `/etc` directory for a file `pam.conf` or a `pam.d` directory; if either exists, you must provide some minimal PAM support. (Alternatively, run `ldd` on your `login` executable; if the output includes `libpam.so`, you need PAM.)

Fortunately, security is usually of no concern with bootdisks, since anyone who has physical access to a machine can usually do anything they want anyway. Therefore, you can essentially disable PAM by creating a simple `/etc/pam.conf` file in your root filesystem that looks like this:

```
OTHER    auth       optional      /lib/security/pam_permit.so
OTHER    account    optional      /lib/security/pam_permit.so
OTHER    password   optional      /lib/security/pam_permit.so
OTHER    session    optional      /lib/security/pam_permit.so
```

Also copy the file `/lib/security/pam_permit.so` to your root filesystem. This library is only about 8K so it imposes minimal overhead.

Note that this configuration allows anyone complete access to the files and services on your machine. If you care about security on your bootdisk for some reason, you'll have to copy some or all of your hard disk's PAM setup to your root filesystem. Be sure to read the PAM documentation carefully, and copy any libraries needed in `/lib/security` onto your root filesystem.

You must also include `/lib/libpam.so` on your bootdisk. But you already know this since you ran ldd on `/bin/login`, which showed this dependency.

4.4.2 NSS (Name Service Switch).

If you are using glibc (aka libc6), you will have to make provisions for name services or you will not be able to log in. The file `/etc/nsswitch.conf` controls database lookups for various servies. If you don't plan to access services from the network (eg, DNS or NIS lookups), you need only prepare a simple `nsswitch.conf` file that looks like this:

```
passwd:      files
shadow:      files
group:       files
hosts:       files
services:    files
networks:    files
protocols:   files
rpc:         files
ethers:      files
netmasks:    files
bootparams:  files
automount:   files
aliases:     files
netgroup:    files
publickey:   files
```

This specifies that every service be provided only by local files. You will also need to include `/lib/libnss_files.so.1`, which will be loaded dynamically to handle the file lookups.

If you plan to access the network from your bootdisk, you may want to create a more elaborate `nsswitch.conf` file. See the `nsswitch` man page for details. Keep in mind that you must include a file `/lib/libnss_service.so.1` for each *service* you specify.

4.5 Modules.

If you have a modular kernel, you must consider which modules you may want to load from your bootdisk after booting. You might want to include `ftape` and `zftape` modules if your backup tapes are on floppy tape, modules for SCSI devices if you have them, and possibly modules for PPP or SLIP support if you want to access the net in an emergency.

These modules may be placed in `/lib/modules`. You should also include `insmod`, `rmmod` and `lsmod`. Depending on whether you want to load modules automatically, you might also include `modprobe`, `depmod` and `swapout`. If you use `kerneld`, include it along with `/etc/conf.modules`.

However, the main advantage to using modules is that you can move non-critical modules to a utility disk and load them when needed, thus using less space on your root disk. If you may have to deal with many different devices, this approach is preferable to building one huge kernel with many drivers built in.

Note that in order to boot a compressed ext2 filesystem, you must have ramdisk and ext2 support built-in. They cannot be supplied as modules.

4.6 Some final details.

Some system programs, such as `login`, complain if the file `/var/run/utmp` and the directory `/var/log` do not exist. So:

```
mkdir -p /mnt/var/{log,run}
touch /mnt/var/run/utmp
```

Finally, after you have set up all the libraries you need, run `ldconfig` to remake `/etc/ld.so.cache` on the root filesystem. The cache tells the loader where to find the libraries. To remake `ld.so.cache`, issue the following commands:

```
chdir /mnt; chroot /mnt /sbin/ldconfig
```

The `chroot` is necessary because `ldconfig` always remakes the cache for the root filesystem.

4.7 Wrapping it up.

Once you have finished constructing the root filesystem, unmount it, copy it to a file and compress it:

```
umount /mnt
dd if=DEVICE bs=1k | gzip -v9 > rootfs.gz
```

When this finishes you will have a file `rootfs.gz` that is your compressed root filesystem. You should check its size to make sure it will fit on a diskette; if it doesn't you'll have to go back and remove some files. Section 8.1 (Reducing root filesystem size) has some hints for reducing the size of the root filesystem.

5 Choosing a kernel.

At this point you have a complete compressed root filesystem. The next step is to build or select a kernel. In most cases it would be possible to copy your current kernel and boot the diskette from that. However, there may be cases where you wish to build a separate one.

One reason is size. If you are building a single boot/root diskette, the kernel will be one of the largest files on the diskette so you will have to reduce the size of the kernel as much as possible. To reduce kernel size, build it with the minumum set of facilities necessary to support the desired system. This means leaving out everything you don't need. Networking is a good thing to leave out, as well as support for any disk drives and other devices which you don't need when running your boot/root system. As stated before, your kernel *must* have ramdisk and ext2 support built into it.

Having worked out a minimum set of facilities to include in a kernel, you then need to work out what to add back in. Probably the most common uses for a boot/root diskette system would be to examine and restore a corrupted root file system, and to do this you may need kernel support. For example, if your backups are all held on tape using Ftape to access your tape drive, then, if you lose your current root drive and drives containing Ftape, then you will not be able to restore from your backup tapes. You will have to reinstall Linux, download and reinstall ftape, and then try to read your backups.

The point here is that, whatever I/O support you have added to your kernel to support backups should also be added into your boot/root kernel.

The procedure for actually building the kernel is described in the documentation that comes with the kernel. It is quite easy to follow, so start by looking in `/usr/src/linux`. If you have trouble building a kernel, you should probably not attempt to build boot/root systems anyway. Remember to compress the kernel with "`make zImage`".

6 Putting them together: Making the diskette(s).

At this point you have a kernel and a compressed root filesystem. If you are making a boot/root disk, check their sizes to make sure they will both fit on one disk. If you are making a two disk boot+root set, check the root filesystem to make sure it will fit on a single diskette.

You should decide whether to use LILO to boot the bootdisk kernel. The alternative is to copy the kernel directly to the diskette and boot without LILO. The advantage of using LILO is that it enables you to supply some parameters to the kernel which may be necessary to initialize your hardware (Check the file `/etc/lilo.conf` on your system. If it exists and has a line like "`append=...`", you probably need this feature). The disadvantage of using LILO is that building the bootdisk is more complicated, and takes slightly more space. You will have to set up a small separate filesystem, which we shall call the **kernel filesystem**, where you transfer the kernel and a few other files that LILO needs.

If you are going to use LILO, read on; if you are going to transfer the kernel directly, skip ahead to the section 6.2 (Without using LILO).

6.1 Transferring the kernel with LILO .

The first thing you must do is create a small configuration file for LILO. It should look like this:

```
boot       =/dev/fd0
install    =/boot/boot.b
map        =/boot/map
read-write
backup     =/dev/null
compact
image      = KERNEL
label      = Bootdisk
root       =/dev/fd0
```

For an explanation of these parameters, see LILO's user documentation. You will probably also want to add an `append=...` line to this file from your hard disk's `/etc/lilo.conf` file.

Save this file as `bdlilo.conf`.

You now have to create a small filesystem, which we shall call a **kernel filesystem**, to distinguish it from the root filesystem.

First, figure out how large the filesystem should be. Take the size of your kernel in blocks (the size shown by "`ls -l KERNEL`" divided by 1024 and rounded up) and add 50. Fifty blocks is approximately the space needed for inodes plus other files. You can calculate this number exactly if you want to, or just use 50. If you're creating a two-disk set, you may as well overestimate the space since the first disk is only used for the kernel anyway. Call this number `KERNEL_BLOCKS`.

Put a floppy diskette in the drive (for simplicity we'll assume `/dev/fd0`) and create an ext2 kernel filesystem on it:

```
mke2fs -i 8192 -m 0 /dev/fd0 KERNEL_BLOCKS
```

The "`-i 8192`" specifies that we want one inode per 8192 bytes. Next, mount the filesystem, remove the `lost+found` directory, and create `dev` and `boot` directories for LILO:

```
mount /dev/fd0 /mnt
rm -rf /mnt/lost+found
mkdir /mnt/{boot,dev}
```

Next, create devices `/dev/null` and `/dev/fd0`. Instead of looking up the device numbers, you can just copy them from your hard disk using `-R`:

```
cp -R /dev/{null,fd0} /mnt/dev
```

LILO needs a copy of its boot loader, `boot.b`, which you can take from your hard disk. It is usually kept in the `/boot` directory.

```
cp /boot/boot.b /mnt/boot
```

Finally, copy in the LILO configuration file you created in the last section, along with your kernel. Both can be put in the root directory:

```
cp bdlilo.conf KERNEL /mnt
```

Everything LILO needs is now on the kernel filesystem, so you are ready to run it. LILO's `-r` flag is used for installing the boot loader on some other root:

```
lilo -v -C bdlilo.conf -r /mnt
```

LILO should run without error, after which the kernel filesystem should look something like this:

```
total 361
    1 -rw-r--r--   1 root     root         176 Jan 10 07:22 bdlilo.conf
    1 drwxr-xr-x   2 root     root        1024 Jan 10 07:23 boot/
    1 drwxr-xr-x   2 root     root        1024 Jan 10 07:22 dev/
  358 -rw-r--r--   1 root     root      362707 Jan 10 07:23 vmlinuz
boot:
total 8
    4 -rw-r--r--   1 root     root        3708 Jan 10 07:22 boot.b
    4 -rw-------   1 root     root        3584 Jan 10 07:23 map
dev:
total 0
    0 brw-r-----   1 root     root       2,   0 Jan 10 07:22 fd0
    0 crw-r--r--   1 root     root       1,   3 Jan 10 07:22 null
```

Do not worry if the file sizes are slightly different from yours.

Now leave the disk in the drive and go to section 6.3 (Setting the ramdisk word).

6.2 Transferring the kernel without LILO.

If you are *not* using LILO, transfer the kernel to the bootdisk with the `dd` command:

```
% dd if=KERNEL of=/dev/fd0 bs=1k
353+1 records in
353+1 records out
```

In this example, `dd` wrote 353 complete records + 1 partial record, so the kernel occupies the first 354 blocks of the diskette. Call this number KERNEL_BLOCKS and remember it for use in the next section.

Finally, set the root device to be the diskette itself, then set the root to be loaded read/write:

```
rdev /dev/fd0 /dev/fd0
rdev -R /dev/fd0 0
```

Be careful to use a capital `-R` in the second `rdev` command.

6.3 Setting the ramdisk word.

Inside the kernel image is the **ramdisk word** that specifies where the root filesystem is to be found, along with other options. The word is defined in `/usr/src/linux/arch/i386/kernel/setup.c` and is interpreted as follows:

```
bits  0-10:    Offset to start of ramdisk, in 1024 byte blocks
bits 11-13:    unused
bit     14:    Flag indicating that ramdisk is to be loaded
bit     15:    Flag indicating to prompt before loading rootfs
```

If bit 15 is set, on boot-up you will be prompted to place a new floppy diskette in the drive. This is necessary for a two-disk boot set.

There are two cases, depending on whether you are building a single boot/root diskette or a double "boot+root" diskette set.

1. If you are building a single disk, the compressed root filesystem will be placed right after the kernel, so the offset will be the first free block (which should be the same as KERNEL_BLOCKS). Bit 14 will be set to 1, and bit 15 will be zero.

2. If you are building a two-disk set, the root filesystem will begin at block zero of the second disk, so the offset will be zero. Bit 14 will be set to 1, and bit 15 will be 1.

After carefully calculating the value for the ramdisk word, set it with `rdev -r`. Be sure to use the *decimal* value. If you used LILO, the argument to `rdev` here should be the *mounted kernel path*, e.g. `/mnt/vmlinuz`; if you copied the kernel with `dd`, instead use the floppy device name (*e.g.*, `/dev/fd0`).

```
rdev -r KERNEL_OR_FLOPPY_DRIVE  VALUE
```

If you used LILO, unmount the diskette now.

HOWTO

6.4   Transferring the root filesystem.

The last step is to transfer the root filesystem.

- If the root filesystem will be placed on the *same* disk as the kernel, transfer it using dd with the seek option, which specifies how many blocks to skip:

> dd if=rootfs.gz of=/dev/fd0 bs=1k seek=KERNEL_BLOCKS

- If the root filesystem will be placed on a *second* disk, remove the first diskette, put the second diskette in the drive, then transfer the root filesystem to it:

> dd if=rootfs.gz of=/dev/fd0 bs=1k

Congratulations, you are done! *You should always test a bootdisk before putting it aside for an emergency!* If it fails to boot, read on.

7   Troubleshooting, or The Agony of Defeat.

When building bootdisks, the first few tries often will not boot. The general approach to building a root disk is to assemble components from your existing system, and try and get the diskette-based system to the point where it displays messages on the console. Once it starts talking to you, the battle is half over because you can see what it is complaining about, and you can fix individual problems until the system works smoothly. If the system just hangs with no explanation, finding the cause can be difficult. To get a system to boot to the stage where it will talk to you requires several components to be present and correctly configured. The recommended procedure for investigating the problem where the system will not talk to you is as follows:

- Check that the root disk actually contains the directories you think it does. It is easy to copy at the wrong level so that you end up with something like /rootdisk/bin instead of /bin on your root diskette.
- Check that there is a /lib/libc.so with the same link that appears in your /lib directory on your hard disk.
- Check that any symbolic links in your /dev directory in your existing system also exist on your root diskette filesystem, where those links are to devices which you have included in your root diskette. In particular, /dev/console links are essential in many cases.
- Check that you have included /dev/tty1, /dev/null, /dev/zero, /dev/mem, /dev/ram and /dev/kmem files.
- Check your kernel configuration – support for all resources required up to login point must be built in, not modules. So *ramdisk and ext2 support must be built-in.*
- Check that your kernel root device and ramdisk settings are correct.

Once these general aspects have been covered, here are some more specific files to check:

1. Make sure init is included as /sbin/init or /bin/init. Make sure it is executable.
2. Run ldd init to check init's libraries. Usually this is just libc.so, but check anyway. Make sure you included the necessary libraries and loaders.
3. Make sure you have the right loader for your libraries – ld.so for a.out or ld-linux.so for ELF.
4. Check the /etc/inittab on your bootdisk filesystem for the calls to getty (or some getty-like program, such as agetty, mgetty or getty_ps). Double-check these against your hard disk inittab. Check the man pages of the program you use to make sure these make sense. inittab is possibly the trickiest part because its syntax and content depend on the init program used and the nature of the system. The only way to tackle it is to read the man pages for init and inittab and work out exactly what your existing system is doing when it boots. Check to make sure /etc/inittab has a system initialisation entry. This should contain a command to execute the system initialization script, which must exist.

5. As with `init`, run `ldd` on your `getty` to see what it needs, and make sure the necessary library files and loaders were included in your root filesystem.

6. Be sure you have included a shell program (e.g., `bash` or `ash`) capable of running all of your rc scripts.

7. If you have a `/etc/ld.so.cache` file on your rescue disk, remake it.

If `init` starts, but you get a message like:

```
Id xxx respawning too fast: disabled for 5 minutes
```

it is coming from `init`, usually indicating that `getty` or `login` is dying as soon as it starts up. Check the `getty` and `login` executables and the libraries they depend upon. Make sure the invocations in `/etc/inittab` are correct. If you get strange messages from `getty`, it may mean the calling form in `/etc/inittab` is wrong. The options of the *getty* programs are variable; even different versions of `agetty` are reported to have different incompatible calling forms.

If you get a login prompt, and you enter a valid login name but the system prompts you for another login name immediately, the problem may be with PAM or NSS. See Section 4.4 (PAM and NSS). The problem may also be that you use shadow passwords and didn't copy `/etc/shadow` to your bootdisk.

If you try to run some executable, such as `df`, which is on your rescue disk but you yields a message like: `df:    not found`, check two things: (1) Make sure the directory containing the binary is in your PATH, and (2) make sure you have libraries (and loaders) the program needs.

8 Miscellaneous topics.

8.1 Reducing root filesystem size.

Sometimes a root filesystem is too large to fit on a diskette even after compression. Here are some ways to reduce the filesystem size, listed in decreasing order of effectiveness:

Increase the disk density

By default, floppy diskettes are formatted at 1440K, but higher density formats are available. `fdformat` will format disks for the following sizes: 1600, 1680, 1722, 1743, 1760, 1840, and 1920. Most 1440K drives will support 1722K, and this is what I always use for bootdisks. See the `fdformat` man page and `/usr/src/linux/Documentation/devices.txt`.

Replace your shell

Some of the popular shells for Linux, such as `bash` and `tcsh`, are large and require many libraries. Light-weight alternatives exist, such as `ash`, `lsh`, `kiss` and `smash`, which are much smaller and require few (or no) libraries. Most of these replacement shells are available from `<http://sunsite.unc.edu/pub/Linux/system/shells/>`. Make sure any shell you use is capable of running commands in all the `rc` files you include on your bootdisk.

Strip libraries and binaries

Many libraries and binaries are typically unstripped (include debugging symbols). Running `'file'` on these files will tell you `'not stripped'` if so. When copying binaries to your root filesystem, it is good practice to use:

```
objcopy --strip-all FROM TO
```

When copying libraries, use:

```
objcopy --strip-debug FROM TO
```

Move non-critical files to a utility disk

If some of your binaries are not needed immediately to boot or login, you can move them to a utility disk. See section 8.3 (Building a utility disk) for details. You may also consider moving modules to a utility disk as well.

8.2   Non-ramdisk root filesystems.

Section 4 (Building a root filesystem) gave instructions for building a compressed root filesystem which is loaded to ramdisk when the system boots. This method has many advantages so it is commonly used. However, some systems with little memory cannot afford the RAM needed for this, and they must use root filesystems mounted directly from the diskette.

Such filesystems are actually easier to build than compressed root filesystems because they can be built on a diskette rather than on some other device, and they do not have to be compressed. We will outline the procedure as it differs from the instructions above. If you choose to do this, keep in mind that you will have *much less space* available.

1. Calculate how much space you will have available for root files.

   If you are building a single boot/root disk, you must fit all blocks for the kernel plus all blocks for the root filesystem on the one disk.

2. Using mke2fs, create a root filesystem on a diskette of the appropriate size.

3. Populate the filesystem as described above.

4. When done, unmount the filesystem and transfer it to a disk file but *do not compress it*.

5. Transfer the kernel to a floppy diskette, as described above. When calculating the ramdisk word, **set bit 14 to zero**, to indicate that the root filesystem is not to be loaded to ramdisk. Run the rdev's as described.

6. Transfer the root filesystem as before.

There are several shortcuts you can take. If you are building a two-disk set, you can build the complete root filesystem directly on the second disk and you need not transfer it to a hard disk file and then back. Also, if you are building a single boot/root disk and using LILO, you can build a *single* filesystem on the entire disk, containing the kernel, LILO files and root files, and simply run LILO as the last step.

8.3   Building a utility disk.

Building a utility disk is relatively easy – simply create a filesystem on a formatted disk and copy files to it. To use it with a bootdisk, mount it manually after the system is booted.

In the instructions above, we mentioned that the utility disk could be mounted as /usr. In this case, binaries could be placed into a /bin directory on your utility disk, so that placing /usr/bin in your path will access them. Additional libraries needed by the binaries are placed in /lib on the utility disk.

There are several important points to keep in mind when designing a utility disk:

1. Do not place critical system binaries or libraries onto the utility disk, since it will not be mountable until after the system has booted.

2. You cannot access a floppy diskette and a floppy tape drive simultaneously. This means that if you have a floppy tape drive, you will not be able to access it while your utility disk is mounted.

3. Access to files on the utility disk will be slow.

Appendix 14 (Sample utility disk directory listing) shows a sample of files on a utility disk. Here are some ideas for files you may find useful: programs for examining and manipulating disks (format, fdisk) and filesystems (mke2fs, fsck, debugfs, isofs.o), a lightweight text editor (elvis, jove), compression and archive utilities (gzip, tar, cpio, afio), tape utilities (mt, tob, taper), communications utilities (ppp.o, slip.o, minicom) and utilities for devices (setserial, mknod).

9 How the pros do it.

You may notice that the bootdisks used by major distributions such as Slackware, RedHat or Debian, seem more sophisticated than what is described in this document. Professional distribution bootdisks are based on the same principles outlined here, but employ various tricks because their bootdisks have additional requirements. First, they must be able to work with a wide variety of hardware, so they must be able to interact with the user and load various device drivers. Second, they must be prepared to work with many different installation options, with varying degrees of automation. Finally, distribution bootdisks usually combine installation and rescue capabilities.

Some bootdisks use a feature called **initrd** (**initial ramdisk**). This feature was introduced around 2.0.x and allows a kernel to boot in two phases. When the kernel first boots, it loads an initial ramdisk image from the boot disk. This initial ramdisk is a root filesystem containing a program that runs before the real root fs is loaded. This program usually inspects the environment and/or asks the user to select various boot options, such as the device from which to load the real rootdisk. It typically loads additional modules not built in to the kernel. When this initial program exits, the kernel loads the real root image and booting continues normally. For further information on initrd, see /usr/src/ linux/Documentation/initrd.txt and <ftp://elserv.ffm.fgan.de/pub/linux/loadlin-1. 6/initrd-example.tgz>

The following are summaries of how each distribution's installation disks seem to work, based on inspecting their filesystems and/or source code. We do not guarantee that this information is completely accurate, or that they have not changed since the versions noted.

Slackware (v.3.1) uses a straightforward LILO boot similar to what is described in section 6.1 (Transferring the kernel with LILO). The Slackware bootdisk prints a bootup message ("Welcome to the Slackware Linux bootkernel disk!") using LILO's message parameter. This instructs the user to enter a boot parameter line if necessary. After booting, a root filesystem is loaded from a second disk. The user invokes a setup script which starts the installation. Instead of using a modular kernel, Slackware provides many different kernels and depends upon the user to select the one matching his or her hardware requirements.

RedHat (v.4.0) also uses a LILO boot. It loads a compressed ramdisk on the first disk, which runs a custom init program. This program queries for drivers, and loads additional files from a supplemental disk if necessary.

Debian (v.1.3) is probably the most sophisticated of the installation disk sets. It uses the SYSLINUX loader to arrange various load options, then uses an initrd image to guide the user through installation. It appears to use both a customized init and a customized shell.

10 Frequently asked question (FAQ) list.

Q. I boot from my boot/root disks and nothing happens. What do I do?

See section 3.10 (Troubleshooting), above.

Q. How does the Slackware/Debian/RedHat bootdisk work?

See section 9 (What the pros do), above.

Q. How can I make a boot disk with a XYZ driver?

The easiest way is to obtain a Slackware kernel from your nearest Slackware mirror site. Slackware kernels are generic kernels which atttempt to include drivers for as many devices as possible, so if you have a SCSI or IDE controller, chances are that a driver for it is included in the Slackware kernel.

Go to the a1 directory and select either IDE or SCSI kernel depending on the type of controller you have. Check the xxxxkern.cfg file for the selected kernel to see the drivers which have been included in that kernel. If the device you want is in that list, then the corresponding kernel should boot your computer. Download the xxxxkern.tgz file and copy it to your boot diskette as described above in the section on making boot disks.

You must then check the root device in the kernel, using the rdev command:

```
rdev zImage
```

`rdev` will then display the current root device in the kernel. If this is not the same as the root device you want, then use `rdev` to change it. For example, the kernel I tried was set to `/dev/sda2`, but my root SCSI partition is `/dev/sda8`. To use a root diskette, you would have to use the command:

```
rdev zImage /dev/fd0
```

If you want to know how to set up a Slackware root disk as well, that's outside the scope of this HOWTO, so I suggest you check the Linux Install Guide or get the Slackware distribution. See the section in this HOWTO titled "References".

Q. How do I update my boot diskette with a new kernel?

Just copy the kernel to your boot diskette using the dd command for a boot diskette without a filesystem, or the cp command for a boot/root disk. Refer to the section in this HOWTO titled "Boot" for details on creating a boot disk. The description applies equally to updating a kernel on a boot disk.

Q. How do I update my root diskette with new files?

The easiest way is to copy the filesystem from the rootdisk back to the DEVICE you used (from section 4.2 (Creating the filesystem), above). Then mount the filesystem and make the changes. You have to remember where your root filesystem started and how many blocks it occupied:

```
dd if=/dev/fd0 bs=1k skip=ROOTBEGIN count=BLOCKS | gunzip > DEVICE
mount -t ext2 DEVICE /mnt
```

After making the changes, proceed as before (in Section 4.7 (Wrapping it up)) and transfer the root filesystem back to the disk. You should not have to re-transfer the kernel or re-compute the ramdisk word if you do not change the starting position of the new root filesystem.

Q. How do I remove LILO so that I can use DOS to boot again?

This is not really a Bootdisk topic, but it is asked often. Within Linux, you can run:

```
/sbin/lilo -u
```

You can also use the dd command to copy the backup saved by LILO to the boot sector. Refer to the LILO documentation if you wish to do this.

Within DOS and Windows you can use the DOS command:

```
FDISK /MBR
```

MBR stands for Master Boot Record, and it replaces the boot sector with a clean DOS one, without affecting the partition table. Some purists disagree with this, but even the author of LILO, Werner Almesberger, suggests it. It is easy, and it works.

Q. How can I boot if I've lost my kernel *and* my boot disk?

If you don't have a boot disk standing by, probably the easiest method is to obtain a Slackware kernel for your disk controller type (IDE or SCSI) as described above for "How do I make a boot disk with a XXX driver?". You can then boot your computer using this kernel, then repair whatever damage there is.

The kernel you get may not have the root device set to the disk type and partition you want. For example, Slackware's generic SCSI kernel has the root device set to `/dev/sda2`, whereas my root Linux partition happens to be `/dev/sda8`. In this case the root device in the kernel will have to be changed.

You can still change the root device and ramdisk settings in the kernel even if all you have is a kernel, and some other operating system, such as DOS.

rdev changes kernel settings by changing the values at fixed offsets in the kernel file, so you can do the same if you have a hex editor available on whatever systems you do still have running – for example, Norton Utilities Disk Editor under DOS. You then need to check and if necessary change the values in the kernel at the following offsets:

```
HEX      DEC   DESCRIPTION
0x01F8   504   Low byte of RAMDISK word
0x01F9   505   High byte of RAMDISK word
0x01FC   508   Root minor device number - see below
0X01FD   509   Root major device number - see below
```

The interpretation of the ramdisk word was described in Section 6.3 (Setting the ramdisk word), above.

The major and minor device numbers must be set to the device you want to mount your root filesystem on. Some useful values to select from are:

```
DEVICE        MAJOR MINOR
/dev/fd0        2     0    1st floppy drive
/dev/hda1       3     1    partition 1 on 1st IDE drive
/dev/sda1       8     1    partition 1 on 1st SCSI drive
/dev/sda8       8     8    partition 8 on 1st SCSI drive
```

Once you have set these values then you can write the file to a diskette using either Norton Utilities Disk Editor, or a program called rawrite.exe. This program is included in all distributions. It is a DOS program which writes a file to the "raw" disk, starting at the boot sector, instead of writing it to the file system. If you use Norton Utilities you must write the file to a physical disk starting at the beginning of the disk.

Q. How can I make extra copies of boot/root diskettes?

Because magnetic media may deteriorate over time, you should keep several copies of your rescue disk, in case the original is unreadable.

The easiest way of making copies of any diskettes, including bootable and utility diskettes, is to use the dd command to copy the contents of the original diskette to a file on your hard drive, and then use the same command to copy the file back to a new diskette. Note that you do not need to, and should not, mount the diskettes, because dd uses the raw device interface.

To copy the original, enter the command:

```
dd if=DEVICENAME of=FILENAME
where   DEVICENAME is the device name of the diskette drive
and     FILENAME is the name of the (hard-disk) output file
```

Omitting the count parameter causes dd to copy the whole diskette (2880 blocks if high-density).

To copy the resulting file back to a new diskette, insert the new diskette and enter the reverse command:

```
dd if=FILENAME of=DEVICENAME
```

Note that the above discussion assumes that you have only one diskette drive. If you have two of the same type, you can copy diskettes using a command like:

```
dd if=/dev/fd0 of=/dev/fd1
```

HOWTO

Q. How can I boot without typing in "ahaxxxx=nn,nn,nn" every time?

Where a disk device cannot be autodetected it is necessary to supply the kernel with a command device parameter string, such as:

```
aha152x=0x340,11,3,1
```

This parameter string can be supplied in several ways using LILO:

- By entering it on the command line every time the system is booted via LILO. This is boring, though.
- By using the LILO "`lock`" keyword to make it store the command line as the default command line, so that LILO will use the same options every time it boots.
- By using the `append=` statement in the LILO config file. Note that the parameter string must be enclosed in quotes.

For example, a sample command line using the above parameter string would be:

```
zImage  aha152x=0x340,11,3,1 root=/dev/sda1 lock
```

This would pass the device parameter string through, and also ask the kernel to set the root device to `/dev/sda1` and save the whole command line and reuse it for all future boots.

A sample APPEND statement is:

```
APPEND = "aha152x=0x340,11,3,1"
```

Note that the parameter string must NOT be enclosed in quotes on the command line, but it MUST be enclosed in quotes in the APPEND statement.

Note also that for the parameter string to be acted on, the kernel must contain the driver for that disk type. If it does not, then there is nothing listening for the parameter string, and you will have to rebuild the kernel to include the required driver. For details on rebuilding the kernel, cd to `/usr/src/linux` and read the README, and read the Linux FAQ and Installation HOWTO. Alternatively you could obtain a generic kernel for the disk type and install that.

Readers are strongly urged to read the LILO documentation before experimenting with LILO installation. Incautious use of the BOOT statement can damage partitions.

Q. At boot time, I get error "A: cannot execute B". Why?

There are several cases of program names being hardcoded in various utilities. These cases do not occur everywhere, but they may explain why an executable apparently cannot be found on your system even though you can see that it is there. You can find out if a given program has the name of another hardcoded by using the `strings` command and piping the output through `grep`.

Known examples of hardcoding are:

- Shutdown in some versions has `/etc/reboot` hardcoded, so `reboot` must be placed in the `/etc` directory.
- `init` has caused problems for at least one person, with the kernel being unable to find `init`.

To fix these problems, either move the programs to the correct directory, or change configuration files (e.g. `inittab`) to point to the correct directory. If in doubt, put programs in the same directories as they are on your hard disk, and use the same `inittab` and `/etc/rc.d` files as they appear on your hard disk.

Q. My kernel has ramdisk support, but initializes ramdisks of 0K

Where this occurs, a kernel message like this will appear as the kernel is booting:

```
Ramdisk driver initialized : 16 ramdisks of 0K size
```

This is probably because the size has been set to 0 by kernel parameters at boot time. This could possibly be because of an overlooked LILO configuration file parameter:

```
ramdisk= 0
```

This was included in sample LILO configuration files in some older distributions, and was put there to override any previous kernel setting. If you have such a line, remove it.

Note that if you attempt to use a ramdisk which has been set to 0K the behaviour can be unpredictable, and can result in kernel panics.

11 Resources and pointers.

When retrieving a package, always get the latest version unless you have good reasons for not doing so.

11.1 Pre-made bootdisks.

These are sources for distribution bootdisks. *Please use one of the mirror sites to reduce the load on these machines.*

- *Slackware bootdisks* <http://sunsite.unc.edu/pub/Linux/distributions/slackware/bootdsks.144/> and *Slackware mirror sites* <http://sunsite.unc.edu/pub/Linux/distributions/slackware/MIRRORS.TXT>

- *RedHat bootdisks* <http://sunsite.unc.edu/pub/Linux/distributions/redhat/current/i386/images/> and *Red Hat mirror sites* <http://www.redhat.com/ftp.html>

- *Debian bootdisks* <ftp://ftp.debian.org/pub/debian/dists/stable/main/disks-i386/current/> and *Debian mirror sites* <ftp://ftp.debian.org/pub/debian/README.mirrors.html>

In addition to the distribution bootdisks, the following rescue disk images are available. Unless otherwise specified, these are available in the directory <http://sunsite.unc.edu/pub/Linux/system/recovery/>

- tomsrtbt, by Tom Oehser, is a single-disk boot/root disk based on kernel 2.0.33, with a large list of features and support programs. It supports IDE, SCSI, tape, network adaptors, PCMCIA and more. About 100 utility programs and tools are included for fixing and restoring disks. The package also includes scripts for disassembling and reconstructing the images so that new material can be added if necessary.

- rescue02, by John Comyns, is a rescue disk based on kernel 1.3.84, with support for IDE and Adaptec 1542 and NCR53C7,8xx. It uses ELF binaries but it has enough commands so that it can be used on any system. There are modules that can be loaded after booting for all other SCSI cards. It probably won't work on systems with 4 mb of ram since it uses a 3 mb ram disk.

- resque_disk-2.0.22, by Sergei Viznyuk, is a full-featured boot/root disk based on kernel 2.0.22 with built-in support for IDE, many difference SCSI controllers, and ELF/AOUT. Also includes many modules and useful utilities for repairing and restoring a hard disk.

- cramdisk images, based on the 2.0.23 kernel, available for 4 meg and 8 meg machines. They include math emulation and networking (PPP and dialin script, NE2000, 3C509), or support for the parallel port ZIP drive. These diskette images will boot on a 386 with 4MB RAM. MSDOS support is included so you can download from the net to a DOS partition. <http://sunsite.unc.edu/pub/Linux/system/recovery/images>

11.2   Rescue packages.

Several packages for creating rescue disks are available on sunsite.unc.edu. With these packages you generally specify a set of files for inclusion and the software automates (to varying degrees) the creation of a bootdisk. See <http://sunsite.unc.edu/pub/Linux/system/recovery/!INDEX.html> for more information. **Check the file dates carefully** – some of these packages have not been updated in several years and will not support the creation of a compressed root filesystem loaded into ramdisk. To the best of our knowledge, Yard is the only package that will.

11.3   Graham Chapman's shell scripts

Graham Chapman has written a set of scripts that may be useful as examples of how to create bootdisks. In previous versions of this HOWTO the scripts appeared in an appendix, but they have been deleted from the documented and placed on a web page:

<http://www.zeta.org.au/grahamc/linux.html>

You may find it convenient to use these scripts, but if so, read the instructions carefully – for example, if you specify the wrong swap device, you will find your root filesystem has been throroughly and permanently erased. Be sure you have it correctly configured before you use it!

11.4   LILO – the Linux loader.

Written by Werner Almesberger. Excellent boot loader, and the documentation includes information on the boot sector contents and the early stages of the boot process.

Ftp from <ftp://tsx-11.mit.edu/pub/linux/packages/lilo/>. It is also available on Sunsite and mirrors.

11.5   Linux FAQ and HOWTOs.

These are available from many sources. Look at the usenet newsgroups news.answers and comp.os.linux.announce.

The FAQ is available from <http://sunsite.unc.edu/pub/Linux/docs/faqs/linux-faq> and the HOWTOs from <http://sunsite.unc.edu/pub/Linux/docs/HOWTO>.

Most documentation for Linux may be found at *The Linux Documentation Project homepage* <http://sunsite.unc.edu/LDP/ldp.html>.

If desperate, send mail to mail-server@rtfm.mit.edu with the word "help" in the message, then follow the mailed instructions.

11.6   Ramdisk usage.

An excellent description of the how the new ramdisk code works may be found with the documentation supplied with the Linux kernel. See /usr/src/linux/Documentation/ramdisk.txt. It is written by Paul Gortmaker and includes a section on creating a compressed ramdisk.

11.7   The Linux boot process.

For more detail on the Linux boot process, here are some pointers:

- The Linux System Administrators' Guide has a section on booting, See <http://sunsite.unc.edu/LDP/LDP/sag/node68.html>

- The LILO "Technical overview" <http://sunsite.unc.edu/pub/Linux/system/boot/lilo/lilo-t-20.ps.gz> has the definitive technical, low-level description of the boot process, up to where the kernel is started.

- The source code is the ultimate guide. Below are some kernel files related to the boot process. If you have the Linux kernel source code, you can find these under /usr/src/linux on your machine; alternatively, Shigio Yamaguchi (shigio@wafu.netgate.net) has a very nice hypertext kernel browser at <http://wafu.netgate.net/linux/>. Here are some relevant files:

  arch/i386/boot/bootsect.S,setup.S

  Contain assembly code for the bootsector.

  arch/i386/boot/compressed/misc.c

  Contains code for uncompressing the kernel.

  arch/i386/kernel/

  Directory containing kernel initialization code. setup.c contains the ramdisk word.

  drivers/block/rd.c

  Contains the ramdisk driver. The procedures rd_load and rd_load_image load blocks from a device into a ramdisk. The procedure identify_ramdisk_image determines what kind of filesystem is found and whether it is compressed.

12   LILO boot error codes.

Questions about these errors are asked so often on Usenet that we include them here as a public service. This summary is excerpted from Werner Almsberger's LILO User Documentation, available at <http://sunsite.unc.edu/pub/Linux/system/boot/lilo/lilo-u-20.ps.gz>.

When LILO loads itself, it displays the word "LILO". Each letter is printed before or after performing some specific action. If LILO fails at some point, the letters printed so far can be used to identify the problem.

(nothing)

No part of LILO has been loaded. LILO either isn't installed or the partition on which its boot sector is located isn't active.

L

The first stage boot loader has been loaded and started, but it can't load the second stage boot loader. The two-digit error codes indicate the type of problem. (See also section "Disk error codes".) This condition usually indicates a media failure or a geometry mismatch (e.g. bad disk parameters)

LI

The first stage boot loader was able to load the second stage boot loader, but has failed to execute it. This can either be caused by a geometry mismatch or by moving /boot/boot.b without running the map installer.

LIL

The second stage boot loader has been started, but it can't load the descriptor table from the map file. This is typically caused by a media failure or by a geometry mismatch.

LIL?

The second stage boot loader has been loaded at an incorrect address. This is typically caused by a subtle geometry mismatch or by moving /boot/boot.b without running the map installer.

LIL-

The descriptor table is corrupt. This can either be caused by a geometry mismatch or by moving /boot/map without running the map installer.

LILO

All parts of LILO have been successfully loaded.

If the BIOS signals an error when LILO is trying to load a boot image, the respective error code is displayed. These codes range from 0x00 through 0xbb. See the LILO User Guide for an explanation of these.

13 Sample rootdisk directory listings.

Here are the contents of a sample root filesystem and a utility diskette.

```
Root directory:
drwx--x--x  2 root    root      1024 Nov  1 15:39 bin
drwx--x--x  2 root    root      4096 Nov  1 15:39 dev
drwx--x--x  3 root    root      1024 Nov  1 15:39 etc
drwx--x--x  4 root    root      1024 Nov  1 15:39 lib
drwx--x--x  5 root    root      1024 Nov  1 15:39 mnt
drwx--x--x  2 root    root      1024 Nov  1 15:39 proc
drwx--x--x  2 root    root      1024 Nov  1 15:39 root
drwx--x--x  2 root    root      1024 Nov  1 15:39 sbin
drwx--x--x  2 root    root      1024 Nov  1 15:39 tmp
drwx--x--x  7 root    root      1024 Nov  1 15:39 usr
drwx--x--x  5 root    root      1024 Nov  1 15:39 var

/bin:
-rwx--x--x  1 root    root     62660 Nov  1 15:39 ash
-rwx--x--x  1 root    root      9032 Nov  1 15:39 cat
-rwx--x--x  1 root    root     10276 Nov  1 15:39 chmod
-rwx--x--x  1 root    root      9592 Nov  1 15:39 chown
-rwx--x--x  1 root    root     23124 Nov  1 15:39 cp
-rwx--x--x  1 root    root     23028 Nov  1 15:39 date
-rwx--x--x  1 root    root     14052 Nov  1 15:39 dd
-rwx--x--x  1 root    root     14144 Nov  1 15:39 df
-rwx--x--x  1 root    root     69444 Nov  1 15:39 egrep
-rwx--x--x  1 root    root       395 Nov  1 15:39 false
-rwx--x--x  1 root    root     69444 Nov  1 15:39 fgrep
-rwx--x--x  1 root    root     69444 Nov  1 15:39 grep
-rwx--x--x  3 root    root     45436 Nov  1 15:39 gunzip
-rwx--x--x  3 root    root     45436 Nov  1 15:39 gzip
-rwx--x--x  1 root    root      8008 Nov  1 15:39 hostname
-rwx--x--x  1 root    root     12736 Nov  1 15:39 ln
-rws--x--x  1 root    root     15284 Nov  1 15:39 login
-rwx--x--x  1 root    root     29308 Nov  1 15:39 ls
-rwx--x--x  1 root    root      8268 Nov  1 15:39 mkdir
-rwx--x--x  1 root    root      8920 Nov  1 15:39 mknod
-rwx--x--x  1 root    root     24836 Nov  1 15:39 more
-rws--x--x  1 root    root     37640 Nov  1 15:39 mount
-rwx--x--x  1 root    root     12240 Nov  1 15:39 mt
-rwx--x--x  1 root    root     12932 Nov  1 15:39 mv
-r-x--x--x  1 root    root     12324 Nov  1 15:39 ps
-rwx--x--x  1 root    root      5388 Nov  1 15:39 pwd
-rwx--x--x  1 root    root     10092 Nov  1 15:39 rm
lrwxrwxrwx  1 root    root         3 Nov  1 15:39 sh -> ash
-rwx--x--x  1 root    root     25296 Nov  1 15:39 stty
-rws--x--x  1 root    root     12648 Nov  1 15:39 su
-rwx--x--x  1 root    root      4444 Nov  1 15:39 sync
-rwx--x--x  1 root    root    110668 Nov  1 15:39 tar
-rwx--x--x  1 root    root     19712 Nov  1 15:39 touch
-rwx--x--x  1 root    root       395 Nov  1 15:39 true
-rws--x--x  1 root    root     19084 Nov  1 15:39 umount
-rwx--x--x  1 root    root      5368 Nov  1 15:39 uname
-rwx--x--x  3 root    root     45436 Nov  1 15:39 zcat
```

```
/dev:
lrwxrwxrwx   1 root     root                6 Nov  1 15:39 cdrom -> cdu31a
brw-rw-r--   1 root     root           15,   0 May  5  1998 cdu31a
crw-------   1 root     root            4,   0 Nov  1 15:29 console
crw-rw-rw-   1 root     uucp            5,  64 Sep  9 19:46 cua0
crw-rw-rw-   1 root     uucp            5,  65 May  5  1998 cua1
crw-rw-rw-   1 root     uucp            5,  66 May  5  1998 cua2
crw-rw-rw-   1 root     uucp            5,  67 May  5  1998 cua3
brw-rw----   1 root     floppy          2,   0 Aug  8 13:54 fd0
brw-rw----   1 root     floppy          2,  36 Aug  8 13:54 fd0CompaQ
brw-rw----   1 root     floppy          2,  84 Aug  8 13:55 fd0D1040
brw-rw----   1 root     floppy          2,  88 Aug  8 13:55 fd0D1120
brw-rw----   1 root     floppy          2,  12 Aug  8 13:54 fd0D360
brw-rw----   1 root     floppy          2,  16 Aug  8 13:54 fd0D720
brw-rw----   1 root     floppy          2, 120 Aug  8 13:55 fd0D800
brw-rw----   1 root     floppy          2,  32 Aug  8 13:54 fd0E2880
brw-rw----   1 root     floppy          2, 104 Aug  8 13:55 fd0E3200
brw-rw----   1 root     floppy          2, 108 Aug  8 13:55 fd0E3520
brw-rw----   1 root     floppy          2, 112 Aug  8 13:55 fd0E3840
brw-rw----   1 root     floppy          2,  28 Aug  8 13:54 fd0H1440
brw-rw----   1 root     floppy          2, 124 Aug  8 13:55 fd0H1600
brw-rw----   1 root     floppy          2,  44 Aug  8 13:55 fd0H1680
brw-rw----   1 root     floppy          2,  60 Aug  8 13:55 fd0H1722
brw-rw----   1 root     floppy          2,  76 Aug  8 13:55 fd0H1743
brw-rw----   1 root     floppy          2,  96 Aug  8 13:55 fd0H1760
brw-rw----   1 root     floppy          2, 116 Aug  8 13:55 fd0H1840
brw-rw----   1 root     floppy          2, 100 Aug  8 13:55 fd0H1920
lrwxrwxrwx   1 root     root                7 Nov  1 15:39 fd0H360 -> fd0D360
lrwxrwxrwx   1 root     root                7 Nov  1 15:39 fd0H720 -> fd0D720
brw-rw----   1 root     floppy          2,  52 Aug  8 13:55 fd0H820
brw-rw----   1 root     floppy          2,  68 Aug  8 13:55 fd0H830
brw-rw----   1 root     floppy          2,   4 Aug  8 13:54 fd0d360
brw-rw----   1 root     floppy          2,   8 Aug  8 13:54 fd0h1200
brw-rw----   1 root     floppy          2,  40 Aug  8 13:54 fd0h1440
brw-rw----   1 root     floppy          2,  56 Aug  8 13:55 fd0h1476
brw-rw----   1 root     floppy          2,  72 Aug  8 13:55 fd0h1494
brw-rw----   1 root     floppy          2,  92 Aug  8 13:55 fd0h1600
brw-rw----   1 root     floppy          2,  20 Aug  8 13:54 fd0h360
brw-rw----   1 root     floppy          2,  48 Aug  8 13:55 fd0h410
brw-rw----   1 root     floppy          2,  64 Aug  8 13:55 fd0h420
brw-rw----   1 root     floppy          2,  24 Aug  8 13:54 fd0h720
brw-rw----   1 root     floppy          2,  80 Aug  8 13:55 fd0h880
brw-rw----   1 root     disk            3,   0 May  5  1998 hda
brw-rw----   1 root     disk            3,   1 May  5  1998 hda1
brw-rw----   1 root     disk            3,   2 May  5  1998 hda2
brw-rw----   1 root     disk            3,   3 May  5  1998 hda3
brw-rw----   1 root     disk            3,   4 May  5  1998 hda4
brw-rw----   1 root     disk            3,   5 May  5  1998 hda5
brw-rw----   1 root     disk            3,   6 May  5  1998 hda6
brw-rw----   1 root     disk            3,  64 May  5  1998 hdb
brw-rw----   1 root     disk            3,  65 May  5  1998 hdb1
brw-rw----   1 root     disk            3,  66 May  5  1998 hdb2
brw-rw----   1 root     disk            3,  67 May  5  1998 hdb3
brw-rw----   1 root     disk            3,  68 May  5  1998 hdb4
```

```
brw-rw----    1 root     disk      3,   69 May   5  1998 hdb5
brw-rw----    1 root     disk      3,   70 May   5  1998 hdb6
crw-r-----    1 root     kmem      1,    2 May   5  1998 kmem
crw-r-----    1 root     kmem      1,    1 May   5  1998 mem
lrwxrwxrwx    1 root     root          12 Nov   1 15:39 modem -> ../dev/ttyS1
lrwxrwxrwx    1 root     root          12 Nov   1 15:39 mouse -> ../dev/psaux
crw-rw-rw-    1 root     root      1,    3 May   5  1998 null
crwxrwxrwx    1 root     root     10,    1 Oct   5 20:22 psaux
brw-r-----    1 root     disk      1,    1 May   5  1998 ram
brw-rw----    1 root     disk      1,    0 May   5  1998 ram0
brw-rw----    1 root     disk      1,    1 May   5  1998 ram1
brw-rw----    1 root     disk      1,    2 May   5  1998 ram2
brw-rw----    1 root     disk      1,    3 May   5  1998 ram3
brw-rw----    1 root     disk      1,    4 May   5  1998 ram4
brw-rw----    1 root     disk      1,    5 May   5  1998 ram5
brw-rw----    1 root     disk      1,    6 May   5  1998 ram6
brw-rw----    1 root     disk      1,    7 May   5  1998 ram7
brw-rw----    1 root     disk      1,    8 May   5  1998 ram8
brw-rw----    1 root     disk      1,    9 May   5  1998 ram9
lrwxrwxrwx    1 root     root           4 Nov   1 15:39 ramdisk -> ram0
***   I have only included devices for the IDE partitions I use.
***   If you use SCSI, then use the /dev/sdXX devices instead.
crw-------    1 root     root      4,    0 May   5  1998 tty0
crw--w----    1 root     tty       4,    1 Nov   1 15:39 tty1
crw-------    1 root     root      4,    2 Nov   1 15:29 tty2
crw-------    1 root     root      4,    3 Nov   1 15:29 tty3
crw-------    1 root     root      4,    4 Nov   1 15:29 tty4
crw-------    1 root     root      4,    5 Nov   1 15:29 tty5
crw-------    1 root     root      4,    6 Nov   1 15:29 tty6
crw-------    1 root     root      4,    7 May   5  1998 tty7
crw-------    1 root     tty       4,    8 May   5  1998 tty8
crw-------    1 root     tty       4,    9 May   8 12:57 tty9
crw-rw-rw-    1 root     root      4,   65 Nov   1 12:17 ttyS1
crw-rw-rw-    1 root     root      1,    5 May   5  1998 zero

/etc:
-rw-------    1 root     root         164 Nov   1 15:39 conf.modules
-rw-------    1 root     root         668 Nov   1 15:39 fstab
-rw-------    1 root     root          71 Nov   1 15:39 gettydefs
-rw-------    1 root     root         389 Nov   1 15:39 group
-rw-------    1 root     root         413 Nov   1 15:39 inittab
-rw-------    1 root     root          65 Nov   1 15:39 issue
-rw-r--r--    1 root     root         746 Nov   1 15:39 ld.so.cache
***   ld.so.cache is created by ldconfig and caches library locations.
***   Many things break at boot time if ld.so.cache is missing.
***   You can either remake it after creating the bootdisk, or
***   include ldconfig on the bootdisk and run it from an rc.x script
***   to update the cache.
-rw-------    1 root     root          32 Nov   1 15:39 motd
-rw-------    1 root     root         949 Nov   1 15:39 nsswitch.conf
drwx--x--x    2 root     root        1024 Nov   1 15:39 pam.d
-rw-------    1 root     root         139 Nov   1 15:39 passwd
-rw-------    1 root     root         516 Nov   1 15:39 profile
-rwx--x--x    1 root     root         387 Nov   1 15:39 rc
-rw-------    1 root     root          55 Nov   1 15:39 shells
```

```
-rw-------     1 root      root          774 Nov  1 15:39 termcap
-rw-------     1 root      root           78 Nov  1 15:39 ttytype
lrwxrwxrwx     1 root      root           15 Nov  1 15:39 utmp -
> ../var/run/utmp
lrwxrwxrwx     1 root      root           15 Nov  1 15:39 wtmp -
> ../var/log/wtmp

/etc/pam.d:
-rw-------     1 root      root          356 Nov  1 15:39 other

/lib:
*** I have an ELF system with glibc, so I need the ld-2.so loader.
-rwxr-xr-x     1 root      root        45415 Nov  1 15:39 ld-2.0.7.so
lrwxrwxrwx     1 root      root           11 Nov  1 15:39 ld-linux.so.2 -> ld-
2.0.7.so
-rwxr-xr-x     1 root      root       731548 Nov  1 15:39 libc-2.0.7.so
lrwxrwxrwx     1 root      root           13 Nov  1 15:39 libc.so.6 -> libc-
2.0.7.so
lrwxrwxrwx     1 root      root           17 Nov  1 15:39 libcom_err.so.2 -
> libcom_err.so.2.0
-rwxr-xr-x     1 root      root         6209 Nov  1 15:39 libcom_err.so.2.0
-rwxr-xr-x     1 root      root       153881 Nov  1 15:39 libcrypt-2.0.7.so
lrwxrwxrwx     1 root      root           17 Nov  1 15:39 libcrypt.so.1 -
> libcrypt-2.0.7.so
-rwxr-xr-x     1 root      root        12962 Nov  1 15:39 libdl-2.0.7.so
lrwxrwxrwx     1 root      root           14 Nov  1 15:39 libdl.so.2 -> libdl-
2.0.7.so
lrwxrwxrwx     1 root      root           16 Nov  1 15:39 libext2fs.so.2 -
> libext2fs.so.2.4
-rwxr-xr-x     1 root      root        81382 Nov  1 15:39 libext2fs.so.2.4
-rwxr-xr-x     1 root      root        25222 Nov  1 15:39 libnsl-2.0.7.so
lrwxrwxrwx     1 root      root           15 Nov  1 15:39 libnsl.so.1 -> lib-
nsl-2.0.7.so
-rwx--x--x     1 root      root       178336 Nov  1 15:39 libnss_files-2.0.7.so
lrwxrwxrwx     1 root      root           21 Nov  1 15:39 libnss_files.so.1 -
> libnss_files-2.0.7.so
lrwxrwxrwx     1 root      root           14 Nov  1 15:39 libpam.so.0 -
> libpam.so.0.64
-rwxr-xr-x     1 root      root        26906 Nov  1 15:39 libpam.so.0.64
lrwxrwxrwx     1 root      root           19 Nov  1 15:39 libpam_misc.so.0 -
> libpam_misc.so.0.64
-rwxr-xr-x     1 root      root         7086 Nov  1 15:39 libpam_misc.so.0.64
-r-xr-xr-x     1 root      root        35615 Nov  1 15:39 libproc.so.1.2.6
lrwxrwxrwx     1 root      root           15 Nov  1 15:39 libpwdb.so.0 -
> libpwdb.so.0.54
-rw-r--r--     1 root      root       121899 Nov  1 15:39 libpwdb.so.0.54
lrwxrwxrwx     1 root      root           19 Nov  1 15:39 libtermcap.so.2 -
> libtermcap.so.2.0.8
-rwxr-xr-x     1 root      root        12041 Nov  1 15:39 libtermcap.so.2.0.8
-rwxr-xr-x     1 root      root        12874 Nov  1 15:39 libutil-2.0.7.so
lrwxrwxrwx     1 root      root           16 Nov  1 15:39 libutil.so.1 -> libu-
til-2.0.7.so
lrwxrwxrwx     1 root      root           14 Nov  1 15:39 libuuid.so.1 -
> libuuid.so.1.1
-rwxr-xr-x     1 root      root         8039 Nov  1 15:39 libuuid.so.1.1
```

HOWTO

```
drwx--x--x   3 root      root         1024 Nov  1 15:39 modules
drwx--x--x   2 root      root         1024 Nov  1 15:39 security

/lib/modules:
drwx--x--x   4 root      root         1024 Nov  1 15:39 2.0.35

/lib/modules/2.0.35:
drwx--x--x   2 root      root         1024 Nov  1 15:39 block
drwx--x--x   2 root      root         1024 Nov  1 15:39 cdrom

/lib/modules/2.0.35/block:
-rw-------   1 root      root         7156 Nov  1 15:39 loop.o

/lib/modules/2.0.35/cdrom:
-rw-------   1 root      root        24108 Nov  1 15:39 cdu31a.o

/lib/security:
-rwx--x--x   1 root      root         8771 Nov  1 15:39 pam_permit.so

***  Directory stubs for mounting
/mnt:
drwx--x--x   2 root      root         1024 Nov  1 15:39 SparQ
drwx--x--x   2 root      root         1024 Nov  1 15:39 cdrom
drwx--x--x   2 root      root         1024 Nov  1 15:39 floppy

/proc:

/root:
-rw-------   1 root      root          176 Nov  1 15:39 .bashrc
-rw-------   1 root      root          182 Nov  1 15:39 .cshrc
-rw-------   1 root      root           47 Nov  1 15:39 .glintrc
-rwx--x--x   1 root      root          455 Nov  1 15:39 .profile
-rw-------   1 root      root         4014 Nov  1 15:39 .tcshrc

/sbin:
-rwx--x--x   1 root      root        23976 Nov  1 15:39 depmod
-rwx--x--x   2 root      root       274600 Nov  1 15:39 e2fsck
-rwx--x--x   1 root      root        41268 Nov  1 15:39 fdisk
-rwx--x--x   1 root      root         9396 Nov  1 15:39 fsck
-rwx--x--x   2 root      root       274600 Nov  1 15:39 fsck.ext2
-rwx--x--x   1 root      root        29556 Nov  1 15:39 getty
-rwx--x--x   1 root      root         6620 Nov  1 15:39 halt
-rwx--x--x   1 root      root        23116 Nov  1 15:39 init
-rwx--x--x   1 root      root        25612 Nov  1 15:39 insmod
-rwx--x--x   1 root      root        10368 Nov  1 15:39 kerneld
-rwx--x--x   1 root      root       110400 Nov  1 15:39 ldconfig
-rwx--x--x   1 root      root         6108 Nov  1 15:39 lsmod
-rwx--x--x   2 root      root        17400 Nov  1 15:39 mke2fs
-rwx--x--x   1 root      root         4072 Nov  1 15:39 mkfs
-rwx--x--x   2 root      root        17400 Nov  1 15:39 mkfs.ext2
-rwx--x--x   1 root      root         5664 Nov  1 15:39 mkswap
-rwx--x--x   1 root      root        22032 Nov  1 15:39 modprobe
lrwxrwxrwx   1 root      root            4 Nov  1 15:39 reboot -> halt
-rwx--x--x   1 root      root         7492 Nov  1 15:39 rmmod
-rwx--x--x   1 root      root        12932 Nov  1 15:39 shutdown
```

```
lrwxrwxrwx   1 root      root             6 Nov  1 15:39 swapoff -> swapon
-rwx--x--x   1 root      root          5124 Nov  1 15:39 swapon
lrwxrwxrwx   1 root      root             4 Nov  1 15:39 telinit -> init
-rwx--x--x   1 root      root          6944 Nov  1 15:39 update

/tmp:

/usr:
drwx--x--x   2 root      root          1024 Nov  1 15:39 bin
drwx--x--x   2 root      root          1024 Nov  1 15:39 lib
drwx--x--x   3 root      root          1024 Nov  1 15:39 man
drwx--x--x   2 root      root          1024 Nov  1 15:39 sbin
drwx--x--x   3 root      root          1024 Nov  1 15:39 share
lrwxrwxrwx   1 root      root            10 Nov  1 15:39 tmp -> ../var/tmp

/usr/bin:
-rwx--x--x   1 root      root         37164 Nov  1 15:39 afio
-rwx--x--x   1 root      root          5044 Nov  1 15:39 chroot
-rwx--x--x   1 root      root         10656 Nov  1 15:39 cut
-rwx--x--x   1 root      root         63652 Nov  1 15:39 diff
-rwx--x--x   1 root      root         12972 Nov  1 15:39 du
-rwx--x--x   1 root      root         56552 Nov  1 15:39 find
-r-x--x--x   1 root      root          6280 Nov  1 15:39 free
-rwx--x--x   1 root      root          7680 Nov  1 15:39 head
-rwx--x--x   1 root      root          8504 Nov  1 15:39 id
-r-sr-xr-x   1 root      bin           4200 Nov  1 15:39 passwd
-rwx--x--x   1 root      root         14856 Nov  1 15:39 tail
-rwx--x--x   1 root      root         19008 Nov  1 15:39 tr
-rwx--x--x   1 root      root          7160 Nov  1 15:39 wc
-rwx--x--x   1 root      root          4412 Nov  1 15:39 whoami

/usr/lib:
lrwxrwxrwx   1 root      root            17 Nov  1 15:39 libncurses.so.4 -
> libncurses.so.4.2
-rw-r--r--   1 root      root        260474 Nov  1 15:39 libncurses.so.4.2

/usr/sbin:
-r-x--x--x   1 root      root         13684 Nov  1 15:39 fuser
-rwx--x--x   1 root      root          3876 Nov  1 15:39 mklost+found

/usr/share:
drwx--x--x   4 root      root          1024 Nov  1 15:39 terminfo

/usr/share/terminfo:
drwx--x--x   2 root      root          1024 Nov  1 15:39 l
drwx--x--x   2 root      root          1024 Nov  1 15:39 v

/usr/share/terminfo/l:
-rw-------   1 root      root          1552 Nov  1 15:39 linux
-rw-------   1 root      root          1516 Nov  1 15:39 linux-m
-rw-------   1 root      root          1583 Nov  1 15:39 linux-nic

/usr/share/terminfo/v:
-rw-------   2 root      root          1143 Nov  1 15:39 vt100
-rw-------   2 root      root          1143 Nov  1 15:39 vt100-am
```

```
/var:
drwx--x--x  2 root     root        1024 Nov  1 15:39 log
drwx--x--x  2 root     root        1024 Nov  1 15:39 run
drwx--x--x  2 root     root        1024 Nov  1 15:39 tmp

/var/log:
-rw-------  1 root     root           0 Nov  1 15:39 wtmp

/var/run:
-rw-------  1 root     root           0 Nov  1 15:39 utmp

/var/tmp:
```

14   Sample utility disk directory listing.

```
total 579
-rwxr-xr-x  1 root     root       42333 Jul 28 19:05 cpio*
-rwxr-xr-x  1 root     root       32844 Aug 28 19:50 debugfs*
-rwxr-xr-x  1 root     root      103560 Jul 29 21:31 elvis*
-rwxr-xr-x  1 root     root       29536 Jul 28 19:04 fdisk*
-rw-r--r--  1 root     root      128254 Jul 28 19:03 ftape.o
-rwxr-xr-x  1 root     root       17564 Jul 25 03:21 ftmt*
-rwxr-xr-x  1 root     root       64161 Jul 29 20:47 grep*
-rwxr-xr-x  1 root     root       45309 Jul 29 20:48 gzip*
-rwxr-xr-x  1 root     root       23560 Jul 28 19:04 insmod*
-rwxr-xr-x  1 root     root         118 Jul 28 19:04 lsmod*
lrwxrwxrwx  1 root     root           5 Jul 28 19:04 mt -> mt-st*
-rwxr-xr-x  1 root     root        9573 Jul 28 19:03 mt-st*
lrwxrwxrwx  1 root     root           6 Jul 28 19:05 rmmod -> insmod*
-rwxr-xr-x  1 root     root      104085 Jul 28 19:05 tar*
lrwxrwxrwx  1 root     root           5 Jul 29 21:35 vi -> elvis*
```

Part IX

"DNS HOWTO" Nicolai Langfeldt

janl@math.uio.no
v2.2, 11 February 1999
HOWTO become a totally small time DNS admin.

Contents

1 Preamble

Keywords: DNS, bind, bind-4, bind-8, named, dialup, ppp, slip, isdn, Internet, domain, name, hosts, resolving, caching.

This document is part of the Linux Documentation Project.

1.1 Legal stuff

(C)opyright 1995-1999 Nicolai Langfeldt. Do not modify without amending copyright, distribute freely but retain copyright message.

1.2 Credits and request for help.

I want to thank Arnt Gulbrandsen whom I cause to suffer through the drafts to this work and whom provided many useful suggestions. I also want to thank the numerous people that have e-mailed suggestions and notes.

This will never be a finished document, please send me mail about your problems and successes, it can make this a better HOWTO. So please send comments and/or questions or money to janl@math.uio.no. If you send e-mail and want an answer please show the simple courtesy of *making sure* that the return address is correct and working. Also, **please** read the 8 (QnA) section before mailing me. Another thing, I can only understand Norwegian and English.

If you want to translate this HOWTO please notify me so I can keep track of what languages it has been published in, and also I can notify you when the HOWTO has been updated.

1.3 Dedication

This HOWTO is dedicated to Anne Line Norheim Langfeldt. Though she will probably never read it since she's not that kind of girl.

2 Introduction.

What this is and isn't.

DNS is is the Domain Name System. DNS converts machine names to the IP addresses that all machines on the net have. It maps from name to address and from address to name, and some other things. This HOWTO documents how to define such mappings using a Linux system. A mapping is simply a association between two things, in this case a machine name, like `ftp.linux.org`, and the machines IP number (or address) `199.249.150.4`.

DNS is, to the uninitiated (you ;-), one of the more opaque areas of network administration. This HOWTO will try to make a few things clearer. It describes how to set up a *simple* DNS name server. Starting with a caching only server and going on to setting up a primary DNS server for a domain. For more complex setups you can check the 8 (QnA) section of this document. If it's not described there you will need to *read* the Real Documentation. I'll get back to what this Real Documentation consists of in 9 (the last chapter).

Before you start on this you should configure your machine so that you can telnet in and out of it, and successfully make all kinds of connections to the net, and you should especially be able to do `telnet 127.0.0.1` and get your own machine (test it now!). You also need a good `/etc/nsswitch.conf` (or `/etc/host.conf`), `/etc/resolv.conf` and `/etc/hosts` files as a starting point, since I will not explain their function here. If you don't already have all this set up and working the NET-3-HOWTO and/or the PPP-HOWTO explains how to set it up. Read them.

When I say 'your machine' I mean the machine you are trying to set up DNS on. Not any other machine you might have that's involved in your networking effort.

I assume you're not behind any kind of firewall that blocks name queries. If you are you will need a special configuration, see the section on 8 (QnA).

Name serving on Unix is done by a program called `named`. This is a part of the "bind" package which is coordinated by Paul Vixie for The Internet Software Consortium. `Named` is included in most Linux distributions and is usually installed as `/usr/sbin/named`. If you have a named you can probably use it; if you don't have one you can get a binary off a Linux ftp site, or get the latest and greatest source from *ftp.isc.org:/isc/bind/src/cur/bind-8/*. This HOWTO is about bind version 8. The old version of the HOWTO, about bind 4 is still available at *http://www.math.uio.no/~janl/DNS/* in case you use bind 4. If the named man page talks about (at the very end, the FILES section) `named.conf` you have bind 8, if it talks about `named.boot` you have bind 4. If you have 4 and are security conscious you really ought to upgrade to a recent 8.

DNS is a net-wide database. Take care about what you put into it. If you put junk into it, you, and others will get junk out of it. Keep your DNS tidy and consistent and you will get good service from it. Learn to use it, admin it, debug it and you will be another good admin keeping the net from falling to it's knees by mismanagement.

In this document I state flatly a couple of things that are not completely true (they are at least half truths though). All in the interest of simplification. Things will (probably ;-) work if you believe what I say.

Tip: Make backup copies of all the files I instruct you to change if you already have them, so if after going through this nothing works you can get it back to your old, working state.

3   A caching only name server.

A first stab at DNS config, very useful for dialup users.

A caching only name server will find the answer to name queries and remember the answer the next time you need it. This will shorten the waiting time the next time significantly, especially if you're on a slow connection.

First you need a file called `/etc/named.conf`. This is read when named starts. For now it should simply contain:

```
// Config file for caching only name server

options {
        directory "/var/named";

        // Uncommenting this might help if you have to go through a
        // firewall and things are not working out:

        // query-source port 53;
};

zone "." {
        type hint;
        file "root.hints";
};

zone "0.0.127.in-addr.arpa" {
        type master;
        file "pz/127.0.0";
};
```

The 'directory' line tells named where to look for files. All files named subsequently will be relative to this. Thus pz is a directory under `/var/named`, i.e., `/var/named/pz`. `/var/named` is the right directory according to the *Linux File system Standard*.

The file named `/var/named/root.hints` is named in this. `/var/named/root.hints` should contain this:

```
;
; There might be opening comments here if you already have this file.
; If not don't worry.
;
                    6D IN NS        G.ROOT-SERVERS.NET.
                    6D IN NS        J.ROOT-SERVERS.NET.
.                   6D IN NS        K.ROOT-SERVERS.NET.
.                   6D IN NS        L.ROOT-SERVERS.NET.
.                   6D IN NS        M.ROOT-SERVERS.NET.
.                   6D IN NS        A.ROOT-SERVERS.NET.
.                   6D IN NS        H.ROOT-SERVERS.NET.
.                   6D IN NS        B.ROOT-SERVERS.NET.
.                   6D IN NS        C.ROOT-SERVERS.NET.
.                   6D IN NS        D.ROOT-SERVERS.NET.
.                   6D IN NS        E.ROOT-SERVERS.NET.
.                   6D IN NS        I.ROOT-SERVERS.NET.
.                   6D IN NS        F.ROOT-SERVERS.NET.

G.ROOT-SERVERS.NET.     5w6d16h IN A    192.112.36.4
J.ROOT-SERVERS.NET.     5w6d16h IN A    198.41.0.10
K.ROOT-SERVERS.NET.     5w6d16h IN A    193.0.14.129
L.ROOT-SERVERS.NET.     5w6d16h IN A    198.32.64.12
M.ROOT-SERVERS.NET.     5w6d16h IN A    202.12.27.33
A.ROOT-SERVERS.NET.     5w6d16h IN A    198.41.0.4
H.ROOT-SERVERS.NET.     5w6d16h IN A    128.63.2.53
B.ROOT-SERVERS.NET.     5w6d16h IN A    128.9.0.107
C.ROOT-SERVERS.NET.     5w6d16h IN A    192.33.4.12
D.ROOT-SERVERS.NET.     5w6d16h IN A    128.8.10.90
E.ROOT-SERVERS.NET.     5w6d16h IN A    192.203.230.10
I.ROOT-SERVERS.NET.     5w6d16h IN A    192.36.148.17
F.ROOT-SERVERS.NET.     5w6d16h IN A    192.5.5.241
```

The file describes the root name servers in the world. This changes over time and must be maintained. See the 6 (maintenance section) for how to keep it up to date.

The next section in `named.conf` is the last zone. I will explain its use in a later chapter, for now just make this a file named `127.0.0` in the subdirectory pz:

```
@           IN      SOA     ns.linux.bogus. hostmaster.linux.bogus. (
                            1           ; Serial
                            8H          ; Refresh
                            2H          ; Retry
                            1W          ; Expire
                            1D)         ; Minimum TTL
            NS      ns.linux.bogus.
1           PTR     localhost.
```

Next, you need a `/etc/resolv.conf` looking something like this:

```
search subdomain.your-domain.edu your-domain.edu
nameserver 127.0.0.1
```

The 'search' line specifies what domains should be searched for any host names you want to connect to. The 'nameserver' line specifies the address of your nameserver, in this case your own machine since that is where your named runs (127.0.0.1 is right, no matter if your machine has an other address too). If you want to list several name servers put in one 'nameserver' line for each. (Note: Named never reads this file, the resolver that uses named does.)

To illustrate what this file does: If a client tries to look up foo, then foo.subdomain.your-domain.edu is tried first, then foo.your-fomain.edu, finally foo. If a client tries to look up sunsite.unc.edu, sunsite.unc.edu.subdomain.your-domain.edu is tried first (yes, it's silly, but that's the way it works), then sunsite.unc.edu.your-domain.edu, and finally sunsite.unc.edu. You may not want to put in too many domains in the search line, it takes time to search them all.

The example assumes you belong in the domain subdomain.your-domain.edu, your machine then, is probably called your-machine.subdomain.your-domain.edu. The search line should not contain your TLD (Top Level Domain, 'edu' in this case). If you frequently need to connect to hosts in another domain you can add that domain to the search line like this:

```
search subdomain.your-domain.edu your-domain.edu other-domain.com
```

and so on. Obviously you need to put real domain names in instead. Please note the lack of periods at the end of the domain names. This is important, please note the lack of periods at the end of the domain names.

Next, depending on your libc version you either need to fix /etc/nsswitch.conf or /etc/host.conf. If you already have nsswitch.conf that's what we'll fix, if not, we'll fix host.conf.

/etc/nsswitch.conf

This is a long file specifying where to get different kinds of data types, from what file or database. It usually contains helpful comments at the top, which you should consider reading. After that find the line starting with 'hosts:', it should read

```
hosts:        files dns
```

If there is no line starting with 'hosts:' then put in the one above. It says that programs should first look in the /etc/hosts file, then check DNS according to resolv.conf.

/etc/host.conf

It probably contains several lines, one should start with order and it should look like this:

```
order hosts,bind
```

If there is no 'order' line you should add one. It tells the host name resolving routines to first look in /etc/hosts, then ask the name server (which you in resolv.conf said is at 127.0.0.1).

3.1   Starting named

After all this it's time to start named. If you're using a dialup connection connect first. Type 'ndc start', and press return, no options. If that does not work try '/usr/sbin/ndc start' instead. If that back-fires see the 8 (QnA) section. If you view your syslog message file (usually called /var/adm/messages, but another directory to look in is /var/log and another file to look in is syslog) while starting named (do tail -f /var/log/messages) you should see something like:

(the lines ending in \ continue on the next line)

```
    Feb 15 01:26:17 roke named[6091]: starting.  named 8.1.1 Sat Feb 14 \
      00:18:20 MET 1998 ^Ijanl@roke.uio.no:/var/tmp/bind-8.1.1/src/bin/named
    Feb 15 01:26:17 roke named[6091]: cache zone "" (IN) loaded (serial 0)
```

```
Feb 15 01:26:17 roke named[6091]: master zone "0.0.127.in-addr.arpa" \
  (IN) loaded (serial 1)
Feb 15 01:26:17 roke named[6091]: listening [127.0.0.1].53 (lo)
Feb 15 01:26:17 roke named[6091]: listening [129.240.230.92].53 (ippp0)
Feb 15 01:26:17 roke named[6091]: Forwarding source ad-
dress is [0.0.0.0].1040
Feb 15 01:26:17 roke named[6092]: Ready to answer queries.
```

If there are any messages about errors then there is a mistake. Named will name the file it is in (one of named.conf and root.hints I hope :-) Kill named and go back and check the file.

Now you can test your setup. Start nslookup to examine your work.

```
$ nslookup
Default Server:  localhost
Address:  127.0.0.1

>
```

If that's what you get it's working. We hope. Anything else, go back and check everything. Each time you change the named.conf file you need to restart named using the ndc restart command.

Now you can enter a query. Try looking up some machine close to you. pat.uio.no is close to me, at the University of Oslo:

```
> pat.uio.no
Server:  localhost
Address:  127.0.0.1

Name:    pat.uio.no
Address:  129.240.130.16
```

nslookup now asked your named to look for the machine pat.uio.no. It then contacted one of the name server machines named in your root.hints file, and asked its way from there. It might take tiny while before you get the result as it may need to search all the domains you named in /etc/resolv.conf.

If you ask the same again you get this:

```
> pat.uio.no
Server:  localhost
Address:  127.0.0.1

Non-authoritative answer:
Name:    pat.uio.no
Address:  129.240.2.50
```

Note the "Non-authoritative answer:" line we got this time around. That means that named did not go out on the network to ask this time, the information is in the cache now. But the cached information *might* be out of date (stale). So you are informed of this (very slight) possibility by it saying 'Non-authoritative answer:'. When nslookup says this the second time you ask for a host it's a sure sign that named caches the information and that it's working. You exit nslookup by giving the command 'exit'.

3.2 Making it even better

In large, well organized, academic or ISP (Internet Service Provider) networks you will sometimes find that the network people has set up a forwarder hierarchy of DNS servers which helps lighten the internal network load and on the outside servers as well. It's not easy to know if you're inside such a network or not. It is however not important and by using the DNS server of your network provider as a "forwarder" you can make the responses to queries faster and less of a load on your network. If you use a modem this can be quite a win. For the sake of this example we assume that your network provider has two name servers they want you to use, with IP numbers `10.0.0.1` and `10.1.0.1`. Then, in your `named.conf` file, inside the opening section called "options" insert these lines:

```
forward first;
forwarders {
    10.0.0.1;
    10.1.0.1;
};
```

Restart your nameserver and test it with nslookup. Should work fine.

3.3 Congratulations

Now you know how to set up a caching named. Take a beer, milk, or whatever you prefer to celebrate it.

4 A *simple* domain.

How to set up your own domain.

4.1 But first some dry theory

Before we *really* start this section I'm going to serve you some theory on and an example of how DNS works. And you're going to read it because it's good for you. If you don't want to you should at least skim it very quickly. Stop skimming when you get to what should go in your `named.conf` file.

DNS is a hierarchical, tree structured, system. The top is written '.' and pronounced 'root'. Under . there are a number of Top Level Domains (TLDs), the best known ones are ORG, COM, EDU and NET, but there are many more. Just like a tree it has a root and it branches out. If you have any computer science background you will recognize DNS as a search tree, and you will be able to find nodes, leaf nodes and edges.

When looking for a machine the query proceeds recursively into the hierarchy starting at the top. If you want to find out the address of `prep.ai.mit.edu` your name server has to find a name server that serves `edu`. It asks a . server (it already knows the . servers, that's what the `root.hints` file is for), the . server gives a list of `edu` servers:

```
$ nslookup
Default Server: localhost
Address: 127.0.0.1
```

Start asking a root server:

```
> server c.root-servers.net
Default Server: c.root-servers.net
Address: 192.33.4.12
```

Set the Query type to NS (name server records):

```
> set q=ns
```

Ask about `edu`:

```
> edu.
```

The trailing . here is significant, it tells `nslookup` we're asking that `edu` is right under . (and not under any of our `search` domains, it speeds the search).

```
edu        nameserver = A.ROOT-SERVERS.NET
edu        nameserver = H.ROOT-SERVERS.NET
edu        nameserver = B.ROOT-SERVERS.NET
edu        nameserver = C.ROOT-SERVERS.NET
edu        nameserver = D.ROOT-SERVERS.NET
edu        nameserver = E.ROOT-SERVERS.NET
edu        nameserver = I.ROOT-SERVERS.NET
edu        nameserver = F.ROOT-SERVERS.NET
edu        nameserver = G.ROOT-SERVERS.NET
A.ROOT-SERVERS.NET      internet address = 198.41.0.4
H.ROOT-SERVERS.NET      internet address = 128.63.2.53
B.ROOT-SERVERS.NET      internet address = 128.9.0.107
C.ROOT-SERVERS.NET      internet address = 192.33.4.12
D.ROOT-SERVERS.NET      internet address = 128.8.10.90
E.ROOT-SERVERS.NET      internet address = 192.203.230.10
I.ROOT-SERVERS.NET      internet address = 192.36.148.17
F.ROOT-SERVERS.NET      internet address = 192.5.5.241
G.ROOT-SERVERS.NET      internet address = 192.112.36.4
```

This tells us that all `ROOT-SERVERS.NET` servers serves `EDU.`, so we can go on asking any of them. We'll continue asking C. Now we want to know who serves the next level of the domain name: `mit.edu.`:

```
> mit.edu.
Server:  c.root-servers.net
Address:  192.33.4.12

Non-authoritative answer:
mit.edu nameserver = W20NS.mit.edu
mit.edu nameserver = BITSY.mit.edu
mit.edu nameserver = STRAWB.mit.edu

Authoritative answers can be found from:
W20NS.mit.edu   internet address = 18.70.0.160
BITSY.mit.edu   internet address = 18.72.0.3
STRAWB.mit.edu  internet address = 18.71.0.151
```

`steawb`, `w20ns` and `bitsy` all serves `mit.edu`, we select one and inquire about the name one more level up: `ai.mit.edu`:

```
> server W20NS.mit.edu.
```

Host names are not case sensitive, but I use my mouse to cut and paste so it gets copied as-is from the screen.

```
Server:  W20NS.mit.edu
Address:  18.70.0.160

> ai.mit.edu.
Server:  W20NS.mit.edu
Address:  18.70.0.160

Non-authoritative answer:
ai.mit.edu        nameserver = ALPHA-BITS.AI.MIT.EDU
```

```
ai.mit.edu          nameserver = GRAPE-NUTS.AI.MIT.EDU
ai.mit.edu          nameserver = TRIX.AI.MIT.EDU
ai.mit.edu          nameserver = MUESLI.AI.MIT.EDU
ai.mit.edu          nameserver = LIFE.AI.MIT.EDU
ai.mit.edu          nameserver = BEET-CHEX.AI.MIT.EDU
ai.mit.edu          nameserver = MINI-WHEATS.AI.MIT.EDU
ai.mit.edu          nameserver = COUNT-CHOCULA.AI.MIT.EDU
ai.mit.edu          nameserver = MINTAKA.LCS.MIT.EDU

Authoritative answers can be found from:
AI.MIT.EDU          nameserver = ALPHA-BITS.AI.MIT.EDU
AI.MIT.EDU          nameserver = GRAPE-NUTS.AI.MIT.EDU
AI.MIT.EDU          nameserver = TRIX.AI.MIT.EDU
AI.MIT.EDU          nameserver = MUESLI.AI.MIT.EDU
AI.MIT.EDU          nameserver = LIFE.AI.MIT.EDU
AI.MIT.EDU          nameserver = BEET-CHEX.AI.MIT.EDU
AI.MIT.EDU          nameserver = MINI-WHEATS.AI.MIT.EDU
AI.MIT.EDU          nameserver = COUNT-CHOCULA.AI.MIT.EDU
AI.MIT.EDU          nameserver = MINTAKA.LCS.MIT.EDU
ALPHA-BITS.AI.MIT.EDU   internet address = 128.52.32.5
GRAPE-NUTS.AI.MIT.EDU   internet address = 128.52.36.4
TRIX.AI.MIT.EDU internet address = 128.52.37.6
MUESLI.AI.MIT.EDU       internet address = 128.52.39.7
LIFE.AI.MIT.EDU internet address = 128.52.32.80
BEET-CHEX.AI.MIT.EDU    internet address = 128.52.32.22
MINI-WHEATS.AI.MIT.EDU  internet address = 128.52.54.11
COUNT-CHOCULA.AI.MIT.EDU        internet address = 128.52.38.22
MINTAKA.LCS.MIT.EDU     internet address = 18.26.0.36
```

So `museli.ai.mit.edu` is a nameserver for `ai.mit.edu`:

```
> server MUESLI.AI.MIT.EDU
Default Server:  MUESLI.AI.MIT.EDU
Address:  128.52.39.7
```

Now I change query type, we've found the name server so now we're going to ask about everything `wheaties` knows about `prep.ai.mit.edu`.

```
> set q=any
> prep.ai.mit.edu.
Server:  MUESLI.AI.MIT.EDU
Address:  128.52.39.7

prep.ai.mit.edu CPU = dec/decstation-5000.25     OS = unix
prep.ai.mit.edu
        inet address = 18.159.0.42, protocol = tcp
          ftp telnet  smtp  finger
prep.ai.mit.edu preference = 1, mail exchanger = gnu-life.ai.mit.edu
prep.ai.mit.edu internet address = 18.159.0.42
ai.mit.edu          nameserver = beet-chex.ai.mit.edu
ai.mit.edu          nameserver = alpha-bits.ai.mit.edu
ai.mit.edu          nameserver = mini-wheats.ai.mit.edu
ai.mit.edu          nameserver = trix.ai.mit.edu
ai.mit.edu          nameserver = muesli.ai.mit.edu
ai.mit.edu          nameserver = count-chocula.ai.mit.edu
```

```
ai.mit.edu        nameserver = mintaka.lcs.mit.edu
ai.mit.edu        nameserver = life.ai.mit.edu
gnu-life.ai.mit.edu      internet address = 128.52.32.60
beet-chex.ai.mit.edu     internet address = 128.52.32.22
alpha-bits.ai.mit.edu    internet address = 128.52.32.5
mini-wheats.ai.mit.edu   internet address = 128.52.54.11
trix.ai.mit.edu internet address = 128.52.37.6
muesli.ai.mit.edu        internet address = 128.52.39.7
count-chocula.ai.mit.edu        internet address = 128.52.38.22
mintaka.lcs.mit.edu      internet address = 18.26.0.36
life.ai.mit.edu internet address = 128.52.32.80
```

So starting at . we found the successive name servers for the each level in the domain name. If you had used your own DNS server instead of using all those other servers, your named would of-course cache all the information it found while digging this out for you, and it would not have to ask again for a while.

In the tree analogue each "." in the name is a branching point. And each part between the "."s are the names of individual branches in the tree.

We climb the tree by taking the name we want (`prep.ai.mit.edu`) first finding the root (`.`) and then looking for the next branch to climb, in this case `edu`. Once we have found it we climb it by switching to the server that knows about that part of the name. Next we look for the `mit` branch over the `edu` branch (the combined name is `mit.edu`) and climb it by switching to a server that knows about `mit.edu`. Again we look for the next branch, it's `ai.mit.edu` and again we switch to the server that knows about it. Now we have arrived at the right server, at the right branching point. The last part is finding `prep.ai.mit.edu`, which is simple. In computer science we usually call `prep` a *leaf* on the tree.

A much less talked about, but just as important domain is `in-addr.arpa`. It too is nested like the 'normal' domains. `in-addr.arpa` allows us to get the hosts name when we have its address. A important thing here is to note that ip addresses are written in reverse order in the `in-addr.arpa` domain. If you have the address of a machine: `192.128.52.43` named proceeds just like for the `prep.ai.mit.edu` example: find `arpa.` servers. Find `in-addr.arpa.` servers, find `192.in-addr.arpa.` servers, find `128.192.in-addr.arpa.` servers, find `52.128.192.in-addr.arpa.` servers. Find needed records for `43.52.128.192.in-addr.arpa.`. Clever huh? (Say 'yes'.) The reversion of the numbers can be confusing for years though.

I have just told a lie. DNS does not work precisely the way I just told you. But it's close enough.

4.2 Our own domain

Now to define our own domain. We're going to make the domain `linux.bogus` and define machines in it. I use a totally bogus domain name to make sure we disturb no-one Out There.

One more thing before we start: Not all characters are allowed in host names. We're restricted to the characters of the English alphabet: a-z, and numbers: 0-9 and the character '-' (dash). Keep to those characters. Upper and lower-case characters are the same for DNS, so `pat.uio.no` is identical to `Pat.UiO.No`.

We've already started this part with this line in `named.conf`:

```
zone "0.0.127.in-addr.arpa" {
       type master;
       file "pz/127.0.0";
};
```

Please note the lack of '.' at the end of the domain names in this file. This says that now we will define the zone `0.0.127.in-addr.arpa`, that we're the master server for it and that it is stored in a file called `pz/127.0.0`. We've already set up this file, it reads:

```
@               IN      SOA     ns.linux.bogus. hostmaster.linux.bogus. (
                                1       ; Serial
                                8H      ; Refresh
                                2H      ; Retry
                                1W      ; Expire
                                1D)     ; Minimum TTL
                NS      ns.linux.bogus.
1               PTR     localhost.
```

Please note the '.' at the end of all the full domain names in this file, in contrast to the `named.conf` file above. Some people like to start each zone file with a `$ORIGIN` directive, but this is superfluous. The origin (where in the DNS hierarchy it belongs) of a zone file is specified in the zone section of the `named.conf` file, in this case it's `0.0.127.in-addr.arpa`.

This 'zone file' contains 3 'resource records' (RRs): A SOA RR. A NS RR and a PTR RR. SOA is short for Start Of Authority. The '@' is a special notation meaning the origin, and since the 'domain' column for this file says 0.0.127.in-addr.arpa the first line really means

```
    0.0.127.in-addr.arpa.    IN      SOA ...
```

NS is the Name Server RR. There is no '@' at the start of this line, it is implicit since the last line started with a '@'. Saves some typing that. So the NS line could also be written

```
    0.0.127.in-addr.arpa.    IN      NS      ns.linux.bogus
```

It tells DNS what machine is the name server of the domain `0.0.127.in-addr.arpa`, it is `ns.linux.bogus`. 'ns' is a customary name for name-servers, but as with web servers who are customarily named *www.something* the name may be anything.

And finally the PTR record says that the host at address 1 in the subnet `0.0.127.in-addr.arpa`, i.e., 127.0.0.1 is named `localhost`.

The SOA record is the preamble to *all* zone files, and there should be exactly one in each zone file. It describes the zone, where it comes from (a machine called `ns.linux.bogus`), who is responsible for its contents (hostmaster@linux.bogus, you should insert your e-mail address here), what version of the zone file this is (serial: 1), and other things having to do with caching and secondary DNS servers. For the rest of the fields (refresh, retry, expire and minimum) use the numbers used in this HOWTO and you should be safe.

Now restart your named (the command is `ndc restart`) and use nslookup to examine what you've done:

```
    $ nslookup

    Default Server:  localhost
    Address:  127.0.0.1

    > 127.0.0.1
    Server:  localhost
    Address:  127.0.0.1

    Name:     localhost
    Address:  127.0.0.1
```

so it manages to get `localhost` from 127.0.0.1, good. Now for our main task, the `linux.bogus` domain, insert a new 'zone' section in `named.conf`:

```
zone "linux.bogus" {
        notify no;
        type master;
        file "pz/linux.bogus";
};
```

Note again the lack of ending '.' on the domain name in the `named.conf` file.

In the `linux.bogus` zone file we'll put some totally bogus data:

```
;
; Zone file for linux.bogus
;
; The full zone file
;
@       IN      SOA     ns.linux.bogus. hostmaster.linux.bogus. (
                        199802151       ; serial, todays date + todays serial #
                        8H              ; refresh, seconds
                        2H              ; retry, seconds
                        1W              ; expire, seconds
                        1D )            ; minimum, seconds
;
                NS      ns                     ; Inet Address of name server
                MX      10 mail.linux.bogus    ; Primary Mail Exchanger
                MX      20 mail.friend.bogus.  ; Secondary Mail Exchanger
;
localhost       A       127.0.0.1
ns              A       192.168.196.2
mail            A       192.168.196.4
```

Two things must be noted about the SOA record. `ns.linux.bogus` *must* be a actual machine with a A record. It is not legal to have a CNAME record for he machine mentioned in the SOA record. It's name need not be 'ns', it could be any legal host name. Next, hostmaster.linux.bogus should be read as hostmaster@linux.bogus, this should be a mail alias, or a mailbox, where the person(s) maintaining DNS should read mail frequently. Any mail regarding the domain will be sent to the address listed here. The name need not be 'hostmaster', it can be your normal e-mail address, but the e-mail address 'hostmaster' is often expected to work as well.

There is one new RR type in this file, the MX, or Mail eXchanger RR. It tells mail systems where to send mail that is addressed to someone@linux.bogus, namely too `mail.linux.bogus` or `mail.friend.bogus`. The number before each machine name is that MX RRs priority. The RR with the lowest number (10) is the one mail should be sent to if possible. If that fails the mail can be sent to one with a higher number, a secondary mail handler, i.e., `mail.friend.bogus` which has priority 20 here.

Restart named by running `ndc restart`. Examine the results with nslookup:

```
$ nslookup
> set q=any
> linux.bogus
Server:  localhost
Address:  127.0.0.1

linux.bogus
        origin = ns.linux.bogus
        mail addr = hostmaster.linux.bogus
        serial = 199802151
```

```
              refresh  = 28800 (8 hours)
              retry    = 7200 (2 hours)
              expire   = 604800 (7 days)
              minimum ttl = 86400 (1 day)
    linux.bogus      nameserver = ns.linux.bogus
    linux.bogus      preference = 10,
                     mail exchanger = mail.linux.bogus.linux.bogus
    linux.bogus      preference = 20, mail exchanger = mail.friend.bogus
    linux.bogus      nameserver = ns.linux.bogus
    ns.linux.bogus   internet address = 192.168.196.2
    mail.linux.bogus       internet address = 192.168.196.4
```

Upon careful examination you will discover a bug. The line

```
    linux.bogus      preference = 10,
                     mail exchanger = mail.linux.bogus.linux.bogus
```

is all wrong. It should be

```
    linux.bogus      preference = 10, mail exchanger = mail.linux.bogus
```

I deliberately made a mistake so you could learn from it :-) Looking in the zone file we find that the line

```
              MX      10 mail.linux.bogus      ; Primary Mail Exchanger
```

is missing a period. Or has a 'linux.bogus' too many. If a machine name does not end in a period in a zone file the origin is added to its end causing the double `linux.bogus.linux.bogus`. So either

```
              MX      10 mail.linux.bogus.     ; Primary Mail Exchanger
```

or

```
              MX      10 mail                  ; Primary Mail Exchanger
```

is correct. I prefer the latter form, it's less to type. There are some bind experts that disagree, and some that agree with this. In a zone file the domain should either be written out and ended with a '.' or it should not be included at all, in which case it defaults to the origin.

I must stress that in the named.conf file there should *not* be '.'s after the domain names. You have no idea how many times a '.' too many or few have fouled up things and confused the h*ll out of people.

So having made my point here is the new zone file, with some extra information in it as well:

```
;
; Zone file for linux.bogus
;
; The full zone file
;
@       IN      SOA     ns.linux.bogus. hostmaster.linux.bogus. (
                        199802151        ; serial, todays date + todays serial #
                        8H               ; refresh, seconds
                        2H               ; retry, seconds
                        1W               ; expire, seconds
                        1D )             ; minimum, seconds
```

```
;                       TXT     "Linux.Bogus, your DNS consultants"
                        NS      ns              ; Inet Address of name server
                        NS      ns.friend.bogus.
                        MX      10 mail         ; Primary Mail Exchanger
                        MX      20 mail.friend.bogus. ; Secondary Mail Exchanger

localhost               A       127.0.0.1

gw                      A       192.168.196.1
                        HINFO   "Cisco" "IOS"
                        TXT     "The router"

ns                      A       192.168.196.2
                        MX      10 mail
                        MX      20 mail.friend.bogus.
                        HINFO   "Pentium" "Linux 2.0"
www                     CNAME   ns

donald                  A       192.168.196.3
                        MX      10 mail
                        MX      20 mail.friend.bogus.
                        HINFO   "i486"  "Linux 2.0"
                        TXT     "DEK"

mail                    A       192.168.196.4
                        MX      10 mail
                        MX      20 mail.friend.bogus.
                        HINFO   "386sx" "Linux 1.2"

ftp                     A       192.168.196.5
                        MX      10 mail
                        MX      20 mail.friend.bogus.
                        HINFO   "P6" "Linux 2.1.86"
```

There are a number of new RRs here: HINFO (Host INFOrmation) has two parts, it's a good habit to quote each. The first part is the hardware or CPU on the machine, and the second part the software or OS on the machine. The machine called 'ns' has a Pentium CPU and runs Linux 2.0. CNAME (Canonical NAME) is a way to give each machine several names. So www is an alias for ns.

CNAME record usage is a bit controversial. But it's safe to follow the rule that a MX, CNAME or SOA record should *never* refer to a CNAME record, they should only refer to something with a A record, so it is inadvisable to have

```
foobar          CNAME   www                     ; NO!
```

but correct to have

```
foobar          CNAME   ns                      ; Yes!
```

It's also safe to assume that a CNAME is not a legal host name for a e-mail address: webmaster@www.linux.bogus is an illegal e-mail address given the setup above. You can expect quite a few mail admins Out There to enforce this rule even if it works for you. The way to avoid this is to use A records (and perhaps some others too, like a MX record) instead:

www		A	192.168.196.2

A number of the arch-bind-wizards, recommend *not* using CNAME at all. But the discussion of why or why not is beyond this HOWTO.

But as you see, this HOWTO and many sites does not follow this rule.

Load the new database by running `ndc reload`, this causes named to read its files again.

```
$ nslookup
Default Server:  localhost
Address:  127.0.0.1

> ls -d linux.bogus
```

This means that all records should be listed. It results in this:

```
[localhost]
$ORIGIN linux.bogus.
@                       1D IN SOA       ns hostmaster (
                                        199802151       ; serial
                                        8H              ; refresh
                                        2H              ; retry
                                        1W              ; expiry
                                        1D )            ; minimum
                        1D IN NS        ns
                        1D IN NS        ns.friend.bogus.
                        1D IN TXT       "Linux.Bogus, your DNS consultants"
                        1D IN MX        10 mail
                        1D IN MX        20 mail.friend.bogus.
gw                      1D IN A         192.168.196.1
                        1D IN HINFO     "Cisco" "IOS"
                        1D IN TXT       "The router"
mail                    1D IN A         192.168.196.4
                        1D IN MX        10 mail
                        1D IN MX        20 mail.friend.bogus.
                        1D IN HINFO     "386sx" "Linux 1.0.9"
localhost               1D IN A         127.0.0.1
www                     1D IN CNAME     ns
donald                  1D IN A         192.168.196.3
                        1D IN MX        10 mail
                        1D IN MX        20 mail.friend.bogus.
                        1D IN HINFO     "i486" "Linux 1.2"
                        1D IN TXT       "DEK"
ftp                     1D IN A         192.168.196.5
                        1D IN MX        10 mail
                        1D IN MX        20 mail.friend.bogus.
                        1D IN HINFO     "P6" "Linux 1.3.59"
ns                      1D IN A         192.168.196.2
                        1D IN MX        10 mail
                        1D IN MX        20 mail.friend.bogus.
                        1D IN HINFO     "Pentium" "Linux 1.2"
```

That's good. As you see it looks a lot like the zone file itself. Let's check what it says for *www* alone:

```
> set q=any
> www.linux.bogus.
Server:   localhost
Address:   127.0.0.1

www.linux.bogus canonical name = ns.linux.bogus
linux.bogus      nameserver = ns.linux.bogus
linux.bogus      nameserver = ns.friend.bogus
ns.linux.bogus  internet address = 192.168.196.2
```

In other words, the real name of `www.linux.bogus` is `ns.linux.bogus`, and it gives you some of the information it has about ns as well, enough to connect to it if you were a program.

Now we're halfway.

4.3   The reverse zone

Now programs can convert the names in linux.bogus to addresses which they can connect to. But also required is a reverse zone, one making DNS able to convert from an address to a name. This name is used buy a lot of servers of different kinds (FTP, IRC, WWW and others) to decide if they want to talk to you or not, and if so, maybe even how much priority you should be given. For full access to all services on the Internet a reverse zone is required.

Put this in `named.conf`:

```
zone "196.168.192.in-addr.arpa" {
        notify no;
        type master;
        file "pz/192.168.196";
};
```

This is exactly as with the `0.0.127.in-addr.arpa`, and the contents are similar:

```
@       IN       SOA      ns.linux.bogus. hostmaster.linux.bogus. (
                          199802151 ; Serial, todays date + todays serial
                          8H       ; Refresh
                          2H       ; Retry
                          1W       ; Expire
                          1D)      ; Minimum TTL
                 NS       ns.linux.bogus.

1                PTR      gw.linux.bogus.
2                PTR      ns.linux.bogus.
3                PTR      donald.linux.bogus.
4                PTR      mail.linux.bogus.
5                PTR      ftp.linux.bogus.
```

Now you restart your named (`ndc restart`) and examine your work with nslookup again:

```
> 192.168.196.4
Server:   localhost
Address:   127.0.0.1

Name:    mail.linux.bogus
Address:   192.168.196.4
```

so, it looks OK, dump the whole thing to examine that too:

```
> ls -d 196.168.192.in-addr.arpa
[localhost]
$ORIGIN 196.168.192.in-addr.arpa.
@                      1D IN SOA       ns.linux.bogus. hostmas-
ter.linux.bogus. (
                              199802151       ; serial
                              8H              ; refresh
                              2H              ; retry
                              1W              ; expiry
                              1D )            ; minimum

                    1D IN NS        ns.linux.bogus.
1                   1D IN PTR       gw.linux.bogus.
2                   1D IN PTR       ns.linux.bogus.
3                   1D IN PTR       donald.linux.bogus.
4                   1D IN PTR       mail.linux.bogus.
5                   1D IN PTR       ftp.linux.bogus.
@                   1D IN SOA       ns.linux.bogus. hostmas-
ter.linux.bogus. (
                              199802151       ; serial
                              8H              ; refresh
                              2H              ; retry
                              1W              ; expiry
                              1D )            ; minimum
```

Looks good! If your output didn't look like that look for error-messages in your syslog, I explained how to do that at the very beginning of this chapter.

4.4 Words of caution

There are some things I should add here. The IP numbers used in the examples above are taken from one of the blocks of 'private nets', i.e., they are not allowed to be used publicly on the internet. So they are safe to use in an example in a HOWTO. The second thing is the `notify no;` line. It tells named not to notify its secondary (slave) servers when it has gotten a update to one of its zone files. In bind-8 the named can notify the other servers listed in NS records in the zone file when a zone is updated. This is handy for ordinary use, but for private experiments with zones this feature should be off, we don't want the experiment to pollute the Internet do we?

And, of course, this domain is highly bogus, and so are all the addresses in it. For a real example of a real-life domain see the next main-section.

4.5 Why reverse lookups don't work.

There are a couple of "gotchas" that normally are avoided with name lookups that are often seen when setting up reverse zones. Before you go on you need reverse lookups of your machines working on your own nameserver. If it isn't go back and fix it before continuing.

I will discuss two failures of reverse lookups as seen from outside your network:

4.5.1 The reverse zone isn't delegated.

When you ask a service provider for a network-address range and a domain name the domain name is normally delegated as a matter of course. A delegation is the glue NS record that helps you get from one nameserver to another as explained in the dry theory section above. You read that, right? If your reverse zone dosn't work go back and read it. Now.

The reverse zone also needs to be delegated. If you got the `192.168.196` net with the `linux.bogus` domain from your provider they need to put NS records in for your reverse zone as well as for your forward zone. If you follow the chain from `in-addr.arpa` and up to your net you will probably find a break in the chain. Most probably at your service provider. Having found the break in the chain contact your service-provider and ask them to correct the error.

4.5.2 You've got a classless subnet

This is a somewhat advanced topic, but classless subnets are very common these days and you probably have one unless you're a medium sized company.

A classless subnet is what keeps the Internet going these days. Some years ago there was much ado about the shortage of ip numbers. The smart people in IETF (the Internet Engineering Task Force, they keep the Internet working) stuck their heads together and solved the problem. At a price. The price is that you'll get less than a "C" subnet and some things may break. Please see *Ask Mr. DNS at http://www.acmebw.com/askmrdns/00007.htm* for an good explanation of this and how to handle it.

Did you read it? I'm not going to explain it so please read it.

The first part of the problem is that your ISP must understand the technique described by Mr. DNS. Not all small ISPs have a working understanding of this. If so you might have to explain to them and be persistent. But be sure you understand it first ;-). They will then set up a nice reverse zone at their server which you can examine for correctness with nslookup.

The second and last part of the problem is that you must understand the technique. If you're unsure go back and read about it again. Then you can set up your own classless reverse zone as described by Mr. DNS.

There is another trap lurking here. Old resolvers will *not* be able to follow the CNAME trick in the resolving chain and will fail to reverse-resolve your machine. This can result in the service assigning it an incorrect access class, deny access or something along those lines. If you stumble into such a service the only solution (that I know of) is for your ISP to insert your PTR record directly into their trick classless zone file instead of the trick CNAME record.

Some ISPs will offer other ways to handle this, like Web based forms for you to input your reverse-mappings in or other automagical systems.

5   A real domain example

Where we list some *real* zone files

Users have suggested that I include a real example of a working domain as well as the tutorial example.

I use this example with permission from David Bullock of LAND-5. These files were current 24th of September 1996, and were then edited to fit bind 8 restrictions and use extensions by me. So, what you see here differs a bit from what you find if you query LAND-5's name servers now.

5.1   /etc/named.conf (or /var/named/named.conf)

Here we find master zone sections for the two reverse zones needed: the 127.0.0 net, as well as LAND-5's `206.6.177` subnet. And a primary line for land-5's forward zone `land-5.com`. Also note that instead of stuffing the files in a directory called pz, as I do in this HOWTO, he puts them in a directory called `zone`.

```
// Boot file for LAND-5 name server

options {
        directory "/var/named";
};

zone "." {
        type hint;
        file "root.hints";
};

zone "0.0.127.in-addr.arpa" {
        type master;
        file "zone/127.0.0";
};

zone "land-5.com" {
        type master;
        file "zone/land-5.com";
};

zone "177.6.206.in-addr.arpa" {
        type master;
        file "zone/206.6.177";
};
```

If you put this in your named.conf file to play with **PLEASE** put "notify no;" in the zone sections for the two land-5 zones so as to avoid accidents.

5.2 /var/named/root.hints

Keep in mind that this file is dynamic, and the one listed here is old. You're better off using one produced now, with dig, as explained earlier.

```
; <<>> DiG 8.1 <<>> @A.ROOT-SERVERS.NET.
; (1 server found)
;; res options: init recurs defnam dnsrch
;; got answer:
;; ->>HEADER<<- opcode: QUERY, status: NOERROR, id: 10
;; flags: qr aa rd; QUERY: 1, ANSWER: 13, AUTHORITY: 0, ADDITIONAL: 13
;; QUERY SECTION:
;;      ., type = NS, class = IN

;; ANSWER SECTION:
.                      6D IN NS        G.ROOT-SERVERS.NET.
.                      6D IN NS        J.ROOT-SERVERS.NET.
.                      6D IN NS        K.ROOT-SERVERS.NET.
.                      6D IN NS        L.ROOT-SERVERS.NET.
.                      6D IN NS        M.ROOT-SERVERS.NET.
.                      6D IN NS        A.ROOT-SERVERS.NET.
.                      6D IN NS        H.ROOT-SERVERS.NET.
.                      6D IN NS        B.ROOT-SERVERS.NET.
.                      6D IN NS        C.ROOT-SERVERS.NET.
.                      6D IN NS        D.ROOT-SERVERS.NET.
```

```
.                        6D IN NS        E.ROOT-SERVERS.NET.
.                        6D IN NS        I.ROOT-SERVERS.NET.
.                        6D IN NS        F.ROOT-SERVERS.NET.


;; ADDITIONAL SECTION:
G.ROOT-SERVERS.NET.      5w6d16h IN A    192.112.36.4
J.ROOT-SERVERS.NET.      5w6d16h IN A    198.41.0.10
K.ROOT-SERVERS.NET.      5w6d16h IN A    193.0.14.129
L.ROOT-SERVERS.NET.      5w6d16h IN A    198.32.64.12
M.ROOT-SERVERS.NET.      5w6d16h IN A    202.12.27.33
A.ROOT-SERVERS.NET.      5w6d16h IN A    198.41.0.4
H.ROOT-SERVERS.NET.      5w6d16h IN A    128.63.2.53
B.ROOT-SERVERS.NET.      5w6d16h IN A    128.9.0.107
C.ROOT-SERVERS.NET.      5w6d16h IN A    192.33.4.12
D.ROOT-SERVERS.NET.      5w6d16h IN A    128.8.10.90
E.ROOT-SERVERS.NET.      5w6d16h IN A    192.203.230.10
I.ROOT-SERVERS.NET.      5w6d16h IN A    192.36.148.17
F.ROOT-SERVERS.NET.      5w6d16h IN A    192.5.5.241


;; Total query time: 215 msec
;; FROM: roke.uio.no to SERVER: A.ROOT-SERVERS.NET.  198.41.0.4
;; WHEN: Sun Feb 15 01:22:51 1998
;; MSG SIZE  sent: 17  rcvd: 436
```

5.3   /var/named/zone/127.0.0

Just the basics, the obligatory SOA record, and a record that maps 127.0.0.1 to localhost. Both are required. No more should be in this file. It will probably never need to be updated, unless your nameserver or hostmaster address changes.

```
@              IN      SOA     land-5.com. root.land-5.com. (
                               199609203       ; Serial
                               28800     ; Refresh
                               7200      ; Retry
                               604800    ; Expire
                               86400)    ; Minimum TTL
               NS      land-5.com.

1              PTR     localhost.
```

5.4   /var/named/zone/land-5.com

Here we see the mandatory SOA record, the needed NS records. We can see that he has a secondary name server at ns2.psi.net. This is as it should be, *always* have a off site secondary server as backup. We can also see that he has a master host called land-5 which takes care of many of the different Internet services, and that he's done it with CNAMEs (a alternative is using A records).

As you see from the SOA record, the zone file originates at land-5.com, the contact person is root@land-5.com. hostmaster is another oft used address for the contact person. The serial number is in the customary yyyymmdd format with todays serial number appended; this is probably the sixth version of zone file on the 20th of September 1996. Remember that the serial number *must* increase monotonically, here there is only *one* digit for todays serial#, so after 9 edits he has to wait until tomorrow before he can edit the file again. Consider using two digits.

```
@     IN      SOA     land-5.com. root.land-5.com. (
                      199609206         ; serial, todays date + todays serial #
```

```
                            8H              ; refresh, seconds
                            2H              ; retry, seconds
                            1W              ; expire, seconds
                            1D )            ; minimum, seconds
                   NS       land-5.com.
                   NS       ns2.psi.net.
                   MX       10 land-5.com.  ; Primary Mail Exchanger
                   TXT      "LAND-5 Corporation"

localhost          A        127.0.0.1

router             A        206.6.177.1

land-5.com.        A        206.6.177.2
ns                 A        206.6.177.3
www                A        207.159.141.192

ftp                CNAME    land-5.com.
mail               CNAME    land-5.com.
news               CNAME    land-5.com.

funn               A        206.6.177.2

;
;        Workstations
;
ws-177200          A        206.6.177.200
                   MX       10 land-5.com.  ; Primary Mail Host
ws-177201          A        206.6.177.201
                   MX       10 land-5.com.  ; Primary Mail Host
ws-177202          A        206.6.177.202
                   MX       10 land-5.com.  ; Primary Mail Host
ws-177203          A        206.6.177.203
                   MX       10 land-5.com.  ; Primary Mail Host
ws-177204          A        206.6.177.204
                   MX       10 land-5.com.  ; Primary Mail Host
ws-177205          A        206.6.177.205
                   MX       10 land-5.com.  ; Primary Mail Host
; {Many repetitive definitions deleted - SNIP}
ws-177250          A        206.6.177.250
                   MX       10 land-5.com.  ; Primary Mail Host
ws-177251          A        206.6.177.251
                   MX       10 land-5.com.  ; Primary Mail Host
ws-177252          A        206.6.177.252
                   MX       10 land-5.com.  ; Primary Mail Host
ws-177253          A        206.6.177.253
                   MX       10 land-5.com.  ; Primary Mail Host
ws-177254          A        206.6.177.254
                   MX       10 land-5.com.  ; Primary Mail Host
```

If you examine land-5s nameserver you will find that the host names are of the form ws_*number*. As of late bind 4 versions named started enforcing the restrictions on what characters may be used in host names. So that does not work with bind-8 at all, and I substituted '-' (dash) for '_' (underline) for use in this HOWTO.

Another thing to note is that the workstations don't have individual names, but rather a prefix followed by the two last parts of the IP numbers. Using such a convention can simplify maintenance significantly, but can be a bit impersonal, and, in fact, be a source of irritation among your customers.

We also see that `funn.land-5.com` is an alias for `land-5.com`, but using an A record, not a CNAME record. This is a good policy as noted earlier.

5.5   /var/named/zone/206.6.177

I'll comment on this file below

```
@                   IN      SOA     land-5.com. root.land-5.com. (
                                    199609206       ; Serial
                                    28800    ; Refresh
                                    7200     ; Retry
                                    604800   ; Expire
                                    86400)   ; Minimum TTL
                    NS      land-5.com.
                    NS      ns2.psi.net.
;
;       Servers
;
1       PTR     router.land-5.com.
2       PTR     land-5.com.
2       PTR     funn.land-5.com.
;
;       Workstations
;
200     PTR     ws-177200.land-5.com.
201     PTR     ws-177201.land-5.com.
202     PTR     ws-177202.land-5.com.
203     PTR     ws-177203.land-5.com.
204     PTR     ws-177204.land-5.com.
205     PTR     ws-177205.land-5.com.
; {Many repetitive definitions deleted - SNIP}
250     PTR     ws-177250.land-5.com.
251     PTR     ws-177251.land-5.com.
252     PTR     ws-177252.land-5.com.
253     PTR     ws-177253.land-5.com.
254     PTR     ws-177254.land-5.com.
```

The reverse zone is the bit of the setup that seems to cause the most grief. It is used to find the host name if you have the IP number of a machine. Example: you are an IRC server and accept connections from IRC clients. However you are a Norwegian IRC server and so you only want to accept connections from clients in Norway and other Scandinavian countries. When you get a connection from a client the C library is able to tell you the IP number of the connecting machine because the IP number of the client is contained in all the packets that are passed over the network. Now you can call a function called gethostbyaddr that looks up the name of a host given the IP number. Gethostbyaddr will ask a DNS server, which will then traverse the DNS looking for the machine. Supposing the client connection is from ws-177200.land-5.com. The IP number the C library provides to the IRC server is 206.6.177.200. To find out the name of that machine we need to find `200.177.6.206.in-addr.arpa`. The DNS server will first find the `arpa.` servers, then find `in-addr.arpa.` servers, following the reverse trail through 206, then 6 and at last finding the server for the `177.6.206.in-addr.arpa` zone at LAND-5. From which it will finally get the answer that for `200.177.6.206.in-addr.arpa` we have a "PTR ws-177200.land-5.com" record, meaning that the name that goes with `206.6.177.200` is ws-177200.land-5.com. As with the explanation of how `prep.ai.mit.edu` is looked up, this is slightly fictitious.

Getting back to the IRC server example. The IRC server only accepts connections from the Scandinavian countries, i.e., `*.no`, `*.se`, `*.dk`, the name `ws-177200.land-5.com` clearly does not match any of those, and the server will deny the connection. If there was *no* reverse mapping of `206.2.177.200` through the `in-addr.arpa` zone the server would have been unable to find the name at all and would have to settle to comparing `206.2.177.200` with `*.no`, `*.se` and `*.dk`, none of which will match.

Some people will tell you that reverse lookup mappings are only important for servers, or not important at all. Not so: Many ftp, news, IRC and even some http (WWW) servers will *not* accept connections from machines of which they are not able to find the name. So reverse mappings for machines are in fact *mandatory*.

6   Maintenance

Keeping it working.

There is one maintenance task you have to do on nameds, other than keeping them running. That's keeping the `root.hints` file updated. The easiest way is using dig, first run dig with no arguments, you will get the `root.hints` according to your own server. Then ask one of the listed root servers with `dig @rootserver`. You will note that the output looks terribly like a `root.hints` file. Save it to a file (`dig @e.root-servers.net .  ns >root.hints.new`) and replace the old `root.hints` with it.

Remember to reload named after replacing the cache file.

Al Longyear sent me this script, that can be run automatically to update `root.hints`, install a crontab entry to run it once a month and forget it. The script assumes you have mail working and that the mail-alias 'hostmaster' is defined. You must hack it to suit your setup.

```
#!/bin/sh
#
# Update the nameserver cache information file once per month.
# This is run automatically by a cron entry.
#
# Original by Al Longyear
# Updated for bind 8 by Nicolai Langfeldt
# Miscelanious error-conditions reported by David A. Ranch
# Ping test suggested by Martin Foster
#
(
 echo "To: hostmaster <hostmaster>"
 echo "From: system <root>"
 echo "Subject: Automatic update of the root.hints file"
 echo

 PATH=/sbin:/usr/sbin:/bin:/usr/bin:
 export PATH
 cd /var/named

 # Are we online?  Ping a server at your ISP
 case 'ping -qnc some.machine.net' in
   *'100% packet loss'*)
        echo "The network is DOWN. root.hints NOT updated"
        echo
        exit 0
        ;;
 esac
```

```
dig @rs.internic.net . ns >root.hints.new 2>&1

case 'cat root.hints.new' in
  *NOERROR*)
        # It worked
        ;;
  *)
        echo "The root.hints file update has FAILED."
        echo "This is the dig output reported:"
        echo
        cat root.hints.new
        exit 0
        ;;
esac

echo "The root.hints file has been updated to contain the following
information:"
echo
cat root.hints.new

chown root.root root.hints.new
chmod 444 root.hints.new
rm -f root.hints.old
mv root.hints root.hints.old
mv root.hints.new root.hints
ndc restart
echo
echo "The nameserver has been restarted to ensure that the update is complete."
echo "The previous root.hints file is now called
/var/named/root.hints.old."
) 2>&1 | /usr/lib/sendmail -t
exit 0
```

Some of you might have picked up that the root.hints file is also available by ftp from Internic. Please don't use ftp to update root.hints, the above method is much more friendly to the net, and Internic.

7   Converting from version 4 to version 8

This was originally a section on using bind 8 written by David E. Smith (dave@bureau42.ml.org). I have edited it some to fit the new section name.

There's not much to it. Except for using named.conf instead of named.boot, everything is identical. And bind8 comes with a perl script that converts old-style files to new. Example named.boot (old style) for a cache-only name server:

```
directory /var/named
cache   .                              root.hints
primary 0.0.127.IN-ADDR.ARPA           127.0.0.zone
primary localhost                      localhost.zone
```

On the command line, in the bind8/src/bin/named directory (*this assumes you got a source distribution. If you got a binary package the script is probably around, I'm not sure where it would be though. -ed.*), type:

```
./named-bootconf.pl < named.boot > named.conf
```

Which creates named.conf:

```
// generated by named-bootconf.pl

options {
        directory "/var/named";
};

zone "." {
        type hint;
        file "root.hints";
};

zone "0.0.127.IN-ADDR.ARPA" {
        type master;
        file "127.0.0.zone";
};

zone "localhost" {
        type master;
        file "localhost.zone";
};
```

It works for everything that can go into a `named.boot` file, although it doesn't add all of the new enhancements and configuration options that bind8 allows. Here's a more complete `named.conf` that does the same things, but a little more efficiently.

```
// This is a configuration file for named (from BIND 8.1 or later).
// It would normally be installed as /etc/named.conf.
// The only change made from the 'stock' named.conf (aside from this
// comment :) is that the directory line was uncommented, since I
// already had the zone files in /var/named.

options {
        directory "/var/named";
        datasize 20M;
};

zone "localhost" IN {
        type master;
        file "localhost.zone";
};

zone "0.0.127.in-addr.arpa" IN {
        type master;
        file "127.0.0.zone";
};

zone "." IN {
        type hint;
        file "root.hints";
};
```

HOWTO

In the bind 8 distributions directory bind8/src/bin/named/test you find this, and copies of the zone files, that many people can just drop in and use instantly.

The formats for zone files and `root.hints` files are identical, as are the commands for updating them.

8 Questions and Answers

Please read this section before mailing me.

1. My named wants a named.boot file

   You are reading the wrong HOWTO. Please see the old version of this HOWTO, which covers bind 4, at *http://www.math.uio.no/˜janl/DNS/*

2. How do use DNS from inside a firewall?

   A hint: `forward only;`, You will probably also need

   ```
   query-source port 53;
   ```

   inside the "options" part of the `named.conf` file as suggested in the example 3 (caching) section.

3. How do I make DNS rotate through the available addresses for a service, say www.busy.site to obtain a load balancing effect, or similar?

   Make several **A** records for www.busy.site and use bind 4.9.3 or later. Then bind will round-robin the answers. It will *not* work with earlier versions of bind.

4. I want to set up DNS on a (closed) intranet. What do I do?

   You drop the root.hints file and just do zone files. That also means you don't have to get new hint files all the time.

5. How do I set up a secondary (slave) name server?

   If the primary/master server has address 127.0.0.1 you put a line like this in the named.conf file of your secondary:

   ```
   zone "linux.bogus" {
           type slave;
           file "sz/linux.bogus";
           masters { 127.0.0.1; };
   };
   ```

   You may list several alternate master servers the zone can be copied from inside the `masters` list, separated by ';' (semicolon).

6. I want bind running when I'm disconnected from the net.

   There are three items regarding this:

   - I have received this mail from Ian Clark <ic@deakin.edu.au> where he explains his way of doing this:

     ```
     I run named on my 'Masquerading' machine here. I have
     two root.hints files, one called root.hints.real which contains
     the real root server names and the other called root.hints.fake
     which contains...


     ----
     ; root.hints.fake
     ; this file contains no information
     ----
     ```

> When I go off line I copy the root.hints.fake file to root.hints and restart named.
>
> When I go online I copy root.hints.real to root.hints and restart named.
>
> This is done from ip-down & ip-up respectively.
>
> The first time I do a query off line on a domain name named doesn't have details for it puts an entry like this in messages..
>
> Jan 28 20:10:11 hazchem named[10147]: No root nameserver for class IN
>
> which I can live with.
>
> It certainly seems to work for me. I can use the nameserver for local machines while off the 'net without the timeout delay for external domain names and I while on the 'net queries for external domains work normally

- I have also received information about how bind interacts with NFS and the portmapper on a mostly offline machine from Karl-Max Wanger:

> I use to run my own named on all my machines which are only occasionally connected to the Internet by modem. The nameserver only acts as a cache, it has no area of authority and asks back for everything at the name servers in the root.cache file. As is usu-al with
> Slackware, it is started before nfsd and mountd.
>
> With one of my machines (a Libretto 30 notebook) I had the problem that sometimes I could mount it from another system connected to my local LAN, but most of the time it didn't work. I had the same effect regardless of using PLIP, a PCMCIA ethernet card or PPP over a serial interface.
>
> After some time of guessing and experimenting I found out that apparently named messed with the process of registration nfsd and mountd have to carry out with the portmapper upon startup (I start these daemons at boot time as usual). Starting named after nfsd and mountd eliminated this problem completely.
>
> As there are no disadvantages to expect from such a modified boot sequence I'd advise everybody to do it that way to prevent potential trouble.

- Finally, there is HOWTO information about this at *Ask Mr. DNS* at *http://www.acmebw.com/askmrdns/#linux-ns*. It is about bind 4 though, so you have to adapt what he says to bind 8.

7. Where does the caching name server store its cache? Is there any way I can control the size of the cache?

   The cache is completely stored in memory, it is *not* written to disk at any time. Every time you kill named the cache is lost. The cache is *not* controllable in any way. named manages it according to some simple rules and that is it. You cannot control the cache or the cache size in any way for any reason. If you want to you can "fix" this by hacking named. This is however not recommended.

8. Does named save the cache between restarts? Can I make it save it?

No, named does *not* save the cache when it dies. That means that the cache must be built anew each time you kill and restart named. There is *no* way to make named save the cache in a file. If you want you can "fix" this by hacking named. This is however not recommended.

9. How can I get a domian? I want to set up my own domain called (for example) `linux-rules.net`. How can I get the domain I want assigned to me?

Please contact your network service provider. They will be able to help you with this. Please note that in most parts of the world you need to pay money to get a domain.

9   How to become a bigger time DNS admin.

Documentation and tools.

Real Documentation exists. Online and in print. The reading of several of these is required to make the step from small time DNS admin to a big time one. In print the standard book is *DNS and BIND* by C. Liu and P. Albitz from O'Reilly & Associates, Sebastopol, CA, ISBN 0-937175-82-X. I read this, it's excellent, though based on bind 4, this is not a real problem though. There is also a section in on DNS in *TCP/IP Network Administration*, by Craig Hunt from O'Reilly..., ISBN 0-937175-82-X. Another must for Good DNS administration (or good anything for that matter) is *Zen and the Art of Motorcycle Maintenance* by Robert M. Pirsig :-) Available as ISBN 0688052304 and others.

Online you will find stuff on `<http://www.dns.net/dnsrd/>` (DNS Resources Directory), `<http://www.isc.org/bind.html>`; A FAQ, a reference manual (BOG; Bind Operations Guide) as well as papers and protocol definitions and DNS hacks (these, and most, if not all, of the RFCs mentioned below, are also contained in the bind distribution). I have not read most of these, but then I'm not a big-time DNS admin either. Arnt Gulbrandsen on the other hand has read BOG and he's ecstatic about it :-). The newsgroup *comp.protocols.tcp-ip.domains* is about DNS. In addition there are a number of RFCs about DNS, the most important are probably these:

RFC 2052

A. Gulbrandsen, P. Vixie, *A DNS RR for specifying the location of services (DNS SRV)*, October 1996

RFC 1918

Y. Rekhter, R. Moskowitz, D. Karrenberg, G. de Groot, E. Lear, *Address Allocation for Private Internets*, 02/29/1996.

RFC 1912

D. Barr, *Common DNS Operational and Configuration Errors*, 02/28/1996.

RFC 1912 Errors

B. Barr *Errors in RFC 1912*, this is available at `<http://www.cis.ohio-state.edu/~barr/rfc1912-errors.html>`

RFC 1713

A. Romao, *Tools for DNS debugging*, 11/03/1994.

RFC 1712

C. Farrell, M. Schulze, S. Pleitner, D. Baldoni, *DNS Encoding of Geographical Location*, 11/01/1994.

RFC 1183

R. Ullmann, P. Mockapetris, L. Mamakos, C. Everhart, *New DNS RR Definitions*, 10/08/1990.

RFC 1035

P. Mockapetris, *Domain names - implementation and specification*, 11/01/1987.

RFC 1034

P. Mockapetris, *Domain names - concepts and facilities*, 11/01/1987.

RFC 1033

M. Lottor, *Domain administrators operations guide*, 11/01/1987.

RFC 1032

M. Stahl, *Domain administrators guide*, 11/01/1987.

RFC 974

C. Partridge, *Mail routing and the domain system*, 01/01/1986.

## Part X

"The Linux ELF HOWTO" Daniel Barlow

<daniel.barlow@linux.org>

v1.29, 14 July 1996

This document describes how to migrate your Linux system to compile and run programs in the ELF binary format. It falls into three conceptual parts: (1) What ELF is, and why you should upgrade, (2) How to upgrade to ELF-capability, and (3) what you can do then. After a fairly long fallow period in which I have been pretending to do academic work, it has recently been overhauled to give current information for Linux 2.0.

1   What is ELF? An introduction

ELF (Executable and Linking Format) is a binary format originally developed by USL (UNIX System Laboratories) and currently used in Solaris and System V Release 4. Because of its increased flexibility over the older a.out format that Linux previously used, the GCC and C library developers decided last year to move to using ELF as the Linux standard binary format also.

This 'increased flexibility' manifests as essentially two benefits to the average applications progammer:

- It is much simpler to make shared libraries with ELF. Typically, just compile all the object files with -fPIC, then link with a command like

      gcc -shared -Wl,-soname,libfoo.so.y -o libfoo.so.y.x *.o

  If that looks complex, you obviously haven't ever read up on the equivalent procedure for a.out shared libraries, which involves compiling the library twice, reserving space for all the data you think that the library is likely to require in future, and registering that address space with a third party (it's described in a document over 20 pages long — look at <ftp://tsx-11.mit.edu/pub/linux/packages/GCC/src/tools-2.17.tar.gz> for details).

- It makes dynamic loading (ie programs which can load modules at runtime) much simpler. This is used by Perl 5, Python, and Java, among other things (it's a kicker for many kinds of interpreters). Other suggestions for dynamic loading have included super-fast MUDs, where extra code could be compiled and linked into the running executable without having to stop and restart the program.

Against this it must be weighed that ELF is possibly a bit slower. The figures that get bandied around are between 1% and 5%, though all the actual tests that have been conducted so far indicate that the difference is small enough to get lost in the noise of other events happening at the same time. If you have TeX or a Postscript viewer/printer, you can read speed.comp-1.0.tar.gz, which is available from SunSite somewhere.

The slowdown comes from the fact that ELF library code must be position independent (this is what the -fPIC above stands for) and so a register must be devoted to holding offsets. That's one less for holding variables in, and the 80x86 has a paucity of general-purpose registers anyway. Note that the speed difference only applies to code that is part of shared libraries. For applications or kernels there is no speed difference between a.out and ELF.

1.1   What ELF isn't

There are a number of common misconceptions about what ELF will do for your system:

It's not a way to run SVR4 or Solaris programs

Although it's the same binary 'container' as SVR4 systems use, that doesn't mean that SVR4 programs suddenly become runnable on Linux. It's analogous to a disk format — you can keep Linux programs on MSDOS or Minix-format disks, and vice versa, but that doesn't mean that these systems become able to run each others' programs.

It may be possible to run an application for another x86 Unix under Linux (it depends on the application), but following the instructions in this HOWTO will *not* have that effect. Start by looking at the iBCS kernel module (somewhere on `tsx-11.mit.edu`) and see if it fits your needs.

It's not intrinsically smaller or faster

You may well end up with smaller binaries anyway, though, as you can more easily create shared libraries of common code between many programs. In general, if you use the same compiler options and your binaries come out smaller than they did with a.out, it's more likely to be fluke or a different compiler version. As for 'faster', I'd be surprised. Speed increases could turn up if your binaries are smaller, due to less swapping or larger functional areas fitting in cache.

It doesn't require that you replace every binary on your system

At the end of this procedure you have a system capable of compiling and running both ELF and a.out programs. New programs will by default be compiled in ELF, though this can be overridden with a command-line switch. There is admittedly a memory penalty for running a mixed ELF/a.out system — if you have both breeds of program running at once you also have two copies of the C library in core, and so on. I've had reports that the speed difference from this is undetectable in normal use on a 6Mb system though (I certainly haven't noticed much in 8Mb), so it's hardly pressing. You lose far more memory every day by running bloated programs like Emacs and static Mosaic/Netscape binaries :-)

It's nothing to do with Tolkien.

Or at least, not in this context.

1.2 Why you should convert to ELF

There are essentially two reasons to upgrade your system to compile and run ELF programs: the first is the increased flexibility in programming referred to above, and the second is that, due to the first, everyone else will (or has already). Current releases of the C library and GCC are compiled only for ELF, and other developers are moving ELFwards too.

Many people are concerned about stability (justifiably so, even if it's not so much fun). ELF on Linux has existed since August 1994 and has been publically available since May or June 1995; the teething troubles are probably out of the way by now. You should allow for the possibility of breaking things — as you would with any major upgrade — but the technology that you're upgrading to is no longer bleeding edge. For a system on which any development is done, or on which you want to run other people's precompiled binaries, ELF is pretty much a necessity these days. Plan to switch to it when you upgrade to version 2.0 of the kernel.

1.3 How to convert to ELF

When this HOWTO was first written, there was only one way, and it was the way described here. These days there are high-quality upgradable distributions available — unless you have invested significant time in setting up your machine exactly how you like it, you might find that a backup of all your own data and a reinstall from a recent Red Hat or Debian release is more convenient than messing about with the assorted libraries and compilers described here.

I must stress this. The installation described here is a fairly small job in itself (it can be completed in well under an hour, excepting the time taken to download the new software), but there are a multitude of errors that you can make which will probably leave you with an unbootable system. If you are not comfortable with upgrading shared libraries, if the commands `ldconfig` and `ldd` mean nothing to you, or if you're unhappy about building packages from source code, you should consider the 'easy option'. Even if this description isn't you, think about it anyway — if you want a 'fully ELF' system, *somebody* is going to have to recompile all the binaries on it.

Still with us?

2 Installation

2.1 Background

The aim of this conversion is to leave you with a system which can build and run both a.out and ELF programs, with each type of program being able to find its appropriate breed of shared libraries. This obviously requires a bit more intelligence in the library search routines than the simple 'look in /lib, /usr/lib and anywhere else that the program was compiled to search' strategy that some other systems can get away with.

This intelligence is centralised in a *dynamic loader*, which exists in only one — or two — places on the system. For a.out programs, it's called /lib/ld.so, and for ELF programs it's /lib/ld-linux.so.1. The compiler and linker do not encode absolute library pathnames into the programs they output; instead they put the library name and the absolute path to the appropriate dynamic loader in, and leave that to match the library name to the appropriate place at runtime. This has one very important effect — it means that the libraries that a program uses can be moved to other directories *without recompiling the program*, provided that ld.so (ld-linux.so.1; whatever) is told to search the new directory. This is essential functionality for the directory swapping operation that follows.

The corollary of the above, of course, is that any attempt to delete or move ld.so or ld-linux.so.1 may cause *every dynamically linked program on the system to stop working*. This is generally regarded as a Bad Thing.

The basic plan, then, is that ELF development things (compilers, include files and libraries) go into /usr/{bin,lib,include} where your a.out ones currently are, and the a.out things will be moved into /usr/i486-linuxaout/{bin, lib, include}. /etc/ld.so.conf lists all the places on the system where libraries are expected to be found, and ldconfig is intelligent enough to distinguish between ELF and a.out variants.

There are a couple of exceptions to the library placement:

- Some old programs were built without the use of ld.so. These would all cease working if their libraries were moved from under them. Thus, libc.so* and libm.so* must stay where they are in /lib, and the ELF versions have had their major numbers upgraded so that they do not overwrite the a.out ones. Old X libraries (prior to version 6) are best left where they are also, although newer ones (libX*so.6) must be moved. Moving the old ones will apparently break xview programs, and not moving the new ones will cause them to be overwritten when you install ELF X libraries.

  If you have non-ld.so programs that require libraries other than the above (if you know which programs they are, you can run ldd on them to find out which libraries they need *before* breaking them) you have essentially two options. One, you can extract the ELF library tar files into a temporary directory, check whether your precious library would be overwritten, and if so, move the ELF version of the library into, say, /usr/i486-linux/lib instead of /lib. Make sure your ld.so.conf has /usr/i486-linux/lib in it, then run ldconfig and think no more on't. Two, you can recompile or acquire a newer copy of the offending program. This might not be a bad idea, if possible.

- If you have /usr and / on different partitions, any libraries that you move from /lib must end up somewhere else on the root disk, not on /usr. I used /lib-aout in the instructions that follow.

2.2 Before you start — Notes and Caveats

- You will need to be running a post-1.1.52 **kernel with ELF binary format support**. 1.2.13 works. 2.0.0 (the most recent at the time of writing) also works, as do most of the 1.3 series, though the point of running old 'experimental' kernels is anyway questionable now that 2.0 is here.

- You are recommended to prepare or acquire a linux boot/root disk, such as a Slackware rescue disk. You probably won't need it, but if you do and you don't have one, you'll kick yourself. In a similar 'prevention is better than cure' vein, statically linked copies of mv, ln, and maybe other file manipulation commands (though in fact I think you can do everything else you actually *need* to with shell builtins) may help you out of any awkward situations you could end up in.

- If you were following the early ELF development, or you installed certain versions of Slackware (none of the current ones, admittedly) you may have ELF libraries in /lib/elf (usually libc.so.4 and co). Applications that you built using these should be rebuilt, then the directory removed. There is no need for a /lib/elf directory!

HOWTO

- Most Linux installations these days have converged on the 'FSSTND' standard file system, but doubtless there are still installed systems that haven't. If you see references to /sbin/*something* and you don't have a /sbin directory, you'll probably find the program referred to in /bin or /etc/. It is especially important to check this when you install new programs; if you have /etc nearer the front of the search path than /sbin you'll get odd failures due to running the old versions when you weren't expecting to.

- It's a good idea to pick a time when nobody else is using the computer, or to take it single-user. It might be a good idea to reboot it off a floppy so that a mistake doesn't leave you stuck, but personally I like to leave a *small* element of fun ...

2.3 Ingredients

Anything in the following list that I describe as being "on tsx-11" can be found in <ftp://tsx-11.mit.edu/pub/linux/packages/GCC/>, <ftp://sunsite.unc.edu/pub/Linux/GCC/>, and at many mirrors. Please take the time to look up your nearest mirror site and use that instead of the master sites where possible. It's faster for both you and everyone else.

These packages (either the listed version or a later one) are required. Also download and read through the release notes for each of them: these are the files named release.*packagename*. This applies especially if you get newer versions than are listed here, as procedures may have changed.

Even if you habitually compile things from source, I'd advise you to go for the binary versions where I've indicated, unless you *really* have no use for your hair. Most of them are not set up for 'crosscompiling' on an a.out-based system, and you are probably lining yourself up for major grief if you try.

2.3.1 Absolute essentials

- ld.so-1.7.14.tar.gz — the new dynamic linker. Contains both source and binaries. Note that forthcoming versions of this will require kernel ELF support even for a.out binaries; if you get 1.8.1 or later instead of the version listed, make sure that the kernel you're running was compiled with ELF support *before* you install this.

- libc-5.3.12.bin.tar.gz — the ELF shared images for the C and maths libraries, plus the corresponding static libraries and the include files needed to compile programs with them. Source is also available if you like it, but it takes ages to compile, and probably won't at all unless you already have an ELF system.

- gcc-2.7.2.bin.tar.gz — the ELF C compiler package, which also includes an a.out C compiler which understands the new directory layout. If you want to build gcc yourself (which you'll probably find is simpler when you're already running ELF), you're recommended to apply gcc-2.7.2-linux.diff.gz to the GNU sources first.

- binutils-2.6.0.12.bin.tar.gz — the GNU binary utilities patched for Linux. These are programs such as gas, ld, strings and so on, most of which are required to make the C compiler go. Note that the vanilla GNU binutils (e.g. from prep.ai.mit.edu) are not an acceptable substitute; if you really want to compile this yourself you'll need to use the patched-for-Linux binutils-2.6.0.12.tar.gz package instead of the GNU one.

- ncurses-1.9.9e.tar.gz — this is an SVR4-compatible curses library, which is henceforward deemed to be the 'standard curses library' for Linux. The source is available from GNU sites such as <ftp://prep.ai.mit.edu/gnu/> and also from <ftp://ftp.netcom.com/pub/zm/zmbenhal>, and there is a binary package on tsx-11. By the time you get to install this you will have a fully functional ELF development system, so I recommend the source package if you have any kind of compilation horsepower. That may just be me, though.

- gdbm-1.7.3.tar.gz is a set of database routines that use extensible hashing and work similarly to the standard UNIX dbm and ndbm routines. The source is available from GNU sites such as <ftp://prep.ai.mit.edu/gnu/>; you also need a patch <ftp://ftp.uk.linux.org/pub/Linux/libc/non-core/gdbm.patch> to make shared libraries out of it. That patch also fixes a couple of other things (a one-character typo in the Makefile and a predisposition to use the wrong kind of file locking).

2.3.2   Others

These are other libraries and files which aren't strictly essential, but that you might want to get anyway. This list contains only packages that need to be upgraded to work in an ELF-useful fashion. Later in this document is another list of programs which will continue to work but which you'll have to tweak/upgrade if you want to recompile them in ELF. If your net access involves high-latency links (like, say, a five-minute walk with a box of floppy disks), skip forwards and check that one too before you set out :-)

- The **a.out compatibility** library package, `libc.so-4.7.6`. This is listed as 'optional' because your existing a.out libraries of whatever vintage will continue to work fine with your existing binaries. You might find that you need this if you plan to continue developing in a.out for whatever reason.

- **BSD curses**. If you find binaries which require `libcurses.so.1`, this is the old BSD curses library. They're probably quite rare, which is fortunate as I can't presently find a (source code) copy of the library. It's probably best to recompile programs like this to use ncurses; if this is not an option, there is a binary `libcurses.so` in the `libc-5.0.9.bin.tar.gz` on `tsx-11` mirrors.

- **Berkeley db**: the new 4.4BSD `libdb` database routines. The source can be had from `<ftp://ftp.cs. berkeley.edu/ucb/4bsd/db.1.85.tar.gz/>`, and the patch for Linux shared libraries is `<ftp:// ftp.uk.linux.org/pub/Linux/libc/non-core/db.patch>`

- **C++ stuff.** The `gcc` package comes with `g++`, but you'll also need `libg++-2.7.1.4.bin.tar.gz` to compile any useful C++ software. I don't use C++ myself, but I understand that it is nontrivial to build this from source, hence the binary recommendation.

- **GNU-compatible termcap**. The conversion to ncurses din't happen simultaneously with the move to ELF — you might find that you want to run other people's programs that were built using this library, and for some applications you might wish to continue using it. `gdb` is a legitimate example. If you intend to debug shared libraries and you think that gdb is getting confused about the ones that it's linked with itself, you probably want a statically linked copy of it; in this case, you'll find that a real termcap is a lot smaller than the termcap-compatible routines in ncurses.

  `termcap-2.0.8.tar.gz` is available from `tsx-11`. This is *not* GNU Termcap, but it is completely compatible (the differences are in the error checking, apparently). This is a source code package.

- **MAKEDEV**. In some incarnations, this utility removes existing entries for devices before recreating them. This is Bad News if it removes `/dev/zero`, which causes some versions of `ld-linux.so.1` to break. Find a new version at `<ftp://sunsite.unc.edu/pub/Linux/system/Admin/MAKEDEV-C-1.5.tar.gz>` or `<ftp://sunsite.unc.edu/pub/Linux/system/Admin/MAKEDEV-2.2.tar.gz>`.

- `modules-2.0.0`. If you use modules, the upgrade to binutils which you're shortly about to perform will break all versions of the modules utilities older than 1.3.69. New modules utilities can be had from `<http://www. pi.se/blox/>`.

- The **X window system** includes a lot of shared libraries. As your new programs will be ELF, and ELF programs cannot use a.out libraries, you'll need a new X installation if you want to do any X development. XFree86 3.1.2 comes in both a.out and ELF formats. `ftp` to `ftp.xfree86.org`, read the 'too many users' message that you are almost guaranteed to get, and pick the closest mirror site network-wise to you. Once you have the contents of the `common` and `elf` directories, you must edit `/usr/X11R6/lib/X11/config/linux.cf` to change the lines saying

  ```
  #define LinuxElfDefault        NO
  #define UseElfFormat           NO
  ```

  to say `YES` instead. Otherwise an xpm build will attempt to do odd stuff with `jumpas` and its associated relics of the past. Note that XFree86 binaries currently require an ELF shared termcap library (`libtermcap.so.2`) to be installed.

  If you use Motif, you may also need to contact your vendor, to investigate whether they will supply ELF Motif libraries. I don't use it; I can't help here.

- If you're upgrading to Linux 2.0 at the same time as going ELF, don't forget also to check the `Documentation/Changes` file that comes in the kernel source, to find out what else you'll need.

2.4 Rearranging your filesystem

Sooo... Note that in all that follows, when I say 'remove' I naturally mean 'backup then remove' :-). Take a deep breath ...

1. **The essentials — binary installation**

2. Make the new directories that you will move a.out things to

   ```
   mkdir -p /usr/i486-linuxaout/bin
   mkdir -p /usr/i486-linuxaout/include
   mkdir -p /usr/i486-linuxaout/lib
   mkdir /lib-aout
   ```

3. Untar the dynamic linker package `ld.so-1.7.14` in the directory you usually put source code, then read through the `ld.so-1.7.14/instldso.sh` script just unpacked. If you have a really standard system, run it by doing `sh instldso.sh`, but if you have anything at all unusual then do the install by hand instead. 'Anything at all unusual' includes

   - using zsh as a shell (some versions of zsh define `$VERSION`, which seems to confuse `instldso.sh`)

   - having symlinks from `/lib/elf` to `/lib` (which you shouldn't need, but that's scant consolation when you're looking for the rescue disk)

4. Edit `/etc/ld.so.conf` to add the new directory `/usr/i486-linuxaout/lib` (and `/lib-aout` if you're going to need one). Then rerun `/sbin/ldconfig -v` to check that it is picking up the new directories.

5. Move all the a.out libraries in `/usr/lib` and `/usr/*/lib` to `/usr/i486-linuxaout/lib`. Note, I said 'libraries' not 'everything'. That's files matching the specification `lib*.so*`, `lib*.sa*`, or `lib*.a`. Don't start moving `/usr/lib/gcc-lib` or anything silly like that around.

6. Now look at `/lib`. Leave intact `libc.so*`, `libm.so*`, and `libdl.so*`. If you have symlinks to X libraries (`libX*.so.3*`) leave them there too — XView and some other packages may require them. Leave `ld.so*`, `ld-linux.so*` and any other files starting with `ld`. As for the remaining libraries (if there are any others): if you have `/usr` on the root partition, put them in `/usr/i486-linuxaout/lib`. If you have `/usr` mounted separately, put them in `/lib-aout`. Now run `ldconfig -v`

7. Remove the directory `/usr/lib/ldscripts` if it's there, in preparation for installing the binutils (which will recreate it)

8. Remove any copies of `ld` and `as` (*except* for `ld86` and `as86`) that you can find in `/usr/bin`.

9. You need to clean up your `/usr/include` hierarchy. On an average system, some of the files in here are 'core' functionality and come with libc, while others are from other packages that you or your distribution builder have installed. Given this mess, I suggest you remake it from scratch; rename it to `/usr/include.old`, then unpack `libc-5.2.18.bin.tar.gz` by untarring it from the root directory.

10. Install the binutils package. `tar -xvzf binutils-2.6.0.12.bin.tar.gz -C /` is one perfectly good way to do this.

11. The gcc package expects to be untarred from root. It installs some files in `/usr/bin` and lots more in `/usr/lib/gcc-lib/i486-linux/2.7.2` and `/usr/lib/gcc-lib/i486-linuxaout/2.7.2`. Use

    ```
    $ tar ztf gcc-2.7.2.bin.tar.gz
    ```

    to see what's in it, backup anything that it overwrites that you feel you may want to keep (for example, if you have Gnu ADA installed you will probably want to keep `/usr/bin/gcc`), then just do

    ```
    # tar -zxf gcc-2.7.2.bin.tar.gz -C /
    ```

At this point, you should be able to run `gcc -v` and compile test programs. Try

```
$ gcc -v
Reading specs from /usr/lib/gcc-lib/i486-linux/2.7.2/specs
gcc version 2.7.2
$ gcc -v -b i486-linuxaout
Reading specs from /usr/lib/gcc-lib/i486-linuxaout/2.7.2/specs
gcc version 2.7.2
$ ld -V
ld version 2.6 (with BFD 2.6.0.2)
   Supported emulations:
    elf_i386
    i386linux
    i386coff
```

followed of course by the traditional "Hello, world" program. Try it with `gcc` and with `gcc -b i486-linuxaout` to check that both the a.out and ELF compilers are set up correctly.

Finished? Not quite. You still have all the 'non-core' libraries to install, and a fair amount of mucking about with symlinks. Onwards...

Symlinks

12. Some programs (notably various X programs) use `/lib/cpp`, which under Linux is generally a link to `/usr/lib/gcc-lib/i486-linux/`*version*`/cpp`. As the preceding step probably wiped out whatever version of `cpp` it was pointing to, you'll need to recreate the link:

```
# cd /lib
# ln -s /usr/lib/gcc-lib/i486-linux/2.7.2/cpp .
```

13. When you moved `/usr/include` to `/usr/include.old`, you lost the symlinks into the kernel sources. Run

```
# cd /usr/include
# ln -s ../src/linux/include/linux .
# ln -s ../src/linux/include/asm .
```

(assuming you have kernel source in `/usr/src/linux`; if not, season to taste)

14. The FSSTND people have once again justified their keep by moving the `utmp` and `wtmp` files from `/var/adm` to `/var/run` and `/var/log` respectively. You'll need to add some links dependent on where they currently live, and you may need to make the `/var/log` and `/var/adm` directories too. I reproduce below the `ls -l` output of appropriate bits on my system:

```
$ ls -ld /var/adm /var/log /var/run /var/log/*tmp /var/run/*tmp
lrwxrwxrwx  1 root     root          3 May 24 05:53 /var/adm -> log/
drwxr-xr-x  9 root     root       1024 Aug 13 23:17 /var/log/
lrwxrwxrwx  1 root     root         11 Aug 13 23:17 /var/log/utmp -
> ../run/utmp
-rw-r--r--  1 root     root     451472 Aug 13 23:00 /var/log/wtmp
drwxr-xr-x  2 root     root       1024 Aug 13 23:17 /var/run/
-rw-r--r--  1 root     root        448 Aug 13 23:00 /var/run/utmp
```

Check the FSSTND (from LDP archives such as `<ftp://sunsite.unc.edu/pub/Linux/docs/fsstnd/>`) for the full story.

Rejoice!

By this time you should have a (more or less) fully functioning ELF development system. Stand back and celebrate quietly for a few minutes.

Essential source code packages

15. **ncurses installation** is a fairly long job, though most of of the time can be spent reading Usenet while it builds. After unpacking the tar file, read the `INSTALL` file pretending that you are 'a Linux (...) distribution integrator or packager'; that is, you probably want to be configuring it with a command like

```
$ ./configure --with-normal --with-shared --disable-termcap --enable-
overwrite --prefix=/usr
```

Take heed also of the comments about the default terminal type; in 1.3 and 2.0 kernels this is set to `linux` at boot time, but you may find that you need to edit `/etc/inittab` to avoid having it set back to `console` by `getty`.

If you do not have `/usr/lib/terminfo` on the root disk you will have to fiddle with the 'fallback' support in ncurses. This is documented in the `INSTALL` file mentioned above, and is simple but tedious (due to the necessity of building the library twice). If you're happy with having `linux` and `vt100` as fallbacks, there is a ready-prepared `fallback.c` at `<ftp://ftp.uk.linux.org/pub/Linux/libc/non-core/fallback.c>` which you can copy over the existing one.

After you have installed ncurses, you'll have to get messy in `/usr/lib` — it does some non-optimal things that are simplest to clear up by hand. Note the weird discrepancy between the version numbers; this is ugly but not actually detrimental to human health.

(a) `/usr/lib/libncurses.so.1.9.9e` should be moved to `/lib` so that curses programs which run in single-user mode will continue to do so. If you have `/usr/lib` on the root partition, this is unnecessary but will do no harm.

(b) In `/lib`, make a link to `libncurses.so.1.9.9e` called `libncurses.so.3.0`.

(c) You also need links `/usr/lib/libncurses.so`, `/usr/lib/libcurses.so` and `/usr/lib/libtermcap.so` which should all point to `/lib/libncurses.so.3.0`.

In brief for the hard of thinking, that little lot was

```
# cd /lib
# mv /usr/lib/libncurses.so.1.9.9e .
# ln -s libncurses.so.1.9.9e libncurses.so.3.0
# cd /usr/lib
# ln -s /lib/libncurses.so.3.0 libncurses.so
# ln -s /lib/libncurses.so.3.0 libcurses.so
# ln -s /lib/libncurses.so.3.0 libtermcap.so
```

16. **gdbm** installation. Unpack the source code in a source code directory, apply `gdbm.patch`, and look over the `README` and `INSTALL` files.

The build process should go something like:

```
$ tar zxf gdbm-1.7.3.tar.gz
$ patch -p0 < gdbm.patch
$ cd gdbm-1.7.3
$ ./configure --prefix=/usr
$ make
$ make progs
$ su
# make install
# make install-compat
# cd /usr/lib
# ln -s libgdbm.so.1 libgdbm.so
# ln -s libgdbm.so.1 libgdbm.so.2
# ldconfig
```

The last step is for backward-compatibility; some current distributions use `libgdbm.so.2` which is exactly the same code as `libgdbm.so.1`, but misnumbered for historical reasons.

Optional source code packages. In general, you can just install these according to their instructions, so I won't repeat them. There are two exceptions, though:

17. If you want the **GNU-ish termcap** (strictly speaking, optional; in practice, necessary to use XFree86 binaries) it also needs to be built from source, but shouldn't require anything more complex than

```
$ tar zxf termcap-2.0.8.tar.gz
$ cd termcap-2.0.8
$ make
$ su
# cp libtermcap.so.2.0.8 /usr/lib
# ldconfig
```

I recommend that you *don't* make install, as this would overwrite bits of the ncurses installation. If you need to actually compile things against this library, as opposed to just running binaries that were made with it, think about putting the header files and static libraries somewhere nonstandard, and using -I and -L flags when you compile the said things. The vagueness of this description should make it plain that continued use of termcap is 'discouraged' unless you have a good reason.

18. For libdb, it goes something like:

```
$ tar zxf db.1.85.tar.gz
$ patch -p0 <db.patch
$ cd db.1.85/PORT/linux
$ make
$ su
# mkdir /usr/include/db
# ldconfig
# cp libdb.so.1.85.3 /usr/lib ; ( cd /usr/lib && ln -s libdb.so.1 libd-
b.so )
# cp ../../include/*.h /usr/include/db
```

Note that

- you're not applying PORT/linux/OTHER_PATCHES, because it's subsumed by this patch

- you're installing the header files somewhere other than /usr/include — they conflict with the ones that gdbm uses. To compile programs that want libdb you must add -I/usr/include/db to the C compiler's command line.

2.5 What it should look like (outline directory structure)

This is a deliberately vague guide to what the files you have just installed are. It may be useful for troubleshooting or deciding what to delete.

2.5.1 /lib

- Dynamic linkers ld.so (a.out) and ld-linux.so.1 (ELF). Either of these may be symlinks, but make sure that the files they point to do exist.

- Basic shared libraries libc.so.4, libm.so.4 (a.out) These are symlinks, but check that they point to real files.

- Basic shared libraries libc.so.5, libm.so.5, libdl.so.1,libncurses.so.1,libtermcap.so.2, (ELF). Again, these are symlinks. Check the files that they point to.

2.5.2 /usr/lib

- All the non-library files and directories that were there previously.

- libbfd.so*,libdb.so*, libgdbm.so*, ELF shared libraries.

- More symlinks. For each library in /lib or /usr/lib, there should be a symlink in here. The link's name should be the real filename, minus the version number. For example, for libc,

```
lrwxrwxrwx   1 root     root          14 May  2 20:09 /lib/libc.so.5 -
> libc.so.5.3.12
-rwxr-xr-x   1 bin      bin       583795 Apr 25 06:15 /lib/libc.so.5.3.12
lrwxrwxrwx   1 root     root          12 Oct 27  1995 /usr/lib/libc.so -
> /lib/libc.so.5
```

These links are used by `ld` at link time.

- `libbsd.a`, `libgmon.a`, `libmcheck.a`, `libmcheck.a` and one `lib*.a` file for every ELF shared library in `/lib` and `/usr/lib`. ELF static libraries. The ones that duplicate shared libraries may not be tremendously useful for most people — when using ELF, you can use the `gcc -g` switch with shared libraries, so there's not much reason to compile static any longer. You *will* need to keep them if you actually want to debug the libraries themselves.

- `crt0.o`, `gcrt0.o`. a.out 'start of program' files; one of these is linked as the first file in every a.out program you compile, unless you take steps to avoid it.

- `crt1.o`, `crtbegin.o`, `crtbeginS.o`, `crtend.o`, `crtendS.o`, `crti.o`, `crtn.o`, `gcrt1.o`. ELF s-tartup files. These do similar things to `*crt0.o` above for ELF programs.

2.5.3 /usr/lib/ldscripts

- This is where the driver scripts for `ld` live, as the name suggests. It should look like

```
$ ls /usr/lib/ldscripts/
elf_i386.x      elf_i386.xs     i386coff.xn    i386linux.xbn
elf_i386.xbn    elf_i386.xu     i386coff.xr    i386linux.xn
elf_i386.xn     i386coff.x      i386coff.xu    i386linux.xr
elf_i386.xr     i386coff.xbn    i386linux.x    i386linux.xu
```

2.5.4 /usr/i486-linux/bin

- `ar`, `as`, `gasp`, `ld`, `nm`, `ranlib`, `strip`. These are all actually symlinks to the real binutils in `/usr/bin`

2.5.5 /usr/i486-linuxaout/bin

- `as` — the a.out assembler, and `gasp`, its macro preprocessor
- `ar`, `ld`, `nm`, `ranlib`, `strip` — symlinks to the real binutils in `/usr/bin`

2.5.6 /usr/i486-linux/lib

- `ldscripts` is a symlink to `/usr/lib/ldscripts`.

2.5.7 /usr/i486-linuxaout/lib

- `lib*.so*`. a.out shared library images. Needed to run a.out programs

- `lib*.sa`. a.out shared library stubs. Needed to compile a.out programs that use shared libraries. If you don't intend to, you can safely remove these.

- `lib*.a`. a.out static libraries. Needed to compile static a.out programs (eg when compiling with `-g`). Again, you can delete them if you don't intend to do this.

- `ldscripts` is a symbolic link to `/usr/lib/ldscripts`

2.5.8 /usr/lib/gcc-lib/i486-linux/2.7.2

- This directory contains a version of gcc 2.7.2 set up to compile ELF programs.

2.5.9 `/usr/lib/gcc-lib/i486-linuxaout/2.7.2`

- This directory contains a version of gcc 2.7.2 set up to compile a.out programs, which knows about the new directory structure. If you're not going to compile anything in a.out, deleting this may free up around 4Mb. Note that you need to keep it if you want to build unpatched 1.2 series kernels.

2.6 Common errors — Don't Panic!

(in large friendly letters)

You moved the wrong thing and now nothing runs

> You still have a shell running, though, and with a little ingenuity you can do an awful lot with shell builtins. Remember that `echo *` is an acceptable substitute for `ls`, and `echo >>filename` can be used to add lines to a file. Also, don't forget that `ldconfig` is linked static. If you moved, say, `libc.so.4` to `/lib-aout` mistakenly, you can do `echo "lib-aout" >>/etc/ld.so.conf ; ldconfig -v/` and be back up again. If you moved `/lib/ld.so` you may be able to do `sln /silly/place/ld.so /lib/ld.so`, if you have a statically linked ln, and probably be back up again.

bad address

> on attempting to run anything ELF. You're using kernel 1.3.x, where $x<3$. Don't. They're probably the buggiest Linux kernels on the planet anyway. Upgrade to 2.0 or downgrade to 1.2.13. Some people also report kernel panics in similar circumstances; I haven't investigated, chiefly as I can think of no reason for wanting or needing to run development kernels and not keeping up with the releases.

gcc: installation problem, cannot exec *something*: No such file or directory

> when attempting to do a.out compilations (*something* is usually one of `cpp` or `cc1`). Either it's right, or alternatively you typed
>
> ```
> $ gcc -b -i486-linuxaout
> ```
>
> when you should have typed
>
> ```
> $ gcc -b i486-linuxaout
> ```
>
> Note that the 'i486' does *not* start with a dash.

make: * No targets specified and no makefile found. Stop.**

> indicates that you haven't patched and recompiled `make`, or that you still have an old version of it elsewhere on the system.

no such file or directory: /usr/bin/gcc

> (or any other file that you try to run) when you know there *is* such a file. This usually means that the ELF dynamic loader `/lib/ld-linux.so.1` is not installed, or is unreadable for some reason. You should have installed it at around step 2 previously.

not a ZMAGIC file, skipping

> from `ldconfig`. You have an old version of the ld.so package, so get a recent one. Again, see step 2 of the installation.

_setutent: Can't open utmp file

> This message is often seen in multiples of three when you start an xterm. Go and read the FSSTND tirade near the end of the installation procedure.

3 Building programs

3.1 Ordinary programs

To build a program in ELF, use `gcc` as always. To build in a.out, use `gcc -b i486-linuxaout` .

```
$ cat >hello.c
main() { printf("hello, world\n"); }
^D
$ gcc -o hello hello.c
$ file hello
hello: ELF 32-bit LSB executable i386 (386 and up) Version 1
$ ./hello
hello, world
```

This is perhaps an appropriate time to answer the question "if a.out compilers default to producing a program called a.out, what name does an ELF compiler give its output?". Still a.out, is the answer. Boring boring boring ... :-)

3.2 Building libraries

To build libfoo.so as a shared library, the basic steps look like this:

```
$ gcc -fPIC -c *.c
$ gcc -shared -Wl,-soname,libfoo.so.1 -o libfoo.so.1.0 *.o
$ ln -s libfoo.so.1.0 libfoo.so.1
$ ln -s libfoo.so.1 libfoo.so
$ export LD_LIBRARY_PATH='pwd':$LD_LIBRARY_PATH
```

This will generate a shared library called libfoo.so.1.0, and the appropriate links for ld (libfoo.so) and the dynamic linker (libfoo.so.1) to find it. To test, we add the current directory to LD_LIBRARY_PATH.

When you're happpy that the library works, you'll have to move it to, say, /usr/local/lib, and recreate the appropriate links. Note that the libfoo.so link should point to libfoo.so.1, so it doesn't need updating on every minor version number change. The link from libfoo.so.1 to libfoo.so.1.0 is kept up to date by ldconfig, which on most systems is run as part of the boot process.

```
$ su
# cp libfoo.so.1.0 /usr/local/lib
# /sbin/ldconfig
# ( cd /usr/local/lib ; ln -s libfoo.so.1 libfoo.so )
```

3.3 Building in a.out

You may have a need to continue to build programs in the old a.out format. For 'normal' programs all you need to do to use the a.out compiler is specify the flag -b i486-linuxaout when you call gcc, and -m i386linux when (if) you call ld. If you need to build a.out DLL shared libraries still, you have my sympathy. To the best of my knowledge, the short answer is that it doesn't work. Please mail me if you know different.

4   Patches and binaries

At this point in the proceedings, you can, if you like, stop. You have installed everything necessary to compile and run ELF programs.

You may wish to rebuild programs in ELF, either for purposes of 'neatness' or to minimise memory usage. For most end-user applications, this is pretty simple; some packages however do assume too much about the systems they run on, and may fail due to one or more of:

- Different underscore conventions in the assembler: in an a.out executable, external labels get _ prefixed to them; in an ELF executable, they don't. This makes no difference until you start integrating hand-written assembler: all the labels of the form _foo must be translated to foo, or (if you want to be portable about it) to EXTERNAL(foo) where `EXTERNAL` is some macro which returns either its argument (if `__ELF__` is defined) or `_` concatenated with its argument if not.

- Differences in libc 5 from libc 4. The interface to the locale support has changed, for one.

- The application or build process depending on knowledge of the binary format used — emacs, for example, dumps its memory image to disk in executable format, so obviously needs to know what format your executables are in.

- The application consists of or includes shared libraries (X11 is the obvious example). These will obviously need changes to accomodate the different method of shared library creation in ELF.

Anyway, here are two lists: the first is of programs that needed changing for ELF where the changes have been made (i.e. that you will need new versions of to compile as ELF), and the second is of programs that still need third-party patches of some kind.

4.1 Upgrade:

- **Dosemu**. Nowadays, dosemu runs with ELF. You'll need to monkey with the Makefile. Current versions of dosemu are available from `<ftp://tsx-11.mit.edu/pub/linux/ALPHA/dosemu/>`

- **e2fsutils**. The Utilities for the Second Extended File System versions 0.5c and later compile unchanged in ELF.

- **Emacs**. There are two potential problems here. (i) Emacs has a rather odd build procedure that involves running a minimal version of itself, loading in all the useful bits as lisp, then dumping its memory image back to disk as an executable file. (FSF) Emacs 19.29 and XEmacs 19.12 (formerly Lucid Emacs) can both detect whether you are compiling as ELF and Do The Right Thing automatically. (ii) If you build some versions of emacs against ncurses, it will fail unless you first edit `src/s/linux.h` in the emacs distribution to add the line `#define TERMINFO` somewhere near the top. This is not necessary for 19.31, but is for XEmacs 19.13. Apparently it will be fixed in 19.14.

- **gdb 4.16**. Your existing copy of gdb will continue to work just as well as it always has done in the past, but the shared library support in 4.16 is a lot better, so if you want to debug programs that do weird things in that area, this is a good upgrade.

- **The Kernel**. Kernel versions 2.0 and greater work fine with ELF; you have to say 'yes' to both of

```
Kernel support for ELF binaries (CONFIG_BINFMT_ELF) [Y/m/n/?]
Compile kernel as ELF - if your GCC is ELF-GCC (CON-
FIG_KERNEL_ELF) [Y/n/?]
```

when you run `make config` (this is also the case for most of the 1.3 series). If you are using 1.2 still, see the 'patch' list below.

- **perl 5**. Perl 5.001m and later will compile unchanged on an ELF system, complete with dynamic loading. Current versions of Perl are available from CPAN (Comprehensive Perl Archive Network) sites: see `<ftp://ftp.funet.fi/pub/mirrors/perl/CPAN>` for the closest one to you.

- **ps** and **top**. Procps 0.98 and greater will work with ELF (earlier versions also work, but can't read the kernel to find WCHAN names, if you care about them). Note that 2.0 series kernels require procps 0.99a or greater anyway.

- The `cal` program in **util-linux 2.2** doesn't work. Upgrade to *version 2.5* `<ftp://tsx-11.mit.edu/pub/linux/packages/utils>` or later.

- **Mosaic**. I don't have the facilities to build this myself, but the Mosaic 2.7b1 binary available from NCSA comes in ELF. It has been linked against an odd X setup though, with the result that on normal systems it will complain about not finding `libXpm.so.4.5`. The simple fix is to edit it carefully with emacs or another editor that copes with binary files. Find the occurence of the string `libXpm.so.4.5^@` (where `^@` is a NUL — ASCII zero — character), delete the `.5` and add two more characters after the NUL to aviod changing the file length.

4.2 Patch

- **file**. This works anyway, but can be improved: `<ftp://ftp.uk.linux.org/pub/Linux/libc/non-core/file.patch>` adds support for identifying stripped and mixed-endian ELF binaries.

- `make-3.74` — either get the source code from a GNU site and apply the patch that comes with the libc-5.3.12 release notes, or get the binary `make-3.74.gz` from `tsx-11`. There is a bug in GNU make which only manifests with new ELF libc versions — it's actually a dependency on a bug in old versions of the GNU libc, which was also present in Linux libc until recently. If you keep your old a.out `make` program it will continue to work, but if you want an ELF one you need the patch.

  The GNU Make developers know about the bug, and one day will release a fixed version.

- **The 1.2.x Kernel**. You have three options:

  1. Patch the Makefile slightly to use the a.out compiler. `cd /usr/src/linux/`, cut the following patch out, and feed it into `patch -p1`. Or just edit the Makefile manually using this as a guide; it's clear enough (delete the lines marked with a – and add the ones with a +.

     ```
     diff -u linux-1.2.13/Makefile.orig linux/Makefile
     --- linux-1.2.13/Makefile.orig   Wed Aug 16 20:53:26 1995
     +++ linux/Makefile        Fri Dec  8 16:19:49 1995
     @@ -12,9 +12,9 @@
      TOPDIR := $(shell if [ "$$PWD" != "" ]; then echo $$PWD; else p-
     wd; fi)

     -AS        =as
     -LD        =ld
     -HOSTCC  =gcc -I$(TOPDIR)/include
     -CC      =gcc -D__KERNEL__  -I$(TOPDIR)/include
     +AS      =/usr/i486-linuxaout/bin/as
     +LD      =ld  -m i386linux
     +HOSTCC  =gcc -b i486-linuxaout -I$(TOPDIR)/include
     +CC      =gcc -b i486-linuxaout -D__KERNEL__  -I$(TOPDIR)/include
      MAKE    =make
      CPP     =$(CC) -E
      AR      =ar
     ```

     Alternatively,

  2. Apply H J Lu's patch which allows compiling the kernel in ELF (and also adds the ability to do ELF core dumps). This can be had from `<ftp://ftp.cdrom.com/pub/linux/slackware_source/kernel-source/v1.2/linuxelf-1.2.13.diff.gz>`.

     If you are using an ELF distribution (RedHat 2.1, Slackware 3) which comes with a 1.2 series kernel, you will probably find that this patch or one similar has been applied already.

     The best idea, hoever, is probably

  3. Upgrade to 2.0! 1.2 was never really intended for ELF anyway.

  You will have other problems compiling 1.2.13 with gcc 2.7.2 and above; there was a bug in `asm/io.h` which is only detected by gcc 2.7.2. You will need the patch `<ftp://ftp.uk.linux.org/pub/Linux/libc/misc/io.h>`.

5 Further information

- The *GCC-HOWTO* `<GCC-HOWTO.html>` contains much useful information about development on Linux (at least, I think it does; I maintain it). It should be available from the same place as you found this, which is why the link above is relative.

- The `linux-gcc` mailing list (which is also the `linux.dev.gcc` newsgroup, if you have a `linux.*` news feed) is really the best place to see what's happening, usually without even posting to it. Remember, it's not Usenet, so keep the questions down unless you're actually developing. For instructions on joining the mailing list, mail a message containing the word `help` to `majordomo@vger.rutgers.edu`. Archives of the list are at `<http://www.linux.ncm.com/linux-gcc/>`.

- There's a certain amount of information about what the linux-gcc list is doing at my *linux-gcc web page* `<http://ftp.uk.linux.org/~barlow/linux/gcc-list.html>`, when I remember to update it. This also has a link to the latest version of this HOWTO, and the patches it refers to. For US people and others with poor links to UK academic sites (that's nearly everyone outside of UK academia), this is all mirrored at `<http://www.blackdown.org/elf/elf.html>`

- There's also documentation for the file format on *tsx-11* `<ftp://tsx-11.mit.edu/pub/linux/packages/GCC/ELF.doc.tar.gz>`. This is probably of most use to people who want to understand, debug or rewrite programs that deal directly with binary objects.

- H J Lu's document *ELF: From The Programmer's Perspective* `<ftp://tsx-11.mit.edu/pub/linux/packages/GCC/elf.latex.tar.gz>` contains much useful and more detailed information on programming with ELF. If you aren't LaTeX-capable, it is also available as PostScript.

- Information about the **ncurses** library and the terminfo database is available from *Eric Raymond's ncurses resource page* `<http://www.ccil.org/~esr/ncurses.html>`.

- There is a manual page covering `dlopen(3)` and related functions, which is supplied with the `ld.so` package.

6 Miscellanities

6.1 Feedback

is welcomed. Mail me at *daniel.barlow@linux.org*. My PGP public key (ID 5F263625) is available from my *web pages* `<http://ftp.uk.linux.org/~barlow/>`, if you feel the need to be secretive about things.

If you have a question that you feel this document should have answered and doesn't, mail me. If you have a question which probably shouldn't be answered here but you think I might know the answer anyway, you might want to try posting to an appropriate `comp.os.linux.*` newsgroup first; I usually answer mail eventually, but I have been known to lose it on occasion.

Anyone found adding my name to junk email lists will pay dearly for it.

6.2 Translations

If you wish to translate this document, please go right ahead, but do tell me about it! The chances are (sadly) several hundred to one against that I speak the language you wish to translate to, but that aside I am happy to help in whatever way I can.

Translations that I know of are:

- *Italian* `<http://www.psico.unipd.it/ildp/docs/HOWTO/ELF-HOWTO.html>`, by Favro Renata. (Other HOWTOs are also available in Italian from `<http://www.psico.unipd.it/ildp/docs/HOWTO/INDEX.html>`.

- Kojima Mitsuhiro has produced a Japanese translation, available from `<http://jf.gee.kyoto-u.ac.jp/JF/index.html>`.

6.3 Legal bits

All trademarks used in this document are acknowledged as being owned by their respective owners. Yow!

Part XI

"Linux Ethernet-Howto" by Paul Gortmaker

v2.66, 6 July 1998

This is the Ethernet-Howto, which is a compilation of information about which ethernet devices can be used for Linux, and how to set them up. It hopefully answers all the frequently asked questions about using ethernet cards with Linux. Note that this Howto is focused on the hardware and low level driver aspect of the ethernet cards, and does not cover the software end of things like `ifconfig` and `route`. See the Network Howto for that stuff.

Contents

HOWTO

1   Introduction

The Ethernet-Howto covers what cards you should and shouldn't buy; how to set them up, how to run more than one, and other common problems and questions. It contains detailed information on the current level of support for all of the most common ethernet cards available.

It does *not* cover the software end of things, as that is covered in the NET-3 Howto. Also note that general non-Linux specific questions about Ethernet are not (or at least they should not be) answered here. For those types of questions, see the excellent amount of information in the *comp.dcom.lans.ethernet* FAQ. You can FTP it from `rtfm.mit.edu` just like all the other newsgroup FAQs.

This present revision covers distribution kernels up to and including 2.0.34. Some information pertaining to development kernels up to version 2.1.108 is also included.

The Ethernet-Howto is by:

      Paul Gortmaker, `gpg109@rsphy1.anu.edu.au`

The primary source of information for the initial ASCII-only version of the Ethernet-Howto was:

      Donald J. Becker, `becker@cesdis.gsfc.nasa.gov`

who we should thank for writing the vast majority of ethernet card drivers that are presently available for Linux. He also is the original author of the NFS server too. Thanks Donald!

Please see the Disclaimer and Copying information at the end of this document for information about redistribution of this document and the usual 'we are not responsible for what you do...' legal stuff.

1.1   New Versions of this Document

New versions of this document can be retrieved via anonymous FTP from:

Sunsite HOWTO Archive `<ftp://sunsite.unc.edu/pub/Linux/docs/HOWTO/>`

and various Linux ftp mirror sites. Updates will be made as new information and/or drivers becomes available. If this copy that you are reading is more than 6 months old, it is either out of date, or it means that I have been lazy and haven't updated it.

If you have sent me an update and it is not included in the next release, it probably means I've lost it amongst the ton of junk e-mail I get. Please re-send it (along with an abusive message) and I will try and make sure it gets included in the next release.

This document was produced by using the SGML system that was specifically set up for the Linux Howto project, and there are various output formats available, including, postscript, dvi, ascii, html, and soon TeXinfo.

I would recommend viewing it in the html (via a WWW browser) or the Postscript/dvi format. Both of these contain cross-references that are lost in the ascii format.

If you want to get the latest copy off sunsite, here is URL.

Ethernet-HOWTO <http://sunsite.unc.edu/mdw/HOWTO/Ethernet-HOWTO.html>

1.2   Using the Ethernet-Howto

As this guide is getting bigger and bigger, you probably don't want to spend the rest of your afternoon reading the whole thing. And the good news is that you don't *have* to read it all.

Chances are you are reading this document beacuse you can't get things to work and you don't know what to do or check. The next section (1.3 (HELP - It doesn't work!)) is aimed at newcomers to linux and will point you in the right direction.

Typically the same problems and questions are asked *over and over* again by different people. Chances are your specific problem or question is one of these frequently asked questions, and is answered in the FAQ portion of this document . (3 (The FAQ section)). Everybody should have a look through this section before posting for help.

If you haven't got an ethernet card, then you will want to start with deciding on a card. (2 (What card should I buy...))

If you have already got an ethernet card, but are not sure if you can use it with Linux, then you will want to read the section which contains specific information on each manufacturer, and their cards. (5 (Vendor Specific...))

If you are interested in some of the technical aspects of the Linux device drivers, then you can have a browse of the section with this type of information. (8 (Technical Information))

1.3   HELP - It doesn't work!

Okay, don't panic. This will lead you through the process of getting things working, even if you have no prior background in linux or ethernet hardware.

First thing you need to do is figure out what model your card is so you can determine if Linux has a driver for that particular card. Different cards typically have different ways of being controlled by the host computer, and the linux driver (if there is one) contains this control information in a format that allows linux to use the card. If you don't have any manuals or anything of the sort that tell you anything about the card model, then you can try the section on helping with mystery cards (reference section: 5.40 (Identifying an Unknown Card)).

Now that you know what type of card you have, read through the details of your particular card in the card specific section (reference section: 5 (Vendor Specific...)) which lists in alphabetical order, card manufacturers, individual model numbers and whether it has a linux driver or not. If it lists it as 'Not Supported' you can pretty much give up here. If you can't find your card in that list, then check to see if your card manual lists it as being 'compatible' with another known card type. For example there are hundreds, if not thousands of different cards made to be compatible with the original Novell NE2000 design.

Assuming you have found out that a linux driver exists for your card, you now have to find it and make use of it. Just because linux has a driver for your card does *not* mean that it is built into every kernel. (The kernel is the core operating system that is first loaded at boot, and contains drivers for various pieces of hardware, among other things.) Depending on who made the particular linux distribution you are using, there may be only a few pre-built kernels, and a whole bunch of drivers as smaller separate modules, or there may be a whole lot of kernels, covering a vast combination of built-in driver combinations.

Most linux distributions now ship with a bunch of small modules that are the various drivers. The required modules are typically loaded late in the boot process, or on-demand as a driver is needed to access a particualr device. You will need to

HOWTO

attach this module to the kernel after it has booted up. See the information that came with your distribution on installing and using modules, along with the module section in this document. (10.2 (Using the Ethernet Drivers as Modules))

If you didn't find either a pre-built kernel with your driver, or a module form of the driver, chances are you have a typically uncommon card, and you will have to build your own kernel with that driver included. Once you have linux installed, building a custom kernel is not difficult at all. You essentially answer yes or no to what you want the kernel to contain, and then tell it to build it. There is a Kernel-HowTo that will help you along.

At this point you should have somehow managed to be booting a kernel with your driver built in, or be loading it as a module. About half of the problems people have are related to not having driver loaded one way or another, so you may find things work now.

If it still doesn't work, then you need to verify that the kernel is indeed detecting the card. To do this, you need to type `dmesg | more` when logged in after the system has booted and all modules have been loaded. This will allow you to review the boot messages that the kernel scrolled up the screen during the boot process. If the card has been detected, you should see somewhere in that list a message from your card's driver that starts with `eth0`, mentions the driver name and the hardware parameters (interrupt setting, input/output port address, etc) that the card is set for. If you don't see a message like this, then the driver didn't detect your card, and that is why things aren't working. See the FAQ (3 (The FAQ Section)) for what to do if your card is not detected. If you have a NE2000 compatible, there is also some NE2000 specific tips on getting a card detected in the FAQ section as well.

If the card is detected, but the detection message reports some sort of error, like a resource conflict, then the driver probably won't have initialized properly and the card still wont be useable. Most common error messages of this sort are also listed in the FAQ section, along with a solution.

If the detection message seems okay, then double check the card resources reported by the driver against those that the card is physically set for (either by little black jumpers on the card, or by a software utility supplied by the card manufacturer.) These must match exactly. For example, if you have the card jumpered or configured to IRQ 15 and the driver reports IRQ 10 in the boot messages, things will not work. The FAQ section discusses the most common cases of drivers incorrectly detecting the configuration information of various cards.

At this point, you have managed to get you card detected with all the correct parameters, and hopefully everything is working. If not, then you either have a software configuration error, or a hardware configuration error. A software configuration error is not setting up the right network addresses for the `ifconfig` and `route` commands, and details of how to do that are fully described in the Network HowTo and the 'Network Administrator's Guide' which both probably came on the CD-ROM you installed from.

A hardware configuration error is when some sort of resource conflict or mis-configuration (that the driver didn't detect at boot) that stops the card from working properly. This typically can be observed in one of three different ways. (1) You get an error message when `ifconfig` tries to open the device for use, such as "SIOCSFFLAGS: Try again". (2) The driver reports `eth0` error messages (viewed by `dmesg | more`) or strange inconsistencies for each time it tries to send or receive data. (3) Typing `cat /proc/net/dev` shows non-zero numbers in one of the errs, drop, fifo, frame or carrier columns for `eth0`. Most of the typical hardware configuration errors are also discussed in the FAQ section.

Well, if you have got to this point and things still aren't working, read the FAQ section of this document, read the vendor specific section detailing your particular card, *and if it still doesn't work* then you may have to resort to posting to an appropriate newsgroup for help. If you do post, please detail all relevant information in that post, such as the card brand, the kernel version, the driver boot messages, the output from `cat /proc/net/dev`, a clear description of the problem, and of course what you have already tried to do in an effort to get things to work.

You would be surprised at how many people post useless things like "Can someone help me? My ethernet doesn't work." and nothing else. Readers of the newsgroups tend to ignore such silly posts, whereas a detailed and informational problem description may allow a 'linux-guru' to spot your problem right away.

2 What card should I buy for Linux?

The answer to this question depends heavily on exactly what you intend on doing with your net connection, and how much traffic it will see.

If you only expect a single user to be doing the occasional ftp session or WWW connection, then even an old 8 bit ISA card will probably keep you happy.

If you intend to set up a server, and you require the CPU overhead of Rx'ing and Tx'ing network data to be kept to a minimum, you probably want to look at one of the newer PCI cards that has bus-mastering capapbility, such as with the DEC tulip (21xxx) chip, or the AMD PCnet-PCI chip.

If you fall somewhere in the middle of the above, then any one of the 16 bit ISA cards with stable drivers will do the job for you.

2.1 So What Drivers are Stable?

Of the 16 bit ISA cards, the following drivers are very mature, and you shouldn't have any problems if you buy a card that uses these drivers.

SMC-Ultra/EtherEZ, SMC-Elite (WD80x3), 3c509, Lance, NE2000.

This is not to say that all the other drivers are unstable. It just happens that the above are the oldest and most used of all the linux drivers, making them the safest choice.

Note that some el-cheapo motherboards can have trouble with the bus-mastering that the ISA Lance cards do, and some el-cheapo NE2000 clones can have trouble getting detected at boot.

The most commonly used linux PCI drivers are probably the 3Com Vortex/Boomerang (3c59x/3c9xx), the DEC tulip (21xxx), and the Intel EtherExpressPro 100. The various PCI-NE2000 clone cards are also extremely common, but purchasing a PCI-NE2000 clone card is not recommended unless the lowest possible price is more important than having a modern high-performace design card.

2.2 Eight bit vs 16 bit Cards

You probably can't buy a new 8 bit ISA ethercard anymore, but you will find lots of them turning up at computer swap meets and the like for the next few years, at very low prices. This will make them popular for "home-ethernet" systems. The above holds true for 16 bit ISA cards now as well, since PCI cards are now very common.

Some 8 bit cards that will provide adequate performance for light to average use are the wd8003, the 3c503 and the ne1000. The 3c501 provides poor performance, and these poor 12 year old relics of the XT days should be avoided.

The 8 bit data path doesn't hurt performance that much, as you can still expect to get about 500 to 800kB/s ftp download speed to an 8 bit wd8003 card (on a fast ISA bus) from a fast host. And if most of your net-traffic is going to remote sites, then the bottleneck in the path will be elsewhere, and the only speed difference you will notice is during net activity on your local subnet.

2.3 32 Bit (VLB/EISA/PCI) Ethernet Cards

Note that a 10Mbs network typically doesn't justify requiring a 32 bit interface. See 2.6 (Programmed I/O vs. ...) as to why having a 10Mbps ethercard on an 8MHz ISA bus is really not a bottleneck. Even though having the ethercard on a fast bus won't necessarily mean faster transfers, it will usually mean reduced CPU overhead, which is good for multi-user systems.

Of course for 100Mbps networks, which are now commonplace, the 32 bit interface is a must to make use of the full bandwidth. AMD has the 32 bit PCnet-VLB and PCnet-PCI chips. See 5.4.2 (AMD PCnet-32) for info on the 32 bit versions of the LANCE / PCnet-ISA chip.

The DEC 21xxx PCI 'tulip' chip is another option (see 5.17.4 (DEC 21040)) for power-users. Many manufacturers produce cards that use this chip, and the prices of such no-name cards is usually quite cheap.

3Com's 'Vortex' and 'Boomerang' PCI cards are also another option, and the price is quite cheap if you can get one under their evaluation deal while it lasts. (see 5.1.14 (3c590/3c595))

Intel's EtherExpress Pro 10/100 PCI cards have also been reported to work well with linux. (see 5.22.4 (EtherExpress))

Various clone manufacturers have started making PCI NE2000 clones based on a RealTek or Winbond chip. These cards are also supported by the linux ne2000 driver for v2.0.31 and newer kernels. However you only benefit from the faster bus interface, as the card is still using the age-old ne2000 driver interface. As of v2.0.34 (and above) a separate PCI-specific driver for these cards `ne2k-pci.c` is also available, which will be sightly more efficient than the ISA `ne.c` driver.

2.4   Available 100Mbs Cards and Drivers

The present list of supported 100Mbs hardware is as follows: cards with the DEC 21140 chip; the 3c595/3c90x Vortex cards; and the HP 100VG ANY-LAN. The drivers for the first two are quite stable, but feedback on the HP driver has been low so far.

The EtherExpressPro10/100B now also has a driver in the current v2.0 kenrel. For updates and/or support, see the relevant section in this document.

The 21140 100Base-? chip is supported with the same driver as its 10Mbs counterpart, the 21040. SMC's 100Mbs EtherPower PCI card uses this chip. As with the 21040, you have a choice of two drivers to pick from.

Also have a look at the information on Donald's WWW site, at the following URL:

100Mbs Ethernet `<http://cesdis.gsfc.nasa.gov/linux/misc/100mbs.html>`

Donald had done a fair bit of work with the SMC EtherPower-10/100 cards, and reported getting about 4.6MB/s application to application with TCP on P5-100 Triton machines.

(See 5.1.14 (3c595) and 5.17.4 (DEC 21140) for more details.)

For 100VG information, see the following section, and this URL on Donald's Site:

Donald's 100VG Page `<http://cesdis.gsfc.nasa.gov/linux/drivers/100vg.html>`

You may also be interested in looking at:

Dan Kegel's Fast Ethernet Page `<http://alumni.caltech.edu/dank/fe/>`

2.5   100VG versus 100BaseT

100BaseT is much more prominent than 100VG, and the following blurb from an older one of Donald's informative comp.os.linux postings summarizes the situation quite well:

"For those not in the know, there are two competing 100Mbs ethernet standards, 100VG (aka 100baseVG and 100VG-AnyLAN) and 100baseT (with 100baseTx, 100baseT4 and 100baseFx cable types).

100VG was on the market first, and I feel that it is better engineered than 100baseTx. I was rooting for it to win, but it clearly isn't going to. HP et al. made several bad choices:

1) Delaying the standard so that they could accommodate IBM and support token ring frames. It 'seemed like a good idea at the time', since it would enable token ring shops to upgrade without the managers having to admit they made a very expensive mistake committing to the wrong technology. But there was nothing to be gained, as the two frame types couldn't coexist on a network, token ring is a morass of complexity, and IBM went with 100baseT anyway.

2) Producing only ISA and EISA cards. (A PCI model was only recently announced.) The ISA bus is too slow for 100mbs, and relatively few EISA machines exist. At the time VLB was common, fast, and cheap with PCI a viable choice. But "old-timer" wisdom held that servers would stay with the more expensive EISA bus.

3) Not sending me a databook. Yes, this action was the real reason for the 100VGs downfall :-). I called all over for programming info, and all I could get was a few page color glossy brochure from AT&T describing how wonderful the Regatta chipset was."

2.6 Programmed I/O vs. Shared Memory vs. DMA

If you can already send and receive back-to-back packets, you just can't put more bits over the wire. Every modern ethercard can receive back-to-back packets. The Linux DP8390 drivers (wd80x3, SMC-Ultra, 3c503, ne2000, etc) come pretty close to sending back-to-back packets (depending on the current interrupt latency) and the 3c509 and AT1500 hardware have no problem at all automatically sending back-to-back packets.

The ISA bus can do 5.3MB/sec (42Mb/sec), which sounds like more than enough for 10Mbps ethernet. In the case of the 100Mbps cards, you clearly need a faster bus to take advantage of the network bandwidth.

2.6.1 Programmed I/O (e.g. NE2000, 3c509)

Pro: Doesn't use any constrained system resources, just a few I/O registers, and has no 16M limit.

Con: Usually the slowest transfer rate, the CPU is waiting the whole time, and interleaved packet access is usually difficult to impossible.

2.6.2 Shared memory (e.g. WD80x3, SMC-Ultra, 3c503)

Pro: Simple, faster than programmed I/O, and allows random access to packets. The linux drivers compute the checksum of incoming IP packets as they are copied off the card, resulting in a further reduction of CPU usage vs. an equivalent PIO card.

Con: Uses up memory space (a big one for DOS users, essentially a non-issue under Linux), and it still ties up the CPU.

2.6.3 Slave (normal) Direct Memory Access (e.g. none for Linux!)

Pro: Frees up the CPU during the actual data transfer.

Con: Checking boundary conditions, allocating contiguous buffers, and programming the DMA registers makes it the slowest of all techniques. It also uses up a scarce DMA channel, and requires aligned low memory buffers.

2.6.4 Bus Master Direct Memory Access (e.g. LANCE, DEC 21040)

Pro: Frees up the CPU during the data transfer, can string together buffers, can require little or no CPU time lost on the ISA bus. Most of the bus-mastering linux drivers now use a 'copybreak' scheme where large packets are put directly into a kernel networking buffer by the card, and small packets are copied by the CPU which primes the cache for subsequent processing.

Con: (Only applicable to ISA bus cards) Requires low-memory buffers and a DMA channel for cards. Any bus-master will have problems with other bus-masters that are bus-hogs, such as some primitive SCSI adaptors. A few badly-designed motherboard chipsets have problems with bus-masters. And a reason for not using *any* type of DMA device is using a 486 processor designed for plug-in replacement of a 386: these processors must flush their cache with each DMA cycle. (This includes the Cx486DLC, Ti486DLC, Cx486SLC, Ti486SLC, etc.)

2.7 Type of cable that your card should support

If you are setting up a small "personal" network, you will probably want to use thinnet or thin ethernet cable. This is the style with the standard BNC connectors. See 6 (Cables, Coax...) for other concerns with different types of ethernet cable.

Most ethercards also come in a 'Combo' version for only $10-$20 more. These have both twisted pair and thinnet transceiver built-in, allowing you to change your mind later.

The twisted pair cables, with the RJ-45 (giant phone jack) connectors is technically called 10BaseT. You may also hear it called UTP (Unsheilded Twisted Pair).

The thinnet, or thin ethernet cabling, (RG-58 coaxial cable) with the BNC (metal push and turn-to-lock) connectors is technically called 10Base2.

The older thick ethernet (10mm coaxial cable) which is only found in older installations is called 10Base5.

Large corporate installations will most likely use 10BaseT instead of 10Base2. 10Base2 does not offer an easy upgrade path to the new upcoming 100Base-whatever.

3 Frequently Asked Questions

Here are some of the more frequently asked questions about using Linux with an Ethernet connection. Some of the more specific questions are sorted on a 'per manufacturer basis'. However, since this document is basically 'old' by the time you get it, any 'new' problems will not appear here instantly. For these, I suggest that you make efficient use of your newsreader. For example, nn users would type

```
nn -xX -s'3c'
```

to get all the news articles in your subscribed list that have '3c' in the subject. (ie. 3com, 3c509, 3c503, etc.) The moral: Read the man page for your newsreader.

3.1 Alpha Drivers – Getting and Using them

I heard that there is an updated or alpha driver available for my card. Where can I get it?

The newest of the 'new' drivers can be found on Donald's ftp site: cesdis.gsfc.nasa.gov in the /pub/linux/ area. Things change here quite frequently, so just look around for it. Alternatively, it may be easier to use a WWW browser on:

Don's Linux Home Page <http://cesdis.gsfc.nasa.gov/pub/linux/linux.html>

to locate the driver that you are looking for. (Watch out for WWW browsers that silently munge the source by replacing TABs with spaces and so on - use ftp, or at least an FTP URL for downloading if unsure.)

Now, if it really is an alpha, or pre-alpha driver, then please treat it as such. In other words, don't complain because you can't figure out what to do with it. If you can't figure out how to install it, then you probably shouldn't be testing it. Also, if it brings your machine down, don't complain. Instead, send us a well documented bug report, or even better, a patch!

Note that some of the 'useable' experimental/alpha drivers have been included in the standard kernel source tree. When running make config one of the first things you will be asked is whether to "Prompt for development and/or incomplete code/drivers". You will have to answer 'Y' here to get asked about including any alpha/experiemntal drivers.

3.2 Using More than one Ethernet Card per Machine

What needs to be done so that Linux can run two ethernet cards?

With the Driver as a Module: Most linux distributions use modular drivers now (as opposed to having the driver built into the kernel). In the case of PCI drivers, the module will typically detect all of the installed cards of that brand model automatically. However, for ISA cards, probing for a card is not a safe operation, and hence you typically need to supply the I/O base address of the card so the module knows where to look. This information is typically stored in the file /etc/conf.modules.

As an example, consider a user that has two ISA NE2000 cards, one at `0x300` and one at `0x240` and what lines they would have in their `/etc/conf.modules` file:

```
alias eth0 ne
alias eth1 ne
options ne io=0x240,0x300
```

What this does: This says that if the administrator (or the kernel) does a `modprobe eth0` or a `modprobe eth1` then the `ne.o` driver should be loaded for either `eth0` or `eth1`. Furthermore, when the `ne.o` module is loaded, it should be loaded with the options `io=0x240,0x300` so that the driver knows where to look for the cards. Note that the `0x` is important - things like `300h` as commonly used in the DOS world won't work. Switching the order of the `0x240` and the `0x300` will switch which physical card ends up as `eth0` and `eth1`.

Most of the ISA module drivers can take multiple comma separated i/o values like this example to handle multiple cards. However, some (older?) drivers, such as the 3c501.o module are currently only able to handle one card per module load. In this case you can load the module twice to get both cards detected. The `/etc/conf.modules` file in this case would look like:

```
alias eth0 3c501
alias eth1 3c501
options eth0 -o 3c501-0 io=0x280 irq=5
options eth1 -o 3c501-1 io=0x300 irq=7
```

In this example the `-o` option has been used to give each instance of the module a unique name, since you can't have two modules loaded with the same name. The `irq=` option has also been used to to specify the hardware IRQ setting of the card. (This method can also be used with modules that accept comma separated i/o values, but it is less efficient since the module ends up being loaded twice when it doesn't really need to be.)

As a final example, consider a user with one 3c503 card at `0x350`and one SMC Elite16 (wd8013) card at `0x280`. They would have:

```
alias eth0 wd
alias eth1 3c503
options wd io=0x280
options 3c503 io=0x350
```

For PCI cards, you typically only need the `alias` lines to correlate the `ethN` interfaces with the appropriate driver name, since the I/O base of a PCI card can be safely detected.

The available modules are typically stored in `/lib/modules/'uname -r'/net` where the `uname -r` command gives the kernel version (e.g. 2.0.34). You can look in there to see which one matches your card. Once you have the correct settings in your `conf.modules` file, you can test things out with:

```
modprobe ethN
dmesg | tail
```

where 'N' is the number of the ethernet interface you are testing.

With the Driver Compiled into the Kernel: If you have the driver compiled into the kernel, then the hooks for multiple ethercards are all there. However, note that at the moment only *one* ethercard is auto-probed for by default. This helps to avoid possible boot time hangs caused by probing sensitive cards.

There are two ways that you can enable auto-probing for the second (and third, and...) card. The easiest method is to pass boot-time arguments to the kernel, which is usually done by LILO. Probing for the second card can be achieved by using a boot-time argument as simple as `ether=0,0,eth1`. In this case `eth0` and `eth1` will be assigned in the order that the cards are found at boot. Say if you want the card at `0x300` to be `eth0` and the card at `0x280` to be `eth1` then you could use

```
LILO: linux ether=5,0x300,eth0 ether=15,0x280,eth1
```

The `ether=` command accepts more than the IRQ + i/o + name shown above. Please have a look at 10.1 (Passing Ethernet Arguments...) for the full syntax, card specific parameters, and LILO tips.

These boot time arguments can be made permanent so that you don't have to re-enter them every time. See the LILO configuration option 'append' in the LILO manual.

The second way (not recommended) is to edit the file `Space.c` and replace the `0xffe0` entry for the i/o address with a zero. The `0xffe0` entry tells it not to probe for that device – replacing it with a zero will enable autoprobing for that device.

Note that if you are intending to use Linux as a gateway between two networks, you will have to re-compile a kernel with IP forwarding enabled. Usually using an old AT/286 with something like the 'kbridge' software is a better solution.

If you are viewing this while *net-surfing*, you may wish to look at a mini-howto Donald has on his WWW site. Check out *Multiple Ethercards* `<http://cesdis.gsfc.nasa.gov/linux/misc/multicard.html>`.

3.3   Poor NE2000 Clones

Here is a list of some of the NE-2000 clones that are known to have various problems. Most of them aren't fatal. In the case of the ones listed as 'bad clones' – this usually indicates that the cards don't have the two NE2000 identifier bytes. NEx000-clones have a Station Address PROM (SAPROM) in the packet buffer memory space. NE2000 clones have `0x57,0x57` in bytes `0x0e,0x0f` of the SAPROM, while other supposed NE2000 clones must be detected by their SA prefix.

This is not a comprehensive list of all the NE2000 clones that don't have the `0x57,0x57` in bytes `0x0e,0x0f` of the SAPROM. There are probably hundreds of them. If you get a card that causes the driver to report an 'invalid signature' then you will have to add your cards signature to the driver. The process for doing this is described below.

Accton NE2000 – might not get detected at boot, see below.

Artisoft LANtastic AE-2 – OK, but has flawed error-reporting registers.

AT-LAN-TEC NE2000 – clone uses Winbond chip that traps SCSI drivers

ShineNet LCS-8634 – clone uses Winbond chip that traps SCSI drivers

Cabletron E10**, E20**, E10**-x, E20**-x – bad clones, but the driver checks for them. See 5.11.1 (E10**).

D-Link Ethernet II – bad clones, but the driver checks for them. See 5.15.1 (DE-100 / DE-200).

DFI DFINET-300, DFINET-400 – bad clones, but the driver checks for them. See 5.16.1 (DFI-300 / DFI-400)

EtherNext UTP8, EtherNext UTP16 – bad clones, but the driver checks for them.

3.4   Problems with NE1000 / NE2000 cards (and clones)

Problem: PCI NE2000 clone card is not detected at boot with v2.0.x.

Reason: The `ne.c` driver up to v2.0.30 only knows about the PCI ID number of RealTek 8029 based clone cards. Since then, several others have also released PCI NE2000 clone cards, with different PCI ID numbers, and hence the driver doesn't detect them.

Solution: The easiest solution is to upgrade to a v2.0.31 (or newer) version of the linux kernel. It knows the ID numbers of about five different NE2000-PCI chips, and will detect them automatically at boot or at module loading time. If you upgrade to 2.0.34 (or newer) there is a PCI-only specific NE2000 driver that is slightly smaller and more efficient than the original ISA/PCI driver.

Problem: PCI NE2000 clone card is reported as an ne1000 (8 bit card!) at boot or when I load the ne.o module for v2.0.x, and hence doesn't work.

Reason: Some PCI clones don't implement byte wide access (and hence are not truly 100% NE2000 compatible). This causes the probe to think they are NE1000 cards.

Solution: You need to upgrade to v2.0.31 (or newer) as described above. The driver(s) now check for this hardware bug.

Problem: PCI NE2000 card gets terrible performance, even when reducing the window size as described in the Performance Tips section.

Reason: The spec sheets for the original 8390 chip, desgined and sold over ten years ago, noted that a dummy read from the chip was required before each write operation for maximum reliablity. The driver has the facility to do this but it has been disabled by default since the v1.2 kernel days. One user has reported that re-enabling this 'mis-feature' helped their performance with a cheap PCI NE2000 clone card.

Solution: Since it has only been reported as a solution by one person, don't get your hopes up. Re-enabling the read before write fix is done by simply editing the file `linux/drivers/net/ne.c`, uncommenting the line containing `NE_RW_BUGFIX` and then rebuilding the kernel or module as appropriate. Please send an e-mail describing the performance difference and type of card/chip you have if this helps you. (The same can be done for the `ne2k-pci.c` driver as well).

Probem: ISA Plug and Play NE2000 (such as RealTek 8019) is not detected.

Reason: The original NE2000 specification (and hence the linux NE2000 driver) does not have support for Plug and Play.

Solution: Use the DOS configuration disk that came with the card to disable PnP, and to set the card to a specified I/O address and IRQ. Add a line to `/etc/conf.modules` like `options ne io=0xNNN` where `0xNNN` is the hex I/O address you set the card to. (This assumes you are using a modular driver; if not then use an `ether=0,0xNNN,eth0` argument at boot). Alternatively, if you need to leave PnP enabled for compatibility with some other operating system, then look into the *isapnptools* package. Try `man isapnp` to see if it is already installed on your system. If not, then have a look at the following URL:

ISA PNP Tools <http://www.roestock.demon.co.uk/isapnptools/>

Problem: NE*000 card hangs machine, sometimes with a 'DMA conflict' message, sometimes completely silently.

Reason: There were some bugs in the driver and the upper networking layers that caused this. They have been fixed long ago, in kernels v1.2.9 and above. Upgrade your kernel.

Problem: NE*000 card hangs machine during NE probe, or can not read station address properly.

Reason: Kernels previous to v1.3.7 did not fully reset the card after finding it at boot. Some cheap cards are not left in a reasonable state after power-up and need to be fully reset before any attempt is made to use them. Also, a previous probe may have upset the NE card prior to the NE probe taking place. In that case, look in to using the "reserve=" boot keyword to protect the card from other probes.

Problem: NE*000 driver reports 'not found (no reset ack)' during boot probe.

Reason: This is related to the above change. After the initial verification that an 8390 is at the probed i/o address, the reset is performed. When the card has completed the reset, it is supposed to acknowedge that the reset has completed. Your card doesn't, and so the driver assumes that no NE card is present.

Solution: You can tell the driver that you have a bad card by using an otherwise unused mem_end hexidecimal value of 0xbad at boot time. You *have* to also supply a non-zero i/o base for the card when using the 0xbad override. For example, a card that is at 0x340 that doesn't ack the reset would use something like:

```
LILO: linux ether=0,0x340,0,0xbad,eth0
```

This will allow the card detection to continue, even if your card doesn't ACK the reset. If you are using the driver as a module, then you can supply the option `bad=0xbad` just like you supply the I/O address. Note that v2.0.x modules won't understand the `bad=` option, as it was added during the v2.1 development.

Problem: NE*000 card hangs machine at first network access.

Reason: This problem has been reported for kernels as old as 1.1.57 to the present. It appears confined to a few software configurable clone cards. It appears that they expect to be initialized in some special way.

Solution: Several people have reported that running the supplied DOS software config program and/or the supplied DOS driver prior to warm booting (i.e. loadlin or the 'three-finger-salute') into linux allowed the card to work. This would indicate that these cards need to be initialized in a particular fashion, slightly different than what the present Linux driver does.

Problem: NE*000 ethercard at `0x360` doesn't get detected anymore.

Reason: Kernels (> 1.1.7X) have more sanity checks with respect to overlapping i/o regions. Your NE2000 card is `0x20` wide in i/o space, which makes it hit the parallel port at `0x378`. Other devices that could be there are the second floppy controller (if equipped) at `0x370` and the secondary IDE controller at `0x376-0x377`. If the port(s) are already registered by another driver, the kernel will not let the probe happen.

Solution: Either move your card to an address like `0x280, 0x340, 0x320` or compile without parallel printer support.

Problem: Network 'goes away' every time I print something (NE2000)

Reason: Same problem as above, but you have an older kernel that doesn't check for overlapping i/o regions. Use the same fix as above, and get a new kernel while you are at it.

Problem: NE*000 ethercard probe at 0xNNN: 00 00 C5 ... not found. (invalid signature yy zz)

Reason: First off, do you have a NE1000 or NE2000 card at the addr. 0xNNN? And if so, does the hardware address reported look like a valid one? If so, then you have a poor NE*000 clone. All NE*000 clones are supposed to have the value `0x57` in bytes 14 and 15 of the SA PROM on the card. Yours doesn't – it has 'yy zz' instead.

Solution: There are two ways to get around this. The easiest is to use an `0xbad` mem_end value as described above for the 'no reset ack' problem. This will bypass the signature check, as long as a non-zero i/o base is also given. This way no recompilation of the kernel is required.

The second method involves changing the driver itself, and then recompiling your kernel. The driver (/usr/src/linux/drivers/net/ne.c) has a "Hall of Shame" list at about line 42. This list is used to detect poor clones. For example, the DFI cards use 'DFI' in the first 3 bytes of the PROM, instead of using 0x57 in bytes 14 and 15, like they are supposed to.

You can determine what the first 3 bytes of your card PROM are by adding a line like:

```
printk("PROM prefix: %2.2x %2.2x %2.2x\n",SA_prom[0],SA_prom[1],SA_prom[2]);
```

into the driver, right after the error message you got above, and just before the "return ENXIO" at line 227.

Reboot with this change in place, and after the detection fails, you will get the three bytes from the PROM like the DFI example above. Then you can add your card to the bad_clone_list[] at about line 43. Say the above line printed out:

```
PROM prefix:  0x3F 0x2D 0x1C
```

after you rebooted. And say that the 8 bit version of your card was called the "FOO-1k" and the 16 bit version the "FOO-2k". Then you would add the following line to the bad_clone_list[]:

```
{"FOO-1k", "FOO-2k", {0x3F, 0x2D, 0x1C,}},
```

Note that the 2 name strings you add can be anything – they are just printed at boot, and not matched against anything on the card. You can also take out the "printk()" that you added above, if you want. It shouldn't hit that line anymore anyway. Then recompile once more, and your card should be detected.

Problem: Errors like `DMA address mismatch`

Is the chip a real NatSemi 8390? (DP8390, DP83901, DP83902 or DP83905)? If not, some clone chips don't correctly implement the transfer verification register. MS-DOS drivers never do error checking, so it doesn't matter to them. (Note: The DMA address check is not done by default as of v1.2.4 for performance reasons. Enable it with the 'NE_SANITY' define in `ne.c` if you want the check done.)

Are most of the messages off by a factor of 2? If so: Are you using the NE2000 in a 16 bit slot? Is it jumpered to use only 8 bit transfers?

The Linux driver expects a NE2000 to be in a 16 bit slot. A NE1000 can be in either size slot. This problem can also occur with some clones, notably older D-Link 16 bit cards, that don't have the correct ID bytes in the station address PROM.

Are you running the bus faster than 8Mhz? If you can change the speed (faster or slower), see if that makes a difference. Most NE2000 clones will run at 16MHz, but some may not. Changing speed can also mask a noisy bus.

What other devices are on the bus? If moving the devices around changes the reliability, then you have a bus noise problem – just what that error message was designed to detect. Congratulations, you've probably found the source of other problems as well.

Problem: The machine hangs during boot right after the '8390...' or 'WD....' message. Removing the NE2000 fixes the problem.

Solution: Change your NE2000 base address to something like `0x340`. Alternatively, you can use the "reserve=" boot argument in conjunction with the "ether=" argument to protect the card from other device driver probes.

Reason: Your NE2000 clone isn't a good enough clone. An active NE2000 is a bottomless pit that will trap any driver autoprobing in its space. Changing the NE2000 to a less-popular address will move it out of the way of other autoprobes, allowing your machine to boot.

Problem: The machine hangs during the SCSI probe at boot.

Reason: It's the same problem as above, change the ethercard's address, or use the reserve/ether boot arguments.

Problem: The machine hangs during the soundcard probe at boot.

Reason: No, that's really during the silent SCSI probe, and it's the same problem as above.

Problem: NE2000 not detected at boot - no boot messages at all

Solution: There is no 'magic solution' as there can be a number of reasons why it wasn't detected. The following list should help you walk through the possible problems.

1) Build a new kernel with only the device drivers that you need. Verify that you are indeed booting the fresh kernel. Forgetting to run lilo, etc. can result in booting the old one. (Look closely at the build time/date reported at boot.) Sounds obvious, but we have all done it before. Make sure the driver is in fact included in the new kernel, by checking the `System.map` file for names like `ne_probe`.

2) Look at the boot messages carefully. Does it ever even mention doing a ne2k probe such as 'NE*000 probe at 0xNNN: not found (blah blah)' or does it just fail silently. There is a big difference. Use `dmesg|more` to review the boot messages after logging in, or hit Shift-PgUp to scroll the screen up after the boot has completed and the login prompt appears.

3) After booting, do a `cat /proc/ioports` and verify that the full iospace that the card will require is vacant. If you are at `0x300` then the ne2k driver will ask for `0x300-0x31f`. If any other device driver has registered even one port

anywhere in that range, the probe will not take place at that address and will silently continue to the next of the probed addresses. A common case is having the lp driver reserve `0x378` or the second IDE channel reserve `0x376` which stops the ne driver from probing `0x360-0x380`.

4) Same as above for `cat /proc/interrupts`. Make sure no other device has registered the interrupt that you set the ethercard for. In this case, the probe will happen, and the ether driver will complain loudly at boot about not being able to get the desired IRQ line.

5) If you are still stumped by the silent failure of the driver, then edit it and add some printk() to the probe. For example, with the ne2k you could add/remove lines (marked with a '+' or '-') in net/ne.c like:

```
      int reg0 = inb_p(ioaddr);

+     printk("NE2k probe - now checking %x\n",ioaddr);
-     if (reg0 == 0xFF)
+     if (reg0 == 0xFF) {
+         printk("NE2k probe - got 0xFF (vacant i/o port)\n");
          return ENODEV;
+     }
```

Then it will output messages for each port address that it checks, and you will see if your card's address is being probed or not.

6) You can also get the ne2k diagnostic from Don's ftp site (mentioned in the howto as well) and see if it is able to detect your card after you have booted into linux. Use the '`-p 0xNNN`' option to tell it where to look for the card. (The default is `0x300` and it doesn't go looking elsewhere, unlike the boot-time probe.) The output from when it finds a card will look something like:

```
Checking the ethercard at 0x300.
  Register 0x0d (0x30d) is 00
  Passed initial NE2000 probe, value 00.
8390 registers: 0a 00 00 00 63 00 00 00 01 00 30 01 00 00 00 00
SA PROM   0: 00 00 00 00 c0 c0 b0 b0 05 05 65 65 05 05 20 20
SA PROM 0x10: 00 00 07 07 0d 0d 01 01 14 14 02 02 57 57 57 57

        NE2000 found at 0x300, using start page 0x40 and end page 0x80.
```

Your register values and PROM values will probably be different. Note that all the PROM values are doubled for a 16 bit card, and that the ethernet address (00:00:c0:b0:05:65) appears in the first row, and the double `0x57` signature appears at the end of the PROM.

The output from when there is no card installed at `0x300` will look something like this:

```
Checking the ethercard at 0x300.
  Register 0x0d (0x30d) is ff
  Failed initial NE2000 probe, value ff.
8390 registers: ff ff ff ff ff ff ff ff ff ff ff ff ff ff ff ff
SA PROM      0: ff ff ff ff ff ff ff ff ff ff ff ff ff ff ff ff
SA PROM 0x10: ff ff ff ff ff ff ff ff ff ff ff ff ff ff ff ff

  Invalid signature found, wordlength 2.
```

The `0xff` values arise because that is the value that is returned when one reads a vacant i/o port. If you happen to have some other hardware in the region that is probed, you may see some non `0xff` values as well.

7) Try warm booting into linux from a DOS boot floppy (via loadlin) after running the supplied DOS driver or config program. It may be doing some extra (i.e. non-standard) "magic" to initialize the card.

8) Try Russ Nelson's ne2000.com packet driver to see if even it can see your card – if not, then things do not look good. Example:

```
A:> ne2000 0x60 10 0x300
```

The arguments are software interrupt vector, hardware IRQ, and i/o base. You can get it from any msdos archive in pktdrv11.zip – The current version may be newer than 11.

3.5   Problems with SMC Ultra/EtherEZ and WD80*3 cards

Problem: You get messages such as the following:

```
eth0: bogus packet size: 65531, status=0xff, nxpg=0xff
```

Reason: There is a shared memory problem.

Solution: The most common reason for this is PCI machines that are not configured to map in ISA memory devices. Hence you end up reading the PC's RAM (all `0xff` values) instead of the RAM on the card that contains the data from the received packet.

Other typical problems that are easy to fix are board conflicts, having cache or 'shadow ROM' enabled for that region, or running your ISA bus faster than 8Mhz. There are also a surprising number of memory failures on ethernet cards, so run a diagnostic program if you have one for your ethercard.

Problem: SMC EtherEZ doesn't work in non-shared memory (PIO) mode.

Reason: Older versions of the Ultra driver only supported the card in the shared memory mode of operation.

Solution: The driver in kernel version 2.0 and above also supports the programmed i/o mode of operation. Upgrade to v2.0, or get the drop-in replacement for kernel v1.2.13 from Donald's ftp/www site.

Problem: Old wd8003 and/or jumper-settable wd8013 always get the IRQ wrong.

Reason: The old wd8003 cards and jumper-settable wd8013 clones don't have the EEPROM that the driver can read the IRQ setting from. If the driver can't read the IRQ, then it tries to auto-IRQ to find out what it is. And if auto-IRQ returns zero, then the driver just assigns IRQ 5 for an 8 bit card or IRQ 10 for a 16 bit card.

Solution: Avoid the auto-IRQ code, and tell the kernel what the IRQ that you have jumpered the card to is via a boot time argument. For example, if you are using IRQ 9, using the following should work.

```
LILO: linux ether=9,0,eth0
```

Problem: SMC Ultra card is detected as wd8013, but the IRQ and shared memory base is wrong.

Reason: The Ultra card looks a lot like a wd8013, and if the Ultra driver is not present in the kernel, the wd driver may mistake the ultra as a wd8013. The ultra probe comes before the wd probe, so this usually shouldn't happen. The ultra stores the IRQ and mem base in the EEPROM differently than a wd8013, hence the bogus values reported.

Solution: Recompile with only the drivers you need in the kernel. If you have a mix of wd and ultra cards in one machine, and are using modules, then load the ultra module first.

3.6   Problems with 3Com cards

Problem: The 3c503 picks IRQ N, but this is needed for some other device which needs IRQ N. (eg. CD ROM driver, modem, etc.) Can this be fixed without compiling this into the kernel?

HOWTO

Solution: The 3c503 driver probes for a free IRQ line in the order {5, 9/2, 3, 4}, and it should pick a line which isn't being used. The driver chooses when the card is ifconfig'ed into operation.

If you are using a modular driver, you can use module parameters to set various things, including the IRQ value.

The following selects IRQ9, base location 0x300, <ignored value>, and if_port #1 (the external transceiver).

```
io=0x300 irq=9 xcvr=1
```

Alternately, if the driver is compiled into the kernel, you can set the same values at boot by passing parameters via LILO.

```
LILO: linux ether=9,0x300,0,1,eth0
```

The following selects IRQ3, probes for the base location, <ignored value>, and the default if_port #0 (the internal transceiver)

```
LILO: linux ether=3,0,0,0,eth0
```

Problem: 3c503: configured interrupt X invalid, will use autoIRQ.

Reason: The 3c503 card can only use one of IRQ{5, 2/9, 3, 4} (These are the only lines that are connected to the card.) If you pass in an IRQ value that is not in the above set, you will get the above message. Usually, specifying an interrupt value for the 3c503 is not necessary. The 3c503 will autoIRQ when it gets ifconfig'ed, and pick one of IRQ{5, 2/9, 3, 4}.

Solution: Use one of the valid IRQs listed above, or enable autoIRQ by not specifying the IRQ line at all.

Problem: The supplied 3c503 drivers don't use the AUI (thicknet) port. How does one choose it over the default thinnet port?

Solution: The 3c503 AUI port can be selected at boot-time for in-kernel drivers, and at module insertion for modular drivers. The selection is overloaded onto the low bit of the currently-unused dev->rmem_start variable, so a boot-time parameter of:

```
LILO: linux ether=0,0,0,1,eth0
```

should work for in-kernel drivers.

To specify the AUI port when loading as a module, just append xcvr=1 to the module options line along with your i/o and irq values.

3.7 FAQs Not Specific to Any Card.

3.7.1 Ethercard is Not Detected at Boot.

The usual reason for this is that people are using a kernel that does not have support for their particular card built in. For a modular kernel, it usually means that the required module has not been requested for loading, or that an I/O address needs to be specified as a module option.

If you are using a modular based kernel, such as those installed by most of the linux distributions, then try and use the configuration utility for the distribution to select the module for your card. For ISA cards, it is a good idea to determine the I/O address of the card and add it as an option (e.g. io=0x340) if the configuration utility asks for any options. If there is no configuration utility, then you will have to add the correct module name (and options) to /etc/conf.modules – see man modprobe for more details.

If you are using a pre-compiled kernel that is part of a distribution set, then check the documentation to see which kernel you installed, and if it was built with support for your particular card. If it wasn't, then your options are to try and get one that has support for your card, or build your own.

It is usually wise to build your own kernel with only the drivers you need, as this cuts down on the kernel size (saving your precious RAM for applications!) and reduces the number of device probes that can upset sensitive hardware. Building a kernel is not as complicated as it sounds. You just have to answer yes or no to a bunch of questions about what drivers you want, and it does the rest.

The next main cause is having another device using part of the i/o space that your card needs. Most cards are 16 or 32 bytes wide in i/o space. If your card is set at 0x300 and 32 bytes wide, then the driver will ask for 0x300-0x31f. If any other device driver has registered even one port anywhere in that range, the probe will not take place at that address and the driver will silently continue to the next of the probed addresses. So, after booting, do a `cat /proc/ioports` and verify that the full iospace that the card will require is vacant.

Another problem is having your card jumpered to an i/o address that isn't probed by default. There is a list 8.1 (probed addresses) for each card in this document. Even if the i/o setting of your card is not in the list of probed addresses, you can supply it at boot (for in-kernel drivers) with the `ether=` command as described in 10.1 (Passing Ethernet Arguments...) Modular drivers can make use of the `io=` option to specify an address that isn't probed by default.

3.7.2 `ifconfig` reports the wrong i/o address for the card.

No it doesn't. You are just interpreting it incorrectly. This is *not* a bug, and the numbers reported are correct. It just happens that some 8390 based cards (wd80x3, smc-ultra, etc) have the actual 8390 chip living at an offset from the first assigned i/o port. This is the value stored in `dev->base_addr`, and is what `ifconfig` reports. If you want to see the full range of ports that your card uses, then try `cat /proc/ioports` which will give the numbers you expect.

3.7.3 PCI machine detects card but driver fails probe.

Newer PCI BIOSes may not enable all PCI cards at power-up, especially if the BIOS option 'PNP OS' is enabled. This mis-feature is to support the next release of Windows which still uses some real-mode drivers. Either disable this option, or try and upgrade to a newer driver which has the code to enable a disabled card.

3.7.4 Shared Memory ISA cards in PCI Machine dont work (0xffff)

This will usually show up as reads of lots of `0xffff` values. No shared memory cards of any type will work in a PCI machine unless you have the PCI ROM BIOS/CMOS SETUP configuration set properly. You have to set it to allow shared memory access from the ISA bus for the memory region that your card is trying to use. If you can't figure out which settings are applicable then ask your supplier or local computer guru. For AMI BIOS, there is usually a "Plug and Play" section where there will be an "ISA Shared Memory Size" and "ISA Shared Memory Base" settings. For cards like the wd8013 and SMC Ultra, change the size from the default of 'Disabled' to 16kB, and change the base to the shared memory address of your card.

3.7.5 NexGen machine gets 'mismatched read page pointers' errors.

A quirk of the NexGen CPU caused all users with 8390 based cards (wd80x3, 3c503, SMC Ultra/EtherEZ, ne2000, etc.) to get these error messages. Kernel versions 2.0 and above do not have these problems. Upgrade your kernel.

3.7.6 Asynchronous Transfer Mode (ATM) Support

Werner Almesberger has been working on ATM support for linux. He has been working with the Efficient Networks ENI155p board (*Efficient Networks* <http://www.efficient.com/>) and the Zeitnet ZN1221 board (*Zeitnet* <http://www.zeitnet.com/>).

Werner says that the driver for the ENI155p is rather stable, while the driver for the ZN1221 is presently unfinished.

Check the latest/updated status at the following URL:

Linux ATM Support <http://lrcwww.epfl.ch/linux-atm/>

3.7.7 Gigabyte Ethernet Support

Is there any gigabyte ethernet support for Linux?

A driver for the Packet Engines G-NIC PCI Gigabit Ethernet adapter is due to be added into the upcoming release of kernel v2.0.34. For more details, support, and driver updates, see:

```
http://cesdis.gsfc.nasa.gov/linux/drivers/yellowfin.html
```

3.7.8 FDDI Support

Is there FDDI support for Linux?

Yes. Larry Stefani has written a driver for v2.0 with Digital's DEFEA (FDDI EISA) and DEFPA (FDDI PCI) cards. This was included into the v2.0.24 kernel. Currently no other cards are supported though.

3.7.9 Full Duplex Support

Will Full Duplex give me 20MBps? Does Linux support it?

Cameron Spitzer writes the following about full duplex 10Base-T cards: "If you connect it to a full duplex switched hub, and your system is fast enough and not doing much else, it can keep the link busy in both directions. There is no such thing as full duplex 10BASE-2 or 10BASE-5 (thin and thick coax). Full Duplex works by disabling collision detection in the adapter. That's why you can't do it with coax; the LAN won't run that way. 10BASE-T (RJ45 interface) uses separate wires for send and receive, so it's possible to run both ways at the same time. The switching hub takes care of the collision problem. The signalling rate is 10 Mbps."

So as you can see, you still will only be able to receive or transmit at 10Mbps, and hence don't expect a 2x performance increase. As to whether it is supported or not, that depends on the card and possibly the driver. Some cards may do auto-negotiation, some may need driver support, and some may need the user to select an option in a card's EEPROM configuration. Only the serious/heavy user would notice the difference between the two modes anyway.

3.7.10 Ethernet Cards for Linux on Alpha/AXP PCI Boards

As of v2.0, only the 3c509, depca, de4x5 lance32, and all the 8390 drivers (wd, smc-ultra, ne, 3c503, etc.) have been made 'architecture independent' so as to work on the DEC Alpha CPU based systems. Other updated PCI drivers from Donald's WWW page may also work as these have been written with architecture independence in mind.

Note that the changes that are required to make a driver architecture independent aren't that complicated. You only need to do the following:

-multiply all `jiffies` related values by HZ/100 to account for the different HZ value that the Alpha uses. (i.e `timeout=2;` becomes `timeout=2*HZ/100;`)

-replace any i/o memory (640k to 1MB) pointer dereferences with the appropriate readb() writeb() readl() writel() calls, as shown in this example.

```
-        int *mem_base = (int *)dev->mem_start;
-        mem_base[0] = 0xba5eba5e;
+        unsigned long mem_base = dev->mem_start;
+        writel(0xba5eba5e, mem_base);
```

-replace all memcpy() calls that have i/o memory as source or target destinations with the appropriate one of `mem-cpy_fromio()` or `memcpy_toio()`.

Details on handling memory accesses in an architecture independent fashion are documented in the file `linux/Documentation/IO-mapping.txt` that comes with recent kernels.

3.7.11 Ethernet for Linux on SUN/Sparc Hardware.

For the most up to date information on Sparc stuff, try the following URL:

Linux Sparc <http://www.geog.ubc.ca/sparc>

Note that some Sparc ethernet hardware gets its MAC address from the host computer, and hence you can end up with multiple interfaces all with the same MAC address. If you need to put more than one interface on the same net then use the hw option to ifconfig to assign unique MAC address.

Issues regarding porting PCI drivers to the Sparc platform are similar to those mentioned above for the AXP platform. In addition there may be some endian issues, as the Sparc is big endian, and the AXP and ix86 are little endian.

3.7.12 Linking 10BaseT without a Hub

Can I link 10BaseT (RJ45) based systems together without a hub?

You can link 2 machines easily, but no more than that, without extra devices/gizmos. See 6.2 (Twisted Pair) – it explains how to do it. And no, you can't hack together a hub just by crossing a few wires and stuff. It's pretty much impossible to do the collision signal right without duplicating a hub.

3.7.13 SIOCSIFxxx: No such device

I get a bunch of 'SIOCSIFxxx: No such device' messages at boot, followed by a 'SIOCADDRT: Network is unreachable' What is wrong?

Your ethernet device was not detected at boot/module insertion time, and when ifconfig and route are run, they have no device to work with. Use dmesg | more to review the boot messages and see if there are any messages about detecting an ethernet card.

3.7.14 SIOCSFFLAGS: Try again

I get 'SIOCSFFLAGS: Try again' when I run 'ifconfig' – Huh?

Some other device has taken the IRQ that your ethercard is trying to use, and so the ethercard can't use the IRQ. You don't necessairly need to reboot to resolve this, as some devices only grab the IRQs when they need them and then release them when they are done. Examples are some sound cards, serial ports, floppy disk driver, etc. You can type cat /proc/interrupts to see which interrupts are presently *in use*. Most of the Linux ethercard drivers only grab the IRQ when they are opened for use via 'ifconfig'. If you can get the other device to 'let go' of the required IRQ line, then you should be able to 'Try again' with ifconfig.

3.7.15 Using 'ifconfig' and Link UNSPEC with HW-addr of 00:00:00:00:00:00

When I run ifconfig with no arguments, it reports that LINK is UNSPEC (instead of 10Mbs Ethernet) and it also says that my hardware address is all zeros.

This is because people are running a newer version of the 'ifconfig' program than their kernel version. This new version of ifconfig is not able to report these properties when used in conjunction with an older kernel. You can either upgrade your kernel, 'downgrade' ifconfig, or simply ignore it. The kernel knows your hardware address, so it really doesn't matter if ifconfig can't read it.

You may also get strange information if the ifconfig program you are using is a lot older than the kernel you are using.

3.7.16 Huge Number of RX and TX Errors

When I run ifconfig with no arguments, it reports that I have a huge error count in both rec'd and transmitted packets. It all seems to work ok – What is wrong?

Look again. It says RX packets *big number* **PAUSE** errors 0 **PAUSE** dropped 0 **PAUSE** overrun 0. And the same for the TX column. Hence the big numbers you are seeing are the total number of packets that your machine has rec'd and transmitted. If you still find it confusing, try typing cat /proc/net/dev instead.

3.7.17 Entries in /dev/ for Ethercards

I have /dev/eth0 as a link to /dev/xxx. Is this right?

Contrary to what you have heard, the files in /dev/* are not used. You can delete any /dev/wd0, /dev/ne0 and similar entries.

3.7.18 Linux and "trailers"

Should I disable trailers when I 'ifconfig' my ethercard?

You can't disable trailers, and you shouldn't want to. 'Trailers' are a hack to avoid data copying in the networking layers. The idea was to use a trivial fixed-size header of size 'H', put the variable-size header info at the end of the packet, and allocate all packets 'H' bytes before the start of a page. While it was a good idea, it turned out to not work well in practice. If someone suggests the use of '-trailers', note that it is the equivalent of sacrificial goats blood. It won't do anything to solve the problem, but if problem fixes itself then someone can claim deep magical knowledge.

3.7.19 Access to the raw Ethernet Device

How do I get access to the raw ethernet device in linux, without going through TCP/IP and friends?

```
int s=socket(AF_INET,SOCK_PACKET,htons(ETH_P_ALL));
```

This gives you a socket receiving every protocol type. Do recvfrom() calls to it and it will fill the sockaddr with device type in sa_family and the device name in the sa_data array. I don't know who originally invented SOCK_PACKET for Linux (its been in for ages) but its superb stuff. You can use it to send stuff raw too via sendto() calls. You have to have root access to do either of course.

4   Performance Tips

Here are some tips that you can use if you are suffering from low ethernet throughput, or to gain a bit more speed on those ftp transfers.

The ttcp.c program is a good test for measuring raw throughput speed. Another common trick is to do a ftp> get large_file /dev/null where large_file is > 1MB and residing in the buffer cache on the Tx'ing machine. (Do the 'get' at least twice, as the first time will be priming the buffer cache on the Tx'ing machine.) You want the file in the buffer cache because you are not interested in combining the file access speed from the disk into your measurement. Which is also why you send the incoming data to /dev/null instead of onto the disk.

4.1   General Concepts

Even an 8 bit card is able to receive back-to-back packets without any problems. The difficulty arises when the computer doesn't get the Rx'd packets off the card quick enough to make room for more incoming packets. If the computer does not quickly clear the card's memory of the packets already received, the card will have no place to put the new packet.

In this case the card either drops the new packet, or writes over top of a previously received packet. Either one seriously interrupts the smooth flow of traffic by causing/requesting re-transmissions and can seriously degrade performance by up to a factor of 5!

Cards with more onboard memory are able to "buffer" more packets, and thus can handle larger bursts of back-to-back packets without dropping packets. This in turn means that the card does not require as low a latency from the the host computer with respect to pulling the packets out of the buffer to avoid dropping packets.

Most 8 bit cards have an 8kB buffer, and most 16 bit cards have a 16kB buffer. Most Linux drivers will reserve 3kB of that buffer (for two Tx buffers), leaving only 5kB of receive space for an 8 bit card. This is room enough for only three full sized (1500 bytes) ethernet packets.

4.2 ISA Bus Speed

As mentioned above, if the packets are removed from the card fast enough, then a drop/overrun condition won't occur even when the amount of Rx packet buffer memory is small. The factor that sets the rate at which packets are removed from the card to the computer's memory is the speed of the data path that joins the two – that being the ISA bus speed. (If the CPU is a dog-slow 386sx-16, then this will also play a role.)

The recommended ISA bus clock is about 8MHz, but many motherboards and peripheral devices can be run at higher frequencies. The clock frequency for the ISA bus can usually be set in the CMOS setup, by selecting a divisor of the mainboard/CPU clock frequency.

For example, here are some receive speeds as measured by the TTCP program on a 40MHz 486, with an 8 bit WD8003EP card, for different ISA bus speeds.

```
        ISA Bus Speed (MHz)        Rx TTCP (kB/s)
        -------------------        --------------
        6.7                        740
        13.4                       970
        20.0                       1030
        26.7                       1075
```

You would be hard pressed to do better than 1075kB/s with *any* 10Mb/s ethernet card, using TCP/IP. However, don't expect every system to work at fast ISA bus speeds. Most systems will not function properly at speeds above 13MHz. (Also, some PCI systems have the ISA bus speed fixed at 8MHz, so that the end user does not have the option of increasing it.)

In addition to faster transfer speeds, one will usually also benefit from a reduction in CPU usage due to the shorter duration memory and i/o cycles. (Note that hard disks and video cards located on the ISA bus will also usually experience a performance increase from an increased ISA bus speed.)

Be sure to back up your data prior to experimenting with ISA bus speeds in excess of 8MHz, and thouroughly test that all ISA peripherals are operating properly after making any speed increases.

4.3 Setting the TCP Rx Window

Once again, cards with small amounts of onboard RAM and relatively slow data paths between the card and the computer's memory run into trouble. The default TCP Rx window setting is 32kB, which means that a fast computer on the same subnet as you can dump 32k of data on you without stopping to see if you received any of it okay.

Recent versions of the `route` command have the ability to set the size of this window on the fly. Usually it is only for the local net that this window must be reduced, as computers that are behind a couple of routers or gateways are 'buffered' enough to not pose a problem. An example usage would be:

```
        route add <whatever> ... window <win_size>
```

where `win_size` is the size of the window you wish to use (in bytes). An 8 bit 3c503 card on an ISA bus operating at a speed of 8MHz or less would work well with a window size of about 4kB. Too large a window will cause overruns and dropped packets, and a drastic reduction in ethernet throughput. You can check the operating status by doing a `cat /proc/net/dev` which will display any dropped or overrun conditions that occurred.

HOWTO

4.4 Increasing NFS performance

Some people have found that using 8 bit cards in NFS clients causes poorer than expected performance, when using 8kB (native Sun) NFS packet size.

The possible reason for this could be due to the difference in on board buffer size between the 8 bit and the 16 bit cards. The maximum ethernet packet size is about 1500 bytes. Now that 8kB NFS packet will arrive as about 6 back to back maximum size ethernet packets. Both the 8 and 16 bit cards have no problem Rx'ing back to back packets. The problem arises when the machine doesn't remove the packets from the cards buffer in time, and the buffer overflows. The fact that 8 bit cards take an extra ISA bus cycle per transfer doesn't help either. What you *can* do if you have an 8 bit card is either set the NFS transfer size to 2kB (or even 1kB), or try increasing the ISA bus speed in order to get the card's buffer cleared out faster. I have found that an old WD8003E card at 8MHz (with no other system load) can keep up with a large receive at 2kB NFS size, but not at 4kB, where performance was degraded by a factor of three.

5 Vendor/Manufacturer/Model Specific Information

The following lists many cards in alphabetical order by vendor name and then product identifier. Beside each product ID, you will see either 'Supported', 'Semi-Supported' or 'Not Supported'.

Supported means that a driver for that card exists, and many people are happily using it and it seems quite reliable.

Semi-Supported means that a driver exists, but at least one of the following descriptions is true: (1) The driver and/or hardware are buggy, which may cause poor performance, failing connections or even crashes. (2) The driver is new or the card is fairly uncommon, and hence the driver has seen very little use/testing and the driver author has had very little feedback. Obviously (2) is preferable to (1), and the individual description of the card/driver should make it clear which one holds true. In either case, you will probably have to answer 'Y' when asked "Prompt for development and/or incomplete code/drivers?" when running `make config`.

Not Supported means there is not a driver currently available for that card. This could be due to a lack of interest in hardware that is rare/uncommon, or because the vendors won't release the hardware documentation required to write a driver.

Note that the difference between 'Supported' and 'Semi-Supported' is rather subjective, and is based on user feedback observed in newsgroup postings and mailing list messages. (After all, it is impossible for one person to test all drivers with all cards for each kernel version!!!) So be warned that you may find a card listed as semi-supported works perfectly for you (which is great), or that a card listed as supported gives you no end of troubles and problems (which is not so great).

5.1 3Com

If you are not sure what your card is, but you think it is a 3Com card, you can probably figure it out from the assembly number. 3Com has a document 'Identifying 3Com Adapters By Assembly Number' (ref 24500002) that would most likely clear things up. See 8.6 (Technical Information from 3Com) for info on how to get documents from 3Com.

Also note that 3Com has a FTP site with various goodies: `ftp.3Com.com` that you may want to check out.

For those of you browsing this document by a WWW browser, you can try 3Com's WWW site as well.

5.1.1 3c501

Status – *Semi-Supported*

Too brain-damaged to use. Available surplus from many places. Avoid it like the plague. Again, do not purchase this card, even as a joke. It's performance is horrible, and it breaks in many ways.

For those not yet convinced, the 3c501 can only do one thing at a time – while you are removing one packet from the single-packet buffer it cannot receive another packet, nor can it receive a packet while loading a transmit packet. This was fine for a network between two 8088-based computers where processing each packet and replying took 10's of msecs, but modern networks send back-to-back packets for almost every transaction.

AutoIRQ works, DMA isn't used, the autoprobe only looks at `0x280` and `0x300`, and the debug level is set with the third boot-time argument.

Once again, the use of a 3c501 is *strongly discouraged*! Even more so with a IP multicast kernel, as you will grind to a halt while listening to *all* multicast packets. See the comments at the top of the source code for more details.

5.1.2   EtherLink II, 3c503, 3c503/16

Status – *Supported*

The 3c503 does not have "EEPROM setup", so a diagnostic/setup program isn't needed before running the card with Linux. The shared memory address of the 3c503 is set using jumpers that are shared with the boot PROM address. This is confusing to people familiar with other ISA cards, where you always leave the jumper set to "disable" unless you have a boot PROM.

These cards should be about the same speed as the same bus width WD80x3, but turn out to be actually a bit slower. These shared-memory ethercards also have a programmed I/O mode that doesn't use the 8390 facilities (their engineers found too many bugs!) The Linux 3c503 driver can also work with the 3c503 in programmed-I/O mode, but this is slower and less reliable than shared memory mode. Also, programmed-I/O mode is not as well tested when updating the drivers. You shouldn't use the programmed-I/O mode unless you need it for MS-DOS compatibility.

The 3c503's IRQ line is set in software, with no hints from an EEPROM. Unlike the MS-DOS drivers, the Linux driver has capability to autoIRQ: it uses the first available IRQ line in {5,2/9,3,4}, selected each time the card is ifconfig'ed. (Older driver versions selected the IRQ at boot time.) The ioctl() call in 'ifconfig' will return EAGAIN if no IRQ line is available at that time.

Some common problems that people have with the 503 are discussed in 3.6 (Problems with...).

If you intend on using this driver as a loadable module you should probably see 10.2 (Using the Ethernet Drivers as Modules) for module specific information.

Note that some old diskless 386 workstations have an on board 3c503 (made by 3Com and sold under different names, like 'Bull') but the vendor ID is not a 3Com ID and so it won't be detected. More details can be found in the Etherboot package, which you will need anyways to boot these diskless boxes.

5.1.3   3c505

Status – *Semi-Supported*

This is a driver that was written by Craig Southeren `geoffw@extro.ucc.su.oz.au`. These cards also use the i82586 chip. There are not that many of these cards about. It is included in the standard kernel, but it is classed as an alpha driver. See 3.1 (Alpha Drivers) for important information on using alpha-test ethernet drivers with Linux.

There is also the file `/usr/src/linux/drivers/net/README.3c505` that you should read if you are going to use one of these cards. It contains various options that you can enable/disable. Technical information is available in 8.5 (Programming the Intel chips).

5.1.4   3c507

Status – *Semi-Supported*

This card uses one of the Intel chips, and the development of the driver is closely related to the development of the Intel Ether Express driver. The driver is included in the standard kernel release, but as an alpha driver.

See 3.1 (Alpha Drivers) for important information on using alpha-test ethernet drivers with Linux. Technical information is available in 8.5 (Programming the Intel chips).

5.1.5   3c509 / 3c509B

Status – *Supported*

This card is fairly inexpensive and has good performance for a non-bus-master design. The drawbacks are that the original 3c509 requires very low interrupt latency. The 3c509B shouldn't suffer from the same problem, due to having a larger buffer. (See below.) These cards use PIO transfers, similar to a ne2000 card, and so a shared memory card such as a wd8013 will be more efficient in comparison.

The original 3c509 has a small packet buffer (4kB total, 2kB Rx, 2kB Tx), causing the driver to occasionally drop a packet if interrupts are masked for too long. To minimize this problem, you can try unmasking interrupts during IDE disk transfers (see `man hdparm`) and/or increasing your ISA bus speed so IDE transfers finish sooner.

The newer model 3c509B has 8kB on board, and the buffer can be split 4/4, 5/3 or 6/2 for Rx/Tx. This setting is changed with the DOS configuration utility, and is stored on the EEPROM. This should alleviate the above problem with the original 3c509.

3c509B users should use the supplied DOS utility to disable the *plug and play* support, *and* to set the output media to what they require. The linux driver currently does *not* support the Autodetect media setting, so you *have* to select 10Base-T or 10Base-2 or AUI.

With regards to the media detection features, Cameron said: "Autoselect is a feature of the commercial drivers for 3C509(B). AFAIK nobody ever claimed the Linux driver attempts it. When drivers/net/3c509.c recognizes my 3C509B at boot time, it says: `eth0:   3c509 at 0x300 tag 1, 10baseT port, ...` revealing that the card is configured for 10BASE-T. It finds that out by reading the little EEPROM, which IMHO is the Right Way To Do It."

As for the plug-and-pray stuff, Cameron adds: "It was a marketing decision to turn PnP on as a factory default setting. If it caused you a hassle, or not, please take the time to say so when you mail in your warranty card. The more info they have, the better decisions they can make. Also, check with your motherboard supplier to see if you need a BIOS upgrade."

Note that to turn off PnP entirely, you should do a `3C5X9CFG /PNP:DISABLE` and then follow that with a hard reset to ensure that it takes effect.

Some people ask about the "Server or Workstation" and "Highest Modem Speed" settings presented in the DOS configuration utility. Donald writes "These are only hints to the drivers, and the Linux driver does not use these parameters: it always optimizes for high throughput rather than low latency ('Server'). Low latency was critically important for old, non-windowed, IPX throughput. To reduce the latency the MS-DOS driver for the 3c509 disables interrupts for some operations, blocking serial port interrupts. Thus the need for the 'modem speed' setting. The Linux driver avoids the need to disable interrupts for long periods by operating only on whole packets e.g. by not starting to transmit a packet until it is completely transferred to the card."

Note that the ISA card detection uses a different method than most cards. Basically, you ask the cards to respond by sending data to an ID_PORT (port `0x100` to `0x1ff` on intervals of `0x10`). This detection method means that a particular card will *always* get detected first in a multiple ISA 3c509 configuration. The card with the lowest hardware ethernet address will *always* end up being `eth0`. This shouldn't matter to anyone, except for those people who want to assign a 6 byte hardware address to a particular interface. If you have multiple 3c509 cards, it is best to append `ether=0,0,ethN` commands without the i/o port specified (i.e. use i/o=zero) and allow the probe to sort out which card is first. Using a non-zero i/o value will ensure that it does not detect all your cards, so don't do it.

If this really bothers you, have a look at Donald's latest driver, as you may be able to use a `0x3c509` value in the unused mem address fields to order the detection to suit.

5.1.6   3c515

Status – *Not Supported*

This is 3Com's farily recent ISA 100Mbps offering, codenamed "CorkScrew". Donald is working on support for these cards, and it will probably appear in the near future on his WWW driver page. The driver will be incorporated into the

3c59x/3c90x driver, so you should probably expect to look for it on the Vortex page:

Vortex `<http://cesdis.gsfc.nasa.gov/linux/drivers/vortex.html>`

5.1.7   3c523

Status – *Semi-Supported*

This MCA bus card uses the i82586, and Chris Beauregard has modified the ni52 driver to work with these cards. The driver for it can be found in the v2.1 kernel source tree.

More details can be found on the MCA-Linux page at `http://glycerine.cetmm.uni.edu/mca/`

5.1.8   3c527

Status – *Not Supported*

Yes, another MCA card. No, not too much interest in it. Better chances with the 3c529 if you are stuck with MCA.

5.1.9   3c529

Status – *Semi-Supported*

This card actually uses the same chipset as the 3c509. Donald actually put hooks into the 3c509 driver to check for MCA cards after probing for EISA cards, and before probing for ISA cards. But it hasn't evolved much further than that. Donald writes:

"I don't have access to a MCA machine (nor do I fully understand the probing code) so I never wrote the `mca_adaptor_select_mode()` or `mca_adaptor_id()` routines. If you can find a way to get the adaptor I/O address that assigned at boot time, you can just hard-wire that in place of the commented-out probe. Be sure to keep the code that reads the IRQ, if_port, and ethernet address."

Darrell Frappier (aa822@detroit.freenet.org) reports that you can get the i/o address from running the PS/2 reference diskette, and once you put that directly into the driver, it does actually work.

The required MCA probe code will probably appear in the driver in a development kernel sometime soon, now that MCA support is in the kernel.

More details can be found on the MCA-Linux page at `http://glycerine.cetmm.uni.edu/mca/`

5.1.10   3c562

Status – *Supported*

This PCMCIA card is the combination of a 3c589B ethernet card with a modem. The modem appears as a standard modem to the end user. The only difficulty is getting the two separate linux drivers to share one interrupt. There are a couple of new registers and some hardware interrupt sharing support. You need to use a v2.0 or newer kernel that has the support for interrupt sharing.

As a side note, the modem part of the card has been reported to be not well documented for the end user (the manual just says 'supports the AT command set') and it may not connect as well as other name brand modems. The recommendation is to buy a 3c589B instead, and then get a PCMCIA modem card from a company that specializes in modems.

Thanks again to Cameron for getting a sample unit and documentation sent off to David Hinds. Look for support in David's PCMCIA package release.

See 9.3 (PCMCIA Support) for more info on PCMCIA chipsets, socket enablers, etc.

5.1.11 3c575

Status – *Not Supported*

A driver for this PCMCIA card is under development and hopefully will be included in David's PCMCIA package within a few months.

5.1.12 3c579

Status – *Supported*

The EISA version of the 509. The current EISA version uses the same 16 bit wide chip rather than a 32 bit interface, so the performance increase isn't stunning. Make sure the card is configured for EISA addressing mode. Read the above 3c509 section for info on the driver.

5.1.13 3c589 / 3c589B

Status – *Semi-Supported*

Many people have been using this PCMCIA card for quite some time now. Note that support for it is not (at present) included in the default kernel source tree. You will also need a supported PCMCIA controller chipset. There are drivers available on Donald's ftp site:

```
cesdis.gsfc.nasa.gov:/pub/linux/pcmcia/README.3c589
cesdis.gsfc.nasa.gov:/pub/linux/pcmcia/3c589.c
cesdis.gsfc.nasa.gov:/pub/linux/pcmcia/dbether.c
```

Or for those that are *net-surfing* you can try:

Don's PCMCIA Stuff <http://cesdis.gsfc.nasa.gov/linux/pcmcia.html>

You will still need a PCMCIA socket enabler as well.

See 9.3 (PCMCIA Support) for more info on PCMCIA chipsets, socket enablers, etc.

The "B" in the name means the same here as it does for the 3c509 case.

5.1.14 3c590 / 3c595

Status – *Supported*

These "Vortex" cards are for PCI bus machines, with the '590 being 10Mbps and the '595 being 3Com's 100Mbs offering. Also note that you can run the '595 as a '590 (i.e. in a 10Mbps mode). The driver is included in the v2.0 kernel source, but is also continually being updated. If you have problems with the driver in the v2.0 kernel, you can get an updated driver from the following URL:

Vortex <http://cesdis.gsfc.nasa.gov/linux/drivers/vortex.html>

Note that there are two different 3c590 cards out there, early models that had 32kB of on-board memory, and later models that only have 8kB of memory. Chances are you won't be able to buy a new 3c59x for much longer, as it is being replaced with the 3c90x card. If you are buying a used one off somebody, try and get the 32kB version. The 3c595 cards have 64kB, as you can't get away with only 8kB RAM at 100Mbps!

A thanks to Cameron Spitzer and Terry Murphy of 3Com for sending cards and documentation to Donald so he could write the driver.

Donald has set up a mailing list for Vortex driver support. To join the list, just do:

```
echo subscribe | /bin/mail linux-vortex-request@cesdis.gsfc.nasa.gov
```

5.1.15   3c592 / 3c597

Status – *Supported*

These are the EISA versions of the 3c59x series of cards. The 3c592/3c597 (aka Demon) should work with the vortex driver discussed above.

5.1.16   3c900 / 3c905 / 3c905B

Status – *Supported*

These cards (aka 'Boomerang', aka EtherLink III XL) have been released to take over the place of the 3c590/3c595 cards.

The support for the Cyclone 'B' revision was only recently added. To use this card with older v2.0 kernels, you must obtain the updated `3c59x.c` driver from Donald's site at:

Vortex-Page <http://cesdis.gsfc.nasa.gov/linux/drivers/vortex.html>

If in doubt about anything then check out the above WWW page. Donald has set up a mailing list for Vortex driver support announcements and etc. To join the list, just do:

```
echo subscribe | /bin/mail linux-vortex-request@cesdis.gsfc.nasa.gov
```

5.2   Accton

5.2.1   Accton MPX

Status – *Supported*

Don't let the name fool you. This is still supposed to be a NE2000 compatible card, and should work with the ne2000 driver.

5.2.2   Accton EN1203, EN1207, EtherDuo-PCI

Status – *Supported*

This is another implementation of the DEC 21040 PCI chip. The EN1207 card has the 21140, and also has a 10Base-2 connector, which has proved troublesome for some people in terms of selecting that media. Using the card with 10Base-T and 100Base-T media have worked for others though. So as with all purchases, you should try and make sure you can return it if it doesn't work for you.

See 5.17.4 (DEC 21040) for more information on these cards, and the present driver situation.

5.2.3   Accton EN2209 Parallel Port Adaptor (EtherPocket)

Status – *Semi-Supported*

A driver for these parallel port adapters is available but not yet part of the 2.0 or 2.1 kernel source. You have to get the driver from:

```
http://www.unix-ag.uni-siegen.de/~nils/accton_linux.html
```

5.2.4   Accton EN2212 PCMCIA Card

Status – *Semi-Supported*

David Hinds has been working on a driver for this card, and you are best to check the latest release of his PCMCIA package to see what the present status is.

5.3 Allied Telesyn/Telesis

5.3.1 AT1500

Status –*Supported*

These are a series of low-cost ethercards using the 79C960 version of the AMD LANCE. These are bus-master cards, and hence one of the faster ISA bus ethercards available.

DMA selection and chip numbering information can be found in 5.4.1 (AMD LANCE).

More technical information on AMD LANCE based Ethernet cards can be found in 8.7 (Notes on AMD...).

5.3.2 AT1700

Status – *Supported*

Note that to access this driver during `make config` you still have to answer 'Y' when asked "Prompt for development and/or incomplete code/drivers?" at the first. This is simply due to lack of feedback on the driver stability due to it being a relatively rare card. This will probably be changed for v2.1 kernels.

The Allied Telesis AT1700 series ethercards are based on the Fujitsu MB86965. This chip uses a programmed I/O interface, and a pair of fixed-size transmit buffers. This allows small groups of packets to be sent back-to-back, with a short pause while switching buffers.

A unique feature is the ability to drive 150ohm STP (Shielded Twisted Pair) cable commonly installed for Token Ring, in addition to 10baseT 100ohm UTP (unshielded twisted pair). A fibre optic version of the card (AT1700FT) exists as well.

The Fujitsu chip used on the AT1700 has a design flaw: it can only be fully reset by doing a power cycle of the machine. Pressing the reset button doesn't reset the bus interface. This wouldn't be so bad, except that it can only be reliably detected when it has been freshly reset. The solution/work-around is to power-cycle the machine if the kernel has a problem detecting the AT1700.

Some production runs of the AT1700 had another problem: they are permanently wired to DMA channel 5. This is undocumented, there are no jumpers to disable the "feature", and no driver dares use the DMA capability because of compatibility problems. No device driver will be written using DMA if installing a second card into the machine breaks both, and the only way to disable the DMA is with a knife.

5.3.3 AT2450

Status – *Supported*

This is the PCI version of the AT1500, and it doesn't suffer from the problems that the Boca 79c970 PCI card does. DMA selection and chip numbering information can be found in 5.4.1 (AMD LANCE).

More technical information on AMD LANCE based Ethernet cards can be found in 8.7 (Notes on AMD...).

5.3.4 AT2540FX

Status – *Semi-Supported*

This card uses the i82557 chip, and hence may/should work with the eepro100 driver. If you try this please send in a report so this information can be updated.

5.4 AMD / Advanced Micro Devices

Carl Ching of AMD was kind enough to provide a very detailed description of all the relevant AMD ethernet products which helped clear up this section.

5.4.1 AMD LANCE (7990, 79C960/961/961A, PCnet-ISA)

Status – *Supported*

There really is no AMD ethernet card. You are probably reading this because the only markings you could find on your card said AMD and the above number. The 7990 is the original 'LANCE' chip, but most stuff (including this document) refer to all these similar chips as 'LANCE' chips. (...incorrectly, I might add.)

These above numbers refer to chips from AMD that are the heart of many ethernet cards. For example, the Allied Telesis AT1500 (see 5.3.1 (AT1500)) and the NE1500/2100 (see 5.27.4 (NE1500)) use these chips.

The 7990/79c90 have long been replaced by newer versions. The 79C960 (a.k.a. PCnet-ISA) essentially contains the 79c90 core, along with all the other hardware support required, which allows a single-chip ethernet solution. The 79c961 (PCnet-ISA+) is a jumperless Plug and Play version of the '960. The final chip in the ISA series is the 79c961A (PCnet-ISA II), which adds full duplex capabilities. All cards with one of these chips should work with the lance.c driver, with the exception of very old cards that used the original 7990 in a shared memory configuration. These old cards can be spotted by the lack of jumpers for a DMA channel.

One common problem people have is the 'busmaster arbitration failure' message. This is printed out when the LANCE driver can't get access to the bus after a reasonable amount of time has elapsed (50us). This usually indicates that the motherboard implementation of bus-mastering DMA is broken, or some other device is hogging the bus, or there is a DMA channel conflict. If your BIOS setup has the 'GAT option' (for Guaranteed Access Time) then try toggling/altering that setting to see if it helps.

Also note that the driver only looks at the addresses: `0x300`, `0x320`, `0x340`, `0x360` for a valid card, and any address supplied by an `ether=` boot argument is silently ignored (this will be fixed) so make sure your card is configured for one of the above I/O addresses for now.

The driver will still work fine, even if more than 16MB of memory is installed, since low-memory 'bounce-buffers' are used when needed (i.e. any data from above 16MB is copied into a buffer below 16MB before being given to the card to transmit.)

The DMA channel can be set with the low bits of the otherwise-unused dev->mem_start value (a.k.a. PARAM_1). (see 10.1.1 (PARAM_1)) If unset it is probed for by enabling each free DMA channel in turn and checking if initialization succeeds.

The HP-J2405A board is an exception: with this board it's easy to read the EEPROM-set values for the IRQ, and DMA.

See 8.7 (Notes on AMD...) for more info on these chips.

5.4.2 AMD 79C965 (PCnet-32)

Status – *Supported*

This is the PCnet-32 – a 32 bit bus-master version of the original LANCE chip for VL-bus and local bus systems. chip. While these chips can be operated with the standard `lance.c` driver, a 32 bit version (`lance32.c`) is also available that does not have to concern itself with any 16MB limitations associated with the ISA bus.

5.4.3 AMD 79C970/970A (PCnet-PCI)

Status – *Supported*

This is the PCnet-PCI – similar to the PCnet-32, but designed for PCI bus based systems. Please see the above PCnet-32 information. This means that you need to build a kernel with PCI BIOS support enabled. The '970A adds full duplex support along with some other features to the original '970 design.

Note that the Boca implementation of the 79C970 fails on fast Pentium machines. This is a hardware problem, as it affects DOS users as well. See the Boca section for more details.

HOWTO

5.4.4   AMD 79C971 (PCnet-FAST)

Status – *Supported*

This is AMD's 100Mbit chip for PCI systems, which also supports full duplex operation. It was introduced in June 1996.

5.4.5   AMD 79C974 (PCnet-SCSI)

Status – *Supported*

This is the PCnet-SCSI – which is basically treated like a '970 from an Ethernet point of view. Also see the above information. Don't ask if the SCSI half of the chip is supported – this is the *Ethernet-HowTo*, not the SCSI-HowTo.

5.5   Ansel Communications

5.5.1   AC3200 EISA

Status – *Semi-Supported*

Note that to access this driver during `make config` you still have to answer 'Y' when asked "Prompt for development and/or incomplete code/drivers?" at the first. This is simply due to lack of feedback on the driver stability due to it being a relatively rare card.

This driver is included in the present kernel as an alpha test driver. It is based on the common NS8390 chip used in the ne2000 and wd80x3 cards. Please see 3.1 (Alpha Drivers) in this document for important information regarding alpha drivers.

If you use it, let one of us know how things work out, as feedback has been low, even though the driver has been in the kernel since v1.1.25.

If you intend on using this driver as a loadable module you should probably see 10.2 (Using the Ethernet Drivers as Modules) for module specific information.

5.6   Apricot

5.6.1   Apricot Xen-II On Board Ethernet

Status – *Supported*

This on board ethernet uses an i82596 bus-master chip. It can only be at i/o address `0x300`. The author of this driver is Mark Evans. By looking at the driver source, it appears that the IRQ is hardwired to 10.

Earlier versions of the driver had a tendency to think that anything living at `0x300` was an apricot NIC. Since then the hardware address is checked to avoid these false detections.

5.7   Arcnet

Status – *Supported*

With the very low cost and better performance of ethernet, chances are that most places will be giving away their Arcnet hardware for free, resulting in a lot of home systems with Arcnet.

An advantage of Arcnet is that all of the cards have identical interfaces, so one driver will work for everyone. It also has built in error handling so that it supposedly never loses a packet. (Great for UDP traffic!)

Avery Pennarun's arcnet driver has been in the default kernel sources since 1.1.80. The arcnet driver uses 'arc0' as its name instead of the usual 'eth0' for ethernet devices. Bug reports and success stories can be mailed to:

apenwarr@foxnet.net

There are information files contained in the standard kernel for setting jumpers and general hints.

Supposedly the driver also works with the 100Mbs ARCnet cards as well!

5.8 AT&T

Note that AT&T's StarLAN is an orphaned technology, like SynOptics LattisNet, and can't be used in a standard 10Base-T environment, without a hub that 'speaks' both.

5.8.1 AT&T T7231 (LanPACER+)

Status – *Not Supported*

These StarLAN cards use an interface similar to the i82586 chip. At one point, Matthijs Melchior (`matthijs.n.melchior@att.com`) was playing with the 3c507 driver, and almost had something useable working. Haven't heard much since that.

5.9 AT-Lan-Tec / RealTek

5.9.1 AT-Lan-Tec / RealTek Pocket adaptor

Status – *Supported*

This is a generic, low-cost OEM pocket adaptor being sold by AT-Lan-Tec, and (likely) a number of other suppliers. A driver for it is included in the standard kernel. Note that there is substantial information contained in the driver source file 'atp.c'.

Note that the device name that you pass to `ifconfig` is *not* `eth0` but `atp0` for this device.

5.9.2 RealTek 8009

Status – *Supported*

This is an ISA NE2000 clone, and is reported to work fine with the linux NE2000 driver. The `rset8009.exe` program can be obtained from RealTek's WWW site at `http://www.realtek.com.tw` - or via ftp from the same site.

5.9.3 RealTek 8019

Status – *Supported*

This is a Plug and Pray version of the above. Use the DOS software to disable PnP and enable jumperless configuration; set the card to a sensible i/o address and IRQ and you should be ready to go. (If using the driver as a module, don't forget to add an `io=0xNNN` option to `/etc/conf.modules`). The `rset8019.exe` program can be obtained from RealTek's WWW site at `http://www.realtek.com.tw` - or via ftp from the same site.

5.9.4 RealTek 8029

Status – *Supported*

This is a PCI single chip implementation of a NE2000 clone. Various vendors are now selling cards with this chip. See 5.27.2 (NE2000-PCI) for information on using any of these cards.

5.9.5 RealTek 8129/8139

Status – *Semi-Supported*

Another PCI single chip ethernet solution from RealTek. A driver for cards based upon this chip is due to be included in the v2.0.34 release of linux. For more information, see:

`http://cesdis.gsfc.nasa.gov/linux/drivers/rtl8139.html`

HOWTO

5.10 Boca Research

Yes, they make more than just multi-port serial cards. :-)

5.10.1 Boca BEN (ISA, VLB, PCI)

Status – *Supported*

These cards are based on AMD's PCnet chips. Perspective buyers should be warned that many users have had endless problems with these VLB/PCI cards. Owners of fast Pentium systems have been especially hit. Note that this is not a driver problem, as it hits DOS/Win/NT users as well. Boca's technical support number is (407) 241-8088, and you can also reach them at `75300.2672@compuserve.com`. The older ISA cards don't appear to suffer the same problems.

Donald did a comparitive test with a Boca PCI card and a similar Allied Telsyn PCnet/PCI implementation, which showed that the problem lies in Boca's implementation of the PCnet/PCI chip. These test results can be accessed on Don's www server.

Linux at CESDIS `<http://cesdis.gsfc.nasa.gov/linux/>`

Boca is offering a 'warranty repair' for affected owners, which involves adding one of the missing capacitors, but it appears that this fix doesn't work 100 percent for most people, although it helps some.

If you are *still* thinking of buying one of these cards, then at least try and get a 7 day unconditional return policy, so that if it doesn't work properly in your system, you can return it.

More general information on the AMD chips can be found in 5.4.1 (AMD LANCE).

More technical information on AMD LANCE based Ethernet cards can be found in 8.7 (Notes on AMD...).

5.11 Cabletron

Donald writes: 'Yes, another one of these companies that won't release its programming information. They waited for months before actually confirming that all their information was proprietary, deliberately wasting my time. Avoid their cards like the plague if you can. Also note that some people have phoned Cabletron, and have been told things like 'a D. Becker is working on a driver for linux' – making it sound like I work for them. This is NOT the case.'

Apparently Cabletron has changed their policy with respect to programming information (like Xircom) since Donald made the above comment several years ago – send e-mail to `support@ctron.com` if you want to verify this or ask for programming information. However, at this point in time, there is little demand for modified/updated drivers for the older E20xx and E21xx cards.

5.11.1 E10**, E10**-x, E20**, E20**-x

Status – *Semi-Supported*

These are NEx000 almost-clones that are reported to work with the standard NEx000 drivers, thanks to a ctron-specific check during the probe. If there are any problems, they are unlikely to be fixed, as the programming information is unavailable.

5.11.2 E2100

Status – *Semi-Supported*

Again, there is not much one can do when the programming information is proprietary. The E2100 is a poor design. Whenever it maps its shared memory in during a packet transfer, it maps it into the *whole 128K region!* That means you **can't** safely use another interrupt-driven shared memory device in that region, including another E2100. It will work most of the time, but every once in a while it will bite you. (Yes, this problem can be avoided by turning off interrupts while transferring packets, but that will almost certainly lose clock ticks.) Also, if you mis-program the board, or halt the machine at just the wrong moment, even the reset button won't bring it back. You will *have* to turn it off and *leave* it off for about 30 seconds.

Media selection is automatic, but you can override this with the low bits of the dev->mem_end parameter. See 10.1.1 (PARAM_2). Module users can specify an xcvr=N value as an option in the /etc/conf.modules file.

Also, don't confuse the E2100 for a NE2100 clone. The E2100 is a shared memory NatSemi DP8390 design, roughly similar to a brain-damaged WD8013, whereas the NE2100 (and NE1500) use a bus-mastering AMD LANCE design.

There is an E2100 driver included in the standard kernel. However, seeing as programming info isn't available, don't expect bug-fixes. Don't use one unless you are already stuck with the card.

If you intend on using this driver as a loadable module you should probably see 10.2 (Using the Ethernet Drivers as Modules) for module specific information.

5.11.3 E22**

Status – *Semi-Supported*

According to information in a Cabletron Tech Bulletin, these cards use the standard AMD PC-Net chipset (see 5.4.1 (AMD PC-Net)) and should work with the generic lance driver.

5.12 Cogent

Here is where and how to reach them:

```
Cogent Data Technologies, Inc.
175 West Street, P.O. Box 926
Friday Harbour, WA 98250, USA.

Cogent Sales
15375 S.E. 30th Place, Suite 310
Bellevue, WA 98007, USA.

Technical Support:
Phone (360) 378-2929 between 8am and 5pm PST
Fax (360) 378-2882
Compuserve GO COGENT
Bulletin Board Service (360) 378-5405
Internet: support@cogentdata.com
```

5.12.1 EM100-ISA/EISA

Status – *Semi-Supported*

These cards use the SMC 91c100 chip and may work with the SMC 91c92 driver, but this has yet to be verified.

5.12.2 Cogent eMASTER+, EM100-PCI, EM400, EM960, EM964

Status – *Supported*

These are yet another DEC 21040 implementation that should hopefully work fine with the standard 21040 driver.

The EM400 and the EM964 are four port cards using a DEC 21050 bridge and 4 21040 chips.

See 5.17.4 (DEC 21040) for more information on these cards, and the present driver situation.

HOWTO

5.13 Compaq

Compaq aren't really in the business of making ethernet cards, but a lot of their systems have embedded ethernet controllers on the motherboard.

5.13.1 Compaq Deskpro / Compaq XL (Embedded AMD Chip)

Status – *Supported*

Machines such as the XL series have an AMD 79c97x PCI chip on the mainboard that can be used with the standard LANCE driver. But before you can use it, you have to do some trickery to get the PCI BIOS to a place where Linux can see it. Frank Maas was kind enough to provide the details:

" The problem with this Compaq machine however is that the PCI directory is loaded in high memory, at a spot where the Linux kernel can't (won't) reach. Result: the card is never detected nor is it usable (sideline: the mouse won't work either) The workaround (as described thoroughly in http://www-c724.uibk.ac.at/XL/) is to load MS-DOS, launch a little driver Compaq wrote and then load the Linux kernel using LOADLIN. Ok, I'll give you time to say 'yuck, yuck', but for now this is the only working solution I know of. The little driver simply moves the PCI directory to a place where it is normally stored (and where Linux can find it)."

More general information on the AMD chips can be found in 5.4.1 (AMD LANCE).

5.14 Danpex

5.14.1 Danpex EN9400

Status – *Supported*

Yet another card based on the DEC 21040 chip, reported to work fine, and at a relatively cheap price.

See 5.17.4 (DEC 21040) for more information on these cards, and the present driver situation.

5.15 D-Link

5.15.1 DE-100, DE-200, DE-220-T, DE-250

Status – *Supported*

Some of the early D-Link cards didn't have the `0x57` PROM signature, but the ne2000 driver knows about them. For the software configurable cards, you can get the config program from `www.dlink.com`. The DE2** cards were the most widely reported as having the spurious transfer address mismatch errors with early versions of linux. Note that there are also cards from Digital (DEC) that are also named DE100 and DE200, but the similarity stops there.

5.15.2 DE-520

Status – *Supported*

This is a PCI card using the PCI version of AMD's LANCE chip. DMA selection and chip numbering information can be found in 5.4.1 (AMD LANCE).

More technical information on AMD LANCE based Ethernet cards can be found in 8.7 (Notes on AMD...).

5.15.3 DE-530

Status – *Supported*

This is a generic DEC 21040 PCI chip implementation, and is reported to work with the generic 21040 tulip driver.

See 5.17.4 (DEC 21040) for more information on these cards, and the present driver situation.

5.15.4   DE-600

Status – *Supported*

Laptop users and other folk who might want a quick way to put their computer onto the ethernet may want to use this. The driver is included with the default kernel source tree. Bjorn Ekwall bj0rn@blox.se wrote the driver. Expect about 180kb/s transfer speed from this via the parallel port. You should read the README.DLINK file in the kernel source tree.

Note that the device name that you pass to ifconfig is *now* eth0 and not the previously used dl0.

If your parallel port is *not* at the standard 0x378 then you will have to recompile. Bjorn writes: "Since the DE-620 driver tries to sqeeze the last microsecond from the loops, I made the irq and port address constants instead of variables. This makes for a usable speed, but it also means that you can't change these assignements from e.g. lilo; you _have_ to recompile..." Also note that some laptops implement the on-board parallel port at 0x3bc which is where the parallel ports on monochrome cards were/are.

5.15.5   DE-620

Status – *Supported*

Same as the DE-600, only with two output formats. Bjorn has written a driver for this model, for kernel versions 1.1 and above. See the above information on the DE-600.

5.15.6   DE-650

Status – *Semi-Supported*

Some people have been using this PCMCIA card for some time now with their notebooks. It is a basic 8390 design, much like a NE2000. The LinkSys PCMCIA card and the IC-Card Ethernet (available from Midwest Micro) are supposedly DE-650 clones as well. Note that at present, this driver is *not* part of the standard kernel, and so you will have to do some patching.

See 9.3 (PCMCIA Support) in this document, and if you can, have a look at:

Don's PCMCIA Stuff <http://cesdis.gsfc.nasa.gov/linux/pcmcia.html>

5.16   DFI

5.16.1   DFINET-300 and DFINET-400

Status – *Supported*

These cards are now detected (as of 0.99pl15) thanks to Eberhard Moenkeberg emoenke@gwdg.de who noted that they use 'DFI' in the first 3 bytes of the prom, instead of using 0x57 in bytes 14 and 15, which is what all the NE1000 and NE2000 cards use. (The 300 is an 8 bit pseudo NE1000 clone, and the 400 is a pseudo NE2000 clone.)

5.17   Digital / DEC

5.17.1   DEPCA, DE100/1, DE200/1/2, DE210, DE422

Status – *Supported*

As of linux v1.0, there is a driver included as standard for these cards. It was written by David C. Davies. There is documentation included in the source file 'depca.c', which includes info on how to use more than one of these cards in a machine. Note that the DE422 is an EISA card. These cards are all based on the AMD LANCE chip. See 5.4.1 (AMD LANCE) for more info. A maximum of two of the ISA cards can be used, because they can only be set for 0x300 and 0x200 base I/O address. If you are intending to do this, please read the notes in the driver source file depca.c in the standard kernel source tree.

HOWTO

This driver will also work on Alpha CPU based machines, and there are various ioctl()s that the user can play with.

5.17.2 Digital EtherWorks 3 (DE203, DE204, DE205)

Status – *Supported*

Included into kernels v1.1.62 and above is this driver, also by David C. Davies of DEC. These cards use a proprietary chip from DEC, as opposed to the LANCE chip used in the earlier cards like the DE200. These cards support both shared memory or programmed I/O, although you take about a 50%performance hit if you use PIO mode. The shared memory size can be set to 2kB, 32kB or 64kB, but only 2 and 32 have been tested with this driver. David says that the performance is virtually identical between the 2kB and 32kB mode. There is more information (including using the driver as a loadable module) at the top of the driver file `ewrk3.c` and also in `README.ewrk3`. Both of these files come with the standard kernel distribution. This driver has Alpha CPU support like depca.c does.

The standard driver has a number of interesting ioctl() calls that can be used to get or clear packet statistics, read/write the EEPROM, change the hardware address, and the like. Hackers can see the source code for more info on that one.

David has also written a configuration utility for this card (along the lines of the DOS program `NIC-SETUP.EXE`) along with other tools. These can be found on `sunsite.unc.edu` in the directory `/pub/Linux/system/Network/management` – look for the file `ewrk3tools-X.XX.tar.gz`.

5.17.3 DE425 (EISA), DE434, DE435, DE500

Status – *Supported*

These cards are based on the 21040 chip mentioned below. Included into kernels v1.1.86 and above is this driver, also by David C. Davies of DEC. It sure is nice to have support from someone on the inside ;-) The DE500 uses the newer 21140 chip to provide 10/100Mbs ethernet connections. Have a read of the 21040 section below for extra info.

Note that as of 1.1.91, David has added a compile time option that will allow non-DEC cards to work with this driver. Have a look at `README.de4x5` for details.

All the Digital cards will autoprobe for their media (except, temporarily, the DE500 due to a patent issue).

This driver is also ALPHA CPU ready and supports being loaded as a module. Users can access the driver internals through ioctl() calls - see the 'ewrk3' tools and the de4x5.c sources for information about how to do this.

5.17.4 DEC 21040, 21041, 2114x, Tulip

Status – *Supported*

The DEC 21040 is a bus-mastering single chip ethernet solution from Digital, similar to AMD's PCnet chip. The 21040 is specifically designed for the PCI bus architecture. SMC's new EtherPower PCI card uses this chip.

You have a choice of *two* drivers for cards based on this chip. There is the DE425 driver discussed above, and the generic 21040 driver that Donald has written.

Warning: Even though your card may be based upon this chip, *the drivers may not work for you*. David C. Davies writes:

"There are no guarantees that either 'tulip.c' OR 'de4x5.c' will run any DC2114x based card other than those they've been written to support. WHY?? You ask. Because there is a register, the General Purpose Register (CSR12) that (1) in the DC21140A is programmable by each vendor and they all do it differently (2) in the DC21142/3 this is now an SIA control register (a la DC21041). The only small ray of hope is that we can decode the SROM to help set up the driver. However, this is not a guaranteed solution since some vendors (e.g. SMC 9332 card) don't follow the Digital Semiconductor recommended SROM programming format."

In non-technical terms, this means that if you aren't sure that an unknown card with a DC2114x chip will work with the linux driver(s), then make sure you can return the card to the place of purchase *before* you pay for it.

The updated 21041 chip is also found in place of the 21040 on most of the later SMC EtherPower cards. The 21140 is for supporting 100Base-? and works with the Linux drivers for the 21040 chip. To use David's `de4x5` driver with non-DEC cards, have a look at `README.de4x5` for details.

Donald has used SMC EtherPower-10/100 cards to develop the 'tulip' driver. Note that the driver that is in the standard kernel tree at the moment is not the most up to date version. If you are having trouble with this driver, you should get the newest version from Donald's ftp/WWW site.

Tulip Driver `<http://cesdis.gsfc.nasa.gov/linux/drivers/tulip.html>`

The above URL also contains a (non-exhaustive) list of various cards/vendors that use the 21040 chip.

Also note that the tulip driver is still considered an *alpha* driver (see 3.1 (Alpha Drivers)) at the moment, and should be treated as such. To use it, you will have to edit `arch/i386/config.in` and uncomment the line for `CONFIG_DEC_ELCP` support.

Donald has even set up a mailing list for tulip driver support announcements, etc. To join it just type:

```
echo subscribe | /bin/mail linux-tulip-request@cesdis.gsfc.nasa.gov
```

5.18 Farallon

Farallon sells EtherWave adaptors and transceivers. This device allows multiple 10baseT devices to be daisy-chained.

5.18.1 Farallon Etherwave

Status – *Supported*

This is reported to be a 3c509 clone that includes the EtherWave transceiver. People have used these successfully with Linux and the present 3c509 driver. They are too expensive for general use, but are a great option for special cases. Hublet prices start at $125, and Etherwave adds $75-$100 to the price of the board – worth it if you have pulled one wire too few, but not if you are two network drops short.

5.19 Hewlett Packard

The 272** cards use programmed I/O, similar to the NE*000 boards, but the data transfer port can be 'turned off' when you aren't accessing it, avoiding problems with autoprobing drivers.

Thanks to Glenn Talbott for helping clean up the confusion in this section regarding the version numbers of the HP hardware.

5.19.1 27245A

Status – *Supported*

8 Bit 8390 based 10BaseT, not recommended for all the 8 bit reasons. It was re-designed a couple years ago to be highly integrated which caused some changes in initialization timing which only affected testing programs, not LAN drivers. (The new card is not 'ready' as soon after switching into and out of loopback mode.)

If you intend on using this driver as a loadable module you should probably see 10.2 (Using the Ethernet Drivers as Modules) for module specific information.

5.19.2 HP EtherTwist, PC Lan+ (27247, 27252A)

Status – *Supported*

The HP PC Lan+ is different to the standard HP PC Lan card. This driver was added to the list of drivers in the standard kernel during the v1.1.x development cycle. It can be operated in either a PIO mode like a ne2000, or a shared memory mode like a wd8013.

The 47B is a 16 Bit 8390 based 10BaseT w/AUI, and the 52A is a 16 Bit 8390 based ThinLAN w/AUI. These cards have 32K onboard RAM for Tx/Rx packet buffering instead of the usual 16KB, and they both offer LAN connector autosense.

If you intend on using this driver as a loadable module you should probably see 10.2 (Using the Ethernet Drivers as Modules) for module specific information.

5.19.3   HP-J2405A

Status – *Supported*

These are lower priced, and slightly faster than the 27247/27252A, but are missing some features, such as AUI, ThinLAN connectivity, and boot PROM socket. This is a fairly generic LANCE design, but a minor design decision makes it incompatible with a generic 'NE2100' driver. Special support for it (including reading the DMA channel from the board) is included thanks to information provided by HP's Glenn Talbott.

More technical information on LANCE based cards can be found in 8.7 (Notes on AMD...)

5.19.4   HP-Vectra On Board Ethernet

Status – *Supported*

The HP-Vectra has an AMD PCnet chip on the motherboard. Earlier kernel versions would detect it as the HP-J2405A but that would fail, as the Vectra doesn't report the IRQ and DMA channel like the J2405A. Get a kernel newer than v1.1.53 to avoid this problem.

DMA selection and chip numbering information can be found in 5.4.1 (AMD LANCE).

More technical information on LANCE based cards can be found in 8.7 (Notes on AMD...)

5.19.5   HP 10/100 VG Any Lan Cards (27248B, J2573, J2577, J2585)

Status – *Supported*

As of early 1.3.x kernels, this driver was made available by Jaroslav Kysela, (perex@pf.jcu.cz). Due to the newness of the driver and the relatively small number of VG cards in use, feedback on this driver has been low.

Donald has also written a driver for these cards. Unlike the above, it is not presently in the standard kernel source tree. Check out the following URL for more information on Donald's 100VG work.

Donald's 100VG Page <http://cesdis.gsfc.nasa.gov/linux/drivers/100vg.html>

5.19.6   HP NetServer 10/100TX PCI (D5013A)

Status – *Supported*

Apparently these are just a rebadged Intel EtherExpress Pro 10/100B card. See the Intel section for more information.

5.20   IBM / International Business Machines

5.20.1   IBM Thinkpad 300

Status – *Supported*

This is compatible with the Intel based Zenith Z-note. See 5.38.1 (Z-note) for more info.

Supposedly this site has a comprehensive database of useful stuff for newer versions of the Thinkpad. I haven't checked it out myself yet.

Thinkpad-info <http://peipa.essex.ac.uk/html/linux-thinkpad.html>

For those without a WWW browser handy, try peipa.essex.ac.uk:/pub/tp750/

5.20.2   IBM Credit Card Adaptor for Ethernet

Status – *Semi-Supported*

People have been using this PCMCIA card with Linux as well. Similar points apply, those being that you need a supported PCMCIA chipset on your notebook, and that you will have to patch the PCMCIA support into the standard kernel.

See 9.3 (PCMCIA Support) in this document, and if you can, have a look at:

Don's PCMCIA Stuff `<http://cesdis.gsfc.nasa.gov/linux/pcmcia.html>`

5.20.3   IBM Token Ring

Status – *Semi-Supported*

To support token ring requires more than only writing a device driver, it also requires writing the source routing routines for token ring. It is the source routing that would be the most time comsuming to write.

Peter De Schrijver has been spending some time on Token Ring lately. and has worked with IBM ISA and MCA token ring cards.

The present token ring code has been included into the first of the 1.3.x series kernels.

Peter says that it was originally tested on an MCA 16/4 Megabit Token Ring board, but it should work with other Tropic based boards.

5.21   ICL Ethernet Cards

5.21.1   ICL EtherTeam 16i/32

Status – *Supported*

Mika Kuoppala (miku@pupu.elt.icl.fi) wrote this driver, and it was included into early 1.3.4x kernels. It uses the Fujitsu MB86965 chip that is also used on the at1700 cards.

5.22   Intel Ethernet Cards

Note that the naming of the various Intel cards is ambiguous and confusing at best. If in doubt, then check the `i8xxxx` number on the main chip on the card or for PCI cards, use the PCI information in the `/proc` directory and then compare that to the numbers listed here.

5.22.1   Ether Express

Status – *Supported*

This card uses the intel i82586. Earlier versions of this driver (in v1.2 kernels) were classed as alpha-test, as it didn't work well for most people. The driver in the v2.0 kernel seems to work much better for those who have tried it. The comments at the top of the driver source list some of the problems associated with these cards.

There is also some technical information available on the i82586 in 8.5 (Programming the Intel Chips) and also in the source code for the driver 'eexpress.c'. Don't be afraid to read it. ;-)

5.22.2   Ether Express PRO/10

Status – *Supported*

Bao Chau Ha has written a driver for these cards that has been included into early 1.3.x kernels. It may also work with some of the Compaq built-in ethernet systems that are based on the i82595 chip.

5.22.3 Ether Express PRO/10 PCI (EISA)

Status – *Semi-Supported*

John Stalba (stalba@ultranet.com) has written a driver for the PCI version. These cards use the PLX9036 PCI interface chip with the Intel i82596 LAN controller chip. If your card has the i82557 chip, then you *don't* have this card, but rather the version discussed next, and hence want the EEPro100 driver instead.

You can get the alpha driver for the PRO/10 PCI card, along with instructions on how to use it at:

EEPro10 Driver <http://www.ultranet.com/~stalba/eep10pci.html>

If you have the EISA card, you will probably have to hack the driver a bit to account for the different (PCI vs. EISA) detection mechanisms that are used in each case.

5.22.4 Ether Express PRO 10/100B

Status – *Supported*

A driver for this card is included in the current v2.0 and v2.1 kernel source tree. Note that this driver will *not* work with the older 100A cards. The chip numbers listed in the driver are i82557/i82558.

For driver updates and/or driver support, have a look at:

EEPro-100B Page <http://cesdis.gsfc.nasa.gov/linux/drivers/eepro100.html>

To subscribe to the mailing list relating to this driver, do:

```
echo subscribe | /bin/mail linux-eepro100-request@cesdis.gsfc.nasa.gov
```

Apparently Donald had to sign a non-disclosure agreement that stated he could actually disclose the driver source code! How is that for sillyness on intel's part?

5.23 Kingston

Kingston make various cards, including NE2000+, AMD PCnet based cards, and DEC tulip based cards. Most of these cards should work fine with their respective driver. See *Kingston Web Page* <http://www.kingston.com>

The KNE40 DEC 21041 tulip based card is reported to work fine with the generic tulip driver.

5.24 LinkSys

LinkSys make a handful of different NE2000 clones, some straight ISA cards, some ISA plug and play and some even ne2000-PCI clones based on one of the supported ne2000-PCI chipsets. There are just too many models to list here.

Linux gets a mention in their WWW support page. Have a look at:

http://www.linksys.com/support/solution/nos/linux.htm

if you are having trouble using one of their cards with linux.

5.24.1 LinkSys Etherfast 10/100 Cards.

Status – *Supported*

Beware with these cards - apparently some use the DEC chipset, and some use a proprietary PNIC chipset. The drivers for the DEC chips will *not* work with the PNIC cards. Thanks to Blake Wright for reporting this useful bit of information.

The DEC/tulip based cards are reported to work fine though.

5.24.2 LinkSys Pocket Ethernet Adapter Plus (PEAEPP)

Status – *Supported*

This is supposedly a DE-620 clone, and is reported to work well with that driver. See 5.15.5 (DE-620) for more information.

5.24.3 LinkSys PCMCIA Adaptor

Status – *Supported*

This is supposed to be a re-badged DE-650. See 5.15.6 (DE-650) for more information.

5.25 Microdyne

5.25.1 Microdyne Exos 205T

Status – *Semi-Supported*

Another i82586 based card. Dirk Niggemann dirk-n@dircon.co.uk has written a driver that he classes as "pre-alpha" that he would like people to test. Mail him for more details.

5.26 Mylex

Mylex can be reached at the following numbers, in case anyone wants to ask them anything.

```
MYLEX CORPORATION, Fremont
Sales:  800-77-MYLEX, (510) 796-6100
FAX:    (510) 745-8016.
```

They also have a web site: *Mylex WWW Site* <http://www.mylex.com>

5.26.1 Mylex LNE390A, LNE390B

Status – *Supported*

These are fairly old EISA cards that make use of a shared memory implementation similar to the wd80x3. A driver for these cards is available in the current 2.1.x series of kernels.

5.26.2 Mylex LNP101

Status – *Supported*

This is a PCI card that is based on DEC's 21040 chip. It is selectable between 10BaseT, 10Base2 and 10Base5 output. The LNP101 card has been verified to work with the generic 21040 driver.

See the section on the 21040 chip (5.17.4 (DEC 21040)) for more information.

5.26.3 Mylex LNP104

Status – *Semi-Supported*

The LNP104 uses the DEC 21050 chip to deliver *four* independent 10BaseT ports. It should work with recent 21040 drivers that know how to share IRQs, but nobody has reported trying it yet (that I am aware of).

5.27   Novell Ethernet, NExxxx and associated clones.

The prefix 'NE' came from Novell Ethernet. Novell followed the cheapest NatSemi databook design and sold the manufacturing rights (spun off?) Eagle, just to get reasonably-priced ethercards into the market. (The now ubiquitous NE2000 card.)

5.27.1   NE1000, NE2000

Status – *Supported*

NOTE: If you are using a kernel that is older than v1.2.9, it is *strongly* recommended that you upgrade to a newer version. There was an important bugfix made to the ne driver in 1.2.7, and another important bugfix made to the upper layers (dev.c) in 1.2.9. Both of these bugs can cause a ne2000 card to hang your computer.

The ne2000 is now a generic name for a bare-bones design around the NatSemi 8390 chip. They use programmed I/O rather than shared memory, leading to easier installation but slightly lower performance and a few problems. Again, the savings of using an 8 bit NE1000 over the NE2000 are only warranted if you expect light use. Some problems can arise with poor NE2000 clones. You should see 3.4 (Problems with...), and 3.3 (Poor NE2000 Clones)

Some recently introduced NE2000 clones use the National Semiconductor 'AT/LANTic' 83905 chip, which offers a shared memory mode similar to the wd8013 and EEPROM software configuration. The shared memory mode will offer less CPU usage (i.e. more efficient) than the programmed i/o mode.

In general it is not a good idea to put a NE2000 clone at I/O address 0×300 because nearly *every* device driver probes there at boot. Some poor NE2000 clones don't take kindly to being prodded in the wrong areas, and will respond by locking your machine. Also 0×320 is bad because SCSI drivers probe into 0×330.

Donald has written a NE2000 diagnostic program (ne2k.c) for all ne2000 cards. See 7.2 (Diagnostic Programs) for more information.

If you intend on using this driver as a loadable module you should probably see 10.2 (Using the Ethernet Drivers as Modules) for module specific information.

5.27.2   NE2000-PCI (RealTek/Winbond/Compex)

Status – *Supported*

Yes, believe it or not, people are making PCI cards based on the ten year old interface design of the ne2000. At the moment nearly all of these cards are based on the RealTek 8029 chip, or the Winbond 89c940 chip. The Compex, KTI, VIA and Netvin cards apparently also use these chips, but have a different PCI ID. The linux kernel v2.0.33 has support to automatically detect all these cards and use them. (If you are using a kernel v2.0.30 or older, you should upgrade to ensure your card will be detected.)

Note that you have to say 'Y' to the 'Other ISA cards' option when running `make config` as you are actually using the same NE2000 driver as the ISA cards use. (That should also give you a hint that these cards aren't anywhere as intelligent as say a DEC 21040 card...) In the future, a PCI-only NE2000 driver will be included in the kernel source for these cards. The driver is currently available for testing at:

`http://cesdis.gsfc.nasa.gov/linux/drivers/ne2k-pci.html`

Some newer motherboards don't enable all the PCI cards at power-up, and this generally causes the card to be detected, but to fail the probe. Code to enable such cards is due to be added to the v2.0.34 `ne.c` driver, based on that which is in the above PCI-only driver.

If you have a NE2000 PCI card that is *not* detected by the driver, please contact the maintainer of the NE2000 driver as listed in `/usr/src/linux/MAINTAINERS` along with the output from a `cat /proc/pci` and `dmesg` so that support for your card can also be added to the driver.

5.27.3 NE-10/100

Status – *Not Supported*

These are ISA 100Mbps cards based on the National Semiconductor DP83800 and DP83840 chips. There is currently no driver support, nor has anyone reported that they are working on a driver.

5.27.4 NE1500, NE2100

Status – *Supported*

These cards use the original 7990 LANCE chip from AMD and are supported using the Linux lance driver. Newer NE2100 clones use the updated PCnet/ISA chip from AMD.

Some earlier versions of the lance driver had problems with getting the IRQ line via autoIRQ from the original Novell/Eagle 7990 cards. Hopefully this is now fixed. If not, then specify the IRQ via LILO, and let us know that it still has problems.

DMA selection and chip numbering information can be found in 5.4.1 (AMD LANCE).

More technical information on LANCE based cards can be found in 8.7 (Notes on AMD...)

5.27.5 NE3200

Status – *Not Supported*

This card uses a lowly 8MHz 80186, and hence you are better off using a cheap NE2000 clone. Even if a driver was available, the NE2000 card would most likely be faster.

5.27.6 NE5500

Status – *Supported*

These are just AMD PCnet-PCI cards ('970A) chips. More information on LANCE/PCnet based cards can be found in 5.4.1 (AMD LANCE).

5.28   Proteon

5.28.1   Proteon P1370-EA

Status – *Supported*

Apparently this is a NE2000 clone, and works fine with Linux.

5.28.2   Proteon P1670-EA

Status – *Supported*

This is yet another PCI card that is based on DEC's Tulip chip. It has been reported to work fine with Linux.

See the section on the 21040 chip (5.17.4 (DEC 21040)) for more driver information.

5.29   Pure Data

5.29.1   PDUC8028, PDI8023

Status – *Supported*

The PureData PDUC8028 and PDI8023 series of cards are reported to work, thanks to special probe code contributed by Mike Jagdis `jaggy@purplet.demon.co.uk`. The support is integrated with the WD driver.

5.30 Racal-Interlan

Racal Interlan can be reached via WWW at `www.interlan.com`. I believe they were also known as MiCom-Interlan at one point in the past.

5.30.1 ES3210

Status – *Semi-Supported*

This is an EISA 8390 based shared memory card. An experimetal driver for v2.0 is available (from me, pg). It is reported to work fine, but the EISA IRQ and shared memory address detection appears not to work with (at least) the early revision cards. In that case, you have to supply them at boot; e.g. `ether=5,0,0xd0000,eth0` for IRQ 5 and shared memory at `0xd0000`. The i/o base is automatically detected and hence a value of zero should be used.

This driver will appear in the v2.1 kernels at some time in the near future.

5.30.2 NI5010

Status – *Semi-Supported*

This driver, by Jan-Pascal van Best (jvbest@qv3pluto.leidenuniv.nl) supports the old 8 bit MiCom-Interlan cards. You can get the driver from:

NI5010 Driver `<http://qv3pluto.leidenuniv.nl/jvbest/ni5010/ni5010.html>`

Jan-Pascal has got very little feedback on this driver and would appreciate it if you dropped him a note saying if it worked or not.

5.30.3 NI5210

Status – *Semi-Supported*

Michael Hipp has written a driver for this card. It is included in the standard kernel as an 'alpha' driver. Michael would like to hear feedback from users that have this card. See 3.1 (Alpha Drivers) for important information on using alpha-test ethernet drivers with Linux.

Michael says that "the internal sysbus seems to be slow. So we often lose packets because of overruns while receiving from a fast remote host."

This card also uses one of the Intel chips. See 8.5 (Programming the Intel Chips) for more technical information.

5.30.4 NI6510 (not EB)

Status – *Semi-Supported*

There is also a driver for the LANCE based NI6510, and it is also written by Michael Hipp. Again, it is also an 'alpha' driver. For some reason, this card is not compatible with the generic LANCE driver. See 3.1 (Alpha Drivers) for important information on using alpha-test ethernet drivers with Linux.

5.30.5 EtherBlaster (aka NI6510EB)

Status – *Supported*

As of kernel 1.3.23, the generic LANCE driver had a check added to it for the `0x52,  0x44` NI6510EB specific signature. Others have reported that this signature is not the same for all NI6510EB cards however, which will cause the lance driver to not detect your card. If this happens to you, you can change the probe (at about line 322 in lance.c) to printk() out what the values are for your card and then use them instead of the `0x52,  0x44` defaults.

The cards should probably be run in 'high-performance' mode and not in the NI6510 compatible mode when using the lance driver.

5.31   Sager

5.31.1   Sager NP943

Status – *Semi-Supported*

This is just a 3c501 clone, with a different S.A. PROM prefix. I assume it is equally as brain dead as the original 3c501 as well. Kernels 1.1.53 and up check for the NP943 I.D. and then just treat it as a 3c501 after that. See 5.1.1 (3Com 3c501) for all the reasons as to why you really don't want to use one of these cards.

5.32   Schneider & Koch

5.32.1   SK G16

Status – *Supported*

This driver was included into the v1.1 kernels, and it was written by PJD Weichmann and SWS Bern. It appears that the SK G16 is similar to the NI6510, in that it is based on the first edition LANCE chip (the 7990). Once again, it appears as though this card won't work with the generic LANCE driver.

5.33   SEEQ

5.33.1   SEEQ 8005

Status – *Supported*

This driver was included into early 1.3.x kernels, and was written by Hamish Coleman. There is little information about the card included in the driver, and hence little information to be put here. If you have a question, you are probably best off e-mailing hamish@zot.apana.org.au

5.34   SMC (Standard Microsystems Corp.)

Please see 5.36 (Western Digital) for information on SMC cards. (SMC bought out Western Digital's network card section quite a while ago.)

5.35   Thomas Conrad

5.35.1   Thomas Conrad TC-5048

This is yet another PCI card that is based on DEC's 21040 chip.

See the section on the 21040 chip (5.17.4 (DEC 21040)) for more information.

5.36   Western Digital / SMC

The ethernet part of Western Digital has been bought out by SMC. One common mistake people make is that the relatively new SMC Elite Ultra is the same as the older SMC Elite16 models – this is **not** the case. They have separate drivers.

Here is how to contact SMC (not that you should need to.)

> SMC / Standard Microsystems Corp., 80 Arkay Drive, Hauppage, New York, 11788, USA.

Technical Support via phone:

```
800-992-4762 (USA)
800-433-5345 (Canada)
516-435-6250 (Other Countries)
```

HOWTO

Literature requests:

```
800-SMC-4-YOU (USA)
800-833-4-SMC (Canada)
516-435-6255  (Other Countries)
```

Technical Support via E-mail:

```
techsupt@ccmail.west.smc.com
```

FTP Site:

```
ftp.smc.com
```

WWW Site: *SMC* <http://www.smc.com>

5.36.1 WD8003, SMC Elite

Status – *Supported*

These are the 8-bit versions of the card. The 8 bit 8003 is slightly less expensive, but only worth the savings for light use. Note that some of the non-EEPROM cards (clones with jumpers, or old *old* old wd8003 cards) have no way of reporting the IRQ line used. In this case, auto-irq is used, and if that fails, the driver silently assings IRQ 5. You can get the SMC setup/driver disks from SMC's ftp site. Note that some of the newer SMC 'SuperDisk' programs will fail to detect the real old EEPROM-less cards. The file SMCDSK46.EXE seems to be a good all-round choice. Also the jumper settings for all their cards are in an ascii text file in the aforementioned archive. The latest (greatest?) version can be obtained from ftp.smc.com.

As these are basically the same as their 16 bit counterparts (WD8013 / SMC Elite16), you should see the next section for more information.

5.36.2 WD8013, SMC Elite16

Status – *Supported*

Over the years the design has added more registers and an EEPROM. (The first wd8003 cards appeared about ten years ago!) Clones usually go by the '8013' name, and usually use a non-EEPROM (jumpered) design. Late model SMC cards will have the SMC 83c690 chip instead of the original Nat Semi DP8390 found on earlier cards. The shared memory design makes the cards a bit faster than PIO cards, especially with larger packets. More importantly, from the driver's point of view, it avoids a few bugs in the programmed-I/O mode of the 8390, allows safe multi-threaded access to the packet buffer, and it doesn't have a programmed-I/O data register that hangs your machine during warm-boot probes.

Non-EEPROM cards that can't just read the selected IRQ will attempt auto-irq, and if that fails, they will silently assign IRQ 10. (8 bit versions will assign IRQ 5)

Cards with a non standard amount of memory on board can have the memory size specified at boot (or as an option in /etc/conf.modules if using modules). The standard memory size is 8kB for an 8bit card and 16kB for a 16bit card. For example, the older WD8003EBT cards could be jumpered for 32kB memory. To make full use of that RAM, you would use something like (for i/o=0x280 and IRQ 9):

```
LILO: linux ether=9,0x280,0xd0000,0xd8000,eth0
```

Also see 3.5 (8013 problems) for some of the more common problems and frequently asked questions that pop up often.

If you intend on using this driver as a loadable module you should probably see 10.2 (Using the Ethernet Drivers as Modules) for module specific information.

5.36.3   SMC Elite Ultra

Status – *Supported*

This ethercard is based on a new chip from SMC, the 83c790, which has a few new features. While it has a mode that is similar to the older SMC ethercards, it's not entirely compatible with the old WD80*3 drivers. However, in this mode it shares most of its code with the other 8390 drivers, while operating slightly faster than a WD8013 clone.

Since part of the Ultra *looks like* an 8013, the Ultra probe is supposed to find an Ultra before the wd8013 probe has a chance to mistakenly identify it.

Donald mentioned that it is possible to write a separate driver for the Ultra's 'Altego' mode which allows chaining transmits at the cost of inefficient use of receive buffers, but that will probably not happen.

Bus-Master SCSI host adaptor users take note: In the manual that ships with Interactive UNIX, it mentions that a bug in the SMC Ultra will cause data corruption with SCSI disks being run from an aha-154X host adaptor. This will probably bite aha-154X compatible cards, such as the BusLogic boards, and the AMI-FastDisk SCSI host adaptors as well.

SMC has acknowledged the problem occurs with Interactive, and older Windows NT drivers. It is a hardware conflict with early revisions of the card that can be worked around in the driver design. The current Ultra driver protects against this by only enabling the shared memory during data transfers with the card. Make sure your kernel version is at least 1.1.84, or that the driver version reported at boot is at least `smc-ultra.c:v1.12` otherwise you are vulnerable.

If you intend on using this driver as a loadable module you should probably see 10.2 (Using the Ethernet Drivers as Modules) for module specific information.

5.36.4   SMC Elite Ultra32 EISA

Status – *Supported*

This EISA card shares a lot in common with its ISA counterpart. A working (and stable) driver is included in v2.0.33 kernels. The driver will be included with a future release of the v2.1.x linux kernel as well. Thanks go to Leonard Zubkoff for purchasing some of these cards so that Leonard and myself could add linux support for them.

5.36.5   SMC EtherEZ (8416)

Status – *Supported*

This card uses SMC's 83c795 chip and supports the Plug 'n Play specification. It also has an *SMC Ultra* compatible mode, which allows it to be used with the Linux Ultra driver. Be sure to set your card for this compatibility mode. See the above information for notes on the Ultra driver.

For v1.2 kernels, the card had to be configured for shared memory operation. However v2.0 kernels can use the card in shared memory or programmed i/o mode. Shared memory mode will be slightly faster, and use considerably less CPU resources as well.

Note that the EtherEZ specific checks were added to the SMC Ultra driver in 1.1.84, and hence earlier kernel versions will not detect or handle these cards correctly.

5.36.6   SMC EtherPower PCI (8432)

Status – *Supported*

NB: The EtherPower II is an entirely different card. See below! These cards are a basic DEC 21040 implementation, i.e. one big chip and a couple of transceivers. Donald has used one of these cards for his development of the generic 21040 driver (aka `tulip.c`). Thanks to Duke Kamstra, once again, for supplying a card to do development on.

Some of the later revisons of this card use the newer DEC 21041 chip, which may cause problems with older versions of the tulip driver. If you have problems, make sure you are using the latest driver release, which may not yet be included in the current kernel source tree.

HOWTO

See 5.17.4 (DEC 21040) for more details on using one of these cards, and the current status of the driver.

Apparently, the latest revision of the card, the EtherPower-II uses the 9432 chip. It is unclear at the moment if this one will work with the present driver. As always, if unsure, check that you can return the card if it doesn't work with the linux driver *before* paying for the card.

5.36.7 SMC EtherPower II PCI (9432)

Status – *Semi-Supported*

These cards, based upon the SMC 83c170 chip, are entirely different than the Tulip based cards. A new alpha-test driver named `epic100.c` is due to be included in kernel v2.0.34 to support these cards. For more details, see:

```
http://cesdis.gsfc.nasa.gov/linux/drivers/epic100.html
```

5.36.8 SMC 3008

Status – *Not Supported*

These 8 bit cards are based on the Fujitsu MB86950, which is an ancient version of the MB86965 used in the Linux at1700 driver. Russ says that you could probably hack up a driver by looking at the at1700.c code and his DOS packet driver for the Tiara card (tiara.asm). They are not very common.

5.36.9 SMC 3016

Status – *Not Supported*

These are 16bit i/o mapped 8390 cards, much similar to a generic NE2000 card. If you can get the specifications from SMC, then porting the NE2000 driver would probably be quite easy. They are not very common.

5.36.10 SMC-9000 / SMC 91c92/4

Status – *Supported*

The SMC9000 is a VLB card based on the 91c92 chip. The 91c92 appears on a few other brand cards as well, but is fairly uncommon. Erik Stahlman (erik@vt.edu) has written this driver which is in v2.0 kernels, but not in the older v1.2 kernels. You may be able to drop the driver into a v1.2 kernel source tree with minimal difficulty.

5.36.11 SMC 91c100

Status – *Semi-Supported*

The SMC 91c92 driver is supposed to work for cards based on this 100Base-T chip, but at the moment this is unverified.

5.37 Xircom

For the longest time, Xircom wouldn't release the programming information required to write a driver, unless you signed your life away. Apparently enough linux users have pestered them for driver support (they claim to support all popular networking operating systems...) so that they have changed their policy to allow documentation to be released without having to sign a non-disclosure agreement, and apparently they will release the source code to the SCO driver as well. If you want to verify that this is the case, you can reach Xircom at 1-800-874-7875, 1-800-438-4526 or +1-818-878-7600.

However, at the moment nobody has rushed forth offering to write any drivers, so most of their products are still unsupported, with the exception of a few PCMCIA devices.

5.37.1 PE1, PE2, PE3-10B*

Status – *Not Supported*

Not to get your hopes up, but if you have one of these parallel port adaptors, you may be able to use it in the DOS emulator with the Xircom-supplied DOS drivers. You will have to allow DOSEMU access to your parallel port, and will probably have to play with SIG (DOSEMU's Silly Interrupt Generator).

5.38 Zenith

5.38.1 Z-Note

Status – *Supported*

The built-in Z-Note network adaptor is based on the Intel i82593 using *two* DMA channels. There is an (alpha?) driver available in the present kernel version. As with all notebook and pocket adaptors, it is under the 'Pocket and portable adaptors' section when running `make config`. See 8.5 (Programming the Intel chips) for more technical information. Also note that the IBM ThinkPad 300 is compatible with the Z-Note.

5.39 Znyx

5.39.1 Znyx ZX342 (DEC 21040 based)

Status – *Supported*

You have a choice of *two* drivers for cards based on this chip. There is the DE425 driver written by David, and the generic 21040 driver that Donald has written.

Note that as of 1.1.91, David has added a compile time option that may allow non-DEC cards (such as the Znyx cards) to work with this driver. Have a look at `README.de4x5` for details.

See 5.17.4 (DEC 21040) for more information on these cards, and the present driver situation.

5.40 Identifying an Unknown Card

Okay, so your uncle's cousin's neighbour's friend had a brother who found an old ISA ethernet card in the AT case he was using as a cage for his son's pet hampster. Somehow you ended up with the card and want to try and use it with linux, but nobody has a clue what the card is and there isn't any documentation.

First of all, look for any obvious model numbers that might give a clue. Any model number that contains 2000 will most likely be a NE2000 clone. Any cards with 8003 or 8013 on them somewhere will be Western/Digital WD80x3 cards or SMC Elite cards or clones of them.

5.40.1 Identifying the Network Interface Controller

Look for the biggest chip on the card. This will be the network controller (NIC) itself, and most can be identified by the part number. If you know which NIC is on the card, the following might be able to help you figure out what card it is.

Probably still the most common NIC is the National Semiconductor DP8390 aka NS32490 aka DP83901 aka DP83902 aka DP83905 aka DP83907. And those are just the ones made by National! Other companies such as Winbond and UMC make DP8390 and DP83905 clone parts, such as the Winbond 89c904 (DP83905 clone) and the UMC 9090. If the card has some form of 8390 on it, then chances are it is a ne1000 or ne2000 clone card. The second most common 8390 based card are wd80x3 cards and clones. Cards with a DP83905 can be configured to be an ne2000 *or* a wd8013. Never versions of the genuine wd80x3 and SMC Elite cards have an 83c690 in place of the original DP8390. The SMC Ultra cards have an 83c790, and use a slightly different driver than the wd80x3 cards. The SMC EtherEZ cards have an 83c795, and use the same driver as the SMC Ultra. All BNC cards based on some sort of 8390 or 8390 clone will usually have an 8392 (or 83c692, or XXX392) 16 pin DIP chip very close to the BNC connector.

Another common NIC found on older cards is the Intel i82586. Cards having this NIC include the 3c505, 3c507, 3c523, Intel EtherExpress-ISA, Microdyne Exos-205T, and the Racal-Interlan NI5210.

The original AMD LANCE NIC was numbered AM7990, and newer revisions include the 79c960, 79c961, 79c965, 79c970, and 79c974. Most cards with one of the above will work with the Linux LANCE driver, with the exception of the old Racal-Interlan NI6510 cards that have their own driver.

Newer PCI cards having a DEC 21040, 21041, 21140, or similar number on the NIC should be able to use the linux tulip or de4x5 driver.

Other PCI cards having a big chip marked RTL8029 are ne2000 clone cards, and the ne driver in linux version v2.0 and up should automatically detect these cards at boot.

5.40.2 Identifying the Ethernet Address

Each ethernet card has its own six byte address that is unique to that card. The first three bytes of that address are the same for each card made by that particular manufacturer. For example all SMC cards start with `00:00:c0`. The last three are assigned by the manufacturer uniquely to each individual card as they are produced.

If your card has a sticker on it giving all six bits of its address, you can look up the vendor from the first three. However it is more common to see only the last three bytes printed onto a sticker attached to a socketed PROM, which tells you nothing.

You can determine which vendors have which assigned addresses from RFC-1340. Apparently there is a more up to date listing available in various places as well. Try a WWW or FTP search for `EtherNet-codes` or `Ethernet-codes` and you will find something.

5.40.3 Tips on Trying to Use an Unknown Card

If you are still not sure what the card is, but have at least narrowed it down some, then you can build a kernel with a whole bunch of drivers included, and see if any of them autodetect the card at boot.

If the kernel doesn't detect the card, it may be that the card is not configured to one of the addresses that the driver probes when looking for a card. In this case, you might want to try getting `scanport.tar.gz` from your local linux ftp site, and see if that can locate where your card is jumpered for. It scans ISA i/o space from 0x100 to 0x3ff looking for devices that aren't registered in `/proc/ioports`. If it finds an unknown device starting at some particular address, you can then explicity point the ethernet probes at that address with an `ether=` boot argument.

If you manage to get the card detected, you can then usually figure out the unknown jumpers by changing them one at a time and seeing at what i/o base and IRQ that the card is detected at. The IRQ settings can also usually be determined by following the traces on the back of the card to where the jumpers are soldered through. Counting the 'gold fingers' on the backside, from the end of the card with the metal bracket, you have IRQ 9, 7, 6, 5, 4, 3, 10, 11, 12, 15, 14 at fingers 4, 21, 22, 23, 24, 25, 34, 35, 36, 37, 38 respectively. Eight bit cards only have up to finger 31.

Jumpers that appear to do nothing usually are for selecting the memory address of an optional boot ROM. Other jumpers that are located near the BNC or RJ-45 or AUI connectors are usually to select the output media. These are also typically near the 'black box' voltage converters marked YCL, Valor, or Fil-Mag.

A nice collection of jumper settings for various cards can be found at the following URL:

Ethercard Settings `<http://www.slug.org.au/NIC/>`

5.41 Drivers for Non-Ethernet Devices

There are a few other drivers that are in the linux source that present an *ethernet-like* device to network programs, while not really being ethernet. These are briefly listed here for completeness.

`dummy.c` - The purpose of this driver is to provide a device to point a route through, but not to actually transmit packets.

`eql.c` - Load Equalizer, enslaves multiple devices (usually modems) and balances the Tx load across them while presenting a single device to the network programs.

`ibmtr.c` - IBM Token Ring, which is not really ethernet. Broken-Ring requires source routing and other uglies.

`loopback.c` - Loopback device, for which all packets from your machine and destined for your own machine go. It essentially just moves the packet off the Tx queue and onto the Rx queue.

`pi2.c` - Ottawa Amateur Radio Club PI and PI2 interface.

`plip.c` - Parallel Line Internet Protocol, allows two computers to send packets to each other over two joined parallel ports in a point-to-point fashion.

`ppp.c` - Point-to-Point Protocol (RFC1331), for the Transmission of Multi-protocol Datagrams over a Point-to-Point Link (again usually modems).

`slip.c` - Serial Line Internet Protocol, allows two computers to send packets to each other over two joined serial ports (usually via modems) in a point-to-point fashion.

`tunnel.c` - Provides an IP tunnel through which you can tunnel network traffic transparently across subnets

`wavelan.c` - An Ethernet-like radio transceiver controlled by the Intel 82586 coprocessor which is used on other ethercards such as the Intel EtherExpress.

6   Cables, Coax, Twisted Pair

If you are starting a network from scratch, it's considerably less expensive to use thin ethernet, RG58 co-ax cable with BNC connectors, than old-fashioned thick ethernet, RG-5 cable with N connectors, or 10baseT, twisted pair telco-style cables with RJ-45 eight wire 'phone' connectors. See 2.7 (Type of cable...) for an introductory look at cables.

Also note that the FAQ from *comp.dcom.lans.ethernet* has a lot of useful information on cables and such. Look in *Usenet FAQs* <ftp://rtfm.mit.edu/pub/usenet-by-hierarchy/> for the FAQ for that newsgroup.

6.1   Thin Ethernet (thinnet)

Thin ethernet is the 'ether of choice'. The cable is inexpensive. If you are making your own cables solid-core RG58A is \$0.27/m. and stranded RG58AU is \$0.45/m. Twist-on BNC connectors are < \$2 ea., and other misc. pieces are similarly inexpensive. It is essential that you properly terminate each end of the cable with 50 ohm terminators, so budget \$2 ea. for a pair. It's also vital that your cable have no 'stubs' – the 'T' connectors must be attached directly to the ethercards.

The only drawback is that if you have a big loop of machines connected together, and some bonehead breaks the loop by taking one cable off the side of his tee, the whole network goes down because it sees an infinite impedance (open circuit) instead of the required 50 ohm termination. Note that you can remove the tee piece from the card itself without killing the whole subnet, as long as you don't remove the cables from the tee itself. Of course this will disturb the machine that you pull the actual tee off of. 8-) And if you are doing a small network of two machines, you *still* need the tees and the 50 ohm terminators – you *can't* just cable them together!

Note that there are a few cards out there with 'on-board termination'. These cards have a jumper which when closed, puts a 50 ohm resistor across the BNC input. With these cards, you can use a BNC T and terminator like normal, or put the cable directly onto the card and close the jumper to enable the on-board termination.

There are also some fancy cable systems which *look like* a single lead going to the card, but the lead is actually a loop, with the two runs of cable laying side-by-side covered by an outer sheath, giving the lead an oval shaped cross-section. At the turnaround point of the loop, a BNC connector is spliced in which connects to your card. So you have the equivalent of two runs of cable and a BNC T, but in this case, it is impossible for the user to remove a cable from one side of the T and disturb the network.

6.2 Twisted Pair

Twisted pair networks require active hubs, which start around $50, and the raw cable cost can actually be higher than thinnet. You can pretty much ignore claims that you can use your existing telephone wiring as it is a rare installation where that turns out to be the case.

On the other hand, all 100Mb/sec ethernet proposals use twisted pair, and most new business installations use twisted pair. (This is probably to avoid the problem with idiots messing with the BNC's as described above.) Also, Russ Nelson adds that 'New installations should use Category 5 wiring. Anything else is a waste of your installer's time, as 100Base-whatever is going to require Cat 5.'

Some gizmos are floating around which allow you to daisy-chain machines together, and the like. For example, Farallon sells EtherWave adaptors and transceivers. This device allows multiple 10baseT devices to be daisy-chained. They also sell a 3c509 clone that includes the EtherWave transceiver. The drawback is that it's more expensive and less reliable than a cheap mini-hub and another ethercard. You probably should either go for the hub approach or switch over to 10base2 thinnet.

If you are only connecting two machines, it is possible to avoid using a hub, by swapping the Rx and Tx pairs (1-2 and 3-6).

If you hold the RJ-45 connector facing you (as if you were going to plug it into your mouth) with the lock tab on the top, then the pins are numbered 1 to 8 from left to right. The pin usage is as follows:

```
Pin Number              Assignment
----------              ----------
1                       Output Data (+)
2                       Output Data (-)
3                       Input Data (+)
4                       Reserved for Telephone use
5                       Reserved for Telephone use
6                       Input Data (-)
7                       Reserved for Telephone use
8                       Reserved for Telephone use
```

If you want to make a cable, the following should spell it out for you. Differential signal pairs must be on the same twisted pair to get the required minimal impedance/loss of a UTP cable. If you look at the above table, you will see that 1+2 and 3+6 are the two sets of differential signal pairs. Not 1+3 and 2+6 !!!!!! At 10MHz, with short lengths, you *may* get away with such errors, if it is only over a short length. Don't even think about it at 100MHz.

For a normal patch cord, with ends 'A' and 'B', you want straight through pin-to-pin mapping, with the input and output each using a pair of twisted wires (for impedance issues). That means 1A goes to 1B, 2A goes to 2B, 3A goes to 3B and 6A goes to 6B. The wires joining 1A-1B and 2A-2B must be a twisted pair. Also the wires joining 3A-3B and 6A-6B must be another twisted pair.

Now if you don't have a hub, and want to make a 'null cable', what you want to do is make the input of 'A' be the output of 'B' and the output of 'A' be the input of 'B', without changing the polarity. Tha means connecting 1A to 3B (out+ A to in+ B) and 2A to 6B (out- A to in- B). These two wires must be a twisted pair. They carry what card/plug 'A' considers output, and what is seen as input for card/plug 'B'. Then connect 3A to 1B (in+ A to out+ B) and also connect 6A to 2B (in- A to out- B). These second two must also be a twisted pair. They carry what card/plug 'A' considers input, and what card/plug 'B' considers output.

So, if you consider a normal patch cord, chop one end off of it, swap the places of the Rx and Tx twisted pairs into the new plug, and crimp it down, you then have a 'null' cable. Nothing complicated. You just want to feed the Tx signal of one card into the Rx of the second and vice versa.

Note that before 10BaseT was ratified as a standard, there existed other network formats using RJ-45 connectors, and the same wiring scheme as above. Examples are SynOptics's LattisNet, and AT&T's StarLAN. In some cases, (as with early

3C503 cards) you could set jumpers to get the card to talk to hubs of different types, but in most cases cards designed for these older types of networks will not work with standard 10BaseT networks/hubs. (Note that if the cards also have an AUI port, then there is no reason as to why you can't use that, combined with an AUI to 10BaseT transceiver.)

6.3   Thick Ethernet

Thick ethernet is mostly obsolete, and is usually used only to remain compatible with an existing implementation. You can stretch the rules and connect short spans of thick and thin ethernet together with a passive $3 N-to-BNC connector, and that's often the best solution to expanding an existing thicknet. A correct (but expensive) solution is to use a repeater in this case.

7   Software Configuration and Card Diagnostics

In most cases, if the configuration is done by software, and stored in an EEPROM, you will usually have to boot DOS, and use the supplied DOS program to set the cards IRQ, I/O, mem_addr and whatnot. Besides, hopefully it is something you will only be setting once. If you don't have the DOS software for your card, try looking on the WWW site of your card manufacturer. If you don't know the site name, take a guess at it, i.e. 'www.my_vendor.com' where 'my_vendor' is the name of your card manufacturer. This works for SMC, 3Com, and many *many* other manufacturers.

There are some cards for which Linux versions of the config utils exist, and they are listed here. Donald has written a few small card diagnostic programs that run under Linux. Most of these are a result of debugging tools that he has created while writing the various drivers. Don't expect fancy menu-driven interfaces. You will have to read the source code to use most of these. Even if your particular card doesn't have a corresponding diagnostic, you can still get some information just by typing cat /proc/net/dev – assuming that your card was at least detected at boot.

In either case, you will have to run most of these programs as root (to allow I/O to the ports) and you probably want to shut down the ethercard before doing so by typing ifconfig eth0 down (Note: replace eth0 with atp0 or whatever when appropriate.)

7.1   Configuration Programs for Ethernet Cards

7.1.1   WD80x3 Cards

For people with wd80x3 cards, there is the program wdsetup which can be found in wdsetup-0.6a.tar.gz on Linux ftp sites. I am not sure if it is being actively maintained or not, as it has not been updated for quite a while. If it works fine for you then great, if not, use the DOS version that you should have got with your card. If you don't have the DOS version, you will be glad to know that the SMC setup/driver disks are available at SMC's ftp site. Of course, you *have* to have an EEPROM card to use this utility. Old, *old* wd8003 cards, and some wd8013 clones use jumpers to set up the card instead.

7.1.2   Digital / DEC Cards

The Digital EtherWorks 3 card can be configured in a similar fashion to the DOS program NICSETUP.EXE. David C. Davies wrote this and other tools for the EtherWorks 3 in conjunction with the driver. Look on sun-site.unc.edu in the directory /pub/linux/system/Network/management for the file that is named ewrk3tools-X.XX.tar.gz.

7.1.3   NE2000+ or AT/LANTIC Cards

Some Nat Semi DP83905 implementations (such as the AT/LANTIC and the NE2000+) are software configurable. (Note that these cards can also emulate a wd8013 card!) You can get the file /pub/linux/setup/atlantic.c from Donald's ftp server, cesdis.gsfc.nasa.gov to configure this card. In addition, the configuration programs for the Kingston DP83905 cards seem to work with all cards, as they don't check for a vendor specific address before allowing you to use them. Follow the following URL: *Kingston Software* <http://www.kingston.com/download/etherx/etherx.htm> and get 20XX12.EXE and INFOSET.EXE.

HOWTO

Be careful when configuring NE2000+ cards, as you can give them bad setting values which can cause problems. A typical example is accidentally enabling the boot ROM in the EEPROM (even if no ROM is installed) to a setting that conflicts with the VGA card. The result is a computer that just beeps at you (AMI beep eight times for VGA failure) when you turn it on and nothing appears on the screen.

You can typically recover from this by doing the following: Remove the card from the machine, and then boot and enter the CMOS setup. Change the 'Display Adapter' to 'Not Installed' and change the default boot drive to 'A:' (your floppy drive). Also change the 'Wait for F1 if any Error' to 'Disabled'. This way, the computer should boot without user intervention. Now create a bootable DOS floppy ('format a: /s /u') and copy the program `default.exe` from the `20XX12.EXE` archive above onto that floppy. Then type `echo default > a:autoexec.bat` so that the program to set the card back to sane defaults will be run automatically when you boot from this floppy. Shut the machine off, re-install the ne2000+ card, insert your new boot floppy, and power it back up. It will still probably beep at you, but eventually you should see the floppy light come on as it boots from the floppy. Wait a minute or two for the floppy to stop, indicating that it has finished running the `default.exe` program, and then power down your computer. When you then turn it on again, you should hopefully have a working display again, allowing you to change your CMOS settings back, and to change the card's EEPROM settings back to the values you want.

Note that if you don't have DOS handy, you can do the whole method above with a linux boot disk that automatically runs Donald's `atlantic` program (with the right command line switches) instead of a DOS boot disk that automatically runs the `default.exe` program.

7.1.4   3Com Cards

The 3Com Etherlink III family of cards (i.e. 3c5x9) can be configured by using another config utility from Donald. You can get the file `/pub/linux/setup/3c5x9setup.c` from Donald's ftp server, `cesdis.gsfc.nasa.gov` to configure these cards. (Note that the DOS 3c5x9B config utility may have more options pertaining to the new "B" series of the Etherlink III family.)

7.2   Diagnostic Programs for Ethernet Cards

Any of the diagnostic programs that Donald has written can be obtained from this URL.

Ethercard Diagnostics `<http://cesdis.gsfc.nasa.gov/pub/linux/diag/diagnostic.html>`

Allied Telesis AT1700 – look for the file `/pub/linux/diag/at1700.c` on `cesdis.gsfc.nasa.gov`.

Cabletron E21XX – look for the file `/pub/linux/diag/e21.c` on `cesdis.gsfc.nasa.gov`.

HP PCLAN+ – look for the file `/pub/linux/diag/hp+.c` on `cesdis.gsfc.nasa.gov`.

Intel EtherExpress – look for the file `/pub/linux/diag/eexpress.c` on `cesdis.gsfc.nasa.gov`.

NE2000 cards – look for the file `/pub/linux/diag/ne2k.c` on `cesdis.gsfc.nasa.gov`. There is also a PCI version for the now common NE2000-PCI clones.

RealTek (ATP) Pocket adaptor – look for the file `/pub/linux/diag/atp-diag.c` on `cesdis.gsfc.nasa.gov`.

All Other Cards – try typing `cat /proc/net/dev` and `dmesg` to see what useful info the kernel has on the card in question.

8   Technical Information

For those who want to play with the present drivers, or try to make up their own driver for a card that is presently unsupported, this information should be useful. If you do not fall into this category, then perhaps you will want to skip this section.

8.1 Probed Addresses

While trying to determine what ethernet card is there, the following addresses are autoprobed, assuming the type and specs of the card have not been set in the kernel. The file names below are in /usr/src/linux/drivers/net/

3c501.c	0x280, 0x300
3c503.c:	0x300, 0x310, 0x330, 0x350, 0x250, 0x280, 0x2a0, 0x2e0
3c505.c:	0x300, 0x280, 0x310
3c507.c:	0x300, 0x320, 0x340, 0x280
3c509.c:	Special ID Port probe
apricot.c	0x300
at1700.c:	0x300, 0x280, 0x380, 0x320, 0x340, 0x260, 0x2a0, 0x240
atp.c:	0x378, 0x278, 0x3bc
depca.c	0x300, 0x200
de600.c:	0x378
de620.c:	0x378
eexpress.c:	0x300, 0x270, 0x320, 0x340
hp.c:	0x300, 0x320, 0x340, 0x280, 0x2C0, 0x200, 0x240
hp-plus.c	0x200, 0x240, 0x280, 0x2C0, 0x300, 0x320, 0x340
lance.c:	0x300, 0x320, 0x340, 0x360
ne.c:	0x300, 0x280, 0x320, 0x340, 0x360
ni52.c	0x300, 0x280, 0x360, 0x320, 0x340
ni65.c	0x300, 0x320, 0x340, 0x360
smc-ultra.c:	0x200, 0x220, 0x240, 0x280, 0x300, 0x340, 0x380
wd.c:	0x300, 0x280, 0x380, 0x240

There are some NE2000 clone ethercards out there that are waiting black holes for autoprobe drivers. While many NE2000 clones are safe until they are enabled, some can't be reset to a safe mode. These dangerous ethercards will hang any I/O access to their 'dataports'. The typical dangerous locations are:

Ethercard jumpered base	Dangerous locations (base + 0x10 - 0x1f)
0x300 *	0x310-0x317
0x320	0x330-0x337
0x340	0x350-0x357
0x360	0x370-0x377

* The 0x300 location is the traditional place to put an ethercard, but it's also a popular place to put other devices (often SCSI controllers). The 0x320 location is often the next one chosen, but that's bad for for the AHA1542 driver probe. The 0x360 location is bad, because it conflicts with the parallel port at 0x378. If you have two IDE controllers, or two floppy controlers, then 0x360 is also a bad choice, as a NE2000 card will clobber them as well.

Note that kernels > 1.1.7X keep a log of who uses which i/o ports, and will not let a driver use i/o ports registered by an earlier driver. This may result in probes silently failing. You can view who is using what i/o ports by typing cat /proc/ioports if you have the proc filesystem enabled.

To avoid these lurking ethercards, here are the things you can do:

- Probe for the device's BIOS in memory space. This is easy and always safe, but it only works for cards that always have BIOSes, like primary SCSI controllers.

- Avoid probing any of the above locations until you think you've located your device. The NE2000 clones have a reset range from <base>+0x18 to <base>+0x1f that will read as 0xff, so probe there first if possible. It's also safe to probe in the 8390 space at <base>+0x00 - <base>+0x0f, but that area will return quasi-random values

- If you must probe in the dangerous range, for instance if your target device has only a few port locations, first check that there isn't an NE2000 there. You can see how to do this by looking at the probe code in /usr/src/linux/net/inet/ne.c

- Use the 'reserve' boot time argument to protect volatile areas from being probed. See the information on using boot time arguments with LILO in 10.1.2 (The reserve command)

8.2   Writing a Driver

The only thing that one needs to use an ethernet card with Linux is the appropriate driver. For this, it is essential that the manufacturer will release the technical programming information to the general public without you (or anyone) having to sign your life away. A good guide for the likelihood of getting documentation (or, if you aren't writing code, the likelihood that someone else will write that driver you really, really need) is the availability of the Crynwr (nee Clarkson) packet driver. Russ Nelson runs this operation, and has been very helpful in supporting the development of drivers for Linux. *Net-surfers* can try this URL to look up Russ' software.

Russ Nelson's Packet Drivers `<http://www.crynwr.com/crynwr/home.html>`

Given the documentation, you can write a driver for your card and use it for Linux (at least in theory). Keep in mind that some old hardware that was designed for XT type machines will not function very well in a multitasking environment such as Linux. Use of these will lead to major problems if your network sees a reasonable amount of traffic.

Most cards come with drivers for MS-DOS interfaces such as NDIS and ODI, but these are useless for Linux. Many people have suggested directly linking them in or automatic translation, but this is nearly impossible. The MS-DOS drivers expect to be in 16 bit mode and hook into 'software interrupts', both incompatible with the Linux kernel. This incompatibility is actually a feature, as some Linux drivers are considerably better than their MS-DOS counterparts. The '8390' series drivers, for instance, use ping-pong transmit buffers, which are only now being introduced in the MS-DOS world.

(Ping-pong Tx buffers means using at least 2 max-size packet buffers for Tx packets. One is loaded while the card is transmitting the other. The second is then sent as soon as the first finished, and so on. In this way, most cards are able to continuously send back-to-back packets onto the wire.)

OK. So you have decided that you want to write a driver for the Foobar Ethernet card, as you have the programming information, and it hasn't been done yet. (...these are the two main requirements ;-) You should start with the skeleton network driver that is provided with the Linux kernel source tree. It can be found in the file /usr/src/linux/drivers/net/skeleton.c in all recent kernels. Also have a look at the Kernel Hackers Guide, at the following URL: *KHG* `<http://www.redhat.com:8080/HyperNews/get/khg.html>`

8.3   Driver interface to the kernel

Here are some notes on the functions that you would have to write if creating a new driver. Reading this in conjunction with the above skeleton driver may help clear things up.

8.3.1   Probe

Called at boot to check for existence of card. Best if it can check un-obtrsively by reading from memory, etc. Can also read from i/o ports. Initial writing to i/o ports in a probe is *not good* as it may kill another device. Some device initialization is usually done here (allocating i/o space, IRQs,filling in the dev->??? fields etc.) You need to know what io ports/mem the card can be configured to, how to enable shared memory (if used) and how to select/enable interrupt generation, etc.

8.3.2   Interrupt handler

Called by the kernel when the card posts an interrupt. This has the job of determining why the card posted an interrupt, and acting accordingly. Usual interrupt conditions are data to be rec'd, transmit completed, error conditions being reported. You need to know any relevant interrupt status bits so that you can act accordingly.

8.3.3   Transmit function

Linked to dev->hard_start_xmit() and is called by the kernel when there is some data that the kernel wants to put out over the device. This puts the data onto the card and triggers the transmit. You need to know how to bundle the data and how to get it onto the card (shared memory copy, PIO transfer, DMA?) and in the right place on the card. Then you need to know how to tell the card to send the data down the wire, and (possibly) post an interrupt when done. When the hardware can't accept additional packets it should set the dev->tbusy flag. When additional room is available, usually during a transmit-complete interrupt, dev->tbusy should be cleared and the higher levels informed with mark_bh(INET_BH).

8.3.4   Receive function

Called by the kernel interrupt handler when the card reports that there is data on the card. It pulls the data off the card, packages it into a sk_buff and lets the kernel know the data is there for it by doing a netif_rx(sk_buff). You need to know how to enable interrupt generation upon Rx of data, how to check any relevant Rx status bits, and how to get that data off the card (again sh mem, PIO, DMA, etc.)

8.3.5   Open function

linked to dev->open and called by the networking layers when somebody does ifconfig eth0 up - this puts the device on line and enables it for Rx/Tx of data. Any special initialization incantations that were not done in the probe sequence (enabling IRQ generation, etc.) would go in here.

8.3.6   Close function (optional)

This puts the card in a sane state when someone does ifconfig eth0 down. It should free the IRQs and DMA channels if the hardware permits, and turn off anything that will save power (like the transceiver).

8.3.7   Miscellaneous functions

Things like a reset function, so that if things go south, the driver can try resetting the card as a last ditch effort. Usually done when a Tx times out or similar. Also a function to read the statistics registers of the card if so equipped.

8.4   Interrupts and Linux

There are two kinds of interrupt handlers in Linux: fast ones and slow ones. You decide what kind you are installing by the flags you pass to irqaction(). The fast ones, such as the serial interrupt handler, run with _all_ interrupts disabled. The normal interrupt handlers, such as the one for ethercard drivers, runs with other interrupts enabled.

There is a two-level interrupt structure. The 'fast' part handles the device register, removes the packets, and perhaps sets a flag. After it is done, and interrupts are re-enabled, the slow part is run if the flag is set.

The flag between the two parts is set by:

```
mark_bh(INET_BH);
```

Usually this flag is set directly by the device driver during a transmit-complete interrupt.

You might wonder why all interrupt handlers cannot run in 'normal mode' with other interrupts enabled. Ross Biro uses this scenario to illustrate the problem:

- You get a serial interrupt, and start processing it. The serial interrupt is now masked.

- You get a network interrupt, and you start transferring a maximum-sized 1500 byte packet from the card.

- Another character comes in, but this time the interrupts are masked!

The 'fast' interrupt structure solves this problem by allowing bounded-time interrupt handlers to run without the risk of leaving their interrupt lines masked by another interrupt request.

There is an additional distinction between fast and slow interrupt handlers – the arguments passed to the handler. A 'slow' handler is defined as

```
static void
handle_interrupt(int reg_ptr)
{
    int irq = -(((struct pt_regs *)reg_ptr)->orig_eax+2);
    struct device *dev = irq2dev_map[irq];
    ...
```

While a fast handler gets the interrupt number directly

```
static void
handle_fast_interrupt(int irq)
{
    ...
```

A final aspect of network performance is latency. The only board that really addresses this is the 3c509, which allows a predictive interrupt to be posted. It provides an interrupt response timer so that the driver can fine-tune how early an interrupt is generated.

8.5   Programming the Intel chips (i82586 and i82593)

These chips are used on a number of cards, namely the 3c507 ('86), the Intel EtherExpress 16 ('86), Microdyne's exos205t ('86), the Z-Note ('93), and the Racal-Interlan ni5210 ('86).

Russ Nelson writes: 'Most boards based on the 82586 can reuse quite a bit of their code. More, in fact, than the 8390-based adapters. There are only three differences between them:

- The code to get the Ethernet address,
- The code to trigger CA on the 82586, and
- The code to reset the 82586.

The Intel EtherExpress 16 is an exception, as it I/O maps the 82586. Yes, I/O maps it. Fairly clunky, but it works.

Garrett Wollman did an AT&T driver for BSD that uses the BSD copyright. The latest version I have (Sep '92) only uses a single transmit buffer. You can and should do better than this if you've got the memory. The AT&T and 3c507 adapters do; the ni5210 doesn't.

The people at Intel gave me a very big clue on how you queue up multiple transmit packets. You set up a list of NOP-> XMIT-> NOP-> XMIT-> NOP-> XMIT-> beginning) blocks, then you set the 'next' pointer of all the NOP blocks to themselves. Now you start the command unit on this chain. It continually processes the first NOP block. To transmit a packet, you stuff it into the next transmit block, then point the NOP to it. To transmit the next packet, you stuff the next transmit block and point the previous NOP to *it*. In this way, you don't have to wait for the previous transmit to finish, you can queue up multiple packets without any ambiguity as to whether it got accepted, and you can avoid the command unit start-up delay.'

8.6 Technical information from 3Com

If you are interested in working on drivers for 3Com cards, you can get technical documentation from 3Com. Cameron has been kind enough to tell us how to go about it below:

3Com's Ethernet Adapters are documented for driver writers in our 'Technical References' (TRs). These manuals describe the programmer interfaces to the boards but they don't talk about the diagnostics, installation programs, etc that end users can see.

The Network Adapter Division marketing department has the TRs to give away. To keep this program efficient, we centralized it in a thing called 'CardFacts.' CardFacts is an automated phone system. You call it with a touch-tone phone and it faxes you stuff. To get a TR, call CardFacts at 408-727-7021. Ask it for Developer's Order Form, document number 9070. Have your fax number ready when you call. Fill out the order form and fax it to 408-764-5004. Manuals are shipped by Federal Express 2nd Day Service.

After you get a manual, if you still can't figure out how to program the board, try our 'CardBoard' BBS at 1-800-876-3266, and if you can't do that, write Andy_Chan@3Mail.3com.com and ask him for alternatives. If you have a real stumper that nobody has figured out yet, the fellow who needs to know about it is Steve_Lebus@3Mail.3com.com.

There are people here who think we are too free with the manuals, and they are looking for evidence that the system is too expensive, or takes too much time and effort. That's why it's important to try to use CardFacts *before* you start calling and mailing the people I named here.

There are even people who think we should be like Diamond and Xircom, requiring tight 'partnership' with driver writers to prevent poorly performing drivers from getting written. So far, 3Com customers have been really good about this, and there's no problem with the level of requests we've been getting. We need your continued cooperation and restraint to keep it that way.

```
Cameron Spitzer, 408-764-6339
3Com NAD
Santa Clara
work: camerons@nad.3com.com
home: cls@truffula.sj.ca.us
```

8.7 Notes on AMD PCnet / LANCE Based cards

The AMD LANCE (Local Area Network Controller for Ethernet) was the original offering, and has since been replaced by the 'PCnet-ISA' chip, otherwise known as the 79C960. A relatively new chip from AMD, the 79C960, is the heart of many new cards being released at present. Note that the name 'LANCE' has stuck, and some people will refer to the new chip by the old name. Dave Roberts of the Network Products Division of AMD was kind enough to contribute the following information regarding this chip:

'As for the architecture itself, AMD developed it originally and reduced it to a single chip – the PCnet(tm)-ISA – over a year ago. It's been selling like hotcakes ever since.

Functionally, it is equivalent to a NE1500. The register set is identical to the old LANCE with the 1500/2100 architecture additions. Older 1500/2100 drivers will work on the PCnet-ISA. The NE1500 and NE2100 architecture is basically the same. Initially Novell called it the 2100, but then tried to distinguish between coax and 10BASE-T cards. Anything that was 10BASE-T only was to be numbered in the 1500 range. That's the only difference.

Many companies offer PCnet-ISA based products, including HP, Racal-Datacom, Allied Telesis, Boca Research, Kingston Technology, etc. The cards are basically the same except that some manufacturers have added 'jumperless' features that allow the card to be configured in software. Most have not. AMD offers a standard design package for a card that uses the PCnet-ISA and many manufacturers use our design without change. What this means is that anybody who wants to write drivers for most PCnet-ISA based cards can just get the data-sheet from AMD. Call our literature distribution center at (800)222-9323 and ask for the Am79C960, PCnet-ISA data sheet. It's free.

A quick way to understand whether the card is a 'stock' card is to just look at it. If it's stock, it should just have one large chip on it, a crystal, a small IEEE address PROM, possibly a socket for a boot ROM, and a connector (1, 2, or 3, depending on the media options offered). Note that if it's a coax card, it will have some transceiver stuff built onto it as well, but that should be near the connector and away from the PCnet-ISA.'

There is also some info regarding the LANCE chip in the file lance.c which is included in the standard kernel.

A note to would-be card hackers is that different LANCE implementations do 'restart' in different ways. Some pick up where they left off in the ring, and others start right from the beginning of the ring, as if just initialised. This is a concern when setting the multicast list.

8.8   Multicast and Promiscuous Mode

Another one of the things Donald has worked on is implementing multicast and promiscuous mode hooks. All of the *released* (i.e. **not** ALPHA) ISA drivers now support promiscuous mode.

Donald writes: 'At first I was planning to do it while implementing either the /dev/* or DDI interface, but that's not really the correct way to do it. We should only enable multicast or promiscuous modes when something wants to look at the packets, and shut it down when that application is finished, neither of which is strongly related to when the hardware is opened or released.

I'll start by discussing promiscuous mode, which is conceptually easy to implement. For most hardware you only have to set a register bit, and from then on you get every packet on the wire. Well, it's almost that easy; for some hardware you have to shut the board (potentially dropping a few packet), reconfigure it, and then re-enable the ethercard. This is grungy and risky, but the alternative seems to be to have every application register before you open the ethercard at boot-time.

OK, so that's easy, so I'll move on something that's not quite so obvious: Multicast. It can be done two ways:

1. Use promiscuous mode, and a packet filter like the Berkeley packet filter (BPF). The BPF is a pattern matching stack language, where you write a program that picks out the addresses you are interested in. Its advantage is that it's very general and programmable. Its disadvantage is that there is no general way for the kernel to avoid turning on promiscuous mode and running every packet on the wire through every registered packet filter. See 8.9 (The Berkeley Packet Filter) for more info.

2. Using the built-in multicast filter that most etherchips have.

I guess I should list what a few ethercards/chips provide:

```
Chip/card   Promiscuous  Multicast filter
----------------------------------------
Seeq8001/3c501  Yes      Binary filter (1)
3Com/3c509      Yes      Binary filter (1)
8390            Yes      Autodin II six bit hash (2) (3)
LANCE           Yes      Autodin II six bit hash (2) (3)
i82586          Yes      Hidden Autodin II six bit hash (2) (4)
```

1. These cards claim to have a filter, but it's a simple yes/no 'accept all multicast packets', or 'accept no multicast packets'.

2. AUTODIN II is the standard ethernet CRC (checksum) polynomial. In this scheme multicast addresses are hashed and looked up in a hash table. If the corresponding bit is enabled, this packet is accepted. Ethernet packets are laid out so that the hardware to do this is trivial – you just latch six (usually) bits from the CRC circuit (needed anyway for error checking) after the first six octets (the destination address), and use them as an index into the hash table (six bits – a 64-bit table).

3. These chips use the six bit hash, and must have the table computed and loaded by the host. This means the kernel must include the CRC code.

4. The 82586 uses the six bit hash internally, but it computes the hash table itself from a list of multicast addresses to accept.

Note that none of these chips do perfect filtering, and we still need a middle-level module to do the final filtering. Also note that in every case we must keep a complete list of accepted multicast addresses to recompute the hash table when it changes.

My first pass at device-level support is detailed in the outline driver `skeleton.c`

It looks like the following:

```
#ifdef HAVE_MULTICAST
static void set_multicast_list(struct device *dev, int num_addrs,
                void *addrs);
#endif
.
.
.
ethercard_open() {
...
#ifdef HAVE_MULTICAST
        dev->set_multicast_list = &set_multicast_list;
#endif
...

#ifdef HAVE_MULTICAST
/* Set or clear the multicast filter for this adaptor.
    num_addrs -- -1      Promiscuous mode, receive all packets
    num_addrs -- 0       Normal mode, clear multicast list
    num_addrs > 0        Multicast mode, receive normal and
            MC packets, and do best-effort filtering.
  */
static void
set_multicast_list(struct device *dev, int num_addrs, void *addrs)
{
...
```

Any comments, criticism, etc. are welcome.'

8.9   The Berkeley Packet Filter (BPF)

The general idea of the developers is that the BPF functionality should not be provided by the kernel, but should be in a (hopefully little-used) compatibility library.

For those not in the know: BPF (the Berkeley Packet Filter) is an mechanism for specifying to the kernel networking layers what packets you are interested in. It's implemented as a specialized stack language interpreter built into a low level of the networking code. An application passes a program written in this language to the kernel, and the kernel runs the program on each incoming packet. If the kernel has multiple BPF applications, each program is run on each packet.

The problem is that it's difficult to deduce what kind of packets the application is really interested in from the packet filter program, so the general solution is to always run the filter. Imagine a program that registers a BPF program to pick up a low data-rate stream sent to a multicast address. Most ethernet cards have a hardware multicast address filter implemented as a 64 entry hash table that ignores most unwanted multicast packets, so the capability exists to make this a very inexpensive operation. But with the BFP the kernel must switch the interface to promiscuous mode, receive _all_ packets, and run them through this filter. This is work, BTW, that's very difficult to account back to the process requesting the packets.

9 Networking with a Laptop/Notebook Computer

There are currently only a few ways to put your laptop on a network. You can use the SLIP code (and run at serial line speeds); you can buy one of the few laptops that come with a NE2000-compatible ethercard; you can get a notebook with a supported PCMCIA slot built-in; you can get a laptop with a docking station and plug in an ISA ethercard; or you can use a parallel port Ethernet adapter such as the D-Link DE-600.

9.1 Using SLIP

This is the cheapest solution, but by far the most difficult. Also, you will not get very high transmission rates. Since SLIP is not really related to ethernet cards, it will not be discussed further here. See the NET-2 Howto.

9.2 Built in NE2000

This solution severely limits your laptop choices and is fairly expensive. Be sure to read the specifications carefully, as you may find that you will have to buy an additional non-standard transceiver to actually put the machine on a network. A good idea might be to boot the notebook with a kernel that has ne2000 support, and make sure it gets detected and works before you lay down your cash.

9.3 PCMCIA Support

As this area of Linux development is fairly young, I'd suggest that you join the LAPTOPS mailing channel. See 10.3 (Mailing lists...) which describes how to join a mailing list channel.

Try and determine exactly what hardware you have (ie. card manufacturer, PCMCIA chip controller manufacturer) and then ask on the LAPTOPS channel. Regardless, don't expect things to be all that simple. Expect to have to fiddle around a bit, and patch kernels, etc. Maybe someday you will be able to type 'make config' 8-)

At present, the two PCMCIA chipsets that are supported are the Databook TCIC/2 and the intel i82365.

There is a number of programs on tsx-11.mit.edu in /pub/linux/packages/laptops/ that you may find useful. These range from PCMCIA Ethercard drivers to programs that communicate with the PCMCIA controller chip. Note that these drivers are usually tied to a specific PCMCIA chip (ie. the intel 82365 or the TCIC/2)

For NE2000 compatible cards, some people have had success with just configuring the card under DOS, and then booting linux from the DOS command prompt via `loadlin`.

For those that are *net-surfing* you can try:

Don's PCMCIA Stuff `<http://cesdis.gsfc.nasa.gov/linux/pcmcia.html>`

Anyway, the PCMCIA driver problem isn't specific to the Linux world. It's been a real disaster in the MS-DOS world. In that world people expect the hardware to work if they just follow the manual. They might not expect it to interoperate with any other hardware or software, or operate optimally, but they do expect that the software shipped with the product will function. Many PCMCIA adaptors don't even pass this test.

Things are looking up for Linux users that want PCMCIA support, as substantial progress is being made. Pioneering this effort is David Hinds. His latest PCMCIA support package can be obtained from `cb-iris.stanford.edu` in the directory `/pub/pcmcia/`. Look for a file like `pcmcia-cs-X.Y.Z.tgz` where X.Y.Z will be the latest version number. This is most likely uploaded to `tsx-11.mit.edu` as well.

Note that Donald's PCMCIA enabler works as a user-level process, and David Hinds' is a kernel-level solution. You may be best served by David's package as it is much more widely used.

9.4 ISA Ethercard in the Docking Station.

Docking stations for laptops typically cost about $250 and provide two full-size ISA slots, two serial and one parallel port. Most docking stations are powered off of the laptop's batteries, and a few allow adding extra batteries in the docking station if you use short ISA cards. You can add an inexpensive ethercard and enjoy full-speed ethernet performance.

9.5 Pocket / parallel port adaptors.

The 'pocket' ethernet adaptors may also fit your need. Until recently they actually costed more than a docking station and cheap ethercard, and most tie you down with a wall-brick power supply. At present, you can choose from the D-Link, or the RealTek adaptor. Most other companies treat the programming information as a trade secret, so support will likely be slow in coming. (if ever!) Xircom (see 5.37 (Xircom)) apparently are now releasing their specs, but nobody is currently working on a driver.

Note that the transfer speed will not be all that great (perhaps 200kB/s tops?) due to the limitations of the parallel port interface.

See 5.15.4 (DE-600 / DE-620) and 5.9.1 (RealTek) for supported pocket adaptors.

You can sometimes avoid the wall-brick with the adaptors by buying or making a cable that draws power from the laptop's keyboard port. (See 5.9.1 (keyboard power))

10 Miscellaneous.

Any other associated stuff that didn't fit in anywhere else gets dumped here. It may not be relevant, and it may not be of general interest but it is here anyway.

10.1 Passing Ethernet Arguments to the Kernel

Here are two generic kernel commands that can be passed to the kernel at boot time. This can be done with LILO, loadlin, or any other booting utility that accepts optional arguments.

For example, if the command was 'blah' and it expected 3 arguments (say 123, 456, and 789) then, with LILO, you would use:

```
LILO: linux blah=123,456,789
```

Note: PCI cards have their i/o and IRQ assigned by the BIOS at boot. This means that any boot time arguments for a PCI card's IRQ or i/o ports are usually ignored.

For more information on (and a complete list of) boot time arguments, please see the *BootPrompt-HOWTO* <http://sunsite.unc.edu/mdw/HOWTO/BootPrompt-HOWTO.html>

10.1.1 The `ether` command

In its most generic form, it looks something like this:

```
ether=IRQ,BASE_ADDR,PARAM_1,PARAM_2,NAME
```

All arguments are optional. The first non-numeric argument is taken as the NAME.

IRQ: Obvious. An IRQ value of '0' (usually the default) means to autoIRQ. It's a historical accident that the IRQ setting is first rather than the base_addr – this will be fixed whenever something else changes.

BASE_ADDR: Also obvious. A value of '0' (usually the default) means to probe a card-type-specific address list for an ethercard.

PARAM_1: It was orginally used as an override value for the memory start for a shared-memory ethercard, like the WD80*3. Some drivers use the low four bits of this value to set the debug message level. 0 – default, 1-7 – level 1..7, (7 is maximum verbosity) 8 – level 0 (no messages). Also, the LANCE driver uses the low four bits of this value to select the DMA channel. Otherwise it uses auto-DMA.

PARAM_2: The 3c503 driver uses this to select between the internal and external transceivers. 0 – default/internal, 1 – AUI external. The Cabletron E21XX card also uses the low 4 bits of PARAM_2 to select the output media. Otherwise it detects automatically.

NAME: Selects the network device the values refer to. The standard kernel uses the names 'eth0', 'eth1', 'eth2' and 'eth3' for bus-attached ethercards, and 'atp0' for the parallel port 'pocket' ethernet adaptor. The arcnet driver uses 'arc0' as its name. The default setting is for a single ethercard to be probed for as 'eth0'. Multiple cards can only be enabled by explicitly setting up their base address using these LILO parameters. The 1.0 kernel has LANCE-based ethercards as a special case. LILO arguments are ignored, and LANCE cards are always assigned 'eth<n>' names starting at 'eth0'. Additional non-LANCE ethercards must be explicitly assigned to 'eth<n+1>', and the usual 'eth0' probe disabled with something like 'ether=0,-1,eth0'. (Yes, this is bug.)

10.1.2 The `reserve` command

This next lilo command is used just like 'ether=' above, ie. it is appended to the name of the boot select specified in lilo.conf

```
reserve=IO-base,extent{,IO-base,extent...}
```

In some machines it may be necessary to prevent device drivers from checking for devices (auto-probing) in a specific region. This may be because of poorly designed hardware that causes the boot to *freeze* (such as some ethercards), hardware that is mistakenly identified, hardware whose state is changed by an earlier probe, or merely hardware you don't want the kernel to initialize.

The `reserve` boot-time argument addresses this problem by specifying an I/O port region that shouldn't be probed. That region is reserved in the kernel's port registration table as if a device has already been found in that region. Note that this mechanism shouldn't be necessary on most machines. Only when there is a problem or special case would it be necessary to use this.

The I/O ports in the specified region are protected against device probes. This was put in to be used when some driver was hanging on a NE2000, or misidentifying some other device as its own. A correct device driver shouldn't probe a reserved region, unless another boot argument explicitly specifies that it do so. This implies that `reserve` will most often be used with some other boot argument. Hence if you specify a `reserve` region to protect a specific device, you must generally specify an explicit probe for that device. Most drivers ignore the port registration table if they are given an explicit address.

For example, the boot line

```
LILO: linux reserve=0x300,32 ether=0,0x300,eth0
```

keeps all device drivers except the ethercard drivers from probing 0x300-0x31f.

As usual with boot-time specifiers there is an 11 parameter limit, thus you can only specify 5 reserved regions per `reserve` keyword. Multiple `reserve` specifiers will work if you have an unusually complicated request.

10.2 Using the Ethernet Drivers as Modules

Most of the linux distributions now ship kernels that have very few drivers built-in. The drivers are instead supplied as a bunch of independent dynamically loadable modules. These modular drivers are typically loaded by the administrator with the `modprobe(8)` command, or in some cases they are automatically loaded by the kernel through 'kerneld' (in 2.0) or 'kmod' (in 2.1) which then calls `modprobe`.

You particular distribution may offer nice graphical configuration tools for setting up ethernet modules. If possible you should try and use them first. The description that follows here gives information on what underlies any fancy configuration program, and what these programs change.

The information that controls what modules are to be used and what options are supplied to each module is usually stored in the file `/etc/conf.modules`. The two main options of interest (for ethernet cards) that will be used in this file are `alias` and `options`. The `modprobe` command consults this file for module information.

The actual modules themselves are typically stored in a directory named `/lib/modules/'uname -r'/net` where the `uname -r` command gives the kernel version (e.g. 2.0.34). You can look in there to see which module matches your card.

The first thing you need in your `conf.modules` file is something to tell `modprobe` what driver to use for the `eth0` (and `eth1` and...) network interface. You use the `alias` command for this. For example, if you have an ISA SMC EtherEZ card which uses the `smc-ultra.o` driver module, you need to `alias` this driver to `eth0` by adding the line:

```
alias eth0 smc-ultra
```

The other thing you may need is an `options` line indicating what options are to be used with a particular module (or module alias). Continuing with the above example, if you only used the single `alias` line with no `options` line, the kernel would warn you (see `dmesg`) that autoprobing for ISA cards is not a good idea. To get rid of this warning, you would add another line telling the module what I/O base the card is configured to, in this case say the hexidecimal address `0x280` for example.

```
options smc-ultra io=0x280
```

Most ISA modules accept parameters like `io=0x340` and `irq=12` on the `insmod` command line. It is *REQUIRED* or at least *STRONGLY ADVISED* that you supply these parameters to avoid probing for the card. Unlike PCI and EISA devices, there is no real safe way to do auto-probing for most ISA devices, and so it should be avoided when using drivers as modules.

A list of all the options that each module accepts can be found in the file:

`/usr/src/linux/Documentation/networking/net-modules.txt`

It is recommended that you read that to find out what options you can use for your particular card. Note that some modules support comma separated value lists for modules that have the capability to handle multiple devices from a single module, such as all the 8390 based drivers, and the PLIP driver. For exemple:

```
options 3c503 io=0x280,0x300,0x330,0x350 xcvr=0,1,0,1
```

The above would have the one module controlling four 3c503 cards, with card 2 and 4 using external transcievers. Don't put spaces around the '=' or commas.

Also note that a *busy* module can't be removed. That means that you will have to `ifconfig eth0 down` (shut down the ethernet card) before you can remove the module(s).

The command `lsmod` will show you what modules are loaded, whether they are in use, and `rmmod` will remove them.

10.3 Mailing Lists and the Linux Newsgroups

If you have questions about your ethernet card, please READ this document first. You may also want to join the NET channel of the Linux mailing lists by sending mail to `majordomo@vger.rutgers.edu` to get help with what lists are available, and how to join them.

Furthermore keep in mind that the NET channel is for development discussions only. General questions on how to configure your system should be directed to comp.os.linux.setup unless you are actively involved in the development of part of the networking for Linux. We ask that you *please* respect this general guideline for content.

Also, the news groups *comp.sys.ibm.pc.hardware.networking* and *comp.dcom.lans.ethernet* should be used for questions that are not Linux specific.

10.4   Related Documentation

Much of this info came from saved postings from the comp.os.linux groups, which shows that it is a valuable resource of information. Other useful information came from a bunch of small files by Donald himself. Of course, if you are setting up an Ethernet card, then you will want to read the NET-2 Howto so that you can actually configure the software you will use. Also, if you fancy yourself as a bit of a hacker, you can always scrounge some additional info from the driver source files as well. There is usually a paragraph or two in there describing any important points before any actual code starts..

For those looking for information that is not specific in any way to Linux (i.e. what is 10BaseT, what is AUI, what does a hub do, etc.) I strongly recommend the **Ethernet-FAQ** that is posted regularly to the newsgroup *comp.dcom.lans.ethernet*. You can grab it from RTFM which holds all the newsgroup FAQs at the following URL:

Usenet FAQs `<ftp://rtfm.mit.edu/pub/usenet-by-hierarchy/>`

You can also have a look at the 'Ethernet-HomePage' so to speak, which is at the following URL:

Ethernet-HomePage `<http://wwwhost.ots.utexas.edu/ethernet/ethernet-home.html>`

10.5   Contributors

Other people who have contributed (directly or indirectly) to the Ethernet-Howto are, in alphabetical order:

```
Ross Biro            <bir7@leland.stanford.edu>
Alan Cox             <iialan@www.linux.org.uk>
David C. Davies      <davies@wanton.enet.dec.com>
Bjorn Ekwall         <bj0rn@blox.se>
David Hinds          <dhinds@allegro.stanford.edu>
Michael Hipp         <mhipp@student.uni-tuebingen.de>
Mike Jagdis          <jaggy@purplet.demon.co.uk>
Duke Kamstra         <kamstra@ccmail.west.smc.com>
Russell Nelson       <nelson@crynwr.com>
Cameron Spitzer      <camerons@NAD.3Com.com>
Dave Roberts         <david.roberts@amd.com>
Glenn Talbott        <gt@hprnd.rose.hp.com>
```

These mail addresses are intentionally not 'mailto' links so as to protect these people from WWW 'spam-bot' filters. Many thanks to the above people, and all the other unmentioned testers out there.

10.6   Disclaimer and Copyright

This document is *not* gospel. However, it is probably the most up to date info that you will be able to find. Nobody is responsible for what happens to your hardware but yourself. If your ethercard or any other hardware goes up in smoke (...nearly impossible!) we take no responsibility. ie. THE AUTHORS ARE NOT RESPONSIBLE FOR ANY DAMAGES INCURRED DUE TO ACTIONS TAKEN BASED ON THE INFORMATION INCLUDED IN THIS DOCUMENT.

This document is Copyright (c) 1993-1997 by Paul Gortmaker. Permission is granted to make and distribute verbatim copies of this manual provided the copyright notice and this permission notice are preserved on all copies.

If you are intending to incorporate this document into a published work, please make contact (vai e-mail) so that you can be supplied with the most up to date information available. In the past, out of date versions of the Linux HowTo documents have been published, which caused the developers undue grief from being plagued with questions that were already answered in the up to date versions.

10.7 Closing

If you have found any glaring typos, or outdated info in this document, please send an e-mail. It's getting big, and it is easy to overlook stuff. If you have e-mailed about a change, and it hasn't been included in the next version, please don't hesitate to send it again, as it might have got lost amongst the usual sea of SPAM and junk mail.

Thanks!

HOWTO

Part XII

"Firewalling and Proxy Server HOWTO" Mark Grennan

markg@netplus.net
v0.4, 8 November 1996
This document is designed to teach the basics of firewall systems and give you some detail on setting up both a filtering and proxy firewall on a Linux based PC. An HTML version of this document is available at *http://okcforum.org/~markg/Firewall-HOWTO.html*

Contents

1 Introduction

This original Firewall-HOWTO was written by David Rudder, **drig@execpc.com**. I'd like to thank him for allowing me to update his work.

Firewalls have gained great fame recently as the ultimate in Internet Security. Like most things that gain fame, with that fame has come misunderstanding. This HOWTO will go over the basics of what a firewall is, how to set one up, what proxy servers are, how to set up proxy servers, and the applications of this technology outside of the security realm.

1.1 Feedback

Any feedback is very welcome. **PLEASE REPORT ANY INACCURACIES IN THIS PAPER!!!** I am human, and prone to making mistakes. If you find any, fixing them is of my highest interest. I will try to answer all e-mail, but I am busy, so don't get insulted if I don't.

*My email address is **markg@netplus.net***

1.2 Disclaimer

I AM NOT RESPONSIBLE FOR ANY DAMAGES INCURRED DUE TO ACTIONS TAKEN BASED ON THIS DOCUMENT. This document is meant as an introduction to how firewalls and proxy servers work. I am not, nor do I pretend to be, a security expert. I am just some guy who has read to much and likes computers more than most people. Please, I am writing this to help get people acquainted with this subject, and I am not ready to stake my life on the accuracy of what is in here.

1.3 Copyright

In short, we wish to promote dissemination of this information through as many channels as possible. However, we do wish to retain copyright on the HOWTO documents, and would like to be notified of any plans to redistribute the HOWTOs.

If you have any questions, please contact Mark Grennan at <markg@netplus.net>.

1.4 My Reasons for Writing This

Even though there were a lot of discussions on comp.os.linux.* over the past year about firewalling, I found it difficult to find the information I needed to setup a firewall. The original version of this HOWTO was helpful but still lacking. I hope this beefed up version of David Rudder's Firewall HOWTO will give everyone the information they need to create a functioning firewall in hours, not weeks.

I also feel I should return something to the Linux community.

1.5 TODO

- Give some instructions on how to setup the clients
- Find a good UDP proxy server that works with Linux

1.6 Further Readings

- The NET-2 HOWTO
- The Ethernet HOWTO
- The Multiple Ethernet Mini HOWTO
- Networking with Linux
- The PPP HOWTO
- TCP/IP Network Administrator's Guide by O'Reilly and Associates
- The Documentation for the TIS Firewall Toolkit

Trusted Information System's (TIS) web site has a great collection of documentation on firewalls and related meterial. **http://www.tis.com/**

Also, I am working on a security project called I am calling *Secure Linux*. On the *Secure Linux* web site I am gathering all the information, documemtation and programs you need to create a trusted Linux system. Email me if you would like information.

2 Understanding Firewalls

A firewall is a term used for a part of a car. In cars, firewalls are physical objects that separate the engine from the passengers. They are meant to protect the passenger in case the car's engine catches fire while still providing the driver access to the engine's controls.

A firewall in computers is a device that protects a private network from the public part (the internet as a whole).

The firewall computer, from now on named "firewall", can reach both the protected network and the internet. The protected network can't reach the internet, and the internet can not reach the protected network.

For someone to reach the internet from inside the protected network, they must telnet to firewall, and use the internet from there.

The simplest form of a firewall is a dual homed system. (a system with two network connections) If you can TRUST ALL your users, you can simple setup a Linux (compile it with IP forwarding/gatewaying turned OFF!) and give everyone accounts on it. The can then login to this system and telnet, FTP, read mail, and use any other service you provided. With this setup, the only computer on your private network that knows anything about the outside world is the firewall. The other system on your protected network dont even need a default route.

This needs re-stating. For the above firewall to work **YOU MUST TRUST ALL YOUR USERS!** I don't recommend it.

2.1 Drawbacks with Firewalls

The problem with filtering firewalls are they inhibit the access to your network from the internet. Only services on systems that have pass filters can be accessed. With a proxy server users can login to the firewall and then access any system within the private network they have access to.

Also, new types of network clients and servers a coming out almost daily. When they do you must find a new way to allow controled access before these services can be used.

2.2 Types of Firewalls

There are two types of firewalls.

1. IP or Filtering Firewalls - that block all but selected network traffic.
2. Proxy Servers - that make the network connections for you.

2.2.1 IP Filtering Firewalls

An IP filtering firewall works at the packet level. It is designed to control the flow of packets based the source, destination, port and packet type information contained in each packet.

This type of firewall is very secure but lacks any sort of useful logging. It can block people from accessing private system but it will not tell you who accessed your public systems or who accessed the internet from the inside.

Filtering firewalls are absolute filters. Even if you want to give someone on outside access to your private servers you can not without giving everyone access to the servers.

Linux has included packet filtering software in the kernel starting with version 1.3.x.

2.2.2 Proxy Servers

Proxy servers allow indirect internet access through the firewall. The best example of how this works is a person telneting to a system and then telneting from there to another. Only with a proxy server the process is automatic. When you connect to a proxy server with your client software, the proxy server starts it's client (proxy) software and passes you the data.

Because proxy servers are duplicating all the communications they can log every thing they do.

The great thing about proxy servers is that they are completely secure, when configured correctly. They will not allow someone in through them. There are no direct IP routes.

3 Setting up the Firewall

3.1 Hardware requirements

For our example, the computer is a 486-DX66 with 16 meg of memory and a 500 meg Linux partition. This system has two network cards one connected to our private LAN and the other connected to the a lan we will call the de-militarized zone (DMZ). The DMZ has a router connected to it with a connection to the internet.

This is a pretty standard setup for a business. You could use one network card and a modem with PPP to the internet. The point is, the firewall must have two IP network numbers.

I know a lot of people have small LANs at home with two or three computers on them. Something you might consider is putting all your modems in on Linux box (maybe an old 386) and connecting all of them to the internet with load balancing. With this setup when only one person was pulling data they would get both modems doubling the throughput. :-)

4 Firewalling Software

4.1 Available packages

If all you want is a filtering firewall, you only need Linux and the basic networking packages. One package that might not come with your distribution is the IP Firewall Administration tool.

(IPFWADM) Comes from **http://www.xos.nl/linux/ipfwadm/**

If you want to setup a poxy server you will need one of these packages.

1. SOCKS
2. TIS Firewall Toolkit (FWTK)

4.2 The TIS Firewall Toolkit vs SOCKS

Trusted Information System (**http://www.tis.com**) has put out a collection of programs designed to facilitate firewalling. The programs do basically the same thing as the SOCKS package, but with a different design strategy. Where Socks has one program that covers all Internet transactions, TIS has provided one program for each utility that wishes to use the firewall.

To contrast the two, let's use the example of world wide web and Telnet access. With SOCKS, you set up one configuration file and one daemon. Through this file and daemon, both telnet and WWW are enabled, as well as any other service that you have not disabled.

With the TIS toolkit, you set up one daemon for each WWW and telnet, as well as configuration files for each. After you have done this, other internet access is still prohibited until explicitly set up. If a daemon for a specific utility has not been provided (like talk), there is a " plug-in " daemon, but it is neither as flexible, nor as easy to set up, as the other tools.

This might seem a minor, but it makes a major difference. SOCKS allows you to be sloppy. With a poorly set up SOCKS server, someone from the inside could gain more access to the internet than was originally intended. With the TIS toolkit, the people on the inside have only the access the system administrator wants them to have.

SOCKS is easier to set up, easier to compile and allows for greater flexibility. The TIS toolkit is more secure if you want to regulate the users inside the protected network. Both provide absolute protection from the outside.

I will cover the installation and setup of both.

5 Preparing the Linux system

5.1 Compiling the Kernel

Start with a clean installation of your Linux distribution. (I used RedHat 3.0.3 and the examples here are based on this distribution.) The less software you have loaded the less holes, backdoors and/or bugs there will be to introduce security problems in your system, so load only a minimal set of applications.

Pick a stable kernel. I used the Linux 2.0.14 kernel for my system. So this documentation is based on it's settings.

You well need to recompile the Linux kernel with the appropriate options. At this point, you should look at the Kernel HOWTO, the Ethernet HOWTO, and the NET-2 HOWTO if you haven't done this before.

Here are the network related setting I know work in 'make config'

1. Under General setup

   (a) Turn Networking Support ON

2. Under Networking Options

   (a) Turn Network firewalls ON

   (b) Turn TCP/IP Networking ON

   (c) Turn IP forwarding/gatewaying OFF (UNLESS you wish to use IP filtering)

   (d) Turn IP Firewalling ON

   (e) Turn IP firewall packet loggin ON (this is not required but it is a good idea)

   (f) Turn IP: masquerading OFF (I am not covering this subject here.)

   (g) Turn IP: accounting ON

   (h) Turn IP: tunneling OFF

   (i) Turn IP: aliasing OFF

   (j) Turn IP: PC/TCP compatibility mode OFF

   (k) Turn IP: Reverse ARP OFF

   (l) Turn Drop source routed frames ON

3. Under Network device support

   (a) Turn Network device support ON

   (b) Turn Dummy net driver support ON

   (c) Turn Ethernet (10 or 100Mbit) ON

   (d) Select your network card

Now you can recompile, reinstall the kernel and reboot. Your network card/s should show up in the boot-up sequence. If not, go over the other HOWTOs again until it is working.

5.2 Configuring two network cards

If you have two network cards in your computer, you most likely will need to add an append statement to your /etc/lilo.conf file to describe the IRQ and address of both cards. My lilo append statement looks like this:

```
append="ether=12,0x300,eth0 ether=15,0x340,eth1"
```

5.3 Configuring the Network Addresses

This is the real interesting part. Now you have a few decisions to make. Since we don't want the internet to have access to any part of the private network, we do not need to use real addresses. There are a number of internet addresses set aside for private networks. Because everyone needs more addresses and because these addresses can not cross the Internet they are a good choice.

Of these, 192.168.2.xxx, is set aside and we will use it in our examples.

Your proxy firewall will be a member of both networks and so it can pass the data through to and from the private network.

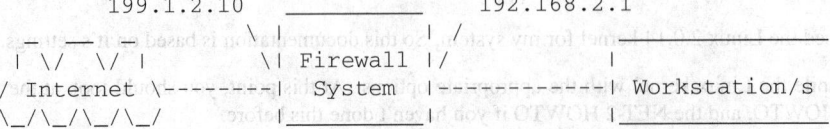

```
        199.1.2.10    _____    192.168.2.1
                         \ |         | /
 __ __ __ __              \| Firewall |/
|  \/  \/  |              \| System  |/              |            |
/ Internet \------------| System  |------------| Workstation/s |
\_/\_/\_/\_/              |_____|                |_____|
```

If your going to use a filtering firewall you can still use these numbers. You will need to use IP masquerading to make this happen. With this process the firewall will forward packets and translate them into "REAL " " IP address to travel on the Internet.

You must assign the real IP address to the network card on the Internet (out) side. And, assign 192.168.2.1 to the Ethernet card on inside. This will be your proxy/gateway IP address. You can assign all the other machines in the protected network some number in that 192.168.2.xxx range. (192.168.2.2 through 192.168.2.254)

Since I use RedHat Linux (Hey guys, want to give me a copy for the plugs? ;-) to configure the network at boot time I added a 'ifcfg-eth1' file in the /etc/sysconfig/network-scripts directory. This file is read during the boot process to set your network and routing tables.

Here is what my ifcfg-eth1 looks like;

```
#!/bin/sh
#>>>Device type: ethernet
#>>>Variable declarations:
DEVICE=eth1
IPADDR=192.168.2.1
NETMASK=255.255.255.0
NETWORK=192.168.2.0
BROADCAST=192.168.2.255
GATEWAY=199.1.2.10
ONBOOT=yes
#>>>End variable declarations
```

You can also use these scripts to automatically connect by modem to your provider. Look at the ipup-ppp script.

If your going to use a modem for your internet connection your outside IP address will be assigned for you by your provider at connect time.

5.4   Testing your network

Start by checking ifconfig and route. If you have two network cards your ifconfig should look something like:

```
#ifconfig
lo         Link encap:Local Loopback
           inet addr:127.0.0.0  Bcast:127.255.255.255  Mask:255.0.0.0
           UP BROADCAST LOOPBACK RUNNING  MTU:3584  Metric:1
           RX packets:1620 errors:0 dropped:0 overruns:0
           TX packets:1620 errors:0 dropped:0 overruns:0

eth0       Link encap:10Mbps Ethernet  HWaddr 00:00:09:85:AC:55
           inet addr:199.1.2.10 Bcast:199.1.2.255  Mask:255.255.255.0
           UP BROADCAST RUNNING MULTICAST  MTU:1500  Metric:1
           RX packets:0 errors:0 dropped:0 overruns:0
           TX packets:0 errors:0 dropped:0 overruns:0
           Interrupt:12 Base address:0x310

eth1       Link encap:10Mbps Ethernet  HWaddr 00:00:09:80:1E:D7
           inet addr:192.168.2.1  Bcast:192.168.2.255  Mask:255.255.255.0
           UP BROADCAST RUNNING MULTICAST  MTU:1500  Metric:1
           RX packets:0 errors:0 dropped:0 overruns:0
           TX packets:0 errors:0 dropped:0 overruns:0
           Interrupt:15 Base address:0x350
```

and your route table sould look like:

```
#route -n
Kernel routing table
Destination      Gateway       Genmask          Flags MSS   Window Use Iface
199.1.2.0        *             255.255.255.0    U     1500  0      15 eth0
192.168.2.0      *             255.255.255.0    U     1500  0       0 eth1
127.0.0.0        *             255.0.0.0        U     3584  0       2 lo
default          199.1.2.10    *                UG    1500  0      72 eth0
```

Note: 199.1.2.0 is the Internet side of this firewall and 192.168.2.0 is the private side.

Now try to ping the internet from the firewall. I used to use nic.ddn.mil as my test point. It's still a good test, but has proven to be less reliable than I had hoped. If it doesn't work at first, try pinging a couple other places that are not connected to your LAN. If this doesn't work, then your PPP is incorrectly setup. Reread the Net-2 HOWTO, and try again.

Next, try pinging a host within the protected network from the firewall. All the computers should be able to ping each other. If not, go over the NET-2 HOWTO again and work on the network some more.

Then, try to ping the outside address of firewall from inside the protected network. (NOTE: this is not any of the 192.168.2.xxx IP numbers.) If you can, then you have not turned off IP Forwarding. Make sure this is the way you want it. If you leave it turned on you will have to go through the IP filtering section of this document as well.

Now try pinging the internet from behind your firewall. Use the same address that worked for you before. (I.E. nic.ddn.mil) Again, if you have IP Forwarding turned off, this should not work. But, if you have it turned on, it should.

If have IP Forwarding turned on and your using a "REAL" (not 192.168.2.*) IP address for your private network, and you can't ping the internet but you can ping the internet side your firewall, check if the next router up stream is routing packets for your private network address. (Your provider may have to do this for you.)

If you have assigned your protected network to 192.168.2.*, then no can packets can be routed to it anyway. If you have skipped ahead and you already have IP masquerading turn on, this test should work.

Now, you have your basic system setup.

5.5   Securing the Firewall

A firewall isn't any good if it is left wide open to attacks through a unused service. A "bad guy" could gain access to the firewall and modify it for their own needs.

Start by turning off any unneeded services. Look at /etc/inetd.conf file. This file controls what are called the "super server". It controls a bunch of the server daemons and starts them as they are requested.

Definitely turn off netstat, systat, tftp, bootp, and finger. To turn a service off, put # as the first character of the service line. When your done, send a SIG-HUP to the process by typing "**kill -HUP** <**pid**>", where <pid> is the process number of inetd. This will make inetd re-read its configuration file (inetd.conf) and restart.

Test it out by telneting to port 15 on firewall, the netstat port. If you get an output of netstat, you have not restarted it correctly.

6   IP filtering setup (IPFWADM)

To start, you should have IP Forwarding turned on in your kernel and your system should be up and forwarding everything you send it. Your routing tables should be in place and you should be able to access everything, both from the inside out and from the outside in.

But, we're building a firewall so we need to start chocking down what everyone has access to.

In my system I created a couple of scripts to set the firewall forwarding policy and accounting policy. I call theses scripts from the /etc/rc.d scripts so my system is configured at boot time.

By default the IP Forwarding system in the Linux kernel forwards everything. Because of this, your firewall script should start by denying access to everything and flushing any ipfw rules in place from the last time it was run. This script will do the trick.

```
#
# setup IP packet Accounting and Forwarding
#
#    Forwarding
#
# By default DENY all services
ipfwadm -F -p deny
# Flush all commands
ipfwadm -F -f
ipfwadm -I -f
ipfwadm -O -f
```

Now we have the ultimate firewall. Nothing can get through. No doubt you have some services you need to forward so here are a few examples you should find useful.

```
# Forward email to your server
ipfwadm -F -a accept -b -P tcp -S 0.0.0.0/0 1024:65535 -D 192.1.2.10 25

# Forward email connections to outside email servers
ipfwadm -F -a accept -b -P tcp -S 196.1.2.10 25 -D 0.0.0.0/0 1024:65535

# Forward Web connections to your Web Server
/sbin/ipfwadm -F -a accept -b -P tcp -S 0.0.0.0/0 1024:65535 -D 196.1.2.11 80

# Forward Web connections to outside Web Server
/sbin/ipfwadm -F -a accept -b -P tcp -S 196.1.2.* 80 -D 0.0.0.0/0 1024:65535

# Forward DNS traffic
/sbin/ipfwadm -F -a accept -b -P udp -S 0.0.0.0/0 53 -D 196.1.2.0/24
```

You might also be interested in accounting for traffic going through your firewall. This script will count ever packet. You could add a line or to to account for packets going to just a single system.

```
# Flush the current accounting rules
ipfwadm -A -f
# Accounting
/sbin/ipfwadm -A -f
/sbin/ipfwadm -A out -i -S 196.1.2.0/24 -D 0.0.0.0/0
/sbin/ipfwadm -A out -i -S 0.0.0.0/0 -D 196.1.2.0/24
/sbin/ipfwadm -A in -i -S 196.1.2.0/24 -D 0.0.0.0/0
/sbin/ipfwadm -A in -i -S 0.0.0.0/0 -D 196.1.2.0/24
```

If all you wanted was a filtering firewall you can stop here. Enjoy :-)

7 Installing the TIS Proxy server

7.1 Getting the software

The TIS FWTK is avaible at **ftp://ftp.tis.com/**.

Don't make the mistake I did. When you ftp files from TIS, READ THE README's. The TIS fwtk is locked up in a hidden directory on their server. TIS requires you **send email to fwtk-request@tis.com** with only the word **SEND** in the body of the message to learn the name of this hidden directory. No subject is needed in the message. Their system will then mails you back the directory name (good for 12 hours) to download the source.

As I'm writing this TIS is releasing version 2.0 (beta) of the FWTK. This version seems to compile well (with a few exceptions) and everything is working for me. This is the version I will be covering here. When they release the final code I'll update the HOWTO.

To install the FWTK, create a fwtk-2.0 directory in your /usr/src directory. Move your copy of the FWTK (fwtk-2.0.tar.gz) to your this directory and untar it (tar zxf fwtk-2.0.tar.gz).

The FWTK does not proxy SSL web documents but there is an addon for it written by Jean-Christophe Touvet. It is avaible at **ftp://ftp.edelweb.fr/pub/contrib/fwtk/ssl-gw.tar.Z**. Touvet does not support this code.

I am using a modified version that includes access to Netscape secure news servers written by Eric Wedel. It is available at **ftp://mdi.meridian-data.com/pub/tis.fwtk/ssl-gw/ssl-gw2.tar.Z**.

In our example I will use Eric Wedel's version.

To install it, simply create a ssl-gw directory in your /usr/src/fwtk-2.0 directory and put the files in it.

When I installed this gateway it required a few changes before it would compile with the rest of the toolkit.

The first change was to the ssl-gw.c file. I found it didn't include a needed include file.

```
#if defined(__linux)
#include        <sys/ioctl.h>
#endif
```

Second it didn't come with a Makefile. I copied one out of the other gateway directories and replaced the gateway's name with ssl-gw.

7.2 Compiling the TIS FWTK

Version 2.0 of the FWTK compiles much easier then any of the older versions. I still found a couple of things that needed to be changed before the BETA version would compile cleanly. Hopefully these changes will be make in the final version.

To fix it up, start by changing to the /usr/src/fwtk/fwtk directory and coping the Makefile.config.linux file over the Makefile.config file.

DON'T RUN FIXMAKE. The instructions tell you to run this. If you do it will break the makefiles in each directory.

I do have a fix for fixmake. The problem is the sed script add a '.' and " to the include line of ever Makefile. This sed script works.

```
sed 's/^include[        ]*\([^ ].*\)/include \1/' $name .proto > $name
```

Next we need to edit the Makefile.config file. There are two changes you may need to make.

The author set the source directory to his home directory. We are compiling our code in /usr/src so you should changed the FWTKSRCDIR variable to reflect this.

```
FWTKSRCDIR=/usr/src/fwtk/fwtk
```

Second, at least some Linux system us the gdbm database. The Makefile.config is using dbm. You might need to change this. I had to for RedHat 3.0.3.

```
DBMLIB=-lgdbm
```

The last fix is in the x-gw. The bug in the BETA version is in the socket.c code. To fix it remove these lines of code.

```
#ifdef SCM_RIGHTS   /* 4.3BSD Reno and later */
                    + sizeof(un_name->sun_len) + 1
#endif
```

If you added the ssl-gw to your FWTK source directory you will need to add it to the list of directory in the Makefile.

```
DIRS=   smap smapd netacl plug-gw ftp-gw tn-gw rlogin-gw http-gw x-gw ssl-gw
```

Now run **make**.

7.3 Installing the TIS FWTK

Run **make install**.

The default installation directory is /usr/local/etc. You could change this (I didn't) to a more secure directory. I chose to change the access to this directory to 'chmod 700'.

All last is left now is to configure the firewall.

7.4 Configuring the TIS FWTK

Now the fun realy begins. We must teach the system to call theses new services and create the tables to control them.

I'm not going to try to re-write the TIS FWTK manual here. I will show you the setting I found worked and explain the problems I ran into and how I got around them.

There are three files that make up these controls.

- /etc/services

  - Tells the system what ports a services is on.

- /etc/inetd.conf

  - Tells inetd what program to call when someone knocks on a service port.

- /usr/local/etc/netperm-table

  - Tells the FWTK services who to allow and deny service to.

To get the FWTK functioning, you should edit these files from the bottom up. Editing the services file without the inetd.conf or netperm-table file set correctly could make your system inaccessible.

7.4.1 The netperm-table file

This file controls who can access the services of the TIS FWTK. You should think about the traffic using the firewall from both sides. People outside your network should identify themselves before gaining access, but the people inside your network might be allowed to just pass through.

So people can identify themselves, the firewall uses a program called **authsrv** to keep a database of user IDs and passwords. The authentication section of the netperm-table controls where the database is keep and who can access it.

I had some trouble closing the access to this service. Note the premit-hosts line I show uses a '*' to give everyone access. The correct setting for this line is " authsrv: premit-hosts localhost if you can get it working.

```
#
# Proxy configuration table
#
# Authentication server and client rules
authsrv:        database /usr/local/etc/fw-authdb
authsrv:        permit-hosts *
authsrv:        badsleep 1200
authsrv:        nobogus true
# Client Applications using the Authentication server
*:              authserver 127.0.0.1 114
```

To initialize the database, su to root, and run **./authsrv** in the /var/local/etc directory to create the administrative user record. Here is a sample session.

Read the FWTK documentation to learn how to add users and groups.

```
#
# authsrv
authsrv# list
authsrv# adduser admin "Auth DB admin"
ok - user added initially disabled
authsrv# ena admin
enabled
authsrv# proto admin pass
changed
authsrv# pass admin "plugh"
Password changed.
authsrv# superwiz admin
set wizard
authsrv# list
Report for users in database
user    group  longname          ok?    proto  last
------  ------ ----------------- -----  ------ -----
admin          Auth DB admin     ena    passw  never
authsrv# display admin
Report for user admin (Auth DB admin)
Authentication protocol: password
Flags: WIZARD
authsrv# ^D
EOT
#
```

The telnet gateway (tn-gw) controls are straight forward and the first you should set up.

In my example, I premit host from inside the private network to pass through without authenticating themselves. (permit-hosts 19961.2.* -passok) But, any other user must enter their user ID and password to use the proxy. (permit-hosts * -auth)

I also allow one other system (196.1.2.202) to access the firewall directly without going through the firewall at all. The two inetacl-in.telnetd lines do this. I will explain how these lines are called latter.

The Telnet timeout should be keep short.

```
# telnet gateway rules:
tn-gw:                  denial-msg           /usr/local/etc/tn-deny.txt
tn-gw:                  welcome-msg          /usr/local/etc/tn-welcome.txt
tn-gw:                  help-msg             /usr/local/etc/tn-help.txt
tn-gw:                  timeout 90
tn-gw:                  permit-hosts 196.1.2.* -passok -xok
tn-gw:                  permit-hosts * -auth
# Only the Administrator can telnet directly to the Firewall via Port 24
netacl-in.telnetd: permit-hosts 196.1.2.202 -exec /usr/sbin/in.telnetd
```

The r-commands work the same way as telnet.

```
# rlogin gateway rules:
rlogin-gw:    denial-msg     /usr/local/etc/rlogin-deny.txt
rlogin-gw:    welcome-msg    /usr/local/etc/rlogin-welcome.txt
rlogin-gw:    help-msg       /usr/local/etc/rlogin-help.txt
rlogin-gw:    timeout 90
rlogin-gw:    permit-hosts 196.1.2.* -passok -xok
rlogin-gw:    permit-hosts * -auth -xok
# Only the Administrator can telnet directly to the Firewall via Port
netacl-rlogind: permit-hosts 196.1.2.202 -exec /usr/libexec/rlogind -a
```

You shouldn't have anyone accessing your firewall directly and that includes FTP so don't put an FTP, server on you firewall.

Again, the permit-hosts line allows anyone in the protected network free access to the Internet and all others must authenticate themselves. I included logging of every file sent and received to my controls. (-log { retr stor })

The ftp timeout controls how long it will take to drop a bad connections as well as how long a connection will stay open with out activity.

```
# ftp gateway rules:
ftp-gw:                 denial-msg           /usr/local/etc/ftp-deny.txt
ftp-gw:                 welcome-msg          /usr/local/etc/ftp-welcome.txt
ftp-gw:                 help-msg             /usr/local/etc/ftp-help.txt
ftp-gw:                 timeout 300
ftp-gw:                 permit-hosts 196.1.2.* -log { retr stor }
ftp-gw:                 permit-hosts * -authall -log { retr stor }
```

Web, gopher and browser based ftp are contorted by the http-gw. The first two lines create a directory to store ftp and web documents as they are passing through the firewall. I make these files owned by root and put the in a directory accessible only by root.

The Web connection should be kept short. It controls how long the user will wait on a bad connections.

```
# www and gopher gateway rules:
http-gw:      userid            root
```

HOWTO

```
http-gw:       directory         /jail
http-gw:       timeout 90
http-gw:       default-httpd     www.afs.net
http-gw:       hosts             196.1.2.* -log { read write ftp }
http-gw:       deny-hosts        *
```

The ssl-gw is really just a pass anything gateway. Be carefull with it. In this example I allow anyone inside the protected network to connect to any server outside the network except the addresses 127.0.0.* and 192.1.1.* and then only on ports 443 through 563. Ports 443 through 563 are known SSL ports.

```
# ssl gateway rules:
ssl-gw: timeout 300
ssl-gw: hosts   196.1.2.* -dest { !127.0.0.* !192.1.1.* *:443:563 }
ssl-gw: deny-hosts        *
```

Here is an example of how to use the plug-gw to allow connections to a news server. In this example I allow anyone inside the protected network to connect to only one system and only to it's news port.

The seconded line allows the news server to pass its data back to the protected network.

Because most clients expect to stay connected while the user read news, the timeout for a news server should be long.

```
# NetNews Pluged gateway
plug-gw:          timeout 3600
plug-gw: port nntp 196.1.2.* -plug-to 199.5.175.22 -port nntp
plug-gw: port nntp 199.5.175.22 -plug-to 196.1.2.* -port nntp
```

The finger gateway is simple. Anyone inside the protected network must login first and then we allow them to use the finger program on the firewall. Anyone else just gets a message.

```
# Enable finger service
netacl-fingerd: permit-hosts 196.1.2.* -exec /usr/libexec/fingerd
netacl-fingerd: permit-hosts * -exec /bin/cat /usr/local/etc/finger.txt
```

I haven't setup the Mail and X-windows services so I'm not including examples. If anyone has a working example, please send me email.

7.4.2   The inetd.conf file

Here is a complete /etc/inetd.conf file. All un-needed services have been commented out. I have included the complete file to show what to turn off, as well as how to setup the new firewall services.

```
#echo stream   tcp  nowait  root         internal
#echo dgram    udp  wait    root         internal
#discard       stream  tcp  nowait  root      internal
#discard       dgram   udp  wait    root      internal
#daytime       stream  tcp  nowait  root      internal
#daytime       dgram   udp  wait    root      internal
#chargen       stream  tcp  nowait  root      internal
#chargen       dgram   udp  wait    root      internal
# FTP firewall gateway
ftp-gw         stream  tcp  nowait.400  root  /usr/local/etc/ftp-gw  ftp-gw
# Telnet firewall gateway
```

```
telnet          stream  tcp  nowait     root  /usr/local/etc/tn-gw /us-
r/local/etc/tn-gw
# local telnet services
telnet-a      stream  tcp  nowait      root  /usr/local/etc/netacl in.telnetd
# Gopher firewall gateway
gopher          stream  tcp  nowait.400  root  /usr/local/etc/http-gw /us-
r/local/etc/http-gw
# WWW firewall gateway
http  stream  tcp  nowait.400  root  /usr/local/etc/http-gw /us-
r/local/etc/http-gw
# SSL firewall gateway
ssl-gw  stream  tcp    nowait  root  /usr/local/etc/ssl-gw  ssl-gw
# NetNews firewall proxy (using plug-gw)
nntp       stream  tcp    nowait  root    /usr/local/etc/plug-gw plug-gw nntp
#nntp stream  tcp     nowait  root    /usr/sbin/tcpd  in.nntpd
# SMTP (email) firewall gateway
#smtp stream  tcp      nowait  root    /usr/local/etc/smap smap
#
# Shell, login, exec and talk are BSD protocols.
#
#shell       stream  tcp     nowait  root    /usr/sbin/tcpd  in.rshd
#login       stream  tcp     nowait  root    /usr/sbin/tcpd  in.rlogind
#exec stream  tcp     nowait  root    /usr/sbin/tcpd  in.rexecd
#talk dgram   udp     wait    root    /usr/sbin/tcpd  in.talkd
#ntalk        dgram   udp     wait    root    /usr/sbin/tcpd  in.ntalkd
#dtalk        stream  tcp     waut    nobody  /usr/sbin/tcpd  in.dtalkd
#
# Pop and imap mail services et al
#
#pop-2   stream  tcp  nowait  root  /usr/sbin/tcpd    ipop2d
#pop-3   stream  tcp  nowait  root  /usr/sbin/tcpd    ipop3d
#imap    stream  tcp  nowait  root  /usr/sbin/tcpd    imapd
#
# The Internet UUCP service.
#
#uucp    stream  tcp  nowait  uucp  /usr/sbin/tcpd  /usr/lib/uucp/uucico -l
#
# Tftp service is provided primarily for booting.  Most sites
# run this only on machines acting as "boot servers." Do not uncomment
# this unless you *need* it.
#
#tftp dgram   udp     wait    root    /usr/sbin/tcpd  in.tftpd
#bootps       dgram   udp     wait    root    /usr/sbin/tcpd  bootpd
#
# Finger, systat and netstat give out user information which may be
# valuable to potential "system crackers."  Many sites choose to disable
# some or all of these services to improve security.
#
# cfinger is for GNU finger, which is currently not in use in RHS Linux
#
finger          stream  tcp  nowait  root  /usr/sbin/tcpd  in.fingerd
#cfinger        stream  tcp  nowait  root  /usr/sbin/tcpd  in.cfingerd
#systat         stream  tcp  nowait  guest /usr/sbin/tcpd  /bin/ps -auwwx
#netstat        stream  tcp  nowait  guest /usr/sbin/tcpd  /bin/netstat -f inet
#
```

HOWTO

```
# Time service is used for clock syncronization.
#
#time stream  tcp nowait  root  /usr/sbin/tcpd  in.timed
#time dgram   udp wait    root  /usr/sbin/tcpd  in.timed
#
# Authentication
#
auth          stream tcp wait    root  /usr/sbin/tcpd  in.identd -w -t120
authsrv       stream tcp nowait  root  /usr/local/etc/authsrv authsrv
#
# End of inetd.conf
```

7.4.3   The /etc/services file

This is where it all begins. When a client connects to the firewall it connects on a known port (less then 1024). For example telnet connects on port 23. The inetd deamon hears this connection and looks up the name of these service in the /etc/services file. It then calls the program assigned to the name in the /etc/inetd.conf file.

Some of the services we are creating are not normally in the /etc/services file. You can assign some of them to any port you want. For example, I have assigned the administrator's telnet port (telnet-a) to port 24. You could assign it to port 2323 if you wished. For the administrator (YOU) to connect directly to the firewall you will need to telnet to port 24 not 23 and if you setup your netperm-table file, like I did, you will only be able to to this from one system inside your protected network.

```
telnet-a     24/tcp
ftp-gw       21/tcp              # this named changed
auth         113/tcp    ident    # User Verification
ssl-gw       443/tcp
```

8   The SOCKS Proxy Server

8.1   Setting up the Proxy Server

The SOCKS proxy server available from **ftp://sunsite.unc.edu/pub/Linux/system/Network/misc/socks-linux- src.tgz**. There is also an example config file in that directory called "socks-conf". Uncompress and untar the files into a directory on your system, and follow the instructions on how to make it. I had a couple problems when I made it. Make sure that your Makefiles are correct.

One important thing to note is that the proxy server needs to be added to /etc/inetd.conf. You must add a line:

```
socks  stream  tcp  nowait  nobody  /usr/local/etc/sockd  sockd
```

to tell the server to run when requested.

8.2   Configuring the Proxy Server

The SOCKS program needs two separate configuration files. One to tell the access allowed, and one to route the requests to the appropriate proxy server. The access file should be housed on the server. The routing file should be housed on every Un*x machine. The DOS and, presumably, Macintosh computers will do their own routing.

8.2.1   The Access File

With socks4.2 Beta, the access file is called "sockd.conf". It should contain 2 lines, a permit and a deny line. Each line will have three entries:

- The Identifier (permit/deny)
- The IP address
- The address modifier

The identifier is either permit or deny. You should have both a permit and a deny line.

The IP address holds a four byte address in typical IP dot notation. I.E. 192.168.2.0.

The address modifier is also a typical IP address four byte number. It works like a netmask. Envision this number to be 32 bits (1s or 0s). If the bit is a 1, the corresponding bit of the address that it is checking must match the corresponding bit in the IP address field. For instance, if the line is:

```
permit 192.168.2.23 255.255.255.255
```

it will permit only the IP address that matches every bit in 192.168.2.23, eg, only 192.168.2.3. The line:

```
permit 192.168.2.0 255.255.255.0
```

will permit every number within group 192.168.2.0 through 192.168.2.255, the whole C Class domain. One should not have the line:

```
permit 192.168.2.0 0.0.0.0
```

as this will permit every address, regardless.

So, first permit every address you want to permit, and then deny the rest. To allow everyone in the domain 192.168.2.xxx, the lines:

```
permit 192.168.2.0 255.255.255.0
deny 0.0.0.0 0.0.0.0
```

will work nicely. Notice the first "0.0.0.0" in the deny line. With a modifier of 0.0.0.0, the IP address field does not matter. All 0's is the norm because it is easy to type.

More than one entry of each is allowed.

Specific users can also be granted or denied access. This is done via ident authentication. Not all systems support ident, including Trumpet Winsock, so I will not go into it here. The documentation with socks is quite adequate on this subject.

8.2.2 The Routing File

The routing file in SOCKS is poorly named "socks.conf". I say "poorly named" because it is so close to the name of the access file that it is easy to get the two confused.

The routing file is there to tell the SOCKS clients when to use socks and when not to. For instance, in our network, 192.168.2.3 will not need to use socks to talk with 192.168.2.1, firewall. It has a direct connection in via Ethernet. It defines 127.0.0.1, the loopback, automatically. Of course you do not need SOCKS to talk to yourself. There are three entries:

- deny
- direct
- sockd

Deny tells SOCKS when to reject a request. This entry has the same three fields as in sockd.conf, identifier, address and modifier. Generally, since this is also handled by sockd.conf, the access file, the modifier field is set to 0.0.0.0. If you want to preclude yourself from calling any place, you can do it here.

The direct entry tells which addresses to not use socks for. These are all the addresses that can be reached without the proxy server. Again we have the three fields, identifier, address and modifier. Our example would have

```
direct 192.168.2.0 255.255.255.0
```

Thus going direct for any on our protected network.

The sockd entry tells the computer which host has the socks server daemon on it. The syntax is:

```
sockd @=<serverlist> <IP address> <modifier>
```

Notice the @= entry. This allows you to set the IP addresses of a list of proxy servers. In our example, we only use one proxy server. But, you can have many to allow a greater load and for redundancy in case of failure.

The IP address and modifier fields work just like in the other examples. You specify which addresses go where through these. 6.2.3. DNS from behind a Firewall

Setting up Domain Name service from behind a firewall is a relatively simple task. You need merely to set up the DNS on the firewalling machine. Then, set each machine behind the firewall to use this DNS.

8.3   Working With a Proxy Server

8.3.1   Unix

To have your applications work with the proxy server, they need to be "sockified". You will need two different telnets, one for direct communication, one for communication via the proxy server. SOCKS comes with instructions on how to SOCKify a program, as well as a couple pre-SOCKified programs. If you use the SOCKified version to go somewhere direct, SOCKS will automatically switch over to the direct version for you. Because of this, we want to rename all the programs on our protected network and replace them with the SOCKified programs. "Finger" becomes "finger.orig", "telnet" becomes "telnet.orig", etc. You must tell SOCKS about each of these via the include/socks.h file.

Certain programs will handle routing and sockifying itself. Netscape is one of these. You can use a proxy server under Netscape by entering the server's address (192.168.2.1 in our case) in the SOCKs field under Proxies. Each application will need at least a little messing with, regardless of how it handles a proxy server.

8.3.2   MS Windows with Trumpet Winsock

Trumpet Winsock comes with built in proxy server capabilities. In the "setup" menu, enter the IP address of the server, and the addresses of all the computers reachable directly. Trumpet will then handle all outgoing packets.

8.3.3   Getting the Proxy Server to work with UDP Packets

The SOCKS package works only with TCP packets, not UDP. This makes it quite a bit less useful. Many useful programs, such as talk and Archie, use UDP. There is a package designed to be used as a proxy server for UDP packets called UDPrelay, by Tom Fitzgerald <fitz@wang.com>. Unfortunately, at the time of this writing, it is not compatible with Linux.

8.4   Drawbacks with Proxy Servers

The proxy server is, above all, a security device. Using it to increase internet access with limited IP addresses will have many drawbacks. A proxy server will allow greater access from inside the protected network to the outside, but will keep the inside completely unaccessible from the outside. This means no servers, talk or archie connections, or direct mailing to the inside computers. These drawbacks might seem slight, but think of it this way:

- You have left a report you are doing on your computer inside a firewall protected network. You are at home, and decide that you would like to go over it. You can not. You can not reach your computer because it is behind the firewall. You try to log into `firewall` first, but since everyone has proxy server access, no one has set up an account for you on it.

- Your daughter goes to college. You want to email her. You have some private things to talk about, and would rather have your mail sent directly to your machine. You trust your systems administrator completely, but still, this is private mail.

- The inability to use UDP packets represents a big drawback with the proxy servers. I imagine UDP capabilities will be coming shortly.

FTP causes another problem with a proxy server. When getting or doing an `ls`, the FTP server opens a socket on the client machine and sends the information through it. A proxy server will not allow this, so FTP doesn't particularly work.

And, proxy servers run slow. Because of the greater overhead, almost any other means of getting this access will be faster.

Basically, if you have the IP addresses, and you are not worried about security, do not use a firewall and/or proxy servers. If you do not have the IP addresses, but you are also not worried about security, you might also want to look into using an IP emulator, like Term, Slirp or TIA. Term is available from **ftp://sunsite.unc.edu**, Slirp is available from **ftp://blitzen.canberra.edu.au/pub/slirp**, and TIA is available from marketplace.com. These packages will run faster, allow better connections, and provide a greater level of access to the inside network from the internet. Proxy servers are good for those networks which have a lot of hosts that will want to connect to the internet on the fly, with one setup and little work after that.

9 Advanced Configurations

There is one configuration I would like to go over before wrapping this document up. The one I have just outlined will probably suffice for most people. However, I think the next outline will show a more advanced configuration that can clear up some questions. If you have questions beyond what I have just covered, or are just interested in the versatility of proxy servers and firewalls, read on.

9.1 A large network with emphasis on security

Say, for instance, you are the leader of millisha and you wish to network your site. You have 50 computers and a subnet of 32 (5 bits) IP numbers. You need various levels of access within your network because you tell your followers different things. Therefore, you'll need to protect certain parts of the network from the rest.

The levels are:

1. The external level. This is the level that gets shown to everybody. This is where you rant and rave to get new volunteers.

2. **Troop** This is the level of people who have gotten beyond the external level. Here is where you teach them about the evail goverment and how to make bombs.

3. **Mercenary** Here is where the *real* plans are keep. In this level is stored all the information on how the 3rd world goverment is going to take over the world, your plans involving Newt Gingrich, Oklahoma City, lown care products and what realy is stored in that hangers at area 51.

9.1.1 The Network Setup

The IP numbers are arranged as:

- 1 number is 192.168.2.255, which is the broadcast address and is not usable.

- 23 of the 32 IP addresses are allocated to 23 machines that will be accessible to the internet.

- 1 extra IP goes to a linux box on that network

- 1 extra goes to a different linux box on that network.
  - 2 IP #'s go to the router
  - 4 are left over, but given domain names paul, ringo, john, and george, just to confuse things a bit.
- The protected networks both have the addresses 192.168.2.xxx

Then, two separate networks are built, each in different rooms. They are routed via infrared Ethernet so that they are completely invisible to the outside room. Luckily, infrared ethernet works just like normal ethernet.

These networks are each connected to one of the linux boxes with an extra IP address.

There is a file server connecting the two protected networks. This is because the plans for taking over the world involves some of the higher Troops. The file server holds the address 192.168.2.17 for the Troop network and 192.168.2.23 for the Mercenary network. It has to have different IP addresses because it has to have different Ethernet cards. IP Forwarding on it is turned off.

IP Forwarding on both Linux boxes is also turned off. The router will not forward packets destined for 192.168.2.xxx unless explicitly told to do so, so the internet will not be able to get in. The reason for turning off IP Forwarding here is so that packets from the Troop's network will not be able to reach the Mercenary network, and vica versa.

The NFS server can also be set to offer different files to the different networks. This can come in handy, and a little trickery with symbolic links can make it so that the common files can be shared with all. Using this setup and another ethernet card can offer this one file server for all three networks.

9.1.2 The Proxy Setup

Now, since all three levels want to be able to monitor the network for their own devious purposes, all three need to have net access. The external network is connected directly into the internet, so we don't have to mess with proxy servers here. The Mercenary and Troop networks are behind firewalls, so it is necessary to set up proxy servers here.

Both networks will be setup very similarly. They both have the same IP addresses assigned to them. I will throw in a couple of parameters, just to make things more interesting though.

1. No one can use the file server for internet access. This exposes the file server to viruses and other nasty things, and it is rather important, so its off limits.
2. We will not allow troop access to the World Wide Web. They are in training, and this kind of information retrieval power might prove to be damaging.

So, the sockd.conf file on the Troop's linux box will have this line:

```
deny 192.168.2.17 255.255.255.255
```

and on the Mercenary machine:

```
deny 192.168.2.23 255.255.255.255
```

And, the Troop's linux box will have this line

```
deny 0.0.0.0 0.0.0.0 eq 80
```

This says to deny access to all machines trying to access the port equal (eq) to 80, the http port. This will still allow all other services, just deny Web access.

Then, both files will have:

```
permit 192.168.2.0 255.255.255.0
```

to allow all the computers on the 192.168.2.xxx network to use this proxy server except for those that have already been denied (ie. the file server and Web access from the Troop network).

The Troop's sockd.conf file will look like:

```
deny 192.168.2.17 255.255.255.255
deny 0.0.0.0 0.0.0.0 eq 80
permit 192.168.2.0 255.255.255.0
```

and the Mercenary file will look like:

```
deny 192.168.2.23 255.255.255.255
permit 192.168.2.0 255.255.255.0
```

This should configure everything correctly. Each network is isolated accordingly, with the proper amount of interaction. Everyone should be happy.

Now, take over the world!

HOWTO

Part XIII

"The Linux GCC HOWTO" Daniel Barlow

<dan@detached.demon.co.uk>

v1.17, 28 February 1996

This document covers how to set up the GNU C compiler and development libraries under Linux, and gives an overview of compiling, linking, running and debugging programs under it. Most of the material in it has been taken from Mitch D'Souza's GCC-FAQ, which it replaces, or the ELF-HOWTO, which it will eventually largely replace. This is the first publically released version (despite the version number; that's an artifact of RCS). Feedback is welcomed.

1 Preliminaries

1.1 ELF vs. a.out

Linux development is in a state of flux right now. Briefly, there are two formats for the binaries that Linux knows how to execute, and depending on how your system is put together, you may have either. When reading this HOWTO, it helps to know which.

How to tell? Use the 'file' utility (eg `file /bin/bash`). For an ELF program it will say something with ELF in, for an a.out program it will say something involving `Linux/i386`.

The differences between ELF and a.out are covered (extensively) later in this document. ELF is the newer format, and generally accepted as better.

1.2 Administrata

The copyright information and like legalese can be found at the *end* of this document, together with the statutory warnings about asking dumb questions on Usenet, revealing your ignorance of the C language by reporting bugs which aren't, and picking your nose while chewing gum.

1.3 Typography

If you're reading this in Postscipt, dvi, or html format, you get to see a little more font variation than people with the plain text version. In particular, filenames, commands, command output and source code excerpts are set in some form of `typewriter` font, whereas 'variables' and random things that need emphasizing are *empasized*.

You also get a usable index. In dvi or postscript, the numbers in the index are section numbers. In HTML they're just sequentially assigned numbers that you can click on. In the plain text version, they really are just numbers. Get an upgrade!

The Bourne (rather than C) shell syntax is used in examples. C shell users will want to use

```
% setenv FOO bar
```

where I have written

```
$ FOO=bar; export FOO
```

If the prompt shown is # rather than $, the command shown will probably only work as root. Of course, I accept no responsibility for anything that happens to your system as a result of trying these examples. Have a nice day : -)

HOWTO

2   Where to get things

2.1   This document

This document is one of the Linux HOWTO series, so is available from all Linux HOWTO repositories, such as <http://sunsite.unc.edu/pub/linux/docs/HOWTO/>. The HTML version can also be found (possibly in a slightly newer version) from <http://ftp.linux.org.uk/~barlow/howto/gcc-howto.html>.

2.2   Other documentation

The official documentation for gcc is in the source distribution (see below) as texinfo files, and as .info files. If you have a fast network connection, a cdrom, or a reasonable amount of patience, you can just untar it and copy the relevant bits into /usr/info. If not, you may find them at *tsx-11* <ftp://tsx-11.mit.edu:/pub/linux/packages/GCC/>, but not necessarily always the latest version.

There are two source of documentation for libc. GNU libc comes with info files which describe Linux libc fairly accurately except for stdio. Also, the *manpages* <ftp://sunsite.unc.edu/pub/Linux/docs/> archive are written for Linux and describe a lot of system calls (section 2) and libc functions (section 3).

2.3   GCC

There are two answers.

(a) The official Linux GCC distribution can always be found in binary (ready-compiled) form at <ftp://tsx-11.mit.edu:/pub/linux/packages/GCC/>. At the time of writing, 2.7.2 (gcc-2.7.2.bin.tar.gz) is the latest version.

(b) The latest source distribution of GCC from the Free Software Foundation can be had from *GNU archives* <ftp://prep.ai.mit.edu/pub/gnu/>. This is not necessarily always the same version as above, though it is just now. The Linux GCC maintainer(s) have made it easy for you to compile the latest version available yourself — the configure script should set it all up for you. Check *tsx-11* <ftp://tsx-11.mit.edu:/pub/linux/packages/GCC/> as well, for patches which you may want to apply.

To compile anything non-trivial (and quite a few trivial things also) you will also need the

2.4   C library and header files

What you want here depends on (i) whether your system is ELF or a.out, and (ii) which you want it to be. If you're upgrading from libc 4 to libc 5, you are recommended to look at the ELF-HOWTO from approximately the same place as you found this document.

These are available from *tsx-11* <ftp://tsx-11.mit.edu:/pub/linux/packages/GCC/> as above:

libc-5.2.18.bin.tar.gz

— ELF shared library images, static libraries and include files for the C and maths libraries.

libc-5.2.18.tar.gz

— Source for the above. You will also need the .bin. package for the header files. If you are deliberating whether to compile the C library yourself or use the binaries, the right answer in nearly all cases is to use the binaries. You will however need to roll your own if you want NYS or shadow password support.

libc-4.7.5.bin.tar.gz

— a.out shared library images and static libraries for version 4.7.5 of the C library and friends. This is designed to coexist with the libc 5 package above, but is only really necessary if you wish to keep using/developing a.out format programs.

2.5   Associated tools (as, ld, ar, strings etc)

From *tsx-11* `<ftp://tsx-11.mit.edu:/pub/linux/packages/GCC/>`, just like everything else so far. The current version is `binutils-2.6.0.2.bin.tar.gz`.

Note that the binutils are only available in ELF, the current libc version is in ELF and the a.out libc is happiest when used in conjunction with an ELF libc. C library development is moving emphatically ELFwards, and unless you have really good reasons for needing a.out things you're encouraged to follow suit.

3   GCC installation and setup

3.1   GCC versions

You can find out what GCC version you're running by typing `gcc -v` at the shell prompt. This is also a fairly reliable way to find out whether you are set up for ELF or a.out. On my system it does

```
$ gcc -v
Reading specs from /usr/lib/gcc-lib/i486-box-linux/2.7.2/specs
gcc version 2.7.2
```

The key things to note here are

- `i486`. This indicates that the gcc you are using was built for a 486 processor — you might have 386 or 586 instead. All of these chips can run code compiled for each of the others; the difference is that the 486 code has added padding in some places so runs faster on a 486. This has no detrimental performance effect on a 386, but does make the binaries slightly larger.

- `box`. This is *not* at all important, and may say something else (such as `slackware` or `debian`) or nothing at all (so that the complete directory name is `i486-linux`). If you build your own gcc, you can set this at build time for cosmetic effect. Just like I did :-)

- `linux`. This may instead say `linuxelf` or `linuxaout`, and, confusingly, the meaning of each varies according to the version that you are using.

  - `linux` means ELF if the version is 2.7.0 or newer, a.out otherwise.

  - `linuxaout` means a.out. It was introduced as a target when the definition of `linux` was changed from a.out to ELF, so you won't see any `linuxaout` gcc older than 2.7.0.

  - `linuxelf` is obsolete. It is generally a version of gcc 2.6.3 set to produce ELF executables. Note that gcc 2.6.3 has known bugs when producing code for ELF — an upgrade is advisable.

- `2.7.2` is the version number.

So, in summary, I have gcc 2.7.2 producing ELF code. Quelle surprise.

3.2   Where did it go?

If you installed gcc without watching, or if you got it as part of a distribution, you may like to find out where it lives in the filesystem. The key bits are

- `/usr/lib/gcc-lib/`*target*`/`*version*`/` (and subdirectories) is where most of the compiler lives. This includes the executable programs that do actual compiling, and some version-specific libraries and include files.

- `/usr/bin/gcc` is the compiler driver — the bit that you can actually run from the command line. This can be used with multiple versions of gcc provided that you have multiple compiler directories (as above) installed. To find out the default version it will use, type `gcc -v`. To force it to another version, type `gcc -V` *version*. For example

HOWTO

```
# gcc -v
Reading specs from /usr/lib/gcc-lib/i486-box-linux/2.7.2/specs
gcc version 2.7.2
# gcc -V 2.6.3 -v
Reading specs from /usr/lib/gcc-lib/i486-box-linux/2.6.3/specs
gcc driver version 2.7.2 executing gcc version 2.6.3
```

- /usr/*target*/(bin|lib|include)/. If you have multiple targets installed (for example, a.out and elf, or a cross-compiler of some sort, the libraries, binutils (as, ld and so on) and header files for the non-native target(s) can be found here. Even if you only have one kind of gcc installed you might find anyway that various bits for it are kept here. If not, they're in /usr/(bin|lib|include).

- /lib/,/usr/lib and others are library directories for the native system. You will also need /lib/cpp for many applications (X makes quite a lot of use of it) — either copy it from /usr/lib/gcc-lib/*target*/*version*/ or make a symlink pointing there.

3.3   Where are the header files?

Apart from whatever you install yourself under /usr/local/include, there are three main sources of header files in Linux:

- Most of /usr/include/ and its subdirectories are supplied with the libc binary package from H J Lu. I say 'most' because you may also have files from other sources (curses and dbm libraries, for example) in here, especially if you are using the newest libc distribution (which doesn't come with curses or dbm, unlike the older ones).

- /usr/include/linux and /usr/include/asm (for the files <linux/*.h> and <asm/*.h>) should be symbolic links to the directories linux/include/linux and linux/include/asm in the kernel source distribution. You need to install these if you plan to do *any* non-trivial development; they are not just there for compiling the kernel.

  You might find also that you need to do make config in the kernel directory after unpacking the sources. Many files depend on <linux/autoconf.h> which otherwise may not exist, and in some kernel versions asm is a symbolic link itself and only created at make config time.

  So, if you unpack your kernel sources under /usr/src/linux, that's

  ```
  $ cd /usr/src/linux
  $ su
  # make config
  [answer the questions.  Unless you're going to go on and build the kernel
  it doesn't matter _too_ much what you say]
  # cd /usr/include
  # ln -s ../src/linux/include/linux .
  # ln -s ../src/linux/include/asm .
  ```

- Files such as <float.h>, <limits.h>, <varargs.h>, <stdarg.h> and <stddef.h> vary according to the compiler version, so are found in /usr/lib/gcc-lib/i486-box-linux/2.7.2/include/ and places of that ilk.

3.4   Building cross compilers

3.4.1   Linux as the target platform

Assuming you have obtained the source code to gcc, usually you can just follow the instructions given in the INSTALL file for GCC. A configure -target=i486-linux -host=XXX on platform XXX followed by a make should do the trick. Note that you will need the Linux includes, the kernel includes, and also to build the cross assembler and cross linker from the sources in <ftp://tsx-11.mit.edu/pub/linux/packages/GCC/>.

3.4.2 Linux as the source platform, MSDOS as the target

Ugh. Apparently this is somewhat possible by using the "emx" package or the "go" extender. Please look at `<ftp://sunsite.unc.edu/pub/Linux/devel/msdos>`.

I have not tested this and cannot vouch for its abilities.

4 Porting and Compiling

4.1 Automatically defined symbols

You can find out what symbols your version of gcc defines automatically by running it with the `-v` switch. For example, mine does:

```
$ echo 'main(){printf("hello world\n");}' | gcc -E -v -
Reading specs from /usr/lib/gcc-lib/i486-box-linux/2.7.2/specs
gcc version 2.7.2
 /usr/lib/gcc-lib/i486-box-linux/2.7.2/cpp -lang-c -v -undef
-D__GNUC__=2 -D__GNUC_MINOR__=7 -D__ELF__ -Dunix -Di386 -Dlinux
-D__ELF__ -D__unix__ -D__i386__ -D__linux__ -D__unix -D__i386
-D__linux -Asystem(unix) -Asystem(posix) -Acpu(i386)
-Amachine(i386) -D__i486__ -
```

If you are writing code that uses Linux-specific features, it is a good idea to enclose the nonportable bits in

```
#ifdef __linux__
/* ... funky stuff ... */
#endif /* linux */
```

Use `__linux__` for this purpose, *not* `linux`. Although the latter is defined, it is not POSIX compliant.

4.2 Compiler invocation

The documentation for compiler switches is the gcc info page (in Emacs, use `C-h i` then select the 'gcc' option). Your distributor may not have packed this with your system, or you may have an old version; the best thing to do in this case is to download the gcc source archive from `<ftp://prep.ai.mit.edu/pub/gnu>` or one of its mirrors, and copy them out of it.

The gcc manual page (`gcc.1`) is, generally speaking, out of date. It will warn you of this when you try to look at it.

4.2.1 Compiler flags

gcc can be made to optimize its output code by adding `-On` to its command line, where *n* is an optional small integer. Meaningful values of *n*, and their exact effect, vary according to the exact version, but typically it ranges from 0 (no optimization) to 2 (lots) or 3 (lots and lots).

Internally, gcc translates these to a series of `-f` and `-m` options. You can see exactly which `-O` levels map to which options by running gcc with the `-v` flag and the (undocumented) `-Q` flag. For example, for `-O2`, mine says

```
enabled: -fdefer-pop -fcse-follow-jumps -fcse-skip-blocks
-fexpensive-optimizations
        -fthread-jumps -fpeephole -fforce-mem -ffunction-cse -finline
-fcaller-saves -fpcc-struct-return -frerun-cse-after-loop
-fcommon -fgnu-linker -m80387 -mhard-float -mno-soft-float
        -mno-386 -m486 -mieee-fp -mfp-ret-in-387
```

Using an optimization level higher than your compiler supports (e.g. -O6) will have exactly the same effect as using the highest level that it *does* support. Distributing code which is set to compile this way is a poor idea though — if further optimisations are incorporated into future versions, you (or your users) may find that they break your code.

Users of gcc 2.7.0 thru 2.7.2 should note that there is a bug in -O2 on these. Specifically, strength reduction doesn't work. A patch can be had to fix this if you feel like recompiling gcc, otherwise make sure that you always compile with -fno-strength-reduce

Processor-specific There are other -m flags which aren't turned on by any variety of -O but are nevertheless useful. Chief among these are -m386 and -m486, which tell gcc to favour the 386 or 486 respectively. Code compiled with one of these will still work on the other; 486 code is bigger, but otherwise not slower on the 386.

There is currently no -mpentium or -m586. Linus suggests using -m486 -malign-loops=2 -malign-jumps=2 -malign-functions=2, to get 486 code optimisations but without the big gaps for alignment (which the pentium doesn't need). Michael Meissner (of Cygnus) says

> My hunch is that -mno-strength-reduce also results in faster code on the x86 (note, I'm not talking about the strength reduction bug, which is another issue). This is because the x86 is rather register starved (and GCC's method of grouping registers into spill registers vs. other registers doesn't help either). Strength reduction typically results in using additional registers to replace multiplications with addition. I also suspect -fcaller-saves may also be a loss.

> Another hunch is that -fomit-frame-pointer might or might not be a win. On the one hand, it can mean that another register is available for allocation. On the other hand, the way the x86 encodes its instruction set, means that stack relative addresses take more space instead of frame relative addresses, which means slightly less Icache availble to the program. Also, -fomit-frame-pointer, means that the compiler has to constantly adjust the stack pointer after calls, while with a frame, it can let the stack accumulate for a few calls.

The final word on this subject is from Linus again:

> Note that if you want to get optimal performance, don't believe me: test. There are lots of gcc compiler switches, and it may be that a particular set gives the best optimizations for you.

4.2.2 Internal compiler error: cc1 got fatal signal 11

Signal 11 is SIGSEGV, or 'segmentation violation'. Usually it means that the program got its pointers confused and tried to write to memory it didn't own. So, it could be a gcc bug.

gcc is however, a well tested and reliable piece of software, for the most part. It also uses a large number of complex data structures, and an awful lot of pointers. In short, it's the pickiest RAM tester commonly available. If you *can't duplicate the bug* — if it doesn't stop in the same place when you restart the compilation — it's almost certainly a problem with your hardware (CPU, memory, motherboard or cache). **Don't** claim it as a bug because your computer passes the power-on checks or runs Windows ok or whatever; these 'tests' are commonly and rightly held to be worthless. And don't claim it's a bug because a kernel compile always stops during 'make zImage' — of course it will! 'make zImage' is probably compiling over 200 files; we're looking for a slightly *smaller* place than that.

If you can duplicate the bug, and (better) can produce a short program that exhibits it, you can submit it as a bug report to the FSF, or to the linux-gcc mailing list. See the gcc documentation for details of exactly what information they need.

4.3 Portability

It has been said that, these days, if something hasn't been ported to Linux then it is not worth having :-)

Seriously though, in general only minor changes are needed to the sources to get over Linux's 100% POSIX compliance. It is also worthwhile passing back any changes to authors of the code such that in the future only 'make' need be called to provide a working executable.

4.3.1 BSDisms (including `bsd_ioctl`, `daemon` and `<sgtty.h>`)

You can compile your program with `-I/usr/include/bsd` and link it with `-lbsd` (i.e. add `-I/usr/include/bsd` to `CFLAGS` and `-lbsd` to the `LDFLAGS` line in your Makefile). There is *no* need to add `-D__USE_BSD_SIGNAL` any more if you want BSD type signal behavior, as you get this automatically when you have `-I/usr/include/bsd` and include `<signal.h>`.

4.3.2 'Missing' signals (`SIGBUS`, `SIGEMT`, `SIGIOT`, `SIGTRAP`, `SIGSYS` etc)

Linux is POSIX compliant. These are not POSIX-defined signals — ISO/IEC 9945-1:1990 (IEEE Std 1003.1-1990), paragraph B.3.3.1.1 sez:

> "The signals SIGBUS, SIGEMT, SIGIOT, SIGTRAP, and SIGSYS were omitted from POSIX.1 because their behavior is implementation dependent and could not be adequately categorized. Conforming implementations may deliver these signals, but must document the circumstances under which they are delivered and note any restrictions concerning their delivery."

The cheap and cheesy way to fix this is to redefine these signals to `SIGUNUSED`. The *correct* way is to bracket the code that handles them with appropriate `#ifdefs`:

```
#ifdef SIGSYS
/* ... non-posix SIGSYS code here .... */
#endif
```

4.3.3 K & R Code

GCC is an ANSI compiler; much existing code is not ANSI. There's really not much that can be done about this, except to add `-traditional` to the compiler flags. There is a certain amount of finer-grained control over which varieties of brain damage to emulate; consult the gcc info page.

Note that `-traditional` has effects beyond just changing the language that gcc accepts. For example, it turns on `-fwritable-strings`, which moves string constants into data space (from text space, where they cannot be written to). This increases the memory footprint of the program.

4.3.4 Preprocessor symbols conflict with prototypes in the code

One of the most frequent problems is that some common functions are defined as macros in Linux's header files and the preprocessor will refuse to parse similar prototype definitions in the code. Common ones are `atoi()` and `atol()`.

4.3.5 `sprintf()`

Something to be aware of, especially when porting from SunOS, is that `sprintf(string, fmt, ...)` returns a pointer to `string` on many unices, whereas Linux (following ANSI) returns the number of characters which were put into the string.

4.3.6 `fcntl` and friends. Where are the definitions of `FD_*` stuff ?

In `<sys/time.h>`. If you are using `fcntl` you probably want to include `<unistd.h>` too, for the actual prototype.

Generally speaking, the manual page for a function lists the necessary `#include`s in its SYNOPSIS section.

4.3.7 The `select()` timeout. Programs start busy-waiting.

Once upon a time, the timeout parameter to `select()` was used read-only. Even then, manual pages warned:

> select() should probably return the time remaining from the original timeout, if any, by modifying the time value in place. This may be implemented in future versions of the system. Thus, it is unwise to assume that the timeout pointer will be unmodified by the select() call.

The future has arrived! At least, it has here. On return from a `select()`, the timeout argument will be set to the remaining time that it would have waited had data not arrived. If no data had arrived, this will be zero, and future calls using the same timeout structure will immediately return.

To fix, put the timeout value into that structure every time you call `select()`. Change code like

```
struct timeval timeout;
timeout.tv_sec = 1; timeout.tv_usec = 0;
while (some_condition)
        select(n,readfds,writefds,exceptfds,&timeout);
```

to, say,

```
struct timeval timeout;
while (some_condition) {
        timeout.tv_sec = 1; timeout.tv_usec = 0;
        select(n,readfds,writefds,exceptfds,&timeout);
}
```

Some versions of Mosaic were at one time notable for this problem. The speed of the spinning globe animation was inversely related to the speed that the data was coming in from the network at!

4.3.8 Interrupted system calls.

Symptom: When a program is stopped using Ctrl-Z and then restarted - or in other situations that generate signals: Ctrl-C interruption, termination of a child process etc. - it complains about "interrupted system call" or "write: unknown error" or things like that.

Problem: POSIX systems check for signals a bit more often than some older unices. Linux may execute signal handlers —

- asynchronously (at a timer tick)
- on return from any system call
- during the execution of the following system calls: `select()`, `pause()`, `connect()`, `accept()`, `read()` on terminals, sockets, pipes or files in `/proc`, `write()` on terminals, sockets, pipes or the line printer, `open()` on FIFOs, PTYs or serial lines, `ioctl()` on terminals, `fcntl()` with command `F_SETLKW`, `wait4()`, `syslog()`, any TCP or NFS operations.

For other operating systems you may have to include the system calls `creat()`, `close()`, `getmsg()`, `putmsg()`, `msgrcv()`, `msgsnd()`, `recv()`, `send()`, `wait()`, `waitpid()`, `wait3()`, `tcdrain()`, `sigpause()`, `semop()` to this list.

If a signal (that the program has installed a handler for) occurs during a system call, the handler is called. When the handler returns (to the system call) it detects that it was interrupted, and immediately returns with -1 and `errno = EINTR`. The program is not expecting that to happen, so bottles out.

You may choose between two fixes.

(1) For every signal handler that you install, add `SA_RESTART` to the sigaction flags. For example, change

```
signal (sig_nr, my_signal_handler);
```

to

```
        signal (sig_nr, my_signal_handler);
    { struct sigaction sa;
        sigaction (sig_nr, (struct sigaction *)0, &sa);
#ifdef SA_RESTART
        sa.sa_flags |= SA_RESTART;
#endif
#ifdef SA_INTERRUPT
        sa.sa_flags &= ~ SA_INTERRUPT;
#endif
        sigaction (sig_nr, &sa, (struct sigaction *)0);
    }
```

Note that while this applies to most system calls, you must still check for `EINTR` yourself on `read()`, `write()`, `ioctl()`, `select()`, `pause()` and `connect()`. See below.

(2) Check for `EINTR` explicitly, yourself:

Here are two examples for `read()` and `ioctl()`,

Original piece of code using `read()`

```
    int result;
    while (len > 0) {
      result = read(fd,buffer,len);
      if (result < 0) break;
      buffer += result; len -= result;
    }
```

becomes

```
    int result;
    while (len > 0) {
      result = read(fd,buffer,len);
      if (result < 0) { if (errno != EINTR) break; }
      else { buffer += result; len -= result; }
    }
```

and a piece of code using `ioctl()`

```
    int result;
    result = ioctl(fd,cmd,addr);
```

becomes

```
    int result;
    do { result = ioctl(fd,cmd,addr); }
    while ((result == -1) && (errno == EINTR));
```

Note that in some versions of BSD Unix the default behaviour is to restart system calls. To get system calls interrupted you have to use the `SV_INTERRUPT` or `SA_INTERRUPT` flag.

4.3.9   Writable strings (program seg faults randomly)

GCC has an optimistic view of its users, believing that they intend string constants to be exactly that — constant. Thus, it stores them in the text (code) area of the program, where they can be paged in and out from the program's disk image (instead of taking up swapspace), and any attempt to rewrite them will cause a segmentation fault. This is a feature!

It may cause a problem for old programs that, for example, call `mktemp()` with a string constant as argument. `mktemp()` attempts to rewrite its argument in place.

To fix, either (a) compile with `-fwritable-strings`, to get gcc to put constants in data space, or (b) rewrite the offending parts to allocate a non-constant string and strcpy the data into it before calling.

4.3.10 Why does the `execl()` call fail?

Because you're calling it wrong. The first argument to `execl` is the program that you want to run. The second and subsequent arguments become the `argv` array of the program you're calling. Remember: `argv[0]` is traditionally set even when a program is run with 'no' arguments. So, you should be writing

```
execl("/bin/ls","ls",NULL);
```

not just

```
execl("/bin/ls", NULL);
```

Executing the program with no arguments at all is construed as an invitation to print out its dynamic library dependencies, at least using a.out. ELF does things differently.

(If you want this library information, there are simpler interfaces; see the section on dynamic loading, or the manual page for `ldd`).

5 Debugging and Profiling

5.1 Preventative maintenance (lint)

There is no widely-used lint for Linux, as most people are satisfied with the warnings that gcc can generate. Probably the most useful is the `-Wall` switch — this stands for 'Warnings, all' but probably has more mnemonic value if thought of as the thing you bang your head against.

There is a public domain lint available from `<ftp://larch.lcs.mit.edu/pub/Larch/lclint>`. I don't know how good it is.

5.2 Debugging

5.2.1 How do I get debugging information into a program ?

You need to compile and link all its bits with the `-g` switch, and without the `-fomit-frame-pointer` switch. Actually, you don't need to recompile all of it, just the bits you're interested in debugging.

On a.out configurations the shared libraries are compiled with `-fomit-frame-pointer`, which gdb won't get on with. Giving the `-g` option when you link should imply static linking; this is why.

If the linker fails with a message about not finding libg.a, you don't have `/usr/lib/libg.a`, which is the special debugging-enabled C library. It may be supplied in the libc binary package, or (in newer C library versions) you may need to get the libc source code and build it yourself. You don't actually *need* it though; you can get enough information for most purposes simply by symlinking it to `/usr/lib/libc.a`

How do I get it out again? A lot of GNU software comes set up to compile and link with `-g`, causing it to make very big (and often static) executables. This is not really such a hot idea.

If the program has an autoconf generated `configure` script, you can usually turn off debugging information by doing `./configure CFLAGS=` or `./configure CFLAGS=-O2`. Otherwise, check the Makefile. Of course, if you're using ELF, the program is dynamically linked regardless of the `-g` setting, so you can just `strip` it.

5.2.2 Available software

Most people use **gdb**, which you can get in source form from *GNU archive sites* `<ftp://prep.ai.mit.edu/pub/gnu>`, or as a binary from *tsx-11* `<ftp://tsx-11.mit.edu/pub/linux/packages/GCC>` or sunsite. **xxgdb** is an X debugger based on this (i.e. you need gdb installed first). The source may be found at `<ftp://ftp.x.org/contrib/xxgdb-1.08.tar.gz>`

Also, the **UPS** debugger has been ported by Rick Sladkey. It runs under X as well, but unlike xxgdb, it is not merely an X front end for a text based debugger. It has quite a number of nice features, and if you spend any time debugging stuff, you probably should check it out. The Linux precompiled version and patches for the stock UPS sources can be found in `<ftp://sunsite.unc.edu/pub/Linux/devel/debuggers/>`, and the original source at `<ftp://ftp.x.org/contrib/ups-2.45.2.tar.Z>`.

Another tool you might find useful for debugging is '**strace**', which displays the system calls that a process makes. It has a multiplicity of other uses too, including figuring out what pathnames were compiled into binaries that you don't have the source for, exacerbating race conditions in programs that you suspect contain them, and generally learning how things work. The latest version of strace (currently 3.0.8) can be found at `<ftp://ftp.std.com/pub/jrs/>`.

5.2.3 Background (daemon) programs

Daemon programs typically execute `fork()` early, and terminate the parent. This makes for a short debugging session. The simplest way to get around this is to set a breakpoint for `fork`, and when the program stops, force it to return 0.

```
(gdb) list
1       #include <stdio.h>
2
3       main()
4       {
5         if(fork()==0) printf("child\n");
6         else printf("parent\n");
7       }
(gdb) break fork
Breakpoint 1 at 0x80003b8
(gdb) run
Starting program: /home/dan/src/hello/./fork
Breakpoint 1 at 0x400177c4

Breakpoint 1, 0x400177c4 in fork ()
(gdb) return 0
Make selected stack frame return now? (y or n) y
#0  0x80004a8 in main ()
    at fork.c:5
5         if(fork()==0) printf("child\n");
(gdb) next
Single stepping until exit from function fork,
which has no line number information.
child
7       }
```

5.2.4 Core files

When Linux boots it is usually configured not to produce core files. If you like them, use your shell's builtin command to re-enable them: for C-shell compatibles (e.g. tcsh) this is

```
% limit core unlimited
```

while Bourne-like shells (sh, bash, zsh, pdksh) use

```
$ ulimit -c unlimited
```

If you want a bit more versatility in your core file naming (for example, if you're trying to conduct a post-mortem using a debugger that's buggy itself) you can make a simple mod to your kernel. Look for the code in `fs/binfmt_aout.c` and `fs/binfmt_elf.c` (in newer kernels, you'll have to grep around a little in older ones) that says

```
        memcpy(corefile,"core.",5);
#if 0
        memcpy(corefile+5,current->comm,sizeof(current->comm));
#else
        corefile[4] = '\0';
#endif
```

and change the 0s to 1s.

5.3   Profiling

Profiling is a way to examine which bits of a program are called most often or run for longest. It is a good way to optimize code and look at where time is being wasted. You must compile all object files that you require timing information for with `-p`, and to make sense of the output file you will also need `gprof` (from the binutils package). See the `gprof` manual page for details.

6   Linking

Between the two incompatible binary formats, the static vs shared library distinction, and the overloading of the verb 'link' to mean both 'what happens after compilation' and 'what happens when a compiled program is invoked' (and, actually, the overloading of the word 'load' in a comparable but opposite sense), this section is complicated. Little of it is much more complicated than that sentence, though, so don't worry too much about it.

To alleviate the confusion somewhat, we refer to what happens at runtime as 'dynamic loading' and cover it in the next section. You will also see it described as 'dynamic linking', but not here. This section, then, is exclusively concerned with the kind of linking that happens at the end of a compilation.

6.1   Shared vs static libraries

The last stage of building a program is to 'link' it; to join all the pieces of it together and see what is missing. Obviously there are some things that many programs will want to do — open files, for example, and the pieces that do these things are provided for you in the form of libraries. On the average Linux system these can be found in `/lib` and `/usr/lib/`, among other places.

When using a static library, the linker finds the bits that the program modules need, and physically copies them into the executable output file that it generates. For shared libraries, it doesn't — instead it leaves a note in the output saying 'when this program is run, it will first have to load this library'. Obviously shared libraries tend to make for smaller executables; they also use less memory and mean that less disk space is used. The default behaviour of Linux is to link shared if it can find the shared libraries, static otherwise. If you're getting static binaries when you want shared, check that the shared library files (`*.sa` for a.out, `*.so` for ELF) are where they should be, and are readable.

On Linux, static libraries have names like `libname.a`, while shared libraries are called `libname.so.x.y.z` where `x.y.z` is some form of version number. Shared libraries often also have links pointing to them, which are important, and (on a.out configurations) associated `.sa` files. The standard libraries come in both shared and static formats.

You can find out what shared libraries a program requires by using `ldd` (List Dynamic Dependencies)

```
$ ldd /usr/bin/lynx
        libncurses.so.1 => /usr/lib/libncurses.so.1.9.6
        libc.so.5 => /lib/libc.so.5.2.18
```

This shows that on my system the WWW browser 'lynx' depends on the presence of `libc.so.5` (the C library) and `libncurses.so.1` (used for terminal control). If a program has no dependencies, `ldd` will say 'statically linked' or 'statically linked (ELF)'.

6.2 Interrogating libraries ('which library is `sin()` in?')

`nm` *libraryname* should list all the symbols that *libraryname* has references to. It works on both static and shared libraries. Suppose that you want to know where `tcgetattr()` is defined: you might do

```
$ nm libncurses.so.1 |grep tcget
        U tcgetattr
```

The U stands for 'undefined' — it shows that the ncurses library uses but does not define it. You could also do

```
$ nm libc.so.5 | grep tcget
00010fe8 T __tcgetattr
00010fe8 W tcgetattr
00068718 T tcgetpgrp
```

The 'W' stands for 'weak', which means that the symbol is defined, but in such a way that it can be overridden by another definition in a different library. A straightforward 'normal' definition (such as the one for `tcgetpgrp`) is marked by a 'T'

The short answer to the question in the title, by the way, is `libm.(so|a)`. All the functions defined in `<math.h>` are kept in the maths library; thus you need to link with `-lm` when using any of them.

6.3 Finding files

`ld: Output file requires shared library 'libfoo.so.1'`

The file search strategy of ld and friends varies according to version, but the only default you can reasonably assume is `/usr/lib`. If you want libraries elsewhere to be searched, specify their directories with the `-L` option to gcc or ld.

If that doesn't help, check that you have the right file in that place. For a.out, linking with `-lfoo` makes ld look for `libfoo.sa` (shared stubs), and if unsuccessful then for `libfoo.a` (static). For ELF, it looks for `libfoo.so` then `libfoo.a`. `libfoo.so` is usually a symbolic link to `libfoo.so.x`.

6.4 Building your own libraries

6.4.1 Version control

As any other program, libraries tend to have bugs which get fixed over time. They also may introduce new features, change the effect of existing ones, or remove old ones. This could be a problem for programs using them; what if it was depending on that old feature?

So, we introduce library versioning. We categorise the changes that might be made to a library as 'minor' or 'major', and we rule that a 'minor' change is not allowed to break old programs that are using the library. You can tell the version of a library by looking at its filename (actually, this is, strictly speaking, a lie for ELF; keep reading to find out why) : `libfoo.so.1.2` has major version 1, minor version 2. The minor version number can be more or less anything — libc puts a 'patchlevel' in it, giving library names like `libc.so.5.2.18`, and it's also reasonable to put letters, underscores, or more or less any printable ASCII in it.

One of the major differences between ELF and a.out format is in building shared libraries. We look at ELF first, because it's simpler.

6.4.2   ELF? What is it then, anyway?

ELF (Executable and Linking Format) is a binary format originally developed by USL (UNIX System Laboratories) and currently used in Solaris and System V Release 4. Because of its increased flexibility over the older a.out format that Linux was using, the GCC and C library developers decided last year to move to using ELF as the Linux standard binary format also.

Come again?   This section is from the document '/news-archives/comp.sys.sun.misc'.

> ELF ("Executable Linking Format) is the "new, improved" object file format introduced in SVR4. ELF is much more powerful than straight COFF, in that it *is* user-extensible. ELF views an object-file as an arbitrarily long list of sections (rather than an array of fixed size entities), these sections, unlike in COFF, do not HAVE to be in a certain place and do not HAVE to come in any specific order etc. Users can add new sections to object-files if they wish to capture new data. ELF also has a far more powerful debugging format called DWARF (Debugging With Attribute Record Format) - not currently fully supported on linux (but work is underway). A linked list of DWARF DIEs (or Debugging Information Entries) forms the .debug section in ELF. Instead of being a collection of small, fixed-size information records, DWARF DIEs each contain an arbitrarily long list of complex attributes and are written out as a scope-based tree of program data. DIEs can capture a large amount of information that the COFF .debug section simply couldn't (like C++ inheritance graphs etc.).

> ELF files are accessed via the SVR4 (Solaris 2.0 ?) ELF access library, which provides an easy and fast interface to the more gory parts of ELF. One of the major boons in using the ELF access library is that you will never need to look at an ELF file qua. UNIX file, it is accessed as an Elf *, after an elf_open() call and from then on, you perform elf_foobar() calls on its components instead of messing about with its actual on-disk image (something many COFFers did with impunity).

The case for/against ELF, and the necessary contortions to upgrade an a.out system to support it, are covered in the ELF-HOWTO and I don't propose to cut/paste them here. The HOWTO should be available in the same place as you found this one.

ELF shared libraries   To build `libfoo.so` as a shared library, the basic steps look like this:

```
$ gcc -fPIC -c *.c
$ gcc -shared -Wl,-soname,libfoo.so.1 -o libfoo.so.1.0 *.o
$ ln -s libfoo.so.1.0 libfoo.so.1
$ ln -s libfoo.so.1 libfoo.so
$ LD_LIBRARY_PATH='pwd':$LD_LIBRARY_PATH ; export LD_LIBRARY_PATH
```

This will generate a shared library called `libfoo.so.1.0`, and the appropriate links for ld (`libfoo.so`) and the dynamic loader (`libfoo.so.1`) to find it. To test, we add the current directory to `LD_LIBRARY_PATH`.

When you're happpy that the library works, you'll have to move it to, say, `/usr/local/lib`, and recreate the appropriate links. The link from `libfoo.so.1` to `libfoo.so.1.0` is kept up to date by `ldconfig`, which on most systems is run as part of the boot process. The `libfoo.so` link must be updated manually. If you are scrupulous about upgrading all the parts of a library (e.g. the header files) at the same time, the simplest thing to do is make `libfoo.so` -> `libfoo.so.1`, so that ldconfig will keep both links current for you. If you *aren't*, you're setting yourself up to have *all kinds of weird things* happen at a later date. Don't say you weren't warned.

```
$ su
# cp libfoo.so.1.0 /usr/local/lib
# /sbin/ldconfig
# ( cd /usr/local/lib ; ln -s libfoo.so.1 libfoo.so )
```

Version numbering, sonames and symlinks   Each library has a *soname*. When the linker finds one of these in a library it is searching, it embeds the soname into the binary instead of the actual filename it is looking at. At runtime, the dynamic loader will then search for a file with the name of the soname, not the library filename. Thus a library called `libfoo.so` could have a soname `libbar.so`, and all programs linked to it would look for `libbar.so` instead when they started.

This sounds like a pointless feature, but it is key to understanding how multiple versions of the same library can coexist on a system. The de facto naming standard for libraries in Linux is to call the library, say, `libfoo.so.1.2`, and give it a soname of `libfoo.so.1`. If it's added to a 'standard' library directory (e.g. `/usr/lib`), `ldconfig` will create a symlink `libfoo.so.1 -> libfoo.so.1.2` so that the appropriate image is found at runtime. You also need a link `libfoo.so -> libfoo.so.1` so that ld will find the right soname to use at link time.

So, when you fix bugs in the library, or add new functions (any changes that won't adversely affect existing programs), you rebuild it, keeping the soname as it was, and changing the filename. When you make changes to the library that would break existing binaries, you simply increment the number in the soname — in this case, call the new version `libfoo.so.2.0`, and give it a soname of `libfoo.so.2`. Now switch the `libfoo.so` link to point to the new version and all's well with the world again.

Note that you don't *have* to name libraries this way, but it's a good convention. ELF gives you the flexibility to name libraries in ways that will confuse the pants off people, but that doesn't mean you have to use it.

Executive summary: supposing that you observe the tradition that major upgrades may break compatibility, minor upgrades may not, then link with

```
gcc -shared -Wl,-soname,libfoo.so.major -o libfoo.so.major.minor
```

and everything will be all right.

6.4.3   a.out. Ye olde traditional format

The ease of building shared libraries is a major reason for upgrading to ELF. That said, it's still possible in a.out. Get `<ftp://tsx-11.mit.edu/pub/linux/packages/GCC/src/tools-2.17.tar.gz>` and read the 20 page document that you will find after unpacking it. I hate to be so transparently partisan, but it should be clear from context that I never bothered myself :-)

ZMAGIC vs QMAGIC   QMAGIC is an executable format just like the old a.out (also known as ZMAGIC) binaries, but which leaves the first page unmapped. This allows for easier NULL dereference trapping as no mapping exists in the range 0-4096. As a side effect your binaries are nominally smaller as well (by about 1K).

Obsolescent linkers support ZMAGIC only, semi-obsolescent support both formats, and current versions support QMAGIC only. This doesn't actually matter, though, as the kernel can still run both formats.

Your 'file' command should be able to identify whether a program is QMAGIC.

File Placement   An a.out (DLL) shared library consists of two real files and a symlink. For the 'foo' library used throughout this document as an example, these files would be `libfoo.sa` and `libfoo.so.1.2`; the symlink would be `libfoo.so.1` and would point at the latter of the files. What are these for?

At compile time, `ld` looks for `libfoo.sa`. This is the 'stub' file for the library, and contains all exported data and pointers to the functions required for run time linking.

At run time, the dynamic loader looks for `libfoo.so.1`. This is a symlink rather than a real file so that libraries can be updated with newer, bugfixed versions without crashing any application that was using the library at the time. After the new version — say, `libfoo.so.1.3` — is completely there, running ldconfig will switch the link to point to it in one atomic operation, leaving any program which had the old version still perfectly happy.

DLL libraries (I know that's a tautology — so sue me) often appear bigger than their static counterparts. They reserve space for future expansion in the form of 'holes' which can be made to take no disk space. A simple cp call or using the program `makehole` will achieve this. You can also strip them after building, as the addresses are in fixed locations. **Do not attempt to strip ELF libraries**.

"libc-lite"? A libc-lite is a light-weight version of the libc library built such that it will fit on a floppy and suffice for all of the most menial of UNIX tasks. It does *not* include curses, dbm, termcap etc code. If your `/lib/libc.so.4` is linked to a lite lib, you are advised to replace it with a full version.

6.4.4 Linking: common problems

Send me your linking problems! I probably won't do anything about them, but I will write them up if I get enough ...

Programs link static when you wanted them shared

Check that you have the right links for `ld` to find each shared library. For ELF this means a `libfoo.so` symlink to the image, for a.out a `libfoo.sa` file. A lot of people had this problem after moving from ELF binutils 2.5 to 2.6 — the earlier version searched more 'intelligently' for shared libraries, so they hadn't created all the links. The intelligent behaviour was removed for compatibility with other architectures, and because quite often it got its assumptions wrong and caused more trouble than it solved.

The DLL tool 'mkimage' fails to find libgcc, or

As of `libc.so.4.5.x` and above, libgcc is no longer shared. Hence you must replace occurrences of '`-lgcc`' on the offending line with '`gcc -print-libgcc-file-name`' (complete with the backquotes).

Also, delete all `/usr/lib/libgcc*` files. This is important.

`__NEEDS_SHRLIB_libc_4` multiply defined messages

are another consequence of the same problem.

"Assertion failure" message when rebuilding a DLL ?

This cryptic message most probably means that one of your jump table slots has overflowed because too little space has been reserved in the original `jump.vars` file. You can locate the culprit(s) by running the '`getsize`' command provided in the tools-2.17.tar.gz package. Probably the only solution, though, is to bump the major version number of the library, forcing it to be backward incompatible.

`ld: output file needs shared library libc.so.4`

This usually happens when you are linking with libraries other than libc (e.g. X libraries), and use the `-g` switch on the link line without also using `-static`.

The `.sa` stubs for the shared libraries usually have an undefined symbol `_NEEDS_SHRLIB_libc_4` which gets resolved from the `libc.sa` stub. However with `-g` you end up linking with `libg.a` or `libc.a` and thus this symbol never gets resolved, leading to the above error message.

In conclusion, add `-static` when compiling with the `-g` flag, or don't link with `-g`. Quite often you can get enough debugging information by compiling the individual files with `-g`, and linking *without* it.

7 Dynamic Loading

This section is a tad short right now; it will be expanded over time as I gut the ELF howto

7.1 Concepts

Linux has shared libraries, as you will by now be sick of hearing if you read the whole of the last section at a sitting. Some of the matching-names-to-places work which was traditionally done at link time must be deferred to load time.

7.2 Error messages

Send me your link errors! I won't do anything about them, but I might write them up ...

```
can't load library:   /lib/libxxx.so, Incompatible version
```

(a.out only) This means that you don't have the correct major version of the xxx library. No, you can't just make a symlink to another version that you do have; if you are lucky this will cause your program to segfault. Get the new version. A similar situation with ELF will result in a message like

```
ftp: can't load library 'libreadline.so.2'
```

```
warning using incompatible library version xxx
```

(a.out only) You have an older minor version of the library than the person who compiled the program used. The program will still run. Probably. An upgrade wouldn't hurt, though.

7.3 Controlling the operation of the dynamic loader

There are a range of environment variables that the dynamic loader will respond to. Most of these are more use to `ldd` than they are to the average user, and can most conveniently be set by running ldd with various switches. They include

- `LD_BIND_NOW` — normally, functions are not 'looked up' in libraries until they are called. Setting this flag causes all the lookups to happen when the library is loaded, giving a slower startup time. It's useful when you want to test a program to make sure that everything is linked.

- `LD_PRELOAD` can be set to a file containing 'overriding' function definitions. For example, if you were testing memory allocation strategies, and wanted to replace 'malloc', you could write your replacement routine, compile it into `malloc.o` and then

  ```
  $ LD_PRELOAD=malloc.o; export LD_PRELOAD
  $ some_test_program
  ```

  `LD_ELF_PRELOAD` and `LD_AOUT_PRELOAD` are similar, but only apply to the appropriate type of binary. If `LD_something_PRELOAD` and `LD_PRELOAD` are set, the more specific one is used.

- `LD_LIBRARY_PATH` is a colon-separated list of directories in which to look for shared libraries. It does *not* affect `ld`; it only has effect at runtime. Also, it is disabled for programs that run setuid or setgid. Again, `LD_ELF_LIBRARY_PATH` and `LD_AOUT_LIBRARY_PATH` can also be used to direct the search differently for different flavours of binary. `LD_LIBRARY_PATH` shouldn't be necessary in normal operation; add the directories to `/etc/ld.so.conf/` and rerun ldconfig instead.

- `LD_NOWARN` applies to a.out only. When set (e.g. with `LD_NOWARN=true; export LD_NOWARN`) it stops the loader from issuing non-fatal warnings (such as minor version incompatibility messages).

- `LD_WARN` applies to ELF only. When set, it turns the usually fatal "Can't find library" messages into warnings. It's not much use in normal operation, but important for ldd.

- `LD_TRACE_LOADED_OBJECTS` applies to ELF only, and causes programs to think they're being run under `ldd`:

  ```
  $ LD_TRACE_LOADED_OBJECTS=true /usr/bin/lynx
          libncurses.so.1 => /usr/lib/libncurses.so.1.9.6
          libc.so.5 => /lib/libc.so.5.2.18
  ```

7.4 Writing programs with dynamic loading

This is very close to the way that Solaris 2.x dynamic loading support works, if you're familiar with that. It is covered extensively in H J Lu's ELF programming document, and the `dlopen(3)` manual page, which can be found in the ld.so package. Here's a nice simple example though: link it with `-ldl`

```
#include <dlfcn.h>
#include <stdio.h>

main()
{
  void *libc;
```

```
    void (*printf_call)();

if(libc=dlopen("/lib/libc.so.5",RTLD_LAZY))
{
    printf_call=dlsym(libc,"printf");
    (*printf_call)("hello, world\n");
}

}
```

8 Contacting the developers

8.1 Bug reports

Start by **narrowing the problem down**. Is it specific to Linux, or does it happen with gcc on other systems? Is it specific to the kernel version? Library version? Does it go away if you link static? Can you trim the program down to something **short** that demonstrates the bug?

Having done that, you'll know what program(s) the bug is in. For GCC, the bug reporting procedure is explained in the info file. For ld.so or the C or maths libraries, send mail to linux-gcc@vger.rutgers.edu. If possible, include a short and self-contained program that exhibits the bug, and a description both of what you want it to do, and what it actually does.

8.2 Helping with development

If you want to help with the development effort for GCC or the C library, the first thing to do is join the linux-gcc@vger.rutgers.edu mailing list. If you just want to see what the discussion is about, there are list archives at <http://homer.ncm.com/linux-gcc/>. The second and subsequent things depend on what you want to do!

9 The Remains

9.1 The Credits

> Only presidents, editors, and people with tapeworms have the right to use the editorial "we".

(Mark Twain)

This HOWTO is based very closely on Mitchum DSouza's GCC-FAQ; most of the information (not to mention a reasonable amount of the text) in it comes directly from that document. Instances of the first person pronoun in this HOWTO could refer to either of us; generally the ones that say "I have not tested this; don't blame me if it toasts your hard disk/system/spouse" apply to both of us.

Contributors to this document have included (in ASCII ordering by first name) Andrew Tefft, Axel Boldt, Bill Metzenthen, Bruce Evans, Bruno Haible, Daniel Barlow, Daniel Quinlan, David Engel, Dirk Hohndel, Eric Youngdale, Fergus Henderson, H.J. Lu, Jens Schweikhardt, Kai Petzke, Michael Meissner, Mitchum DSouza, Olaf Flebbe, Paul Gortmaker, Rik Faith, Steven S. Dick, Tuomas J Lukka, and of course Linus Torvalds, without whom the whole exercise would have been pointless, let alone impossible :-)

Please do not feel offended if your name has not appeared here and you have contributed to this document (either as HOWTO or as FAQ). Email me and I will rectify it.

9.2   Translations

At this time, there are no known translations of this work. If you wish to produce one, please go right ahead, but do tell me about it! The chances are (sadly) several hundred to one against that I speak the language you wish to translate to, but that aside I am happy to help in whatever way I can.

9.3   Feedback

is welcomed. Mail me at *dan@detached.demon.co.uk*. My PGP public key (ID 5F263625) is available from my *web pages* `<http://ftp.linux.org.uk/~barlow/>`, if you feel the need to be secretive about things.

9.4   Legalese

All trademarks used in this document are acknowledged as being owned by their respective owners.

This document is copyright (C) 1996 Daniel Barlow `<dan@detached.demon.co.uk>` It may be reproduced and distributed in whole or in part, in any medium physical or electronic, as long as this copyright notice is retained on all copies. Commercial redistribution is allowed and encouraged; however, the author would like to be notified of any such distributions.

All translations, derivative works, or aggregate works incorporating any Linux HOWTO documents must be covered under this copyright notice. That is, you may not produce a derivative work from a HOWTO and impose additional restrictions on its distribution. Exceptions to these rules may be granted under certain conditions; please contact the Linux HOWTO coordinator at the address given below.

In short, we wish to promote dissemination of this information through as many channels as possible. However, we do wish to retain copyright on the HOWTO documents, and would like to be notified of any plans to redistribute the HOWTOs.

If you have questions, please contact Tim Bynum, the Linux HOWTO coordinator, at `linux-howto@sunsite.unc.edu` via email.

10   Index

Entries starting with a non-alphabetical character are listed in ASCII order.

- `-fwritable-strings` 4.3.3 (39) 4.3.9 (56)
- /lib/cpp 3.2 (16)
- a.out 1.1 (1)
- `ar` 2.5 (10)
- `as` 2.5 (8)
- <asm/*.h> 3.3 (19)
- `atoi()` 4.3.4 (40)
- `atol()` 4.3.4 (41)
- binaries too big 5.2.1 (63) 6.1 (65) 6.4.4 (77)
- chewing gum 1.2 (3)
- `cos()` 6.2 (68)
- debugging 5.2 (59)
- `dlopen()` 7.4 (82)
- `dlsym()` 7.4 (83)

- SIGSEGV 4.2.2 (31) 4.3.9 (53)
- SIGSEGV, in gcc 4.2.2 (32)
- SIGSYS 4.3.2 (38)
- SIGTRAP 4.3.2 (37)
- sin() 6.2 (67)
- soname 6.4.2 (73)
- sprintf() 4.3.5 (42)
- statically linked binaries, unexpected 6.1 (66) 6.4.4 (78)
- <stdarg.h> 3.3 (23)
- <stddef.h> 3.3 (24)
- strings 2.5 (11)
- <sys/time.h> 4.3.6 (48)
- <unistd.h> 4.3.6 (49)
- <varargs.h> 3.3 (22)
- version numbers 3.1 (12) 6.4.2 (74)
- weird things 6.4.2 (72)
- ZMAGIC 6.4.3 (75)

HOWTO

## Part XIV

"Glibc 2 HOWTO" Eric Green

ejg3@cornell.edu
v1.5, 8 February 1998
The glibc 2 HOWTO covers installing and using the GNU C Library version 2 (libc 6) on Linux systems.

Contents

HOWTO

1   Introduction.

1.1   About glibc 2.

Glibc 2 is the latest version of the GNU C Library. It currently runs unmodified on GNU Hurd systems and Linux i386, m68k, and alpha systems. Support for Linux PowerPC, MIPS, Sparc, Sparc 64, and Arm will be in version 2.1. In the future support for other architectures and operating systems will be added.

On Linux, glibc 2 is used as the libc with major version 6, the successor of the Linux libc 5. It is intended by the Linux libc developers to eventually replace libc 5. As of 2.0.6, glibc is considered production quality. Version 2.1 (due out in the near future) will be ready for main stream use along with adding more ports and features.

There are three optional add-ons available for glibc 2:

Crypt

    The UFC-crypt package. It is seperate because of export restrictions.

LinuxThreads

    An implementation of the Posix 1003.1c "pthread" interface.

Locale data

    Contains the data needed to build the locale data files to use the internationalization features of the glibc.

The crypt and LinuxThreads add-ons are strongly recommended... not using them risks to be incompatible with the libraries of other systems. (If you do not wish to use them, you must add the option –disable-sanity-checks when you run configure.)

1.2   About this document.

This HOWTO covers installing the glibc 2 library on an existing Linux system. It is tailored for users of Intel based systems currently using libc 5, but users of other systems and alternate libraries (such as glibc 1) should be able to use this information by substituting the proper filenames and architecture names in the appropriate places.

The latest copy of this HOWTO can be found as part of the *Linux Documentation Project* <http://sunsite.unc. edu/LDP> or from <http://www.imaxx.net/~thrytis/glibc/Glibc2-HOWTO.html>.

1.3 Recent changes in this document.

Differences between version 1.5 and 1.4:

- Indexing added Ed Bailey.
- Changed my email address.

Differences between version 1.4 and 1.3:

- Changed current status from experimental to production.
- Updated list of developmental ports.
- Updated latest version to 2.0.6.

2 Choosing your installation method.

There are a few ways to install glibc. You can install the libraries as a test, using the existing libraries as the default but letting you try the new libraries by using different options when compiling your program. Installing in this way also makes it easy to remove glibc in the future (though any program linked with glibc will no longer work after the libraries are removed). Using glibc as a test library requires you to compile the libraries from source. There is no binary distribution for installing libraries this way. This installation is described in 4 (Installing as a test library).

The other way described in this document to install is using glibc as your primary library. All new programs that you compile on your system will use glibc, though you can link programs with your old libraries using different options while compiling. You can either install the libraries from binaries, or compile the library yourself. If you want to change optimization or configuration options, or use an add-on which is not distributed as a binary package, you must get the source distribution and compile. This installation procedure is described in 5 (Installing as the primary C library).

Frodo Looijaard describes yet another way of installing glibc. His method involves installing glibc as a secondary library and setting up a cross compiler to compile using glibc. The installation procedure for this method is more complicated then the test library install described in this document, but allows for easier compiling when linking to glibc. This method is described in his *Installing glibc-2 on Linux* <http://huizen.dds.nl/~frodol/glibc/> document.

If you are currently running Debian 1.3 but do not want to upgrade to the unstable version of Debian to use glibc, the *Debian libc5 to libc6 Mini-HOWTO* <http://www.gate.net/~storm/FAQ/libc5-libc6-Mini-HOWTO. html> describes how to use Debian packages to upgrade your system.

If you are installing glibc 2 on an important system, you might want to use the test install. Even if there are no bugs, some programs will need to be modified before they will compile due to changes in function prototypes and types.

3 Getting the library.

The glibc 2 consists of the glibc package and three optional add-on packages, LinuxThreads, Locale, and Crypt. The source can be found at

- <ftp://prep.ai.mit.edu/pub/gnu/glibc-2.0.6.tar.gz>
- <ftp://prep.ai.mit.edu/pub/gnu/glibc-linuxthreads-2.0.6.tar.gz>
- <ftp://prep.ai.mit.edu/pub/gnu/glibc-localedata-2.0.6.tar.gz>
- <ftp://prep.ai.mit.edu/pub/gnu/glibc-crypt-2.0.6.tar.gz>

It will take about 150 MB of disk space for the full compile and install. The basic binary install of just the core library package is about 50 MB.

Binary packages for 2.0.6 are not available. Version 2.0.4 binary packages are available for i386 and m68k, and version 2.0.1 for the alpha can be found at

HOWTO

- Intel x86:
  - `<ftp://prep.ai.mit.edu/pub/gnu/glibc-2.0.4.bin.i386.tar.gz>`
  - `<ftp://prep.ai.mit.edu/pub/gnu/glibc-crypt-2.0.4.bin.i386.tar.gz>`
- Alpha:
  - `<ftp://prep.ai.mit.edu/pub/gnu/glibc-2.0.1.bin.alpha-linux.tar.gz>`
  - `<ftp://prep.ai.mit.edu/pub/gnu/glibc-crypt-2.0.1.bin.alpha-linux.tar.gz>`
- m68k:
  - `<ftp://prep.ai.mit.edu/pub/gnu/glibc-2.0.4-m68k-linux.bin.tar.gz>`
  - `<ftp://prep.ai.mit.edu/pub/gnu/glibc-crypt-2.0.4-m68k-linux.bin.tar.gz>`

There are export restrictions on the crypt add-on. Non-US users should get it from `<ftp://ftp.ifi.uio.no/pub/gnu>`.

If you are running a Red Hat distribution, you can get rpms for glibc 2 from `<ftp://ftp.redhat.com/pub/redhat/>`. Glibc 2 is the primary C library for the new Red Hat distribution 5.0.

If you are running a Debian distribution, you can get the packages for glibc 2 from `<ftp://ftp.debian.org/debian/dists/unstable/main/>`. The files are named libc6. Glibc 2 is now part of the base package of the hamm version of Debian, and will be the primary libc when Debian 2.0 is released.

4 Installing as a test library.

This section covers installing glibc 2 as a test library. Anything you compile will be linked to your existing libraries unless you give some extra parameters to link to the new libraries. It appears that the paths are compiled into quite a few files, so you probably have to install the library from source.

4.1 Compiling and installing.

4.1.1 Prerequisites.

- About 150 MB free disk space
- GNU make 3.75
- gcc >= 2.7.2 (better 2.7.2.1)
- binutils 2.8.1 (for alpha you need a snapshot)
- bash 2.0
- autoconf 2.12 (if you change configure.in)
- texinfo 3.11

On an i586@133 with 64 MB of RAM, it takes about 3 hours to compile with full libraries with add-ons. On a loaded i686@200, it takes about half an hour.

4.1.2 Extracting the source.

You need to extract the source from the archives so you can compile it. The best way to do this is:

```
tar xzf glibc-2.0.6.tar.gz
cd glibc-2.0.6
tar xzf ../glibc-linuxthreads-2.0.6.tar.gz
tar xzf ../glibc-crypt-2.0.6.tar.gz
tar xzf ../glibc-localedata-2.0.6.tar.gz
```

This will put linuxthreads, crypt, and localedata directories in the glibc-2.0.6 directory where configure can find these add-ons.

4.1.3 Configuring.

In the glibc-2.0.6 directory, create a directory named compile, and cd into it. All work will be done in this directory, which will simplify cleaning up. (The developers have not been very concerned with getting 'make clean' perfect yet.)

```
mkdir compile
cd compile
```

Run `../configure`. To use the add-on packages, you need to specify them with –enable-add-ons, such as –enable-add-ons=linuxthreads,crypt,localedata. You also need to choose a destination directory to install to. /usr/i486-linuxglibc2 is a good choice. The configure line for this would be:

```
../configure --enable-add-ons=linuxthreads,crypt,localedata --
prefix=/usr/i486-linuxglibc2
```

4.1.4 Compiling and installing.

To compile and verify, run:

```
make
make check
```

If the 'make check' succeeds, install the library:

```
make install
```

4.2 Updating the dynamic loader.

1. Create a link from the new `ld.so` to `/lib/ld-linux.so.2`:

   ```
   ln -s /usr/i486-linuxglibc2/lib/ld-linux.so.2 /lib/ld-linux.so.2
   ```

   This is the only library where the location is fixed once a program is linked, and using a link in `/lib` will ease upgrading to glibc as your primary C library when the stable version is released.

2. Edit `/etc/ld.so.conf`. You need to add path to the lib directory the new libraries reside in at the end of the file, which will be `<prefix>/lib`, such as `/usr/i486-linuxglibc2/lib` for the choice above. After you have modified `/etc/ld.so.conf`, run

   ```
   ldconfig -v
   ```

4.3 Configuring for gcc.

The last step of installation is updating `/usr/lib/gcc-lib` so gcc knows how to use the new libraries. First you need to duplicate the existing configuration. To find out which configuration is current, use the -v option of gcc:

```
% gcc -v
Reading specs from /usr/lib/gcc-lib/i486-unknown-linux/2.7.2.2/specs
gcc version 2.7.2.2
```

In this case, i486-unknown-linux is the system, and 2.7.2.2 is the version. You need to copy the `/usr/lib/gcc-lib/<system>` to the new test system directory:

```
cd /usr/lib/gcc-lib/
cp -r i486-unknown-linux i486-linuxglibc2
```

Change into your new test system directory and version directory

```
cd /usr/lib/gcc-lib/i486-linuxglibc2/2.7.2.2
```

and edit the file `specs` found in this directory. In this file, change `/lib/ld-linux.so.1` to `/lib/ld-linux.so.2`. You also need to remove all expressions `%{...:-lgmon}` in the file, since glibc does not use the gmon library for profiling. A sample specs file can be found in the 9 (Sample specs file) section.

4.4 Updating header file links.

You need create links in your new include directory to other include directories:

```
cd /usr/i486-linuxglibc2/include
ln -s /usr/src/linux/include/linux
ln -s /usr/src/linux/include/asm
ln -s /usr/X11R6/include/X11
```

You might also have other libraries such as ncurses which need their header files put in this directory. You should copy or link the files from `/usr/include`. (Some libraries may need to be recompiled with glibc2 in order to work with it. In these cases, just compile and install the package to `/usr/i486-linuxglibc2`.)

4.5 Testing your installation.

To test the installation, create the following program in a file glibc.c:

```
#include <stdio.h>

main()
{
    printf("hello world!\n");
}
```

and compile with the options of "`-b <base install directory> -nostdinc -I<install directory>/include -I/usr/lib/gcc-lib/<new system dir>/<gcc version>/include`":

```
% gcc -b i486-linuxglibc2 -nostdinc -I/usr/i486-linuxglibc2/include -
I/usr/lib/gcc-lib/i486-linuxglibc2/2.7.2.2/include glibc.c -o glibc
```

Use ldd to verify the program was linked with glibc2, and not your old libc:

```
% ldd glibc
libc.so.6 => /usr/i486-linuxglibc2/lib/libc-2.0.6.so (0x4000d000)
/lib/ld-linux.so.2 => /lib/ld-linux.so.2 (0x40000000)
```

If it compiles, the links check out, and it generates "hello world!" when run, the installation succeeded.

5   Installing as the primary C library.

This section covers installing glibc 2 as your primary C library. Any new programs you compile will be linked with this library, unless you use special compile options to link with another version.

If you are are using Redhat or Debian and have downloaded the appropriate rpm or deb files, see the Redhat or Debian installion instructions. You can then skip this section.

5.1   Building the library from source.

This section explains how to compile glibc 2 and add-ons from the sources. You must compile the library if you want to change optimization or configuration options or use a package you do not have the binaries for.

5.1.1   Prerequisites.

- About 150 MB free disk space

- GNU make 3.75

- gcc >= 2.7.2 (better 2.7.2.1)

- binutils 2.8.1 (for alpha you need a snapshot)

- bash 2.0

- autoconf 2.12 (if you change configure.in)

- texinfo 3.11

On an i586@133 with 64 MB of RAM, it takes about 3 hours to compile with full libraries with add-ons. On a loaded i686@200, it takes about half an hour.

5.1.2   Extracting the source.

You need to extract the source from the archives so you can compile it. The best way to do this is:

```
tar xzf glibc-2.0.6.tar.gz
cd glibc-2.0.6
tar xzf ../glibc-linuxthreads-2.0.6.tar.gz
tar xzf ../glibc-crypt-2.0.6.tar.gz
tar xzf ../glibc-localedata-2.0.6.tar.gz
```

This will put linuxthreads, crypt, and localedata directories in the glibc-2.0.6 directory where configure can find these add-ons.

5.1.3 Configuring.

In the `glibc-2.0.6` directory, create a directory named compile, and cd into it. All work will be done in this directory, which will simplify cleaning up. (The developers have not been very concerned with getting 'make clean' perfect yet.)

```
mkdir compile
cd compile
```

Run `../configure`. To use the add-on packages, you need to specify them with –enable-add-ons, such as –enable-add-ons=linuxthreads,crypt,localedata. You probably will also want to specify paths where it will be installed. To match the standard linux distributions, specify –prefix=/usr. (When a prefix of /usr is specified on a linux system, configure knows to adjust other paths to place libc.so and other important libraries in /lib.) The whole configure line would be:

```
../configure --enable-add-ons=linuxthreads,crypt,localedata --prefix=/usr
```

5.1.4 Compiling.

To compile and verify, run:

```
make
make check
```

5.2 Preparing for installation.

Now you need to move some files around to prepare for the new library, whether you are installing from source or binaries. Any new program compiled will be linked to glibc, but old programs which are not statically linked will still depend on libc 5, so you can not just overwrite the old version.

1. Create a new directory to hold the old files to:

   ```
   mkdir -p /usr/i486-linuxlibc5/lib
   ```

2. The old header files must be evacuated from /usr/include:

   ```
   mv /usr/include /usr/i486-linuxlibc5/include
   ```

3. Create a new include directory and set up the links to other include directories:

   ```
   mkdir /usr/include

   ln -s /usr/src/linux/include/linux /usr/include/linux
   ln -s /usr/src/linux/include/asm /usr/include/asm
   ln -s /usr/X11R6/include/X11 /usr/include/X11
   ln -s /usr/lib/g++-include /usr/include/g++
   ```

   The links may need adjusting according to your distribution. At least Slackware puts g++ headers in /usr/local/g++-include, while Debian puts the headers in /usr/include/g++, and links /usr/lib/g++-include to /usr/include/g++. In the later case, you probably will want to move the original g++ include directory back to /usr/include.

4. Restore any extra header files and links. Some non-standard libraries such as ncurses put files in /usr/include or put a link to their include directories in the /usr/include. These files and links need to be restored in order to use the extra libraries properly.

5. Add your new library directory (such as `/usr/i486-linuxlibc5/lib`) *at the top* of your `/etc/ld.so.conf` file. You should have ld.so 1.8.8 or better installed to avoid getting strange messages once glibc is installed.

6. Move/copy all the old C libraries into the new directory.

```
mv /usr/lib/libbsd.a /usr/i486-linuxlibc5/lib
mv /usr/lib/libc.a /usr/i486-linuxlibc5/lib
mv /usr/lib/libgmon.a /usr/i486-linuxlibc5/lib
mv /usr/lib/libm.a /usr/i486-linuxlibc5/lib
mv /usr/lib/libmcheck.a /usr/i486-linuxlibc5/lib
mv /usr/lib/libc.so /usr/i486-linuxlibc5/lib
mv /usr/lib/libm.so /usr/i486-linuxlibc5/lib
cp /lib/libm.so.5.* /usr/i486-linuxlibc5/lib
cp /lib/libc.so.5.* /usr/i486-linuxlibc5/lib
```

`libm.so.5` and `libc.so.5` should be copied and not moved if `/usr` is a seperate partition from `/`, because they are required by programs used to start linux and must be located on the root drive partition.

7. Move the `/usr/lib/*.o` files into the new directory.

```
mv /usr/lib/crt1.o /usr/i486-linuxlibc5/lib
mv /usr/lib/crti.o /usr/i486-linuxlibc5/lib
mv /usr/lib/crtn.o /usr/i486-linuxlibc5/lib
mv /usr/lib/gcrt1.o /usr/i486-linuxlibc5/lib
```

8. Update your library cache after your libraries are moved.

```
ldconfig -v
```

5.3 Installing from the binary package.

If you are installing glibc from precompiled binaries, you must:

```
cd /
gzip -dc glibc-2.0.bin.i386.tar.gz | tar tvvf -
gzip -dc glibc-crypt-2.0.bin.i386.tar.gz | tar tvvf -
ldconfig -v
```

If you have a different architecture or version, substitute the proper file names.

5.4 Installing from the source.

To install the library from source, run:

```
make install
ldconfig -v
```

5.5 Updating the gcc specs.

The final step of the installation (for both binary and source installs) is to update the gcc `specs` file so you can link your programs properly. To determine which specs file is the one used by gcc, use:

```
% gcc -v
reading specs from /usr/lib/gcc-lib/i486-unknown-linux/2.7.2.2/specs
gcc version 2.7.2.2
```

In this case, i486-unknown-linux is the system, and 2.7.2.2 is the version. You need to copy the /usr/lib/gcc-lib/<system> to the old system directory:

```
cd /usr/lib/gcc-lib/
cp -r i486-unknown-linux i486-linuxlibc5
```

Change into the original directory and version directory

```
cd /usr/lib/gcc-lib/i486-unknown-linux/2.7.2.2
```

and edit the file specs found in this directory. In this file, change /lib/ld-linux.so.1 to /lib/ld-linux.so.2. You also need to remove all expressions %{...:-lgmon} in the file, since glibc does not use the gmon library for profiling. A sample specs file can be found in the 9 (Sample specs file) section.

5.6   Testing your installation.

To test the installation, create the following program in a file glibc.c:

```
#include <stdio.h>

main()
{
    printf("hello world!\n");
}
```

and compile the program.

```
% gcc glibc.c -o glibc
```

Use ldd to verify the program was linked with glibc2, and not your old libc:

```
% ldd glibc
libc.so.6 => /lib/libc.so.6 (0x4000e000)
/lib/ld-linux.so.2 => /lib/ld-linux.so.2 (0x40000000)
```

If this compiles and generates "hello world!" when run, the installation was successful.

6   Compiling with the non-primary libc.

There are times you will want to use an alternate library to compile your programs with. This section explains how to accomplish this, using the directories and installation names used in the examples in the previous two sections. Remember to change the names to fit your setup.

6.1   A warning when using non-primary libcs.

Before compiling any programs which is used in the system boot process, remember that if the program is dynamically linked and is used before the non-root partitions are mounted, all linked libraries must be on the root partition. Following the installation process in the previous section for installing glibc as your primary C library, the old libc is left in /lib, which will be on your root partition. This means all of your programs will still work during booting. However, if /usr is on a different partition and you install glibc as a test library in /usr/i486-linuxglibc2, any new programs you compile with glibc will not work until your /usr partition is mounted.

6.2   Compiling programs with a test glibc.

To compile a program with a test-install glibc, you need to reset the include paths to point to the glibc includes. Specifying "-nostdinc" will negate the normal paths, and "-I/usr/i486-linuxglibc2/include" will point to the glibc includes.   You will also need to specify the gcc includes, which are found in /usr/lib/gcc-lib/i486-linuxglibc2/2.7.2.2/include (assuming you installed the test lib in i486-linuxglibc2 with gcc version 2.7.2.2).

To link a program with a test-install glibc, you need to specify the gcc setup. This is done by using the option "-b i486-linuxglibc2".

For most programs, you can specify these new options by adding them to the $CFLAGS and $LDFLAGS makefile options:

```
    CFLAGS = -nostdinc -I/usr/i486-linuxglibc2/include -I/usr/lib/gcc-lib/i486-
    linuxglibc2/2.7.2.2/include -b i486-linuxglibc2
    LDFLAGS = -b i486-linuxglibc2
```

If you are using a configure script, define the $CFLAGS and $LDFLAGS shell variables (by using env/setenv for c-sh/tcsh, or set/export for sh/bash/etc) before running configure. The makefiles generated by this should contain the proper $CFLAGS and $LDFLAGS. Not all configure scripts will pick up the variables, so you should check after running configure and edit the makefiles by hand if necessary.

If the programs you are compiling only call gcc (and not cpp or binutils directly), you can use the following script to save having to specify all of the options each time:

```
    #!/bin/bash
    /usr/bin/gcc -b i486-linuxglibc2 -nostdinc \
                -I/usr/i486-linuxglibc2/include \
                -I/usr/lib/gcc-lib/i486-linuxglibc2/2.7.2.2/include "$@"
```

You can then use this script instead of "gcc" when compiling.

6.3   Compiling programs with libc 5 when glibc is primary library.

To compile a program with your old libraries when you have installed glibc as your main library, you need to reset the include paths to the old includes. Specifying "-nostdinc" will negate the normal paths, and "-I/usr/i486-linuxlibc5/include" will point to the glibc includes.   You must also specify "-I/usr/lib/gcc-lib/i486-linuxlibc5/2.7.2.2/include" to include the gcc specific includes. Remember to adjust these paths based on the what you named the new directories and your gcc version.

To link a program with your old libc, you need to specify the gcc setup. This is done by using the option "-b i486-linuxlibc5".

For most programs, you can specify these new options by appending them to the $CFLAGS and $LDFLAGS makefile options:

HOWTO

```
     CFLAGS = -nostdinc -I/usr/i486-linuxlibc5/include -I/usr/lib/gcc-lib/i486-
     linuxlibc5/2.7.2.2/include -b i486-linuxlibc5
     LDFLAGS = -b i486-linuxlibc5
```

If you are using a configure script, define the $CFLAGS and $LDFLAGS shell variables (by using env/setenv for c-sh/tcsh, or set/export for sh/bash/etc) before running configure. The makefiles generated by this should contain the proper $CFLAGS and $LDFLAGS. Not all configure scripts will pick up the variables, so you should check after running configure and edit the makefiles by hand if necessary.

If the programs you are compiling only call gcc (and not cpp or binutils directly), you can use the following script to save having to specify all of the options each time:

```
#!/bin/bash
/usr/bin/gcc -b i486-linuxlibc5 -nostdinc \
             -I/usr/i486-linuxlibc5/include \
             -I/usr/lib/gcc-lib/i486-linuxlibc5/2.7.2.2/include "$@"
```

You can then use this script instead of "gcc" when compiling.

7 Compiling C++ programs.

Libg++ uses parts of the math library, so is link to libm. Since your existing libg++ will be compiled with your old library, you will have to recompile libg++ with glibc or get a binary copy. The latest source for libg++ along with a binary linked with glibc (for x86) can be found at <ftp://ftp.yggdrasil.com/private/hjl/>.

7.1 Installing libg++ for a test glibc install.

If you have installed glibc as a test library, you need to install the files into the directory you installed glibc into (such as /usr/i486-linuxglibc2 for the example in the previous sections). If you are installing from the binary package (which i would recommend, since i never had any luck compiling libg++ this way), you need to extract the files into a temporary directory and move all the usr/lib/ files into the <install directory>/lib/ directory, the usr/include/ files into the <install directory>/include/ directory (remember to delete your include/g++ link first!), and the usr/bin/ files into the <install directory>/bin/ directory.

7.2 Installing libg++ for a primary glibc install.

If you have installed glibc as the primary library, you first need to move your old libg++ files into your old libc directory if you still want to be able to compile g++ programs with your old libc. Probably the easiest way to do this is by installing a new copy of the libg++ compiled with libc 5 as in the previous section, and then installing the glibc version normally.

7.3 Compiling C++ programs with the non-primary libc.

If you are trying to compile a C++ program with a non-primary libc, you will need to include the g++ include dir, which in the examples above would be /usr/i486-linuxglibc2/include/g++ for a test glibc install or /usr/i486-linuxlibc5/include/g++ for a primary glibc install. This can usually be done by appending the $CXXFLAGS variable:

```
     CXXFLAGS = -nostdinc -I/usr/i486-linuxglibc2/include -I/usr/lib/gcc-
     lib/i486-linuxglibc2/2.7.2.2/include -I/usr/i486-linuxlibc5/include/g++ -
     b i486-linuxglibc2
```

8 Reporting bugs.

If you think the lib is buggy, please read first the FAQ. It might be that others had the same problem and there's an easy solution. You should also check the section "Recommended Tools to Install the GNU C Library" in the `INSTALL` file since some bugs are bugs of the tools and not of glibc.

Once you've found a bug, make sure it's really a bug. A good way to do this is to see if the GNU C library behaves the same way some other C library does. If so, probably you are wrong and the libraries are right (but not necessarily). If not, one of the libraries is probably wrong.

Next, go to `<http://www-gnats.gnu.org:8080/cgi-bin/wwwgnats.pl>`, and look through the bug database. Check here to verify the problem has not already been reported. You should also look at the file `BUGS` (distributed with libc) to check for known bugs.

Once you're sure you've found a new bug, try to narrow it down to the smallest test case that reproduces the problem. In the case of a C library, you really only need to narrow it down to one library function call, if possible. This should not be too difficult.

The final step when you have a simple test case is to report the bug. When reporting a bug, send your test case, the results you got, the results you expected, what you think the problem might be (if you've thought of anything), your system type, the versions of the GNU C library, the GNU CC compiler, and the GNU Binutils which you are using. Also include the files `config.status` and `config.make` which are created by running `configure`; they will be in whatever directory was current when you ran `configure`.

All bug reports for the GNU C library should be sent using the `glibcbug` shell script which comes with the GNU libc to `<bugs@gnu.org>` (the older address `<bugs@gnu.ai.mit.edu>` is still working), or submitted through the GNATS web interface at `<http://www-gnats.gnu.org:8080/cgi-bin/wwwgnats.pl>`.

Suggestions and questions should be sent to the mailing list at `<bugs-glibc@prep.ai.mit.edu>`. If you don't read the gnewsgroup gnu.bug.glibc, you can subscribe to the list by asking `<bug-glibc-request@prep.ai.mit.edu>`.

Please DO NOT send bug report for the GNU C library to `<bug-gcc@prep.ai.mit.edu>`. That list is for bug reports for GNU CC. GNU CC and the GNU C library are separate entities maintained by separate people.

9 Sample specs file.

Included here is a sample `specs` file for glibc 2 which is used by gcc for compiling and linking. It should be found in the directory `/usr/lib/gcc-lib/<new system dir>/<gcc version>`. If you are running an x86 system, you probably can copy this section to the file exactly.

```
*asm:
%{V} %{v:%{!V:-V}} %{Qy:} %{!Qn:-Qy} %{n} %{T} %{Ym,*} %{Yd,*} %{Wa,*:%*}

*asm_final:
%{pipe:-}

*cpp:
%{fPIC:-D__PIC__ -D__pic__} %{fpic:-D__PIC__ -D__pic__} %{!m386:-
D__i486__} %{posix:-D_POSIX_SOURCE} %{pthread:-D_REENTRANT}

*cc1:
%{profile:-p}

*cc1plus:
```

HOWTO

```
*endfile:
%{!shared:crtend.o%s} %{shared:crtendS.o%s} crtn.o%s

*link:
-m elf_i386 %{shared:-shared}   %{!shared:   %{!ibcs:   %{!stat-
ic:     %{rdynamic:-export-dynamic}    %{!dynamic-linker:-dynamic-
linker /lib/ld-linux.so.2}} %{static:-static}}}

*lib:
%{!shared: %{pthread:-lpthread}          %{profile:-lc_p} %{!profile: -lc}}

*libgcc:
-lgcc

*startfile:
%{!shared: %{pg:gcrt1.o%s} %{!pg:%{p:gcrt1.o%s} %{!p:%{profile:gcrt1.o%s} \
%{!profile:crt1.o%s}}}} crti.o%s %{!shared:crtbegin.o%s} \
%{shared:crtbeginS.o%s}

*switches_need_spaces:


*signed_char:
%{funsigned-char:-D__CHAR_UNSIGNED__}

*predefines:
-D__ELF__ -Dunix -Di386 -Dlinux -Asystem(unix) -Asystem(posix) -
Acpu(i386) -Amachine(i386)

*cross_compile:
0

*multilib:
. ;
```

10 Miscellanea.

10.1 Further information.

10.1.1 Web pages.

- *FSF's GNU C Library Home Page* <http://www.gnu.org/software/libc/libc.html>
- *Using GNU Libc 2 with Linux* <http://www.imaxx.net/~thrytis/glibc/>
- *Installing glibc-2 on Linux* <http://huizen.dds.nl/~frodol/glibc/>.
- *Debian   libc5   to   libc6   Mini-HOWTO*   <http://www.gate.net/~storm/FAQ/libc5-libc6-Mini-HOWTO.html>.

10.1.2 Newgroups.

- *comp.os.linux.development.system*
- *comp.os.linux.development.apps*

- *linux.dev.kernel*
- *gnu.bugs.glibc*

10.1.3 Mailing lists.

Glibc 2 Linux discussion list.

This list is intended for discussion among Linux users who have installed glibc2, the new GNU C libraries. Topics might include compatibility issues and questions about the compilation of code in a Linux/glibc setting. To subscribe, send mail to *Majordomo@ricardo.ecn.wfu.edu* <mailto:Majordomo@ricardo.ecn.wfu.edu> with a body of "subscribe glibc-linux <your email address>.

10.2 Credits.

Most of this information was stolen from the *GNU Libc web page* <http://www.gnu.org/software/libc/libc.html> and from Ulrich Drepper's <drepper@gnu.ai.mit.edu> glibc 2 announcement and his comments. Andreas Jaeger <aj@arthur.rhein-neckar.de> provided some of the Reporting bugs section.

The following people have provided information and feedback for this document:

- Allex <allex@ms2.accmail.com.tw>
- Mark Brown <M.A.Brown-4@sms.ed.ac.uk>
- Ulrich Drepper <drepper@gnu.ai.mit.edu>
- Scott K. Ellis <ellis@valueweb.net>
- Aron Griffis <agriffis@coat.com>
- Andreas Jaeger <aj@arthur.rhein-neckar.de>
- Frodo Looijaard <frodol@dds.nl>
- Ryan McGuire <rmcguire@freenet.columbus.oh.us>
- Shaya Potter <spotter@capaccess.org>
- Les Schaffer <godzilla@futuris.net>
- Andy Sewell <puck@pookhill.demon.co.uk>
- Gary Shea <shea@gtsdesign.com>
- Stephane <sr@adb.fr>
- Jan Vandenbos <jan@imaxx.net>

Translations of this document are being done by:

- Chinese: Allex <allex@ms2.accmail.com.tw>
- French: Olivier Tharan <tharan@int-evry.fr>
- Japanese: Kazuyuki Okamoto <ikko-@pacific.rim.or.jp>

10.3 Feedback.

Besides writing this HOWTO, maintaining the *glibc 2 for Linux* <http://www.imaxx.net/~thrytis/glibc> page, and using it on my machine, I have nothing to do with the glibc project. I am far from knowledgeable on this topic, though I try to help with problems mailed to me. I welcome any feedback, corrections, or suggestions you have to offer. Please send them to *ejg3@cornell.edu* <mailto:ejg3@cornell.edu>.

10.4 Copyright.

Copyright (c) 1997 by Eric Green. This document may be distributed under the terms set forth in the LDP license.

HOWTO

Part XV

"Linux IPCHAINS-HOWTO" Paul Russell

Paul.Russell@rustcorp.com.au
v1.0.5, 27 October 1998
This document aims to describe how to obtain, install and configure the enhanced IP firewalling chains software for Linux, and some ideas on how you might use them.

Contents

HOWTO

1 Introduction

This is the Linux IPCHAINS-HOWTO. You should read the Linux NET-3-HOWTO as well. The IP-Masquerading HOWTO, the PPP-HOWTO, the Ethernet-HOWTO and the Firewall HOWTO might make interesting reading. (Then again, so might the alt.fan.bigfoot FAQ).

If packet filtering is passe to you, read Section 1.2 (Why?), Section 2.3 (How?), and scan through the titles in Section 4 (IP Firewalling Chains).

If you are converting from ipfwadm, read Section 2 (Introduction), Section 2.3 (How?), and Appendices in section 7 (Differences between ipchains and ipfwadm) and section 8 (Using the 'ipfwadm-wrapper' script).

1.1 What?

Linux ipchains is a rewrite of the Linux IPv4 firewalling code (which was mainly stolen from BSD) and a rewrite of ipfwadm, which was a rewrite of BSD's ipfw, I believe. It is required to administer the IP packet filters in Linux kernel versions 2.1.102 and above.

1.2 Why?

The older Linux firewalling code doesn't deal with fragments, has 32-bit counters (on Intel at least), doesn't allow specification of protocols other than TCP, UDP or ICMP, can't make large changes atomically, can't specify inverse rules, has some quirks, and can be tough to manage (making it prone to user error).

1.3 How?

Currently the code is in the mainstream kernel from 2.1.102. For the 2.0 kernel series, you will need to download a kernel patch from the web page. If your 2.0 kernel is more recent than the supplied patch, the older patch should be OK; this part of the 2.0 kernels is fairly stable (eg. the 2.0.34 kernel patch works just fine on the 2.0.35 kernel). Since the 2.0 patch is incompatible with the ipportfw and ipautofw patches, I don't recommend applying it unless you really need some functionality that ipchains offers.

1.4 Where?

The official page is *The Linux IP Firewall Chains Page* `<http://www.adelaide.net.au/~rustcorp/linux/ipchains>`

There is a mailing list for bug reports, discussion, development and usage. Join the mailing list by sending a message containing the word "subscribe" to ipchains-request at wantree.com.au. To mail to the list use 'ipchains' instead of 'ipchains-request'.

2 Packet filtering basics.

2.1 What?

All traffic through a network is sent in the form of **packets**. For example, downloading this package (say it's 50k long) might cause you to receive 36 or so packets of 1460 bytes each, (to pull numbers at random).

The start of each packet says where it's going, where it came from, the type of the packet, and other administrative details. This start of the packet is called the **header**. The rest of the packet, containing the actual data being transmitted, is usually called the **body**.

Some protocols, such **TCP**, which is used for web traffic, mail, and remote logins, use the concept of a 'connection' – before any packets with actual data are sent, various setup packets (with special headers) are exchanged saying 'I want to connect', 'OK' and 'Thanks'. Then normal packets are exchanged.

A packet filter is a piece of software which looks at the *header* of packets as they pass through, and decide the fate of the entire packet. It might decide to **deny** the packet (ie. discard the packet as if it had never received it), **accept** the packet (ie. let the packet go through), or **reject** the packet (like deny, but tell the source of the packet that it has done so).

Under Linux, packet filtering is built into the kernel, and there are a few trickier things we can do with packets, but the general principle of looking at the headers and deciding the fate of the packet is still there.

2.2 Why?

Control. Security. Watchfulness.

Control:
> when you are using a Linux box to connect your internal network to another network (say, the Internet) you have an opportunity to allow certain types of traffic, and disallow others. For example, the header of a packet contains the destination address of the packet, so you can prevent packets going to a certain part of the outside network. As another example, I use Netscape to access the Dilbert archives. There are advertisements from doubleclick.net on the page, and Netscape wastes my time by cheerfully downloading them. Telling the packet filter not to allow any

packets to or from the addresses owned by doubleclick.net solves that problem (there are better ways of doing this though).

Security:

> when your Linux box is the only thing between the chaos of the Internet and your nice, orderly network, it's nice to know you can restrict what comes tromping in your door. For example, you might allow anything to go out from your network, but you might be worried about the well-known 'Ping of Death' coming in from malicious outsiders. As another example, you might not want outsiders telnetting to your Linux box, even though all your accounts have passwords; maybe you want (like most people) to be an observer on the Internet, and not a server (willing or otherwise) – simply don't let anyone connect in, by having the packet filter reject incoming packets used to set up connections.

Watchfulness:

> sometimes a badly configured machine on the local network will decide to spew packets to the outside world. It's nice to tell the packet filter to let you know if anything abnormal occurs; maybe you can do something about it, or maybe you're just curious by nature.

2.3   How?

2.3.1   A kernel with packet filtering.

You need a kernel which has the new IP firewall chains in it. You can tell if the kernel you are running right now has this installed by looking for the file '/proc/net/ip_fwchains'. If it exists, you're in.

If not, you need to make a kernel that has IP firewall chains. First, download the source to the kernel you want. If you have a kernel numbered 2.1.102 or higher, you won't need to patch it (it's in the mainstream kernel now). Otherwise, apply the patch from the web page listed above, and set the configuration as detailed below. If you don't know how to do this, don't panic – read the Kernel-HOWTO.

The configuration options you will need to set *for the 2.0-series kernel* are:

```
CONFIG_EXPERIMENTAL=y
CONFIG_FIREWALL=y
CONFIG_IP_FIREWALL=y
CONFIG_IP_FIREWALL_CHAINS=y
```

For the *2.1 or 2.2 series kernels*:

```
CONFIG_FIREWALL=y
CONFIG_IP_FIREWALL=y
```

The tool `ipchains` talks to the kernel and tells it what packets to filter. Unless you are a programmer, or overly curious, this is how you will control the packet filtering.

2.3.2   `ipchains`.

This tool replaces `ipfwadm` used for the old IP Firewall code. The package also contains a shell script called `ipfwadm-wrapper` which allows you to do packet filtering as it was done before. You should *not* use this script unless you want a quick way of upgrading a system which uses `ipfwadm` (it's slower, and doesn't check arguments, etc). In that case, you don't need this HOWTO much either. See Appendix 7 (Differences between ipchains and ipfwadm) and Appendix 8 (Using the 'ipfwadm-wrapper' script) for more details on `ipfwadm` issues.

3   I'm confused! Routing, masquerading, portforwarding, ipautofw...

This HOWTO is about packet filtering. This means deciding whether a packet should be allowed to pass or not. However, Linux being the hacker's playground that it is, you probably want to do more than that.

One problem is that the same tool ("ipchains") is used to control both masquerading and transparent proxying, although these are notionally separate from packet filtering (the current Linux implementation blurs these together unnaturally, leaving the impression that they are closely related).

Masquerading and proxying are covered by separate HOWTOs, and the auto forwarding and port forwarding features are controlled by separate tools, but since so many people keep asking me about it, I'll include a set of common scenarios and indicate when each one should be applied. The security merits of each setup will not be discussed here.

3.1   Gratuitous Promotion: WatchGuard Rules

You can buy off-the-shelf firewalls. An excellent one is WatchGuard's FireBox. It's excellent because I like it, it's secure, it's Linux-based, and because they are funding the maintenance of ipchains as well as the new firewalling code (aimed for 2.3). In short, WatchGuard are paying for me to eat while I work for you. So please consider their stuff.

http://www.watchguard.com <http://www.watchguard.com>

3.2   Common Firewall-like Setups

You run littlecorp.com. You have an internal network, and a single dialup (PPP) connection to the Internet (firewall-1.littlecorp.com which is 1.2.3.4). You run Ethernet on your local network, and your personal machine is called "myhost".

3.3   Private Network: Traditional proxies.

In this scenario, packets from the private network never traverse the Internet, and vice versa. The IP addresses of the private network should be assigned from the RFC1597 Private Network Allocations (ie. 10.*.*.*, 172.16.*.* or 192.168.*.*).

The only way things ever connect to the Internet is by connecting to the firewall, which is the only machine on both networks, which connects onwards. You run a program (on the firewall) called a proxy to do this (there are proxies for FTP, web access, telnet, RealAudio, Usenet News and other services). See the Firewall HOWTO.

Any services you wish the Internet to access must be on the firewall. (But see 3.7 (Limited Internal Services) below).

Example: Allowing web access from private network to the Internet.

1. The private network is assigned 192.168.1.* addresses, with myhost being 192.168.1.100, and the firewall's Ethernet interface being assigned 192.168.1.1.

2. A web proxy (eg. "squid") is installed and configured on the firewall, say running on port 8080.

3. Netscape on the private network is configured to use the firewall port 8080 as a proxy.

4. DNS does not need to be configured on the private network.

5. DNS does need to be configured on the firewall.

6. No default route (aka gateway) needs to be configured on the private network.

Netscape on myhost reads http://slashdot.org.

1. Netscape connects to the firewall port 8080, using port 1050 on myhost. It asks for the web page of "http://slashdot.org".

2. The proxy looks up the name "slashdot.org", and gets 207.218.152.131. It then opens a connection to that IP address (using port 1025 on the firewall's external interface), and asks the web server (port 80) for the web page.

3. As it receives the web page from its connection to the web server, it copies the data to the connection from Netscape.

4. Netscape renders the page.

ie. From slashdot.org's point of view, the connection is made from 1.2.3.4 (firewall's PPP interface) port 1025 to 207.218.152.131 (slashdot.org) port 80. From myhost's point of view, the connection is made from 192.168.1.100 (myhost) port 1050, to 192.168.1.1 (firewall's Ethernet interface) port 8080.

3.4 Private Network: Transparent proxies.

In this scenario, packets from the private network never traverse the Internet, and vice versa. The IP addresses of the private network should be assigned from the RFC1597 Private Network Allocations (ie. 10.*.*.*, 172.16.*.* or 192.168.*.*).

The only way things ever connect to the Internet is by connecting to the firewall, which is the only machine on both networks, which connects onwards. You run a program (on the firewall) called a transparent proxy to do this; the kernel sends outgoing packets to the transparent proxy instead of sending them onwards (ie. it bastardizes routing).

Transparent proxying means that the clients don't need to know there is a proxy involved.

Any services you wish the Internet to access must be on the firewall. (But see 3.7 (Limited Internal Services) below).

Example: Allowing web access from private network to the Internet.

1. The private network is assigned 192.168.1.* addresses, with myhost being 192.168.1.100, and the firewall's Ethernet interface being assigned 192.168.1.1.

2. A transparent web proxy (I believe there are patches for squid to allow it to operate in this manner, or try "transproxy") is installed and configured on the firewall, say running on port 8080.

3. The kernel is told to redirect connections to port 80 to the proxy, using ipchains.

4. Netscape on the private network is configured to connect directly.

5. DNS needs to be configured on the private network (ie. you need to run a DNS server as a proxy on the firewall).

6. The default route (aka gateway) needs to be configured on the private network, to send packets to the firewall.

Netscape on myhost reads http://slashdot.org.

1. Netscape looks up the name "slashdot.org", and gets 207.218.152.131. It then opens a connection to that IP address, using local port 1050, and asks the web server (port 80) for the web page.

2. As the packets from myhost (port 1050) to slashdot.org (port 80) pass through the firewall, they are redirected to the waiting transparent proxy on port 8080. The transparent proxy opens a connection (using local port 1025) to 207.218.152.131 port 80 (which is where the original packets were going).

3. As the proxy receives the web page from its connection to the web server, it copies the data to the connection from Netscape.

4. Netscape renders the page.

ie. From slashdot.org's point of view, the connection is made from 1.2.3.4 (firewall's PPP interface) port 1025 to 207.218.152.131 (slashdot.org) port 80. From myhost's point of view, the connection is made from 192.168.1.100 (myhost) port 1050, to 207.218.152.131 (slashdot.org) port 80, but it's actually talking to the transparent proxy.

3.5 Private Network: Masquerading.

In this scenario, packets from the private network never traverse the Internet without special treatment, and vice versa. The IP addresses of the private network should be assigned from the RFC1597 Private Network Allocations (ie. 10.*.*.*, 172.16.*.* or 192.168.*.*).

Instead of using a proxy, we use a special kernel facility called "masquerading". Masquerading rewrites packets as they pass through the firewall, so that they always seem to come from the firewall itself. It then rewrites the responses so that they look like they are going to the original recipient.

Masquerading has separate modules to handle "tricky" protocols, such as FTP, RealAudio, Quake, etc. For really hard-to-handle protocols, the "auto forwarding" facility can handle some of them by automatically setting up port forwarding for related sets of ports: look for "ipportfw" (2.0 kernels) or "ipmasqadm" (2.1 kernels).

Any services you wish the Internet to access must be on the firewall. (But see 3.7 (Limited Internal Services) below).

Example: Allowing web access from private network to the Internet.

1. The private network is assigned 192.168.1.* addresses, with myhost being 192.168.1.100, and the firewall's Ethernet interface being assigned 192.168.1.1.

2. The firewall is set up to masquerade any packets coming from the private network and going to port 80 on an Internet host.

3. Netscape is configured to connect directly.

4. DNS must be configured correctly on the private network.

5. The firewall should be the default route (aka gateway) for the private network.

Netscape on myhost reads http://slashdot.org.

1. Netscape looks up the name "slashdot.org", and gets 207.218.152.131. It then opens a connection to that IP address, using local port 1050, and asks the web server (port 80) for the web page.

2. As the packets from myhost (port 1050) to slashdot.org (port 80) pass through the firewall, they are rewritten to come from the PPP interface of the firewall, port 65000. The firewall has a valid Internet address (1.2.3.4) so reply packets from www.linuxhq.com get routed back OK.

3. As packets from slashdot.org (port 80) to firewall.littlecorp.com (port 65000) come in, they are rewritten to go to myhost, port 1050. This is the real magic of masquerading: it remembers when it rewrites outgoing packets to it can write them back as replies come in.

4. Netscape renders the page.

ie. From the slashdot.org's point of view, the connection is made from 1.2.3.4 (firewall's PPP interface) port 65000 to 207.218.152.131 (slashdot.org) port 80. From the myhost's point of view, the connection is made from 192.168.1.100 (myhost) port 1050, to 207.218.152.131 (slashdot.org) port 80.

3.6 Public Network.

In this scenario, your personal network is a part of the Internet: packets can flow without change across both networks. The IP addresses of the internal network must be assigned by applying for a block of IP addresses, so the rest of the network will know how to get packets to you. This implies a permanent connection

In this role, packet filtering is used to restrict which packets can be forwarded between your network and the rest of the Internet, eg. to restrict the rest of the Internet to only accessing your internal web servers.

Example: Allowing web access from private network to the Internet.

1. Your internal network is assigned according to the IP address block you have registered, (say 1.2.3.*).

2. The firewall is set up to allow all traffic.

3. Netscape is configured to connect directly.

4. DNS must be configured correctly on your network.

5. The firewall should be the default route (aka gateway) for the private network.

Netscape on myhost reads http://slashdot.org.

1. Netscape looks up the name "slashdot.org", and gets 207.218.152.131. It then opens a connection to that IP address, using local port 1050, and asks the web server (port 80) for the web page.

HOWTO

2. Packets pass through your firewall, just as they pass through several other routers between you and slashdot.org.

3. Netscape renders the page.

ie. There is only one connection: from 1.2.3.100 (myhost) port 1050, to 207.218.152.131 (slashdot.org) port 80.

3.7 Limited Internal Services

There are a few tricks you can pull to allow the Internet to access your internal services, rather than running the services on the firewall. These will work with either a proxy or masquerading based approach for external connections.

The simplest approach is to run a "redirector", which is a poor-man's proxy which waits for a connection on a given port, and then open a connection a fixed internal host and port, and copies data between the two connections. An example of this is the "redir" program. From the Internet point of view, the connection is made to your firewall. >From your internal server's point of view, the connection is made from the internal interface of the firewall to the server.

Another approach (which requires a 2.0 kernel patched for ipportfw, or a 2.1 or later kernel) is to use port forwarding in the kernel. This does the same job as "redir" in a different way: the kernel rewrites packets as they pass through, changing their destination address and ports to point them at an internal host and port. From the Internet's point of view, the connection is made to your firewall. From your internal server's point of view, a direct connection is made from the Internet host to the server.

4 IP firewalling chains.

This section describes all you really need to know to build a packet filter that meets your needs.

4.1 How packets traverse the filters.

The kernel starts with three lists of rules; these lists are called **firewall chains** or just **chains**. The three chains are called **input**, **output** and **forward**. When a packet comes in (say, through the Ethernet card) the kernel uses the `input` chain to decide its fate. If it survives that step, then the kernel decides where to send the packet next (this is called **routing**). If it is destined for another machine, it consults the `forward` chain. Finally, just before a packet is to go out, the kernel consults the `output` chain.

A chain is a checklist of **rules**. Each rule says 'if the packet header looks like this, then here's what to do with the packet'. If the rule doesn't match the packet, then the next rule in the chain is consulted. Finally, if there are no more rules to consult, then the kernel looks at the chain **policy** to decide what to do. In a security-conscious system, this policy usually tells the kernel to reject or deny the packet.

For ASCII-art fans, this shown the complete path of a packet coming into a machine.

```
       -----------------------------------------------------------------------
       |                  ACCEPT/                                 lo interface |
       v                  REDIRECT                                             |
--> C --> S --> _____ --> D --> ~~~~~~~~ --> local? -----> _____   -->
    h   -> a   |input |    e   {Routing }     |_____|     |output |ACCEPT
    e   | n    |Chain |    m   {Decision}    |forward|---->|Chain  |
    c   | i    |_____|    a   ~~~~~~~~      |Chain  |   ^ |_____|
    k   | t       |       s       |  ^      |_____|   |     |
    s   | y       |       q       |  |          |      |     |
    u   | |       v       e       v  |          v      |     v
    m   | |     DENY/     r  Local Process      v      |   DENY/
    |   | v     REJECT    a       |          DENY/      |   REJECT
    |   |DENY            d        |          REJECT      |
    v.  |                e  -------+----------------------
   DENY |
```

Here is a blow-by-blow description of each stage:

Checksum:

This is a test that the packet hasn't been corrupted in some way. If it has, it is denied.

Sanity:

There is actually one of these sanity checks before each firewall chain, but the input chain's is the most important. Some malformed packets might confuse the rule-checking code, and these are denied here (a message is printed to the syslog if this happens).

input chain:

This is the first firewall chain against which the packet will be tested. If the verdict of the chain is not DENY or REJECT, the packet continues on.

Demasquerade:

If the packet is a reply to a previously masqueraded packet, it is demasqueraded, and skips straight to the output chain. If you don't use IP Masquerading, you can mentally erase this from the diagram.

Routing decision:

The destination field is examined by the routing code, to decide if this packet should go to a local process (see Local process below) or forwarded to a remote machine (see forward chain below).

Local process:

A process running on the machine can receive packets after the Routing Decision step, and can send packets (which go through the Routing Decision step, then traverse the output chain).

lo interface:

If packets from a local process are destined for a local process, they will go through the output chain with interface set to 'lo', then return through the input chain with interface also 'lo'. The lo interface is usually called the loopback interface.

local:

If the packet was not created by a local process, then the forward chain is checked, otherwise the packet goes to the output chain.

forward chain:

This chain is traversed for any packets which are attempting to pass through this machine to another.

output chain:

This chain is traversed for all packets just before they are sent out.

4.1.1 Using `ipchains`.

First, check that you have the version of ipchains that this document refers to:

```
$ ipchains --version
ipchains 1.3.8, 27-Oct-1998
```

ipchains has a fairly detailed manual page (man ipchains), and if you need more detail on particulars, you can check out the programming interface (man 4 ipfw), or the file net/ipv4/ip_fw.c in the 2.1.x kernel source, which is (obviously) authoritative.

There is also an excellent quick reference card by Scott Bronson in the source package, in both A4 and US Letter PostScript(TM).

There are several different things you can do with ipchains. First the operations to manage whole chains. You start with three built-in chains input, output and forward which you can't delete.

1. Create a new chain (-N).

2. Delete an empty chain (-X).

3. Change the policy for a built-in chain. (-P).

4. List the rules in a chain (-L).

5. Flush the rules out of a chain (-F).

6. Zero the packet and byte counters on all rules in a chain (-Z).

There are several ways to manipulate rules inside a chain:

1. Append a new rule to a chain (-A).

2. Insert a new rule at some position in a chain (-I).

3. Replace a rule at some position in a chain (-R).

4. Delete a rule at some position in a chain (-D).

5. Delete the first rule that matches in a chain (-D).

There are a few operations for masquerading, which are in `ipchains` for want of a good place to put them:

1. List the currently masqueraded connections (-M -L).

2. Set masquerading timeout values (-M -S). (But see 6.8 (I can't set masquerading timeouts!)).

The final (and perhaps the most useful) function allows you to check what would happen to a given packet if it were to traverse a given chain.

4.1.2 Operations on a single rule.

This is the bread-and-butter of ipchains; manipulating rules. Most commonly, you will probably use the append (-A) and delete (-D) commands. The others (-I for insert and -R for replace) are simple extensions of these concepts.

Each rule specifies a set of conditions the packet must meet, and what to do if it meets them (a 'target'). For example, you might want to deny all ICMP packets coming from the IP address 127.0.0.1. So in this case our conditions are that the protocol must be ICMP and that the source address must be 127.0.0.1. Our target is 'DENY'.

127.0.0.1 is the 'loopback' interface, which you will have even if you have no real network connection. You can use the 'ping' program to generate such packets (it simply sends an ICMP type 8 (echo request) which all cooperative hosts should obligingly respond to with an ICMP type 0 (echo reply) packet). This makes it useful for testing.

```
# ping -c 1 127.0.0.1
PING 127.0.0.1 (127.0.0.1): 56 data bytes
64 bytes from 127.0.0.1: icmp_seq=0 ttl=64 time=0.2 ms

--- 127.0.0.1 ping statistics ---
1 packets transmitted, 1 packets received, 0% packet loss
round-trip min/avg/max = 0.2/0.2/0.2 ms
# ipchains -A input -s 127.0.0.1 -p icmp -j DENY
# ping -c 1 127.0.0.1
PING 127.0.0.1 (127.0.0.1): 56 data bytes

--- 127.0.0.1 ping statistics ---
1 packets transmitted, 0 packets received, 100% packet loss
#
```

You can see here that the first ping succeeds (the '-c 1' tells ping to only send a single packet).

Then we append (-A) to the 'input' chain, a rule specifying that for packets from 127.0.0.1 ('-s 127.0.0.1') with protocol ICMP ('-p ICMP') we should jump to DENY ('-j DENY').

Then we test our rule, using the second ping. There will be a pause before the program gives up waiting for a response that will never come.

We can delete the rule in one of two ways. Firstly, since we know that it is the only rule in the input chain, we can use a numbered delete, as in:

```
# ipchains -D input 1
#
```

To delete rule number 1 in the input chain.

The second way is to mirror the -A command, but replacing the -A with -D. This is useful when you have a complex chain of rules and you don't want to have to count them to figure out that it's rule 37 that you want to get rid of. In this case, we would use:

```
# ipchains -D input -s 127.0.0.1 -p icmp -j DENY
#
```

The syntax of -D must have exactly the same options as the -A (or -I or -R) command. If there are multiple identical rules in the same chain, only the first will be deleted.

4.1.3 Filtering specifications.

We have seen the use of '-p' to specify protocol, and '-s' to specify source address, but there are other options we can use to specify packet characteristics. What follows is an exhaustive compendium.

Specifying source and destination IP addresses. Source (-s) and destination (-d) IP addresses can be specified in four ways. The most common way is to use the full name, such as 'localhost' or 'www.linuxhq.com'. The second way is to specify the IP address such as '127.0.0.1'.

The third and fourth ways allow specification of a group of IP addresses, such as '199.95.207.0/24' or '199.95.207.0/255.255.255.0'. These both specify any IP address from 192.95.207.0 to 192.95.207.255 inclusive; the digits after the '/' tell which parts of the IP address are significant. '/32' or '/255.255.255.255' is the default (match all of the IP address). To specify any IP address at all '/0' can be used, like so:

```
# ipchains -A input -s 0/0 -j DENY
#
```

This is rarely used, as the effect above is the same as not specifying the '-s' option at all.

Specifying inversion. Many flags, including the '-s' and '-d' flags can have their arguments preceded by '!' (pronounced 'not') to match addresses NOT equal to the ones given. For example. '-s ! localhost' matches any packet not coming from localhost.

Specifying protocol. The protocol can be specified with the '-p' flag. Protocol can be a number (if you know the numeric protocol values for IP) or a name for the special cases of 'TCP', 'UDP' or 'ICMP'. Case doesn't matter, so 'tcp' works as well as 'TCP'.

The protocol name can be prefixed by a '!', to invert it, such as '-p ! TCP'.

Specifying UDP and TCP ports. For the special case where a protocol of TCP or UDP is specified, there can be an extra argument indicating the TCP or UDP port, or an (inclusive) range of ports (but see 4.1.3 (Handling Fragments) below). A range is represented using a ':' character, such as '6000:6010', which covers 11 port numbers, from 6000 to 6010 inclusive. If the lower bound is omitted, it defaults to 0. If the upper bound is omitted, it defaults to 65535. So to specify TCP connections coming from ports under 1024, the syntax would be as '-p TCP -s 0.0.0.0/0 :1023'. Port numbers can be specified by name, eg. 'www'.

Note that the port specification can be preceded by a '!', which inverts it. So to specify every TCP packet BUT a WWW packet, you would specify

```
-p TCP -d 0.0.0.0/0 ! www
```

It is important to realize that the specification

```
-p TCP -d ! 192.168.1.1 www
```

is very different from

```
-p TCP -d 192.168.1.1 ! www
```

The first specifies any TCP packet to the WWW port on any machine but 192.168.1.1. The second specifies any TCP connection to any port on 192.168.1.1 but the WWW port.

Finally, this case means not the WWW port and not 192.168.1.1:

```
-p TCP -d ! 192.168.1.1 ! www
```

Specifying ICMP type & code. ICMP also allows an optional argument, but as ICMP doesn't have ports, (ICMP has a **type** and a **code**) they have a different meaning.

You can specify them as ICMP names (use `ipchains -h icmp` to list the names) after the '-s' option, or as a numeric ICMP type and code, where the type follows the '-s' option and the code follows the '-d' option.

The ICMP names are fairly long: you only need use enough letters to make the name distinct from any other.

Here is a small table of some of the most common ICMP packets:

```
Number  Name                      Required by

0       echo-reply                ping
3       destination-unreachable   Any TCP/UDP traffic.
5       redirect                  routing if not running routing daemon
8       echo-request              ping
11      time-exceeded             traceroute
```

Note that the ICMP names cannot be preceded by '!' at the moment.

DO NOT DO NOT DO NOT block all ICMP type 3 messages! (See 5.2.1 (ICMP Packets) below).

Specifying an interface. The '-i' option specifies the name of an **interface** to match. An interface is the physical device the packet came in on, or is going out on. You can use the `ifconfig` command to list the interfaces which are 'up' (ie. working at the moment).

The interface for incoming packets (ie. packets traversing the `input` chain) is considered to be the interface they came in on. Logically, the interface for outgoing packets (packets traversing the `output` chain) is the interface they will go out on. The interface for packets traversing the `forward` chain is also the interface they will go out on; a fairly arbitrary decision it seems to me.

It is perfectly legal to specify an interface that currently does not exist; the rule will not match anything until the interface comes up. This is extremely useful for dial-up PPP links (usually interface `ppp0`) and the like.

As a special case, an interface name ending with a '+' will match all interfaces (whether they currently exist or not) which begin with that string. For example, to specify a rule which matches all PPP interfaces, the `-i ppp+` option would be used.

The interface name can be preceded by a '!' to match a packet which does NOT match the specified interface(s).

Specifying TCP SYN packets only.   It is sometimes useful to allow TCP connections in one direction, but not the other. For example, you might want to allow connections to an external WWW server, but not connections from that server.

The naive approach would be to block TCP packets coming from the server. Unfortunately, TCP connections require packets going in both directions to work at all.

The solution is to block only the packets used to request a connection. These packets are called **SYN** packets (ok, technically they're packets with the SYN flag set, and the FIN and ACK flags cleared, but we call them SYN packets). By disallowing only these packets, we can stop attempted connections in their tracks.

The '-y' flag is used for this: it is only valid for rules which specify TCP as their protocol. For example, to specify TCP connection attempts from 192.168.1.1:

```
-p TCP -s 192.168.1.1 -y
```

Once again, this flag can be inverted by preceding it with a '!', which means every packet other than the connection initiation.

Handling fragments.   Sometimes a packet is too large to fit down a wire all at once. When this happens, the packet is divided into **fragments**, and sent as multiple packets. The other end reassembles the fragments to reconstruct the whole packet.

The problem with fragments is that some of the specifications listed above (in particular, source port, destinations port, ICMP type, ICMP code, or TCP SYN flag) require the kernel to peek at the start of the packet, which is only contained in the first fragment.

If your machine is the only connection to an external network, then you can tell the Linux kernel to reassemble all fragments which pass through it, by compiling the kernel with `IP: always defragment` set to 'Y'. This sidesteps the issue neatly.

Otherwise, it is important to understand how fragments get treated by the filtering rules. Any filtering rule that asks for information we don't have will *not* match. This means that the first fragment is treated like any other packet. Second and further fragments won't be. Thus a rule `-p TCP -s 192.168.1.1 www` (specifying a source port of 'www') will never match a fragment (other than the first fragment). Neither will the opposite rule `-p TCP -s 192.168.1.1 ! www`.

However, you can specify a rule specifically for second and further fragments, using the '-f' flag. Obviously, it is illegal to specify a TCP or UDP port, ICMP type, ICMP code or TCP SYN flag in such a fragment rule.

It is also legal to specify that a rule does *not* apply to second and further fragments, by preceding the '-f' with '!'.

Usually it is regarded as safe to let second and further fragments through, since filtering will effect the first fragment, and thus prevent reassembly on the target host, however, bugs have been known to allow crashing of machines simply by sending fragments. Your call.

Note for network-heads: malformed packets (TCP, UDP and ICMP packets too short for the firewalling code to read the ports or ICMP code and type) are treated as fragments as well. Only TCP fragments starting at position 8 are explicitly dropped by the firewall code (a message should appear in the syslog if this occurs).

As an example, the following rule will drop any fragments going to 192.168.1.1:

```
# ipchains -A output -f -D 192.168.1.1 -j DENY
#
```

4.1.4   Filtering side effects.

OK, so now we know all the ways we can match a packet using a rule. If a packet matches a rule, the following things happen:

1. The byte counter for that rule is increased by the size of the packet (header and all).
2. The packet counter for that rule is incremented.
3. If the rule requests it, the packet is logged.
4. If the rule requests it, the packet's Type Of Service field is changed.
5. If the rule requests it, the packet is marked (not in 2.0 kernel series).
6. The rule target is examined to decide what to do to the packet next.

For variety, I'll address these in order of importance.

Specifying a target.   A **target** tells the kernel what to do with a packet that matches a rule. ipchains uses '-j' (think 'jump-to') for the target specification.

The simplest case is when there is no target specified. This type of rule (often called an 'accounting' rule) is useful for simply counting a certain type of packet. Whether this rule matches or not, the kernel simply examines the next rule in the chain. For example, to count the number of packets from 192.168.1.1, we could do this:

```
# ipchains -A input -s 192.168.1.1
#
```

(Using 'ipchains -L -v' we can see the byte and packet counters associated with each rule).

There are six special targets. The first three, ACCEPT, REJECT and DENY are fairly simple. ACCEPT allows the packet through. DENY drops the packet as if it had never been received. REJECT drops the packet, but (if it's not an ICMP packet) generates an ICMP reply to the source to tell it that the destination was unreachable.

The next one, MASQ tells the kernel to masquerade the packet. For this to work, your kernel needs to be compiled with IP Masquerading enabled. For details on this, see the Masquerading-HOWTO and the Appendix 7 (Differences between ipchains and ipfwadm). This target is only valid for packets traversing the forward chain.

The other major special target is REDIRECT which tells the kernel to send a packet to a local port instead of wherever it was heading. This can only be specified for rules specifying TCP or UDP as their protocol. Optionally, a port (name or number) can be specified following '-j REDIRECT' which will cause the packet to be redirected to that particular port, even if it was addressed to another port. This target is only valid for packets traversing the input chain.

The final special target is RETURN which is identical to falling off the end of the chain immediately. (See 4.1.4 (Setting Policy) below).

Any other target indicates a user-defined chain (as described in 4.1.4 (Operations on an Entire Chain) below). The packet will begin traversing the rules in that chain. If that chain doesn't decide the fate of the packet, then once traversal on that chain has finished, traversal resumes on the next rule in the current chain.

Time for more ASCII art. Consider two (silly) chains: input (the built-in chain) and Test (a user-defined chain).

```
          'input'                        'Test'
     ----------------------------   ----------------------------
     | Rule1: -p ICMP -j REJECT |   | Rule1: -s 192.168.1.1    |
     |--------------------------|   |--------------------------|
```

```
| Rule2: -p TCP -j Test   |   | Rule2: -d 192.168.1.1   |
|-------------------------|   -------------------------
| Rule3: -p UDP -j DENY   |
-------------------------
```

Consider a TCP packet coming from 192.168.1.1, going to 1.2.3.4. It enters the `input` chain, and gets tested against Rule1 - no match. Rule2 matches, and its target is `Test`, so the next rule examined is the start of `Test`. Rule1 in `Test` matches, but doesn't specify a target, so the next rule is examined, Rule2. This doesn't match, so we have reached the end of the chain. We return to the `input` chain, where we had just examined Rule2, so we now examine Rule3, which doesn't match either.

So the packet path is:

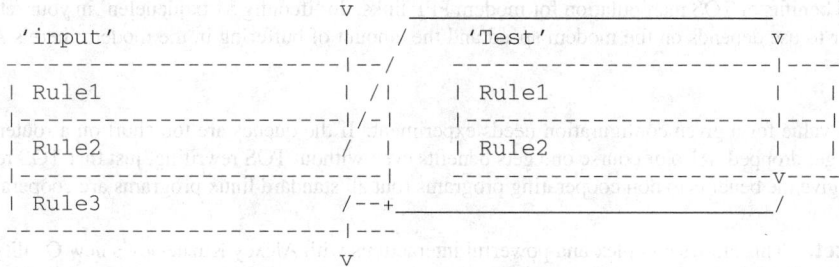

```
                        v        _____
  'input'                       /    'Test'              v
-----------------------|--/     -----------------------|----
| Rule1               | /|      | Rule1               |   |
|---------------------|/-|      |---------------------|---|
| Rule2               / |       | Rule2               |   |
|---------------------|         -----------------------v----
| Rule3              /--+_____/
-----------------------|---
                        v
```

See the section 5.1 (How to Organise Your Firewall Rules) for ways to use user-defined chains effectively.

Logging packets.   This is a side effect that matching a rule can have; you can have the matching packet logged using the '-l' flag. You will usually not want this for routine packets, but it is a useful feature if you want to look for exceptional events (see `man klogd` or `man dmesg`).

Manipulating the Type Of Service   There are four seldom-used bits in the IP header, called the **Type of Service** (TOS) bits. They effect the way packets are treated; the four bits are "Minimum Delay", "Maximum Throughput", "Maximum Reliability" and "Minimum Cost". Only one of these bits is allowed to be set. Rob van Nieuwkerk, the author of the TOS-mangling code, puts it as follows:

> Especially the "Minimum Delay" is important for me. I switch it on for "interactive" packets in my upstream (Linux) router. I'm behind a 33k6 modem link. Linux prioritizes packets in 3 queues. This way I get acceptable interactive performance while doing bulk downloads at the same time. (It could even be better if there wasn't such a big queue in the serial driver, but latency is kept down 1.5 seconds now).

The most common use is to set telnet & ftp control connections to "Minimum Delay" and FTP data to "Maximum Throughput". This would be done as follows:

```
ipchains -A output -p tcp -d 0.0.0.0/0 telnet -t 0x01 0x10
ipchains -A output -p tcp -d 0.0.0.0/0 ftp -t 0x01 0x10
ipchains -A output -p tcp -s 0.0.0.0/0 ftp-data -t 0x01 0x08
```

The '-t' flag takes two extra parameters, both in hexadecimal. These allow complex twiddling of the TOS bits: the first mask is ANDed with the packet's current TOS, and then the second mask is XORed with it. If this is too confusing, just use the following table:

```
TOS Name              Value           Typical Uses

Minimum Delay         0x01 0x10       ftp, telnet
Maximum Throughput    0x01 0x08       ftp-data
```

```
Maximum Reliability    0x01  0x04      snmp
Minimum Cost           0x01  0x02      nntp
```

Andi Kleen goes on to point out the following (mildly edited for posterity):

> Maybe it would be useful to add an reference to the txqueuelen parameter of ifconfig to the discussion of TOS bits. The default device queue length is tuned for ethernet cards, on modems it is too long and makes the 3 band scheduler (which queues based on TOS) work suboptimally. It is a good idea to set it to a value between 4-10 on modem or single b channel ISDN links: on bundled devices a longer queue is needed. This is a 2.0 and 2.1 problem, but in 2.1 it is a ifconfig flag (with recent nettools), while in 2.0 it requires source patches in the device drivers to change.

So, to see maximal benifits of TOS manipulation for modem PPP links, do 'ifconfig $1 txqueuelen' in your /etc/ppp/ip-up script. The number to use depends on the modem speed and the amount of buffering in the modem; here's Andi setting me straight again:

> The best value for a given configuration needs experiment. If the queues are too short on a router then packets will get dropped. Also of course one gets benefits even without TOS rewriting, just that TOS rewriting helps to give the benefits to non cooperating programs (but all standard linux programs are cooperating).

Marking a packet. This allows complex and powerful interactions with Alexey Kuznetsov's new Quality of Service implementation, as well as the mark-based forwarding in later 2.1 series kernels. More news as it comes to hand. This option is ignored altogether in the 2.0 kernel series.

Operations on an entire chain. A very useful feature of ipchains is the ability to group related rules into chains. You can call the chains whatever you want, as long as the names don't clash with the built-in chains (`input`, `output` and `forward`) or the targets (`MASQ`, `REDIRECT`, `ACCEPT`, `DENY`, `REJECT` or `RETURN`). I suggest avoiding upper-case labels entirely, since I may use these for future extensions. The chain name can be up to 8 characters long.

Creating a new chain. Let's create a new chain. Because I am such an imaginative fellow, I'll call it `test`.

```
# ipchains -N test
#
```

It's that simple. Now you can put rules in it as detailed above.

Deleting a chain. Deleting a chain is simple as well.

```
# ipchains -X test
#
```

Why '-X'? Well, all the good letters were taken.

There are a couple of restrictions to deleting chains: they must be empty (see 4.1.4 (Flushing a Chain) below) and they must not be the target of any rule. You can't delete any of the three built-in chains.

Flushing a chain. There is a simple way of emptying all rules out of a chain, using the '-F' command.

```
# ipchains -F forward
#
```

If you don't specify a chain, then *all* chains will be flushed.

Listing a chain.   You can list all the rules in a chain by using the '-L' command.

```
# ipchains -L input
Chain input (refcnt = 1): (policy ACCEPT)
target     prot opt    source                    destination              ports
ACCEPT     icmp -----   anywhere                  anywhere                 any
# ipchains -L test
Chain test (refcnt = 0):
target     prot opt    source                    destination              ports
DENY       icmp -----   localnet/24               anywhere                 any
#
```

The 'refcnt' listed for `test` is the number of rules which have `test` as their target. This must be zero (and the chain be empty) before this chain can be deleted.

If the chain name is omitted, all chains are listed, even empty ones.

There are three options which can accompany '-L'. The '-n' (numeric) option is very useful as it prevents `ipchains` from trying to lookup the IP addresses, which (if you are using DNS like most people) will cause large delays if your DNS is not set up properly, or you have filtered out DNS requests. It also causes ports to be printed out as numbers rather than names.

The '-v' options shows you all the details of the rules, such as the the packet and byte counters, the TOS masks, the interface, and the packet mark. Otherwise these values are omitted. For example:

```
# ipchains -v -L input
Chain input (refcnt = 1): (policy ACCEPT)
pkts bytes target prot opt tosa tosx ifname mark source destination ports
  10   840 ACCEPT icmp --- 0xFF 0x00  lo            anywhere anywhere   any
```

Note that the packet and byte counters are printed out using the suffixes 'K', 'M' or 'G' for 1000, 1,000,000 and 1,000,000,000 respectively. Using the '-x' (expand numbers) flag as well prints the full numbers, no matter how large they are.

Resetting (zeroing) counters.   It is useful to be able to reset the counters. This can be done with the '-Z' (zero counters) option. For example:

```
# ipchains -v -L input
Chain input (refcnt = 1): (policy ACCEPT)
pkts bytes target prot opt tosa tosx ifname mark source destination ports
  10   840 ACCEPT icmp --- 0xFF 0x00  lo            anywhere anywhere  any
# ipchains -Z input
# ipchains -v -L input
Chain input (refcnt = 1): (policy ACCEPT)
pkts bytes target prot opt tosa tosx ifname mark source destination ports
   0     0 ACCEPT icmp --- 0xFF 0x00  lo            anywhere anywhere  any
#
```

The problem with this approach is that sometimes you need to know the counter values immediately before they are reset. In the above example, some packets could pass through between the '-L' and '-Z' commands. For this reason, you can use the '-L' and '-Z' *together*, to reset the counters while reading them. Unfortunately, if you do this, you can't operate on a single chain: you have to list and zero all the chains at once.

```
# ipchains -L -v -Z
Chain input (policy ACCEPT):
pkts bytes target prot opt tosa tosx ifname mark source destination ports
```

```
     0     0 ACCEPT icmp --- 0xFF 0x00  lo                anywhere anywhere   any
Chain forward (refcnt = 1): (policy ACCEPT)
Chain output (refcnt = 1): (policy ACCEPT)
Chain test (refcnt = 0):
     0     0 DENY  icmp --- 0xFF 0x00  lo    ppp0 localnet/24 anywhere   any
# ipchains -L -v
Chain input (policy ACCEPT):
pkts bytes target prot opt tosa tosx ifname mark source destination ports
    10   840 ACCEPT icmp --- 0xFF 0x00  lo                anywhere anywhere   any

Chain forward (refcnt = 1): (policy ACCEPT)
Chain output (refcnt = 1): (policy ACCEPT)
Chain test (refcnt = 0):
     0     0 DENY  icmp --- 0xFF 0x00  lo    ppp0 localnet/24 anywhere   any
#
```

Setting policy.   We glossed over what happens when a packet hits the end of a built-in chain when we discussed how a packet walks through chains in 4.1.4 (Specifying a Target) above. In this case, the **policy** of the chain determines the fate of the packet. Only built-in chains (`input`, `output` and `forward`) have policies, because if a packet falls off the end of a user-defined chain, traversal resumes at the previous chain.

The policy can be any of the first four special targets: `ACCEPT`, `DENY`, `REJECT` or `MASQ`. `MASQ` is only valid for the 'forward' chain.

It is also important to note that a `RETURN` target in a rule in one of the built-in chains is useful to explicitly target the chain policy when a packet matches a rule.

4.1.5   Operations on masquerading.

There are several parameters you can tweak for IP Masquerading. They are bundled with `ipchains` because it's not worth writing a separate tool for them (although this will change).

The IP Masquerading command is '-M', and it can be combined with '-L' to list currently masqueraded connections, or '-S' to set the masquerading parameters.

The '-L' command can be accompanied by '-n' (show numbers instead of hostnames and port names) or '-v' (show deltas in sequence numbers for masqueraded connection, just in case you care).

The '-S' command should be followed by three timeout values, each in seconds: for TCP sessions, for TCP sessions after a FIN packet, and for UDP packets. If you don't want to change one of these values, simply give a value of '0'.

The default values are listed in '/usr/include/net/ip_masq.h', currently 15 minutes, 2 minutes and 5 minutes respectively.

The most common value to change is the first one, for FTP (see 5.2.3 (FTP Nightmares) below).

Note the problems with setting timeouts listed in 6.8 (I can't set masquerading timeouts!).

4.1.6   Checking a packet.

Sometimes you want to see what happens when a certain packet enters your machine, such as for debugging your firewall chains. `ipchains` has the '-C' command to allow this, using the exact same routines that the kernel uses to diagnose real packets.

You specify which chain to test the packet on by following the '-C' argument with its name. Whereas the kernel always starts traversing on the `input`, `output` or `forward` chains, you are allowed to begin traversing on any chain for testing purposes.

The details of the 'packet' are specified using the same syntax used to specify firewall rules. In particular, a protocol ('-p'), source address ('-s'), destination address ('-d') and interface ('-i') are compulsory. If the protocol is TCP or UDP, then a single source and a single destination port must be specified, and a ICMP type and code must be specified for the ICMP protocol (unless the '-f' flag is specified to indicate a fragment rule, in which case these options are illegal).

If the protocol is TCP (and the '-f' flag is not specified), the '-y' flag may be specified, to indicate that the test packet should have the SYN bit set.

Here is an example of testing a TCP SYN packet from 192.168.1.1 port 60000 to 192.168.1.2 port www, coming in the eth0 interface, entering the 'input' chain. (This is a classic incoming WWW connection initiation):

```
# ipchains -C input -p tcp -y -i eth0 -s 192.168.1.1 60000 -
d 192.168.1.2 www
packet accepted
#
```

4.1.7 Multiple rules at once and watching what happens.

Sometimes a single command line can result in multiple rules being effected. This is done in two ways. Firstly, if you specify a hostname which resolves (using DNS) to multiple IP addresses, `ipchains` will act as if you had typed multiple commands with each combination of addresses.

So if the hostname 'www.foo.com' resolves to three IP addresses, and the hostname 'www.bar.com' resolves to two IP addresses, then the command 'ipchains -A input -j reject -s www.bar.com -d www.foo.com' would append six rules to the `input` chain.

The other way to have `ipchains` perform multiple actions is to use the bidirectional flag ('-b'). This flag makes `ipchains` behave as if you had typed the command twice, the second time with the '-s' and '-d' arguments reversed. So, to avoid forwarding either to or from 192.168.1.1, you could do the following:

```
# ipchains -b -A forward -j reject -s 192.168.1.1
#
```

Personally, I don't like the '-b' option much; if you want convenience, see 4.2.1 (Using ipchains-save) below.

The -b option can be used with the insert ('-I'), delete ('-D') (but not the variation which takes a rule number), append ('-A') and check ('-C') commands.

Another useful flag is '-v' (verbose) which prints out exactly what `ipchains` is doing with your commands. This is useful if you are dealing with commands that may effect multiple rules. For example, here we check the behaviour of fragments between 192.168.1.1 and 192.168.1.2.

```
# ipchains -v -b -C input -p tcp -f -s 192.168.1.1 -d 192.168.1.2 -i lo
   tcp opt    ---f- tos 0xFF 0x00  via lo    192.168.1.1  -
> 192.168.1.2    * ->   *
packet accepted
   tcp opt    ---f- tos 0xFF 0x00  via lo    192.168.1.2  -
> 192.168.1.1    * ->   *
packet accepted
#
```

4.2 Useful Examples

I have a dialup PPP connection (-i ppp0). I grab news (-p TCP -s news.virtual.net.au nntp) and mail (-p TCP -s mail.virtual.net.au pop-3) every time I dial up. I use Debian's FTP method to update my machine regularly (-p TCP -y -s ftp.debian.org.au ftp-data). I surf the web through my ISP's proxy while this is going on (`-p TCP -d proxy.virtual.net.au 8080`), but hate the ads from doubleclick.net on the Dilbert Archive (`-p TCP -y -d 199.95.207.0/24` & `-p TCP -y -d 199.95.208.0/24`).

I don't mind people trying to ftp to my machine while I'm online (`-p TCP -d $LOCALIP ftp`), but don't want anyone outside pretending to have an IP address of my internal network (`-s 192.168.1.0/24`). This is commonly called IP spoofing, and there is a better way to protect yourself from it in the 2.1.x kernels and above: see 5.7 (How do I set up IP spoof protection?).

This setup is fairly simple, because there are currently no other boxes on my internal network.

I don't want any local process (ie. Netscape, lynx etc.) to connect to doubleclick.net:

```
# ipchains -A output -d 199.95.207.0/24 -j REJECT
# ipchains -A output -d 199.95.208.0/24 -j REJECT
#
```

Now I want to set priorities on various outgoing packets (there isn't much point in doing it on incoming packets). Since I have a fair number of these rules, it makes sense to put them all in a single chain, called `ppp-out`.

```
# ipchains -N ppp-out
# ipchains -A output -i ppp0 -j ppp-out
#
```

Minimum delay for web traffic & telnet.

```
# ipchains -A ppp-out -p TCP -d proxy.virtual.net.au 8080 -t 0x01 0x10
# ipchains -A ppp-out -p TCP -d 0.0.0.0 telnet -t 0x01 0x10
#
```

Low cosr for ftp data, nntp, pop-3:

```
# ipchains -A ppp-out -p TCP -d 0.0.0.0/0 ftp-data -t 0x01 0x02
# ipchains -A ppp-out -p TCP -d 0.0.0.0/0 nntp -t 0x01 0x02
# ipchains -A ppp-out -p TCP -d 0.0.0.0/0 pop-3 -t 0x01 0x02
#
```

There are a few restrictions on packets coming in the ppp0 interface: let's create a chain called 'ppp-in':

```
# ipchains -N ppp-in
# ipchains -A input -i ppp0 -j ppp-in
#
```

Now, no packets coming in ppp0 should be claiming a source address of 192.168.1.*, so we log and deny them:

```
# ipchains -A ppp-in -s 192.168.1.0/24 -l -j DENY
#
```

I allow UDP packets in for DNS (I run a caching nameserver which forwards all requests to 203.29.16.1, so I expect DNS replies from them only), incoming ftp, and return ftp-data only (which should only be going to a port above 1023, and not the X11 ports around 6000).

```
# ipchains -A ppp-in -p UDP -s 203.29.16.1 -d $LOCALIP dns -j ACCEPT
# ipchains -A ppp-in -p TCP -s 0.0.0.0/0 ftp-data -d $LOCALIP 1024:5999 -
j ACCEPT
# ipchains -A ppp-in -p TCP -s 0.0.0.0/0 ftp-data -d $LOCALIP 6010: -
j ACCEPT
```

```
# ipchains -A ppp-in -p TCP -d $LOCALIP ftp -j ACCEPT
#
```

Finally, local-to-local packets are OK:

```
# ipchains -A input -i lo -j ACCEPT
#
```

Now, my default policy on the `input` chain is DENY, so everything else gets dropped:

```
# ipchains -P input DENY
#
```

NOTE: I wouldn't set up my chains in this order, as packets might get through while I'm setting up. Safest is usually to set the policy to DENY first, then insert the rules. Of course, if your rules require DNS lookups to resolve hostnames, you could be in trouble.

4.2.1 Using `ipchains-save`.

Setting up firewall chains just the way you want them, and then trying to remember the commands you used so you can do them next time is a pain.

So, `ipchains-save` is a script which reads your current chains setup and saves it to a file. For the moment I'll keep you in suspense with regards to what `ipchains-restore` does.

`ipchains-save` can save a single chain, or all chains (if no chain name is specified). The only option currently permitted is '-v' which prints the rules (to stderr) as they are saved. The policy of the chain is also saved for `input`, `output` and `forward` chains.

```
$ ipchains-save > my_firewall
Saving 'input'.
Saving 'output'.
Saving 'forward'.
Saving 'ppp-in'.
Saving 'ppp-out'.
$
```

4.2.2 Using `ipchains-restore`.

`ipchains-restore` restores chains as saved with `ipchains-save`. It can take two options: '-v' which describes each rule as it is added, and '-f' which forces flushing of user-defined chains if they exist, as described below.

If a user-defined chain is found in the input, `ipchains-restore` checks if that chain already exists. If it does, then you will be prompted whether the chains should be flushed (cleared of all rules) or whether restoring this chain should be skipped. If you specified '-f' on the command line, you will not be prompted; the chain will be flushed.

You must be root to run this script; it uses `ipchains` to attempt to restore the rules.

For example:

```
# ipchains-restore < my_firewall
Restoring 'input'.
Restoring 'output'.
Restoring 'forward'.
Restoring 'ppp-in'.
Chain 'ppp-in' already exists. Skip or flush? [S/f]? s
Skipping 'ppp-in'.
```

```
Restoring 'ppp-out'.
Chain 'ppp-out' already exists. Skip or flush? [S/f]? f
Flushing 'ppp-out'.
#
```

5 Miscellaneous.

This section contains all the information and FAQs that I couldn't fit inside the structure above.

5.1 How to Organize Your Firewall Rules.

This question requires some thought. You can try to organize them to optimize speed (minimize the number of rule-checks for the most common packets) or to increase manageability.

If you have an intermittent link, say a PPP link, you might want to set the first rule in the input chain to be set to '-i ppp0 -j DENY' at boot time, then have something like this in your `ip-up` script:

```
# Re-create the 'ppp-in' chain.
ipchains-restore -f < ppp-in.firewall

# Replace DENY rule with jump to ppp-handling chain.
ipchains -R input 1 -i ppp0 -j ppp-in
```

Your `ip-down` script would look like:

```
ipchains -R input 1 -i ppp0 -j DENY
```

5.2 What *not* to filter out.

There are some things you should be aware of before you start filtering out everything you don't want.

5.2.1 ICMP packets.

ICMP packets are used (among other things) to indicate failure for other protocols (such as TCP and UDP). 'destination-unreachable' packets in particular. Blocking these packets means that you will never get 'Host unreachable' or 'No route to host' errors; any connections will just wait for a reply that never comes. This is irritating, but rarely fatal.

A worse problem is the role of ICMP packets in MTU discovery. All good TCP implementations (Linux included) use MTU discovery to try to figure out what the largest packet that can get to a destination without being fragmented (fragmentation slows performance, especially when occasional fragments are lost). MTU discovery works by sending packets with the "Don't Fragment" bit set, and then sending smaller packets if it gets an ICMP packet indicating "Fragmentation needed but DF set" ('fragmentation-needed'). This is a type of 'destination-unreachable' packet, and if it is never received, the local host will not reduce MTU, and performance will be abysmal or non-existent.

5.2.2 TCP connections to DNS (nameservers).

If you're trying to block outgoing TCP connections, remember that DNS doesn't always use UDP; if the reply from the server exceeds 512 bytes, the client uses a TCP connection (still going to port number 53) to get the data.

This can be a trap because DNS will 'mostly work' if you disallow such TCP transfers; you may experience strange long delays and other occasional DNS problems if you do.

If your DNS queries are always directed at the same external source (either directly by using the `nameserver` line in `/etc/resolv.conf` or by using a caching nameserver in forward mode), then you need only allow TCP connections to port `domain` on that nameserver from the local `domain` port (if using a caching nameserver) or from a high port (> 1023) if using `/etc/resolv.conf`.

5.2.3 FTP nightmares.

The classic packet filtering problem is FTP. FTP has two **modes**; the traditional one is called **active mode** and the more recent one is called **passive mode**. Web browsers usually default to passive mode, but command-line FTP programs usually default to active mode.

In active mode, when the remote end wants to send a file (or even the results of an `ls` or `dir` command) it tries to open a TCP connection to the local machine. This means you can't filter out these TCP connections without breaking active FTP.

If you have the option of using passive mode, then fine; passive mode makes data connections from client to server, even for incoming data. Otherwise, it is recommended that you only allow TCP connections to ports above 1024 and not between 6000 and 6010 (6000 is used for X-Windows).

5.3 Filtering out Ping of Death.

Linux boxes are now immune to the famous **Ping of Death**, which involves sending an illegally-large ICMP packet which overflows buffers in the TCP stack on the receiver and causes havoc.

If you are protecting boxes which might be vulnerable, you could simply block ICMP fragments. Normal ICMP packets aren't large enough to require fragmentation, so you won't break anything except big pings. I have heard (unconfirmed) reports that some systems required only the last fragment of an oversize ICMP packet to corrupt them, so blocking only the first fragment is not recommended.

While the exploit programs I have seen all use ICMP, there is no reasons that TCP or UDP fragments (or an unknown protocol) could not be used for this attack, so blocking ICMP fragments is only a temporary solution.

5.4 Filtering out Teardrop and Bonk.

Teardrop and Bonk are two attacks (mainly against Microsoft Windows NT machines) which rely on overlapping fragments. Having your Linux router do defragmentation, or disallowing all fragments to your vulnerable machines are the other options.

5.5 Filtering out Fragment Bombs.

Some less-reliable TCP stacks are said to have problems dealing with large numbers of fragments of packets when they don't receive all the fragments. Linux does not have this problem. You can filter out fragments (which might break legitimate uses) or compile your kernel with 'IP: always defragment' set to 'Y' (only if your Linux box is the only possible route for these packets).

5.6 Changing firewall rules.

There are some timing issues involved in altering firewall rules. If you are not careful, you can let packets through while you are half-way through your changes. A simplistic approach is to do the following:

```
# ipchains -I input 1 -j DENY
# ipchains -I output 1 -j DENY
# ipchains -I forward 1 -j DENY

... make changes ...

# ipchains -D input 1
# ipchains -D output 1
# ipchains -D forward 1
#
```

This drops all packets for the duration of the changes.

If you changes are restricted to a single chain, you might want to create a new chain with the new rules, and then replace ('-R') the rule that pointed to the old chain with one that points to the new chain: then you can delete the old chain. This replacement will occur atomically.

5.7 How do I set up IP spoof protection?

IP spoofing is a technique where a host sends out packets which claim to be from another host. Since packet filtering makes decisions based on this source address, IP spoofing is uses to fool packet filters. It is also used to hide the identity of attackers using SYN attacks, Teardrop, Ping of Death and the like (don't worry if you don't know what they are).

The best way to protect from IP spoofing is called Source Address Verification, and it is done by the routing code, and not firewalling at all. Look for a file called `/proc/sys/net/ipv4/conf/all/rp_filter`. If this exists, then turning on Source Address Verification at every boot is the right solution for you. To do that, insert the following lines somewhere in your init scripts, before any network interfaces are initialized (eg. Debian users would put them in /etc/init.d/netbase if they are not already there):

```
# This is the best method: turn on Source Address Verification and get
# spoof protection on all current and future interfaces.
if [ -e /proc/sys/net/ipv4/conf/all/rp_filter ]; then
    echo -n "Setting up IP spoofing protection..."
    for f in /proc/sys/net/ipv4/conf/*/rp_filter; do
        echo 1 > $f
    done
    echo "done."
else
    echo PROBLEMS SETTING UP IP SPOOFING PROTECTION.  BE WORRIED.
    echo "CONTROL-D will exit from this shell and continue system startup."
    echo
    # Start a single user shell on the console
    /sbin/sulogin $CONSOLE
fi
```

If you cannot do this, you can manually insert rules to protect every interface. This requires knowledge of each interface. The 2.1 kernels automatically reject packets claiming to come from the 127.* addresses (reserved for the local loopback interface, lo).

For example, say we have three interfaces, `eth0`, `eth1` and `ppp0`. We can use `ifconfig` to tell us the address and netmask of the interfaces. Say `eth0` was attached to a network 192.168.1.0 with netmask 255.255.255.0, `eth1` was attached to a network 10.0.0.0 with netmask 255.0.0.0, and `ppp0` connected to the Internet (where any address except the reserved private IP addresses are allowed), we would insert the following rules:

```
# ipchains -A input -i eth0 -s ! 192.168.1.0/255.255.255.0 -j DENY
# ipchains -A input -i ! eth0 -s 192.168.1.0/255.255.255.0 -j DENY
# ipchains -A input -i eth1 -s ! 10.0.0.0/255.0.0.0 -j DENY
# ipchains -A input -i ! eth1 -s 10.0.0.0/255.0.0.0 -j DENY
#
```

This approach is not as good as the Source Address Verification approach, because if your network changes, you have to change your firewalling rules to keep up.

If you are running a 2.0 series kernel, you might want to protect the loopback interface as well, using a rule like this:

```
# ipchains -A input -i ! lo -s 127.0.0.0/255.0.0.0 -j DENY
#
```

5.8 Advanced projects.

There is a userspace library I have written which is included with the source distribution called 'libfw'. It uses the ability of IP Chains 1.3 and above to copy a packet to userspace (using the IP_FIREWALL_NETLINK config option).

Things such as **stateful inspection** (I prefer the term dynamic firewalling) can be implemented in userspace using this library. Other nifty ideas include controlling packets on a per-user basis by doing a lookup in a userspace daemon. This should be pretty easy.

The 'mark' capability of the firewalls is underutilized: it could easily be used to represent a priority for the Quality of Service code, which would make it simple to control packet priorities.

5.9 Future enhancements.

Firewalling and NAT are being redesigned for 2.3. Plans and discussions are available on the netdev archive. These enhancements should clear up many outstanding usability issues (really, firewalling and masquerading shouldn't be *this hard*), and allow growth for far more flexible firewalling.

6 Common problems.

6.1 ipchains -L freezes! You're probably blocking DNS lookups; it will eventually time out. Try using the '-n' (numeric) flag to ipchains, which suppresses the lookup of names.

6.2 Masquerading/forwarding doesn't work!

Make sure that packet forwarding is enabled (in recent kernels it is disabled by default, meaning that packets never even try to traverse the 'forward' chain). You can override this (as root) by typing

```
# echo 1 > /proc/sys/net/ipv4/ip_forward
#
```

If this works for you, you can put this somewhere in your bootup scripts so it is enabled every time; you'll want to set up your firewalling before this command runs though, otherwise there's an opportunity for packets to slip through.

6.3 Wildcard interfaces don't work!

There was a bug in versions 2.1.102 and 2.1.103 of the kernel (and some old patches I produced) which made ipchains commands which specified a wildcard interface (such as -i ppp+) fail.

This is fixed in recent kernels, and in the 2.0.34 patch on the web site. You can also fix it by hand in the kernel source by changing line 63 or so in include/linux/ip_fw.h:

```
#define IP_FW_F_MASK    0x002F  /* All possible flag bits mask   */
```

This should read "0x003F". Fix this and recompile the kernel.

6.4 TOS doesn't work!

This was my mistake: setting the Type of Service field did not actually set the Type of Service in kernel versions 2.1.102 through 2.1.111. This problem was fixed in 2.1.112.

6.5 `ipautofw` and `ipportfw` don't work!

For 2.0.x, this is true; I haven't time to create and maintain a jumbo patch for ipchains and ipautofw/ipportfw.

For 2.1.x, download ipmasqadm from

```
<url url="http://juanjox.home.ml.org/"
     name="http://juanjox.home.ml.org/">
```

and use it exactly as you would have used `ipautofw` or `ipportfw`, except instead of `ipportfw` you type `ipmasqadm portfw`, and instead of `ipautofw` you type `ipmasqadm autofw`.

6.6 xosview is broken!

Upgrade to version 1.6.0 or above, which doesn't require any firewall rules at all for 2.1.x kernels. This seems to have broken again in the 1.6.1 release; please bug the author (it's not my fault!).

6.7 Segmentation fault with `-j` `REDIRECT`!

This was a bug in ipchains version 1.3.3. Please upgrade.

6.8 I can't set masquerading timeouts!

True (for 2.1.x kernels) up to 2.1.123. In 2.1.124, trying to set the masquerading timeouts causes a kernel lockup (change `return` to `ret` = on line 1328 of net/ipv4/ip_fw.c). In 2.1.125, it works fine.

6.9 I want to firewall IPX!

So do a number of others, it seems. My code only covers IP, unfortunately. On the good side, all the hooks are there to firewall IPX! You just need to write the code; I will happily help where possible.

7 Appendix: Differences between `ipchains` and `ipfwadm`

Some of these changes are a result of kernel changes, and some a result of `ipchains` being different from `ipfwadm`.

1. Many arguments have been remapped: capitals now indicates a command, and lower case now indicates an option.

2. Arbitrary chains are supported, so even built-in chains have full names instead of flags (eg. 'input' instead of '-I').

3. The '-k' option has vanished: use '! -y'.

4. The '-b' option actually inserts/appends/deletes two rules, rather than a single 'bidirectional' rule.

5. The '-b' option can be passed to '-C' to do two checks (one in each direction).

6. The '-x' option to '-l' has been replaced by '-v'.

7. Multiple source and destination ports are not supported anymore. Hopefully being able to negate the port range will somewhat make up for that.

8. Interfaces can only be specified by name (not address). The old semantics got silently changed in the 2.1 kernel series anyway.

9. Fragments are examined, not automatically allowed through.

10. Explicit accounting chains have been done away with.

11. Arbitrary protocols over IP can be tested for.

12. The old behavior of SYN and ACK matching (which was previously ignored for non-TCP packets) has changed; the SYN option is not valid for non-TCP-specific rules.

13. Counters are now 64-bit on 32-bit machines, not 32-bit.

14. Inverse options are now supported.

15. ICMP codes are now supported.

16. Wildcard interfaces are now supported.

17. TOS manipulations are now sanity-checked: the old kernel code would silently stop you from (illegally) manipulating the 'Must Be Zero' TOS bit; ipchains now returns an error if you try, as well as for other illegal cases.

7.1 Quick-Reference table.

[Mainly, command arguments are UPPER CASE, and option arguments are lower case]

One thing to note, masquerading is specified by '-j MASQ'; it is completely different from '-j ACCEPT', and not treated as merely a side-effect, unlike ipfwadm does.

```
=================================================================
| ipfwadm        | ipchains           | Notes
-----------------------------------------------------------------
| -A [both]      | -N acct            | Create an 'acct' chain
|                |& -I 1 input -j acct | and have output and input
|                |& -I 1 output -j acct | packets traverse it.
|                |& acct              |
-----------------------------------------------------------------
| -A in          | input              | A rule with no target
-----------------------------------------------------------------
| -A out         | output             | A rule with no target
-----------------------------------------------------------------
| -F             | forward            | Use this as [chain].
-----------------------------------------------------------------
| -I             | input              | Use this as [chain].
-----------------------------------------------------------------
| -O             | output             | Use this as [chain].
-----------------------------------------------------------------
| -M -l          | -M -L              |
-----------------------------------------------------------------
| -M -s          | -M -S              |
-----------------------------------------------------------------
| -a policy      | -A [chain] -j POLICY | (but see -r and -m).
-----------------------------------------------------------------
| -d policy      | -D [chain] -j POLICY | (but see -r and -m).
-----------------------------------------------------------------
| -i policy      | -I 1 [chain] -j POLICY| (but see -r and -m).
-----------------------------------------------------------------
| -l             | -L                 |
-----------------------------------------------------------------
| -z             | -Z                 |
-----------------------------------------------------------------
| -f             | -F                 |
-----------------------------------------------------------------
| -p             | -P                 |
-----------------------------------------------------------------
| -c             | -C                 |
-----------------------------------------------------------------
| -P             | -p                 |
-----------------------------------------------------------------
```

HOWTO

-S	-s	Only takes one port or range, not multiples.
-D	-d	Only takes one port or range, not multiples.
-V	\<none\>	Use -i [name].
-W	-i	
-b	-b	Now actually makes 2 rules.
-e	-v	
-k	! -y	Doesn't work unless -p tcp also specified.
-m	-j MASQ	
-n	-n	
-o	-l	
-r [redirpt]	-j REDIRECT [redirpt]	
-t	-t	
-v	-v	
-x	-x	
-y	-y	Doesn't work unless -p tcp also specified.

7.2 Examples of translated ipfwadm commands

Old command: ipfwadm -F -p deny

New command: ipchains -P forward DENY

Old command: ipfwadm -F -a m -S 192.168.0.0/24 -D 0.0.0.0/0

New command: ipchains -A forward -j MASQ -s 192.168.0.0/24 -d 0.0.0.0/0

Old command: ipfwadm -I -a accept -V 10.1.2.1 -S 10.0.0.0/8 -D 0.0.0.0/0

New command: ipchains -A input -j ACCEPT -i eth0 -s 10.0.0.0/8 -d 0.0.0.0/0

(Note that there is no equivalent for specifying interfaces by address: use the interface name. On this machine, 10.1.2.1 corresponds to eth0).

8 Appendix: Using the `ipfwadm-wrapper` script.

The `ipfwadm-wrapper` shell script should be a plug-in replacement of `ipfwadm` for backwards compatibility with ipfwadm 2.3a.

The only feature it can't really handle is the '-V' option. When this is used, a warning is given. If the '-W' option is also used, the '-V' option is ignored. Otherwise, the script tries to find the interface name associated with that address, using `ifconfig`. If that fails (such as for an interface which is down) then it will exit with an error message.

This warning can be suppressed by either changing the '-V' to a '-W', or directing the standard output of the script to /dev/null.

If you should find any mistakes in this script, or any changes between the real ipfwadm and this script, *please* report a bug to me: send an Email to ipchains@wantree.com.au with "BUG-REPORT" in the subject. Please list your old version of `ipfwadm` (`ipfwadm -h`), your version of `ipchains` (`ipchains -version`), the version of the ipfwadm wrapper script (`ipfwadm-wrapper -version`). Also send the output of `ipchains-save`. Thanks in advance.

Mix `ipchains` with this `ipfwadm-wrapper` script at your own peril.

9 Appendix: thanks.

Many thanks have to go to Michael Neuling, who wrote the first releasable cut of the IP chains code while working for me. Public apologies for nixing his result-caching idea, which Alan Cox later proposed and I have finally begun implementing, having seen the error of my ways.

Thanks to Alan Cox for his 24-hour EMail tech support, and encouragement.

Thanks to all the authors of the ipfw and ipfwadm code, especially Jos Vos. Standing on the shoulders of giants and all that... This applies to Linus Torvalds and all the kernel and userspace hackers as well.

Thanks to the diligent beta testers and bughunters, especially Jordan Mendelson, Shaw Carruthers, Kevin Moule, Dr. Liviu Daia, Helmut Adams, Franck Sicard, Kevin Littlejohn, Matt Kemner, John D. Hardin, Alexey Kuznetsov, Leos Bitto, Jim Kunzman, Gerard Gerritsen, Serge Sivkov, Andrew Burgess, Steve Schmidtke, Richard Offer, Bernhard Weisshuhn and Pavel Krauz for beating sense into me on the TCP DNS stuff.

HOWTO

Part XVI

"Linux IPX-HOWTO" Kevin Thorpe

kevin@pricetrak.com
v2.3, 06 May 1998
This document aims to describe how to obtain, install and configure various tools available for the the Linux operating system that use the Linux kernel IPX protocol support.

Contents

HOWTO

1 Introduction.

This is the Linux IPX-HOWTO. You should read the Linux NET-3-HOWTO in conjunction with this document.

1.1 Changes from the previous release.

```
Change of author:
        Many thanks to Terry Dawson for passing on this document and
        congratulations on becoming a father :-).

Additions:
        Addition of a brief explanation of IPX. This is in response to
        many baffled queries on the discussion lists.

Corrections/Updates:
        New version of ncpfs which now supports NDS logins. This is early
        beta test and may be prohibited in your country due to the use of
        patented technology.

        Addition of support for trustee rights in mars_nwe. This is still
        in beta test.
```

1.2 Introduction.

The Linux Kernel has a completely new network implementation as compared to other Unix like operating systems. The ability to take a fresh approach to developing the kernel networking software has led to the Linux kernel having support for a range of non tcp/ip protocols being built. The IPX protocol is one of those that have been included.

The Linux kernel supports the IPX protocol only. It does not yet support protocols such as IPX/RIP, SAP or NCP, these are supported by other software such as that documented elsewhere in this document.

The IPX support was originally developed by Alan Cox <alan@lxorguk.ukuu.org.uk> and has been significantly enhanced by Greg Page <greg@caldera.com>.

2 Disclaimer.

I do not and cannot know everything there is to know about the Linux network software. Please accept and be warned that this document probably does contain errors. Please read any README files that are included with any of the various pieces of software described in this document for more detailed and accurate information. I will attempt to keep this document as error-free and up-to-date as possible. Versions of software are current as at time of writing.

In no way do I or the authors of the software in this document offer protection against your own actions. If you configure this software, even as described in this document and it causes problems on your network then you alone must carry the responsibility. I include this warning because IPX network design and configuration is not always a simple matter and sometimes undesirable interaction with other routers and fileservers can result if you do not design or configure your network carefully. I also include this warning because I was asked to by someone unfortunate enough to have discovered this lesson the hard way.

3 Related Documentation.

This document presumes you understand how to build a Linux kernel with the appropriate networking options selected and that you understand how to use the basic network tools such as *ifconfig* and *route*. If you do not, then you should read the *NET-3-HOWTO* <NET-3-HOWTO.html> in conjunction with this document as it describes these.

Other Linux HOWTO documents that might be useful are:

The *Ethernet-HOWTO* <Ethernet-HOWTO.html>, which describes the details of configuring an Ethernet device for Linux.

The *PPP-HOWTO* <PPP-HOWTO.html> as IPX support is available for version 2.2.0d and later of the Linux PPP implementation.

3.1 New versions of this document.

If your copy of this document is more than two months old then I strongly recommend you obtain a newer version. The networking support for Linux is changing very rapidly with new enhancements and features, so this document also changes fairly frequently. The latest released version of this document can always be retrieved by anonymous ftp from:

ftp:/sunsite.unc.edu/pub/Linux/docs/HOWTO/IPX-HOWTO>/

or:

ftp:/sunsite.unc.edu/pub/Linux/docs/HOWTO/other-formats/IPX-HOWTO{-html.tar,ps,dvi}.gz>/

via the World Wide Web from the *Linux Documentation Project Web Server* <http://sunsite.unc.edu/ LDP/linux.html>, at page: *IPX-HOWTO* <http://sunsite.unc.edu/LDP/HOWTO/IPX-HOWTO.html> or directly from me, <kevin@pricetrak.com>. It may also be posted to the newsgroups: comp.os.linux.networking, comp.os.linux.answers and news.answers from time to time.

3.2   Feedback.

Please send any comments, updates, or suggestions to me, <kevin@pricetrak.com>. The sooner I get feedback, the sooner I can update and correct this document. If you find any problems with it, please mail me directly as I can miss info posted to the newsgroups.

3.3   Mailing list support.

There is a mailing list established for discussion of the various Linux IPX software packages described in this document. You can subscribe to it by sending a mail message to 'listserv@sh.cvut.cz' with 'add linware' in the body of the message. To post to the list your send your mail to 'linware@sh.cvut.cz'. I regularly watch this list.

The mailing list is archived at *www.kin.vslib.cz* <http://www.kin.vslib.cz/hypermail/linware/>.

4   Some of the terms used in this document.

You will often see the terms `client` and `server` used in this document. They are normally fairly specific terms but in this document I have generalized their definitions a little so that they mean the following:

client
> The machine or program that initiates an action or a connection for the purpose of gaining use of some service or data.

server
> The machine or program that accepts incoming connections from multiple remote machines and provides a service or data to those.

These definitions are not very reliable either, but they provide a means of distinguishing the ends of peer to peer systems such as *SLIP* or *PPP* which truly do not actually have clients and servers.

Other terms you will see are:

Bindery
> The *bindery* is a specialised database storing network configuration information on a Novell fileserver. Netware clients may query the *bindery* to obtain information on available services, routing and user information.

Frame Type
> is a term used to describe that actual protocol used to carry the IPX (and IP) datagrams across your ethernet style network segments. There are four common ones. They are:

Ethernet_II
> This is a refined version of the original DIX ethernet standard. Novell has been allocated a formal protocol id and this means that both IPX and IP can coexist happily in an Ethernet_II environment quite happily. This is commonly used in Novell environments and is a good choice.

802.3
> This is an I.E.E.E. protocol defining a Carrier Sense Multiple Access with Collision Detection (CSMA/CD) mechanism. It was based on the original DIX Ethernet standard, with an important modification, the type (protocol id) field was converted into a length field instead. It is for this reason that IPX really shouldn't be run here. IEEE 802.3 was designed to carry IEEE 802.2 frames **only** but there are implementations that use it to carry IPX frames directly and remarkably it does work. Avoid it unless you are trying to interwork with a network already configured to use it.

802.2
> This is an I.E.E.E. protocol that defines a set of Logical Link Control procedures. It provides a simplistic way of allowing different protocols to coexist, but is quite limited in this respect. Novell uses an unofficial Service Address Point (like a protocol id) but since everyone else uses it as well, that hasn't yet presented too much of a problem.

SNAP

SNAP is the Sub Network Access Protocol. This protocol is designed ride on top of 802.3 and 802.2. It expands the multiprotocol capability of 802.2 and provides some measure of compatability with existing Ethernet and Ethernet_II frame types.

IPX

Internet Packet eXchange is a protocol used by the Novell corporation to provide internetworking support for their NetWare(tm) product. IPX is similar in functionality to the IP protocol used by the tcp/ip community.

IPX network address

This is a number which uniquely identifies a particular IPX network. The usual notation for this address is in hexadecimal. An example might look like: `0x23a91002`.

IPX Internal network

This is a virtual IPX network. It is virtual because it does not correspond to a physical network. This is used to provide a means of uniquely identifying and addressing a particular IPX host. This is generally only useful to IPX hosts that exist on more than one physical IPX network such as fileservers. The address is coded in the same form as for a physical IPX network.

RIP

Routing Information Protocol is a protocol used to automatically propagate network routes in an IPX network. It is functionally similar to the RIP used within the tcp/ip community.

NCP

NetWare Core Protocol is a networked filesystem protocol designed by the Novell Corporation for their NetWare(tm) product. NCP is functionally similar to the NFS used in the tcp/ip community.

SAP

Service Advertisement Protocol is a protocol designed by the Novell Corporation that is used to advertise network services in a NetWare(tm) environment.

Hardware address

This is a number that uniquely identifies a host in a physical network at the media access layer. Examples of this are *Ethernet Addresses*. An Ethernet address is generally coded as six hexadecimal values separated by colon characters eg. `00:60:8C:C3:3C:0F`.

route

The *route* is the path that your packets take through the network to reach their destination.

5   A brief discussion of IPX network topology

This is a much simplified explanation for people new to IPX. Large networks will probably break lots of the rules explained here. In complex IPX networks the administrator should always be consulted.

IPX networking revolves around a scheme of numbered *networks* unlike IP which places more emphasis on the *interface* addresses. A network is a collection of equipment connected to the same LAN segment and *using the same frame type*. Different frame types on the same LAN segment are treated as seperate networks.

Each network must be allocated a number which is unique across the entire internetwork. This is usually performed by a NetWare(tm) server, but can easily be performed by Linux. IPX clients are given this number by the server when starting, they only require to know the correct frame type.

Routing between networks is usually performed by putting two network cards in a server. This server then runs the RIP protocol which holds a routing table for the internetwork. Periodic broadcasts of this routing table are exchanged between servers. Within a short time each server 'discovers' the topology of the internetwork.

If you only wish to use the services of an existing NetWare server, you can use `ipx_configure` (section 7.1) to automatically define the IPX interfaces by using broadcast queries to look for a server. If this fails, or you wish to provide IPX services, you will need to define the interfaces manually using `ipx_interface` or `mars_nwe`.

HOWTO

6 The IPX related files in the `/proc` filesystem.

There are a number of files related to the Linux IPX support that are located within the `/proc` filesystem. They are:

/proc/net/ipx_interface

This file contains information about the IPX interfaces configured on your machine. These may have been configured manually by command or automatically detected and configured.

/proc/net/ipx_route

This file contains a list of the routes that exist in the IPX routing table. These routes may have been added manually by command or automatically by an IPX routing daemon.

/proc/net/ipx

This file is a list of the IPX sockets that are currently open for use on the machine.

7 Greg Pages IPX tools.

Greg Page <greg@caldera.com of Caldera Incorporated has written a suite of IPX configuration tools and enhanced the Linux IPX kernel support.

The kernel enhancements allow linux to be configured as a fully featured IPX bridge or router. The enhanced IPX support has already been fed back into the mainstream kernel distribution so you will probably already have it.

The network configuration tools provide you with the capability to configure your network devices to support IPX and allow you to configure IPX routing and other facilities under Linux. The Linux IPX network tools are available from: *sunsite.unc.edu* <ftp://sunsite.unc.edu/pub/Linux/system/filesystems/ncpfs/ipx.tgz>.

7.1 The IPX tools in more detail.

ipx_interface

This command is used to manually add, delete or check ipx capability to an existing network device. Normally the network device would be an Ethernet device such at eth0. At least one IPX interface must be designated the *primary* interface and the *-p* flag to this command does this. For example to enable Ethernet device eth0 for IPX capability as the primary IPX interface using the IEEE 802.2 frame type and IPX network address 39ab0222 you would use:

```
# ipx_interface add -p eth0 802.2 0x39ab0222
```

If the frame type differs from NetWare(tm) servers on this network, they will studiously ignore you. If the frame type is correct but the network number differs, they will still ignore you but complain frequently on the NetWare server console. The latter is guaranteed to gain you flames from your NetWare administrator and may disrupt existing NetWare clients.

If you get an error while running this program and you happen to not have already configured tcp/ip, then you will find that you need to manually start the eth0 interface using the command:

```
# ifconfig eth0 up
```

ipx_configure

This command enables or disables the automatic setting of the interface configuration and primary interface settings.

-auto_interface

allows you to select whether new network devices should be automatically configured as IPX devices or not.

-auto_primary

allows you to select whether the IPX software should automatically select a primary interface or not. Problems have been noted using this with Windows 95 clients on the network.

A typical example would be to enable both automatic interface configuration and automatic primary interface setting with the following command:

```
# ipx_configure --auto_interface=on --auto_primary=on
```

ipx_internal_net

This command allows you to configure or deconfigure an internal network address. An internal network address is optional, but when it is configured it will always be the primary interface. To configure an IPX network address of `ab000000` on IPX node 1 you would use:

```
# ipx_internal_net add 0xab000000 1
```

ipx_route

The command allows you to manually modify the IPX routing table. For example to add a route to IPX network `39ab0222` via a router with node number `00608CC33C0F` on IPX network `39ab0108`:

```
# ipx_route add 0x39ab0222 0x39ab0108 0x00608CC33C0F
```

8   Configuring your Linux machine as an IPX router.

If you have a number of IPX segments that you wish to internetwork you need the services of a router. In the Novell environment there are two pieces of information which are necessary to be propagated around the network. They are the network routing information propagated using Novell RIP, and the service advertisement information propagated using Novell SAP. Any router must support both of these protocols to be useful in most situations.

Linux has support for both of these protocols and can be fairly easily made to function as a fully Novell compliant router.

The Linux kernel IPX support actually manages the IPX packet forwarding across interfaces, but it does this according to the rules coded into the IPX routing table. Linux needs a program to implement the Novell RIP and SAP to ensure that the IPX routing table is built correctly and updated periodically to reflect changes in the network status.

Volker Lendecke <lendecke@namu01.gwdg.de> has developed a routing daemon *ipxripd* that will do this for you. The *mars_nwe* package mentioned later includes an alternative routing daemon.

You can find *ipxripd* at:

sunsite.unc.edu   <ftp://sunsite.unc.edu/pub/Linux/system/filesystems/ncpfs/ipxripd-0.
7.tgz>

or at Volkers home site at:

ftp.gwdg.de <ftp://ftp.gwdg.de/pub/linux/misc/ncpfs/ipxripd-0.7.tgz>

Configuring your Linux machine to act as a router is very straightforward. The steps you must take are:

1. Build your kernel with IPX, Ethernet and /proc support.

2. Obtain, compile and install the *ipxd* daemon program.

3. Boot the new kernel and ensure that each of the Ethernet cards has been properly detected and there are no hardware conflicts.

4. Enable the IPX protocol on each of the interfaces using the *ipx_interface* command described above.

5. Start the *ipxd* daemon program.

Consider the following simple network:

```
IPX Addr: 0x01000000  802.2
|-------------------------|
```

```
                                               Linux Router
  IPX Addr: 0x02000000   802.2           \
|-------------------------|               \    eth0/-----------\
                |                          \   \--====|          |
                \                           \        | IPX route |
                 \                           \  eth1 | Table     |
  IPX Addr: 0x03000000   etherII             \----====|          |
|-------------------------|                       |          ^   |
                |                                  |          |   |
                \                             eth2 |  IPXd        |
                 _____/ ====|         |
                                              |          |   |
  IPX Addr: 0x04000000   etherII         eth3 |  SAPd        |
|-------------------------|                   / ====|         |
                |                             |    _____ |
                 _____/            \___/
```

The configuration for the above network would look like:

```
# ipx_interface add eth0 802.2 0x0100000000
# ipx_interface add eth1 802.2 0x0200000000
# ipx_interface add eth2 etherii 0x0300000000
# ipx_interface add eth3 etherii 0x0400000000
# ipxd
```

You should then wait a moment or two and check your `/proc/net/ipx_route` file and you should see it populated with the IPX routes relevant to your configuration and any learned from any other routers in the network.

8.1   Do I need to configure an internal network ?

Novell has a feature called an internal network, which it uses to simplify routing in situations where a host has more than one network device connected. This is useful in the case of a fileserver connected to multiple networks as it means that only one route needs to be advertised to reach the server regardless of which network you are attempting from.

In the case of a configuration where you are not running a fileserver and your machine acting only as an IPX router the question is not as simple to answer. It has been reported that configuring for IPX/PPP works 'better' if you also configure an internal network.

In any case it is easy to do, but may require a rebuild of your kernel. When you are working through the kernel `make config` you must answer `y` when asked `Full internal IPX network` as illustrated:

```
    ...
    ...
    Full internal IPX network (CONFIG_IPX_INTERN) [N/y/?] y
    ...
    ...
```

To configure the internal network interface, use the *ipx_internal_net* command described earlier in the IPX tools section. The main precaution to take is to ensure that they IPX network address you assign is unique on your network and that no other machine or network is using it.

9   Configuring your Linux machine as an NCP client.

If you are a user of a mixed technology network that comprises both IP and IPX protocols it is likely that at some time or another you have wanted to have your Linux machine access data stored on a Novell fileserver on your network. Novell have long offered an NFS server package for their fileservers that would allow this, but if you are a small site or have only a small number of people interested in doing this it is difficult to justify the cost of the commercial package.

Volker Lendecke <lendecke@namu01.gwdg.de> has written a Linux filesystem kernel module that supports a subset of the Novell NCP that will allow you to mount Novell volumes into your Linux filesystem without requiring any additional products for your fileserver. Volker has called the package *ncpfs* and derived the necessary information mainly from the book "Netzwerkprogrammierung in C" by Manfred Hill and Ralf Zessin (further details of the book are contained within the README file in the *ncpfs* package).

The software causes Linux to emulate a normal Novell workstation for file services. It also includes a small print utility that allows you to print to Novell print queues (This is documented in the Print Client section later). The *ncpfs* package will work with Novell fileservers of version 3.x and later, it will not work the Novell 2.x. The *ncpfs* client will also work with close Novell compatible products, but unfortunately some products that claim to be compatible aren't compatible enough. To use *ncpfs* with Novell 4.x fileservers, it is preferred to use the Novell server in *bindery* emulation mode. The NDS support is a very recent early beta addition to *ncpfs* and additionally its use may be prohibited in your country due to the inclusion of patented technology.

9.1 Obtaining *ncpfs*.

The latest *ncpfs* package was designed to be built against the version 1.2.13 kernel or kernels later than 1.3.71 (this includes 2.x.x). If you not using a kernel in either of these categories then you will have to upgrade your kernel. The *Kernel-HOWTO* <Kernel-HOWTO.html> describes how to do this in detail.

You can obtain the *ncpfs* package by anonymous ftp from Volker's home site at: *ftp.gwdg.de* <ftp://ftp.gwdg.de/pub/linux/misc/ncpfs/> or *sunsite.unc.edu* <ftp://sunsite.unc.edu/pub/Linux/system/filesystems/ncpfs> or mirror sites. The current version at the time of writing was:

ncpfs-2.0.11.tgz or ncpfs-2.2.0.tgz which adds the NDS support.

9.2 Building *ncpfs* for kernel 1.2.13.

Build a kernel with Ethernet and IPX support

The first thing you need to do is ensure that your kernel has been built with IPX support enabled. In the 1.2.13 version kernel you need only ensure that you have answered Y to the question: 'The IPX protocol' as illustrated:

```
...
...
Assume subnets are local (CONFIG_INET_SNARL) [y]
Disable NAGLE algorithm (normally enabled) (CONFIG_TCP_NAGLE_OFF) [n]
The IPX protocol (CONFIG_IPX) [n] y
*
* SCSI support
...
...
```

You will also need to ensure that you include an appropriate driver for your Ethernet card. If you do not know how to do this then you should read the *Ethernet-HOWTO* <Ethernet-HOWTO.html>.

You can then proceed to build your kernel. Make sure you remember to run *lilo* to install it when you have finished.

Untar the *ncpfs* software

```
# cd /usr/src
# tar xvfz ncpfs-2.0.11.tgz
# cd ncpfs
```

Check the Makefile

If you intend to use *kerneld* to autoload the *ncpfs* kernel module then you must uncomment the line in the `Make-file` that refers to: `KERNELD`. If you are unsure what this means then you should read the *Kernel-HOWTO* `<Kernel-HOWTO.html>` to familiarise yourself with kernel module configuration.

Make the *ncpfs* software

The software should compile cleanly with no other configuration necessary:

```
# make
```

Copy the IPX tools somewhere useful if you don't already have them.

After the *make* has completed you should find all of the tools you need in the `ncpfs/bin` directory. You can use:

```
# make install
```

to install the tools in Volkers choice of directories. If you are running on an ELF based system then you will need to rerun `'ldconfig -v'` to ensure that the shared library is able to be found.

Copy the *ncpfs.o* module somewhere useful if necessary.

If you are compiling for a `1.2.*` kernel then you will find a file called `ncpfs.o` in the `ncpfs/bin` directory after the *make* has completed. This is the *ncpfs* kernel module. You should copy this somewhere useful. On my *debian* system I have copied it to the `/lib/modules/1.2.13/fs` directory and added `ncpfs` to the `/etc/modules` file so that it will be automatically started at boot time. If you are using some other distribution you should find where it keeps its modules and copy it there, or just copy it to your `/etc` directory. To load the modules manually you need to use the command:

```
# insmod ncpfs.o
```

9.3   Building *ncpfs* for kernels 1.3.71++/2.0.*.

For the latest version of *ncpfs* you must use kernel `1.3.71` or newer, this includes the `2.0.*` kernels.

If you intend using a kernel that is version `1.3.71` or newer then the *ncpfs* kernel code has been included in the standard kernel distribution. You need only answer `Y` to:

```
Networking options   --->
    ...
    ...
    <*> The IPX protocol
    ...
Filesystems   --->
    ...
    ...
    <*> NCP filesystem support (to mount NetWare volumes)
    ...
```

You will still need to follow the instructions for building for kernels `1.2.*` so that you can build the tools but there will not be a module file for you to install.

9.4   Configuring and using *ncpfs*.

Configure the IPX network software

There are two ways of configuring the IPX network software. You can manually configure all of your IPX network information or you can choose to let the software determine for itself some reasonable settings using the command:

```
# ipx_configure --auto_interface=on --auto_primary=on
```

This should be reasonable in most circumstances, but if it doesn't work for you then read the 'IPX tools' section above to configure your software manually. Problems have been noted using this on networks containing Windows '95 clients.

Test the configuration

After your IPX network is configured you should be able to use the *slist* command to see a list of all of the Novell fileserver on your network:

```
# slist
```

If the slist command displays a message like: `ncp_connect:  Invalid argument` then your kernel probably does not support IPX. Check that you have actually booted off the appropriate kernel. When you boot you should see messages about 'IPX' and 'ncpfs' in the system startup messages. If the *slist* command does not list all of your fileservers then you may need to use the manual network configuration method.

Mount a Novell(tm) server or volume.

If your IPX network software is working ok you should now be able to mount a Novell fileserver or volume into your Linux filesystem. The *ncpmount* command is used for this purpose and requires that you specify at least the following information:

1. The fileserver name

2. (optionally) The fileserver directory to mount

3. The fileserver login id. If it has a password you will also need that.

4. The mount point ie. where you want the mount to go. This will be an existing directory on your machine.

There is an equivalent *ncpumount* command to unmount a mounted NCP filesystem. The NCP filesystems will be unmounted cleanly if you shutdown your machine normally, so you needn't worry about *ncpumount*ing your filesystems manually before a *halt* or *shutdown*.

An example command to mount fileserver ACCT_FS01, with a login id of guest with no password, under the /mnt/Accounts directory might look like the following:

```
# ncpmount -S ACCT_FS01 /mnt/Accounts -U guest -n
```

Note the use of the `-n` option to indicate that no password is required for the login. The same login specifying a password of secret would look like:

```
# ncpmount -S ACCT_FS01 /mnt/Accounts -U guest -P secret
```

If you don't specify either the `-n` or the `-P` options you will be prompted for a password.

Check the mount

If the mount is successful you will find all the volumes accessible to the userid used for login listed as directories under the mount point. You should then also be able to traverse the directory structure to find other files. You may alternatively use the `-V` option to mount a single volume.

NCP does not provide uid or gid ownership of files. All the files will have the permission and ownership assigned to the mount point directory restricted by trustee permissions on the Novell server. Bear this in mind when sharing mounts between Linux users.

Configure mounts to be automatically performed.

If you have some need to permanently have an ncp mount then you will want to configure the commands above into your *rc* files so that they occur automatically at boot time. If your distribution doesn't already provide some way of configuring IPX like debian then I recommend you place them in your /etc/rc.local file if you have one. You might use something like:

```
#
# Start the ncp filesystem

/sbin/insmod /lib/modules/1.2.13/fs/ncpfs.o

# configure the IPX network
ipx_configure --auto_interface=on --auto_primary=on

# guest login to the Accounting fileserver
```

HOWTO

```
ncpmount -S ACCT_FS01 /mnt/Accounts -U guest -n
#
```

There is another means of configuring NCP mounts and that is by building a $HOME/.nwclient file. This file contains details of temporary or user specific NCP mounts that would be performed regularly. It allows you to store the details of mounts so that you can recreate them without having to specify all of the detail each time. Its format is quite straightforward:

```
# The first entry is the 'preferred server' entry and is
# used whenever you do not specify a server explicitly.
#
# User TERRY login to DOCS_FS01 fileserver with password 'password'
DOCS_FS01/TERRY password
#
# Guest login to the ACCT_FS01 fileserver with no password.
ACCT_FS01/GUEST -
```

To activate these mounts you could use:

```
$ ncpmount /home/terry/docs
```

to mount: DOCS_FS01 with a login of TERRY under the /home/terry/docs directory. Note that this entry was chosen because no fileserver was specified in the mount command. If the following command were used:

```
$ ncpmount -S ACCT_FS01 /home/terry/docs
```

then a GUEST login to ACCT_FS01 would be mounted there instead.

Note: for this mechanism to work the permissions of the $HOME/.nwclient file must be 0600 so you would need to use the command:

```
$ chmod 0600 $HOME/.nwclient
```

If non-root users are to be allowed to use this mechanism then the *ncpmount* command must be Set Userid Root, so you would need to give it permissions:

```
# chmod 4755 ncpmount
```

Try out the *nsend* utility

a utility to send messages to Novell users is also included in the package, it is called *nsend* and is used as follows:

```
# nsend rod hello there
```

would send the message "hello there" to a logged in user "rod" on your "primary" fileserver (the first one appearing in your .nwclient file. You can specify another fileserver with the same syntax as for the *ncpmount* command.

10   Configuring your Linux machine as an NCP server.

There are two packages available that allow Linux to provide the functions of a Novell Fileserver. They both allow you to share files on your linux machine with users using Novell NetWare client software. Users can attach and map filesystems to appear as local drives on their machines just as they would to a real Novell fileserver. You may want to try both to see which best serves your intended purpose.

10.1   The *mars_nwe* package.

Martin Stover <mstover@freeway.de> developed *mars_nwe* to enable linux to provide both file and print services for NetWare clients.

In case you are wondering about the name: *mars_nwe* is Martin Stovers Netware Emulator.

10.1.1 Capability of *mars_nwe*.

mars_nwe implements a subset of the full Novell NCP for file services, disk based bindery and also print services. It is likely to contain bugs but there are many people using it now and the number of bugs is steadily decreasing as new versions are released.

10.1.2 Obtaining *mars_nwe*.

You can obtain *mars_nwe* from *ftp.gwdg.de* `<ftp://ftp.gwdg.de/pub/linux/misc/ncpfs/>` or from `<ftp://sunsite.unc.edu/pub/Linux/system/filesystems/ncpfs/>`.

The version current at the time of writing was: `mars_nwe-0.99.pl10.tgz`.

10.1.3 Building the *mars_nwe* package.

Build a kernel with Ethernet and IPX Support

In the `1.2.13` version kernel you need only ensure that you have answered `Y` to the question: 'The IPX protocol' and `N` to the question: 'Full internal IPX network' as illustrated:

```
...
...
The IPX protocol (CONFIG_IPX) [n] y
...
...
Full internal IPX network (CONFIG_IPX_INTERN) [N/y/?] n
...
...
```

In newer kernels a similar process is adopted but the actual text of the prompt may have changed slightly.

You will also need to ensure that you include an appropriate driver for your Ethernet card. If you do not know how to do this then you should read the *Ethernet-HOWTO* `<Ethernet-HOWTO.html>`.

You can then proceed to build your kernel. Make sure you remember to run *lilo* to install it when you have finished.

Untar the *mars_nwe* package.

```
# cd /usr/src
# tar xvfz mars_nwe-0.99.pl10.tgz
```

Make *mars_nwe*.

To make the package is very simple. The first step is to simply run `make`, this will create a `config.h` file for you. Next you should look at and edit the `config.h` file if necessary. It allows you to configure items such as the installation directories that will be used and the maximum number of sessions and volumes that the server will support. The really important entries to look at are:

```
FILENAME_NW_INI          the location of the initialisation file
PATHNAME_PROGS           where the executable support programs will be found.
PATHNAME_BINDERY         where the 'bindery' files will go.
PATHNAME_PIDFILES        the directory for the 'pid' files to be written.
MAX_CONNECTIONS          the maximum number of simultaneous connection-
s allowed.
MAX_NW_VOLS              the maximum number of volumes mars_nwe will support.
MAX_FILE_HANDLES_CONN    the maximum number of open files per connection.
WITH_NAME_SPACE_CALLS    if you want to support ncpfs clients.
INTERNAL_RIP_SAP         whether you want mars_nwe to provide rip/sap routing.
SHADOW_PWD               whether you use shadow passwords or not.
```

The defaults will probably be ok but you should check anyway.

When this is done:

HOWTO

```
# make
# make install
```

will build the servers and install them in the appropriate directory. The installation script also installs the configuration file /etc/nwserv.conf.

Configure the server.

Configuration is fairly simple. You need to edit the /etc/nwserv.conf file. The format of this file may at first look a little cryptic, but it is fairly straightforward. The file contains a number of single line configuration items. Each line is whitespace delimited and begins with a number that indicates the contents of the line. All characters following a '#' character are considered a comment and ignored. Martin supplies an example configuration file in the package, but I'll present what I consider to be a simplified example to offer an alternative for you.

```
# VOLUMES (max. 5)
# Only the SYS volume is compulsory. The directory containing the SYS
# volume must contain the directories: LOGIN, PUBLIC, SYSTEM, MAIL.
# The 'i' option ignores case.
# The 'k' option converts all filenames in NCP requests to lowercase.
# The 'm' option marks the volume as removable (useful for cdroms etc.)
# The 'r' option set the volume to read-only.
# The 'o' option indicates the volume is a single mounted filesystem.
# The 'P' option allows commands to be used as files.
# The 'O' option allows use of the OS/2 namespace
# The 'N' option allows use of the NFS namespace
# The default is upper case.
# Syntax:
#    1 <Volumename> <Volumepath>    <Options>

1   SYS       /home/netware/SYS/              # SYS
1   DATA      /home/netware/DATA/      k      # DATA
1   CDROM     /cdrom                   kmr    # CDROM

# SERVER NAME
# If not set then the linux hostname will be converted to upper case
# and used. This is optional, the hostname will be used if this is not
# configured.
# Syntax:
#    2 <Servername>

2   LINUX_FS01

# INTERNAL NETWORK ADDRESS
# The Internal IPX Network Address is a feature that simplifies
# IPX routing for multihomed hosts (hosts that have ports on more
# than one IPX network).
# Syntax:
#    3 <Internal Network Address> [<Node Number>]
# or:
#    3 auto
#
# If you use 'auto' then your host IP address will be used. NOTE: this
# may be dangerous, please be sure you pick a number unique to your
# network. Addresses are 4byte hexadecimal (the leading 0x is required).

3   0x49a01010  1
```

```
# NETWORK DEVICE(S)
# This entry configures your IPX network. If you already have your
# IPX network configured then you do not need this. This is the same as
# using ipx_configure/ipx_interface before you start the server.
# Syntax:
#    4 <IPX Network Number> <device_name> <frametype> [<ticks>]
#                           Frame types: ethernet_ii, 802.2, 802.3, SNAP

4  0x39a01010  eth0  802.3  1

# SAVE IPX ROUTES AFTER SERVER IS DOWNED
# Syntax:
#    5 <flag>
#        0 = don't save routes, 1 = do save routes

5 0

# NETWARE VERSION
# Syntax:
#    6 <version>
#        0 = 2.15, 1 = 3.11

6 1

# PASSWORD HANDLING
# Real Novell DOS clients support a feature which encypts your
# password when changing it. You can select whether you want your
# mars server to support this feature or not.
# Syntax
#    7 <flag>
#    <flag> is:
#        0 to force password encryption. (Clients can't change password)
#        1 force password encryption, allow unencrypted password change.
#        7 allow non-encrypted password but no empty passwords.
#        8 allow non-encrypted password including empty passwords.
#        9 completely unencrypted passwords (doesn't work with OS/2)

7 1

# MINIMAL GID UID rights
# permissions used for attachments with no login. These permissions
# will be used for the files in your primary server attachment.
# Syntax:
#    10 <gid>
#    11 <uid>
#    <gid> <uid> are from /etc/passwd, /etc/groups

10  200
11  201

# SUPERVISOR password
# May be removed after the server is started once. The server will
# encrypt this information into the bindery file after it is run.
# You should avoid using the 'root' user and instead use another
# account to administer the mars fileserver.
```

HOWTO

```
#
# This entry is read and encrypted into the server bindery files, so
# it only needs to exist the first time you start the server to ensure
# that the password isn't stolen.
#
# Syntax:
#    12 <Supervisor-Login> <Unix username> [<password>]

12  SUPERVISOR  terry  secret

# USER ACCOUNTS
# This associates NetWare logins with unix accounts. Password are
# optional.
# Syntax:
#      13 <User Login> <Unix Username> [<password>]

13  MARTIN martin
13  TERRY  terry

# LAZY SYSTEM ADMIN CONFIGURATION
# If you have a large numbers of users and could not be bothered using
# type 13 individual user mappings, you can automatically map mars_nwe
# logins to linux user names. BUT, there is currently no means of making
# use of the linux login password so all users configured this way are
# will use the single password supplied here. My recommendation is not
# to do this unless security is absolutely no concern to you.
# Syntax:
#    15 <flag> <common-password>
#    <flag> is: 0  - don't automatically map users.
#               1  - do automatically map users not configured above.
#               99 - automatically map every user in this way.

15  0  duzzenmatta

# SANITY CHECKING
# mars_nwe will automatically ensure that certain directories exist if
# you set this flag.
# Syntax:
#    16 <flag>
#    <flag> is 0 for no, don't, or 1 for yes, do.

16  0

# PRINT QUEUES
# This associates NetWare printers with unix printers. The queue
# directories must be created manually before printing is attempted.
# The queue directories are NOT lpd queues.
# Syntax:
#    21 <queue_name> <queue_directory> <unix_print_cmd>

21  EPSON  SYS:/PRINT/EPSON lpr -h
21  LASER  SYS:/PRINT/LASER lpr -Plaser

# DEBUG FLAGS
# These are not normally needed, but may be useful if are you debugging
```

```
# a problem.
# Syntax:
#     <debug_item> <debug_flag>
#
#     100 = IPX KERNEL
#     101 = NWSERV
#     102 = NCPSERV
#     103 = NWCONN
#     104 = start NWCLIENT
#     105 = NWBIND
#     106 = NWROUTED
#                   0 = disable debug, 1 = enable debug

100 0
101 0
102 0
103 0
104 0
105 0
106 0


# RUN NWSERV IN BACKGROUND AND USE LOGFILE
# Syntax:
#     200 <flag>
#         0 = run NWSERV in foreground and don't use logfile
#         1 = run NWSERV in background and use logfile

200  1


# LOGFILE NAME
# Syntax:
#     201 <logfile>

201  /tmp/nw.log


# APPEND LOG OR OVERWRITE
# Syntax:
#     202 <flag>
#         0 = append to existing logfile
#         1 = overwrite existing logfile

202  1


# SERVER DOWN TIME
# This item sets the time after a SERVER DOWN is issued that the
# server really goes down.
# Syntax:
#     210 <time>
#         in seconds. (defaults 10)

210  10


# ROUTING BROADCAST INTERVAL
# The time is seconds between server broadcasts
# Syntax:
```

```
#     211 <time>
#           in seconds. (defaults 60)

211  60


# ROUTING LOGGING INTERVAL
# Set how many broadcasts take place before logging of routing
# information occurs.
# Syntax:
#     300   <number>

300  5


# ROUTING LOGFILE
# Set the name of the routing logfile
# Syntax:
#     301 <filename>

301  /tmp/nw.routes


# ROUTING APPEND/OVERWRITE
# Set whether you want to append to an existing log file or
# overwrite it.
# Syntax:
#     302 <flag>
#           <flag> is 0 for append, 1 for create/overwrite

302  1


# WATCHDOG TIMING
# Set the timing for watchdog messages that ensure the network is
# still alive.
# Syntax:
#     310 <value>
#           <value> =   0 - always send watchdogs
#                     < 0 - (-ve) for disable watchdogs
#                     > 0 - send watchdogs when network traffic
#                           drops below 'n' ticks

310  7


# STATION FILE
# Set the filename for the stations file which determine which
# machines this fileserver will act as the primary fileserver for.
# The syntax of this file is described in the 'examples' directory
# of the source code.
# Syntax:
#     400 <filename>

400  /etc/nwserv.stations


# GET NEAREST FILESERVER HANDLING
# Set how SAP Get Nearest Fileserver Requests are handled.
# Syntax:
#     401 <flag>
```

```
#              <flag> is: 0 - disable 'Get Nearest Fileserver' requests.
#                         1 - The 'stations' file lists station-
s to be excluded.
#                         2 - The 'stations' file lists station-
s to be included.

401  2
```

Start the server

If you've configured the server to expect external programs to configure your network and/or provide the routing function then you should start those before starting the server. Presuming you have configured the server so that it will configure your interfaces for you and provide the routing services you need only issue the command:

```
# nwserv
```

Test the server

To test the server you should first try to attach and login from a NetWare client on your network. You then set a CAPTURE from the client and attempt a print. If both of these are successful then the server is working.

10.2 The *lwared* package.

Ales Dryak <A.Dryak@sh.cvut.cz> developed *lwared* to allow Linux to function as an NCP based fileserver.

Ales has called the package *lwared*, an abbreviation for *LinWare Daemon*.

10.2.1 Capability of *lwared*.

The *lwared* server is capable of providing a subset of the full function of the Novell NCP. It incorporates messaging but it does not provide any printing facilities at all. It does not currently work very well with either Windows95 or Windows NT clients. The *lwared* server relies on external programs to build and update the IPX routing and SAP tables. Misbehaving clients can cause the server to crash. Importantly, filename translation facilities have not been included.

The server does work for NETX and VLM NetWare shells.

10.2.2 Obtaining *lwared*

The *lwared* package can be built for any kernel newer than 1.2.0, I recommend you use version 1.2.13 as no kernel patches are required if you do. Some of the IPX functionality has changed with the version 1.3.* kernels and this means that patches are now required to make it work properly. Appropriate patches are included for the new kernels, so if you must use an alpha kernel you should still be able to get *lwared* to work properly for you.

You can obtain the *lwared* package by anonymous ftp from: *klokan.sh.cvut.cz* <ftp://klokan.sh.cvut.cz/pub/linux/linware/>

or from:

sunsite.unc.edu <ftp://sunsite.unc.edu/pub/Linux/system/network/daemons> or mirror sites. The current version at the time of writing was: lwared-0.95.tar.gz

10.2.3 Building *lwared*

Untar the *lwared* package

Something like:

```
# cd /usr/src
# tar xvpfz lwared-0.95.tar.gz
```

HOWTO

Build a kernel with Ethernet and IPX support

If you are using an alpha `1.3.*` kernel then you should try and use kernel version `1.3.17` or newer because the supplied patches were built against it. `1.3.*` kernels older than `1.3.17` will require hand patching to install. (*some information on how to do this is included in the* `INSTALL` *file in the package.*). To install the patches against a `1.3.17` kernel or newer you should try:

```
# make patch
```

After applying the patches if necessary, the next thing you need to do is ensure that your kernel has been built with IPX support enabled. In the `1.2.13` version kernel you need only ensure that you have answered `Y` to the question: 'The IPX protocol' as illustrated:

```
    . . .
    . . .
Assume subnets are local (CONFIG_INET_SNARL) [y]
Disable NAGLE algorithm (normally enabled) (CONFIG_TCP_NAGLE_OFF) [n]
The IPX protocol (CONFIG_IPX) [n] y
 *  SCSI support
    . . .
    . . .
```

In newer kernels a similar process is adopted by the actual text of the prompt may have changed slightly.

You will also need to ensure that you include an appropriate driver for your Ethernet card. If you do not know how to do this then you should read the *Ethernet-HOWTO* `<Ethernet-HOWTO.html>`.

You can then proceed to build your kernel. Make sure you remember to run *lilo* to install it when you have finished.

Compile and install *lwared*.

To compile *lwared* you should first check, edit if necessary, the `server/config.h` file. This file contains various settings that will govern the way your server will behave when it is running. The defaults are reasonable, though you might want to check that the directories specified for the log files and configuration files suit your system.

```
# make depend
# make
# make install
```

I found that the 'make depend' complained about not finding the `float.h` file on my system but appeared to work anyway. I also found that when I tried compiling with gcc `2.6.3` I found I had to change the line:

```
#include <net/route.h>
```

to

```
#include <net/if_route.h>
```

in `lib/ipxkern.c` as this file changed name sometime.

The 'make install' will attempt to install the server and routing daemon programs into your `/usr/sbin` directory, the *lwpasswd* program into your `/usr/bin` directory, the IPX utility programs will be installed into your `/sbin` directory and last but not least the manual pages will go into the `/usr/man` directory structure. If any of these locations are not suitable for your system then you should edit the relevant `Makefile` and change the target directories to suit.

10.2.4   Configuring and using *lwared*

Now the fun bit!

Configuring the IPX network

The first thing you must do is configure your Ethernet interfaces to support the IPX networks your server will support. To do this you will need to know the IPX network addresses for each of your LAN segments, which

Ethernet device (eth0, eth1 etc.) is on which segment, what frame type (802.3, EtherII etc.) each LAN segment uses and what Internal Network address your server should use (this is really needed if your server will service more than one LAN segment). A configuration for a server that is on two dis-similar segments with IPX network addresses 23a91300 and 23a91301 and internal network address bdefaced might look like:

```
# ipx_internal_net add BDEFACED 1
# ipx_interface add eth0 802.3 23a91300
# ipx_interface add eth1 etherii 23a91301
```

Start the routing daemons

The kernel software itself actually does the IPX packet forwarding as it does for IP, but the kernel requires additional programs to manage the routing table updates. In the case of IPX two daemons are needed and both are supplied with *lwared*: *ipxripd* manages the IPX routing information and *ipxsapd* manages the SAP information. To start the daemons you need only specify the location of where they should write their log messages:

```
# ipxripd /var/adm/ipxrip
# ipxsapd /var/adm/ipxsap
```

Configure the *lwared* server

There are two files that you must manually configure to allow user login to your *lwared* server. They are:

/etc/lwpasswd

This is where LinWare user account information is kept. The *lwpasswd* program is to keep it up to date. In its simplest form the /etc/lwpasswd file looks like:

```
ales:
terryd:
guest:
```

Its format is a simple list of login id followed by a ':' character and then the encrypted version of the login passwd. A couple of important caveats here: No encrypted password means no password, LinWare users must have Linux accounts, that is any user you place in /etc/lwpasswd must also appear in /etc/passwd and root is the only account that can change the password of another LinWare user. If you are logged in as root you can change the password of a LinWare user as this transcript demonstrates:

```
# lwpasswd rodg
Changing password for RODG
Enter new password:
Re-type new password:
Password changed.
```

/etc/lwvtab

This is the LinWare volume tables and it stores information about what directories should be made available to LinWare users (this file is similar in nature to the NFS /etc/exports file). A simple example of its format is as follows:

```
SYS                    /lwfs/sys
DATA                   /lwfs/data
HOME                   /home
```

The format is simple: Volume name followed by whitespace followed by Linux directory to export. You must have at **least** an entry for the SYS volume for the server to start. If you intend your DOS based users to be able use your LinWare server as their primary server then you must install a standard SYS volume directory structure underneath the directory you export as your SYS volume. Since these files are proprietary and copyright to the Novell corporation you should have a license for these. If you users will be using a Novell fileserver as their primary server then this will not be necessary.

Start the *lwared* server.

tada!

```
# lwared
```

It is almost an anticlimax isn't it ? Ok so you've got a question, right? What is the fileserver name that is being advertised ? If you started the server as shown then the LinWare server name being advertised will be based on what is returned by the Linux *hostname*. If you'd like it to be something else then you can give the server the name when you start it, for example:

```
# lwared -nlinux00
```

would start the server with the name `linux00`.

Test the *lwared* server.

The very first thing to test is that your LinWare server appears in an *slist* from a DOS client on your network. The *slist* program is stored on the `SYS` volume of a Novell fileserver so you must do this from a machine that is already logged in somewhere. If this is not successful then check that *ipxsapd* and *lwared* are both running. If the *slist* is successful then you should try attaching to the server and mapping a volume:

```
C:> attach linux00/ales
   ...
   ...
C:> map l:=linux00/data:
C:> l:
```

You should then be able to treat the new map just like any other map. The file permissions you will have will be based on those allowed to the *linux* account that parallels your LinWare login.

11   Configuring your Linux machine as a Novell Print Client.

The *ncpfs* package includes two small programs that allow you to handle printing from you Linux machine to a printer attached to a Novell print server. The *nprint* command allows you to print to a file to a NetWare print queue. The *pqlist* command allows you the list the available print queues on a NetWare server.

To obtain and install these commands just follow the instructions relating to the NCP client described earlier.

Both commands require that you supply username and password so you might normally consider building some shell scripts to make the task of printing easier.

An example might look like:

```
# pqlist -S ACCT_FS01 -U guest -n
# nprint -S ACCT_FS01 -q LASER -U guest -n filename.txt
```

The login syntax is similar to the *ncpmount* command. The examples above assume that fileserver `ACCT_FS01` has a `guest` account with no password, that a print queue called `LASER` exists and that `guest` is allowed to print to it.

On my Linux boxen I have a short shell script for each Novell printer. This can then be used as a print filter to allow printing using the standard Linux spooler.

12   Configuring your Linux machine as a Novell Print Server.

A program to allow your Linux machine to act as a print server on a Netware network is included in the *ncpfs* package. For instructions on how to obtain and build, it follow the directions in the 'Netware client' section above. Alternatively, support is included in the *mars_nwe* package.

12.1   Prerequisites

Configuration is quite straightforward but relies on you already having your printer configuration completed and working under Linux. This is covered in the *Printing-HOWTO* `<Printing-HOWTO.html>` in some depth.

12.2 Configuration

When you have a working printer configuration, and you have built and installed the *pserver* utility then you need to add commands to start it into your `rc` files.

Exactly what command will use will depend on depend on exactly how you want it to operate, but in its simplest form something like the following will work:

```
# pserver -S ACCT_01 -U LASER -P secret -q LASERJET
```

This example asks the *pserver* utility to login in to the `ACCT_01` fileserver with username `LASER` and password `secret` and to take jobs from the `LASERJET` print queue. When an incoming print job is received it will use the default print command of *lpr* to feed the print job to the Linux print daemon. The print queue must already be defined on the fileserver and the username must have server priveliges for the queue.

You could if you wished use any Linux command to accept and print the print job. The `-c` argument allows you to specify the exact print command. For example:

```
# pserver -S ACCT_01 -U LASER -P secret -q LASERJET -c "lpr -Plaserjet"
```

would do exactly the same as the previous example except it would send the job to the `laserjet` *printcap* configuration instead of the default one.

13 An overview of the *ncpfs* user and adminstration commands

Recent versions of Volker's *ncpfs* package include a range of user and administration commands that you might want to use. The tools are built and installed as part of the *ncpfs* installation process, so if you haven't already, follow the instructions supplied in the Novell Client section above to build and install them.

Detailed information is available in the supplied *man* pages but a brief summary of the commands is as follows;

13.1 User commands.

ncopy

Network Copy - allows efficient file copies to be performed by using a Netware function rather than a copy across the network.

nprint

Network Print - allows you to print a file to a Netware print queue on a Netware server.

nsend

Network Send - allows you to send messages to other users on a Netware server.

nwbols

List Bindery Objects - allows you to list the bindery contents of a Netware server.

nwboprops

List Properties of a Bindery Object - allows you to the properties of a Netware bindery object.

nwbpset

Set Bindery Property - allows you to set the properties of a Netware bindery object.

nwbpvalues

Print Netware Bindery Objects Property Contents - allows you to print the contents of a Netware bindery property.

nwfsinfo

Fileserver Information - prints some summary information about a Netware server.

nwpasswd

> Netware Password - allows you to change a Netware users password.

nwrights

> Netware Rights - displays the rights associated with a particular file or directory.

nwuserlist

> Userlist - lists the users currently logged into a Netware fileserver.

pqlist

> Print Queue List - displays the contents of a Netware print queue.

slist

> Server List - displays a list of know Netware fileserver.

13.2   Administration tools.

nwbocreate

> Create a Bindery Object - allows you to create a Netware bindery object.

nwborm

> Remove Bindery Object - allows you to delete a Netware bindery object.

nwbpadd

> Add Bindery Property - allows you to set the value of an existing property of a Netware bindery object.

nwbpcreate

> Create Bindery Property - allows you to create a new property for an existing Netware bindery object.

nwbprm

> Remove Bindery Property - allows you to remove a property from a Netware bindery object.

nwgrant

> Grant Trustee Rights - allows you to assign trustee rights to a directory on a Netware fileserver.

nwrevoke

> Revoke Trustee Rights - allows you to remove trustee rights from a directory on a Netware fileserver.

14   Configuring PPP for IPX support.

New versions of the *pppd* PPP daemon for Linux have support that allows you to carry IPX packets across a PPP serial link. You need at least version `ppp-2.2.0d` of the daemon. See the *PPP-HOWTO* `<PPP-HOWTO.html>` for details on where to find it. When you compile *pppd* you must ensure you enable the IPX support by adding the following two lines:

```
IPX_CHANGE = 1
USE_MS_DNS = 1
```

to: `/usr/src/linux/pppd-2.2.0f/pppd/Makefile.linux`.

The `IPX_CHANGE` is what configures the IPX support into PPP. The `USE_MS_DNS` define allows Microsoft Windows95 machines to do Name Lookups.

The real trick to getting it to work in knowing how to configure it.

There are many ways of doing this, but I'm only going to describe the two that I've received any information on. I've tried neither yet, so consider this section experimental, and if you get something to work, please let me know.

14.1 Configuring an IPX/PPP server.

The first thing you need to do is configure your Linux machine as an IP/PPP server. Don't panic! This isn't difficult. Again, follow the instructions in the *PPP-HOWTO* <PPP-HOWTO.html> and you should be pretty much ok. When you have this done there are a couple of simple modifications you need to make to get IPX working over the same configuration.

14.1.1 First steps.

One of the first steps you must take is to configure your linux machine as an IPX router as described in the appropriate section earlier in this document. You won't need to use the *ipx_route* command for the ppp interface because *pppd* will configure these for you as it does for IP. When you have the *ipxd* daemon running it will automatically detect any new IPX interfaces and propogates routes for them. In this way your dialup hosts will be seen by other machines automatically when they connect.

14.1.2 Design.

When you are running as a server it will normally be your responsibility to assign network address to each of the PPP links when they are established. This is an important point, each PPP link will be an IPX network and will have a unique IPX network address. This means that you must decide how you will allocate addresses and what what they will be. A simple convention is to allocate one IPX network address to each serial device that will support IPX/PPP. You could allocate IPX network addresses based on the login id of the connecting user, but I don't see any particularly good reason to do so.

I will assume that this is what you have done, and that there are two serial devices (modems) that we will use. The addresses I've assigned in this contrived example are:

```
device  IPX Network Address
------  -------------------
ttyS0   0xABCDEF00
ttyS1   0xABCDEF01
```

14.1.3 Configure *pppd*.

Configure your /etc/ppp/options.ttyS0 file as follows:

```
ipx-network 0xABCDEF00
ipx-node 2:0
ipxcp-accept-remote
```

and your /etc/ppp/options.ttyS1 file as:

```
ipx-network 0xABCDEF01
ipx-node 3:0
ipxcp-accept-remote
```

These will ask *pppd* to allocate the appropriate IPX network addresses to the link when the link is established, set the local node number to 2 or 3 and will let the remote node overwrite what the remote node number with what it thinks it is. Note that each of the addresses are hexadecimal numbers and that 0x is required at the start of the network address, but not required at the start of the node address.

There are other places this information could be configured. If you have only one dialin modem then an entry could go into the /etc/ppp/options file. Alternatively this information can be passed on the command line to *pppd*.

14.1.4   Test the server configuration.

To test the configuration you will need to have a client configuration that is known to work. When the caller dials in, logs in and *pppd* starts it will assign the network address, advise the client of the servers node number and negotiate the clients node number. When this has completed, and after *ipxd* has detected the new interface the client should be able to establish IPX connections to remote hosts.

14.2   Configuring an IPX/PPP client.

In a client configuration, whether or not you configure your Linux machine as an IPX router depends on whether you have a local LAN that you wish to act as an IPX router for. If you are a standalone machine connecting to an IPX/PPP dialin server then you won't need to run *ipxd*, but if you have a LAN and wish all of the machines on the LAN to make use of the IPX/PPP route then you must configure and run *ipxd* as described. This configuration is much simpler because you do not have multiple serial devices to configure.

14.2.1   Configuring *pppd*

The simplest configuration is one that allows the server to supply all of the IPX network configuration information. This configuration would be compatible with the server configuration described above.

Again you need to add some options to your `/etc/ppp/options` file, they are:

```
ipxcp-accept-network
ipxcp-accept-remote
ipxcp-accept-local
```

These options tell *pppd* to act completely passively and accept all of the configuration details from the server. You could supply default values here for servers that don't supply details by adding `ipx-network` and `ipx-node` entries similar to the server configuration.

14.2.2   Testing the IPX/PPP client.

To test the client you will need a known working server to dial into. After you have dialled in and pppd has run you should see the IPX details configured on your `ppp0` device when you run the *ifconfig* command and you should be able to use *ncpmount*.

I'm not sure whether you will have to manually add IPX routes so that you can reach distant fileserver or not. This seems likely. If anyone running this configuration could tell me I'd be grateful.

15   IPX tunnel over IP

Many of you will be in a situation where you have two Novell Local Area Netorks with only an IP connection between them. How do you play multiplayer deathmatch DOOM for DOS via this arrangement you might ask ? Andreas Godzina <ag@agsc.han.de> has an answer for you in the form of *ipxtunnel*.

ipxtunnel provides a bridge-like facility for IPX by allowing IPX packets to be encapsulated with tcp/ip datagrams so that they can be carried by a tcp/ip connection. It listens for IPX packets and when it hears one it wraps it within a tcp/ip datagram and routes it to a remote IP address that you specify. For this to work of course the machine that you route the encapsulated IPX must also be running a copy of the same version of *ipxtunnel* as you.

15.1   Obtaining *ipxtunnel*

You can obtain *ipxtunnel* from *sunsite.unc.edu* <ftp://sunsite.unc.edu/pub/Linux/system/network/daemons> or mirror sites.

15.2 Building *ipxtunnel*

ipxtunnel built cleanly for me using the following commands:

```
# cd /usr/src
# tar xvfz .../ipxtunnel.tgz
# cd ipxtunnel
# make
```

15.3 Configuring *ipxtunnel*

Configuration for *ipxtunnel* is easy. Lets say that your friends machine is `gau.somewhere.com` and your machine is called `gim.sw.edu`. *ipxtunnel* uses a configuration file called `/etc/ipxtunnel.conf`. This file allows you to specify the default UDP port to use for the tcp/ip connection, where to send the encapsulated data and which of your local interfaces *ipxtunnel* should listen on and deliver IPX packets to.

A simple configuration file would look like the following:

```
#
# /etc/ipxtunnel.conf for gim.sw.edu
#
# The UDP port to use:                        (default 7666)
port 7777
#
# The remote machine to send IPX packets to: (no default)
remote gau.somewhere.com
#
# The local interfaces to listen for IPX on: (default eth0)
interface eth0
interface eth1
```

Obviously the other machine would have a similar configuration file specifying this machine as a `remote` host.

15.4 Testing and using *ipxtunnel*

ipxtunnel acts **like** an IPX bridge, so the IPX networks at either end of the link should probably be the same. Andreas has never tested the *ipxtunnel* in an environment that actually supports Novell file servers so if you do try this in a real environment let Andreas know if it works or not.

If the *ipxtunnel* is working you should be able to start your DOOM machines up at each end of the link running IPX mode and they should see each other.

Andreas has only used this code over good high speed lines and he makes no claim as to its performance when your link is low speed. Again, let him know what works for you and what doesn't.

16 Commercial IPX support for Linux.

16.1 Caldera'a Network Desktop

Caldera Inc., produce a Linux distribution that features a range of commercially supported enhancements including fully functional Novell NetWare client support. The base distribution is the well respected Red Hat Linux Distribution and Caldera have added their "Network Desktop" products to this. The NetWare support provides a fully featured Novell NetWare client built on technology licensed from Novell Corporation. The client provides full client access to Novell 3.x and 4.x fileservers and includes features such as NetWare Directory Service (NDS) and RSA encryption.

You can obtain much more information and ordering details from the: *Caldera Inc Web Server* `<http://www.caldera.com/>`.

If you work within a Netware 4.x and/or NDS environment then the Caldera Netware Client is the only solution available.

If you have a business critical application for Novell support for Linux then the Caldera product should be something you take a close look at.

17   Some Frequently Asked Questions

Where can I find commercially supported IPX software for Linux ?

The Caldera Corporation offers a fully licensed and fully supported Netware 3.x and 4.x client. You can obtain information about it from the *Caldera Inc Web Server* `<http://www.caldera.com/>`.

Does the IPX software work with Arcnet/Token Ring/etc. ?

The Linux IPX software does work with ArcNet and Token Ring interfaces. I haven't heard of anyone trying it with AX.25 yet. Configuration is the same as for configuring for ethernet except you will have to substitute appropriate device names in place of 'eth0' and appopriate hardware addresses where necessary.

How do I configure more than one IPX interface ?

If you have more than one interface in your machine you should use the *ipx_interface* command to manually configure each one, you should not use the 'plug n play' configuration.

How do I choose IPX addresses ?

IPX networking is similar, but not identical to, IP networking. A major difference is the way that addresses are used. IPX does not use the concept of subnetworking and so the sort of associations that you have between network addresses and networks is different. The rules are fairly simple:

- Every IPX network address must be unique on a wide area network. This includes Internal Network Addresses. Many organisations using IPX over a wide area network will have some sort of addressing standard that you should follow.

- Every Host address on an individual network must be unique. This means that every host on each IPX network must have a uniquely assigned address. In the case of ethernet network this isn't difficult as the cards each have a unique address. In the case of IPX/PPP this means you must ensure that you allocate unique addresses to all hosts on the network, irrespective of which end of the link(s) they are connected. Host address do not need to be unique across a wide area network as the network address is used in combination with the host address to uniquely identify a host.

What are frame types, which should I use ?

There are a variety of frame types in use over which you can run IPX. The most common of these are described in the 'common terms' section of this document (under the '`Frame Type` entry').

If you are installing your machine on an existing network then you must use whatever is already in use to allow you to interwork with the other hosts on the network, but if the installation is a brand new network you can use any of a range of protocols to carry your IPX traffic. My recommendation if you are configuring a brand new network and you need to carry both IPX and IP traffic is to use the `Ethernet_II` frame type.

My Windows95 machines mess up my frame type autodetection ?

Apparently they can, yeah. I could make nasty comments, but instead I'll just suggest that you use the manual frame type configuration instead of the automatic one. It is probably the better way anyway.

Why do I get the message 'invalid argument' when I configure IPX ?

You are probably not running a kernel that supports IPX, either recompile your kernel so it does, or double check that you have actually used lilo to install and run the new kernel.

Why do I get the message 'package not installed' when I configure IPX ?

You are probably not running a kernel that supports IPX, either recompile your kernel so it does, or double check that you have actually used lilo to install and run the new kernel.

Why do I get the message 'IPX support not in kernel' from *pppd* ?

You've probably compiled IPX as a module and not ensured that it was loaded before started *pppd*.

How do I NFS export a mounted NCP filesystem ?

To use NFS to export an NCP filesystem you must mount it using the *ncpmount* -V option. This option allows you to mount only one volume of a fileserver instead of the usual mounting of all of them. When you do this your NFS daemon will allow you to export that filesystem in the usual way.

Why doesn't slist work when I have an internel network with mars_nwe ?

You must have the get nearest server enabled. That is, entry 401 in /etc/nwserv.conf should be 0 unless you have a reason for not responding to get nearest servers. If you just want slist to work and not respond to every get nearest server request, include your internal network and node number in /etc/nwserv.stations and set entry 401 in /etc/nwserv.conf to 2.

Does ncpfs package work with mars_nwe ?

Martin and Volker's code is slowly beginning to converge. Recent versions of *mars_nwe* have an option to enable it to work with *ncpfs*. You must enable the WITH_NAME_SPACE_CALLS in the *mars_nwe* config.h file.

Is there any free DOS software to work with mars_nwe ?

A contrived question deserves a contrived answer. I'm glad you asked, Martin has a package that he distributes alongside his *mars_nwe* package that offers free DOS client support for the *mars_nwe* server. You can find it at the same sites as the server, and it will be called mars_dosutils-0.01.tgz. It includes C source code for programs such as *slist.exe*, *login.exe*, *map.exe* etc. The source is compilable with Borland(tm) C.

18   Copyright Message.

The IPX-HOWTO, a guide to software supporting the IPX protocol for Linux. Copyright (c) 1995 Terry Dawson.

This program is free software; you can redistribute it and/or modify it under the terms of the GNU General Public License as published by the Free Software Foundation; either version 2 of the License, or (at your option) any later version.

This program is distributed in the hope that it will be useful, but WITHOUT ANY WARRANTY; without even the implied warranty of MERCHANTABILITY or FITNESS FOR A PARTICULAR PURPOSE. See the GNU General Public License for more details.

You should have received a copy of the GNU General Public License along with this program; if not, write to the:

Free Software Foundation, Inc., 675 Mass Ave, Cambridge, MA 02139, USA.

19   Miscellaneous and Acknowledgements.

Terry Dawson <terry@perf.no.itg.telstra.com.au> for the original document

David E. Storey <dave@tamos.gmu.edu> and Volker Lendecke <lendecke@namu01.gwdg.de> both assisted greatly by supplying me with information for this document. Gilbert Callaghan <gilbert@pokey.inviso.com>, David Higgins <dave@infra.com> and Chad Robinson <chadr@brtgate.brttech.com> each contributed information on configuring IPX/PPP. Bennie Venter <bjv@Gil-galad.paradigm-sa.com> contributed some useful information relating to frame types. Christopher Wall <vergil@idir.net contributed some useful suggestions to improve the readability and layout of the document. Axel Boldt <boldt@math.ucsb.edu> contributed some useful suggestions and feedback. Erik D. Olson <eriko@wrq.com> provided some useful feedback and information on configuring PPP for IPX. Brian King <root@brian.library.dal.ca> contributed a question for the FAQ section.

"NetWare" is a registered trademark of the *Novell Corporation* <http://www.novell.com/>. "Caldera" is a registered trademark of the *Caldera Corporation* <http://www.caldera.com/>.

regards Kevin Thorpe.

<kevin@pricetrak.com>

## Part XVII

"The Linux Intranet Server HOWTO" Pramod Karnad

karnad@indiamail.com
v2.11, 7 August 1997

This document describes how to setup an Intranet using Linux as the server which binds Unix, Netware, NT and Windows together. Hence by just establishing the connection to the Linux box you are provided transparent access to all the various platforms. Detailed explanations are provided for setting up HTTP using the NCSA server and connect to it using TCP/IP clients from Novell, Microsoft under Windows3.1, WFWG,Win95 and WinNT and MacTCP on the Apple PowerMac.

Contents

HOWTO

1 Introduction

In simple terms, the **Intranet** is the descriptive term being used for the implementation of Internet technologies within a corporate organisation, rather than for external connection to the global Internet. This implementation is performed in such a way as to transparently deliver the immense informational resources of an organisation to each individuals desktop with minimal cost, time and effort. This document attempts to explain in simple terms how to setup an Intranet using tools which are readily available and are generally costing little or are free.

This document assumes that you already know how to install TCP/IP on your Linux server and connect it physically to your LAN using an Ethernet network card. This also assumes you have some basic knowledge of Netware, WinNT and Mac systems. The configuration of the Netware server has been shown using version 3.1x as the basis. You can also use INETCFG to achieve the same result. On the client side the discussion is with respect to Windows 3.1x, Windows for Workgroups and Win95, WinNT and the Apple PowerMac.

I am using the private network addresses (RFC-1918) of 172.16.0.0 and 172.17.0.0 only as examples. You may choose suitable addresses depending on your configuration.

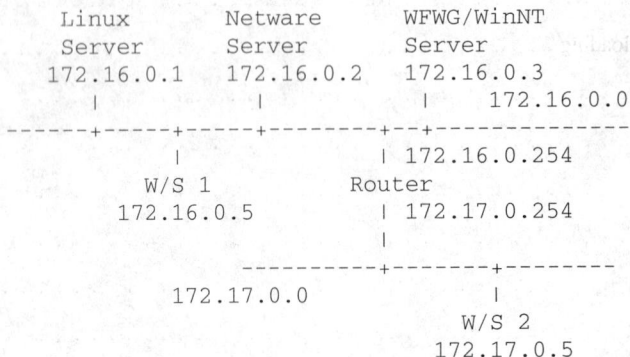

1.1 What is required

You will need the following software before attempting the installation.

- the HTTP server software which can be downloaded from OneStep NCSA HTTPd Downloader at *http://hoohoo.ncsa.uiuc.edu/docs/setup/OneStep.html* page.

- The Novell Netware Client available from *HTTP://support.novell.com/* (The TCP/IP files are included with the client).

- The Microsoft TCP/IP client available from *HTTP://www.microsoft.com/*

- The Apple MacTCP client available from *HTTP://www.apple.com/*

- WWW Browsers like Netscape at *HTTP://home.netscape.com/* or MS Internet Explorer at *HTTP://www.microsoft.com/* or NCSA Mosaic from *http://www.ncsa.uiuc.edu/SDG/Software/Mosaic/NCSAMosaicHome.html*

1.2 New versions of this document

New versions of the Linux Intranet Server HOWTO will be periodically posted to comp.os.linux.announce and comp.os.linux.help. They will also be uploaded to various Linux FTP sites, including sunsite.unc.edu.

The Latest version of this document is available in HTML format at *http://www.inet.co.th/cyberclub/karnadp/http.html*

1.3 Feedback

If you have questions or comments about this document, please feel free to mail Pramod Karnad, at *karnad@indiamail.com*. Suggestions, criticism and mail are always welcome. If you find a mistake with this document, please let me know so I can correct it in the next version. Thanx.

2 Install the HTTP server

When you download the server you have two options: To get the source and compile it yourself, or get the precompiled binaries. The precompiled binaries for Linux (ELF) version are available at NCSA but not the older versions.

2.1 Preparation before downloading

The server at NCSA will guide you through the steps for configuration options and prepare the various files for you. But before you attempt to download HTTPd be prepared with answers to the following questions

2.1.1 The Operating System

First, you must choose whether to download the source or a pre-compiled version of the software. If your particular system doesn't appear in the menu, then you will have to get the default source, and compile it yourself.

To check the version of your Linux go to the command prompt on your Linux machine and type

```
linux:~$  uname -a
```

which will respond with a line which looks similar to this

```
linux:~$  uname -a
Linux linux 2.0.29 #4 Tue Sep 13 04:05:51 CDT 1994 i586
linux:~$
```

The version of Linux is 2.0.29.

The remaining parameters can be specified before downloading or configured later by modifying the file `srm.conf` in the `/usr/local/etc/httpd/conf` directory. The names of the actual directives that appear in the file `httpd.conf` are shown in brackets. The only exception is the directive DocumentRoot which appears in the file `srm.conf`

2.1.2 Process type (ServerType)

This specifies how your machine will run your HTTPd server. The preferred method is "standalone". This makes the HTTP daemon to be running constantly. If you choose to load HTTPd under "inetd", the server binary will be reloaded into memory for every request, which may slow your server down.

2.1.3 Binding Port (Port)

This specifies which port of your machine that the HTTPd daemon will bind to and listen for HTTP requests. If you can login as "root", use the default setting of 80. Otherwise choose a setting between 1025 and 65535.

2.1.4 Server user identity (User)

This is the user id the server will change to when answering requests and acting on files.This question needs to be answered only if you are running the server as `"standalone"`. If you are someone without root permissions, just use your own login name. If you are system administrator, you might want to create a special user so you can control file permissions.

2.1.5 Server group identity (Group)

This is the group id the server will change to when answering requests and acting on files. This is similar to Server User identity and is applicable only if you are running the server as standalone.

If you do not have root permissions, just use the name of your primary group. You can find out your group by typing **groups** at the Linux command prompt.

2.1.6 Server administrator email address (ServerAdmin)

This is the email address that the user should send an email message to when reporting a problem with the server. You can put your personal e-mail address.

2.1.7 Location of server directory (ServerRoot)

This is where the server resides on your system. If you have root permissions leave it in its recommended location `/usr/local/etc/httpd`. If you cannot login as root, choose a subdirectory in your home path. You can find out the path of your home directory with the **pwd** command.

2.1.8 Location of HTML files (DocumentRoot)

This is where the HTML files to be served are located. The default location is `/usr/local/etc/httpd/htdocs`. You could however set it to be the home directory of the special user you chose in Server user identity, or a subdirectory in your home directory if you can't login as root.

When in doubt, use the default settings. Now that you have answers to the above questions you can Download NCSA HTTPd at *http://hoohoo.ncsa.uiuc.edu/docs/setup/OneStep.html*. You should read the HTTPd Documentation at *http://hoohoo.ncsa.uiuc.edu/docs/* before you attempt installation. If you are planning to compile the code then you need to modify the makefiles in each of the th ree directories `support`, `src`, `cgi-src`. If your version of Linux is already supported then you just have to type **make linux** at the top level directory (i.e. `/usr/local/etc/httpd`)

2.2 Compiling HTTPd

Compiling is simple, just type `make linux` at the prompt in the server root directory. **Note:** Users of pre-ELF Linux have to uncomment `#define NO_PASS` in file `portability.h` and set `DBM_LIBS= -ldbm` in the `Makefile` before compiling HTTPd.

3 Testing HTTPd

After you have installed HTTPd, login as root and start it by typing **httpd &** . (assuming you have installed as standalone) You should now be able to see it in the list generated by **ps**. The simplest way to test HTTPd is by Telnet. At the Linux command prompt type

```
linux:~$  telnet 172.16.0.1 80
```

where 80 is the default port for HTTP. If you have configured `"Port"` as something different then type that number instead. You should get a response which looks like this

```
Trying 172.16.0.1...
Connected to linux.mydomain.
Escape character is '^]'.
```

Now if you type in any character and press Enter you should get a response similar to the one shown below.

```
HTTP/1.0 400 Bad Request
Date: Wed, 10 Jan 1996 10:24:37 GMT
Server: NCSA/1.5
Content-type: text/html

<HEAD><TITLE>400 Bad Request < /TITLE> < /HEAD>
<BODY><H1>400 Bad Request < /H1>
Your client sent a query that this server could
not understand.<P>
Reason: Invalid or unsupported method.<P>
< /BODY>
```

Now we are ready to connect to this server using another PC and a WWW Browser.

4 Connecting to the Linux Server

Please refer to the diagram shown in the chapter 1 (Introduction) for the addressing scheme used. Workstation 1 (W/S1) is on network 172.16.0.0 and can access the Linux server directly whereas Workstation 2 (W/S2) is on network 172.17.0.0 and needs to use the gateway (router) 172.17.0.254 to access the Linux box. This gateway information needs to be provided while configuring the clients only on W/S2. Netware refers to the gateway as 'ip_router'.

I am using W/S2 to illustrate the client setup. To setup W/S1 just change the address 172.17.0.5 to 172.16.0.5 and ignore all references to the gateway/router.

If you do not have a router you can skip the next section and proceed to

- 4.2 (Setup Netware Server) if you use a Netware server.
- 4.4 (Setup MS Windows Client) if you use the Microsoft Client.

4.1 Setup the Linux server

You may skip this section if you do not have a router.

You have to configure the Linux server to recognise the router thus allowing Workstation 2 to connect to the Web server. In order to setup the Linux server you should login as root. At the server prompt type

```
route add gw default 172.16.0.254
```

To use this gateway everytime you boot the Linux server edit the file /etc/rc.d/rc.inet1 and change the line containing the gateway definition to GATEWAY = "172.16.0.254". Make sure the line for adding the gateway is not commented out.

ALT: You can add routes to the networks on the other side of the router. This would be done as

```
route add -net 172.17.0.0 gw 172.16.0.254
```

To add this route everytime you boot Linux add the command to your /etc/rc.d/rc.local file.

4.2 Setup the Netware server

In order to setup the Netware server you should have Supervisor permissions or atleast Console operator permissions. If these cannot be got, try asking your Network Administrator to help you with the setup. At the Server enable the Ethernet_II frame type on the LAN by typing these commands or include them in the AUTOEXEC.ncf file.

```
load NE2000 frame=Ethernet_II name=IPNET
load TCPIP
bind IP to IPNET addr=172.16.0.2 mask=FF.FF.FF.0
```

You might have to specify the slot or board number while loading the NE2000 driver depending on your machine configuration. (eg: load NE2000 slot=3 frame=.....)

4.3 Setup the Netware Client

On the PC you have the choice of Win3.1,WFWG or Win95. The installation procedure differs between Win95 and the older windows if you are using the 32bit client from Microsoft or Novell. If you are going to use the 16bit client, the procedure is the same and you can refer to the Windows 3.x installation instructions. For installing the 32bit client for Win95 skip to 4.3.2 (Windows 95 installation).

4.3.1 Windows 3.x

If you are using Win3.1 or WFWG you can install the Netware Client (VLMs) and some additional files which are provided with the TCP/IP diskette, namely

TCPIP.exe, VTCPIP.386, WINSOCK.dll and WLIBSOCK.dll

Note that the WINSOCK.dll file is different from the ones provided with Win95 and Trumpet. Install the Netware Client with the support for windows. Copy VTCPIP.386, WINSOCK.dll and WLIBSOCK.dll to the SYSTEM directory and TCPIP.exe to the NWCLIENT directory. Now modify the STARTNET.bat in the NWCLIENT directory to

```
lsl
ne2000       ---> your network card driver
c:\windows\odihlp.exe     ---->if you are using WFWG
ipxodi
tcpip        ---> add this line
nwip         ---> if you use Netware/IP
vlm
```

Create a subdirectory (say) \NET\TCP and copy the files HOSTS, NETWORKS, PROTOCOLS and SERVICES from /etc on your Linux server or the directory SYS:ETC on your Netware server. Edit the copied HOSTS file to add the line for your new Linux server. This will enable you to refer to the Linux server as http://linux.mydomain/ instead of http://172.16.0.1/ in your WWW browser

```
127.0.0.1      localhost
172.16.0.1      linux.mydomain
```

Edit the NET.cfg file in NWCLIENT directory

```
Link Driver NE2000
    port 300
    int 3
    MEM D0000
    FRAME Ethernet_802.2

; ---- add these lines ----
```

```
            FRAME Ethernet_II

      Protocol TCPIP
         PATH TCP_CFG C:\NET\TCP
         ip_address  172.17.0.5
         ip_netmask  255.255.255.0
         ip_router   172.17.0.254   ---> add the address of your gateway only
                                     ---> if you have to use this
                                     ---> gateway to reach your HTTP server


      Link Support
         MemPool 6192      ---> the minimum is 1024. Try with different values
         Buffers 10 1580   ---> this again can be fine tuned

   ;---------------------------------
   ; You may need to add lines like these if you are using Netware/IP
   ;
      NWIP
         NWIP_DOMAIN_NAME  mydomain
         NSQ_BROADCAST     ON
         NWIP1_1 COMPATIBILITY   OFF
         AUTORETRIES       1
         AUTORETRY SECS    10
```

Edit the SYSTEM.ini file in the WINDOWS directory and add this entry for VTCPIP.386

```
      [386Enh]
      .....
      network=*vnetbios, vipx.386, vnetware.386, VTCPIP.386
      .....
```

Reboot your PC, run STARTNET.bat and you can now use your favorite WWW browser to access your Web pages. You need not login to Netware and you don't have to run TCPMAN (if you use Trumpet Winsock).

4.3.2   Windows 95

This section explains how to install the 32bit client on Win95. Firstly you must install the following

```
      Client for Netware Networks (from Microsoft or Novell)
      Microsoft TCP/IP Protocol
      Network Adapter
```

To install these items, click on My Computer, Control Panel, Networks. Click Add. You will now be in a window that displays Client, Adapter, Protocol and Service. To install the Client for Netware Networks:

```
      1. DoubleClick on Client
      2. Click on Microsoft or Novell
      3. DoubleClick on Client for Netware Networks
```

To install the TCP/IP Protocol:

```
      1. DoubleClick on Protocol
      2. Click on Microsoft
      3. DoubleClick on TCP/IP
```

Windows 95 by default installs several other protocols automatically. Remove them by clicking on them and clicking the Remove button. Typically Win95 installs the Microsoft NetBeui protocol, and IPX/SPX compatible protocol. You can delete the NetBEUI protocol, but you will need the IPX/SPX protocol if you wish to login to the Netware Server.

To setup TCP/IP click on TCP/IP, click on Properties, click on the tab IP address

```
Enter your IP address in the "Specify an IP address "
                     box as 172.17.0.5
In the Subnet Mask box enter 255.255.255.0
```

select the tab Gateway

```
Enter your gateway (router) address in the box New gateway
   as 172.17.0.254
Click the Add button
```

The gateway address should now appear under the installed gateways box. Now Click OK.

You should get a message to reboot. Do so. You should now be able to use the Browser to connect to your HTTP Server.

4.4 Setup Microsoft Client

If you are using the Microsoft Client for accessing your network, then this section details how to install TCP/IP for

- 4.4.1 (Windows for Workgroups (WFWG))
- 4.4.2 (Windows 95)
- 4.4.3 (Windows NT 4.0)

Note: To enable you to refer to the Linux server as `http://linux.mydomain/` instead of `http://172.16.0.1/` in the WWW browser and all your intranet commands you need to edit the `hosts` file. You can add more entries for each of your other hosts (Netware, Unix, WinNT) as well. The Windows family keeps its HOSTS file in `\WINDOWS` or in `\WINDOWS\SYSTEM` depending on the version. Edit this file and add a line for your Linux server as:

```
127.0.0.1       localhost
172.16.0.1      linux.mydomain

172.16.0.2      netware.mydomain
172.16.0.3      winNT.mydomain
172.16.0.5      ws_1
```

4.4.1 Windows for Workgroups

This section explains how to install the 32bit client on WFWG. Firstly you must download the TCP/IP drivers for Windows from Microsoft. The current version is 3.11b and is available at *ftp://ftp.microsoft.com* or other sites as `tcp32b.exe`. Make sure that you have load Win32s before trying to load the TCP/IP-32bit driver.

Having expanded the TCP/IP files into a temporary directory (say `C:\TEMP`), check your `\WINDOWS\SYSTEM` directory for copies of `OEMSETUP.INF`. If there are any, rename them. Now copy the `OEMSETUP.INF` file from the TEMP directory to the `\WINDOWS\SYSTEM` directory. If you have loaded any other TCP/IP stacks on your system, please remove them before you proceed.

Start Network Setup or Windows Setup/Change Network settings

```
Click the Networks button
Click Install Microsoft Windows Network.
  Choose support for additional networks (if required)
Click OK
```

You should be prompted for your network adapter - select the appropriate one. If you are not prompted, then

```
Click the Adapter button
    select an adapter (say NE2000)
    Click OK
Click the Protocol button
    select the MS TCP/IP-32 protocol
    click OK
```

You will now be prompted to configure the TCP/IP protocol stack. You can always reconfigure this by highlighting the TCP/IP protocol shown in the box Adapters and clicking the Setup button.

```
In the IP address box enter 172.17.0.5
In the Subnet Mask box enter 255.255.255.0
Enter your gateway (router) address in the box default gateway
    as 172.17.0.254
```

Click OK. The computer will ask you to restart. Do so. You should now be able to use the Browser to connect to your HTTP Server.

4.4.2 Windows 95

This section explains how to install the 32bit client for Microsoft on Win95. Firstly you must install the following

```
Client for Microsoft Networks
Microsoft TCP/IP Protocol
Network Adapter
```

To install these items, click on My Computer, Control Panel, Networks. Click Add. You will now be in a window that displays Client, Adapter, Protocol and Service. To install the Client for Microsoft Networks:

```
1. DoubleClick on Client
2. Click on Microsoft
3. DoubleClick on Client for Microsoft Networks
```

To install the TCP/IP Protocol:

```
1. DoubleClick on Protocol
2. Click on Microsoft
3. DoubleClick on TCP/IP
```

Windows 95 by default installs several protocols automatically. Remove them by clicking on them and clicking the Remove button. Typically Win95 installs the Microsoft NetBeui protocol.

To setup TCP/IP click on TCP/IP, click on Properties, click on the tab IP address

```
Enter your IP address in the "Specify an IP address "
                box as 172.17.0.5
In the Subnet Mask box enter 255.255.255.0
```

select the tab Gateway

```
Enter your gateway (router) address in the box New gateway
     as 172.17.0.254
Click the Add button
```

The gateway address should now appear under the installed gateways box. Now Click OK.

You should get a message to reboot. Do so. You should now be able to use the Browser to connect to your HTTP Server.

4.4.3   Windows NT

This section details how to Install the TCP/IP client for WinNT 4.0. Start Control Panel/ Network

```
Select the Adapter tab.
     Click Add to add a new adapter (if you don't have one)
```

You should be prompted for your network adapter - select the appropriate one. To add the protocols.

```
Select the Protocols tab
     Click Add
     Select the TCP/IP protocol
     Click OK
```

You will now be prompted to configure the TCP/IP protocol stack. You can always reconfigure this by highlighting the TCP/IP protocol and clicking the Properties button.

```
Select the tab IP Address
     Mark the checkbox 'Specify an IP address'
     In the IP address box enter 172.17.0.5
     In the Subnet Mask box enter 255.255.255.0
     Enter your gateway (router) address in the box Default Gateway
          as 172.17.0.254
```

Click OK. The computer will ask you to restart. You can now use any Browser to connect to your HTTP Server.

4.5   Setup TCP/IP on Macintosh

If you are using the Macintosh for accessing your network, then this section details how to install MacTCP for the PowerMacs.

Note: To enable you to refer to the Linux server as `http://linux.mydomain/` instead of `http://172.16.0.1/` in the WWW browser and all your intranet commands you need to edit the `hosts` file. The format of the hosts file is different from the one used in Unix. The Mac hosts file is based on RFC-1035. You can add more entries for each of your other hosts (Netware, Unix, WinNT) as well. The MacOS keeps its HOSTS file in the `Preferences folder` under the `System folder`. Edit this file and add a line for your Linux server as:

```
linux.mydomain     A   172.16.0.1

netware.mydomain   A   172.16.0.2
winNT.mydomain     A   172.16.0.3
ws_1               A   172.16.0.5
```

4.5.1   MacTCP

This section explains how to install MacTCP. Firstly you must download the MacTCP files from Apple or install it from the Internet Connection CD. To configure MacTCP, click the Apple Menu/ Control Panels/ TCP/IP. In the screen change the setting for 'Connect via:' to 'Ethernet'

Change the 'Configure' setting to 'Manually'

```
In the IP address box enter 172.17.0.5
In the Subnet Mask box enter 255.255.255.0
Enter your gateway (router) address in the box
    Router address as 172.17.0.254
```

Click OK. You should now be able to use the Browser to connect to your HTTP Server.

5   Setting up the Intranet

An Intranet cannot be complete without sharing the resources on the different platforms. You will need support for other filesystems, so that you can access the data available on them. This document provides instructions to connect Linux to the following popular filesystems.

- 5.1 (NCP filesystem for Netware)
- 5.2 (SMB filesystem for Windows)
- 5.3 (NFS filesystem for Unix)

These filesystems can be compiled into the Linux kernel or added as modules, depending on the version of Linux.   If you are not familiar with compiling the kernel you can refer to the K-ernel   HOWTO   *http://sunsite.unc.edu/mdw/HOWTO/Kernel-HOWTO.html*   and   the   Module   HOWTO *http://sunsite.unc.edu/mdw/HOWTO/Module-HOWTO.html* for compiling the kernel with modules.

5.1   NCPFS

To share the files on the Netware server you will need support for NCP (ncpfs). NCPFS works with kernel version 1.2.x and 1.3.71 upwards. It does not work with any earlier 1.3.x kernel. It cannot access the NDS database in Netware 4.x, but can make use of the bindery. If you are using Netware 4.x you can enable bindery support for specific containers using the command Set Bindery Context at the console as:

```
set Bindery Context = CORP.MYDOM;WEBUSER.MYDOM
```

In the above example two containers have bindery support enabled.

You   will   need   to   download   the   NCP   filesystem   utilities   using   the   URL   *ft-p://sunsite.unc.edu/pub/Linux/system/filesystems/ncpfs/ncpfs.tgz* (currently ncpfs-2.0.10) from Sunsite.

5.1.1   Installation

To install the ncpfs utilities, type

```
zcat ncpfs.tgz | tar xvf -
```

to expand the files into its own directory. In this case you will get a directory ncpfs-2.0.10 Change your directory to this ncpfs directory before proceeding with the installation. Read the README and edit the Makefile if necessary.

The installation of ncpfs depends on the kernel version you are using. For kernel 1.2, you should simply type 'make'. Subsequently typing 'make install' will install the executables and man pages.

If you use Kernel 1.3.71 or later, you might have to recompile your kernel. With these kernels, the kernel part of ncpfs is already included in the main source tree. To check if the kernel needs to be recompiled type

```
cat /proc/filesystems
```

It should show you a line saying that the kernel knows ncpfs.

If ncpfs is not there, you can either recompile the kernel or add ncpfs as a module. For recompiling the kernel you should type 'make config' and when it asks you for

```
The IPX protocol (CONFIG_IPX) [N/y/?]
```

simply answer 'y'. Probably you do not need the full internal net that you are asked for next. Once the kernel is successfully installed, reboot, check `/proc/filesystems` and if everything is OK proceed with the installation of the ncpfs utilities. Change directory to the location holding your downloaded ncpfs files, and type 'make'. After the compilation is finished type 'make install' to install the various utilities and man pages.

5.1.2 Mounting NCPFS

To check the installation type

```
ipx_configure --auto_interface=on --auto_primary=on
```

....wait for 10 seconds and type

```
slist
```

You should be able to see a list of your Netware servers. Now we are ready to share files from the Netware server.

Suppose we need to access HTML files from directory \home\htmldocs on volume VOL1: on the server MY-DOM_NW, I recommend that you create a new user (say) 'EXPORT' with password 'EXP123' on this server to whom you grant appropriate access rights to this directory using SYSCON or NWADMIN.

On the Linux machine create a new directory /mnt/MYDOM_NW. Now type the command

```
ncpmount -S MYDOM_NW -U EXPORT -P EXP123 /mnt/MYDOM_NW
```

to mount the netware file system. Typing the command

```
ls /mnt/MYDOM_NW/vol1/home/htmldocs
```

will show you a list of all the files in MYDOM_NW/VOL1:\HOME\HTMLDOCS (using Netware file notation). If you have any problems please read the IPX HOWTO at *http://sunsite.unc.edu/mdw/HOWTO/IPX-HOWTO.html* for more insights into the IPX system.

5.2 SMBFS

To share the files on the Windows server you will need support for SMB (smbfs).

You will need to download the SMB filesystem utilities from

ftp://sunsite.unc.edu/pub/Linux/system/filesystems/smbfs/smbfs.tgz

(currently smbfs-2.0.1) from Sunsite.

5.2.1 Installation

To install the smbfs utilities, type

```
zcat smbfs.tgz | tar xvf -
```

to expand the files into its own directory. In this case you will get a directory `smbfs-2.0.1` Change your directory to this smbfs directory before proceeding with the installation. Read the README and edit the Makefile if necessary.

The installation of smbfs depends on the kernel version you are using. For kernel 1.2, you should simply type 'make'. Subsequently typing 'make install' will install the executables and man pages.

If you use Kernel 2.0 or later, you might have to recompile your kernel. With these kernels, the kernel part of smbfs is already included in the main source tree. To check if the kernel needs to be recompiled type

```
cat /proc/filesystems
```

It should show you a line saying that the kernel knows smbfs.

If smbfs is not there, you can either recompile the kernel or add smbfs as a module. For recompiling the kernel you should type 'make config' and when it asks you for adding SMB filesystem support simply answer yes. Once the kernel is successfully installed, reboot, check `/proc/filesystems` and if everything is OK proceed with the installation of the smbfs utilities. Change directory to the location holding your downloaded smbfs files, and type 'make'. After the compilation is finished type 'make install' to install the various utilities and man pages.

5.2.2 Mounting SMBFS

In our example let us assume that the WinNT server is called 'MYDOM_NT' and is sharing its directory `C:\PUB\HTMLDOCS` with a share name of 'HTMLDOCS' without a password. On the Linux machine create a new directory `/mnt/MYDOM_NT`. Now type the command

```
smbmount //MYDOM_NT/HTMLDOCS /mnt/MYDOM_NT -n
```

to mount the SMB (windows share) file system. If this does not work try

```
smbmount //MYDOM_NT/COMMON /mnt/MYDOM_NT -n -I 172.16.0.3
```

Typing the command

```
ls /mnt/MYDOM_NT
```

will show you a list of all the files in `bsol;bsol;MYDOM_NT\PUB\HTMLDOCS` (using Windows file notation).

5.3 NFS

First you will need a kernel with the NFS file system either compiled in or available as a module.

Suppose you have a Unix host running NFS with the name MYDOM_UNIX and an IP address of 172.16.0.4. You can check the directories that are being exported (shared) by this host by typing the command

```
showmount -e 172.16.0.4
```

Once we know the exported directories you can mount them by entering a appropriate mount command. I recommend that you create a subdirectory under '/mnt' (say) 'MYDOM_UNIX' and use that as your mount point.

```
mount -o rsize=1024,wsize=1024 172.16.0.4:/pub/htmldocs /mnt/MYDOM_UNIX
```

The rsize and wsize may have to be changed depending on your environment.

If you have any problems please read the NFS HOWTO at *http://sunsite.unc.edu/mdw/HOWTO/NFS-HOWTO.html* for more insights into the NFS system.

6 Accessing the Web

Now that we have setup the HTTP server, the clients and interconnected the Linux server with the other servers, we need to make some small adjustments on the Linux server to be able to access these mounted filesystems from the Web Browser.

6.1 Accessing the mounted filesystems

To access the mounted directories in your HTML pages you have two methods:

- Create a link in DocumentRoot (`/usr/local/etc/httpd/htdocs`) to refer to the mounted directory as

```
ln -s /mnt/MYDOM_NW/vol1/home/htmldocs netware
            or

ln -s /mnt/MYDOM_NT      winNT
            or

ln -s /mnt/MYDOM_UNIX      unix
```

- to edit the file `srm.conf` in your `/usr/local/etc/httpd/conf` directory and add a new alias.

```
# Alias fakename realname
Alias /icons/       /usr/local/etc/httpd/icons/

# alias for netware server
Alias /netware/     /mnt/MYDOM_NW/vol1/home/htmldocs/
Alias /winNT/       /mnt/MYDOM_NT/
Alias /unix/        /mnt/MYDOM_UNIX
```

And restart your HTTPd. You can access the documents on the netware server by referring to them as `http://linux.mydomain/netware/index.htm` for the netware files and similar notations for the others.

6.2 Connecting to the Internet

You can finally connect your Intranet to the Internet to access E-Mail and all the wonderful information out there. I propose to write a brief note on how to do this in a future revision. Detailed explanations are available in the ISP Hookup HOWTO from *http://sunsite.unc.edu/mdw/HOWTO/ISP-Hookup-HOWTO.html* and Diald mini HOWTO at *http://sunsite.unc.edu/mdw/HOWTO/mini/Diald* for setting up these connections.

6.3 Other uses

The HTTP server can be used in the office to provide transparent access to information residing on different servers, at several locations and directories. The data can be simple documents in Word, Lotus spreadsheets, or complex databases.

The application of this technology is being typically used as follows:-

- Publishing corporate documentsThese documents can include newsletters, annual reports, maps, company facilities, price lists, product information literature, and any document which is of value within the corporate entity.
- Access into searchable directoriesRapid access to corporate phone books and the like. This data can be mirrored at a Web site or, via CGI scripts, the Web server can serve as a gateway to back-end pre-existing or new applications. This means that, using the same standard access mechanisms, information can be made more widely available and in a simpler manner. This means that it can be used to create an interface with RDBMS like ORACLE and SYBASE for generating real-time information. Here is a list of links to such sites on the Web.
  - Web Access - *http://cscsun1.larc.nasa.gov/~beowulf/db/web_access.html* - CGI gateways - *HTTP://www.w3.org/hypertext/WWW/RDBGate/Overview.html*

- Corporate/Department/Individual pagesAs cultures change within organistions to the point where even each department moves towards their own individual mission statements, the Intranet technology provides the ideal medium to communicate current information to the Department or Individual. Powerful search engines provide the means for people to find the group or individual who has the answers to the continuous questions which arise in the normal day-to-day course of doing business.

- Simple Groupware applicationsWith HTML forms support, sites can provide sign-up sheets, surveys and simple scheduling.

- Software distributionAdministrators can use the Intranet to deliver software and up-dates on-demand to users across the corporate network . This can be done with 'Java' which allows the creation and transparent distribution of objects on-demand rather than just data or applications. This is indeed possible more easily with the newer versions of Linux which has builtin support for Java.

- MailWith the move to the use of Intranet mail products with standard and simple methods for attachment of documents, sound, vision and other multimedia between individuals, mail is being pushed further forward as a simple, de facto communications method. Mail is essentially individual to individual, or individual to small group, communication. Several utilities are available on the Linux platform to setup an E-mail system like **sendmail, pop3d, imapd**.

- User InterfaceThe Intranet technology is evolving so rapidly that the tools available, in particular HTML, can be used to dramatically change the way we interface with systems. With HTML you can build an Interface which is only limited by the creators imagination. The beauty about using Intranet technologies for this is that it is so simple. Clicking a hyperlink from HTML can take you to another page, it could ring an alarm, run a yearend procedure or anything else that a computer program can do.

7 More things to do

Here is a list of other interesting things to do with your Linux Intranet server. All the software mentioned below is freeware or shareware.

- Browse the Linux server using Network Neighbourhood in Win95/ NT; Setup a WINS like NBT server. Check out the SAMBA Web page at *http://lake.canberra.edu.au/pub/samba/samba.html*

- Implement a search engine on your Intranet. Connect to ht://Dig at *http://htdig.sdsu.edu/*

- Use CUSeeMe by setting up a local reflector. Refer to their page at Cornell *http://cu-seeme.cornell.edu/*

- Setup Web Conferencing. Use COW from *http://thecity.sfsu.edu/COW/*

- Deploy a SQL database. Refer to the mSQL Home page at *http://Hughes.com.au/*

- Setup FTP,Gopher,Finger,Bootp servers on the Netware server. Get them at *http://mft.ucs.ed.ac.uk/*

- Emulate a Netware server. Check out the NCP Utilities at *ftp://sunsite.unc.edu/pub/Linux/system/filesystems/ncpfs/*

If you find other interesting things to do with your Linux Intranet server, please feel free to mail me.

8 Credits and Legalities

8.1 Thanks

Thanks to the people at NCSA for providing such excellent documentation, David Anderson and all others for trying out this HOWTO and sending in their comments. The details on Netware/IP are courtesy Romel Flores (rom@mnl.sequel.net).

8.2 Copyright information

This document is copyrighted © 1996,1997 Pramod Karnad and distributed under the following terms:

Part XVIII

"Java CGI HOWTO" by David H. Silber

javacgi-document@orbits.com
v0.5, 1 December 1998

This HOWTO document explains how to set up your server to allow CGI programs written in Java and how to use Java to write CGI programs. Although HOWTO documents are targetted towards use with the Linux operating system, this particular one is not dependant on the particular version of unix used.

Contents

HOWTO

1 Introduction

Because of the way that Java is designed the programmer does not have easy access to the system's environment variables. Because of the way that the Java Development Kit (JDK) is set up, it is necessary to use multiple tokens to invoke a program, which does not mesh very well with the standard HTML forms/CGI manner of operations. There are ways around these limitations, and I have implemented one of them. Read further for details.

Since I wrote the previous paragraph in 1996, there have been many changes in the Java technology. It is likely that a better solution to running server-side Java programs is now available – perhaps you should take a look at servlets.

1.1 Prior Knowledge

I am assuming that you have a general knowledge of HTML and CGI concepts and at least a minimal knowledge of your HTTP server. You should also know how to program in Java, or a lot of this will not make sense.

1.2 This Document

The latest version of this document can be read at *http://www.orbits.com/software/Java_CGI.html*.

1.3 The Package

The latest version of the package described here can be accessed via anonymous FTP at *ftp://ftp.orbits.com/pub/software/java_cgi-0.5.tgz*. The package distribution includes SGML source for this document.

The package is distributed under the terms of the GNU Library General Public License. This document can be distributed under the terms of the Linux HOWTO copyright notice.

If you use this software, please make some reference to *http://www.orbits.com/software/Java_CGI.html*, so that others will be able to find the Java CGI classes.

I have run out of time to maintain and support this package, so this will probably be its final release. If anyone out there is sufficiently enamoured of this software that they wish to take over the maintenace of it, please contact me at `javacgi-document@orbits.com`.

1.4 The Mailing List

I have created a majordomo list to allow people to help each-other work through their mutual problems in installing and using this software. Send a message to `javacgi-request@orbits.com`, containing the word *subscribe*.

2 Setting Up Your Server to Run Java CGI Programs (With Explanations)

This section will lead you through installing my *Java CGI* package with copious explanations so that you know what the effects of your actions will be. If you just want to install the programs and don't care about the whys & wherefores, skip to 3 (Setting Up Your Server to Run Java CGI Programs (The Short Form)).

2.1 System Requirements

This software should work on any unix-like web server that has the Java Development Kit installed. I am using it on a *Debian Linux* system running *apache* as the HTTP daemon. If you find that it does not run on your server, please contact the mailing list. See 1.4 (The Mailing List) for details.

Unfortunatly, the Java run-time interpreter seems to be something of a memory hog – you may want to throw another few megabytes of RAM onto your server if you will be using Java CGI programs a lot.

2.2 Java CGI Add-On Software

The software that I wrote to aid in this is called *Java CGI*. You can get it from *ftp://ftp.orbits.com/pub/software/java_cgi-0.5.tgz*. (The version number may have changed.)

2.3 Unpacking the Source

Find a convenient directory to unpack this package into. (If you don't already have a standard place to put packages, I suggest that you use `/usr/local/src`.) Unpack the distribution with this command:

```
gzip -dc java_cgi-0.5.tgz | tar -xvf -
```

This will create a directory called `java_cgi-0.5`. In there you will find the files referenced in the rest of this document. (If the version number has changed, use the instructions from within that distribution from this point on.)

2.4 Decide On Your Local Path Policies

You need to decide where you want your Java CGI programs to live. Generally, you will want to put them in a directory in parallel with your `cgi-bin` directory. My *apache* server came configured to use `/var/www/cgi-bin` as the `cgi-bin` directory, so I use `/var/www/javacgi` as the directory to put Java CGI programs in. You probably do not want to put your Java CGI programs into one of the existing `CLASSPATH` directories. Edit the Makefile to reflect your system configuration. Make sure that you are logged in as the root user and run `make install`. This will compile the Java programs, modify the `java.cgi` script to fit in with your system and install the programs in the appropriate places. If you want the HTML version of this documentation and an HTML test document in addition, run `make all` instead.

2.5 Testing your installation.

Installed from the distribution are HTML documents called `javacgitest.html`, `javaemailtest.html` and `javahtmltest.html`. If you installed `all` in the previous section, it will be in the directory you specified for WEB-DIR in the `Makefile`. If you didn't, you can run `make test` to build them from `javacgitest.html-dist`, `javaemailtest.html-dist` and `javahtmltest.html-dist`.

When you are sure that your installation is working correctly, you may wish to remove `CGI_Test.class`, `E-mail_Test.class` and `HTML_Test.class` from your JAVACGI directory and `javacgitest.html`, `javaemailtest.html` and `javahtmltest.html` from your WEBDIR directory as they show the user information that is normally only available to the server.

3 Setting Up Your Server to Run Java CGI Programs (The Short Form)

- Get the *Java CGI* package from *ftp://ftp.orbits.com/pub/software/java_cgi-0.5.tgz*. (The version number may have changed.)

HOWTO

- Unpack the distribution with this command:

```
gzip -dc java_cgi-0.5.tgz | tar -xvf -
```

(If the version number has changed, use the instructions from within that distribution from this point on.)

- Edit the `Makefile` you will find in the newly created directory `java_cgi-0.5` as appropriate to your system.

- As root, run `make install`. This will compile the Java programs, apply your system-specific information and install the various files. If you want the HTML version of this documentation and an HTML test document, run `make all` instead.

- You should be ready to go.

4 Executing a Java CGI Program

4.1 Obstacles to Running Java Programs Under the CGI Model

There are two main problems in running a Java program from a web server:

4.1.1 You can't run Java programs like ordinary executables.

You need to run the Java run-time interpreter and provide the initial class (program to run) on the command-line. With an HTML form, there is no provision for sending a command-line to the web server.

4.1.2 Java does not have general access to the environment.

Every environment variable that will be needed by the Java program must be explicitly passed in. There is no method similar to the **C** `getenv()` function.

4.2 Overcoming Problems in Running Java CGI Programs

To deal with these obstacles, I wrote a shell CGI program that provides the information needed by the Java interpreter.

4.2.1 The java.cgi script.

This shell script manages the interaction between the HTTP daemon and the Java CGI program that you wish to use. It extracts the name of the program that you want to run from the server-provided data. It collects all of the environment data into a temporary file. Then, it runs the Java run-time interpreter with the name of the file of environment information and the program name added to the command-line.

The `java.cgi` script was configured and installed in 2.4 (Decide On Your Local Path Policies).

4.2.2 Invoking java.cgi from an HTML form.

My forms that use Java CGI programs specify a form action as follows:

```
<form action="/cgi-bin/java.cgi/CGI_Test" method="POST">
```

Where `/cgi-bin/` is your local CGI binary directory, `java.cgi` is the Java front-end that allows us to run Java programs over the web and `CGI_Test` is an example of the name of the Java program to run.

5 Using the Java CGI Classes.

There are currently three main classes supported – 5.1 (CGI), 5.3 (Email) and 5.5 (HTML). I am considering adding classes to deal with MIME-formatted input and output – MIMEin & MIMEout, respectively.

There are also a few support and test classes. 5.2 (CGI_Test), 5.4 (Email_Test) and 5.4 (HTML_Test) are intended to be used to test your installation. They can also be used as a starting-point for your own Java programs which use this class library. The 5.7 (Text) class is the superclass for both the `Email` and the `HTML` classes.

5.1 CGI

5.1.1 Class Syntax

```
public class CGI
```

5.1.2 Class Description

The CGI class holds the "CGI Information" – Environment variables set by the web server and the name/value sent from a form when its **submit** action is selected. All information is stored in a `Properties` class object.

This class is in the "Orbits.net" package.

5.1.3 Member Summary

```
CGI()         //  Constructor.
getNames()    //  Get the list of names.
getValue()    //  Get form value by specifying name.
```

5.1.4 See Also

`CGI_Test`.

5.1.5 CGI()

Purpose

Constructs an object which contains the available CGI data.

Syntax

```
public CGI()
```

Description

When a CGI object is constructed, all available CGI information is sucked-up into storage local to the new object.

5.1.6 getNames()

Purpose

List the names which are defined to have corresponding values.

Syntax

```
public Enumeration getKeys ()
```

Description

Provides the full list of names for which coresponding values are defined.

Returns

An `Enumeration` of all the names defined.

5.1.7 getValue()

Purpose

Retrieves the **value** associated with the **name** specified.

Syntax

```
public String getValue ( String name )
```

Description

This method provides the corespondence between the `names` and `values` sent from an HTML form.

Parameter

name

The key by which values are selected.

Returns

A `String` containing the value.

5.2 CGI_Test

This class provides both an example of how to use the `CGI` class and a test program which can be used to confirm that the *Java CGI* package is functioning correctly.

5.2.1 Member Summary

main()	// Program main().

5.2.2 See Also

CGI.

5.2.3 main()

Purpose

Provide a `main()` method.

Syntax

```
public static void main( String argv[] )
```

Description

This is the entry point for a CGI program which does nothing but return a list of the available name/value pairs and their current values.

Parameter

argv[]

Arguments passed to the program by the `java.cgi` script. Currently unused.

5.3 Email

5.3.1 Class Syntax

```
public class Email extends Text
```

5.3.2 Class Description

Messages are built up with the `Text` class `add*()` methods and the e-mail-specific methods added by this class. When complete, the message is sent to its destination.

This class is in the "Orbits.net" package.

5.3.3   Member Summary

```
Email()      //  Constructor.
send()       //  Send the e-mail message.
sendTo()     //  Add a destination for message.
subject()    //  Set the Subject: for message.
```

5.3.4   See Also

Email_Test, Text.

5.3.5   Email()

Purpose

Constructs an object which will contain an email message.

Syntax

```
public Email()
```

Description

Sets up an empty message to be completed by the Email methods.

See Also

Text.

5.3.6   send()

Purpose

Send the e-mail message.

Syntax

```
public void send ()
```

Description

This formats and sends the message. If no destination address has been set, there is no action taken.

5.3.7   sendTo()

Purpose

Add a destination for this message.

Syntax

```
public String sendTo ( String address )
```

Description

Add address to the list of destinations for this method. There is no set limit to the number of destinations an e-mail message may have. I'm sure that if you build up the list large enough, you can exceed the size of the parameter list that the *Mail Transport Agent* can accept or use up your memory.

Parameter/

address

A destination to send this message to.

5.3.8   subject()

Purpose

Set the subject for this message.

Syntax

```
public void subject ( String subject )
```

Description

This method sets the text for the e-mail's `Subject:` line. If called more than once, the latest subject set is the one that is used.

Parameter

subject

The text of this message's `Subject:` line.

5.4   Email_Test

This class provides both an example of how to use the `Email` class and a test program which can be used to confirm that the *Java CGI* package is functioning correctly.

5.4.1   Member Summary

```
        main()       //  Program main().
```

5.4.2   See Also

`Email`.

5.4.3   main()

Purpose

Provide a `main()` method.

Syntax

```
public static void main( String argv[] )
```

Description

This is the entry point for a CGI program which returns a list of the available name/value pairs and their current values. It will also send this list to the address specified in the `Email` variable.

Parameter

argv[]

Arguments passed to the program by the `java.cgi` script. Currently unused.

5.5   HTML

5.5.1   Class Syntax

```
public class HTML extends Text
```

5.5.2   Class Description

Messages are built up with the `Text` class `add*()` methods and the HTML-specific methods added by this class. When complete, the message is sent to its destination.

Currently, there is no error checking to confirm that the list-building methods are being used in a correct order, so the programmer must take pains not to violate HTML syntax.

This class is in the "Orbits.net" package.

5.5.3   Member Summary

```
HTML()                   //  Constructor.
author()                 //  Set the name of the document author.
definitionList()         //  Start a definition list.
definitionListTerm()     //  Add a term to a definition list.
endList()                //  End a list.
listItem()               //  Add an entry to a list.
send()                   //  Send the HTML message.
title()                  //  Set the text for the document title.
```

5.5.4   See Also

HTML_Test, Text.

5.5.5   HTML()

Purpose

Constructs an object which will contain an HTML message.

Syntax

```
public HTML()
```

Description

Sets up an empty message to be completed by the HTML methods.

See Also

Text.

5.5.6   author()

Purpose

Set the name of the document author.

Syntax

```
public void author ( String author )
```

Description

Set the name of the document author to author.

Parameter/

author

The text to use as the author of this message.

See Also

title().

5.5.7   definitionList()

Purpose

Start a definition list.

Syntax

```
public void definitionList ()
```

Description

Start a definition list. A *definition list* is a list specialized so that each entry in the list is a *term* followed by the definition *text* for that term. The start of a definition list should be followed by the creation of (at least) one term/text pair and a call to the endList() method. *Note that, currently, lists cannot be nested.*

See Also

definitionListTerm(), endList(), listItem().

5.5.8 definitionListTerm()

Purpose

Add a term to a definition list.

Syntax

```
public void definitionListTerm ()
```

Description

Add a term to a definition list. The text for the term part of the current list entry should be appended to the message after this method is called and before a corresponding `listItem` method is called.

See Also

```
definitionList(),listItem().
```

5.5.9 endList()

Purpose

End a list.

Syntax

```
public void endList ()
```

Description

End a list. This method closes out a list. *Note that, currently, lists cannot be nested.*

See Also

```
definitionList().
```

5.5.10 listItem()

Purpose

Add an entry to a list.

Syntax

```
public void listItem ()

public void listItem ( String item )

public boolean listItem ( String term, String item )
```

Description

Add an entry to a list. If the first form is used, the text for the current list item should be appended to the message after this method is called and before any other list methods are called. In the second and third forms, the `item` text is specified as a parameter to the method instead of (or in addition to) being appended to the message. The third form is specific to definition lists and provides both the term and the definition of the list entry.

Parameters

item

The text of this list entry.

term

The text of this definition list entry's term part.

See Also

```
definitionList(),definitionListTerm(),endList().
```

5.5.11   send()

Purpose

Send the HTML message.

Syntax

```
public void send ()
```

Description

Send the HTML message.

5.5.12   title()

Purpose

Set the text for the document title.

Syntax

```
public void title ( String title )
```

Description

Set the text for the document title.

Parameter

title

The text of this message's title.

See Also

```
author().
```

5.6   HTML_Test

This class provides both an example of how to use the HTML class and a test program which can be used to confirm that the *Java CGI* package is functioning correctly.

5.6.1   Member Summary

```
main()       //  Program main().
```

5.6.2   See Also

HTML.

5.6.3   main()

Purpose

Provide a main() method.

Syntax

```
public static void main( String argv[] )
```

Description

This is the entry point for a CGI program which returns a list of the available name/value pairs in an HTML document, with each name/value pair displayed in a definition list element.

Parameter

argv[]

Arguments passed to the program by the java.cgi script. Currently unused.

HOWTO

5.7 Text

5.7.1 Class Syntax

```
public abstract class Text
```

5.7.2 Class Description

This class is the superclass of the `Email` and `HTML` classes. Messages are built up with the methods in this class and completed and formatted with the methods in subclasses.

This class is in the "Orbits.text" package.

5.7.3 Member Summary

```
Text()             //  Constructor.
add()              //  Add text to this object.
addLineBreak()     //  Add a line break.
addParagraph()     //  Add a paragraph break.
```

5.7.4 See Also

`Email`, `HTML`.

5.7.5 add()

Purpose

Add text to this item.

Syntax

```
public void add ( char addition )

public void add ( String addition )

public void add ( StringBuffer addition )
```

Description

Add `addition` to the contents of this text item.

Parameter

addition

Text to be added to the text item.

See Also

`addLineBreak()`, `addParagraph()`.

5.7.6 addLineBreak()

Purpose

Force a line break at this point in the text.

Syntax

```
public void addLineBreak ()
```

Description

Add a line break to the text at the current point.

See Also

`add()`, `addParagraph()`.

5.7.7 addParagraph()

Purpose

Start a new paragaph.

Syntax

```
public void add ()
```

Description

Start a new paragraph at this point in the text flow.

See Also

```
add(),addLineBreak().
```

6 Future Plans

- Add to the Email class:

  Email(int capacity)

  Used when we know how much space the message will need to have allocated.

  sendTo(String [] address)

  Add a list of primary destinations to the e-mail message.

  sendCc(String address)

  Add a Carbon-Copy destination to the e-mail message.

  sendCc(String [] address)

  Add a list of Carbon-Copy destinations to the e-mail message.

  sendBcc(String address)

  Add a Blind Carbon-Copy destination to the e-mail message.

  sendBcc(String [] address)

  Add a list of Blind Carbon-Copy destinations to the e-mail message.

- Add to the HTML class:

  HTML(int capacity)

  Used when we know how much space the message will need to have allocated.

  public void unorderedList()

  Start an unordered list.

  public void orderedList()

  Start an ordered list.

  public void directoryList()

  Start a directory list.

  public void menuList()

  Start a menu list.

  void anchor(String anchorName)

  Specify an anchor.

  void link(String url, String text)

  Specify a link.

  void applet(String url, String altText)

  Specify an applet link.

- Allow HTML lists to be nested.

- Add error checking code to enforce correct ordering of HTML list formatting codes.
- The location of the file of environment data should be configurable from the `Makefile`.
- Get rid of the spurious empty name/value pair that appears in the list when we are dealing with the GET method of data transfer.
- Consider having CGI implement the java.util.Enumeration interface to successively provide variable names.
- Add a `Test` class, which would use every method in this package.
- Document how `CGI_Test`, `Email_Test` and `HTML_Test` build on each other to provide incremental tests for debugging purposes.
- Document how Test uses every feature available in this package.

7 Changes

7.1 Changes from 0.4 to 0.5

- Changed documentation and comments to reflect the final nature of this release.

7.2 Changes from 0.3 to 0.4

- Fleshed out the HTML class to provide minimal functionality.
- Wrote the HTML_Test class and javahtmltest.html-dist.
- Added the HTML methods to deal with a definition list.

7.3 Changes from 0.2 to 0.3

- Added the Text and Email classes. HTML was also added, but it is merely a stub at this point.
- Put the various classes into packages. The main classes are in `Orbits.net.*`, the support class `Text` is in `Orbits.text.Text`.
- Changed `CGItest` to `CGI_Test`.
- Added the `Email_Test` class.

7.4 Changes from 0.1 to 0.2

- The environment variables are put into a temporary file instead of being crammed into the Java inperpreter command-line. The `CGI` class and `java.cgi` had to be modified.
- The `javacgitest.html` document is made part of the distribution.
- The text files which are modified by `make` upon installation are provided with names that end with *-dist*.

## Part XIX

"The Linux Kernel HOWTO" Brian Ward

bri@blah.math.tu-graz.ac.at
v0.80, 26 May 1997
This is a detailed guide to kernel configuration, compilation, upgrades, and troubleshooting for ix86-based systems.

Contents

HOWTO

1 Introduction

Should you read this document? Well, see if you've got any of the following symptoms:

- "Arg! This wizzo-46.5.6 package says it needs kernel release 1.8.193 and I still only have release 1.0.9!"

- There's a device driver in one of the newer kernels that you just gotta have

- You really have no idea at all how to compile a kernel

- "Is this stuff in the README *really* the whole story?"

- You came, you tried, it didn't work

- You need something to give to people who insist on asking you to install their kernels for them

1.1 Read this first! (I mean it)

Some of the examples in this document assume that you have GNU `tar`, `find`, and `xargs`. These are quite standard; this should not cause problems. It is also assumed that you know your system's filesystem structure; if you don't, it is critical that you keep a written copy of the `mount` command's output during normal system operation (or a listing of `/etc/fstab`, if you can read it). This information is important, and does not change unless you repartition your disk, add a new one, reinstall your system, or something similar.

The latest "production" kernel version at the time of this writing was 2.0.30, meaning that the references and examples correspond to that release. Even though I try to make this document as version-independent as possible, the kernel is constantly under development, so if you get a newer release, it will inevitably have some differences. Again, this should not cause major problems, but it may create some confusion.

There are two versions of the linux kernel source, "production" and "development." Production releases begin with 1.0.x and are currently the even-numbered releases; 1.0.x was production, 1.2.x is production, as well as 2.0.x. These kernels are considered to be the most stable, bug-free versions available at the time of release. The development kernels (1.1.x, 1.3.x, etc) are meant as testing kernels, for people willing to test out new and possibly very buggy kernels. You have been warned.

1.2 A word on style

`Text that looks like this` is either something that appears on your screen, a filename, or something that can be directly typed in, such as a command, or options to a command (if you're looking at a plain-text file, it doesn't look any different). Commands and other input are frequently quoted (with ' '), which causes the following classic punctuation problem: if such an item appears at the end of a sentence in quotes, people often type a '.' along with the command, because the American quoting style says to put the period inside of the quotation marks. Even though common sense (and unfortunately, this assumes that the one with the "common sense" is used to the so-called American style of quotation) should tell one to strip off the punctuation first, many people simply do not remember, so I will place it outside the quotation marks in such cases. In other words, when indicating that you should type "`make config`" I would write '`make config`', not '`make config`.'

2 Important questions and their answers

2.1 What does the kernel do, anyway?

The Unix kernel acts as a mediator for your programs and your hardware. First, it does (or arranges for) the memory management for all of the running programs (processes), and makes sure that they all get a fair (or unfair, if you please) share of the processor's cycles. In addition, it provides a nice, fairly portable interface for programs to talk to your hardware.

There is certainly more to the kernel's operation than this, but these basic functions are the most important to know.

2.2 Why would I want to upgrade my kernel?

Newer kernels generally offer the ability to talk to more types of hardware (that is, they have more device drivers), they can have better process management, they can run faster than the older versions, they could be more stable than the older versions, and they fix silly bugs in the older versions. Most people upgrade kernels because they want the device drivers and the bug fixes.

2.3 What kind of hardware do the newer kernels support?

See the Hardware-HOWTO. Alternatively, you can look at the `config.in` file in the linux source, or just find out when you try `make config`. This shows you all hardware supported by the standard kernel distribution, but not everything that linux supports; many common device drivers (such as the PCMCIA drivers and some tape drivers) are loadable modules maintained and distributed separately.

2.4 What version of gcc and libc do I need?

Linus recommends a version of gcc in the README file included with the linux source. If you don't have this version, the documentation in the recommended version of gcc should tell you if you need to upgrade your libc. This is not a difficult procedure, but it is important to follow the instructions.

2.5 What's a loadable module?

These are pieces of kernel code which are not linked (included) directly in the kernel. One compiles them separately, and can insert and remove them into the running kernel at almost any time. Due to its flexibility, this is now the preferred way to code certain kernel features. Many popular device drivers, such as the PCMCIA drivers and the QIC-80/40 tape driver, are loadable modules.

2.6 How much disk space do I need?

It depends on your particular system configuration. First, the compressed linux source is nearly 6 megabytes large at version 2.0.10. Most sites keep this even after unpacking. Uncompressed, it takes up 24 MB. But that's not the end – you need more to actually compile the thing. This depends on how much you configure into your kernel. For example, on one particular machine, I have networking, the 3Com 3C509 driver, and three filesystems configured, using close to 30 MB. Adding the compressed linux source, you need about 36 MB for this particular configuration. On another system, without network device support (but still with networking support), and sound card support, it consumes even more. Also, a newer kernel is certain to have a larger source tree than an older one, so, in general, if you have a lot of hardware, make sure that you have a big enough hard disk in that mess (and at today's prices, I cannot help but to recommend getting another disk space as an answer to your storage problems).

2.7 How long does it take?

For most people, the answer is "fairly long." The speed of your system and the amount of memory you have ultimately determines the time, but there is a small bit to do with the amount of stuff you configure into the kernel. On a 486DX4/100 with 16 MB of RAM, on a v1.2 kernel with five filesystems, networking support, and sound card drivers, it takes around 20 minutes. On a 386DX/40 (8 MB RAM) with a similar configuration, compilation lasts nearly 1.5 hours. It is a generally good recommendation to make a little coffee, watch some TV, knit, or whatever you do for fun while your machine compiles the kernel. You can have someone else with a faster machine compile it for you if you really have a slow machine.

3   How to actually configure the kernel

3.1   Getting the source

You can obtain the source via anonymous ftp from `ftp.funet.fi` in `/pub/Linux/PEOPLE/Linus`, a mirror, or other sites. It is typically labelled `linux-x.y.z.tar.gz`, where `x.y.z` is the version number. Newer (better?) versions and the patches are typically in subdirectories such as 'v1.1' and 'v1.2' The highest number is the latest version, and is usually a "test release," meaning that if you feel uneasy about beta or alpha releases, you should stay with a major release.

I *strongly* suggest that you use a mirror ftp site instead of ftp.funet.fi. Here is a short list of mirrors and other sites:

```
USA:        sunsite.unc.edu:/pub/Linux/kernel
USA:        tsx-11.mit.edu:/pub/linux/sources/system
UK:         sunsite.doc.ic.ac.uk:/pub/unix/Linux/sunsite.unc-mirror/kernel
Austria:    ftp.univie.ac.at:/systems/linux/sunsite/kernel
Germany:    ftp.Germany.EU.net:/pub/os/Linux/Local.EUnet/Kernel/Linus
Germany:    sunsite.informatik.rwth-aachen.de:/pub/Linux/PEOPLE/Linus
France:     ftp.ibp.fr:/pub/linux/sources/system/patches
Australia:  sunsite.anu.edu.au:/pub/linux/kernel
```

In general, a mirror of `sunsite.unc.edu` is a good place to look. The file `/pub/Linux/MIRRORS` contains a list of known mirrors. If you do not have ftp access, a list of BBS systems which carry linux is posted periodically to comp.os.linux.announce; try to obtain this.

If you were looking for general Linux information and distributions, try `http://www.linux.org`.

3.2   Unpacking the source

Log in as or `su` to 'root', and `cd` to `/usr/src`. If you installed kernel source when you first installed linux (as most do), there will already be a directory called 'linux' there, which contains the entire old source tree. If you have the disk space and you want to play it safe, preserve that directory. A good idea is to figure out what version your system runs now and rename the directory accordingly. The command 'uname -r' prints the current kernel version. Therefore, if 'uname -r' said '1.0.9', you would rename (with 'mv') 'linux' to 'linux-1.0.9'. If you feel mildly reckless, just wipe out the entire directory. In any case, make certain there is no 'linux' directory in `/usr/src` before unpacking the full source code.

Now, in `/usr/src`, unpack the source with 'tar zxpvf linux-x.y.z.tar.gz' (if you've just got a .tar file with no .gz at the end, 'tar xpvf linux-x.y.z.tar' works.). The contents of the source will fly by. When finished, there will be a new 'linux' directory in `/usr/src`. cd to linux and look over the README file. There will be a section with the label 'INSTALLING the kernel'. Carry out the instructions when appropriate – symbolic links that should be in place, removal of stale .o files, etc.

3.3   Configuring the kernel

Note: Some of this is reiteration/clarification of a similar section in Linus' README file.

The command 'make config' while in `/usr/src/linux` starts a configure script which asks you many questions. It requires bash, so verify that bash is `/bin/bash`, `/bin/sh`, or `$BASH`.

There are some alternatives to 'make config' and you may very well find them easier and more comfortable to use. For those "running X," you can try 'make xconfig' if you have Tk installed ('click-o-rama' - Nat). 'make menuconfig' is for those who have (n)curses and would prefer a text-based menu. These interfaces have one clear advantage: If you goof up and make a wrong choice during configuration, it is simple to go back and fix it.

You are ready to answer the questions, usually with 'y' (yes) or 'n' (no). Device drivers typically have an 'm' option. This means "module," meaning that the system will compile it, but not directly into the kernel, but as a loadable module. A more comical way to describe it is as "maybe." Some of the more obvious and non-critical options are not described here; see the section "Other configuration options" for short descriptions of a few others.

In 2.0.x and later, there is a '?' option, which provides a brief description of the configuration parameter. That information is likely to be the most up-to-date.

3.3.1 Kernel math emulation

If you don't have a math coprocessor (you have a bare 386 or 486SX), you must say 'y' to this. If you do have a coprocessor and you still say 'y', don't worry too much – the coprocessor is still used and the emulation ignored. The only consequence is that the kernel will be larger (costing RAM). I have been told that the math emulation is slow; although this does not have much to do with this section, it might be something to keep in mind when faced with sluggish X window system performance.

3.3.2 Normal (MFM/RLL) disk and IDE disk/cdrom support

You probably need to support this; it means that the kernel will support standard PC hard disks, which most people have. This driver does not include SCSI drives; they come later in the configuration.

You will then be asked about the "old disk-only" and "new IDE" drivers. You want to choose one of them; the main difference is that the old driver only supports two disks on a single interface, and the new one supports a secondary interface and IDE/ATAPI cdrom drives. The new driver is 4k larger than the old one and is also supposedly "improved," meaning that aside from containing a different number of bugs, it might improve your disk performance, especially if you have newer (EIDE-type) hardware.

3.3.3 Networking support

In principle, you would only say 'y' if your machine is on a network such as the internet, or you want to use SLIP, PPP, term, etc to dial up for internet access. However, as many packages (such as the X window system) require networking support even if your machine does not live on a real network, you should say 'y'. Later on, you will be asked if you want to support TCP/IP networking; again, say 'y' here if you are not absolutely sure.

3.3.4 Limit memory to low 16MB

There exist buggy 386 DMA controllers which have problems with addressing anything more than 16 MB of RAM; you want to say 'y' in the (rare) case that you have one.

3.3.5 System V IPC

One of the best definitions of IPC (Interprocess Communication) is in the Perl book's glossary. Not surprisingly, some Perl programmers employ it to let processes talk to each other, as well as many other packages (DOOM, most notably), so it is not a good idea to say n unless you know exactly what you are doing.

3.3.6 Processor type (386, 486, Pentium, PPro)

(in older kernels: Use -m486 flag for 486-specific optimizations)

Traditionally, this compiled in certain optimizations for a particular processor; the kernels ran fine on other chips, but the kernel was perhaps a bit larger. In newer kernels, however, this is no longer true, so you should enter the processor for which you are compiling the kernel. A "386" kernel will work on all machines.

3.3.7 SCSI support

If you have SCSI devices, say 'y'. You will be prompted for further information, such as support for CD-ROM, disks, and what kind of SCSI adapter you have. See the SCSI-HOWTO for greater detail.

3.3.8 Network device support

If you have a network card, or you would like to use SLIP, PPP, or a parallel port adapter for connecting to the Internet, say 'y'. The config script will prompt for which kind of card you have, and which protocol to use.

3.3.9 Filesystems

The configure script then asks if you wish to support the following filesystems:

Standard (minix) - Newer distributions don't create minix filesystems, and many people don't use it, but it may still be a good idea to configure this one. Some "rescue disk" programs use it, and still more floppies may have a minix filesystem, since the minix filesystem is less painful to use on a floppy.

Extended fs - This was the first version of the extended filesystem, which is no longer in widespread use. Chances are that you'll know it if you need it and that if you are doubt, you do not need it.

Second extended - This is widely used in new distributions. You probably have one of these, and need to say 'y'.

xiafs filesystem - At one time, this was not uncommon, but at the time of this writing, I did not know of anyone using it.

msdos - If you want to use your MS-DOS hard disk partitions, or mount MS-DOS formatted floppy disks, say 'y'.

umsdos - This filesystem expands an MS-DOS filesystem with usual Unix-like features such as long filenames. It is not useful for people (like me) who "don't do DOS."

/proc - Another one of the greatest things since powdered milk (idea shamelessly stolen from Bell Labs, I guess). One doesn't make a proc filesystem on a disk; this is a filesystem interface to the kernel and processes. Many process listers (such as 'ps') use it. Try 'cat /proc/meminfo' or 'cat /proc/devices' sometime. Some shells (rc, in particular) use /proc/self/fd (known as /dev/fd on other systems) for I/O. You should almost certainly say 'y' to this; many important linux tools depend on it.

NFS - If your machine lives on a network and you want to use filesystems which reside on other systems with NFS, say 'y'.

ISO9660 - Found on most CD-ROMs. If you have a CD-ROM drive and you wish to use it under Linux, say 'y'.

OS/2 HPFS - At the time of this writing, a read-only fs for OS/2 HPFS.

System V and Coherent - for partitions of System V and Coherent systems (These are other PC Unix variants).

But I don't know which filesystems I need!   Ok, type 'mount'. The output will look something like this:

```
blah# mount
/dev/hda1 on / type ext2 (defaults)
/dev/hda3 on /usr type ext2 (defaults)
none on /proc type proc (defaults)
/dev/fd0 on /mnt type msdos (defaults)
```

Look at each line; the word next to 'type' is the filesystem type. In this example, my / and /usr filesystems are second extended, I'm using /proc, and there's a floppy disk mounted using the msdos (bleah) filesystem.

You can try 'cat /proc/filesystems' if you have /proc currently enabled; it will list your current kernel's filesystems.

The configuration of rarely-used, non-critical filesystems can cause kernel bloat; see the section on modules for a way to avoid this and the "Pitfalls" section on why a bloated kernel is undesirable.

3.3.10 Character devices

Here, you enable the drivers for your printer (parallel printer, that is), busmouse, PS/2 mouse (many notebooks use the PS/2 mouse protocol for their built-in trackballs), some tape drives, and other such "character" devices. Say 'y' when appropriate.

Note: Selection is a program which allows the use of the mouse outside of the X window system for cut and paste between virtual consoles. It's fairly nice if you have a serial mouse, because it coexists well with X, but you need to do special tricks for others. Selection support was a configuration option at one time, but is now standard.

Note 2: Selection is now considered obsolete. "gpm" is the name of the new program. It can do fancier things, such translate mouse protocols, handle multiple mice, ..

3.3.11 Sound card

If you feel a great desire to hear `biff` bark, say 'y', and later on, another config program will compile and ask you all about your sound board. (A note on sound card configuration: when it asks you if you want to install the full version of the driver, you can say 'n' and save some kernel memory by picking only the features which you deem necessary.) I highly recommend looking at the Sound-HOWTO for more detail about sound support if you have a sound card.

3.3.12 Other configuration options

Not all of the configuration options are listed here because they change too often or fairly self-evident (for instance, 3Com 3C509 support to compile the device drive for this particular ethernet card). There exists a fairly comprehensive list of all the options (plus a way to place them into the `Configure` script) put together by Axel Boldt (axel@uni-paderborn.de) with the following URL:

> `http://math-www.uni-paderborn.de/~axel/config_help.html`

or via anonymous FTP at:

> `ftp://sunsite.unc.edu/pub/Linux/kernel/config/krnl_cnfg_hlp.x.yz.tgz`

where the `x.yz` is the version number.

For later (2.0.x and later) kernels, this has been integrated into the source tree.

3.3.13 Kernel hacking

>From Linus' README:

the "kernel hacking" configuration details usually result in a bigger or slower kernel (or both), and can even make the kernel less stable by configuring some routines to actively try to break bad code to find kernel problems (kmalloc()). Thus you should probably answer 'n' to the questions for a "production" kernel.

3.4 Now what? (The Makefile)

After you `make config`, a message tells you that your kernel has been configured, and to "check the top-level `Makefile` for additional configuration," etc.

So, look at the `Makefile`. You probably will not need to change it, but it never hurts to look. You can also change its options with the 'rdev' command once the new kernel is in place.

4 Compiling the kernel

4.1 Cleaning and depending

When the configure script ends, it also tells you to 'make dep' and (possibly) 'clean'. So, do the 'make dep'. This insures that all of the dependencies, such the include files, are in place. It does not take long, unless your computer is fairly slow to begin with. For older versions of the kernel, when finished, you should do a 'make clean'. This removes all of the object files and some other things that an old version leaves behind. In any case, *do not* forget this step before attempting to recompile a kernel.

4.2 Compile time

After depending and cleaning, you may now 'make zImage' or 'make zdisk' (this is the part that takes a long time.). 'make zImage' will compile the kernel, and leave a file in arch/i386/boot called 'zImage' (among other things). This is the new compressed kernel. 'make zdisk' does the same thing, but also places the new zImage on a floppy disk which you hopefully put in drive "A:". 'zdisk' is fairly handy for testing new kernels; if it bombs (or just doesn't work right), just remove the floppy and boot with your old kernel. It can also be a handy way to boot if you accidentally remove your kernel (or something equally as dreadful). You can also use it to install new systems when you just dump the contents of one disk onto the other ("all this and more! NOW how much would you pay?").

All even halfway reasonably recent kernels are compressed, hence the 'z' in front of the names. A compressed kernel automatically decompresses itself when executed.

4.3 Other "make"ables

'make mrproper' will do a more extensive 'clean'ing. It is sometimes necessary; you may wish to do it at every patch. 'make mrproper' will also delete your configuration file, so you might want to make a backup of it (.config) if you see it as valuable.

'make oldconfig' will attempt to configure the kernel from an old configuration file; it will run through the 'make config' process for you. If you haven't ever compiled a kernel before or don't have an old config file, then you probably shouldn't do this, as you will most likely want to change the default configuration.

See the section on modules for a description of 'make modules'.

4.4 Installing the kernel

After you have a new kernel that seems to work the way you want it to, it's time to install it. Most people use LILO (Linux Loader) for this. 'make zlilo' will install the kernel, run LILO on it, and get you all ready to boot, BUT ONLY if lilo is configured in the following way on your system: kernel is /vmlinuz, lilo is in /sbin, and your lilo config (/etc/lilo.conf) agrees with this.

Otherwise, you need to use LILO directly. It's a fairly easy package to install and work with, but it has a tendency to confuse people with the configuration file. Look at the config file (either /etc/lilo/config for older versions or /etc/lilo.conf for new versions), and see what the current setup is. The config file looks like this:

```
image = /vmlinuz
    label = Linux
    root = /dev/hda1
    ...
```

The 'image =' is set to the currently installed kernel. Most people use /vmlinuz. 'label' is used by lilo to determine which kernel or operating system to boot, and 'root' is the / of that particular operating system. Make a backup copy of your old kernel and copy the zImage which you just made into place (you would say 'cp zImage /vmlinuz' if you use '/vmlinuz'). Then, rerun lilo – on newer systems, you can just run 'lilo', but on older stuff, you might have to do an /etc/lilo/install or even an /etc/lilo/lilo -C /etc/lilo/config.

If you would like to know more about LILO's configuration, or you don't have LILO, get the newest version from your favorite ftp site and follow the instructions.

To boot one of your old kernels off the hard disk (another way to save yourself in case you screw up the new kernel), copy the lines below (and including) 'image = xxx' in the LILO config file to the bottom of the file, and change the 'image = xxx' to 'image = yyy', where 'yyy' is the full pathname of the file you saved your backup kernel to. Then, change the 'label = zzz' to 'label = linux-backup' and rerun lilo. You may need to put a line in the config file saying 'delay=x', where x is an amount in tenths of a second, which tells LILO to wait that much time before booting, so that you can interrupt it (with the shift key, for example), and type in the label of the backup boot image (in case unpleasant things happen).

5 Patching the kernel

5.1 Applying a patch

Incremental upgrades of the kernel are distributed as patches. For example, if you have version 1.1.45, and you notice that there's a 'patch46.gz' out there for it, it means you can upgrade to version 1.1.46 through application of the patch. You might want to make a backup of the source tree first ('make clean' and then 'cd /usr/src; tar zcvf old-tree.tar.gz linux' will make a compressed tar archive for you.).

So, continuing with the example above, let's suppose that you have 'patch46.gz' in /usr/src. cd to /usr/src and do a 'zcat patch46.gz | patch -p0' (or 'patch -p0 < patch46' if the patch isn't compressed). You'll see things whizz by (or flutter by, if your system is that slow) telling you that it is trying to apply hunks, and whether it succeeds or not. Usually, this action goes by too quickly for you to read, and you're not too sure whether it worked or not, so you might want to use the -s flag to patch, which tells patch to only report error messages (you don't get as much of the "hey, my computer is actually doing something for a change!" feeling, but you may prefer this..). To look for parts which might not have gone smoothly, cd to /usr/src/linux and look for files with a .rej extension. Some versions of patch (older versions which may have been compiled with on an inferior filesystem) leave the rejects with a # extension. You can use 'find' to look for you;

```
find .  -name '*.rej' -print
```

prints all files who live in the current directory or any subdirectories with a .rej extension to the standard output.

If everything went right, do a 'make clean', 'config', and 'dep' as described in sections 3 and 4.

There are quite a few options to the patch command. As mentioned above, patch -s will suppress all messages except the errors. If you keep your kernel source in some other place than /usr/src/linux, patch -p1 (in that directory) will patch things cleanly. Other patch options are well-documented in the manual page.

5.2 If something goes wrong

(Note: this section refers mostly to quite old kernels)

The most frequent problem that used to arise was when a patch modified a file called 'config.in' and it didn't look quite right, because you changed the options to suit your machine. This has been taken care of, but one still might encounter it with an older release. To fix it, look at the config.in.rej file, and see what remains of the original patch. The changes will typically be marked with '+' and '−' at the beginning of the line. Look at the lines surrounding it, and remember if they were set to 'y' or 'n'. Now, edit config.in, and change 'y' to 'n' and 'n' to 'y' when appropriate. Do a

```
patch -p0 < config.in.rej
```

and if it reports that it succeeded (no fails), then you can continue on with a configuration and compilation. The `config.in.rej` file will remain, but you can get delete it.

If you encounter further problems, you might have installed a patch out of order. If patch says 'previously applied patch detected: Assume -R?', you are probably trying to apply a patch which is below your current version number; if you answer 'y', it will attempt to degrade your source, and will most likely fail; thus, you will need to get a whole new source tree (which might not have been such a bad idea in the first place).

To back out (unapply) a patch, use 'patch -R' on the original patch.

The best thing to do when patches really turn out wrong is to start over again with a clean, out-of-the-box source tree (for example, from one of the `linux-x.y.z.tar.gz` files), and start again.

5.3   Getting rid of the .orig files

After just a few patches, the `.orig` files will start to pile up. For example, one 1.1.51 tree I had was once last cleaned out at 1.1.48. Removing the .orig files saved over a half a meg.

```
find .  -name '*.orig' -exec rm -f {} ';'
```

will take care of it for you. Versions of `patch` which use # for rejects use a tilde instead of `.orig`.

There are better ways to get rid of the `.orig` files, which depend on GNU `xargs`:

```
find .  -name '*.orig' | xargs rm
```

or the "quite secure but a little more verbose" method:

```
find . -name '*.orig' -print0 | xargs --null rm --
```

5.4   Other patches

There are other patches (I'll call them "nonstandard") than the ones Linus distributes. If you apply these, Linus' patches may not work correctly and you'll have to either back them out, fix the source or the patch, install a new source tree, or a combination of the above. This can become very frustrating, so if you do not want to modify the source (with the possibility of a very bad outcome), back out the nonstandard patches before applying Linus', or just install a new tree. Then, you can see if the nonstandard patches still work. If they don't, you are either stuck with an old kernel, playing with the patch or source to get it to work, or waiting (possibly begging) for a new version of the patch to come out.

How common are the patches not in the standard distribution? You will probably hear of them. I used to use the noblink patch for my virtual consoles because I hate blinking cursors (This patch is (or at least was) frequently updated for new kernel releases.). With most newer device drivers being developed as loadable modules, though, the frequecy of "nonstandard" patches is decreasing significantly.

6   Additional packages

Your linux kernel has many features which are not explained in the kernel source itself; these features are typically utilized through external packages. Some of the most common are listed here.

6.1   kbd

The linux console probably has more features than it deserves. Among these are the ability to switch fonts, remap your keyboard, switch video modes (in newer kernels), etc. The kbd package has programs which allow the user to do all of this, plus many fonts and keyboard maps for almost any keyboard, and is available from the same sites that carry the kernel source.

6.2 util-linux

Rik Faith (`faith@cs.unc.edu`) put together a large collection of linux utilities which are, by odd coincidence, called util-linux. These are now maintained by Nicolai Langfeldt (`util-linux@math.uio.no`). Available via anonymous ftp from sunsite.unc.edu in `/pub/Linux/system/misc`, it contains programs such as `setterm`, `rdev`, and `ctr-laltdel`, which are relevant to the kernel. As Rik says, *do not install without thinking;* you do not need to install everything in the package, and it could very well cause serious problems if you do.

6.3 hdparm

As with many packages, this was once a kernel patch and support programs. The patches made it into the official kernel, and the programs to optimize and play with your hard disk are distributed separately.

6.4 gpm

gpm stands for general purpose mouse. This program allows you to cut and paste text between virtual consoles and do other things with a large variety of mouse types.

7 Some pitfalls

7.1 make clean

If your new kernel does really weird things after a routine kernel upgrade, chances are you forgot to `make clean` before compiling the new kernel. Symptoms can be anything from your system outright crashing, strange I/O problems, to crummy performance. Make sure you do a `make dep`, too.

7.2 Huge or slow kernels

If your kernel is sucking up a lot of memory, is too large, and/or just takes forever to compile even when you've got your new 786DX6/440 working on it, you've probably got lots of unneeded stuff (device drivers, filesystems, etc) configured. If you don't use it, don't configure it, because it does take up memory. The most obvious symptom of kernel bloat is extreme swapping in and out of memory to disk; if your disk is making a lot of noise and it's not one of those old Fujitsu Eagles that sound like like a jet landing when turned off, look over your kernel configuration.

You can find out how much memory the kernel is using by taking the total amount of memory in your machine and subtracting from it the amount of "total mem" in `/proc/meminfo` or the output of the command '`free`'. You can also find out by doing a '`dmesg`' (or by looking at the kernel log file, wherever it is on your system). There will be a line which looks like this:

```
Memory:  15124k/16384k available (552k kernel code, 384k reserved, 324k data)
```

My 386 (which has slightly less junk configured) says this:

```
Memory:  7000k/8192k available (496k kernel code, 384k reserved, 312k data)
```

If you 'just gotta' have a big kernel but the system won't let you, you can try '`make bzimage`'. You may very well have to install a new version of LILO if you do this.

7.3 Kernel doesn't compile

If it does not compile, then it is likely that a patch failed, or your source is somehow corrupt. Your version of gcc also might not be correct, or could also be corrupt (for example, the include files might be in error). Make sure that the symbolic links which Linus describes in the README are set up correctly. In general, if a standard kernel does not compile, something is seriously wrong with the system, and reinstallation of certain tools is probably necessary.

Or perhaps you're compiling a 1.2.x kernel with an ELF compiler (gcc 2.6.3 and higher). If you're getting a bunch of `so-and-so undefined` messages during the compilation, chances are that this is your problem. The fix is in most cases very simple. Add these lines to the top of `arch/i386/Makefile`:

```
AS=/usr/i486-linuxaout/bin/as
LD=/usr/i486-linuxaout/bin/ld -m i386linux
CC=gcc -b i486-linuxaout -D__KERNEL__ -I$(TOPDIR)/include
```

Then `make dep` and `zImage` again.

In rare cases, gcc can crash due to hardware problems. The error message will be something like "xxx exited with signal 15" and it will generally look very mysterious. I probably would not mention this, except that it happened to me once - I had some bad cache memory, and the compiler would occasionally barf at random. Try reinstalling gcc first if you experience problems. You should only get suspicious if your kernel compiles fine with external cache turned off, a reduced amount of RAM, etc.

It tends to disturb people when it's suggested that their hardware has problems. Well, I'm not making this up. There is an FAQ for it – it's at `http://www.bitwizard.nl/sig11/`.

7.4   New version of the kernel doesn't seem to boot

You did not run LILO, or it is not configured correctly. One thing that "got" me once was a problem in the config file; it said '`boot = /dev/hda1`' instead of '`boot = /dev/hda`' (This can be really annoying at first, but once you have a working config file, you shouldn't need to change it.).

7.5   You forgot to run LILO, or system doesn't boot at all

Ooops! The best thing you can do here is to boot off of a floppy disk and prepare another bootable floppy (such as '`make zdisk`' would do). You need to know where your root (`/`) filesystem is and what type it is (e.g. second extended, minix). In the example below, you also need to know what filesystem your `/usr/src/linux` source tree is on, its type, and where it is normally mounted.

In the following example, `/` is `/dev/hda1`, and the filesystem which holds `/usr/src/linux` is `/dev/hda3`, normally mounted at `/usr`. Both are second extended filesystems. The working kernel image in `/usr/src/linux/arch/i386/boot` is called `zImage`.

The idea is that if there is a functioning `zImage`, it is possible to use that for the new floppy. Another alternative, which may or may not work better (it depends on the particular method in which you messed up your system) is discussed after the example.

First, boot from a boot/root disk combo or rescue disk, and mount the filesystem which contains the working kernel image:

```
mkdir /mnt
mount -t ext2 /dev/hda3 /mnt
```

If `mkdir` tells you that the directory already exists, just ignore it. Now, `cd` to the place where the working kernel image was. Note that

`/mnt + /usr/src/linux/arch/i386/boot - /usr = /mnt/src/linux/arch/i386/boot`

Place a formatted disk in drive "A:" (not your boot or root disk!), dump the image to the disk, and configure it for your root filesystem:

```
cd /mnt/src/linux/arch/i386/boot
dd if=zImage of=/dev/fd0
```

```
rdev /dev/fd0 /dev/hda1
```

cd to / and unmount the normal /usr filesystem:

```
cd /
umount /mnt
```

You should now be able to reboot your system as normal from this floppy. Don't forget to run lilo (or whatever it was that you did wrong) after the reboot!

As mentioned above, there is another common alternative. If you happened to have a working kernel image in / (/vmlinuz for example), you can use that for a boot disk. Supposing all of the above conditions, and that my kernel image is /vmlinuz, just make these alterations to the example above: change /dev/hda3 to /dev/hda1 (the / filesystem), /mnt/src/linux to /mnt, and if=zImage to if=vmlinuz. The note explaining how to derive /mnt/src/linux may be ignored.

Using LILO with big drives (more than 1024 cylinders) can cause problems. See the LILO mini-HOWTO or documentation for help on that.

7.6 It says 'warning: bdflush not running'

This can be a severe problem. Starting with a kernel release after 1.0 (around 20 Apr 1994), a program called 'update' which periodically flushes out the filesystem buffers, was upgraded/replaced. Get the sources to 'bdflush' (you should find it where you got your kernel source), and install it (you probably want to run your system under the old kernel while doing this). It installs itself as 'update' and after a reboot, the new kernel should no longer complain.

7.7 It says stuff about undefined symbols and does not compile

You probably have an ELF compiler (gcc 2.6.3 and up) and the 1.2.x (or earlier) kernel source. The usual fix is to add these three lines to the top of arch/i386/Makefile:

```
AS=/usr/i486-linuxaout/bin/as
LD=/usr/i486-linuxaout/bin/ld -m i386linux
CC=gcc -b i486-linuxaout -D__KERNEL__ -I$(TOPDIR)/include
```

This will compile a 1.2.x kernel with the a.out libraries.

7.8 I can't get my IDE/ATAPI CD-ROM drive to work

Strangely enough, lots of people cannot get their ATAPI drives working, probably because there are a number of things that can go wrong.

If your CD-ROM drive is the only device on a particular IDE interface, it must be jumpered as "master" or "single." Supposedly, this is the most common error.

Creative Labs (for one) has put IDE interfaces on their sound cards now. However, this leads to the interesting problem that while some people only have one interface to being with, many have two IDE interfaces built-in to their motherboards (at IRQ15, usually), so a common practice is to make the soundblaster interface a third IDE port (IRQ11, or so I'm told).

This causes problems with linux in that versions 1.2.x don't support a third IDE interface (there is support in starting somewhere in the 1.3.x series but that's development, remember, and it doesn't auto-probe). To get around this, you have a few choices.

If you have a second IDE port already, chances are that you are not using it or it doesn't already have two devices on it. Take the ATAPI drive off the sound card and put it on the second interface. You can then disable the sound card's interface, which saves an IRQ anyway.

If you don't have a second interface, jumper the sound card's interface (not the sound card's sound part) as IRQ15, the second interface. It should work.

If for some reason it absolutely has to be on a so-called "third" interface, or there are other problems, get a 1.3.x kernel (1.3.57 has it, for example), and read over `drivers/block/README.ide`. There is much more information here.

7.9   It says weird things about obsolete routing requests

Get new versions of the `route` program and any other programs which do route manipulation. `/usr/include/linux/route.h` (which is actually a file in `/usr/src/linux`) has changed.

7.10   Firewalling not working in 1.2.0

Upgrade to at least version 1.2.1.

7.11   "Not a compressed kernel Image file"

Don't use the `vmlinux` file created in `/usr/src/linux` as your boot image; `[..]/arch/i386/boot/zImage` is the right one.

7.12   Problems with console terminal after upgrade to 1.3.x

Change the word `dumb` to `linux` in the console termcap entry in `/etc/termcap`. You may also have to make a terminfo entry.

7.13   Can't seem to compile things after kernel upgrade

The linux kernel source includes a number of include files (the things that end with `.h`) which are referenced by the standard ones in `/usr/include`. They are typically referenced like this (where `xyzzy.h` would be something in `/usr/include/linux`):

```
    #include <linux/xyzzy.h>
```

Normally, there is a link called `linux` in `/usr/include` to the `include/linux` directory of your kernel source (`/usr/src/linux/include/linux` in the typical system). If this link is not there, or points to the wrong place, most things will not compile at all. If you decided that the kernel source was taking too much room on the disk and deleted it, this will obviously be a problem. Another way it might go wrong is with file permissions; if your `root` has a umask which doesn't allow other users to see its files by default, and you extracted the kernel source without the p (preserve filemodes) option, those users also won't be able to use the C compiler. Although you could use the `chmod` command to fix this, it is probably easier to re-extract the include files. You can do this the same way you did the whole source at the beginning, only with an additional argument:

```
    blah# tar zxvpf linux.x.y.z.tar.gz linux/include
```

Note: "`make config`" will recreate the `/usr/src/linux` link if it isn't there.

7.14   Increasing limits

The following few *example* commands may be helpful to those wondering how to increase certain soft limits imposed by the kernel:

```
echo 4096 > /proc/sys/kernel/file-max
echo 12288 > /proc/sys/kernel/inode-max
echo 300 400 500 > /proc/sys/vm/freepages
```

8   Note for upgrade to version 2.0.x

Kernel version 2.0.x introduced quite a bit of changes for kernel installation. The file `Documentation/Changes` in the 2.0.x source tree contains information that you should know when upgrading to version 2.0.x. You will most likely need to upgrade several key packages, such as gcc, libc, and SysVInit, and perhaps alter some system files, so expect this. Don't panic, though.

9   Modules

Loadable kernel modules can save memory and ease configuration. The scope of modules has grown to include filesystems, ethernet card drivers, tape drivers, printer drivers, and more.

9.1   Installing the module utilities

The module utilities are available from wherever you got your kernel source as `modules-x.y.z.tar.gz`; choose the highest patchlevel `x.y.z` that is equal to or below that of your current kernel. Unpack it with 'tar zxvf `modules-x.y.z.tar.gz`', `cd` to the directory it creates (`modules-x.y.z`), look over the `README`, and carry out its installation instructions (which is usually something simple, such as `make install`). You should now have the programs `insmod`, `rmmod`, `ksyms`, `lsmod`, `genksyms`, `modprobe`, and `depmod` in `/sbin`. If you wish, test out the utilities with the "hw" example driver in `insmod`; look over the `INSTALL` file in that subdirectory for details.

`insmod` inserts a module into the running kernel. Modules usually have a `.o` extension; the example driver mentioned above is called `drv_hello.o`, so to insert this, one would say '`insmod drv_hello.o`'. To see the modules that the kernel is currently using, use `lsmod`. The output looks like this:

```
blah# lsmod
Module:         #pages:  Used by:
drv_hello          1
```

'drv_hello' is the name of the module, it uses one page (4k) of memory, and no other kernel modules depend on it at the moment. To remove this module, use '`rmmod drv_hello`'. Note that `rmmod` wants a *module name,* not a filename; you get this from `lsmod`'s listing. The other module utilities' purposes are documented in their manual pages.

9.2   Modules distributed with the kernel

As of version 2.0.30, most of everything is available as a loadable modules. To use them, first make sure that you don't configure them into the regular kernel; that is, don't say `y` to it during '`make config`'. Compile a new kernel and reboot with it. Then, `cd` to `/usr/src/linux` again, and do a '`make modules`'. This compiles all of the modules which you did not specify in the kernel configuration, and places links to them in `/usr/src/linux/modules`. You can use them straight from that directory or execute '`make modules_install`', which installs them in `/lib/modules/x.y.z`, where `x.y.z` is the kernel release.

This can be especially handy with filesystems. You may not use the minix or msdos filesystems frequently. For example, if I encountered an msdos (shudder) floppy, I would `insmod /usr/src/linux/modules/msdos.o`, and then `rmmod msdos` when finished. This procedure saves about 50k of RAM in the kernel during normal operation. A small note is in order for the minix filesystem: you should *always* configure it directly into the kernel for use in "rescue" disks.

10   Other configuration options

This section contains descriptions of selected kernel configuration options (in `make config`) which are not listed in the configuration section. Most device drivers are not listed here.

10.1   General setup

`Normal floppy disk support` - is exactly that.   You may wish to read over the file `driver-s/block/README.fd`; this is especially important for IBM Thinkpad users.

`XT harddisk support` - if you want to use that 8 bit XT controller collecting dust in the corner.

`PCI bios support` - if you have PCI, you may want to give this a shot; be careful, though, as some old PCI motherboards could crash with this option. More information about the PCI bus under linux is found in the PCI-HOWTO.

`Kernel support for ELF binaries` - ELF is an effort to allow binaries to span architectures and operating systems; linux seems is headed in that direction and so you most likely want this.

`Set version information on all symbols for modules` - in the past, kernel modules were recompiled along with every new kernel. If you say y, it will be possible to use modules compiled under a different patchlevel. Read `README.modules` for more details.

10.2   Networking options

Networking options are described in the NET-3-HOWTO (or NET-something-HOWTO).

11   Tips and tricks

11.1   Redirecting output of the make or patch commands

If you would like logs of what those 'make' or 'patch' commands did, you can redirect output to a file. First, find out what shell you're running: 'grep root /etc/passwd' and look for something like '/bin/csh'.

If you use sh or bash,

        (command) 2>&1 | tee (output file)

will place a copy of (command)'s output in the file '(output file)'.

For csh or tcsh, use

        (command) |& tee (output file)

For rc (Note: you probably do not use rc) it's

        (command) >[2=1] | tee (output file)

11.2   Conditional kernel install

Other than using floppy disks, there are several methods of testing out a new kernel without touching the old one. Unlike many other Unix flavors, LILO has the ability to boot a kernel from anywhere on the disk (if you have a large (500 MB or above) disk, please read over the LILO documentation on how this may cause problems). So, if you add something similar to

        image = /usr/src/linux/arch/i386/boot/zImage
          label = new_kernel

to the end of your LILO configuration file, you can choose to run a newly compiled kernel without touching your old /vmlinuz (after running `lilo`, of course). The easiest way to tell LILO to boot a new kernel is to press the shift key at bootup time (when it says LILO on the screen, and nothing else), which gives you a prompt. At this point, you can enter 'new_kernel' to boot the new kernel.

If you wish to keep several different kernel source trees on your system at the same time (this can take up a *lot* of disk space; be careful), the most common way is to name them /usr/src/linux-x.y.z, where x.y.z is the kernel version. You can then "select" a source tree with a symbolic link; for example, 'ln -sf linux-1.2.2 /usr/src/linux' would make the 1.2.2 tree current. Before creating a symbolic link like this, make certain that the last argument to ln is not a real directory (old symbolic links are fine); the result will not be what you expect.

11.3   Kernel updates

Russell Nelson (nelson@crynwr.com) summarizes the changes in new kernel releases. These are short, and you might like to look at them before an upgrade. They are available with anonymous ftp from ftp.emlist.com in pub/kchanges or through the URL

```
http://www.crynwr.com/kchanges
```

12   Other relevant HOWTOs that might be useful

- Sound-HOWTO: sound cards and utilities
- SCSI-HOWTO: all about SCSI controllers and devices
- NET-2-HOWTO: networking
- PPP-HOWTO: PPP networking in particular
- PCMCIA-HOWTO: about the drivers for your notebook
- ELF-HOWTO: ELF: what it is, converting..
- Hardware-HOWTO: overview of supported hardware
- Module-HOWTO: more on kernel modules
- Kerneld mini-HOWTO: about kerneld
- BogoMips mini-HOWTO: in case you were wondering

13   Misc

13.1   Author

The author and maintainer of the Linux Kernel-HOWTO is Brian Ward (bri@blah.math.tu-graz.ac.at). Please send me any comments, additions, corrections (Corrections are, in particular, the most important to me.).

You can take a look at my 'home page' at one of these URLs:

```
http://www.math.psu.edu/ward/
http://blah.math.tu-graz.ac.at/~bri/
```

Even though I try to be attentive as possible with mail, please remember that I get a *lot* of it every day, so it may take a little time to get back to you. Especially when emailing me with a question, please try extra hard to be clear and detailed in your message. If you're writing about non-working hardware (or something like that), I need to know what your hardware configureation is. If you report an error, don't just say "I tried this but it gave an error;" I need to know what the error was. I would also like to know what versions of the kernel, gcc, and libc you're using. If you just tell me you're using this-or-that distribution, it won't tell me much at all. I don't care if you ask simple questions; remember, if you don't ask, you may never get an answer! I'd like to thank everyone who has given me feedback.

If you mailed me and did not get an answer within a resonable amount of time (three weeks or more), then chances are that I accidentally deleted your message or something (sorry). Please try again.

I get a lot of mail about thing which are actually hardware problems or issues. That's OK, but please try to keep in mind that I'm not familiar with all of the hardware in the world and I don't know how helpful I can be; I personally use machines with IDE and SCSI disks, SCSI CD-ROMs, 3Com and WD ethernet cards, serial mice, motherboards with PCI, NCR 810 SCSI controllers, AMD 386DX40 w/Cyrix copr., AMD 5x86, AMD 486DX4, and Intel 486DX4 processors (This is an overview of what I use and am familiar with, certainly not a recommendation, but if you want that, you're more than welcome to ask :-)).

Version -0.1 was written on October 3, 1994. This document is available in SGML, PostScript, TeX, roff, and plain-text formats.

13.2   To do

The "Tips and tricks" section is a little small. I hope to expand on it with suggestions from others.

So is "Additional packages."

More debugging/crash recovery info needed.

13.3   Contributions

A small part of Linus' README (kernel hacking options) is inclusive. (Thanks, Linus!)

uc@brian.lunetix.de (Ulrich Callmeier): patch -s and xargs.

quinlan@yggdrasil.com (Daniel Quinlan): corrections and additions in many sections.

nat@nat@nataa.fr.eu.org (Nat Makarevitch): mrproper, tar -p, many other things

boldt@math.ucsb.edu (Axel Boldt): collected descriptions of kernel configuration options on the net; then provided me with the list

lembark@wrkhors.psyber.com (Steve Lembark): multiple boot suggestion

kbriggs@earwax.pd.uwa.edu.au (Keith Briggs): some corrections and suggestions

rmcguire@freenet.columbus.oh.us (Ryan McGuire): makeables additions

dumas@excalibur.ibp.fr (Eric Dumas): French translation

simazaki@ab11.yamanashi.ac.jp (Yasutada Shimazaki): Japanese translation

jjamor@lml.ls.fi.upm.es (Juan Jose Amor Iglesias): Spanish translation

mva@sbbs.se (Martin Wahlen): Swedish translation

jzp1218@stud.u-szeged.hu (Zoltan Vamosi): Hungarian translation

bart@mat.uni.torun.pl (Bartosz Maruszewski): Polish translation

donahue@tiber.nist.gov (Michael J Donahue): typos, winner of the "sliced bread competition"

rms@gnu.ai.mit.edu (Richard Stallman): "free" documentation concept/distribution notice

dak@Pool.Informatik.RWTH-Aachen.DE (David Kastrup): NFS thing

esr@snark.thyrsus.com (Eric Raymond): various tidbits

The people who have sent me mail with questions and problems have also been quite helpful.

HOWTO

13.4   Copyright notice, License, and all that stuff

Part XX

"RedHat Linux KickStart HOWTO" Martin Hamilton

<martinh@gnu.org>
v0.2, 11 January 1999

This HOWTO briefly describes how to use the RedHat Linux *KickStart* system to rapidly install large numbers of identical Linux boxes. For advanced users, we describe how to modify the KickStart installation procedure to do your own thing, and give a quick guide to building RPM packages of your own.

Contents

1   Copyright

2 Homepage

If you got this document from a Linux HOWTO mirror site or a CD-ROM, you might want to check back to the *KickStart HOWTO home page* <http://wwwcache.ja.net/dev/kickstart/> to see if there's a newer version around.

3 Introduction

RedHat Linux version 5 comes with a a little-known (and until now, not hugely documented) feature called *KickStart*. This lets you automate most/all of a RedHat Linux installation, including:

- Language selection
- Network configuration and distribution source selection
- Keyboard selection
- Boot loader installation (e.g. lilo)
- Disk partitioning and filesystem creation
- Mouse selection
- X Window system server configuration
- Timezone selection
- Selection of an (initial) root password
- Which packages to install

Eagle eyed RedHat users will probably have realised by now that these are essentially the main steps involved in the manual installation of a RedHat Linux system. KickStart makes it possible for you to script the regular installation process, by putting the information you would normally type at the keyboard into a configuration file.

But wait - there's more :-)

Having finished the normal installation process, KickStart also lets you specify a list of shell level commands which you would like to be executed. This means that you can automatically install extra local software not distributed as part of RedHat Linux (yes, there are even more free software programs than the ones you get with the RedHat distribution. Some can't be distributed by RedHat on legal grounds, e.g. the ssh and PGP encryption systems) and carry out any tidying up you may need to do in order to get a fully operational system.

4 Prerequisites

There are two approaches to a KickStart install - one is to simply copy your KickStart configuration file to a RedHat boot floppy. The other is to use a regular boot floppy and get your KickStart config file off the network.

In both cases, you'll need:

1. Intel (i386) class machines - KickStart appears to only work on these at the time of writing.
2. KickStart config file - we'll talk about this in the next section.
3. RedHat boot disk - preferably from the *updates* directory, to take advantage of any fixes/driver updates.
4. DNS entries for the IP addresses you'll be using - optional, but will stop the installation from prompting you for your machine's domain name.

If you want to fetch your config file over the network, you'll need to export it via NFS - this is the only access method supported at the moment. The config file lets you specify a different NFS server to fetch the RedHat distribution itself from.

You can configure a static IP address for your machine - e.g. a special one reserved for KickStart installations. Alternatively, if you don't want to hard code an IP address in the config file you can tell KickStart to use a BOOTP/DHCP server to fetch this. Some servers will allocate new addresses in a given range automatically, e.g. *the CMU BOOTP server with dynamic addressing extensions* <ftp://ftp.ntplx.net/pub/networking/bootp>.

More information on NFS and BOOTP/DHCP is in Appendix A.

5 Setting up a boot floppy

Essentially, all you have to do is copy your KickStart config file to */ks.cfg* on the RedHat boot floppy, e.g.

```
mcopy ks.cfg a:
```

However - the RedHat boot floppy is pretty full, and you may find that you have to delete some of the other files to make room for the KickStart config file. I was able to make enough room for mine by deleting the various message files normally displayed by the SYSLINUX boot loader, e.g.

```
mdel a:\*.msg
```

Another approach would be to throw away the drivers for some of the hardware you don't have - see the section on modifying the boot floppy below.

You may also want to edit *syslinux.cfg*, the SYSLINUX config file. This also lives in the top level directory of the RedHat boot floppy. For instance, the following *syslinux.cfg* will cause KickStart mode to be entered into automatically as the machine boots up, without the normal delay:

```
default ks
prompt 0
label ks
   kernel vmlinuz
   append ks=floppy initrd=initrd.img
```

Note that you almost probably want to base your boot and supplementary floppies on the most recent disk images available in the *updates/i386* on your local RedHat mirror site. Older images may be buggy or have driver support for less hardware.

6 The KickStart config file

There are three main sections to the config file:

1. System info, e.g. disk partitioning and network config
2. RedHat packages to install
3. Post-installation shell commands to run

There are some other possibilities which we won't talk about here, but **might** work. For more information check out the sample KickStart config in *misc/src/install/ks.samp* and *doc/README.ks* under the top level *i386* RedHat distribution directory on your CD-ROM or local RedHat mirror site.

6.1 System info

The available directives which I've been using are:

lang

Language configuration, e.g. for English

```
        lang en
```

network

Network configuration, e.g. to use BOOTP/DHCP

```
        network --bootp
```

nfs

NFS server and directory to install from, e.g.

```
        nfs --server chicken.swedish-chef.org /mnt/cdrom
```

to use the NFS server *chicken.swedish-chef.org* and try to mount the RedHat distribution from the directory */mnt/cdrom*.

keyboard

Select keyboard type, e.g. for UK keyboards

```
        keyboard uk
```

zerombr

Clear the Master Boot Record - removes any existing operating system boot loader from your disk

clearpart

Clear existing partitions - e.g. to remove all existing disk partitions prior to installation

```
        clearpart --all
```

part

Partition the disk, e.g. to make a root filesystem of 500MB

```
        part / --size 500
```

install

Make a fresh installation of RedHat Linux.

mouse

Set the mouse being used, e.g. for a PS/2 or compatible "bus mouse"

```
        mouse ps/2
```

timezone

Set the timezone, e.g. for local time in the UK

```
        timezone --utc Europe/London
```

rootpw

Set the initial root password, based on a previously derived encrypted password

```
        rootpw --iscrypted XaacoeGPmf/A.
```

lilo

Install the LILO boot loader, e.g. in the Master Boot Record

```
        lilo --location mbr
```

%packages

Packages to install - see below.

%post

Post-installation shell commands - see below.

Note that the directory where KickStart is looking for the RedHat distribution should have a subdirectory *RedHat*, which contains the RedHat distribution tree for the platform in question. In the above example, we should see something like the following files and directories:

```
/mnt/cdrom/RedHat
/mnt/cdrom/RedHat/base
/mnt/cdrom/RedHat/contents
/mnt/cdrom/RedHat/i386
/mnt/cdrom/RedHat/instimage
/mnt/cdrom/RedHat/RPMS
/mnt/cdrom/RPM-PGP-KEY
```

If you're installing off a CD-ROM rather than off the network, the contents should look something like this:

```
RedHat
RedHat/base
RedHat/contents
RedHat/i386
RedHat/instimage
RedHat/RPMS
RPM-PGP-KEY
```

If you have the RedHat distribution for multiple architectures (e.g. on an NFS server - they're too big to fit more than one architecture's version onto a single CD-ROM), you'll notice that each distribution has the same files and directories under a subdirectory, e.g.

```
alpha/RPM-PGP-KEY
i386/RPM-PGP-KEY
sparc/RPM-PGP-KEY
```

There should be a file architecture/Redhat/architecture, e.g. *i386/Redhat/i386*.

If you want to create your own encrypted passwords, it's very easy using Perl, e.g.

```
% perl -e 'print crypt("schmurrdegurr", "Xa") . "\n";'p
```

Other options (or mooted options), which I've not tried:

cdrom

Install off CD-ROM rather than network.

device

Explicitly declare device details, e.g.

```
device ethernet 3c509 --opts "io=0x330, irq=7"
```

Alternative values of device include scsi for SCSI controllers and cdrom for proprietary CD-ROM drives.

upgrade

Upgrade an existing installation rather than make a fresh installation.

xconfig

Configure X Window server, graphics card and monitor. e.g.

```
xconfig --server "Mach64" --monitor "tatung cm14uhe"
```

I've not delved too deeply into this last one, because I'm not ever planning to run X on the console of any of my KickStarted machines. I'm told that running xconfig within KickStart itself is a bit flaky, but the same functionality is also available from the command line via Xconfigurator - so you might be best off leaving this to the post-installation script.

Here's how this first part of a KickStart config file looks when we put all the bits together:

HOWTO

```
lang en
network --static --ip 198.168.254.253 --netmask 255.255.255.0
  --gateway 198.168.254.1 --nameserver 198.168.254.2
nfs --server chicken.swedish-chef.org /mnt/cdrom
keyboard uk
zerombr yes
clearpart --all
part / --size 500
part swap --size 120
install
mouse ps/2
timezone --utc Europe/London
rootpw --iscrypted XaacoeGPmf/A.
lilo --location mbr
```

Note that some of the RedHat documentation refers to an invocation of the `network` directive which doesn't actually work in practice: `network -option`. The correct invocation is to put `network` followed by `-static`, `-bootp` or `-dhcp`. Be aware that the BOOTP and DHCP options are different - to the extent that they even use different code.

You can add the `-grow` parameter to a `part` directive to indicate that it's OK to grow the partition beyond the size you specify. It probably only makes sense to have one partition tagged with `-grow`.

6.2 Packages to install

The start of the packages section of the KickStart config file is indicated by the presence of a `%packages` directive on a line of its own. This is followed by one or both of two types of package specifier - individual packages may be installed by giving the name of their RPM (excluding the version and platform information), and groups of packages may be installed by giving their group name.

Here's a sample `packages` section for a KickStart config file:

```
%packages
@ Base
netkit-base
bind-utils
ncftp
rdate
tcp_wrappers
traceroute
cmu-snmp
```

So, what are these groups ? Well, there are a number of groups defined by default in a file called *base/comps* under the RedHat distribution's top level directory. Here are the ones which were current at the time of writing:

- Base
- Printer Support
- X Window System
- Mail/WWW/News Tools
- DOS/Windows Connectivity
- File Managers
- Graphics Manipulation
- X Games
- Console Games

- X multimedia support
- Console Multimedia
- Print Server
- Networked Workstation
- Dialup Workstation
- News Server
- NFS Server
- SMB (Samba) Connectivity
- IPX/Netware(tm) Connectivity
- Anonymous FTP/Gopher Server
- Web Server
- DNS Name Server
- Postgres (SQL) Server
- Network Management Workstation
- TeX Document Formatting
- Emacs
- Emacs with X windows
- C Development
- Development Libraries
- C++ Development
- X Development
- Extra Documentation

You'll notice that they correspond to the various configurations which you're prompted for during a manual installation. Note that some of the packages in a given package group are duplicated in other groups, and that you can install multiple groups of packages without this causing problems. Each group's entry in the *comps* listing looks similar to this:

```
0 Extra Documentation
sag
lpg
howto
faq
man-pages
end
```

It seems that groups with a *1* next to their name (the first line above) are selected for installation by default. You can customise the Linux installation process even further by creating your own groups or redefine existing ones by editing this file.

6.3   Post-installation shell commands

This is probably the best feature of all, and something which there is no direct equivalent to in the manual installation process. What we can do here is specify a sequence of shell level commands which should be executed after the main installation (disk partitioning, package installation, and so on) is complete.

The beginning of this section is signified by the `%post` directive in the KickStart config file. In what follows you can take advantage of all of the utilities which have been installed on your newly built Linux system, e.g.

HOWTO

```
%post
ln -s /etc/rc.d/init.d /etc/init.d
ln -s /etc/rc.d/rc.local /etc/rc.local
ln -s /usr/bin/md5sum /usr/bin/md5
ln -s /usr/bin/perl /usr/local/bin/perl
chmod ug-s /bin/linuxconf
mkdir /var/tmp/tmp
perl -spi -e 's!image=/boot/vmlinuz-.*!image=/boot/vmlinuz!' /etc/lilo.conf
rm /etc/rc.d/rc*.d/*sendmail
```

You can also use I/O redirection and here documents:

```
cat <<EOF >>/etc/passwd
squid:*:102:3500:Squid Proxy:/usr/squid:/bin/bash
EOF

cat <<EOF >>/etc/group
cache:x:3500:
EOF
```

Modify the run-time startup scripts:

```
cat <<EOF >>/etc/rc.local
echo 8192 > /proc/sys/kernel/file-max
echo 32768 > /proc/sys/kernel/inode-max

[ -x /usr/sbin/sshd ] && /usr/sbin/sshd
[ -x /usr/sbin/cfd ] && /usr/sbin/cfd

EOF
```

Set up *crontab* entries:

```
cat <<EOF >/tmp/crontab.root
# Keep the time up to date
0,15,30,45 * * * * /usr/sbin/ntpdate -s eggtimer 2>&1 >/dev/null
# Recycle Exim log files
1 0 * * * /usr/exim/bin/exicyclog
# Flush the Exim queue
0,15,30,45 * * * * /usr/exim/bin/exim -q
EOF

crontab /tmp/crontab.root
rm /tmp/crontab.root
```

And even install other RPMs which you made yourself:

```
rpm -i ftp://chicken.swedish-chef.org/rpms/squid.rpm
rpm -i ftp://chicken.swedish-chef.org/rpms/ssh.rpm
rpm -i ftp://chicken.swedish-chef.org/rpms/exim.rpm
rpm -i ftp://chicken.swedish-chef.org/rpms/cfengine.rpm
rpm -i ftp://chicken.swedish-chef.org/rpms/linux.rpm

ssh-keygen -b 1024 -f /etc/ssh_host_key -N ""
depmod -a
```

Note that you can achieve the same effect by making your own RPMs containing the commands you want executed - see below for more information. Give them a carefully chosen name and you can force them to be installed first (e.g. name starts with 'aaa') or last (e.g. name starts with 'zzz').

Be aware that a less painful way of doing root crontab entries is to create them as files in one or more of the directories */etc/cron.hourly*, */etc/cron.daily*, */etc/cron.weekly* and */etc/cron.monthly*.

More information about making your own RPMs is available in Appendix B.

7   Installation itself

Boot the to-be-installed machine off your RedHat boot floppy as usual, but instead of pressing RETURN at the SYSLINUX prompt, type linux ks.

If you're lucky, this will be all you have to type!

If you customised your RedHat boot floppy as outlined above, you won't even need to do this bit :-)

Since we're really just automating the normal steps involved in a RedHat installation, the normal dialogs may appear if/when KickStart gets confused about what to do next. The most likely case is that your network interface won't be detected automatically, and you'll be prompted for its IRQ and I/O address space. KickStart tends to need help for ISA bus cards, but detects PCI bus cards automatically.

You can keep an eye on what KickStart is doing by by switching virtual consoles as usual:

- Alt-F1 - installation dialog
- Alt-F2 - shell prompt
- Alt-F3 - install log (messages from install program)
- Alt-F4 - system log (messages from kernel, etc.)
- Alt-F5 - other messages

8   Mounting the boot/supp disks

The RedHat boot disk *boot.img* is in MS-DOS format, using the SYSLINUX program to boot up. The supplementary disk *supp.img* is a Linux ext2 filesystem. If you have support for the loopback filesystem in your Linux kernel, you can mount both of these files in your filesystem and hack at them:

```
# mkdir -p /mnt/boot /mnt/supp
# mount -o loop -t msdos boot.img /mnt/boot
# mount -o loop supp.img /mnt/supp
```

Now you should be able to see and manipulate the files on the boot and supplementary disk under */mnt/boot* and */mnt/supp* respectively. Phew! Note that older versions of mount may not be able to handle the -o loop option. In these cases you'll need to explicitly use losetup to configure the loopback device for each file, e.g.

```
# losetup /dev/loop0 boot.img
# mount -t msdos /dev/loop0 /mnt/boot
```

You might also need to explicitly use the -t ext2 option when mounting an ext2 filesystem like the one on the supplementary disk. But, it looks like people with modern Linux distributions shouldn't have to worry about this.

Of course, if you don't want to mess around too much, you can cut a corner and manipulate actual floppy disks rather than these floppy disk images. If time is important, you'll probably prefer to use the loopback devices, since you can hack around with the disk images without incurring the latency associated with a genuine floppy disk read/write.

9 Modifying the RedHat installer

If you want to mess around with the installation procedure itself, the source code can be found on the RedHat CD-ROM or your local RedHat mirror site. It's in *misc/src/install* under the *i386* distribution top level directory.

If you examine the RedHat boot disk you'll see that, in addition to the Linux kernel *vmlinuz*, there's a large file *initrd.img*:

```
- -rwxr-xr-x  1 root    root        559 May 11 15:48 boot.msg
- -rwxr-xr-x  1 root    root        668 May 11 15:48 expert.msg
- -rwxr-xr-x  1 root    root        986 May 11 15:48 general.msg
- -rwxr-xr-x  1 root    root     968842 May 11 15:48 initrd.img
- -rwxr-xr-x  1 root    root       1120 May 11 15:48 kickit.msg
- -r-xr-xr-x  1 root    root       5352 May 11 15:48 ldlinux.sys
- -rwxr-xr-x  1 root    root        875 May 11 15:48 param.msg
- -rwxr-xr-x  1 root    root       1239 May 11 15:48 rescue.msg
- -rwxr-xr-x  1 root    root        402 May 11 15:48 syslinux.cfg
- -rwxr-xr-x  1 root    root     444602 May 11 15:48 vmlinuz
```

You guessed it, this is another `ext2` filesystem saved as a file - - but with a twist. It's actually compressed as well. You can uncompress it and then mount the result, e.g.

```
# gzip -dc /mnt/boot/initrd.img >/tmp/initrd.ext2
# mkdir /mnt/initrd
# mount -o loop /tmp/initrd.ext2 /mnt/initrd
```

Probably the most important part of this filesystem is the collection of loadable kernel modules which are included with the boot disk. If you need to merge in a new version of a driver, you'll need to either replace *vmlinuz* with a new kernel which has this statically linked, or replace it in the modules collection. What's more, you may need to throw other modules away to make room.

The modules collection is the file *modules/modules.cgz*. Wondering what that might be ? It's actually a compressed `cpio` archive, believe it or not! And you thought nobody used `cpio` any more... Actually RPM itself uses `cpio` internally, too. Here's how to hack around with it:

```
# gzip -dc /mnt/initrd/modules/modules.cgz >/tmp/modules.cpio
# cpio -itv <modules.cpio >modules.listing
# mkdir modules
# cpio -idumv <../modules.cpio
```

I don't believe that there is currently a way under Linux (at least in mainstream distributions) to transparently access compressed filesystems. Let me know if you know better!

If you change anything, remember to:

1. Use `cpio` to recreate the archive. How to do this is left as an exercise for the reader...
2. Use `gzip` to compress the resulting archive.
3. Copy it to */mnt/initrd*, or wherever you put the uncompressed *initrd.img* archive.
4. Unmount */mnt/initrd* (or whatever you called it).
5. Compress the new *initrd.img* using `gzip` again.
6. Copy the resulting archive onto the boot disk image - */mnt/boot/initrd.img* in our example.
7. Unmount the boot disk image, e.g. */mnt/boot*.

Finally, you can now create new boot floppies using this modified boot disk setup, e.g.

```
# cat boot.img >/dev/fd0
```

10   FAQs/Wish list

Q: After KickStart installation, my machine won't boot up. The BIOS complains with a message like `Missing operating system`.

A: Sounds like the partition with the root filesystem on isn't bootable. Use `fdisk` to toggle its bootable status.

Q: After the floppy boots, I get the message: `Error opening files for kickstart copy:  File exists`.

A: Use a more recent version of *boot.img* and *supp.img* - look in the *updates* directory of your local RedHat mirror site. There was a bug in some older versions of these for RedHat 5.1.

Q: Can you have all outstanding patches (update RPMs) applied automatically too ? How ?

A1: Copy the RPMs you want installing to the RPMS directory from which the installation is going to take place, get rid of the older RPMs, and update the file *RedHat/base/hdlist* with the new RPM details. See Appendix C for a script from Eric Doutreleau to do this for you. If you do this yourself, remember to run *genhdlist* afterwards!

A2: Try this Perl script: *patchup* `<http://wwwcache.ja.net/dev/patchup/>`. This compares the RPMs your system has installed with those in a nominated directory and reports on the ones it thinks need updating. It can even install them for you if you trust it to.

A3: *rpm2hml* `<http://rufus.w3.org/linux/rpm2html/>` has a much more powerful (12MB of C code vs. a page of Perl!) version of A2.

Q: A single config file on the install server for all of the clients, perhaps as a fallback after trying *IPADDR-kickstart* ?

A1: Use the BOOTP/DHCP 'boot file' parameter *bf* to set the filename.

A2: Add a a record `bf=/kickstart/ks.cfg` to the relevant entry in */etc/bootptab*.

Q: More flexibility when things go wrong - e.g. prompt for alternate locations if distribution not found on CD-ROM.

A: ?

Q: Explicit exclusion of packages - e.g. everything apart from *sendmail*.

A: Rebuild the **BASE** package without sendmail.

Q: Choose which services are started automatically on boot-up by the run-level scripts under */etc/rc.d/*.

A: The *chkconfig* utility lets you configure which services are run automatically on boot-up. You can run this in your post-installation script section, e.g. to run *ypbind* in run levels 3, 4 and 5:

```
chkconfig --level 345 ypbind on
```

and it will start the ypbind level on the 345 level.

Q: When executing the shell commands in the `%post` section, bring any output up in another virtual console rather than overwriting the main screen. *Could be done in the shell commands section using* open*?*.

A: No problem - do something like this:

```
exec >/dev/tty5
```

Q: Does the filesystem creation code check for bad blocks ?

A: If you switch to the virtual console where the filesystem creation output is being displayed, you won't see any mention of the 'read-only' test being performed. Looks like the answer is no.

Q: Can I arrange things so some of my machines are configured differently from others ?

A: You could move the host dependent stuff into the scripted section of the KickStart config - e.g. only install a given RPM if on a given machine. It would be useful to have a conditional installation feature in the packages section of the config file, e.g. switching on architecture, or hostname/domain name/IP address.

Q: Are there any changes between RedHat 5.1 and 5.2 ?

A1: Lots of changes in the installer, but mostly bug fixes or cosmetic improvements. No impact on KickStart as far as I can tell - from a *diff -rcs* of the two *misc/src/install* directories.

A2: RH5.2 now apparently includes the automatic IP allocation/DHCP patches to `bootpd`, but they have left out the documentation which tells you how to use it.

Q: (How) can you clear a specific partition or partitions ? e.g. to leave */home* but zap */.*

A: You can't - yet!

Q: Can you arrange to have your partitions created across multiple drives ? e.g. */* on `sda` and */home* on `sdb`.

A: Don't think so - looks like you only get access to the first drive from the partitioning tool.

Q: Is it possible to specify existing partitions to be included in the mount table, or is it only possible to specify the creation of new partitions that will then be included?

A: ?

Q: After running `mkkickstart`, where is the file it creates?

A: It doesn't create a file - it dumps the KickStart config to `stdout`.

Q: In virtual console 4 (Alt-F4) I get `Unable to load NLS charset cp437(nls_cp437)`. What does this mean ? Should I be worried ?

A: Sounds like you're trying to mount a CD-ROM burned with the Joliet (Unicode extensions to ISO 9660. In theory the filenames on the CD-ROM might get munched and not make it through to Linux correctly. In practice it doesn't seem to cause any problems - could be a spurious dependency ?

Q: Why am i getting the X Window System installed ? I didn't put it in my list of packages.

A: The `XFree86-VGA16` RPM is a 'base' component, and as such always gets installed - unless you change the definition of the base class.

Q: In my post-installation script, can I use the packages which have been installed by now to do funky things not possible with the limited tools on the floppies ?

A: Yep - e.g. if you chose to install Perl when you put your KickStart config together, almost anything is possible in about five lines :-)

11 Credits

Thanks to Eric Doutreleau for the info about *chkconfig*, the `SYSLINUX` config file hack, and the Perl script for updating your distribution server's RPMs. Thanks to Robert Kaminsky for extensive investigations. Thanks to Piete Brooks, Flavia Regina Munhoz, Tom Toffoli, Bob Robbins, Charlie Brady and Ragen Herrington, for their comments and questions.

12 Appendix A - Configuring BOOTP/DHCP and NFS

If you're wondering what on earth this BOOTP and DHCP stuff is, more information is available at *the DHCP WWW site* <http://www.dhcp.org/>. NFS is documented separately in detail in the NFS HOWTO, and there's a DHCP mini-HOWTO too. I've tried to provide enough details here to help you get started, whilst not treating the topics in depth - let me know if you think this is overkill.

In the BOOTP/DHCP + NFS configuration we're discussing, the KickStart config file should be NFS mountable by the machine being installed from */kickstart/IPADDR-kickstart* on the BOOTP/DHCP server, where *IPADDR* is the IP address of the new machine, e.g. */kickstart/198.168.254.254-kickstart* for the machine *198.168.254.254*.

You should be able to override this location by returning the `bf` parameter (boot file) in your BOOTP/DHCP response. It may even be possible to have this NFS mounted off another machine entirely.

To NFS export some directories from an existing Linux box, create the file */etc/exports* with contents something like:

```
/kickstart  *.swedish-chef.org(ro,no_root_squash)
/mnt/cdrom  *.swedish-chef.org(ro,no_root_squash)
```

Note that if you didn't register the IP addresses you're going to be using in the DNS, you may be told to get lost by the NFS server and/or the RPC portmapper. In this you can probably get away with putting IP address/netmask pairs in the config files, e.g.

```
/kickstart  198.168.254.0/255.255.255.0(ro,no_root_squash)
```

and in */etc/hosts.allow*:

```
ALL: 194.82.103.0/255.255.255.0: ALLOW
```

This is because most Linux distributions use TCP wrappers to do access control for some or all of the NFS related daemons. Be aware that the */etc/exports* syntax tends to be different on other Unix variants - the NFS servers bundled with Linux distributions tend to offer a much wider range of options than the ones shipped with other versions of Unix.

Be aware that if you include a root password in your KickStart config file, or NFS export directories containing sensitive information, you should take care to expose this information to as few people as possible. This can be done by making the NFS export permissions as fine grained as you can, e.g. by specifying a particular host or subnet to export to rather than a whole domain. If you keep a special IP address free for KickStart installations, everything's nice and simple, but you'll have to change it later - or reconfigure the machine to get its IP address via BOOTP/DHCP.

Most NFS servers require you to tell `mountd` and `nfsd` (on some versions of Unix they're prefixed with a `rpc.`) that the */etc/exports* file has changed - usually by sending a `SIGHUP`. There's often a program or script called `exportfs`, which will do this for you, e.g.

```
# exportfs -a
```

If you didn't have NFS up and running when this machine was booted, the directories may not be exported automatically. Try rebooting, or running the following programs as root:

```
# portmap
# rpc.nfsd
# rpc.mountd
```

As noted, on some systems the `rpc.` prefix isn't used. In most modern Unix distributions, these programs can be found in the */usr/sbin* or */usr/libexec* directories. These might not be in your path already, e.g. if you used `su` to become *root*. The `portmap` program is also sometimes called `rpcbind`, e.g. on Solaris, some versions of `nfsd` require a command line argument specifying the number of instances of the server to run, and you may find you also need to run another daemon called `biod`. The above should suffice on most (all?) Linux systems.

If you're using the CMU BOOTP server with DHCP and dynamic addressing extensions referred to earlier, a sample */etc/bootptab* entry (*/etc/bootptab* is the normal location of the BOOTP/DHCP configuration file) would look something like this:

```
.dynamic-1:ip=198.168.254.128:T254=0x30:T250="ds=198.168.254.2:
    dn=swedish-chef.org:sm=255.255.255.0:gw=198.168.254.1:
    dl=0xFFFFFFFF":
```

(wrapped for clarity)

This says to allocate IP addresses dynamically on encountering new machines, starting at *198.168.254.128* and continuing for the next 48 (the hexadecimal value *30*) addresses. Each client will be passed back the value of *T250*. In this case that sets:

- the DNS server ds to *198.168.254.2*
- the domain name dn to *swedish-chef.org*
- the subnet mask sm to *255.255.255.0*
- the default gateway gw to *198.168.254.1*
- the lease length dl (how long the address is valid for) to "forever"

There seem to be a number of other versions of this server kicking around which do not support dynamic addressing. For these, you would have to list the hardware (typically Ethernet MAC) address of each to-be-installed machine in */etc/bootptab*, and the entries would look something like this:

```
bork.swedish-chef.org:ip=198.168.254.128:ha=0000E8188E56:
    ds=198.168.254.2:dn=swedish-chef.org:sm=255.255.255.0:
    gw=198.168.254.1:dl=0xFFFFFFFF":
```

(wrapped for clarity)

Note that the parameter ha corresponds to the hardware address of the machine being installed.

13   Appendix B - Making your own RPMs

The RPM package format is already very well documented, particularly in the book *Maximum RPM* by Ed Bailey, which you can download from the *RPM WWW site* <http://www.rpm.org/> - also available from all good book stores! This is just a couple of quick hints for people in a hurry.

RPM packages are built from a *spec* file. This consists (in a similar fashion to the KickStart config file) of a recipe of steps that need to be taken in order to build the package - it's expected that you'll have to build it from source, potentially for multiple platforms, and may need to apply patches before compiling. Once built and installed, a binary RPM will be created from the files and directories you specify as being associated with the package. It's important to note that RPM has no idea of which files and directories are related to a given package - you have to tell it.

Here's a sample specification for a custom RPM of the *Squid WWW cache server* <http://squid.nlanr.net/>:

```
Summary: Squid Web Cache server
Name: squid
Version: 1.NOVM.22
Release: 1
Copyright: GPL/Harvest
Group: Networking/Daemons
Source: squid-1.NOVM.22-src.tar.gz
Patch: retry-1.NOVM.20.patch
%description
This is just a first attempt to package up the Squid Web Cache for easy
installation on our RedHat Linux servers
```

```
%prep
%setup
%build
configure --prefix=/usr/squid
perl -spi -e 's!#( -DALLOW_HOSTNAME_UNDERSCORES)!$1!' src/Makefile
make

%install
make install

%files
/usr/squid
```

Here's how to build this RPM:

```
% mkdir -p SOURCES BUILD SRPMS RPMS/i386
% cp ~/squid-1.NOVM.22-src.tar.gz SOURCES
% cp ~/retry-1.NOVM.20.patch SOURCES
% rpm -ba squid-1.NOVM.22+retry-1.spec
```

This will automatically create a subdirectory under the *BUILD* directory, into which it'll unpack the source code and then apply the patch (there are a number of options available for patching - check the book for details). Now, RPM will automatically build the package by running `configure` and then `make`, install it using `make install`, and take a snapshot of the files under */usr/squid*. It's the latter which will form the binary RPM of the Squid software.

Note that we can insert arbitrary shell commands into the unpacking, building and installing processes, e.g. the call to `perl` which tweaks one of Squid's compile-time parameters.

The final binary RPM will be left under the *RPMS* directory in the platform specific subdirectory *i386*. In this case it will be called *squid-1.NOVM.22-1.i386.rpm*. Note that the filename is created by concatenating the values of the following parameters from the spec file: `Name`, `Version` and `Release` - plus the hardware platform in question, *i386* in this case. Try to bear this in mind when creating your own RPMs, to avoid giving them overly long or painful names!

It's also worth bearing in mind that you can build RPMs without having to rebuild the whole software package, e.g.

```
Summary: Linux 2.0.36 kernel + filehandle patch + serial console patch
Name: linux
Version: 2.0.36+filehandle+serial_console
Release: 1
Copyright: GPL
Group: Base/Kernel
Source: linux-2.0.36+filehandle+serial_console.tar.gz
%description
This is just a first attempt to package up the Linux kernel with patches
for installation on our RedHat Linux servers

%prep
echo

%setup
echo

%build
echo

%install
```

```
echo

%post
/sbin/lilo

%files
/lib/modules/2.0.36
/boot/vmlinuz
```

In this case we simply create an RPM based on the */boot/vmlinuz* file and the contents of the directory */lib/modules/2.0.36*, and execute */sbin/lilo* after the package has been installed on a target machine. Let me know if you know much neater way of writing the spec file than this.

14   Appendix C - Munging your own RPMs into the distribution

Here is Eric's script for munging updated RPMs into the RedHat distribution area:

```perl
#!/usr/bin/perl
#
$redhatdir="/cdrom/i386";
$rpmdir="/cdrom/i386/RedHat/RPMS/";
$updatedir="/cdrom/updates/";
@OTHERDIR=($updatedir);
foreach $dir (@OTHERDIR)
        {
        print "update for $dir\n";
        system(" find $dir -name \"*.rpm\" -exec cp {} $rpmdir \\; ");
        }
chdir($contribdir) || die "peux pas aller dans $contribdir $!\n";
system("chmod -R 755 $redhatdir");
chdir($rpmdir) || die "problem to go in $rpmdir $!\n";
#
# remove the old file
#
opendir(DIR,'.');
@package=grep(/\.rpm$/,readdir(DIR));
foreach $file (@package)
        {
        $file =~ /(.*)\-([\d+|\.]+\w*)\-(\d+)\.[i386|noarch].*/;
        $nom=$1;
        $version=$2;
        $buildvers=$3;
        if ($NOM{$nom})
                {
                $version2=$VERSION{$nom};
                $buildver2=$BUILDVERS{$nom};
                $file2=$FILE{$nom};
                $nom2=$NOM{$nom};
                if ( $version2 gt $version )
                        {
                        print "$file2 is newer than $file\n";
                        unlink($file);
                        }
                else
```

```
                                    {
                                    if ( $version2 lt $version )
                                            {
                                            print "$file is newer than $file2\n";
                                            unlink($file2);
                                            $VERSION{$nom}=$version;
                                            $BUILDVERS{$nom}=$buildvers;
                                            $FILE{$nom}=$file;
                                            $NOM{$nom}=$nom;
                                            }
                                    else
                                            {
                                            if ( $buildver2 > $buildvers )
                                                    {
                                                    print "$file2 : $buildver2 es-
t mieux que $file : $buildvers\n";
                                                    unlink($file);
                                                    }
                                            else
                                                    {
                                                print "$file2 : $buildver2 is old-
er than $file : $buildvers\n";
                                                    unlink($file2);
                                                    $VERSION{$nom}=$version;
                                                    $BUILDVERS{$nom}=$buildvers;
                                                    $FILE{$nom}=$file;
                                                    $NOM{$nom}=$nom;
                                                    }
                                            }
                                    }
                        else
                                {
                                $VERSION{$nom}=$version;
                                $BUILDVERS{$nom}=$buildvers;
                                $FILE{$nom}=$file;
                                $NOM{$nom}=$nom;
                                }
                        }

# we do the hard thing here
#
system("$redhatdir/misc/src/install/genhdlist $redhatdir");
```

## Part XXI

"LinuxDoc+Emacs+Ispell-HOWTO" Author: Philippe MARTIN

feloy@wanadoo.fr Translator: Sébastien Blondeel *Sebastien.Blondeel@lifl.fr*
v0.4, 27 February 1998

This document is aimed at writers and translators of Linux HOWTOs or any other paper for the Linux Documentation Project. It gives them hints at using tools including Emacs and Ispell.

Contents

HOWTO

1 Preamble

1.1 Copyright

Copyright Philippe Martin 1998

You may redistribute and/or modify this document as long as you comply with the terms of the GNU General Public Licence, version 2 or later.

1.2 Credits

Special thanks go to Sébastien Blondeel, who is a nasty bugger and asked me so much about Emacs setup. His clever questions have allowed me to understand it better and pass the knowledge to you through this document.

1.3 Comments

Do not hesitate to tell me any thing you think will help make this document better. I will examine your critics thoroughly. Do not hesitate as well to ask me any questions related to topics discussed here. I will be more than happy to answer them, as they may help me further improve this document.[42]

1.4 Versions

This paper is about the following versions:

- Sgml-tools version 0.99,
- Emacs version 19.34,
- Ispell version 3.1,
- All Emacs libraries referred to in this document are distributed with the above Emacs version, apart from `iso-sgml`, which is distributed with XEmacs, and `psgml`, which is a stand-alone library.

2 Introduction

2.1 SGML

Standard Generalised Mark-up Language, or **SGML**, is a language to define document types.

For instance, one may define the document type *recipe*, with a first part presenting the ingredients, a second part introducing the accessories, a third part giving step by step instructions for baking the cake, and a nice final picture to show the outcome of it all.

This is called a *Document Type Definition*. It does not define what the final product will look like, it only defines what it may contain.

To use the same example again, I'm sure that upon reading my idea of a recipe, you recognised yours, or your favourite cook's. Nevertheless, they actually look different: mine have a picture in the upper left corner of the bathroom cupboard, and the ingredients list can be found in the back garden, between the swimming pool and the barbecue. Yours?

Thanks to this standard definition, one can write a document, without taking into account what it will look like in the end to the reader.

---

[42]Translator note: If the English is ugly, well then that goes to me!

2.2 The `LinuxDoc` Type Definition

This type is used to write, as you might have guessed, documents related to Linux.

Such documents are generally built as follows: they start with a title followed by the name of the author, and the version number and date. Then comes the abstract (so you don't have to browse through it before realizing it isn't what you were looking for after all), then the contents which show the structure so that those in a rush can go directly to the part they want to read.

Then comes a list of chapters, sections, paragraphs. Among these, one can insert bits of programs, change the font to emphasise a word or a sentence, insert lists, refer to another part of the document, etc.

To write such a document, you just need to specify at the right time the title, the author, the date, and the document version, the chapters and sections, say when a list is to be inserted, what its elements are etc.

2.3 `SGML-Tools`

SGML-Tools will turn the specification of a document into the final result in the form you prefer. If you want it in your personal library, you will choose *PostScript*. If you want to share it with the world through the Web, it will be *HTML*. If you can't help it and must read it under Windows, you can turn it into *RTF* to be able to read it with any word processor. Or maybe use all three formats to accommodate your changing moods.

SGML-Tools are available via anonymous FTP at *ftp://ftp.lip6.fr/pub/sgml-tools/*

3 Your first document.

3.1 From a text document

If you want to turn a text document into SGML to port it to other formats, this is the way to go:

1. Add the following lines at the very beginning:

   ```
   <!doctype linuxdoc system>
    <article>
     <title>Title Goes Here</title>
     <author>
      name of author, author's e-mail, etc.
     </author>
     <date>
      version and date
     </date>
   ```

2. If you describe briefly the contents of the document in the beginning, surround that paragraph with the `<abstract>` and `</abstract>` tags.

3. Then insert the `<toc>` tag, which stands for *Table Of Contents*.

4. At the beginning of each new chapter, replace the line giving the number and title of the chapter with:

   ```
   <sect>The Title Of The Chapter
   ```

   and add the `</sect>` tag at the end of the chapter.
   Note : You don't have to put the chapter number, this is done automatically.

5. Proceed in the same way for sections. You need to delete their numbers and tag their titles with `<sect1>` and they end with `</sect1>`.

6. You can also define as many as 4 levels of nesting in the sections, using `<sectn>` and `</sectn>` where n= 2, 3, or 4 in a similar way.

7. In the beginning of each paragraph, insert the `<p>` tag.

8. If you need to emphasise some parts, tag them with `<it>` and `</it>` (*italics*), `<bf>` and `</bf>` (**bold face**), or `<tt>` and `</tt>` (typewriter style).

9. To insert a list like the following one:

```
This is a four lines list:

- first line goes here
- second line comes next
- yet another one
- that's it.
```

you must replace it with:

```
This is a four lines list:
<itemize>
<item>first line goes here
<item>second line come next
<item>yet another one
<item>that's it.
</itemize>
```

10. When a whole block is a part of a program, or something else that needs to stick out:

```
<verb>
10 REM Oh my God what's this?
20 REM I thought this had long disappeared!
30 PRINT "I am back to";
40 PRINT "save the world."
50 INPUT "From whom, do you reckon? ",M$
60 IF M$="Bill" THEN PRINT "Thou art wise.":GOTO PARADISE
70 ELSE PRINT "You ain't got a clue...":GOTO RICHMOND
</verb>
```

11. Thus far, your SGML formating skills are fairly decent. If you want to refine your document, you may have a look at the user's guide for **SGML-Tools**, which gives more details about the **LinuxDoc** document type.

4 Configuring `Emacs`

4.1 Accented Characters

If you want to write documents in French or in any other western European language, you will need 8-bit characters. This is how to set Emacs up to tell it to accept such characters.

4.1.1 The displaying of 8-bit characters

To let Emacs display 8-bit characters, you will need the following lines in your `.emacs` file:

```
(standard-display-european 1)
(load-library "iso-syntax")
```

If you are using Emacs on a terminal which has no 8-bit support, you can use the `iso-ascii` library (`(load-library "iso-ascii")`), which tells Emacs to display such characters to its best approximation.

4.1.2 The typing of 8-bit characters

If your keyboard allows you to enter accented characters, no problem. If not here are some remedies:

The `iso-acc` library The Emacs `iso-acc` library will let you type 8-bit characters from a 7-bit keyboard.

To use it, insert the following in your `.emacs` file:

```
(load-library "iso-acc")
```

Then, upon running Emacs and opening the file you need to edit, type `Meta-x iso-accents-mode`.

You can then enter the **é** of the French word *café* typing **'** then e. More generally, you will type an accented character typing the accent first, then the letter to accent (upper or lower case). The following are the accents you may use:

- **'** : Acute
- **'** : Grave
- **^** : Circumflex
- **"** : Dieresis
- **~** : Tilde, cedilla, and other particular cases (cf iso-acc.el).
- **/** : To bar a letter, etc.

If you need one of these characters and not an accented letter, type a space next to it. For instance, to type *l'éléphant*, type l **'** ⟨*spc*⟩ **'** e l **'** e ...

You will find all the possible combinations in the `iso-acc.el` file.

The ⟨*Meta*⟩ key Some terminals will let you type 8-bit characters with the ⟨*Meta*⟩ (or ⟨*Alt*⟩) key. For example, pressing ⟨*Meta*⟩-**i** will get you the **é** character.

But Emacs reserved the ⟨*Meta*⟩ key for other uses, and I know of no library which lets you use it for accented characters.

This is a solution:

```
(global-set-key "\ei" '(lambda () (interactive) (insert ?\351)))
```

Such a line, if inserted in your `.emacs` file, will let you type **é** using the ⟨*Meta*⟩-**i** keystroke. You can redefine in such a way the combinations you need if you replace **i** with the right key and **351** with the right code (the code being taken from the ISO-8859-1 character set).

Warning! Some local modes may redefine such key combinations.

4.1.3 The displaying of 8-bit SGML characters

Under SGML, you can type accented characters with macros. For example, the **é** key is **é**. Generally, the applications that need to read SGML can read 8-bit characters and there is no need to use these macros. But some may not be able to do so. Given that there is a way to solve this problem, it would be a waste to let these crash.

The `iso-sgml` library will let you type accented characters under Emacs, like always, but upon saving your file to the disk, it will turn these 8-bit characters into their SGML equivalent.

It is therefore easy, thanks to this library, to type and reread your document under Emacs, and you can be sure a non 8-bit clean application will accept you document.

To use this library, you just need to add the following lines to your `.emacs` file:

```
(setq sgml-mode-hook
'(lambda () "Defaults for SGML mode."
 (load-library "iso-sgml")))
```

4.2 SGML mode

Upon loading a file with the **.sgml** extension, Emacs enters the **sgml mode** automatically. If it doesn't, you can tell it to do so manually by typing `Meta-x sgml-mode`, or automatically by adding the following lines to your `.emacs` file:

```
(setq auto-mode-alist
(append '(("\.sgml$"  . sgml-mode))
          auto-mode-alist))
```

This mode will let you choose how to insert 8-bit characters for example. With `Meta-x sgml-name-8bit-mode` (or the menu item *SGML/Toggle 8-bit insertion*), you can choose to type 8-bit characters as is, or in SGML form, i.e. in the form **&...;**.

It will as well let you hide or show SGML tags, with `Meta-x sgml-tags-invisible` (or the menu item *SGML/Toggle Tag Visibility*).

4.3 PSGML mode

PSGML mode helps a lot to edit SGML documents with Emacs.

The *psgml-linuxdoc* documentation explains how to install this mode and use it with *LinuxDoc*.

4.4 Miscellaneous

4.4.1 auto-fill mode

In the normal mode, when you type a paragraph and get to the end of the line, you must use the ⟨*Return*⟩ key yourself to get to the next line, or else your line goes on through the whole paragraph. When you use ⟨*Return*⟩ to get to the next line, you get a paragraph with ragged right margins.

If you let some lines go beyond a reasonable width, you won't be able to see them with some editors.

The **auto-fill** mode automates this boring task: when you go further than a certain column (the 70th by default), you are automatically taken to the next line.

This is how to use this mode, and set the width of your lines to 80:

```
(setq sgml-mode-hook
        '(lambda () "Defaults for SGML mode."
            (auto-fill-mode)
            (setq fill-column 80)))
```

5 Ispell

If you want to spell-check your document from within Emacs, you may use the **Ispell** package and its Emacs mode.

5.1 Choosing your default dictionaries

You can set up Emacs so that upon loading a file, it chooses automatically which dictionaries to use (you can use several). The first one, certainly the most important, is the main dictionary, distributed with Ispell. You can choose among several languages. The second one is your personal dictionary, where Ispell will insert words it couldn't find in the main dictionary but you told it to remember.

If you wish to use as a default dictionary the French dictionary that comes with Ispell, and if you wish to use the file `.ispell-dico-perso` in your home directory as a personal dictionary, insert the following lines in your `.emacs` file:

```
(setq sgml-mode-hook
'(lambda () "Defauts for SGML mode."
(setq ispell-personal-dictionary "~/.ispell-dico-perso")
(ispell-change-dictionary "francais")
))
```

5.2 Selecting special dictionaries for certain files

You may have a little problem if you do not spell-check documents in the same language at all times. If you translate documents, it is very likely that you swap languages (and dictionaries) very often.

I don't know of any Lisp way of selecting, either automatically, or with a single mouse click, the main and personal dictionaries associated to the language currently being used. (If you do, please tell me!)

However, it is possible to indicate, at the end of the file, which dictionaries you want to use for the current file (and only this one). It suffices to add them as commentaries, so that Ispell can read them upon launching a spell-check:

```
<!-- Local IspellDict: english -->
<!-- Local IspellPersDict: ~/emacs/.ispell-english -->
```

If you have previously defined, in your `.emacs` file, that your default dictionaries are the French dictionaries, then you can add these lines in the end of any file written in English.

5.3 Spell-checking your document

To spell-check the whole of your document, use, from anywhere in the document the `Meta-x ispell-buffer` command. You may as well only run the checking on a region in your document:

- Mark the beginning of the region with `Ctrl-Spc` (mark-set-command),
- Go to the end of the region to check,
- type `Meta-x ispell-region`.

Emacs then runs Ispell. Upon meeting an unknown word, this one shows you said word (usually highlighted) and prompts you for a key:

- **spc** accepts the word, this time only,
- **i** accepts the word and inserts it in your personal dictionary,

- **a** accepts the word for this session,
- **A** accepts the word for this file, and inserts it in the local file dictionary
- **r** allows you to correct the word by hand
- **R** allows you to correct all the occurrences of the misspelled word,
- **x** stops the checking, and puts the cursor back in place,
- **X** stops the checking and leaves the cursor where it is, letting you correct your file; you will be able to continue the spell-checking later if you type `Meta-x ispell-continue`,
- **?** gives you online help.

If ispell finds one or several words close to the unknown one, it will show them in a little window, each one of them preceded by a digit. Just type this digit to replace the misspelled word with the corresponding word.

5.4 Personal dictionary versus local file dictionary

The **i** key will let you insert a word in your personal dictionary, whereas **A** will let you insert a word in the local file dictionary.

The local file dictionary is a sequence of words inserted at the end of the file, as comments, reread by Ispell each time it is run on the file. This way, you can accept some words, acceptable in this file, but not necessarily acceptable in other files.

As far as I am concerned, I think it is better that the personal dictionary be reserved for words the main dictionary doesn't know but which belong to the language (like hyphenated words), plus some common words like proper nouns or others (like *Linux*), if they don't look too much like a real word of the main dictionary; adding too many words in the personal dictionary, such as first names, may be dangerous, because they may look like a word of the language (one can imagine Ispell being mystified on the following: '*When the going gets tof, the tof get going*[43]'!).

5.5 Typing spell-checking

Ispell can spell-check your file while you're typing. You need to use **ispell-minor-mode** for this. To start it or stop it, type `Meta-x ispell-minor-mode`. Ispell will *beep* you each time you type a word it doesn't know.

If those *beeps* hassle you (or your roommate is taking a nap), you can replace those annoying *beeps* with a flash on the screen, with the command `Meta-x set-variable RET visible-bell RET t RET`. You can add the following line in your `.emacs` and silence Emacs forever:

```
(setq visible-bell t)
```

6 Dirty Tricks

6.1 Inserting a header automatically

Emacs allows you to *hook* some actions to any event (opening of a file, saving, running a new mode, etc).

The **autoinsert** library uses this feature: when you open a new file under Emacs, this library inserts, according to the type of the file, a *standard* header.

In our case, this *standard* header could well be the part declaring the document type (LinuxDoc), the title, the author, and the date.

I will describe here two ways to insert such a header. You could insert a template file containing the information to insert, or you could run an **elisp** routine.

---

[43] *Tof* is a French abbreviation for the first name *Christophe*.

6.1.1 by inserting a file

You must first tell Emacs to run the `auto-insert` when opening a file, then to read the **autoinsert** library which declares the `auto-insert-alist` list which we need to change. This list defines the header to insert for each file type. By default, the file to insert must be in the `~/insert/` directory, but it is possible to redefine the `auto-insert-directory` variable if you want to put it somewhere else.

Add the following lines to your `.emacs` file to insert the `~/emacs/sgml-insert.sgml` file each time you open a new SGML file:

```
(add-hook 'find-file-hooks 'auto-insert)
(load-library "autoinsert")
(setq auto-insert-directory "~/emacs/")
(setq auto-insert-alist
     (append '((sgml-mode .  "sgml-insert.sgml"))
             auto-insert-alist))
```

You can then write in the `~/emacs/sgml-insert.sgml` file your customised header, then re-run Emacs and open some `foobar.sgml` file. Emacs should ask you to confirm the automatic insertion, and if you answer yes, insert your header.

6.1.2 by running a routine

This works like before, but instead of setting the `auto-insert-alist` to a file to insert, you need to set it to a function to execute. This is how to proceed, taking for granted you want to write this function in a file named `~/emacs/sgml-header.el`. (there's no need to burden your `.emacs` file with such a function, as it may turn out to be quite long):

```
(add-hook 'find-file-hooks 'auto-insert)
(load-library "autoinsert")
(add-to-list 'load-path "~/emacs")
(load-library "sgml-header")
(setq auto-insert-alist
     (append '(((sgml-mode .  "SGML Mode") . insert-sgml-header))
             auto-insert-alist))
```

You will find in 7 (appendix) an example of `insert-sgml-header` function.

7 An `insert-sgml-header` function

This function will let the user insert a customised header for a Linux Documentation Project document in a file. It can be called automatically when one opens a new file, or explicitly, by the user.

This function prompts the user, through the *mini-buffer*, for some pieces of information, some of which are necessary, some of which are not.

First comes the title. If none is given, the function returns immediately, and inserts nothing. Then comes the date, the author, his e-mail and home page (these last two are optional).

Then comes a request for the name of the translator. If there is none, just type *Return*, and no further prompting about a hypothetical translator will be done. If there is one, you are asked for his e-mail and home page (optional as well).

This function then prints your request to the current buffer, including of course all the information you typed in a set up form, and including as well the tags which will serve for the abstract and the first chapter. It finally puts the cursor in the place where the abstract needs to be typed.

```
(defun insert-sgml-header ()
  "Inserts the header for a LinuxDoc document"
  (interactive)
  (let (title author email home translator email-translator home-translator date
            starting-point)
    (setq title (read-from-minibuffer "Title: "))
    (if (> (length title) 0)
        (progn
          (setq date (read-from-minibuffer "Date: ")
                author (read-from-minibuffer "Author: ")
                email (read-from-minibuffer "Author e-mail: ")
                home (read-from-minibuffer "Author home page: http://")
                translator (read-from-minibuffer "Translator: "))
          (insert "<!doctype linuxdoc system>\n<article>\n<title>")
          (insert title)
          (insert "</title>\n<author>\nAuthor: ") (insert author) (in-
sert "<newline>\n")
          (if (> (length email) 0)
              (progn
                (insert "<htmlurl url=\"mailto:")
                (insert email) (insert "\" name=\"") (insert email)
                (insert "\"><newline>\n")))
          (if (> (length home) 0)
              (progn
                (insert "<htmlurl url=\"http://")
                (insert home) (insert "\" name=\"") (insert home)
                (insert "\">\n<newline>")))
          (if (> (length translator) 0)
              (progn
                (setq email-translator (read-from-minibuffer "Translator e-
mail: ")
                      home-translator (read-from-minibuffer "Transla-
tor home page: http://"))
                (insert "Translator : ")
                (insert translator)
                (insert "<newline>\n")
                (if (> (length email-translator) 0)
                    (progn
                      (insert "<htmlurl url=\"mailto:")
                      (insert email-translator) (insert "\" name=\"")
                      (insert email-translator)
                      (insert "\"><newline>\n")))
                (if (> (length home-translator) 0)
                    (progn
                      (insert "<htmlurl url=\"http://")
                      (insert home-translator) (insert "\" name=\"")
                      (insert home-translator)
                      (insert "\"><newline>\n")))))
          (insert "</author>\n<date>\n")
          (insert date)
          (insert "\n</date>\n\n<abstract>\n")
          (setq point-beginning (point))
(insert "\n</abstract>\n<toc>\n\n<sect>\n<p>\n\n\n</sect>\n\n</article>\n")
          (goto-char point-beginning)
          ))))
```

Part XXII

"Alpha Miniloader Howto" David A. Rusling

david.rusling@reo.mts.dec.com
v0.84, 6 December 1996
This document describes the Miniloader, a program for Alpha based systems that can be used to initialize the machine and load Linux. The Alpha Linux Miniloader (to give it it's full name) is also known as MILO.

Contents

1   Introduction

This document describes the Miniloader for Linux on Alpha AXP (MILO). This firmware is used to initialize Alpha AXP based systems, load and start Linux and, finally, provide PALcode for Linux.

1.1   Copyright

The Alpha Miniloader (MILO) HOWTO is copyright (C) 1995, 1996 David A Rusling.

Copyright. Like all Linux HOWTO documents, it may be reproduced and distributed in whole or in part, in any medium, physical or electronic, so long as this copyright notice is retained on all copies. Commercial redistribution is allowed and encouraged; however the author would *like* to be notified of such distributions. You may translate this HOWTO into any language whatsover provided that you leave this copyright statement and disclaimer intact, and that you append a notice stating who translated the document.

Disclaimer. While I have tried to include the most correct and up to date information available to me, I cannot guarantee that usage of information in this document does not result in loss of data or equipment. I provide NO WARRENTY about the information in the HOWTO and I cannot be made liable for any consequences resulting from using the information in this HOWTO.

1.2   New Versions of this Document

The latest version of this document can be found in `<ftp://gatekeeper.dec.com/pub/Digital/Linux-Alpha/Miniloader/docs>` and David Mosberger-Tang is kind enough to include the html form of it in his excellent Linux Alpha FAQ site `<http://www.azstarnet.com/~axplinux>`.

2   What is MILO?

On Intel based PC systems, the BIOS firmware sets up the system and then loads the image to be run from the boot block of a DOS file system. This is more or less what MILO does on an Alpha based system, however there are several interesting differences between BIOS firmware and MILO, not least of which is that MILO includes and uses standard Linux device drivers unmodified. MILO is firmware, unlike LILO, which relies on the BIOS firmware to get itself loaded. The main functional parts of MILO are:

1. PALcode,

2. Memory set up code (builds page tables and turns on virtual addressing),

3. Video code (BIOS emulation code and TGA (21030)),

4. Linux kernel code. This includes real Linux kernel code (for example, the interrupt handling) and ersatz or mock Linux kernel,

5. Linux block device drivers (for example, the floppy driver),

6. File system support (ext2, MS-DOS and ISO9660),

7. User inteface code (MILO),

8. Kernel interface code (sets up the HWRPB and memory map for linux),

9. NVRAM code for managing environment variables.

The following paragraphs describe these functional parts in more detail.

PALcode can be thought of as a tiny software layer that tailors the chip to a particular operating system. It runs in a special mode (PALmode) which has certain restrictions but it uses the standard Alpha instruction set with just five extra instructions. In this way, the Alpha chip can run such diverse operating systems as Windows NT, OpenVMS, Digital Unix and, of course, Linux. The PALcode that MILO uses (and therefore Linux itself) is, like the rest of MILO, freeware. It is derived from Digital's Evaluation Board software example Digital Unix PALcode.. The differences between the different PALcodes are because of differences in address mapping and interrupt handling that exist between the Alpha chips (21066 based systems have a different I/O map to 21064+2107x systems) and different Alpha based systems.

For MILO to operate properly it needs to know what memory is available, where Linux will eventually be running from and it must be able to allocate temporary memory for the Linux device drivers. The code maintains a memory map that has entries for permanent and temporary allocated pages. As it boots, MILO uncompresses itself into the correct place in physical memory. When it passes control to the Linux kernel, it reserves memory for the compressed version of itself, the PALcode (which the kernel needs) and some data structures. This leaves most of the memory in the system for Linux itself.

The final act of the memory code is to set up and turn on virtual addressing so that the data structures that Linux expects to see are at the correct place in virtual memory.

MILO contains video code that initialises and uses the video device for the system. It will detect and use a VGA device if there is one, otherwise it will try to use a TGA (21030) video device. Failing that, it will assume that there is no graphics device. The BIOS emulation that the standard, pre-built, images include is Digital's own BIOS emulation which supports most, if not all, of the standard graphics devices available.

Linux device drivers live within the kernel and expect certain services from the kernel. Some of these services are provided directly by Linux kernel code, for example the interrupt handling and some is provided by kernel look-alike routines.

MILO's most powerful feature is that you can embed unaltered Linux device drivers into it. This gives it the potential to support every device that Linux does. MILO includes all of the block devices that are configured into the Linux kernel that it is built against as well as a lot of the block device code (for example, ll_rw_blk()).

MILO loads the Linux kernel from real file systems rather than from boot blocks and other strange places. It understands MSDOS, EXT2 and ISO9660 filesystems. Gzip'd files are supported and these are recommended, particularly if you are loading from floppy which is rather slow. MILO recognises these by their .gz suffix.

Built into MILO is a simple keyboard driver which, together with an equally simple video driver allows it to have a simple user interface. That interface allows you to list file systems on configured devices, boot Linux or run flash update utilities and set environment variables that control the system's booting. Like LILO, you can pass arguments to the Kernel.

MILO must tell the Linux kernel what sort of system this is, how much memory there is and which of that memory is free. It does this using the HWRPB (Hardware Restart Parameter Block) data structure and associated memory cluster descriptions. These are placed at the appropriate place in virtual memory just before control is passed to the Linux kernel.

3   Pre-Built Standard MILO Images.

If you are planning to run Linux on a standard Alpha based system, then there are pre-built "standard" MILO images that you might use. These (along with the sources and other interesting stuff) can be found in `<ftp://gatekeeper.dec.com/pub/Digital/Linux-Alpha/Miniloader>`.

The `images` subdirectory contains a directory per standard system (eg AlphaPC64) with MILO images having the following naming convention:

1. `MILO` - Miniloader executable image, this image can be loaded in a variety of ways,

2. `fmu.gz` - Flash management utility,

3. `MILO.dd` - Boot block floppy disk image. These should be written using rawrite.exe or `dd` on Linux.

The test-images, like the images subdirectory contains a directory per standard system. These images are somewhat experimental but tend to contain all the latest features.

4 How To Build MILO

You build MILO seperately from the Kernel. As MILO requires parts of the kernel to function (for example interrupt handling) you must first configure and build the kernel that matches with MILO that you want to build. Mostly this means building the kernel with the same version number. So, MILO-2.0.25.tar.gz will build against linux-2.0.25.tar.gz. MILO may build against a higher version of the kernel, but there again it may not. Also, now that ELF shared libraries are fully supported, there are two versions of the MILO sources. To build under an ELF system you must first unpack the standard MILO sources and then patch those sources with the same version numbered ELF patch. In the remainder of this discussion, I assume that your kernel sources and object files are stored in the subtree at /usr/src/linux and that the linux kernel has been fully built with the command make boot

To build MILO, change your working directory to the MILO source directory and invoke make with:

```
$    make KSRC=/usr/src/linux config
```

Just like the Linux kernel, you will be asked a series of questions

```
Echo output to the serial port (MINI_SERIAL_ECHO) [y]
```

It's a good idea to echo kernel printk to /dev/ttyS0 if you can. If you can (and want to), then type "y", otherwise "n". All of the standard, pre-built, MILO images include serial port I/O using COM1.

```
Use Digital's BIOS emulation code (not free) (MI-
NI_DIGITAL_BIOS_EMU) [y]
```

This code is included as a library which is freely distributable so long as it is used on an Alpha based system. The sources are not available. If you answer n then the freeware alternative BIOS emulation will be built. It's sources are included with MILO. Note that you cannot right now build choose Digital's BIOS emulation code in an ELF system (the library is not yet ready) and so you must answer no to this question.

```
Build PALcode from sources (Warning this is dangerous) (MI-
NI_BUILD_PALCODE_FROM_SOURCES) [n]
```

You should only do this if you have changed the PALcode sources, otherwise use the standard, pre-built PALcode included with MILO.

You are now all set to build the MILO image itself:

```
$    make KSRC=/usr/src/linux
```

When the build has successfully completed, the MILO image is in the file called milo. There are a lot of images called milo.*, these should be ignored.

5 How To Load MILO

The most commonly supported method of loading MILO is from the Windows NT ARC firmware as most shipping systems support this. However, there are a wide variety of loading MILO. It may be loaded from:

- a failsafe boot block floppy,
- the Windows NT ARC firmware,

- Digital's SRM console,
- an Alpha Evaluation Board Debug Monitor,
- flash/ROM.

5.1 Loading MILO from the Windows NT ARC firmware

Most, if not all, Alpha AXP based systems include the Windows NT ARC firmware and this is the prefered method of booting MILO and thus Linux. Once the Windows NT firmware is running and you have the correct MILO image for your system, this method is completely generic.

The Windows NT ARC firmware is an environment in which programs can run and make callbacks into the firmware to perform actions. The Windows NT OSLoader is a program that does exactly this. Linload.exe is a much simpler program which does just enough to load and execute MILO. It loads the appropriate image file into memory at 0x00000000 and then makes a swap-PAL PALcall to it. MILO, like Linux, uses a different PALcode to Windows NT which is why the swap has to happen. MILO relocates itself to 0x200000 and continues on through the PALcode reset entry point as before.

Before you add a Linux boot option, you will need to copy linload.exe and the appropriate MILO that you wish to load to someplace that the Windows NT ARC firmware can read from. In the following example, I assume that you are booting from a DOS format floppy disk:

1. At the boot menu, select `"Supplementary menu..."`
2. At the `"Supplementary menu"`, select `"Set up the system..."`
3. At the `"Setup menu"`, select `"Manage boot selection menu..."`
4. In the `"Boot selections menu"`, choose `"Add a boot selection"`
5. Choose `"Floppy Disk 0"`
6. Enter `"linload.exe"` as the osloader directory and name
7. Say "yes" to the operating system being on the same partition as the osloader
8. Enter `"\"` as the operating system root directory
9. I usually enter `"Linux"` as the name for this boot selection
10. Say "No" you do not want to initialise the debugger at boot time
11. You should now be back in the `"Boot selections menu"`, choose the `"Change a boot selection option"` and pick the selection you just created as the one to edit
12. Use the down arrow to get `"OSLOADFILENAME"` up and then type in the name of the MILO image that you wish to use, for example `"noname.arc"` followed by return.
13. Press ESC to get back to the `"Boot Selections menu"`
14. Choose `"Setup Menu"` (or hit ESC again) and choose `"Supplementary menu, and save changes"` option
15. ESC will get you back to the `"Boot menu"` and you can attempt to boot MILO. If you do not want Linux as the first boot option, then you can alter the order of the boot options in the `"Boot selections menu"`.

At the end of all this, you should have a boot selection that looks something like:

```
LOADIDENTIFIER=Linux
SYSTEMPARTITION=multi(0)disk(0)fdisk(0)
OSLOADER=multi(0)disk(0)fdisk(0)\linload.exe
OSLOADPARTITION=multi(0)disk(0)fdisk(0)
OSLOADFILENAME=\noname.arc
OSLOADOPTIONS=
```

HOWTO

You can now boot MILO (and then Linux). You can load linload.exe and MILO directly from a file system that Windows NT understands such as NTFS or DOS on a hard disk.

The contents `OSLOADOPTIONS` are passed to MILO which interprets it as a command. So, in order to boot Linux directly from Windows NT without pausing in MILO, you could pass the following in `OSLOADOPTIONS`:

```
boot sda2:vmlinux.gz root=/dev/sda2
```

See 6 (MILO's User Interface) for more information on the commands available.

Another (rather sneaky) way of loading of loading MILO via the WNT ARC firmware is to put MILO onto an MS-DOS floppy and call it `fwupdate.exe` and then choose the "Upgrade Firmware" option.

5.2 Loading MILO from the Evaluation Board Debug Monitor

Evaluation boards (and often designs cloned from them) include support for the Alpha Evaluation Board Debug Monitor. Consult your system document before considering this method of booting MILO. The following systems are *known* to include Debug Monitor support:

- AlphaPC64 (Section 5.6.2 (AlphaPC64))
- EB64+ (Section 5.6.4 (EB64+))
- EB66+ (Section 5.6.3 (EB66+))
- EB164 (Section 5.6.6 (EB164))
- PC164 (Section 5.6.7 (PC164))

Before you consider this method, you should note that the early versions of the Evaluation Board Debug Monitor did not include video or keyboard drivers and so you must be prepared to connect another system via the serial port so that you can use the Debug Monitor. Its interface is very simple and typing help shows a whole heap of commands. The ones that are most interesting include the word `boot` or `load` in them.

The Evaluation Board Debug Monitor can load an image either via the network (netboot) or via a floppy (flboot). In either case, set the boot address to 0x200000 (> `bootadr 200000`) before booting the image.

If the image is on floppy (and note that only DOS formatted floppies are supported), then you will need to type the following command:

```
AlphaPC64> flboot <MILO-image-name>
```

5.3 Loading MILO from a Failsafe Boot Block Floppy

Only the AxpPCI33 is *known* to include failsafe boot block floppy support (Section < id="noname-section" name="Noname">).

If you do not have a standard pre-built MILO .dd image, then you may need to build an SRM boot block floppy. Once you have built MILO, you need to do the following on Digital Unix box:

```
fddisk -fmt /dev/rfd0a
cat mboot bootm > /dev/rfd0a
disklabel -rw rfd0a 'rx23' mboot bootm
```

Or on a Linux box:

```
cat mboot bootm > /dev/fd0
```

If you have a standard MILO image available (say `MILO.dd`) then you would build a boot block floppy using the following command:

```
dd if=MILO.dd of=/dev/fd0
```

5.4 Loading MILO from Flash

There are a number of systems where MILO can be blown into flash and booted directly (instead of via the Windows NT ARC firmware):

- AlphaPC64 (Section 5.6.2 (AlphaPC64))
- Noname (Section 5.6.1 (Noname))
- EB66+ (Section 5.6.3 (EB66+))
- EB164 (Section 5.6.6 (EB164))
- PC164 (Section 5.6.7 (PC164))

5.5 Loading MILO from the SRM Console

The SRM (short for System Reference Manual) Console knows nothing about filesystems or disk-partitions, it simply expects that the secondary bootstrap loader occupies a consecutive range of physical disk sectors starting from a given offset. The information describing the secondary bootstrap loader (its size and offset) is given in the first 512 byte block. To load MILO via the SRM you must generate that structure on a device which the SRM can access (such as a floppy disk). This is what `mboot` and `bootm`, `mboot` is the first block (or boot description) and `mboot` is the `MILO` image rounded up to a 512 byte boundary.

To load MILO from a boot block device, either build `mboot` and `bootm` and push them onto the boot device using the following command:

```
$ cat mboot bootm > /dev/fd0
```

Or, grab the appropriate `MILO.dd` from a web site and write it onto the boot device using either `RAWRITE.EXE` or `dd`.

Once you have done that you can boot the SRM console and use one of its many commands to boot MILO. For example, to boot MILO from a boot block floppy you would use the following command:

```
>>>boot dva0
(boot dva0.0.0.0.1 -flags 0)
block 0 of dva0.0.0.0.1 is a valid boot block
reading 621 blocks from dva0.0.0.0.1
bootstrap code read in
base = 112000, image_start = 0, image_bytes = 4da00
initializing HWRPB at 2000
initializing page table at 104000
initializing machine state
setting affinity to the primary CPU
jumping to bootstrap code
MILO Stub: V1.1
Unzipping MILO into position
Allocating memory for unzip
####...
```

The following systems are *known* to have SRM Console support:

- Noname (Section 5.6.1 (Noname))

- AlphaPC64 (Section 5.6.2 (AlphaPC64))
- EB164 (Section 5.6.6 (EB164))
- PC164 (Section 5.6.7 (PC164))

5.6 System Specific Information

5.6.1 AxpPCI33 (Noname)

The Noname board can load MILO from the Windows NT ARC firmware (Section 5.1 (booting from Windows NT ARC firmware)), from the SRM Console (Section 5.5 (Loading MILO from the SRM Console)). and from a failsafe boot block floppy (Section 5.3 (Loading from a Failsafe Boot Block Floppy)). A flash management utility, runnable from MILO is available so that once MILO is running, it can be blown into flash (Section 7 (running the flash management utility)). However, be warned that once you have done this you will lose the previous image held there as there is only room for one image.

The way that Noname boots is controlled by a set of jumpers on the board, J29 and J28. These look like:

```
                4
    J29    2 x x x 6
           1 x x x 5

    J28    2 x x x 6
           1 x x x 5
                3
```

The two options that we're interested in are J28, pins 1-3 which boots the console/loader from flash and J29, pins 1-3 which boots the console/loader from a boot block floppy. The second option is the one that you need to first boot MILO on the Noname board.

Once you've selected the boot from floppy option via the jumpers, put the SRM boot block floppy containing MILO into the floppy and reboot. In a few seconds (after the floppy light goes out) you should see the screen blank to white and MILO telling you what's going on.

If you are really interested in technical stuff, the Noname loads images off of the floppy into physical address 0x104000 and images from flash into 0x100000. For this reason, MILO is built with it's PALcode starting at 0x200000. When it is first loaded, it moves itself to the correct location (see relocate.S).

5.6.2 AlphaPC64 (Cabriolet)

The AlphaPC64 includes the Windows NT ARC firmware (Section 5.1 (booting from Windows NT ARC firmware)), the SRM Console (Section 5.5 (Loading MILO from the SRM Console)) and the Evaluation Debug Monitor (Section 5.2 (Loading from the Debug Monitor)). These images are in flash and there is room to add MILO so that you can boot MILO directly from flash. A flash management utility, runnable from MILO is available so that once MILO is running, it can be blown into flash (Section 7 (running the flash management utility)). This system supports MILO environment variables.

You select between the boot options (and MILO when it is been put into flash) using a combination of jumpers and a boot option which is saved in the NVRAM of the TOY clock.

The jumper is J2, SP bits 6 and 7 have the following meanings:

- SP bit 6 should always be out. If this jumper is set then the SROM mini-debugger gets booted,
- SP bit 7 in is boot image selected by the boot option byte in the TOY clock,
- SP bit 7 out is boot first image in flash.

So, with bit 7 out, the Debug Monitor will be booted as it is `always` the first image in flash. With bit 7 in, the image selected by the boot option in the TOY clock will be selected. The Debug Monitor, the Windows NT ARC firmware and MILO all support setting this boot option byte but you must be very careful using it. In particular, you cannot set the boot option so that next time the system boots MILO when you are running the Windows NT ARC firmware, it only allows you to set Debug Monitor or Windows NT ARC as boot options.

To get MILO into flash via the Evaluation Board Debug Monitor, you will need a flashable image. The build proceedures make MILO.rom, but you can also make a rom image using the makerom tool in the Debug Monitor software that comes with the board:

```
> makerom -v -i7 -l200000 MILO -o mini.flash
```

(type makerom to find out what the arguments mean, but 7 is a flash image id used by the srom and -l200000 gives the load address for the image as 0x200000).

Load that image into memory (via the Debug Monitor commands flload, netload, and so on) at 0x200000 and then blow the image into flash:

```
AlphaPC64> flash 200000 8
```

(200000 is where the image to be blown is in memory and 8 is the segment number where you put the image. There are 16 1024*64 byte segments in the flash and the Debug Monitor is at seg 0 and the Windows NT ARC firmware is at seg 4).

Set up the image that the srom will boot by writing the number of the image into the TOY clock.

```
AlphaPC64> bootopt 131
```

(131 means boot the 3rd image, 129 = 1st, 130 = 2nd and so on).

Power off, put jumper 7 on and power on and you should see the MILO burst into life. If you don't then take jumper 7 back off and reboot the Debug Monitor.

5.6.3 EB66+

The EB66+, like all of the Alpha Evaluation Boards built by Digital contains the Evaluation Board Debug Monitor and so this is available to load MILO (Section 5.2 (Loading from the Debug Monitor)). Quite often (although not always) boards whose design is derived from these include the Debug Monitor also. Usually, these boards include the Windows NT ARC firmware (Section 5.1 (booting from Windows NT ARC firmware)). A flash management utility, runnable from MILO is available so that once MILO is running, it can be blown into flash (Section 7 (running the flash management utility)). This system supports MILO environment variables.

These systems have several boot images in flash controlled by jumpers. The two jumper banks are J18 and J16 and are located at the bottom of the board in the middle (if the Alpha chip is at the top). You select between the boot options (and MILO when it is been put into flash) using a combination of jumpers and a boot option which is saved in the NVRAM of the TOY clock.

Jumper 7-8 of J18 in means boot the image described by the boot option. Jumper 7-8 of J18 out means boot the Evaluation Board Debug Monitor.

Blowing an image into flash via the Evaluation Board Debug Monitor is exactly the same proceedure as for the AlphaPC64 (Section 5.6.2 (AlphaPC64)).

5.6.4 EB64+/Aspen Alpine

This system is quite like the AlphaPC64 except that it does not contain flash which MILO can be loaded from. The EB64+ has two ROMs, one of which contains the Windows NT ARC firmware (Section 5.1 (booting from Windows NT

HOWTO

ARC firmware)). and the other contains the Evaluation Board Debug Monitor (Section 5.2 (Loading from the Debug Monitor)).

The Aspen Alpine is a little different in that it only has one ROM; this contains the Windows NT ARC firmware.

5.6.5 Universal Desktop Box (Multia)

This is a very compact pre-packaged 21066 based system that includes a TGA (21030) graphics device. Although you can *just* fit a half height PCI graphics card in the box you are better off waiting for full TGA support in XFree86. It includes the Windows NT ARC firmware and so booting from that is the prefered method (Section 5.1 (Loading from Windows NT)).

5.6.6 EB164

The EB164, like all of the Alpha Evaluation Boards built by Digital contains the Evaluation Board Debug Monitor and so this is available to load MILO (Section 5.2 (Loading from the Debug Monitor)). Quite often (although not always) boards whose design is derived from these include the Debug Monitor also. Usually, these boards include the Windows NT ARC firmware (Section 5.1 (booting from Windows NT ARC firmware)). The SRM console is also available (Section 5.5 (Loading MILO from the SRM Console)). A flash management utility, runnable from MILO is available so that once MILO is running, it can be blown into flash (Section 7 (running the flash management utility)). This system supports MILO environment variables.

These systems have several boot images in flash controlled by jumpers. The two jumper bank is J1 and is located at the bottom of the board on the left (if the Alpha chip is at the top). You select between the boot options (and MILO when it is been put into flash) using a combination of jumpers and a boot option which is saved in the NVRAM of the TOY clock.

Jumper SP-11 of J1 in means boot the image described by the boot option. Jumper SP-11 of J1 out means boot the Evaluation Board Debug Monitor.

Blowing an image into flash via the Evaluation Board Debug Monitor is exactly the same proceedure as for the AlphaPC64 (Section 5.6.2 (AlphaPC64)).

5.6.7 PC164

The PC164, like all of the Alpha Evaluation Boards built by Digital contains the Evaluation Board Debug Monitor and so this is available to load MILO (Section 5.2 (Loading from the Debug Monitor)). Quite often (although not always) boards whose design is derived from these include the Debug Monitor also. Usually, these boards include the Windows NT ARC firmware (Section 5.1 (booting from Windows NT ARC firmware)). The SRM console is also available (Section 5.5 (Loading MILO from the SRM Console)). A flash management utility, runnable from MILO is available so that once MILO is running, it can be blown into flash (Section 7 (running the flash management utility)). This system supports MILO environment variables.

These systems have several boot images in flash controlled by jumpers. The main jumper block, J30, contains the system configuration jumpers and jumper CF6 in means that the system will boot the Debug Monitor, the default is out.

Blowing an image into flash via the Evaluation Board Debug Monitor is exactly the same proceedure as for the AlphaPC64 (Section 5.6.2 (AlphaPC64)).

5.6.8 XL266

The XL266 is one of a family of systems that are known as Avanti. It has a riser card containing the Alpha chip and cache which plugs into the main board at right angles. This board can replace the equivalent Pentium board.

Some of these systems ship with the SRM console but others, notably the XL266 ship with only the Windows NT ARC firmware (Section 5.1 (booting from Windows NT ARC firmware)).

Here is my list of compatible systems:

- AlphaStation 400 (Avanti),

- AlphaStation 250,

- AlphaStation 200 (Mustang),

- XL. There are two flavours, XL266 and XL233 with the only difference being in processor speed and cache size.

Note The system that I use to develop and test MILO is an XL266 and so this is the only one that I can guarentee will work. However, technically, all of the above systems are equivalent; they have the same support chipsets and the same interrupt handling mechanisms.

5.6.9   Platform2000

This is a 233Mhz 21066 based system.

6   MILO's User Interface

Once you have correctly installed/loaded/run MILO you will see the MILO (for MIniLOader) prompt displayed on your screen. There is a very simple interface that you must use in order to boot a particular Linux kernel image. Typing "help" is a good idea as it gives a useful summary of the commands.

6.1   The "help" Command

Probably the most useful command that MILO has:

```
MILO> help
MILO command summary:

ls [-t fs] [dev:[dir]]
                     - List files in directory on device
boot [-t fs] [dev:file] [boot string]
                     - Boot Linux from the specified device and file
run [-t fs] dev:file
                     - Run the standalone program dev:file
show                 - Display all known devices and file systems
set VAR VALUE        - Set the variable VAR to the specified VALUE
unset VAR            - Delete the specified variable
reset                - Delete all variables
print                - Display current variable settings
help [var]           - Print this help text

Devices are specified as: fd0, hda1, hda2, sda1...
Use the '-t filesystem-name' option if you want to use
  anything but the default filesystem  ('ext2').
Use the 'show' command to show known devices and filesystems.
Type 'help var' for a list of variables.
```

Note that the `bootopt` command only appears on AlphaPC64 (and similar) systems. Refer to the board's dcoumentation to find out just what it means.

Devices. Until you use a command that needs to make use of a device, no device inititalisation will take place. The first `show`, `ls`, `boot` or `run` commands all cause the devices within MILO to be initialised. Devices are named in the same way (exactly) that Linux itself will name them. So, the first IDE disk will be called 'hda' and it's first partition will be 'hda1'. Use the `show` command to show what devices are available.

HOWTO

File Systems. MILO supports three file systems, MSDOS, EXT2 and ISO9660. So long as a device is available to it, MILO can `listboot` or `run` an image stored on one of these file systems. MILO's default file system is EXT2 and so you have tell MILO that the file system is something other than that. All of the commands that use filenames allow you to pass the file system using the `-t [filesystem]` option. So, if you wanted to list the contents of a SCSI CD ROM, you might type the following:

```
MILO> ls -t iso9660 scd0:
```

Variables. MILO contains some settable variables that help the boot process. If you are loading via the Windows NT ARC firmware, then MILO makes use of the boot option environment variables set up by that firmware. For some systems, MILO (for example, the AlphaPC64) maintains its own set of environment variables that do not change from boot to boot. These variables are:

```
MILO> help var
Variables that MILO cares about:
  MEMORY_SIZE       - System memory size in megabytes
  BOOT_DEV          - Specifies the default boot device
  BOOT_FILE         - Specifies the default boot file
  BOOT_STRING       - Specifies the boot string to pass to the kernel
  SCSIn_HOSTID      - Specifies the host id of the n-th SCSI controller.
  AUTOBOOT          - If set, MILO attempts to boot on powerup
                      and enters command loop only on failure.
  AUTOBOOT_TIMEOUT  - Seconds to wait before auto-booting on powerup.
```

6.2   Booting Linux

The `boot` command boots a linux kernel from a device. You will need to have a linux kernel image on an EXT2 formated disk (SCSI, IDE or floppy) or an ISO9660 formatted CD available to MILO. The image can be gzip'd and in this case MILO will recognise that it is gzip'd by the .gz suffix.

You should note that the version of MILO does not usually have to match the version of the Linux kernel that you are loading. You boot Linux using the following command syntax:

```
MILO> boot [-t file-system] device-name:file-name [[boot-option] [boot-
option] ...]
```

Where `device-name` is the name of the device that you wish to use and `file-name` is the name of the file containing the Linux kernel. All arguments supplied after the file name are passed directly to the Linux kernel.

If you are installing Red Hat, then you will need to specify a root device and so on. So you would use:

```
MILO> boot fd0:vmlinux.gz root=/dev/fd0 load_ramdisk=1
```

MILO will automatically contain the block devices that you configure into your vmlinux. I have tested the floppy driver, the IDE driver and a number of SCSI drivers (for example, the NCR 810), and these work fine. Also, it is important to set the host id of the SCSI controller to a reasonable value. By default, MILO will initialize it to the highest possible value (7) which should normally work just fine. However, if you wish, you can explicitly set the host id of the n-th SCSI controller in the system by setting environment variable SCSIn_HOSTID to the appropriate value. For example, to set the hostid of the first SCSI controller to 7, you can issue the following command at the MILO prompt:

```
setenv SCSI0_HOSTID 7
```

6.3 Rebooting Linux

You may want to reboot a running Linux system using the `shutdown -r now` command. In this case, the Linux kernel returns control to MILO (via the HALT CallPAL entrypoint). MILO leaves a compressed copy of itself in memory for just this reason and detects that the system is being rebooted from information held in the HWRPB (Hardware Restart Parameter Block). In this case it starts to reboot using exactly the same command that was used to boot the Linux kernel the last time. There is a 30 second timeout that allows you to interrupt this process and boot whatever kernel you wish in whatever way you wish.

6.4 The "bootopt" command

For flash based systems such as the AlphaPC64, EB164 and the EB66+, there are a number of possible boot options and these are changed using the `bootopt` command. This has one argument, a decimal number which is the type of the image to be booted the next time the system is power cycled or reset:

0 Boot the Evaluation Board Debug Monitor,

1 Boot the Windows NT ARC firmware.

In order to tell the boot code to boot the MILO firmware from flash then you need a boot option that means boot the N'th image. For this, you need to 128 plus N, so if MILO is the third image, you would use the command:

```
MILO> bootopt 131
```

Note: Be very careful with this command. A good rule is never to set bootopt to 0 (the Evaluation Board Debug Monitor), but instead use the system's jumpers to achieve the same thing.

7 Running the Flash Management Utility

The `run` command is used to run the flash management utility. Before you start you will need a device available to MILO that contains the updateflash program. This (like vmlinux) can be gzip'd. You need to run the flash management utility program from the MILO using the (`run`) command:

```
MILO> run fd0:fmu.gz
```

Once it has loaded and initialised, the flash management utility will tell you some information about the flash device and give you a command prompt. Again the `help` command is most useful.

```
Linux MILO Flash Management Utility V1.0

Flash device is an Intel 28f008SA
  16 segments, each of 0x10000 (65536) bytes
Scanning Flash blocks for usage
Block 12 contains the environment variables
FMU>
```

Note that on systems where environment variables may be stored and where there is more than one flash block (for example, the AlphaPC64) the flash management utility will look for a block to hold MILO's environment variables. If such a block already exists, the flash management utility will tell you where it is. Otherwise, you must use the `environment` command to set a block and initialise it. In the above example, flash block 12 contains MILO's environment variables.

7.1   The "help" command

```
FMU> help
FMU command summary:

list                    - List the contents of flash
program                 - program an image into flash
quit                    - Quit
environment             - Set which block should contain the environmen-
t variables
bootopt num             - Select firmware type to use on next power up
help                    - Print this help text
FMU>
```

Note that the `environment` and `bootopt` commands are only available on the EB66+, the AlphaPC64, EB164 and PC164 systems (and their clones).

7.2   The "list" command

The "list" command shows the current usage of the flash memory. Where there is more than one flash block, the usage of each flash block is shown. In the example below you can see that Windows NT ARC is using blocks 4:7 and block 15.

```
FMU> list
Flash blocks:  0:DBM  1:DBM  2:DBM  3:WNT  4:WNT  5:WNT  6:WNT  7:WN-
T  8:MILO
          9:MILO 10:MILO 11:MILO 12:MILO 13:U 14:U 15:WNT
Listing flash Images
  Flash image starting at block 0:
    Firmware Id:  0 (Alpha Evaluation Board Debug Monitor)
    Image size is 191248 bytes (3 blocks)
    Executing at 0x300000
  Flash image starting at block 3:
    Firmware Id:  1 (Windows NT ARC)
    Image size is 277664 bytes (5 blocks)
    Executing at 0x300000
  Flash image starting at block 8:
    Firmware Id:  7 (MILO/Linux)
    Image size is 217896 bytes (4 blocks)
    Executing at 0x200000
FMU>
```

7.3   The "program" command

The flash management utility contains a compressed copy of a flash image of MILO. The "program" command allows you to blow this image into flash. The command allows you to back out, but before you run it you should use the "list" command to see where to put MILO. If MILO is already in flash, then the flash management utility will offer to overwrite it.

```
FMU> program
Image is:
    Firmware Id:  7 (MILO/Linux)
    Image size is 217896 bytes (4 blocks)
    Executing at 0x200000
Found existing image at block 8
Overwrite existing image? (N/y)? y
```

```
Do you really want to do this (y/N)? y
Deleting blocks ready to program: 8 9 10 11
Programming image into flash
Scanning Flash blocks for usage
FMU>
```

Wait until it has completed before powering off your system.

Note: I cannot emphasise just how careful you must be here not to overwrite an existing flash image that you might need or render your system useless. A very good rule is never to overwrite the Debug Monitor.

7.4   The "environment" command

This selects a flash block to contain MILO's environment variables.

7.5   The "bootopt" command

This is just the same as MILO's "bootopt" command, see (Section 6.4 (The "bootopt" command)).

7.6   The "quit" command

This is really pretty meaningless. The only way back to MILO (or anything else) once the flash management utility has run is to reboot the system.

8   Restrictions.

Unfortunately this is not a perfect world and there, as always, some restrictions that you should be aware of.

MILO is not meant to load operating systems other than Linux, although it can load images linked to run at the same place in memory as Linux (which is 0xFFFFFC0000310000). This is how the flash management utilities can be run.

The PALcode sources included in `miniboot/palcode/`*blah* are correct, however there are problems when they are built using the latest `gas`. They *do* build if you use the ancient a.out gas that's supplied in the Alpha Evaluation Board toolset (and that's how they were built). I'm trying to get someone to fix the new gas. Meanwhile, as a workaround, I have provided pre-built PALcode for the supported boards and David Mosberger-Tang has a fixed gas on his ftp site.

9   Problem Solving.

Here are some common problems that people have seen, together with the solutions.

Reading MS-DOS floppies from the Evaluation Board Debug Monitor.

Some of the older versions of the Evaluation Board Debug Monitor (pre-version 2.0) have a problem with DOS format flopies generated from Linux. Usually, the Debug Monitor can load the first few sectors all right, but then goes into an endless loop complaining about "bad sectors." Apparently, there is an incompatibility between the DOS file system as expected by the Debug Monitor and the Linux implementation of DOSFS. To make the long story short: if you run into this problem, try using DOS to write the floppy disk. For example, if loading the file MILO.cab doesn't work, use a DOS machine, insert the floppy and then do:

```
copy a:MILO.cab c:
copy c:MILO.cab a:
del c:MILO.cab
```

Then try booting from that floppy again. This normally solves the problem.

MILO displays a long sequence of O> and does not accept input.

This usually happens when MILO was built to use COM1 as a secondary console device. In such a case, MILO echo output to COM1 and accepts input from there also. This is great for debugging but not so great if you have a device other than a terminal connected. If this happens, disconnect the device or power it down until the Linux kernel has booted. Once Linux is up and running, everything will work as expected.

MILO complains that the kernel image has the wrong magic number

Older versions of MILO did not support the ELF object file format and so could not recognise an ELF image and this might be your problem. If this is reported, upgrade to the latest MILO that you can find. All 2.0.20 and beyond MILOs support ELF. On the other hand it could be that the image is indeed damaged. You should also note that MILO does not yet automatically distinquish between GZIP'd and non-GZIP'd images; you need to add the ".gz" suffix to the file name.

MILO prints "...turning on virtual addressing and jumping to the Linux Kernel" and nothing else happens

One obvious problem is that the kernel image is wrongly built or is built for another Alpha system altogether. Another is that the video board is a TGA (Zlxp) device and the kernel has been built for a VGA device (or vice versa). It is worth building the kernel to echo to COM1 and then connecting a terminal to that serial port or retrying the kernel that came with the Linux distribution that you installed.

MILO does not recognise the SCSI device

The standard MILO images include as many device drivers as are known to be stable for Alpha (as of now that includes the NCR 810, QLOGIC ISP, Buslogic and Adaptec 2940s and 3940 cards). If your card is not included, it may be that the driver is not stable enough on an Alpha system yet. Again, the latest MILO images are worth trying. You can tell which SCSI devices a MILO image has built into it by using the "show" command.

10   Acknowledgements.

I would like to thank:

- Eric Rasmussen and Eileen Samberg the authors of the PALcode,
- Jim Paradis for the keyboard driver and the original MILO interface,
- Jay Estabrook for his help and bugfixes,
- David Mosberger-Tang for the freeware BIOS emulation and his support and encouragement,
- Last (and not least) Linus Torvalds for the timer code and his kernel.

There are a number of things that still need doing to MILO, if you want to add something yourself, then do let me know *david.rusling@reo.mts.dec.com* <mailto:david.rusling@reo.mts.dec.com> so that we do not duplicate our efforts.

Finally, a big thank you to Digital for producing such a wonderful chip (and paying me to do this).

Part XXIII

"Linux MIPS HOWTO" Ralf Bächle

ralf@gnu.org

v0.1, 13 March 1998
This HOWTO describes the MIPS port of the Linux operating system, common problems and their solutions, availability and more. It also tries to be a little helpful to other people who might read this FAQ in an attempt to find information that actually should be covered elsewhere.

Contents

HOWTO

1 What is Linux/MIPS?

Linux/MIPS is a port of the widespread UNIX clone Linux to the MIPS architecture. Linux/MIPS is running on a large number of technically very different systems ranging from little embedded systems and servers to large desktop machines and servers that, at least at the time when they were introduced into the market, were the best of their class.

Linux/MIPS advantages over other operating systems at this time are

- The entire Linux system consists only of Free Software.
- Excellent Price/Performance ratio.
- Availability of large amounts of software of which a large part again is Free Software.
- Binary compatibility across a growing number of platforms.
- Small footprint making Linux/MIPS suitable for many embedded systems.

In short, Linux has been designed and ships with Fahrvergnügen. However as usual your mileage may vary and you should examine Linux's suitability for your purpose which purpose this document tries to serve.

2 What hardware does Linux/MIPS support?

2.1 Hardware platforms

Many machines are available with a number of different CPU options of which not all are currently supported. Please check section 2.2 (Processor Types) to make sure your CPU type is supported. This is a listing of machines that are running Linux/MIPS, systems to which Linux/MIPS could be ported or systems that people have an interest in running Linux/MIPS.

2.1.1 Acer PICA

The *Acer PICA* is derived from the *Mips Magnum 4000* design. It has a R4400PC CPU running at 133Mhz or optionally 150Mhz plus a 512kb (optionally 2mb) second level cache; the Magnum's G364 gfx card was replaced with a S3 968 based one. The system is supported with the exception of the X server.

2.1.2 Baget/MIPS series

The Baget series includes several boxes which have R3000 processors: Baget 23, Baget 63, and Baget 83. Baget 23 and 63 have BT23-201 or BT23-202 motherboards with R3500A (which is basically a R3000A chip) at 25 MHz and R3081E at 50 MHz respectively. The BT23-201 board has VME bus and VIC068, VAC068 chips as system controllers. The BT23-202 board has PCI as internal bus and VME as internal. Support for BT23-201 board has been done by *Gleb Raiko (rajko@mech.math.msu.su)* and *Vladimir Roganov (vroganov@msiu.ru)* with a bit help from *Serguei Zimin (zimin@msiu.ru)*. Support for BT23-202 is under development along with Baget 23B which consists of 3 BT23-201 boards with shared VME bus.

Baget 83 is mentioned here for completeness only. It has only 2mb RAM and it's too small to run Linux. The Baget/MIPS code has been merged with the DECstation port; source for both is available at `<http://decstation.unix-ag.org/>`.

2.1.3 Cobalt Qube and Raq

The Cobalt Qube product series are low cost headless server systems based on a IDT R5230. Cobalt has developed its own Linux/MIPS variant to fit the special requirements of the Qube as well as possible. Basically the Qube kernel has been derived from Linux/MIPS 2.1.56, then backported to 2.0.30 for stability's sake, then optimized. Cobalt kernels are available from Cobalt's ftp site `<http://www.cobaltnet.com>`. The Cobalt Qube support has never been integrated into the official Linux/MIPS 2.1.x kernels.

2.1.4 Netpower 100

The *Netpower 100* is apparently an *Acer PICA* in disguise. It should therefore be supported but this is untested. If there is a problem then it is probably the machine detection.

2.1.5 Nintendo 64

The *Nintendo 64* is R4300 based game console with 4mb RAM. Its graphics chips were developed by Silicon Graphics for Nintendo. Right now this port has pipe dream status and will continue to be in that state until Nintendo decides to publish the necessary technical information. The question remains as to whether this is a good idea.

2.1.6 Silicon Graphics Indy

The Indy is currently the only (mostly) supported Silicon Graphics machine. The only supported graphics card is the Newport card aka "XL" graphics. The Indy is available with a large number of CPU options at various clock rates all of which are supported. There is currently no X server available for the Indy; *Alan Cox (alan@lxorguk.ukuu.org.uk)* is working on one.

Strange numbers of available memory   On bootup the kernel on the Indy will report available memory with a message like

```
Memory: 27976k/163372k available (1220k kernel code, 2324k data)
```

The large difference between the first pair of numbers is caused by a 128mb area in the Indy's memory address space which mirrors up to the first 128mb of memory. The difference between the two numbers will always be about 128mb and does not indicate a problem of any kind.

Indy PROM related problems   Several people have reported these problems with their machines after upgrading them typically from surplus parts. There are several PROM versions for the Indy available. Machines with old PROM versions which have been upgraded to newer CPU variants like a R4600SC or R5000SC module can crash during the self test with an error message like

```
Exception: <vector=Normal>
Status register: 0x30004803<CU1,CU0,IM7,IM4,IPL=???,MODE=KERNEL,EXL,IE>
Cause register: 0x4000<CE=0,IP7,EXC=INT>
Exception PC: 0xbfc0b598
Interrupt exception
CPU Parity Error Interrupt
Local I/O interrupt register 1: 0x80 <VR/GIO2>
CPU parity error register: 0x80b<B0,B1,B3,SYSAD_PAR>
CPU parity error: address: 0x1fc0b598
NESTED EXCEPTION #1 at EPC: 9fc3df00; first exception at PC: bfc0b598
```

In that case you'll have to upgrade your machine's PROMs to a newer version or go back to an older CPU version. Usually R4000SC or R4400SC modules should work in that case. Just to be clear, this is a problem which is unrelated to Linux. It's only mentioned here because several Linux users have asked about it.

ELF support in old PROM versions   Old PROM versions don't know about the ELF binary format which the Linux kernel uses, that is can't boot Linux directly. The preferable solution for this is of course a PROM upgrade. Alternatively you can use Sash of IRIX 5 or newer to boot the kernel. Sash knows how to load ELF binaries and doesn't care if it's an IRIX or Linux kernel. Simply type "Sash" to the prom monitor. You should get another shell prompt, this time from Sash. Now launch Linux as usual.

Sash can read EFS or XFS filesystems or read the kernel from bootp / tftp. That means if you intend to use Sash for booting the kernel from local disk you'll still have to have a minimal IRIX installation on your system.

Why is so much memory reserved on my Indy?   On bootup the 'Memory: ...' message on an Indy says that there is 128mb of RAM reserved. That is ok; just like the PC architecture has a gap in its memory address space between 640kb and 1024kb, the Indy has a 128mb-sized area in its memory map where the first 128mb of its memory is mirrored. Linux knows about it and just ignores that memory, thus this message.

2.1.7   Silicon Graphics Challenge S

This machine is very similar to the Indy; the difference is that it doesn't have a keyboard and a GFX card but has an additional SCSI WD33C95 based adapter. This WD33C95 hostadapter is currently not supported.

2.1.8   Silicon Graphics Indigo

This machine is only being mentioned here because occasionally people have confused it with Indys. The Indigo series is a different architecture however and therefore yet unsupported. *Andrew R. Baker (andrewb@uab.edu)* announced a university project to port Linux to the Indigo on January 2, 1999.

2.1.9   Serial console on SGI machines

Make sure the kernel you're using includes the appropriate driver for a serial interface and serial console. Set the *console* ARC environment variable to either the value *d1* or *d2* for Indy and Challenge S depending on which serial interface you're going to use as console.

If you have the problem that all kernel messages appear on the serial console on bootup but everything is missing from the point when init starts, then you probably have the wrong setup for your /dev/console. You can find more information about this in the Linux kernel source documentation; it's in /usr/src/linux/Documentation/serial-console.txt if you have the kernel source installed.

2.1.10 Motorola 68k based machines like the Iris 3000

These are *very* old machines, probably more than ten years old by now. As these machines are not based on MIPS processors this document is the wrong place to search for information. However, in order to make things easy, these machines are currently not supported.

2.1.11 SGI VisPC

This is actually an x86 based system, therefore not covered by this FAQ. But to make your search for answers simple, here it is. *Ken Klingman (kck@mailbox.esd.sgi.com)* posted on January 17, 1999 to SGI's Linux mailing list:

```
We are working on it.  We're actually close to getting
the base level system support into the 2.2 release.
Software-only X and OpenGL should follow relatively
shortly, but hardware-accelerated OpenGL is still
some time off.  See www.precisioninsight.com for
news about hardware-accelerated OpenGL.
```

For more information see the Documentation/ of Linux kernel versions from 2.2.0 and newer. There is additional information available on the web on `<http://www.linux.sgi.com/intel/>`. Note that the SGI/MIPS and SGI/Intel people are working independently of each other, therefore the sources in the anonymous CVS on linus.linux.sgi.com may or may not work for Intel machines; we don't test this.

2.1.12 Other Silicon Graphics machines

At this time no other Silicon Graphics machine is supported. This also applies to the *very* old Motorola 68k based systems.

2.1.13 Sony Playstation

The Sony Playstation is based on an R3000 derivative and uses a set of graphics chips developed by Sony themselves. While the machine in theory would be capable of running Linux, a port is difficult, since Sony so far hasn't provided the necessary technical information. This still leaves the question of whether the port would be worthwhile. So in short, nothing has happend yet even though many people have shown their interest in trying Linux on a Playstation so far.

2.1.14 SNI RM200C

In contrast to the RM200 (see below) this machine has EISA and PCI slots. The RM200 is supported with the exception of the availability of the onboard NCR53c810A SCSI controller.

2.1.15 SNI RM200

If your machine has both EISA and PCI slots, then it is an RM200C; please see above. Due to the slight architectural differences of the RM200 and the RM200C this machine isn't currently supported in the official sources. *Michael Engel (engel@numerik.math.uni-siegen.de)* has managed to get his RM200 working partially but the patches haven't yet been included in the official Linux/MIPS sources.

2.1.16 SNI RM300C

The RM300 is technically very similar to the RM200C. It should be supported by the current Linux kernel, but we haven't yet received any reports.

2.1.17 SNI RM400

The RM400 isn't supported.

2.1.18 Algorithmics P4032

The Algorithmics P4032 port is at the time of this writing still running Linux 2.1.36.

2.1.19 Algorithmics P5064

The P5064 is basically an R5000-based 64bit variant of the P4032. It's not yet supported but a Linux port will be quite easy.

2.1.20 DECstation series

Support for DECstations is under development, started by Paul M. Antoine. These days most of the work is done by *Harald Koerfgen (harald.koerfgen@netcologne.de)* and others. On the Internet, DECstation-related information can be found at `<http://decstation.unix-ag.org/>`. The intention is to support all different flavours of DECstations that exist.

These are the DECstation models we know about:

- 2100, codename PMAX
- 3100, Is identical to the 2100 except the R2000A/R2010A @ 16 MHz
- 5000/xx (Personal DECstation), codename MAXine
- 5000/1xx, codename 3MIN
- 5000/200, codename 3MAX
- 5000/2x0, codename 3MAX+
- 5100, codename MIPSMATE

The 2100 has a R2000A/R2010A processor at 12 MHz, the 5000/240 a R3040 processor at 40 MHz (what has a 5k/260 ?) and the 5100 a R3000A processor at 20 MHz. The other mentioned 5000's have R3000A/R3010A processor at 20, 25 or 33 MHz. The MAXine and the 3MIN have the processor and cache on a separate daughterboard that can be exchanged for a R4000 processor at 50 MHz.

At the moment of this writing serial and ethernet device drivers for the on-board IC's are being developed, the 3MIN is booting single user.

2.1.21 Mips Magnum 4000 / Olivetti M700-10

These two machines are almost completely identical. Back during the ACE initiative Olivetti licensed the Jazz design and marketed the machine with Windows NT as OS. MIPS Computer Systems, Inc. itself bought the Jazz design and marketed it as the MIPS Magnum 4000 series of machines. Magnum 4000 systems were marketed with Windows NT and RISC/os as operating systems.

The firmware on the machine depended on the operating system which was installed. Linux/MIPS supports only the little endian firmware on these two types of machines. Since the M700-10 was only marketed as an NT machine all M700-10 machines have this firmware installed. The MIPS Magnum case is somewhat more complex. If your machine has been configured big endian for RISC/os then you need to reload the little endian firmware. This firmware was originally included on a floppy with the delivery of every Magnum. If you don't have the floppy anymore you can download it via anonymous ftp from `<ftp://ftp.fnet.fr>`.

It is possible to reconfigure the M700 for headless operation by setting the firmware environment variables ConsoleIn and ConsoleOut to multi()serial(0)term(). Also try the command *listdev* which will show the available ARC devices.

In some cases, like where the G364 graphics card is missing but the console is still configured to use normal graphics it will be necessary to set the configuration jumper JP2 on the board. After the next reset the machine will reboot with the console on COM2.

2.1.22 MIPS Magnum 4000SC

The Mips Magnum 4000SC is the same as a Magnum 4000 (see above) with the exception that it uses an R4000SC CPU.

2.1.23 VaxStation

As the name already implies this machine is a member of Digital Equipment's VAX family. It's mentioned here because people often confuse it with Digital's MIPS based DECstation family due to the similar type numbers. These two families of architectures share little technical similarities. Unfortunately the VaxStation, like the entire VAX family, is currently unsupported.

2.2 Processor types

2.2.1 R2000, R3000 family

The R2000 is the original MIPS processor. It's a 32 bit processor which was clocked at 8MHz back in '85 when the first MIPS processors came to the market. Later versions were clocked faster: for instance, the R3000 is a 100% compatible redesign of the R2000, just clocked faster. Because of their high compatibility, where this document mentions the R3000, in most cases the same facts also apply to the R2000.

The R3000 is basically an R2000 plus an R3010 FPU and 64k cache running at up to 40Mhz and integrated into the same chip. Support for the R3000 processor is currently in the works by various people. *Harald Koerfgen (harald.koerfgen@netcologne.de)* and *Gleb O. Raiko (raiko@niisi.msk.ru)* have both independently worked on patches which haven't yet been integrated into the official Linux/MIPS sources.

2.2.2 R6000

Sometimes people confuse the R6000, a MIPS processor, with RS6000, a series of workstations made by IBM. So if you're reading this in hope of finding out more about Linux on IBM machines you're reading the wrong document.

The R6000 is currently not supported. It is a 32-bit MIPS ISA 2 processor and a pretty interesting and weird piece of silicon. It was developed and produced by a company named *BIT Technology*. Later NEC took over the semiconductor production. It was built in ECL technology, the same technology that was and still is being used to build extremely fast chips like those used in some Cray computers. The processor had its TLB implemented as part of the last couple of lines of the external primary cache, a technology called *TLB slice*. That means its MMU is substantially different from those of the R3000 or R4000 series, which is also one of the reasons why the processor isn't supported.

2.2.3 R4000 and R5000 family

Linux supports many of the members of the R4000 family. Currently these are R4000PC, R4400PC, R4300, R4600, R4700, R5000, R5230, R5260. Many others are probably working as well.

Not supported are R4000MC and R4400MC CPUs (that is multiprocessor systems) as well R5000 systems with a CPU controlled second level cache. This means where the cache is controlled by the R5000 itself in contrast to some external external cache controller. The difference is important because, unlike other systems, especially PCs, on MIPS the cache is architecturally visible and needs to be controlled by software.

Special credit goes to *Ulf Carlsson (grim@zigzegv.ml.org)* who provided the CPU module for debugging the R4000SC / R4400SC support.

2.2.4 R8000

The R8000 is currently unsupported partly because this processor is relatively rare and has only been used in a few SGI machines, partly because the Linux/MIPS developers don't have such a machine.

The R8000 is a pretty interesting piece of silicon. Unlike the other members of the MIPS family it is a set of seven chips. Its cache and TLB architecture is pretty different from the other members of the MIPS family. It was born as a hack to get the floating point crown back to Silicon Graphics before the R10000 is finished.

HOWTO

2.2.5 R10000

The R10000 is currently unsupported because the Linux/MIPS developers don't have an R10000 machine.

3 Linux distributions.

3.1 RedHat

For MIPSeb, there's Rough Cuts Linux, previously known as Hard Hat Linux, which is most of Red Hat Linux 5.1 ported for MIPSeb. You can get this at `<ftp://ftp.linux.sgi.com/pub/hardhat>`.

It is also bundled along with M68k, UltraSparc and PowerPC in a package called "Rough Cuts" pressed by Red Hat, and available wherever Red Hat products are sold. This is a very convenient way to get it without having to download 280MB. You can order Rough Cuts directly from Red Hat at `<http://www.redhat.com/product.phtml/RC1000>`.

As well, there's a distribution based on Red Hat 5.2 that's targetting the Cobalt Qubes; those binaries will work perfectly on other MIPSel architectures available at `<ftp://intel.cleveland.lug.net/pub/Mipsel>`.

4 Linux/MIPS net resources.

4.1 Anonymous FTP servers.

The two primary anonymous FTP servers for Linux/MIPS are

ftp.linux.sgi.com

> This server should satisfy almost all your Linux/MIPS related ftp desires. Really.

ftp.fnet.fr

> This server is currently pretty outdated; it's included here mostly for completeness and for people with interest in prehistoric software.

On all these ftp servers there is a list of mirror sites you may want to use for faster access.

4.2 Anonymous CVS servers.

For those who always want to stay on the bleeding edge and want to avoid having to download patch files or full tarballs we also have an anonymous CVS server. Using CVS you can checkout the Linux/MIPS source tree with the following commands:

```
cvs -d :pserver:cvs@linus.linux.sgi.com:/cvs login
(Only needed the first time you use anonymous CVS, the password is "cvs")
cvs -d :pserver:cvs@linus.linux.sgi.com:/cvs co <repository>
```

where you insert linux, libc, or gdb for <repository>.

The other important CVS archive of the Linux community is vger.rutgers.edu where a lot of code is being collected before being sent to Linus for distribution. Although vger itself no longer offers anonymous access, there are mirror sites which do provide anonymous access. For details how to access them see . The modules which are of interest are "linux", "modutils", "pciutils", "netutils".

4.3   Web servers.

The two primary anonymous web servers for Linux/MIPS are

www.linux.sgi.com

This server covers most of Linux/MIPS; it's somewhat SGI centric but since Linux/MIPS tries to be the same on every platform most of its information is of interest to all users.

lena.fnet.fr

This server is currently pretty outdated; it's included here mostly for completeness.

All these servers have mirrors scattered all over the world; you may want to use one for best performance.

4.4   Mailing lists.

There are three Linux/MIPS oriented mailing lists:

linux-mips@fnet.fr

This mailing list is used for most non-SGI related communication of all kinds. Subscription is handled by a human; send your subscription requests to *linux-mips-mips@fnet.fr*. You can unsubscribe from this mailing list by sending *unsubscribe <your-email-address>* to the same address.

linux@engr.sgi.com

This mailing list currently has the most traffic. It's somewhat SGI-centric but is nevertheless of interest especially to developers as a good number of SGI engineers are subscribed to this list. Subscription to this list is handled via *Majordomo (majordomo@engr.sgi.com)*; just send an email with the words *subscribe linux-mips*. In order to unsubscribe send *unsubscribe linux-mips*. Note that you have to be subscribed if you want to post; the growth of spam forced us into that policy.

linux-mips@vger.rutgers.edu

This mailing list has only very low traffic as most people tend to use one of the above mailing lists. Subscription is handled via *Majordomo (majordomo@vger.rutgers.edu)*; just send an email with the words *subscribe linux-mips*. In order to unsubscribe send *unsubscribe linux-mips*.

5   Installation of Linux/MIPS and common problems.

5.1   NFS booting fails.

Usually the reason for this is that people have unpacked the tar archive under IRIX, not Linux. Since the representation of device files over NFS is not standardized between various Unices, this fails. The symptom is that the system dies with the error message "Warning: unable to open an initial console." right after mounting the NFS filesystem.

For now the workaround is to use a Linux system (doesn't need to be MIPS) to unpack the installation archive onto the NFS server. The NFS server itself may be any type of UNIX.

5.2   Self compiled kernels crash when booting.

When I build my own kernel, it crashes. On an Indy the crash message looks like the following; the same problem hits other machines as well but may look completely different.

```
Exception: <vector=UTLB Miss>
Status register: 0x300004803<CU1,CU0,IM4,IPL=???,MODE=KERNEL,EXL,IE>
Cause register: 0x8008<CE=0,IP8,EXC=RMISS>
Exception PC: 0x881385cc, Exception RA: 0x88002614
exception, bad address: 0x47c4
```

```
Local I/O interrupt register 1: 0x80 <VR/GIO2>
Saved user regs in hex (&gpda 0xa8740e48, &_regs 0xa8741048):
  arg: 7 8bfff938 8bfffc4d 880025dc
  tmp: 8818c14c 8818c14c 10 881510c4 14 8bfad9e0 0 48
  sve: 8bfdf3e8 8bfffc40 8bfb2720 8bfff938 a8747420 9fc56394 0 9fc56394
  t8 48 t9 8bfffee66 at 1 v0 0 v1 8bfff890 k1 bad11bad
  gp 881dfd90 fp 9fc4be88 sp 8bfff8b8 ra 88002614

PANIC: Unexpected exception
```

This problem is caused by a still unfixed bug in Binutils newer than version 2.7. As a workaround, change the following line in arch/mips/Makefile from:

```
LINKFLAGS        = -static -N
```

to:

```
LINKFLAGS        = -static
```

5.3   Booting the kernel on the Indy fails with PROM error messages

```
>> boot bootp()/vmlinux
73264+592+11520+331680+27848d+3628+5792 entry: 0x8df9a960
Setting $netaddres to 192.168.1.5 (from server deadmoon)
Obtaining /vmlinux from server deadmoon

Cannot load bootp()/vmlinux
Illegal f_magic number 0x7f45, expected MIPSELMAGIC or MIPSEBMAGIC.
```

This problem only happens for Indys with very old PROM versions which cannot handle the ELF binary format which Linux uses. A solution for this problem is in the works.

5.4   Where can I get the little endian firmware for my SNI?

SNI's system can be operated in both big and little endian modes. At this time Linux/MIPS only supports the little endian firmware. This is somewhat unlucky since SNI hasn't shipped that firmware for quite some time, since they dropped NT.

When running in big endian mode the firmware looks similar to an SGI Indy which is already supported, therefore fixing the SNI support will be relativly easy. Interested hackers should contact *Ralf Bächle (ralf@gnu.org)*.

5.5   ld dies with signal 6

```
collect2: ld terminated with signal 6 [Aborted]
```

This is a known bug in older binutils versions. You will have to upgrade to binutils 2.8.1 plus very current patches.

6   Milo

Milo is the boot loader used to boot the little endian MIPS systems with ARC firmware, currently the Jazz family and the SNI RM 200. While Milo uses the same name and has a similar purpose to the Alpha version of Milo, these two Milos have nothing else in common. They were developed by different people, don't share any code, and work on different hardware platforms. The fact that both have the same name is just a kind of historic "accident".

Plans are to remove the need for Milo in the near future.

6.1   Building Milo

The building procedure of Milo is described in detail in the README files in the Milo package. Since Milo has some dependencies to kernel header files which have changed over time Milo often cannot be built easily; however the Milo distribution includes binaries for both Milo and Pandora.

6.2   Pandora

Pandora is a simple debugger. It has been primarily developed in order to analyze undocumented systems. Pandora includes a dissassembler, memory dump functions and more. If you only want to use Linux there is no need to install Pandora. It's small though.

7   Loadable Modules

Using modules on Linux/MIPS is quite easy; it should work as expected for people who have used it on other Linux systems. If you want to run a module-based system then you should have at least kernel version 980919 and modutils newer than version 2.1.121 installed. Older versions won't work.

8   How do I setup a crosscompiler?

First of all go and download the following source packages:

- binutils-2.8.1.tar.gz
- egcs-1.0.2.tar.gz
- glibc-2.0.6.tar.gz
- glibc-crypt-2.0.6.tar.gz
- glibc-localedata-2.0.6.tar.gz
- glibc-linuxthreads-2.0.6.tar.gz

These are the currently recommended versions. Older versions may or may not be working. If you're trying to use older versions please don't send bug reports; we don't care. When installing please install things in the order binutils, egcs, then glibc. Unless you have older versions already installed, changing the order *will* fail. The installation description below mentions a number of patches which you can get from the respective SRPM packages on *ftp.linux.sgi.com*. However since these SRPM packages are intended to be compiled natively it's not possible to just rebuild them.

8.1   Diskspace requirements

For the installation you'll have to choose a directory for installation. I'll refer to that directory below with <prefix>. To avoid a certain problem it's best to use the same value for <prefix> as your native gcc. For example if your gcc is installed in /usr/bin/gcc then choose /usr for <prefix>. You must use the same <prefix> value for all the packages that you're going to install.

During compilation you'll need about 31mb diskspace for binutils; for installation you'll need 7mb diskspace for on <prefix>'s partition. Building egcs requires 71mb and installation 14mb. GNU libc requires 149mb diskspace during compilation and 33mb for installation. Note these numbers are just a guideline and may differ significantly for different processor and operating system architectures.

8.2 Byte order

One of the special features of the MIPS architecture is that all processors except the R8000 can be configured to run either in big or in little endian mode. Byte order means the way the processor stores multibyte numbers in memory. Big endian machines store the byte with the highest value digits at the lowest address while little endian machines store it at the highest address. Think of it as writing multi-digit numbers from left to right or vice versa.

In order to setup your crosscompiler correctly you have to know the byte order of the crosscompiler target. If you don't already know, check the section 2.1 (Hardware Platforms) for your machine's byteorder.

8.3 Configuration names

Many of the packages based on autoconf support many different architectures and operating systems. In order to differentiate between these many configurations, names are constructed with <cpu>-<company>-<os> or even <cpu>-<company>-<kernel>-<os>. Expressed this way the configuration names of Linux/MIPS are mips-unknown-linux-gnu for big endian targets or mipsel-unknown-linux-gnu for little endian targets. These names are a bit long and are allowed to be abbreviated to mips-linux or mipsel-linux. You *must* use the same configuration name for all packages that comprise your crosscompilation environment. Also, while other names like mips-sni-linux or mipsel-sni-linux are legal configuration names, use mips-linux or mipsel-linux instead; these are the configuration names known to other packages like the Linux kernel sources and they'd otherwise have to be changed for crosscompilation.

I'll refer to the target configuration name below with <target>.

8.4 Installation of GNU Binutils.

This is the first and simplest part - at least as long as you're trying to install on any halfway-sane UNIX flavour. Just cd into a directory with enough free space and do the following:

```
gzip -cd binutils-<version>.tar.gz | tar xf -
cd binutils-<version>
patch -p1 < ../binutils-<version>-mips.patch
./configure --prefix=<prefix> --target=<target>
make CFLAGS=-O2
make install
```

This usually works very easily. On certain machines using GCC 2.7.x as compiler is known to dump core. This is a known bug in GCC and can be fixed by upgrading to GCC 2.8.1 or egcs.

8.5 Assert.h

Some people have an old assert.h headerfile installed, probably a leftover from an old crosscompiler installation. This file may cause autoconf scripts to fail silently; it was never necessary and was only installed because of a bug in older GCC versions. Check to see if the file <prefix>/<target>/include/assert.h exists in your installation. If so, just delete the it: it should never have been installed.

8.6 First installation of egcs

Now the not-so-funny part begins: there is a so-called bootstrap problem. In our case that means the installation process of egcs needs an already- installed glibc, but we cannot compile glibc because we don't have a working crosscompiler yet. Luckily you'll only have to go through this once when you install a crosscompiler for the first time. Later when you already have glibc installed things will be much smoother. So now do:

```
gzip -cd egcs-<version>.tar.gz | tar xf -
cd egcs-<version>
for i in egcs-1.0.2-libio.patch egcs-1.0.2-hjl.patch \
    egcs-1.0.2-rth1.patch egcs-1.0.2-rth2.patch egcs-1.0.2-rth3.patch \
    egcs-1.0.2-rth4.patch egcs-1.0.2-hjl2.patch egcs-1.0.2-jim.patch \
    egcs-1.0.2-haifa.patch egcs-1.0.1-objcbackend.patch \
    egcs-1.0.2-mips.patch; do patch -p1 -d < ../$i; done
./configure --prefix=<prefix> --with-newlib --target=<target>
cd gcc
make LANGUAGES="c"
```

Note that we deliberately don't build gcov, protoize, unprotoize and the libraries. Gcov doesn't make sense in a cross-compiler environment and protoize and unprotoize might even overwrite your native programs - this is a bug in the gcc makefiles. Finally we cannot build the libraries because we don't have glibc installed yet. If everything went successfully, install with:

```
make LANGUAGES="c" install
```

8.7 float.h

Another bootstrap problem is that building GCC requires running programs on the machine for which GCC will generate code, but since a crosscompiler is running on a different type of machine this cannot work. When building GCC this happens for the header file float.h. Luckily there is a simple solution: download the header file from one of the Linux/MIPS ftp servers or rip it from one of the native Linux/MIPS binary packages. Later when recompiling or upgrading egcs usually the already-installed float.h file will do because float.h changes rarely. Install it with:

```
cp float.h <prefix>/<target/<version>/include/float.h
```

where <version> is the internal version number of the egcs version you're using. For egcs 1.0.2 for example you would use egcs-2.90.27 for <version>. If not sure - ls is your friend.

8.8 Installing the kernel sources

Installing the kernel sources is simple. Just place them into some directory of your choice and configure them such that some files which are generated by the procedure will be installed. This works the same as you're used to when configuring the kernel sources for native compilation. The only problem you may run into is that you may need to install some required GNU programs like bash or have to override the manufacturer-provided versions of programs by placing the GNU versions earlier in the PATH variable. When configuring you should answer the question "Are you using a crosscompiler", that is the option CONFIG_CROSSCOMPILE, with "yes". When you're done with configuring type make clean; make depend; make. The last make command will generate the header file <linux/version.h> which compiling some programs depends on. This file is generated right at the beginning of the make command, so if you're not interested in actually building a kernel you may interrupt the compilation after this file has been built. It may be a good idea, however, to compile the kernel as a test for your newly-built crosscompiler.

If you only want the crosscompiler for building the kernel, you're done. Crosscompiling libc is only required to be able to compile user applications.

8.9 Installing GNU libc

Do:

```
gzip -cd glibc-2.0.6.tar.gz | tar xf -
cd glibc-2.0.6
gzip -cd glibc-crypt-2.0.6.tar.gz | tar xf -
gzip -cd glibc-localedata-2.0.6.tar.gz | tar xf -
gzip -cd glibc-linuxthreads-2.0.6.tar.gz | tar xf -
patch -p1 < ../glibc-2.0.6-mips.patch
mkdir build
cd build
CC=<target>-gcc BUILD_CC=gcc AR=<target>-ar RANLIB=<target>-ranlib \
        ../configure --prefix=/usr --host=<target> \
        --enable-add-ons=crypt,linuxthreads,localedata --enable-profile
make
```

You now have a compiled GNU libc which still needs to be installed. Do *not* just type make install. That would overwrite your host system's files with Linux/MIPS-specific files with disastrous effects. Instead install GNU libc into some other arbitrary directory <somedir> from which we'll move the parts we need for crosscompilation into the actual target directory:

```
make install_root=<somedir> install
```

Now cd into <somedir> and finally install GNU libc manually:

```
cd usr/include
find . -print | cpio -pumd <prefix>/<target>/include
cd ../../lib
find . -print | cpio -pumd <prefix>/<target>/lib
cd ../usr/lib
find . -print | cpio -pumd <prefix>/<target>/lib
```

GNU libc also contains extensive online documentation. Your systems might already have a version of this documentation installed, so if you don't want to install the info pages, which will save you a less than a megabyte, or already have them installed, skip the next step:

```
cd ../info
gzip -9 *.info*
find . -name \*.info\* -print | cpio -pumd <prefix>/info
```

If you're not bootstrapping your installation is now finished.

8.10 Building egcs again

The first attempt of building egcs was stopped by lack of a GNU libc. Since we now have libc installed we can rebuild egcs but this time as complete as a crosscompiler installation can be:

```
gzip -cd egcs-<version>.tar.gz | tar xf -
cd egcs-<version>
```

```
for i in egcs-1.0.2-libio.patch egcs-1.0.2-hjl.patch \
      egcs-1.0.2-rth1.patch egcs-1.0.2-rth2.patch egcs-1.0.2-rth3.patch \
      egcs-1.0.2-rth4.patch egcs-1.0.2-hjl2.patch egcs-1.0.2-jim.patch \
      egcs-1.0.2-haifa.patch egcs-1.0.1-objcbackend.patch \
      egcs-1.0.2-mips.patch; do patch -p1 < ../$i; done
./configure --prefix=<prefix> --target=<target>
make LANGUAGES="c c++ objective-c f77"
```

As you can see the procedure is the same as the first time with the exception that we dropped the –with-newlib option. This option was necessary to avoid the libgcc build breaking due to the lack of libc. Now install with:

```
make LANGUAGES="c c++ objective-c f77" install
```

You're almost finished. All you have left to do now is to reinstall float.h, which has been overwritten by the last make install command. You'll have to do this every time you reinstall egcs as a crosscompiler. If you think you don't need the Objective C or F77 compilers you can omit them from above commands; each will save you about 3mb. Do not build gcov, protoize or unprotoize.

8.11   Should I build the C++, Objective C or F77 compilers?

The answer to this question largely depends on your use of your crosscompiler environment. If you only intend to rebuild the Linux kernel then you have no need for the full blown setup and can safely omit the Objective C and F77 compilers. You must, however, build the C++ compiler, because building the libraries included with the egcs distribution requires C++.

8.12   GDB

Building GDB as crossdebugger is only of interest to kernel developers; for them GDB may be a life saver. Such a remote debugging setup always consists of two parts: the remote debugger GDB running on one machine and the target machine running the Linux/MIPS kernel being debugged. The machines are typically interconnected with a serial line. The target machine's kernel needs to be equipped with a "debugging stub" which communicates with the GDB host machine using the remote serial protocol.

Depending on the target's architecture you may have to implement the debugging stub yourself. In general you'll only have to write very simple routines for serial. The task is further simplified by the fact that most machines are using similar serial hardware typically based on the 8250, 16450 or derivatives.

9   Related Literature

9.1   See MIPS Run

author Dominic Sweetman, published Morgan Kaufmann, ISBN 1-55860-410-3.

This is intended as a pretty comprehensive guide to programming MIPS, wherever it's different from programming any other 32-bit CPU. It's the first time anyone tried to write a readable and comprehensive explanation and account of the wide range of MIPS CPUs available, and should be very helpful for anyone programming MIPS who isn't insulated by someone else's operating system. And the author is a free-unix enthusiast who subscribes to the Linux/MIPS mailing list!

John Hennessey, father of the MIPS architecture, was kind enough to write in the foreword: " ... this book is the best combination of completeness and readability of any book on the MIPS architecture ..."

It includes some context about RISC CPUs, a description of the architecture and instruction set including the "co-processor 0" instructions used for CPU control; sections on caches, exceptions, memory management and floating point. There's a detailed assembly language guide, some stuff about porting, and some fairly heavy-duty software examples.

Available from:

- `<http://www.algor.co.uk/algor/info/seemipsrun.html>` (europe)
- `<http://www.mkp.com/books_catalog/1-55860-410-3.asp>` (US)

and from good bookshops anywhere. It's 512 pages and costs around $50 in the US, £39.95 in the UK.

I'd be inclined to list two other books too, both from Morgan Kaufmann and available from www.mkp.com or any good bookshop:

9.2 The MIPS Programmer's Handbook

authors Farquhar and Bunce, published by Morgan Kaufmann, ISBN 1-55860-297-6.

A readable introduction to the practice of programming MIPS at the low level, by the author of PMON. Strengths: lots of examples; weakness: leaves out some big pieces of the architecture (such as memory management, floating point and advanced caches) because they didn't feature in the LSI "embedded" products this book was meant to partner.

9.3 Computer Architecture - A Quantitative Approach

authors Hennessy & Patterson, published Morgan Kaufmann, ISBN 1-58860-329-8.

The bible of modern computer architecture and a must-read if you want to understand what makes programs run slow or fast. Is it about MIPS? Well, it's mostly about something very *like* MIPS... Its sole defect is its size and weight - but unlike most big books it's worth every page.

10 Linux/MIPS news

Some of this chapter is pretty historic ...

04-Dec-98

Ariel Faigon announces that SGI has joined Linux International.

13-Oct-98

Ralf Bächle fixes the support for R4000SC / R4400SC CPUs.

12-Oct-98

Vladimir Roganov reports that his R3000 system is now stable enough to compile GDB.

03-Oct-98

Harald Körfgen reports that his DECstation 5000/133 is now running single user. Congratulations!

29-Sep-98

Ralf starts rewriting this FAQ to fit with reality.

10-Jun-98

ftp.linux.sgi.com now offers anonymous CVS access.

01-Feb-98

First commercial Linux/MIPS based product accounced.

26-Jan-98

One more timewarp in this list because the maintainer is lazy^H^H^H^H busy coding. The driver for the NCR53c8xx has been modified and has been successfully tested with several machines, most notably the SNI RM200. Even better, the initial version seems to be reliable.

Already some time ago Thomas Bogendörfer implemented the necessary changes to the NCR53C9x driver aka ESP driver, so there is now SCSI support for the builtin hostadapters in the Mips Magnum 4000, Olivetti M700-10 and Acer PICA.

28-Nov-97

First public release of X11 client binaries.

30-Aug-97

Duh, time warp in this page once again. A lot has happend in the meantime and the maintainer of this pages is a lazy person that rather prefers to code and hack than write docs...

SGI now has its own Linux/MIPS server reachable as http://www.linux.sgi.com, with lots of SGI specific information and many links. The server is also reachable under ftp.linux.sgi.com. In addition to binaries, sources and docs specific to Silicon Graphic machines this server also has all the other Linux/MIPS stuff in stock. Only available on this server is the developers' cvs archive for download. Sorry, no anonymous CVS yet.

Silicon Graphics has supported some of the Linux key developers' work on Linux/MIPS with hardware. As a result the work is now advancing more quickly and Ralf is no longer the lone workhorse ...

Already available for some time the Indy port is now in the standard kernel source tree.

Long missing, but finally there: Thomas Bogendoerfer contributed patches to the NCR53C9x driver for Mips Magnum 4000, Olivetti M700 and Acer PICA.

Many more packages of a RedHat port to MIPS are now available for ftp download. Installing is still more a thing for experts ... but we're working on it!

Eeecmacs lovers will be pleased to hear that this FAQ has been edited by Emacs running on a Linux/MIPS machine.

6-May-97

David Monro releases version 1.01 of bfsd. bfsd is a daemon that can be used to boot the machines built by Mips Computersystems, Inc. over a network.

10-Jun-96

Release of Linux/MIPS kernel 2.0.4. This release features a partially rewritten signal handler that should match POSIX.1.

3-Jun-96

First release of shared libraries for Linux/MIPS based on GNU libc snapshot 960619.

Release of Linux/MIPS kernel 2.0.1.

25-May-96

David S. Miller starts working on SGI support at Silicon Graphics.

20-May-96

Release 1.3.98 of the kernel adds support for the SNI RM200 PCI.

27-Mar-96

Linux/MIPS works as NFS server.

The IDE CD driver now also supports Linux/MIPS.

24-Mar-96

Added reference to literature available online form SGI to the FAQ.

23-Mar-96

New chapter in the FAQ about the ARC standard.

27-Jan-96

Release of Milo 0.26 and a kernel patch to use it. This release passes parameters to the kernel in a completely different way that makes porting Linux/MIPS to another architecture a lot easier.

HOWTO

24-Jan-96

Release of crosscompiler binaries based on the FSF's Binutils version 2.6. This release brings lots of new features and many bugfixes.

21-Jan-96

Warner Losh started working on a port of Linux/MIPS to Deskstation rPC44.

20-Jan-96

Linux/MIPS kernel updated to version 1.3.58.

Patch gcc-2.7.2-1.diffs.gz has been released.

Patch binutils-2.6-1.diffs.gz has been released. This patch contains lots of bugfixes. The Linux kernel Makefiles will automatically detect whether Binutils 2.6 or an older version is installed and use the new features resulting in a much smaller kernel executable which is especially useful for bootdisks.

15-Jan-96

Release of a complete root and /usr filesystem that can be NFS mounted to use a Linux/MIPS system as a diskless client. A native development kit based on GCC 2.7.2, Binutils 2.6 and GNU libc snapshot 951218 is included as well as many of the standard utilities.

25-Dec-95

Linux/MIPS boots off an NFS filesystem as a diskless client. This also means that the rest of Linux/MIPS networking is operational now.

7-Jan-95

Soft-N-Hard GMBH and SNI sign a contract. SNI will loan an RM200 to Soft-N-Hard for porting Linux/MIPS to it.

22-Sep-95

The Linux/MIPS FTP archive and mailing list have been moved to fnet.fr. (There is much more news I currently have no time to document)

18-Jul-95

New crossdevelopment tools released. GCC-2.6.3-2 and Binutils-2.5.2-2 for Linux/i386 need kernels with ELF support and libc-5.0.9 installed. The new crossdev tools are required for Linux/MIPS kernels above 1.2.9. A.out versions of the crossdev tools will follow soon.

14-Jul-95

We have a working shell!

12-Jul-95

Patches 2.6.3-2 for Linux/MIPS GCC released. This compiler better complies with the MIPS standard of symbol names.

10-Jul-95

Linux/MIPS kernel 1.2.9 released.

9-Jun-95

Milo 0.24 released. This version features improved machine type detection and many cleanups and bugfixes.

24-May-95

Linux/MIPS kernel 1.2.8 released. This version features many bugfixes and has the Magnum 4000 specific changes from Linux-1.2.7 integrated.

Milo 0.23 released. This version features built-in support for Olivetti M700 machines. Milo is now split into two binaries: A simple bootloader and a standalone debugger/monitor with boot capability.

23-5-95

Linux/MIPS kernel 1.2.7 on Olivetti M700 mounts root file system.

22-May-95

Linux/MIPS kernel 1.2.7 on Mips Magnum 4000 mounts root file system.

Added NEC RiscStation and RiscServer to target list.

Milo 0.22 successfully tested on NEC RiscStation and RiscServer.

18-May-95

Linux/MIPS kernel 1.2.7 released. This release features initial Magnum 4000 support and tons of bugfixes.

12-May-95

Milo 0.22 released. This version contains some cleanups and several bugfixes.

5-May-95

The Linux/MIPS archive is now also available from ftp://ftp.mcc.ac.uk/pub/linux/MIPS.

3-May-95

Milo 0.21 released. This version features more built-in debugger/monitor commands and contains some important bug fixes.

30-Apr-95

Milo 0.20 released. This version features a built-in debugger/monitor and a lot of new library functions.

Port to Olivetti M700 started.

26-Apr-95

Linux/MIPS kernel 1.2.6 released.

13-Apr-95

Milo 0.19 released. This version includes some minor fixes plus initial support for kernels in ELF format.

13-Apr-95

Milo 0.18b released. This version includes support for Mips Magnum 4000. Port to Mips Magnum 4000 started.

27-Mar-95

Linux/MIPS kernel 1.2.2 released. Kernel now mounts its root file system.

22-Mar-95

Milo 0.18 released. This version includes support for Deskstation rPC44 systems.

Port to DeskStation rPC44 started.

Part XXIV

"The Linux Electronic Mail HOWTO" Guylhem Aznar

<guylhem at oeil.qc.ca>
v2.2, January 1999
This document describes the setup, care and feeding of Electronic Mail (e-mail) under Linux. You need to read this if you plan to communicate locally or to remote sites via electronic mail. You probably do *not* need to read this document if don't exchange electronic mail with other users on your system or with other sites.

Contents

HOWTO

1   Introduction, copyright and standard disclaimer

1.1   Email and spamming

First, convert all "at" in Emails address to "@".

It's simple for humans, but not for bots searching the web to spam ; therefore it's enough to protect generous contributors from being spammed !

1.2   Goals

The intent of this document is to answer some of the questions and comments that appear to meet the definition of "frequently asked questions" about e-mail software under Linux in general and the version in the Linux Debian and RedHat distributions in particular.

1.3   New versions

New versions of this document will be periodically posted to comp.os.linux.announce, comp.answers and mail.answers. They will also be added to the various anonymous ftp sites who archive such information including *sunsite.unc.edu:/pub/Linux/docs/HOWTO*.

In addition, you should be generally able to find this document on the Linux WorldWideWeb home page at *http://sunsite.unc.edu/mdw/linux.html*.

1.4   Feedback

I am interested in any feedback, positive or negative, regarding the content of this document via e-mail. Definitely contact me if you find errors or obvious omissions.

I read, but do not necessarily respond to, all e-mail I receive. Requests for enhancements will be considered and acted upon based on that day's combination of available time, merit of the request and daily blood pressure :-)

Flames will quietly go to /dev/null so don't bother.

Feedback concerning the actual format of the document should go to the HOWTO coordinator : Greg Hankins (`gregh at sunsite.unc.edu`).

1.5   Copyright

The Mail-HOWTO is copyrighted (c) 1998 Guylhem Aznar. Distributed under LDP copyright license. If you have questions, please contact Greg Hankins, the Linux HOWTO coordinator, at `gregh at sunsite.unc.edu`.

1.6   Limited warranty

Of course, I disavow any potential liability for the contents of this document. Use of the concepts, examples, and/or other content of this document is entirely at your own risk.

2 Other sources of information

2.1 USENET

There is nothing "special" about configuring and running mail software under Linux (any more). Accordingly, you almost certainly do *NOT* want to be posting generic mail-related questions to the comp.os.linux.* newsgroups.

Don't post in comp.os.linux hierarchy unless it's really linux specific, for example : "Which options was Debian 1.2 sendmail compiled with ?" or "RedHat 5.0 smail crashes when I run it".

Let me repeat that.

There is virtually no reason to post anything mail-related in the comp.os.linux hierarchy any more. There are existing newsgroups in the comp.mail.* hierarchy to handle *ALL* your questions.

IF YOU POST TO COMP.OS.LINUX. FOR NON-LINUX-SPECIFIC QUESTIONS, YOU ARE LOOKING IN THE WRONG PLACE FOR HELP. THE MAIL EXPERTS HANG OUT IN THE PLACES INDICATED ABOVE AND GENERALLY DO NOT RUN LINUX.*

POSTING TO THE LINUX HIERARCHY FOR NON-LINUX-SPECIFIC QUESTIONS WASTES YOUR TIME AND EVERYONE ELSE'S AND IT FREQUENTLY DELAYS YOUR GETTING THE ANSWER TO YOUR QUESTION.

GOOD PLACES are :

```
comp.mail.elm           the ELM mail system.
comp.mail.mh            The Rand Message Handling system.
comp.mail.mime          Multipurpose Internet Mail Extensions.
comp.mail.misc          General discussions about computer mail.
comp.mail.multi-media   Multimedia Mail.
comp.mail.mush          The Mail User's Shell (MUSH).
comp.mail.sendmail      the BSD sendmail agent.
comp.mail.smail         the smail mail agent.
comp.mail.uucp          Mail in the uucp environment.
```

2.2 Mailing Lists

There are many sendmail, smail and qmail mailing lists.

You can find addresses in /usr/doc/the_one_you_have_chosen.

2.3 Other documents from LDP

There is plenty of excellent material provided in the other Linux HOWTO documents and from the Linux DOC project.

In particular, you might want to take a look at the following:

- on your own computer in /usr/doc/ :-)
- the Linux Networking Administrators' Guide
- the Serial Communications HOWTO
- the Ethernet HOWTO
- the UUCP HOWTO if you're fed via UUCP

2.4 Books

The following is a non-inclusive set of books that will help:

- "Managing UUCP and USENET" from O'Reilly and Associates is in my opinion the best book out there for figuring out the programs and protocols involved in being a USENET site.

- "Unix Communications" from The Waite Group contains a nice description of all the pieces (and more) and how they fit together.

- "Sendmail" from O'Reilly and Associates looks to be the definitive reference on sendmail-v8 and sendmail+IDA. It's a "must have" for anybody hoping to make sense out of sendmail without bleeding in the process.

- "The Internet Complete Reference" from Osborne is a fine reference book that explains the various services available on Internet and is a great source for information on news, mail and various other Internet resources.

- "The Linux Networking Administrators' Guide" from Olaf Kirch of the Linux Documentation Project is available on the net and is also published by (at least) O'Reilly and SSC.

  It makes a fine one-stop shopping to learn about everything you ever imagined you'd need to know about Unix networking.

3 Requirements

3.1 Hardware

There are no specific hardware requirements for mail under Linux.

You'll need some sort of 'transport' software to connect to remote systems, which means either TCP/IP or uucp.

This could mean that you need a modem or ethernet card, depending on your setup. In most cases, you'll want the fastest modem you can afford, i.e. V90 57 600 bps currently. In general, you want to have a 16550 UART on your serial board or built into your modem to handle speeds of above 9600 baud.

If you don't know what that last sentence means, please consult the comp.dcom.modems group or the various fine modem and serial communications FAQs and periodic postings on USENET.

3.2 Software

Well, the problem is here. Which mail software will you choose ?

There is currently qmail, smail, vmail and sendmail.

Each has its own features, but the better compromise is qmail, for high security (even is vmail is more secure), high speed (even is smail is faster for local uses) and ease of configuration.

Of course, feel free to choose any mail software, informations provided here shall only help you in your choice.

Sendmail can be nice for many sites with complicated options, but I think its configuration is too hard for beginners while it is not very secure or very fast, so there is only a **really** outdated sendmail section in this HOWTO.

If you know what you're doing, choose sendmail (and you shouldn't be reading this HOWTO !); otherwise I generally recommend qmail.

4 Qmail v1.03

Secured, fast and easy to use, this is my preferred MTA (mail transport agent).

Currently, no distribution comes with qmail, so we will focus on compiling and installing qmail, since this is the only tricky part : configuration is really straightforward.

4.1 Getting qmail

Go to www.qmail.org to download latest version.

4.2 Uncompressing sources

Then decompress it running :

```
mv qmail.tar.gz /usr/local/src
cd /usr/local/src ; tar -zxvf qmail.tar.gz
```

If you find a bz2 version (new and better compression format), just replace tar by :

```
bunzip2 qmail.tar.bz2
tar -xvf qmail.tar
```

4.3 Preparing compilation

Now enter qmail dir to check configuration defaults :

```
cd qmail; more conf-*
```

You shouldn't need to change any default, but you can for example specify an alternate installation dir or better compilation flags.

Now run :

```
mkdir /var/qmail
```

to create target dir.

If you haven't installed a Debian distribution, you'll need to add qmail own users : qmail's high security depends on that.

Nobody will be able to break your whole mail system or gain root access since qmail is divided into modules running each under their own UID.

So run :

```
# groupadd nofiles
# useradd -g nofiles -d /var/qmail/alias alias
# useradd -g nofiles -d /var/qmail qmaild
# useradd -g nofiles -d /var/qmail qmaill
# useradd -g nofiles -d /var/qmail qmailp
# groupadd qmail
# useradd -g qmail -d /var/qmail qmailq
# useradd -g qmail -d /var/qmail qmailr
# useradd -g qmail -d /var/qmail qmails
```

or hand-edit /etc/passwd and /etc/group to add these users by yourself : for example you can respectively add :

```
qmail:*:2107:
nofiles:*:2108:
```

```
          alias:*:7790:2108::/var/qmail/alias:/bin/true
          qmaild:*:7791:2108::/var/qmail/:/bin/true
          qmaill:*:7792:2108::/var/qmail/:/bin/true
          qmailp:*:7793:2108::/var/qmail/:/bin/true
          qmailq:*:7794:2107::/var/qmail/:/bin/true
          qmailr:*:7795:2107::/var/qmail/:/bin/true
          qmails:*:7796:2107::/var/qmail/:/bin/true
```

Now you can run

```
   make setup check
```

to check your configuration, then :

```
   ./config
```

to configure qmail.

Now you must install some aliases, since /etc/alias is not used by qmail unless you compile and install some optional package.

Here's my setup :

```
   File : ".qmail-MAILER-DAEMON"
   &postmaster
   File : ".qmail-bin"
   &root
   File : ".qmail-daemon"
   &root
   File : ".qmail-decode"
   &root
   File : ".qmail-dumper"
   &root
   File : ".qmail-games"
   &root
   File : ".qmail-ingres"
   &root
   File : ".qmail-mailer-daemon"
   &postmaster
   File : ".qmail-manager"
   &root
   File : ".qmail-news"
   &root
   File : ".qmail-nobody"
   &root
   File : ".qmail-operator"
   &root
   File : ".qmail-postmaster"
   &root
   File : ".qmail-root"
   &guylhem
   File : ".qmail-system"
   &root
   File : ".qmail-toor"
   &root
   File : ".qmail-uucp"
```

```
&root
File : ".qmail-uucp-default"
|preline -dr /usr/bin/uux - -r -gC -a"${SENDER:-MAILER-
DAEMON}" lm!rmail "($DEFAULT@$HOST)"
```

You need to create each of these file in ~alias, replacing &guylhem in .qmail-root by your own login to get root mail.

ATTENTION UUCP USERS !

DO NOT TRUST QMAIL FAQ FOR UUCP, USE MY .qmail-uucp-default INSTEAD ! ELSE YOU WILL NOT BE ABLE TO SEND ANY MAIL BY YOUR UUCP CONNEXION !

Now you'll need to decide in which format your users will get their mail.

Here's my suggestion :

- For NFS mounted home dirs, use MAILDIR format with a patch for local mail readers (patchs are available on www.qmail.org)

- If no patch is available, prefer MAILFILE format : any mail reader can read a file containing mail, people will only need to create an alias (for bash) or a setenv (for csh) for their mail reader

- Avoid /var/spool/mail/$USER format, too unsecure

To fix default format, read each file in /var/qmail/boot then copy the one you best like to /var/qmail/rc.

home or proc are safe choices, but prefer home for security reasons.

4.4   Configuring qmail

In /var/qmail/control, edit :

4.4.1   defaultdomain, me, plusdomain

- me is you local FQDN (full qualified domain name), for example on my machine it is barber-ouge.linux.lmm.com

- defaultdomain will be added to any host name without dots, including defaulthost, for example you can set it to localnetwork so any mail sent to joe@hisbox will be completed to be sent to joe@hisbox.localnetwork instead

- plusdomain is the exception : is is added to any host name that ends with a plus sign, including defaulthost (set in me) if it ends with a plus sign.

These 3 examples shows you the power and ease of configuration of qmail !

4.4.2   locals, rcpthosts

If you want to support virtual domain names, just put additional names in these files.

Any mail you receive for these names will be handled locally.

The difference between locals and rcpthosts is the latter isn't considered as a local alias, which is useful if you receive mail from some free email address like yahoo.com or lemel.fr while you also send mail to other users of these non local services, i.e. you don't want to handle locally mail send to someone@yahoo.com !

4.4.3   virtualdomains

There can you specify defaut outgoing mode, for example :

```
#:alias-uucp
```

if you don't want to send outgoing mail by uucp but by smtp (default) or

```
:alias-ucp
```

if you send your outgoing mail by uucp.

4.5   Testing qmail

Now it is configured, try :

```
sh -cf '/var/qmail/rc &'
```

to launch qmail (it won't interfere with your local MTA), then :

```
echo to: mylogin | /var/qmail/bin/qmail-inject
```

You should receive this mail in the format you've chosen in /var/qmail/boot/.

4.6   Removing your other MTA

If this test was successful, just kill your previous MTA :

killall -STOP daemon_name ; if any children are running, you should killall -CONT their_name, wait, killall -STOP again, and repeat ad nauseam.

If there aren't any children, killall -TERM and then killall -CONT.

Remove it (how you can do this depends on the distribution you installed, for example rpm -e –nodeps on RedHat, Caldera and Suse, or dpkg -r –force-depends on Debian) then run :

```
# ln -s /var/qmail/bin/sendmail /usr/lib/sendmail
# ln -s /var/qmail/bin/sendmail /usr/sbin/sendmail
```

Now set up qmail-smtpd in /etc/inetd.conf (all on one line):

```
smtp stream tcp nowait qmaild /var/qmail/bin/tcp-env tcp-
env /var/qmail/bin/qmail-smtpd
```

If you are using a old non-SYSV-init distribution like redhat, just add to your boot scripts :

```
sh -cf '/var/qmail/rc &'
```

Usually /etc/rc.local but your mileage may vary.

For actual SYSV-init compliant distributions (RedHat, Caldera, Suse, Debian), add this script to /etc/init.d/ :

DEBIAN version :

```
#!/bin/sh

test -x /var/qmail/rc || exit 0

case "$1" in
  start)
      echo -n "Starting mta: "
      sh -cf '/var/qmail/rc &'
      echo "qmail."
      ;;
  stop)
      echo -n "Stopping mta: "
      killall qmail-lspawn
      echo "qmail."
      ;;
  restart)
      echo -n "Restarting mta: "
      killall -HUP qmail-lspawn
      killall -ALRM qmail-lspawn
      echo "qmail."
      ;;
  *)
      echo "Usage: /etc/init.d/qmail {start|stop|restart}"
      exit 1
esac

exit 0
```

REDHAT version :

```
#!/bin/sh
#
# qmail        This shell script takes care of starting and stopping qmail.
#
# description: qmail is a Mail Transport Agent, which is the program \
#              that moves mail from one machine to another.
# processname: qmail
# config: /var/qmail/control/

# Source function library.
. /etc/rc.d/init.d/functions

# Source networking configuration.
. /etc/sysconfig/network

export PATH=$PATH:/var/qmail/bin

# Check that networking is up.
[ ${NETWORKING} = "no" ] && exit 0

[ -f /usr/sbin/sendmail ] || exit 0

# See how we were called.
case "$1" in
  start)
```

```
            # Start daemons.
            echo -n "Starting qmail: "
            qmail-start '|preline procmail' splogger qmail &
            touch /var/lock/subsys/qmail
            echo
            ;;
    stop)
            # Stop daemons.
            echo -n "Shutting down qmail: "
            killproc qmail-lspawn
            echo
            rm -f /var/lock/subsys/qmail
            ;;
    restart)
            $0 stop
            $0 start
            ;;
    status)
            status qmail
            ;;
    *)
            echo "Usage: qmail {start|stop|restart|status}"
            exit 1
    esac

    exit 0
```

And make symlinks to each /etc/rcN.d/, for example :

```
    ln -sf /etc/init.d/qmail /etc/rc1.d/K19qmail
```

If the first letter is K, you will kill qmail on this runlevel (1 for single mode or 6 for boot), but if the first letter is S, you will start qmail on this runlevel (each others runlevel).

- How to decide whether you should put a K or a S ? Do what the majority of dæmons in this runlevel do !
- What number should you put after K or S ? The number next to your network daemon.

RedHat, Caldera and Suze will use /etc/rc.d/ instead of plain /etc/ for Debian distribution, i.e. /etc/rc.d/rc1.d or /etc/rc.d/init.d for example.

4.7   That's all, folks !

No need to reboot (remember, you're using linux, not some other cheap OS !) for the modifications to take effect, just run :

```
    killall inetd
    init 1
```

To go to single user mode, then :

```
    init 2
```

to go back to your default runlevel (indicated in /etc/inittab with initdefault label).

You could also hand-start qmail script but "init" method will show you if qmail script is well positioned, i.e. launched after network scripts but before any program depend on email to warn you (like inn).

5 Smail v3.1

Smail3.1 seems to be a de-facto standard transport agent for uucp-only sites and for some smtp sites. It's easy to configure, it compiles without patching from the sources and it's fairly secure.

5.1 Configuring smail

Install smail binary from your distribution (I recommand you choose this) or get smail sources and build smail. If you're building smail from sources, you need to have the following in your os/linux file so that 'sed' gives you shell scripts that work properly.

```
CASE_NO_NEWLINES=true
```

Once it's installed, config. files will certainly go in /etc/smail (but your mileage may vary if you use old distributions); let's start editing them !

5.2 "config" file

```
# From
smart_path=polux
smart_transport=uux

# To
hostname=barberouge
domains=linux.lmm.com

visible_name=barberouge.linux.lmm.com
uucp_name=barberouge.linux.lmm.com

# max_message_size=512k
# auth_domains=foo.bar
# more_hostnames=barberouge.polux.freenix.fr
```

Well, first, who is feeding you ? I'm fed by "polux" via uucp (i.e. uux transport); naturally you need to change this file according to your own situation. For example, you could by fed by "bargw.bar.foobar.com" via "smtp", in that case you don't need a transport file and can define "-transport_file " to indicate you don't need one.

You can also use "postmaster_address = yourname", hide the network topology in outgoing addresses (if you're a gateway) using "visible_name", set which aliases address can also be used for the email you receive, using "more_hostnames".

See smail documentation for more details or the examples in /usr/doc/smail/examples to see if any match your situation.

5.3 "directors" file

```
# aliasinclude - expand ":include:filename" addresses pro-
duced by alias files
# This entry and the next one are pretty much boiler-plate.  Reasons
# for making significant changes are few.  The sole purpose of these
# is to match and expand addresses of the form:
#       :include:pathname
# which may occur in alias files or mailing-list/forward files
# (produced by any director with a driver of forwardfile).
aliasinclude:
        driver = aliasinclude,          # use this special-case driver
```

```
                nobody;                          # associate nobody us-
er with addresses

                                                 #  when mild permission violations
                                                 #  are encountered
           copysecure,                           # get permission-
s from alias director
           copyowners,                           # get owners from alias director



# forwardinclude - expand ":include:filename" addrs produced by for-
ward files
forwardinclude:
           driver = forwardinclude,              # use this special-case driver
           nobody;
           copysecure,                           # get perms from forwarding director
           copyowners,                           # get owners from forward-
ing director



# aliases - search for alias expansions stored in a database
# This is the standard aliases file.  It is used for generic things,
# like mapping root, postmaster, MAILER-DAEMON and uucp to site
# admins, creating some small system alias expansions, and such.  In
# this site configuration, the aliases file is used mostly for
# machine-specific aliasing/forwarding information.  Global forwarding
# information should be put in the "forward" database.
aliases:
           driver=aliasfile,                     # general-purpose aliasing director
           -nobody,                              # all addresses are associated
                                                 # with nobody by default, so setting
                                                 # this is not useful.

           sender_okay,                          # don't remove sender from expansions
           owner=owner-$user;                    # problems go to an owner address
           file=/etc/aliases,
           modemask=002,                         # should not be globally writable
           optional,                             # ignore if file does not exist
           proto=1search,                        # unsorted ASCII file


# forward - search for expansions stored in a forwarding database
# This is the subdomain-wide user forwarding database.  Entries are
# maintained here for current or past users, to forward their mail to
# their preferred mail-reading machine.  The forward database is
# shipped around the TCP/IP network as changes are made, to keep the
# network consistent.
#forward:
#          driver = aliasfile,                   # general-purpose aliasing director
#          -nobody,                              # all addresses are associated
#                                                # with nobody by default, so setting
#                                                # this is not useful.
#          owner = real-$user;                   # problems go to an owner address
#
#          file = /etc/forward,
#          modemask = 002,
```

```
#          proto = dbm,                          # use dbm(3X) library for access


# dotforward - expand .forward files in user home directories
# For users that have an entry in the "forward" database, a ".forward"
# file is only used if it is on the "home" machine, as identified in
# the forward database.  If used, it is treated as a list of addresses
# to which mail should be delivered, rather than (or in addition to)
# the user identified in the local address.
dotforward:
        driver = forwardfile,              # general-purpose forward-
ing director
        owner = postmaster, nobody, sender_okay;

        file = ~/.forward,                 # .forward file in home directories
        checkowner,                        # the user can own this file
        owners = root,                     # or root can own the file
        modemask = 002,                    # it should not be globally writable
        caution = daemon:root,             # don't run things as root or daemon
        # be extra careful of remotely accessible home directories
        unsecure = "~uucp:/tmp:/usr/tmp:/var/tmp"


# forwardto - expand a "Forward to " in user mailbox files
# This emulates the V6/V7/System-V forwarding mechanism which uses a
# line of forward addresses stored at the beginning of user mailbox files
# prefixed with the string "Forward to "
forwardto:
        driver = forwardfile,
        owner = postmaster, nobody, sender_okay;

        file = /var/spool/mail/${lc:user},        # point at user mail-
box files
        forwardto,                         # enable "Forward to " function
        checkowner,                        # the user can own this file
        owners = root,                     # or root can own the file
        modemask = 0002,                   # under Sys-
tem V, group mail can write
        caution = daemon:root              # don't run things as root or daemon


# user - match users on the local host with delivery to their mailboxes
user:   driver = user;                     # driver to match usernames
        transport = local                  # local transport goes to mailboxes


# real_user - match usernames when prefixed with the string "real-"
# This is useful for allowing an address which explicitly delivers to a
# user's mailbox file.  For example, errors in a .forward file expansion
# could be delivered here, or forwarding loops between multiple machines
# can be resolved by using a real-username address.  Also, users that
# wish to use mail as a means of transferring data to a machine that
# is not their "home" machine can mail to real-login-name@remote.host.
real_user:
        driver = user;
```

```
            transport = local,
            prefix = "real-"                      # for example, match real-root


    # lists - expand mailing lists stored in a list directory
    # mailing lists can be created simply by creating a file in the
    # /etc/smail/lists directory.
    lists:  driver = forwardfile,
            caution,                               # flag all addresses with caution
            nobody,                                # and then associate the nobody user
            owner = owner-$user;                   # system V sites may wish to use
                                                   # o-$user, as owner-$user may be
                                                   # too long for a 14-char filename.
            file = lists/${lc:user}                # lists is under $smail_lib_dir


    # owners - expand mailing lists stored in a list owner directory
    # mailing lists owner lists can be created simply by creating a file
    # in the /etc/smail/lists/owner directory.  Mailing list owners
    # are sent locally generated errors dealing with a mailing list of the
    # same name.  To create an owner list for a mailing list, create a
    # file with the name of the list in /etc/smail/lists/owner.  This
    # will create a list address of owner-listname, as is used by the
    # "lists" director above.
    owners: driver = forwardfile,
            caution,                               # flag all addresses with caution
            nobody,                                # and then associate the nobody user
            owner = postmaster;                    # system V sites may wish to use
                                                   # o-$user, as owner-$user may be
                                                   # too long for a 14-char filename.
            prefix = "owner-",
            file = lists/owner/${lc:user}    # lists is under $smail_lib_dir


    # request - expand mailing lists stored in a list request directory
    # mailing lists request lists can be created simply by creating a file
    # in the /etc/smail/lists/request directory.  Request addresses
    # are typically used as a standard address for queries about a mailing
    # list.  For example, requests for additions or deletions to a list
    # will generally be sent to "list-request", which should be set up to
    # forward to the appropriate person or persons.
    request: driver = forwardfile,
            caution,                               # flag all addresses with caution
            nobody,                                # and then associate the nobody user
            owner = postmaster;                    # system V sites may wish to use
                                                   # o-$user, as owner-$user may be
                                                   # too long for a 14-char filename.
            suffix = "-request",
            file = lists/request/${lc:user} # lists is under $smail_lib_dir
```

You shouldn't need to change anything here, only mailing list options if you intend to run some using smail, or forwards options if, for example, you want to disable forwarding.

5.4 "fidopaths" file

```
.f105.n324.z2.fidonet.org        f105.n324.z2.fidonet.org!%s
.n324.z2.fidonet.org             f105.n324.z2.fidonet.org!%s
.z2.fidonet.org                  f105.n324.z2.fidonet.org!%s
.fidonet.org                     f105.n324.z2.fidonet.org!%s
```

Create such a file only if you're using ifmail and FIDO.

5.5 "routers" file

```
# forces - force certain paths
# This database exists as a means of hardcoding the paths to various
# machines or domains.  It is for use in creating temporary tweaks to
# the other routing databases.  To change the database, edit the file
# maps/force.path and type "make" in the maps/ subdirectory.
forces:
        driver = pathalias,            # router to search paths file
        method = /etc/smail/maps/table; # transports are in this file
        file = forcepaths,             # file containing force path info
        proto = lsearch,               # use the sorted path file
        optional,
        reopen                         # close when not being used


uucp_neighbors:
        driver=uuname,                 # use a program which return-
s neighbors
        transport=uux;
        cmd="/usr/bin/uuname -a",      # specifically, use the uu-
name program
#        domain=uucp                   # strip ending ".uucp"


# smart_host - a partially specified smarthost director
# If the config file attribute smart_path is defined as a path from the
# local host to a remote host, then hostnames not matched otherwise will
# be sent off to the stated remote host.  The config file attribute
# smart_transport can be used to specify a different transport.
# If the smart_path attribute is not defined, this router is ignored.
smart_host:
        driver = smarthost,            # special-case driver
        transport = uux                # by default deliver over UUCP
#       path=phreak


# ifmail - to send mails to fidonet and vice versa
ifmail:
        driver=pathalias,
        transport=ifmail;
        file=fidopaths,
        proto=lsearch
```

You should only include ifmail chapter if you use ifmail for FIDO mails. Note you can also change transport mode from "uux" (ie UUCP) to, for example, "smtp" or even 'hardcode the paths to various machines or domains' in "/etc/smail/maps/table".

This is useful if you want outgoing mail for your local network to be delivered immediately, since there's no need for it to be routed to your uucp connexion of your internet access.

5.6   "transports" file

```
# local - deliver mail to local users
# Tell smail to append directly to user mailbox files in the /var/spool/mail
# directory.
#local: driver = appendfile,              # append message to a file
#       -return_path,                     # include a Return-Path: field
#       local,                            # use local forms for delivery
#       from,                             # supply a From_ envelope line
#       unix_from_hack;                   # insert > before From in body
#
#       file = /var/spool/mail/${lc:user},      # use this loca-
tion for Linux
#                                         # Note, mail spool must be 1777
#       file = ~/mailfile,                # use this location for bet-
ter security
#       group = mail,                     # group to own file for System V
#       mode = 0660,                      # under Sys-
tem V, group mail can access
#       suffix = "\n",                    # append an extra newline
#       append_as_user,


# This allows each user to have a ~/.procmailrc file to control filtering
# of mail and saving mail from mail lists in separate mailbox-
es if they wish.
local:  +inet,
        -uucp,
        driver = pipe,                    # append message to a file
        return_path,                      # include a Return-Path: field
        local,                            # use local forms for delivery
        from,                             # supply a From_ envelope line
        unix_from_hack;                   # insert > before From in body

        cmd = "/usr/bin/procmail",        # use procmail for local delivery
        parent_env,                       # environment info from parent addr
        pipe_as_user,                     # use user-id associat-
ed with address
        umask = 0022,                     # umask for child process
#       -ignore_status,                   # exit status should be believed
#       -ignore_write_errors,             # retry on broken pipes


# pipe - deliver mail to shell commands
# This is used implicitly when smail encounters addresses which begin with
# a vertical bar character, such as "|/usr/lib/news/recnews talk.bizarre".
# The vertical bar is removed from the address before being given to the
# transport.
#pipe:  driver = pipe,                    # pipe message to another program
#       return_path, local, from, unix_from_hack;
#
#       cmd = "/bin/sh -c $user",         # send address to the Bourne Shell
```

```
#        parent_env,                    # environment info from parent addr
#        pipe_as_user,                  # use user-id associat-
ed with address
#        umask = 0022,                  # umask for child process
#        -log_output,                   # do not log stdout/stderr
#        ignore_status,                 # exit status may be bogus, ig-
nore it
#        ignore_write_errors,           # ignore broken pipes


# file - deliver mail to files
# This is used implicitly when smail encounters addresses which begin with
# a slash or squiggle character, such as "/usr/info/list_messages" or
# perhaps "~/Mail/inbox".
#file: driver = appendfile,
#        return_path, local, from, unix_from_hack;
#
#        file = $user,                  # file is taken from address
#        append_as_user,                # use user-id associat-
ed with address
#        expand_user,                   # expand ~ and $ within address
#        check_path,
#        suffix = "\n",
#        mode = 0644


# uux - deliver to the rmail program on a remote UUCP site
#
# As many as five recipient addresses will be delivered to the remote
# host in one UUCP transaction.
uux:    driver = pipe,
        -uucp,
        inet,
#        uucp,                          # use UUCP-style addressing forms
        from,                           # supply a From_ envelope line
        max_addrs = 5,                  # at most 5 addresses per invocation
        max_chars = 200;                # at most 200 chars of addresses
# the -r flag prevents immediate delivery, parentheses around the
# $user variable prevent special interpretation by uux.
        cmd = "/usr/bin/uux - -r -g$grade $host!rmail $((${strip:user})$)",
#         cmd="/usr/bin/uux - $host!rmail $(($user)$)",
        ignore_write_errors,           # ignore broken pipes
        umask = 0022,
#        pipe_as_sender,


# uux_one_addr - deliver mail over UUCP to a remote host that can take
#                one address at a time.
# This is often necessary when delivering to a site running an unmodified
# version of 4.1BSD.
uux_one_addr:
        driver = pipe,
        uucp,                           # use UUCP-style addressing forms
        from;                           # supply a From_ envelope line
# the -r flag prevents immediate delivery
```

```
            cmd = "/usr/bin/uux - -r -g$grade $host!rmail (${strip:user})",
            umask = 0022,
            pipe_as_sender


queueonly:
            driver = pipe;                      # send the message to a pipe
            cmd = "/usr/lib/sendmail -Q -f $sender -bm $user",
                                                # use getmail for local delivery
            user=root,                          # execute getmail as "root"
            group=mail,                         # execute getmail as "mail"
            parent_env,                         # environment info from parent addr
            -pipe_as_user,                      # use user-id associat-
ed with address
            umask = 0007,                       # umask for child process

# to deliver the message.  The smtp transport is included only if BSD
# networking exists.
# The uucp attribute can be specified for transfers within the UUCP
# zone.  The inet attribute must be specified for transfers within the
# Internet.
# NOTE: This is hardly optimal, a backend should exist which can handle
#       multiple messages per connection.
# ALSO: It may be necessary to restrict max_addrs to 100, as this is the
#       lower limit SMTP requires an implementation to handle for one
#       message.
smtp:       driver=tcpsmtp,
            inet,                               # if UUCP_ZONE is not defined
#           uucp,                               # if UUCP_ZONE is defined
            -max_addrs, -max_chars;             # no limit on number of addresses

            short_timeout=5m,                   # timeout for short operations
            long_timeout=2h,                    # timeout for longer SMTP operations
            service=smtp,                       # connect to this service port
# For internet use: uncomment the below 4 lines
            use_bind,                           # resolve MX and multiple A records
            defnames,                           # use standard domain searching
            defer_no_connect,                   # try again if the nameserver is down
            local_mx_okay,                      # fail an MX to the local host


ifmail:
            from,received,max_addrs=5,max_chars=200,
            driver=pipe;
            pipe_as_sender,
            cmd="/usr/local/bin/ifmail -x9 -r$host $((${strip:user})$)"
```

You should include an ifmail chapter only if you use ifmail for FIDO mails. Apart from that, you shouldn't need to edit anything in this file which defines transport agents (like uux, smtp ...) you can use as parameters in other config. files.

Note I commented out some parts, like "pipes" or "file", to enhance security.

5.7   "maps/" directory

It contains map and table files :

First, map file

```
#N       foo.bar foo2.bar2
#S       AT 486/RedHat Linux 1.2.13
#O       organization
#C       contact
#E       administration (email)
#T       phone
#P       address
#R
#U       hosts connected via uucp
#W       created/edited by
#
hname polux

hname linux.eu.org

hname = polux
hname = polux.linux.eu.org
```

Once again, edit this file to match you situation (I'm fed by polux.linux.eu.org).

Now table file

```
*        uux
```

You can define different transports to different path, for exemple "smtp" for the machines in your local network, "uux" (i.e. uucp) for the rest of the world or vice-versa (I'm using uucp for any outgoing mail, therefore I use "*" !).

5.8 Other good examples

The previous files are the one I currently use for my site, you shouldn't encounter any problem using them as samples/basis for your own files.

The following files are provided only as good exemples to configure smail a different way.

```
#ident "@(#) transports,v 1.2 1990/10/24 05:20:46 tron Exp"

# See smail(5) for a complete description of the contents of this file.

# local - deliver mail to local users
#
# Tell smail to append directly to user mailbox files in the /usr/mail
# directory.
local:  driver = appendfile,          # append message to a file
        return_path,                  # include a Return-Path: field
        local,                        # use local forms for delivery
        from,                         # supply a From_ envelope line
        unix_from_hack;               # insert > before From in body

        file = /usr/mail/${lc:user},  # use this location for System V
        group = mail,                 # group to own file for System V
        mode = 0660,                  # under Sys-
tem V, group mail can access
```

```
        suffix = "\n",                      # append an extra newline
        append_as_user,

# pipe - deliver mail to shell commands
#
# This is used implicitly when smail encounters addresses which begin with
# a vertical bar character, such as "|/usr/lib/news/recnews talk.bizarre".
# The vertical bar is removed from the address before being given to the
# transport.
pipe:   driver = pipe,                      # pipe message to another program
        return_path, local, from, unix_from_hack;

        cmd = "/bin/sh -c $user",           # send address to the Bourne Shell
        parent_env,                         # environment info from parent addr
        pipe_as_user,                       # use user-id associat-
ed with address
        umask = 0022,                       # umask for child process
        -log_output,                        # do not log stdout/stderr
        ignore_status,                      # exit status may be bogus, ig-
nore it
        ignore_write_errors,                # ignore broken pipes

# file - deliver mail to files
#
# This is used implicitly when smail encounters addresses which begin with a
# slash or squiggle character, such as "/usr/info/list_messages" or perhaps
# "~/Mail/inbox".
file:   driver = appendfile,
        return_path, local, from, unix_from_hack;

        file = $user,                       # file is taken from address
        append_as_user,                     # use user-id associat-
ed with address
        expand_user,                        # expand ~ and $ within address
        suffix = "\n",
        mode = 0644

# uux - deliver to the rmail program on a remote UUCP site
#
# As many as five recipient addresses will be delivered to the re-
mote host in
# one UUCP transaction.
uux:    driver = pipe,
        uucp,                               # use UUCP-style addressing forms
        from,                               # supply a From_ envelope line
        max_addrs = 5,                      # at most 5 addresses per invocation
        max_chars = 200;                    # at most 200 chars of addresses

        # the -r flag prevents immediate delivery, parentheses around the
        # $user variable prevent special interpretation by uux.
        cmd = "/usr/bin/uux - -r -g$grade $host!rmail $((${strip:user})$)",
        umask = 0022,
        pipe_as_sender

# uux_one_addr - deliver mail over UUCP to a remote host that can take one
```

```
# address at a time.
#
# This is often necessary when delivering to a site running an unmodified
# version of 4.1BSD.
uux_one_addr:
        driver = pipe,
        uucp,                                  # use UUCP-style addressing forms
        from;                                  # supply a From_ envelope line

        # the -r flag prevents immediate delivery
        cmd = "/usr/bin/uux - -r -g$grade $host!rmail (${strip:user})",
        umask = 0022, pipe_as_sender

# demand - deliver to a remote rmail program, polling on demand
demand: driver = pipe,
        uucp, from, max_addrs = 5, max_chars = 200;

        # with no -r flag, try to contact remote site immediately
        cmd = "/usr/bin/uux - -g$grade $host!rmail $(($user)$)",
        umask = 0022, pipe_as_sender

# uusmtp - deliver to the rsmtp program on a remote UUCP site
#
# Deliver using a simple Batched SMTP protocol to the remote machine.
# This allows much more arbitrary addresses to be used.  It also
# removes the limit on recipient addresses per invocation of uux.
uusmtp: driver = pipe,
        bsmtp,                                 # send batched SMTP commands
        -max_addrs,                            # there is no limit on the number or
        -max_chars;                            #   total size of recipien-
t addresses.

        # supply -r to prevent immediate delivery, the recipient addresses
        # are stored in the data sent to the standard input of rsmtp.
        cmd = "/usr/bin/uux - -r -g$grade $host!rsmtp",
        umask = 0022, pipe_as_sender

# demand_uusmtp - deliver to a remote rsmtp program, polling on demand
demand_uusmtp:
        driver = pipe,
        bsmtp, -max_addrs, -max_chars;

        # with no -r flag, try to contact remote site immediately
        cmd = "/usr/bin/uux - -g$grade $host!rsmtp",
        umask = 0022, pipe_as_sender

# smtp - deliver using SMTP over TCP/IP
#
# Connect to a remote host using TCP/IP and initiate an SMTP conversation to
# deliver the message.  The smtp transport is included only if BS-
D networking
# exists.

# NOTE: It may be necessary to restrict max_addrs to 100, as this is the
#       lower limit SMTP requires an implementation to handle for one
```

```
#          message.
smtp:      driver = smtp,
           -max_addrs,
           -max_chars


#ident "@(#) table,v 1.2 1990/10/24 05:20:31 tron Exp"

# This file names the transports that are to be used in delivering
# to specific hosts from bargw.

#host              transport
#--------          ---------
curdsgw            demand_uusmtp    # deliver using batched SMTP
oldbsd             uux_one_addr     # 4.1BSD sites cannot take more than one addr
sun                demand           # call sun when their is mail to send
*                  uux              # for all others, poll at intervals
```

5.9   Restarting inetd

To run smail as a smtp daemon, add one of the following to /etc/inetd.conf:

```
        smtp stream tcp nowait  root  /usr/bin/smtpd smtpd
```

or:

```
        smtp stream tcp nowait  root  /usr/sbin/tcpd  /usr/sbin/in.smtpd
```

Outgoing mail gets sent automatically, when using elm.

5.10   Smail with smtp

Generally, ISPs use smtp, therefore you shouldn't have any problems sending your mail. If your internet link is down when you send mail, then the mail sits in "/var/spool/smail/input". When the link next comes up, "runq" is run which causes the mail to be sent. However, receiving mail is **the** problem since your provider has many clients to look after, not only you !

Usually, you can retreive your mail via the POP protocol, see POP section below.

6   OUTDATED SECTION : Sendmail+IDA

For big sites, sendmail is worth choosing, due to the "incredible ease of use", (very relative feeling when you know qmail) but you must decide which you want between sendmail+IDA and sendmail 8.x :

- If you use an old kernel (1.0) : sendmail+IDA
- If you use a not so old kernel (1.2) : sendmail+IDA and source code editing
- Recent kernel (2.0) will choose sendmail 8.x

Remember, linux newbies or people concerned by security / ease of configuration should rather try using smail or qmail, which are easier to use and safer.

HOWTO

6.1 Source installation

If your distribution doesn't provide you with a ready-to-install sendmail package (.rpm for RedHat, Caldera and Suse, .deb for Debian) just download the sources and run :

- cd / ; tar -zxvf sendmail5.67b+IDA1.5.tpz

- cd to /usr/local/lib/mail/CF and copy the sample.m4 local.m4 file to "yourhostname.m4".

Edit out the distributed hostname, aliases, smarthost and put in the correct one for your site. The default file is for a uucp-only site who has domainized headers and who talks to a smart host. Then "make yourhostname.cf" and move the resulting file to /etc/sendmail.cf

- if you are uucp-only, you do *NOT* need to create any of the tables mentioned in the README.linux file.

You'll just have to touch the files so that the Makefile works. Just edit the .m4 file, make sendmail.cf and start testing it.

- if you're uucp-only and you talk to sites in addition to your "smart-host", you'll need to add uucpxtable entries for each (or mail to them will also go through the smart host) and run dbm against the revised uucpxtable.

- If you run Rich Braun's original binary distribution of 5.67a, you'll need to freeze the configuration if you change your .cf file with "/usr/lib/sendmail -bz" to make the changes take effect.

You should also update your version to at least 5.67b since there is a nasty security hole in 5.67a and earlier. Another nice thing is that if you have mail.debug set and you run syslogd, your incoming and outgoing mail messages will get logged. See the "/etc/syslog.conf" file for details.

The sources for sendmail+IDA can be found at vixen.cso.uiuc.edu ; they require no patching to run under Linux if you're running something like a kernel of 1.00.

If you're running a kernel > 1.1.50, you get the fun of reversing most of the Linux-specific patches that are now in the vanilla sources. (I *did* told you this sendmail was only for old kernels :-)

It's extremely obvious where this needs to be done : just type "make" and when it blows up, go to that line in the sources and comment out the Linux-specific code that's in there.

If you're going to run sendmail+IDA, I strongly recommend you go to the sendmail5.67b+IDA1.5 version since all required Linux-specific patches are now in the vanilla sources and several security holes have been plugged that WERE (!!!) in the older version you may have grabbed or built before about December 1st, 1993.

Now linux kernel is 2.0, you should use sendmail 8.x insted of sendmail+IDA, but I told you'd better choose sendmail 8.x :-)

6.2 The sendmail.m4 file

Sendmail+IDA requires you to set up a `sendmail.m4` file rather than editing the `sendmail.cf` file directly. The nice thing about this is that it is simple to set up mail configurations that are extremely difficult (if not totally impossible for most people to set up correctly) in smail or traditional sendmail.

The sendmail.m4 file that corresponds to the above smail example looks like the following:

```
dnl #------------------ SAMPLE SENDMAIL.M4 FILE ------------------
dnl #
dnl # (the string 'dnl' is the m4 equivalent of commenting out a line)
dnl #
dnl # you generally don't want to override LIBDIR from the compiled in paths
```

```
dnl #define(LIBDIR,/usr/local/lib/mail)dnl      # where all support files go
define(LOCAL_MAILER_DEF, mailers.linux)dnl      # mailer for local delivery
define(POSTMASTERBOUNCE)dnl                     # postmaster gets bounces
define(PSEUDODOMAINS, BITNET UUCP)dnl           # don't try DNS on these
dnl #
dnl #-------------------------------------------------------------
dnl #
dnl # names we're known by
define(PSEUDONYMS, myhostname.subdomain.domain myhostname.UUCP)
dnl #
dnl # our primary name
define(HOSTNAME, myhostname.subdomain.domain)
dnl #
dnl # our uucp name
define(UUCPNAME, myhostname)dnl
dnl #
dnl #-------------------------------------------------------------
dnl #
define(UUCPNODES, |uuname|sort|uniq)dnl         # our uucp neighbors
define(BANGIMPLIESUUCP)dnl                      # make certain that uucp
define(BANGONLYUUCP)dnl                         #  mail is treated correctly
define(RELAY_HOST, my_uucp_neighbor)dnl         # our smart relay host
define(RELAY_MAILER, UUCP-A)dnl                 # we reach moria via uucp
dnl #
dnl #-------------------------------------------------------------
dnl #
dnl # the various dbm lookup tables
dnl #
define(ALIASES, LIBDIR/aliases)dnl              # system aliases
define(DOMAINTABLE, LIBDIR/domaintable)dnl      # domainize hosts
define(PATHTABLE, LIBDIR/pathtable)dnl          # paths database
define(GENERICFROM, LIBDIR/generics)dnl         # generic from addresses
define(MAILERTABLE, LIBDIR/mailertable)dnl      # mailers per host or domain
define(UUCPXTABLE, LIBDIR/uucpxtable)dnl        # paths to hosts we feed
define(UUCPRELAYS, LIBDIR/uucprelays)dnl        # short-circuit paths
dnl #
dnl #-------------------------------------------------------------
dnl #
dnl # include the 'real' code that makes it all work
dnl # (provided with the source code)
dnl #
include(Sendmail.mc)dnl                         # REQUIRED ENTRY !!!
dnl #
dnl #------------ END OF SAMPLE SENDMAIL.M4 FILE -------
```

6.3   Defining a local mailer

Unlike most Unix distributions, Linux does not come with a local mail delivery agent by default. Now, deliver or procmail is generally installed, so no complexity will be added to this already very complex setup. I recommend using the commonly available `deliver` or `procmail` programs, which can be optional packages in a some Linux distributions.

In order to do so, you need to define a `LOCAL_MAILER_DEF` in the `sendmail.m4` file that points to a file that looks like:

```
# -- /usr/local/lib/mail/mailers.linux --
#     (local mailers for use on Linux )
Mlocal, P=/usr/bin/deliver, F=SlsmFDMP, S=10, R=25/10, A=deliver $u
Mprog,  P=/bin/sh,          F=lsDFMeuP,  S=10, R=10,    A=sh -c $u
```

There is a also built-in default for `deliver` in the `Sendmail.mc` file that gets included into the `sendmail.cf` file. To specify it, you would not use the `mailers.linux` file but would instead define the following in your sendmail.m4 file:

```
dnl --- (in sendmail.m4) ---
define(LOCAL_MAILER_DEF, DELIVER)dnl          # mailer for local delivery
```

Unfortunately, Sendmail.mc assumes deliver is installed in /bin, which is not the case with Slackware1.1.1 (which installs it in /usr/bin). In that case you'd need to either fake it with a link or rebuild deliver from sources so that it resides in /bin. Please note procmail is generally better than deliver, for example for mail filtering.

6.4   The sendmail+IDA dbm tables

Setting up special behavior for sites or domains is done through a number of optional dbm tables rather than editing the `sendmail.cf` file directly.

Refer to the July-1994 issue of `Linux Journal` (if you can still find it :-), to the docs in the sources, or to the sendmail chapter in the newest version of the Linux DOC Project `Networking Administration Guide` which will be available real-soon-now for more details.

- mailertable - defines special behavior for remote hosts or domains.
- uucpxtable - forces UUCP delivery of mail to hosts that are in DNS format.
- pathtable - defines UUCP bang-paths to remote hosts or domains.
- uucprelays - short-circuits the pathalias path to well-known remote hosts.
- genericfrom - converts internal addresses into generic ones visible to the outside world.
- xaliases - converts generic addresses to/from valid internal ones.
- decnetxtable - converts RFC-822 addresses to DECnet-style addresses.

6.5   So which entries are really required?

When not using any of the optional dbm tables, sendmail delivers mail via the RELAY_HOST and RELAY_MAILER) defined in the sendmail.m4 file used to generate sendmail.cf. It is easily possible to override this behavior through entries in the domaintable or uucpxtable.

A generic site that is on Internet and speaks Domain Name Service, or one that is UUCP-only and forwards all mail via UUCP through a smart RELAY_HOST, probably does not need any specific table entries at all.

Virtually all systems should set the DEFAULT_HOST and PSEUDONYMS macros, which define the canonical site name and aliases it is known by.

If all you have is a relay host and relay mailer, you don't need to set these defaults since it works automagically. UUCP hosts will probably also need to set UUCPNAME to their official UUCP name.

They will also probably set RELAY_MAILER and RELAY_HOST which enable smart-host routing through a mail relay.

The mail transport to be used is defined in RELAY_MAILER and should usually be UUCP-A for UUCP sites. If your site is SMTP-only and talks 'Domain Name Service', you would change the RELAY_MAILER.

If you're a SLIP site, you might want to take the easy way out and just forward all outgoing mail to your service provider to do the right thing with. To do so, you'd want to define ISOLATED_DOMAINS and VALIDATION_DOMAINS to be your domain, you'd also want to define RELAY_HOST to be your service provider and RELAY_MAILER to be TCP. Of course, you want to ask permission before you set any system up as your general purpose relay.

6.6   Sendmail 8.x

Sendmail 8.7.x from Berkeley was the latest major revision after sendmail5. It had wonderful built-in support for building under Linux : just "make linux" and all was set.

You'll probably be best served by grabbing one of the various binary distributions off of the usual Linux archive sites rather than fighting things like Berkeley dbm yourself.

There's a nice distribution of sendmail 8.6.12 from Jason Haar - `j.haar at lazerjem.demon.co.uk` on sunsite.unc.edu in /pub/Linux/system/Mail/delivery/sendmail-8.6.12-bin.tgz that has the source documentation and a very nice quickie description of how to run sendmail v8 for common configurations.

The bottom line with sendmail v8 is that you want to configure the bare minimum necessary to get the job done ; the following is an example that should get you close at least.

6.7   A sample 8.7.x mc file

Much like sendmail+IDA, sendmail v8 uses m4 to process a config file into a full sendmail.cf that sendmail uses. The following is my current mc file for my site (ppp to Internet for outgoing mail, uucp for incoming mail).

```
dnl divert(-1)
#-------------------------------------------------------------------
#
# this is the .mc file for a linux host that's set up as follows:
#
#        - connected to Internet for outbound mail (ppp here)
#        - connected via UUCP for incoming mail
#        - domainized headers
#        - no local mailer (use 'deliver' instead)
#        - no DNS running so don't canonicalize outgoing via DNS
#        - all non-local outbound mail goes to the RELAY_HOST over smtp
#          (we run ppp and let our service provider do the work)
#
#                                          vds 3/31/95
#
#-------------------------------------------------------------------
include('../m4/cf.m4')
VERSIONID('linux nodns relays to slip service provider smarthost')dnl
Cwmyhostname.myprimary.domain myhostname.UUCP localhost
OSTYPE(linux)
FEATURE(nodns)dnl
FEATURE(always_add_domain)dnl
FEATURE(redirect)
FEATURE(nocanonify)
dnl MAILER(local)dnl
MAILER(smtp)dnl
MAILER(uucp)dnl
define('RELAY_HOST', smtp:my.relay.host.domain)
define('SMART_HOST', smtp:my.relay.host.domain)
define('UUCP_RELAY', smtp:my.relay.host.domain)
define('LOCAL_MAILER_PATH', '/bin/deliver')
define('LOCAL_MAILER_ARGS', 'deliver $u')
```

6.8 Sendmail v8 tidbits

There are a few differences I suppose to the 'IDA bigots' among us. So far, I've found the following:

Instead of 'runq', you type 'sendmail -q' to run the queue !

6.9 Local Delivery Agents

Unlike most operating systems, Linux did not have mail "built-in" : you needed a program to deliver the local mail, like "lmail", "procmail" or "deliver".

However, every recent distribution includes a local mailer now !

Documentation for how to use either for local delivery is in the sendmail5.67b+IDA1.5 binary release (on sunsite) mentioned above.

7 POP mail

This section also concerns IMAP, not very different from POP.

7.1 History

On a workstation network, mail has always been a problem:

- Either you use "user@computer.foo.com" with problems when "computer" is down, making your network known to the people outside, having different addresses for a same person switching to another computer, ...
- Either you take a mail hub, "mailhost.foo.com" with rules for rewriting, so every user seems to post from the same address, even if they are on different computers.

But in that case, how can user read their mail ?

Using a rsh with elm ? :-)

It would overload our mail hub ! One method was forwarding or UUCP, smtp, etc. but it's too complicated.

Then came POP/IMAP, both with security problems at the beginning, now fixed using ssh on new versions) : a mail program has sometimes to be set locally (like qmail, smail or vmail if, for example, you use elm, but mozilla will avoid that !) however, getting and sending Email is simpler.

7.2 Getting mail

Here come POP's main drawbacks : the password is sent as a clear text on the network, and some mail readers just don't know POP : you must choose a POP-aware mailer, like Pine, Emacs, Netscape, Mutt ...

Password problem can be solved creating a crypted "channel" to have POP on it or using APOP or RPOP extensions. The mail reader problem can be solved either by changing mail reader (mozilla is POP ready, as are Emacs and pine) or by using a POP "mail sucker" with a local mail program.

Here're some pop programs worth trying :

- gwpop (a Good Way to POP) is very protected since it creates a crypted "channel" and puts mail directly in the "spool" ; however, it depends on Perl.
- popclient, simple to use :
  For example if your login is john and your password PrettySecret, you will run :

```
$ popclient -3 -v mail.acme.net -u john -p "PrettySecret" -k -o JOHN-
INET-MAIL
```

- fetchmail, which is actively supported and incredibly simple to use : it is configured in ~/.fetchmailrc, so you only need to run fetchmail when you want to retrive your mail.

    Here's my .fetchmailrc :

```
poll mail.server protocol pop3:
        forcecr
        password PrettySecret;
```

Please note forcecr option is needed to use fetchmail with qmail which strictly respects RFCs.

7.3   Sending mail

For this, you must use smtp-aware mail software, like qmail, smail, vmail or mozilla (this one does everything : mail reader, POP receive, smtp send !)

Go to one of the previous sections to install and configure the one you like best. Then, will you will reach "Testing", try to send some mail to a local account on the mail hub.

7.4   Reading mail

If your program doesn't do everything itself, you can install elm, pgp, mush, pine ... many good programs are freely available for linux platforms !

7.5   Testing

To check your mail server has pop, try :

```
$ telnet mailhost 110
```

If it works, you will get something like "OK Pop server (...) starting" : type "quit" !

To install a ssh crypted "channel", first test your mail server typing :

```
$ ssh mailhost date
```

If you get the date, you should be OK. Please note ssh will not ask for a password, therefore you must create a ".shosts" file on the mail server, containing client's name. To test ssh port redirection (which gwpop uses), type :

```
$ ssh -n -f -L 12314:localhost:110 mailhost sleep 30
```

then

```
$ telnet localhost 12314
```

Then will you hopefully see mail hub's pop banner. If you don't use ssh, don't forget to comment out $ssh on gwpop script. To check whether procmail is running, try "procmail -v"

7.6 Using

Now you can edit gwpop Perl script to check everything is ok, then run gwpop :

```
$ gwpop -v your-username
POP password on mailhost: yoursecretpasword
```

If gwpop "error messages" are normal, the mail from mail hub will be downloaded to your local machine wherever you told gwpop to put it. (please test with some mail !).

You can also use gwpop as a daemon :

```
$ gwpop -d $HOME/tmp your-username
```

gwpop messages are then sent to syslog and gwpop will run endlessly ; a "HUP" signal will force gwpop to get your mail.

You can get POP software here used on :

```
ftp://ftp.pasteur.fr/pub/Network/gwpop
ftp://ftp.informatik.rwth-aachen.de/pub/packages/procmail
http://www.cs.hut.fi/ssh/
```

8 Mail "user agents"

This section contains information related to "user agents", which means the software the user sees and uses. This software relies on the "transport agents" mentioned above. Many other mail "User Agents" are available now (pine, mush ...) but I haven't found any linux-specific information to tell on them. Please tell me if I'm missing something !

8.1 Mutt

You should have no problem to compile, install or run mutt ; qmail users will either get qmail patch or run it with -f flag to read their local mail folder.

If mutt bothers you with an "unknown terminal error" after a distribution upgrading, just recompile it.

8.2 Elm

Elm compiles, installs and runs flawlessly under Linux. For more information, see the elm sources and installation instructions. Elm and filter need to be mode 2755 (group mail) with /var/spool/mail mode 775 and group mail.

Qmail users will get a patch to use nifty qmail features, or will run elm with -f flag to point to their local mail folder.

If you use a binary distribution, you'll need to create a "/usr/local/lib/elm/elm.rc" file to override the compiled-in hostname and domain information:

- replace "subdomain.domain" with your domain name replace
- "myhostname" with you un-domainized hostname replace

```
#---------- /usr/local/lib/elm/elm.rc ------------------
#
# this is the unqualified hostname
hostname = myhostname
#
# this is the local domain
hostdomain = subdomain.domain
```

```
#
# this is the fully qualified hostname
hostfullname = myhostname.subdomain.domain
#
#-------------------------------------------------------------
```

One thing you want to be aware of is that if you have Elm compiled to be MIME enabled, you need metamail installed and in your path or Elm will not be able to read MIME mail you've received. Metamail is available on `thumper.bellcore.com` and of course via "archie".

In the "too cool to be true" category, there is a distribution of Elm-2.4.24 that is "PGP-aware". To try it, grab the file `ftp://ftp.viewlogic.com/pub/elm-2.4pl24pgp3.tar.gz`, which is elm2.4.24 with PGP hooks added. You configure and build it the same way you do normal Elm, which means you probably need to add the patches mentioned above. For what it's worth, I run it here and like it a lot. Of course, there must be more recent versions available, including elm-ME+.

While this item is not Linux-specific, it's perceived (wrongly) to be a nagging Elm bug nevertheless. We've heard that Elm sometimes fails with a message that it's unable to malloc() some massive number of bytes. The identified workaround is to remove the post-processed global mail aliases (aliases.dir and aliases.pag).

THIS IS NOT A BUG IN ELM, it's an error in configuration of Elm by whomever you got your binary distribution of Elm from.

Elm has an enhanced and non-compatible, format for aliases ; you need to ensure that the path Elm uses for aliases is different from the path sendmail/smail uses. From the volume of reports of this problem, it's apparent that at least one major distribution 'on the street' has in the past been misconfigured. (from `scot at catzen.gun.de` (Scot W. Stevenson))

The current metamail package requires csh for some of its scripts. Failure to have csh (or tcsh) will cause most interesting errors...

8.3 Mailx

If you don't have a local `mailx` program, save yourself the pain : just go and grab the mailx kit from Slackware 2.1.0 or later, which has a nice implementation of mailx5.5. If you're into building from sources, mailx v5.5 compiles without patching under Linux if you have `"pmake"` installed.

If anybody is still using it, I strongly recommend removing the old "edmail" stuff from SLS1.00 and replacing it with mailx.

8.4 Other user agents

The following also are known to run under Linux. Consult "archie" for details regarding how to find them...

- mutt - by far better than elm, very easy to use
- pine - from the Univ. of Washington
- metamail - allows MIME support
- mh - yet another way to handle mail
- deliver - file/process mail based on rules
- procmail - file/process mail based on rules
- majordomo - manages e-mail lists
- mserv - provide files-by-mail

HOWTO

9 Acknowledgements

The following people have helped in the assembly of the information and experience that helped make this document possible:

Steve Robbins, Ian Kluft, Rich Braun, Ian Jackson, Syd Weinstein, Ralf Sauther, Martin White, Matt Welsh, Ralph Sims, Phil Hughes, Scot Stevenson, Neil Parker, Stephane Bortzmayer and especially many thanks to Vince Skahan for his huge contribution.

If I forgot anybody, my apologies : just Email me !

Part XXV

"Modem-HOWTO" David S.Lawyer

bf347@lafn.org

Help with selecting, connecting, configuring, trouble-shooting, and understanding modems for a PC. See Serial-HOWTO for multiport serial boards. Contains much info from Serial-HOWTO by Greg Hankins

Contents

HOWTO

HOWTO

1 Introduction

This covers conventional modems for PC's, mainly modems on the ISA bus (although much of this should also apply to the PCI bus). For modems on the PCMCIA bus see the PCMCIA-HOWTO: PCMCIA serial and modem devices.

1.1 Copyright, Trademarks, Disclaimer, & Credits

1.1.1 Copyright

Copyright (c) 1998 by David S. Lawyer and Greg Hankins. Please freely copy and distribute (sell or give away) this document. You may create derivative works and distribute them provided you:

I. For the case of minor changes and corrections where there exists a current maintainer:
Send your proposed changes to the current maintainer first. You may distribute (per II. below) only if the current maintainer neglects to incorporate your changes in a timely manner. If the changes are only to correct typos, you need not wait for a reply from the maintainer before you distribute.

II. In all other cases:

1. Make a good faith effort to insure that a copy of the derivative work (including any master copy) gets on the Internet at a well-known (and mirrored) site for free downloading.

2. If you change the license, license the work in the spirit of this license, or use GPL (Free Software Foundation).

3. The major authors become the copyright owners (not to exceed 3). Minor contributions do not make you an author.

4. Make a good faith effort to contact the maintainer (or principal copyright owners if there is no maintainer) to let them know what you have done. If the changes are extensive, then you should also attempt to make more such contacts (including prior to your project).

5. Give full credit to significant previous authors and contributors although the credits section need not exceed 1% of the length of the document.

1.1.2 Trademarks

If certain words are trademarks, the context should make it clear to whom they belong. For example "MS Windows" (or just "Windows") implies that "Windows" belongs to Microsoft (MS). "Hayes" is a trademark of Microcomputer Products Inc. I use "winmodem" to mean any modem which requires MS-Windows and not in the trademark sense.

1.1.3 Disclaimer

Much of the info in this HOWTO was obtained from the previous Serial-HOWTO, the Internet, etc. and may be unreliable. While I haven't intentionally tried to mislead you, there are likely a number of errors in this document. Please let me know about them. Since this is free documentation, it should be obvious that neither I nor previous authors can be held legally responsible for any errors.

1.1.4 Credits

The following is only a rough approximation of how this document was created: About 1/3 of the material here was lifted directly from Serial-HOWTO v. 1.11 by Greg Hankins. <mailto:gregh@cc.gatech.edu> (with his permission). About another 1/3 was taken from that Serial-HOWTO and revised. The remaining 1/3 is newly created by the author: David S. Lawyer <mailto:bf347@lafn.org>.

1.2   Future Plans, You Can Help

An explanation of how to set up modems for dial-in is lacking in this version but should be included in the next. Please let me know of any errors in facts, opinions, logic, spelling, grammar, clarity, links, etc. But first, if the date is over a months old, check to see that you have the latest version. Please send me any other info that you think belongs in this document. The French "Modems-HOWTO" needs to be somehow merged with this document (but I don't know French).

1.3   New Versions of this HOWTO

New versions of this Modem-HOWTO come out every month or so since modem situation is rapidly changing (and since I'm still learning). Your problem might be solved in the latest version. It will be available to browse and/or download at LDP mirror sites. For a list of such sites see: <http://sunsite.unc.edu/LDP/mirrors.html> If you only want to quickly check the date of the latest version you may not want to use a mirror site so check out: <http://sunsite.unc.edu/LDP/HOWTO/Modem-HOWTO.html>.

1.4   What is a Modem ?

A modem is a device that lets one send digital signals over ordinary telephone lines not designed for digital signals. If telephone lines were all digital then you wouldn't need a modem. It permits your computer to connect to and communicate with the rest of the world. When you use a modem, you normally use a communication program or web browser (which includes such a program) to utilize the modem and dial-out on a telephone line. Advanced modem users can set things up so that others may phone in to them and use their computer. This is called "dial-in".

There are two basic types of modems for a PC: external and internal. The external sets on your desk outside the PC while the internal is not visible since it's inside the PC. The external modem plugs into a connector on the back of the PC known as a "serial port". The internal modem is a card that is inserted inside the computer and has an (invisible) serial port built into it. For a more detailed comparison see 4.1 (External vs. Internal). Thus when you get an internal modem, you also get a dedicated serial port (which can only be used with the modem and not with anything else such as another modem or a printer). In Linux, the serial ports are named ttyS0, ttyS1, etc. (corresponding respectively to COM1, COM2, etc. in Dos/Windows).

The serial port is not to be confused with the "Universal Serial Bus" (USB) which uses a special modular connector and may be used with modems in the future. See 2 (Modem & Serial Port Basics) for more details on modems and serial ports.

1.5   Quick Install

1.5.1   External Modem Install

With a straight-thru or modem cable, connect the modem to an unused serial port on the PC. Make sure you know the name of the serial port: COM1 is ttyS0, COM2 is ttyS1. You may need to check the BIOS to determine this. Plug in the power cord to provide power to the modem. See 1.5.3 (All Modems) for further instructions.

1.5.2   Internal Modems (on ISA bus)

(See 4.5.3 (PCI Modems) for the PCI bus) If the modem says it will only work under MS Windows, you are out of luck. If you already have 2 serial ports, make this the 3rd serial port (ttyS2 = COM3). Find an unused IRQ number to use. An unused one is often IRQ5 for the 2nd parallel port or a sound card (which you may not have). Then set the jumpers (or the like) on the internal modem to the unused IRQ and I/O address 3E8 (ttyS2) .

"Or the like" (in the previous sentence) may be a bit tricky. If the modem is a Plug and Play (PnP) for the ISA bus, the equivalent probably can be done using the "isapnp" program which comes with "isapnptools". See "man isapnp". Another possible alternate way to set the IRQ and 3E8 is (if possible) to configure it under Windows. If you have a PnP BIOS, then configuring under Windows should put the configuration into the PnP BIOS so that it will be used at boot-time for Linux (provided you tell CMOS that you don't have a PnP operating system when you use Linux). For Windows 3.x use the ICU utility. There may even be a way to disable PnP using software that came with the modem.

HOWTO

Finally you must also find the file where "setserial" is run and add a line something like: "setserial /dev/ttyS2 irq5". See 1.5.3 (All Modems) for further instructions.

1.5.3 All Modems

Plug the modem into a telephone line. Then start up a communication program such as minicom and go to the configuration menu for the serial port. Assign it a high baud rate a few times higher than the bit rate of your modem. See 9.4 (Speed Table) for the "best" speeds to use. Tell it the full name of your serial port such as /dev/ttyS1. Set hardware flow control (RTS/CTS). Now you need to save these settings and exit minicom. Then start minicom again, type AT to see if your modem is there and responds with OK. Then go to the dial directory (or menu) and dial a number.

2 Modem & Serial Port Basics

You don't have to understand the basics to use and install a modem. But understanding it may help to determine what is wrong if you run into problems. After reading this section, if you want to understand it even better you may want to see 16 (How Modems Work) in this document (not yet complete). A future version of Serial-HOWTO (expected by Feb. 1999). should cover more on the serial port itself.

2.1 Modem Converts Digital to Analog (and conversely)

Most all telephone main lines are digital already but the lines leading to your house (or business) are usually analog which means that they were designed to transmit a voltage wave which is an exact replica of the sound wave coming out of your mouth. Such a voltage wave is called "analog". If viewed on an oscilloscope it looks like a sine wave of varying frequency and amplitude. A digital signal is like a square wave. For example 3 v (volts) might be a 1-bit and 0 v could be a 0-bit. For most serial ports (used by external modems) +12 v is a 0-bit and -12 v is a 1-bit (some are + or - 5 v).

To send data from your computer over the phone line, the modem takes the digital signal from your computer and converts it to "analog". It does this by both creating an analog sine wave and then "MODulating" it. Since the result still represents digital data, it could also be called a digital signal instead of analog. But it looks something like an analog signal and almost everyone calls it analog. At the other end of the phone line another modem "DEModulates" this signal and the pure digital signal is recovered. Put together the "mod" and "dem" parts of the two words above and you get "modem" (if you drop one of the two d's). A "modem" is thus a MODulator-DEModulator. Just what modulation is may be found in the section 16.1 (Modulation Details).

2.2 What is a Serial Port ?

2.2.1 Intro to Serial

Since modems have a serial port between them and the computer, it's necessary to understand the serial port as well as the modem. The serial port is an I/O (Input/Output) device. Most PC's have one or two serial ports. Each has a 9-pin connector (sometimes 25-pin) on the back of the computer. Computer programs can send data (bytes) to the transmit pin (output) and receive bytes from the receive pin (input). The other pins are for control purposes and ground.

The serial port is much more than just a connector. It converts the data from parallel to serial and changes the electrical representation of the data. Inside the computer, data bits flow in parallel (using many wires at the same time). Serial flow is a stream of bits over a single wire (such as on the transmit or receive pin of the serial connector). For the serial port to create such a flow, it must convert data from parallel (inside the computer) to serial on the transmit pin (and conversely).

Most of the electronics of the serial port is found in a computer chip (or a section of a chip) known as a UART. For more details on UARTs see the section 11 (What Are UARTs? How Do They Affect Performance?). But you may want to finish this section first so that you will hopefully understand how the UART fits into the overall scheme of things.

2.2.2 Pins and Wires

Old PC's used 25 pin connectors but only about 9 pins were actually used, so today most connectors are only 9-pin. Each of the 9 pins connects to a wire. Besides the two wires used for transmitting and receiving data, another pin (wire) is signal ground. The voltage on any wire is measured with respect to this ground. There are still more wires which are for control purposes (signalling) only and not for sending bytes. All of these signals could have been sent on a single wire, but instead, there is a separate dedicated wire for every type of signal. Some (or all) these control wires are called "modem control lines". These control wires are either in the asserted state (on) of +12 volts or in the negated state (off) of -12 volts. There is a wire to signal the computer to stop sending bytes to the modem. Conversely, another wire signals the modem to stop sending bytes to the computer. Other wires may tell the modem to hang up the telephone line or tell the computer that a connection has been made or that the telephone line is ringing (someone is attempting to call in).

2.2.3   Internal Modem Contains Serial Port

For an internal modem there is no 9-pin connector but the behavior is exactly as if the above mentioned cable wires existed. Instead of a a 12 volt signal in a wire giving the state of a modem control line, the internal modem may just use a status bit in its own memory (a register) to determine the state of this non-existent "wire". The internal modem's serial port looks just like a real serial port to the computer. It even includes the speed limits that one may set at ordinary serial ports such as 115200 bits/sec. Unfortunately today, many internal modems don't work exactly this way but instead use MS Windows software to help do their job and will not work under Linux. See 4.4 (Avoid: winmodems).

2.3   I/O Address & IRQ

Since the computer needs to communicate with each serial port, the operating system (OS) must know that the serial port exists, where it is (its I/O address) and what wire (IRQ number) the serial port is to use to request service from the computer's CPU. Thus every serial port device must store in its non-volatile memory both its I/O address and its Interrupt ReQuest number: IRQ. The IRQ determines what wire is used to request service using interrupt signals. See 2.4 (Interrupts).

The serial ports are labeled ttyS0, ttyS1, etc. (corresponding to COM1, COM2, etc. in DOS). There is also an obsolete set of names: cua0, cua1, etc which are almost the same as ttyS0, ttyS1, etc. See 5.4 (The cua Device). Which one of these names refers to certain physical serial port is determined (in part) by the I/O address stored inside the hardware chip of the physical port. This mapping of names (such as ttyS1) to I/O addresses and IRQ's may be set by the "setserial" command. 6.2 (What is Setserial). This does not set the I/O address and IRQ on the hardware itself (which is set by jumpers or by plug-and-play).

2.4   Interrupts

Bytes come in over the phone line to the modem, are converted from analog to digital by the modem and passed along to the serial port on their way to their destination inside your computer. When the serial port gets say 8 bytes from the modem (may be set to 1, 4, 8, or 14) it signals the CPU to fetch them by sending an electrical signal known as an interrupt on a dedicated conductor. Old serial ports would always send an interrupt for every byte received.

Each interrupt conductor (inside the computer) has a number (IRQ) and the serial port must know which conductor to use to signal on. For example, ttyS0 normally uses IRQ number 4 known as IRQ4 (or IRQ 4). A list of them and more will be found in "man setserial" (search for "Configuring Serial Ports"). Interrupts are issued whenever the serial port needs to get the CPU's attention. It's important to do this in a timely manner since the buffer inside the serial port can hold only 16 (1 in old modems) incoming bytes. If the CPU fails to remove such received bytes promptly, then there will not be any space left for any more incoming bytes and the small buffer may overflow (overrun). Bytes will be lost. For an external modem, there is no way to stop the flow rapidly enough to prevent this. For an internal modem the 16-byte buffer is on the same card and a good modem will not write to it if it's full. Thus a good internal modem will not overrun the 16-byte buffers and this is one advantage of an internal modem.

Interrupts are also issued when the serial port has just sent out all 16 of it bytes from its small transmit buffer to the modem. It then has space for 16 more outgoing bytes. The interrupt is to notify the CPU of that fact so that it may put more bytes in the small transmit buffer to be transmitted. Also, when a modem control line changes state an interrupt is issued.

The buffers mentioned above are all hardware buffers. The serial port also has large buffers in main memory. This will be explained later

HOWTO

Interrupts convey a lot of information but only indirectly. The interrupt itself just tells a chip called the interrupt controller that a certain serial port needs attention. The interrupt controller then signals the CPU. The CPU runs a special program to service the serial port. That program is called an interrupt service routine (part of the serial driver software). It tries to find out what has happened at the serial port and then deals with the problem such a transferring bytes from (or to) the serial port's hardware buffer. This program can easily find out what has happened since the serial port has registers at I/O addresses known to the the serial driver software. These registers contain status information about the serial port. The software reads these registers and by inspecting the contents, finds out what has happened and takes appropriate action.

2.5   Data Compression (by the Modem)

Before continuing with the basics of the serial port, one needs to understand about something done by the modem: data compression. In some cases this task is actually done by software run on the computer's CPU but unfortunately at present, such software only works for MS Windows. The discussion here will be for the case where the modem itself does the compression since this is what must happen in order for the modem to work under Linux.

In order to send data faster over the phone line, one may compress (encode it) using a custom encoding scheme which itself depends on the data. The encoded data is smaller than the original (less bytes) and can be sent over the Internet in less time. This process is called "data compression".

If you download files from the Internet, they are likely already compressed and it is not feasible for the modem to try to compress them further. Your modem may sense that what is passing thru has already been compressed and refrain from trying a compress it any more. If you are receiving data which has been compressed by the other modem, your modem will decompress it and create many more bytes than were sent over the phone line. Thus the flow of data from your modem into your computer will be higher than the flow over the phone line to you. The ratio of this flow is called the compression ratio. Compression ratios as high as 4 are possible, but not very likely.

2.6   Error Correction

Similar to data compression, modems may be set to do error correction. While there is some overhead cost involved which slows down the byte/sec flow rate, the fact that error correction strips off start and stop bits actually increases the data byte/sec flow rate.

For the serial port's interface with the external world, each 8-bit byte has 2 extra bits added to it: a start-bit and a stop-bit. Without error correction, these extra stop and stop bits usually go right thru the modem and out over the phone lines. But when error correction is enabled, these extra bits are stripped off and the 8-bit bytes are put into packets. This is more efficient and results in higher byte/sec flow in spite of the fact that there are a few more bytes added for packet headers and error correction purposes.

2.7   Data Flow (Speeds)

Data (bytes representing letters, pictures, etc.) flows from your computer to your modem and then out on the telephone line (and conversely). Flow rates (such as 56k (56000) bits/sec) are (incorrectly) called "speed". But almost everyone says "speed" instead of "flow rate". If there were no data compression the flow rate from the computer to the modem would be about the same as the flow rate over the telephone line.

Actually there are two different speeds to consider at your end of the phone line:

- The speed on the phone line itself (DCE speed) modem-to-modem
- The speed from your computer's serial port to your modem (DTE speed)

When you dial out and connect to another modem on the other end of the phone line, your modem often sends you a message like "CONNECT 28800" or "CONNECT 115200". What do these mean? Well, its either the DCE speed or the DTE speed. If it's higher than the advertised modem speed it must be the DTE modem-to-computer speed. This is the case for the 115200 speed shown above. The 28800 must be a DCE (modem-to-modem) speed since the serial port has no such speed. One may configure the modem to report either speed. Some modems report both speeds and report the modem-to-modem speed as (for example): CARRIER 28800.

If you have an internal modem you would not expect that there would be any speed limit on the DTE speed from your modem to your computer since you modem is inside your computer and is almost part of your computer. But there is since the modem contains a dedicated serial port within it.

It's important to understand that the average speed is often less than the specified speed, especially on the short DTE computer-to-modem line. Waits (or idle time) result in a lower average speed. These waits may include long waits of perhaps a second due to 2.8 (Flow Control). At the other extreme there may be very short waits (idle time) of several micro-seconds separating the end of one byte and the start of the next byte. In addition, modems will fallback to lower speeds if the telephone line conditions are less than pristine.

For a discussion of what DTE speed is best to use see section 9 (What Speed Should I Use).

2.8   Flow Control

Flow control means the ability to stop the flow of bytes in a wire. It also includes provisions to restart the flow without any loss of bytes. Flow control is needed for modems to allow a jump in flow rates.

2.8.1   Flow Control Explained by an Example

For example, consider the case where your 33.6k modem is not doing any data compression or error correction. You have set the serial port speed to 115,200 bits/sec (bps). You are sending data from your computer to the phone line. Then the flow from the your computer to your modem is at 115.2k bps. However the flow from your modem out the phone line is at best only 33.6k bps. Since a faster flow (115.2k) is going into your modem than is coming out of it, the modem is storing the excess flow (115.2k -33.6k = 81.6k) in one of its buffers. This buffer would eventually overrun (run out of storage space) unless the 115.2k flow is stopped.

But now flow control comes to the rescue. When the modem's buffer is almost full, the modem sends a stop signal to the serial port. The serial port passes on the stop signal to the device driver and the 115.2k bps flow is halted. Then the modem continues to send out data at 33.6k bps drawing on the data it previous accumulated in its buffer. Since nothing is coming into the buffer, the level of bytes in it starts to drop. When almost no bytes are left in the buffer, the modem sends a start signal to the serial port and the 115.2k flow from the computer to the modem resumes. In effect, flow control creates an average flow rate (in this case 33.6k) which is significantly less than the "on" flow rate of 115.2k bps. This is "start-stop" flow control.

The above is an example of flow control for flow from the computer to the modem , but there is also flow control which is used for the opposite direction of flow: from a modem to a computer. You don't often need it in this direction (for flow from a modem to PC), but a for complex example of a case where it's needed see 2.10 (Complex Flow Control Example). But if you don't have a high enough speed set between the modem and the computer (serial port speed) then you do need to slow down the flow from the modem to the PC. To do this you must stop the incoming flow of bytes over the telephone line. Your modem must tell the other modem to stop sending. See 2.8.4 (Modem-to-Modem Flow Control) More details on flow control may eventually be put into the Serial-HOWTO.

2.8.2   Symptoms of No Flow Control

Understanding flow-control theory can be of practical use. For example I used my modem to access the Internet and it seemed to work fine. But after a few months I tried to send long files from my PC to an ISP and a huge amount of retries and errors resulted (but eventually Kermit could send a long file after many retries). Receiving in the other direction (from my ISP to me) worked fine. The problem turned out to be a hardware defect in my modem that had resulted in disabling flow control. My modem's buffer was overflowing (overrunning) on long outgoing files since no "stop" signal was ever sent to the computer to halt sending to the modem. There was no problem in the direction from the modem to my computer since the capacity (say 115.2k) was always higher than the flow over the telephone line. The fix was to enable flow control by putting an enable-flow-control command for the modem last in the init string.

2.8.3 Hardware vs. Software Flow Control

For modems, it's best to use "hardware" flow control that uses two dedicated "modem control" wires to send the "stop" and "start" signals. Software flow control uses the main receive and transmit wires to send the start and stop signals. It uses the ASCII control characters DC1 (start) and DC3 (stop) for this purpose. They are just inserted into the regular stream of data. Software flow control is not only slower in reacting but also does not allow the sending of binary data thru the modem unless special precautions are taken. Since binary data will likely contain DC1 and DC3, special means must be taken to distinguish between a DC3 that means a flow control stop and a DC3 that is part of the binary code. Likewise for DC1. To get software flow control to work for binary data requires both modem (hardware) and software support.

2.8.4 Modem-to-Modem Flow Control

This is the flow control of the data sent over the telephone lines between two modems. Practically speaking, it only exists when you have error correction set. Actually, even without error correction it's possible to enable software flow control between modems but it may interfere with sending binary data so it's not often used.

2.9 Data Flow Path; Buffers

Although much has been explained about this including flow control, a pair of 16-byte serial port buffers (in the hardware), and a pair of larger buffers inside the modem, there is still another pair of buffers. These are large buffers (perhaps 8k) in main memory also known as serial port buffers. When an application program sends bytes to the serial port (and modem), they first get stashed in the the transmit serial port buffer in main memory. The pair consists of both this transmit buffer and a receive buffer for the opposite direction of byte-flow.

The serial device driver takes out say 16 bytes from this transmit buffer, one byte at a time and puts them into the 16-byte transmit buffer in the serial hardware for transmission. Once in that transmit buffer, there is no way to stop them from being transmitted. They are then transmitted to the modem which also has a fair sized (say 1k) buffer. When the device driver (on orders from flow control) stops the flow of outgoing bytes from the computer, what it actually stops is the flow of outgoing bytes from the large transmit buffer in main memory. Even after this has happened and the flow to the modem has stopped, an application program may keep sending bytes to the 8k transmit buffer until it becomes fill. When it gets fill, the application program can't send any more bytes to it (a "write" statement in a C_program blocks) and the application program temporarily stops running and waits until some buffer space becomes available. Thus a flow control "stop" is ultimately able to stop the program that is sending the bytes. Even though this program stops, the computer does not necessarily stop computing. It may switch to running other processes while it's waiting at a flow control stop. The above was a little oversimplified since there is another alternative of having the application program itself do something else while it is waiting to "write".

2.10 Complex Flow Control Example

For many situations, there is a transmit path involving several links, each with its own flow control. For example, I type at a text-terminal connected to a PC. Inside the PC is a modem to access a BBS. For this I use the application program "minicom" which deals with 2 serial ports: one connected to the modem and another connected to the text-terminal. What I type at the text terminal goes into the first serial port to minicom, then from minicom out the second serial port to the modem, and then onto the telephone line to the BBS. The text-terminal has a limit to the speed at which bytes can be displayed on its screen and issues a flow control "stop" from time to time to slow down the flow. What happens when such a "stop" is issued? Let's consider a case where the "stop" is long enough to get thru to the BBS and stop the program at the BBS which is sending out the bytes.

Let's trace out the flow of this "stop" (which may be "hardware" on some links and "software" on others). First, suppose I'm "capturing" a long file from the BBS which is being sent simultaneously to both my text-terminal and a to file on my hard-disk. The bytes are coming in faster than the terminal can handle them so it sends a "stop" out its serial port to the first serial port on my PC. The device driver detects it and stops sending bytes from the 8k serial buffer (in main memory) to the terminal. Now minicom still keeps sending out bytes for the terminal into this 8k buffer.

When this 8k transmit buffer (on the first serial port) is full, minicom must stop writing to it. Minicom stops and waits. But this also causes minicom to stop reading from the 8k receive buffer on the 2nd serial port connected to the modem.

Flow from the modem continues until this 8k buffer too fills up and sends a different "stop" to the modem. Now the modem's buffer ceases to send to the serial port and also fills up. The modem (assuming error correction is enabled) sends a "stop signal" to the other modem at the BBS. This modem stops sending bytes out of its buffer and when its buffer gets fill, another stop signal is sent to the serial port of the BBS. At the BBS, the 8-k (or whatever) buffer fills up and the program at the BBS can't write to it anymore and thus temporarily halts.

Thus a stop signal from a text terminal has halted a programs on a BBS computer. What a Rube Goldberg (complex) sequence of events! Note that the stop signal passed thru 4 serial ports, 2 modems, and one application program (minicom). This counts the serial port attached to the terminal. Each serial port has 2 buffers (in one direction of flow): the 8k one and the hardware 16-byte one. The application program may have a buffer in main memory as specified in its C-code. This adds up to 11 different buffers the data is passing thru. Note that the small serial hardware buffers do not participate directly in flow control.

If the terminal speed limitation is the bottleneck in the flow from the BBS to the terminal, then its flow control "stop" is actually stopping the program that is sending from the BBS as explained above. But you may ask, how can a "stop" last so long that 11 buffers (some of them large) all get filled up? It can actually happen this way if all the buffers were near their upper limits when the terminal sent out the "stop".

But if you were to run a simulation on it you would discover that it's usually more complicated than this. At an instant of time some links are flowing and others are stopped (due to flow control). A "stop" from the terminal seldom propagates back to the BBS neatly as described above. It may take a few "stops" from the terminal to result in a "stop" at the BBS. To understand what is going on you really need to observe a simulation which can be done for a simple case with coins on a table. Use only a few buffers and set the upper level for each buffer at only a few coins.

Does one really need to understand all this? Well, understanding this explained to me why capturing text from a BBS was loosing text. The situation was exactly the above example but modem-to-modem flow control was disabled. Chunks of captured text that were supposed to get to the hard-disk never got there because of an overflow (overrun) at the modem buffer due to flow control "stops" from the terminal. Even though the BBS had a flow path to the hard-disk without bottlenecks, the overflow due to the terminal happened on this path and chunks of text were lost.

2.11   Modem Commands

Commands to the modem are sent to it from the communication software over the same conductor as used to send data. The commands are short ASCII strings. Examples are "AT&K3" for enabling hardware flow control (RTS/CTS) between your computer and modem; and "ATDT5393401 for Dialing the number 5393401. Note all commands are prefaced by "AT". Some commands such as enabling flow control help configure the modem. Other commands such as dialing a number actually do something. There are about a hundred or so different possible commands. When your communication software starts running, it first sends an "init" string of commands to the modem to configure it. All commands are sent on the ordinary data line before the modem dials (or receives a call).

Once the modem is connected to another modem (on-line mode), everything that is sent from your computer to your modem goes directly to the other modem and is not interpreted by the modem as a command. There is a way to "escape" from this mode of operation and go back to command mode where everything sent to the modem will be interpreted as a command. The computer just sends "+++" with a specified time spacing before and after it. If this time spacing is correct, the modem reverts to command mode. Another way to do this is by a signal on a certain modem control line.

There are a number of lists of modem commands on the Internet. The section 15.5 (Web Sites) has links to a couple of such web-sites. Different models and brands of modems do not use exactly the same set of such commands. So what works for one modem might not work for another. Some common command (not guaranteed to work on all modems) are listed in this HOWTO in the section 3.5 (Modem Configuration)

3   Configuring Modems (including the serial port)

If you want to use a modem only for MS Windows/Dos, then you can just install almost any modem and it will work OK. With a Linux PC it's not usually this easy unless you use an external modem. All external modems should work OK (even if they are labeled "Plug and Play") But most new internal modems are Plug-and-Play (PnP) and have PnP serial ports.

HOWTO

You may need to use the Linux "isapnp" program to configure these PnP serial ports. See the Plug-and-Play-HOWTO for more information.

3.1 Configuring Overview

Since each modem has an associated serial port there are two parts to configuring a modem:

- Configuring the modem itself: Done by the communication program
- Configuring the modem's serial port: Done only partly by the communication program

Most of the above configuring (but not necessarily most of the effort) is done by the communication program that you use with the modem such as `minicom` or `seyon`, or by the PPP part of your Web Browser. If you use the modem for dial-in, then the `getty` program which you use to present outsiders with a login-prompt, will help configure. Thus to configure the modem (and much of the serial port) you need to configure the communication program (or PPP or `getty`). The documentation for these programs and/or the PPP-HOWTO should be helpful.

But note that not all of the configuration of the serial port is done by the communication program (or getty). The remaining configuring is simple to state (but sometimes difficult to do). It mainly consists of setting the I/O address of the port and its IRQ number. In fact, plug-and-play could set these without you doing a thing. But there's a serious problem: Linux (as of early 1999) doesn't support plug-and-play very well. This may create a difficult problem for you.

3.2 Configuring the IRQ and IO-Address of the Serial Port

Prior to firing up (and configuring) your communication program, you must do the configuring that your communication program can't do. Oversimplified, this consists only of identifying the serial port on which the modem resides: Is it ttyS2 (=COM3) or ttyS1 (=COM2) etc.? If you know the answer for sure (and there are no IRQ conflicts), then there is nothing to do and you may start your communication program .

Otherwise, you must establish the serial port identification and assign it an IRQ number. This is done by putting two values (an IRQ number and I/O address) into two places:

1. A memory register of the serial port hardware itself
2. the device driver (often by running "`setserial`" at boot-time)

Both of the above are supposed to by done by a plug-and-play operating system (OS). For item 1. setting these numbers in a modem card (or for the serial port in the case of an external modem) was formerly done by jumpers. Today it's supposed to be done at boot-time by plug-and-play (PnP).

For item 2. if you accept the default settings there is no need to use `setserial`. But if you use "`setserial`" the IRQ and IO address you tell it must be exactly the same as what is set inside the serial port hardware (or will be set via PnP). We might call all of this "io-irq" configuring for short. In the Wintel world, the I/O address and IRQ are called "resources" and we are thus configuring certain resources.

3.2.1 Plug-and-Play

Plug-and-Play was designed to automate this io-irq configuring, but for Linux at present, it has made life more complicated. The standard kernels for Linux don't support plug-and-play very well. If you use a patch to the Linux kernel to covert it to a plug-and-play operating system, then all of the above should be handled automatically by the OS. But when you want to use this to automate configuring devices other that the serial port, you may find that you'll still have to configure the drivers manually since many Linux drivers are not written to support a Linux PnP OS. If you use `isapnptools` or the BIOS for configuring plug-and-play this will only put the two values into the registers of the serial port section of the modem card and you will likely still need to set up setserial. None of this is easy or very well documented as of early 1999. See Plug-and-Play-HOWTO and the isapnptools FAQ.

3.2.2 Using a PnP BIOS to IO-IRQ Configure

While the explanation of how to use a PnP OS or isapnp for io-irq configuring should come with such software, this is not the case if you want to let a PnP BIOS do such configuring. The BIOS usually has a CMOS menu for setting up the first two serial ports. There is often little to choose from. Unless otherwise indicated in menus, the standard I/O addresses and IRQ's should be used by the BIOS. See 5.1 (Serial Port Device Names & Numbers)

Whether you like it or not, when you start up a PC the PnP BIOS starts to do PnP (io-irq) configuring of hardware devices. It may do the job partially and turn the rest over to a PnP OS (which you don't have) or if thinks you don't have a PnP OS it may fully configure all the PnP devices but not configure the device drivers. This is what you want but it's not always easy to figure out exactly what the PnP BIOS has done.

If you tell the BIOS that you don't have a PnP OS, then the PnP BIOS should do the configuring of all PnP serial ports –not just the first two. If you have MS Windows on the same PC, the BIOS should have saved the io-irq configuration used for MS Windows in its non-volatile memory and use the same configuration for Linux. In this case if you can find out how MS Windows has set up io-irq then it should be the same under Linux.

If you add a new PnP device, the BIOS should change its PnP configuration to accommodate it. It could even change the io-irq of existing devices if required to avoid any conflicts. For this purpose, it keeps a list of non-PnP devices provided that you have told the BIOS how these non-PnP devices are io-irq configured. One way to tell the BIOS this is by running a program called ICU under MS Windows.

But how do you find out what the BIOS has done so that you set up the device drivers with this info? It would be nice be the BIOS's CMOS menus provided this info but they probably don't (except for COM1 and COM2). So it may be quite a hassle to find out. See 3.3.2 (What is set in my serial port hardware?)

3.2.3 External Modem Configure

If you use an external modem and plug it into say the ttyS1 connector, then there's (usually) no io-irq configuring to do since ttyS1 has likely already been io-irq configured. Your CMOS BIOS may have a menu to do this for COM1 and COM2.

3.2.4 If More Than 2 Serial Ports

Normally you don't need to configure the first two serial ports that your computer comes with since the default configuration works fine. The Linux distribution you get probably has these defaults built into it so you have nothing to do. Everything is different when you want to add a third serial port. The io-irq configuring of it uses the same principles as for the first two serial ports but this time (unless you use a plug-and-play operating system) you have to do it yourself. To do this (as already mentioned) you'll need to run setserial: 6.2 (What is Setserial) and also set the io-irq data into the modem card by PnP methods (or by physical jumpers or switches on old cards).

3.2.5 Methods for Setting I/O Addresses and IRQs

Here's a summary of what was just discussed (and more). The modem is entirely configured by sending commands to it from the computer (via the communication program) as is much of the serial port (such as the baud rate and hardware flow control). For more details on the PnP options see Plug-and-Play-HOWTO. You configure the io-irq of the serial port by:

1. Setting the IRQ number and the I/O address in the port hardware (io-irq) by doing one of the following:

   - Doing nothing for an external modem where the existing io-irq is OK
   - Using a PnP BIOS CMOS setup menu for an external modem (usually only for ttyS0 (Com1) and ttyS1 (Com2))
   - Doing nothing if you have both a PnP internal modem and a PnP Linux operating system.
   - Setting jumpers (if they exist) on an internal modem, old serial card, or old motherboard
   - Using `isapnp` for a PnP internal modem (non-PCI)

HOWTO

- Letting a PnP BIOS automatically configure a PnP internal modem (but it may be difficult to determine just what that configuration is). See 3.2.2 (Using a PnP BIOS to I0-IRQ Configure)
- Using a setup program which comes with the modem (run under MS Windows) that disables PnP

2. Run "setserial": Assigns say ttyS2 to an I/O address and IRQ number. Except that you probably don't need to run it if you have only 1 or 2 serial ports total or if you use a PnP operating system.

3.2.6 Avoiding I/O Address Conflicts of IBM 8514 Video Board

The I/O address of the IBM 8514 video board (and it's clones) is allegedly 0x2e8, the same as the I/O address of ttyS3. That is bad news if you try to use ttyS3 at this I/O address.

3.3 What is the current I/O address and IRQ of my Serial Port ?

There are two answers to this question: 1. What the device driver thinks has been set (This is what setserial "sets"). 2. What is actually set in the hardware. They both should be the same. If you're having trouble (including communication programs that can't communicate) it may mean that these two items are not set the same. In other words, this means that the driver has incorrect info on the serial port. If the driver has the wrong I/O address it will try to send data to a non-existing serial port –or even worse, to an actual device that is not a serial port. If it has the wrong IRQ it will not get interrupt service requests from the serial port, resulting in the possible overflow of the serial port's buffer and in very slow response (due to fallback to very slow "polling" methods instead of interrupts). If it has the wrong model of UART there is also apt to be trouble.

3.3.1 What does the device driver think?

How do you insure that the device driver has the correct info? Well, if everything seems OK then there's no need to look into this. But otherwise, it's easy to see what the device driver thinks. One way is to just type "setserial -g /dev/ttyS*". At boot-time, a message on the console should show this. You may look at /proc/ioports but it only shows the same I/O address which setserial has "set" but are not necessarily the way its actually set in the hardware. To see the IRQs used by currently running processes (that have devices open) look at /proc/interrupts. It also shows how many actual interrupts have been issued (often thousands). None of the above tests show what is actually set in the device. But if everything works fine, the devices are likely actually set up that way in the hardware.

3.3.2 What is set in my serial port hardware?

But how do you find out what I/O address and IRQ are actually set in the device hardware? For Plug-and-Play (PnP) modems (or PnP serial ports) on the ISA bus one may try the pnpdump program (part of isapnptools). If you use the –dumpregs option then it should tell you the actual I/O address and IRQ set in the modem card. The address it "trys" is not the device's I/O address, but a special read-port used only for PnP purposes.

For an older card, the jumper setting may tell you how its set. If the modem is PCI look at /proc/pci or /proc/bus/pci/devices. One crude method is try probing with setserial using the "autoconfig" option. You'll need to guess the addresses to probe at. See 6.2 (What is Setserial).

Another approach is to see how it's configured under MS-Windows (if you have it on the same machine). How it's configured under MS-Windows may not be the same as for Linux, but it's likely the same if you let a PnP BIOS automatically do the configuring when you start Linux (and have told the BIOS that you don't have a PnP operating system when running Linux).

3.4 Other Configuring

3.4.1 Configuring Hardware Flow Control (RTS/CTS)

See 2.8 (Flow Control) for an explanation of it. You should always use hardware flow control if possible. Your communication program or "getty" should have an option for setting it (and if you're in luck it might be enabled by default). It needs to be set both inside your modem (by an init string or default) and in the device driver. Your communication program should set both of these (if you configure it right).

If none of the above will fully enable hardware flow control. Then you must do it yourself. For the modem, make sure that it's either done by the init string or is on by default. If you need to tell the device driver to do it is best done on startup by putting a file that runs at boot-time. See the subsection 6.2.3 (Boot-time Configuration) You need to add the following to such a file for each serial port (example is ttyS2) you want to enable hardware flow control on:

```
stty crtscts < /dev/ttyS2
```

If you want to see if flow control is enabled do the following: In minicom (or the like) type AT&V to see how the modem is configured and look for &K3 which means hardware flow control. Then see if the device driver knows about it by typing: stty -a < /dev/ttyS2 Look for "crtscts" (without a disabling minus sign).

3.5 Modem Configuration (excluding serial port)

3.5.1 AT Commands

While the serial port on which a modem resides requires configuring, so does the modem itself. The modem is configured by sending AT commands (or the like) to it on the same serial line that is used to send data.

Most modems use an AT command set. These are cryptic and short ASCII commands where all command strings are prefaced by the letters AT. For example: ATZ&K3 There are two commands here Z and &K3. Unfortunately there are many different variations of the AT command set so that what works for one modem may or may not work for another modem. Thus there is no guarantee that the AT commands given in this section will work on your modem. Another point is that to get the modem to act on the AT command string, a return character must be sent at the end of the string. Sometimes the AT is prefaced by a return character and sometimes there are symbols added to the string (such as) which only tell the communication program to pause for a tiny interval of time at that point.

If you have a manual for your modem you can likely look up the AT command set in it. Otherwise, you may try to find it on the Internet. One may use a search engine and include some actual commands in the search terms to avoid finding sites that just talk about such commands but fail to list them. You might also try a few of the sites listed in the subsection 15.5 (Web Sites)

3.5.2 The Init String

The examples given in this subsection are from the Hayes AT modem command set. All command strings must be prefaced by the two letters AT. When a modem is powered on, it automatically configures itself with one of the configurations it has stored in its non-volatile memory. If this configuration is satisfactory there is nothing further to do.

If it's not satisfactory, then one may either alter it or reconfigure the modem by sending it a string of commands known as an "init string" (= initialization string). Most of the time, an init string is automatically sent to the modem when you start up a communication program (will depend on how you configured the program or what script you wrote for it if you use Kermit). You can usually edit the init string and change it to whatever you want. Sometimes the communications program will let you select the model of your modem and then use an init string that it thinks is best for that modem.

So there is both a default "string" (called a profile) stored inside the modem and another (the init string) that the communications program sends it. The modem will wind up configured like the default set it except that it will be modified by the commands included in the init string. If the init string is empty then it will of course use the default configuration.

Actually there is more than one "default" configuration (or profile) stored in the modem's non-volatile memory (it's still there when you turn it off). In my modem there are two factory profiles (0 and 1, neither of which can be changed) and two user defined profiles (0 and 1) that the user may set and store. Your modem may have more. Which one of these user-defined profiles is used at power-up depends on another item stored in the profile. If the command &Y0 is given then in the future profile 0 will be used at power-on. If it's a 1 instead of a 0 then profile 1 will be used at power-on.

There are also commands to recall (use it now) any of the 4 stored profiles. One may put such a command in an init string. Of course if it recalls the same profile as was automatically loaded at power-up, nothing is changed (unless the init string is sent after the modem has been in use for a while and had it's configuration changed by software, etc.) It's a good idea to use some kind of an init string so that it may be reset by sending it the init string after it's been in use for a while (and may have had it's initial configuration modified).

Recalling a saved profile (use 1 instead of 0 for profile 1):
Z0 recalls user-defined profile 0 and resets (hangs up, etc.)
&F0 recalls factory profile 0

Once you have sent commands to the modem to configure it the way you want (including recalling a factory profile and modifying it a little) you may save this as a user-defined profile:
&W0 saves the current configuration to user-profile 0

Many people don't bother saving a good configuration in their modem, but instead, send the modem a longer init string each time the modem is used. Another method is to restore the factory default at the start of the init string and then modify it a little by adding a few other commands to the end of the init string. This way no one can cause problems by modifying the user-defined profile which is loaded at power-on.

You may pick an init string supplied by someone else that they think is right for your modem. Some communication programs have a library of init strings to select from. The most difficult method (and one which will teach you the most about modems) is to study the modem manual and write one yourself. You could save this configuration inside the modem so that you don't need an init string. A third alternative is to start with an init string someone else wrote, but improve on it a little yourself.

3.5.3 Other Modem Commands

Future editions of Modem-HOWTO may contain more AT commands but the rest of this section is what was in the old Serial-HOWTO. All strings must start with AT. Here's a few Hayes AT codes that should be in the string (if they are not set by using a factory default or by a saved configuration).

```
E1          command echo ON
Q0          result codes are reported
V1          verbose ON
S0=0        never answer (uugetty does this with the WAITFOR option)
```

Here's some more codes concerning modem control lines DCD and DSR:

```
&C1         DCD is on after connect only
&S0         DSR is always on
```

These affect what your modem does when calls start and end. What DTR does may also be set up but it's more complicated.

If your modem does not support a stored profile, you can set these through the INIT string in a config file (or the like). Some older modems come with DIP switches that affect register settings. Be sure these are set correctly, too.

Greg Hankins has a collection of modem setups for different types of modems. If you would like to send him your working configuration, please do so: <mailto:gregh@cc.gatech.edu> You can get these setups at ftp://ftp.cc.gatech.edu/pub/people/gregh/modem-configs.

Note: to get his USR Courier V.34 modem to reset correctly when DTR drops, Greg Hankins had to set &D2 and S13=1 (this sets bit 0 of register S13). This has been confirmed to work on USR Sportster V.34 modems as well.

Note: some Supra modems treat DCD differently than other modems. If you are using a Supra, try setting &C0 and *not* &C1. You must also set &D2 to handle DTR correctly.

4 Modems for a Linux PC

4.1 External vs. Internal

A modem for a PC may be either internal or external. The internal one is installed inside of your PC (you must remove screws, etc. to install it) and the external one just plugs into a serial port connector on a PC. Internal modems are less expensive, are less likely to overrun, usually use less electricity, and use up no space on your desk. External modems are much easier to install, require less configuration, and have lights which may give you a clue as to what is happening. External modems are easy to move to another computer. Most external modems have no switch to turn off the power supply when not in use and thus are likely to consume a little electricity even when turned off (unless you unplug the power supply from the wall). Each watt they draw costs you about $1/yr. Another possible disadvantage of an external is that you will be forced to use an existing serial port which may not support a speed of over 115,200 k (although as of late 1998 most new internal modems don't either –but some do). If a new internal modem had a 16650 UART it would put less load on the CPU (but almost none do as of late 1998).

Internal modems present a special problem for Linux, but will work just as well as external modems provided you avoid the high percentage of them that will work only for MS Windows, and also provided that you spend time (sometimes a lot of time) to configure them correctly. Some of the modems which will work only under MS Windows are, unfortunately, not labeled as such. If you buy a new one, make sure that you can return it for a refund if it will not work under Linux.

While most new modems are plug-and-play you have various ways to deal with them:

- Use the "isapnp" program

- Have a PnP BIOS do the configuring

- Patch the kernel to create a PnP Linux

Each of the above has shortcomings. Isapnp documentation is difficult to understand although reading the Plug-and-Play-HOWTO (at present incomplete) will aid in understanding it. If you want the PnP BIOS to do the configuring, all you need to do is to make sure that it knows you don't have a PnP operating system. But you may have trouble trying to determine how it set things up. See 3.3.2 (What is set in my serial port hardware?). Patching the kernel can be complicated too. There are a lot of device drivers that don't cooperate with the patch (so you will need to manually configure them).

There are many Linux users that say that it's a lot simpler just to get an external modem and plug it in. But since new peripherals are all PnP today, you may eventually need to deal with it, so why not now? It may be easier to deal with PnP under Linux in the future but pioneers are needed to lead the way today in spite of the old adage that "Pioneering doesn't pay".

4.2 External Modems

4.2.1 PnP External Modems

Many external modems are labeled "Plug and Play" (PnP) but they should all work fine as non-PnP modems. Since you usually plug the modem into a serial port which has its own IRQ number and I/O address, the modem needs no PnP features to set these up. However, the serial port itself may need to be configured (IRQ number and I/O address) unless the default configuration is OK.

How can an external modem be called PnP since it can't be configured by PnP? Well, it has a special PnP identification built into it that can be read (thru the serial port) by a PnP operating system. Such an operating system would then know that you have a modem on a certain port and would also know the model number. Then you might not need to configure application programs by telling them what port the modem is on (such as /dev/ttyS2 or COM3). But if you don't have such a PnP operating system you will need to configure your application program manually by giving it the /dev id (such as /dev/ttyS2).

4.2.2 Cabling & Installation

Connecting an external modem is simple compared to connecting most other devices to a serial port that require various types of "null modem" cables. Modems use straight through cable, with no pins crossed over. Most computer stores should have these. Make sure you get the correct gender. If you are using the DB9 or DB25 serial port at your computer, it will always be male which means that the connector on the cable should be female. Hook up your modem to one of your serial ports. If you are willing to accept the default IRQ and I/O address of the port you connect it to, then you are ready to start your communication program and configure the modem itself.

4.2.3 What the Lights (LED's) Mean

- TM Test Modem
- AA Auto Answer (If on, your modem will answer an incoming call)
- RD Receive Data line = RxD
- SD Send Data line = TxD
- TR data Terminal Ready = DTR (set by your PC)
- RI Ring Indicator (If on, someone is "ringing" your modem)
- OH Off Hook (If off, your modem has hung up the phone line)
- MR Modem Ready = DSR ??
- EC Error Correction
- DC Data Compression
- HS High Speed (for this modem)

4.3 Internal Modems

An internal modem is installed in a PC by taking off the cover of the PC and inserting the modem card into a vacant slot on the motherboard. There are modems for the ISA slots and others for the PCI slots. While external modems plug into the serial port (via a short cable) the internal modems have the serial port built into the modem. In other words, the modem card is both a serial port and a modem.

Setting the I/O address and IRQ for a serial port was formerly done by jumpers on the card. These are little black rectangular "cubes" about 5x4x2 mm in size which push in over pins on the card. Plug-and-Play modems (actually the serial port part of the modems) don't use jumpers for setting these but instead are configured by sending configuration commands to them (via I/O address space on the ISA bus inside the computer). Such configuration commands can be sent by a PnP BIOS, the isapnp program (for the ISA bus only) or by a PnP operating system. The configuring of them is built into Windows 95/98 OS. Under Linux you have a choice of ways (none of which is always easy) to io-irq configure them:

1. Use "isapnp" which may be run automatically at every boot-time
2. Use a PnP BIOS alone (which runs at every boot-time)
3. Patch Linux to make it a PnP operating system

4.4 Internal Modems You Must Avoid (winmodems, etc.)

A majority of internal modems made after about mid-1998 *don't* work with Linux since they are "winmodems" or the like. Names used include: HSP, HCF, and soft-... modem. Such modems turn over much (or even almost all) of the work of the modem to the main processor (CPU) chip of your computer (such as a Pentium chip). Since only Windows (and not Linux) software is provided to do this, it will not work under Linux. A list of modems which do and don't work under Linux is at *Linux modem list* <http://www.o2.net/~gromitkc/winmodem.html>

A better term for "winmodem" might be "software modem" or "soft-modem". But since this software is only for MS Windows, the term "winmodem" is now a good one since it also implies it's "Windows-only". The term "Winmodem" is a trademark for a certain type of "winmodem". Here is some more precise terminology regarding "winmodems":

HSP (Host Signal Processor) means that the host processor (your CPU chip) creates the code needed to produce the electrical signal on the phone line. The modem itself just creates whatever electrical waveshape the CPU tells it to. In contrast to this, a "controllerless" modem can create the waveshapes on its own (but can't control the modem). It contains no facilities to deal with bytes being sent and received. It can't compress strings of bytes; it can't check for errors; it can't put them into packets. In other words it can't control the modem but instead has the CPU do all this work using a program for Windows. The Rockwell HCF (stands for ??) scheme does this. If the software that does all this could be ported to Linux and then there wouldn't be this problem. Besides the above, a modem which doesn't simulate a serial port will not work under Linux.

How do you determine if an internal modem will work under Linux? If you don't know the model of the modem and you also have Windows on your Linux PC, click on the "Modem" icon in the "Control Panel". First check out the modem list on the Web mentioned 3 paragraphs above. If that doesn't work (or isn't feasible), you can look at the package it came in (or a manual) find the section on the package that says something like "Minimum System Requirements" or just "System Requirements". It may be in fine print. Read it closely. If Windows is listed as one of the requirements then it will likely not work under Linux.

Otherwise, it may work under Linux if it fails to state explicitly that you must have Windows. By saying it's "designed for Windows" it may only mean that it fully supports Microsoft's plug-and-play which is OK since Linux uses the same plug-and-play specs (but doesn't support them very well as yet). Being "designed for Windows" thus gives no clue as to whether or not it will work under Linux. You might check the Website of the manufacturer or inquire via email. I once saw a web-page that specifically stated that one model worked under Linux while implying that another model didn't.

As far as the author knows, there is no effort currently underway to support winmodems in Linux. You might request that modem manufacturers port their code to Linux (or the like).

4.5 Which Internal Modems are Best to Avoid ?

- 4.4 (Avoid: winmodems) or the like. They will NOT work at all
- 4.5.3 (PCI Modems) often don't work under Linux
- 4.5.1 (MWave and DSP Modems) might work, but only if you first start Windows/Dos each time you power on your PC
- Modems with 4.5.2 (RPI (Rockwell)) drivers work but with reduced performance

4.5.1 MWave and DSP Modems

Such modems use DSP's (Digital Signal Processors) which are programmed by algorithms which must be downloaded from the hard disk to the DSP's memory just before using the modem. Unfortunately, the downloading is done by Dos/Windows programs so one can't do it from Linux. Ordinary modems that work with Linux often have a DSP too (and may mention this on the packaging), but the program that runs it is stored inside the modem. This is not a "DSP modem" in the sense of this section and should work OK under Linux.

If a DSP modem modem simulates a serial port, then it is usable with Linux which communicates with modems via the serial port. If you also have Dos/Windows on the same PC you may be able to use the modem: First start Dos/Windows (make sure the modem gets initialized) and then without turning off the computer, go into Linux. One way to do this may be to press CTRL-ALT-DEL. An example of a DSP modem is IBM's Aptiva MWAVE.

4.5.2 Rockwell (RPI) Drivers

Modems that require Rockwell RPI drivers are not fully usable since the driver software doesn't work on Linux. The RPI does compression and error correction using MS Windows software on your computer's CPU. If you are willing to operate the modem without using the RPI (and have no compression nor error correction) then you may easily disable RPI by sending the modem (via the initialization string) a command to do so each time you power on your modem. On

HOWTO

my modem this command is +H0. Not having data compression available may not be much of a handicap since most long files which you download from the Internet are already compressed and attempts at further compression may only slow things down a bit.

4.5.3 PCI Modems

A PCI modem card is one which inserts into a PCI-bus slot on the motherboard of a PC. Unfortunately, it seems that most PCI modems will not work under Linux. But since some people have gotten PCI modems to work under Linux it seems that a small minority of such modems will work under Linux.

After you install a PCI modem, look at /proc/pci. If you see a high main memory address (like 0xfebfff00), it probably works by shared memory which is not supported by Linux. If there is no such high memory address and the only address you see is an I/O address under 0xffff ??, then it might work OK. I'm not really sure of the /proc/pci signature to look for to determine whether or not the modem will work under Linux. If this request is still in the latest version of this HOWTO, please send me info on what /proc/pci looks like for PCI modems that work under Linux or let me know what signatures to look for in /proc/pci to determine whether or not the modem will work with Linux.

5 Serial Port Devices /dev/ttySN

5.1 Serial Port Device Names & Numbers

Devices in Linux have major and minor numbers. Each serial port may have 4 possible names, only 2 of which are official and found in the /dev directory: ttyS and cua. The cua name is deprecated and may not be used in the future. See 5.4 (The cua Device). Dos/Windows use the COM name while the setserial program uses tty00, tty01, etc. Don't confuse dev/tty0, dev/tty1, etc. which are used for the console (your PC monitor) but are not serial ports.

dos	set-serial		major	minor		major	minor	I/O address
COM1	tty00	/dev/ttyS0	4,	64;	/dev/cua0	5,	64	3F8
COM2	tty01	/dev/ttyS1	4,	65;	/dev/cua1	5,	65	2F8
COM3	tty02	/dev/ttyS2	4,	66;	/dev/cua2	5,	66	3E8
COM4	tty03	/dev/ttyS3	4,	67;	/dev/cua3	5,	67	2E8

Note that all distributions should come with ttyS devices (and cua devices until cua is finally abolished) already made correctly. You can verify this by typing:

```
linux% ls -l /dev/cua*
linux% ls -l /dev/ttyS*
```

5.2 Creating Devices In the /dev directory

If you don't have a device, you will need to create it with the mknod command. Example, suppose you needed to create devices for ttyS0:

```
linux# mknod -m 666 /dev/cua0 c 5 64
linux# mknod -m 666 /dev/ttyS0 c 5 64
```

You can use the MAKEDEV script, which lives in /dev. See the man page for it. This simplifies the making of devices. For example, if you needed to make the devices for ttyS0 you would type:

```
linux# cd /dev
linux# ./MAKEDEV ttyS0
```

This handles the devices creation and should set the correct permissions.

5.3 Link ttySN to /dev/modem ?

On some installations, two extra devices will be created, /dev/modem for your modem and /dev/mouse for your mouse. Both of these are symbolic links to the appropriate device in /dev which you specified during the installation (unless you have a bus mouse, then /dev/mouse will point to the bus mouse device).

There has been some discussion on the merits of /dev/mouse and /dev/modem. The use of these links is discouraged. In particular, if you are planning on using your modem for dialin you may run into problems because the lock files may not work correctly if you use /dev/modem. Use them if you like, but *be sure they point to the right device*. However, if you change or remove this link, some applications might need reconfiguration.

5.4 The cua Device

Each ttyS device has a corresponding cua device. It is planned to eventually abolish cua so it's best to use ttyS (unless cua is required). There is a difference between cua and ttyS but a savvy programmer can make a ttyS port behave just like a cua port so there is no real need for the cua anymore. Except some older programs may need to use the cua.

What's the difference? The main difference between cua and ttyS has to do with what happens in a C-program when an ordinary "open" command tries to open the port. If a cua port has been set to check modem control signals, the port can be opened even if the DCD modem control signal says not to. Astute programming (by adding additional lines to the program) can force a ttyS port to behave this way also. But a cua port can be more easily programmed to open for dialing out on a modem even when the modem fails to assert DCD (since no one has called into it and there's no carrier). That's why cua was once used for dial-out and ttyS used for dial-in.

Starting with Linux kernel 2.2, a warning message will be put in the kernel log when one uses cua. This is an omen that cua will sometime disappear.

6 Interesting Programs You Should Know About

6.1 What is getty?

"getty" is a program that handles the login process when you log into a Linux box. You will need to use some type of "getty" if you want others to be able to dial in to your Linux PC with a modem. You do not need to use getty if you only want to dial out with your modem. There are three getty versions that modems may use with Linux: mgetty, getty_ps, and agetty. agetty is the simplest (and weakest) of the three and some consider it mainly for text-terminals. The syntax for these programs differs, so be sure to check that you are using the correct syntax for whatever getty you use. If this sentence appears in the latest version of this howto, then if you can write a few paragraphs comparing mgetty with getty_ps, etc. please submit it so that it can be included here. Mgetty is only a few years old and seems to be more popular for new installations than the older getty_ps.

6.1.1 About mgetty

mgetty is a version of getty mainly for use with modems. It may be used for hard-wired terminals but the documentation is about 99% related to modems. In addition to allowing dialup logins, mgetty also provides FAX support and auto PPP detection. There is a supplemental program called vgetty which handles voicemail for some modems. mgetty documentation (supplied in texinfo format) is good, and does not need supplementing. Please refer to it for installation instructions. You can find the latest information on mgetty at *http://www.leo.org/~doering/mgetty/* and <http://alpha.greenie.net/mgetty>

6.1.2 About getty_ps

getty_ps contains two programs: getty is used for console and terminal devices, and uugetty for modems. Greg Hankins (former author of Serial-HOWTO) used uugetty so his writings about it are included here. See 8 (Uugetty). The other gettys are well covered by the documentation that comes with them.

HOWTO

6.1.3 About agetty and mingetty

agetty is the third variation of getty. It's a simple, completely functional implementation of getty which is best suited for virtual consoles or terminals rather than modems. But it works fine with modems under favorable conditions.

mingetty is a small getty that will work only for consoles (monitors). While the previous 3 variations of getty will work for both real terminals and dial-in modems, mingetty will not do this.

6.2 What is Setserial ?

6.2.1 Intro to Setserial

setserial is a program which allows you to tell the device driver software the I/O address of the serial port, which IRQ is set in the port's hardware, etc. With appropriate options, it can also probe (at a given I/O address) for a serial port but you must guess the I/O address (or it may use whatever address the driver thinks your /dev/ttySx is at). Setserial does not set either IRQ's nor I/O addresses in the serial port hardware itself. You must tell setserial the identical values that have been set in the hardware. It's set in the hardware either by jumpers or by plug-and-play. Do not just invent some values that you think would be nice to use. However, if you know the I/O address but don't know the IRQ you may command setserial to attempt to determine it.

You can see a list of possible commands to use (but not the one-letter options such as -v for verbose –which you should normally use when troubleshooting) by typing setserial with no arguments. Note that setserial calls an I/O address a "port". If the argument to setserial is for example just /dev/ttyS1, then you'll see some info about how that device driver is configured for that port. But this doesn't tell you if the hardware actually has these values set in it. If fact, you can run setserial and assign a purely fictitious I/O address, any IRQ, and whatever uart type you would like to have. Then the next time you type "setserial ..." it will display these bogus values without complaint. Note that assignments made by setserial are lost when the PC is powered down so it is usually run automatically somewhere each time that Linux is booted.

6.2.2 Probing

In order to try to find out if you have a certain piece of serial hardware you must first know its I/O address (or the device driver must have an I/O address for it, likely previously set by setserial). To try to detect the physical hardware use the -v (verbose) and autoconfig command to setserial. If the resulting message shows a uart type such as 16550A, then you're OK. If instead it shows "unknown" for the uart type, then there is likely no serial port at all at that I/O address. Some cheap serial ports don't identify themselves correctly so if you see "unknown" you still might have something there. See the file in which "setserial" is run at boot-time. Besides auto-probing for uart type, setserial can auto-probe for IRQ's but this doesn't always work right either.

6.2.3 Boot-time Configuration

There is usually a file somewhere that runs setserial at boot-time. If it's not run at boot-time then your Linux system will automatically configure only ttyS{0-3} using the default IRQs of 4 and 3 (with the default IRQ conflicts). In 1998 it was (temporarily ?) changed to only ttyS{0-1}. So if you have more than 2 serial ports, or want to have control over how the ports are configured you should configure using setserial. In fact, your distribution may have set things up so that the setserial program runs automatically at boot-time.

The file that runs setserial at boot-time is likely somewhere in the /etc directory-tree. You might use "locate" to find a file named: rc.serial, or 0setserial (Debian), etc. This supplied file which runs setserial at start-up may contain a number of commented-out examples. By uncommenting some of these and/or modifying them, you may be able to set things up correctly or run some tests. You could copy a few of them to another file and then execute it as a shell script but don't forget to also copy any capitalized definitions needed such as SETSERIAL=/bin/setserial.

If you use setserial you could test it on the command line first, and then when you have it working, put it into the file which runs it at boot-time: /etc/rc.d/rc.serial or /etc/rc.boot/0setserial so that it is run at startup. If those files don't exist try /etc/rc.d/rc.local (someone reported that with one kernel, rc.local was executed too late after the serial port had already been opened). Or you could just edit one of the above files and cross your fingers. Make sure that you are using a valid path for setserial, and a valid device name.

6.2.4 IRQs

By default, both ttyS0 and ttyS2 share IRQ 4, while ttyS0 and ttyS3 share IRQ 3. But sharing serial interrupts is not permitted unless you have kernel 2.2 or better. If you don't have this modern kernel but only have two serial ports ttyS0 and ttyS1 you're still OK since IRQ sharing conflicts don't exist for non-existent devices.

But if you do have more than 2 serial ports, then for kernels < 2.2 such sharing may be dangerous if the two devices with the same IRQ are being used at the same time. If you add an internal modem and retain ttyS0 and ttyS1, then you should attempt to find an unused IRQ and set it both on your modem card (or serial port) and then use setserial to assign it to your device driver. If IRQ 5 is not being used for a sound card, this may be one you can use for a modem. To set the IRQ in hardware you may need to use isapnp, a PnP BIOS (See 3.2.2 (Using a PnP BIOS to I0-IRQ Configure)) or patch Linux to make it PnP. To help you determine which spare IRQ's you might have, type "man setserial" and search for say: "IRQ 11".

6.3 What is isapnp ?

isapnp is a program to configure Plug-and-Play (PnP) devices on the ISA bus including internal modems. It comes in a package called "isapnptools" and includes another program, "pnpdump" which finds all your ISA PnP devices and shows you options for configuring them in a format which may be added to the PnP configuration file: /etc/isapnp.conf. It may also be used with the –dumpregs option to show the current I/O address and IRQ of the modem's serial port. The isapnp command may be put into a startup file so that it runs each time you start the computer and thus will configure ISA PnP devices. It is able to do this even if your BIOS doesn't support PnP. See Plug-and-Play-HOWTO.

7 Trying Out Your Modem (Dialing Out)

7.1 Are You Ready to Dial Out ?

Once you've plugged in your modem and know which serial port it's on you're ready to try using it. Before you try to get the Internet on it or have people call in to you, first try something simpler like dialing out to some number to see if your modem is working OK. Find a phone number that is connected to a modem. It you don't know what number to call, ask at computer stores for such phone numbers of bulletin boards, etc. or see if a local library has a phone number for their on-line catalog.

Then make sure you are ready to phone. Do you know what serial port (such as ttyS2) your modem is on? You should have found this out when you io-irq configured your serial ports. Have you decided what speed you are going to use for this port? See 9.4 (Speed Table) for a quick selection or 9 (What Speed Should I Use) for more details. If you have no idea what speed to set, just set it a few times faster than the advertised speed of your modem. Also remember that if you see a menu where an option is "hardware flow control" and/or "RTS/CTS" or the like, select it. Is a live telephone cable plugged in to your modem? You may want to connect the cable to a real telephone to make sure that it can produce a dial tone.

Now you need to select a communication (dialing) program to use to dial out. Dialing programs include: minicom, seyon (X-windows), and kermit. See section 10 (Communications Programs) about some communications programs. Two examples are presented next: 7.2 (Dialing Out with Minicom) and 7.3 (Dialing Out with Kermit)

7.2 Dialing Out with Minicom

Minicom comes with most Linux distributions. To configure it you should be the root user. Type "minicom -s" to configure. This will take you directly to the configuration (set-up) menus. Alternatively you could just run "minicom" and then type ^A to see the bottom status line. This shows to type ^A Z for help (you've already typed the ^A so just type z). From the help menu go to the Configuration menu.

Most of the options don't need to be set for just simply dialing out. To configure you have to supply a few basic items: the name of the serial port your modem is on such as /dev/ttyS2 and the speed such as 115200. These are set at the serial port menu. Go to it and set them. Also (if possible) set hardware flow control (RTS/CTS). Then save them. When typing in the speed, you should also see something like "8N1" which you should leave alone. It means: 8-bit bytes, No parity, 1 stop-bit appended to each byte. If you can't find the speed you want, a lower speed will always work for a test. Exit (hit return) when done and save the configuration as default (dfl) using the menu. You may want to exit minicom and start it again so it can now find the serial port and initialize the modem, or you could go to help and tell minicom to initialize the modem.

Now you are ready to dial. But first at the main screen you get after you first type "minicom" make sure there's a modem there by typing AT and then hit the "enter/return" key. It should display OK. If it doesn't something is wrong and there is no point of trying to dial.

If you got the "OK" go back to help and select the dialing directory. You may edit it and type in a phone number, etc. into the directory and then select "dial" to dial it. Alternatively, you may just dial manually (by selecting "manual" and then type the number at the keyboard). If it doesn't work, carefully note any error messages and try to figure out what went wrong.

7.3   Dialing Out with Kermit

You can find the latest version of `kermit` at *http://www.columbia.edu/kermit/*. For example, say your modem was on ttyS3, and it's speed was 115200 bps. You would do the following:

```
linux# kermit
C-Kermit 6.0.192, 6 Sep 96, for Linux
 Copyright (C) 1985, 1996,
   Trustees of Columbia University in the City of New York.
Default file-transfer mode is BINARY
Type ? or HELP for help.
C-Kermit>set line /dev/ttyS3
C-Kermit>set carrier-watch off
C-Kermit>set speed 115200
/dev/ttyS3, 115200 bps
C-Kermit>c
Connecting to /dev/ttyS3, speed 115200.
The escape character is Ctrl-\ (ASCII 28, FS)
Type the escape character followed by C to get back,
or followed by ? to see other options.
ATE1Q0V1                     ; you type this and then the Enter key
OK                           ; modem should respond with this
```

If your modem responds to AT commands, you can assume your modem is working correctly on the Linux side. Now try calling another modem by typing:

```
ATDT7654321
```

where 7654321 is a phone number. Use ATDP instead of ATDT if you have a pulse line. If the call goes through, your modem is working.

To get back to the `kermit` prompt, hold down the Ctrl key, press the backslash key, then let go of the Ctrl key, then press the C key:

```
Ctrl-\-C
(Back at linux)
C-Kermit>quit
linux#
```

This was just a test using the primitive "by-hand" dialing method. The normal method is to let `kermit` do the dialing for you with its built-in modem database and automatic dialing features, for example using a US Robotics (USR) modem:

```
linux# kermit
C-Kermit 6.0.192, 6 Sep 1997, for Linux
 Copyright (C) 1985, 1996,
  Trustees of Columbia University in the City of New York.
Default file-transfer mode is BINARY
Type ? or HELP for help
C-Kermit>set modem type usr        ; Select modem type
C-Kermit>set line /dev/ttyS3       ; Select communication device
C-Kermit>set speed 115200          ; Set the dialing speed
C-Kermit>dial 7654321              ; Dial
 Number: 7654321
 Device=/dev/ttyS3, modem=usr, speed=115200
 Call completed.<BEEP>
Connecting to /dev/ttyS3, speed 115200
The escape character is Ctrl-\ (ASCII 28, FS).
Type the escape character followed by C to get back,
or followed by ? to see other options.

Welcome to ...

login:
```

8   Uugetty for Dial-In (from the old Serial-HOWTO)

8.1   Installing getty_ps

Since uugetty is part of getty_ps you'll first have to install getty_ps. If you don't have it, get the latest version from *sunsite.unc.edu:/pub/Linux/system/serial*. In particular, if you want to use high speeds (57600 and 115200 bps), you must get version 2.0.7j or later. You must also have libc 5.x or greater.

By default, `getty_ps` will be configured to be Linux FSSTND (File System Standard) compliant, which means that the binaries will be in `/sbin`, and the config files will be named `/etc/conf.{uu}getty.tty`*S*N. This is not apparent from the documentation! It will also expect lock files to go in `/var/lock`. Make sure you have the `/var/lock` directory.

If you don't want FSSTND compliance, binaries will go in `/etc`, config files will go in `/etc/default/{uu}getty.tty`*S*N, and lock files will go in `/usr/spool/uucp`. I recommend doing things this way if you are using UUCP, because UUCP will have problems if you move the lock files to where it isn't looking for them.

`getty_ps` can also use `syslogd` to log messages. See the man pages for `syslogd(1)` and `syslog.conf(5)` for setting up `syslogd`, if you don't have it running already. Messages are logged with priority LOG_AUTH, errors use LOG_ERR, and debugging uses LOG_DEBUG. If you don't want to use `syslogd` you can edit `tune.h` in the `getty_ps` source files to use a log file for messages instead, namely `/var/adm/getty.log` by default.

Decide on if you want FSSTND compliance and syslog capability. You can also choose a combination of the two. Edit the `Makefile`, `tune.h` and `config.h` to reflect your decisions. Then compile and install according to the instructions included with the package.

>From this point on, all references to `getty` will refer to `getty_ps`. References to `uugetty` will refer to the `uugetty` that comes with the `getty_ps` package. These instructions will not work for `mgetty` or `agetty`.

8.2 Setting up uugetty

Make sure that you have an outgoing and incoming device for the serial port your modem is on. If you have your modem on `ttyS3` you will need the `/dev/cua3`, and `/dev/ttyS3` devices. If you don't have the correct devices, see section 5.2 (Creating Devices In <tt>/dev</tt>) on how to create devices, and create the devices. If you want to be able to dial out with your modem while `uugetty` is watching the port for logins, use the `/dev/cuaN` device instead of the `/dev/ttySN` device [One wouldn't need cua if the software was written to avoid it.]

`uugetty` does important lock file checking. Update `/etc/gettydefs` to include an entry for your modem. When you are done editing `/etc/gettydefs`, you can verify that the syntax is correct by doing:

```
linux# getty -c /etc/gettydefs
```

8.2.1 Modern Modems

If you have a 9600 bps or faster modem with data compression, you can lock your serial port to one speed. For example:

```
# 115200 fixed speed
F115200# B115200 CS8 # B115200 SANE -ISTRIP HUPCL #@S @L @B login: #F115200
```

If you have your modem set up to do RTS/CTS hardware flow control, you can add `CRTSCTS` to the entries:

```
# 115200 fixed speed with hardware flow control
F115200# B115200 CS8 CRTSCTS # B115200 SANE -ISTRIP HUPCL CRTSCT-
S #@S @L @B login: #F115200
```

8.2.2 Old slow modems

If you have a slow modem (under 9600 bps) Then, instead of one line for a single speed, your need several lines to try a number of speeds. Note the these lines are linked to each other by the last "word" in the line such as #38400. Blank lines are needed between each entry.

```
# Modem entries
115200# B115200 CS8 # B115200 SANE -ISTRIP HUPCL #@S @L @B login: #57600

57600# B57600 CS8 # B57600 SANE -ISTRIP HUPCL #@S @L @B login: #38400

38400# B38400 CS8 # B38400 SANE -ISTRIP HUPCL #@S @L @B login: #19200

19200# B19200 CS8 # B19200 SANE -ISTRIP HUPCL #@S @L @B login: #9600

9600# B9600 CS8 # B9600 SANE -ISTRIP HUPCL #@S @L @B login: #2400

2400# B2400 CS8 # B2400 SANE -ISTRIP HUPCL #@S @L @B login: #115200
```

8.2.3 Login Banner

If you want, you can make `uugetty` print interesting things in the login banner. In Greg's examples, he has the system name, the serial line, and the current bps rate. You can add other things:

```
@B    The current (evaluated at the time the @B is seen) bps rate.
@D    The current date, in MM/DD/YY.
@L    The serial line to which getty is attached.
@S    The system name.
@T    The current time, in HH:MM:SS (24-hour).
```

```
@U     The number of currently signed-on users.  This is  a
       count of the number of entries in the /etc/utmp file
       that have a non-null ut_name field.
@V     The value of VERSION, as given in the defaults file.
To display a single '@' character, use either '\@' or '@@'.
```

8.3   Customizing uugetty

There are lots of parameters you can tweak for each port you have. These are implemented in separate config files for each port. The file /etc/conf.uugetty will be used by *all* instances of uugetty, and /etc/conf.uugetty.tty*SN* will only be used by that one port. Sample default config files can be found with the getty_ps source files, which come with most Linux distributions. Due to space concerns, they are not listed here. Note that if you are using older versions of getty (older than 2.0.7e), or aren't using FSSTND, then the default file will be /etc/default/uugetty.tty*SN*. Greg's /etc/conf.uugetty.ttyS3 looked like this:

```
# sample uugetty configuration file for a Hayes compatible modem to allow
# incoming modem connections
#
# alternate lock file to check... if this lock file exists, then uugetty is
# restarted so that the modem is re-initialized
ALTLOCK=cua3
ALTLINE=cua3
# line to initialize
INITLINE=cua3
# timeout to disconnect if idle...
TIMEOUT=60
# modem initialization string...
# format: <expect> <send> ... (chat sequence)
INIT="" AT\r OK\r\n
WAITFOR=RING
CONNECT="" ATA\r CONNECT\s\A
# this line sets the time to delay before sending the login banner
DELAY=1
#DEBUG=010
```

Add the following line to your /etc/inittab, so that uugetty is run on your serial port (substituting in the correct information for your environment - config file location, port, speed, and default terminal type):

```
S3:456:respawn:/sbin/uugetty -d /etc/default/uugetty.ttyS3 t-
tyS3 F115200 vt100
```

Restart init:

```
linux# init q
```

For the speed parameter in your /etc/inittab, you want to use the highest bps rate that your modem supports.

Now Linux will be watching your serial port for connections. Dial in from another machine and login to you Linux system.

uugetty has a lot more options, see the man page for getty(1m) for a full description. Among other things there is a scheduling feature, and a ringback feature.

9   What Speed Should I Use with My Modem?

By "speed" we really mean the "data flow rate" but almost everybody incorrectly calls it speed. For all modern modems you have no choice of the speed that the modem uses on the telephone line since it will automatically choose the highest possible speed that is possible under the circumstances. But you do have a choice as to what speed will be used between your modem and your computer. This is sometimes called "DTE speed" where "DTE" stands for Data Terminal Equipment (Your computer is a DTE.) You need to set this speed high enough so this part of the signal path will not be a bottleneck. The setting for the DTE speed is the maximum speed of this link. Most of the time it will likely operate at lower speeds.

For an external modem, DTE speed is the speed (in bits/sec) of the flow over the cable between you modem and PC. For an internal modem, it's the same idea since the modem also emulates a serial port. It may seem ridiculous having a speed limit on communication between a computer and a modem card that is directly connected inside the computer to a much higher speed bus. But it's that way since the modem card probably includes a dedicated serial port which does have speed limits (and settable speeds).

9.1   Speed and Data Compression

What speed do you choose? If it were not for "data compression" one might try to choose a DTE speed exactly the same as the modem speed. Data compression takes the bytes sent to the modem from your computer and encodes them into a fewer number of bytes. For example, if the flow (speed) from the PC to the modem was 20,000 bytes/sec (bps) and the compression ratio was 2 to 1, then only 10,000 bytes/sec would flow over the telephone line. Thus for a 2:1 compression ratio you need to set the speed double the maximum modem speed on the phone line. If the compression ratio is 3 to 1 you need to set it 3 times faster.

9.2   Where do I Set Speed ?

This DTE speed is normally set by a menu in your communications program or by an option given to the getty command if someone is dialing in. You can't set the DCE modem-to-modem speed.

9.3   Can't Set a High Enough Speed

You need to find out the highest speed supported by your hardware. As of late 1998 most hardware only supported speeds up to 115.2K bps. A few 56K internal modems support 230.4K bps. If you have a communications programs that doesn't show high enough speeds in its menu, then there are some options you can give to the setserial command so that a low speed command from the communication program will actually result in a higher speed. With these options, when you set the speed for 38400 the actual speed will be much higher. See the man page for "setserial" and search for spd_hi, spd_vhi, spd_cust, baud_base, and divisor. Note that you must set baud_base to the actual maximum speed of the hardware. This speed is usually lower than the frequency of the crystal oscillator in the hardware since the crystal frequency is often divided by 16 in the hardware to get the actual top speed. The reason the crystal frequency needs to be higher is so that this high crystal speed can be used to take a number of samples of each bit to determine if it's a 1 or a 0. To get a speed of 230400 (if this is what your serial port hardware supports –few do) on ttyS2 you could use:

```
setserial /dev/ttyS2 spd_cust baud_base 230400 divisor 1
```
In some cases this works when "stty 230400" doesn't. If you've used spd_cust you'll have to claim the speed is 38400 somewhere else to obtain the actual speed of 230400. This method of setting speed is sort of a hack and when applications catch up to higher speeds it might not be needed anymore.

9.4   Speed Table

It's best to have at least a 16650 UART for a 56K modem but few modems support it. Second best is a 16550 that has been tweaked to give 230,400 bps. Here are some suggested speeds to set your serial line if your modem speed is:

- 56K (V.90) use 115200 bps or 230400 bps (a few % faster ?)

- 28.8K (V.34), 33.6K (V.34) use 115200 bps
- 14400 bps (V.32bis), with V.42bis data compression, use 57600 bps
- 9600 bps (V.32), with V.42bis data compression, use 38400 bps
- slower than a 9600 bps (V.32) modem, set your speed to the highest speed your modem supports.

10 Communications Programs And Utilities

PPP is by far the most widely used. It's used for Internet access. For dialing out to public libraries, bulletin boards, etc. `minicom` is the most popular followed by `Seyon` (X-Windows only) and `Kermit`.

10.1 Minicom vs. Kermit

Minicom is only a communications program while Kermit is both a communications program and a file transfer protocol. But one may use the Kermit protocol from within Minicom (provided one has Kermit installed on one's PC). Minicom is menu based while Kermit is command line based (interactive at the special Kermit prompt). While the Kermit program is free software, the documentation is not all free. There is no detailed manual supplied and it is suggested that you purchase a book as the manual. However Kermit has interactive online help which tells all but lacks tutorial explanations for the beginner. Commands may be put in a script file so you don't have to type them over again each time. Kermit (as a communications program) is more powerful than Minicom.

Although all Minicom documentation is free, it's not as extensive as Kermit's. Since permission is required to include Kermit in a commercial distribution, and since the documentation is not entirely free, some distributions don't include Kermit. In my opinion it's easier to set up Minicom and there is less to learn.

10.2 Lists of Programs

Here is a list of some communication software you can choose from, available via FTP, if they didn't come with your distribution. I would like comparative comments on the dialout programs. Are the least popular ones obsolete?

10.2.1 Least Popular Dialout

- `ecu` - a communications program
- `pcomm` - `procomm`-like communications program with zmodem
- `xc` - xcomm communication package

10.2.2 Most Popular Dialout

- `minicom` - `telix`-like communications program. Supports scripts, zmodem, kermit
- *C-Kermit* `<http://www.columbia.edu/kermit/>` - portable, scriptable, serial and TCP/IP communications including file transfer, character-set translation, and zmodem support
- `seyon` - X based communication program

10.2.3 Fax

- `efax` a small fax program
- `hylafax` a large fax program based on the client-server model.
- `mgetty+fax` handles fax stuff and login for dial-ins

10.2.4 Voicemail

- *mvm* `<http://www-internal.alphanet.ch/~schafer/mvm>` is a Minimal VoiceMail for Linux
- vgetty is an extension to mgetty that handles voicemail for some modems. It should come with recent releases of mgetty.

10.2.5 Dial-in (uses getty)

- `mgetty+fax` is for modems and is well documented. It also handles fax stuff and provides an alternative to `uugetty`. It's incorporating `callback` and voicemail (using vgetty) features. See 6.1.1 (About mgetty)

- `uugetty` is for modems. It comes as a part of the `ps_getty` package. See 6.1.2 (About getty_ps)

10.2.6 Other

- `callback` is where you dial out to a remote modem and then that modem hangs up and calls you back (to save on phone bills).

- `SLiRP` and `term` provide a PPP-like service that you can run in user space on a remote computer with a shell account. See 10.3 (term and SLiRP) for more details

- `ZyXEL` is a control program for ZyXEL U-1496 modems. It handles dialin, dialout, dial back security, FAXing, and voice mailbox functions.

- SLIP and PPP software can be found at

  ftp://sunsite.unc.edu/pub/Linux/system/network/serial.

- Other things can be found on *ftp://sunsite.unc.edu/pub/Linux/system/serial* and *ft-p://sunsite.unc.edu/pub/Linux/apps/serialcomm* or one of the many mirrors. These are the directories where serial programs are kept.

10.3   SLiRP and term

`SLiRP` and `term` are programs which are of use if you only have a dial-up shell account on a Unix-like machine and want to get the equivalent of a PPP account (or the like) without being authorized to have it (possibly because you don't want to pay extra for it, etc.). `SLiRP` is more popular than `term` which is almost obsolete.

To use `SLiRP` you install it in your shell account on the remote computer. Then you dial up the account and run SLiRP on the remote and PPP on your local PC. You now have a PPP connection over which you may run a web browser on your local PC such as Netscape, etc. There may be some problems as SLiRP is not as good as a real PPP account. Some accounts may provide SLiRP since it saves on IP addresses (You have no IP address while using SLiRP).

`term` is something like SLiRP only you need to run `term` on both the local and remote computer. There is no PPP on the phone line since `term` uses its own protocol. To use `term` from your PC you need to use a term-aware version of ftp to do ftp, etc. Thus it's easier to use SLiRP since the ordinary version of ftp works fine with SLiRP. There is an unmaintained Term HOWTO.

11   What Are UARTs? How Do They Affect Performance?

UARTs (**U**niversal **A**synchronous **R**eceiver **T**ransmitter) are serial chips on your PC motherboard (or on an internal modem card). The UART function may also be done on a chip that does other things as well. On older computers like many 486's, the chips were on the disk I/O controller card. Still older computer have dedicated serial boards.

The UART's purpose is to convert bytes from the PC's parallel bus to a serial bit-stream. The cable going out of the serial port is serial and has only one wire for each direction of flow. The serial port sends out a stream of bits, one bit at a time. Conversely, the bit stream that enters the serial port via the external cable is converted to parallel bytes that the computer can understand. UARTs deal with data in byte sized pieces, which is conveniently also the size of ASCII characters.

Say you have a terminal hooked up to your PC. When you type a character, the terminal gives that character to it's transmitter (also a UART). The transmitter sends that byte out onto the serial line, one bit at a time, at a specific rate. On the PC end, the receiving UART takes all the bits and rebuilds the (parallel) byte and puts it in a buffer.

There are two basic types of UARTs: dumb UARTS and FIFO UARTS. Dumb UARTs are the 8250, 16450, early 16550, and early 16650. They are obsolete but if you understand how they work it's easy to understand how the modern ones work with FIFO UARTS (late 16550, 16550A, 16c552, late 16650, 16750, and 16C950).

There is some confusion regarding 16550. Early models had a bug and worked properly only as 16450's. Later models with the bug fixed were named 16550A but many manufacturers did not accept the name change and continued calling it a 16550. Most all 16550's in use today are like 16550A's. Linux will report it as being a 16550A even though your hardware manual (or a label note) says it's a 16550. A similar situation exists for the 16650 (only it's worse since the manufacturer allegedly didn't admit anything was wrong). Linux will report a late 16650 as being a 16650V2. If it reports it as 16650 it is bad news and only is used as if it had a one-byte buffer.

To understand the differences between dumb and FIFO (First In, First Out queue discipline) first let's examine what happens when a UART has sent or received a byte. The UART itself can't do anything with the data passing thru it, it just receives and sends it. For the original dumb UARTS, the CPU gets an interrupt from the serial device every time a byte has been sent or received. The CPU then moves the received byte out of the UART's buffer and into memory somewhere, or gives the UART another byte to send. The 8250 and 16450 UARTs only have a 1 byte buffer. That means, that every time 1 byte is sent or received, the CPU is interrupted. At low transfer rates, this is OK. But, at high transfer rates, the CPU gets so busy dealing with the UART, that is doesn't have time to adequately tend to other tasks. In some cases, the CPU does not get around to servicing the interrupt in time, and the byte is overwritten, because they are coming in so fast. This is called an "overrun" or "overflow".

That's where the FIFO UARTs are useful. The 16550A (or 16550) FIFO chip comes with 16 byte FIFO buffers. This means that it can receive up to 14 bytes (or send 16 bytes) before it has to interrupt the CPU. Not only can it wait for more bytes, but the CPU then can transfer all 14 (or more) bytes at a time. Although the interrupt threshold (trigger level) may be set at 8 instead of 14, this is still a significant advantage over the other UARTs, which only have 1 byte buffers. The CPU receives less interrupts, and is free to do other things. Data is not lost, and everyone is happy.

While most PC's only have a 16550 with 16-byte buffers, better UARTS have even larger buffers. Note that the interrupt is issued slightly before the buffer get full (at say a "trigger level" of 14 bytes for a 16-byte buffer). This allows room for a few more bytes to be received during the time that the interrupt is being serviced. The trigger level may be set to various permitted values by kernel software. A trigger level of 1 will be almost like a dumb UART (except that it still has room for 15 more bytes after it issues the interrupt).

If you type something while visiting a BBS, the characters you type go out thru the serial port. Your typed characters that you see on the screen are what was echoed back thru the telephone line thru your modem and then thru your serial port to the screen. If you had a 16-byte buffer on the serial port which held back characters until it had 14 of them, you would need to type many characters before you could see what you typed (before they appeared on the screen). This would be very confusing but there is a "timeout" to prevent this. Thus you normally see a character on the screen just as soon as you type it.

The "timeout" works like this for the receive UART buffer: If characters arrive one after another, then an interrupt is issued only when say the 14th character reaches the buffer. But if a character arrives and the next character doesn't arrive soon thereafter, then an interrupt is issued. This happens even though there are not 14 characters in the buffer (there may only be one character in it). Thus when what you type goes thru this buffer, it acts almost like a 1-byte buffer even though it is actually a 16-byte buffer (unless your typing speed is a hundred times faster than normal). There is also "timeout" for the transmit buffer as well.

Here's a list of UARTs. *TL* is *T*rigger *L*evel

- 8250, 16450, early 16550: Obsolete with 1-byte buffers
- 16550, 16550A, 16c552: 16-byte buffers, TL=1,4,8,14
- 16650: 32-byte buffers. Speed up to 460.8 Kbps
- 16750: 64-byte buffer for send, 56-byte for receive. Speed up to 921.6 Kbps
- Hayes ESP: 1K-byte buffers.

The obsolete ones are only good for modems no higher than 14.4k (DTE speeds up to 38400 bps). For modern modems you need at least a 16550 (and not an early 16550). For V.90 56k modems, it may be a several percent faster with a 16650 (especially if you are downloading uncompressed files). The main advantage of the 16650 is its larger buffer size as the extra speed isn't needed unless the modem compression ratio is high. Some 56k internal modems may come with a 16650 ??

HOWTO

Non-UART, and intelligent multiport boards use DSP chips to do additional buffering and control, thus relieving the CPU even more. For example, the Cyclades Cyclom, and Stallion EasyIO boards use a Cirrus Logic CD1400 RISC UART, and many boards use 80186 CPUs or even special RISC CPUs, to handle the serial I/O.

Most newer PC's (486's, Pentiums, or better) come with 16550A's (usually called just 16550's). If you have something really old the chip may unplug so that you may be able to upgrade by buying a 16550A chip and replacing your existing 16450 UART. If the functionality has been put on another type of chip, you are out of luck. If the UART is socketed, then upgrading is easy (if you can find a replacement). The new and old are pin-to-pin compatible. It may be more feasible to just buy a new serial board on the Internet (few retail stores stock them today).

12 Troubleshooting

12.1 Software

- `modemstat` and `statserial` show the current state of various modem signal lines (such as DTR, CTS, etc.)

- `irqtune` will give serial port interrupts higher priority to improve performance.

- `hdparm` for hard-disk tuning may help some more.

12.2 My Modem is Physically There but Can't be Found

For the PCI bus look at /proc/pci. Otherwise see 3.3 (What is the current I/O address and IRQ of my Serial Port ?) Here are some common mistakes people make:

- setserial: They run it (without the "autoconfig" option) or see it displayed on the screen at boot-time, and erroneously think that the result shows how their hardware is actually configured.

- /proc/interrupts: When their modem isn't in use they don't see their modem's interrupt there, and erroneously conclude that their modem can't be found (or doesn't have an interrupt set).

- /proc/ioports: People think this shows the hardware configuration when it only shows about the same data (possibly erroneous) as setserial.

You may probe for the modem's serial port using "setserial" with the "autoconfig" argument at the I/O address you think the modem is at. If it shows "unknown" for UART type there may be nothing there. See 6.2 (What is setserial). Your problem could be due to a winmodem (or the like) which can't be used with Linux. See 4.4 (Avoid: winmodems).

12.3 "Operation not supported by device" (error message) for ttySx

This means that an operation requested by setserial, stty, etc. couldn't be done because the kernel doesn't support doing it. A common reason is that the "serial" module wasn't loaded at the time. "lsmod" will show you if it's now loaded but it sometimes is automatically loaded when needed so it may be loaded now but wasn't loaded when you got the error message. The "serial" module should be listed in the file: /etc/modules.conf. The actual module should reside in: /lib/modules/.../misc/serial.o.

12.4 Slow. Text appears on the screen slowly after long delays

This will happen from the very start of using the modem. One symptom happens when you are manually typing to your modem: You type but the screen remains blank (until after several seconds when you finally might see what you typed). Another symptom is that only a few words at a time appear on the screen (possibly with missing text).

This may be due to a mis-set IRQ. This means that the IRQ used by the device driver does not correspond to the IRQ set in hardware (IRQ mis-set). With a mis-set IRQ you may loose received data and get "input overrun" error messages (or find them in logs). See 14.1 (Interrupt Mis-set) for more details.

It could also be an interrupt conflict. See 14.2 (Interrupt Conflicts) Make sure there are no IRQs being shared. Check all your boards (serial, ethernet, SCSI, etc...). Make sure the jumper (or PnP) settings, and the `setserial` parameters are correct for all your serial devices. Also check `/proc/ioports` and `/proc/interrupts` and `/proc/pci` for conflicts.

12.5 Uploading (downloading) files is broken/slow

Flow control (both at your PC and/or modem) may not be enabled. If you have set a high DTE speed (like 115.2K) then flow from your modem to your PC may work OK but a lot of flow in the other direction will not all get thru due to the telephone line bottleneck. This will result in many errors and the resending of packets. It may thus take far too long to send a file. In some cases, files don't make it thru at all. If you're downloading long uncompressed files or web pages (and your modem uses data compression) or you've set a low DTE speed, then downloading may also be broken due to no flow control.

12.6 For Dial-in I Keep Getting "line NNN of inittab invalid"

Make sure you are using the correct syntax for your version of `init`. The different `init`'s that are out there use different syntax in the `/etc/inittab` file. Make sure you are using the correct syntax for your version of `getty`.

12.7 When I Try To Dial Out, It Says "/dev/ttySN: Device or resource busy"

This problem can arise when DCD or DTR are not implemented correctly. DCD should only be on (asserted) when there is an actual connection (ie someone has dialed in), not when `getty` is watching the port. Check to make sure that your modem is configured to only assert DCD when there is a connection. DTR should be on (asserted) whenever something is using, or watching the line, like `getty`, `kermit`, or some other comm program.

Another common cause of "device busy" errors, is that you set up your serial port with an interrupt already taken by something else. As each device initializes, it asks Linux for permission to use its hardware interrupt. Linux keeps track of which interrupt is assigned to whom, and if your interrupt is already taken, your device won't be able to initialize properly. The device really doesn't have much of any way to tell you that this happened, except that when you try to use it, it will return a "device-busy" error. Check the interrupts on all of your boards (serial, ethernet, SCSI, etc.). Look for IRQ conflicts.

12.8 I Keep Getting "Getty respawning too fast: disabled for 5 minutes"

Make sure your modem is configured correctly. Look at registers E and Q. This can occur when your modem is chatting with `getty`.

Make sure you are calling `getty` correctly from your `/etc/inittab`. Using the wrong syntax or device names will cause serious problems.

For uugetty, verify that your `/etc/gettydefs` syntax is correct by doing the following:

```
linux# getty -c /etc/gettydefs
```

This can also happen when the `uugetty` initialization is failing. See section 12.10 (uugetty Still Doesn't Work).

12.9 My Modem is Hosed after Someone Hangs Up, or uugetty doesn't respawn

This can happen when your modem doesn't reset when DTR is dropped. Greg Hankins saw his RD and SD LEDs go crazy when this happened. You need to have your modem reset. Most Hayes compatible modems do this with `&D3`, but on his USR Courier, he had to set `&D2` and `S13=1`. Check your modem manual (if you have one).

HOWTO

12.10   uugetty Still Doesn't Work

There is a DEBUG option that comes with `getty_ps`. Edit your config file `/etc/conf.{uu}getty.tty`*SN* and add `DEBUG=`*NNN*. Where *NNN* is one of the following combination of numbers according to what you are trying to debug:

```
D_OPT     001          option settings
D_DEF     002          defaults file processing
D_UTMP    004          utmp/wtmp processing
D_INIT    010          line initialization (INIT)
D_GTAB    020          gettytab file processing
D_RUN     040          other runtime diagnostics
D_RB      100          ringback debugging
D_LOCK    200          uugetty lockfile processing
D_SCH     400          schedule processing
D_ALL     777          everything
```

Setting `DEBUG=010` is a good place to start.

If you are running `syslogd`, debugging info will appear in your log files. If you aren't running `syslogd` info will appear in `/tmp/getty:tty`*SN* for debugging `getty` and `/tmp/uugetty:tty`*SN* for uugetty, and in `/var/adm/getty.log`. Look at the debugging info and see what is going on. Most likely, you will need to tune some of the parameters in your config file, and reconfigure your modem.

You could also try `mgetty`. Some people have better luck with it.

13   Flash Upgrades

Many modems can be upgraded by reprogramming their flash memories with an upgrade program which you get from the Internet. By sending this "program" via the serial port to the modem, the modem will store this program in its non-volatile memory (it's still there when the power is turned off). The instructions on installing it are usually on how to do in under Windows so you'll need to figure out how to do the equivalent under Linux (unless you want to install the upgrade under Windows).

If the latest version of this HOWTO still contains this request (see 1.3 (New Versions of this HOWTO)) please send me your experiences with installing such upgrades that will be helpful to others.

If you need to send a file (program) to your modem, how do you do it? First, there may be a command that you need to send your modem to tell it that what follows is a flash ROM upgrade. In one case this was AT** Next, you need to send the file directly to the modem. Communication programs often use zmodem or kermit to send files to the modem (and beyond) but these put the file into packets which append headers and you want the exact file, not a modified one. But the kermit program has a "transmit" command that will send the file directly (without using the kermit packets) so this is one way to send a file directly. Another way would be to escape from the communication program to the shell (in minicom this is ^aj) and then: `cat upgrade_file_name > /dev/ttyS2` . Then go back to the communication program (type fg at the command line prompt in minicom) to see what happened.

14   Problems Explained

While the section 12 (Troubleshooting) lists problems by symptom, this section explains what will happen if something is set incorrectly. This section helps you understand what caused the symptom and what other symptoms might be due to the same problem.

14.1   Interrupt Mis-set

If you don't understand what an interrupt does see 2.4 (Interrupts). If a serial port has one IRQ set in the hardware but a different one set in the device driver, the device driver will not receive any interrupts sent by the serial port. Since the serial port uses interrupts to tell its driver when it needs service (fetching bytes from it's 16-byte receive buffer or putting another 16-bytes in its transmit buffer) one might expect that the serial port would not work at all.

But it still may work anyway –sort of. Why? Well, besides the interrupt method of servicing the port there's a polling method that doesn't need interrupts. The way it works is that every so often the device driver checks the serial port to see if it needs anything such as if it has some bytes that need fetching from its receive buffer. If interrupts don't work, the serial driver falls back to this polling method. But this polling method was not intended to be used a substitute for interrupts. It's so slow that it's not practical to use and may cause buffer overruns. Its purpose may have been to get things going again if just one interrupt is lost or fails to do the right thing. It's also useful in showing you that interrupts have failed.

For the 16-byte transmit buffer, 16 bytes will be transmitted and then it will wait until the next polling takes place (several seconds later) before the next 16 bytes is sent out. Thus transmission is very slow and in small chunks. Receiving is slow too since bytes that are received by the receive buffer are likely to remain there for several seconds until it is polled.

This explains why it takes so long before you see what you typed. When you type say AT to the modem, the AT goes out the serial port to the modem. The modem then echos the AT back thru the serial port to the screen. Thus the AT characters had to pass twice thru the serial port. Normally this happens so fast that AT seems to appear on the screen at the same time that you hit the keys on the keyboard. With polling delays thru the serial port, you don't see what you typed until many seconds later.

What about overruns of the 16-byte receive buffer? This will happen with an external modem since the modem just sends to the serial port at high speed which is likely to overrun the 16-byte buffer. But for an internal modem, the serial port is on the same card and it's likely to check that this receive buffer has room for more bytes before putting received bytes into it. In this case there will be no overrun of this receive buffer, but text will just appear on your screen in 16-byte chunks at intervals of several seconds.

Even with an external modem you might not get overruns. If just a few characters (under 16) are sent you don't get overruns since the buffer likely has room for them. But attempts to send a larger number of bytes from your modem to your screen may result in overruns. However, more than 16 (with no gaps) can get thru OK if the timing is right. For example, if 32 bytes were received (and no more bytes followed), the polling might just happen after the first 16 bytes had been received. Then there would be space for the next 16 bytes so that 32 bytes gets thru OK. Similar conditions might pass between 16 to 31 bytes thru OK. But it's also likely that only an occasional 16-byte chunk will get thru and huge gaps of missing data will be lost.

If you have an obsolete serial port with only a 1-byte buffer (or it's been incorrectly set to work like a 1-byte buffer) then the situation will be much worse than described above and only one character will occasionally make it thru the port. This character is likely to be just a line-feed since this is often the last character to be transmitted in a burst of characters sent to your screen. Thus you may type AT to the modem but never see AT on the screen. All you see several seconds later is that the cursor drops down one line. This has happened to me even with a 16-byte buffer that was somehow behaving like a 1-byte buffer.

When a communication program starts up, it expects interrupts to be working. It's not geared to using this slow polling-like mode of operation. Thus all sorts of mistakes may be made such as setting up the serial port and/or modem incorrectly. It may fail to realize when a connection has been made. If a script is being used for login, it may fail (caused by timeout) due to the polling delays.

14.2   Interrupt Conflicts

When two devices have the same IRQ number it's called sharing interrupts. Under some conditions this sharing works out OK. Starting with kernel version 2.2, serial ports may share interrupts with other serial ports. Devices on the PCI bus may share the same IRQ interrupt with other devices on the PCI bus. In other cases where there is potential for conflict, there should be no problem if no two devices with the same IRQ are ever "in use" at the same time. More precisely, "in use" really means "open" (in programmer jargon). In cases other than the exceptions mentioned above (unless special software permits sharing), sharing is not allowed and conflicts arise if sharing is attempted.

Even if two processes with conflicting IRQs run at the same time, one of the devices will likely have its interrupts sent to its device driver and will work OK. The other device will not have its interrupts sent to the correct driver and will likely behave just like a process with mis-set interrupts. See 14.1 (Interrupt Mis-set) for more details.

15 Other Sources of Information

15.1 Misc

- man pages for: `agetty(8)`, `getty(1m)`, `gettydefs(5)`, `init(1)`, `isapnp(8)`, `login(1)`, `mgetty(8)`, `setserial(8)`

- Your modem manual (if it exists). Some modems come without manuals.

- The Linux serial mailing list. To join, send email to *majordomo@vger.rutgers.edu*, with "subscribe linux-serial" in the message body. If you send "help" in the message body, you get a help message. The server also serves many other Linux lists. Send the "lists" command for a list of mailing lists.

15.2 Books

I've been unable to find a good up-to-date book on modems.

- The Complete Modem Reference by Gilbert Held, 1997. Contains too much info about obsolete topics. More up-to-date info may be found on the Internet.

- Modems For Dummies by Tina Rathbone, 1996. (Have never seen it.)

15.3 HOWTOs

- Cable-Modem mini-howto
- ISDN Howto (not a LDP Howto) <http://www.suse.de/Support/sdb_e/isdn.html>: drivers for ISDN "Modems"; Much related info on this is in German
- Modems-HOWTO: In French (Not used in creating this Modem-HOWTO)
- NET-3-HOWTO: all about networking, including SLIP, CSLIP, and PPP
- PPP-HOWTO: help with PPP including modem set-up
- Serial-HOWTO has info on Multiport Serial Cards used for both terminals and banks of modems. Technical info on the serial port will appear in the next revision of it.
- Serial-Programming-HOWTO: for some aspects of serial-port programming
- Text-Terminal-HOWTO: (including connecting up with modems)
- UUCP-HOWTO: for information on setting up UUCP

15.4 Usenet newsgroups

- comp.os.linux.answers FAQs, How-To's, READMEs, etc. about Linux.
- comp.os.linux.hardware Hardware compatibility with the Linux operating system.
- comp.os.linux.setup Linux installation and system administration.
- comp.dcom.modems Modems for all OS's

15.5 Web Sites

- Hayes AT modem commands *Technical Reference for Hayes (tm) Modem Users* <http://www.hayes.com/TechSupport/techref/>

- *Rockwell-based modem commands* <http://www.rss.rockwell.com/techinfo/>

- A white paper discussing serial communications and multiport serial boards is available from Cyclades at *http://www.cyclades.com*.

- Modem FAQs:
  Navas 28800 Modem FAQ <http://web.aimnet.com/jnavas/modem/faq.html>

- *Curt's High Speed Modem Page* <http://www.teleport.com/curt/modems.html>

- Much info on 56k modems *56k Modem = v.Unreliable* <http://808hi.com/56k/>

- *Links to modem manufacturers* <http://www.56k.com/links/Modem_Manufacturers/>

- *Identifying modems by FCC ID* <http://www.sbsdirect.com/fccenter.html>

- Partial list of modems which work/don't_work under Linux *modem list* <http://www.o2.net/~gromitkc/winmodem.html>

16   Appendix A: How Modems Work (technical) (unfinished)

16.1   Modulation Details

16.1.1   Intro to Modulation

Modulation is the conversion of a digital signal represented by binary bits (0 or 1) into an analog signal something like a sine wave. The modulated signal consists pure sine wave "carrier" signal which is modified to convey information. A pure carrier sine wave, unchanging in frequency and voltage, provides no flow of information at all (except that a carrier is present). To make it convey information we modify (or modulate) this carrier. There are 3 basic types of modulation: frequency, amplitude, and phase. They will be explained next.

16.1.2   Frequency Modulation

The simplest modulation method is frequency modulation. Frequency is measured in cycles per second (of a sine wave). It's the count of the number of times the sine wave shape repeats itself in a second. This is the same as the number of times it reaches it peak value in a second. The word "Hertz" (abbreviated Hz) is used to mean "cycles per second".

A simple example of frequency modulation is where one frequency means a 0 and another means a 1. For example, for some obsolete 300 baud modems 1070 Hz meant a binary 0 while 1270 Hz meant a binary 1. This was called "frequency shift keying". Instead of just two possible frequencies, more could be used to allow more information to be transmitted. If we had 4 different frequencies (call them A, B, C, and D) then each frequency could stand for a pair of bits. For example, to send 00 one would use frequency A. To send 01, use frequency B; for 10 use C; for 11 use D. In like manner, by using 8 different frequencies we could send 3 bits with each shift in frequency. Each time we double the number of possible frequencies we increase the number of bits it can represent by 1.

16.1.3   Amplitude Modulation

Once one understands frequency modulation example above including the possibilities of representing a few bits by a single shift in frequency, it's easier to understand both amplitude modulation and phase modulation. For amplitude modulation, one just changes the height (voltage) of the sine wave analogous to changing the frequency of the sine wave. For a simple case there could only be 2 allowed amplitude levels, one representing a 0-bit and another representing a 1-bit. As explained for the case of frequency modulation, having more possible amplitudes will result in more information being transmitted.

16.1.4 Phase Modulation

To change the phase of a sine wave at a certain instant of time, we stop sending this old sine wave and immediately begin sending a new sine wave of the same frequency and amplitude. If we started sending the new sine wave at the same voltage level (and slope) as existed when we stopped sending the old sine wave, there would be no change in phase (and no detectable change at all). But suppose that we started up the new sine wave at a different point on the sine wave curve. Then there would likely be a sudden voltage jump at the point in time where the old sine wave stopped and the new sine wave began. This is a phase shift and it's measured in degrees (deg.) A 0 deg. (or a 360 deg.) phase shift means no change at all while a 180 deg. phase shift just reverses the voltage (and slope) of the sine wave. Put another way, a 180 deg. phase shift just skips over a half-period (180 deg.) at the point of transition. Of course we could just skip over say 90 deg. or 135 deg. etc. As in the example for frequency modulation, the more possible phase shifts, the more bits a single shift in phase can represent.

16.1.5 Combination Modulation

Instead of just selecting either frequency, amplitude, or phase modulation, we may chose to combine modulation methods. Suppose that we have 256 possible frequencies and thus can send a byte (8 bits) for each shift in frequency (since 2 to the 8 power is 256). Suppose also that we have another 256 different amplitudes so that each shift in amplitude represents a byte. Also suppose there are 256 possible phase shifts. Then a certain points in time we may make a shift in all 3 things: frequency, amplitude and phase. This would send out 3 bytes for each such transition.

No modulation method in use today actually does this. It's not practical due to the relatively long time it would take to detect all 3 types of changes. But what is quite common is the simultaneous change in both phase and amplitude. This is called phase-amplitude modulation (sometimes also called quadrature amplitude modulation = QAM). This method is used for the common modem speeds of 14.4k, 28.8k, and 33.6k. The only significant case where this modulation method is not used today is for 56k modems. But even 56k modems exclusively use QAM (phase-amplitude modulation) in the direction from your PC out the telephone line. Sometimes even the other direction will also fall back to QAM when line conditions are not good enough. Thus QAM (phase-amplitude modulation) still remains the most widely used method on ordinary telephone lines.

16.1.6 56k Modems (v.90)

The modulation method used above 33.6k is entirely different than the common phase-amplitude modulation. The details of exactly how it works seem to be obscure and I couldn't find them on the Internet as of late 1998. But the basic idea behind it is easy to understand. Since ordinary telephone calls are converted to digital signals at the local offices of the telephone company, the fastest speed that you can send digital data by an ordinary telephone call is the same speed that the telephone company uses over its digital portion of the phone call transmission. What is this speed? Well, in the USA it's exactly 56k! In other countries it may be slightly higher.

Thus in the USA 56k is the absolute top speed possible for an ordinary telephone call using the digital portion of the circuit that was designed to send digital encodings of the human voice. In order to use 56k, the modem must know exactly how the telephone company is doing its digital encoding of the analog signals. This task is far too complicated if both sides of a telephone call have only an analog interface to the telephone company. But if one side has a digital interface, then it's possible (at least in one direction). Thus if your ISP has a digital interface to the phone company, the ISP may send out a certain digital signal over the phone lines toward your PC. The digital signal from the ISP gets converted to analog at the local telephone office near your PC's location (perhaps near your home). Then it's your modem's task to try to figure out exactly what that digital signal was. If it can do this then transmission at 56k (the speed of the telephone company's digital signal) is possible in this direction.

What method does the telephone company use to digitally encode analog signals? It uses a method of sampling the amplitude of the analog signal at a rate of 8000 samples per second. Each sample amplitude is encoded as a 7-bit (ASCII-like) byte. (Note: 7 x 8000 = 56k) This is called "Pulse Code Modulation" = PCM. These bytes are then sent digitally on the telephone company's digital circuits where many calls share a single circuit using a time-sharing scheme known as "time division multiplexing". Then finally at the local telephone office near your home, the digital signal is de-multiplexed resulting in the same digital signal as was originally created by PCM. This signal is then converted back to analog and sent to your home. Each 7-bit byte creates a certain amplitude of the analog signal. Your modem's task is to determine just what that PCM 7-bit byte was based on the amplitude it detects.

This is (sort of) "amplitude demodulation" but not really. It's not amplitude demodulation because there is no carrier. Actually, it's called "modulus conversion" which is the inverse of PCM. In order to determine the digital codes the telephone Co. used to create the analog signal, the modem must sample this analog signal amplitude at exactly the same points in time the phone Co. used when it created the analog signal. In order to get the modem to do this correctly the modem must go thru "training" periods where the ISP's modem sends out known digital signals and the modem trains itself to recognize those signals. (At least that's the way I think it works ??)

Note that the digital part of the telephone network is bi-directional. Two such circuits are used for a phone call, one in each direction. Also, while 7-bit bytes are used to encode the amplitude, the bytes sent are 8-bit ones with the extra bit used by the telephone company for its signalling purposes. The telephone users have no control over this extra bit. This means that while the digital signal is actually 64k bits/sec, only 56k can be controlled by the user.

17 Appendix B: "baud" vs. "bps"

17.1 A simple example

"baud" and "bps" are perhaps one of the most misused terms in the computing and telecommunications field. Many people use these terms interchangeably, when in fact they are not! bps is simply the number of bits transmitted per second. The baud rate is a measure of how many times per second a signal changes (or could change). For a typical serial port a 1-bit is -12 volts and a 0-bit is +12 v (volts). If the bps is 38,400 a sequence of 010101... would also be 38,400 baud since the voltage shifts back and forth from positive to negative to positive ... and there are 38,400 shifts per second. For another sequence say 111000111... there will be fewer shifts of voltage since for three 1's in sequence the voltage just stays at -12 volts yet we say that its still 38,400 baud since there is a possibility that the number of changes per second will be that high.

Looked at another way, put an imaginary tic mark separating each bit (even thought the voltage may not change). 38,400 baud then means 38,400 tic marks per second. The tic marks at at the instants of permitted change and are actually marked by a synchronized clock signal generated in the hardware but not sent over the external cable.

Suppose that a "change" may have more than the two possible outcomes of the previous example (of +- 12 v). Suppose it has 4 possible outcomes, each represented by a unique voltage level. Each level may represent a pair of bits (such as 01). For example, -12v could be 00, -6v 01, +6v 10 and +12v 11. Here the bit rate is double the baud rate. For example, 3000 changes per second will generate 2 bits for each change resulting in 6000 bits per second (bps). In other words 3000 baud results in 6000 bps.

17.2 Real examples

The above example is overly simple. Real examples are more complicated but based on the same idea. This explains how a modem running at 2400 baud, can send 14400 bps (or higher). The modem achieves a bps rate greater than baud rate by encoding many bits in each signal change (or transition). Thus, when 2 or more bits are encoded per baud, the bps rate exceeds the baud rate. If your modem-to-modem connection is at 14400 bps, it's going to be sending 6 bits per signal transition at 2400 baud. A speed of 28800 bps is obtained by 3200 baud at 9 bits/baud. When people misuse the word baud, they may mean the modem speed (such as 33.6K).

Common modem bps rates were formerly 50, 75, 110, 300, 1200, 2400, 9600. These were also the bps rates over the serial_port-to-modem cables. Today the bps modem-to-modem rates are 14.4K, 28.8K, 33.6K, and 56K, but the rates over the serialPort-to-modem cables are not the same but are: 19.2K, 38.4K, 57.6K and 115.2K). Using modems with V.42bis compression (max 4:1 compression), rates up to 115.2K bps are possible for 33.6K modems (230.4K is possible for 56K modems).

Except for the 56k modems, most modems run at 2400, 3000, or 3200 baud. Because of the bandwidth limitations on voice-grade phone lines, baud rates greater than 2400 are harder to achieve, and only work under conditions of pristine phone line quality.

How did this confusion between bps and baud start? Well, back when antique low speed modems were high speed modems, the bps rate actually did equal the baud rate. One bit would be encoded per phase change. People would use bps and baud interchangeably, because they were the same number. For example, a 300 bps modem also had a baud rate of 300. This all changed when faster modems came around, and the bit rate exceeded the baud rate. "baud" is named after Emile Baudot, the inventor of the asynchronous telegraph printer.

18 Appendix C: Terminal Server Connection

This section was adapted from Text-Terminal-HOWTO.

A terminal server is something like an intelligent switch that can connect many modems (or terminals) to one or more computers. It's not a mechanical switch so it may change the speeds and protocols of the streams of data that go thru it. A number of companies make terminal servers: Xyplex, Cisco, 3Com, Computone, Livingston, etc. There are many different types and capabilities. Another HOWTO is needed to compare and describe them (including the possibility of creating your own terminal server with a Linux PC). Most are used for modem connections rather than directly connected terminals.

One use for them is to connect many modems (or terminals) to a high speed network which connects to host computers. Of course the terminal server must have the computing power and software to run network protocols so it is in some ways like a computer. The terminal server may interact with the user and ask what computer to connect to, etc. or it may connect without asking. One may sometimes send jobs to a printer thru a terminal server.

A PC today has enough computing power to act like a terminal server except that each serial port should have its own hardware interrupt. PC's only have a few spare interrupts for this purpose and since they are hard-wired you can't create more by software. A solution is to use an advanced multiport serial card which has its own system of interrupts (or on lower cost models, shares one of the PC's interrupts between a number of ports). See Serial-HOWTO for more info. If such a PC runs Linux with getty running on many serial ports it might be thought of as a terminal server. It is in effect a terminal server if it's linked to other PC's over a network and if its job is mainly to pass thru data and handle the serial port interrupts every 14 (or so) bytes. Software called "radius" is sometimes used.

Today real terminal servers serve more than just terminals. They also serve PC's which emulate terminals, and are sometimes connected to a bank of modems connected to phone lines. Some even include built-in modems. If a terminal (or PC emulating one) is connected directly to a modem, the modem at the other end of the line could be connected to a terminal server. In some cases the terminal server by default expects the callers to use PPP packets, something that real text terminals don't generate.

19 Appendix D: Other Types of Modems

This HOWTO currently only deals with the common type of modem used to connect PC's to ordinary analog telephone lines. There are various other types of modems, including devices called modems that are not really modems.

19.1 Digital-to-Digital "Modems"

The standard definition of a modem is sometimes broadened to include "digital" modems. Today direct digital service is now being provided to many homes and offices so a computer there sends out digital signals directly (well almost) into the telephone lines. But a device is still needed to convert the computer digital signal into type allowed on telephone circuits and this device is sometimes called a modem. The next 2 sections: ISDN and DSL concern digital-to-digital "modems".

19.2 ISDN "Modems"

The "modem" is really a Terminal Adapter (TA). A Debian package "isdnutils" is available. There is a ISDN Howto in German with an English translation: <http://www.suse.de/Support/sdb_e/isdn.html>. It's put out by the SuSE distribution of Linux and likely is about drivers available in that distribution. There is an isdn4linux package and a newsgroup: de.alt.comm.isdn4linux. Many of the postings are in German. You might try using a search engine (such as DejaNews) to find "isdn4linux".

19.3 Digital Subscriber Line (DSL)

DSL uses the existing twisted pair line from your home (etc.) to the local telephone office. This can be used if your telephone line can accept higher speeds than an ordinary modem (say 56k) sends over it. It replaces the analog-to-digital converter at the local telephone office with a converter which can accept a much faster flow of data (in a different format of course). The device which converts the digital signals from your computer to the signal used to represent digital data on the local telephone line is also called a modem. This document presently does not cover the special aspects of these modems.

END OF Modem-HOWTO

HOWTO

## Part XXVI

"HOWTO: Multi Disk System Tuning" Stein Gjoen

sgjoen@nyx.net

v0.17, 3 February 1998

This document describes how best to use multiple disks and partitions for a Linux system. Although some of this text is Linux specific the general approach outlined here can be applied to many other multi tasking operating systems.

Contents

HOWTO

1   Introduction

For strange and artistic reasons this brand new release is code named the **Daybreak** release.

New code names will appear as per industry standard guidelines to emphasize the state-of-the-art-ness of this document.

This document was written for two reasons, mainly because I got hold of 3 old SCSI disks to set up my Linux system on and I was pondering how best to utilise the inherent possibilities of parallelizing in a SCSI system. Secondly I hear there is a prize for people who write documents...

This is intended to be read in conjunction with the Linux Filesystem Structure Standard (FSSTND). It does not in any way replace it but tries to suggest where physically to place directories detailed in the FSSTND, in terms of drives, partitions, types, RAID, file system (fs), physical sizes and other parameters that should be considered and tuned in a Linux system, ranging from single home systems to large servers on the Internet.

Even though it is now more than a year since last release of the FSSTND work is still continuing, under a new name, and will encompass more than Linux, fill in a few blanks hinted at in FSSTND version 1.2 as well as other general improvements. The development mailing list is currently private but a general release is hopefully in the near future. The new issue will be named Filesystem Hierarchy Standard (FHS) and will cover more than Linux alone. Very recently FHS version 2.0 was released but there are still a few issues to be dealt with and even longer before this new standard will have an impact on actual distribusions.

It is also a good idea to read the Linux Installation guides thoroughly and if you are using a PC system, which I guess the majority still does, you can find much relevant and useful information in the FAQs for the newsgroup comp.sys.ibm.pc.hardware especially for storage media.

This is also a learning experience for myself and I hope I can start the ball rolling with this HOWTO and that it perhaps can evolve into a larger more detailed and hopefully even more correct HOWTO.

First of all we need a bit of legalese. Recent development shows it is quite important.

1.1   Copyright

This HOWTO is copyrighted 1996 Stein Gjoen.

Unless otherwise stated, Linux HOWTO documents are copyrighted by their respective authors. Linux HOWTO documents may be reproduced and distributed in whole or in part, in any medium physical or electronic, as long as this copyright notice is retained on all copies. Commercial redistribution is allowed and encouraged; however, the author would like to be notified of any such distributions.

All translations, derivative works, or aggregate works incorporating any Linux HOWTO documents must be covered under this copyright notice. That is, you may not produce a derivative work from a HOWTO and impose additional restrictions on its distribution. Exceptions to these rules may be granted under certain conditions; please contact the Linux HOWTO coordinator at the address given below.

In short, we wish to promote dissemination of this information through as many channels as possible. However, we do wish to retain copyright on the HOWTO documents, and would like to be notified of any plans to redistribute the HOWTOs.

If you have questions, please contact Tim Bynum, the Linux HOWTO coordinator, at linux-howto@sunsite.unc.edu via email.

1.2 Disclaimer

Use the information in this document at your own risk. I disavow any potential liability for the contents of this document. Use of the concepts, examples, and/or other content of this document is entirely at your own risk.

All copyrights are owned by their owners, unless specifically noted otherwise. Use of a term in this document should not be regarded as affecting the validity of any trademark or service mark.

Naming of particular products or brands should not be seen as endorsements.

You are strongly recommended to take a backup of your system before major installation and backups at regular intervals.

1.3 News

The most recent news is that FHS version 2.0 is released and the work is picing up momentum. No linux distributions using FHS has been announced yet but when that happens there will have to be a few rewrites to this HOWTO. And speaking of HOWTO, I have now dropped all pretenses and removed the 'mini' prefix, as this was becoming something of a joke.

A recent addition is a new section on how best to get help should you find yourself unable to solve your problems as well as more suggestion on maintenance.

Due to an enormous amount of spam I have been forced to mangle all e-mail addresses herein in order to fool the e-mail harvesters that scan through the net for victims to be put on the lists. Feedbeck tells me some damage has already happened, this is very unfortunate. Mangiling is done by replacing the @ character with (at)

A number of pointers to relevant mailing lists are also added.

Since the 0.14 version was released there have been too many changes to list here. I have received much input and a substantial patch from kris (at) koentopp.de that adds many new details. The document has grown a lot, actually beyond expectations.

I have also upgraded my system to Debian 1.2.6 and have replaced the old Slackware values with the Debian values for disk space requirements for the various directory. I will use Debian as a base for discussions and examples here, though the HOWTO is equally applicable to other distributions, even other operating systems. At the time of writing this Debian 1.3 is out in beta and will soon be used as the test bench for further versions of this document.

More news: there has been a fair bit of interest in new kinds of file systems in the comp.os.linux newsgroups, in particular logging, journaling and inherited file systems. Watch out for updates. Projects on volume management is also under way. The old defragmentation program for ext2fs is being updated and there is continuing interests for compression.

The latest version number of this document can be gleaned from my plan entry if you *finger* <finger:sgjoen@nox.nyx.net> my Nyx account.

Also, the latest version will be available on my web space on nyx: *The Multi Disk System Tuning HOWTO Homepage* <http://www.nyx.net/sgjoen/disk.html>.

A text-only version as well as the SGML source can also be downloaded there. A nicely formatted postscript version is also available now. In order to save disk space and bandwidth it has been compressed using gzip.

Also planned is a series of URLs to helpful software referred to in this document. A mirror in Europe will be announced soon.

I have very recently changed jobs, address etc so there will be a few delays in updates before I get the time for a more systematic updates.

From version 0.15 onward this document is primarily handled as an SGML document which means future printouts should look nicer than the old text based version. This also means that it has more or less grown into a full HOWTO. With respect to size it must be admitted it is a long time since there was anything "mini" about it.

1.4 Credits

In this version I have the pleasure of acknowledging even more people who have contributed in one way or another:

```
ronnej (at ) ucs.orst.edu
cm (at) kukuruz.ping.at
armbru (at) pond.sub.org
R.P.Blake (at) open.ac.uk
neuffer (at) goofy.zdv.Uni-Mainz.de
sjmudd (at) redestb.es
nat (at) nataa.fr.eu.org
sundbyk (at) horten.geco-prakla.slb.com
gjoen (at) sn.no
mike (at) i-Connect.Net
roth (at) uiuc.edu
phall (at) ilap.com
szaka (at) mirror.cc.u-szeged.hu
CMckeon (at) swcp.com
kris (at) koentopp.de
edick (at) idcomm.com
pot (at) fly.cnuce.cnr.it
earl (at) sbox.tu-graz.ac.at
ebacon (at) oanet.com
vax (at) linkdead.paranoia.com
```

Special thanks go to nakano (at) apm.seikei.ac.jp for doing the *Japanese translation* <http://jf. linux.or.jp/JF/JF-ftp/other-formats/Disk-HOWTO/html/Disk-HOWTO.html>, general contributions as well as contributing an example of a computer in an academic setting, which is included at the end of this document.

Not many still, so please read through this document, make a contribution and join the elite. If I have forgotten anyone, please let me know.

New in this version is an appendix with a few tables you can fill in for your system in order to simplify the design process.

Any comments or suggestions can be mailed to my mail address on nyx: *sgjoen@nyx.net*.

So let's cut to the chase where swap and /tmp are racing along hard drive...

2 Structure

As this type of document is supposed to be as much for learning as a technical reference document I have rearranged the structure to this end. For the designer of a system it is more useful to have the information presented in terms of the goals of this exercise than from the point of view of the logical layer structure of the devices themselves. Nevertheless this document would not be complete without such a layer structure the computer field is so full of, so I will include it here as an introduction to how it works.

It is a long time since the *mini* in mini-HOWTO could be defended as proper but I am convinced that this document is as long as it needs to be in order to make the right design decisions, and not longer.

2.1 Logical structure

This is based on how each layer access each other, traditionally with the application on top and the physical layer on the bottom. It is quite useful to show the interrelationship between each of the layers used in controlling drives.

```
|__      File structure          ( /usr /tmp etc)      __|
|__      File system             (ext2fs, vfat etc)    __|
|__      Volume management       (AFS)                 __|
|__      RAID, concatenation     (md)                  __|
|__      Device driver           (SCSI, IDE etc)       __|
|__      Controller              (chip, card)          __|
|__      Connection              (cable, network)      __|
|__      Drive                   (magnetic, optical etc) __|
-----------------------------------------------------------------
```

In the above diagram both volume management and RAID and concatenation are optional layers. The 3 lower layers are in hardware. All parts are discussed at length later on in this document.

2.2 Document structure

Most users start out with a given set of hardware and some plans on what they wish to achieve and how big the system should be. This is the point of view I will adopt in this document in presenting the material, starting out with hardware, continuing with design constraints before detailing the design strategy that I have found to work well. I have used this both for my own personal computer at home, a multi purpose server at work and found it worked quite well. In addition my Japanese co-worker in this project have applied the same strategy on a server in an academic setting with similar success.

Finally at the end I have detailed some configuration tables for use in your own design. If you have any comments regarding this or notes from your own design work I would like to hear from you so this document can be upgraded.

3 Drive technologies

A far more complete discussion on drive technologies for IBM PCs can be found at the home page of *The Enhanced IDE/Fast-ATA FAQ* <http://thef-nym.sci.kun.nl/pieterh/storage.html> which is also regularly posted on Usenet News. Here I will just present what is needed to get an understanding of the technology and get you started on your setup.

3.1 Drives

This is the physical device where your data lives and although the operating system makes the various types seem rather similar they can in actual fact be very different. An understanding of how it works can be very useful in your design work. Floppy drives fall outside the scope of this document, though should there be a big demand I could perhaps be persuaded to add a little here.

3.2 Geometry

Physically disk drives consists of one or more platters containing data that is read in and out using sensors mounted on movable heads that are fixed with respects to themselves. Data transfers therefore happens across all surfaces simultaneously which defines a cylinder of tracks. The drive is also divided into sectors containing a number of data fields.

Drives are therefore often specified in terms of its geometry: the number of Cylinders, Heads and Sectors (CHS).

For various reasons there is now a number of translations between

- the physical CHS of the drive itself
- the logical CHS the drive reports to the BIOS or OS
- the logical CHS used by the OS

Basically it is a mess and a source of much confusion. For more information you are strongly recommended to read the *Large Disk mini-HOWTO*

3.3 Media

The media technology determines important parameters such as read/write rates, seek times, storage size as well as if it is read/write or read only.

3.3.1 Magnetic Drives

This is the typical read-write mass storage medium, and as everything else in the computer world, comes in many flavours with different properties. Usually this is the fastest technology and offers read/write capability. The platter rotates with a constant angular velocity (CAV) with a variable physical sector density for more efficient magnetic media area utilisation. In other words, the number of bits per unit length is kept roughly constant by increasing the number of logical sectors for the outer tracks.

Typical values for rotational speeds are 4500 and 5400 rpm, though 7200 is also used. Very recently also 10000 rpm has entered the mass market. Seek times are around 10ms, transfer rates quite variable from one type to another but typically 4-40 MB/s. With the extreme high performance drives you should remember that performance costs more electric power which is dissipated as heat, see the point on 16.6 (Power and Heating).

Note that there are several kinds of transfers going on here, and that these are quoted in different units. First of all there is the platter-to-drive cache transfer, usually quoted in Mbits/s. Typical values here is about 50-250 Mbits/s. The second stage is from the built in drive cache to the adapter, and this is typically quoted in MB/s, and typical quoted values here is 3-40 MB/s. Note, however, that this assumed data is already in the cache and hence for maximum readout speed from the drive the effective transfer rate will decrease dramatically.

3.3.2 Optical drives

Optical read/write drives exist but are slow and not so common. They were used in the NeXT machine but the low speed was a source for much of the complaints. The low speed is mainly due to the thermal nature of the phase change that represents the data storage. Even when using relatively powerful lasers to induce the phase changes the effects are still slower than the magnetic effect used in magnetic drives.

Today many people use CD-ROM drives which, as the name suggests, is read-only. Storage is about 650 MB, transfer speeds are variable, depending on the drive but can exceed 1.5 MB/s. Data is stored on a spiraling single track so it is not useful to talk about geometry for this. Data density is constant so the drive uses constant linear velocity (CLV). Seek is also slower, about 100ms, partially due to the spiraling track. Recent, high speed drives, use a mix of CLV and CAV in order to maximize performance. This also reduces access time caused by the need to reach correct rotational speed for readout.

A new type (DVD) is on the horizon, offering up to about 18 GB on a single disk.

3.3.3 Solid State Drives

This is a relatively recent addition to the available technology and has been made popular especially in portable computers as well as in embedded systems. Containing no movable parts they are very fast both in terms of access and transfer rates. The most popular type is flash RAM, but also other types of RAM is used. A few years ago many had great hopes for magnetic bubble memories but it turned out to be relatively expensive and is not that common.

In general the use of RAM disks are regarded as a bad idea as it is normally more sensible to add more RAM to the motherboard and let the operating system divide the memory pool into buffers, cache, program and data areas. Only in very special cases, such as real time systems with short time margins, can RAM disks be a sensible solution.

Flash RAM is today available in several 10's of megabytes in storage and one might be tempted to use it for fast, temporary storage in a computer. There is however a huge snag with this: flash RAM has a finite life time in terms of the number of times you can rewrite data, so putting swap, /tmp or /var/tmp on such a device will certainly shorten its lifetime dramatically. Instead, using flash RAM for directories that are read often but rarely written to, will be a big performance win.

In order to get the optimum life time out of flash RAM you will need to use special drivers that will use the RAM evenly and minimize the number of block erases.

This example illustrates the advantages of splitting up your directory structure over several devices.

Solid state drives have no real cylinder/head/sector addressing but for compatibility reasons this is simulated by the driver to give a uniform interface to the operating system.

3.4 Interfaces

There is a plethora of interfaces to chose from widely ranging in price and performance. Most motherboards today include IDE interface or better, Intel supports it through the Triton PCI chip set which is very popular these days. Many motherboards also include a SCSI interface chip made by NCR and that is connected directly to the PCI bus. Check what you have and what BIOS support you have with it.

3.4.1 MFM and RLL

Once upon a time this was the established technology, a time when 20 MB was awesome, which compared to todays sizes makes you think that dinosaurs roamed the Earth with these drives. Like the dinosaurs these are outdated and are slow and unreliable compared to what we have today. Linux does support this but you are well advised to think twice about what you would put on this. One might argue that an emergency partition with a suitable vintage of DOS might be fitting.

3.4.2 ESDI

Actually, ESDI was an adaptation of the very widely used SMD interface used on "big" computers to the cable set used with the ST506 interface, which was more convenient to package than the 60-pin + 26-pin connector pair used with SMD. The ST506 was a "dumb" interface which relied entirely on the controller and host computer to do everything from computing head/cylinder/sector locations and keeping track of the head location, etc. ST506 required the controller to extract clock from the recovered data, and control the physical location of detailed track features on the medium, bit by bit. It had about a 10-year life if you include the use of MFM, RLL, and ERLL/ARLL modulation schemes. ESDI, on the other hand, had intelligence, often using three or four separate microprocessors on a single drive, and high-level commands to format a track, transfer data, perform seeks, and so on. Clock recovery from the data stream was accomplished at the drive, which drove the clock line and presented its data in NRZ, though error correction was still the task of the controller. ESDI allowed the use of variable bit density recording, or, for that matter, any other modulation technique, since it was locally generated and resolved at the drive. Though many of the techniques used in ESDI were later incorporated in IDE, it was the increased popularity of SCSI which led to the demise of ESDI in computers. ESDI had a life of about 10 years, though mostly in servers and otherwise "big" systems rather than PC's.

3.4.3 IDE and ATA

Progress made the drive electronics migrate from the ISA slot card over to the drive itself and Integrated Drive Electronics was borne. It was simple, cheap and reasonably fast so the BIOS designers provided the kind of snag that the computer industry is so full of. A combination of an IDE limitation of 16 heads together with the BIOS limitation of 1024 cylinders gave us the infamous 504 MB limit. Following the computer industry traditions again, the snag was patched with a kludge and we got all sorts of translation schemes and BIOS bodges. This means that you need to read the installation documentation very carefully and check up on what BIOS you have and what date it has as the BIOS has to tell Linux what size drive you have. Fortunately with Linux you can also tell the kernel directly what size drive you have with the drive parameters, check the documentation for LILO and Loadlin, thoroughly. Note also that IDE is equivalent to ATA, AT Attachment. IDE uses CPU-intensive Programmed Input/Output (PIO) to transfer data to and from the drives and has no capability for the more efficient Direct Memory Access (DMA) technology. Highest transfer rate is 8.3 MB/s.

HOWTO

3.4.4 EIDE, Fast-ATA and ATA-2

These 3 terms are roughly equivalent, fast-ATA is ATA-2 but EIDE additionally includes ATAPI. ATA-2 is what most use these days which is faster and with DMA. Highest transfer rate is increased to 16.6 MB/s.

3.4.5 Ultra-ATA

A new, faster DMA mode that is approximately twice the speed of EIDE PIO-Mode 4 (33 MB/s). Disks with and without Ultra-ATA can be mixed on the same cable without speed penalty for the faster adapters. The Ultra-ATA interface is electrically identical with the normal Fast-ATA interface, including the maximum cable length.

3.4.6 ATAPI

The ATA Packet Interface was designed to support CD-ROM drives using the IDE port and like IDE it is cheap and simple.

3.4.7 SCSI

The Small Computer System Interface is a multi purpose interface that can be used to connect to everything from drives, disk arrays, printers, scanners and more. The name is a bit of a misnomer as it has traditionally been used by the higher end of the market as well as in work stations since it is well suited for multi tasking environments.

The standard interface is 8 bits wide and can address 8 devices. There is a wide version with 16 bit that is twice as fast on the same clock and can address 16 devices. The host adapter always counts as a device and is usually number 7. It is also possible to have 32 bit wide busses but this usually requires a double set of cables to carry all the lines.

The old standard was 5 MB/s and the newer fast-SCSI increased this to 10 MB/s. Recently ultra-SCSI, also known as Fast-20, arrived with 20 MB/s transfer rates for an 8 bit wide bus.

The higher performance comes at a cost that is usually higher than for (E)IDE. The importance of correct termination and good quality cables cannot be overemphasized. SCSI drives also often tend to be of a higher quality than IDE drives. Also adding SCSI devices tend to be easier than adding more IDE drives: Often it is only a matter of plugging or unplugging the device; some people do this without powering down the system. This feature is most convenient when you have multiple systems and you can just take the devices from one system to the other should one of them fail for some reason.

There is a number of useful documents you should read if you use SCSI, the SCSI HOWTO as well as the SCSI FAQ posted on Usenet News.

SCSI also has the advantage you can connect it easily to tape drives for backing up your data, as well as some printers and scanners. It is even possible to use it as a very fast network between computers while simultaneously share SCSI devices on the same bus. Work is under way but due to problems with ensuring cache coherency between the different computers connected, this is a non trivial task.

3.5 Cabling

I do not intend to make too many comments on hardware but I feel I should make a little note on cabling. This might seem like a remarkably low technological piece of equipment, yet sadly it is the source of many frustrating problems. At todays high speeds one should think of the cable more of a an RF device with its inherent demands on impedance matching. If you do not take your precautions you will get a much reduced reliability or total failure. Some SCSI host adapters are more sensitive to this than others.

Shielded cables are of course better than unshielded but the price is much higher. With a little care you can get good performance from a cheap unshielded cable.

- For Fast-ATA and Ultra-ATA, the maximum cable length is specified as 45cm (18"). The data lines of both IDE channels are connected on many boards, though, so they count as **one** cable. In any case EIDE cables should be as short as possible. If there are mysterious crashes or spontaneous changes of data, it is well worth investigating your cabling. Try a lower PIO mode or disconnect the second channel and see if the problem still occurs.

- Use as short cable as possible, but do not forget the 30 cm minimum separation for ultra SCSI.

- Avoid long stubs between the cable and the drive, connect the plug on the cable directly to the drive without an extension.

- Use correct termination for SCSI devices and at the correct position: the end of the SCSI chain.

- Do not mix shielded or unshielded cabling, do not wrap cables around metal, try to avoid proximity to metal parts along parts of the cabling. Any such discontinuities can cause impedance mismatching which in turn can cause reflection of signals which increases noise on the cable. This problems gets even more severe in the case of multi channel controllers. Recently someone suggested wrapping bubble plastic around the cables in order to avoid too close proximity to metal, a real problem inside crowded cabinets.

3.6   Host Adapters

This is the other end of the interface from the drive, the part that is connected to a computer bus. The speed of the computer bus and that of the drives should be roughly similar, otherwise you have a bottleneck in your system. Connecting a RAID 0 disk-farm to a ISA card is pointless. These days most computers come with 32 bit PCI bus capable of 132 MB/s transfers which should not represent a bottleneck for most people in the near future.

As the drive electronic migrated to the drives the remaining part that became the (E)IDE interface is so small it can easily fit into the PCI chip set. The SCSI host adapter is more complex and often includes a small CPU of its own and is therefore more expensive and not integrated into the PCI chip sets available today. Technological evolution might change this.

Some host adapters come with separate caching and intelligence but as this is basically second guessing the operating system the gains are heavily dependent on which operating system is used. Some of the more primitive ones, that shall remain nameless, experience great gains. Linux, on the other hand, have so much smarts of its own that the gains are much smaller.

Mike Neuffer, who did the drivers for the DPT controllers, states that the DPT controllers are intelligent enough that given enough cache memory it will give you a big push in performance and suggests that people who have experienced little gains with smart controllers just have not used a sufficiently intelligent caching controller.

3.7   Multi Channel Systems

In order to increase throughput it is necessary to identify the most significant bottlenecks and then eliminate them. In some systems, in particular where there are a great number of drives connected, it is advantageous to use several controllers working in parallel, both for SCSI host adapters as well as IDE controllers which usually have 2 channels built in. Linux supports this.

Some RAID controllers feature 2 or 3 channels and it pays to spread the disk load across all channels. In other words, if you have two SCSI drives you want to RAID and a two channel controller, you should put each drive on separate channels.

3.8   Multi Board Systems

In addition to having both a SCSI and an IDE in the same machine it is also possible to have more than one SCSI controller. Check the SCSI-HOWTO on what controllers you can combine. Also you will most likely have to tell the kernel it should probe for more than just a single SCSI or a single IDE controller. This is done using kernel parameters when booting, for instance using LILO. Check the HOWTOs for SCSI and LILO for how to do this.

3.9   Speed Comparison

The following tables are given just to indicate what speeds are possible but remember that these are the theoretical maximum speeds. All transfer rates are in MB per second and bus widths are measured in bits.

3.9.1 Controllers

```
IDE          :        8.3 - 16.7
Ultra-ATA    :        33

SCSI         :
                      Bus width (bits)

Bus Speed (MHz)       |        8       16      32
----------------------------------------------------
  5                   |        5       10      20
 10   (fast)          |       10       20      40
 20   (fast-20 / ultra)  |     20       40      80
 40   (fast-40 / ultra-2) |    40       80      --
----------------------------------------------------
```

3.9.2 Bus types

```
ISA          :        8-12
EISA         :        33
VESA         :        40      (Sometimes tuned to 50)

PCI
                      Bus width (bits)

Bus Speed (MHz)       |        32      64
----------------------------------------------------
33                    |       132     264
66                    |       264     528
----------------------------------------------------
```

3.10   Benchmarking

This is a very, very difficult topic and I will only make a few cautious comments about this minefield. First of all, it is more difficult to make comparable benchmarks that have any actual meaning. This, however, does not stop people from trying...

Instead one can use benchmarking to diagnose your own system, to check it is going as fast as it should, that is, not slowing down. Also you would expect a significant increase when switching from a simple file system to RAID, so a lack of performance gain will tell you something is wrong.

When you try to benchmark you should not hack up your own, instead look up `iozone` and `bonnie` and read the documentation very carefully. More information about this is coming soon.

3.11   Comparisons

SCSI offers more performance than EIDE but at a price. Termination is more complex but expansion not too difficult. Having more than 4 (or in some cases 2) IDE drives can be complicated, with wide SCSI you can have up to 15 per adapter. Some SCSI host adapters have several channels thereby multiplying the number of possible drives even further.

RLL and MFM is in general too old, slow and unreliable to be of much use.

3.12 Future Development

SCSI-3 is under way and will hopefully be released soon. Faster devices are already being announced, most recently an 80 MB/s monster specification has been proposed. This is based around the ultra-2 standard (which used a 40MHz clock) combined with a 16 bit cable.

Some manufacturers already announce SCSI-3 devices but this is currently rather premature as the standard is not yet firm. As the transfer speeds increase the saturation point of the PCI bus is getting closer. Currently the 64 bit version has a limit of 264 MB/s. The PCI transfer rate will in the future be increased from the current 33MHz to 66MHz, thereby increasing the limit to 528 MB/s.

Another trend is for larger and larger drives. I hear it is possible to get 55 GB on a single drive though this is rather expensive. Currently the optimum storage for your money is about 6.4 GB but also this is continuously increasing. The introduction of DVD will in the near future have a big impact, with nearly 20 GB on a single disk you can have a complete copy of even major FTP sites from around the world. The only thing we can be reasonably sure about the future is that even if it won't get any better, it will definitely be bigger.

Addendum: soon after I first wrote this I read that the maximum useful speed for a CD-ROM was 20x as mechanical stability would be too great a problem at these speeds. About one month after that again the first commercial 24x CD-ROMs were available...

3.13 Recommendations

My personal view is that EIDE is the best way to start out on your system, especially if you intend to use DOS as well on your machine. If you plan to expand your system over many years or use it as a server I would strongly recommend you get SCSI drives. Currently wide SCSI is a little more expensive. You are generally more likely to get more for your money with standard width SCSI. There is also differential versions of the SCSI bus which increases maximum length of the cable. The price increase is even more substantial and cannot therefore be recommended for normal users.

In addition to disk drives you can also connect some types of scanners and printers and even networks to a SCSI bus.

Also keep in mind that as you expand your system you will draw ever more power, so make sure your power supply is rated for the job and that you have sufficient cooling. Many SCSI drives offer the option of sequential spin-up which is a good idea for large systems. See also the point on 16.6 (Power and Heating).

4 Considerations

The starting point in this will be to consider where you are and what you want to do. The typical home system starts out with existing hardware and the newly converted Linux user will want to get the most out of existing hardware. Someone setting up a new system for a specific purpose (such as an Internet provider) will instead have to consider what the goal is and buy accordingly. Being ambitious I will try to cover the entire range.

Various purposes will also have different requirements regarding file system placement on the drives, a large multiuser machine would probably be best off with the /home directory on a separate disk, just to give an example.

In general, for performance it is advantageous to split most things over as many disks as possible but there is a limited number of devices that can live on a SCSI bus and cost is naturally also a factor. Equally important, file system maintenance becomes more complicated as the number of partitions and physical drives increases.

4.1 File system features

The various parts of FSSTND have different requirements regarding speed, reliability and size, for instance losing root is a pain but can easily be recovered. Losing /var/spool/mail is a rather different issue. Here is a quick summary of some essential parts and their properties and requirements. Note that this is just a guide, there can be binaries in etc and lib directories, libraries in bin directories and so on.

4.1.1 Swap

Speed

Maximum! Though if you rely too much on swap you should consider buying some more RAM. Note, however, that on many PC motherboards the cache will not work on RAM above 128 MB.

Size

Similar as for RAM. Quick and dirty algorithm: just as for tea: 16 MB for the machine and 2 MB for each user. Smallest kernel run in 1 MB but is tight, use 4 MB for general work and light applications, 8 MB for X11 or GCC or 16 MB to be comfortable. (The author is known to brew a rather powerful cuppa tea...)

Some suggest that swap space should be 1-2 times the size of the RAM, pointing out that the locality of the programs determines how effective your added swap space is. Note that using the same algorithm as for 4BSD is slightly incorrect as Linux does not allocate space for pages in core.

Also remember to take into account the type of programs you use. Some programs that have large working sets, such as finite element modeling (FEM) have huge data structures loaded in RAM rather than working explicitly on disk files. Data and computing intensive programs like this will cause excessive swapping if you have less RAM than the requirements.

Other types of programs can lock their pages into RAM. This can be for security reasons, preventing copies of data reaching a swap device or for performance reasons such as in a real time module. Either way, locking pages reduces the remaining amount of swappable memory and can cause the system to swap earlier then otherwise expected.

In `man 8 mkswap` it is explained that each swap partition can be a maximum of just under 128 MB in size.

Reliability

Medium. When it fails you know it pretty quickly and failure will cost you some lost work. You save often, don't you?

Note 1

Linux offers the possibility of interleaved swapping across multiple devices, a feature that can gain you much. Check out "`man 8 swapon`" for more details. However, software raiding `swap` across multiple devices adds more overheads than you gain.

Thus the `/etc/fstab` file might look like this:

```
/dev/sda1          swap            swap     pri=1                0        0
/dev/sdc1          swap            swap     pri=1                0        0
```

Remember that the `fstab` file is *very* sensitive to the formatting used, read the man page carefully and do *not* just cut and paste the lines above.

Note 2

Some people use a RAM disk for swapping or some other file systems. However, unless you have some very unusual requirements or setups you are unlikely to gain much from this as this cuts into the memory available for caching and buffering.

4.1.2 Temporary storage (`/tmp` and `/var/tmp`)

Speed

Very high. On a separate disk/partition this will reduce fragmentation generally, though `ext2fs` handles fragmentation rather well.

Size

Hard to tell, small systems are easy to run with just a few MB but these are notorious hiding places for stashing files away from prying eyes and quota enforcements and can grow without control on larger machines. Suggested: small home machine: 8 MB, large home machine: 32 MB, small server: 128 MB, and large machines up to 500 MB (The machine used by the author at work has 1100 users and a 300 MB `/tmp` directory). Keep an eye on these directories, not only for hidden files but also for old files. Also be prepared that these partitions might be the first reason you might have to resize your partitions.

Reliability

Low. Often programs will warn or fail gracefully when these areas fail or are filled up. Random file errors will of course be more serious, no matter what file area this is.

Files

Mostly short files but there can be a huge number of them. Normally programs delete their old `tmp` files but if somehow an interruption occurs they could survive. Many distributions have a policy regarding cleaning out `tmp` files at boot time, you might want to check out what your setup is.

Note

In FSSTND there is a note about putting `/tmp` on RAM disk. This, however, is not recommended for the same reasons as stated for swap. Also, as noted earlier, do not use flash RAM drives for these directories. One should also keep in mind that some systems are set to automatically clean `tmp` areas on rebooting.

(* That was 50 lines, I am home and dry! *)

4.1.3 Spool areas (`/var/spool/news` and `/var/spool/mail`)

Speed

High, especially on large news servers. News transfer and expiring are disk intensive and will benefit from fast drives. Print spools: low. Consider RAID0 for news.

Size

For news/mail servers: whatever you can afford. For single user systems a few MB will be sufficient if you read continuously. Joining a list server and taking a holiday is, on the other hand, not a good idea. (Again the machine I use at work has 100 MB reserved for the entire `/var/spool`)

Reliability

Mail: very high, news: medium, print spool: low. If your mail is very important (isn't it always?) consider RAID for reliability.

Files

Usually a huge number of files that are around a few KB in size. Files in the print spool can on the other hand be few but quite sizable.

Note

Some of the news documentation suggests putting all the `.overview` files on a drive separate from the news files, check out all news FAQs for more information.

4.1.4 Home directories (`/home`)

Speed

Medium. Although many programs use `/tmp` for temporary storage, others such as some news readers frequently update files in the home directory which can be noticeable on large multiuser systems. For small systems this is not a critical issue.

Size

Tricky! On some systems people pay for storage so this is usually then a question of finance. Large systems such as *nyx.net* <http://www.nyx.net/> (which is a free Internet service with mail, news and WWW services) run successfully with a suggested limit of 100 KB per user and 300 KB as enforced maximum. Commercial ISPs offer typically about 5 MB in their standard subscription packages.

If however you are writing books or are doing design work the requirements balloon quickly.

Reliability

Variable. Losing `/home` on a single user machine is annoying but when 2000 users call you to tell you their home directories are gone it is more than just annoying. For some their livelihood relies on what is here. You do regular backups of course?

HOWTO

Files

Equally tricky. The minimum setup for a single user tends to be a dozen files, 0.5 - 5 KB in size. Project related files can be huge though.

Note1

You might consider RAID for either speed or reliability. If you want extremely high speed and reliability you might be looking at other operating system and hardware platforms anyway. (Fault tolerance etc.)

Note2

Web browsers often use a local cache to speed up browsing and this cache can take up a substantial amount of space and cause much disk activity. There are many ways of avoiding this kind of performance hits, for more information see the sections on 8.6.1 (Home Directories) and 8.6.3 (WWW).

Note3

Users often tend to use up all available space on the /home partition. The Linux Quota subsystem is capable of limiting the number of blocks and the number of inode a single user ID can allocate on a per-filesystem basis. See the *Linux Quota mini-HOWTO* <http://sunsite.unc.edu/LDP/mini> by *Albert M.C. Tam* <mailto: bertie(at)scn.org> for details on setup.

4.1.5 Main binaries (/usr/bin and /usr/local/bin)

Speed

Low. Often data is bigger than the programs which are demand loaded anyway so this is not speed critical. Witness the successes of live file systems on CD ROM.

Size

The sky is the limit but 200 MB should give you most of what you want for a comprehensive system. A big system, for software development or a multi purpose server should perhaps reserve 500 MB both for installation and for growth.

Reliability

Low. This is usually mounted under root where all the essentials are collected. Nevertheless losing all the binaries is a pain...

Files

Variable but usually of the order of 10 - 100 kB.

4.1.6 Libraries (/usr/lib and /usr/local/lib)

Speed

Medium. These are large chunks of data loaded often, ranging from object files to fonts, all susceptible to bloating. Often these are also loaded in their entirety and speed is of some use here.

Size

Variable. This is for instance where word processors store their immense font files. The few that have given me feedback on this report about 70 MB in their various lib directories. A rather complete Debian 1.2 installation can take as much as 250 MB which can be taken as an realistic upper limit. The following ones are some of the largest disk space consumers: GCC, Emacs, TeX/LaTeX, X11 and perl.

Reliability

Low. See point 4.1.5 (Main binaries).

Files

Usually large with many of the order of 100 kB in size.

Note

For historical reasons some programs keep executables in the lib areas. One example is GCC which have some huge binaries in the /usr/lib/gcc/lib hierarchy.

4.1.7   Root

Speed

> Quite low: only the bare minimum is here, much of which is only run at startup time.

Size

> Relatively small. However it is a good idea to keep some essential rescue files and utilities on the root partition and some keep several kernel versions. Feedback suggests about 20 MB would be sufficient.

Reliability

> High. A failure here will possibly cause a fair bit of grief and you might end up spending some time rescuing your boot partition. With some practice you can of course do this in an hour or so, but I would think if you have some practice doing this you are also doing something wrong.
>
> Naturally you do have a rescue disk? Of course this is updated since you did your initial installation? There are many ready made rescue disks as well as rescue disk creation tools you might find valuable. Presumably investing some time in this saves you from becoming a root rescue expert.

Note 1

> If you have plenty of drives you might consider putting a spare emergency boot partition on a separate physical drive. It will cost you a little bit of space but if your setup is huge the time saved, should something fail, will be well worth the extra space.

Note 2

> For simplicity and also in case of emergencies it is not advisable to put the root partition on a RAID level 0 system. Also if you use RAID for your boot partition you have to remember to have the md option turned on for your emergency kernel.

4.1.8   DOS etc.

At the danger of sounding heretical I have included this little section about something many reading this document have strong feelings about. Unfortunately many hardware items come with setup and maintenance tools based around those systems, so here goes.

Speed

> Very low. The systems in question are not famed for speed so there is little point in using prime quality drives. Multitasking or multi-threading are not available so the command queueing facility found in SCSI drives will not be taken advantage of. If you have an old IDE drive it should be good enough. The exception is to some degree Win95 and more notably NT which have multi-threading support which should theoretically be able to take advantage of the more advanced features offered by SCSI devices.

Size

> The company behind these operating systems is not famed for writing tight code so you have to be prepared to spend a few tens of MB depending on what version you install of the OS or Windows. With an old version of DOS or Windows you might fit it all in on 50 MB.

Reliability

> Ha-ha. As the chain is no stronger than the weakest link you can use any old drive. Since the OS is more likely to scramble itself than the drive is likely to self destruct you will soon learn the importance of keeping backups here.
>
> Put another way: "Your mission, should you choose to accept it, is to keep this partition working. The warranty will self destruct in 10 seconds..."
>
> Recently I was asked to justify my claims here. First of all I am not calling DOS and Windows sorry excuses for operating systems. Secondly there are various legal issues to be taken into account. Saying there is a connection between the last two sentences are merely the ravings of the paranoid. Surely. Instead I shall offer the esteemed reader a few key words: DOS 4.0, DOS 6.x and various drive compression tools that shall remain nameless.

4.2 Explanation of terms

Naturally the faster the better but often the happy installer of Linux has several disks of varying speed and reliability so even though this document describes performance as 'fast' and 'slow' it is just a rough guide since no finer granularity is feasible. Even so there are a few details that should be kept in mind:

4.2.1 Speed

This is really a rather woolly mix of several terms: CPU load, transfer setup overhead, disk seek time and transfer rate. It is in the very nature of tuning that there is no fixed optimum, and in most cases price is the dictating factor. CPU load is only significant for IDE systems where the CPU does the transfer itself but is generally low for SCSI, see SCSI documentation for actual numbers. Disk seek time is also small, usually in the millisecond range. This however is not a problem if you use command queueing on SCSI where you then overlap commands keeping the bus busy all the time. News spools are a special case consisting of a huge number of normally small files so in this case seek time can become more significant.

There are two main parameters that are of interest here:

Seek
is usually specified in the average time take for the read/write head to seek from one track to another. This parameter is important when dealing with a large number of small files such as found in spool files. There is also the extra seek delay before the desired sector rotates into position under the head. This delay is dependent on the angular velocity of the drive which is why this parameter quite often is quoted for a drive. Common values are 4500, 5400 and 7200 rpm (rotations per minute). Higher rpm reduces the seek time but at a substantial cost. Also drives working at 7200 rpm have been known to be noisy and to generate a lot of heat, a factor that should be kept in mind if you are building a large array or "disk farm". Very recently drives working at 10000 rpm has entered the market and here the cooling requirements are even stricter and minimum figures for air flow are given.

Transfer
is usually specified in megabytes per second. This parameter is important when handling large files that have to be transferred. Library files, dictionaries and image files are examples of this. Drives featuring a high rotation speed also normally have fast transfers as transfer speed is proportional to angular velocity for the same sector density.

It is therefore important to read the specifications for the drives very carefully, and note that the maximum transfer speed quite often is quoted for transfers out of the on board cache (burst speed) and *not* directly from the platter (sustained speed). See also section on 16.6 (Power and Heating).

4.2.2 Reliability

Naturally no-one would want low reliability disks but one might be better off regarding old disks as unreliable. Also for RAID purposes (See the relevant information) it is suggested to use a mixed set of disks so that simultaneous disk crashes become less likely.

So far I have had only one report of total file system failure but here unstable hardware seemed to be the cause of the problems.

4.2.3 Files

The average file size is important in order to decide the most suitable drive parameters. A large number of small files makes the average seek time important whereas for big files the transfer speed is more important. The command queueing in SCSI devices is very handy for handling large numbers of small files, but for transfer EIDE is not too far behind SCSI and normally much cheaper than SCSI.

4.3 Technologies

In order to decide how to get the most of your devices you need to know what technologies are available and their implications. As always there can be some tradeoffs with respect to speed, reliability, power, flexibility, ease of use and complexity.

4.3.1 RAID

This is a method of increasing reliability, speed or both by using multiple disks in parallel thereby decreasing access time and increasing transfer speed. A checksum or mirroring system can be used to increase reliability. Large servers can take advantage of such a setup but it might be overkill for a single user system unless you already have a large number of disks available. See other documents and FAQs for more information.

For Linux one can set up a RAID system using either software (the `md` module in the kernel), a Linux compatible controller card (PCI-to-SCSI) or a SCSI-to-SCSI controller. Check the documentation for what controllers can be used. A hardware solution is usually faster, and perhaps also safer, but comes at a significant cost.

SCSI-to-SCSI controllers are usually implemented as complete cabinets with drives and a controller that connects to the computer with a second SCSI bus. This makes the entire cabinet of drives look like a single large, fast SCSI drive and requires no special RAID driver. The disadvantage is that the SCSI bus connecting the cabinet to the computer becomes a bottleneck.

PCI-to-SCSI are as the name suggests, connected to the high speed PCI bus and is therefore not suffering from the same bottleneck as the SCSI-to-SCSI controllers. These controllers require special drivers but you also get the means of controlling the RAID configuration over the network which simplifies management.

Currently the only supported SCSI RAID controller cards are the SmartCache I/III/IV and SmartRAID I/III/IV controller families from DPT. These controllers are supported by the EATA-DMA driver in the standard kernel. This company also has an informative *home page* `<http://www.dpt.com>` which also describes various general aspects of RAID and SCSI in addition to the product related information.

More information from the author of the DPT controller drivers (EATA* drivers) can be found at his pages on *SCSI* `<http://www.uni-mainz.de/neuffer/scsi>` and *DPT* `<http://www.uni-mainz.de/neuffer/scsi/dpt>`.

SCSI-to-SCSI-controllers are small computers themselves, often with a substantial amount of cache RAM. To the host system they mask themselves as a gigantic, fast and reliable SCSI disk whereas to their disks they look like the computer's SCSI host adapter. Some of these controllers have the option to talk to multiple hosts simultaneously. Since these controllers look to the host as a normal, albeit large SCSI drive they need no special support from the host system. Usually they are configured via the front panel or with a vt100 terminal emulator connected to their on-board serial interface.

Very recently I have heard that Syred also makes SCSI-to-SCSI controllers that are supported under Linux. I have no more information about this yet but will come back with more information soon. In the mean time check out their *home* `<http://www.syred.com>` pages for more information.

RAID comes in many levels and flavours which I will give a brief overview of this here. Much has been written about it and the interested reader is recommended to read more about this in the RAID FAQ.

- RAID *0* is not redundant at all but offers the best throughput of all levels here. Data is striped across a number of drives so read and write operations take place in parallel across all drives. On the other hand if a single drive fail then everything is lost. Did I mention backups?

- RAID *1* is the most primitive method of obtaining redundancy by duplicating data across all drives. Naturally this is massively wasteful but you get one substantial advantage which is fast access. The drive that access the data first wins. Transfers are not any faster than for a single drive, even though you might get some faster read transfers by using one track reading per drive.

  Also if you have only 2 drives this is the only method of achieving redundancy.

- RAID *2* and *4* are not so common and are not covered here.

- RAID *3* uses a number of disks (at least 2) to store data in a striped RAID 0 fashion. It also uses an additional redundancy disk to store the XOR sum of the data from the data disks. Should the redundancy disk fail, the system can continue to operate as if nothing happened. Should any single data disk fail the system can compute the data on this disk from the information on the redundancy disk and all remaining disks. Any double fault will bring the whole RAID set off-line.

RAID 3 makes sense only with at least 2 data disks (3 disks including the redundancy disk). Theoretically there is no limit for the number of disks in the set, but the probability of a fault increases with the number of disks in the RAID set. Usually the upper limit is 5 to 7 disks in a single RAID set.

Since RAID 3 stores all redundancy information on a dedicated disk and since this information has to be updated whenever a write to any data disk occurs, the overall write speed of a RAID 3 set is limited by the write speed of the redundancy disk. This, too, is a limit for the number of disks in a RAID set. The overall read speed of a RAID 3 set with all data disks up and running is that of a RAID 0 set with that number of data disks. If the set has to reconstruct data stored on a failed disk from redundant information, the performance will be severely limited: All disks in the set have to be read and XOR-ed to compute the missing information.

- RAID *5* is just like RAID 3, but the redundancy information is spread on all disks of the RAID set. This improves write performance, because load is distributed more evenly between all available disks.

There are also hybrids available based on RAID 1 and one other level. Many combinations are possible but I have only seen a few referred to. These are more complex than the above mentioned RAID levels.

RAID *0/1* combines striping with duplication which gives very high transfers combined with fast seeks as well as redundancy. The disadvantage is high disk consumption as well as the above mentioned complexity.

RAID *1/5* combines the speed and redundancy benefits of RAID5 with the fast seek of RAID1. Redundancy is improved compared to RAID 0/1 but disk consumption is still substantial. Implementing such a system would involve typically more than 6 drives, perhaps even several controllers or SCSI channels.

4.3.2 AFS, Veritas and Other Volume Management Systems

Although multiple partitions and disks have the advantage of making for more space and higher speed and reliability there is a significant snag: if for instance the /tmp partition is full you are in trouble even if the news spool is empty, as it is not easy to retransfer quotas across partitions. Volume management is a system that does just this and AFS and Veritas are two of the best known examples. Some also offer other file systems like log file systems and others optimised for reliability or speed. Note that Veritas is not available (yet) for Linux and it is not certain they can sell kernel modules without providing source for their proprietary code, this is just mentioned for information on what is out there. Still, you can check their *home page* <http://www.veritas.com> to see how such systems function.

Derek Atkins, of MIT, ported AFS to Linux and has also set up the *Linux AFS mailing List* for this which is open to the public. Requests to join the list should go to *Request* and finally bug reports should be directed to *Bug Reports*.

Important: as AFS uses encryption it is restricted software and cannot easily be exported from the US. AFS is now sold by Transarc and they have set up a www site. The directory structure there has been reorganized recently so I cannot give a more accurate URL than just the *Transarc Home Page* <http://www.transarc.com> which lands you in the root of the web site. There you can also find much general information as well as a FAQ.

The is now also development based on the last free sources of AFS.

Volume management is for the time being an area where Linux is lacking. Someone has recently started a virtual partition system project that will reimplement many of the volume management functions found in IBM's AIX system.

4.3.3 Linux md Kernel Patch

There is however one kernel project that attempts to do some of this, md, which has been part of the kernel distributions since 1.3.69. Currently providing spanning and RAID it is still in early development and people are reporting varying degrees of success as well as total wipe out. Use with caution.

Currently it offers linear mode and RAID levels 0,1,4,5; all in various stages of development and reliability with linear mode and RAID levels 0 and 1 being the most stable. It is also possible to stack some levels, for instance mirroring (RAID 1) two pairs of drives, each pair set up as striped disks (RAID 0), which offers the speed of RAID 0 combined with the reliability of RAID 1.

Think very carefully what drives you combine so you can operate all drives in parallel, which gives you better performance and less wear. Read more about this in the documentation that comes with md.

4.3.4   General File System Consideration

In the Linux world `ext2fs` is well established as a general purpose system. Still for some purposes others can be a better choice. News spools lend themselves to a log file based system whereas high reliability data might need other formats. This is a hotly debated topic and there are currently few choices available but work is underway. Log file systems also have the advantage of very fast file checking. Mail servers in the 100 GB class can suffer file checks taking several days before becoming operational after rebooting.

The `Minix` file system is the oldest one, used in some rescue disk systems but otherwise very little used these days. At one time the `Xiafs` was a strong contender to the standard for Linux but seems to have fallen behind these days.

Adam Richter from Yggdrasil posted recently that they have been working on a compressed log file based system but that this project is currently on hold. Nevertheless a non-working version is available on their FTP server. Check out *the Yggdrasil ftp server* <ftp://ftp.yggdrasil.com/private/adam> where special patched versions of the kernel can be found. Hopefully this will be rolled into the mainstream kernel in the near future.

As of July, 23th 1997 *Hans Reiser* <mailto:reiser(at)RICOCHET.NET> has put up the source to his tree based *reiserfs* <http://idiom.com/beverly/reiserfs.html> on the web. While his filesystem has some very interesting features and is much faster than `ext2fs`, it is still very experimental and difficult to integrate with the standard kernel. Expect some interesting developments in the future - this is different from your "average log based file system for Linux" project, because Hans already has working code.

There is room for access control lists (ACL) and other unimplemented features in the existing `ext2fs`, stay tuned for future updates.

There is also an encrypted file system available but again as this is under export control from the US, make sure you get it from a legal place.

File systems is an active field of academic and industrial research and development, the results of which are quite often freely available. Linux has in many cases been a development tool in such activities so you can expect a lot of continuous work in this field, stay tuned for the latest development.

4.3.5   CD-ROM File Systems

There has been a number of file systems available for use on CD-ROM systems and one of the earliest one was the *High Sierra* format, supposedly named after the hotel where the final agreement took place. This was the precursor to the *ISO 9660* format which is supported by Linux. Later there were the *Rock Ridge* extensions which added file system features such as long filenames, permissions and more.

The Linux iso9660 file system supports both High Sierra as well as Rock Ridge extensions.

However, once again Microsoft decided it should create another standard and their latest effort here is called *Joliet* and offers some internationalisation features. This is at the time of writing not yet available in the standard kernel releases but exists in beta versions. Hopefully this should soon work its way into the standard kernel.

In a recent Usenet News posting hpa (at) transmeta.com (H. Peter Anvin) writes the following the following interesting piece of trivia:

```
Actually, Joliet is a city outside Chicago; best known for being the
site of the prison where Elwood was locked up in the movie "Blues
Brothers."  Rock Ridge (the UNIX extensions to ISO 9660) is named
after the (fictional) town in the movie "Blazing Saddles."
```

4.3.6   Compression

Disk versus file compression is a hotly debated topic especially regarding the added danger of file corruption. Nevertheless there are several options available for the adventurous administrators. These take on many forms, from kernel modules and patches to extra libraries but note that most suffer various forms of limitations such as being read-only.

HOWTO

As development takes place at neck breaking speed the specs have undoubtedly changed by the time you read this. As always: check the latest updates yourself. Here only a few references are given.

- DouBle features file compression with some limitations.
- Zlibc adds transparent on-the-fly decompression of files as they load.
- there are many modules available for reading compressed files or partitions that are native to various other operating systems though currently most of these are read-only.
- dmsdos (currently in version 0.8.0a) offer many of the compression options available for DOS and Windows. It is not yet complete but work is ongoing and new features added regularly.
- e2compr is a package that extends `ext2fs` with compression capabilities. It is still under testing and will therefore mainly be of interest for kernel hackers but should soon gain stability for wider use. Check the *e2compr homepage* `<http://netspace.net.au/~reiter/e2compr.html>` for more information. I have reports of speed and good stability which is why it is mentioned here.

4.3.7 Other filesystems

Also there is the user file system (`userfs`) that allows FTP based file system and some compression (`arcfs`) plus fast prototyping and many other features. The `docfs` is based on this filesystem.

Recent kernels feature the loop or loopback device which can be used to put a complete file system within a file. There are some possibilities for using this for making new file systems with compression, tarring, encryption etc.

Note that this device is unrelated to the network loopback device.

There is a number of other ongoing file system projects, but these are in the experimental stage and fall outside the scope of this HOWTO.

4.3.8 Physical Track Positioning

This trick used to be very important when drives were slow and small, and some file systems used to take the varying characteristics into account when placing files. Although higher overall speed, on board drive and controller caches and intelligence has reduced the effect of this.

Nevertheless there is still a little to be gained even today. As we know, "*world dominance*" is soon within reach but to achieve this "*fast*" we need to employ all the tricks we can use .

To understand the strategy we need to recall this near ancient piece of knowledge and the properties of the various track locations. This is based on the fact that transfer speeds generally increase for tracks further away from the spindle, as well as the fact that it is faster to seek to or from the central tracks than to or from the inner or outer tracks.

Most drives use disks running at constant angular velocity but use (fairly) constant data density across all tracks. This means that you will get much higher transfer rates on the outer tracks than on the inner tracks; a characteristics which fits the requirements for large libraries well.

Newer disks use a logical geometry mapping which differs from the actual physical mapping which is transparently mapped by the drive itself. This makes the estimation of the "middle" tracks a little harder.

In most cases track 0 is at the outermost track and this is the general assumption most people use. Still, it should be kept in mind that there are no guarantees this is so.

Inner
tracks are usually slow in transfer, and lying at one end of the seeking position it is also slow to seek to.
This is more suitable to the low end directories such as DOS, root and print spools.

Middle
tracks are on average faster with respect to transfers than inner tracks and being in the middle also on average faster to seek to.
This characteristics is ideal for the most demanding parts such as `swap`, `/tmp` and `/var/tmp`.

Outer

> tracks have on average even faster transfer characteristics but like the inner tracks are at the end of the seek so statistically it is equally slow to seek to as the inner tracks.

> Large files such as libraries would benefit from a place here.

Hence seek time reduction can be achieved by positioning frequently accessed tracks in the middle so that the average seek distance and therefore the seek time is short. This can be done either by using `fdisk` or `cfdisk` to make a partition on the middle tracks or by first making a file (using `dd`) equal to half the size of the entire disk before creating the files that are frequently accessed, after which the dummy file can be deleted. Both cases assume starting from an empty disk.

The latter trick is suitable for news spools where the empty directory structure can be placed in the middle before putting in the data files. This also helps reducing fragmentation a little.

This little trick can be used both on ordinary drives as well as RAID systems. In the latter case the calculation for centring the tracks will be different, if possible. Consult the latest RAID manual.

5 Other Operating Systems

Many Linux users have several operating systems installed, often necessitated by hardware setup systems that run under other operating systems, typically DOS or some flavour of Windows. A small section on how best to deal with this is therefore included here.

5.1 DOS

Leaving aside the debate on weather or not DOS qualifies as an operating system one can in general say that it has little sophistication with respect to disk operations. The more important result of this is that there can be severe difficulties in running various versions of DOS on large drives, and you are therefore strongly recommended in reading the *Large Drives mini-HOWTO*. One effect is that you are often better off placing DOS on low track numbers.

Having been designed for small drives it has a rather unsophisticated file system (*FAT*) which when used on large drives will allocate enormous block sizes. It is also prone to block fragmentation which will after a while cause excessive seeks and slow effective transfers.

One solution to this is to use a defragmentation program regularly but it is strongly recommended to back up data and verify the disk before defragmenting. All versions of DOS have `chkdsk` that can do some disk checking, newer versions also have `scandisk` which is somewhat better. There are many defragmentation programs available, some versions have one called `defrag`. Norton Utilities have a large suite of disk tools and there are many others available too.

As always there are snags, and this particular snake in our drive paradise is called *hidden files*. Some vendors started to use these for copy protection schemes and would not take kindly to being moved to a different place on the drive, even if it remained in the same place in the directory structure. The result of this was that newer defragmentation programs will not touch any hidden file, which in turn reduces the effect of defragmentation.

Being a single tasking, single threading and single most other things operating system there is very little gains in using multiple drives unless you use a drive controller with built in RAID support of some kind.

There are a few utilities called `join` and `subst` which can do some multiple drive configuration but there is very little gains for a lot of work. Some of these commands have been removed in newer versions.

In the end there is very little you can do, but not all hope is lost. Many programs need fast, temporary storage, and the better behaved ones will look for environment variables called `TMPDIR` or `TEMPDIR` which you can set to point to another drive. This is often best done in `autoexec.bat`.

```
SET TMPDIR=E:/TMP
```

HOWTO

Not only will this possibly gain you some speed but also it can reduce fragmentation.

There have been reports about difficulties in removing multiple primary partitions using the `fdisk` program that comes with DOS. Should this happen you can instead use a Linux rescue disk with Linux `fdisk` to repair the system.

5.2 Windows

Most of the above points are valid for Windows too, with the exception of Windows95 which apparently has better disk handling, which will get better performance out of SCSI drives.

A useful thing is the introduction of long filenames, to read these from Linux you will need the `vfat` file system for mounting these partitions.

The most important thing is the introduction of the new file system `FAT32` which is better suited to large drives. The snag is that there is very little support for this today, not even in NT 4.0 or many drive utility systems. A stable driver for Linux is coming soon but is not yet ready for prime time. Stay tuned for updates.

Disk fragmentation is still a problem. Some of this can be avoided by doing a defragmentation immediately before and immediately after installing large programs or systems. I use this scheme at work and have found it to work quite well. Purging unused files and emptying the waste basket first can improve defragmentation further.

Windows also use swap drives, redirecting this to another drive can give you some performance gains. There are several mini-HOWTOs telling you how best to share swap space between various operating systems.

Very recently someone started a project supporting `ext2fs` support for Win95 which you can read about at this *web site* `<http://www.globalxs.nl/home/p/pvs/>`.

The trick of setting `TEMPDIR` can still be used but not all programs will honour this setting. Some do, though. To get a good overview of the settings in the control files you can run `sysedit` which will open a number of files for editing, one of which is the `autoexec` file where you can add the `TEMPDIR` settings.

Much of the temporary files are located in the `/windows/temp` directory and changing this is more tricky. To achieve this you can use `regedit` which is rather powerful and quite capable of rendering your system in a state you will not enjoy, or more precisely, in a state much les enjoyable than windows in general. Registry database error is a message that means seriously bad news. Also you will see that many programs have their own private temporary directories scattered around the system.

Setting the swap file to a separate partition is a better idea and much less risky. Keep in mind that this partition cannot be used for anything else, even if there should appear to be space left there.

5.3 OS/2

The only special note here is that you can get a file system driver for OS/2 that can read an `ext2fs` partition.

5.4 NT

This is a more serious system featuring most buzzwords known to marketing. It is well worth noting that it features software striping and other more sophisticated setups. Check out the drive manager in the control panel. I do not have easy access to NT, more details on this can take a bit of time.

One important snag was recently reported by acahalan at cs.uml.edu : (reformatted from a Usenet News posting)

NT DiskManager has a serious bug that can corrupt your disk when you have several (more than one?) extended partitions. Microsoft provides an emergency fix program at their web site. See the *knowledge base* `<http://www.microsoft.com/kb/>` for more. (This affects Linux users, because Linux users have extra partitions)

5.5   Sun OS

There is a little bit of confusion in this area between Sun OS vs. Solaris. Strictly speaking Solaris is just Sun OS 5.x packaged with Openwindows and a few other things. If you run Solaris, just type uname -a to see your version. Parts of the reason for this confusion is that Sun Microsystems used to use an OS from the BSD family, albeight with a few bits and pieces from elsewhere as well as things made by themselves. This was the situation up to Sun OS 4.x.y when they did a "strategic roadmap decision" and decided to switch over to the official Unix, System V, Release 4 (aka SVR5), and Sun OS 5 was created. This made a lot of people unhappy. Also this was bundled with other things and marketed under the name Solaris, which currently stands at release 2.6 .

5.5.1   Sun OS 4

This is quite familiar to most Linux users. Note however that the file system structure is quite different and does not conform to FSSTND so any planning must be based on the traditional structure. You can get some information by the man page on this: man hier. This is, like most manpages, rather brief but should give you a good start. If you are still confused by the structure it will at least be at a higher level.

5.5.2   Sun OS 5 (aka Solaris)

This comes with a snazzy installation system that runs under Openwindows, it will help you in partitioning and formatting the drives before installing the system from CD-ROM. It will also fail if your drive setup is too far out, and as it takes a complete installation run from a full CD-ROM in a 1x only drive this failure will dawn on you after too long time. That is the experience we had where I used to work. Instead we installed everything onto one drive and then moved directories across.

The default settings are sensible for most things, yet there remains a little oddity: swap drives. Even though the official manual recommends multiple swap drives (which are used in a similar fashion as on Linux) the default is to use only a single drive. It is recommended to change this as soon as possible.

Sun OS 5 offers also a file system especially designed for temporary files, tmpfs. This is a kind of souped up RAM disk, and like ordinary RAM disks the contents is lost when the power goes. If space is scarce parts of the pseudo drive is swapped out, so in effect you store temporary files on the swap partition. Linux does not have such a file system; it has been discussed in the past but opinions were mixed. I would be interested in hearing comments on this.

The only comment so far is: don't! Under Solaris 2.0 it seem that creating too big files in /tmp can cause a out of swap space kernel panic trap. As the evidence of what has happened is as lost as any data on a RAMdisk after powering down it can be hard to find out what has happened. What is worse, it seems that user space processes can cause this kernel panic and unless this problem is taken care of it is best not to use tmpfs.

Also see the note on 16.1 (Combining swap and /tmp).

Trivia: There is a movie also called Solaris, a science fiction movie that is very, very long, slow and incomprehensible. This was often pointed out at the time Solaris (the OS) appeared...

6   Clusters

In this section I will briefly touch on the ways machines can be connected together but this is so big a topic it could be a separate HOWTO in its own right, hint, hint. Also, strictly speaking, this section lies outside the scope of this HOWTO, so if you feel like getting fame etc. *you* could contact me and take over this part and turn it into a new document.

These days computers gets outdated at an incredible rate. There is however no reason why old hardware could not be put to good use with Linux. Using an old and otherwise outdated computer as a network server can be both useful in its own right as well as a valuable educational exercise. Such a local networked cluster of computers can take on many forms but to remain within the charter of this HOWTO I will limit myself to the disk strategies. Nevertheless I would hope someone else could take on this topic and turn it into a document on its own.

This is an exciting area of activity today, and many forms of clustering is available today, ranging from automatic workload balancing over local network to more exotic hardware such as Scalable Coherent Interface (SCI) which gives a tight integration of machines, effectively turning them into a single machine. Various kinds of clustering has been available for larger machines for some time and the VAXcluster is perhaps a well known example of this. Clustering is done usually in order to share resources such as disk drives, printers and terminals etc, but also processing resources equally transparently between the computational nodes.

There is no universal definition of clustering, in here it is taken to mean a network of machines that combine their resources to serve users. Admittedly this is a rather loose definition but this will change later.

These days also Linux offers some clustering features but for a starter I will just describe a simple local network. It is a good way of putting old and otherwise unusable hardware to good use, as long as they can run Linux or something similar.

One of the best ways of using an old machine is as a network server in which case the effective speed is more likely to be limited by network bandwidth rather than pure computational performance. For home use you can move the following functionality off to an older machine used as a server:

- news
- mail
- web proxy
- printer server
- modem server (PPP, SLIP, FAX, Voice mail)

You can also NFS mount drives from the server onto your workstation thereby reducing drive space requirements. Still read the FSSTND to see what directories should *not* be exported. The best candidates for exporting to all machines are /usr and /var/spool and possibly /usr/local but probably not /var/spool/lpd.

Most of the time even slow disks will deliver sufficient performance. On the other hand, if you do processing directly on the disks on the server or have very fast networking, you might want to rethink your strategy and use faster drives. Searching features on a web server or news database searches are two examples of this.

Such a network can be an excellent way of learning system administration and building up your own toaster network, as it often is called. You can get more information on this in other HOWTOs but there are two important things you should keep in mind:

- Do not pull IP numbers out of thin air. Configure your inside net using IP numbers reserved for private use, and use your network server as a router that handles this IP masquerading.

- Remember that if you additionally configure the router as a firewall you might not be able to get to your own data from the outside, depending on the firewall configuration.

The *nyx* network provides an example of a cluster in the sense defined here. It consists of the following machines:

nyx
    is one of the two user login machines and also provides some of the networking services.

nox
    (aka nyx10) is the main user login machine and is also the mail server.

noc
    is a dedicated news server. The news spool is made accessible through NFS mounting to nyx and nox.

arachne
    (aka www) is the web server. Web pages are written by NFS mounting onto nox.

There are also some more advanced clustering projects going, notably

- *The Beowolf Project* <http://cesdis.gsfc.nasa.gov/linux/beowulf/beowulf.html>

- *The Genoa Active Message Machine (GAMMA)* <http://www.disi.unige.it/project/gamma/>

High-tech clustering requires high-tech interconnect, and SCI is one of them. To find out more you can either look up the home page of *Dolphin Interconnect Solutions* <http://www.dolphinics.no/> which is one of the main actors in this field, or you can have a look at *scizzl* <http://www.scizzl.com/>.

7 Mount Points

In designing the disk layout it is important not to split off the directory tree structure at the wrong points, hence this section. As it is highly dependent on the FSSTND it has been put aside in a separate section, and will most likely have to be totally rewritten when FHS is released. Nobody knows when that will happen, and at the time of writing this a debate of near-religious qualities is taking place on the mailing list. In the meanwhile this will do.

Remember that this is a list of where a separation *can* take place, not where it *has* to be. As always, good judgement is always required.

Again only a rough indication can be given here. The values indicate

```
0=don't separate here
1=not recommended
  ...
4=useful
5=recommended
```

In order to keep the list short, the uninteresting parts are removed.

```
Directory     Suitability
/
|
+-bin          0
+-boot         0
+-dev          0
+-etc          0
+-home         5
+-lib          0
+-mnt          0
+-proc         0
+-root         0
+-sbin         0
+-tmp          5
+-usr          5
|  \
|  +-X11R6      3
|  +-bin        3
|  +-lib        4
|  +-local      4
|  | \
|  | +bin          2
|  | +lib          4
|  +-src        3
|
+-var          5
```

HOWTO

```
        \
        +-adm         0
        +-lib         2
        +-lock        1
        +-log         1
        +-preserve    1
        +-run         1
        +-spool       4
        | \
        | +-mail       3
        | +-mqueue     3
        | +-news       5
        | +-smail      3
        | +-uucp       3
        +-tmp         5
```

There is of course plenty of adjustments possible, for instance a home user would not bother with splitting off the
/var/spool hierarchy but a serious ISP should. The key here is *usage*.

8 Disk Layout

With all this in mind we are now ready to embark on the layout. I have based this on my own method developed when I
got hold of 3 old SCSI disks and boggled over the possibilities.

The tables in the appendices are designed to simplify the mapping process. They have been designed to help you go
through the process of optimizations as well as making an useful log in case of system repair. A few examples are also
given.

8.1 Selection for partitioning

Determine your needs and set up a list of all the parts of the file system you want to be on separate partitions and sort
them in descending order of speed requirement and how much space you want to give each partition.

The table in Appendix A (section 17 ( )) is a useful tool to select what directories you should put on different partitions.
It is sorted in a logical order with space for your own additions and notes about mounting points and additional systems.
It is therefore NOT sorted in order of speed, instead the speed requirements are indicated by bullets ('o').

If you plan to RAID make a note of the disks you want to use and what partitions you want to RAID. Remember various
RAID solutions offers different speeds and degrees of reliability.

(Just to make it simple I'll assume we have a set of identical SCSI disks and no RAID)

8.2 Mapping partitions to drives

Then we want to place the partitions onto physical disks. The point of the following algorithm is to maximise parallelizing
and bus capacity. In this example the drives are A, B and C and the partitions are 987654321 where 9 is the partition with
the highest speed requirement. Starting at one drive we 'meander' the partition line over and over the drives in this way:

```
        A :  9  4  3
        B :  8  5  2
        C :  7  6  1
```

This makes the 'sum of speed requirements' the most equal across each drive.

Use the table in Appendix B (section 18 ( )) to select what drives to use for each partition in order to optimize for parallelicity.

Note the speed characteristics of your drives and note each directory under the appropriate column. Be prepared to shuffle directories, partitions and drives around a few times before you are satisfied.

8.3 Sorting partitions on drives

After that it is recommended to select partition numbering for each drive.

Use the table in Appendix C (section 19 ( )) to select partition numbers in order to optimize for track characteristics. At the end of this you should have a table sorted in ascending partition number. Fill these numbers back into the tables in appendix A and B.

You will find these tables useful when running the partitioning program (`fdisk` or `cfdisk`) and when doing the installation.

8.4 Optimizing

After this there are usually a few partitions that have to be 'shuffled' over the drives either to make them fit or if there are special considerations regarding speed, reliability, special file systems etc. Nevertheless this gives what this author believes is a good starting point for the complete setup of the drives and the partitions. In the end it is actual use that will determine the real needs after we have made so many assumptions. After commencing operations one should assume a time comes when a repartitioning will be beneficial.

For instance if one of the 3 drives in the above mentioned example is very slow compared to the two others a better plan would be as follows:

```
A : 9 6 5
B : 8 7 4
C : 3 2 1
```

8.4.1 Optimizing by characteristics

Often drives can be similar in apparent overall speed but some advantage can be gained by matching drives to the file size distribution and frequency of access. Thus binaries are suited to drives with fast access that offer command queueing, and libraries are better suited to drives with larger transfer speeds where IDE offers good performance for the money.

8.4.2 Optimizing by drive parallelising

Avoid drive contention by looking at tasks: for instance if you are accessing `/usr/local/bin` chances are you will soon also need files from `/usr/local/lib` so placing these at separate drives allows less seeking and possible parallel operation and drive caching. It is quite possible that choosing what may appear less than ideal drive characteristics will still be advantageous if you can gain parallel operations. Identify common tasks, what partitions they use and try to keep these on separate physical drives.

Just to illustrate my point I will give a few examples of task analysis here.

Office software

  such as editing, word processing and spreadsheets are typical examples of low intensity software both in terms of CPU and disk intensity. However, should you have a single server for a huge number of users you should not forget that most such software have auto save facilities which cause extra traffic, usually on the home directories. Splitting users over several drives would reduce contention.

News

  readers also feature auto save features on home directories so ISPs should consider separating home directories

News spools are notorious for their deeply nested directories and their large number of very small files. Loss of a news spool partition is not a big problem for most people, too, so they are good candidates for a RAID 0 setup with many small disks to distribute the many seeks among multiple spindles. It is recommended in the manuals and FAQs for the INN news server to put news spool and `.overview` files on separate drives for larger installations.

There is also a web page dedicated to *INN optimising* `<http://www.spinne.com/usenet/inn-perf.html>` well worth reading.

Database

applications can be demanding both in terms of drive usage and speed requirements. The details are naturally application specific, read the documentation carefully with disk requirements in mind. Also consider RAID both for performance and reliability.

E-mail

reading and sending involves home directories as well as in- and outgoing spool files. If possible keep home directories and spool files on separate drives. If you are a mail server or a mail hub consider putting in- and outgoing spool directories on separate drives.

Losing mail is an extremely bad thing, if you are and ISP or major hub. Think about RAIDing your mail spool and consider frequent backups.

Software development

can require a large number of directories for binaries, libraries, include files as well as source and project files. If possible split as much as possible across separate drives. On small systems you can place `/usr/src` and project files on the same drive as the home directories.

Web browsing

is becoming more and more popular. Many browsers have a local cache which can expand to rather large volumes. As this is used when reloading pages or returning to the previous page, speed is quite important here. If however you are connected via a well configured proxy server you do not need more than typically a few megabytes per user for a session. See also the sections on 8.6.1 (Home Directories) and 8.6.3 (WWW).

8.5 Usage requirements

When you get a box of 10 or so CD-ROMs with a Linux distribution and the entire contents of the big FTP sites it can be tempting to install as much as your drives can take. Soon, however, one would find that this leaves little room to grow and that it is easy to bite over more than can be chewed, at least in polite company. Therefore I will make a few comments on a few points to keep in mind when you plan out your system. Comments here are actively sought.

Testing

Linux is simple and you don't even need a hard disk to try it out, if you can get the boot floppies to work you are likely to get it to work on your hardware. If the standard kernel does not work for you, do not forget that often there can be special boot disk versions available for unusual hardware combinations that can solve your initial problems until you can compile your own kernel.

Learning

about operating system is something Linux excels in, there is plenty of documentation and the source is available. A single drive with 50 MB is enough to get you started with a shell, a few of the most frequently used commands and utilities.

Hobby

use or more serious learning requires more commands and utilities but a single drive is still all it takes, 500 MB should give you plenty of room, also for sources and documentation.

Serious

software development or just serious hobby work requires even more space. At this stage you have probably a mail and news feed that requires spool files and plenty of space. Separate drives for various tasks will begin to show a benefit. At this stage you have probably already gotten hold of a few drives too. Drive requirements gets harder to estimate but I would expect 2-4 GB to be plenty, even for a small server.

Servers

come in many flavours, ranging from mail servers to full sized ISP servers. A base of 2 GB for the main system should be sufficient, then add space and perhaps also drives for separate features you will offer. Cost is the main limiting factor here but be prepared to spend a bit if you wish to justify the "S" in ISP. Admittedly, not all do it.

8.6 Servers

Big tasks require big drives and a separate section here. If possible keep as much as possible on separate drives. Some of the appendices detail the setup of a small departmental server for 10-100 users. Here I will present a few consideration for the higher end servers. In general you should not be afraid of using RAID, not only because it is fast and safe but also because it can make growth a little less painful. All the notes below come as additions to the points mentioned earlier.

Popular servers rarely just happens, rather they grow over time and this demands both generous amounts of disk space as well as a good net connection. In many of these cases it might be a good idea to reserve entire SCSI drives, in singles or as arrays, for each task. This way you can move the data should the computer fail. Note that transferring drives across computers is not simple and might not always work, especially in the case of IDE drives. Drive arrays require careful setup in order to reconstruct the data correctly, so you might want to keep a paper copy of your `fstab` file as well as a note of SCSI IDs.

8.6.1 Home directories

Estimate how many drives you will need, if this is more than 2 I would recommend RAID, strongly. If not you should separate users across your drives dedicated to users based on some kind of simple hashing algorithm. For instance you could use the first 2 letters in the user name, so `jbloggs` is put on `/u/j/b/jbloggs` where `/u/j` is a symbolic link to a physical drive so you can get a balanced load on your drives.

8.6.2 Anonymous FTP

This is an essential service if you are serious about service. Good servers are well maintained, documented, kept up to date, and immensely popular no matter where in the world they are located. The big server `ftp.funet.fi` is an excellent example of this.

In general this is not a question of CPU but of network bandwidth. Size is hard to estimate, mainly it is a question of ambition and service attitudes. I believe the big archive at ftp.cdrom.com is a *BSD machine with 50 GB disk. Also memory is important for a dedicated FTP server, about 256 MB RAM would be sufficient for a very big server, whereas smaller servers can get the job done well with 64 MB RAM. Network connections would still be the most important factor.

8.6.3 WWW

For many this is the main reason to get onto the Internet, in fact many now seem to equate the two. In addition to being network intensive there is also a fair bit of drive activity related to this, mainly regarding the caches. Keeping the cache on a separate, fast drive would be beneficial. Even better would be installing a caching proxy server. This way you can reduce the cache size for each user and speed up the service while at the same time cut down on the bandwidth requirements.

With a caching proxy server you need a fast set of drives, RAID0 would be ideal as reliability is not important here. Higher capacity is better but about 2 GB should be sufficient for most. Remember to match the cache period to the capacity and demand. Too long periods would on the other hand be a disadvantage, if possible try to adjust based on the URL. For more information check up on the most used servers such as `Harvest`, *Squid* `<http://www.nlanr.net/Squid>` and the one from Netscape.

8.6.4 Mail

Handling mail is something most machines do to some extent. The big mail servers, however, come into a class of their own. This is a demanding task and a big server can be slow even when connected to fast drives and a good net feed. In the Linux world the big server at `vger.rutgers.edu` is a well known example. Unlike a news service which is distributed and which can partially reconstruct the spool using other machines as a feed, the mail servers are centralised. This makes safety much more important, so for a major server you should consider a RAID solution with emphasize on reliability. Size is hard to estimate, it all depends on how many lists you run as well as how many subscribers you have.

8.6.5 News

This is definitely a high volume task, and very dependent on what news groups you subscribe to. On Nyx there is a fairly complete feed and the spool files consume about 17 GB. The biggest groups are no doubt in the `alt.binary.*` hierarchy, so if you for some reason decide not to get these you can get a good service with perhaps 12 GB. Still others, that shall remain nameless, feel 2 GB is sufficient to claim ISP status. In this case news expires so fast I feel the spelling IsP is barely justified. A full newsfeed means a traffic of a few GB every day and this is an ever growing number.

8.6.6 Others

There are many services available on the net and even though many have been put somewhat in the shadows by the web. Nevertheless, services like *archie*, *gopher* and *wais* just to name a few, still exist and remain valuable tools on the net. If you are serious about starting a major server you should also consider these services. Determining the required volumes is hard, it all depends on popularity and demand. Providing good service inevitably has its costs, disk space is just one of them.

8.7 Pitfalls

The dangers of splitting up everything into separate partitions are briefly mentioned in the section about volume management. Still, several people have asked me to emphasize this point more strongly: when one partition fills up it cannot grow any further, no matter if there is plenty of space in other partitions.

In particular look out for explosive growth in the news spool (`/var/spool/news`). For multi user machines with quotas keep an eye on `/tmp` and `/var/tmp` as some people try to hide their files there, just look out for filenames ending in gif or jpeg...

In fact, for single physical drives this scheme offers very little gains at all, other than making file growth monitoring easier (using `'df'`) and physical track positioning. Most importantly there is no scope for parallel disk access. A freely available volume management system would solve this but this is still some time in the future. However, when more specialised file systems become available even a single disk could benefit from being divided into several partitions.

8.8 Compromises

One way to avoid the aforementioned pitfalls is to only set off fixed partitions to directories with a fairly well known size such as swap, `/tmp` and `/var/tmp` and group together the remainders into the remaining partitions using symbolic links.

Example: a slow disk (`slowdisk`), a fast disk (`fastdisk`) and an assortment of files. Having set up `swap` and `tmp` on `fastdisk`; and `/home` and root on slowdisk we have (the fictitious) directories `/a/slow`, `/a/fast`, `/b/slow` and `/b/fast` left to allocate on the partitions `/mnt.slowdisk` and `/mnt.fastdisk` which represents the remaining partitions of the two drives.

Putting `/a` or `/b` directly on either drive gives the same properties to the subdirectories. We could make all 4 directories separate partitions but would lose some flexibility in managing the size of each directory. A better solution is to make these 4 directories symbolic links to appropriate directories on the respective drives.

Thus we make

```
/a/fast point to /mnt.fastdisk/a/fast    or    /mnt.fastdisk/a.fast
/a/slow point to /mnt.slowdisk/a/slow    or    /mnt.slowdisk/a.slow
/b/fast point to /mnt.fastdisk/b/fast    or    /mnt.fastdisk/b.fast
/b/slow point to /mnt.slowdisk/b/slow    or    /mnt.slowdisk/b.slow
```

and we get all fast directories on the fast drive without having to set up a partition for all 4 directories. The second (right hand) alternative gives us a flatter files system which in this case can make it simpler to keep an overview of the structure.

The disadvantage is that it is a complicated scheme to set up and plan in the first place and that all mount point and partitions have to be defined before the system installation.

9 Implementation

Having done the layout you should now have a detailed description on what goes where. Most likely this will be on paper but hopefully someone will make a more automated system that can deal with everything from the design, through partitioning to formatting and installation. This is the route one will have to take to realise the design.

Modern distributions come with installation tools that will guide you through partitioning and formatting and also set up /etc/fstab for you automatically. For later modifications, however, you will need to understand the underlying mechanisms.

9.1 Drives and Partitions

When you start DOS or the like you will find all partitions labeled C: and onwards, with no differentiation on IDE, SCSI, network or whatever type of media you have. In the world of Linux this is rather different. During booting you will see partitions described like this:

```
Dec  6 23:45:18 demos kernel: Partition check:
Dec  6 23:45:18 demos kernel:  sda: sda1
Dec  6 23:45:18 demos kernel:  hda: hda1 hda2
```

SCSI drives are labelled sda, sdb, sdc etc, and (E)IDE drives are labelled hda, hdb, hdc etc. There are also standard names for all devices, full information can be found in /dev/MAKEDEV and /usr/src/linux/Documentation/devices.txt.

Partitions are labelled numerically for each drive hda1, hda2 and so on. On SCSI drives there can be 15 partitions per drive, on EIDE drives there can be 63 partitions per drive. Both limits exceed what is currently useful for most disks.

These are then mounted according to the file /etc/fstab before they appear as a part of the file system.

9.2 Partitioning

First you have to partition each drive into a number of separate partitions. Under Linux there are two main methods, fdisk and the more screen oriented cfdisk. These are complex programs, read the manual *very* carefully. Under DOS there are other choices, mainly the version of fdisk that is bundled with for instance DOS, or fips. The latter has the unique advantage here that it can repartition a drive without necessarily damaging existing data, unlike all the other partitioning programs.

In order to get the most out of fips you should first defragment your drive. This way you can allocate more space to other partitions.

Nevertheless, it is important you do a full backup of all your valued data before partitioning.

Partitions come in 3 flavours, primary, extended and logical. You have to use primary partitions for booting, but there is a maximum of 4 primary partitions. If you want more you have to define an extended partition within which you define your logical partitions.

Each partition has an identifier number which tells the operating system what it is, for Linux the types swap and ext2fs are the ones you will need to know.

There is a readme file that comes with fdisk that gives more in-depth information on partitioning.

Someone has just made a *Partitioning HOWTO* which contains excellent, in depth information on the nitty-gritty of partitioning. Rather than repeating it here and bloating this document further, I will instead refer you to it instead.

9.3   Multiple devices (md)

Being in a state of flux you should make sure to read the latest documentation on this kernel feature. It is not yet stable, beware.

Briefly explained it works by adding partitions together into new devices md0, md1 etc. using mdadd before you activate them using mdrun. This process can be automated using the file /etc/mdtab.

Then you then treat these like any other partition on a drive. Proceed with formatting etc. as described below using these new devices.

There is now also a HOWTO in development for RAID using md you should read.

9.4   Formatting

Next comes partition formatting, putting down the data structures that will describe the files and where they are located. If this is the first time it is recommended you use formatting with verify. Strictly speaking it should not be necessary but this exercises the I/O hard enough that it can uncover potential problems, such as incorrect termination, before you store your precious data. Look up the command mkfs for more details.

Linux can support a great number of file systems, rather than repeating the details you can read the manpage for fs which describes them in some details. Note that your kernel has to have the drivers compiled in or made as modules in order to be able to use these features. When the time comes for kernel compiling you should read carefully through the file system feature list. If you use make menuconfig you can get online help for each file system type.

Note that some rescue disk systems require minix, msdos and ext2fs to be compiled into the kernel.

Also swap partitions have to be prepared, and for this you use mkswap.

9.5   Mounting

Data on a partition is not available to the file system until it is mounted on a mount point. This can be done manually using mount or automatically during booting by adding appropriate lines to /etc/fstab. Read the manual for mount and pay close attention to the tabulation.

10   Maintenance

It is the duty of the system manager to keep an eye on the drives and partitions. Should any of the partitions overflow, the system is likely to stop working properly, no matter how much space is available on other partitions, until space is reclaimed.

Partitions and disks are easily monitored using df and should be done frequently, perhaps using a cron job or some other general system management tool.

Do not forget the swap partitions, these are best monitored using one of the memory statistics programs such as free, procinfo or top.

Drive usage monitoring is more difficult but it is important for the sake of performance to avoid contention - placing too much demand on a single drive if others are available and idle.

It is important when installing software packages to have a clear idea where the various files go. As previously mentioned GCC keeps binaries in a library directory and there are also other programs that for historical reasons are hard to figure out, X11 for instance has an unusually complex structure.

When your system is about to fill up it is about time to check and prune old logging messages as well as hunt down core files. Proper use of `ulimit` in global shell settings can help saving you from having core files littered around the system.

10.1 Backup

The observant reader might have noticed a few hints about the usefulness of making backups. Horror stories are legio about accidents and what happened to the person responsible when the backup turned out to be non-functional or even non existent. You might find it simpler to invest in proper backups than a second, secret identity.

There are many options and also a mini-HOWTO (`Backup-With-MSDOS`) detailling what you need to know. In addition to the DOS specifics it also contains general information and further leads.

In addition to making these backups you should also make sure you can restore the data. Not all systems verify that the data written is correct and many administrators have started restoring the system after an accident happy in the belief that everything is working, only to discover to their horror that the backups were useless. Be careful.

10.2 Defragmentation

This is very dependent on the file system design, some suffer fast and nearly debilitating fragmentation. Fortunately for us, `ext2fs` does not belong to this group and therefore there has been very little talk about making a defragmentation tool.

If for some reason you feel this is necessary, the quick and easy solution is to do a backup and a restore. If only a small area is affected, for instance the home directories, you could `tar` it over to a temporary area on another partition, *verify* the archive, delete the original and then untar it back again.

10.3 Deletions

Quite often disk space shortages can be remedied simply by deleting unnecessary files that accumulate around the system. Quite often programs that terminate abnormally cause all kinds of mess lying around the oddest places. Normally a core dump results after such an incident and unless you are going to debug it you can simply delete it. These can be found everywhere so you are advised to do a global search for them now and then.

Unexpected termination can also cause all sorts of temporary files remaining in places like `/tmp` or `/var/tmp`, files that are automatically removed when the program ends normally. Rebooting cleans up some of these areas but not necessary all and if you have a long uptime you could end up with a lot of old junk. If space is short you have to delete with care, make sure the file is not in active use first. Utilities like `file` can often tell you what kind of file you are looking at.

Many things are logged when the system is running, mostly to files in the `/var/log` area. In particular the file `/var/log/messages` tends to grow until deleted. It is a good idea to keep a small archive of old log files around for comparison should the system start to behave oddly.

If the mail or news system is not working properly you could have excessive growth in their spool areas, `/var/spool/mail` and `/var/spool/news` respectively. Beware of the overview files as these have a leading dot which makes them invisible to `ls -l`, it is always better to use `ls -Al` which will reveal them.

User space overflow is a particularly tricky topic. Wars have been waged between system administrators and users. Tact, diplomacy and a generous budget for new drives is what is needed. Make use of the message-of-the-day feature, information displayed during login from the `/etc/motd` file to tell users when space is short. Setting the default shell settings to prevent core files being dumped can save you a lot of work too.

Certain kinds of people try to hide files around the system, usually trying to take advantage of the fact that files with a leading dot in the name are invisible to the `ls` command. One common example are files that look like `...` that normally either are not seen, or, when using `ls -al` disappear in the noise of normal files like `.` or `..` that are in every directory. There is however a countermeasure to this, use `ls -Al` that suppresses `.` or `..` but shows all other dot-files.

10.4 Upgrades

No matter how large your drives, time will come when you will find you need more. As technology progresses you can get ever more for your money. At the time of writing this, it appears that 6.4 GB drives gives you the most bang for your bucks.

Note that with IDE drives you might have to remove an old drive, as the maximum number supported on your mother board is normally only 2 or some times 4. With SCSI you can have up to 7 for narrow (8-bit) SCSI or up to 15 for wide (15 bit) SCSI, per channel. Some host adapters can support more than a single channel and in any case you can have more than one host adapter per system. My personal recommendation is that you will most likely be better off with SCSI in the long run.

The question comes, where should you put this new drive? In many cases the reason for expansion is that you want a larger spool area, and in that case the fast, simple solution is to mount the drive somewhere under /var/spool. On the other hand newer drives are likely to be faster than older ones so in the long run you might find it worth your time to do a full reorganizing, possibly using your old design sheets.

If the upgrade is forced by running out of space in partitions used for things like /usr or /var the upgrade is a little more involved. You might consider the option of a full re-installation from your favourite (and hopefully upgraded) distribution. In this case you will have to be careful not to overwrite your essential setups. Usually these things are in the /etc directory. Proceed with care, fresh backups and working rescue disks. The other possibility is to simply copy the old directory over to the new directory which is mounted on a temporary mount point, edit your /etc/fstab file, reboot with your new partition in place and check that it works. Should it fail you can reboot with your rescue disk, re-edit /etc/fstab and try again.

Until volume management becomes available to Linux this is both complicated and dangerous. Do not get too surprised if you discover you need to restore your system from a backup.

The Tips-HOWTO gives the following example on how to move an entire directory structure across:

```
(cd /source/directory; tar cf - . ) | (cd /dest/directory; tar xvfp -)
```

While this approach to moving directory trees is portable among many Unix systems, it is inconvenient to remember. Also, it fails for deeply nested directory trees when pathnames become to long to handle for tar (GNU tar has special provisions to deal with long pathnames).

If you have access to GNU cp (which is always the case on Linux systems), you could as well use

```
cp -av /source/directory /dest/directory
```

GNU cp knows specifically about symbolic links, FIFOs and device files and will copy them correctly.

11 Advanced Issues

Linux and related systems offer plenty of possibilities for fast, efficient and devastating destruction. This document is no exception. With power comes dangers and the following sections describe a few more esoteric issues that should not be attempted before reading and understanding the documentation, the issues and the dangers. You should also make a backup. Also remember to try to restore the system from scratch from your backup at least once. Otherwise you might not be the first to be found with a perfect backup of your system and no tools available to reinstall it (or, even more embarrassing, some critical files missing on tape).

The techniques described here are rarely necessary but can be used for very specific setups. Think very clearly through what you wish to accomplish before playing around with this.

11.1 Hard Disk Tuning

The hard drive parameters can be tuned using the `hdparms` utility. Here the most interesting parameter is probably the read-ahead parameter which determines how much prefetch should be done in sequential reading.

If you want to try this out it makes most sense to tune for the characteristic file size on your drive but remember that this tuning is for the *entire* drive which makes it a bit more difficult. Probably this is only of use on large servers using dedicated news drives etc.

For safety the default hdparm settings are rather conservative. The disadvantage is that this mean you can get lost interrupts if you have a high frequency of IRQs as you would when using the serial port and an IDE disk as IRQs from the latter would mask other IRQs. THis would be noticable as less then ideal performance when downloading data from the net to disk. Setting `hdparm -u1 device` would prevent this masking and either improve your performance or, depending on hardware, corrupt the data on your disk. Experiment with caution and fresh backups.

11.2 File System Tuning

Most file systems come with a tuning utility and for `ext2fs` there is the `tune2fs` utility. Several parameters can be modified but perhaps the most useful parameter here is what size should be reserved and who should be able to take advantage of this which could help you getting more useful space out of your drives, possibly at the cost of less room for repairing a system should it crash.

11.3 Spindle Synchronizing

This should not in itself be dangerous, other than the peculiar fact that the exact details of the connections remain unclear for many drives. The theory is simple: keeping a fixed phase difference between the different drives in a RAID setup makes for less waiting for the right track to come into position for the read/write head. In practice it now seems that with large read-ahead buffers in the drives the effect is negligible.

Spindle synchronisation should not be used on RAID0 or RAID 0/1 as you would then lose the benefit of having the read heads over different areas of the mirrored sectors.

12 Further Information

There is wealth of information one should go through when setting up a major system, for instance for a news or general Internet service provider. The FAQs in the following groups are useful:

12.1 News groups

Some of the most interesting news groups are:

- *Storage* <news:comp.arch.storage>.
- *PC storage* <news:comp.sys.ibm.pc.hardware.storage>.
- *AFS* <news:alt.filesystems.afs>.
- *SCSI* <news:comp.periphs.scsi>.
- *Linux setup* <news:comp.os.linux.setup>.

Most newsgroups have their own FAQ that are designed to answer most of your questions, as the name Frequently Asked Questions indicate. Fresh versions should be posted regularly to the relevant newsgroups. If you cannot find it in your news spool you could go directly to the *FAQ main archive FTP site* <ftp://rtfm.mit.edu>. The WWW versions can be browsed at *FAQ main archive WWW site* <http://www.cis.ohio-state.edu/hypertext/faq/usenet/FAQ-List.html>.

Some FAQs have their own home site, of particular interest here are

HOWTO

- *SCSI FAQ* <http://www.paranoia.com/filipg/HTML/LINK/F_SCSI.html> and

- *comp.arch.storage FAQ* <http://alumni.caltech.edu/rdv/comp_arch_storage/FAQ-1.html>.

12.2 Mailing lists

These are low noise channels mainly for developers. Think twice before asking questions there as noise delays the development. Some relevant lists are linux-raid, linux-scsi and linux-ext2fs. Many of the most useful mailing lists run on the vger.rutgers.edu server but this is notoriously overloaded, so try to find a mirror. There are some lists mirrored at *The Redhat Home Page* <http://www.redhat.com>. Many lists are also accessible at *linuxhq* <http://www.linuxhq.com/lnxlists>, and the rest of the web site is a gold mine of useful information.

If you want to find out more about the lists available you can send a message with the line lists to the *list server at vger.rutgers.edu* <mailto:majordomo@vger.rutgers.edu>. If you need help on how to use the mail server just send the line help to the same address. Due to the popularity of this server it is likely it takes a bit to time before you get a reply or even get messages after you send a subscribe command.

There is also a number of other majordomo list servers that can be of interest such as the *EATA driver list* <mailto:linux-eata@mail.uni-mainz.de> and the *Intelligent IO list* <mailto:linux-i2o@dpt.com>.

Mailing lists are in a state of flux but you can find links to a number of interesting lists from the *Linux Documentation Homepage* <http://sunsite.unc.edu/LDP>.

12.3 HOWTO

These are intended as the primary starting points to get the background information as well as show you how to solve a specific problem. Some relevant HOWTOs are Bootdisk, Installation, SCSI and UMSDOS. The main site for these is the *LDP archive* <http://sunsite.unc.edu/LDP> at Sunsite.

There is a a new HOWTO out that deals with setting up a DPT RAID system, check out the *DPT RAID HOWTO homepage* <http://www.ram.org/computing/linux/dpt_raid.html>.

12.4 Mini-HOWTO

These are the smaller free text relatives to the HOWTOs. Some relevant mini-HOWTOs are Backup-With-MSDOS, Diskless, LILO, Linux+DOS+Win95+OS2, Linux+OS2+DOS, Linux+Win95, NFS-Root, Win95+Win+Linux, ZIP Drive . You can find these at the same place as the HOWTOs, usually in a sub directory called mini. Note that these are scheduled to be converted into SGML and become proper HOWTOs in the near future.

The old Linux Large IDE mini-HOWTO is no longer valid, instead read /usr/src/linux/drivers/block/README.ide or /usr/src/linux/Documentation/ide.txt.

12.5 Local resources

In most distributions of Linux there is already a document directory already, have a look in the *document archive* <file:///usr/doc> where most packages store their main documentation and README files etc. Also you will here find the *HOWTO archive* <file:///usr/doc/HOWTO> of ready formatted HOWTOs and also the *mini-HOWTO archive* <file:///usr/doc/HOWTO/mini> of plain text documents.

Many of the configuration files mentioned earlier can be found in the *etc* <file:///etc> directory. In particular you will want to work with the *fstab* <file:///etc/fstab> file that sets up the mounting of partitions and possibly also *mdtab* <file:///etc/mdtab> file that is used for the md system to set up RAID.

The *kernel source* `<file:///usr/src/linux>` is, of course, the ultimate documentation. In other words, *use the source, Luke*. It should also be pointed out that the kernel comes not only with source code which is even commented (well, partially at least) but also an informative *documentation directory* `<file:///usr/src/linux/Documentation>`. If you are about to ask any questions about the kernel you should read this first, it will save you and many others a lot of time and possibly embarrassment.

Also have a look in your *system log file* `<file:///var/log/messages>` to see what is going on and in particular how the booting went if too much scrolled off your screen. Using `tail -f /var/log/messages` in a separate window or screen will give you a continuous update of what is going on in your system.

You can also take advantage of the */proc* `<file:///proc>` file system that is a window into the inner workings of your system. Use `cat` rather than `more` to view the files as they are reported as being zero length.

Much of the work here is based on the Filesystem Structure Standard (FSSTND). It has changed name to File Hierarchy Standard (FHS) and is less Linux specific. The maintainer has set up a *home page* `<http://www.pathname.com/fhs>` which tells you how to join the currently private mailing list, where the development takes place.

12.6   Web pages

There is a huge number of informative web pages out there and by their very nature they change quickly so don't be too surprised if these links become quickly outdated.

A good starting point is of course the Sunsite *LDP archive* `<http://sunsite.unc.edu/LDP/>` that is a information-tion central for documentation, project pages and much, much more.

- Mike Neuffer, the author of the DPT caching RAID controller drivers, has some interesting pages on *SCSI* `<http://www.uni-mainz.de/neuffer/scsi>` and *DPT* `<http://www.uni-mainz.de/neuffer/scsi/dpt>`.

- Software RAID 1 development information can be found at *RAID 1 development page* `<http://www.nuclecu.unam.mx/miguel/raid>`.

- Disk related information on benchmarking, RAID, reliability and much, much more can be found at *Linas Vepstas* `<http://linas.org>` project page.

- There is also information available on how to *RAID the root partition* `<ftp://ftp.bizsystems.com/pub/raid/Root-RAID-HOWTO.html>` and what software packages are needed to achieve this.

- In depth documentation on *ext2fs* `<http://step.polymtl.ca/ldd/ext2fs/ext2fs_toc.html>` is also available.

- Mark D. Roth has information on *VPS* `<http://www.uiuc.edu/ph/www/roth>`

- A similar kind of project on an *Enhanced File System* `<http://www.virtual.net.au/rjh/enh-fs.html>`

- People who are awaiting support for VFAT32 and Joliet could have a look at the *development page* `<http://bmrc.berkeley.edu/people/chaffee/index.html>` for a preview. These drivers are now entering the 2.1.x kernel development series.

- There is an ongoing compression project that integrates in `ext2fs` and is called `e2compr`. For more information check out the *e2compr homepage* `<http://netspace.net.au/~reiter/e2compr.html>`.

- For more information on booting and also some BSD information have a look at *booting information* `<http://www.paranoia.com/~vax/boot.html>` page.

For diagrams and information on all sorts of disk drives, controllers etc. both for current and discontinued lines *The Ref* `<http://theref.c3d.rl.af.mil>` is the site you need. There is a lot of useful information here, a real treasure trove. You can also download the database using *FTP* `<ftp://theref.c3d.rl.af.mil/public>`.

Please let me know if you have any other leads that can be of interest.

12.7 Search engines

Remember you can also use the web search engines and that some, like

- *Altavista* <http://www.altavista.digital.com>

- *Excite* <http://www.excite.com>

- *Hotbot* <http://www.hotbot.com>

can also search usenet news.

Also remember that *Dejanews* <http://www.dejanews.com> is a dedicated news searcher that keeps a news spool from early 1995 and onwards.

If you have to ask for help you are most likely to get help in the comp.os.linux.setup news group. Due to large workload and a slow network connection I am not able to follow that newsgroup so if you want to contact me you have to do so by e-mail.

13 Getting Help

In the end you might find yourself unable to solve your problems and need help from someone else. The most efficient way is either to ask someone local or in your nearest Linux user group, search the web for the nearest one.

Another possibility is to ask on Usenet News in one of the many, many newsgroups available. The problem is that these have such a high volume and noise (called low signal-to-noise ratio) that your question can easily fall through unanswered.

No matter where you ask it is important to ask well or you will not be taken seriously. Saying just *my disk does not work* is not going to help you and instead the noise level is increased even further and if you are lucky someone will ask you to clarify.

Instead you are recommended to describe your problems in some detail that will enable people to help you. The problem could lie somewhere you did not expect. Therefore you are advised to list up the following information on your system:

Hardware

- Processor

- Chip set (Triton, Saturn etc)

- Bus (ISA, VESA, PCI etc)

- Expansion cards used (Disk controllers, video, io etc)

Software

- BIOS (On motherboard and possibly SCSI host adapters)

- LILO, if used

- Linux kernel version as well as possible modifications and patches

- Kernel parameters, if any

- Software that shows the error (with version number or date)

Peripherals

- Type of disk drives with manufacturer name, version and type

- Other relevant peripherals connected to the same busses

As an example of how interrelated these problems are: an old chip set caused problems with a certain combination of video controller and SCSI host adapter.

Remember that booting text is logged to `/var/log/messages` which can answer most of the questions above. Obviously if the drives fail you might not be able to get the log saved to disk but you can at least scroll back up the screen using the `SHIFT` and `PAGE UP` keys. It may also be useful to include part of this in you request for help but do not go overboard, keep it *brief* as a complete log file dumped to Usenet News is more than a little annoying.

14   Concluding Remarks

Disk tuning and partition decisions are difficult to make, and there are no hard rules here. Nevertheless it is a good idea to work more on this as the payoffs can be considerable. Maximizing usage on one drive only while the others are idle is unlikely to be optimal, watch the drive light, they are not there just for decoration. For a properly set up system the lights should look like Christmas in a disco. Linux offers software RAID but also support for some hardware base SCSI RAID controllers. Check what is available. As your system and experiences evolve you are likely to repartition and you might look on this document again. Additions are always welcome.

14.1   Coming Soon

There are a few more important things that are about to appear here. In particular I will add more example tables as I am about to set up two fairly large and general systems, one at work and one at home. These should give some general feeling on how a system can be set up for either of these two purposes. Examples of smooth running existing systems are also welcome.

There is also a fair bit of work left to do on the various kinds of file systems and utilities.

There will be a big addition on drive technologies coming soon as well as a more in depth description on using `fdisk` or `cfdisk`. The file systems will be beefed up as more features become available as well as more on RAID and what directories can benefit from what RAID level.

Recently I received an information pack from DPT, who made the first hardware RAID supported by Linux. Their leaflets now carry the familiar penguin logo to show they support Linux. More in-depth information will come soon.

There is some minor overlapping with the Linux Filesystem Structure Standard that I hope to integrate better soon, which will probably mean a big reworking of all the tables at the end of this document. When the new version is released there will be a substantial rewrite of some of the sections in this HOWTO but no release date has been announced yet.

When the new standard appear various details such as directory names, sizes and file placements will be changed.

I have made the assumption that the first partition starts at track 0 and that this track is the innermost track. That, however, is looking more and more like an unwarranted assumption, and not only because of the logical re-mapping that takes place. More on this when information becomes available.

As more people start reading this I should get some more comments and feedback. I am also thinking of making a program that can automate a fair bit of this decision making process and although it is unlikely to be optimum it should provide a simpler, more complete starting point.

14.2   Request for Information

It has taken a fair bit of time to write this document and although most pieces are beginning to come together there are still some information needed before we are out of the beta stage.

- More information on swap sizing policies is needed as well as information on the largest swap size possible under the various kernel versions.
- How common is drive or file system corruption? So far I have only heard of problems caused by flaky hardware.
- References to speed and drives is needed.

HOWTO

- Are any other Linux compatible RAID controllers available?

- Leads to file system, volume management and other related software is welcome.

- What relevant monitoring, management and maintenance tools are available?

- General references to information sources are needed, perhaps this should be a separate document?

- Usage of /tmp and /var/tmp has been hard to determine, in fact what programs use which directory is not well defined and more information here is required. Still, it seems at least clear that these should reside on different physical drives in order to increase parallelicity.

14.3   Suggested Project Work

Now and then people post on comp.os.linux.*, looking for good project ideas. Here I will list a few that comes to mind that are relevant to this document. Plans about big projects such as new file systems should still be posted in order to either find co-workers or see if someone is already working on it.

Planning tools

that can automate the design process outlines earlier would probably make a medium sized project, perhaps as an exercise in constraint based programming.

Partitioning tools

that take the output of the previously mentioned program and format drives in parallel and apply the appropriate symbolic links to the directory structure. It would probably be best if this were integrated in existing system installation software. The drive partitioning setup used in Solaris is an example of what it can look like.

Surveillance tools

that keep an eye on the partition sizes and warn before a partition overflows.

Migration tools

that safely lets you move old structures to new (for instance RAID) systems. This could probably be done as a shell script controlling a back up program and would be rather simple. Still, be sure it is safe and that the changes can be undone.

15   Questions and Answers

This is just a collection of what I believe are the most common questions people might have. Give me more feedback and I will turn this section into a proper FAQ.

- Q:How many physical disk drives (spindles) does a Linux system need? A: Linux can run just fine on one drive (spindle). Having enough RAM (around 32 MB, and up to 64 MB) to support swapping is a better price/performance choice than getting a second disk. (E)IDE disk is usually cheaper (but a little slower) than SCSI.

- Q: I have a single drive, will this HOWTO help me? A: Yes, although only to a minor degree. Still, the section on 4.3.8 (Physical Track Positioning) will offer you some gains.

- Q: Are there any disadvantages in this scheme? A: There is only a minor snag: if even a single partition overflows the system might stop working properly. The severity depends of course on what partition is affected. Still this is not hard to monitor, the command df gives you a good overview of the situation. Also check the swap partition(s) using free to make sure you are not about to run out of virtual memory.

- Q: OK, so should I split the system into as many partitions as possible for a single drive? A: No, there are several disadvantages to that. First of all maintenance becomes needlessly complex and you gain very little in this. In fact if your partitions are too big you will seek across larger areas than needed. This is a balance and dependent on the number of physical drives you have.

- Q: Does that mean more drives allows more partitions? A: To some degree, yes. Still, some directories should not be split off from root, check out the file system standard (soon released under the name File Hierarchy Standard) for more details.

- Q: What if I have many drives I want to use? A: If you have more than 3-4 drives you should consider using RAID of some form. Still, it is a good idea to keep your root partition on a simple partition without RAID, see the section on 4.3.1 (RAID) for more details.

- Q: I have installed the latest Windows95 but cannot access this partition from within the Linux system, what is wrong? A: Most likely you are using `FAT32` in your windows partition. It seems that Microsoft decided we needed yet another format, and this was introduced in their latest version of Windows95, called OSR2. The advantage is that this format is better suited to large drives. Unfortunately there is no stable driver for Linux out *yet* . A test version is out but not yet in the standard kernel.

  You might also be interested to hear that Microsoft NT 4.0 does not support it yet either.

  Until a stable version is available you can avoid this problem by installing Windows95 over an existing FAT16 partition, made for instance by an older installation of DOS. This forces the Windows95 to use FAT16 which *is* supported by Linux.

- Q: I cannot get the disk size and partition sizes to match, something is missing. What has happened? A:It is possible you have mounted a partition onto a mount point that was not an empty directory. Mount points are directories and if it is not empty the mounting will mask the contents. If you do the sums you will see the amount of disk space used in this directory is missing from the observed total.

  To solve this you can boot from a rescue disk and see what is hiding behind your mount points and remove or transfer the contents by mounting th offending partition on a temporary mounting point. You might find it useful to have "spare" emergency mounting points ready made.

- Q: What is this nyx that is mentioned several times here? A: It is a large free Unix system with currently about 10000 users. I use it for my web pages for this HOWTO as well as a source of ideas for a setup of large Unix systems. It has been running for many years and has a quite stable setup. For more information you can view the *Nyx homepage* <http://www.nyx.net> which also gives you information on how to get your own free account.

16   Bits and Pieces

This is basically a section where I stuff all the bits I have not yet decided where should go, yet that I feel is worth knowing about. It is a kind of transient area.

16.1   Combining `swap` and `/tmp`

Recently there have been discussions in the various linux related news groups about specialized file systems for temporary storage. This is partly inspired by the `tmpfs` on *BSD* and Solaris, as well as `swapfs` on the NeXT machines.

The rationale is that these are temporary storage that normally does not require much space, yet in normal systems you need to reserve a certain amount of space for these. Elementary statistical knowledge tells you (very simplified) that when you sum a number of variables the relative statistical uncertainty decreases. So combining `swap` and `/tmp` you do not need to reserve as much space as you otherwise would need.

This specialized file system is nothing more than a swappable RAM disk that are swapped out to disk when and only when space is limited, thus effectively putting temporary files on the swap partition.

There is, however, a snag. This scheme prevents you from getting parallel activity on `swap` and `/tmp` drives so under heavy activity the system takes a bigger performance hit. Put another way, you trade speed to get space. Interleaving across multiple drives reduces this somewhat.

16.2   Interleaved `swap` drives.

This is not striping across several drives, instead drives are accessed in a round robin fashion in order to spread the load in a crude fashion. In Linux you additionally have a priority parameter you can adjust for tuning your system, especially useful if your disks differs significantly in speed. Check `man 8 swapon` as well as `man 2 swapon` for more information.

16.3 Swap partition: to use or not to use

In many cases you do not need a swap partition, for instance if you have plenty of RAM, say, more than 64 MB, and you are the sole user of the machine. In this case you can experiment running without a swap partition and check the system logs to see if you ran out of virtual memory at any point.

Removing swap partitions have two advantages:

- you save disk space (rather obvious really)
- you save seek time as swap partitions otherwise would lie in the middle of your disk space.

In the end, having a swap partition is like having a heated toilet: you do not use it very often, but you sure appreciate it when you require it.

16.4 Mount point and /mnt

In an earlier version of this document I proposed to put all permanently mounted partitions under /mnt. That, however, is not such a good idea as this itself can be used as a mount point, which leads to all mounted partitions becoming unavailable. Instead I will propose mounting straight from root using a meaningful name like /mnt.descriptive-name.

Lately I have become aware that some Linux distributions use mount points at subdirectories *under* /mnt, such as /mnt/floppy and /mnt/cdrom, which just shows how confused the whole issue is. Hopefully FHS should clarify this.

16.5 SCSI id numbers and names

Partitions are labeled in the order they are found, *not* depending on the SCSI id number. This means that if you add a drive with an id number inserted in the previous order of numbers, or change id number in any other way, the partition names will be messed up. This is important if you use removable media. In order to save yourself from some unpleasant experiences, you are recommended to use low numbers for fixed media and reserve the last number(s) for removable media drives.

Many have been bitten by this misfeature and there is a strong call for something to be done about it. Nobody knows how soon this will be fixed so in the meantime it is wise to take this into consideration when you design your system. For instance it may be a good idea to use the lowest SCSI id number for you root disk so that it has the least probability of being renumbered should one drive fail.

16.6 Power and Heating

Not many years ago a machine with the equivalent power of a modern PC required 3-phase power and cooling, usually by air conditioning the machine room but some times also by water cooling. Technology has progressed very quickly giving not only high speed but also low power components. Still, there is a definite limit to the technology, something one should keep in mind as the system is expanded with yet another disk drive or PCI card. When the power supply is running at full rated power, keep in mind that all this energy is going somewhere, mostly into heat. Unless this is dissipated using fans you will get a serious heating inside the cabinet followed by a reduced reliability and also life time of the electronics. Manufacturers state minimum cooling requirements for their drives, usually in terms of cubic feet per minute (CFM). You are well advised to take this serious.

Keep air flow passages open, clean out dust and check the temperature of your system running. If it is too hot to touch it is probably running too hot.

If possible use sequential spin up for the drives. It is during spin up, when the drive platters accelerate up to normal speed, that a drive consumes maximum power and if all drives start up simultaneously you could go beyond the rated power maximum of your power supply.

16.7 Dejanews

This is an Internet system that no doubt most of you are familiar with. It searches and serves *Usenet News* articles from 1995 and to the latest postings and also offers a web based reading and posting interface. There is a lot more, check out *Dejanews* `<http://www.dejanews.com>` for more information.

What perhaps is less known, is that they use about 20 Linux SMP computers each of which uses the md module to manage between 4 and 24 Gig of disk space (over 150 Gig altogether) for this service. The system is continuously growing but at the time of writing they use mostly dual Pentium Pro 200MHz systems with 256 MB RAM.

A production machine normally has 1 disk for the operating system and between 4 and 6 disks managed by the md module where the articles are archived. The drives are connected to BusLogic Model BT-946C PCI SCSI adapters, usually two to a machine.

Just in case: this is not an advertisement, it is stated as an example of how much is required for what is a major Internet service.

16.8 File system structure

There are many file system structures in existence, differing with FSSTND (and soon FHS) to varying degree both in terms of philosophy, strategy and implementation. It is not possible to detail all here, instead the interested reader should read the relevant manual page, `man hier` which is available on many platforms and implementations.

16.9 Track numbering and optimizing schemes

In the old days the file system used to take advantage of knowing the physical drive parameters in order to optimize transfers, for instance by endeavouring to keep a file within a single track if possible which saves track-to-track seek time. These days with logical drive parameters, drive cache and schemes to map out bad sectors, such optimizations become meaningless and might even cost more than it would gain. As most Linux installations use modern file systems these schemes are not used, however, some other operating systems have retained such schemes.

17 Appendix A: Partitioning layout table: mounting and linking

The following table is designed to make layout a simpler paper and pencil exercise. It is probably best to print it out (using NON PROPORTIONAL fonts) and adjust the numbers until you are happy with them.

Mount point is what directory you wish to mount a partition on or the actual device. This is also a good place to note how you plan to use symbolic links.

The size given corresponds to a fairly big Debian 1.2.6 installation. Other examples are coming later.

Mainly you use this table to select what structure and drives you will use, the partition numbers and letters will come from the next two tables.

Directory	Mount point	speed	seek	transfer	size	SIZE
swap	_____	ooooo	ooooo	ooooo	32	_____
/	_____	o	o	o	20	_____
/tmp	_____	oooo	oooo	oooo		_____
/var	_____	oo	oo	oo	25	_____
/var/tmp	_____	oooo	oooo	oooo		_____
/var/spool	_____					_____

/var/spool/mail	_____	o	o	o
/var/spool/news	_____	ooo	ooo	oo
/var/spool/____	_____			
/home	_____	oo		oo
/usr	_____			500
/usr/bin	_____	o	o	250
/usr/lib	_____	oo	ooo	200
/usr/local	_____	oo		
/usr/local/bin	_____	o	oo	o
/usr/local/lib	_____	oo	oo	ooo
/usr/local/____	_____			
/usr/src	_____	o	oo	o	50
DOS	_____	o	o	o
Win	_____	oo	oo	oo
NT	_____	ooo	ooo	ooo
/mnt.____	_____			
/mnt.____	_____			
/mnt.____	_____			
/____	_____			
/____	_____			
/____	_____			

Total capacity: _____

18 Appendix B: Partitioning layout table: numbering and sizing

This table follows the same logical structure as the table above where you decided what disk to use. Here you select the physical tracking, keeping in mind the effect of track positioning mentioned earlier in 4.3.8 (Physical Track Positioning).

The final partition number will come out of the table after this.

Drive	sda	sdb	sdc	hda	hdb	hdc	
SCSI ID		__	__				
Directory							
swap							
/							
/tmp							
/var	:	:	:	:	:	:	:
/var/tmp							
/var/spool	:	:	:	:	:	:	:
/var/spool/mail							
/var/spool/news	:	:	:	:	:	:	:
/var/spool/____							

```
/home            :|      |       |      |       |       |      |

/usr             :|      |       |      |       |       |      |
/usr/bin         :       :       :      :       :       :      :
/usr/lib         |       |       |      |       |       |      |
/usr/local       :       :       :      :       :       :      :
/usr/local/bin   |       |       |      |       |       |      |
/usr/local/lib   :       :       :      :       :       :      :
/usr/local/____  |       |       |      |       |       |      |
/usr/src         |       |       |      |       |       |      |

DOS              |       |       |      |       |       |      |
Win              :       :       :      :       :       :      :
NT               |       |       |      |       |       |      |

/mnt.____/_____  :|      |       |      |       |       |      |
/mnt.____/_____  :|      |       |      |       |       |      |
/mnt.____/_____  :|      |       |      |       |       |      |
/_____   :       :       :      :       :       :      :
/_____   |       |       |      |       |       |      |
/_____   :       :       :      :       :       :      :


Total capacity:
```

19   Appendix C: Partitioning layout table: partition placement

This is just to sort the partition numbers in ascending order ready to input to fdisk or cfdisk. Here you take physical track positioning into account when finalizing your design. Unless you get specific information otherwise, you can assume track 0 is the outermost track.

These numbers and letters are then used to update the previous tables, all of which you will find very useful in later maintenance.

In case of disk crash you might find it handy to know what SCSI id belongs to which drive, consider keeping a paper copy of this.

```
           Drive :   sda     sdb     sdc     hda     hdb     hdc     ___

Total capacity: |   ___  |   ___  |   ___  |  ___ |   ___  |   ___  |   ___
SCSI ID         |   ___  |   ___  |   ___  |


Partition

1                       |       |       |      |       |       |      |
2                       :       :       :      :       :       :      :
3                       |       |       |      |       |       |      |
4                       :       :       :      :       :       :      :
5                       |       |       |      |       |       |      |
6                       :       :       :      :       :       :      :
7                       |       |       |      |       |       |      |
8                       :       :       :      :       :       :      :
9                       |       |       |      |       |       |      |
10                      :       :       :      :       :       :      :
```

11	|	|	|	|	|	|	|
12	:	:	:	:	:	:	:
13	|	|	|	|	|	|	|
14	:	:	:	:	:	:	:
15	|	|	|	|	|	|	|
16	:	:	:	:	:	:	:

20   Appendix D: Example: Multipurpose server

The following table is from the setup of a medium sized multipurpose server where I work. Aside from being a general Linux machine it will also be a network related server (DNS, mail, FTP, news, printers etc.) X server for various CAD programs, CD ROM burner and many other things. The files reside on 3 SCSI drives with a capacity of 600, 1000 and 1300 MB.

Some further speed could possibly be gained by splitting `/usr/local` from the rest of the `/usr` system but we deemed the further added complexity would not be worth it. With another couple of drives this could be more worthwhile. In this setup drive sda is old and slow and could just a well be replaced by an IDE drive. The other two drives are both rather fast. Basically we split most of the load between these two. To reduce dangers of imbalance in partition sizing we have decided to keep `/usr/bin` and `/usr/local/bin` in one drive and `/usr/lib` and `/usr/local/lib` on another separate drive which also affords us some drive parallelizing.

Even more could be gained by using RAID but we felt that as a server we needed more reliability than was then afforded by the md patch and a dedicated RAID controller was out of our reach.

21   Appendix E: Example: mounting and linking

Directory	Mount point	speed	seek	transfer	size	SIZE
swap	sdb2, sdc2	ooooo	ooooo	ooooo	32	2x64
/	sda2	o	o	o	20	100
/tmp	sdb3	oooo	oooo	oooo		300
/var	_____	oo	oo	oo		_____
/var/tmp	sdc3	oooo	oooo	oooo		300
/var/spool	sdb1					436
/var/spool/mail	_____	o	o	o		_____
/var/spool/news	_____	ooo	ooo	oo		_____
/var/spool/____	_____					_____
/home	sda3	oo	oo	oo		400
/usr	sdb4				230	200
/usr/bin	_____	o	oo	o	30	_____
/usr/lib	-> libdisk	oo	oo	ooo	70	_____
/usr/local	_____					_____
/usr/local/bin	_____	o	oo	o		_____
/usr/local/lib	-> libdisk	oo	oo	ooo		_____
/usr/local/____	_____					_____
/usr/src	->/home/usr.src	o	oo	o	10	_____
DOS	sda1	o	o	o		100

```
Win             _____      oo      oo      oo
NT              _____      ooo     ooo     ooo          ___

/mnt.libdisk    sdc4            oo      oo      ooo          226
/mnt.cd         sdc1            o       o       oo           710


Total capacity: 2900 MB
```

22   Appendix F: Example: numbering and sizing

Here we do the adjustment of sizes and positioning.

```
Directory         sda     sdb     sdc

swap            |       |  64  |  64  |

/               |  100  |       |       |

/tmp            |       |  300 |       |

/var            :       :       :       :
/var/tmp        |       |       |  300  |
/var/spool      :       :  436  :       :
/var/spool/mail |       |       |       |
/var/spool/news :       :       :       :
/var/spool/____ |       |       |       |

/home           |  400  |       |       |

/usr            |       |  200  |       |
/usr/bin        :       :       :       :
/usr/lib        |       |       |       |
/usr/local      :       :       :       :
/usr/local/bin  |       |       |       |
/usr/local/lib  :       :       :       :
/usr/local/____ |       |       |       |
/usr/src        :       :       :       :

DOS             |  100  |       |       |
Win             :       :       :       :
NT              |       |       |       |

/mnt.libdisk    |       |       |  226  |
/mnt.cd         :       :       :  710  :
/mnt.___/_____  |       |       |       |


Total capacity: |  600  | 1000 | 1300  |
```

23 Appendix G: Example: partition placement

This is just to sort the partition numbers in ascending order ready to input to fdisk or cfdisk. Remember to optimize for physical track positioning (not done here).

```
        Drive :    sda     sdb     sdc

Total capacity: |   600 |  1000 |  1300 |

Partition

1               |   100 |   436 |   710 |
2               :   100 :    64 :    64 :
3               |   400 |   300 |   300 |
4               :       :   200 :   226 :
```

24 Appendix H: Example II

The following is an example of a server setup in an academic setting, and is contributed by nakano (at) apm.seikei.ac.jp. I have only done minor editing to this section.

/var/spool/delegate is a directory for storing logs and cache files of an WWW proxy server program, "delegated". Since I don't notice it widely, there are 1000–1500 requests/day currently, and average disk usage is 15–30% with expiration of caches each day.

/mnt.archive is used for data files which are big and not frequently referenced such a s experimental data (especially graphic ones), various source archives, and Win95 backups (growing very fast...).

/mnt.root is backup root file system containing rescue utilities. A boot floppy is also prepared to boot with this partition.

```
=====================================================
Directory               sda     sdb     hda

swap                |    64 |    64 |       |
/                   |       |       |    20 |
/tmp                |       |       |   180 |

/var                :   300 :       :       :
/var/tmp            |       |   300 |       |
/var/spool/delegate |   300 |       |       |

/home               |       |       |   850 |
/usr                |   360 |       |       |
/usr/lib            -> /mnt.lib/usr.lib
/usr/local/lib      -> /mnt.lib/usr.local.lib

/mnt.lib            |       |   350 |       |
/mnt.archive        :       :  1300 :       :
/mnt.root           |       |    20 |       |

Total capacity:        1024    2034    1050
```

```
===================================================
      Drive :        sda    sdb    hda
Total capacity:    | 1024 | 2034 | 1050 |

Partition
1                  |  300 |   20 |   20 |
2                  :   64 : 1300 :  180 :
3                  |  300 |   64 |  850 |
4                  :  360 :  ext :      :
5                  |      |  300 |      |
6                  :      :  350 :      :


Filesystem          1024-blocks  Used Available Capacity Mounted on
/dev/hda1              19485    10534      7945     57%   /
/dev/hda2             178598       13    169362      0%   /tmp
/dev/hda3             826640   440814    343138     56%   /home
/dev/sda1             306088    33580    256700     12%   /var
/dev/sda3             297925    47730    234807     17%   /var/spool/delegate
/dev/sda4             363272   170872    173640     50%   /usr
/dev/sdb5             297598        2    282228      0%   /var/tmp
/dev/sdb2            1339248   302564    967520     24%   /mnt.archive
/dev/sdb6             323716    78792    228208     26%   /mnt.lib
```

Apparently `/tmp` and `/var/tmp` is too big. These directories shall be packed together into one partition when disk space shortage comes.

`/mnt.lib` is also seemed to be, but I plan to install newer TeX and ghostscript archives, so `/usr/local/lib` may grow about 100 MB or so (since we must use Japanese fonts!).

Whole system is backed up by Seagate Tapestore 8000 (Travan TR-4, 4G/8G).

25   Appendix I: Example III: SPARC Solaris

The following section is the basic design used at work for a number of Sun SPARC servers running Solaris 2.5.1 in an industrial development environment. It serves a number of database and cad applications in addition to the normal services such as mail.

Simplicity is emphasized here so `/usr/lib` has not been split off from `/usr`.

This is the basic layout, planned for about 100 users.

```
    Drive:      SCSI 0                        SCSI 1

    Partition   Size (MB)   Mount point       Size (MB)   Mount point

    0           160         swap              160         swap
    1           100         /tmp              100         /var/tmp
    2           400         /usr
    3           100         /
    4            50         /var
    5
    6           remainder   /local0           remainder   /local1
```

Due to specific requirements at this place it is at times necessary to have large partitions available on a short notice. Therefore drive 0 is given as many tasks as feasible, leaving a large `/local1` partition.

HOWTO

This setup has been in use for some time now and found satisfactorily.

For a more general and balanced system it would be better to swap `/tmp` and `/var/tmp` and then move `/var` to drive 1.

## Part XXVII

"Multicast over TCP/IP HOWTO"
Juan-Mariano de Goyeneche

<jmseyas@dit.upm.es>

v1.0, 20 March 1998

This HOWTO tries to cover most aspects related to multicast over TCP/IP networks. So, a lot of information within it is not Linux-specific (just in case you don't use GNU/Linux... yet). Multicast is currently an active area of research and, at the time of writing, many of the "standards" are merely drafts. Keep it in mind while reading the lines that follow.

Contents

HOWTO

1 Introduction.

I'll try to give here the most wide range, up to date and accurate information related to multicasting over TCP/IP networks that I can. Any feedback is very welcome. If you find any mistakes in this document, have any comments about its contents or an update or addition, please send them to me at the address listed at the top of this howto.

1.1 What is Multicast.

Multicast is... a need. Well, at least in some scenarios. If you have information (a *lot* of information, usually) that should be transmitted to various (but usually not *all*) hosts over an internet, then Multicast is the answer. One common situation in which it is used is when distributing real time audio and video to the set of hosts which have joined a distributed conference.

Multicast is much like radio or TV in the sense that only those who have tuned their receivers (by selecting a particular frequency they are interested on) receive the information. That is: you hear the channel you are interested in, but not the others.

1.2 The problem with Unicast.

Unicast is anything that is not broadcast nor multicast. All right, the definition is not very bright... When you send a packet and there is only one sender process -yours- and one recipient process (the *one* you are sending the packet to), then this is unicast. TCP is, by its own nature, unicast oriented. UDP supports a lot more paradigms, but if you are sending UDP packets and there is only one precess supposed to receive them, this is unicast too.

For years unicast transmissions proved to be enough for the Internet. It was not until 1993 when the first implementation of multicast saw the light in the 4.4 BSD release. It seems nobody needed it until then. Which were those new problems that multicast addressed?

Needless to say that the Internet has changed a lot since the "early days". Particularly, the appearance of the Web strongly transformed the situation: people didn't just want connections to remote hosts, mail and FTP. First they wanted to see the pictures people placed in their home pages, but later they also wanted to *see* and *hear* that people.

With today's technology it is possible to afford the "cost" of making a unicast connection with everyone who wants to see your web page. However, if you are to send audio and video, which needs a *huge* amount of bandwidth compared with web applications, you have -you *had*, until multicast came into scene- two options: to establish a separate unicast connection with *each* of the recipients, or to use broadcast. The first solution is not affordable: if we said that a *single* connection sending audio/video consumes a huge bandwidth, imagine having to establish hundreds or, may be, thousands of those connections. Both the sending computer and your network would collapse.

Broadcast seems to be *a* solution, but it's not certainly *the* solution. If you want all the hosts in your LAN to attend the conference, you may use broadcast. Packets will be sent only once and every host will receive them as they are sent to the broadcast address. The problem is that perhaps only a *few* of the hosts and not *all* are interested in those packets. Furthermore: perhaps some hosts are really interested in your conference, but they are outside of your LAN, a few routers away. And you know that broadcast works fine inside a LAN, but problems arise when you want broadcast packets to be routed across different LANs.

The best solution seems to be one in which you send packets to a certain special address (a certain frequency in radio/TV transmissions). Then, all hosts which have decided to join the conference will be aware of packets with that destination address, read them when they traverse the network, and pass them to the IP layer to be demultiplexed. This is similar to broadcasting in that you send only one broadcast packet and all the hosts in the network recognize and read it; it differs, however, in that not all multicast packets are read and processed, but only those that were previously registered in the kernel as being "of interest".

Those special packets are routed at kernel level like any packet because they *are* IP packets. The only difference might reside in the routing algorithm which tells the kernel where to route or not to route them.

2 Multicast Explained.

2.1 Multicast addresses.

As you probably know, the range of IP addresses is divided into "classes" based on the high order bits of a 32 bits IP address:

```
Bit -->  0                               31        Address Range:
        +-+--------------------------+
        |0|      Class A Address      |        0.0.0.0 - 127.255.255.255
        +-+--------------------------+
        +-+-+-------------------------+
        |1 0|     Class B Address      |      128.0.0.0 - 191.255.255.255
        +-+-+-------------------------+
        +-+-+-+------------------------+
        |1 1 0|   Class C Address       |     192.0.0.0 - 223.255.255.255
        +-+-+-+------------------------+
        +-+-+-+-+-----------------------+
        |1 1 1 0|  MULTICAST Address     |     224.0.0.0 - 239.255.255.255
        +-+-+-+-+-----------------------+
        +-+-+-+-+-+----------------------+
        |1 1 1 1 0|    Reserved          |     240.0.0.0 - 247.255.255.255
        +-+-+-+-+-+----------------------+
```

The one which concerns us is the "Class D Address". Every IP datagram whose destination address starts with "1110" is an IP Multicast datagram.

The remaining 28 bits identify the multicast "*group*" the datagram is sent to. Following with the previous analogy, you have to tune your radio to hear a program that is transmitted at some specific frequency, in the same way you have to "tune" your kernel to receive packets sent to an specific multicast group. When you do that, it's said that the host has *joined* that group in the interface you specified. More on this later.

There are some special multicast groups, say "well known multicast groups", you should not use in your particular applications due the special purpose they are destined to:

- 224.0.0.1 is the *all-hosts* group. If you ping that group, all multicast capable hosts on the network should answer, as every multicast capable host *must* join that group at start-up on all it's multicast capable interfaces.

- 224.0.0.2 is the *all-routers* group. All multicast routers must join that group on all it's multicast capable interfaces.

- 224.0.0.4 is the *all DVMRP routers*, 224.0.0.5 the *all OSPF routers*, 224.0.013 the *all PIM routers*, etc.

All this special multicast groups are regularly published in the "Assigned Numbers" RFC.

In any case, range 224.0.0.0 through 224.0.0.255 is reserved for local purposes (as administrative and maintenance tasks) and datagrams destined to them are never forwarded by multicast routers. Similarly, the range 239.0.0.0 to

239.255.255.255 has been reserved for "administrative scoping" (see section 2.3.1 for information on administrative scoping).

2.2 Levels of conformance.

Hosts can be in three different levels of conformance with the Multicast specification, according to the requirements they meet.

Level 0 is the "no support for IP Multicasting" level. Lots of hosts and routers in the Internet are in this state, as multicast support is not mandatory in IPv4 (it is, however, in IPv6). Not too much explanation is needed here: hosts in this level can neither send nor receive multicast packets. They must ignore the ones sent by other multicast capable hosts.

Level 1 is the "support for sending but not receiving multicast IP datagrams" level. Thus, note that it is not necessary to join a multicast group to be able to send datagrams to it. Very few additions are needed in the IP module to make a "Level 0" host "Level 1-compliant", as shown in section 2.3.

Level 2 is the "full support for IP multicasting" level. Level 2 hosts must be able to both send and receive multicast traffic. They must know the way to join and leave multicast groups and to propagate this information to multicast routers. Thus, they must include an Internet Group Management Protocol (IGMP) implementation in their TCP/IP stack.

2.3 Sending Multicast Datagrams.

By now, it should be obvious that multicast traffic is handled at the transport layer with UDP, as TCP provides point-to-point connections, not feasibles for multicast traffic. (Heavy research is taking place to define and implement new multicast-oriented transport protocols. See section 9 (Multicast Transport Protocols) for details).

In principle, an application just needs to open a UDP socket and fill with a class D multicast address the destination address where it wants to send data to. However, there are some operations that a sending process must be able to control.

2.3.1 TTL.

The TTL (Time To Live) field in the IP header has a double significance in multicast. As always, it controls the live time of the datagram to avoid it being looped forever due to routing errors. Routers decrement the TTL of every datagram as it traverses from one network to another and when its value reaches 0 the packet is dropped.

The TTL in IPv4 multicasting has also the meaning of "threshold". Its use becomes evident with an example: suppose you set a long, bandwidth consuming, video conference between all the hosts belonging to your department. You want that huge amount of traffic to remain in your LAN. Perhaps your department is big enough to have various LANs. In that case you want those hosts belonging to each of *your* LANs to attend the conference, but in any case you want to collapse the entire Internet with your multicast traffic. There is a need to limit how "long" multicast traffic will expand across routers. That's what the TTL is used for. Routers have a TTL threshold assigned to each of its interfaces, and only datagrams with a TTL greater than the interface's threshold are forwarded. Note that when a datagram traverses a router with a certain threshold assigned, the datagram's TTL is *not* decremented by the value of the threshold. Only a comparison is made. (As before, the TTL is decremented by 1 each time a datagram passes across a router).

A list of TTL thresholds and their associated scope follows:

```
TTL      Scope
---------------------------------------------------------------------------
   0     Restricted to the same host. Won't be output by any interface.
   1     Restricted to the same subnet. Won't be forwarded by a router.
 <32     Restricted to the same site, organization or department.
 <64     Restricted to the same region.
<128     Restricted to the same continent.
<255     Unrestricted in scope. Global.
```

Nobody knows what "site" or "region" mean exactly. It is up to the administrators to decide what this limits apply to.

The TTL-trick is not always flexible enough for all needs, specially when dealing with overlapping regions or trying to establish geographic, topologic and bandwidth limits simultaneously. To solve this problems, administratively scoped IPv4 multicast regions were established in 1994. (see D. Meyer's *"Administratively Scoped IP Multicast"* Internet draft). It does scoping based on multicast addresses rather than on TTLs. The range 239.0.0.0 to 239.255.255.255 is reserved for this administrative scoping.

2.3.2   Loopback.

When the sending host is Level 2 conformant and is also a member of the group datagrams are being sent to, a copy is looped back by default. This does not mean that the interface card reads its own transmission, recognizes it as belonging to a group the interface belongs to, and reads it from the network. On the contrary, is the IP layer which, by default, recognizes the to-be-sent datagram and copies and queues it on the IP input queue before sending it.

This feature is desirable in some cases, but not in others. So the sending process can turn it on and off at wish.

2.3.3   Interface selection.

Hosts attached to more than one network should provide a way for applications to decide which network interface will be used to output the transmissions. If not specified, the kernel chooses a default one based on system administrator's configuration.

2.4   Receiving Multicast Datagrams.

2.4.1   Joining a Multicast Group.

Broadcast is (in comparison) easier to implement than multicast. It doesn't require processes to give the kernel some rules regarding what to do with broadcast packets. The kernel just knows what to do: read and deliver *all* of them to the proper applications.

With multicast, however, it is necessary to advise the kernel which multicast groups we are interested in. That is, we have to ask the kernel to "join" those multicast groups. Depending on the underlying hardware, multicast datagrams are filtered by the hardware or by the IP layer (and, in some cases, by both). Only those with a destination group previously registered via a join are accepted.

Essentially, when we join a group we are telling the kernel: "OK. I know that, by default, you ignore multicast datagrams, but remember that I am interested in *this* multicast group. So, do read and deliver (to any process interested in them, not only to me) any datagram that you see in this network interface with this multicast group in its destination field".

Some considerations: first, note that you don't just join a group. You join a group *on* a particular network interface. Of course, it is possible to join the same group on more than one interface. If you don't specify a concrete interface, then the kernel will choose it based on its routing tables when datagrams are to be sent. It is also possible that more than one process joins the same multicast group on the same interface. They will all receive the datagrams sent to that group via that interface.

As said before, any multicast-capable hosts join the *all-hosts* group at start-up , so "pinging" 224.0.0.1 returns all hosts in the network that have multicast enabled.

Finally, consider that for a process to receive multicast datagrams it has to ask the kernel to join the group *and* bind the port those datagrams were being sent to. The UDP layer uses both the destination address and port to demultiplex the packets and decide which socket(s) deliver them to.

2.4.2 Leaving a Multicast Group.

When a process is no longer interested in a multicast group, it informs the kernel that *it* wants to leave that group. It is important to understand that this doesn't mean that the kernel will no longer accept multicast datagrams destined to that multicast group. It will still do so if there are more precesses who issued a "multicast join" petition for that group and are still interested. In that case *the host* remains member of the group, until all the processes decide to leave the group.

Even more: if you leave the group, but remain bound to the port you were receiving the multicast traffic on, and there are more processes that joined the group, you will still receive the multicast transmissions.

The idea is that joining a multicast group only tells the IP and data link layer (which in some cases explicitly tells the hardware) to accept multicast datagrams destined to that group. It is not a per-process membership, but a per-host membership.

2.4.3 Mapping of IP Multicast Addresses to Ethernet/FDDI addresses.

Both Ethernet and FDDI frames have a 48 bit destination address field. In order to avoid a kind of multicast ARP to map multicast IP addresses to ethernet/FDDI ones, the IANA reserved a range of addresses for multicast: every ethernet/FDDI frame with its destination in the range 01-00-5e-00-00-00 to 01-00-5e-ff-ff-ff (hex) contains data for a multicast group. The prefix 01-00-5e identifies the frame as multicast, the next bit is always 0 and so only 23 bits are left to the multicast address. As IP multicast groups are 28 bits long, the mapping can not be one-to-one. Only the 23 least significant bits of the IP multicast group are placed in the frame. The remaining 5 high-order bits are ignored, resulting in 32 different multicast groups being mapped to the same ethernet/FDDI address. This means that the ethernet layer acts as an imperfect filter, and the IP layer will have to decide whether to accept the datagrams the data-link layer passed to it. The IP layer acts as a definitive perfect filter.

Full details on IP Multicasting over FDDI are given in RFC 1390: "*Transmission of IP and ARP over FDDI Networks*". For more information on mapping IP Multicast addresses to ethernet ones, you may consult `draft-ietf-mboned-intro-multicast-03.txt`: "*Introduction to IP Multicast Routing*".

If you are interested in IP Multicasting over Token-Ring Local Area Networks, see RFC 1469 for details.

3   Kernel requirements and configuration.

Linux is, of course (you doubted it?), full Level-2 Multicast-Compliant. It meets all requirements to send, receive and act as a router (mrouter) for multicast datagrams.

If you want just to send and receive, you must say yes to "*IP: multicasting*" when configuring your kernel. If you also want your Linux box to act as a multicast router (mrouter) you also need to enable multicast routing in the kernel by selecting "*IP: forwarding/gatewaying*", "*IP: multicast routing*" and "*IP: tunneling*", the latter because new versions of `mrouted` relay on IP tunneling to send multicast datagrams encapsulated into unicast ones. This is necessary when establishing tunnels between multicast hosts separated by unicast-only networks and routers. (The `mrouted` is a daemon that implements the multicast routing algorithm -the routing policy- and instructs the kernel on how to route multicast datagrams).

Some kernel versions label multicast routing as "*EXPERIMENTAL*", so you should enable "*Prompt for development and/or incomplete code/drivers*" in the "*Code maturity level options*" section.

If, when running the `mrouted`, traffic generated in the same network your Linux box is connected to is correctly forwarded to the other network, but you can't see the other's network traffic on your local network, check whether you are receiving ICMP protocol error messages. Almost sure you forgot to turn on IP tunneling in your Linux router. It's a kind of stupid error when you know it but, believe me, its quite time-consuming when you don't, and there is no apparent reason that explains what is going wrong. A sniffer proves to be quite useful in these situations!

(You can see more on multicast routing on section 8 (Routing Policies and Forwarding Techniques); `mrouted` and tunnels are also explained in sections 4 (The MBone) and 5 (Multicast applications)).

Once you have compiled and installed your new kernel, you should provide a default route for multicast traffic. The goal is to add a route to the network 224.0.0.0.

The problem most people seem to face in this stage of the configuration is with the value of the mask to supply. If you have read Terry Dawson's excellent NET-3-HOWTO, it should not be difficult to guess the correct value, though. As explained there, the netmask is a 32 bit number filled with all-1s in the network part of your IP address, and with all-0s in the host part. Recall from section 2.1 that a class D multicast address has no netwok/host sections. Instead it has a 28-bit group identifier and a 4-bit class D identifier. Well, this 4 bits are the network part and the remaining 28 the host part. So the netmask needed is 11110000000000000000000000000000 or, easier to read: 240.0.0.0. Then, the full command should be:

```
route add 224.0.0.0 netmask 240.0.0.0 dev eth0
```

Depending on how old your `route` program is, you might need to add the `-net` flag after the `add`.

Here we supposed that `eth0` was multicast-capable and that, when not otherwise specified, we wanted multicast traffic to be output there. If this is not your case, change the `dev` parameter as appropriate.

The `/proc` filesystem proves here to be useful once again: you can check `/proc/net/igmp` to see the groups your host is currently subscribed to.

4   The MBone.

Using a new technology usually carries some advantages and disadvantages. The advantages of multicast are -I think- clear. The main disadvantage is that hundreds of hosts and, specially, routers don't support it yet. As a consequence, people who started working on multicast, bought new equipment, modified their operating systems, and built *multicast islands* in their local places. Then they discovered that it was difficult to communicate with people doing similar things because if only one of the routers between them didn't support multicast there was nothing to do...

The solution was clear: they decided to build a *virtual multicast network* in the top of the Internet. That is: sites with multicast routers between them could communicate directly. But sites joined across unicast routers would send their island's multicast traffic encapsulated in unicast packets to other multicast islands. Routers in the middle would not have problems, as they would be dealing with unicast traffic. Finally, in the receiving site, traffic would be de-encapsulated, and sent to the island in the original multicast way. Two ends converting from multicast to unicast, and then again to multicast define what is called a multicast *tunnel*.

The *MBone* or *Multicast Backbone* is that virtual multicast network based on multicast islands connected by multicast tunnels.

Several activities take place in the MBone daily, but it deserves to be remarked the profusion of tele-conferences with real time audio and video taking place across the whole Internet. As an example, it was recently transmitted (live) the talk Linus Torvalds gave to the Silicon Valley Linux Users Group.

For more information on the MBone, see:

`<http://www.mediadesign.co.at/newmedia/more/mbone-faq.html>`

5   Multicast applications.

Most people dealing with multicast, sooner or later decide to connect to the MBone, and then they usually need an `mrouted`. You'll also need it if you don't have a multicast-capable router and you want multicast traffic generated in one of your subnets to be "heard" on another. `mrouted` does circunvect the problem of sending multicast traffic across unicast routers -it encapsulates multicast datagrams into unicast ones (IP into IP)- but this is not the only feature it provides. Most important, it instructs the kernel on how to route (or not-to-route) multicast datagrams based on their source and destination. So, even having a multicast capable router, `mrouted` can be used to tell it *what* to do with the datagrams (note I said *what*, and not *how*; `mrouted` says "forward this to the network connected to that interface", but actual forwarding is performed by the kernel). This distinction between actual-forwarding and the algorithm that decides who and how to forward is very useful as it allows to write forwarding code only once and place it into the kernel. Forwarding algorithms and policies are then implemented in user space daemons, so it is very easy to change from one policy to another without the need of kernel re-compilation.

You can get a version of *mrouted* ported to Linux from:

`<ftp://www.video.ja.net/mice/mrouted/Linux/>`. This site is mirrored all across the world. Be sure to read the `<ftp://www.video.ja.net/mice/README.mirrors>` file to choose the one nearest you.

Next, we'll focus specially on multicast applications written to connect to the MBone, which have been ported to Linux. The list is picked up from Michael Esler's "Linux Multicast Information" page `<http://www.cs.virginia.edu/~mke2e/multicast/>`. I recommend you that page for lots of information and resources on multicast and Linux.

Audio Conferencing

- NeVoT - Network Voice Terminal `<http://www.fokus.gmd.de/step/nevot>`
- RAT - UCL Robust-Audio Tool `<http://www-mice.cs.ucl.ac.uk/mice/rat>`
- vat - LBL visual audio tool `<http://www-nrg.ee.lbl.gov/vat/>`

Video Conferencing

- ivs - Inria video conferencing system `<http://www.inria.fr/rodeo/ivs.html>`
- nv - Network video tool `<ftp://ftp.parc.xerox.com/pub/net-research/>`
- nv w/ Meteor - Release of nv w/ support for the Matrox Meteor (UVa) `<ftp://ftp.cs.virginia.edu/pub/gwtts/Linux/nv-meteor.tar.gz>`
- vic - LBL video conferencing tool `<http://www-nrg.ee.lbl.gov/vic/>`
- vic w/ Meteor - Release of vic w/ support for the Matrox Meteor (UVa) `<ftp://ftp.cs.virginia.edu/pub/gwtts/Linux/vic2.7a38-meteor.tar.gz>`

Other Utilities

- mmphone Multimedia phone service `<http://www.eit.com/software/mmphone/phoneform.html>`
- wb - LBL shared white board `<http://www-nrg.ee.lbl.gov/wb/>`
- webcast - Reliable multicast application for linking Mosaic browsers `<http://www.ncsa.uiuc.edu/SDG/Software/XMosaic/CCI/webcast.html>`

Session Tools

I placed session tools later because I think they deserve some explanation. When a conference takes places, several multicast groups and ports are assigned to each service you want for your conference (audio, video, shared white-boards, etc...) Announces of the conferences that will take place, along with information on multicast groups, ports and programs that will be used (vic, vat, ...) are periodically multicasted to the MBone. Session tools "hear" this information and present you in an easy way which conferences are taking (or will take) place, so you can decide which interest you. Also, they facilitate the task of joining a session. Instead of launching each program that will be used and telling which multicast group/port to join, you usually just need to click and the session tool launches the proper programs suppling them all information needed to join the conference. Session tools usually let you announce your own conferences on the MBone.

- gwTTS - University of Virginia tele-tutoring system `<http://www.cs.Virginia.EDU/~gwtts>`
- isc - Integrated session controller `<http://www.fokus.gmd.de/step/isc>`
- mmcc - Multimedia conference control `<ftp://ftp.isi.edu/confctrl/mmcc>`
- sd - LBL session directory tool `<ftp://ftp.ee.lbl.gov/conferencing/sd>`
- sd-snoop - Tenet Group session directory snoop utility `<ftp://tenet.berkeley.edu/pub/software>`
- sdr - UCL's next generation session directory `<ftp://cs.ucl.ac.uk/mice/sdr>`

6 Multicast programming.

Multicast programming... or writing your own multicast applications.

Several extensions to the programming API are needed in order to support multicast. All of them are handled via two system calls: `setsockopt()` (used to pass information to the kernel) and `getsockopt()` (to retrieve information regarded multicast behavior). This does *not* mean that 2 new system calls were added to support multicast. The pair `setsockopt()`/`getsockopt()` has been there for years. Since 4.2 BSD at least. The addition consists on a new set of options (multicast options) that are passed to these system calls, that the kernel must understand.

The following are the `setsockopt()`/`getsockopt()` function prototypes:

```
int getsockopt(int s, int level, int optname, void* optval, int* optlen);

int setsockopt(int s, int level, int optname, const void* optval, in-
    t optlen);
```

The first parameter, `s`, is the socket the system call applies to. For multicasting, it must be a socket of the family `AF_INET` and its type may be either `SOCK_DGRAM` or `SOCK_RAW`. The most common use is with `SOCK_DGRAM` sockets, but if you plan to write a routing daemon or modify some existing one, you will probably need to use `SOCK_RAW` ones.

The second one, `level`, identifies the layer that is to handle the option, message or query, whatever you want to call it. So, `SOL_SOCKET` is for the socket layer, `IPPROTO_IP` for the IP layer, etc... For multicast programming, `level` will always be `IPPROTO_IP`.

`optname` identifies the option we are setting/getting. Its value (either supplied by the program or returned by the kernel) is `optval`. The optnames involved in multicast programming are the following:

	setsockopt()	getsockopt()
IP_MULTICAST_LOOP	yes	yes
IP_MULTICAST_TTL	yes	yes
IP_MULTICAST_IF	yes	yes
IP_ADD_MEMBERSHIP	yes	no
IP_DROP_MEMBERSHIP	yes	no

`optlen` carries the size of the data structure `optval` points to. Note that in `getsockopt()` it is a value-result rather than a value: the kernel writes the value of `optname` in the buffer pointed by `optval` and informs us of that value's size via `optlen`.

Both `setsockopt()` and `getsockopt()` return 0 on success and -1 on error.

6.1 IP_MULTICAST_LOOP.

You have to decide, as the application writer, whether you want the data you send to be looped back to your host or not. If you plan to have more than one process or user "listening", loopback must be enabled. On the other hand, if you are sending the images your video camera is producing, you probably don't want loopback, even if you want to see yourself on the screen. In that latter case, your application will probably receive the images from a device attached to the computer and send them to the socket. As the application already "has" that data, it is improbable it wants to receive it again on the socket. Loopback is by default enabled.

Regard that `optval` is a pointer. You can't write:

```
setsockopt(socket, IPPROTO_IP, IP_MULTICAST_LOOP, 0, 1);
```

to disable loopback. Instead write:

```
u_char loop;
setsockopt(socket, IPPROTO_IP, IP_MULTICAST_LOOP, &loop, sizeof(loop));
```

and set `loop` to 1 to enable loopback or 0 to disable it.

To know whether a socket is currently looping-back or not use something like:

```
u_char loop;
int size;

getsockopt(socket, IPPROTO_IP, IP_MULTICAST_LOOP, &loop, &size)
```

6.2   IP_MULTICAST_TTL.

If not otherwise specified, multicast datagrams are sent with a default value of 1, to prevent them to be forwarded beyond the local network. To change the TTL to the value you desire (from 0 to 255), put that value into a variable (here I name it "ttl") and write somewhere in your program:

```
u_char ttl;
setsockopt(socket, IPPROTO_IP, IP_MULTICAST_TTL, &ttl, sizeof(ttl));
```

The behavior with `getsockopt()` is similar to the one seen on IP_MULTICAST_LOOP.

6.3   IP_MULTICAST_IF.

Usually, the system administrator specifies the default interface multicast datagrams should be sent from. The programmer can override this and choose a concrete outgoing interface for a given socket with this option.

```
struct in_addr interface_addr;
setsockopt (socket, IPPROTO_IP, IP_MULTICAST_IF, &inter-
face_addr, sizeof(interface_addr));
```

>From now on, all multicast traffic generated in this socket will be output from the interface chosen. To revert to the original behavior and let the kernel choose the outgoing interface based on the system administrator's configuration, it is enough to call `setsockopt()` with this same option and `INADDR_ANY` in the interface field.

In determining or selecting outgoing interfaces, the following `ioctls` might be useful: `SIOCGIFADDR` (to get an interface's address), `SIOCGIFCONF` (to get the list of all the interfaces) and `SIOCGIFFLAGS` (to get an interface's flags and, thus, determine whether the interface is multicast capable or not -the `IFF_MULTICAST` flag-).

If the host has more than one interface and the IP_MULTICAST_IF option is not set, multicast transmissions are sent from the default interface, although the remaining interfaces might be used for multicast *forwarding* if the host is acting as a multicast router.

6.4   IP_ADD_MEMBERSHIP.

Recall that you need to tell the kernel which multicast groups you are interested in. If no process is interested in a group, packets destined to it that arrive to the host are discarded. In order to inform the kernel of your interests and, thus, become a member of that group, you should first fill a `ip_mreq` structure which is passed later to the kernel in the `optval` field of the `setsockopt()` system call.

The ip_mreq structure (taken from `/usr/include/linux/in.h`) has the following members:

```
struct ip_mreq
{
```

```
            struct in_addr imr_multiaddr;     /* IP multicast address of group */
            struct in_addr imr_interface;     /* local IP address of interface */
   };
```

(Note: the "physical" definition of the structure is in the file above specified. Nonetheless, you should not include `<linux/in.h>` if you want your code to be portable. Instead, include `<netinet/in.h>` which, in turn, includes `<linux/in.h>` itself).

The first member, `imr_multiaddr`, holds the group address you want to join. Remember that memberships are also associated with interfaces, not just groups. This is the reason you have to provide a value for the second member: `imr_interface`. This way, if you are in a multihomed host, you can join the same group in several interfaces. You can always fill this last member with the wildcard address (`INADDR_ANY`) and then the kernel will deal with the task of choosing the interface.

With this structure filled (say you defined it as: `struct ip_mreq mreq;`) you just have to call `setsockopt()` this way:

```
   setsockopt (socket, IPPROTO_IP, IP_ADD_MEMBERSHIP, &mreq, sizeof(mreq));
```

Notice that you can join several groups to the same socket, not just one. The limit to this is `IP_MAX_MEMBERSHIPS` and, as of version 2.0.33, it has the value of 20.

6.5 IP_DROP_MEMBERSHIP.

The process is quite similar to joining a group:

```
   struct ip_mreq mreq;
   setsockopt (socket, IPPROTO_IP, IP_DROP_MEMBERSHIP, &mreq, sizeof(mreq));
```

where `mreq` is the same structure with the same data used when joining the group. If the `imr_interface` member is filled with `INADDR_ANY`, the first matching group is dropped.

If you have joined a lot of groups to the same socket, you don't need to drop memberships in all of them in order to terminate. When you close a socket, all memberships associated with it are dropped by the kernel. The same occurs if the process that opened the socket is killed.

Finally, keep in mind that a process dropping membership for a group does not imply that the host will stop receiving datagrams for that group. If another socket joined that group in that same interface previously to this `IP_DROP_MEMBERSHIP`, *the host* will keep being a member of that group.

Both ADD_MEMBERSHIP and DROP_MEMBERSHIP are nonblocking operations. They should return immediately indicating either success or failure.

7   The internals.

This section's aim is to provide some information, not needed to reach a basic understanding on how multicast works nor to be able to write multicast programs, but which is very interesting, gives some insight on the underlying multicast protocols and implementations, and may be useful to avoid common errors and misunderstandings.

7.1   IGMP.

When talking about `IP_ADD_MEMBERSHIP` and `IP_DROP_MEMBERSHIP`, we said that the information provided by this "commands" was used by the kernel to choose which multicast datagrams accept or discard. This is true, but it is not all the truth. Such a simplification would imply that multicast datagrams for *all* multicast groups around the world would be received by our host, and then it would check the memberships issued by processes running on it to decide whether to pass the traffic to them or to throw it out. As you can imagine, this is a complete bandwidth waste.

What actually happens is that hosts instruct their routers telling them which multicast groups they are interested in; then, those routers tell their up-stream routers they want to receive that traffic, and so on. Algorithms employed for making the decision of *when* to ask for a group's traffic or saying that it is not desired anymore, vary a lot. There's something, however, that never changes: *how* this information is transmitted. **IGMP** is used for that. It stands for Internet Group Management Protocol. It is a new protocol, similar in many aspects to ICMP, with a protocol number of 2, whose messages are carried in IP datagrams, and which all level 2-compliant host are required to implement.

As said before, it is used both by hosts giving membership information to its routers, and by routers to communicate between themselves. In the following I'll cover only the hosts-routers relationships, mainly because I was unable to find information describing router to router communication other than the mrouted source code (rfc 1075 describing the Distance Vector Multicast Routing Protocol is now obsoleted, and `mrouted` implements a modified DVMRP not yet documented).

IGMP version 0 is specified in RFC-988 which is now obsoleted. Almost no one uses version 0 now.

IGMP version 1 is described in RFC-1112 and, although it is updated by RFC-2236 (IGMP version 2) it is in wide use still. The Linux kernel implements the full IGMP version 1 and parts of version 2 requirements, but not all.

Now I'll try to give an informal description of the protocol. You can check RFC-2236 for an in-proof formal description, with lots of state diagrams and time-out boundaries.

All IGMP messages have the following structure:

```
 0                   1                   2                   3
 0 1 2 3 4 5 6 7 8 9 0 1 2 3 4 5 6 7 8 9 0 1 2 3 4 5 6 7 8 9 0 1
+-+-+-+-+-+-+-+-+-+-+-+-+-+-+-+-+-+-+-+-+-+-+-+-+-+-+-+-+-+-+-+-+
|     Type      | Max Resp Time |           Checksum            |
+-+-+-+-+-+-+-+-+-+-+-+-+-+-+-+-+-+-+-+-+-+-+-+-+-+-+-+-+-+-+-+-+
|                         Group Address                         |
+-+-+-+-+-+-+-+-+-+-+-+-+-+-+-+-+-+-+-+-+-+-+-+-+-+-+-+-+-+-+-+-+
```

IGMP version 1 (hereinafter IGMPv1) labels the "Max Resp Time" as "Unused", zeroes it when sent, and ignores it when received. Also, it brakes the "Type" field in two 4-bits wide fields: "Version" and "Type". As IGMPv1 identifies a "Membership Query" message as 0x11 (version 1, type 1) and IGMPv2 as 0x11 too, the 8 bits have the same effective interpretation.

I think it is more instructive to give first the IGMPv1 description and next point out the IGMPv2 additions, as they are mainly that, additions.

For the following discussions it is important to remember that multicast routers receive *all* IP multicast datagrams.

7.1.1 IGMP version 1.

Routers periodically send *IGMP Host Membership Queries* to the all-hosts group (224.0.0.1) with a TTL of 1 (once every minute or two). All multicast-capable hosts hear them, but don't answer immediately to avoid an IGMP Host Membership Report storm. Instead, they start a random delay timer for each group they belong to *on the interface* they received the query.

Sooner or later, the timer expires in one of the hosts, and it sends an IGMP *Host Membership Report* (also with TTL 1) to the multicast address of the group being reported. As it is sent to the group, all hosts that joined the group -and which are currently waiting for their own timer to expire- receive it, too. Then, they stop their timers and don't generate any other report. Just one is generated -by the host that chose the smaller timeout-, and that is enough for the router. It only needs to know that there are members for that group in the subnet, not how many nor which.

When no reports are received for a given group after a certain number of queries, the router assumes that no members are left, and thus it doesn't have to forward traffic for that group on that subnet. Note that in IGMPv1 there are no "Leave Group messages".

When a host joins a *new* group, the kernel sends a report for that group, so that the respective process needs not to wait a minute or two until a new membership query is received. As you can see this IGMP packet is generated by the kernel as a response to the IP_ADD_MEMBERSHIP command, seen in section 6.4 (IP_ADD_MEMBERSHIP). Note the emphasis in the adjective "new": if a process issues an IP_ADD_MEMBERSHIP command for a group the host is already a member of, no IGMP packets are sent as we must already be receiving traffic for that group; instead, a counter for that group's use is incremented. IP_DROP_MEMBERSHIP generates no datagrams in IGMPv1.

Host Membership Queries are identified by Type 0x11, and Host Membership Reports by Type 0x12.

No reports are sent for the all-hosts group. Membership in this group is permanent.

7.1.2 IGMP version 2.

One important addition to the above is the inclusion of a *Leave Group* message (Type 0x17). The reason is to reduce the bandwidth waste between the time the last host in the subnet drops membership and the time the router times-out for its queries and decides there are no more members present for that group (leave latency). Leave Group messages should be addressed to the all-routers group (224.0.0.2) rather than to the group being left, as that information is of no use for other members (kernel versions up to 2.0.33 send them to the group; although it does no harm to the hosts, it's a waste of time as they have to process them, but don't gain useful information). There are certain subtle details regarding when and when-not to send Leave Messages; if interested, see the RFC.

When an IGMPv2 router receives a Leave Message for a group, it sends *Group-Specific Queries* to the group being left. This is another addition. IGMPv1 has no group-specific queries. All queries are sent to the all-hosts group. The Type in the IGMP header does not change (0x11, as before), but the "Group Address" is filled with the address of the multicast group being left.

The "Max Resp Time" field, which was set to 0 in transmission and ignored on reception in IGMPv1, is meaningful only in "Membership Query" messages. It gives the maximum time allowed before sending a report in units of 1/10 second. It is used as a tune mechanism.

IGMPv2 adds another message type: 0x16. It is a "Version 2 Membership Report" sent by IGMPv2 hosts if they detect an IGMPv2 router is present (an IGMPv2 host knows an IGMPv1 router is present when it receives a query with the "Max Response" field set to 0).

When more than one router claims to act as querier, IGMPv2 provides a mechanism to avoid "discussions": the router with the lowest IP address is designed to be querier. The other routers keep timeouts. If the router with lower IP address crashes or is shutdown, the decision of who will be the querier is taken again after the timers expire.

7.2 Kernel corner.

This sub-section gives some start-points to study the multicast implementation of the Linux kernel. It does not explain that implementation. It just says where to find things.

The study was carried over version 2.0.32, so it could be a bit outdated by the time you read it (network code seems to have changed *A LOT* in 2.1.x releases, for instance).

Multicast code in the Linux kernel is always surrounded by #ifdef CONFIG_IP_MULTICAST / #endif pairs, so that you can include/ exclude it from your kernel based on your needs (this inclusion/exclusion is done at compile time, as you probably know if reading that section... #ifdefs are handled by the preprocessor. The decision is made based in what you selected when doing either a make config, make menuconfig or make xconfig).

You might want multicast features, but if your Linux box is not going to act as a multicast router you will probably not want multicast router features included in your new kernel. For this you have the multicast routing code surrounded by #ifdef CONFIG_IP_MROUTE / #endif pairs.

Kernel sources are usually placed in /usr/src/linux. However, the place may change so, both for accuracy and brevity, I will refer to the root directory of the kernel sources as just LINUX. Then, something like LINUX/net/ipv4/udp.c should be the same as /usr/src/linux/net/ipv4/udp.c if you unpacked the kernel sources in the /usr/src/linux directory.

All multicast interfaces with user programs shown in the section devoted to multicast programming were driven across the setsockopt()/ getsockopt() system calls. Both of them are implemented by means of functions that make some tests to verify the parameters passed to them and which, in turn, call another function that makes some additional tests, demultiplexes the call based on the level parameter to either system call, and then calls another function which... (if interested in all this jumps, you can follow them in LINUX/net/socket.c (functions sys_socketcall() and sys_setsockopt(), LINUX/net/ipv4/af_inet.c (function inet_setsockopt()) and LINUX/net/ipv4/ip_sockglue.c (function ip_setsockopt())).

The one which interests us is LINUX/net/ipv4/ip_sockglue.c. Here we find ip_setsockopt() and ip_getsockopt() which are mainly a switch (after some error checking) verifying each possible value for optname. Along with unicast options, all multicast ones seen here are handled: IP_MULTICAST_TTL, IP_MULTICAST_LOOP, IP_MULTICAST_IF, IP_ADD_MEMBERSHIP and IP_DROP_MEMBERSHIP. Previously to the switch, a test is made to determine whether the options are multicast router specific, and if so, they are routed to the ip_mroute_setsockopt() and ip_mroute_getsockopt() functions (file LINUX/net/ipv4/ipmr.c).

In LINUX/net/ipv4/af_inet.c we can see the default values we talked about in previous sections (loopback enabled, TTL=1) provided when the socket is created (taken from function inet_create() in this file):

```
#ifdef CONFIG_IP_MULTICAST
        sk->ip_mc_loop=1;
        sk->ip_mc_ttl=1;
        *sk->ip_mc_name=0;
        sk->ip_mc_list=NULL;
#endif
```

Also, the assertion of "closing a socket makes the kernel drop all memberships this socket had" is corroborated by:

```
#ifdef CONFIG_IP_MULTICAST
                /* Applications forget to leave groups before exiting */
                ip_mc_drop_socket(sk);
#endif
```

taken from inet_release(), on the same file as before.

Device independent operations for the Link Layer are kept in LINUX/net/core/dev_mcast.c.

Two important functions are still missing: the processing of input and output multicast datagrams. As any other datagrams, incoming datagrams are passed from the device drivers to the ip_rcv() function (LINUX/net/ipv4/ip_input.c). In this function is where the perfect filtering is applied to multicast packets that crossed the devices layer (recall that lower layers only perform best-effort filtering and is IP who 100% knows whether we are interested in that multicast group or not). If the host is acting as a multicast router, this function decides too whether the datagram should be forwarded and calls ipmr_forward() appropriately. (ipmr_forward() is implemented in LINUX/net/ipv4/ipmr.c).

Code in charge of out-putting packets is kept in LINUX/net/ipv4/ip_output.c. Here is where the IP_MULTICAST_LOOP option takes effect, as it is checked to see whether to loop back the packets or not (function ip_queue_xmit()). Also the TTL of the outgoing packet is selected based on whether it is a multicast or unicast one. In the former case, the argument passed to the IP_MULTICAST_TTL option is used (function (ip_build_xmit()).

While working with `mrouted` (a program which gives the kernel information about how to route multicast datagrams), we detected that all multicast packets originated on the local network were properly routed..., except the ones from the Linux box that was acting as the multicast router!! ip_input.c was working OK, but it seemed ip_output.c wasn't. Reading the source code for the output functions, we found that outgoing datagrams were not being passed to `ipmr_forward()`, the function that had to decide whether they should be routed or not. The packets were outputed to the local network but, as network cards are usually unable to read their own transmissions, those datagrams were never routed. We added the necessary code to the `ip_build_xmit()` function and everything was OK again. (Having the sources for your kernel is not a luxury or pedantry; it's a need!)

`ipmr_forward()` has been mentioned a couple of times. It is an important function as it solves one important misunderstanding that appears to be widely expanded. When routing multicast traffic, it is *not* `mrouted` who makes the copies and sends them to the proper recipients. `mrouted` receives all multicast traffic and, based on that information, computes the multicast routing tables and *tells the kernel* how to route: "datagrams for this group coming from that interface should be forwarded to those interfaces". This information is passed to the kernel by calls to `setsockopt()` on a raw socket opened by the `mrouted` daemon (the protocol specified when the raw socket was created *must* be `IPPROTO_IGMP`). This options are handled in the `ip_mroute_setsockopt()` function from `LINUX/net/ipv4/ipmr.c`. The first option (would be better to call them commands rather than options) issued on that socket must be `MRT_INIT`. All other commands are ignored (returning `-EACCES`) if `MRT_INIT` is not issued first. Only one instance of `mrouted` can be running at the same time in the same host. To keep track of this, when the first `MRT_INIT` is received, an important variable, `struct sock* mroute_socket`, is pointed to the socket `MRT_INIT` was received on. If `mroute_socket` is not null when attending an `MRT_INIT` this means another mrouted is already running and `-EADDRINUSE` is returned. All resting commands (`MRT_DONE`, `MRT_ADD_VIF`, `MRT_DEL_VIF`, `MRT_ADD_MFC`, `MRT_DEL_MFC` and `MRT_ASSERT`) return `-EACCES` if they come from a socket different than `mroute_socket`.

As routed multicast datagrams can be received/sent across either physical interfaces or tunnels, a common abstraction for both was devised: VIFs, Virtual InterFaces. `mrouted` passes vif structures to the kernel, indicating physical or tunnel interfaces to add to its routing tables, and multicast forwarding entries saying where to forward datagrams.

VIFs are added with `MRT_ADD_VIF` and deleted with `MRT_DEL_VIF`. Both pass a `struct vifctl` to the kernel (defined in `/usr/include/linux/mroute.h`) with the following information:

```
struct vifctl {
        vifi_t  vifc_vifi;                   /* Index of VIF */
        unsigned char vifc_flags;           /* VIFF_ flags */
        unsigned char vifc_threshold;       /* ttl limit */
        unsigned int vifc_rate_limit;       /* Rate limiter values (NI) */
        struct in_addr vifc_lcl_addr;       /* Our address */
        struct in_addr vifc_rmt_addr;       /* IPIP tunnel addr */
};
```

With this information a `vif_device` structure is built:

```
struct vif_device
{
        struct device   *dev;                       /* Device we are using */
        struct route    *rt_cache;                  /* Tunnel route cache */
        unsigned long   bytes_in,bytes_out;
        unsigned long   pkt_in,pkt_out;             /* Statistics */
        unsigned long   rate_limit;                 /* Traffic shaping (NI) */
        unsigned char   threshold;                  /* TTL threshold */
        unsigned short  flags;                      /* Control flags */
        unsigned long   local,remote;               /* Address-
es(remote for tunnels)*/
};
```

Note the dev entry in the structure. The device structure is defined in /usr/include/linux/netdevice.h file. It is a big structure, but the field that interests us is is:

```
struct ip_mc_list*     ip_mc_list;    /* IP multicast filter chain     */
```

The ip_mc_list structure -defined in /usr/include/linux/igmp.h- is as follows:

```
struct ip_mc_list
{
        struct device *interface;
        unsigned long multiaddr;
        struct ip_mc_list *next;
        struct timer_list timer;
        short tm_running;
        short reporter;
        int users;
};
```

So, the ip_mc_list member from the dev structure is a pointer to a linked list of ip_mc_list structures, each containing an entry for each multicast group the network interface is a member of. Here again we see membership is associated to interfaces. LINUX/net/ipv4/ip_input.c traverses this linked list to decide whether the received datagram is destined to any group the interface that received the datagram belongs to:

```
#ifdef CONFIG_IP_MULTICAST
                if(!(dev->flags&IFF_ALLMULTI) && brd==IS_MULTICAST
                   && iph->daddr!=IGMP_ALL_HOSTS
                   && !(dev->flags&IFF_LOOPBACK))
                {
                        /*
                         *      Check it is for one of our groups
                         */
                        struct ip_mc_list *ip_mc=dev->ip_mc_list;
                        do
                        {
                                if(ip_mc==NULL)
                                {
                                        kfree_skb(skb, FREE_WRITE);
                                        return 0;
                                }
                                if(ip_mc->multiaddr==iph->daddr)
                                        break;
                                ip_mc=ip_mc->next;
                        }
                        while(1);
                }
#endif
```

The users field in the ip_mc_list structure is used to implement what was said in section 7.1.1 (IGMP version 1): if a process joins a group and the interface is already a member of that group (ie, another process joined that same group in that same interface before) only the count of members (users) is incremented. No IGMP messages are sent, as you can see in the following code (taken from `ip_mc_inc_group()`, called by `ip_mc_join_group()`, both in `LINUX/net/ipv4/igmp.c`):

```
        for(i=dev->ip_mc_list;i!=NULL;i=i->next)
        {
                if(i->multiaddr==addr)
                {
                        i->users++;
                        return;
                }
        }
```

When dropping memberships, the counter is decremented and additional operations are performed only when the count reaches 0 (`ip_mc_dec_group()`).

`MRT_ADD_MFC` and `MRT_DEL_MFC` set or delete forwarding entries in the multicast routing tables. Both pass a `struct mfcctl` to the kernel (also defined in `/usr/include/linux/mroute.h`) with this information:

```
struct mfcctl
{
        struct in_addr mfcc_origin;         /* Origin of mcast     */
        struct in_addr mfcc_mcastgrp;       /* Group in question   */
        vifi_t  mfcc_parent;                /* Where it arrived    */
        unsigned char mfcc_ttls[MAXVIFS];   /* Where it is going   */
};
```

With all this information in hand, `ipmr_forward()` "walks" across the VIFs, and if a matching is found *it* duplicates the datagram and calls `ipmr_queue_xmit()` which, in turn, uses the output device specified by the routing table and the proper destination address if the packet is to be sent across a tunnel (ie, the unicast destination address of the other end of the tunnel).

Function `ip_rt_event()` (not directly related to output, but which is in ip_output.c too) receives events related to a network device, like the device going up. This function assures that then the device joins the ALL-HOSTS multicast group.

IGMP functions are implemented in `LINUX/net/ipv4/igmp.c`. Important information for that functions appears in `/usr/include/linux/igmp.h` and `/usr/include/linux/mroute.h`. The IGMP entry in the `/proc/net` directory is created with `ip_init()` in `LINUX/net/ipv4/ip_output.c`.

8 Routing Policies and Forwarding Techniques.

One trivial algorithm to make worldwide multicast traffic available everywhere could be to send it... everywhere, despite someone wants it or not. As this does not seem quite optimized, several routing algorithms and forwarding techniques have been implemented.

DVMRP (Distance Vector Multicast Routing Protocol) is, perhaps, the one most multicast routers use now. It is a *dense mode* routing protocol, that is, it performs well in environments with high bandwidth and densely distributed members. However, in *sparse mode* scenarios, it suffers from scalability problems.

Together with DVMRP we can find other dense mode routing protocols, such as **MOSPF** (Multicast Extensions to OSPF -Open Shortest Path First-) and PIM-DM (Protocol-Independent Multicast Dense Mode).

To perform routing in sparse mode environments, we have **PIM-SM** (Protocol Independent Multicast Sparse Mode) and **CBT** (Core Based Trees).

OSPF version 2 is explained in RFC 1583, and MOSPF in RFC 1584. PIM-SM and CBT specifications can be found in RFC 2117 and 2201, respectively.

All this routing protocols use some type of multicast forwarding, such as *flooding*, *Reverse Path Broadcasting* (RPB), *Truncated Reverse Path Broadcasting* (TRPB), *Reverse Path Multicasting* (RPM) or *Shared Trees*.

It would be too long to explain them here and, as short descriptions for them are publicly available, I'll just recommend reading the `draft-ietf-mboned-in.txt` text. You can find it in the same places RFCs are available, and it explains in some detail all the above techniques and policies.

9   Multicast Transport Protocols.

So far we have been talking about multicast transmissions using UDP. This is the usual practice, as it is impossible to do it with TCP. However, intense research is taking place since a couple of years in order to develop some new multicast transport protocols.

Several of these protocols have been implemented and are being tested. A good lesson from them is that it seems no multicast transport protocol is general and good enough for all types of multicast applications.

If transport protocols are complex and difficult to tune, imagine dealing with delays (in multimedia conferences), data loss, ordering, retransmissions, flow and congestion control, group management, etc, when the receiver is not one, but perhaps hundreds or thousands of sparse hosts. Here scalability is an issue, and new techniches are implemented, such as not giving acknowledges for every packet received but, instead, send *negative acknowledges* (NACKs) for data not received. RFC 1458 gives the proposed requirements for multicast protocols.

Giving descriptions of those multicast protocols is out of the scope of this section. Instead, I'll give you the names of some of them and point you to some sources of information: Real-Time Transport Protocol (RTP) is concerned with multi-partite multimedia conferences, **Scalable Reliable Multicast** (SRM) is used by the wb (the distributed White-Board tool, see section 5 (Multicast applications)), **Uniform Reliable Group Communication Protocol** (URGC) enforces reliable and ordered transactions based in a centralized control, **Muse** was developed as an application specific protocol: to multicast news articles over the MBone, the **Multicast File Transfer Protocol** (MFTP) is quite descriptive by itself and people "join" to file transmission (previously announced) much in the same way they would join a conference, **Log-Based Receiver-reliable Multicast** (LBRM) is a curious protocol that keeps track of all packets sent in a logging server that tells the sender whether it has to retransmit the data or can drop it safely as all receivers got it. One protocol with a funny name -especially for a multicast protocol- is STORM (**STructure-Oriented Resilient Multicast**). Lots and lots of multicast protocols can be found searching the Web, along with some interesting papers proposing new activities for multicast (for instance, www page distribution using multicast).

A good page providing comparisons between reliable multicast protocols is

`<http://www.tascnets.com/mist/doc/mcpCompare.html>`.

A very good and up-to-date site, with lots of interesting links (Internet drafts, RFCs, papers, links to other sites) is:

`<http://research.ivv.nasa.gov/RMP/links.html>`.

`<http://hill.lut.ac.uk/DS-Archive/MTP.html>` is also a good source of information on the subject.

Katia Obraczka's "*Multicast Transport Protocols: A Survey and Taxonomy*" article gives short descriptions for each protocol and tries to classify them according to different features. You can read it in the IEEE Communications magazine, January 1998, vol. 36, No. 1.

10   References.

10.1   RFCs.

- RFC 1112 "Host Extensions for IP Multicasting". Steve Deering. August 1989.

- RFC 2236 "Internet Group Management Protocol, version 2". W. Fenner. November 1997.
- RFC 1458 "Requirements for Multicast Protocols". Braudes, R and Zabele, S. May 1993.
- RFC 1469 "IP Multicast over Token-Ring Local Area Networks". T. Pusateri. June 1993.
- RFC 1390 "Transmission of IP and ARP over FDDI Networks". D. Katz. January 1993.
- RFC 1583 "OSPF Version 2". John Moy. March 1994.
- RFC 1584 "Multicast Extensions to OSPF". John Moy. March 1994.
- RFC 1585 "MOSPF: Analysis and Experience". John Moy. March 1994.
- RFC 1812 "Requirements for IP version 4 Routers". Fred Baker, Editor. June 1995
- RFC 2117 "Protocol Independent Multicast-Sparse Mode (PIM-SM): Protocol Specification". D. Estrin, D. Farinacci, A. Helmy, D. Thaler; S. Deering, M. Handley, V. Jacobson, C. Liu, P. Sharma, and L. Wei. July 1997.
- RFC 2189 "Core Based Trees (CBT version 2) Multicast Routing". A. Ballardie. September 1997.
- RFC 2201 "Core Based Trees (CBT) Multicast Routing Architecture". A. Ballardie. September 1997.

10.2   Internet Drafts.

- "Introduction to IP Multicast Routing". `draft-ietf-mboned-intro- multicast- 03.txt`. T. Maufer, C. Semeria. July 1997.
- "Administratively Scoped IP Multicast". `draft-ietf-mboned-admin-ip- space-03.txt`. D. Meyer. June 10, 1997.

10.3   Web pages.

- Linux Multicast Homepage. `<http://www.cs.virginia.edu/~mke2e/multicast.html>`
- Linux Multicast FAQ. `<http://andrew.triumf.ca/pub/linux/multicast-FAQ>`
- Multicast and MBONE on Linux. `<http://www.teksouth.com/linux/multicast/>`
- Christian Daudt's MBONE-Linux Page. `<http://www.microplex.com/~csd/linux/mbone.html>`
- Reliable Multicast Links `<http://research.ivv.nasa.gov/RMP/links.html>`
- Multicast Transport Protocols `<http://hill.lut.ac.uk/DS-Archive/MTP.html>`

10.4   Books.

- "TCP/IP Illustrated: Volume 1 The Protocols". Stevens, W. Richard. Addison Wesley Publishing Company, Reading MA, 1994
- "TCP/IP Illustrated: Volume 2, The Implementation". Wright, Gary and W. Richard Stevens. Addison Wesley Publishing Company, Reading MA, 1995
- "UNIX Network Programming Volume 1. Networking APIs: Sockets and XTI". Stevens, W. Richard. Second Edition, Prentice Hall, Inc. 1998.
- "Internetworking with TCP/IP Volume 1 Principles, Protocols, and Architecture". Comer, Douglas E. Second Edition, Prentice Hall, Inc. Englewood Cliffs, New Jersey, 1991

11   Copyright and Disclaimer.

HOWTO

12   Acknowledgements.

This is the best opportunity I've ever had to thank so *many* people I feel grateful to. So, I'm afraid this is going to be a large section... It is, in any case, the most important one of this paper (for me, at least...).

First, I want to thank Elena Apolinario Fernández de Sousa (yes, Elena is the first name; the REST is THE surname ;-)). I tried to reflect in this Howto all the knowledge I collected while working with her in connecting our Department to the MBone and debugging problems with locally generated CSCW software across multicast tunnels. She was of invaluable help in finding and correcting network problems, discovering and fixing kernel bugs that puzzled us for days, ... and keeping the sense of humor alive while problems appeared and appeared, but solutions didn't. She also read and corrected the drafts for this document and provided important ideas and suggestions. If this howto is here and is usefull for somebody, it will be, in many aspects, thanks to her. Thanks, Elena!

There is something I have been lucky enough to find all my (still-not-too-long) live, but, despite being repetitive, has never stopped amazing me. I'm talking about people that altruistically employ part of their time and/or resources to help other people learn new things; and, what is better, they enjoy doing it. This is not only (but also, too) explain things they already know, but lend their books, provide access to their sources and facilitate you the way to learn all things they know; sometimes, even more... I know quite a few of that people, and I'd like to thank them for all their help.

Pablo Basterrechea was my "first source of documentation" while I was in my pre-Internet stage. I learned assembly and advanced structured programming entirely from his books (well, the latter also from his programs...). Thanks for all, Pablo.

In my first course at the University that "primary source of documentation" moved to Pepe Mañas. He was teaching then Computer Programming there, and soon I became addict to his bookshelf. He lent me his books lots of times without asking for a minimum sign that could assure that I was going to return them back to him, not even my name! My first approach to TCP/IP was also by his hand: he lent me Comer's "Internetworking with TCP/IP, Volume 1" for the whole summer. He did not even know my name by then, but he lent me the book... That book influenced me a lot, and TCP/IP has become one of my primary fields of interest since that summer.

If there are two persons I must thank most, these are (in alphabetic order ;-)), José Manuel and Paco Moya. Nobody I asked more things more times (C, C++, Linux, security, Web, OSs, signals & systems, electronics, ... anything!) and, despite my persistence, I always got throughly and friendly responses and help. If I'm using GNU/Linux now, this is, again, thanks to them. I feel particularly lucky with friends like them. THANKS.

Iñigo Mascaraque also helped (from him I got my first System Administration book) and encouraged me in my beginnings, but never stopped reminding me that, although this was a fascinating world and an important part of my career, I should not forget the other, less-interesting, parts. (I don't forget, I$!).

As I am on the topic, I'd like to thank my parents, too. They always tried to make the best opportunities available for me. Many thanks for all.

I also feel grateful to Joaquín Seoane, the first who trusted me enough to give me a root password in the time I was learning system administration by myself, and Santiago Pavón, the one who gave me my first opportunity here at DIT.

W. Richard Stevens' books have been a real revelation for me (it's a pity they are so expensive...). If he ever reads this paper, I'd like to thank him for them, and encourage him to keep on writing. Anything that comes out of his hands will

-undoubtedly- be good for all of us.

Finally I'd like to thank Richard Stallman, Linus Torvalds, Alan Cox and all contributors to the Linux kernel and the free software in general, for giving us such a great OS.

I'm sure I'm forgetting someone here... Sorry. I'm certain they know I'm grateful to them too, so if they tell me, everybody will know it... :-)

HOWTO

Part XXVIII

"Linux NET-3-HOWTO, Linux Networking." Terry Dawson (main author), VK2KTJ; Alessandro Rubini (maintainer)

alessandro.rubini@linux.it

v1.4, August 1998

The Linux Operating System boasts kernel based networking support written almost entirely from scratch. The performance of the tcp/ip implementation in recent kernels makes it a worthy alternative to even the best of its peers. This document aims to describe how to install and configure the Linux networking software and associated tools.

Contents

HOWTO

1   Changes from version 1.3 (April 1998)

```
Additions:
        Traffic Shaper.
        Plip for new kernels

Corrections/Updates:
        Maintainer address for netkit.
        Descriptions of domain names revised.
        General reordering of sections.
        2.0 and 2.2 differences are marked, although some 2.2 info is missing.
        Fixed many references to external documents.
ToDo:
        Describe new routing algorithm
        Add IPv6 kernel compile options
        Describe /proc/sys/net/* entries.
        WanRouter device
        Describe the new firewalling commands for 2.2
```

2   Introduction.

The original NET-FAQ was written by Matt Welsh and Terry Dawson to answer frequently asked questions about networking for Linux at a time before the Linux Documentation Project had formally started. It covered the very early development versions of the Linux Networking Kernel. The NET-2-HOWTO superceded the NET-FAQ and was one of the original LDP HOWTO documents, it covered what was called version 2 and later version 3 of the Linux kernel Networking software. This document in turn supercedes it and relates only to version 3 of the Linux Networking Kernel.

Previous versions of this document became quite large because of the enormous amount of material that fell within its scope. To help reduce this problem a number of HOWTO's dealing with specific networking topics have been produced. This document will provide pointers to them where relevant and cover those areas not yet covered by other documents.

HOWTO

In April 1998 Terry left as NET-3 maintainer, due to his high load. Alessandro Rubini is the new maintainer and would like to keep the document as good as before, although he's new in this kind of stuff.

2.1 Feedback

I always appreciate feedback and especially value contributions. Please direct any feedback or contributions to me by email (*rubini@linux.it* `<mailto:rubini@linux.it>`.

3 How to use this HOWTO document (NET-3-HOWTO howto?).

This document is organized top-down. The first sections include informative material and can be skipped if you are not interested; what follows is a generic discussion of networking issues, and you must ensure you understand this before proceeding to more specific parts. The rest, "technology specific" information is grouped in three main sections: Ethernet and IP-related information, technologies pertaining to widespread PC hardware and seldom-used technologies.

The suggested path through the document is thus the following:

Read the generic sections

> These sections apply to every, or nearly every, technology described later and so are very important for you to understand. On the other hand, I expect many of the readers to be already confident with this material.

Consider your network

> You should know how your network is, or will be, designed and exactly what hardware and technology types you will be implementing.

Read the "Ethernet and IP" section if you are directly connected a LAN or the Internet

> This section describes basic Ethernet configuration and the various features that Linux offers for IP networks, like firewalling, advanced routing and so on.

Read the next section if you are interested in low-cost local networks or dial-up connections

> The section describes PLIP, PPP, SLIP and ISDN, the widespread technologies used on personal workstations.

Read the technology specific sections related to your requirements

> If your needs differ from IP and/or common hardware, the final section covers details specific to non-IP protocols and peculiar communication hardware.

Do the configuration work

> You should actually try to configure your network and take careful note of any problems you have.

Look for further help if needed

> If you experience problems that this document does not help you to resolve then read the section related to where to get help or where to report bugs.

Have fun!

> Networking is fun, enjoy it.

3.1 Conventions used in this document

No special convention is used here, but you must be warned about the way commands are shown. Following the classic Unix documentation, any command you should type to your shell is prefixed by a prompt. This howto shows `"user%"` as the prompt for commands that do not require superuser privileges, and `"root#"` as the prompt for commands that need to run as root. I chose to use `"root#"` instead of a plain `"#"` to prevent confusion with snapshots from shell scripts, where the hash mark is used to define comment lines.

When "Kernel Compile Options" are shown, they are represented in the format used by *menuconfig*. They should be understandable even if you (like me) are not used to *menuconfig*. If you are in doubt about the options' nesting, running the program once can't but help.

Note that any link to other HOWTO's is local to help you browsing your local copy of the LDP documents, in case you are using the html version of this document. If you don't have a complete set of documents, every HOWTO can be retrieved from `sunsite.unc.edu` (directory `/pub/Linux/HOWTO`) and its countless mirrors.

4 General Information about Linux Networking.

4.1 A brief history of Linux Networking Kernel Development.

Developing a brand new kernel implementation of the tcp/ip protocol stack that would perform as well as existing implementations was not an easy task. The decision not to port one of the existing implementations was made at a time when there was some uncertainty as to whether the existing implementations may become encumbered by restrictive copyrights because of the court case put by U.S.L. and when there was a lot of fresh enthusiasm for doing it differently and perhaps even better than had already been done.

The original volunteer to lead development of the kernel network code was Ross Biro <biro@yggdrasil.com>. Ross produced a simple and incomplete but mostly usable implementation set of routines that were complemented by an ethernet driver for the WD-8003 network interface card. This was enough to get many people testing and experimenting with the software and some people even managed to connect machines in this configuration to live internet connections. The pressure within the Linux community driving development for networking support was building and eventually the cost of a combination of some unfair pressure applied to Ross and his own personal commitments outweighed the benefit he was deriving and he stepped down as lead developer. Ross's efforts in getting the project started and accepting the responsibility for actually producing something useful in such controversial circumstances were what catalyzed all future work and were therefore an essential component of the success of the current product.

Orest Zborowski <obz@Kodak.COM> produced the original BSD socket programming interface for the Linux kernel. This was a big step forward as it allowed many of the existing network applications to be ported to linux without serious modification.

Somewhere about this time Laurence Culhane <loz@holmes.demon.co.uk> developed the first drivers for Linux to support the SLIP protocol. These enabled many people who did not have access to Ethernet networking to experiment with the new networking software. Again, some people took this driver and pressed it into service to connect them to the Internet. This gave many more people a taste of the possibilities that could be realized if Linux had full networking support and grew the number of users actively using and experimenting with the networking software that existed.

One of the people that had also been actively working on the task of building networking support was Fred van Kempen <waltje@uwalt.nl.mugnet.org>. After a period of some uncertainty following Ross's resignation from the lead developer position Fred offered his time and effort and accepted the role essentially unopposed. Fred had some ambitious plans for the direction that he wanted to take the Linux networking software and he set about progressing in those directions. Fred produced a series of networking code called the 'NET-2' kernel code (the 'NET' code being Ross's) which many people were able to use pretty much usefully. Fred formally put a number of innovations on the development agenda, such as the dynamic device interface, Amateur Radio AX.25 protocol support and a more modularly designed networking implementation. Fred's NET-2 code was used by a fairly large number of enthusiasts, the number increasing all the time as word spread that the software was working. The networking software at this time was still a large number of patches to the standard release of kernel code and was not included in the normal release. The NET-FAQ and subsequent NET-2-HOWTO's described the then fairly complex procedure to get it all working. Fred's focus was on developing innovations to the standard network implementations and this was taking time. The community of users was growing impatient for something that worked reliably and satisfied the 80% of users and, as with Ross, the pressure on Fred as lead developer rose.

Alan Cox <iialan@www.uk.linux.org> proposed a solution to the problem designed to resolve the situation. He proposed that he would take Fred's NET-2 code and debug it, making it reliable and stable so that it would satisfy the impatient user base while relieving that pressure from Fred allowing him to continue his work. Alan set about doing this, with some good success and his first version of Linux networking code was called 'Net-2D(ebugged)'. The code worked reliably in many typical configurations and the user base was happy. Alan clearly had ideas and skills of his own to contribute to the project and many discussions relating to the direction the NET-2 code was heading ensued. There developed two distinct schools within the Linux networking community, one that had the philosophy of 'make it work first, then make it better' and the other of 'make it better first'. Linus ultimately arbitrated and offered his support to Alan's development efforts and included Alan's code in the standard kernel source distribution. This placed Fred in a difficult position. Any continued development would lack the large user base actively using and testing the code and this would mean progress would be slow and difficult. Fred continued to work for a short time and eventually stood down and Alan came to be the new leader of the Linux networking kernel development effort.

Donald Becker <becker@cesdis.gsfc.nasa.gov> soon revealed his talents in the low level aspects of networking and produced a huge range of ethernet drivers, nearly all of those included in the current kernels were developed by Donald. There have been other people that have made significant contributions, but Donald's work is prolific and so warrants special mention.

Alan continued refining the NET-2-Debugged code for some time while working on progressing some of the matters that remained unaddressed on the 'TODO' list. By the time the Linux 1.3.* kernel source had grown its teeth the kernel networking code had migrated to the NET-3 release on which current versions are based. Alan worked on many different aspects of the networking code and with the assistance of a range of other talented people from the Linux networking community grew the code in all sorts of directions. Alan produced dynamic network devices and the first standard AX.25 and IPX implementations. Alan has continued tinkering with the code, slowly restructuring and enhancing it to the state it is in today.

PPP support was added by Michael Callahan <callahan@maths.ox.ac.uk> and Al Longyear <longyear@netcom.com> this too was critical to increasing the number of people actively using linux for networking.

Jonathon Naylor <jsn@cs.nott.ac.uk> has contributed by significantly enhancing Alan's AX.25 code, adding NetRom and Rose protocol support. The AX.25/NetRom/Rose support itself is quite significant, because no other operating system can boast standard native support for these protocols beside Linux.

There have of course been hundreds of other people who have made significant contribution to the development of the Linux networking software. Some of these you will encounter later in the technology specific sections, other people have contributed modules, drivers, bug-fixes, suggestions, test reports and moral support. In all cases each can claim to have played a part and offered what they could. The Linux kernel networking code is an excellent example of the results that can be obtained from the Linux style of anarchic development, if it hasn't yet surprised you, it is bound to soon enough, the development hasn't stopped.

4.2 Where to get other information about Linux Networking.

There are a number of places where you can find good information about Linux networking.

Alan Cox, the current maintainer of the Linux kernel networking code maintains a world wide web page that contains highlights of current and new developments in linux Networking at: *www.uk.linux.org* <http://www.uk.linux.org/NetNews.html>.

Another good place is a book written by Olaf Kirch entitled the Network Administrators Guide. It is a work of the *Linux Documentation Project* <http://sunsite.unc.edu/LDP/> and you can read it interactively at *Network Administrators Guide HTML version* <http://sunsite.unc.edu/LDP/LDP/nag/nag.html> or you can obtain it in various formats by ftp from the *sunsite.unc.edu LDP ftp archive* <ftp://sunsite.unc.edu/pub/Linux/docs/LDP/network-guide/>. Olaf's book is quite comprehensive and provides a good high level overview of network configuration under linux.

There is a newsgroup in the Linux news hierarchy dedicated to networking and related matters, it is: *comp.os.linux.networking* <news:comp.os.linux.networking>

There is a mailing list to which you can subscribe where you may ask questions relating to Linux networking. To subscribe you should send a mail message:

```
To: majordomo@vger.rutgers.edu
Subject: anything at all
Message:
```

```
subscribe linux-net
```

On the various IRC networks there are often #linux channels on which people will be able to answer questions on linux networking.

Please remember when reporting any problem to include as much relevant detail about the problem as you can. Specifically you should specify the versions of software that you are using, especially the kernel version, the version of tools such as *pppd* or *dip* and the exact nature of the problem you are experiencing. This means taking note of the exact syntax of any error messages you receive and of any commands that you are issuing.

4.3 Where to get some non-linux-specific network information.

If you are after some basic tutorial information on tcp/ip networking generally, then I recommend you take a look at the following documents:

tcp/ip introduction

> this document comes as both a *text version* <ftp://athos.rutgers.edu/runet/tcp-ip-intro.doc> and a *postscript version* <ftp://athos.rutgers.edu/runet/tcp-ip-intro.ps>.

tcp/ip administration

> this document comes as both a *text version* <ftp://athos.rutgers.edu/runet/tcp-ip-admin.doc> and a *postscript version* <ftp://athos.rutgers.edu/runet/tcp-ip-admin.ps>.

If you are after some more detailed information on tcp/ip networking then I highly recommend:

> *Internetworking with TCP/IP, Volume 1: principles, protocols and architecture*, by Douglas E. Comer, ISBN 0-13-227836-7, Prentice Hall publications, Third Edition, 1995.

If you are wanting to learn about how to write network applications in a Unix compatible environment then I also highly recommend:

> *Unix Network Programming*, by W. Richard Stevens, ISBN 0-13-949876-1, Prentice Hall publications, 1990.

A second edition of this book is appearing on the bookshelves; the new book is made up of three volumes: check *Prenice-Hall's web site* <http://www.phptr.com/> to probe further.

You might also try the *comp.protocols.tcp-ip* <news:comp.protocols.tcp-ip> newsgroup.

An important source of specific technical information relating to the Internet and the tcp/ip suite of protocols are RFC's. RFC is an acronym for 'Request For Comment' and is the standard means of submitting and documenting Internet protocol standards. There are many RFC repositories. Many of these sites are ftp sites and other provide World Wide Web access with an associated search engine that allows you to search the RFC database for particular keywords.

One possible source for RFC's is at *Nexor RFC database* <http://pubweb.nexor.co.uk/public/rfc/index/rfc.html>.

5 Generic Network Configuration Information.

The following subsections you will pretty much need to know and understand before you actually try to configure your network. They are fundamental principles that apply regardless of the exact nature of the network you wish to deploy.

5.1 What do I need to start ?

Before you start building or configuring your network you will need some things. The most important of these are:

HOWTO

5.1.1 Current Kernel source.

Because the kernel you are running now might not yet have support for the network types or cards that you wish to use you will probably need the kernel source so that you can recompile the kernel with the appropriate options.

You can always obtain the latest kernel source from *ftp.kernel.org* `<ftp://ftp.kernel.org/pub/linux/kernel>`. Please remember that ftp.kernel.org is seriously overloaded: the preferred way to get current sources is by downloading patches instead of whole tar files; moreover, you should first try to reach mirrors of the main ftp site, like *ftp.funet.fi* `<ftp://ftp.funet.fi//mirrors/ftp.kernel.org/pub/linux/kernel>`; also remember that every Linux site usually carries updated kernel sources).

Normally the kernel source will be untarred into the `/usr/src/linux` directory. For information on how to apply patches and build the kernel you should read the *Kernel-HOWTO* `<Kernel-HOWTO.html>`. For information on how to configure kernel modules you should read the "Modules mini-HOWTO". Also, the `README` file found in the kernel sources and the `Documentation` directory are very informative for the brave reader.

Unless specifically stated otherwise, I recommend you stick with the standard kernel release (the one with the even number as the second digit in the version number). Development release kernels (the ones with the odd second digit) may have structural or other changes that may cause problems working with the other software on your system. If you are uncertain that you could resolve those sorts of problems in addition to the potential for there being other software errors, then don't use them.

On the other hand, some of the features described here have been introduced during the development of 2.1 kernels, so you must take your choice: you can stick to 2.0 while wait for 2.2 and an updated distribution with every new tool, or you can get 2.1 and look around for the various support programs needed to exploit the new features. As I write this paragraph, in August 1998, 2.1.115 is current and 2.2 is expected to appear pretty soon.

5.1.2 Current Network tools.

The network tools are the programs that you use to configure linux network devices. These tools allow you to assign addresses to devices and configure routes for example.

Most modern linux distributions are supplied with the network tools, so if you have installed from a distribution and haven't yet installed the network tools then you should do so.

If you haven't installed from a distribution then you will need to source and compile the tools yourself. This isn't difficult.

The network tools are now maintained by Bernd Eckenfels and are available at: *ftp.inka.de* `<ftp://ftp.inka.de/pub/comp/Linux/networking/NetTools/>` and are mirrored at: *ftp.uk.linux.org* `<ftp://ftp.uk.linux.org/pub/linux/Networking/base/>`.

Be sure to choose the version that is most appropriate for the kernel you wish to use and follow the instructions in the package to install.

To install and configure the version current at the time of the writing you need do the following:

```
user% tar xvfz net-tools-1.33.tar.gz
user% cd net-tools-1.33
user% make config
user% make
root# make install
```

Additionally, if you intend configuring a firewall or using the IP masquerade feature you will require the *ipfwadm* command. The latest version of it may be obtained from: *ftp.xos.nl* `<ftp:ftp.xos.nl/pub/linux/ipfwadm>`. Again there are a number of versions available. Be sure to pick the version that most closely matches your kernel. Note that the firewalling features of Linux changed during 2.1 development. This only applies to version 2.0 of the kernel.

To install and configure the version current at the time of the writing you need do the following:

```
user% tar xvfz ipfwadm-2.3.0.tar.gz
user% cd ipfwadm-2.3.0
user% make
root# make install
```

Note that if you run version 2.2 (or late 2.1) of the kernel, *ipfwadm* is not the right tool to configure firewalling. This version of the NET-3-HOWTO currently doesn't deal with the new firewalling setup.

5.1.3 Network Application Programs.

The network application programs are programs such as *telnet* and *ftp* and their respective server programs. David Holland has been managing a distribution of the most common of these, which is now maintained by net-bug@ftp.uk.linux.org. You may obtain the distribution from: *ftp.uk.linux.org* <ftp://ftp.uk.linux.org/pub/linux/Networking/base>.

In March 1997 the package has been split to several smaller packages, but in May 1997 the most basic programs has been merged into a package called netkit-base-0.10. You might need to get the base package and/or additional packages.

To install and configure the version current at the time of the writing you need do the following:

```
user% tar xvfz netkit-base-0.10
user% cd netkit-base-0.10
user% more README
user% vi MCONFIG
user% make
root# make install
```

5.1.4 Addresses.

Internet Protocol Addresses are composed of four bytes. The convention is to write addresses in what is called 'dotted decimal notation'. In this form each byte is converted to a decimal number (0-255) dropping any leading zero's unless the number is zero and written with each byte separated by a '.' character. By convention each interface of a host or router has an IP address. It is legal for the same IP address to be used on each interface of a single machine in some circumstances but usually each interface will have its own address.

Internet Protocol Networks are contiguous sequences of IP addresses. All addresses within a network have a number of digits within the address in common. The portion of the address that is common amongst all addresses within the network is called the 'network portion' of the address. The remaining digits are called the 'host portion'. The number of bits that are shared by all addresses within a network is called the netmask and it is role of the netmask to determine which addresses belong to the network it is applied to and which don't. For example, consider the following:

```
-----------------    ---------------
Host Address         192.168.110.23
Network Mask         255.255.255.0
Network Portion      192.168.110.
Host portion                    .23
-----------------    ---------------
Network Address      192.168.110.0
Broadcast Address    192.168.110.255
-----------------    ---------------
```

Any address that is 'bitwise anded' with its netmask will reveal the address of the network it belongs to. The network address is therefore always the lowest numbered address within the range of addresses on the network and always has the host portion of the address coded all zeroes.

The broadcast address is a special address that every host on the network listens to in addition to its own unique address. This address is the one that datagrams are sent to if every host on the network is meant to receive it. Certain types of data like routing information and warning messages are transmitted to the broadcast address so that every host on the network can receive it simultaneously. There are two commonly used standards for what the broadcast address should be. The most widely accepted one is to use the highest possible address on the network as the broadcast address. In the example above this would be 192.168.110.255. For some reason other sites have adopted the convention of using the network address as the broadcast address. In practice it doesn't matter very much which you use but you must make sure that every host on the network is configured with the same broadcast address.

For administrative reasons some time early in the development of the IP protocol some arbitrary groups of addresses were formed into networks and these networks were grouped into what are called classes. These classes provide a number of standard size networks that could be allocated. The ranges allocated are:

```
-------------------------------------------------------------
| Network | Netmask       | Network Addresses               |
| Class   |               |                                 |
-------------------------------------------------------------
|    A    | 255.0.0.0     | 0.0.0.0   - 127.255.255.255     |
|    B    | 255.255.0.0   | 128.0.0.0 - 191.255.255.255     |
|    C    | 255.255.255.0 | 192.0.0.0 - 223.255.255.255     |
|Multicast| 240.0.0.0     | 224.0.0.0 - 239.255.255.255     |
-------------------------------------------------------------
```

What addresses you should use depends on exactly what it is that you are doing. You may have to use a combination of the following activities to get all the addresses you need:

Installing a linux machine on an existing IP network

If you wish to install a linux machine onto an existing IP network then you should contact whoever administers the network and ask them for the following information:

- Host IP Address
- IP network address
- IP broadcast address
- IP netmask
- Router address
- Domain Name Server Address

You should then configure your linux network device with those details. You can not make them up and expect your configuration to work.

Building a brand new network that will never connect to the Internet

If you are building a private network and you never intend that network to be connected to the Internet then you can choose whatever addresses you like. However, for safety and consistency reasons there have been some IP network addresses that have been reserved specifically for this purpose. These are specified in RFC1597 and are as follows:

```
-------------------------------------------------------------
|            RESERVED PRIVATE NETWORK ALLOCATIONS           |
-------------------------------------------------------------
| Network | Netmask      | Network Addresses                |
| Class   |              |                                  |
```

```
-------------------------------------------------------------
|     A      |  255.0.0.0      | 10.0.0.0     -  10.255.255.255   |
|     B      |  255.255.0.0    | 172.16.0.0   -  172.31.255.255   |
|     C      |  255.255.255.0  | 192.168.0.0  -  192.168.255.255  |
-------------------------------------------------------------
```

You should first decide how large you want your network to be and then choose as many of the addresses as you require.

5.2   Where should I put the configuration commands ?

There are a few different approaches to Linux system boot procedures. After the kernel boots, it always executes a program called '*init*'. The *init* program then reads its configuration file called /etc/inittab and commences the boot process. There are a few different flavours of *init* around, although everyone is now converging to the System V (Five) flavour, developed by Miguel van Smoorenburg.

Despite the fact that the *init* program is always the same, the setup of system boot is organized in a different way by each distribution.

Usually the /etc/inittab file contains an entry looking something like:

```
si::sysinit:/etc/init.d/boot
```

This line specifies the name of the shell script file that actually manages the boot sequence. This file is somewhat equivalent to the AUTOEXEC.BAT file in MS-DOS.

There are usually other scripts that are called by the boot script and often the network is configured within one of many of these.

The following table may be used as a guide for your system:

```
-----------------------------------------------------------------------
Distrib. | Interface Config/Routing        | Server Initialization
-----------------------------------------------------------------------
Debian   | /etc/init.d/network             | /etc/rc2.d/*
-----------------------------------------------------------------------
Slackware| /etc/rc.d/rc.inet1              | /etc/rc.d/rc.inet2
-----------------------------------------------------------------------
RedHat   | /etc/rc.d/init.d/network        | /etc/rc.d/rc3.d/*
-----------------------------------------------------------------------
```

Note that Debian and Red Hat use a whole directory to host scripts that fire up system services (and usually information does not lie within these files, for example Red Hat systems store all of system configuration in files under /etc/sysconfig, whence it is retrieved by boot scripts). If you want to grasp the details of the boot process, my suggestion is to check */etc/inittab* and the documentation that accompanies *init*. Linux Journal is also going to publish an article about system initialization, and this document will point to it as soon as it is available on the web.

Most modern distributions include a program that will allow you to configure many of the common sorts of network interfaces. If you have one of these then you should see if it will do what you want before attempting a manual configuration.

```
------------------------------------------------
Distrib  | Network configuration program
------------------------------------------------
RedHat   | /usr/bin/netcfg
Slackware | /sbin/netconfig
```

HOWTO

5.3   Creating your network interfaces.

In many Unix operating systems the network devices have appearances in the */dev* directory. This is not so in Linux. In Linux the network devices are created dynamically in software and do not require device files to be present.

In the majority of cases the network device is automatically created by the device driver while it is initializing and has located your hardware. For example, the ethernet device driver creates `eth[0..n]` interfaces sequentially as it locates your ethernet hardware. The first ethernet card found becomes `eth0`, the second `eth1` etc.

In some cases though, notably *slip* and *ppp*, the network devices are created through the action of some user program. The same sequential device numbering applies, but the devices are not created automatically at boot time. The reason for this is that unlike ethernet devices, the number of active *slip* or *ppp* devices may vary during the uptime of the machine. These cases will be covered in more detail in later sections.

5.4   Configuring a network interface.

When you have all of the programs you need and your address and network information you can configure your network interfaces. When we talk about configuring a network interface we are talking about the process of assigning appropriate addresses to a network device and to setting appropriate values for other configurable parameters of a network device. The program most commonly used to do this is the *ifconfig* (interface configure) command.

Typically you would use a command similar to the following:

```
root# ifconfig eth0 192.168.0.1 netmask 255.255.255.0 up
```

In this case I'm configuring an ethernet interface 'eth0' with the IP address '192.168.0.1' and a network mask of '255.255.255.0'. The '*up*' that trails the command tells the interface that it should become active, but can usually be omitted, as it is the default. To shutdown an interface, you can just call "`ifconfig eth0 down`".

The kernel assumes certain defaults when configuring interfaces. For example, you may specify the network address and broadcast address for an interface, but if you don't, as in my example above, then the kernel will make reasonable guesses as to what they should be based on the netmask you supply and if you don't supply a netmask then on the network class of the IP address configured. In my example the kernel would assume that it is a class-C network being configured on the interface and configure a network address of '192.168.0.0' and a broadcast address of '192.168.0.255' for the interface.

There are many other options to the *ifconfig* command. The most important of these are:

up

    this option activates an interface (and is the default).

down

    this option deactivates an interface.

[- arp]

    this option enables or disables use of the address resolution protocol on this interface

[- allmulti]

    this option enables or disables the reception of all hardware multicast packets. Hardware multicast enables groups of hosts to receive packets addressed to special destinations. This may be of importance if you are using applications like desktop videoconferencing but is normally not used.

mtu N

    this parameter allows you to set the *MTU* of this device.

netmask <addr>

> this parameter allows you to set the network mask of the network this device belongs to.

irq <addr>

> this parameter only works on certain types of hardware and allows you to set the IRQ of the hardware of this device.

[- broadcast [addr]]

> this parameter allows you to enable and set the accepting of datagrams destined to the broadcast address, or to disable reception of these datagrams.

[- pointopoint [addr]]

> this parameter allows you to set the address of the machine at the remote end of a point to point link such as for *slip* or *ppp*.

hw <type> <addr>

> this parameter allows you to set the hardware address of certain types of network devices. This is not often useful for ethernet, but is useful for other network types such as AX.25.

You may use the *ifconfig* command on any network interface. Some user programs such as *pppd* and *dip* automatically configure the network devices as they create them, so manual use of *ifconfig* is unnecessary.

5.5   Configuring your Name Resolver.

The '*Name Resolver*' is a part of the linux standard library. Its prime function is to provide a service to convert human-friendly hostnames like '`ftp.funet.fi`' into machine friendly IP addresses such as `128.214.248.6`.

5.5.1   What's in a name ?

You will probably be familiar with the appearance of Internet host names, but may not understand how they are constructed, or deconstructed. Internet domain names are hierarchical in nature, that is, they have a tree-like structure. A '*domain*' is a family, or group of names. A '*domain*' may be broken down into '*subdomain*'. A '*toplevel domain*' is a domain that is not a subdomain. The Top Level Domains are specified in RFC-920. Some examples of the most common top level domains are:

COM

> Commercial Organizations

EDU

> Educational Organizations

GOV

> Government Organizations

MIL

> Military Organizations

ORG

> Other organizations

NET

> Internet-Related Organizations

Country Designator

> these are two letters codes that represent a particular country.

For historical reasons most domains belonging to one of the non-country based top level domains were used by organizations within the United States, although the United States also has its own country code '`.us`'. This is not true any more for `.com` and `.org` domains, which are commonly used by non-us companies.

HOWTO

Each of these top level domains has subdomains. The top level domains based on country name are often next broken down into subdomains based on the `com`, `edu`, `gov`, `mil` and `org` domains. So for example you end up with: `com.au` and `gov.au` for commercial and government organizations in Australia; note that this is not a general rule, as actual policies depend on the naming authority for each domain.

The next level of division usually represents the name of the organization. Further subdomains vary in nature, often the next level of subdomain is based on the departmental structure of the organization but it may be based on any criterion considered reasonable and meaningful by the network administrators for the organization.

The very left-most portion of the name is always the unique name assigned to the host machine and is called the '*hostname*', the portion of the name to the right of the hostname is called the '*domainname*' and the complete name is called the '*Fully Qualified Domain Name*'.

To use Terry's host as an example, the fully qualified domain name is '`perf.no.itg.telstra.com.au`'. This means that the host name is '`perf`' and the domain name is '`no.itg.telstra.com.au`'. The domain name is based on a top level domain based on his country, Australia and as his email address belongs to a commercial organization, '`.com`' is there as the next level domain. The name of the company is (was) '`telstra`' and their internal naming structure is based on organizational structure, in this case the machine belongs to the Information Technology Group, Network Operations section.

Usually, the names are fairly shorter; for example, my ISP is called "`systemy.it`" and my non-profit organization is called "`linux.it`", without any `com` and `org` subdomain, so that my own host is just called "`morgana.systemy.it`" and `rubini@linux.it` is a valid email address. Note that the owner of a domain has the rights to register hostnames as well as subdomains; for example, the LUG I belong to uses the domain `pluto.linux.it`, because the owners of `linux.it` agreed to open a subdomain for the LUG.

5.5.2 What information you will need.

You will need to know what domain your hosts name will belong to. The name resolver software provides this name translation service by making requests to a '*Domain Name Server*', so you will need to know the IP address of a local nameserver that you can use.

There are three files you need to edit, I'll cover each of these in turn.

5.5.3 /etc/resolv.conf

The `/etc/resolv.conf` is the main configuration file for the name resolver code. Its format is quite simple. It is a text file with one keyword per line. There are three keywords typically used, they are:

domain
> this keyword specifies the local domain name.

search
> this keyword specifies a list of alternate domain names to search for a hostname

nameserver
> this keyword, which may be used many times, specifies an IP address of a domain name server to query when resolving names

An example `/etc/resolv.conf` might look something like:

```
domain maths.wu.edu.au
search maths.wu.edu.au wu.edu.au
nameserver 192.168.10.1
nameserver 192.168.12.1
```

This example specifies that the default domain name to append to unqualified names (ie hostnames supplied without a domain) is `maths.wu.edu.au` and that if the host is not found in that domain to also try the `wu.edu.au` domain directly. Two nameservers entry are supplied, each of which may be called upon by the name resolver code to resolve the name.

5.5.4   /etc/host.conf

The `/etc/host.conf` file is where you configure some items that govern the behaviour of the name resolver code. The format of this file is described in detail in the '`resolv+`' man page. In nearly all circumstances the following example will work for you:

```
order hosts,bind
multi on
```

This configuration tells the name resolver to check the `/etc/hosts` file before attempting to query a nameserver and to return all valid addresses for a host found in the `/etc/hosts` file instead of just the first.

5.5.5   /etc/hosts

The `/etc/hosts` file is where you put the name and IP address of local hosts. If you place a host in this file then you do not need to query the domain name server to get its IP Address. The disadvantage of doing this is that you must keep this file up to date yourself if the IP address for that host changes. In a well managed system the only hostnames that usually appear in this file are an entry for the loopback interface and the local hosts name.

```
# /etc/hosts
127.0.0.1        localhost loopback
192.168.0.1      this.host.name
```

You may specify more than one host name per line as demonstrated by the first entry, which is a standard entry for the loopback interface.

5.5.6   Running a name server

If you want to run a local nameserver, you can do it easily. Please refer to the *DNS-HOWTO* `<DNS-HOWTO.html>` and to any documents included in your version of *BIND* (Berkeley Internet Name Domain).

5.6   Configuring your loopback interface.

The '`loopback`' interface is a special type of interface that allows you to make connections to yourself. There are various reasons why you might want to do this, for example, you may wish to test some network software without interfering with anybody else on your network. By convention the IP address '`127.0.0.1`' has been assigned specifically for loopback. So no matter what machine you go to, if you open a telnet connection to `127.0.0.1` you will always reach the local host.

Configuring the loopback interface is simple and you should ensure you do (but note that this task is usually performed by the standard initialization scripts).

```
root# ifconfig lo 127.0.0.1
root# route add -host 127.0.0.1 lo
```

We'll talk more about the *route* command in the next section.

5.7 Routing.

Routing is a big topic. It is easily possible to write large volumes of text about it. Most of you will have fairly simple routing requirements, some of you will not. I will cover some basic fundamentals of routing only. If you are interested in more detailed information then I suggest you refer to the references provided at the start of the document.

Let's start with a definition. What is IP routing ? Here is one that I'm using:

> IP Routing is the process by which a host with multiple network connections decides where to deliver IP datagrams it has received.

It might be useful to illustrate this with an example. Imagine a typical office router, it might have a PPP link off the Internet, a number of ethernet segments feeding the workstations and another PPP link off to another office. When the router receives a datagram on any of its network connections, routing is the mechanism that it uses to determine which interface it should send the datagram to next. Simple hosts also need to route, all Internet hosts have two network devices, one is the loopback interface described above and the other is the one it uses to talk to the rest of the network, perhaps an ethernet, perhaps a PPP or SLIP serial interface.

Ok, so how does routing work ? Each host keeps a special list of routing rules, called a routing table. This table contains rows which typically contain at least three fields, the first is a destination address, the second is the name of the interface to which the datagram is to be routed and the third is optionally the IP address of another machine which will carry the datagram on its next step through the network. In linux you can see this table by using the following command:

```
user% cat /proc/net/route
```

or by using either of the following commands:

```
user% /sbin/route -n
user% netstat -r
```

The routing process is fairly simple: an incoming datagram is received, the destination address (who it is for) is examined and compared with each entry in the table. The entry that best matches that address is selected and the datagram is forwarded to the specified interface. If the gateway field is filled then the datagram is forwarded to that host via the specified interface, otherwise the destination address is assumed to be on the network supported by the interface.

To manipulate this table a special command is used. This command takes command line arguments and converts them into kernel system calls that request the kernel to add, delete or modify entries in the routing table. The command is called 'route'.

A simple example. Imagine you have an ethernet network. You've been told it is a class-C network with an address of 192.168.1.0. You've been supplied with an IP address of 192.168.1.10 for your use and have been told that 192.168.1.1 is a router connected to the Internet.

The first step is to configure the interface as described earlier. You would use a command like:

```
root# ifconfig eth0 192.168.1.10 netmask 255.255.255.0 up
```

You now need to add an entry into the routing table to tell the kernel that datagrams for all hosts with addresses that match 192.168.1.* should be sent to the ethernet device. You would use a command similar to:

```
root# route add -net 192.168.1.0 netmask 255.255.255.0 eth0
```

Note the use of the '-net' argument to tell the route program that this entry is a network route. Your other choice here is a '-host' route which is a route that is specific to one IP address.

This route will enable you to establish IP connections with all of the hosts on your ethernet segment. But what about all of the IP hosts that aren't on your ethernet segment ?

It would be a very difficult job to have to add routes to every possible destination network, so there is a special trick that is used to simplify this task. The trick is called the 'default' route. The default route matches every possible destination, but poorly, so that if any other entry exists that matches the required address it will be used instead of the default route. The idea of the default route is simply to enable you to say "and everything else should go here". In the example I've contrived you would use an entry like:

```
root# route add default gw 192.168.1.1 eth0
```

The 'gw' argument tells the route command that the next argument is the IP address, or name, of a gateway or router machine which all datagrams matching this entry should be directed to for further routing.

So, your complete configuration would look like:

```
root# ifconfig eth0 192.168.1.10 netmask 255.255.255.0 up
root# route add -net 192.168.1.0 netmask 255.255.255.0 eth0
root# route add default gw 192.168.1.1 eth0
```

If you take a close look at your network 'rc' files you will find that at least one of them looks very similar to this. This is a very common configuration.

Let's now look at a slightly more complicated routing configuration. Let's imagine we are configuring the router we looked at earlier, the one supporting the PPP link to the Internet and the lan segments feeding the workstations in the office. Lets imagine the router has three ethernet segments and one PPP link. Our routing configuration would look something like:

```
root# route add -net 192.168.1.0 netmask 255.255.255.0 eth0
root# route add -net 192.168.2.0 netmask 255.255.255.0 eth1
root# route add -net 192.168.3.0 netmask 255.255.255.0 eth2
root# route add default ppp0
```

Each of the workstations would use the simpler form presented above, only the router needs to specify each of the network routes separately because for the workstations the default route mechanism will capture all of them letting the router worry about splitting them up appropriately. You may be wondering why the default route presented doesn't specify a 'gw'. The reason for this is simple, serial link protocols such as PPP and slip only ever have two hosts on their network, one at each end. To specify the host at the other end of the link as the gateway is pointless and redundant as there is no other choice, so you do not need to specify a gateway for these types of network connections. Other network types such as ethernet, arcnet or token ring do require the gateway to be specified as these networks support large numbers of hosts on them.

5.7.1 So what does the *routed* program do ?

The routing configuration described above is best suited to simple network arrangements where there are only ever single possible paths to destinations. When you have a more complex network arrangement things get a little more complicated. Fortunately for most of you this won't be an issue.

The big problem with 'manual routing' or 'static routing' as described, is that if a machine or link fails in your network then the only way you can direct your datagrams another way, if another way exists, is by manually intervening and executing the appropriate commands. Naturally this is clumsy, slow, impractical and hazard prone. Various techniques have been developed to automatically adjust routing tables in the event of network failures where there are alternate routes, all of these techniques are loosely grouped by the term 'dynamic routing protocols'.

You may have heard of some of the more common dynamic routing protocols. The most common are probably RIP (Routing Information Protocol) and OSPF (Open Shortest Path First Protocol). The Routing Information Protocol is very common on small networks such as small-medium sized corporate networks or building networks. OSPF is more modern and more capable at handling large network configurations and better suited to environments where there is a large number of possible paths through the network. Common implementations of these protocols are: '*routed*' - RIP and '*gated*' - RIP, OSPF and others. The '*routed*' program is normally supplied with your Linux distribution or is included in the 'NetKit' package detailed above.

An example of where and how you might use a dynamic routing protocol might look something like the following:

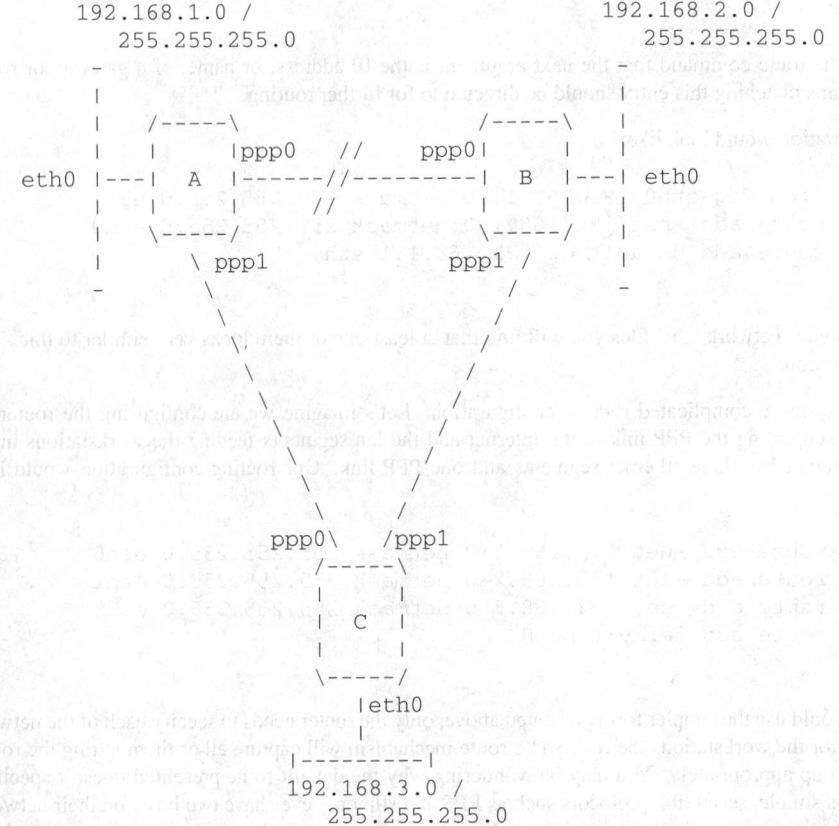

We have three routers A, B and C. Each supports one ethernet segment with a Class C IP network (netmask 255.255.255.0). Each router also has a PPP link to each of the other routers. The network forms a triangle.

It should be clear that the routing table at router A could look like:

```
root# route add -net 192.168.1.0 netmask 255.255.255.0 eth0
root# route add -net 192.168.2.0 netmask 255.255.255.0 ppp0
root# route add -net 192.168.3.0 netmask 255.255.255.0 ppp1
```

This would work just fine until the link between router A and B should fail. If that link failed then with the routing entry shown above hosts on the ethernet segment of A could not reach hosts on the ethernet segment on B because their datagram would be directed to router A's ppp0 link which is broken. They could still continue to talk to hosts on the ethernet segment of C and hosts on the C's ethernet segment could still talk to hosts on B's ethernet segment because the link between B and C is still intact.

But wait, if A can talk to C and C can still talk to B, why shouldn't A route its datagrams for B via C and let C send them to B ? This is exactly the sort of problem that dynamic routing protocols like RIP were designed to solve. If each of the routers A, B and C were running a routing daemon then their routing tables would be automatically adjusted to reflect the new state of the network should any one of the links in the network fail. To configure such a network is simple, at each router you need only do two things. In this case for Router A:

```
root# route add -net 192.168.1.0 netmask 255.255.255.0 eth0
root# /usr/sbin/routed
```

The '*routed*' routing daemon automatically finds all active network ports when it starts and sends and listens for messages on each of the network devices to allow it to determine and update the routing table on the host.

This has been a very brief explanation of dynamic routing and where you would use it. If you want more information then you should refer to the suggested references listed at the top of the document.

The important points relating to dynamic routing are:

1. You only need to run a dynamic routing protocol daemon when your Linux machine has the possibility of selecting multiple possible routes to a destination.

2. The dynamic routing daemon will automatically modify your routing table to adjust to changes in your network.

3. RIP is suited to small to medium sized networks.

5.8 Configuring your network servers and services.

Network servers and services are those programs that allow a remote user to make user of your Linux machine. Server programs listen on network ports. Network ports are a means of addressing a particular service on any particular host and are how a server knows the difference between an incoming telnet connection and an incoming ftp connection. The remote user establishes a network connection to your machine and the server program, the network daemon program, listening on that port accepts the connection and executes. There are two ways that network daemons may operate. Both are commonly employed in practice. The two ways are:

standalone

the network daemon program listens on the designated network port and when an incoming connection is made it manages the network connection itself to provide the service.

slave to the *inetd* server

the *inetd* server is a special network daemon program that specializes in managing incoming network connections. It has a configuration file which tells it what program needs to be run when an incoming connection is received. Any service port may be configured for either of the tcp or udp protcols. The ports are described in another file that we will talk about soon.

There are two important files that we need to configure. They are the /etc/services file which assigns names to port numbers and the /etc/inetd.conf file which is the configuration file for the *inetd* network daemon.

5.8.1 /etc/services

The /etc/services file is a simple database that associates a human friendly name to a machine friendly service port. Its format is quite simple. The file is a text file with each line representing and entry in the database. Each entry is comprised of three fields separated by any number of whitespace (tab or space) characters. The fields are:

HOWTO

```
name            port/protocol      aliases        # comment
```

name

a single word name that represents the service being described.

port/protocol

this field is split into two subfields.

port

a number that specifies the port number the named service will be available on. Most of the common services have assigned service numbers. These are described in `RFC-1340`.

protocol

this subfield may be set to either `tcp` or `udp`.

It is important to note that an entry of `18/tcp` is very different from an entry of `18/udp` and that there is no technical reason why the same service needs to exist on both. Normally common sense prevails and it is only if a particular service is available via both `tcp` and `udp` that you will see an entry for both.

aliases

other names that may be used to refer to this service entry.

Any text appearing in a line after a '#' character is ignored and treated as a comment.

An example `/etc/services` file. All modern linux distributions provide a good `/etc/services` file. Just in case you happen to be building a machine from the ground up, here is a copy of the `/etc/services` file supplied with an old *Debian* <http://www.debian.org/> distribution:

```
# /etc/services:
# $Id: services,v 1.3 1996/05/06 21:42:37 tobias Exp $
#
# Network services, Internet style
#
# Note that it is presently the policy of IANA to assign a single well-known
# port number for both TCP and UDP; hence, most entries here have t-
wo entries
# even if the protocol doesn't support UDP operations.
# Updated from RFC 1340, ''Assigned Numbers'' (July 1992).  Not all ports
# are included, only the more common ones.

tcpmux          1/tcp                             # TCP port ser-
vice multiplexer
echo            7/tcp
echo            7/udp
discard         9/tcp           sink null
discard         9/udp           sink null
systat          11/tcp          users
daytime         13/tcp
daytime         13/udp
netstat         15/tcp
qotd            17/tcp          quote
msp             18/tcp                            # message send protocol
msp             18/udp                            # message send protocol
chargen         19/tcp          ttytst source
chargen         19/udp          ttytst source
ftp-data        20/tcp
```

```
ftp              21/tcp
ssh              22/tcp                            # SSH Remote Login Protocol
ssh              22/udp                            # SSH Remote Login Protocol
telnet           23/tcp
# 24 - private
smtp             25/tcp         mail
# 26 - unassigned
time             37/tcp         timserver
time             37/udp         timserver
rlp              39/udp         resource           # resource location
nameserver       42/tcp         name               # IEN 116
whois            43/tcp         nicname
re-mail-ck       50/tcp                            # Remote Mail Check-
ing Protocol
re-mail-ck       50/udp                            # Remote Mail Check-
ing Protocol
domain           53/tcp         nameserver         # name-domain server
domain           53/udp         nameserver
mtp              57/tcp                            # deprecated
bootps           67/tcp                            # BOOTP server
bootps           67/udp
bootpc           68/tcp                            # BOOTP client
bootpc           68/udp
tftp             69/udp
gopher           70/tcp                            # Internet Gopher
gopher           70/udp
rje              77/tcp         netrjs
finger           79/tcp
www              80/tcp         http               # WorldWideWeb HTTP
www              80/udp                            # HyperText Trans-
fer Protocol
link             87/tcp         ttylink
kerberos         88/tcp         kerberos5 krb5     # Kerberos v5
kerberos         88/udp         kerberos5 krb5     # Kerberos v5
supdup           95/tcp
# 100 - reserved
hostnames        101/tcp        hostname           # usually from sri-nic
iso-tsap         102/tcp        tsap               # part of ISODE.
csnet-ns         105/tcp        cso-ns             # also used by C-
SO name server
csnet-ns         105/udp        cso-ns
rtelnet          107/tcp                           # Remote Telnet
rtelnet          107/udp
pop-2            109/tcp        postoffice         # POP version 2
pop-2            109/udp
pop-3            110/tcp                           # POP version 3
pop-3            110/udp
sunrpc           111/tcp        portmapper         # RPC 4.0 portmapper TCP
sunrpc           111/udp        portmapper         # RPC 4.0 portmapper UDP
auth             113/tcp        authentication tap ident
sftp             115/tcp
uucp-path        117/tcp
nntp             119/tcp        readnews untp      # USENET News Trans-
fer Protocol
ntp              123/tcp
```

HOWTO

```
ntp                123/udp                          # Network Time Protocol
netbios-ns         137/tcp                          # NETBIOS Name Service
netbios-ns         137/udp
netbios-dgm        138/tcp                          # NETBIOS Datagram Service
netbios-dgm        138/udp
netbios-ssn        139/tcp                          # NETBIOS session service
netbios-ssn        139/udp
imap2              143/tcp                          # Interim Mail Access Pro-
to v2
imap2              143/udp
snmp               161/udp                          # Simple Net Mgmt Proto
snmp-trap          162/udp       snmptrap           # Traps for SNMP
cmip-man           163/tcp                          # ISO mgmt over IP (CMOT)
cmip-man           163/udp
cmip-agent         164/tcp
cmip-agent         164/udp
xdmcp              177/tcp                          # X Display Mgr. Con-
trol Proto
xdmcp              177/udp
nextstep           178/tcp       NeXTStep NextStep       # NeXTStep window
nextstep           178/udp       NeXTStep NextStep       # server
bgp                179/tcp                          # Border Gateway Proto.
bgp                179/udp
prospero           191/tcp                          # Cliff Neuman's Prospero
prospero           191/udp
irc                194/tcp                          # Internet Relay Chat
irc                194/udp
smux               199/tcp                          # SNMP Unix Multiplexer
smux               199/udp
at-rtmp            201/tcp                          # AppleTalk routing
at-rtmp            201/udp
at-nbp             202/tcp                          # AppleTalk name binding
at-nbp             202/udp
at-echo            204/tcp                          # AppleTalk echo
at-echo            204/udp
at-zis             206/tcp                          # AppleTalk zone information
at-zis             206/udp
z3950              210/tcp       wais               # NISO Z39.50 database
z3950              210/udp       wais
ipx                213/tcp                          # IPX
ipx                213/udp
imap3              220/tcp                          # Interactive Mail Access
imap3              220/udp                          # Protocol v3
ulistserv          372/tcp                          # UNIX Listserv
ulistserv          372/udp
#
# UNIX specific services
#
exec               512/tcp
biff               512/udp       comsat
login              513/tcp
who                513/udp       whod
shell              514/tcp       cmd                # no passwords used
syslog             514/udp
printer            515/tcp       spooler            # line printer spooler
```

```
talk              517/udp
ntalk             518/udp
route             520/udp      router routed    # RIP
timed             525/udp      timeserver
tempo             526/tcp      newdate
courier           530/tcp      rpc
conference        531/tcp      chat
netnews           532/tcp      readnews
netwall           533/udp                       # -for emergency broadcasts
uucp              540/tcp      uucpd             # uucp daemon
remotefs          556/tcp      rfs_server rfs    # Brunhoff remote filesystem
klogin            543/tcp                        # Kerberized 'rlogin' (v5)
kshell            544/tcp      krcmd             # Kerberized 'rsh' (v5)
kerberos-adm      749/tcp                        # Kerberos 'kadmin' (v5)
#
webster           765/tcp                        # Network dictionary
webster           765/udp
#
# From ''Assigned Numbers'':
#
#> The Registered Ports are not controlled by the IANA and on most systems
#> can be used by ordinary user processes or programs executed by ordinary
#> users.
#
#> Ports are used in the TCP [45,106] to name the ends of logical
#> connections which carry long term conversations.  For the purpose of
#> providing services to unknown callers, a service contact port is
#> defined.  This list specifies the port used by the server process as its
#> contact port.  While the IANA can not control uses of these ports it
#> does register or list uses of these ports as a convenience to the
#> community.
#
ingreslock        1524/tcp
ingreslock        1524/udp
prospero-np       1525/tcp                       # Prospero non-privileged
prospero-np       1525/udp
rfe               5002/tcp                        # Radio Free Ethernet
rfe               5002/udp                        # Actually uses UDP only
bbs               7000/tcp                        # BBS service
#
#
# Kerberos (Project Athena/MIT) services
# Note that these are for Kerberos v4 and are unofficial.  Sites running
# v4 should uncomment these and comment out the v5 entries above.
#
kerberos4         750/udp      kdc               # Kerberos (server) udp
kerberos4         750/tcp      kdc               # Kerberos (server) tcp
kerberos_master   751/udp                        # Kerberos authentication
kerberos_master   751/tcp                        # Kerberos authentication
passwd_server     752/udp                        # Kerberos passwd server
krb_prop          754/tcp                        # Kerberos slave propagation
krbupdate         760/tcp      kreg              # Kerberos registration
kpasswd           761/tcp      kpwd              # Kerberos "passwd"
kpop              1109/tcp                        # Pop with Kerberos
knetd             2053/tcp                        # Kerberos de-multiplexor
```

```
zephyr-srv      2102/udp                # Zephyr server
zephyr-clt      2103/udp                # Zephyr serv-hm connection
zephyr-hm       2104/udp                # Zephyr hostmanager
eklogin         2105/tcp                # Kerberos encrypted rlogin
#
# Unofficial but necessary (for NetBSD) services
#
supfilesrv      871/tcp                 # SUP server
supfiledbg      1127/tcp                # SUP debugging
#
# Datagram Delivery Protocol services
#
rtmp            1/ddp                   # Routing Table Maintenance Protocol
nbp             2/ddp                   # Name Binding Protocol
echo            4/ddp                   # AppleTalk Echo Protocol
zip             6/ddp                   # Zone Information Protocol
#
# Debian GNU/Linux services
rmtcfg          1236/tcp                # Gracilis Packeten remote con-
fig server
xtel            1313/tcp                # french minitel
cfinger         2003/tcp                # GNU Finger
postgres        4321/tcp                # POSTGRES
mandelspawn     9359/udp        mandelbrot      # network mandelbrot

# Local services
```

In the real world, the actual file is always growing as new services are being created. If you fear your own copy is incomplete, I'd suggest to copy a new /etc/services from a recent distribution.

5.8.2 /etc/inetd.conf

The /etc/inetd.conf file is the configuration file for the *inetd* server daemon. Its function is to tell *inetd* what to do when it receives a connection request for a particular service. For each service that you wish to accept connections for you must tell *inetd* what network server daemon to run and how to run it.

Its format is also fairly simple. It is a text file with each line describing a service that you wish to provide. Any text in a line following a '#' is ignored and considered a comment. Each line contains seven fields separated by any number of whitespace (tab or space) characters. The general format is as follows:

```
service  socket_type  proto  flags  user  server_path  server_args
```

service

    is the service relevant to this configuration as taken from the /etc/services file.

socket_type

    this field describes the type of socket that this entry will consider relevant, allowable values are: stream, dgram, raw, rdm, or seqpacket. This is a little technical in nature, but as a rule of thumb nearly all tcp based services use stream and nearly all udp based services use dgram. It is only very special types of server daemons that would use any of the other values.

proto

    the protocol to considered valid for this entry. This should match the appropriate entry in the /etc/services file and will typically be either tcp or udp. Sun RPC (Remote Procedure Call) based servers will use rpc/tcp or rpc/udp.

flags

> there are really only two possible settings for this field. This field setting tells *inetd* whether the network server program frees the socket after it has been started and therefore whether *inetd* can start another one on the next connection request, or whether *inetd* should wait and assume that any server daemon already running will handle the new connection request. Again this is a little tricky to work out, but as a rule of thumb all `tcp` servers should have this entry set to `nowait` and most `udp` servers should have this entry set to `wait`. Be warned there are some notable exceptions to this, so let the example guide you if you are not sure.

user

> this field describes which user account from `/etc/passwd` will be set as the owner of the network daemon when it is started. This is often useful if you want to safeguard against security risks. You can set the user of an entry to the `nobody` user so that if the network server security is breached the possible damage is minimized. Typically this field is set to `root` though, because many servers require root privileges in order to function correctly.

server_path

> this field is pathname to the actual server program to execute for this entry.

server_args

> this field comprises the rest of the line and is optional. This field is where you place any command line arguments that you wish to pass to the server daemon program when it is launched.

An example `/etc/inetd.conf`   As for the `/etc/services` file all modern distributions will include a good `/etc/inetd.conf` file for you to work with. Here, for completeness is the `/etc/inetd.conf` file from the *Debian* <http://www.debian.org/> distribution.

```
# /etc/inetd.conf:  see inetd(8) for further informations.
#
# Internet server configuration database
#
#
# Modified for Debian by Peter Tobias <tobias@et-inf.fho-emden.de>
#
# <service_name> <sock_type> <proto> <flags> <user> <server_path> <args>
#
# Internal services
#
#echo           stream  tcp     nowait  root    internal
#echo           dgram   udp     wait    root    internal
discard         stream  tcp     nowait  root    internal
discard         dgram   udp     wait    root    internal
daytime         stream  tcp     nowait  root    internal
daytime         dgram   udp     wait    root    internal
#chargen        stream  tcp     nowait  root    internal
#chargen        dgram   udp     wait    root    internal
time            stream  tcp     nowait  root    internal
time            dgram   udp     wait    root    internal
#
# These are standard services.
#
telnet  stream  tcp     nowait  root    /usr/sbin/tcpd  /usr/sbin/in.telnetd
ftp     stream  tcp     nowait  root    /usr/sbin/tcpd  /usr/sbin/in.ftpd
#fsp    dgram   udp     wait    root    /usr/sbin/tcpd  /usr/sbin/in.fspd
#
# Shell, login, exec and talk are BSD protocols.
#
shell   stream  tcp     nowait  root    /usr/sbin/tcpd  /usr/sbin/in.rshd
```

```
login    stream  tcp      nowait  root   /usr/sbin/tcpd  /usr/sbin/in.rlogind
#exec    stream  tcp      nowait  root   /usr/sbin/tcpd  /usr/sbin/in.rexecd
talk     dgram   udp      wait    root   /usr/sbin/tcpd  /usr/sbin/in.talkd
ntalk    dgram   udp      wait    root   /usr/sbin/tcpd  /usr/sbin/in.ntalkd
#
# Mail, news and uucp services.
#
smtp     stream  tcp      nowait  root   /usr/sbin/tcpd  /usr/sbin/in.smtpd
#nntp    stream  tcp      nowait  news   /usr/sbin/tcpd  /usr/sbin/in.nntpd
#uucp    stream  tcp      nowait  uucp   /usr/sbin/tcpd  /usr/lib/uucp/uucico
#comsat  dgram   udp      wait    root   /usr/sbin/tcpd  /usr/sbin/in.comsat
#
# Pop et al
#
#pop-2   stream  tcp      nowait  root   /usr/sbin/tcpd  /usr/sbin/in.pop2d
#pop-3   stream  tcp      nowait  root   /usr/sbin/tcpd  /usr/sbin/in.pop3d
#
# 'cfinger' is for the GNU finger server available for Debian.
# (NOTE: The current implementation of the 'finger' daemon allows
#  it to be run as 'root'.)
#
#cfinger stream tcp      nowait  root   /usr/sbin/tcpd  /usr/sbin/in.cfingerd
#finger stream tcp       nowait  root   /usr/sbin/tcpd  /usr/sbin/in.fingerd
#netstat         stream  tcp     nowait nobody /usr/sbin/tcpd  /bin/netstat
#systat stream tcp       nowait  nobody /usr/sbin/tcpd  /bin/ps -auwwx
#
# Tftp service is provided primarily for booting.  Most sites
# run this only on machines acting as "boot servers."
#
#tftp    dgram   udp      wait    nobody /usr/sbin/tcpd  /usr/sbin/in.tftpd
#tftp    dgram   udp      wait    nobody /usr/sbin/tcpd  /us-
r/sbin/in.tftpd /boot
#bootps dgram   udp      wait    root   /usr/sbin/bootpd         bootpd -i -
t 120
#
# Kerberos authenticated services (these probably need to be corrected)
#
#klogin          stream  tcp     nowait root   /usr/sbin/tcpd  /us-
r/sbin/in.rlogind -k
#eklogin         stream  tcp     nowait root   /usr/sbin/tcpd  /us-
r/sbin/in.rlogind -k -x
#kshell          stream  tcp     nowait root   /usr/sbin/tcpd  /us-
r/sbin/in.rshd -k
#
# Services run ONLY on the Kerberos server (these proba-
bly need to be corrected)
#
#krbupdate       stream tcp      nowait root   /us-
r/sbin/tcpd  /usr/sbin/registerd
#kpasswd         stream tcp      nowait root   /us-
r/sbin/tcpd  /usr/sbin/kpasswdd
#
# RPC based services
#
#mountd/1        dgram  rpc/udp wait    root   /us-
```

```
r/sbin/tcpd  /usr/sbin/rpc.mountd
#rstatd/1-3    dgram  rpc/udp wait    root    /us-
r/sbin/tcpd  /usr/sbin/rpc.rstatd
#rusersd/2-3   dgram  rpc/udp wait    root    /us-
r/sbin/tcpd  /usr/sbin/rpc.rusersd
#walld/1       dgram  rpc/udp wait    root    /us-
r/sbin/tcpd  /usr/sbin/rpc.rwalld
#
# End of inetd.conf.
ident          stream tcp    nowait nobody /usr/sbin/identd    i-
dentd -i
```

5.9   Other miscellaneous network related configuration files.

There are a number of miscellaneous files relating to network configuration under linux that you might be interested in. You may never have to modify these files, but it is worth describing them so you know what they contain and what they are for.

5.9.1 /etc/protocols

The /etc/protocols file is a database that maps protocol id numbers against protocol names. This is used by programmers to allow them to specify protocols by name in their programs and also by some programs such as *tcpdump* to allow them to display names instead of numbers in their output. The general syntax of the file is:

```
    protocolname  number  aliases
```

The /etc/protocols file supplied with the *Debian* <http://www.debian.org/> distribution is as follows:

```
# /etc/protocols:
# $Id: protocols,v 1.1 1995/02/24 01:09:41 imurdock Exp $
#
# Internet (IP) protocols
#
#       from: @(#)protocols    5.1 (Berkeley) 4/17/89
#
# Updated for NetBSD based on RFC 1340, Assigned Numbers (July 1992).

ip      0     IP          # internet protocol, pseudo protocol number
icmp    1     ICMP        # internet control message protocol
igmp    2     IGMP        # Internet Group Management
ggp     3     GGP         # gateway-gateway protocol
ipencap 4     IP-ENCAP    # IP encapsulated in IP (officially ''IP'')
st      5     ST          # ST datagram mode
tcp     6     TCP         # transmission control protocol
egp     8     EGP         # exterior gateway protocol
pup     12    PUP         # PARC universal packet protocol
udp     17    UDP         # user datagram protocol
hmp     20    HMP         # host monitoring protocol
xns-idp 22    XNS-IDP     # Xerox NS IDP
rdp     27    RDP         # "reliable datagram" protocol
iso-tp4 29    ISO-TP4     # ISO Transport Protocol class 4
xtp     36    XTP         # Xpress Tranfer Protocol
ddp     37    DDP         # Datagram Delivery Protocol
idpr-cmtp 39      IDPR-CMTP       # IDPR Control Message Transport
```

```
rspf    73    RSPF        # Radio Shortest Path First.
vmtp    81    VMTP        # Versatile Message Transport
ospf    89    OSPFIGP     # Open Shortest Path First IGP
ipip    94    IPIP        # Yet Another IP encapsulation
encap   98    ENCAP       # Yet Another IP encapsulation
```

5.9.2 /etc/networks

The /etc/networks file has a similar function to that of the /etc/hosts file. It provides a simple database of network names against network addresses. Its format differs in that there may be only two fields per line and that the fields are coded as:

```
networkname networkaddress
```

An example might look like:

```
loopnet    127.0.0.0
localnet   192.168.0.0
amprnet    44.0.0.0
```

When you use commands like the *route* command, if a destination is a network and that network has an entry in the /etc/networks file then the route command will display that network name instead of its address.

5.10 Network Security and access control.

Let me start this section by warning you that securing your machine and network against malicious attack is a complex art. I do not consider myself an expert in this field at all and while the following mechanisms I describe will help, if you are serious about security then I recommend you do some research of your own into the subject. There are many good references on the Internet relating to the subject, including the *Security-HOWTO* <Security-HOWTO.html>

An important rule of thumb is: **'Don't run servers you don't intend to use'**. Many distributions come configured with all sorts of services configured and automatically started. To ensure even a minimum level of safety you should go through your /etc/inetd.conf file and comment out (*place a '#' at the start of the line*) any entries for services you don't intend to use. Good candidates are services such as: shell, login, exec, uucp, ftp and informational services such as finger, netstat and systat.

There are all sorts of security and access control mechanisms, I'll describe the most elementary of them.

5.10.1 /etc/ftpusers

The /etc/ftpusers file is a simple mechanism that allows you to deny certain users from logging into your machine via ftp. The /etc/ftpusers file is read by the ftp daemon program (*ftpd*) when an incoming ftp connection is received. The file is a simple list of those users who are disallowed from logging in. It might looks something like:

```
# /etc/ftpusers - users not allowed to login via ftp
root
uucp
bin
mail
```

5.10.2 /etc/securetty

The `/etc/securetty` file allows you to specify which `tty` devices `root` is allowed to login on. The `/etc/securetty` file is read by the login program (usually */bin/login*). Its format is a list of the tty devices names allowed, on all others `root` login is disallowed:

```
# /etc/securetty - tty's on which root is allowed to login
tty1
tty2
tty3
tty4
```

5.10.3 The *tcpd* hosts access control mechanism.

The *tcpd* program you will have seen listed in the same `/etc/inetd.conf` provides logging and access control mechanisms to services it is configured to protect.

When it is invoked by the *inetd* program it reads two files containing access rules and either allows or denies access to the server it is protecting accordingly.

It will search the rules files until the first match is found. If no match is found then it assumes that access should be allowed to anyone. The files it searches in sequence are: `/etc/hosts.allow`, `/etc/hosts.deny`. I'll describe each of these in turn. For a complete description of this facility you should refer to the appropriate *man* pages (`hosts_access(5)` is a good starting point).

/etc/hosts.allow The `/etc/hosts.allow` file is a configuration file of the */usr/sbin/tcpd* program. The `hosts.allow` file contains rules describing which hosts are *allowed* access to a service on your machine.

The file format is quite simple:

```
# /etc/hosts.allow
#
# <service list>: <host list> [: command]
```

service list

is a comma delimited list of server names that this rule applies to. Example server names are: `ftpd`, `telnetd` and `fingerd`.

host list

is a comma delimited list of host names. You may also use IP addresses here. You may additionally specify hostnames or addresses using wildcard characters to match groups of hosts. Examples include: `g-w.vk2ktj.ampr.org` to match a specific host, `.uts.edu.au` to match any hostname ending in that string, `44.` to match any IP address commencing with those digits. There are some special tokens to simplify configuration, some of these are: `ALL` matches every host, `LOCAL` matches any host whose name does not contain a '.' ie is in the same domain as your machine and `PARANOID` matches any host whose name does not match its address (name spoofing). There is one last token that is also useful. The `EXCEPT` token allows you to provide a list with exceptions. This will be covered in an example later.

command

is an optional parameter. This parameter is the full pathname of a command that would be executed everytime this rule is matched. It could for example run a command that would attempt to identify who is logged onto the connecting host, or to generate a mail message or some other warning to a system administrator that someone is attempting to connect. There are a number of expansions that may be included, some common examples are: `%h` expands to the name of the connecting host or address if it doesn't have a name, `%d` the daemon name being called.

An example:

```
# /etc/hosts.allow
#
# Allow mail to anyone
in.smtpd: ALL
# All telnet and ftp to only hosts within my domain and my host at home.
telnetd, ftpd: LOCAL, myhost.athome.org.au
# Allow finger to anyone but keep a record of who they are.
fingerd: ALL: (finger @%h | mail -s "finger from %h" root)
```

/etc/hosts.deny The /etc/hosts.deny file is a configuration file of the */usr/sbin/tcpd* program. The hosts.deny file contains rules describing which hosts are *disallowed* access to a service on your machine.

A simple sample would look something like this:

```
# /etc/hosts.deny
#
# Disallow all hosts with suspect hostnames
ALL: PARANOID
#
# Disallow all hosts.
ALL: ALL
```

The PARANOID entry is really redundant because the other entry traps everything in any case. Either of these entry would make a reasonable default depending on your particular requirement.

Having an ALL: ALL default in the /etc/hosts.deny and then specifically enabling on those services and hosts that you want in the /etc/hosts.allow file is the safest configuration.

5.10.4   /etc/hosts.equiv

The hosts.equiv file is used to grant certain hosts and users access rights to accounts on your machine without having to supply a password. This is useful in a secure environment where you control all machines, but is a security hazard otherwise. Your machine is only as secure as the least secure of the trusted hosts. To maximize security, don't use this mechanism and encourage your users not to use the .rhosts file as well.

5.10.5   Configure your *ftp* daemon properly.

Many sites will be interested in running an anonymous *ftp* server to allow other people to upload and download files without requiring a specific userid. If you decide to offer this facility make sure you configure the *ftp* daemon properly for anonymous access. Most *man* pages for ftpd(8) describe in some length how to go about this. You should always ensure that you follow these instructions. An important tip is to not use a copy of your /etc/passwd file in the anonymous account /etc directory, make sure you strip out all account details except those that you must have, otherwise you will be vulnerable to brute force password cracking techniques.

5.10.6   Network Firewalling.

Not allowing datagrams to even reach your machine or servers is an excellent means of security. This is covered in depth in the *Firewall-HOWTO* <Firewall-HOWTO.html>, and (more concisely) in a later section of this document.

5.10.7   Other suggestions.

Here are some other, potentially religious suggestions for you to consider.

sendmail

despite its popularity the *sendmail* daemon appears with frightening regularity on security warning announcements. Its up to you, but I choose not to run it.

NFS and other Sun RPC services

be wary of these. There are all sorts of possible exploits for these services. It is difficult finding an option to services like NFS, but if you configure them, make sure you are careful with who you allow mount rights to.

6 IP- and Ethernet-Related Information

This section covers information specific to Ethernet and IP. These subsections have been grouped together because I think they are the most interesting ones in the formerly-called "Technology Specific" Section. Anyone with a LAN should be able to benefit from these goodies.

6.1 Ethernet

Ethernet device names are 'eth0', 'eth1', 'eth2' etc. The first card detected by the kernel is assigned 'eth0' and the rest are assigned sequentially in the order they are detected.

By default, the Linux kernel only probes for one Ethernet device, you need to pass command line arguments to the kernel in order to force detection of furter boards.

To learn how to make your ethernet card(s) working under Linux you should refer to the *Ethernet-HOWTO* <Ethernet-HOWTO.html>.

Once you have your kernel properly built to support your ethernet card then configuration of the card is easy.

Typically you would use something like (which most distributions already do for you, if you configured them to support your ethernet):

```
root# ifconfig eth0 192.168.0.1 netmask 255.255.255.0 up
root# route add -net 192.168.0.0 netmask 255.255.255.0 eth0
```

Most of the ethernet drivers were developed by Donald Becker, becker@CESDIS.gsfc.nasa.gov.

6.2 EQL - multiple line traffic equaliser

The EQL device name is 'eql'. With the standard kernel source you may have only one EQL device per machine. EQL provides a means of utilizing multiple point to point lines such as PPP, slip or plip as a single logical link to carry tcp/ip. Often it is cheaper to use multiple lower speed lines than to have one high speed line installed.

Kernel Compile Options:

```
Network device support  --->
    [*] Network device support
    <*> EQL (serial line load balancing) support
```

To support this mechanism the machine at the other end of the lines must also support EQL. Linux, Livingstone Portmasters and newer dial-in servers support compatible facilities.

To configure EQL you will need the eql tools which are available from: *sunsite.unc.edu* <ftp://sunsite.unc.edu/pub/linux/system/Serial/eql-1.2.tar.gz>.

Configuration is fairly straightforward. You start by configuring the eql interface. The eql interface is just like any other network device. You configure the IP address and mtu using the *ifconfig* utility, so something like:

```
        root# ifconfig eql 192.168.10.1 mtu 1006
```

Next you need to manually initiate each of the lines you will use. These may be any combination of point to point network devices. How you initiate the connections will depend on what sort of link they are, refer to the appropriate sections for further information.

Lastly you need to associate the serial link with the EQL device, this is called 'enslaving' and is done with the *eql_enslave* command as shown:

```
        root# eql_enslave eql sl0 28800
        root# eql_enslave eql ppp0 14400
```

The '*estimated speed*' parameter you supply *eql_enslave* doesn't do anything directly. It is used by the EQL driver to determine what share of the datagrams that device should receive, so you can fine tune the balancing of the lines by playing with this value.

To disassociate a line from an EQL device you use the *eql_emancipate* command as shown:

```
        root# eql_emancipate eql sl0
```

You add routing as you would for any other point to point link, except your routes should refer to the `eql` device rather than the actual serial devices themselves, typically you would use:

```
        root# route add default eql
```

The EQL driver was developed by Simon Janes, `simon@ncm.com`.

6.3   IP Accounting (for Linux-2.0)

The IP accounting features of the Linux kernel allow you to collect and analyze some network usage data. The data collected comprises the number of packets and the number of bytes accumulated since the figures were last reset. You may specify a variety of rules to categorize the figures to suit whatever purpose you may have. This option has been removed in kernel 2.1.102, because the old ipfwadm-based firewalling was replaced by "ipfwchains".

Kernel Compile Options:

```
        Networking options  --->
            [*] IP: accounting
```

After you have compiled and installed the kernel you need to use the *ipfwadm* command to configure IP accounting. There are many different ways of breaking down the accounting information that you might choose. I've picked a simple example of what might be useful to use, you should read the *ipfwadm* man page for more information.

Scenario: You have a ethernet network that is linked to the internet via a PPP link. On the ethernet you have a machine that offers a number of services and that you are interested in knowing how much traffic is generated by each of ftp and world wide web traffic, as well as total tcp and udp traffic.

You might use a command set that looks like the following, which is shown as a shell script:

```
#!/bin/sh
#
# Flush the accounting rules
ipfwadm -A -f
#
# Set shortcuts
localnet=44.136.8.96/29
any=0/0
# Add rules for local ethernet segment
ipfwadm -A in   -a -P tcp -D $localnet ftp-data
ipfwadm -A out  -a -P tcp -S $localnet ftp-data
ipfwadm -A in   -a -P tcp -D $localnet www
ipfwadm -A out  -a -P tcp -S $localnet www
ipfwadm -A in   -a -P tcp -D $localnet
ipfwadm -A out  -a -P tcp -S $localnet
ipfwadm -A in   -a -P udp -D $localnet
ipfwadm -A out  -a -P udp -S $localnet
#
# Rules for default
ipfwadm -A in   -a -P tcp -D $any ftp-data
ipfwadm -A out  -a -P tcp -S $any ftp-data
ipfwadm -A in   -a -P tcp -D $any www
ipfwadm -A out  -a -P tcp -S $any www
ipfwadm -A in   -a -P tcp -D $any
ipfwadm -A out  -a -P tcp -S $any
ipfwadm -A in   -a -P udp -D $any
ipfwadm -A out  -a -P udp -S $any
#
# List the rules
ipfwadm -A -l -n
#
```

The names "ftp-data" and "www" refer to lines in /etc/services. The last command lists each of the Accounting rules and displays the collected totals.

An important point to note when analyzing IP accounting is that **totals for all rules that match will be incremented** so that to obtain differential figures you need to perform appropriate maths. For example if I wanted to know how much data was not ftp nor www I would substract the individual totals from the rule that matches all ports.

```
root# ipfwadm -A -l -n
IP accounting rules
 pkts bytes dir prot source              destination           ports
    0     0 in  tcp  0.0.0.0/0           44.136.8.96/29        * -> 20
    0     0 out tcp  44.136.8.96/29      0.0.0.0/0             20 -> *
   10  1166 in  tcp  0.0.0.0/0           44.136.8.96/29        * -> 80
   10   572 out tcp  44.136.8.96/29      0.0.0.0/0             80 -> *
  252 10943 in  tcp  0.0.0.0/0           44.136.8.96/29        * -> *
  231 18831 out tcp  44.136.8.96/29      0.0.0.0/0             * -> *
    0     0 in  udp  0.0.0.0/0           44.136.8.96/29        * -> *
    0     0 out udp  44.136.8.96/29      0.0.0.0/0             * -> *
    0     0 in  tcp  0.0.0.0/0           0.0.0.0/0             * -> 20
    0     0 out tcp  0.0.0.0/0           0.0.0.0/0             20 -> *
   10  1166 in  tcp  0.0.0.0/0           0.0.0.0/0             * -> 80
   10   572 out tcp  0.0.0.0/0           0.0.0.0/0             80 -> *
```

```
253 10983 in  tcp  0.0.0.0/0           0.0.0.0/0              *  ->  *
231 18831 out tcp  0.0.0.0/0           0.0.0.0/0              *  ->  *
  0     0 in  udp  0.0.0.0/0           0.0.0.0/0              *  ->  *
  0     0 out udp  0.0.0.0/0           0.0.0.0/0              *  ->  *
```

6.4 IP Accounting (for Linux-2.2)

The new accounting code is accessed via "IP Firewall Chains". See *the IP chanins home page* `<http://www.adelaide.net.au/~rustcorp/ipfwchains/ipfwchains.html>` for more information. Among other things, you'll now need to use *ipchains* instead of `ipfwadm` to configure your filters. (From `Documentation/Changes` in the latest kernel sources).

6.5 IP Aliasing

There are some applications where being able to configure multiple IP addresses to a single network device is useful. Internet Service Providers often use this facility to provide a 'customized' to their World Wide Web and ftp offerings for their customers. You can refer to the "IP-Alias mini-HOWTO" for more information than you find here.

Kernel Compile Options:

```
Networking options  --->
    ....
    [*] Network aliasing
    ....
    <*> IP: aliasing support
```

After compiling and installing your kernel with IP_Alias support configuration is very simple. The aliases are added to virtual network devices associated with the actual network device. A simple naming convention applies to these devices being `<devname>:<virtual dev num>`, e.g. `eth0:0`, `ppp0:10` etc. Note that the the ifname:number device can only be configured *after* the main interface has been set up.

For example, assume you have an ethernet network that supports two different IP subnetworks simultaneously and you wish your machine to have direct access to both, you could use something like:

```
root# ifconfig eth0 192.168.1.1 netmask 255.255.255.0 up
root# route add -net 192.168.1.0 netmask 255.255.255.0 eth0

root# ifconfig eth0:0 192.168.10.1 netmask 255.255.255.0 up
root# route add -net 192.168.10.0 netmask 255.255.255.0 eth0:0
```

To delete an alias you simply add a '-' to the end of its name and refer to it and is as simple as:

```
root# ifconfig eth0:0- 0
```

All routes associated with that alias will also be deleted automatically.

6.6 IP Firewall (for Linux-2.0)

IP Firewall and Firewalling issues are covered in more depth in the *Firewall-HOWTO* `<Firewall-HOWTO.html>`. IP Firewalling allows you to secure your machine against unauthorized network access by filtering or allowing datagrams from or to IP addresses that you nominate. There are three different classes of rules, incoming filtering, outgoing filtering and forwarding filtering. Incoming rules are applied to datagrams that are received by a network device. Outgoing rules are applied to datagrams that are to be transmitted by a network device. Forwarding rules are applied to datagrams that are received and are not for this machine, ie datagrams that would be routed.

Kernel Compile Options:

```
Networking options  --->
    [*] Network firewalls
    ....
    [*] IP: forwarding/gatewaying
    ....
    [*] IP: firewalling
    [ ] IP: firewall packet logging
```

Configuration of the IP firewall rules is performed using the *ipfwadm* command. As I mentioned earlier, security is not something I am expert at, so while I will present an example you can use, you should do your own research and develop your own rules if security is important to you.

Probably the most common use of IP firewall is when you are using your linux machine as a router and firewall gateway to protect your local network from unauthorized access from outside your network.

The following configuration is based on a contribution from Arnt Gulbrandsen, <agulbra@troll.no>.

The example describes the configuration of the firewall rules on the Linux firewall/router machine illustrated in this diagram:

```
  -                               -
   \                             |  172.16.37.0
    \                            |    /255.255.255.0
     \          ---------        |
    |  172.16.174.30 | Linux |   |
NET =================| f/w   |------|    ..37.19
    |     PPP        | router|   |   --------
   /            ---------    |---| Mail |
  /                          |   | /DNS |
 /                           |   --------
  -                          |
                               -
```

The following commands would normally be placed in an `rc` file so that they were automatically started each time the system boots. For maximum security they would be performed after the network interfaces are configured, but before the interfaces are actually brought up to prevent anyone gaining access while the firewall machine is rebooting.

```
#!/bin/sh

# Flush the 'Forwarding' rules table
# Change the default policy to 'accept'
#
/sbin/ipfwadm -F -f
/sbin/ipfwadm -F -p accept
#
# .. and for 'Incoming'
#
/sbin/ipfwadm -I -f
/sbin/ipfwadm -I -p accept

# First off, seal off the PPP interface
```

```
          # I'd love to use '-a deny' instead of '-a reject -y' but then it
          # would be impossible to originate connections on that inter-
face too.
          # The -o causes all rejected datagrams to be logged. This trades
          # disk space against knowledge of an attack of configuration error.
          #
          /sbin/ipfwadm -I -a reject -y -o -P tcp -S 0/0 -D 172.16.174.30

          # Throw away certain kinds of obviously forged packets right away:
          # Nothing should come from multicast/anycast/broadcast addresses
          #
          /sbin/ipfwadm -F -a deny -o -S 224.0/3 -D 172.16.37.0/24
          #
          # and nothing coming from the loopback network should ever be
          # seen on a wire
          #
          /sbin/ipfwadm -F -a deny -o -S 127.0/8 -D 172.16.37.0/24

          # accept incoming SMTP and DNS connections, but only
          # to the Mail/Name Server
          #
          /sbin/ipfwadm -F -a accept -P tcp -S 0/0 -D 172.16.37.19 25 53
          #
          # DNS uses UDP as well as TCP, so allow that too
          # for questions to our name server
          #
          /sbin/ipfwadm -F -a accept -P udp -S 0/0 -D 172.16.37.19 53
          #
          # but not "answers" coming to dangerous ports like NFS and
          # Larry McVoy's NFS extension.  If you run squid, add its port here.
          #
          /sbin/ipfwadm -F -a deny -o -P udp -S 0/0 53 \
                  -D 172.16.37.0/24 2049 2050

          # answers to other user ports are okay
          #
          /sbin/ipfwadm -F -a accept -P udp -S 0/0 53 \
                  -D 172.16.37.0/24 53 1024:65535

          # Reject incoming connections to identd
          # We use 'reject' here so that the connecting host is told
          # straight away not to bother continuing, otherwise we'd experience
          # delays while ident timed out.
          #
          /sbin/ipfwadm -F -a reject -o -P tcp -S 0/0 -D 172.16.37.0/24 113

          # Accept some common service connections from the 192.168.64 and
          # 192.168.65 networks, they are friends that we trust.
          #
          /sbin/ipfwadm -F -a accept -P tcp -S 192.168.64.0/23 \
                  -D 172.16.37.0/24 20:23

          # accept and pass through anything originating inside
          #
          /sbin/ipfwadm -F -a accept -P tcp -S 172.16.37.0/24 -D 0/0
```

```
# deny most other incoming TCP connections and log them
# (append 1:1023 if you have problems with ftp not working)
#
/sbin/ipfwadm -F -a deny -o -y -P tcp -S 0/0 -D 172.16.37.0/24

# ... for UDP too
#
/sbin/ipfwadm -F -a deny -o -P udp -S 0/0 -D 172.16.37.0/24
```

Good firewall configurations are a little tricky. This example should be a reasonable starting point for you. The *ipfwadm* manual page offers some assistance in how to use the tool. If you intend to configure a firewall, be sure to ask around and get as much advice from sources you consider reliable and get someone to test/sanity check your configuration from the outside.

6.7 IP Firewall (for Linux-2.2)

The new firewalling code is accessed via "IP Firewall Chains". See *the IP chanins home page* <http://www.adelaide.net.au/~rustcorp/ipfwchains/ipfwchains.html> for more information. Among other things, you'll now need to use *ipchains* instead of `ipfwadm` to configure your filters. (From `Documentation/Changes` in the latest kernel sources).

6.8 IPIP Encapsulation

Why would you want to encapsulate IP datagrams within IP datagrams? It must seem an odd thing to do if you've never seen an application of it before. Ok, here are a couple of common places where it is used: Mobile-IP and IP-Multicast. What is perhaps the most widely spread use of it though is also the least well known, Amateur Radio.

Kernel Compile Options:

```
Networking options  --->
    [*] TCP/IP networking
    [*] IP: forwarding/gatewaying
    ....
    <*> IP: tunneling
```

IP tunnel devices are called 'tun10', 'tun11' etc.

"But why ?". Ok, ok. Conventional IP routing rules mandate that an IP network comprises a network address and a network mask. This produces a series of contiguous addresses that may all be routed via a single routing entry. This is very convenient, but it means that you may only use any particular IP address while you are connected to the particular piece of network to which it belongs. In most instances this is ok, but if you are a mobile netizen then you may not be able to stay connected to the one place all the time. IP/IP encapsulation (IP tunneling) allows you to overcome this restriction by allowing datagrams destined for your IP address to be wrapped up and redirected to another IP address. If you know that you're going to be operating from some other IP network for some time you can set up a machine on your home network to accept datagrams to your IP address and redirect them to the address that you will actually be using temporarily.

6.8.1 A tunneled network configuration.

As always, I believe a diagram will save me lots of confusing text, so here is one:

192.168.1/24   192.168.2/24

```
 -                                        -
|      ppp0 =              ppp0 =         |
|  aaa.bbb.ccc.ddd   fff.ggg.hhh.iii      |
|                                         |
|    /-----\                  /-----\     |
|   |       |        //      |       |    |
|---|   A   |------//--------|   B   |---|
|   |       |      //        |       |    |
|    \-----/                  \-----/     |
|                                  |
 -                                        -
```

The diagram illustrates another possible reason to use IPIP encapsulation, virtual private networking. This example presupposes that you have two machines each with a simple dial up internet connection. Each host is allocated just a single IP address. Behind each of these machines are some private local area networks configured with reserved IP network addresses. Suppose that you want to allow any host on network A to connect to any host on network B, just as if they were properly connected to the Internet with a network route. IPIP encapsulation will allow you to do this. Note, encapsulation does not solve the problem of how you get the hosts on networks A and B to talk to any other on the Internet, you still need tricks like IP Masquerade for that. Encapsulation is normally performed by machine functioning as routers.

Linux router 'A' would be configured with a script like the following:

```
#!/bin/sh
PATH=/sbin:/usr/sbin
mask=255.255.255.0
remotegw=fff.ggg.hhh.iii
#
# Ethernet configuration
ifconfig eth0 192.168.1.1 netmask $mask up
route add -net 192.168.1.0 netmask $mask eth0
#
# ppp0 configuration (start ppp link, set default route)
pppd
route add default ppp0
#
# Tunnel device configuration
ifconfig tun0 192.168.1.1 up
route add -net 192.168.2.0 netmask $mask gw $remotegw tun0
```

Linux router 'B' would be configured with a similar script:

```
#!/bin/sh
PATH=/sbin:/usr/sbin
mask=255.255.255.0
remotegw=aaa.bbb.ccc.ddd
#
# Ethernet configuration
ifconfig eth0 192.168.2.1 netmask $mask up
route add -net 192.168.2.0 netmask $mask eth0
#
# ppp0 configuration (start ppp link, set default route)
pppd
```

```
route add default ppp0
#
# Tunnel device configuration
ifconfig tun0 192.168.2.1 up
route add -net 192.168.1.0 netmask $mask gw $remotegw tun0
```

The command:

```
route add -net 192.168.1.0 netmask $mask gw $remotegw tun0
```

reads: 'Send any datagrams destined for `192.168.1.0/24` inside an IPIP encap datagram with a destination address of `aaa.bbb.ccc.ddd`'.

Note that the configurations are reciprocated at either end. The tunnel device uses the '`gw`' in the route as the *destination* of the IP datagram in which it will place the datagram it has received to route. That machine must know how to decapsulate IPIP datagrams, that is, it must also be configured with a tunnel device.

6.8.2   A tunneled host configuration.

It doesn't have to be a whole network you route. You could for example route just a single IP address. In that instance you might configure the `tun1` device on the 'remote' machine with its home IP address and at the A end just use a host route (and Proxy Arp) rather than a network route via the tunnel device. Let's redraw and modify our configuration appropriately. Now we have just host 'B' which to want to act and behave as if it is both fully connected to the Internet and also part of the remote network supported by host 'A':

```
192.168.1/24


 -
 |         ppp0 =                 ppp0 =
 |     aaa.bbb.ccc.ddd        fff.ggg.hhh.iii
 |
 |     /-----\                  /-----\
 |    |       |        //      |       |
 |---|   A   |------//--------|   B   |
 |    |       |     //         |       |
 |     \-----/                  \-----/
 |                                         also: 192.168.1.12
 -
```

Linux router 'A' would be configured with:

```
#!/bin/sh
PATH=/sbin:/usr/sbin
mask=255.255.255.0
remotegw=fff.ggg.hhh.iii
#
# Ethernet configuration
ifconfig eth0 192.168.1.1 netmask $mask up
route add -net 192.168.1.0 netmask $mask eth0
#
# ppp0 configuration (start ppp link, set default route)
pppd
route add default ppp0
```

```
#
# Tunnel device configuration
ifconfig tunl0 192.168.1.1 up
route add -host 192.168.1.12 gw $remotegw tunl0
#
# Proxy ARP for the remote host
arp -s 192.168.1.12 xx:xx:xx:xx:xx:xx pub
```

Linux host 'B' would be configured with:

```
#!/bin/sh
PATH=/sbin:/usr/sbin
mask=255.255.255.0
remotegw=aaa.bbb.ccc.ddd
#
# ppp0 configuration (start ppp link, set default route)
pppd
route add default ppp0
#
# Tunnel device configuration
ifconfig tunl0 192.168.1.12 up
route add -net 192.168.1.0 netmask $mask gw $remotegwtunl0
```

This sort of configuration is more typical of a Mobile-IP application. Where a single host wants to roam around the Internet and maintain a single usable IP address the whole time. You should refer to the Mobile-IP section for more information on how that is handled in practice.

6.9 IP Masquerade (for Linux-2.0)

Many people have a simple dialup account to connect to the Internet. Nearly everybody using this sort of configuration is allocated a single IP address by the Internet Service Provider. This is normally enough to allow only one host full access to the network. IP Masquerade is a clever trick that enables you to have many machines make use of that one IP address, by causing the other hosts to look like, hence the term masquerade, the machine supporting the dialup connection. There is a small caveat and that is that the masquerade function nearly always works only in one direction, that is the masqueraded hosts can make calls out, but they cannot accept or receive network connections from remote hosts. This means that some network services do not work such as *talk* and others such as *ftp* must be configured to operate in passive (PASV) mode to operate. Fortunately the most common network services such as *telnet*, World Wide Web and *irc* do work just fine.

Kernel Compile Options:

```
Code maturity level options  --->
    [*] Prompt for development and/or incomplete code/drivers
Networking options  --->
    [*] Network firewalls
    ....
    [*] TCP/IP networking
    [*] IP: forwarding/gatewaying
    ....
    [*] IP: masquerading (EXPERIMENTAL)
```

Normally you have your linux machine supporting a slip or PPP dialup line just as it would if it were a standalone machine. Additionally it would have another network device configured, perhaps an ethernet, configured with one of the reserved network addresses. The hosts to be masqueraded would be on this second network. Each of these hosts would have the IP address of the ethernet port of the linux machine set as their default gateway or router.

A typical configuration might look something like this:

```
    _                                            _
     \                                          |  192.168.1.0
      \                                         |   /255.255.255.0
       \                 ---------              |
        |               | Linux | .1.1 |
 NET ================| masq  |------|
        |    PPP/slip   | router|              |   --------
       /                 ---------             |--| host |
      /                                        |  |      |
     /                                         |   --------
    _                                           _
```

The most relevant commands for this configuration are:

```
# Network route for ethernet
route add -net 192.168.1.0 netmask 255.255.255.0 eth0
#
# Default route to the rest of the internet.
route add default ppp0
#
# Cause all hosts on the 192.168.1/24 network to be masqueraded.
ipfwadm -F -a m -S 192.168.1.0/24 -D 0.0.0.0/0
```

If you are minimalist and a lazy typist, like me, and your masquerading host has only two interfaces (so that every packet being forwarded must be masqueraded), the following command will suffice:

```
root# /sbin/ipfwadm -F -a accept -m
```

You can get more information on the Linux IP Masquerade feature from the *IP Masquerade Resource Page* <http://www.hwy401.com/achau/ipmasq/>. Also, a *very* detailed document about masquesrading is the "IP-Masquerade mini-HOWTO" (which also intructs to configure other OS's to run with a Linux masquerade server).

6.10 IP Transparent Proxy

IP transparent proxy is a feature that enables you to redirect servers or services destined for another machine to those services on this machine. Typically this would be useful where you have a linux machine as a router and also provides a proxy server. You would redirect all connections destined for that service remotely to the local proxy server.

Kernel Compile Options:

```
Code maturity level options  --->
    [*] Prompt for development and/or incomplete code/drivers
Networking options  --->
    [*] Network firewalls
    ....
    [*] TCP/IP networking
    ....
    [*] IP: firewalling
```

```
    . . . .
    [*] IP: transparent proxy support (EXPERIMENTAL)
```

Configuration of the transparent proxy feature is performed using the *ipfwadm* command

An example that might be useful is as follows:

```
root# ipfwadm -I -a accept -D 0/0 telnet -r 2323
```

This example will cause any connection attempts to port `telnet` (23) on any host to be redirected to port 2323 on this host. If you run a service on that port, you could forward telnet connections, log them or do whatever fits your need.

A more interesting example is redirecting all `http` traffic through a local cache. However, the protocol used by proxy servers is different from native http: where a client connects to `www.server.com:80` and asks for `/path/page`, when it connects to the local cache it contacts `proxy.local.domain:8080` and asks for `www.server.com/path/page`.

To filter an `http` request through the local proxy, you need to adapt the protocol by inserting a small server, called `transproxy` (you can find it on the world wide web). You can choose to run `transproxy` on port 8081, and issue this command:

```
root# ipfwadm -I -a accept -D 0/0 80 -r 8081
```

The `transproxy` program, then, will receive all connections meant to reach external servers and will pass them to the local proxy after fixing protocol differences.

6.11   IPv6

Just when you thought you were beginning to understand IP networking the rules get changed! IPv6 is the shorthand notation for version 6 of the Internet Protocol. IPv6 was developed primarily to overcome the concerns in the Internet community that there would soon be a shortage of IP addresses to allocate. IPv6 addresses are 16 bytes long (128 bits). IPv6 incorporates a number of other changes, mostly simplifications, that will make IPv6 networks more managable than IPv4 networks.

Linux already has a working, but not complete, IPv6 implementation in the `2.1.*` series kernels.

If you wish to experiment with this next generation Internet technology, or have a requirement for it, then you should read the IPv6-FAQ which is available from *www.terra.net* `<http://www.terra.net/ipv6/>`.

6.12   Mobile IP

The term "IP mobility" describes the ability of a host that is able to move its network connection from one point on the Internet to another without changing its IP address or losing connectivity. Usually when an IP host changes its point of connectivity it must also change its IP address. IP Mobility overcomes this problem by allocating a fixed IP address to the mobile host and using IP encapsulation (tunneling) with automatic routing to ensure that datagrams destined for it are routed to the actual IP address it is currently using.

A project is underway to provide a complete set of IP mobility tools for Linux. The Status of the project and tools may be obtained from the: *Linux Mobile IP Home Page* `<http://anchor.cs.binghamton.edu/~mobileip/>`.

6.13 Multicast

IP Multicast allows an arbitrary number of IP hosts on disparate IP networks to have IP datagrams simultaneously routed to them. This mechanism is exploited to provide Internet wide "broadcast" material such as audio and video transmissions and other novel applications.

Kernel Compile Options:

```
Networking options  --->
        [*] TCP/IP networking
        ....
        [*] IP: multicasting
```

A suite of tools and some minor network configuration is required. Please check the *Multicast-HOWTO* <Multicast-HOWTO.html> for more information on Multicast support in Linux.

6.14 NAT - Network Address Translation

The IP Network Address Translation facility is pretty much the standardized big brother of the Linux IP Masquerade facility. It is specified in some detail in RFC-1631 at your nearest RFC archive. NAT provides features that IP-Masquerade does not that make it eminently more suitable for use in corporate firewall router designs and larger scale installations.

An alpha implementation of NAT for Linux 2.0.29 kernel has been developed by Michael.Hasenstein, Michael.Hasenstein@informatik.tu-chemnitz.de. Michaels documentation and implementation are available from:

Linux IP Network Address Web Page <http://www.csn.tu-chemnitz.de/HyperNews/get/linux-ip-nat.html>

Newer Linux 2.1.* kernels also include some NAT functionality in the routing algorithm.

6.15 Traffic Shaper - Changing allowed bandwidth

The traffic shaper is a driver that creates new interface devices, those devices are traffic-limited in a user-defined way, they rely on physical network devices for actual transmission and can be used as outgoing routed for network traffic.

The shaper was introduced in Linux-2.1.15 and was backported to Linux-2.0.36 (it appeared in 2.0.36-pre-patch-2 distributed by Alan Cox, the author of the shaper device and maintainer of Linux-2.0).

The traffic shaper can only be compiled as a module and is configured by the *shapecfg* program with commands like the following:

```
shapecfg attach shaper0 eth1
shapecfg speed shaper0 64000
```

The shaper device can only control the bandwidth of outgoing traffic, as packets are transmitted via the shaper only according to the routing tables; therefore, a "route by source address" functionality could help in limiting the overall bandwidth of specific hosts using a Linux router.

Linux-2.1 already has support for such routing, if you need it for Linux-2.0 please check the patch by Mike McLagan, at ftp.invlogic.com. Refer to Documentationnetworking/shaper.txt for further information about the shaper.

If you want to try out a (tentative) shaping for incoming packets, try out rshaper-1.01 (or newer), from *ftp.systemy.it* <ftp://ftp.systemy.it/pub/develop>.

HOWTO

6.16   Routing in Linux-2.2

The latest versions of Linux-2.1 offer a lot of flexibility in routing policy. Unfortunately, you have to wait for the next version of this howto, or go read the kernel sources.

7   Using common PC hardware

7.1   ISDN

The Integrated Services Digital Network (ISDN) is a series of standards that specify a general purpose switched digital data network. An ISDN 'call' creates a synchronous point to point data service to the destination. ISDN is generally delivered on a high speed link that is broken down into a number of discrete channels. There are two different types of channels, the 'B Channels' which will actually carry the user data and a single channel called the 'D channel' which is used to send control information to the ISDN exchange to establish calls and other functions. In Australia for example, ISDN may be delivered on a 2Mbps link that is broken into 30 discrete 64kbps B channels with one 64kbps D channel. Any number of channels may be used at a time and in any combination. You could for example establish 30 separate calls to 30 different destinations at 64kbps each, or you could establish 15 calls to 15 different destinations at 128kbps each (two channels used per call), or just a small number of calls and leave the rest idle. A channel may be used for either incoming or outgoing calls. The original intention of ISDN was to allow Telecommunications companies to provide a single data service which could deliver either telephone (via digitised voice) or data services to your home or business without requiring you to make any special configuration changes.

There are a few different ways to connect your computer to an ISDN service. One way is to use a device called a 'Terminal Adaptor' which plugs into the Network Terminating Unit that you telecommunications carrier will have installed when you got your ISDN service and presents a number of serial interfaces. One of those interfaces is used to enter commands to establish calls and configuration and the others are actually connected to the network devices that will use the data circuits when they are established. Linux will work in this sort of configuration without modification, you just treat the port on the Terminal Adaptor like you would treat any other serial device. Another way, which is the way the kernel ISDN support is designed for allows you to install an ISDN card into your Linux machine and then has your Linux software handle the protocols and make the calls itself.

Kernel Compile Options:

```
ISDN subsystem  --->
        <*> ISDN support
        [ ] Support synchronous PPP
        [ ] Support audio via ISDN
        < > ICN 2B and 4B support
        < > PCBIT-D support
        < > Teles/NICCY1016PC/Creatix support
```

The Linux implementation of ISDN supports a number of different types of internal ISDN cards. These are those listed in the kernel configuration options:

- ICN 2B and 4B
- Octal PCBIT-D
- Teles ISDN-cards and compatibles

Some of these cards require software to be downloaded to them to make them operational. There is a separate utility to do this with.

Full details on how to configure the Linux ISDN support is available from the /usr/src/linux/Documentation/isdn/ directory and an FAQ dedicated to *isdn4linux* is available at *www.lrz-*

muenchen.de `<http://www.lrz-muenchen.de/~ui161ab/www/isdn/>`. (You can click on the english flag to get an english version).

A note about PPP. The PPP suite of protocols will operate over either asynchronous or synchronous serial lines. The commonly distributed PPP daemon for Linux '*pppd*' supports only asynchronous mode. If you wish to run the PPP protocols over your ISDN service you need a specially modified version. Details of where to find it are available in the documentation referred to above.

7.2 PLIP for Linux-2.0

PLIP device names are 'plip0', 'plip1 and plip2.

Kernel Compile Options:

```
Network device support   --->
    <*> PLIP (parallel port) support
```

plip (Parallel Line IP), is like SLIP, in that it is used for providing a *point to point* network connection between two machines, except that it is designed to use the parallel printer ports on your machine instead of the serial ports (a cabling diagram in included in the cabling diagram section later in this document). Because it is possible to transfer more than one bit at a time with a parallel port, it is possible to attain higher speeds with the *plip* interface than with a standard serial device. In addition, even the simplest of parallel ports, printer ports, can be used in lieu of you having to purchase comparatively expensive 16550AFN UART's for your serial ports. PLIP uses a lot of CPU compared to a serial link and is most certainly not a good option if you can obtain some cheap ethernet cards, but it will work when nothing else is available and will work quite well. You should expect a data transfer rate of about 20 kilobytes per second when a link is running well.

The PLIP device drivers competes with the parallel device driver for the parallel port hardware. If you wish to use both drivers then you should compile them both as modules to ensure that you are able to select which port you want to use for PLIP and which ports want for the printer driver. Refer to the "Mudules mini-HOWTO" for more information on kernel module configuration.

Please note that some laptops use chipsets that will not work with PLIP because they do not allow some combinations of signals that PLIP relies on, that printers don't use.

The Linux *plip* interface is compatible with the *Crynwyr Packet Driver PLIP* and this will mean that you can connect your Linux machine to a DOS machine running any other sort of tcp/ip software via *plip*.

In the 2.0.* series kernel the plip devices are mapped to i/o port and IRQ as follows:

```
device  i/o    IRQ
------  -----  ---
plip0   0x3bc  5
plip1   0x378  7
plip2   0x278  2
```

If your parallel ports don't match any of the above combinations then you can change the IRQ of a port using the *ifconfig* command using the 'irq' parameter (be sure to enable IRQ's on your printer ports in your ROM BIOS if it supports this option). As an alternative, you can specify "io=" annd "irq=" options on the *insmod* command line, if you use modules. For example:

```
root# insmod plip.o io=0x288 irq=5
```

PLIP operation is controlled by two timeouts, whose default values are probably ok in most cases. You will probably need to increase them if you have an especially slow computer, in which case the timers to increase are actually on the **other** computer. A program called *plipconfig* exists that allows you to change these timer settings without recompiling your kernel. It is supplied with many Linux distributions.

To configure a *plip* interface, you will need to invoke the following commands (or **add** them to your initialization scripts):

```
root# /sbin/ifconfig plip1 localplip pointopoint remoteplip
root# /sbin/route add remoteplip plip1
```

Here, the port being used is the one at I/O address 0x378; *localplip* amd *remoteplip* are the names or IP addresses used over the PLIP cable. I personally keep them in my `/etc/hosts` database:

```
# plip entries
192.168.3.1    localplip
192.168.3.2    remoteplip
```

The *pointopoint* parameter has the same meaning as for SLIP, in that it specifies the address of the machine at the other end of the link.

In almost all respects you can treat a *plip* interface as though it were a *SLIP* interface, except that neither *dip* nor *slattach* need be, nor can be, used.

Further information on PLIP may be obtained from the "PLIP mini-HOWTO".

7.3 PLIP for Linux-2.2

During development of the 2.1 kernel versions, support for the parallel port was changed to a better setup.

Kernel Compile Options:

```
General setup  --->
    [*] Parallel port support
Network device support  --->
    <*> PLIP (parallel port) support
```

The new code for PLIP behaves like the old one (use the same *ifconfig* and *route* commands as in the previous section, but initialization of the device is different due to the advanced parallel port support.

The "first" PLIP device is always called "plip0", where first is the first device detected by the system, similarly to what happens for Ethernet devices. The actual parallel port being used is one of the available ports, as shown in `/proc/parport`. For example, if you have only one parallel port, you'll only have a directory called `/proc/parport/0`.

If your kernel didn't detect the IRQ number used by your port, "`insmod plip`" will fail; in this case just write the right number to `/proc/parport/0/irq` and reinvoke *insmod*.

Complete information about parallel port management is available in the file `Documentation/parport.txt`, part of your kernel sources.

7.4 PPP

PPP devices names are 'ppp0', 'ppp1, etc. Devices are numbered sequentially with the first device configured receiving '0'.

Kernel Compile Options:

```
Networking options  --->
    <*> PPP (point-to-point) support
```

PPP configuration is covered in detail in the *PPP-HOWTO* `<PPP-HOWTO.html>`.

7.4.1 Maintaining a permanent connection to the net with *pppd*.

If you are fortunate enough to have a semi permanent connection to the net and would like to have your machine automatically redial your PPP connection if it is lost then here is a simple trick to do so.

Configure PPP such that it can be started by the `root` user by issuing the command:

```
# pppd
```

Be sure that you have the '-detach' option configured in your `/etc/ppp/options` file. Then, insert the following line into your `/etc/inittab` file, down with the *getty* definitions:

```
pd:23:respawn:/usr/sbin/pppd
```

This will cause the *init* program to spawn and monitor the *pppd* program and automatically restart it if it dies.

7.5 SLIP client

SLIP devices are named 'sl0', 'sl1' etc. with the first device configured being assigned '0' and the rest incrementing sequentially as they are configured.

Kernel Compile Options:

```
Network device support  --->
    [*] Network device support
    <*> SLIP (serial line) support
    [ ]   CSLIP compressed headers
    [ ]   Keepalive and linefill
    [ ]   Six bit SLIP encapsulation
```

SLIP (Serial Line Internet Protocol) allows you to use tcp/ip over a serial line, be that a phone line with a dialup modem, or a leased line of some sort. Of course to use SLIP you need access to a *SLIP-server* in your area. Many universities and businesses provide SLIP access all over the world.

Slip uses the serial ports on your machine to carry IP datagrams. To do this it must take control of the serial device. Slip device names are named *sl0, sl1* etc. How do these correspond to your serial devices ? The networking code uses what is called an *ioctl* (i/o control) call to change the serial devices into SLIP devices. There are two programs supplied that can do this, they are called *dip* and *slattach*

7.5.1 dip

dip (Dialup IP) is a smart program that is able to set the speed of the serial device, command your modem to dial the remote end of the link, automatically log you into the remote server, search for messages sent to you by the server and extract information for them such as your IP address and perform the *ioctl* necessary to switch your serial port into SLIP mode. *dip* has a powerful scripting ability and it is this that you can exploit to automate your logon procedure.

You can find it at: *sunsite.unc.edu* `<ftp://sunsite.unc.edu/pub/Linux/system/Network/serial/dip/dip337o-uri.tgz>`.

To install it, try the following:

```
user% tar xvzf dip337o-uri.tgz
user% cd dip-3.3.7o
user% vi Makefile
root# make install
```

The `Makefile` assumes the existence of a group called *uucp*, but you might like to change this to either *dip* or *SLIP* depending on your configuration.

7.5.2   slattach

slattach as contrasted with *dip* is a very simple program, that is very easy to use, but does not have the sophistication of *dip*. It does not have the scripting ability, all it does is configure your serial device as a SLIP device. It assumes you have all the information you need and the serial line is established before you invoke it. *slattach* is ideal to use where you have a permanent connection to your server, such as a physical cable, or a leased line.

7.5.3   When do I use which ?

You would use *dip* when your link to the machine that is your SLIP server is a dialup modem, or some other temporary link. You would use *slattach* when you have a leased line, perhaps a cable, between your machine and the server and there is no special action needed to get the link working. See section 'Permanent Slip connection' for more information.

Configuring SLIP is much like configuring an Ethernet interface (read section 'Configuring an ethernet device' above). However there are a few key differences.

First of all, SLIP links are unlike ethernet networks in that there is only ever two hosts on the network, one at each end of the link. Unlike an ethernet that is available for use as soon are you are cabled, with SLIP, depending on the type of link you have, you may have to initialize your network connection in some special way.

If you are using *dip* then this would not normally be done at boot time, but at some time later, when you were ready to use the link. It is possible to automate this procedure. If you are using *slattach* then you will probably want to add a section to your *rc.inet1* file. This will be described soon.

There are two major types of SLIP servers: Dynamic IP address servers and static IP address servers. Almost every SLIP server will prompt you to login using a username and password when dialing in. *dip* can handle logging you in automatically.

7.5.4   Static SLIP server with a dialup line and DIP.

A static SLIP server is one in which you have been supplied an IP address that is exclusively yours. Each time you connect to the server, you will configure your SLIP port with that address. The static SLIP server will answer your modem call, possibly prompt you for a username and password, and then route any datagrams destined for your address to you via that connection. If you have a static server, then you may want to put entries for your hostname and IP address (since you know what it will be) into your `/etc/hosts`. You should also configure some other files such as: `rc.inet2`, `host.conf`, `resolv.conf`, `/etc/HOSTNAME` and `rc.local`. Remember that when configuring `rc.inet1`, you don't need to add any special commands for your SLIP connection since it is *dip* that does all of the hard work for you in configuring your interface. You will need to give *dip* the appropriate information and it will configure the interface for you after commanding the modem to establish the call and logging you into your SLIP server.

If this is how your SLIP server works then you can move to section 'Using Dip' to learn how to configure *dip* appropriately.

7.5.5   Dynamic SLIP server with a dialup line and DIP.

A *dynamic* SLIP server is one which allocates you an IP address randomly, from a pool of addresses, each time you logon. This means that there is no guarantee that you will have any particular address each time, and that address may well be used by someone else after you have logged off. The network administrator who configured the SLIP server will have assigned a pool of address for the SLIP server to use, when the server receives a new incoming call, it finds the first unused address, guides the caller through the login process and then prints a welcome message that contains the IP address it has allocated and will proceed to use that IP address for the duration of that call.

Configuring for this type of server is similar to configuring for a static server, except that you must add a step where you obtain the IP address that the server has allocated for you and configure your SLIP device with that.

Again, *dip* does the hard work and new versions are smart enough to not only log you in, but to also be able to automatically read the IP address printed in the welcome message and store it so that you can have it configure your SLIP device with it.

If this is how your SLIP server works then you can move to section 'Using Dip' to learn how to configure *dip* appropriately.

7.5.6 Using DIP.

As explained earlier, *dip* is a powerful program that can simplify and automate the process of dialing into the SLIP server, logging you in, starting the connection and configuring your SLIP devices with the appropriate *ifconfig* and *route* commands.

Essentially to use *dip* you'll write a 'dip script', which is basically a list of commands that *dip* understands that tell *dip* how to perform each of the actions you want it to perform. See `sample.dip` that comes supplied with *dip* to get an idea of how it works. *dip* is quite a powerful program, with many options. Instead of going into all of them here you should look at the *man* page, README and sample files that will have come with your version of *dip*.

You may notice that the `sample.dip` script assumes that you're using a static SLIP server, so you know what your IP address is beforehand. For dynamic SLIP servers, the newer versions of *dip* include a command you can use to automatically read and configure your SLIP device with the IP address that the dynamic server allocates for you. The following sample is a modified version of the `sample.dip` that came supplied with *dip337j-uri.tgz* and is probably a good starting point for you. You might like to save it as `/etc/dipscript` and edit it to suit your configuration:

```
#
# sample.dip    Dialup IP connection support program.
#
#                This file (should show) shows how to use the DIP
#        This file should work for Annex type dynamic servers, if you
#        use a static address server then use the sample.dip file that
#        comes as part of the dip337-uri.tgz package.
#
#
# Version:      @(#)sample.dip  1.40    07/20/93
#
# Author:       Fred N. van Kempen, <waltje@uWalt.NL.Mugnet.ORG>
#

main:
# Next, set up the other side's name and address.
# My dialin machine is called 'xs4all.hacktic.nl' (== 193.78.33.42)
get $remote xs4all.hacktic.nl
# Set netmask on sl0 to 255.255.255.0
netmask 255.255.255.0
# Set the desired serial port and speed.
port cua02
speed 38400


# Reset the modem and terminal line.
```

```
# This seems to cause trouble for some people!
reset

# Note! "Standard" pre-defined "errlevel" values:
#  0 - OK
#  1 - CONNECT
#  2 - ERROR
#
# You can change those grep'ping for "addchat()" in *.c...

# Prepare for dialing.
send ATQ0V1E1X4\r
wait OK 2
if $errlvl != 0 goto modem_trouble
dial 555-1234567
if $errlvl != 1 goto modem_trouble

# We are connected.  Login to the system.
login:
sleep 2
wait ogin: 20
if $errlvl != 0 goto login_trouble
send MYLOGIN\n
wait ord: 20
if $errlvl != 0 goto password_error
send MYPASSWD\n
loggedin:

# We are now logged in.
wait SOMEPROMPT 30
if $errlvl != 0 goto prompt_error

# Command the server into SLIP mode
send SLIP\n
wait SLIP 30
if $errlvl != 0 goto prompt_error

# Get and Set your IP address from the server.
#   Here we assume that after commanding the SLIP server into SLIP
#   mode that it prints your IP address
get $locip remote 30
if $errlvl != 0 goto prompt_error

# Set up the SLIP operating parameters.
get $mtu 296
# Ensure "route add -net default xs4all.hacktic.nl" will be done
default

# Say hello and fire up!
done:
print CONNECTED $locip ---> $rmtip
mode CSLIP
goto exit

prompt_error:
```

```
print TIME-OUT waiting for sliplogin to fire up...
goto error

login_trouble:
print Trouble waiting for the Login: prompt...
goto error

password:error:
print Trouble waiting for the Password: prompt...
goto error

modem_trouble:
print Trouble occurred with the modem...
error:
print CONNECT FAILED to $remote
quit

exit:
exit
```

The above example assumes you are calling a *dynamic* SLIP server, if you are calling a *static* SLIP server, then the `sample.dip` file that comes with *dip337j-uri.tgz* should work for you.

When *dip* is given the *get $local* command it searches the incoming text from the remote end for a string that looks like an IP address, ie strings numbers separated by '.' characters. This modification was put in place specifically for *dynamic* SLIP servers, so that the process of reading the IP address granted by the server could be automated.

The example above will automatically create a default route via your SLIP link, if this is not what you want, you might have an ethernet connection that should be your default route, then remove the *default* command from the script. After this script has finished running, if you do an *ifconfig* command, you will see that you have a device *sl0*. This is your SLIP device. Should you need to, you can modify its configuration manually, after the *dip* command has finished, using the *ifconfig* and *route* commands.

Please note that *dip* allows you to select a number of different protocols to use with the `mode` command, the most common example is *cSLIP* for SLIP with compression. Please note that both ends of the link must agree, so you should ensure that whatever you select agrees with what your server is set to.

The above example is fairly robust and should cope with most errors. Please refer to the *dip* man page for more information. Naturally you could, for example, code the script to do such things as redial the server if it doesn't get a connection within a prescribed period of time, or even try a series of servers if you have access to more than one.

7.5.7 Permanent SLIP connection using a leased line and slattach.

If you have a cable between two machines, or are fortunate enough to have a leased line, or some other permanent serial connection between your machine and another, then you don't need to go to all the trouble of using *dip* to set up your serial link. *slattach* is a very simple to use utility that will allow you just enough functionality to configure your connection.

Since your connection will be a permanent one, you will want to add some commands to your `rc.inet1` file. In essence all you need to do for a permanent connection is ensure that you configure the serial device to the correct speed and switch the serial device into SLIP mode. *slattach* allows you to do this with one command. **Add** the following to your `rc.inet1` file:

```
#
# Attach a leased line static SLIP connection
#
#  configure /dev/cua0 for 19.2kbps and cslip
/sbin/slattach -p cslip -s 19200 /dev/cua0 &
```

HOWTO

```
      /sbin/ifconfig sl0 IPA.IPA.IPA.IPA pointopoint IPR.IPR.IPR.IPR up
      #
      # End static SLIP.
```

Where:

IPA.IPA.IPA.IPA

> represents your IP address.

IPR.IPR.IPR.IPR

> represents the IP address of the remote end.

slattach allocates the first unallocated SLIP device to the serial device specified. *slattach* starts with *sl0*. Therefore the first *slattach* command attaches SLIP device *sl0* to the serial device specified and *sl1* the next time, etc.

slattach allows you to configure a number of different protocols with the -p argument. In your case you will use either *SLIP* or *cSLIP* depending on whether you want to use compression or not. Note: both ends must agree on whether you want compression or not.

7.6 SLIP server.

If you have a machine that is perhaps network connected, that you'd like other people be able to dial into and provide network services, then you will need to configure your machine as a server. If you want to use SLIP as the serial line protocol, then currently you have three options as to how to configure your Linux machine as a SLIP server. My preference would be to use the first presented, *sliplogin*, as it seems the easiest to configure and understand, but I will present a summary of each, so you can make your own decision.

7.6.1 Slip Server using *sliplogin*.

sliplogin is a program that you can use in place of the normal login shell for SLIP users that converts the terminal line into a SLIP line. It allows you to configure your Linux machine as either a *static address server*, users get the same address everytime they call in, or a *dynamic address server*, where users get an address allocated for them which will not necessarily be the same as the last time they called.

The caller will login as per the standard login process, entering their username and password, but instead of being presented with a shell after their login, *sliplogin* is executed which searches its configuration file (/etc/slip.hosts) for an entry with a login name that matches that of the caller. If it locates one, it configures the line as an 8bit clean line, and uses an *ioctl* call to convert the line discipline to SLIP. When this process is complete, the last stage of configuration takes place, where *sliplogin* invokes a shell script which configures the SLIP interface with the relevant ip address, netmask and sets appropriate routing in place. This script is usually called /etc/slip.login, but in a similar manner to *getty*, if you have certain callers that require special initialization, then you can create configuration scripts called /etc/slip.login.loginname that will be run instead of the default specifically for them.

There are either three or four files that you need to configure to get *sliplogin* working for you. I will detail how and where to get the software and how each is configured in detail. The files are:

- /etc/passwd, for the dialin user accounts.
- /etc/slip.hosts, to contain the information unique to each dial-in user.
- /etc/slip.login, which manages the configuration of the routing that needs to be performed for the user.
- /etc/slip.tty, which is required only if you are configuring your server for *dynamic address allocation* and contains a table of addresses to allocate
- /etc/slip.logout, which contains commands to clean up after the user has hung up or logged out.

Where to get *sliplogin* You may already have the *sliplogin* package installed as part of your distribution, if not then *sliplogin* can be obtained from: *sunsite.unc.edu* `<ftp://sunsite.unc.edu/pub/linux/system/Network/serial/sliplogin-2.1.1.tar.gz>`. The tar file contains both source, precompiled binaries and a *man* page.

To ensure that only authorized users will be able to run *sliplogin* program, you should add an entry to your `/etc/group` file similar to the following:

```
..
slip::13:radio,fred
..
```

When you install the *sliplogin* package, the `Makefile` will change the group ownership of the *sliplogin* program to `slip`, and this will mean that only users who belong to that group will be able to execute it. The example above will allow only users `radio` and `fred` to execute *sliplogin*.

To install the binaries into your `/sbin` directory and the *man* page into section 8, do the following:

```
# cd /usr/src
# gzip -dc .../sliplogin-2.1.1.tar.gz | tar xvf -
# cd sliplogin-2.1.1
# <..edit the Makefile if you don't use shadow passwords..>
# make install
```

If you want to recompile the binaries before installation, add a `make clean` before the `make install`. If you want to install the binaries somewhere else, you will need to edit the `Makefile` *install* rule.

Please read the `README` files that come with the package for more information.

Configuring `/etc/passwd` for Slip hosts. Normally you would create some special logins for Slip callers in your `/etc/passwd` file. A convention commonly followed is to use the *hostname* of the calling host with a capital 'S' prefixing it. So, for example, if the calling host is called `radio` then you could create a `/etc/passwd` entry that looked like:

```
Sradio:FvKurok73:1427:1:radio SLIP login:/tmp:/sbin/sliplogin
```

It doesn't really matter what the account is called, so long as it is meaningful to you.

Note: the caller doesn't need any special home directory, as they will not be presented with a shell from this machine, so `/tmp` is a good choice. Also note that *sliplogin* is used in place of the normal login shell.

Configuring `/etc/slip.hosts` The `/etc/slip.hosts` file is the file that *sliplogin* searches for entries matching the login name to obtain configuration details for this caller. It is this file where you specify the ip address and netmask that will be assigned to the caller and configured for their use. Sample entries for two hosts, one a static configuration for host `radio` and another, a dynamic configuration for user host `albert` might look like:

```
#
Sradio    44.136.8.99    44.136.8.100    255.255.255.0    normal        -1
Salbert   44.136.8.99    DYNAMIC         255.255.255.0    compressed    60
#
```

The `/etc/slip.hosts` file entries are:

1. the login name of the caller.
2. ip address of the server machine, ie this machine.
3. ip address that the caller will be assigned. If this field is coded `DYNAMIC` then an ip address will be allocated based on the information contained in your `/etc/slip.tty` file discussed later. **Note:** you must be using at least version 1.3 of sliplogin for this to work.

4. the netmask assigned to the calling machine in dotted decimal notation eg 255.255.255.0 for a Class C network mask.

5. the slip mode setting which allows you to enable/disable compression and slip other features. Allowable values here are "`normal`" or "`compressed`".

6. a timeout parameter which specifies how long the line can remain idle (no datagrams received) before the line is automatically disconnected. A negative value disables this feature.

7. optional arguments.

Note: You can use either hostnames or IP addresses in dotted decimal notation for fields 2 and 3. If you use hostnames then those hosts must be resolvable, that is, your machine must be able to locate an ip address for those hostnames, otherwise the script will fail when it is called. You can test this by trying trying to telnet to the hostname, if you get the '*Trying nnn.nnn.nnn...*' message then your machine has been able to find an ip address for that name. If you get the message '*Unknown host*', then it has not. If not, either use ip addresses in dotted decimal notation, or fix up your name resolver configuration (See section `Name Resolution`).

The most common slip modes are:

normal

> to enable normal uncompressed SLIP.

compressed

> to enable van Jacobsen header compression (cSLIP)

Naturally these are mutually exclusive, you can use one or the other. For more information on the other options available, refer to the *man* pages.

Configuring the /etc/slip.login file. After *sliplogin* has searched the `/etc/slip.hosts` and found a matching entry, it will attempt to execute the `/etc/slip.login` file to actually configure the SLIP interface with its ip address and netmask.

The sample `/etc/slip.login` file supplied with the *sliplogin* package looks like this:

```
#!/bin/sh -
#
#       @(#)slip.login  5.1 (Berkeley) 7/1/90
#
# generic login file for a SLIP line.  sliplogin invokes this with
# the parameters:
#     $1          $2        $3    $4, $5, $6 ...
#   SLIPunit ttyspeed    pid   the arguments from the slip.host entry
#
/sbin/ifconfig $1 $5 pointopoint $6 mtu 1500 -trailers up
/sbin/route add $6
arp -s $6 <hw_addr> pub
exit 0
#
```

You will note that this script simply uses the *ifconfig* and *route* commands to configure the SLIP device with its ipaddress, remote ip address and netmask and creates a route for the remote address via the SLIP device. Just the same as you would if you were using the *slattach* command.

Note also the use of *Proxy ARP* to ensure that other hosts on the same ethernet as the server machine will know how to reach the dial-in host. The `<hw_addr>` field should be the hardware address of the ethernet card in the machine. If your server machine isn't on an ethernet network then you can leave this line out completely.

Configuring the /etc/slip.logout file. When the call drops out, you want to ensure that the serial device is restored to its normal state so that future callers will be able to login correctly. This is achieved with the use of the /etc/slip.logout file. It is quite simple in format and is called with the same argument as the /etc/slip.login file.

```
#!/bin/sh -
#
#                   slip.logout
#
/sbin/ifconfig $1 down
arp -d $6
exit 0
#
```

All it does is 'down' the interface which will delete the manual route previously created. It also uses the *arp* command to delete any proxy arp put in place, again, you don't need the *arp* command in the script if your server machine does not have an ethernet port.

Configuring the /etc/slip.tty file. If you are using dynamic ip address allocation (have any hosts configured with the DYNAMIC keyword in the /etc/slip.hosts file, then you must configure the /etc/slip.tty file to list what addresses are assigned to what port. You only need this file if you wish your server to dynamically allocate addresses to users.

The file is a table that lists the *tty* devices that will support dial-in SLIP connections and the ip address that should be assigned to users who call in on that port.

Its format is as follows:

```
# slip.tty    tty -> IP address mappings for dynamic SLIP
# format: /dev/tty?? xxx.xxx.xxx.xxx
#
/dev/ttyS0      192.168.0.100
/dev/ttyS1      192.168.0.101
#
```

What this table says is that callers that dial in on port /dev/ttyS0 who have their remote address field in the /etc/slip.hosts file set to DYNAMIC will be assigned an address of 192.168.0.100.

In this way you need only allocate one address per port for all users who do not require an dedicated address for themselves. This helps you keep the number of addresses you need down to a minimum to avoid wastage.

7.6.2   Slip Server using *dip*.

Let me start by saying that some of the information below came from the *dip* man pages, where how to run Linux as a SLIP server is briefly documented. Please also beware that the following has been based on the *dip337o-uri.tgz* package and probably will not apply to other versions of *dip*.

dip has an input mode of operation, where it automatically locates an entry for the user who invoked it and configures the serial line as a SLIP link according to information it finds in the /etc/diphosts file. This input mode of operation is activated by invoking *dip* as *diplogin*. This therefore is how you use *dip* as a SLIP server, by creating special accounts where *diplogin* is used as the login shell.

The first thing you will need to do is to make a symbolic link as follows:

```
# ln -sf /usr/sbin/dip /usr/sbin/diplogin
```

You then need to add entries to both your `/etc/passwd` and your `/etc/diphosts` files. The entries you need to make are formatted as follows:

To configure Linux as a SLIP server with *dip*, you need to create some special SLIP accounts for users, where *dip* (in input mode) is used as the login shell. A suggested convention is that of having all SLIP accounts begin with a capital 'S', eg 'Sfredm'.

A sample `/etc/passwd` entry for a SLIP user looks like:

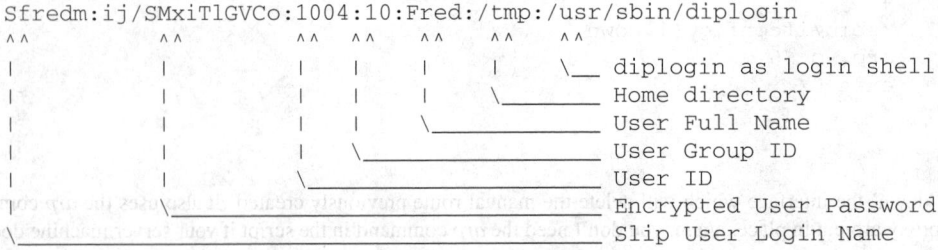

```
Sfredm:ij/SMxiTlGVCo:1004:10:Fred:/tmp:/usr/sbin/diplogin
       ^^         ^^      ^^   ^^   ^^    ^^   ^^
       |          |        |    |    |     |    \__ diplogin as login shell
       |          |        |    |    |     _____ Home directory
       |          |        |    |    _____ User Full Name
       |          |        |    _____ User Group ID
       |          |        _____ User ID
       |          _____ Encrypted User Password
       _____ Slip User Login Name
```

After the user logs in, the *login* program, if it finds and verifies the user ok, will execute the *diplogin* command. *dip*, when invoked as *diplogin* knows that it should automatically assume that it is being used a login shell. When it is started as *diplogin* the first thing it does is use the *getuid()* function call to get the userid of whoever has invoked it. It then searches the `/etc/diphosts` file for the first entry that matches either the userid or the name of the *tty* device that the call has come in on and configures itself appropriately. By judicious decision as to whether to give a user an entry in the `diphosts` file, or whether to let the user be given the default configuration you can build your server in such a way that you can have a mix of static and dynamically assigned address users.

dip will automatically add a 'Proxy-ARP' entry if invoked in input mode, so you do not need to worry about manually adding such entries.

Configuring `/etc/diphosts` `/etc/diphosts` is used by *dip* to lookup preset configurations for remote hosts. These remote hosts might be users dialing into your linux machine, or they might be for machines that you dial into with your linux machine.

The general format for `/etc/diphosts` is as follows:

```
    ..
Suwalt::145.71.34.1:145.71.34.2:255.255.255.0:SLIP uwalt:CSLIP,1006
ttyS1::145.71.34.3:145.71.34.2:255.255.255.0:Dynamic ttyS1:CSLIP,296
    ..
```

The fields are:

1. `login name`: as returned by getpwuid(getuid()) or tty name.
2. `unused`: compat. with passwd
3. `Remote Address`: IP address of the calling host, either numeric or by name
4. `Local Address`: IP address of this machine, again numeric or by name
5. `Netmask`: in dotted decimal notation
6. `Comment field`: put whatever you want here.
7. `protocol`: Slip, CSlip etc.
8. `MTU`: decimal number

An example `/etc/net/diphosts` entry for a remote SLIP user might be:

```
Sfredm::145.71.34.1:145.71.34.2:255.255.255.0:SLIP uwalt:SLIP,296
```

which specifies a SLIP link with remote address of 145.71.34.1 and MTU of 296, or:

```
Sfredm::145.71.34.1:145.71.34.2:255.255.255.0:SLIP uwalt:CSLIP,1006
```

which specifies a cSLIP-capable link with remote address 145.71.34.1 and MTU of 1006.

Therefore, all users who you wish to be allowed a statically allocated dial-up IP access should have an entry in the /etc/diphosts. If you want users who call a particular port to have their details dynamically allocated then you must have an entry for the `tty` device and do not configure a user based entry. You should remember to configure at least one entry for each `tty` device that your dialup users use to ensure that a suitable configuration is available for them regardless of which modem they call in on.

When a user logs in they will receive a normal login and password prompt at which they should enter their SLIP-login userid and password. If these verify ok then the user will see no special messages and they should just change into SLIP mode at their end. The user should then be able to connect ok and be configured with the relevant parameters from the `diphosts` file.

7.6.3 SLIP server using the *dSLIP* package.

Matt Dillon <dillon@apollo.west.oic.com> has written a package that does not only dial-in but also dial-out SLIP. Matt's package is a combination of small programs and scripts that manage your connections for you. You will need to have *tcsh* installed as at least one of the scripts requires it. Matt supplies a binary copy of the *expect* utility as it too is needed by one of the scripts. You will most likely need some experience with *expect* to get this package working to your liking, but don't let that put you off.

Matt has written a good set of installation instructions in the README file, so I won't bother repeating them.

You can get the *dSLIP* package from its home site at:

apollo.west.oic.com

```
/pub/linux/dillon_src/dSLIP203.tgz
```

or from:

sunsite.unc.edu

```
/pub/Linux/system/Network/serial/dSLIP203.tgz
```

Read the README file and create the /etc/passwd and /etc/group entries **before** doing a make install.

8   Other Network Technologies

The following subsections are specific to particular network technologies. The information contained in these sections does not necessarily apply to any other type of network technology. The topics are sorted alphabetically.

8.1   ARCNet

ARCNet device names are 'arc0e', 'arc1e', 'arc2e' etc. or 'arc0s', 'arc1s', 'arc2s' etc. The first card detected by the kernel is assigned 'arc0e' or 'arc0s' and the rest are assigned sequentially in the order they are detected. The letter at the end signifies whether you've selected ethernet encapsulation packet format or RFC1051 packet format.

Kernel Compile Options:

```
Network device support   --->
    [*] Network device support
    <*> ARCnet support
    [ ]    Enable arc0e (ARCnet "Ether-Encap" packet format)
    [ ]    Enable arc0s (ARCnet RFC1051 packet format)
```

Once you have your kernel properly built to support your ethernet card then configuration of the card is easy.

Typically you would use something like:

```
root# ifconfig arc0e 192.168.0.1 netmask 255.255.255.0 up
root# route add -net 192.168.0.0 netmask 255.255.255.0 arc0e
```

Please refer to the /usr/src/linux/Documentation/networking/arcnet.txt and /usr/src/linux/Documentation/networking/arcnet-hardware.txt files for further information.

ARCNet support was developed by Avery Pennarun, apenwarr@foxnet.net.

8.2 Appletalk (`AF_APPLETALK`)

The Appletalk support has no special device names as it uses existing network devices.

Kernel Compile Options:

```
Networking options   --->
    <*> Appletalk DDP
```

Appletalk support allows your Linux machine to interwork with Apple networks. An important use for this is to share resources such as printers and disks between both your Linux and Apple computers. Additional software is required, this is called *netatalk*. Wesley Craig netatalk@umich.edu represents a team called the 'Research Systems Unix Group' at the University of Michigan and they have produced the *netatalk* package which provides software that implements the Appletalk protocol stack and some useful utilities. The *netatalk* package will either have been supplied with your Linux distribution, or you will have to ftp it from its home site at the *University of Michigan* <ftp://terminator.rs.itd.umich.edu/unix/netatalk/>

To build and install the package do something like:

```
user% tar xvfz .../netatalk-1.4b2.tar.Z
user% make
root# make install
```

You may want to edit the 'Makefile' before calling *make* to actually compile the software. Specifically, you might want to change the DESTDIR variable which defines where the files will be installed later. The default of /usr/local/atalk is fairly safe.

8.2.1 Configuring the Appletalk software.

The first thing you need to do to make it all work is to ensure that the appropriate entries in the /etc/services file are present. The entries you need are:

```
rtmp   1/ddp   # Routing Table Maintenance Protocol
nbp    2/ddp   # Name Binding Protocol
echo   4/ddp   # AppleTalk Echo Protocol
zip    6/ddp   # Zone Information Protocol
```

The next step is to create the Appletalk configuration files in the `/usr/local/atalk/etc` directory (or wherever you installed the package).

The first file to create is the `/usr/local/atalk/etc/atalkd.conf` file. Initially this file needs only one line that gives the name of the network device that supports the network that your Apple machines are on:

```
eth0
```

The Appletalk daemon program will add extra details after it is run.

8.2.2   Exporting a Linux filesystems via Appletalk.

You can export filesystems from your linux machine to the network so that Apple machine on the network can share them.

To do this you must configure the `/usr/local/atalk/etc/AppleVolumes.system` file. There is another configuration file called `/usr/local/atalk/etc/AppleVolumes.default` which has exactly the same format and describes which filesystems users connecting with guest privileges will receive.

Full details on how to configure these files and what the various options are can be found in the *afpd* man page.

A simple example might look like:

```
/tmp Scratch
/home/ftp/pub "Public Area"
```

Which would export your `/tmp` filesystem as AppleShare Volume 'Scratch' and your ftp public directory as AppleShare Volume 'Public Area'. The volume names are not mandatory, the daemon will choose some for you, but it won't hurt to specify them anyway.

8.2.3   Sharing your Linux printer across Appletalk.

You can share your linux printer with your Apple machines quite simply. You need to run the *papd* program which is the Appletalk Printer Access Protocol Daemon. When you run this program it will accept requests from your Apple machines and spool the print job to your local line printer daemon for printing.

You need to edit the `/usr/local/atalk/etc/papd.conf` file to configure the daemon. The syntax of this file is the same as that of your usual `/etc/printcap` file. The name you give to the definition is registered with the Appletalk naming protocol, NBP.

A sample configuration might look like:

```
TricWriter:\
    :pr=lp:op=cg:
```

Which would make a printer named 'TricWriter' available to your Appletalk network and all accepted jobs would be printed to the linux printer 'lp' (as defined in the `/etc/printcap` file) using *lpd*. The entry 'op=cg' says that the linux user 'cg' is the operator of the printer.

HOWTO

8.2.4 Starting the appletalk software.

Ok, you should now be ready to test this basic configuration. There is an *rc.atalk* file supplied with the *netatalk* package that should work ok for you, so all you should have to do is:

```
root# /usr/local/atalk/etc/rc.atalk
```

and all should startup and run ok. You should see no error messages and the software will send messages to the console indicating each stage as it starts.

8.2.5 Testing the appletalk software.

To test that the software is functioning properly, go to one of your Apple machines, pull down the Apple menu, select the Chooser, click on AppleShare, and your Linux box should appear.

8.2.6 Caveats of the appletalk software.

- You may need to start the Appletalk support before you configure your IP network. If you have problems starting the Appletalk programs, or if after you start them you have trouble with your IP network, then try starting the Appletalk software before you run your `/etc/rc.d/rc.inet1` file.

- The *afpd* (Apple Filing Protocol Daemon) severely messes up your hard disk. Below the mount points it creates a couple of directories called ".AppleDesktop" and `Network Trash Folder`. Then, for each directory you access it will create a `.AppleDouble` below it so it can store resource forks, etc. So think twice before exporting `/`, you will have a great time cleaning up afterwards.

- The *afpd* program expects clear text passwords from the Macs. Security could be a problem, so be very careful when you run this daemon on a machine connected to the Internet, you have yourself to blame if somebody nasty does something bad.

- The existing diagnostic tools such as *netstat* and *ifconfig* don't support Appletalk. The raw information is available in the `/proc/net/` directory if you need it.

8.2.7 More information

For a much more detailed description of how to configure Appletalk for Linux refer to Anders Brownworth *Linux Netatalk-HOWTO* page at *thehamptons.com* <http://thehamptons.com/anders/netatalk/>.

8.3 ATM

Werner Almesberger <werner.almesberger@lrc.di.epfl.ch> is managing a project to provide Asynchronous Transfer Mode support for Linux. Current information on the status of the project may be obtained from: *lrcwww.epfl.ch* <http://lrcwww.epfl.ch/linux-atm/>.

8.4 AX25 (AF_AX25)

AX.25 device names are 's10', 's11', etc. in 2.0.* kernels or 'ax0', 'ax1', etc. in 2.1.* kernels.

Kernel Compile Options:

```
Networking options  --->
    [*] Amateur Radio AX.25 Level 2
```

The AX25, Netrom and Rose protocols are covered by the *AX25-HOWTO* <AX25-HOWTO.html>. These protocols are used by Amateur Radio Operators world wide in packet radio experimentation.

Most of the work for implementation of these protocols has been done by Jonathon Naylor, jsn@cs.nott.ac.uk.

8.5 DECNet

Support for DECNet is currently being worked on. You should expect it to appear in a late `2.1.*` kernel.

8.6 FDDI

FDDI device names are 'fddi0', 'fddi1', 'fddi2' etc. The first card detected by the kernel is assigned 'fddi0' and the rest are assigned sequentially in the order they are detected.

Larry Stefani, `lstefani@ultranet.com`, has developed a driver for the Digital Equipment Corporation FDDI EISA and PCI cards.

Kernel Compile Options:

```
Network device support   --->
    [*] FDDI driver support
    [*] Digital DEFEA and DEFPA adapter support
```

When you have your kernel built to support the FDDI driver and installed, configuration of the FDDI interface is almost identical to that of an ethernet interface. You just specify the appropriate FDDI interface name in the *ifconfig* and *route* commands.

8.7 Frame Relay

The Frame Relay device names are 'dlci00', 'dlci01' etc for the DLCI encapsulation devices and 'sdla0', 'sdla1' etc for the FRAD(s).

Frame Relay is a new networking technology that is designed to suit data communications traffic that is of a 'bursty' or intermittent nature. You connect to a Frame Relay network using a Frame Relay Access Device (FRAD). The Linux Frame Relay supports IP over Frame Relay as described in RFC-1490.

Kernel Compile Options:

```
Network device support   --->
    <*> Frame relay DLCI support (EXPERIMENTAL)
    (24)    Max open DLCI
    (8)     Max DLCI per device
    <*>     SDLA (Sangoma S502/S508) support
```

Mike McLagan, `mike.mclagan@linux.org`, developed the Frame Relay support and configuration tools.

Currently the only FRAD supported are the *Sangoma Technologies* `<http://www.sangoma.com/>` S502A, S502E and S508.

To configure the FRAD and DLCI devices after you have rebuilt your kernel you will need the Frame Relay configuration tools. These are available from *ftp.invlogic.com* `<ftp://ftp.invlogic.com/pub/linux/fr/frad-0.15.tgz>`. Compiling and installing the tools is straightforward, but the lack of a top level Makefile makes it a fairly manual process:

```
user% tar xvfz .../frad-0.15.tgz
user% cd frad-0.15
user% for i in common dlci frad; make -C $i clean; make -C $i; done
root# mkdir /etc/frad
root# install -m 644 -o root -g root bin/*.sfm /etc/frad
root# install -m 700 -o root -g root frad/fradcfg /sbin
```

```
rppt# install -m 700 -o root -g root dlci/dlcicfg /sbin
```

Note that the previous commands use *sh* syntax, if you use a *csh* flavour instead (like *tcsh*), the *for* loop will look different.

After installing the tools you need to create an /etc/frad/router.conf file. You can use this template, which is a modified version of one of the example files:

```
# /etc/frad/router.conf
# This is a template configuration for frame relay.
# All tags are included. The default values are based on the code
# supplied with the DOS drivers for the Sangoma S502A card.
#
# A '#' anywhere in a line constitutes a comment
# Blanks are ignored (you can indent with tabs too)
# Unknown [] entries and unknown keys are ignored
#

[Devices]
Count=1                     # number of devices to configure
Dev_1=sdla0                 # the name of a device
#Dev_2=sdla1                # the name of a device

# Specified here, these are applied to all devices and can be overridden for
# each individual board.
#
Access=CPE
Clock=Internal
KBaud=64
Flags=TX
#
# MTU=1500                  # Maximum transmit IFrame length, default is 4096
# T391=10                   # T391 value    5 - 30, default is 10
# T392=15                   # T392 value    5 - 30, default is 15
# N391=6                    # N391 value    1 - 255, default is 6
# N392=3                    # N392 value    1 - 10, default is 3
# N393=4                    # N393 value    1 - 10, default is 4

# Specified here, these set the defaults for all boards
# CIRfwd=16                 # CIR forward    1 - 64
# Bc_fwd=16                 # Bc forward     1 - 512
# Be_fwd=0                  # Be forward     0 - 511
# CIRbak=16                 # CIR backward   1 - 64
# Bc_bak=16                 # Bc backward    1 - 512
# Be_bak=0                  # Be backward    0 - 511


#
#
# Device specific configuration
#
#


#
# The first device is a Sangoma S502E
```

```
#
[sdla0]
Type=Sangoma              # Type of the device to configure, currently only
                          # SANGOMA is recognized
#
# These keys are specific to the 'Sangoma' type
#
# The type of Sangoma board - S502A, S502E, S508
Board=S502E
#
# The name of the test firmware for the Sangoma board
# Testware=/usr/src/frad-0.10/bin/sdla_tst.502
#
# The name of the FR firmware
# Firmware=/usr/src/frad-0.10/bin/frm_rel.502
#
Port=360                  # Port for this particular card
Mem=C8                    # Address of memory window, A0-EE, depending on card
IRQ=5                     # IRQ number, do not supply for S502A
DLCIs=1                   # Number of DLCI's attached to this device
DLCI_1=16                 # DLCI #1's number, 16 - 991
# DLCI_2=17
# DLCI_3=18
# DLCI_4=19
# DLCI_5=20
#
# Specified here, these apply to this device only,
# and override defaults from above
#
# Access=CPE              # CPE or NODE, default is CPE
# Flags=TXIgnore,RXIgnore,BufferFrames,DropAborted,Stats,MCI,AutoDLCI
# Clock=Internal          # External or Internal, default is Internal
# Baud=128                # Specified baud rate of attached CSU/DSU
# MTU=2048                # Maximum transmit IFrame length, default is 4096
# T391=10                 # T391 value    5 - 30, default is 10
# T392=15                 # T392 value    5 - 30, default is 15
# N391=6                  # N391 value    1 - 255, default is 6
# N392=3                  # N392 value    1 - 10, default is 3
# N393=4                  # N393 value    1 - 10, default is 4


#
# The second device is some other card
#
# [sdla1]
# Type=FancyCard          # Type of the device to configure.
# Board=                  # Type of Sangoma board
# Key=Value               # values specific to this type of device


#
# DLCI Default configuration parameters
# These may be overridden in the DLCI specific configurations
#
CIRfwd=64                 # CIR forward    1 - 64
# Bc_fwd=16               # Bc forward     1 - 512
```

```
# Be_fwd=0             # Be forward    0 - 511
# CIRbak=16            # CIR backward   1 - 64
# Bc_bak=16            # Bc backward    1 - 512
# Be_bak=0             # Be backward    0 - 511


#
# DLCI Configuration
# These are all optional. The naming convention is
# [DLCI_D<devicenum>_<DLCI_Num>]
#

[DLCI_D1_16]
# IP=
# Net=
# Mask=
# Flags defined by Sangoma: TXIgnore,RXIgnore,BufferFrames
# DLCIFlags=TXIgnore,RXIgnore,BufferFrames
# CIRfwd=64
# Bc_fwd=512
# Be_fwd=0
# CIRbak=64
# Bc_bak=512
# Be_bak=0

[DLCI_D2_16]
# IP=
# Net=
# Mask=
# Flags defined by Sangoma: TXIgnore,RXIgnore,BufferFrames
# DLCIFlags=TXIgnore,RXIgnore,BufferFrames
# CIRfwd=16
# Bc_fwd=16
# Be_fwd=0
# CIRbak=16
# Bc_bak=16
# Be_bak=0
```

When you've built your `/etc/frad/router.conf` file the only step remaining is to configure the actual devices themselves. This is only a little trickier than a normal network device configuration, you need to remember to bring up the FRAD device before the DLCI encapsulation devices. These commands are best hosted in a shell script, due to their number:

```
#!/bin/sh
# Configure the frad hardware and the DLCI parameters
/sbin/fradcfg /etc/frad/router.conf || exit 1
/sbin/dlcicfg file /etc/frad/router.conf
#
# Bring up the FRAD device
ifconfig sdla0 up
#
# Configure the DLCI encapsulation interfaces and routing
ifconfig dlci00 192.168.10.1 pointopoint 192.168.10.2 up
route add -net 192.168.10.0 netmask 255.255.255.0 dlci00
#
ifconfig dlci01 192.168.11.1 pointopoint 192.168.11.2 up
```

```
route add -net 192.168.11.0 netmask 255.255.255.0 dlci00
#
route add default dev dlci00
#
```

8.8   IPX (`AF_IPX`)

The IPX protocol is most commonly utilized in Novell NetWare(tm) local area network environments. Linux includes support for this protocol and may be configured to act as a network endpoint, or as a router for IPX.

Kernel Compile Options:

```
Networking options   --->
        [*] The IPX protocol
        [ ] Full internal IPX network
```

The IPX protocol and the NCPFS are covered in greater depth in the *IPX-HOWTO* <IPX-HOWTO.html>.

8.9   NetRom (`AF_NETROM`)

NetRom device names are 'nr0', 'nr1', etc.

Kernel Compile Options:

```
Networking options   --->
        [*] Amateur Radio AX.25 Level 2
        [*] Amateur Radio NET/ROM
```

The AX25, Netrom and Rose protocols are covered by the *AX25-HOWTO* <AX25-HOWTO.html>. These protocols are used by Amateur Radio Operators world wide in packet radio experimentation.

Most of the work for implementation of these protocols has been done by Jonathon Naylor, jsn@cs.nott.ac.uk.

8.10   Rose protocol (`AF_ROSE`)

Rose device names are 'rs0', 'rs1', etc. in 2.1.* kernels. Rose is available in the 2.1.* kernels.

Kernel Compile Options:

```
Networking options   --->
        [*] Amateur Radio AX.25 Level 2
        <*> Amateur Radio X.25 PLP (Rose)
```

The AX25, Netrom and Rose protocols are covered by the *AX25-HOWTO* <AX25-HOWTO.html>. These protocols are used by Amateur Radio Operators world wide in packet radio experimentation.

Most of the work for implementation of these protocols has been done by Jonathon Naylor, jsn@cs.nott.ac.uk.

HOWTO

8.11 SAMBA - 'NetBEUI', 'NetBios' support.

SAMBA is an implementation of the Session Management Block protocol. Samba allows Microsoft and other systems to mount and use your disks and printers.

SAMBA and its configuration are covered in detail in the *SMB-HOWTO* `<SMB-HOWTO.html>`.

8.12 STRIP support (Starmode Radio IP)

STRIP device names are 'st0', 'st1', etc.

Kernel Compile Options:

```
Network device support  --->
        [*] Network device support
        ....
        [*] Radio network interfaces
        < > STRIP (Metricom starmode radio IP)
```

STRIP is a protocol designed specifically for a range of Metricom radio modems for a research project being conducted by Stanford University called the *MosquitoNet Project* `<http://mosquitonet.Stanford.EDU/mosquitonet.html>`. There is a lot of interesting reading here, even if you aren't directly interested in the project.

The Metricom radios connect to a serial port, employ spread spectrum technology and are typically capable of about 100kbps. Information on the Metricom radios is available from the: *Metricom Web Server* `<http://www.metricom.com/>`.

At present the standard network tools and utilities do not support the STRIP driver, so you will have to download some customized tools from the MosquitoNet web server. Details on what software you need is available at the: *MosquitoNet STRIP Page* `<http://mosquitonet.Stanford.EDU/strip.html>`.

A summary of configuration is that you use a modified *slattach* program to set the line discipline of a serial tty device to STRIP and then configure the resulting 'st[0-9]' device as you would for ethernet with one important exception, for technical reasons STRIP does not support the ARP protocol, so you must manually configure the ARP entries for each of the hosts on your subnet. This shouldn't prove too onerous.

8.13 Token Ring

Token ring device names are 'tr0', 'tr1' etc. Token Ring is an IBM standard LAN protocol that avoids collisions by providing a mechanism that allows only one station on the LAN the right to transmit at a time. A 'token' is held by one station at a time and the station holding the token is the only station allowed to transmit. When it has transmitted its data it passes the token onto the next station. The token loops amongst all active stations, hence the name 'Token Ring'.

Kernel Compile Options:

```
Network device support  --->
        [*] Network device support
        ....
        [*] Token Ring driver support
        < > IBM Tropic chipset based adaptor support
```

Configuration of token ring is identical to that of ethernet with the exception of the network device name to configure.

8.14   X.25

X.25 is a circuit based packet switching protocol defined by the `C.C.I.T.T.` (a standards body recognized by T-elecommunications companies in most parts of the world). An implementation of X.25 and LAPB are being worked on and recent `2.1.*` kernels include the work in progress.

Jonathon Naylor `jsn@cs.nott.ac.uk` is leading the development and a mailing list has been established to discuss Linux X.25 related matters. To subscribe send a message to: `majordomo@vger.rutgers.edu` with the text `"subscribe linux-x25"` in the body of the message.

Early versions of the configuration tools may be obtained from Jonathon's ftp site at *ftp.cs.nott.ac.uk* `<ftp://ftp.cs.nott.ac.uk/jsn/>`.

8.15   WaveLan Card

Wavelan device names are 'eth0', 'eth1', etc.

Kernel Compile Options:

```
Network device support  --->
        [*] Network device support
        ....
        [*] Radio network interfaces
        ....
        <*> WaveLAN support
```

The WaveLAN card is a spread spectrum wireless lan card. The card looks very like an ethernet card in practice and is configured in much the same way.

You can get information on the Wavelan card from *Wavelan.com* `<http://www.wavelan.com/>`.

9   Cables and Cabling

Those of you handy with a soldering iron may want to build your own cables to interconnect two linux machines. The following cabling diagrams should assist you in this.

9.1   Serial NULL Modem cable

Not all NULL modem cables are alike. Many null modem cables do little more than trick your computer into thinking all the appropriate signals are present and swap transmit and receive data. This is ok but means that you must use software flow control (XON/XOFF) which is less efficient than hardware flow control. The following cable provides the best possible signalling between machines and allows you to use hardware (RTS/CTS) flow control.

```
Pin Name  Pin                                      Pin
Tx Data   2   ----------------------------------- 3
Rx Data   3   ----------------------------------- 2
RTS       4   ----------------------------------- 5
CTS       5   ----------------------------------- 4
Ground    7   ----------------------------------- 7
DTR       20  -\----------------------------------- 8
DSR       6   -/
RLSD/DCD  8   -----------------------------------/- 20
                                               \- 6
```

9.2 Parallel port cable (PLIP cable)

If you intend to use the PLIP protocol between two machines then this cable will work for you irrespective of what sort of parallel ports you have installed.

```
Pin Name       pin           pin
STROBE         1*
D0->ERROR      2  ----------- 15
D1->SLCT       3  ----------- 13
D2->PAPOUT     4  ----------- 12
D3->ACK        5  ----------- 10
D4->BUSY       6  ----------- 11
D5             7*
D6             8*
D7             9*
ACK->D3        10 ----------- 5
BUSY->D4       11 ----------- 6
PAPOUT->D2     12 ----------- 4
SLCT->D1       13 ----------- 3
FEED           14*
ERROR->D0      15 ----------- 2
INIT           16*
SLCTIN         17*
GROUND         25 ----------- 25
```

Notes:

- Do not connect the pins marked with an asterisk '*'.
- Extra grounds are 18,19,20,21,22,23 and 24.
- If the cable you are using has a metallic shield, it should be connected to the metallic DB-25 shell at **one end only**.

Warning: A miswired PLIP cable can destroy your controller card. Be very careful and double check every connection to ensure you don't cause yourself any unnecessary work or heartache.

While you may be able to run PLIP cables for long distances, you should avoid it if you can. The specifications for the cable allow for a cable length of about 1 metre or so. Please be very careful when running long plip cables as sources of strong electromagnetic fields such as lightning, power lines and radio transmitters can interfere with and sometimes even damage your controller. If you really want to connect two of your computers over a large distance you really should be looking at obtaining a pair of thin-net ethernet cards and running some coaxial cable.

9.3 10base2 (thin coax) Ethernet Cabling

10base2 is an ethernet cabling standard that specifies the use of 52 ohm coaxial cable with a diameter of about 5 millimeters. There are a couple of important rules to remember when interconnecting machines with 10base2 cabling. The first is that you must use terminators at **both ends** of the cabling. A terminator is a 52 ohm resistor that helps to ensure that the signal is absorbed and not reflected when it reaches the end of the cable. Without a terminator at each end of the cabling you may find that the ethernet is unreliable or doesn't work at all. Normally you'd use 'T pieces' to interconnect the machines, so that you end up with something that looks like:

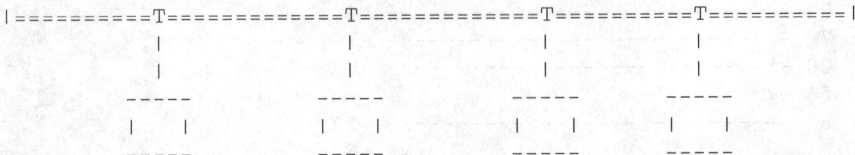

where the '|' at either end represents a terminator, the '======' represents a length of coaxial cable with BNC plugs at either end and the 'T' represents a 'T piece' connector. You should keep the length of cable between the 'T piece' and the actual ethernet card in the PC as short as possible, ideally the 'T piece' will be plugged directly into the ethernet card.

9.4 Twisted Pair Ethernet Cable

If you have only two twisted pair ethernet cards and you wish to connect them you do not require a hub. You can cable the two cards directly together. A diagram showing how to do this is included in the *Ethernet-HOWTO* `<Ethernet-HOWTO.html>`

10 Glossary of Terms used in this document.

The following is a list of some of the most important terms used in this document.

ARP

> This is an acronym for the *Address Resolution Protocol* and this is how a network machine associates an IP Address with a hardware address.

ATM

> This is an acronym for *Asynchronous Transfer Mode*. An ATM network packages data into standard size blocks which it can convey efficiently from point to point. ATM is a circuit switched packet network technology.

client

> This is usually the piece of software at the end of a system where the user is. There are exceptions to this, for example, in the X11 window system it is actually the server with the user and the client runs on the remote machine. The client is the program or end of a system that is receiving the service provided by the server. In the case of *peer to peer* systems such as *slip* or *ppp* the client is taken to be the end that initiates the connection and the remote end, being called, is taken to be the server.

datagram

> A datagram is a discrete package of data and headers which contain addresses, which is the basic unit of transmission across an IP network. You might also hear this called a 'packet'.

DLCI

> The DLCI is the Data Link Connection Identifier and is used to identify a unique virtual point to point connection via a Frame Relay network. The DLCI's are normally assigned by the Frame Relay network provider.

Frame Relay

> Frame Relay is a network technology ideally suited to carrying traffic that is of bursty or sporadic nature. Network costs are reduced by having many Frame Relay customer sharing the same network capacity and relying on them wanting to make use of the network at slightly different times.

Hardware address

> This is a number that uniquely identifies a host in a physical network at the media access layer. Examples of this are *Ethernet Addresses* and *AX.25 Addresses*.

ISDN

> This is an acronym for *Integrated Services Digital Network*. ISDN provides a standardized means by which T-elecommunications companies may deliver either voice or data information to a customers premises. Technically ISDN is a circuit switched data network.

ISP

> This is an acronym of Internet Service Provider. These are organizations or companies that provide people with network connectivity to the Internet.

IP address

> This is a number that uniquely identifies a TCP/IP host on the network. The address is 4 bytes long and is usually represented in what is called the "dotted decimal notation", where each byte is represented in decimal from with dots '.' between them.

HOWTO

MSS

The Maximum Segment Size (*MSS*) is the largest quantity of data that can be transmitted at one time. If you want to prevent local fragmentation MSS would equal MTU-IP header.

MTU

The Maximum Transmission Unit (*MTU*) is a parameter that determines the largest datagram than can be transmitted by an IP interface without it needing to be broken down into smaller units. The MTU should be larger than the largest datagram you wish to transmit unfragmented. Note, this only prevents fragmentation locally, some other link in the path may have a smaller MTU and the datagram will be fragmented there. Typical values are 1500 bytes for an ethernet interface, or 576 bytes for a SLIP interface.

route

The *route* is the path that your datagrams take through the network to reach their destination.

server

This is usually the piece of software or end of a system remote from the user. The server provides some service to one or many clients. Examples of servers include *ftp*, *Networked File System*, or *Domain Name Server*. In the case of *peer to peer* systems such as *slip* or *ppp* the server is taken to be the end of the link that is called and the end calling is taken to be the client.

window

The *window* is the largest amount of data that the receiving end can accept at a given point in time.

11   Linux for an ISP ?

If you are interested in using Linux for ISP purposes the I recommend you take a look at the *Linux ISP homepage* <http://www.anime.net/linuxisp/> for a good list of pointers to information you might need and use.

12   Acknowledgements

I'd like to thank the following people for their contributions to this document (in no particular order): Terry Dawson, Axel Boldt, Arnt Gulbrandsen, Gary Allpike, Cees de Groot, Alan Cox, Jonathon Naylor, Claes Ensson, Ron Nessim, John Minack, Jean-Pierre Cocatrix, Erez Strauss.

13   Copyright.

The NET-3-HOWTO, information on how to install and configure networking support for Linux. Copyright (c) 1997 Terry Dawson, 1998 Alessandro Rubini

This program is free software; you can redistribute it and/or modify it under the terms of the GNU General Public License as published by the Free Software Foundation; either version 2 of the License, or (at your option) any later version.

This program is distributed in the hope that it will be useful, but WITHOUT ANY WARRANTY; without even the implied warranty of MERCHANTABILITY or FITNESS FOR A PARTICULAR PURPOSE. See the GNU General Public License for more details.

You should have received a copy of the GNU General Public License along with this program; if not, write to the:

Free Software Foundation, Inc., 675 Mass Ave, Cambridge, MA 02139, USA.

## Part XXIX

"NFS HOWTO" Nicolai Langfeldt

janl@math.uio.no
v0.7, 3 November 1997
HOWTO set up NFS clients and servers.

Contents

HOWTO

1   Preamble

1.1   Legal stuff

(C)opyright 1997 Nicolai Langfeldt. Do not modify without amending copyright, distribute freely but retain this paragraph. The FAQ section is based on a NFS FAQ compiled by Alan Cox. The Checklist section is based on a mount problem checklist compiled by the IBM Corporation.

1.2   Other stuff

This will never be a finished document, please send me mail about your problems and successes, it can make this a better HOWTO. Please send money, comments and/or questions to janl@math.uio.no. If you send E-mail please *make sure* that the return address is correct and working, I get *a lot* of E-mail and figuring out your e-mail address can be a lot of work. Please.

If you want to translate this HOWTO please notify me so I can keep track of what languages I have been published in :-).

Curses and Thanks to Olaf Kirch who got me to write this and then gave good suggestions for it :-)

This HOWTO covers NFS in the 2.0 versions of the kernel. There are significant enhancements, and changes, of NFS in the 2.1 versions of the kernel.

1.3   Dedication

This HOWTO is dedicated to Anne Line Norheim Langfeldt. Though she will probably never read it since she's not that kind of girl.

2   README.first

NFS, the Network File System has three important characteristics:

- It makes sharing of files over a network possible.
- It mostly works well enough.
- It opens a can of security risks that are well understood by crackers, and easily exploited to get access (read, write and delete) to all your files.

I'll say something on both issues in this HOWTO. Please make sure you read the security section of this HOWTO, and you will be vulnerable to fewer silly security risks. The passages about security will at times be pretty technical and require some knowledge about IP networking and the terms used. If you don't recognize the terms you can either go back and check the networking HOWTO, wing it, or get a book about TCP/IP network administration to familiarize yourself with TCP/IP. That's a good idea anyway if you're administrating UNIX/Linux machines. A very good book on the subject is *TCP/IP Network Administration* by Craig Hunt, published by O'Reilly & Associates, Inc. And after you've read it and understood it you'll have higher value on the job market, you can't loose ;-)

There are two sections to help you troubleshoot NFS, called *Mount Checklist* and *FAQs*. Please refer to them if something dosn't work as advertized.

3   Setting up a NFS server

3.1   Prerequisites

Before you continue reading this HOWTO you will need to be able to telnet back and forth between the machine you're using as server and the client. If that does not work you need to check the networking/NET-2 HOWTO and set up networking properly.

3.2   First step

Before we can do anything else we need a NFS server set up. If you're part of a department or university network there are likely numerous NFS servers already set up. If they will let you get access to them, or indeed, if you're reading this HOWTO to get access to one of them you obviously don't need to read this section and can just skip ahead to the section on 4 (setting up a NFS client)

If you need to set up a non-Linux box as server you will have to read the system manual(s) to discover how to enable NFS serving and export of file systems through NFS. There is a separate section in this HOWTO on how to do it on many different systems. After you have figured all that out you can continue reading the next section of this HOWTO. Or read more of this section since some of the things I will say are relevant no matter what kind of machine you use as server.

Those of you still reading will need to set up a number of programs.

3.3   The portmapper

The portmapper on Linux is called either `portmap` or `rpc.portmap`. The man page on my system says it is a "DARPA port to RPC program number mapper". It is the first security holes you'll open reading this HOWTO. Description of how to close one of the holes is in the 6 (security section). Which I, again, urge you to read.

Start the portmapper. It's either called `portmap` or `rpc.portmap` and it should live in the `/usr/sbin` directory (on some machines it's called rpcbind). You can start it by hand now, but it will need to be started every time you boot your machine so you need to make/edit the rc scripts. Your rc scripts are explained more closely in the init man page, they usually reside in `/etc/rc.d`, `/etc/init.d` or `/etc/rc.d/init.d`. If there is a script called something like `inet` it's probably the right script to edit. But, what to write or do is outside the scope of this HOWTO. Start portmap, and check that it lives by running `ps aux`. It does? Good.

3.4   Mountd and nfsd

The next programs we need running are mountd and nfsd. But first we'll edit another file. `/etc/exports` this time. Say I want the file system `/mn/eris/local` which lives on the machine `eris` to be available to the machine called `apollon`. Then I'd put this in `/etc/exports` on eris:

```
/mn/eris/local  apollon(rw)
```

The above line gives apollon read/write access to `/mn/eris/local`. Instead of `rw` it could say `ro` which means read only (if you put nothing it defaults to read only). There are other options you can give it, and I will discuss some security related ones later. They are all enumerated in the `exports` man page which you should have read at least once in your life. There are also better ways than listing all the hosts in the exports file. You can for example use net groups if you are running NIS (or NYS) (NIS was known as YP), and always specify domain wild cards and IP-subnets as hosts that are allowed to mount something. But you should consider who can get access to the server in unauthorized ways if you use such blanket authorizations.

Note: This exports file is not the same syntax that other Unixes use. There is a separate section in this HOWTO about other Unixes `exports` files.

Now we're set to start mountd (or maybe it's called `rpc.mountd` and then nfsd (which could be called `rpc.nfsd`). They will both read the exports file.

If you edit `/etc/exports` you will have to make sure nfsd and mountd knows that the files have changed. The traditonal way is to run `exportfs`. Many Linux distributions lack a exportfs program. If you're exportfs-less you can install this script on your machine:

```
#!/bin/sh
killall -HUP /usr/sbin/rpc.mountd
killall -HUP /usr/sbin/rpc.nfsd
echo re-exported file systems
```

Save it in, say, `/usr/sbin/exportfs`, and don't forget to `chmod a+rx` it. Now, whenever you change your exports file, you run exportfs after, as root.

Now you should check that mountd and nfsd are running properly. First with `rpcinfo -p`. It should show something like this:

```
program vers proto    port
100000    2   tcp     111    portmapper
100000    2   udp     111    portmapper
100005    1   udp     745    mountd
100005    1   tcp     747    mountd
100003    2   udp    2049    nfs
100003    2   tcp    2049    nfs
```

As you see the portmapper has announced it's services, and so has mountd and nfsd.

If you get `rpcinfo: can't contact portmapper: RPC: Remote system error - Connection refused` or something similar instead then the portmapper isn't running. Fix it. If you get `No remote programs registered.` then either the portmapper doesn't want to talk to you, or something is broken. Kill nfsd, mountd, and the portmapper and try the ignition sequence again.

After checking that the portmapper reports the services you can check with ps too. The portmapper will continue to report the services even after the programs that extend them have crashed. So a ps check can be smart if something seems broken.

Of course, you will need to modify your system rc files to start mountd and nfsd as well as the portmapper when you boot. It is very likely that the scripts already exist on your machine, you just have to uncomment the critical section or activate it for the correct init run levels.

Man pages you should be familiar with now: portmap, mountd, nfsd, and exports.

Well, if you did everything exactly like I said you should you're all set to start on the NFS client.

4 Setting up a NFS client

First you will need a kernel with the NFS file system either compiled in or available as a module. This is configured before you compile the kernel. If you have never compiled a kernel before you might need to check the kernel HOWTO and figure it out. If you're using a very cool distribution (like Red Hat) and you've never fiddled with the kernel or modules on it (and thus ruined it ;-), nfs is likely automagicaly available to you.

You can now, at a root prompt, enter a appropriate mount command and the file system will appear. Continuing the example in the previous section we want to mount `/mn/eris/local` from eris. This is done with this command:

```
mount -o rsize=1024,wsize=1024 eris:/mn/eris/local /mnt
```

(We'll get back to the rsize and wsize options.) The file system is now available under /mnt and you can cd there, and ls in it, and look at the individual files. You will notice that it's not as fast as a local file system, but a lot more convenient than ftp. If, instead of mounting the file system, mount produces a error message like mount: eris:/mn/eris/local failed, reason given by server: Permission denied then the exports file is wrong, or you forgot to run exportfs after editing the exports file. If it says mount clntudp_create: RPC: Program not registered it means that nfsd or mountd is not running on the server.

To get rid of the file system you can say

```
umount /mnt
```

To make the system mount a nfs file system upon boot you edit /etc/fstab in the normal manner. For our example a line such as this is required:

```
# device          mountpoint      fs-type      options              dump fsckorder
...
eris:/mn/eris/local  /mnt      nfs          rsize=1024,wsize=1024 0     0
...
```

That's all there is too it, almost. Read on please.

4.1 Mount options

There are some options you should consider adding at once. They govern the way the NFS client handles a server crash or network outage. One of the cool things about NFS is that it can handle this gracefully. If you set up the clients right. There are two distinct failure modes:

soft

> The NFS client will report and error to the process accessing a file on a NFS mounted file system. Some programs can handle this with composure, most won't. I cannot recommend using this setting.

hard

> The program accessing a file on a NFS mounted file system will hang when the server crashes. The process cannot be interrupted or killed unless you also specify intr. When the NFS server is back online the program will continue undisturbed from where it were. This is probably what you want. I recommend using hard,intr on all NFS mounted file systems.

Picking up the previous example, this is now your fstab entry:

```
# device          mountpoint      fs-type      options              dump fsckorder
...
eris:/mn/eris/local  /mnt      nfs          rsize=1024,wsize=1024,hard,intr 0 0
...
```

4.2 Optimizing NFS

Normally, if no rsize and wsize options are specified NFS will read and write in chunks of 4096 or 8192 bytes. Some combinations of Linux kernels and network cards cannot handle that large blocks, and it might not be optimal, anyway. So we'll want to experiment and find a rsize and wsize that works and is as fast as possible. You can test the speed of your options with some simple commands. Given the mount command above and that you have write access to the disk you can do this to test the sequential write performance:

```
time dd if=/dev/zero of=/mnt/testfile bs=16k count=4096
```

This creates a 64Mb file of zeroed bytes (which should be large enough that caching is no significant part of any performance perceived, use a larger file if you have a lot of memory). Do it a couple (5-10?) of times and average the times. It is the 'elapsed' or 'wall clock' time that's most interesting in this connection. Then you can test the read performance by reading back the file:

```
time dd if=/mnt/testfile of=/dev/null bs=16k
```

do that a couple of times and average. Then umount, and mount again with a larger rsize and wsize. They should probably be multiples of 1024, and not larger than 16384 bytes since that's the maximum size in NFS version 2. Directly after mounting with a larger size cd into the mounted file system and do things like ls, explore the fs a bit to make sure everything is as it should. If the rsize/wsize is too large the symptoms are *very* odd and not 100% obvious. A typical symptom is incomplete file lists when doing 'ls', and no error messages. Or reading files failing mysteriously with no error messages. After establishing that the given rsize/wsize works you can do the speed tests again. Different server platforms are likely to have different optimal sizes. SunOS and Solaris is reputedly a lot faster with 4096 byte blocks than with anything else.

Newer Linux kernels (since 1.3 sometime) perform read-ahead for rsizes larger or equal to the machine page size. On Intel CPUs the page size is 4096 bytes. Read ahead will *significantly* increase the NFS read performance. So on a Intel machine you will want 4096 byte rsize if at all possible.

Remember to edit /etc/fstab to reflect the rsize/wsize you found.

A trick to increase NFS write performance is to disable synchronous writes on the server. The NFS specification states that NFS write requests shall not be considered finished before the data written is on a non-volatile medium (normally the disk). This restricts the write performance somewhat, asynchronous writes will speed NFS writes up. The Linux nfsd has never done synchronous writes since the Linux file system implementation does not lend itself to this, but on non-Linux servers you can increase the performance this way with this in your exports file:

```
/dir    -async,access=linuxbox
```

or something similar. Please refer to the exports man page on the machine in question. Please note that this increases the risk of data loss.

5 NFS over slow lines

Slow lines include Modems, ISDN and quite possibly other long distance connections.

This section is based on knowledge about the used protocols but no actual experiments. My home computer has been down for 6 months (bad HD, low on cash) and so I have had no modem connection to test this with. Please let me hear from you if try this :-)

The first thing to remember is that NFS is a slow protocol. It has high overhead. Using NFS is almost like using kermit to transfer files. It's *slow*. Almost anything is faster than NFS. FTP is faster. HTTP is faster. rcp is faster. ssh is faster.

Still determined to try it out? Ok.

NFS' default parameters are for quite fast, low latency, lines. If you use these default parameters over high latency lines it can cause NFS to report errors, abort operations, pretend that files are shorter than they really are, and act mysteriously in other ways.

The first thing to do is *not* to use the soft mount option. This will cause timeouts to return errors to the software, which will, most likely not handle the situation at all well. This is a good way to get for mysterious failures. Instead use the hard mount option. When `hard` is active timeouts causes infinite retries instead of aborting whatever it was the software wanted to do. This is what you want. Really.

The next thing to do is to tweak the timeo and retrans mount options. They are described in the nfs(5) man page, but here is a copy:

> timeo=n   The value in tenths of a second before
>   sending the first retransmission after an
>   RPC timeout.   The default value is 7 tenths
>   of a second. After the first timeout, the
>   timeout is doubled after each successive
>   timeout until a maximum timeout of 60 sec-
>   onds is reached or the enough retransmis-
>   sions have occured to cause a major time-
>   out. Then, if the filesystem is hard
>   mounted, each new timeout cascade restarts
>   at twice the initial value of the previous
>   cascade, again doubling at each retransmis-
>   sion. The maximum timeout is always 60
>   seconds. Better overall performance may be
>   achieved by increasing the timeout when
>   mounting on a busy network, to a slow
>   server, or through several routers or gate-
>   ways.
>
> retrans=n   The number of minor timeouts and retrans-
>   missions that must occur before a major
>   timeout occurs. The default is 3 timeouts.
>   When a major timeout occurs, the file oper-
>   ation is either aborted or a "server not
>   responding" message is printed on the con-
>   sole.

In other words: If a reply is not received within the 0.7 second (700ms) timeout the NFS client will repeat the request and double the timeout to 1.4 seconds. If the reply does not appear within the 1.4 seconds the request is repeated again and the timeout doubled again, to 2.8 seconds.

A lines speed can be measured with ping with the same packet size as your rsize/wsize options.

```
$ ping -s 8192 lugulbanda
PING lugulbanda.uio.no (129.240.222.99): 8192 data bytes
8200 bytes from 129.240.222.99: icmp_seq=0 ttl=64 time=15.2 ms
8200 bytes from 129.240.222.99: icmp_seq=1 ttl=64 time=15.9 ms
8200 bytes from 129.240.222.99: icmp_seq=2 ttl=64 time=14.9 ms
8200 bytes from 129.240.222.99: icmp_seq=3 ttl=64 time=14.9 ms
8200 bytes from 129.240.222.99: icmp_seq=4 ttl=64 time=15.0 ms

--- lugulbanda.uio.no ping statistics ---
5 packets transmitted, 5 packets received, 0% packet loss
round-trip min/avg/max = 14.9/15.1/15.9 ms
```

The time here is how long the ping packet took to get back and forth to lugulbanda. 15ms is quite fast. Over a 28.000 bps line you can expect something like 4000-5000ms, and if the line is otherwise loaded this time will be even higher, easily double. When this time is high we say that there is 'high latency'. Generally, for larger packets and for more loaded lines the latency will tend to increase. Increase timeo suitably for your line and load. And since the latency increases when you use the line for other things: If you ever want to use FTP and NFS at the same time you should try measuring ping times while using FTP to transfer files.

6 Security and NFS

I am by no means a computer security expert. But I do have a *little* advice for the security conscious. But be warned: This is by no means a complete list of NFS related problems and if you think you're safe once you're read and implemented all this I have a bridge I want to sell you.

This section is probably of no concern if you are on a *closed* network where you trust all the users, and no-one you don't trust can get access to machines on the network. I.e., there should be no way to dial into the network, and it should in no way be connected to other networks where you don't trust everyone using it as well as the security. Do you think I sound paranoid? I'm not at all paranoid. This is just *basic* security advice. And remember, the things I say here is just the start of it. A *secure* site needs a diligent and knowledgeable admin that knows where to find information about current and potential security problems.

NFS has a basic problem in that the client, if not told otherwise, will trust the NFS server and vice versa. This can be bad. It means that if the server's root account is broken into it can be quite easy to break into the client's root account as well. And vice versa. There are a couple of coping strategies for this, which we'll get back to.

Something you should read is the CERT advisories on NFS, most of the text below deals with issues CERT has written advisories about. See *ftp.cert.org/01-README* for a up to date list of CERT advisories. Here are some NFS related advisories:

```
CA-91:21.SunOS.NFS.Jumbo.and.fsirand                      12/06/91
     Vulnerabilities concerning Sun Microsystems, Inc. (Sun) Network
     File System (NFS) and the fsirand program.  These vulnerabilities
     affect SunOS versions 4.1.1, 4.1, and 4.0.3 on all architectures.
     Patches are available for SunOS 4.1.1.  An initial patch for SunOS
     4.1 NFS is also available. Sun will be providing complete patches
     for SunOS 4.1 and SunOS 4.0.3 at a later date.

CA-94:15.NFS.Vulnerabilities                              12/19/94
     This advisory describes security measures to guard against several
     vulnerabilities in the Network File System (NFS). The advisory was
     prompted by an increase in root compromises by intruders using tools
     to exploit the vulnerabilities.

CA-96.08.pcnfsd                                           04/18/96
     This advisory describes a vulnerability in the pcnfsd program (also
     known as rpc.pcnfsd). A patch is included.
```

6.1 Client Security

On the client we can decide that we don't want to trust the server too much a couple of ways with options to mount. For example we can forbid suid programs to work off the NFS file system with the `nosuid` option. This is a good idea and you should consider using this with all NFS mounted disks. It means that the server's root user cannot make a suid-root program on the file system, log in to the client as a normal user and then use the suid-root program to become root on the client too. We could also forbid execution of files on the mounted file system altogether with the `noexec` option. But this is more likely to be impractical than `nosuid` since a file system is likely to at least contain *some* scripts or programs that needs to be executed. You enter these options in the options column, with the `rsize` and `wsize`, separated by commas.

6.2   Server security: nfsd

On the server we can decide that we don't want to trust the client's root account. We can do that by using the root_squash option in exports:

```
/mn/eris/local apollon(rw,root_squash)
```

Now, if a user with UID 0 on the client attempts to access (read, write, delete) the file system the server substitutes the UID of the servers 'nobody' account. Which means that the root user on the client can't access or change files that only root on the server can access or change. That's good, and you should probably use `root_squash` on all the file systems you export. "But the root user on the client can still use 'su' to become any other user and access and change that users files!" say you. To which the answer is: Yes, and that's the way it is, and has to be with Unix and NFS. This has one important implication: All important binaries and files should be owned by `root`, and not `bin` or other non-root account, since the only account the clients root user cannot access is the servers root account. In the NFSd man page there are several other squash options listed so that you can decide to mistrust whomever you (don't) like on the clients. You also have options to squash any UID and GID range you want to. This is described in the Linux NFSd man page.

root_squash is in fact the default with the Linux NFSd, to grant root access to a filesystem use `no_root_squash`.

Another important thing is to ensure that nfsd checks that all it's requests comes from a privileged port. If it accepts requests from any old port on the client a user with no special privileges can run a program that's is easy to obtain over the Internet. It talks nfs protocol and will claim that the user is anyone the user wants to be. Spooky. The Linux nfsd does this check by default, on other OSes you have to enable this check yourself. This should be described in the nfsd man page for the OS.

Another thing. Never export a file system to 'localhost' or 127.0.0.1. Trust me.

6.3   Server security: the portmapper

The basic portmapper, in combination with nfsd has a design problem that makes it possible to get to files on NFS servers without any privileges. Fortunately the portmapper Linux uses is relatively secure against this attack, and can be made more secure by configuring up access lists in two files.

First we edit `/etc/hosts.deny`. It should contain the line

```
portmap: ALL
```

which will deny access to *everyone*. That's a bit drastic perhaps, so we open it again by editing `/etc/hosts.allow`. But first we need to figure out what to put in it. It should basically list all machines that should have access to your portmapper. On a run of the mill Linux system there are very few machines that need any access for any reason. The portmapper administrates nfsd, mountd, ypbind/ypserv, pcnfsd, and 'r' services like ruptime and rusers. Of these only nfsd, mountd, ypbind/ypserv and perhaps pcnfsd are of any consequence. All machines that needs to access services on your machine should be allowed to do that. Let's say that your machines address is 129.240.223.254 and that it lives on the subnet 129.240.223.0 should have access to it (those are terms introduced by the networking HOWTO, go back and refresh your memory if you need to). Then we write

```
portmap: 129.240.223.0/255.255.255.0
```

in `hosts.allow`. This is the same as the network address you give to route and the subnet mask you give to ifconfig. For the device `eth0` on this machine `ifconfig` should show

```
...
eth0      Link encap:10Mbps Ethernet  HWaddr 00:60:8C:96:D5:56
          inet addr:129.240.223.254  Bcast:129.240.223.255  Mask:255.255.255.0
```

```
        UP BROADCAST RUNNING MULTICAST  MTU:1500  Metric:1
        RX packets:360315 errors:0 dropped:0 overruns:0
        TX packets:179274 errors:0 dropped:0 overruns:0
        Interrupt:10 Base address:0x320
...
```

and `netstat -rn` should show

```
Kernel routing table
Destination    Gateway         Genmask         Flags Metric Ref Use    Iface
...
129.240.223.0  0.0.0.0         255.255.255.0   U     0         0   174412 eth0
...
```

(Network address in first column).

The `hosts.deny` and `hosts.allow` files are described in the manual pages of the same names.

IMPORTANT: Do *not* put *anything* but *IP NUMBERS* in the portmap lines of these files. Host name lookups can indirectly cause portmap activity which will trigger host name lookups which can indirectly cause portmap activity which will trigger...

The above things should make your server tighter. The only remaining problem (Yeah, right!) is someone breaking root (or boot MS-DOS) on a trusted machine and using that privilege to send requests from a secure port as any user they want to be.

6.4   NFS and firewalls

It's a very good idea to firewall the nfs and portmap ports in your router or firewall. The nfsd operates at port 2049, both udp and tcp protocols. The portmapper at port 111, tcp and udp, and mountd at port 745 and and 747, tcp and udp. Normally. You should check the ports with the `rpcinfo -p` command.

If on the other hand you want NFS to go through a firewall there are options for newer NFSds and mountds to make them use a specific (nonstandard) port which can be open in the firewall.

6.5   Summary

If you use the hosts.allow/deny, root_squash, nosuid and privileged port features in the portmapper/nfs software you avoid many of the presently known bugs in nfs and can almost feel secure about *that* at least. But still, after all that: When an intruder has access to your network, s/he can make strange commands appear in your `.forward` or mailbox file when `/home` or `/var/spool/mail` are mounted over NFS. For the same reason, you should never access your PGP private key over nfs. Or at least you should know the risk involved. And now you know a bit of it.

NFS and the portmapper makes up a complex subsystem and therefore it's not totally unlikely that new bugs will be discovered, either in the basic design or the implementation we use. There might even be holes known now, which someone is abusing. But that's life. To keep abreast of things like this you should at least read the newsgroups *comp.os.linux.announce* and *comp.security.announce* at a absolute minimum.

7   Mount Checklist

This section is based on IBM Corp. NFS mount problem checklist. My thanks to them for making it available for this HOWTO. If you experience a problem mounting a NFS filesystem please refer to this list before posting your problem. Each item describes a failure mode and the fix.

1. File system not exported, or not exported to the client in question.

   Fix: Export it

2. Name resolution doesn't jibe with the exports list.

   e.g.: export list says export to `johnmad` but `johnmad`'s name is resolved as `johnmad.austin.ibm.com`. mount permission is denied.

   Fix: Export to both forms of the name.

   It can also happen if the client has 2 interfaces with different names for each of the two adapters and the export only specifies one.

   Fix: export both interfaces.

   This can also happen if the server can't do a lookuphostbyname or lookuphostbyaddr (these are library functions) on the client. Make sure the client can do `host <name>`; `host <ip_addr>`; and that both shows the same machine.

   Fix: straighten out name resolution.

3. The file system was mounted after NFS was started (on that server). In that case the server is exporting underlying mount point, not the mounted filesystem.

   Fix: Shut down NFSd and then restart it.

   Note: The clients that had the underlying mount point mounted will get problems accessing it after the restart.

4. The date is wildly off on one or both machines (this can mess up make)

   Fix: Get the date set right.

   The HOWTO author recommends using NTP to synchronize clocks. Since there are export restrictions on NTP in the US you have to get NTP for debian, redhat or slackware from ftp://ftp.hacktic.nl/pub/replay/pub/linux or a mirror.

5. The server can not accept a mount from a user that is in more than 8 groups.

   Fix: decrease the number of groups the user is in or mount via a different user.

8 FAQs

This is the FAQ section. Most of it was written by Alan Cox.

1. I get a lot of 'stale nfs handle' errors when using Linux as a nfs server.

   This is caused by a bug in some oldish nfsd versions. It is fixed in nfs-server2.2beta16 and later.

2. When I try to mount a file system I get

   ```
   can't register with portmap: system error on send
   ```

   You are probably using a Caldera system. There is a bug in the rc scripts. Please contact Caldera to obtain a fix.

3. Why can't I execute a file after copying it to the NFS server?

   The reason is that nfsd caches open file handles for performance reasons (remember, it runs in user space). While nfsd has a file open (as is the case after writing to it), the kernel won't allow you to execute it. Nfsds newer than spring 95 release open files after a few seconds, older ones would cling to them for days.

4. My NFS files are all read only

   The Linux NFS server defaults to read only. RTFM the "exports" and nfsd manual pages. You will need to alter `/etc/exports`.

5. I mount from a linux nfs server and while ls works I can't read or write files.

   On older versions of Linux you must mount a NFS servers with `rsize=1024,wsize=1024`.

6. I mount from a Linux NFS server with a block size of between 3500-4000 and it crashes the Linux box regularly

   Basically don't do it then.

HOWTO

7. Can Linux do NFS over TCP

   No, not at present.

8. I get loads of strange errors trying to mount a machine from a Linux box.

   Make sure your users are in 8 groups or less. Older servers require this.

9. When I reboot my machine it sometimes hangs when trying to unmount a hung NFS server.

   Do **not** unmount NFS servers when rebooting or halting, just ignore them, it will not hurt anything if you don't unmount them. The command is `umount -avt nonfs`.

10. Linux NFS clients are very slow when writing to Sun and BSD systems

    NFS writes are normally synchronous (you can disable this if you don't mind risking losing data). Worse still BSD derived kernels tend to be unable to work in small blocks. Thus when you write 4K of data from a Linux box in the 1K packets it uses BSD does this

```
read 4K page
alter 1K
write 4K back to physical disk
read 4K page
alter 1K
write 4K page back to physical disk
etc..
```

9 Exporting filesystems

The way to export filesytems with NFS is not completely consistent across platforms of course. In this case Linux and Solaris 2 are the deviants. This section lists, superficially the way to do it on most systems. If the kind of system you have is not covered you must check your OS man-pages. Keywords are: nfsd, system administration tool, rc scripts, boot scripts, boot sequence, /etc/exports, exportfs. I'll use one example throughout this section: How to export /mn/eris/local to apollon read/write.

9.1 IRIX, HP-UX, Digital-UNIX, Ultrix, SunOS 4 (Solaris 1), AIX

These OSes use the traditional Sun export format. In `/etc/exports` write:

```
/mn/eris/local -rw=apollon
```

The complete documentation is in the `exports` man page. After editing the file run `exportfs -av` to export the filesystems.

How strict the exportfs command is about the syntax varies. On some OSes you will find that previously entered lines reads:

```
/mn/eris/local apollon
```

or even something degenerate like:

```
/mn/eris/local rw=apollon
```

I recommend being formal. You risk that the next version of `exportfs` if much stricter and then suddenly everything will stop working.

9.2 Solaris 2

Sun completely re-invented the wheel when they did Solaris 2. So this is completely different from all other OSes. What you do is edit the file `/etc/dfs/dfstab`. In it you place share commands as documented in the share(1M) man page. Like this:

```
share -o rw=apollon -d "Eris Local" /mn/eris/local
```

After editing run the program `shareall` to export the filesystems.

10 PC-NFS

You should not run PC-NFS. You should run samba.

Sorry: I don't know anything about PC-NFS. If someone feels like writing something about it please do and I'll include it here.

HOWTO

## Part XXX

"The Linux NIS(YP)/NYS/NIS+ HOWTO"
Thorsten Kukuk

v1.0, 9 March 1999

This document describes how to configure Linux as NIS(YP) or NIS+ client and how to install as NIS server.

Contents

HOWTO

1   Introduction

More and more, Linux machines are installed as part of a network of computers. To simplify network administration, most networks (mostly Sun-based networks) run the Network Information Service. Linux machines can take full advantage of existing NIS service or provide NIS service themselves. Linux machines can also act as full NIS+ clients, this support is in beta stage.

This document tries to answer questions about setting up NIS(YP) and NIS+ on your Linux machine. Don't forget to read the section 5 (The RPC Portmapper).

The NIS-Howto is edited and maintained by

```
        Thorsten Kukuk, <kukuk@suse.de>
```

The primary source of the information for the initial NIS-Howto was from:

```
    Andrea Dell'Amico        <adellam@ZIA.ms.it>
    Mitchum DSouza           <Mitch.DSouza@NetComm.IE>
    Erwin Embsen             <erwin@nioz.nl>
    Peter Eriksson           <peter@ifm.liu.se>
```

who we should thank for writing the first versions of this document.

1.1   New Versions of this Document

You can always view the latest version of this document on the World Wide Web via the URL *http://www.suse.de/˜kukuk/linux/HOWTO/NIS-HOWTO.html* `<http://www.suse.de/~kukuk/linux/HOWTO/NIS-HOWTO.html>`.

New versions of this document will also be uploaded to various Linux WWW and FTP sites, including the LDP home page.

Links to translations of this document could be found at *http://www.suse.de/˜kukuk/linux/nis-howto.html* `<http://www.suse.de/~kukuk/linux/nis-howto.html>`.

1.2   Disclaimer

Although this document has been put together to the best of my knowledge it may, and probably does contain errors. Please read any README files that are bundled with any of the various pieces of software described in this document for more detailed and accurate information. I will attempt to keep this document as error free as possible.

1.3   Feedback and Corrections

If you have questions or comments about this document, please feel free to mail Thorsten Kukuk, at *kukuk@suse.de*. I welcome any suggestions or criticisms. If you find a mistake with this document, please let me know so I can correct it in the next version. Thanks.

Please do *not* mail me questions about special problems with your Linux Distribution! I don't know every Linux Distribution. But I will try to add every solution you send me.

1.4   Acknowledgements

We would like to thank all the people who have contributed (directly or indirectly) to this document. In alphabetical order:

```
Byron A Jeff             <byron@cc.gatech.edu>
Markus Rex              <msrex@suse.de>
Miquel van Smoorenburg  <miquels@cistron.nl>
```

Theo de Raadt is responsible for the original yp-clients code. Swen Thuemmler ported the yp-clients code to Linux and also ported the yp-routines in libc (again based on Theo's work). Thorsten Kukuk has written the NIS(YP) and NIS+ routines for GNU libc 2.x from scratch.

2   Glossary and General Information

2.1   Glossary of Terms

In this document a lot of acronyms are used. Here are the most important acronyms and a brief explanation:

DBM

DataBase Management, a library of functions which maintain key-content pairs in a data base.

DLL

Dynamically Linked Library, a library linked to an executable program at run-time.

domainname

A name "key" that is used by NIS clients to be able to locate a suitable NIS server that serves that domainname key. Please note that this does not necessarily have anything at all to do with the DNS "domain" (machine name) of the machine(s).

FTP

File Transfer Protocol, a protocol used to transfer files between two computers.

libnsl

Name services library, a library of name service calls (getpwnam, getservbyname, etc...) on SVR4 Unixes. GNU libc uses this for the NIS (YP) and NIS+ functions.

libsocket

Socket services library, a library for the socket service calls (socket, bind, listen, etc...) on SVR4 Unixes.

NIS

Network Information Service, a service that provides information, that has to be known throughout the network, to all machines on the network. There is support for NIS in Linux's standard libc library, which in the following text is referred to as "traditional NIS".

NIS+

Network Information Service (Plus :-), essentially NIS on steroids. NIS+ is designed by Sun Microsystems Inc. as a replacement for NIS with better security and better handling of _large_ installations.

NYS

This is the name of a project and stands for NIS+, YP and Switch and is managed by Peter Eriksson <peter@ifm.liu.se>. It contains among other things a complete reimplementation of the NIS (= YP) code that uses the Name Services Switch functionality of the NYS library.

NSS

Name Service Switch. The /etc/nsswitch.conf file determines the order of lookups performed when a certain piece of information is requested.

RPC

Remote Procedure Call. RPC routines allow C programs to make procedure calls on other machines across the network. When people talk about RPC they most often mean the Sun RPC variant.

YP

Yellow Pages(tm), a registered trademark in the UK of British Telecom plc.

TCP-IP

Transmission Control Protocol/Internet Protocol. It is the data communication protocol most often used on Unix machines.

2.2   Some General Information

The next four lines are quoted from the Sun(tm) System & Network Administration Manual:

```
"NIS was formerly known as Sun Yellow Pages (YP) but
 the name Yellow Pages(tm) is a registered trademark
 in the United Kingdom of British Telecom plc and may
 not be used without permission."
```

NIS stands for Network Information Service. Its purpose is to provide information, that has to be known throughout the network, to all machines on the network. Information likely to be distributed by NIS is:

- login names/passwords/home directories (/etc/passwd)
- group information (/etc/group)

If, for example, your password entry is recorded in the NIS passwd database, you will be able to login on all machines on the network which have the NIS client programs running.

Sun is a trademark of Sun Microsystems, Inc. licensed to SunSoft, Inc.

3   NIS, NYS or NIS+ ?

3.1   libc 4/5 with traditional NIS or NYS ?

The choice between "traditional NIS" or the NIS code in the NYS library is a choice between laziness and maturity vs. flexibility and love of adventure.

The "traditional NIS" code is in the standard C library and has been around longer and sometimes suffers from its age and slight inflexibility.

The NIS code in the NYS library requires you to recompile the libc library to include the NYS code into it (or maybe you can get a precompiled version of libc from someone who has already done it).

Another difference is that the traditional NIS code has some support for NIS Netgroups, which the NYS code doesn't. On the other hand the NYS code allows you to handle Shadow Passwords in a transparent way. The "traditonal NIS" code doesn't support Shadow Passwords over NIS.

3.2 glibc 2 and NIS/NIS+

Forgot all this if you use the new GNU C Library 2.x (aka libc6). It has real NSS (name switch service) support, which makes it very flexible, and contains support for the following NIS/NIS+ maps: aliases, ethers, group, hosts, netgroups, networks, protocols, publickey, passwd, rpc, services and shadow. The GNU C Library has no problems with shadow passwords over NIS.

3.3 NIS or NIS+ ?

The choice between NIS and NIS+ is easy - use NIS if you don't have to use NIS+ or have severe security needs. NIS+ is _much_ more problematic to administer (it's pretty easy to handle on the client side, but the server side is horrible). Another problem is that the support for NIS+ under Linux is still under developement - you need the latest glibc 2.1. There is an unsupported port of the glibc NIS+ support for libc5 as dropin replacement.

4 How it works

4.1 How NIS works

Within a network there must be at least one machine acting as a NIS server. You can have multiple NIS servers, each serving different NIS "domains" - or you can have cooperating NIS servers, where one is the master NIS server, and all the other are so-called slave NIS servers (for a certain NIS "domain", that is!) - or you can have a mix of them...

Slave servers only have copies of the NIS databases and receive these copies from the master NIS server whenever changes are made to the master's databases. Depending on the number of machines in your network and the reliability of your network, you might decide to install one or more slave servers. Whenever a NIS server goes down or is too slow in responding to requests, a NIS client connected to that server will try to find one that is up or faster.

NIS databases are in so-called DBM format, derived from ASCII databases. For example, the files /etc/passwd and /etc/group can be directly converted to DBM format using ASCII-to-DBM translation software ("makedbm", included with the server software). The master NIS server should have both, the ASCII databases and the DBM databases.

Slave servers will be notified of any change to the NIS maps, (via the "yppush" program), and automatically retrieve the necessary changes in order to synchronize their databases. NIS clients do not need to do this since they always talk to the NIS server to read the information stored in it's DBM databases.

Old ypbind versions do a broadcast to find a running NIS server. This is insecure, due the fact that anyone may install a NIS server and answer the broadcast queries. Newer Versions of ypbind (ypbind-3.3 or ypbind-mt) are able to get the server from a configuration file - thus no need to broadcast.

4.2 How NIS+ works

NIS+ is a new version of the network information nameservice from Sun. The biggest difference between NIS and NIS+ is that NIS+ has support for data encryption and authentication over secure RPC.

The naming model of NIS+ is based upon a tree structure. Each node in the tree corresponds to an NIS+ object, from which we have six types: directory, entry, group, link, table and private.

The NIS+ directory that forms the root of the NIS+ namespace is called the root directory. There are two special NIS+ directories: org_dir and groups_dir. The org_dir directory consists of all administration tables, such as passwd, hosts, and mail_aliases. The groups_dir directory consists of NIS+ group objects which are used for access control. The collection of org_dir, groups_dir and their parent directory is referred to as an NIS+ domain.

5   The RPC Portmapper

To run any of the software mentioned below you will need to run the program /usr/sbin/portmap. Some Linux distributions already have the code in the /sbin/init.d/ or /etc/rc.d/ files to start up this daemon. All you have to do is to activate it and reboot your Linux machine. Read your Linux Distribution Documentation how to do this.

The RPC portmapper (portmap(8)) is a server that converts RPC program numbers into TCP/IP (or UDP/IP) protocol port numbers. It must be running in order to make RPC calls (which is what the NIS/NIS+ client software does) to RPC servers (like a NIS or NIS+ server) on that machine. When an RPC server is started, it will tell portmap what port number it is listening to, and what RPC program numbers it is prepared to serve. When a client wishes to make an RPC call to a given program number, it will first contact portmap on the server machine to determine the port number where RPC packets should be sent.

Normally, standard RPC servers are started by inetd(8), so portmap must be running before inetd is started.

For secure RPC, the portmapper needs the Time service. Make sure, that the Time service is enabled in /etc/inetd.conf on all hosts:

```
#
# Time service is used for clock syncronization.
#
time    stream  tcp     nowait  root    internal
time    dgram   udp     wait    root    internal
```

IMPORTANT: Don't forget to restart inetd after changes on its configuration file !

6   What do you need to set up NIS?

6.1   Determine whether you are a Server, Slave or Client.

To answer this question you have to consider two cases:

1. Your machine is going to be part of a network with existing NIS servers

2. You do not have any NIS servers in the network yet

In the first case, you only need the client programs (ypbind, ypwhich, ypcat, yppoll, ypmatch). The most important program is ypbind. This program must be running at all times, which means, it should always appear in the list of processes. It is a daemon process and needs to be started from the system's startup file (eg. /etc/init.d/nis, /sbin/init.d/ypclient, /etc/rc.d/init.d/ypbind, /etc/rc.local). As soon as ypbind is running your system has become a NIS client.

In the second case, if you don't have NIS servers, then you will also need a NIS server program (usually called ypserv). Section 8 (Setting up a NIS Server) describes how to set up a NIS server on your Linux machine using the "ypserv" implementation by Peter Eriksson and Thorsten Kukuk. Note that from version 0.14 this implementation supports the master-slave concept talked about in section 4.1.

There is also another free NIS server available, called "yps", written by Tobias Reber in Germany which does support the master-slave concept, but has other limitations and isn't supported since a long time.

6.2 The Software

The system library "/usr/lib/libc.a" (version 4.4.2 and better) or the shared library "/lib/libc.so.x" contain all necessary system calls to succesfully compile the NIS client and server software. For the GNU C Library 2 (glibc 2.x), you also need /lib/libnsl.so.1.

Some people reported that NIS only works with "/usr/lib/libc.a" version 4.5.21 and better so if you want to play it safe don't use older libc's. The NIS client software can be obtained from:

```
Site                  Directory                    File Name

ftp.kernel.org        /pub/linux/utils/net/NIS     yp-tools-2.2.tar.gz
ftp.kernel.org        /pub/linux/utils/net/NIS     ypbind-mt-
1.4.tar.gz
ftp.kernel.org        /pub/linux/utils/net/NIS     ypbind-3.3.tar.gz
ftp.kernel.org        /pub/linux/utils/net/NIS     ypbind-3.3-
glibc5.diff.gz
ftp.uni-paderborn.de  /linux/local/yp              yp-clients-
2.2.tar.gz
```

Once you obtained the software, please follow the instructions which come with the software. yp-clients 2.2 are for use with libc4 and libc5 until 5.4.20. libc 5.4.21 and glibc 2.x needs yp-tools 1.4.1 or later. The new yp-tools 2.2 should work with every Linux libc. Since there was a bug in the NIS code, you shouldn't use libc 5.4.21-5.4.35. Use libc 5.4.36 or later instead, or the most YP programs will not work. ypbind 3.3 will work with all libraries, too. If you use gcc 2.8.x or greater, egcs or glibc 2.x, you should add the ypbind-3.3-glibc5.diff patch to ypbind 3.3. Please never use the ypbind from yp-clients 2.2. ypbind-mt is a new, multithreaded daemon. It needs a Linux 2.2 kernel, and glibc 2.1 or later.

6.3 The ypbind daemon

After you have succesfully compiled the software you are now ready to install it. A suitable place for the ypbind daemon is the directory /usr/sbin. Some people may tell you that you don't need ypbind on a system with NYS. This is wrong. ypwhich and ypcat need it always.

You must do this as root of course. The other binaries (ypwhich, ypcat, yppasswd, yppoll, ypmatch) should go in a directory accessible by all users, normally /usr/bin.

Newer ypbind versions have a configuration file called /etc/yp.conf. You can hardcode a NIS server there - for more info see the manual page for ypbind(8). You also need this file for NYS. An example:

```
ypserver voyager
ypserver defiant
ypserver ds9
```

If the system cam resolv the hostnames without NIS, you may use the name, otherwise you have to use the IP address. ypbind 3.3 has a bug and will only use the last entry (ypserver ds9 in the example). All other entries are ignored. ypbind-mt handle this correct and uses that one, which answerd at first.

It might be a good idea to test ypbind before incorporating it in the startup files. To test ypbind do the following:

- Make sure you have your YP-domain name set. If it is not set then issue the command:

  ```
  /bin/domainname nis.domain
  ```

  where `nis.domain` should be some string _NOT_ normally associated with the DNS-domain name of your machine! The reason for this is that it makes it a little harder for external crackers to retreive the password database from your NIS servers. If you don't know what the NIS domain name is on your network, ask your system/network administrator.

- Start up "/usr/sbin/portmap" if it is not already running.

- Create the directory "/var/yp" if it does not exist.

- Start up "/usr/sbin/ypbind"

- Use the command "rpcinfo -p localhost" to check if ypbind was able to register its service with the portmapper. The output should look like:

```
program vers proto   port
100000    2   tcp    111  portmapper
100000    2   udp    111  portmapper
100007    2   udp    637  ypbind
100007    2   tcp    639  ypbind
```

or

```
program vers proto   port
100000    2   tcp    111  portmapper
100000    2   udp    111  portmapper
100007    2   udp    758  ypbind
100007    1   udp    758  ypbind
100007    2   tcp    761  ypbind
100007    1   tcp    761  ypbind
```

Depending on the ypbind version you are using.

- You may also run "rpcinfo -u localhost ypbind". This command should produce something like:

```
program 100007 version 2 ready and waiting
```

or

```
program 100007 version 1 ready and waiting
program 100007 version 2 ready and waiting
```

The output depends on the ypbind version you have installed. Important is only the "version 2" message.

At this point you should be able to use NIS client programs like ypcat, etc... For example, "ypcat passwd.byname" will give you the entire NIS password database.

IMPORTANT: If you skipped the test procedure then make sure you have set the domain name, and created the directory

```
/var/yp
```

This directory MUST exist for ypbind to start up succesfully.

To check if the domainname is set correct, use the /bin/ypdomainname from yp-tools 2.2. It uses the yp_get_default_domain() function which is more restrict. It doesn't allow for example the "(none)" domainname, which is the default under Linux and makes a lot of problems.

If the test worked you may now want to change your startupd files so that ypbind will be started at boot time and your system will act as a NIS client. Make sure that the domainname will be set before you start ypbind.

Well, that's it. Reboot the machine and watch the boot messages to see if ypbind is actually started.

6.4   Setting up a NIS Client using Traditional NIS

For host lookups you must set (or add) "nis" to the lookup order line in your /etc/host.conf file. Please read the manpage "resolv+.8" for more details.

Add the following line to /etc/passwd on your NIS clients:

```
+::::::
```

You can also use the + and - characters to include/exclude or change users. If you want to exclude the user guest just add -guest to your /etc/passwd file. You want to use a different shell (e.g. ksh) for the user "linux"? No problem, just add "+linux::::::/bin/ksh" (without the quotes) to your /etc/passwd. Fields that you don't want to change have to be left empty. You could also use Netgroups for user control.

For example, to allow login-access only to miquels, dth and ed, and all members of the sysadmin netgroup, but to have the account data of all other users available use:

```
+miquels::::::
+ed::::::
+dth::::::
+@sysadmins::::::
-ftp
+:*::::::/etc/NoShell
```

Note that in Linux you can also override the password field, as we did in this example. We also remove the login "ftp", so it isn't known any longer, and anonymous ftp will not work.

The netgroup would look like

```
sysadmins (-,software,) (-,kukuk,)
```

IMPORTANT: The netgroup feature is implemented starting from libc 4.5.26. If you have a version of libc earlier than 4.5.26, every user in the NIS password database can access your linux machine if you run "ypbind" !

6.5   Setting up a NIS Client using NYS

All that is required is that the NIS configuration file (/etc/yp.conf) points to the correct server(s) for its information. Also, the Name Services Switch configuration file (/etc/nsswitch.conf) must be correctly set up.

You should install ypbind. It isn't needed by the libc, but the NIS(YP) tools need it.

If you wish to use the include/exclude user feature (+/-guest/+@admins), you have to use "passwd: compat" and "group: compat" in nsswitch.conf. Note that there is no "shadow: compat"! You have to use "shadow: files nis" in this case.

The NYS sources are part of the libc 5 sources. When run configure, say the first time "NO" to the "Values correct" question, then say "YES" to "Build a NYS libc from nys".

6.6   Setting up a NIS Client using glibc 2.x

The glibc uses "traditional NIS", so you need to start ypbind.   The Name Services Switch configuration file (/etc/nsswitch.conf) must be correctly set up. If you use the compat mode for passwd, shadow or group, you have to add the "+" at the end of this files and you can use the include/exclude user feature. The configuration is excatly the same as under Solaris 2.x.

HOWTO

6.7   The nsswitch.conf File

The Network Services switch file /etc/nsswitch.conf determines the order of lookups performed when a certain piece of information is requested, just like the /etc/host.conf file which determines the way host lookups are performed. For example, the line

```
hosts: files nis dns
```

specifies that host lookup functions should first look in the local /etc/hosts file, followed by a NIS lookup and finally through the domain name service (/etc/resolv.conf and named), at which point if no match is found an error is returned. This file must be readable for every user! You can find more information in the man-page nsswitch.5 or nsswitch.conf.5.

A good /etc/nsswitch.conf file for NIS is:

```
#
# /etc/nsswitch.conf
#
# An example Name Service Switch config file. This file should be
# sorted with the most-used services at the beginning.
#
# The entry '[NOTFOUND=return]' means that the search for an
# entry should stop if the search in the previous entry turned
# up nothing. Note that if the search failed due to some other reason
# (like no NIS server responding) then the search continues with the
# next entry.
#
# Legal entries are:
#
#       nisplus              Use NIS+ (NIS version 3)
#       nis                  Use NIS (NIS version 2), also called YP
#       dns                  Use DNS (Domain Name Service)
#       files                Use the local files
#       db                   Use the /var/db databases
#       [NOTFOUND=return]    Stop searching if not found so far
#

passwd:     compat
group:      compat
# For libc5, you must use shadow: files nis
shadow:     compat

passwd_compat: nis
group_compat: nis
shadow_compat: nis

hosts:      nis files dns

services:   nis [NOTFOUND=return] files
networks:   nis [NOTFOUND=return] files
protocols:  nis [NOTFOUND=return] files
rpc:        nis [NOTFOUND=return] files
ethers:     nis [NOTFOUND=return] files
netmasks:   nis [NOTFOUND=return] files
netgroup:   nis
bootparams: nis [NOTFOUND=return] files
```

```
    publickey:   nis [NOTFOUND=return] files
    automount:   files
    aliases:     nis [NOTFOUND=return] files
```

passwd_compat, group_compat and shadow_compat are only supported by glibc 2.x. If there are no shadow rules in /etc/nsswitch.conf, glibc will use the passwd rule for lookups. There are some more lookup module for glibc like hesoid. For more information, read the glibc documentation.

6.8   Shadow Passwords with NIS

Shadow passwords over NIS are always a bad idea. You loose the security, which shadow gives you, and it is supported by only some few Linux C Libraries. A good way to avoid shadow passwords over NIS is, to put only the local system users in /etc/shadow. Remove the NIS user entries from the shadow database, and put the password back in passwd. So you can use shadow for the root login, and normal passwd for NIS user. This has the advantage that it will work with every NIS client.

6.8.1   Linux

The only Linux libc which supports shadow passwords over NIS, is the GNU C Library 2.x. Linux libc5 has no support for it. Linux libc5 compiled with NYS enabled has some code for it. But this code is badly broken in some cases and doesn't work with all correct shadow entries.

6.8.2   Solaris

Solaris does not support shadow passwords over NIS.

6.8.3   PAM

PAM does not support Shadow passwords over NIS, especially pam_pwdb/libpwdb. This is a big problem for RedHat 5.x users. If you have glibc and PAM, you need to change the /etc/pam.d/* entries. Replace all pam_pwdb rules through pam_unix_* modules. Due a bug in the pam_unix_auth.so module this will not always work.

An example /etc/pam.d/login file looks like:

```
    #%PAM-1.0
    auth       required     /lib/security/pam_securetty.so
    auth       required     /lib/security/pam_unix_auth.so
    auth       required     /lib/security/pam_nologin.so
    account    required     /lib/security/pam_unix_acct.so
    password   required     /lib/security/pam_unix_passwd.so
    session    required     /lib/security/pam_unix_session.so
```

For auth you need to use the pam_unix_auth.so module, for account the pam_unix_acct.so, for password the pam_unix_passwd.so and for session the pam_unix_session.so module.

7   What do you need to set up NIS+ ?

7.1   The Software

The Linux NIS+ client code was developed for the GNU C library 2. There is also a port for Linux libc5, since most commercial Applications are linked against this library, and you cannot recompile them for using glibc. There are problems with libc5 and NIS+: static programs cannot be linked with it, and programs compiled with this library will not work with other libc5 versions.

You need to retrieve and compile the GNU C Library 2.1 for Intel based platforms, or GNU C Library 2.1.1 for 64bit platforms. As base System you need a glibc based Distribution like Debian 2.x, RedHat 5.x or SuSE Linux 6.x.

HOWTO

For every distribution, you need to recompile the gcc/g++ compiler, libstdc++ and ncures. For Redhat, you need to make a lot of changes of the PAM configuration. For SuSE Linux 6.0, you need to recompile the shadow package.

The NIS+ client software can be obtained from:

Site	Directory	File Name
ftp.funet.fi	/pub/gnu/funet	libc-*, glibc-crypt-*, glibc-linuxthreads-*
ftp.kernel.org	/pub/linux/utils/net/NIS+	nis-utils-19990223.tar.gz
ftp.kernel.org	/pub/linux/utils/net/NIS+	pam_keylogin-1.2.tar.gz

Distributions based on glibc can be fetched from:

Site	Directory
ftp.debian.org	/pub/debian/dists/slink
ftp.redhat.com	/pub/redhat/redhat-5.2
ftp.suse.de	/pub/SuSE-Linux/6.0

For compilation of the GNU C Library please follow the instructions which come with the software. You cam find the patched libc5, based on NYS, and the sources as drop in replacement for the standart libc5 at:

Site	Directory	File Name
ftp.kernel.org	/pub/linux/utils/net/NIS+	libc-5.4.44-nsl-0.4.10.tar.gz

You should also have a look at *http://www.suse.de/~kukuk/linux/nisplus.html* <http://www.suse.de/~kukuk/linux/nisplus.html> for more information and the latest sources.

7.2   Setting up a NIS+ client

IMPORTANT: For setting up a NIS+ client read your Solaris NIS+ docs what to do on the server side! This document only describes what to do on the client side!

After installing the new libc and nis-tools, create the credentials for the new client on the NIS+ server. Make sure portmap is running. Then check if your Linux PC has the same time as the NIS+ Server. For secure RPC, you have only a small window from about 3 minutes, in which the credentials are valid. A good idea is to run xntpd on every host. After this, run

```
domainname nisplus.domain.
nisinit -c -H <NIS+ server>
```

to initialize the cold start file. Read the nisinit man page for more options. Make sure that the domainname will always be set after a reboot. If you don't know what the NIS+ domain name is on your network, ask your system/network administrator.

Now you should change your /etc/nsswitch.conf file. Make sure that the only service after publickey is nisplus ("publickey: nisplus"), and nothing else!

Then start keyserv and make sure, that it will always be started as first daemon after portmap at boot time. Run

```
keylogin -r
```

to store the root secretkey on your system. (I hope you have added the publickey for the new host on the NIS+ Server?).

"niscat passwd.org_dir" should now show you all entries in the passwd database.

7.3 NIS+, keylogin, login and PAM

When the user logs in, he need to set his secretkey to keyserv. This is done by calling "keylogin". The login from the shadow package will do this for the user, if it was compiled against glibc 2.1. For a PAM aware login, you have to install pam_keylogin-1.2.tar.gz and change the /etc/pam.d/login file to use pam_unix_auth, not pwdb, which doesn't support NIS+. An example:

```
#%PAM-1.0
auth        required      /lib/security/pam_securetty.so
auth        required      /lib/security/pam_keylogin.so
auth        required      /lib/security/pam_unix_auth.so
auth        required      /lib/security/pam_nologin.so
account     required      /lib/security/pam_unix_acct.so
password    required      /lib/security/pam_unix_passwd.so
session     required      /lib/security/pam_unix_session.so
```

7.4 The nsswitch.conf File

The Network Services switch file /etc/nsswitch.conf determines the order of lookups performed when a certain piece of information is requested, just like the /etc/host.conf file which determines the way host lookups are performed. For example, the line

```
hosts: files nisplus dns
```

specifies that host lookup functions should first look in the local /etc/hosts file, followed by a NIS+ lookup and finally through the domain name service (/etc/resolv.conf and named), at which point if no match is found an error is returned.

A good /etc/nsswitch.conf file for NIS+ is:

```
#
# /etc/nsswitch.conf
#
# An example Name Service Switch config file. This file should be
# sorted with the most-used services at the beginning.
#
# The entry '[NOTFOUND=return]' means that the search for an
# entry should stop if the search in the previous entry turned
# up nothing. Note that if the search failed due to some other reason
# (like no NIS server responding) then the search continues with the
# next entry.
#
# Legal entries are:
#
#       nisplus             Use NIS+ (NIS version 3)
#       nis                 Use NIS (NIS version 2), also called YP
#       dns                 Use DNS (Domain Name Service)
#       files               Use the local files
#       db                  Use the /var/db databases
#       [NOTFOUND=return]   Stop searching if not found so far
#

passwd:     compat
# for libc5: passwd: files nisplus
group:      compat
# for libc5: group: files nisplus
```

```
shadow:        compat
# for libc5: shadow: files nisplus

passwd_compat: nisplus
group_compat:  nisplus
shadow_compat: nisplus

hosts:         nisplus files dns

services:      nisplus [NOTFOUND=return] files
networks:      nisplus [NOTFOUND=return] files
protocols:     nisplus [NOTFOUND=return] files
rpc:           nisplus [NOTFOUND=return] files
ethers:        nisplus [NOTFOUND=return] files
netmasks:      nisplus [NOTFOUND=return] files
netgroup:      nisplus
bootparams:    nisplus [NOTFOUND=return] files
publickey:     nisplus
automount:     files
aliases:       nisplus [NOTFOUND=return] files
```

8 Setting up a NIS Server

8.1 The Server Program ypserv

This document only describes how to set up the "ypserv" NIS server.

The NIS server software can be found on:

Site	Directory	File Name
ftp.kernel.org	/pub/linux/utils/net/NIS	ypserv-1.3.6.tar.gz

You could also look at *http://www.suse.de/~kukuk/linux/nis.html* <http://www.suse.de/~kukuk/linux/nis.html> for more information.

The server setup is the same for both traditional NIS and NYS.

Compile the software to generate the ypserv and makedbm programs. You can configure ypserv to use the securenets file or the tcp_wrappers. The tcp_wrapper is much more flexible, but a lot of people have big problems with it. And some configuration files for tcp_wrappers may cause a memory leak. If you have problems with ypserv compiled for tcp_wrapper, recompile it using the securenets file. ypserv –version tells you, which version you have.

If you run your server as master, determine what files you require to be available via NIS and then add or remove the appropriate entries to the "all" rule in /var/yp/Makefile. You always should look at the Makefile and edit the Options at the beginning of the file.

There was one big change between ypserv 1.1 and ypserv 1.2. Since version 1.2, the file handles are cached. This means you have to call makedbm always with the -c option if you create new maps. Make sure, you are using the new /var/yp/Makefile from ypserv 1.2 or later, or add the -c flag to makedbm in the Makefile. If you don't do that, ypserv will continue to use the old maps, and not the updated one.

Now edit /var/yp/securenets and /etc/ypserv.conf. For more information, read the ypserv(8) and ypserv.conf(5) manual pages.

Make sure the portmapper (portmap(8)) is running, and start the server ypserv. The command

```
% rpcinfo -u localhost ypserv
```

should output something like

```
program 100004 version 1 ready and waiting
program 100004 version 2 ready and waiting
```

The "version 1" line could be missing, depending on the ypserv version and configuration you are using. It is only necessary if you have old SunOS 4.x clients.

Now generate the NIS (YP) database. On the master, run

```
% /usr/lib/yp/ypinit -m
```

On a slave make sure that ypwhich -m works. This means, that your slave must be configured as NIS client before you could run

```
% /usr/lib/yp/ypinit -s masterhost
```

to install the host as NIS slave.

That's it, your server is up and running.

If you have bigger problems, you could start ypserv and ypbind in debug mode on different xterms. The debug output should show you what goes wrong.

If you need to update a map, run make in the /var/yp directory on the NIS master. This will update a map if the source file is newer, and push the files to the slave servers. Please don't use ypinit for updating a map.

You might want to edit root's crontab *on the slave* server and add the following lines:

```
20 *     * * *     /usr/lib/yp/ypxfr_1perhour
40 6     * * *     /usr/lib/yp/ypxfr_1perday
55 6,18 * * *     /usr/lib/yp/ypxfr_2perday
```

This will ensure that most NIS maps are kept up-to-date, even if an update is missed because the slave was down at the time the update was done on the master.

You can add a slave at every time later. At first, make sure that the new slave server has permissions to contact the NIS master. Then run

```
% /usr/lib/yp/ypinit -s masterhost
```

on the new slave. On the master server, add the new slave server name to /var/yp/ypservers and run make in /var/yp to update the map.

If you want to restrict access for users to your NIS server, you'll have to setup the NIS server as a client as well by running ypbind and adding the plus-entries to /etc/passwd _halfway_ the password file. The library functions will ignore all normal entries after the first NIS entry, and will get the rest of the info through NIS. This way the NIS access rules are maintained. An example:

```
root:x:0:0:root:/root:/bin/bash
daemon:*:1:1:daemon:/usr/sbin:
bin:*:2:2:bin:/bin:
sys:*:3:3:sys:/dev:
sync:*:4:100:sync:/bin:/bin/sync
games:*:5:100:games:/usr/games:
```

HOWTO

```
man:*:6:100:man:/var/catman:
lp:*:7:7:lp:/var/spool/lpd:
mail:*:8:8:mail:/var/spool/mail:
news:*:9:9:news:/var/spool/news:
uucp:*:10:50:uucp:/var/spool/uucp:
nobody:*:65534:65534:noone at all,,,,:/dev/null:
+miquels::::::
+:*:::::/etc/NoShell
[ All normal users AFTER this line! ]
tester:*:299:10:Just a test account:/tmp:
miquels:1234567890123:101:10:Miquel van Smoorenburg:/home/miquels:/bin/zsh
```

Thus the user "tester" will exist, but have a shell of /etc/NoShell. miquels will have normal access.

Alternatively, you could edit the `/var/yp/Makefile` file and set NIS to use another source password file. On large systems the NIS password and group files are usually stored in `/etc/yp/`. If you do this the normal tools to administrate the password file such as `passwd`, `chfn`, `adduser` will not work anymore and you need special homemade tools for this.

However, `yppasswd`, `ypchsh` and `ypchfn` will work of course.

8.2   The Server Program yps

To set up the "yps" NIS server please refer to the previous paragraph. The "yps" server setup is similar, _but_ not exactly the same so beware if you try to apply the "ypserv" instructions to "yps"! "yps" is not supported by any author, and contains some security leaks. You really shouldn't use it !

The "yps" NIS server software can be found on:

Site	Directory	File Name
ftp.lysator.liu.se	/pub/NYS/servers	yps-0.21.tar.gz
ftp.kernel.org	/pub/linux/utils/net/NIS	yps-0.21.tar.gz

8.3   The Program rpc.ypxfrd

rpc.ypxfrd is used for speed up the transfer of very large NIS maps from a NIS master to NIS slave servers. If a NIS slave server receives a message that there is a new map, it will start ypxfr for transfering the new map. ypxfr will read the contents of a map from the master server using the yp_all() function. This process can take several minutes when there are very large maps which have to store by the database library.

The rpc.ypxfrd server speeds up the transfer process by allowing NIS slave servers to simply copy the master server's map files rather than building their own from scratch. rpc.ypxfrd uses an RPC-based file transfer protocol, so that there is no need for building a new map.

rpc.ypxfrd can be started by inetd. But since it starts very slow, it should be started with ypserv. You need to start rpc.ypxfrd only on the NIS master server.

8.4   The Program rpc.yppasswdd

Whenever users change their passwords, the NIS password database and probably other NIS databases, which depend on the NIS password database, should be updated. The program "rpc.yppasswdd" is a server that handles password changes and makes sure that the NIS information will be updated accordingly. rpc.yppasswdd is now integrated in ypserv. You don't need the older, separate yppasswd-0.9.tar.gz or yppasswd-0.10.tar.gz, and you shouldn't use them any longer. The rpc.yppasswdd in ypserv 1.3.2 has full shadow support. yppasswd is now part of yp-tools-2.2.tar.gz.

You need to start rpc.yppasswdd only on the NIS master server. By default, users are not allowed to change their full name or the login shell. You can allow this with the -e chfn or -e chsh option.

If your passwd and shadow files are not in another directory then /etc, you need to add the -D option. For example, if you have put all source files in /etc/yp and wish to allow the user to change his shell, you need to start rpc.yppasswdd with the following parameters:

```
rpc.yppasswdd -D /etc/yp -e chsh
```

or

```
rpc.yppasswdd -s /etc/yp/shadow -p /etc/yp/passwd -e chsh
```

There is nothing more to do. You just need to make sure, that `rpc.yppasswdd` uses the same files as `/var/yp/Makefile`. Errors will be logged using syslog.

9   Verifying the NIS/NYS Installation

If everything is fine (as it should be), you should be able to verify your installation with a few simple commands. Assuming, for example, your passwd file is being supplied by NIS, the command

```
% ypcat passwd
```

should give you the contents of your NIS passwd file. The command

```
% ypmatch userid passwd
```

(where userid is the login name of an arbitrary user) should give you the user's entry in the NIS passwd file. The "ypcat" and "ypmatch" programs should be included with your distribution of traditional NIS or NYS.

If a user cannot log in, run the following program on the client:

```
#include <stdio.h>
#include <pwd.h>
#include <sys/types.h>

int
main(int argc, char *argv[])
{
   struct passwd *pwd;

   if(argc != 2)
      {
         fprintf(stderr,"Usage: getwpnam username\n");
         exit(1);
      }

   pwd=getpwnam(argv[1]);

   if(pwd != NULL)
      {
         printf("name.....: [%s]\n",pwd->pw_name);
         printf("password.: [%s]\n",pwd->pw_passwd);
         printf("user id..: [%d]\n", pwd->pw_uid);
```

```
        printf("group id.: [%d]\n",pwd->pw_gid);
        printf("gecos....: [%s]\n",pwd->pw_gecos);
        printf("directory: [%s]\n",pwd->pw_dir);
        printf("shell....: [%s]\n",pwd->pw_shell);
    }
  else
    fprintf(stderr,"User \"%s\" not found!\n",argv[1]);

  exit(0);
}
```

Running this program with the username as parameter will print all the information the getpwnam function gives back for this user. This should show you which entry is incorrect. The most common problem is, that the password field is overwritten with a "*".

GNU C Library 2.1 (glibc 2.1) comes with a tool called getent. Use this program instead the above on such a system. You could try:

```
    getent passwd
```

or

```
    getent passwd login
```

10   Common Problems and Troubleshooting NIS

Here are some common problems reported by various users:

1. The libraries for 4.5.19 are broken. NIS won't work with it.

2. If you upgrade the libraries from 4.5.19 to 4.5.24 then the su command breaks. You need to get the su command from the slackware 1.2.0 distribution. Incidentally that's where you can get the updated libraries.

3. When a NIS server goes down and comes up again ypbind starts complaining with messages like:

```
    yp_match: clnt_call:
            RPC: Unable to receive; errno = Connection refused
```

and logins are refused for those who are registered in the NIS database. Try to login as root and kill ypbind and start it up again. An update to ypbind 3.3 or higher should also help.

4. After upgrading the libc to a version greater then 5.4.20, the YP tools will not work any longer. You need yp-tools 1.2 or later for libc >= 5.4.21 and glibc 2.x. For earlier libc version you need yp-clients 2.2. yp-tools 2.x should work for all libraries.

5. In libc 5.4.21 - 5.4.35 yp_maplist is broken, you need 5.4.36 or later, or some YP programs like ypwhich will segfault.

6. libc 5 with traditional NIS doesn't support shadow passwords over NIS. You need libc5 + NYS or glibc 2.x.

7. ypcat shadow doesn't show the shadow map. This is correct, the name of the shadow map is shadow.byname, not shadow.

8. Solaris doesn't use always privileged ports. So don't use password mangling if you have a Solaris client.

11 Frequently Asked Questions

Most of your questions should be answered by now. If there are still questions unanswered you might want to post a message to

```
comp.os.linux.networking
```

Part XXXI

"Oracle Database HOWTO" Paul Haigh

paul@nailed.demon.co.uk
v1.2, 4 August 1998
A guide to installing and configuring the Oracle Database Server on a Linux system

Contents

HOWTO

1   Introduction

1.1   Version History

- v0.1 - 21 Feb 1998 - Paul Haigh - Original Version.
- v0.2 - 01 Mar 1998 - Paul Haigh - Comments From Proofreaders Added.
- v1.0 - 10 Mar 1998 - Paul Haigh - First Release to LDP.
- v1.1 - 20 Jun 1998 - Paul Haigh - Added troubleshooting section & general tidyup.
- v1.2 - 04 Aug 1998 - Paul Haigh - Added Oracle Corp News & Removed Section on Future Enhancements.

1.2   Copyright

The Oracle Database HOWTO copyright (c) 1998, Paul Haigh.

Like all Linux HOWTO documents, this may be reproduced and distributed in whole or in part, in any medium, physical or electronic, so long as this copyright notice is retained on all copies.

Commercial redistribution is allowed and encouraged; however the author would like to be notified of such distributions. You may translate this HOWTO into any language whatsoever provided that you leave this copyright statement and disclaimer intact, and that you append a notice stating who translated the document.

1.3   Disclaimer

While I have tried to include the most correct and up to date information available to me, I cannot guarantee that usage of information in this document does not result in loss of data or equipment. I provide NO WARRANTY about the information in the HOWTO and I cannot be made liable for any consequences resulting from using the information in this HOWTO.

1.4   Aim of the HOWTO

In this HOWTO I will attempt to cover installation and basic admin of an Oracle database running on a Linux machine. In particular I will cover Oracle server installation, SQL*Net configuration and client configuration.

This document is not an in depth tutorial on using or administering an Oracle database, if that is what you are looking for there are great books on those subjects published by O'Reilly and others.

I am also not going to cover the development of Oracle programs under UNIX. If this is absolutley necessary to you then I would recommend that you purchase the SCO development system (with OpenServer 5.x) from SCO, which I am told can be obtained for a very reasonable US $19, from `www.sco.com`.

1.5 Requirements

I am assuming a number of items that you will need for following the HOWTO.

- **Oracle Server CD for SCO Openserver (Version 7.3.3.0.0.)**

  This **must** be a legal copy. Remember that Oracle are a profit making company and charge for their products. If you want a free SQL compliant database use PostgresSQL or similar.

  It is also possible to install oracle, using a 60 day evaluation licence, from a downloadable `tar` file from the Oracle web site. I have not personally tried this and it is completely unverified.

- **A Linux Server**

  You wouldn't be reading this without one...would you?

- **Kernel 2.0.30+**

  I cannot guarantee that these instructions will be accurate for any other Kernel. (Not that I am guaranteeing it for 2.0.30 either...).

- **iBCS**

  It is very important to have this installed and working with the latest possible version for your platform. (I am using iBCS-2.0-10.i386.rpm from Redhat Linux).

- **Lots of disc space**

  600 Mb+ is a reasonable amount. It is possible to install with less but you need to make some sacrifices, and I never like starting with those. However, I will attempt to point out areas in which space can be freed up.

- **32Mb+ Ram**

  I know that this sounds like a lot, especially in Linux terms, but remember that Oracle is a complex piece of software. You wouldn't have the same reservations on SCO!

  I am not saying that Oracle doesn't work with less, just that it is less than Oracle recommend and I wouldn't suggest it.

- **Licenses from Oracle**

  I know that I have already mentioned this but I want to be clear that this is important. Using software from Oracle without a license is illegal.

1.6 News From Oracle Corporation

Oracle have bowed into pressure from the Linux community. Oracle Corporation have decided to **officially** support Oracle 8 on the Linux (i386) platform. This should be released in December 1998, according to the Oracle website.

Better still Oracle will also be porting `Oracle Applications` to the linux platform. This should be available in the first half of 1999, according to the Oracle website.

References:

- *http://www.oracle.com/html/linux.html*
- *http://www.news.com/News/Item/0,4,24436,00.html*
- *http://www.zdnet.com/pcweek/news/0720/20morac.html*

2 Installing the Oracle Software

2.1 Server Preparation

2.1.1 Creating an Oracle User

Unsurprisingly we require a user to hold the Oracle database. Since we have no desire to relink the Oracle kernel (more about that later) we have to accept the Oracle defaults for user name and group name. This includes the user ORACLE and the group DBA.

1. Login as Root

2. Create the oracle user and the group dba.

```
$ groupadd dba
$ useradd  oracle
```

3. Ensure a home directory is created for the user oracle.

```
$ mkdir /home/oracle
$ mkdir /home/oracle/7.3.3.0.0 (Version of Oracle)
$ chown -R oracle.dba /home/oracle
```

2.2 Installing from CDROM

Unfortunately the Oracle Installer on the SCO disc will not work. A variety of problems can be experienced, from core dumps to hangs. As a result we need to copy the files from the CDROM manually and uncompress them:

(Ensure the CDROM is mounted on the system).

1. Log on as Oracle

2. Change directory to `/home/oracle/7.3.3.0.0.`

3. Copy all install files from CDROM

```
$ cp -a /mnt/cdrom/* .
```

4. Un-compress all Oracle files on CDROM.

```
$ find . -name *_ -exec ~/7.3.3.0.0/orainst/oiuncomp {} \;
```

2.3 Post Installation Tasks

2.3.1 Tasks for Root

Add the following lines to `/etc/profile` or add to the `.profile` for each user who is going to use Oracle.

```
# Oracle Specific
ORACLE_HOME=/home/oracle/7.3.3.0.0
ORACLE_SID=orcl
ORACLE_TERM=vt100
export ORACLE_HOME ORACLE_SID ORACLE_TERM

# Alter path for Oracle
PATH="$PATH:$ORACLE_HOME/bin"
```

We also need to change the owner and permissions of the Oracle ulimit increase utility.

```
$ chown root.root $ORACLE_HOME/bin/osh
$ chmod u+s $ORACLE_HOME/bin/osh
```

2.3.2 Tasks for Oracle

Change permissions for the Oracle files to ensure correct operation.

```
$ chmod +x $ORACLE_HOME/bin/*
$ chmod u+s $ORACLE_HOME/bin/oracle
```

Oracle tools require the messages to be in the $ORACLE_HOME/tool_name/mesg directory. So, move the msb files from the msg_ship directories to the mesg directories.

```
$ mv $ORACLE_HOME/plsql/mesg/mesg_ship/* $ORACLE_HOME/plsql/mesg/.
$ mv $ORACLE_HOME/rdbms/mesg/mesg_ship/* $ORACLE_HOME/rdbms/mesg/.
$ mv $ORACLE_HOME/svrmgr/mesg/mesg_ship/* $ORACLE_HOME/svrmgr/mesg/.
```

Create the following directories if they do not exist:

```
$ mkdir $ORACLE_HOME/rdbms/log
$ mkdir $ORACLE_HOME/rdbms/audit
$ mkdir $ORACLE_HOME/network/log
```

2.3.3 Things you can remove

The following directories can safely be removed:

- $ORACLE_HOME/guicommon2/
- $ORACLE_HOME/ctx/
- $ORACLE_HOME/md/
- $ORACLE_HOME/mlx/
- $ORACLE_HOME/precomp/
- $ORACLE_HOME/slax/

3 Creating a Database

Now the Oracle server is installed we need to create a database to test the installation.

```
If you are using Oracle 7.2.x or earlier, please read the troubleshooting sec-
tion below.
```

3.1 Create the Initialisation File

Copy the $ORACLE_HOME/dbs/init.ora to $ORACLE_HOME/dbs/initorcl.ora:

```
$ cd $ORACLE_HOME/dbs
$ cp init.ora initorcl.ora
```

Modify it by adding the following lines:

```
db_name = orcl
COMPATIBLE=7.3.3.0.0
```

3.2   Creating the Database Install Script

Create a script file called makedb.sql in the $ORACLE_HOME/dbs directory:

```
connect internal
startup nomount
set echo on
spool makedb.log
create database orcl
        maxinstances 1
        maxlogfiles  8
        datafile '$ORACLE_HOME/dbs/orcl_syst_01.dbf' size 40M reuse
        logfile
                '$ORACLE_HOME/dbs/orcl_redo_01.dbf' size 1M reuse,
                '$ORACLE_HOME/dbs/orcl_redo_02.dbf' size 1M reuse,
                '$ORACLE_HOME/dbs/orcl_redo_03.dbf' size 1M reuse;
@$ORACLE_HOME/rdbms/admin/catalog.sql
create tablespace rollback
        datafile '$ORACLE_HOME/dbs/orcl_roll_01.dbf' size 8.5M reuse;
create tablespace temp
        datafile '$ORACLE_HOME/dbs/orcl_temp_01.dbf' size 5M reuse
        temporary;
create tablespace users
        datafile '$ORACLE_HOME/dbs/orcl_user_01.dbf' size 10M reuse;
create rollback segment r1 tablespace rollback
        storage ( optimal 5M );
alter rollback segment r1 online;
connect system/manager
@$ORACLE_HOME/rdbms/admin/catdbsyn.sql
connect internal
@$ORACLE_HOME/rdbms/admin/catproc.sql
connect system/manager
@$ORACLE_HOME/sqlplus/admin/pupbld.sql
spool off
exit
```

3.3   Running the Database Installation Script

Start svrmgrl and run the script:

```
$ cd $ORACLE_HOME/dbs
$ svrmgrl

Oracle Server Manager Release 2.3.3.0.0 - Production

Copyright (c) Oracle Corporation 1994, 1995. All rights reserved.

Oracle7 Server Release 7.3.3.0.0 - Production Release
PL/SQL Release 2.3.3.0.0 - Production

SVRMGR> connect internal
Connected.
SVRMGR> startup nomount
ORACLE instance started.
Total System Global Area       4313312 bytes
Fixed Size                       41876 bytes
```

```
Variable Size              4140364 bytes
Database Buffers           122880 bytes
Redo Buffers                  8192 bytes
SVRMGR> @makedb
<loads of messages>
SVRMGR> exit
Server Manager complete.
```

3.4   Starting the Database

Firstly, we need to bring up the database by hand (we will automate this later on). To startup an Oracle database we need to issue the `startup` command when connected internally:

```
$ svrmgrl

Oracle Server Manager Release 2.3.3.0.0 - Production

Copyright (c) Oracle Corporation 1994, 1995. All rights reserved.

Oracle7 Server Release 7.3.3.0.0 - Production Release
PL/SQL Release 2.3.3.0.0 - Production

SVRMGR> connect internal
Connected.
SVRMGR> startup
ORACLE instance started.
Total System Global Area      4313316 bytes
Fixed Size                      41876 bytes
Variable Size                 4140368 bytes
Database Buffers               122880 bytes
Redo Buffers                     8192 bytes
Database mounted.
Database opened.
SVRMGR> exit
Server Manager complete.
```

3.5   Stopping the Database

It is worth mentioning here that restarting a Linux server without shutting down the Oracle database first there is a high risk of corrupting the database.

So, before we issue the Linux `shutdown` command it is wise to bring down the database:

```
$ svrmgrl

Oracle Server Manager Release 2.3.3.0.0 - Production

Copyright (c) Oracle Corporation 1994, 1995. All rights reserved.

Oracle7 Server Release 7.3.3.0.0 - Production Release
PL/SQL Release 2.3.3.0.0 - Production

SVRMGR> connect internal
Connected.
SVRMGR> shutdown
Database closed.
```

HOWTO

```
Database dismounted.
ORACLE instance shut down.
SVRMGR> exit
Server Manager complete.
```

3.6 Create a Default User

The database, as created, has a two special users which are automatically created. These are:

Username	Password
SYSTEM	MANAGER
SYS	change_on_install

These users are typically used to hold the standard data dictionary information for the database. It is a good idea to change the passwords from the defaults as soon as possible.

This can be achieved by:

```
sqlplus system/manager

SQL*Plus: Release 3.3.3.0.0 - Production on Sat Feb 21 12:43:33 1998

Copyright (c) Oracle Corporation 1979, 1996.  All rights reserved.


Connected to:
Oracle7 Server Release 7.3.3.0.0 - Production Release

SQL> alter user system identified by <newpassword>;

User altered.

SQL> alter user sys identified by <newpassword>;

User altered.

SQL> exit;
Disconnected from Oracle7 Server Release 7.3.3.0.0 - Production Release
PL/SQL Release 2.3.3.0.0 - Production
```

Since the user `system/manager` is similar to using `root` on a UNIX machine, we need to create a user with less ability to cause damage. (remember to bring up the database before attempting to create a user)

Connect to SQL*Plus and create a user:

```
$ sqlplus system/manager

SQL*Plus: Release 3.3.3.0.0 - Production on Sat Feb 21 12:43:33 1998

Copyright (c) Oracle Corporation 1979, 1996.  All rights reserved.


Connected to:
Oracle7 Server Release 7.3.3.0.0 - Production Release
PL/SQL Release 2.3.3.0.0 - Production
```

```
SQL> create user <user> identified by <psw>
  2  default tablespace users
  3  temporary tablespace temp;

User created.

SQL> grant connect, resource to <user>

Grant succeeded.

SQL> exit
Disconnected from Oracle7 Server Release 7.3.3.0.0 - Production Release
PL/SQL Release 2.3.3.0.0 - Production
```

Now that you have a new user on the system you can play with the new system. To login to the Oracle database:

```
$ sqlplus <user>/<password>
```

If this completes with no error messages then you have a working Oracle database. If you never want to connect to this database from anywhere but this server then the job is complete, enjoy!

If, however, like most people you want to configure the networking software so that you can connect from other machines, keep on reading.

4 Configuring SQL*Net on the Server

All of these files configure the Oracle networking software (SQL*Net, aka Net8 for Oracle8). These files should all be created on the server in the $ORACLE_HOME/network/admin directory.

4.1 tnsnames.ora

The TNSNAMES.ORA file identifies services available from the machine. On our instance here we will describe all databases that the server has mounted. For each database instance on your server add a section like below:

```
orcl.world =
  (DESCRIPTION =
    (ADDRESS_LIST =
      (ADDRESS =
        (COMMUNITY = tcp.world)
        (PROTOCOL = TCP)
        (Host = <INSERT HOST NAME OF SERVER HERE> )
        (Port = 1521)
      )
      (ADDRESS =
        (COMMUNITY = tcp.world)
        (PROTOCOL = TCP)
        (Host = <INSERT HOST NAME OF SERVER HERE> )
        (Port = 1526)
      )
    )
    (CONNECT_DATA = (SID = ORCL)
    )
  )
```

4.2 `listener.ora`

The `listener.ora` file contains the descriptions of the services that other machines are allowed to connect to and any configuration that is required for the server listener.

It contains sections for the listener name, listener address, databases served by the listener and configuration parameters.

Here is an example:

```
# Name of listener and addresses to listen on
LISTENER =
        ( ADDRESS_LIST =
                (ADDRESS =
                        (PROTOCOL=tcp)
                        (HOST=<INSERT HOST>)
                        (PORT=1521)
                        (COMMUNITY=UK_SUP_TCPIP)
                )
                (ADDRESS =
                        (PROTOCOL=ipc)
                        (KEY=700)
                        (COMMUNITY=UK_SUP_TCPIP)
                )
        )

# List of services served by this listener
SID_LIST_LISTENER=
        (SID_LIST=
                (SID_DESC=
                        (SID_NAME=orcl)
                        (ORACLE_HOME=/home/oracle/7.3.3.0.0)
                )
        )

# Start of configuration parameters.
TRACE_LEVEL_LISTENER=OFF
TRACE_FILE_LISTENER = "listener"
LOG_FILE_LISTENER = "listener"
CONNECT_TIMEOUT_LISTENER = 10
STOP_LISTENER = YES
DBA_GROUP = dba
```

4.3 `sqlnet.ora`

The `sqlnet.ora` file contains configuration for the particular node of the network. This is independent of the number of databases or the number of listeners. The most important thing in this file is the `Dead Connection Timeout` configuration variable.

Dead connection timeout checks every incoming process to a database instance and ensures that the client end of it is still responding. If the client (of whatever type) is not responding then the Oracle server shadow process is killed.

This is very useful if you have many clients accessing a database, especially during a developmental phase when those clients are more likely to be failing to exit cleanly from the Oracle database.

Below is a copy of my own `sqlnet.ora` file for you to puruse:

```
TRACE_LEVEL_CLIENT = OFF
```

```
sqlnet.expire_time = 30          # The number of seconds between clien-
t checks.
names.default_domain = world
name.default_zone = world
```

4.4 Starting and Stopping the Listeners

Now that the configuration of the listeners and SQL*Net is complete we can attempt to connect to the database using the networking software. (Before we were using direct links to the database, whereas here we are simulating a connection from a remote client machine).

To start the listener using the above configuration:

```
$ lsnrctl

LSNRCTL for SCO System V/386: Version 2.3.3.0.0 - Production on 23-FEB-
98 20:38:25

Copyright (c) Oracle Corporation 1994.  All rights reserved.

Welcome to LSNRCTL, type "help" for information.

LSNRCTL> start
Starting /home/oracle/7.3.3.0.0/bin/tnslsnr: please wait...

TNSLSNR for SCO System V/386: Version 2.3.3.0.0 - Production
System parameter file is /home/oracle/7.3.3.0.0/network/admin/listener.ora
Log messages written to /home/oracle/7.3.3.0.0/network/log/listener.log
Listening on: (ADDRESS=(PROTOCOL=tcp)(DEV=6)(HOST=192.168.1.1)(PORT=1521))
Listening on: (ADDRESS=(PROTOCOL=ipc)(DEV=10)(KEY=700))

Connecting to (ADDRESS=(PROTOCOL=tcp)(HOST=magic.com)(PORT=1521)
(COMMUNITY=UK_SUP_TCPIP))
STATUS of the LISTENER
------------------------
Alias                    LISTENER
Version                  TNSLSNR for SCO System V/386: Version 2.3.3.0.0 -
Production
Start Date               23-FEB-98 20:38:50
Uptime                   0 days 0 hr. 0 min. 0 sec
Trace Level              off
Security                 OFF
SNMP                     ON
Listener Parameter File  /home/oracle/7.3.3.0.0/network/admin/listener.ora
Listener Log File        /home/oracle/7.3.3.0.0/network/log/listener.log
Services Summary...
  orcl          has 1 service handler(s)
The command completed successfully
LSNRCTL> exit
```

To stop the listeners:

```
$ lsnrctl

LSNRCTL for SCO System V/386: Version 2.3.3.0.0 - Production on 23-FEB-
98 20:43:20
```

HOWTO

```
Copyright (c) Oracle Corporation 1994.  All rights reserved.

Welcome to LSNRCTL, type "help" for information.

LSNRCTL> stop
Connecting to (ADDRESS=(PROTOCOL=tcp)(HOST=magic.com)(PORT=1521)
(COMMUNITY=UK_SUP_TCPIP))
The command completed successfully
LSNRCTL> exit
```

If you have a DNS setup which doesn't return the IP address for the hostname specified then starting and stopping the listener can take some time (2-3 mins. dependant on the DNS timeout variable). If this is the case, don't worry, be patient.

5   Client Configuration

5.1   Windows Clients

SQL*Net configuration on the PC using newer versions of the Oracle Client Software is very easy. The best (and easiest) way of achiving a fully working client installation is to use the `SQL*Net Easy Configuration` tool supplied by Oracle.

This toolhas a wizard type interface to take you through the installation of the `tnsnames.ora` and `sqlnet.ora` files.

Select "Add Database Alias" and enter a name for the alias when prompted. This alias is the name you will refer to the database instance as, and as such should be the same as the instance name (orcl in this case).

Select TCP/IP as the protocol, and when prompted the hostname of the machine hosting the database and the instance name of the database.

That's it.

However, if you do not have the `SQL*Net Easy Configuration` Tool then don't worry. You can simply create the `tnsnames.ora` and the `sqlnet.ora` files in the `$ORACLE_HOME/network/admin` directory on the client exactly as they are on the server. This will provide an alias the same as on the server (always a good idea anyway).

5.2   Unix Clients

UNIX clients are not very different that windows clients. If you have the `Network Manager` from Oracle then user that in the same way as above, if not then you can, again, just use the same configuration files as the server in the `$ORACLE_HOME/network/admin` directory.

6   Automatic Startup and Shutdown

6.1   `dbstart` & `dbstop`

The automatic startup and shutdown of the Oracle database can be achieved (in 7.3.3.0.0) with the files dbstart and dbshut both provided by Oracle. These files rely on the existance of the file /etc/oratab to work (although by altering the dbshut and dbstart files this can be moved).

The format of the /etc/oratab file is as follows:

```
SID:ORACLE_HOME:AUTO
```

An example:

```
orcl:/home/oracle/7.3.3.0.0:Y
leaveup:/home/oracle/7.3.2.1.0:N
```

6.2 init.d & rc.d

To start and stop the database when the machine comes up and goes down by modifying the startup routines for the Linux machine. This is quite easy, although I should point out here that this may change depending on which flavour of Linux (slackware, debian, redhat, etc). I will show examples which work for Redhat Linux 5.0. To modify these for your own flavour of Linux, please see your Linux documentation sets. (Although it should hold true for any Sys V type UNIX).

Firstly, we need to create the script which will run `dbshut` and `dbstart` in the `/etc/rc.d/init.d` directory. Create the following file as `/etc/rc.d/init.d/oracle`:

```
#!/bin/sh
#
# /etc/rc.d/init.d/oracle
# Description: Starts and stops the Oracle database and listeners
# See how we were called.
case "$1" in
  start)
        echo -n "Starting Oracle Databases: "
        echo "----------------------------------------------------
" >> /var/log/oracle
        date +"! %T %a %D : Starting Oracle Databases as part of sys-
tem up." >> /var/log/oracle
        echo "----------------------------------------------------
" >> /var/log/oracle
        su - oracle -c dbstart >> /var/log/oracle
        echo "Done."
        echo -n "Starting Oracle Listeners: "
        su - oracle -c "lsnrctl start" >> /var/log/oracle
        echo "Done."
        echo ""
        echo "----------------------------------------------------
" >> /var/log/oracle
        date +"! %T %a %D : Finished." >> /var/log/oracle
        echo "----------------------------------------------------
" >> /var/log/oracle
        touch /var/lock/subsys/oracle
        ;;
  stop)
        echo -n "Shutting Down Oracle Listeners: "
        echo "----------------------------------------------------
" >> /var/log/oracle
        date +"! %T %a %D : Shutting Down Oracle Databases as part of sys-
tem down." >> /var/log/oracle
        echo "----------------------------------------------------
" >> /var/log/oracle
        su - oracle -c "lsnrctl stop" >> /var/log/oracle
        echo "Done."
        rm -f /var/lock/subsys/oracle
        echo -n "Shutting Down Oracle Databases: "
        su - oracle -c dbshut >> /var/log/oracle
        echo "Done."
        echo ""
```

HOWTO

```
        echo "----------------------------------------------------
" >> /var/log/oracle
        date +"! %T %a %D : Finished." >> /var/log/oracle
        echo "----------------------------------------------------
" >> /var/log/oracle
        ;;
restart)
        echo -n "Restarting Oracle Databases: "
        echo "----------------------------------------------------
" >> /var/log/oracle
        date +"! %T %a %D : Restarting Oracle Databases as part of sys-
tem up." >> /var/log/oracle
        echo "----------------------------------------------------
" >> /var/log/oracle
        su - oracle -c dbstop >> /var/log/oracle
        su - oracle -c dbstart >> /var/log/oracle
        echo "Done."
        echo -n "Restarting Oracle Listeners: "
        su - oracle -c "lsnrctl stop" >> /var/log/oracle
        su - oracle -c "lsnrctl start" >> /var/log/oracle
        echo "Done."
        echo ""
        echo "----------------------------------------------------
" >> /var/log/oracle
        date +"! %T %a %D : Finished." >> /var/log/oracle
        echo "----------------------------------------------------
" >> /var/log/oracle
        touch /var/lock/subsys/oracle
        ;;
    *)
        echo "Usage: oracle {start|stop|restart}"
        exit 1
esac
```

It is worth checking that this file actually correctly stops and starts the databases for your system. Check the log file, `/var/log/oracle` for error messages.

Once this script is working we need to create start and kill symbolic links in the appropriate runlevel directories `/etc/rc.d/rcX.d`.

The following commands will ensure that the databases will come up in runlevels 2,3 and 4:

```
$ ln -s ../init.d/oracle /etc/rc.d/rc2.d/S99oracle
$ ln -s ../init.d/oracle /etc/rc.d/rc3.d/S99oracle
$ ln -s ../init.d/oracle /etc/rc.d/rc4.d/S99oracle
```

To stop the databases on reboot or restart we need the following links:

```
$ ln -s ../init.d/oracle /etc/rc.d/rc0.d/K01oracle      # Halting
$ ln -s ../init.d/oracle /etc/rc.d/rc6.d/K01oracle      # Rebooting
```

7   Other Bits

7.1   Intelligent Agent

If you have a need for the `Oracle Intelligent Agent`, I found that you can run it without any configuration changes. To start the IA try:

```
$ lsnrctl dbsnmp_start
```

To stop the IA try:

```
$ lsnrctl dbsnmp_stop
```

There do not appear to be any messages indicating a sucessful or otherwise start or stop of the intelligent agent. However, the IA responded to Enterprise manager on the client side so I can only assume that it is working.

8 Troubleshooting

See below for various troubleshooting hints.

8.1 I cannot create a database when using Oracle 7.2.x.

The files shipped by Oracle in the 7.2.x product are incorrect in assuming that you want to setup a parallel server configuration. The shipped `init.ora` file has the following line in it:

```
# define parallel server (multi-instance) parameters
ifile = ora_system:initps.ora
```

To fix the problem simply comment it out:

```
# define parallel server (multi-instance) parameters
#ifile = ora_system:initps.ora
```

8.2 I'm getting segmentation faults in `svrmgrl` under version 7.3.4.x.

I've had this problem reported to me by a number of people. Gerald Weber gerald_weber@master.co.at solved it:

```
Hi Paul,

first of all thanks for your help,but none of the possible problems you are
thinking about were responsible for my problem.
The problem is the iBCS-emulator itself.
It seems that Oracle performs an sysconf-calls which isn't supported in the
current version of iBCS.
Look at the trace :

<7>[22]615 sysconf(34)
<7>iBCS2 unsupported sysconf call 34
<7>[22]615 sysconf error return linux=-22 -> ibcs=22 <Invalid argument>
<7>[24]615 sysconf(34)
<7>iBCS2 unsupported sysconf call 34
<7>[24]615 sysconf error return linux=-22 -> ibcs=22 <Invalid argument>

Solution:  patching the iBCS-source.apply the following diff-pach :


--- sysconf.c    Sun Apr 19 19:19:15 1998
+++ sysconf.c.ori     Sun Apr 19 19:28:45 1998
@@ -60,7 +60,6 @@
 #define _SC_JOB_CONTROL        5
 #define _SC_SAVED_IDS  6
```

HOWTO

```
 #define _SC_VERSION     7
-#define _SC_HACK_FOR_ORACLE 34

 #define _SC_PAGESIZE    11

@@ -97,11 +96,6 @@
                case _SC_SAVED_IDS: {
                        return (1);
                }
-
-               case _SC_HACK_FOR_ORACLE: {
-                  return (1);
-               }
-

                case _SC_PAGESIZE: {
                  return PAGE_SIZE;
```

9   Credits

This document was based on a document written by Bob Withers, bwit@pobox.com. Additional information taken from documents written by Georg Rehfeld, rehfeld@wmd.de and David Mansfield, david@claremont.com.

Additional proof reading done by Bob Withers, Mark Watling, mwatling@mjw-ltd.demon.co.uk, Peter Sodhi, petersodhi@unn.unisys.com and Greg Hankins, greg.hankins@cc.gatech.edu.

My thanks go to the tremendous support from all the people involved in this document and the research that has gone into it. Particular thanks to Bob Withers and Mark Watling for the additional comments and help they have provided.

Part XXXII

"Linux PCI-HOWTO" by Michael Will

Michael.Will@student.uni-tuebingen.de
v0.6g, 30 March 1997
Information on what works with Linux and PCI-boards and what does not. Please get the latest version of this document at *The Linux Documentation Project* <http://sunsite.unc.edu/LDP/linux.html>

Contents

HOWTO

1   Introduction

Many people, including me, would like to run Linux on a PCI-based machine. Since it is not obvious which PCI motherboards and PCI cards will work with Linux and which do not, I conducted a survey and spent some hours to compile the information contained herein.

If you have information to add, please mail me. If you have questions, feel free to ask.

Help with my style/grammar/language is welcome as well. I am not a native- speaker of English and expect to make occasional mistakes.

Note: "on-board chip" refers to a SCSI chip integrated onto the motherboard rather than on a PCI expansion card.

Also, "quotes" herein may have slight context editing.

2   Why PCI?

2.1   General overview

The PC-architecture has several BUS-Systems to choose from:

ISA

> 16 or 8bit, cheap, slow (usually 8Mhz), standard, many cards available>

EISA

> 32bit, expensive, fast, few cards available, fading>

MCA

> 32 or 16bit ex-IBM-proprietary, fast, becoming rare>

VESA-Local-Bus

> 32bit, based on 486 architecture, cheap, fast, many cards available>

PCI-Local-Bus

> 32bit (64 bit coming), cheap, fast, many cards available, nowadays standard>

MCA worked fine, but never achieved much market, being used on only some early IBM PS/2 machines. There were very few cards.

EISA was reliable, but rather expensive, and intended more for servers, than for the average user. It has the next fewest cards available.

VESA-Local-Bus (VLB) had some problems with high bus-speeds, and was not very reliable, but mainly due to its low price and better-than-ISA performance, sold very well. Technically, it's almost a direct map of the 486 processor bus. Most VESA boards should be stable by now. At the beginning of 1996, many 486 motherboards still support VESA, but PCI is growing. VESA busses are tied directly to the speed of the memory bus for 486's, or half the speed for Pentiums.

PCI now has the advantage. Like EISA it is not proprietary. It is as faster than EISA or MCA, and cheaper. Most current Pentium motherboards use the PCI bus; VESA is fading. Virtualy all PCI motherboards and cards sold at the beginning of 1996 are 32 bit, and run at 0-33 MHz.

Currently, most Pentium motherboards run the PCI bus at 1/2 the memory speed (ie: 33 MHz for the 66 MHz memory bus on the P66,P100,P133,P166; 30 MHz for the 60 MHz memory bus on the P60,P90,P120,P150; and 25 Mhz on the 50 MHz memory bus of the P75). This is probably true of Cyrix 6x86 motherboards too. NexGen 5x86 implemention isn't known. The PCI spec does allow the PCI bus to be run asynchronously from the processor, (eg: 33 Mhz bus on P75), but this is not common yet.

PCI 2.1 has been defined, allowing 64 bit PCI, and/or 0-66 MHz operations, but no x86 chipsets yet support these options. 64 bit PCI will probably appear first, in 32/64 bit dual compatible versions. That is, you will be able to mix 32 and 64 bit cards. 66 MHz PCI will take longer, as it's technically demanding, can only support one or maybe two slots per bridge, and may not work well with 33 MHz cards.

PCI is not processor dependent like the VESA Local-Bus. This means you can use the winner-1000-PCI in an Alpha-driven-PCI computer as well as in a i486/Pentium-driven PCI computer, with the appropriate BIOS and software. Beside Intel and DEC Alpha platforms, PCI is used on some PowerPC's.

Some PCI variations to be aware of: some implementations support "Bus Master" cards in all PCI slots, some in only one slot, and some not at all; some implementations support "bridging" on cards and some do not.

2.2 Performance

taken from Craig Sutphin's early Pro-PCI-Propaganda

> Unlike some local buses, which are aimed at speeding up graphics alone, the PCI Local Bus is a total system solution, providing increased performance for networks, disk drives, full-motion video, graphics and the full range of high-speed peripherals. At 33 MHz, the synchronous PCI Local Bus transfers 32 bits of data at up to 132 Mbytes/sec. A transparent 64-bit extension of the 32-bit data and address buses can double the bus bandwidth (264 Mbytes/sec) and offer forward and backwards compatibility for 32 and 64-bit PCI Local Bus peripherals. Because it is processor-independent, the PCI Local Bus is optimized for I/O functions, enabling the local bus to operate concurrent with the processor/memory subsystem. For users of high-end desktop PC's, PCI makes high reliability, high performance and ease of use more affordable than ever before; no trivial task at 33 MHz bus-clock rates. Variable length linear or toggle mode bursting for both reads and writes improves write dependent graphics performance. By comprehending the loading and frequency requirements of the local bus at the component level, buffers and glue logic are eliminated.

See the chapter about Benchmarks for some crude (and perhaps meaningless) benchmarks on ASUS PCI Boards with 486 and 586.

2.3 The onboard-SCSI-II-chip NCR53c810

One very nice feature of some PCI mother boards is the NCR onboard-SCSI-II-chip, which is said to be as fast as the EISA-Adaptec-1742, but much cheaper. Drivers for DOS/OS2 are available. Drew Eckard has released his version of his NCR53c810-driver, which is in the standard kernel since v1.2.

This works so well I sold my adaptec-1542B-ISA soon after I bought the ASUS SP3-saturn-chipset II PCI board, and found the onboard NCR-SCSI controller to be much faster.

The NCR53c810-chip is onboard on some PCI-motherboards. There are add-on-boards available too, for about US$ 70.00.

There is only one thing I noticed did not work with the NCR-drivers when I tried them. Disconnect/Reconnect did not work, so using a SCSI-tape could be a pain, especially when using "mt erase" or the like blocks the whole SCSI-bus until it has finished. Since this was very unsatisfying for me, I bought one of these nice but expensive DPT PCI SCSI controller and had no such problems anymore.

People have reported this problem has been solved by Drew by now.

FreeBSD does support the NCR53c810 for quite a long time already, including Tagged Command Queues, FAST, WIDE and Disconnect for NCR 53c810, 815, 825. Drew said, it would be possible to adapt the FreeBSD driver to Linux. I somewhere saw some patches to do exactly this, any pointer to the location?

I personaly have the impression there are some important wheels invented more than once because of the differently evolving of FreeBSD and Linux. Some more cooperation could do both systems very well...

2.4 Drew Eckhardt on PCI-SCSI:

Drew said on end of March 95 about the SCSI on PCI: (slightly edited for clarity in context)

The Adaptec 2940, Buslogic BT946, BT946W, DPT PCI boards, Future Domain 3260, NCR53c810, NCR53c815, N-CR53c820, and NCR53c825 all work for some definition of the word works.

- The Adaptec 2940 suffers from the same cabling sensitivity that plagues all recent boards, but otherwise works fine.
- The Future Domain boards are not busmasters, and the driver doesn't support multiple simultaenous commands. If you don't (currently) need multiple simultaneous commands, get a NCR board, which will be cheaper and is busmastering. If you need multiple simultaneous commands, get a Buslogic.
- The Buslogic BT956W will do WIDE SCSI with the Linux drivers (although you can't use targets 8-15), the Adaptec 2940W (with one line patch to the 2940 driver) won't, nor will the NCR53c820 and NCR53c825.
- The NCR boards are dirt cheap (< $ 70 US), are generally quite fast, but the driver currently doesn't support multiple simultaenous commands. Alpha which do neat things like disconnect/reconnect and synchronous transfer are now publicly available, see below.
- Emulux, Forex, and other unmentioned PCI SCSI controllers will not work.

2.5 New Alpha Version of the NCR driver

Well, this is not exactly *that* new anymore, please try to he versions which are in the kernel by version 2.0.x before going for this entry.

Alpha versions of the NCR driver which do neat things like disconnect/reconnect and synchronous transfers are now publically available. Any one interested in playing with them should

- Join the NCR mailing list, by sending mail to majordomo@colorado.edu with subscribe ncr53c810 in the text.
- Get all of the readmes, and latest diffs file from ftp://tsx-11.mit.edu/pub/ALPHA/linux/SCSI/ncr53c810

2.6 The EATA-DMA driver and the PCI SCSI controllers from DPT

The EATA-DMA scsi driver has undergone extensive changes and now also supports PCI SCSI controllers, multiple controllers and all SCSI channels on the multichannel SmartCache/Raid boards in all combinations of WIDE, FAST-20 (ULTRA) and DIFFERENTIAL.

The driver supports all EATA-DMA Protocol (CAM document CAM/89-004 rev. 2.0c) compliant SCSI controllers and has been tested with many of those controllers in mixed combinations.

```
Those are:              (ISA)    (EISA)  (PCI)
      DPT Smartcache: PM2011   PM2012B
      Smartcache III: PM2021   PM2022   PM2024
                               PM2122   PM2124
                               PM2322
      Smartcache IV:  PM2041   PM2042   PM2044
                               PM2142   PM2144
                               PM2322
      SmartRAID     : PM3021   PM3122
                               PM3222   PM3224
                                        PM3334
      and some controllers from NEC, AT&T, SNI, AST, Olivetti and Alphatronix.
```

On a "base" DPT card (no caching or RAID module), a MC680x0 controls the bus-mastering DMA chip(s) and the SCSI controller chip. The DPT SCSI card almost works like a SCSI coprocessor.

The DPT card also will emulate an IDE controller/drive (ST506 interface), which enables you to use it with all operating systems even if they don't have an EATA driver.

On a card with the caching module, the 680x0 maintains and manages the on-board cacheing. The DPT card supports up to 64 MB RAM for disk-cacheing.

On a card with the RAID module, the 680x0 also performs the management of the RAID, doing the mirroring on RAID-1, doing the striping and ECC info generation on RAID-5, etc.

The entry level boards utilize a Motorola 68000, the high-end, more raid specific DPT cards use a 68020, 68030 or 68040/40MHz processor.

Official list prices range from $ 265 to $1.645 (January 18, 1996)

Since I've been asked numerous times where you can buy those boards in Europe, I asked DPT to send me a list of their official European distributors. Here is a small excerpt:

```
Austria: Macrotron GmbH          Tel:+43 1 408 15430  Fax:+43 1 408 1545
Denmark: Tallgrass Technologies A/S Tel:+45 86 14 7000  Fax:+45 86 14 7333
Finland: Computer 2000 Finnland OY Tel:+35 80 887 331   Fax:+35 80 887 333 43
France : Chip Technologies        Tel:+33 1 49 60 1011  Fax:+33 1 49 599350
Germany: Akro Datensysteme GmbH   Tel:+49 (0)89 3178701 Fax:+49 (0)89 31787299
Russia : Soft-tronik             Tel:+7 812 315 92 76   Fax:+7 812 311 01 08
U.K.   : Ambar Systems Ltd.      Tel:+44 1296 311 300   Fax:+44 296 479 461
```

"IMHO, the DPT cards are the best-designed SCSI cards available for a PC. And I've written code for just about every type of SCSI card for the PC. (Although, in retrospect, I don't know why!) ;-)" Jon R. Taylor (jtaylor@magicnet.net) President, Visionix, Inc.

The latest version of the EATA-DMA driver and a Slackware bootdisk is available on: ftp.i-Connect.Net:/pub/Local/EATA

Since patchlevel 1.1.81 the driver is included in the standard kernel distribution.

The author can be reached under these addresses: neuffer@mail.uni-mainz.de or mike@i-Connect.Net

2.7 BT-946C fully supported with kernel 1.3.x and newer

There is a driver in the 1.3.x kernels (available as a patch for the 1.2.13 kernel) written by someone associated with buslogic that fully supports the 946C and ALL of it's features including strict round robin, tagged queueing, multiple scatter/gather, multiple mailboxes, IRQ sharing, and yes, 15 devices on Fast/Wide. It is no longer necessary to use any ISA emulation with the driver (no DMA channel, no ISA address), and the driver is /fast/ and /stable/ (it's out of BETA and into full release).

The driver is available on ftp.dandelion.com (the newest version can always be got by doing "get BusLogic*"). It supports ALL BusLogic controllers with the exception of the FlashPoint LT, which uses a different interface. The driver is included in the 1.3.x kernels as standard for BusLogic devices.

2.8 Future Domain TMC-3260 PCI SCSI

Rik Faith (faith@cs.unc.edu) informed me on Wed, 1 Feb 1995 about the Future Domain TMC-3260 PCI SCSI card being supported by the Future Domain 16x0 SCSI driver. Newer information might be contained in the SCSI-HOWTO.

- Detection is not done well, and does not use standard PCI BIOS detection methods (someone who has a PCI board needs to send me patches to fix this problem). So, you might have to fiddle with the detection routine in the kernel to get it detected.

- The driver still does not support multiple outstanding commands, so your system will hang while your tape rewinds.

- The driver does not support the enhanced pseudo-32bit transfer mode supported by recent Future Domain chips, so you will not get transfer rates as high as under DOS.

- The driver only supports the SCSI-I protocol, so your really fast hard disks will not get used at the highest possible throughput. (Again, fixes for all these problems are solicited – no one is working on them at this time.)

2.9   other thoughts on scsi

James Soutter (J.K.Soutter1@lut.ac.uk) asked me to add the following information on Fast-Wide-SCSI-2:

> Fast Wide SCSI-2 is sometimes incorrectly called SCSI-3. It differs from the normal Fast SCSI-2 (like the Adapted 1542B?) because it uses a 16 bit data bus rather than the more usual 8 bit bus. This improves the maximum transfer rate from 10 MB/s to 20 MB/s but requires the use of special Fast Wide SCSI-2 drives. The added performance of Fast Wide SCSI-2 will not necessarily improve the speed of your system. Most hard disk drives have a maximum internal transfer rate of less than 10 MB/s and so one drive alone can not flood a FAST SCSI-2 bus.
>
> In Seagate's Oct 1993 product overview, only one Fast Wide SCSI-2 drive has an internal transfer rate of more than 10 MB/s (the ST12450W). Most of the drives have a maximum internal transfer rate of 6 MB/s or less, although the ST12450W is not the only exception to the rule. In conclusion, Fast Wide SCSI is designed for the file server market and will not necessarily benefit a single user workstation style system.
>
> Rather than buying a PCI system with a SCSI interface on the motherboard, or rather than waiting for the NCR driver, you could purchase a separate PCI based SCSI card. According to Drew, the only PCI SCSI option that stands a chance of working is the Buslogic 946. It purports to be Adaptec 1540 compatible, like the EISA/VESA/ISA boards in the series.
>
> Drew commented that other PCI based SCSI controllers are unlikely to be supported under Linux or the BSD's because the NCR based controllers are cheaper and more prevalent.

I definitely recommend reading the SCSI HOWTO in regards to newer information about PCI SCSI drivers.

Ernst Kloecker (ernst@cs.tu-berlin.de) wrote: (edited)

> Talus Corporation has finished a NS/FIP driver for PCI boards with NCR SCSI. It will be shipping very soon, might even be free because a third party might pay for the work and donate the driver to NeXT.

Not every PCI-Board has got the chip. The old ASUS do, and one of the J-Bond boards does, too. (Most of the boards nowadays (6/95) do expect you to buy the NCR53c810 seperately.) Some vendors provide an alternative as you can read in Drew's text...

The NCR-Chip is clever enough to work with drives formatted by other controllers, and should be no problem.

3   ASUS-Boards

3.1   ASUS and the NMI (Parity) – impact on Gravis-Ultrasound

The newer trition PCI-Mainboards in 1995 did not seem to support parity-SIMMS anymore. Since I usualy took the cheaper nonparity-SIMMS anyway, I did not consider this a problem until I put the Gravis-Ultrasound into my machine. Under DOS the SBOS-Driver and Setup/Test utility does complain about "nmi procedure disabled on this p.c.". The manual says I'd better get a better mainboard in that case, not very helpful.

The gravis-ultrasound did work nice in the ASUS-SP3 and ASUS-SP4, inspite of this, but the gravis-ultrasound-max I have here got gmod to kernel panic on both boards, and sometimes when playing au-files via /dev/audio did strange things, like playing the rest of an older, previously played sound after the new one. The sounddriver does recommend a buffer of 65536 with the GUS Max instead of the small one like the GUS - why I do not know. I do not have such a problem with the newer ASUS TP4 XE boards, though. Both are equipped with 1M DRAM onboard. These problems are probably not related to the NMI-problem, but because of the sounddriver?

I heard not only ASUS but most of the newer PCI-Mainboards are lacking in parity/NMI-support.

Strange enough - the ASUS-TP4 (Trition Chipset) does work with the GUS Max - it does load the SBOS-Driver. I have to admit, I am confused.

3.2   Various types of ASUS Boards

3.2.1   ASUS SP3 with saturn chipset I (rev. 2) for 486,

- 2 x rs232 with 16550
- NCR53c810 onboard,
- slightly broken saturn-chipset I (rev. 2)

3.2.2   ASUS SP3G with saturn chipset II (rev. 4) for 486,

like SP3, but less buggy saturn chipset

3.2.3   ASUS SP3-SiS chipset, for 486

like AP4, but newer, SiS chipset, green functions and all the EIDE, rs232 with 2 16550 and centronics. Only 2 SIMM Slots, Does seem to work with AMD486DX4/120, but was not very reliably on NCR53c810 and various operating systems (Windows-NT, Windows95, OS2), after upgrading to a PentiumBoard ASUS SP4, all the problems vanished, so it must have been the board. Still does seem to work nice for Linux, though.

3.2.4   ASUS AP4, for 486, with PCI/ISA/VesaLocalbus

green functions, 1VL, 3 ISA, 4 PCI slots, only EIDE onboard, no fd-controller, no rs232/centronics. Very small size.

does recognice AMD486DX2/66 as DX4/100 only. This can be corrected with soldering one pin (which?) to ground, but I would not recommend a board like this anyway.

The one I tested was broken for OS2 and Linux, but people are said to use it for both.

The VesaLocalbus-Slot is expected to be slower than the normal vesa-localbus boards because of the PCI2VL bridge, but without penalty to the PCI section.

3.2.5   ASUS SP4-SiS, for Pentium90, PCI/ISA

like SP3-SiS, but for Pentium90/100.

3.2.6   ASUS TP4 with Triton chipset and EDO-Support

has the Triton-Chipset for better performance and supports normal PS2-Simms as well as Fast-Page-Mode and EDO modules.

3.2.7   ASUS TP4XE with Triton chipset and additional SRAM/EDORAM support

supports the new EDORAM and upcoming SRAM standards. At least SRAM is said to considerabely increase performance. Did for some reason not accept the 8M PS2-SIMMS working ok in ASUS SP4, after changing them against others, bigger looking ones, (16 chips instead of 8 if I remember right) it worked ok. Has been tested with P90 and P100.

3.2.8   ...and many others now.

if you have new information on problems with them, please report.

3.3 Benchmarks on ASUS Mainboards

I tried to compare the speed of CPUs in two ASUS Mainboards: for 486 I tested the SP3 SiS (the one with one vesa-local-bus slot) and for 586 I tested the ASUS TP4/XE, each with 16M RAM, always the same unloaded system with another CPU, with whetstone and dhrystone.

I must admit, I have not read the benchmarks-faq yet, and will probably edit the section a loot soon. If you have any comments, please mail me.

I am especially confused about the amd486DX4/100 being faster on dhrystones than the DX4/120 version? I did not see that kind of inconsistency on comparing the P90 and P100.

Perhaps this was at fault: when I plugged in the amdDX4-100, I had the board jumpered for DX2-66. While the BIOS did report it as an DX4-100, the board might have used the wrong clockspeeds... but since DX2-66 uses 33Mhz * 2 and DX4 uses 33Mhz * 3, this would have been correct?

The board running with DX4-120 is jumpered to 40Mhz * 3 = 120 Mhz.

Another thing I wonder about is why the whetstones-result does yield so even numbers on some machines?

3.3.1 ASUS SP3 with amd486DX4-100

- Dhrystone time for 500000 passes = 7 by 63559 dhrystones/second
- Whetstone time for 1000 passes = 5 by 200.0000 Whetstones/second

3.3.2 ASUS SP3 with amd486DX4-120

- Dhrystone time for 500000 passes = 8 by 56074 dhrystones/second
- Whetstone time for 1000 passes = 4 by 250.0000 Whetstones/second

3.3.3 ASUS SP3 with intel486DX2-66

- Dhrystone time for 500000 passes = 9 by 50761 dhrystones/second
- Whetstone time for 1000 passes = 7 by 142.8571 Whetstones/second

3.3.4 ASUS TP4/XE with intel586-90

- Dhrystone time for 500000 passes = 4 by 101010 dhrystones/second
- Whetstone time for 1000 passes = 3 by 333.3333 Whetstones/second

3.3.5 ASUS TP4/XE with intel586-100

- Dhrystone time for 500000 passes = 4 by 102040 dhrystones/second
- Whetstone time for 1000 passes = 2 by 500.0000 Whetstones/second

3.4 Detailed information on the old ASUS PCI-I-SP3 with saturn chipset from heinrich@zsv.gmd.de:

- 3 PCI, 4 ISA Slots (3x16, 1x8 Bit)
- ZIF Socket for the CPU
- room for 4 72pin-SIMMs (max. 128M)
- Award BIOS in Flash-Eprom
- Onboard: NCR-SCSI, 1par, 2ser (with FIFO), AT-Bus, Floppy

The board does like most in that price class – write-through cache, no write-back. This should not be significant, maybe 3% of performance.

The BIOS supports scsi-drives under DOS/Windows without additional drivers, but with the board come additional drivers which are said to give better performance, for DOS/Windows(ASPI), OS2, Windows-NT, SCO-Unix, Netware (3.11 and 4, if interpreted correctly)

Gert Doering (gert@greenie.muc.de) was saying the SCO-Unix-driver for the onboard-SCSI-Chip was not working properly. After two or three times doing: "time dd if=/dev/rhd20 of=/dev/null bs=100k count=500" it kernel-paniced...

The trouble some people experienced with this board might be due to them using an outboard Adaptec-SCSI-Controller with "sync negotiation" turned on. (This predates the NCR driver release; hence the use of the Adaptec.) Please check that in the BIOS-Setup of the Adaptec-1542C if you use one and have problems with occasional hangups!

There is a new version of the ASUS-Board which should have definitely less problems. It is called ASUS-PCI-I/SP3G, the G is important. It has the new Saturn-chipset rev. 4 and the bugs should be gone. They use the Saturn-ZX-variant and the new SP3G has fully PCI conforming level-triggered (thus shareable), BIOS-configurable interrupts. It has an on-board PS/2-mouseport, EPA-power-saving-modes and DX4-support, too. It performs excellently. If you can get the German computer magazine C't from July (?), you will find a test report where the ASUS-Board is the best around.

Latest information about ASUS-SP3-G: You might experience crashes when using PCI-to-Memory-Posting. If you disable this, all works perfect. jw@peanuts.informatik.uni-tuebingen.de said he believed it to be a problem of the current Linux-kernel rather than the hardware, because part of the system still works when crashing, looking like a deadlock in the swapper, and OS2/DOS/WINDOZE don't crash at all.

Someone else with a very old ASUS-SP3 (saturn-I chipset) reported crashes with using XFree86, which went away when he installed the very latest betaversion which seems to work around a bit of the problems.

3.5   Pat Dowler (dowler@pt1B1106.FSH.UVic.CA) with ASUS SP3G

- ASUS SP3G board (it is rev.4 == saturn II)
- AMD DX4-100 CPU (need to set jumper 36 to 1&2 rather than 2&3, otherwise it's set the same as other 486DXn chips)
- 256K cache (comes with 15ns cache :-)
- 16meg RAM (2x8meg)
- ET4000 ISA video card
- quantum IDE hard drive
- SMC Elitel16 combo ethernet card

Unlike some other reports, I find the mouse pointer moves very smoothly under X (just like the ol' 386) - it is jumpy under some, but not all, DOS games though...

Performance is great!! I ran some large floating point tests and found the performance in 3x33 (100MHz) mode to be almost 1.5x that in 2x (66MHz) mode (large being 500x500 doubles - 4meg or so)... I was a little dubious about clock-tripling but I seem to be getting full benefit :-)

The heavily configurable energy star stuff doesn't work with the current AMD DX4 chips - you need an SL chip

I really need a SCSI disk and a PCI video card :-)

(I had a phonecall by a person who had this problem with the buggy SMC FIFO chipset, after using X-window they hung.)

4   confusion about saturn chipsets

Pat Duffy (duffy@theory.chem.ubc.ca) said:

Saturn I: these are revisions 1 and 2 of the Saturn chipsets.
Saturn II: This is also called rev. 4 of the Saturn chipsets.

As far as I know, rev. 3 never actually shipped, and (from a few people who
have it) the SP3G now has rev. 4 (or Saturn II) in it.

Confused? Well, the only real definitive answer is to get ahold of the board
and run the debug script in the PCI chipset list on it. As far as I know,
though, the SP3G board is indeed shipping with rev. 4 (Saturn II).

5 Video-Cards

Linux people have successfully used # 9 XGE Level 12, ELSA Winner 1000, and S3-928 video cards. The XFree86(tm)-3.1.1 does support boards with the tseng et4000/w32 in accelerated mode, as well as S3 Vision 864 and 964 chipsets including boards like the ELSA Winner 1000Pro and 2000Pro, Number Nine GXE64 and GXE64Pro, Miro Crystal 20SV). Support in the S3 Server for the Chrontel8391 clock chip has been added.

Trio32 and Trio64 S3 Boards like the SPEA V7 Mirage P64 PCI and MIRO Crystal 40SV, are also supported, the Mach32 and Mach64 are supported in accelerated mode, too.

The SVGA Driver

16bpp mode (65K colors instead of the usual 256) support for Mach32 boards as well as 32bpp for some S3 boards and the P9000 boards has been added.

tldraben@teleport.com reported:

- Diamond Stealth W32 (et4000/W32) – Text mode works, X11 suffered from "pixel dust", unbearable never got it to work and returned it.
- # 9GXE L12 – Works, virtual consoles corrupted when switched, fixed this with disabling the "fast dram mode" feature in his BIOS. Does not get a dot clock above 85, though.

Genoa Phantom 8900PCI card seems to work well. Genoa Phantom/W32 2MB does not work in an ASUS-Board. Tseng 3000/W32i chipset seems to work well. Spea-v7 mercury-lite works perfectly since XFree86(tm)-2.1.

Spea V7 Mirage P64 PCI 2M with Trio64 works nice since XFree86(tm)-3.1.1

ATI Graphics Ultra Pro for PCI with 2MB VRAM and an ATI68875C DAC run well as dem@skyline.dayton.oh.us tells us: "It's humming right along at 1280x1024 w/256 colors @74Hz non-interlaced. Looks great."

Paradise WD90C33 PCI did lock up on screensaver/X - this has been solved in the newer versions of the kernel. jbauer@badlands.NoDak.edu (John Edward Bauer)

miroChrystal 8S/PCI (1MB) S3 - no problem.

Stephen Tweedie reported his Cirrus Logics 5434 PCI card works well. It is a 64bit with 2M and runs perfectly with the SVGA driver in 8, 16 and 32 bit per pixel.

6 Ethernet Cards

Of course the ISA-ethernet-cards still work, but people are asking for PCI-based ones. The author of many (if not most) ethernet- drivers said the following some time ago (unfortunately I have not managed to contact him about new information):

From: Donald Becker (becker@cesdis.gsfc.nasa.gov) Subject: PCI ethernet cards supported? The LANCE code has been extended to handle the PCI version. I hope to get the PCI probe code (about a dozen extra lines in the LANCE driver) into the next kernel version. I'm working on the 32 bit mode code. I haven't yet started the 21040 code.

I'll write drivers for the PCnet32 mode and the DEC 21040. That will cover most of the PCI ethercard market.

file://cesdis.gsfc.nasa.gov/pub/people/becker/whoiam.html

In the new testkernels of 1.1.50 and above, the AMD-singlechip ethernetadapters are supported. With a pentium, they ought to then see 900K/second ftps +(assuming an NCR PCI scsi controller) at about 20% cpu load. (AMD Lance).

Anything based on the AMD PCnet/PCI chip should work at the time being. In the US the Boca board costs under US$ 70

Geoffry Coram reported in the news that he got his 3com 590 TPO to work. He had to get the alpha driver from http://cesdis.gsfc.nasa.gov/linux/drivers. Other drivers would be there as well. Note http://cesdis.gsfc.nasa.gov/linux/drivers/vortex.html

Donald Holmgren said he successfully attached his DEC DE435 (PCI) card to the local network on thin coax (BNC). The DE435 driver checks the twisted pair connection first, then switches to the alternate port (jumper selectable as AUI or BNC) if the 10BaseT port fails.

Jim Cusick uses the Boca BEN 1PI card on a thin coax network. It works just fine. You might want to check out: http://cesdis.gsfc.nasa.gov/linux/misc/boca-failure.html for details on the early failures of this card. My second card, after sending one back for replacement, was marked "PN 4186". The old one that did not work was "PN 4185". Mandate this newer model when you order from you vendor. At $ 70, the card is a good deal.

Dave Platt recommends to stay off the Boca BEN1PI card at all costs. It would be unreliable due to design flaws, and Boca seems unable to really fix the problem. The 3Com 3c590 "Vortex" PCI card is available in a combo version (10BaseT, thin coax, and AUI). The Linux driver for this card is not yet part of the release kernel, but is available from http://cesdis.gsfc.nasa.gov/linux/drivers/vortex.html and can be patched into the later 1.2.x kernels (as well as 1.3.x) without much difficulty. The Linux driver does not support the interface autodetect feature of this card - you must use the DOS utility to configure the card for the interface you wish to use (thin coax in this case). Once you've done that, the Linux driver will use the correct interface.

He has been using a 3c590 for several weeks, and it is working fine.

Dave Kennedy said he got two of the above Boca boards and they work fine under light load, but under heavy work like ftping two 16M files into both directions, they failed. He sent the boards back to Boca for a hardwarefix. After they soldered a couple of things (diodes/resistors) onto the card and sent them back, the cards worked fine regardless of load. The two cards have been in 7/24 use in two P90 systems without problems for 6 months now.

Craig does not recommend it since Boca seems not to follow the AMD specs but he has been running them for 2 weeks without problems. He tested his NFS performance and has been moving large files to and from server (16M, 8M). He also tried to do all his workin localy using his data files mounted by NFS and has had no problems. Performance seems to be 100 percent better (wrt to NFS performance) over his NE2000 ISA board. (editors note: but so would probably have been the ISA SMC Elite Ultra?)

6.1 3com-3c590-tpo

Someone on usenet mentioned ht used the 3Com-3C590-TPO (EtherLink III - PCI). He had to get the "3c59x.c" driver and "vortex.patch" to make it work with his 1.2.8 Linux kernel.

6.2 DEC435 PCI NIC

The DEC435 PCI NIC is said to work great with the drivers included in the Slackwaredistribution - I'd say they are in the standard-kernel?

HOWTO

7 Motherboards

The people who answered were using the following boards:

7.1 ASUS

- Ruediger.Funck@Physik.TU-Muenchen.DE - successful.
- strauss@dagoba.escape.de - half-successful, works, but...
- krypton@netzservice.de (Ulrich Teichert), - successful.
- heinrich@zsv.gmd.de - successful
- CARSTEN@AWORLD.aworld.de - successful
- egooch@mc.com - successful - but trouble with the serial port
- archie@CS.Berkeley.EDU and his friend - successful after solving IDE-puzzle
- Lars Heinemann (lars@uni-paderborn.de) successful
- Michael Will (Michael.Will@student.uni-tuebingen.de) - successful.

7.2 Micronics P54i-90

root@intellibase.gte.com succesful bill.foster@mccaw.com successful karpens@ncssm-server.ncssm.edu successful

7.3 SA486P AIO-II

ah@doc.ic.ac.uk successful

7.4 Sirius SPACE

hi86@rz.uni-karlsruhe.de - successful

7.5 Gateway-2000

kenf@clark.net - no problems except the soundcard he tries to swap dmarples@comms.eee.strathclyde.ac.uk - successful, but... robert logan (rl@de-montfort.ac.uk) - flawless. James D. Levine (jdl@netcom.com) - flawless.

7.6 Intel-Premiere

grif@cs.ucr.edu - successful jeromem@amiserv.xnet.com - successful demarest@rerf.or.jp - successful (Premier-II)

7.7 DELL Poweredge SP4100 gbelow@pmail.sams.ch - successful

7.8 DELL OptiPlex Gl+ 575 torsten@videonetworks.com - successful when turning off plug and play

7.9 Comtrade Best Buy PCI / PCI48X MB Rev 1.0

tldraben@Teleport.Com - "Works, I believe it has buggy Saturn chipset. I would also like to add: I strongly recommend not buying from Contrade. Their service is horrible. "

7.10 IDeal PCI / PCI48X MB Rev 1.0

tldraben@Teleport.Com - "Did not work with PCI48X motherboard"

7.11   CMD Tech. PCI IDE / CSA-6400C

tldraben@TelePort.com - "Works"

7.12   GA-486iS (Gigabyte)

Stefan.Dalibor@informatik.uni-erlangen.de - success with problems.

7.13   GA-586-ID (Gigabyte) 90 Mhz Pentium PCI/EISA Board

kkeyte@esoc.bitnet - succesful

7.14   ESCOM 486dx2/66 - which board?

Works perfect except the ftape-streamer (archive)

7.15   J-Bond with i486dx2/66

Drew Eckhardt (drew@kinglear.cs.Colorado.EDU) uses Diamond Stealth 64 VRAM with 4M of memory (964 based). It works great, he usualy runs it at 1024x768 72hz in 32bpp; 16 and 8bpp also work. He needed to get the X311u2S3.tgz server from ftp.xfree86.org; people with 968 based Diamond boards will definately need to do this.

7.16   super micro 011895 03:50 SUPER P54CI-PCI rev 1.3 (Opti)

Manuel de Vega Barreiro

- board super micro 011895 03:50 SUPER P54CI-PCI rev 1.3

- Opti chipset: 82c557,82c556,82c558,82c621.

- 4 PCI, 4 ISA Slots (4x16 Bit)

- ZIF Socket for CPU (120,100,90,75 mHz)

- 4 72 pin-SIMMs (max 128Mb)

- cache 256,512,1024 Kb L2-cache

- Ami WinBIOS in Flash-Eprom (101094-VIPER-P)

- onboard: EIDE for 4 drives

- Pentium with 90Mhz, 8M (now 16M) RAM and 256K L2-cache.

- 1 maxtor 540 Mb, 1 st3122A 1Gb

- Number Nine 9GXE64pro with 2Mb

- Sound blaster 16 + cdrom Matsushita

- 17" microscan 5ep ADI monitor

I run linux 1.1.57 (now 1.2.1) without problems. dosemu0.53 work fine (com. software like kermit and xtalk) XFree86 3.1 at 1024x768 resolution

8 reports on success

8.1 GigaByte GA486-AM with AMD Am5x86-133-WB @ 160MHz (40MHz PCI)

GigaByte GA486-AM

- AMD Am5x86-133-WB @ 160MHz (40MHz PCI)
- BIOS as of 11/07/95 (Rev.A)
- 256KB 2nd level cache (15ns)
- 48MB RAM (Mixed 60/70ns)

Hercules Terminator 64/VIDEO (S3 765 or "Trio 64V+")

Sound Blaster 16

- Panasonic CR563 CD-ROM drive

Silicon 4Ser/3Par I/O

- Mouse
- Terminal
- Terminal
- Modem (14k4)
- HP Laserjet III

Mitsumi CD-ROM controller

- FX001D drive

Longshine 1MBit Floppy controller

- IOMega Tape Insider 250
- 3,5" Floppy
- 5,25" Floppy

No Network card, because the 4 ISA slots are full, and I don't have a PCI card. I (now) use kernel 2.0.22 with APM enabled, and the hard drives power down and up properly without panics. The system is 24hrs up a day and still running. Kernel compilation takes between 5 and 7 minutes, depending on options.

8.2 California Graphics - Sunray II Pro

Guido Trentalancia (guido@gulliver.unian.it) reported the California Graphics - Sunray II Pro with Triton chipset to work well with Pentium100, Hd: Conner cfs420a, Conner cfs210a, crunching numbers at 147492 dhrystones/second.

8.3 Micronics P54i-90 (root@intellibase.gte.com)

Pentium with 90Mhz, 32M RAM and 512K L2-cache. Works extremely well (a kernel recompile takes 10 minutes :-).

The board includes:

- UART - two 16550A high speed UARTS

- ECP - one enhanced parallel port
- Onboard IDE controller
- Onboard floppy controller

Pros: Currently, I'm using it with an Adaptec 1542CF and a 1G Seagate drive, No problems. Graphics is ATI Graphics Pro Turbo (PCI). Very fast. The serial ports can keep up with a TeleBit T3000 modem (38400) without overruns. Caching above 16M does occur. There are 3 banks of SIMM slots (2 SIMM's per bank), with each bank capable of 64M each (2 32M 72-pin SIMM's). Each bank must be filled completely to be used (I'm only using bank 0 with 2 16Mx72-pin SIMM's). The CPU socket is a ZIF type socket. The BIOS is Phoenix, FLASH type.

Drawbacks: RAM is expandable to 192M, but the L2 cache is maxed at 512K. While the graphics are very fast, there is currently no XF86 server for the Mach64 (well, actually there is, but it doesn't use any of the accelerator features; it's just an SVGA server). I don't know if the onboard IDE hard drive controller works; I'm prejudiced against a standard that won't allow my peripherals to operate across platforms, so I didn't buy an IDE disk; instead, I got a Seagate 31200N and a NEC 3Xi.

Mitch

8.4 Angelo Haritsis (ah@doc.ic.ac.uk) about SA486P AIO-II:

The motherboard I eventually bought (in the UK) is one supporting 486 SX/DX/DX2/DX4 chips. It is called SA486P AIO-II. Features include:

- Intel Saturn v2 chipset
- Phoenix BIOS (flash eprom option)
- NCR scsi BIOS v 3.04.00
- 256K 15ns cache (max 512) write back and write through
- 4 72-pin SIMM slots in 2 banks
- 3 PCI slots, 4 ISA
- On-board NCR 53c810 scsi controller
- On-board IDE / floppy / 2 x 16550A uarts / enhanced parallel

I bought it from a company (UK) called ICS, (note I have no connections whatsoever with the company, just a happy customer). I use a 486/DX2-66 CPU.

Before I had a VLB 486 m/board with a buslogic BT-445S controller that I was borrowing. I have 2 scsi devices: 1 barracuda 2.1GB ST12550N disk and a Wangtek 5525ES tape drive. I was expecting a lot of adventures by switching to the new motherboard, esp after hearing all these non-success stories on the net. To my surprise everything worked flawlessly on the 1st boot! (1.1.50). And it has been doing so for about a month now. I did not even have to repartition the disk: apparently the disk geometry bios translation of the 2 controllers is the same. Linux has had no problems at all. SCSI is visibly much faster as well (sorry, I have no actual performance measurements).

The only problems (related to Drew's linux ncr53c7,810 scsi driver - thanks for the good work Drew!) are:

- no synchronous transfers are yet supported => performance hit
- disconnect/reconnect is disabled => disk scsi ops "hold" during certain slow scsi device opeartions (eg tape rewind)
- tagged queuing is not there (?) => performance hit

If you get Windows complainingg about 32-bit disk driver problems, just disable 32-bit disk access via Control Panel. This should not hurt performance. (What I did is remove the WDCTRL driver from my SYSTEM.INI).

All else is fine. I tried the serial ports with some dos/windows s/w and worked ok. The IDE/floppy work ok as well. I have not tried the parallel yet. The motherboard is quite fast and so far I am very pleased with the upgrade. I have not yet tried a PCI graphics board. I will later on. I am using an old ISA S3 which is fine at the moment.

PS: the NCR drivers in the 2.0.x kernels should have no problems of that kind anymore. please consult the SCSI-HOWTO for further and hopefully more uptodate information.

8.5   bill.foster@mccaw.com about his Micronics M5Pi

Micronics M5Pi motherboard with 60 MHz Pentium, PCI bus having the following components:

```
16Mb RAM/512k cache
onboard IDE, parallel, 16550A UARTS
2 X 340MB Maxtor IDE Hard Drives
Soundblaster 16 SCSI-II
Toshiba 3401B SCSI CD-ROM
Archive Viper 525MB SCSI Tape Drive
Viewsonic 17 monitor
Cardex Challenger PCI video card (ET4000/W32P)
A4-Tech Serial Mouse
```

Everything works great, Slackware installation was very easy, I can run Quicken 7 for DOS under DOSEMU. I run X at 1152x900 resolution at 67Hz.

8.6   Simon Karpen (karpens@ncssm-server.ncssm.edu) with Micronics M54pi

I have had no problems with the above board, the on-board PCI IDE (hopefully soon will also have SCSI), and an ATI Mach32 (GUP) with 2MB of VRAM.

8.7   Goerg von Below (gbelow@pmail.sams.ch) about DELL Poweredge

```
- Intel 486DX4/100
- 16 MB RAM
- DELL SCSI array (DSA) with Firmware A07, DSA-Manager 1.7
- 1 GB SCSI HD DIGITAL
- NEC SCSI CD-ROM
- 2 GB internal SCSI streamer
- 3-Com C579 EISA Ethernet card
- ATI 6800AX PCI VGA subsystem, 1024 MB RAM
```

```
CAVE! DELL SCSI Array controller (DSA) runs only with firmware Rev. A07 !
A06 is buggy, impossible to reboot !
To get it: ftp dell.com , file is /dellbbs/dsa/dsaman17.zip
```

Apart from this firmware-problem there where no problems for the last 2 months, running with linux 1.1.42 as primary nameserver, newsserver and www-server on internet.

8.8   zenon@resonex.com about Gateway2000 P-66

Gateway2000's P5-66 system with Intel's PCI motherboard, with 5 ISA slots and 3 PCI slots. The only PCI card I am using is the # 9 GXe level 12 PCI card (2 MB VRAM and 1 MB DRAM). This card was bought from Dell. Under Linux I am using the graphics in the 80x25 mode only (I am waiting for some XFree86 refinements before using it in 1280x1024 resolution), but under DOS/Windows I have used the card in 1280x1024x256 mode without problems. Etherlink 3C509

Ethernet card, Mitsumi bus-interface card, Adaptec 1542C SCSI interface card and additional serial/parallel ports card (which makes the total of serial ports 3).

I have total of 32 MB RAM (recognized and used by both Linux and DOS). There is also a bus mouse (Microsoft in the PS2 mode).

No problems so far.

8.9   James D. Levine (jdl@netcom.com) with Gateway2000

Gateway 2000 P5-60 with an Intel Mercury motherboard, AMI-Flash-BIOS, (1.00.03.AF1, (c)'92) 16M RAM, on-board IDE controller and an ATI AX0 (Mach32 Ultra XLR) PCI display adapter. He had absolutely no problems with the hardware so far but has not tried anything fancy, such as accelerated IDE drivers or SCSI support.

8.10   hi86@rz.uni-karlsruhe.de with SPACE

SPACE-board, 8MB RAM, S3 805 1MB DRAM PCI 260MB Seagate IDE-hard disk because of lack of NCR53c810-Driver, 0.99pl15d, does seem to work well.

8.11   grif@cs.ucr.edu with INTEL

17 machines running a 60Mhz-i586 on Intel-Premier-PCI-Board

8.12   Jermoe Meyers (jeromem@amiserv.xnet.com) with Intel Premiere

Motherboard - Intel Premiere Plato-babyAT 90mhz with Buslogic bt946c w/4.86 mcode w/4.22 autoSCSI firmware, (note, mine came with 4.80 mcode and 4.17 autoSCSI firmware. (interrupt pins A,B,C conform to respective PCI slots!) ATI Xpression (Mach64) - using driver from sunsite, (running AcerView 56L monitor).

The motherboard has 4 IDE drives, Linux (Slackware 2.0) sees the first two and everything on the Buslogic as it emulates an adaptec 1542. Uh, yes, Dos sees them all. Buslogic is VERY accomodating in regards to shipping upgraded chips (you will have to know how to change PLCC (plastic leaded chip carrier) chips, 3 of them. Though, don't let that scare you :-) it's not that tough. Get a low end PLCC removal tool, and your in business. You also might want to "flash upgrade" your system bios from Intel's IPAN BBS, a trivial process. Whats even more interesting is I also have a Sound Blaster SCSI-2 running a scsi CDROM drive off it's adaptech 1522 onboard controller. So thats 4 IDE drives (2 under Linux) and 2 SCSI-2 controllers.

I hope this helps others who are struggling with PCI technology use Linux! Jerry (jeromem@xnet.com)

8.13   Timothy Demarest (demarest@rerf.or.jp) Intel Plato Premiere II

My system is configured as follows: 16Mb 60ns RAM, 3Com Etherlink-III 53C809 ethernet card (using 10base2), ATI Mach 64 2Mb VRAM, Toshiba 2x SCSI CDROM, NCR 53c810 PCI SCSI, Syquest 3270 270Mb Cartridge Drive, Viewsonic 17 monitor, Pentium-90 (FDIV Bug Free). Running Slackware 2.1.0, Kernel 1.2.0, with other misc patches/upgrades.

Everything is functioning flawlessly. I dont recommend the Syquest drives. I have used the 3105 and the 3270 and both a very, very fragile. Also, the cartridges are easily damaged and I have had frequent problems with them. I am in the process of looking for alternative removable storage (MO, Zip, Minidisc, etc).

Some information you might need:

HOWTO

8.13.1 Flash Bios upgrades

Flash Bios updates can be ftp'd from wuarchive.wustl.edu:/pub/MSDOS_UPLOADS/plato. The current version is 1.00.12.AX1. The BIOS upgrades *must* be done in order. 1.00.03.AZ1 to 1.00.06.AX1 to 1.00.08.AX1 to 1.00.10.AX1 to 1.00.12.AX1. The Flash BIOS updates can also be downloaded from the Intel BBS. I do not have that number right now.

8.13.2 NCR 53c810 BIOSless PCI SCSI

If you are using an NCR 53c810 BIOSless PCI SCSI card in the Plato, you may have trouble getting the card to be recognized. I had to change one of the jumpers on the NCR card: the jumper that controls whether there is 1 or 2 NCR SCSI cards in your system must be set to "2". I dont know why, but this is how I got it to work. The other jumper controls the INT setting (A,B,C,D). I left mine at A (the default).

8.13.3 apart from that - plug and play!

There are no settings in the motherboard BIOS for setting the NCR 53c810. Dont worry - once the card is jumpered correctly, it will be recognized! So much for PCI Plug-n-Play!

8.14 heinrich@zsv.gmd.de with ASUS

ASUS-PCI-Board (SP3) having:

- – Asus PCI-Board with AMD 486/dx2-66 and 16M RAM
- – Fujitsu 2196ESA 1G SCSI-II
- – Future Domain 850MEX Controller (cheap-SCSI-Controller, almost a clone to Seagate's ST01... want's to use ncr53c810 as soon as the driver comes out
- – ATI Graphics Ultra (the older one with Mach-8 Chip, ISA-Bus)
- – Slackware 1.1.1

He just exchanged the boards, plugged his cards in, connected the cables, and it worked perfect. He does not use any PCI-Cards yet, though.

8.15 CARSTEN@AWORLD.aworld.de with ASUS

ASUS-PCI-Board with 486DX66/2, miro-crystal 8s PCI driven by the S3-drivers of XFree86-2.0, using the onboard SCSI-Chip. No problems with compatibility at all.

8.16 Lars Heinemann (lars@uni-paderborn.de) with ASUS

ASUS PCI/I-486SP3 Motherboard w/ 486DX2/66 and 16M RAM (2x8), miroChrystal 8S/PCI (1MB) S3, Soundblaster PRO, Adaptec 1542b (3.20 ROM) SCSI host adapter with two hard disks (Fujitsu M2694ESA u. Quantum LPS52) and a QIC-150 Streamer attached. No problems at all!

8.17 Ruediger.Funck@Physik.TU-Muenchen.DE with ASUS

ASUS PCI/I-486SP3 / i486DX2-66 / 8 MB PS/2 70 ns BIOS: Award v 4.50 CPU TO DRAM write buffer: enabled CPU TO PCI write buffer: enabled PCI TO DRAM write buffer: disabled, unchangeable CPU TO PCI burst write: enabled Miro Crystal 8s PCI - S3 P86C805 - 1MB DRAM

Quantum LPS 540S SCSI-Harddisk on NCR53c810-controller.

8.18 robert logan (rl@de-montfort.ac.uk with GW/2000)

Gateway 2000 4DX2-66P 16 Megs RAM, PCI ATI AX0 2MB DRAM (ATI GUP). WD 2540 Hard Disk (528 Megs) CrystalScan 1776LE 17inch. (Runs up to 1280x1024) Slackware 1.1.2 (0.99pl15f)

It is giving no problems. He uses SLIP for networking and an Orchid-Soundwave-32 for niceties, awaiting the NCR-Driver. The only problem he has is that the IDE-Drive could be much faster on the PCI-IDE. It is one of the new Western Digital fast drives and in DOS/WfW it absolutely screams - on Linux it is just as slow as a good IDE-Drive.

8.19 archie@CS.Berkeley.EDU and his friend use ASUS

Archie and his friend have rather similar configurations:

- ASUS PCI-SP3 board (4 ISA, 3 PCI)
- Intel 486DX2/66
- Genoa Phantom 8900PCI card (friend: Tseng 3000/W32i chipset)
- Maxtor 345 MB IDE hard drive
- Supra 14.4 internal modem
- ViewSonic 6e monitor (Archie)
- NEC Multisync 4fge (friend)
- Slackware 1.2.0

The onboard-SCSI is disabled. First there were problems with the IDE-drive: "on the board there's a jumper which selects whether IRQ14 comes from the ISA bus or the PCI bus. The manual has an example where they show connecting it to PCI INT-A. Well, we did that just like the example... but then later our IDE drive would not work (the IDE controller is on board). Had to take it back. The guys at NCA were puzzled, then traced it back to this jumper. I guess the IDE controller uses IRQ14 or something? That's not documented anywhere in the manual. Other than that, seems to be kicking ass nicely now. Running X, modeming, etc. (for the Supra you have to explicitly tell the kernel that the COM port has a 16550A using setserial (in Slackware /etc/rc.d/rc.serial))".

8.20 Michael Will with ASUS-SP3 486 (the old one)

used the following:

- ASUS PCI-SP3-Board with 486dx2/66 and 16M RAM
- NCR53c810-SCSI-II chip driving a 1GB-Seagate-SCSI-II disk and a Wangtec-tape
- ATI-GUP PCI Mach32 Graphics card with 2M VRAM running perfectly with XFree86(tm)-3.1 8bpp and 16bpp
- Linux kernel 1.1.69

It runs perfectly and I am content with the speed, the ATI-GUP-PCI (Mach32) does not give as good benchmarks as expected, though. Since I got the money by now, I got me an ASUS-SP4 with P90 which gives me better throughput on Mach32-PCI... If I had even more money I'd get me another 16M of RAM and a Mach64-PCI with 4M RAM, though... I still keep on dreaming :-)

8.21 Mike Frisch (mfrisch@saturn.tlug.org) Giga-Byte 486IM

- Motherboard: Giga-Byte 486IM
- Configuration: 4 ISA slots (2 double as VLB) and 4 PCI slots
- CPU: Intel 486DX/33
- BIOS: Award 4.50G

HOWTO

- PCI EIDE Disk Controller: Giga-Byte GA-107 (CMD 640x PCI Multi-I/O)

- PCI Video card: ATI Graphics eXpression PCI 2MB DRAM

- Linux Kernel: 1.2.9

- Linux Dist'n: Highly modified Slackware 2.2.0

I have been running this board 24 hours a day for the past 5-6 months. It has worked flawlessly for me under DOS/Windows, OS/2 Warp, and Linux (with Linux being run usually 24 hours a day).

8.22 Karl Keyte (kkeyte@esoc.bitnet) Gigabyte GA586 Pentium

- PCI/EISA Board Gigabyte GA586-ID 90MHz Pentium (dual processor, one fitted)

- 32M RAM

- SCSI - no scsi-NCR-chip on-board, using Adaptec 1542C,

- PCI ATI GUP 2M VRAM

- Adaptec 1742 EISA SCSI controller

- Soundblaster 16

- usual I/O

Everything under DOS AND Linux works perfectly. No problem whatsoever. A VERY fast machine! BYTE Unix benchmarks place it about the same as a Sun SuperSPARC-20 running Solaris 2.3. The PC is faster for integer arithmetic and process stuff (including context switching). The SPARC is faster for floating point and one of the disk benchmarks.

8.23 kenf@clark.net with G/W 2000

He uses a Gateway 2000 with no problems, except the soundcard (which one?). He is trading it in for a genuine sound-blaster in hopes that will help.

8.24 Joerg Wedeck (jw@peanuts.informatik.uni-tuebingen.de) / ESCOM

originaly buyed a 486 DX2/66 from ESCOM (which board?) with onboard IDE and without (!) onboard NCR-SCSI-chip. ISA-adaptec 1542cf scsi-controller instead spea v7 mercury lite (s3, PCI, 1MB), ISA-Soundblaster-16, mitsumi-cdrom (the slower one). Everything except the archive-streamer works with no problems. The spea-v7 works perfectly since XFree86-2.1.

He abandoned the Intel-board in favour of an ASUS-SP3-g and has some problems with PCI-to-Memory burstmode which is crashing only on Linux, "looking like a deadlock in the swapper". If you have any information on this, please eMail the maintainer of the PCI-HOWTO.

After turning off the PCI-to-Memory posting feature it just works perfect.

Rather than sending him mail please read his http-homepage at "http://wsiserv.informatik.uni-tuebingen.de/ jw" where he keeps information about his PCI-system, too.

8.25 Ulrich Teichert / ASUS

ASUS-PCI board with AMD486dx40 (but actually running at 33Mhz?!) His ISA-ET3000 Optima 1024A ISA works nice. No problems with Quantum540S SCSI Harddisk attached to the onboard NCR53c810.

9 Reports of problems

9.1 Compaq PCI systems, especially Presarios

Patrick Yaner (p_yaner@eos.ncsu.edu) reported a Compaq-speciality to me. It seems they are mapping the PCI BIOS data area to an obscure area of memory, one that Linux (or OS2) cannot access. It can usually find it, but it can't get in, and gives a message on startup (something like "pcibios_init: entry in high memory area, unable to access"). Although this is alright with the display (which is on the PCI bus) and the IDE controller (also PCI), it means any other PCI devices – such as an Ethernet card – cannot be detected by Linux.

Compaq offers a driver for DOS at ftp://ftp.compaq.com/pub/softpaq/Drivers/SP1116.ZIP

but using this with linux would mean using the program that boots linux from DOS, instead of LILO. Note that Compaq occasionally updates the software in this archive, so the file ftp://ftp.compaq.com/pub/softpaq/allfiles.html (also available as allfiles.txt) might be handy in checking to see that they haven't upgraded.

Oddly, this information can also be found in the SCSI HOWTO, although the Pressarios come with IDE built in.

9.2 VLSI Wildcat PCI chipset like in Zeos P120 box

Paul Bame (bame@sde.hp.com) reported:

The Wildcat PCI chipset works fine in late 1.3 and all 2.0 kernels.

9.3 dmarples@comms.eee.strathclyde.ac.uk G/W 2000

Gateway 2000 G/W 2000 4DX2/66 PCI ATI-Graphics-Ultra-Pro IDE of indeterminate make

It works well - only the IDE-Card runs in ISA-compatibility-mode, and works a lot faster when switched into PCI-Mode by a DOS-program... thus it's not that fast in Linux, and a patch would be nice.

9.4 cip574@wpax01.physik.uni-wuerzburg.de (Frank Hofmann) / ASUS

He uses the ASUS-board with 16MB-RAM, ISA-based S3/928, and the onboard-IDE-controller with a Seagate ST4550A harddisk. He's had no trouble with the newer Linux-kernels.

His problem:

```
using X, my mouse is not responding the way I was used to before.  It's
sometimes behind movement and makes jumps if moved quickly.  I think
this was discussed In a Linux newsgroup before (I don't know which one)
and is due to the use of 16550 serial chips for the onboard serial in-
terfaces.  After two weeks, I got used to it :-)
```

Reducing the threshold of the 16550 should help. There should be a patch to setserial available somewhere, but I do not know where.

9.5 axel@avalanche.cs.tu-berlin.de (Axel Mahler) / ASUS

ASUS PCI/I-486SP3 Motherboard (Award BIOS 4.50), 16 MB RAM the on-Board NCR Chip is disabled, he had the Genoa Phantom/W32 2MB for PCI and a Adaptec AHA-1542CF (BIOS v2.01) connected to:

- an IBM 1.05 GB Harddisk
- a Toshiba CD-ROM (XM4101-B)
- a HP DAT-Streamer (2GB)

when creating the filesystems, 'mke2fs' (0.4, v. 1.11.93) hung and installation was impossible. After replacing the Genoa Phantom/W32 2MB PCI with an ELSA Winner 1000 2MB PCI it worked perfectly. He tested it with an old Eizo VGA-ISA and it worked as well, so the problem was in the Genoa-PCI-card.

9.6 Frank Strauss (strauss@dagoba.escape.de) / ASUS

ASUS SP3 Board i486DX2/66 NCR53c810 disabled Adaptec 1542B in ISA Slot with 2 hard drives (200MB Maxtor, 420MB Fijutsu), SyQuest 88MB and Tandberg Streamer ELSA Winner 1000 PCI, 1MB-VRAM Soundblaster Pro in ISA Slot at IRQ 5 Onboard IDE disabled Onboard serial, parallel, FD enabled

After a reset, the machine sometimes 'hangs' (soft and hard-reset the same) - this is probably not related to the Adaptec and the Soundcard, because even without these the system sometimes fails to come up. But if it runs, (and the ELSA-WINNER-1000-PCI-message appears) it runs ok.

The two serial ports are detected as 16550 as they should, but at some mailbox-sessions there was heavy data-loss at V42bis... The problem seems to be in the hardware...

CPU>-PCI-Burst seems to work well with DOS/MS-Windows

CPU->PCI-Burst does not work properly with linux0.99p15, Messing up when switching the virtual-consoles, crashing completely when calling big apps like ghostview, or xdvi, leaving the SCSI-LED on (!).

(I suspect these apps would be using a lot of CPU->PCI-burst because of the big heap of data to transmit to the PCI-Winner-1000)

After disabling CPU->PCI-Burst, it works well, the Winner-1000 at 1152x846 (not much font cache with 1MB) does 93k xstones. OpaqueMove with twm is more than just endureable :-)

He has got a SATURN.EXE which he loads under DOS before starting Linux, helping to turn on burst without hangs...

Someone stated that these problems might go away when turning off "sync negotiation" on the Adaptec - I do not know if this is possible with the adaptec1542B too? But I guess so.

With CPU->PCI-Burst it yielded 95k xstones, so he considers it as not too grave to do without. His only problem is that he would like to run his Winner-1000 at 1152x900 which fails because it seems to take any x-resolution higher than 1024pixels as a 1280pixel-resolution, thus wasting a lot end resulting in a y-resolution of 816pixels... but this is probably no PCI-related problem. It should have gone away with XFree86-2.1

9.7 egooch@mc.com / ASUS

- BOARD ASUS PCI/I-486 SP3 RAM: 16MB (4x4M-SIMM)
- CPU 486DX33 CPU
- BIOS Ver. 4.50 (12/30/93)
- Floppy Two floppy drives (1.2 and 1.44), using ASUS on-board floppy controller
- SCSI tried both WD7000 SCSI controller and Adaptec 1542CF and worked.
- Two SCSI 320M hard drives
- SCSI NEC84 CDROM drive
- SCSI QIC150 Archive tape drive
- Video - Tseng ET4000 ISA graphics card
- Sound PAS16 sound card
- Printer attached to on-board ASUS parallel port

He has nothing in the PCI-Slots yet, but wants to buy a PCI-Video-Card, currently uses WD7000 SCSI controller but will switch to the NCR-Chip onboard as soon as the driver is out.

Everything works perfectly - the first serial port which has a 14.4K-Modem attached does hang occasionally when reconnecting with the modem after having used it previously. He says that would not be unique to ASUS but rather a bug in the SMC-LSI device with its 16550UART. The logitech-serial-mouse on the second port works fine. Setting down the threshold of the 16550 for the mouseport would definitely help, one does seem to need a special patched setserial for that? I have not got the information yet, please contact me if you know more!

9.8 Stefan.Dalibor@informatik.uni-erlangen.de / GigaByte

- Board - GA-486iS from Gigabyte w/ 256Kb 2L-Cache, i486-DX2
- Bios - AMI, 93/8
- SCSI - no scsi-NCR-chip on-board, using Adaptec 1542C,
- Video - ELSA Winner 1000
- Linux 0.99pl14 + SCSI-Clustering-Patches / Slackware 1.1.1

All seems to go well, but he has not tried neither networking, printing or a streamer yet. Before applying the clustering-patches he had some problems with hangs triggered by "find", but this no longer is the case - perhaps it was an older kernel-bug.

The ELSA-Winner-1000 sometimes hangs, with very strange patterns on the screen resolved only by rebooting... The dealer has told him it was a bug in the ELSA-Card, but the manufacturer claims it had solved the problem. The bug is not reproducible so he does not plan to take any action at the moment.

All in all the machine seems to work very well under heavy text processing (emacs, LaTeX, xfig, ghostview) usage. Interaction is surprisingly responsive, little difference between it and the 3-4X as expensive Sun he works on...

CPU->PCI-Burst is still disabled because the bios does not support the PCI-things well?

A problem with his new modem (v32 terbo) arose: it looses characters. Especially when using SLIP it complains a lot about RX and TX errors. As soon as he runs X it gets unusable. He said he activated FIFO and RTS/CTS with stty, but to no avail...

9.9 Steve Durst (sdurst@burns.rl.af.mil) with UMC 8500 mainboard

Running Linux 1.2.12 on the UMC8500-100Mhz motherboard with the dreaded CMD PCIO640B (E)IDE controller, when booting the screen wiggles a few seconds, as if the Diamond Stealth64-DRAM (S3 864) has to warm up first, but he can live with that.

9.10 Tom Drabenstott (tldraben@Teleport.Com) with Comtrade / PCI48IX

PCI48IX Motherboard Rev. 1.0. Made by ??? documentation copyrighted by "exrc". The BIOS says not very much about PCI.

His E-315E Super IDE UMC (863+865) ISA-Controller-card does have problems. (It is a multifunction controller-card). It seems to work well under DOS/OS2 but not under Linux.

10 General tips for PCI-Motherboard + Linux NCR PCI SCSI

This was compiled by Angelo Haritsis (ah@doc.ic.ac.uk) from various people's postings:

10.1 DON'Ts:

Do *NOT* go for combination VLB/PCI motherboards. They usually have a lot of problems. Get a plain PCI version (with ISA slots as well of course). A lot of bad things have been heard about OPTI chipset PCI motherboards. Someone hints: "Avoid the OPTi (82C596/82C597/82C822) chipset based motherboards like the TMC PCI54PV".

(I know of at least one person having no problems with his TMC PCI54PV motherboard. He just had to put the N-CR53c810 addonboard into slot-A which is the only slot capable of busmastering as it seems.)

Rumours say that Intel chipset PCI motherboards will have problems with more than one bus-mastering PCI board. I have not tried this one yet on mine and have nothing to suggest. I also heard that the Saturn II chipset is problematic, but this is the one I use and it is perfectly ok! Advice: Try to negotiate a 1-2 week money back agreement with your supplier, in case the motherboard you get has problems with the use you plan for it.

10.2   SIMM slots

Go for 72-pin only SIMMs for speed: Some (all?) of the mainboards which take 30 pin SIMMs use a 32 bit main memory interface, and will be significantly slower than the Intel based boards which all use a 64 bit or permanently interleaved memory interface. You might want to keep that in mind.

10.3   Praised PCI Pentium motherboard

The P90 Intel motherboard with the Intel Premiere II chipset (aka Plato). Get the latest BIOS which has concatenated NCR scsi BIOS 3.04.00. Otherwise DOS won't see your scsi disk(s) if you use a BIOS-less 53c810 based controller. NCR SCSI BIOS exists in the AMI BIOS of the plato after version 1.00.08 (or maybe verion 1.00.06). This BIOS is FLASH upgradeable so you should be able to get the upgrade on a floppy from your supplier. The current version is 1.00.10 and has all early problems fixed.

(Bios files should be available at ftp.demon.co.uk:/pub/ibmpc/intel, but I did not check that myself. the Autor.)

10.4   irq-lines

The value in the interrupt line PCI configuration register is usually set manually (for compatability with legacy ISA boards) in the extended CMOS setup screens on a per-slot or per-device basis. Older PCI mainboards also force you to set jumpers for each PCI slot/device which select how PCI INTA and perhaps INTB, INTC, and INTD are mapped to an 8259 IRQ line, Obviously, if these jumpers exist on your board, they must match the settings in the extended CMOS setup. Also note that some boards (notably Viglens) have silkscreens and instruction manuals which disagree with the wiring, and some experimentation may be in order.

10.5   Info about the different NCR 8xx family scsi chips:

All NCR 8XX Chips are dircet connect PCI bus mastering devices, that have no preformance difference wether on motherboard or add in option card. All devices comply with PCI 2.0 Specification, and can burst 32 bit data at the full 33 MHz (133Mbytes/Sec)

10.5.1   53C810

53C810 = 8 bit Fast SCSI-2 (10 MB/Sec) Single ended only Requires Integrated Mother board BIOS 100 pin Quad Flat Pack (PQFP) Worlds first PCI SCSI Chip, Volumes make it the most inexpensive.

10.5.2   53C815

53C815 = 8 bit Fast SCSI-2 (10 MB/Sec) Single Ended only Support ROM BIOS interface, which makes it ideal for add-in card Designs. 128 Pin QFP

10.5.3   53C825

53C825 = 8 bit Fast SCSI-2, Single ended or Differential 16 bit Fast SCSI-2 (20 MB/Sec), Single ended or Differetial Also has support for external Rom, making it a good candidate for add in cards. 160 pin QFP Not supported by linux yet. (See section below on news about the 825). Must have devices with wide or differential scsi to use these features.

10.6 future of 53c8xx

There are 4 new devices planned for announcement late this year and into early next year. Footprint compitible with 810 and 825 with some new features.

All the Chips require a BIOS in DOS/Intel applications. The 810 is the only chip that needs it resident on the motherboard. Latest NCR SCSI BIOS version: 3.04.00 The bios supports disks >1GB, indeed up to 8G under MS-LOSS.

10.7 Performance of the 53c810

C't magazine's DOS benchmarks showed that it was significantly faster than the Buslogic BT-946, one user noted a 10-15% performance increase versus an Adaptec 2940, and with a very fast disk it may be 2.5X as fast as an Adaptec 1540.

10.8 News about NCR53c825 support

works. period.

10.9 Frederic POTTER (Frederic.Potter@masi.ibp.fr) about Pentium+NCR+Strap_bug

On some Intel Plato board, the NCR bios doesn't recognize the board, because it needs to see the board as a "secondary SCSI controller", and because on most SCSI board the jumper to select between primary/secondary has been ironed to primary (to spare 1 cent, presumably).

Solution:

```
near the NCR chip, they are 3 via ( kind of holes ) with a strap like
that
          O--O  O

     this mean primary is selected as default setting. For the Plato Intel
     Mainboard, it should be like that

          O  O--O

     The best solution is to get rid of the strap and to put a 2 position
     jumper instead.
```

10.10 PCIprobe in the latest Linux Kernels by Frederic Potter

Frederic Potter has added a PCI-Probe into the latest kernels. If you do a "cat /proc/pci" it should list all your cards. If you own cards which are not properly recogniced, please contact him via mail as "Frederic.Potter@masi.ibp.fr".

See arch/i386/kernel/bios32.c and include/linux/pci.h in the kernel source for more information on PCI-Probe-Stuff.

10.11 Other PCI Devices

What other PCI-cards are supported? Apart from various graphicscards, I would like to know about other cards like ethernet, framegrabber, or the TSET boards Cyclades is about to beta-test at the moment:

10.11.1 Cyclades: a 16-port PCI RISC-based multiport card.

The product is called Cyclom-Ye, and has the following characteristics:

HOWTO

- PCI host card based on the PLX chip-set. This host card supports 8 to 32 serial ports, utilizing 8 or 16-port external boxes.

- SCSI II cable.

- 8 or 16-port external boxes with RJ45 or DB25 connectors (your choice). You can start with 8 ports and expand to 32, by just adding more boxes. Each external box contains 2 or 4 CD-1400 RISC Serial controllers (each CD-1400 controls 4 serial ports).

- Up to 4 Host cards can be installed in the PC system, allowing a maximum of 128 serial ports per system.

The product is being in the beta-test phase at July the 26th, 1995, and should be available by Octobre or something. eMail them at sales@cyclades.com.

11 Conclusion

If you have some moneny to put into your machine, you'd be well off with a Pentium90, ASUS-SP4, which is what I use at the moment. If you can afford 32M RAM that would be much better than 16M RAM.

Real soon now the upcoming standard will be the Triton Chipset with support for special SIMMS called EDODRAM, and SRAM. Both will be more expensive than PS2-RAM, and at the time of writing (28-June-1995) SRAM is not available. While EDO-DRAM is more expensive, this is not because of the production costs, they are said to be the same.

For a highperformance system I would still choose an ASUS-TP4/XE with EDO-DRAM, but if you do not need to use it at the moment, I d rather wait some more.

For Graphic-boards I'd say the best cheap board fitting perfectly on a good Multisync-15 like the Samsung SyncMaster 15Gli, is the SPEA V7 Mirage P64 with Trio64 Chipset and 2M DRAM. For more sophisticated Display like the Iiyama-IDEK 8617A-T I think the PCI Mach64 ATI-GUP-Turbo (not the cheaper GUP-Turbo-Windows) would be a good choice, with 4M RAM you can have truecolor in higher resolutions. It is well supported in the XFree86(tm)-3.1.1, and there are commercial X-Servers available of which I'd recommend Accelerated/X by Roell, which supports the Mach64 very well and fast.

For SCSI I'd take the DPT rather than the (much cheaper and very fast) NCR53c810 in case you plan to use SCSI-Tapes a lot. The NCR53c810 driver on Linux does lack disconnect/reconnect support, thus blocking the SCSIbus on operations like "mt rewind", "mt fsf" etc. It bears a performance penalty on tar-operations - but check out Drews new alpha drivers before making a decision, perhaps it does solve all the problems.

For building servers, the DPT would be the controller of choice anyway because of all the nifty hardware cache (with elevator sorting on accesses, so cache it is not a silly thing even in a Linux enviroment where the OS does the caching) and RAID-Support up to raid level 5.

If you do not want to spend that much money on computer equipment (e.g.: you are having a life) you might go for an ASUS-SP3-SiS with AMD-DX2/66 or DX4/100. The SPEA V7 Mirage P64 PCI with 2M DRAM would be a good choice, since it uses the Trio64 S3 Chip, which is well supported by XFree86(tm)-3.1.1, quite cheap to buy and fast, too.

Another fine card since XFree86(tm)-3.1 is the fast and cheap et4000/w32-PCI-card.

12 Thanks

I want to thank the following people for supporting this document:

- David Lesher (wb8foz@netcom.com) for extensive help with the english language

- Nathanael MAKAREVITCH (nat@nataa.frmug.fr.net) for translating into french

- Jun Morimoto (morimoto@lab.imagica.co.jp) for translating into japanese

- Marco Melgazzi (marco@vcldec1.polito.it) for translating into italian

- Donald Becker (becker@cesdis.gsfc.nasa.gov) for ethernet-informations

- Drew Eckhardt (drew@kinglear.cs.Colorado.EDU) for SCSI-informations

- Zhahai Stewart (zhahai@hisys.com) for help with the intro section

and many more peole adding information mostly by mail and by posts, some of them will be named here:

```
CARSTEN@AWORLD.aworld.de,
dmarples@comms.eee.strathclyde.ac.uk,
drew@kinglear.cs.Colorado.EDU (Working at the PCI-NCR53c810-Driver),
duncan@spd.eee.strathclyde.ac.uk,
fm3@irz.inf.tu-dresden.de,
grif@ucrengr.ucr.edu,
heinrich@zsv.gmd.de,
hm@ix.de (iX-Magazine),
hm@seneca.ix.de,
kebsch.pad@sni.de,
kenf@clark.net,
matthias@penthouse.boerde.de,
ortloff@omega.informatik.uni-dortmund.de,
preberle@cip.informatik.uni-erlangen.de,
rob@me62.lbl.gov,
rsi@netcom.com,
sk001sp@unidui.uni-duisburg.de,
strauss@dagoba.escape.de,
strauss@dagoba.priconet.de,
hi86@rz.uni-karlsruhe.de,
Ulrich Teichert, krypton@netzservice.de,
Stefan.Dalibor@informatik.uni-erlangen.de,
tldraben@teleport.com
mundkur@eagle.ece.uci.edu,
ooch@jericho.mc.com,
Gert Doering (gert@greenie.muc.de),
James D. Levine (jdl@netcom.com),
Georg von Below (gbelow@pmail.sams.ch),
Jerome Meyers (jeromem@quake.xnet.com),
Angelo Haritsis (ah@doc.ic.ac.uk),
archie@CS.Berkeley.EDU and his friend kenf@clark.net.
```

13 copyright/legalese

(c)opyright 1993,94 by Michael Will - the GPL (Gnu Public License) applies. See last section about this.

If you sell this HOWTO on a CD or in a book I would be happy to have a copy for reference.

(Michael.Will@student.uni-tuebingen.de)

Contact me, either via eMail or call +49-7071-969063.

Trademarks are owned by their owners. There is no warranty on the information in this document.

For german users I am offering tested, preinstalled / preconfigured and supported Linux-PCI-machines. Call me at 07071-969063.

HOWTO

14 GPL - Gnu Public License

```
            GNU GENERAL PUBLIC LICENSE
               Version 2, June 1991
```

                         Preamble

  The licenses for most software are designed to take away your
freedom to share and change it. By contrast, the GNU General Public
License is intended to guarantee your freedom to share and change free
software--to make sure the software is free for all its users. This
General Public License applies to most of the Free Software
Foundation's software and to any other program whose authors commit to
using it. (Some other Free Software Foundation software is covered by
the GNU Library General Public License instead.) You can apply it to
your programs, too.

  When we speak of free software, we are referring to freedom, not
price. Our General Public Licenses are designed to make sure that you
have the freedom to distribute copies of free software (and charge for
this service if you wish), that you receive source code or can get it
if you want it, that you can change the software or use pieces of it
in new free programs; and that you know you can do these things.

  To protect your rights, we need to make restrictions that forbid
anyone to deny you these rights or to ask you to surrender the rights.
These restrictions translate to certain responsibilities for you if you
distribute copies of the software, or if you modify it.

  For example, if you distribute copies of such a program, whether
gratis or for a fee, you must give the recipients all the rights that
you have. You must make sure that they, too, receive or can get the
source code. And you must show them these terms so they know their
rights.

  We protect your rights with two steps: (1) copyright the software, and
(2) offer you this license which gives you legal permission to copy,
distribute and/or modify the software.

  Also, for each author's protection and ours, we want to make certain
that everyone understands that there is no warranty for this free
software. If the software is modified by someone else and passed on, we
want its recipients to know that what they have is not the original, so
that any problems introduced by others will not reflect on the original
authors' reputations.

  Finally, any free program is threatened constantly by software
patents. We wish to avoid the danger that redistributors of a free
program will individually obtain patent licenses, in effect making the
program proprietary. To prevent this, we have made it clear that any

patent must be licensed for everyone's free use or not licensed at all.

The precise terms and conditions for copying, distribution and modification follow.

GNU GENERAL PUBLIC LICENSE
TERMS AND CONDITIONS FOR COPYING, DISTRIBUTION AND MODIFICATION

0. This License applies to any program or other work which contains a notice placed by the copyright holder saying it may be distributed under the terms of this General Public License. The "Program", below, refers to any such program or work, and a "work based on the Program" means either the Program or any derivative work under copyright law: that is to say, a work containing the Program or a portion of it, either verbatim or with modifications and/or translated into another language. (Hereinafter, translation is included without limitation in the term "modification".) Each licensee is addressed as "you".

Activities other than copying, distribution and modification are not covered by this License; they are outside its scope. The act of running the Program is not restricted, and the output from the Program is covered only if its contents constitute a work based on the Program (independent of having been made by running the Program). Whether that is true depends on what the Program does.

1. You may copy and distribute verbatim copies of the Program's source code as you receive it, in any medium, provided that you conspicuously and appropriately publish on each copy an appropriate copyright notice and disclaimer of warranty; keep intact all the notices that refer to this License and to the absence of any warranty; and give any other recipients of the Program a copy of this License along with the Program.

You may charge a fee for the physical act of transferring a copy, and you may at your option offer warranty protection in exchange for a fee.

2. You may modify your copy or copies of the Program or any portion of it, thus forming a work based on the Program, and copy and distribute such modifications or work under the terms of Section 1 above, provided that you also meet all of these conditions:

  a) You must cause the modified files to carry prominent notices stating that you changed the files and the date of any change.

  b) You must cause any work that you distribute or publish, that in whole or in part contains or is derived from the Program or any part thereof, to be licensed as a whole at no charge to all third parties under the terms of this License.

  c) If the modified program normally reads commands interactively when run, you must cause it, when started running for such interactive use in the most ordinary way, to print or display an announcement including an appropriate copyright notice and a notice that there is no warranty (or else, saying that you provide a warranty) and that users may redistribute the program under

HOWTO

these conditions, and telling the user how to view a copy of this
License. (Exception: if the Program itself is interactive but
does not normally print such an announcement, your work based on
the Program is not required to print an announcement.)

These requirements apply to the modified work as a whole. If
identifiable sections of that work are not derived from the Program,
and can be reasonably considered independent and separate works in
themselves, then this License, and its terms, do not apply to those
sections when you distribute them as separate works. But when you
distribute the same sections as part of a whole which is a work based
on the Program, the distribution of the whole must be on the terms of
this License, whose permissions for other licensees extend to the
entire whole, and thus to each and every part regardless of who wrote it.

Thus, it is not the intent of this section to claim rights or contest
your rights to work written entirely by you; rather, the intent is to
exercise the right to control the distribution of derivative or
collective works based on the Program.

In addition, mere aggregation of another work not based on the Program
with the Program (or with a work based on the Program) on a volume of
a storage or distribution medium does not bring the other work under
the scope of this License.

  3. You may copy and distribute the Program (or a work based on it,
under Section 2) in object code or executable form under the terms of
Sections 1 and 2 above provided that you also do one of the following:

  a) Accompany it with the complete corresponding machine-readable
  source code, which must be distributed under the terms of Sections
  1 and 2 above on a medium customarily used for software interchange; or,

  b) Accompany it with a written offer, valid for at least three
  years, to give any third party, for a charge no more than your
  cost of physically performing source distribution, a complete
  machine-readable copy of the corresponding source code, to be
  distributed under the terms of Sections 1 and 2 above on a medium
  customarily used for software interchange; or,

  c) Accompany it with the information you received as to the offer
  to distribute corresponding source code. (This alternative is
  allowed only for noncommercial distribution and only if you
  received the program in object code or executable form with such
  an offer, in accord with Subsection b above.)

The source code for a work means the preferred form of the work for
making modifications to it. For an executable work, complete source
code means all the source code for all modules it contains, plus any
associated interface definition files, plus the scripts used to
control compilation and installation of the executable. However, as a
special exception, the source code distributed need not include
anything that is normally distributed (in either source or binary
form) with the major components (compiler, kernel, and so on) of the
operating system on which the executable runs, unless that component

itself accompanies the executable.

If distribution of executable or object code is made by offering access to copy from a designated place, then offering equivalent access to copy the source code from the same place counts as distribution of the source code, even though third parties are not compelled to copy the source along with the object code.

4. You may not copy, modify, sublicense, or distribute the Program except as expressly provided under this License. Any attempt otherwise to copy, modify, sublicense or distribute the Program is void, and will automatically terminate your rights under this License. However, parties who have received copies, or rights, from you under this License will not have their licenses terminated so long as such parties remain in full compliance.

5. You are not required to accept this License, since you have not signed it. However, nothing else grants you permission to modify or distribute the Program or its derivative works. These actions are prohibited by law if you do not accept this License. Therefore, by modifying or distributing the Program (or any work based on the Program), you indicate your acceptance of this License to do so, and all its terms and conditions for copying, distributing or modifying the Program or works based on it.

6. Each time you redistribute the Program (or any work based on the Program), the recipient automatically receives a license from the original licensor to copy, distribute or modify the Program subject to these terms and conditions. You may not impose any further restrictions on the recipients' exercise of the rights granted herein. You are not responsible for enforcing compliance by third parties to this License.

7. If, as a consequence of a court judgment or allegation of patent infringement or for any other reason (not limited to patent issues), conditions are imposed on you (whether by court order, agreement or otherwise) that contradict the conditions of this License, they do not excuse you from the conditions of this License. If you cannot distribute so as to satisfy simultaneously your obligations under this License and any other pertinent obligations, then as a consequence you may not distribute the Program at all. For example, if a patent license would not permit royalty-free redistribution of the Program by all those who receive copies directly or indirectly through you, then the only way you could satisfy both it and this License would be to refrain entirely from distribution of the Program.

If any portion of this section is held invalid or unenforceable under any particular circumstance, the balance of the section is intended to apply and the section as a whole is intended to apply in other circumstances.

It is not the purpose of this section to induce you to infringe any patents or other property right claims or to contest validity of any such claims; this section has the sole purpose of protecting the integrity of the free software distribution system, which is

HOWTO

implemented by public license practices. Many people have made
generous contributions to the wide range of software distributed
through that system in reliance on consistent application of that
system; it is up to the author/donor to decide if he or she is willing
to distribute software through any other system and a licensee cannot
impose that choice.

This section is intended to make thoroughly clear what is believed to
be a consequence of the rest of this License.

8. If the distribution and/or use of the Program is restricted in
certain countries either by patents or by copyrighted interfaces, the
original copyright holder who places the Program under this License
may add an explicit geographical distribution limitation excluding
those countries, so that distribution is permitted only in or among
countries not thus excluded. In such case, this License incorporates
the limitation as if written in the body of this License.

9. The Free Software Foundation may publish revised and/or new versions
of the General Public License from time to time. Such new versions will
be similar in spirit to the present version, but may differ in detail to
address new problems or concerns.

Each version is given a distinguishing version number. If the Program
specifies a version number of this License which applies to it and "any
later version", you have the option of following the terms and conditions
either of that version or of any later version published by the Free
Software Foundation. If the Program does not specify a version number of
this License, you may choose any version ever published by the Free Software
Foundation.

10. If you wish to incorporate parts of the Program into other free
programs whose distribution conditions are different, write to the author
to ask for permission. For software which is copyrighted by the Free
Software Foundation, write to the Free Software Foundation; we sometimes
make exceptions for this. Our decision will be guided by the two goals
of preserving the free status of all derivatives of our free software and
of promoting the sharing and reuse of software generally.

NO WARRANTY

11. BECAUSE THE PROGRAM IS LICENSED FREE OF CHARGE, THERE IS NO WARRANTY
FOR THE PROGRAM, TO THE EXTENT PERMITTED BY APPLICABLE LAW. EXCEPT WHEN
OTHERWISE STATED IN WRITING THE COPYRIGHT HOLDERS AND/OR OTHER PARTIES
PROVIDE THE PROGRAM "AS IS" WITHOUT WARRANTY OF ANY KIND, EITHER EXPRESSED
OR IMPLIED, INCLUDING, BUT NOT LIMITED TO, THE IMPLIED WARRANTIES OF
MERCHANTABILITY AND FITNESS FOR A PARTICULAR PURPOSE. THE ENTIRE RISK AS
TO THE QUALITY AND PERFORMANCE OF THE PROGRAM IS WITH YOU. SHOULD THE
PROGRAM PROVE DEFECTIVE, YOU ASSUME THE COST OF ALL NECESSARY SERVICING,
REPAIR OR CORRECTION.

12. IN NO EVENT UNLESS REQUIRED BY APPLICABLE LAW OR AGREED TO IN WRITING
WILL ANY COPYRIGHT HOLDER, OR ANY OTHER PARTY WHO MAY MODIFY AND/OR
REDISTRIBUTE THE PROGRAM AS PERMITTED ABOVE, BE LIABLE TO YOU FOR DAMAGES,
INCLUDING ANY GENERAL, SPECIAL, INCIDENTAL OR CONSEQUENTIAL DAMAGES ARISING

OUT OF THE USE OR INABILITY TO USE THE PROGRAM (INCLUDING BUT NOT LIMITED
TO LOSS OF DATA OR DATA BEING RENDERED INACCURATE OR LOSSES SUSTAINED BY
YOU OR THIRD PARTIES OR A FAILURE OF THE PROGRAM TO OPERATE WITH ANY OTHER
PROGRAMS), EVEN IF SUCH HOLDER OR OTHER PARTY HAS BEEN ADVISED OF THE
POSSIBILITY OF SUCH DAMAGES.

END OF TERMS AND CONDITIONS

Appendix: How to Apply These Terms to Your New Programs

If you develop a new program, and you want it to be of the greatest
possible use to the public, the best way to achieve this is to make it
free software which everyone can redistribute and change under these terms.

To do so, attach the following notices to the program. It is safest
to attach them to the start of each source file to most effectively
convey the exclusion of warranty; and each file should have at least
the "copyright" line and a pointer to where the full notice is found.

    <one line to give the program's name and a brief idea of what it does.>
    Copyright (C) 19yy (name of author)

    This program is free software; you can redistribute it and/or modify
    it under the terms of the GNU General Public License as published by
    the Free Software Foundation; either version 2 of the License, or
    (at your option) any later version.

    This program is distributed in the hope that it will be useful,
    but WITHOUT ANY WARRANTY; without even the implied warranty of
    MERCHANTABILITY or FITNESS FOR A PARTICULAR PURPOSE. See the
    GNU General Public License for more details.

    You should have received a copy of the GNU General Public License
    along with this program; if not, write to the Free Software
    Foundation, Inc., 675 Mass Ave, Cambridge, MA 02139, USA.

Also add information on how to contact you by electronic and paper mail.

If the program is interactive, make it output a short notice like this
when it starts in an interactive mode:

    Gnomovision version 69, Copyright (C) 19yy name of author
    Gnomovision comes with ABSOLUTELY NO WARRANTY; for details type 'show w'.
    This is free software, and you are welcome to redistribute it
    under certain conditions; type 'show c' for details.

The hypothetical commands 'show w' and 'show c' should show the appropriate
parts of the General Public License. Of course, the commands you use may
be called something other than 'show w' and 'show c'; they could even be
mouse-clicks or menu items--whatever suits your program.

You should also get your employer (if you work as a programmer) or your
school, if any, to sign a "copyright disclaimer" for the program, if
necessary. Here is a sample; alter the names:

HOWTO

Yoyodyne, Inc., hereby disclaims all copyright interest in the program 'Gnomovision' (which makes passes at compilers) written by James Hacker.

(signature of Ty Coon), 1 April 1989
Ty Coon, President of Vice

This General Public License does not permit incorporating your program into proprietary programs. If your program is a subroutine library, you may consider it more useful to permit linking proprietary applications with the library. If this is what you want to do, use the GNU Library General Public License instead of this License.

## Part XXXIII

"Linux Parallel Processing HOWTO" Hank Dietz

pplinux@ecn.purdue.edu

v980105, 5 January 1998

Parallel Processing refers to the concept of speeding-up the execution of a program by dividing the program into multiple fragments that can execute simultaneously, each on its own processor. A program being executed across N processors might execute N times faster than it would using a single processor. This document discusses the four basic approaches to parallel processing that are available to Linux users: SMP Linux systems, clusters of networked Linux systems, parallel execution using multimedia instructions (i.e., MMX), and attached (parallel) processors hosted by a Linux system.

Contents

1   Introduction

Parallel Processing refers to the concept of speeding-up the execution of a program by dividing the program into multiple fragments that can execute simultaneously, each on its own processor. A program being executed across n processors might execute n times faster than it would using a single processor.

Traditionally, multiple processors were provided within a specially designed "parallel computer"; along these lines, Linux now supports **SMP** systems (often sold as "servers") in which multiple processors share a single memory and bus interface within a single computer. It is also possible for a group of computers (for example, a group of PCs each running Linux) to be interconnected by a network to form a parallel-processing **cluster**. The third alternative for parallel computing using Linux is to use the **multimedia instruction extensions** (i.e., MMX) to operate in parallel on vectors of integer data. Finally, it is also possible to use a Linux system as a "host" for a specialized **attached** parallel processing compute engine. All these approaches are discussed in detail in this document.

1.1   Is Parallel Processing What I Want?

Although use of multiple processors can speed-up many operations, most applications cannot yet benefit from parallel processing. Basically, parallel processing is appropriate only if:

- Your application has enough parallelism to make good use of multiple processors. In part, this is a matter of identifying portions of the program that can execute independently and simultaneously on separate processors, but you will also find that some things that *could* execute in parallel might actually slow execution if executed in parallel using a particular system. For example, a program that takes four seconds to execute within a single machine might be able to execute in only one second of processor time on each of four machines, but no speedup would be achieved if it took three seconds or more for these machines to coordinate their actions.

- Either the particular application program you are interested in already has been **parallelized** (rewritten to take advantage of parallel processing) or you are willing to do at least some new coding to take advantage of parallel processing.

- You are interested in researching, or at least becoming familiar with, issues involving parallel processing. Parallel processing using Linux systems isn't necessarily difficult, but it is not familiar to most computer users, and there isn't any book called "Parallel Processing for Dummies"... at least not yet. This HOWTO is a good starting point, not all you need to know.

The good news is that if all the above are true, you'll find that parallel processing using Linux can yield supercomputer performance for some programs that perform complex computations or operate on large data sets. What's more, it can do that using cheap hardware... which you might already own. As an added bonus, it is also easy to use a parallel Linux system for other things when it is not busy executing a parallel job.

If parallel processing is *not* what you want, but you would like to achieve at least a modest improvement in performance, there are still things you can do. For example, you can improve performance of sequential programs by moving to a faster processor, adding memory, replacing an IDE disk with fast wide SCSI, etc. If that's all you are interested in, jump to section 6.2; otherwise, read on.

1.2   Terminology

Although parallel processing has been used for many years in many systems, it is still somewhat unfamiliar to most computer users. Thus, before discussing the various alternatives, it is important to become familiar with a few commonly used terms.

SIMD:

SIMD (Single Instruction stream, Multiple Data stream) refers to a parallel execution model in which all processors execute the same operation at the same time, but each processor is allowed to operate upon its own data. This model naturally fits the concept of performing the same operation on every element of an array, and is thus often associated with vector or array manipulation. Because all operations are inherently synchronized, interactions among SIMD processors tend to be easily and efficiently implemented.

MIMD:

MIMD (Multiple Instruction stream, Multiple Data stream) refers to a parallel execution model in which each processor is essentially acting independently. This model most naturally fits the concept of decomposing a program for parallel execution on a functional basis; for example, one processor might update a database file while another processor generates a graphic display of the new entry. This is a more flexible model than SIMD execution, but it is achieved at the risk of debugging nightmares called **race conditions**, in which a program may intermittently fail due to timing variations reordering the operations of one processor relative to those of another.

SPMD:

SPMD (Single Program, Multiple Data) is a restricted version of MIMD in which all processors are running the same program. Unlike SIMD, each processor executing SPMD code may take a different control flow path through the program.

Communication Bandwidth:

The bandwidth of a communication system is the maximum amount of data that can be transmitted in a unit of time... once data transmission has begun. Bandwidth for serial connections is often measured in **baud** or **bits/second (b/s)**, which generally correspond to 1/10 to 1/8 that many **Bytes/second (B/s)**. For example, a 1,200 baud modem transfers about 120 B/s, whereas a 155 Mb/s ATM network connection is nearly 130,000 times faster, transferring about about 17 MB/s. High bandwidth allows large blocks of data to be transferred efficiently between processors.

Communication Latency:

The latency of a communication system is the minimum time taken to transmit one object, including any send and receive software overhead. Latency is very important in parallel processing because it determines the minimum useful **grain size**, the minimum run time for a segment of code to yield speed-up through parallel execution. Basically, if a segment of code runs for less time than it takes to transmit its result value (i.e., latency), executing that code segment serially on the processor that needed the result value would be faster than parallel execution; serial execution would avoid the communication overhead.

Message Passing:

Message passing is a model for interactions between processors within a parallel system. In general, a message is constructed by software on one processor and is sent through an interconnection network to another processor, which then must accept and act upon the message contents. Although the overhead in handling each message (latency) may be high, there are typically few restrictions on how much information each message may contain. Thus, message passing can yield high bandwidth making it a very effective way to transmit a large block of data from one processor to another. However, to minimize the need for expensive message passing operations, data

HOWTO

structures within a parallel program must be spread across the processors so that most data referenced by each processor is in its local memory... this task is known as **data layout**.

Shared Memory:

Shared memory is a model for interactions between processors within a parallel system. Systems like the multi-processor Pentium machines running Linux **physically** share a single memory among their processors, so that a value written to shared memory by one processor can be directly accessed by any processor. Alternatively, **logically** shared memory can be implemented for systems in which each processor has it own memory by converting each non-local memory reference into an appropriate inter-processor communication. Either implementation of shared memory is generally considered easier to use than message passing. Physically shared memory can have both high bandwidth and low latency, but only when multiple processors do not try to access the bus simultaneously; thus, data layout still can seriously impact performance, and cache effects, etc., can make it difficult to determine what the best layout is.

Aggregate Functions:

In both the message passing and shared memory models, a communication is initiated by a single processor; in contrast, aggregate function communication is an inherently parallel communication model in which an entire group of processors act together. The simplest such action is a **barrier synchronization**, in which each individual processor waits until every processor in the group has arrived at the barrier. By having each processor output a datum as a side-effect of reaching a barrier, it is possible to have the communication hardware return a value to each processor which is an arbitrary function of the values collected from all processors. For example, the return value might be the answer to the question "did any processor find a solution?" or it might be the sum of one value from each processor. Latency can be very low, but bandwidth per processor also tends to be low. Traditionally, this model is used primarily to control parallel execution rather than to distribute data values.

Collective Communication:

This is another name for aggregate functions, most often used when referring to aggregate functions that are constructed using multiple message-passing operations.

SMP:

SMP (Symmetric Multi-Processor) refers to the operating system concept of a group of processors working together as peers, so that any piece of work could be done equally well by any processor. Typically, SMP implies the combination of MIMD and shared memory. In the IA32 world, SMP generally means compliant with MPS (the Intel MultiProcessor Specification); in the future, it may mean "Slot 2"....

SWAR:

SWAR (SIMD Within A Register) is a generic term for the concept of partitioning a register into multiple integer fields and using register-width operations to perform SIMD-parallel computations across those fields. Given a machine with k-bit registers, data paths, and function units, it has long been known that ordinary register operations can function as SIMD parallel operations on as many as n, k/n-bit, field values. Although this type of parallelism can be implemented using ordinary integer registers and instructions, many high-end microprocessors have recently added specialized instructions to enhance the performance of this technique for multimedia-oriented tasks. In addition to the Intel/AMD/Cyrix **MMX** (MultiMedia eXtensions), there are: Digital Alpha **MAX** (MultimediA eXtensions), Hewlett-Packard PA-RISC **MAX** (Multimedia Acceleration eXtensions), MIPS **MDMX** (Digital Media eXtension, pronounced "Mad Max"), and Sun SPARC V9 **VIS** (Visual Instruction Set). Aside from the three vendors who have agreed on MMX, all of these instruction set extensions are roughly comparable, but mutually incompatible.

Attached Processors:

Attached processors are essentially special-purpose computers that are connected to a **host** system to accelerate specific types of computation. For example, many video and audio cards for PCs contain attached processors designed, respectively, to accelerate common graphics operations and audio **DSP** (Digital Signal Processing). There is also a wide range of attached **array processors**, so called because they are designed to accelerate arithmetic operations on arrays. In fact, many commercial supercomputers are really attached processors with workstation hosts.

RAID:

RAID (Redundant Array of Inexpensive Disks) is a simple technology for increasing both the bandwidth and reliability of disk I/O. Although there are many different variations, all have two key concepts in common. First, each data block is **striped** across a group of $n+k$ disk drives such that each drive only has to read or write $1/n$ of the data... yielding n times the bandwidth of one drive. Second, redundant data is written so that data can be recovered if a disk drive fails; this is important because otherwise if any one of the $n+k$ drives were to fail, the entire file system could be lost. A good overview of RAID in general is given at <http://www.dpt.com/uraiddoc.html>, and information about RAID options for Linux systems is at <http://linas.org/linux/raid.html>. Aside from specialized RAID hardware support, Linux also supports software RAID 0, 1, 4, and 5 across multiple disks hosted by a single Linux system; see the Software RAID mini-HOWTO and the Multi-Disk System Tuning mini-HOWTO for details. RAID across disk drives *on multiple machines in a cluster* is not directly supported.

IA32:

IA32 (Intel Architecture, 32-bit) really has nothing to do with parallel processing, but rather refers to the class of processors whose instruction sets are generally compatible with that of the Intel 386. Basically, any Intel x86 processor after the 286 is compatible with the 32-bit flat memory model that characterizes IA32. AMD and Cyrix also make a multitude of IA32-compatible processors. Because Linux evolved primarily on IA32 processors and that is where the commodity market is centered, it is convenient to use IA32 to distinguish any of these processors from the PowerPC, Alpha, PA-RISC, MIPS, SPARC, etc. The upcoming IA64 (64-bit with EPIC, Explicitly Parallel Instruction Computing) will certainly complicate matters, but Merced, the first IA64 processor, is not scheduled for production until 1999.

COTS:

Since the demise of many parallel supercomputer companies, COTS (Commercial Off-The-Shelf) is commonly discussed as a requirement for parallel computing systems. Being fanatically pure, the only COTS parallel processing techniques using PCs are things like SMP Windows NT servers and various MMX Windows applications; it really doesn't pay to be that fanatical. The underlying concept of COTS is really minimization of development time and cost. Thus, a more useful, more common, meaning of COTS is that at least most subsystems benefit from commodity marketing, but other technologies are used where they are effective. Most often, COTS parallel processing refers to a cluster in which the nodes are commodity PCs, but the network interface and software are somewhat customized... typically running Linux and applications codes that are freely available (e.g., copyleft or public domain), but not literally COTS.

1.3 Example Algorithm

In order to better understand the use of the various parallel programming approaches outlined in this HOWTO, it is useful to have an example problem. Although just about any simple parallel algorithm would do, by selecting an algorithm that has been used to demonstrate various other parallel programming systems, it becomes a bit easier to compare and contrast approaches. M. J. Quinn's book, *Parallel Computing Theory And Practice*, second edition, McGraw Hill, New York, 1994, uses a parallel algorithm that computes the value of Pi to demonstrate a variety of different parallel supercomputer programming environments (e.g., nCUBE message passing, Sequent shared memory). In this HOWTO, we use the same basic algorithm.

The algorithm computes the approximate value of Pi by summing the area under x squared. As a purely sequential C program, the algorithm looks like:

```
#include <stdlib.h>;
#include <stdio.h>;

main(int argc, char **argv)
{
  register double width, sum;
  register int intervals, i;

  /* get the number of intervals */
  intervals = atoi(argv[1]);
  width = 1.0 / intervals;

  /* do the computation */
```

```
sum = 0;
for (i=0; i<intervals; ++i) {
  register double x = (i + 0.5) * width;
  sum += 4.0 / (1.0 + x * x);
}
sum *= width;

printf("Estimation of pi is %f\n", sum);

return(0);
}
```

However, this sequential algorithm easily yields an "embarrassingly parallel" implementation. The area is subdivided into intervals, and any number of processors can each independently sum the intervals assigned to it, with no need for interaction between processors. Once the local sums have been computed, they are added together to create a global sum; this step requires some level of coordination and communication between processors. Finally, this global sum is printed by one processor as the approximate value of Pi.

In this HOWTO, the various parallel implementations of this algorithm appear where each of the different programming methods is discussed.

1.4   Organization Of This Document

The remainder of this document is divided into five parts. Sections 2, 3, 4, and 5 correspond to the three different types of hardware configurations supporting parallel processing using Linux:

- Section 2 discusses SMP Linux systems. These directly support MIMD execution using shared memory, although message passing also is implemented easily. Although Linux supports SMP configurations up to 16 processors, most SMP PC systems have either two or four identical processors.

- Section 3 discusses clusters of networked machines, each running Linux. A cluster can be used as a parallel processing system that directly supports MIMD execution and message passing, perhaps also providing logically shared memory. Simulated SIMD execution and aggregate function communication also can be supported, depending on the networking method used. The number of processors in a cluster can range from two to thousands, primarily limited by the physical wiring constraints of the network. In some cases, various types of machines can be mixed within a cluster; for example, a network combining DEC Alpha and Pentium Linux systems would be a **heterogeneous cluster**.

- Section 4 discusses SWAR, SIMD Within A Register. This is a very restrictive type of parallel execution model, but on the other hand, it is a built-in capability of ordinary processors. Recently, MMX (and other) instruction set extensions to modern processors have made this approach even more effective.

- Section 5 discusses the use of Linux PCs as hosts for simple parallel computing systems. Either as an add-in card or as an external box, attached processors can provide a Linux system with formidable processing power for specific types of applications. For example, inexpensive ISA cards are available that provide multiple DSP processors offering hundreds of MFLOPS for compute-bound problems. However, these add-in boards are *just* processors; they generally do not run an OS, have disk or console I/O capability, etc. To make such systems useful, the Linux "host" must provide these functions.

The final section of this document covers aspects that are of general interest for parallel processing using Linux, not specific to a particular one of the approaches listed above.

As you read this document, keep in mind that we haven't tested everything, and a lot of stuff reported here "still has a research character" (a nice way to say "doesn't quite work like it should" ;-). However, parallel processing using Linux is useful now, and an increasingly large group is working to make it better.

The author of this HOWTO is Hank Dietz, Ph.D., currently Associate Professor of Electrical and Computer Engineering at Purdue University, in West Lafayette, IN, 47907-1285. Dietz retains rights to this document as per the Linux Documentation Project guidelines. Although an effort has been made to ensure the correctness and fairness of this presentation, neither Dietz nor Purdue University can be held responsible for any problems or errors, and Purdue University does not endorse any of the work/products discussed.

2 SMP Linux

This document gives a brief overview of how to use *SMP Linux* <http://www.uk.linux.org/SMP/title.html> systems for parallel processing. The most up-to-date information on SMP Linux is probably available via the SMP Linux project mailing list; send email to *majordomo@vger.rutgers.edu* with the text `subscribe linux-smp` to join the list.

Does SMP Linux really work? In June 1996, I purchased a brand new (well, new off-brand ;-) two-processor 100MHz Pentium system. The fully assembled system, including both processors, Asus motherboard, 256K cache, 32M RAM, 1.6G disk, 6X CDROM, Stealth 64, and 15" Acer monitor, cost a total of $1,800. This was just a few hundred dollars more than a comparable uniprocessor system. Getting SMP Linux running was simply a matter of installing the "stock" uniprocessor Linux, recompiling the kernel with the `SMP=1` line in the makefile uncommented (although I find setting `SMP` to `1` a bit ironic ;-), and informing `lilo` about the new kernel. This system performs well enough, and has been stable enough, to serve as my primary workstation ever since. In summary, SMP Linux really does work.

The next question is how much high-level support is available for writing and executing shared memory parallel programs under SMP Linux. Through early 1996, there wasn't much. Things have changed. For example, there is now a very complete POSIX threads library.

Although performance may be lower than for native shared-memory mechanisms, an SMP Linux system also can use most parallel processing software that was originally developed for a workstation cluster using socket communication. Sockets (see section 3.3) work within an SMP Linux system, and even for multiple SMPs networked as a cluster. However, sockets imply a lot of unnecessary overhead for an SMP. Much of that overhead is within the kernel or interrupt handlers; this worsens the problem because SMP Linux generally allows only one processor to be in the kernel at a time and the interrupt controller is set so that only the boot processor can process interrupts. Despite this, typical SMP communication hardware is so much better than most cluster networks that cluster software will often run better on an SMP than on the cluster for which it was designed.

The remainder of this section discusses SMP hardware, reviews the basic Linux mechanisms for sharing memory across the processes of a parallel program, makes a few observations about atomicity, volatility, locks, and cache lines, and finally gives some pointers to other shared memory parallel processing resources.

2.1 SMP Hardware

Although SMP systems have been around for many years, until very recently, each such machine tended to implement basic functions differently enough so that operating system support was not portable. The thing that has changed this situation is Intel's Multiprocessor Specification, often referred to as simply **MPS**. The MPS 1.4 specification is currently available as a PDF file at <http://www.intel.com/design/pro/datashts/242016.htm>, and there is a brief overview of MPS 1.1 at <http://support.intel.com/oem_developer/ial/support/9300.HTM>, but be aware that Intel does re-arrange their WWW site often. A wide range of *vendors* <http://www.uruk.org/~erich/mps-hw.html> are building MPS-compliant systems supporting up to four processors, but MPS theoretically allows many more processors.

The only non-MPS, non-IA32, systems supported by SMP Linux are Sun4m multiprocessor SPARC machines. SMP Linux supports most Intel MPS version 1.1 or 1.4 compliant machines with up to sixteen 486DX, Pentium, Pentium MMX, Pentium Pro, or Pentium II processors. Unsupported IA32 processors include the Intel 386, Intel 486SX/SLC processors (the lack of floating point hardware interferes with the SMP mechanisms), and AMD & Cyrix processors (they require different SMP support chips that do not seem to be available at this writing).

HOWTO

It is important to understand that the performance of MPS-compliant systems can vary widely. As expected, one cause for performance differences is processor speed: faster clock speeds tend to yield faster systems, and a Pentium Pro processor is faster than a Pentium. However, MPS does not really specify how hardware implements shared memory, but only how that implementation must function from a software point of view; this means that performance is also a function of how the shared memory implementation interacts with the characteristics of SMP Linux and your particular programs.

The primary way in which systems that comply with MPS differ is in how they implement access to physically shared memory.

2.1.1 Does each processor have its own L2 cache?

Some MPS Pentium systems, and all MPS Pentium Pro and Pentium II systems, have independent L2 caches. (The L2 cache is packaged within the Pentium Pro or Pentium II modules.) Separate L2 caches are generally viewed as maximizing compute performance, but things are not quite so obvious under Linux. The primary complication is that the current SMP Linux scheduler does not attempt to keep each process on the same processor, a concept known as **processor affinity**. This may change soon; there has recently been some discussion about this in the SMP Linux development community under the title "processor binding." Without processor affinity, having separate L2 caches may introduce significant overhead when a process is given a timeslice on a processor other than the one that was executing it last.

Many relatively inexpensive systems are organized so that two Pentium processors share a single L2 cache. The bad news is that this causes contention for the cache, seriously degrading performance when running multiple independent sequential programs. The good news is that many parallel programs might actually benefit from the shared cache because if both processors will want to access the same line from shared memory, only one had to fetch it into cache and contention for the bus is averted. The lack of processor affinity also causes less damage with a shared L2 cache. Thus, for parallel programs, it isn't really clear that sharing L2 cache is as harmful as one might expect.

Experience with our dual Pentium shared 256K cache system shows quite a wide range of performance depending on the level of kernel activity required. At worst, we see only about 1.2x speedup. However, we also have seen up to 2.1x speedup, which suggests that compute-intensive SPMD-style code really does profit from the "shared fetch" effect.

2.1.2 Bus configuration?

The first thing to say is that most modern systems connect the processors to one or more PCI busses that in turn are "bridged" to one or more ISA/EISA busses. These bridges add latency, and both EISA and ISA generally offer lower bandwidth than PCI (ISA being the lowest), so disk drives, video cards, and other high-performance devices generally should be connected via a PCI bus interface.

Although an MPS system can achieve good speed-up for many compute-intensive parallel programs even if there is only one PCI bus, I/O operations occur at no better than uniprocessor performance... and probably a little worse due to bus contention from the processors. Thus, if you are looking to speed-up I/O, make sure that you get an MPS system with multiple independent PCI busses and I/O controllers (e.g., multiple SCSI chains). You will need to be careful to make sure SMP Linux supports what you get. Also keep in mind that the current SMP Linux essentially allows only one processor in the kernel at any time, so you should choose your I/O controllers carefully to pick ones that minimize the kernel time required for each I/O operation. For really high performance, you might even consider doing raw device I/O directly from user processes, without a system call... this isn't necessarily as hard as it sounds, and need not compromise security (see section 3.3 for a description of the basic techniques).

It is important to note that the relationship between bus speed and processor clock rate has become very fuzzy over the past few years. Although most systems now use the same PCI clock rate, it is not uncommon to find a faster processor clock paired with a slower bus clock. The classic example of this was that the Pentium 133 generally used a faster bus than a Pentium 150, with appropriately strange-looking performance on various benchmarks. These effects are amplified in SMP systems; it is even more important to have a faster bus clock.

2.1.3 Memory interleaving and DRAM technologies?

Memory interleaving actually has nothing whatsoever to do with MPS, but you will often see it mentioned for MPS systems because these systems are typically more demanding of memory bandwidth. Basically, two-way or four-way interleaving organizes RAM so that a block access is accomplished using multiple banks of RAM rather than just one. This provides higher memory access bandwidth, particularly for cache line loads and stores.

The waters are a bit muddied about this, however, because EDO DRAM and various other memory technologies tend to improve similar kinds of operations. An excellent overview of DRAM technologies is given in `<http://www.pcguide.com/ref/ram/tech.htm>`.

So, for example, is it better to have 2-way interleaved EDO DRAM or non-interleaved SDRAM? That is a very good question with no simple answer, because both interleaving and exotic DRAM technologies tend to be expensive. The same dollar investment in more ordinary memory configurations generally will give you a significantly larger main memory. Even the slowest DRAM is still a heck of a lot faster than using disk-based virtual memory....

2.2 Introduction To Shared Memory Programming

Ok, so you have decided that parallel processing on an SMP is a great thing to do... how do you get started? Well, the first step is to learn a little bit about how shared memory communication really works.

It sounds like you simply have one processor store a value into memory and another processor load it; unfortunately, it isn't quite that simple. For example, the relationship between processes and processors is very blurry; however, if we have no more active processes than there are processors, the terms are roughly interchangeable. The remainder of this section briefly summarizes the key issues that could cause serious problems, if you were not aware of them: the two different models used to determine what is shared, atomicity issues, the concept of volatility, hardware lock instructions, cache line effects, and Linux scheduler issues.

2.2.1 Shared Everything Vs. Shared Something

There are two fundamentally different models commonly used for shared memory programming: **shared everything** and **shared something**. Both of these models allow processors to communicate by loads and stores from/into shared memory; the distinction comes in the fact that shared everything places all data structures in shared memory, while shared something requires the user to explicitly indicate which data structures are potentially shared and which are **private** to a single processor.

Which shared memory model should you use? That is mostly a question of religion. A lot of people like the shared everything model because they do not really need to identify which data structures should be shared at the time they are declared... you simply put locks around potentially-conflicting accesses to shared objects to ensure that only one process(or) has access at any moment. Then again, that really isn't all that simple... so many people prefer the relative safety of shared something.

Shared Everything The nice thing about sharing everything is that you can easily take an existing sequential program and incrementally convert it into a shared everything parallel program. You do not have to first determine which data need to be accessible by other processors.

Put simply, the primary problem with sharing everything is that any action taken by one processor could affect the other processors. This problem surfaces in two ways:

- Many libraries use data structures that simply are not sharable. For example, the UNIX convention is that most functions can return an error code in a variable called `errno`; if two shared everything processes perform various calls, they would interfere with each other because they share the same `errno`. Although there is now a library version that fixes the `errno` problem, similar problems still exist in most libraries. For example, unless special precautions are taken, the X library will not work if calls are made from multiple shared everything processes.

- Normally, the worst-case behavior for a program with a bad pointer or array subscript is that the process that contains the offending code dies. It might even generate a `core` file that clues you in to what happened. In shared everything parallel processing, it is very likely that the stray accesses will bring the demise of *a process other than the one at fault*, making it nearly impossible to localize and correct the error.

Neither of these types of problems is common when shared something is used, because only the explicitly-marked data structures are shared. It also is fairly obvious that shared everything only works if all processors are executing the exact same memory image; you cannot use shared everything across multiple different code images (i.e., can use only SPMD, not general MIMD).

The most common type of shared everything programming support is a **threads library**. *Threads* <http://liinwww. ira.uka.de/bibliography/Os/threads.html> are essentially "light-weight" processes that might not be scheduled in the same way as regular UNIX processes and, most importantly, share access to a single memory map. The POSIX *Pthreads* <http://www.mit.edu:8001/people/proven/pthreads.html> package has been the focus of a number of porting efforts; the big question is whether any of these ports actually run the threads of a program in parallel under SMP Linux (ideally, with a processor for each thread). The POSIX API doesn't require it, and versions like <http://www.aa.net/~mtp/PCthreads.html> apparently do not implement parallel thread execution - all the threads of a program are kept within a single Linux process.

The first threads library that supported SMP Linux parallelism was the now somewhat obsolete bb_threads library, <ftp://caliban.physics.utoronto.ca/pub/linux/>, a very small library that used the Linux clone() call to fork new, independently scheduled, Linux processes all sharing a single address space. SMP Linux machines can run multiple of these "threads" in parallel because each "thread" is a full Linux process; the trade-off is that you do not get the same "light-weight" scheduling control provided by some thread libraries under other operating systems. The library used a bit of C-wrapped assembly code to install a new chunk of memory as each thread's stack and to provide atomic access functions for an array of locks (mutex objects). Documentation consisted of a README and a short sample program.

More recently, a version of POSIX threads using clone() has been developed. This library, *LinuxThreads* <http://pauillac.inria.fr/~xleroy/linuxthreads/>, is clearly the preferred shared everything library for use under SMP Linux. POSIX threads are well documented, and the *LinuxThreads README* <http://pauillac.inria.fr/~xleroy/linuxthreads/README> and *LinuxThreads FAQ* <http://pauillac.inria.fr/~xleroy/linuxthreads/faq.html> are very well done. The primary problem now is simply that POSIX threads have a lot of details to get right and LinuxThreads is still a work in progress. There is also the problem that the POSIX thread standard has evolved through the standardization process, so you need to be a bit careful not to program for obsolete early versions of the standard.

Shared Something Shared something is really "only share what needs to be shared." This approach can work for general MIMD (not just SPMD) provided that care is taken for the shared objects to be allocated at the same places in each processor's memory map. More importantly, shared something makes it easier to predict and tune performance, debug code, etc. The only problems are:

- It can be hard to know beforehand what really needs to be shared.
- The actual allocation of objects in shared memory may be awkward, especially for what would have been stack-allocated objects. For example, it may be necessary to explicitly allocate shared objects in a separate memory segment, requiring separate memory allocation routines and introducing extra pointer indirections in each reference.

Currently, there are two very similar mechanisms that allow groups of Linux processes to have independent memory spaces, all sharing only a relatively small memory segment. Assuming that you didn't foolishly exclude "System V IPC" when you configured your Linux system, Linux supports a very portable mechanism that has generally become known as "System V Shared Memory." The other alternative is a memory mapping facility whose implementation varies widely across different UNIX systems: the mmap() system call. You can, and should, learn about these calls from the manual pages... but a brief overview of each is given in sections 2.5 and 2.6 to help get you started.

2.2.2 Atomicity And Ordering

No matter which of the above two models you use, the result is pretty much the same: you get a pointer to a chunk of read/write memory that is accessible by all processes within your parallel program. Does that mean I can just have my parallel program access shared memory objects as though they were in ordinary local memory? Well, not quite....

Atomicity refers to the concept that an operation on an object is accomplished as an indivisible, uninterruptible, sequence. Unfortunately, sharing memory access does not imply that all operations on data in shared memory occur atomically. Unless special precautions are taken, only simple load or store operations that occur within a single bus transaction (i.e., aligned 8, 16, or 32-bit operations, but not misaligned nor 64-bit operations) are atomic. Worse still, "smart" compilers like GCC will often perform optimizations that could eliminate the memory operations needed to ensure that other processors can see what this processor has done. Fortunately, both these problems can be remedied... leaving only the relationship between access efficiency and cache line size for us to worry about.

However, before discussing these issues, it is useful to point-out that all of this assumes that memory references for each processor happen in the order in which they were coded. The Pentium does this, but also notes that future Intel processors might not. So, for future processors, keep in mind that it may be necessary to surround some shared memory accesses with instructions that cause all pending memory accesses to complete, thus providing memory access ordering. The CPUID instruction apparently is reserved to have this side-effect.

2.2.3 Volatility

To prevent GCC's optimizer from buffering values of shared memory objects in registers, all objects in shared memory should be declared as having types with the volatile attribute. If this is done, all shared object reads and writes that require just one word access will occur atomically. For example, suppose that *p* is a pointer to an integer, where both the pointer and the integer it will point at are in shared memory; the ANSI C declaration might be:

```
volatile int * volatile p;
```

In this code, the first volatile refers to the int that p will eventually point at; the second volatile refers to the pointer itself. Yes, it is annoying, but it is the price one pays for enabling GCC to perform some very powerful optimizations. At least in theory, the -traditional option to GCC might suffice to produce correct code at the expense of some optimization, because pre-ANSI K&R C essentially claimed that all variables were volatile unless explicitly declared as register. Still, if your typical GCC compile looks like cc -O6 ..., you really will want to explicitly mark things as volatile only where necessary.

There has been a rumor to the effect that using assembly-language locks that are marked as modifying all processor registers will cause GCC to appropriately flush all variables, thus avoiding the "inefficient" compiled code associated with things declared as volatile. This hack appears to work for statically allocated global variables using version 2.7.0 of GCC... however, that behavior is *not* required by the ANSI C standard. Still worse, other processes that are making only read accesses can buffer the values in registers forever, thus *never* noticing that the shared memory value has actually changed. In summary, do what you want, but only variables accessed through volatile are *guaranteed* to work correctly.

Note that you can cause a volatile access to an ordinary variable by using a type cast that imposes the volatile attribute. For example, the ordinary int i; can be referenced as a volatile by *((volatile int *) &i); thus, you can explicitly invoke the "overhead" of volatility only where it is critical.

2.2.4 Locks

If you thought that ++i; would always work to add one to a variable i in shared memory, you've got a nasty little surprise coming: even if coded as a single instruction, the load and store of the result are separate memory transactions, and other processors could access i between these two transactions. For example, having two processes both perform ++i; might only increment i by one, rather than by two. According to the Intel Pentium "Architecture and Programming Manual," the LOCK prefix can be used to ensure that any of the following instructions is atomic relative to the data memory location it accesses:

```
BTS, BTR, BTC                      mem, reg/imm
XCHG                               reg, mem
XCHG                               mem, reg
ADD, OR, ADC, SBB, AND, SUB, XOR   mem, reg/imm
NOT, NEG, INC, DEC                 mem
CMPXCHG, XADD
```

However, it probably is not a good idea to use all these operations. For example, XADD did not even exist for the 386, so coding it may cause portability problems.

The XCHG instruction *always* asserts a lock, even without the LOCK prefix, and thus is clearly the preferred atomic operation from which to build higher-level atomic constructs such as semaphores and shared queues. Of course, you can't get GCC to generate this instruction just by writing C code... instead, you must use a bit of in-line assembly code. Given a word-size volatile object *obj* and a word-size register value *reg*, the GCC in-line assembly code is:

```
__asm__ __volatile__ ("xchgl %1,%0"
                      :"=r" (reg), "=m" (obj)
                      :"r" (reg), "m" (obj));
```

Examples of GCC in-line assembly code using bit operations for locking are given in the source code for the *bb_threads library* <ftp://caliban.physics.utoronto.ca/pub/linux/>.

It is important to remember, however, that there is a cost associated with making memory transactions atomic. A locking operation carries a fair amount of overhead and may delay memory activity from other processors, whereas ordinary references may use local cache. The best performance results when locking operations are used as infrequently as possible. Further, these IA32 atomic instructions obviously are not portable to other systems.

There are many alternative approaches that allow ordinary instructions to be used to implement various synchronizations, including **mutual exclusion** - ensuring that at most one processor is updating a given shared object at any moment. Most OS textbooks discuss at least one of these techniques. There is a fairly good discussion in the Fourth Edition of *Operating System Concepts*, by Abraham Silberschatz and Peter B. Galvin, ISBN 0-201-50480-4.

2.2.5 Cache Line Size

One more fundamental atomicity concern can have a dramatic impact on SMP performance: cache line size. Although the MPS standard requires references to be coherent no matter what caching is used, the fact is that when one processor writes to a particular line of memory, every cached copy of the old line must be invalidated or updated. This implies that if two or more processors are both writing data to different portions of the same line a lot of cache and bus traffic may result, effectively to pass the line from cache to cache. This problem is known as **false sharing**. The solution is simply to try to *organize data so that what is accessed in parallel tends to come from a different cache line for each process*.

You might be thinking that false sharing is not a problem using a system with a shared L2 cache, but remember that there are still separate L1 caches. Cache organization and number of separate levels can both vary, but the Pentium L1 cache line size is 32 bytes and typical external cache line sizes are around 256 bytes. Suppose that the addresses (physical or virtual) of two items are a and b and that the largest per-processor cache line size is c, which we assume to be a power of two. To be very precise, if `((int) a) & ~(c - 1)` is equal to `((int) b) & ~(c - 1)`, then both references are in the same cache line. A simpler rule is that if shared objects being referenced in parallel are at least c bytes apart, they should map to different cache lines.

2.2.6 Linux Scheduler Issues

Although the whole point of using shared memory for parallel processing is to avoid OS overhead, OS overhead can come from things other than communication per se. We have already said that the number of processes that should be constructed is less than or equal to the number of processors in the machine. But how do you decide exactly how many processes to make?

For best performance, *the number of processes in your parallel program should be equal to the expected number of your program's processes that simultaneously can be running on different processors*. For example, if a four-processor SMP typically has one process actively running for some other purpose (e.g., a WWW server), then your parallel program should use only three processes. You can get a rough idea of how many other processes are active on your system by looking at the "load average" quoted by the uptime command.

Alternatively, you could boost the priority of the processes in your parallel program using, for example, the renice command or nice() system call. You must be privileged to increase priority. The idea is simply to force the other processes out of processors so that your program can run simultaneously across all processors. This can be accomplished somewhat more explicitly using the prototype version of SMP Linux at <http://luz.cs.nmt.edu/~rtlinux/>, which offers real-time schedulers.

If you are not the only user treating your SMP system as a parallel machine, you may also have conflicts between the two or more parallel programs trying to execute simultaneously. This standard solution is **gang scheduling** - i.e., manipulating scheduling priority so that at any given moment, only the processes of a single parallel program are running. It is useful to recall, however, that using more parallelism tends to have diminishing returns and scheduler activity adds overhead. Thus, for example, it is probably better for a four-processor machine to run two programs with two processes each rather than gang scheduling between two programs with four processes each.

There is one more twist to this. Suppose that you are developing a program on a machine that is heavily used all day, but will be fully available for parallel execution at night. You need to write and test your code for correctness with the full number of processes, even though you know that your daytime test runs will be slow. Well, they will be *very* slow if you have processes **busy waiting** for shared memory values to be changed by other processes that are not currently running (on other processors). The same problem occurs if you develop and test your code on a single-processor system.

The solution is to embed calls in your code, wherever it may loop awaiting an action from another processor, so that Linux will give another process a chance to run. I use a C macro, call it `IDLE_ME`, to do this: for a test run, compile with `cc -DIDLE_ME=usleep(1); ...`; for a "production" run, compile with `cc -DIDLE_ME={} ....` The `usleep(1)` call requests a 1 microsecond sleep, which has the effect of allowing the Linux scheduler to select a different process to run on that processor. If the number of processes is more than twice the number of processors available, it is not unusual for codes to run ten times faster with `usleep(1)` calls than without them.

2.3 bb_threads

The bb_threads ("Bare Bones" threads) library, `<ftp://caliban.physics.utoronto.ca/pub/linux/>`, is a remarkably simple library that demonstrates use of the Linux `clone()` call. The `gzip tar` file is only 7K bytes! Although this library is essentially made obsolete by the LinuxThreads library discussed in section 2.4, bb_threads is still usable, and it is small and simple enough to serve well as an introduction to use of Linux thread support. Certainly, it is far less daunting to read this source code than to browse the source code for LinuxThreads. In summary, the bb_threads library is a good starting point, but is not really suitable for coding large projects.

The basic program structure for using the bb_threads library is:

1. Start the program running as a single process.
2. You will need to estimate the maximum stack space that will be required for each thread. Guessing large is relatively harmless (that is what virtual memory is for ;-), but remember that *all* the stacks are coming from a single virtual address space, so guessing huge is not a great idea. The demo suggests 64K. This size is set to b bytes by `bb_threads_stacksize(b)`.
3. The next step is to initialize any locks that you will need. The lock mechanism built-into this library numbers locks from 0 to `MAX_MUTEXES`, and initializes lock i by `bb_threads_mutexcreate(i)`.
4. Spawning a new thread is done by calling a library routine that takes arguments specifying what function the new thread should execute and what arguments should be transmitted to it. To start a new thread executing the `void`-returning function f with the single argument *arg*, you do something like `bb_threads_newthread(f, &arg)`, where f should be declared something like `void f(void *arg, size_t dummy)`. If you need to pass more than one argument, pass a pointer to a structure initialized to hold the argument values.
5. Run parallel code, being careful to use `bb_threads_lock(n)` and `bb_threads_unlock(n)` where n is an integer identifying which lock to use. Note that the lock and unlock operations in this library are very basic spin locks using atomic bus-locking instructions, which can cause excessive memory-reference interference and do not make any attempt to ensure fairness.

   The demo program packaged with bb_threads did not correctly use locks to prevent `printf()` from being executed simultaneously from within the functions `fnn` and `main`... and because of this, the demo does not always work. I'm not saying this to knock the demo, but rather to emphasize that this stuff is *very tricky*; also, it is only slightly easier using LinuxThreads.
6. When a thread executes a `return`, it actually destroys the process... but the local stack memory is not automatically deallocated. To be precise, Linux doesn't support deallocation, but the memory space is not automatically added back to the `malloc()` free list. Thus, the parent process should reclaim the space for each dead child by `bb_threads_cleanup(wait(NULL))`.

The following C program uses the algorithm discussed in section 1.3 to compute the approximate value of Pi using two bb_threads threads.

```c
#include <stdio.h>
#include <stdlib.h>
#include <unistd.h>
#include <sys/types.h>
#include <sys/wait.h>
#include "bb_threads.h"

volatile double pi = 0.0;
volatile int intervals;
volatile int pids[2];          /* Unix PIDs of threads */

void
do_pi(void *data, size_t len)
{
  register double width, localsum;
  register int i;
  register int iproc = (getpid() != pids[0]);

  /* set width */
  width = 1.0 / intervals;

  /* do the local computations */
  localsum = 0;
  for (i=iproc; i<intervals; i+=2) {
    register double x = (i + 0.5) * width;
    localsum += 4.0 / (1.0 + x * x);
  }
  localsum *= width;

  /* get permission, update pi, and unlock */
  bb_threads_lock(0);
  pi += localsum;
  bb_threads_unlock(0);
}

int
main(int argc, char **argv)
{
  /* get the number of intervals */
  intervals = atoi(argv[1]);

  /* set stack size and create lock... */
  bb_threads_stacksize(65536);
  bb_threads_mutexcreate(0);

  /* make two threads... */
  pids[0] = bb_threads_newthread(do_pi, NULL);
  pids[1] = bb_threads_newthread(do_pi, NULL);

  /* cleanup after two threads (really a barrier sync) */
  bb_threads_cleanup(wait(NULL));
  bb_threads_cleanup(wait(NULL));
```

```
  /* print the result */
  printf("Estimation of pi is %f\n", pi);

  /* check-out */
  exit(0);
}
```

2.4   LinuxThreads

LinuxThreads `<http://pauillac.inria.fr/~xleroy/linuxthreads/>` is a fairly complete and solid implementation of "shared everything" as per the POSIX 1003.1c threads standard. Unlike other POSIX threads ports, LinuxThreads uses the same Linux kernel threads facility (`clone()`) that is used by bb_threads. POSIX compatibility means that it is relatively easy to port quite a few threaded applications from other systems and various tutorial materials are available. In short, this is definitely the threads package to use under Linux for developing large-scale threaded programs.

The basic program structure for using the LinuxThreads library is:

1. Start the program running as a single process.
2. The next step is to initialize any locks that you will need. Unlike bb_threads locks, which are identified by numbers, POSIX locks are declared as variables of type `pthread_mutex_t lock`. Use `pthread_mutex_init(&lock,val)` to initialize each one you will need to use.
3. As with bb_threads, spawning a new thread is done by calling a library routine that takes arguments specifying what function the new thread should execute and what arguments should be transmitted to it. However, POSIX requires the user to declare a variable of type `pthread_t` to identify each thread. To create a thread `pthread_t thread` running `f()`, one calls `pthread_create(&thread,NULL,f,&arg)`.
4. Run parallel code, being careful to use `pthread_mutex_lock(&lock)` and `pthread_mutex_unlock(&lock)` as appropriate.
5. Use `pthread_join(thread,&retval)` to clean-up after each thread.
6. Use `-D_REENTRANT` when compiling your C code.

An example parallel computation of Pi using LinuxThreads follows. The algorithm of section 1.3 is used and, as for the bb_threads example, two threads execute in parallel.

```
#include <stdio.h>
#include <stdlib.h>
#include "pthread.h"

volatile double pi = 0.0;  /* Approximation to pi (shared) */
pthread_mutex_t pi_lock;   /* Lock for above */
volatile double intervals; /* How many intervals? */

void *
process(void *arg)
{
  register double width, localsum;
  register int i;
  register int iproc = (*((char *) arg) - '0');

  /* Set width */
  width = 1.0 / intervals;
```

```
  /* Do the local computations */
  localsum = 0;
  for (i=iproc; i<intervals; i+=2) {
    register double x = (i + 0.5) * width;
    localsum += 4.0 / (1.0 + x * x);
  }
  localsum *= width;

  /* Lock pi for update, update it, and unlock */
  pthread_mutex_lock(&pi_lock);
  pi += localsum;
  pthread_mutex_unlock(&pi_lock);

  return(NULL);
}

int
main(int argc, char **argv)
{
  pthread_t thread0, thread1;
  void * retval;

  /* Get the number of intervals */
  intervals = atoi(argv[1]);

  /* Initialize the lock on pi */
  pthread_mutex_init(&pi_lock, NULL);

  /* Make the two threads */
  if (pthread_create(&thread0, NULL, process, "0") ||
      pthread_create(&thread1, NULL, process, "1")) {
    fprintf(stderr, "%s: cannot make thread\n", argv[0]);
    exit(1);
  }

  /* Join (collapse) the two threads */
  if (pthread_join(thread0, &retval) ||
      pthread_join(thread1, &retval)) {
    fprintf(stderr, "%s: thread join failed\n", argv[0]);
    exit(1);
  }

  /* Print the result */
  printf("Estimation of pi is %f\n", pi);

  /* Check-out */
  exit(0);
}
```

2.5   System V Shared Memory

The System V IPC (Inter-Process Communication) support consists of a number of system calls providing message queues, semaphores, and a shared memory mechanism. Of course, these mechanisms were originally intended to be used for multiple processes to communicate within a uniprocessor system. However, that implies that it also should work to communicate between processes under SMP Linux, no matter which processors they run on.

Before going into how these calls are used, it is important to understand that although System V IPC calls exist for things like semaphores and message transmission, you probably should not use them. Why not? These functions are generally slow and serialized under SMP Linux. Enough said.

The basic procedure for creating a group of processes sharing access to a shared memory segment is:

1. Start the program running as a single process.

2. Typically, you will want each run of a parallel program to have its own shared memory segment, so you will need to call `shmget()` to create a new segment of the desired size. Alternatively, this call can be used to get the ID of a pre-existing shared memory segment. In either case, the return value is either the shared memory segment ID or -1 for error. For example, to create a shared memory segment of *b* bytes, the call might be `shmid = shmget(IPC_PRIVATE, b, (IPC_CREAT | 0666))`.

3. The next step is to attach this shared memory segment to this process, literally adding it to the virtual memory map of this process. Although the `shmat()` call allows the programmer to specify the virtual address at which the segment should appear, the address selected must be aligned on a page boundary (i.e., be a multiple of the page size returned by `getpagesize()`, which is usually 4096 bytes), and will override the mapping of any memory formerly at that address. Thus, we instead prefer to let the system pick the address. In either case, the return value is a pointer to the base virtual address of the segment just mapped. The code is `shmptr = shmat(shmid, 0, 0)`.

   Notice that you can allocate all your static shared variables into this shared memory segment by simply declaring all shared variables as members of a `struct` type, and declaring *shmptr* to be a pointer to that type. Using this technique, shared variable *x* would be accessed as *shmptr->x*.

4. Since this shared memory segment should be destroyed when the last process with access to it terminates or detaches from it, we need to call `shmctl()` to set-up this default action. The code is something like `shmctl(shmid, IPC_RMID, 0)`.

5. Use the standard Linux `fork()` call to make the desired number of processes... each will inherit the shared memory segment.

6. When a process is done using a shared memory segment, it really should detach from that shared memory segment. This is done by `shmdt(shmptr)`.

Although the above set-up does require a few system calls, once the shared memory segment has been established, any change made by one processor to a value in that memory will automatically be visible to all processes. Most importantly, each communication operation will occur without the overhead of a system call.

An example C program using System V shared memory segments follows. It computes Pi, using the same algorithm given in section 1.3.

```
#include <stdio.h>
#include <stdlib.h>
#include <unistd.h>
#include <sys/types.h>
#include <sys/stat.h>
#include <fcntl.h>
#include <sys/ipc.h>
#include <sys/shm.h>

volatile struct shared { double pi; int lock; } *shared;

inline extern int xchg(register int reg,
volatile int * volatile obj)
{
   /* Atomic exchange instruction */
__asm__ __volatile__ ("xchgl %1,%0"
```

```
                        :"=r" (reg), "=m" (*obj)
                        :"r" (reg), "m" (*obj));
    return(reg);
}

main(int argc, char **argv)
{
    register double width, localsum;
    register int intervals, i;
    register int shmid;
    register int iproc = 0;;

    /* Allocate System V shared memory */
    shmid = shmget(IPC_PRIVATE,
                   sizeof(struct shared),
                   (IPC_CREAT | 0600));
    shared = ((volatile struct shared *) shmat(shmid, 0, 0));
    shmctl(shmid, IPC_RMID, 0);

    /* Initialize... */
    shared->pi = 0.0;
    shared->lock = 0;

    /* Fork a child */
    if (!fork()) ++iproc;

    /* get the number of intervals */
    intervals = atoi(argv[1]);
    width = 1.0 / intervals;

    /* do the local computations */
    localsum = 0;
    for (i=iproc; i<intervals; i+=2) {
        register double x = (i + 0.5) * width;
        localsum += 4.0 / (1.0 + x * x);
    }
    localsum *= width;

    /* Atomic spin lock, add, unlock... */
    while (xchg((iproc + 1), &(shared->lock))) ;
    shared->pi += localsum;
    shared->lock = 0;

    /* Terminate child (barrier sync) */
    if (iproc == 0) {
        wait(NULL);
        printf("Estimation of pi is %f\n", shared->pi);
    }

    /* Check out */
    return(0);
}
```

In this example, I have used the IA32 atomic exchange instruction to implement locking. For better performance and portability, substitute a synchronization technique that avoids atomic bus-locking instructions (discussed in section 2.2).

When debugging your code, it is useful to remember that the `ipcs` command will report the status of the System V IPC facilities currently in use.

2.6 Memory Map Call

Using system calls for file I/O can be very expensive; in fact, that is why there is a user-buffered file I/O library (`getchar()`, `fwrite()`, etc.). But user buffers don't work if multiple processes are accessing the same writeable file, and the user buffer management overhead is significant. The BSD UNIX fix for this was the addition of a system call that allows a portion of a file to be mapped into user memory, essentially using virtual memory paging mechanisms to cause updates. This same mechanism also has been used in systems from Sequent for many years as the basis for their shared memory parallel processing support. Despite some very negative comments in the (quite old) man page, Linux seems to correctly perform at least some of the basic functions, and it supports the degenerate use of this system call to map an anonymous segment of memory that can be shared across multiple processes.

In essence, the Linux implementation of `mmap()` is a plug-in replacement for steps 2, 3, and 4 in the System V shared memory scheme outlined in section 2.5. To create an anonymous shared memory segment:

```
shmptr =
    mmap(0,                          /* system assigns address */
         b,                          /* size of shared memory segment */
         (PROT_READ | PROT_WRITE),   /* access rights, can be rwx */
         (MAP_ANON | MAP_SHARED),    /* anonymous, shared */
         0,                          /* file descriptor (not used) */
         0);                         /* file offset (not used) */
```

The equivalent to the System V shared memory `shmdt()` call is `munmap()`:

```
munmap(shmptr, b);
```

In my opinion, there is no real benefit in using `mmap()` instead of the System V shared memory support.

3 Clusters Of Linux Systems

This section attempts to give an overview of cluster parallel processing using Linux. Clusters are currently both the most popular and the most varied approach, ranging from a conventional network of workstations (**NOW**) to essentially custom parallel machines that just happen to use Linux PCs as processor nodes. There is also quite a lot of software support for parallel processing using clusters of Linux machines.

3.1 Why A Cluster?

Cluster parallel processing offers several important advantages:

- Each of the machines in a cluster can be a complete system, usable for a wide range of other computing applications. This leads many people to suggest that cluster parallel computing can simply claim all the "wasted cycles" of workstations sitting idle on people's desks. It is not really so easy to salvage those cycles, and it will probably slow your co-worker's screen saver, but it can be done.

- The current explosion in networked systems means that most of the hardware for building a cluster is being sold in high volume, with correspondingly low "commodity" prices as the result. Further savings come from the fact that only one video card, monitor, and keyboard are needed for each cluster (although you may need to swap these into each machine to perform the initial installation of Linux, once running, a typical Linux PC does not need a "console"). In comparison, SMP and attached processors are much smaller markets, tending toward somewhat higher price per unit performance.

- Cluster computing can *scale to very large systems*. While it is currently hard to find a Linux-compatible SMP with many more than four processors, most commonly available network hardware easily builds a cluster with up to 16 machines. With a little work, hundreds or even thousands of machines can be networked. In fact, the entire Internet can be viewed as one truly huge cluster.

- The fact that replacing a "bad machine" within a cluster is trivial compared to fixing a partly faulty SMP yields much higher availability for carefully designed cluster configurations. This becomes important not only for particular applications that cannot tolerate significant service interruptions, but also for general use of systems containing enough processors so that single-machine failures are fairly common. (For example, even though the average time to failure of a PC might be two years, in a cluster with 32 machines, the probability that at least one will fail within 6 months is quite high.)

OK, so clusters are free or cheap and can be very large and highly available... why doesn't everyone use a cluster? Well, there are problems too:

- With a few exceptions, network hardware is not designed for parallel processing. Typically latency is very high and bandwidth relatively low compared to SMP and attached processors. For example, SMP latency is generally no more than a few microseconds, but is commonly hundreds or thousands of microseconds for a cluster. SMP communication bandwidth is often more than 100 MBytes/second; although the fastest network hardware (e.g., "Gigabit Ethernet") offers comparable speed, the most commonly used networks are between 10 and 1000 times slower.

  The performance of network hardware is poor enough as an *isolated cluster network*. If the network is not isolated from other traffic, as is often the case using "machines that happen to be networked" rather than a system designed as a cluster, performance can be substantially worse.

- There is very little software support for treating a cluster as a single system. For example, the `ps` command only reports the processes running on one Linux system, not all processes running across a cluster of Linux systems.

Thus, the basic story is that clusters offer great potential, but that potential may be very difficult to achieve for most applications. The good news is that there is quite a lot of software support that will help you achieve good performance for programs that are well suited to this environment, and there are also networks designed specifically to widen the range of programs that can achieve good performance.

3.2   Network Hardware

Computer networking is an exploding field... but you already knew that. An ever-increasing range of networking technologies and products are being developed, and most are available in forms that could be applied to make a parallel-processing cluster out of a group of machines (i.e., PCs each running Linux).

Unfortunately, no one network technology solves all problems best; in fact, the range of approach, cost, and performance is at first hard to believe. For example, using standard commercially-available hardware, the cost per machine networked ranges from less than $5 to over $4,000. The delivered bandwidth and latency each also vary over four orders of magnitude.

Before trying to learn about specific networks, it is important to recognize that these things change like the wind (see `<http://www.uk.linux.org/NetNews.html>` for Linux networking news), and it is very difficult to get accurate data about some networks.

Where I was particularly uncertain, I've placed a *?*. I have spent a lot of time researching this topic, but I'm sure my summary is full of errors and has omitted many important things. If you have any corrections or additions, please send email to *pplinux@ecn.purdue.edu*.

Summaries like the LAN Technology Scorecard at `<http://web.syr.edu/~jmwobus/comfaqs/lan-technology.html>` give some characteristics of many different types of networks and LAN standards. However, the summary in this HOWTO centers on the network properties that are most relevant to construction of Linux clusters. The section discussing each network begins with a short list of characteristics. The following defines what these entries mean.

Linux support:

If the answer is *no*, the meaning is pretty clear. Other answers try to describe the basic program interface that is used to access the network. Most network hardware is interfaced via a kernel driver, typically supporting TCP/UDP communication. Some other networks use more direct (e.g., library) interfaces to reduce latency by bypassing the kernel.

Years ago, it used to be considered perfectly acceptable to access a floating point unit via an OS call, but that is now clearly ludicrous; in my opinion, it is just as awkward for each communication between processors executing a parallel program to require an OS call. The problem is that computers haven't yet integrated these communication mechanisms, so non-kernel approaches tend to have portability problems. You are going to hear a lot more about this in the near future, mostly in the form of the new **Virtual Interface (VI) Architecture**, <http://www.viarch.org/>, which is a standardized method for most network interface operations to bypass the usual OS call layers. The VI standard is backed by Compaq, Intel, and Microsoft, and is sure to have a strong impact on SAN (System Area Network) designs over the next few years.

Maximum bandwidth:

This is the number everybody cares about. I have generally used the theoretical best case numbers; your mileage *will* vary.

Minimum latency:

In my opinion, this is the number everybody should care about even more than bandwidth. Again, I have used the unrealistic best-case numbers, but at least these numbers do include *all* sources of latency, both hardware and software. In most cases, the network latency is just a few microseconds; the much larger numbers reflect layers of inefficient hardware and software interfaces.

Available as:

Simply put, this describes how you get this type of network hardware. Commodity stuff is widely available from many vendors, with price as the primary distinguishing factor. Multiple-vendor things are available from more than one competing vendor, but there are significant differences and potential interoperability problems. Single-vendor networks leave you at the mercy of that supplier (however benevolent it may be). Public domain designs mean that even if you cannot find somebody to sell you one, you or anybody else can buy parts and make one. Research prototypes are just that; they are generally neither ready for external users nor available to them.

Interface port/bus used:

How does one hook-up this network? The highest performance and most common now is a PCI bus interface card. There are also EISA, VESA local bus (VL bus), and ISA bus cards. ISA was there first, and is still commonly used for low-performance cards. EISA is still around as the second bus in a lot of PCI machines, so there are a few cards. These days, you don't see much VL stuff (although <http://www.vesa.org/> would beg to differ).

Of course, any interface that you can use without having to open your PC's case has more than a little appeal. IrDA and USB interfaces are appearing with increasing frequency. The Standard Parallel Port (SPP) used to be what your printer was plugged into, but it has seen a lot of use lately as an external extension of the ISA bus; this new functionality is enhanced by the IEEE 1284 standard, which specifies EPP and ECP improvements. There is also the old, reliable, slow RS232 serial port. I don't know of anybody connecting machines using VGA video connectors, keyboard, mouse, or game ports... so that's about it.

Network structure:

A bus is a wire, set of wires, or fiber. A hub is a little box that knows how to connect different wires/fibers plugged into it; switched hubs allow multiple connections to be actively transmitting data simultaneously.

Cost per machine connected:

Here's how to use these numbers. Suppose that, not counting the network connection, it costs $2,000 to purchase a PC for use as a node in your cluster. Adding a Fast Ethernet brings the per node cost to about $2,400; adding a Myrinet instead brings the cost to about $3,800. If you have about $20,000 to spend, that means you could have either 8 machines connected by Fast Ethernet or 5 machines connected by Myrinet. It also can be very reasonable to have multiple networks; e.g., $20,000 could buy 8 machines connected by both Fast Ethernet and TTL_PAPERS. Pick the network, or set of networks, that is most likely to yield a cluster that will run your application fastest.

By the time you read this, these numbers will be wrong... heck, they're probably wrong already. There may also be quantity discounts, special deals, etc. Still, the prices quoted here aren't likely to be wrong enough to lead you to a totally inappropriate choice. It doesn't take a PhD (although I do have one ;-) to see that expensive networks only make sense if your application needs their special properties or if the PCs being clustered are relatively expensive.

Now that you have the disclaimers, on with the show....

3.2.1 ArcNet

- Linux support: *kernel drivers*
- Maximum bandwidth: *2.5 Mb/s*
- Minimum latency: *1,000 microseconds?*
- Available as: *multiple-vendor hardware*
- Interface port/bus used: *ISA*
- Network structure: *unswitched hub or bus (logical ring)*
- Cost per machine connected: *$200*

ARCNET is a local area network that is primarily intended for use in embedded real-time control systems. Like Ethernet, the network is physically organized either as taps on a bus or one or more hubs, however, unlike Ethernet, it uses a token-based protocol logically structuring the network as a ring. Packet headers are small (3 or 4 bytes) and messages can carry as little as a single byte of data. Thus, ARCNET yields more consistent performance than Ethernet, with bounded delays, etc. Unfortunately, it is slower than Ethernet and less popular, making it more expensive. More information is available from the ARCNET Trade Association at `<http://www.arcnet.com/>`.

3.2.2 ATM

- Linux support: *kernel driver, AAL* library*
- Maximum bandwidth: *155 Mb/s* (soon, *1,200 Mb/s*)
- Minimum latency: *120 microseconds*
- Available as: *multiple-vendor hardware*
- Interface port/bus used: *PCI*
- Network structure: *switched hubs*
- Cost per machine connected: *$3,000*

Unless you've been in a coma for the past few years, you have probably heard a lot about how ATM (Asynchronous Transfer Mode) *is* the future... well, sort-of. ATM is cheaper than HiPPI and faster than Fast Ethernet, and it can be used over the very long distances that the phone companies care about. The ATM network protocol is also designed to provide a lower-overhead software interface and to more efficiently manage small messages and real-time communications (e.g., digital audio and video). It is also one of the highest-bandwidth networks that Linux currently supports. The bad news is that ATM isn't cheap, and there are still some compatibility problems across vendors. An overview of Linux ATM development is available at `<http://lrcwww.epfl.ch/linux-atm/>`.

3.2.3 CAPERS

- Linux support: *AFAPI library*
- Maximum bandwidth: *1.2 Mb/s*
- Minimum latency: *3 microseconds*
- Available as: *commodity hardware*
- Interface port/bus used: *SPP*
- Network structure: *cable between 2 machines*
- Cost per machine connected: *$2*

CAPERS (Cable Adapter for Parallel Execution and Rapid Synchronization) is a spin-off of the PAPERS project, `<http://garage.ecn.purdue.edu/~papers/>`, at the Purdue University School of Electrical and Computer Engineering. In essence, it defines a software protocol for using an ordinary "LapLink" SPP-to-SPP cable to implement the PAPERS library for two Linux PCs. The idea doesn't scale, but you can't beat the price. As with T-TL_PAPERS, to improve system security, there is a minor kernel patch recommended, but not required: `<http://garage.ecn.purdue.edu/~papers/giveioperm.html>`.

3.2.4 Ethernet

- Linux support: *kernel drivers*
- Maximum bandwidth: *10 Mb/s*
- Minimum latency: *100 microseconds*
- Available as: *commodity hardware*
- Interface port/bus used: *PCI*
- Network structure: *switched or unswitched hubs, or hubless bus*
- Cost per machine connected: *$100* (hubless, *$50*)

For some years now, 10 Mbits/s Ethernet has been the standard network technology. Good Ethernet interface cards can be purchased for well under $50, and a fair number of PCs now have an Ethernet controller built-into the motherboard. For lightly-used networks, Ethernet connections can be organized as a multi-tap bus without a hub; such configurations can serve up to 200 machines with minimal cost, but are not appropriate for parallel processing. Adding an unswitched hub does not really help performance. However, switched hubs that can provide full bandwidth to simultaneous connections cost only about $100 per port. Linux supports an amazing range of Ethernet interfaces, but it is important to keep in mind that variations in the interface hardware can yield significant performance differences. See the Hardware Compatibility HOWTO for comments on which are supported and how well they work; also see `<http://cesdis1.gsfc.nasa.gov/linux/drivers/>`.

An interesting way to improve performance is offered by the 16-machine Linux cluster work done in the Beowulf project, `<http://cesdis.gsfc.nasa.gov/linux/beowulf/beowulf.html>`, at NASA CESDIS. There, Donald Becker, who is the author of many Ethernet card drivers, has developed support for load sharing across multiple Ethernet networks that shadow each other (i.e., share the same network addresses). This load sharing is built-into the standard Linux distribution, and is done invisibly below the socket operation level. Because hub cost is significant, having each machine connected to two or more hubless or unswitched hub Ethernet networks can be a very cost-effective way to improve performance. In fact, in situations where one machine is the network performance bottleneck, load sharing using shadow networks works much better than using a single switched hub network.

3.2.5 Ethernet (Fast Ethernet)

- Linux support: *kernel drivers*
- Maximum bandwidth: *100 Mb/s*
- Minimum latency: *80 microseconds*
- Available as: *commodity hardware*
- Interface port/bus used: *PCI*
- Network structure: *switched or unswitched hubs*
- Cost per machine connected: *$400?*

Although there are really quite a few different technologies calling themselves "Fast Ethernet," this term most often refers to a hub-based 100 Mbits/s Ethernet that is somewhat compatible with older "10 BaseT" 10 Mbits/s devices and cables. As might be expected, anything called Ethernet is generally priced for a volume market, and these interfaces are generally a small fraction of the price of 155 Mbits/s ATM cards. The catch is that having a bunch of machines dividing the bandwidth of a single 100 Mbits/s "bus" (using an unswitched hub) yields performance that might not even be as good on average as using 10 Mbits/s Ethernet with a switched hub that can give each machine's connection a full 10 Mbits/s.

Switched hubs that can provide 100 Mbits/s for each machine simultaneously are expensive, but prices are dropping every day, and these switches do yield much higher total network bandwidth than unswitched hubs. The thing that makes ATM switches so expensive is that they must switch for each (relatively short) ATM cell; some Fast Ethernet switches take advantage of the expected lower switching frequency by using techniques that may have low latency through the switch, but take multiple milliseconds to change the switch path... if your routing pattern changes frequently, avoid those switches. See <http://cesdis1.gsfc.nasa.gov/linux/drivers/> for information about the various cards and drivers.

Also note that, as described for Ethernet, the Beowulf project, <http://cesdis.gsfc.nasa.gov/linux/beowulf/beowulf.html>, at NASA has been developing support that offers improved performance by load sharing across multiple Fast Ethernets.

3.2.6 Ethernet (Gigabit Ethernet)

- Linux support: *kernel drivers*
- Maximum bandwidth: *1,000 Mb/s*
- Minimum latency: *300 microseconds?*
- Available as: *multiple-vendor hardware*
- Interface port/bus used: *PCI*
- Network structure: *switched hubs or FDRs*
- Cost per machine connected: *$2,500?*

I'm not sure that Gigabit Ethernet, <http://www.gigabit-ethernet.org/>, has a good technological reason to be called Ethernet... but the name does accurately reflect the fact that this is intended to be a cheap, mass-market, computer network technology with native support for IP. However, current pricing reflects the fact that Gb/s hardware is still a tricky thing to build.

Unlike other Ethernet technologies, Gigabit Ethernet provides for a level of flow control that should make it a more reliable network. FDRs, or Full-Duplex Repeaters, simply multiplex lines, using buffering and localized flow control to improve performance. Most switched hubs are being built as new interface modules for existing gigabit-capable switch fabrics. Switch/FDR products have been shipped or announced by at least <http://www.acacianet.com/>, <http://www.baynetworks.com/>, <http://www.cabletron.com/>, <http://www.networks.digital.com/>, <http://www.extremenetworks.com/>, <http://www.foundrynet.com/>, <http://www.gigalabs.com/>, <http://www.packetengines.com/>. <http://www.plaintree.com/>, <http://www.prominet.com/>, <http://www.sun.com/>, and <http://www.xlnt.com/>.

There is a Linux driver, <http://cesdis.gsfc.nasa.gov/linux/drivers/yellowfin.html>, for the Packet Engines "Yellowfin" G-NIC, <http://www.packetengines.com/>. Early tests under Linux achieved about 2.5x higher bandwidth than could be achieved with the best 100 Mb/s Fast Ethernet; with gigabit networks, careful tuning of PCI bus use is a critical factor. There is little doubt that driver improvements, and Linux drivers for other NICs, will follow.

3.2.7 FC (Fibre Channel)

- Linux support: *no*
- Maximum bandwidth: *1,062 Mb/s*
- Minimum latency: *?*
- Available as: *multiple-vendor hardware*
- Interface port/bus used: *PCI?*
- Network structure: *?*
- Cost per machine connected: *?*

The goal of FC (Fibre Channel) is to provide high-performance block I/O (an FC frame carries a 2,048 byte data payload), particularly for sharing disks and other storage devices that can be directly connected to the FC rather than connected through a computer. Bandwidth-wise, FC is specified to be relatively fast, running anywhere between 133 and 1,062 Mbits/s. If FC becomes popular as a high-end SCSI replacement, it may quickly become a cheap technology; for now, it is not cheap and is not supported by Linux. A good collection of FC references is maintained by the Fibre Channel Association at `<http://www.amdahl.com/ext/CARP/FCA/FCA.html>`

3.2.8 FireWire (IEEE 1394)

- Linux support: *no*

- Maximum bandwidth: *196.608 Mb/s* (soon, *393.216 Mb/s*)

- Minimum latency: *?*

- Available as: *multiple-vendor hardware*

- Interface port/bus used: *PCI*

- Network structure: *random without cycles (self-configuring)*

- Cost per machine connected: *$600*

FireWire, `<http://www.firewire.org/>`, the IEEE 1394-1995 standard, is destined to be the low-cost high-speed digital network for consumer electronics. The showcase application is connecting DV digital video camcorders to computers, but FireWire is intended to be used for applications ranging from being a SCSI replacement to interconnecting the components of your home theater. It allows up to 64K devices to be connected in any topology using busses and bridges that does not create a cycle, and automatically detects the configuration when components are added or removed. Short (four-byte "quadlet") low-latency messages are supported as well as ATM-like isochronous transmission (used to keep multimedia messages synchronized). Adaptec has FireWire products that allow up to 63 devices to be connected to a single PCI interface card, and also has good general FireWire information at `<http://www.adaptec.com/serialio/>`.

Although FireWire will not be the highest bandwidth network available, the consumer-level market (which should drive prices very low) and low latency support might make this one of the best Linux PC cluster message-passing network technologies within the next year or so.

3.2.9 HiPPI And Serial HiPPI

- Linux support: *no*

- Maximum bandwidth: *1,600 Mb/s* (serial is *1,200 Mb/s*)

- Minimum latency: *?*

- Available as: *multiple-vendor hardware*

- Interface port/bus used: *EISA, PCI*

- Network structure: *switched hubs*

- Cost per machine connected: *$3,500* (serial is *$4,500*)

HiPPI (High Performance Parallel Interface) was originally intended to provide very high bandwidth for transfer of huge data sets between a supercomputer and another machine (a supercomputer, frame buffer, disk array, etc.), and has become the dominant standard for supercomputers. Although it is an oxymoron, **Serial HiPPI** is also becoming popular, typically using a fiber optic cable instead of the 32-bit wide standard (parallel) HiPPI cables. Over the past few years, HiPPI crossbar switches have become common and prices have dropped sharply; unfortunately, serial HiPPI is still pricey, and that is what PCI bus interface cards generally support. Worse still, Linux doesn't yet support HiPPI. A good overview of HiPPI is maintained by CERN at `<http://www.cern.ch/HSI/hippi/>`; they also maintain a rather long list of HiPPI vendors at `<http://www.cern.ch/HSI/hippi/procintf/manufact.htm>`.

3.2.10 IrDA (Infrared Data Association)

- Linux support: *no?*
- Maximum bandwidth: *1.15 Mb/s* and *4 Mb/s*
- Minimum latency: *?*
- Available as: *multiple-vendor hardware*
- Interface port/bus used: *IrDA*
- Network structure: *thin air* ;-)
- Cost per machine connected: *$0*

IrDA (Infrared Data Association, <http://www.irda.org/>) is that little infrared device on the side of a lot of laptop PCs. It is inherently difficult to connect more than two machines using this interface, so it is unlikely to be used for clustering. Don Becker did some preliminary work with IrDA.

3.2.11 Myrinet

- Linux support: *library*
- Maximum bandwidth: *1,280 Mb/s*
- Minimum latency: *9 microseconds*
- Available as: *single-vendor hardware*
- Interface port/bus used: *PCI*
- Network structure: *switched hubs*
- Cost per machine connected: *$1,800*

Myrinet <http://www.myri.com/> is a local area network (LAN) designed to also serve as a "system area network" (SAN), i.e., the network within a cabinet full of machines connected as a parallel system. The LAN and SAN versions use different physical media and have somewhat different characteristics; generally, the SAN version would be used within a cluster.

Myrinet is fairly conventional in structure, but has a reputation for being particularly well-implemented. The drivers for Linux are said to perform very well, although shockingly large performance variations have been reported with different PCI bus implementations for the host computers.

Currently, Myrinet is clearly the favorite network of cluster groups that are not too severely "budgetarily challenged." If your idea of a Linux PC is a high-end Pentium Pro or Pentium II with at least 256 MB RAM and a SCSI RAID, the cost of Myrinet is quite reasonable. However, using more ordinary PC configurations, you may find that your choice is between *N* machines linked by Myrinet or *2N* linked by multiple Fast Ethernets and TTL_PAPERS. It really depends on what your budget is and what types of computations you care about most.

3.2.12 Parastation

- Linux support: *HAL or socket library*
- Maximum bandwidth: *125 Mb/s*
- Minimum latency: *2 microseconds*
- Available as: *single-vendor hardware*
- Interface port/bus used: *PCI*
- Network structure: *hubless mesh*
- Cost per machine connected: *> $1,000*

The ParaStation project `<http://wwwipd.ira.uka.de/parastation>` at University of Karlsruhe Department of Informatics is building a PVM-compatible custom low-latency network. They first constructed a two-processor ParaPC prototype using a custom EISA card interface and PCs running BSD UNIX, and then built larger clusters using DEC Alphas. Since January 1997, ParaStation has been available for Linux. The PCI cards are being made in cooperation with a company called Hitex (see `<http://www.hitex.com:80/parastation/>`). Parastation hardware implements both fast, reliable, message transmission and simple barrier synchronization.

3.2.13 PLIP

- Linux support: *kernel driver*
- Maximum bandwidth: *1.2 Mb/s*
- Minimum latency: *1,000 microseconds?*
- Available as: *commodity hardware*
- Interface port/bus used: *SPP*
- Network structure: *cable between 2 machines*
- Cost per machine connected: *$2*

For just the cost of a "LapLink" cable, PLIP (Parallel Line Interface Protocol) allows two Linux machines to communicate through standard parallel ports using standard socket-based software. In terms of bandwidth, latency, and scalability, this is not a very serious network technology; however, the near-zero cost and the software compatibility are useful. The driver is part of the standard Linux kernel distributions.

3.2.14 SCI

- Linux support: *no*
- Maximum bandwidth: *4,000 Mb/s*
- Minimum latency: *2.7 microseconds*
- Available as: *multiple-vendor hardware*
- Interface port/bus used: *PCI, proprietary*
- Network structure: *?*
- Cost per machine connected: *> $1,000*

The goal of SCI (Scalable Coherent Interconnect, ANSI/IEEE 1596-1992) is essentially to provide a high performance mechanism that can support coherent shared memory access across large numbers of machines, as well various types of block message transfers. It is fairly safe to say that the designed bandwidth and latency of SCI are both "awesome" in comparison to most other network technologies. The catch is that SCI is not widely available as cheap production units, and there isn't any Linux support.

SCI primarily is used in various proprietary designs for logically-shared physically-distributed memory machines, such as the HP/Convex Exemplar SPP and the Sequent NUMA-Q 2000 (see `<http://www.sequent.com/>`). However, SCI is available as a PCI interface card and 4-way switches (up to 16 machines can be connected by cascading four 4-way switches) from Dolphin, `<http://www.dolphinics.com/>`, as their CluStar product line. A good set of links overviewing SCI is maintained by CERN at `<http://www.cern.ch/HSI/sci/sci.html>`.

3.2.15 SCSI

- Linux support: *kernel drivers*
- Maximum bandwidth: *5 Mb/s to over 20 Mb/s*
- Minimum latency: *?*
- Available as: *multiple-vendor hardware*
- Interface port/bus used: *PCI, EISA, ISA card*

- Network structure: *inter-machine bus sharing SCSI devices*
- Cost per machine connected: *?*

SCSI (Small Computer Systems Interconnect) is essentially an I/O bus that is used for disk drives, CD ROMS, image scanners, etc. There are three separate standards SCSI-1, SCSI-2, and SCSI-3; Fast and Ultra speeds; and data path widths of 8, 16, or 32 bits (with FireWire compatibility also mentioned in SCSI-3). It is all pretty confusing, but we all know a good SCSI is somewhat faster than EIDE and can handle more devices more efficiently.

What many people do not realize is that it is fairly simple for two computers to share a single SCSI bus. This type of configuration is very useful for sharing disk drives between machines and implementing **fail-over** - having one machine take over database requests when the other machine fails. Currently, this is the only mechanism supported by Microsoft's PC cluster product, WolfPack. However, the inability to scale to larger systems renders shared SCSI uninteresting for parallel processing in general.

3.2.16 ServerNet

- Linux support: *no*
- Maximum bandwidth: *400 Mb/s*
- Minimum latency: *3 microseconds*
- Available as: *single-vendor hardware*
- Interface port/bus used: *PCI*
- Network structure: *hexagonal tree/tetrahedral lattice of hubs*
- Cost per machine connected: *?*

ServerNet is the high-performance network hardware from Tandem, `<http://www.tandem.com>`. Especially in the online transation processing (OLTP) world, Tandem is well known as a leading producer of high-reliability systems, so it is not surprising that their network claims not just high performance, but also "high data integrity and reliability." Another interesting aspect of ServerNet is that it claims to be able to transfer data from any device directly to any device; not just between processors, but also disk drives, etc., in a one-sided style similar to that suggested by the MPI remote memory access mechanisms described in section 3.5. One last comment about ServerNet: although there is just a single vendor, that vendor is powerful enough to potentially establish ServerNet as a major standard... Tandem is owned by Compaq.

3.2.17 SHRIMP

- Linux support: *user-level memory mapped interface*
- Maximum bandwidth: *180 Mb/s*
- Minimum latency: *5 microseconds*
- Available as: *research prototype*
- Interface port/bus used: *EISA*
- Network structure: *mesh backplane (as in Intel Paragon)*
- Cost per machine connected: *?*

The SHRIMP project, `<http://www.CS.Princeton.EDU/shrimp/>`, at the Princeton University Computer Science Department is building a parallel computer using PCs running Linux as the processing elements. The first SHRIMP (Scalable, High-Performance, Really Inexpensive Multi-Processor) was a simple two-processor prototype using a dual-ported RAM on a custom EISA card interface. There is now a prototype that will scale to larger configurations using a custom interface card to connect to a "hub" that is essentially the same mesh routing network used in the Intel Paragon (see `<http://www.ssd.intel.com/paragon.html>`). Considerable effort has gone into developing low-overhead "virtual memory mapped communication" hardware and support software.

3.2.18 SLIP

- Linux support: *kernel drivers*
- Maximum bandwidth: *0.1 Mb/s*
- Minimum latency: *1,000 microseconds?*
- Available as: *commodity hardware*
- Interface port/bus used: *RS232C*
- Network structure: *cable between 2 machines*
- Cost per machine connected: *$2*

Although SLIP (Serial Line Interface Protocol) is firmly planted at the low end of the performance spectrum, SLIP (or CSLIP or PPP) allows two machines to perform socket communication via ordinary RS232 serial ports. The RS232 ports can be connected using a null-modem RS232 serial cable, or they can even be connected via dial-up through a modem. In any case, latency is high and bandwidth is low, so SLIP should be used only when no other alternatives are available. It is worth noting, however, that most PCs have two RS232 ports, so it would be possible to network a group of machines simply by connecting the machines as a linear array or as a ring. There is even load sharing software called EQL.

3.2.19 TTL_PAPERS

- Linux support: *AFAPI library*
- Maximum bandwidth: *1.6 Mb/s*
- Minimum latency: *3 microseconds*
- Available as: *public-domain design, single-vendor hardware*
- Interface port/bus used: *SPP*
- Network structure: *tree of hubs*
- Cost per machine connected: *$100*

The PAPERS (Purdue's Adapter for Parallel Execution and Rapid Synchronization) project, <http://garage.ecn.purdue.edu/~papers/>, at the Purdue University School of Electrical and Computer Engineering is building scalable, low-latency, aggregate function communication hardware and software that allows a parallel supercomputer to be built using unmodified PCs/workstations as nodes.

There have been over a dozen different types of PAPERS hardware built that connect to PCs/workstations via the SPP (Standard Parallel Port), roughly following two development lines. The versions called "PAPERS" target higher performance, using whatever technologies are appropriate; current work uses FPGAs, and high bandwidth PCI bus interface designs are also under development. In contrast, the versions called "TTL_PAPERS" are designed to be easily reproduced outside Purdue, and are remarkably simple public domain designs that can be built using ordinary TTL logic. One such design is produced commercially, <http://chelsea.ios.com:80/~hgdietz/sbm4.html>.

Unlike the custom hardware designs from other universities, TTL_PAPERS clusters have been assembled at many universities from the USA to South Korea. Bandwidth is severely limited by the SPP connections, but PAPERS implements very low latency aggregate function communications; even the fastest message-oriented systems cannot provide comparable performance on those aggregate functions. Thus, PAPERS is particularly good for synchronizing the displays of a video wall (to be discussed further in the upcoming Video Wall HOWTO), scheduling accesses to a high-bandwidth network, evaluating global fitness in genetic searches, etc. Although PAPERS clusters have been built using IBM PowerPC AIX, DEC Alpha OSF/1, and HP PA-RISC HP-UX machines, Linux-based PCs are the platforms best supported.

User programs using TTL_PAPERS AFAPI directly access the SPP hardware port registers under Linux, without an OS call for each access. To do this, AFAPI first gets port permission using either `iopl()` or `ioperm()`. The problem with these calls is that both require the user program to be privileged, yielding a potential security hole. The solution is an optional kernel patch, <http://garage.ecn.purdue.edu/~papers/giveioperm.html>, that allows a privileged process to control port permission for any process.

3.2.20   USB (Universal Serial Bus)

- Linux support: *kernel driver*
- Maximum bandwidth: *12 Mb/s*
- Minimum latency: *?*
- Available as: *commodity hardware*
- Interface port/bus used: *USB*
- Network structure: *bus*
- Cost per machine connected: *$5?*

USB (Universal Serial Bus, `<http://www.usb.org/>`) is a hot-pluggable conventional-Ethernet-speed, bus for up to 127 peripherals ranging from keyboards to video conferencing cameras. It isn't really clear how multiple computers get connected to each other using USB. In any case, USB ports are quickly becoming as standard on PC motherboards as RS232 and SPP, so don't be surprised if one or two USB ports are lurking on the back of the next PC you buy. Development of a Linux driver is discussed at `<http://peloncho.fis.ucm.es/~inaky/USB.html>`.

In some ways, USB is almost the low-performance, zero-cost, version of FireWire that you can purchase today.

3.2.21   WAPERS

- Linux support: *AFAPI library*
- Maximum bandwidth: *0.4 Mb/s*
- Minimum latency: *3 microseconds*
- Available as: *public-domain design*
- Interface port/bus used: *SPP*
- Network structure: *wiring pattern between 2-64 machines*
- Cost per machine connected: *$5*

WAPERS (Wired-AND Adapter for Parallel Execution and Rapid Synchronization) is a spin-off of the PAPERS project, `<http://garage.ecn.purdue.edu/~papers/>`, at the Purdue University School of Electrical and Computer Engineering. If implemented properly, the SPP has four bits of open-collector output that can be wired together across machines to implement a 4-bit wide wired AND. This wired-AND is electrically touchy, and the maximum number of machines that can be connected in this way critically depends on the analog properties of the ports (maximum sink current and pull-up resistor value); typically, up to 7 or 8 machines can be networked by WAPERS. Although cost and latency are very low, so is bandwidth; WAPERS is much better as a second network for aggregate operations than as the only network in a cluster. As with TTL_PAPERS, to improve system security, there is a minor kernel patch recommended, but not required: `<http://garage.ecn.purdue.edu/~papers/giveioperm.html>`.

3.3   Network Software Interface

Before moving on to discuss the software support for parallel applications, it is useful to first briefly cover the basics of low-level software interface to the network hardware. There are really only three basic choices: sockets, device drivers, and user-level libraries.

3.3.1   Sockets

By far the most common low-level network interface is a socket interface. Sockets have been a part of unix for over a decade, and most standard network hardware is designed to support at least two types of socket protocols: UDP and TCP. Both types of socket allow you to send arbitrary size blocks of data from one machine to another, but there are several important differences. Typically, both yield a minimum latency of around 1,000 microseconds, although performance can be far worse depending on network traffic.

These socket types are the basic network software interface for most of the portable, higher-level, parallel processing software; for example, PVM uses a combination of UDP and TCP, so knowing the difference will help you tune performance. For even better performance, you can also use these mechanisms directly in your program. The following is just a simple overview of UDP and TCP; see the manual pages and a good network programming book for details.

UDP Protocol (SOCK_DGRAM)   **UDP** is the User Datagram Protocol, but you more easily can remember the properties of UDP as Unreliable Datagram Processing. In other words, UDP allows each block to be sent as an individual message, but a message might be lost in transmission. In fact, depending on network traffic, UDP messages can be lost, can arrive multiple times, or can arrive in an order different from that in which they were sent. The sender of a UDP message does not automatically get an acknowledgment, so it is up to user-written code to detect and compensate for these problems. Fortunately, UDP does ensure that if a message arrives, the message contents are intact (i.e., you never get just part of a UDP message).

The nice thing about UDP is that it tends to be the fastest socket protocol. Further, UDP is "connectionless," which means that each message is essentially independent of all others. A good analogy is that each message is like a letter to be mailed; you might send multiple letters to the same address, but each one is independent of the others and there is no limit on how many people you can send letters to.

TCP Protocol (SOCK_STREAM)   Unlike UDP, **TCP** is a reliable, connection-based, protocol. Each block sent is not seen as a message, but as a block of data within an apparently continuous stream of bytes being transmitted through a connection between sender and receiver. This is very different from UDP messaging because each block is simply part of the byte stream and it is up to the user code to figure-out how to extract each block from the byte stream; there are no markings separating messages. Further, the connections are more fragile with respect to network problems, and only a limited number of connections can exist simultaneously for each process. Because it is reliable, TCP generally implies significantly more overhead than UDP.

There are, however, a few pleasant surprises about TCP. One is that, if multiple messages are sent through a connection, TCP is able to pack them together in a buffer to better match network hardware packet sizes, potentially yielding better-than-UDP performance for groups of short or oddly-sized messages. The other bonus is that networks constructed using reliable direct physical links between machines can easily and efficiently simulate TCP connections. For example, this was done for the ParaStation's "Socket Library" interface software, which provides TCP semantics using user-level calls that differ from the standard TCP OS calls only by the addition of the prefix `PSS` to each function name.

3.3.2   Device Drivers

When it comes to actually pushing data onto the network or pulling data off the network, the standard unix software interface is a part of the unix kernel called a device driver. UDP and TCP don't just transport data, they also imply a fair amount of overhead for socket management. For example, something has to manage the fact that multiple TCP connections can share a single physical network interface. In contrast, a device driver for a dedicated network interface only needs to implement a few simple data transport functions. These device driver functions can then be invoked by user programs by using `open()` to identify the proper device and then using system calls like `read()` and `write()` on the open "file." Thus, each such operation could transport a block of data with little more than the overhead of a system call, which might be as fast as tens of microseconds.

Writing a device driver to be used with Linux is not hard... if you know *precisely* how the device hardware works. If you are not sure how it works, don't guess. Debugging device drivers isn't fun and mistakes can fry hardware. However, if that hasn't scared you off, it may be possible to write a device driver to, for example, use dedicated Ethernet cards as dumb but fast direct machine-to-machine connections without the usual Ethernet protocol overhead. In fact, that's pretty much what some early Intel supercomputers did.... Look at the Device Driver HOWTO for more information.

3.3.3   User-Level Libraries

If you've taken an OS course, user-level access to hardware device registers is exactly what you have been taught never to do, because one of the primary purposes of an OS is to control device access. However, an OS call is at least tens of microseconds of overhead. For custom network hardware like TTL_PAPERS, which can perform a basic network operation in just 3 microseconds, such OS call overhead is intolerable. The only way to avoid that overhead is to have user-level code - a user-level library - directly access hardware device registers. Thus, the question becomes one of how a user-level library can access hardware directly, yet not compromise the OS control of device access rights.

On a typical system, the only way for a user-level library to directly access hardware device registers is to:

1. At user program start-up, use an OS call to map the page of memory address space containing the device registers into the user process virtual memory map. For some systems, the mmap() call (first mentioned in section 2.6) can be used to map a special file which represents the physical memory page addresses of the I/O devices. Alternatively, it is relatively simple to write a device driver to perform this function. Further, this device driver can control access by only mapping the page(s) containing the specific device registers needed, thereby maintaining OS access control.

2. Access device registers without an OS call by simply loading or storing to the mapped addresses. For example, *((char *) 0x1234) = 5; would store the byte value 5 into memory location 1234 (hexadecimal).

Fortunately, it happens that Linux for the Intel 386 (and compatible processors) offers an even better solution:

1. Using the ioperm() OS call from a privileged process, get permission to access the precise I/O port addresses that correspond to the device registers. Alternatively, permission can be managed by an independent privileged user process (i.e., a "meta OS") using the *giveioperm() OS call* <http://garage.ecn.purdue.edu/~papers/giveioperm.html> patch for Linux.

2. Access device registers without an OS call by using 386 port I/O instructions.

This second solution is preferable because it is common that multiple I/O devices have their registers within a single page, in which case the first technique would not provide protection against accessing other device registers that happened to reside in the same page as the ones intended. Of course, the down side is that 386 port I/O instructions cannot be coded in C - instead, you will need to use a bit of assembly code. The GCC-wrapped (usable in C programs) inline assembly code function for a port input of a byte value is:

```
extern inline unsigned char
inb(unsigned short port)
{
    unsigned char _v;
__asm__ __volatile__ ("inb %w1,%b0"
                      :"=a" (_v)
                      :"d" (port), "0" (0));
    return _v;
}
```

Similarly, the GCC-wrapped code for a byte port output is:

```
extern inline void
outb(unsigned char value,
unsigned short port)
{
__asm__ __volatile__ ("outb %b0,%w1"
                      :/* no outputs */
                      :"a" (value), "d" (port));
}
```

3.4   PVM (Parallel Virtual Machine)

PVM (Parallel Virtual Machine) is a freely-available, portable, message-passing library generally implemented on top of sockets. It is clearly established as the de-facto standard for message-passing cluster parallel computing.

PVM supports single-processor and SMP Linux machines, as well as clusters of Linux machines linked by socket-capable networks (e.g., SLIP, PLIP, Ethernet, ATM). In fact, PVM will even work across groups of machines in which a variety of different types of processors, configurations, and physical networks are used - **Heterogeneous Clusters** - even to the scale of treating machines linked by the Internet as a parallel cluster. PVM also provides facilities for parallel job control across a cluster. Best of all, PVM has long been freely available (currently from `<http://www.epm.ornl.gov/pvm/ pvm_home.html>`), which has led to many programming language compilers, application libraries, programming and debugging tools, etc., using it as their "portable message-passing target library." There is also a network newsgroup, *comp.parallel.pvm*.

It is important to note, however, that PVM message-passing calls generally add significant overhead to standard socket operations, which already had high latency. Further, the message handling calls themselves do not constitute a particularly "friendly" programming model.

Using the same Pi computation example first described in section 1.3, the version using C with PVM library calls is:

```c
#include <stdlib.h>
#include <stdio.h>
#include <pvm3.h>

#define NPROC    4

main(int argc, char **argv)
{
  register double lsum, width;
  double sum;
  register int intervals, i;
  int mytid, iproc, msgtag = 4;
  int tids[NPROC];  /* array of task ids */

  /* enroll in pvm */
  mytid = pvm_mytid();

  /* Join a group and, if I am the first instance,
     iproc=0, spawn more copies of myself
  */
  iproc = pvm_joingroup("pi");

  if (iproc == 0) {
    tids[0] = pvm_mytid();
    pvm_spawn("pvm_pi", &argv[1], 0, NULL, NPROC-1, &tids[1]);
  }
  /* make sure all processes are here */
  pvm_barrier("pi", NPROC);

  /* get the number of intervals */
  intervals = atoi(argv[1]);
  width = 1.0 / intervals;

  lsum = 0.0;
  for (i = iproc; i<intervals; i+=NPROC) {
    register double x = (i + 0.5) * width;
    lsum += 4.0 / (1.0 + x * x);
  }

  /* sum across the local results & scale by width */
```

HOWTO

```
sum = lsum * width;
pvm_reduce(PvmSum, &sum, 1, PVM_DOUBLE, msgtag, "pi", 0);

/* have only the console PE print the result */
if (iproc == 0) {
    printf("Estimation of pi is %f\n", sum);
}

/* Check program finished, leave group, exit pvm */
pvm_barrier("pi", NPROC);
pvm_lvgroup("pi");
pvm_exit();
return(0);
}
```

3.5 MPI (Message Passing Interface)

Although PVM is the de-facto standard message-passing library, MPI (Message Passing Interface) is the relatively new official standard. The home page for the MPI standard is `<http://www.mcs.anl.gov:80/mpi/>` and the news-group is *comp.parallel.mpi*.

However, before discussing MPI, I feel compelled to say a little bit about the PVM vs. MPI religious war that has been going on for the past few years. I'm not really on either side. Here's my attempt at a relatively unbiased summary of the differences:

Execution control environment.

Put simply, PVM has one and MPI doesn't specify how/if one is implemented. Thus, things like starting a PVM program executing are done identically everywhere, while for MPI it depends on which implementation is being used.

Support for heterogeneous clusters.

PVM grew-up in the workstation cycle-scavenging world, and thus directly manages heterogeneous mixes of machines and operating systems. In contrast, MPI largely assumes that the target is an MPP (Massively Parallel Processor) or a dedicated cluster of nearly identical workstations.

Kitchen sink syndrome.

PVM evidences a unity of purpose that MPI 2.0 doesn't. The new MPI 2.0 standard includes a lot of features that go way beyond the basic message passing model - things like RMA (Remote Memory Access) and parallel file I/O. Are these things useful? Of course they are... but learning MPI 2.0 is a lot like learning a complete new programming language.

User interface design.

MPI was designed after PVM, and clearly learned from it. MPI offers simpler, more efficient, buffer handling and higher-level abstractions allowing user-defined data structures to be transmitted in messages.

The force of law.

By my count, there are still significantly more things designed to use PVM than there are to use MPI; however, porting them to MPI is easy, and the fact that MPI is backed by a widely-supported formal standard means that using MPI is, for many institutions, a matter of policy.

Conclusion? Well, there are at least three independently developed, freely available, versions of MPI that can run on clusters of Linux systems (and I wrote one of them):

- LAM (Local Area Multicomputer) is a full implementation of the MPI 1.1 standard. It allows MPI programs to be executed within an individual Linux system or across a cluster of Linux systems using UDP/TCP socket communication. The system includes simple execution control facilities, as well as a variety of program development and debugging aids. It is freely available from `<http://www.osc.edu/lam.html>`.

- MPICH (MPI CHameleon) is designed as a highly portable full implementation of the MPI 1.1 standard. Like LAM, it allows MPI programs to be executed within an individual Linux system or across a cluster of Linux systems using UDP/TCP socket communication. However, the emphasis is definitely on promoting MPI by providing an efficient, easily retargetable, implementation. To port this MPI implementation, one implements either the five functions of the "channel interface" or, for better performance, the full MPICH ADI (Abstract Device Interface). MPICH, and lots of information about it and porting, are available from `<http://www.mcs.anl.gov/mpi/mpich/>`.

- AFMPI (Aggregate Function MPI) is a subset implementation of the MPI 2.0 standard. This is the one that I wrote. Built on top of the AFAPI, it is designed to showcase low-latency collective communication functions and RMAs, and thus provides only minimal support for MPI data types, communicators, etc. It allows C programs using MPI to run on an individual Linux system or across a cluster connected by AFAPI-capable network hardware. It is freely available from `<http://garage.ecn.purdue.edu/~papers/>`.

No matter which of these (or other) MPI implementations one uses, it is fairly simple to perform the most common types of communications.

However, MPI 2.0 incorporates several communication paradigms that are fundamentally different enough so that a programmer using one of them might not even recognize the other coding styles as MPI. Thus, rather than giving a single example program, it is useful to have an example of each of the fundamentally different communication paradigms that MPI supports. All three programs implement the same basic algorithm (from section 1.3) that is used throughout this HOWTO to compute the value of Pi.

The first MPI program uses basic MPI message-passing calls for each processor to send its partial sum to processor 0, which sums and prints the result:

```
#include <stdlib.h>
#include <stdio.h>
#include <mpi.h>

main(int argc, char **argv)
{
  register double width;
  double sum, lsum;
  register int intervals, i;
  int nproc, iproc;
  MPI_Status status;

  if (MPI_Init(&argc, &argv) != MPI_SUCCESS) exit(1);
  MPI_Comm_size(MPI_COMM_WORLD, &nproc);
  MPI_Comm_rank(MPI_COMM_WORLD, &iproc);
  intervals = atoi(argv[1]);
  width = 1.0 / intervals;
  lsum = 0;
  for (i=iproc; i<intervals; i+=nproc) {
    register double x = (i + 0.5) * width;
    lsum += 4.0 / (1.0 + x * x);
  }
  lsum *= width;
  if (iproc != 0) {
    MPI_Send(&lbuf, 1, MPI_DOUBLE, 0, 0, MPI_COMM_WORLD);
  } else {
    sum = lsum;
    for (i=1; i<nproc; ++i) {
      MPI_Recv(&lbuf, 1, MPI_DOUBLE, MPI_ANY_SOURCE,
               MPI_ANY_TAG, MPI_COMM_WORLD, &status);
```

HOWTO

```
      sum += lsum;
    }
    printf("Estimation of pi is %f\n", sum);
  }
  MPI_Finalize();
  return(0);
}
```

The second MPI version uses collective communication (which, for this particular application, is clearly the most appropriate):

```
#include <stdlib.h>
#include <stdio.h>
#include <mpi.h>

main(int argc, char **argv)
{
  register double width;
  double sum, lsum;
  register int intervals, i;
  int nproc, iproc;

  if (MPI_Init(&argc, &argv) != MPI_SUCCESS) exit(1);
  MPI_Comm_size(MPI_COMM_WORLD, &nproc);
  MPI_Comm_rank(MPI_COMM_WORLD, &iproc);
  intervals = atoi(argv[1]);
  width = 1.0 / intervals;
  lsum = 0;
  for (i=iproc; i<intervals; i+=nproc) {
    register double x = (i + 0.5) * width;
    lsum += 4.0 / (1.0 + x * x);
  }
  lsum *= width;
  MPI_Reduce(&lsum, &sum, 1, MPI_DOUBLE,
             MPI_SUM, 0, MPI_COMM_WORLD);
  if (iproc == 0) {
    printf("Estimation of pi is %f\n", sum);
  }
  MPI_Finalize();
  return(0);
}
```

The third MPI version uses the MPI 2.0 RMA mechanism for each processor to add its local lsum into sum on processor 0:

```
#include <stdlib.h>
#include <stdio.h>
#include <mpi.h>

main(int argc, char **argv)
{
  register double width;
  double sum = 0, lsum;
  register int intervals, i;
```

```
int nproc, iproc;
MPI_Win sum_win;

if (MPI_Init(&argc, &argv) != MPI_SUCCESS) exit(1);
MPI_Comm_size(MPI_COMM_WORLD, &nproc);
MPI_Comm_rank(MPI_COMM_WORLD, &iproc);
MPI_Win_create(&sum, sizeof(sum), sizeof(sum),
               0, MPI_COMM_WORLD, &sum_win);
MPI_Win_fence(0, sum_win);
intervals = atoi(argv[1]);
width = 1.0 / intervals;
lsum = 0;
for (i=iproc; i<intervals; i+=nproc) {
  register double x = (i + 0.5) * width;
  lsum += 4.0 / (1.0 + x * x);
}
lsum *= width;
MPI_Accumulate(&lsum, 1, MPI_DOUBLE, 0, 0,
               1, MPI_DOUBLE, MPI_SUM, sum_win);
MPI_Win_fence(0, sum_win);
if (iproc == 0) {
  printf("Estimation of pi is %f\n", sum);
}
MPI_Finalize();
return(0);
}
```

It is useful to note that the MPI 2.0 RMA mechanism very neatly overcomes any potential problems with the corresponding data structure on various processors residing at different memory locations. This is done by referencing a "window" that implies the base address, protection against out-of-bound accesses, and even address scaling. Efficient implementation is aided by the fact that RMA processing may be delayed until the next `MPI_Win_fence`. In summary, the RMA mechanism may be a strange cross between distributed shared memory and message passing, but it is a very clean interface that potentially generates very efficient communication.

3.6 AFAPI (Aggregate Function API)

Unlike PVM, MPI, etc., the AFAPI (Aggregate Function Application Program Interface) did not start life as an attempt to build a portable abstract interface layered on top of existing network hardware and software. Rather, AFAPI began as the very hardware-specific low-level support library for PAPERS (Purdue's Adapter for Parallel Execution and Rapid Synchronization; see `<http://garage.ecn.purdue.edu/~papers/>`).

PAPERS was discussed briefly in section 3.2; it is a public domain design custom aggregate function network that delivers latencies as low as a few microseconds. However, the important thing about PAPERS is that it was developed as an attempt to build a supercomputer that would be a better target for compiler technology than existing supercomputers. This is qualitatively different from most Linux cluster efforts and PVM/MPI, which generally focus on trying to use standard networks for the relatively few sufficiently coarse-grain parallel applications. The fact that Linux PCs are used as components of PAPERS systems is simply an artifact of implementing prototypes in the most cost-effective way possible.

The need for a common low-level software interface across more than a dozen different prototype implementations was what made the PAPERS library become standardized as AFAPI. However, the model used by AFAPI is inherently simpler and better suited for the finer-grain interactions typical of code compiled by parallelizing compilers or written for SIMD architectures. The simplicity of the model not only makes PAPERS hardware easy to build, but also yields surprisingly efficient AFAPI ports for a variety of other hardware systems, such as SMPs.

AFAPI currently runs on Linux clusters connected using TTL_PAPERS, CAPERS, or WAPERS. It also runs (without OS calls or even bus-lock instructions, see section 2.2) on SMP systems using a System V Shared Memory library called SHMAPERS. A version that runs across Linux clusters using UDP broadcasts on conventional networks (e.g., Ethernet) is under development. All released versions are available from `<http://garage.ecn.purdue.edu/~papers/>`. All versions of the AFAPI are designed to be called from C or C++.

The following example program is the AFAPI version of the Pi computation described in section 1.3.

```
#include <stdlib.h>
#include <stdio.h>
#include "afapi.h"

main(int argc, char **argv)
{
  register double width, sum;
  register int intervals, i;

  if (p_init()) exit(1);

  intervals = atoi(argv[1]);
  width = 1.0 / intervals;

  sum = 0;
  for (i=IPROC; i<intervals; i+=NPROC) {
    register double x = (i + 0.5) * width;
    sum += 4.0 / (1.0 + x * x);
  }

  sum = p_reduceAdd64f(sum) * width;

  if (IPROC == CPROC) {
    printf("Estimation of pi is %f\n", sum);
  }

  p_exit();
  return(0);
}
```

3.7 Other Cluster Support Libraries

In addition to PVM, MPI, and AFAPI, the following libraries offer features that may be useful in parallel computing using a cluster of Linux systems. These systems are given a lighter treatment in this document simply because, unlike PVM, MPI, and AFAPI, I have little or no direct experience with the use of these systems on Linux clusters. If you find any of these or other libraries to be especially useful, please send email to me at *pplinux@ecn.purdue.edu* describing what you've found, and I will consider adding an expanded section on that library.

3.7.1 Condor (process migration support)

Condor is a distributed resource management system that can manage large heterogeneous clusters of workstations. Its design has been motivated by the needs of users who would like to use the unutilized capacity of such clusters for their long-running, computation-intensive jobs. Condor preserves a large measure of the originating machine's environment on the execution machine, even if the originating and execution machines do not share a common file system and/or password mechanisms. Condor jobs that consist of a single process are automatically checkpointed and migrated between workstations as needed to ensure eventual completion.

Condor is available at `<http://www.cs.wisc.edu/condor/>`. A Linux port exists; more information is available at `<http://www.cs.wisc.edu/condor/linux/linux.html>`. Contact *condor-admin@cs.wisc.edu* for details.

3.7.2 DFN-RPC (German Research Network - Remote Procedure Call)

The DFN-RPC, a (German Research Network Remote Procedure Call) tool, was developed to distribute and parallelize scientific-technical application programs between a workstation and a compute server or a cluster. The interface is optimized for applications written in fortran, but the DFN-RPC can also be used in a C environment. It has been ported to Linux. More information is at `<ftp://ftp.uni-stuttgart.de/pub/rus/dfn_rpc/README_dfnrpc.html>`.

3.7.3 DQS (Distributed Queueing System)

Not exactly a library, DQS 3.0 (Distributed Queueing System) is a job queueing system that has been developed and tested under Linux. It is designed to allow both use and administration of a heterogeneous cluster as a single entity. It is available from `<http://www.scri.fsu.edu/~pasko/dqs.html>`.

There is also a commercial version called CODINE 4.1.1 (COmputing in DIstributed Network Environments). Information on it is available from `<http://www.genias.de/genias_welcome.html>`.

3.8 General Cluster References

Because clusters can be constructed and used in so many different ways, there are quite a few groups that have made interesting contributions. The following are references to various cluster-related projects that may be of general interest. This includes a mix of Linux-specific and generic cluster references. The list is given in alphabetical order.

3.8.1 Beowulf

The Beowulf project, `<http://cesdis1.gsfc.nasa.gov/beowulf/>`, centers on production of software for using off-the-shelf clustered workstations based on commodity PC-class hardware, a high-bandwidth cluster-internal network, and the Linux operating system.

Thomas Sterling has been the driving force behind Beowulf, and continues to be an eloquent and outspoken proponent of Linux clustering for scientific computing in general. In fact, many groups now refer to their clusters as "Beowulf class" systems - even if the cluster isn't really all that similar to the official Beowulf design.

Don Becker, working in support of the Beowulf project, has produced many of the network drivers used by Linux in general. Many of these drivers have even been adapted for use in BSD. Don also is responsible for many of these Linux network drivers allowing load-sharing across multiple parallel connections to achieve higher bandwidth without expensive switched hubs. This type of load sharing was the original distinguishing feature of the Beowulf cluster.

3.8.2 Linux/AP+

The Linux/AP+ project, `<http://cap.anu.edu.au/cap/projects/linux/>`, is not exactly about Linux clustering, but centers on porting Linux to the Fujitsu AP1000+ and adding appropriate parallel processing enhancements. The AP1000+ is a commercially available SPARC-based parallel machine that uses a custom network with a torus topology, 25 MB/s bandwidth, and 10 microsecond latency... in short, it looks a lot like a SPARC Linux cluster.

3.8.3 Locust

The Locust project, `<http://www.ecsl.cs.sunysb.edu/~manish/locust/>`, is building a distributed virtual shared memory system that uses compile-time information to hide message-latency and to reduce network traffic at run time. Pupa is the underlying communication subsystem of Locust, and is implemented using Ethernet to connect 486 PCs under FreeBSD. Linux?

3.8.4 Midway DSM (Distributed Shared Memory)

Midway, `<http://www.cs.cmu.edu/afs/cs.cmu.edu/project/midway/WWW/HomePage.html>`, is a software-based DSM (Distributed Shared Memory) system, not unlike TreadMarks. The good news is that it uses compile-time aids rather than relatively slow page-fault mechanisms, and it is free. The bad news is that it doesn't run on Linux clusters.

3.8.5 Mosix

MOSIX modifies the BSDI BSD/OS to provide dynamic load balancing and preemptive process migration across a networked group of PCs. This is nice stuff not just for parallel processing, but for generally using a cluster much like a scalable SMP. Will there be a Linux version? Look at `<http://www.cs.huji.ac.il/mosix/>` for more information.

3.8.6 NOW (Network Of Workstations)

The Berkeley NOW (Network Of Workstations) project, `<http://now.cs.berkeley.edu/>`, has led much of the push toward parallel computing using networks of workstations. There is a lot work going on here, all aimed toward "demonstrating a practical 100 processor system in the next few years." Alas, they don't use Linux.

3.8.7 Parallel Processing Using Linux

The parallel processing using Linux WWW site, `<http://yara.ecn.purdue.edu/~pplinux/>`, is the home of this HOWTO and many related documents including online slides for a full-day tutorial. Aside from the work on the PAPERS project, the Purdue University School of Electrical and Computer Engineering generally has been a leader in parallel processing; this site was established to help others apply Linux PCs for parallel processing.

Since Purdue's first cluster of Linux PCs was assembled in February 1994, there have been many Linux PC clusters assembled at Purdue, including several with video walls. Although these clusters used 386, 486, and Pentium systems (no Pentium Pro systems), Intel recently awarded Purdue a donation which will allow it to construct multiple large clusters of Pentium II systems (with as many as 165 machines planned for a single cluster). Although these clusters all have/will have PAPERS networks, most also have conventional networks.

3.8.8 Pentium Pro Cluster Workshop

In Des Moines, Iowa, April 10-11, 1997, AMES Laboratory held the Pentium Pro Cluster Workshop. The WWW site from this workshop, `<http://www.scl.ameslab.gov/workshops/PPCworkshop.html>`, contains a wealth of PC cluster information gathered from all the attendees.

3.8.9 TreadMarks DSM (Distributed Shared Memory)

DSM (Distributed Shared Memory) is a technique whereby a message-passing system can appear to behave as an SMP. There are quite a few such systems, most of which use the OS page-fault mechanism to trigger message transmissions. TreadMarks, `<http://www.cs.rice.edu/~willy/TreadMarks/overview.html>`, is one of the more efficient of such systems and does run on Linux clusters. The bad news is "TreadMarks is being distributed at a small cost to universities and nonprofit institutions." For more information about the software, contact *treadmarks@ece.rice.edu*.

3.8.10 U-Net (User-level NETwork interface architecture)

The U-Net (User-level NETwork interface architecture) project at Cornell, `<http://www2.cs.cornell.edu/U-Net/Default.html>`, attempts to provide low-latency and high-bandwidth using commodity network hardware by by virtualizing the network interface so that applications can send and receive messages without operating system intervention. U-Net runs on Linux PCs using a DECchip DC21140 based Fast Ethernet card or a Fore Systems PCA-200 (not PCA-200E) ATM card.

3.8.11 WWT (Wisconsin Wind Tunnel)

There is really quite a lot of cluster-related work at Wisconsin. The WWT (Wisconsin Wind Tunnel) project, <http://www.cs.wisc.edu/~wwt/>, is doing all sorts of work toward developing a "standard" interface between compilers and the underlying parallel hardware. There is the Wisconsin COW (Cluster Of Workstations), Cooperative Shared Memory and Tempest, the Paradyn Parallel Performance Tools, etc. Unfortunately, there is not much about Linux.

4 SIMD Within A Register (e.g., using MMX)

SIMD (Single Instruction stream, Multiple Data stream) Within A Register (SWAR) isn't a new idea. Given a machine with k-bit registers, data paths, and function units, it has long been known that ordinary register operations can function as SIMD parallel operations on n, k/n-bit, integer field values. However, it is only with the recent push for multimedia that the 2x to 8x speedup offered by SWAR techniques has become a concern for mainstream computing. The 1997 versions of most microprocessors incorporate hardware support for SWAR:

- *AMD K6 MMX (MultiMedia eXtensions)*
- *Cyrix M2 MMX (MultiMedia eXtensions)*
- *Digital Alpha MAX (MultimediA eXtensions)*
- *Hewlett-Packard PA-RISC MAX (Multimedia Acceleration eXtensions)*
- *Intel Pentium II & Pentium with MMX (MultiMedia eXtensions)*
- *Microunity Mediaprocessor SIGD (Single Instruction on Groups of Data)*
- *MIPS Digital Media eXtension (MDMX, pronounced Mad Max)*
- *Sun SPARC V9 VIS (Visual Instruction Set)*

There are a few holes in the hardware support provided by the new microprocessors, quirks like only supporting some operations for some field sizes. It is important to remember, however, that you don't need any hardware support for many SWAR operations to be efficient. For example, bitwise operations are not affected by the logical partitioning of a register.

4.1 SWAR: What Is It Good For?

Although *every* modern processor is capable of executing with at least some SWAR parallelism, the sad fact is that even the best SWAR-enhanced instruction sets do not support very general-purpose parallelism. In fact, many people have noticed that the performance difference between Pentium and "Pentium with MMX technology" is often due to things like the larger L1 cache that coincided with appearance of MMX. So, realistically, what is SWAR (or MMX) good for?

- Integers only, the smaller the better. Two 32-bit values fit in a 64-bit MMX register, but so do eight one-byte characters or even an entire chess board worth of one-bit values.

  Note: there *will be a floating-point version of MMX*, although very little has been said about it at this writing. Cyrix has posted a set of slides, <ftp://ftp.cyrix.com/developr/mpf97rm.pdf>, that includes a few comments about **MMFP**. Apparently, MMFP will support two 32-bit floating-point numbers to be packed into a 64-bit MMX register; combining this with two MMFP pipelines will yield four single-precision FLOPs per clock.

- SIMD or vector-style parallelism. The same operation is applied to all fields simultaneously. There are ways to nullify the effects on selected fields (i.e., equivalent to SIMD enable masking), but they complicate coding and hurt performance.

- Localized, regular (preferably packed), memory reference patterns. SWAR in general, and MMX in particular, are terrible at randomly-ordered accesses; gathering a vector x[y] (where y is an index array) is prohibitively expensive.

These are serious restrictions, but this type of parallelism occurs in many parallel algorithms - not just multimedia applications. For the right type of algorithm, SWAR is more effective than SMP or cluster parallelism... and it doesn't cost anything to use it.

HOWTO

4.2 Introduction To SWAR Programming

The basic concept of SWAR, SIMD Within A Register, is that operations on word-length registers can be used to speed-up computations by performing SIMD parallel operations on n k/n-bit field values. However, making use of SWAR technology can be awkward, and some SWAR operations are actually more expensive than the corresponding sequences of serial operations because they require additional instructions to enforce the field partitioning.

To illustrate this point, let's consider a greatly simplified SWAR mechanism that manages four 8-bit fields within each 32-bit register. The values in two registers might be represented as:

```
         PE3        PE2        PE1        PE0
      +--------+--------+--------+--------+
Reg0  | D 7:0  | C 7:0  | B 7:0  | A 7:0  |
      +--------+--------+--------+--------+
Reg1  | H 7:0  | G 7:0  | F 7:0  | E 7:0  |
      +--------+--------+--------+--------+
```

This simply indicates that each register is viewed as essentially a vector of four independent 8-bit integer values. Alternatively, think of A and E as values in Reg0 and Reg1 of processing element 0 (PE0), B and F as values in PE1's registers, and so forth.

The remainder of this document briefly reviews the basic classes of SIMD parallel operations on these integer vectors and how these functions can be implemented.

4.2.1 Polymorphic Operations

Some SWAR operations can be performed trivially using ordinary 32-bit integer operations, without concern for the fact that the operation is really intended to operate independently in parallel on these 8-bit fields. We call any such SWAR operation *polymorphic*, since the function is unaffected by the field types (sizes).

Testing if any field is non-zero is polymorphic, as are all bitwise logic operations. For example, an ordinary bitwise-and operation (C's & operator) performs a bitwise and no matter what the field sizes are. A simple bitwise and of the above registers yields:

```
         PE3          PE2          PE1          PE0
      +----------+----------+----------+----------+
Reg2  | D&H 7:0  | C&G 7:0  | B&F 7:0  | A&E 7:0  |
      +----------+----------+----------+----------+
```

Because the bitwise and operation always has the value of result bit k affected only by the values of the operand bit k values, all field sizes are supported using the same single instruction.

4.2.2 Partitioned Operations

Unfortunately, lots of important SWAR operations are not polymorphic. Arithmetic operations such as add, subtract, multiply, and divide are all subject to carry/borrow interactions between fields. We call such SWAR operations *partitioned*, because each such operation must effectively partition the operands and result to prevent interactions between fields. However, there are actually three different methods that can be used to achieve this effect.

Partitioned Instructions Perhaps the most obvious approach to implementing partitioned operations is to provide hardware support for "partitioned parallel instructions" that cut the carry/borrow logic between fields. This approach can yield the highest performance, but it requires a change to the processor's instruction set and generally places many restrictions on field size (e.g., 8-bit fields might be supported, but not 12-bit fields).

The AMD/Cyrix/Intel MMX, Digital MAX, HP MAX, and Sun VIS all implement restricted versions of partitioned instructions. Unfortunately, these different instruction set extensions have significantly different restrictions, making algorithms somewhat non-portable between them. For example, consider the following sampling of partitioned operations:

Instruction	AMD/Cyrix/Intel MMX	DEC MAX	HP MAX	Sun VIS
Absolute Difference		8		8
Merge Maximum		8, 16		
Compare	8, 16, 32			16, 32
Multiply	16			8x16
Add	8, 16, 32		16	16, 32

In the table, the numbers indicate the field sizes, in bits, for which each operation is supported. Even though the table omits many instructions including all the more exotic ones, it is clear that there are many differences. The direct result is that high-level languages (HLLs) really are not very effective as programming models, and portability is generally poor.

Unpartitioned Operations With Correction Code   Implementing partitioned operations using partitioned instructions can certainly be efficient, but what do you do if the partitioned operation you need is not supported by the hardware? The answer is that you use a series of ordinary instructions to perform the operation with carry/borrow across fields, and then correct for the undesired field interactions.

This is a purely software approach, and the corrections do introduce overhead, but it works with fully general field partitioning. This approach is also fully general in that it can be used either to fill gaps in the hardware support for partitioned instructions, or it can be used to provide full functionality for target machines that have no hardware support at all. In fact, by expressing the code sequences in a language like C, this approach allows SWAR programs to be fully portable.

The question immediately arises: precisely how inefficient is it to simulate SWAR partitioned operations using unpartitioned operations with correction code? Well, that is certainly the $64k question... but many operations are not as difficult as one might expect.

Consider implementing a four-element 8-bit integer vector add of two source vectors, x+y, using ordinary 32-bit operations.

An ordinary 32-bit add might actually yield the correct result, but not if any 8-bit field carries into the next field. Thus, our goal is simply to ensure that such a carry does not occur. Because adding two k-bit fields generates an at most $k+1$ bit result, we can ensure that no carry occurs by simply "masking out" the most significant bit of each field. This is done by bitwise anding each operand with $0x7f7f7f7f$ and then performing an ordinary 32-bit add.

```
t = ((x & 0x7f7f7f7f) + (y & 0x7f7f7f7f));
```

That result is correct... except for the most significant bit within each field. Computing the correct value for each field is simply a matter of doing two 1-bit partitioned adds of the most significant bits from x and y to the 7-bit carry result which was computed for t. Fortunately, a 1-bit partitioned add is implemented by an ordinary exclusive or operation. Thus, the result is simply:

```
(t ^ ((x ^ y) & 0x80808080))
```

Ok, well, maybe that isn't so simple. After all, it is six operations to do just four adds. However, notice that the number of operations is not a function of how many fields there are... so, with more fields, we get speedup. In fact, we may get speedup anyway simply because the fields were loaded and stored in a single (integer vector) operation, register availability may be improved, and there are fewer dynamic code scheduling dependencies (because partial word references are avoided).

Controlling Field Values While the other two approaches to partitioned operation implementation both center on getting the maximum space utilization for the registers, it can be computationally more efficient to instead control the field values so that inter-field carry/borrow events should never occur. For example, if we know that all the field values being added are such that no field overflow will occur, a partitioned add operation can be implemented using an ordinary add instruction; in fact, given this constraint, an ordinary add instruction appears polymorphic, and is usable for any field sizes without correction code. The question thus becomes how to ensure that field values will not cause carry/borrow events.

One way to ensure this property is to implement partitioned instructions that can restrict the range of field values. The Digital MAX vector minimum and maximum instructions can be viewed as hardware support for clipping field values to avoid inter-field carry/borrow.

However, suppose that we do not have partitioned instructions that can efficiently restrict the range of field values... is there a sufficient condition that can be cheaply imposed to ensure carry/borrow events will not interfere with adjacent fields? The answer lies in analysis of the arithmetic properties. Adding two k-bit numbers generates a result with at most $k+1$ bits; thus, a field of $k+1$ bits can safely contain such an operation despite using ordinary instructions.

Thus, suppose that the 8-bit fields in our earlier example are now 7-bit fields with 1-bit "carry/borrow spacers":

```
                PE3              PE2              PE1              PE0
      +----+-------+----+--------+----+--------+----+--------+
Reg0  | D' | D 6:0 | C' | C 6:0  | B' | B 6:0  | A' | A 6:0  |
      +----+-------+----+--------+----+--------+----+--------+
```

A vector of 7-bit adds is performed as follows. Let us assume that, prior to the start of any partitioned operation, all the carry spacer bits (A', B', C', and D') have the value 0. By simply executing an ordinary add operation, all the fields obtain the correct 7-bit values; however, some spacer bit values might now be 1. We can correct this by just one more conventional operation, masking-out the spacer bits. Our 7-bit integer vector add, x+y, is thus:

```
((x + y) & 0x7f7f7f7f)
```

This is just two instructions for four adds, clearly yielding good speedup.

The sharp reader may have noticed that setting the spacer bits to 0 does not work for subtract operations. The correction is, however, remarkably simple. To compute x-y, we simply ensure the initial condition that the spacers in x are all 1, while the spacers in y are all 0. In the worst case, we would thus get:

```
(((x | 0x80808080) - y) & 0x7f7f7f7f)
```

However, the additional bitwise or operation can often be optimized out by ensuring that the operation generating the value for x used | 0x80808080 rather than & 0x7f7f7f7f as the last step.

Which method should be used for SWAR partitioned operations? The answer is simply "whichever yields the best speedup." Interestingly, the ideal method to use may be different for different field sizes within the same program running on the same machine.

4.2.3 Communication & Type Conversion Operations

Although some parallel computations, including many operations on image pixels, have the property that the ith value in a vector is a function only of values that appear in the ith position of the operand vectors, this is generally not the case. For example, even pixel operations such as smoothing require values from adjacent pixels as operands, and transformations like FFTs require more complex (less localized) communication patterns.

It is not difficult to efficiently implement 1-dimensional nearest neighbor communication for SWAR using unpartitioned shift operations. For example, to move a value from PEi to PE(i+1), a simple shift operation suffices. If the fields are 8-bits in length, we would use:

```
(x << 8)
```

Still, it isn't always quite that simple. For example, to move a value from PE*i* to PE(*i*-1), a simple shift operation might suffice... but the C language does not specify if shifts right preserve the sign bit, and some machines only provide signed shift right. Thus, in the general case, we must explicitly zero the potentially replicated sign bits:

```
((x >> 8) & 0x00ffffff)
```

Adding "wrap-around connections" is also reasonably efficient using unpartitioned shifts. For example, to move a value from PE*i* to PE(*i*+1) with wraparound:

```
((x << 8) | ((x >> 24) & 0x000000ff))
```

The real problem comes when more general communication patterns must be implemented. Only the HP MAX instruction set supports arbitrary rearrangement of fields with a single instruction, which is called `Permute`. This `Permute` instruction is really misnamed; not only can it perform an arbitrary permutation of the fields, but it also allows repetition. In short, it implements an arbitrary `x[y]` operation.

Unfortunately, `x[y]` is very difficult to implement without such an instruction. The code sequence is generally both long and inefficient; in fact, it is sequential code. This is very disappointing. The relatively high speed of `x[y]` operations in the MasPar MP1/MP2 and Thinking Machines CM1/CM2/CM200 SIMD supercomputers was one of the key reasons these machines performed well. However, `x[y]` has always been slower than nearest neighbor communication, even on those supercomputers, so many algorithms have been designed to minimize the need for `x[y]` operations. In short, without hardware support, it is probably best to develop SWAR algorithms as though `x[y]` wasn't legal... or at least isn't cheap.

4.2.4 Recurrence Operations (Reductions, Scans, etc.)

A recurrence is a computation in which there is an apparently sequential relationship between values being computed. However, if these recurrences involve associative operations, it may be possible to recode the computation using a tree-structured parallel algorithm.

The most common type of parallelizable recurrence is probably the class known as associative reductions. For example, to compute the sum of a vector's values, one commonly writes purely sequential C code like:

```
t = 0;
for (i=0; i<MAX; ++i) t += x[i];
```

However, the order of the additions is rarely important. Floating point and saturation math can yield different answers if the order of additions is changed, but ordinary wrap-around integer additions will yield the same results independent of addition order. Thus, we can re-write this sequence into a tree-structured parallel summation in which we first add pairs of values, then pairs of those partial sums, and so forth, until a single final sum results. For a vector of four 8-bit values, just two addition steps are needed; the first step does two 8-bit adds, yielding two 16-bit result fields (each containing a 9-bit result):

```
t = ((x & 0x00ff00ff) + ((x >> 8) & 0x00ff00ff));
```

The second step adds these two 9-bit values in 16-bit fields to produce a single 10-bit result:

```
((t + (t >> 16)) & 0x000003ff)
```

HOWTO

Actually, the second step performs two 16-bit field adds... but the top 16-bit add is meaningless, which is why the result is masked to a single 10-bit result value.

Scans, also known as "parallel prefix" operations, are somewhat harder to implement efficiently. This is because, unlike reductions, scans produce partitioned results. For this reason, scans can be implemented using a fairly obvious sequence of partitioned operations.

4.3   MMX SWAR Under Linux

For Linux, IA32 processors are our primary concern. The good news is that AMD, Cyrix, and Intel all implement the same MMX instructions. However, MMX performance varies; for example, the K6 has only one MMX pipeline - the Pentium with MMX has two. The only really bad news is that Intel is still running those stupid MMX commercials.... ;-)

There are really three approaches to using MMX for SWAR:

1. Use routines from an MMX library. In particular, Intel has developed several "performance libraries," <http://developer.intel.com/drg/tools/ad.htm>, that offer a variety of hand-optimized routines for common multimedia tasks. With a little effort, many non-multimedia algorithms can be reworked to enable some of the most compute-intensive portions to be implemented using one or more of these library routines. These libraries are not currently available for Linux, but could be ported.

2. Use MMX instructions directly. This is somewhat complicated by two facts. The first problem is that MMX might not be available on the processor, so an alternative implementation must also be provided. The second problem is that the IA32 assembler generally used under Linux does not currently recognize MMX instructions.

3. Use a high-level language or module compiler that can directly generate appropriate MMX instructions. Such tools are currently under development, but none is yet fully functional under Linux. For example, at Purdue University (<http://dynamo.ecn.purdue.edu/~hankd/SWAR/>) we are currently developing a compiler that will take functions written in an explicitly parallel C dialect and will generate SWAR modules that are callable as C functions, yet make use of whatever SWAR support is available, including MMX. The first prototype module compilers were built in Fall 1996, however, bringing this technology to a usable state is taking much longer than was originally expected.

In summary, MMX SWAR is still awkward to use. However, with a little extra effort, the second approach given above can be used now. Here are the basics:

1. You cannot use MMX if your processor does not support it. The following GCC code can be used to test if MMX is supported on your processor. It returns 0 if not, non-zero if it is supported.

```
inline extern
int mmx_init(void)
{
        int mmx_available;

        __asm__ __volatile__ (
                /* Get CPU version information */
                "movl $1, %%eax\n\t"
                "cpuid\n\t"
                "andl $0x800000, %%edx\n\t"
                "movl %%edx, %0"
                : "=q" (mmx_available)
                : /* no input */
        );
        return mmx_available;
}
```

2. An MMX register essentially holds one of what GCC would call an `unsigned long long`. Thus, memory-based variables of this type become the communication mechanism between your MMX modules and the C programs that call them. Alternatively, you can declare your MMX data as any 64-bit aligned data structure (it is convenient to ensure 64-bit alignment by declaring your data type as a `union` with an `unsigned long long` field).

3. If MMX is available, you can write your MMX code using the `.byte` assembler directive to encode each instruction. This is painful stuff to do by hand, but not difficult for a compiler to generate. For example, the MMX instruction `PADDB MM0,MM1` could be encoded as the GCC in-line assembly code:

```
__asm__ __volatile__ (".byte 0x0f, 0xfc, 0xc1\n\t");
```

Remember that MMX uses some of the same hardware that is used for floating point operations, so code intermixed with MMX code must not invoke any floating point operations. The floating point stack also should be empty before executing any MMX code; the floating point stack is normally empty at the beginning of a C function that does not use floating point.

4. Exit your MMX code by executing the `EMMS` instruction, which can be encoded as:

```
__asm__ __volatile__ (".byte 0x0f, 0x77\n\t");
```

If the above looks very awkward and crude, it is. However, MMX is still quite young.... future versions of this document will offer better ways to program MMX SWAR.

5 Linux-Hosted Attached Processors

Although this approach has recently fallen out of favor, it is virtually impossible for other parallel processing methods to achieve the low cost and high performance possible by using a Linux system to host an attached parallel computing system. The problem is that very little software support is available; you are pretty much on your own.

5.1 A Linux PC Is A Good Host

In general, attached parallel processors tend to be specialized to perform specific types of functions.

Before becoming discouraged by the fact that you are somewhat on your own, it is useful to understand that, although it may be difficult to get a Linux PC to appropriately host a particular system, a Linux PC is one of the few platforms well suited to this type of use.

PCs make a good host for two primary reasons. The first is the cheap and easy expansion capability; resources such as more memory, disks, networks, etc., are trivially added to a PC. The second is the ease of interfacing. Not only are ISA and PCI bus prototyping cards widely available, but the parallel port offers reasonable performance in a completely non-invasive interface. The IA32 separate I/O space also facilitates interfacing by providing hardware I/O address protection at the level of individual I/O port addresses.

Linux also makes a good host OS. The free availability of full source code, and extensive "hacking" guides, obviously are a tremendous help. However, Linux also provides good near-real-time scheduling, and there is even a true real-time version of Linux at <http://luz.cs.nmt.edu/~rtlinux/>. Perhaps even more important is the fact that while providing a full UNIX environment, Linux can support development tools that were written to run under Microsoft DOS and/or Windows. MSDOS programs can execute within a Linux process using `dosemu` to provide a protected virtual machine that can literally run MSDOS. Linux support for Windows 3.xx programs is even more direct: free software such as `wine`, <http://www.linpro.no/wine/>, simulates Windows 3.11 well enough for most programs to execute correctly and efficiently within a UNIX/X environment.

The following two sections give examples of attached parallel systems that I'd like to see supported under Linux....

5.2 Did You DSP That?

There is a thriving market for high-performance DSP (Digital Signal Processing) processors. Although these chips were generally designed to be embedded in application-specific systems, they also make great attached parallel computers. Why?

- Many of them, such as the Texas Instruments (<http://www.ti.com/>) TMS320 and the Analog Devices (<http://www.analog.com/>) SHARC DSP families, are designed to construct parallel machines with little or no "glue" logic.

- They are cheap, especially per MIP or MFLOP. Including the cost of basic support logic, it is not unheard of for a DSP processor to be one tenth the cost of a PC processor with comparable performance.

- They do not use much power nor generate much heat. This means that it is possible to have a bunch of these chips powered by a conventional PC's power supply - and enclosing them in your PC's case will not turn it into an oven.

- There are strange-looking things in most DSP instruction sets that high-level (e.g., C) compilers are unlikely to use well - for example, "Bit Reverse Addressing." Using an attached parallel system, it is possible to straightforwardly compile and run most code on the host, while running the most time-consuming few algorithms on the DSPs as carefully hand-tuned code.

- These DSP processors are not really designed to run a UNIX-like OS, and generally are not very good as stand-alone general-purpose computer processors. For example, many do not have memory management hardware. In other words, they work best when hosted by a more general-purpose machine... such as a Linux PC.

Although some audio cards and modems include DSP processors that Linux drivers can access, the big payoff comes from using an attached parallel system that has four or more DSP processors.

Because the Texas Instruments TMS320 series, <http://www.ti.com/sc/docs/dsps/dsphome.htm>, has been very popular for a long time, and it is trivial to construct a TMS320-based parallel processor, there are quite a few such systems available. There are both integer-only and floating-point capable versions of the TMS320; older designs used a somewhat unusual single-precision floating-point format, but the new models support IEEE formats. The older TMS320C4x (aka, 'C4x) achieves up to 80 MFLOPS using the TI-specific single-precision floating-point format; in contrast, a single 'C67x will provide up to 1 GFLOPS single-precision or 420 MFLOPS double-precision for IEEE floating point calculations, using a VLIW-based chip architecture called VelociTI. Not only is it easy to configure a group of these chips as a multiprocessor, but in a single chip, the 'C8x multiprocessor will provide a 100 MFLOPS IEEE floating-point RISC master processor along with either two or four integer slave DSPs.

The other DSP processor family that has been used in more than a few attached parallel systems lately is the SHARC (aka, ADSP-2106x) from Analog Devices <http://www.analog.com/>. These chips can be configured as a 6-processor shared memory multiprocessor without external glue logic, and larger systems also can be configured using six 4-bit links/chip. Most of the larger systems seem targeted to military applications, and are a bit pricey. However, Integrated Computing Engines, Inc., <http://www.iced.com/>, makes an interesting little two-board PCI card set called GreenICE. This unit contains an array of 16 SHARC processors, and is capable of delivering a peak speed of about 1.9 GFLOPS using a single-precision IEEE format. GreenICE costs less than $5,000.

In my opinion, attached parallel DSPs really deserve a lot more attention from the Linux parallel processing community....

5.3 FPGAs And Reconfigurable Logic Computing

If parallel processing is all about getting the highest speedup, then why not build custom hardware? Well, we all know the answers; it costs too much, takes too long to develop, becomes useless when we change the algorithm even slightly, etc. However, recent advances in electrically reprogrammable FPGAs (Field Programmable Gate Arrays) have nullified most of those objections. Now, the gate density is high enough so that an entire simple processor can be built within a single FPGA, and the time to reconfigure (reprogram) an FPGA has also been dropping to a level where it is reasonable to reconfigure even when moving from one phase of an algorithm to the next.

This stuff is not for the weak of heart: you'll have to work with hardware description languages like VHDL for the FPGA configuration, as well as writing low-level code to interface to programs on the Linux host system. However, the cost of

FPGAs is low, and especially for algorithms operating on low-precision integer data (actually, a small superset of the stuff SWAR is good at), FPGAs can perform complex operations just about as fast as you can feed them data. For example, simple FPGA-based systems have yielded better-than-supercomputer times for searching gene databases.

There are other companies making appropriate FPGA-based hardware, but the following two companies represent a good sample.

Virtual Computer Company offers a variety of products using dynamically reconfigurable SRAM-based Xilinx FPGAs. Their 8/16 bit "Virtual ISA Proto Board" `<http://www.vcc.com/products/isa.html>` is less than $2,000.

The Altera ARC-PCI (Altera Reconfigurable Computer, PCI bus), `<http://www.altera.com/html/new/pressrel/pr_arc-pci.html>`, is a similar type of card, but uses Altera FPGAs and a PCI bus interface rather than ISA.

Many of the design tools, hardware description languages, compilers, routers, mappers, etc., come as object code only that runs under Windows and/or DOS. You could simply keep a disk partition with DOS/Windows on your host PC and reboot whenever you need to use them, however, many of these software packages may work under Linux using `dosemu` or Windows emulators like `wine`.

6 Of General Interest

The material covered in this section applies to all four parallel processing models for Linux.

6.1 Programming Languages And Compilers

I am primarily known as a compiler researcher, so I'd like to be able to say that there are lots of really great compilers automatically generating efficient parallel code for Linux systems. Unfortunately, the truth is that it is hard to beat the performance obtained by expressing your parallel program using various explicit communication and other parallel operations within C code that is compiled by GCC.

The following language/compiler projects represent some of the best efforts toward producing reasonably efficient code from high-level languages. Generally, each is reasonably effective for the kinds of programming tasks it targets, but none is the powerful general-purpose language and compiler system that will make you forever stop writing C programs to compile with GCC... which is fine. Use these languages and compilers as they were intended, and you'll be rewarded with shorter development times, easier debugging and maintenance, etc.

There are plenty of languages and compilers beyond those listed here (in alphabetical order). A list of freely available compilers (most of which have nothing to do with Linux parallel processing) is at `<http://www.idiom.com/free-compilers/>`.

6.1.1 Fortran 66/77/PCF/90/HPF/95

At least in the scientific computing community, there will always be Fortran. Of course, now Fortran doesn't mean the same thing it did in the 1966 ANSI standard. Basically, Fortran 66 was pretty simple stuff. Fortran 77 added tons of features, the most noticeable of which were the improved support for character data and the change of DO loop semantics. PCF (Parallel Computing Forum) Fortran attempted to add a variety of parallel processing support features to 77. Fortran 90 is a fully-featured modern language, essentially adding C++-like object-oriented programming features and parallel array syntax to the 77 language. HPF (High-Performance Fortran, `<http://www.crpc.rice.edu/HPFF/home.html>`), which has itself gone through two versions (HPF-1 and HPF-2), is essentially the enhanced, standardized, version of what many of us used to know as CM Fortran, MasPar Fortran, or Fortran D; it extends Fortran 90 with a variety of parallel processing enhancements, largely focussed on specifying data layouts. Finally, Fortran 95 represents a relatively minor enhancement and refinement of 90.

What works with C generally can also work with `f2c`, `g77` (a nice Linux-specific overview is at `<http://linux.uni-regensburg.de/psi_linux/gcc/html_g77/g77_91.html>`), or the commercial Fortran 90/95 products from `<http://extweb.nag.co.uk/nagware/NCNJNKNM.html>`. This is because all of these compilers eventually come down to the same code-generation used in the back-end of GCC.

Commercial Fortran parallelizers that can generate code for SMPs are available from `<http://www.kai.com/>` and `<http://www.psrv.com/vast/vast_parallel.html>`. It is not clear if these compilers will work for SMP Linux, but it should be possible given that the standard POSIX threads (i.e., LinuxThreads) work under SMP Linux.

The Portland Group, `<http://www.pgroup.com/>`, has commercial parallelizing HPF Fortran (and C, C++) compilers that generate code for SMP Linux; they also have a version targeting clusters using MPI or PVM. FORGE/spf/xHPF products at `<http://www.apri.com/>` might also be useful for SMPs or clusters.

Freely available parallelizing Fortrans that might be made to work with parallel Linux systems include:

- ADAPTOR (Automatic DAta Parallelism TranslaTOR, `<http://www.gmd.de/SCAI/lab/adaptor/adaptor_home.html>`), which can translate HPF into Fortran 77/90 code with MPI or PVM calls, but does not mention Linux.

- Fx `<http://www.cs.cmu.edu/~fx/Fx>` at Carnegie Mellon targets some workstation clusters, but Linux?

- HPFC (prototype HPF Compiler, `<http://www.cri.ensmp.fr/~coelho/hpfc.html>`) generates Fortran 77 code with PVM calls. Is it usable on a Linux cluster?

- Can PARADIGM (PARAllelizing compiler for DIstributed-memory General-purpose Multicomputers, `<http://www.crhc.uiuc.edu/Paradigm/>`) be used with Linux?

- The Polaris compiler, `<http://ece.www.ecn.purdue.edu/~eigenman/polaris/>`, generates Fortran code for shared memory multiprocessors, and may soon be retargeted to PAPERS Linux clusters.

- PREPARE, `<http://www.irisa.fr/EXTERNE/projet/pampa/PREPARE/prepare.html>`, targets MPI clusters... it is not clear if it can generate code to run on IA32 processors.

- Combining ADAPT and ADLIB, shpf (Subset High Performance Fortran compilation system, `<http://www.ccg.ecs.soton.ac.uk/Projects/shpf/shpf.html>`) is public domain and generates Fortran 90 with MPI calls... so, if you have a Fortran 90 compiler under Linux....

- SUIF (Stanford University Intermediate Form, see `<http://suif.stanford.edu/>`) has parallelizing compilers for both C and Fortran. This is also the focus of the National Compiler Infrastructure Project... so, is anybody targeting parallel Linux systems?

I'm sure that I have omitted many potentially useful compilers for various dialects of Fortran, but there are so many that it is difficult to keep track. In the future, I would prefer to list only those compilers known to work with Linux. Please email comments and/or corrections to *pplinux@ecn.purdue.edu*.

6.1.2   GLU (Granular Lucid)

GLU (Granular Lucid) is a very high-level programming system based on a hybrid programming model that combines intensional (Lucid) and imperative models. It supports both PVM and TCP sockets. Does it run under Linux? More information is available at `<http://www.csl.sri.com/GLU.html>`.

6.1.3   Jade And SAM

Jade is a parallel programming language that extends C to exploit coarse-grain concurrency in sequential, imperative programs. It assumes a distributed shared memory model, which is implemented by SAM for workstation clusters using PVM. More information is available at `<http://suif.stanford.edu/~scales/sam.html>`.

6.1.4   Mentat And Legion

Mentat is an object-oriented parallel processing system that works with workstation clusters and has been ported to Linux. Mentat Programming Language (MPL) is an object-oriented programming language based on C++. The Mentat run-time system uses something vaguely resembling non-blocking remote procedure calls. More information is available at `<http://www.cs.virginia.edu/~mentat/>`.

Legion `<http://www.cs.virginia.edu/~legion/>` is built on top on Mentat, providing the appearance of a single virtual machine across wide-area networked machines.

6.1.5 MPL (MasPar Programming Language)

Not to be confused with Mentat's MPL, this language was originally developed as the native parallel C dialect for the MasPar SIMD supercomputers. Well, MasPar isn't really in that business any more (they are now NeoVista Solutions, <http://www.neovista.com>, a data mining company), but their MPL compiler was built using GCC, so it is still freely available. In a joint effort between the University of Alabama at Huntsville and Purdue University, MasPar's MPL has been retargeted to generate C code with AFAPI calls (see section 3.6), and thus runs on both Linux SMPs and clusters. The compiler is, however, somewhat buggy... see <http://www.math.luc.edu/~laufer/mspls/papers/cohen.ps>.

6.1.6 PAMS (Parallel Application Management System)

Myrias is a company selling a software product called PAMS (Parallel Application Management System). PAMS provides very simple directives for virtual shared memory parallel processing. Networks of Linux machines are not yet supported. See <http://www.myrias.com/> for more information.

6.1.7 Parallaxis-III

Parallaxis-III is a structured programming language that extends Modula-2 with "virtual processors and connections" for data parallelism (a SIMD model). The Parallaxis software comprises compilers for sequential and parallel computer systems, a debugger (extensions to the gdb and xgbd debugger), and a large variety of sample algorithms from different areas, especially image processing. This runs on sequential Linux systems... an old version supported various parallel targets, and the new version also will (e.g., targeting a PVM cluster). More information is available at <http://www.informatik.uni-stuttgart.de/ipvr/bv/p3/p3.html>.

6.1.8 pC++/Sage++

pC++/Sage++ is a language extension to C++ that permits data-parallel style operations using "collections of objects" from some base "element" class. It is a preprocessor generating C++ code that can run under PVM. Does it run under Linux? More information is available at <http://www.extreme.indiana.edu/sage/>.

6.1.9 SR (Synchronizing Resources)

SR (Synchronizing Resources) is a concurrent programming language in which resources encapsulate processes and the variables they share; operations provide the primary mechanism for process interaction. SR provides a novel integration of the mechanisms for invoking and servicing operations. Consequently, all of local and remote procedure call, rendezvous, message passing, dynamic process creation, multicast, and semaphores are supported. SR also supports shared global variables and operations.

It has been ported to Linux, but it isn't clear what parallelism it can execute with. More information is available at <http://www.cs.arizona.edu/sr/www/index.html>.

6.1.10 ZPL And IronMan

ZPL is an array-based programming language intended to support engineering and scientific applications. It generates calls to a simple message-passing interface called IronMan, and the few functions which constitute this interface can be easily implemented using nearly any message-passing system. However, it is primarily targeted to PVM and MPI on workstation clusters, and Linux is supported. More information is available at <http://www.cs.washington.edu/research/projects/orca3/zpl/www/>.

6.2   Performance Issues

There are a lot of people who spend a lot of time benchmarking particular motherboards, network cards, etc., trying to determine which is the best. The problem with that approach is that by the time you've been able to benchmark something, it is no longer the best available; it even may have been taken off the market and replaced by a revised model with entirely different properties.

Buying PC hardware is like buying orange juice. Usually, it is made with pretty good stuff no matter what company name is on the label. Few people know, or care, where the components (or orange juice concentrate) came from. That said, there are some hardware differences that you should pay attention to. My advice is simply that you be aware of what you can expect from the hardware under Linux, and then focus your attention on getting rapid delivery, a good price, and a reasonable policy for returns.

An excellent overview of the different PC processors is given in `<http://www.pcguide.com/ref/cpu/fam/>`; in fact, the whole WWW site `<http://www.pcguide.com/>` is full of good technical overviews of PC hardware. It is also useful to know a bit about performance of specific hardware configurations, and the Linux Benchmarking HOWTO `<http://sunsite.unc.edu/LDP/HOWTO/Benchmarking-HOWTO.html>` is a good place to start.

The Intel IA32 processors have many special registers that can be used to measure the performance of a running system in exquisite detail. Intel VTune, `<http://developer.intel.com/design/perftool/vtune/>`, uses the performance registers extensively in a very complete code-tuning system... that unfortunately doesn't run under Linux. A loadable module device driver, and library routines, for accessing the Pentium performance registers is available from `<http://www.cs.umd.edu/users/akinlar/driver.html>`. Keep in mind that these performance registers are different on different IA32 processors; this code works only with Pentium, not with 486, Pentium Pro, Pentium II, K6, etc.

Another comment on performance is appropriate, especially for those of you who want to build big clusters and put them in small spaces. At least some modern processors incorporate thermal sensors and circuits that are used to slow the internal clock rate if operating temperature gets too high (an attempt to reduce heat output and improve reliability). I'm not suggesting that everyone should go buy a peltier device (heat pump) to cool each CPU, but you should be aware that high operating temperature does not just shorten component life - it also can directly reduce system performance. Do not arrange your computers in physical configurations that block airflow, trap heat within confined areas, etc.

Finally, performance isn't just speed, but also reliability and availability. High reliability means that your system almost never crashes, even when components fail... which generally requires special features like redundant power supplies and hot-swap motherboards. That usually isn't cheap. High availability refers to the concept that your system is available for use nearly all the time... the system may crash when components fail, but the system is quickly repaired and rebooted. There is a High-Availability HOWTO that discusses many of the basic issues. However, especially for clusters, high availablity can be achieved simply by having a few spares. I recommend at least one spare, and prefer to have at least one spare for every 16 machines in a large cluster. Discarding faulty hardware and replacing it with a spare can yield both higher availability and lower cost than a maintenance contract.

6.3   Conclusion - It's Out There

So, is anybody doing parallel processing using Linux? Yes!

It wasn't very long ago that a lot of people were wondering if the death of many parallel-processing supercomputer companies meant that parallel processing was on its way out. I didn't think it was dead then (see `<http://dynamo.ecn.purdue.edu/~hankd/Opinions/pardead.html>` for a fun overview of what I think really happened), and it seems quite clear now that parallel processing is again on the rise. Even Intel, which just recently stopped making parallel supercomputers, is proud of the parallel processing support in things like MMX and the upcoming IA64 EPIC (Explicitly Parallel Instruction Computer).

If you search for "Linux" and "parallel" with your favorite search engine, you'll find quite a few places are involved in parallel processing using Linux. In particular, Linux PC clusters seem to be popping-up everywhere. The appropriateness of Linux, combined with the low cost and high performance of PC hardware, have made parallel processing using Linux a popular approach to supercomputing for both small, budget-constrained, groups and large, well-funded, national research laboratories.

Various projects listed elsewhere in this document maintain lists of "kindred" research sites that have similar parallel Linux configurations. However, at `<http://yara.ecn.purdue.edu/~pplinux/Sites/>`, there is a hypertext document intended to provide photographs, descriptions, and contact information for all the various sites using Linux systems for parallel processing. To have information about your site posted there:

- You must have a "permanent" parallel Linux site: an SMP, cluster of machines, SWAR system, or PC with attached processor, which is configured to allow users to *execute parallel programs under Linux*. A Linux-based software environment (e.g., PVM, MPI, AFAPI) that directly supports parallel processing must be installed on the system. However, the hardware need not be dedicated to parallel processing under Linux, and may be used for completely different purposes when parallel programs are not being run.

- Request that your site be listed. Send your site information to *pplinux@ecn.purdue.edu*. Please follow the format used in other entries for your site information. *No site will be listed without an explicit request from the contact person for that site.*

There are 14 clusters in the current listing, but we are aware of at least several dozen Linux clusters world-wide. Of course, listing does not imply any endorsement, etc.; our hope is simply to increase awareness, research, and collaboration involving parallel processing using Linux.

HOWTO

Part XXXIV

"Database-SQL-RDBMS HOW-TO document for Linux (PostgreSQL Object Relational Database System)" Al Dev (Alavoor Vasudevan)

alavoor@yahoo.com

v11.0, 8 January 1999

This document is a "practical guide" to very quickly setup a SQL Database engine and front end tools on a Unix system. It also discusses the International standard language ANSI/ISO SQL and reviews the merits/advantages of the SQL database engine developed by the world-wide internet in an "open development" environment. It is about HOW-TO setup a next generation Object Relational SQL Database "PostgreSQL" on Unix system which can be used as a Application Database Server or as a Web Database Server. PostgreSQL implements a subset of International ISO/ANSI SQL standards of years 1998,92,89. This document also gives information on the database interface programs like Front End GUIs, RAD tools (Rapid Application Development), ODBC, JDBC drivers, "C", "C++", Java, Perl programming interfaces and Web Database Tools. Information given here applies to all Unix platforms and to all other SQL databases. It will be very useful for people who are new to Databases, SQL language and PostgreSQL. This document also has SQL tutorial, SQL syntax which would be very helpful for beginners. Experienced people will find this document as a useful reference guide. For students, the information given here will enable them to get the source code for PostgreSQL relational database system, from which they can learn as to how a RDBMS SQL database engine is created.

Contents

HOWTO

1   Introduction

The purpose of this document is to provide comprehensive list of pointers/URLs to quickly setup PostgreSQL and also to advocate the benefits of Open Source Code system like PostgreSQL, Linux.

Each and every computer system in the world needs a database to store/retrieve the information. The primary reason you use the computer is to store, retrieve and process information and do all these very quickly, thereby saving you time. At the same time, the system must be simple, robust, fast, reliable, economical and very easy to use. Database is the most **VITAL SYSTEM** as it stores mission critical information of every company in this world. The most popular database systems are based on the International Standard Organisation (ISO) SQL specifications, which in turn is based on ANSI SQL (American) standards. The most current specifications widely used in the industry are ISO/ANSI SQL 1992. Upcoming standard is the SQL 1998/99 which is also called SQL-3 is still under development. Popular database like Oracle, Sybase and Informix systems are based on these standards or are trying to implement these standards.

There are more than 20 varieties of commercial/internet database systems which are being used in the world and many more will be coming in the near future. Without a standard like ANSI/ISO SQL, it would be very difficult for the customer to develop a application once and run on all the database systems. Customer wants to develop an application ONCE using ISO SQL, ODBC, JDBC and deploy on all varieties of database systems in the world.

The world's most popular FREE Database which implements some of the ISO SQL, ANSI SQL/98, SQL/92 and ANSI SQL/89 RDBMS is PostgreSQL. PostgreSQL is next generation Object relational database and the future ANSI SQL standards like SQL 1998 (SQL-3) and beyond will increasingly deal with Object databases and Object data types. PostgreSQL is the only free RDBMS in the world which supports Object databases and SQL. This document will tell you how-to install the database, how to set up the Web database, application database, front end GUIs and interface programs. It is strongly advised that you MUST write your database applications 100 % compliant to standards of ISO/ANSI SQL, ODBC, JDBC so that your application is portable across multiple databases like PostgreSQL, Oracle, Sybase, Informix etc.

You get the highest quality, and lot many features with PostgreSQL as it follows 'Open Source Code development model'. Open Source Code model is the one where the complete source code is given to you and the development takes place on the internet by a extremely vast network of human brains. Future trend shows that most of the software development will take place on the so called "Information Super-Highway" which spans the whole globe. In the coming years, internet growth will be explosive which will further fuel rapid adoption of PostgreSQL by the database community.

By applying the principles of statistics, mathematics and science to software quality, you get the best quality of software only in a 'Open Source Code System' like PostgreSQL, wherein the source code is open to a very vast number of human brains inter-connected by the information super-highway. Greater the number of human brains working, the better will be the quality of software. Open Source Code model will also prevent **RE-INVENTION OF WHEELS**, eliminates **DUPLICATION OF WORK** and will be very economical, saves time in distribution and follows the modern economic laws of optimizing the national and global resources. Once a software work is done by others, than you **DO NOT** need to re-do that again. You will not be wasting your valuable time on something which had already been **WELL DONE**. Your time is extremely precious and it must be utilized efficiently, because you have only 8 hours per day for doing work!! As we will be entering the 21st century, there will be a change in the way that you get software for your use. Customers will give first preference for the open systems software like PostgreSQL, Linux, etc...

If you buy binaries, you will not get any equity and ownership of source code. Source code is a very valuable asset and binaries have no value. Buying software *may* become a thing of the past. You only need to buy good hardware, it is worth spending money on the hardware and get the software from internet. Important point is that it is the computer hardware which is **doing bulk of the work**. Hardware is the real work horse and software is just driving it. Computer hardware is so much more complex that only 6 nations out of 180 countries in the world so far have demonstrated the capability of designing and manufacturing computer chips/hardware. Design and manufacturing of computer chips is a advanced technology. It is a very complex process, capital intensive, requires large investments in plant and production machines which deal with 0.18 micron technology. On a single small silicon chip millions of transistors/circuits are densely packed. Companies like Applied Material, AMD, Intel, Cyrix, Hitachi, IBM and others spent significant number of man-years to master the high-technology like Chip Design, Micro-electronics and Nano-electronics. Micro means (one-millionth of meter 10^{-6}), Nano means (one-billionth of meter 10^{-9}). Current technology uses micro-electronics of about 0.35 micron using aluminum as conductors and 0.25 micron sizes using copper as conductors of electrons. In near future the technology of 0.10 micron with copper and even nano-electronics will be used to make computer chips. Aluminum conductors will be phased out by copper on computer chips, as copper is a better conductor of electrons. In photolithography process extreme ultraviolet, X-ray or electron-beam techniques will be used to etch circuits for feature size less than 0.15 micron. In about 20 years from now, silicon chips will be phased out by molecular computers and bio chips which will be billions of times faster than silicon chips. Molecules are a group of atoms. And atoms are tiny particles which makes up everything that you see in this world. Molecular computers will use the molecules of matter as ultra-fast electronic on/off switches. When the switch is ON it indicates 1, and when it is OFF it indicates 0. All the computer programs in this world are based on binary (numbers 1 and 0). Table below shows the progress and future advancement trends of computer chips.

```
              Advancement of chip capabilities in future
              ********************************************
```

Item/Year	1997	1999	2001	2003	2012	2020
Feature size(micron)	0.25	0.18	0.15	0.13	0.05	<.00001
Wafer size(mm)	200	300	300	300	450	Mol/Bio
Min Operating Volt.	1.8-2.5	1.5-1.8	1.2-1.5	1.2-1.5	0.5-0.6	<0.001
Max power dissip.	70	90	110	130	175	600
On-chip freq. (MHz)	750	1,250	1,500	2,100	10,000	>50,000
DRAM capacity	256 MB	1 GB	2 GB	4 GB	256 GB	>1000GB

As you can see, it is hardware that is high technology and important and software is a less difficult technology. Hence, manufacturing hardware/hard-goods is vital for national economy! Companies like Compaq, Dell, Sun Microsystems, HP, IBM who manufacture computers are major contributors to U.S economy today and in the future!!

On other hand, each and every country in the world develops/makes software. In fact, any person in this world with a small low-cost PC can create a Oracle database server system. But it would take him about 10 years (Oracle database server is about 10 man-years of work). One man-year is one person working full-time for one full year. If 10 people work for a year than it is 10 man-years spent.

Databases like Oracle, Informix, Sybase, IBM DB2 (Unix) are written using the "C" language and binaries are created by compiling the source code and than they are shipped out to customers. Oracle, Sybase, Informix databases are 100 % "C" programs!!

Since a lot of work had been done on PostgreSQL for the past 12 years, it does not make sense to re-create from scratch another database system which satisfies ANSI/ISO SQL. It will be a great advantage to take the existing code and add missing features or enhancements to PostgreSQL and start using it immediately.

PostgreSQL is not just a free database but it is a good quality 'Internet Product'. Prediction is that demand for "Made in Internet" products will grow exponentially as it is capable of maintaining a high quality, low cost, extremely large user-base and developer-base. Those nations who do not use the 'Made in Internet' products will be seriously missing "World-wide Internet Revolution" and will be left far behind other countries. The reason is "Internet" itself is the world's **LARGEST** software company!

2   Other Formats of this Document

This document is published in 10 different formats namely - DVI, Postscript, Latex, LyX, GNU-info, HTML, RTF(Rich Text Format), Plain-text, Unix man pages and SGML.

- You can get this HOWTO document as a single file tar ball in HTML, DVI, Postscript or SGML formats from - `<ftp://sunsite.unc.edu/pub/Linux/docs/HOWTO/other-formats/>`
- Plain text format is in: `<ftp://sunsite.unc.edu/pub/Linux/docs/HOWTO>`
- Translations to other languages like French, German, Spanish, Chinese, Japanese are in `<ftp://sunsite.unc.edu/pub/Linux/docs/HOWTO>` Any help from you to translate to other languages is welcome.

The document is written using a tool called "SGML tool" which can be got from - `<http://www.xs4all.nl/~cg/sgmltools/>` Compiling the source you will get the following commands like

- sgml2html databasehowto.sgml (to generate html file)
- sgml2rtf databasehowto.sgml (to generate RTF file)
- sgml2latex databasehowto.sgml (to generate latex file)

This document is located at -

- `<http://sunsite.unc.edu/LDP/HOWTO/PostgreSQL-HOWTO.html>`

Also you can find this document at the following mirrors sites -

- `<http://www.caldera.com/LDP/HOWTO/PostgreSQL-HOWTO.html>`
- `<http://www.WGS.com/LDP/HOWTO/PostgreSQL-HOWTO.html>`
- `<http://www.cc.gatech.edu/linux/LDP/HOWTO/PostgreSQL-HOWTO.html>`
- `<http://www.redhat.com/linux-info/ldp/HOWTO/PostgreSQL-HOWTO.html>`
- Other mirror sites near you (network-address-wise) can be found at `<http://sunsite.unc.edu/LDP/hmirrors.html>` select a site and go to directory /LDP/HOWTO/PostgreSQL-HOWTO.html

In order to view the document in dvi format, use the xdvi program. The xdvi program is located in tetex-xdvi*.rpm package in Redhat Linux which can be located through ControlPanel | Applications | Publishing | TeX menu buttons.

```
        To read dvi document give the command -
              xdvi -geometry 80x90 howto.dvi
        And resize the window with mouse. See man page on xdvi.
          To navigate use Arrow keys, Page Up, Page Down keys, also
```

```
you can use 'f', 'd', 'u', 'c', 'l', 'r', 'p', 'n' letter
keys to move up, down, center, next page, previous page etc.
To turn off expert menu press 'x'.
```

You can read postscript file using the program 'gv' (ghostview) or 'ghostscript'. The ghostscript program is in ghostscript*.rpm package and gv program is in gv*.rpm package in Redhat Linux which can be located through ControlPanel | Applications | Graphics menu buttons. The gv program is much more user friendly than ghostscript. Also ghostscript and gv are available on other platforms like OS/2, Windows 95 and NT, you view this document even on those platforms.

```
To read postscript document give the command -
       gv howto.ps

To use ghostscript give -
       ghostscript howto.ps
```

CAUTION: This document is large, total number of pages (postscript) if printed will be approximately 113 pages.

You can read HTML format document using Netscape Navigator, Microsoft Internet explorer, Redhat Baron Web browser or any of the 10 other web browsers.

You can read the latex, LyX output using LyX a X-Windows front end to latex.

3   Laws of Physics applies to Software!

In this chapter, it will be shown how science plays a important role in the creation of various objects like software, this universe, mass, atoms, energy and even yourself! This chapter also shows why knowledge of science is very important BEFORE you start using the products of science. Objects include everything - for example PostgreSQL, time, mass, energy, planets, sun, moon, stars, galaxies, super-clusters, humans etc... are objects made by science. This chapter also shows how laws of science and statistics favour the open-source code system like PostgreSQL and Linux. As the internet speed is increasing everyday, and internet is becoming more and MORE reliable, the open-source code system will gain very rapid momentum. And, if rules of statistics and laws of physics are correct than the closed source-code systems will eventually VANISH from this planet.

The paragraphs given below will show you - "how vast science is, how important it is for man and how it impacts software projects like PostgreSQL, Linux".

Developing a project like PostgreSQL requires resources like energy and time, hence PostgreSQL is a product of energy and time. Since energy and time can be explained only by science, there is a direct co-relation between physics and software projects like PostgreSQL, Linux.

Laws of science (Physics) applies everywhere and at all the times, to anything that you do, even while you are developing the software projects. Physics is in action even while you are talking (sound waves), walking (friction between ground and your feet), reading a book or writing software. Various branches of sciences like physics, chemistry etc all merge into one grand region called Mathematics (which is also known as the Queen of all Sciences). Everything in this world has a deep root in mathematics, including PostgreSQL. PostgreSQL uses 'Modern Algebra' which is a tiny branch of mathematics. Modern algebra deals with 'Set Theory', 'Relational Algebra', science of Groups, Rings, Collections, Sets, Unions, Intersections, Exclusions, Domains, Lists, etc...

The software like PostgreSQL is existing today because of the energy and time. It is the energy which made this world, human brains and many other things! And mass and energy are ONE and the **SAME** entity! The fact that mass and energy are same was unknown to people 100 years ago!

Cells in the human brains consume energy while processing (creating software), by converting the chemical energy from food into electrical and heat energy. Even while you are reading this paragraph, the cells in your brain are burning out the fuel and are using tiny amounts of energy. So STOP READING NOW ! The energy activity of neurons (brain cells) can be measured in the laboratory. For example, there are many instruments like 'Lie Detectors' and other medical instruments which can measure the energy activities of brain. All of these implies that human brain is a thermodynamic heat engine. Because human brain is a thermodynamic engine, the laws of thermodynamics applies to brain and hence thermodynamics has indirect effects on software like PostgreSQL.

As per science, it is impossible to build any system or theory (including a database software system) which will be 100 % perfect and bug free. It is like chasing a mirage, we will **NEVER** reach the goal of perfect system or theory. Detailed mathematical equations/discussions to prove that 'perfect system' (as well as 'imperfect system') is impossible, is a advanced topic and is beyond the scope of this document. And such a mathematical discussion deals with infinite number of dimensions (as well as primary dimensions) which are existing in nature. Unfortunately humans can see or feel only 4 dimensions but mathematics can easily explore many other dimensions. Other dimensions are **'infinitely smaller'** than the atoms and atoms themselves are very minute which human eyes cannot see them! Mathematics is very powerful as it can analyze and explain the birth/death of our universe. Our universe is almost **zero size** if you look from other universe and vice versa. That is, our universe is not visible (does not exist) for persons in other universe! And vice versa!! Theoretically, you can exit out of our universe and travel vast distances (billions of light years) in zero time and re-enter universe at a different point of space-time! Distance between our universe and other universes is actually zero!

Even though there are infinite number of dimensions, they all can be derived/generated from a small number of PRIMARY dimensions. That is, infinite number of dimensions can combine and collapse into primary dimensions. Primary dimensions simply absorb other dimensions without themselves getting destroyed. Mathematicians use these primary dimensions to understand the birth and death of universes. The universe where you are currently living started with a **BIG BANG** billions of years ago (roughly 20 billion years ago) which was caused by the interactions of atomic particles of other dimensions. Just before the big bang there was a tiny point where length, breadth, height and time was ZERO (that is, our universe was NOT THERE!!) and other universes and primary dimensions were existing. Time itself was NOT there and atoms, stars, planets, galaxies were NOT there! The atoms inside your body were NOT there!! So many things happened even BEFORE the time was born!

Big bang and hence birth of our universe was caused by few atoms of primary dimensions. **SOMEONE** (something?) caused the dashing of few tiny atoms of other dimensions to create our universe, and new dimensions time, length, breadth, height was born! We see someone's hand in this process. That process is **not very well understood** by man. Man is trying to generate another universe in the lab by simulating the big bang event (Huge accelerator is under construction in Europe, another construction in Dallas, USA was stopped by US congress due to budget cuts). There are atoms of other dimensions just as we have atoms in our universe. Theoretically, you can create/generate infinite number of universes! This process is reversible, that is our universe can completely close down and vanish into few atoms of other dimensions! It is similar in anology as to how YOU were born from two tiny cells which DASHED against each other to create one single cell. That single tiny cell divided and multiplied into 6 trillion cells to become a 6 foot tall human (that is you!). There are some similarities between humans and universes, universes are born and later die, very much similar to humans.

Since PERFECT state (as well as IMPERFECT state) is impossible, universes like ours are born and later die down in a cyclic process. BUT there can NO PERFECT death, only transformation is permitted by science! Our universe is currently expanding at a tremendous rate, it is not static but is very dynamic. This universe will keep expanding untill something interferes to collapse this universe by applying pressures with external dimensions to aborb and annihilate our universe!! Two possibilities are - removing the mass from our universe via black holes (a slow process), or injecting more mass into our universe via white holes (a rapid big crunch process). There can be millions of universes in existence but there can be very few universes which are built from primary dimensions. You are not only made up of atoms of this universe but also by atoms of other dimensions! In black holes the atoms and particles from our universe get sucked into and are completely transformed and converted to particles of other dimensions! In the center of black hole time is zero and length, breadth, height is zero! And black hole is EXIT/ENTRY door to and from other universes. Entry/Exit doors to other universes can open up anywhere, even inside your body!

There can be infinite number of colors, computer langauages, computer chip designs and theories but there CANNOT be ONE SINGLE PERFECT color, computer language, design or system! What you can have is only a NEAR PERFECT color(wavelength), system, database, or theory! Nature is like a Kaliedoscope.

By combining the energies of millions of people around the world via internet it is possible to achieve a **NEAR PERFECT** system (including a database software system). Individually, the energy of each person will be minute, but by networking a large number of people, the total energy will be huge which can be focused on a project to generate a near perfect system. Human beings are creatures of finite energy and resources, frequently guilty of errors ranging from the trivial to the profound. Because of our propensity for error varies broadly with particular skills, particular experience and the vagaries of the moment, the discovery and elimination of software bugs produced by ordinary human error can be greatly facilitated by bringing a great many minds to bear on the problem. In addition, more individuals represent extra person hours of code and its asocciated function.

It is very clear that internet can network a vast number of people, which implies internet has a lot of energy and time which can produce much higher quality software products in much shorter time as compared to commercial companies. Even big companies like Microsoft, IBM cannot overpower and overrule the laws of Physics but will eventually **SURRENDER UNTO** laws of science!

Today, there are too many SQL RDBMS databases in the world aiming at only one specification ANSI/ISO SQL. **Man must not waste his time creating too many SIMILAR/IDENTICAL software packages** and there are many other topics in science which need good attention.

Conclusion is - because of laws of science, 'open source code' system like PostgreSQL, Linux will be always much better than 'closed source code' system and it is possible to prove this statement scientifically.

4   What is PostgreSQL ?

PostgreSQL Version 6.4 is a free database, complete source code is given to you and is a Object-Relational Database System near compliant (getting closer) with ANSI SQL1998,92,89 and runs on diverse hardware platforms and Operating systems.

```
Sometimes emergency bug fix patches are released after the
GA release of PostgreSQL. You can apply these optional patches
depending upon the needs of your application. Follow these
steps to apply the patches -
Change directory to postgresql source directory
        cd /usr/src/postgresql6.4
        patch -p0 < patchfile
        make clean
        make
See also manual page do 'man patch'
```

The patch files are located in

*   PostgreSQL patches : `<ftp://ftp.postgresql.org/pub/patches>`

The ultimate objective and the final goal of PostgreSQL is to become 100 % compliant to ANSI/ISO SQL and also to become the number ONE open generic Database in the world. PostgreSQL will also guide, steer, control, monitor and dictate the future of ANSI/ISO SQL. That is, the implementation and ideas first take place in PostgreSQL and than later be incorporated into the ANSI/ISO SQL.

Informix Universal server (released 1997) is based on earlier version of PostgreSQL because Informix bought Illustra Inc. and integrated with Informix. Illustra database was completely based on Postgres (earlier version of PostgreSQL).

PostgreSQL is an enhancement of the POSTGRES database management system, a next-generation DBMS research prototype. While PostgreSQL retains the powerful data model and rich data types of POSTGRES, it replaces the PostQuel query language with an extended subset of SQL.

PostgreSQL development is being performed by a team of Internet developers who all subscribe to the PostgreSQL development mailing list. The current coordinator is Marc G. Fournier

*   *scrappy@postgreSQL.org*

HOWTO

This team is now responsible for all current and future development of PostgreSQL. Ofcourse, the database customer himself is the developer of PostgreSQL! The development load is distributed among a very large number of database end-users on internet.

The authors of PostgreSQL 1.01 were Andrew Yu and Jolly Chen. Many others have contributed to the porting, testing, debugging and enhancement of the code. The original Postgres code, from which PostgreSQL is derived, was the effort of many graduate students, undergraduate students, and staff programmers working under the direction of Professor Michael Stonebraker at the University of California, Berkeley.

The original name of the software at Berkeley was Postgres. When SQL functionality was added in 1995, its name was changed to Postgres95. The name was changed at the end of 1996 to PostgreSQL.

Millions of PostgreSQL is installed as Database servers, Web database servers and Application data servers. It is much more advanced and is a object oriented relational database (ORDBMS).

PostgreSQL can store more data types than traditional datatypes like integer, characters, etc. - you get to create user-defined types, functions, inheritance etc. PostgreSQL runs on Solaris, SunOS, HPUX, AIX, Linux, Irix, Digital Unix, BSDi,NetBSD, FreeBSD, SCO unix, NEXTSTEP, Unixware and all and every flavor of Unix. Port to Windows 95/NT is underway.

- Title: PostgreSQL SQL RDBMS Database (Object Relational Database Management System)
- Current Version: 6.4
- Age: PostgreSQL is 12 years old. Developed since 1985
- Authors: Developed by millions/universities/companies on internet for the past 12 YEARS

PostgreSQL and related items in this document are subject to the following COPYRIGHT.

5 Where to get it ?

You can buy Redhat Linux CDROM, Debian Linux CDROM or Slackware Linux CDROM which already contains the Postgresql in package form (both source code and binaries) from :

- Linux System Labs Web site: <http://www.lsl.com/> 7 (U.S. dollars)

- Cheap Bytes Inc Web site: `<http://www.cheapbytes.com/>` 7 (U.S. dollars)
- Debian Main Web site : `<http://www.debian.org/vendors.html>`

PostgreSQL organisation is also selling 'PostgreSQL CDROM' which contains the complete source code and binaries for many Unix operating systems as well as full documentation.

- PostgreSQL CDROM from main Web site at : `<http://www.postgresql.org>` 30 (U.S. dollars)

Binaries only distribution of PostgreSQL:

- You can run PostgreSQL without compiling the source. Get binaries for Intel-Linux from `<ftp://www.redhat.com/pub/contrib/i386/>` file is postgresql-6.4.i386.rpm. This is in the redhat package 'rpm' format and it contains both source and binaries for PostgreSQL.
- Binaries site for Solaris, HPUX, AIX, IRIX, Linux : `<ftp://ftp.postgresql.org/pub/bindist>` If you compile on any platform please upload to site, so that it will be useful for others.
- ftp site : Get binaries for Intel-Linux from `<ftp://ftp.redhat.com/pub/contrib/i386/>` file is postgresql-6.4.i386.rpm. This is in the redhat package 'rpm' format and it contains both source and binaries for PostgreSQL.

WWW Web sites:

- Primary Web site: `<http://www.postgresql.org/>`
- Secondary Web site: `<http://logical.thought.net/postgres95/>`
- `<http://www.itm.tu-clausthal.de/mirrors/postgres95/>`
- `<http://s2k-ftp.cs.berkeley.edu:8000/postgres95/>`
- `<http://xenium.pdi.net/PostgreSQL/>`
- `<http://s2k-ftp.cs.berkeley.edu:8000/postgres95/>`

The ftp sites are listed below :-

- Primary FTP: `<ftp://ftp.postgresql.org/pub>`
- Secondary FTP: `<ftp://ftp.chicks.net/pub/postgresql>`
- `<ftp://ftp.emsi.priv.at/pub/postgres/>`
- `<ftp://ftp.itm.tu-clausthal.de/pub/mirrors/postgres95>`
- `<ftp://rocker.sch.bme.hu/pub/mirrors/postgreSQL>`
- `<ftp://ftp.jaist.ac.jp/pub/dbms/postgres95>`
- `<ftp://ftp.luga.or.at/pub/postgres95>`
- `<ftp://postgres95.vnet.net:/pub/postgres95>`
- `<ftp://ftpza.co.za/mirrors/postgres>`
- `<ftp://sunsite.auc.dk/pub/databases/postgresql>`
- `<ftp://ftp.task.gda.pl/pub/software/postgresql>`
- `<ftp://xenium.pdi.net/pub/PostgreSQL>`

PostgreSQL source code is also available at all the mirror sites of sunsite unc (total of about 1000 sites around the globe). It is inside the Red Hat Linux distribution in /pub/contrib/i386/postgresql.rpm file.

- For list of mirror sites go to `<ftp://sunsite.unc.edu>`

6 PostgreSQL Supports Extremely Large Databases greater than 200 Gig

Performance of 32-bit cpu machines will decline rapidly when the database size exceeds 5 GigaByte. You can run 30 gig database on 32-bit cpu but the performance will be degraded. Machines with 32-bit cpu imposes a limitation of 2 GB on RAM, 2 GB on file system sizes and other limitations on the operating system.

For extremely large databases, it is strongly advised to use 64-bit machines like Digital Alpha cpu, Sun Ultra-sparc 64-bit cpu, Silicon graphics 64-bit cpu, Intel Merced IA-64 cpu, HPUX 64bit machines or IBM 64-bit machines. Compile PostgreSQL under 64-bit cpu and it can support huge databases and large queries. Performance of PostgreSQL for queries on large tables and databases will be several times faster than PostgreSQL on 32-bit cpu machines. Advantage of 64-bit machines are that you get very large memory addressing space and the operating system can support very large file-systems, provide better performance with large databases, support much larger memory (RAM), have more capabilities etc..

7 How can I trust PostgreSQL ? Regression Test Package builds customer confidence

To validate PostgreSQL, regression test package (src/test/regress) is included in the distribution. Regression test package will verify the standard SQL operations as well as the extensibility capabilities of PostgreSQL. The test package already contains hundreds of SQL test programs.

You should use the computer's high-speed power to validate the PostgreSQL, instead of using human brain power. Computers can carry out software regression tests millions or even billions of times faster than humans can. Modern computers can run billions of SQL tests in a very short time. In the near future the speed of computer will be several zillion times faster than human brain! Hence, it makes sense to use the power of computer to validate the software.

You can add more tests just in case you need to, and can upload to the primary PostgreSQL web site if you feel that it will be useful to others on internet. Regression test package helps build customer confidence and trust in PostgreSQL and facilitates rapid deployment of PostgreSQL on production systems.

Regression test package can be taken as a **"VERY SOLID"** technical document mutually agreed upon between the developers and end-users. PostgreSQL developers extensively use the regression test package during development period and also before releasing the software to public to ensure good quality.

Capablilities of PostgreSQL are directly reflected by the regression test package. If a functionality, syntax or feature exists in the regression package than it is supported, and all others which are NOT listed in the package MAY not be supported by PostgreSQL!! You may need to verify those and add it to regression package.

8 GUI FrontEnd Tool for PostgreSQL (Graphical User Interface)

PostgreSQL has Tcl/Tk interface library in the distribution called 'pgTcl'. Tcl/Tk is a Rapid Application Development tool and is a scripting language. Using Tcl/TK, you can develop applications once and run it everywhere on NT, Win 95, Linux, Apple Macintosh iMac, OS/2 and all unixes. Tcl stands for 'Tool Command Language' and Tk is 'Tool Kit'. There is a IDE (integrated development environment) for Tcl/Tk called SpecTcl. Check for this rpm package under Redhat linux distribution or at the sunscript site given below.

Perl is strongly recommended as a scripting language, since it is the most widely used and very powerful and is available on every hardware and OS platforms. Perl-Tk or Perl-Qt or C++ QtEZ or C++ Lesstiff is strongly recommended. A combination of Perl, C and Tk will satisfy the needs of most projects, considering the time resources, speed of executable and ease of programming. Note that Java programs run very slow. Even C++ programs run slower than C programs. The C programs run the fastest as compared to other languages. Perl programs can be converted to "C" program using Perl2C program and than compiled which will run fast.

Perl is used for programming 90 % of internet scripts in the world. So you will have only one language ("Perl") for all your needs - in applications as well as internet. See Perl Database Interface of this document at 11 ()

You should ponder over the strong points of Perl vis-a-vis Tcl/Tk before starting any project on Tcl. Tcl/TK is usually shipped with every linux cdrom. Also you can get it from these sites -

- Tcl/Tk `<http://www.scriptics.com>`
- Object oriented extension of Tcl called INCR at `<http://www.tcltk.com>`
- Visual TCL site `<http://www.neuron.com>`
- Visual TCL Redhat rpm at `<ftp://ftp.redhat.com/pub/contrib/i386/visualtcl*.rpm>`
- `<http://sunscript.sun.com/>`
- `<http://sunscript.sun.com/TclTkCore/>`
- `<ftp://ftp.sunlabs.com/pub/tcl/tcl8.0a2.tar.Z>`
- Reference text book: Many textbooks on TCL/TK are available in the market.

9 Integrated Development Environment Tools for PostgreSQL (GUI IDE)

Check out the following development tools which you can use in conjunction with ODBC/JDBC drivers. These are similar to Borland C++ Builder, Borland JBuilder.

Vibe is a Java and C++ IDE (Integrated Development Environment) that won Unix Review's IDE of the year.

- More information on Vibe is at `<http://www.LinuxMall.com/products/00487.html>`
- 'QT' an application framework for Windows95/NT and Unix available at `<http://www.troll.no>` and ftp site is at `<ftp://ftp.troll.no>`

You can also use Borland C++ Builder, Delphi, Borland JBuilder, PowerBuilder on Windows95 connecting to PostgreSQL on unix box through ODBC/JDBC drivers.

See also **PERL** Database Interface of this document at 11 () Perl and C/C++ is strongly recommended as the choice of langauge for IDE.

Free of cost IDE Tools -

Check the CDROM of redhat linux distribution.

- Lesstiff Motif tool `<ftp://ftp.redhat.com/pub/contrib/i386/lesstiff*.rpm>`
- FreeBuilder `<ftp://ftp.redhat.com/pub/contrib/i386/free*.rpm>`
- SpecTCL `<ftp://ftp.redhat.com/pub/contrib/i386/spec*.rpm>`
- JccWarrior `<ftp://ftp.redhat.com/pub/contrib/i386/jcc*.rpm>`
- Kanchenjunga Java RAD Tool for PostgreSQL `<http://www.man.ac.uk/~whaley/kj/kanch.html>`
- Applixware Tool `<http://www.redhat.com>`
- XWPE X Windows Programming Environment `<http://www.rpi.edu/~payned/xwpe/>` `<ftp://ftp.redhat.com/pub/contrib/i386/xwpe*.rpm>`
- XWB X Windows Work Bench `<ftp://ftp.redhat.com/pub/contrib/i386/xwb*.rpm>`
- NEdit `<ftp://ftp.redhat.com/pub/contrib/i386/nedit*.rpm>`

HOWTO

10 Interface Drivers for PostgreSQL

10.1 ODBC Drivers for PostgreSQL

ODBC stands for 'Open DataBase Connectivity' is a popular standard for accessing information from various databases from different vendors. Applications written using the ODBC drivers are guaranteed to work with various databases like PostgreSQL, Oracle, Sybase, Informix etc..

- PostODBC is already included in the distribution. See main web site `<http://www.postgresql.org>`. It is included on the PostgreSQL CDROM.

- `<http://www.openlinksw.com>` Open Link Software Corporation is selling ODBC for PostgreSQL and other databases. Open Link also is giving away free ODBC (limited seats) check them out.

- Insight ODBC for PostgreSQL `<http://www.insightdist.com/psqlodbc>` This is the official PostODBC site.

There is a project called the FreeODBC Pack Package . There's no PostgreSQL Version there, maybe you can help.

- `<http://www.ids.net/~bjepson/freeODBC/>` This is a free of cost version of ODBC.

10.2 UDBC Drivers for PostgreSQL

UDBC is a static version of ODBC independent of driver managers and DLL support, used to embed database connectivity support directly into applications.

- `<http://www.openlinksw.com>` Open Link Software Corporation is selling UDBC for PostgreSQL and other databases. Open Link also is giving away free UDBC (limited seats) check them out.

10.3 JDBC Drivers for PostgreSQL

JDBC stands for 'Java DataBase Connectivity'. Java is a platform independent programming language developed by Sun Microsystems. Java programmers are encouraged to write database applications using the JDBC to facilitate portability across databases like PostgreSQL, Oracle, informix, etc. If you write Java applications you can get JDBC drivers for PostgreSQL from the following sites:

JDBC driver is already included in the PostgreSQL distribution.

- `<http://www.demon.co.uk/finder/postgres/index.html>` Sun's Java connectivity to PostgreSQL

- `<ftp://ftp.ai.mit.edu/people/rst/rst-jdbc.tar.gz>`

- `<http://www.openlinksw.com>` Open Link Software Corporation is selling JDBC for PostgreSQL and other databases. Open Link also is giving away free JDBC (limited seats) check them out.

- JDBC UK site `<http://www.retep.org.uk/postgres>`

- JDBC FAQ site `<http://eagle.eku.edu/tools/jdbc/faq.html>`

The JDBC home, guide and FAQ are located at -

- JDBC HOME `<http://splash.javasoft.com/jdbc>`

- JDBC guide `<http://www.javasoft.com/products/jdk/1.1/docs/guide/jdbc>`

- JDBC FAQ `<http://javanese.yoyoweb.com/JDBC/FAQ.txt>`

10.4 Java for PostgreSQL

Java programmers can find these for PostgreSQL very useful.

- `<ftp://ftp.redhat.com/pub/contrib/i386>` and see postgresql-jdbc-*.rpm
- `<http://www.blackdown.org>`

11 Perl Database Interface (DBI) Driver for PostgreSQL

11.1 Perl 5 interface for PostgreSQL

PERL is an acronym for 'Practical Extraction and Report Language'. Perl is available on each and every operating system and hardware platform in the world. You can use Perl on Windows95/NT, Apple Macintosh iMac, all flavors of Unix (Solaris, HPUX, AIX, Linux, Irix, SCO etc..), mainframe MVS, desktop OS/2, OS/400, Amdahl UTS and many others. Perl runs **EVEN** on many unpopular or generally-unknown operating systems and hardware!! So do not be surprised if you see perl running on a very rarely used operating system. You can imagine the vast extent of the user base and developer base of Perl.

Perl interface for PostgreSQL is included in the distribution of PostgreSQL. Check in src/pgsql_perl5 directory.

- Pgsql_perl5 contact Email: *E.Mergl@bawue.de*
- Another source from - `<ftp://ftp.kciLink.com/pub/PostgresPerl-1.3.tar.gz>`
- Perl Home page : `<http://www.perl.com/perl/index.html>`
- Perl tutorial, look for Tutorial title at : `<http://reference.perl.com/>`
- Perl FAQ is at : `<http://www.yahoo.com/Computers_and_Internet/Programming_Languages/Perl/>`
- Perl GUI User Interfaces Perl-Qt rpm : `<ftp://ftp.redhat.com/pub/contrib/i386>` and look for PerlQt-1.06-1.i386.rpm
- Perl GUI User Interfaces Perl-Qt : `<http://www.accessone.com/~jql/perlqt.html>`
- Perl GUI User Interfaces Perl-XForms : `<ftp://ftp.redhat.com/pub/contrib/i386>` and look for Xforms4Perl-0.8.4-1.i386.rpm
- Perl GUI User Interfaces Perl-Tk : `<ftp://ftp.redhat.com/pub/contrib/i386>`
- Perl GUIkits : `<http://reference.perl.com/query.cgi?ui>`
- Perl Database Interfaces : `<http://reference.perl.com/query.cgi?database>`
- Perl to "C" translator : `<http://www.perl.com/CPAN-local/modules/by-module/B/>` and look for Compiler-a3.tar.gz
- Bourne shell to Perl translator : `<http://www.perl.com/CPAN/authors/id/MERLYN/sh2perl-0.02.tar.gz>`
- awk to Perl a2p and sed to Perl s2p is included with the PERl distribution.
- See also the newsgroups for PERL at comp.lang.perl.*

11.2 Perl Database Interface DBI

11.2.1 WHAT IS DBI ?

The Perl Database Interface (DBI) is a database access Application Programming Interface (API) for the Perl Language. The Perl DBI API specification defines a set of functions, variables and conventions that provide a consistent database interface independent of the actual database being used. The information for this DBI section is obtained from 'DBI FAQ' doc whose author is Alligator Descartes and reproduced here with his permission.

- Alligator Descartes Hermetica is at *descarte@hermetica.com*

11.2.2 DBI driver for PostgreSQL DBD-Pg-0.89

Get DBD-Pg-0.89.tar.gz from below

- DBD-Pg-0.89: `<http://www.perl.com/CPAN/modules/by-module/DBD/>`
- Comprehensive Perl Archive Network CPAN `<http://www.perl.com/CPAN>`
- DBI drivers list and DBI module pages `<http://www.hermetica.com/technologia/perl/DBI>`
- DBI information is at `<http://www.fugue.com/dbi/>`
- Primary ftp site `<ftp://ftp.demon.co.uk/pub/perl/db>`
- Miscellaneous DBI link `<http://www-ccs.cs.umass.edu/db.html>`
- Miscellaneous DBI link `<http://www.odmg.org/odmg93/updates_dbarry.html>`
- Miscellaneous DBI link `<http://www.jcc.com/sql_stnd.html>`
- PostgreSQL database `<http://www.postgresql.org>`

REQUIREMENTS:

- - build, test and install Perl 5 (at least 5.002)
- - build, test and install the DBI module (at least 0.89)
- - build, test and install PostgreSQL (at least 6.2)

11.2.3 Technical support for DBI

Please send comments and bug-reports to

- *E.Mergl@bawue.de*

Please include the output of perl -v, and perl -V, the version of PostgreSQL, the version of DBD-Pg, and the version of DBI in your bug-report.

11.2.4 What is DBI, DBperl, Oraperl and *perl?

To quote Tim Bunce, the architect and author of DBI:

"DBI is a database access Application Programming Interface (API) for the Perl Language. The DBI API Specification defines a set of functions, variables and conventions that provide a consistent database interface independent of the actual database being used."

In simple language, the DBI interface allows users to access multiple database types transparently. So, if you connecting to an Oracle, Informix, mSQL, Sybase or whatever database, you don't need to know the underlying mechanics of the 3GL layer. The API defined by DBI will work on all these database types.

A similar benefit is gained by the ability to connect to two different databases of different vendor within the one perl script, ie, I want to read data from an Oracle database and insert it back into an Informix database all within one program. The DBI layer allows you to do this simply and powerfully.

DBperl is the old name for the interface specification. It's usually now used to denote perl4 modules on database interfacing, such as, oraperl, isqlperl, ingperl and so on. These interfaces didn't have a standard API and are generally not supported.

Here's a list of DBperl modules, their corresponding DBI counterparts and support information. DBI driver queries should be directed to the dbi-users mailing list.

```
Module Name  Database Required   Author        DBI
-----------  -----------------   ------        ---
Sybperl      Sybase              Michael Peppler DBD::Sybase
                                 <mpeppler@datamig.com>
                                 http://www.mbay.net/~mpeppler
Oraperl      Oracle 6 & 7        Kevin Stock     DBD::Oracle
                                 <dbi-users@fugue.com>
Ingperl      Ingres              Tim Bunce &     DBD::Ingres
                                 Ted Lemon
                                 <dbi-users@fugue.com>
Interperl    Interbase           Buzz Moschetti  DBD::Interbase
                                 <buzz@bear.com>
Uniperl      Unify 5.0           Rick Wargo      None
                                 <rickers@coe.drexel.edu>
Pgperl       Postgres            Igor Metz       DBD::Pg
                                 <metz@iam.unibe.ch>
Btreeperl    NDBM                John Conover    SDBM?
                                 <john@johncon.com>
Ctreeperl    C-Tree              John Conover    None
                                 <john@johncon.com>
Cisamperl    Informix C-ISAM     Mathias Koerber None
                                 <mathias@unicorn.swi.com.sg>
Duaperl      X.500 Directory     Eric Douglas    None
             User Agent
```

However, some DBI modules have DBperl emulation layers, so, DBD::Oracle comes with an Oraperl emulation layer, which allows you to run legacy oraperl scripts without modification. The emulation layer translates the oraperl API calls into DBI calls and executes them through the DBI switch.

Here's a table of emulation layer information:

```
Module           Emulation Layer    Status
------           ---------------    ------
DBD::Oracle      Oraperl            Complete
DBD::Informix    Isqlperl           Under development
DBD::Sybase      Sybperl            Working? ( Needs verification )
DBD::mSQL        Msqlperl           Experimentally released with
                                    DBD::mSQL-0.61
```

The Msqlperl emulation is a special case. Msqlperl is a perl5 driver for mSQL databases, but does not conform to the DBI Specification. It's use is being deprecated in favour of DBD::mSQL. Msqlperl may be downloaded from CPAN via:

- `<http://www.perl.com/cgi-bin/cpan_mod?module=Msqlperl>`

11.2.5 DBI specifications

There are a few information sources on DBI.

- DBI Specification `<http://www.hermetica.com/technologia/perl/DBI/doc/dbispec>`

There are two specifications available at this link, the new DBI Draft Specification which is a rapidly changing document as the development team drive towards a stable interface, and the old historical DBperl Specification out of which the current DBI interface evolved.

The later document should be regarded as being of historical interest only and should not serve as a programming manual, or authoratative in any sense. However, it is still a very useful reference source.

HOWTO

POD documentation PODs are chunks of documentation usually embedded within perl programs that document the code "in place", providing a useful resource for programmers and users of modules. POD for DBI and drivers is beginning to become more commonplace, and documentation for these modules can be read with the following commands.

The DBI Specification The POD for the DBI Specification can be read with the command

perldoc DBI

Oraperl Users of the Oraperl emulation layer bundled with DBD::Oracle, may read up on how to program with the Oraperl interface by typing:

perldoc Oraperl

This will produce an updated copy of the original oraperl man page written by Kevin Stock for perl4. The oraperl API is fully listed and described there.

DBD::mSQL Users of the DBD::mSQL module may read about some of the private functions and quirks of that driver by typing:

perldoc DBD::mSQL

Frequently Asked Questions The Frequently Asked Questions is also available as POD documentation. Read this by typing:

perldoc DBI::FAQ

This may be more convenient to people not permanently, or conveniently, connected to the Internet.

POD in general Information on writing POD, and on the philosophy of POD in general, can be read by typing:

perldoc perlpod

Users with the Tk module installed may be interested to learn there is a Tk-based POD reader available called tkpod, which formats POD in a convenient and readable way.

Rambles, Tidbits and Observations : There are a series of occasional rambles from various people on the DBI mailing lists.

- `<http://www.hermetica.com/technologia/perl/DBI/tidbits>`

"DBI – The perl5 Database Interface" This is an article written by Alligator Descartes and Tim Bunce on the structure of DBI. It was published in issue 5 of "The Perl Journal". It's extremely good. Go buy the magazine. In fact, buy all of them. "The Perl Journal"'s WWW site is:

- `<http://www.tpj.com>`

"DBperl" This article, published in the November 1996 edition of "Dr. Dobbs Journal" concerned DBperl.

"The Perl5 Database Interface" This item is a book to be written by Alligator Descartes and published by O'Reilly and Associates.

Mailing Lists There are three mailing lists for DBI run by Ted Lemon. These can all be subscribed to and unsubscribed from via the World Wide Web at

- Mailing lists `<http://www.fugue.com/dbi>`

The lists that users may participate in are:

dbi-announce This mailing list is for announcements only. If you cannot successfully use the form on the above WWW page, please subscribe to the list in the following manner:

- Email: *dbi-announce-request@fugue.com* with a message body of 'subscribe'

dbi-dev This mailing list is intended for the use of developers discussing ideas and concepts for the DBI interface, API and driver mechanics. Only any use for developers, or interested parties. If you cannot successfully use the form on the above WWW page, please subscribe to the list in the following manner:

- Email: *dbi-dev-request@fugue.com* with a message body of 'subscribe'

dbi-users This mailing list is a general discussion list used for bug reporting, problem discussion and general enquiries. If you cannot successfully use the form on the above WWW page, please subscribe to the list in the following manner:

- Email: *dbi-users-request@fugue.com* with a message body of 'subscribe'

Mailing List Archives

- US Mailing List Archives `<http://outside.organic.com/mail-archives/dbi-users/>`
- European Mailing List Archives `<http://www.rosat.mpe-garching.mpg.de/mailing-lists/ PerlDB-Interest>`

11.2.6 Compilation problems or "It fails the test"

If you have a core dump, try the Devel::CoreStack module for generating a stack trace from the core dump. Devel::CoreStack can be found on CPAN at:

- `<http://www.perl.com/cgi-bin/cpan_mod?module=Devel::CoreStack>`

Email the dbi-users Mailing List stack trace, module versions, perl version, test cases, operating system versions and any other pertinent information. The more information you send, the quicker developers can track problems down. If you send us nothing, expect nothing back.

11.2.7 Is DBI supported under Windows 95 / NT platforms?

The DBI and DBD::Oracle Win32 ports are now a standard part of DBI, so, downloading DBI of version higher than 0.81 should work fine. You can access Microsoft Access and SQL-Server databases from DBI via ODBC. Supplied with DBI-0.79 (and later) is an experimental DBI 'emulation layer' for the Win32::ODBC module. It's called DBI::W32ODBC. You will need the Win32::ODBC module.

- Win32 DBI `<http://www.hermetica.com/technologia/perl/DBI/win32>`
- Win32 ODBC `<http://www.roth.net>`

11.2.8 What's DBM? And why use DBI instead ?

UNIX was originally blessed with simple file-based "databases", namely the dbm system. dbm lets you store data in files, and retrieve that data quickly. However, it also has serious drawbacks.

File Locking

The dbm systems did not allow particularly robust file locking capabilities, nor any capability for correcting problems arising through simultaneous writes [to the database].

Arbitrary Data Structures

The dbm systems only allows a single fixed data structure: key-value pairs. That value could be a complex object, such as a [C] struct, but the key had to be unique. This was a large limitation on the usefulness of dbm systems.

However, dbm systems still provide a useful function for users with simple datasets and limited resources, since they are fast, robust and extremely well-tested. Perl modules to access dbm systems have now been integrated into the core Perl distribution via the AnyDBM_File module.

To sum up, DBM is a perfectly satisfactory solution for essentially read-only databases, or small and simple datasets. However, for more powerful and scaleable datasets, not to mention robust transactional locking, users are recommended to use DBI.

11.2.9   Is < insert feature here > supported in DBI?

Given that we're making the assumption that the feature you have requested is a non-standard database-specific feature, then the answer will be no.

DBI reflects a generic API that will work for most databases, and has no database-specific functionality.

However, driver authors may, if they so desire, include hooks to database-specific functionality through the func method defined in the DBI API. Script developers should note that use of functionality provided via the func methods is unlikely to be portable across databases.

11.2.10   Is DBI any use for CGI programming?

In a word, yes! DBI is hugely useful for CGI programming! In fact, CGI programming is one of two top uses for DBI.

DBI confers the ability to CGI programmers to power WWW-fronted databases to their users, which provides users with vast quantities of ordered data to play with. DBI also provides the possibility that, if a site is receiving far too much traffic than their database server can cope with, they can upgrade the database server behind the scenes with no alterations to the CGI scripts.

11.2.11   How do I get faster connection times with DBD Oracle and CGI?

The Apache httpd maintains a pool of httpd children to service client requests. Using the Apache mod_perl module by Doug MacEachern, the perl interpreter is embedded with the httpd children. The CGI, DBI, and your other favorite modules can be loaded at the startup of each child. These modules will not be reloaded unless changed on disk. For more information on Apache, see the Apache Project's WWW site:

- Apache Project WWW site `<http://www.apache.org>`
- Mod_perl module `<http://www.perl.com/cgi-bin/cpan_mod?module=mod_perl>`

11.2.12   How do I get persistent connections with DBI and CGI?

Using Edmund Mergl's Apache::DBI module, database logins are stored in a hash with each of these httpd child. If your application is based on a single database user, this connection can be started with each child. Currently, database connections cannot be shared between httpd children. Apache::DBI can be downloaded from CPAN via:

- `<http://www.perl.com/cgi-bin/cpan_mod?module=Apache::DBI>`

11.2.13   "When I run a perl script from the command line, it works, but, when I run it under the httpd, it fails!" Why?

Basically, a good chance this is occurring is due to the fact that the user that you ran it from the command line as has a correctly configured set of environment variables, in the case of DBD::Oracle, variables like $ORACLE_HOME, $ORACLE_SID or TWO_TASK. The httpd process usually runs under the user id of nobody, which implies there is no configured environment. Any scripts attempting to execute in this situation will correctly fail. To solve this problem, set the environment for your database in a BEGIN ( ) block at the top of your script. This will solve the problem. Similarly, you should check your httpd error logfile for any clues, as well as the "Idiot's Guide To Solving Perl / CGI Problems" and "Perl CGI Programming FAQ" for further information. It is unlikely the problem is DBI-related. Read BOTH these documents carefully!

- Idiot's Guide to Solving Perl / CGI problems `<http://www.perl.com/perl/faq/index.html>`

11.2.14   Can I do multi-threading with DBI?

As of the current date, no. Perl does not support multi-threading. However, multi-threading is expected to become part of the perl core distribution as of version 5.005, which implies that DBI may support multi-threading fairly soon afterwards. For some OCI example code for Oracle that has multi-threaded SELECT statements, see:

- `<http://www.hermetica.com/technologia/oracle/oci/orathreads.tar.gz>`

11.2.15   How can I invoke stored procedures with DBI?

Assuming that you have created a stored procedure within the target database, eg, an Oracle database, you can use $dbh->do to immediately execute the procedure. For example,

$dbh->do("BEGIN someProcedure END");

11.2.16   How can I get return values from stored procedures with DBI?

Remember to perform error checking, though!

```
$sth = $dbh->prepare( "BEGIN foo(:1, :2, :3); END;" );
$sth->bind_param(1, $a);
$sth->bind_param_inout(2, \$path, 2000);
$sth->bind_param_inout(3, \$success, 2000);
$sth->execute;
```

11.2.17   How can I create or drop a database with DBI?

Database creation and deletion are concepts that are entirely too abstract to be adequately supported by DBI. For example, Oracle does not support the concept of dropping a database at all! Also, in Oracle, the database server essentially is the database, whereas in mSQL, the server process runs happily without any databases created in it. The problem is too disparate to attack. Some drivers, therefore, support database creation and deletion through the private func methods. You should check the documentation for the drivers you are using to see if they support this mechanism.

11.2.18   How are NULL values handled by DBI?

NULL values in DBI are specified to be treated as the value undef. NULLs can be inserted into databases as NULL, for example:

```
$rv = $dbh->do( "INSERT INTO table VALUES( NULL )" );
```

but when queried back, the NULLs should be tested against undef. This is standard across all drivers.

11.2.19   What are these func methods all about?

The func method is defined within DBI as being an entry point for database-specific functionality, eg, the ability to create or drop databases. Invoking these driver-specific methods is simple, for example, to invoke a createDatabase method that has one argument, we would write:

```
$rv = $dbh->func( 'argument', 'createDatabase' );
```

Software developers should note that the func methods are non-portable between databases.

11.2.20 Commercial Support and Training

The Perl5 Database Interface is FREE software. IT COMES WITHOUT WARRANTY OF ANY KIND. However, some organizations are providing either technical support or training programs on DBI.

PERL CLINIC : The Perl Clinic can arrange commercial support contracts for Perl, DBI, DBD::Oracle and Oraperl. Support is provided by the company with whom Tim Bunce, author of DBI, works. For more information on their services, please see :

- <http://www.perl.co.uk/tpc>

12 PostgreSQL Management Tools

12.1 PGACCESS - A GUI Tool for PostgreSQL Management

PgAccess is a Tcl/Tk interface to PostgreSQL. It is already included in the distribution of PostgreSQL. You may want to check out this web site for a newer copy

- <http://www.flex.ro/pgaccess>
- If you have any comment, suggestion for improvements, please feel free to e-mail to : *teo@flex.ro*

Features of PgAccess

PgAccess windows - Main window, Table builder, Table(query) view, Visual query builder.

Tables

- opening tables for viewing, max 200 records (changed by preferences menu)
- column resizing, dragging the vertical grid line (better in table space rather than in the table header)
- text wrap in cells - layout saved for every table
- import/export to external files (SDF,CSV)
- filter capabilities (enter filter like (price>3.14)
- sort order capabilities (enter manually the sort field(s))
- editing in place
- improved table generator assistant
- improved field editing

Queries

- define , edit and stores "user defined queries"
- store queries as views
- execution of queries
- viewing of select type queries result
- query deleting and renaming
- Visual query builder with drag & drop capabilities. For any of you who had installed the Tcl/Tk plugin for Netscape Navigator, you can see it at work clicking here

Sequences

- defines sequences, delete them and inspect them Functions

- define, inspect and delete functions in SQL language

Future implementation will have

- table design (add new fields, renaming, etc.)
- function definition
- report generator
- basic scripting

If you have any comment, suggestion for improvements e-mail to :

- *teo@flex.ro*

Information about libgtcl

You will need the PostgreSQL to Tcl interface library libgtcl, lined as a Tcl/Tk 'load'-able module. The libpgtcl and the source is located in the PostgreSQL directory /src/interfaces/libpgtcl. Specifically, you will need a libpgtcl library that is 'load'-able from Tcl/Tk. This is technically different from an ordinary PostgreSQL loadable object file, because libpgtcl is a collection of object files. Under Linux, this is called libpgtcl.so. You can download from the above site a version already compiled for Linux i386 systems. Just copy libpgtcl.so into your system library director (/usr/lib). One of the solutions is to remove from the source the line containing load libpgtcl.so and to load pgaccess.tcl not with wish, but with pgwish (or wishpg) that wish that was linked with libpgtcl library.

12.2   Windows Interactive Query Tool for PostgreSQL (WISQL or MPSQL)

MPSQL provides users with a graphical SQL interface to PostgreSQL. MPSQL is similar to Oracle's SQL Worksheet and Microsoft SQL Server's query tool WISQL. It has nice GUI and has history of commands. Also you can cut and paste and it has other nice features to improve your productivity.

- `<http://www.troubador.com/~keidav/index.html>`
- Email: *keidav@whidbey.com*
- `<http://www.ucolick.org/~de/>` in file tcl_syb/wisql.html
- `<http://www.troubador.com/~keidav/index.html>`
- Email: *de@ucolick.org*

12.3   Interactive Query Tool (ISQL) for PostgreSQL called PSQL

ISQL is For Character command line terminals. This is included in the distribution, and is called PSQL. Very similar to Sybase ISQL, Oracle SQLplus. At unix prompt give command 'psql' which will put you in psql> prompt.

```
Type \h to see help of commands.
```

Very user friendly and easy to use. Can also be accessed from shell scripts.

12.4   MPMGR - A Database Management Tool for PostgreSQL

MPMGR will provide a graphical management interface for PostgresSQL. You can find it at

- `<http://www.mutinybaysoftware.com/>`
- Email: *keidav@mutinybaysoftware.com*
- `<http://www.troubador.com/~keidav/index.html>`

- Email: *keidav@whidbey.com*
- <http://www.ucolick.org/~de> in file tcl_syb/wisql.html
- WISQL for PostgreSQL <http://www.ucolick.org/~de/Tcl/pictures>
- Email: *de@ucolick.org*

13 Setting up multi-boxes PostgreSQL with just one monitor

You can stack up the cpu-boxes and connect to just one monitor and use the KVM (Keyboard, Video, Monitor) switch box to select the host. This saves space and you eliminate monitor, keyboard and the mouse (saving anywhere from 100 to 500 US dollars per set) and also avoid lot of clutter.

Using this switch box, you can stack up many PostgreSQL servers (development, test, production), Web servers, ftp servers, Intranet servers, Mail servers, News servers in a tower shelf. The switch box can be used for controlling Windows 95/NT or OS/2 boxes as well.

Please check out these sites:

- DataComm Warehouse Inc Call 24 hours a day, 7 days a week at 1-800-328-2261. They supply all varieties of computer hardware <http://www.warehouse.com> 4-port Manual KVM switch (PS/2) is about $89.99 Part No. DDS1354
- Network Technologies Inc <http://www.networktechinc.com/servswt.html> (120 dollars/PC 8 ports) which lists 'Server Switches' and 'Video only switches'
- Scene Double Inc, England <http://www.scene.demon.co.uk/qswitch.htm>
- Cybex corporation <http://www.cybex.com>
- Raritan Inc <http://www.raritan.com>
- RealStar Solutions Inc <http://www.real-star.com/kvm.htm>
- Belkin Inc <http://www.belkin.com>
- Better Box Communications Ltd. <http://www.betterbox.com/info.html>
- Go to nearest hardware store and ask for "Server Switch" also known as "KVM Auto Switches".

Search engine yahoo to find more companies with "Server Switches" or "KVM Switches".

It is strongly recommended to have a dedicated unix box for each PostgreSQL data-server for better performance. No other application program/processes should run on this box. See the Business section of your local newspapers for local vendors selling only intel box, 13" monochrome monitor (very low cost monitor). Local vendors sell just the hardware **without** any Microsoft Windows/DOS (saves you about $ 150). You do not need a color monitor for the database server, as you can do remote administration from color PC workstation. Get RedHat (or some other distribution of) Linux cdrom from below -

- Linux System Labs Web site: <http://www.lsl.com/> 7 (U.S. dollars)
- Cheap Bytes Inc Web site: <http://www.cheapbytes.com/> 7 (U.S. dollars)

Make sure that the hardware you purchase is supported by Redhat Linux. Check the ftp site of Redhat for recommended hardware like SCSI adapters, video cards before buying. For just $ 600 you will get a powerful intel box with Redhat Linux running PostgreSQL. Use odbc/jdbc/perl/tcl to connect to PostgreSQL from Windows95, OS/2, Unix Motif or web browser (e.g. Redbaron, Opera, Netscape, 20 others). (Web browsers are very fast becoming the standard client).

Using this idea you can control many cpu boxes by just one monitor and one keyboard!

Below is the **extract from networktechnic Inc** for the "Server Switches"

Order now call 800-742-8324 (toll free in USA)

To receive our catalog please Email your address to: sales@networktechinc.com

CONTROL MULTIPLE PC'S with one keyboard monitor & mouse These electronic switches will allow one keyboard, monitor & mouse to control up to 64 PC's. Embedded microcomputers simulate the presence of keyboard, monitor & mouse to all attached PC's 100% of the time.

Features and Applications

- Keyboard, front panel or remote control
- 9 pin D Serial or 6 pin miniDIN mouse support
- 5 pin DIN or 6 pin miniDIN keyboard support
- 1600x1200 video resolution with no degradation
- Uses standard cables
- Desktop or rackmount

Specifications - Keyboard

- All connectors are female
- 5 pin DIN or 6 pin miniDIN
- Will hard or soft boot all PC's 100% of the time

Controls - Buttons on Front

- Touch a button and be connected to that PC
- Hold any button in for more than 0.5 second and go into SCAN, BROADCAST or COMMAND mode
- LEDs on front indicate mode of operation Keyboard
- Type CTRL+* and go into COMMAND mode
- SCAN, BROADCAST or COMMAND are available

Mouse

* 9 pin D serial

- o NTI switch emulates Microsoft serial mouse to all PC's
- o 9 pin D male for mouse
- o 9 pin D female for PC's

* 6 pin miniDIN

- o NTI switch emulates IBM PS/2 style mouse to all PC's
- o All connectors are female

Wired remote

- Optional–must be purchased
- Operates same as "Buttons on Front"

Monitor-VGA

- Bandwidth is 150 MHz
- 1600X1200 resolution with no degradation
- All connectors are female

HOWTO

14 Applications and Tools for PostgreSQL

14.1 PostgreSQL 4GL for web database applications - AppGEN Development System

AppGEN can be downloaded from

- `<http://www.man.ac.uk/~whaley/ag/appgen.html>`
- `<ftp://ftp.mcc.ac.uk/pub/linux/ALPHA/AppGEN>`.

AppGEN is a high level fourth generation language and application generator for producing World Wide Web (WWW) based applications. These applications are typically used over the internet or within a corporate intranet. AppGEN applications are implemented as C scripts conforming to the Common Gateway Interface (CGI) standard supported by most Web Servers.

To use AppGEN you will need the following :-

PostgresSQL, relational database management system

A CGI compatible web server such as NCSA's HTTPD

An ansi C compiler such as GCC

AppGEN consists of the following Unix (Linux) executables :-

- defgen, which produces a basic template application from a logical data structure. The applications are capable of adding, updating, deleting and searching for records within the database whilst automatically maintaining referential integrity.
- appgen, the AppGEN compiler which compiles the appgen source code into CGI executable C source and HTML formatted documents ready for deployment on a web server.
- dbf2sql, a utility fo converting dBase III compatible .dbf files into executable SQL scripts. This enables data stored in most DOS/Windows based database packages to be migrated to a SQL server such as PostgresSQL.
- In addition, AppGEN comprises of a collection of HTML documents, GIF files and Java applets which are used at runtime by the system. And of course, like all good software, the full source code is included.

The author, Andrew Whaley, can be contacted on

- *andrew@arthur.smuht.nwest.nhs.uk*

14.2 WWW Web interface for PostgresSQL - DBENGINE

dbengine a plug 'n play Web interface for PostgreSQL created by Ingo Ciechowski. It is at

- `<http://www.cis-computer.com/dbengine/>`

About DBENGINE : dbengine is an interface between the WWW and Postgres95 which provides simple access to any existing database within just a few minutes.

PHP 3 gives you a Perl like language in your documents, but no real Perl while AppGen and wdb-p95 require that you create some configuration file for each of your databases – sound's like you'll first of all have to learn some sort of new mata language before you can get started.

Unlike other tools you don't have to learn any special programming or scripting language to get started with dbengine. Also there's no configuration file for each database, so you don't have to get familiar with such a new structure. However - in case you want to gain access to the full features of dbengine it'd be a good idea to know the Perl language.

The whole system can be configured by simple manipulations of an additional database that contains closer information about how to visualize your database access. You can even specify virtual Fields which are calculated on the fly right before they're displayed on the screen.

License : dbengine is free software under the same terms as Perl. Read its licence if you aren't sure what you can or can't do. The bottom line is that this is a kinder and gentler version of the GNU licence – one that doesn't infect your work if you care to borrow from dbengine or package up pieces of it as part of a commercial product.

14.3   Apache Webserver Module for PostgreSQL - NeoSoft NeoWebScript

Apache is a well-known Web Server. And a module to interface PostgreSQL to Apache Webserver is at -

- <http://www.neosoft.com/neowebscript/>

NeoWebScript is a programming language that allows both simple and complex programs to be embedded into HTML files.

When an HTML page containing embedded NeoWebScript is requested, the NeoWebScript-enabled webserver executes the embedded script(s), producing a webpage containing customized content created by the program.

NeoWebScript is a fast, secure, easy to learn way to do powerful, server-based interactive programming directly in the HTML code in web pages. With NeoWebScript, counters, email forms, graffiti walls, guest books and visitor tracking are all easy, even for a beginning programmer. See how well NeoWebScript holds its' own vs. PERL and JavaScript.

If you'd like to install NeoWebScript on your webserver, your Webmaster needs to read our Sysop FAQ to get started. Theory of Operations will explain how NeoWebScript works, while installation will take them through the steps. Management deals with configuration issues and running the server, tests let you verify correct NeoWebScript operation, and troubleshooting deals with server problems.

There is no cost to you to use NeoWebScript-2.2 for your ISP, your intranet, or your extranet. You'll see a full license when you register to download, but it costs $ 99 if you want to embed it in your own product or use it in a commerce (eg. SSL) server.

NeoWebScript is a module for the Apache webserver that allows you to embed the Tcl/Tk programming language in your webpages as a scripting tool. It was invented by Karl Lehenbauer, NeoSoft's Chief Technical Officer, and documented, enhanced and extended by NeoSoft's programmers and technical writers.

The Apache webserver is the world's most popular webserver, accounting for 68 % of the sites polled.

Tcl/Tk is the powerful, free, cross-platform scripting language developed by Dr. John Ousterhout. In his own words

"Tcl/Tk lets software developers get the job done ten times faster than with toolkits based on C or C++. It's also a great glue language for making existing applications work together and making them more graphical and Internet-aware."

Karl Lehenbauer, Founder and Chief Technical Officer of NeoSoft, has been part of Tcl/Tk development from the very beginning. Together with Mark Diehkans, they authored Extended Tcl, also known as TclX or NeoSoft Tcl, a powerful set of extensions to the language. Many of the current core Tcl commands originated in Extended Tcl, and were then imported into the core language by Dr. Ousterhout.

NeoSoft Inc., 1770 St. James Place, Suite 500, Houston, TX 77056 USA

14.4   HEITML server side extension of HTML and a 4GL language for PostgreSQL

Tool heitml is another way to interface postgres with the world wide web. For more details contact

```
Helmut Emmelmann H.E.I. Informationssyteme GmbH
Wimpfenerstrasse 23 Tel. 49-621-795141
68259 Mannheim Germany Fax. 49-621-795161
```

- E-mail Mr.Helmut Emmelmann at *emmel@h-e-i.de*

- Heitml main web site `<http://www.heitml.com>`

- Heitml secondary web site `<http://www.h-e-i.deom>`

heitml is a server side extension of HTML and a 4GL language at the same time. People can write web applications in the HTML style by using new HTML-like tags.

heitml (pronounced "Hi"-TML) is an extension of HTML and a full-featured 4th generation language that enables Web-based Applications to interact with data stored in SQL databases, without resorting to complex CGI scripts.

heitml extends HTML on the sever side, dynamically converting ".hei" files to HTML format and so is compatible with any web browser.It embraces the familiar, easy-to-use HTML syntax and provides a large assortment of pre-developed Tags and Libraries to take care of tasks that formerly required CGI. As XML, heitml provides user defined tags. With heitml the user defined markup can be translated to HTML and send to a browser.

heitml targets both HTML designers and professional programmers alike. HTML designers can use heitml Tags to build dynamic web pages, access SQL databases, or create complete web applications. Counters, registration databases, search forms, email forms, or hierarchical menues can all be created simply by using the pre-developed HTML-like Tags found in the many Component Libraries.

For programmers heitml embeds a complete forth generation language in HTML

```
(e.g. <if>, <while>, and <let> Tags),
```

plus powerful expression evaluation with integer, real, boolean, string, and tuple data types. Tuples have reference semantics as in modern object oriented languages and are stored on a heap. heitml variables including all complex data structures stored on the heap maintain their values between pages using the Session Mode. It is possible to define your own tags or environment tags and even re-define HTML-tags.

heitml makes it possible to

- - - develop Web Sites in a structured and modular way, drastically reducing maintenance overhead.

- - - develop intelligent and interactive Web Sites, with content that dynamically adapts itself to user needs.

- - - show the content of SQL databases with no programming other than to use our library of prefined "dba" Tags.

- - - develop complex database and Catalog Shopping applications using Session Variables

heitml runs on Linux with any Web Server using the CGI interface, and is especially fast (avoiding the CGI overhead) within the APACHE Web Server using the apache API. Currently MSQL (Version 1 and 2), PostgreSQL (Version 6), mysql, and the yard databases are supported). heitml also works on Linux, BSDi, Solaris and SunOS, as well as Windows NT with CGI and ISAPI and ODBC and Windows 95.

heitml (on linux) is free for research, non-commercial and private usage. Commercial Web Sites must pay a licensing fee. The fully operational version of heitml is available for a trial period downloaded freely. (Note, however, that each ".hei" Web Page you develop will display a message identifying it as the version for non-commercial use. After registration, you will receive a key to switch off the message without having to re-install the program.)

heitml (pronounced "Hi"-TML) significantly extends and enhances the functionality of HTML by definable tags and full programming features. This makes dynamic content and database applications possible simply within the HTML world, without CGI and without external scripting or programming languages. This means you, as an HTML author, can embed applications in your web pages, simply by using some new tags without CGI and without programming. As an advanced user or programmer on the other hand you can create and program powerful tag libraries. This approach makes heitml suitable for HTML newcomers and professional programmers alike. heitml runs on the web server and dynamically generates HTML, so heitml is compatible with the internet standards and with any web browser. It allows full access to databases while shielding the user from any unneccessary CGI complexity. heitml has been developed according to the newst research and in compiler construction and transaction systems.

heitml pages are developed just the same way as HTML pages, with a text editor or HTML editor, and placed on the web server as usual. However now pages can contain dynamic heitml tags and access tag libraries. You can use these tags to access the database, to create dynamic content, to send emails, and even to create powerful applications like registration databases and shopping systems.

HTML newcomers and professional programmers alike will be amazed at how quickly and easily they can design exciting applications like our Interactive Guestbook without resorting to complex and difficult to learn CGI scripts, simply by using the tools provided in our dba Library.

heitml is accompanied by a wide range of tag libraries, to create guestbooks, database maintenance applications, extensible query forms, powerful email forms or structure your web site using a hierarchic menu. These tools are ready to go, just add the corresponding tags to your web site.

As an experienced programmer you can make fully use of the heitml persistent dynamic tuple architecture : heitml is not just a scripting language with dynamic typing, full power expression evaluation, recursive procedures and extensive parameter passing features, but it also features persistent dynamic tuples to automatically keep session data of any size.

14.5 America On-line AOL Web server for PostgreSQL

The no-cost commercial webserver, AOLserver version 2.3 supports database connections to PostgreSQL 6.2.1 and higher. for more info see

- AOL Web Server `<http://www.aolserver.com>`

14.6 Problem/Project Tracking System Application Tool for PostgreSQL

This is at

- `<http://www.homeport.org/~shevett/pts/>`

14.7 Convert dbase dbf files to PostgreSQL

The program dbf2msql works fine with mSQL and PostgreSQL. You can find it at

- `<ftp://ftp.nerosworld.com/pub/SQL/dbf2sql/>`
- `<ftp://ftp.postgresql.org/pub/incoming/dbf2pg-3.0.tar.gz>`

This program was written by Maarten Boekhold, Faculty of Electrical Engineering TU Delft, NL Computer Architecture and Digital Technique section

- *M.Boekhold@et.tudelft.nl*

You can also use a python method to read dbf files and load into a postgres database.

- See `<http://www.python.org>`

15 Web Database Design/Implementation tool for PostgreSQL - EARP

- `<http://www.oswego.edu/Earp>`
- `<ftp://ftp.oswego.edu>` in the directory 'pub/unix/earp'.

15.1   What is EARP ?

The "Easily Adjustable Response Program" (EARP) created by David Dougherty.   EARP is a Web Database Design/Implementation tool, built on top of the PostgreSQL database system. Its functionality includes:

- A Visual Design System.
- A sendmail interface. (can handle incoming and outgoing mail)
- An Enhanced Security Mechanism.
- A cgi driver.

15.2   Implementation

The main implementation of EARP is a CGI binary which runs under the http daemon to provide access to the database server. All of the design tools are built into the driver, no design takes place over anything but the web. The tools themselves require a graphical browser, the compatibility of objects designed with the tools is implementation independent, based on designing individuals preferences.

15.3   What you need to run EARP

EARP will likely run on a variety of platforms with little or no porting. The known working platforms consist of the following:

- Solaris 2.5
- Linux 1.2.13+
- GNU C++
- PostgreSQL (Version 1.01 / 1.02)
- netsite server
- NCSA httpd

- GNU C++
- PostgreSQL (Version 1.01 / 1.02)
- NCSA httpd
- Apache httpd

The current (1.3) release of Earp was designed on top of the libpq release that came with PostgreSQL v1.01/1.02. If you are using a more recent version of Postgres, expect that the program will require some porting to work correctly. In the development version (Earp 2.0), libpq support is being incorporated as a module.

15.4   How does it work ?

One of the main features of EARP is that it uses an Object Oriented approach to producing html pages which interface to the database. Most pages will consist of several objects. Each object is produced by some sort of tool and given a name, objects are then linked together in a callable sequence by the page tool. Objects are also reusable across multiple pages. Basic tools exist for HTML, Querys, Grabbing input from forms, Extendable Formatting of Query and Input objects, and Linking together of objects into other objects. More advanced tools include the mail tool and the multithreaded query tool.

Another feature of EARP is advanced security. Access to various areas of the EARP system can be limited in a variety of ways. To facilitate its advanced security, EARP performs checks for each connection to the system, determining what ids and groups the connecting agent belongs to. Access to areas is defined seperately, and the combination decides if access to a specific area of Earp is allowed. Moreover, all that is required to implement the security features is an http server that supports basic (or better) user authentication.

15.5 Where to get EARP ?

EARP is available via anonymous ftp from

- `<ftp://ftp.oswego.edu>` in the directory 'pub/unix/earp'.

16 PHP Hypertext Preprocessor - Server-side html-embedded scripting language for PostgreSQL

WWW Interface Tool is at -

- `<http://www.php.net>`
- `<http://www.vex.net/php>`

Old name is Professional Home Pages (PHP 3) and new name is PHP Hypertext Pre-Processor

- Mirror sites are in many countries like www.COUNTRYCODE.php.net
- `<http://www.fe.de.php.net>`
- `<http://www.sk.php.net>`
- `<http://php.iquest.net/>`

Questions e-mail to :

- *rasmus@lerdorf.on.ca*

PHP 3 is a server-side html-embedded scripting language. It lets you write simple scripts right in your .HTML files much like JavaScript does, except, unlike JavaScript PHP 3 is not browser-dependant. JavaScript is a client-side html-embedded language while PHP 3 is a server-side language. PHP 3 is similar in concept to Netscape's LiveWire Pro product. If you have the money, you run Netscape's Commerce Server and you run one of the supported operating systems, you should probably have a look at LiveWire Pro. If you like free fast-moving software that comes with full source code you will probably like PHP 3.

16.1 Major Features

Standard CGI, FastCGI and Apache module Support As a standard CGI program, PHP 3 can be installed on any Unix machine running any Unix web server. With support for the new FastCGI standard, PHP 3 can take advantage of the speed improvements gained through this mechanism. As an Apache module, PHP 3 becomes an extremely powerful and lightning fast alternative to CGI programmimg.

- Access Logging With the access logging capabilities of PHP 3, users can maintain their own hit counting and logging. It does not use the system's central access log files in any way, and it provides real-time access monitoring. The Log Viewer Script provides a quick summary of the accesses to a set of pages owned by an individual user. In addition to that, the package can be configured to generate a footer on every page which shows access information. See the bottom of this page for an example of this.
- Access Control A built-in web-based configuration screen handles access control configuration. It is possible to create rules for all or some web pages owned by a certain person which place various restrictions on who can view these pages and how they will be viewed. Pages can be password protected, completely restricted, logging disabled and more based on the client's domain, browser, e-mail address or even the referring document.
- Postgres Support Postgres is an advanced free RDBMS. PHP 3 supports embedding Postgres95 and PostgreSQL SQL queries directly in .html files.

- RFC-1867 File Upload Support File Upload is a new feature in Netscape 2.0. It lets users upload files to a web server. PHP 3 provides the actual Mime decoding to make this work and also provides the additional framework to do something useful with the uploaded file once it has been received.

- HTTP-based authentication control PHP 3 can be used to create customized HTTP-based authentication mechanisms for the Apache web server.

- Variables, Arrays, Associative Arrays PHP 3 supports typed variables, arrays and even Perl-like associative arrays. These can all be passed from one web page to another using either GET or POST method forms.

- Conditionals, While Loops PHP 3 supports a full-featured C-like scripting language. You can have if/then/elseif/else/endif conditions as well as while loops and switch/case statements to guide the logical flow of how the html page should be displayed.

- Extended Regular Expressions Regular expressions are heavily used for pattern matching, pattern substitutions and general string manipulation. PHP 3 supports all common regular expression operations.

- Raw HTTP Header Control The ability to have web pages send customized raw HTTP headers based on some condition is essential for high-level web site design. A frequent use is to send a Location: URL header to redirect the calling client to some other URL. It can also be used to turn off cacheing or manipulate the last update header of pages.

- On-the-fly GIF image creation PHP 3 has support for Thomas Boutell's GD image library which makes it possible to generate GIF images on the fly.

- ISP "Safe Mode" support PHP 3 supports a unique "Safe Mode" which makes it safe to have multiple users run PHP scripts on the same server.

- It's Free! One final essential feature. The package is completely free. It is licensed under the GPL which allows you to use the software for any purpose, commercial or otherwise. See the GNU Public License document for complete details.

16.2 Credits

* Large parts of this code were developed at and for the University of Toronto. Many thanks to Lee Oattes of the Network Development Department at the university for constant constructive criticism.

* The PostgreSQL support code was written by Adam Sussman

- *asussman@vidya.com*

* Countless others have helped test and debug the package.

16.3 PHP 3 - Brief History

PHP began life as a simple little cgi wrapper written in Perl. It was never intended to go beyond own private use. The name of this first package was Personal Home Page Tools, which later became Personal Home Page Construction Kit.

A tool was written to easily embed SQL queries into web pages. It was basically another CGI wrapper that parsed SQL queries and made it easy to create forms and tables based on these queries. This tool was named FI (Form Interpreter).

PHP/FI version 2.0 is a complete rewrite of these two packages combined into a single program. It has now evolved to the point where it is a simple programming language embedded inside HTML files. The original acronym, PHP, has stuck. It isn't really appropriate any longer. PHP/FI is used more for entire web sites today than for small Personal Home Page setups. By whatever name, it eliminates the need for numerous small Perl cgi programs by allowing you to place simple scripts directly in your HTML files. This speeds up the overall performance of your web pages since the overhead of forking Perl several times has been eliminated. It also makes it easier to manage large web sites by placing all components of a web page in a single html file. By including support for various databases, it also makes it trivial to develop database enabled web pages. Many people find the embedded nature much easier to deal with than trying to create separate HTML and CGI files.

Throughout this documentation any references to PHP, FI or PHP/FI all refer to the same thing. The difference between PHP and FI is only a conceptual one. Both are built from the same source distribution. Now PHP/FI is renamed as PHP 3.

16.4   So, what can I do with PHP/FI ?

The first thing you will notice if you run a page through PHP/FI is that it adds a footer with information about the number of times your page has been accessed (if you have compiled access logging into the binary). This is just a very small part of what PHP/FI can do for you. It serves another very important role as a form interpreter cgi, hence the FI part of the name. For example, if you create a form on one of your web pages, you need something to process the information on that form. Even if you just want to pass the information to another web page, you will have to have a cgi program do this for you. PHP/FI makes it extremely easy to take form data and do things with it.

16.5   A simple example

Suppose you have a form:

```
<FORM ACTION="/cgi-bin/php.cgi/~userid/display.html" METHOD=POST>
<INPUT TYPE="text" name="name">
<INPUT TYPE="text" name="age">
<INPUT TYPE="submit">
<FORM>
```

Your display.html file could then contain something like:

```
< ?echo "Hi $ name, you are $ age years old!<p>" >
```

It's that simple! PHP/FI automatically creates a variable for each form input field in your form. You can then use these variables in the ACTION URL file.

The next step once you have figured out how to use variables is to start playing with some logical flow tags in your pages. For example, if you wanted to display different messages based on something the user inputs, you would use if/else logic. In our above example, we can display different things based on the age the user entered by changing our display.html to:

```
<?
    if($age>50);
        echo "Hi $name, you are ancient!<p>";
    elseif($age>30);
        echo "Hi $name, you are very old!<p>";
    else;
        echo "Hi $name.";
    endif;
>
```

PHP/FI provides a very powerful scripting language which will do much more than what the above simple example demonstrates. See the section on the PHP/FI Script Language for more information.

You can also use PHP/FI to configure who is allowed to access your pages. This is done using a built-in configuration screen. With this you could for example specify that only people from certain domains would be allowed to see your pages, or you could create a rule which would password protect certain pages. See the Access Control section for more details.

PHP/FI is also capable of receiving file uploads from any RFC-1867 compliant web browser. This feature lets people upload both text and binary files. With PHP/FI's access control and logical functions, you have full control over who is allowed to upload and what is to be done with the file once it has been uploaded. See the File Upload section for more details.

HOWTO

PHP/FI has support for the PostgreSQL database package. It supports embedded SQL queries in your .HTML files. See the section on PostgreSQL Support for more information.

PHP/FI also has support for the mysql database package. It supports embedded SQL queries in your .HTML files. See the section on mysql Support for more information.

16.6   CGI Redirection

16.6.1   Apache 1.0.x Notes

A good way to run PHP/FI is by using a cgi redirection module with the Apache server. Please note that you do not need to worry about redirection modules if you are using the Apache module version of PHP/FI. There are two of these redirection modules available. One is developed by Dave Andersen

- *angio@aros.net*

and it is available at

- `<ftp://ftp.aros.net/pub/util/apache/mod_cgi_redirect.c>`

and the other comes bundled with Apache and is called mod_actions.c. The modules are extremely similar. They differ slightly in their usage. Both have been tested and both work with PHP/FI.

Check the Apache documentation on how to add a module. Generally you add the module name to a file called Configuration. The line to be added if you want to use the mod_actions module is:

Module action_module mod_actions.o

If you are using the mod_cgi_redirect.c module add this line:

Module cgi_redirect_module mod_cgi_redirect.o

Then compile your httpd and install it. To configure the cgi redirection you need to either create a new mime type in your mime.types file or you can use the AddType command in your srm.conf file to add the mime type. The mime type to be added should be something like this:

        application/x-httpd-php phtml

If you are using the mod_actions.c module you need to add the following line to your srm.conf file:

        Action application/x-httpd-php /cgi-bin/php.cgi

If you are using mod_cgi_redirect.c you should add this line to srm.conf:

        CgiRedirect application/x-httpd-php /cgi-bin/php.cgi

Don't try to use both mod_actions.c and mod_cgi_redirect.c at the same time.

Once you have one of these cgi redirection modules installed and configured correctly, you will be able to specify that you want a file parsed by php/fi simply by making the file's extension .phtml. Furthermore, if you add index.phtml to your DirectoryIndex configuration line in your srm.conf file then the top-level page in a directory will be automatically parsed by php if your index file is called index.phtml.

16.6.2   Netscape HTTPD

You can automatically redirect requests for files with a given extension to be handled by PHP/FI by using the Netscape Server CGI Redirection module. This module is available in the File Archives on the PHP/FI Home Page. The README in the package explicitly explains how to configure it for use with PHP/FI.

16.6.3 NCSA HTTPD

NCSA does not currently support modules, so in order to do cgi redirection with this server you need to modify your server source code. A patch to do this with NCSA 1.5 is available in the PHP/FI file archives.

16.7 Running PHP/FI from the command line

If you build the CGI version of PHP/FI, you can use it from the command line simply typing: php.cgi filename where filename is the file you want to parse. You can also create standalone PHP/FI scripts by making the first line of your script look something like:

```
#!/usr/local/bin/php.cgi -q
```

The "-q" suppresses the printing of the HTTP headers. You can leave off this option if you like.

17 Python Interface for PostgreSQL

Python in an interpreted, object orientated scripting language. It is simple to use (light syntax, simple and straighforward statements), and has many extensions for building GUIs, interfacing with WWW, etc. An intelligent web browser (Hot-Java like) is currently under development (november 1995), and this should open programmers many doors. Python is copyrighted by Stichting S Mathematisch Centrum, Amsterdam, The Netherlands, and is freely distributable. It contains support for dynamic loading of objects, classes, modules, and exceptions. Adding interfaces to new system libraries through C code is straightforward, making Python easy to use in custom settings. Python is a very high level scripting language with X interface. Python package is distributed on Linux cdroms includes most of the standard Python modules, along with modules for interfacing to the Tix widget set for Tk.

PyGreSQL is a python module that interfaces to a PostgreSQL database. It embeds the PostgreSQL query library to allow easy use of the powerful PostgreSQL features from a Python script. PyGreSQL is written by D'Arcy J.M. Cain and Pascal Andre.

- New site of PyGreSQL `<http://www.druid.net/pygresql/>`
- Maintained by D'Arcy at `<http://www.druid.net/~darcy/>`
- Old site is at `<ftp://ftp.via.ecp.fr/pub/python/contrib/Database/PyGres95.README>`
- D'Arcy J.M. Cain *darcy@druid.net*
- Pascal Andre *andre@chimay.via.ecp.fr*
- Pascal Andre *andre@via.ecp.fr*

17.1 Where to get PyGres ?

The home sites of the differents packages are:

- Python `<ftp://ftp.python.org:/pub/www.python.org/1.5/python1.5b2.tar.gz>`
- PyGreSQL `<ftp://ftp.druid.net/pub/distrib/PyGreSQL-2.1.tgz>`
- Old site `<ftp://ftp.via.ecp.fr/pub/python/contrib/Database/PyGres95-1.0b.tar.gz>`

You should anyway try to find some mirror site closer of your site. Refer to the information sources to find these sites. PyGreSQL should reside in the contrib directories of Python and PostgreSQL sites.

HOWTO

17.2   Information and support

If you need information about these packages please check their web sites:

- Python : `<http://www.python.org/>`
- PostgreSQL : `<http://epoch.cs.berkeley.edu:8000/postgres95/index.html>`
- PyGreSQL `<ftp://ftp.druid.net/pub/distrib/PyGreSQL-2.1.tgz>`
- Old site PyGreSQL : `<http://www.via.ecp.fr/via/products/pygres.html>`

For support :

- Mailing list for PyGreSQL. You can join by sending email to *majordomo@vex.net* with the line "subscribe pygresql name@domain" in the body replacing "name@domain" with your own email address.
- Newsgroup for Python : newsgroup comp.lang.python
- PyGreSQL : contact Andre at *andre@via.ecp.fr* for bug reports, ideas, remarks

18   Gateway between PostgreSQL and the WWW - WDB-P95

18.1   About wdb-p95

WDB-P95 - A Web interface to PostgreSQL Databases was created by J. Douglas Dunlop It is at

- New WDB from J Rowe is at `<http://www.lava.net/beowulf/programming/wdb>`
- New versions of WWW-WDB is at `<http://www.eol.ists.ca/~dunlop/wdb-p95/>`
- For questions or to join Mailing lists contact *dunlop@eol.ists.ca*

This is a modified version of wdb-1.3a2 which provides a gateway to a the WWW for PostgreSQL. This version also requires a Browser that is capable of handling HTML Tables for the tabular output. This is not required by the original wdb and can be fairly easily reverted.

You can try out CASI Tape and Image Query. You can have a peek at the Form Definition File (FDF) which is used to create the CASI Tape and Image Query too, which includes a JOIN of 2 tables.

This release contains all files necessary to install and run WDB-P95 as an interface to your PostgreSQL databases. To port this system to other database should be relatively easy - provided that it supports standard SQL and has a Perl interface.

18.2   Does the PostgreSQL server, pgperl, and httpd have to be on the same host?

No - the PostgreSQL server does not have to be on the same host. As WDB-P95 is called by the http daemon, they have to be on the same host. - And as WDB-P95 was written to use Pg.pm - pgperl has to be on the same host too. Pgperl was written using the libpq library, so it will be able to access any PostgreSQL server anywhere in the net, just like any other PostgreSQL client. As illustrated below

(WWW Client (Netscape)) => (HTTP Server (NCSA's http) + WDB-P95 + pgperl + libpq)=> (PostgreSQL server)

Curly brackets () represent machines.

Each machine can be of a different type : NT, SUN, HP, ... but you need the libpq interface library for the machine type where you plan to use WDB-P95, as you need it to compile pgperl. (The system was designed to use HTML tables so a recent WWW client is best)

19   "C", "C++", ESQL/C language Interfaces and Bitwise Operators for PostgreSQL

19.1   "C" interface

It is included in distribution and is called 'libpq'. Similar to Oracle OCI, Sybase DB-lib, Informix CLI libraries.

19.2   "C++" interface

It is included in distribution and is called 'libpq++'.

19.3   ESQL/C

ESQL/C 'Embedded C Pre-compiler' for PostgreSQL ESQL/C is like Oracle Pro*C, Informix ESQL/C. The PostgreSQL ESQL/C is an SQL application-programming interface (API) enables the C programmer to create custom applications with database-management capabilities. The PostgreSQL ESQL/C allows you to use a third-generation language with which you are familiar and still take advantage of the Structured Query Language (SQL).

ESQL/C consists of the following pieces of software:

- The ESQL/C libraries of C functions provide access to the database server.
- The ESQL/C header files provide definitions for the data structures, constants, and macros useful to the ESQL/C program.
- The ESQL/C preprocessor, is a source-code preprocessor that converts a C file containing SQL statements into an executable file.

It is at

- ESQL/C for PostgreSQL is already included in the distribution.
- Main site <ftp://ftp.lysator.liu.se/pub/linus>
- Email : *linus@epact.se*

19.4   BitWise Operators for PostgreSQL

Bitwise operators was written by Nicolas Moldavsky

- *nico@overnet.com.ar*

"C" functions that implement bitwise operators (AND, OR, XOR, bit complement) on pgsql. Get them by anonymous FTP from

- <ftp://ftp.overnet.com.ar/pub/utils/linux/bitpgsql.tgz>

Makefile for Linux is included.

20   Japanese Kanji Code for PostgreSQL

It is at the following site

- <ftp://ftp.sra.co.jp/pub/cmd/postgres/>

HOWTO

21 PostgreSQL Port to Windows 95/Windows NT

Port to Windows 95/Windows NT is underway. Porting is being done using gcc, gmake for Win NT/95. To compile source code on win32 gnu-win32 program is used. GNU gcc is available for win32. Check this site -

- <http://www.cygnus.com/misc/gnu-win32/>

At this site and get the file cdk.exe (self-extractor file for gnu-win32)

Porting can also be done using the following "Unix-Emulator on NT" tool from

- <http://www.softway.com>

22 Mailing Lists

22.1 Get a Free e-mail account

Check out the free deals offered - get free e-mail accounts from

- In Yahoo <http://www.yahoo.com> click on e-mail
- In Lycos <http://www.lycos.com> click on new e-mail accounts
- In hotmail <http://www.hotmail.com> click on new e-mail accounts

Subscribe to PostgreSQL mailing list and Yahoo has additional feature of creating a seperate folder for PostgreSQL e-mails, so that your regular e-mail is not cluttered. Select menu Email- > Options- > Filters and pick seperate folder for email. With this e-mail account you can access mail from anywhere in the world as long as you have access to a web page.

If you have any other e-mail, you can use "Mail Filters" to receive automatically the PostgreSQL mails into a seperate folder. This will avoid mail cluttering.

22.2 English Mailing List

See the Mailing Lists Item on the main web page at :

- <http://www.postgresql.org/>
- Email questions to: *pgsql-questions@postgresql.org*
- Developers *pgsql-hackers@postgresql.org*
- Port specific questions *pgsql-ports@postgresql.org*
- Documentation questions *pgsql-docs@postgresql.org*

You will get the answers/replies back by e-mail in less than a day!!

You can also subscribe to mailing lists. See also the section 'Get a Free e-mail account' above. To subscribe or unsubscribe from the list, send mail to

- *pgsql-questions-request@postgresql.org*
- *pgsql-hackers-request@postgresql.org*
- *pgsql-ports-request@postgresql.org*
- *pgsql-docs-request@postgresql.org*

The body of the message should contain the single line

subscribe

(or)

unsubscribe

22.3 Archive of Mailing List

Also mailing lists are archived in html format at the following location -

- Date-wise listing available via MHonarc via the WWW at `<http://www.postgresql.org/mhonarc/pgsql-questions>`
- `<ftp://ftp.postgresql.org>` directory is /pub/majordomo

22.4 Spanish Mailing List

Now there is an "unofficial" list of postgreSQL in Spanish. See also the section 'Free Account to Organise your PostgreSQL e-mails' above. To subscribe the user has to send a message to:

- *majordomo@tlali.iztacala.unam.mx*

The body of the message should contain the single line:

inscripcion pgsql-ayuda

23 Documentation and Reference Books

23.1 User Guides and Manuals

The following are included in the PostgreSQL distribution in the postscript, HTML formats and unix man-pages. If you have access to internet, you can find the documents listed below at `<http://www.postgresql.org/docs>`

- "Installation Guide"
- "User Guide" for PostgreSQL
- "Implementation Guide" detailing database internals of PostgreSQL.
- Online manuals.
- Online manuals in HTML formats.
- Also manuals in Postscript format for printing hard copies.

23.2 Online Documentation

- Listing and description of default data types and operators

      ```
      Is a a part of PSQL command in the release 6.4.
      ```

- Listing of supported SQL keywords

      ```
      There is a script in the /tools directory to do that
      ```

- Listings of supported statements -

      ```
      Use the command psql \h
      ```

HOWTO

- Basic relational database concepts under PostgreSQL (implementation) and several online examples (queries) -

  ```
  Look at the regression tests at src/test. There y-
  ou can find the directories
  regress/sql and suite/*.sql.
  ```

- Tutorial for PostgreSQL.

  ```
  SQL tutorial scripts is in the directory src/tutorial
  ```

  See also "SQL Tutorial for beginners" in Appendix B of this document 32 ()

23.3   Useful Reference Textbooks

- "Understanding the New SQL: A Complete Guide" - by Jim Melton and Alan R.Simon

  ```
  Morgan Kaufman Publisher is one of best SQL books. This deal-
  s with SQL92.
  ```

- "A Guide to THE SQL STANDARD" - by C.J.Date

  ```
  Addison-Wesley Publishing company is also a good book. Very popu-
  lar book for SQL.
  ```

- SQL - The Standard Handbook, November 1992

  ```
  Stephen Cannan and Gerard Otten
  McGraw-Hill Book Company Europe , Berkshire, SL6 2QL, England
  ```

- SQL Instant Reference, 1993

  ```
  Martin Gruber, Technical Editor: Joe Celko
  SYBEX Inc.  2021 Challenger Drive Alameda, CA 94501
  ```

- C.J.Date, "An introduction to Database Systems" (6th Edition), Addison-Wesley, 1995, ISBN 0-201-82458-2

  ```
  This book is the Bible of Database Management Systems.
  The book details normalization, SQL, recovery, concurrency, security,
  integrity, and extensions to the original relational model, curren-
  t issues
  like client/server systems and the Object Oriented model(s). Many
  references are included for further reading. Recommended for most users.
  ```

- Stefan Stanczyk, "Theory and Practice of Relational Databases", UCL Press Ltd, 1990, ISBN 1-857-28232-9

  ```
  Book details theory of relational databases, relational alge-
  bra, calculus
  and normalisation. But it does not cover real world issues and examples
  beyond simple examples. Recommended for most users.
  ```

- "The Practical SQL Handbook" Third Edition, Addison Wesley Developers Press ISBN 0-201-44787-8

  ```
  Recommended for most users.
  ```

- Michael Stonebraker, "Readings in Database Systems", Morgan Kaufmann, 1988, ISBN 0-934613-65-6

  ```
  This book is a collection of papers that have been published over the
  years on databases. It's not for the casual user but it is really a
  reference for advanced (post-graduate) students or database system
  developers.
  ```

- C.J.Date, "Relational Database - Selected Readings", Addison-Wesley, 1986, ISBN 0-201-14196-5

> This book is a collection of papers that have been published over the
> years on databases. It's not for the casual user but it is really a
> reference for advanced (post-graduate) students or database system
> developers.

- Nick Ryan and Dan Smith, "Database Systems Engineering", International Thomson Computer Press, 1995, ISBN 1-85032-115-9

> This book goes into the details of access methods, storage techniques.

- Bipin C. Desai, "An introduction to Database Systems", West Publishing Co., 1990, ISBN 0-314-66771-7

> It's not for the casual user but it is for advanced (post-graduate)
> students or database system developers.

- Joe Celko "INSTANT SQL Programming"

> Wrox Press Ltd.
> Unit 16, 20 James Road, Tyseley
> Birmingham, B11 2BA, England
> 1995

- Michael Gorman "Database Management Systems: Understanding and Applying Database"

> Technology
> QED and John Wiley
> 1991

- Michael Gorman "Enterprise Database for a Client/Server Environment" QED and John Wiley

> Presents the requirements of building client/server database
> applications via repository metamodels and the use of ANSI standard SQL
> 1993

Hundreds of other titles on SQL are available! Check out a bookstore.

23.4   ANSI/ISO SQL Specifications documents - SQL 1992, SQL 1998

ANSI/ISO SQL specifications documents can be found at these sites listed below -

- <http://www.naiua.org/std-orgs.html>
- <http://www.ansi.org/docs> and click on file cat_c.html and search with "Database SQL"
- SQL92 standard <http://www.jcc.com> and click on file sql_stnd.html
- ANSI/ISO SQL specifications <http://www.contrib.andrew.cmu.edu/~shadow/sql.html> You will find SQL Reference here.

23.5   Syntax of ANSI/ISO SQL 1992

See Appendix A of this document 31 ()

23.6   Syntax of ANSI/ISO SQL 1998

The SQL 1998 (SQL 3) specification is still under development. See 'Electronic Access to the SQL3 Working Draft' of this document at 23.9 ()

23.7   SQL Tutorial for beginners

See Appendix B of this document 32 ()

23.8   Temporal Extension to SQL92

- Document for Temporal Extension to SQL-92 `<ftp://FTP.cs.arizona.edu/tsql/tsql2/>`
- Temporal SQL-3 specification `<ftp://FTP.cs.arizona.edu/tsql/tsql2/sql3/>`

This directory contains the language specification for a temporal extension to the SQL-92 language standard. This new language is designated TSQL2.

The language specification present here is the final version of the language.

Correspondence may be directed to the chair of the TSQL2 Language Design Committee, Richard T.Snodgrass, Department of Computer Science, University of Arizona, Tucson, AZ 85721,

- *rts@cs.arizona.edu*

The affiliations and e-mail addresses of the TSQL2 Language Design Committee members may be found in a separate section at the end of the language specification.

The contents of this directory are as follows.

spec.dvi,.ps TSQL2 Language Specification, published in September, 1994

bookspec.ps TSQL2 Language Specification, as it appears in the TSQL2 book, published in September, 1995 (see below).

sql3 change proposals submitted to the ANSI and ISO SQL3 committees.

Associated with the language specification is a collection of commentaries which discuss design decisions, provide examples, and consider how the language may be implemented. These commentaries were originally proposals to the TSQL2 Language Design Committee. They now serve a different purpose: to provide examples of the constructs, motivate the many decisions made during the language design, and compare TSQL2 with the many other language proposals that have been made over the last fifteen years. It should be emphasized that these commentaries are not part of the TSQL2 language specification per se, but rather supplement and elaborate upon it. The language specification proper is the final word on TSQL2.

The commentaries, along with the language specification, several indexes, and other supporting material, has been published as a book:

Snodgrass, R.T., editor, The TSQL2 Temporal Query Language, Kluwer Academic Publishers, 1995, 674+xxiv pages.

The evaluation commentary appears in the book in an abbreviated form; the full commentary is provided in this directory as file eval.ps

The file tl2tsql2.pl is a prolog program that tranlates allowed temporal logic to TSQL2. This program was written by Michael Boehlen

- *boehlen@iesd.auc.dk*

He may be contacted for a paper that describes this translation. This is a rather dated version of that program. Newer versions are available at

- `<http://www.cs.auc.dk/general/DBS/tdb/TimeCenter/Software>`

(the TimeDB and Tiger systems).

23.9   Part 0 - Acquiring ISO/ANSI SQL Documents

This document shows you how to (legally) acquire a copy of the SQL-92 standard and how to acquire a copy of the "current" SQL3 Working Draft.

The standard is copyrighted ANSI standard by ANSI, the ISO standard by ISO.

There are two (2) current SQL standards, an ANSI publication and an ISO publication. The two standards are word-for-word identical except for such trivial matters as the title of the document, page headers, the phrase "International Standard" vs "American Standard", and so forth.

Buying the SQL-92 Standard

The ISO standard, ISO/IEC 9075:1992, Information Technology - Database Languages - SQL, is currently (March, 1993) available and in stock from ANSI at:

```
American National Standards Institute
1430 Broadway
New York, NY 10018 (USA)
Phone (sales): +1.212.642.4900
```

at a cost of US$230.00. The ANSI version, ANSI X3.135-1992, American National Standard for Information Systems - Database Language SQL, was not available from stock at this writing, but was expected to be available by some time between late March and early May, 1993). It is expected to be be priced at US$225.00.

If you purchase either document from ANSI, it will have a handling charge of 7% added to it (that is, about US$9.10). Overseas shipping charges will undoubtedly add still more cost. ANSI requires a hardcopy of a company purchase order to accompany all orders; alternately, you can send a check drawn on a US bank in US dollars, which they will cash and clear before shipping your order. (An exception exists: If your organization is a corporate member of ANSI, then ANSI will ship the documents and simply bill your company.)

The ISO standard is also available outside the United States from local national bodies (country standardization bodies) that are members of either ISO (International Organization for Standardization) or IEC (International Electrotechnical Commission). Copies of the list of national bodies and their addresses are available from ANSI or from other national bodies. They are also available from ISO:

```
International Organization for Standardization
Central Secretariat
1, rue de Varembi
CH-1211 Genhve 20
Switzerland
```

If you prefer to order the standard in a more convenient and quick fashion, you'll have to pay for the privilege. You can order ISO/IEC 9075:1992, Information Technology - Database Languages - SQL, from:

```
Global Engineering Documents
2805 McGaw Ave
Irvine, CA 92714 (USA)
USA
Phone (works from anywhere): +1.714.261.1455
Phone (only in the USA): (800)854-7179
```

for a cost of US$308.00. I do not know if that includes shipping or not, but I would guess that international shipping (at least) would cost extra. They will be able to ship you a document fairly quickly and will even accept "major credit cards". Global does not yet have the ANSI version nor do they have a price or an expected date (though I would expect it within a few weeks following the publication by ANSI and at a price near US$300.00).

Buying a copy of the SQL3 Working Draft

You can purchase a hardcopy of the SQL3 working draft from the ANSI X3 Secretariat, CBEMA (Computer and Business Equipment Manufacturers Association). They intend to keep the "most recent" versions of the SQL3 working draft available and sell them for about US$60.00 to US$65.00. You can contact CBEMA at:

```
        CBEMA, X3 Secretariat
        Attn: Lynn Barra
        1250 Eye St.
        Suite 200
        Washington, DC 20005 (USA)
```

Lynn Barra can also be reached by telephone at +1.202.626.5738 to request a copy, though mail is probably more courteous.

Electronic Access to the SQL3 Working Draft

The most recent version (as of the date of this writing) of the SQL3 (both ANSI and ISO) working draft (and all of its Parts) is available by "anonymous ftp" or by "ftpmail" on:

```
        gatekeeper.dec.com
```

at

```
        /pub/standards/sql/
```

In this directory are a number of files. There are PostScript. files and "plain text" (not prettily formatted, but readable on a screen without special software).

In general, you can find files with names like:

```
        sql-bindings-mar94.ps
        sql-bindings-mar94.txt
        sql-cli-mar94.ps
        sql-cli-mar94.txt
        sql-foundation-mar94.ps
        sql-foundation-mar94.txt
        sql-framework-mar94.ps
        sql-framework-mar94.txt
        sql-psm-mar94.ps
        sql-psm-mar94.txt
```

As new versions of the documents are produced, the "mar94" will change to indicate the new date of publication (e.g., "aug94" is the expected date of the next publication after "mar94").

In addition, for those readers unable to get a directory listing by FTP, we have placed a file with the name:

```
        ls
```

into the same directory. This file (surprise!) contains a directory listing of the directory.

Retrieving Files Directly Using ftp

This is a sample of how to use FTP. Specifically, it shows how to connect to gatekeeper.dec.com, get to the directory where the base document is kept, and transfer the document to your host. Note that your host must have Internet access to do this. The login is 'ftp' and the password is your email address (this is sometimes referred to as 'anonymous ftp'). The command 'type binary' is used to ensure that no bits are stripped from the file(s) received. 'get' gets one file at a time. Comments in the script below are inside angle brackets < like so > .

```
% ftp gatekeeper.dec.com
Connected to gatekeeper.dec.com.
220- *** /etc/motd.ftp ***
```

```
            Gatekeeper.DEC.COM is an unsupported service of DEC Corpo-
    rate Research.
            <...this goes on for a while...>
     220 gatekeeper.dec.com FTP server (Version 5.83 Sat ... 1992) ready.
     Name (gatekeeper.dec.com:<yourlogin here>): ftp  <anonymous also works>
     331 Guest login ok, send ident as password.
     Password: <enter your email address here >
     230 Guest login ok, access restrictions apply.
     Remote system type is UNIX.  <or whatever>
     Using binary mode to transfer files.
     ftp> cd pub/standards/sql
     250 CWD command successful.
     ftp> dir
     200 PORT command successful.
     150 Opening ASCII mode data connection for /bin/ls.
     total 9529
     -r--r--r--  1 root      system      357782 Feb 25 10:18 x3h2-93-081.ps
     -r--r--r--  1 root      system      158782 Feb 25 10:19 x3h2-93-081.txt
     -r--r--r--  1 root      system      195202 Feb 25 10:20 x3h2-93-082.ps
     -r--r--r--  1 root      system       90900 Feb 25 10:20 x3h2-93-082.txt
     -r--r--r--  1 root      system     5856284 Feb 25 09:55 x3h2-93-091.ps
     -r--r--r--  1 root      system     3043687 Feb 25 09:57 x3h2-93-091.txt
     226 Transfer complete.
     ftp> type binary
     200 Type set to I.
     ftp> get x3h2-93-082.txt
     200 PORT command successful.
     150 Opening BINARY mode data connection for x3h2-93-082.txt (90900 bytes).
     226 Transfer complete.
     90900 bytes received in 0.53 seconds (166.11 Kbytes/s)
     ftp> quit
     % <the file is now in your directory as x3h2-93-082.txt>
```

Retrieving Files Without Direct ftp Support

Digital Equipment Corporation, like several other companies, provides ftp email service. The response can take several days, but it does provide a service equivalent to ftp for those without direct Internet ftp access. The address of the server is:

ftpmail@decwrl.dec.com

The following script will retrieve the PostScript for the latest version of the SQL3 document:

```
        reply joe.programmer@imaginary-corp.com
        connect gatekeeper.dec.com anonymous
        binary
        compress
```

The following script will retrieve the PostScript for the latest version of the SQL3 document:

```
        reply joe.programmer@imaginary-corp.com
        connect gatekeeper.dec.com anonymous
        binary
        compress
        uuencode
        chdir /pub/standards/sql
```

HOWTO

```
get x3h2-93-091.ps
quit
```

The first line in the script commands the server to return the requested files to you; you should replace "joe.programmer@imaginary-corp.com" with your Internet address. The file in this example, x3h2-93-091.ps, is returned in "compress"ed "uuencode"d format as 34 separate email messages. If your environment does not provide tools for reconstructing such files, then you could retrieve the file as plain text with the following script:

```
reply joe.programmer@imaginary-corp.com
connect gatekeeper.dec.com anonymous
chdir /pub/standards/sql
get x3h2-93-091.ps
quit
```

But be warned, the .ps file will probably be sent to you in more than 70 parts!

To retrieve any particular file, other than x3h2-93-091.ps, simply replace "x3h2-93-091.ps" with the name of the desired file. To get a directory listing of all files available, replace "get x3h2-93-091.ps" with "dir".

23.10   Part 1 - ISO/ANSI SQL Current Status

This chapter is a source of information about the SQL standards process and its current state.

Current Status:

Development is currently underway to enhance SQL into a computationally complete language for the definition and management of persistent, complex objects. This includes: generalization and specialization hierarchies, multiple inheritance, user defined data types, triggers and assertions, support for knowledge based systems, recursive query expressions, and additional data administration tools. It also includes the specification of abstract data types (ADTs), object identifiers, methods, inheritance, polymorphism, encapsulation, and all of the other facilities normally associated with object data management.

In the fall of 1996, several parts of SQL3 went through a ISO CD ballot. Those parts were SQL/Framework, SQL/Foundation, and SQL/Bindings. Those ballots failed (as expected) with 900 or so comments. In Late January, there was an ISO DBL editing meeting that processed a large number of problem solutions that were either included with ballot comments or submitted as separate papers. Since the DBL editing meeting was unable to process all of the comments, the editing meeting has been extended. The completion of the editing meeting is scheduled for the end of July, 1997, in London.

Following the July editing meeting, the expectation is that a Final CD ballot will be requested for these parts of SQL. The Final CD process will take about 6 months and a DBL editing meeting, after which there will be a DIS ballot and a fairly quick IS ballot.

The ISO procedures have changed since SQL/92, so the SQL committees are still working through the exact details of the process.

If everything goes well, these parts of SQL3 will become an official ISO/IEC standard in late 1998, but the schedule is very tight.

In 1993, the ANSI and ISO development committees decided to split future SQL development into a multi-part standard. The Parts are:

- Part 1: Framework A non-technical description of how the document is structured.
- Part 2: Foundation The core specification, including all of the new ADT features.
- Part 3: SQL/CLI The Call Level Interface.
- Part 4: SQL/PSM The stored procedures specification, including computational completeness.

- Part 5: SQL/Bindings The Dynamic SQL and Embedded SQL bindings taken from SQL-92.

- Part 6: SQL/XA An SQL specialization of the popular XA Interface developed by X/Open

- Part 7:SQL/TemporalAdds time related capabilities to the SQL standards.

In the USA, the entirety of SQL3 is being processed as both an ANSI Domestic ("D") project and as an ISO project. The expected time frame for completion of SQL3 is currently 1999.

The SQL/CLI and SQL/PSM are being processed as fast as possible as addendums to SQL-92. In the USA, these are being processed only as International ("I") projects. SQL/CLI was completed in 1995. SQL/PSM should be completed sometime in late 1996.

In addition to the SQL3 work, a number of additional projects are being persued:

- SQL/MM An ongoing effort to define standard multi-media packages using the SQL3 ADT capabilities.

- Remote Data Access (RDA)

Standards Committee and Process

There are actually a number of SQL standards committees around the world. There is an international SQL standards group as a part of ISO. A number of countries have committees that focus on SQL. These countries (usually) send representatives to ISO/IEC JTC1/SC 21/WG3 DBL meetings. The countries that actively participate in the ISO SQL standards process are:

- Australia

- Brazil

- Canada

- France

- Germany

- Japan

- Korea

- The Netherlands

- United Kingdom

- United States

NIST Validation

SQL implementations are validated (in the Unites States) by the National Institute of Standards and Testing (NIST). NIST currently has a validation test suite for entry level SQL-92. The exact details of the NIST validation requirements are defined as a Federal Information Processing Standard (FIPS). The current requirements for SQL are defined in FIPS 127-2. The Postscript and Text versions of this document can be retrieved from NIST. The current SQL Validated Products List can also be retrieved from NIST.

Standard SQL Publications and Articles

There are two versions of the SQL standard. Both are available from ANSI:

- ISO/IEC 9075:1992, "Information Technology — Database Languages — SQL"

- ANSI X3.135-1992, "Database Language SQL"

The two versions of the SQL standard are identical except for the front matter and references to other standards. Both versions are available from:

```
         American National Standards Institute
         1430 Broadway
         New York, NY 10018
         USA
         Phone (sales): +1.212.642.4900
```

In additon to the SQL-92 standard, there is now a Technical Corrigendum (bug fixes):

```
         * Technical Corrigendum 1:1994 to ISO/IEC 9075:1992
```

TC 1 should also be available from ANSI. There is only an ISO version of TC 1 – it applies both to the ISO and ANSI versions of SQL-92.

In addition to the standards, several books have been written about the 1992 SQL standard. These books provide a much more readable description of the standard than the actual standard.

Related Standards

A number of other standards are of interest to the SQL community. This section contains pointers to information on those efforts. These pointers will be augmented as additional information becomes available on the web.

- SQL Environments (FIPS 193)
- Next Generation Repository Systems (X3H4) - a News Release calling for particpation in "Developing Standards for the Next Generation Repository Systems."

23.11   Part 2 - ISO/ANSI SQL Foundation

A significant portion of the SQL3 effort is in the SQL Foundation document:

- Base SQL/PSM capabilities (moved form SQL/PSM-92)
- New data types
- Triggers
- Subtables
- Abstract Data Types (ADT)
- Object Oriented Capabilities

There are several prerequisites to the object oriented capabilities:

- Capability of defining complex operations
- Store complex operations in the database
- External procedure calls ■ Some operations may not be in SQL, or may require external interactions

These capabilities are defined as a part of SQL/PSM

A great deal of work is currently being done to refine the SQL-3 object model and align it with the object model proposed by ODMG. This effort is described in the X3H2 and ISO DBL paper: Accomodating SQL3 and ODMG. A recent update on the SQL3/OQL Merger is also available.

SQL3 Timing

Work on SQL3 is well underway, but the final standards is several years away.

- International ballot to progress SQL3 Foundation from Working Draft to Committee Draft (CD) taking place fall, 1996.

- Ballot is expected to generate numerous comments
- A second CD ballot is likely to be required
- Draft International Standard ballot is likely to be take place in mid 1998
- International Standard could be completed by mid 1999.

The ANSI version of the standard will be on a similar schedule.

23.12   Part 3 - ISO/ANSI SQL Call Level Interface

The SQL/CLI is a programing call level interface to SQL databases. It is designed to support database access from shrink-wrapped applications. The CLI was originally created by a subcommittee of the SQL Access Group (SAG). The SAG/CLI specification was published as the Microsoft Open DataBase Connectivity (ODBC) specification in 1992. In 1993, SAG submitted the CLI to the ANSI and ISO SQL committees. (The SQL Access Group has now merged with X/Open consortium.)

SQL/CLI provides an international standard for:

- Implementation-independent CLI to access SQL databases
- Client-server tools can easily access database through dynamic Link Libraries
- Supports and encourages rich set of Client-server tools

SQL/CLI Timing

For the standards process, SQL/CLI is being processed with blinding speed.

- SQL/CLI is an addendum to 1992 SQL standard (SQL-92)
- Completed as an ISO standard in 1995
- ISO/IEC 9075-3:1995 Information technology – Database languages – SQL – Part 3: Call-Level Interface (SQL/CLI)
- Current SQL/CLI effort is adding support for SQL3 features

23.13   Part 4 - ISO/ANSI SQL Persistent Stored Modules

SQL/PSM expands SQL by adding:

- Procedural language extensions
- Multi-statement and Stored Procedures
- External function and procedure calls

In addition to being a valuable application development tool, SQL/PSM provides the foundation support for the object oriented capabilities in SQL3.

Multi-statement and Stored Procedures

Multi-statement and stored procedures offer a variety of advantages in a client/server environment:

- Performance - Since a stored procedure can perform multiple SQL statements, network interaction with the client are reduced.
- Security - A user can be given the right to call a stored procedure that updates a table or set of tables but denied the right to update the tables directly
- Shared code - The code in a stored procedure does not have to be rewritten and retested for each client tool that accesses the database.

- Control - Provides a single point of definition and control for application logic.

Procedural Language Extensions

Procedural language add the power of a traditional programming language to SQL through flow control statements and a variety of other programming constructs.

Flow Control Statements

- If-then-else
- Looping constructs
- Exception handling
- Case statement
- Begin-End blocks

The procedural language extensions include other programming language constructs:

- Variable declarations
- Set statements for value assignment
- Get diagnostics for process and status information

In addition, all of the traditional SQL statements can be included in multi-statement procedures.

External Procedure and Function Calls

One feature frequently mentioned in the wish lists for many database products, and implemented in some, is a capability augmenting the built-in features with calls to user-written procedures external to the database software.

- Allows a particular site or application to add their own database functions
- Can be used throughout the database applications

The benefit of this capability is that it gives the database (and therefore database applications) access to a rich set of procedures and functions too numerous to be defined by a standards committee.

SQL/PSM Timing

SQL/PSM is proceeding quickly:

- SQL/PSM is an addendum to SQL-92
- International ballot to progress SQL/PSM from a Draft International Standard to an International Standard ended January, 1996.
- Editing meeting in May, 1996 did not resolve all of the comments
- Continuation of PSM Editing meeting is scheduled for September 30 through October 4, 1996
- The schedule is tight but there is a chance that PSM will be published with a 1996 date.
- The official designation will be: ISO/IEC DIS 9075-4:199? Information technology – Database languages – SQL – Part 4: SQL Persistent Stored Modules (SQL/PSM)
- Work is well underway on adding SQL/PSM support for SQL3 features.

23.14   Part 5 - ISO/ANSI SQL/Bindings

For ease of reference, the programming language bindings have been pulled out into a separate document. The current version is simply an extract of the dynamic and embedded bindings from SQL-92.

A variety of issues remain unresolved for the programming language bindings.

For traditional programming language, mappings exist for the SQL-92 datatypes. However, mappings must be defined between SQL objects and programming language variables.

For object oriented languages, mapping must be defined for the current SQL datatypes and between the SQL object model and the object model of the object-oriented language.

The object model needs to stabilize before these can be addressed.

The language bindings will be completed as a part of SQL3.

23.15   Part 6 - ISO/ANSI SQL XA Interface Specialization (SQL/XA)

This specification would standardize an application program interface (API) between a global Transaction Manager and an SQL Resource Manager. It would standardize the function calls, based upon the semantics of ISO/IEC 10026, "Distributed Transaction Processing", that an SQL Resource Manager would have to support for two-phase commit. The base document is derived from an X/Open publication, with X/Open permission, that specifies explicit input and output parameters and semantics, in terms of SQL data types, for the following functions: xa_close, xa_commit, xa_complete, xa_end, xa_forget, xa_open, xa_prepare, xa_recover, xa_rollback, and xa_start.

ISO is currently attempting to fast-track the X/Open XA specification. The fast-track process adopts a current industry specification with no changes. The XA fast-track ballot at the ISO SC21, JTC 1 level started on April 27, 1995 and ends on October 27, 1995. If the XA specification is approved by 75% of the votes, and by 2/3 of the p-members of JTC 1, it will become an International Standard. If the fast-track ballot is approved, SQL/XA could become a standard in 1996.

23.16   Part 7 - ISO/ANSI SQL Temporal

Temporal SQL deals with time-related data. The concept is that it is useful to query data to discover what it looked like at a particular point in time. Temporal SQL is a December, 1994 paper by Rick Snodgrass describing the concepts.

X3 Announces the Approval of a New Project, ISO/IEC 9075 Part 7: SQL/Temporal is a press release related to SQL/Temporal.

```
--------------------------------------------------------------------
                           Temporal SQL
                           ***********
       Rick Snodgrass (chair of the TSQL2 committee)
       31-Dec-1994
```

Several people have questioned the need for additional support for time in SQL3 (as proposed by DBL RIO-75, requesting a new part of SQL to support temporal databases). The claim is that abstract data types (ADT's) are sufficient for temporal support. In this informational item, I argue, using concrete examples, that using columns typed with abstract data types is inadequate for temporal queries. In particular, many common temporal queries are either difficult to simulate in SQL, or require embedding SQL in a procedural language. Alternatives are expressed in TSQL2, a temporal extension to SQL-92.

23.16.1   INTRODUCTION

Valid-time support goes beyond that of a temporal ADT. With the later, a column is specified as of a temporal domain, such as DATE or INTERVAL (examples will be given shortly). With valid time, the rows of a table vary over time, as reality changes. The timestamp associated with a row of a valid-time table is interpreted by the query language as the time when the combination of values of the columns in the row was valid. This implicit timestamp allows queries to be expressed succinctly and intuitively.

HOWTO

23.16.2   A CASE STUDY - STORING CURRENT INFORMATION

The University of Arizona's Office of Appointed Personnel has some information in a database, including each employee's name, their current salary, and their current title. This can be represented by a simple table.

```
Employee(Name, Salary, Title)
```

Given this table, finding an employee's salary is easy.

```
SELECT Salary
FROM Employee
WHERE Name = 'Bob'
```

Now the OAP wishes to record the date of birth. To do so, a column is added to the table, yielding the following schema.

```
Employee(Name, Salary, Title, DateofBirth DATE)
```

Finding the employee's date of birth is analogous to determining the salary.

```
SELECT DateofBirth
FROM Employee
WHERE Name = 'Bob'
```

23.16.3   A CASE STUDY - STORING HISTORY INFORMATION

The OAP wishes to computerize the employment history. To do so, they append two columns, one indicating when the information in the row became valid, the other indicating when the information was no longer valid.

Employee (Name, Salary, Title, DateofBirth, Start DATE, Stop DATE)

To the data model, these new columns are identical to DateofBirth. However, their presence has wide-ranging consequences.

23.16.4   A CASE STUDY - PROJECTION

To find an employee's current salary, things are more difficult.

```
SELECT Salary
FROM Employee
WHERE Name = 'Bob' AND Start <= CURRENT_DATE AND CURREN-
T_DATE <= Stop
```

This query is more complicated than the previous one. The culprit is obviously the two new columns. The OAP wants to distribute to each employee their salary history. Specifically, for each person, the maximal intervals at each salary needs to be determined. Unfortunately, this is not possible in SQL. An employee could have arbitrarily many title changes between salary changes.

Name	Salary	Title	DateofBirth	Start	Stop
Bob	60000	Assistant Provost	1945-04-09	1993-01-01	1993-05-30
Bob	70000	Assistant Provost	1945-04-09	1993-06-01	1993-09-30
Bob	70000	Provost	1945-04-09	1993-10-01	1994-01-31
Bob	70000	Professor	1945-04-09	1994-02-01	1994-12-31

Figure 1

Note that there are three rows in which Bob's salary remained constant at $70,000. Hence, the result should be two rows for Bob.

```
Name    Salary  Start        Stop
----    ------  -----        ----
Bob     60000   1993-01-01   1993-05-30
Bob     70000   1993-06-01   1994-12-31
```

One alternative is to give the user a printout of Salary and Title information, and have user determine when his/her salary changed. This alternative is not very appealing or realistic. A second alternative is to use SQL as much as possible.

```
CREATE TABLE Temp(Salary, Start, Stop)
AS       SELECT Salary, Start, Stop
         FROM Employee;
```

repeat

```
        UPDATE Temp T1
        SET (T1.Stop) = (SELECT MAX(T2.Stop)
                        FROM Temp AS T2
                        WHERE T1.Salary = T2.Salary AND T1.Start < T2.Start
                                AND T1.Stop >= T2.Start AND T1.Stop < T2.Stop)
        WHERE EXISTS (SELECT *
                        FROM Temp AS T2
                        WHERE T1.Salary = T2.Salary AND T1.Start < T2.Start
                                AND T1.Stop >= T2.Start AND T1.Stop < T2.Stop)
        until no rows updated;

DELETE FROM Temp T1

WHERE EXISTS (SELECT *
                FROM Temp AS T2
                WHERE T1.Salary = T2.Salary
                        AND ((T1.Start > T2.Start AND T1.Stop <= T2.Stop)
                        OR (T1.Start >= T2.Start AND T1.Stop < T2.Stop)
```

The loop finds those intervals that overlap or are adjacent and thus should be merged. The loop is executed in the worst case, where N is the number of rows in a chain of overlapping or adjacent value-equivalent row can simulate the query on the example table to convince him/herself of its correctness.

A third alternative is to use SQL only to open a cursor on the table. A linked list of periods is maint salary. This linked list should be initialized to empty.

```
DECLARE emp_cursor CURSOR FOR
        SELECT Salary, Title, Start, Stop
        FROM Employee;
OPEN emp_cursor;
loop:
        FETCH emp_cursor INTO :salary, :start, :stop;
        if no-data returned then goto finished;
        find position in linked list to insert this in
        goto loop;
finished:
CLOSE emp_cursor;
```

iterate through linked list, printing out dates and salaries

The linked list may not be necessary in this case if the cursor is ORDER BY Start.

In any case, the query, a natural one, is quite difficult to express using the facilities present in SQL-92. The query is trivial in TSQL2.

```
SELECT Salary
FROM Employee
```

23.16.5 A CASE STUDY - JOIN

A more drastic approach is to avoid the problem of extracting the salary history by reorganizing the schema to separate salary, title, and date of birth information (in the following, we ignore the date of birth, for simplicity).

```
Employee1 (Name, Salary, Start DATE, Stop DATE)
Employee2 (Name, Title, Start DATE, Stop DATE)
```

The Employee1 table is as follows.

Name	Salary	Start	Stop
Bob	60000	1993-01-01	1993-05-30
Bob	70000	1993-06-01	1993-12-31

Here is the example Employee2 table.

Name	Title	Start	Stop
Bob	Assistant Provost	1993-01-01	1993-09-30
Bob	Provost	1993-10-01	1994-01-31
Bob	Professor	1994-02-01	1994-12-31

ith this change, getting the salary information for an employee is now easy.

```
SELECT Salary, Start, Stop
FROM Employee1
WHERE Name = 'Bob'
```

if the OAP wants a table of salary, title intervals (that is, suppose the OAP wishes a table to be computed in f Figure 1)? One alternative is to print out two tables, and let the user figure out the combinations. A second ds to use SQL entirely. Unfortunately, this query must do a case analysis of how each row of Employee1 h row of Employee2; there are four possible cases.

```
 Employee1.Name, Salary, Dept, Employee1.Start, Employee1.Stop
ployee1, Employee2
ployee1.Name = Employee2.Name
  Employee2.Start <= Employee1.Start AND Employ-
   < Employee2.Stop

  loyee1.Name, Salary, Dept, Employee1.Start, Employee2.Stop
   ee1, Employee2
   ee1.Name = Employee2.Name
    oyee1.Start >= Employee2.Start AND Employ-
     ployee1.Stop
```

```
                    AND Employee1.Start < Employee2.Stop
UNION
SELECT Employee1.Name, Salary, Dept, Employee2.Start, Employee1.Stop
FROM Employee1, Employee2
WHERE Employee1.Name = Employee2.Name
      AND Employee2.Start > Employee1.Start AND Employ-
ee1.Stop < Employee2.Stop
           AND Employee2.Start < Employee1.Stop
UNION
SELECT Employee1.Name, Salary, Dept, Employee2.Start, Employee2.Stop
FROM Employee1, Employee2
WHERE Employee1.Name = Employee2.Name
      AND Employee2.Start > Employee1.Start AND Employ-
ee2.Stop < Employee1.Stop
```

Getting all the cases right is a challenging task. In TSQL2, performing a temporal join is just what one would expect.

```
SELECT Employee1.Name, Salary, Dept
FROM Employee1, Employee2
WHERE Employee1.Name = Employee2.Name
```

23.16.6 A CASE STUDY - AGGREGATES

Now the OAP is asked, what is the maximum salary? Before adding time, this was easy.

```
SELECT MAX(Salary)
FROM Employee
```

Now that the salary history is stored, we'd like a history of the maximum salary over time. The problem, of course, is that SQL does not provide temporal aggregates. The easy way to do this is to print out the information, and scan manually for the maximums. An alternative is to be tricky and convert the snapshot aggregate query into a non-aggregate query, then convert that into a temporal query. The non-aggregate query finds those salaries for which a greater salary does not exist.

```
SELECT Salary
FROM Employee AS E1
WHERE NOT EXISTS (SELECT *
                  FROM Employee AS E2
                  WHERE E2.Salary > E1.Salary)
```

Converting this query into a temporal query is far from obvious. The following is one approach.

```
CREATE TABLE Temp (Salary, Start, Stop)
AS   SELECT Salary, Start, Stop
     FROM Employee;
INSERT INTO Temp
     SELECT T.Salary, T.Start, E.Start
     FROM Temp AS T, Employee AS E
     WHERE E.Start >= T.Start AND E.Start < T.Stop AND E.Salary > T.Salary;

INSERT INTO Temp
     SELECT T.Salary, T.Stop, E.Stop
     FROM Temp AS T, Employee AS E
     WHERE E.Stop > T.Start AND E.Stop <= T.Stop AND E.Salary > T.Salary;
DELETE FROM Temp T
WHERE EXISTS (SELECT *
```

HOWTO

```
                 FROM Employee AS E
                 WHERE ((T.Start => E.Start AND T.Start < E.Stop)
                        OR (E.Start >= T.Start AND E.Start < T.Stop))
                 AND E.Salary > T.Salary;
```

This approach creates an auxiliary table. We add to this table the lower period of a period subtraction and the upper period of a period subtraction. We then delete all periods that overlap with some row defined by the subquery, thereby effecting the NOT EXISTS. Finally we generate from the auxiliary table maximal periods, in the same way that the salary information was computed above. As one might imagine, such SQL code is extremely inefficient to execute, given the complex nested queries with inequality predicates.

A third alternative is to use SQL as little as possible, and instead compute the desired maximum history in a host language using cursors.

The query in TSQL2 is again straightforward and intuitive.

```
                 SELECT MAX(Salary)
                 FROM Employee
```

23.16.7 SUMMARY

Time-varying data is manipulated in most database applications. Valid-time support is absent in SQL. Many common temporal queries are either difficult to simulate in SQL, or require embedding SQL in a procedural language, due to SQL's lack of support for valid-time tables in its data model and query constructs.

Elsewhere, we showed that adding valid-time support requires few changes to the DBMS implementation, can dramatically simplify some queries and enable others, and can later enable optimizations in storage structures, indexing methods, and optimization strategies that can yield significant performance improvements.

With a new part of SQL3 supporting time-varying information, we can begin to address such applications, enabling SQL3 to better manage temporal data.

```
------------------------------------------------------------------------
            Accredited Standards Committee* X3, Information Technology
 NEWS RELEASE

 Doc. No.:       PR/96-0002

 Reply to:       Barbara Bennett at bbennett@itic.nw.dc.us

            X3 Announces the Approval of a New Project, ISO/IEC

                 9075 Part 7:   SQL/Temporal

 Washington D.C., January 1996
------------------------------------------------------------------------
```

– Accredited Standards Committee X3, Information Technology is announcing the approval of a new project on SQL/Temporal Support, ISO/IEC 9075 Part 7, with the work being done in Technical Committee X3H2, Database. The scope of this proposed standard specifies a new Part of the emerging SQL3 standard, e.g., Part 7, Temporal SQL, to be extensions to the SQL language supporting storage, retrieval, and manipulation of temporal data in an SQL database environment. The next X3H2 meeting is scheduled for March 11-14, 1996 in Kansas.

Inquiries regarding this project should be sent to the

```
            Chairman of X3H2,
            Dr. Donald R. Deutsch,
```

```
Sybase, Inc., Suite 800,
6550 Rock Spring
Drive, Bethesda, MD  20817.
Email: deutsch@sybase.com.
```

An initial call for possible patents and other pertinent issues (copyrights, trademarks) is now being issued. Please submit information on these issues to the

```
X3 Secretariat at
1250 Eye Street
NW, Suite 200,
Washington DC  20005.
Email: x3sec@itic.nw.dc.us
FAX:  (202)638-4922.
```

23.17   Part 8 - ISO/ANSI SQL MULTIMEDIA (SQL/MM)

A new ISO/IEC international standardization project for development of an SQL class library for multimedia applications was approved in early 1993. This new standardization activity, named SQL Multimedia (SQL/MM), will specify packages of SQL abstract data type (ADT) definitions using the facilities for ADT specification and invocation provided in the emerging SQL3 specification. SQL/MM intends to standardize class libraries for science and engineering, full-text and document processing, and methods for the management of multimedia objects such as image, sound, animation, music, and video. It will likely provide an SQL language binding for multimedia objects defined by other JTC1 standardization bodies (e.g. SC18 for documents, SC24 for images, and SC29 for photographs and motion pictures).

The Project Plan for SQL/MM indicates that it will be a multi-part standard consisting of an evolving number of parts. Part 1 will be a Framework that specifies how the other parts are to be constructed. Each of the other parts will be devoted to a specific SQL application package. The following SQL/MM Part structure exists as of August 1994:

- Part 1: Framework A non-technical description of how the document is structured.
- Part 2: Full Text Methods and ADTs for text data processing. About 45 pages.
- Part 3: Spatial Methods and ADTs for spatial data management. About 200 pages with active contributions from Spatial Data experts from 3 national bodies.
- Part 4: General Purpose Methods and ADTs for complex numbers, Facilities include trig and exponential functions, vectors, sets, etc. Currently about 90 pages.

There are a number of standards efforts in the area of Spatial and Geographic information:

- ANSI X3L1 - Geographic Information Systems. Mark Ashworth of Unisys is the liason between X3L1 and ANSI X3H2. He is also the editor for parts 1, 3, and 4 of the SQL/MM draft.
- ISO TC 211 - Geographic information/Geomatics

24   Technical support for PostgreSQL

If you have any technical question or encounter any problem you can e-mail to:

- *pgsql-questions@postgresql.org*

and expect e-mail answer in less than a day. As the user-base of internet product is very vast, and users support other users, internet will be capable of giving technical support to billions of users easily. Email support is much more convenient than telephone support as you can cut and paste error messages, program output etc.. and easily transmit to mailing list/newsgroup.

In the near future, PostgreSQL organisation will be selling technical support to large/small companies, the revenue generated will be used for maintaining several mirror sites (web and ftp) around the world. The revenue will also be used to produce printed documentation, guides, textbooks which will help the customers.

You can also take help from professional consulting firms like Anderson, WGS (Work Group Solutions). Contact them for help, since they have very good expertise in "C", "C++" (PostgreSQL is written in "C") -

- Work Group Solutions <http://www.wgs.com>
- Anderson Consulting <http://www.ac.com>

25 Economic and Business Aspects

Commercial databases pay many taxes like federal, state, sales, employment, social security, medicare taxes, health care for employees, bunch of benefits for employees, marketing and advertisement costs. All these costs do not go directly for the development of the database. When you buy a commercial database, some portion of the amount goes for overheads like taxes, expenses and balance for database R&D costs.

Also commercial databases have to pay for buildings/real-estates and purchase Unix machines, install and maintain them. All of these costs are passed onto customers.

PostgreSQL has the advantage over commercial databases as there is no direct tax since it is made on the internet. A very vast group of people contribute to the development of the PostgreSQL. For example, in a hypothetical case, if there are one million companies in U.S.A and each contribute about $ 10 (worth of software to PostgreSQL) than each and every company will get ten million dollars!! This is the **GREAT MAGIC** of software development on internet.

Currently, PostgreSQL source code is about 2,00,000 lines of "C", "C++" code. If cost of each line of "C" code is $ 2 than the total cost of PostgreSQL as of today is $ 4,00,000 (four hundred thousand dollars!).

Many companies already develop in-house vast amount of "C", "C++" code. Hence by taking in the source code of PostgreSQL and collaborating with other companies on internet will greatly benefit the company saving time and efforts.

26 List of Other Databases

Listed below are other SQL databases for Unix, Linux.

- Click and go to Applications->databases. <http://www.caldera.com/tech-ref/linuxapps/linapps.html>
- Click and go to Applications->databases. <http://www.xnet.com/~blatura/linapps.shtml>
- Database resources <http://linas.org/linux/db.html> This was written by Linas Vepstas: *linas@fc.net*
- Free Database List <http://cuiwww.unige.ch:80/~scg/FreeDB/FreeDB.list.html>
- Browne's RDBMS List <http://www.hex.net/~cbbrowne/rdbms.html> written by Christopher B. Browne *cbbrowne@hex.net*
- SAL's List of Relational DBMS <http://SAL.KachinaTech.COM/H/1/>
- SAL's List of Object-Oriented DBMS <http://SAL.KachinaTech.COM/H/2/>
- SAL's List of Utilites and Other Databases <http://SAL.KachinaTech.COM/H/3/>
- ACM SIGMOD Index of Publicly Available Database Software <http://bunny.cs.uiuc.edu/sigmod/databaseSoftware/>

27 Internet World Wide Web Searching Tips

Internet is very vast and it has vast number of software and has a ocean of information underneath. It is growing at the rate of 300% annually world wide. It is estimated that there are about 10 million Web sites world wide!

To search for a information you would use search engines like "Yahoo", "Netscape", "Lycos" etc. Go to Yahoo, click on search. Use filtering options to narrow down your search criteria. The default search action is "Intelligent search" which is more general and lists all possiblities. Click on "Options" to select "EXACT phrase" search, "AND" search, "OR" search, etc.. This way you would find the information you need much faster. Also in the search menu, there are radio-buttons for searching in Usenet, Web-sites and Yahoo sites.

28 Conclusion

After researching all the available databases which are **free** and source code is available, it was found that ONLY PostgreSQL is the MOST mature, most widely used and robust RDBMS SQL free database (object relational) in the world.

PostgreSQL is very appealing since lot of work had already been done. It has ODBC and JDBC drivers, using these it is possible to write applications independent of the databases. The applications written in PostgreSQL using ODBC, JDBC drivers are easily portable to other databases like Oracle, Sybase and Informix and vice versa.

You may ask "But why PostgreSQL ?" The answer is, since it takes lot more time to develop a database system from scratch, it makes sense to pick up a database system which satisfies the following conditions -

A database system

- Whose source code is available - Must be a 'Open Source Code' system
- Has no license strings, no ownership strings attached to it
- Which can be distributed on internet
- Which had been on development for several years.
- Which satisfies standards like ISO/ANSI SQL 92 (and SQL 89)
- Which can satisfy future needs like SQL 3 (SQL 98)
- Which has advanced capabilities

And it just happens to be 'PostgreSQL' which satisfies all these conditions and is an appropriate software for this situation.

29 FAQ - Questions on PostgreSQL

Please refer to the latest version of FAQ for General, Linux and Irix at

- <http://www.postgresql.org/docs/faq-english.shtml>

30 Copyright Notice

31 Appendix A - Syntax of ANSI/ISO SQL 1992

```
This file contains a depth-first tree traversal of the BNF
for the  language done at about 27-AUG-1992 11:03:41.64.
The specific version of the BNF included here is:  ANSI-only, SQL2-only.


<SQL terminal character> ::=
     <SQL language character>
   | <SQL embedded language character>


<SQL language character> ::=
     <simple Latin letter>
   | <digit>
   | <SQL special character>

<simple Latin letter> ::=
     <simple Latin upper case letter>
   | <simple Latin lower case letter>

<simple Latin upper case letter> ::=
        A | B | C | D | E | F | G | H | I | J | K | L | M | N | O
   | P | Q | R | S | T | U | V | W | X | Y | Z

<simple Latin lower case letter> ::=
        a | b | c | d | e | f | g | h | i | j | k | l | m | n | o
   | p | q | r | s | t | u | v | w | x | y | z

<digit> ::=
     0 | 1 | 2 | 3 | 4 | 5 | 6 | 7 | 8 | 9

<SQL special character> ::=
        <space>
   | <double quote>
   | <percent>
   | <ampersand>
   | <quote>
   | <left paren>
   | <right paren>
   | <asterisk>
   | <plus sign>
   | <comma>
   | <minus sign>
   | <period>
   | <solidus>
   | <colon>
   | <semicolon>
   | <less than operator>
   | <equals operator>
   | <greater than operator>
```

```
        | <question mark>
        | <underscore>
        | <vertical bar>

<space> ::= !! <EMPHASIS>(space character in character set in use)

<double quote> ::= "

<percent> ::= %

<ampersand> ::= &

<quote> ::= '

<left paren> ::= (

<right paren> ::= )

<asterisk> ::= *

<plus sign> ::= +

<comma> ::= ,

<minus sign> ::= -

<period> ::= .

<solidus> ::= /

<colon> ::= :

<semicolon> ::= ;

<less than operator> ::= <

<equals operator> ::= =

<greater than operator> ::= >

<question mark> ::= ?

<underscore> ::= _

<vertical bar> ::= |

<SQL embedded language character> ::=
        <left bracket>
        | <right bracket>

<left bracket> ::= [

<right bracket> ::= ]

<token> ::=
```

```
            <nondelimiter token>
        | <delimiter token>

<nondelimiter token> ::=
        <regular identifier>
      | <key word>
      | <unsigned numeric literal>
      | <national character string literal>
      | <bit string literal>
      | <hex string literal>

<regular identifier> ::= <identifier body>

<identifier body> ::=
      <identifier start> [ ( <underscore> | <identifier part> )... ]

<identifier start> ::= <EMPHASIS>(!! See the Syntax Rules)

<identifier part> ::=
        <identifier start>
      | <digit>

<key word> ::=
        <reserved word>
      | <non-reserved word>

<reserved word> ::=
        ABSOLUTE | ACTION | ADD | ALL
      | ALLOCATE | ALTER | AND
      | ANY | ARE
      | AS | ASC
      | ASSERTION | AT
      | AUTHORIZATION | AVG
      | BEGIN | BETWEEN | BIT | BIT_LENGTH
      | BOTH | BY
      | CASCADE | CASCADED | CASE | CAST
      | CATALOG
      | CHAR | CHARACTER | CHAR_LENGTH
      | CHARACTER_LENGTH | CHECK | CLOSE | COALESCE
      | COLLATE | COLLATION
      | COLUMN | COMMIT
      | CONNECT
      | CONNECTION | CONSTRAINT
      | CONSTRAINTS | CONTINUE
      | CONVERT | CORRESPONDING | COUNT | CREATE | CROSS
      | CURRENT
      | CURRENT_DATE | CURRENT_TIME
      | CURRENT_TIMESTAMP | CURRENT_USER | CURSOR
      | DATE | DAY | DEALLOCATE | DEC
      | DECIMAL | DECLARE | DEFAULT | DEFERRABLE
      | DEFERRED | DELETE | DESC | DESCRIBE | DESCRIPTOR
      | DIAGNOSTICS
      | DISCONNECT | DISTINCT | DOMAIN | DOUBLE | DROP
      | ELSE | END | END-EXEC | ESCAPE
      | EXCEPT | EXCEPTION
```

```
        | EXEC | EXECUTE | EXISTS
        | EXTERNAL | EXTRACT
        | FALSE | FETCH | FIRST | FLOAT | FOR
        | FOREIGN | FOUND | FROM | FULL
        | GET | GLOBAL | GO | GOTO
        | GRANT | GROUP
        | HAVING | HOUR
        | IDENTITY | IMMEDIATE | IN | INDICATOR
        | INITIALLY | INNER | INPUT
        | INSENSITIVE | INSERT | INT | INTEGER | INTERSECT
        | INTERVAL | INTO | IS
        | ISOLATION
        | JOIN
        | KEY
        | LANGUAGE | LAST | LEADING | LEFT
        | LEVEL | LIKE | LOCAL | LOWER
        | MATCH | MAX | MIN | MINUTE | MODULE
        | MONTH
        | NAMES | NATIONAL | NATURAL | NCHAR | NEXT | NO
        | NOT | NULL
        | NULLIF | NUMERIC
        | OCTET_LENGTH | OF
        | ON | ONLY | OPEN | OPTION | OR
        | ORDER | OUTER
        | OUTPUT | OVERLAPS
        | PAD | PARTIAL | POSITION | PRECISION | PREPARE
        | PRESERVE | PRIMARY
        | PRIOR | PRIVILEGES | PROCEDURE | PUBLIC
        | READ | REAL | REFERENCES | RELATIVE | RESTRICT
        | REVOKE | RIGHT
        | ROLLBACK | ROWS
        | SCHEMA | SCROLL | SECOND | SECTION
        | SELECT
        | SESSION | SESSION_USER | SET
        | SIZE | SMALLINT | SOME | SPACE | SQL | SQLCODE
        | SQLERROR | SQLSTATE
        | SUBSTRING | SUM | SYSTEM_USER
        | TABLE | TEMPORARY
        | THEN | TIME | TIMESTAMP
        | TIMEZONE_HOUR | TIMEZONE_MINUTE
        | TO | TRAILING | TRANSACTION
        | TRANSLATE | TRANSLATION | TRIM | TRUE
        | UNION | UNIQUE | UNKNOWN | UPDATE | UPPER | USAGE
        | USER | USING
        | VALUE | VALUES | VARCHAR | VARYING | VIEW
        | WHEN | WHENEVER | WHERE | WITH | WORK | WRITE
        | YEAR
        | ZONE

<non-reserved word> ::=

        ADA
        | C | CATALOG_NAME
        | CHARACTER_SET_CATALOG | CHARACTER_SET_NAME
        | CHARACTER_SET_SCHEMA | CLASS_ORIGIN | COBOL | COLLATION_CATALOG
```

```
       | COLLATION_NAME | COLLATION_SCHEMA | COLUMN_NAME | COMMAND_FUNCTION
       | COMMITTED
       | CONDITION_NUMBER | CONNECTION_NAME | CONSTRAIN-
T_CATALOG | CONSTRAINT_NAME
       | CONSTRAINT_SCHEMA | CURSOR_NAME
       | DATA | DATETIME_INTERVAL_CODE
       | DATETIME_INTERVAL_PRECISION | DYNAMIC_FUNCTION
       | FORTRAN
       | LENGTH
       | MESSAGE_LENGTH | MESSAGE_OCTET_LENGTH | MESSAGE_TEXT | MORE | MUMPS
       | NAME | NULLABLE | NUMBER
       | PASCAL | PLI
| REPEATABLE | RETURNED_LENGTH | RETURNED_OCTET_LENGTH | RETURNED_SQLSTATE
       | ROW_COUNT
       | SCALE | SCHEMA_NAME | SERIALIZABLE | SERVER_NAME | SUBCLASS_ORIGIN
       | TABLE_NAME | TYPE
       | UNCOMMITTED | UNNAMED

<unsigned numeric literal> ::=
       <exact numeric literal>
     | <approximate numeric literal>

<exact numeric literal> ::=
       <unsigned integer> [ <period> [ <unsigned integer> ] ]
     | <period> <unsigned integer>

<unsigned integer> ::= <digit>...

<approximate numeric literal> ::= <mantissa> E <exponent>

<mantissa> ::= <exact numeric literal>

<exponent> ::= <signed integer>

<signed integer> ::= [ <sign> ] <unsigned integer>

<sign> ::= <plus sign> | <minus sign>

<national character string literal> ::=
     N <quote> [ <character representation>... ] <quote>
       [ ( <separator>... <quote> [ <character representa-
tion>... ] <quote> )... ]

<character representation> ::=
       <nonquote character>
     | <quote symbol>

<nonquote character> ::= !! <EMPHASIS>(See the Syntax Rules.)

<quote symbol> ::= <quote><quote>

<separator> ::= ( <comment> | <space> | <newline> )...

<comment> ::=
     <comment introducer> [ <comment character>... ] <newline>
```

```
<comment introducer> ::= <minus sign><minus sign>[<minus sign>...]

<comment character> ::=
      <nonquote character>
    | <quote>

<newline> ::= !! <EMPHASIS>(implementation-defined end-of-line indicator)

<bit string literal> ::=
    B <quote> [ <bit>... ] <quote>
    [ ( <separator>... <quote> [ <bit>... ] <quote> )... ]

<bit> ::= 0 | 1

<hex string literal> ::=
    X <quote> [ <hexit>... ] <quote>
    [ ( <separator>... <quote> [ <hexit>... ] <quote> )... ]

<hexit> ::= <digit> | A | B | C | D | E | F | a | b | c | d | e | f

<delimiter token> ::=
      <character string literal>
    | <date string>
    | <time string>
    | <timestamp string>
    | <interval string>
    | <delimited identifier>
    | <SQL special character>
    | <not equals operator>
    | <greater than or equals operator>
    | <less than or equals operator>
    | <concatenation operator>
    | <double period>
    | <left bracket>
    | <right bracket>

<character string literal> ::=
    [ <introducer><character set specification> ]
    <quote> [ <character representation>... ] <quote>
      [ ( <separator>... <quote> [ <character representa-
tion>... ] <quote> )... ]

<introducer> ::= <underscore>

<character set specification> ::=
      <standard character repertoire name>
    | <implementation-defined character repertoire name>
    | <user-defined character repertoire name>
    | <standard universal character form-of-use name>
    | <implementation-defined universal character form-of-use name>

<standard character repertoire name> ::= <character set name>

<character set name> ::= [ <schema name> <period> ]
```

HOWTO

```
    <SQL language identifier>

<schema name> ::=
    [ <catalog name> <period> ] <unqualified schema name>

<catalog name> ::= <identifier>

<identifier> ::=
    [ <introducer><character set specification> ] <actual identifier>

<actual identifier> ::=
      <regular identifier>
    | <delimited identifier>

<delimited identifier> ::=
    <double quote> <delimited identifier body> <double quote>

<delimited identifier body> ::= <delimited identifier part>...

<delimited identifier part> ::=
      <nondoublequote character>
    | <doublequote symbol>

<nondoublequote character> ::= <EMPHASIS>(!! See the Syntax Rules)

<doublequote symbol> ::= <double quote><double quote>

<unqualified schema name> ::= <identifier>

<SQL language identifier> ::=
    <SQL language identifier start>
       [ ( <underscore> | <SQL language identifier part> )... ]

<SQL language identifier start> ::= <simple Latin letter>

<SQL language identifier part> ::=
      <simple Latin letter>
    | <digit>

<implementation-defined character repertoire name> ::=
    <character set name>

<user-defined character repertoire name> ::= <character set name>

<standard universal character form-of-use name> ::=
    <character set name>

<implementation-defined universal character form-of-use name> ::=
    <character set name>

<date string> ::=
    <quote> <date value> <quote>

<date value> ::=
    <years value> <minus sign> <months value>
```

```
                    <minus sign> <days value>

<years value> ::= <datetime value>

<datetime value> ::= <unsigned integer>

<months value> ::= <datetime value>

<days value> ::= <datetime value>

<time string> ::=
    <quote> <time value> [ <time zone interval> ] <quote>

<time value> ::=
    <hours value> <colon> <minutes value> <colon> <seconds value>

<hours value> ::= <datetime value>

<minutes value> ::= <datetime value>

<seconds value> ::=
      <seconds integer value> [ <period> [ <seconds fraction> ] ]

<seconds integer value> ::= <unsigned integer>

<seconds fraction> ::= <unsigned integer>

<time zone interval> ::=
    <sign> <hours value> <colon> <minutes value>

<timestamp string> ::=
    <quote> <date value> <space> <time value>
        [ <time zone interval> ] <quote>

<interval string> ::=
    <quote> ( <year-month literal> | <day-time literal> ) <quote>

<year-month literal> ::=
        <years value>
    | [ <years value> <minus sign> ] <months value>

<day-time literal> ::=
        <day-time interval>
    | <time interval>

<day-time interval> ::=
    <days value>
        [ <space> <hours value> [ <colon> <minutes value>
        [ <colon> <seconds value> ] ] ]

<time interval> ::=
        <hours value> [ <colon> <minutes value> [ <colon> <seconds value> ] ]
    | <minutes value> [ <colon> <seconds value> ]
    | <seconds value>
```

HOWTO

```
<not equals operator> ::= <>

<greater than or equals operator> ::= >=

<less than or equals operator> ::= <=

<concatenation operator> ::= ||

<double period> ::= ..

<module> ::=
    <module name clause>
    <language clause>
    <module authorization clause>
    [ <temporary table declaration>... ]
    <module contents>...

<module name clause> ::=
    MODULE [ <module name> ]
      [ <module character set specification> ]

<module name> ::= <identifier>

<module character set specification> ::=
    NAMES ARE <character set specification>

<language clause> ::=
    LANGUAGE <language name>

<language name> ::=
    ADA | C | COBOL | FORTRAN | MUMPS | PASCAL | PLI

<module authorization clause> ::=
      SCHEMA <schema name>
    | AUTHORIZATION <module authorization identifier>
    | SCHEMA <schema name>
          AUTHORIZATION <module authorization identifier>

<module authorization identifier> ::=
    <authorization identifier>

<authorization identifier> ::= <identifier>

<temporary table declaration> ::=
    DECLARE LOCAL TEMPORARY TABLE
        <qualified local table name>
      <table element list>
      [ ON COMMIT ( PRESERVE | DELETE ) ROWS ]

<qualified local table name> ::=
    MODULE <period> <local table name>

<local table name> ::= <qualified identifier>

<qualified identifier> ::= <identifier>
```

```
<table element list> ::=
      <left paren> <table element> [ ( <comma> <table elemen-
t> )... ] <right paren>

<table element> ::=
      <column definition>
    | <table constraint definition>

<column definition> ::=
    <column name> ( <data type> | <domain name> )
    [ <default clause> ]
    [ <column constraint definition>... ]
    [ <collate clause> ]

<column name> ::= <identifier>

<data type> ::=
      <character string type>
          [ CHARACTER SET <character set specification> ]
    | <national character string type>
    | <bit string type>
    | <numeric type>
    | <datetime type>
    | <interval type>

<character string type> ::=
      CHARACTER [ <left paren> <length> <right paren> ]
    | CHAR [ <left paren> <length> <right paren> ]
    | CHARACTER VARYING <left paren> <length> <right paren>
    | CHAR VARYING <left paren> <length> <right paren>
    | VARCHAR <left paren> <length> <right paren>

<length> ::= <unsigned integer>

<national character string type> ::=
      NATIONAL CHARACTER [ <left paren> <length> <right paren> ]
    | NATIONAL CHAR [ <left paren> <length> <right paren> ]
    | NCHAR [ <left paren> <length> <right paren> ]
    | NATIONAL CHARACTER VARYING <left paren> <length> <right paren>
    | NATIONAL CHAR VARYING <left paren> <length> <right paren>
    | NCHAR VARYING <left paren> <length> <right paren>

<bit string type> ::=
      BIT [ <left paren> <length> <right paren> ]
    | BIT VARYING <left paren> <length> <right paren>

<numeric type> ::=
      <exact numeric type>
    | <approximate numeric type>

<exact numeric type> ::=
      NUMERIC [ <left paren> <precision> [ <comma> <scale> ] <right paren> ]
    | DECIMAL [ <left paren> <precision> [ <comma> <scale> ] <right paren> ]
    | DEC [ <left paren> <precision> [ <comma> <scale> ] <right paren> ]
```

HOWTO

```
      | INTEGER
      | INT
      | SMALLINT

<precision> ::= <unsigned integer>

<scale> ::= <unsigned integer>

<approximate numeric type> ::=
      FLOAT [ <left paren> <precision> <right paren> ]
    | REAL
    | DOUBLE PRECISION

<datetime type> ::=
      DATE
    | TIME [ <left paren> <time precision> <right paren> ]
          [ WITH TIME ZONE ]
    | TIMESTAMP [ <left paren> <timestamp precision> <right paren> ]
          [ WITH TIME ZONE ]

<time precision> ::= <time fractional seconds precision>

<time fractional seconds precision> ::= <unsigned integer>

<timestamp precision> ::= <time fractional seconds precision>

<interval type> ::= INTERVAL <interval qualifier>

<interval qualifier> ::=
      <start field> TO <end field>
    | <single datetime field>

<start field> ::=
    <non-second datetime field>
        [ <left paren> <interval leading field precision> <right paren> ]

<non-second datetime field> ::= YEAR | MONTH | DAY | HOUR
    | MINUTE

<interval leading field precision> ::= <unsigned integer>

<end field> ::=
      <non-second datetime field>
    | SECOND [ <left paren> <interval fractional seconds preci-
sion> <right paren> ]

<interval fractional seconds precision> ::= <unsigned integer>

<single datetime field> ::=
      <non-second datetime field>
          [ <left paren> <interval leading field precision> <right paren> ]
    | SECOND [ <left paren> <interval leading field precision>
          [ <comma> <interval fractional seconds preci-
sion> ] <right paren> ]
```

```
<domain name> ::= <qualified name>

<qualified name> ::=
    [ <schema name> <period> ] <qualified identifier>

<default clause> ::=
      DEFAULT <default option>

<default option> ::=
      <literal>
    | <datetime value function>
    | USER
    | CURRENT_USER
    | SESSION_USER
    | SYSTEM_USER
    | NULL

<literal> ::=
      <signed numeric literal>
    | <general literal>

<signed numeric literal> ::=
    [ <sign> ] <unsigned numeric literal>

<general literal> ::=
      <character string literal>
    | <national character string literal>
    | <bit string literal>
    | <hex string literal>
    | <datetime literal>
    | <interval literal>

<datetime literal> ::=
      <date literal>
    | <time literal>
    | <timestamp literal>

<date literal> ::=
    DATE <date string>

<time literal> ::=
    TIME <time string>

<timestamp literal> ::=
    TIMESTAMP <timestamp string>

<interval literal> ::=
    INTERVAL [ <sign> ] <interval string> <interval qualifier>

<datetime value function> ::=
      <current date value function>
    | <current time value function>
    | <current timestamp value function>

<current date value function> ::= CURRENT_DATE
```

```
<current time value function> ::=
      CURRENT_TIME [ <left paren> <time precision> <right paren> ]

<current timestamp value function> ::=
      CURRENT_TIMESTAMP [ <left paren> <timestamp precision> <right paren> ]

<column constraint definition> ::=
    [ <constraint name definition> ]
    <column constraint>
      [ <constraint attributes> ]

<constraint name definition> ::= CONSTRAINT <constraint name>

<constraint name> ::= <qualified name>

<column constraint> ::=
      NOT NULL
    | <unique specification>
    | <references specification>
    | <check constraint definition>

<unique specification> ::=
    UNIQUE | PRIMARY KEY

<references specification> ::=
    REFERENCES <referenced table and columns>
      [ MATCH <match type> ]
      [ <referential triggered action> ]

<referenced table and columns> ::=
      <table name> [ <left paren> <reference column list> <right paren> ]

<table name> ::=
      <qualified name>
    | <qualified local table name>

<reference column list> ::= <column name list>

<column name list> ::=
    <column name> [ ( <comma> <column name> )... ]

<match type> ::=
      FULL
    | PARTIAL

<referential triggered action> ::=
      <update rule> [ <delete rule> ]
    | <delete rule> [ <update rule> ]

<update rule> ::= ON UPDATE <referential action>

<referential action> ::=
      CASCADE
    | SET NULL
```

```
                | SET DEFAULT
                | NO ACTION

    <delete rule> ::= ON DELETE <referential action>

    <check constraint definition> ::=
        CHECK
            <left paren> <search condition> <right paren>

    <search condition> ::=
            <boolean term>
        | <search condition> OR <boolean term>

    <boolean term> ::=
            <boolean factor>
        | <boolean term> AND <boolean factor>

    <boolean factor> ::=
        [ NOT ] <boolean test>

    <boolean test> ::=
        <boolean primary> [ IS [ NOT ]
            <truth value> ]

    <boolean primary> ::=
            <predicate>
        | <left paren> <search condition> <right paren>

    <predicate> ::=
            <comparison predicate>
        | <between predicate>
        | <in predicate>
        | <like predicate>
        | <null predicate>
        | <quantified comparison predicate>
        | <exists predicate>
        | <unique predicate>
        | <match predicate>
        | <overlaps predicate>

    <comparison predicate> ::=
        <row value constructor> <comp op>
            <row value constructor>

    <row value constructor> ::=
            <row value constructor element>
        | <left paren> <row value constructor list> <right paren>
        | <row subquery>

    <row value constructor element> ::=
            <value expression>
        | <null specification>
        | <default specification>

    <value expression> ::=
```

```
          <numeric value expression>
        | <string value expression>
        | <datetime value expression>
        | <interval value expression>

<numeric value expression> ::=
          <term>
        | <numeric value expression> <plus sign> <term>
        | <numeric value expression> <minus sign> <term>

<term> ::=
          <factor>
        | <term> <asterisk> <factor>
        | <term> <solidus> <factor>

<factor> ::=
        [ <sign> ] <numeric primary>

<numeric primary> ::=
          <value expression primary>
        | <numeric value function>

<value expression primary> ::=
          <unsigned value specification>
        | <column reference>
        | <set function specification>
        | <scalar subquery>
        | <case expression>
        | <left paren> <value expression> <right paren>
        | <cast specification>

<unsigned value specification> ::=
          <unsigned literal>
        | <general value specification>

<unsigned literal> ::=
          <unsigned numeric literal>
        | <general literal>

<general value specification> ::=
          <parameter specification>
        | <dynamic parameter specification>
        | <variable specification>
        | USER
        | CURRENT_USER
        | SESSION_USER
        | SYSTEM_USER
        | VALUE

<parameter specification> ::=
        <parameter name> [ <indicator parameter> ]

<parameter name> ::= <colon> <identifier>

<indicator parameter> ::=
```

```
    [ INDICATOR ] <parameter name>

<dynamic parameter specification> ::= <question mark>

<variable specification> ::=
    <embedded variable name> [ <indicator variable> ]

<embedded variable name> ::=
    <colon><host identifier>

<host identifier> ::=
      <Ada host identifier>
    | <C host identifier>
    | <COBOL host identifier>
    | <Fortran host identifier>
    | <MUMPS host identifier>
    | <Pascal host identifier>
    | <PL/I host identifier>

<Ada host identifier> ::= !! <EMPHASIS>(See the Syntax Rules.)

<C host identifier> ::=
    !! <EMPHASIS>(See the Syntax Rules.)

<COBOL host identifier> ::= !! <EMPHASIS>(See the Syntax Rules.)

<Fortran host identifier> ::= !! <EMPHASIS>(See the Syntax Rules.)

<MUMPS host identifier> ::= !! <EMPHASIS>(See the Syntax Rules.)

<Pascal host identifier> ::= !! <EMPHASIS>(See the Syntax Rules.)

<PL/I host identifier> ::= !! <EMPHASIS>(See the Syntax Rules.)

<indicator variable> ::=
    [ INDICATOR ] <embedded variable name>

<column reference> ::= [ <qualifier> <period> ] <column name>

<qualifier> ::=
      <table name>
    | <correlation name>

<correlation name> ::= <identifier>

<set function specification> ::=
      COUNT <left paren> <asterisk> <right paren>
    | <general set function>

<general set function> ::=
      <set function type>
          <left paren> [ <set quantifier> ] <value expression> <right paren>

<set function type> ::=
    AVG | MAX | MIN | SUM | COUNT
```

HOWTO

```
<set quantifier> ::= DISTINCT | ALL

<scalar subquery> ::= <subquery>

<subquery> ::= <left paren> <query expression> <right paren>

<query expression> ::=
     <non-join query expression>
   | <joined table>

<non-join query expression> ::=
     <non-join query term>
   | <query expression> UNION  [ ALL ]
       [ <corresponding spec> ] <query term>
   | <query expression> EXCEPT [ ALL ]
       [ <corresponding spec> ] <query term>

<non-join query term> ::=
     <non-join query primary>
   | <query term> INTERSECT [ ALL ]
       [ <corresponding spec> ] <query primary>

<non-join query primary> ::=
     <simple table>
   | <left paren> <non-join query expression> <right paren>

<simple table> ::=
     <query specification>
   | <table value constructor>
   | <explicit table>

<query specification> ::=
   SELECT [ <set quantifier> ] <select list> <table expression>

<select list> ::=
     <asterisk>
   | <select sublist> [ ( <comma> <select sublist> )... ]

<select sublist> ::=
     <derived column>
   | <qualifier> <period> <asterisk>

<derived column> ::= <value expression> [ <as clause> ]

<as clause> ::= [ AS ] <column name>

<table expression> ::=
   <from clause>
   [ <where clause> ]
   [ <group by clause> ]
   [ <having clause> ]

<from clause> ::= FROM <table reference>
   [ ( <comma> <table reference> )... ]
```

```
<table reference> ::=
    <table name> [ [ AS ] <correlation name>
        [ <left paren> <derived column list> <right paren> ] ]
  | <derived table> [ AS ] <correlation name>
        [ <left paren> <derived column list> <right paren> ]
  | <joined table>

<derived column list> ::= <column name list>

<derived table> ::= <table subquery>

<table subquery> ::= <subquery>

<joined table> ::=
    <cross join>
  | <qualified join>
  | <left paren> <joined table> <right paren>

<cross join> ::=
    <table reference> CROSS JOIN <table reference>

<qualified join> ::=
    <table reference> [ NATURAL ] [ <join type> ] JOIN
        <table reference> [ <join specification> ]

<join type> ::=
    INNER
  | <outer join type> [ OUTER ]
  | UNION

<outer join type> ::=
    LEFT
  | RIGHT
  | FULL

<join specification> ::=
    <join condition>
  | <named columns join>

<join condition> ::= ON <search condition>

<named columns join> ::=
    USING <left paren> <join column list> <right paren>

<join column list> ::= <column name list>

<where clause> ::= WHERE <search condition>

<group by clause> ::=
    GROUP BY <grouping column reference list>

<grouping column reference list> ::=
    <grouping column reference>
        [ ( <comma> <grouping column reference> )... ]
```

```
<grouping column reference> ::=
    <column reference> [ <collate clause> ]

<collate clause> ::= COLLATE <collation name>

<collation name> ::= <qualified name>

<having clause> ::= HAVING <search condition>

<table value constructor> ::=
    VALUES <table value constructor list>

<table value constructor list> ::=
    <row value constructor> [ ( <comma> <row value constructor> )... ]

<explicit table> ::= TABLE <table name>

<query term> ::=
      <non-join query term>
    | <joined table>

<corresponding spec> ::=
    CORRESPONDING [ BY <left paren> <corresponding colum-
n list> <right paren> ]

<corresponding column list> ::= <column name list>

<query primary> ::=
      <non-join query primary>
    | <joined table>

<case expression> ::=
      <case abbreviation>
    | <case specification>

<case abbreviation> ::=
      NULLIF <left paren> <value expression> <comma>
          <value expression> <right paren>
    | COALESCE <left paren> <value expression>
          ( <comma> <value expression> )... <right paren>

<case specification> ::=
      <simple case>
    | <searched case>

<simple case> ::=
    CASE <case operand>
      <simple when clause>...
      [ <else clause> ]
    END

<case operand> ::= <value expression>

<simple when clause> ::= WHEN <when operand> THEN <result>
```

```
<when operand> ::= <value expression>

<result> ::= <result expression> | NULL

<result expression> ::= <value expression>

<else clause> ::= ELSE <result>

<searched case> ::=
    CASE
       <searched when clause>...
       [ <else clause> ]
    END

<searched when clause> ::= WHEN <search condition> THEN <result>

<cast specification> ::=
    CAST <left paren> <cast operand> AS
        <cast target> <right paren>

<cast operand> ::=
        <value expression>
    | NULL

<cast target> ::=
        <domain name>
    | <data type>

<numeric value function> ::=
        <position expression>
    | <extract expression>
    | <length expression>

<position expression> ::=
    POSITION <left paren> <character value expression>
        IN <character value expression> <right paren>

<character value expression> ::=
        <concatenation>
    | <character factor>

<concatenation> ::=
    <character value expression> <concatenation operator>
        <character factor>

<character factor> ::=
    <character primary> [ <collate clause> ]

<character primary> ::=
        <value expression primary>
    | <string value function>

<string value function> ::=
        <character value function>
```

HOWTO

```
        | <bit value function>

<character value function> ::=
        <character substring function>
    | <fold>
    | <form-of-use conversion>
    | <character translation>
    | <trim function>

<character substring function> ::=
    SUBSTRING <left paren> <character value expression> FROM <start posi-
tion>
                [ FOR <string length> ] <right paren>

<start position> ::= <numeric value expression>

<string length> ::= <numeric value expression>

<fold> ::= ( UPPER | LOWER )
        <left paren> <character value expression> <right paren>

<form-of-use conversion> ::=
    CONVERT <left paren> <character value expression>
        USING <form-of-use conversion name> <right paren>

<form-of-use conversion name> ::= <qualified name>

<character translation> ::=
    TRANSLATE <left paren> <character value expression>
        USING <translation name> <right paren>

<translation name> ::= <qualified name>

<trim function> ::=
    TRIM <left paren> <trim operands> <right paren>

<trim operands> ::=
    [ [ <trim specification> ] [ <trim character> ] FROM ] <trim source>

<trim specification> ::=
        LEADING
    | TRAILING
    | BOTH

<trim character> ::= <character value expression>

<trim source> ::= <character value expression>

<bit value function> ::=
    <bit substring function>

<bit substring function> ::=
    SUBSTRING <left paren> <bit value expression> FROM <start position>
        [ FOR <string length> ] <right paren>
```

```
<bit value expression> ::=
      <bit concatenation>
    | <bit factor>

<bit concatenation> ::=
      <bit value expression> <concatenation operator> <bit factor>

<bit factor> ::= <bit primary>

<bit primary> ::=
      <value expression primary>
    | <string value function>

<extract expression> ::=
    EXTRACT <left paren> <extract field>
        FROM <extract source> <right paren>

<extract field> ::=
      <datetime field>
    | <time zone field>

<datetime field> ::=
      <non-second datetime field>
    | SECOND

<time zone field> ::=
      TIMEZONE_HOUR
    | TIMEZONE_MINUTE

<extract source> ::=
      <datetime value expression>
    | <interval value expression>

<datetime value expression> ::=
      <datetime term>
    | <interval value expression> <plus sign> <datetime term>
    | <datetime value expression> <plus sign> <interval term>
    | <datetime value expression> <minus sign> <interval term>

<interval term> ::=
      <interval factor>
    | <interval term 2> <asterisk> <factor>
    | <interval term 2> <solidus> <factor>
    | <term> <asterisk> <interval factor>

<interval factor> ::=
    [ <sign> ] <interval primary>

<interval primary> ::=
      <value expression primary> [ <interval qualifier> ]

<interval term 2> ::= <interval term>

<interval value expression> ::=
      <interval term>
```

```
          | <interval value expression 1> <plus sign> <interval term 1>
          | <interval value expression 1> <minus sign> <interval term 1>
          | <left paren> <datetime value expression> <minus sign>
               <datetime term> <right paren> <interval qualifier>

<interval value expression 1> ::= <interval value expression>

<interval term 1> ::= <interval term>

<datetime term> ::=
     <datetime factor>

<datetime factor> ::=
     <datetime primary> [ <time zone> ]

<datetime primary> ::=
     <value expression primary>
   | <datetime value function>

<time zone> ::=
    AT <time zone specifier>

<time zone specifier> ::=
     LOCAL
   | TIME ZONE <interval value expression>

<length expression> ::=
     <char length expression>
   | <octet length expression>
   | <bit length expression>

<char length expression> ::=
    ( CHAR_LENGTH | CHARACTER_LENGTH )
         <left paren> <string value expression> <right paren>

<string value expression> ::=
     <character value expression>
   | <bit value expression>

<octet length expression> ::=
    OCTET_LENGTH <left paren> <string value expression> <right paren>

<bit length expression> ::=
    BIT_LENGTH <left paren> <string value expression> <right paren>

<null specification> ::=
    NULL

<default specification> ::=
    DEFAULT

<row value constructor list> ::=
    <row value constructor element>
         [ ( <comma> <row value constructor element> )... ]
```

```
<row subquery> ::= <subquery>

<comp op> ::=
      <equals operator>
    | <not equals operator>
    | <less than operator>
    | <greater than operator>
    | <less than or equals operator>
    | <greater than or equals operator>

<between predicate> ::=
    <row value constructor> [ NOT ] BETWEEN
        <row value constructor> AND <row value constructor>

<in predicate> ::=
    <row value constructor>
        [ NOT ] IN <in predicate value>

<in predicate value> ::=
        <table subquery>
    | <left paren> <in value list> <right paren>

<in value list> ::=
    <value expression> ( <comma> <value expression> )...

<like predicate> ::=
    <match value> [ NOT ] LIKE <pattern>
        [ ESCAPE <escape character> ]

<match value> ::= <character value expression>

<pattern> ::= <character value expression>

<escape character> ::= <character value expression>

<null predicate> ::= <row value constructor>
    IS [ NOT ] NULL

<quantified comparison predicate> ::=
    <row value constructor> <comp op> <quantifier> <table subquery>

<quantifier> ::= <all> | <some>

<all> ::= ALL

<some> ::= SOME | ANY

<exists predicate> ::= EXISTS <table subquery>

<unique predicate> ::= UNIQUE <table subquery>

<match predicate> ::=
    <row value constructor> MATCH [ UNIQUE ]
        [ PARTIAL | FULL ] <table subquery>
```

HOWTO

```
<overlaps predicate> ::=
    <row value constructor 1> OVERLAPS <row value constructor 2>

<row value constructor 1> ::= <row value constructor>

<row value constructor 2> ::= <row value constructor>

<truth value> ::=
      TRUE
    | FALSE
    | UNKNOWN

<constraint attributes> ::=
      <constraint check time> [ [ NOT ] DEFERRABLE ]
    | [ NOT ] DEFERRABLE [ <constraint check time> ]

<constraint check time> ::=
      INITIALLY DEFERRED
    | INITIALLY IMMEDIATE

<table constraint definition> ::=
    [ <constraint name definition> ]
    <table constraint> [ <constraint attributes> ]

<table constraint> ::=
      <unique constraint definition>
    | <referential constraint definition>
    | <check constraint definition>

<unique constraint definition> ::=
             <unique specification> even in SQL3)
    <unique specification>
      <left paren> <unique column list> <right paren>

<unique column list> ::= <column name list>

<referential constraint definition> ::=
    FOREIGN KEY
        <left paren> <referencing columns> <right paren>
        <references specification>

<referencing columns> ::=
    <reference column list>

<module contents> ::=
      <declare cursor>
    | <dynamic declare cursor>
    | <procedure>

<declare cursor> ::=
    DECLARE <cursor name> [ INSENSITIVE ] [ SCROLL ] CURSOR
      FOR <cursor specification>

<cursor name> ::= <identifier>
```

```
<cursor specification> ::=
    <query expression> [ <order by clause> ]
      [ <updatability clause> ]

<order by clause> ::=
    ORDER BY <sort specification list>

<sort specification list> ::=
    <sort specification> [ ( <comma> <sort specification> )... ]

<sort specification> ::=
    <sort key> [ <collate clause> ] [ <ordering specification> ]

<sort key> ::=
      <column name>
    | <unsigned integer>

<ordering specification> ::= ASC | DESC

<updatability clause> ::=
    FOR
        ( READ ONLY |
          UPDATE [ OF <column name list> ] ) )

<dynamic declare cursor> ::=
    DECLARE <cursor name> [ INSENSITIVE ] [ SCROLL ] CURSOR
        FOR <statement name>

<statement name> ::= <identifier>

<procedure> ::=
    PROCEDURE <procedure name>
        <parameter declaration list> <semicolon>
      <SQL procedure statement> <semicolon>

<procedure name> ::= <identifier>

<parameter declaration list> ::=
      <left paren> <parameter declaration>
          [ ( <comma> <parameter declaration> )... ] <right paren>
    | <parameter declaration>...

<parameter declaration> ::=
      <parameter name> <data type>
    | <status parameter>

<status parameter> ::=
    SQLCODE | SQLSTATE

<SQL procedure statement> ::=
      <SQL schema statement>
    | <SQL data statement>
    | <SQL transaction statement>
    | <SQL connection statement>
    | <SQL session statement>
```

```
     | <SQL dynamic statement>
     | <SQL diagnostics statement>

<SQL schema statement> ::=
      <SQL schema definition statement>
    | <SQL schema manipulation statement>

<SQL schema definition statement> ::=
      <schema definition>
    | <table definition>
    | <view definition>
    | <grant statement>
    | <domain definition>
    | <character set definition>
    | <collation definition>
    | <translation definition>
    | <assertion definition>

<schema definition> ::=
    CREATE SCHEMA <schema name clause>
       [ <schema character set specification> ]
       [ <schema element>... ]

<schema name clause> ::=
        <schema name>
    | AUTHORIZATION <schema authorization identifier>
    | <schema name> AUTHORIZATION
          <schema authorization identifier>

<schema authorization identifier> ::=
    <authorization identifier>

<schema character set specification> ::=
    DEFAULT CHARACTER
        SET <character set specification>

<schema element> ::=
        <domain definition>
    | <table definition>
    | <view definition>
    | <grant statement>
    | <assertion definition>
    | <character set definition>
    | <collation definition>
    | <translation definition>

<domain definition> ::=
    CREATE DOMAIN <domain name>
        [ AS ] <data type>
       [ <default clause> ]
       [ <domain constraint>... ]
       [ <collate clause> ]

<domain constraint> ::=
    [ <constraint name definition> ]
```

```
        <check constraint definition> [ <constraint attributes> ]

<table definition> ::=
    CREATE [ ( GLOBAL | LOCAL ) TEMPORARY ] TABLE
        <table name>
      <table element list>
      [ ON COMMIT ( DELETE | PRESERVE ) ROWS ]

<view definition> ::=
    CREATE VIEW <table name> [ <left paren> <view column list>
                                <right paren> ]
      AS <query expression>
      [ WITH [ <levels clause> ] CHECK OPTION ]

<view column list> ::= <column name list>

<levels clause> ::=
    CASCADED | LOCAL

<grant statement> ::=
    GRANT <privileges> ON <object name>
      TO <grantee> [ ( <comma> <grantee> )... ]
        [ WITH GRANT OPTION ]

<privileges> ::=
        ALL PRIVILEGES
    | <action list>

<action list> ::= <action> [ ( <comma> <action> )... ]

<action> ::=
        SELECT
    | DELETE
    | INSERT [ <left paren> <privilege column list> <right paren> ]
    | UPDATE [ <left paren> <privilege column list> <right paren> ]
    | REFERENCES [ <left paren> <privilege column list> <right paren> ]
    | USAGE

<privilege column list> ::= <column name list>

<object name> ::=
        [ TABLE ] <table name>
    | DOMAIN <domain name>
    | COLLATION <collation name>
    | CHARACTER SET <character set name>
    | TRANSLATION <translation name>

<grantee> ::=
        PUBLIC
    | <authorization identifier>

<assertion definition> ::=
    CREATE ASSERTION <constraint name> <assertion check>
      [ <constraint attributes> ]
```

```
<assertion check> ::=
    CHECK
        <left paren> <search condition> <right paren>

<character set definition> ::=
    CREATE CHARACTER SET <character set name>
        [ AS ]
      <character set source>
      [ <collate clause> | <limited collation definition> ]

<character set source> ::=
      GET <existing character set name>

<existing character set name> ::=
        <standard character repertoire name>
    | <implementation-defined character repertoire name>
    | <schema character set name>

<schema character set name> ::= <character set name>

<limited collation definition> ::=
    COLLATION FROM <collation source>

<collation source> ::=
      <collating sequence definition>
    | <translation collation>

<collating sequence definition> ::=
        <external collation>
    | <schema collation name>
    | DESC <left paren> <collation name> <right paren>
    | DEFAULT

<external collation> ::=
EXTERNAL <left paren> <quote> <external collation name> <quote> <right paren>

<external collation name> ::=
        <standard collation name>
    | <implementation-defined collation name>

<standard collation name> ::= <collation name>

<implementation-defined collation name> ::= <collation name>

<schema collation name> ::= <collation name>

<translation collation> ::=
      TRANSLATION <translation name>
          [ THEN COLLATION <collation name> ]

<collation definition> ::=
    CREATE COLLATION <collation name> FOR
        <character set specification>
      FROM <collation source>
          [ <pad attribute> ]
```

```
<pad attribute> ::=
      NO PAD
   | PAD SPACE

<translation definition> ::=
    CREATE TRANSLATION <translation name>
      FOR <source character set specification>
        TO <target character set specification>
      FROM <translation source>

<source character set specification> ::= <character set specification>

<target character set specification> ::= <character set specification>

<translation source> ::=
      <translation specification>

<translation specification> ::=
      <external translation>
   | IDENTITY
   | <schema translation name>

<external translation> ::=
    EXTERNAL <left paren> <quote> <external transla-
tion name> <quote> <right paren>

<external translation name> ::=
      <standard translation name>
   | <implementation-defined translation name>

<standard translation name> ::= <translation name>

<implementation-defined translation name> ::= <translation name>

<schema translation name> ::= <translation name>

<SQL schema manipulation statement> ::=
      <drop schema statement>
   | <alter table statement>
   | <drop table statement>
   | <drop view statement>
   | <revoke statement>
   | <alter domain statement>
   | <drop domain statement>
   | <drop character set statement>
   | <drop collation statement>
   | <drop translation statement>
   | <drop assertion statement>

<drop schema statement> ::=
    DROP SCHEMA <schema name> <drop behavior>

<drop behavior> ::= CASCADE | RESTRICT
```

HOWTO

```
<alter table statement> ::=
    ALTER TABLE <table name> <alter table action>

<alter table action> ::=
      <add column definition>
    | <alter column definition>
    | <drop column definition>
    | <add table constraint definition>
    | <drop table constraint definition>

<add column definition> ::=
    ADD [ COLUMN ] <column definition>

<alter column definition> ::=
    ALTER [ COLUMN ] <column name> <alter column action>

<alter column action> ::=
      <set column default clause>
    | <drop column default clause>

<set column default clause> ::=
    SET <default clause>

<drop column default clause> ::=
    DROP DEFAULT

<drop column definition> ::=
    DROP [ COLUMN ] <column name> <drop behavior>

<add table constraint definition> ::=
    ADD <table constraint definition>

<drop table constraint definition> ::=
    DROP CONSTRAINT <constraint name> <drop behavior>

<drop table statement> ::=
    DROP TABLE <table name> <drop behavior>

<drop view statement> ::=
    DROP VIEW <table name> <drop behavior>

<revoke statement> ::=
    REVOKE [ GRANT OPTION FOR ]
        <privileges>
        ON <object name>
      FROM <grantee> [ ( <comma> <grantee> )... ] <drop behavior>

<alter domain statement> ::=
    ALTER DOMAIN <domain name> <alter domain action>

<alter domain action> ::=
      <set domain default clause>
    | <drop domain default clause>
    | <add domain constraint definition>
    | <drop domain constraint definition>
```

```
<set domain default clause> ::= SET <default clause>

<drop domain default clause> ::= DROP DEFAULT

<add domain constraint definition> ::=
    ADD <domain constraint>

<drop domain constraint definition> ::=
    DROP CONSTRAINT <constraint name>

<drop domain statement> ::=
    DROP DOMAIN <domain name> <drop behavior>

<drop character set statement> ::=
    DROP CHARACTER SET <character set name>

<drop collation statement> ::=
    DROP COLLATION <collation name>

<drop translation statement> ::=
    DROP TRANSLATION <translation name>

<drop assertion statement> ::=
    DROP ASSERTION <constraint name>

<SQL data statement> ::=
      <open statement>
    | <fetch statement>
    | <close statement>
    | <select statement: single row>
    | <SQL data change statement>

<open statement> ::=
    OPEN <cursor name>

<fetch statement> ::=
    FETCH [ [ <fetch orientation> ] FROM ]
      <cursor name> INTO <fetch target list>

<fetch orientation> ::=
      NEXT
    | PRIOR
    | FIRST
    | LAST
    | ( ABSOLUTE | RELATIVE ) <simple value specification>

<simple value specification> ::=
      <parameter name>
    | <embedded variable name>
    | <literal>

<fetch target list> ::=
    <target specification> [ ( <comma> <target specification> )... ]
```

```
<target specification> ::=
      <parameter specification>
    | <variable specification>

<close statement> ::=
    CLOSE <cursor name>

<select statement: single row> ::=
    SELECT [ <set quantifier> ] <select list>
      INTO <select target list>
        <table expression>

<select target list> ::=
    <target specification> [ ( <comma> <target specification> )... ]

<SQL data change statement> ::=
      <delete statement: positioned>
    | <delete statement: searched>
    | <insert statement>
    | <update statement: positioned>
    | <update statement: searched>

<delete statement: positioned> ::=
    DELETE FROM <table name>
      WHERE CURRENT OF <cursor name>

<delete statement: searched> ::=
    DELETE FROM <table name>
      [ WHERE <search condition> ]

<insert statement> ::=
    INSERT INTO <table name>
      <insert columns and source>

<insert columns and source> ::=
      [ <left paren> <insert column list> <right paren> ]
          <query expression>
    | DEFAULT VALUES

<insert column list> ::= <column name list>

<update statement: positioned> ::=
    UPDATE <table name>
      SET <set clause list>
        WHERE CURRENT OF <cursor name>

<set clause list> ::=
    <set clause> [ ( <comma> <set clause> )... ]

<set clause> ::=
    <object column> <equals operator> <update source>

<object column> ::= <column name>

<update source> ::=
```

```
        <value expression>
    | <null specification>
    | DEFAULT

<update statement: searched> ::=
    UPDATE <table name>
      SET <set clause list>
      [ WHERE <search condition> ]

<SQL transaction statement> ::=
        <set transaction statement>
    | <set constraints mode statement>
    | <commit statement>
    | <rollback statement>

<set transaction statement> ::=
    SET TRANSACTION <transaction mode>
        [ ( <comma> <transaction mode> )... ]

<transaction mode> ::=
        <isolation level>
    | <transaction access mode>
    | <diagnostics size>

<isolation level> ::=
    ISOLATION LEVEL <level of isolation>

<level of isolation> ::=
        READ UNCOMMITTED
    | READ COMMITTED
    | REPEATABLE READ
    | SERIALIZABLE

<transaction access mode> ::=
        READ ONLY
    | READ WRITE

<diagnostics size> ::=
    DIAGNOSTICS SIZE <number of conditions>

<number of conditions> ::= <simple value specification>

<set constraints mode statement> ::=
    SET CONSTRAINTS <constraint name list>
        ( DEFERRED | IMMEDIATE )

<constraint name list> ::=
        ALL
    | <constraint name> [ ( <comma> <constraint name> )... ]

<commit statement> ::=
    COMMIT [ WORK ]

<rollback statement> ::=
    ROLLBACK [ WORK ]
```

```
<SQL connection statement> ::=
      <connect statement>
    | <set connection statement>
    | <disconnect statement>

<connect statement> ::=
    CONNECT TO <connection target>

<connection target> ::=
      <SQL-server name>
        [ AS <connection name> ]
          correspondence with Tony Gordon)
        [ USER <user name> ]
    | DEFAULT

<SQL-server name> ::= <simple value specification>

<connection name> ::= <simple value specification>

<user name> ::= <simple value specification>

<set connection statement> ::=
    SET CONNECTION <connection object>

<connection object> ::=
      DEFAULT
    | <connection name>

<disconnect statement> ::=
    DISCONNECT <disconnect object>

<disconnect object> ::=
      <connection object>
    | ALL
    | CURRENT

<SQL session statement> ::=
      <set catalog statement>
    | <set schema statement>
    | <set names statement>
    | <set session authorization identifier statement>
    | <set local time zone statement>

<set catalog statement> ::=
    SET CATALOG <value specification>

<value specification> ::=
      <literal>
    | <general value specification>

<set schema statement> ::=
    SET SCHEMA <value specification>

<set names statement> ::=
```

```
        SET NAMES <value specification>

<set session authorization identifier statement> ::=
    SET SESSION AUTHORIZATION
        <value specification>

<set local time zone statement> ::=
    SET TIME ZONE
        <set time zone value>

<set time zone value> ::=
        <interval value expression>
    | LOCAL

<SQL dynamic statement> ::=
        <system descriptor statement>
    | <prepare statement>
    | <deallocate prepared statement>
    | <describe statement>
    | <execute statement>
    | <execute immediate statement>
    | <SQL dynamic data statement>

<system descriptor statement> ::=
        <allocate descriptor statement>
    | <deallocate descriptor statement>
    | <set descriptor statement>
    | <get descriptor statement>

<allocate descriptor statement> ::=
    ALLOCATE DESCRIPTOR <descriptor name>
        [ WITH MAX <occurrences> ]

<descriptor name> ::=
    [ <scope option> ] <simple value specification>

<scope option> ::=
        GLOBAL
    | LOCAL

<occurrences> ::= <simple value specification>

<deallocate descriptor statement> ::=
    DEALLOCATE DESCRIPTOR <descriptor name>

<set descriptor statement> ::=
    SET DESCRIPTOR <descriptor name>
        <set descriptor information>

<set descriptor information> ::=
        <set count>
    | VALUE <item number>
        <set item information> [ ( <comma> <set item information> )... ]

<set count> ::=
```

```
     COUNT <equals operator> <simple value specification 1>

<simple value specification 1> ::= <simple value specification>

<item number> ::= <simple value specification>

<set item information> ::=
    <descriptor item name> <equals operator> <simple value specification 2>

<descriptor item name> ::=
      TYPE
    | LENGTH
    | OCTET_LENGTH
    | RETURNED_LENGTH
    | RETURNED_OCTET_LENGTH
    | PRECISION
    | SCALE
    | DATETIME_INTERVAL_CODE
    | DATETIME_INTERVAL_PRECISION
    | NULLABLE
    | INDICATOR
    | DATA
    | NAME
    | UNNAMED
    | COLLATION_CATALOG
    | COLLATION_SCHEMA
    | COLLATION_NAME
    | CHARACTER_SET_CATALOG
    | CHARACTER_SET_SCHEMA
    | CHARACTER_SET_NAME

<simple value specification 2> ::= <simple value specification>

<item number> ::= <simple value specification>

<get descriptor statement> ::=
    GET DESCRIPTOR <descriptor name> <get descriptor information>

<get descriptor information> ::=
      <get count>
    | VALUE <item number>
        <get item information> [ ( <comma> <get item information> )... ]

<get count> ::=
    <simple target specification 1> <equals operator>
        COUNT

<simple target specification 1> ::= <simple target specification>

<simple target specification> ::=
      <parameter name>
    | <embedded variable name>

<get item information> ::=
    <simple target specification 2> <equals operator> <descriptor item name>>
```

```
<simple target specification 2> ::= <simple target specification>

<prepare statement> ::=
    PREPARE <SQL statement name> FROM <SQL statement variable>

<SQL statement name> ::=
      <statement name>
    | <extended statement name>

<extended statement name> ::=
    [ <scope option> ] <simple value specification>

<SQL statement variable> ::= <simple value specification>

<deallocate prepared statement> ::=
    DEALLOCATE PREPARE <SQL statement name>

<describe statement> ::=
      <describe input statement>
    | <describe output statement>

<describe input statement> ::=
    DESCRIBE INPUT <SQL statement name> <using descriptor>

<using descriptor> ::=
    ( USING | INTO ) SQL DESCRIPTOR <descriptor name>

<describe output statement> ::=
    DESCRIBE [ OUTPUT ] <SQL statement name> <using descriptor>

<execute statement> ::=
    EXECUTE <SQL statement name>
    [ <result using clause> ]
    [ <parameter using clause> ]

<result using clause> ::= <using clause>

<using clause> ::=
      <using arguments>
    | <using descriptor>

<using arguments> ::=
    ( USING | INTO ) <argument> [ ( <comma> <argument> )... ]

<argument> ::= <target specification>

<parameter using clause> ::= <using clause>

<execute immediate statement> ::=
    EXECUTE IMMEDIATE <SQL statement variable>

<SQL dynamic data statement> ::=
      <allocate cursor statement>
    | <dynamic open statement>
```

```
        | <dynamic fetch statement>
        | <dynamic close statement>
        | <dynamic delete statement: positioned>
        | <dynamic update statement: positioned>

<allocate cursor statement> ::=
    ALLOCATE <extended cursor name> [ INSENSITIVE ]
        [ SCROLL ] CURSOR
      FOR <extended statement name>

<extended cursor name> ::=
    [ <scope option> ] <simple value specification>

<dynamic open statement> ::=
    OPEN <dynamic cursor name> [ <using clause> ]

<dynamic cursor name> ::=
        <cursor name>
      | <extended cursor name>

<dynamic fetch statement> ::=
    FETCH [ [ <fetch orientation> ] FROM ] <dynamic cursor name>
        <using clause>

<dynamic close statement> ::=
    CLOSE <dynamic cursor name>

<dynamic delete statement: positioned> ::=
    DELETE FROM <table name>
      WHERE CURRENT OF
          <dynamic cursor name>

<dynamic update statement: positioned> ::=
    UPDATE <table name>
      SET <set clause>
          [ ( <comma> <set clause> )... ]
        WHERE CURRENT OF
            <dynamic cursor name>

<SQL diagnostics statement> ::=
    <get diagnostics statement>

<get diagnostics statement> ::=
    GET DIAGNOSTICS <sql diagnostics information>

<sql diagnostics information> ::=
        <statement information>
      | <condition information>

<statement information> ::=
    <statement information item> [ ( <comma> <statement informa-
tion item> )... ]

<statement information item> ::=
    <simple target specification> <equals operator> <statement informa-
```

```
tion item name>

<statement information item name> ::=
      NUMBER
    | MORE
    | COMMAND_FUNCTION
    | DYNAMIC_FUNCTION
    | ROW_COUNT

<condition information> ::=
    EXCEPTION <condition number>
      <condition information item> [ ( <comma> <condition informa-
tion item> )... ]

<condition number> ::= <simple value specification>

<condition information item> ::=
    <simple target specification> <equals operator> <condition informa-
tion item name>

<condition information item name> ::=
      CONDITION_NUMBER
    | RETURNED_SQLSTATE
    | CLASS_ORIGIN
    | SUBCLASS_ORIGIN
    | SERVER_NAME
    | CONNECTION_NAME
    | CONSTRAINT_CATALOG
    | CONSTRAINT_SCHEMA
    | CONSTRAINT_NAME
    | CATALOG_NAME
    | SCHEMA_NAME
    | TABLE_NAME
    | COLUMN_NAME
    | CURSOR_NAME
    | MESSAGE_TEXT
    | MESSAGE_LENGTH
    | MESSAGE_OCTET_LENGTH

<embedded SQL host program> ::=
      <embedded SQL Ada program>
    | <embedded SQL C program>
    | <embedded SQL COBOL program>
    | <embedded SQL Fortran program>
    | <embedded SQL MUMPS program>
    | <embedded SQL Pascal program>
    | <embedded SQL PL/I program>

<embedded SQL Ada program> ::= !! <EMPHASIS>(See the Syntax Rules.)

<embedded SQL C program> ::=
      !! <EMPHASIS>(See the Syntax Rules.)

<embedded SQL COBOL program> ::= !! <EMPHASIS>(See the Syntax Rules.)
```

```
<embedded SQL Fortran program> ::=
    !! <EMPHASIS>(See the Syntax Rules.)

<embedded SQL MUMPS program> ::= !! <EMPHASIS>(See the Syntax Rules.)

<embedded SQL Pascal program> ::=
    !! <EMPHASIS>(See the Syntax Rules.)

<embedded SQL PL/I program> ::= !! <EMPHASIS>(See the Syntax Rules.)

<embedded SQL declare section> ::=
      <embedded SQL begin declare>
        [ <embedded character set declaration> ]
        [ <host variable definition>... ]
      <embedded SQL end declare>
    | <embedded SQL MUMPS declare>

<embedded SQL begin declare> ::=
    <SQL prefix> BEGIN DECLARE SECTION
        [ <SQL terminator> ]

<SQL prefix> ::=
      EXEC SQL
    | <ampersand>SQL<left paren>

<SQL terminator> ::=
      END-EXEC
    | <semicolon>
    | <right paren>

<embedded character set declaration> ::=
    SQL NAMES ARE <character set specification>

<host variable definition> ::=
      <Ada variable definition>
    | <C variable definition>
    | <COBOL variable definition>
    | <Fortran variable definition>
    | <MUMPS variable definition>
    | <Pascal variable definition>
    | <PL/I variable definition>

<Ada variable definition> ::=
    <Ada host identifier> [ ( <comma> <Ada host identifier> )... ] :
    <Ada type specification> [ <Ada initial value> ]

<Ada type specification> ::=
      <Ada qualified type specification>
    | <Ada unqualified type specification>

<Ada qualified type specification> ::=
      SQL_STANDARD.CHAR [ CHARACTER SET
        [ IS ] <character set specification> ]
          <left paren> 1 <double period> <length> <right paren>
    | SQL_STANDARD.BIT
```

```
                    <left paren> 1 <double period> <length> <right paren>
        | SQL_STANDARD.SMALLINT
        | SQL_STANDARD.INT
        | SQL_STANDARD.REAL
        | SQL_STANDARD.DOUBLE_PRECISION
        | SQL_STANDARD.SQLCODE_TYPE
        | SQL_STANDARD.SQLSTATE_TYPE
        | SQL_STANDARD.INDICATOR_TYPE

<Ada unqualified type specification> ::=
        CHAR
            <left paren> 1 <double period> <length> <right paren>
        | BIT
            <left paren> 1 <double period> <length> <right paren>
        | SMALLINT
        | INT
        | REAL
        | DOUBLE_PRECISION
        | SQLCODE_TYPE
        | SQLSTATE_TYPE
        | INDICATOR_TYPE

<Ada initial value> ::=
        <Ada assignment operator> <character representation>...

<Ada assignment operator> ::= <colon><equals operator>

<C variable definition> ::=
        [ <C storage class> ]
        [ <C class modifier> ]
        <C variable specification>
     <semicolon>

<C storage class> ::=
        auto
     | extern
     | static

<C class modifier> ::= const | volatile

<C variable specification> ::=
        <C numeric variable>
     | <C character variable>
     | <C derived variable>

<C numeric variable> ::=
     ( long | short | float | double )
        <C host identifier> [ <C initial value> ]
            [ ( <comma> <C host identifier> [ <C initial value> ] )... ]

<C initial value> ::=
        <equals operator> <character representation>...

<C character variable> ::=
     char [ CHARACTER SET
```

```
                [ IS ] <character set specification> ]
          <C host identifier>
            <C array specification> [ <C initial value> ]
          [ ( <comma> <C host identifier>
            <C array specification>
                    [ <C initial value> ] )... ]

<C array specification> ::=
    <left bracket> <length> <right bracket>

<C derived variable> ::=
      <C VARCHAR variable>
    | <C bit variable>

<C VARCHAR variable> ::=
    VARCHAR [ CHARACTER SET [ IS ]
        <character set specification> ]
        <C host identifier>
          <C array specification> [ <C initial value> ]
        [ ( <comma> <C host identifier>
          <C array specification>
                    [ <C initial value> ] )... ]

<C bit variable> ::=
    BIT <C host identifier>
        <C array specification> [ <C initial value> ]
      [ ( <comma> <C host identifier>
        <C array specification>
                    [ <C initial value> ] )... ]

<COBOL variable definition> ::=
    (01|77) <COBOL host identifier> <COBOL type specification>
        [ <character representation>... ] <period>

<COBOL type specification> ::=
      <COBOL character type>
    | <COBOL bit type>
    | <COBOL numeric type>
    | <COBOL integer type>

<COBOL character type> ::=
    [ CHARACTER SET [ IS ]
          <character set specification> ]
    ( PIC | PICTURE ) [ IS ] ( X [ <left paren> <length> <right paren> ] )...

<COBOL bit type> ::=
    ( PIC | PICTURE ) [ IS ]
        ( B [ <left paren> <length> <right paren> ] )...

<COBOL numeric type> ::=
    ( PIC | PICTURE ) [ IS ]
      S <COBOL nines specification>
    [ USAGE [ IS ] ] DISPLAY SIGN LEADING SEPARATE

<COBOL nines specification> ::=
```

```
            <COBOL nines> [ V [ <COBOL nines> ] ]
          | V <COBOL nines>

   <COBOL nines> ::= ( 9 [ <left paren> <length> <right paren> ] )...

   <COBOL integer type> ::=
          <COBOL computational integer>
        | <COBOL binary integer>

   <COBOL computational integer> ::=
          ( PIC | PICTURE ) [ IS ] S<COBOL nines>
          [ USAGE [ IS ] ] ( COMP | COMPUTATIONAL )

   <COBOL binary integer> ::=
          ( PIC | PICTURE ) [ IS ] S<COBOL nines>
          [ USAGE [ IS ] ] BINARY

   <Fortran variable definition> ::=
        <Fortran type specification>
        <Fortran host identifier>
          [ ( <comma> <Fortran host identifier> )... ]

   <Fortran type specification> ::=
        CHARACTER [ <asterisk> <length> ]
            [ CHARACTER SET [ IS ]
                  <character set specification> ]
      | BIT [ <asterisk> <length> ]
      | INTEGER
      | REAL
      | DOUBLE PRECISION

   <MUMPS variable definition> ::=
        ( <MUMPS numeric variable> | <MUMPS character variable> )
            <semicolon>

   <MUMPS numeric variable> ::=
        <MUMPS type specification>
        <MUMPS host identifier> [ ( <comma> <MUMPS host identifier> )... ]

   <MUMPS type specification> ::=
          INT
        | DEC
            [ <left paren> <precision> [ <comma> <scale> ] <right paren> ]
        | REAL

   <MUMPS character variable> ::=
        VARCHAR <MUMPS host identifier> <MUMPS length specification>
          [ ( <comma> <MUMPS host identifier> <MUMPS length specifica-
   tion> )... ]

   <MUMPS length specification> ::=
        <left paren> <length> <right paren>

   <Pascal variable definition> ::=
        <Pascal host identifier> [ ( <comma> <Pascal host identifi-
```

```
er> )... ] <colon>
        <Pascal type specification> <semicolon>

<Pascal type specification> ::=
        PACKED ARRAY
            <left bracket> 1 <double period> <length> <right bracket>
          OF CHAR
            [ CHARACTER SET [ IS ]
                    <character set specification> ]
      | PACKED ARRAY
            <left bracket> 1 <double period> <length> <right bracket>
          OF BIT
      | INTEGER
      | REAL
      | CHAR [ CHARACTER SET
                                [ IS ] <character set specification> ]
      | BIT

<PL/I variable definition> ::=
      (DCL | DECLARE)
          (    <PL/I host identifier>
          | <left paren> <PL/I host identifier>
                [ ( <comma> <PL/I host identifier> )... ] <right paren> )
      <PL/I type specification>
      [ <character representation>... ] <semicolon>

<PL/I type specification> ::=
          ( CHAR | CHARACTER ) [ VARYING ]
              <left paren><length><right paren>
              [ CHARACTER SET
                  [ IS ] <character set specification> ]
      | BIT [ VARYING ] <left paren><length><right paren>
      | <PL/I type fixed decimal> <left paren> <precision>
              [ <comma> <scale> ] <right paren>
      | <PL/I type fixed binary> [ <left paren> <precision> <right paren> ]
      | <PL/I type float binary> <left paren> <precision> <right paren>

<PL/I type fixed decimal> ::=
        ( DEC | DECIMAL ) FIXED
      | FIXED ( DEC | DECIMAL )

<PL/I type fixed binary> ::=
        ( BIN | BINARY ) FIXED
      | FIXED ( BIN | BINARY )

<PL/I type float binary> ::=
        ( BIN | BINARY ) FLOAT
      | FLOAT ( BIN | BINARY )

<embedded SQL end declare> ::=
      <SQL prefix> END DECLARE SECTION
          [ <SQL terminator> ]

<embedded SQL MUMPS declare> ::=
      <SQL prefix>
```

```
        BEGIN DECLARE SECTION
          [ <embedded character set declaration> ]
          [ <host variable definition>... ]
        END DECLARE SECTION
      <SQL terminator>

<embedded SQL statement> ::=
      <SQL prefix>
        <statement or declaration>
      [ <SQL terminator> ]

<statement or declaration> ::=
          <declare cursor>
      | <dynamic declare cursor>
      | <temporary table declaration>
      | <embedded exception declaration>
      | <SQL procedure statement>

<embedded exception declaration> ::=
      WHENEVER <condition> <condition action>

<condition> ::=
      SQLERROR | NOT FOUND

<condition action> ::=
      CONTINUE | <go to>

<go to> ::=
      ( GOTO | GO TO ) <goto target>

<goto target> ::=
          <host label identifier>
      | <unsigned integer>
      | <host PL/I label variable>

<host label identifier> ::= !!<EMPHASIS>(See the Syntax Rules.)

<host PL/I label variable> ::= !!<EMPHASIS>(See the Syntax Rules.)

<preparable statement> ::=
          <preparable SQL data statement>
      | <preparable SQL schema statement>
      | <preparable SQL transaction statement>
      | <preparable SQL session statement>
      | <preparable implementation-defined statement>

<preparable SQL data statement> ::=
          <delete statement: searched>
      | <dynamic single row select statement>
      | <insert statement>
      | <dynamic select statement>
      | <update statement: searched>
      | <preparable dynamic delete statement: positioned>
      | <preparable dynamic update statement: positioned>
```

```
<dynamic single row select statement> ::= <query specification>

<dynamic select statement> ::= <cursor specification>

<preparable dynamic delete statement: positioned> ::=
    DELETE [ FROM <table name> ]
        WHERE CURRENT OF <cursor name>

<preparable dynamic update statement: positioned> ::=
    UPDATE [ <table name> ]
        SET <set clause list>
        WHERE CURRENT OF <cursor name>

<preparable SQL schema statement> ::=
        <SQL schema statement>

<preparable SQL transaction statement> ::=
        <SQL transaction statement>

<preparable SQL session statement> ::=
        <SQL session statement>

<preparable implementation-defined statement> ::=
    !! <EMPHASIS>(See the Syntax Rules.)

<direct SQL statement> ::=
    <directly executable statement> <semicolon>

<directly executable statement> ::=
        <direct SQL data statement>
    | <SQL schema statement>
    | <SQL transaction statement>
    | <SQL connection statement>
    | <SQL session statement>
    | <direct implementation-defined statement>

<direct SQL data statement> ::=
        <delete statement: searched>
    | <direct select statement: multiple rows>
    | <insert statement>
    | <update statement: searched>
    | <temporary table declaration>

<direct select statement: multiple rows> ::=
    <query expression> [ <order by clause> ]

<direct implementation-defined statement> ::=
    !!<EMPHASIS>(See the Syntax Rules)

<SQL object identifier> ::=
    <SQL provenance> <SQL variant>

<SQL provenance> ::= <arc1> <arc2> <arc3>

<arc1> ::= iso | 1 | iso <left paren> 1 <right paren>
```

```
<arc2> ::= standard | 0 | standard <left paren> 0 <right paren>

<arc3> ::= 9075

<SQL variant> ::= <SQL edition> <SQL conformance>

<SQL edition> ::= <1987> | <1989> | <1992>

<1987> ::= 0 | edition1987 <left paren> 0 <right paren>

<1989> ::= <1989 base> <1989 package>

<1989 base> ::= 1 | edition1989 <left paren> 1 <right paren>

<1989 package> ::= <integrity no> | <integrity yes>

<integrity no> ::= 0 | IntegrityNo <left paren> 0 <right paren>

<integrity yes> ::= 1 | IntegrityYes <left paren> 1 <right paren>

<1992> ::= 2 | edition1992 <left paren> 2 <right paren>

<SQL conformance> ::= <low> | <intermediate> | <high>

<low> ::= 0 | Low <left paren> 0 <right paren>

<intermediate> ::= 1 | Intermediate <left paren> 1 <right paren>

<high> ::= 2 | High <left paren> 2 <right paren>
```

32 Appendix B - SQL Tutorial for beginners

32.1 Tutorial for PostgreSQL

SQL tutorial is also distributed with PostgreSQL. The SQL tutorial scripts is in the directory src/tutorial

32.2 Internet URL pointers

The SQL tutorial for beginners can be found at

- <http://w3.one.net/~jhoffman/sqltut.htm>

Comments or suggestions? Mail to

- Jim Hoffman *jhoffman@one.net*

The following are the sites suggested by John Hoffman:

- SQL Reference <http://www.contrib.andrew.cmu.edu/~shadow/sql.html>
- Ask the SQL Pro <http://www.inquiry.com/techtips/thesqlpro/>
- SQL Pro's Relational DB Useful Sites <http://www.inquiry.com/techtips/thesqlpro/usefulsites.html>

- Programmer's Source <http://infoweb.magi.com/~steve/develop.html>
- DBMS Sites <http://info.itu.ch/special/wwwfiles> Go here and see file comp_db.html
- DB Ingredients <http://www.compapp.dcu.ie/databases/f017.html>
- Web Authoring <http://www.stars.com/Tutorial/CGI/>
- Computing Dictionary <http://wfn-shop.princeton.edu/cgi-bin/foldoc>
- DBMS Lab/Links <http://www-ccs.cs.umass.edu/db.html>
- SQL FAQ <http://epoch.CS.Berkeley.EDU:8000/sequoia/dba/montage/FAQ> Go here and see file SQL_TOC.html
- SQL Databases <http://chaos.mur.csu.edu.au/itc125/cgi/sqldb.html>
- RIT Database Design Page <http://www.it.rit.edu/~wjs/IT/199602/icsa720/icsa720postings.html>
- Database Jump Site <http://www.pcslink.com/~ej/dbweb.html>
- Programming Tutorials on the Web <http://www.eng.uc.edu/~jtilley/tutorial.html>
- Development Resources <http://www.ndev.com/ndc2/support/resources.htp>
- Query List <http://ashok.pair.com/sql.htm>
- IMAGE SQL Miscellaneous <http://jazz.external.hp.com/training/sqltables/main.html>
- Internet Resource List <http://www.eit.com/web/netservices.html>

33   Appendix C - Linux Quick Install Instructions

If you are planning to use PostgreSQL on Linux, and need help in installing Linux, then please visit the pointers given in this Appendix. They cover the following topics -

- Salient Features of Linux - Why Linux is better as a database server when compared with Windows 95/NT
- 10 minutes Linux Quick Install Instructions
- Microsoft-Linux Analogy List
- Quick Steps to Recompile the Linux Kernel

- Main Site is at <http://members.spree.com/technology/aldev/>
- Mirror site <http://aldev.8m.com>
- Mirror site <http://aldev.webjump.com>
- Mirror site <http://homepages.infoseek.com/~aldev1/index.html>
- Mirror site <http://www3.bcity.com/aldev/>

Part XXXV

"Root RAID HOWTO cookbook" Michael A. Robinton

michael@bzs.org <mailto:michael@bzs.org>

v1.07, 25 March 1998

This document provides a cookbook for creating a root mounted raid filesystem and companion fallback rescue system using linux initrd. There are complete step-by-step instruction for both raid1 and raid5 md0 devices. Each step is accompanied by an explanation of it's purpose. Included with this revision is a generic **linuxrc** initrd file which may be configured with a single three line 4.13 (/etc/raidboot.conf) file for raid1 and raid5 configurations.

Contents

1 Introduction

The reader is assumed to be familiar with the various types of raid implementations, their advantages and drawbacks. This is not a tutorial, just a set of instructions on how to implement root mounted raid on a linux system. All of the information necessary to become familiar with linux raid is listed here directly or by reference, please read it before send e-mail questions.

1.1 Where to get Up-to-date copies of this document.

Root-RAID-HOWTO

Available in LaTeX (for DVI and PostScript), plain text, and HTML.

sunsite.unc.edu/mdw/HOWTO/ <http://sunsite.unc.edu/mdw/HOWTO/>

Available in SGML and HTML.

ftp.bizsystems.com/pub/raid/ <ftp://ftp.bizsystems.com/pub/raid/>

1.2 Bugs

As of this writing, the problem of stopping a root mounted RAID device has not yet been solved in a satisfactory way. A work-around proposed by Ed Welbon and implemented by Bohumil Chalupa is incorporated into this document which eliminates the need for a long ckraid at each boot for raid1 and raid5 devices. Without the workaround, it is necessary to **ckraid** the **md** device each time the system is re-booted. On a large array this can cause a severe availability performance degradation. On my 6 gig RAID1 device running on a Pentium 166 with 128 megs of ram, it takes well over half an hour to ckraid :-(after each re-boot. It takes over an hour on my 13 gig RAID5 array with a 20mb/sec scsi adaptor.

The workaround stores the status of the array at shutdown on the **real** boot device and compares it to a reference status placed there when the system is first built. If the status's match at reboot, the superblock on the array is rebuilt on the next boot, otherwise the operator is notified of the status error and the rescue system is left running with all the raid tools available.

Rebuilding the superblock causes the system to ignore that the array was powered down without mdstop by marking all the drives as **OK**, as if nothing happened. This only works if all the drives are OK at shutdown. If the array was operating with a bad drive, the operator must remove the bad drive prior to restarting the md device or the data can be corrupted.

None of this applies to raid0 which does not have to be mdstopped before shutdown.

Final proposed solutions to this problem include a **finalrd** similar to **initrd**, and **mdrootstop** which writes the **clean** flags to the array during shutdown when it is mounted read only. I am sure there are others.

In the mean time, the problem has been by-passed for now Please let me know when this problem is solved more cleanly!!!

1.3 Acknowledgements

The writings and e-mail from the following individuals helped to make this document possible. Many of the ideas were *stolen* from the helpful work of others, I have just tried to put it all in **COOKBOOK** form so that it is straightforward to use. My thanks to:

- *Linas Vepstas* <mailto:linas@linas.org> *for the RAID howto that explained most of this to me.*
- *Gadi Oxman* <mailto:gadio@netvision.net.il> *for answering my dumb 'newbie' questions.*
- *Ed Welbon* <mailto:welbon@bga.com> *for the execellent* **initrd.md** *package that inspired me to write this.*
- *Bohumil Chalupa* <mailto:bochal@apollo.karlov.mff.cuni.cz> *for implementing the re-boot 'workaround' that allows* **root-mounted-raid** *to work in a production environment.*
- and many others who contributed to this work in one way or another.

HOWTO

1.4   Copyright Notice

This document is GNU copyleft by Michael Robinton *michael@bzs.org* `<mailto:michael@bzs.org>`.

Permission to use, copy, distribute this document for any purpose is hereby granted, provided that the author's / editor's name and this notice appear in all copies and/or supporting documents; and that an unmodified version of this document is made freely available. This document is distributed in the hope that it will be useful, but WITHOUT ANY WARRANTY, either expressed or implied. While every effort has been taken to ensure the accuracy of the information documented herein, the author / editor / maintainer assumes NO RESPONSIBILITY for any errors, or for any damages, direct or consequential, as a result of the use of the information documented herein.

2   What you need BEFORE YOU START

The packages you need and the documentation that answers the most common questions about setting up and running raid are listed below. Please review them throughly.

2.1   Required Packages

You need to obtain the most recent versions of these packages.

- a linux kernel that supports raid, initrd and /dev/loopx

    I used *linux-2.0.33* `<ftp://sunsite.unc.edu/pub/Linux/kernel/>` from sunsite

- *raid145-971022-2.0.31* `<ftp://ftp.kernel.org/pub/linux/daemons/raid/>` patch adds support for raid1/4/5

- *raidtools-pre3-0.42* `<ftp://ftp.kernel.org/pub/linux/daemons/raid/>` tools to create and maintain raid devices (documentation too).

- 12 (Gadi's raid stop patch) in Appendix E.

- *linuxthreads-0.71* `<ftp://ftp.inria.fr/INRIA/Projects/cristal/Xavier.Leroy>` required threads package. Use ftp, browser doesn't work ftp.inria.fr/INRIA/Projects/cristal/Xavier.Leroy

- A Linux distribution, ready to install.

    I used *Slackware-3.4* `<ftp://ftp.cdrom.com/pub/linux>`

Helpful but not required

- *raidboot-0.01.tar.gz* `<ftp://ftp.bizsystems.com/pub/raid/>` pre-built raid rescue/boot system.

The detailed instructions in this document are based on the above packages. If the packages have been updated or you use a different linux distribution, you may have to modify the procedures you find here.

The patches, tool assortment, etc... may vary with 2.1 kernels. Please check the most recent documentation at:

    ftp.kernel.org/pub/linux/daemons/raid/   `<ftp://ftp.kernel.org/pub/linux/daemons/raid/>`

2.2   Other similar implementations.

I chose to include in the kernel all of the pieces necessary to run from boot without loading any modules. My kernel image is a little over 300k compressed.

Take a look at *Ed Welbon's* `<mailto:welbon@bga.com>` **initrd.md.tar.gz** for another way to make a bootable raid device. He uses loadable modules. A look at his concise scripts will show you how it is done if you need a very small kernel with modules.

http://www.realtime.net/~welbon/initrd.md.tar.gz `<http://www.realtime.net/~welbon/`
`initrd.md.tar.gz>`

2.3 Documentation – Recommended Reading

Please read:

/usr/src/linux/Documentation/initrd.txt

as well as the documentation and man pages that accompany the raidtools set. In particular, read **man mdadd** as well as the **QuickStart.RAID** document included in the raidtools package.

You may also wish to review:

- *BootPrompt-HOWTO* `<http://sunsite.unc.edu/mdw/HOWTO/BootPrompt-HOWTO.html>`
- **man lilo**
- **man lilo.conf**

2.4 RAID resources

- *sunsite.unc.edu/mdw/HOWTO/mini/Software-RAID* `<http://sunsite.unc.edu/mdw/HOWTO/mini/`
  `Software-RAID>`
- *www.ssc.com/lg/issue17/raid.html* `<http://www.ssc.com/lg/issue17/raid.html>`
- *linas.org/linux/raid.html* `<http://linas.org/linux/raid.html>`
- *ftp.kernel.org/pub/linux/daemons/raid/* `<ftp://ftp.kernel.org/pub/linux/daemons/raid/>`
- *www.realtime.net/~welbon/initrd.md.tar.gz* `<http://www.realtime.net/~welbon/initrd.md.tar.`
  `gz>`
- *luthien.nuclecu.unam.mx/~miguel/raid/* `<http://luthien.nuclecu.unam.mx/~miguel/raid/>`

Mailing lists can be joined at:

- *majordomo@nuclecu.unam.mx* `<mailto:majordomo@nuclecu.unam.mx>`*send a message to* **subscribe raiddev**send mail to: *raiddev@nuclecu.unam.mx* `<mailto:raiddev@nuclecu.unam.mx>`
- *majordomo@vger.rutgers.edu* `<mailto:majordomo@vger.rutgers.edu>`*send a message to* **subscribe linux-raid**send mail to: *linux-raid@vger.rutgers.edu* `<mailto:linux-raid@vger.rutgers.edu>` *(this seems to be the most active list)*

3 Quick Start for ROOT RAID

If you don't want to try and build and debug the rescue system, you can get a generic one created from Slackware-3.4 from:

ftp.bizsystems.com/pub/raid/raidboot-0.01.tar.gz `<ftp://ftp.bizsystems.com/pub/raid/>`

Perform the following steps:

- Compile the raid enabled kernel with built in support for your disk subsystem
- Test that the raid array will configure and mount correctly
- Build your OS on the raid system

- Correct the entries in **fstab** to show **/dev/md0** as the root device. Make sure that the partition(s) you use for booting are included in **fstab**.

- Modify your shutdown halt and reboot script(s) (mine is /etc/rc.d/rc.6) as shown in 4.12 (Modifying the rc-scripts for SHUTDOWN)

- Copy the following from you development filesystem to the rescue system AND the new raid system

```
cd /root/raidboot
mkdir mnt
gzip -d rescue.clean
losetup /dev/loop0  rescue.clean
mount /dev/loop0    mnt
```

copy these files

```
cp -p /etc/*       mnt/etc
cp -p /etc/rc.d/*  mnt/etc/rc.d
        {or as appropriate for your system}
cp -a /lib/modules/* mnt/lib/modules
```

Correct the entries in **fstab** to show **/dev/md0** as the root device. Make sure that the partition(s) you use for booting is included in **fstab**.

Create **/etc/raidboot.conf** which describes the raid boot configuration. This file may **NOT** contain comments in the first three lines, after that it doesn't matter.

raidboot.conf

```
/dev/sda1 /dev/sda2
raidboot
raid5.conf
# comments may only be placed 'after' the three
# configuration lines.
#
# This is 'raidboot.conf'
#
# line one, the partition(s) containing the 'initrd' raid-rescue system
#       It is not necessary to boot from these partitions, however,
#       since the rescue system will not fit on floppy, it is necessary
#       to know which partitions are to be used to load the rescue system
#
# line two, the path to the raidboot config information
#       Where the shutdown status, etc... is located at boot time
#       It does NOT include the mount point information, only 'path'
#       /mntpoint/'path'
#
# line -3-, name of the raid configuration file
#       Current raid configuration file i.e. raid1.conf, raid5.conf
```

A few more things to do and the raid systems is ready to boot.

Create 13 (rc.raidown), as described in Appendix F, and copy it to /etc/rc.d on the rescue, development, and raid system. Unmount the rescue system and zip it.

```
umount mnt
losetup -d /dev/loop0
mv rescue.clean rescue
```

```
        gzip rescue
```

Copy the rescue file to the raidboot partitions.

```
        cp rescue.gz /mnt_point(1)/raidboot
        cp rescue.gz /mnt_point(2)/raidboot
```

Activate the raid array.

```
        mdadd -ar
```

Save the **good** reference status to the raidboot partition

```
        cat /proc/mdstat | grep md0 > /mnt_point(1)/raidboot/raidgood.ref
        cat /proc/mdstat | grep md0 > /mnt_point(1)/raidboot/raidgood.ref
```

Lastly, configure the boot program as outlined in 4.13 (Boot Time Configuration Parameters) and reboot your system onto the raid array.

4   initrd- Cookbook for root mounted RAID

This is the procedure to make an 'initrd' ramdisk with rescue tools for raid.

Specifically, this document referrs to RAID1 and RAID5 implementations.

4.1   Security Reminder

The rescue file system may be used stand alone. Should your raid array fail to mount, you are left with the rescue system mounted and running. TAKE THE APPROPRIATE SECURITY PRECAUTIONS!!!

4.2   Build the Kernel and Raid Tools

The first thing that must be done is to patch and build your kernel and become familiar with the raid tools. Make sure and include 12 (Gadi's raid stop patch) in Appendix E. Configure, mount and test your raid device(s). The details of how to do this are included in the **raidtools** package and briefly reviewed later in this document.

4.3   Build the *initrd* Rescue and Boot filesystem

I used the **Slackware-3.4** distribution to build both the Rescue/Boot filesystem and the filesystem for the production machine. Any linux distribution should work fine. If you use a different distribution, review the Slackware specific portion of this procedure and modify it to suit your needs.

I use loadlin to boot the kernel image and ramdisk from a dos partition simply because there are oddball devices in my system that have dos configuration software. Lilo will work just as well and a small linux partition can be used instead containing only the raid/boot files and the **lilo** record.

For the raid boot/rescue system, I chose to create a minimum ramdisk system using the Slackware 'setup' script followed by installing the 'linuxthreads' package and 'raidtools' over the clean Slackware installation on my ramdisk. I used the *identical* procedure to build the production system. So the rescue and production systems are very similar.

This installation process gives me a 'bare' system (save a copy of the file) to which I overlay

```
        /lib/modules/2.x.x......
        /etc .... with a modified fstab, mdtab, raidX.conf, raidboot.conf
```

```
/etc/rc.d
/dev/md*
```

from my current system to customize it for the particular kernel and machine that it is/will-be running on.

This makes the boot/rescue system the same system that is running on the root mounted raid device, just skinnyed down a bit, while allowing the library, etc... revisions to always be current.

4.4   Start the STEP by STEP instructions

From the root home directory (/root):

```
cd /root
mkdir raidboot
cd raidboot
```

Create a mountpoints to work on

```
mkdir mnt
mkdir mnt2
```

Make a file large enough to do the file system install. This will be a lot larger than the final rescue file system. I chose 24 megs since 16 megs is not large enough

```
dd if=/dev/zero of=build bs=1024k count=24
```

associate the file with a loop device and generate an ext2 file system on the file

```
losetup /dev/loop0 build
mke2fs -v -m0 -L initrd /dev/loop0
mount /dev/loop0 mnt
```

4.5   Install the distribution - Slackware Specific

4.6 (...skip Slackware Specific stuff) and go to next section.

Now that an empty filesystem is created and mounted, run "setup".

```
Specify             /root/raidboot/mnt
```

as the **'target'**. The source is whatever you normally install from. Select the packages you wish to install and proceed but **DO NOT** configure.

Choose 'EXPERT' prompting mode.

I chose 'A', 'AP, and 'N' installing only the minimum to run the system plus an editor I am familiar with (vi, jed, joe) that is reasonably compact.

```
lqqqqqqqq SELECTING PACKAGES FROM SERIES A (BASE LINUX SYSTEM) qqqqqqqqk
x lqqqqqqqqqqqqqqqqqqqqqqqqqqqqqqqqqqqqqqqqqqqqqqqqqqqqqqqqqqqqqqqqqqqqk x
x x   [X] aaa_base  Basic filesystem, shell, and utils - REQUIRED    x x
x x   [X] bash      GNU bash-1.14.7 shell - REQUIRED                 x x
x x   [X] devs      Device files found in /dev - REQUIRED            x x
x x   [X] etc       System config files & utilities - REQUIRED       x x
x x   [X] shadow    Shadow password suite - REQUIRED                 x x
```

```
x x    [ ] ide       Linux 2.0.30 no SCSI (YOU NEED 1 KERNEL)     x x
x x    [ ] scsi      Linux 2.0.30 with SCSI (YOU NEED 1 KERNEL)   x x
x x    [ ] modules   Modular Linux device drivers                 x x
x x    [ ] scsimods  Loadable SCSI device drivers                 x x
x x    [X] hdsetup   Slackware setup scripts - REQUIRED           x x
x x    [ ] lilo      Boots Linux (not UMSDOS), DOS, OS/2, etc.    x x
x x    [ ] bsdlpr    BSD lpr - printer spooling system            x x
x x    [ ] loadlin   Boots Linux (UMSDOS too!) from MS-DOS        x x
x x    [ ] pnp       Plug'n'Play configuration tool               x x
x x    [ ] umsprogs  Utilities needed to use the UMSDOS filesystem x x
x x    [X] sysvinit  System V-like INIT programs - REQUIRED       x x
x x    [X] bin       GNU fileutils 3.12, elvis, etc. - REQUIRED   x x
x x    [X] ldso      Dynamic linker/loader - REQUIRED             x x
x x    [ ] ibcs2     Runs SCO/SysVr4 binaries                     x x
x x    [X] less      A text pager utility - REQUIRED              x x
x x    [ ] pcmcia    PCMCIA card services support                 x x
x x    [ ] getty     Getty_ps 2.0.7e - OPTIONAL                   x x
x x    [X] gzip      The GNU zip compression - REQUIRED           x x
x x    [X] ps        Displays process info - REQUIRED             x x
x x    [X] aoutlibs  a.out shared libs - RECOMMENDED              x x
x x    [X] elflibs   The ELF shared C libraries - REQUIRED        x x
x x    [X] util      Util-linux utilities - REQUIRED              x x
x x    [ ] minicom   Serial transfer and modem comm package       x x
x x    [ ] cpio      The GNU cpio backup/archiving utility        x x
x x    [X] e2fsbn    Utilities for the ext2 file system           x x
x x    [X] find      GNU findutils 4.1                            x x
x x    [X] grep      GNU grep 2.0                                 x x
x x    [ ] kbd       Change keyboard mappings                     x x
x x    [X] gpm       Cut and paste text with your mouse           x x
x x    [X] sh_utils  GNU sh-utils 1.16 - REQUIRED                 x x
x x    [X] sysklogd  Logs system and kernel messages              x x
x x    [X] tar       GNU tar 1.12 - REQUIRED                      x x
x x    [ ] tcsh      Extended C shell version 6.07                x x
x x    [X] txtutils  GNU textutils-1.22 - REQUIRED                x x
x x    [ ] zoneinfo  Configures your time zone                    x x
x mqqqqqqqqqqqqqqqqqqqqqqqqqqqqqqqqqqqqqqqqqqqqqqqqqqqqqqqqqqqqqqqqj x
```

HOWTO

From the 'AP series, I use only 'JOE', and editor I like, and 'MC' a small and useful file management tool. You choose the utilities you will need on your system.

```
lqqqqqqqqq SELECTING PACKAGES FROM SERIES AP (APPLICATIONS) qqqqqqqqqk
x x      [ ] ispell   The International version of ispell        x x
x x      [ ] jove     Jonathan's Own Version of Emacs text editor x x
x x      [ ] manpgs   More man pages (online documentation)      x x
x x      [ ] diff     GNU diffutils                              x x
x x      [ ] sudo     Allow special users limited root access    x x
x x      [ ] ghostscr GNU Ghostscript version 3.33               x x
x x      [ ] gsfonts1 Ghostscript fonts (part one)               x x
x x      [ ] gsfonts2 Ghostscript fonts (part two)               x x
x x      [ ] gsfonts3 Ghostscript fonts (part three)             x x
x x      [ ] jed      JED programmer's editor                    x x
x x      [X] joe      joe text editor, version 2.8               x x
x x      [ ] jpeg     JPEG image compression utilities           x x
x x      [ ] bc       GNU bc - arbitrary precision math language x x
x x      [ ] workbone a text-based audio CD player               x x
```

```
x x      [X] mc        The Midnight Commander file manager           x x
x x      [ ] mt_st     mt ported from BSD - controls tape drive      x x
x x      [ ] groff     GNU troff document formatting system          x x
x x      [ ] quota     User disk quota utilities                     x x
x x      [ ] sc        The 'sc' spreadsheet                          x x
x x      [ ] texinfo   GNU texinfo documentation system              x x
x x      [ ] vim       Improved vi clone                             x x
x x      [ ] ash       A small /bin/sh type shell - 62K              x x
x x      [ ] zsh       Zsh - a custom *nix shell                     x x
x mqqqqqqqqqqqqqqqqqqqqqqqqqqqqqqqqqqqqqqqqqqqqqqqqqqqqqqqqqqqqqqqqqqj x
```

From the 'N' package I only loaded TCPIP. This isn't really necessary, but is very handy and allows access to the network while working on a repair or update with the root raid array dismounted. TCPIP also contains 'biff' which is used by some of the applications in 'A'. If you don't install 'N' you might want to install the biff package anyway.

```
lqqqq SELECTING PACKAGES FROM SERIES N (NETWORK/NEWS/MAIL/UUCP) qqqqqk
x lqqqqqqqqqqqqqqqqqqqqqqqqqqqqqqqqqqqqqqqqqqqqqqqqqqqqqqqqqqqqqqqqqqqk x
x x      [ ] apache    Apache WWW (HTTP) server                      x x
x x      [ ] procmail  Mail delivery/filtering utility               x x
x x      [ ] dip       Handles SLIP/CSLIP connections                x x
x x      [ ] ppp       Point-to-point protocol                       x x
x x      [ ] mailx     The mailx mailer                              x x
x x      [X] tcpip     TCP/IP networking programs                    x x
x x      [ ] bind      Berkeley Internet Name Domain server          x x
x x      [ ] rdist     Remote file distribution utility              x x
x x      [ ] lynx      Text-based World Wide Web browser             x x
x x      [ ] uucp      Taylor UUCP 1.06.1 with HDB && Taylor configs x x
x x      [ ] elm       Menu-driven user mail program                 x x
x x      [ ] pine      Pine menu-driven mail program                 x x
x x      [ ] sendmail  The sendmail mail transport agent             x x
x x      [ ] metamail  Metamail multimedia mail extensions           x x
x x      [ ] smailcfg  Extra configuration files for sendmail        x x
x x      [ ] cnews     Spools and transmits Usenet news              x x
x x      [ ] inn       InterNetNews news transport system            x x
x x      [ ] tin       The 'tin' news reader (local or NNTP)         x x
x x      [ ] trn       'trn' for /var/spool/news                     x x
x x      [ ] trn-nntp  'trn' for NNTP (install 1 'trn' maximum)      x x
x x      [ ] nn-spool  'nn' for /var/spool/news                      x x
x x      [ ] nn-nntp   'nn' for NNTP (install 1 'nn' maximum)        x x
x x      [ ] netpipes  Network pipe utilities                        x x
x mqqqqqqqqqqqqqqqqqqqqqqqqqqqqqqqqqqqqqqqqqqqqqqqqqqqqqqqqqqqqqqqqqqj x
```

With the installation complete, say no to everything else (no to all configuration requests) and exit the script.

4.6 Install linux pthreads

Now you must install the 'linuxthreads-0.71' library. I have included this diff for the linuxthreads Makefile rather than explain the details of the installation by hand. Save the original Makefile, apply the diff and then:

```
        cd /usr/src/linuxthreads-0.71
    patch
        make
        make install
```

```
-------------------diff Makefile.old  Makefile.raid-----------------
2a3,13
> # If you are building "linuxthreads" for installation on a mount
> # point which is not the "root" partition, redefine 'BUILDIR' to
> # the mount point to use as the "root" directory
> # You may wish to do this if you are building an 'initial ram disk'
> # such as used with bootable root raid devices.
> # REQUIRES ldconfig version 1.9.5 or better
> # do ldconfig -v to check
> #
> BUILDIR=/root/raidboot/mnt
> #BUILDIR=
>
81,82c92,93
<       install pthread.h $(INCLUDEDIR)/pthread.h
<       install semaphore.h $(INCLUDEDIR)/semaphore.h
---
>       install pthread.h $(BUILDIR)$(INCLUDEDIR)/pthread.h
>       install semaphore.h $(BUILDIR)$(INCLUDEDIR)/semaphore.h
84c95
<       test -f /usr/include/sched.h || install sched.h $(INCLUDEDIR)/sched.h
---
>       test -f $(BUILDIR)/usr/include/sched.h || instal-
l sched.h $(BUILDIR)$(INCLUDEDIR)/sched.h
86,89c97,103
<       install $(LIB) $(LIBDIR)/$(LIB)
<       install $(SHLIB) $(SHAREDLIBDIR)/$(SHLIB)
<       rm -f $(LIBDIR)/$(SHLIB0)
<       ln -s $(SHAREDLIBDIR)/$(SHLIB) $(LIBDIR)/$(SHLIB0)
---
>       install $(LIB) $(BUILDIR)$(LIBDIR)/$(LIB)
>       install $(SHLIB) $(BUILDIR)$(SHAREDLIBDIR)/$(SHLIB)
>       rm -f $(BUILDIR)$(LIBDIR)/$(SHLIB0)
>       ln -s $(SHAREDLIBDIR)/$(SHLIB) $(BUILDIR)$(LIBDIR)/$(SHLIB0)
> ifneq ($(BUILDIR),)
>       ldconfig -r ${BUILDIR} -n $(SHAREDLIBDIR)
> else
91c105,106
<       cd man; $(MAKE) MANDIR=$(MANDIR) install
---
> endif
>       cd man; $(MAKE) MANDIR=$(BUILDIR)$(MANDIR) install
```

4.7 Install Raid Tools

The next step is the installation of the raid tools. raidtools-0.42

You must run the "configure" script to point the Makefile at the build directory for the ramdisk files

```
cd /usr/src/raidtools-0.42
configure --sbindir=/root/raidboot/mnt/sbin --prefix=/root/raidboot/mnt/usr
make
make install
```

Now!! the Makefile for install is not quite right so do the following to clean up. This will be fixed in future releases so that the re-linking will not be necessary.

> Fix the make install error

The file links specified in the Makefile at 'LINKS' must be removed and re-linked to operate properly.

```
cd /root/raidboot/mnt/sbin
ln -fs mdadd mdrun
ln -fs mdadd mdstop
```

4.8   Remove un-needed directories and files from new filesystem.

Delete the following directories from filesystem (CAUTION DON'T DELETE FROM YOUR RUNNING SYSTEM) it's easy to do, guess how I found out!!!

```
cd /root/raidboot/mnt
rm -r home/ftp/*
rm -r lost+found
rm -r usr/doc
rm -r usr/info
rm -r usr/local/man
rm -r usr/man
rm -r usr/openwin
rm -r usr/share/locale
rm -r usr/X*
rm -r var/man
rm -r var/log/packages
rm -r var/log/setup
rm -r var/log/disk_contents
```

4.9   Create /dev/mdx

The last step simply copies the /dev/md* devices from the current file system onto the rescue file system. You could create these with mknode.

```
cp -a /dev/md* /root/raidboot/mnt/dev
```

4.10   Create a bare filesystem suitable for *initrd*

Now you have a clean re-useable filesystem ready for customization. Once customized, this file system can be used for rescue should the raid device(s) become corrupted and the raid tools needed to fix them. It will also be used to boot and root-mount the raid device by adding the linuxrc file which will be discussed next.

Copy the file system to a smaller device for the initrd file, 16 megs should be large enough.

Create the smaller file system and mount it

```
cd /root/raidboot
dd if=/dev/zero of=bare.fs bs=1024k count=16
```

associate the file with a loop device and generate a ext2 file system on the file

```
losetup /dev/loop1 bare.fs
mke2fs -v -m0 -L initrd /dev/loop1
```

```
        mount /dev/loop1 mnt2
```

Copy the 'build' file system to 'bare.fs'

```
        cp -a mnt/* mnt2
```

Save the 'bare.fs' system before customization so later update is easy. The 'build' file system is no longer needed and may be deleted.

```
        cd /root/raidboot
        umount mnt
        umount mnt2
        losetup -d /dev/loop0
        losetup -d /dev/loop1
        rm build
        cp bare.fs rescue
        gzip -9 bare.fs
```

4.10.1 Create the BOOT/RESCUE *initrd* filesystem

Now copy the system dependent items that match the kernel from the development platform, or you can manually modify the files in the rescue file system to match your target system.

```
        losetup /dev/loop0 rescue
        mount /dev/loop0 mnt
```

Make sure your etc directory is clean of *~, core and log files. The next 2 commands creates some warning messages, ignore them.

```
        cp -dp /etc/* mnt/etc
        cp -dp /etc/rc.d/* mnt/etc/rc.d

        mkdir  mnt/lib/modules
        cp -a  /lib/modules/2.x.x mnt/lib/modules <--- your current 2.x.x
```

Edit the following files to correct them for your rescue system.

```
        cd mnt
```

```
Non-network
        etc/fstab
        etc/mdtab          should work OK
Network
        etc/hosts
        etc/resolv.conf
        etc/hosts.equiv          and related files
        etc/rc.d/rc.inet1        correct ip#, mask, gateway, etc...
        etc/rc.d/rc.S            remove entire section on file system status
                from:
                        # Test to see if the root partition isread-only
                to but not including:
                        # remove /etc/mtab* so that mount will .....
                            This avoids the annoying warning that
                            the ramdisk is mounted rw.
```

```
        etc/rc.d/rc.xxxxx        others as required, see later on in this doc
        root/.rhosts             if present
        home/xxxx/xxxx           others as required
```

```
WARNING:    The above procedure moves your password and shadow
            files onto the rescue disk!!!!!

WARNING:    You may not wish to do this for security reasons.
```

Create any directories for mounting /dev/disk... as may be required that are unique to your system. These are the mountpoints for booting the system (boot partition and backup boot partition). My system boot from dos using **loadlin**, however linux partition(s) and lilo will work fine. My system uses:

```
        cd /root/raidboot/mnt         <--- initrd root
        mkdir dosa                    dos partition mount point
        mkdir dosb                    dos mirror mount point
```

The rescue file system is complete!

You will note upon examination of the files in the rescue file system, that there are still many files that could be deleted. I have not done this since it would overly complicate this procedure and most raid systems have adequate disk and memory. If you wish to skinny down the file system, go to it!

4.11   Making 'initrd' boot the RAID device - linuxrc

To make the rescue disk boot the raid device, you need only copy the executable script file:

   linuxrc

to the root of the device.

The theory of operation for this **linuxrc** file is discussed in 14 (Appendix G, linuxrc theory of operation).

A very simple and much easier to understand (working) linuxrc is included in 11 (Appendix D), *obsolete linuxrc and shutdown scripts*. Copy the following text to **linuxrc** and save in your development area.

```
-------------------- linuxrc --------------------
#!/bin/sh
# ver 1.13 3-6-98
#
############### BEGIN 'linuxrc' #################
#               DEFINE FUNCTIONS               #
################################################
# Define 'Fault' function in the event something
# goes wrong during the execution of 'linuxrc'
#
FaultExit () {
# correct fstab to show '/dev/ram0' for rescue system
    /bin/cat /etc/fstab | {
    while read Line
    do
        if [ -z "$( echo ${Line} | /usr/bin/grep md0 )" ]; then
            echo ${Line}
        else
            echo "/dev/ram0 / ext2 defaults 1 1"
```

```
            fi
        done
        } > /etc/tmp.$$
        /bin/mv /etc/tmp.$$ /etc/fstab
#           point root at /dev/ram0 (the rescue system)
            echo 0x100>/proc/sys/kernel/real-root-dev
            /bin/umount /proc
            exit
}

# Define 'Warning' procdure to print banner on boot terminal
#
Warning () {
    echo '*******************************'
    echo -e " $*"
    echo '*******************************'
}

# Define 'SplitKernelArg' to help extract 'Raid' related kernel arguments
SplitKernelArg () { eval $1='$( IFS=,; echo $2)' }

#Define 'SplitConfArgs' to help extract system configuration arguments
SplitConfArgs () {
    RaidBootType=$1
    RaidBootDevice=$2
    RaidConfigPath=$3
}
#######################################################
################## MAIN linuxrc #######################
#######################################################
# mount the proc file system
/bin/mount /proc

# Get the boot partition and configuration location from command line
CMDLINE='/bin/cat /proc/cmdline'
for Parameter in $CMDLINE; do
    Parameter=$( IFS='='; echo ${Parameter} )
    case $Parameter in
        Raid*) SplitKernelArg $Parameter;;
    esac
done

# check for 'required raid boot'
if [ -z "${Raid_Conf}" ]; then
    Warning Kernel command line \'Raid_Conf\' missing
    FaultExit
fi
SplitConfArgs $Raid_Conf

# tmp mount the boot partition
/bin/mount -t ${RaidBootType} ${RaidBootDevice} /mnt

# get etc files from primary raid system
pushd /etc
```

HOWTO

```
# this will un-tar into 'etc' (see rc.6)
if [ ! -f /mnt/${RaidConfigPath}/raidboot.etc ]; then
# bad news, this file should be here
    Warning required file \'raidboot.etc\' \
    missing from ${RaidBootDevice}/${RaidConfigPath} \\n \
    \\tUsing rescue system defaults
else
    /bin/tar -xf /mnt/${RaidConfigPath}/raidboot.etc
fi
# get 'real' raidboot device for this boot
# status path, and name of raidX.conf
if [ ! -f /mnt/${RaidConfigPath}/raidboot.cfg ]; then
# bad news, this file should be here
    Warning required file 'raidboot.cfg' \
    missing from ${RaidBootDevice}/${RaidConfigPath}\\n \
    \\tUsing rescue system defaults
# Get the first raidX.conf file name in $RArg1
    RaidBootDevs=$RaidBootDevice
    RaidStatusPath=$RaidConfigPath
    for RaidConfigEtc in $( ls raid*.conf )
    do break; done
else
    {
    read RaidBootDevs
    read RaidStatusPath
    read RaidConfigEtc
    } < /mnt/${RaidConfigPath}/raidboot.cfg


fi
popd
/bin/umount /mnt

# Set a flag in case the raid status file is not found
#
RAIDOWN="raidboot.ro not found"
RAIDREF="raidgood.ref not found"
echo "Reading md0 shutdown status."


# search for raid shutdown status
for Device in ${RaidBootDevs}
do
#     these filesystem types should be in 'fstab' since
#     the partitions must be mounted for a clean raid shutdown
    /bin/mount ${Device} /mnt
    if [ -f /mnt/${RaidStatusPath}/raidboot.ro ]; then
        RAIDOWN='/bin/cat /mnt/${RaidStatusPath}/raidboot.ro'
        RAIDREF='/bin/cat /mnt/${RaidStatusPath}/raidgood.ref'
        /bin/umount /mnt
        break
    fi
    /bin/umount /mnt
done
# Test for a clean shutdown with array matching reference
if [ "${RAIDOWN}" != "${RAIDREF}" ]; then
    Warning shutdown ERROR ${RAIDOWN}
```

```
        FaultExit
fi

# The raid array is clean, remove shutdown status files
for Device in ${RaidBootDevs}
do
    /bin/mount ${Device} /mnt
    /bin/rm -f /mnt/${RaidStatusPath}/raidboot.ro
    /bin/umount /mnt
done

# Write a clean superblock on all raid devices

echo "write clean superblocks"
/sbin/mkraid -f --only-superblock /etc/${RaidConfigEtc}

# Activate raid array(s)
if [ -z "$Raid_ALT" ]; then
    /sbin/mdadd -ar
else
    /sbin/mdadd $Raid_ALT
fi

#  If there are errors - BAIL OUT and leave rescue running
if [ $? -ne 0 ]; then
    Warning some RAID device has errors
    FaultExit
fi

# Everything is fine, let the kernel mount /dev/md0
# tell the kernel to switch to /dev/md0 as the /root device
# The 0x900 value is the device number calculated by:
#  256*major_device_number + minor_device number
echo "/dev/md0 mounted on root"
echo 0x900>/proc/sys/kernel/real-root-dev
# umount /proc to deallocate initrd device ram space
/bin/umount /proc
exit
#----------------- end linuxrc -----------------------
```

Add 'linuxrc' to initrd boot device

```
        cd /root/raidboot
        chmod 777 linuxrc
        cp -p linuxrc mnt
```

4.12   Modifying the rc-scripts for SHUTDOWN

To complete the installation, modify the rc scripts to save the md status to the real root device when shutdown occurs.

```
In slackware this is rc.0 -> rc.6
In debian 'bo' this is in both 'halt' and 'reboot'

If you implement this in another distribution, please e-mail
```

the instructions and sample files so they can be included here.

I have modified Bohumil Chalupa's raid stop work-around slightly. His original solution is presented in 8 (Appendix A).

Since there are no linux partitions left on the production system except **md0**, the boot partitions are used to store the **raidOK readonly** status. I chose to write a file to each of the duplicate boot partitions containing the status of the md array at shutdown and signifying that the md device has been remounted RO. This allows the system to be fail safe when any of the hard drives die.

The shutdown script is modified to call 13 (rc.raidown) which saves the necessary information to successfully reboot and mount the raid device. Examples of shutdown scripts for various linux distributions are shown in 9 (Appendix B).

To capture the raid array shutdown status insert a call to 13 (rc.raidown) after any **case** statements (if present) but before the actual shutdown (kills, status saves, etc...) begins and before the file systems are dismounted.

```
############## Save raid boot and status info ##############
#
  if [ -x /etc/rc.d/rc.raidown ]; then
    /etc/rc.d/rc.raidown
  fi
################# end raid boot ########################
```

After all the file systems are dismounted (the root file system 'will not' dismount) but before any powerfail status check add:

```
############### for raid arrays ########################
# Stop all known raid arrays (except root which won't stop)
  if [ -x /sbin/mdstop ]; then
    echo "Stopping raid"
    /sbin/mdstop -a
  fi
##########################################################
```

This will cleanly stop all raid devices except root. Root status is passed to the next boot in **raidstat.ro**.

Copy the rc file to your new raid array, the rescue file system that is still mounted on **/root/raidboot/mnt** and the development system if it is on the same machine.

Modify rescue **etc/fstab** as needed and make sure rescue **mdtab** is correct.

Now copy the rescue disk to your dos partition and everything should be ready to boot the raid device as root.

```
        umount mnt
        losetup -d /dev/loop0
        gzip -9 rescue
```

Copy rescue.gz to your boot partitions.

All that remains is to creat the configuration file **raidboot.conf** and test the new file system by rebooting.

4.13   Configuring RAIDBOOT - raidboot.conf

The comments following the example configuration file explain each of the three lines. This example file is for a 4 drive raid5 scsii array with duplicate boot partitions on drives sda1 and sdb1. Put the paramaters descriptive of your file systems here instead.

```
/dev/sda1 /dev/sdb1
linux
raid5.conf
# comments may only be placed 'after' the three
# configuration lines.
#
# This is 'raidboot.conf'
#
# line one, the partition(s) containing the 'initrd' raid-rescue system
#       It is not necessary to boot from these partitions, however,
#       since the rescue system will not fit on floppy, it is necessary
#       to know which partitions are to be used to load the rescue system
#
# line two, the path to the raidboot config information
#       Where the shutdown status, etc... is located at boot time
#       It does NOT include the mount point information, only 'path'
#       /mntpoint/'path'
#
# line -3-, name of the raid configuration file
#       Current raid configuration file i.e. raid1.conf, raid5.conf
```

4.14   Kernel 'loadlin and lilo' variables for RESCUE and RAID

There are two kernel variables for the RESCUE and RAID system, only the first need be specified.

- Raid_Conf=msdos,/dev/sda1,raidboot

    This variable points to raid boot device and configuration file. For floppy rescue boot, you may want to specify this on the kernel command line or in the loadlin or lilo boot file

    format: `'filesystem-type,device,path-to-config-from-mountpoint'`

- Raid_ALT=-r,-p5,/dev/md0,/dev/sda3 /dev/sdb3 /dev/sdc3 /dev/sdd3

    Alternate mdadd parameters necessary when booting with non-redundant raid array. These are the comma separated command line parameters for **mdadd**. Unless they are needed to start a failed/non-redundant array, COMMENT OUT OR SPECIFY WITH A 'NULL'.

    i.e. Raid_ALT=

Either of these parameters may be specified in the lilo or loadlin boot parameter file or on the loadlin kernel command line. Care must be taken that the maximum line length is not exceeded, however, if the command line is used (128 characters).

When booting with **lilo**, the parameters are included in the lilo config file in the form:

```
append="Raid_Conf=msdos,/dev/sda1,raidboot"
append="Raid_ALT=-r,-p5,/dev/md0,/dev/sda3 /dev/sdb3 /dev/sdc3 /dev/sdd3"
```

See **man lilo.conf** for more detailed information.

Since I have some hardware that requires DOS configuration utilities, I have a small dos partition on the system. Therefore, I used loadlin to boot the raid5 system from the dos partition with a mirror (copy) on the companion disk. An identical method is used for the raid1 system. The example below uses loadlin, but the procedure is very similar for lilo.

My dos root system contains a small editor among the utilities so I can modify the boot parameters of loadlin if necessary, allowing me to reboot the linux system on my swap disk while testing.

The dos system contains this tree for linux

HOWTO

```
c:\raidboot.bat
c:\raidboot\loadlin.exe
c:\raidboot\zimage
c:\raidboot\rescue.gz
c:\raidboot\raidboot.cfg
c:\raidboot\raidboot.etc
c:\raidboot\raidgood.ref
c:\raidboot\raidstat.ro (only at shutdown)
```

linux.bat contains:

```
-------------------- linux.bat --------------------
echo "Start the LOADLIN process:"
c:\raidboot\loadlin @c:\raidboot\boot.par
-------------------- end linux.bat --------------------
```

boot.par contains:

```
# loadlin boot parameter file
#
# version 1.02 3-6-98

# linux kernel image
c:\linux\zimage

# target root device
root=/dev/md0
#root=/dev/ram0
#root=/dev/sdc5

# mount root device as 'ro'
ro

# size of ram disk
ramdisk_size=16384

# initrd file name
initrd=c:\raidboot\rescue.gz
#noinitrd

# memory ends here
mem=131072k

# points to raid boot device, configuration file
# for floppy rescue boot, you may want to specify
# this on the command line instead of here
# format 'filesystem-type,device,path-to-config-frm_mntpnt'
Raid_Conf=msdos,/dev/sda1,raidboot

# Alternate mdadd parameters
# necessary when boot with non-redundant raid
# otherwise, COMMENT OUT OR SPECIFY 'NULL'
#Raid_ALT=-r,-p5,/dev/md0,/dev/sda3 /dev/sdb3 /dev/sdc3 /dev/sdd3

# ethernet devices
```

```
                    ether=10,0x300,eth0
```

```
***** >> NOTE!! the only difference between forcing the rescue system to
          run and the raid device mounting, is the loadlin parameter
```

```
               root=/dev/ram0          for the rescue system
               root=/dev/md0           for RAID

               With root=/dev/ram0 the RAID device will not mount
               and the rescue system will run unconditionally.
```

If the RAID array fails, the rescue system is left mounted and running.

5 Configuring the Production RAID system.

5.1 System specs. Two systems with identical motherboards were configured.

		Raid-1	Raid-5
Motherboard:	Iwill P55TU	dual ide	adaptec scsi
Processor:	Intel P200		
Disks:		2ea 7 gig	4 ea Segate 4.2 gig
		Maxtors	wide scsii

The disk drives are designated by linux as 'sda' through 'sdd' on the raid5 system and 'hda' and 'hdc' on the raid1 system.

5.2 Partitioning the hard drives.

Since testing a large root mountable RAID array is difficult because of the ckraid re-boot problem, I re-partitioned my swap space to include a smaller RAID partition for testing purposes, sda6,sdb6,sdc6,sdd6, and a small root and /usr/src partition pair for developing and testing the raid kernel and tools. You may find this helpful.

```
        <bf/DEVELOPMENT SYSTEM - RAID5/
   Device         System         Size     Purpose

   /dev/sda1      dos boot       16 meg   boot partition
 * /dev/sda2      extended       130 meg  (see below)
   /dev/sda3      linux native   4 gig    primary raid5-1
---------------------sda2--------------------------------
 * /dev/sda5      linux swap     113 meg  SWAP space
 * /dev/sda6      linux native   16 meg   test raid5-1
========================================================
   /dev/sdb1      dos boot       16 meg   boot partition duplicate
 * /dev/sdb2      extended       130 meg  (see below)
   /dev/sdb3      linux native   4 gig    primary raid5-2
---------------------sdb2--------------------------------
 * /dev/sdb5      linux swap     113 meg  SWAP space
 * /dev/sdb6      linux native   16 meg   test raid5-2
========================================================
 * /dev/sdc2      extended       146 meg  (see below)
   /dev/sdc3      linux native   4 gig    primary raid5-3
---------------------sdc2--------------------------------
 * /dev/sdc5      linux swap     130 meg  development root partition
 * /dev/sdc6      linux native   16 meg   test raid5-3
```

HOWTO

```
=============================================================
* /dev/sdd2       extended          146 meg (see below)
  /dev/sdd3       linux native      4 gig   primary raid5-4
---------------------sdd2-------------------------------
* /dev/sdd5       linux swap        130 meg development /usr/src
* /dev/sdd6       linux native      16 meg  test raid5-4


          <bf/DEVELOPMENT SYSTEM - RAID1/
  Device          System          Size    Purpose

  /dev/hda1       dos             16meg   boot partition
* /dev/hda2       extended        126m    (see below)
  /dev/hda3       linux           126m    development root partition
  /dev/hda4       linux           6+gig   raid1-1
---------------------hda2-------------------------------
* /dev/hda5       linux           26m     test raid1-1
* /dev/hda6       linux swap      100m
=============================================================

  /dev/hdc1       is simply an exact copy of hda1 so the
                  partion can be made active if hda fails
* /dev/hdc2       extended        126m    (see below)
  /dev/hdc3       linux           126m    development /usr/src
  /dev/hdc4       linux           6+gig   raid1-2
---------------------hdc2-------------------------------
* /dev/hdc5       linux           26m     test raid1-2
* /dev/hdc6       linux swap      100m
```

The sdx2 and hdx3 partitions were switched to 'swap' after developing this utility. I could have done it on another machine, however, the libraries and kernels are all about a year or more out of date on my other linux boxes and I preferred to build it on the target machine.

The partitioning scheme was chosen so that in the event that any one of the drives fails catastrophically, the system will continue to run and be bootable with minimum effort and NO data loss.

- If any single hard drive fails, the boot will abort, and the rescue system will run. Examination of the screen message or /dosx/raidboot/raidstat.ro will tell the operator the status of the failed array.

- If sda1 (raid5) or hda1 (raid1) fails, the dos backup boot partition must be made 'active' and the bios must recognize the new partition as the boot device or it must be physically be moved to the xda position. Alternatively, the system could be booted from a floppy disk using the initrd image on the remaining backup boot drive. The raid system can then be made active again by issuing:

      "/sbin/mkraid /etc/raid<it/x/.conf -f --only-superblock"

  to rebuild the remaining superblock(s).

- Once this is done, then

      mdadd -ar

- Examine the status of the array to verify that everything is OK then replace the good array reference with the current status until the failed disk can be repaired or replaced.

      cat /proc/mdstat | grep md0 > /dosx/raidboot/raidgood.ref

      shutdown -r now

  to do a clean reboot, and the system is up again.

6 Building the RAID file system.

This description is for my RAID systems described in the system specs. Your system may have a different RAID architecture, so modify as appropriate. Please read the man pages and QuickStart.RAID that come with the raidtools-0.42

6.1 /etc/raid5.conf

```
# raid-5 configuration
raiddev                    /dev/md0
raid-level                 5
nr-raid-disks              4
chunk-size                 32

# Parity placement algorithm
parity-algorithm           left-symmetric

# Spare disks for hot reconstruction
#nr-spare-disks            0

device                     /dev/sda3
raid-disk                  0

device                     /dev/sdb3
raid-disk                  1

device                     /dev/sdc3
raid-disk                  2

device                     /dev/sdd3
raid-disk                  3
```

6.2 /etc/raid1.conf

```
# raid-1 configuration
raiddev                    /dev/md0
raid-level                 1
nr-raid-disks              2
nr-spare-disks             0

device                     /dev/hda4
raid-disk                  0

device                     /dev/hdc4
raid-disk                  1
```

6.3 Step by Step procedures for building production RAID file system.

For my RAID5 system I did a complete install of:

```
Slackware-3.4              any current distribution should work OK
linuxthreads-0.71
raidtools-0.42
linux-2.0.33 with raid145 patch and Gadi's patch
```

Create and format the raid device.

```
mkraid /etc/raid5.conf
mdcreate raid5 /dev/md0 /dev/sda3 /dev/sdb3 /dev/sdc3 /dev/sdd3
mdadd -ar
mke2fs /dev/md0
mkdir /md
mount -t ext2 /dev/md0 /md
```

Create the reference files that reboot will use, this may be different on your system.

```
cat /proc/mdstat | grep md0 > /dosa/raidboot/raidgood.ref
cat /proc/mdstat | grep md0 > /dosb/raidboot/raidgood.ref
```

Use Slackware-3.4 or another distribution to build your OS

```
setup
```

Specify '/md' as the target, and the source whatever your normally use. Select and install the disksets of interest except for the kernel. Configure the system, but skip the section on lilo and kernel booting. Exit setup.

Install 'pthreads'

```
cd /usr/src/linuxthreads-0.71
```

edit the Makefile and specify

```
BUILDIR=/md

make
make install
```

Install 'raidtools'

```
cd /usr/src/raidtools-0.42
configure --sbindir=/md/sbin --prefix=/md/usr
```

fix the raidtools make install error

```
cd /md/sbin
rm mdrun
rm mdstop
ln -s mdadd mdrun
ln -s mdadd mdstop
```

Create /dev/mdx

```
cp -a /dev/md* /md/dev
```

Add the system configuration from the current system (ignore errors).

```
cp -dp /etc/* mnt/etc
cp -dp /etc/rc.d/* mnt/etc/rc.d          (include the new rc.6)
mkdir  mnt/lib/modules
```

```
      cp -a  /lib/modules/2.x.x mnt/lib/modules <--- your current 2.x.x
```

Edit the following files to correct them for your file system

```
      cd /md
```

Non-network

```
      etc/fstab        correct for real root and raid devices.
      etc/mdtab        should work OK
```

Network

```
      etc/hosts
      etc/resolv.conf
      etc/hosts.equiv      and related files
      etc/rc.d/rc.inet1    correct ip#, mask, gateway, etc...
      etc/rc.d/rc.S        remove entire section on file system status
            from:
                     # Test to see if the root partition isread-only
            to but not including:
                     # remove /etc/mtab* so that mount will .....
                     This avoids the annoying warning that
                     the ramdisk is mounted rw.
      etc/rc.d/rc.xxxxx    others as required
      root/.rhosts         if present
      home/xxxx/xxxx       others as required
```

```
   WARNING:   The above procedure moves your password and shadow
              files onto the new file system!!!!!

   WARNING:   You may not wish to do this for security reasons.
```

Create any directories for mounting /dev/disk... as may be required that are unique to your system. Mine need:

```
      cd /md         <--- new file system root
      mkdir dosa              dos partition mount point
      mkdir dosb              dos mirror mount point
```

The new file system is complete. Make sure and save the md reference status to the 'real' root device and you are ready to boot.

mount the dos partitions on dosa and dosb

```
      cat /proc/mdstat | grep md0 > /dosa/raidboot/raidgood.ref
      cat /proc/mdstat | grep md0 > /dosb/raidboot/raidgood.ref

      mdstop /dev/md0
```

7 One last thought.

Remember that an expert is someone who knows at least 1% more than you do about a subject. Bear this in mind when you e-mail me for help. I'll try, but I've only done this once for raid1 and once for raid5!

Michael Robinton *Michael@bzs.org* <mailto:michael@bzs.org>

8 Appendix A. - Bohumil Chalupa's md0 shutdown

Bohumil Chalupa's post to the linux raid list on the work around for the raid1 + 5 mdstop problem. His solution does not address the possibility of the raid device being corrupt at shutdown. So I have added a simple status comparison to a good reference status at boot. This allows the operator to intervene if something is wrong with a disk in the array. The description of this is in the main body of this document.

```
> From: Bohumil Chalupa <bochal@apollo.karlov.mff.cuni.cz>
>
> I can now boot initrd and use linuxrc to start the RAID1 array,
> then successfully switch root to /dev/md0.
>
> I don't know, however, any way how to cleanly _stop_ the array.

Well. I have to answer myself :-)

> Date: Mon, 29 Dec 1997 02:21:38 -0600 (CST)
> From: Edward Welbon <welbon@bga.com>
> Subject: Re: dismounting root raid device
>
> For md devices other than raid0, there is probably state that needs to
> be saved that is only known once all writes have completed.  Such state
> of course can't be saved to root once it is mounted readonly.  In that
> case, you would have to be able to mount a writeable filesystem "X"
> on the readonly root and be able to write to "X" (I recall doing this
> during "rescue" operations, but not as an automated procedure).
>
> The filesystem "X" would presumably be a boot device from which the raid
> (during linuxrc exection via initrd) would pickup it's initial state from.
> Fortunately raid0 isn't required to write out any state (though it would
> be pleasant to be able to write the check sums to mdtab after an mdstop).
> Eventually, I will fiddle with this but it doesn't seem difficult though
> the "devil" is always in the "details".

Yes, that's it.
I had this idea in mind for some time already, but had no time to try it.
Yesterday I did, and it works.

With my RAID1 (mirror), I don't save any checksums or raid superblock data.
I only save an information on the "real" boot partition, that the root md
volume was remounted readonly during shutdown. Then, during boot, the
linuxrc script runs mkraid --only-superblock  when it finds this
information; otherwise, it runs ckraid.
This means, that the raid superblock information is not updated during
shutdown; it's updated at the boot time.
It is not very clean, I'm afraid,  :-(   but it works.

I'm using Slackware and initrd.md by Edward Welbon to boot the root raid
device.
As far as I remember now, the only modified files are
mkdisk and linuxrc, and /etc/rc.d/rc.6 shutdown script.
And lilo.conf, of course.

I'm appending the important parts.
```

Bohumil Chalupa

```
-------------- my.linuxrc follows ----------------
#!/bin/sh
# we need /proc
/bin/mount /proc
# start up the md0 device. let the /etc/rc.d scripts get the rest of them
# we should do as little as possible here
# _____
# root raid1 shutdown test & recreation
# /start must be created on the rd image in my.mkdisk
echo "preparing md0: mounting /start"
/bin/mount /dev/sda2 /start -t ext2
echo "reading saved md0 state from /start"
if [ -f /start/root.raid.ok ]; then
 echo "raid ok, modyfying superblock"
 rm /start/root.raid.ok
 /sbin/mkraid /etc/raid1.conf -f --only-superblock
else
 echo "raid not clean, runing ckraid --fix"
 /sbin/ckraid --fix /etc/raid1.conf
fi
echo "unmounting /start"
/bin/umount /start
# _____
#
echo "adding md0 for root file system"
/sbin/mdadd /dev/md0 /dev/sda1 /dev/sdb1
echo "starting md0"
/sbin/mdrun -p1 /dev/md0
# tell kernel we want to switch to /dev/md0 as root device, the 0x900 value
# is arrived at via 256*major_device_number + minor_device number.
echo "setting real-root-dev"
/bin/echo 0x900>/proc/sys/kernel/real-root-dev
#  unmount /proc so that the ram disk can be deallocated.
echo "unmounting /proc"
/bin/umount /proc
/bin/echo "We are hopefully ready to mount /dev/md0 (major 9, minor 0) as
root"
exit
-------------- end of my.linuxrc ----------------------------------


----------- extract from /etc/rc.d/rc.6 follows ----------------
  # Turn off swap, then unmount local file systems.
  echo "Turning off swap."
  swapoff -a
  echo "Unmounting local file systems."
  umount -a -tnonfs
  # Don't remount UMSDOS root volumes:
  if [ ! "'mount | head -1 | cut -d ' ' -f 5'" = "umsdos" ]; then
    mount -n -o remount,ro /
  fi

  # Save raid state
```

HOWTO

```
   echo "Saving RAID state"
   /bin/mount -n /dev/sda2 /start -t ext2
   touch /start/root.raid.ok
   /bin/umount -n /start


-------------- end of excerpt from rc.6 ----------------------


------------------ part of my.mkdisk follows ----------------------
#
#  now we have the filesystem ready to be populated, we need to
#  get a few important directories.  I had endless trouble till
#  I created a pristine mtab.  In my case, it is convenient that
#  /etc/mdtab is copied over, this way I can activate md with
#  a simple "/sbin/mdadd -ar" in linuxrc.
#
cp -a $ROOT/etc $MOUNTPNT 2>cp.stderr 1>cp.stdout
rm -rf $MOUNTPNT/etc/mtab
rm -rf $MOUNTPNT/etc/ppp*
rm -rf $MOUNTPNT/etc/termcap
rm -rf $MOUNTPNT/etc/sendmail*
rm -rf $MOUNTPNT/etc/rc.d
rm -rf $MOUNTPNT/etc/dos*
cp -a $ROOT/sbin $ROOT/dev $ROOT/lib $ROOT/bin $MOUNTPNT 2>>cp.stderr
1>>cp.stdout
# _____
#  RAID: will need mkraid and ckraid
cp -a $ROOT/usr/sbin/mkraid $ROOT/usr/sbin/ckraid $MOUNTPNT/sbin
2>>cp.stderr 1>>cp.stdout
# ----------------------------------------------------------------
#  it seems that init wont come out to play unless it has utmp.   this can
#  probably be pruned back alot.  no telling what the real bug was 8-).
#
mkdir $MOUNTPNT/var $MOUNTPNT/var/log $MOUNTPNT/var/run $MOUNTPNT/initrd
touch $MOUNTPNT/var/run/utmp $MOUNTPNT/etc/mtab
chmod a+r $MOUNTPNT/var/run/utmp $MOUNTPNT/etc/mtab
ln -s /var/run/utmp $MOUNTPNT/var/log/utmp
ln -s /var/log/utmp $MOUNTPNT/etc/utmp
ls -lstrd $MOUNTPNT/etc/utmp $MOUNTPNT/var/log/utmp $MOUNTPNT/var/run/utmp
#
#  since I wanted to change the mount point, I needed this though
#  I suppose that I could have done a "mkdir /proc" in linuxrc.
#
mkdir $MOUNTPNT/proc
chmod 555 $MOUNTPNT/proc
#
# ---------------------------------------------------------
#  we'll mount the real boot device to /start temporarily
#  to check the root raid state saved at shutdown time
#
mkdir $MOUNTPNT/start
# ---------------------------------------------------------
#
#  need linuxrc  (it is, after all, the point of this exercise).
#
```

```
if [ -x ./my.linuxrc ]; then
  cp -a ./my.linuxrc $MOUNTPNT/linuxrc
  chmod 777 $MOUNTPNT/linuxrc
else
  ln -s /bin/sh $MOUNTPNT/linuxrc
fi
#
----------------- part of my.mkdisk ends -----------------
```

9 Appendix B. - Sample SHUTDOWN scripts

- 9.1 (Slackware)
- 9.2 (Debian)

9.1 Slackware - /etc/rc.d/rc.6

```
#! /bin/sh
#
# rc.6          This file is executed by init when it goes into runlevel
#               0 (halt) or runlevel 6 (reboot). It kills all processes,
#               unmounts file systems and then either halts or reboots.
#
# Version:      @(#)/etc/rc.d/rc.6      1.50    1994-01-15
#
# Author:       Miquel van Smoorenburg <miquels@drinkel.nl.mugnet.org>
# Modified by:  Patrick J. Volkerding, <volkerdi@ftp.cdrom.com>
#
# Modified by:  Michael A. Robinton < michael@bizsystems.com >
#               to add call to rc.raidown
  # Set the path.
  PATH=/sbin:/etc:/bin:/usr/bin

  # Set linefeed mode to avoid staircase effect.
  stty onlcr

  echo "Running shutdown script $0:"

  # Find out how we were called.
  case "$0" in
      *0)
              message="The system is halted."
              command="halt"
              ;;
      *6)
              message="Rebooting."
              command=reboot
              ;;
      *)
              echo "$0: call me as \"rc.0\" or \"rc.6\" please!"
              exit 1
              ;;
  esac

############ Save raid boot and status info #############
```

```
#
if [ -x /etc/rc.d/rc.raidown ]; then
    /etc/rc.d/rc.raidown
fi
################## end raid boot ##########################

  # Kill all processes.
  # INIT is supposed to handle this entirely now, but this didn't always
  # work correctly without this second pass at killing off the processes.
  # Since INIT already notified the user that processes were being killed,
  # we'll avoid echoing this info this time around.
  if [ "$1" != "fast" ]; then # shutdown did not already kill all processes
    killall5 -15
    killall5 -9
  fi

  # Try to turn off quota and accounting.
  if [ -x /usr/sbin/quotaoff ]
  then
        echo "Turning off quota."
        /usr/sbin/quotaoff -a
  fi
  if [ -x /sbin/accton ]
  then
        echo "Turning off accounting."
        /sbin/accton
  fi

  # Before unmounting file systems write a reboot or halt record to wtmp.
  $command -w

  # Save localtime
  [ -e /usr/lib/zoneinfo/localtime ] && cp /usr/lib/zoneinfo/localtime /etc

  # Asynchronously unmount any remote filesystems:
  echo "Unmounting remote filesystems."
  umount -a -tnfs &

  # Turn off swap, then unmount local file systems.
  echo "Turning off swap."
  swapoff -a
  echo "Unmounting local file systems."
  umount -a -tnonfs
  # Don't remount UMSDOS root volumes:
  if [ ! "`mount | head -1 | cut -d ' ' -f 5`" = "umsdos" ]; then
    mount -n -o remount,ro /
  fi

############### for raid arrays #########################
# Stop all known raid arrays (except root which won't stop)
if [ -x /sbin/mdstop ]; then
  echo "Stopping raid"
  /sbin/mdstop -a
fi
########################################################
```

```
# See if this is a powerfail situation.
if [ -f /etc/powerstatus ]; then
  echo "Turning off UPS, bye."
  /sbin/powerd -q
  exit 1
fi

# Now halt or reboot.
echo "$message"
[ ! -f /etc/fastboot ] && echo "On the next boot fsck will be FORCED."
$command -f
############## end rc.6 #############################
```

9.2 Debian bo - /etc/init.d/halt and /etc/init.d/reboot

The modifications shown here for Debian bo halt and reboot files are NOT TESTED. When you test this, please e-mail me so I can remove this comment.

9.2.1 /etc/init.d/halt

```
#! /bin/sh
#
# halt          The commands in this script are executed as the last
#               step in runlevel 0, ie halt.
#
# Version:      @(#)halt  1.10  26-Apr-1997  miquels@cistron.nl
#

PATH=/sbin:/bin:/usr/sbin:/usr/bin

############ Save raid boot and status info #############
#
if [ -x /etc/rc.d/rc.raidown ]; then
   /etc/rc.d/rc.raidown
fi
################# end raid boot #######################

# Kill all processes.
echo -n "Sending all processes the TERM signal... "
killall5 -15
echo "done."
sleep 5
echo -n "Sending all processes the KILL signal... "
killall5 -9
echo "done."

# Write a reboot record to /var/log/wtmp.
halt -w

# Save the random seed between reboots.
/etc/init.d/urandom stop

echo -n "Deactivating swap... "
swapoff -a
```

```
echo "done."

echo -n "Unmounting file systems... "
umount -a
echo "done."

mount -n -o remount,ro /

################ for raid arrays #########################
# Stop all known raid arrays (except root which won't stop)
if [ -x /sbin/mdstop ]; then
  echo "Stopping raid"
  /sbin/mdstop -a
fi
##########################################################

# See if we need to cut the power.
if [ -x /etc/init.d/ups-monitor ]
then
        /etc/init.d/ups-monitor poweroff
fi

halt -d -f
############# end halt ###################
```

9.2.2 /etc/init.d/reboot

```
#! /bin/sh
#
# reboot        The commands in this script are executed as the last
#               step in runlevel 6, ie reboot.
#
# Version:      @(#)reboot  1.9  02-Feb-1997  miquels@cistron.nl
#

PATH=/sbin:/bin:/usr/sbin:/usr/bin

############ Save raid boot and status info #############
#
if [ -x /etc/rc.d/rc.raidown ]; then
   /etc/rc.d/rc.raidown
fi
################## end raid boot #########################

# Kill all processes.
echo -n "Sending all processes the TERM signal... "
killall5 -15
echo "done."
sleep 5
echo -n "Sending all processes the KILL signal... "
killall5 -9
echo "done."

# Write a reboot record to /var/log/wtmp.
halt -w
```

```
# Save the random seed between reboots.
/etc/init.d/urandom stop

echo -n "Deactivating swap... "
swapoff -a
echo "done."

echo -n "Unmounting file systems... "
umount -a
echo "done."

mount -n -o remount,ro /

################ for raid arrays ########################
# Stop all known raid arrays (except root which won't stop)
if [ -x /sbin/mdstop ]; then
  echo "Stopping raid"
  /sbin/mdstop -a
fi
##########################################################

echo -n "Rebooting... "
reboot -d -f -i
```

10   Appendix C. - other setup files

10.1   linuxrc 4.11 (linuxrc file)

10.2   loadlin – linux.bat file - boot.par 4.14 (linux.bat file - boot.par)

10.3   linuxthreads Makefile.diff 4.6 (linuxthreads Makefile.diff)

10.4   raid1.conf 6.2 (raid1.conf)

10.5   raid5.conf 6.1 (raid5.conf)

10.6   raidboot.conf 4.13 (raidboot.conf)

10.7   rc.raidown 13 (rc.raidown)

11   Appendix D. - obsolete linuxrc and shutdown scripts

11.1   Obsolete working - linuxrc

This linuxrc file works fine with the shutdown procedure in the next subsection.

```
--------------------- linuxrc ---------------------
#!/bin/sh
# ver 1.07 2-12-98
# linuxrc - for raid1 using small dos partition and loadlin
#
```

```
# mount the proc file system
/bin/mount /proc

# This may vary for your system.
# Mount the dos partitions, try both
# in case one disk is dead
/bin/mount /dosa
/bin/mount /dosc

# Set a flag in case the raid status file is not found
# then check both drives for the status file
RAIDOWN="raidstat.ro not found"
/bin/echo "Reading md0 shutdown status."
if [ -f /dosa/raidboot/raidstat.ro ]; then
  RAIDOWN='/bin/cat /dosa/raidboot/raidstat.ro'
  RAIDREF='/bin/cat /dosc/raidboot/raidgood.ref'
else
  if [ -f /dosc/raidboot/raidstat.ro ]; then
    RAIDOWN='/bin/cat /dosc/raidboot/raidstat.ro'
    RAIDREF='/bin/cat /dosc/raidboot/raidgood.ref'
  fi
fi

# Test for a clean shutdown with all disks operational
if [ "${RAIDOWN} != ${RAIDREF}" ]; then
  echo "ERROR ${RAIDOWN}"
# Use the next 2 lines to BAIL OUT and leave rescue running
  /bin/echo 0x100>/proc/sys/kernel/real-root-dev
  exit                      # leaving the error files in dosa/raidboot,etc...
fi

# The raid array is clean, proceed by removing
# status file and writing a clean superblock
/bin/rm /dosa/raidboot/raidstat.ro
/bin/rm /dosc/raidboot/raidstat.ro
/sbin/mkraid /etc/raid1.conf -f --only-superblock

/bin/umount /dosa
/bin/umount /dosc

# Mount raid array
echo "Mounting md0, root filesystem"
/sbin/mdadd -ar

# If there are errors - BAIL OUT and leave rescue running
if [ $? -ne 0 ]; then
   echo "RAID device has errors"
# Use the next 3 lines to BAIL OUT
   /bin/rm /etc/mtab            # remove bad mtab
   /bin/echo 0x100>/proc/sys/kernel/real-root-dev
   exit
fi

# else tell the kernel to switch to /dev/md0 as the /root device
```

```
# The 0x900 value the device number calculated by:
#  256*major_device_number + minor_device number
/bin/echo 0x900>/proc/sys/kernel/real-root-dev

# umount /proc to deallocate initrd device ram space
/bin/umount /proc
/bin/echo "/dev/md0 mounted as root"
exit
#----------------- end linuxrc ---------------------
```

11.2   Obsolete working - shutdown scripts

This shutdown procedure works fine with the preceeding **linuxrc**

To capture the raid array shutdown status, just before the file systems are dismounted insert:

```
RAIDSTATUS='/bin/cat /proc/mdstat | /usr/bin/grep md0'
```

After all the file systems are dismounted (the root file system 'will not' dismount) add:

```
# root device remains mounted RO
# mount dos file systems RW
mount -n -o remount,ro /
echo "Writing RAID read-only boot FLAG(s)."
mount -n /dosa
mount -n /dosc
# create raid mounted RO flag in duplicate
# containing the shutdown status of the raid array
echo ${RAIDSTATUS} > /dosa/raidboot/raidstat.ro
echo ${RAIDSTATUS} > /dosc/raidboot/raidstat.ro

umount -n /dosa
umount -n /dosc

# Stop all the raid arrays (except root)
echo "Stopping raid"
mdstop -a
```

This will cleanly stop all raid devices except root. Root status is passed to the next boot in **raidstat.ro**.

The complete shutdown script from my old raid1 Slackware system follows, I have switched raid1 to the new procedure with the /etc/raidboot.conf file.

```
#! /bin/sh
#
# rc.6         This file is executed by init when it goes into runlevel
#              0 (halt) or runlevel 6 (reboot). It kills all processes,
#              unmounts file systems and then either halts or reboots.
#
# Version:     @(#)/etc/rc.d/rc.6    1.50    1994-01-15
#
# Author:      Miquel van Smoorenburg <miquels@drinkel.nl.mugnet.org>
# Modified by: Patrick J. Volkerding, <volkerdi@ftp.cdrom.com>
# Modified by: Michael A. Robinton, <michael@bzs.org> for RAID shutdown
```

HOWTO

```
# Set the path.
PATH=/sbin:/etc:/bin:/usr/bin

# Set linefeed mode to avoid staircase effect.
stty onlcr

echo "Running shutdown script $0:"

# Find out how we were called.
case "$0" in
    *0)
                message="The system is halted."
                command="halt"
                ;;
    *6)
                message="Rebooting."
                command=reboot
                ;;
    *)
                echo "$0: call me as \"rc.0\" or \"rc.6\" please!"
                exit 1
                ;;
esac

# Kill all processes.
# INIT is supposed to handle this entirely now, but this didn't always
# work correctly without this second pass at killing off the processes.
# Since INIT already notified the user that processes were being killed,
# we'll avoid echoing this info this time around.
if [ "$1" != "fast" ]; then # shutdown did not already kill all processes
  killall5 -15
  killall5 -9
fi

# Try to turn off quota and accounting.
if [ -x /usr/sbin/quotaoff ]
then
      echo "Turning off quota."
      /usr/sbin/quotaoff -a
fi
if [ -x /sbin/accton ]
then
      echo "Turning off accounting."
      /sbin/accton
fi

# Before unmounting file systems write a reboot or halt record to wtmp.
$command -w

# Save localtime
[ -e /usr/lib/zoneinfo/localtime ] && cp /usr/lib/zoneinfo/localtime /etc

# Asynchronously unmount any remote filesystems:
echo "Unmounting remote filesystems."
umount -a -tnfs &
```

```
# you must have issued
# 'cat /proc/mdstat | grep md0 > {your boot vol}/raidboot/raidgood.ref'
# before linuxrc will execute properly with this info
RAIDSTATUS='/bin/cat /proc/mdstat | /usr/bin/grep md0 # capture raid status'

# Turn off swap, then unmount local file systems.
# clearing mdtab as well
echo "Turning off swap."
swapoff -a
echo "Unmounting local file systems."
umount -a -tnonfs

# Don't remount UMSDOS root volumes:
if [ ! "'mount | head -1 | cut -d ' ' -f 5'" = "umsdos" ]; then
  mount -n -o remount,ro /
fi

# root device remains mounted
# mount dos file systems RW
echo "Writing RAID read-only boot FLAG(s)."
mount -n /dosa
mount -n /dosc
# create raid mounted RO flag in duplicate
# containing the shutdown status of the raid array
echo ${RAIDSTATUS} > /dosa/raidboot/raidstat.ro
echo ${RAIDSTATUS} > /dosc/raidboot/raidstat.ro

umount -n /dosa
umount -n /dosc

# Stop all the raid arrays (except root)
echo "Stopping raid"
mdstop -a

# See if this is a powerfail situation.
if [ -f /etc/power_is_failing ]; then
  echo "Turning off UPS, bye."
  /sbin/powerd -q
  exit 1
fi

# Now halt or reboot.
echo "$message"
[ ! -f /etc/fastboot ] && echo "On the next boot fsck will be FORCED."
$command -f
```

12   Appendix E. - Gadi's raid stop patch for the linux kernel

```
--- linux/drivers/block/md.c.old        Fri Nov 21 13:37:11 1997
+++ linux/drivers/block/md.c     Sat Dec  6 13:34:28 1997
@@ -622,8 +622,13 @@
       return do_md_run (minor, (int) arg);
```

```
      case STOP_MD:
-        return do_md_stop (minor, inode);
-
+        err = do_md_stop(minor, inode);
+        if (err) {
+           printk("md: enabling auto mdstop for %s\n",
kdevname(inode->i_rdev));
+           md_dev[minor].auto_mdstop = 1;
+        }
+        return err;
+
      case BLKGETSIZE:    /* Return device size */
        if (!arg) return -EINVAL;
        err=verify_area (VERIFY_WRITE, (long *) arg, sizeof(long));
@@ -692,6 +697,10 @@

   sync_dev (inode->i_rdev);
   md_dev[minor].busy--;
+  if (!md_dev[minor].busy && md_dev[minor].auto_mdstop) {
+      do_md_stop(minor, inode);
+      md_dev[minor].auto_mdstop = 0;
+  }
  }

 static int md_read (struct inode *inode, struct file *file,
--- linux/include/linux/md.h~   Fri Nov 21 13:29:14 1997
+++ linux/include/linux/md.h    Fri Nov 21 13:29:14 1997
@@ -260,6 +260,7 @@
   int              repartition;
   int              busy;
   int              nb_dev;
+  int              auto_mdstop;
   void             *private;
 };
```

13   Appendix F. - rc.raidown

Copy the following text into the script file **rc.raidown** and save it in **/etc/rc.d**.

```
#! /bin/sh
#
# rc.raidown    This file is executed by init when it goes into runlevel
#               0 (halt) or runlevel 6 (reboot). It saves the status of
#               a root mounted raid array for subsequent re-boot
#
# Version:      1.08   3-25-98 Michael A. Robinton < michael@bizsystems.com >
#
############ Save raid boot and status info #############
if [ -f /etc/raidboot.conf ]
then
  {
  read RaidBootDevs
  read RaidStatusPath
  read RaidConfigEtc
```

```
      } < /etc/raidboot.conf

# you must have issued
#        cat /proc/mdstat | grep md0 >
#                  {your boot vol mnt(s)}/{RaidStatusPath}/raidgood.ref
# before linuxrc will execute properly with this info
#
#        capture raid status
    RAIDSTATUS='/bin/cat /proc/mdstat | /usr/bin/grep md0'
    mkdir /tmp/raid$$
    echo "Writing RAID read-only boot FLAG(s)."
    for Device in ${RaidBootDevs}
    do
# get mount point for raid boot device or use tmp
    RBmount=$( cat /proc/mounts | /usr/bin/grep ${Device} )
    if [ -n ${RBmounts} ]; then
        RBmount=$( echo ${RBmount} | cut -f 2 -d ' ' )
    else
        RBmount="/tmp/raid$$"
        mount ${Device} ${RBmount}
    fi
    if [ -d ${RBmount}/${RaidStatusPath} ]; then
# Create raid mounted RO flag = shutdown status of raid array
        echo ${RAIDSTATUS} > ${RBmount}/${RaidStatusPath}/raidboot.ro
# Don't propagate 'fstab' from ramdisk
        if [ -f /linuxrc ]; then
            FSTAB=
        else
            FSTAB=fstab
        fi
        pushd /etc
# Save etc files for rescue system
        /bin/tar --ignore-failed-read \
            -cf ${RBmount}/${RaidStatusPath}/raidboot.etc \
            raid*.conf mdtab* ${FSTAB} lilo.conf
        popd
# Create new raidboot.cfg
        {
        /bin/echo ${RaidBootDevs}
        /bin/echo ${RaidStatusPath}
        /bin/echo ${RaidConfigEtc}
        } > ${RBmount}/${RaidStatusPath}/raidboot.cfg
        /bin/umount ${RBmount}
    fi
    done
    rmdir /tmp/raid$$
    echo "Raid boot armed"
fi
################ end raid boot ########################
```

14 Appendix G. - linuxrc theory of operation

This is the complex form of the linuxrc file for root mounted raid. It must be processed with 'bash' or another shell that recognizes shell functions.

The advantage is that it is generic and is not dependent on startup files and parameters located in the **initrd** image.

A **Raid_Conf** parameter passed to **linuxrc** by the kernel at boot from lilo or loadlin contains a pointer to the boot devices and location the of initial 2 raidboot files needed by **linuxrc** (*raidboot.etc and raidboot.cfg placed by the shutdown script*).

> **raidboot.etc** containing the 'tar'ed files:

```
raid*
mdtab*
fstab
lilo.conf                ( if applicable )
```

from the primary system that are transferred to the initrd **/etc**etc directory at startup. With care, this file may be edited if necessary when your system 'really' crashes. **raidboot.cfg** contains the name of the boot partition in use and applicable backup(s) as well as the path to the rest of the raid start up file used by **linuxrc**. This file is normally created by the shutdown file and may be created manually if necessary.

> **raidboot.cfg** is of the form, 3 lines - no comments

```
/dev/bootdev1 /dev/bootdev2 [/dev/bootdev3 ... and so on]
raid-status/path
name_of_raidX.conf_file
```

> the **raid-status/path** does not include the name of the mountpoint the **raidX.conf** filename is that one found in /etc and normally used for **ckraid** and **mkraid**.

The following additional files reside on the permanent raid boot partitions. This is usually the same as above, but in emergency situations may be loaded from anywhere they are available, such as a floppy boot disk.

- **raidgood.ref** created by the command cat /proc/mdstat | grep md0 > /{raid_status_path}/raidgood.ref
  See the 4.12 (shutdown scripts) for saving this file and the next

- **raidstat.ro** created at each shutdown by the shutdown rc file, saving the exit status of the raid array.

"The Linux SCSI programming HOWTO"
Heiko Eißfeldt

heiko@colossus.escape.de
v1.5, 7 May 1996
This document deals with programming the Linux generic SCSI interface.

Contents

HOWTO

1   What's New?

Newer kernels have changed the interface a bit. This affects a section formerly entitled 'rescanning the devices'. Now it is possible to add/remove SCSI devices on the fly.

Since kernel 1.3.98 some important header files have been moved/split (sg.h and scsi.h).

Some stupid bugs have been replaced by newer ones.

Editor's note: the interfaces in this document remain the same in kernel version 2.2.5 released in February, 1999.

2   Introduction

This document is a guide to the installation and programming of the Linux generic SCSI interface.

It covers kernel prerequisites, device mappings, and basic interaction with devices. Some simple C programming examples are included. General knowledge of the SCSI command set is required; for more information on the SCSI standard and related information, see the appendix to this document.

Note the plain text version of this document lacks cross references (they show up as "").

3   What Is The Generic SCSI Interface?

The generic SCSI interface has been implemented to provide general SCSI access to (possibly exotic) pieces of SCSI hardware. It was developed by Lawrence Foard (entropy@world.std.com) and sponsored by Killy Corporation (see the comments in `scsi/sg.h`).

The interface makes special device handling possible from user level applications (i.e. outside the kernel). Thus, kernel driver development, which is more risky and difficult to debug, is not necessary.

However, if you don't program the driver properly it is possible to hang the SCSI bus, the driver, or the kernel. Therefore, it is important to properly program the generic driver and to first back up all files to avoid losing data. Another useful thing to do before running your programs is to issue a `sync` command to ensure that any buffers are flushed to disk, minimizing data loss if the system hangs.

Another advantage of the generic driver is that as long as the interface itself does not change, all applications are independent of new kernel development. In comparison, other low-level kernel drivers have to be synchronized with other internal kernel changes.

Typically, the generic driver is used to communicate with new SCSI hardware devices that require special user applications to be written to take advantage of their features (e.g. scanners, printers, CD-ROM jukeboxes). The generic interface allows these to be written quickly.

4   What Are The Requirements To Use It?

4.1   Kernel Configuration

You must have a supported SCSI controller, obviously. Furthermore, your kernel must have controller support as well as generic support compiled in. Configuring the Linux kernel (via `make config` under /usr/src/linux) typically looks like the following:

```
    ...
  *
  * SCSI support
  *
  SCSI support? (CONFIG_SCSI) [n] y
  *
  * SCSI support type (disk, tape, CDrom)
  *
    ...
  Scsi generic support (CONFIG_CHR_DEV_SG) [n] y
  *
  * SCSI low-level drivers
  *
    ...
```

If available, modules can of course be build instead.

4.2   Device Files

The generic SCSI driver uses its own device files, separate from those used by the other SCSI device drivers. They can be generated using the `MAKEDEV` script, typically found in the `/dev` directory. Running `MAKEDEV sg` produces these files:

```
        crw-------   1 root      system    21,    0 Aug 20 20:09 /dev/sga
        crw-------   1 root      system    21,    1 Aug 20 20:09 /dev/sgb
        crw-------   1 root      system    21,    2 Aug 20 20:09 /dev/sgc
        crw-------   1 root      system    21,    3 Aug 20 20:09 /dev/sgd
        crw-------   1 root      system    21,    4 Aug 20 20:09 /dev/sge
        crw-------   1 root      system    21,    5 Aug 20 20:09 /dev/sgf
```

```
crw-------   1 root     system    21,   6 Aug 20 20:09 /dev/sgg
crw-------   1 root     system    21,   7 Aug 20 20:09 /dev/sgh
                                    |     |
                         major,    minor device numbers
```

Note that these are character devices for raw access. On some systems these devices may be called
/dev/{sg0,sg1,...}, depending on your installation, so adjust the following examples accordingly.

4.3   Device Mapping

These device files are dynamically mapped to SCSI id/LUNs on your SCSI bus (LUN = logical unit). The mapping
allocates devices consecutively for each LUN of each device on each SCSI bus found at time of the SCSI scan, beginning
at the lower LUNs/ids/buses. It starts with the first SCSI controller and continues without interruption with all following
controllers. This is currently done in the initialisation of the SCSI driver.

For example, assuming you had three SCSI devices hooked up with ids 1, 3, and 5 on the first SCSI bus (each having one
LUN), then the following mapping would be in effect:

```
/dev/sga -> SCSI id 1
/dev/sgb -> SCSI id 3
/dev/sgc -> SCSI id 5
```

If you now add a new device with id 4, then the mapping (after the next rescan) will be:

```
/dev/sga -> SCSI id 1
/dev/sgb -> SCSI id 3
/dev/sgc -> SCSI id 4
/dev/sgd -> SCSI id 5
```

Notice the change for id 5 – the corresponding device is no longer mapped to /dev/sgc but is now under /dev/sgd.

Luckily newer kernels allow for changing this order.

4.3.1   Dynamically insert and remove SCSI devices

If a newer kernel and the /proc file system is running, a non-busy device can be removed and installed 'on the fly'.

To remove a SCSI device:

```
echo "scsi remove-single-device a b c d" > /proc/scsi/scsi
```

and similar, to add a SCSI device, do

```
echo "scsi add-single-device a b c d" > /proc/scsi/scsi
```

where

```
        a == hostadapter id (first one being 0)
        b == SCSI channel on hostadapter (first one being 0)
        c == ID
        d == LUN (first one being 0)
```

So in order to swap the /dev/sgc and /dev/sgd mappings from the previous example, we could do

```
echo "scsi remove-single-device 0 0 4 0" > /proc/scsi/scsi
echo "scsi remove-single-device 0 0 5 0" > /proc/scsi/scsi
echo "scsi add-single-device 0 0 5 0" > /proc/scsi/scsi
echo "scsi add-single-device 0 0 4 0" > /proc/scsi/scsi
```

since generic devices are mapped in the order of their insertion.

When adding more devices to the scsi bus keep in mind there are limited spare entries for new devices. The memory has been allocated at boot time and has room for 2 more devices.

5   Programmers Guide

The following sections are for programmers who want to use the generic SCSI interface in their own applications. An example will be given showing how to access a SCSI device with the INQUIRY and the TESTUNITREADY commands.

When using these code examples, note the following:

- the location of the header files sg.h and scsi.h has changed in kernel version 1.3.98. Now these files are located at /usr/src/linux/include/scsi, which is hopefully linked to /usr/include/scsi. Previously they were in /usr/src/linux/drivers/scsi. We assume a newer kernel in the following text.

- the generic SCSI interface was extended in kernel version 1.1.68; the examples require at least this version. But please avoid kernel version 1.1.77 up to 1.1.89 and 1.3.52 upto 1.3.56 since they had a broken generic scsi interface.

- the constant DEVICE in the header section describing the accessed device should be set according to your available devices (see section 8 ()).

6   Overview Of Device Programming

The header file include/scsi/sg.h contains a description of the interface (this is based on kernel version 1.3.98):

```
struct sg_header
  {
  int pack_len;
                   /* length of incoming packet (including header) */
  int reply_len;   /* maximum length of expected reply */
  int pack_id;     /* id number of packet */
  int result;      /* 0==ok, otherwise refer to errno codes */
  unsigned int twelve_byte:1;
                   /* Force 12 byte command length for group 6 & 7 commands   */
  unsigned int other_flags:31;              /* for future use */
  unsigned char sense_buffer[16]; /* used only by reads */
  /* command follows then data for command */
  };
```

This structure describes how a SCSI command is to be processed and has room to hold the results of the execution of the command. The individual structure components will be discussed later in section 8 ().

The general way of exchanging data with the generic driver is as follows: to send a command to an opened generic device, write() a block containing these three parts to it:

```
struct sg_header
SCSI command
data to be sent with the command
```

To obtain the result of a command, read() a block with this (similar) block structure:

```
struct sg_header
data coming from the device
```

This is a general overview of the process. The following sections describe each of the steps in more detail.

NOTE: Up to recent kernel versions, it is necessary to block the SIGINT signal between the `write()` and the corresponding `read()` call (i.e. via `sigprocmask()`). A return after the `write()` part without any `read()` to fetch the results will block on subsequent accesses. This signal blocking has not yet been included in the example code. So better do not issue SIGINT (a la ^C) when running these examples.

7 Opening The Device

A generic device has to be opened for read and write access:

$$\text{int fd = open (device\_name, O\_RDWR);}$$

(This is the case even for a read-only hardware device such as a cdrom drive.)

We have to perform a `write` to send the command and a `read` to get back any results. In the case of an error the return code is negative (see section 21 () for a complete list).

8 The Header Structure

The header structure `struct sg_header` serves as a controlling layer between the application and the kernel driver. We now discuss its components in detail.

int pack_len

defines the size of the block written to the driver. This is defined within the kernel for internal use.

int reply_len

defines the size of the block to be accepted at reply. This is defined from the application side.

int pack_id

This field helps to assign replies to requests. The application can supply a unique id for each request. Suppose you have written several commands (say 4) to one device. They may work in parallel, one being the fastest. When getting replies via 4 reads, the replies do not have to have the order of the requests. To identify the correct reply for a given request one can use the `pack_id` field. Typically its value is incremented after each request (and wraps eventually). The maximum amount of outstanding requests is limited by the kernel to SG_MAX_QUEUE (eg 4).

int result

the result code of a `read` or `write` call. This is (sometimes) defined from the generic driver (kernel) side. It is safe to set it to null before the `write` call. These codes are defined in `errno.h` (0 meaning no error).

unsigned int twelve_byte:1

This field is necessary only when using non-standard vendor specific commands (in the range 0xc0 - 0xff). When these commands have a command length of 12 bytes instead of 10, this field has to be set to one before the write call. Other command lengths are not supported. This is defined from the application side.

unsigned char sense_buffer[16]

This buffer is set after a command is completed (after a `read()` call) and contains the SCSI sense code. Some command results have to be read from here (e.g. for TESTUNITREADY). Usually it contains just zero bytes. The value in this field is set by the generic driver (kernel) side.

The following example function interfaces directly with the generic kernel driver. It defines the header structure, sends the command via `write`, gets the result via `read` and does some (limited) error checking. The sense buffer data is available in the output buffer (unless a NULL pointer has been given, in which case it's in the input buffer). We will use it in the examples which follow.

Note: Set the value of DEVICE to your device descriptor.

```
#define DEVICE "/dev/sgc"

/* Example program to demonstrate the generic SCSI interface */
#include <stdio.h>
#include <unistd.h>
#include <string.h>
#include <fcntl.h>
#include <errno.h>
#include <scsi/sg.h>


#define SCSI_OFF sizeof(struct sg_header)
static unsigned char cmd[SCSI_OFF + 18];        /* SCSI command buffer */
int fd;                                 /* SCSI device/file descriptor */

/* process a complete SCSI cmd. Use the generic SCSI interface. */
static int handle_SCSI_cmd(unsigned cmd_len,          /* command length */
                           unsigned in_size,          /* input data size */
                           unsigned char *i_buff,     /* input buffer */
                           unsigned out_size,         /* output data size */
                           unsigned char *o_buff      /* output buffer */
                           )
{
    int status = 0;
    struct sg_header *sg_hd;

    /* safety checks */
    if (!cmd_len) return -1;            /* need a cmd_len != 0 */
    if (!i_buff) return -1;             /* need an input buffer != NULL */
#ifdef SG_BIG_BUFF
    if (SCSI_OFF + cmd_len + in_size > SG_BIG_BUFF) return -1;
    if (SCSI_OFF + out_size > SG_BIG_BUFF) return -1;
#else
    if (SCSI_OFF + cmd_len + in_size > 4096) return -1;
    if (SCSI_OFF + out_size > 4096) return -1;
#endif

    if (!o_buff) out_size = 0;       /* no output buffer, no output size */

    /* generic SCSI device header construction */
    sg_hd = (struct sg_header *) i_buff;
    sg_hd->reply_len   = SCSI_OFF + out_size;
    sg_hd->twelve_byte = cmd_len == 12;
    sg_hd->result = 0;
#if      0
    sg_hd->pack_len    = SCSI_OFF + cmd_len + in_size; /* not necessary */
    sg_hd->pack_id;         /* not used */
    sg_hd->other_flags; /* not used */
#endif
```

```
                /* send command */
                status = write( fd, i_buff, SCSI_OFF + cmd_len + in_size );
                if ( status < 0 || status != SCSI_OFF + cmd_len + in_size ||
                                sg_hd->result ) {
                    /* some error happened */
                    fprintf( stderr, "write(generic) result = 0x%x cmd = 0x%x\n",
                            sg_hd->result, i_buff[SCSI_OFF] );
                    perror("");
                    return status;
                }

                if (!o_buff) o_buff = i_buff;        /* buffer pointer check */

                /* retrieve result */
                status = read( fd, o_buff, SCSI_OFF + out_size);
                if ( status < 0 || status != SCSI_OFF + out_size || sg_hd->result ) {
                    /* some error happened */
                    fprintf( stderr, "read(generic) status = 0x%x, result = 0x%x, "
                                "cmd = 0x%x\n",
                                status, sg_hd->result, o_buff[SCSI_OFF] );
                    fprintf( stderr, "read(generic) sense "
                        "%x %x %x %x %x %x %x %x %x %x %x %x %x %x %x %x\n",
                        sg_hd->sense_buffer[0],          sg_hd->sense_buffer[1],
                        sg_hd->sense_buffer[2],          sg_hd->sense_buffer[3],
                        sg_hd->sense_buffer[4],          sg_hd->sense_buffer[5],
                        sg_hd->sense_buffer[6],          sg_hd->sense_buffer[7],
                        sg_hd->sense_buffer[8],          sg_hd->sense_buffer[9],
                        sg_hd->sense_buffer[10],         sg_hd->sense_buffer[11],
                        sg_hd->sense_buffer[12],         sg_hd->sense_buffer[13],
                        sg_hd->sense_buffer[14],         sg_hd->sense_buffer[15]);
                    if (status < 0)
                        perror("");
                }
                /* Look if we got what we expected to get */
                if (status == SCSI_OFF + out_size) status = 0; /* got them all */

                return status;  /* 0 means no error */
        }
```

While this may look somewhat complex at first appearance, most of the code is for error checking and reporting (which is useful even after the code is working).

Handle_SCSI_cmd has a generalized form for all SCSI commands types, falling into each of these categories:

```
        Data Mode                  | Example Command
==================================================
neither input nor output data | test unit ready
 no input data, output data   | inquiry, read
 input data, no output data   | mode select, write
   input data, output data    | mode sense
```

9 Inquiry Command Example

One of the most basic SCSI commands is the INQUIRY command, used to identify the type and make of the device. Here is the definition from the SCSI-2 specification (for details refer to the SCSI-2 standard).

Table 44: INQUIRY Command

Bit Byte	7	6	5	4	3	2	1	0
0	Operation Code (12h)							
1	Logical Unit Number			Reserved				EVPD
2	Page Code							
3	Reserved							
4	Allocation Length							
5	Control							

The output data are as follows:

Table 45: Standard INQUIRY Data Format

Bit Byte	7	6	5	4	3	2	1	0
0	Peripheral Qualifier			Peripheral Device Type				
1	RMB	Device-Type Modifier						
2	ISO Version		ECMA Version			ANSI-Approved Version		
3	AENC	TrmIOP	Reserved		Response Data Format			
4	Additional Length (n-4)							
5	Reserved							
6	Reserved							
7	RelAdr	WBus32	WBus16	Sync	Linked	Reserved	CmdQue	SftRe
8 15	(MSB) Vendor Identification (LSB)							
16 31	(MSB) Product Identification (LSB)							
32 35	(MSB) Product Revision Level (LSB)							
36	Vendor Specific							

```
| 55 |                                                                    |
|-----+--------------------------------------------------------------------|
| 56 |                                                                    |
|- - -+---                    Reserved                              ---|
| 95 |                                                                    |
|=====+====================================================================|
|     |                  Vendor-Specific Parameters                        |
|=====+====================================================================|
| 96 |                                                                    |
|- - -+---                 Vendor Specific                         ---|
| n   |                                                                    |
+=====+====================================================================+
```

The next example uses the low-level function handle_SCSI_cmd to perform the Inquiry SCSI command.

We first append the command block to the generic header, then call handle_SCSI_cmd. Note that the output buffer size argument for the handle_SCSI_cmd call excludes the generic header size. After command completion the output buffer contains the requested data, unless an error occurred.

```c
#define INQUIRY_CMD       0x12
#define INQUIRY_CMDLEN    6
#define INQUIRY_REPLY_LEN 96
#define INQUIRY_VENDOR    8        /* Offset in reply data to vendor name */

/* request vendor brand and model */
static unsigned char *Inquiry ( void )
{
  unsigned char Inqbuffer[ SCSI_OFF + INQUIRY_REPLY_LEN ];
  unsigned char cmdblk [ INQUIRY_CMDLEN ] =
      { INQUIRY_CMD,  /* command */
                  0,  /* lun/reserved */
                  0,  /* page code */
                  0,  /* reserved */
    INQUIRY_REPLY_LEN,  /* allocation length */
                  0 };/* reserved/flag/link */

  memcpy( cmd + SCSI_OFF, cmdblk, sizeof(cmdblk) );

  /*
   * +------------------+
   * | struct sg_header | <- cmd
   * +------------------+
   * | copy of cmdblk   | <- cmd + SCSI_OFF
   * +------------------+
   */

  if (handle_SCSI_cmd(sizeof(cmdblk), 0, cmd,
                    sizeof(Inqbuffer) - SCSI_OFF, Inqbuffer )) {
      fprintf( stderr, "Inquiry failed\n" );
      exit(2);
  }
  return (Inqbuffer + SCSI_OFF);
}
```

The example above follows this structure. The Inquiry function copies its command block behind the generic header (given by SCSI_OFF). Input data is not present for this command. Handle_SCSI_cmd will define the header structure.

We can now implement the function `main` to complete this working example program.

```
void main( void )
{
  fd = open(DEVICE, O_RDWR);
  if (fd < 0) {
    fprintf( stderr, "Need read/write permissions for "DEVICE".\n" );
    exit(1);
  }

  /* print some fields of the Inquiry result */
  printf( "%s\n", Inquiry() + INQUIRY_VENDOR );
}
```

We first open the device, check for errors, and then call the higher level subroutine. Then we print the results in human readable format including the vendor, product, and revision.

Note: There is more information in the Inquiry result than this little program gives. You may want to extend the program to give device type, ANSI version etc. The device type is of special importance, since it determines the mandatory and optional command sets for this device. If you don't want to program it yourself, you may want to use the scsiinfo program from Eric Youngdale, which requests nearly all information about an SCSI device. Look at tsx-11.mit.edu in pub/Linux/ALPHA/scsi.

10   The Sense Buffer

Commands with no output data can give status information via the sense buffer (which is part of the header structure). Sense data is available when the previous command has terminated with a CHECK CONDITION status. In this case the kernel automatically retrieves the sense data via a REQUEST SENSE command. Its structure is:

```
+=====-========-========-========-========-========-========-========-========+
| Bit|   7    |   6    |   5    |   4    |   3    |   2    |   1    |   0    |
|Byte |        |        |        |        |        |        |        |        |
|=====+========+=========================================================|
| 0   | Valid  |              Error Code (70h or 71h)                      |
|-----+---------------------------------------------------------------------|
| 1   |                      Segment Number                                 |
|-----+---------------------------------------------------------------------|
| 2   |Filemark|  EOM   |  ILI   |Reserved|           Sense Key             |
|-----+---------------------------------------------------------------------|
| 3   | (MSB)                                                               |
|- - -+---                    Information                              ---|
| 6   |                                                            (LSB) |
|-----+---------------------------------------------------------------------|
| 7   |                 Additional Sense Length (n-7)                       |
|-----+---------------------------------------------------------------------|
| 8   | (MSB)                                                               |
|- - -+---              Command-Specific Information                  ---|
| 11  |                                                            (LSB) |
|-----+---------------------------------------------------------------------|
| 12  |                   Additional Sense Code                             |
|-----+---------------------------------------------------------------------|
| 13  |               Additional Sense Code Qualifier                       |
|-----+---------------------------------------------------------------------|
| 14  |                  Field Replaceable Unit Code                        |
```

```
|-----+---------------------------------------------------------------|
| 15  |  SKSV  |                                                        |
|- - -+------------               Sense-Key Specific            ---|
| 17  |                                                               |
|-----+---------------------------------------------------------------|
| 18  |                                                               |
|- - -+---                  Additional Sense Bytes               ---|
| n   |                                                               |
+===============================================================+
```

Note: The most useful fields are Sense Key (see section 21.3 ()), Additional Sense Code and Additional Sense Code Qualifier (see section 22 ()). The latter two are used combined as a pair.

11   Example Using Sense Buffer

Here we will use the TEST UNIT READY command to check whether media is loaded into our device. The header declarations and function `handle_SCSI_cmd` from the inquiry example will be needed as well.

Table 73: TEST UNIT READY Command

Bit Byte	7	6	5	4	3	2	1	0
0	Operation Code (00h)							
1	Logical Unit Number			Reserved				
2	Reserved							
3	Reserved							
4	Reserved							
5	Control							

Here is the function which implements it:

```
#define TESTUNITREADY_CMD 0
#define TESTUNITREADY_CMDLEN 6

#define ADD_SENSECODE 12
#define ADD_SC_QUALIFIER 13
#define NO_MEDIA_SC 0x3a
#define NO_MEDIA_SCQ 0x00

int TestForMedium ( void )
{
  /* request READY status */
  static unsigned char cmdblk [TESTUNITREADY_CMDLEN] = {
      TESTUNITREADY_CMD, /* command */
                  0, /* lun/reserved */
                  0, /* reserved */
                  0, /* reserved */
```

```
                                    0, /* reserved */
                                    0};/* control */

    memcpy( cmd + SCSI_OFF, cmdblk, sizeof(cmdblk) );

    /*
     * +------------------+
     * | struct sg_header | <- cmd
     * +------------------+
     * | copy of cmdblk   | <- cmd + SCSI_OFF
     * +------------------+
     */

    if (handle_SCSI_cmd(sizeof(cmdblk), 0, cmd,
                                0, NULL)) {
        fprintf (stderr, "Test unit ready failed\n");
        exit(2);
    }

    return
     *(((struct sg_header*)cmd)->sense_buffer +ADD_SENSECODE) !=
                                        NO_MEDIA_SC ||
     *(((struct sg_header*)cmd)->sense_buffer +ADD_SC_QUALIFIER) !=
                                        NO_MEDIA_SCQ;
}
```

Combined with this main function we can do the check.

```
void main( void )
{
    fd = open(DEVICE, O_RDWR);
    if (fd < 0) {
        fprintf( stderr, "Need read/write permissions for "DEVICE".\n" );
        exit(1);
    }

    /* look if medium is loaded */

    if (!TestForMedium()) {
        printf("device is unloaded\n");
    } else {
        printf("device is loaded\n");
    }
}
```

The file generic_demo.c from the appendix contains both examples.

12   Ioctl Functions

There are two ioctl functions available:

- ioctl(fd, SG_SET_TIMEOUT, &Timeout); sets the timeout value to Timeout * 10 milliseconds.
  Timeout has to be declared as int.

- `ioctl(fd, SG_GET_TIMEOUT, &Timeout);` gets the current timeout value. `Timeout` has to be declared as int.

13 Driver Defaults

13.1 Transfer Lengths

Currently (at least up to kernel version 1.1.68) input and output sizes have to be less than or equal than 4096 bytes unless the kernel has been compiled with `SG_BIG_BUFF` defined, if which case it is limited to `SG_BIG_BUFF` (e.g. 32768) bytes. These sizes include the generic header as well as the command block on input. `SG_BIG_BUFF` can be safely increased upto (131072 - 512). To take advantage of this, a new kernel has to be compiled and booted, of course.

13.2 Timeout And Retry Values

The default timeout value is set to one minute (`Timeout` = 6000). It can be changed through an ioctl call (see section 12 ()). The default number of retries is one.

14 Obtaining The Scsi Specifications

There are standards entitled SCSI-1 and SCSI-2 (and possibly soon SCSI-3). The standards are mostly upward compatible.

The SCSI-1 standard is (in the author's opinion) mostly obsolete, and SCSI-2 is the most widely used. SCSI-3 is very new and very expensive. These standardized command sets specify mandatory and optional commands for SCSI manufacturers and should be preferred over the vendor specific command extensions which are not standardized and for which programming information is seldom available. Of course sometimes there is no alternative to these extensions.

Electronic copies of the latest drafts are available via anonymous ftp from:

- ftp.cs.tulane.edu:pub/scsi
- ftp.symbios.com:/pub/standards
- ftp.cs.uni-sb.de:/pub/misc/doc/scsi

(I got my SCSI specification from the Yggdrasil Linux CD-ROM in the directory /usr/doc/scsi-2 and /usr/doc/scsi-1).

The SCSI FAQ also lists the following sources of printed information:

The SCSI specification: Available from:

```
        Global Engineering Documents
        15 Inverness Way East
        Englewood Co  80112-5704
        (800) 854-7179
          SCSI-1: X3.131-1986
          SCSI-2: X3.131-199x
          SCSI-3 X3T9.2/91-010R4 Working Draft

(Global Engineering Documentation in Irvine, CA (714)261-1455??)

SCSI-1: Doc \# X3.131-1986 from ANSI, 1430 Broadway, NY, NY 10018

IN-DEPTH EXPLORATION OF SCSI can be obtained from
Solution Technology, Attn: SCSI Publications, POB 104, Boulder Creek,
```

```
CA 95006, (408)338-4285, FAX (408)338-4374

THE SCSI ENCYCLOPEDIA and the SCSI BENCH REFERENCE can be obtained from
ENDL Publishing, 14426 Black Walnut Ct., Saratoga, CA 95090,
(408)867-6642, FAX (408)867-2115

SCSI: UNDERSTANDING THE SMALL COMPUTER SYSTEM INTERFACE was published
by Prentice-Hall, ISBN 0-13-796855-8
```

15 Related Information Sources

15.1 HOWTOs and FAQs

The Linux **SCSI-HOWTO** by Drew Eckhardt covers all supported SCSI controllers as well as device specific questions. A lot of troubleshooting hints are given. It is available from sunsite.unc.edu in /pub/Linux/docs/LDP and its mirror sites.

General questions about SCSI are answered in the **SCSI-FAQ** from the newsgroup Comp.Periphs.Scsi (available on tsx-11 in pub/linux/ALPHA/scsi and mirror sites).

15.2 Mailing list

There is a **mailing list** for bug reports and questions regarding SCSI development under Linux. To join, send email to majordomo@vger.rutgers.edu with the line subscribe linux-scsi in the body of the message. Messages should be posted to linux-scsi@vger.rutgers.edu. Help text can be requested by sending the message line "help" to majordomo@vger.rutgers.edu.

15.3 Example code

sunsite.unc.edu: apps/graphics/hpscanpbm-0.3a.tar.gz

This package handles a HP scanjet scanner through the generic interface.

tsx-11.mit.edu: BETA/cdrom/private/mkisofs/cdwrite-1.3.tar.gz

The cdwrite package uses the generic interface to write a cd image to a cd writer.

sunsite.unc.edu: apps/sound/cds/cdda2wav*.src.tar.gz

A shameless plug for my own application, which copies audio cd tracks into wav files.

16 Other useful stuff

Things that may come in handy. I don't have no idea if there are newer or better versions around. Feedback is welcome.

16.1 Device driver writer helpers

These documents can be found at the sunsite.unc.edu ftp server and its mirrors.

/pub/Linux/docs/kernel/kernel-hackers-guide

The LDP kernel hackers guide. May be a bit outdated, but covers the most fundamental things.

/pub/Linux/docs/kernel/drivers.doc.z

This document covers writing character drivers.

/pub/Linux/docs/kernel/tutorial.doc.z

Tutorial on writing a character device driver with code.

HOWTO

/pub/Linux/docs/kernel/scsi.paper.tar.gz

> A Latex document describing howto write a SCSI driver.

/pub/Linux/docs/hardware/DEVICES

> A list of device majors and minors used by Linux.

16.2   Utilities

tsx-11.mit.edu: ALPHA/scsi/scsiinfo*.tar.gz

> Program to query a scsi device for operating parameters, defect lists, etc. An X-based interface is available which requires you have Tk/Tcl/wish installed. With the X-based interface you can easily alter the settings on the drive.

tsx-11.mit.edu: ALPHA/kdebug

> A gdb extension for kernel debugging.

17   Other SCSI Access Interfaces

In Linux there is also another SCSI access method via SCSI_IOCTL_SEND_COMMAND ioctl calls, which is deprecated. Special tools like 'scsiinfo' utilize it.

There are some other similar interfaces in use in the un*x world, but not available for Linux:

1. CAM (Common Access Method) developed by Future Domain and other SCSI vendors. Linux has little support for a SCSI CAM system yet (mainly for booting from hard disk). CAM even supports target mode, so one could disguise ones computer as a peripheral hardware device (e.g. for a small SCSI net).

2. ASPI (Advanced SCSI Programming Interface) developed by Adaptec. This is the de facto standard for MS-DOS machines.

There are other application interfaces from SCO(TM), NeXT(TM), Silicon Graphics(TM) and SUN(TM) as well.

18   Final Comments

The generic SCSI interface bridges the gap between user applications and specific devices. But rather than bloating a lot of programs with similar sets of low-level functions, it would be more desirable to have a shared library with a generalized set of low-level functions for a particular purpose. The main goal should be to have independent layers of interfaces. A good design would separate an application into low-level and hardware independent routines. The low-level routines could be put into a shared library and made available for all applications. Here, standardized interfaces should be followed as much as possible before making new ones.

By now you should know more than I do about the Linux generic SCSI interface. So you can start developing powerful applications for the benefit of the global Linux community now...

19   Acknowledgments

Special thanks go to Jeff Tranter for proofreading and enhancing the text considerably as well as to Carlos Puchol for useful comments. Drew Eckhardt's and Eric Youngdale's help on my first (dumb) questions about the use of this interface has been appreciated.

20 Appendix

21 Error handling

The functions `open`, `ioctl`, `write` and `read` can report errors. In this case their return value is -1 and the global variable errno is set to the error number. The errno values are defined in `/usr/include/errno.h`. Possible values are:

```
Function | Error        | Description
=========|==============|===================================================
open     | ENXIO        | not a valid device
         | EACCES       | access mode is not read/write (O_RDWR)
         | EBUSY        | device was requested for nonblocking access,
         |              | but is busy now.
         | ERESTARTSYS  | this indicates an internal error. Try to
         |              | make it reproducible and inform the SCSI
         |              | channel (for details on bug reporting
         |              | see Drew Eckhardts SCSI-HOWTO).
ioctl    | ENXIO        | not a valid device
read     | EAGAIN       | the device would block. Try again later.
         | ERESTARTSYS  | this indicates an internal error. Try to
         |              | make it reproducible and inform the SCSI
         |              | channel (for details on bug reporting
         |              | see Drew Eckhardts SCSI-HOWTO).
write    | EIO          | the length is too small (smaller than the
         |              | generic header struct). Caution: Currently
         |              | there is no overlength checking.
         | EAGAIN       | the device would block. Try again later.
         | ENOMEM       | memory required for this request could not be
         |              | allocated. Try later again unless you
         |              | exceeded the maximum transfer size (see above)
select   |              | none
close    |              | none
```

For read/write positive return values indicate as usual the amount of bytes that have been successfully transferred. This should equal the amount you requested.

21.1 Error status decoding

Furthermore a detailed reporting is done via the kernels `hd_status` and the devices `sense_buffer` (see section 10 ()) both from the generic header structure.

The meaning of `hd_status` can be found in `drivers/scsi/scsi.h`: This `unsigned int` is composed out of different parts:

```
lsb    |     ...     |     ...     | msb
=======|=============|=============|============
status | sense key   | host code   | driver byte
```

These macros from `drivers/scsi/scsi.h` are available, but unfortunately cannot be easily used due to weird header file interdependencies. This has to be cleaned.

```
        Macro            | Description
=========================|=======================================================
```

```
status_byte(hd_status)  | The SCSI device status. See section Status codes
msg_byte(hd_status)     | From the device. See section SCSI sense keys
host_byte(hd_status)    | From the kernel. See section Hostcodes
driver_byte(hd_status)  | From the kernel. See section midlevel codes
```

21.2   Status codes

The following status codes from the SCSI device (defined in scsi/scsi.h) are available.

```
Value | Symbol
======|=====================
0x00  | GOOD
0x01  | CHECK_CONDITION
0x02  | CONDITION_GOOD
0x04  | BUSY
0x08  | INTERMEDIATE_GOOD
0x0a  | INTERMEDIATE_C_GOOD
0x0c  | RESERVATION_CONFLICT
```

Note that these symbol values have been **shifted right once**. When the status is CHECK_CONDITION, the sense data in the sense buffer is valid (check especially the additional sense code and additional sense code qualifier).

These values carry the meaning from the SCSI-2 specification:

Table 27: Status Byte Code

```
+==========================================================================+
|       Bits of Status Byte      | Status                                  |
| 7   6   5   4   3   2   1   0  |                                         |
|--------------------------------+-----------------------------------------|
| R   R   0   0   0   0   0   R  | GOOD                                    |
| R   R   0   0   0   0   1   R  | CHECK CONDITION                         |
| R   R   0   0   0   1   0   R  | CONDITION MET                           |
| R   R   0   0   1   0   0   R  | BUSY                                    |
| R   R   0   1   0   0   0   R  | INTERMEDIATE                            |
| R   R   0   1   0   1   0   R  | INTERMEDIATE-CONDITION MET              |
| R   R   0   1   1   0   0   R  | RESERVATION CONFLICT                    |
| R   R   1   0   0   0   1   R  | COMMAND TERMINATED                      |
| R   R   1   0   1   0   0   R  | QUEUE FULL                              |
|                                |                                         |
|       All Other Codes          | Reserved                                |
|--------------------------------------------------------------------------|
| Key: R = Reserved bit                                                    |
+==========================================================================+
```

```
A definition of the status byte codes is given below.

GOOD.  This status indicates that the target has successfully completed the
command.

CHECK CONDITION.  This status indicates that a contingent alle-
giance condition
has occurred (see 6.6).
```

CONDITION MET. This status or INTERMEDIATE-CONDITION MET is returned whenever
the requested operation is satisfied (see the SEARCH DATA and PRE-FETCH
commands).

BUSY. This status indicates that the target is busy. This status shall be
returned whenever a target is unable to accept a command from an otherwise
acceptable initiator (i.e., no reservation conflicts). The recommended
initiator recovery action is to issue the command again at a later time.

INTERMEDIATE. This status or INTERMEDIATE-CONDITION MET shall be returned for
every successfully completed command in a series of linked commands (except
the last command), unless the command is terminated with CHECK CONDITION,
RESERVATION CONFLICT, or COMMAND TERMINATED status. If INTERMEDIATE or
INTERMEDIATE-CONDITION MET status is not returned, the series of linked
commands is terminated and the I/O process is ended.

INTERMEDIATE-CONDITION MET. This status is the combination of the CONDITION
MET and INTERMEDIATE statuses.

RESERVATION CONFLICT. This status shall be returned whenever an initiator
attempts to access a logical unit or an extent within a logical unit that is
reserved with a conflicting reservation type for another SCSI device (see the
RESERVE and RESERVE UNIT commands). The recommended initiator recovery action
is to issue the command again at a later time.

COMMAND TERMINATED. This status shall be returned whenever the target
terminates the current I/O process after receiving a TERMINATE I/O PROCESS
message (see 5.6.22). This status also indicates that a contingen-
t allegiance
condition has occurred (see 6.6).

QUEUE FULL. This status shall be implemented if tagged queuing is
implemented. This status is returned when a SIMPLE QUEUE TAG, ORDERED QUEUE
TAG, or HEAD OF QUEUE TAG message is received and the command queue is full.
The I/O process is not placed in the command queue.

21.3   SCSI Sense Keys

These kernel symbols (from `scsi/scsi.h`) are predefined:

```
Value | Symbol
======|=================
0x00  | NO_SENSE
0x01  | RECOVERED_ERROR
0x02  | NOT_READY
0x03  | MEDIUM_ERROR
0x04  | HARDWARE_ERROR
0x05  | ILLEGAL_REQUEST
0x06  | UNIT_ATTENTION
0x07  | DATA_PROTECT
0x08  | BLANK_CHECK
```

HOWTO

```
0x0a  | COPY_ABORTED
0x0b  | ABORTED_COMMAND
0x0d  | VOLUME_OVERFLOW
0x0e  | MISCOMPARE
```

A verbatim list from the SCSI-2 doc follows (from section 7.2.14.3):

```
                Table 69: Sense Key (0h-7h) Descriptions
+========-===========================================================+
| Sense | Description                                                |
|  Key  |                                                            |
|-------+----------------------------------------------------------|
|   0h  | NO SENSE.  Indicates that there is no specific sense key   |
|       | information to be reported for the designated logical unit.|
|       | This would be the case for a successful command or a command|
|       | that received CHECK CONDITION or COMMAND TERMINATED status |
|       | because one of the filemark, EOM, or ILI bits is set to one.|
|-------+----------------------------------------------------------|
|   1h  | RECOVERED ERROR.  Indicates that the last command completed |
|       | successfully with some recovery action performed by the target.|
|       | Details may be determinable by examining the additional sense|
|       | bytes and the information field.  When multiple recovered errors|
|       | occur during one command, the choice of which error to report|
|       | (first, last, most severe, etc.) is device specific.      |
|-------+----------------------------------------------------------|
|   2h  | NOT READY.  Indicates that the logical unit addressed cannot be|
|       | accessed.  Operator intervention may be required to correct this|
|       | condition.                                                 |
|-------+----------------------------------------------------------|
|   3h  | MEDIUM ERROR.  Indicates that the command terminated with a non-|
|       | recovered error condition that was probably caused by a flaw in|
|       | the medium or an error in the recorded data.  This sense key may|
|       | also be returned if the target is unable to distinguish between a|
|       | flaw in the medium and a specific hardware failure (sense key 4h)|
|-------+----------------------------------------------------------|
|   4h  | HARDWARE ERROR.  Indicates that the target detected a non-|
|       | recoverable hardware failure (for example, controller failure,|
|       | device failure, parity error, etc.) while performing the command|
|       | or during a self test.                                     |
|-------+----------------------------------------------------------|
|   5h  | ILLEGAL REQUEST.  Indicates that there was an illegal parameter|
|       | in the command descriptor block or in the additional parameters|
|       | supplied as data for some commands (FORMAT UNIT, SEARCH DATA,|
|       | etc.).  If the target detects an invalid parameter in the command|
|       | descriptor block, then it shall terminate the command without|
|       | altering the medium.  If the target detects an invalid parameter|
|       | in the additional parameters supplied as data, then the target|
|       | may have already altered the medium.  This sense key may also|
|       | indicate that an invalid IDENTIFY message was received (5.6.7). |
|-------+----------------------------------------------------------|
|   6h  | UNIT ATTENTION.  Indicates that the removable medium may have|
|       | been changed or the target has been reset.  See 6.9 for more|
|       | detailed information about the unit attention condition.   |
|-------+----------------------------------------------------------|
|   7h  | DATA PROTECT.  Indicates that a command that reads or writes the|
```

```
|            |   medium was attempted on a block that is protected from this   |
|            |   operation.  The read or write operation is not performed.    |
+==============================================================================+
```

Table 70: Sense Key (8h-Fh) Descriptions

```
+==============================================================================+
| Sense |  Description                                                         |
| Key   |                                                                      |
|-------+----------------------------------------------------------------------|
|  8h   |  BLANK CHECK.  Indicates that a write-once device or a sequential-   |
|       |  access device encountered blank medium or format-defined end-of-   |
|       |  data indication while reading or a write-once device encountered    |
|       |  a non-blank medium while writing.                                   |
|-------+----------------------------------------------------------------------|
|  9h   |  Vendor Specific.  This sense key is available for reporting         |
|       |  vendor specific conditions.                                         |
|-------+----------------------------------------------------------------------|
|  Ah   |  COPY ABORTED.  Indicates a COPY, COMPARE, or COPY AND VERIFY        |
|       |  command was aborted due to an error condition on the source         |
|       |  device, the destination device, or both.  (See 7.2.3.2 for         |
|       |  additional information about this sense key.)                       |
|-------+----------------------------------------------------------------------|
|  Bh   |  ABORTED COMMAND.  Indicates that the target aborted the command.    |
|       |  The initiator may be able to recover by trying the command again.   |
|-------+----------------------------------------------------------------------|
|  Ch   |  EQUAL.  Indicates a SEARCH DATA command has satisfied an equal      |
|       |  comparison.                                                         |
|-------+----------------------------------------------------------------------|
|  Dh   |  VOLUME OVERFLOW.  Indicates that a buffered peripheral device has   |
|       |  reached the end-of-partition and data may remain in the buffer      |
|       |  that has not been written to the medium.  A RECOVER BUFFERED DATA   |
|       |  command(s) may be issued to read the unwritten data from the        |
|       |  buffer.                                                             |
|-------+----------------------------------------------------------------------|
|  Eh   |  MISCOMPARE.  Indicates that the source data did not match the       |
|       |  data read from the medium.                                          |
|-------+----------------------------------------------------------------------|
|  Fh   |  RESERVED.                                                           |
+==============================================================================+
```

21.4 Host codes

The following host codes are defined in `drivers/scsi/scsi.h`. They are set by the kernel driver.

```
Value | Symbol          | Description
======|=================|=======================================
0x00  | DID_OK          | No error
0x01  | DID_NO_CONNECT  | Couldn't connect before timeout period
0x02  | DID_BUS_BUSY    | BUS stayed busy through time out period
0x03  | DID_TIME_OUT    | TIMED OUT for other reason
0x04  | DID_BAD_TARGET  | BAD target
0x05  | DID_ABORT       | Told to abort for some other reason
0x06  | DID_PARITY      | Parity error
0x07  | DID_ERROR       | internal error
0x08  | DID_RESET       | Reset by somebody
```

HOWTO

```
0x09  | DID_BAD_INTR  | Got an interrupt we weren't expecting
```

21.5 Driver codes

The midlevel driver categorizes the returned status from the lowlevel driver based on the sense key from the device. It suggests some actions to be taken such as retry, abort or remap. The routine scsi_done from scsi.c does a very differentiated handling based on host_byte(), status_byte(), msg_byte() and the suggestion. It then sets the driver byte to show what it has done. The driver byte is composed out of two nibbles: the driver status and the suggestion. Each half is composed from the below values being 'or'ed together (found in scsi.h).

```
Value | Symbol          | Description of Driver status
======|===============|=====================================
0x00  | DRIVER_OK       | No error
0x01  | DRIVER_BUSY     | not used
0x02  | DRIVER_SOFT     | not used
0x03  | DRIVER_MEDIA    | not used
0x04  | DRIVER_ERROR    | internal driver error
0x05  | DRIVER_INVALID  | finished (DID_BAD_TARGET or DID_ABORT)
0x06  | DRIVER_TIMEOUT  | finished with timeout
0x07  | DRIVER_HARD     | finished with fatal error
0x08  | DRIVER_SENSE    | had sense information available


Value | Symbol          | Description of suggestion
======|===============|=====================================
0x10  | SUGGEST_RETRY   | retry the SCSI request
0x20  | SUGGEST_ABORT   | abort the request
0x30  | SUGGEST_REMAP   | remap the block (not yet implemented)
0x40  | SUGGEST_DIE     | let the kernel panic
0x80  | SUGGEST_SENSE   | get sense information from the device
0xff  | SUGGEST_IS_OK   | nothing to be done
```

22 Additional sense codes and additional sense code qualifiers

When the status of the executed SCSI command is CHECK_CONDITION, sense data is available in the sense buffer. The additional sense code and additional sense code qualifier are contained in that buffer.

From the SCSI-2 specification I include two tables. The first is in lexical, the second in numerical order.

22.1 ASC and ASCQ in lexical order

The following table list gives a list of descriptions and device types they apply to.

```
+==============================================================================+
|              D - DIRECT ACCESS DEVICE                                        |
|             .T - SEQUENTIAL ACCESS DEVICE                                    |
|             . L - PRINTER DEVICE                                            |
|             .  P - PROCESSOR DEVICE                                          |
|             .  .W - WRITE ONCE READ MULTIPLE DEVICE                          |
|             .  . R - READ ONLY (CD-ROM) DEVICE                               |
|             .  .  S - SCANNER DEVICE                                         |
|             .  .  .O - OPTICAL MEMORY DEVICE                                 |
|             .  .  . M - MEDIA CHANGER DEVICE                                 |
|             .  .  .  C - COMMUNICATION DEVICE                                |
|             .  .  .  .                                                       |
```

ASC	ASCQ	DTLPWRSOMC	DESCRIPTION
13h	00h	D W O	ADDRESS MARK NOT FOUND FOR DATA FIELD
12h	00h	D W O	ADDRESS MARK NOT FOUND FOR ID FIELD
00h	11h	R	AUDIO PLAY OPERATION IN PROGRESS
00h	12h	R	AUDIO PLAY OPERATION PAUSED
00h	14h	R	AUDIO PLAY OPERATION STOPPED DUE TO ERROR
00h	13h	R	AUDIO PLAY OPERATION SUCCESSFULLY COMPLETED
00h	04h	T S	BEGINNING-OF-PARTITION/MEDIUM DETECTED
14h	04h	T	BLOCK SEQUENCE ERROR
30h	02h	DT WR O	CANNOT READ MEDIUM - INCOMPATIBLE FORMAT
30h	01h	DT WR O	CANNOT READ MEDIUM - UNKNOWN FORMAT
52h	00h	T	CARTRIDGE FAULT
3Fh	02h	DTLPWRSOMC	CHANGED OPERATING DEFINITION
11h	06h	WR O	CIRC UNRECOVERED ERROR
30h	03h	DT	CLEANING CARTRIDGE INSTALLED
4Ah	00h	DTLPWRSOMC	COMMAND PHASE ERROR
2Ch	00h	DTLPWRSOMC	COMMAND SEQUENCE ERROR
2Fh	00h	DTLPWRSOMC	COMMANDS CLEARED BY ANOTHER INITIATOR
2Bh	00h	DTLPWRSO C	COPY CANNOT EXECUTE SINCE HOST CANNOT DISCONNECT
41h	00h	D	DATA PATH FAILURE (SHOULD USE 40 NN)
4Bh	00h	DTLPWRSOMC	DATA PHASE ERROR
11h	07h	W O	DATA RESYNCHRONIZATION ERROR
16h	00h	D W O	DATA SYNCHRONIZATION MARK ERROR
19h	00h	D O	DEFECT LIST ERROR
19h	03h	D O	DEFECT LIST ERROR IN GROWN LIST
19h	02h	D O	DEFECT LIST ERROR IN PRIMARY LIST
19h	01h	D O	DEFECT LIST NOT AVAILABLE
1Ch	00h	D O	DEFECT LIST NOT FOUND
32h	01h	D W O	DEFECT LIST UPDATE FAILURE
40h	NNh	DTLPWRSOMC	DIAGNOSTIC FAILURE ON COMPONENT NN (80H-FFH)
63h	00h	R	END OF USER AREA ENCOUNTERED ON THIS TRACK
00h	05h	T S	END-OF-DATA DETECTED
14h	03h	T	END-OF-DATA NOT FOUND
00h	02h	T S	END-OF-PARTITION/MEDIUM DETECTED
51h	00h	T O	ERASE FAILURE
0Ah	00h	DTLPWRSOMC	ERROR LOG OVERFLOW
11h	02h	DT W SO	ERROR TOO LONG TO CORRECT
03h	02h	T	EXCESSIVE WRITE ERRORS
3Bh	07h	L	FAILED TO SENSE BOTTOM-OF-FORM
3Bh	06h	L	FAILED TO SENSE TOP-OF-FORM
00h	01h	T	FILEMARK DETECTED
14h	02h	T	FILEMARK OR SETMARK NOT FOUND
09h	02h	WR O	FOCUS SERVO FAILURE
31h	01h	D L O	FORMAT COMMAND FAILED
58h	00h	O	GENERATION DOES NOT EXIST

Table 71: (continued)

ASC	ASCQ	DTLPWRSOMC	DESCRIPTION
1Ch	02h	D O	GROWN DEFECT LIST NOT FOUND
00h	06h	DTLPWRSOMC	I/O PROCESS TERMINATED
10h	00h	D W O	ID CRC OR ECC ERROR

```
| 22h  00h  D          ILLEGAL FUNCTION(SHOULD USE 20 00, 24 00, OR 26 00)|
| 64h  00h       R     ILLEGAL MODE FOR THIS TRACK                        |
| 28h  01h         M   IMPORT OR EXPORT ELEMENT ACCESSED                  |
| 30h  00h  DT WR OM   INCOMPATIBLE MEDIUM INSTALLED                      |
| 11h  08h  T          INCOMPLETE BLOCK READ                              |
| 48h  00h  DTLPWRSOMC INITIATOR DETECTED ERROR MESSAGE RECEIVED          |
| 3Fh  03h  DTLPWRSOMC INQUIRY DATA HAS CHANGED                          |
| 44h  00h  DTLPWRSOMC INTERNAL TARGET FAILURE                           |
| 3Dh  00h  DTLPWRSOMC INVALID BITS IN IDENTIFY MESSAGE                  |
| 2Ch  02h        S    INVALID COMBINATION OF WINDOWS SPECIFIED          |
| 20h  00h  DTLPWRSOMC INVALID COMMAND OPERATION CODE                    |
| 21h  01h         M   INVALID ELEMENT ADDRESS                           |
| 24h  00h  DTLPWRSOMC INVALID FIELD IN CDB                              |
| 26h  00h  DTLPWRSOMC INVALID FIELD IN PARAMETER LIST                   |
| 49h  00h  DTLPWRSOMC INVALID MESSAGE ERROR                             |
| 11h  05h      WR O   L-EC UNCORRECTABLE ERROR                          |
| 60h  00h        S    LAMP FAILURE                                      |
| 5Bh  02h  DTLPWRSOM  LOG COUNTER AT MAXIMUM                            |
| 5Bh  00h  DTLPWRSOM  LOG EXCEPTION                                     |
| 5Bh  03h  DTLPWRSOM  LOG LIST CODES EXHAUSTED                         |
| 2Ah  02h  DTL WRSOMC LOG PARAMETERS CHANGED                           |
| 21h  00h  DT WR OM   LOGICAL BLOCK ADDRESS OUT OF RANGE                |
| 08h  00h  DTL WRSOMC LOGICAL UNIT COMMUNICATION FAILURE                |
| 08h  02h  DTL WRSOMC LOGICAL UNIT COMMUNICATION PARITY ERROR           |
| 08h  01h  DTL WRSOMC LOGICAL UNIT COMMUNICATION TIME-OUT               |
| 4Ch  00h  DTLPWRSOMC LOGICAL UNIT FAILED SELF-CONFIGURATION            |
| 3Eh  00h  DTLPWRSOMC LOGICAL UNIT HAS NOT SELF-CONFIGURED YET          |
| 04h  01h  DTLPWRSOMC LOGICAL UNIT IS IN PROCESS OF BECOMING READY      |
| 04h  00h  DTLPWRSOMC LOGICAL UNIT NOT READY, CAUSE NOT REPORTABLE      |
| 04h  04h  DTL    O   LOGICAL UNIT NOT READY, FORMAT IN PROGRESS        |
| 04h  02h  DTLPWRSOMC LOGICAL UNIT NOT READY, INIT COMMAND REQUIRED     |
| 04h  03h  DTLPWRSOMC LOGICAL UNIT NOT READY, MANUAL FIX REQUIRED       |
| 25h  00h  DTLPWRSOMC LOGICAL UNIT NOT SUPPORTED                        |
| 15h  01h  DTL WRSOM  MECHANICAL POSITIONING ERROR                      |
| 53h  00h  DTL WRSOM  MEDIA LOAD OR EJECT FAILED                        |
| 3Bh  0Dh         M   MEDIUM DESTINATION ELEMENT FULL                   |
| 31h  00h  DT W  O    MEDIUM FORMAT CORRUPTED                           |
| 3Ah  00h  DTL WRSOM  MEDIUM NOT PRESENT                                |
| 53h  02h  DT WR OM   MEDIUM REMOVAL PREVENTED                          |
| 3Bh  0Eh         M   MEDIUM SOURCE ELEMENT EMPTY                       |
| 43h  00h  DTLPWRSOMC MESSAGE ERROR                                     |
| 3Fh  01h  DTLPWRSOMC MICROCODE HAS BEEN CHANGED                       |
| 1Dh  00h  D  W  O    MISCOMPARE DURING VERIFY OPERATION                |
| 11h  0Ah  DT    O    MISCORRECTED ERROR                                |
| 2Ah  01h  DTL WRSOMC MODE PARAMETERS CHANGED                          |
| 07h  00h  DTL WRSOM  MULTIPLE PERIPHERAL DEVICES SELECTED              |
| 11h  03h  DT W SO    MULTIPLE READ ERRORS                              |
| 00h  00h  DTLPWRSOMC NO ADDITIONAL SENSE INFORMATION                   |
| 00h  15h       R     NO CURRENT AUDIO STATUS TO RETURN                 |
| 32h  00h  D  W  O    NO DEFECT SPARE LOCATION AVAILABLE                |
| 11h  09h  T          NO GAP FOUND                                      |
| 01h  00h  D  W  O    NO INDEX/SECTOR SIGNAL                            |
| 06h  00h  D  WR OM   NO REFERENCE POSITION FOUND                       |
+=======================================================================+
```

```
Table 71: (continued)
+==============================================================================+
| ASC  ASCQ  DTLPWRSOMC  DESCRIPTION                                           |
| ---  ----              ------------------------------------------------      |
| 02h  00h   D  WR OM    NO SEEK COMPLETE                                      |
| 03h  01h   T           NO WRITE CURRENT                                      |
| 28h  00h   DTLPWRSOMC  NOT READY TO READY TRANSITION, MEDIUM CHANGED         |
| 5Ah  01h   DT WR OM    OPERATOR MEDIUM REMOVAL REQUEST                       |
| 5Ah  00h   DTLPWRSOM   OPERATOR REQUEST OR STATE CHANGE INPUT                |
| 5Ah  03h   DT W  O     OPERATOR SELECTED WRITE PERMIT                        |
| 5Ah  02h   DT W  O     OPERATOR SELECTED WRITE PROTECT                       |
| 61h  02h        S      OUT OF FOCUS                                          |
| 4Eh  00h   DTLPWRSOMC  OVERLAPPED COMMANDS ATTEMPTED                         |
| 2Dh  00h   T           OVERWRITE ERROR ON UPDATE IN PLACE                    |
| 3Bh  05h   L           PAPER JAM                                             |
| 1Ah  00h   DTLPWRSOMC  PARAMETER LIST LENGTH ERROR                           |
| 26h  01h   DTLPWRSOMC  PARAMETER NOT SUPPORTED                               |
| 26h  02h   DTLPWRSOMC  PARAMETER VALUE INVALID                               |
| 2Ah  00h   DTL WRSOMC  PARAMETERS CHANGED                                    |
| 03h  00h   DTL W SO    PERIPHERAL DEVICE WRITE FAULT                         |
| 50h  02h   T           POSITION ERROR RELATED TO TIMING                      |
| 3Bh  0Ch        S      POSITION PAST BEGINNING OF MEDIUM                     |
| 3Bh  0Bh        S      POSITION PAST END OF MEDIUM                           |
| 15h  02h   DT WR O     POSITIONING ERROR DETECTED BY READ OF MEDIUM          |
| 29h  00h   DTLPWRSOMC  POWER ON, RESET, OR BUS DEVICE RESET OCCURRED         |
| 42h  00h   D           POWER-ON OR SELF-TEST FAILURE (SHOULD USE 40 NN)      |
| 1Ch  01h   D        O  PRIMARY DEFECT LIST NOT FOUND                         |
| 40h  00h   D           RAM FAILURE (SHOULD USE 40 NN)                        |
| 15h  00h   DTL WRSOM   RANDOM POSITIONING ERROR                              |
| 3Bh  0Ah        S      READ PAST BEGINNING OF MEDIUM                         |
| 3Bh  09h        S      READ PAST END OF MEDIUM                               |
| 11h  01h   DT W  SO    READ RETRIES EXHAUSTED                                |
| 14h  01h   DT WR O     RECORD NOT FOUND                                      |
| 14h  00h   DTL WRSO    RECORDED ENTITY NOT FOUND                             |
| 18h  02h   D  WR O     RECOVERED DATA - DATA AUTO-REALLOCATED                |
| 18h  05h   D  WR O     RECOVERED DATA - RECOMMEND REASSIGNMENT               |
| 18h  06h   D  WR O     RECOVERED DATA - RECOMMEND REWRITE                    |
| 17h  05h   D  WR O     RECOVERED DATA USING PREVIOUS SECTOR ID               |
| 18h  03h        R      RECOVERED DATA WITH CIRC                              |
| 18h  01h   D  WR O     RECOVERED DATA WITH ERROR CORRECTION AND RETRIES      |
| 18h  00h   DT WR O     RECOVERED DATA WITH ERROR CORRECTION APPLIED          |
| 18h  04h        R      RECOVERED DATA WITH L-EC                              |
| 17h  03h   DT WR O     RECOVERED DATA WITH NEGATIVE HEAD OFFSET              |
| 17h  00h   DT WRSO     RECOVERED DATA WITH NO ERROR CORRECTION APPLIED       |
| 17h  02h   DT WR O     RECOVERED DATA WITH POSITIVE HEAD OFFSET              |
| 17h  01h   DT WRSO     RECOVERED DATA WITH RETRIES                           |
| 17h  04h      WR O     RECOVERED DATA WITH RETRIES AND/OR CIRC APPLIED       |
| 17h  06h   D  W  O     RECOVERED DATA WITHOUT ECC - DATA AUTO-REALLOCATED    |
| 17h  07h   D  W  O     RECOVERED DATA WITHOUT ECC - RECOMMEND REASSIGNMENT   |
| 17h  08h   D  W  O     RECOVERED DATA WITHOUT ECC - RECOMMEND REWRITE        |
| 1Eh  00h   D  W  O     RECOVERED ID WITH ECC CORRECTION                      |
| 3Bh  08h   T           REPOSITION ERROR                                      |
| 36h  00h   L           RIBBON, INK, OR TONER FAILURE                         |
| 37h  00h   DTL WRSOMC  ROUNDED PARAMETER                                     |
| 5Ch  00h   D        O  RPL STATUS CHANGE                                     |
```

HOWTO

```
| 39h  00h  DTL WRSOMC  SAVING PARAMETERS NOT SUPPORTED                        |
| 62h  00h        S     SCAN HEAD POSITIONING ERROR                            |
| 47h  00h  DTLPWRSOMC  SCSI PARITY ERROR                                      |
| 54h  00h        P     SCSI TO HOST SYSTEM INTERFACE FAILURE                  |
| 45h  00h  DTLPWRSOMC  SELECT OR RESELECT FAILURE                             |
+==============================================================================+
```

Table 71: (concluded)

```
+==============================================================================+
| ASC ASCQ  DTLPWRSOMC  DESCRIPTION                                            |
| --- ----  ----------  -----------------------------------------------------  |
| 3Bh  00h  TL          SEQUENTIAL POSITIONING ERROR                          |
| 00h  03h  T           SETMARK DETECTED                                       |
| 3Bh  04h   L          SLEW FAILURE                                           |
| 09h  03h      WR O    SPINDLE SERVO FAILURE                                  |
| 5Ch  02h  D       O   SPINDLES NOT SYNCHRONIZED                              |
| 5Ch  01h  D       O   SPINDLES SYNCHRONIZED                                  |
| 1Bh  00h  DTLPWRSOMC  SYNCHRONOUS DATA TRANSFER ERROR                        |
| 55h  00h        P     SYSTEM RESOURCE FAILURE                                |
| 33h  00h  T           TAPE LENGTH ERROR                                      |
| 3Bh  03h    L         TAPE OR ELECTRONIC VERTICAL FORMS UNIT NOT READY       |
| 3Bh  01h  T           TAPE POSITION ERROR AT BEGINNING-OF-MEDIUM             |
| 3Bh  02h  T           TAPE POSITION ERROR AT END-OF-MEDIUM                   |
| 3Fh  00h  DTLPWRSOMC  TARGET OPERATING CONDITIONS HAVE CHANGED               |
| 5Bh  01h  DTLPWRSOM   THRESHOLD CONDITION MET                                |
| 26h  03h  DTLPWRSOMC  THRESHOLD PARAMETERS NOT SUPPORTED                     |
| 2Ch  01h        S     TOO MANY WINDOWS SPECIFIED                             |
| 09h  00h  DT  WR O    TRACK FOLLOWING ERROR                                  |
| 09h  01h      WR O    TRACKING SERVO FAILURE                                 |
| 61h  01h        S     UNABLE TO ACQUIRE VIDEO                                |
| 57h  00h          R   UNABLE TO RECOVER TABLE-OF-CONTENTS                    |
| 53h  01h  T           UNLOAD TAPE FAILURE                                    |
| 11h  00h  DT  WRSO    UNRECOVERED READ ERROR                                 |
| 11h  04h  D   W   O   UNRECOVERED READ ERROR - AUTO REALLOCATE FAILED        |
| 11h  0Bh  D   W   O   UNRECOVERED READ ERROR - RECOMMEND REASSIGNMENT        |
| 11h  0Ch  D   W   O   UNRECOVERED READ ERROR - RECOMMEND REWRITE THE DATA|
| 46h  00h  DTLPWRSOMC  UNSUCCESSFUL SOFT RESET                                |
| 59h  00h          O   UPDATED BLOCK READ                                     |
| 61h  00h        S     VIDEO ACQUISITION ERROR                                |
| 50h  00h  T           WRITE APPEND ERROR                                     |
| 50h  01h  T           WRITE APPEND POSITION ERROR                            |
| 0Ch  00h  T     S     WRITE ERROR                                            |
| 0Ch  02h  D   W   O   WRITE ERROR - AUTO REALLOCATION FAILED                 |
| 0Ch  01h  D   W   O   WRITE ERROR RECOVERED WITH AUTO REALLOCATION           |
| 27h  00h  DT  W   O   WRITE PROTECTED                                        |
|                                                                              |
| 80h  XXh     \                                                               |
| THROUGH       >       VENDOR SPECIFIC.                                       |
| FFh  XX      /                                                               |
|                                                                              |
| XXh  80h     \                                                               |
| THROUGH       >       VENDOR SPECIFIC QUALIFICATION OF STANDARD ASC.         |
| XXh  FFh     /                                                               |
|                       ALL CODES NOT SHOWN ARE RESERVED.                      |
|------------------------------------------------------------------------------|
```

22.2 ASC and ASCQ in numerical order

Table 364: ASC and ASCQ Assignments

```
+==============================================================================+
|             D - DIRECT ACCESS DEVICE                                         |
|            .T - SEQUENTIAL ACCESS DEVICE                                     |
|            . L - PRINTER DEVICE                                              |
|            .  P - PROCESSOR DEVICE                                           |
|            .  .W - WRITE ONCE READ MULTIPLE DEVICE                           |
|            .  . R - READ ONLY (CD-ROM) DEVICE                                |
|            .  .  S - SCANNER DEVICE                                          |
|            .  .  .O - OPTICAL MEMORY DEVICE                                  |
|            .  .  . M - MEDIA CHANGER DEVICE                                  |
|            .  .  .  C - COMMUNICATION DEVICE                                 |
|            .  .  .  .                                                        |
| ASC ASCQ  DTLPWRSOMC  DESCRIPTION                                            |
| --- ----  ----------  ------------------------------------------------- |
|  00  00   DTLPWRSOMC  NO ADDITIONAL SENSE INFORMATION                       |
|  00  01   T           FILEMARK DETECTED                                     |
|  00  02   T      S    END-OF-PARTITION/MEDIUM DETECTED                      |
|  00  03   T           SETMARK DETECTED                                      |
|  00  04   T      S    BEGINNING-OF-PARTITION/MEDIUM DETECTED               |
|  00  05   T      S    END-OF-DATA DETECTED                                  |
|  00  06   DTLPWRSOMC  I/O PROCESS TERMINATED                                |
|  00  11        R      AUDIO PLAY OPERATION IN PROGRESS                      |
|  00  12        R      AUDIO PLAY OPERATION PAUSED                           |
|  00  13        R      AUDIO PLAY OPERATION SUCCESSFULLY COMPLETED          |
|  00  14        R      AUDIO PLAY OPERATION STOPPED DUE TO ERROR            |
|  00  15        R      NO CURRENT AUDIO STATUS TO RETURN                     |
|  01  00   DW     O    NO INDEX/SECTOR SIGNAL                                |
|  02  00   DWR   OM    NO SEEK COMPLETE                                      |
|  03  00   DTL W  SO   PERIPHERAL DEVICE WRITE FAULT                         |
|  03  01    T          NO WRITE CURRENT                                      |
|  03  02    T          EXCESSIVE WRITE ERRORS                                |
|  04  00   DTLPWRSOMC  LOGICAL UNIT NOT READY, CAUSE NOT REPORTABLE         |
|  04  01   DTLPWRSOMC  LOGICAL UNIT IS IN PROCESS OF BECOMING READY         |
|  04  02   DTLPWRSOMC  LOGICAL UNIT NOT READY, INIT COMMAND REQUIRED        |
|  04  03   DTLPWRSOMC  LOGICAL UNIT NOT READY, MANUAL FIX REQUIRED          |
|  04  04   DTL    O    LOGICAL UNIT NOT READY, FORMAT IN PROGRESS           |
|  05  00   DTL WRSOMC  LOGICAL UNIT DOES NOT RESPOND TO SELECTION           |
|  06  00   DWR  OM NO  REFERENCE POSITION FOUND                             |
|  07  00   DTL WRSOM   MULTIPLE PERIPHERAL DEVICES SELECTED                 |
|  08  00   DTL WRSOMC  LOGICAL UNIT COMMUNICATION FAILURE                   |
|  08  01   DTL WRSOMC  LOGICAL UNIT COMMUNICATION TIME-OUT                  |
|  08  02   DTL WRSOMC  LOGICAL UNIT COMMUNICATION PARITY ERROR              |
|  09  00   DT  WR O    TRACK FOLLOWING ERROR                                |
|  09  01       WR O    TRA CKING SERVO FAILURE                              |
|  09  02       WR O    FOC US SERVO FAILURE                                 |
|  09  03       WR O    SPI NDLE SERVO FAILURE                               |
+==============================================================================+
```

Table 364: (continued)

```
+==============================================================================+
|             D - DIRECT ACCESS DEVICE                                         |
```

HOWTO

```
|          .T - SEQUENTIAL ACCESS DEVICE                                       |
|          . L - PRINTER DEVICE                                                |
|          . P - PROCESSOR DEVICE                                             |
|          . .W - WRITE ONCE READ MULTIPLE DEVICE                            |
|          . . R - READ ONLY (CD-ROM) DEVICE                                 |
|          . . S - SCANNER DEVICE                                            |
|          . . .O - OPTICAL MEMORY DEVICE                                    |
|          . . . M - MEDIA CHANGER DEVICE                                    |
|          . . . . C - COMMUNICATION DEVICE                                  |
|          . . . .                                                           |
| ASC ASCQ  DTLPWRSOMC  DESCRIPTION                                          |
| --- ----  ----------  ------------------------------------------------- |
|  0A  00   DTLPWRSOMC  ERROR LOG OVERFLOW                                  |
|  0B  00                                                                    |
|  0C  00    T     S    WRITE ERROR                                         |
|  0C  01    D    W O   WRITE ERROR RECOVERED WITH AUTO REALLOCATION        |
|  0C  02    D    W O   WRITE ERROR - AUTO REALLOCATION FAILED              |
|  0D  00                                                                    |
|  0E  00                                                                    |
|  0F  00                                                                    |
|  10  00    D    W O   ID CRC OR ECC ERROR                                 |
|  11  00    DT   WRSO  UNRECOVERED READ ERROR                              |
|  11  01    DT   W SO  READ RETRIES EXHAUSTED                              |
|  11  02    DT   W SO  ERROR TOO LONG TO CORRECT                           |
|  11  03    DT   W SO  MULTIPLE READ ERRORS                                |
|  11  04    D    W O   UNRECOVERED READ ERROR - AUTO REALLOCATE FAILED     |
|  11  05         WR O  L-EC UNCORRECTABLE ERROR                            |
|  11  06         WR O  CIRC UNRECOVERED ERROR                              |
|  11  07          W O  DATA RESYNCHRONIZATION ERROR                        |
|  11  08    T          INCOMPLETE BLOCK READ                               |
|  11  09    T          NO GAP FOUND                                        |
|  11  0A    DT     O   MISCORRECTED ERROR                                  |
|  11  0B    D    W O   UNRECOVERED READ ERROR - RECOMMEND REASSIGNMENT     |
|  11  0C    D    W O   UNRECOVERED READ ERROR - RECOMMEND REWRITE THE DATA |
|  12  00    D    W O   ADDRESS MARK NOT FOUND FOR ID FIELD                 |
|  13  00    D    W O   ADDRESS MARK NOT FOUND FOR DATA FIELD               |
|  14  00    DTL  WRSO  RECORDED ENTITY NOT FOUND                           |
|  14  01    DT   WR O  RECORD NOT FOUND                                    |
|  14  02    T          FILEMARK OR SETMARK NOT FOUND                       |
|  14  03    T          END-OF-DATA NOT FOUND                               |
|  14  04    T          BLOCK SEQUENCE ERROR                                |
|  15  00    DTL  WRSOM RANDOM POSITIONING ERROR                            |
|  15  01    DTL  WRSOM MECHANICAL POSITIONING ERROR                        |
|  15  02    DT   WR O  POSITIONING ERROR DETECTED BY READ OF MEDIUM        |
|  16  00    DW     O   DATA SYNCHRONIZATION MARK ERROR                     |
|  17  00    DT   WRSO  RECOVERED DATA WITH NO ERROR CORRECTION APPLIED     |
|  17  01    DT   WRSO  RECOVERED DATA WITH RETRIES                         |
|  17  02    DT   WR O  RECOVERED DATA WITH POSITIVE HEAD OFFSET            |
|  17  03    DT   WR O  RECOVERED DATA WITH NEGATIVE HEAD OFFSET            |
|  17  04         WR O  RECOVERED DATA WITH RETRIES AND/OR CIRC APPLIED     |
|  17  05    D    WR O  RECOVERED DATA USING PREVIOUS SECTOR ID             |
|  17  06    D    W O   RECOVERED DATA WITHOUT ECC - DATA AUTO-REALLOCATED  |
|  17  07    D    W O   RECOVERED DATA WITHOUT ECC - RECOMMEND REASSIGNMENT |
|  17  08    D    W O   RECOVERED DATA WITHOUT ECC - RECOMMEND REWRITE      |
|  18  00    DT   WR O  RECOVERED DATA WITH ERROR CORRECTION APPLIED        |
```

```
|  18  01   D   WR O    RECOVERED DATA WITH ERROR CORRECTION AND RETRIES  |
|  18  02   D   WR O    RECOVERED DATA - DATA AUTO-REALLOCATED             |
|  18  03       R       RECOVERED DATA WITH CIRC                           |
|  18  04       R       RECOVERED DATA WITH LEC                            |
|  18  05   D   WR O    RECOVERED DATA - RECOMMEND REASSIGNMENT            |
|  18  06   D   WR O    RECOVERED DATA - RECOMMEND REWRITE                 |
+=========================================================================+
```

Table 364: (continued)

```
+=========================================================================+
|            D - DIRECT ACCESS DEVICE                                      |
|            .T - SEQUENTIAL ACCESS DEVICE                                 |
|            . L - PRINTER DEVICE                                          |
|            .  P - PROCESSOR DEVICE                                       |
|            .  .W - WRITE ONCE READ MULTIPLE DEVICE                       |
|            .  . R - READ ONLY (CD-ROM) DEVICE                            |
|            .  .  S - SCANNER DEVICE                                      |
|            .  .  .O - OPTICAL MEMORY DEVICE                              |
|            .  .  . M - MEDIA CHANGER DEVICE                              |
|            .  .  .  C - COMMUNICATION DEVICE                             |
|            .  .  .  .                                                    |
| ASC ASCQ  DTLPWRSOMC  DESCRIPTION                                        |
| --- ----  ----------  ------------------------------------------------- |
|  19  00   D        O  DEFECT LIST ERROR                                  |
|  19  01   D        O  DEFECT LIST NOT AVAILABLE                          |
|  19  02   D        O  DEFECT LIST ERROR IN PRIMARY LIST                  |
|  19  03   D        O  DEFECT LIST ERROR IN GROWN LIST                    |
|  1A  00   DTLPWRSOMC  PARAMETER LIST LENGTH ERROR                        |
|  1B  00   DTLPWRSOMC  SYNCHRONOUS DATA TRANSFER ERROR                    |
|  1C  00   D        O  DEFECT LIST NOT FOUND                             |
|  1C  01   D        O  PRIMARY DEFECT LIST NOT FOUND                      |
|  1C  02   D        O  GROWN DEFECT LIST NOT FOUND                        |
|  1D  00   D   W    O  MISCOMPARE DURING VERIFY OPERATION                 |
|  1E  00   D   W    O  RECOVERED ID WITH ECC                              |
|  1F  00                                                                  |
|  20  00   DTLPWRSOMC  INVALID COMMAND OPERATION CODE                     |
|  21  00   DT  WR OM   LOGICAL BLOCK ADDRESS OUT OF RANGE                 |
|  21  01          M    INVALID ELEMENT ADDRESS                            |
|  22  00   D           ILLEGAL FUNCTION SHOULD USE 20 00, 24 00, OR 26 00)|
|  23  00                                                                  |
|  24  00   DTLPWRSOMC  INVALID FIELD IN CDB                               |
|  25  00   DTLPWRSOMC  LOGICAL UNIT NOT SUPPORTED                         |
|  26  00   DTLPWRSOMC  INVALID FIELD IN PARAMETER LIST                    |
|  26  01   DTLPWRSOMC  PARAMETER NOT SUPPORTED                            |
|  26  02   DTLPWRSOMC  PARAMETER VALUE INVALID                            |
|  26  03   DTLPWRSOMC  THRESHOLD PARAMETERS NOT SUPPORTED                 |
|  27  00   DT  W   O   WRITE PROTECTED                                    |
|  28  00   DTLPWRSOMC  NOT READY TO READY TRANSITION(MEDIUM CHANGED)      |
|  28  01          M    IMPORT OR EXPORT ELEMENT ACCESSED                  |
|  29  00   DTLPWRSOMC  POWER ON, RESET, OR BUS DEVICE RESET OCCURRED      |
|  2A  00   DTL WRSOMC  PARAMETERS CHANGED                                 |
|  2A  01   DTL WRSOMC  MODE PARAMETERS CHANGED                            |
|  2A  02   DTL WRSOMC  LOG PARAMETERS CHANGED                             |
|  2B  00   DTLPWRSO C  COPY CANNOT EXECUTE SINCE HOST CANNOT DISCONNECT   |
|  2C  00   DTLPWRSOMC  COMMAND SEQUENCE ERROR                             |
```

HOWTO

```
| 2C  01        S      TOO MANY WINDOWS SPECIFIED                       |
| 2C  02        S      INVALID COMBINATION OF WINDOWS SPECIFIED         |
| 2D  00      T        OVERWRITE ERROR ON UPDATE IN PLACE               |
| 2E  00                                                                |
| 2F  00  DTLPWRSOMC   COMMANDS CLEARED BY ANOTHER INITIATOR            |
| 30  00  DT  WR OM    INCOMPATIBLE MEDIUM INSTALLED                    |
| 30  01  DT  WR O     CANNOT READ MEDIUM - UNKNOWN FORMAT              |
| 30  02  DT  WR O     CANNOT READ MEDIUM - INCOMPATIBLE FORMAT         |
| 30  03  DT           CLEANING CARTRIDGE INSTALLED                     |
| 31  00  DT  W  O     MEDIUM FORMAT CORRUPTED                          |
| 31  01  D L    O     FORMAT COMMAND FAILED                            |
| 32  00  D   W  O     NO DEFECT SPARE LOCATION AVAILABLE               |
| 32  01  D   W  O     DEFECT LIST UPDATE FAILURE                       |
| 33  00      T        TAPE LENGTH ERROR                                |
| 34  00                                                                |
| 35  00                                                                |
| 36  00      L        RIBBON, INK, OR TONER FAILURE                    |
+===============================================================================+
```

Table 364: (continued)

```
+===============================================================================+
|         D - DIRECT ACCESS DEVICE                                      |
|         .T - SEQUENTIAL ACCESS DEVICE                                 |
|         . L - PRINTER DEVICE                                          |
|         . P - PROCESSOR DEVICE                                        |
|         . .W - WRITE ONCE READ MULTIPLE DEVICE                        |
|         . . R - READ ONLY (CD-ROM) DEVICE                             |
|         . . . S - SCANNER DEVICE                                      |
|         . . .O - OPTICAL MEMORY DEVICE                                |
|         . . . M - MEDIA CHANGER DEVICE                                |
|         . . . C - COMMUNICATION DEVICE                                |
|         . . .                                                         |
| ASC ASCQ  DTLPWRSOMC  DESCRIPTION                                     |
| --- ----  ----------  -----------------------------------------------|
| 37  00  DTL WRSOMC   ROUNDED PARAMETER                                |
| 38  00                                                                |
| 39  00  DTL WRSOMC   SAVING PARAMETERS NOT SUPPORTED                  |
| 3A  00  DTL WRSOM    MEDIUM NOT PRESENT                               |
| 3B  00    TL         SEQUENTIAL POSITIONING ERROR                     |
| 3B  01    T          TAPE POSITION ERROR AT BEGINNING-OF-MEDIUM       |
| 3B  02    T          TAPE POSITION ERROR AT END-OF-MEDIUM             |
| 3B  03     L         TAPE OR ELECTRONIC VERTICAL FORMS UNIT NOT READY |
| 3B  04     L         SLEW FAILURE                                     |
| 3B  05     L         PAPER JAM                                        |
| 3B  06     L         FAILED TO SENSE TOP-OF-FORM                      |
| 3B  07     L         FAILED TO SENSE BOTTOM-OF-FORM                   |
| 3B  08    T          REPOSITION ERROR                                 |
| 3B  09          S    READ PAST END OF MEDIUM                          |
| 3B  0A          S    READ PAST BEGINNING OF MEDIUM                    |
| 3B  0B          S    POSITION PAST END OF MEDIUM                      |
| 3B  0C          S    POSITION PAST BEGINNING OF MEDIUM                |
| 3B  0D            M  MEDIUM DESTINATION ELEMENT FULL                  |
| 3B  0E            M  MEDIUM SOURCE ELEMENT EMPTY                      |
| 3C  00                                                                |
| 3D  00  DTLPWRSOMC   INVALID BITS IN IDENTIFY MESSAGE                 |
```

```
|  3E   00   DTLPWRSOMC   LOGICAL UNIT HAS NOT SELF-CONFIGURED YET          |
|  3F   00   DTLPWRSOMC   TARGET OPERATING CONDITIONS HAVE CHANGED          |
|  3F   01   DTLPWRSOMC   MICROCODE HAS BEEN CHANGED                        |
|  3F   02   DTLPWRSOMC   CHANGED OPERATING DEFINITION                      |
|  3F   03   DTLPWRSOMC   INQUIRY DATA HAS CHANGED                          |
|  40   00   D            RAM FAILURE (SHOULD USE 40 NN)                    |
|  40   NN   DTLPWRSOMC   DIAGNOSTIC FAILURE ON COMPONENT NN (80H-FFH)      |
|  41   00   D            DATA PATH FAILURE (SHOULD USE 40 NN)              |
|  42   00   D            POWER-ON OR SELF-TEST FAILURE (SHOULD USE 40 NN)  |
|  43   00   DTLPWRSOMC   MESSAGE ERROR                                     |
|  44   00   DTLPWRSOMC   INTERNAL TARGET FAILURE                           |
|  45   00   DTLPWRSOMC   SELECT OR RESELECT FAILURE                        |
|  46   00   DTLPWRSOMC   UNSUCCESSFUL SOFT RESET                           |
|  47   00   DTLPWRSOMC   SCSI PARITY ERROR                                 |
|  48   00   DTLPWRSOMC   INITIATOR DETECTED ERROR MESSAGE RECEIVED         |
|  49   00   DTLPWRSOMC   INVALID MESSAGE ERROR                             |
|  4A   00   DTLPWRSOMC   COMMAND PHASE ERROR                               |
|  4B   00   DTLPWRSOMC   DATA PHASE ERROR                                  |
|  4C   00   DTLPWRSOMC   LOGICAL UNIT FAILED SELF-CONFIGURATION            |
|  4D   00                                                                  |
|  4E   00   DTLPWRSOMC   OVERLAPPED COMMANDS ATTEMPTED                     |
|  4F   00                                                                  |
|  50   00   T            WRITE APPEND ERROR                                |
|  50   01   T            WRITE APPEND POSITION ERROR                       |
|  50   02   T            POSITION ERROR RELATED TO TIMING                  |
|  51   00   T        O   ERASE FAILURE                                     |
|  52   00   T            CARTRIDGE FAULT                                   |
+=========================================================================+
```

Table 364: (continued)

```
+=========================================================================+
|            D - DIRECT ACCESS DEVICE                                       |
|            .T - SEQUENTIAL ACCESS DEVICE                                  |
|            . L - PRINTER DEVICE                                           |
|            .  P - PROCESSOR DEVICE                                        |
|            .  .W - WRITE ONCE READ MULTIPLE DEVICE                        |
|            .  . R - READ ONLY (CD-ROM) DEVICE                             |
|            .  .  S - SCANNER DEVICE                                       |
|            .  .  .O - OPTICAL MEMORY DEVICE                               |
|            .  .  . M - MEDIA CHANGER DEVICE                               |
|            .  .  .  C - COMMUNICATION DEVICE                              |
|            .  .  .  .                                                     |
| ASC  ASCQ  DTLPWRSOMC   DESCRIPTION                                       |
| ---  ----              ------------------------------------------------- |
|  53   00   DTL WRSOM    MEDIA LOAD OR EJECT FAILED                        |
|  53   01   T            UNLOAD TAPE FAILURE                               |
|  53   02   DT  WR OM    MEDIUM REMOVAL PREVENTED                          |
|  54   00        P       SCSI TO HOST SYSTEM INTERFACE FAILURE             |
|  55   00        P       SYSTEM RESOURCE FAILURE                           |
|  56   00                                                                  |
|  57   00            R   UNABLE TO RECOVER TABLE-OF-CONTENTS               |
|  58   00   O            GENERATION DOES NOT EXIST                         |
|  59   00   O            UPDATED BLOCK READ                                |
|  5A   00   DTLPWRSOM    OPERATOR REQUEST OR STATE CHANGE INPUT(UNSPECIFIED)|
|  5A   01   DT  WR OM    OPERATOR MEDIUM REMOVAL REQUEST                   |
```

HOWTO

```
|    5A   02    DT   W   O     OPERATOR SELECTED WRITE PROTECT                     |
|    5A   03    DT   W   O     OPERATOR SELECTED WRITE PERMIT                      |
|    5B   00    DTLPWRSOM      LOG EXCEPTION                                       |
|    5B   01    DTLPWRSOM      THRESHOLD CONDITION MET                             |
|    5B   02    DTLPWRSOM      LOG COUNTER AT MAXIMUM                              |
|    5B   03    DTLPWRSOM      LOG LIST CODES EXHAUSTED                            |
|    5C   00    D        O     RPL STATUS CHANGE                                   |
|    5C   01    D        O     SPINDLES SYNCHRONIZED                               |
|    5C   02    D        O     SPINDLES NOT SYNCHRONIZED                           |
|    5D   00                                                                       |
|    5E   00                                                                       |
|    5F   00                                                                       |
|    60   00            S      LAMP FAILURE                                        |
|    61   00            S      VIDEO ACQUISITION ERROR                             |
|    61   01            S      UNABLE TO ACQUIRE VIDEO                             |
|    61   02            S      OUT OF FOCUS                                        |
|    62   00            S      SCAN HEAD POSITIONING ERROR                         |
|    63   00           R       END OF USER AREA ENCOUNTERED ON THIS TRACK          |
|    64   00           R       ILLEGAL MODE FOR THIS TRACK                         |
|    65   00                                                                       |
|    66   00                                                                       |
|    67   00                                                                       |
|    68   00                                                                       |
|    69   00                                                                       |
|    6A   00                                                                       |
|    6B   00                                                                       |
|    6C   00                                                                       |
|    6D   00                                                                       |
|    6E   00                                                                       |
|    6F   00                                                                       |
+=================================================================================+
```

Table 364: (concluded)

```
+=================================================================================+
|            D - DIRECT ACCESS DEVICE                                              |
|            .T - SEQUENTIAL ACCESS DEVICE                                         |
|            . L - PRINTER DEVICE                                                  |
|            .  P - PROCESSOR DEVICE                                               |
|            .  .W - WRITE ONCE READ MULTIPLE DEVICE                               |
|            .  . R - READ ONLY (CD-ROM) DEVICE                                    |
|            .  .  S - SCANNER DEVICE                                              |
|            .  .  .O - OPTICAL MEMORY DEVICE                                      |
|            .  .  . M - MEDIA CHANGER DEVICE                                      |
|            .  .  .  C - COMMUNICATION DEVICE                                     |
|            .  .  .  .                                                            |
| ASC ASCQ  DTLPWRSOMC  DESCRIPTION                                                |
| --- ----             ---------------------------------------------------------- |
|    70   00                                                                       |
|    71   00                                                                       |
|    72   00                                                                       |
|    73   00                                                                       |
|    74   00                                                                       |
|    75   00                                                                       |
|    76   00                                                                       |
|    77   00                                                                       |
```

```
|    78   00                                                                |
|    79   00                                                                |
|    7A   00                                                                |
|    7B   00                                                                |
|    7C   00                                                                |
|    7D   00                                                                |
|    7E   00                                                                |
|    7F   00                                                                |
|                                                                           |
|    80   xxh \                                                             |
|     THROUGH >   VENDOR SPECIFIC.                                          |
|    FF   xxh /                                                             |
|                                                                           |
|    xxh 80 \                                                               |
|    THROUGH >   VENDOR SPECIFIC QUALIFICATION OF STANDARD ASC.             |
|    xxh FF /                                                               |
|                 ALL CODES NOT SHOWN OR BLANK ARE RESERVED.                |
+===========================================================================+
```

23   A SCSI command code quick reference

Table 365 is a numerical order listing of the command operation codes.

Table 365: SCSI-2 Operation Codes

```
+===========================================================================+
|            D - DIRECT ACCESS DEVICE              Device Column Key        |
|            .T - SEQUENTIAL ACCESS DEVICE         M = Mandatory            |
|            . L - PRINTER DEVICE                  O = Optional             |
|            .  P - PROCESSOR DEVICE               V = Vendor Specific      |
|            .  .W - WRITE ONCE READ MULTIPLE DEVICE   R = Reserved         |
|            .  . R - READ ONLY (CD-ROM) DEVICE                             |
|            .  .  S - SCANNER DEVICE                                       |
|            .  .  .O - OPTICAL MEMORY DEVICE                               |
|            .  .  . M - MEDIA CHANGER DEVICE                               |
|            .  .  . C - COMMUNICATION DEVICE                               |
|            .  .  .  .                                                     |
|         OP DTLPWRSOMC Description                                         |
|-----------+----------+----------------------------------------------------|
|         00 MMMMMMMMMM TEST UNIT READY                                     |
|         01 M          REWIND                                             |
|         01 O V OO OO  REZERO UNIT                                        |
|         02 VVVVVV  V                                                     |
|         03 MMMMMMMMMM REQUEST SENSE                                      |
|         04   O        FORMAT                                            |
|         04 M        O FORMAT UNIT                                       |
|         05 VMVVVV  V  READ BLOCK LIMITS                                 |
|         06 VVVVVV  V                                                    |
|         07          O INITIALIZE ELEMENT STATUS                         |
|         07 OVV O  OV  REASSIGN BLOCKS                                   |
|         08          M GET MESSAGE(06)                                   |
|         08 OMV OO OV  READ(06)                                          |
|         08   O        RECEIVE                                           |
|         09 VVVVVV  V                                                    |
```

```
|   0A    M          PRINT                                                  |
|   0A           M   SEND MESSAGE(06)                                       |
|   0A    M          SEND(06)                                               |
|   0A OM O   OV     WRITE(06)                                              |
|   0B O   OO OV     SEEK(06)                                              |
|   0B   O           SLEW AND PRINT                                         |
|   0C VVVVVV  V                                                            |
|   0D VVVVVV  V                                                            |
|   0E VVVVVV  V                                                            |
|   0F VOVVVV  V     READ REVERSE                                           |
|   10   O O         SYNCHRONIZE BUFFER                                     |
|   10 VM VVV        WRITE FILEMARKS                                        |
|   11 VMVVVV        SPACE                                                  |
|   12 MMMMMMMMMM    INQUIRY                                                |
|   13 VOVVVV        VERIFY(06)                                             |
|   14 VOOVVV        RECOVER BUFFERED DATA                                  |
|   15 OMO OOOOOO    MODE SELECT(06)                                        |
|   16 M   MM MO     RESERVE                                                |
|   16   MM  M       RESERVE UNIT                                           |
|   17 M   MM MO     RELEASE                                                |
|   17   MM  M       RELEASE UNIT                                           |
|   18 OOOOOOOO      COPY                                                   |
|   19 VMVVVV        ERASE                                                  |
|   1A OMO OOOOOO    MODE SENSE(06)                                         |
|   1B O             LOAD UNLOAD                                            |
|   1B        O      SCAN                                                   |
|   1B O             STOP PRINT                                             |
|   1B O   OO O      STOP START UNIT                                        |
+==========================================================================+
```

Table 365: (continued)

```
+==========================================================================+
|           D - DIRECT ACCESS DEVICE                Device Column Key       |
|           .T - SEQUENTIAL ACCESS DEVICE           M = Mandatory           |
|           . L - PRINTER DEVICE                    O = Optional            |
|           . P - PROCESSOR DEVICE                  V = Vendor Specific     |
|           . .W - WRITE ONCE READ MULTIPLE DEVICE  R = Reserved            |
|           . . R - READ ONLY (CD-ROM) DEVICE                               |
|           . . S - SCANNER DEVICE                                          |
|           . . .O - OPTICAL MEMORY DEVICE                                  |
|           . . . M - MEDIA CHANGER DEVICE                                  |
|           . . . C - COMMUNICATION DEVICE                                  |
|           . . . .                                                         |
|       OP DTLPWRSOMC Description                                           |
|-----------+----------+---------------------------------------------------|
|   1C OOOOOOOOOO RECEIVE DIAGNOSTIC RESULTS                                |
|   1D MMMMMMMMMM SEND DIAGNOSTIC                                           |
|   1E OO  OO OO  PREVENT ALLOW MEDIUM REMOVAL                              |
|   1F                                                                      |
|   20 V   VV V                                                             |
|   21 V   VV V                                                             |
|   22 V   VV V                                                             |
|   23 V   VV V                                                             |
|   24 V   VVM    SET WINDOW                                                |
|   25       O    GET WINDOW                                                |
```

```
|   25 M    M  M     READ CAPACITY                                        |
|   25         M     READ CD-ROM CAPACITY                                 |
|   26 V    VV                                                            |
|   27 V    VV                                                            |
|   28            O GET MESSAGE(10)                                       |
|   28 M    MMMM     READ(10)                                             |
|   29 V    VV O     READ GENERATION                                      |
|   2A            O SEND MESSAGE(10)                                      |
|   2A         O     SEND(10)                                             |
|   2A M    M  M     WRITE(10)                                            |
|   2B  O            LOCATE                                               |
|   2B            O POSITION TO ELEMENT                                   |
|   2B O    OO O     SEEK(10)                                             |
|   2C V       O     ERASE(10)                                           |
|   2D V    O  O     READ UPDATED BLOCK                                   |
|   2E O    O  O     WRITE AND VERIFY(10)                                 |
|   2F O    OO O     VERIFY(10)                                           |
|   30 O    OO O     SEARCH DATA HIGH(10)                                 |
|   31         O     OBJECT POSITION                                      |
|   31 O    OO O     SEARCH DATA EQUAL(10)                                |
|   32 O    OO O     SEARCH DATA LOW(10)                                  |
|   33 O    OO O     SET LIMITS(10)                                       |
|   34         O     GET DATA BUFFER STATUS                               |
|   34 O    OO O     PRE-FETCH                                            |
|   34  O            READ POSITION                                        |
|   35 O    OO O     SYNCHRONIZE CACHE                                    |
|   36 O    OO O     LOCK UNLOCK CACHE                                    |
|   37 O       O     READ DEFECT DATA(10)                                 |
|   38      O  O     MEDIUM SCAN                                          |
|   39 OOOOOOOO      COMPARE                                              |
|   3A OOOOOOOO      COPY AND VERIFY                                      |
|   3B OOOOOOOOOO WRITE BUFFER                                            |
|   3C OOOOOOOOOO READ BUFFER                                             |
|   3D      O  O     UPDATE BLOCK                                         |
|   3E O    OO O     READ LONG                                            |
|   3F O    O  O     WRITE LONG                                           |
+===========================================================================+


Table 365: (continued)
+===========================================================================+
|          D - DIRECT ACCESS DEVICE              Device Column Key |
|          .T - SEQUENTIAL ACCESS DEVICE         M = Mandatory     |
|          . L - PRINTER DEVICE                  O = Optional      |
|          .  P - PROCESSOR DEVICE               V = Vendor Specific|
|          . .W - WRITE ONCE READ MULTIPLE DEVICE R = Reserved     |
|          . . R - READ ONLY (CD-ROM) DEVICE                       |
|          . .  S - SCANNER DEVICE                                 |
|          . . .O - OPTICAL MEMORY DEVICE                          |
|          . . . M - MEDIA CHANGER DEVICE                          |
|          . . .  C - COMMUNICATION DEVICE                         |
|          . . .  .                                               |
|       OP DTLPWRSOMC Description                                  |
|----------+----------+-----------------------------------------------|
|   40 OOOOOOOOOO CHANGE DEFINITION                               |
|   41 O            WRITE SAME                                     |
```

HOWTO

```
|    42     O       READ SUB-CHANNEL                                          |
|    43     O       READ TOC                                                  |
|    44     O       READ HEADER                                               |
|    45     O       PLAY AUDIO(10)                                            |
|    46                                                                       |
|    47     O       PLAY AUDIO MSF                                            |
|    48     O       PLAY AUDIO TRACK INDEX                                    |
|    49     O       PLAY TRACK RELATIVE(10)                                   |
|    4A                                                                       |
|    4B     O       PAUSE RESUME                                              |
|    4C 0000000000  LOG SELECT                                                |
|    4D 0000000000  LOG SENSE                                                 |
|    4E                                                                       |
|    4F                                                                       |
|    50                                                                       |
|    51                                                                       |
|    52                                                                       |
|    53                                                                       |
|    54                                                                       |
|    55 000 000000  MODE SELECT(10)                                           |
|    56                                                                       |
|    57                                                                       |
|    58                                                                       |
|    59                                                                       |
|    5A 000 000000  MODE SENSE(10)                                            |
|    5B                                                                       |
|    5C                                                                       |
|    5D                                                                       |
|    5E                                                                       |
|    5F                                                                       |
+============================================================================+


Table 365: (concluded)
+============================================================================+
|        D - DIRECT ACCESS DEVICE                      Device Column Key |
|        .T - SEQUENTIAL ACCESS DEVICE                 M = Mandatory     |
|        . L - PRINTER DEVICE                          O = Optional      |
|        .  P - PROCESSOR DEVICE                       V = Vendor Specific|
|        . .W - WRITE ONCE READ MULTIPLE DEVICE        R = Reserved      |
|        . . R - READ ONLY (CD-ROM) DEVICE                              |
|        . . . S - SCANNER DEVICE                                       |
|        . . . .O - OPTICAL MEMORY DEVICE                               |
|        . . . . M - MEDIA CHANGER DEVICE                               |
|        . . . . . C - COMMUNICATION DEVICE                             |
|        . . . . . .                                                    |
|        OP DTLPWRSOMC Description                                       |
|----------+----------+-------------------------------------------------|
|    A0                                                                 |
|    A1                                                                 |
|    A2                                                                 |
|    A3                                                                 |
|    A4                                                                 |
|    A5          M  MOVE MEDIUM                                         |
|    A5          O     PLAY AUDIO(12)                                   |
|    A6          O     EXCHANGE MEDIUM                                  |
```

```
|          A7                                                                    |
|          A8              O GET MESSAGE(12)                                      |
|          A8      OO  O    READ(12)                                              |
|          A9       O       PLAY TRACK RELATIVE(12)                               |
|          AA              O SEND MESSAGE(12)                                      |
|          AA      O   O    WRITE(12)                                             |
|          AB                                                                     |
|          AC          O    ERASE(12)                                             |
|          AD                                                                     |
|          AE      O   O    WRITE AND VERIFY(12)                                   |
|          AF      OO  O    VERIFY(12)                                            |
|          B0      OO  O    SEARCH DATA HIGH(12)                                   |
|          B1      OO  O    SEARCH DATA EQUAL(12)                                  |
|          B2      OO  O    SEARCH DATA LOW(12)                                    |
|          B3      OO  O    SET LIMITS(12)                                        |
|          B4                                                                     |
|          B5                                                                     |
|          B5           O   REQUEST VOLUME ELEMENT ADDRESS                         |
|          B6                                                                     |
|          B6           O   SEND VOLUME TAG                                        |
|          B7           O   READ DEFECT DATA(12)                                   |
|          B8                                                                     |
|          B8           O   READ ELEMENT STATUS                                    |
|          B9                                                                     |
|          BA                                                                     |
|          BB                                                                     |
|          BC                                                                     |
|          BD                                                                     |
|          BE                                                                     |
|          BF                                                                     |
+================================================================================+
```

24   Example programs

Here is the C example program, which requests manufacturer/model and reports if a medium is loaded in the device.

```c
#define DEVICE "/dev/sgc"
/* Example program to demonstrate the generic SCSI interface */
#include <stdio.h>
#include <unistd.h>
#include <string.h>
#include <fcntl.h>
#include <errno.h>
#include <scsi/sg.h>

#define SCSI_OFF sizeof(struct sg_header)
static unsigned char cmd[SCSI_OFF + 18];        /* SCSI command buffer */
int fd;                                  /* SCSI device/file descriptor */

/* process a complete scsi cmd. Use the generic scsi interface. */
static int handle_scsi_cmd(unsigned cmd_len,         /* command length */
                           unsigned in_size,         /* input data size */
                           unsigned char *i_buff,    /* input buffer */
                           unsigned out_size,        /* output data size */
```

```
                              unsigned char *o_buff       /* output buffer */
                              )
{
    int status = 0;
    struct sg_header *sg_hd;

    /* safety checks */
    if (!cmd_len) return -1;              /* need a cmd_len != 0 */
    if (!i_buff) return -1;               /* need an input buffer != NULL */
#ifdef SG_BIG_BUFF
    if (SCSI_OFF + cmd_len + in_size > SG_BIG_BUFF) return -1;
    if (SCSI_OFF + out_size > SG_BIG_BUFF) return -1;
#else
    if (SCSI_OFF + cmd_len + in_size > 4096) return -1;
    if (SCSI_OFF + out_size > 4096) return -1;
#endif

    if (!o_buff) out_size = 0;

    /* generic scsi device header construction */
    sg_hd = (struct sg_header *) i_buff;
    sg_hd->reply_len   = SCSI_OFF + out_size;
    sg_hd->twelve_byte = cmd_len == 12;
    sg_hd->result = 0;
#if      0
    sg_hd->pack_len   = SCSI_OFF + cmd_len + in_size; /* not necessary */
    sg_hd->pack_id;      /* not used */
    sg_hd->other_flags; /* not used */
#endif

    /* send command */
    status = write( fd, i_buff, SCSI_OFF + cmd_len + in_size );
    if ( status < 0 || status != SCSI_OFF + cmd_len + in_size ||
                    sg_hd->result ) {
        /* some error happened */
        fprintf( stderr, "write(generic) result = 0x%x cmd = 0x%x\n",
                    sg_hd->result, i_buff[SCSI_OFF] );
        perror("");
        return status;
    }

    if (!o_buff) o_buff = i_buff;         /* buffer pointer check */

    /* retrieve result */
    status = read( fd, o_buff, SCSI_OFF + out_size);
    if ( status < 0 || status != SCSI_OFF + out_size || sg_hd->result ) {
        /* some error happened */
        fprintf( stderr, "read(generic) result = 0x%x cmd = 0x%x\n",
                sg_hd->result, o_buff[SCSI_OFF] );
        fprintf( stderr, "read(generic) sense "
                "%x %x %x %x %x %x %x %x %x %x %x %x %x %x %x %x\n",
                sg_hd->sense_buffer[0],           sg_hd->sense_buffer[1],
                sg_hd->sense_buffer[2],           sg_hd->sense_buffer[3],
                sg_hd->sense_buffer[4],           sg_hd->sense_buffer[5],
                sg_hd->sense_buffer[6],           sg_hd->sense_buffer[7],
```

```
                        sg_hd->sense_buffer[8],           sg_hd->sense_buffer[9],
                        sg_hd->sense_buffer[10],          sg_hd->sense_buffer[11],
                        sg_hd->sense_buffer[12],          sg_hd->sense_buffer[13],
                        sg_hd->sense_buffer[14],          sg_hd->sense_buffer[15]);
            if (status < 0)
                perror("");
        }
        /* Look if we got what we expected to get */
        if (status == SCSI_OFF + out_size) status = 0; /* got them all */

        return status;  /* 0 means no error */
}

#define INQUIRY_CMD       0x12
#define INQUIRY_CMDLEN    6
#define INQUIRY_REPLY_LEN 96
#define INQUIRY_VENDOR    8        /* Offset in reply data to vendor name */

/* request vendor brand and model */
static unsigned char *Inquiry ( void )
{
  unsigned char Inqbuffer[ SCSI_OFF + INQUIRY_REPLY_LEN ];
  unsigned char cmdblk [ INQUIRY_CMDLEN ] =
      { INQUIRY_CMD,  /* command */
                  0,  /* lun/reserved */
                  0,  /* page code */
                  0,  /* reserved */
  INQUIRY_REPLY_LEN,  /* allocation length */
                  0 };/* reserved/flag/link */

  memcpy( cmd + SCSI_OFF, cmdblk, sizeof(cmdblk) );

  /*
   * +-------------------+
   * | struct sg_header  | <- cmd
   * +-------------------+
   * | copy of cmdblk    | <- cmd + SCSI_OFF
   * +-------------------+
   */

  if (handle_scsi_cmd(sizeof(cmdblk), 0, cmd,
                      sizeof(Inqbuffer) - SCSI_OFF, Inqbuffer )) {
      fprintf( stderr, "Inquiry failed\n" );
      exit(2);
  }
  return (Inqbuffer + SCSI_OFF);
}

#define TESTUNITREADY_CMD 0
#define TESTUNITREADY_CMDLEN 6

#define ADD_SENSECODE 12
#define ADD_SC_QUALIFIER 13
#define NO_MEDIA_SC 0x3a
#define NO_MEDIA_SCQ 0x00
```

HOWTO

```c
int TestForMedium ( void )
{
  /* request READY status */
  static unsigned char cmdblk [TESTUNITREADY_CMDLEN] = {
       TESTUNITREADY_CMD, /* command */
                       0, /* lun/reserved */
                       0, /* reserved */
                       0, /* reserved */
                       0, /* reserved */
                       0};/* reserved */

  memcpy( cmd + SCSI_OFF, cmdblk, sizeof(cmdblk) );

  /*
   * +-------------------+
   * | struct sg_header  | <- cmd
   * +-------------------+
   * | copy of cmdblk    | <- cmd + SCSI_OFF
   * +-------------------+
   */

  if (handle_scsi_cmd(sizeof(cmdblk), 0, cmd,
                            0, NULL)) {
      fprintf (stderr, "Test unit ready failed\n");
      exit(2);
  }

  return
   *(((struct sg_header*)cmd)->sense_buffer +ADD_SENSECODE) !=
                                         NO_MEDIA_SC ||
   *(((struct sg_header*)cmd)->sense_buffer +ADD_SC_QUALIFIER) !=
                                         NO_MEDIA_SCQ;

}


void main( void )
{
  fd = open(DEVICE, O_RDWR);
  if (fd < 0) {
    fprintf( stderr, "Need read/write permissions for "DEVICE".\n" );
    exit(1);
  }

  /* print some fields of the Inquiry result */
  printf( "%s\n", Inquiry() + INQUIRY_VENDOR );

  /* look if medium is loaded */
  if (!TestForMedium()) {
    printf("device is unloaded\n");
  } else {
    printf("device is loaded\n");
  }
}
```

Part XXXVII

"SMB HOWTO" David Wood

dwood@plugged.net.au
v1.0, 10 August 1996
This is the SMB HOWTO. This document describes how to use the Session Message Block (SMB) protocol, also called the NetBIOS or LanManager protocol, with Linux.

Contents

HOWTO

1   Introduction

This is the SMB HOWTO. This document describes how to use the Session Message Block (SMB) protocol, also called the NetBIOS or LanManager protocol, with Linux.

This document is maintained by David Wood (*dwood@plugged.net.au*). Additions, modifications or corrections may be mailed there for inclusion in the next release.

The SMB protocol is used by Microsoft Windows 3.11, NT and 95 to share disks and printers. Using the Samba suite of tools by Andrew Tridgell, UNIX (including Linux) machines can share disk and printers with Windows hosts.

There are four things that one can do with Samba:

1. Share a linux drive with Windows machines.

2. Share a Windows drive with linux machines.

3. Share a linux printer with Windows machines.

4. Share a Windows printer with linux machines.

All of these are covered in this document.

Disclaimer: The procedures and scripts either work for the author or have been reported to work by the people that provided them. Different configurations may not work with the information given here. If you encounter such a situation, you may e-mail the author with suggestions for improvement in this document, but the author guarantees nothing. What did you expect? The author is, after all, a consultant...

2   Further Information

This HOWTO attempts to explain how to configure basic SMB file and print services on a linux machine. Samba is a very complex and complete package. There would be no point in attempting to duplicate all of the documentation for Samba here.

For further information, please see the following documents:

- The Samba documentation, available as part of the Samba distribution. The distribution is available at: *ftp://nimbus.anu.edu.au/pub/tridge/samba/* `<ftp://nimbus.anu.edu.au/pub/tridge/samba/>`
- The linux Printing HOWTO.
- The Print2Win Mini-HOWTO.

3   Installation

The latest source version of Samba is available from:

ftp://nimbus.anu.edu.au/pub/tridge/samba/ `<ftp://nimbus.anu.edu.au/pub/tridge/samba/>`

However, if you have installed the Redhat distribution of linux, you have the option of installing it as a package. Some other distributions also include the Samba binaries.

The following two daemons are required for the Samba package. They are typically installed in /usr/sbin and run either on boot from the systems startup scripts or from inetd. Example scripts are shown in 4 (Running the Daemons).

```
smbd (The SMB daemon)
nmbd (Provides NetBIOS nameserver support to clients)
```

Typically, the following Samba binaries are installed in /usr/bin, although the location is optional.

```
smbclient       (An SMB client for UNIX machines)
smbprint        (A script to print to a printer on an SMB host)
smbprint.sysv   (As above, but for SVR4 UNIX machines)
smbstatus       (Lists the cuurent SMB connections for the local host)
smbrun          (A 'glue' script to facilitate runnning applciations
                 on SMB hosts)
```

Additionally, a script called 'print' is included with this HOWTO, which serves as a usefull front end to the smbprint script.

The Samba package is simple to install. Simply retrieve the source from the location mentioned above, and read the file README in the distribution. There is also a file called docs/INSTALL.txt in the distribution that provides a simple step-by-step set of instructions.

Following installation, place the daemons in /usr/sbin and the binaries in /usr/bin. Install the man pages in /usr/local/man.

When you made the Samba package, you would have specified in the Makefile the location for the configuration file, smb.conf. This is generally in /etc, but you can put it anywhere you like. For these directions, we will presume that you specified the location of the configuration file as /etc/smb.conf, the log file location as log file = /var/log/samba-log.%m and the lock directory as lock directory = /var/lock/samba.

Install the configuration file, smb.conf. Go to the directory where Samba was built. Look in the subdirectory examples/simple and read the file README. Copy the file smb.conf found in that directory to /etc. BE CAREFUL! If you have a linux distribution that already has Samba installed, you may already have a Samba configuration file in /etc. You should probably start with that one.

If you don't want to have your configuration file in /etc, put it wherever you want to, then put a symlink in /etc:

```
ln -s /path/to/smb.conf /etc/smb.conf
```

4 Running The Daemons

The two SMB daemons are /usr/sbin/smbd and /usr/sbin/nmbd.

You can run the Samba daemons from inetd or as stand-alone processes. If you are configuring a permanent file server, they should be run from inetd so that they will be restarted if they die. If you just want to use SMB services occasionally or to assist with systems administration, you can start them with an /etc/rc.d/init.d script or even by hand when you need them.

To run the daemons from inetd, place the following lines in the inetd configuration file, /etc/inetd.conf:

```
# SAMBA NetBIOS services (for PC file and print sharing)
netbios-ssn stream tcp nowait root /usr/sbin/smbd smbd
netbios-ns dgram udp wait root /usr/sbin/nmbd nmbd
```

Then restart the inetd daemon by running the command:

```
kill -HUP 1
```

To run the daemons from the system startup scripts, put the following script in file called /etc/rc.d/init.d/smb and symbolically link it to the files specified in the comments:

```
#!/bin/sh

#
# /etc/rc.d/init.d/smb - starts and stops SMB services.
#
# The following files should be synbolic links to this file:
# symlinks: /etc/rc.d/rc1.d/K35smb   (Kills SMB services on shutdown)
#           /etc/rc.d/rc3.d/S91smb   (Starts SMB services in multius-
er mode)
#           /etc/rc.d/rc6.d/K35smb   (Kills SMB services on reboot)
#

# Source function library.
. /etc/rc.d/init.d/functions

# Source networking configuration.
. /etc/sysconfig/network

# Check that networking is up.
[ ${NETWORKING} = "no" ] && exit 0

# See how we were called.
case "$1" in
  start)
```

HOWTO

```
              echo -n "Starting SMB services: "
              daemon smbd -D
              daemon nmbd -D
              echo
              touch /var/lock/subsys/smb
              ;;
       stop)
              echo -n "Shutting down SMB services: "
              killproc smbd
              killproc nmbd
              rm -f /var/lock/subsys/smb
              echo ""
              ;;
       *)
              echo "Usage: smb {start|stop}"
              exit 1
       esac
```

5   General Configuration (/etc/smb.conf)

Samba configuration on a linux (or other UNIX machine) is controlled by a single file, /etc/smb.conf. This file determines which system resources you want to share with the outside world and what restrictions you wish to place on them.

Since the following sections will address sharing linux drives and printers with Windows machines, the smb.conf file shown in this section is as simple as you can get, just for introductory purposes.

Don't worry about the details, yet. Later sections will introduce the major concepts.

Each section of the file starts with a section header such as [global], [homes], [printers], etc.

The [global] section defines a few variables that Samba will use to define sharing for all resources.

The [homes] section allows a remote users to access their (and only their) home directory on the local (linux) machine. That is, if a Windows user trys to connect to this share from their Windows machines, they will be connected to their personal home directory. Note that to do this, they must have an account on the linux box.

The sample smb.conf file below allows remote users to get to their home directories on the local machine and to write to a temporary directory. For a Windows user to see these shares, the linux box has to be on the local network. Then the user simply connects a network drive from the Windows File Manager or Windows Explorer.

Note that in the following sections, additional entries for this file will be given to allow more resources to be shared.

```
; /etc/smb.conf
;
; Make sure and restart the server after making changes to this file, ex:
; /etc/rc.d/init.d/smb stop
; /etc/rc.d/init.d/smb start

[global]
; Uncomment this if you want a guest account
; guest account = nobody
   log file = /var/log/samba-log.%m
   lock directory = /var/lock/samba
   share modes = yes

[homes]
   comment = Home Directories
```

```
      browseable = no
      read only = no
      create mode = 0750

[tmp]
      comment = Temporary file space
      path = /tmp
      read only = no
      public = yes
```

6   Sharing A Linux Drive With Windows Machines

As shown in the simple smb.conf above, sharing linux drives with Windows users is easy. However, like everything else with Samba, you can control things to a large degree. Here are some examples:

To share a directory with the public, create a clone of the [tmp] section above by adding something like this to smb.conf:

```
[public]
      comment = Public Stuff
      path = /home/public
      public = yes
      writable = yes
      printable = yes
```

To make the above directory readable by the public, but only writable by people in group staff, modify the entry like this:

```
[public]
      comment = Public Stuff
      path = /home/public
      public = yes
      writable = yes
      printable = no
      write list = @staff
```

For other tricks to play with drive shares, see the Samba documentation or man pages.

7   Sharing A Windows Drive With Linux Machines

An SMB client program for UNIX machines is included with the Samba distribution. It provides an ftp-like interface on the command line. You can uyse this utility to transfer files between a Windows 'server' and a linux client.

To see which shares are available on a given host, run:

```
/usr/sbin/smbclient -L host
```

where 'host' is the name of the machine that you wish to view. this will return a list of 'service' names - that is, names of drives or printers that it can share with you. Unless the SMB server has no security configured, it will ask you for a password. Get it the password for the 'guest' account or for your personal account on that machine.

For example:

```
smbclient -L zimmerman
```

The output of this command should look something like this:

HOWTO

```
Server time is Sat Aug 10 15:58:27 1996
Timezone is UTC+10.0
Password:
Domain=[WORKGROUP] OS=[Windows NT 3.51] Server=[NT LAN Manager 3.51]

Server=[ZIMMERMAN] User=[] Workgroup=[WORKGROUP] Domain=[]

        Sharename      Type        Comment
        ---------      ----        -------
        ADMIN$         Disk        Remote Admin
        public         Disk        Public
        C$             Disk        Default share
        IPC$           IPC         Remote IPC
        OReilly        Printer     OReilly
        print$         Disk        Printer Drivers


This machine has a browse list:

        Server                 Comment
        ---------              -------
        HOPPER                 Samba 1.9.15p8
        KERNIGAN               Samba 1.9.15p8
        LOVELACE               Samba 1.9.15p8
        RITCHIE                Samba 1.9.15p8
        ZIMMERMAN
```

The browse list shows other SMB servers with resources to share on the network.

To use the client, run:

```
/usr/sbin/smbclient service <password>
```

where 'service' is a machine and share name. For example, if you are trying to reach a directory that has been shared as 'public' on a machine called zimmerman, the service would be called \\zimmerman\public. However, due to shell restrictions, you will need to escape the backslashes, so you end up with something like this:

```
/usr/sbin/smbclient \\\\zimmerman\\public mypasswd
```

where 'mypasswd' is the literal string of your password.

You will get the smbclient prompt:

```
Server time is Sat Aug 10 15:58:44 1996
Timezone is UTC+10.0
Domain=[WORKGROUP] OS=[Windows NT 3.51] Server=[NT LAN Manager 3.51]
smb: \>
```

Type 'h' to get help using smbclient:

```
smb: \> h
ls             dir          lcd          cd           pwd
get            mget         put          mput         rename
more           mask         del          rm           mkdir
```

md	rmdir	rd	prompt	recurse
translate	lowercase	print	printmode	queue
cancel	stat	quit	q	exit
newer	archive	tar	blocksize	tarmode
setmode	help	?	!	

smb: \>

If you can use ftp, you shouldn't need the man pages for smbclient.

8   Sharing A Linux Printer With Windows Machines

To share a linux printer with Windows machines, you need to make certain that your printer is set up to work under linux. If you can print from linux, setting up an SMB share of the printer is stright forward.

See the Printing HOWTO to set up local printing.

Since the author uses a printer connected to a Windows NT machine, this section should not be taken as definitive, but merely a suggestion. Anyone with details to share, please send them to *dwood@plugged.net.au* so this section can be completed.

Add printing configuration to your smb.conf:

```
[global]
    printing = bsd
    printcap name = /etc/printcap
    load printers = yes
    log file = /var/log/samba-log.%m
    lock directory = /var/lock/samba

[printers]
    comment = All Printers
    security = server
    path = /var/spool/lpd/lp
    browseable = no
    printable = yes
    public = yes
    writable = no
    create mode = 0700

[ljet]
    security = server
    path = /var/spool/lpd/lp
    printer name = lp
    writable = yes
    public = yes
    printable = yes
    print command = lpr -r -h -P %p %s
```

Make certain that the printer path (in this case under [ljet]) matches the spool directory in /etc/printcap!

NOTE: There are some problems sharing printers on UNIX boxes with Windows NT machines using Samba. One problem is with NT seeing the shared printer properly. To fix this, see the notes in the Samba distribution in the file docs/WinNT.txt. The other deals with password problems. See the comments in the same file for an annoying gain of understanding and failure to fix the problem.

9   Sharing A Windows Printer With Linux Machines

To share a printer on a Windows machine, you must do the following:

a) You must have the proper entries in /etc/printcap and they must correspond to the local directory structure (for the spool directory, etc)

b) You must have the script /usr/bin/smbprint. This comes with the Samba source, but not with all Samba binary distributions. A slightly modifed copy is discussed below.

c) If you want to convert ASCII files to Postscript, you must have nenscript, or its equivalent. nenscript is a Postscript converter and is generally installed in /usr/bin.

d) you may wish to make Samba printing easier by having an easy-to-use front end. A simple perl script to handle ASCII, Postscript or created Postscript is given below.

The /etc/printcap entry below is for an HP 5MP printer on a Windows NT host. The entries are as follows:

```
cm - comment
lp - device name to open for output
sd - the printer's spool directory (on the local machine)
af - the accounting file
mx - the maximum file size (zero is unlimited)
if - name of the input filter (script)
```

For more information, see the Printing HOWTO or the man page for printcap.

```
# /etc/printcap
#
# //zimmerman/oreilly via smbprint
#
lp:\
        :cm=HP 5MP Postscript OReilly on zimmerman:\
        :lp=/dev/lp1:\
        :sd=/var/spool/lpd/lp:\
        :af=/var/spool/lpd/lp/acct:\
        :mx#0:\
        :if=/usr/bin/smbprint:
```

Make certain that the spool and accounting directories exist and are writable. Ensure that the 'if' line holds the proper path to the smbprint script (given below) and make sure that the proper device is pointed to (the /dev speical file).

Next is the smbprint script itself. It is usually placed in /usr/bin and is attributable to Andrew Tridgell, the person who created Samba as far as I know. It comes with the Samba source distribution, but is absent from some binary distributions, so I have recreated it here.

You may wish to look at this carefully. There are some minor alterations that have shown themselves to be useful.

```
#!/bin/sh -x

# This script is an input filter for printcap printing on a unix machine. It
# uses the smbclient program to print the file to the specified smb-based
# server and service.
# For example you could have a printcap entry like this
#
# smb:lp=/dev/null:sd=/usr/spool/smb:sh:if=/usr/local/samba/smbprint
#
```

```
# which would create a unix printer called "smb" that will print via this
# script. You will need to create the spool directory /usr/spool/smb with
# appropriate permissions and ownerships for your system.

# Set these to the server and service you wish to print to
# In this example I have a WfWg PC called "lapland" that has a printer
# exported called "printer" with no password.

#
# Script further altered by hamiltom@ecnz.co.nz (Michael Hamilton)
# so that the server, service, and password can be read from
# a /usr/var/spool/lpd/PRINTNAME/.config file.
#
# In order for this to work the /etc/printcap entry must include an
# accounting file (af=...):
#
#    cdcolour:\
#        :cm=CD IBM Colorjet on 6th:\
#        :sd=/var/spool/lpd/cdcolour:\
#        :af=/var/spool/lpd/cdcolour/acct:\
#        :if=/usr/local/etc/smbprint:\
#        :mx=0:\
#        :lp=/dev/null:
#
# The /usr/var/spool/lpd/PRINTNAME/.config file should contain:
#    server=PC_SERVER
#    service=PR_SHARENAME
#    password="password"
#
# E.g.
#    server=PAULS_PC
#    service=CJET_371
#    password=""

#
# Debugging log file, change to /dev/null if you like.
#
logfile=/tmp/smb-print.log
# logfile=/dev/null


#
# The last parameter to the filter is the accounting file name.
#
spool_dir=/var/spool/lpd/lp
config_file=$spool_dir/.config

# Should read the following variables set in the config file:
#    server
#    service
#    password
#    user
eval 'cat $config_file'

#
```

```
# Some debugging help, change the >> to > if you want to same space.
#
echo "server $server, service $service" >> $logfile


(
# NOTE You may wish to add the line 'echo translate' if you want automatic
# CR/LF translation when printing.
        echo translate
        echo "print -"
        cat
) | /usr/bin/smbclient "\\\\$server\\$service" $password -U $user -N -
P >> $logfile
```

Most linux distributions come with nenscript for converting ASCII documents to Postscript. The following perl script makes life easier be providing a simple interface to linux printing via smbprint.

```
Usage: print [-a|c|p] <filename>
       -a prints <filename> as ASCII
       -c prints <filename> formatted as source code
       -p prints <filename> as Postscript
        If no switch is given, print attempts to
        guess the file type and print appropriately.
```

Using smbprint to print ASCII files tends to truncate long lines. This script breaks long lines on whitespace (instead of in the middle of a word), if possible.

The source code formatting is done with nenscript. It takes an ASCII file and foramts it in 2 columns with a fancy header (date, filename, etc). It also numbers the lines. Using this as an example, other types of formatting can be accomplished.

Postscript documents are already properly formatted, so they pass through directly.

```
#!/usr/bin/perl

# Script:    print
# Authors:   Brad Marshall, David Wood
#            Plugged In Communications
# Date:      960808
#
# Script to print to oreilly which is currently on zimmerman
# Purpose:   Takes files of various types as arguments and
# processes them appropriately for piping to a Samba print script.
#
# Currently supported file types:
#
# ASCII      - ensures that lines longer than $line_length character-
s wrap on
#              whitespace.
# Postscript - Takes no action.
# Code       - Formats in Postscript (using nenscript) to display
#              properly (landscape, font, etc).
#


# Set the maximum allowable length for each line of ASCII text.
$line_length = 76;
```

```perl
# Set the path and name of the Samba print script
$print_prog = "/usr/bin/smbprint";

# Set the path and name to nenscript (the ASCII-->Postscript converter)
$nenscript = "/usr/bin/nenscript";

unless ( -f $print_prog ) {
        die "Can't find $print_prog!";
}
unless ( -f $nenscript ) {
        die "Can't find $nenscript!";
}

&ParseCmdLine(@ARGV);

# DBG
print "filetype is $filetype\n";

if ($filetype eq "ASCII") {
        &wrap($line_length);
} elsif ($filetype eq "code") {
        &codeformat;
} elsif ($filetype eq "ps") {
        &createarray;
} else {
        print "Sorry..no known file type.\n";
        exit 0;
}
# Pipe the array to smbprint
open(PRINTER, "|$print_prog") || die "Can't open $print_prog: $!\n";
foreach $line (@newlines) {
        print PRINTER $line;
}
# Send an extra linefeed in case a file has an incomplete last line.
print PRINTER "\n";
close(PRINTER);
print "Completed\n";
exit 0;


# ---------------------------------------------------- #
#         Everything below here is a subroutine        #
# ---------------------------------------------------- #

sub ParseCmdLine {
        # Parses the command line, finding out what file type the file is

        # Gets $arg and $file to be the arguments (if the exists)
        # and the filename
        if ($#_ < 0) {
                &usage;
        }
        # DBG
#       foreach $element (@_) {
#               print "*$element* \n";
#       }
```

```
        $arg = shift(@_);
        if ($arg =~ /\-./) {
                $cmd = $arg;
        # DBG
#       print "\$cmd found.\n";

                $file = shift(@_);
        } else {
                $file = $arg;
        }

        # Defining the file type
        unless ($cmd) {
                # We have no arguments

                if ($file =~ /\.ps$/) {
                        $filetype = "ps";
                } elsif ($file =~ /\.java$|\.c$|\.h$|\.pl$|\.sh$|\
                        \.csh$|\.m4$|\.inc$|\.html$|\.htm$/) {
                        $filetype = "code";
                } else {
                        $filetype = "ASCII";
                }

                # Process $file for what type is it and return $filetype
        } else {
                # We have what type it is in $arg
                if ($cmd =~ /^-p$/) {
                        $filetype = "ps";
                } elsif ($cmd =~ /^-c$/) {
                        $filetype = "code";
                } elsif ($cmd =~ /^-a$/) {
                        $filetype = "ASCII"
                }
        }
}

sub usage {
        print "
Usage: print [-a|c|p] <filename>
        -a prints <filename> as ASCII
        -c prints <filename> formatted as source code
        -p prints <filename> as Postscript
        If no switch is given, print attempts to
        guess the file type and print appropriately.\n
";
        exit(0);
}

sub wrap {
        # Create an array of file lines, where each line is < the
        # number of characters specified, and wrapped only on whitespace

        # Get the number of characters to limit the line to.
```

```perl
$limit = pop(@_);

# DBG
#print "Entering subroutine wrap\n";
#print "The line length limit is $limit\n";

# Read in the file, parse and put into an array.
open(FILE, "<$file") || die "Can't open $file: $!\n";
while(<FILE>) {
        $line = $_;

        # DBG
        #print "The line is:\n$line\n";

        # Wrap the line if it is over the limit.
        while ( length($line) > $limit ) {

                # DBG
                #print "Wrapping...";

                # Get the first $limit +1 characters.
                $part = substr($line,0,$limit +1);

                # DBG
                #print "The partial line is:\n$part\n";

                # Check to see if the last character is a space.
                $last_char = substr($part,-1, 1);
                if ( " " eq $last_char ) {
                    # If it is, print the rest.

                    # DBG
                    #print "The last character was a space\n";

                    substr($line,0,$limit + 1) = "";
                    substr($part,-1,1) = "";
                    push(@newlines,"$part\n");
                } else {
                    # If it is not, find the last space in the
                    # sub-line and print up to there.

                    # DBG
                    #print "The last character was not a space\n";

                    # Remove the character past $limit
                    substr($part,-1,1) = "";
                    # Reverse the line to make it easy to find
                    # the last space.
                    $revpart = reverse($part);
                    $index = index($revpart," ");
                    if ( $index > 0 ) {
                      substr($line,0,$limit-$index) = "";
                      push(@newlines,substr($part,0,$limit-$index)
                        . "\n");
                    } else {
```

```
                                        # There was no space in the line, so
                                        # print it up to $limit.
                                        substr($line,0,$limit) = "";
                                        push(@newlines,substr($part,0,$limit)
                                           . "\n");
                                }
                        }
                }
                push(@newlines,$line);
        }
        close(FILE);
}

sub codeformat {
        # Call subroutine wrap then filter through nenscript
        &wrap($line_length);

        # Pipe the results through nenscript to create a Postscript
        # file that adheres to some decent format for printing
        # source code (landscape, Courier font, line numbers).
        # Print this to a temporary file first.
        $tmpfile = "/tmp/nenscript$$";
        open(FILE, "|$nenscript -2G -i$file -N -p$tmpfile -r") ||
                die "Can't open nenscript: $!\n";
        foreach $line (@newlines) {
                print FILE $line;
        }
        close(FILE);

        # Read the temporary file back into an array so it can be
        # passed to the Samba print script.
        @newlines = ("");
        open(FILE, "<$tmpfile") || die "Can't open $file: $!\n";
        while(<FILE>) {
                push(@newlines,$_);
        }
        close(FILE);
        system("rm $tmpfile");
}

sub createarray {
        # Create the array for postscript
        open(FILE, "<$file") || die "Can't open $file: $!\n";
        while(<FILE>) {
                push(@newlines,$_);
        }
        close(FILE);
}
```

10 Copyright

11 Acknowledgements

As soon as you mail me with suggestions, I'll acknowledge you here in the next release.

HOWTO

Part XXXVIII

"SRM Firmware Howto" David Mosberger

davidm@azstarnet.com
v0.5, 17 August 1996

This document describes how to boot Linux/Alpha using the SRM firmware, which is the firmware normally used to boot DEC Unix. Generally, it is preferable to use MILO instead of aboot since MILO is perfectly adapted to the needs of Linux. However, MILO is not always available for a particular system and MILO does not presently have the ability to boot over the network. In either case, using the SRM console may be the right solution.

Contents

Unless you're interested in technical details, you may want to skip right to Section 3 ().

1   How Does SRM Boot an OS?

All versions of SRM can boot from SCSI disks and the versions for recent platforms, such as the Noname or AlphaStations can boot from floppy disks as well. Network booting via bootp is supported. Note that older SRM versions (notably the one for the Jensen) *cannot* boot from floppy disks. Also, booting from IDE disk drives is unsupported.

Booting Linux with SRM is a two step process: first, SRM loads and transfers control to the secondary bootstrap loader. Then the secondary bootstrap loader sets up the environment for Linux, reads the kernel image from a disk filesystem and finally transfers control to Linux.

Currently, there are two secondary bootstrap loaders for Linux: the *raw* loader that comes with the Linux kernel and aboot which is distributed separately. These two loaders are described in more detail below.

1.1 Loading The Secondary Bootstrap Loader

SRM knows nothing about filesystems or disk-partitions. It simply expects that the secondary bootstrap loader occupies a consecutive range of physical disk sector, starting from a given offset. The information on the size of the secondary bootstrap loader and the offset of its first disk sector is stored in the first 512 byte sector. Specifically, the long integer at offset 480 stores the *size* of the secondary bootstrap loader (in 512-byte blocks) and the long at offset 488 gives the *sector number* at which the secondary bootstrap loader starts. The first sector also stores a flag-word at offset 496 which is always 0 and a checksum at offset 504. The checksum is simply the sum of the first 63 long integers in the first sector.

If the checksum in the first sector is correct, SRM goes ahead and reads the *size* sectors starting from the sector given in the *sector number* field and places them in *virtual* memory at address 0x20000000. If the reading completes successfully, SRM performs a jump to address 0x20000000.

2 The Raw Loader

The sources for this loader can be found in directory

```
linux/arch/alpha/boot
```

of the Linux kernel source distribution. It loads the Linux kernel by reading START_SIZE bytes starting at disk offset BOOT_SIZE+512 (also in bytes). The constants START_SIZE and BOOT_SIZE are defined in linux/include/asm-alpha/system.h. START_SIZE must be at least as big as the kernel image (i.e., the size of the .text, .data, and .bss segments). Similarly, BOOT_SIZE must be at least as big as the image of the raw bootstrap loader. Both constants should be an integer multiple of the sector size, which is 512 bytes. The default values are currently 2MB for START_SIZE and 16KB for BOOT_SIZE. Note that if you want to boot from a 1.44MB floppy disk, you have to reduce START_SIZE to 1400KB and make sure that the kernel you want to boot is no bigger than that.

To build a raw loader, simply type make rawboot in /usr/src/linux. This should produce the following files in arch/alpha/boot:

tools/lxboot:
> The first sector on the disk. It contains the offset and size of the next file in the format described above.

tools/bootlx:
> The raw boot loader that will load the file below.

vmlinux.nh:
> The raw kernel image consisting of the .text, .data, and .bss segments of the object file in /usr/src/linux/vmlinux. The extension .nh indicates that this file has no object-file header.

The concatenation of these three files should be written to the disk from which you want to boot. For example, to boot from a floppy, insert an empty floppy disk in, say, /dev/fd0 and then type:

```
cat tools/lxboot tools/bootlx vmlinux >/dev/fd0
```

You can then shutdown the system and boot from the floppy by issueing the command boot dva0.

3 The aboot Loader

When using the SRM firmware, aboot is the preferred way of booting Linux. It supports:

- direct booting from various filesystems (ext2, ISO9660, and UFS, the DEC Unix filesystem)
- booting of executable object files (both ELF and ECOFF)
- booting compressed kernels

- network booting (using bootp)

- partition tables in DEC Unix format (which is compatible with BSD Unix partition tables)

- interactive booting and default configurations for SRM consoles that cannot pass long option strings

3.1 Getting and Building aboot

The latest sources for `aboot` are available in *this ftp directory* `<ftp://ftp.azstarnet.com/pub/linux/axp/aboot>`. The description in this manual applies to `aboot` version 0.5 or newer.

Once you downloaded and extracted the latest tar file, take a look at the `README` and `INSTALL` files for installation hints. In particular, be sure to adjust the variables in `Makefile` and in `include/config.h` to match your environment. Normally, you won't need to change anything when building under Linux, but it is always a good idea to double check. If you're satisfied with the configuration, simply type `make` to build it (if you're not building under Linux, be advised that `aboot` requires GNU `make`).

After running `make`, the `aboot` directory should contain the following files:

aboot

This is the actual `aboot` executable (either an ECOFF or ELF object file).

bootlx

Same as above, but it contains only the text, data and bss segments—that is, this file is not an object file.

sdisklabel/writeboot

Utility to install `aboot` on a hard disk.

tools/e2writeboot

Utility to install `aboot` on an ext2 filesystem (usually used for floppies only).

tools/isomarkboot

Utility to install `aboot` on a iso9660 filesystem (used by CD-ROM distributors).

tools/abootconf

Utility to configure an installed `aboot`.

3.2 Floppy Installation

The bootloader can be installed on a floppy using the `e2writeboot` command (note: this can't be done on a Jensen since its firmware does *not* support booting from floppy). This command requires that the disk is not overly fragmented as it needs to find enough contiguous file blocks to store the entire `aboot` image (currently about 90KB). If `e2writeboot` fails because of this, reformat the floppy and try again (e.g., with `fdformat(1)`). For example, the following steps install `aboot` on floppy disk assuming the floppy is in drive `/dev/fd0`:

```
fdformat /dev/fd0
mke2fs /dev/fd0
e2writeboot /dev/fd0 bootlx
```

3.3 Harddisk Installation

Since the `e2writeboot` command may fail on highly fragmented disks and since reformatting a harddisk is not without pain, it is generally safer to install `aboot` on a harddisk using the `swriteboot` command. `swriteboot` requires that the first few sectors are reserved for booting purposes. We suggest that the disk be partitioned such that the first partition starts at an offset of 2048 sectors. This leaves 1MB of space for storing `aboot`. On a properly partitioned disk, it is then possible to install `aboot` as follows (assuming the disk is `/dev/sda`):

```
swriteboot /dev/sda bootlx
```

HOWTO

On a Jensen, you will want to leave some more space, since you need to write a kernel to this place, too—2MB should be sufficient when using compressed kernels. Use `swriteboot` as described in Section 3.6 () to write `bootlx` together with the Linux kernel.

3.4 CD-ROM Installation

To make a CD-ROM bootable by SRM, simply build `aboot` as described above. Then, make sure that the `bootlx` file is present on the iso9660 filesystem (e.g., copy `bootlx` to the directory that is the filesystem master, then run `mkisofs` on that directory). After that, all that remains to be done is to mark the filesystem as SRM bootable. This is achieved with a command of the form:

```
isomarkboot filesystem bootlx
```

The command above assumes that `filesystem` is a file containing the iso9660 filesystem and that `bootlx` has been copied into the root directory of that filesystem. That's it!

3.5 Building the Linux Kernel

A bootable Linux kernel can be built with the following steps. During the `make config`, be sure to answer "yes" to the question whether you want to boot the kernel via SRM.

```
cd /usr/src/linux
make config
make dep
make boot
```

The last command will build the file `arch/alpha/boot/vmlinux.gz` which can then be copied to the disk from which you want to boot from. In our floppy disk example above, this would entail:

```
mount /dev/fd0 /mnt
cp arch/alpha/boot/vmlinux.gz /mnt
umount /mnt
```

3.6 Booting Linux

With the SRM firmware and `aboot` installed, Linux is generally booted with a command of the form:

```
boot devicename -fi filename -fl flags
```

The *filename* and *flags* arguments are optional. If they are not specified, SRM uses the default values stored in environment variables `BOOT_OSFILE` and `BOOT_OSFLAGS`. The syntax and meaning of these two arguments is described in more detail below.

3.6.1 Boot Filename

The filename argument takes the form:

   [*n*/]*filename*

n is a single digit in the range 1..8 that gives the partition number from which to boot from. *filename* is the path of the file you want boot. For example to boot from the second partition of SCSI device 6, you would enter:

```
boot dka600 -file 2/vmlinux.gz
```

Or to boot from floppy drive 0, you'd enter:

```
boot dva0 -file vmlinux.gz
```

If a disk has no partition table , aboot pretends the disk contains one ext2 partition starting at the first diskblock. This allows booting from floppy disks.

As a special case, partition number 0 is used to request booting from a disk that does not (yet) contain a file system. When specifying "partition" number 0, aboot assumes that the Linux kernel is stored right behind the aboot image. Such a layout can be achieved with the swriteboot command. For example, to setup a filesystem-less boot from /dev/sda, one could use the command:

```
swriteboot /dev/sda bootlx vmlinux.gz
```

Booting a system in this way is not normally necessary. The reason this feature exists is to make it possible to get Linux installed on a systems that can't boot from a floppy disk (e.g., the Jensen).

3.6.2 Boot Flags

A number of bootflags can be specified. The syntax is:

```
-flags "options..."
```

Where "options..." is any combination the following options (separated by blanks). There are many more bootoptions, depending on what drivers your kernel has installed. The options listed below are therefore just examples to illustrate the general idea:

load_ramdisk=1

> Copy root file system from a (floppy) disk to the RAM disk before starting the system. The RAM disk will be used in lieu of the root device. This is useful to bootstrap Linux on a system with only one floppy drive.

floppy=*str*

> Sets floppy configuration to *str*.

root=*dev*

> Select device *dev* as the root-file system. The device can be specified as a major/minor hex number (e.g., 0x802 for /dev/sda2) or one of a few canonical names (e.g., /dev/fd0, /dev/sda2).

single

> Boot system in single user mode.

kgdb

> Enable kernel-gdb (works only if CONFIG_KGDB is enabled; a second Alpha system needs to be connected over the serial port in order to make this work)

Some SRM implementations (e.g., the one for the Jensen) are handicapped and allow only short option strings (e.g., at most 8 characters). In such a case, aboot can be booted with the single-character boot flag "i". With this flag, aboot will prompt the user to intercively enter a boot option string of up to 256 characters. For example:

```
boot dka0 -fl i
aboot> 3/vmlinux.gz root=/dev/sda3 single
```

Since booting in that manner quickly becomes tedious, aboot allows to define short-hands for frequently used commandlines. In particular, a single digit option (0-9) requests that aboot uses the corresponding option string stored in file /etc/aboot.conf. A sample aboot.conf is shown below:

```
#
# aboot default configurations
#
0:3/vmlinux.gz root=/dev/sda3
1:3/vmlinux.gz root=/dev/sda3 single
2:3/vmlinux.new.gz root=/dev/sda3
3:3/vmlinux root=/dev/sda3
8:- root=/dev/sda3           # fs-less boot of raw kernel
9:0/vmlinux.gz root=/dev/sda3 # fs-less boot of (compressed) ECOFF kernel
```

With this configuration file, the command

```
boot dka0 -fl 1
```

corresponds exactly to the boot command shown above. It is quite easy to forget what number corresponds to what option string. To alleviate this problem, boot with option "h" and `aboot` will print the contents of `/etc/aboot.conf` before issueing the prompt for the full option string.

Finally, whenever `aboot` prompts for an option string, it is possible to enter one of the single character flags ("i", "h", or "0"-"9") to get the same effect as if that flag had been specified in the boot command line. For example, you could boot with flag "i" and then type "h" (followed by return) to remind yourself of the contents of `/etc/aboot.conf`

Selecting the Partition of /etc/aboot.conf When installed on a harddisk, `aboot` needs to know what partition to search for the `/etc/aboot.conf` file. A newly compiled `aboot` will search the *second* partition (e.g., `/dev/sda2`). Since it would be inconvenient to have to recompile `aboot` just to change the partition number, `abootconf` allows to directly modify an installed `aboot`. Specifically, if you want to change `aboot` to use the *third* partition on disk `/dev/sda`, you'd use the command:

```
abootconf /dev/sda 3
```

You can verify the current setting by simply omitting the partition number. That is: `abootconf /dev/sda` will print the currently selected partition number. Note that `aboot` does have to be installed already for this command to succeed. Also, when installing a new `aboot`, the partition number will fall back to the default (i.e., it will be necessary to rerun `abootconf`).

Since `aboot` version 0.5, it is also possible to select the `aboot.conf` partition via the boot command line. This can be done with a command line of the form $a:b$ where a is the partition that holds `/etc/aboot.conf` and b is a single-letter option as described above (0-9, i, or h). For example, if you type `boot -fl "3:h" dka100` the system boots from SCSI ID 1, loads `/etc/aboot.conf` from the third partition, prints its contents on the screen and waits for you to enter the boot options.

3.7   Booting Over the Network

Two prelimenary steps are necessary before Linux can be booted via a network. First, you need to set the SRM environment variables to enable booting via the bootp protocol and second you need to setup another machine as the your boot server. Please refer to the SRM documentation that came with your machine for information on how to enable bootp. Setting up the boot server is obviously dependent on what operating system that machine is running, but typically it involves starting the program `bootpd` in the background after configuring the `/etc/bootptab` file. The `bootptab` file has one entry describing each client that is allowed to boot from the server. For example, if you want to boot the machine `myhost.cs.arizona.edu`, then an entry of the following form would be needed:

```
myhost.cs.arizona.edu:\
        :hd=/remote/:bf=vmlinux.bootp:\
        :ht=ethernet:ha=08012B1C51F8:hn:vm=rfc1048:\
        :ip=192.12.69.254:bs=auto:
```

This entry assumes that the machine's Ethernet address is `08012B1C51F8` and that its IP address is 192.12.69.254. The Ethernet address can be found with the `show device` command of the SRM console or, if Linux is running, with the `ifconfig` command. The entry also defines that if the client does not specify otherwise, the file that will be booted is `vmlinux.bootp` in directory `/remote`. For more information on configuring `bootpd`, please refer to its man page.

Next, build `aboot` with with the command `make netboot`. Make sure the kernel that you want to boot has been built already. By default, the `aboot Makefile` uses the kernel in `/usr/src/linux/arch/alpha/boot/vmlinux.gz` (edit the `Makefile` if you want to use a different path). The result of `make netboot` is a file called `vmlinux.bootp` which contains `aboot` *and* the Linux kernel, ready for network booting.

Finally, copy `vmlinux.bootp` to the bootsever's directory. In the example above, you'd copy it into `/remote/vmlinux.bootp`. Next, power up the client machine and boot it, specifying the Ethernet adapter as the boot device. Typically, SRM calls the first Ethernet adapter ewa0, so to boot from that device, you'd use the command:

```
boot ewa0
```

The `-fi` and `-fl` options can be used as usual. In particular, you can ask `aboot` to prompt for Linux kernel arguments by specifying the option `-fl i`.

4 Sharing a Disk With DEC Unix

Unfortunately, DEC Unix doesn't know anything about Linux, so sharing a single disk between the two OSes is not entirely trivial. However, it is not a difficult task if you heed the tips in this section. The section assumes you are using `aboot` version 0.5 or newer.

4.1 Partitioning the disk

First and foremost: *never* use any of the Linux partitioning programs (`minlabel` or `fdisk`) on a disk that is also used by DEC Unix. The Linux `minlabel` program uses the same partition table format as DEC Unix `disklabel`, but there are some incompatibilities in the data that `minlabel` fills in, so DEC Unix will simply refuse to accept a partition table generated by `minlabel`. To setup a Linux `ext2` partition under DEC Unix, you'll have to change the disktab entry for your disk. For the purpose of this discussion, let's assume that you have an rz26 disk (a common 1GB drive) on which you want to install Linux. The disktab entry under DEC Unix v3.2 looks like this (see file `/etc/disktab`):

```
rz26|RZ26|DEC RZ26 Winchester:\
        :ty=winchester:dt=SCSI:ns#57:nt#14:nc#2570:\
        :oa#0:pa#131072:ba#8192:fa#1024:\
        :ob#131072:pb#262144:bb#8192:fb#1024:\
        :oc#0:pc#2050860:bc#8192:fc#1024:\
        :od#393216:pd#552548:bd#8192:fd#1024:\
        :oe#945764:pe#552548:be#8192:fe#1024:\
        :of#1498312:pf#552548:bf#8192:ff#1024:\
        :og#393216:pg#819200:bg#8192:fg#1024:\
        :oh#1212416:ph#838444:bh#8192:fh#1024:
```

The interesting fields here are o?, and p?, where ? is a letter in the range a-h (first through 8-th partition). The o value gives the starting offset of the partition (in sectors) and the p value gives the size of the partition (also in sectors). See `disktab(4)` for more info. Note that DEC Unix likes to define overlapping partitions. For the entry above, the partition layout looks like this (you can verify this by adding up the various o and p values):

```
      a         b            d             e            f
|---|-------|-----------|------------|-----------|
```

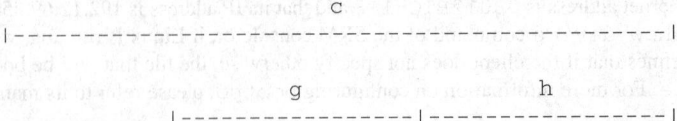

DEC Unix insists that partition a starts at offset 0 and that partition c spans the entire disk. Other than that, you can setup the partition table any way you like.

Let's suppose you have DEC Unix using partition g and want to install Linux on partition h with partition b being a (largish) swap partition. To get this layout without destroying the existing DEC Unix partition, you need to set the partition types explicitly. You can do this by adding a t field for each partition. In our case, we add the following line to the above disktab entry.

```
:ta=unused:tb=swap:tg=4.2BSD:th=resrvd8:
```

Now why do we mark partition h as "resrvd8" instead of "ext2"? Well, DEC Unix doesn't know about Linux. It so happens that partition type "ext2" corresponds to a numeric value of 8, and DEC Unix uses the string "resrvd8" for that value. Thus, in DEC Unix speak, "resrvd8" means "ext2". OK, this was the hard part. Now we just need to install the updated disktab entry on the disk. Let's assume the disk has SCSI id 5. In this case, we'd do:

```
disklabel -rw /dev/rrz5c rz26
```

You can verify that everything is all right by reading back the disklabel with disklabel -r /dev/rrz5c. At this point, you may want to reboot DEC Unix and make sure the existing DEC Unix partition is still alive and well. If that is the case, you can shut down the machine and start with the Linux installation. Be sure to skip the disk partitioning step during the install. Since we already installed a good partition table, you should be able to proceed and select the 8th partition as the Linux root partition and the 2nd partition as the swap partition. If the disk is, say, the second SCSI disk in the machine, then the device name for these partitions would be /dev/sdb8 and /dev/sdb2, respectively (note that Linux uses letters to name the drives and numbers to name the partitions, which is exactly reversed from what DEC Unix does; the Linux scheme makes more sense, of course ;-).

4.2 Installing aboot

First big caveat: with the SRM firmware, you can boot one and only one operating system per disk. For this reason, it is generally best to have at least two SCSI disks in a machine that you want to dualboot between Linux and DEC Unix. Of course, you could also boot Linux from a floppy if speed doesn't matter or over the network, if you have a bootp-capable server. But in this section we assume you want to boot Linux from a disk that contains one or more DEC Unix partitions.

Second big caveat: installing aboot on a disk shared with DEC Unix renders the first and third partition unusable (since those *must* have a starting offset of 0). For this reason, we recommend that you change the size of partition a to something that is just big enough to hold aboot (1MB should be plenty).

Once these two caveats are taken care of, installing aboot is almost as easy as usual: since partition a and c will overlap with aboot, we need to tell swriteboot that this is indeed OK. We can do this under Linux with a command line of the following form (again, assuming we're trying to install aboot on the second SCSI disk):

```
swriteboot -f1 -f3 /dev/sdb bootlx
```

The -f1 means that we want to force writing bootlx even though it overlaps with partition 1. The corresponding applies for partition 3.

This is it. You should now be able to shutdown the system and boot Linux from the harddisk. In our example, the SRM command line to do this would be:

```
boot dka5 -fi 8/vmlinux.gz -fl root=/dev/sdb8
```

Part XXXIX

"Linux Security HOWTO" Kevin Fenzi and Dave Wreski

kevin@scrye.com and dave@nic.com

v0.9.11, 1 May 1998

This document is a general overview of security issues that face the administrator of Linux systems. It covers general security philosophy and a number of specific examples of how to better secure your Linux system from intruders. Also included are pointers to security related material and programs. NOTE: This is a beta version of this document. Improvements, constructive criticism, additions and corrections are gratefully accepted. Please mail your feedback to both authors. Be sure and include "Linux", "security" or "HOWTO" in the subject line of your mail to avoid spam filters and to bring your mail to the quick attention of the authors.

Contents

1   Introduction

This document covers some of the main security issues that affect Linux security. General philosophy and net born resources are discussed.

A number of other HOWTO documents overlap with security issues, and those have been pointed to wherever appropriate.

This document is NOT meant to be a up to date exploits document. Large numbers of new exploits happen all the time. This document will tell you where to look for such up to date information, and some general methods to prevent such exploits from taking place.

1.1   New Versions of this Document

New versions of this document will be periodically posted to *comp.os.linux.answers*. They will also be added to the various anonymous FTP sites who archive such information, including:

`ftp://sunsite.unc.edu/pub/Linux/docs/HOWTO`

In addition, you should generally be able to find this document on the Linux Worldwide Web home page via:

`http://sunsite.unc.edu/mdw/linux.html`

Finally, the very latest version of this document should also be available in various formats from:

`http://scrye.com/~kevin/lsh/`

1.2 Feedback

All comments, error reports, additional information and criticism of all sorts should be directed to:

kevin@scrye.com

and

dave@nic.com

NOTE: Please send your feedback to _both_ authors. Also, be sure and include "Linux" "security" or "HOWTO" in your subject to avoid kevin's spam filter.

1.3 Disclaimer

No liability for the contents of this documents can be accepted. Use the concepts, examples and other content at your own risk. Additionally, this is an early version, with many possibilities for inaccuracies and errors.

A number of the examples and descriptions use the RedHat(tm) package layout and system setup. Your mileage may vary.

As far as we know, only programs that under certain terms may be used or evaluated for personal purposes will be described. Most of the programs will be available complete with source under GNU-like terms.

1.4 Copyright Information

This document is copyrighted (c)1998 Kevin Fenzi and Dave Wreski, and distributed under the following terms:

- Linux HOWTO documents may be reproduced and distributed in whole or in part, in any medium physical or electronic, as long as this copyright notice is retained on all copies. Commercial redistribution is allowed and encouraged; however, the authors would like to be notified of any such distributions.

- All translations, derivative works, or aggregate works incorporating any Linux HOWTO documents must be covered under this copyright notice. That is, you may not produce a derivative work from a HOWTO and impose additional restrictions on its distribution. Exceptions to these rules may be granted under certain conditions; please contact the Linux HOWTO coordinator at the address given below.

- If you have questions, please contact Tim Bynum, the Linux HOWTO coordinator, at

linux-howto@sunsite.unc.edu

2 Overview

This document will attempt to explain some procedures and commonly used software to help your Linux system be more secure. It is important to discuss some of the basic concepts first, and create a security foundatation before we get started.

2.1 Why Do We Need Security?

In the ever-changing world of global data communications, inexpensive Internet connections, and fast-paced software development, security is becomming more and more of an issue. Security is now a basic requirement because global computing is inherently insecure. As your data goes from point A to point B on the Internet, for example, it may pass through several other points along the way, giving other users the opportunity to intercept, and even alter, your data. Even other users on your system may maliciously transform your data into something you did not intend. Unauthorized access to your system may be obtained by intruders, also known as "crackers", who then use advanced knowledge to impersonate you, steal information from you, or even deny you access to your own resources. If you're still wondering what the difference is between a "Hacker" and a "Cracker", see Eric Raymond's document, "How to Become A Hacker", available at *http://sagan.earthspace.net/~esr/faqs/hacker-howto.html*.

2.2 How Secure Is Secure?

First, keep in mind that no computer system can ever be "completely secure". All you can do is make it increasingly difficult for someone to compromise your system. For the average home Linux user, not much is required to keep the casual cracker at bay. For high profile Linux users (banks, telecommunications companies, etc), much more work is required.

Another factor to take into account is that the more secure your system is the more intrusive your security becomes. You need to decide where in this balancing act your system is still usable and yet secure for your purposes. For instance, you could require everyone dialing into your system to use a call back modem to call them back at their home number. This is more secure, but if someone is not at home, it makes it difficult for them to login. You could also setup your Linux system with no network or connection to the Internet, but this makes it harder to surf the web.

If you are a large to medium-sized site, you should establish a "Security Policy" stating how much security is required by your site and what auditing is in place to check it. You can find a well-known security policy example at *http://ds.internic.net/rfc/rfc2196.txt*. It has been recently updated, and contains a great framework for establishing a security policy for your company.

2.3 What Are You Trying to Protect?

Before you attempt to secure your system, you should determine what level of threat you have to protect against, what risks you should or should not take, and how vulnerable your system is as a result. You should analyze your system to know what you're protecting, why you're protecting it, what value it has, and who has responsibility for your data and other assets.

- Risk is the possibility that an intruder may be successful in attempting to access your computer. Can an intruder read, write files, or execute programs that could cause damage? Can they delete critical data? Prevent you or your company from getting important work done? Don't forget, someone gaining access to your account, or your system, can also impersonate you. Additionally, having one insecure account on your system can result in your entire network being compromised. A single user that is allowed to login using an rhosts file, or allowing the use of an insecure service, such as tftp, you risk an intruder using this to 'get his foot in the door'. Once the intruder has a user account on your system, or someone else's system, it can be used to gain access to another system, or another account.

- Threat is typically from someone with motivation to gain unauthorized access to your network, or computer. You must decide who you trust to have access to your system, and what threat they could impose. There are several types of intruders, and it is useful to keep the different characteristics in mind as you are securing your systems.

  - **The Curious** - This type of intruder is basically interested in finding out what type of system and data, you have.

  - **The Malicious** - This type of intruder is out to either bring down your systems, or deface your web page, or otherwise cause you time and money to recover.

  - **The High-Profile Intruder** - This type of intruder is trying to use your system to gain popularity and infamy. He might use your high-profile system to advertise his abilities.

  - **The Competition** - This type of intruder is interested in what data you have on your system. It might be someone who thinks you have something that could benefit him financially, or otherwise.

- Vulnerability describes how well protected your computer is from another network, and the potential for someone gaining unauthorized access. What's at stake if someone breaks into your system? Of course the concerns of a dynamic PPP home user will be different than those of a company connecting their machine to the Internet, or another large network.

  How much time would it take to retrieve/recreate any data that was lost? An initial time investment now can save ten times more time later if you have to recreate data that was lost. Have you checked your backup strategy, and verified your data lately?

2.4   Developing A Security Policy

Create a simple, generic policy for your system that your users can readily understand and follow. It should protect the data you're safeguarding, as well as the privacy of the users. Some things to consider adding are who has access to the system (Can my friend use my account?), who's allowed to install software on the system, who owns what data, disaster recovery, and appropriate use of the system.

A generally accepted security policy starts with the phrase:

> **"That which is not permitted is prohibited"**

This means that unless you grant access to a service for a user, that user shouldn't be using that service until you do grant access. Make sure the policies work on your regular user account, Saying, "Ah, I can't figure this permissions problem out, I'll just do it as root" can lead to security holes that are very obvious, and even ones that haven't been exploited yet.

2.5   Means of Securing Your Site

This document will discuss various means in which you can secure the assets you have worked hard for: your local machine, data, users, network, even your reputation. What would happen to your reputation if an intruder deleted some of your user's data? Or defaced your web site? Or published your company's corporate project plan for next quarter? If you are planning a network installation, there are many factors you must take into account before adding a single machine to your network.

Even if you have a single dialup PPP account, or just a small site, this does not mean intruders won't be interested in your systems. Large, high profile sites are not the only targets, many intruders simply want to exploit as many sites as possible, regardless of their size. Additionally, they may use a security hole in your site to gain access to other sites you're connected to.

Intruders have a lot of time on their hands, and can avoid guessing how you've obscured your system just by trying all the possibilities. There are also several reasons an intruder may be interested in your systems, which we will discuss later.

2.5.1   Host Security

Perhaps the area of most concentration on security is done with host-based security. This typically involves making sure your own system is secure, and hoping everyone else on your network does the same. Choosing good passwords, securing your host's local network services, keeping good accounting records, and upgrading programs with known security exploits are among the things the local security administrator is responsible for doing. Although this is absolutely necessary, it can become a daunting task once your network of machines becomes larger.

2.5.2   Your Network Security

Network security is also as necessary as local host security. With your single system, or a distributed computing network, the Internet, or hundreds, if not thousands or more computers on the same network, you can't rely on each one of those systems being secure. Making sure authorized users are the only ones permitted to use your network resources, building firewalls, using strong encryption, and ensuring there are no rogue, or unsecured, machines on your network are all part of the network security administrator's duties.

This document will discuss some of the techniques used to secure your site, and hopefully show you some of the ways to prevent an intruder from gaining access to what you are trying to protect.

2.5.3   Security Through Obscurity

One type of security that must be discussed is "security through obscurity". This means that by doing something like changing the login name from 'root' to 'toor', for example, to try and obscure someone from breaking into your system as root is only a false sense of security, and will result in very unpleasant consequences. Rest assured that any system attacker will quickly see through such empty security measures. Simply because you may have a small site, or relatively low profile does not mean an intruder won't be interested in what you have. We'll discuss what your protecting in the next sections.

2.6 Organization of This Document

This document has been segregated into a number of sections. They cover several broad kinds of security issues. The first, physical security, covers how you need to protect your physical machine from tampering. The second describes how to protect your system from tampering by local users. The third, files and filesystem security show you how to setup your filesystems and premissions on your files. The next, password security and encryption discusses how to use encryption to better secure your machine and network. Kernel security discusses what kernel options you should set or be aware of for a more secure machine. network security, describes how to better secure your Linux system from network attacks. Security preperation discusses how to prepair your machine(s) before bringing the on-line. The next discusses what to do when you detect a system compromise in progress or detect one that has recently happened. Then links to other security resources are enumerated, and finally some questions and answers and a few closing words.

The two main points to realize when reading this document are:

- Be aware of your system. Check system logs such as /var/log/messages and keep an eye on your system, and

- Two, keep your system up to date by making sure you have installed the current versions of software and have upgraded per security alerts. Just doing this will help make your system markedly more secure.

3   Physical Security

The first "layer" of security you need to take into account is the physical security of your computer systems. Who has direct physical access to your machine? Should they? Can you protect your machine from their tampering? Should you?

How much physical security you need on your system is very dependent on your situation, and/or budget.

If you are a home user, you probably don't need a lot (although you might need to protect your machine from tampering by children or annoying relatives). If you are in a Lab environment, you need considerably more, but users will still need to be able to get work done on the machines. Many of the following sections will help out. If you are in a Office, you may or may not need to secure your machine off hours or while you are away. At some companies, leaving your console unsecured is a termination offense.

Obvious physical security methods such as locks on doors, cables, locked cabinets, and video survailance are all a good idea, but beyond the scope of this document. :)

3.1   Computer locks

Many more modern pc cases include a "locking" feature. Usually this will be a socket on the front of the case that allows you to turn an included key to a locked or unlocked position. Case locks can help prevent someone from stealing your pc, or opening up the case and directly manipulating/stealing your hardware. They can also sometimes prevent someone from rebooting your computer on their own floppy or other hardware.

These case locks do different things according to the support in the motherboard and how the case is constructed. On many pc's they make it so you have to break the case to get the case open. On some others they make it so that it will not let you plug in new keyboards and mice. Check your motherboard or case instructions for more information. This can sometimes be a very useful feature, even though the locks are usually very low quality and can easily be defeated by attackers with locksmithing.

Some cases (most notably sparcs and macs) have a dongle on the back that if you put a cable through attackers would have to cut the cable or break the case to get into it. Just putting a padlock or combo lock through these can be a good deterrent to someone stealing your machine.

3.2   BIOS Security

The BIOS is the lowest level of software that configures or manipulates your x86 based hardware. LILO and other Linux boot methods access the BIOS to determine how to boot up your Linux machine. Other hardware that Linux runs on has similar software (OpenFirmware on macs and new suns, sun boot prom, etc...). You can use your BIOS to prevent attackers from rebooting your machine and manipulating your linux system.

Under Linux/x86 many PC BIOSs let you set a boot password. This doesn't provide all that much security (bios can be reset, or removed if someone can get into the case), but might be a good deterant (ie it will take time and leave traces of tampering).

Many x86 bioses also allow you to specify various other good security settings. Check your bios manual or look at it the next time you boot up. Some examples are: disallow booting from floppy drives and passwords to access some bios features.

On Linux/Sparc, your SPARC EEPROM can be set to require a boot-up password. This might slow attackers down.

NOTE: If you have a server machine, and you setup a boot password, your machine will not boot up unattended. Keep in mind that you will need to come in and supply the password in the even of a power failure. ;(

3.3 Boot Loader Security

The various Linux boot loaders also can have a boot password set. Using lilo, take a look at the "restricted" and "password" settings. "password" allows you to set a bootup password. "restricted" will let the machine boot _unless_ someone specifies options at the lilo: prompt (like 'single').

Keep in mind when setting all these passwords that you need to remember them. :) Also remember that these passwords will mearly slow the determined attacker. This won't prevent someone from booting from a floppy, and mounting your root partition. If you are using security in conjunction with a boot loader, you might as well disable booting from a floppy in your computer's BIOS, as well as password-protecting your computer's BIOS.

If anyone has security related information from a different boot loader, we would love to hear it. (grub, silo, milo, linload, etc).

NOTE: If you have a server machine, and you setup a boot password, your machine will not boot up unattended. Keep in mind that you will need to come in and supply the password in the even of a power failure. ;(

3.4 xlock and vlock

If you wander away from your machine from time to time, it is nice to be able to "lock" your console so that no one tampers with or looks at your work. Two programs that do this are: xlock and vlock.

Xlock is a X display locker. It should be included in any Linux distributions that support X. Check out the man page for it for more options, but in general you can run xlock from any xterm on your console and it will lock the display and require your password to unlock.

vlock is a simple little program that allows you to lock some or all of the virtual consoles on your Linux box. You can lock just the one you are working in or all of them. If you just lock one, others can come in and use the console, they will just not be able to use your vty until you unlock it. vlock ships with redhat Linux, but your mileage may vary.

Of course locking your console will prevent someone from tampering with your work, but does not prevent them from rebooting your machine or otherwise disrupting your work. It also does not prevent them from accessing your machine from another machine on the network and causing problems.

3.5 Detecting Physical Security Compromises

The first thing to always note is when your machine was rebooted. Since Linux is a robust and stable OS, the only times your machine should reboot is when YOU take it down for OS upgrades, hardware swapping, or the like. If your machine has rebooted without you doing it, a trouble light should go on. Many of the ways that your machine can be compromised require the intruder to reboot or power off your machine.

Check for signs of tampering on the case and computer area. Although many intruders clean traces of their presence out of logs, it's a good idea to check through them all and note any discrepancy.

Some things to check for in your logs:

- Short or incomplete logs.
- Logs containing strange timestamps.
- Logs with incorrect permissions or ownership.
- Records of reboots or restarting of services.
- missing logs.
- su entries or logins from strange places.

We will discuss system log data later in the HOWTO.

4 Local Security

The next thing to take a look at is the security in your system against attacks from local users. Did we just say _local_ users? yes.

Getting access to a local user is one of the first things that system intruders attempt, while on their way to exploiting the root account. With lax local security, they can then "upgrade" their normal user access to root access using a variety of bugs and poorly setup local services. If you make sure your local security is tight, then the intruder will have another hurdle to jump.

Local users can also cause a lot of havoc with your system even (especially) if they really are who they say they are. Providing accounts to people you don't know or have no contact information for is a very bad idea.

4.1 Creating New Accounts

You should make sure to provide user accounts with only the minimal requirements for the task they need to do. If you provide your son (age 10) with an account, you might want them to only have access to a word processor or drawing program, but be unable to delete data that is not his.

Several good rules of thumb when allowing other people legitimate access to your Linux machine:

- Give them the minimal amount of privileges they need.
- Be aware when/where they login from, or should be logging in from.
- Make sure and remove their account when they no longer need the access.

Many local user accounts that are used in security compromises are ones that have not been used in months or years. Since no one is using them they provide the ideal attack vehicle.

4.2 Root Security

The most sought-after account on your machine is the superuser account. This account has authority over the entire machine, which may also include authority over other machines on the network. Remember that you should only use the root account for very short specific tasks and should mostly run as a normal user. Running as root all the time is a very very very bad idea.

Several tricks to avoid messing up your own box as root:

- When doing some complex command, try running it first in a non destructive way...especially commands that use globbing: ie, you are going to do a "rm foo*.bak", instead, first do: "ls foo*.bak" and make sure you are going to delete the files you think you are. Using echo in place of destructive commands also sometimes works.

HOWTO

- Some people find it helpfull to do a "touch /-i" on their systems. This will make commands like: "rm -rf *" ask you if you really want to delete all the files. (It does this by your shell resolving the "-i" file first, and treating it as the -i option to rm.) This will not help with rm statements with no * in them. ;(

- Only become root to do single specific tasks. If you find yourself trying to figure out how to do something, go back to a normal user shell until you are **sure** what needs to be done by root.

- The command path for the root user is very important. The command path, or the PATH environment variable, defines the location the shell searches for programs. Try and limit the command path for the root user as much as possible, and never use '.', meaning 'the current directory', in your PATH statement. Additionally, never have writable directories in your search path, as this can allow attackers to modify or place new binaries in your search path, allowing them to run as root the next time you run that command.

- Never use the rlogin/rsh/rexec (called the r-utilities) suite of tools as root. They are subject to many sorts of attacks, and are downright dangerous run as root. Never create a .rhosts file for root.

- The /etc/securetty file contains a list of terminals that root can login from. By default (on Red Hat Linux) this is set to only the local virtual consoles(vtys). Be very careful of adding anything else to this file. You should be able to login remotely as your regular user account and then 'su' if you need to (hopefully over ssh or other encrypted channel), so there is no need to be able to login directly as root.

- Always be slow and deliberate running as root. Your actions could affect a lot of things. Think before you type!

If you absolutely positively need to allow someone (hopefully very trusted) to have superuser access to your machine, there are a few tools that can help. Sudo allows users to use their password to access a limited set of commands as root. This would allow you to, for instance, let a user be able to eject and mount removable media on your Linux box, but have no other root privileges. sudo also keeps a log of all successfull and unsuccessful sudo attempts, allowing you to track down who used what command to do what. For this reason sudo works well even in places where a number of people have root access, but use sudo so you can keep track of changes made.

Although sudo can be used to give specific users specific privileges for specific tasks, it does have several shortcomings. It should be used only for a limited set of tasks, like restarting a server, or adding new users. Any program that offers a shell escape will give the user root access. This includes most editors, for example. Also, a program as innocous as /bin/cat can be used to overwrite files, which could allow root to be exploited. Consider sudo as a means for accountability, and don't expect it to replace the root user yet be secure.

5   Files and Filesystem Security

A few minutes of preparation and planning ahead before putting your systems online can help to protect your system, and the data that is stored on them.

- There should never be a reason for user's home directories to allow SUID/SGID programs to be run from there. Use the 'nosuid' option in /etc/fstab for partitions that are writable by others than root. You may also wish to use 'nodev' and 'noexec' on user's home partitions, as well as /var, which prohibit execution of programs, and creation of character or block devices, which should never be necessary anyway.

- If you are exporting filesystems using NFS, be sure to configure /etc/exports with the most restrictive access possible. This means not using wildcards, not allowing root write access, and mounting read-only wherever possible.

- Configure your user's file-creation umask to be as restrictive as possible. Commonly used settings are 022, 033, and the most restrictive 077, and are added to /etc/profile.

- Set filesystem limits instead of allowing 'unlimited' as is the default. You can control the per-user limits using the resource-limits PAM module and /etc/pam.d/limits.conf. For example, limits for group 'users' might look like this:

```
@users          hard    core    0
@users          hard    nproc   50
@users          hard    rss     5000
```

This says to prohibit the creation of core files, restrict the number of processes to 50, and restrict memory usage per user to 5M.

- The /var/log/wtmp and /var/run/utmp files contain the login records for all users on your system. Its integrity must be maintained because it can be used to determine when and from where a user (or potential intruder) has entered your system. These files should also have 644 permissions, without affecting normal system operation.

- The immutable bit can be used to prevent accidentally deleting or overwriting a file that must be protected. It also prevents someone from creating a symbolic link to this file, which has been the source of attacks involving deleting /etc/passwd or /etc/shadow. See the chattr(1) man page for information on the immutable bit.

- SUID and SGID files on your system are a potential security risk, and should be monitored closely. Because these programs grant special privileges to the user who is executing them, it is necessary to ensure that insecure programs are not installed. A favorite trick of crackers is to exploit SUID "root" programs, then leave a SUID program as a backdoor to get in the next time, even if the original hole is plugged. Find all SUID/SGID programs on your system, and keep track of what they are, so you are aware of any changes which could indicate a potential intruder. Use the following command to find all SUID/SGID programs on your system:

```
root#  find / -type f \( -perm -04000 -o -perm -02000 \)
```

You can descriminitely remove the SUID or SGID permissions on a suspicious program with chmod(1), then change it back if you absolutely feel it is necessary.

- World-writable files, particularly system files, can be a security hole if a cracker gains access to your system and modifies them. Additionally, world-writable directories are dangerous, since they allow a cracker to add or delete files as he wishes. To locate all world-writable files on your system, use the following command:

```
root# find / -perm -2 -print
```

and be sure you know why those files are writable. In the normal course of operation, several files will be writable, including some from /dev, and symbolic links.

- Unowned files may also be an indication an intruder has accessed your system. You can locate files on your system that do not have an owner, or belong to a group with the command:

```
root# find / -nouser -o -nogroup -print
```

- Finding .rhosts Files should be a part of your regular system administration duties, as these files should not be permitted on your system. Remember, a cracker only needs one insecure account to potentially gain access to your entire network. You can locate all .rhosts files on your system with the following command:

```
root# find /home -name .rhosts -print
```

- Finally, before changing permissions on any system files, make sure you understand what you are doing. Never change permissions on a file because it seems like the easy way to get things working. Always determine why the file has that permission before changing it.

5.1 Umask Settings

The umask command can be used to determine the default file creation mode on your system. It is the octal complement of the desired file mode. If files are created without any regard to their permissions settings, the user could inadvertantly give read or write permission to someone that should not have this permission. Typically umask settings include 022, 027, and 077, which is the most restrictive. Normally the umask is set in /etc/profile, so it applies to all users on the system. For example, you may have a line that looks like this:

```
# Set the user's default umask
umask 033
```

Be sure to make root's umask 077, which will disable read, write, and execute permission for other users, unless explicitly changed using chmod(1).

If you are using Red Hat, and adhered to their user and group ID creation scheme (User Private Groups), it is only necessary to use 002 for a umask. This is due to the fact that the default configuration is one user per group.

5.2 File Permissions

It's important to insure that your system files are not open for casual editing by users and groups who shouldn't be doing such system maintance.

UNIX seperates access control on files and directories according to three characteristics: owner, group, and other. There is always exactly one owner, any number of members of the group, and everyone else.

A quick explanation of unix permissions:

Ownership - Which user(s) and group(s) retain(s) control of the permission settings of the node and parent of the node

Permissions - Bits capable of being set or reset to allow certain types of access to it. Permissions for directories may have a different meaning than the same set of permissions on files.

Read:

- To be able to view contents of a file
- To be able to read a directory

Write:

- To be able to add to or change a file
- To be able to delete or move files in a directory

Execute:

- To be able to run a binary program or shell script
- To be able to search in a directory, combined with read permission

Save Text Attribute: (For directories)

The sticky bit also has a different meaning when applied to directories. If the sticky bit is set on a directory, then a user may only delete files that the user owns or for which he has explicit write permission granted, even when he has write access to the directory. This is designed for directories like /tmp, which are world-writable, but where it may not be desirable to allow any user to delete files at will. The sticky bit is seen as a 't' in a long directory listing.

SUID Attribute: (For Files)

This describes set-user-id permissions on the file. When the set user ID access mode is set in the owner permissions, and the file is executable, processes which run it are granted access to system resources based on the user who created the process. This is the cause of many 'buffer overflow' exploits.

SGID Attribute: (For Files)

If set in the group permissions, this bit controls the "set group id" status of a file. This behaves the same way as SUID, except the group is affected instead. The file must also be executable for this to have any effect.

SGID Attribute: (For directories)

If you set the SGID bit on a directory (with "chmod g+s directory"), files created in that directory will have their group set to the directory's group.

You - The owner of the file

Group - The group you belong to

Everyone - Anyone on the system that is not the owner or a member of the group

File Example:

```
        -rw-r--r--  1 kevin  users         114 Aug 28  1997 .zlogin
     1st bit - directory?                (no)
       2nd bit - read by owner?          (yes, by kevin)
        3rd bit - write by owner?        (yes, by kevin)
         4th bit - execute by owner?     (no)
          5th bit - read by group?       (yes, by users)
           6th bit - write by group?     (no)
            7th bit - execute by group?  (no)
             8th bit - read by everyone?    (yes, by everyone)
              9th bit - write by everyone?  (no)
               10th bit - execute by everyone?  (no)
```

The following lines are examples of the minimum set of the permissions that are required to perform the access described. You may want to give more permission than what's listed, but this should describe what these minimum permissions on files do:

```
-r--------  Allow read access to the file by owner
--w-------  Allows the owner to modify or delete the file
---x------  The owner can execute this program, but not shell scripts,
              which still need read permission
---s------  Will execute with effective user ID = owner
-------s--  Will execute with effective user ID = group
-rw------T  No update of "last modified time".  Usually used for swap
              files
---t------  No effect.  (formerly sticky bit)
```

Directory Example:

```
        drwxr-xr-x  3 kevin  users        512 Sep 19 13:47 .public_html/
     1st bit - directory?                (yes, it contains many files)
       2nd bit - read by owner?          (yes, by kevin)
        3rd bit - write by owner?        (yes, by kevin)
         4th bit - execute by owner?     (yes, by kevin)
          5th bit - read by group?       (yes, by users
           6th bit - write by group?     (no)
            7th bit - execute by group?  (yes, by users)
             8th bit - read by everyone?    (yes, by everyone)
              9th bit - write by everyone?  (no)
               10th bit - execute by everyone?  (yes, by everyone)
```

The following lines are examples of the minimum set of the permissions that are required to perform the access described. You may want to give more permission than what's listed, but this should describe what these minimum permissions on directories do:

```
dr--------  The contents can be listed, but file attributes can't be read
d--x------  The directory can be entered, and used in full execution
              paths
dr-x------  File attributes can now be read by owner
d-wx------  Files can now be created/deleted, even if the directory
              isn't the current one
d------x-t  Prevents files from deletion by others with write
              access. Used on /tmp
```

```
d---s--s--  No effect
```

System configuration files (usually in /etc) are usually mode 640 (-rw-r——), and owned by root. Depending on your sites security requirements, you might adjust this. Never leave any system files writable by a group or everyone. Some configuration files, including /etc/shadow, should only be readable by root, and directories in /etc should at least not be accessible by others.

SUID Shell Scripts

SUID shell scripts are a serious security risk, and for this reason the kernel will not honor them. Regardless of how secure you think the shell script is, it can be exploited to give the cracker a root shell.

5.3 Integrity Checking with Tripwire

Another very good way to detect local (and also network) attacks on your system is to run an integrity checker like Tripwire. Tripwire runs a number of checksums on all your important binaries and config files and compares them against a database of former, known-good values as a reference. Thus, any changes in the files will be flagged.

It's a good idea to install tripwire onto a floppy, and then physically set the write protect on the floppy. This way intruders can't tamper with tripwire itself or change the database. Once you have tripwire setup, it's a good idea to run it as part of your normal security administration duties to see if anything has changed.

You can even add a crontab entry to run tripwire from your floppy every night and mail you the results in the morning. Something like:

```
# set mailto
MAILTO=kevin
# run tripwire
15 05 * * * root /usr/local/adm/tcheck/tripwire
```

will mail you a report each morning at 5:15am.

Tripwire can be a godsend to detecting intruders before you would otherwise notice them. Since a lot of files change on the average system, you have to be careful what is cracker activity and what is your own doing.

5.4 Trojan Horses

A Trojan Horse is named after the fabled ploy in Homers great literary work. The idea is that you put up a program or binary that sounds great, and get other people to download it and run it as root. Then, you can compromise their system while they are not paying attention. While they think the binary they just pulled down does one thing (and it might very well), it also compromises their security.

You should take care of what programs you install on your machine. redhat provides MD5 checksums, and PGP signs, RPM files so you can verify you are installing the real thing. Other distributions have similar methods. You should never run any binary you don't have the source for or a well known binary as root! Few attackers are willing to release source code to public scrutiny.

Although it can be complex, make sure you are getting the source for some program from it's real distribution site. If the program is going to run as root make sure either you or someone you trust has looked over the source and verified it.

6 Password Security & Encryption

One of the most important security features used today are passwords. It is important for both you and all your users to have secure, unguessable passwords. Most of the more recent Linux distributions include 'passwd' programs that do not allow you to set a easily guessable password. Make sure your passwd program is up to date and has these features.

In depth discussion of encryption is beyond the scope of this document, but a introduction is in order. Encryption is very useful, possibly even nessessary in this day and age. There are all sorts of methods of encrypting data, each with their own set of characteristics.

Most unicies (and Linux is no exception) primarily use a one-way encryption algorithm, called DES (Data Encryption Standard) to encrypt your passwords. This encrypted password is then stored in (typically) /etc/passwd (or less commonly) /etc/shadow. When you attempt to login, whatever you type in is encrypted again and compared with the entry in the file that stores your passwords. If they match, it must be the same password, and you are allowed access. Although DES is a two-way encryption algorithm (you can code and then decode a message, given the right keys), the variant that most unicies use is one-way. This means that it should not be possible to reverse the encryption to get the password from the contents of /etc/passwd (or /etc/shadow).

Brute force attacks, such as "Crack" or "John the Ripper" (see below) can often guess passwords unless your password is sufficently random. PAM modules (see below) allow you to use a different encryption routine with your passwords (MD5 or the like).

You can go to *http://consult.cern.ch/writeup/security/security_3.html* for information on how to choose a good password.

6.1 PGP and Public Key Cryptography

Public Key Cryptography, such as that which is used for PGP, involves cryptography that uses one key for encryption, and one key for decryption. Traditionally, cryptography involves using the same key for encryption that is used for decryption. This "private key" must be known to both parties, and somehow transferred from one another securely.

Public key encryption alleviates the need to securely transmit the key that is used for encryption by using two seperate keys, a public key and a private key. Each person's public key is available by anyone to do the encryption, while at the same time each person keeps his or her private key to decrypt messages encrypted with the correct public key.

There are advantages to both public key and private key cryptography, and you can read about those differences in the RSA Cryptography FAQ, listed at the end of this section.

PGP (Pretty Good Privacy) is well supported on Linux. Versions 2.6.2 and 5.0 are known to work well. For a good primer on PGP and how to use it, take a look a the PGP FAQ. *http://www.pgp.com/service/export/faq/55faq.cgi* Be sure to use the version that is applicable to your country, as due to export restrictions by the US Government, strong-encryption is considered a military weapon, and prohibited from being transferred in electronic form outside the country.

There is also a step-by-step guide for configuring PGP on Linux available at *http://mercury.chem.pitt.edu/~angel/LinuxFocus/English/November1997/article7.html* It was written for the International version of PGP, but is easily adaptable to the United States version. You may also need a patch for some of the latest versions of Linux, which is available at *ftp://sunsite.unc.edu/pub/Linux/apps/crypto*.

More information on cryptography can be found in the RSA cryptography FAQ, available at *http://www.rsa.com/rsalabs/newfaq/*. Here you will find information on such terms as "Diffie-Hellman", "public-key cryptography", "Digital Certificates", etc.

6.2 SSL, S-HTTP, HTTPS and S/MIME

Often times users ask about the differences between the various security and encryption protocols, and how to use them. While this isn't an encryption document, it is a good idea to explain briefly what each are, and where to find more information.

- **SSL:** - SSL, or Secure Sockets Layer, is an encryption method developed by Netscape to provide security over the Internet. It supports several different encryption protocols, and provides client and server authentication. SSL operates at the transport layer, creates a secure encrypted channel of data, and thus can seamlessly encrypt data of many types. This is most commonly seen when going to a secure site to view a secure online document with Communicator, and serves as the basis for secure communications with Communicator, as well as many other Netscape

Communications data encryption. More information can be found at *http://www.consensus.com/security/ssl-talk-faq.html*. Information on Netscape's other security implementations, and a good starting point for these protocols is available at *http://home.netscape.com/info/security-doc.html*.

- **S-HTTP:** - S-HTTP is another protocol that provides security services across the Internet. It was designed to provide confidentiality, authenticity, integrity, and non-repudiability [cannot be mistaken for someone else] while supporting multiple key management mechanisms and cryptographic algorithms via option negotiation between the parties involved in each transaction. S-HTTP is limited to the specific software that is implementing it, and encrypts each message individually. [From RSA Cryptography FAQ, page 138]

- **S/MIME:** - S/MIME, or Secure Multipurpose Internet Mail Extension, is an encryption standard used to encrypt electronic mail, or other types of messages on the Internet. It is an open standard developed by RSA, so it is hopefully likely we will see it on Linux one day soon. More information on S/MIME can be found at *http://home.netscape.com/assist/security/smime/overview.html*.

6.3   Linux x-kernel IPSEC Implementation

Along with CIPE, and other forms of data encryption, there is also an implemention of IPSEC for Linux. IPSEC is an effort by the IETF to create cryptographically secure communications at the IP network level, which also provides authentication, integrity, access control, and confidentiality. Information on IPSEC and Internet draft can be found at *http://www.ietf.org/html.charters/ipsec-charter.html*. You can also find links to other protocols involving key management, and an IPSEC mailing list and archives.

The Linux implementation, which is being developed at the University of Arizona, uses an object-based framework for implementing network protocols called x-kernel, and can be found at *http://www.cs.arizona.edu/xkernel/hpcc-blue/linux.html*. Most simply, the x-kernel is a method of passing messages at the kernel level, which makes for an easier implementation.

As with other forms of cryptography, it is not distributed with the kernel by default due to export restrictions.

6.4   SSH (Secure Shell), stelnet

SSH and stelnet are programs that allow you to login to remote systems and have a encrypted connection.

SSH is a suite of programs used as a secure replacement for rlogin, rsh and rcp. It uses public-key cryptography to encrypt communications between two hosts, as well as for user authentication. This can be used to securely login to a remote host or copy data between hosts, while preventing man-in-the-middle attacks (session hijacking) and DNS spoofing. It will perform data compression on your connections, and secure X11 communications between hosts. The SSH home page can be found at *http://www.cs.hut.fi/ssh/*

You can also use SSH from your Windows workstation to your Linux SSH server. There are several freely available Windows client implementations, including the one at *http://guardian.htu.tuwien.ac.at/therapy/ssh/* as well as a commercial implementation from DataFellows, at *http://www.datafellows.com*.

SSLeay is a free implmentation of Netscape's Secure Sockets Layer protocol, including several applications, such as Secure telnet, a module for Apache, several databases, as well as several algorithms including DES, IDEA and Blowfish.

Using this library, a secure telnet replacement has been created that does encryption over a telnet connection. Unlike SSH, stelnet uses SSL, the Secure Sockets Layer protocol developed by Netscape. You can find Secure telnet and Secure FTP by starting with the SSLeay FAQ, available at *http://www.psy.uq.oz.au/˜ftp/Crypto/*

6.5   PAM - Pluggable Authentication Modules

Newer versions of the Red Hat Linux distribution ship with a unified authentication scheme called "PAM". PAM allows you to change on the fly your authentication methods, requirements, and encapsulate all local authentication methods without re-compiling any of your binaries. Configuration of PAM is beyond the scope of this document, but be suer to take a look at the PAM web site for more information. *http://www.kernel.org/pub/linux/libs/pam/index.html*

Just a few of the things you can do with PAM:

- Use a non DES encryption for your passwords. (Making them harder to brute force decode)

- Set resource limits on all your users so they can't perform denial of service attacks (number of processes, amount of memory, etc)

- Enable shadow passwords (see below) on the fly

- allow specific users to login only at specific times from specific places

Within a few hours of installing and configuring your system, you can prevent many attacks before they even occur. For example, use PAM to disable the system-wide usage of dot-rhosts files in user's home directories by adding these lines to /etc/pam.d/login:

```
#
# Disable rsh/rlogin/rexec for users
#
login auth required pam_rhosts_auth.so no_rhosts
```

6.6   Cryptographic IP Encapsulation (CIPE)

The primary goal of this software is to provide a facility for secure (against eavesdropping, including traffic analysis, and faked message injection) subnetwork interconnection across an insecure packet network such as the Internet.

CIPE encrypts the data at the network level. Packets travelling between hosts on the network are encrypted. The encryption engine is placed near the driver which sends and receives packets.

This is unlike SSH, which encrypts the data by connection, at the socket level. A logical connection between programs running on different hosts is encrypted.

CIPE can be used in tunnelling, in order to create a Virtual Private Network. Low-level encryption has the advantage that it can be made to work transparently between the two networks connected in the VPN, without any change to application software.

Summarized from the CIPE documentation:

The IPSEC standards define a set of protocols which can be used (among other things) to build encrypted VPNs. However, IPSEC is a rather heavyweight and complicated protocol set with a lot of options, implementations of the full protocol set are still rarely used and some issues (such as key management) are still not fully resolved. CIPE uses a simpler approach, in which many things which can be parameterized (such as the choice of the actual encryption algorithm used) are an install-time fixed choice. This limits flexibility, but allows for a simple (and therefore efficient, easy to debug...) implementation.

Further information can be found at *http://www.inka.de/~bigred/devel/cipe.html*

As with other forms of cryptography, it is not distributed with the kernel by default due to export restrictions.

6.7   Kerberos

Kerberos is an authentication system developed by the Athena Project at MIT. When a user logs in, Kerberos authenticates that user (using a password), and provides the user with a way to prove her identity to other servers and hosts scattered around the network.

This authentication is then used by programs such as rlogin to allow the user to login to other hosts without a password (in place of the .rhosts file). The authentication is also used by the mail system in order to guarantee that mail is delivered to the correct person, as well as to guarantee that the sender is who he claims to be.

HOWTO

The overall effect of installing Kerberos and the numerous other programs that go with it is to virtually eliminate the ability of users to "spoof" the system into believing they are someone else. Unfortunately, installing Kerberos is very intrusive, requiring the modification or replacement of numerous stanard programs.

You can find more information on kerberos at *http://www.veritas.com/common/f/97042301.htm* and the code can be found at *http://nii.isi.edu/info/kerberos/*

[From: Stein, Jennifer G., Clifford Neuman, and Jeffrey L. Schiller. "Kerberos: An Authentication Service for Open Network Systems." USENIX Conference Proceedings, Dallas, Texas, Winter 1998.]

6.8   Shadow Passwords.

Shadow passwords are a means of keeping your encrypted password information secret from normal users. Normally this encrypted password is stored in your /etc/passwd file for all to read. They can then run password guesser programs on it and attempt to determine what it is. Shadow passwords save this information to a /etc/shadow file that only privileged users can read. In order to run shadow passwords you need to make sure all your utilities that need access to password information are recompiled to support it. PAM (above) also allows you to just plug in a shadow module and doesn't require re-compilation of executables. You can refer to the Shadow-Password HOWTO for further information if necessary. It is available at *http://sunsite.unc.edu/LDP/HOWTO/Shadow-Password-HOWTO.html* It is rather dated now, and will not be required for distributions supporting PAM.

6.9   Crack and John the Ripper

If for some reason your passwd program is not enforcing non easily guessable passwords, you might want to run a password cracking program and make sure your users passwords are secure.

Password cracking programs work on a simple idea. They try every word in the dictionary, and then variations on those words. They encrypt each one and check it against your encrypted password. If they get a match they are in.

There are a number of programs out there...the two most notable of which are "Crack" and "John the Ripper" *http://www.false.com/security/john/index.html* . They will take up a lot of your cpu time, but you should be able to tell if an attacker could get in using them by running them first yourself and notifying users with weak passwords. Note that an attacker would have to use some other hole first in order to get your passwd (unix /etc/passwd) file, but these are more common than you might think.

6.10   CFS - Cryptographic File System and TCFS - transparent cryptographic File System

CFS is a way of encrypting an entire file system and allow users to store encrypted files on them. It uses a NFS server running on the local machine. rpms are avail at *http://www.replay.com/redhat/* and more information on how it all works is at: *ftp://ftp.research.att.com/dist/mab/*

TCFS improves on CFS, adding more integration with the file system, so that it's transparent to any users using the file system that it's encrypted. more information at: *http://edu-gw.dia.unisa.it/tcfs/*

6.11   X11, SVGA and display security

6.11.1   X11

It's important for you to secure your graphical display to prevent attackers from doing things like: grabbing your passwords as you type them without you knowing it, reading documents or information you are reading on your screen, or even using a hole to gain superuser access. Running remote X applications over a network also can be fraught with peril, allowing sniffers to see all your interaction with the remote system.

X has a number of access control mechanisms. The simplest of them is host based. You can use xhost to specify what hosts are allowed access to your display. This is not very secure at all. If someone has access to your machine they can xhost + their machine and get in easily. Also, if you have to allow access from an untrusted machine, anyone there can compromise your display.

When using xdm (x display manager) to login, you get a much better access method: MIT-MAGIC-COOKIE-1. A 128bit cookie is generated and stored in your .Xauthorty file. If you need to allow a remote machine access to your display, you can use the xauth command and the information in your .Xauthority file to provide only that connection access. See the Remote-X-Apps mini-howto, available at *http://sunsite.unc.edu/LDP/HOWTO/mini/Remote-X-Apps.html*.

You can also use ssh (see ssh, above) to allow secure X connections. This has the advantage of also being transparent to the end user, and means that no un-encrypted data flows across the network.

Take a look at the Xsecurity man page for more information on X security. The safe bet is to use xdm to login to your console and then use ssh to go to remote sites you wish to run X programs off of.

6.11.2 SVGA

SVGAlib programs are typically SUID-root in order to access all your Linux machines video hardware. This makes them very dangerous. If they crash, you typically need to reboot your machine to get a usable console back. Make sure any SVGA programs you are running are authentic, and can at least be somewhat trusted. Even better, don't run them at all.

6.11.3 GGI (Generic Graphics Interface project)

The Linux GGI project is trying to solve several of the problems with video interfaces on Linux. GGI will move a small piece of the video code into the Linux kernel, and then control access to the video system. This means GGI will be able to restore your console at any time to a known good state. They will also allow a secure attention key, so you can be sure that there is no Trojan horse login program running on your console. *http://synergy.caltech.edu/~ggi/*

7 Kernel Security

This is a description of the kernel configuration options that relate to security, and an explanation of what they do, and how to use them.

As the kernel controls your computer's networking, it is important that the kernel is very secure, and the kernel itself won't be compromised. To prevent some of the latest networkworking attacks, you should try and keep your kernel version current. You can find new kernels at ftp://ftp.kernel.org.

7.1 Kernel Compile Options

- IP: Drop source routed frames (CONFIG_IP_NOSR) This option should be enabled. Source routed frames contain the entire path to their destination inside of the packet. This means that routers the packet goes thru does not need to inspect the packet, and just forwards it on. This could lead to data entering your system that may be a potential exploit.

- IP: Firewalling (CONFIG_IP_FIREWALL) This option is necessary if you are going to configure your machine as a firewall, do masquerading, or wish to protect your dial-up workstation from someone entering via your PPP dial-up interface.

- IP: forwarding/gatewaying (CONFIG_IP_FORWARD) If you enable IP forwarding, your Linux box essentially becomes a router. If your machine is on a network, you could be forwarding data from one network to another, and perhaps subverting a firewall that was put there to prevent this from happening. Normal dial-up users will want to disable this, and other users should concentrate on the security implications of doing this. Firewall machines will want this enabled, and used in conjunction with firewall software.

  You can enable and disable IP forwarding dynamically using the following command:

  ```
  root#  echo 1 > /proc/sys/net/ipv4/ip_forward
  ```

  and disable it with the command:

  ```
  root#  echo 0 > /proc/sys/net/ipv4/ip_forward
  ```

This file (and many other files in /proc) will always appear to be zero length, but in fact aren't. This is a newly introduced kernel feature, so be sure your using a kernel 2.0.33 or later.

- IP: firewall packet logging (CONFIG_IP_FIREWALL_VERBOSE) This option gives you information about packets your firewall received, like sender, receipient, port, etc.

- IP: always defragment (CONFIG_IP_ALWAYS_DEFRAG) Generally this option is disabled, but if you are building a firewall or a masquerading host, you will want to enable it. When data is sent from one host to another, it does not always get sent as a single packet of data, but rather it is fragmented into several pieces. The problem with this is that the port numbers are only stored in the first fragment. This means that someone can insert information into the remaining packets for your connection that aren't supposed to be there.

- IP: syn cookies (CONFIG_SYN_COOKIES) SYN Attack is a denial of service (DoS) attack that consumes all the resources on your machine, forcing you to reboot. We can't think of a reason you wouldn't normally enable this.

- Packet Signatures (CONFIG_NCPFS_PACKET_SIGNING) This is an option that is available in the 2.1 kernel series that will sign NCP packets for stronger security. Normally you can leave it off, but it is there if you do need it.

- IP: Firewall packet netlink device (CONFIG_IP_FIREWALL_NETLINK) This is a really neat option that allows you to analyze the first 128 bytes of the packets in a userspace program, to determine if you would like to accept or deny the packet, based on its validity.

7.2 Kernel Devices

There are a few block and character devices available on Linux that will also help you with security.

The two devices /dev/random and /dev/urandom are provided by the kernel to retrieve random data at any time.

Both /dev/random and /dev/urandom should be secure enough to use in generating PGP keys, SSH challenges, and other applications where secure random numbers are requisite. Attackers should be unable to predict the next number given any initial sequence of numbers from these sources. There has been a lot of effort put in to ensuring that the numbers you get from these sources are random in every sense of the word random.

The only difference is that /dev/random runs out of random bytes and it makes you wait for more to be accumulated. Note that on some systems, it can block for a long time waiting for new user-generated entry to be entered into the system. So you have to use care before using /dev/random. (Perhaps the best thing to do is to use it when you're generating sensitive keying information, and you tell the user to pound on the keyboard repeatedly until you print out "OK, enough".)

/dev/random is high quality entropy, generated from measuring the inter-interrupt times etc. It blocks until enough bits of random data are available.

/dev/urandom is similar, but when the store of entropy is running low, it'll return a cryptographically strong hash of what there is. This isn't as secure, but it's enough for most applications.

You might read from the devices using something like:

```
root#  head -c 6 /dev/urandom | uuencode -
```

This will print six random characters on the console, suitable for password generation.

See /usr/src/linux/drivers/char/random.c for a description of the algorithm.

Thanks to Theodore Y. Ts'o, Jon Lewis, and others from Linux-kernel for helping me (Dave) with this.

8 Network Security

Network security is becoming more and more important as people spend more and more time connected. Compromising network security is often much easier than physical or local, and is much more common.

There are a number of good tools to assist with network security, and more and more of them are shipping with Linux distributions.

8.1 Packet Sniffers

One of the most common ways intruders gain access to more systems on your network is by employing a packet sniffer on a already compromised host. This "sniffer" just listens on the Ethernet port for things like "Password" and "Login" and "su" in the packet stream and then logs the traffic after that. This way, attackers gain passwords for systems they are not even attempting to break into. Clear text passwords are very vulnerable to this attack.

EXAMPLE: host A has been compromised. Attacker installs a sniffer. Sniffer picks up admin logging into host B from Host C. It gets the admins personal password as they login to B. Then, the admin does a 'su' to fix a problem. They now have the root password for Host B. Later the admin lets someone telnet from his account to host Z on another site. Now the attacker has a password/login on host Z.

In this day and age, the attacker doesn't even need to compromise a system to do this, they could also bring a laptop or pc into a building and tap into your net.

Using ssh or other encrypted password methods thwarts this attack. Things like APOP for pop accounts also prevents this attack. (Normal pop logins are very vulnerable to this, as is anything that sends clear text passwords over the wire.)

8.2 System services and tcp_wrappers

As soon as you put your Linux system on ANY network the first thing to look at is what services you need to offer. Services that you do not need to offer should be disabled so that you have one less thing to worry about and attackers have one less place to look for a hole.

There are a number of ways to disable services under Linux. You can look at your /etc/inetd.conf file and see what services are being offered by your inetd. Disable any that you do not need by commenting them out (# at the beginning of the line), and then sending your inetd process a SIGHUP.

You can also remove (or comment out) services in your /etc/services file. This will mean that local clients will also be unable to find the service (ie, if you remove ftp, and try and ftp to a remote site from that machine it will fail with an unknown service message). It's usually not worth the trouble to remove services, since it provides no additional security. If a local person wanted to use ftp even tho you had commented it out, they would make their own client that use the common ftp port and would still work fine.

Some of the services you will want to leave enabled are:

- ftp
- telnet
- mail, such as pop-3 or imap
- identd
- time

If you know you are not going to use some particular package, you can also delete it entirely. rpm -e under the Red Hat distribution will erase an entire package. Under debian dpkg likely does the same thing.

Additionally, you really want to disable the rsh/rlogin/rcp utilities, including login (used by rlogin), shell (used by rcp), and exec (used by rsh) from being started in /etc/inetd.conf. These protocols are extremely insecure and have been the cause of exploits in the past.

You should check your /etc/rc.d/rcN.d, where N is your systems run level and see if any of the servers started in that directory are not needed. The files in /etc/rc.d/rcN.d are actually symbolic links to the directory /etc/rc.d/init.d. Renaming the files in the init.d directory has the effect of disabling all the symbolic links in /etc/rc.d/rcN.d. If you only wish to disable a service for a particular runlevel, rename the appropriate file with a lower-case 's', instead of the upper-case 'S', such as in S45dhcpd.

If you have BSD style rc files, you will want to check /etc/rc* for programs you don't need.

Most Linux distributions ship with tcp_wrappers "wrapping" all your tcp services. A tcp_wrapper (tcpd) is invoked from inetd instead of the real server. tcpd then checks the host that is requesting the service and either executes the real server or denies access from that host. tcpd allows you to restrict access to your tcp services. You should make a /etc/hosts.allow and add in only those hosts that need to have access to your machines services.

If you are a home dialup user, we suggest you deny ALL. tcpd also logs failed attempts to access services, so this can give you an idea that you are under attack. If you add new services, you should be sure to configure it to use tcp_wrappers TCP based. For example, a normal dial-up user can prevent outsiders from connecting to your machine, yet still have the ability to retrieve mail, and make network connections to the Internet. To do this, you might add the following to your /etc/hosts.allow:

ALL: 127.

And of course /etc/hosts.deny would contain:

ALL: ALL

which will prevent external connections to your machine, yet still allow you from the inside to connect to servers on the Internet.

8.3   Verify Your DNS Information

Keeping up-to-date DNS information about all hosts on your network can help to increase security. In the event of an unauthorized host becomes connected to your network, you can recognize it by its lack of a DNS entry. Many services can be configured to not accept connections from hosts that do not have valid DNS entries.

8.4   identd

identd is a small program that typically runs out of your inetd. It keeps track of what user is running what tcp service, and then reports this to whoever requests it.

Many people misunderstand the usefulness of identd, and so disable it or block all off site requests for it. identd is not there to help out remote sites. There is no way of knowing if the data you get from the remote identd is correct or not. There is no authentication in identd requests.

Why would you want to run it then? Because it helps _you_ out, and is another data-point in tracking. If your identd is un compromised, then you know it's telling remote sites the user-name or uid of people using tcp services. If the admin at a remote site comes back to you and tells you user so and so was trying to hack into their site, you can easily take action against that user. If you are not running identd, you will have to look at lots and lots of logs, figure out who was on at the time, and in general take a lot more time to track down the user.

The identd that ships with most distributions is more configurable than many people think. You can disable identd for specific users (they can make a .noident file), you can log all identd requests (I recommend it), you can even have identd return a uid instead of a user name or even NO-USER.

8.5   SATAN , ISS, and Other Network Scanners

There are a number of different software packages out there that do port and service based scanning of machines or networks. SATAN and ISS are two of the more well known ones. This software connects to the target machine (or all the target machines on a network) on all the ports it can, and tries to determine what service is running there. Based on this information, you could find out the machine is vulnerable to a specific exploit on that server.

SATAN (Security Administrators Tool for Analyzing Networks) is a port scanner with a web interface. It can be configured to do light, medium, or strong checks on a machine or a network of machines. It's a good idea to get SATAN and scan your machine or network, and fix the problems it finds. Make sure you get the copy of SATAN from sun-site or a reputable FTP or web site. There was a Trojan copy of SATAN that was distributed out on the net. *http://www.trouble.org/~zen/satan/satan.html*

ISS (Internet Security Scanner) is another port based scanner. It is faster than Satan, and thus might be better for large networks. However, SATAN tends to provide more information.

Abacus-Sentry is a commercial port scanner from www.psionic.com. Look at it's home page on the web for more information. *http://www.psionic.com*

Detecting Port scans.

There are some tools designed to alert you to probes by Satan and ISS and other scanning software, However liberal use of tcp_wrappers and making sure to look over your log files regularly, you should be able to notice such probes. Even on the lowest setting, Satan still leaves traces in the logs on a stock Red Hat system.

8.6 Sendmail, qmail and MTA's.

One of the most important services you can provide is a mail server. Unfortunately, it is also one of the most vulnerable to attack, simply due to the number of tasks it must perform and the privileges it typically needs.

If you are using sendmail it is very important to keep up on current versions. Sendmail has a long long history of security exploits. Always make sure you are running the most recent version. *http://www.sendmail.org*

If you are tired of upgrading your version of sendmail every week, you might consider switching over to qmail. qmail was designed with security in mind from the ground up. It's fast and stable and secure. *http://www.qmail.org*

8.7 Denial of Service Attacks

A Denial of service attack is one where the attacker tries to make some resource too busy to answer legitimate requests, or to deny legitimate users access to your machine.

Denial of service attacks have increased greatly in recent years. Some of the more popular and recent ones are listed below. Note that new ones show up all the time, so this is just a few examples. Read the Linux security lists and the bugtraq list and archives for more current information.

- **SYN Flooding** - SYN flooding is a network denial of service attack. It takes advantage of a "loophole" in the way TCP connections are created. The newer Linux kernels (2.0.30 and up) have several configurable options to prevent SYN flood attacks from denying people access to your machine or services. See the section on kernel security for proper kernel protection options.

- **Pentium "F00F" Bug** - It was recently discovered that a series of assembly codes send to a genuine Intel Pentium processor would reboot the machine. This affects every machine with a Pentium processor (not clones, not Pentium Pro or PII), no matter what operating system it's running. Linux kernel 2.0.32 and up contain a work around for this bug, preventing it from locking your machine. Kernel 2.0.33 has an improved version of the kernel fix, and is suggested over 2.0.32. If you are running on a Pentium, you should upgrade now!

- **Ping Flooding** - Ping flooding is a simple brute force denial of service attack. The attacker sends a "flood" of ICMP packets to your machine. If they are doing this from a host with better bandwidth than yours, your machine will be unable to send anything on the network. A variation on this attack, called "smurfing", sends ICMP packets to a host with _your_ machines return IP, allowing them to flood you less detectably. You can find more information about the "smurf" attack at *http://www.quadrunner.com/~chuegen/smurf.txt* If you are ever under a ping flood attack, use a tool like tcpdump to determine where the packets are coming from (or appear to be coming from), then contact your provider with this information. Ping floods can most easily be stopped at the router level or by using a firewall.

- **Ping o' Death** - The Ping o' Death attack is a result of incoming ICMP ECHO REQUEST packets being larger than the kernel data structures that store this information can hold. Because sending a single, large (65,510 bytes) "ping" packet to many systems will cause them to hang or even crash, this problem was quickly dubbed the "Ping o' Death." This one has long been fixed, and is no longer anything to worry about.

- **Teardrop / New Tear** - One of the most recent exploits involves a bug present in the IP fragmentation code on Linux and Windows platforms. It is fixed in kernel version 2.0.33, and does not require selecting any kernel compile-time options to utilize the fix. Linux is apparently not vulnerable to the 'newtear' exploit.

You can find most exploit code, and a more in-depth description of how they work at *http://www.rootshell.com* using their search engine.

8.8   NFS (Network File System) Security.

NFS is a very widely used file sharing protocol. It allows servers running nfsd and mountd to "export" entire filesystems to other machines with nfs filesystem support builtin to their kernels (or some other client support if they are non Linux machines). Mountd keeps track of mounted filesystems in /etc/mtab, and can display them with 'showmount'.

Many sites use NFS to serve home directories to users, so that no matter what machine in the cluster they login to, they will have all their home files.

There is some small amount of "security" allowed in exporting filesystems. You can make your nfsd map the remote root user (uid=0) to the nobody user, denying them total access to the files exported. However, since individual users have access to their own (or at least the same uid) files, the remote superuser can login or su to their account and have total access to their files. This is only a small hindrance to an attacker that has access to mount your remote filesystems.

If you must use NFS, make sure you export to only those machines that you really need to export only. Never export your entire root directory, export only directories you need to export.

See the NFS HOWTO for more information on NFS: *NFS HOWTO*

8.9   NIS (Network Information Service) (formerly YP).

Network Information service (formerly YP) is a means of distributing information to a group of machines. The NIS master holds the information tables and converts them into NIS map files. These maps are then served over the network, allowing NIS client machines to get login, password, home directory and shell information (all the information in a standard /etc/passwd file). This allows users to change their password once and have it take affect on all the machines in the NIS domain.

NIS is not at all secure. It was never meant to be. It was meant to be handy and usefull. Anyone that can guess the name of your NIS domain (anywhere on the net) can get a copy of your passwd file, and use crack and john the ripper against your users passwords. Also, it is possible to spoof NIS and do all sorts of nasty tricks. If you must use NIS, make sure you are aware of the dangers.

There is a much more secure replacement for NIS, called NIS+. Check out the NIS HOWTO for more information: *http://sunsite.unc.edu/mdw/HOWTO/NIS-HOWTO.html*

8.10   Firewalls

Firewalls are a means of restricting what information is allowed into and out of your local network. Typically the firewall host is connected to the Internet and your local lan, and the only access from your lan to the Internet is through the firewall. This way the firewall can control what passes back and forth from the Internet and your lan.

There are a number of types and methods of setting up firewalls. Linux machines make pretty good low cost firewalls. Firewall code can be built right into 2.0 and higher kernels. The ipfwadm user space tool allows you to change what types of network traffic you allow on the fly. You can also log particular types of network traffic.

Firewalls are a very usefull and important technique in securing your network. It is important to realize that you should never think that because you have a firewall, you don't need to secure the machines behind it. This is a fatal mistake.

Check out the very good Firewall-HOWTO at your latest sunsite archive for more information on firewalls and Linux. *http://sunsite.unc.edu/mdw/HOWTO/Firewall-HOWTO.html*

More information can also be found in the IP-Masquerade mini-howto: *http://sunsite.unc.edu/mdw/HOWTO/mini/IP-Masquerade.html*

More information on ipfwadm (The tool that lets you change settings on your firewall, can be found at it's home page: *http://www.xos.nl/linux/ipfwadm/*

9 Security Preparation (before you go on-line)

Ok, so you have checked over your system, and determined its as secure as feasible, and are ready to put it online. There are a few things you should now do in order to be prepared in case an intrusion actually does happen, so you can quickly disable the intruder, and get back up and running.

9.1 Make a Full Backup of Your Machine

Discussion of backup methods and storage is beyond the scope of this document, but a few words relating to backups and security:

If you have less than 650mb of data to store on a partition, a CD-R copy of your data is a good way to go (as it's hard to tamper with later, and if stored properly can last a long time). Tapes and other re-writable media should be write protected as soon as your backup is complete and verified to prevent tampering. Make sure you store your backups in a secure off line area. A good backup will ensure that you have a known good point to restore your system from.

9.2 Choosing a Good Backup Schedule

A six-tape cycle is an easy one to maintain. This includes four tapes for during the week, one tape for even Friday's, and one tape for odd Friday's. Perform an incremental backup every day, and a full backup on the appropriate Friday tape. If you make some particular important changes or add some important data to your system, a backup might well be in order.

9.3 Backup Your RPM or Debian File Database

In the event of an intrusion, you can use your RPM database like you would use tripwire, but only if you can be sure it too hasn't been modified. You should copy the RPM database to a floppy, and keep this copy off-line at all times. The Debian distribution likely has something similar.

Specifically, the files /var/lib/rpm/fileindex.rpm and /var/lib/rpm/packages.rpm most likely won't fit on a single floppy. Compressed, each should fit on a seperate floppy.

Now, when your system is compromised, you can use the command:

```
root#  rpm -Va
```

to verify each file on the system. See the RPM man page, as there are a few other options that can be included to make it less verbose.

This means that every time a new RPM is added to the system, the RPM database will need to be rearchived. You will have to decide the advantages versus drawbacks.

9.4 Keep Track of Your System Accounting Data

It is very important that the information that comes from syslog has not been compromised. Making the files in /var/log readable and writable by a limited number of users is a good start.

Be sure to keep an eye on what gets written there, especially under the 'auth' facility. Multiple login failures, for example, can indicate an attempted break-in.

Where to look for your log file will depend on your distribution. In a Linux system that conforms to the "Linux Filesystem Standard", such as Red Hat, you will want to look in /var/log and check messages, mail.log, and others.

You can find out where your distribution is logging to by looking at your /etc/syslog.conf file. This is the file that tells syslogd (the system logging daemon) where to log various messages.

You might also want to configure your log-rotating script or daemon to keep logs around longer so you have time to examine them. Take a look at the 'logrotate' package un recent Red Hat distributions. Other distributions likely have a similar process.

If your log files have been tampered with, see if you can determine when the tampering started, and what sort of things they appeared to tamper with. Are there large periods of time that cannot be accounted for? Checking backup tapes (if you have any) for untampered log files is a good idea.

Log files are typically modified by the intruder in order to cover his tracks, but they should still be checked for strange happenings. You may notice the intruder attempting to gain entrance, or exploit a program in order to obtain the root account. You might see log entries before the intruder has time to modify them.

You should also be sure to seperate the 'auth' facility from other log data, including attempts to switch users using 'su', login attempts, and other user accounting information.

If possible, configure syslog to send a copy of the most important data to a secure system. This will prevent an intruder from covering his tracks by deleting his login/su/ftp/etc attempts. See the syslog.conf man page, and refer to the '@' option.

Finally, log files are much less useful when no one is reading them. Take some time out every once in a while to look over your log files, and get a feeling for what the look like on a normal day. Knowing this can help make unusual things stand out.

9.5 Apply All New System Updates.

Most Linux users install from a CDROM. Due to the fast paced nature of security fixes, new (fixed) programs are always being released. Before you connect your machine to the network, it's a good idea to check with your distribution's ftp site (ftp.redhat.com for example) and get all the updated packages since you received your distribution CDROM. Many times these packages contain important security fixes, so it's a good idea to get them installed.

10 What To Do During and After a Breakin

So you have followed some of the advice here (or elsewhere) and have detected a breakin? The first thing to do is to remain calm. Hasty actions can cause more harm than the attacker would have.

10.1 Security Compromise under way.

Spotting a security compromise under way can be a tense undertaking. How you react can have large consequences.

If the compromise you are seeing is a physical one, odds are you have spotted someone who has broken into your home, office or lab. You should notify your local authorities. In a lab setting you might have spotted someone trying to open a case or reboot a machine. Depending on your authority and procedures, you might ask them to stop, or contact your local security people.

If you have detected a local user trying to compromise your security, the first thing to do is confirm they are in fact who you think they are. Check the site they are logging in from. Is it the site they are normally in from? no? Then use a non electronic means of getting in touch. For instance, call them on the phone or walk over to their office/house and talk to them. If they agree that they are on, you can ask them to explain what they were doing or tell them to cease doing it. If they are not on, and have no idea what you are talking about, odds are this incident requires further investigation. Look into such incidents , and have lots of information before making any accusations.

If you have detected a network compromise, the first thing to do (if you are able) is to disconnect your network. If they are connected via modem, unplug the modem cable, if they are connected via ethernet, unplug the ethernet cable. This will prevent them from doing any further damage, and they will probably see it as a network problem rather than detection.

If you are unable to disconnect the network (if you have a busy site, or you do not have physical control of your machines), the next best step is to use something like tcp_wrappers or ipfwadm to deny access from the intruders site.

If you can't deny all people from the same site as the intruder, locking the users account will have to do. Note that locking an account is not an easy thing. You have to keep in mind .rhosts files, FTP access, and a host of backdoors).

After you have done one of the above (disconnected network, denied access from their site, and/or disabled their account), you need to kill all their user processes and log them off.

You should monitor your site well for the next few minutes, as the attacker will try and get back in. Perhaps using a different account, and/or from a different network address.

10.2 Security Compromise has already happened

So you have either detected a compromise that has already happened or you have detected it and locked (hopefully) the offending attacker out of your system. Now what?

10.2.1 Closing the Hole

If you are able to determine what means the attacker used to get into your system, you should try and close that hole. For instance, perhaps you see several FTP entries just before the user logged in. Disable the FTP service and check and see if there is an updated version or any of the lists know of a fix.

Check all your log files, and make a visit to your security lists and pages and see if there are any new common exploits you can fix. You can find Caldera security fixes here *http://www.caldera.com/tech-ref/security/*. Red Hat has not yet seperated their security fixes from bugfixes, but their distribution errata is available at *http://www.redhat.com/errata* It is very likely that if one vendor has released a security update, that most other Linux vendors will as well.

If you don't lock the attacker out, they will likely be back. Not just back on your machine, but back somewhere on your network. If they were running a packet sniffer, odds are good they have access to other local machines.

10.2.2 Assessing the Damage

The first thing is to assess the damage. What has been compromised? If you are running an Integrity Checker like Tripwire you can make a tripwire run and it should tell you. If not, you will have to look around at all your important data.

Since Linux systems are getting easier and easier to install, you might consider saving your config files and then wiping your disk(s) and reinstalling, then restoring your user files from backups and your config files. This will insure that you have a new clean system. If you have to backup files from the compromised system, be especially cautious of any binaries that you restore as they may be trojan horses placed there by the intruder.

10.2.3 Backups, Backups, Backups!

Having regular backups is a godsend for security matters. If your system is compromised, you can restore the data you need from backups. Of course some data is valuable to the attacker to, and they will not only destroy it, they will steal it and have their own copies, but at least you will still have the data.

You should check several backups back into the past before restoring a file that has been tampered with. The intruder could have compromised your files long ago, and you could have made many successful backups of the compromised file!!!

HOWTO

Of course, there are also a raft of security concerns with backups. Make sure you are storing them in a secure place. Know who has access to them. (If an attacker can get your backups, they can have access to all your data without you ever knowing it.)

10.2.4   Tracking Down the Intruder.

Ok, you have locked the intruder out, and recovered your system, but you're not quite done yet. While it is unlikely that most intruders will ever be caught, you should report the attack.

You should report the attack to the admin contact at the site where the attacker attacked your system. You can look up this contact with "whois" or the internic database. You might send them an email with all applicable log entries and dates and times. If you spotted anything else distinctive about your intruder, you might mention that too. After sending the email, you should (if you are so inclined) follow up with a phone call. If that admin in turn spots your attacker, they might be able to talk to the admin of the site where they are coming from and so on.

Good hackers often use many intermediate systems. Some (or many) of which may not even know they have been compromised. Trying to track a cracker back to their home system can be difficult. Being polite to the admins you talk to can go a long way to getting help from them.

You should also notify any security organizations you are a part of (CERT or similar).

11   Security Sources

There are a LOT of good sites out there for UNIX security in general and Linux security specifically. It's very important to subscribe to one (or more) of the security mailing lists and keep current on security fixes. Most of these lists are very low volume, and very informative.

11.1   FTP sites

CERT is the Computer Emergency Response Team. They often send out alerts of current attacks and fixes. *cert.org*

Replay has archives of many security programs. Since they are outside the US, they don't need to obey US crypto restrictions. *replay.com*

Matt Blaze is the author of CFS and a great security advocate. *Matt Blaze's stuff*

tue.nl is a great security ftp site in the Netherlands. *ftp.win.tue.nl*

11.2   Web Sites

The Hacker FAQ is a FAQ about hackers: *The Hacker FAQ*

The COAST archive has a large number of unix security programs and information: *COAST*

Rootshell.com is a great site for seeing what exploits are currently being used by crackers: *rootshell.com exploits*

BUGTRAQ puts out advisories on security issues: *BUGTRAQ archives*

CERT, the Computer Emergency Response Team, puts out advisories on common attacks on unix platforms: *CERT home*

Dan Farmer is the author of SATAN and many other security tools, his home site has some interesting security survey information as well as security tools: *Dan Farmers trouble.org*

The Linux security WWW is a good site for Linux security information: *Linux Security WWW*

Reptile has lots of good Linux security information on his site: *Reptiles Linux Security Page*

Infilsec has a vulnerability engine that can tell you what vulnerabilities affect a specific platform: *Infilsec vulnerability engine*

CIAC sends out periodic security bulitins on common exploits: *CIAC bulitins*

A good starting point for Linux Pluggable Authentication modules can be found at *http://www.kernel.org/pub/linux/libs/pam/*.

11.3 Mailing Lists

Bugtraq: To subscribe to bugtraq, send mail to listserv@netspace.org containing the message body subscribe bugtraq. (see links above for archives).

CIAC: Send e-mail to: majordomo@tholia.llnl.gov In the BODY (not subject) of the message put (either or both): subscribe ciac-bulletin

11.4 Books - Printed Reading Material.

There are a number of good security books out there. This section lists a few of them. In addition to the security specify books, security is covered in a number of other books on system administration.

Building Internet Firewalls By D. Brent Chapman & Elizabeth D. Zwicky

1st Edition September 1995

ISBN: 1-56592-124-0

Practical UNIX & Internet Security, 2nd Edition By Simson Garfinkel & Gene Spafford

2nd Edition April 1996

ISBN: 1-56592-148-8

Computer Security Basics By Deborah Russell & G.T. Gangemi, Sr.

1st Edition July 1991

ISBN: 0-937175-71-4

Linux Network Administrator's Guide By Olaf Kirch

1st Edition January 1995

ISBN: 1-56592-087-2

PGP: Pretty Good Privacy By Simson Garfinkel

1st Edition December 1994

ISBN: 1-56592-098-8

Computer Crime A Crimefighter's Handbook By David Icove, Karl Seger & William VonStorch (Consulting Editor Eugene H. Spafford)

1st Edition August 1995

ISBN: 1-56592-086-4

12 Glossary

- **Host:** A computer system attached to a network
- **Firewall:** A component or set of components that restricts access between a protected network and the Internet, or between other sets of networks.

- **Bastion Host:** A computer system that must be highly secured because it is vulnerable to attack, usually because it is exposed to the Internet and is a main point of contact for users of internal networks. It gets its name from the highly fortified projects on the outer walls of medieval castles. Bastions overlook critical areas of defense, usually having strongs walls, room for extra troops, and the occasional useful tub of boiling hot oil for discouraging attackers.

- **Dual-homed Host:** A general-purpose computer system that has at least two network interfaces.

- **Packet:** The fundamental unit of communication on the Internet.

- **Packet Filtering:** The action a device takes to selectively control the flow of data to and from a network. Packet filters allow or block packets, usually while routing them from one network to another (most often from the Internet to an internal network, and vice-versa). accomplish packet filtering, you set up a set of rules that specifiy what types of packets (those to or from a particular IP address or port) are to be allowed and what types are to be blocked.

- **Perimeter network:** A network added between a protected network and an external network, in order to provide an additional layer of security. A perimeter network is sometimes called a DMZ.

- **Proxy server:** A program that deals with external servers on behalf of internal clients. Proxy clients talk to proxy servers, which relay approved client requests on to real servers, and relay answers back to clients.

- **Denial of Service:** A denial of service attack is when an attacker consumes the resources on your computer for things it was not intended to be doing, thus preventing normal use of your network resources to legimite purposes.

- **Buffer Overflow:** Common coding style is never to allocate buffers "large enough" and not checking for overflows. When such buffers are overflows, the executing program (daemon or set-uid program) can be tricked in doing some other things. Generally this works by overwriting a function's return address on the stack to point to another location.

- **IP Spoofing:** IP-Spoofing is a complex technical attack that is made up of several components. It is a security exploit that works by tricking computers in a trust-relationship that you are someone that you really aren't. There is an extensive paper written by daemon9, route, and infinity in the Volume Seven, Issue Fourty-Eight issue of Phrack Magazine.

- **Authentication:** The property of knowing that the data received is the same as the data that was sent and that the claimed sender is in fact the actual sender.

- **Non-repudiation:** The property of a receiver being able to prove that the sender of some data did in fact send the data even though the sender might later desire to deny ever having sent that data.

13 Frequently Asked Questions

1. Is it more secure to compile driver support directly into the kernel, instead of making it a module? Answer: Some people think it is better to disable the ability to load device drivers using modules, because an intruder could load a trojan module or himself load a module that could affect system security.

   However, in order to load modules, you must be root. The module object files are also only writable by root. This means the intruder would need root access to insert a module. If the intruder gains root access, there are more serious things to worry about than whether he will load a module.

   Modules are for dynamically loading support for a particular device that may be infrequently used. On server machines, or firewalls for instance, this is very unlikely to happen. For this reason, it would make more sense to compile support directly into the kernel for machines acting as a server. Modules are also slower than support compiled directly in the kernel.

2. Logging in as root from a remote machine always fails. Answer: See the section on Root security. This is done intentionally to prevent remote users from attempting to connect via telnet to your machine as root, which is a serious security vulnerability. Don't forget, potential intruders have time on their side, and can run automated programs to find your password.

3. How do I enable shadow passwords on my Red Hat 4.2 or 5.0 Linux box? Answer: Shadow passwords is a mechanism for storing your password in a file other than the normal /etc/passwd file. This has several advantages. The first one is that the shadow file, /etc/shadow, is only readable by root, unlike /etc/passwd, which must remain

readable by everyone. The other advantage is that as the administrator, you can enable or disable accounts without everyone knowing the status of other users accounts.

The /etc/passwd file is then used to store user and group names, used by programs like '/bin/ls' to map the user ID to the proper username in a directory listing.

The /etc/shadow file then only contains the username and his/her password, and perhaps accounting information, like when the account expires, etc.

To enable shadow passwords, run 'pwconv' as root, and /etc/shadow should now exist, and be used by applications. Since you are using RH 4.2 or above, the PAM modules will automatically adapt to the change from using normal /etc/passwd to shadow passwords without any other change.

Since your interested in securing your passwords, perhaps you would also be interested in generating good passwords to begin with. For this you can use the 'pam_cracklib' module, which is part of PAM. It runs your password against the Crack libraries to help you decide if it is too easily guessable by password cracking programs.

4. How can I enable the Apache SSL extensions? Answer:

1.Get SSLeay 0.8.0 or later from ftp://ftp.psy.uq.oz.au/pub/Crypto/SSL

2.Build and test and install it!

3.Get Apache 1.2.5 source

4.Get Apache SSLeay extensions from *here* `<ftp://ftp.ox.ac.uk/pub/crypto/SSL/apache_1.2.5+ssl_1.13.tar.gz>`

5.Unpack it in the apache-1.2.5 source directory and patch Apache as per the README.

6.Configure and build it.

You might also try *Replay Associates* which has many pre-built packages, and is located outside of the United States.

5. How can I manipulate user accounts, and still retain security? Answer: The Red Hat distribution, especially RH5.0, contains a great number of tools to change the properties of user accounts.

- The pwconv and unpwconv programs can be used to convert back and forth between shadow and non-shadowed passwords

- The pwck and grpck programs can be used to verify proper organization of the passwd and group files.

- The programs useradd, usermod, and userdel can be used to add, delete and modify user accounts. The programs groupadd, groupmod, and groupdel will do the same for groups.

- Group passwords can be created using gpasswd.

All these programs are 'shadow-aware' – that is; if you enable shadow it will use /etc/shadow for password information, otherwise it won't.

See the respective man pages for further information.

6. How can I password protect specific HTML documents using Apache? I bet you didn't know about *http://www.apacheweek.org* did you?

You can find information on User Authentication at *http://www.apacheweek.com/features/userauth* as well as other web server security tips from *http://www.apache.org/docs/misc/security_tips.html*

14   Conclusion

By subscribing to the security alert mailing lists, and keeping current, you can do a lot towards securing your machine. If you pay attention to your log files and run something like tripwire regularly, you can do even more.

A reasonable level of computer security is not difficult to maintain on a home machine. More effort is required on business machines, but Linux can indeed be a secure platform. Due to the nature of Linux development, security fixes often come out much faster than they do on commercial operating systems, making Linux an ideal platform when security is a requirement.

HOWTO

15 Thanks to

Information here is collected from many sources. Thanks to the following that either indirectly or directly have contributed:

```
Rob Riggs <rob@DevilsThumb.com>
S. Coffin <scoffin@netcom.com>
Viktor Przebinda <viktor@CRYSTAL.MATH.ou.edu>
Roelof Osinga <roelof@eboa.com>
Kyle Hasselbacher <kyle@carefree.quux.soltec.net>
"David S. Jackson" <dsj@dsj.net>
"Todd G. Ruskell" <ruskell@boulder.nist.gov>
Rogier Wolff <R.E.Wolff@BitWizard.nl>
```

Part XL

"The Linux Serial Programming HOWTO" by Peter H. Baumann

Peter.Baumann@dlr.de
v1.0, 22 January 1998
This document describes how to program communications with devices over a serial port on a Linux box.

Contents

1   Introduction

This is the Linux Serial Programming HOWTO. All about how to program communications with other devices / computers over a serial line under Linux. Different techniques are explained: Canonical I/O (only complete lines are transmitted/received), asyncronous I/O, and waiting for input from multiple sources.

This document does not describe how to set up serial ports, because this has been described by Greg Hankins in the Serial-HOWTO.

I have to emphasize that I am not an expert in this field, but have had problems with a project that involved such communication. The code examples presented here were derived from the miniterm code available from the LDP programmers guide (`ftp://sunsite.unc.edu/pub/Linux/docs/LDP/programmers-guide/lpg-0.4.tar.gz` and mirrors) in the examples directory.

Since I wrote this document in June 1997, I have moved to WinNT to satisfy customers need, so I have not built up more in depth knowledge. If anybody has any comments, I will gladly incorporate them into this document (see sect. Feedback). If someone would like to take over and do a better job, please e-mail me.

All examples were tested using a i386 Linux Kernel 2.0.29.

1.1 Copyright

The Linux Serial-Programming-HOWTO is copyright (C) 1997 by Peter Baumann. Linux HOWTO documents may be reproduced and distributed in whole or in part, in any medium physical or electronic, as long as this copyright notice is retained on all copies. Commercial redistribution is allowed and encouraged; however, the author would *like* to be notified of any such distributions.

All translations, derivative works, or aggregate works incorporating any Linux HOWTO documents must be covered under this copyright notice. That is, you may not produce a derivative work from a HOWTO and impose additional restrictions on its distribution. Exceptions to these rules may be granted under certain conditions; please contact the Linux HOWTO coordinator at the address given below.

In short, we wish to promote dissemination of this information through as many channels as possible. However, we do wish to retain copyright on the HOWTO documents, and would *like* to be notified of any plans to redistribute the HOWTOs.

If you have questions, please contact Tim Bynum, the Linux HOWTO coordinator, at *linux-howto@sunsite.unc.edu* via email.

1.2 New Versions Of This Document

New versions of the Serial-Programming-HOWTO will be available at *ftp://sunsite.unc.edu:/pub/Linux/docs/HOWTO/Serial-Programming-HOWTO* and mirror sites. There are other formats, such as PostScript and DVI versions in the other-formats directory. The Serial-Programming-HOWTO is also available at *http://sunsite.unc.edu/LDP/HOWTO/Serial-Programming-HOWTO.html* and will be posted to *comp.os.linux.answers* monthly.

1.3 Feedback

Please send me any corrections, questions, comments, suggestions, or additional material. I would like to improve this HOWTO! Tell me exactly what you don't understand, or what could be clearer. You can reach me at *Peter.Baumann@dlr.de* via email. Please include the version number of the Serial-Programming-HOWTO when writing, this is version 0.3.

2 Getting started

2.1 Debugging

The best way to debug your code is to set up another Linux box, and connect the two computers via a null-modem cable. Use miniterm (available from the LDP programmers guide (ftp://sunsite.unc.edu/pub/Linux/docs/LDP/programmers-guide/lpg-0.4.tar.gz in the examples directory) to transmit characters to your Linux box. Miniterm can be compiled very easily and will transmit all keyboard input raw over the serial port. Only the define statement #define MODEMDEVICE "/dev/ttyS0" has to be checked. Set it to ttyS0 for COM1, ttyS1 for COM2, etc.. It is essential for testing, that *all* characters are transmitted raw (without output processing) over the line. To test your connection, start miniterm on both computers and just type away. The characters input on one computer should appear on the other computer and vice versa. The input will not be echoed to the attached screen.

To make a null-modem cable you have to cross the TxD (transmit) and RxD (receive) lines. For a description of a cable see sect. 7 of the Serial-HOWTO.

It is also possible to perform this testing with only one computer, if you have two unused serial ports. You can then run two miniterms off two virtual consoles. If you free a serial port by disconnecting the mouse, remember to redirect /dev/mouse if it exists. If you use a multiport serial card, be sure to configure it correctly. I had mine configured wrong and everything worked fine as long as I was testing only on my computer. When I connected to another computer, the port started loosing characters. Executing two programs on one computer just isn't fully asynchronous.

2.2 Port Settings

The devices /dev/ttyS* are intended to hook up terminals to your Linux box, and are configured for this use after startup. This has to be kept in mind when programming communication with a raw device. E.g. the ports are configured to echo characters sent from the device back to it, which normally has to be changed for data transmission.

All parameters can be easily configured from within a program. The configuration is stored in a structure struct termios, which is defined in <asm/termbits.h>:

```
#define NCCS 19
struct termios {
        tcflag_t c_iflag;               /* input mode flags */
        tcflag_t c_oflag;               /* output mode flags */
        tcflag_t c_cflag;               /* control mode flags */
        tcflag_t c_lflag;               /* local mode flags */
        cc_t c_line;                    /* line discipline */
        cc_t c_cc[NCCS];                /* control characters */
};
```

This file also includes all flag definitions. The input mode flags in c_iflag handle all input processing, which means that the characters sent from the device can be processed before they are read with read. Similarly c_oflag handles the output processing. c_cflag contains the settings for the port, as the baudrate, bits per character, stop bits, etc.. The local mode flags stored in c_lflag determine if characters are echoed, signals are sent to your program, etc.. Finally the array c_cc defines the control characters for end of file, stop, etc.. Default values for the control characters are defined in <asm/termios.h>. The flags are described in the manual page termios(3). The structure termios contains the c_line (line discipline) element, which is not used in POSIX compliant systems.

2.3 Input Concepts for Serial Devices

Here three different input concepts will be presented. The appropriate concept has to be chosen for the intended application. Whenever possible, do not loop reading single characters to get a complete string. When I did this, I lost characters, whereas a read for the whole string did not show any errors.

2.3.1 Canonical Input Processing

This is the normal processing mode for terminals, but can also be useful for communicating with other dl input is processed in units of lines, which means that a read will only return a full line of input. A line is by default terminated by a NL (ASCII LF), an end of file, or an end of line character. A CR (the DOS/Windows default end-of-line) will not terminate a line with the default settings.

Canonical input processing can also handle the erase, delete word, and reprint characters, translate CR to NL, etc..

2.3.2 Non-Canonical Input Processing

Non-Canonical Input Processing will handle a fixed amount of characters per read, and allows for a character timer. This mode should be used if your application will always read a fixed number of characters, or if the connected device sends bursts of characters.

2.3.3 Asynchronous Input

The two modes described above can be used in synchronous and asynchronous mode. Synchronous is the default, where a `read` statement will block, until the read is satisfied. In asynchronous mode the `read` statement will return immediatly and send a signal to the calling program upon completion. This signal can be received by a signal handler.

2.3.4 Waiting for Input from Multiple Sources

This is not a different input mode, but might be useful, if you are handling multiple devices. In my application I was handling input over a TCP/IP socket and input over a serial connection from another computer quasi-simultaneously. The program example given below will wait for input from two different input sources. If input from one source becomes available, it will be processed, and the program will then wait for new input.

The approach presented below seems rather complex, but it is important to keep in mind that Linux is a multi-processing operating system. The `select` system call will not load the CPU while waiting for input, whereas looping until input becomes available would slow down other processes executing at the same time.

3 Program Examples

All examples have been derived from `miniterm.c`. The type ahead buffer is limited to 255 characters, just like the maximum string length for canonical input processing (`<linux/limits.h>` or `<posix1_lim.h>`).

See the comments in the code for explanation of the use of the different input modes. I hope that the code is understandable. The example for canonical input is commented best, the other examples are commented only where they differ from the example for canonical input to emphasize the differences.

The descriptions are not complete, but you are encouraged to experiment with the examples to derive the best solution for your application.

Don't forget to give the appropriate serial ports the right permissions (e. g.: `chmod a+rw /dev/ttyS1`)!

3.1 Canonical Input Processing

```
#include <sys/types.h>
#include <sys/stat.h>
#include <fcntl.h>
#include <termios.h>
#include <stdio.h>

/* baudrate settings are defined in <asm/termbits.h>, which is
included by <termios.h> */
#define BAUDRATE B38400
/* change this definition for the correct port */
#define MODEMDEVICE "/dev/ttyS1"
#define _POSIX_SOURCE 1 /* POSIX compliant source */

#define FALSE 0
#define TRUE 1

volatile int STOP=FALSE;

main()
{
  int fd,c, res;
  struct termios oldtio,newtio;
  char buf[255];
```

```
/*
   Open modem device for reading and writing and not as controlling tty
   because we don't want to get killed if linenoise sends CTRL-C.
*/
fd = open(MODEMDEVICE, O_RDWR | O_NOCTTY );
if (fd <0) {perror(MODEMDEVICE); exit(-1); }

tcgetattr(fd,&oldtio); /* save current serial port settings */
bzero(&newtio, sizeof(newtio)); /* clear struct for new port settings */

/*
   BAUDRATE: Set bps rate. You could also use cfsetispeed and cfsetospeed.
   CRTSCTS : output hardware flow control (only used if the cable has
             all necessary lines. See sect. 7 of Serial-HOWTO)
   CS8     : 8n1 (8bit,no parity,1 stopbit)
   CLOCAL  : local connection, no modem contol
   CREAD   : enable receiving characters
*/
newtio.c_cflag = BAUDRATE | CRTSCTS | CS8 | CLOCAL | CREAD;

/*
   IGNPAR  : ignore bytes with parity errors
   ICRNL   : map CR to NL (otherwise a CR input on the other computer
             will not terminate input)
   otherwise make device raw (no other input processing)
*/
newtio.c_iflag = IGNPAR | ICRNL;

/*
Raw output.
*/
newtio.c_oflag = 0;

/*
   ICANON  : enable canonical input
   disable all echo functionality, and don't send signals to calling program
*/
newtio.c_lflag = ICANON;

/*
   initialize all control characters
   default values can be found in /usr/include/termios.h, and are given
   in the comments, but we don't need them here
*/
newtio.c_cc[VINTR]    = 0;     /* Ctrl-c */
newtio.c_cc[VQUIT]    = 0;     /* Ctrl-\ */
newtio.c_cc[VERASE]   = 0;     /* del */
newtio.c_cc[VKILL]    = 0;     /* @ */
newtio.c_cc[VEOF]     = 4;     /* Ctrl-d */
newtio.c_cc[VTIME]    = 0;     /* inter-character timer unused */
newtio.c_cc[VMIN]     = 1;     /* blocking read until 1 character ar-
rives */
newtio.c_cc[VSWTC]    = 0;     /* '\0' */
newtio.c_cc[VSTART]   = 0;     /* Ctrl-q */
newtio.c_cc[VSTOP]    = 0;     /* Ctrl-s */
```

```
newtio.c_cc[VSUSP]    = 0;     /* Ctrl-z */
newtio.c_cc[VEOL]     = 0;     /* '\0' */
newtio.c_cc[VREPRINT] = 0;     /* Ctrl-r */
newtio.c_cc[VDISCARD] = 0;     /* Ctrl-u */
newtio.c_cc[VWERASE]  = 0;     /* Ctrl-w */
newtio.c_cc[VLNEXT]   = 0;     /* Ctrl-v */
newtio.c_cc[VEOL2]    = 0;     /* '\0' */

/*
  now clean the modem line and activate the settings for the port
*/
tcflush(fd, TCIFLUSH);
tcsetattr(fd,TCSANOW,&newtio);

/*
  terminal settings done, now handle input
  In this example, inputting a 'z' at the beginning of a line will
  exit the program.
*/
while (STOP==FALSE) {      /* loop until we have a terminating condition */
/* read blocks program execution until a line terminating character is
   input, even if more than 255 chars are input. If the number
   of characters read is smaller than the number of chars available,
   subsequent reads will return the remaining chars. res will be set
   to the actual number of characters actually read */
   res = read(fd,buf,255);
   buf[res]=0;                 /* set end of string, so we can printf */
   printf(":%s:%d\n", buf, res);
   if (buf[0]=='z') STOP=TRUE;
}
/* restore the old port settings */
tcsetattr(fd,TCSANOW,&oldtio);
}
```

3.2   Non-Canonical Input Processing

In non-canonical input processing mode, input is not assembled into lines and input processing (erase, kill, delete, etc.) does not occur. Two parameters control the behavior of this mode: `c_cc[VTIME]` sets the character timer, and `c_cc[VMIN]` sets the minimum number of characters to receive before satisfying the read.

If MIN > 0 and TIME = 0, MIN sets the number of characters to receive before the read is satisfied. As TIME is zero, the timer is not used.

If MIN = 0 and TIME > 0, TIME serves as a timeout value. The read will be satisfied if a single character is read, or TIME is exceeded (t = TIME *0.1 s). If TIME is exceeded, no character will be returned.

If MIN > 0 and TIME > 0, TIME serves as an inter-character timer. The read will be satisfied if MIN characters are received, or the time between two characters exceeds TIME. The timer is restarted every time a character is received and only becomes active after the first character has been received.

If MIN = 0 and TIME = 0, read will be satisfied immediately. The number of characters currently available, or the number of characters requested will be returned. According to Antonino (see contributions), you could issue a `fcntl(fd, F_SETFL, FNDELAY);` before reading to get the same result.

By modifying `newtio.c_cc[VTIME]` and `newtio.c_cc[VMIN]` all modes described above can be tested.

```
#include <sys/types.h>
#include <sys/stat.h>
#include <fcntl.h>
#include <termios.h>
#include <stdio.h>

#define BAUDRATE B38400
#define MODEMDEVICE "/dev/ttyS1"
#define _POSIX_SOURCE 1 /* POSIX compliant source */
#define FALSE 0
#define TRUE 1

volatile int STOP=FALSE;

main()
{
  int fd,c, res;
  struct termios oldtio,newtio;
  char buf[255];

 fd = open(MODEMDEVICE, O_RDWR | O_NOCTTY );
 if (fd <0) {perror(MODEMDEVICE); exit(-1); }

  tcgetattr(fd,&oldtio); /* save current port settings */

  bzero(&newtio, sizeof(newtio));
  newtio.c_cflag = BAUDRATE | CRTSCTS | CS8 | CLOCAL | CREAD;
  newtio.c_iflag = IGNPAR;
  newtio.c_oflag = 0;

  /* set input mode (non-canonical, no echo,...) */
  newtio.c_lflag = 0;

  newtio.c_cc[VTIME]    = 0;   /* inter-character timer unused */
  newtio.c_cc[VMIN]     = 5;   /* blocking read until 5 chars received */

  tcflush(fd, TCIFLUSH);
  tcsetattr(fd,TCSANOW,&newtio);


  while (STOP==FALSE) {        /* loop for input */
    res = read(fd,buf,255);    /* returns after 5 chars have been input */
    buf[res]=0;                /* so we can printf... */
    printf(":%s:%d\n", buf, res);
    if (buf[0]=='z') STOP=TRUE;
  }
  tcsetattr(fd,TCSANOW,&oldtio);
}
```

3.3 Asynchronous Input

```
#include <termios.h>
#include <stdio.h>
#include <unistd.h>
#include <fcntl.h>
```

```
#include <sys/signal.h>
#include <sys/types.h>

#define BAUDRATE B38400
#define MODEMDEVICE "/dev/ttyS1"
#define _POSIX_SOURCE 1 /* POSIX compliant source */
#define FALSE 0
#define TRUE 1

volatile int STOP=FALSE;

void signal_handler_IO (int status);    /* definition of signal handler */
int wait_flag=TRUE;                     /* TRUE while no signal received */

main()
{
  int fd,c, res;
  struct termios oldtio,newtio;
  struct sigaction saio;              /* definition of signal action */
  char buf[255];

  /* open the device to be non-blocking (read will return immediatly) */
  fd = open(MODEMDEVICE, O_RDWR | O_NOCTTY | O_NONBLOCK);
  if (fd <0) {perror(MODEMDEVICE); exit(-1); }

  /* install the signal handler before making the device asynchronous */
  saio.sa_handler = signal_handler_IO;
  saio.sa_mask = 0;
  saio.sa_flags = 0;
  saio.sa_restorer = NULL;
  sigaction(SIGIO,&saio,NULL);

  /* allow the process to receive SIGIO */
  fcntl(fd, F_SETOWN, getpid());
  /* Make the file descriptor asynchronous (the manual page says only
     O_APPEND and O_NONBLOCK, will work with F_SETFL...) */
  fcntl(fd, F_SETFL, FASYNC);

  tcgetattr(fd,&oldtio); /* save current port settings */
  /* set new port settings for canonical input processing */
  newtio.c_cflag = BAUDRATE | CRTSCTS | CS8 | CLOCAL | CREAD;
  newtio.c_iflag = IGNPAR | ICRNL;
  newtio.c_oflag = 0;
  newtio.c_lflag = ICANON;
  newtio.c_cc[VMIN]=1;
  newtio.c_cc[VTIME]=0;
  tcflush(fd, TCIFLUSH);
  tcsetattr(fd,TCSANOW,&newtio);

  /* loop while waiting for input. normally we would do something
     useful here */
  while (STOP==FALSE) {
    printf(".\n");usleep(100000);
    /* after receiving SIGIO, wait_flag = FALSE, input is available
       and can be read */
```

```
            if (wait_flag==FALSE) {
               res = read(fd,buf,255);
               buf[res]=0;
               printf(":%s:%d\n", buf, res);
               if (res==1) STOP=TRUE; /* stop loop if only a CR was input */
               wait_flag = TRUE;      /* wait for new input */
            }
        }
        /* restore old port settings */
        tcsetattr(fd,TCSANOW,&oldtio);
    }

    /**************************************************************************
     * signal handler. sets wait_flag to FALSE, to indicate above loop that    *
     * characters have been received.                                          *
     **************************************************************************/

    void signal_handler_IO (int status)
    {
      printf("received SIGIO signal.\n");
      wait_flag = FALSE;
    }
```

3.4   Waiting for Input from Multiple Sources

This section is kept to a minimum. It is just intended to be a hint, and therefore the example code is kept short. This will not only work with serial ports, but with any set of file descriptors.

The select call and accompanying macros use a fd_set. This is a bit array, which has a bit entry for every valid file descriptor number. select will accept a fd_set with the bits set for the relevant file descriptors and returns a fd_set, in which the bits for the file descriptors are set where input, output, or an exception occurred. All handling of fd_set is done with the provided macros. See also the manual page select(2).

```
    #include <sys/time.h>
    #include <sys/types.h>
    #include <unistd.h>

    main()
    {
        int   fd1, fd2;  /* input sources 1 and 2 */
        fd_set readfs;   /* file descriptor set */
        int    maxfd;    /* maximum file desciptor used */
        int    loop=1;   /* loop while TRUE */

        /* open_input_source opens a device, sets the port correctly, and
           returns a file descriptor */
        fd1 = open_input_source("/dev/ttyS1");   /* COM2 */
        if (fd1<0) exit(0);
        fd2 = open_input_source("/dev/ttyS2");   /* COM3 */
        if (fd2<0) exit(0);
        maxfd = MAX (fd1, fd2)+1;  /* maximum bit entry (fd) to test */

        /* loop for input */
        while (loop) {
          FD_SET(fd1, &readfs);  /* set testing for source 1 */
```

```
    FD_SET(fd2, &readfs);  /* set testing for source 2 */
    /* block until input becomes available */
    select(maxfd, &readfs, NULL, NULL, NULL);
    if (FD_ISSET(fd1))          /* input from source 1 available */
       handle_input_from_source1();
    if (FD_ISSET(fd2))          /* input from source 2 available */
       handle_input_from_source2();
  }


}
```

The given example blocks indefinitely, until input from one of the sources becomes available. If you need to timeout on input, just replace the select call by:

```
int res;
struct timeval Timeout;

/* set timeout value within input loop */
Timeout.tv_usec = 0;  /* milliseconds */
Timeout.tv_sec  = 1;  /* seconds */
res = select(maxfd, &readfs, NULL, NULL, &Timeout);
if (res==0)
/* number of file descriptors with input = 0, timeout occurred. */
```

This example will timeout after 1 second. If a timeout occurs, select will return 0, but beware that `Timeout` is decremented by the time actually waited for input by `select`. If the timeout value is zero, select will return immediatly.

4   Other Sources of Information

- The Linux Serial-HOWTO describes how to set up serial ports and contains hardware information.
- *Serial Programming Guide for POSIX Compliant Operating Systems* <http://www.easysw.com/~mike/serial>, by Michael Sweet. This link is obsolete and I could not find a new location for it. Does somebody know where we can find it again? It was a well prepared document!
- The manual page `termios(3)` describes all flags for the `termios` structure.

5   Contributions

As mentioned in the introduction, I am no expert in this field, but had problems myself, and found a solution with the help of others. Thanks for the help from Mr. Strudthoff from the European Transonic Windtunnel, Cologne, Michael Carter (mcarter@rocke.electro.swri.edu, and Peter Waltenberg (p.waltenberg@karaka.chch.cri.nz)

Antonino Ianella (antonino@usa.net wrote the Serial-Port-Programming Mini HOWTO, at the same time I prepared this document. Greg Hankins asked me to incorporate Antonino's Mini-HOWTO into this document.

The structure of this document and SGML formatting was derived from the Serial-HOWTO by Greg Hankins. Thanks also for various corrections made by : Dave Pfaltzgraff (Dave_Pfaltzgraff@patapsco.com), Sean Lincolne (slincol@tpgi.com.au), Michael Wiedmann (mw@miwie.in-berlin.de), and Adrey Bonar (andy@tipas.lt).

"Linux Shadow Password HOWTO" Michael H. Jackson

mhjack@tscnet.com

v1.3, 3 April 1996

This document aims to describe how to obtain, install, and configure the Linux password *Shadow Suite*. It also discusses obtaining, and reinstalling other software and network daemons that require access to user passwords. This other software is not actually part of the Shadow Suite, but these programs will need to be recompiled to support the *Shadow Suite*. This document also contains a programming example for adding shadow support to a program. Answers to some of the more frequently asked questions are included near the end of this document.

Contents

HOWTO

1 Introduction.

This is the Linux Shadow-Password-HOWTO. This document describes why and how to add shadow password support on a Linux system. Some examples of how to use some of the *Shadow Suite's* features is also included.

When installing the *Shadow Suite* and when using many of the utility programs, you must be logged in as *root*. When installing the *Shadow Suite* you will be making changes to system software, and it is highly recommended that you make backup copies of programs as indicated. I also recommend that you read and understand all the instructions before you begin.

1.1 Changes from the previous release.

```
Additions:
        Added a sub-section on why you might not want to install shadow
        Added a sub-section on updating the xdm program
        Added a section on how to put Shadow Suite features to work
        Added a section containing frequently asked questions

Corrections/Updates:
        Corrected html references on Sunsite
        Corrected section on wu-ftp to reflect adding -lshadow to the Makefile
        Corrected minor spelling and verbiage errors
        Changed section on wu-ftpd to support ELF
        Updated to reflect security problems in various login programs
        Updated to recommend the Linux Shadow Suite by Marek Michalkiewicz
```

1.2 New versions of this document.

The latest released version of this document can always be retrieved by anonymous FTP from:

sunsite.unc.edu

/pub/Linux/docs/HOWTO/Shadow-Password-HOWTO

or:

/pub/Linux/docs/HOWTO/other-formats/Shadow-Password-HOWTO{-html.tar,ps,dvi}.gz

or via the World Wide Web from the *Linux Documentation Project Web Server* <http://sunsite.unc. edu/mdw/linux.html>, at page: *Shadow-Password-HOWTO* <http://sunsite.unc.edu/linux/HOWTO/ Shadow-Password-HOWTO.html> or directly from me, <mhjack@tscnet.com>. It will also be posted to the newsgroup: comp.os.linux.answers

This document is now packaged with the Shadow-YYDDMM packages.

1.3 Feedback.

Please send any comments, updates, or suggestions to me: *Michael H. Jackson <mhjack@tscnet.com>* The sooner I get feedback, the sooner I can update and correct this document. If you find any problems with it, please mail me directly as I very rarely stay up-to-date on the newsgroups.

2 Why shadow your passwd file?

By default, most current Linux distributions do not contain the *Shadow Suite* installed. This includes Slackware 2.3, Slackware 3.0, and other popular distributions. One of the reasons for this is that the copyright notices in the original *Shadow Suite* were not clear on redistribution if a fee was charged. Linux uses a GNU Copyright (sometimes refereed to as a Copyleft) that allows people to package it into a convenient package (like a CD-ROM distribution) and charge a fee for it.

The current maintainer of the *Shadow Suite, Marek Michalkiewicz <marekm@i17linuxb.ists.pwr.wroc.pl>* received the source code from the original author under a BSD style copyright that allowed redistribution. Now that the copyright issues are resolved, it is expected that future distributions will contain password shadowing by default. Until then, you will need to install it yourself.

If you installed your distribution from a CD-ROM, you may find that, even though the distribution did not have the *Shadow Suite* installed, some of the files you need to install the *Shadow Suite* may be on the CD-ROM.

However, Shadow Suite versions 3.3.1, 3.3.1-2, and shadow-mk all have security problems with their login program and several other suid root programs that came with them, and should no longer be used.

All of the necessary files may be obtained via anonymous FTP or through the World Wide Web.

On a Linux system without the *Shadow Suite* installed, user information including passwords is stored in the `/etc/passwd` file. The password is stored in an *encrypted* format. If you ask a cryptography expert, however, he or she will tell you that the password is actually in an *encoded* rather than *encrypted* format because when using crypt(3), the text is set to null and the password is the key. Therefore, from here on, I will use the term *encoded* in this document.

The algorithm used to encode the password field is technically referred to as a *one way hash function*. This is an algorithm that is easy to compute in one direction, but very difficult to calculate in the reverse direction. More about the actual algorithm used can be found in section 2.4 or your crypt(3) manual page.

When a user picks or is assigned a password, it is encoded with a randomly generated value called the *salt*. This means that any particular password could be stored in 4096 different ways. The *salt* value is then stored with the encoded password.

When a user logs in and supplies a password, the *salt* is first retrieved from the stored encoded password. Then the supplied password is *encoded* with the *salt* value, and then compared with the *encoded* password. If there is a match, then the user is authenticated.

It is computationally difficult (but not impossible) to take a randomly *encoded* password and recover the original password. However, on any system with more than just a few users, at least some of the passwords will be common words (or simple variations of common words).

System crackers know all this, and will simply encrypt a dictionary of words and common passwords using all possible 4096 *salt* values. Then they will compare the encoded passwords in your `/etc/passwd` file with their database. Once they have found a match, they have the password for another account. This is referred to as a *dictionary attack*, and is one of the most common methods for gaining or expanding unauthorized access to a system.

If you think about it, an 8 character password encodes to 4096 * 13 character strings. So a dictionary of say 400,000 common words, names, passwords, and simple variations would easily fit on a 4GB hard drive. The attacker need only sort them, and then check for matches. Since a 4GB hard drive can be had for under $1000.00, this is well within the means of most system crackers.

Also, if a cracker obtains your `/etc/passwd` file first, they only need to encode the dictionary with the `salt` values actually contained in your `/etc/passwd` file. This method is usable by your average teenager with a couple of hundred spare Megabytes and a 486 class computer.

Even without lots of drive space, utilities like crack(1) can usually break at least a couple of passwords on a system with enough users (assuming the users of the system are allowed to pick their own passwords).

The `/etc/passwd` file also contains information like user ID's and group ID's that are used by many system programs. Therefore, the `/etc/passwd` file *must* remain world readable. If you were to change the `/etc/passwd` file so that nobody can read it, the first thing that you would notice is that the `ls -l` command now displays user ID's instead of names!

The *Shadow Suite* solves the problem by relocating the passwords to another file (usually `/etc/shadow`). The `/etc/shadow` file is set so that it cannot be read by just anyone. Only *root* will be able to read and write to the `/etc/shadow` file. Some programs (like xlock) don't need to be able to change passwords, they only need to be able to verify them. These programs can either be run *suid root* or you can set up a group *shadow* that is allowed read only access to the `/etc/shadow` file. Then the program can be run *sgid shadow*.

By moving the passwords to the `/etc/shadow` file, we are effectively keeping the attacker from having access to the encoded passwords with which to perform a *dictionary attack*.

Additionally, the *Shadow Suite* adds lots of other nice features:

- A configuration file to set login defaults (`/etc/login.defs`)
- Utilities for adding, modifying, and deleting user accounts and groups
- Password aging and expiration
- Account expiration and locking
- Shadowed group passwords (optional)
- Double length passwords (16 character passwords— NOT RECOMMENDED)
- Better control over user's password selection
- Dial-up passwords
- Secondary authentication programs (NOT RECOMMENDED)

Installing the *Shadow Suite* contributes toward a more secure system, but there are many other things that can also be done to improve the security of a Linux system, and there will eventually be a series of Linux Security HOWTO's that will discuss other security measures and related issues.

For current information on other Linux security issues, including warnings on known vulnerabilities see the *Linux Security home page.* <http://bach.cis.temple.edu/linux/linux-security/>

2.1 Why you might NOT want to shadow your passwd file.

There are a few circumstances and configurations in which installing the *Shadow Suite* would *NOT* be a good idea:

- The machine does not contain user accounts.
- Your machine is running on a LAN and is using NIS (Network Information Services) to get or supply user names and passwords to other machines on the network. (This can actually be done, but is beyond the scope of this document, and really won't increase security much anyway)
- Your machine is being used by terminal servers to verify users via NFS (Network File System), NIS, or some other method.
- Your machine runs other software that validates users, and there is no shadow version available, and you don't have the source code.

2.2 Format of the /etc/passwd file

A non-shadowed `/etc/passwd` file has the following format:

```
username:passwd:UID:GID:full_name:directory:shell
```

Where:

username
> The user (login) name

passwd
> The encoded password

UID
> Numerical user ID

GID

Numerical default group ID

full_name

The user's full name - Actually this field is called the GECOS (General Electric Comprehensive Operating System) field and can store information other than just the full name. The Shadow commands and manual pages refer to this field as the comment field.

directory

User's home directory (Full pathname)

shell

User's login shell (Full Pathname)

For example:

```
username:Npge08pfz4wuk:503:100:Full Name:/home/username:/bin/sh
```

Where Np is the salt and ge08pfz4wuk is the *encoded* password. The encoded salt/password could just as easily have been kbeMVnZM0oL7I and the two are exactly the same password. There are 4096 possible encodings for the same password. (The example password in this case is 'password', a really *bad* password).

Once the shadow suite is installed, the /etc/passwd file would instead contain:

```
username:x:503:100:Full Name:/home/username:/bin/sh
```

The x in the second field in this case is now just a place holder. The format of the /etc/passwd file really didn't change, it just no longer contains the *encoded* password. This means that any program that reads the /etc/passwd file but does not actually need to verify passwords will still operate correctly.

The passwords are now relocated to the shadow file (usually /etc/shadow file).

2.3 Format of the shadow file

The /etc/shadow file contains the following information:

```
username:passwd:last:may:must:warn:expire:disable:reserved
```

Where:

username

The User Name

passwd

The Encoded password

last

Days since Jan 1, 1970 that password was last changed

may

Days before password may be changed

must

Days after which password must be changed

warn

Days before password is to expire that user is warned

expire

>   Days after password expires that account is disabled

disable

>   Days since Jan 1, 1970 that account is disabled

reserved

>   A reserved field

The previous example might then be:

```
username:Npge08pfz4wuk:9479:0:10000::::
```

2.4   Review of crypt(3).

From the crypt(3) manual page:

"*crypt* is the password encryption function. It is based on the *Data Encryption Standard* algorithm with variations intended (among other things) to discourage use of hardware implementations of a key search.

The key is a user's typed password. (The encoded string is all NULLs)

The *salt* is a two-character string chosen from the set (a-zA-Z0-9./). This string is used to perturb the algorithm in one of 4096 different ways.

By taking the lowest 7 bits of each character of the key, a 56-bit key is obtained. This 56-bit key is used to encrypt repeatedly a constant string (usually a string consisting of all zeros). The returned value points to the encrypted password, a series of 13 printable ASCII characters (the first two characters represent the salt itself). The return value points to static data whose content is overwritten by each call.

Warning: The key space consists of 2**56 equal 7.2e16 possible values. Exhaustive searches of this key space **are possible** using massively parallel computers. Software, such as `crack(1)`, is available which will search the portion of this key space that is generally used by humans for passwords. Hence, password selection should, at minimum, avoid common words and names. The use of a `passwd(1)` program that checks for crackable passwords during the selection process is recommended.

The DES algorithm itself has a few quirks which make the use of the `crypt(3)` interface a very poor choice for anything other than password authentication. If you are planning on using the `crypt(3)` interface for a cryptography project, don't do it: get a good book on encryption and one of the widely available DES libraries."

Most *Shadow Suites* contain code for doubling the length of the password to 16 characters. Experts in des recommend against this, as the encoding is simply applied first to the left half and then to the right half of the longer password. Because of the way crypt works, this may make for a *less* secure encoded password then if double length passwords were not used in the first place. Additionally, it is less likely that a user will be able to remember a 16 character password.

There is development work under way that would allow the authentication algorithm to be replaced with something more secure and with support for longer passwords (specifically the MD5 algorithm) and retain compatibility with the crypt method.

If you are looking for a good book on encryption, I recommend:

```
"Applied Cryptography: Protocols, Algorithms, and Source Code in C"
by Bruce Schneier <schneier@chinet.com>
ISBN: 0-471-59756-2
```

3   Getting the Shadow Suite.

3.1   History of the Shadow Suite for Linux

DO NOT USE THE PACKAGES IN THIS SECTION, THEY HAVE SECURITY PROBLEMS

The original *Shadow Suite* was written by `John F. Haugh II`.

There are several versions that have been used on Linux systems:

- `shadow-3.3.1` is the original.
- `shadow-3.3.1-2` is Linux specific patch made by *Florian La Roche <flla@stud.uni-sb.de>* and contains some further enhancements.
- `shadow-mk` was specifically packaged for Linux.

The `shadow-mk` package contains the `shadow-3.3.1` package distributed by `John F. Haugh II` with the `shadow-3.3.1-2 patch` installed, a few fixes made by *Mohan Kokal <magnus@texas.net>* that make installation a lot easier, a patch by `Joseph R.M. Zbiciak` for `login1.c` (login.secure) that eliminates the -f, -h security holes in /bin/login, and some other miscellaneous patches.

The `shadow.mk` package was the *previously* recommended package, but should be replaced due to a *security problem* with the `login` program.

There are *security problems* with Shadow versions 3.3.1, 3.3.1-2, and shadow-mk involving the `login` program. This `login` bug involves not checking the length of a login name. This causes the buffer to overflow causing crashes or worse. It has been rumored that this buffer overflow can allow someone with an account on the system to use this bug and the shared libraries to gain *root* access. I won't discuss exactly how this is possible because there are a lot of Linux systems that are affected, but systems with these *Shadow Suites* installed, and most pre-ELF distributions *without* the *Shadow Suite* are vulnerable!

For more information on this and other Linux security issues, see the *Linux Security home page (Shared Libraries and login Program Vulnerability)* `<http://bach.cis.temple.edu/linux/linux-security/ Linux-Security-FAQ/Linux-telnetd.html>`

3.2   Where to get the Shadow Suite.

The only recommended *Shadow Suite* is still in BETA testing, however the latest versions are safe in a production environment and don't contain a vulnerable `login` program.

The package uses the following naming convention:

```
shadow-YYMMDD.tar.gz
```

where `YYMMDD` is the issue date of the Suite.

This version will eventually be *Version 3.3.3* when it is released from Beta testing, and is maintained by *Marek Michalkiewicz <marekm@i17linuxb.ists.pwr.wroc.pl>*. It's available as: *shadow-current.tar.gz* `<ftp://i17linuxb. ists.pwr.wroc.pl/pub/linux/shadow/shadow-current.tar.gz>`.

The following mirror sites have also been established:

- *ftp://ftp.icm.edu.pl/pub/Linux/shadow/shadow-current.tar.gz*
- *ftp://iguana.hut.fi/pub/linux/shadow/shadow-current.tar.gz*
- *ftp://ftp.cin.net/usr/ggallag/shadow/shadow-current.tar.gz*
- *ftp://ftp.netural.com/pub/linux/shadow/shadow-current.tar.gz*

You should use the currently available version.

You should NOT use a version *older* than shadow-960129 as they also have the login security problem discussed above.

When this document refers to the *Shadow Suite* I am referring to the this package. It is assumed that this is the package that you are using.

For reference, I used shadow-960129 to make these installation instructions.

If you were previously using shadow-mk, you should upgrade to this version and rebuild everything that you originally compiled.

3.3 What is included with the Shadow Suite.

The *Shadow Suite* contains replacement programs for:

su, login, passwd, newgrp, chfn, chsh, and id

The package also contains the new programs:

chage, newusers, dpasswd, gpasswd, useradd, userdel, usermod, groupadd, groupdel, groupmod, groups, pwck, grpck, lastlog, pwconv, and pwunconv

Additionally, the library: libshadow.a is included for writing and/or compiling programs that need to access user passwords.

Also, manual pages for the programs are also included.

There is also a configuration file for the login program which will be installed as /etc/login.defs.

4 Compiling the programs.

4.1 Unpacking the archive.

The first step after retrieving the package is unpacking it. The package is in the tar (tape archive) format and compressed using gzip, so first move it to /usr/src, then type:

```
tar -xzvf shadow-current.tar.gz
```

This will unpack it into the directory: /usr/src/shadow-YYMMDD

4.2 Configuring with the config.h file

The first thing that you need to do is to copy over the Makefile and the config.h file:

```
cd /usr/src/shadow-YYMMDD
cp Makefile.linux Makefile
cp config.h.linux config.h
```

You should then take a look at the config.h file. This file contains definitions for some of the configuration options. If you are using the *recommended* package, I recommend that you disable group shadow support for your first time around.

By default shadowed group passwords are enabled. To disable these edit the config.h file, and change the #define SHADOWGRP to #undef SHADOWGRP. I recommend that you disable them to start with, and then if you really want group passwords and group administrators that you enable it later and recompile. If you leave it enabled, you *must* create the file /etc/gshadow.

Enabling the long passwords option is NOT recommended as discussed above.

Do NOT change the setting: #undef AUTOSHADOW

The AUTOSHADOW option was originally designed so that programs that were shadow ignorant would still function. This sounds good in theory, but does not work correctly. If you enable this option, and the program runs as root, it may call getpwnam() as root, and later write the modified entry back to the /etc/passwd file (with the *no-longer-shadowed password*). Such programs include chfn and chsh. (You can't get around this by swapping real and effective uid before calling getpwnam() because root may use chfn and chsh too.)

The same warning is also valid if you are building libc, it has a SHADOW_COMPAT option which does the same thing. It *should NOT* be used! If you start getting encoded passwords back in your /etc/passwd file, this is the problem.

If you are using a libc version prior to 4.6.27, you will need to make a couple more changes to config.h and the Makefile. To config.h edit and change:

    #define HAVE_BASENAME

to:

    #undef HAVE_BASENAME

And then in the Makefile, change:

```
SOBJS = smain.o env.o entry.o susetup.o shell.o \
        sub.o mail.o motd.o sulog.o age.o tz.o hushed.o

SSRCS = smain.c env.c entry.c setup.c shell.c \
        pwent.c sub.c mail.c motd.c sulog.c shadow.c age.c pw-
pack.c rad64.c \
        tz.c hushed.c

SOBJS = smain.o env.o entry.o susetup.o shell.o \
        sub.o mail.o motd.o sulog.o age.o tz.o hushed.o basename.o

SSRCS = smain.c env.c entry.c setup.c shell.c \
        pwent.c sub.c mail.c motd.c sulog.c shadow.c age.c pw-
pack.c rad64.c \
        tz.c hushed.c basename.c
```

These changes add the code contained in basename.c which is contained in libc 4.6.27 and later.

4.3   Making backup copies of your original programs.

It would also be a good idea to track down and make backup copies of the programs that the shadow suite will replace. On a Slackware 3.0 system these are:

- /bin/su
- /bin/login
- /usr/bin/passwd
- /usr/bin/newgrp
- /usr/bin/chfn
- /usr/bin/chsh
- /usr/bin/id

The BETA package has a *save* target in the Makefile, but it's commented out because different distributions place the programs in different places.

You should also make a backup copy of your `/etc/passwd` file, but be careful to name it something else if you place it in the same directory so you don't overwrite the `passwd` command.

4.4 Running make

You need to be logged as root to do most of the installation.

Run make to compile the executables in the package:

```
make all
```

You may see the warning: `rcsid defined but not used`. This is fine, it just happens because the author is using a version control package.

5 Installing

5.1 Have a boot disk handy in case you break anything.

If something goes terribly wrong, it would be handy to have a boot disk. If you have a boot/root combination from your installation, that will work, otherwise see the *Bootdisk-HOWTO* `<http://sunsite.unc.edu/mdw/HOWTO/ Bootdisk-HOWTO.html>`, which describes how to make a bootable disk.

5.2 Removing duplicate man pages

You should also move the manual pages that are about to be replaced. Even if you are brave enough install the Shadow Suite without making backups, you will still want to remove the old manual pages. The new manual pages won't normally overwrite the old ones because the old ones are probably compressed.

You can use a combination of: `man -aW command` and `locate command` to locate the manual pages that need to be (re)moved. It's generally easier to figure out which are the older pages before you run `make install`.

If you are using the Slackware 3.0 distribution, then the manual pages you want to remove are:

- /usr/man/man1/chfn.1.gz
- /usr/man/man1/chsh.1.gz
- /usr/man/man1/id.1.gz
- /usr/man/man1/login.1.gz
- /usr/man/man1/passwd.1.gz
- /usr/man/man1/su.1.gz
- /usr/man/man5/passwd.5.gz

There may also be man pages of the same name in the `/var/man/cat[1-9]` subdirectories that should also be deleted.

5.3 Running make install

You are now ready to type: (do this as root)

```
make install
```

This will install the new and replacement programs and fix-up the file permissions. It will also install the man pages.

This also takes care of installing the Shadow Suite include files in the correct places in /usr/include/shadow.

Using the BETA package you must manually copy the file login.defs to the /etc subdirectory and make sure that only *root* can make changes to it.

```
cp login.defs /etc
chmod 700 /etc/login.defs
```

This file is the configuration file for the *login* program. You should review and make changes to this file for your particular system. This is where you decide which tty's root can login from, and set other security policy settings (like password expiration defaults).

5.4   Running pwconv

The next step is to run pwconv. This must also be done as *root*, and is best done from the /etc subdirectory:

```
cd /etc
/usr/sbin/pwconv
```

pwconv takes your /etc/passwd file and strips out the fields to create two files: /etc/npasswd and /etc/nshadow.

A pwunconv program is also provided if you need to make a normal /etc/passwd file out of an /etc/passwd and /etc/shadow combination.

5.5   Renaming npasswd and nshadow

Now that you have run pwconv you have created the files /etc/npasswd and /etc/nshadow. These need to be copied over to /etc/passwd and /etc/shadow. We also want to make a backup copy of the original /etc/passwd file, and make sure only root can read it. We'll put the backup in root's home directory:

```
cd /etc
cp passwd ~passwd
chmod 600 ~passwd
mv npasswd passwd
mv nshadow shadow
```

You should also ensure that the file ownerships and permissions are correct. If you are going to be using *X-Windows*, the xlock and xdm programs need to be able to read the shadow file (but not write it).

There are two ways that this can be done. You can set xlock to suid root (xdm is usually run as root anyway). Or you can make the shadow file owned by root with a group of shadow, but before you do this, make sure that you have a shadow group (look in /etc/group). None of the users on the system should actually be in the shadow group.

```
chown root.root passwd
chown root.shadow shadow
chmod 0644 passwd
chmod 0640 shadow
```

Your system now has the password file shadowed. You *should* now pop over to another virtual terminal and verify that you can login.

Really, do this now!

If you can't, then something is wrong! To get back to a non-shadowed state, do the following the following:

```
cd /etc
cp ~passwd passwd
chmod 644 passwd
```

You would then restore the files that you saved earlier to their proper locations.

6   Other programs you may need to upgrade or patch

Even though the shadow suite contains replacement programs for most programs that need to access passwords, there are a few additional programs on most systems that require access to passwords.

If you are running a *Debian Distribution* (or even if you are not), you can obtain Debian sources for the programs that need to be rebuild from: ftp://ftp.debian.org/debian/stable/source/

The remainder of this section discusses how to upgrade `adduser`, `wu_ftpd`, `ftpd`, `pop3d`, `xlock`, `xdm` and `sudo` so that they support the shadow suite.

See the section 8 (Adding Shadow Support to a C program) for a discussion on how to put shadow support into any other program that needs it (although the program must then be run SUID root or SGID shadow to be able to actually access the shadow file).

6.1   Slackware adduser program

Slackware distributions (and possibly some others) contain a interactive program for adding users called `/s-bin/adduser`. A shadow version of this program can be obtained from *ftp://sunsite.unc.edu/pub/Linux/system/Admin/accounts/adduser.shadow-1.4.tar.gz.*

I would encourage you to use the programs that are supplied with the *Shadow Suite* (`useradd`, `usermod`, and `userdel`) instead of the slackware `adduser` program. They take a little time to learn how to use, but it's well worth the effort because you have much more control and they perform proper file locking on the `/etc/passwd` and `/etc/shadow` file (`adduser` doesn't).

See the section on 7 (Putting the Shadow Suite to use) for more information.

But if you gotta have it, here is what you do:

```
tar -xzvf adduser.shadow-1.4.tar.gz
cd adduser
make clean
make adduser
chmod 700 adduser
cp adduser /sbin
```

6.2   The wu_ftpd Server

Most Linux systems some with the `wu_ftpd` server. If your distribution does not come with shadow installed, then your `wu_ftpd` will not be compiled for shadow. `wu_ftpd` is launched from `inetd/tcpd` as a *root* process. If you are running an old `wu_ftpd` daemon, you will want to upgrade it anyway because older ones had a bug that would allow the *root* account to be compromised (For more info see the *Linux security home page* <http://bach.cis.temple.edu/linux/linux-security/Linux-Security-FAQ/Linux-wu.ftpd-2.4-Update.html>).

Fortunately, you only need to get the source code and recompile it with shadow enabled.

If you are not running an ELF system, The `wu_ftp` server can be found on Sunsite as *wu-ftp-2.4-fixed.tar.gz* <ftp://sunsite.unc.edu/pub/Linux/system/Network/file-transfer/wu-ftpd-2.4-fixed.tar.gz>

Once you retrieve the server, put it in /usr/src, then type:

```
cd /usr/src
tar -xzvf wu-ftpd-2.4-fixed.tar.gz
cd wu-ftpd-2.4-fixed
cp ./src/config/config.lnx.shadow ./src/config/config.lnx
```

Then edit ./src/makefiles/Makefile.lnx, and change the line:

```
LIBES     = -lbsd -support
```

to:

```
LIBES     = -lbsd -support -lshadow
```

Now you are ready to run the build script and install:

```
cd /usr/src/wu-ftpd-2.4-fixed
/usr/src/wu-ftp-2.4.fixed/build lnx
cp /usr/sbin/wu.ftpd /usr/sbin/wu.ftpd.old
cp ./bin/ftpd /usr/sbin/wu.ftpd
```

This uses the Linux shadow configuration file, compiles and installs the server.

On my Slackware 2.3 system I also had to do the following before running build:

```
cd /usr/include/netinet
ln -s in_systm.h in_system.h
cd -
```

Problems have been reported compiling this package under ELF systems, but the Beta version of the next release works fine. It can be found as *wu-ftp-2.4.2-beta-10.tar.gz* <ftp://tscnet.com/pub/linux/network/ftp/wu-ftpd-2.4.2-beta-10.tar.gz>

Once you retrieve the server, put it in /usr/src, then type:

```
cd /usr/src
tar -xzvf wu-ftpd-2.4.2-beta-9.tar.gz
cd wu-ftpd-beta-9
cd ./src/config
```

Then edit config.lnx, and change:

```
#undef SHADOW.PASSWORD
```

to:

```
#define SHADOW.PASSWORD
```

Then,

```
cd ../Makefiles
```

and edit the file Makefile.lnx and change:

```
LIBES = -lsupport -lbsd # -lshadow
```

to:

```
LIBES = -lsupport -lbsd -lshadow
```

Then build and install:

```
cd ..
build lnx
cp /usr/sbin/wu.ftpd /usr/sbin/wu.ftpd.old
cp ./bin/ftpd /usr/sbin/wu.ftpd
```

Note that you should check your /etc/inetd.conf file to make sure that this is where your wu.ftpd server really lives. It has been reported that some distributions place the server daemons in different places, and then wu.ftpd in particular may be named something else.

6.3   Standard ftpd

If you are running the standard ftpd server, I would recommend that you upgrade to the wu_ftpd server. Aside from the known bug discussed above, it's generally thought to be more secure.

If you insist on the standard one, or you need *NIS* support, Sunsite has *ftpd-shadow-nis.tgz* <ftp://sunsite.unc.edu/pub/Linux/system/Network/file-transfer/ftpd-shadow-nis.tgz>

6.4   pop3d (Post Office Protocol 3)

If you need to support the third *Post Office Protocol (POP3)*, you will need to recompile a pop3d program. pop3d is normally run by inetd/tcpd as root.

There are two versions available from Sunsite: *pop3d-1.00.4.linux.shadow.tar.gz* <ftp://sunsite.unc.edu/pub/Linux/system/Mail/pop/pop3d-1.00.4.linux.shadow.tar.gz> and *pop3d+shadow+elf.tar.gz* <ftp://sunsite.unc.edu/pub/Linux/system/Mail/pop/pop3d+shadow+elf.tar.gz>

Both of these are fairly straight forward to install.

6.5   xlock

If you install the shadow suite, and then run *X Windows System* and lock the screen without upgrading your xlock, you will have to use CNTL-ALT-Fx to switch to another *tty*, login, and kill the xlock process (or use CNTL-ALT-BS to kill the X server). Fortunately it's fairly easy to upgrade your xlock program.

If you are running XFree86 Versions 3.x.x, you are probably using xlockmore (which is a great screen-saver in addition to a lock). This package supports *shadow* with a recompile. If you have an older xlock, I recommend that you upgrade to this one.

xlockmore-3.5.tgz is available at: <ftp://sunsite.unc.edu/pub/Linux/X11/xutils/screensavers/xlockmore-3.7.tgz>

Basically, this is what you need to do:

Get the xlockmore-3.7.tgz file and put it in /usr/src unpack it:

```
tar -xzvf xlockmore-3.7.tgz
```

Edit the file: /usr/X11R6/lib/X11/config/linux.cf, and change the line:

```
#define HasShadowPasswd     NO

to

#define HasShadowPasswd     YES
```

Then build the executables:

```
cd /usr/src/xlockmore
xmkmf
make depend
make
```

Then move everything into place and update file ownerships and permissions:

```
cp xlock /usr/X11R6/bin/
cp XLock /var/X11R6/lib/app-defaults/
chown root.shadow /usr/X11R6/bin/xlock
chmod 2755 /usr/X11R6/bin/xlock
chown root.shadow /etc/shadow
chmod 640 /etc/shadow
```

Your xlock will now work correctly.

6.6   xdm

xdm is a program that presents a login screen for X-Windows. Some systems start xdm when the system is told to goto a specified run level (see /etc/inittab.

With the *Shadow Suite* install, xdm will need to be updated. Fortunately it's fairly easy to upgrade your xdm program.

xdm.tar.gz is available at: `<ftp://sunsite.unc.edu/pub/Linux/X11/xutils/xdm.tar.gz>`

Get the xdm.tar.gz file and put it in /usr/src, then to unpack it:

```
tar -xzvf xdm.tar.gz
```

Edit the file: /usr/X11R6/lib/X11/config/linux.cf, and change the line:

```
#define HasShadowPasswd     NO

to

#define HasShadowPasswd     YES
```

Then build the executables:

```
cd /usr/src/xdm
xmkmf
make depend
make
```

Then move everything into place:

```
cp xdm /usr/X11R6/bin/
```

xdm is run as *root* so you don't need to change it file permissions.

6.7 sudo

The program sudo allows a system administrator to let users run programs that would normally require root access. This is handy because it lets the administrator limit access to the root account itself while still allowing users to do things like mounting drives.

sudo needs to read passwords because it verifies the users password when it's invoked. sudo already runs SUID root, so accessing the /etc/shadow file is not a problem.

sudo for the shadow suite, is available as at: `<ftp://sunsite.unc.edu/pub/Linux/system/Admin/ sudo-1.2-shadow.tgz>`

Warning: When you install sudo your /etc/sudoers file will be replaced with a default one, so you need to make a backup of it if you have added anything to the default one. (you could also edit the Makefile and remove the line that copies the default file to /etc).

The package is already setup for shadow, so all that's required is to recompile the package (put it in /usr/src):

```
cd /usr/src
tar -xzvf sudo-1.2-shadow.tgz
cd sudo-1.2-shadow
make all
make install
```

6.8 imapd (E-Mail pine package)

imapd is an e-mail server similar to pop3d. imapd comes with the *Pine E-mail* package. The documentation that comes with the package states that the default for Linux systems is to include support for shadow. However, I have found that this is not true. Furthermore, the build script / Makefile combination on this package is makes it very difficult to add the libshadow.a library at compile time, so I was unable to add shadow support for imapd.

If anyone has this figured out, please E-mail me, and I'll include the solution here.

6.9 pppd (Point-to-Point Protocol Server)

The pppd server can be setup to use several types of authentication: *Password Authentication Protocol* (PAP) and *Cryptographic Handshake Authentication Protocol* (CHAP). The pppd server usually reads the password strings that it uses from /etc/ppp/chap-secrets and/or /etc/ppp/pap-secrets. If you are using this default behavior of pppd, it is not necessary to reinstall pppd.

pppd also allows you to use the *login* parameter (either on the command line, or in the configuration or options file). If the *login* option is given, then pppd will use the /etc/passwd file for the username and passwords for the *PAP*. This, of course, will no longer work now that our password file is shadowed. For pppd-1.2.1d this requires adding code for shadow support.

The example given in the next section is adding shadow support to pppd-1.2.1d (an older version of pppd).

pppd-2.2.0 already contains shadow support.

7 Putting the Shadow Suite to use.

This section discusses some of the things that you will want to know now that you have the *Shadow Suite* installed on your system. More information is contained in the manual pages for each command.

7.1 Adding, Modifying, and deleting users

The *Shadow Suite* added the following command line oriented commands for adding, modifying, and deleting users. You may also have installed the `adduser` program.

7.1.1 useradd

The `useradd` command can be used to add users to the system. You also invoke this command to change the default settings.

The first thing that you should do is to examine the default settings and make changes specific to your system:

```
useradd -D
```

```
GROUP=1
HOME=/home
INACTIVE=0
EXPIRE=0
SHELL=
SKEL=/etc/skel
```

The defaults are probably not what you want, so if you started adding users now you would have to specify all the information for each user. However, we can and should change the default values.

On my system:

- I want the default group to be 100
- I want passwords to expire every 60 days
- I don't want to lock an account because the password is expired
- I want to default shell to be `/bin/bash`

To make these changes I would use:

```
useradd -D -g100 -e60 -f0 -s/bin/bash
```

Now running `useradd -D` will give:

```
GROUP=100
HOME=/home
INACTIVE=0
EXPIRE=60
SHELL=/bin/bash
SKEL=/etc/skel
```

Just in case you wanted to know, these defaults are stored in the file `/etc/default/useradd`.

Now you can use `useradd` to add users to the system. For example, to add the user `fred`, using the defaults, you would use the following:

```
useradd -m -c "Fred Flintstone" fred
```

This will create the following entry in the `/etc/passwd` file:

```
fred:*:505:100:Fred Flintstone:/home/fred:/bin/bash
```

And the following entry in the /etc/shadow file:

```
fred:!:0:0:60:0:0:0:0
```

fred's home directory will be created and the contents of /etc/skel will be copied there because of the -m switch.

Also, since we did not specify a UID, the next available one was used.

fred's account is created, but fred still won't be able to login until we unlock the account. We do this by changing the password.

```
passwd fred
```

```
Changing password for fred
Enter the new password (minimum of 5 characters)
Please use a combination of upper and lower case letters and numbers.
New Password: *******
Re-enter new password: *******
```

Now the /etc/shadow will contain:

```
fred:J0C.WDR1amIt6:9559:0:60:0:0:0:0
```

And fred will now be able to login and use the system. The nice thing about useradd and the other programs that come with the *Shadow Suite* is that they make changes to the /etc/passwd and /etc/shadow files atomically. So if you are adding a user, and another user is changing their password at the same time, both operations will be performed correctly.

You should use the supplied commands rather than directly editing /etc/passwd and /etc/shadow. If you were editing the /etc/shadow file, and a user were to change his password while you are editing, and then you were to save the file you were editing, the user's password change would be lost.

Here is a small interactive script that adds users using useradd and passwd:

```
#!/bin/bash
#
# /sbin/newuser - A script to add users to the system using the Shadow
#                 Suite's useradd and passwd commands.
#
# Written my Mike Jackson <mhjack@tscnet.com> as an example for the Linux
# Shadow Password Howto.  Permission to use and modify is expressly granted.
#
# This could be modified to show the defaults and allow modification similar
# to the Slackware Adduser program.  It could also be modified to disallow
# stupid entries.  (i.e. better error checking).
#
##
#  Defaults for the useradd command
##
GROUP=100       # Default Group
HOME=/home      # Home directory location (/home/username)
SKEL=/etc/skel  # Skeleton Directory
INACTIVE=0      # Days after password expires to disable account (0=never)
EXPIRE=60       # Days that a passwords lasts
SHELL=/bin/bash # Default Shell (full path)
```

HOWTO

```
##
#   Defaults for the passwd command
##
PASSMIN=0          # Days between password changes
PASSWARN=14        # Days before password expires that a warning is given
##
#   Ensure that root is running the script.
##
WHOAMI='/usr/bin/whoami'
if [ $WHOAMI != "root" ]; then
        echo "You must be root to add news users!"
        exit 1
fi
##
#   Ask for username and fullname.
##
echo ""
echo -n "Username: "
read USERNAME
echo -n "Full name: "
read FULLNAME
#
echo "Adding user: $USERNAME."
#
# Note that the "" around $FULLNAME is required because this field is
# almost always going to contain at least on space, and without the "'s
# the useradd command would think that you we moving on to the next
# parameter when it reached the SPACE character.
#
/usr/sbin/useradd -c"$FULLNAME" -d$HOME/$USERNAME -e$EXPIRE \
        -f$INACTIVE -g$GROUP -m -k$SKEL -s$SHELL $USERNAME
##
#   Set password defaults
##
/bin/passwd -n $PASSMIN -w $PASSWARN $USERNAME >/dev/null 2>&1
##
#   Let the passwd command actually ask for password (twice)
##
/bin/passwd $USERNAME
##
#   Show what was done.
##
echo ""
echo "Entry from /etc/passwd:"
echo -n "        "
grep "$USERNAME:" /etc/passwd
echo "Entry from /etc/shadow:"
echo -n "        "
grep "$USERNAME:" /etc/shadow
echo "Summary output of the passwd command:"
echo -n "        "
passwd -S $USERNAME
echo ""
```

Using a script to add new users is really much more preferable than editing the /etc/passwd or /etc/shadow files directly or using a program like the Slackware `adduser` program. Feel free to use and modify this script for your particular system.

For more information on the `useradd` see the online manual page.

7.1.2 usermod

The `usermod` program is used to modify the information on a user. The switches are similar to the `useradd` program.

Let's say that you want to change `fred`'s shell, you would do the following:

```
usermod -s /bin/tcsh fred
```

Now `fred`'s `/etc/passwd` file entry would be change to this:

```
fred:*:505:100:Fred Flintstone:/home/fred:/bin/tcsh
```

Let's make `fred`'s account expire on 09/15/97:

```
usermod -e 09/15/97 fred
```

Now `fred`'s entry in `/etc/shadow` becomes:

```
fred:J0C.WDR1amIt6:9559:0:60:0:0:10119:0
```

For more information on the `usermod` command see the online manual page.

7.1.3 userdel

`userdel` does just what you would expect, it deletes the user's account. You simply use:

```
userdel -r username
```

The `-r` causes all files in the user's home directory to be removed along with the home directory itself. Files located in other file system will have to be searched for and deleted manually.

If you want to simply lock the account rather than delete it, use the `passwd` command instead.

7.2 The passwd command and passwd aging.

The `passwd` command has the obvious use of changing passwords. Additionally, it is used by the *root* user to:

- Lock and unlock accounts (`-l` and `-u`)
- Set the maximum number of days that a password remains valid (`-x`)
- Set the minimum days between password changes (`-n`)
- Sets the number of days of warning that a password is about to expire (`-w`)
- Sets the number of days after the password expires before the account is locked (`-i`)
- Allow viewing of account information in a clearer format (`-S`)

For example, let look again at `fred`

```
passwd -S fred
fred P 03/04/96 0 60 0 0
```

This means that `fred`'s password is valid, it was last changed on 03/04/96, it can be changed at any time, it expires after 60 days, fred will not be warned, and and the account won't be disabled when the password expires.

This simply means that if `fred` logs in after the password expires, he will be prompted for a new password at login.

If we decide that we want to warn `fred` 14 days before his password expires and make his account inactive 14 days after he lets it expire, we would need to do the following:

```
passwd -w14 -i14 fred
```

Now `fred` is changed to:

```
fred P 03/04/96 0 60 14 14
```

For more information on the `passwd` command see the online manual page.

7.3   The login.defs file.

The file `/etc/login` is the configuration file for the `login` program and also for the *Shadow Suite* as a whole.

`/etc/login` contains settings from what the prompts will look like to what the default expiration will be when a user changes his password.

The `/etc/login.defs` file is quite well documented just by the comments that are contained within it. However, there are a few things to note:

- It contains flags that can be turned on or off that determine the amount of logging that takes place.
- It contains pointers to other configuration files.
- It contains defaults assignments for things like password aging.

From the above list you can see that this is a rather important file, and you should make sure that it is present, and that the settings are what you desire for your system.

7.4   Group passwords.

The `/etc/groups` file may contain passwords that permit a user to become a member of a particular group. This function is enabled if you define the constant `SHADOWGRP` in the `/usr/src/shadow-YYMMDD/config.h` file.

If you define this constant and then compile, you must create an `/etc/gshadow` file to hold the group passwords and the group administrator information.

When you created the `/etc/shadow`, you used a program called `pwconv`, there no equivalent program to create the `/etc/gshadow` file, but it really doesn't matter, it takes care of itself.

To create the initial `/etc/gshadow` file do the following:

```
touch /etc/gshadow
chown root.root /etc/gshadow
chmod 700 /etc/gshadow
```

Once you create new groups, they will be added to the `/etc/group` and the `/etc/gshadow` files. If you modify a group by adding or removing users or changing the group password, the `/etc/gshadow` file will be changed.

The programs `groups`, `groupadd`, `groupmod`, and `groupdel` are provided as part of the *Shadow Suite* to modify groups.

The format of the `/etc/group` file is as follows:

```
groupname:!:GID:member,member,...
```

Where:

groupname

 The name of the group

!

 The field that normally holds the password, but that is now relocated to the `/etc/gshadow` file.

GID

 The numerical group ID number

member

 List of group members

The format of the `/etc/gshadow` file is as follows:

```
groupname:password:admin,admin,...:member,member,...
```

Where:

groupname

 The name of the group

password

 The encoded group password.

admin

 List of group administrators

member

 List of group members

The command `gpasswd` is used only for adding or removing administrators and members to or from a group. `root` or someone in the list of administrators may add or remove group members.

The groups password can be changed using the `passwd` command by *root* or anyone listed as an administrator for the group.

Despite the fact that there is not currently a manual page for `gpasswd`, typing `gpasswd` without any parameters gives a listing of options. It's fairly easy to grasp how it all works once you understand the file formats and the concepts.

7.5 Consistency checking programs

7.5.1 pwck

The program `pwck` is provided to provide a consistency check on the `/etc/passwd` and `/etc/shadow` files. It will check each username and verify that it has the following:

- the correct number of fields
- unique user name
- valid user and group identifier
- valid primary group
- valid home directory
- valid login shell

It will also warn of any account that has no password.

It's a good idea to run `pwck` after installing the *Shadow Suite*. It's also a good idea to run it periodically, perhaps weekly or monthly. If you use the `-r` option, you can use `cron` to run it on a regular basis and have the report mailed to you.

7.5.2   grpck

`grpck` is the consistency checking program for the `/etc/group` and `/etc/gshadow` files. It performs the following checks:

- the correct number of fields
- unique group name
- valid list of members and administrators

It also has the `-r` option for automated reports.

7.6   Dial-up passwords.

Dial-up passwords are another optional line of defense for systems that allow dial-in access. If you have a system that allows many people to connect locally or via a network, but you want to limit who can dial in and connect, then dial-up passwords are for you. To enable dial-up passwords, you must edit the file `/etc/login.defs` and ensure that `DIALUPS_CHECK_ENAB` is set to `yes`.

Two files contain the dial-up information, `/etc/dialups` which contains the ttys (one per line, with the leading "/dev/" removed). If a tty is listed then dial-up checks are performed.

The second file is the `/etc/d_passwd` file. This file contains the fully qualified path name of a shell, followed by an optional password.

If a user logs into a line that is listed in `/etc/dialups`, and his shell is listed in the file `/etc/d_passwd` he will be allowed access only by suppling the correct password.

Another useful purpose for using dial-up passwords might be to setup a line that only allows a certain type of connect (perhaps a PPP or UUCP connection). If a user tries to get another type of connection (i.e. a list of shells), he must know a password to use the line.

Before you can use the dial-up feature, you must create the files.

The command `dpasswd` is provided to assign passwords to the shells in the `/etc/d_passwd` file. See the manual page for more information.

8   Adding shadow support to a C program

Adding shadow support to a program is actually fairly straightforward. The only problem is that the program must be run by root (or SUID root) in order for the the program to be able to access the `/etc/shadow` file.

This presents one big problem: very careful programming practices must be followed when creating SUID programs. For instance, if a program has a shell escape, this must not occur as root if the program is SUID root.

For adding shadow support to a program so that it can check passwords, but otherwise does need to run as root, it's a lot safer to run the program SUID shadow instead. The `xlock` program is an example of this.

In the example given below, `pppd-1.2.1d` already runs SUID as root, so adding shadow support should not make the program any more vulnerable.

8.1 Header files

The header files should reside in `/usr/include/shadow`. There should also be a `/usr/include/shadow.h`, but it will be a symbolic link to `/usr/include/shadow/shadow.h`.

To add shadow support to a program, you need to include the header files:

```
#include <shadow/shadow.h>
#include <shadow/pwauth.h>
```

It might be a good idea to use compiler directives to conditionally compile the shadow code (I do in the example below).

8.2 libshadow.a library

When you installed the *Shadow Suite* the `libshadow.a` file was created and installed in `/usr/lib`.

When compiling shadow support into a program, the linker needs to be told to include the `libshadow.a` library into the link.

This is done by:

```
gcc program.c -o program -lshadow
```

However, as we will see in the example below, most large programs use a `Makefile`, and usually have a variable called `LIBS=...` that we will modify.

8.3 Shadow Structure

The `libshadow.a` library uses a structure called `spwd` for the information it retrieves from the `/etc/shadow` file. This is the definition of the `spwd` structure from the `/usr/include/shadow/shadow.h` header file:

```
struct spwd
{
  char *sp_namp;                  /* login name */
  char *sp_pwdp;                  /* encrypted password */
  sptime sp_lstchg;               /* date of last change */
  sptime sp_min;                  /* minimum number of days between changes */
  sptime sp_max;                  /* maximum number of days between changes */
  sptime sp_warn;                 /* number of days of warning before password
                                     expires */
  sptime sp_inact;                /* number of days after password expires
                                     until the account becomes unusable. */
  sptime sp_expire;               /* days since 1/1/70 until account expires
*/
  unsigned long sp_flag;          /* reserved for future use */
};
```

The *Shadow Suite* can put things into the `sp_pwdp` field besides just the encoded passwd. The password field could contain:

```
username:Npge08pfz4wuk;@/sbin/extra:9479:0:10000::::
```

This means that in addition to the password, the program `/sbin/extra` should be called for further authentication. The program called will get passed the username and a switch that indicates why it's being called. See the file `/usr/include/shadow/pwauth.h` and the source code for `pwauth.c` for more information.

What this means is that we should use the function `pwauth` to perform the actual authentication, as it will take care of the secondary authentication as well. The example below does this.

The author of the *Shadow Suite* indicates that since most programs in existence don't do this, and that it may be removed or changed in future versions of the *Shadow Suite*.

8.4   Shadow Functions

The `shadow.h` file also contains the function prototypes for the functions contained in the `libshadow.a` library:

```
extern void setspent __P ((void));
extern void endspent __P ((void));
extern struct spwd *sgetspent __P ((__const char *__string));
extern struct spwd *fgetspent __P ((FILE *__fp));
extern struct spwd *getspent __P ((void));
extern struct spwd *getspnam __P ((__const char *__name));
extern int putspent __P ((__const struct spwd *__sp, FILE *__fp));
```

The function that we are going to use in the example is: `getspnam` which will retrieve for us a `spwd` structure for the supplied name.

8.5   Example

This is an example of adding shadow support to a program that needs it, but does not have it by default.

This example uses the *Point-to-Point Protocol Server* (pppd-1.2.1d), which has a mode in which it performs *PAP* authentication using user names and passwords from the `/etc/passwd` file instead of the *PAP* or *CHAP* files. You would not need to add this code to `pppd-2.2.0` because it's already there.

This feature of pppd probably isn't used very much, but if you installed the *Shadow Suite*, it won't work anymore because the passwords are no longer stored in `/etc/passwd`.

The code for authenticating users under `pppd-1.2.1d` is located in the `/usr/src/pppd-1.2.1d/pppd/auth.c` file.

The following code needs to be added to the top of the file where all the other `#include` directives are. We have surrounded the `#includes` with conditional directives (i.e. only include if we are compiling for shadow support).

```
#ifdef HAS_SHADOW
#include <shadow.h>
#include <shadow/pwauth.h>
#endif
```

The next thing to do is to modify the actual code. We are still making changes to the `auth.c` file.

Function `auth.c` before modifications:

```
/*
 * login - Check the user name and password against the system
 * password database, and login the user if OK.
 *
 * returns:
 *      UPAP_AUTHNAK: Login failed.
 *      UPAP_AUTHACK: Login succeeded.
 * In either case, msg points to an appropriate message.
```

```
 */
static int
login(user, passwd, msg, msglen)
    char *user;
    char *passwd;
    char **msg;
    int *msglen;
{
    struct passwd *pw;
    char *epasswd;
    char *tty;

    if ((pw = getpwnam(user)) == NULL) {
        return (UPAP_AUTHNAK);
    }
     /*
      * XXX If no passwd, let them login without one.
      */
    if (pw->pw_passwd == '\0') {
        return (UPAP_AUTHACK);
    }

    epasswd = crypt(passwd, pw->pw_passwd);
    if (strcmp(epasswd, pw->pw_passwd)) {
        return (UPAP_AUTHNAK);
    }

    syslog(LOG_INFO, "user %s logged in", user);

    /*
     * Write a wtmp entry for this user.
     */
    tty = strrchr(devname, '/');
    if (tty == NULL)
        tty = devname;
    else
        tty++;
    logwtmp(tty, user, "");                   /* Add wtmp login entry */
    logged_in = TRUE;

    return (UPAP_AUTHACK);
}
```

The user's password is placed into pw->pw_passwd, so all we really need to do is add the function getspnam. This will put the password into spwd->sp_pwdp.

We will add the function pwauth to perform the actual authentication. This will automatically perform secondary authentication if the shadow file is setup for it.

Function auth.c after modifications to support shadow:

```
/*
 * login - Check the user name and password against the system
 * password database, and login the user if OK.
 *
```

```
* This function has been modified to support the Linux Shadow Password
* Suite if USE_SHADOW is defined.
*
* returns:
*        UPAP_AUTHNAK: Login failed.
*        UPAP_AUTHACK: Login succeeded.
* In either case, msg points to an appropriate message.
*/
static int
login(user, passwd, msg, msglen)
    char *user;
    char *passwd;
    char **msg;
    int *msglen;
{
    struct passwd *pw;
    char *epasswd;
    char *tty;

#ifdef USE_SHADOW
    struct spwd *spwd;
    struct spwd *getspnam();
#endif

    if ((pw = getpwnam(user)) == NULL) {
        return (UPAP_AUTHNAK);
    }

#ifdef USE_SHADOW
        spwd = getspnam(user);
        if (spwd)
                pw->pw_passwd = spwd->sp-pwdp;
#endif

    /*
     * XXX If no passwd, let NOT them login without one.
     */
    if (pw->pw_passwd == '\0') {
        return (UPAP_AUTHNAK);
    }
#ifdef HAS_SHADOW
    if ((pw->pw_passwd && pw->pw_passwd[0] == '@'
        && pw_auth (pw->pw_passwd+1, pw->pw_name, PW_LOGIN, NULL))
        || !valid (passwd, pw)) {
        return (UPAP_AUTHNAK);
    }
#else
    epasswd = crypt(passwd, pw->pw_passwd);
    if (strcmp(epasswd, pw->pw_passwd)) {
        return (UPAP_AUTHNAK);
    }
#endif

    syslog(LOG_INFO, "user %s logged in", user);
```

```
  /*
   * Write a wtmp entry for this user.
   */
  tty = strrchr(devname, '/');
  if (tty == NULL)
      tty = devname;
  else
      tty++;
  logwtmp(tty, user, "");                    /* Add wtmp login entry */
  logged_in = TRUE;

  return (UPAP_AUTHACK);
}
```

Careful examination will reveal that we made another change as well. The original version allowed access (returned UPAP_AUTHACK if there was NO password in the /etc/passwd file. This is *not* good, because a common use of this login feature is to use one account to allow access to the PPP process and then check the username and password supplied by PAP with the username in the /etc/passwd file and the password in the /etc/shadow file.

So if we had set the original version up to run as the shell for a user i.e. ppp, then anyone could get a ppp connection by setting their PAP to user ppp and a password of null.

We fixed this also by returning UPAP_AUTHNAK instead of UPAP_AUTHACK if the password field was empty.

Interestingly enough, pppd-2.2.0 has the same problem.

Next we need to modify the Makefile so that two things occur: USE_SHADOW must be defined, and libshadow.a needs to be added to the linking process.

Edit the Makefile, and add:

```
  LIBS = -lshadow
```

Then we find the line:

```
  COMPILE_FLAGS = -I.. -D_linux_=1 -DGIDSET_TYPE=gid_t
```

And change it to:

```
  COMPILE_FLAGS = -I.. -D_linux_=1 -DGIDSET_TYPE=gid_t -DUSE_SHADOW
```

Now make and install.

9   Frequently Asked Questions.

Q: I used to control which tty's *root* could log into using the file /etc/securettys, but it doesn't seem to work anymore, what's going on?

A: The file /etc/securettys does absolutely nothing now that the *Shadow Suite* is installed. The tty's that *root* can use are now located in the login configuration file /etc/login.defs. The entry in this file may point to another file.

Q: I installed the *Shadow Suite*, but now I can't login, what did I miss?

A: You probably installed the Shadow programs, but didn't run pwconv or you forgot to copy /etc/npasswd to /etc/passwd and /etc/nshadow to /etc/shadow. Also, you may need to copy login.defs to /etc.

Q: In the section on xlock, it said to change the group ownership of the `/etc/shadow` file to `shadow`. I don't have a `shadow` group, what do I do?

A: You can add one. Simply edit the `/etc/group` file, and insert a line for the shadow group. You need to ensure that the group number is not used by another group, and you need to insert it before the `nogroup` entry. Or you can simply suid `xlock` to root.

Q: Is there a mailing list for the Linux Shadow Password Suite?

A: Yes, but it's for the development and beta testing of the next Shadow Suite for Linux. You can get added to the list by mailing to: `shadow-list-request@neptune.cin.net` with a subject of: `subscribe`. The list is actually for discussions of the Linux `shadow-YYMMSS` series of releases. You should join if you want to get involved in further development or if you install the Suite on your system and want to get information on newer releases.

Q: I installed the *Shadow Suite*, but when I use the `userdel` command, I get "userdel: cannot open shadow group file", what did I do wrong?

A: You compiled the *Shadow Suite* with the `SHADOWGRP` option enabled, but you don't have an `/etc/gshadow` file. You need to either edit the `config.h` file and recompile, or create an `/etc/group` file. See the section on shadow groups.

Q: I installed the *Shadow Suite* but now I'm getting encoded passwords back in my `/etc/passwd` file, what's wrong?

A: You either enabled the `AUTOSHADOW` option in the Shadow `config.h` file, or your `libc` was compiled with the `SAHDOW_COMPAT` option. You need to determine which is the problem, and recompile.

10 Copyright Message.

The Linux Shadow Password HOWTO is Copyright (c) 1996 Michael H. Jackson.

Permission is granted to make and distribute verbatim copies of this document provided the copyright notice and this permission notice are preserved on all copies.

Permission is granted to copy and distribute modified versions of this document under the conditions for verbatim copies above, provided a notice clearly stating that the document is a modified version is also included in the modified document.

Permission is granted to copy and distribute translations of this document into another language, under the conditions specified above for modified versions.

Permission is granted to convert this document into another media under the conditions specified above for modified versions provided the requirement to acknowledge the source document is fulfilled by inclusion of an obvious reference to the source document in the new media. Where there is any doubt as to what defines 'obvious' the copyright owner reserves the right to decide.

11 Miscellaneous and Acknowledgments.

The code examples for `auth.c` are taken from pppd-1.2.1d and ppp-2.1.0e, Copyright (c) 1993 and The Australian National University and Copyright (c) 1989 Carnegie Mellon University.

Thanks to Marek Michalkiewicz <marekm@i17linuxb.ists.pwr.wroc.pl> for writing and maintaining the *Shadow Suite* for Linux, and for his review and comments on this document.

Thanks to Ron Tidd <rtidd@tscnet.com> for his helpful review and testing.

Thanks to everyone who has sent me feedback to help improve this document.

Please, if you have any comments or suggestions then mail them to me.

regards

Michael H. Jackson <mhjack@tscnet.com>

"Software Release Practice HOWTO" Eric S. Raymond

<esr@thyrsus.com>

1.0, 21 November 1998

This HOWTO describes good release practices for Linux open-source projects. By following these practices, you will make it as easy as possible for users to build your code and use it, and for other developers to understand your code and cooperate with you to improve. This document is a must-read for novice developers. Experienced developers should review it when they are about to release a new project. It will be revised periodically to reflect the evolution of good-practice standards.

Contents

HOWTO

1 Introduction

1.1 Why this document?

There is a large body of good-practice traditions for open-source code that helps other people port, use, and cooperate with developing it. Some of these conventions are traditional in the Unix world and predate Linux; others have developed recently in response to particular new tools and technologies such as the World Wide Web.

This document will help you learn good practice. It is organized into topic sections, each containing a series of checklist items. Think of these as a pre-flight checklist for your distribution.

1.2 New versions of this document

This document will be posted monthly to the newsgroups `comp.os.linux.answers`. The document is archived on a number of Linux FTP sites, including `sunsite.unc.edu` in `pub/Linux/docs/HOWTO`.

You can also view the latest version of this HOWTO on the World Wide Web via the URL `<http://sunsite.unc.edu/LDP/HOWTO/Software-Release-Practice.html>`.

Feel free to mail any questions or comments about this HOWTO to Eric S. Raymond, *esr@snark.thyrsus.com* `<mailto:esr@snark.thyrsus.com>`.

2 Good project- and archive- naming practice

As the load on maintainers of archives like Sunsite, the PSA site and CPAN increases, there is an increasing trend for submissions to be processed partly or wholly by programs (rather than entirely by a human).

This makes it more important for project and archive-file names to fit regular patterns that computer programs can parse and understand.

2.1 Use GNU-style names with a stem and major.minor.patch numbering.

It's helpful to everybody if your archive files all have GNU-like names – all-lower-case alphanumeric stem prefix, followed by a dash, followed by a version number, extension, and other suffixes.

Let's suppose you have a project you call 'foobar' at version 1, release 2, level 3. If it's got just one archive part (presumably the sources), here's what its names should look

foobar-1.2.3.tar.gz

> The source archive

foobar.lsm

> The LSM file (assuming you're submitting to Sunsite).

Please *don't* use these:

foobar123.tar.gz

> This looks to many programs like an archive for a project called'foobar123' with no version number.

foobar1.2.3.tar.gz

> This looks to many programs like an archive for a project called 'foobar1' at version 2.3.

foobar-v1.2.3.tar.gz

> Many programs think this goes with a project called 'foobar-v1'.

foo_bar-1.2.3.tar.gz

> The underscore is hard for people to speak, type, and remember

FooBar-1.2.3.tar.gz

Unless you *like* looking like a marketing weenie. This is also hard for people to speak, type, and remember.

If you have to differentiate between source and binary archives, or between different kinds of binary, or express some kind of build option in the file name, please treat that as a file extension to go *after* the version number. That is, please do this:

foobar-1.2.3.src.tar.gz

sources

foobar-1.2.3.bin.tar.gz

binaries, type not specified

foobar-1.2.3.bin.ELF.tar.gz

ELF binaries

foobar-1.2.3.bin.ELF.static.tar.gz

ELF binaries statically linked

foobar-1.2.3.bin.SPARC.tar.gz

SPARC binaries

Please *don't* use names like 'foobar-ELF-1.2.3.tar.gz', because programs have a hard time telling type infixes (like '-ELF') fromn the stem.

A good general form of name has these parts in order:

1. project prefix
2. dash
3. version number
4. dot
5. "src" or "bin" (optional)
6. dot or dash (dot preferred)
7. binary type and options (optional)
8. archiving and compression extensions

2.2 Try hard to choose a name prefix that is unique and easy to type

The stem prefix should be common to all a project's files, and it should be easy to read, type, and remember. So please don't use underscores. And don't capitalize or BiCapitalize without extremely good reason – it messes up the natural human-eyeball search order and looks like some marketing weenie trying to be clever.

It confuses people whe twon different projects have the same stem name. So try to check for collisions before your first release. A good place to check is the *index file of Sunsite* <http://sunsite.unc.edu/pub/Linux>.

3   Good development practice

Most of these are concerned with ensuring portability, not only across Linuxes but to other Unixes as well. Being portable to other Unixes is not just a worthy form of professionalism and hackerly politeness, it's valuable insurance against future changes in Linux itself.

Finally, other people *will* try to build your code on non-Linux systems; portability minimizes the number of annoying perplexed email messages you will get.

3.1 Write either pure ANSI C or a portable scripting language

For portability and stability, you should write either in ANSI C or a scripting language that is guaranteed portable because it has just one cross-platform implementation.

Scripting languages that qualify include Python, Perl, Tcl, and Emacs Lisp. Plain old shell does *not* qualify; there are too many different implementations with subtle idiosyncracies, and the shell environment is subject to disruption by user customizations such as shell aliases.

Java holds promise as a portable language, but the Linux-available implementations are still scratchy and poorly integrated with Linux. Java is still a bleeding-edge choice, though one likely to become more popular as it matures.

3.2 Follow good C portability practices

If you are writing C, do feel free to use the full ANSI features – including function prototypes, which will help you spot cross-module inconsistancies. The old-style K&R compilers are history.

On the other hand, do *not* assume that GCC-specific features such as the '-pipe' option or nested functions are available. These will come around and bite you the second somebody ports to a non-Linux, non-GCC system.

3.3 Use autoconf/automake/autoheader

If you're writing C, use autoconf/automake/autoheader to handle portability issues, do system-configuration probes, and tailor your makefiles. People building from sources today expect to be able to type "configure; make" and get a clean build – and rightly so.

3.4 Sanity-check your code before release

If you're writing C, test-compile with -Wall and clean up the errors at least once before each release. This catches a surprising number of errors. For real thoroughness, compile with -pedantic as well.

If you're writing Perl, check your code with perl -c, perl -w, and perl -T before each release (see the Perl documentation for discussion).

4 Good distribution-making practice

These guidelines describe how your distribution should look when someone downloads, retrieves and unpacks it.

4.1 Make sure tarballs always unpack into a single new directory

The single most annoying mistake newbie developers make is to build tarballs that unpack the files and directories in the distribution into the current directory, potentially stepping on files already located there. *Never do this!*

Instead, make sure your archive files all have a common directory part named after the project, so they will unpack into a single top-level directory directly *beneath* the current one.

Here's a makefile trick that, assuming your distribution directory is named 'foobar' and SRC contains a list of your distribution files, accomplishes this. It requires GNU tar 1.13

```
VERS=1.0
foobar-$(VERS).tar.gz:
        tar --name-prefix='foobar-$(VERS)/' -czf foobar-$(VERS).tar.gz $(SRC)
```

If you have an older tar program, do something like this:

```
foobar-$(VERS).tar.gz:
        @ls $(SRC) | sed s:^:foobar-$(VERS)/: >MANIFEST
        @(cd ..; ln -s foobar foobar-$(VERS))
        (cd ..; tar -czvf foobar/foobar-$(VERS).tar.gz 'cat foobar/MANIFEST')
        @(cd ..; rm foobar-$(VERS))
```

4.2 Have a README

Have a file called README or READ.ME that is a roadmap of your source distribution. By ancient convention, this is the first file intrepid explorers will read after unpacking the source.

Good things to have in the README include:

- A brief description of the project.
- A pointer to the project website (if it has one)
- Notes on the developer's build environment and potential portability problems.
- A roadmap describing important files and subdirectories.
- Either build/installation instructions or a pointer to a file containing same (usually INSTALL).
- Either a maintainers/credits list or a pointer to a file containing same (usually CREDITS).
- Either recent project news or a pointer to a file containing same (usually NEWS).

4.3 Respect and follow standard file naming practices

Before even looking at the README, your intrepid explorer will have scanned the filenames in the top-level directory of your unpacked distribution. Those names can themselves convey information. By adhering to certain standard naming practices, you can give the explorer valuable clues about what to look in next.

Here are some standard top-level file names and what they mean. Not every distribution needs all of these.

README or READ.ME
> the roadmap file, to be read first

INSTALL
> configuration, build, and installation instructions

CREDITS
> list of project contributers

NEWS
> recent project news

HISTORY
> project history

COPYING
> project license terms (GNU convention)

LICENSE
> project license terms

MANIFEST
> list of files in the distribution

FAQ
> plain-text Frequently-Asked-Questions document for the project

TAGS
> generated tag file for use by Emacs or vi

Note the overall convention that filenames with all-caps names are human-readable metainformation about the package, rather than build components.

5 Good communication practice

Your software won't do the world much good if nobody but you knows it exists. Also, developing a visible presence for the project on the Internet will assist you in recruiting users and co-developers. Here are the standard ways to do that.

5.1 Announce to c.o.l.a

Announce new releases to *comp.os.linux.announce* <news:comp.os.linux.announce>. Besides being widely read itself, this group is a major feeder for web-based what's-new sites like *Freshmeat* <http://www.freshmeat.net>.

5.2 Announce to a relevant topic newsgroup

Find USENET topics group directly relevant to your application, and announce there as well. Post only where the *function* of the code is relevant, and exercise restraint.

If (for example) you are releasing program written in Perl that queries IMAP servers, you should certainly post to comp.mail.imap. But you should probably not post to comp.lang.perl unless the program is also an instructive example of cutting-edge Perl techniques.

Your announcement should include the URL of a project website.

5.3 Have a website

If you intend try to build any substantial user or developer community around your project, it should have a website. Standard things to have on the website include:

- The project charter (why it exists, who the audience is, etc).
- Download links for the project sources.
- Instructions on how to join the project mailing list(s).
- A FAQ (Frequently Asked Questions) list.
- HTMLized versions of the project documentation
- Links to related and/or competing projects.

Some project sites even have URLs for anonymous access to the master source tree.

5.4 Host project mailing lists

It's standard practice to have a private development list through which project collaborators can communicate and exchange patches. You may also want to have an announcements list for people who want to be kept informed of the project's process

5.5 Release to major archives

For the last several years, the *Sunsite archive* <http://www.sunsite/unc.edu/pub/Linux/> has been the most important interchange location for Linux software.

Other important locations include:

- the *Python Software Activity* <http://www.python.org> site (for software written in Python).
- the *CPAN* <http://language.perl.com/CPAN>, the Comprehensive Perl Archive Network, (for software written in Perl).

5.6 Provide RPMs

The de-facto standard format for installable binary packages is that used by the Red Hat Package manager, RPM. It's featured in the most popular Linux distribution, and supported by effectively all other Linux distributions (except Debian a Slackware).

Accordingly, it's a good idea for your project site to provide installable RPMs as well as source tarballs.

Part XLIII

"The teTeX HOWTO: The Linux-teTeX Local Guide" Robert Kiesling

v3.7, 9 November 1998
This document covers the basic installation and usage of the teTeX TeX and LaTeX implementation under the major U.S. Linux distributions, and auxiliary packages like Ghostscript. Contents of the teTeX HOWTO: The Linux-teTeX Local Guide are Copyright (C) 1997, 1998 by Robert A. Kiesling. The exact terms of copying are given in the introduction and the appendices. Registered trademarks are the property of their respective owners. Please send all complaints, suggestions, errata, and any miscellany to *kiesling@ix.netcom.com*, so I can keep this document as complete and up to date as possible.

Contents

1   Introduction.

1.1 Copyright.

The teTeX-HOWTO is copyright (C) 1997, 1998 by Robert Kiesling. Permission is granted to make and distribute verbatim copies of this manual provided that the copyright notice and this permission notice are preserved on all copies.

Permission is granted to copy and distribute modified versions of this manual under the conditions for verbatim copying, provided also that the sections entitled, "Distribution," and, "GNU General Public License," are included exactly as in the original, and provided that the entire resulting derived work is distributed under the terms of a permission notice identical to this one.

Permission is granted to copy and distribute translations of this manual into another language, under the above conditions for modified versions. except that the sections entitled, "Distribution," and, "GNU General Public License," may be included in a translation approved by the Free Software Foundation instead of in the original English. Please refer to Section 1.2 (Distribution and Copyright) for terms of copying.

1.2 Software described in this document.

TeX handles only the formatting part of the document preparation. Generating output from TeX is like compiling source code into object code, which still needs to be linked. You prepare an input file with a text editor——what most people think of as "word processing"—— and format the input file document with TeX to produce a device-independent output file, called a `.dvi` file.

You also need a program or two to translate TeX's `.dvi` output for your screen and printer. These programs are collectively known as "dviware." For example, TeX itself only makes requests for fonts. It is up to the `.dvi` output translator to provide the actual font for the output regardless of whether the medium is a video screen or paper. This extra step may seem overly complicated, but the abstraction allows documents to display the same on different devices with little or no change to the original document.

1.2.1 teTeX.

TeX is implemented for practically every serious computer system in the world—and quite a few "non-serious" ones—so implementors must provide the installation facilities for all of them. This accounts in part for teTeX's complexity, in addition to the inherent complexity of any TeX installation. It also accounts for the fact that installing the system yourself is a significant task, and unless you are already familiar with TeX, it is easy to get lost in the numerous executable programs, TeX files, documentation, and fonts.

Fortunately, teTeX is part of the GNU/Linux distribution. You can install the package much more easily using GNU/Linux installation tools. You may already have teTeX installed on your system. If so, you can skip ahead to Section 2 (Using teTeX).

However, if you want to install the package, the archives necessary for a workable teTeX installation are on the CTAN archive network. There is a list of these sites in Section 8 (CTAN site list).

CTAN is the Comprehensive TeX Archive Network, a series of anonymous FTP sites that archive TeX programs, macros, fonts, and documentation. In the course of using TeX you'll probably become familiar with at least one CTAN site. In this document, a pathname like `~CTAN/contrib/pstricks` means "look in the directory `contrib/pstricks` of your nearest CTAN site."

The installation of the generic teTeX distribution described in Section 9 (Installing the CTAN teTeX distribution) concentrates on the Intel versions of Linux. Installing teTeX on other hardware should require only substituting the appropriate executable program archive in the installation process.

In addition to the executable programs, the distribution includes all of the TeX and LaTeX package, `metafont` and its sources, `bibtex`, `makeindex`, and *all* of the documentation... more than 4 megabytes' worth. The documentation covers everything you will forseeably need to know to get started. So, you should install all of the documents. Not only will you eventually read them, the documents themselves provide many examples of "live" TeX and LaTeX code.

TeX was written by Professor Donald Knuth of Stanford University. It is a lower-level typesetting language for all of the higher-level packages like LaTeX. Essentially, LaTeX is a set of TeX macros that provide convenient, predefined document formats for end users. If you like the formats provided by LaTeX, you may never need to learn bare-bones TeX programming. The difference between the two languages is like the difference between assembly language and C. You can have the speed and flexibility of TeX, or the convenience of LaTeX.

By the way, the letters of the word "TeX" are Greek, tau-epsilon-chi. It is not a fraternity, but the root of the Greek word, *techne,* which means art and/or science. "TeX" is not pronounced like the first syllable in "Texas." The *chi* has no English equivalent, but TeX is generally pronounced so that it rhymes with "yecch," to use Professor Knuth's example from *The TeXBook,* which is one of the standard TeX references. When writing, "TeX," on character devices, always use the standard capitalization, or the `\TeX{}` macro in typesetting.

1.2.2 Text editors.

Any of the editors that work under Linux—`jed`, `joe`, `jove`, `vi`, `vim`, `stevie`, Emacs, and microemacs—will work to prepare a TeX input file, as long as the editor reads and writes plain-vanilla ASCII text. My preference is GNU Emacs. There are several reasons for this:

- You can format, preview and print documents with Emacs's TeX and LaTeX modes.

- Emacs can automatically insert TeX-style, "curly quotes," as you type, rather than the `"ASCII-vanilla"` kind.

- Emacs has integrated support for Texinfo, a hypertext documentation system.

- Emacs is widely supported. Versions 19.34 and later, for example, are included in the major U.S. Linux distributions. The most recent version from the GNU archives is 20.3.

- Emacs does everything except butter the toast in the morning.

- Emacs is free.

1.2.3 `dvips`.

Tomas Rokicki's `dvips` generates Postscript from a `.dvi` file. In addition, it runs Metafont if necessary to generate the bit mapped fonts it needs or uses Postscript fonts for the output. It can also crop and resize pages and perform graphics translations from instructions in a TeX or LaTeX file,

The `dvips` program is part of the teTeX distribution. It is discussed fully in Section 6 (Mixing text and graphics with <tt>dvips</tt>)

1.2.4 Fonts.

Much of TeX's, and therefore LaTeX's, complexity, arises from its implementation of various font systems, and the way these fonts are specified. A major improvement of LaTeX 2e over its predecessor was the way users specify fonts, the former New Font Selection Scheme. They're discussed in Section 4.2 (Characters and type styles), Section 3.2 (TeX Font Commands), and Section 7 (Using Postscript fonts).)

teTeX comes distributed with about a dozen standard fonts preloaded, which is enough to get you started. Also provided are the font metrics descriptions, in .tfm (TeX font metric) files. To generate the other fonts that you need, it is simply a matter of installing the metafont sources. teTeX's .dvi utilities will invoke metafont automatically and generate the Computer Modern fonts you need.

2   Using teTeX.

Theoretically, at least, everything is installed correctly and is ready to run. teTeX is a very large software package. As with any complex software package, you'll want to start by learning teTeX slowly, instead of being overwhelmed by its complexity.

At the same time, we want the software to do something useful. So instead of watching TeX typeset

```
''Hello, World!''
```

as Professor Knuth suggests, we'll produce a couple of teTeX's own documents in order to test it.

2.1   Printing the documentation.

You should be logged in as root the first few times you run teTeX. If you aren't, Metafont may not be able to create the necessary directories for its fonts. The texconfig program includes an option to make the font directories world-writable, but if you're working on a multi-user system, security considerations may make this option impractical or undesirable.

In either instance, if you don't have the appropriate permissions to write to the directories where the fonts are stored, Metafont will complain loudly because it can't make the directories. You won't see any output because you have a bunch of zero-length font characters. This is no problem. Simply log out, re-login as root, and repeat the offending operation.

The nice thing about teTeX is that, if you blow it, no real harm is done. It's not like a compiler, where, say, you will trash the root partition if a pointer goes astray. What, you haven't read the teTeX manual yet? Of course you haven't. It's still in the distribution, in source code form, waiting to be output.

So, without further delay, you will want to read the teTeX manual. It's located in the directory

```
/usr/lib/teTeX/texmf/doc/tetex.
```

The LaTeX source for the manual is called TETEXDOC.tex. (The .tex extension is used for both TeX and LaTeX files. Some editors, like Emacs, can tell the difference.) There is also a file TETEXDOC.dvi included with the distribution, which you might want to keep in a safe place—say, another directory —in case you want to test your .dvi drivers later. With that out of the way, type

```
latex TETEXDOC.tex
```

LaTeX will print several warnings. The first,

```
LaTeX Warning: Label(s) may have changed. Rerun to get the
cross-references right.
```

is standard. It's common to build a document's Table of Contents by LaTeXing the document twice. So, repeat the command. The other warnings can be safely ignored. They simply are informing you that some of the FTP paths mentioned in the documentation are too wide for their alloted spaces. Sections 3.3 (Paragraph styles and dimensions) and 3.3.1 (Tolerances) describe horizontal spacing in more detail.

teTeX will have generated several files from `TETEXDOC.tex`. The one that we're interested in is `TETEXDOC.dvi`. This is the device-independent output which you can send either to the screen or the printer. If you're running teTeX under the X Windows System, you can preview the document with `xdvi`.

For the present, let's assume that you have a HP LaserJet II. You would give the command

```
dvilj2 TETEXDOC.dvi
```

which writes a PCL output file from `TETEXDOC.dvi`, including soft fonts which will be downloaded to the LaserJet. This is *not* a feature of TeX or LaTeX, but a feature provided by `dvilj2`. Other `.dvi` drivers provide features that are relevant to the devices they support. `dvilj2` tries to fill the font requests which were made in the original LaTeX document with the the closest equivalents available on the system. In the case of a plain text document like `TETEXDOC.tex`, there isn't much difficulty. All of the fonts requested by `TETEXDOC.tex` will be generated by `metafont`, which is automatically invoked by `dvilj2`, if the fonts aren't already present. (If you're running `dvilj2` for the first time, the program may need to generate all of the fonts.) There are several options that control font generation via `dvilj2`. They're outlined in the manual page. At this point, you shouldn't need to operate `metafont` directly. If you do, then something has gone awry with your installation. All of the `.dvi` drivers will invoke `metafont` directly via the kpathsea path-searching library—the discussion of which is beyond the scope of this document—and you don't need to do any more work with `metafont` for the present—all of the `metafont` sources for the Computer Modern font library are provided.

You can print `TETEXDOC.lj` with the command

```
lpr TETEXDOC.lj
```

You may also need to install a printer filter that understands PCL.

The nine-page *teTeX Guide* provides some useful information for further configuring your system, some of which I have mentioned, much that this document doesn't cover.

Some of the information in the next section I haven't been able to test, because I have a non-Postscript HP Deskjet 400 color ink jet printer connected to the computer's parallel port. However, not owning a Postscript printer is no barrier to printing text and graphics from your text documents. Ghostscript is available in most Linux distributions and it could already be installed on your system.

3 TeX commands.

Preparing documents for TeX typesetting is easy. Make sure there's a blank line between the paragraphs of a plain text file, and run file through the TeX program with the command

```
tex your_text_file
```

The result will be a file of the same base name and the extension `.dvi`. TeX formats the text in 10-point, Computer Modern Roman, single-spaced, with justified left and right margins. If you receive error messages from special characters like dollar signs, escape them with a backslash character, \, and run TeX on the file again. You should be able to process the resulting file with the `.dvi` file translator of your choice (see above) to get printed output.

One peculiarity of TeX input is that you must use opening and closing quotes, which are denoted in the input file with the grave accent and single quote characters. Emacs' TeX mode does this for you automatically.

```
"These are ASCII-type quotes."
``These are 'TeX-style' quotes.''
```

3.1   Command overview.

Commands in TeX start with a backslash ("\"). For example, the command to change the spacing between lines is

```
\baselineskip=24pt
```

The baseline is the bottom of the characters on a line, not counting descenders. The distance between the baseline of one line and the next is the \baselineskip, and is assigned a value of 24 points.

Measurements or dimensions in TeX are often given in the following units:

```
pt      % Point            1/72 in.
pc      % Pica:            12 pt.
in      % Inch:            72.27 pt.
cm      % Centimeter:      2.54 cm = 1 in.
mm      % Millimeter:      10 mm = 1 cm.
```

Some commands do not take assignments. For example:

```
\smallskip     % Approximately 3 pt.
\medskip       % Two \smallskips.
\bigskip       % Two \medskips.
```

A \smallskip inserts a 3 pt. vertical space in the document. The measurements are approximate because TeX needs to adjust the dimensions for page breaks, section headings, and other units of vertical space. This is true for horizontal spacing as well.

```
\hsize=6.5in
```

This command sets the line length to a width of 6.5 inches. TeX tries to fill the line by adjusting the spacing between words, and some letters. If TeX cannot fill a line to within its tolerances, it produces a warning message, and adjusts the horizontal spacing within the line as best it can. Formatting tolerances are discussed in Section 3.3.1 (Tolerances).

There are many other commands that specify horizontal and vertical dimensions and tolerances, and the most commonly use commands are described below.

3.2   Font commands.

In TeX, the default font is 10 pt. Computer Modern Roman. To specify a typeface, like italic, bold, or monospaced, use the following commands.

```
\rm        % Roman (the default).
\it        % Italics.
\bf        % Bold.
\tt        % Monospaced (teletype).
\sl        % Oblique (slanted).
```

The commands change the typeface where they appear in the text, as in this example.

```
This text is Roman, \it and this text is italic.  \bf This text is
bold, and \rm this text is in Roman again.
```

To specify a font for your document, use the \font command.

```
\font\romantwelve=cmr12
```

This creates the font command \romantwelve, which, when used in the text, changes the font to Computer Modern Roman, 12 point.

```
\romantwelve
This is the Computer Modern Roman font at 12 points.
```

For information about the fonts in the teTeX distribution look at the file:

```
/usr/lib/teTeX/texmf/doc/fonts/fontname/fontname.dvi
```

If you want to print a sample of a font, TeX the file

```
/usr/lib/teTeX/texmf/tex/plain/base/fontchart.tex
```

and fill in the name of the font you want to print at the prompt.

You can also change the size of a font to get different effects. Font magnification is exponential, and specified with the scaled \magstep command, which is placed after the font specification.

```
\font\sfmedium=cmss12 scaled \magstep 1
```

This command will give you a sans serif font that is 120 percent the size of the 12-point Computer Modern sans serif font. Fonts can be magnified in steps from 0 to 5. Each step provides and additional 120 percent magnification.

3.3   Paragraph styles and dimensions.

As mentioned above, TeX typesets text in 10-point Computer Modern Roman by default. The length of a line is the value of \hsize, which defaults to 6.5 in. If you want to change the value of \hsize to 5.5 in. for example, use this command.

```
\hsize=5.5in
```

In TeX a *dimension* is an adjustable unit of length, either horizontal or vertical. The amount by which a dimension can be increased or decreased can be specified in its definition. Closely related to a dimension is a *skip*, which is a dimension that is placed in one of TeX's internal registers. Skips are defined with the \newskip command. The \smallskip dimension, as defined by TeX is:

```
\newskip\smallskipamount \smallskipamount=3pt plus 1pt minus 1pt
```

The \smallskip command is shorthand for:

```
\vskip\smallskipamount
```

There are a number of dimensions that control the page layout. They are summarized in Section 3.4 (Page layout).

TeX formats paragraphs with justified left and right margins. If you want the text to be left justified only, use this command:

```
\raggedright
```

To typeset a line that is justified to the right margin, use the \rightline command:

```
\rightline{This is the line to be typeset.}
```

The \line command typesets the text of its argument to fill the entire line.

```
\line{This text will be spaced to fit the entire line.}
```

The \hfil command adds space to fill out the line where it occurs. So, for example, the \rightline command is equivalent to:

```
\line{\hfilThis line will be right justified.}
```

To typeset a line that is centered, use the \centerline command.

```
\centerline{This is the line to be centered.}
```

To change the left margin, set the value of \hoffset, as in this example:

```
\hoffset=1.5in
```

The \parindent command specifies the amount that the first line of every paragraph is indented.

```
\parindent=.5in
```

Two other dimensions, \leftskip and \rightskip, will indent the right and left margins, respectively, of the paragraphs that come after them.

```
\leftskip=.5in
\rightskip=.5in
```

The control word \narrower is equivalent to:

```
\leftskip=\parindent
\rightskip=\parindent
```

That is, \narrower narrows the paragraph margins by the value of \parindent

As mentioned in the previous section, the \baselineskip specifies the distance between lines. The default is 12 pt. To approximate double-spaced text, use the following command.

```
\baselineskip=\baselineskip*1.6
```

The \parskip command specifies the distance in addition to \baselineskip between paragraphs. By default, no extra space is added, but the distance between paragraphs can stretch as much as 1 pt. to fill the page correctly. To put a blank line between paragraphs, use this command:

```
\parskip=\baselineskip
```

3.3.1 Tolerances. (What are those black rectangles after every line?)

TeX normally formats text to strict tolerances. If, for some reason, text cannot be formatted to within those tolerances, TeX produces a warning message and formats the text the best it can. If the text must be stretched too much to fit the line, TeX warns you that the \hbox is underfull. Text that must be squeezed to fit in the line produces an overfull \hbox warning.

For each overfull \hbox, TeX places a *slug*, a black rectangle, after the line. The slug indicates that the line could not be formatted to within the specifications set by the \hbadness parameter.

The fit of the text within its specified dimensions is measured by its *badness*, which is a number between 0 and 10000. A badness of 0 is a perfect fit, and a badness of 10000 means that the line probably will never fit. The default value of \hbadness is 1000. If you set \hbadness to 10000, TeX does not report underfull lines.

Sometimes TeX allows a line to extend past the right margin. This is an aesthetic decision on the part of TeX's author. The amount is determined by the \hfuzz parameter, which defaults to 0.1 pt. If the text does not fit within the line, the \tolerance parameter determines how TeX will handle the overfull \hbox. The default value of \tolerance is 200. Setting \tolerance to 1000 suppresses overfull \hbox warnings and the printing of slugs.

3.4   Page layout.

In addition to the left margin and line length dimensions that are described in the previous section, TeX also lets you specify top and bottom margins, and vertical spacing.

Like the \hsize and \hoffset dimensions described in the previous section, TeX also provides the \vsize and \voffset commands. The default for \vsize is 8.9 in., and \voffset defaults to 0.

Normally, teTeX places the beginning of the first line of text 1 in. below the top of the paper and 1 in. from the left edge. You can start the text closer to the top of the page with the command:

\voffset=-0.5in

If you want to add vertical space in a document, the commands \smallskip, \medskip, and \bigskip will add approximately 3, 6, and 12 points of blank vertical space. These measurements are approximate; TeX will adjust them by as much as 1 pt. so the page is filled correctly.

The \vfill command adds an adjustable vertical space between paragraphs on a page. It is infinitely stretchable, so it will add vertical space to fill as much of the rest of the page as possible. If you want to specify a dimension, use \vskip as in:

\vskip 10pt

The commands \hss and \vss are similar to \hfil and \vfill, but they provide dimensions that are infinitely shrinkable as well as infinitely stretchable.

The \vskip and \vfill commands produce flexible lengths. They do not add space where no text exists; for example, at the top of a page. Use \vglue if you want to add an absolute space.

TeX fills the \vsize dimension with as much text as possible before it starts a new page. To force a page break, use the \vfill \eject sequence. If \vfill is not used, the text before the \break will be spaced to fill the page.

If you want TeX to be more flexible about its vertical page sizing, place the \raggedbottom command in your document. TeX will then adjust the bottom margin of each page slightly to make vertical spacing more consistent.

3.5   Page numbers, headers, and footers.

teTeX by default places the page number at the bottom center of the page. If you want to change the location and style of the page number, you can specify alternate headers and footers by changing definitions of \headline and \footline. The default value for \footline contains the \folio command, which prints the page number. The default value for \headline is \hfil, so a blank line is printed.

The \pageno command is a synonym for TeX's internal page counter. You can change the page number by changing the value of \pageno. If \pageno is negative, the numbers are printed as Roman numerals.

```
\pageno=10
\pageno=-1
```

The command \nopagenumbers is shorthand for:

```
\headline={\hfil}
\footline={\hfil}
```

The default footline also contains the font command \tenrm, which sets the page number's font to 10-point Roman. If you want to print the page number in 12-point Roman, for example, you would first define a 12-point Roman font, and use that in the definition of \footline. Font commands are discussed in Section 3.2 (Font commands).

```
\font\twelvrm=cmr12
\footline={\hss\twelvrm\folio\hss}
```

You can put a *rule*, a horizontal line, at the top of each page by redefining \headline as:

```
\headline={\hrulefill}
```

To specify different headers for even and odd pages use the \ifodd command, which has the form:

```
\ifodd[condition][true-action]\else[false-action]
```

An example \headline that uses different headers for even and odd pages would be:

```
\headline={\ifodd\pageno odd-page-header \else even-page-header}
```

The \ifodd statement uses the first argument if the page number is odd, and the second argument otherwise.

3.6   Titles and macros.

TeX provides only the \beginsection macro for section headings. It leaves a space above its argument, prints the text of the heading in bold type, adds a \smallskip after the text of the heading, and starts the next paragraph with no indent.

The LaTeX chapter and section commands described below add section numbering, and will print the section names and numbers in the page headings, and automatically add the sections to the Table of Contents.

In plain TeX, you must write these functions yourself. The \def command allows you to define new commands. Suppose you want to print a chapter title. First you define the font that you want to use. A large, sans serif font for chapter titles would be defined like this:

```
\font\chapterfontsans=cmss12 scaled \magstep 4
```

You can use the \chapterfontsans command anywhere you want to switch to this font, which is approximately 24 points in height. However, in this example, it will be used primarily in the command \chaptertitlesans. Here is its definition:

```
\def\chaptertitlesans#1{\hbox{}\bigskip\bigskip
  \noindent{\leftline{\chapterfontsans#1}}
  \par\bigskip\bigskip\noindent}
```

The first line, \hbox{}\bigskip, anchors a 12-point space at the top of the page by placing an empty \hbox{} there. The line with the chapter title is not indented, nor is the paragraph which immediately follows it. If you place a blank line between the \sschaptertitle macro and the next paragraph, the final \noindent applies to the blank line, not the text of the following paragraph. To format correctly, use the \sschaptertitle as in this example:

The #1 statement in the definition is replaced by the first argument to \chaptertitlesans; that is, the title of the chapter. Parameters TeX definitions are declared with #1, #2, #3, and so on. An example usage of \chaptertitlesans would be:

```
\chaptertitlesans{Chapter 1}
This is the starting text of the first paragraph of the chapter.
The paragraph will not be indented.  The chapter's title is
"Chapter 1."
```

4 LaTeX commands.

4.1 Document structure.

Documents formatted for LaTeX have a few more rules, but with complex documents, LaTeX can greatly simplify the formatting process.

Essentially, LaTeX is a document markup language which tries to separate the output style from the document's logical content. For example, formatting a section heading with TeX would require specifying 36 points of white space above the heading, then the heading itself set in bold, 24-point type, then copying the heading text and page number to the Table of Contents, then leaving 24 points of white space after the heading. By contrast, LaTeX has the \section{} command, which does all of the work for you. If you need to change the format of the section headings throughout your document, you can change the definition of \section{} instead of the text in the document. You can see where this would save hours of reformatting for documents of more than a dozen pages in length.

All LaTeX documents have three sections: a *preamble*, the *body* text, and a *postamble*. These terms are standard jargon and are widely used by TeXperts.

The preamble, at a minimum, specifies the type of document to be produced—the *document class*—and a statement which signals the beginning of the document's body text. For example:

```
\documentclass{article}
%\begin{document}
```

The document's postamble is usually very simple. Except in specialized cases, it contains only the statement:

```
%\end{document}
```

Note the \begin{document} and \end{document} pairing. In LaTeX, this is called an *environment*. All text must appear within an environment, and many commands are effective only in the environments in which they're called. The document environment is the only instance where LaTeX enforces this convention, however. That is, it's the only environment that is required in a document. (An exception is letter class, which also requires you to declare \begin{letter} and \end{letter}. See the section 4.4.2 (Letters).) However, many formatting features are specified as environments. They're described in the following sections.

The document classes can be called with arguments. For example, instead of the default, 10-point type used as the base point size, as in the previous example, we could have specified

```
\documentclass[letterpaper]{article}
```

to produce the document using 12 points as the base point size. The document class, *article,* makes the necessary adjustments.

There are a few document classes which are commonly used. They're described below. The *report* class is similar to *article* class, but produces a title page and starts each section on a new page. The *letter* class includes special definitions for addresses, salutations, and closings, a few of which are described below.

You can include canned LaTeX code, commonly known as a *package,* with the \usepackage{} command.

```
\usepackage{fancyhdr}
```

The command above would include the LaTeX style file `fancyhdr.sty` from one of the TEXINPUTS directories, which you and teTeX specified during installation and setup processes.

```
\documentclass{article}
\usepackage{fancyhdr}
%\begin{document}
```

Note that the \usepackage{} declarations are given before the \begin{document} statement; that is, in the document preamble.

`fancyhdr.sty` extends the \pagestyle{} command so that you can create custom headers and footers. Most LaTeX document classes provide headers and footers of the following standard page styles:

```
\pagestyle{plain}        % default pages style -- page number centered at
                         % the bottom of the page.
\pagestyle{empty}        % no headers or footers
\pagestyle{headings}     % print section number and page number at the
                         % top of the page.
\pagestyle{myheadings}   % print custom information in the page heading.
```

Everything on a line to the right of the percent sign is a comment.

The \pagestyle{} command doesn't take effect until the following page. To change the headers and footers on the current page, use the command

```
\thispagestyle{the_pagestyle}
```

4.2   Characters and type styles.

Character styles are partially a function of the fonts specified in the document. However, bold and italic character emphasis should be available for every font present on the system. Underlining, too, can be used, though its formatting presents special problems. See section 5 (LaTeX extension packages and other resources), below.

You can specify text to be emphasized in several ways. The most portable is the \em command. All text within its scope is italicized by default. For example:

```
This word will be {\em emphasized.}
```

If you have italicized text that runs into text which is not italicized, you can specify an italic correction factor to be used. The command for this is \/; that is, a backslash and a forward slash.

```
This example {\em will\/} print correctly.
```

```
This example will {\em not} print correctly.
```

Slightly less portable, but still acceptable in situations where they're used singly, are the commands \it, \bf, and \tt, which specify that the characters within their scope be printed using italic, bold, and monospaced (teletype) typefaces, respectively.

```
{\tt This text will be printed monospaced,}
{\it this text will be italic,} and
{\bf this text will be bold\dots} all in one paragraph.
```

The command \dots prints a series of three periods for ellipses, which will not break across a line.

The most recent version of LaTeX, which is what you have, includes commands which account for instances where one emphasis command would supersede another.

```
This is {\it not {\bf bold italic!}}
```

What happens is that teTeX formats the text with the italic typeface until it encounters the \bf command, at which point it switches to boldface type.

To get around this, the NFSS scheme of selecting font shapes requires three parameters for each typeface: shape, series, and family. Not all font sets will include all of these styles. LaTeX will print a warning, however, if it needs to substitute another font.

You can specify the following font shapes:

```
\textup{text}               % upright shape (the default)
\textit{text}               % italic
\textsl{text}               % slanted
\textsc{text}               % small caps
```

These are the two series that most fonts have:

```
\textmd{text}               % medium series (the default)
\textbf{text}               % boldface series.
```

There are generally three families of type available.

```
\textrm{text}               % Roman (the default)
\textsf{text}               % sans serif
\texttt{text}               % typewriter (monospaced, Courier-like)
```

Setting font styles using these parameters, you can combine effects.

```
\texttt{\textit{This example likely will result in a font
substitution, because many fonts don't include a typewriter italic
typeface.}}
```

The font family defaults to Computer Modern, which is a bit-mapped font. Other font families are usually Postscript-format Type 1 fonts. See section 7 (Using PostScript fonts) for details on how to specify them.

There are also many forms of accents and special characters which are available for typesetting. This is only a few of them. (Try typesetting these on your own printer.)

```
\'{o}   \'{e}   \^{o}   \"{u}   \={o}   \c{c}   '? '!
\copyright      \pounds        \dag
```

Finally, there are characters which are used as meta- or escape characters in TeX and LaTeX. One of them, the dollar sign, is mentioned above. The complete set of meta characters, which need to be escaped with a backslash to be used literally, is:

```
# $ % & _ { }
```

There are also different alphabets available, like Greek and Cyrillic. LaTeX provides many facilities for setting non-English text, which are covered by some of the other references mentioned here

4.3   Margins and line spacing.

Changing margins in a TeX or LaTeX document is not a straightforward task. A lot depends on the relative indent of the text you're trying to adjust the margin for. The placement of the margin-changing command is also significant.

For document-wide changes to LaTeX documents, the \evensidemargin and \oddsidemargin commands are available. They affect the left-hand margins of the even-numbered and odd-numbered pages, respectively. For example,

```
\evensidemargin=1in
\oddsidemargin=1in
```

adds on inch to the left-hand margin of the even and odd pages *in addition* to the standard one-inch, left-hand margin. These commands affect the entire document and will shift the entire body of the text right and left across a page, regardless of any local indent, so they're safe to use with LaTeX environments like `verse` and `list`.

Below is a set of margin-changing macros which I wrote. They have a different effect than the commands mentioned above. Because they use plain TeX commands, they're not guaranteed to honor the margins of any LaTeX environments which may be in effect, but you can place them anywhere in a document and change the margins from that point on.

```
%%   margins.sty -- v. 0.1    by Robert Kiesling
%%   Copies of this code may be freely distributed in verbatim form.
%%
%%   Some elementary plain TeX margin-changing commands. Lengths are
%%   in inches:
%%   \leftmargin{1}    %% sets the document's left margin in 1 inch.
%%   \leftindent{1}    %% sets the following paragraphs' indent in
%%                         1 inch.
%%   \rightindent{1}   %% sets the following paragraphs' right margins
%%                     %% in 1 inch.
%%   \llength{3}       %% sets the following lines' lengths to 3 inches.
%%
\message{Margins macros...}
\def\lmargin#1{\hoffset = #1 in}
\def\lindent#1{\leftskip = #1 in}
\def\rindent#1{\rightskip = #1 in}
\def\llength#1{\hsize = #1 in}
%%
%% (End of margins macros.)
```

Place this code in a file called `margins.sty` in your local `$TEXINPUTS` directory. The commands are explained in the commented section of the file. To include them in a document, use the command

```
\usepackage{margins}
```

in the document preamble.

While we're on the subject, if you don't want the right margin to be justified, which is the default, you can tell LaTeX to use ragged right margins by giving the command:

```
\raggedright
```

Setting line spacing also has its complexities.

The *baselineskip* measurement is the distance between lines of text. It is given as an absolute measurement. For example,

```
\baselineskip=24pt
```

or even better:

```
\setlength{\baselineskip}{24pt}
```

The difference between the two forms is that *setlength* will respect any scoping rules that may be in effect when you use the command.

The problem with using baselineskip is that it also affects the distance between section headings, footnotes, and the like. You need to take care that baselineskip is correct for whatever text elements you're formatting. There are, however, LaTeX macro packages, like `setspace.sty`, which will help you in these circumstances. See section 5 (LaTeX extension packages and other resources).

4.4 Document classes.

LaTeX provides document classes which provide standardized formats for documents. They provide environments to format lists, quotations, footnotes, and other text elements. Commonly used document classes are covered in the following sections.

4.4.1 Articles and reports.

As mentioned above, the `article` class and the `report` class are similar. The main differences are that the report class creates a title page by default and begins each section on a new page. Mostly, though, the two document classes are similar.

To create titles, abstracts, and bylines in these document classes, you can type, for example,

```
\title{The Breeding Habits of Cacti}
\author{John Q. Public}
{Description of how common desert cacti search
for appropriate watering holes to perform their breeding
rituals.}
```

in the document preamble. Then, the command

```
%\maketitle
```

given at the start of the text, will generate either a title page in the report class, or the title and abstract at the top of the first page, in the article class.

Sections can be defined with commands that include the following:

```
\section
\subsection
\subsubsection
```

These commands will produce the standard, numbered sections used in technical documents. For unnumbered sections, use

```
\section*
\subsection*
\subsubsection*
```

and so on.

LaTeX provides many environments for formatting displayed material. You can include quoted text with the `quotation` environment.

```
\begin{quotation}
Start of paragraph to be quoted...

... end of paragraph.
\end{quotation}
```

For shorter quotes, you can use the `quote` environment.

To format verse, use the `verse` environment.

```
\begin{verse}
Because I could not stop for death\\
He kindly stopped for me
\end{verse}
```

Notice that you must use the double backslashes to break lines in the correct places. Otherwise, LaTeX fills the lines in a verse environment, just like any other environment.

Lists come in several flavors. To format a bulleted list, the `list` environment is used:

```
\begin{list}
\item
This is the first item of the list.
\item
This is the second item of the list...
\item
... and so on.
\end{list}
```

A numbered list uses the `enumerate` environment:

```
\begin{enumerate}
\item
Item No. 1.
\item
Item No. 2.
\item
\dots
\end{enumerate}
```

A descriptive list uses the `description` environment.

```
\begin{description}
```

```
\item{Oven} Dirty, needs new burner.
\item{Refrigerator}  Dirty.  Sorry.
\item{Sink and drainboard}  Stained, drippy, cold water faucet.
\end{description}
```

4.4.2   Letters.

The letter class uses special definitions to format business letters.

The letter environment takes one argument, the address of the letter's addressee. The address command, which must appear in the document preamble, defines the return address. The signature command defines the sender's name as it appears after the closing.

The LaTeX source of a simple business letter might look like this.

```
\documentclass[letterpaper]{letter}
\signature{John Q. Public}
\address{123 Main St.\\Los Angeles, CA.  96005\\Tel: 123/456-7890}
%\begin{document}
\begin{letter}{ACME Brick Co.\\100 Ash St.\\San Diego, CA 96403}
\opening{Dear Sir/Madam:}

With regard to one of your bricks that I found on my living room
carpet surrounded by shards of my broken front window...

(Remainder of the body of the letter.)

\closing{Sincerely,}

\end{letter}
%\end{document}
```

Note that the addresses include double backslashes, which specify where the line breaks should occur.

5   LaTeX extension packages and other resources.

We mentioned above that using underlining as a form of text emphasis presents special problems. Actually, TeX has no problem underlining text, because it is a convention of mathematical typesetting. In LaTeX, you can underline words with the command:

```
\underline{text to be underlined}
```

The problem is that underlining will not break across lines, and, in some circumstances, underlining can be uneven. However, there is a LaTeX macro package, ready-made, that makes underlining the default mode of text emphasis. It's called ulem.sty, and is one of the many contributed LaTeX packages that are freely available via the Internet.

To use ulem.sty, include the command:

```
\usepackage{ulem}
```

in the document preamble.

The packages which are available for LaTeX include:

ifthen

Include conditional statements in your documents.

initials

Defines a font for initial dropped capitals.

sanskrit

Font and preprocessor for producing documents in Sanskrit.

recipe

A LaTeX2e class to typeset recipes.

refman

Variant report and article styles.

To make the path given in the Catalogue into a fully-qualified URL, concatenate the path to the host name URL and top-level path of the CTAN archive you wish to contact. For example, the top-level CTAN directory of the site *ftp.tex.ac.uk* is `ctan/tex-archive`. The complete URL of the directory of the **refman** package would be:

```
ftp://ftp.tex.ac.uk/ctan/tex-archive/    +
macros/latex/contrib/supported/refman    =

ftp://ftp.tex.ac.uk/ctan/tex-archive/macros/latex/contrib/supported/refman/
```

Some packages have more than one file, so only the path to the package's directory is given.

When you have the URL in hand, you can retrieve the package from one of the CTAN archive sites listed in section 8 (Appendix A). You can download a complete list of the archive's contents as the file `FILES.byname`, in the archive's top-level directory. You can also search the archive on line for a keyword with the `ftp` command

```
quote site index <keyword>
```

6   Mixing text and graphics with `dvips`.

In general, this section applies to any TeX or LaTeX document which mixes text and graphics. teTeX, like most other TeX distributions, is configured to request Computer Modern fonts by default. When printing documents with Type 1 scalable fonts or graphics, font and graphics imaging is the job of `dvips`. `dvips` can use either Computer Modern bit mapped fonts or Type 1 scalable fonts, or any combination of the two. First, let's concentrate on printing and previewing some graphics.

You will probably want to follow this procedure any time a LaTeX source document has the statement

```
\includepackage{graphics}
```

in the document preamble. This statement tells LaTeX to include the text of the `graphics.sty` package in the source document. There are other commands to perform graphics operations, and the statements in plain-TeX documents may not clue you in whether you need to use `dvips`. The difference will be apparent in the output, though, when the document is printed with missing figures and other graphics.

So, for now, we'll concentrate on printing documents which use the LaTeX `graphics.sty` package. You might want to take a look at the original TeX input. It isn't included in the teTeX distribution, but it is available at

```
~CTAN/macros/latex/packages/graphics/grfguide.tex.
```

What the teTeX distribution does include is the `.dvi` output file, and it is already TeXed for you. There is a reason for this, and it has to do with the necessity of including Type 1 fonts in the output in order for the document to print properly.

If you want to LaTeX `grfguide.tex`, see the next section. For now, however, we'll work on getting usable output using `dvips`.

The file `grfguide.dvi` is located in the directory

```
texmf/doc/latex/graphics
```

The first step in outputting `grfguide.dvi` is to translate it to Postscript. The program `dvips` is used for this. It does just exactly what its name implies. There are many options available for invoking `dvips`, but the simplest (nearly) form is

```
dvips -f -r <grfguide.dvi >grfguide.ps
```

The `-f` command switch tells `dvips` to operate as a filter, reading from standard input and writing to standard output. `dvips` output can be configured so its output defaults to `lpr`.

If you can print Postscript directly to your printer via `lpr`, you can simply type

```
dvips -r grfguide.dvi
```

The `-r` option tells dvips to output the pages in reverse order so they stack correctly when they exit a printer. Use it or not, as appropriate for your output device.

Depending on whether you still have the fonts that `dvilj2` generated from the last document, `dvips` and metafont may or may not need to create new fonts needed by `grfguide.dvi`. Eventually, though, `dvips` will output a list of the pages translated to Postscript, and you will have your Postscript output ready to be rendered on whatever output device you have available.

If you're lucky (and rich), then you have a Postscript-capable printer already and will be able to print `grfguide.ps` directly. You can either spool the output to the printer using `lpr`. If for some reason your printer software doesn't work right with Postscript files, you can, in a pinch, simply dump the file to printer, with

```
cat grfguide.ps >/dev/lp0
```

or whichever port your printer is attached to, though this is not recommended for everyday use.

If you want or need to invoke Ghostscript manually, this is the standard procedure for its operation. The first thing you want to do is invoke Ghostscript to view its command line arguments, like this:

```
gs -help | less
```

You'll see a list of supported output devices and sundry other commands. Pick the output device which most nearly matches your printer. I generally produce black-and-white text and use the `cdjmono` driver, which drives a color Deskjet in monochrome (black and white) mode.

The command line I would use is:

```
gs -dNOPAUSE -sDEVICE=cdjmono -sOutputFile=/tmp/gs.out grfguide.ps -c quit
```

This will produce my HP-compatible output in the `/tmp` directory. It's a good idea to use a directory like `/tmp`, because `gs` can be particular about access permissions, and you can't (and shouldn't) always count on being logged in as `root` to perform these steps. Now you can print the file:

```
lpr /tmp/gs.out
```

Obviously, this can all go into a shell script. On my system, I have two simple scripts written, `pv` and `pr`, which simply outputs the Postscript file either to the display or the printer. Screen previewing is possible without X, but it's far from ideal. So, it's definitely worth the effort to install XFree86 to view the output on the screen..

The order of commands in a `gs` command line is significant, because some of the options tell Ghostscript to look for pieces of Postscript code from its library.

The important thing to remember is that `grfguide.dvi` makes requests for both Computer Modern bit mapped and Type 1 scaled fonts. If you can mix scalable and bit mapped fonts in a document, you're well on the way to becoming a TeXpert.

6.1 What if my printer isn't supported?

The teTeX distribution comes with only a limited selection of DVI output drivers: `dvips`, drivers for Hewlett Packard LaserJets, and nothing else. You have two options if you have a printer which isn't LaserJet-compatible: You can use `dvips` and Ghostscript, which I would recommend anyway, for reasons already mentioned, or you can investigate other dviware sources.

A limited number of DVI drivers have been ported to Linux and are available as pre-built binaries. They are located in the Linux archives at *ftp://sunsite.unc.edu/pub/Linux/apps/tex/dvi/*.

The master dviware libraries are maintained at the University of Utah archives. If you can't find a DVI driver there that supports your printer, chances are that it doesn't exist. You can also write your *own* DVI driver using the templates available there. The library's URL is *ftp://ftp.math.utah.edu/pub/tex/dvi/*.

7 Using Postscript fonts.

It used to be that public domain, Type 1 fonts were much poorer quality than Computer Modern bit mapped fonts. This situation has improved in the last several years, though, but matching the fonts is up to you. Having several different font systems on one machine can seem redundant and an unnecessary waste of disk space. And the Computer Modern fonts can seem, well, a little too *formal* to be suitable for everyday use. It reminds me sometimes of bringing out the good China to feed the dog. At least you don't need to spend a bundle on professional quality fonts any longer.

One of the major improvements of LaTeX2e over its predecessor was the inclusion of the New Font Selection Scheme. (It's now called PSNFSS.) Formerly, TeX authors would specify fonts with commands like

```
\font=bodyroman = cmr10 scaled \magstep 1
```

which provides precision but requires the skills of a type designer and mathematician to make good use of. Also, it's not very portable. If another system didn't have the font `cmr10` (this is TeX nomenclature for Computer Modern Roman, 10 point, with the default medium stroke weight), somebody would have to re-code the fonts specifications for the entire document. PSNFSS, however, allows you specify fonts by family (Computer Modern, URW Nimbus, Helvetica, Utopia, and so forth), weight (light, medium, bold), orientation (upright or oblique), face (Roman, Italic), and base point size. (See the section 4.2 (Characters and type styles) for a description of the commands to specify typefaces.) Many fonts are packaged as families. For example, a Roman-type font may come packaged with a sans serif font, like Helvetica, and a monospaced font, like Courier. You, as the author of a LaTeX document, can specify an entire font family with one command.

There are, as I said, several high-quality font sets available in the public domain. One of them is Adobe Utopia. Another is Bitstream Charter. Both are commercial quality fonts which have been donated to the public domain.

These happen to be two of my favorites. If you look around one of the CTAN sites, you will find these and other fonts archived there. There are enough fonts around that you'll be able to design documents the way you want them to look, and not just English text, either. TeX was originally designed for mathematical typesetting, so there is a full range of mathematical fonts available, as well as Cyrillic, Greek, Kana, and other alphabets too numerous to mention.

The important thing to look for is files which have either the `.pfa` or `.pfb` extension. They indicate that these are the scalable fonts themselves, not simply the metrics files. Type 1 fonts use `.pfm` metric files, as opposed to the `.tfm` metric files which bit mapped fonts use. The two font sets I mentioned above are included in teTeX distributions, as well as separately.

What I said above, concerning the ease of font selection under PSNFSS, is true in this instance. If we want to use the Charter fonts in our document instead of Computer Modern bit mapped, all that is necessary is include the LaTeX statement

```
\renewcommand{\familydefault}{bch}
```

in the document preamble, where "bch" is the common designation for Bitstream Charter. The Charter fonts reside in the directory

```
/usr/lib/teTeX/texmf/fonts/type1/bitstrea/charter
```

There you'll see the `.pfb` files of the Charter fonts: `bchb8a.pfb` for Charter Bold, `bchr8a.pfb` for Charter Roman, `bchbi8a.pfb` for Charter Bold Italic. The "8a" in the font names indicates the character encoding. At this point you shouldn't need to worry much about them, because the encodings mostly differ for 8-bit characters, which have numeric values above 128 decimal. They mostly define accents and non-English characters. The Type 1 font encodings generally work well for Western alphabets because they conform to the ISO 8859 standards for international character sets, so this is an added benefit of using them.

To typeset a document which has Charter fonts selected, you would give the command

```
pslatex document.tex
```

`pslatex` is a variant of teTeX's standard `latex` command which defines the directories where the Type 1 fonts are, as well as some additional LaTeX code to load. You'll see the notice screen for `pslatex` followed by the status output of the TeX job itself. In a moment, you'll have a `.dvi` file which includes the Charter font requests. You can then print the file with `dvips`, and `gs` if necessary.

Installing a Type 1 font set is not difficult, as long as you follow a few basic steps. You should unpack the fonts in a subdirectory of the `/usr/lib/teTeX/texmf/fonts/type1` directory, where your other Type 1 fonts are located, and then run `texhash` to let the directory search routines know that the fonts have been added. Then you need to add the font descriptions to the file `psfonts.map` so `dvips` knows they're on the system. The format of the `psfonts.map` file is covered in a couple different places in the references mentioned above. Again, remember to run the `texhash` program to update the teTeX directory database.

It is definitely an advantage to use the X Windows System with teTeX— XFree86 under Linux—because it allows for superior document previewing. It's not required, but in general, anything that allows for easier screen previewing is going to benefit your work, in terms of the quality of the output. However, there is a tradeoff with speed of editing, which is much quicker on character-mode displays.

8 Appendix A: CTAN site list.

This is the text of the file `CTAN.sites`, which is available in the top-level directory of each CTAN archive or mirror site.

```
In order to reduce network load, it is recommended that you use the
Comprehensive TeX Archive Network (CTAN) host which is located in the
closest network proximity to your site.  Alternatively, you may wish to
obtain a copy of the CTAN via CD-ROM (see help/CTAN.cdrom for details).

Known mirrors of the CTAN reside on (alphabetically):
```

```
cis.utovrm.it (Italia)                    /TeX
ctan.unsw.edu.au (NSW, Australia)         /tex-archive
dongpo.math.ncu.edu.tw (Taiwan)           /tex-archive
ftp.belnet.be (Belgium)                   /packages/TeX
ftp.ccu.edu.tw (Taiwan)                   /pub/tex
ftp.cdrom.com (West coast, USA)           /pub/tex/ctan
ftp.comp.hkbu.edu.hk (Hong Kong)          /pub/TeX/CTAN
ftp.cs.rmit.edu.au  (Australia)           /tex-archive
ftp.cs.ruu.nl (The Netherlands)           /pub/tex-archive
ftp.cstug.cz (The Czech Republic)         /pub/tex/CTAN
ftp.duke.edu (North Carolina, USA)        /tex-archive
ftp.funet.fi (Finland)                    /pub/TeX/CTAN
ftp.gwdg.de (Deutschland)                 /pub/dante
ftp.jussieu.fr (France)                   /pub4/TeX/CTAN
ftp.kreonet.re.kr (Korea)                 /pub/CTAN
ftp.loria.fr (France)                     /pub/unix/tex/ctan
ftp.mpi-sb.mpg.de (Deutschland)           /pub/tex/mirror/ftp.dante.de
ftp.nada.kth.se (Sweden)                  /pub/tex/ctan-mirror
ftp.oleane.net (France)                   /pub/mirrors/CTAN/
ftp.rediris.es (Espa\~na)                 /mirror/tex-archive
ftp.rge.com (New York, USA)               /pub/tex
ftp.riken.go.jp (Japan)                   /pub/tex-archive
ftp.tu-chemnitz.de (Deutschland)          /pub/tex
ftp.u-aizu.ac.jp (Japan)                  /pub/tex/CTAN
ftp.uni-augsburg.de (Deutschland)         /tex-archive
ftp.uni-bielefeld.de (Deutschland)        /pub/tex
ftp.unina.it (Italia)                     /pub/TeX
ftp.uni-stuttgart.de (Deutschland)        /tex-archive (/pub/tex)
ftp.univie.ac.at (\"Osterreich)           /packages/tex
ftp.ut.ee (Estonia)                       /tex-archive
ftpserver.nus.sg (Singapore)              /pub/zi/TeX
src.doc.ic.ac.uk (England)                /packages/tex/uk-tex
sunsite.auc.dk (Denmark)                  /pub/tex/ctan
sunsite.cnlab-switch.ch (Switzerland)     /mirror/tex
sunsite.icm.edu.pl (Poland)               /pub/CTAN
sunsite.unc.edu (North Carolina, USA)     /pub/packages/TeX
wuarchive.wustl.edu (Missouri, USA)       /packages/TeX
```

Known partial mirrors of the CTAN reside on (alphabetically):
```
ftp.adfa.oz.au (Australia)                /pub/tex/ctan
ftp.fcu.edu.tw (Taiwan)                   /pub2/tex
ftp.germany.eu.net (Deutschland)          /pub/packages/TeX
ftp.gust.org.pl (Poland)                  /pub/TeX
ftp.jaist.ac.jp (Japan)                   /pub/TeX/tex-archive
ftp.uu.net (Virginia, USA)                /pub/text-processing/TeX
nic.switch.ch (Switzerland)               /mirror/tex
sunsite.dsi.unimi.it (Italia)             /pub/TeX
sunsite.snu.ac.kr (Korea)                 /shortcut/CTAN
```

Please send updates to this list to <ctan@urz.uni-heidelberg.de>.

The participating hosts in the Comprehensive TeX Archive Network are:
```
ftp.dante.de  (Deutschland)
     -- anonymous ftp                     /tex-archive (/pub/tex /pub/archive)
     -- gopher on node gopher.dante.de
```

```
-- e-mail via ftpmail@dante.de
-- World Wide Web access on www.dante.de
-- Administrator: <ftpmaint@dante.de>

ftp.tex.ac.uk (England)
-- anonymous ftp                    /tex-archive (/pub/tex /pub/archive)
-- gopher on node gopher.tex.ac.uk
-- NFS mountable from nfs.tex.ac.uk:/public/ctan/tex-archive
-- World Wide Web access on www.tex.ac.uk
-- Administrator: <ctan-uk@tex.ac.uk>
```

9   Appendix B: Installing the CTAN teTeX distribution.

The generic, teTeX distribution isn't any harder to install than the Linux packages. See section 9.3 (Generic CTAN distribution), below.

You should consider installing the generic teTeX distribution from the CTAN archives if:

- Your system isn't based on one of the standard Linux distributions.

- You don't have root privileges on your system.

- You want or need to have the very latest version of teTeX, or LaTeX.

- You don't have enough disk space available for a full installation.

- You want to install teTeX somewhere instead of the /usr file system.

- You would like to share your teTeX installation with other UNIX variants or platforms on a network. In this case, you should strongly consider installing from the *source* distribution. See section 9.3 (Installing the source distribution), below.

- You want the latest versions of teTeX's public domain Type 1 fonts, which are significantly better than the fonts included in earlier releases.

A complete installation of the binary distribution requires 40-50 Mb of disk space, and building the distribution from the source code takes about 75 Mb, so you should make sure that the disk space is available before you start. You don't need to have the GCC compiler or the X Windows System installed (although X certainly helps because it is much easier to preview documents on-screen). All you need is an editor that is capable of producing plain ASCII, text (see section 2). What could be simpler?

You can retrieve the files from one of the CTAN archives listed in section 8 (Appendix A). In the examples below, the files were retrieved from the CTAN archive at *ftp.tex.ac.uk*.

9.1   Installing the binary distribution.

9.1.1   Minimal installation.

First, FTP to *ftp.tex.ac.uk* and cd to the directory

```
ctan/tex-archive/systems/unix/teTeX/distrib/
```

Retrieve the files

```
INSTALL.bin
install.sh
```

and place them in the top-level directory where you want to install teTeX, for example, `/var/teTeX` if you plan to install teTeX in the `/var` file system.

Print out the `INSTALL.bin` file. Keep this file handy, because it describes how to install a minimal teTeX installation. The minimal installation requires only 10-15 MB of disk space, but it is recommended that you install the complete teTeX package if at all possible. For a minimum installation, you'll need the files

```
ctan/tex-archive/systems/unix/teTeX/distrib/base/latex-base.tar.gz
ctan/tex-archive/systems/unix/teTeX/distrib/base/tetex-base.tar.gz
```

You'll also need one of two archives which contain the executable teTeX programs. Retrieve the archive file

```
ctan/tex-archive/systems/unix/teTeX/distrib/binaries/i386-linux.tar.gz
```

if your system uses the Linux ELF shared libraries, `ld.so` of at least version 1.73, and clibs of at least version 5.09. If it doesn't, retrieve the archive

```
ctan/tex-archive/systems/unix/teTeX/distrib/binaries/i386-linuxaout.tar.gz
```

which is compiled for systems that use the older, a.out-format static libraries.

Then, following the instructions in the file `INSTALL.bin`, execute the command

```
sh ./install.sh
```

while in the top-level teTeX installation directory. (Make sure that the teTeX archives are located there, too.) After a few moments, the installation program will warn you that you are missing some of the teTeX packages. However, if you're planning only a minimal teTeX installation, you should ignore the warnings and proceed. To configure the basic teTeX system, see section 9.2 (Base system configuration), below.

To install the remaining packages, see the next section.

9.1.2 Complete installation.

To perform a complete teTeX installation, retrieve the archive files listed in the previous section, as well as the following files:

```
ctan/tex-archive/systems/unix/teTeX/distrib/doc/ams-doc.tar.gz
ctan/tex-archive/systems/unix/teTeX/distrib/doc/bibtex-doc.tar.gz
ctan/tex-archive/systems/unix/teTeX/distrib/doc/eplain-doc.tar.gz
ctan/tex-archive/systems/unix/teTeX/distrib/doc/fonts-doc.tar.gz
ctan/tex-archive/systems/unix/teTeX/distrib/doc/general-doc.tar.gz
ctan/tex-archive/systems/unix/teTeX/distrib/doc/generic-doc.tar.gz
ctan/tex-archive/systems/unix/teTeX/distrib/doc/latex-doc.tar.gz
ctan/tex-archive/systems/unix/teTeX/distrib/doc/makeindex-doc.tar.gz
ctan/tex-archive/systems/unix/teTeX/distrib/doc/metapost-doc.tar.gz
ctan/tex-archive/systems/unix/teTeX/distrib/doc/programs-doc.tar.gz
ctan/tex-archive/systems/unix/teTeX/distrib/fonts/ams-fonts.tar.gz
ctan/tex-archive/systems/unix/teTeX/distrib/fonts/dc-fonts.tar.gz
ctan/tex-archive/systems/unix/teTeX/distrib/fonts/ec-fonts.tar.gz
ctan/tex-archive/systems/unix/teTeX/distrib/fonts/misc-fonts.tar.gz
ctan/tex-archive/systems/unix/teTeX/distrib/fonts/postscript-fonts.tar.gz
ctan/tex-archive/systems/unix/teTeX/distrib/fonts/sauter-fonts.tar.gz
ctan/tex-archive/systems/unix/teTeX/distrib/goodies/amstex.tar.gz
ctan/tex-archive/systems/unix/teTeX/distrib/goodies/bibtex.tar.gz
```

```
ctan/tex-archive/systems/unix/teTeX/distrib/goodies/eplain.tar.gz
ctan/tex-archive/systems/unix/teTeX/distrib/goodies/latex-extra.tar.gz
ctan/tex-archive/systems/unix/teTeX/distrib/goodies/metapost.tar.gz
ctan/tex-archive/systems/unix/teTeX/distrib/goodies/pictex.tar.gz
ctan/tex-archive/systems/unix/teTeX/distrib/goodies/pstricks.tar.gz
ctan/tex-archive/systems/unix/teTeX/distrib/goodies/texdraw.tar.gz
ctan/tex-archive/systems/unix/teTeX/distrib/goodies/xypic.tar.gz
```

All of these files should be placed in the top-level directory where you want teTeX to reside. As with the minimal installation, execute the command

```
sh ./install.sh
```

9.2 Base system configuration.

The `install.sh` script, after determining which teTeX archive series are present, will present you with a menu of options. The only setting you need to make at this point is to set the top-level directory where you want teTeX installed, by selecting the "D" option. You must, of course, choose a directory in whose parent directory you have write permissions. For example, if you are installing teTeX in your home directory, you would specify the teTeX installation directory as

```
/home/john.q.public/teTeX
```

and, after returning to the main menu, select "I" to proceed with the installation. Note that the directory must not exist already: the `install.sh` script must be able to create it.

An option which you should consider enabling, is setting an alternative directory for generated fonts. Even if you plan to use only Postscript-format, Type 1 scalable fonts, occasionally you'll process a file that requires the Computer Modern fonts. Enabling this option requires that you enter the directory to use. You must have write permissions for the parent directory. Following the example above, you could specify

```
/home/john.q.public/texfonts
```

or, if you want the generated fonts to be accessible by all users on the system, specify a directory like

```
/var/texfonts
```

I would recommend that you *not,* however, use the default `/var/tmp/texfonts` directory for this option, because the generated fonts could be deleted after the next reboot, and the fonts will need to be generated again the next time they're needed.

After you've selected the option "I", and `install.sh` has installed the archives, set various permissions, and generated its links and format files, the program will exit with a message telling you to add the teTeX binary directory to your `$PATH` environment variable, and the directories where the man pages and info files reside to your `$MANPATH` and `$INFOPATH` environment variables. For example, add the statements

```
export PATH=$PATH:"/home/john.q.public/teTeX/bin"
export MANPATH=$MANPATH":/home/john.q.public/teTeX/man"
export INFOPATH$=INFOPATH":/home/john.q.public/teTeX/info"
```

to your `~/.bash_profile` if you use `bash` as your shell, or to your `~/.profile` if you use another shell for logins.

Log out, and then log in again, so the environment variables are registered. Then, run the command

```
texconfig confall
```

HOWTO

to insure that the installation is correct.

Next, you can configure teTeX for you specific hardware. See section 9.4 (Post-installation configuration details), below.

9.3   Installing the CTAN source distribution.

To install teTeX V. 0.4 from the source code, `ftp` to a CTAN site like *ftp://ftp.tex.ac.uk* and retrieve the files

```
ctan/tex-archive/systems/unix/teTeX/distrib/INSTALL.src
ctan/tex-archive/systems/unix/teTeX/distrib/sources/README.texmf-src
ctan/tex-archive/systems/unix/teTeX/distrib/sources/teTeX-lib-0.4pl8.tar.gz
ctan/tex-archive/systems/unix/teTeX/distrib/sources/teTeX-src-0.4pl7.tar.gz
```

Read over the instructions in `INSTALL.src`, then `su` to root and unpack the files in a directory for which you have read-write-execute permissions.

Remember to use the `p` argument to `tar`, and also remember to unset the `noclobber` option of `bash`. You can do this with the counterintuitive command

```
set +o noclobber
```

Note that the argument `+o` to `set` *un*sets a variable, just exactly backwards from what you might expect.

The file `teTeX-lib-0.4pl8.tar.gz` will create the directory `./teTeX`. The file `teTeX-src-0.4pl7.tar.gz` will create the directory `teTeX-src-0.4` Print out the file `INSTALL.src` and keep it nearby for the following steps. `cd` to the `./teTeX-src-0.4` directory, and, per the instructions in the `INSTALL.src` file, edit `./Makefile`. You need to set the `TETEXDIR` variable to the absolute path of the parent teTeX directory. This will be the subdirectory `teTeX` of the directory where you unpacked the source and library archives. For example, if you unpacked the archives in your home directory, you would set `TETEXDIR` to

```
/home/john.q.public/teTeX
```

The rest of the `Makefile` options are pretty generic. With GCC version 2.7.2 and later, you should not need to make any further adjustments unless you have a non-standard compiler and library setup, or want the compiler to perform some further optimizations, or for some other reason. Check that the `USE_DIALOG`, `USE_NCURSES`, and `HAVE_NCURSES` variables are set correctly for your system, because the `dialog` program needs the ncurses library to be installed. A `ncurses` library is included in the source distribution, so the default values in the `Makefile` should work fine. If you can't get `ncurses` to compile or link, `texconfig` can also be run from the command line.

If you've done everything correctly up to this point, you should be able to type `make world` in the top-level source directory, and relax until the teTeX executables are built. This can take a few hours.

After the build has completed, set the environment variables `$PATH`, `$MANPATH`, and `$INFOPATH` to include the teTeX directories. The statements which would be added to the file `~/.bash_profile`, in the example, above, would be

```
export PATH=$PATH":/home/john.q.public/teTeX/bin/i386-linux"
export MANPATH=$MANPATH":/home/john.q.public/teTeX/man"
export INFOPATH=$INFOPATH":/home/john.q.public/teTeX/info"
```

The `$PATH` variable is different in the source distribution than in the binary distribution. Note that here the path to the binaries is `teTeX/bin/i386-linux` instead of simply `teTeX/bin` as in the binary distribution.

At this point you can run `texconfig confall` to ensure that the paths have been set correctly, and then proceed to configure teTeX as in the binary distribution. See the section 9.4 (Post-installation configuration details), below.

9.4 Post-installation configuration details.

The first thing you want to do is look at Thomas Esser's README file. It contains a lot of hints on how to configure teTeX for your output device (i.e., printer). The README file is located in the directory

```
/usr/lib/teTeX/texmf/doc/tetex
```

Read the file over with the command (the path in the following examples is that of the Slackware distribution):

```
less /usr/lib/teTeX/texmf/doc/tetex/README
```

or, print it out with the command

```
cat /usr/lib/teTeX/texmf/doc/tetex/README >/dev/lp0
```

assuming that your printer is connected to /dev/lp0. Substitute the device driver file that your printer is connected to, as appropriate.

Or, better still, print it using the lpr command:

```
lpr /usr/lib/teTeX/texmf/doc/tetex/README
```

You should have installed the printer daemon that is included with your distribution of Linux. If not, do that now, per the instructions that come with the package.

Print out the teTeX-FAQ. Keep the FAQ handy because it contains useful hints for configuring teTeX's output drivers for your printer. We'll get to that in a moment. In more recent releases of teTeX, the teTeX-FAQ is viewable via the texconfig utility.

Next, you want to define a directory to store your own TeX format files. teTeX searches the directories listed by the $TEXINPUTS environment variable for local TeX input files:

```
export TEXINPUTS=".:~/texinputs:"
```

to the system-wide /etc/profile file. Individual users can set their own local $TEXINPUTS directory, by adding the line in their ~/.profile or ~/.bash_profile if bash is the default shell. The $TEXINPUTS environment variable tells teTeX to look for users' individual TeX style files in the ~/texinputs directories under each user's home directory. It is *critical* that a colon appear before and after this directory. teTeX is going to append its own directory searches to your own. You want to have teTeX search the local format files first, so it uses the local versions of any of the standard files you have edited.

Add the /usr/lib/teTeX/bin directory to the system-wide path if you're installing teTeX as root. Again, if you're installing a personal copy of teTeX, add the directory where the teTeX binaries are located to *the front* your $PATH with the following line in your ~/.profile or ~/.bash_profile:

```
export PATH="~/tetex/bin:"$PATH
```

Now, log in as root and run texconfig per the instructions in the teTeX-FAQ and choose the printer that is attached to your system. Make sure that you configure teTeX for both the correct printer and printer resolution.

Finally, run the texhash program. This ensures that teTeX's internal database is up to date. The database is actually a ls-lR file. You *must* run texhash every time you change the system configuration, or teTeX will not be able to locate your changes.

10 Appendix C: Distribution and Copyright.

10.1 Distribution.

teTeX is *free software;* this means everyone is free to use the software and free to redistribute it on certain conditions. The package is not in the public domain. It is copyrighted and there are restrictions on its distribution, but these restrictions are designed to permit everything that a good cooperating citizen would want to do. What is not allowed is to try to prevent others from further sharing any version of free software that they might get from you. The precise conditions are found in the GNU General Public License that comes with many of the software packages and also appears following this section.

One way to get a copy of the package is from someone else who has it. You need not ask for our permission to do so, or tell any one else; just copy it. If you have access to the Internet, you can get the latest distribution versions by anonymous FTP. See the chapter "Sources" for more information.

You may also receive the software when you buy a computer. Computer manufacturers are free to distribute copies on the same terms that apply to everyone else. These terms require them to give you the full sources, including whatever changes they may have made, and to permit you to redistribute these packages received from them under the usual terms of the General Public License. In other words, the program must be free for you when you get it, not just free for the manufacturer.

You can also order copies of GNU software from the Free Software Foundation on CD-ROM. This is a convenient and reliable way to get a copy; it is also a good way to help fund our work. (The Foundation has always received most of its funds in this way.) An order form is included many distribution, and on our web site in http://www.gnu.ai.mit.edu/order/order.html. For further information, write to

```
Free Software Foundation
59 Temple Place, Suite 330
Boston, MA  02111-1307 USA
USA
```

The income from distribution fees goes to support the foundation's purpose: the development of new free software, and improvements to our existing programs.

If you use GNU software at your workplace, please suggest that the company make a donation. If company policy is unsympathetic to the idea of donating to charity, you might instead suggest ordering a CD-ROM from the Foundation occasionally, or subscribing to periodic updates.

10.2 GNU GENERAL PUBLIC LICENSE

Version 2, June 1991

Copyright (C) 1989, 1991 Free Software Foundation, Inc. 59 Temple Place, Suite 330, Boston, MA 02111-1307 USA

Everyone is permitted to copy and distribute verbatim copies of this license document, but changing it is not allowed.

Preamble.

The licenses for most software are designed to take away your freedom to share and change it. By contrast, the GNU General Public License is intended to guarantee your freedom to share and change free software—to make sure the software is free for all its users. This General Public License applies to most of the Free Software Foundation's software and to any other program whose authors commit to using it. (Some other Free Software Foundation software is covered by the GNU Library General Public License instead.) You can apply it to your programs, too.

When we speak of free software, we are referring to freedom, not price. Our General Public Licenses are designed to make sure that you have the freedom to distribute copies of free software (and charge for this service if you wish), that you receive source code or can get it if you want it, that you can change the software or use pieces of it in new free programs; and that you know you can do these things.

To protect your rights, we need to make restrictions that forbid anyone to deny you these rights or to ask you to surrender the rights. These restrictions translate to certain responsibilities for you if you distribute copies of the software, or if you modify it.

For example, if you distribute copies of such a program, whether gratis or for a fee, you must give the recipients all the rights that you have. You must make sure that they, too, receive or can get the source code. And you must show them these terms so they know their rights.

We protect your rights with two steps: (1) copyright the software, and (2) offer you this license which gives you legal permission to copy, distribute and/or modify the software.

Also, for each author's protection and ours, we want to make certain that everyone understands that there is no warranty for this free software. If the software is modified by someone else and passed on, we want its recipients to know that what they have is not the original, so that any problems introduced by others will not reflect on the original authors' reputations.

Finally, any free program is threatened constantly by software patents. We wish to avoid the danger that redistributors of a free program will individually obtain patent licenses, in effect making the program proprietary. To prevent this, we have made it clear that any patent must be licensed for everyone's free use or not licensed at all.

The precise terms and conditions for copying, distribution and modification follow.

TERMS AND CONDITIONS FOR COPYING, DISTRIBUTION AND MODIFICATION

- This License applies to any program or other work which contains a notice placed by the copyright holder saying it may be distributed under the terms of this General Public License. The "Program" below, refers to any such program or work, and a "work based on the Program" means either the Program or any derivative work under copyright law: that is to say, a work containing the Program or a portion of it, either verbatim or with modifications and/or translated into another language. (Hereinafter, translation is included without limitation in the term, "modification.") Each licensee is addressed as "you."

  Activities other than copying, distribution and modification are not covered by this License; they are outside its scope. The act of running the Program is not restricted, and the output from the Program is covered only if its contents constitute a work based on the Program (independent of having been made by running the Program). Whether that is true depends on what the Program does.

- You may copy and distribute verbatim copies of the Program's source code as you receive it, in any medium, provided that you conspicuously and appropriately publish on each copy an appropriate copyright notice and disclaimer of warranty; keep intact all the notices that refer to this License and to the absence of any warranty; and give any other recipients of the Program a copy of this License along with the Program.

  You may charge a fee for the physical act of transferring a copy, and you may at your option offer warranty protection in exchange for a fee.

- You may modify your copy or copies of the Program or any portion of it, thus forming a work based on the Program, and copy and distribute such modifications or work under the terms of Section 1 above, provided that you also meet all of these conditions:

  1. You must cause the modified files to carry prominent notices stating that you changed the files and the date of any change.

  2. You must cause any work that you distribute or publish, that in whole or in part contains or is derived from the Program or any part thereof, to be licensed as a whole at no charge to all third parties under the terms of this License.

  3. If the modified program normally reads commands interactively when run, you must cause it, when started running for such interactive use in the most ordinary way, to print or display an announcement including an appropriate copyright notice and a notice that there is no warranty (or else, saying that you provide a warranty) and that users may redistribute the program under these conditions, and telling the user how to view a copy of this License.

(Exception: if the Program itself is interactive but does not normally print such an announcement, your work based on the Program is not required to print an announcement.)

These requirements apply to the modified work as a whole. If identifiable sections of that work are not derived from the Program, and can be reasonably considered independent and separate works in themselves, then this License, and its terms, do not apply to those sections when you distribute them as separate works. But when you distribute the same sections as part of a whole which is a work based on the Program, the distribution of the whole must be on the terms of this License, whose permissions for other licensees extend to the entire whole, and thus to each and every part regardless of who wrote it.

Thus, it is not the intent of this section to claim rights or contest your rights to work written entirely by you; rather, the intent is to exercise the right to control the distribution of derivative or collective works based on the Program.

In addition, mere aggregation of another work not based on the Program with the Program (or with a work based on the Program) on a volume of a storage or distribution medium does not bring the other work under the scope of this License.

- You may copy and distribute the Program (or a work based on it, under Section 2) in object code or executable form under the terms of Sections 1 and 2 above provided that you also do one of the following:

1. Accompany it with the complete corresponding machine-readable source code, which must be distributed under the terms of Sections 1 and 2 above on a medium customarily used for software interchange; or,

2. Accompany it with a written offer, valid for at least three years, to give any third party, for a charge no more than your cost of physically performing source distribution, a complete machine-readable copy of the corresponding source code, to be distributed under the terms of Sections 1 and 2 above on a medium customarily used for software interchange; or,

3. Accompany it with the information you received as to the offer to distribute corresponding source code. (This alternative is allowed only for noncommercial distribution and only if you received the program in object code or executable form with such an offer, in accord with Subsection b above.)

The source code for a work means the preferred form of the work for making modifications to it. For an executable work, complete source code means all the source code for all modules it contains, plus any associated interface definition files, plus the scripts used to control compilation and installation of the executable. However, as a special exception, the source code distributed need not include anything that is normally distributed (in either source or binary form) with the major components (compiler, kernel, and so on) of the operating system on which the executable runs, unless that component itself accompanies the executable.

If distribution of executable or object code is made by offering access to copy from a designated place, then offering equivalent access to copy the source code from the same place counts as distribution of the source code, even though third parties are not compelled to copy the source along with the object code.

- You may not copy, modify, sublicense, or distribute the Program except as expressly provided under this License. Any attempt otherwise to copy, modify, sublicense or distribute the Program is void, and will automatically terminate your rights under this License. However, parties who have received copies, or rights, from you under this License will not have their licenses terminated so long as such parties remain in full compliance.

- You are not required to accept this License, since you have not signed it. However, nothing else grants you permission to modify or distribute the Program or its derivative works. These actions are prohibited by law if you do not accept this License. Therefore, by modifying or distributing the Program (or any work based on the Program), you indicate your acceptance of this License to do so, and all its terms and conditions for copying, distributing or modifying the Program or works based on it.

- Each time you redistribute the Program (or any work based on the Program), the recipient automatically receives a license from the original licensor to copy, distribute or modify the Program subject to these terms and conditions. You may not impose any further restrictions on the recipients' exercise of the rights granted herein. You are not responsible for enforcing compliance by third parties to this License.

- If, as a consequence of a court judgment or allegation of patent infringement or for any other reason (not limited to patent issues), conditions are imposed on you (whether by court order, agreement or otherwise) that contradict the conditions of this License, they do not excuse you from the conditions of this License. If you cannot distribute so as to satisfy simultaneously your obligations under this License and any other pertinent obligations, then as a consequence you may not distribute the Program at all. For example, if a patent license would not permit royalty-free redistribution of the Program by all those who receive copies directly or indirectly through you, then the only way you could satisfy both it and this License would be to refrain entirely from distribution of the Program.

If any portion of this section is held invalid or unenforceable under any particular circumstance, the balance of the section is intended to apply and the section as a whole is intended to apply in other circumstances.

It is not the purpose of this section to induce you to infringe any patents or other property right claims or to contest validity of any such claims; this section has the sole purpose of protecting the integrity of the free software distribution system, which is implemented by public license practices. Many people have made generous contributions to the wide range of software distributed through that system in reliance on consistent application of that system; it is up to the author/donor to decide if he or she is willing to distribute software through any other system and a licensee cannot impose that choice.

This section is intended to make thoroughly clear what is believed to be a consequence of the rest of this License.

- If the distribution and/or use of the Program is restricted in certain countries either by patents or by copyrighted interfaces, the original copyright holder who places the Program under this License may add an explicit geographical distribution limitation excluding those countries, so that distribution is permitted only in or among countries not thus excluded. In such case, this License incorporates the limitation as if written in the body of this License.

- The Free Software Foundation may publish revised and/or new versions of the General Public License from time to time. Such new versions will be similar in spirit to the present version, but may differ in detail to address new problems or concerns.

Each version is given a distinguishing version number. If the Program specifies a version number of this License which applies to it and "any later version," you have the option of following the terms and conditions either of that version or of any later version published by the Free Software Foundation. If the Program does not specify a version number of this License, you may choose any version ever published by the Free Software Foundation.

- If you wish to incorporate parts of the Program into other free programs whose distribution conditions are different, write to the author to ask for permission. For software which is copyrighted by the Free Software Foundation, write to the Free Software Foundation; we sometimes make exceptions for this. Our decision will be guided by the two goals of preserving the free status of all derivatives of our free software and of promoting the sharing and reuse of software generally.

NO WARRANTY

- BECAUSE THE PROGRAM IS LICENSED FREE OF CHARGE, THERE IS NO WARRANTY FOR THE PROGRAM, TO THE EXTENT PERMITTED BY APPLICABLE LAW. EXCEPT WHEN OTHERWISE STATED IN WRITING THE COPYRIGHT HOLDERS AND/OR OTHER PARTIES PROVIDE THE PROGRAM "AS IS" WITHOUT WARRANTY OF ANY KIND, EITHER EXPRESSED OR IMPLIED, INCLUDING, BUT NOT LIMITED TO, THE IMPLIED WARRANTIES OF MERCHANTABILITY AND FITNESS FOR A PARTICULAR PURPOSE. THE ENTIRE RISK AS TO THE QUALITY AND PERFORMANCE OF THE PROGRAM IS WITH YOU. SHOULD THE PROGRAM PROVE DEFECTIVE, YOU ASSUME THE COST OF ALL NECESSARY SERVICING, REPAIR OR CORRECTION.

- IN NO EVENT UNLESS REQUIRED BY APPLICABLE LAW OR AGREED TO IN WRITING WILL ANY COPYRIGHT HOLDER, OR ANY OTHER PARTY WHO MAY MODIFY AND/OR REDISTRIBUTE THE PROGRAM AS PERMITTED ABOVE, BE LIABLE TO YOU FOR DAMAGES, INCLUDING ANY GENERAL, SPECIAL, INCIDENTAL OR CONSEQUENTIAL DAMAGES ARISING OUT OF THE USE OR INABILITY TO USE THE PROGRAM (INCLUDING BUT NOT LIMITED TO LOSS OF DATA OR DATA BEING RENDERED INACCURATE OR LOSSES SUSTAINED BY YOU OR THIRD PARTIES OR A FAILURE OF THE PROGRAM TO OPERATE WITH ANY OTHER PROGRAMS), EVEN IF SUCH HOLDER OR OTHER PARTY HAS BEEN ADVISED OF THE POSSIBILITY OF SUCH DAMAGES.

END OF TERMS AND CONDITIONS

10.3   How to Apply These Terms to Your New Programs

If you develop a new program, and you want it to be of the greatest possible use to the public, the best way to achieve this is to make it free software which everyone can redistribute and change under these terms.

To do so, attach the following notices to the program. It is safest to attach them to the start of each source file to most effectively convey the exclusion of warranty; and each file should have at least the "copyright" line and a pointer to where the full notice is found.

HOWTO

Part XLIV

"The UPS Howto" Harvey J. Stein

hjstein@bfr.co.il
v2.42, 18 November 1997

Contents

HOWTO

1   Introduction

This HOWTO covers connecting a UPS to a computer running Linux. The idea is to connect the two in such a way that Linux can shutdown cleanly when the power goes out, and before the UPS's battery gives out.

This includes pointing out the existence of software packages which aid in establishing such communications, and detailing exactly how such communications are carried out. The latter often is unnecessary if you can find a software package that's already been configured for your UPS. Otherwise, you'll have to read on.

To a large extent this document is even more redundant than when I originally wrote it three years ago. All the basic information has always been contained in the `powerd` man page that comes with the `SysVinit` package. Whereas three years ago one could commonly find Linux distributions which didn't even include this man page, I don't believe this is the case any longer.

Furthermore, when I first wrote this Howto, there was no software other than `powerd.c` for Linux/UPS communications and control. Today there are quite afew UPS control packages available in *Sunsite's UPS directory* `<http://sunsite.unc.edu:/pub/Linux/system/ups>`.

None the less, I'm continuing to maintain the UPS Howto. Why bother? Well,

- An additional general overview might help to understand how to connect a Linux system to a UPS, even if it's just the same information written differently.

- The HOWTO is serving as a repository for UPS specific data - there are many UPSs that haven't yet been incorporated into the general packages.

- The HOWTO contains additional details that aren't available in other documents.

- Some of the UPS software packages available in *Sunsite's UPS directory* `<http://sunsite.unc.edu:/pub/Linux/system/ups>` seem to be quite sparsely documented. You might need to read this before you can understand how to use them.

- This thing seems to have a life of it's own now. It's clear when a Howto should be born. It's less clear when it should be put to sleep.

1.1   Contributors

I am forever indebted to those from whom I've received help, suggestions, and UPS specific data. The list includes:

- Hennus Bergman (*hennus@sky.owl.nl*)
- Charli (*mefistos@impsat1.com.ar*)
- Ciro Cattuto (*Ciro Cattuto*)

- Nick Christenson (*npc@minotaur.jpl.nasa.gov*)

- Lam Dang (*angit@netcom.com*)

- Markus Eiden (*Markus@eiden.de*)

- Dan Fandrich (*dan@fch.wimsey.bc.ca*)

- Ben Galliart (*bgallia@orion.it.luc.edu*)

- Danny ter Haar (*dth@cistron.nl*)

- Christian G. Holtje (*docwhat@uiuc.edu*)

- Raymond A. Ingles (*inglesra@frc.com*)

- Peter Kammer (*pkammer@ics.uci.edu*)

- Marek Michalkiewicz (*ind43@sun1000.ci.pwr.wroc.pl*)

- Jim Ockers (*ockers@umr.edu*)

- Evgeny Stambulchik (*fnevgeny@plasma-gate.weizmann.ac.il*)

- Clive A. Stubbings (*cas@vjet.demon.co.uk*)

- Miquel van Smoorenburg (*miquels@cistron.nl*)

- Slavik Terletsky (*ts@polynet.lviv.ua*)

- Tom Webster (*webster@kaiwan.com*)

Note that email addresses appearing below as excerpts from email messages can be out of date. The above is probably out of date too, but some of it's more recent than what's below.

Also, many apologies to anyone whom I've failed to note in this list. Please email me and I'll add you.

1.2 Important disclaimer

I really can't guarantee that any of this will work for you. Connecting a UPS to a computer can be a tricky business. One or the other or both might burn out, blow up, catch fire, or start World War Three. Furthermore, I only have direct experience with the Advice 1200 A UPS, and a 5kva Best Ferrups, and I didn't have to make a cable. So, BE CAREFUL. GATHER ALL INFORMATION YOU CAN ON YOUR UPS. THINK FIRST. DON'T IMPLICITLY TRUST ANYTHING YOU READ HERE OR ANYWHERE ELSE.

On the other hand, I managed to get everything working with my UPSs, without much information from the manufacturer, and without blowing anything up, so it is possible.

1.3 Other documents

This document does not cover the general features and capabilities of UPSs. For that type of information, you might turn to *The UPS FAQ* <ftp://navigator.jpl.nasa.gov/pub/doc/faq/UPS.faq>. It can also be found at *ftp://rtfm.mit.edu/pub/usenet-by-hierarchy/comp/answers/UPS-faq*. It is maintained by Nick Christenson (*n-pc@minotaur.jpl.nasa.gov*), but seems to have last been updated in 1995. In email to him, he'd like that you put UPS or UPS FAQ or something along these lines in the Subject line of the message.

There're also more and more UPS manufactures sprouting up on the net. Some of them actually supply useful information on their web sites. A convenient list of UPS manufacturers' web sites is available at *The UPS Directory* <http://www.upssystems.uk.com/upsdir.html>. Said site also has a *UPS FAQ* <http://www.upssystems.uk.com/upsfaqs.html>.

2 Important note on obsolete information

I've just discovered that some of the documentation below is obsolete. In particular, the `init` daemon that comes with *the latest sysvinit package* <http://sunsite.unc.edu/pub/Linux/system/daemons/init/sysvinit-2.64.tar.gz> is more sophisticated than I've portrayed it to be. Although it seems that the current version is backward compatible with what's written here, it looks like it has some undocumented features which are **very important** for UPS support.

The control mechanism outlined below only allows `powerd` to give `init` one of two messages, namely `powerfail` or `powerok`. `init` runs one command when it receives `powerfail`, and another when it receives `powerok`. This leads to complicated `powerd` logic for dealing with low battery signals and other sorts of special situations.

Newer versions of `init` (as of version 2.58, it seems) are more sophisticated. These versions can be signaled to run one of `three` scripts. Thus, `init` can have a `powerfail` script for announcing a power outage, a `powerfailnow` script for doing an immediate shutdown, and a `powerok` script for halting any pending shutdowns. This is much cleaner than the gyrations one would have to go through with the mechanisms detailed below.

Although most of the discussion here assumes the old `init` communication method, I just added two new sections where the authors uses the new communcation method. These are sections 8.3 (Trust Energy Protector 400/650) and 8.13.2 (APC Smart-UPS 700). The former is especially detailed. Both include a `powerd.c` which signals `init` to do an immediate shutdown when a low battery signal is received, as well as the relevant `/etc/inittab` lines to make this work. Other than this, all I can tell you is to look at the source code for `init`.

Also, for all I know, many of the software packages listed below also use this newer communication method.

3 Smart and dumb UPSs.

UPSs fall into two categories, which I'll call "smart" and "dumb". The difference between the two is the amount of information one can get from the UPS and the amount of control one can exert over the UPS.

Dumb UPS

- Connects to the computer via serial port.
- Uses modem control lines to communicate with the computer.
- Can signal whether or not the power is out.
- Typically can signal whether or not the battery is low.
- The computer can usually signal the UPS to turn itself off.

Smart UPS

- Connects to the computer via serial port.
- Communicates with the computer via normal data transfer through the serial port.
- Typically has some sort of command language that the computer can use to get various pieces of information from the UPS, to set various operating parameters for the UPS, and to control the UPS (such as turning it off).

Usually smart UPSs can be operated in dumb mode. This is useful because as far as I know, the company which manufactures the most popular smart UPS (namely APC) will only disclose the communication protocol for their UPSs to people who sign a non-disclosure agreement.

As far as I know, the only smart UPS available which is easy to communicate with under Linux are those made by Best. Furthermore, BEST fully documents the smart mode (and the dumb mode) of their UPSs. BEST also supplies source code for programs which can communicate with their UPSs.

All the packages listed in section 4 (Software) will communicate with a UPS in dumb mode. This is all you really need. The ones specifically for the APC UPSs make various claims as to being usable in smart mode, but I don't know exactly what they permit. A full implementation would give you a pop-up window with all sorts of fun gauges displaying various statistics for the UPS, such as load, internal temperature, fault history, input voltage, output voltage, etc. It seems like the `smupsd-0.9-1.i386.rpm` package (section 4 (Software)) approaches this. I'm not sure about the others.

The rest of this document is pretty much confined to configuring your system to work with a dumb UPS. The general idea is about the same with a smart UPS, but the details of how `powerd` would need to work and what kind of cable you need are different for a smart UPS.

4 Software

Basically, all you need is a working `powerd` binary, usually found in `/sbin/powerd`. This is usually part of the `SysVinit` package. As far as I know, all current Linux distributions include a recent version of `SysVinit`. Very old versions didn't include `powerd`.

The only problem you might have is that your cable might not match how `powerd` is set up, in which case you'll have to either rewire your cable, or pick up a copy of `powerd.c` and modify it to work with your cable. Or, for that matter, you can always pick up one of the following packages, most of which allow you to configure them to match your cable.

As mentioned, an alternative to using the `powerd` that comes with the `SysVinit` package would be to use one of the UPS packages now available. There are many packages currently available to aid in setting up computer/ups communications. None of this was available when I first wrote this Howto, which is why I had to write it. In fact, there's a good chance that you might be able to use one of these software packages, and avoid this Howto entirely!

As of 15 March 1997 or so, *Sunsite's UPS directory* <http://sunsite.unc.edu:/pub/Linux/system/ups> had quite a few packages available. Other sites seem to have UPS control packages available too. Here's what I've found to date (all but two from sunsite):

Enhanced_APC_BackUPS.tar.gz

> http://sunsite.unc.edu:/pub/Linux/system/ups/Enhanced_APC_BackUPS.tar.gz
>
> A package for controlling APC Smart UPSs. Seems to basically follow the BUPS Howto (included here), but also seems to have some low battery warning support.

Enhanced_APC_UPSD-v1.4.tar.gz

> http://sunsite.unc.edu:/pub/Linux/system/ups/Enhanced_APC_UPSD-v1.4.tar.gz
>
> The `.lsm` file says that it's formerly the above package, but it actually includes the above package as a `.tar.gz` file inside of this `tar.gz` file! The documentation is spotty. It seems to support APC UPSs in both smart mode and dumb mode, but I can't be sure.

apcd-0.5.tar.gz

> http://sunsite.unc.edu:/pub/Linux/system/ups/apcd-0.5.tar.gz
>
> Another package for controlling APC Smart UPSs. Seems to include some sort of master/slave support (i.e. - one machine signals others to shut down when the power goes out). Seems to use the UPS in smart mode, as opposed to via modem signal line toggling.

smupsd-0.9-1.i386.rpm

> ftp://ftp.redhat.com/pub/contrib/i386/smupsd-0.9-1.i386.rpm
>
> The author (*David E. Myers, dem@netsco.com*) writes:
>
> smupsd monitors an *APC Smart-UPS[TM]* under *Red Hat[TM] Linux*. Should power fail, smupsd will power down the system and the UPS in an orderly fashion.
>
> smupsd has the following features:
>
> - Shuts down the system and the UPS based on either remaining UPS battery charge or elapsed time since power failure.
>
> - UPS parameters can be monitored live from any host with the graphical monitor program upsmon, written in Java(TM).

- UPS parameters can be logged to a file for analysis and reporting.

- When additional systems share the same UPS, instances of smupsd running on these systems can read UPS parameters from the one running on the system serially connected to the UPS (master/slave).

- Network access from remote hosts can be controlled via the `/etc/hosts.allow` file.

genpower-1.0.1.tgz

http://sunsite.unc.edu:/pub/Linux/system/ups/genpower-1.0.1.tgz

A general UPS handling package. Includes configurations for many UPSs - two TrippLite configurations, and three APC configurations. Includes good documentation. A best buy.

powerd-2.0.tar.gz

http://sunsite.unc.edu:/pub/Linux/system/ups/powerd-2.0.tar.gz

A replacement for the `powerd` that comes with the `SysVinit` package. As opposed to comments included in the documentation it doesn't seem to have been merged into the `SysVinit` package as of version 2.62. Its advantages are that it can act as a server for other `powerd`s running on other machines (for when you have a network of machines hanging off a single UPS), and it can be configured by config file - the source code doesn't have to be edited and recompiled.

upsd-1.0.tgz

http://sunsite.unc.edu:/pub/Linux/system/ups/upsd-1.0.tgz

Another replacement for `powerd`. Seems to be quite comparable in features to powerd-2.0.tar.gz.

checkups.tar

http://www.bestpower.com/section/software/checkups.tar

This package is for controlling Best UPSs. It's direct from Best's web site. Includes binaries for lots of `unix` flavors, but more importantly, it includes source code, so you can try it out under Linux, and if it doesn't work, you can try to fix it. The source code includes both "basic checkups" which controls the UPS in dumb mode, and "advanced checkups" which is a little more sophisticated - it will signal a shutdown when the UPS says it has X minutes of power remaining instead of just shutting down X minutes after the power goes out. The advanced checkups program also will shut down when the UPS registers various alarms such as High Ambient Temperature, Near Low Battery, Low AC Out, or User Test Alarm.

bestups-0.9.tar.gz

http://sunsite.unc.edu:/pub/Linux/system/ups/bestups-0.9.tar.gz

A package that might very well be on sunsite by the time you read this. It's a pair of communications module which works with Best Ferrups UPSs. It operates the UPS in smart mode. It inter-operates well with powerd-2.0 - useful if you have a big Best Ferrups UPS keeping up all the machines on a network.

NOTE - This package has yet to be uploaded to Sunsite. I keep begging the author to finish and upload it, but he has yet to find the time.

LanSafe III

http://www.deltecpower.com/soft.html

Deltec Electronics (and Exide) sell a software package called LanSafe III. They have a Linux version. It comes with their UPSs. They also say that it works with other UPSs (on the dumb level).

apcupsd-2.8.tar.gz

http://sunsite.unc.edu:/pub/Linux/system/ups/apcupsd-2.8.tar.gz

The author (*Andre Hedrick, hedrick@astro.dyer.vanderbilt.edu*) writes:

apcupsd-2.1.tar.gz replaces Enhanced-APC-UPSD.tar.gz

It is a very complete package for APC UPSs. There is support for the entire range of UPSs in their product line. I have now added smart mode signaling to the package and support with APC's own cables or a custom cable if you don't have an APC cable that is supported to date.

smartups-1.1.tgz

http://sunsite.unc.edu:/pub/Linux/system/ups/smartups-1.1.tgz

From the LSM:

A powerd and an X11 graphing utility which shows you the voltages, frequencies, load percentage and battery level in realtime. The protocol that the "Safeware" software uses, and "Tripplite" UPSs are supported. Source + ELF binaries.

ups.tar.gz

http://sunsite.unc.edu:/pub/Linux/system/ups/ups.tar.gz

From the LSM:

Program to interact with battery backups (Powerbox UPS).

usvd-2.0.0.tgz

http://sunsite.unc.edu:/pub/Linux/system/usvd-2.0.0/usvd-2.0.0.tgz

From the LSM:

usvd is a daemon that monitors the state of an uninterrupted power supply and reacts upon state changes (line fail, line back, battery low situations). You can write your own scripts that are called in these cases. It does *not* require SYSVINIT.

Note that I've only glanced at these packages. I haven't used them. We were just about to start using *bestups-0.9.tar.gz* <http://sunsite.unc.edu:/pub/Linux/system/ups/bestups-0.9.tar.gz> in conjunction with *powerd-2.0.tar.gz* <http://sunsite.unc.edu:/pub/Linux/system/ups/powerd-2.0.tar.gz>, but we never quite got around to it.

5   Do it yourself guide

This discussion is specifically tailored for dumb UPS control. However, most of the process is about the same for dumb UPSs and smart UPSs. The biggest difference is in the details of how the UPS monitoring daemon (typically `powerd`) communicates with the UPS.

Before doing anything, I suggest the following algorithm:

- Skim this document.
- Download and investigate all packages which seem specifically tailored to your UPS.
- Download and investigate the more generic packages. Note that some of the more generic packages are actually more powerful, better documented, and easier to use than their more specific counterparts.
- If you still can't get things working, or if points are still unclear, read this document more carefully, and hack away...

5.1   What you need to do (summary)

- Plug the computer into the UPS.
- Connect the computer's serial port to the UPS with a special cable.
- Run `powerd` (or some sort of equivalent) on the computer.
- Setup your `init` to do something reasonable on powerfail and powerok events (like start a `shutdown` and kill any currently running `shutdowns`, respectively, for example).

5.2   How it's supposed to work

UPS's job

When the power goes out, the UPS continues to power the computer and signals that the power went out by throwing a relay or turning on an opticoupler on it's control port.

Cable's job

The cable is designed so that when the UPS throws said relay, this causes a particular serial port control line (typically DCD) to go high.

Powerd's job

The powerd daemon monitors the serial port. Keeps raised/lowered whatever serial port control lines the UPS needs to have raised/lowered (typically, DTR must be kept high and whatever line shuts off the UPS must be kept low). When powerd sees the UPS control line go high, it writes FAIL to /etc/powerstatus and sends the init process a SIGPWR signal. (Older versions of powerd and initd wrote to /etc/powerfail.) When the control line goes low again, it writes OK to /etc/powerstatus and sends init a SIGPWR signal.

Init's job (aside from everything else it does)

When it receives a SIGPWR, it looks at /etc/powerstatus. If it contains FAIL it runs the powerfail entry from /etc/inittab. If it contains OK it runs the powerokwait entry from inittab.

5.3 How to set things up

The following presupposes that you have a cable that works properly with powerd. If you're not sure that your cable works (or how it works), see section 6.2 (Reverse-engineering cables and hacking powerd.c) for information on dealing with poorly described cables and reconfiguring powerd.c. Sections 6.3 (Serial port pin assignments) and 6.4 (Ioctl to RS232 correspondence) will also be useful.

If you need to make a cable, see section 6.1 (How to make a cable) for the overall details, and the subsection of section 8 (Info on selected UPSs) that refers to your UPS. The latter might also include information on manufacturer supplied cables. You may want to at least skim all of section 8 (Info on selected UPSs) because each section has a few additional generally helpful details.

- Edit /etc/inittab. Put in something like this:

```
# What to do when power fails (Halt system & drain battery :):
pf::powerfail:/etc/powerfailscript +5

# If power is back before shutdown, cancel the running shutdown.
pg:0123456:powerokwait:/etc/powerokscript
```

- Write scripts /etc/powerfailscript and /etc/powerokscript to shutdown in 5 minutes (or whatever's appropriate) and kill any existing shutdown, respectively. Depending on the version of shutdown that you're using, this will be either so trivial that you'll dispense with the scripts, or be a 1 line bash script, something along the lines of:

```
kill 'ps -aux | grep "shutdown" | grep -v grep | awk '{print $2}''
```

and you'll keep the scripts. (In case it doesn't come out right, the first single quote on the above line is a backquote, the second and third are single quotes, and the last is also a backquote.)

- Tell init to re-process the inittab file with the command:

```
telinit q
```

- Edit rc.local so that powerd gets run upon startup. The syntax is:

```
powerd <line>
```

  Replace <line> with the serial port that the UPS is connected, such as /dev/cua1.

- Connect computer's serial port to UPS's serial port. DO NOT PLUG THE COMPUTER INTO UPS YET.

- Plug a light into the UPS.

- Turn on the UPS and the light.

- Run powerd.

- Test the setup:

- Yank the UPS's plug.

    * Check that the light stays on.
    * Check that `/etc/powerfailscript` runs.
    * Check that `shutdown` is running.

- Plug the UPS back in.

    * Check that the light stays on.
    * Check that `/etc/powerokscript` runs.
    * Check that `/etc/powerfailscript` is not running.
    * Check that `shutdown` is no longer running.

- Yank the UPS's plug again. Leave it out and make sure that the computer shuts down properly in the proper amount of time.

- **The Dangerous Part.** After everything seems to be proper, power down the computer and plug it into the UPS. Run a script that sync's the hard disk every second or so. Simultaneously run a second script that keeps doing a find over your entire hard disk. The first is to make this a little safer and the second is to help draw lots of power. Now, pull the plug on the UPS, check again that `shutdown` is running and wait. Make sure that the computer shuts down cleanly before the battery on the UPS gives out. This is dangerous because if the power goes out before the computer shuts down, you can end up with a corrupt file system, and maybe even lose all your files. You'll probably want to do a full backup before this test, and set the shutdown time extremely short to begin with.

Congratulations! You now have a Linux computer that's protected by a UPS and will shutdown cleanly when the power goes out!

5.4   User Enhancements

- Hack `powerd.c` to monitor the line indicating that the batteries are low. When the batteries get low, do an **immediate** shutdown.

- Modify the shutdown procedure so that if it's shutting down in a `powerfail` situation, then it turns off the UPS after doing everything necessary.

6   Hardware notes

6.1   How to make a cable

This section is just from messages I've seen on the net. I haven't done it so I can't write from experience. If anyone has, please write this section for me :). See also the message about the GPS1000 contained in section 8.11 (GPS1000 from ACCODATA), not to mention all the UPS specific data in section 8 (Info on selected UPSs).

```
>From miquels@caution.cistron.nl.mugnet.org Wed Jul 21 14:26:33 1993
Newsgroups: comp.os.linux
Subject: Re: UPS interface for Linux?
From: miquels@caution.cistron.nl.mugnet.org (Miquel van Smoorenburg)
Date: Sat, 17 Jul 93 18:03:37
Distribution: world
Organization: Cistron Electronics.

In article <1993Jul15.184450.5193@excaliber.uucp>
joel@rac1.wam.umd.edu (Joel M. Hoffman) writes:
>I'm in the process of buying a UPS (Uninteruptable Power Supply), and
>notice that some of them have interfaces for LAN's to signal the LAN
>when the power fails.
```

HOWTO

```
>
>Is there such an interface for Linux?
>
>Thanks.
>
>-Joel
>(joel@wam.umd.edu)
>
```

When I worked on the last versioon of SysVinit (Now version 2.4),
I temporarily had a UPS on my computer, so I added support for it.
You might have seen that in the latest <signal.h> header files there
is a #define SIGPWR 30 now :-). Anyway, I did not have such a special
interface but the output of most UPS's is just a relais that makes or breaks
on power interrupt. I thought up a simple way to connect this to the
DCD line of the serial port. In the SysVinit package there is a daemon
called 'powerd' that keeps an eye on that serial line and sends SIGPWR
to init when the status changes, so that init can do something (such as
bringing the system down within 5 minutes). How to connect the UPS to
the serial line is described in the source "powerd.c", but I will
draw it here for explanation:

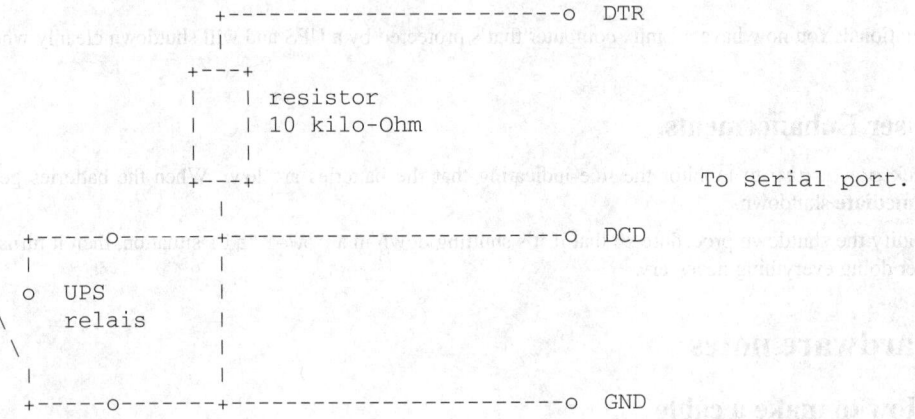

Nice drawing eh?

Hope this helps.
SysVinit can be found on sunsite (and tsx-11 probably) as
SysVinit2.4.tar.z

Mike.

--

Miquel van Smoorenburg, <miquels@cistron.nl.mugnet.org>
Ibmio.com: cannot open CONFIG.SYS: file handle broke off.

>From danny@caution.cistron.nl.mugnet.org Wed Jul 21 14:27:04 1993
Newsgroups: comp.os.linux
Subject: Re: UPS interface for Linux?

```
From: danny@caution.cistron.nl.mugnet.org (Danny ter Haar)
Date: Mon, 19 Jul 93 11:02:14
Distribution: world
Organization: Cistron Electronics.

In article <9307174330@caution.cistron.nl.mugnet.org>
miquels@caution.cistron.nl.mugnet.org (Miquel van Smoorenburg) writes:
>How to connect the UPS to the serial line is described in the source
>"powerd.c", but I will draw it here for explanation:

The drawing wasn't really clear, please use this one in stead !
>
>                          +-----------------------o DTR
>                          |
>                        +---+
>                        |   | resistor
>                        |   | 10 kilo-Ohm
>                        |   |
>                        +---+                       To serial port.
>                          |
>          +-----o-------+-----------------------o DCD
>          |
>          o  UPS
>          \    relais
>           \
>           |
>          +-----o-----------------------------o GND
>
```

```
The DTR is kept high, when the UPS's power input is gone it
will close the relais . The computer is monitoring
the DCD input port to go LOW . When this happens it will start a
shutdown sequence...
```

```
_____
Danny

--
<======================================================================>
Danny ter Haar   <dannyth@hacktic.nl> or <danny@cistron.nl.mugnet.org>
Robins law #103: 'a couple of lightyears can't part good friends'
```

6.2 Reverse-engineering cables and hacking powerd.c

Try to get documentation for the cables that your UPS seller supplies. In particular find out:

- What lines need to be kept high.
- What line(s) turn off the UPS.
- What lines the UPS toggles to indicate that:
  - Power is out.
  - Battery is low.

You then need to either hack `powerd.c` appropriately, or use one of the above configurable packages (see the packages `genpower-1.0.1.tgz`, `powerd-2.0.tar.gz`, or `upsd-1.0.tgz` described in section 4 (Software)). If you use one of the packages, follow the instructions there. If you want to hack `powerd.c`, keep reading.

If you have trouble getting the above information, or just want to check it (a *good* idea) the following program might help. It's a hacked version of `powerd.c`. It allows you to set the necessary port flags from the command line and then monitors the port, displaying the control lines every second. I used it as "upscheck /dev/cua1 2" (for example) to set the 2nd bit (DTR) and to clear the other bits. The number base 2 indicates which bits to set, so for example to set bits 1, 2 and 3, (and clear the others) use 7. See the code for details.

Here's the (untested) upscheck.c program. It's untested because I edited the version I originally used to make it clearer, and can't test the new version at the moment.

```
/*
 * upscheck      Check how UPS & computer communicate.
 *
 * Usage:        upscheck <device> <bits to set>
 *               For example, upscheck /dev/cua4 4 to set bit 3 &
 *               monitor /dev/cua4.
 *
 * Author:       Harvey J. Stein <hjstein@math.huji.ac.il>
 *               (but really just a minor modification of Miquel van
 *               Smoorenburg's <miquels@drinkel.nl.mugnet.org> powerd.c
 *
 * Version:      1.0 19940802
 *
 */
#include <sys/types.h>
#include <sys/ioctl.h>
#include <fcntl.h>
#include <errno.h>
#include <stdlib.h>
#include <unistd.h>
#include <stdio.h>
#include <signal.h>

/* Main program. */
int main(int argc, char **argv)
{
  int fd;

/*  These TIOCM_* parameters are defined in <linux/termios.h>, which  */
/*  is indirectly included here.                                      */
  int dtr_bit = TIOCM_DTR;
  int rts_bit = TIOCM_RTS;
  int set_bits;
  int flags;
  int status, oldstat = -1;
  int count = 0;
  int pc;

  if (argc < 2) {
        fprintf(stderr, "Usage: upscheck <device> <bits-to-set>\n");
        exit(1);
  }

  /* Open monitor device. */
  if ((fd = open(argv[1], O_RDWR | O_NDELAY)) < 0) {
```

```
            fprintf(stderr, "upscheck: %s: %s\n", argv[1], sys_errlist[errno]);
            exit(1);}

    /* Get the bits to set from the command line. */
    sscanf(argv[2], "%d", &set_bits);

    while (1) {
        /* Set the command line specified bits (& only the command line */
        /* specified bits).                                             */
        ioctl(fd, TIOCMSET, &set_bits);
        fprintf(stderr, "Setting %o.\n", set_bits);

        sleep(1);

        /* Get the current line bits */
        ioctl(fd, TIOCMGET, &flags);
        fprintf(stderr, "Flags are %o.\n", flags);

/*  Fiddle here by changing TIOCM_CTS to some other TIOCM until    */
/*  this program detects that the power goes out when you yank     */
/*  the plug on the UPS.  Then you'll know how to modify powerd.c. */
        if (flags & TIOCM_CTS)
            {
                pc = 0 ;
                fprintf(stderr, "power is up.\n");
            }
        else
            {
                pc = pc + 1 ;
                fprintf(stderr, "power is down.\n");
            }
    }

    close(fd);
}
```

6.3   Serial port pin assignments

The previous section presupposes knowledge of the correspondence between terminal signals and serial port pins. Here's a reference for that correspondence, taken from David Tal's "Frequently Used Cables and Connectors" document. I'm including a diagram illustrating the connectors, and a table listing the correspondence between pin numbers and terminal line signals.

If you need a general reference for cable wiring, connectors, etc, then David Tal's would be a good one, but I can't seem to locate this document on the net any more. But I've found a good replacement. It's *The Hardware Book* <http://www.blackdown.org/~hwb/hwb.html>.

Other useful sites:

- *Yost Serial Device Wiring Standard* <http://star.sols.pt/docs/yost.html> which contains interesting information on how to use RJ-45 jacks and eight wire cables for all serial port connections.

- *Stokely Consulting* <http://www.stokely.com/stokely> for general Unix info, and in particular their Unix Serial Port Resources.

- *Unix Workstation System Administration Education Certification* <http://www.uwsg.indiana.edu/usail/edcert/> which contains *RS-232: Connectors and Cabling* <http://www.uwsg.indiana.edu/

```
usail/peripherals/serial/rs232/>
```

Incidentally, it seems that the Linuxdoc-sgml package still doesn't format tables very well in the `html` output. If you want to be able to read the following table, you're probably going to have to look at either the DVI version or the plain text version of this document.

```
DB-25   | DB-9| Name   |   EIA  |  CCITT | DTE-DCE| Description
-------------------------------------------------------------------------
  1     |     |   FG   |   AA   |  101   |  ---   | Frame Ground/Chassis GND
  2     | 3   |   TD   |   BA   |  103   |  --->  | Transmitted Data, TxD
  3     | 2   |   RD   |   BB   |  104   |  <---  | Received Data, RxD
  4     | 7   |   RTS  |   CA   |  105   |  --->  | Request To Send
  5     | 8   |   CTS  |   CB   |  106   |  <---  | Clear To Send
  6     | 6   |   DSR  |   CC   |  107   |  <---  | Data Set Ready
  7     | 5   |   SG   |   AB   |  102   |  ---   | Signal Ground, GND
  8     | 1   |   DCD  |   CF   |  109   |  <---  | Data Carrier Detect
  9     |     |   --   |   --   |   -    |   -    | Positive DC test voltage
 10     |     |   --   |   --   |   -    |   -    | Negative DC test voltage
 11     |     |   QM   |   --   |   -    |  <---  | Equalizer mode
 12     |     |   SDCD |   SCF  |  122   |  <---  | Secondary Data Carri-
er Detect
 13     |     |   SCTS |   SCB  |  121   |  <---  | Secondary Clear To Send
 14     |     |   STD  |   SBA  |  118   |  --->  | Secondary Transmitted Data
 15     |     |   TC   |   DB   |  114   |  <---  | Transmitter (signal) Clock
 16     |     |   SRD  |   SBB  |  119   |  <---  | Secondary Receiver Clock
 17     |     |   RC   |   DD   |  115   |  --->  | Receiver (signal) Clock
 18     |     |   DCR  |   --   |   -    |  <---  | Divided Clock Receiver
 19     |     |   SRTS |   SCA  |  120   |  --->  | Secondary Request To Send
 20     | 4   |   DTR  |   CD   |  108.2 |  --->  | Data Terminal Ready
 21     |     |   SQ   |   CG   |  110   |  <---  | Signal Quality Detect
 22     | 9   |   RI   |   CE   |  125   |  <---  | Ring Indicator
 23     |     |   --   |   CH   |  111   |  --->  | Data rate selector
 24     |     |   --   |   CI   |  112   |  <---  | Data rate selector
 25     |     |   TC   |   DA   |  113   |  <---  | Transmitted Clock
```

Pin Assignment for the Serial Port (RS-232C), 25-pin and 9-pin

```
       1                         13     1         5
     _____      _____
     \ . . . . . . . . . . . . . /     \ . . . . . /    RS232-connectors
      \ . . . . . . . . . . . . /       \ . . . . /     seen from outside
       ---------------------------       ----------     of computer.
       14                    25          6       9
```

```
DTE : Data Terminal Equipment (i.e. computer)
DCE : Data Communications Equipment (i.e. modem)
RxD : Data received; 1 is transmitted "low", 0 as "high"
TxD : Data sent; 1 is transmitted "low", 0 as "high"
DTR : DTE announces that it is powered up and ready to communicate
DSR : DCE announces that it is ready to communicate; low=modem hangup
RTS : DTE asks DCE for permission to send data
CTS : DCE agrees on RTS
RI  : DCE signals the DTE that an establishment of a connection is attempted
DCD : DCE announces that a connection is established
```

6.4 Ioctl to RS232 correspondence

Since you also might need to modify `powerd.c` to raise and lower the correct lines, you might also need the numeric values of different terminal signals. The can be found in `/usr/include/linux/termios.h`, but are reproduced here for reference. Since they could change, you're best off confirming these values against said file.

```
/* modem lines */
#define TIOCM_LE       0x001
#define TIOCM_DTR      0x002
#define TIOCM_RTS      0x004
#define TIOCM_ST       0x008
#define TIOCM_SR       0x010
#define TIOCM_CTS      0x020
#define TIOCM_CAR      0x040
#define TIOCM_RNG      0x080
#define TIOCM_DSR      0x100
#define TIOCM_CD       TIOCM_CAR
#define TIOCM_RI       TIOCM_RNG
```

Note that the 3rd column is in Hex.

7 What to do when you're really stuck

Here's a novel solution to UPS control for when the UPS and the computer just aren't on speaking terms. I must say that every time I read this, I'm struck by how clever a solution it is.

```
From: " Raymond A. Ingles" <inglesra@frc.com>
To: hjstein@math.huji.ac.il
Subject: UPS HOWTO tip
Date: Mon, 24 Feb 1997 11:48:32 -0500 (EST)


    I don't know if others would find this useful, but I thought I might
pass this along for possible inclusion in the HOWTO. Thanks for
maintaining a HOWTO that I found very useful!

-----------------

  My fiancee bought me a UPS as a present, a Tripp-Lite 400, I believe. It
was very welcome and seems to operate as expected, but unfortunately
doesn't have a serial interface to let the computer know the line power
has failed. It's apparently intended for home or office use where the
computer will not be left unattended.

  This, of course, was unacceptable and I began working on a line monitor,
planning on opening up the case and figuring out how to add the hardware
that the manufacturer had left out. Then I realized that there was a
quicker and simpler and cheaper (if somewhat less functional) way.

  I had an old 2400 baud modem that I wasn't using, and hooked it up to an
unused serial port on my computer. I then plugged the modem into a surge
supressor plugged into the wall power. I set up powerd with the options
as follows:
```

```
-----
serialline    /dev/ttyS1
monitor       DCD
failwhen      low
-----
```

 Now, when the wall power fails (or, since that hasn't happened lately,
when I pull the surge supressor from the wall to test this setup) the modem
fails but the UPS starts supplying power to the computer. When powerd
notices the modem has dropped DCD, it triggers the powerfail sequence.

 Obviously, this has some limitations. You can't tell from the modem when
the battery is low and so on. You can only tell that the wall power has
failed. Still, it's certainly cheap and I hate to see functioning
computer equipment lie unused. These days you should be able to get a
2400 baud modem for very nearly free.

 I'd still suggest getting a real UPS with full communication capability.
But if you're stuck with a less-functional one, this may at least make it
useful.

 Sincerely,

 Ray Ingles   (810) 377-7735   inglesra@frc.com

 "Anybody who has ever seen a photograph showing the kind of damage that
a trout traveling that fast can inflict on the human skull knows that
such photographs are very valuable. I paid $20 for mine." - Dave Barry

8   Info on selected UPSs

This section contains UPS specific information. What I'd like is to have the UPS control port information (what each pin does and needs to have done), information on the manufacturer supplied cable (what it connects where), and a hacked version of powerd.c which works with the UPS. What I currently have is fairly complete descriptions of setting up each UPS. I'd try to distill out the relevant information, but since I can't test each UPS, it's hard to decide exactly what's relevant. Furthermore, each UPS seems to have some additional quirks that are nicely described by the authors of each section. So for now I'm leaving everything in. Makes for a hefty Howto.

Please send me your experiences for inclusion here.

8.1   General Experiences.

I've been saving peoples comments, but haven't gotten permission yet to include them here. Here's a general summary of what I've heard from people.

APC: Won't release info on their smart mode without your signature on a non-disclosure agreement. Thus, people are forced to run their smart UPSs in the dumb mode as outlined above. Various people have had varying amounts of success reverse engineering

Best: Helpful and friendly. Supply source code and documentation both for dumb modes and smart modes.

TrippLite: One person reported that TrippLite won't release info either.

Upsonic: One person reported that Upsonic has discussed technical details over the phone, answered questions via fax and are generally helpful.

8.2   Advice 1200 A

UPS from Advice Electronics, Tel Aviv Israel (they stick their own name on the things).

I don't recommend them. Our experiences with them have been very bad. We've twice had a 17" monitor fry when the power failed. We've had computers spontaneously reboot when the power failed.

None the less, for completeness, here's he UPS Control Port's pin specifications.

- 2 - Power Fail.
- 5 - Battery Low.
- 6 - Shut Down UPS.
- 4 - Common ground for pin 2, 5, 6.

They also gave me the following picture which didn't help me, but may help you if you want to build a cable yourself:

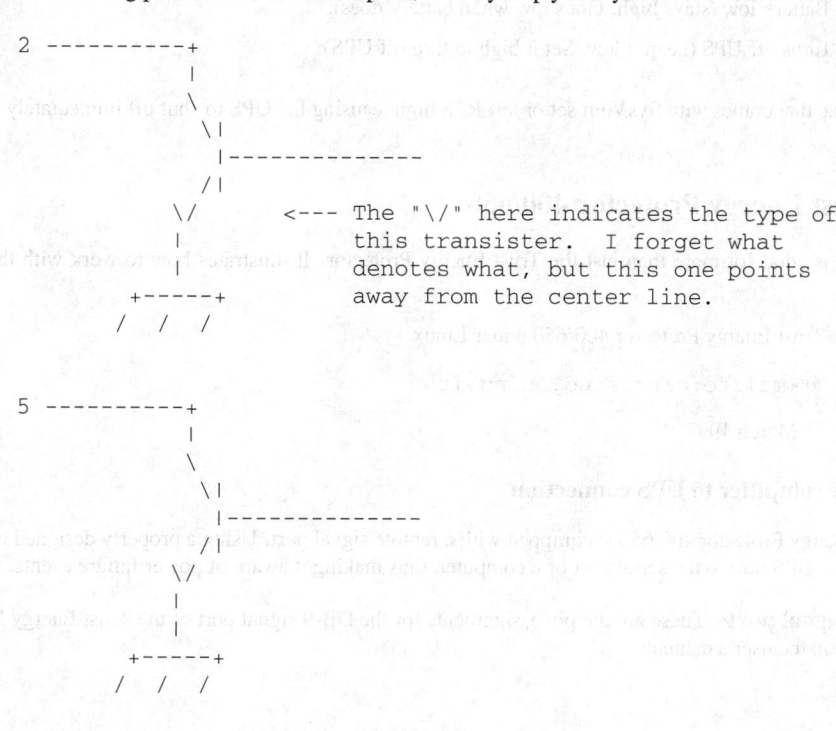

```
2 ----------+
            |
             \
            \ |
             |--------------
            / |
           \/        <--- The "\/" here indicates the type of
            |             this transister.  I forget what
            |             denotes what, but this one points
       +-----+           away from the center line.
       / / /


5 ---------+
           |
            \
           \ |
            |--------------
           / |
          \/
           |
           |
       +-----+
       / / /
```

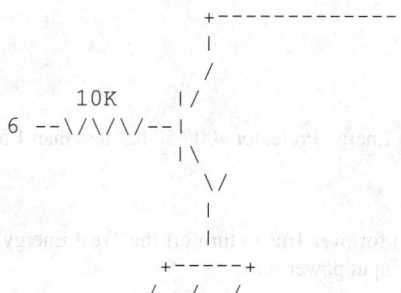

```
            +--------------
            |
            /
   10K    | /
6 --\/\/\/--|
          | \
           \/
            |
       +-----+
       / / /
```

```
4  ----------+
           |
       +-----+
      /  /  /
```

Cable supplied

They first gave me a cable that was part of a DOS UPS control package called RUPS. I used this for testing. When I was satisfied, they gave me a cable they use for Netware servers connected to UPSs. It functioned identically. Here are the details:

- DTR - Powers cable (make powerd.c keep it high).
- CTS - Power out (stays high and goes low when power goes out).
- DSR - Battery low (stays high. Goes low when battery does).
- RTS - Turns off UPS (keep it low. Set it high to turn off UPS).

(The powerd.c that comes with SysVinit set or left RTS high, causing the UPS to shut off immediately when powerd was started up!)

8.3 Trust Energy Protector 400/650

This section is good for more than just the Trust Energy Protector. It illustrates how to work with the new features of `init`.

How to use a Trust Energy Protector 400/650 under Linux

by *Ciro Cattuto* <mailto:ciro@stud.unipg.it>

Version 1.0 - 31 March 1997

8.3.1 The computer to UPS connection

The Trust Energy Protector 400/650 is equipped with a remote signal port. Using a properly designed cable, it is possible to connect the UPS port to the serial port of a computer, thus making it aware of power failure events.

The UPS signal port These are the pin assignments for the DB-9 signal port of the Trust Energy Protector 400/650, as described in the user's manual:

pin 2

The relay will close when input power fails.

pin 4

Common for pins 2 and 5.

pin 5

The relay will close when the battery inside the Trust Energy Protector 400/650 has less than 1.5 minutes of backup time left.

pin 6

The user may send a high level signal (+5V - +12V) for over 1ms to turn off the Trust Energy Protector 400/650. However this option can only be activated when the input power fails.

pin 7

Common for pin 6.

The Cable This is the cable I used to connect the UPS to the serial port of my computer:

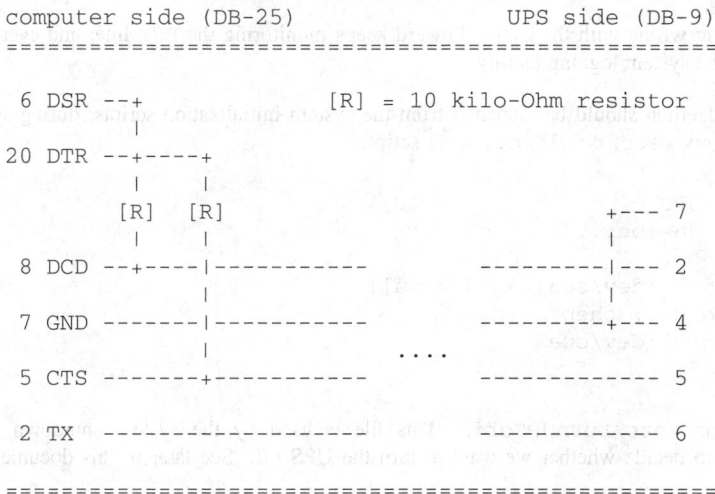

```
computer side (DB-25)                    UPS side (DB-9)
=====================================================

  6 DSR --+              [R] = 10 kilo-Ohm resistor
          |
 20 DTR --+----+
          |    |
        [R]   [R]                          +--- 7
          |    |                           |
  8 DCD --+----|-----------      ----------|--- 2
               |                           |
  7 GND -------|-----------      ----------+--- 4
               |               . . . .
  5 CTS -------+-----------      ------------ 5

  2 TX  --------------------      ------------ 6


=====================================================
```

In the case of a DB-9 serial port, the pins 6,20,8,7,5,2 are mapped to pins 6,4,1,5,8,3.

How the cable works The computer raises DTR and checks whether DSR is high, to ensure that the cable is connected to the computer. While the power is good, DCD and CTS are both high (because of the pull-up resistors).

When the power fails, the relay between pins 2 and 4 of the UPS port closes, and DCD becomes low, signalling the failure condition.

Similarly, when the UPS batteries are getting low, the relay between pins 5 and 4 closes, thus lowering CTS.

During a power failure the computer is able to turn off the UPS by raising TX for over 1ms. This can be easily accomplished sending a 0xFF byte to the serial port, at a low baud rate.

8.3.2   The powerd daemon

To make use of the information available at the serial port we need to run a program which monitors the port, decodes the signals and sends the appropriate messages to the operating system, i.e. to the init process. The init process can execute scripts and programs designed to handle (gracefully!) the power failure event.

Compiling powerd In Appendix A you'll find the source code of powerd, the daemon I use to monitor the Trust Energy Protector 400/650. To compile it you will need the source code of the sysvinit package (I used the code from sysvinit-2.60). Just overwrite the original powerd.c and compile it.

How powerd works As soon as powerd starts it opens the serial device connected to the UPS and forces DTR high. It then forks a daemon and exits, leaving the daemon running. The powerd daemon can be in one of three states:

State 0 - POWER IS GOOD

In this state powerd reads the serial port every T0_SLEEP seconds (see the #define lines at the beginning of the code). If DCD drops, powerd switches to state 1. If CTS drops powerd switches to state 2 (this shouldn't happen without DCD dropping before, but I decided to stay on the safe side).

State 1 - POWER FAILURE

A power failure was detected. DCD is low and powerd reads the UPS port every T1_SLEEP seconds. If DCD becomes high, it switches to state 0. If CTS drops, it switches to state 2.

State 2 - POWER CRITICAL

UPS batteries are low. The powerd daemon will remain in this state.

HOWTO

Each time `powerd` changes state, it notifies the init process, so that the appropriate action can be taken. These events are logged using the system logging facility.

If DSR is low there must be something wrong with the cable. Powerd keeps monitoring the DSR line, and every two minutes sends a warning message to the system logging facility.

Running powerd   The `powerd` daemon should be launched from the system initialization scripts, during system startup. I added the following lines to my `/etc/rc.d/rc.local` script:

```
# Add support for the UPS
echo "Starting powerd daemon..."
rm -f /etc/turnUPSoff
stty -crtscts speed 75 < /dev/cua3 > /dev/null
if [ -x /usr/sbin/powerd ]; then
        /usr/sbin/powerd /dev/cua3
fi
```

First we remove (if present) the file `/etc/turnUPSoff`. This file is used by the system shutdown script (`/etc/rc.d/rc.0`, in my case) to decide whether we want to turn the UPS off. See later in this document for more information.

Then we disable hardware flow control on the serial device connected to the UPS, and set its baud rate to 75. Now we're confident that the TX signal will stay high for a time long enough to turn the UPS off, if we send a character to the serial port (again, see later).

Finally we launch the `powerd` daemon, specifying the serial port to monitor. Notice that we're not going to read characters from the serial device, so don't worry if you have interrupt conflicts - they'll do no harm.

8.3.3   The inittab file and the shutdown scripts

The `powerd` process is now running, and it will send signals to `init` whenever a power failure occurs. Now we have to configure the system so that it can react in a useful way when those signals are received.

Modifying inittab   Add the following lines near the beginning of your /etc/inittab file:

```
# What to do when power fails (delayed shutdown).
pf::powerfail:/etc/powerfail_script

# If power is back before shutdown, cancel the running shutdown.
pg::powerokwait:/etc/powerokay_script

# If UPS batteries are getting low, do an immediate shutdown.
pc::powerfailnow:/etc/powerfailnow_script
```

The scripts   The scripts `powerfail_script`, `powerokay_script` and `powerfailnow_script` are executed when `init` receives the corresponding signal. They have the responsibility of shutting down the system in a clean way or cancelling a running shutdown in case power comes back. These are the scripts I'm currently using:

`/etc/powerfail_script`:

```
#!/bin/sh
/bin/sync
/usr/bin/sleep 10m
kill -9 'ps auxw | grep "shutdown" | grep -v grep | awk '{print $2}''
> /etc/turnUPSoff
/sbin/shutdown -t30 -h +3 "POWER FAILURE"
```

My Trust Energy Protector 400 powers only the computer, so I have quite a long backup time. Since power failures only last for some minutes in my zone, the system responds to a blackout in the following way: it waits for 10 minutes (usually the power comes back before) and then halts the system, allowing the users to close their applications and leave the machine. Before issuing the shutdown command, I make sure that there are no running shutdowns. I also create the file /etc/turnUPSoff, so that the system will turn off the UPS.

/etc/powerokay_script:

```
#!/bin/sh
kill 'ps auxw | grep "powerfail_script" | grep -v grep | awk '{print $2}''
kill -9 'ps auxw | grep "shutdown" | grep -v grep | awk '{print $2}''
rm -f /etc/turnUPSoff
```

If power comes back, we kills the running powerfail_script and any running shutdown. We also remove /etc/turnUPSoff.

/etc/powerfailnow_script:

```
#!/bin/sh
kill -9 'ps auxw | grep "shutdown" | grep -v grep | awk '{print $2}''
> /etc/turnUPSoff
/sbin/shutdown -h now "UPS batteries low. IMMEDIATE SHUTDOWN."
```

If batteries are getting low, we make sure that there are no running shutdowns, create the /etc/turnUPSoff file and then shutdown the system immediately.

The system shutdown script When system shutdown is complete, we can turn off the UPS raising the TX signal of the serial port for over 1ms. The serial device is already properly configured (see the stty command in the rc.local script). If the file /etc/turnUPSoff is present, we send the byte 0xff (all '1' bits) to the serial port.

To do this, add the following lines near the bottom of your system shutdown script (/etc/rc.d/rc.0, in my case). The proper place depends on the way your system is configured, but it should be okay to insert the lines before the echo command which prints the "System is halted" message.

```
# Is this a powerfail situation?
if [ -f /etc/turnUPSoff ]; then
  echo "Turning off UPS. Bye."
  sleep 5
  echo -e "\377" > /dev/cua3
  exit 1
fi
```

8.3.4 General remarks

This document contains things I learned while trying to configure *my* Linux system to use the Trust Energy Protector 400. Some informations (the path of the system inizialization scripts, for example) may be specific to my system, and you probably will need some customization. However, I hope this document will be a useful trace for those trying to use a Trust Energy Protector 400/650 under Linux. If you experience difficulties, look for general information in the rest of this UPS-Howto. Good luck!

Feedback I would greatly appreciate receiving feedback about this document, so that I can polish it and correct possible mistakes (I know the English is not very good, but I'm Italian after all!). Direct any comments/suggestions/critics to the following e-mail address:

ciro@stud.unipg.it

If you have problems using Trust Energy Protector 400/650 under Linux, feel free to contact me. I'll try to help you.

Legal Issues   I have no relation at all with Trust Networking Products.

The information contained in this document comes "as is". Use it at your own risk. I can't be held responsible for any damage or loss of data resulting from the use of the code and information given here.

Ciro Cattuto

8.3.5   Appendix A - Source code for the powerd daemon

`powerd.c`:

```
/*
 * powerd        Catch power failure signals from
 *               a Trust Energy Protector 400/650
 *               and notify init
 *
 * Usage:        powerd /dev/cua3 (or any other serial device)
 *
 * Author:       Ciro Cattuto <ciro@stud.unipg.it>
 *
 * Version 1.0 - 31 March 1997
 *
 * This code is heavily based on the original powerd.c code
 * by Miquel van Smoorenburg <miquels@drinkel.ow.org>.
 *
 * This program is free software; you can redistribute it and/or
 * modify it under the terms of the GNU General Public License
 * as published by the Free Software Foundation; either version
 * 2 of the License, or (at your option) any later version.
 *
 */

/* state 0 - power is good */
#define T0_SLEEP        10      /* interval between port reads, in second-
s */
#define T0_DCD           3      /* number of seconds DCD has to be high
                                   to cause an action                    */
#define T0_CTS           3      /* number of seconds CTS has to be high
                                   to cause an action                    */
/* state 1 - power is failing */
#define T1_SLEEP         2      /* interval between ports read-
s         */
#define T1_DCD           3      /* same as T0_DCD                        */
#define T1_CTS           3      /* same as T0_CTS                        */

#define DSR_SLEEP        2
#define DSR_TRIES       60

/* Use the new way of communicating with init. */
#define NEWINIT

#include <sys/types.h>
#include <sys/stat.h>
#include <sys/ioctl.h>
```

```
#include <fcntl.h>
#include <errno.h>
#include <stdlib.h>
#include <unistd.h>
#include <stdio.h>
#include <signal.h>
#include <syslog.h>
#include <string.h>
#include "paths.h"
#ifdef NEWINIT
#include "initreq.h"
#endif

#ifndef SIGPWR
#  define SIGPWR SIGUSR1
#endif

#ifdef NEWINIT
void alrm_handler()
{
}
#endif

/* Tell init that the power has gone (1), is back (0),
   or the UPS batteries are low (2). */
void powerfail(int event)
{
  int fd;
#ifdef NEWINIT
  struct init_request req;

  /* Fill out the request struct. */
  memset(&req, 0, sizeof(req));
  req.magic = INIT_MAGIC;
  switch (event)
        {
        case 0:
                req.cmd = INIT_CMD_POWEROK;
                break;
        case 1:
                req.cmd = INIT_CMD_POWERFAIL;
                break;
        case 2:
        default:
                req.cmd = INIT_CMD_POWERFAILNOW;
        }

  /* Open the fifo (with timeout) */
  signal(SIGALRM, alrm_handler);
  alarm(3);
  if ((fd = open(INIT_FIFO, O_WRONLY)) >= 0
                && write(fd, &req, sizeof(req)) == sizeof(req)) {
        close(fd);
        return;
  }
```

```
        /* Fall through to the old method.. */
#endif

   /* Create an info file for init. */
   unlink(PWRSTAT);
   if ((fd = open(PWRSTAT, O_CREAT|O_WRONLY, 0644)) >= 0) {
   switch (event)
           {
           case 0:
                   write(fd, "OK\n", 3);
                   break;

           case 1:
                   write(fd, "FAIL\n", 5);
                   break;

           case 2:
           default:
                   write(fd, "LOW\n", 4);
                   break;
           }
   close(fd);
   }

   kill(1, SIGPWR);
}

/* Main program. */
int main(int argc, char *argv[])
{
   int fd;
   int dtr_bit = TIOCM_DTR;
   int flags;
   int DCD, CTS;
   int status = -1;
   int DCD_count = 0, CTS_count = 0;
   int tries;

   if (argc < 2) {
           fprintf(stderr, "Usage: powerd <device>\n");
           exit(1);
   }

   /* Start syslog. */
   openlog("powerd", LOG_CONS|LOG_PERROR, LOG_DAEMON);

   /* Open monitor device. */
   if ((fd = open(argv[1], O_RDWR | O_NDELAY)) < 0) {
           syslog(LOG_ERR, "%s: %s", argv[1], sys_errlist[errno]);
           closelog();
           exit(1);
   }

   /* Line is opened, so DTR is high. Force it anyway to be sure. */
   ioctl(fd, TIOCMBIS, &dtr_bit);
```

```
/* Daemonize. */
switch(fork()) {
      case 0: /* Child */
              closelog();
              setsid();
              break;
      case -1: /* Error */
              syslog(LOG_ERR, "can't fork.");
              closelog();
              exit(1);
      default: /* Parent */
              closelog();
              exit(0);
}

/* Restart syslog. */
openlog("powerd", LOG_CONS, LOG_DAEMON);

/* Now sample the DCD line. */
while(1) {
      /* Get the status. */
      ioctl(fd, TIOCMGET, &flags);

      /* Check the connection: DSR should be high. */
      tries = 0;
      while((flags & TIOCM_DSR) == 0) {
              /* Keep on trying, and warn every two minutes. */
              if ((tries % DSR_TRIES) == 0)
                  syslog(LOG_ALERT, "UPS connection error");
              sleep(DSR_SLEEP);
              tries++;
              ioctl(fd, TIOCMGET, &flags);
      }
      if (tries > 0)
              syslog(LOG_ALERT, "UPS connection OK");

      /* Calculate present status. */
      DCD = flags & TIOCM_CAR;
      CTS = flags & TIOCM_CTS;

      if (status == -1)
              {
              status = (DCD != 0) ? 0 : 1;
              if (DCD == 0)
                      {
                      syslog(LOG_ALERT, "Power Failure. UPS active.");
                      powerfail(1);
                      }
              }

      switch (status)
              {
              case 0:
                      if ((DCD != 0) && (CTS != 0))
```

```
                            {
                            DCD_count = 0;
                            CTS_count = 0;
                            sleep(T0_SLEEP);
                            continue;
                            }
                    if (DCD == 0)
                            DCD_count++;
                    if (CTS == 0)
                            CTS_count++;
                    if ((DCD_count < T0_DCD) && (CTS_count < T0_CTS))
                            {
                            sleep(1);
                            continue;
                            }
                    if (CTS_count == T0_CTS)
                            {
                            status = 2;
                            syslog(LOG_ALERT, "UPS batteries low!");
                            break;
                            }
                    status = 1;
                    DCD_count = 0;
                    syslog(LOG_ALERT, "Power Failure. UPS active.");
                    break;

            case 1:
                    if ((DCD == 0) && (CTS != 0))
                            {
                            DCD_count = 0;
                            CTS_count = 0;
                            sleep(T1_SLEEP);
                            continue;
                            }
                    if (DCD != 0)
                            DCD_count++;
                    if (CTS == 0)
                            CTS_count++;
                    if ((DCD_count < T1_DCD) && (CTS_count < T1_CTS))
                            {
                            sleep(1);
                            continue;
                            }
                    if (CTS_count == T1_CTS)
                            {
                            status = 2;
                            syslog(LOG_ALERT, "UPS batteries low!");
                            break;
                            }
                    status = 0;
                    DCD_count = 0;
                    CTS_count = 0;
                    syslog(LOG_ALERT, "Power okay.");
                    break;
```

```
                        case 2:
                                sleep(1);
                                continue;

                        default:
                                break;
                }

        powerfail(status);
    }
    /* Never happens */
    return(0);
}
```

8.4   Trust UPS 400-A

I received a submission about the Trust UPS 400-A. I don't know if it's the same as the Trust Energy Protector 400, so I'm including the submission.

```
From: "Marcel Ammerlaan" <marcel@ch.twi.tudelft.nl>
To: hjstein@math.huji.ac.il
Subject: UPS addition
Date: Wed, 16 Jul 1997 01:17:11 +100

Hello Harvey,

I've got an addition to your UPS Howto. I've got a
"Trust UPS 400-A" which isn't listed. This product doesn't seem
to be manufactured anymore by it's producer (www.trust.box.nl).
But that doesn't mean it's not available anymore, I've got mine
really cheap just a month ago. Also this company just relabels
products so maybe there are others that have got the same UPS.

I have included a picture of the UPS in case anybody got such a beast
under another label.

The cable was easily constructed based on the original powerd cable
and the documentation from trust.
It clearly describes which pins of the D-shell connector of the UPS
carry which signal.

It extends the original design with 2 extra functions:
1) Battery low indication
2) Power down UPS

The cable I created looks like (see the other attachement).

This cable has been tested with powergend by Tom Webster and did work
completely (although your milage may vary).

Type:              "pleur"
Cable Power:       {TIOCM_DTR,0}
Inverter Kill:     {TIOCM_RTS,1}
Inverter Kill Time: 5
Power Check:       {TIOCM_CTS,0}
```

```
Battery Check:          {TIOCM_CAR,0}
Cable Check:            {TIOCM_RI,0}
```

Although (just as the powerd cable) the cable check function isn't
used because the UPS doesn't seem to support it.

Well that's about it I guess. If you need more information about the
UPS the cable or the software feel free to contact me.

And remember, everything described here works for me but I don't
guarantee it will for you.

Marcel Ammerlaan
CEO Pleursoft (explains the cablename doesn't it :-)
The Netherlands

<RSA implemented in 3 lines of perl deleted by the editor ;)>

```
Marcel Ammerlaan    | <m.j.ammerlaan@twi.tudelft.nl>
Paardenmarkt 78     | Just another nerd on the loose
2611 PD Delft       |
The Netherlands     |
```

8.5   Sustainer S-40a

Information on the Sustainer S-40a.

```
From: fnevgeny@plasma-gate.weizmann.ac.il (Evgeny Stambulchik)
To: hjstein@math.huji.ac.il, hjstein@math.huji.ac.il,
        hjstein@math.huji.ac.il, hjstein@math.huji.ac.il
Subject: UPS-HowTo add-ons
Date: Sun, 10 Sep 1995 13:09:50 +0300 (IST)
```

Hi Harvey,

This is an addition to your UPS-HowTo. I'm using Sustainer S-40a UP-
S for a few
months with unipower package (now it's called genpower) and home-made cable
constructed as follows (I've sent all this stuff to Tom Webster, author of the
package, too, and it should appear in the next version):

```
        UPS SIDE                                    LINUX SIDE


            2 POWER FAIL                              1(8)
 +-----------o----------------------------+---------------o  DCD
 |                                        |
 o                                        |
  /                                       |
 /                                        |
 |          4 COMMON                      |               5(7)
 +-----------o------+-----------------|---------------o  GND
 |                  |                 |
  \                 |                 |
```

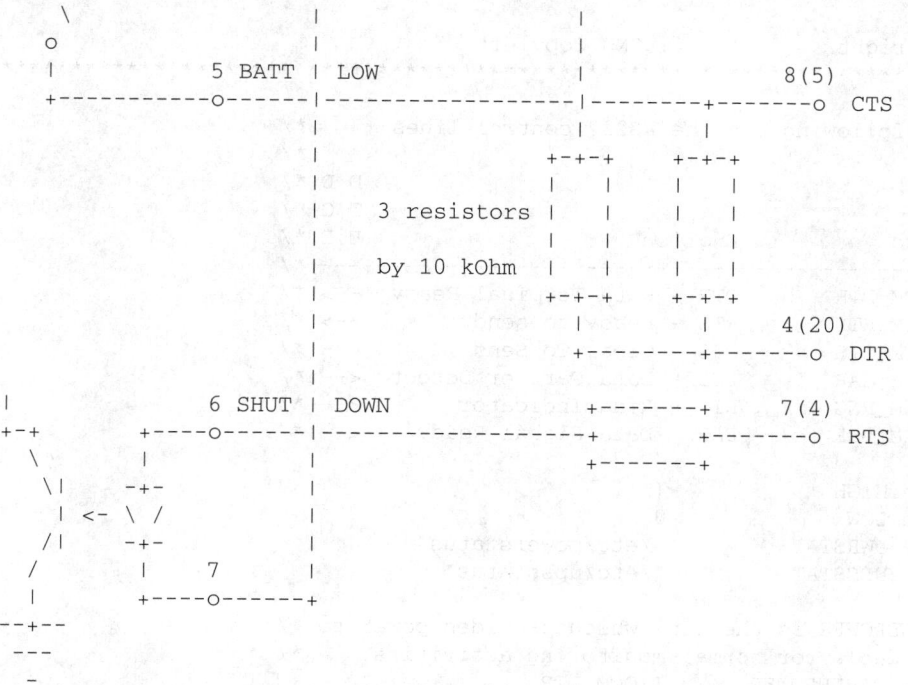

```
            \                   |                   |
            o                   |                   |
            |      5 BATT |  LOW                    |              8(5)
         +-----------o------|------------------|--------+-------o  CTS
         |                  |                   |        |
         |                  |                   +-+-+    +-+-+
         |                  |                   | | |    | | |
         |                  |      3 resistors  | | |    | | |
         |                  |                   | | |    | | |
         |                  |      by 10 kOhm   | -|-    | | |
         |                  |                   +-+-+    +-+-+
         |                  |                    | |      |      4(20)
         |                  |                    +--------+-------o  DTR
         |                  |
         |      6 SHUT |  DOWN                   +-------+      7(4)
       +-+       +----o------|------------------+       +-------o  RTS
        \        |           |                  +-------+
         \|    -+-           |
          | <- \ /           |
         /|    -+-           |
        /        |     7      |
         |       +----o------+
      --+--
       ---
        -
```

NOTE!!!: Shutdown pins in the tech info supplied with UP-
S (4 and 6) are given
incorrectly! The valid ones are 6 and 7, as shown above.
Note2: Pin numbers on the PC side in the brackets are for 25-pin connector,
outside - for 9-pin one.

Here's the unipowerd.h file I used:


```
/***************************************************************************/
/* File Name            : unipowerd.h                                      */
/* Program Name         : unipowerd                    Version: 1.0.0      */
/* Author               : Tom Webster <webster@kaiwan.com>                 */
/* Created              : 1994/04/20                                       */
/* Last Modified By     : Tom Webster                  Date: 1995/04/09    */
/* Last Modified By     : Evgeny Stambulchik (for Sustainer UPS)           */
/*                                                                         */
/* Compiler (created)   : GCC 2.5.8                                        */
/* Compiler (env)       : Linux 1.0.9                                      */
/* ANSI C Compatable    : No                                               */
/* POSIX Compatable     : Yes?                                             */
/*                                                                         */
/* Purpose              : Header file for unipowerd.                       */
/*                      : Contains the configuration information for       */
/*                      : unipowerd.  Edit this file as indicated          */
/*                      : below to activate features and to customize      */
/*                      : unipowerd for your UPS.                          */
```

```
/*                                                                       */
/* Copyright           : GNU Copyleft                                    */
/***********************************************************************/

/* The following are the RS232 control lines      */
/*                                                 */
/*                                          D D */
/*                                          T C */
/* Macro             English                E E */
/* ----------------------------------------------- */
/* TIOCM_DTR         DTR - Data Terminal Ready  --> */
/* TIOCM_RTS         RTS - Ready to send        --> */
/* TIOCM_CTS         CTS - Clear To Send        <-- */
/* TIOCM_CAR         DCD - Data Carrier Detect  <-- */
/* TIOCM_RNG         RI  - Ring Indicator       <-- */
/* TIOCM_DSR         DSR - Data Signal Ready    <-- */

#define HIGH               (1)
#define LOW                0
#define PWRSTAT            "/etc/powerstatus"
#define UPSSTAT            "/etc/upsstatus"

/* CABLEPOWER is the line which provides power to */
/* the cable for normal monitoring activities.    */
#define CABLEPOWER         TIOCM_DTR

#define POWERBIT           TIOCM_CAR
#define POWEROK            HIGH

/* Define CABLECHECK as 1 to check for low battery */
/* Define CABLECHECK as 0 value to skip            */
#define CABLECHECK         0
#define CABLEBIT           TIOCM_RNG
#define CABLEOK            HIGH

/* Define BATTCHECK as 1 to check for low battery  */
/* Define BATTCHECK as 0 value to skip.            */
#define BATTCHECK          1
#define BATTBIT            TIOCM_CTS
#define BATTOK             HIGH

/* Define INVERTERKILL as 1 to hndle killing the inverter */
/* Define INVERTERKILL as 0 value to skip.                */
/* INVERTERBIT is the line which will kill the inverter   */
/*    while the UPS is in powerfail mode.                 */
/* INVERTERTIME is the time in seconds to hold the line   */
/*    defiined by INVERTERBIT high to kill the inverter.  */
#define INVERTERKILL       1
#define INVERTERBIT        TIOCM_RTS
#define INVERTERTIME       5

/***********************************************************************/
/* End of File unipowerd.h                                             */
/***********************************************************************/
```

```
I'm aware that current name of the package is genpow-
er. I haven't try it yet as
see no reason to switch to the new version meantime; the former seem-
s to work
very stable. Nevertheless, here is the add-on for genpower-
1.0.1's genpowerd.h
file (hopefully, I "translated" unipowerd.h correctly):
Add-on for genpower-1.0.1's genpowerd.h file:

/* Evgeny's Sustainer S-40A */
 {"sustainer",   {TIOCM_DTR,0}, {TIOCM_RTS,1},  5, {TIOCM_CAR,0}, {TI-
OCM_CTS,0},
 {0,0}}

Evgeny
```

8.6   Systel

Another Israeli company. I never ended up purchasing a UPS from them, but they were very good about getting me detailed documentation on their communication port. It should be easy enough to control their UPS. Their phone number is 972-8-409-019 (972-8-407-216 for fax).

8.7   Deltec Power, Fiskars Power Systems and Exide.

Fiskars <http://www.fiskars.fi/> is a Finnish holding company. They used to own *Deltec Power* <http://www.deltecpower.com>. In March of 1996 Fiskars sold Deltec Power to *Exide Electronics Group* <http://www.exide.com/exide>. At that time, Deltec Power was one of the world's largest makers of UPSs.

Under Fiskars, Deltec used to make the PowerServers 10, 20, 30, and 40. The Deltec Power home page mentions other UPSs.

Exide now bundles UPS control software with their UPSs that works under Linux. They also sell the software separately. They say that their software works with other UPSs too.

I'd like to hear from people using their software.

Here's the advertisement they emailed me:

Exide Electronics announces LanSafe III UPS Power Management Software for Linux.

LanSafe III is a UPS Power Management application. It provides automatic orderly shutdown functionality incase of an extended power failure that should outlast the UPS battery run time.

LanSafe III enables broadcast messages and e-mail to be sent according to user defined power condition changes. The shutdown procedure can also be customized.

LanSafe III works together with the vast majority of all Exide Electronics UPS models. It goes even one step further by supporting basic shutdown functionality also with other manufacturers UPSs.

LanSafe III for Linux runs on Intel based Linux systems. Both character based and X11/Motif based user interfaces are provided.

LanSafe III supports all the major OS platforms: Linux, IBM AIX, HP UX, Digital UNIX, SCO UNIX, Solaris, SunOS, AT&T UNIX, all Windows platforms, OS/2, Novell and Macintosh among others.

LanSafe III is bundled with the following Exide Electronics UPSs: OneUPS Plus, NetUPS, PowerWare Prestige, Power-Ware Profile, PowerWare Plus 5xx.

HOWTO

It also ships with FPS Power Systems UPSs: PowerRite Plus, PowerRite Max, PowerWorks A30, PowerWorks A40, Series 9000 and Series 10000.

It is also possible to purchase a separate software license to use with a previous UPS model or an other manufactures UPS. Regular licenses are S$149, with site licenses also available.

For details please visit our Web sites at www.exide.com, www.fiskarsUPS.com and www.deltecpower.com.

Incidentally, when I tried to connect to www.fiskarsUPS.com, it prompted me for a username and password.

8.8   Beaver model UB500 UPS

dan@fch.wimsey.bc.ca (Dan Fandrich) writes:

I seem to have gotten my old Beaver model UB500 UPS working with genpower. The interface uses RS-232 compatible voltage levels, so installing it is a snap. There is a DE-9 female connector on the back which plugs directly into a 9-pin PC serial port using a plain 9-pin video monitor extension cable.

The DIP switches allow quite versatile pinouts. To emulate genpower's apc1-nt type of UPS, they must be set as follows:

```
1  | on  | (CTS = power fail)
2  | off | (CTS = low battery)
3  | off | (DSR = power fail)
4  | off | (DSR = low battery)
5  | off | (CD  = power fail)
6  | on  | (CD  = low battery)
7  | off | (RI  = power fail)
8  | off | (RI  = low battery)
9  | on  | (DTR = inverter off)
10 | off | (RTS = inverter off)
```

DIP switch SW601 for Beaver model UB500 UPS.

The switches form groups of adjacent pairs for each output pin. They are mutually exclusive–don't try to turn on both switch 5 and 6 simultaneously, for example, or you'll be shorting the low battery and power fail signals.

That's all there is to it. Feel free to add this do your documentation.

8.9   Sendom

Documentation on using the Sendom UPS.

```
From: charli <mefistos@impsat1.com.ar>
To: hjstein@math.huji.ac.il
Subject: ups howto contribution
Date: Wed, 13 Nov 1996 19:07:41 -0200


hjstein@math.huji.ac.il


sir:


i connected a sendom ups with the help of your UPS-howto and man powerd
and discovered something useful. perhaps this thing extends to some
other ups.
im using slackware 3.0 distribution. i has the soft configuration in
/etc/inittab already done. its only needed to add the /rc.local powerd
```

```
/cuaX

i used the man powerd diagram:
        9pin    25pin

DTR     4       20      ---------
                                |       >
DSR     6       6       --              < 10k
                                        >
DCD     1       8       -------------------------
                                                        relais
GND     5       7       -------------------------
```

```
the fact is that the sendom ups dont use relais but some electronic
solid state device, and it works one way BUT NO THE OTHER. so if you
make the cable and doesnt work, first try inverting the cable in the
ups "relais"

i hope this can be useful, if you want to include this somewhere, feel
free to correct my english. please aknowledge this mail even with an
empty
mail so i know it arrived
end
```

8.10   Best

Information on Best UPSs is available on at the *Best Power* <http://www.bestpower.com/index.html> web-site. Their website includes the checkups.tar (section 4 (Software)) package for communicating with Best UPSs, both in smart mode and in dumb mode, and it includes source code, so you can compile it under Linux.

8.10.1   Best Fortress - Using Best's software

Linux Best Power UPS Mini-HOWTO by Michael Stutz (*stutz@dsl.org*, and *http://dsl.org/m/*) v1.0, 14 Aug 97

0.0 Disclaimer

Copyright 1997 by Michael Stutz; this information is free; it may be redistributed and/or modified under the terms of the GNU General Public License, either Version 2 of the License, or (at your preference) any later version, and as long as this sentence remains; this information comes WITHOUT ANY WARRANTY; without even the implied warranty of MERCHANTABILITY or FITNESS FOR A PARTICULAR PURPOSE; see the GNU General Public License for more details.

1.0 Introduction

Best Power <http://www.bestpower.com> are the makers of high quality UPS products, with their Fortress line in particular being well-suited for typical Linux users. Although their products are not currently priced as low as some (such as APC), Best Power provide source code for their UPS software and have been very respondent to queries from Linux users. Furthermore, their hardware seems to be highly regarded, making Best Power a winning choice for Linux users.

This document describes the installation of a Best Power Fortress UPS (model used was a 1996-model 660a with accom-panying Best Power CD-ROM) to a Linux box.

2.0 Installation

2.1 Hardware

Install the hardware as indicated in the instructions. The Best Power "Fortress" series comes with an RS-232 cable that should attach to a spare serial port on the back of the computer.

2.2 Software

This is where it differs from the manual, which does not currently have Linux-specific instructions. The accompanying Fortress CD-ROM, however, does come with source code for the UPS software, so getting it up and running on a Linux system is a trivial task.

To do this, follow these steps, and use the manual as a reference to get an overall feel for how the software works. I took the liberty of making a few changes in this HOWTO from the way the Fortress software is set up on other UNIX systems that I feel are better suited for a Linux system. For example, I eliminated the need for an /etc/best directory and put the executables in /usr/local/sbin, which I feel is a more appropriate place.

- First, create the "upsdown" script that is executed during a power outage. This one will halt the system:

```
cat > /etc/upsdown << EOF
#!/bin/sh
shutdown -h now < /dev/console &
EOF
```

- Now, make directories for the documentation and the source code:

```
mkdir /usr/doc/best
mkdir /usr/local/src/best
```

- Mount the CD-ROM, and untar the unix/checkups.tar file into the /tmp directory or somewhere similar:

```
cd /tmp
tar /cdrom/unix/checkups.tar
```

- Change into the etc/best/advanced directory that should have been extracted from the checkups tarball.
- Copy the documentation and UPS script files to their proper place in the sytem:

```
cp README /usr/doc/best
cp manual.txt /usr/doc/best
cp bestsend /etc
cp source/*.c /usr/local/src/best
```

- Clean up the /tmp mess and compile the software:

```
cd /usr/local/src/best
rm -R /tmp/etc
gcc -o checkups checkups.c
gcc -o mftalk mftalk.c
mv checkups /usr/local/sbin
mv mftalk /usr/local/sbin
```

- Test the UPS. Replace ttySx with the serial port of your choice. If you have a good connection, you should see a row of characters print across the screen:

```
mftalk /dev/ttySx
```

- Make the checkups program run at startup for testing. This can be done in several different ways (described in the manual). The way I did it is by adding this line to /etc/inittab:

```
ups:234:once:/usr/local/sbin/checkups -c500 /dev/ttyS1
```

- Test it. Do this by taking out power to UPS by pulling out the fuse connected to the UPS, and wait a couple of minutes. It print a warning messages and then halt the system after a few mintues.

- If that works, take out the "-c500" from the line in your inittab (which basically means shut down the system right away instead of when the UPS power runs out), and you're good to go!

3.0 Conclusions

I welcome suggestions for improving this document or the techniques described herein. As of this writing, Best Power seemed interested in including this or other information in their documentation to help Linux users with their product, so this is definitely a company to support. Let them know how you feel at *sales@bestpower.com* and *support@bestpower.com*.

8.10.2 Best Fortress LI-950

Some comments on the Best Fortress.

```
From lnz@dandelion.com Wed May 31 19:53:09 1995
Newsgroups: comp.os.linux.hardware
Subject: Re: UPS for use with Linux?
From: Leonard N. Zubkoff <lnz@dandelion.com>
Date: 25 May 1995 16:27:55 -0700
Organization: Dandelion Digital
NNTP-Posting-Host: dandelion.com
NNTP-Posting-User: root
In-reply-to: nautix@community.net's message of 23 May 1995 09:41:40 -0700

In article <3pt384$sic@odin.community.net> nautix@community.net writes:

    Ditto what Craig says.  APC was very uncooperative, but I have only
    good things to say about Best.  I use their Fortress LI 660 model;
    660 VA, lots of status features on the front, etc.  The CheckUPS
    software costs extra and needs some hacking to fit into my
    FSSTND-ish file system (the directories and file names are hard-coded
    to fit into SunOS 4.1.x).  I'd be happy to send you my diffs, if
    you want them.  (I love it when a vendor ships the source as
    a normal business practice!)

    The CheckUPS software is limited to doing automagic shutdowns, though.
    The UPS can give lots of status information; CheckUPS only asks for
    ''If the power has failed, how much battery time remains?''

    Best follows up on their customer satisfaction cards, too.
    I indicated that I was dissappointed that CheckUPS didn't do more
    status reporting (like input voltage, output voltage, percent load,
    etc.), which is available from the UPS.  I asked for a the
    spec on the interface lingo; they said ''sure'' and had it to me in
    2 days, free.  A full-featured UPS status checker is on my back burner.
    Does anyone see a demand for such a utility?

Let me add yet another recommendation for Best Power.  I just purchased a
Fortress LI-950, though I declined on the CheckUPS software.  Unlike some
other brands, a simple three wire cable is all that's needed to connect the
Fortress to a serial port -- no need for pull-up circuitry in the cabling.
A few minutes hacking and I had program to act as both a shutdown monitor
daemon, and to kill the inverter output when the system is shutdown while
on battery power.

I may eventually want to use the smarter serial communication mode rather
```

than the simple contact mode, so I asked Best technical support for the documentation, and it arrived today, a week after I called them. Once I peruse the documentation I'll decide if a smarter interface is really worthwhile, especially since at some point I'll need to shut down two networked machines sharing the UPS.

Leonard

8.10.3 Best Ferrups

In addition to the doumentation and softare on Best's web site, you could also use the `bestups-0.9.tar.gz` (section 4 (Software)) package. We've just started testing it with our 5kva FERRUPS.

The basic idea is that there are two modules. One which fields information requests on a network port, relays those requests to the UPS, and returns the results. The second module talks to the first, interprets the results, and responds with either OK or FAIL.

This is sufficient to allow the `powerd-2.0.tar.gz` package (section 4 (Software)) to do the rest of the work.

The details can be gotten from the `bestups-0.9.tar.gz` package (section 4 (Software)).

Incidentally, our 5kva Ferrups has performed flawlessly in keeping our 10 computers and 30 screens humming.

8.11 GPS1000 from ACCODATA

```
>From hennus@sky.nl.mugnet.org Thu Mar 10 15:10:22 1994
Newsgroups: comp.os.linux.help
Subject: Re: auto-shutdown with UPS
From: hennus@sky.nl.mugnet.org (Hennus Bergman)
Date: Tue, 1 Mar 1994 22:17:45 GMT
Distribution: world
Organization: The Organization For Removal Of On-Screen Logos


In article <CRAFFERT.94Feb28125452@nostril.lehman.com>,
Colin Owen Rafferty <craffert@nostril.lehman.com> wrote:
>I am about to buy an Uninterruptable Power Supply for my machine, and
>I would like to get one that has the "auto-shutdown" feature.
>
I just got one of those real cheap :-)
It's a GPS1000 by ACCODATA. Anybody know how good the output
signal of these things is? (Don't have a scope myself :-()


>I assume that these each have some kind of serial connection that
>tells the system information about it.
>
I took it apart to find out how it worked. There were three optocouplers
(two output, one input) connected to a 9 pin connector at the back.
One turns on when the power fails, and goes off again when the power
returns. While the power is off, you can use the 'input' to shut the
battery off. (It releases the power-relay.) The third one is some kind
of feedback to tell that it did accepted the 'shut-down command'.
I think the interface for my UPS was designed to be connected to TTL-
level
    signals, but with some resistors it could be connected to serial port.
It's wired in such a way that using a RS-232 port you cannot use both
output optocouplers; but the shutdown feedback is not necessary anyway,
```

```
just use the important one. ;-)
(Note that it is possible to blow the transistor part in optocouplers
with RS-232 levels if you wire it the wrong way round ;-))

I was hoping I would be able to connect it to my unused game port,
but that doesn't have an output, does it?
I'll probably end up getting an extra printer port for this.

Not all UPS' use optocouplers, some use simple relays, which are
less critical to connect, but of course not as 'nice'.

>Has anyone written a package that watches the UPS and does a shutdown
>(or something) when the power is off?
SysVinit-2.4 (and probably 2.5 as well) has a 'powerd' daemon that
continually watches a serial port for presence of the CD (Carrier
Detect) line and signals init when it drops. Init then activates
shutdown with a time delay. If the power returns within a few minutes
the shutdown is cancelled. Very Nice.
The only problem I had with it is that it doesn't actually tell the
UPS to turn off when the shutdown is complete. It just sits there with
a root prompt. I'll probably write a small program to shut it down
>from /etc/brc. RSN.

>    Colin Rafferty, Lehman Brothers <craffert@lehman.com>

Hennus Bergman
```

8.12 TrippLite BC750LAN (Standby UPS)

Tom Webster (*webster@kaiwan.com*, the author of the genpower package) sent me information on the TrippLite BC750LAN. If you have one of these, your probably best off using his package.

But, for completeness, here's his cable wiring diagram (done by trial and error, and without documentation):

```
        UPS                 System
        DB-25               DB-25
          1 <--------------> 1        Ground

          2 <--------------> 4        Power Fail
          8 <--------------> 8        Sensing Circuit

          3 <--------------> 2        Inverter Shutdown
         20 <--------------> 22       Circuit
```

8.13 APC

If the above plethora of APC packages doesn't get you running, maybe the following sections will help.

8.13.1 APC Back-UPS

There seems to be some controversy as to the accuracy of the information here on APC Back-UPSs. So, please be careful. I'm prefacing this section with one message of caution I received. It might not make a lot of sense before the rest of this section is read, but this way, at least you're more likely to see it. And again, since I don't have any APC UPS units, I can't verify the accuracy of either of these messages.

A message of caution

```
From ind43@sun1000.ci.pwr.wroc.pl Sun Oct  9 11:00:42 1994
Newsgroups: comp.os.linux.admin
Subject: BUPS-HOWTO warning
From: ind43@sun1000.ci.pwr.wroc.pl (Marek Michalkiewicz)
Date: 6 Oct 1994 18:38:15 GMT
Organization: Technical Univeristy of Wroclaw
NNTP-Posting-Host: ci3ux.ci.pwr.wroc.pl
X-Newsreader: TIN [version 1.2 PL2]


If you want to connect the APC Back-UPS to your Linux box, this might
be of interest to you.

There is a good BUPS-HOWTO which describes how to do this. But it has
one "bug".

The RTS serial port signal is used to shut down the UPS. The UPS will
shut down only if it operates from its battery. The manual says that
the shutdown signal must be high for at least 0.5s. But few milliseconds
is enough, at least for my APC Back-UPS 600.

Using RTS to shut down the UPS can be dangerous, because the RTS goes
high when the serial device is opened. The backupsd program then turns
RTS off, but it is on (high) for a moment. This kills the power when
backupsd is first started and there is a power failure at this time.
This can happen for example when the UPS is shut down, unattended,
and the power comes back for a while.

Either start backupsd before mounting any filesystems for read-write,
or (better) use TX (pin 3) instead of RTS (pin 7) to shut down the
UPS (pin numbers are for 9-pin plug). Use ioctl(fd, TCSBRKP, 10);
to make TX high for one second, for example. Using TX should be safe.
Maybe I will post the diffs if time permits...

-- Marek Michalkiewicz
ind43@ci3ux.ci.pwr.wroc.pl
```

BUPS-HOWTO   Luminated Software Group Presents

HOWTO use Back-UPS (by APC) (to keep your linux box from frying)

Version: 1.01 BETA

Document by: Christian G. Holtje <docwhat@uiuc.edu> Cabling info and help: Ben Galliart <bgallia@orion.it.luc.edu>

This document, under one condition, is placed in Public Domain. The one condition is that credit is given where credit is due. Modify this as much as you want, just give some credit to us who worked.

** Warning!   I, nor any of us who have written or helped with this document, make and guarantees or claims for this text/source/hints.   If anything is damaged, we take NO RESPONSIBILITY! This works to the BEST OF OUR KNOWLEDGE, but we may have made mistakes.   So be careful! **

Al right, you just bought (or are going to buy) a Back-UPS from APC. (Other brands might be able to use this info, with little or no modification, but we don't know) You've looked at the price of the Power-Chute software/cabling, and just are not sure it's worth the price. Well, I made my own cable, and my own software and am using it to automatically shut off the power to my linux box when a power failure hits. Guess what? You can too!

*** The Cable ***

This was the hardest part to figure out (I know little about hardware, so Ben did the most work for this). To build one, you need to buy from your local radio shack (or other part supplier) this stuff:

```
1 9-Position Male D-Subminature Connector (solder-type)
      [Radio Shack cat. no. 276-1537c]
1 9-Position Female D-Subminature Connector (solder-type)
      [Radio Shack cat. no. 276-1538c]
2 casings for the above plugs (usually sold separately)
Some stranded wire (wire made of strands, not solid wire)
```

You also need, but may be able to borrow:

```
1 soldering iron
solder
```

Okay...this is how you connect it up!

These diagrams are looking into the REVERSE SIDE (the side where you solder the wire onto the plugs) The letters G, R, and B represent the colors of the wires I used, and help to distinguish one line from the next. (NOTE: I'm use standard rs-232 (as near as we can tell) numbering. The APC book uses different numbers. Ignore them! Use ours...I already changed the numbers for you!)

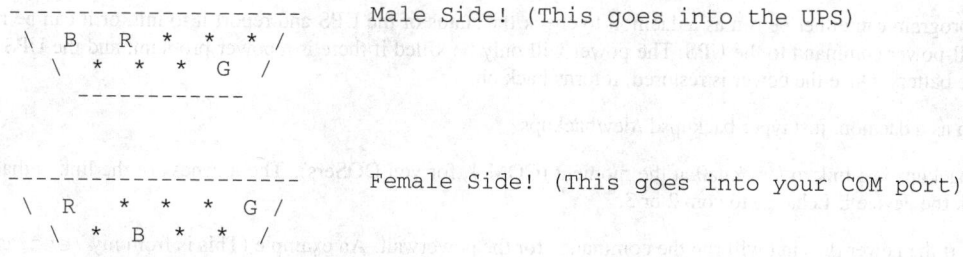

```
    ---------------------       Male Side! (This goes into the UPS)
    \  B   R   *   *   *  /
      \  *   *   *   G  /
        -----------

    --------------------        Female Side! (This goes into your COM port)
    \  R   *   *   *   G /
      \  *   B   *   *  /
        -----------
```

For those who like the numbers better:

```
        Male            Female
    ---------------------------------------
         1               7          Black
         2               1          Red
         9               5          Green
```

————Aside: What the rs-232 pins are for!———— Since we had to dig this info up anyway:

>From the REAR (the soldering side) the pins are numbered so:

```
    ---------------------
    \  1   2   3   4   5 /
      \  6   7   8   9  /
        -----------
```

The pins mean:

Number	Name	Abbr. (Sometimes writ- ten with D prefix)
1	Carrier Detect	CD
2	Receive Data	RD
3	Transmit Data	TD(?)
4	Data Terminal Ready	DTR
5	Signal Ground	Gnd
6	Data Set Ready	DSR
7	Request to Send	RTS(?)
8	Clear to Send	CS
9	Ring Indicator	RI

What we did is connect the UPS's RS-232 Line Fail Output to the CD, the UPS's chassis to Gnd, and the UPS's RS-232 Shut Down Input to RTS. Easy now that we told you, no?

I have no idea if the software below will work, if you purchase the cable from APC. It might, and it might not.

*** The Software ***

Okay, I use the SysVInit package by Miquel van Smoorenburg for Linux. (see end for file locations, credits, email addresses, etc.) I don't know what would have to be changed to use someone elses init, but I know this code (following) will work with Miquel's stuff. Just so I give credit where credit's due. I looked at Miquel's code to figure out how ioctl()'s worked. If I didn't have that example, I'd have been in trouble. I also used the powerfail() routine (verbatim, I think), since it must interact with his init, I thought that he should know best. The .c file is at the end of this document, and just needs to be clipped off. To clip the file, edit away and extra '.sigs' and junk. This document should end on the line /* End of File */.....cut the rest.

This program can either be run as a daemon to check the status of the UPS and report it to init, or it can be run to send the kill-power command to the UPS. The power will only be killed if there is a power problem, and the UPS is running off the battery. Once the power is restored, it turns back on.

To run as a daemon, just type: backupsd /dev/backups

/dev/backups is a link to /dev/cua0 at the moment (COM 1, for you DOSers). The niceness of the link is that I can just re-link the device if I change to com 2 or 3.

Then, if the power dies init will run the commands for the powerwait. An example (This is from my /etc/inittab):

```
#Here are the actions for powerfailure.
pf::powerwait:/etc/rc.d/rc.power start
po::powerokwait:/etc/rc.d/rc.power stop
```

The powerwait will run, if the power goes down, and powerokwait will run if the power comes back up.

Here is my entire rc.power:

```
#! /bin/sh
#
# rc.power       This file is executed by init when there is a powerfailure.
#
# Version:       @(#)/etc/rc.d/rc.power   1.50    1994-08-10
#
# Author:        Christian Holtje, <docwhat@uiuc.edu>
#
```

```
    # Set the path.
    PATH=/sbin:/etc:/bin:/usr/bin:/sbin/dangerous

    # Find out how we were called.
    case "$1" in
            start)
                    echo "Warning there is Power problems."  | wall
                    # Save current Run Level
                    ps | gawk '{ if (($5 == "init") && ($1 == "1")) print $6 }' \
                            | cut -f2 -d[ | cut -f1 -d] \
                                > /tmp/run.level.power
                    /sbin/shutdown -h +1m
                    ;;
            stop)
                    echo "Power is back up.  Attempting to halt shut-
    down." | wall
                    shutdown -c
                    ;;
            *)
                    echo "Usage:  $0 [start|stop]"
                    exit 1
                    ;;
    esac
```

Pretty nifty, no? Actually, there is a problem here...I haven't had time to figure it out...If there is a 'sh' wizard out there....

There is one little detail left, that is having the UPS turn off the power if it was halted with the power out. This is accomplished by adding this line into the end of your halt script:

```
    /sbin/backupsd /dev/backups killpower
```

This will only kill the power if there is no power being supplied to your UPS.

*** Testing the stuff ***

This is just a short section saying this:

BE CAREFUL!

I recommend backing up your linux partitions, syncing several times before testing and just being careful in general. Of course, I'm just recommending this. I wasn't careful at all, and had to clean my partition several times testing my config. But it works. :)

*** Where to Get It ***

Miquel van Smoorenburg's SysVInit can be gotten at:

```
sunsite.unc.edu:/pub/Linux/system/Daemons/SysVinit-2.50.tgz
```

and a fix for some bash shells is right next-door as:

```
sunsite.unc.edu:/pub/Linux/system/Daemons/SysVinit-2.50.patch1
```

As to getting this HOWTO, you can email me. docwhat@uiuc.edu with the subject saying 'request' and the keyword 'backups' in body of the letter. (I may automate this, and other stuff)

*** Credit Where Credit's Due Dept. ***

Thanks to Miquel van Smoorenburg <miquels@drinkel.nl.mugnet.org> for his wonderful SysVInit package and his powerd.c which helped me very much.

Christian Holtje <docwhat@uiuc.edu> Documentation backupsd.c (what wasn't Miquel's) rc.power

Ben Galliart <bgallia@orion.it.luc.edu> The cable Information for the RS-232 standard Lousy Jokes (none quoted here)

```c
/*  backupsd.c -- Simple Daemon to catch power failure signals from a
 *                Back-UPS (from APC).
 *
 *  Parts of the code are from Miquel van Smoorenburg's powerd.c
 *  Other parts are original from Christian Holtje <docwhat@uiuc.edu>
 *  I believe that it is okay to say that this is Public Domain, just
 *  give credit, where credit is due.
 *
 *  Disclaimer:  We make NO claims to this software, and take no
 *               resposibility for it's use/misuse.
 */

#include <sys/types.h>
#include <sys/ioctl.h>
#include <fcntl.h>
#include <errno.h>
#include <stdlib.h>
#include <unistd.h>
#include <stdio.h>
#include <signal.h>

/* This is the file needed by SysVInit */
#define PWRSTAT          "/etc/powerstatus"

void powerfail(int fail);

/* Main program. */
int main(int argc, char **argv)
{
  int fd;
  int killpwr_bit = TIOCM_RTS;
  int flags;
  int status, oldstat = -1;
  int count = 0;

  if (argc < 2) {
        fprintf(stderr, "Usage: %s <device> [killpower]\n", argv[0]);
        exit(1);
  }

  /* Open the the device */
  if ((fd = open(argv[1], O_RDWR | O_NDELAY)) < 0) {
        fprintf(stderr, "%s: %s: %s\n", argv[0], argv[1],
                sys_errlist[errno]);
        exit(1);
  }

  if ( argc >= 3  && (strcmp(argv[2], "killpower")==0) )
        {
```

```
            /* Let's kill the power! */
            fprintf(stderr, "%s: Attempting to kill the power!\n",argv[0] );
            ioctl(fd, TIOCMBIS, &killpwr_bit);
            /* Hmmm..... If you have a power outtage, you won't make it! */
            exit(0);
        }
    else
        /* Since we don't want to kill the power, clear the RTS. (killp-
wr_bit) */
        ioctl(fd, TIOCMBIC, &killpwr_bit);

/* Become a daemon. */
  switch(fork()) {
  case 0: /* I am the child. */
            setsid();
            break;
  case -1: /* Failed to become daemon. */
            fprintf(stderr, "%s: can't fork.\n", argv[0]);
            exit(1);
  default: /* I am the parent. */
            exit(0);
  }


  /* Now sample the DCD line. */
  while(1) {
      ioctl(fd, TIOCMGET, &flags);
      status = (flags & TIOCM_CD);
      /* Did DCD jumps to high? Then the power has failed. */
      if (oldstat == 0 && status != 0) {
          count++;
          if (count > 3) powerfail(0);
          else { sleep(1); continue; }
      }
      /* Did DCD go down again? Then the power is back. */
      if (oldstat > 0 && status == 0) {
          count++;
          if (count > 3) powerfail(1);
          else { sleep(1); continue; }
      }
      /* Reset count, remember status and sleep 2 seconds. */
      count = 0;
      oldstat = status;
      sleep(2);
  }
  /* Error! (shouldn't happen) */
  return(1);
}


/* Tell init the power has either gone or is back. */
void powerfail(ok)
int ok;
{
  int fd;
```

```
/* Create an info file needed by init to shutdown/cancel shutdown */
unlink(PWRSTAT);
if ((fd = open(PWRSTAT, O_CREAT|O_WRONLY, 0644)) >= 0) {
      if (ok)
              write(fd, "OK\n", 3);
      else
              write(fd, "FAIL\n", 5);
      close(fd);
}
kill(1, SIGPWR);
}

/* End of File */
```

More notes

```
From ockers@carnot02.maem.umr.edu Mon Jan 16 15:27:29 1995
Newsgroups: comp.os.linux.hardware
Subject: Back-UPS, backupsd, and low battery signal
From: ockers@carnot02.maem.umr.edu (Jim Ockers)
Date: 12 Jan 1995 04:22:44 GMT
Reply-To: ockers@umr.edu
Organization: the all-male wasteland of Rolla, MO
NNTP-Posting-Host: carnot02.maem.umr.edu
X-Newsreader: TIN [version 1.2 PL2]
```

Hello all,

I use the backupsd on my linux system and I like it a lot. I also
run Windows NT when I have to and it has a UPS daemon too. The pinouts
required by Windows NT are different from the ones you specify in the
program but that is easily changed since I have the source for your
program..

Anyways I was browsing through the Windows NT knowledge base (KB) and
found something interesting. If you look in the documentation for your
Back-UPS under "computer interface port" you will see that this UPS will
send a Low Battery signal at least two minutes before the battery fails.

At least the manual for my Back-UPS 400 says that...

However they also speak some Electrical Engineering gibberish ("Outputs ...
are actually open collector outputs which must be pulled up to a common
referenced supply no greater than +40 Vdc. The transistors are capable
of a maximum non-inductive load of 25mAdc.)

Well that means nothing to me, but what I discovered in the NT KB was
that it is possible to use the low battery signal in the same manner that
the other signals are used. The output from pin 5 on the UPS should go
to the pin on which you are reading the LowBatt signal into the computer.
When that line goes high, the battery is running out of charge. When
the situation is normal, that line will be low. (Hi/Lo in a standard
RS-232 signal, just like the other lines.)

What they don't tell you in the APC manual, and they should, is that
you need to buy a 10 KOhm resistor (50 cents at Radio Shack) and connect
pins 5 and 8 on the UPS side using the resistor. Pin 8 provides the
"common referenced supply no greater than 40vdc". Here's how you would
make the cable (the 1st three lines are the same as the HOWTO):

```
          PC side                        UPS side
pin     7 <----------------------------> 1              ShutDownUPS
        1 <----------------------------> 2              LineFail
        5 <----------------------------> 4 (same as 9 ) GND
        ? your choice  <---------------> 5              LowBatt
                                         |
                                       > 10
                                       <   KOhm
                                         |
                                         8
```

So then when the LowBatt line is HIGH then the computer has 2 minutes
to shut down before the battery runs out.

This is not mentioned in the Back-UPS HOWTO nor is it addressed in the
backupsd source. However I would think that it would be a Good Thing
to have in there; especially since a power failure would not require
a shutdown unless the UPS batteries were low. In most cases it would
mean that the backupsd could send a warning to everyone if the LineFails,
and give everyone a one (or two) minute warning when the batteries start
running down.

As far as I know this applies to all the APC Back-UPS and Smart-UPS
products. These instructions were for a Smart-UPS 900,1250, and 2000
according to the NT KB. However they have been tested with a Back-UPS
400 running Windows NT and everything works properly...

I'd sure like to have a backupsd that handled the LowBatt situation too.
Does anyone feel like modifying the backupsd.c source so that it will do
this too? (I can't program in C yet...)

P.S. The APC manual says to use only pin 4 as the common and even though
in the diagram it says that pin 9 is connected to pin 4 you might want to
be sure and use pin 4 . This differs from the instructions in the HOWTO.

P.P.S. I mailed this to the Back-UPS HOWTO authors.

--
Jim   (ockers@umr.edu)   Ask me about Linux!
http://www.umr.edu/~ockers/ - home page

From: Peter Kammer <pkammer@liege.ICS.UCI.EDU>
To: "Harvey J. Stein" <hjstein@math.huji.ac.il>
cc: "Christian G. Holtje" <docwhat@uiuc.edu>
Subject: UPS-Howto--minor correction
Date: Mon, 07 Oct 1996 12:00:16 -0700

Mr. Stein,

Let me first thank you for putting together and maintaining the
Linux UPS-HowTo document. I recently attached a APC Back-UPS 400 to a
a Linux box and the document turned out to be very helpful.

I would like to suggest a correction to the the text diagrams which
accompany the description in section 11.5.2. The diagrams are presented as
being the rear of the plug. This in mind, the diagram of the male is
backwards:

```
      ---------------------      Male Side! (This goes into the UPS)
      \  B   R  *   *   * /
       \  *   *   *  G  /
        ------------
```

From the rear, the pins on the male connector are numbered
right-to-left. The correct diagram should be:

```
      ---------------------      Male Side! (This goes into the UPS)
      \  *   *   *  R  B /
       \  G  *   *   * /
        ------------
```

Similarly, the numbered diagram should be labeled as for the rear of the
female plug.

```
        ----------------------
        \  1   2   3   4   5 /
         \  6   7   8   9  /
          ------------
```

The rear of the male is numbered the reverse:

```
        ----------------------
        \  5   4   3   2   1 /
         \  9   8   7   6  /
          ------------
```

This caused us some confusion until we realized our mistake. With four
different configurations to be aware of (front, rear) x (male, female) it
is easy to get confused. Even now, reference in hand, I keep reexamining
my diagrams.

It might also be helpful to add a reference to the APC technical document
for the Back-UPS line which is available on-line at:

    http://www.apcc.com/english/techs/techref4/224e.htm

Once we corrected our wiring, setting up the software was relatively simple
thanks to your documentation. We used the alternative (using TD to kill
the UPS power rather than RTS) wiring scheme and ran into few problems.
Your efforts in maintaining this information are much appreciated.

```
------------
Peter Kammer                       Dept. of Information and Computer Science
pkammer@ics.uci.edu                University of California
http://www.ics.uci.edu/~pkammer/   Irvine, CA 92697-3425
```

APC Back-UPS Pro 650

```
From: Troy Muller <tmuller@agora.rdrop.com>
Sender: tmuller@napalm.it.wsu.edu
To: abel@netvision.net.il
Subject: APC Back-UPS Pro 650
Date: Sun, 06 Apr 1997 12:50:40 -0700

Dear Mr. Stein,

I have a Back-UPS Pro 650 from APC and finally got it working with a
standard APC cable.

I used cable number 940-0023A and Enhanced_APC_BackUPS software.  My
only grudge is the software broadcasts every 2 seconds, but hacking the
dowall.c code to sleep 10 sec before broadcasting seems to limit it to
every 10 seconds with a 2-3 message queued to be printed (ie. much more
acceptable).
```

8.13.2   APC Smart-UPS

Many people have APC Smart UPSs. There seem to be packages for using them in smart modes (see the afore mentioned packages `Enhanced_APC_UPSD-v1.4.tar.gz`, `apcd-0.5.tar.gz`, and `smupsd-0.7-1.i386.rpm` described in section 4 (Software)). I don't know how the support in each package is. It seems that APC **still** refuses to release the protocol for the "smart" mode without a non-disclosure agreement, so everyone's left reverse engineering it.

The general consensus is to buy from a brand which does release the information, such as Best.

Another possibility is to run the SCO Unix version of APC's Powerchute UPS control software under Linux via the iBCS compatibility package. I'm told by Clive A. Stubbings (*cas@vjet.demon.co.uk*) that this works nicely after some install script adjustments. He says that the only problem is "the GUI stuff seems to have difficulty controlling non-local UPSs across the net".

If you have an APC Smart-UPS, and you can't get any of the above software to work in smart mode, you can still use it in dumb mode. The following sections detail how to do that. In particular, I've received messages from people regarding the Model 600, the Model 700, and the model 1400. You'll probably have to hack `powerd.c` as outlined in section 6.2 (Reverse-engineering cables and hacking powerd.c).

APC Smart-UPS, Model 600

```
From dangit@netcom.com Mon Aug 22 10:16:23 1994
Newsgroups: comp.os.linux.misc
Subject: UPS Monitoring Cable For APC
From: dangit@netcom.com (Lam Dang)
Date: Fri, 19 Aug 1994 11:56:28 GMT
Organization: NETCOM On-line Communication Services (408 261-4700 guest)
X-Newsreader: TIN [version 1.2 PL1]

[Didn't make it the first time.]

A few netters have asked about UPS monitoring cables.  This is what I
```

found when I made one for my APC Smart-UPS, Model 600. A disclaimer is in order. This is just an experimenter's report; use it at your own risks. Please read the User's Manual first, especially Section 6.4, Computer Interface Port.

The cable is to run between a 9-pin female connector on the UPS and a 25-pin male connector on the PC. Since I cut off one end of a 9-pin cable and replaced it with a 25-pin connector, I had to be VERY CAREFUL ABOUT PIN NUMBERS. The 25-pin hood is big enough to contain a voltage regulator and two resistors. I got all the materials (listed below) from Radio Shack for less than 10 bucks. As required by Windows NT Advanced Server 3.5 (Beta 2), the "interface" between the UPS connector and the PC connector is as follows:

```
   UPS (9-pin)              PC (25-pin)

   1 (Shutdown)             20 (DTR)
   3 (Line Fail)            5 (CTS)
   4 (Common)               7 (GND)
   5 (Low Battery)          8 (DCD)
   9 (Chassis Ground)       1 (Chassis Ground)
```

This is pretty straightforward. You can use UPS pin 6 instead of 3 (they're the inverse of each other). The complication is in pulling up UPS open collector pins 3 (or 6) and 5.

This APC model provides an unregulated output of 24 Vdc at UPS pin 8. The output voltage is available all the time (at least until some time after Low Battery has been signalled). The supply is limited to 40 mA. To pull up, UPS pin 8 is input to a +5 Vdc voltage regulator. The output of the regulator goes into two 4.7K resistors. The other end of one resistor connects both UPS pin 3 (Line Fail) and PC pin 5 (CTS). That of the other resistor connects both UPS pin 5 (Low Battery) and PC pin 8 (DCD). The two resistors draw about 2 mA when closed.

Test your cable without connecting it to the PC. When the UPS is on line, pins 5 (CTS) and 8 (DCD) at the PC end of the cable should be very close to 5 Vdc, and applying a high to pin 20 (DTR) for 5 seconds should have no effect. Now pull the power plug to put the UPS on battery. Pin 5 (CTS) should go down to zero Vdc, pin 8 (DCD) should stay the same at 5 Vdc, and applying a high to pin 20 (DTR), e.g., by shorting pins 8 and 20, should shut down the UPS after about 15 seconds.

Keep the UPS on battery until Low Battery is lighted on its front panel. Now pin 8 (DCD) should go down to zero Vdc too. Wait until the UPS battery is recharged. Then connect your cable to the PC, disable the UPS option switches by turning all of them ON, and run your favorite UPS monitoring software.

For those who want to run it with Windows NT Advanced Server, the UPS interface voltages are NEGATIVE for both power failure (using UPS pin 3) and low battery conditions, and POSITIVE for remote shutdown. Serial line parameters such as baud rate don't matter.

I haven't tested my cable with Linux powerd. When you do, please let us

know. I run NT as often as Linux on the same PC. I must conform to NT's
UPS scheme. Perhaps somebody can modify powerd to work with it and post
the source code here.

List of materials:

        1 shielded D-sub connector hood (Radio Shack 276-1510)
        1 25-pin female D-sub crimp-type connector (276-1430)
        1 7805 +5Vdc voltage regulator (276-1770)
        2 4.7K resistors
        1 component perfboard (276-148)
        1 cable with at least one 9-pin male connector.

You'll need a multimeter, a soldering iron, and a couple of hours.

Hope this helps.

Regards,

--
Lam Dang
dangit@netcom.com

APC Smart-UPS 700   Here're some details for running an APC Smart-UPS 700 in dumb mode.

It has a clever usage of a transistor in the cable so that the UPS will turn off when the computer is turned off. And it
includes a powerd.c which also does a fast low battery shutdown.

Also, note that Markus' is also using init's new capabilities. So we have here another illustration of how to use the new
init to your advantage.

    From: Markus Eiden <Markus@eiden.de>
    Sender: eiden@eiden.de
    To: "Harvey J. Stein" <abel@netvision.net.il>
    Subject: Re: APC Smart-UPS
    Date: Sun, 30 Mar 1997 16:21:05 +0200

    I'm using an APC Smart-UPS 700 for my Linux box, running 2.0.21 on an
    ASUS-Board.

    To use some features of the UPS you need four things:

    1) You have to build a RS232-cable with a small interface.
    2) You need the powerd-source from the sysvinit-package (I use version 2.65
       from Miquel van Smoorenburg). Then you have to patch his powerd.
    3) You have to change your /etc/inittab
    4) You need a script to run some commands if the power is down or battery
       is low.

    Some features:

    When the power goes down, a script will start and a syslog-entry is done.

    If the battery is low, an other script will start

(which shutdown your computer of course) and a syslog-entry is done.

If you shutdown your computer and the power is down, the UPS will be shut down too.

1)Let's start with the cable:
=================================

If you have a look at the back side of you UPS you will see a female connector like this:

```
            8                    1: Shutdown the UPS when the power is down and
                                    pin 1 is high.
    X   X   X   X                 3: Goes low on "Linefail"
  X   X   X   X   X               4: GND
                                  5: Goes low on  "Low battery"
  1       3   4   5               8: +24V
```

On the other hand at the back side of your PC there exist a male connector like this:

```
      8       6                  1: DCD
    X   X   X   X                 4: DTR
  X   X   X   X   X               5: GND
  5   4           1               6: DSR
                                  8: CTS
```

You have to build the following interface between these connectors:

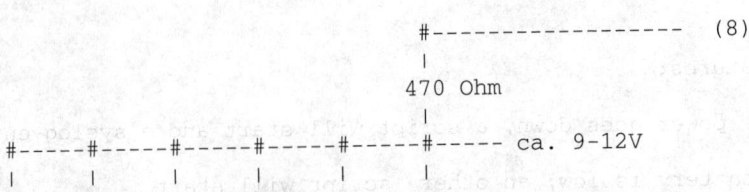

```
PC                                                                UPS


                                    #------------------ (8)
                                    |
                                    470 Ohm
                                    |
    #-----#-----#-----#-----#-----#----- ca. 9-12V
    |     |     |     |     |     |
```

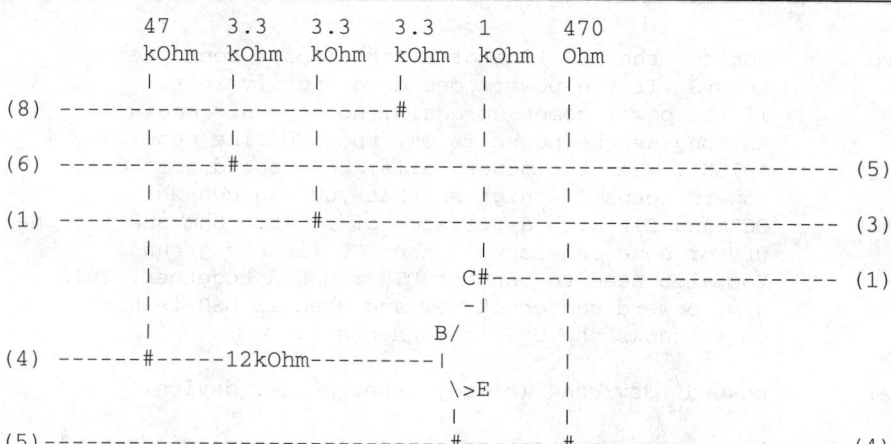

```
                    47    3.3   3.3   3.3   1     470
                    kOhm  kOhm  kOhm  kOhm  kOhm  Ohm
                     |     |     |     |     |     |
    (8) ------------------------#     |     |     |
                     |     |     |     |     |     |
    (6) ------------#----------------------------------------------- (5)
                     |     |     |     |     |     |
    (1) ------------------#--------------------------------------- (3)
                     |     |     |           |     |
                     |     |     |          C#------------------------- (1)
                     |     |     |          -|     |
                     |     |     |          B/     |
    (4) ------#-----12kOhm---------|              |
                                   \>E     |     |
                                    |     |
    (5)---------------------------------#-------#------------------- (4)
```

-I use a "BC140" - transistor, but nearly any simple NPN-transistor
 should work ;-)

-The transistor works as an "inverter". If you shutdown your PC,
 AND the power ist down, then pin 4(PC) goes low and 1(UPS) goes
 high. This shuts down the UPS for saving batteries power.

 2) The powerd-Source:
 =========================

I patched the powerd-source very little (so it is really the source
of Miquel).

(a) Give an "alert" to the syslogd if 8(PC, CTS) is down (Cause
     the cable is not connected)

(b) DCD droped to zero => power has failed => call powerfail(0)
     => Give INIT_CMD_POWERFAIL to the init-process

(c) DCD comes up again => power is back => call powerfail(1)
     => Give INIT_CMD_POWEROK to the init-process

(d) DSR and DCD are dropped to zero => power has failed and
     battery is low => call powerfail(2) => Give
     INIT_CMD_POWERFAILNOW to the init-process

 Thats it.

--------------------------->8---- Schnipp ----------------------------

```c
/*
 * powerd       Monitor the DCD line of a serial port connected to
 *              an UPS. If the power goes down, notify init.
 *              If the power comes up again, notify init again.
 *              As long as the power is OK, the DCD line should be
 *              "HIGH". When the power fails, DCD should go "LOW".
 *              Powerd keeps DTR high so that you can connect
 *              DCD and DTR with a resistor of 10 Kilo Ohm and let the
 *              UPS or some relais pull the DCD line to ground.
 *              You also need to connect DTR and DSR together. This
 *              way, powerd can check now and then if DSR is high
 *              so it knows the UPS is connected!!
 *
 * Usage:       powerd /dev/cua4 (or any other serial device).
 *
 * Author:      Miquel van Smoorenburg, <miquels@drinkel.cistron.nl>.
 *              Some minor changes by Markus Eiden, <Markus@Eiden.de>
 *              for the APC-Smart-UPS-powerd.
 *
 * Version:     1.31,  29-Feb-1996.
 *
 *              This program was originally written for my employer,
 *                      ** Cistron Electronics **
 *              who has given kind permission to release this program
 *              for general puppose.
 *
 *              Copyright 1991-1996 Cistron Electronics.
 *
 *              This program is free software; you can redistrib-
ute it and/or
 *              modify it under the terms of the GNU General Public License
 *              as published by the Free Software Foundation; either version
 *              2 of the License, or (at your option) any later version.
 *
 *              Some minor changes for the APC-powerd by Markus Eiden
 *              Markus@Eiden.de
 */

/* Use the new way of communicating with init. */
#define NEWINIT

#include <sys/types.h>
#include <sys/stat.h>
#include <sys/ioctl.h>
#include <fcntl.h>
#include <errno.h>
#include <stdlib.h>
#include <unistd.h>
#include <stdio.h>
#include <signal.h>
#include <syslog.h>
#include <string.h>
#include "paths.h"
#ifdef NEWINIT
#include "initreq.h"
```

```
#endif

#ifndef SIGPWR
#   define SIGPWR SIGUSR1
#endif

#ifdef NEWINIT
void alrm_handler()
{
}
#endif

/* Tell init the power has either gone or is back. */
void powerfail(ok)
int ok;
{
  int fd;
#ifdef NEWINIT
  struct init_request req;

  /* Fill out the request struct. */
  memset(&req, 0, sizeof(req));
  req.magic = INIT_MAGIC;


  /* INIT_CMD_* are definied in initreq.h               *
   * Have a look at  init.c and /etc/inittab            *
   *                                                    *
   * ok=0 -> INIT_CMD_POWERFAIL      -> powerwait       *
   * ok=1 -> INIT_CMD_POWEROK        -> powerokwait     *
   * ok=2 -> INIT_CMD_POWERFAILNOW   -> powerfailnow    */


  switch (ok) {
    case 0 : req.cmd = INIT_CMD_POWERFAIL;
             /* Linefail -> warning */
             break;
    case 1 : req.cmd = INIT_CMD_POWEROK;
             /* Power is back -> cancel warning */
             break;
    case 2 : req.cmd = INIT_CMD_POWERFAILNOW;
             /* Linefail and LowBatt -> reboot */
             break;
             }

  /* Open the fifo (with timeout) */
  signal(SIGALRM, alrm_handler);
  alarm(3);
  if ((fd = open(INIT_FIFO, O_WRONLY)) >= 0
                && write(fd, &req, sizeof(req)) == sizeof(req)) {
        close(fd);
        return;
  }
  /* Fall through to the old method.. */
#endif
```

```
        /* Create an info file for init. */
        unlink(PWRSTAT);
        if ((fd = open(PWRSTAT, O_CREAT|O_WRONLY, 0644)) >= 0) {
                if (ok)
                        write(fd, "OK\n", 3);
                else
                        write(fd, "FAIL\n", 5);
                close(fd);
        }
        kill(1, SIGPWR);
}

/* Main program. */
int main(int argc, char **argv)
{
    int fd;
    int dtr_bit = TIOCM_DTR;
    int flags;
    int status, oldstat = -1;
    int count = 0;
    int tries = 0;
    int powerfailed = 0;
    int rebootnow   = 0;

    if (argc < 2) {
            fprintf(stderr, "Usage: powerd <device>\n");
            exit(1);
    }

    /* Start syslog. */
    openlog("powerd", LOG_CONS|LOG_PERROR, LOG_DAEMON);

    /* Open monitor device. */
    if ((fd = open(argv[1], O_RDWR | O_NDELAY)) < 0) {
            syslog(LOG_ERR, "%s: %s", argv[1], sys_errlist[errno]);
            closelog();
            exit(1);
    }

    /* Line is opened, so DTR is high. Force it anyway to be sure. */

    /* USE: low Batt -> Reboot -> DTR goes low               *
     * transistor is open -> shutdown-pin  of the UPS goes   *
     * high -> UPS goes down after about 20s. If there is a  *
     * linefail and the computer is off, the                 *
     * UPS goes down. If the power is back, the              *
     * UPS goes on, the computer boots, and powerd           *
     * is startet.                                           */

    /* Verwendung: Die UPS meldet low Batt -> Reboot -> DTR geht    *
     * auf Low -> Transistor oeffnet -> Shutdown der UPS geht auf   *
     * High -> UPS schaltet sich nach circa 20s aus. Bei jedem      *
     * Linefail und ausgeschaltetem Computer, schaltet sich die     *
     * UPS aus. Kommt der Strom zurueck, dann schaltet sich die     *
```

```
 * UPS selbstaendig ein, der Computer bootet, und der powerd   *
 * wird gestartet.                                             */

ioctl(fd, TIOCMBIS, &dtr_bit);




/* Daemonize. */
switch(fork()) {
     case 0: /* Child */
             closelog();
             setsid();
             break;
     case -1: /* Error */
             syslog(LOG_ERR, "can't fork.");
             closelog();
             exit(1);
     default: /* Parent */
             closelog();
             exit(0);
}


/* Restart syslog. */
openlog("powerd", LOG_CONS, LOG_DAEMON);

 syslog(LOG_INFO, "APCpowerd started...");

/* Now sample the DCD line. */
while(1) {
     /* Get the status. */
     ioctl(fd, TIOCMGET, &flags);

     /* Check the connection: CTS should be high. */
     tries = 0;
     /* TIOCM_*- have a look at   .../ams/termios.h */
     while((flags & TIOCM_CTS) == 0) {
             /* Keep on trying, and warn every two minutes. */
             if ((tries % 60) == 0)
                 syslog(LOG_ALERT, "UPS connection error");
             sleep(2);
             tries++;
             ioctl(fd, TIOCMGET, &flags);
     }
     if (tries > 0)
             syslog(LOG_ALERT, "UPS connection OK");

     /* Calculate present status. */
     status = (flags & TIOCM_CAR);

     /* Did DCD drop to zero? Then the power has failed. */
     if (oldstat != 0 && status == 0) {
             count++;
             if (count > 3) {
                     powerfailed = 1;
```

HOWTO

```
                        powerfail(0);
                        }
            else {
                        sleep(1);
                        continue;
                }
        }
        /* Did DCD come up again? Then the power is back. */
        if (oldstat == 0 && status > 0) {
                count++;
                if (count > 3) {
                        powerfailed = 0;

                        /* eigentlich unnoetig: */
                        rebootnow = 0;

                        powerfail(1);
                        }
                else {
                        sleep(1);
                        continue;
                }
        }

        /* Low battery and Linefail ? */
        if (rebootnow==0)
        if (powerfailed==1)
        if ((flags & TIOCM_DSR) == 0)
        {
            rebootnow=1;
            powerfail(2);

        }

        /* Reset count, remember status and sleep 2 seconds. */
        count = 0;
        oldstat = status;
        sleep(2);
    }
    /* Never happens */
    return(0);
}
```

------------------- schnap ------------ 8<-----------------------------

3) Change your inittab:
=========================

Init gets the INIT_CMDs and will start a script:

```
pf::powerwait:/sbin/init.d/powerfail    start
pn::powerfailnow:/sbin/init.d/powerfail now
po::powerokwait:/sbin/init.d/powerfail  stop
```

(Which means for example: if the power has failed (powerwait) start the
script /sbin/init.d/powerfail with the parameter "start".)

4) The powerfail-Script
==========================

----------------- 8< ------- schnipp ---------------

```
#! /bin/sh
# Copyright (c) 1997 Markus Eiden, Markus@Eiden.de
#

case "$1" in
    start)
        echo "THE POWER IS DOWN!" | wall
        logger "Powerfail"
        ;;
    now)
        echo "BATTERY IS LOW! Shutdown in 1 minute" | wall
        logger "Battery is low, shutdown in 1 minute"
        sync
        /sbin/shutdown -r -t 5 +1
        ;;
    stop)
        echo "THE POWER IS BACK!!" | wall
        logger "Power is back"

        /sbin/shutdown -c >/dev/null 2>/dev/null

        ;;
  *)
        echo "Usage: $0 {start|now|stop}"
        exit 1
        ;;
esac

exit 0
```

-------------------- >8 ---------- schnapp -------------

Well, that should be easy ;-)

You are ready now, but be careful: It works for me, but I really can't
guarantee that any of this will work for you.

Some advice at the end: If /sbin/init.d/powerfail shuts down your
PC then DTR goes down, so the shutdown pin (UPS) goes high.
>From that time it takes about 20 or 30 seconds for the UPS to shut down.

It is your job to prevent your Linux-box from booting within these 20 seconds (in particular to mount the filesystem). On my system it was no problem. There are four easy ways to prevent the PC from the fast booting:

1) The BIOS should do some routines (Like searching the number of tracks of your floppydisk if you have one)

2) If you have LILO installed, tell him to wait.

3) You do nothing (like I did)

4) You buy some more memory so that counting the memory takes 30 seconds. That should be about 1024 Megabytes ;-).

Markus Eiden

Markus@Eiden.de


```
--
-----------------------------------------------------------------------
StR Dipl.-Ing. Markus Eiden  \\://              Markus@eiden.de
Am alten Sportplatz 3            (o -)      http://www.rp.schule.de/eiden/
D-67599 Gundheim         ---ooO-(_)-Ooo---         NIC-HDL: ME256-RIPE
```

APC Smart-UPS 1400   Another day, another APC. This is for the Smart-UPS 1400, in dumb mode.

```
From: "Slavik Terletsky" <ts@polynet.lviv.ua>
To: hjstein@math.huji.ac.il
Subject: my contribution to UPS HOWTO
Date: Mon, 27 Jan 1997 21:10:16 +0000


Hello
I just hacked ups daemon, if you want, you may enclose it
in your UPS HOWTO document (i used some info from).
Please replay.
--

UPS daemon for FreeBSD (2.1.5 - tested).
Interacts with APC Smart-UPS 1400.

Connection scheme:

UPS (pin, signal name)              PC (pin, signal name)
----------------------              ---------------------

1 Shutdown          >------------>  4 Data Terminal Ready
2 Line Failed       >------------>  8 Clear To Send
4 Common            >------------>  5 Ground
5 Battery Low       >--------+-->  1 Data Carrier Detector
8 Battery (+24V)    >--|10K|-+

UPSD DESCRIPTION
```

```
usage: upsd <device> [wait [script]]

device  - device name upsd interacts thru (e.g. /dev/cuaa1)
wait    - time (secs) to wait before running script, (default value 0 sec).
script  - system shutdown script (default /etc/rc.shutdown).

Actions:
upsd logs all the changes of UPS status (power {up,down}, battery {low,ok}).
When "power down" and "battery low" upsd activates UPS SHUTDOWN signal,
waits for a <wait> seconds, and then runs system shutdown script - <script>.

Script sample:

#!/bin/sh
# Script is executed when system is going down.

PATH=/sbin:/bin:/usr/sbin:/usr/bin

echo "System is going DOWN right NOW" | wall

reboot


Upsd source:
/* UPS daemon
 * Copyright 1997 Slavik Terletsky. All rights reserved.
 * Author: Slavik Terletsky <ts@polynet.lviv.ua>
 * System: FreeBSD
 */
#include <stdio.h>
#include <stdlib.h>
#include <signal.h>
#include <syslog.h>
#include <unistd.h>
#include <varargs.h>
#include <fcntl.h>
#include <errno.h>
#include <sys/uio.h>
#include <sys/types.h>
#include <sys/ioctl.h>
#include <sys/ttycom.h>

int status;
int wait = 0;
FILE *fd;
char *scr = "/etc/rc.shutdown";
char *idf = "/var/run/upsd.pid";

void upsterm();
void upsdown(int);

int main(int argc, char *argv[]) {
 int pd;
 int zero = 0;
 char d5, d6, d7;
```

```
char low = 0;
char pow = 1;

/* check arguments */
switch(argc) {
case  4:
scr = argv[3];
case  3:
wait = atoi(argv[2]);
case  2:
break;
default:
fprintf(stderr, "usage: %s <device> [wait [script]]\n", argv[0]);
exit(1);
}

/* check if script exists */
if(!(fd = fopen(scr, "r"))) {
fprintf(stderr, "fopen: %s: %s\n", scr, sys_errlist[errno]);
exit(1);
}
fclose(fd);

/* check if upsd is already running */
if(fd = fopen(idf, "r")) {
fprintf(stderr, "fopen: %s: File already exists\n", idf);
exit(1);
}

/* become a daemon */
switch(fork()) {
case -1:        /* error */
fprintf(stderr, "fork: %s\n", sys_errlist[errno]);
exit(1);
case  0:        /* child */
break;
default:        /* parent */
exit(0);
}

/* save the pid */
if(!(fd = fopen(idf, "w"))) {
fprintf(stderr, "fopen: %s: %s\n", idf, sys_errlist[errno]);
exit(1);
}
fprintf(fd, "%d\n", (int)getpid());
fclose(fd);

/* open monitor device */
if((pd = open(argv[1], O_RDWR | O_NDELAY)) < 0) {
fprintf(stderr, "open: %s: %s\n", argv[1], sys_errlist[errno]);
exit(1);
}

/* daemon is alive */
```

```
openlog("upsd", LOG_PID, LOG_DAEMON);
syslog(LOG_INFO, "daemon started");

/* signal reaction */
(void)signal(SIGTERM, upsterm);

/* monitor device */
while(1) {
/* clear bits */
if(ioctl(pd, TIOCMSET, &zero) < 0) {
 fprintf(stderr, "ioctl: %s\n", sys_errlist[errno]);
 exit(1);
}

/* get device status */
if(ioctl(pd, TIOCMGET, &status) < 0) {
 fprintf(stderr, "ioctl: %s\n", sys_errlist[errno]);
 exit(1);
}

/* determin status */
d5 = status & 0x20;
d6 = status & 0x40;
d7 = status & 0x80;

/* power up */
if(!(d7 + d5)) {
 if(!pow) {
  syslog(LOG_CRIT, "power up");
  pow = 1;
 }
/* power down */
} else {
 if(pow) {
  syslog(LOG_CRIT, "power down");
  pow = 0;
 }
}

/* battery low */
if(!d6 && !low) {
 syslog(LOG_ALERT, "battery low");
 low = 1;

 /* down ups */
 if(!pow) {
  upsdown(pd);
 }
}

/* battery ok */
if(d6 && low) {
 syslog(LOG_CRIT, "battery ok");
 low = 0;
}
```

```
    sleep(1);
    }

    /* not reached */
    return 0;

}

void upsterm() {
    /* log termination message */
    syslog(LOG_INFO, "daemon terminated");

    /* remove pid file */
    unlink(idf);

    exit(0);
}

void upsdown(int pd) {
    /* log shutdown message */
    syslog(LOG_ALERT, "system is going down");

    /* remove pid file */
    unlink(idf);

    /* save our filesystem */
    system("/bin/sync");
    system("/bin/sync");
    system("/bin/sync");

    /* shutdown ups */
    status = TIOCM_DTR;
    if(ioctl(pd, TIOCMSET, &status) < 0) {
    fprintf(stderr, "ioctl: %s\n", sys_errlist[errno]);
    exit(1);
    }

    /* wait and then run script */
    sleep(wait);
    system(scr);
}
# Slavik Terletsky       # University "Lvivska Poytechnika" #
# Network Administrator # mailto:ts@polynet.lviv.ua         #
```

9 How to shutdown other machines on the same UPS

Some people (myself included) have several computers running Linux connected to one UPS. One computer monitors the UPS and needs to get the other computers to shut down when the power goes out.

We assume the computers can communicate over a network. Call the computer that monitors the UPS the master and the other computers the slaves.

In the old days this required some fancy programming.

These days, the best thing to do is to pick up either the `powerd-2.0.tar.gz` package or the `upsd-1.0.tgz` package (see section 4 (Software)), and follow the instructions. Both are able to run on the slaves in a mode where they connect over the network to a `powerd` or `upsd` process running on the master to query the status of the UPS. Some of the APC specific packages seem to have this ability too.

Note, though, that if your network is insecure, you might want to add a little security to this, lest someone spoof the slave `powerd` processes into thinking that the power is out.

Another possibility is to go for SNMP (Simple Network Management Protocol). Detailing the use of SNMP is beyond the scope of this document, not to mention currently being beyond me.

HOWTO

Part XLV

"The Linux UUCP HOWTO" Guylhem Aznar

<guylhem at oeil.qc.ca>

v2.0, 6 February 1998

This document describes the setup, care & feeding of UUCP under Linux. You need to read this if you plan to connect to remote sites via UUCP via a modem, via a direct-connection, or via Internet. You probably do *not* need to read this document if don't talk UUCP or if you don't know what it means.

Contents

HOWTO

1   Introduction, copyright & standard disclaimer

1.1   Email & spamming

First, convert all "at" in Emails addresses given in this document into "@".

It's simple for humans, but not for bots searching the web to spam ; therefore it's enough to protect generous contributors from being spammed.

1.2   Goals

The intent of this document is to answer some of the questions & comments that appear to meet the definition of "frequently asked questions" about UUCP software under Linux genrally & the version in the Linux Debian and RedHat distributions in particular.

1.3   New versions

New versions of this document will be periodically posted to comp.os.linux.announce, comp.answers & news.answers. They will also be added to the various anonymous ftp sites who archive such information including *sunsite FTP* <http://sunsite.unc.edu:/pub/Linux/docs/HOWTO>.

In addition, you should be generally able to find this document on the Linux WorldWideWeb home page at *the LDP page* <http://sunsite.unc.edu/LDP/>.

1.4   Feedback

I am interested in any feedback (please e-mail), positive or negative, regarding the content of this document. Definitely contact me if you find errors or obvious omissions.

I read, but do not necessarily respond to, all e-mail I receive. Requests for enhancements will be considered & acted upon based on that day's combination of available time, merit of the request & daily blood pressure :-)

Flames will quietly go to /dev/null so don't bother.

Feedback concerning the actual format of the document should go to the HOWTO coordinator: Greg Hankins (`gregh at sunsite.unc.edu`).

1.5   Copyright

The UUCP-HOWTO is copyrighted (c)1997 Guylhem Aznar. Distributed under LDP copyright license. If you have questions, please contact Greg Hankins, the Linux HOWTO coordinator, at `gregh at sunsite.unc.edu`.

1.6   Limited warranty

Of course, I disavow any potential liability for the contents of this document. Use of the concepts, examples, &/ or other content of this document is entirely at your own risk.

2   Other sources of information

2.1   USENET

There is nothing "special" about configuring & running UUCP under Linux (any more). Accordingly, you almost certainly do *NOT* want to be posting generic UUCP-related questions to the comp.os.linux.* newsgroups.

Don't post in comp.os.linux hierarchy unless it's really linux specific, for example: "What's wrong with Debian 1.2 uucp?" or "RedHat 5.0 uucp crashes when I run it" ...

Let me repeat that.

There is virtually no reason to post anything uucp-related in the comp.os.linux hierarchy any more. There are existing newsgroups in the comp.mail.* hierarchy to handle *ALL* your questions.

IF YOU POST TO COMP.OS.LINUX. FOR NON-LINUX-SPECIFIC QUESTIONS, YOU ARE LOOKING IN THE WRONG PLACE FOR HELP. THE UUCP EXPERTS HANG OUT IN THE PLACES INDICATED ABOVE AND GENERALLY DO NOT RUN LINUX.*

POSTING TO THE LINUX HIERARCHY FOR NON-LINUX-SPECIFIC QUESTIONS WASTES YOUR TIME AND EVERYONE ELSE'S AND IT FREQUENTLY DELAYS YOU FROM GETTING THE ANSWER TO YOUR QUESTION.

The GOOD PLACE is `comp.mail.uucp` since you can get answers for most of your UUCP questions.

2.2   Mailing Lists

There is a Taylor UUCP mailing list.

To join (or get off) the list, send mail to

> `taylor-uucp-request@gnu.ai.mit.edu`

This request goes to a person, not to a program, so please make sure that you include the address at which you want to receive mail in the text of the message.

To send a message to the list, send it to

> `taylor-uucp@gnu.ai.mit.edu`

2.3   Other documents from LDP

There is plenty of exceptional material provided in the other Linux HOWTO documents & from the Linux DOC project.

In particular, you might want to take a look at the following:

- on your own computer in /usr/doc/uucp & /usr/info/uucp* :-)
- the Linux Networking Administrators' Guide
- the Serial Communications HOWTO
- the Ethernet HOWTO
- the News HOWTO
- the Mail HOWTO

2.4   Books

HDB & V2 versions of UUCP are documented in about every vendor's documentation as well as in almost all *nix communications books.

Taylor config. files are currently only documented in the info files provided with the sources (& in your distribution hopefully). The following is a non-inclusive set of books that will help.

- `"Managing UUCP & USENET"` from O'Reilly & Associates is in my opinion the best book out there for figuring out the programs & protocols involved in being a USENET site.
- `"Unix Communications"` from The Waite Group contains a nice description of all the pieces (& more) & how they fit together.
- `"Practical Unix Security"` from O'Reilly & Associates has a nice discussion of how to secure UUCP.
- `"The Internet Complete Reference"` from Osborne is a fine reference book that explains the various services available on Internet & is a great source for information on news, mail & various other Internet resources.
- `"The Linux Networking Administrators' Guide"` from Olaf Kirch of the Linux DOC Project is available on the net & is also published by (at least) O'Reilly & SSC. It makes a fine *one-stop shopping* to learn about everything you ever imagined you'd need to know about Unix networking.

3   Requirements

3.1   Hardware

There are no specific hardware requirements for UUCP under Linux. Basically any Hayes-compatible modem works painlessly with UUCP.

In most cases, you'll want the fastest modem you can afford, i.e. 56000 bps actually. In general, you want to have a 16550 UART on your serial board or built into your modem to handle speeds of above 9600 baud.

If you don't know what that last sentence means, please consult the *comp.dcom.modems* group or the various fine modem & serial communications FAQs & periodic postings on USENET.

3.2   Software

UUCP for linux is available everywhere, for example on sunsite.unc.edu. But before trying to get any version, try to install & make your current uucp work ; there're many little differences between each linux distribution, therefore it's easier for you to configure/install your distribution's UUCP package rather than editing sources for some options, setting the right paths & permissions, installing, etc.

But if you prefer sources ...

1) Unpack

To extract a gzip'd tar archive, I do the following:

```
gunzip -c filename.tar.z | tar xvf -
```

A "modern" tar can just do a:

```
tar -zxvf filename.tgz
```

2) Run "configure"

Type "`sh configure`".

The configure script will compile a number of test programs to see what is available on your system & will calculate many things.

The configure script will create `conf.h` from conf.h.in & `Makefile` from Makefile.in. It will also create config.status, which is a shell script which actually creates the files.

3) Decide where to install

Rather than editing the Makefile.in file in the sources you can get the same effect by:

```
"configure --prefix=/usr/lib"
```

4) Edit "policy.h" for your local system

- - set the type of lockfiles you want (HAVE_HDB_LOCKFILES)
- - set the type of config files you want built in (HAVE_TAYLOR_CONFIG, HAVE_V2_CONFIG, HAVE_HDB_CONFIG)
- - set the type of spool directory structure you want (SPOOLDIR_HDB)
- - set the type of logging you want (HAVE_HDB_LOGGING)
- - set the default search path for commands (I added /usr/local/bin to mine)

5) Then compile & install the software

- Type "`make`" to compile.
- Type "`make install`" to install.

4   Setting up the config files

I recommend you start by installing the attached known-good config. files included in the document.

4.1   Installing config. files

Put these file in their "standard" location: `/etc/uucp` on recent linux distributions or `/usr/lib/uucp` on older ones.

Then make sure that the `permissions` of the files are

```
(guylhem@barberouge:uucp)$ ls -l
total 11
-rw-r--r--   1 uucp      uucp       501 Jan 23 11:33 Poll
-rw-r-----   1 uucp      uucp       589 Jan 23 11:34 call
-rw-r-----   1 uucp      uucp      1184 Jan 23 12:06 config
-rw-r-----   1 uucp      uucp       476 Jan 23 12:31 crontab
-rw-r-----   1 uucp      uucp      1256 Jan 23 11:47 dial
-rw-r-----   1 uucp      uucp       486 Jan 23 11:48 passwd
-rw-r-----   1 uucp      uucp       810 Jan 23 11:55 port
-rw-r--r--   1 uucp      uucp      1690 Jan 23 12:04 sys
(guylhem@barberouge:uucp)$
```

To change file owner, as root, type:

```
(root@barberouge:uucp)$ chown uucp.uucp *
```

Then you must change file permissions; as root once again, type:

```
(root@barberouge:uucp)# chmod 640 *
(root@barberouge:uucp)# chmod +r Poll sys
```

4.2 "Poll" file

This file is used to set polling timetables for any system.

```
schedule polux 01
poll      polux 01
```

My machine calls polux at 01:00, that's all!

You can add more line if you must call many other machines, but don't forget to put the 2 lines (schedule & poll) for each.

4.3 "call" file

It contains your login/password for each system you poll:

```
polux uudan password
```

My machine uses "uudan" login & "password" password :-) when it polls "polux".

As for Poll, adapt this to your situation.

4.4 "config" file

```
nodename barberouge                      # The UUCP name of this system

spool /var/spool/uucp                    # The UUCP spool directory
pubdir /var/spool/uucppublic             # The UUCP public directory
logfile /var/log/uucp/log                # The UUCP log file
statfile /var/log/uucp/stats             # The UUCP statistics file
debugfile /var/log/uucp/debug            # The UUCP debugging file

#sysfile        /etc/uucp/sys            # Default "sys"
#portfile       /etc/uucp/port           # Default "port"
```

```
#dialfile          /etc/uucp/dial        # Default "dial"
#dialcodefile      /etc/uucp/dialcode     # Default "dialcode"
#callfile          /etc/uucp/call         # Default "call"
#passwdfile        /etc/uucp/passwd       # Default "passwd"

# No commands may be executed by unknowns (empty list of permitted commands)
# Upload is authorized in /var/spool/uucp
unknown commands
unknown pubdir /var/spool/uucp
unknown remote-send ~ !~/upload
unknown remote-receive ~/upload
```

Here just replace "barberouge" by your system name ; run "hostname" if you can't remind it.

4.5 "crontab" file

```
# Every day just before morning generate reports.
#
0 7 * * *          /usr/lib/uucp/uudemon.day root
#
# Every hour start the uudemon.hr. To actually poll a remote system,
# enter its name in /etc/uucp/Poll. You are encouraged to change the "8".
#
8 * * * *          /usr/lib/uucp/uudemon.hr
```

Just run "crontab -u uucp /etc/uucp/crontab" to add it to the others crontabs.

4.6 "dial" file

```
# 1) expect nothing (i.e., continue with step 2)
# 2) send "ATZ", then a carriage return, then sleep for 1 to 2 seconds.
# The \c means to not send a final carriage return.
# 3) wait until the modem echoes "OK", then do the the same for "ATX4" & "OK"
# 4) send "ATDT", then the telephone number (after translat-
ing any dialcodes).
# 5) wait until the modem echoes "CONNECT"
# 6) if we get "BUSY", "NO CARRIER" ... during the chat scrip-
t we abort dialing
# 7) when the call is over, we make sure we hangup the modem


dialer hayes
chat "" ATZ\r\d\c OK\r \dATX4\r\d\c OK\r ATDT\D CONNECT
chat-fail RING
chat-fail NO\sCARRIER
chat-fail ERROR
chat-fail NO\sDIALTONE
chat-fail BUSY
chat-fail NO\sANSWER
chat-fail VOICE
complete \d\d+++\d\dATH\r\c
abort \d\d+++\d\dATH\r\c


# You can also add other dialers: inetd, nullmodem ...
#dialer nullmodem
```

HOWTO

```
#complete \d\dexit\r\c
#abort \d\dexit\r\c
```

Syntax is complicated ... you'd rather not touch anything here but "ATZ" & "ATX4" which are my modem init string.

4.7 "passwd" file

```
#uuguest                    guestpassword
```

If you allow uucp dialin, just add system/passwords in this file.

It's *that* simple.

But it's recommended for security reasons to make sure each have a separate account & home directory so you can track things.

4.8 "port" file

```
# Description for the modem entry
# Debianers, make SURE this device is root:dialout, mode 0660 (crw-rw---)

port ACU
type modem
device /dev/ttyS0
dialer hayes
speed 57600
# hardflow n


# Description for the TCP port - pretty trivial. DON'T DELETE.
# Change service number if non standard, cf /etc/services

port TCP
type tcp
#service 540


# Description for the nullmodem entry
# (ttyS1 means COM2)

port nullmodem
type direct
device /dev/ttyS1
dialer nullmodem
speed 115200
```

You shouldn't change anything here ... except your modem port.

On recent distributions with mgetty, it's /dev/ttySN while on older distributions it's /dev/cuaN, where N is you serial port:

N starts at 0 & ttyS(N) means COM(N+1), for example, my null-modem is on ttyS1 (COM2) while my modem is on ttyS0 (COM1).

Most of recent modems support hardware flow control, if your doesn't, just uncomment the line "# hardflow n".

4.9   "sys" file

```
# First some defaults. These are for ALL other entries (unless overridden).
#
protocol gvG
protocol-parameter G packet-size 1024
# protocol-parameter G window 7
protocol-parameter G short-packets


#
# Our remote uucp connection.
#
system polux
call-login *
call-password *
local-send /
local-receive /var/spool/uucppublic
remote-send /
remote-receive /var/spool/uucppublic
time any
phone 0111111110
port ACU
chat "" \r\c ogin:-BREAK-ogin:-BREAK- \L word: \P
#chat "" \d\d\r\c ogin: \d\L word: \P

# This is an alternate - it means that if a connection using the above
# "system polux" fails it falls through to this entry.
# Only useful if your service provider has more then one phone num-
ber for UUCP.
#
#alternate polux-2
#alias polux-2
#phone 0222222220


# Here's another alternate - we poll the system over TCP/IP.
# This is useful if we have a PPP connection to our provider.
# The first two entries will fail because the modem is busy & we will poll
# over TCP/IP.
#
#alternate polux-tcp
#alias polux-tcp
#time any
#address uucp.polux
#port TCP
#protocol t


#
# Last example - a system that we poll over TCP/IP.
#
#system horizon
#call-login *
#call-password *
#time any
#chat "" \d\d\r\c ogin: \d\L word: \P
#address uucp.horizon.nl
```

```
#port TCP
#protocol t
```

Here, you must change "polux" by the name of the system you poll & "0111111110" by its phone number.

"polux-2", "polux-tcp" & "horizon" are just examples of user specific needs ; if the system you poll has more than one line, define it as "itsname-2" ; if you call it by PPP sometimes, just define "itsname-tcp" also.

It's useful when chat script fail (busy ...)

4.10   Now let's test all this

First run:

```
(root@barberouge:uucp)# su uucp
(uucp@barberouge:uucp)# /usr/lib/uucp/uuchk
Local node name barberouge
Spool directory /var/spool/uucp
Public directory /var/spool/uucppublic
Lock directory /var/lock
Log file /var/log/uucp/log
Statistics file /var/log/uucp/stats
Debug file /var/log/uucp/debug
Global debugging level
uucico -l will strip login names and passwords
uucico will strip UUCP protocol commands
Start uuxqt once per uucico invocation


System: polux
  When called using any login name
  Call out using port ACU
  The possible ports are:
   Port name ACU
    Port type modem
    Device /dev/ttyS0
    Speed 57600
    Carrier available
    Hardware flow control available
    Dialer hayes
     Chat script "" ATZ\r\d\c OK\r \dATX4\r\d\c OK\r ATDT\D CONNECT
     Chat script timeout 60
     Chat failure strings RING NO\sCARRIER ERROR NO\sDIALTONE BUSY
                  NO\sANSWER VOICE
     Chat script incoming bytes stripped to seven bits
     Wait for dialtone ,
     Pause while dialing ,
     Carrier available
     Wait 60 seconds for carrier
     When complete chat script "" \d\d+++\d\dATH\r\c
     When complete chat script timeout 60
     When complete chat script incoming bytes stripped to seven bits
     When aborting chat script "" \d\d+++\d\dATH\r\c
     When aborting chat script timeout 60
     When aborting chat script incoming bytes stripped to seven bits
  Phone number 0111111110
```

```
       Chat script "" \r\c ogin:-BREAK-ogin:-BREAK- \L word: \P
       Chat script timeout 10
       Chat script incoming bytes stripped to seven bits
       Login name uudan
       Password your_password_here
       At any time may call if any work
       May retry the call up to 26 times
       May make local requests when calling
       May make local requests when called
       May send by local request: /
       May send by remote request: /
       May accept by local request: /var/spool/uucppublic
       May receive by remote request: /var/spool/uucppublic
       May execute /usr/bin/uucp /usr/bin/rmail /usr/bin/rnews
       Execution path /bin /usr/bin /usr/local/bin /usr/sbin
       Will leave 50000 bytes available
       Public directory is /var/spool/uucppublic
       Will use protocols gvG
       For protocol G will use the following parameters
        packet-size 1024
        short-packets
```

to check if all the informations you've set are correct.

Warning: your mileage may vary ; different distributions use different paths, regardless Linux FSSTD!

If everything is correct, run:

```
        /usr/sbin/uucico -r 1 -x 9 -s remote_system_name
```

The -x 9 will have maximum debugging information written to the /var/log/uucp/debug file for help in initial setup.

I normally run -x 4 here since that level logs details that help me with login problems. Obviously, this text contains clear informations from your systems file (account/password) so protect it against world-read.

4.11   Additional informations

>From *Pierre.Beyssac at emeraude.syseca.fr*

Taylor has more logging levels. Use -x all to get the highest level possible.

Also, do a "tail -f /var/log/uucp/debug" while debugging to watch things happen on the fly.

5   It doesn't work - now what?

In general, you can refer to the documentation mentioned above if things don't work.

You can also refer to your more experienced UUCP neighbors for help. Usually, it's something like a typo anyway.

6 Frequently Asked Questions about Linux UUCP

6.1 Why is all the info here for UUCPs configured in "Taylor" rather than "HDB" mode?

(religious mode on - I know some people are just as religious about "ease of use" as I am about "being standard". That's why they make source code you can build your own from :-))

Because IMHO it's the de-facto standard UUCP implementation at this time. There are thousands of sites with experienced admins & there are many places you can get incredibly good information concerning the HDB setup.

Moreover, if you know what HDB is, you shouldn't be reading this HOWTO :-)

Use the `uuconv` utility in /usr/sbin to convert config files from one mode to another.

6.2 Why do I get "timeout" on connections when I upgraded to uucp-1.04?

- from *Ed Carp - erc at apple.com* If you use a "Direct" device in the Devices file, there's now a 10 second timeout compiled in. Make the name of the Device anything other than "Direct". If you tweak the example /etc/uucp files provided, you won't have problems with this one.

- from *Greg Naber - greg at squally.halcyon.com* If you get chat script timeouts, you can tweak the sources by editing at line 323 in uuconf/syssub.c & changing the default timeouts from 10 seconds to something larger.

- from *Ed Rodda - ed at orca.wimsey.bc.ca* If you get chat script timeouts, typically connecting to other Taylor sites, a pause after login can fix this.

```
feed Any ACU,ag 38400 5551212 ogin: \c\d "" yourname word: passwd
```

- from *Dr. Eberhard W. Lisse - el at lisse.NA* Some kernels experience modems hanging up after a couple of seconds. The following patch sent by Ian Taylor might help.

```
*** conn.c.orig Mon Feb 22 20:25:24 1993
--- conn.c      Mon Feb 22 20:33:10 1993
***************
*** 204,209 ****
--- 204,212 ----

      /* Make sure any signal reporting has been done before we set
         fLog_sighup back to TRUE.  */
+     /* SMR: it seems to me if we don't care about SIGHUP-
S, we should clear
+        the flag before we return */
+     afSignal[INDEXSIG_SIGHUP] = FALSE;
      ulog (LOG_ERROR, (const char *) NULL);
      fLog_sighup = TRUE;
```

6.3 Why doesn't HDB anonymous uucp seem to work?

Taylor in HDB mode seems to be sensitive to white space & blank lines. To be safe, make sure that there are no blank lines or trailing spaces in the Permissions file.

Lastly, make sure that you have a file called `remote.unknown` in /usr/lib/uucp or /etc/uucp & that it's *NOT* executable.

See the O'Reilly & Associates book `"Managing UUCP & USENET"` for details regarding this file.

6.4   What does "no matching ports found" mean?

In all probability, you are attempting to use a dialer that doesn't exist, or the dialer you've specified in the port files doesn't match up with any valid devices in the dial file.

6.5   What are known good config files for HDB mode?

The following are "known-good" config files for Taylor 1.05 under Linux in HoneyDanBer mode. They work on kernels of 0.99-8 or later. All files should be in /usr/lib/uucp or /etc/uucp unless you've tweaked the sources to put the uucp library elsewhere.

If you *HAVE* put things in non-standard places, be aware that things like sendmail might get very confused. You need to ensure that all communications-related programs agree on your idea of "standard" paths.

```
#-------------- Devices -------------
# make sure the device (cua1 here) matches your system
# cua N = COM N+1
#
# here "scout" is the Digicom Scout Plus 19.2 modem I use
# tbfast etc. is for a Telebit Trailblazer Plus modem's various speeds
#
ACU cua1 - 19200 scout
ACU cua1 - 9600 tbfast
ACU cua1 - 1200 tbslow
ACU cua1 - 2400 tbmed


#-------------- dialers --------------
# note the setting of the Trailblazer registers "on the fly"
# "scout" is a Digicom Scout Plus (Hayes-like) modem I use here
#
scout    =W-,    "" ATM0DT\T CONNECT
tbfast   =W-,    "" A\pA\pA\pT OK ATS50=255DT\T CONNECT\sFAST
tbslow   =W-,    "" A\pA\pA\pT OK ATS50=2DT\T CONNECT\s1200
tbmed    =W-,    "" A\pA\pA\pT OK ATS50=3DT\T CONNECT\s2400


#-------------- Systems -------------
# this is a very generic entry that will work for most systems
#
# the Any;1 means that you can call once per minute with using -f (force)
# the ACU,g means force "g" protocol rather than Taylor's default "i"
#
fredsys Any;1 ACU,g 19200 scout5555555 "" \r ogin:--ogin: uanon word: uanon


#------------------------------- Permissions -------------------------

# Taylor UUCP in HDB mode appears to be sensitive to blank lines.
# Make sure all Permissions lines are real or commented out.
#
# this is a anonymous uucp entry
#
LOGNAME=nuucp MACHINE=OTHER \
READ=/var/spool/uucp/nuucp \
WRITE=/var/spool/uucp/nuucp \
SENDFILES=yes REQUEST=yes \
COMMANDS=/bin/rmail
```

HOWTO

```
# # this is a normal setup for a remote system that talks to us
# note the absolute path to rnews since this site puts things
# in locations that aren't "standard"
#
LOGNAME=fredsys MACHINE=fredsys \
READ=/var/spool/uucp/fredsys:/var/spool/uucp/uucppublic:/files \
WRITE=/var/spool/uucp/fredsys:/var/spool/uucppublic \
SENDFILES=yes REQUEST=yes \
COMMANDS=/bin/rmail:/usr/bin/rnews
#-------------------------------------------------------------------
```

6.6   Getting uucico to call alternate numbers

The new v1.05 has an added '-z' switch to uucico that will try alternate numbers for a remote system.

You can else use Taylor mode & "systemyouarecalling-2" (see "sys" in config. files section for more details)

7   Acknowledgements

The following people have helped in the assembly of the information & experience that helped make this document possible:

Ed Carp, Steve Robbins, Ian Taylor, Greg Naber, Matt Welsh, Pierre Beyssac & especially many thanks to Vince Skahan for his huge contribution.

If I forgot anybody, my apologies: just email me.

Part XLVI

"VME Howto" John Huggins and Michael Wyrick

vmelinux@va.net
v0.8a, 30 July 1998
This document came about to show the embedded system community how to run Linux on their VMEbus Pentium and other PCI local bus based VMEbus processor designs.

Contents

1   Introduction

1.1 Knowledge Required

Using Linux on an embedded VMEbus processor board is not very difficult. However, more than fundamental knowledge is required. This document is not a primer on how to fully configure a Linux machine.

In order to understand this HOWTO document it is assumed that you are thoroughly familiar with the following:

- Configuring and compiling a Linux kernel to operate the various peripherals on your board. *Kernel-HOWTO*
- Setting up and configuring of network devices *NET-3 HOWTO*
- Setting up of inetd *NET-3 HOWTO*
- Setting up and use of the Tundra Universe PCI to VME Bridge Chip *Tundra Universe*. The new VMEUtils program makes knowledge of the Universe unnecessary for those who do not wish to deal with register level Universe access.
- Compiling and installing various network packages like *Apache Site Wu-Ftpd FAQ*
- The VMEbus Rev. D and VME64. Excellent information may be found at the *VMEbus International Trade Association (VITA)*.

If you are uncertain of how to proceed with any of the above it is STRONGLY recommended that you use the links provided to familiarize yourself with all packages. We may not reply to any mail regarding any of the above. Please direct any questions to the appropriate author of the HOWTO or consult the respective hardware manufacturer.

This document describes the installation and use of VMELinux on a Xycom XVME-655 6U VME processor board. Other brands of VME boards that use a Pentium and the Tundra Universe chip should be capable of running VMELinux. Please consult the Board Support Section of the VMELinux web site for tested boards. *VMELinux Project Web Site*

1.2 Why use Linux on VMEbus systems?

Operating systems for VMEbus computers are usually Real-time Operating Systems (RTOS) which have high cost and a significant learning curve. In return the RTOS offers quick response to real world events for control of machinery or response to a process.

The VMEbus provides a rugged computer enclosure and interconnection system. Many system integrators require this ruggedness and also need very fast real-time response. However, there are many times when there is little need for real-time response, but the software still needs:

- networking capability,
- remote access via telnet or similar program,
- file transfer via FTP or similar programs,
- remote booting via BOOTP or similar method,
- a way to respond to system interrupts.

Linux has all these capabilities. Thus, the VMELinux Project exists.

1.3 Purpose

The purpose of VMELinux is to give the VME system integrator another choice in operating systems. Rich in features, high in reliability and low in cost, Linux offers benefits to the embedded computer industry. High cost operating systems economically prohibit the use of VME in many applications. With Linux and the VMELinux drivers, the rugged VMEbus has new possibilities.

The purpose of the VMELinux Project is to:

- Maintain and improve the free VMELinux Kernel Driver software,
- Offer added value software components such as the VMEUtils program and VMEShell utilities.
- Test the software on various makes and brands of manufacturer supplied VME processor boards,
- Maintain web based documentation on each tested brand and make of boards,
- Maintain this HOWTO.
- Integrate user suggested and user supplied improvements into the virgin code so we may all benefit from the programming talents of others.
- Become the original source for all the above software so VMELinux users can be assured of original code from the authors.

HOWTO

1.4 Feedback

As VMELinux is tested in the field, we encourage comments about how well or how bad it works. Please feel free to send comments to *The VMELinux Project*

As we get experience about each brand of VME CPU, we will list the different configurations in this HOWTO. For now we will describe only the Xycom board.

1.5 VMELinux Revision History

Linux Kernel Driver

- November, 1997, v0.2 - Initial version on Xycom Board
- December, 1997, v0.3 - Useable version used for actual work with project.
- February, 1998, v0.6 - DMA mode added to VME access modes.
- June, 1998, v0.8 - Fixed a few things to allow the new VMEUtils to work.
- June 24, 1998, v0.8a - Current version made available on the website.

VMEUtils Program

- February, 1998, v0.6 - Created a command line interpreter to access the VMEbus
- June, 1998, v0.8 - Fixed several issues to allow VMEShell Utilities to function
- June 24, 1998, v0.8a - Current version made available on the website.

VMEShell Utilities

- June, 1998, v0.8 - Created command line utilities that allow access to the VMEbus from the Linux shell prompt. These shell programs interface with the VMEUtils program.
- June 24, 1998, v0.8a - Changed the name of all the shell programs so they all begin with "vme." Current version made available on the website.

1.6 Copyright/Distribution

This document is Copyright 1997-1998 by John Huggins and the VMELinux Project.

A verbatim copy may be reproduced or distributed in any medium physical or electronic without permission of the author. Translations are similarly permitted without express permission if it includes a notice on who translated it. Commercial redistribution is allowed and encouraged; however please notify *The VMELinux Project* of any such distributions.

Excerpts from the document may be used without prior consent provided that the derivative work contains the verbatim copy or a pointer to a verbatim copy.

Permission is granted to make and distribute verbatim copies of this document provided the copyright notice and this permission notice are preserved on all copies.

In short, we wish to promote dissemination of this information through as many channels as possible. However, we wish to retain copyright on this HOWTO document, and would like to be notified of any plans to redistribute this HOWTO.

2 Installation of the VMELinux Kernel Driver

2.1 Download the Source

Download the distribution from the *VMELinux Web Site*.

2.2 Install the source to the software

Place the file in a directory reserved for VME usage; We suggest /universe. Untar the zipped/tarred file by typing...

```
tar -xzf VMELinux_08a.tar.gz
```

You should see three directories and one link to ca91c042

```
ca91c042
vmeshell
vmeutils
driver
```

In ca91c042 you should find:

```
ca91c042/
ca91c042/Makefile
ca91c042/ca91c042.c
ca91c042/ca91c042.h
ca91c042/README
ca91c042/e
ca91c042/ins
ca91c042/stat
ca91c042/uns
```

In vmeshell you should find:

```
vmeshell/vmer
vmeshell/README
vmeshell/vmeseek
vmeshell/cmd.vme
vmeshell/vmew
vmeshell/vmeregw
vmeshell/vmeregr
vmeshell/vmefa
vmeshell/vmecall
vmeshell/e
vmeshell/ec
vmeshell/fa.vme
vmeshell/map.vme
vmeshell/tmp.vme
vmeshell/vmedb
vmeshell/vmedl
vmeshell/vmedw
vmeshell/vmemap
vmeshell/vmerb
vmeshell/vmerf
vmeshell/vmerl
vmeshell/vmerw
vmeshell/vmewb
vmeshell/vmewf
vmeshell/vmewl
vmeshell/vmeww
```

In the vmeutils directory you should find:

```
vmeutils/commands.cpp
vmeutils/commands.h
vmeutils/universe.h
vmeutils/Makefile
vmeutils/vmeutils.h
vmeutils/unilib.h
vmeutils/unilib.cpp
vmeutils/vmeutils.cpp
vmeutils/README
```

2.3   Compile the VMELinux components

Enter the "ca91c042" directory and make the VMELinux device driver module.

```
make
```

Now you must create the several /dev driver files. Type:

```
make devices
```

Once made, you should see the file "ca91c042.o" in the directory. This is a loadable module. See below for loading information. Plus, you should find several "vme..." files in the /dev directory.

Once the devices are made in the /dev directory you must change their permissions. Type:

```
cd /dev
chmod 666 vme*
```

Here is how the files should look:

```
hostname:/dev# ls -l vme*
crw-rw-rw-   1 root      root      70,   8 Jul 30 10:51 vme_ctl
crw-rw-rw-   1 root      root      70,   0 Jul 30 10:51 vme_m0
crw-rw-rw-   1 root      root      70,   1 Jul 30 10:51 vme_m1
crw-rw-rw-   1 root      root      70,   2 Jul 30 10:51 vme_m2
crw-rw-rw-   1 root      root      70,   3 Jul 30 10:51 vme_m3
crw-rw-rw-   1 root      root      70,   4 Jul 30 10:51 vme_s0
crw-rw-rw-   1 root      root      70,   5 Jul 30 10:51 vme_s1
crw-rw-rw-   1 root      root      70,   6 Jul 30 10:51 vme_s2
crw-rw-rw-   1 root      root      70,   7 Jul 30 10:51 vme_s3
hostname:/dev#
```

Change to the "vmeutils" directory and type make there.

```
make
```

This will compile the "vmeutils" program. This program directly speaks to the kernel driver. It is a reference work for those of you who wish to write your own programs to directly speak with the driver.

Copy the program "vmeutils" to your user binary directory. On our system this is "/usr/local/bin." Alternatively, you can create a link in the user bin directory to the "vmeutils" program.

Change to the "vmeshell" directory. There are no files to be compiled here. These are shell programs that use the "vmeutils" program to access the VMEbus. All the files beginning with "vme" should with have a link made or be copied to the "/usr/local/bin" directory.

You are now ready to try the driver.

2.4 Load the VMELinux Kernel Module

Make sure you are root and insert "load" the VMELinux Kernel Module for the Universe chip by typing...

```
insmod ca91c042
```

Or just type "ins" to let the shell script do this for you. Once complete, type...

```
stat
```

You should see a list of registers displayed on your screen. Something like this...

```
Universe driver info:
  Control Pointer = 0000
  Stats  reads = 0  writes = 0  ioctls = 0
  LSI0_CTL = 00800000    LSI1_CTL = 00800000
  LSI0_BS  = C0000000    LSI1_BS  = 00000000
  LSI0_BD  = C0010000    LSI1_BD  = 00000000
  LSI0_TO  = 40009000    LSI1_TO  = 00000000
  LSI2_CTL = 00800000    LSI3_CTL = 00800000
  LSI2_BS  = 00000000    LSI3_BS  = 00000000
  LSI2_BD  = 00000000    LSI3_BD  = 00000000
  LSI2_TO  = 00000000    LSI3_TO  = 00000000
  image_va0   = 00000000     image_va1   = 00000000
  image_va2   = 00000000     image_va3   = 00000000

Driver Program Status:
  DMACTL 0    = 00000000 DMACTL 1    = 00000000
  DMACTL 2    = 00000000 DMACTL 3    = 00000000
  OkToWrite 0 = 0        OkToWrite 1 = 0
  OkToWrite 2 = 0        OkToWrite 3 = 0
  Mode 0      = 0        Mode 1      = 0
  Mode 2      = 0        Mode 3      = 0
```

If not, something went wrong.

2.5 Difficulties

The Universe driver does a good job of finding the Universe chip on a PCI bus, but differences in board design may prevent this. We tested all our routines on a Xycom XVME-655 board. There is little reason why this should not work on any other Intel board with a PCI bus and the Universe PCI-VME bridge chip. If you encounter problems, please let us know at the *The VMELinux Project*

3 How to talk to the VMEbus with the VMEUtils and the VMEShell Packages

3.1 What is the VMEUtils program

This program can be run as is. Once started, you will see a command prompt. Type ? And you will see a list of commands. While useful, I think you will find the VMEShell scripts a better way to go. They do use this program to speak with the kernel driver so it is necessary to have this program available in the current PATH.

The source code for "vmeutils" is also instruction on how to speak directly to the kernel driver. For those of you who wish to create programs that directly speak with the driver, these source files are good examples.

3.2 What are the VMEShell Scripts

The VMEShell programs are unix shell scripts. They offer the operator a simple way to access the data on a VMEbus. Using these commands creates temporary files in the user's working directory which store information on the last access you did. This is nice because it will be possible to log off the machine, log back in and proceed from where you left off without having to re-enter VMEbus information again. Plus, these files are stored in the current working directory, so you can have different VME access configuration just by setting up different directories for each VME board of interest.

Assuming you placed the shell programs and the "vmeutils" program in the /usr/local/bin directory, you should be able to log in as a regular user and run them. What follows assumes exactly this.

3.3 The "vmemap" command.

Login as a regular user and create a directory to experiment with. Once in this directory type:

```
vmemap
```

You should get a help screen like this...

```
Usage:  map address count space size type
  where address is VME Address to set Universe image to

    Space = 0 CR/CSR    Space = 1 A16
    Space = 2 A24       Space = 3 A32

    Size  = 1 8 bit     Size  = 2 16 bit
    Size  = 3 32 bit    Size  = 4 64 bit

    Type  = 0 USR/DATA  Type  = 1 USR/PRG
    Type  = 2 SUP/DATA  Type  = 3 SUP/PRG
```

This is where you tell VMELinux how you want to access the VMEbus. We assume you already know about the VMEbus' many modes of operation, but here is a short list to help you.

- **address** is the actual VMEbus address you wish to see. This should be set to the lower most value of the address range of interest.
- **count** is the number of bytes you consider a valid range to view. This is the number of bytes starting at the address specified above.
- **space** is the addressing space (mode). For those of you who do not know what we are talking about here, the VMEbus has four overlapping address spaces that can be called independant of each other. A16 is a 64 KiloByte space. A24 is a 16 MegaByte space. A32 is a 4 GigaByte space. There is an A64 space defined the VME specification, but the Universe does not support it.

- **Size** refers to the maximum datawidth allowed for the VME board you are accessing. Some VMEbus board only handle 8 bit data paths. Others transfer 32 bits (four bytes) at a time. Some can handle a special VME block mode which can move 64 bits per transaction. The Universe can handle all these modes allowing you to mix inexpensive serial port boards with hugh memory arrays.

- **Type** is the type of VME transaction performed. Some VME boards make a distinction between "User" access (USR) and "Supervisior" access (SUP). Also, some boards allow access to two "pages" of memory: Program (PRG) and Data. The Universe supports all modes.

Typing...

```
vmemap 0x8000 0x100 1 2 0
```

sets up the VMELinux driver to access an A16 board at base address 8000 Hex with a range of 100H bytes with 16 bit data width and USR/DATA mode.

You will find two new files in your current directory.

- fa.vme
- map.vme

fa.vme stores a "fixed adder" value that will be added to all subsequent accesses with the programs below.

map.vme store the parameters above so you do not have to enter them every time.

All the following shell utilities read values from these two files to performs VME accesses.

3.4   Read Byte, Word or Long

Syntax:

- vmerb -[options] address size
- vmerw -[options] address size
- vmerl -[options] address size

3.5   Write Byte, Word or Long

Syntax:

- vmewb -[options] address value
- vmeww -[options] address value
- vmewl -[options] address value

3.6   Read the VMEbus to a file

Syntax:

- vmerf -[options] address size filename

3.7   Write a file to the VMEbus

Syntax:

- vmewf -[options] address filename

HOWTO

3.8 Parameters

There are several parameters used with these commands: address, size and filename.

- address - The actual hexadecimal VMEbus address you wish to read. If the map command is set to access A16 VME address space, the address should be 0xABCD. If the space is A24 then use 0xABCDEF. For A32 space use 0xABCDEFGH.
- size - The number of bytes to read. This value is always the number of bytes regardless of the data word size read. For example, if you want to read 16 bytes of information and use vmerl, the display will show 16 bytes displayed as 4 long words.
- filename - The name of the file to send "read" VMEbus data to or "write" VMEbus data from.
- value - a hex value written as "0xXXXX."

3.9 Options

Available options are defined with a single dash with the any combination of the following:

- q - Hides details on the access to the vmeutils program (default)
- Q - Shows details on the access to the vmeutils program
- p - Single access PCI addressing mode (opposite of d) (default)
- d - DMA access PCI addressing mode (opposite of p) (very fast access to the VMEbus)
- 0, 1, 2, or 3 - Which Universe chip "Image" to use (defaults to 0)
- b - binary mode off (default)
- B - binary mode on
- v - turn off verbose parameter printing (default)
- V - turn on verbose parameter printing to see how the driver is begin used

3.10 A Note about DMA mode.

VMELinux offers access to all the features of the Universe Chip. Especially useful is access to the DMA engine on the chip. With this feature the Universe chip transfers data on the PCI bus by becoming a PCI master. This is nice, but the real benefit comes from the VMEbus accesses. Even if the VMEbus interface is not using block mode transfers, the Universe chip can complete VMEbus transfers under 400 nanoseconds sustained. This is the direct result of the Universe taking complete control of both the PCI bus and the VMEbus. Thus, it is possible to access non block mode VMEbus peripherals much faster than older technologies.

4 How to talk to the Tundra Universe PCI-VME bridge using the devices drivers.

4.1 The device drivers used with VMELinux

- /dev/vme_ioctl
- /dev/vme_m0
- /dev/vme_m1
- /dev/vme_m2
- /dev/vme_m3
- /dev/vme_s0
- /dev/vme_s1
- /dev/vme_s2
- /dev/vme_s3

4.2 VMEMaster Device Drivers

/dev/vme_m* are drivers used to access the VMEbus as a bus master.

The Universe chip offers the programmer four VMEMaster windows to the VMEbus. These windows are called Images. The details of the registers within these windows is beyond the scope of this Howto. Please refer to the Universe documentation for details. *Tundra Universe*

4.3 VMESlave Device Drivers

/dev/vme_s* are drivers used to allow another VMEbus master to access this device.

The Universe chip offers the programmer four VMESlave windows to the VMEbus. These windows are called Images. The details of the registers within these windows is beyond the scope of this Howto. Please refer to the Universe documentation for details. *Tundra Universe*

Slave VME modes are not yet supported by VMELinux.

4.4 Direct Control of the Universe Registers

/dev/vme_ioctl allows read and write access to the Universe registers.

For experienced users, this device allows direct access to the Universe chip's internal registers. Explanation of these registers and what they do is beyond the scope of this howto. Please consult the Universe documentation available from *Tundra Universe*

4.5 read()

n = read(vme_handle,buf,len);

Where:

- vme_handle = The value returned by "open,"
- buf = pointer to data block,
- len = number of bytes to read from the VMEbus.

4.6 write()

write(vme_handle,buf,len);

Where:

- vme_handle = The value returned by "open,"
- buf = pointer to data block,
- len = number of bytes to write to the VMEbus.

4.7 lseek()

lseek(vme_handle,vme_pnt,Seek_Type);

Where:

- vme_handle = The value returned by "open,"
- vme_pnt = The actual VME address to access,
- Seek_Type = SEEK_SET or SEEK_CUR

4.8   ioctl()

ioctl(vme_handle, command, argument);

Where:

- vme_handle = The value returned by "open,"
- command = IOCTL_SET_CTL or IOCTL_SET_MODE or IOCTL_SET_BS or IOCTL_SET_BD or IOCTL_SET_TO
- argument to be sent

And:

- IOCTL_SET_CTL = Sets the image CTL register to argument. Argument must be 32 bits.
- IOCTL_SET_MODE = "MODE_DMA" or "MODE_PROGRAMMED" - Sets the mode by which the Universe chips communicates to the PCI bus (Not VME Block Mode)
- IOCTL_SET_BS = Sets the image BS register to arguments. NOTE: The BD register must already be set prior to making this call.
- IOCTL_SET_BD = Sets the image BD register to argument.
- IOCTL_SET_TO = Set the image TO register to argument.

4.9   open() and close()

Here is where you open and close the four VMELinux Master or Slave devices plus the Control device. Slave images are not yet supported.

- vme_handle = open("//dev//vme_m0",O_RDWR,0);
- uni_handle = open("//dev//vme_ctl",O_RDWR,0);

- close(vme_handle);
- close(uni_handle);

5   Advantages of the VMEbus, Linux and VMELinux

5.1   Pin and socket connectors

The VMEbus standard uses pin and socket connectors. This is superior to edge connections in that the connection is not exposed to humidity and other environmental conditions. It is a more expensive way of doing things, but offers longer times before failure.

5.2   Eurocard assembly

A VMEboard is either a 3U (160 x 100 mm) or a 6U size (160 x 233.35 mm). These sizes correspond to the Eurocard standard for board modules and card cages. Eurocard is a popular format used by many different busses including CompactPCI. This popularity makes the materials needed for cage assembly inexpensive and easy to obtain.

5.3   Linux is Low Cost

The nature of Linux is in its user supported and freely available format. The number of people using Linux is growing. The number of people contributing to the continued development of the Linux software base is growing. It is unfair to state that Linux is a good value because it is available for little to no charge. Linux is a good value because it works.

5.4   Linux is Stable

There are those who say that Linux us an unstable operating system. It is true that the new Linux kernels in development are experimental and should not be relied on for critical applications. However, stable versions of the Linux OS are always available and provide very stable operation. VMELinux is always based on the stable versions of the kernel source; Today's stable kernels are the 2.0.X series.

5.5   Linux is Dynamic

Because so many people are developing Linux, you do not have to wait long for improvements, fixes or new features to become part of the Linux distribution.

6   Current and planned Board Support

While the VMELinux driver should work with any PCI based design, the following boards have actually run our software.

6.1   Xycom XVME655 Pentium VMEbus Board

- This XyCom board is compatible with the standard VMELinux kernel driver package from *VMELinux Project*
- A prepared kernel will be available soon. It will be based on the newest version of the Linux kernel and will include appropriate drivers for the onboard NE2100 Ethernet interface. Check the website for details.

6.2   XyCom XVME656 Pentium VMEBus Board

- This XyCom board is compatible with the standard VMELinux kernel driver package from *VMELinux Project*
- A prepared kernel will be available soon. It will be based on the newest version of the Linux kernel and will include appropriate drivers for the onboard AHA2940/AIC7000 SCSI and 82558 Intel EtherExpress Ethernet peripherals. Check the website for details.

6.3   Dynatem DPC1-0367

- This board is compatible with the standard VMELinux kernel driver package from *VMELinux Project*
- A prepared kernel will be available soon. It will be based on the newest version of the Linux kernel and will include appropriate drivers for the onboard SCSI and Tulip Ethernet peripherals. Check the website for details.

6.4   Planned Board Support

If you do not see VMELinux support for your board let us know. Maybe the manufacture will lend us a board for development.

7   Conclusion

VMELinux offers the user a low cost way to implement a VMEbus system quickly, reliably and with all the advantages of a unix environment. We are using VMELinux in our projects so you can be sure future developments will come quick. On the drawing board for this year are:

- Implementation of Interrupts and Handling thereof,
- Porting to other brands of Intel VMEbus boards,
- Porting of VMELinux to other processors that use the Universe chip,
- A study of running the VMELinux kernel driver module as a RT-Linux task.

HOWTO

This document outlines the steps you need to install the VMELinux Kernel Driver into the example Xycom XVME-655 Pentium VME board. It is our hope that others will attempt installation of VMELinux into other boards and let us know their success.

Mail any responses to *The VMELinux Project*. If you have a question or an update to the document let us know and we will add it.

8 FAQ

8.1 The Shell utilities return a bunch of stars (*) when I access a board I know is there. What gives?

Check to be sure the /dev/vme... files have their permissions set to 666. If not, the shell utilities will return a * in place of data to indicate an error condition similar to a VME bus error.

8.2 How does VMELinux handle interrupts?

Right now it doesn't. However, we are planning to get that part going soon. Please be patient.

8.3 I have RedHat 5.1 and can't get VMELinux programs to compile.

RedHat 5.1 includes a new compiler. If you manually edit the Makefile in each directory to call up the new egcs compiler, things should compile. We fully intend to support RedHat 5.1 installations, but for now I suggest using 5.0 or Slackware.

Part XLVII

"From VMS to Linux HOWTO" By Guido Gonzato

guido@ibogfs.cineca.it

v1.0.2, 20 April 1998

This HOWTO is aimed at all those who have been using VMS and now need or want to switch to Linux, the free UNIX clone. The transition is made (hopefully) painless with a step–to–step comparison between commands and available tools.

Contents

HOWTO

1   Introduction

1.1   Why Linux?

You've heard that UNIX is difficult and balk at the prospect of leaving VMS, don't you? Don't worry. Linux, one of the finest UNIX clones, is not more difficult to use than VMS; actually, I find it easier. Although VMS aficionados may not agree, in many people's opinion Linux is much more powerful and versatile.

Linux and VMS are both good operating systems and accomplish essentially the same tasks, but Linux' tools are (IMHO) superior, its syntax is often much more concise, and has some features missing in VMS that help save a lot of time. (You'll often hear that VMS and UNIX have a different 'philosophy'.) Moreover, Linux is available for PCs while VMS is not, and modern Pentium-based Linux machines can outperform a VAX. The icing on the cake is the excellent performance of modern video cards, which turn an X11-based Linux box into a fast graphic workstation; nearly always, quicker than dedicated machines.

I have many reasons to believe that the combination Pentium + Linux is preferable to VAX–VMS, but preferences are a strictly personal matter and you may disagree. You'll decide by yourself after a few months.

I imagine you're a university researcher or a student, and that you use VMS for the following everyday tasks:

- writing papers with TeX/LaTeX;
- programming in Fortran;
- doing some graphics;
- using Internet services;
- et cetera.

In the following sections I'm going to explain to you how to do these tasks under Linux, exploiting your experience with VMS. Prerequisites:

- Linux and X Window System are properly installed;
- there's a system administrator to take care of the technical details (please get help from them, not from me ;-)) ;
- your shell—the equivalent of DCL—is `bash` (ask your sysadm).

Please note that this HOWTO is not enough to acquaint you fully with Linux: it only contains the bare essential to get you started. You should learn more about Linux to make the most of it (advanced `bash` features, programming, regular expressions...). From now on, RMP means 'please read the man pages for further details'. The man pages are the equivalent of the command HELP.

The Linux Documentation Project documents, available on *sunsite.unc.edu:/pub/Linux/docs/LDP*, are an important source of information. I suggest that you read Larry Greenfield's "Linux User Guide"—it's invaluable for the novice user.

And now, go ahead.

1.2 Comparing Commands and Files

This table attempts to compare VMS' and Linux' most used commands. Please keep in mind that the syntax is often very different; for more details, refer to the following sections.

```
VMS                        Linux                   Notes
------------------------------------------------------------------------
--

@COMMAND                   command                 must be executable
COPY file1 file2           cp file1 file2
CREATE/DIR [.dirname]      mkdir dirname           only one at a time
CREATE/DIR [.dir1.dir2]    mkdirhier dir/name
DELETE filename            rm filename
DIFF file1 file2           diff -c file1 file2
DIRECTORY                  ls
DIRECTORY [...]file        find . -name file
DIRECTORY/FULL             ls -al
EDIT filename              vi filename,            you won't like it
                           emacs filename,         EDT compatible
                           jed filename            ditto---my favourite
FORTRAN prog.for           g77 prog.f,             no need to do LINK
                           f77 prog.f,
                           fort77 prog.f
HELP command               man command             must speci-
fy 'command'
                           info command            ditto
LATEX file.tex             latex file.tex
LOGIN.COM                  .bash_profile,          'hidden' file
                           .bashrc                 ditto
LOGOUT.COM                 .bash_logout            ditto
MAIL                       mail,                   crude
                           elm,                    much better
                           pine                    better still
PRINT file.ps              lpr file.ps
PRINT/QUEUE=laser file.ps  lpr -Plaser file.ps
PHONE user                 talk user
RENAME file1 file2         mv file1 file2          not for multi-
ple files
RUN progname               progname
SEARCH file "pattern"      grep pattern file
SET DEFAULT [-]            cd ..
SET DEFAULT [.dir.name]    cd dir/name
SET HOST hostname          telnet hostname,        not exactly the same
                           rlogin hostname
SET FILE/OWNER_UIC=joe     chown joe file          completely different
SET NOBROADCAST            mesg
SET PASSWORD               passwd
SET PROT=(perm) file       chmod perm file         completely different
```

SET TERMINAL	export TERM=	different syntax
SHOW DEFAULT	pwd	
SHOW DEVICE	du, df	
SHOW ENTRY	lpq	
SHOW PROCESS	ps -ax	
SHOW QUEUE	lpq	
SHOW SYSTEM	top	
SHOW TIME	date	
SHOW USERS	w	
STOP	kill	
STOP/QUEUE	kill,	for processes
	lprm	for print queues
SUBMIT command	command &	
SUBMIT/AFTER=time command	at time command	
TEX file.tex	tex file.tex	
TYPE/PAGE file	more file	
	less file	much better

But of course it's not only a matter of different command names. Read on.

2   Short Intro

This is what you absolutely need to know before logging in the first time. Relax, it's not much.

2.1   Files

- Under VMS filenames are in the form filename.extension.version;. Under Linux, the version number doesn't exist (big limitation, but see Section 10.2 (RCS in a Nutshell)); the filename has normally a limit of 255 characters and can have as many dots as you like. Example of filename: This.is_a_FILEname.txt.

- Linux distinguishes between upper case and lower case characters: FILENAME.txt and filename.txt are two different files; ls is a command, LS is not.

- A filename starting with a dot is a 'hidden' file (that is, it won't normally show up in dir listings), while filenames ending with a tilde '~' represent backup files.

Now, a table to sum up how to translate commands from VMS to Linux:

```
VMS                                     Linux
-----------------------------------------------------------------

$ COPY file1.txt; file2.txt;           $ cp file1.txt file2.txt
$ COPY [.dir]file.txt;1 []             $ cp dir/file.txt .
$ COPY [.dir]file.txt;1 [-]            $ cp dir/file.txt ..
$ DELETE *.dat.*                        $ rm *dat
$ DIFF file1 file2                      $ diff -c file1 file2
$ PRINT file                            $ lpr file
$ PRINT/queue=queuename file            $ lpr -Pprintername file
$ SEARCH *.tex.* "geology"              $ grep geology *tex
```

For other examples involving directories, see below; for details about protections, ownership, and advanced topics, see Section 8 (Advanced Topics).

2.2   Directories

- Within the same node and device, directories names under VMS are in the form [top.dir.subdir]; under Linux, /top/dir/subdir/. On the top of the directory tree lies the so–called 'root directory' called /; underneath there are other directories like /bin, /usr, /tmp, /etc, and others.

- The directory /home contains the so–called users' 'home directories': e.g. /home/guido, /home/warner, and so on. When a user logs in, they start working in their home dir; it's the equivalent of SYS$LOGIN. There's a shortcut for the home directory: the tilde '~'. So, cd ~/tmp is the same as, say, cd /home/guido/tmp.

- Directory names follow the same rules as file names. Furthermore, each directory has two special entries: one is . and refers to the directory itself (like []), and .. that refers to the parent directory (like [-]).

And now for some other examples:

```
DOS                                         Linux
------------------------------------------------------------------

$ CREATE/DIR [.dirname]                     $ mkdir dirname
$ CREATE/DIR [.dir1.dir2.dir3]              $ mkdirhier dir1/dir2/dir3
  n/a                                       $ rmdir dirname
                                            (if dirname is empty)
                                            $ rm -R dirname
$ DIRECTORY                                 $ ls
$ DIRECTORY [...]file.*.*                   $ find . -name "file*"
$ SET DEF SYS$LOGIN                         $ cd
$ SET DEF [-]                               $ cd ..
$ SET DEF [top.dir.subdir]                  $ cd /top/dir/subdir
$ SET DEF [.dir.subdir]                     $ cd dir/subdir
$ SHOW DEF                                  $ pwd
```

For protections, ownership, and advanced topics, see Section 8 (Advanced Topics).

2.3   Programs

- Commands, compiled programs, and shell scripts (VMS' 'command files') don't have compulsory extensions like .EXE or .COM and can be called whatever you like. Executable files are marked by an asterisk '*' when you issue ls -F.

- To run an executable file, just type its name (no RUN PROGRAM.EXE or @COMMAND). Caveat: it's essential that the file be located in a directory included in the *path of executables*, which is a list of directories. Typically, the path includes dirs like /bin, /usr/bin, /usr/X11R6/bin, and others. If you write your own programs, put them in a directory you have included in the path (see how in Section 9 (Configuring)). As an alternative, you may run a program specifying its complete path: e.g., /home/guido/data/myprog; or ./myprog, if the current directory isn't in the path.

- Command switches are obtained with /OPTION= under VMS, and with -switch or -switch under Linux, where switch is a letter, more letters combined, or a word. In particular, the switch -R (recursive) of many Linux commands performs the same action as [...] under VMS;

- You can issue several commands on the command line:

        $ command1 ; command2 ; ... ; commandn

- Most of the flexibility of Linux comes from two features awkwardly implemented or missing in VMS: I/O redirection and piping. (To be sincere, I have been told that recent versions of IDL support redirection and piping. I don't have that version.) Redirection is a side feature under VMS (remember the switch /OUTPUT= of many commands), or a fastidious process, like:

HOWTO

```
$ DEFINE /USER SYS$OUTPUT OUT
$ DEFINE /USER SYS$INPUT IN
$ RUN PROG
```

which has the simple Linux (UNIX) equivalent:

```
$ prog < in > out
```

Piping is simply impossible under VMS, but has a key role under UNIX. A typical example:

```
$ myprog < datafile | filter_1 | filter_2 >> result.dat 2> errors.log &
```

which means: the program `myprog` gets its input from the file `datafile` (via <), its output is piped (via |) to the program `filter_1` that takes it as input and processes it, the resulting output is piped again to `filter_2` for further processing, the final output is appended (via >>) to the file `result.dat`, and error messages are redirected (via 2>) onto the file `errors.log`. All this in background (& at the end of the command line). More about this in Section 11 (Examples).

For multitasking, 'queues', and the like, see Section 8 (Advanced Topics).

2.4 Quick Tour

Now you are ready to try Linux out. Enter your login name and password *exactly* as they are. For example, if your login name and password are `john` and `My_PassWd`, *don't* type `John` or `my_passwd`. Remember, UNIX distinguishes between capital and small letters.

Once you've logged in, you'll see a prompt; chances are it'll be something like `machinename:$`. If you want to change the prompt or make some programs start automatically, you'll have to edit a 'hidden' file called `.profile` or `.bash_profile` (see example in Section 9 (Configuring)). This is the equivalent of `LOGIN.COM`.

Pressing ALT–F1, ALT–F2, ... ALT–F6 switches between 'virtual consoles'. When one VC is busy with a full–screen application, you can flip over to another and continue to work. Try and log in to another VC.

Now you may want to start X Window System (from now on, X). X is a graphic environment very similar to DECWindows—actually, the latter derives from the former. Type the command `startx` and wait a few seconds; most likely you'll see an open `xterm` or equivalent terminal emulator, and possibly a button bar. (It depends on how your sysadm configured your Linux box.) Click on the desktop (try both mouse buttons) to see a menu.

While in X, to access the text mode ('console') sessions press CTRL–ALT–F1 ... CTRL–ALT–F6. Try it. When in console, go back to X pressing ALT–F7. To quit X, follow the menu instructions or press CTRL–ALT–BS.

Type the following command to list your home dir contents, including the hidden files:

```
$ ls -al
```

Press SHIFT–PAG UP to back-scroll. Now get help about the `ls` command typing:

```
$ man ls
```

pressing 'q' to exit. To end the tour, type `exit` to quit your session. If now you want to turn off your PC, press CTRL–ALT–DEL and wait a few seconds (*never* switch off the PC while in Linux! You could damage the filesystem.)

If you think you're ready to work, go ahead, but if I were you I'd jump to Section 8 (Advanced Topics).

3 Editing Files

Linux doesn't have EDT, but there are scores of editors available. The only one that's guaranteed to be included in every UNIX version is vi—forget it, your sysadm must have installed something better. Probably the most popular editor is emacs, which can emulate EDT to a certain degree; jed is another editor that provides EDT emulation.

These two editors are particularly useful for editing program sources, since they have two features unknown to EDT: syntax hilighting and automatic indentation. Moreover, you can compile your programs from within the editor (command ESC-X compile); in case of a syntax error, the cursor will be positioned on the offending line. I bet that you'll never want to use the true blue EDT again.

If you have emacs: start it, then type ESC-X edt-emulation-on. Pressing ALT–X or ESC-X is emacs' way of issuing commands, like EDT's CTRL–Z. From now on, emacs acts like EDT apart from a few commands. Differences:

- *don't* press CTRL–Z to issue commands (if you did, you stopped emacs. Type fg to resume it);
- there's an extensive on-line help. Press CTRL-H ?, or CTRL-H T to start a tutorial;
- to save a file, press CTRL-X CTRL-S;
- to exit, press CTRL-X CTRL-C;
- to insert a new file in a buffer, press CTRL-X CTRL-F, then CTRL-X B to switch among buffers.

If you have jed: ask your sysadm to configure jed properly. Emulation is already on when you start it; use the normal keypad keys, and press CTRL–H CTRL–H or CTRL-? to get help. Commands are issued in the same way as emacs'. In addition, there are some handy key bindings missing in the original EDT; key bindings can also be tailored to your own taste. Ask your sysadm.

In alternative, you may use another editor with a completely different interface. emacs in native mode is an obvious choice; another popular editor is joe, which can emulate other editors like emacs itself (being even easier to use) or the DOS editor. Invoke the editor as jmacs or jstar and press, respectively, CTRL-X H or CTRL-J to get online help. emacs and jed are *much* more powerful than good ol' EDT.

4 TeXing

TeX and LaTeX are identical to their VMS counterparts—only quicker :-), but the tools to handle the .dvi and .ps files are superior:

- to run a TeX file through TeX, do as usual: tex file.tex;
- to turn a .dvi file into a .ps file, type dvips -o filename.ps filename.dvi;
- to visualize a .dvi file, type within an X session: xdvi filename.dvi &. Click on the page to magnify. This program is smart: if you edit and run TeX producing newer versions of the .dvi file, xdvi will update it automatically;
- to visualize a .ps file, type within an X session: ghostview filename.ps &. Click on the page to magnify. The whole document or selected pages can be printed. A newer and better program is gv.
- to print the .ps: usually the command lpr mypaper.ps will do, but if the PostScript printer is called, say, 'ps' (ask your sysadm) you'll do: lpr -Pps mypaper.ps. For more information about print queues, go to Section 8.4 (Print Queues).

5 Programming

Programming under Linux is *much* better: there are lots of tools that make programming easier and quicker. For instance, the drudgery of editing–saving–exiting–compiling–re-editing can be cut short by using editors like emacs or jed, as seen above.

5.1 Fortran

Not substantial differences here, but note that at the time of writing the available (free) compilers are not 100% compatible with VMS'; expect some minor quirks. (It's actually the VMS compiler which has non-standard extensions.) See `/usr/doc/g77/DOC` or `/usr/doc/f2c/f2c.ps` for details.

Your sysadm has installed a native compiler called g77 (good but, as of version 0.5.21, still not perfectly compatible with DEC Fortran) or possibly the Fortran to C translator, f2c, and one of the front-ends that make it mimic a native compiler. In my experience, the package yaf77 is the one that provides best results.

To compile a Fortran program with g77, edit the source, save it with extension .f, then do:

```
$ g77 myprog.f
```

which creates by default an executable called a.out (you don't have to link anything). To give the executable a different name and do some optimisation:

```
$ g77 -O2 -o myprog myprog.f
```

Beware of optimisations! Ask your sysadm to read the documentation that comes with the compiler and tell you if there are any problems.

To compile a subroutine:

```
$ g77 -c mysub.f
```

This creates a file mysub.o. To link this subroutine to a program, you'll do

```
$ g77 -o myprog myprog.f mysub.o
```

If you have many external subroutines and you want to make a library, do the following:

```
$ cd subroutines/
$ cat *f >mylib.f ; g77 -c mylib.f
```

This will create mylib.o that you can link to your programs.

Finally, to link an external library called, say, libdummy.so:

```
$ g77 -o myprog myprog.f -ldummy
```

If you have f2c, you only have to use f77 or fort77 instead of g77.

Another useful programming tool is make, described below.

5.2 Using make

The utility make is a tool to handle the compilation of programs that are split into several source files.

Let's suppose you have source files containing your routines, file_1.f, file_2.f, file_3.f, and a source file of the main program that uses the routines, myprog.f. If you compile your program manually, whenever you modify one of the source files you have to figure out which file depends on which, which file to recompile first, and so on.

Instead of getting mad, you can write a 'makefile'. This is a text file containing the dependencies between your sources: when one is modified, only the ones that depend on the modified file will be recompiled.

In our example, you'd write a makefile like this:

```
# This is makefile
# Press the <TAB> key where you see <TAB>!
# It's important: don't use spaces instead.

myprog: myprog.o file_1.o file_2.o file_3.o
<TAB>g77 -o myprog myprog.o file_1.o file_2.o file_3.o
# myprog depends on four object files

myprog.o: myprog.f
<TAB>g77 -c myprog.f
# myprog.o depends on its source file

file_1.o: file_1.f
<TAB>g77 -c file_1.f
# file_1.o depends on its source file

file_2.o: file_2.f file_1.o
<TAB>g77 -c file_2.f file_1.o
# file_2.o depends on its source file and an object file

file_3.o: file_3.f file_2.o
<TAB>g77 -c file_3.f file_2.o
# file_3.o depends on its source file and an object file

# end of makefile.
```

Save this file as `Makefile` and type `make` to compile your program; alternatively, save it as `myprog.mak` and type `make -f myprog.mak`. And of course, RMP.

5.3   Shell Scripts

Shell scripts are the equivalent of VMS' command files and, for a change, are much more powerful.

To write a script, all you have to do is write a standard ASCII file containing the commands, save it, then make it executable with the command `chmod +x <scriptfile>`. To execute it, type its name.

Writing scripts under `bash` is such a vast subject it would require a book by itself, and I will not delve into the topic any further. I'll just give you a more-or-less comprehensive and (hopefully) useful example you can extract some basic rules from.

EXAMPLE: sample.sh

```
#!/bin/sh
# sample.sh
# I am a comment
# don't change the first line, it must be there
echo "This system is: 'uname -a'" # use the output of the command
echo "My name is $0" # built-in variables
echo "You gave me the following $# parameters: "$*
echo "First parameter is: "$1
echo -n "What's your name? " ; read your_name
echo notice the difference: "hi $your_name" # quoting with "
echo notice the difference: 'hi $your_name' # quoting with '
DIRS=0 ; FILES=0
```

```
for file in 'ls .' ; do
  if [ -d ${file} ] ; then # if file is a directory
    DIRS='expr $DIRS + 1'  # this means DIRS = DIRS + 1
  elif [ -f ${file} ] ; then
    FILES='expr $FILES + 1'
  fi
  case ${file} in
    *.gif|*.jpg) echo "${file}: graphic file" ;;
    *.txt|*.tex) echo "${file}: text file" ;;
    *.c|*.f|*.for) echo "${file}: source file" ;;
    *) echo "${file}: generic file" ;;
  esac
done
echo "there are ${DIRS} directories and ${FILES} files"
ls | grep "ZxY--!!!WKW"
if [ $? != 0 ] ; then # exit code of last command
  echo "ZxY--!!!WKW not found"
fi
echo "enough... type 'man bash' if you want more info."
```

5.4   C

Linux is an excellent environment to program in C. Taken for granted that you know C, here are a couple of guidelines. To compile your standard `hello.c` you'll use the `gcc` compiler, which comes as part of Linux and has the same syntax as `g77`:

```
$ gcc -O2 -o hello hello.c
```

To link a library to a program, add the switch `-l<libname>`. For example, to link the math library and optimize do

```
$ gcc -O2 -o mathprog mathprog.c -lm
```

(The `-l<libname>` switch forces `gcc` to link the library `/usr/lib/lib<libname>.a`; so `-lm` links `/usr/lib/libm.a`).

When your program is made of several source files, you'll need to use the utility `make` described above. Just use `gcc` and C source files in the makefile.

You can invoke some help about the C functions, that are covered by man pages, section 3; for example,

```
$ man 3 printf
```

There are lots of libraries available out there; among the first you'll want to use are `ncurses`, to handle text mode effects, and `svgalib`, to do graphics.

6   Graphics

Among the scores of graphic packages available, `gnuplot` stands out for its power and ease of use. Go to X and type `gnuplot`, and have two sample data files ready: `2D-data.dat` (two data per line), and `3D-data.dat` (three data per line).

Examples of 2-D graphs:

```
gnuplot> set title "my first graph"
gnuplot> plot '2D-data.dat'
gnuplot> plot '2D-data.dat' with linespoints
gnuplot> plot '2D-data.dat', sin(x)
gnuplot> plot [-5:10] '2D-data.dat'
```

Example of 3-D graphs (each 'row' of X values is followed by a blank line):

```
gnuplot> set parametric ; set hidden3d ; set contour
gnuplot> splot '3D-data.dat' using 1:2:3 with linespoints
```

A single-column datafile (e.g., a time series) can also be plotted as a 2-D graph:

```
gnuplot> plot [-5:15] '2D-data-1col.dat' with linespoints
```

or as a 3-D graph (blank lines in the datafile, as above):

```
gnuplot> set noparametric ; set hidden3d
gnuplot> splot '3D-data-1col.dat' using 1 with linespoints
```

To print a graph: if the command to print on your Postscript printer is `lpr -Pps file.ps`, issue:

```
gnuplot> set term post
gnuplot> set out '| lpr -Pps'
gnuplot> replot
```

then type `set term x11` to restore. Don't get confused—the last print will come out only when you quit `gnuplot`.

For more info, type `help` or see the examples in directory `/usr/lib/gnuplot/demos/`, if you have it.

7 Mail and Internet Tools

Since Internet was born on UNIX machines, you find plenty of nice and easy-to-use applications under Linux. Here are just some:

- **Mail**: use `elm` or `pine` to handle your email; both programs have on-line help. For short messages, you could use `mail`, as in `mail -s "hello mate" user@somewhere < msg.txt`. You may like programs like `xmail` or some such.

- **Newsgroups**: use `tin` or `slrn`, both very intuitive and self-explanatory.

- **ftp**: apart from the usual character-based `ftp`, ask your sysadm to install the full-screen `ncftp` or a graphical ftp client like `xftp`.

- **WWW**: the ubiquitous `netscape`, or `xmosaic`, `chimera`, and `arena` are graphical web browsers; a character-based one is `lynx`, quick and effective.

8 Advanced Topics

Here the game gets tough. Learn these features, then you'll be ready to say that you 'know something about Linux' ;-)

8.1 Permissions and Ownership

Files and directories have permissions ('protections') and ownership, just like under VMS. If you can't run a program, or can't modify a file, or can't access a directory, it's because you don't have the permission to do so, and/or because the file doesn't belong to you. Let's have a look at the following example:

```
$ ls -l /bin/ls
-rwxr-xr-x   1 root      bin          27281 Aug 15  1995 /bin/ls*
```

The first field shows the permissions of the file `ls` (owner root, group bin). There are three types of ownership: owner, group, and others (similar to VMS owner, group, world), and three types of permissions: read, write (and delete), and execute.

From left to right, `-` is the file type (`-` = ordinary file, `d` = directory, `l` = link, etc); `rwx` are the permissions for the file owner (read, write, execute); `r-x` are the permissions for the group of the file owner (read, execute); `r-x` are the permissions for all other users (read, execute).

To change a file's permissions:

```
$ chmod <whoXperm> <file>
```

where who is `u` (user, that is owner), `g` (group), `o` (other), X is either `+` or `-`, perm is `r` (read), `w` (write), or `x` (execute). Examples:

```
$ chmod u+x file
```

this sets the execute permission for the file owner. Shortcut: `chmod +x file`.

```
$ chmod go-wx file
```

this removes write and execute permission for everyone except the owner.

```
$ chmod ugo+rwx file
```

this gives everyone read, write, and execute permission.

A shorter way to refer to permissions is with numbers: `rwxr-xr-x` can be expressed as 755 (every letter corresponds to a bit: `--` is 0, `-x` is 1, `-w-` is 2...).

For a directory, `rx` means that you can `cd` to that directory, and `w` means that you can delete a file in the directory (according to the file's permissions, of course), or the directory itself. All this is only part of the matter—RMP.

To change a file's owner:

```
$ chown username file
```

To sum up, a table:

```
VMS                          Linux                     Notes
----------------------------------------------------------------------------
--

SET PROT=(O:RW) file.txt     $ chmod u+rw file.txt
                             $ chmod 600 file.txt
SET PROT=(O:RWED,W) file     $ chmod u+rwx file
                             $ chmod 700 file
```

```
SET PROT=(O:RWED,W:RE) file        $ chmod 755 file
SET PROT=(O:RW,G:RW,W) file        $ chmod 660 file
SET FILE/OWNER_UIC=JOE file        $ chown joe file
SET DIR/OWNER_UIC=JOE [.dir]       $ chown joe dir/
```

8.2 Multitasking: Processes and Jobs

More about running programs. There are no 'batch queues' under Linux as you're used to; multitasking is handled very differently. Again, this is what the typical command line looks like:

```
$ command -s1 -s2 ... -sn par1 par2 ... parn < input > output &
```

where -s1, ..., -sn are the program switches, par1, ..., parn are the program parameters.

Now let's see how multitasking works. Programs, running in foreground or background, are called 'processes'.

- To launch a process in background:

  ```
  $ progname [-switches] [parameters] [< input] [> output] &
  [1] 234
  ```

  the shell tells you what the 'job number' (the first digit; see below) and PID (Process IDentifier) of the process are. Each process is identified by its PID.

- To see how many processes there are:

  ```
  $ ps -ax
  ```

  This will output a list of currently running processes.

- To kill a process:

  ```
  $ kill <PID>
  ```

  You may need to kill a process when you don't know how to quit it the right way... ;-). Sometimes, a process will only be killed by one of the following:

  ```
  $ kill -15 <PID>
  $ kill -9 <PID>
  ```

In addition to this, the shell allows you to stop or temporarily suspend a process, send a process to background, and bring a process from background to foreground. In this context, processes are called 'jobs'.

- To see how many jobs there are:

  ```
  $ jobs
  ```

  jobs are identified by the numbers the shell gives them, not by their PID.

- To stop a process running in foreground:

  ```
  $ CTRL-C
  ```

  (it doesn't always work)

- To suspend a process running in foreground:

  ```
  $ CTRL-Z
  ```

  (ditto)

- To send a suspended process into background (it becomes a job):

  ```
  $ bg <job>
  ```

- To bring a job to foreground:

    ```
    $ fg <job>
    ```

- To kill a job:

    ```
    $ kill <%job>
    ```

8.3 Files, Revisited

More information about files.

- **stdin, stdout, stderr**: under UNIX, every system component is treated as if it were a file. Commands and programs get their input from a 'file' called `stdin` (standard input; usually, the keyboard), put their output on a 'file' called `stdout` (usually, the screen), and error messages go to a 'file' called `stderr` (usually, the screen).

    Using < and > you redirect input and output to a different file. Moreover, >> appends the output to a file instead of overwriting it; 2> redirects error messages (stderr); 2>&1 redirects stderr to stdout, while 1>&2 redirects stdout to stderr. There's a 'black hole' called `/dev/null`: everything redirected to it disappears;

- **wildcards**: '*' is almost the same. Usage: * matches all files except the hidden ones; .* matches all hidden files; *.* matches only those that have a '.' in the middle, followed by other characters; p*r matches both 'peter' and 'piper'; *c* matches both 'picked' and 'peck'. '%' becomes '?'. There is another wildcard: the []. Usage: [abc]* matches files starting with a, b, c; *[I-N,1,2,3] matches files ending with I, J, K, L, M, N, 1, 2, 3;

- `mv` (RENAME) doesn't work for multiple files; that is, `mv *.xxx *.yyy` won't work;

- use `cp -i` and `mv -i` to be warned when a file is going to be overwritten.

8.4 Print Queues

Your prints are queued, like under VMS. When you issue a print command, you may specify a printer name. Example:

```
$ lpr file.txt          # this goes to the standard printer
$ lpr -Plaser file.ps   # this goes to the printer named 'laser'
```

To handle the print queues, you use the following commands:

```
VMS                              Linux
--------------------------------------------------------------------------
--

$ PRINT file.ps                  $ lpr file.ps
$ PRINT/QUEUE=laser file.ps      $ lpr -Plaser file.ps
$ SHOW QUEUE                     $ lpq
$ SHOW QUEUE/QUEUE=laser         $ lpq -Plaser
$ STOP/QUEUE                     $ lprm <item>
```

9 Configuring

Your sysadm has already provided you with a number of configuration files like `.xinitrc`, `.bash_profile`, `.inputrc`, and many others. The ones you may want to edit are:

- `.bash_profile` or `.profile`: read by the shell at login time. It's like `LOGIN.COM`;

- `.bash_logout`: read by the shell at logout. It's like `LOGOUT.COM`;

- `.bashrc`: read by non–login shells.

- .inputrc: this file customises the key bindings and the behaviour of the shell.

To give you an example, I'll include my .bash_profile (abridged):

```
# $HOME/.bash_profile

# don't redefine the path if not necessary
echo $PATH | grep $LOGNAME > /dev/null
if [ $? != 0 ]
then
  export PATH="$PATH:/home/$LOGNAME/bin"  # add my dir to the PATH
fi

export PS1='LOGNAME:\w\$ '
export PS2='Continued...>'

# aliases

alias bin="cd ~/bin" ; alias cp="cp -i" ; alias d="dir"
alias del="delete" ; alias dir="/bin/ls $LS_OPTIONS --format=vertical"
alias ed="jed" ; alias mv='mv -i'
alias u="cd .." ; alias undel="undelete"

# A few useful functions

inst() # Install a .tar.gz archive in current directory.
{
  gzip -dc $1 | tar xvf -
}
cz() # List the contents of a .zip archive.
{
  unzip -l $*
}
ctgz() # List the contents of a .tar.gz archive.
{
  for file in $* ; do
    gzip -dc ${file} | tar tf -
  done
}
tgz() # Create a .tgz archive a la zip.
{
  name=$1 ; tar -cvf $1 ; shift
  tar -rf ${name} $* ; gzip -S .tgz ${name}
}
```

And this is my .inputrc:

```
# $HOME/.inputrc
# Last modified: 16 January 1997.
#
# This file is read by bash and defines key bindings to be used by the shell;
# what follows fixes the keys END, HOME, and DELETE, plus accented letters.
# For more information, man readline.
```

```
"\e[1~": beginning-of-line
"\e[3~": delete-char
"\e[4~": end-of-line

set bell-style visible
set meta-flag On
set convert-meta Off
set output-meta On
set horizontal-scroll-mode On
set show-all-if-ambiguous On

# (F1 .. F5) are "\e[[A" ... "\e[[E"

"\e[[A": "info "
```

10   Useful Programs

10.1   Browsing Files: `less`

You'll use this file browser every day, so I'll give you a couple of tips to use it at best. First of all, ask your sysadm to configure `less` so as it can display not only plain text files, but also compressed files, archives, and so on.

The main advantage of `less` over TYPE is that you can browse files in both directions. It also accepts several commands that are issued pressing a key. The most useful are:

- first of all, press q to leave the browser;

- h gives you extensive help;

- g to go to beginning of file, G to the end, number+g to go to line 'number' (e.g. 125g), number+% to move to that percentage of the file;

- /`pattern` searches forwards for 'pattern'; n searches forwards for the next match; ?`pattern` and N search backwards;

- m+letter marks current position (e.g. ma); '+letter go to the marked position;

- : e examines a new file;

- !command executes the shell command.

10.2   RCS in a Nutshell

The lack of version numbers in files can be easily overcome by using RCS (Revision Control System). This allows you to maintain several versions of the same file, and offers many more advantages. I'll only explain the very basics of this powerful version control system.

The most important commands are ci and co. The first ("check in") is used to commit the changes you have done to your file, and create a new version. The second ("check out") is used to obtain a working copy of your file from the RCS system, either to modify it or simply use it for browsing, printing, or whatever.

Let's see an example. First of all you create an *initial revision* of your file, using your favourite editor. Let's suppose that the file you'll have under RCS control is called project.tex. Follow these steps:

- make a subdirectory called RCS/ in the directory containing project.tex. RCS/ will contain the revision control file;

- to put project.tex under RCS control, issue the command

```
$ ci project.tex
RCS/project.tex,v  <-- project.tex
enter description, terminated with a single '.' or end of file:
NOTE: This is NOT the log message!
>>
```

- you will write a line or more containing a description of the contents of your file. End it with a line containing a '.' by itself, and you'll see

```
initial revision: 1.1
done
```

Now the file `project.tex` has been taken over by RCS.

10.2.1   Using the latest version

Whenever you want to use, but not modify, the latest version of project.tex, you issue the command

```
$ co project.tex
RCS/project.tex,v  --> project.tex
revision 1.1
done
```

This extracts the latest version (read only) of your file. Now you can browse it, or compile it with tex, but you can't modify it.

10.2.2   Creating a new version

When you want to modify your file, you must obtain a "lock" on it. This means that RCS knows that you're about to make a newer version. In this case, you use the command

```
$ co project.tex
RCS/project.tex,v  --> project.tex
revision 1.1 (locked)
done
```

You now have a working copy you can modify with your editor. When you're done editing it, you check it in again to commit the changes:

```
$ ci project.tex
RCS/project.tex,v  <-- project.tex
new revision 1.2; previous revision: 1.1
enter log message, terminated with a single '.' or end of file:
>> (enter your description here)
>> .
done
```

If you want to change the version number, type `ci -f2.0 project.tex`.

10.2.3   Comparing versions

If you want to see the history of the changes in project.tex, issue

```
$ rlog project.tex
```

10.2.4   Using an old version

To extract an older version of your file (say, version 1.2 when you're working on 1.6), issue

```
$ co -r1.2 project.tex
```

Be aware that this overwrites your existing working file, if you have one. You may do:

```
$ co -r1.2 -p project.tex > project.tex.1.2
```

10.3   Archiving: tar & gzip

Under UNIX there are some widely used applications to archive and compress files. `tar` is used to make archives, that is collections of files. To make a new archive:

```
$ tar -cvf <archive_name.tar> <file> [file...]
```

To extract files from an archive:

```
$ tar -xpvf <archive_name.tar> [file...]
```

To list the contents of an archive:

```
$ tar -tf <archive_name.tar> | less
```

Files can be compressed to save disk space using `compress`, which is obsolete and shouldn't be used any more, or `gzip`:

```
$ compress <file>
$ gzip <file>
```

that creates a compressed file with extension .Z (`compress`) or .gz (`gzip`). These programs don't make archives, but compress files individually. To decompress, use:

```
$ compress -d <file.Z>
$ gzip -d <file.gz>
```

RMP.

The `unarj`, `zip` and `unzip` utilities are also available. Files with extension `.tar.gz` or `.tgz` (archived with `tar`, then compressed with `gzip`) are very common in the UNIX world. Here's how to list the contents of a `.tar.gz` archive:

```
$ gzip -dc <file.tar.gz> | tar tf - | less
```

To extract the files from a `.tar.gz` archive:

```
$ gzip -dc <file.tar.gz> | tar xvf -
```

11 Real Life Examples

UNIX' core idea is that there are many simple commands that can linked together via piping and redirection to accomplish even really complex tasks. Look at the following examples; I'll only explain the most complex ones, for the others, please study the above sections and the man pages.

Problem: ls is too quick and the file names fly away.

Solution:

```
$ ls | less
```

Problem: I have a file containing a list of words. I want to sort it in reverse order and print it.

Solution:

```
$ cat myfile.txt | sort -r | lpr
```

Problem: my datafile has some repeated lines! How do I get rid of them?

Solution:

```
$ sort datafile.dat | uniq > newfile.dat
```

Problem: I have a file called 'mypaper.txt' or 'mypaper.tex' or some such somewhere, but I don't remember where I put it. How do I find it?

Solution:

```
$ find ~ -name "mypaper*"
```

Explanation: find is a very useful command that lists all the files in a directory tree (starting from ~ in this case). Its output can be filtered to meet several criteria, such as -name.

Problem: I have a text file containing the word 'entropy' in this directory, is there anything like SEARCH?

Solution: yes, try

```
$ grep -l 'entropy' *
```

Problem: somewhere I have text files containing the word 'entropy', I'd like to know which and where they are. Under VMS I'd use search entropy [...]*.*.*, but grep can't recurse subdirectories. Now what?

Solution:

```
$ find . -exec grep -l "entropy" {} \; 2> /dev/null
```

Explanation: find . outputs all the file names starting from the current directory, -exec grep -l "entropy" is an action to be performed on each file (represented by {}), \ terminates the command. If you think this syntax is awful, you're right.

In alternative, write the following script:

```
#!/bin/sh
# rgrep: recursive grep
if [ $# != 3 ]
then
```

```
      echo "Usage: rgrep --switches 'pattern' 'directory'"
      exit 1
fi
find $3 -name "*" -exec grep $1 $2 {} \; 2> /dev/null
```

Explanation: `grep` works like `search`, and combining it with `find` we get the best of both worlds.

Problem: I have a data file that has two header lines, then every line has 'n' data, not necessarily equally spaced. I want the 2nd and 5th data of each line. Shall I write a Fortran program...?

Solution: nope. This is quicker:

```
   $ awk 'NL > 2 {print $2, "\t", $5}' datafile.dat > newfile.dat
```

Explanation: the command `awk` is actually a programming language: for each line starting from the third in `datafile.dat`, print out the second and fifth field, separated by a tab. Learn some `awk`—it saves a lot of time.

Problem: I've downloaded an FTP site's `ls-lR.gz` to check its contents. For each subdirectory, it contains a line that reads "total xxxx", where xxxx is size in kbytes of the dir contents. I'd like to get the grand total of all these xxxx values.

Solution:

```
   zcat ls-lR.gz | awk ' $1 == "total" { i += $2 } END {print i}'
```

Explanation: `zcat` outputs the contents of the `.gz` file and pipes to `awk`, whose man page you're kindly requested to read ;-)

Problem: I've written a Fortran program, `myprog`, to calculate a parameter from a data file. I'd like to run it on hundreds of data files and have a list of the results, but it's a nuisance to ask each time for the file name. Under VMS I'd write a lengthy command file, and under Linux?

Solution: a very short script. Make your program look for the data file 'mydata.dat' and print the result on the screen (stdout), then write the following script:

```
#!/bin/sh
# myprog.sh: run the same command on many different files
# usage: myprog.sh *.dat
for file in $*   # for all parameters (e.g. *.dat)
do
  # append the file name to result.dat
  echo -n "${file}:    " >> results.dat
  # copy current argument to mydata.dat, run myprog
  # and append the output to results.dat
  cp ${file} mydata.dat ; myprog >> results.dat
done
```

Problem: I want to replace 'geology' with 'geophysics' in all my text files. Shall I edit them all manually?

Solution: nope. Write this shell script:

```
#!/bin/sh
# replace $1 with $2 in $*
# usage: replace "old-pattern" "new-pattern" file [file...]
OLD=$1            # first parameter of the script
NEW=$2            # second parameter
shift ; shift     # discard first two parameters: the next are the file names
```

```
for file in $*  # for all files given as parameters
do
# replace every occurrence of OLD with NEW, save on a temporary file
  sed "s/$OLD/$NEW/g" ${file} > ${file}.new
# rename the temporary file as the original file
  /bin/mv ${file}.new ${file}
done
```

Problem: I have some data files, I don't know their length and have to remove their last but one and last but two lines. Er... manually?

Solution: no, of course. Write this script:

```
#!/bin/sh
# prune.sh: removes n-1th and n-2th lines from files
# usage: prune.sh file [file...]
for file in $*   # for every parameter
do
  LINES='wc -l $file | awk '{print $1}''  # number of lines in file
  LINES='expr $LINES - 3'                  # LINES = LINES - 3
  head -n $LINES $file > $file.new         # output first LINES lines
  tail -n 1 $file >> $file.new             # append last line
done
```

I hope these examples whetted your appetite...

12   Tips You Can't Do Without

- **Command completion**: pressing <TAB> when issuing a command will complete the command line for you. Example: you have to type less this_is_a_long_name; typing in less thi<TAB> will suffice. (If you have other files that start with the same characters, supply enough characters to resolve any ambiguity.)

- **Back-scrolling**: pressing SHIFT–PAG UP (the grey key) allows you to backscroll a few pages, depending on your PC's video memory.

- **Resetting the screen**: if you happen to more or cat a binary file, your screen may end up full of garbage. To fix things, blind type reset or this sequence of characters: echo CTRL-V ESC c RETURN.

- **Pasting text**: in console, see below; in X, click and drag to select the text in an xterm window, then click the middle button (or the two buttons together if you have a two-button mouse) to paste.

- **Using the mouse**: ask your sysadm to install gpm, a mouse driver for the console. Click and drag to select text, then right click to paste the selected text. It works across different VCs.

13   The End

13.1   Copyright

Unless otherwise stated, Linux HOWTO documents are copyrighted by their respective authors. Linux HOWTO documents may be reproduced and distributed in whole or in part, in any medium physical or electronic, as long as this copyright notice is retained on all copies. Commercial redistribution is allowed and encouraged; however, the author would like to be notified of any such distributions.

All translations, derivative works, or aggregate works incorporating any Linux HOWTO documents must be covered under this copyright notice. That is, you may not produce a derivative work from a HOWTO and impose additional restrictions on its distribution. Exceptions to these rules may be granted under certain conditions; please contact the Linux HOWTO coordinator at the address given below.

In short, we wish to promote dissemination of this information through as many channels as possible. However, we do wish to retain copyright on the HOWTO documents, and would like to be notified of any plans to redistribute the HOWTOs.

If you have questions, please contact Tim Bynum, the Linux HOWTO coordinator, at linux-howto@sunsite.unc.edu via email.

14 Disclaimer

This work was written following the experience we had at the Settore di Geofisica of Bologna University (Italy), where a VAX 4000 is being superseded and replaced by Linux-based Pentium PCs. Most of my colleagues are VMS users, and some of them have switched to Linux.

"From VMS to Linux HOWTO" was written by Guido Gonzato, *guido@ibogfs.cineca.it*, 1997. Many thanks to my colleagues and friends who helped me define the needs and habits of the average VMS user, especially to Dr. Warner Marzocchi.

Please help me improve this HOWTO. I'm not a VMS expert and never will be, so your suggestions and bug reports are more than welcome.

Enjoy,

Guido =8-)

Part XLVIII

"Virtual Services Howto" Brian Ackerman

brian@nycrc.net
v2.1, 15 August 1998
This document came about to satisfy the ever increasing need to know how to virtualize a service.

Contents

HOWTO

1 Introduction

1.1 Knowledge Required

Creating a virtual services machine is not all that difficult, however, more than fundamental knowledge is required. This document is not a primer to how to fully configure a Linux machine.

In order to understand this HOWTO document it is assumed that you are thoroughly familiar with the following:

- Compiling a Linux kernel and adding IP aliasing support *IP alias mini-HOWTO*
- Setting up and configuring of network devices *NET-3 HOWTO*
- Setting up of inetd *NET-3 HOWTO*
- Various network packages like *Sendmail Apache Qmail SAMBA*
- Setting up DNS *DNS HOWTO*
- Understanding basic system administration *Linux Systems Administrators's Guide*
- Understanding how to setup a Web Server *WWW HOWTO*

If you are uncertain of how to proceed with any of the above it is STRONGLY recommended that you use the html links provided to familiarize yourself with all packages. I will NOT reply to mail regarding any of the above. Please direct your questions to the appropriate author of the HOWTO.

1.2 Purpose

The purpose of virtual services is to allow a single machine to recognize multiple IP addresses without multiple network cards. IP aliasing is a kernel option that allows you to assign each network device more than one IP address. The kernel then multiplexes (swaps between them very fast) in the background and to the user it appears like you have more than one server.

This multiplexing allows multiple domains (www.domain1.com, www.domain2.com, etc.) to be hosted by the same machine for the same cost as hosting one domain. Unfortunately, most services (FTP, web, mail) were not designed to handle muliple domains. In order to make them work properly you must modify both configuration files and source code. This document describes how to make these modifications in the setting up of a virtual machine.

A deamon is also required in order to make virtual services function. The source for this daemon (virtuald) is provided later in this document.

1.3 Feedback

This document will expand as packages are updated and source or configuration modifications change. If there are any portions of this document that are unclear please feel free to email me with your suggestions or questions. So that I do not have to go searching through the entire HOWTO please make certain that all comments are as specific as possible and include the section where the uncertainty lies. It is important that all mail be addressed with VIRTSERVICES HOWTO in the subject line. Any other mail will be considered personal and all my friends know that I do not ever read my personal mail so it will probably get discarded with theirs.

Please note that my examples are just that, examples and should not be copied verbatim. You may have to insert your own values. If you are having trouble, send me mail. Include all the pertinent configuration files and the error messages you get when installing and I will look them over and reply with my suggestions.

1.4 Revision History

V1.0

Initial version

V1.1

Fixed error in Virtual Web Section

V1.2

Fixed the date

V2.0

Updated html links.

Web updates.

New Sendmail option.

New Qmail section.

Syslogd updates.

FTP updates.

Virtuald default option.

New SAMBA section.

FAQ updates.

HOWTO

V2.1

Changed all paths to /usr/local.

Added virtuald VERBOSELOG compile option.

Fixed setuid/setgid bug in virtmailfilter.

Fixed execl bug in virtmailfilter.

Fixed capitialization bug in virtmailfilter.

Fixed environment variable sanity check in virtmailfilter.

Removed mbox code from virtmailfilter/virtmaildelivery.

Added tcpserver.init pop section for Qmail.

Added alias domain name question to the FAQ.

Fixed virtmailfilter to send home directory to virtmaildelivery.

1.5 Copyright/Distribution

This document is Copyright (c) 1997 by The Computer Resource Center Inc.

A verbatim copy may be reproduced or distributed in any medium physical or electronic without permission of the author. Translations are similarly permitted without express permission if it includes a notice on who translated it. Commercial redistribution is allowed and encouraged; however please notify *Computer Resource Center* of any such distributions.

Excerpts from the document may be used without prior consent provided that the derivative work contains the verbatim copy or a pointer to a verbatim copy.

Permission is granted to make and distribute verbatim copies of this document provided the copyright notice and this permission notice are preserved on all copies.

In short, we wish to promote dissemination of this information through as many channels as possible. However, I do wish to retain copyright on this HOWTO document, and would like to be notified of any plans to redistribute this HOWTO.

2 IP Aliasing

IP aliasing is a kernel option that needs to be set up in order to run a virtual hosting machine. There is already a mini-HOWTO on *IP aliasing*. Consult that for any questions on how to set it up.

3 Virtuald

3.1 Introduction

Every network connection is made up of two IP address/port pairs. The API (Applications Program Interface) for network programming is called the Sockets API. The socket acts like an open file and by reading/writing to it you can send data over a network connection. There is a function call `getsockname` that will return the IP address of the local socket. Virtuald uses `getsockname` to determine which IP on the local machine is being accessed. Virtuald reads a config file to retrieve the directory associated with that IP. It will `chroot` to that directory and hand the connection off to the service. `Chroot` resets / or the root directory to a new point so everything higher in the directory tree is cut off from the running program. Therefore, each IP address gets their own virtual filesystem. To the network program this is transparent and the program will behave like nothing happened. Virtuald in conjunction with a program like inetd can then be used to virtualize any service.

3.2 Inetd

Inetd is a network super server that listens at multiple ports and when it receives a connection (for example, an incoming pop request), inetd performs the network negotiation and hands the network connection off to the specified program. This prevents services from running idly when they are not needed.

A standard /etc/inetd.conf file looks like this:

```
ftp stream tcp nowait root /usr/sbin/tcpd \
        wu.ftpd -l -a
pop-3 stream tcp nowait root /usr/sbin/tcpd \
        in.qpop -s
```

A virtual /etc/inetd.conf file looks like this:

```
ftp stream tcp nowait root /usr/local/bin/virtuald \
        virtuald /virtual/conf.ftp wu.ftpd -l -a
pop-3 stream tcp nowait root /usr/local/bin/virtuald \
        virtuald /virtual/conf.pop in.qpop -s
```

3.3 Config File

Each service gets a config file that will control what IPs and directories are allowed for that service. You can have one master config file or several config files if you want each service to get a different list of domains. A config file looks like this:

```
# This is a comment and so are blank lines

# Format IP SPACE dir NOSPACES
10.10.10.129 /virtual/domain1.com
10.10.10.130 /virtual/domain2.com
10.10.10.157 /virtual/domain3.com

# Default option for all other IPs
default /
```

3.4 Source

This is the C source code to the virtuald program. Compile it and install it in /usr/local/bin with permission 0755, user root, and group root. The only compile option is VERBOSELOG which will turn on/off logging of connections.

```
#include <netinet/in.h>
#include <sys/socket.h>
#include <arpa/inet.h>
#include <stdarg.h>
#include <unistd.h>
#include <string.h>
#include <syslog.h>
#include <stdio.h>

#undef VERBOSELOG

#define BUFSIZE 8192
```

```
int getipaddr(char **ipaddr)
{
        struct sockaddr_in virtual_addr;
        static char ipaddrbuf[BUFSIZE];
        int virtual_len;
        char *ipptr;

        virtual_len=sizeof(virtual_addr);
        if (getsockname(0,(struct sockaddr *)&virtual_addr,&virtual_len)<0)
        {
                syslog(LOG_ERR,"getipaddr: getsockname failed: %m");
                return -1;
        }
        if (!(ipptr=inet_ntoa(virtual_addr.sin_addr)))
        {
                syslog(LOG_ERR,"getipaddr: inet_ntoa failed: %m");
                return -1;
        }
        strncpy(ipaddrbuf,ipptr,sizeof(ipaddrbuf)-1);
        *ipaddr=ipaddrbuf;
        return 0;
}

int iptodir(char **dir,char *ipaddr,char *filename)
{
        char buffer[BUFSIZE],*bufptr;
        static char dirbuf[BUFSIZE];
        FILE *fp;

        if (!(fp=fopen(filename,"r")))
        {
                syslog(LOG_ERR,"iptodir: fopen failed: %m");
                return -1;
        }
        *dir=NULL;
        while(fgets(buffer,BUFSIZE,fp))
        {
                buffer[strlen(buffer)-1]=0;
                if (*buffer=='#' || *buffer==0)
                        continue;
                if (!(bufptr=strchr(buffer,' ')))
                {
                        syslog(LOG_ERR,"iptodir: strchr failed");
                        return -1;
                }
                *bufptr++=0;
                if (!strcmp(buffer,ipaddr))
                {
                        strncpy(dirbuf,bufptr,sizeof(dirbuf)-1);
                        *dir=dirbuf;
                        break;
                }
                if (!strcmp(buffer,"default"))
                {
                        strncpy(dirbuf,bufptr,sizeof(dirbuf)-1);
```

```
                                        *dir=dirbuf;
                                        break;
                        }
        }
        if (fclose(fp)==EOF)
        {
                syslog(LOG_ERR,"iptodir: fclose failed: %m");
                return -1;
        }
        if (!*dir)
        {
                syslog(LOG_ERR,"iptodir: ip not found in conf file");
                return -1;
        }
        return 0;
}

int main(int argc,char **argv)
{
        char *ipaddr,*dir;

        openlog("virtuald",LOG_PID,LOG_DAEMON);

#ifdef VERBOSELOG
        syslog(LOG_ERR,"Virtuald Starting: $Revision: 1.49 $");
#endif
        if (!argv[1])
        {
                syslog(LOG_ERR,"invalid arguments: no conf file");
                exit(0);
        }
        if (!argv[2])
        {
                syslog(LOG_ERR,"invalid arguments: no program to run");
                exit(0);
        }
        if (getipaddr(&ipaddr))
        {
                syslog(LOG_ERR,"getipaddr failed");
                exit(0);
        }
#ifdef VERBOSELOG
        syslog(LOG_ERR,"Incoming ip: %s",ipaddr);
#endif
        if (iptodir(&dir,ipaddr,argv[1]))
        {
                syslog(LOG_ERR,"iptodir failed");
                exit(0);
        }
        if (chroot(dir)<0)
        {
                syslog(LOG_ERR,"chroot failed: %m");
                exit(0);
        }
#ifdef VERBOSELOG
```

```
                syslog(LOG_ERR,"Chroot dir: %s",dir);
#endif
        if (chdir("/")<0)
        {
                syslog(LOG_ERR,"chdir failed: %m");
                exit(0);
        }
        if (execvp(argv[2],argv+2)<0)
        {
                syslog(LOG_ERR,"execvp failed: %m");
                exit(0);
        }

        closelog();

        exit(0);
}
```

4 Shell Scripts

4.1 Virtfs

Each domain should get their own directory structure. Since you are using `chroot` you will require duplicate copies of the shared libraries, binaries, conf files, etc. I use /virtual/domain1.com for each domain that I create.

I realize that you are taking up more disk space but it is cheaper than a whole new machine and network cards. If you really want to preserve space you can hard link the files together so only one copy of each binary exists. The filesystem that I use takes up a little over 2M. However, this script attempts to copy all the files from the main filesystem in order to be as generic as possible.

Here is a sample virtfs script:

```
#!/bin/sh

echo '$Revision: 1.49 $'

echo -n "Enter the domain name: "
read domain

if [ "$domain" = "" ]
then
        echo Nothing entered: aborting
        exit 0
fi

leadingdir=/virtual

echo -n "Enter leading dir: (Enter for default: $leadingdir): "
read ans

if [ "$ans" != "" ]
then
        leadingdir=$ans
fi
```

```
newdir=$leadingdir/$domain

if [ -d "$newdir" ]
then
        echo New directory: $newdir: ALREADY exists
        exit 0
else
        echo New directory: $newdir
fi

echo Create $newdir
mkdir -p $newdir

echo Create bin
cp -pdR /bin $newdir

echo Create dev
cp -pdR /dev $newdir

echo Create dev/log
ln -f /virtual/log $newdir/dev/log

echo Create etc
mkdir -p $newdir/etc
for i in /etc/*
do
        if [ -d "$i" ]
        then
                continue
        fi
        cp -pd $i $newdir/etc
done

echo Create etc/skel
mkdir -p $newdir/etc/skel

echo Create home
for i in a b c d e f g h i j k l m n o p q r s t u v w x y z
do
        mkdir -p $newdir/home/$i
done

echo Create home/c/crc
mkdir -p $newdir/home/c/crc
chown crc.users $newdir/home/c/crc

echo Create lib
mkdir -p $newdir/lib
for i in /lib/*
do
        if [ -d "$i" ]
        then
                continue
        fi
```

```
        cp -pd $i $newdir/lib
done

echo Create proc
mkdir -p $newdir/proc

echo Create sbin
cp -pdR /sbin $newdir

echo Create tmp
mkdir -p -m 0777 $newdir/tmp
chmod +t $newdir/tmp

echo Create usr
mkdir -p $newdir/usr

echo Create usr/bin
cp -pdR /usr/bin $newdir/usr

echo Create usr/lib
mkdir -p $newdir/usr/lib

echo Create usr/lib/locale
cp -pdR /usr/lib/locale $newdir/usr/lib

echo Create usr/lib/terminfo
cp -pdR /usr/lib/terminfo $newdir/usr/lib

echo Create usr/lib/zoneinfo
cp -pdR /usr/lib/zoneinfo $newdir/usr/lib

echo Create usr/lib/\*.so\*
cp -pdR /usr/lib/*.so* $newdir/usr/lib

echo Create usr/sbin
cp -pdR /usr/sbin $newdir/usr

echo Linking usr/tmp
ln -s /tmp $newdir/usr/tmp

echo Create var
mkdir -p $newdir/var

echo Create var/lock
cp -pdR /var/lock $newdir/var

echo Create var/log
mkdir -p $newdir/var/log

echo Create var/log/wtmp
cp /dev/null $newdir/var/log/wtmp

echo Create var/run
cp -pdR /var/run $newdir/var
```

```
echo Create var/run/utmp
cp /dev/null $newdir/var/run/utmp

echo Create var/spool
cp -pdR /var/spool $newdir/var

echo Linking var/tmp
ln -s /tmp $newdir/var/tmp

echo Create var/www/html
mkdir -p $newdir/var/www/html
chown webmast.www $newdir/var/www/html
chmod g+s $newdir/var/www/html

echo Create var/www/master
mkdir -p $newdir/var/www/master
chown webmast.www $newdir/var/www/master

echo Create var/www/server
mkdir -p $newdir/var/www/server
chown webmast.www $newdir/var/www/server

exit 0
```

4.2 Virtexec

To execute commands in a virtual environment you have to `chroot` to that directory and then run the command. I have written a special shell script called virtexec that handles this for any command:

```
#!/bin/sh

echo '$Revision: 1.49 $'

BNAME='basename $0'
FIRST4CHAR='echo $BNAME | cut -c1-4'
REALBNAME='echo $BNAME | cut -c5-'

if [ "$BNAME" = "virtexec" ]
then
        echo Cannot run virtexec directly: NEED a symlink
        exit 0
fi

if [ "$FIRST4CHAR" != "virt" ]
then
        echo Symlink not a virt function
        exit 0
fi

list=""
num=1
for i in /virtual/*
do
        if [ ! -d "$i" ]
        then
```

```
                continue
        fi
        if [ "$i" = "/virtual/lost+found" ]
        then
                continue
        fi
        list="$list $i $num"
        num='expr $num + 1'
done

if [ "$list" = "" ]
then
        echo No virtual environments exist
        exit 0
fi

dialog --clear --title 'Virtexec' --menu Pick 20 70 12 $list 2> /tmp/menu.$$
if [ "$?" = "0" ]
then
        newdir='cat /tmp/menu.$$'
else
        newdir=""
fi
tput clear
rm -f /tmp/menu.$$

echo '$Revision: 1.49 $'

if [ ! -d "$newdir" ]
then
        echo New directory: $newdir: NOT EXIST
        exit 0
else
        echo New directory: $newdir
fi

echo bname: $BNAME

echo realbname: $REALBNAME

if [ "$*" = "" ]
then
        echo args: none
else
        echo args: $*
fi

echo Changing to $newdir
cd $newdir

echo Running program $REALBNAME

chroot $newdir $REALBNAME $*

exit 0
```

Please note that you must have the `dialog` program installed on your system for this to work. To use virtexec just symlink a program to it. For example,

```
ln -s /usr/local/bin/virtexec /usr/local/bin/virtpasswd
ln -s /usr/local/bin/virtexec /usr/local/bin/virtvi
ln -s /usr/local/bin/virtexec /usr/local/bin/virtpico
ln -s /usr/local/bin/virtexec /usr/local/bin/virtemacs
ln -s /usr/local/bin/virtexec /usr/local/bin/virtmailq
```

Then if you type virtvi or virtpasswd or virtmailq it will allow you to vi a program, change a user's password or check the mail queue on your virtual system. You can create as many virtexec symlinks as you want. Please note that if your program requires a shared library it has to be in the virtual filesystem as well as the binary.

4.3 Notes

I install all the scripts in /usr/local/bin. Anything that I do not want to put on the virtual filesystem I put in /usr/local. The script does not copy any of the files in /usr/local to the virtual filesystem. Any files that are important to not cross virtual filesystems should be removed. For example, ssh is installed on my system and I did not want the private key for the server available on all the virtual filesystems so I remove it from each virtual filesystem after I run virtfs. I also change resolv.conf and remove anything that has the name of another domain on it for legal reasons. For example, /etc/hosts and /etc/HOSTNAME.

The programs that I symlink to virtexec are:

- virtpasswd – change a user password
- virtadduser – create a user
- virtdeluser – delete a user
- virtsmbstatus – see SAMBA status
- virtvi – edit a file
- virtmailq – check out the mailq
- virtnewaliases – rebuild alias tables

5   DNS

You can configure DNS normally. There is a HOWTO on *DNS*.

6   Syslogd

6.1   Problem

Syslogd is the system logging utility commonly used on UNIX systems. Syslogd is a daemon that opens a special file called a FIFO. A FIFO is a special file that acts like a pipe. Anything that is written to the write side will come out the read side. Syslogd waits for data from the read side. There are C functions that write to the write side. If your program uses these C functions your output will go to syslogd.

Remember that we have used a `chroot` environment and the FIFO that syslogd is reading from (/dev/log) is not present. That means all the virtual environments will not log to syslogd.

6.2 Solution

6.2.1 Setup Links

Syslogd can look to a different FIFO if you tell it on the command line so run syslogd with the argument:

```
syslogd -p /virtual/log
```

Then symlink /dev/log to /virtual/log by:

```
ln -sf /virtual/log /dev/log
```

Then hard link all the /dev/log copies to this file by running:

```
ln -f /virtual/log /virtual/domain1.com/dev/log
```

The virtfs script above already does this. Since /virtual is one contiguous disk and the /dev/log's are hard linked they have the same inode number and point to the same data. The `chroot` cannot stop this so all your virtual /dev/log's will now function. Note that all the messages from all the environments will be logged in one place. However, you can write separate programs to filter out the data.

6.2.2 Syslogd.init

This version of the syslogd.init file hard links the /dev/log's each time you start it because syslogd deletes and creates the /dev/log FIFO each time it runs. Here is a modified syslogd.init file:

```
#!/bin/sh

. /etc/rc.d/init.d/functions

case "$1" in
  start)
        echo -n "Starting dev log: "
        ln -sf /virtual/log /dev/log
        echo done
        echo -n "Starting system loggers: "
        daemon syslogd -p /virtual/log
        daemon klogd
        echo
        echo -n "Starting virtual dev log: "
        for i in /virtual/*
        do
                if [ ! -d "$i" ]
                then
                        continue
                fi
                if [ "$i" = "/virtual/lost+found" ]
                then
                        continue
                fi
                ln -f /virtual/log $i/dev/log
                echo -n "."
        done
        echo " done"
        touch /var/lock/subsys/syslogd
```

```
        ;;
stop)
        echo -n "Shutting down system loggers: "
        killproc syslogd
        killproc klogd
        echo
        rm -f /var/lock/subsys/syslogd
        ;;
  *)
        echo "Usage: syslogd {start|stop}"
        exit 1
esac

exit 0
```

6.3   Multiple Syslogd's

6.3.1   One Per Disk

If you run out of space on one filesystem and you have to break up your virtual domains onto different disks remember that hard links will not cross disks. That means you will have to run a separate syslogd for each group of domains on a disk. For example, if you had thirteen domains on /virtual1 and fifteen domains on /virtual2, you would hard link thirteen domains to /virtual1/log and run one syslogd with `syslogd -p /virtual1/log` and hard link fifteen other domains to /virtual2/log with a syslogd running with `syslogd -p /virtual2/log` .

6.3.2   One Per Domain

If you do not want to centralize the logs to one place you could also run one syslogd per domain. This wastes process ID's so I do not recommend it but it is easier to implement. You would have to alter your syslogd.init file to run syslogd as `chroot /virtual/domain1.com syslogd` for each domain. This will run each syslogd within the `chroot` and the logs will be in /virtual/domain1.com/var/log rather than all combined in /var/log. Do not forget to run a syslogd normally `syslogd` for the main system and a kernel logger `klogd` .

7   Virtual FTP

7.1   Inetd

Wu-ftpd comes with built in support to make it virtual. However, you cannot maintain separate password files for each domain. For example, if `bob@domain1.com` and `bob@domain2.com` both want an account you would have to make one of them bob2 or have one of the users choose a different user name. Since you now have a virtual filesystem for each domain you have separate password files and this problem goes away. Just create a virtnewuser script and a virtpasswd script in the way mentioned above and you are all set.

The inetd.conf entries for wu-ftpd:

```
ftp stream tcp nowait root /usr/local/bin/virtuald \
        virtuald /virtual/conf.ftp wu.ftpd -l -a
```

7.2   Anonymous FTP

These are unaffected by the virtuald setup.   For an anonymous user just create the FTP user in /virtual/domain1.com/etc/passwd like you would normally.

```
ftp:x:14:50:Anonymous FTP:/var/ftp:/bin/false
```

Then setup the anonymous FTP directory. You have separate password files for each domain so you can restrict which domain has an anonymous FTP account. Please note that since the FTP server is already `chrooted` into the /virtual/domain1.com directory you do not have to prefix any paths with it.

7.3 Virtual FTP Users

Wu-ftpd supports something called a guest group. This allows you to create different FTP areas for each user. The FTP server does a `chroot` to the specified area so the user cannot go outside that directory tree. If you create the users within a virtual domain this way they will not be able to view the system files.

Add the guest's group to the /virtual/domain1.com/etc/ftpaccess file.

Create an entry in /virtual/domain1.com/etc/passwd with the `chroot` dir and the starting home directory separated by `/./` :

```
guest1:x:8500:51:Guest FTP:/home/g/guest1/./incoming:/bin/false
```

Then setup guest's home like you would for anonymous FTP. You have separate password files for each domain so you can specifiy which domains have guest accounts and which users within a domain are guest users. Please note that since the FTP server is already `chrooted` into the /virtual/domain1.com directory you do not have to prefix any paths with it.

8 Virtual Web

8.1 Running With Virtuald

8.1.1 Not recommended

Apache has their own support for virtual domains. This is the only program I recommend using the internal virtual domain mechanism. When you run something through inetd there is a cost, the program has to start up each time you run it. This results in slower response time, which is perfectly fine for most services but is completely unacceptable for web service. Apache also has a mechanism for stopping connections when too many come in, which can be critical for even medium volume sites.

Simply stated, virtualizing Apache with virtuald is a really bad idea. The whole point of virtuald is to fill the gap created when services DO NOT have their own internal mechanism to do the job. Virtuald is not meant to replace good code that already completes the task at hand.

The above not withstanding here is how to do it for those who are foolhardy enough to do so.

8.1.2 Inetd

Edit /etc/inetd.conf

```
vi /etc/inetd.conf # Add this line
www stream tcp nowait www /usr/local/bin/virtuald \
        virtuald /virtual/conf.www httpd -f /var/www/conf/httpd.conf
```

8.1.3 Httpd.conf

Edit /var/www/conf/httpd.conf

```
vi /var/www/conf/httpd.conf # Or wherever you put the Apache config files
It should say:
ServerType standalone
```

```
Replace it with:
ServerType inetd
```

8.1.4 Configuration

Then configure each instance of the Apache server like you would normally for single domain use.

8.1.5 Httpd.init

An httpd.init file is not needed since the server is run through inetd.

8.2 Running With Apache VirtualHost

Apache has three configuration files `access.conf` , `httpd.conf` , and `srm.conf` . Newer versions of Apache have made the three configuration files unnecessary. However, I find that breaking up the configuration into three sections makes it easier to manage so I will be keeping with that style in this HOWTO document.

8.2.1 Access.conf

This configuration file is used to control the accessibility of directories in the web directory structure. Here is a sample configuration file that shows how to have different options for each domain.

```
# /var/www/conf/access.conf: Global access configuration

# Options are inherited from the parent directory
# Set the main directory with default options
<Directory />
AllowOverride None
Options Indexes
</Directory>

# Give one domain a passwd protected directory
<Directory /virtual/domain1.com/var/www/html/priv>
AuthUserFile /var/www/passwd/domain1.com-priv
AuthGroupFile /var/www/passwd/domain1.com-priv-g
AuthName PRIVSECTION
AuthType Basic
<Limit GET PUT POST>
require valid-user
</Limit>
</Directory>

# Give another domain Server Side Includes
<Directory /virtual/domain2.com/var/www/html>
Options IncludesNOEXEC
</Directory>
```

8.2.2 Httpd.conf

This configuration file is used to control the main options for the Apache server. Here is a sample configuration file that shows how to have different options for each domain.

```
# /var/www/conf/httpd.conf: Main server configuration file
```

```
# Begin: main conf section

# Needed since not using inetd
ServerType standalone

# Port to run on
Port 80

# Log clients with names vs IP addresses
HostnameLookups on

# User to run server as
User www
Group www

# Where server config, error and log files are
ServerRoot /var/www

# Process Id of server in this file
PidFile /var/run/httpd.pid

# Internal server process info
ScoreBoardFile /var/www/logs/apache_status

# Timeout and KeepAlive options
Timeout 400
KeepAlive 5
KeepAliveTimeout 15

# Number of servers to run
MinSpareServers 5
MaxSpareServers 10
StartServers 5
MaxClients 150
MaxRequestsPerChild 30

# End: main conf section

# Begin: virtual host section

# Tell server to accept requests for ip:port
# I have one for each IP needed so you can explicitly ignore certain domains
Listen 10.10.10.129:80
Listen 10.10.10.130:80

# VirtualHost directive allows you to specify another virtual
# domain on your server.  Most Apache options can be specified
# within this section.
<VirtualHost www.domain1.com>

# Mail to this address on errors
ServerAdmin webmaster@domain1.com

# Where documents are kept in the virtual domain
DocumentRoot /virtual/domain1.com/var/www/html
```

```
# Name of the server
ServerName www.domain1.com

# Log files Relative to ServerRoot option
ErrorLog logs/domain1.com-error_log
TransferLog logs/domain1.com-access_log
RefererLog logs/domain1.com-referer_log
AgentLog logs/domain1.com-agent_log

# Use CGI scripts in this domain
ScriptAlias /cgi-bin/ /var/www/cgi-bin/domain1.com/
AddHandler cgi-script .cgi
AddHandler cgi-script .pl
</VirtualHost>

<VirtualHost www.domain2.com>

# Mail to this address on errors
ServerAdmin webmaster@domain2.com

# Where documents are kept in the virtual domain
DocumentRoot /virtual/domain2.com/var/www/html

# Name of the server
ServerName www.domain2.com

# Log files Relative to ServerRoot option
ErrorLog logs/domain2.com-error_log
TransferLog logs/domain2.com-access_log
RefererLog logs/domain2.com-referer_log
AgentLog logs/domain2.com-agent_log

# No CGI's for this host
</VirtualHost>
# End: virtual host section
```

8.2.3 Srm.conf

This configuration file is used to control how requests are serviced and how results are formatted. You do not have to edit anything here for the virtual domains. The sample config file from Apache should work.

8.2.4 Httpd.init

Nothing special has to be done to the httpd.init file. Use a standard one that comes with the Apache configuration.

8.3 File Descriptor Overflow

8.3.1 Warning

This only applies to the standalone style Apache server. A server run through inetd does not interact with the other domains so it has the whole file descriptor table.

Every log file that the Apache server opens is another file descriptor for the process. There is a limit of 256 file descriptors per process in Linux. Since you have multiple domains you are using a lot more file descriptors. If you have too many domains running off of one Apache web server process you can overflow this table. This would mean that certain logs would not work and CGI's would fail.

8.3.2 Multiple Apache Servers

If you assume five file descriptors per domain you can have 50 domains running on your Apache server without any problems. However, if you find your server having problems like this you could create /var/www1 with an Apache server in charge of domain1 - domain25 and /var/www2 with an Apache server in charge of domain26 - domain50 and so on. This would give each server their own configuration, error, and log directory. Each server should be configured separately with their own Listen and VirtualHost directives. Do not forget to run multiple servers in your httpd.init file.

8.4 Sharing Servers With One IP

8.4.1 Saving IPs

The HTTP (HyperText Transfer Protocol) version 1.1 added a feature that communicates the name of the server to the client. This means that the client does not need to look up the server from its IP address. Therefore, two virtual servers could have the same IP address and be different web sites. The Apache configuration is the same as above except that you do not have to put in a different Listen directive since the two domains will have the same IP.

8.4.2 Drawback

The only problem is that virtuald uses IP addresses to distinguish between domains. In its current form virtuald would not be able to `chroot` to different spool directories for each domain. Therefore, mail would only be able to respond as one IP and there no longer be a unique spool directory for each domain. All the web sharing IP clients would have to share that IPs spool directory. That would mean duplicate usernames would be an issue again. However, that is the price you pay for sharing IPs.

8.5 More Information

This HOWTO only shows how to implement virtual support on the Apache web server. Most web servers use a similar interface. For more information on virtual web hosting consult the *WWW HOWTO*, the documentation for Apache at *Apache's Site*, or the documentation at *ApacheWeek*.

9 Virtual Mail/Pop

9.1 Problem

Virtual mail support is in ever increasing demand. Sendmail says it supports virtual mail. What it does support is listening for incoming mail from different domains. You can then specify to have the mail forwarded somewhere. However, if you forward it to the local machine and have incoming mail to bob@domain1.com and bob@domain2.com they will go to the same mail folder. This is a problem since both bob's are different people with different mail.

9.2 Solution

You can make sure that each user name is unique by using a numbering scheme: bob1, bob2, etc or prepending a few characters to each username dom1bob, dom2bob, etc. You could also hack mail and pop to do these conversions behind the scenes but that can get messy. Outgoing mail also has the banner maindomain.com and you want each subdomain's outgoing mail banner to be different.

I have two solutions. One works with sendmail and one works with Qmail. The solution with sendmail should work with a stock install of sendmail. However, it shares all the limitations built into sendmail. It also requires that one sendmail has to be run in queue mode for each domain. Having 50 or more sendmail queue processes that wake up every hour can put a little strain on a machine.

The solution offered with Qmail does not require multiple instances of Qmail and can run out of one queue directory. It does require an extra program since Qmail does not rely on virtuald. I believe a similar procedure can be done with sendmail. However, Qmail lends itself to this solution more readily.

I do not endorse any one program over the other. The sendmail install is a little more straight forward but Qmail is probably the more powerful of the two mail server packages.

9.3   Sendmail Solution

9.3.1   Introduction

Each virtual filesystem gives a domain its own /etc/passwd. This means that bob@domain1.com and bob@domain2.com are different users in different /etc/passwds so mail will be no problem. They also have their own spool directories so the mail folders will be different files on different virtual filesystems.

9.3.2   Create Sendmail Configuration File

Create /etc/sendmail.cf like you would normally through m4. I used:

```
divert(0)
VERSIONID('tcpproto.mc')
OSTYPE(linux)
FEATURE(redirect)
FEATURE(always_add_domain)
FEATURE(use_cw_file)
FEATURE(local_procmail)
MAILER(local)
MAILER(smtp)
```

9.3.3   Edit Sendmail Configuration File

Edit /virtual/domain1.com/etc/sendmail.cf to respond as your virtual domain:

```
vi /virtual/domain1.com/etc/sendmail.cf # Approximately Line 86
It should say:

#Dj$w.Foo.COM

Replace it with:

Djdomain1.com
```

9.3.4   Sendmail Local Delivery

Edit /virtual/domain1.com/etc/sendmail.cw with the local hostnames.

```
vi /virtual/domain1.com/etc/sendmail.cw
mail.domain1.com
domain1.com
domain1
localhost
```

9.3.5   Sendmail Between Virtual Domains: The Hack (PRE8.8.6)

However, sendmail requires one minor source code modification. Sendmail has a file called /etc/sendmail.cw and it contains all machine names that sendmail will deliver mail to locally rather than forwarding to another machine. Sendmail does internal checking of all the devices on the machine to initialize this list with the local IPs. This presents a problem if you are mailing between virtual domains on the same machine. Sendmail will be fooled into thinking another virtual domain is a local address and spool the mail locally. For example, bob@domain1.com sends mail to fred@domain2.com. Since domain1.com's sendmail thinks domain2.com is local, it will spool the mail on domain1.com and never send it to domain2.com. You have to modify sendmail (I did this on v8.8.5 without a problem):

```
vi v8.8.5/src/main.c # Approximately Line 494
It should say:

load_if_names();

Replace it with:

/* load_if_names(); Commented out since hurts virtual */
```

Note only do this if you need to send mail between virtual domains which I think is probable.

This will fix the problem. However, the main ethernet device eth0 is not removed. Therefore, if you send mail from a virtual IP to the one on eth0 on the same box it will delivery locally. Therefore, I just use this as a dummy IP virtual1.maindomain.com (10.10.10.157). I never send mail to this host so neither will the virtual domains. This is also the IP I would use to ssh into the box to check if the system is ok.

9.3.6   Sendmail Between Virtual Domains: New Sendmail Feature (POST8.8.6)

As of Sendmail V8.8.6, there is a new option to disable loading of the extra network interfaces. This means you do NOT have to alter the code in any way. It is called `DontProbeInterfaces` .

Edit /virtual/domain1.com/etc/sendmail.cf

```
vi /virtual/domain1.com/etc/sendmail.cf # Add the line
O DontProbeInterfaces=True
```

9.3.7   Sendmail.init

Sendmail cannot be started stand alone anymore so you have to run it through inetd. This is inefficient and will result in lower start up time but if you had such a high hit site you would not share it on a virtual box with other domains. Note that you are NOT running with the `-bd` flag. Also note that you need a `sendmail -q` running for each domain to queue up undelivered mail. The new sendmail.init file:

```
#!/bin/sh

. /etc/rc.d/init.d/functions

case "$1" in
  start)
        echo -n "Starting sendmail: "
        daemon sendmail -q1h
        echo
        echo -n "Starting virtual sendmail: "
        for i in /virtual/*
        do
                if [ ! -d "$i" ]
                then
                        continue
                fi
                if [ "$i" = "/virtual/lost+found" ]
```

```
then
                continue
        fi
        chroot $i sendmail -q1h
        echo -n "."."
    done
    echo " done"
    touch /var/lock/subsys/sendmail
    ;;
  stop)
        echo -n "Stopping sendmail: "
        killproc sendmail
        echo
        rm -f /var/lock/subsys/sendmail
        ;;
  *)
        echo "Usage: sendmail {start|stop}"
        exit 1
esac

exit 0
```

9.3.8 Inetd Setup

Pop should install normally with no extra effort. It will just need the inetd entry for it with the virtuald part added. The inetd.conf entries for sendmail and pop are:

```
pop-3 stream tcp nowait root /usr/local/bin/virtuald \
        virtuald /virtual/conf.pop in.qpop -s
smtp stream tcp nowait root /usr/local/bin/virtuald \
        virtuald /virtual/conf.mail sendmail -bs
```

9.4 Qmail Solution

9.4.1 Introduction

This solution takes over the delivery responsibilities of qmail-local, so use of the .qmail files in the virtual home directories will not work. However, each domain will still get a domain master user that will control aliasing for the whole domain. Two external programs will be used for that domain masters .qmail-default file. The mail will be passed through these two programs in order to deliver mail for each domain.

Two programs are required since one of them is run setuid root. It is a small program that changes to a non-root user and then runs the second program. Consult your nearest security related site for a discussion as to why this is necessary.

This solution bypasses the need for using virtuald. Qmail is flexible enough to not require a general virtuald setup. Qmail's design utilizes the chaining of programs together to deliver mail. This design makes it very easy to insert the virtual section into the Qmail delivery process without altering a stock install of Qmail.

A note that since you are using one Qmail any unqualified domain name will be expanded with the domain of the main server. This is because you do not have a separate Qmail server for each domain. Therefore, make sure that your client (Eudora, elm, mutt, etc.) knows to expand all of your unqualified domain names.

9.4.2 Setup Virtual Domains

Qmail has to be configured to accept mail for each of the virtual domains you will be serving. Type the following commands.

```
echo "domain1.com:domain1" >> /var/qmail/control/virtualdomains
```

9.4.3   Setup Domain Master User

Add to your main /etc/passwd file the user domain1. I would make the shell /bin/false so that the domain master cannot log in. That user will be able to add .qmail files and all mail for domain1 will route through that account. Note that usernames can only be eight characters long and domain names can be longer. The remaining characters are truncated. That means that user domain12 and domain123 are going to be the same user and Qmail might get confused. So be careful in your master domain user naming convention.

Create the domain master's .qmail files with the following commands. Add any other system aliases at this point. For example, webmaster or hostmaster.

```
echo "user@domain1.com" > /home/d/domain1/.qmail-mailer-daemon
echo "user@domain1.com" > /home/d/domain1/.qmail-postmaster
echo "user@domain1.com" > /home/d/domain1/.qmail-root
```

Create the domain master's .qmail-default file. This will filter all mail to the virtual domain.

```
echo "| /usr/local/bin/virtmailfilter" > /home/d/domain1/.qmail-default
```

9.4.4   Tcpserver

Qmail requires a special pop that can support the Maildir format. The pop program has to be virtualized. The author of Qmail recommends using tcpserver (an inetd replacement) with Qmail so my examples use tcpserver and NOT inetd.

Tcpserver does not require a config file. All the information can be passed to it via the command line. Here is the tcpserver.init file that you would use for the mail daemon and popper:

```
#!/bin/sh

. /etc/rc.d/init.d/functions

QMAILDUSER=`grep qmaild /etc/passwd | cut -d: -f3`
QMAILDGROUP=`grep qmaild /etc/passwd | cut -d: -f4`

# See how we were called.
case "$1" in
  start)
        echo -n "Starting tcpserver: "
        tcpserver -u 0 -g 0 0 pop-3 /usr/local/bin/virtuald \
              /virtual/conf.pop qmail-popup virt.domain1.com \
              /bin/checkpassword /bin/qmail-pop3d Maildir &
        echo -n "pop "
        tcpserver -u $QMAILDUSER -g $QMAILDGROUP 0 smtp \
              /var/qmail/bin/qmail-smtpd &
        echo -n "qmail "
        echo
        touch /var/lock/subsys/tcpserver
        ;;
  stop)
        echo -n "Stopping tcpserver: "
        killall -TERM tcpserver
        echo -n "killing "
        echo
```

```
                rm -f /var/lock/subsys/tcpserver
                ;;
    *)
                echo "Usage: tcpserver {start|stop}"
                exit 1
esac

exit 0
```

9.4.5   Qmail.init

You can use the standard Qmail init script provided. Qmail comes with very good documentation describing how to set this up.

9.4.6   Source

You require two other programs to get virtual mail working with Qmail. They are virtmailfilter and virtmaildelivery. This is the C source to virtmailfilter. It should be installed in /usr/local/bin with permissions 4750, user root, and group nofiles.

```c
#include <sys/wait.h>
#include <unistd.h>
#include <string.h>
#include <stdlib.h>
#include <stdio.h>
#include <ctype.h>
#include <pwd.h>

#define VIRTPRE                 "/virtual"

#define VIRTPWFILE              "etc/passwd"
#define VIRTDELIVERY            "/usr/local/bin/virtmaildelivery"
#define VIRTDELIVERY0           "virtmaildelivery"

#define PERM                    100
#define TEMP                    111
#define BUFSIZE                 8192

int main(int argc,char **argv)
{
        char *username,*usernameptr,*domain,*domainptr,*homedir;
        char virtpath[BUFSIZE];
        struct passwd *p;
        FILE *fppw;
        int status;
        gid_t gid;
        pid_t pid;

        if (!(username=getenv("EXT")))
        {
                fprintf(stdout,"environment variable EXT not set\n");
                exit(TEMP);
        }

        for(usernameptr=username;*usernameptr;usernameptr++)
        {
```

```
                *usernameptr=tolower(*usernameptr);
        }

        if (!(domain=getenv("HOST")))
        {
                fprintf(stdout,"environment variable HOST not set\n");
                exit(TEMP);
        }

        for(domainptr=domain;*domainptr;domainptr++)
        {
                if (*domainptr=='.' && *(domainptr+1)=='.')
                {
                        fprintf(stdout,"environment variable HOST has ..\n");
                        exit(TEMP);
                }
                if (*domainptr=='/')
                {
                        fprintf(stdout,"environment variable HOST has /\n");
                        exit(TEMP);
                }

                *domainptr=tolower(*domainptr);
        }

        for(domainptr=domain;;)
        {
                snprintf(virtpath,BUFSIZE,"%s/%s",VIRTPRE,domainptr);
                if (chdir(virtpath)>=0)
                        break;

                if (!(domainptr=strchr(domainptr,'.')))
                {
                        fprintf(stdout,"domain failed: %s\n",domain);
                        exit(TEMP);
                }

                domainptr++;
        }

        if (!(fppw=fopen(VIRTPWFILE,"r+")))
        {
                fprintf(stdout,"fopen failed: %s\n",VIRTPWFILE);
                exit(TEMP);
        }

        while((p=fgetpwent(fppw))!=NULL)
        {
                if (!strcmp(p->pw_name,username))
                        break;
        }

        if (!p)
        {
                fprintf(stdout,"user %s: not exist\n",username);
```

```
            exit(PERM);
    }

    if (fclose(fppw)==EOF)
    {
            fprintf(stdout,"fclose failed\n");
            exit(TEMP);
    }

    gid=p->pw_gid;
    homedir=p->pw_dir;

    if (setgid(gid)<0 || setuid(p->pw_uid)<0)
    {
            fprintf(stdout,"setuid/setgid failed\n");
            exit(TEMP);
    }

    switch(pid=fork())
    {
            case -1:
                    fprintf(stdout,"fork failed\n");
                    exit(TEMP);
            case 0:
                    if (execl(VIRTDELIVERY,VIRTDELIVERY0,
                        username,homedir,NULL)<0)
                    {
                            fprintf(stdout,"execl failed\n");
                            exit(TEMP);
                    }
            default:
                    if (wait(&status)<0)
                    {
                            fprintf(stdout,"wait failed\n");
                            exit(TEMP);
                    }
                    if (!WIFEXITED(status))
                    {
                            fprintf(stdout,"child did not exit normally\n");
                            exit(TEMP);
                    }
                    break;
    }

    exit(WEXITSTATUS(status));
}
```

9.4.7 Source

You require two other programs to get virtual mail working with Qmail. They are virtmailfilter and virtmaildelivery. This is the C source to virtmaildelivery. It should be installed in /usr/local/bin with permissions 0755, user root, and group root.

```
#include <sys/stat.h>
#include <sys/file.h>
```

```c
#include <stdlib.h>
#include <string.h>
#include <unistd.h>
#include <stdio.h>
#include <errno.h>
#include <time.h>

#define TEMP                    111
#define BUFSIZE                 8192
#define ATTEMPTS                10

int main(int argc,char **argv)
{
        char *user,*homedir,*dtline,*rpline,buffer[BUFSIZE],*p,mail[BUFSIZE];
        char maildir[BUFSIZE],newmaildir[BUFSIZE],host[BUFSIZE];
        int fd,n,nl,i,retval;
        struct stat statp;
        time_t thetime;
        pid_t pid;
        FILE *fp;

        retval=0;

        if (!argv[1])
        {
                fprintf(stdout,"invalid arguments: need username\n");
                exit(TEMP);
        }

        user=argv[1];

        if (!argv[2])
        {
                fprintf(stdout,"invalid arguments: need home directory\n");
                exit(TEMP);
        }

        homedir=argv[2];

        if (!(dtline=getenv("DTLINE")))
        {
                fprintf(stdout,"environment variable DTLINE not set\n");
                exit(TEMP);
        }

        if (!(rpline=getenv("RPLINE")))
        {
                fprintf(stdout,"environment variable RPLINE not set\n");
                exit(TEMP);
        }

        while (*homedir=='/')
                homedir++;
        snprintf(maildir,BUFSIZE,"%s/Maildir",homedir);
        if (chdir(maildir)<0)
```

```
        {
                fprintf(stdout,"chdir failed: %s\n",maildir);
                exit(TEMP);
        }

        time(&thetime);
        pid=getpid();
        if (gethostname(host,BUFSIZE)<0)
        {
                fprintf(stdout,"gethostname failed\n");
                exit(TEMP);
        }

        for(i=0;i<ATTEMPTS;i++)
        {
                snprintf(mail,BUFSIZE,"tmp/%u.%d.%s",thetime,pid,host);
                errno=0;
                stat(mail,&statp);
                if (errno==ENOENT)
                        break;

                sleep(2);
                time(&thetime);
        }
        if (i>=ATTEMPTS)
        {
                fprintf(stdout,"could not create %s\n",mail);
                exit(TEMP);
        }

        if (!(fp=fopen(mail,"w+")))
        {
                fprintf(stdout,"fopen failed: %s\n",mail);
                retval=TEMP; goto unlinkit;
        }

        fd=fileno(fp);

        if (fprintf(fp,"%s",rpline)<0)
        {
                fprintf(stdout,"fprintf failed\n");
                retval=TEMP; goto unlinkit;
        }

        if (fprintf(fp,"%s",dtline)<0)
        {
                fprintf(stdout,"fprintf failed\n");
                retval=TEMP; goto unlinkit;
        }

        while(fgets(buffer,BUFSIZE,stdin))
        {
                for(p=buffer;*p=='>';p++)
                        ;
```

```
                if (!strncmp(p,"From ",5))
                {
                        if (fputc('>',fp)<0)
                        {
                                fprintf(stdout,"fputc failed\n");
                                retval=TEMP; goto unlinkit;
                        }
                }

                if (fprintf(fp,"%s",buffer)<0)
                {
                        fprintf(stdout,"fprintf failed\n");
                        retval=TEMP; goto unlinkit;
                }
        }

        p=buffer+strlen(buffer);
        nl=2;
        if (*p=='\n')
                nl=1;

        for(n=0;n<nl;n++)
        {
                if (fputc('\n',fp)<0)
                {
                        fprintf(stdout,"fputc failed\n");
                        retval=TEMP; goto unlinkit;
                }
        }

        if (fsync(fd)<0)
        {
                fprintf(stdout,"fsync failed\n");
                retval=TEMP; goto unlinkit;
        }

        if (fclose(fp)==EOF)
        {
                fprintf(stdout,"fclose failed\n");
                retval=TEMP; goto unlinkit;
        }

        snprintf(newmaildir,BUFSIZE,"new/%u.%d.%s",thetime,pid,host);
        if (link(mail,newmaildir)<0)
        {
                fprintf(stdout,"link failed: %s %s\n",mail,newmaildir);
                retval=TEMP; goto unlinkit;
        }

unlinkit:
        if (unlink(mail)<0)
        {
                fprintf(stdout,"unlink failed: %s\n",mail);
                retval=TEMP;
        }
```

```
        exit(retval);
}
```

9.5   Acknowledgement

Thank you *Vicente Gonzalez (vince@nycrc.net)* for helping make the Qmail solution possible. You can certainly mail your thanks to Vince, however all questions and comments including issues regarding Qmail, about this HOWTO should continue to be directed to me.

10   Virtual Samba

10.1   Setup

Virtual SAMBA is very simple to install. Make sure that the following files are setup properly:

- /virtual/domain1.com/etc/smb.conf FILE
- /virtual/domain1.com/var/lock/samba DIRECTORY
- /virtual/domain1.com/var/log DIRECTORY
- /usr/local/bin/virtsmbstatus SYMLINK /usr/local/bin/virtexec

10.2   Inetd

Edit /etc/inetd.conf

```
vi /etc/inetd.conf # Add this line
netbios-ssn stream tcp nowait root /usr/local/bin/virtuald \
        virtuald /virtual/conf.smbd smbd
```

10.3   Smb.init

An smb.init file is not needed since the server is run through inetd.

11   Virtual Other

Any other service should be a similar procedure.

- Run virtfs to add the binaries and libraries to the virtual filesystem.
- Add it to /etc/inetd.conf.
- Create a /virtual/conf.service file.
- Create any virtual scripts that need to be made.

12   Conclusion

Those are all the steps you need. Again mail any responses to *Computer Resource Center*. If you have a question or an update to the document let me know and I will add it.

The document has met with a very good response. I thank all the people who sent me questions as they are helping to shape the document to meet the needs of users everywhere. Before you ask a question I urge you to read the FAQ to see if it has been already asked and answered. Thanks again. *Brian*

HOWTO

13 FAQ

Q1. I created sendmail.init and syslogd.init. I put them in /usr/local/bin and tried to run them but I got errors.

A1. These files are called init scripts. They are run by the program init when your computer boots. They do not go with the /usr/local binaries. Consult the Linux System Administrators Guide or the Linux Getting Started Guide for information on how to use the init scripts system.

Q2. I put these lines into /etc/sendmail.cf

```
divert(0)
VERSIONID('tcpproto.mc')
OSTYPE(linux)
FEATURE(redirect)
FEATURE(always_add_domain)
FEATURE(use_cw_file)
FEATURE(local_procmail)
MAILER(local)
MAILER(smtp)
```

And I got really stange output. Why?

A2. You do not put these lines directly in /etc/sendmail.cf. The sendmail.cf file was written to be easy for sendmail to understand and hard for humans to read. Therefore, to make it easy to configure we use a program called m4 and its macro capabilities to create the sendmail.cf file. The FEATURE lines are actually macros that expand to sendmail configuration statements. See the sendmail docs on how to configure sendmail through this method. Also note that you create a main /etc/sendmail.cf file and the virtfs script then copies this to /virtual/domain1.com/etc/sendmail.cf. Then you edit that sendmail.cf file to respond as your domain.

Q3. Where do I get virtuald, what is it, and how do I use it?

A3. Virtuald is C source that I wrote to run a virtual service. It is included with this HOWTO. You compile it like a normal C program `make virtuald` . The resulting binary is placed into /usr/local/bin. Add lines to /etc/inetd.conf that use virtuald as a wrapper to a normal network server program.

Q4. I do not have dialog installed on my system?

A4. Dialog is a program that allows you to put dialog pop up windows into your shell scripts. It is required for my virtual shell script examples to work. You can get a copy of dialog at *sunsite*. It compiles very easily and should be no problem to install.

Q5. How can I know if virtual syslogd is working?

A5. When virtuald runs it should output the following messages to syslogd (/var/log/messages):

```
Nov 19 17:21:07 virtual virtuald[10223]: Virtuald Starting: $Revision: 1.49 $
Nov 19 17:21:07 virtual virtuald[10223]: Incoming ip: 204.249.11.136
Nov 19 17:21:07 virtual virtuald[10223]: Chroot dir: /virtual/domain1.com
```

The `Chroot` dir message is sent by virtuald after the `chroot` system call is performed. If this message appears virtual syslogd is working. If the service you are virtualizing logs messages to syslogd and you see them that is also a sign that virtual syslogd is correctly setup.

Note that if you have not turned on the compile time option VERBOSELOG, virtuald will not log at all. The only way to tell if virtual syslogd is working at that point is if the daemon you are virtualizing independently logs something to syslogd.

Q6. How can I setup quotas across virtual filesystems?

A6. You setup quotas like you would normally. See the *Quota mini-HOWTO*. However, you have to make sure there are no uid conflicts across domains. If there are conflicts you will have users sharing a quota. Set aside a range of uid's that you know will have quota's enabled and tell your domains that they cannot have any users in that range except the ones registered to have a quota.

Q7. What is this \ notation in all the inetd.conf entries?

A7. That is just a method of breaking up config files across two lines. I did that so the line would word wrap in a nice place. You can just ignore the \ and join the two lines back together.

Q8. When I run passwd or other login programs I get `permission denied` . When I run FTP or su I get `no modules loaded for service XXX` . Why?

A8. Those are PAM error messages. I wrote these scripts before PAM was out. My virtfs script does not copy /etc/pam.d, /usr/lib/cracklib_dict.*, /lib/security or any of the other files PAM requires. PAM needs these to function. If you edit my virtfs script to copy these files the problem will go away.

Q9. Can virtuald work with tcpd hosts.allow and hosts.deny files?

A9. Yes it can with some modifications.

First the source has to be changed in two places.

This has to be inserted where the arguments are checked.

```
if (!argv[3])
{
        syslog(LOG_ERR,"invalid arguments: no program to run");
        exit(0);
}
```

The exec line has to be changed from:

```
if (execvp(argv[2],argv+2)<0)
```

to:

```
if (execvp(argv[2],argv+3)<0)
```

Second the inetd.conf lines have to be changed from:

```
ftp stream tcp nowait root /usr/local/bin/virtuald \
        virtuald /virtual/conf.ftp wu.ftpd -l -a
```

to:

```
ftp stream tcp nowait root /usr/local/bin/virtuald \
        virtuald /virtual/conf.ftp tcpd wu.ftpd -l -a
```

Third edit the /virtual/domain1.com/etc/hosts.allow and /virtual/domain1.com/etc/hosts.deny files accordingly.

Q10. Can my virtual hosts run CGI's?

A10. Yes they can but I recommend putting the /cgi-bin in a place outside of the `chroot` that only you have access to. For example, /var/www/cgi-bin/domain1.com. Giving clients access to /cgi-bin is giving them the opportunity to run programs on your sever. This is a big security hole. Be careful. I do not let any cgi run on my systems that I have not personally inspected for bugs.

Q11. My configuration files are different from your examples. What do I do?

A11. There are two basic configuration styles: SystemV and BSD. The examples provided in the HOWTO are based on SystemV style configuration files. Virtual services works equally well on either system. For information on BSD style configuration files consult the origin of your distribution or the nearest LDP site.

Q12. I sent you mail and have not heard a response from you or your response took a long time. Why?

A12. Probably because you did not put VIRTSERVICES HOWTO in your subject header. Please bear in mind that I am a network administrator and that among the other things I do in my 20 hour days is administering my own virtual boxes and those of my clients. Mail that is properly addressed is always responded to within two or three days. Mail that is improperly addressed does not get filtered into my VIRTSERVICES mailbox and can lie around unnoticed for days or weeks.

Q13. Does virtuald work under 100Mbit?

A13 The speed of the network card is unrelated to whether virtuald will work or not. Try making sure that your server works under 10Mbit and that your 100Mbit network card works normally without a virtual server.

Q14. Should I use sendmail's virthost table?

A14. No. That is sendmail's feature to accept info for multiple domains. Virtuald gives each sendmail its own separate `chroot` environment. Install virtuald and then configure sendmail like you would normally for each domain.

Q15. Can I setup virtual telnet on my machine? What about creating a virtual root account so clients can administer their own domains?

A15. These questions come to me quite often and to be honest, I am getting a bit tired of them. The answer, as stated numerous times in the documentation, is that any service run through inetd can be virtualized using virtuald so there is nothing to stop you from doing either of the above. Nothing except common sense. Whatever benefits you might derive from allowing telnet are heavily outweighed by the cost to the virtual box (and thus the sites you are supposed to be hosting in a responsible manner) in terms of security. Here are just a few issues involved:

- In order to completely fool an incoming telnet session you have to hack the kernel to get multiple procs working, reset your source IP address for outgoing connections, fool gethostname so it uses the virtual hostname and not the system hostname, etc. If you are an advanced user then by all means hack the kernel. For the newbie I do not recommend it.

- By allowing users to come into your box via telnet you allow them to run arbitrary programs. Through known hacks you can get root and cause damage to the system.

- Giving a root telnet account on a virtual box is very bad. A root virtual user can still read raw device files which nullifies the `chroot` , shutdown the system, and can kill other processes on the system.

- The programs that these telnet sessions are running take up valuable CPU time that the network services could be using.

- Telnet is an insecure network service. Plain text passwords are sent out over the net. If a malicious user gets this password he/she can use the above mentioned attacks to harm your system.

- Your virtual environments will have to be bigger. You will need more shared libraries, more configuration files, and more binaries. A six gigabyte disk can run out of space really fast.

The bottom line is that allowing login's on a virtual box is a really bad idea. If permitted, every site hosted on that machine is at risk. If you want to allow a site holder to administer users then you are advised to write (not script) the code necessary to run the virtual processes that allow them to add, delete or modify users upon login through ssh. This should be completely menu driven, should never allow a console and should not run as root. In order to accomplish this you will have to change ownership of the pertinent files from root to some other user. If done in this manner it is marginally safe to incorporate into a virtual machine. There is never an acceptable time to allow root login's either through telnet or ssh. Doing so is simply an invitation to disaster. If there is an overwhelming reason to run telnet then the site should be hosted on a dedicated machine where the only risk is to the individual site. No responsible administrator would ever do otherwise and so I will waste no more time on this issue.

Q16. Is there an rpm, tar, web site, mailing list, etc. associated with virtuald and the Virtual-Services HOWTO?

A16. Currently there is nothing like that available. This HOWTO is the only source of information to everything I do concerning this project. I find the HOWTO to be fairly self contained making the need for other pieces of information superfluous.

Q17. When I try to run virtexec as a regular user I get `chroot: operation not permitted`. Why?

A17. `Chroot` is a root restricted system call. Only the superuser can execute it. The virtexec script runs the `chroot` program which is why you need to be root in order to run it.

Q18. I setup pop and sendmail but popping mail does not seem to work. How come?

A18. Some pop programs come with /usr/spool/mail as their place for mail files. I know that qpop has to be manually editted to fix this. Either recompile the source to your program or symlink /virtual/domain1.com/usr/spool to /virtual/domain1.com/var/spool.

Q19. I did not use the program mentioned in your HOWTO, I used program XXX. It does not work. Why?

A19. I tried to make sure to use the most generic of each server in my examples. However, I know that everyone has their favorite version of each server. Send me as much information as possible and I will try to figure out how to solve your problem and document it in the FAQ. The most important piece of information to send me is where to get the version of the software you are running (in the form ftp://ftp.domain1.com/subdir/subdir/file.tgz).

Q20. When I run virtexec is says `symlink not a virt function`. What does this mean and how do I fix it?

A20. Virtexec is a program that will take its zero argument, strip off the first four characters, and run the remaining name in the virtual environment. For example, virtpasswd runs passwd. If the first four characters that it strips off are not `virt` it complains and outputs that error message. Virtexec is written in shell script and should be fairly simple to follow. Refer to the manual pages on bash or whatever shell you run for questions about shell script programming.

Q21. I have a question about Qmail, SAMBA, Apache, etc. that is unrelated to the virtuald setup or how the package interfaces to virtuald.

A21. All the packages described here are fully documented. Some even have full web sites like www.packagename.org dedicated to them. Please consult them about questions dealing with the package that are unrelated to their virtual hosting functionality.

Q22. I have several domain aliases to domain1.com but mail keeps bouncing from the aliases. How come?

A22. Virtmaildelivery relies on the environment variables passed to it to determine which /virtual/domain1.com directory to deliver to. It does not perform any DNS lookups to determine the address of the mail. However, if the address is submail.mail.domain1.com, virtmaildelivery will first try that address and then mail.domain1.com and then domain1.com and then com in that order until either a match happens or there is no domain name left.

However, if you have domain aliases that are not subdomains of one another you have to create symlinks like so:

```
cd /virtual
ln -s domain1.com domain1alias.com
```

That way virtmaildelivery will be fooled into thinking that both directories exist even though one is a symlink and mail will be able to be delivered to user@domain1.com or user@domain1alias.com. Note that virtexec will list both of the domains in the dialog box when your run it. You can choose either one since they will be the same virtual filesystem.

HOWTO

"Linux WWW HOWTO " by Wayne Leister

n3mtr@qis.net
v0.82, 19 November 1997

This document contains information about setting up WWW services under Linux (both server and client). It tries not to be a in detail manual but an overview and a good pointer to further information.

Contents

1   Introduction

Many people are trying Linux because they are looking for a really good *Internet capable* operating system. Also, there are institutes, universities, non-profits, and small businesses which want to set up Internet sites on a small budget. This is where the WWW-HOWTO comes in. This document explains how to set up clients and servers for the largest part of the Internet - *The World Wide Web*.

All prices in this document are stated in US dollars. This document assumes you are running Linux on an Intel platform. Instructions and product availability my vary from platform to platform. There are many links for downloading software in this document. Whenever possible use a mirror site for faster downloading and to keep the load down on the main server.

The US government forbids US companies from exporting encryption stronger than 40 bit in strength. Therefore US companies will usually have two versions of software. The import version will usually support 128 bit, and the export only 40 bit. This applies to web browsers and servers supporting secure transactions. Another name for secure transactions is Secure Sockets Layer (SSL). We will refer to it as SSL for the rest of this document.

1.1   Copyright

This document is Copyright (c) 1997 by Wayne Leister. The original author of this document was Peter Dreuw.(All versions prior to 0.8)

1.2   Feedback

Any feedback is welcome. I do not claim to be an expert. Some of this information was taken from badly written web sites; there are bound to be errors and omissions. But make sure you have the latest version before you send corrections; It may be fixed in the next version (see the next section for where to get the latest version). Send feedback to *n3mtr@qis.net*.

1.3   New versions of this Document

New versions of this document can be retrieved in text format from Sunsite at `<http://sunsite.unc.edu/pub/Linux/docs/HOWTO/WWW-HOWTO>` and almost any Linux mirror site. You can view the latest HTML version on the web at `<http://sunsite.unc.edu/LDP/HOWTO/WWW-HOWTO.html>`. There are also HTML versions available on Sunsite in a tar archive.

2   Setting up WWW client software

The following chapter is dedicated to the setting up web browsers. Please feel free to contact me, if your favorite web browser is not mentioned here. In this version of the document only a few of the browsers have there own section, but I tried to include all of them (all I could find) in the overview section. In the future those browsers that deserve there own section will have it.

The overview section is designed to help you decide which browser to use, and give you basic information on each browser. The detail section is designed to help you install, configure, and maintain the browser.

Personally, I prefer the Netscape; it is the only browser that keeps up with the latest things in HTML. For example, Frames, Java, Javascript, style sheets, secure transactions, and layers. Nothing is worse than trying to visit a web site and finding out that you can't view it because your browser doesn't support some new feature.

However I use Lynx when I don't feel like firing up the X-windows/Netscape monster.

2.1   Overview

5 (Navigator/Communicator)

Netscape Navigator is the only browser mentioned here, which is capable of advanced HTML features. Some of these features are frames, Java, Javascript, automatic update, and layers. It also has news and mail capability. But it is a resource hog; it takes up lots of CPU time and memory. It also sets up a separate cache for each user wasting disk space. Netscape is a commercial product. Companies have a 30 day trial period, but there is no limit for individuals. I would encourage you to register anyway to support Netscape in there efforts against Microsoft (and what is a measly $40US). My guess is if Microsoft wins, we will be forced to use MS Internet Explorer on a Windows platform :(

3 (Lynx)

Lynx is the one of the smallest web browsers. It is the king of text based browsers. It's free and the source code is available under the GNU public license. It's text based, but it has many special features.

Kfm

Kfm is part of the K Desktop Environment (KDE). KDE is a system that runs on top of X-windows. It gives you many features like drag an drop, sounds, a trashcan and a unified look and feel. Kfm is the K File Manager, but it is also a web browser. Don't be fooled by the name, for a young product it is very usable as a web browser. It already supports frames, tables, ftp downloads, looking into tar files, and more. The current version of Kfm is 1.39, and it's free. Kfm can be used without KDE, but you still need the librarys that come with KDE. For more information about KDE and Kfm visit the KDE website at `<http://www.kde.org>`.

4 (Emacs)

Emacs is the one program that does everything. It is a word processor, news reader, mail reader, and web browser. It has a steep learning curve at first, because you have to learn what all the keys do. The X-windows version is easier to use, because most of the functions are on menus. Another drawback is that it's mostly text based. (It can

HOWTO

display graphics if you are running it under X-windows). It is also free, and the source code is available under the GNU public license.

NCSA Mosaic

Mosaic is an X-windows browser developed by the National Center for Supercomputing Applications (NCSA) at the University of Illinois. NCSA spent four years on the project and has now moved on to other things. The latest version is 2.6 which was released on July 7, 1995. Source code is available for non-commercial use. *Spyglass Inc.* `<http://www.spyglass.com>` has the commercial rights to Mosaic. Its a solid X-windows browser, but it lacks the new HTML features. For more info visit the NCSA Mosaic home page at `<http://www.ncsa.uiuc.edu/SDG/Software/Mosaic/>`. The software can be downloaded from `<ftp://ftp.ncsa.uiuc.edu/Mosaic/Unix/binaries/2.6/Mosaic-linux-2.6.Z>`.

Arena

Arena was a X-windows concept browser for the W3C (World Wide Web Consortium) when they were testing HTML 3.0. Hence it supports all the HTML 3.0 standards such as style sheets and tables. Development was taken over by Yggdrasil Computing, with the idea to turn it into a full fledge free X-windows browser. However development has stopped in Feb 1997 with version 0.3.11. Only part of the HTML 3.2 standard has been implemented. The source code is released under the GNU public licence. For more information see the web site at `<http://www.yggdrasil.com/Products/Arena/>`. It can be downloaded from `<ftp://ftp.yggdrasil.com/pub/dist/web/arena/>`.

Amaya

Amaya is the X-windows concept browser for the W3C for HTML 3.2. Therefore it supports all the HTML 3.2 standards. It also supports some of the features of HTML 4.0. It supports tables, forms, client side image maps, put publishing, gifs, jpegs, and png graphics. It is both a browser and authoring tool. The latest public release is 1.0 beta. Version 1.1 beta is in internal testing and is due out soon. For more information visit the Amaya web site at `<http://www.w3.org/Amaya/>`. It can be downloaded from `<ftp://ftp.w3.org/pub/Amaya-LINUX-ELF-1.0b.tar.gz>`.

Red Baron

Red Baron is an X-windows browser made by Red Hat Software. It is bundled with The Official Red Hat Linux distribution. I could not find much information on it, but I know it supports frames, forms and SSL. If you use Red Baron, please help me fill in this section. For more information visit the Red Hat website at `<http://www.redhat.com>`

Chimera

Chimera is a basic X-windows browser. It supports some of the features of HTML 3.2. The latest release is 2.0 alpha 6 released August 27, 1997. For more information visit the Chimera website at `<http://www.unlv.edu/chimera/>`. Chimera can be downloaded from `<ftp://ftp.cs.unlv.edu/pub/chimera-alpha/chimera-2.0a6.tar.gz>`.

Qweb

Qweb is yet another basic X-windows browser. It supports tables, forms, and server site image maps. The latest version is 1.3. For more information visit the Qweb website at `<http://sunsite.auc.dk/qweb/>` The source is available from `<http://sunsite.auc.dk/qweb/qweb-1.3.tar.gz>` The binaries are available in a Red Hat RPM from `<http://sunsite.auc.dk/qweb/qweb-1.3-1.i386.rpm>`

Grail

Grail is an X-windows browser developed by the Corporation for National Research Initiatives (CNRI). Grail is written entirely in Python, a interpreted object-oriented language. The latest version is 0.3 released on May 7, 1997. It supports forms, bookmarks, history, frames, tables, and many HTML 3.2 things.

Internet Explorer

There are rumors, that Microsoft is going to port the Internet Explorer to various Unix platforms - maybe Linux. If its true they are taking their time doing it. If you know something more reliable, please drop me an e-mail.

In my humble opinion most of the above software is unusable for serious web browsing. I'm not trying to discredit the authors, I know they worked very hard on these projects. Just think, if all of these people had worked together on one project, maybe we would have a free browser that would rival Netscape and Internet Explorer.

In my opinion out of all of the broswers, Netscape and Lynx are the best. The runners up would be Kfm, Emacs-W3 and Mosaic.

3 Lynx

Lynx is one of the smaller (around 600 K executable) and faster web browsers available. It does not eat up much bandwidth nor system resources as it only deals with text displays. It can display on any console, terminal or xterm. You will not need an *X Windows system* or additional system memory to run this little browser.

3.1 Where to get

Both the Red Hat and Slackware distributions have Lynx in them. Therefore I will not bore you with the details of compiling and installing Lynx.

The latest version is 2.7.1 and can be retrieved from `<http://www.slcc.edu/lynx/fote/>` or from almost any friendly Linux FTP server like *ftp://sunsite.unc.edu under /pub/Linux/apps/www/broswers/* or mirror site.

For more information on Lynx try these locations:

Lynx Links

> `<http://www.crl.com/~subir/lynx.html>`

Lynx Pages

> `<http://lynx.browser.org>`

Lynx Help Pages

> `<http://www.crl.com/~subir/lynx/lynx_help/lynx_help_main.html>` (the same pages you get from lynx –help and typing ? in lynx)

Note: The Lynx help pages have recently moved. If you have an older version of Lynx, you will need to change your lynx.cfg (in /usr/lib) to point to the new address(above).

I think the most special feature of Lynx against all other web browsers is the capability for batch mode retrieval. One can write a shell script which retrieves a document, file or anything like that via *http, FTP, gopher, WAIS, NNTP* or *file://* - url's and save it to disk. Furthermore, one can fill in data into HTML forms in batch mode by simply redirecting standard input and using the *-post_data* option.

For more special features of Lynx just look at the help files and the man pages. If you use a special feature of Lynx that you would like to see added to this document, let me know.

4 Emacs-W3

There are several different flavors of Emacs. The two most popular are GNU Emacs and XEmacs. GNU Emacs is put out by the Free Software Foundation, and is the original Emacs. It is mainly geared toward text based terminals, but it does run in X-Windows. XEmacs (formerly Lucid Emacs) is a version that only runs on X-Windows. It has many special features that are X-Windows related (better menus etc).

4.1 Where to get

Both the Red Hat and Slackware distributions include GNU Emacs.

The most recent GNU emacs is 19.34. It doesn't seem to have a web site. The FTP site is at `<ftp://ftp.gnu.ai.mit.edu/pub/gnu/>`.

The latest version of XEmacs is 20.2. The XEmacs FTP site is at `<ftp://ftp.xemacs.org/pub/xemacs>`. For more information about XEmacs goto see its web page at `<http://www.xemacs.org>`.

HOWTO

Both are available from the Linux archives at *ftp://sunsite.unc.edu under /pub/Linux/apps/editors/emacs/*

If you got GNU Emacs or XEmacs installed, you probably got the W3 browser running to.

The Emacs W3 mode is a nearly fully featured web browser system written in the Emacs Lisp system. It mostly deals with text, but can display graphics, too - at least - if you run the emacs under the X Window system.

To get XEmacs in to W3 mode, goto the apps menu and select browse the web.

I don't use Emacs, so if someone will explain how to get it into the W3 mode I'll add it to this document. Most of this information was from the original author. If any information is incorrect, please let me know. Also let me know if you think anything else should be added about Emacs.

5 Netscape Navigator/Communicator

5.1 Different versions and options.

Netscape Navigator is the King of WWW browsers. Netscape Navigator can do almost everything. But on the other hand, it is one of the most memory hungry and resource eating program I've ever seen.

There are 3 different versions of the program:

Netscape Navigator includes the web browser, netcaster (push client) and a basic mail program.

Netscape Communicator includes the web browser, a web editor, an advanced mail program, a news reader, netcaster (push client), and a group conference utility.

Netscape Communicator Pro includes everything Communicator has plus a group calendar, IBM terminal emulation, and remote administration features (administrators can update thousands of copies of Netscape from their desk).

In addition to the three versions there are two other options you must pick.

The first is full install or base install. The full install includes everything. The base install includes enough to get you started. You can download the additional components as you need them (such as multimedia support and netcaster). These components can be installed by the Netscape smart update utility (after installing goto help->software updates). At this time the full install is not available for Linux.

The second option is import or export. If you are from the US are Canada you have the option of selecting the import version. This gives you the stronger 128 bit encryption for secure transactions (SSL). The export version only has 40 bit encryption, and is the only version allowed outside the US and Canada.

The latest version of the Netscape Navigator/Communicator/Communicator Pro is 4.03. There are two different versions for Linux. One is for the old 1.2 series kernels and one for the new 2.0 kernels. If you don't have a 2.0 kernel I suggest you upgrade; there are many improvements in the new kernel.

Beta versions are also available. If you try a beta version, they usually expire in a month or so!

5.2 Where to get

The best way to get Netscape software is to go through their web site at `<http://www.netscape.com/download/>`. They have menu's to guide you through the selection. When it ask for the Linux version, it is referring to the kernel (most people should be using 2.0 by now). If your not sure which version kernel you have run 'cat /proc/version'. Going through the web site is the only way to get the import versions.

If you want an export version you can download them directly from the Netscape FTP servers. The FTP servers are also more up to date. For example when I first wrote this the web interface did not have the non-beta 4.03 for Linux yet, but it was on the FTP site. Here are the links to the export Linux 2.0 versions:

Netscape Navigator 4.03 is at `<ftp://ftp.netscape.com/pub/communicator/4.03/ shipping/english/unix/linux20/navigator_standalone/navigator-v403-export. x86-unknown-linux2.0.tar.gz>`

Netscape Communicator 4.03 for Linux 2.0 (kernel) is at `<ftp://ftp.netscape.com/pub/communicator/ 4.03/shipping/english/unix/linux20/base_install/communicator-v403-export. x86-unknown-linux2.0.tar.gz>`

Communicator Pro 4.03 for Linux was not available at the time I wrote this.

These url's will change as new versions come out. If these links break you can find them by fishing around at the FTP site `<ftp://ftp.netscape.com/pub/communicator/>`.

These servers are heavily loaded at times. Its best to wait for off peak hours or select a mirror site. Be prepared to wait, these archives are large. Navigator is almost 8megs, and Communicator base install is 10megs.

5.3 Installing

This section explains how to install version 4 of Netscape Navigator, Communicator, and Communicator Pro.

First unpack the archive to a temporary directory. Then run the `ns-install` script (type `./ns-install`). Then make a symbolic link from the `/usr/local/netscape/netscape` binary to `/usr/local/bin/netscape` (type `ln -s /usr/local/netscape/netscape /usr/local/bin/netscape`). Finally set the system wide environment variable `$MOZILLA_HOME` to `/usr/local/netscape` so Netscape can find its files. If you are using bash for your shell edit your `/etc/profile` and add the lines:

```
MOZILLA_HOME="/usr/local/netscape"
export MOZILLA_HOME
```

After you have it installed the software can automatically update itself with smart update. Just run Netscape as root and goto help->software updates. If you only got the base install, you can also install the Netscape components from there.

Note: This will not remove any old versions of Netscape, you must manually remove them by deleting the Netscape binary and Java class file (for version 3).

6 Setting up WWW server systems

This section contains information on different http server software packages and additional server side tools like script languages for CGI programs etc. There are several dozen web servers, I only covered those that are fully functional. As some of these are commercial products, I have no way of trying them. Most of the information in the overview section was pieced together from various web sites. If there is any incorrect or missing information please let me know.

For a technical description on the http mechanism, take a look at the RFC documents mentioned in the chapter "For further reading" of this HOWTO.

I prefer to use the Apache server. It has almost all the features you would ever need and its free! I will admit that this section is heavily biased toward Apache. I decided to concentrate my efforts on the Apache section rather than spread it out over all the web servers. I may cover other web servers in the future.

6.1 Overview

Cern httpd

This was the first web server. It was developed by the European Laboratory for Particle Physics (CERN). CERN httpd is no longer supported. The CERN httpd server is reported to have some ugly bugs, to be quite slow and resource hungry. The latest version is 3.0. For more information visit the CERN httpd home page at `<http: //www.w3.org/Daemon/Status.html>`. It is available for download at `<ftp://sunsite.unc.edu/`

`pub/Linux/apps/www/servers/httpd-3.0.term.tpz>`(no it is not a typo, the extension is actually .tpz on the site; probably should be .tgz)

NCSA HTTPd

The NCSA HTTPd server is the father to Apache (The development split into two different servers). Therefore the setup files are very similar. NCSA HTTPd is free and the source code is available. This server not covered in this document, although reading the Apache section may give you some help. The NCSA server was once popular, but most people are replacing it with Apache. Apache is a drop in replacement for the NCSA server(same configuration files), and it fixes several shortcomings of the NCSA server. NCSA HTTPd accounts for 4.9% (and falling) of all web servers. (source September 1997 *Netcraft survey* `<http://www.netcraft.com/survey/>`). The latest version is 1.5.2a. For more information see the NCSA website at `<http://hoohoo.ncsa.uiuc.edu>`.

7 (Apache)

Apache is the king of all web servers. Apache and its source code is free. Apache is modular, therefore it is easy to add features. Apache is very flexible and has many, many features. Apache and its derivatives makes up 44% of all web domains (50% if you count all the derivatives). There are over 695,000 Apache servers in operation (source November 1997 *Netcraft survey* `<http://www.netcraft.com/survey/>`).

The official Apache is missing SSL, but there are two derivatives that fill the gap. Stronghold is a commercial product that is based on Apache. It retails for $995; an economy version is available for $495 (based on an old version of Apache). Stronghold is the number two secure server behind Netscape (source *C2 net* `<http://www.c2.net/products/stronghold>` and *Netcraft survey* `<http://www.netcraft.com/survey/>`). For more information visit the Stronghold website at `<http://www.c2.net/products/stronghold/>`. It was developed outside the US, so it is available with 128 bit SSL everywhere.

Apache-SSL is a free implementation of SSL, but it is not for commercial use in the US (RSA has US patents on SSL technology). It can be used for non-commercial use in the US if you link with the free RSAREF library. For more information see the website at `<http://www.algroup.co.uk/Apache-SSL/>`.

Netscape Fast Track Server

Fast Track was developed by Netscape, but the Linux version is put out by Caldera. The Caldera site lists it as Fast Track for OpenLinux. I'm not sure if it only runs on Caldera OpenLinux or if any Linux distribution will do (E-mail me if you have the answer). Netscape servers account for 11.5% (and falling) of all web servers (source September 1997 `<http://www.netcraft.com/survey/>`). The server sells for $295. It is also included with the Caldera OpenLinux Standard distribution which sells for $399 ($199.50 educational). The web pages tell of a nice administration interface and a quick 10 minute setup. The server has support for 40-bit SSL. To get the full 128-bit SSL you need Netscape Enterprise Server. Unfortunately that is not available for Linux :(The latest version available for Linux is 2.0 (Version 3 is in beta, but its not available for Linux yet). To buy a copy goto the Caldera web site at `<http://www.caldera.com/products/netscape/netscape.html>` For more information goto the Fast Track page at `<http://www.netscape.com/comprod/server_central/product/fast_track/>`

WN

WN has many features that make it attractive. First it is smaller than the CERN, NCSA HTTPd, an Apache servers. It also has many built-in features that would require CGI's. For example site searches, enhanced server side includes. It can also decompress/compress files on the fly with its filter feature. It also has the ability to retrieve only part of a file with its ranges feature. It is released under the GNU public license. The current version is 1.18.3. For more information see the WN website at `<http://hopf.math.nwu.edu/>`.

AOLserver

AOLserver is made by America Online. I'll admit that I was surprised by the features of a web server coming from AOL. In addition to the standard features it supports database connectivity. Pages can query a database by Structured Query Language (SQL) commands. The database is access through Open Database Connectivity (ODBC). It also has built-in search engine and TCL scripting. If that is not enough you can add your own modules through the c Application Programming Interface (API). I almost forgot to mention support for 40 bit SSL. And you get all this for free! For more information visit the AOLserver site at `<http://www.aolserver.com/server/>`

Zeus Server

Zeus Server was developed by Zeus Technology. They claim that they are the fastest web server (using WebSpec96 benchmark). The server can be configured and controlled from a web browser! It can limit processor and memory resources for CGI's, and it executes them in a secure environment (whatever that means). It also supports unlimited virtual servers. It sells for $999 for the standard version. If you want the secure server (SSL) the price jumps to $1699. They are based outside the US so 128 bit SSL is available everywhere. For more information visit the Zeus Technology website at <http://www.zeus.co.uk>. The US website is at <http://www.zeus.com>. I'll warn you they are cocky about the fastest web server thing. But they don't even show up under top web servers in the Netcraft Surveys.

CL-HTTP

CL-HTTP stands for Common Lisp Hypermedia Server. If you are a Lisp programmer this server is for you. You can write your CGI scripts in Lisp. It has a web based setup function. It also supports all the standard server features. CL-HTTP is free and the source code is available. For more information visit the CL-HTTP website at <http://www.ai.mit.edu/projects/iiip/doc/cl-http/home-page.html> (could they make that url any longer?).

If you have a commercial purpose (company web site, or ISP), I would strongly recommend that you use Apache. If you are looking for easy setup at the expense of advanced features then the Zeus Server wins hands down. I've also heard that the Netscape Server is easy to setup. If you have an internal use you can be a bit more flexible. But unless one of them has a feature that you just have to use, I would still recommend using one of the three above.

This is only a partial listing of all the servers available. For a more complete list visit Netcraft at <http://www.netcraft.com/survey/servers.html> or Web Compare at <http://webcompare.internet.com>.

7 Apache

The current version of Apache is 1.2.4. Version 1.3 is in beta testing. The main Apache site is at <http://www.apache.org/>. Another good source of information is Apacheweek at <http://www.apacheweek.com/>. The Apache documentation is ok, so I'm not going to go into detail in setting up apache. The documentation is on the website and is included with the source (in HTML format). There are also text files included with the source, but the HTML version is better. The documentation should get a whole lot better once the Apache Documentation Project gets under way. Right now most of the documents are written by the developers. Not to discredit the developers, but they are a little hard to understand if you don't know the terminology.

7.1 Where to get

Apache is included in the Red Hat, Slackware, and OpenLinux distributions. Although they may not be the latest version, they are very reliable binaries. The bad news is you will have to live with their directory choices (which are totally different from each other and the Apache defaults).

The source is available from the Apache web site at <http://www.apache.org/dist/> Binaries are are also available at apache at the same place. You can also get binaries from sunsite at <ftp://sunsite.unc.edu/pub/Linux/apps/www/servers/>. And for those of us running Red Hat the latest binary RPM file can usually be found in the contrib directory at <ftp://ftp.redhat.com/pub/contrib/i386/>.

If your server is going to be used for commercial purposes, it is highly recommended that you get the source from the Apache website and compile it yourself. The other option is to use a binary that comes with a major distribution. For example Slackware, Red Hat, or OpenLinux distributions. The main reason for this is security. An unknown binary could have a back door for hackers, or an unstable patch that could crash your system. This also gives you more control over what modules are compiled in, and allows you to set the default directories. It's not that difficult to compile Apache, and besides you not a real Linux user until you compile your own programs ;)

7.2 Compiling and Installing

First untar the archive to a temporary directory. Next change to the src directory. Then edit the Configuration file if you want to include any special modules. The most commonly used modules are already included. There is no need to change the rules or makefile stuff for Linux. Next run the Configure shell script (`./Configure`). Make sure it says Linux platform and gcc as the compiler. Next you may want to edit the httpd.h file to change the default directories. The server home (where the config files are kept) default is `/usr/local/etc/httpd/`, but you may want to change it to just `/etc/httpd/`. And the server root (where the HTML pages are served from) default is `/usr/local/etc/httpd/htdocs/`, but I like the directory `/home/httpd/html` (the Red Hat default for Apache). If you are going to be using su-exec (see special features below) you may want to change that directory too. The server root can also be changed from the config files too. But it is also good to compile it in, just encase Apache can't find or read the config file. Everything else should be changed from the config files. Finally run make to compile Apache.

If you run in to problems with include files missing, check the following things. Make sure you have the kernel headers (include files) installed for your kernel version. Also make sure you have these symbolic links in place:

```
/usr/include/linux should be a link to /usr/src/linux/include/linux
/usr/include/asm should be a link to /usr/src/linux/include/asm
/usr/src/linux should be a link to the Linux source directory (ex.linux-
2.0.30)
```

Links can be made with `ln -s`, it works just like the cp command except it makes a link (`ln -s source-dir destination-link`)

When make is finished there should be an executable named httpd in the directory. This needs to be moved in to a bin directory. `/usr/sbin` or `/usr/local/sbin` would be good choices.

Copy the conf, logs, and icons sub-directories from the source to the server home directory. Next rename 3 of the files files in the conf sub-directory to get rid of the `-dist` extension (ex. `httpd.conf-dist` becomes `httpd.conf`)

There are also several support programs that are included with Apache. They are in the `support` directory and must be compiled and installed separately. Most of them can be make by using the makefile in that directory (which is made when you run the main `Configure` script). You don't need any of them to run Apache, but some of them make the administrators job easier.

7.3 Configuring

Now you should have four files in your `conf` sub-directory (under your server home directory). The `httpd.conf` sets up the server daemon (port number, user, etc). The `srm.conf` sets the root document tree, special handlers, etc. The `access.conf` sets the base case for access. Finally `mime.types` tells the server what mime type to send to the browser for each extension.

The configuration files are pretty much self-documented (plenty of comments), as long as you understand the lingo. You should read through them thoroughly before putting your server to work. Each configuration item is covered in the Apache documentation.

The `mime.types` file is not really a configuration file. It is used by the server to translate file extensions into mime-types to send to the browser. Most of the common mime-types are already in the file. Most people should not need to edit this file. As time goes on, more mime types will be added to support new programs. The best thing to do is get a new mime-types file (and maybe a new version of the server) at that time.

Always remember when you change the configuration files you need to restart Apache or send it the SIGHUP signal with `kill` for the changes to take effect. Make sure you send the signal to the parent process and not any of the child processes. The parent usually has the lowest process id number. The process id of the parent is also in the `httpd.pid` file in the log directory. If you accidently send it to one of the child processes the child will die and the parent will restart it.

I will not be walking you through the steps of configuring Apache. Instead I will deal with specific issues, choices to be made, and special features.

I highly recommend that all users read through the security tips in the Apache documentation. It is also available from the Apache website at `<http://www.apache.org/docs/mics/security_tips.html>`.

7.4 Hosting virtual websites

Virtual Hosting is when one computer has more than one domain name. The old way was to have each virtual host have its own IP address. The new way uses only one IP address, but it doesn't work correctly with browsers that don't support HTTP 1.1.

My recommendation for businesses is to go with the IP based virtual hosting until most people have browsers that support HTTP 1.1 (give it a year or two). This also gives you a more complete illusion of virtual hosting. While both methods can give you virtual mail capabilities (can someone confirm this?), only IP based virtual hosting can also give you virtual FTP as well.

If it is for a club or personal page, you may want to consider shared IP virtual hosting. It should be cheaper than IP based hosting and you will be saving precious IP addresses.

You can also mix and match IP and shared IP virtual hosts on the same server. For more information on virtual hosting visit Apacheweek at `<http://www.apacheweek.com/features/vhost>`.

7.4.1 IP based virtual hosting

In this method each virtual host has its own IP address. By determining the IP address that the request was sent to, Apache and other programs can tell what domain to serve. This is an incredible waste of IP space. Take for example the servers where my virtual domain is kept. They have over 35,000 virtual accounts, that means 35,000 IP addresses. Yet I believe at last count they had less than 50 servers running.

Setting this up is a two part process. The first is getting Linux setup to accept more than one IP address. The second is setting up apache to serve the virtual hosts.

The first step in setting up Linux to accept multiple IP addresses is to make a new kernel. This works best with a 2.0 series kernel (or higher). You need to include IP networking and IP aliasing support. If you need help with compiling the kernel see the *kernel howto* `<http://sunsite.unc.edu/LDP/HOWTO/Kernel-HOWTO.html>`.

Next you need to setup each interface at boot. If you are using the Red Hat Distribution then this can be done from the control panel. Start X-windows as root, you should see a control panel. Then double click on network configuration. Next goto the interfaces panel and select your network card. Then click alias at the bottom of the screen. Fill in the information and click done. This will need to be done for each virtual host/IP address.

If you are using other distributions you may have to do it manually. You can just put the commands in the `rc.local` file in `/etc/rc.d` (really they should go in with the networking stuff). You need to have a `ifconfig` and `route` command for each device. The aliased addresses are given a sub device of the main one. For example eth0 would have aliases eth0:0, eth0:1, eth0:2, etc. Here is an example of configuring a aliased device:

```
ifconfig eth0:0 192.168.1.57
route add -host 192.168.1.57 dev eth0:0
```

You can also add a broadcast address and a netmask to the ifconfig command. If you have alot of aliases you may want to make a for loop to make it easier. For more information see the *IP alias mini howto* `<http://sunsite.unc.edu/LDP/HOWTO/mini/IP-Alias.html>`.

Then you need to setup your domain name server (DNS) to serve these new domains. And if you don't already own the domain names, you need to contact the *Internic* `<http://www.internic.net>` to register the domain names. See the DNS-howto for information on setting up your DNS.

Finally you need to setup Apache to server the virtual domain correctly. This is in the `httpd.conf` configuration file near the end. They give you an example to go by. All commands specific to that virtual host are put in between the `virtualhost` directive tags. You can put almost any command in there. Usually you set up a different document root, script directory, and log files. You can have almost unlimited number of virtual hosts by adding more `virtualhost` directive tags.

In rare cases you may need to run separate servers if a directive is needed for a virtual host, but is not allowed in the virtual host tags. This is done using the bindaddress directive. Each server will have a different name and setup files. Each server only responds to one IP address, specified by the bindaddress directive. This is an incredible waste of system resources.

7.4.2 Shared IP virtual hosting

This is a new way to do virtual hosting. It uses a single IP address, thus conserving IP addresses for real machines (not virtual ones). In the same example used above those 30,000 virtual hosts would only take 50 IP addresses (one for each machine). This is done by using the new HTTP 1.1 protocol. The browser tells the server which site it wants when it sends the request. The problem is browsers that don't support HTTP 1.1 will get the servers main page, which could be setup to provide a menu of virtual hosts available. That ruins the whole illusion of virtual hosting. The illusion that you have your own server.

The setup is much simpler than the IP based virtual hosting. You still need to get your domain from the Internic and setup your DNS. This time the DNS points to the same IP address as the original domain. Then Apache is setup the same as before. Since you are using the same IP address in the virtualhost tags, it knows you want Shared IP virtual hosting.

There are several work arounds for older browsers. I'll explain the best one. First you need to make your main pages a virtual host (either IP based or shared IP). This frees up the main page for a link list to all your virtual hosts. Next you need to make a back door for the old browsers to get in. This is done using the `ServerPath` directive for each virtual host inside the `virtualhost` directive. For example by adding `ServerPath /mysite/` to www.mysite.com old browsers would be able to access the site by www.mysite.com/mysite/. Then you put the default page on the main server that politely tells them to get a new browser, and lists links to all the back doors of all the sites you host on that machine. When an old browser accesses the site they will be sent to the main page, and get a link to the correct page. New browsers will never see the main page and will go directly to the virtual hosts. You must remember to keep all of your links relative within the web sites, because the pages will be accessed from two different URL's (www.mysite.com and www.mysite.com/mysite/).

I hope I didn't lose you there, but its not an easy workaround. Maybe you should consider IP based hosting after all. A very similar workaround is also explained on the apache website at `<http://www.apache.org/manual/host.html>`.

If anyone has a great resource for Shared IP hosting, I would like to know about it. It would be nice to know what percent of browsers out there support HTTP 1.1, and to have a list of which browsers and versions support HTTP 1.1.

7.5 CGI scripts

There are two different ways to give your users CGI script capability. The first is make everything ending in `.cgi` a CGI script. The second is to make script directories (usually named `cgi-bin`). You could also use both methods. For either method to work the scripts must be world executable (`chmod 711`). By giving your users script access you are creating a big security risk. Be sure to do your homework to minimize the security risk.

I prefer the first method, especially for complex scripting. It allows you to put scripts in any directory. I like to put my scripts with the web pages they work with. For sites with allot of scripts it looks much better than having a directory full of scripts. This is simple to setup. First uncomment the `.cgi` handler at the end of the `srm.conf` file. Then make sure all your directories have the `option ExecCGI` or `All` in the `access.conf` file.

Making script directories is considered more secure. To make a script directory you use the ScriptAlias directive in the `srm.conf` file. The first argument is the Alias the second is the actual directory. For example `ScriptAlias /cgi-bin/ /usr/httpd/cgi-bin/` would make `/usr/httpd/cgi-bin` able to execute scripts. That directory would be used whenever someone asked for the directory `/cgi-bin/`. For security reasons you should also change the properties of the directory to `Options none`, `AllowOveride none` in the `access.conf` (just uncomment the example that is there). Also do not make your script directories subdirectories of your web page directories. For example if you are serving pages from `/home/httpd/html/`, don't make the script directory `/home/httpd/html/cgi-bin`; Instead make it `/home/httpd/cgi-bin`.

If you want your users to have there own script directories you can use multiple `ScriptAlias` commands. Virtual hosts should have there `ScriptAlias` command inside the `virtualhost` directive tags. Does anyone know a simple way to allow all users to have a cgi-bin directory without individual ScriptAlias commands?

7.6   Users Web Directories

There are two different ways to handle user web directories. The first is to have a subdirectory under the users home directory (usually `public_html`). The second is to have an entirely different directory tree for web directories. With both methods make sure set the access options for these directories in the `access.conf` file.

The first method is already setup in apache by default. Whenever a request for `/~bob/` comes in it looks for the `public_html` directory in bob's home directory. You can change the directory with the `UserDir` directive in the `srm.conf` file. This directory must be world readable and executable. This method creates a security risk because for Apache to access the directory the users home directory must be world executable.

The second method is easy to setup. You just need to change the `UserDir` directive in the `srm.conf` file. It has many different formats; you may want to consult the Apache documentation for clarification. If you want each user to have their own directory under `/home/httpd/`, you would use `UserDir /home/httpd`. Then when the request `/~bob/` comes in it would translate to `/home/httpd/bob/`. Or if you want to have a subdirectory under bob's directory you would use `UserDir /home/httpd/*/html`. This would translate to `/home/httpd/bob/html/` and would allow you to have a script directory too (for example `/home/httpd/bob/cgi-bin/`).

7.7   Daemon mode vs. Inetd mode

There are two ways that apache can be run. One is as a daemon that is always running (Apache calls this standalone). The second is from the inetd super-server.

Daemon mode is far superior to inetd mode. Apache is setup for daemon mode by default. The only reason to use the inetd mode is for very low use applications. Such as internal testing of scripts, small company Intranet, etc. Inetd mode will save memory because apache will be loaded as needed. Only the inetd daemon will remain in memory.

If you don't use apache that often you may just want to keep it in daemon mode and just start it when you need it. Then you can kill it when you are done (be sure to kill the parent and not one of the child processes).

To setup inetd mode you need to edit a few files. First in `/etc/services` see if http is already in there. If its not then add it:

```
    http    80/tcp
```

Right after 79 (finger) would be a good place. Then you need to edit the `/etc/inetd.conf` file and add the line for Apache:

```
    http    stream  tcp     nowait  root    /usr/sbin/httpd httpd
```

Be sure to change the path if you have Apache in a different location. And the second httpd is not a typo; the inet daemon requires that. If you are not currently using the inet daemon, you may want to comment out the rest of the lines in the file so you don't activate other services as well (FTP, finger, telnet, and many other things are usually run from this daemon).

If you are already running the inet deamon (`inetd`), then you only need to send it the SIGHUP signal (via kill; see kill's man page for more info) or reboot the computer for changes to take effect. If you are not running `inetd` then you can start it manually. You should also add it to your init files so it is loaded at boot (the `rc.local` file may be a good choice).

7.8 Allowing put and delete commands

The newer web publishing tools support this new method of uploading web pages by http (instead of FTP). Some of these products don't even support FTP anymore! Apache does support this, but it is lacking a script to handle the requests. This script could be a big security hole, be sure you know what you are doing before attempting to write or install one.

If anyone knows of a script that works let me know and I'll include the address to it here.

For more information goto Apacheweek's article at <http://www.apacheweek.com/features/put>.

7.9 User Authentication/Access Control

This is one of my favorite features. It allows you to password protect a directory or a file without using CGI scripts. It also allows you to deny or grant access based on the IP address or domain name of the client. That is a great feature for keeping jerks out of your message boards and guest books (you get the IP or domain name from the log files).

To allow user authentication the directory must have `AllowOverrides AuthConfig` set in the `access.conf` file. To allow access control (by domain or IP address) AllowOverrides Limit must be set for that directory.

Setting up the directory involves putting an `.htaccess` file in the directory. For user authentication it is usually used with an `.htpasswd` and optionally a `.htgroup` file. Those files can be shared among multiple `.htaccess` files if you wish.

For security reasons I recommend that everyone use these directives in there access.conf file:

```
<files ~ "/\.ht">
order deny,allow
deny from all
</files>
```

If you are not the administrator of the system you can also put it in your .htaccess file if AllowOverride Limit is set for your directory. This directive will prevent people from looking into your access control files (.htaccess, .htpasswd, etc).

There are many different options and file types that can be used with access control. Therefore it is beyond the scope of this document to describe the files. For information on how to setup User Authentication see the Apacheweek feature at <http://www.apacheweek.com/features/userauth> or the NCSA pages at <http://hoohoo.ncsa.uiuc.edu/docs-1.5/tutorials/user.html>.

7.10 su-exec

The su-exec feature runs CGI scripts as the user of the owner. Normally it is run as the user of the web server (usually nobody). This allows users to access there own files in CGI scripts without making them world writable (a security hole). But if you are not careful you can create a bigger security hole by using the su-exec code. The su-exec code does security checks before executing the scripts, but if you set it up wrong you will have a security hole.

The su-exec code is not for amateurs. Don't use it if you don't know what you are doing. You could end up with a gaping security hole where your users can gain root access to your system. Do not modify the code for any reason. Be sure to read all the documentation carefully. The su-exec code is hard to setup on purpose, to keep the amateurs out (everything must be done manually, no make file no install scripts).

The su-exec code resides in the `support` directory of the source. First you need to edit the `suexec.h` file for your system. Then you need to compile the su-exec code with this command:

```
gcc suexec.c -o suexec
```

Then copy the suexec executable to the proper directory. The Apache default is `/usr/local/etc/httpd/sbin/`. This can be changed by editing `httpd.h` in the Apache source and recompiling Apache. Apache will only look in this directory, it will not search the path. Next the file needs to be changed to user root (`chown root suexec`) and the suid bit needs to be set (`chmod 4711 suexec`). Finally restart Apache, it should display a message on the console that su-exec is being used.

CGI scripts should be set world executable like normal. They will automaticaly be run as the owner of the CGI script. If you set the SUID (set user id) bit on the CGI scripts they will not run. If the directory or file is world or group writable the script will not run. Scripts owned by system users will not be run (root, bin, etc.). For other security conditions that must be met see the su-exec documentation. If you are having problems see the su-exec log file named `cgi.log`.

Su-exec does not work if you are running Apache from inetd, it only works in daemon mode. It will be fixed in the next version because there will be no inetd mode. If you like playing around in source code, you can edit the http_main.c. You want to get rid of the line where Apache announces that it is using the su-exec wrapper (It wrongly prints this in front of the output of everything).

Be sure and read the Apache documentation on su-exec. It is included with the source and is available on the Apache web site at `<http://www.apache.org/docs/suexec.html>`.

7.11 Imagemaps

Apache has the ability to handle server side imagemaps. Imagemaps are images on webpages that take users to different locations depending on where they click. To enable imagemaps first make sure the imagemap module is installed (its one of the default modules). Next you need to uncomment the `.map` handler at the end of the `srm.conf` file. Now all files ending in `.map` will be imagemap files. Imagemap files map different areas on the image to separate links. Apache uses map files in the standard NCSA format. Here is an example of using a map file in a web page:

```
<a href="/map/mapfile.map">
<img src="picture.gif" ISMAP>
</a>
```

In this example `mapfile.map` is the mapfile, and `picture.gif` is the image to click on.

There are many programs that can generate NCSA compatible map files or you can create them yourself. For a more detailed discussion of imagemaps and map files see the Apacheweek feature at `<http://www.apacheweek.com/features/imagemaps>`.

7.12 SSI/XSSI

Server Side Includes (SSI) adds dynamic content to otherwise static web pages. The includes are embedded in the web page as comments. The web server then parses these includes and passes the results to the web server. SSI can add headers and footers to documents, add date the document was last updated, execute a system command or a CGI script. With the new eXtended Server Side Includes (XSSI) you can do a whole lot more. XSSI adds variables and flow control statements (if, else, etc). Its almost like having an programming language to work with.

Parsing all HTML files for SSI commands would waste allot of system resources. Therefore you need to distinguish normal HTML files from those that contain SSI commands. This is usually done by changing the extension of the SSI enhanced HTML files. Usually the `.shtml` extension is used.

To enable SSI/XSSI first make sure that the includes module is installed. Then edit `srm.conf` and uncomment the `AddType` and `AddHandler` directives for `.shtml` files. Finally you must set `Options Includes` for all directories where you want to run SSI/XSSI files. This is done in the `access.conf` file. Now all files with the extension `.shtml` will be parsed for SSI/XSSI commands.

Another way of enabling includes is to use the `XBitHack` directive. If you turn this on it looks to see if the file is executable by user. If it is and `Options Includes` is on for that directory, then it is treated as an SSI file. This only works for files with the mime type text/html (`.html` `.htm` files). This is not the preferred method.

There is a security risk in allowing SSI to execute system commands and CGI scripts. Therefore it is possible to lock that feature out with the `Option IncludesNOEXEC` instead of Option Includes in the `access.conf` file. All the other SSI commands will still work.

For more information see the Apache mod_includes documentation that comes with the source. It is also available on the website at `<http://www.apache.org/docs/mod/mod_include.html>`.

For a more detailed discussion of SSI/XSSI implementation see the Apacheweek feature at `<http://www.apacheweek.com/features/ssi>`.

For more information on SSI commands see the NCSA documentation at `<http://hoohoo.ncsa.uiuc.edu/docs/tutorials/includes.html>`.

For more information on XSSI commands goto `<ftp://pageplus.com/pub/hsf/xssi/xssi-1.1.html>`.

7.13   Module system

Apache can be extended to support almost anything with modules. There are allot of modules already in existence. Only the general interest modules are included with Apache. For links to existing modules goto the

Apache Module Registry at `<http://www.zyzzyva.com/module_registry/>`.

For module programming information goto `<http://www.zyzzyva.com/module_registry/reference/>`

8   Web Server Add-ons

Sorry this section has not been written yet.

Coming soon: mSQL, PHP/FI, cgiwrap, Fast-cgi, MS frontpage extentions, and more.

9   FAQ

There aren't any frequent asked questions - yet...

10   For further reading

10.1   O'Reilly & Associates Books

In my humble opinion O'Reilly & Associates make the best technical books on the planet. They focus mainly on Internet, Unix and programming related topics. They start off slow with plenty of examples and when you finish the book your an expert. I think you could get by if you only read half of the book. They also add some humor to otherwise boring subjects.

They have great books on HTML, PERL, CGI Programming, Java, JavaScript, C/C++, Sendmail, Linux and much much more. And the fast moving topics (like HTML) are updated and revised about every 6 months or so. So visit the *O'Reilly & Associates* `<http://www.ora.com/>` web site or stop by your local book store for more info.

And remember if it doesn't say O'Reilly & Associates on the cover, someone else probably wrote it.

10.2   Internet Request For Comments (RFC)

- RFC1866 written by T. Berners-Lee and D. Connolly, "Hypertext Markup Language - 2.0", 11/03/1995
- RFC1867 writtenm by E. Nebel and L. Masinter, "Form-based File Upload in HTML", 11/07/1995
- RFC1942 written by D. Raggett, "HTML Tables", 05/15/1996

- RFC1945 by T. Berners-Lee, R. Fielding, H. Nielsen, "Hypertext Transfer Protocol – HTTP/1.0", 05/17/1996.

- RFC1630 by T. Berners-Lee, "Universal Resource Identifiers in WWW: A Unifying Syntax for the Expression of Names and Addresses of Objects on the Network as used in the World-Wide Web", 06/09/1994

- RFC1959 by T. Howes, M. Smith, "An LDAP URL Format", 06/19/1996

HOWTO

Part L

"A mSQL and perl Web Server Mini HOWTO"
Oliver Corff

corff@zedat.fu-berlin.de
v0.1, 17 September 1997

This Mini HOWTO, highly inspired by Michael Schilli's article *Gebunkert: Datenbankbedienung mit Perl und CGI*, published in the german computer magazine iX 8/1997, describes how to build a SQL client/server database using WWW and HTML for the user interface.

Contents

1 About this Document

1.1 Intended Audience

Everybody who wants to install a web server database but does not know which software is necessary and how it is installed should benefit from reading this text. This text provides all information necessary to get a SQL database for a web server going; it does *not* go into any detail of CGI programming, nor does it explain the SQL database language. Excellent books are available on both topics, and it is the intention of this text to provide a working platform based on which a user can then study CGI programming and SQL.

For getting a small scale SQL system running (not the notorious example of a major airline booking system, or space mission management database) it will be sufficient to have the software described in this text and the documentation accompanying it. The user manual of msql (a database introduced in this text) provides sufficient information on SQL for building your own database.

The reader of this text should have a working knowledge of how to obtain files via `ftp` if he has no access to CD-ROMs, and a basic understanding of how to build binaries from sources. Anyway, all steps explained in this text were tested on a real life system and should also work on the reader's system.

1.2 Conventions used in this text

A user command:

```
# make install
```

Screen output from a program:

```
Program installed. Read README for details on how to start.
```

Sample code of a file:

```
# My comment
char letter;
```

2 Introduction

It can be safely assumed that databases with a high volume of data or a complicated relational setup (like, perhaps, a lexical database for a living language) must be accessible to many users and operators at the same time. Ideally, it should be possible to use existing different hardware and software platforms that can be combined into the actual system. In order to reduce the implementation cost, only one system, the database server, needs to be powerful; the user stations typically just display data and accept user commands, but the processing is done on one machine only which led to the name client-server database. In addition, the user interface should be easy to maintain and should require as little as possible on the client side.

A system which meets these criteria can be built around the following items of protocols, concepts and software:

Linux
  supplies the operating system. It is a stable Unix implementation providing true multi-user multi-tasking services with full network (TCP/IP e. a.) support. Except from the actual media and transmission cost, it is available free of charge and comes in form of so-called distributions which usually include everything needed from the basic OS to text processing, scripting, software development, interface builders, etc.

HTML
  is the Hypertext Markup Language used to build interfaces to network systems like Intranets and the WWW, the World Wide Web. HTML is very simple and can be produced with any ASCII-capable text editor.

Browsers

are text-based (e. g. Lynx) or graphical (e. g. Mosaic, Netscape, Arena etc.) applications accepting, evaluating and displaying HTML documents. They are the only piece of software which is directly operated by the database user. Using browsers, it is possible to display various types of data (text, possibly images) and communicate with http servers (see next) on about every popular computer model for which a browser has been made available.

http servers

provide access to the area of a host computer where data intended for public use in a network are stored. They understand the http protocol and procure the information the user requests.

SQL

Structured Query Language is a language for manipulating data in relational databases. It has a very simple grammar and is a standard with wide industry support. SQL-based databases have become the core of the classical client/server database concept. There are many famous SQL systems available, like Oracle, Informix etc., and then there is also msql which comes with a very low or even zero price tag if it is used in academical and educational environments.

CGI

Common Gateway Interface is the programming interface between the system holding the data (in our case an SQL-based system) and the network protocol (HTML, of course). CGIs can be built around many programming languages, but a particularly popular language is perl.

perl

is an extremely powerful scripting language which combines all merits of C, various shell languages, and stream manipulation languages like awk and sed. Perl has a lot of modularized interfaces and can be used to control SQL databases, for example.

3   Installation Procedure

3.1   Hardware Requirements

No general statement can be made about the hardware requirements of a database server. Too much depends on the expected number of users, the kind of application, the network load etc. In a small environment with only a few users and little network traffic a i486-equivalent machine with 16 MB of RAM can be completely sufficient. Linux, the operating system, is very efficient in terms of resources, and can supply enough horse-power for running a broad variety of applications at the same time. Of course, faster processors and more RAM mean more speed, but much more important than the processor is the amount of RAM. The more RAM the system has the less it is forced to swap memory intensive processes to disk in case a bottleneck occurs.

Given anything like 32 MB RAM and a PCI bus, searches and sorting operations can be done without much resorting to swap files etc., resulting in lightening fast speed.

The model installation described in this article was made on a IBM 686 (133Mhz) with 32 MB RAM and a 1.2 GB IDE hard disk. Assuming that the installation process starts from scratch, here is a list of the necessary steps.

3.2   Software Requirements

The software described in this article is available from the Internet or from CD-ROM. The following products were used:

- Red Hat Linux PowerTools: 6 CD's Complete Easy-to-Use Red Hat 4.2, Summer '97; alternatively from `http://www.redhat.com`;
- msql SQL database server: it is now available in two versions. The versions have differences in the number of transactions they can handle, the administration interface, etc. The elder version, 1.0.16, is available from Sunsite mirrors. The ELF executable can be found at `sunsite:apps/database/sql/msql-1.0.16` or on CD-ROM (here: disc 4 of InfoMagic Linux Developer's Resource, 6-CD set, December 1996) or alternatively from the following URL: `http://www.infomagic.com`.

The newer version, 2.0.1, can be directly obtained from Hughes' homepage in Australia (`http://www.hughes.com.au`) or from numerous mirror sites around the world;

- perl from CPAN: The Comprehensive Perl Archive Network. Walnut Creek CDROM, ISBN 1-57176-077-6, May 1997;

- Michael Schilli's CGI example program from computer journal iX 8/1997, pages 150–152, available via ftp from `ftp.uni-paderborn.de:/doc/magazin/iX`;

3.3 Installing the Operating System

Linux is installed in form of the Red Hat Linux Distribution 4.2. In order to install successfully, the machine must either have a DOS-accessible CD-ROM drive, a bootable CD-ROM drive, or else a boot disk must be made following the instructions on the Linux CD.

During installation the user has the choice to select and configure numerous software packages. It is convenient to select the following items now:

- TCP/IP network support,
- the http server Apache, and
- the scripting language perl, and
- the X Window System, as well as
- the browsers Arena (graphical) and Lynx (text-based).

All these packages are provided with the Linux distribution. If you do not install these packages now you still have the chance to do this later with the assistance of glint, the graphical and intuitive software package installation manager. Be sure to be root when installing these packages.

It is beyond the scope of this article to describe the network installation and initialization procedure. Please consult the online (manpages, HTML, texinfo) and printed (Linux Bible, etc. etc.) documentation.

The installation procedure of Red Hat is very mature and requires only little user attention besides the usual choices (like providing host names, etc.). Once the installation ends successfully, the system is basically ready to go.

Installing the X Window System is not mandatory for a pure server but it makes local access and testing much easier. The X installation procedure is done by any of several programs; XF86Setup offers the most extensive self-testing facilities and needs the least handling of hairy details (like video clock programming, etc.). The only requirement is that the software can detect the video adapter. A cheap accelerated graphics adapter (like Trio S64 based cards prior to S64UV+) usually works "out of the box".

At this point we assume that our system is up and running and that Apache, Perl and the X Window System have been successfully installed. We further assume that all standard structures like the file and directory structure are kept as they are defined in the installation. Last but not least we leave the host name as it is, and do at this moment accept the name `localhost`. We'll use this name for testing the installation; once the whole system works the true name can be added. Please note that the network setup also requires editing the files `/etc/hosts`, among others. Ideally this should be done with the administration tools provided to user root.

3.4 The http Server

The http server supplied with Linux is known as Apache to humans and as httpd to the system. The manpage (man httpd) explains how to install and start the http daemon (hence http*d*) but, as mentioned, if the installation went without problems then the server should be running. You can verify the directory tree: there must be a directory `/home/httpd/` with three subdirectories: `../cgi-bin/`, `../html/` and `../icons/`. In `../html/` there must be a file `index.html`. Later we will manipulate or replace this file by our own `index.html`. All configuration information is stored in `/etc/httpd/conf/`. The system is well preconfigured and does not need further setup provided the installation went without error.

3.5   The Browsers

There are essentially three types of browsers available for Linux: pure text-based systems like Lynx, experimental and simple ones like Arena (free!) and commercial ones like Netscape (shareware!) with Java support. While Lynx and Arena come with Linux, Netscape must be procured from other sources. Netscape is available as a precombiled binary for Linux on ix86 architectures and will run "out of the box" as soon as the archive is unpacked.

3.5.1   Configuring Lynx

Once Lynx is started it will look for a 'default URL' which is usually not very meaningful if the system does not have permanent Internet access. In order to change the default URL (and lots of other configuration details) the system administrator should edit `/usr/lib/lynx.cfg`. The file is big, around 57000 bytes and contains occasionally contradicting information. It states its own home as `/usr/local/lib/`. Not far from top is a line beginning with STARTFILE. We replace this line by the following entry: `STARTFILE:http://localhost` and make sure that no spacing etc. is inserted:

```
# STARTFILE:http://www.nyu.edu/pages/wsn/subir/lynx.html
STARTFILE:http://localhost
```

After saving the file, Lynx should now reveal our `index.html` document if started without arguments.

3.5.2   Configuring Arena

Arena first looks for its own default URL when started without arguments. This URL is hard-wired into the executable but can be overrun by the environment variable WWW_HOME. The system administrator can place a line saying `WWW_HOME="http://localhost"` in `/etc/profile`. The variable must then be exported, either by a separate statement (`export WWW_HOME`) or by appending WWW_HOME to the existing export statement:

```
WWW_HOME="http://localhost"
export WWW_HOME
```

After relaunching a login shell, the new default URL is now system-wide known to Arena.

3.5.3   Installing and Configuring Netscape

Netscape is a commercial product and thus not included with the Linux distributions. It is either downloadable from the Internet or available from software collections on CDROM. Netscape comes in form of precompiled binaries for every important hardware platform. For installation purposes, it is useful to create a directory `/usr/local/Netscape/` where the archive is unpacked. The files can be kept in place (except for the Java library: follow the instructions in the README file that comes with the Netscape binary), and it is sufficient to create a soft link in `/usr/local/bin/` by issuing the command

```
# ln -s /usr/local/Netscape/netscape .
```

from within `/usr/local/bin/`.

Netscape is now ready for use and can be configured via the "Options" menu. In "General Preferences" there is a card "Appearance" with the entry "Home Page Location". Enter `http://localhost` here and do not forget to save the options (via "Options" — "Save Options") before exiting Netscape. At the next startup, Netscape will now show the Apache 'homepage'.

3.6 Cooperation of Apache and Browsers

You can now conduct the first real test of both the browser and the http server: simply start any of the available browsers and the `Apache: Red Hat Linux Web Server` page will pop up. This page shows the file locations and other basics of http server installation. If this page is not displayed please check whether the files mentioned above are in place and whether the browser configuration is correct. Close edited configuration files before you start the browser again. If all files are in place and the browsers seem to be configured correctly then examine the network setup of your machine. Either the host name is different from what was entered in the configuration, or the network setup as such is not correct. It is utterly important that `/etc/hosts` contains at least a line like

```
127.0.0.1              localhost localhost.localdomain
```

which implies that you can connect locally to your machine. One can verify this by issuing any network-sensitive command requiring a host name as argument, like `telnet localhost` (provided `telnet` is installed). If that does not work then the network setup must be verified before continuing with the main task.

3.7 The Database Engine and its Installation

Installing the database requires only little more preparation than the previous installation steps. There are a few SQL database engines available with different runtime and administrative requirements, and possibly one of the most straightforward systems is msql, or "Mini-SQL" by David Hughes. msql is shareware. Depending on the version used, commercial sites are charged USD 250.00 and more, private users are charged USD 65.00 and more, and only educational institutions and registered non-profit organizations can use this software free of charge. Please note that the exact figures are provided in the licence notes of the database documentation. The figures given here serve as a rough indicator only.

A few words are in place here why the author chose msql. First of all, there is personal experience. While searching for a database engine the author found msql to be about the easiest to install and maintain, and it provides enough coverage of the SQL language to meet general needs. Only when writing these lines, the author discovered the following words of praise in Alligator Descartes' DBI FAQ (perl database interface FAQ):

> From the current author's point of view, if the dataset is relatively small, being tables of less than 1 million rows, and less than 1000 tables in a given database, then mSQL is a perfectly acceptable solution to your problem. This database is extremely cheap, is wonderfully robust and has excellent support. [...]

Msql is available in two versions now, msql-1.0.16 and msql-2.0.1, which differ in performance (not noticeable in small scale projects) and accompanying software (the newer version comes with more tools, its own scripting language, etc.). We will describe both versions of msql since their installion differs in a few points.

3.7.1 Installing msql-1.0.16

msql is available as source and as compiled executable with ELF support. Using the ELF binaries makes installation easy since the archive file `msql-1.0.16.ELF.tgz` contains a complete absolute directory tree so that all directories are generated properly when unpacked from `/`.

If you decide to compile msql-1.0.16 yourself and are going to use the MsqlPerl package rather than the DBI interface (see a detailed discussion on the difference between these two further down) then be prepared that MsqlPerl might complain during the test suites that some instruction inside msql failed. In this case a patch may be necessary which is described in the MsqlPerl documentation (file `patch.lost.tables`). Notably, this demands including three lines in `msqldb.c` after line 1400 which says `entry->def = NULL;`:

```
*(entry->DB) = 0;
*(entry->table) = 0;
entry->age = 0;
```

The code fragment should now look like

```
            freeTableDef(entry->def);
            safeFree(entry->rowBuf);
            safeFree(entry->keyBuf);
            entry->def = NULL;
            *(entry->DB) = 0;
            *(entry->table) = 0;
            entry->age = 0;
```

Compiling msql involves several steps. After unpacking the source archive, it is necessary to build a target directory. This is done by saying

```
# make target
```

If successful, the system will then answer with

```
    Build of target directory for Linux-2.0.30-i486 complete
```

You must now change into this newly created directory and run a

```
# ./setup
```

command first. The `./` sequence is necessary to make sure that really the command setup in this directory and not another command which happens to have the same name is executed. You will then be asked questions on the location of the source directory and whether a root installation is desired. These questions answered, the system should then run a number of tests checking for available software (compilers, utilities etc.) and finally say

```
    Ready to build mSQL.

    You may wish to check "common/site.h" although the defaults should be
    fine.  When you're ready, type  "make all" to build the software
```

We say

```
# make all
```

If everything went as intended, we'll read:

```
    make[2]: Leaving directory '/usr/local/Minerva/src/msql'
    <-- [msql] done

    Make of mSQL complete.
    You should now mSQL using make install

    NOTE : mSQL cannot be used free of charge at commercial sites.
        Please read the doc/License file to see what you have to do.
    make[1]: Leaving directory '/usr/local/Minerva/src'
```

All binaries must then be made visible to the search paths by creating soft links in /usr/local/bin/. Change to that directory and issue the command

```
# ln -s /usr/local/Minerva/bin/* .
```

after which the links will be properly set.

Mini-HOWTO

3.7.2 Testing msql-1

After the installation it is now possible to test whether the database works. Before anything else is done, the server daemon must be started. The system administrator holding root privileges issues the command

```
# msqld &
```

(do not forget to add the &, otherwise msql won't run in the background.) after which the following screen message appears:

```
mSQL Server 1.0.16 starting ...

Warning : Couldn't open ACL file: No such file or directory
Without an ACL file global access is Read/Write
```

This message tells us that everything so far worked since we did not set up any access restrictions. For the moment it is sufficient to start the msql daemon from within a shell but later we may want to have the system startup automatically execute this command for us. The command must then be mentioned in a suitable rc.d script. Only now the administrator can issue the first genuine database command:

```
# msqladmin create inventur
```

msql replies by saying Database "inventur" created.. As a further proof, we find that the directory /usr/local/Minerva/msqldb/ contains now the empty subdirectory ../inventur/. We could manipulate the newly created database with the administration tools; these procedures are all covered in detail in the msql documentation.

3.7.3 Installing msql-2.0.1

There is now a newer, more powerful version of Hughes' mSQL server available the installation of which is different in a few points. Installing msql-2 from scratch involves the following steps. Copy the archive to your extraction point, e. g. /usr/local/msql-2/, then untar the archive:

```
# tar xfvz msql-2.0.1.tar.gz
```

Change to the root direction of the install tree and issue a

```
# make target
```

Change to targets and look for your machine type. There should be a new subdirectory Linux-*(your version)-(your cpu)/*. Change to that directory and start the setup facility located here:

```
# ./setup
```

There is also a file site.mm which can be edited. Maybe you have got used to the directory name /usr/local/Minerva/ and want to preserve it? In this case change the INST_DIR=... line to your desired target directory. Otherwise, leave everything as it is.

Now you can start building the database:

```
# make
# make install
```

If everything went successfully, we'll see a message like:

```
      [...]

      Installation of mSQL-2 complete.


      *********
      **   This is the commercial, production release of mSQL-2.0
      **   Please see the README file in the top directory of the
      **   distribution for license information.
      *********
```

After all is installed properly we have to take care of the administration details. Here, the real differences from msql-1 begin. First, a user `msql` is created which is responsible for database administration.

```
# adduser msql
```

Then we have to change all ownerships in the mSQL directory to `msql` by saying:

```
# cd /usr/local/Minerva
# chown -R msql:msql *
```

Then we create soft links for all database binaries in `/usr/local/bin/` by saying:

```
# ln -s /usr/local/Minerva/bin/* .
```

3.7.4   Testing msql-2

We can now start the database server by issuing the command `msql2d &` and should get a response similar to this one:

```
      Mini SQL Version 2.0.1
      Copyright (c) 1993-4 David J. Hughes
      Copyright (c) 1995-7 Hughes Technologies Pty. Ltd.
      All rights reserved.


            Loading configuration from '/usr/local/Minerva/msql.conf'.
            Server process reconfigured to accept 214 connections.
            Server running as user 'msql'.
            Server mode is Read/Write.

      Warning : No ACL file.  Using global read/write access.
```

That looks perfect. The database is compiled and in place, and we can now continue with the perl modules since these rely partially on the presence of a working database server for testing.

Accidentally, this is also a good moment to print the complete manual that comes with msql-2.0.1:

```
# gzip -d manual.ps.gz
# lpr manual.ps
```

We can proceed to building the interfaces now, but it is a good idea to keep the newly created SQL server up and running since that makes testing the interface libraries somewhat simpler.

3.8   Choice of Interfaces: DBI/mSQL, MsqlPerl, and Lite

A frequently quoted saying in the Camel Book (the authorative perl documentation) states that there is more than one way to achieve a result when using perl. This, alas, holds true for our model application, too. Basically there are three ways to access an msql database via CGI. First of all the question is whether or not perl shall be used. If we use perl (on which this article focuses) then we still have the choice between two completely different interface models. Besides using perl, we can also employ msql's own scripting language, called Lite, which is reasonably simple and a close clone of C.

3.8.1 DBI and DBD-mSQL

By the time of this writing, using perl's generic database interface called DBI is the method of choice. DBI has a few advantages: It provides unified access control to a number of commercial databases with a single command set. The actual database in use on a given system is then contacted through a driver which effectively hides the pecularities of that database from the programmer. Being such, using DBI provides for a smooth transition between different databases by different makers. In one single script it is even possible to contact several different databases. Please refer to the DBI-FAQ for details. There is, however, one drawback: The DBI interface is still under development and shows rapidly galloping version numbers (sometimes with updates taking place within less than a month). Similarly, the individual database drivers are also frequently updated and may rely on specific versions of the database interface. Users making first-time installations should stick to the version numbers given in this article since other versions may cause compilation and testing problems the trouble shooting of which is nothing for the faint-hearted.

3.8.2 MsqlPerl

MsqlPerl is a library for directly accessing msql from perl scripts. It bypasses the DBI interface and is fairly compact. Though it works fine with both versions of msql, its usage is not promoted anymore in favour of the generalized DBI interface. Nonetheless, in a given installation it may prove to be the interface of choice since it is small and easy to install. Notably, it has less version dependencies than revealed by the interaction of DBI and particular database drivers.

3.8.3 msql's own scripting language: Lite

Last but not least msql-2 comes with its own scripting language: Lite. The language is a close relative of C stripped of its oddities with additional shell-like features (in a way, something like a very specialized version of perl). Lite is a simple language and is well documented in the msql-2 manual. The msql-2 package also comes with a sample application sporting Lite.

We will not describe Lite here because it is well documented but fairly specific to msql-2, and because it is assumed that the readers of this article have a basic interest in and a basic understanding of perl. Nonetheless it is highly recommended to have a closer look at Lite: it may well be the case that Lite offers the solution of choice in an exclusive msql-2 environment (implying no other databases are involved) due to its simplicity and straightforward concept.

3.9 Going the generic way: DBI and DBD-msql

We assume that perl was installed during the system setup or via the package manager mentioned above. No further details will be given here. Nonetheless we first test whether our version of perl is up to date:

```
# perl -v
```

perl should respond with the following message:

```
This is perl, version 5.003 with EMBED
        Locally applied patches:
            SUIDBUF - Buffer overflow fixes for suidperl security

        built under linux at Apr 22 1997 10:04:46
        + two suidperl security patches

Copyright 1987-1996, Larry Wall
[...]
```

So far, everything is fine. The next step includes installing the perl libraries for databases in general (DBI), the msql driver (DBD-mSQL) and CGI. The CGI driver is necessary in any case. The following archives are necessary:

1. DBI-0.81.tar.gz

2. DBD-mSQL-0.65.tar.gz

3. CGI.pm-2.31.tar.gz (or higher)

A caveat is necessary here for beginners: the test installation described here works fine using software with *exactly* these version numbers, and combinations of other versions failed in one or the other way. Debugging flawed version combinations is nothing for those who are not very familiar with the intimate details of the calling conventions etc. of the interfaces. Sometimes only a method is renamed while performing the same task, but sometimes the internal structure changes significantly. So, again, stick with these version numbers if you want to be on the safe side even if you discover that version numbers have increased in the meantime. Frequent updates of these interfaces are the rule rather than the exception, so you should really anticipate problems when installing other versions than those indicated here.

It is very important that the database driver for mSQL (DBD-mSQL) is installed *after* the generic interface DBI.

We start by creating the directory `/usr/local/PerlModules/` as it is very important to keep the original perl directory tree untouched. We could also choose a different directory name since the name is completely uncritical, and unfortunately that is not really mentioned in the README files of the verious perl modules. Having copied the above-mentioned archives to `/usr/local/PerlModules/` we unpack them saying

```
# tar xzvf [archive-file]
```

for every single of the three archives. Do not forget to supply the real archive name to `tar`. The installation process for the three modules is essentially stardardized; only the screen messages showing important steps of individual packages are reproduced here.

3.9.1 Installing perl's Database Interface DBI

The database interface must always be installed before installing the specific database driver. Unpacking the DBI archive creates the directory `/usr/local/PerlModules/DBI-0.81/`. Change to that directory. There are a README file (you should read it) and a perl-specific makefile. Now issue the command

```
# perl Makefile.PL
```

The system should answer with a lengthy message of which the most important part is shown here::

```
[...]
MakeMaker (v5.34)
Checking if your kit is complete...
Looks good
        NAME => q[DBI]
        PREREQ_PM => {  }
        VERSION_FROM => q[DBI.pm]
        clean => { FILES=>q[$(DISTVNAME)/] }
        dist => { DIST_DEFAULT=>q[clean distcheck disttest [...]
Using PERL=/usr/bin/perl

WARNING! By default new modules are installed into your 'site_lib'
directories. Since site_lib directories come after the normal library
directories you MUST delete old DBI files and directories from your
'privlib' and 'archlib' directories and their auto subdirectories.

Writing Makefile for DBI
```

This looks good, as the program says, and we can proceed with the next step:

```
# make
```

If no error message occurs (the detailed protocol dumped on screen is *not* an error message) we test the newly installed library with the command

```
# make test
```

Watch the output for the following lines (you can always scroll back with [Shift]-[PgUp]):

```
[...]
t/basics...........ok
t/dbidrv...........ok
t/examp............ok
All tests successful.
[...]
DBI test application $Revision: 1.20 $
Switch: DBI-0.81 Switch by Tim Bunce, 0.81
Available Drivers: ExampleP, NullP, Sponge
ExampleP: testing 2 sets of 5 connections:
Connecting... 1 2 3 4 5
Disconnecting...
Connecting... 1 2 3 4 5
Disconnecting...
Made 10 connections in  0 secs ( 0.00 usr  0.00 sys =  0.00 cpu)

   test.pl done
```

The final step is to install all files in their proper directories. The following command will take care of it:

```
# make install
```

No more duties are left. If for some reason the installation failed and you want to redo it do not forget to issue

```
# make realclean
```

first. This will remove stale leftovers of the previous installation. You can also remove the files which were installed by copying the screen contents (shown abbreviated)

```
Installing /usr/lib/perl5/site_perl/i386-linux/./auto/DBI/DBIXS.h
Installing /usr/lib/perl5/site_perl/i386-linux/./auto/DBI/DBI.so
Installing /usr/lib/perl5/site_perl/i386-linux/./auto/DBI/DBI.bs
[...]
Writing /usr/lib/perl5/site_perl/i386-linux/auto/DBI/.packlist
Appending installation info to /usr/lib/perl5/i386-linux/5.003/perllocal.pod
```

into a file, replacing every Installing with rm. Provided you named the file uninstall you can then say

```
# . uninstall
```

which will remove the recently installed files.

3.9.2 perl's msql Driver DBD-mSQL

The msql driver can only be installed *after* a successful installation of perl's generic database interface.

The basic steps are the same as above; so first go through

```
# perl Makefile.PL
```

Here, the system should answer with an urgent warning to read the accompanying documentation. It will then detect where msql resides, and asks which version you use:

```
$MSQL_HOME not defined. Searching for mSQL...
Using mSQL in /usr/local/Hughes

 -> Which version of mSQL are you using [1/2]?
```

State your correct version number. Quite a few lines of text will follow. Watch for the following ones:

```
Splendid! Your mSQL daemon is running. We can auto-detect y-
our configuration!

I've auto-detected your configuration to be running on port: 1114
```

You can now test the driver by saying

```
# make test
```

Again, a lengthy output follows. If it ends with

```
Testing: $cursor->func( '_ListSelectedFields' ). This will fail.
        ok: not a SELECT in msqlListSelectedFields!
Re-testing: $dbh->do( 'DROP TABLE testaa' )
        ok
*** Testing of DBD::mSQL complete! You appear to be normal! ***
```

you are on the safe side of life and can install your driver by saying

```
# make install
```

You are now ready to go and can skip the next paragraph.

3.10 The MsqlPerl Interface

If you decide to use the exclusive MsqlPerl interface then no generic database driver is needed, only `MsqlPerl-1.15.tar.gz`, since, as mentioned earlier, MsqlPerl provides a direct interface between perl and the database server without using the DBI interface. Installing and testing is straightforward.

After saying `perl Makefile.PL` the make utility can be started. First you have to answer the question where mSQL resides. If it resides in `/usr/local/Minerva/` the default answer can be confirmed.

Then do a `make test`. Before doing so you must ensure that you have a database named `test` and that you have read and write permissions for it. This can be done by

```
# msqladmin create test
```

3.11 perl's CGI library

Installing perl's CGI part is the simplest of the three steps. Execute the following commands in the given order and everything is done:

```
# perl Makefile.PL
# make
# make install
```

Unlike the previous drivers this interface does not have a test option (# make test) whereas the other modules *should* be tested in any case.

A subdirectory with CGI example scripts is also created. You can copy the contents of this directory into /home/http/cgi-bin/ and use the browser to experiment with the scripts.

3.12 Installation Checklist

We went through the following steps, in this order:

1. Install Linux with networking support
2. Install a http server, e. g. Apache
3. Install a browser, e. g. Arena, lynx or Netscape
4. Install an SQL server, e. g. msql
5. Install a suitable perl SQL interface
6. Install the CGI files

Finally, you can do some clean-up. All source trees for msql and the perl modules can be safely deleted (however, you should not delete your archive files!) since the binaries and documentation are now based in different directories.

4 Running an Example Database

After completing the system installation we can now finally run a model application. Depending on the version of msql installed and the perl database interface used, we have to modify the sample programs in a few points.

First however, the file index.html residing in /home/httpd/html/ must be modified to allow calling a sample database application. We can place our database (which we call database.cgi or inventur.cgi here despite its archive name perl.1st.ck) in /home/httpd/html/test/.

We add one line (of course, depending on your installation choices) similar to the following to index.html:

```
<LI>Test the <A HREF="test/database.cgi">Database, DBI:DBD-mSQL style!</A>
<LI>Test the <A HREF="test/inventur.cgi">Database, MsqlPerl style!</A>
```

Usually you should only pick one of these two choices but if you have both types of database interface installed you can leave both lines here as they are. You can then compare performance, etc.

4.1 Adapting the sample script for MsqlPerl

Our sample script has to be told to use the MsqlPerl interface. The modification takes place in several locations. First, near the beginning of the file, we change the use clause:

```
#
# use DBI;               # Generisches Datenbank-Interface
use Msql;
```

Then, near line 27, the MsqlPerl syntax does not require the mentioning of a specific driver:

```
# $dbh = DBI->connect($host, $database, '', $driver) ||
$dbh = Msql->connect($host, $database) ||
```

Then, from line 33 onward throughout the whole script, we have to change all instances of do against query:

```
# $dbh->do("SELECT * FROM hw") || db_init($dbh);
$dbh->query("SELECT * FROM hw") || db_init($dbh);
```

Finally, in MsqlPerl speak, line 207 can be commented out:

```
# $sth->execute || msg("SQL Error:", $sth->errstr);
```

In addition, it may become necessary to swap all errstr calls like the one in the preceding code fragment against errmsg. This is also version dependent.

After these modifications, the script should run smoothly.

4.2 Adapting the sample script for msql-2

The SQL syntax was redefined during the development of mslq-2. The original script will fail to execute the table initialization statements in lines 45 – 58. The primary key modifier is no longer supported by msql-2, and should simply be skipped:

```
    $dbh->do(<<EOT) || die $dbh->errstr; # Neue Personen-Tabelle
        create table person (
# We do not need the 'primary key' modifier anymore in msql-2!
#           pn          int primary key,  # Personalnummer
            pn          int,              # Personalnummer
            name        char(80),         # Nachname, Vorname
            raum        int               # Raumnummer
        )
EOT
    $dbh->do(<<EOT) || die $dbh->errstr; # Neue Hardware-Tabelle
        create table hw (
# We do not need the 'primary key' modifier anymore in msql-2!
#           asset int primary key,        # Inventurnummer
            asset int,                    # Inventurnummer
            name  char(80),               # Bezeichnung
            person int                    # Besitzer
        )
EOT
```

Unfortunately, this specific script will then accept new entries with identical personnel numbers; the msql-1 modifier primary key intends to prevent exactly this behaviour. The msql-2 documentation shows how to use the CREATE INDEX clause to create unique entries.

5 Conclusion and Outlook

If you have installed msql-2 on your system then you can have a look at the sample programs written in Lite, msql-2's own scripting language.

Either version of msql comes with a basic set of administration tools which allow the user to create and drop tables (`msqladmin`) and examine database structures (`relshow`).

The second generation msql (i.e. msql-2) has a few more genuinely useful utilities: `msqlimport` and `msqlexport`. These allow the dumping of flat line data files into and out of the SQL database. They can be used for loading quantities of existing data *d'un coup* into existing tables, or extract flat data from tables, and the user does not have to deal with writing a *single* line of perl or SQL or whatever code for this task.

If you want to write your own perl scripts dealing with databases you'll find sufficient support in the example files and the extensive on-line documentation that comes with the DBI module.

Anyway, you are now ready to go and present your data to the users of your own network, or even the WWW.

"Linux ADSM Mini-Howto" by Thomas König

Thomas.Koenig@ciw.uni-karlsruhe.de
v, 15 January 1997
This document describes how to install and use a client for the commercial ADSM backup system for Linux/i386.

Contents

1   Introduction

ADSM is a network-based backup system, sold by IBM, in use at many organizations. There are clients for a large variety of systems (different UNIX brands, Windows, Novell, Mac, Windows NT). Unfortunately, at the time of this writing, there is no native Linux version.

You will have to use the SCO binary, and install the iBCS2-emulator for running ADSM. This description is for ADSM v2r1.

At the time if this writing, I am only aware of a version which works with the i386 version of Linux.

2   Installing the iBCS module

The iBCS2 module is available from *ftp://tsx-11.mit.edu/pub/linux/BETA/ibcs2*. If you are running kernel version 1.2.13, get `ibcs-1.2-950721.tar.gz`, unpac it and apply the patches `ibcs-1.2-950808.patch1` and `ibcs-1.2-950828.patch2`. You can then type `"make"` and install the iBCS modlue with `"insmod"`.

For a 2.0 kernel version, get `ibcs-2.0-960610.tar.gz`, unpack it in a suitable place, chdir into that directory, and apply the following patch:

```
--- iBCSemul/ipc.c.orig Wed Jan 15 21:32:15 1997
+++ iBCSemul/ipc.c      Wed Jan 15 21:32:31 1997
@@ -212,7 +212,7 @@
        switch (command) {
                case U_SEMCTL:
                        cmd = ibcs_sem_trans(arg3);
-                       arg4 = (union semun *)get_syscall_parameter (regs, 4);
+                       arg4 = (union semun *)(((unsigned long *) regs-
>esp) + (5));
                        is_p = (struct ibcs_semid_ds *)get_fs_long(arg4->buf);
 #ifdef IBCS_TRACE
                        if ((ibcs_trace & TRACE_API) || ibcs_func_p->trace)
```

Then, copy `CONFIG.i386` to `CONFIG`, and type `make`.

If you don't have them already, create the needed device files by executing

```
# cd /dev
# ln -s null XOR
# ln -s null X0R
# mknod socksys c 30 0
# mknod spx c 30 1
```

3   Installing the ADSM client

The SCO binary is supplied as three tar files, or disks. Change to the root directory, set your umask according to your policies, and unpack them from there (as root). In your Directory /tmp, you will find an installation script; execute that.

You will then have to hand-edit `/usr/adsm/dsm.sys` and `/usr/adsm/dsm.opt`. In `dsm.sys`, important lines to specify are:

Servername
> The name of the server

TCPServeraddress
> The fully qualified host name of the server

NODename
> Your own hostname

In `dsm.opt`, you will have to specify

Server
> As before

Followsymbolic
> Wether or not to follow symbolic links (not a good idea, in general)

SUbdir
> Wether to back up subdirectories (you usually want that)

domain
> The file systems to back up

You will then have to create a SCO-compatible `/etc/mnttab` from your `/etc/fstab`. You can use the following Perl script, `fstab2mnttab`, for this.

```perl
#!/usr/bin/perl

$mnttab_struct = "a32 a32 I L";

open(MTAB, "/etc/mtab") || die "Cannot open /etc/mtab: $!\n";
open(MNTTAB, ">/etc/mnttab") || die "Cannot open /etc/mnttab: $!\n";

while(<MTAB>) {
    next if /pid/;
    chop;
    /^(\S*)\s(\S*)\s(\S*)\s.*$/;
    $device = $1;
    $mountpt = $2;
```

```
        $fstype = $3;
        if($fstype ne "nfs" && $fstype ne "proc") {
            $mnttab_rec =
                pack($mnttab_struct, $device, $mountpt, 0x9d2f, time());
            syswrite(MNTTAB, $mnttab_rec, 72);
            print "Made entry for: $device $mountpt $fstype\n";
        }
    }

    close(MNTTAB);
    exit 0;
```

You do not need to install any shared libraries for these clients; everything is linked statically.

4 Running the client

There are two clients, dsm, which is an X11 interface, and dsmc, a command-line interface. Your computer centre will tell you how to run it. Some startup script at boot, for example

```
dsmc schedule -quiet 2>&1 >/dev/null &
```

will probably be required.

5 Known Problems

Unfortunately, SCO can only deal with hostnames no longer than eight characters. If your hostname is longer, or fully qualified, you may need to specify your hostname on the NODename line in /usr/adsm/dsm.sys.

If you use the DISPLAY variable, you will have to supply the fully qualified host name (i.e. DIS-PLAY=host.full.do.main:0 instead of DISPLAY=host:0).

Mini-HOWTO

"Linux Apache SSL PHP/FI frontpage mini-HOWTO" Marcus Faure

marcus@faure.de
v1.1, July 1998

This document is about building a **multipurpose webserver** that will support dynamic web content via the **PHP/FI** scripting language, secure transmission of data based on Netscape's **SSL**, secure execution of **CGI's** and M$ **Frontpage Server Extensions**

Contents

1 Introduction

Before you start reading: I am not a native speaker, so there are probably spelling/grammatical errors in this document. Feel encouraged to inform me of mistakes.

Mini-HOWTO

1.1 Description of the components

The webserver you hopefully will get after having read this howto is composed of several parts, the original apache sources with some (well, many) patches and some external executables. I recommend using the software versions I tried, they will probably compile without greater problems and result in a fairly stable daemon. If you are courageous, you can try to compile all the latest-stuff-with-tons-of-new-features, but don't blame me if something fails ;-). However, you may report other working configurations to be included in future versions of this document. All of the steps were tested on a linux 2.0.35 box, so the howto is somewhat linux-specific, but you should be able to use it for other unixes as well.

You do not necesserily have to compile in all components. I tried to structure this howto so that you can skip the parts you are not interested in.

The document is neither a user manual to Apache, SSL, PHP/FI nor frontpage. Its prime intention is to save webservice providers some headaches when installing their server and to do my little contribution to the linux community.

PHP is a scripting language that supports dynamic HTML pages. It is a bit like Apache's SSI, but by far more complex and has database modules for many popular dbs. The GD libraries are needed by PHP.

SSL is an implementation of Netscape's Secure Socket Layer that allow secure connections over insecure networks, e.g. to transmit credit card numbers to web based forms.

frontpage is a wysiwyg web authoring tool that makes use of some server-specific extensions called webbots. Some people think frontpage is cool because you can create feedback forms and discussion webs without having to know a bit about html or cgi. It even protects the designer from uploading his/her site via ftp by using a builtin publisher. If you wish to support frontpage but do not like to setup a windows server, the apache server extensions are your choice.

1.2 Working configurations

Though this document has been downloaded some 100 times since I published it, I received only little feedback. In particular, noone told me of other working combinations. Combinations that work for me are:

- Linux 2.0.31, Apache 1.2.4, PHP 2.0.0, SSL 0.8.0, fp 98 3.0.3 (*)
- Linux 2.0.33, Apache 1.2.5, PHP 2.0.1, SSL 0.8.0, fp 98 3.0.3 (*)
- Linux 2.0.35, Apache 1.2.6, PHP 3, SSL 0.8.0, fp 98 3.0.4

(*) version 3.0.3 is 3.6 (not recommended)

1.3 History

v0.0/Apr 98: Preview version

v1.0/Jun 98: Now using Apache 1.2.6, updated fp section, minor corrections

v1.1/Jul 98: Sgmlized and restructered version

You can find the latest version of this document at <http://www.faure.de>

2 Component installation

2.1 Preparations

You will need:

- Apache 1.2.6 <http://www.apache.org/dist/apache_1_2_6.tar.gz>

- PHP/FI Extensions `<http://php.iquest.net/files/download.phtml?/files/php-2.01.tar.gz>`

- GD Library `<http://siva.cshl.org/gd/gd.html>`

- SSL 0.8.0 `<ftp://ftp.ox.ac.uk/pub/crypto/SSL/SSLeay-0.8.0.tar.gz>`

- SSL patch for Apache 1.2.6 `<ftp://ftp.ox.ac.uk/pub/crypto/SSL/apache_1.2.6+ssl_1.17.tar.gz>`

- frontpage 98 server extensions and install script `<http://www.rtr.com/fpsupport/download.htm>`

Get the sources you want. Untar apche, php, gd and ssl to `/usr/src`. Untar the SSL patch to `/usr/src/apache_1.2.6`.

2.2 Adding PHP

cd to /usr/src/gd1.2 and type make. This will build the GD library `libgd.a`, that should be copied to `/usr/lib`. Now cd to `php-2.0.1` and run `./install`.

The relevant questions are:

```
Would you like to compile PHP/FI as an Apache module? [yN] y
Are you compiling for an Apache 1.1 or later server? [Yn] y
Are you using Apache-Stronghold? [yN] y
Does your Apache server support ELF dynamic loading? [yN] y
Apache include directory (which has httpd.h)?

/usr/local/include/apache /usr/src/apache_1.2.6/src

Would you like to build an ELF shared library? [yN] y
Additional directories to search for .h files []: /usr/src/gd1.2
Would you like the bundled regex library? [yN] n
```

Like the frontpage extensions, phtml includes a security problem because it is run under the uid of the webserver. Be sure to turn on safe mode in src/php.h and restrict the search path to a save value. There are some other options in php.h you may want to edit. If you are very concerned about security, compile php as a cgi. However, this will be a performance loss and not as smart as the module version.

Type `make` to build all files. When the compilation is done, copy `mod_php.*` and `libphp.a` to `/usr/src/apache_1.2.6/src` Add a line

```
Module php_module mod_php.o
```

to the end of `/usr/src/apache_1.2.6/src/Configuration`, add

```
-lphp -lm -lgdbm -lgd
```

to the `EXTRA_LIBS` in the same file,

```
application/x-httpd-php phtml
```

to Apache's `mime.types` and

```
AddType application/x-httpd-php .phtml
```

to Apache's `srm.conf`.

You may also want to add `index.phtml` to `DirectoryIndex` in that file so that a file index.phtml is automatically loaded when its directory is requested.

2.3 Adding SSL

`cd /usr/src/SSL-0.8.0; ./Configure linux-elf; make; make rehash` This will create libraries needed by apache. You may issue `make test` to verify the compilation. You have to apply a patch to apache. It is important that you apply it before the frontpage patch, otherwise frontpage will not work. `cd` to `/usr/src/apache_1.2.6/src` and issue `patch < /usr/src/apache_1.2.6/SSLpatch`. Set `SSL_BASE=/usr/src/SSLeay-0.8.0` in `Configuration`. Make sure that `Module proxy_module` is disabled otherwise Apache won't compile. If you are in need of a proxy, go for Squid `<squid.nlanr.net>`

Now `make certificate` to generate `SSLconf/conf/httpsd.pem`.

2.4 Adding frontpage

Rename the `fp30.linux.tar.Z` file to `fp30.linux.tar.gz`, otherwise the install script will not find it. Run `./fp_install` to copy the extension files to `/usr/local/frontpage`. zcat can usually be invoked as /usr/bin/zcat.

You now have to apply the FP patch. `cd` to `/usr/src/apache_1.2.6/src` and type `patch < /usr/src/frontpage/version3.0/apache-fp/fp-patch-apache_1.2.5` This will create the `mod_frontpage.*` files and do some modifications to `Configuration` etc. The 1.2.5 patch will work with both apache 1.2.5 and 1.2.6. Skip the part about installing webs, you can do that later

3 Putting it all together

3.1 Apache modules to try

The modules I use besides SSL, PHP and frontpage are:

```
Module env_module           mod_env.o
Module config_log_module    mod_log_config.o
Module mime_module          mod_mime.o
Module negotiation_module   mod_negotiation.o
Module dir_module           mod_dir.o
Module cgi_module           mod_cgi.o
Module asis_module          mod_asis.o
Module imap_module          mod_imap.o
Module action_module        mod_actions.o
Module alias_module         mod_alias.o
Module rewrite_module       mod_rewrite.o
Module access_module        mod_access.o
Module auth_module          mod_auth.o
Module anon_auth_module     mod_auth_anon.o
Module digest_module        mod_digest.o
Module expires_module       mod_expires.o
Module headers_module       mod_headers.o
Module browser_module       mod_browser.o
```

3.2 Giving CGI's more security

If you are an ISP (you probably are when you read this) you will want to improve security. The suexec utility allows you to do so; it will execute cgi's under the UID of the webowner instead of executing it under the webservers UID. Go to `/usr/src/apache_1.2.6/support` and `make suexec`. `chmod 4711 suxec` and copy it to the location specified in `../src/httpd.h` which is `/usr/local/etc/httpd/sbin/suexec` by default. If the path seems a little cryptic to you - it did to me - edit `httpd.h` and set the path to a more comfortable value.

3.3 Compiling and installing the server daemon

Enter `/usr/src/apache_1.2.6/src` and edit `Configuration` to set all the Modules you want to include in your Apache daemon. When done, run `./Configure` and `make`. This is the last (and most complicated) compilation step, so cross your fingers. If it succeeds, `cp httpsd` to `/usr/sbin`. The daemon is somewhat big, consider this when assembling your webserver. Create the directory `/var/httpd` with subdirectories `cgi-bin`, `conf`, `htdocs`, `icons`, `virt1`, `virt2` and `logs`. In `/usr/src/apache_1.2.6/conf` edit `access.conf-dist`, `mime.types` and `srm.conf-dist` to suit your needs and copy them to `var/httpd/conf/access.conf`, `srm.conf` and `mime.types`. Copy the `httpsd.pem` you created with `make certificate` to `/var/httpd/conf`. Use the following `httpd.conf`:

```
ServerType standalone
Port 80
Listen 80
Listen 443
User wwwrun
Group wwwrun
ServerAdmin webmaster@yourhost.com
ServerRoot /var/httpd
ErrorLog logs/error_log
TransferLog logs/access_log
PidFile logs/httpd.pid
ServerName www.yourhost.com
MinSpareServers 3
MaxSpareServers 20
StartServers 3

SSLCACertificatePath /var/httpd/conf
SSLCACertificateFile /var/httpd/conf/httpsd.pem
SSLCertificateFile /var/httpd/conf/httpsd.pem
SSLLogFile /var/httpd/logs/ssl.log

<VirtualHost www.virt1.com>
SSLDisable
ServerAdmin webmaster@virt1.com
DocumentRoot /var/httpd/virt1
ScriptAlias /cgi-bin/ /var/httpd/virt1/cgi-bin/
ServerName www.virt1.com
ErrorLog logs/virt1-error.log
TransferLog logs/virt1-access.log
User virt1admin
Group users
</VirtualHost>

<VirtualHost www.virt1.com:443>
ServerAdmin webmaster@virt1.com
DocumentRoot /var/httpd/virt1
ScriptAlias /cgi-bin/ /var/httpd/virt1/cgi-bin/
ServerName www.virt1.com
ErrorLog logs/virt1-ssl-error.log
TransferLog logs/virt1-ssl-access.log
```

```
User virt1admin
Group users
SSLCACertificatePath /var/httpd/conf
SSLCACertificateFile /var/httpd/conf/httpsd.pem
SSLCertificateFile /var/httpd/conf/httpsd.pem
SSLLogFile /var/httpd/logs/virt1-ssl.log
SSLVerifyClient 0
SSLFakeBasicAuth
</VirtualHost>


<VirtualHost www.virt2.com>
SSLDisable
ServerAdmin webmaster@virt2.com
DocumentRoot /var/httpd/virt2
ScriptAlias /cgi-bin/ /var/httpd/virt2/cgi-bin/
ServerName www.virt2.com
ErrorLog logs/virt2-error.log
TransferLog logs/virt2-access.log
</VirtualHost>
```

Depending on the modules compiled in, not all directives may be available. You can retrieve a list of available directives with `httpsd -h`.

3.4 Adding frontpage support to a web

Enter `/usr/local/frontpage/version3.0/bin` and load `./fpsrvadm`. Choose `install` and `apache-fp`. The next questions should be answered the following way:

```
Enter server config filename: /var/httpd/conf/httpd.conf
Enter host name for multi-hosting []: www.virt2.com
Starting install, port: www.virt2.com:80, web: ""
Enter user's name []: virt2admin
Enter user's password:
Confirm password:
Creating root web
Recalculate links for root web
Install completed.
```

The user name must be the unix login of the webowner. The password does not necessarily have to match the system password. You have to manually add `sendmailcommand:/usr/sbin/sendmail %r` to `/usr/local/frontpage/www.virt2.com:80.conf`, otherwise your users will not be able to send web-generated eMails. `kill -HUP` your `httpsd` to make fp reread its config. You can now access `www.virt2.com` with your frontpage client.

Under some circumstances `fpsrvadm` complaints that a root web has to be installed first. This is pretty useless, but you should do so to silence `fpsrvadm`.

3.5 Starting the daemon

Start Apache with `httpsd -f /var/httpd/conf/httpd.conf`. You can now access `www.virt1.com` both through http and https which is pretty cool. Of course you have to pay for a real certificate if you want to offer webwide SSL or users might laugh at you.

Copy one of the demo files from the php examples directory to `virt1` to test phtml.

3.6 Some considerations left

Do not use frontpage 97 extensions. They do not work, at least under Linux. When installing specific versions of the c++ libraries, they appear to work but your logs will soon fill with `premature end of script headers` and your mailbox will fill with complaints. Do not use frontpage 98 extensions before version 3.0.2.1330. Do not be confused, version numbers are somewhat inheterogenous. When telnetting to port 80, typing "get / http/1.0" and hitting return twice, you get a version number 3.0.4 for frontpage.

You can find out the more specific version number by executing `/usr/local/frontpage/currentversion/exes/_vti_bin/shtml.exe -version`. Older versions have a nasty bug that requires httpd.conf to be writable by the gid of the webserver. This should make you scream if you are at all concerned about security. Versions since 3.0.2.1330 are more usable.

3.7 Known bugs

When touching `Recalculate Links` in the frontpage client, the server starts a process that consumes 99% cpu cycles and some 10 mb of memory. But even for medium-sized webs and fast machines, the client sometimes recieves a timeout message, though the calculation will be finished correctly. Inform frontpage users to be patient and not to hit `Recalculate Links` several times. Inform yourself to equip the server with at least 64MB.

Please note that at the time of writing both SSL and frontpage work, but not at the same time, that means you can neither publish your web using ssl nor make use of the webbots through https. You can publish your web on port 80 and access it encrypted on port 443, but your counters etc. will be broken. I consider this a bug. This problem shall be fixed in SSL 0.9.0.

3.8 The final word

For those who think the title of this howto is nearly as long as the document: Did you ever listened to Meat Loaf?

O.K. readers, you're done for today. Feel free to send me your feedback, eternal gratitude, flowers, ecash, cars, oil sources etc.

Mini-HOWTO

Part LIII

"Linux Bridge+Firewall Mini-HOWTO version 1.2.0" Peter Breuer

ptb@it.uc3m.es

v, 19 December 1997

Contents

Mini-HOWTO

1 Introduction

You should look at the original *Bridging mini-HOWTO* `<ftp://sunsite.unc.edu/pub/Linux/docs/`
`HOWTO/mini/Bridge>` by Chris Cole for a different perspective on this. He is *chris@polymer.uakron.edu*. The
version of his HOWTO that I have based this document on (alternatively, ripped off) is 1.03 dated Aug 23 1996.

2 What and Why (and How?)

2.1 What

A bridge is an intelligent connecting wire betwen two network cards. A firewall is an intelligent insulator.

2.2 Why

You might want a bridge if you have several computers:

1. to save the price of a new hub when you just happen to have an extra ethernet card available.

2. to save the bother of learning how to do IP-forwarding and other tricks when you _have_ two cards in your computer.

3. to avoid maintenance work in the future when things change around!

"Several computers" might be as few as three if those are routing or bridging or just moving around the room from time
to time! You also might want a bridge just for the fun of finding out what it does. 2 (2) was what I wanted a bridge for.

If you are really interested in 1 (1), you have to be one of the very few. Check the *NET-2-HOWTO* `<ftp://sunsite.`
`unc.edu/pub/Linux/docs/HOWTO/NET-2-HOWTO>` and the *Serial-HOWTO* `<ftp://sunsite.unc.edu/`
`pub/Linux/docs/HOWTO/Serial-HOWTO>` for better tricks.

You want a firewall if

1. you are trying to protect your network from external accesses, or

2. you are trying to deny access to the world outside from your network.

Curiously, I needed 2 (2) here too. Policy at my university presently is that we should not act as internet service providers
to undergraduates.

2.3 How?

I started out bridging the network cards in a firewalling machine and ended up firewalling without having cut the bridge.
It seems to work and is more flexible than either configuration alone. I can take down the firewall and keep bridging or
take down the bridge when I want to be more circumspect.

I would guess that the bridge code lives just above the physical device layer and the firewalling code lives one layer higher
up, so that the bridging and firewalling configurations effectively act as though they are running connected together "in
sequence" and not "in parallel" (ouch!). Diagram:

```
    -> Bridge-in -> Firewall-in -> Kernel -> Firewall-out -> Bridge-out ->
```

There is no other way to explain how one machine can be a "conductor" and an "insulator" at the same time. There are a
few caveats but I'll come to those later. Basically you must route packets that you want to firewall. Anyway, it all seems
to work together nicely for me. Here is what you do ...

3 BRIDGING

3.1 Software

Get the *bridge configuration utility* <ftp://shadow.cabi.net/pub/Linux/BRCFG.tgz> from Alan Cox's home pages. This is the same reference as in Chris' document. I just didn't realize that it was an ftp and not an http URL ...

3.2 Prior Reading.

Read the *Multiple Ethernet HOWTO* <ftp://sunsite.unc.edu/pub/Linux/docs/HOWTO/mini/Multiple-Ethernet> for some advice on getting more than one network card recognized and configured.

Yet more details of the kind of boot magic that you may need are in the *Boot Prompt HOWTO* <ftp://sunsite.unc.edu/pub/Linux/docs/HOWTO/BootPrompt-HOWTO>.

You may be able to get away without the *NET-2 HOWTO* <ftp://sunsite.unc.edu/pub/Linux/docs/HOWTO/NET-2-HOWTO>. It is a good long read and you will have to pick from it the details you need.

3.3 Boot configuration

The reading material above will tell you that you need to prepare the kernel to recognize a second ethernet device at boot up by adding this to your **/etc/lilo.conf**, and then re-run **lilo**:

```
append = "ether=0,0,eth1"
```

Note the "eth1". "eth0" is the first card. "eth1" is the second card. You can always add the boot parameters in your response to the line that lilo offers you. This is for three cards:

```
linux ether=0,0,eth1 ether=0,0,eth2
```

I use **loadlin** to boot my kernel from DOS:

```
loadlin.exe c:\vmlinuz root=/dev/hda3 ro ether=0,0,eth1 ether=0,0,eth2
```

Note that this trick makes the kernel probe at bootup. That will not happen if you load the ethernet drivers as **modules** (for safety since the probe order can't be determined) so if you use modules you will have to add the appropriate IRQ and port parameters for the driver in your **/etc/conf.modules**. I have at least

```
alias eth0 3c509
alias eth1 de620
options 3c509 irq=5 io=0x210
options de620 irq=7 bnc=1
```

You can tell if you use modules by using "ps -aux" to see if **kerneld** is running and checking that there are .o files in a subdirectory of your **/lib/modules** directory. You want the directory named with what uname -r tells you. If you have kerneld and/or you have a foo.o then edit **/etc/conf.modules** and read the man page for depmod carefully.

Note also that until recently (kernel 2.0.25) the **3c509** driver could not be used for more than one card if used as a module. I have seen a patch floating around that fixes the oversight. It may be in the kernel when you read this.

3.4   Kernel configuration

Recompile the kernel with bridging enabled.

```
CONFIG_BRIDGE=y
```

I also compiled with firewalling and IP-forwarding and -masquerading and the rest enabled. Only if you want firewalling too ...

```
CONFIG_FIREWALL=y
CONFIG_NET_ALIAS=y
CONFIG_INET=y
CONFIG_IP_FORWARD=y
CONFIG_IP_MULTICAST=y
CONFIG_IP_FIREWALL=y
CONFIG_IP_FIREWALL_VERBOSE=y
CONFIG_IP_MASQUERADE=y
```

You don't need all of this. What you do need apart from this is the standard net configuration:

```
CONFIG_NET=y
```

and I do not think you need worry about any of the other networking options. I have any options that I did not actually compile into the kernel available through kernel modules that I can add in later.

Install the new kernel in place, rerun lilo and reboot with the new kernel. Nothing should have changed at this point!

3.5   Network addresses

Chris says that a bridge should not have an IP address but that is not the setup to be described here.

You are going to want to use the machine for connecting to the net so you need an address and you need to make sure that you have the loopback device configured in the normal way so that your software can talk to the places they expect to be able to talk to. If loopback is down the name resolver or other net sevices might fail. See the NET-2-HOWTO, but your standard configuration should already have done this bit:

```
ifconfig lo 127.0.0.1 route add -net 127.0.0.0
```

You will have to give addresses to your network cards. I altered the /etc/rc.d/rc.inet1 file in my slackware (3.x) to setup two cards and you should also essentially just look for your net configuration file and double or treble the number of instructions in it. Suppose that you already have an address at

```
192.168.2.100
```

(that is in the private net reserved address space, but never mind - it won't hurt anybody if you use this address by mistake) then you probably already have a line like

```
ifconfig eth0 192.168.2.100 netmask 255.255.255.0 metric 1
```

in your configuration. The first thing you are going to probably want to do is cut the address space reached by this card in half so that you can eventually bridge or firewall the two halves. So add a line which reduces the mask to address a smaller number of machines:

```
ifconfig eth0 netmask 255.255.255.128
```

Try it too. That restricts the card to at most the address space between .0 and .127.

Now you can set your second card up in the other half of the local address space. Make sure that nobody already has the address. For symmetry I set it at 228=128+100 here. Any address will do so long as it is not in the other card's mask, and even then, well, maybe. Avoid special addresses like .0, .1, .128 etc. unless you really know what you are doing.

```
ifconfig eth1 192.168.2.228 netmask 255.255.255.128 metric 1
```

That restricts the second card to addresses between .128 and .255.

3.6   Network routing

This is where I have to announce the caveats in the bridging + firewalling scheme: you cannot firewall packets which are not routed. No routes, no firewall. At least this appears to be true in the 2.0.30 and more recent kernels. The firewalling filters are closely involved with the ip-forwarding code.

That does not mean that you cannot bridge. You can bridge between two cards and firewall them from a third. You can have only two cards and firewall both of them against an outside IP such as a nearby router, provided that the router is routed by you to exactly one of the cards.

In other words, since I will be doing firewalling, so I want to precisely control the physical destination of some packets.

I have the small net of machines attached to a hub hanging off eth0, so I configure a net there:

```
route add -net 192.168.2.128 netmask 255.255.255.128 dev eth0
```

The 128 would be 0 if I had a full class C network there. I don't, by definition, since I just halved the address space. The "dev eth0" is not necessary here because the cards address falls within the mask, but it may be necessary for you. One might need more than one card holding up this subnet (127 machines on one segment, oh yeah) but those cards would be being bridged under the same netmask so that they appear as one to the routing code.

On the other card I have a line going straight through to a big router that I trust.

```
                                          client 129
           __                                 |    __
client 1   \     .0                 .128      |   /    net 1
client 2 --- Hub - eth0 - Kernel - eth1 - Hub - Router --- net 2
client 3 __/     .100               .228      .2 |  \__  net 3
                                              |
                                          client 254
```

I attach the address of the router to that card as a fixed ("static") route because it would otherwise fall within the first cards netmask and the kernel would be thinking wrongly about how to send packets to the big router. I will want to firewall these packets and that is another reason fow wanting to route them specifically.

```
route add 192.168.2.2 dev eth1
```

I don't need it, since I don't have any more machines in that half of the address space, but I declare a net also on the second card. Separating my interfaces into two sets via routing will allow me to do very tight firewalling eventually , but you can get away with far less routing than this.

```
route add -net 192.168.2.128 netmask 255.255.255.128 dev eth1
```

I also need to send all non-local packets out to the world so I tell the kernel to send them to the big router

```
route add default gw 192.168.2.2
```

3.7 Card configuration

So much was standard networking setup, but we are bridging so we also have to listen on both (?) cards for packets that are not aimed at us. The following should go into the network configuration file.

```
ifconfig promisc eth0 ifconfig promisc eth1
```

The man page says allmulti=promisc, but it didn't work for me.

3.8 Additional routing

One thing that I noticed was that I had to put at least the second card into a mode where it would respond to the big router's questions about which machines I was hiding in my local net.

```
ifconfig arp eth1
```

For good measure I did this to the other card too.

```
ifconfig arp eth0.
```

3.9 Bridge Configuration

Put bridging enabling on and into your configuration file:

```
brcfg -enable
```

You should have been trying this out in real time all along, of course! The bridge configure will bring up some numbers. You can experiment with turning on and off the ports one at a time

```
brcfg -port 0 -disable/-enable
brcfg -port 1 -disable/-enable
```

You get status reports anytime by just running

```
brcfg
```

without any parameters. You will see that the bridge listens,learns, and then does forwarding. (I don't understand why the code repeats the same hardware addresses for both my cards, but never mind .. Chris' howto say that is OK)

3.10 Try it out

If you are still up and running as things are, try out your configuration script for real by taking down both cards and then executing it:

```
ifconfig eth0 down ifconfig eth1 down /etc/rc.d/rc.inet1
```

With any luck the various subsystems (**nfs, ypbind**, etc.) won't notice. *Do not try this unless you are sitting at the keyboard!*

If you want to be more careful than this, you should take down as many daemons as possible beforehand, and unmount nfs directories. The worst that can happen is that you have to reboot in single-user mode (the "**single**" parameter to **lilo** or **loadlin**), and take out your changes before rebooting with things the way they were before you started.

3.11 Checks

Verify that there is different traffic on each interface:

```
tcpdump -i eth0
(in one window)
tcpdump -i eth1
(in another window)
```

You should get used to using **tcpdump** to look for things that should not be happening or that are happening and should not.

For instance look for packets that have gone through the bridge to the second card from the internal net. Here I am looking for packets from the machine with address .22:

```
tcpdump -i eth1 -e host 192.168.2.22
```

Then send a ping from the .22 host to the router. You should see the packet reported by tcpdump.

At this stage you should have a bridge ready that also has two network addresses. Test that you can ping them from outside and inside your local net, and that you can telnet and ftp around between inside and outside too.

4 FIREWALLING

4.1 Software and reading

You should read the *Firewall-HOWTO* <ftp://sunsite.unc.edu/pub/Linux/docs/HOWTO/Firewall-HOWTO>.

That will tell you where to get **ipfwadm** if you don't already have it. There are other tools you can get but I made no progress until I tried **ipfwadm**. It is nice and low level! You can see exactly what it is doing.

4.2 Preliminary checks

You have compiled IP-forwarding and masquerading into the kernel so you will want to check that the firewall is in its default (accepting) state with

```
ipfwadm -I -l ipfwadm -O -l ipfwadm -F -l
```

That is respectively, "display the rules affecting the .." incoming or outgoing or forwarding (masquerading) ".. sides of the firewall". The "-l" means "list".

You might have compiled in accounting too:

```
ipfwadm -A -l
```

You should see that there are no rules defined and that the default is to accept every packet. You can get back to this working state anytime with

```
ipfwadm -I -f
ipfwadm -O -f
ipfwadm -F -f
```

The "-f" means "flush". You may need to use that.

4.3   Default rule

I want to cut the world off from my internal net and do nothing else, so I will want to give as a last (default) rule that the firewall should ignore any packets coming in from the internal net and directed to outside. I put all the rules (in this order) into **/etc/rc.d/rc.firewall** and execute it from **/etc/rc.d/rc.local** at bootup.

```
ipfwadm -I -a reject -S 192.168.2.0/255.255.255.128 -D 0.0.0.0/0.0.0.0
```

The "-S" is the source address/mask. The "-D" is the destination address/mask.

This format to is rather long-winded. **Ipfwadm** is intelligent about network names and some common abbreviations. Check the man pages.

It is possibly more convenient to put some or all of these rules on the outgoing half of the firewall by using "-O" instead of "-I", but I'll state the rules here all formulated for the incoming half.

4.4   Holes per address

Before that default rule, I have to place some rules that serve as exceptions to this general denial of external services to internal clients.

I want to treat the firewall machines address on the internal net specially. I will stop people logging in to the firewall machine unless they have special permission, but once they are there they should be allowed to talk to the world.

```
ipfwadm -I -i accept -S 192.168.2.100/255.255.255.255 \
 -D 0.0.0.0/0.0.0.0
```

I also want the internal clients to be able to talk to the firewalling machine. Maybe they can persuade it to let them get out!

```
ipfwadm -I -i accept -S 192.168.2.0/255.255.255.128 \
 -D 192.168.2.100/255.255.255.255
```

Check at this point that you can get in to the clients from outside the firewall via **telnet**, but that you cannot get out. That should mean that you can just about make first contact, but the clients cannot send you any prompts. You should be able to get all the way in if you use the firewall machine as a staging post. Try **rlogin** and **ping** too, with **tcpdump** running on one card or the other. You should be able to make sense of what you see.

4.5   Holes per protocol

I went on to relax the rules protocol by protocol. I want to allow pings from the outside to the inside to get an echo back, for instance, so I inserted the rule:

```
ipfwadm -I -i accept -P icmp -S 192.168.2.0/255.255.255.128 \
 -D 0.0.0.0/0.0.0.0
```

The "-P icmp" works the protocol-specific magic.

Until I get hold of an **ftp** proxy I am also allowing ftp calls out with port-specific relaxations. This targets ports 20 21 and 115 on outside machines.

```
ipfwadm -I -i accept -P tcp -S 192.168.2.0/255.255.255.128 \
 -D 0.0.0.0/0.0.0.0 20 21 115
```

I could not make **sendmail** between the local clients work without a nameserver. Rather than set up a nameserver right then on the firewall, I just lifted the firewall for tcp domain service queries precisely aimed at the nearest existing nameserver and put its address in the clients **/etc/resolv.conf** (`"nameserver 123.456.789.31"` on a separate line).

```
ipfwadm -I -i accept -P tcp -S 192.168.2.0/255.255.255.128 \
 -D 123.456.789.31/255.255.255.255 54
```

You can find which port number and protocol a service requires with **tcpdump**. Trigger the service with a an **ftp** or a **telnet** or whatever to or from the internal machine and then watch for it on the input and output ports of the firewall with **tcpdump**:

```
tcpdump -i eth1 -e host client04
```

for example. The **/etc/services** file is another important source of clues. To let **telnet** and **ftp** IN to the firewall from outside, you have to allow the local clients to call OUT on a specific port. I understand why this is necessary for **ftp** - it's the server that establishes the data stream in the end - but I am not sure why **telnet** also needs this.

```
ipfwadm -I -i accept -P tcp -S 192.168.2.0/255.255.255.128 ftp telnet \
 -D 0.0.0.0/0.0.0.0
```

There is a particular problem with some daemons that look up the hostname of the firewalling machine in order to decide what is their networking address. **Rpc.yppasswdd** is the one I had trouble with. It insists on broadcasting information that says it is outside the firewall (on the second card). That means the clients inside can't contact it.

Rather than start IP aliasing or change the daemon code, I mapped the name to the inside card address on the clients in their **/etc/hosts**.

4.6   Checks

You want to test that you can still **telnet**, **rlogin** and **ping** from the outside. From the inside you should be able to **ping** out. You should also be able to **telnet** to the firewall machine from the inside and the latter should be able to do anything.

That is it. At this point you probably want to learn about **rpc/Y**ellow **P**ages and the interaction with the password file. The firewalled network wants to run without its unprivileged users being able to log on to the firewall - and thus get out. Some other HOWTO!

Mini-HOWTO

"Bridging mini-Howto" Christopher Cole

cole@coledd.com

v1.11, 7 September 1998

This document describes how to setup an ethernet bridge. What is an ethernet bridge? An ethernet bridge is a device that controls data packets within a subnet in an attempt to cut down the amount of traffic. A bridge is usually placed between two separate groups of computers that talk within themselves, but not so much with the computers in the other group. A good example of this is to consider a cluster of Macintoshes and a cluster of unix machines. Both of these groups of machines tend to be quite chatty amongst themselves, and the traffic they produce on the network causes collisions for the other machines who are trying to speak to one another. A bridge would be placed between these groups of computers. The job of the bridge is then to examine the destination of the data packets one at a time and decide whether or not to pass the packets to the other side of the ethernet segment. The result is a faster, quieter network with less collisions.

Contents

1   Setup

1. Get "Bridge Config":

   `<ftp://shadow.cabi.net/pub/Linux/BRCFG.tgz>`

2. Enable multiple ethernet devices on your machine by adding this to your `/etc/lilo.conf`, and re-run `lilo`:

   ```
   append = "ether=0,0,eth1"
   ```

   If you have three interfaces on your bridge, use this line instead:

   ```
   append = "ether=0,0,eth1 ether=0,0,eth2"
   ```

   More interfaces can be found by adding more ether statements. By default a stock Linux kernel probes for a single ethercard, and once one is found the probe ceases. The above append statement tells the kernel to keep probing for more ethernet devices after the first one is found.

   Alternatively, the boot parameter can be used instead:

   ```
   linux ether=0,0,eth1
   ```

   Or, with 3 interfaces, use:

   ```
   linux ether=0,0,eth1 ether=0,0,eth2
   ```

3. Recompile the kernel with `BRIDGING` enabled.

4. A bridge should not have an IP address. It CAN, but a plain bridge doesn't need one. To remove the IP address from your bridge, go to `/etc/sysconfig/network-scripts/` (for a RedHat system) and copy `ifcfg-lo0` to `ifcfg-eth0` & `ifcfg-eth1`. In these 2 eth files, change the line containing "DEVICE=lo" to "DE-VICE=eth0" and "DEVICE=eth1". Other distributions may deviate from this, do what you need to do! If there are more than 2 interfaces to this bridge, be sure to make the corresponding configurations to those, as well.

5. Reboot, so you are running the new kernel with bridging in it, and also to make sure that an IP addresses are not bound to the network interfaces.

6. Once the system is back up, put the ethernet cards into promiscuous mode, so they will look at every packet that passes by its interface:

```
ifconfig eth0 promisc ; ifconfig eth1 promisc
```

All interfaces which are connected to network segments to be bridged are to be put into promiscuous mode.

7. Turn bridging ON using the brcfg program:

```
brcfg -ena
```

8. Verify that there is different traffic on each interface:

```
tcpdump -i eth0      (in one window)
tcpdump -i eth1      (in another window)
```

9. Run a sniffer or tcpdump on another machine to verify the bridge is separating the segment correctly.

2   Common problems

1. **Question**

   I get the message

   ```
   ioctl(SIOCGIFBR) failed: Package not installed
   ```

   What does this mean?

   Answer

   You don't have bridging capability in your kernel. Get a 2.0 or greater kernel, and recompile with the BRIDG-ING option enabled.

2. **Question**

   Machines on one side cannot ping the other side!

   Answer

   - Did you enable bridging using "brcfg -ena"? (brcfg should say "bridging is ENABLED")
   - Did you put the interfaces into promiscuous mode? (issue the "ifconfig" command. The "PROMISC" flag should be on for both interfaces.)
   - If using multiple-media interface adapters, make sure that the correct one is enabled. You may need to use the config/setup program that came with the network interface card.

3. **Question**

   I cannot telnet/ftp from the bridge! Why?

   Answer

   This is because there is no IP address bound to any of bridge interfaces. A bridge is to be a transparent part of a network.

4. **Question**

   What do I need to set up in the way of routing?

   Answer

   Nothing! All routing intelligence is handled by the bridging code in the kernel. To see the ethernet addresses as they are learned by the bridge, use the brcfg program in debug mode:

```
brcfg -deb
```

5. **Question**

   The bridge appears to work, but why doesn't "traceroute" show the bridge as a part of the path?

   Answer

   Due to the nature of a bridge, a "traceroute" should NOT show the bridge as a part of the path. A bridge is to be a transparent component of the network.

6. **Question**

   Is it necessary to compile `IP_FORWARD` into the kernel?

   Answer

   No. The bridging code in the kernel takes care of the packet transport. `IP_FORWARD` is for a gateway which has IP addresses bound to its interfaces.

7. **Question**

   Why are the physical ethernet addresses for port 1 and port 2 the same according to the "`brcfg`" program? Shouldn't they be different?

   Answer

   No. Every port on a bridge intentionally is assigned the same physical ethernet address by the bridging code.

8. **Question**

   Bridging does not appear to be an option when performing a make config on the kernel. How does one enable it?

   Answer

   During the kernel config, answer 'Y' to the question, "Prompt for development and/or incomplete code/drivers (CONFIG_EXPERIMENTAL) [Y/n/?]".

9. **Question**

   Too many hubs (4 or more) chained one after another (in series) cause timing problems on an ethernet. What effect does a bridge have in a subnet that is layered with hubs?

   Answer

   A bridge resets the 3/4/5 hubs rule. A bridge does not deal with packets the way a hub does, and is therefore not a contributor to timing problems on a network.

10. **Question**

    Can a bridge interface to both 10Mb and 100Mb ethernet segments? Will such a configuration slow down the rest of the traffic on the high speed side?

    Answer

    Yes, a bridge can tie together a 10Mb segment with a 100Mb segment. As long as the network card on the fast network is 100Mb capable, TCP takes care of the rest. While it's true that the packets from a host in the 100Mb network communicating to a host in the 10Mb network are moving at only 10Mb/s, the rest of the traffic on the fast ethernet is not slowed down.

Mini-HOWTO

"DHCP mini-HOWTO (DHCPd/DHCPcd)"
Vladimir Vuksan

vuksan@veus.hr

v2.8, 11 February 1998

This document attempts to answer basic questions on how to setup your Linux box to serve as a DHCP server or a DHCP client.

Contents

Mini-HOWTO

1 Introduction

1.1 Standard Disclaimer

No liability for the contents of this documents can be accepted. Use the concepts, examples and other content at your own risk. As this is a new edition of this document, there may be errors and inaccuracies, that may of course be damaging to your system. Proceed with caution, and although this is highly unlikely, I don't take any responsibility for that.

Also bear in mind that this is NOT official information. Much content in this document are assumptions, which appear to work for people. Use the information at your own risk.

1.2 New Versions of this Document

New versions of this document will be periodically posted to *comp.os.linux.answers*. They will also be added to the various anonymous FTP sites who archive such information, including:

In addition, you should generally be able to find this document on the Linux Documentation Project page via:

1.3 Feedback

Feedback is most certaintly welcome for this document. Without your submissions and input, this document wouldn't exist. So, please post your additions, comments and criticisms to `vuksan@veus.hr`.

1.4 Contributors

This document has been modified from the original version by Paul Makeev.

The following people have contributed to this mini-HOWTO.

- Heiko Schlittermann
- Jonathan Smith
- Dan Khabaza
- Hal Sadofsky
- Henrik Stoerner
- Paul Rossington

1.5 Copyright Information

This document is copyrighted (c)1998 Vladimir Vuksan and distributed under the following terms:

- Linux HOWTO documents may be reproduced and distributed in whole or in part, in any medium physical or electronic, as long as this copyright notice is retained on all copies. Commercial redistribution is allowed and encouraged; however, the author would like to be notified of any such distributions.

- All translations, derivative works, or aggregate works incorporating any Linux HOWTO documents must be covered under this copyright notice. That is, you may not produce a derivative work from a HOWTO and impose additional restrictions on its distribution. Exceptions to these rules may be granted under certain conditions; please contact the Linux HOWTO coordinator at the address given below.

  - If you have questions, please contact the Linux HOWTO coordinator at

`linux-howto@sunsite.unc.edu`

2 DHCP protocol

DHCP is Dynamic Host Configuration Protocol. It is used to control vital networking parameters of hosts (running clients) with the help of a server. DHCP is backward compatible with BOOTP. For more information see RFC 2131 (old RFC 1531) and other. (See Internet Resources section at the end of the document). You can also read *DHCP FAQ* (http://web.syr.edu/ jmwobus/comfaqs/dhcp.faq.html).

This mini-HOWTO covers both the DHCP _SERVER_ daemon as well as DHCP _CLIENT_ daemon. Most people need the client daemon which is used by workstations to obtain network information from a remote server. The server daemon is used by system administrators to distribute network information to clients so if you are just a regular user you need the _CLIENT_ daemon.

3 Client Setup

3.1 Downloading Client Daemon

2.0.x kernels

No matter what distribution you are using you will need to download the DHCP client daemon for Linux. The package you need to download is called dhcpcd and the current version is 0.70. You can read the description of the package *here*. (ftp://sunsite.unc.edu/pub/Linux/system/network/daemons/dhcpcd-0.70.lsm)

2.1.x kernels

Due to changes in ipv4 network package in 2.1.x kernels (e.g. way it sets the defaults for several fields) dhcpcd doesn't work properly. Most users don't run experimental kernels so this shouldn't be a problem. If you do you should try dhcpcd 1.3.16 which is a modified version that has been written by Sergei Viznyuk `sergei@phystech.com` in order to avoid mentioned problems. You can fetch it at:

-
-

3.2 Slackware

You can download the latest copy of the DHCPcd from any Sunsite mirror or following:

-
-
- (Primary site in Japan)

Download the latest version of dhcpcd.tar.gz

- Unpack it
  ```
  tar -zxvf dhcpcd-0.70.tar.gz
  ```
- cd into the directory and make dhcpcd
  ```
  cd dhcpcd-0.70
  make
  ```
- Install it (you have to run the following command as root)
  ```
  make install
  ```

This will create the directory /etc/dhcpc where DHCPcd will store the DHCP information and dhcpcd file will be copied into /usr/sbin.

In order to make the system initialize using DHCP during boot type:

```
cd /etc/rc.d
```

```
mv rc.inet1 rc.inet1.OLD
```

This will move the old network initialization script into rc.inet1.OLD. You now need to create the new rc.inet1 script. Following code is all you need:

```
#!/bin/sh
#
# rc.inet1      This shell script boots up the base INET system.

HOSTNAME=`cat /etc/HOSTNAME` #This is probably not necessary but I
                             #will leave it in anyways

# Attach the loopback device.
/sbin/ifconfig lo 127.0.0.1
/sbin/route add -net 127.0.0.0 netmask 255.0.0.0 lo

# IF YOU HAVE AN ETHERNET CONNECTION, use these lines below to configure the
# eth0 interface. If you're only using loopback or SLIP, don't include the
# rest of the lines in this file.

/usr/sbin/dhcpcd
```

Save it and reboot your computer.

When you are finished go the 3.8 (last step)

3.3   RedHat 5.x

DHCPcd configuration under RedHat 5.0+ is really easy. All you need to do is start the Control Panel by typing

```
control-panel
```

- Select "Network Configuration"
- Click on Interfaces
- Click Add
- Select Ethernet
- In the Edit Ethernet/Bus Interface select **"Activate interface at boot time"** as well as select **DHCP** as **Interface configuration protocol**

When you are finished go the 3.8 (last step)

3.4   RedHat 4.x and Caldera OpenLinux 1.1/1.2

DHCPcd is included in the standard RedHat distribution as an RPM and you can find it on your distribution's CD-ROM in RPMS directory or you can download it from:

and install it with

```
rpm -i dhcpcd-0.6-2.i386.rpm
```

Alternatively you can compile your own version by following the steps outlined in the Slackware.

```
This information was provided to me by nothing nothing@cc.gatech.edu
```

```
Removed my static ip and name from /etc/resolv.conf. However, I
did leave in the search line and my two nameserver lines (for some reason my
dhcpcd never creates a /etc/dhcpc/resolv.conf, so I have to use a static
/etc/resolv.conf).
```

```
In /etc/sysconfig/network I removed the HOSTNAME and GATEWAY
entries. I left the other entries as is
(NETWORKING, DOMAINNAME, GATEWAYDEV).
```

```
In /etc/sysconfig/network-scripts/ifcfg-eth0 I removed the IPADDR,
NETMASK, NETWORK, and BROADCAST entries. I left DEVICE and ONBOOT as is.
I changed the BOOTPROTO line to BOOTPROTO=dhcp.
```

```
Save the file. Reboot your computer.
```

When you are finished go the 3.8 (last step)

3.5 Debian

There is a deb package of DHCPcd at

or you can follow the Slackware installation instructions. To unpack the deb package type

```
dpkg -i /where/ever/your/debian/packages/are/dhcpd*deb
```

It appears that there isn't a need for any DHCPcd configuration because:

```
From:  Heiko Schlittermann (heiko@os.inf.tu-dresden.de)
```

The dhcpcd package installs it's startup script as usual for debian packages in /etc/init.d/<package_name>, here as /etc/init.d/dhcpcd, and links this to the various /etc/rc?.d/ directories.

The contents of the /etc/rc?.d/ dirs is then executed at boot time.

If you don't reboot after installing you should consider starting the daemon manually:

```
/etc/init.d/dhcpcd start
```

When you are finished go the 3.8 (last step)

3.6 LinuxPPC and MkLinux

Following section has been written by R. Shapiro

Versions 0.65 and 0.70 of Yoichi Hariguchi's dhcpcd should work properly in MkLinux and in linuxppc kernel 2.1.24, with the following caveats:

* If you want, or need, to build the executable from sources, note that the ppc linux compilers assume that 'char' is 'unsigned char' while the Hariguchi sources assume 'char' is 'signed char'. To build from sources you must edit the Makefile so that CFLAGS includes the option "-fsigned-char".

* The current stable release of linuxppc [aka linux-pmac] is 2.1.24 and requires the

2.1 patch (http://www.cro.net/ vuksan/dhcppatch). Both the DR2.1 and DR3.0 releases of MkLinux use a 2.0 kernel (2.0.33) and do not require this patch, although it's harmless to apply it. Note that the dhcpcd rpm on the linuxppc cd-rom does not include the 2.1 patch and therefore will not work with the linux on that cd! It will work with MkLinux however.

* In linuxppc 2.1.24, you'll see a router warning shortly after dhcpcd starts up. You can ignore this.

* The Hariguchi dhcpcd takes awhile, about 30 seconds, to make its initial connection to the server and to set up routing. In linuxppc 2.1.24, the warning mentioned above is an indication that the routing is ready.

For later linuxppc kernels, no version of the Hariguchi dhcpcd will work: you **must** use Sergei Viznyuk's version instead (current release is 1.3.9: see above for url). Unfortunately the Viznyuk dhcpcd is written for glibc 2, which linuxppc 2.1.1xx isn't. As a result, compiling it is a bit tricky - contact me for details. Once compiled, however, it works fine on late kernels (and not at all in MkLinux or linuxppc 2.1.24).

As far as Viznyuk's version of dhcpcd is concerned I have a Viznyuk dhcpcd (v1.3.7) executable that works in recent linuxppc kernels: 2.1.102, 103, 115, and 119 have been tested. It's possible to build this from sources, but I don't know the details. The Viznyuk dhcpcd doesn't work in 2.1.24, but in that kernel the patched Hariguchi dhcpcd works. The Hariguchi dhcpcd can be built easily from sources.

Short summary:

```
MkLinux:   Hariguchi: yes; Viznyuk, no
2.1.24:    Hariguchi: yes if patched (easy to build); Viznyuk: no
2.1.102+:  Hariguchi: no; Viznyuk: yes (tricky to build)
```

Note that the Viznyuk dhcpcd writes into /etc/resolv.conf directly (after renaming the existing one), so there's no need to copy or link it from /etc/dhcpc. Also note that it's typically installed into /sbin, not /usr/sbin, and that the command lines options are slightly different from the Hariguchi version. These differences may require small changes to ifup, if you're starting dhcpcd that way.

If you want a precompiled dhcpcd for linuxppc, send mail to

reshapiro@mediaone.net.

I've also made binary RPMs available in

Don't use dhcpcd-1.3.8-2.ppc.rpm in that directory, it's broken. The reliable versions here are dhcpcd-0.70-0.ppc.rpm (for linuxppc 2.1.24), and dhcpcd-1.3.8-3.ppc.rpm (linuxppc 2.1.102 and up). An rpm for 1.3.9 should show up shortly. I also have a modified 1.3.9 which includes the -c command-file option, as in 0.65 and 0.70 (the standard Viznyuk dhcpcd doesn't include this.)

3.7   Token Ring networks

If you are trying to run dhcpcd on the Token Ring Network it will not work. This is the solution provided to me by Henrik Stoerner (henrik_stoerner@olicom.dk)

The problem is that dhcpcd only knows about Ethernet cards. If it finds a Token-Ring card, it refuses to do anything with it and reports "interface is not ethernet".

The solution is to apply a simple patch to the dhcpcd sources. I have put up a small web page with the patch, RedHat RPM-files and a precompiled binary at

The patch has been sent to the dhcpcd maintainer, so hopefully it will be included in a future release of dhcpcd.

3.8   Tying it all together

After your machine reboots your network interface should be configured. Type:

```
ifconfig
```

You should get something like this

```
lo        Link encap:Local Loopback
          inet addr:127.0.0.1  Bcast:127.255.255.255  Mask:255.0.0.0
          UP BROADCAST LOOPBACK RUNNING  MTU:3584  Metric:1
          RX packets:302 errors:0 dropped:0 overruns:0 frame:0
          TX packets:302 errors:0 dropped:0 overruns:0 carrier:0 coll:0

eth0      Link encap:Ethernet  HWaddr 00:20:AF:EE:05:45
          inet addr:24.128.53.102  Bcast:24.128.53.255  Mask:255.255.254.0
          ^^^^^^^^^^^^^^^^^^^^^^^^^
          UP BROADCAST NOTRAILERS RUNNING MULTICAST  MTU:1500  Metric:1
          RX packets:24783 errors:1 dropped:1 overruns:0 frame:1
          TX packets:11598 errors:0 dropped:0 overruns:0 carrier:0 coll:96
          Interrupt:10 Base address:0x300
```

If you have some normal number under inet. addr you are set. If you see 0.0.0.0 don't despair, it is a temporary setting before dhcpcd acquires the IP address. If even after few minutes you are seeing 0.0.0.0 please check out 3.10 (troubleshooting). DHCPcd is a daemon and will stay running as long as you have your machine on. Every three hours it will contact the DHCP server and try to renew the IP address lease. It will log all the messages in the syslog (on Slackware /var/adm/syslog, RedHat/OpenLinux /var/log/syslog).

One final thing. You need to specify your nameservers. There are two ways to do it, you can either ask your provider to provide you with the addresses of your name server and then put those in the /etc/resolv.conf or DHCPcd will obtain the list from the DHCP server and will build a resolv.conf in /etc/dhcpc. I decided to use DHCPcds resolv.conf by doing the following:

Back up your old /etc/resolv.conf

```
mv /etc/resolv.conf /etc/resolv.conf.OLD
```

If directory /etc/dhcpc doesn't exist create it

```
mkdir /etc/dhcpc
```

Make a link from /etc/dhcpc/resolv.conf to /etc/resolv.conf

```
ln -s /etc/dhcpc/resolv.conf /etc/resolv.conf
```

If that doesn't work try this (fix suggested by nothing@cc.gatech.edu with a little amendment by Henrik Stoerner)

This last step I had to perform only because my dhcpcd doesn't create an /etc/dhcpc/resolv.conf. In /etc/sysconfig/network-scripts/ifup I made the following changes (which are a very poor hack, but they work for me):

```
elif [ "$BOOTPROTO" = dhcp -a "$ISALIAS" = no ]; then
    echo -n "Using DHCP for ${DEVICE}... "
    /sbin/dhcpcd -c /etc/sysconfig/network-scripts/ifdhcpc-done ${DEVICE}
    echo "echo \$$ > /var/run/dhcp-wait-${DEVICE}.pid; exec sleep 30" | sh

    if [ -f /var/run/dhcp-wait-${DEVICE}.pid ]; then
       ^^^^
        echo "failed."
        exit 1
```

I changed to:

```
elif [ "$BOOTPROTO" = dhcp -a "$ISALIAS" = no ]; then
    echo -n "Using DHCP for ${DEVICE}... "
    /sbin/dhcpcd
    echo "echo \$$ > /var/run/dhcp-wait-${DEVICE}.pid; exec sleep 30" | sh

    if [ ! -f /var/run/dhcp-wait-${DEVICE}.pid ]; then
        ^^^^^^
        echo "failed."
        exit 1
```

Notice the ! (bang) in if [! -f /var/run/dhcp-wait-${DEVICE}.pid];

Now sit back and enjoy :-).

3.9   Various notes

Following step(s) are not necessary but might be useful to some people

a) If you need network connectivity only occasionally you can start dhcpcd from the command line (you have to be root to do this) with:

/usr/sbin/dhcpcd

When you need to down (turn off) the network type

/usr/sbin/dhcpcd -k

3.10   Troubleshooting

If you have followed the steps outlined above and you are unable to access the network there are several possible explanations:

I. Your network card is not configured properly.

During the boot up process your Linux will probe your network card and should say something along these lines:

eth0: 3c509 at 0x300 tag 1, 10baseT port, address 00 20 af ee 11 11, IRQ 10.
3c509.c:1.07 6/15/95 becker@cesdis.gsfc.nasa.gov

If a message like this doesn't appear your ethernet card might not be recognized by your Linux system. If you have a generic ethernet card (a NE2000 clone) you should have received a disk with DOS utilities that you can use to set up the card. Try playing with IRQs until Linux recognizes your card (IRQ 9,10,12 are usually good).

II. Your DHCP server supports RFC 1541/My DHCP server is Windows NT

Try running dhcpcd by typing

dhcpcd -r

Use ifconfig to check if your network interface is configured (wait few seconds for the configuration process, initally it will say Inet.addr=0.0.0.0)

If this solves your problem add the "-r" flag to the boot up scripts ie. instead of /sbin/dhcpcd you will have /s-bin/dhcpcd -r

For example under RedHat edit script /etc/sysconfig/network-scripts/ifup and change the following

```
IFNAME=$[ {DEVICE} \
"/sbin/dhcpcd -r -c /etc/"- etc etc.
```

III. During bootup I get error message "Using DHCP for eth0 ... failed" but my system works fine.

You are most likely using RedHat and you haven't followed instructions carefully :-). You are missing the ! (bang) in one of the if statements. Jump 3.8 (here) and check how to fix it.

IV. My network works for few minutes and then stops responding

There are some reports of gated (gateway daemon) screwing up routing on Linux boxes which results in problem described above. Check if gated is running

```
ps -auxww | grep gate
```

If it is try removing it with RedHat's RPM manager or removing the entry in /etc/rc.d/

V. My ethernet card is recognized during boot up but I still get "NO DHCPOFFER" message in my logs. I also happen to have a PCMCIA ethernet card.

You need to make sure that you have the 10BaseT port ("phone" plug) on your network card activated. Best way to verify it is to check what kind of connector your card is configured for during bootup e.g.

```
eth0: 3c509 at 0x300 tag 1, 10baseT port, address  00 20 af ee 11 11, IRQ 10.
                             ^^^^^^^^^^^^
3c509.c:1.07 6/15/95 becker@cesdis.gsfc.nasa.gov
```

I have received reports of laptop users having this kind of problems due to the PCMCIA utilities (specifically ifport) that would set the connector type to 10Base2 (thinnet). You have to make sure you use 10BaseT for your connection. If you are not reconfigure the card and restart the computer.

VI. My DHCP client broadcasts requests but no one answers (Contributed by Peter Amstutz)

On some systems, you need to include some hostname for your machine as part of the request. With dhcpcd, do this with 'dhcpcd -h foohost' Probably the hostname wanted will be your account username on the network.

VII. I have followed all the steps but still my machine is not able to connect

The cable modem will usually memorize the ethernet address of your network card so if you connect a new computer or switch network cards you will somehow have to "teach" your cable modem to recognize the new computer/card. Usually you can turn of the modem and bring it back up while computer is on or you will have to call tech support and tell them that you have changed a network card in the computer.

You have firewall rules (ipfwadm rules) that disallow port 67/68 traffic used by DHCP to distribute configuration info. Check your firewall rules carefully.

VIII. I have MediaOne Express service and I still can't connect.

It appears that MediaOne has been using adding some things to DHCP that shouldn't be there. Supposedly this is not a problem anymore but if you experience outages check for these things. If you are (un)lucky to have Windows NT on your machine if you go into Event Viewer you will see a warning like this.

DHCP received an unknown option 067 of length 005. The raw option data is given below.

```
0000:  62 61 73 69 63 basic
```

If this is the problem go to and either download a binary or get the source for the change.

4   DHCP Server Setup

4.1   DHCP server for UNIX

There are several DHCP servers available for U*X-like OSes, both commercial and free. One of the more popular free DHCP servers is Paul Vixie/ISC DHCPd. Currently the latest version is 1.0 (suggested for most users) but 2.0 is in beta testing. You can get them from

After you download it you need to unpack it. After you do cd into the distribution directory and type:

```
./configure
```

It will take some time to configure the settings. After it is done type:

```
make
```

and

```
make install
```

4.2   Network Configuration.

When done with installation type ifconfig -a. You should see something like this:

```
eth0      Link encap:10Mbps Ethernet  HWaddr 00:C0:4F:D3:C4:62
          inet addr:183.217.19.43  Bcast:183.217.19.255  Mask:255.255.255.0
          UP BROADCAST RUNNING MULTICAST  MTU:1500  Metric:1
          RX packets:2875542 errors:0 dropped:0 overruns:0
          TX packets:218647 errors:0 dropped:0 overruns:0
          Interrupt:11 Base address:0x210
```

If it doesn't say MULTICAST you should reconfigure your kernel and add multicast support. On most systems you will not need to do this.

Next step is to add route for 255.255.255.255. Quoted from DHCPd README:

"In order for dhcpd to work correctly with picky DHCP clients (e.g., Windows 95), it must be able to send packets with an IP destination address of 255.255.255.255. Unfortunately, Linux insists on changing 255.255.255.255 into the local subnet broadcast address (here, that's 192.5.5.223). This results in a DHCP protocol violation, and while many DHCP clients don't notice the problem, some (e.g., all Microsoft DHCP clients) do. Clients that have this problem will appear not to see DHCPOFFER messages from the server."

Type:

```
route add -host 255.255.255.255 dev eth0
```

If you get a message

```
"255.255.255.255:  Unknown host"
```

You should try adding the following entry to your /etc/hosts file:

```
255.255.255.255 all-ones
```

Then, try:

```
route add -host all-ones dev eth0
```

or

```
route add -net 255.255.255.0 dev eth0
```

eth0 is of course the name of the network device you are using. If it differs change appropriately.

4.3   Options for DHCPd

Now you need to configure DHCPd. In order to do this you will have to create or edit /etc/dhcpd.conf.

Most commonly what you want to do is assign IP addresses randomly. This can be done with settings as follows

```
default-lease-time 600;
max-lease-time 7200;
option subnet-mask 255.255.255.0;
option broadcast-address 192.168.1.255;
option routers 192.168.1.254;
option domain-name-servers 192.168.1.1, 192.168.1.2;
option domain-name "mydomain.org";

subnet 192.168.1.0 netmask 255.255.255.0 {
    range 192.168.1.10 192.168.1.100;
    range 192.168.1.150 192.168.1.200;
}
```

This will result in DHCP server giving a client an IP address from the range 192.168.1.10-192.168.1.100 or 192.168.1.150-192.168.1.200. It will lease an IP address for 600 seconds if the client doesn't ask for specific time frame. Otherwise the maximum (allowed) lease will be 7200 seconds. The server will also "advise" the client that it should use 255.255.255.0 as its subnet mask, 192.168.1.255 as its broadcast address, 192.168.1.254 as the router/gateway and 192.168.1.1 and 192.168.1.2 as its DNS servers.

You can also assign specific IP addresses based on clients ethernet address e.g.

```
host haagen {
    hardware ethernet 08:00:2b:4c:59:23;
    fixed-address 192.168.1.222;
}
```

This will assign IP address 192.168.1.222 to a client with ethernet address 08:00:2b:4c:59:23.

You can also mix and match e.g. you can have certain clients getting "static" IP addresses (e.g. servers) and others being alloted dynamic IPs (e.g. mobile users with laptops). There are a number of other options e.g. wins server addresses, time server etc., if you need any of those options please read the dhcpd.conf man page.

4.4   Starting the server

You can now invoke the DHCP server. Simply type (or include in the bootup scripts)

```
/usr/sbin/dhcpd
```

If you want to verify that everything is working fine you should first turn on the debugging mode and put the server in foreground. You can do this by typing

```
/usr/sbin/dhcpd -d -f
```

Then boot up one of your clients and check out the console of your server. You will see a number of debugging messages coming up.

Mini-HOWTO

" Linux DPT Hardware RAID HOWTO " Ram Samudrala

(me@ram.org)
v1.1, 15 December 1997
How to set up hardware RAID under Linux.

Contents

1 Introduction

This document describes how to set up SCSI hardware RAID, focusing mainly on host-based adapters from DPT, though the principles applied here are fairly general.

Use the information below at your own risk. I disclaim all responsibility for anything you may do after reading this HOW-TO. The latest version of this HOWTO will always be available at *http://www.ram.org/computing/linux/dpt_raid.html*.

2   Supported controllers

Currently the only well-supported host-based hardware RAID controller (i.e, a controller for which there exists a driver under Linux) is one that is made by *DPT* <http://www.dpt.com>. However, there exist other host-based and scsi-to-scsi controller which may work under Linux. These include the ones made by *Syred* <http://www.syred.com>, *ICP-Vortex* <http://www.icp-vortex.com>, and *BusLogic* <http://www.bus-logic.com>. In addition, there exist plenty of SCSI-to-SCSI controllers. See the *RAID solutions for Linux page* <http://linas.org/linux/raid.html> for more info.

If, in the future, there is support for other drivers, I will do my best to incorporate that information into this HOWTO.

3   What hardware should be used?

Given all these options, if you're looking for a RAID solution, you need to think carefully about what you want. Depending on what you want to do, and which RAID level you wish to use, some cards may be better than others. SCSI-to-SCSI adapters may not be as good as host-based adapters, for example (see the *DPT comparison between host-based and SCSI-to-SCSI adapters* <http://www.dpt.com/hstvscsi.html> for why this is the case). Michael Neuffer (*neuffer@kralle.zdv.uni-mainz.de*), the author of the EATA-DMA driver, has a nice discussion about this on his *Linux High Performance SCSI and RAID page* <http://www.uni-mainz.de/~neuffer/scsi/>.

For the purposes of this HOWTO, I am assuming you have only a Linux system running. Also, note that I've only tried this out with the DPT Smartcache VI PM2144UW controller, with the DPT-supplied enclosure (SmartRAID tower), and I have no experience with other set ups. So things may be different for your setup.

4   Installation

4.1   Installing and configuring the hardware

Refer to the instruction manual to install the card and the drives. For DPT, since a storage manager for Linux doesn't exist yet, you need to create a MS-DOS-formatted disk with the system on it (usually created using the command "format \s" at the MS-DOS prompt). You will also be using the DPT storage manager for MS-DOS, which you should probably make a copy of for safety.

Once the hardware is in place, boot using the DOS system disk. Replace the DOS disk with the storage manager. And invoke the storage manager using the command:

```
a:\ dptmgr
```

Wait a minute or so, and you'll get a nice menu of options. Configure the set of disks as a hardware RAID (single logical array). Choose "other" as the operating system.

The MS-DOS storage manager is a lot easier to use with a mouse, and so you might want to have a mouse driver on the initial system disk you create.

Technically, it should be possible to run the SCO storage manager under Linux, but it may be more trouble than its worth. It's probably more easier to run the MS-DOS storage manager under Linux.

4.2   Configuring the kernel

You will need to configure the kernel with SCSI support and the appropriate low level driver. See the *Kernel HOWTO* <http://sunsite.unc.edu/mdw/HOWTO/Kernel-HOWTO.html> for information on how to compile the kernel. Once you choose "yes" for SCSI support, in the low level drivers section, select the driver of your choice (EATA-DMA for most EATA-DMA compliant (DPT) cards, EATA-PIO for the very old PM2001 and PM2012A from DPT). Most drivers, including the EATA-DMA driver, should be available in recent kernel versions.

Once you have the kernel compiled, reboot, and if you've set up everything correctly, you should see the driver recognising the RAID as a single SCSI disk. If you use RAID-5, you will see the size of this disk to be 2/3 of the actual disk space available. The messages you see upon bootup should look something like this:

```
EATA (Extended Attachment) driver version: 2.59b
developed in co-operation with DPT
(c) 1993-96 Michael Neuffer, mike@i-Connect.Net
Registered HBAs:
HBA no. Boardtype    Revis  EATA Bus  BaseIO IRQ DMA Ch ID Pr QS  S/G IS
scsi0 : PM2144UW     v07L.Y 2.0c PCI  0xef90 11  BMST 1  7  N  64 252 Y
scsi0 : EATA (Extended Attachment) HBA driver
scsi : 1 host.
   Vendor: DPT        Model: RAID-5          Rev: 07LY
   Type:   Direct-Access               ANSI SCSI revision: 02
Detected scsi disk sda at scsi0, channel 0, id 8, lun 0
scsi0: queue depth for target 8 on channel 0 set to 64
scsi : detected 1 SCSI disk total.
SCSI device sda: hdwr sector= 512 bytes. Sectors= 35591040 [17378 M-
B] [17.4 GB]
```

(The above display is for a setup with a single DPT SCSI controller, configured as RAID-5, with three disks of 9 GB each.)

5 Usage

5.1 fdisk, mke2fs, mount, etc.

You can now start treating the RAID as a regular disk. The first thing you'll need to do is partition the disk (using fdisk). You'll then need to set up an ext2 filesystem. This can be done by running the command:

```
% mkfs -t ext2 /dev/sdxN
```

where /dev/sdxN is the name of the SCSI partition. Once you do this, you'll be able to mount the partitions and use them as you would any other disk (including adding entries in /etc/fstab).

5.2 Hotswapping

We first tried to test hotswapping by removing a drive and putting it back in the DPT-supplied enclosure/tower (which you buy for an additional cost). Before we could carry this out to completion, one of the disks failed (as I write this, the beeping is driving me crazy). Even though one of the disks failed, all the data on the RAID drive is accessible.

Instead of replacing the drive, we just went through the motions and put the same drive back in. The drive rebuilt itself and everything seems to be okay. During the time the disk had filed, and during the rebuilding process, all the data was accessible. Though it should be noted that if another disk had failed, we'd have been in serious trouble.

5.3 Performance

Here's the output of the Bonnie program, on a 2144 UW with 9x3=17 GB RAID 5 setup. The RAID is on a dual processor Pentium Pro machine running Linux 2.0.32. For comparison, the Bonnie results for the IDE drive on that machine are also given.

```
         -------Sequential Output-------- ---Sequential Input-- --Random--
         -Per Char- --Block--- -Rewrite-- -Per Char- --Block--- --Seeks---
     MB K/sec %CPU K/sec %CPU K/sec %CPU K/sec %CPU K/sec %CPU  /sec  %CPU
```

Mini-HOWTO

```
RAID 100  9210 96.8  1613  5.9   717  5.8  3797 36.1 90931 96.8 4648.2 159.2
IDE  100  3277 32.0  6325 23.5  2627 18.3  4818 44.8 59697 88.0  575.9  16.3
```

It's clear that the RAID is great for block reads and writes (even though write performance is degraded by using RAID-5), but it is not very good at sequential re-writes.

6 Features in the DPT RAID driver

This section describes some of the commands available under Linux to check on the RAID configuration. Again, while references to the eata_dma driver is made, this can be used to check up on any driver.

To see the configuration for your driver, type:

```
% cat /proc/scsi/eata_dma/N
```

where N is the host id for the controller. You should see something like this:

```
EATA (Extended Attachment) driver version: 2.59b
queued commands:        353969
processed interrupts:   353969

scsi0 : HBA PM2144UW
Firmware revision: v07L.Y
Hardware Configuration:
IRQ: 11, level triggered
DMA: BUSMASTER
CPU: MC68020 20MHz
Base IO : 0xef90
Host Bus: PCI
SCSI Bus: WIDE Speed: 10MB/sec.
SCSI channel expansion Module: not present
SmartRAID hardware: present.
    Type: integrated
    Max array groups:            7
    Max drives per RAID 0 array:    7
    Max drives per RAID 3/5 array: 7
Cache Module: present.

    Type: 0
    Bank0: 16MB without ECC
    Bank1: 0MB without ECC
    Bank2: 0MB without ECC
    Bank3: 0MB without ECC
Timer Mod.: present
NVRAM    : present
SmartROM : enabled
Alarm    : on
Host<->Disk command statistics:
        Reads:       Writes:
    1k:          0             0
    2k:          0             0
    4k:          0             0
    8k:          0             0
    16k:         0             0
```

```
   32k:              0              0
   64k:              0              0
  128k:              0              0
  256k:              0              0
  512k:              0              0
 1024k:              0              0
>1024k:              0              0
Sum    :              0              0
```

To get advanced command statistics, type:

```
% echo "eata_dma latency" > /proc/scsi/eata_dma/N
```

Then you can do a:

```
% cat /proc/scsi/eata_dma/N
```

to get more detailed statistics.

To turn off advanced command statistics, type:

```
% echo "eata_dma nolatency" > /proc/scsi/eata_dma/N
```

7   Troubleshooting

7.1   Upon bootup, no SCSI hosts are detected

This could be due to several reasons, but it's probably because the appropriate driver is not configured in the kernel. Check and make sure the appropriate driver (EATA-DMA for most DPT cards) is configured.

7.2   RAID configuration shows up as N different disks

The RAID has not been configured properly. If you're using a DPT storage manager, you need to configure the RAID disks as a single logical array. Michael Neuffer (*neuffer@kralle.zdv.uni-mainz.de*) writes "When you configure the controller with the SM start it with the parameter /FW0 and/or select Solaris as OS. This will cause the array to be setup to be managed internally by the controller."

7.3   If all fails...

Read the SCSI-HOWTO again. Check the cabling and the termination. Try a different machine if you have access to one. The most common cause of problems with SCSI devices and drivers is because of faulty or misconfigured hardware. Finally, you can post to the various newsgroups or e-mail me, and I'll do my best to get back to you.

8   References

The following documents may prove useful to you as you set up RAID:

- *DPT RAID Primer and other RAID/SCSI-related documents* <http://www.dpt.com/techno.html>
- *EATA-DMA homepage* <http://www.uni-mainz.de/~neuffer/scsi/dpt/index.html>
- *Linux Disk HOWTO* <http://sunsite.unc.edu/mdw/HOWTO/Disk-HOWTO.html>
- *Linux Kernel HOWTO* <http://sunsite.unc.edu/mdw/HOWTO/Kernel-HOWTO.html>
- *Linux SCSI HOWTO* <http://sunsite.unc.edu/mdw/HOWTO/SCSI-HOWTO.html>
- *RAID Solutions for Linux* <http://linas.org/linux/raid.html>

Mini-HOWTO

9 Acknowledgements

The following people have been helpful in getting this HOWTO done:

- Boris Fain (*fain@zen.stanford.edu*)
- Jos Vos (*jos@xos.nl*)
- Michael Neuffer (*neuffer@kralle.zdv.uni-mainz.de*)
- Ralph Wallace (*rwallace@rwallace.interaccess.com*)
- Russell Brown (*russell@lutton.lls.com*)
- Syunsuke Ogata (*Syunsuke_Ogata@appear.ne.jp*)

"Diskless Linux Mini Howto" by Robert Nemkin

buci@math.klte.hu
v0.0.3, 12 September 1996
This document describes how to set up a diskless Linux box and copyrighted by Robert Nemkin. Copyright policy is GPL. I whish to thank to Bela Kis <bkis@cartan.math.klte.hu> for translating this document to English.

Contents

1   Changes

- v0.0.3 12 Sep 1996: Some minor error fixes

2   How to set up a diskless Linux box

This document is about setting up a diskless Linux box. Sometimes it might be necessary to run Linux on PC's which have neither hard disks nor floppy drives. If a network, another Unix system with bootp, tftp, an NFS server, and an eprom burner is available then it is possible to set up and operate Linux without hard/floppy disks.

3 Related documents

- NFS-root Mini Howto
- Linux NET-2/3-HOWTO by Terry Dawson, `94004531@postoffice.csu.edu.au`
- `/usr/src/linux/README` about configuring and compiling new kernels

4 Hardware

Whatever is described here was checked on the following configuration

- Sun-OS 4.1.3 as boot server
- Slackware 2.3 + Linux 1.2.8 + wd 8013 ethercard.
- Working Ethernet lan

5 Fundamental ideas

The fundamental idea is as follows: the PC will get its IP address from the boot server via the bootp protocol, using 0.0.0.0 as the initial IP address and its kernel via the tftp protocol. [44]

For this follow the steps below.

5.1 Setting up the PC

Get the nfsboot package (the package is available from your favourite linux mirror site in the `/pub/Linux/system/Linux-boot` directory). It contains a booteprom image for the wd8013 card which can be directly burned in.

There are alternative ways to prepare the PC:

- if your machine is not quite diskless, then you may use the little DOS program, or
- the binary floppy image contained in the same package.

If you choose the latter option you must write the image onto a floppy by the dd command.

These images contain a bootp and tftp client. You need to prepare a linux kernel too, which contains the nfs-root option.

- If you are using the latest stable kernel, linux-1.2.13, then you need to patch the kernel with the patchfile included in the nfsboot package [45]
- If you try to use the latest, but unstable kernel from the linux-1.3.x series, then you have to configure in the nfs-root option.

You may or may not configure block device (floppy or hard disk) support, but you must configure tcp/ip support, wd ethernet card support, nfs filesystem support. Then recompile the kernel as usual.

---

[44] Booting across segments (via router) not a simple question, so either put both the server and the diskless boxes on the same lan segment or configure an UDP helper address in your router to the address of the server. Refer to your router product manual for further info.

[45] Refer to patch(1)

5.2 Setting up a bootpd on the server

It can be found in package `bootpd-2.4.tar.gz` (which can be found on your favourite linux mirror site in the `/pub/Linux/system/Network/boot.net` directory). Get the package, compile and install it. If your other Unix box happens to be a Slackware Linux then you may skip this step for the standard distributions contain a bootpd. The daemon can be run either directly by issuing command

```
bootpd -s
```

or by using inetd. In this case you need to edit:

- /etc/inetd.conf to remove the hashmark from the start of these lines:

```
# tftp    dgram    udp    wait    root    /usr/sbin/in.tftpd    tft-
pd /export
# bootps dgram    udp    wait    root    /usr/sbin/in.bootpd    bootpd
```

- insert or uncomment the following two lines in /etc/services:

```
bootps        67/tcp      # BOOTP server
tftp          69/udp      # TFTP server
```

- restart inetd by

```
kill -HUP <process id of inetd>.
```

5.3 Configure the bootpd on the server.

First of all, bootpd have a config file called bootptab which usually resides in /etc. You must modify it by inserting the IP addresses of your gateway, dns server, and the ethernet address(es) of your diskless machine(s). An example /etc/bootptab:

```
global.prof:\
        :sm=255.255.255.0:\
        :ds=192.168.1.5:\
        :gw=192.168.1.19:\
        :ht=ethernet:\
        :bf=linux:
machine1:hd=/export/root/machine1:tc=global.prof:ha=0000c0863d7a:\
ip=192.168.1.140:
machine2:hd=/export/root/machine2:tc=global.prof:ha=0800110244e1:\
ip=192.168.1.141:
machine3:hd=/export/root/machine3:tc=global.prof:ha=0800110244de:\
ip=192.168.1.142:
```

global.prof is a general template for host entries, where

- sm field contains the subnet mask
- ds field contains the address of the Domain Name Server
- gw field contains the default gateway address
- ht field contains the lan media hardware type
- bf field contains the name of the boot file

After this, every machine must have a line:

- the first field contains the host name,

Mini-HOWTO

- hd field contains the directory of the bootfile,
- the global template can be included with the tc field,
- ha field contains the hardvare address of the ethernet card,
- ip field contains the assigned ip address.

5.4 Understanding tftp

TFTP (`Trivial File Transfer Protocol`) is a file transfer protocol, such as ftp, but it's much simpler to help coding it in EPROMs. TFTP can be used in two ways:

- simple tftp: means that the client can acces to your whole file system. It's simpler but it's a big security hole (anyone can get your password file via tftp).
- secure tftp: the tftp server uses a chroot.2 system call to change it's own root directory. Anything outside the new root directory will be completelly inaccessible. Because of the chroot dir becomes the new root dir, the hd filed in the bootptab must reflect the new situation. For example: when using insecure tftp, the hd field contains the full path to the boot directory: `/export/root/machine1`. When using secure tftp whith /export as root dir, then /export becomes / and the hd field must be `/root/machine1`.

Almost every Unix implementation contains tfpt server, probably you don't need to install your own one.

5.5 Setting up a minimal Linux configuration on the remote server.

This may contain packages a, ap, n, and x of the Slackware distribution. To install more is OK; however the above packages suffice for the purposes of a diskless X terminal. For the installation you need a working Linux system. Find some disk space on the remote machine and export it read-write. Mount the exported directory onto somewhere (e.g. /mnt) on the file system of the Linux box. Start Linux setup and change the root option in the setup from / to /mnt. Then setup the above packages as usual. If you want to run no more than one diskless Linux then no changes are needed. On the other hand, if you plan to use more than one diskless machine then the above setup will not work because some files and directories must be private to the machines. The problem can be bypassed by moving the /usr (it contains no private data) and then create a separate subdir for each diskless machine. For example, if /export/linux/machine1 were mounted to /mnt then the directory structure after the initial setup will look like

```
/export/linux/machine1/bin
/export/linux/machine1/sbin
/export/linux/machine1/lib
/export/linux/machine1/etc
/export/linux/machine1/var
/export/linux/machine1/usr
```

After the changes you will have

```
/export/linux/machine1/bin
/export/linux/machine1/sbin
/export/linux/machine1/lib
/export/linux/machine1/etc
/export/linux/machine1/var
/export/linux/usr
```

Now create the subdirectories for the other machines. Assume for now that your diskless machines are called machine1, machine2, machine3, etc.; then you may use the following bash script to setup the other directories

```
cd /export/linux
for x in machine2 machine3 ; do
        mkdir $x; cd $x
```

```
                    (cd ../machine1; tar cf - *) | tar xvf -
        done
```

Then do the following export:

- /export/linux/usr readonly for everyone.

- /export/liunx/machine1 only to machine1 with rw,root rights.

- /export/liunx/machine2 only to machine2 with rw,root rights.

- /export/liunx/machine3 only to machine3 with rw,root rights.

as follows[46]:

```
# This file is /etc/export
# for remote linux X terminals by Buci
# this line is only once
/export/root/usr            -access=linuxnet
# these lines once for every host
/export/root/machine1       rw=machine1,root=machine1
/export/root/machine2       rw=machine2,root=machine2
/export/root/machine3       rw=machine3,root=machine3
```

Don't forget to run exportfs -a.

5.6   Configuring the tftp server

Now it is time to configure the tftp server. If you do not need secure tftp then everything is quite simple for your clients can be booted from the /export directory.

If a secure tftp is used then you can either make a full /export/linux directory structure under /tftpboot (with a single real kernel and symbolic links for the other machines), or let the /export directory be the boot directory of the secure tftpd. Or, if you have a separate tftpboot directory then, similarly, you need only the original directory structure with a single kernel and symbolic links for the others. You can achieve this setup by typing the following:

```
    mkdir -p /tftpboot/export/linux/machine1
    cd /tftpboot/export/linux/machine1
    cp /export/linux/machine1/<name of the kernel> .
```

Then type the following:

```
    mkdir -p /tftpboot/export/linux/machine2
    cd ../machine2
    ln -s ../machine2/<name of the kernel>
```

5.7   Final work

Finally, you must insert

```
    /sbin/mount nfs_server:/export/linux/usr /usr
```

as the first line of

```
    /export/linux/<machinex>/etc/rc.d/rc.S
```

where <machinex> stands for machine1, machine2, etc.

---

[46]the format of this example follows the SunOs 4.1.3 exports file syntax

Mini-HOWTO

6 Memory and diskspace requirements; speed

. I tested this for only Slackware 2.3; for other distributions/versions the following numbers may vary.

- Diskspace: 28MB + 6.5MB/machine
- RAM: I am using X on 8 MB. For only 4MB swap is needed, I guess, which can be created – separately for each machine – in /tmp. Do not forget to run mkswap.
- Speed: I had no problems on a 486 DX2/66 with 8 Megs.

7 Possible errors

- I found a strange error: in the /dev subdirectory SunOS corrupted the device entries so I needed to rerun MAKEDE-V by mounting the subdirectory onto a disk based Linux box. (The reason was the differences between the linux nfs and the SunOs nfs: both use 32 bit for the Major and Minor device number, but linux uses 16 bit wide fields for both, SunOs uses 14 bit wide field for Major and 18 bit wide filed for Minor device number.)
- When the diskless linux gets booted, there is only one route included in the routing table to the tftp server, so you need to set up correct routing tables. You have two choices here:
  - configure every rc.S for every machine by hand
  - use a bootp client package and write a generalized setup script

8 Errors and possible further expansions of this document

- Correct citation of related documents.
- SunOs is BSD based. Need to include SVR4 (e.g. Solaris) based server configuration.
- Although Linux is quite similar to SunOs as bootp/tftp server, a linux based server example might be usefull.
- Update this document to the current etherboot package.
- Show the differences between the nfs root patched kernel version 1.2.13 and the newest 1.3.x kernel, which contains the nfs-root patch.
- Need to try other ethercards than wd8013
- Include configuration information for bootpc, a bootp client for linux to set up the correct rooting tables.
- Typos and other errors: please, report to buci@math.klte.hu Thank you.

"Linux Ext2fs Undeletion mini-HOWTO" Aaron Crane

<aaronc@pobox.com>

v1.2, 4 August 1997

Picture this. You've spent the last three days with no sleep, no food, not even a shower. Your hacking compulsion has at last paid off: you've finished that program that will bring you world-wide fame and recognition. All that you still need to do is tar it up and put it on Sunsite. Oh, and delete all those Emacs backup files. So you say `rm * ~`. And too late, you notice the extra space in that command. You've just deleted your *magnum opus*! But help is at hand. This document presents a discussion of how to retrieve deleted files from a Second Extended File System. Just maybe, you'll be able to release that program after all...

Contents

1 Introduction

This mini-Howto attempts to provide hints on how to retrieve deleted files from an ext2 filesystem. It also contains a limited amount of discussion of how to avoid deleting files in the first place.

I intend it to be useful certainly for people who have just had, shall we say, a little accident with rm; however, I also hope that people read it anyway. You never know: one day, some of the information in here could save your bacon.

The text assumes a little background knowledge about UNIX filesystems in general; however, I hope that it will be accessible to most Linux users. If you are an outright beginner, I'm afraid that undeleting files under Linux *does* require a certain amount of technical knowledge and persistence, at least for the time being.

You will be unable to recover deleted files from an ext2 filesystem without at least read access to the raw device on which the file was stored. In general, this means that you must be root. You also need debugfs from the e2fsprogs package. This should have been installed by your distribution.

Why have I written this? It stems largely from my own experiences with a particularly foolish and disastrous rm -r command as root. I deleted about 97 JPEG files which I needed and could almost certainly not recover from other sources. Using some helpful tips (see section 15 (Credits and Bibliography)) and a great deal of persistence, I recovered 91 files undamaged. I managed to retrieve at least parts of five of the rest (enough to see what the picture was in each case). Only one was undisplayable, and even for this one, I am fairly sure that no more than 1024 bytes were lost (though unfortunately from the beginning of the file; given that I know nothing about the JFIF file format I had done as much as I could).

I shall discuss further below what sort of recovery rate you can expect for deleted files.

1.1 Revision history

The various publicly-released revisions of this document (and their publication dates) are as follows:

- v1.0 on 18 January 1997
- v1.1 on 23 July 1997 (see section 1.1.1 (Changes in v1.1))
- v1.2 on 4 August 1997 (see section 1.1.2 (Changes in v1.2))

1.1.1 Changes in version 1.1

What changes have been made in this version? First of all, the thinko in the example of file recovery has been fixed. Thankyou to all those who wrote to point out my mistaek; I hope I've learned to be more careful when making up program interaction.

Secondly, the discussion of UNIX filesystem layout has been rewritten to be, I hope, more understandable. I wasn't entirely happy with it in the first place, and some people's comments indicated that it wasn't clear.

Thirdly, the vast uuencoded gzipped tarball of fsgrab in the middle of the file has been removed. The program is now available on *my website* <http://pobox.com/aaronc/tech/fsgrab-1.0.tar.gz> and it should soon make its way onto *Sunsite* <http://sunsite.unc.edu/pub/Linux/utils/disk-management/> (and mirrors).

Fourthly, the document has been translated into the Linux Documentation Project SGML Tools content markup language. This markup language can be easily converted to any of a number of other markup languages (including HTML and LaTeX) for convenient display and printing. One benefit of this is that beautiful typography in paper editions is a much more achievable goal; another is that the document has cross-references and hyperlinks when viewed on the Web.

1.1.2 Changes in v1.2

This revision is very much an incremental change. It's here mainly to include changes suggested by readers, one of which is particularly important.

The first change was suggested by Egil Kvaleberg <*egil@kvaleberg.no*>, who pointed out the dump command in debugfs. Thanks again, Egil.

The second change is to mention the use of chattr for avoiding deleting important files. Thanks to Herman Suijs <*H.P.M.Suijs@kub.nl*> for mentioning this one.

The abstract has been revised. URLs have been added for organisations and software. Various other minor changes have been made (including fixing typos and so on).

1.2 Canonical locations of this document

The latest public release of this document should always be available in plain text format on the *Linux Documentation Project site* <http://sunsite.unc.edu/LDP/> (and mirrors).

The latest release is also kept on *my website* <http://pobox.com/aaronc/> in several formats:

- *SGML source* <http://pobox.com/aaronc/tech/e2-undel/howto.sgml>. This is the source as I have written it, using the SGML Tools package.

- *HTML* <http://pobox.com/aaronc/tech/e2-undel/html/>. This is HTML, automatically generated from the SGML source.

- *Plain text* <http://pobox.com/aaronc/tech/e2-undel/howto.txt>. This is plain text, which is also automatically generated from the SGML source. Note that this file is identical to the one on Sunsite, so if you want the plain text, you are recommended to get it from your favourite LDP mirror (as it will probably be much faster).

2 How not to delete files

It is vital to remember that Linux is unlike MS-DOS when it comes to undeletion. For MS-DOS (and its bastard progeny Windows 95), it is generally fairly straightforward to undelete a file - the 'operating system' (I use the term loosely) even comes with a utility which automates much of the process. For Linux, this is not the case.

So. Rule number one (the prime directive, if you will) is:

> **KEEP BACKUPS**

no matter what. I know, I'm a fine one to talk. I shall merely plead impoverishment (being a student must have *some* perks) and exhort all right-thinking Linux users to go out and buy a useful backup device, work out a decent backup schedule, and to *stick to it*. For more information on this, read Frisch (1995) (see section 15 (Bibliography and Credits)).

In the absence of backups, what then? (Or even in the presence of backups: belt and braces is no bad policy where important data is concerned.)

Try to set the permissions for important files to 440 (or less): denying yourself write access to them means that rm requires an explicit confirmation before deleting. (I find, however, that if I'm recursively deleting a directory with rm -r, I'll interrupt the program on the first or second confirmation request and reissue the command as rm -rf.)

A good trick for selected files is to create a hard link to them in a hidden directory. I heard a story once about a sysadmin who repeatedly deleted /etc/passwd by accident (thereby half-destroying the system). One of the fixes for this was to do something like the following (as root):

```
# mkdir /.backup
# ln /etc/passwd /.backup
```

It requires quite some effort to delete the file contents completely: if you say

```
# rm /etc/passwd
```

then

```
# ln /.backup/passwd /etc
```

will retrieve it. Of course, this does not help in the event that you overwrite the file, so keep backups anyway.

On an ext2 filesystem, it is possible to use ext2 attributes to protect things. These attributes are manipulated with the `chattr` command. There is an 'append-only' attribute: a file with this attribute may be appended to, but may not be deleted, and the existing contents of the file may not be overwritten. If a directory has this attribute, any files or directories within it may be modified as normal, but no files may be deleted. The 'append-only' attribute is set with

```
$ chattr +a FILE...
```

There is also an 'immutable' attribute, which can only be set or cleared by root. A file or directory with this attribute may not be modified, deleted, renamed, or (hard) linked. It may be set as follows:

```
# chattr +i FILE...
```

The ext2fs also provides the 'undeletable' attribute (+u in `chattr`). The intention is that if a file with that attribute is deleted, instead of actually being reused, it is merely moved to a 'safe location' for deletion at a later date. Unfortunately this feature has not yet been implemented in mainstream kernels. However, various kernel patches exist which provide the ability to do reversible deletion; see <*http://www.linuxhq.com/*> if you're interested in patching this facility into your kernel. The most recent patch I know of is by Rogier Wolff <*R.E.Wolff@BitWizard.nl*>, Darren J Moffat <*darren@xarius.demon.co.uk*> and Kurt Huwig <*kurt@huwig.de*>. I would point out though that while this patch implements the feature, it is not an 'undeletion solution' at the moment. Undeletable files are merely moved into another directory; there should be a daemon to periodically clean up that directory.

Some people advocate making `rm` a shell alias or function for `rm -i` (which asks for confirmation on *every* file you delete). Indeed, recent versions of the *Red Hat distribution* <http://www.redhat.com/> do this by default for all users, including root. Personally, I cannot stand software which won't run unattended, so I don't do that. There is also the problem that sooner or later, you'll be running in single-user mode, or using a different shell, or even a different machine, where your `rm` function doesn't exist. If you expect to be asked for confirmation, it is easy to forget where you are and to specify too many files for deletion. Likewise, the various scripts and programs that replace `rm` are, IMHO, very dangerous.

A slightly better solution is to start using a package which handles 'recyclable' deletion by providing a command not named `rm`. For details on these, see Peek, et al (1993) (see section 15 (Bibliography and Credits)).

3   What recovery rate can I expect?

That depends. Among the problems with recovering files on a high-quality, multi-tasking, multi-user operating system like Linux is that you never know when someone wants to write to the disk. So when the operating system is told to delete a file, it assumes that the blocks used by that file are fair game when it wants to allocate space for a new file. (This is a specific example of a general principle for Linux: the kernel and the associated tools assume that the users aren't idiots.) In general, the more usage your machine gets, the less likely you are to be able to recover files successfully.

Also, disk fragmentation can affect the ease of recovering files. If the partition containing the deleted files is very fragmented, you are unlikely to be able to read a whole file.

If your machine, like mine, is effectively a single-user workstation (mine doesn't even have a net connection yet; maybe next year), and you weren't doing anything disk-intensive at the fatal moment of deleting those files, I would expect a recovery rate in the same ball-park as detailed above. I retrieved nearly 94% of the files (and these were binary files, please note) undamaged. If you get 80% or better, you can feel pretty pleased with yourself, I should think.

4 So, how do I undelete a file?

The procedure principally involves finding the data on the raw partition device and making it visible again to the operating system. There are basically two ways of doing this: one is to modify the existing filesystem such that the deleted inodes have their 'deleted' flag removed, and hope that the data just magically falls back into place. The other method, which is safer but slower, is to work out where the data lies in the partition and write it out into a new file.

There are some steps you need to take before beginning to attempt your data recovery; see sections 5 (Unmounting the filesystem), 6 (Preparing to change inodes directly) and 7 (Preparing to write data elsewhere) for details. To find out how to actually retrieve your files, see sections 8 (Finding the deleted inodes), 9 (Obtaining the details of the inodes), 10 (Recovering data blocks) and 11 (Modifying inodes directly).

5 Unmounting the filesystem

Regardless of which method you choose, the first step is to unmount the filesystem containing the deleted files. I strongly discourage any urges you may have to mess around on a mounted filesystem. This step should be performed *as soon as possible* after you realise that the files have been deleted.

The simplest method is as follows: assuming the deleted files were in the /usr partition, say:

```
# umount /usr
```

You may, however, want to keep some things in /usr available. So remount it read-only:

```
# mount -o ro,remount /usr
```

If the deleted files were on the root partition, you'll need to add a -n option to prevent mount from trying to write to /etc/mtab:

```
# mount -n -o ro,remount /
```

Regardless of all this, it is possible that there will be another process using that filesystem (which will cause the unmount to fail with an error such as 'Resource busy'). There is a program which will send a signal to any process using a given file or mount point: fuser. Try this for the /usr partition:

```
# fuser -v -m /usr
```

This lists the processes involved. Assuming none of them are vital, you can say

```
# fuser -k -v -m /usr
```

to send each process a SIGKILL (which is guaranteed to kill it), or for example,

```
# fuser -k -TERM -v -m /usr
```

to give each one a SIGTERM (which will normally make the process exit cleanly).

6 Preparing to change inodes directly

My advice? Don't do it this way. I really don't think it's wise to play with a filesystem at a low enough level for this to work. There are also has problems in that you can only reliably recover the first 12 blocks of each file. So if you have any long files to recover, you'll have to use the other method anyway. (Although see section 12 (Will this get easier in future?) for additional information.)

If you feel you must do it this way, my advice is to copy the raw partition data to an image on a different partition, and then mount this using loopback:

```
# cp /dev/hda5 /root/working
# mount -t ext2 -o loop /root/working /mnt
```

This does, however, require a recent version of `mount`. (Although you should get version 2.6 or newer anyway, as all earlier versions have a major security bug which allows peons to get root access. The major distributions, that is, Debian, RedHat and Slackware, have all been updated with version 2.6 of `mount`.)

Using loopback means that when you completely destroy the filesystem (as you quite possibly will), all you have to do is copy the raw partition back and start again.

7   Preparing to write data elsewhere

You need to make sure you have a rescue partition somewhere. Hopefully, your system has several partitions on it: perhaps a root, a `/usr`, and a `/home`. With all these to choose from, you should have no problem: just create a new directory on one of these.

If you have only a root partition, and store everything on that (like me, until I can get around to repartitioning), things are slightly more awkward. Perhaps you have an MS-DOS or Windows partition you could use? Or you have the ramdisk driver in your kernel, maybe as a module? To use the ramdisk (assuming a kernel more recent than 1.3.48), say the following:

```
# dd if=/dev/zero of=/dev/ram0 bs=1k count=2048
# mke2fs -v -m 0 /dev/ram0 2048
# mount -t ext2 /dev/ram0 /mnt
```

This creates a 2MB ramdisk volume, and mounts it on `/mnt`.

A short word of warning: if you use `kerneld` to automatically load and unload kernel modules, then don't unmount the ramdisk until you've copied any files from it onto non-volatile storage. Once you unmount it, `kerneld` assumes it can unload the module (after the usual waiting period), and once this happens, the memory gets re-used by other parts of the kernel, losing all the painstaking hours you just spent recovering your data.

If you have any of the new 'superfloppy' removable devices, they're probably a good choice for a rescue partition location. Otherwise, you'll just have to stick with floppies.

The other thing you're likely to need is a program which can read the necessary data from the middle of the partition device. At a pinch, `dd` will do the job, but to read from, say, 600 MB into an 800 MB partition, `dd` insists on reading but ignoring the first 600 MB. This takes a not inconsiderable amount of time. My way round this was to write a program which will seek to the middle of the partition. It's called `fsgrab`; you can find the source package on *my website* <http://pobox.com/aaronc/tech/fsgrab-1.0.tar.gz> and it should soon make its way onto *Sunsite* <http://sunsite.unc.edu/pub/Linux/utils/disk-management/> (and mirrors). If you want to use this method, the rest of this mini-Howto assumes that you have `fsgrab`.

If none of the files you are trying to recover were more than 12 blocks long (where a block is usually one kilobyte), then you won't need `fsgrab`.

If you need to use `fsgrab` but don't want to, it is fairly straightforward to translate an `fsgrab` command-line to one for `dd`. If we have

```
fsgrab -c count -s skip device
```

then the corresponding `dd` command is

```
dd bs=1k if=device count=count skip=skip
```

I must warn you that, although fsgrab functioned perfectly for me, I can take no responsibility for how it performs. It was really a very quick and dirty kludge just to get things to work. For more details on the lack of warranty, see the 'No Warranty' section in the COPYING file included with it (the GNU General Public Licence).

8   Finding the deleted inodes

The next step is to ask the filesystem which inodes have recently been freed. This is a task you can accomplish with debugfs. Start debugfs with the name of the device on which the filesystem is stored:

```
# debugfs /dev/hda5
```

If you want to modify the inodes directly, add a -w option to enable writing to the filesystem:

```
# debugfs -w /dev/hda5
```

The debugfs command to find the deleted inodes is lsdel. So, type the command at the prompt:

```
debugfs:  lsdel
```

After much wailing and grinding of disk mechanisms, a long list is piped into your favourite pager (the value of $PAGER). Now you'll want to save a copy of this somewhere else. If you have less, you can type -o followed by the name of an output file. Otherwise, you'll have to arrange to send the output elsewhere. Try this:

```
debugfs:  quit
# echo lsdel | debugfs /dev/hda5 > lsdel.out
```

Now, based only on the deletion time, the size, the type, and the numerical permissions and owner, you must work out which of these deleted inodes are the ones you want. With luck, you'll be able to spot them because they're the big bunch you deleted about five minutes ago. Otherwise, trawl through that list carefully.

I suggest that if possible, you print out the list of the inodes you want to recover. It will make life a lot easier.

9   Obtaining the details of the inodes

debugfs has a stat command which prints details about an inode. Issue the command for each inode in your recovery list. For example, if you're interested in inode number 148003, try this:

```
debugfs:  stat <148003>
Inode: 148003   Type: regular   Mode:  0644   Flags: 0x0   Version: 1
User:   503   Group:   100   Size: 6065
File ACL: 0    Directory ACL: 0
Links: 0   Blockcount: 12
Fragment:  Address: 0    Number: 0    Size: 0
ctime: 0x31a9a574 -- Mon May 27 13:52:04 1996
atime: 0x31a21dd1 -- Tue May 21 20:47:29 1996
mtime: 0x313bf4d7 -- Tue Mar  5 08:01:27 1996
dtime: 0x31a9a574 -- Mon May 27 13:52:04 1996
BLOCKS:
594810 594811 594814 594815 594816 594817
TOTAL: 6
```

Mini-HOWTO

If you have a lot of files to recover, you'll want to automate this. Assuming that your `lsdel` list of inodes to recover in is in `lsdel.out`, try this:

```
# cut -c1-6 lsdel.out | grep "[0-9]" | tr -d " " > inodes
```

This new file `inodes` contains just the numbers of the inodes to recover, one per line. We save it because it will very likely come in handy later on. Then you just say:

```
# sed 's/^.*$/stat <\0>/' inodes | debugfs /dev/hda5 > stats
```

and `stats` contains the output of all the `stat` commands.

10   Recovering data blocks

This part is either very easy or distinctly less so, depending on whether the file you are trying to recover is more than 12 blocks long.

10.1   Short files

If the file was no more than 12 blocks long, then the block numbers of all its data are stored in the inode: you can read them directly out of the `stat` output for the inode. Moreover, `debugfs` has a command which performs this task automatically. To take the example we had before, repeated here:

```
debugfs:  stat <148003>
Inode: 148003   Type: regular   Mode:  0644   Flags: 0x0   Version: 1
User:   503   Group:   100   Size: 6065
File ACL: 0   Directory ACL: 0
Links: 0   Blockcount: 12
Fragment:  Address: 0    Number: 0    Size: 0
ctime: 0x31a9a574 -- Mon May 27 13:52:04 1996
atime: 0x31a21dd1 -- Tue May 21 20:47:29 1996
mtime: 0x313bf4d7 -- Tue Mar  5 08:01:27 1996
dtime: 0x31a9a574 -- Mon May 27 13:52:04 1996
BLOCKS:
594810 594811 594814 594815 594816 594817
TOTAL: 6
```

This file has six blocks. Since this is less than the limit of 12, we get `debugfs` to write the file into a new location, such as `/mnt/recovered.000`:

```
debugfs:   dump <148003> /mnt/recovered.000
```

Of course, this can also be done with `fsgrab`; I'll present it here as an example of using it:

```
# fsgrab -c 2 -s 594810 /dev/hda5 > /mnt/recovered.000
# fsgrab -c 4 -s 594814 /dev/hda5 >> /mnt/recovered.000
```

With either `debugfs` or `fsgrab`, there will be some garbage at the end of `/mnt/recovered.000`, but that's fairly unimportant. If you want to get rid of it, the simplest method is to take the `Size` field from the inode, and plug it into the `bs` option in a `dd` command line:

```
# dd count=1 if=/mnt/recovered.000 of=/mnt/resized.000 bs=6065
```

Of course, it is possible that one or more of the blocks that made up your file has been overwritten. If so, then you're out of luck: that block is gone forever. (But just imagine if you'd unmounted sooner!)

10.2   Longer files

The problems appear when the file has more than 12 data blocks. It pays here to know a little of how UNIX filesystems are structured. The file's data is stored in units called 'blocks'. These blocks may be numbered sequentially. A file also has an 'inode', which is the place where information such as owner, permissions, and type are kept. Like blocks, inodes are numbered sequentially, although they have a different sequence. A directory entry consists of the name of the file and an inode number.

But with this state of affairs, it is still impossible for the kernel to find the data corresponding to a directory entry. So the inode also stores the location of the file's data blocks, as follows:

- The block numbers of the first 12 data blocks are stored directly in the inode; these are sometimes referred to as the *direct block*s.

- The inode contains the block number of an *indirect block*. An indirect block contains the block numbers of 256 additional data blocks.

- The inode contains the block number of a *doubly indirect block*. A doubly indirect block contains the block numbers of 256 additional indirect blocks.

- The inode contains the block number of a *triply indirect block*. A triply indirect block contains the block numbers of 256 additional doubly indirect blocks.

Read that again: I know it's complex, but it's also important.

Now, the current kernel implementation (certainly for all versions up to and including 2.0.30) unfortunately zeroes all indirect blocks (and doubly indirect blocks, and so on) when deleting a file. So if your file was longer than 12 blocks, you have no guarantee of being able to find even the numbers of all the blocks you need, let alone their contents.

The only method I have been able to find thus far is to assume that the file was not fragmented: if it was, then you're in trouble. Assuming that the file was not fragmented, there are several layouts of data blocks, according to how many data blocks the file used:

0 to 12

The block numbers are stored in the inode, as described above.

13 to 268

After the direct blocks, count one for the indirect block, and then there are 256 data blocks.

269 to 65804

As before, there are 12 direct blocks, a (useless) indirect block, and 256 blocks. These are followed by one (useless) doubly indirect block, and 256 repetitions of one (useless) indirect block and 256 data blocks.

65805 or more

The layout of the first 65804 blocks is as above. Then follow one (useless) triply indirect block and 256 repetitions of a 'doubly indirect sequence'. Each doubly indirect sequence consists of a (useless) doubly indirect block, followed by 256 repetitions of one (useless) indirect block and 256 data blocks.

Of course, even if these assumed data block numbers are correct, there is no guarantee that the data in them is intact. In addition, the longer the file was, the less chance there is that it was written to the filesystem without appreciable fragmentation (except in special circumstances).

You should note that I assume throughout that your blocksize is 1024 bytes, as this is the standard value. If your blocks are bigger, some of the numbers above will change. Specifically: since each block number is 4 bytes long, blocksize/4 is the number of block numbers that can be stored in each indirect block. So every time the number 256 appears in the discussion above, replace it with blocksize/4. The 'number of blocks required' boundaries will also have to be changed.

Let's look at an example of recovering a longer file.

```
debugfs:  stat <1387>
Inode: 148004   Type: regular   Mode:  0644   Flags: 0x0   Version: 1
User:    503  Group:    100   Size: 1851347
File ACL: 0    Directory ACL: 0
Links: 0    Blockcount: 3616
Fragment:  Address: 0    Number: 0    Size: 0
ctime: 0x31a9a574 -- Mon May 27 13:52:04 1996
atime: 0x31a21dd1 -- Tue May 21 20:47:29 1996
mtime: 0x313bf4d7 -- Tue Mar  5 08:01:27 1996
dtime: 0x31a9a574 -- Mon May 27 13:52:04 1996
BLOCKS:
8314 8315 8316 8317 8318 8319 8320 8321 8322 8323 8324 8325 8326 8583
TOTAL: 14
```

There seems to be a reasonable chance that this file is not fragmented: certainly, the first 12 blocks listed in the inode (which are all data blocks) are contiguous. So, we can start by retrieving those blocks:

```
# fsgrab -c 12 -s 8314 /dev/hda5 > /mnt/recovered.001
```

Now, the next block listed in the inode, 8326, is an indirect block, which we can ignore. But we trust that it will be followed by 256 data blocks (numbers 8327 through 8582).

```
# fsgrab -c 256 -s 8327 /dev/hda5 >> /mnt/recovered.001
```

The final block listed in the inode is 8583. Note that we're still looking good in terms of the file being contiguous: the last data block we wrote out was number 8582, which is 8327 + 255. This block 8583 is a doubly indirect block, which we can ignore. It is followed by up to 256 repetitions of an indirect block (which is ignored) followed by 256 data blocks. So doing the arithmetic quickly, we issue the following commands. Notice that we skip the doubly indirect block 8583, and the indirect block 8584 immediately (we hope) following it, and start at block 8585 for data.

```
# fsgrab -c 256 -s 8585 /dev/hda5 >> /mnt/recovered.001
# fsgrab -c 256 -s 8842 /dev/hda5 >> /mnt/recovered.001
# fsgrab -c 256 -s 9099 /dev/hda5 >> /mnt/recovered.001
# fsgrab -c 256 -s 9356 /dev/hda5 >> /mnt/recovered.001
# fsgrab -c 256 -s 9613 /dev/hda5 >> /mnt/recovered.001
# fsgrab -c 256 -s 9870 /dev/hda5 >> /mnt/recovered.001
```

Adding up, we see that so far we've written 12 + (7 * 256) blocks, which is 1804. The 'stat' results for the inode gave us a 'blockcount' of 3616; unfortunately these blocks are 512 bytes long (as a hangover from UNIX), so we really want 3616/2 = 1808 blocks of 1024 bytes. That means we need only four more blocks. The last data block written was number 10125. As we've been doing so far, we skip an indirect block (number 10126); we can then write those last four blocks.

```
# fsgrab -c 4 -s 10127 /dev/hda5 >> /mnt/recovered.001
```

Now, with some luck the entire file has been recovered successfully.

11 Modifying inodes directly

This method is, on the surface, much easier. However, as mentioned above, it cannot cope with files longer than 12 blocks.

For each inode you want to recover, you must set the usage count to one, and set the deletion time to zero. This is done with the `mi` (modify inode) command in `debugfs`. Some sample output, modifying inode 148003 from above:

```
debugfs:  mi <148003>
                    Mode  [0100644]
                 User ID  [503]
                Group ID  [100]
                    Size  [6065]
           Creation time  [833201524]
       Modification time  [832708049]
             Access time  [826012887]
           Deletion time  [833201524] 0
              Link count  [0] 1
             Block count  [12]
              File flags  [0x0]
               Reserved1  [0]
                File acl  [0]
           Directory acl  [0]
        Fragment address  [0]
         Fragment number  [0]
           Fragment size  [0]
          Direct Block #0  [594810]
          Direct Block #1  [594811]
          Direct Block #2  [594814]
          Direct Block #3  [594815]
          Direct Block #4  [594816]
          Direct Block #5  [594817]
          Direct Block #6  [0]
          Direct Block #7  [0]
          Direct Block #8  [0]
          Direct Block #9  [0]
         Direct Block #10  [0]
         Direct Block #11  [0]
           Indirect Block  [0]
    Double Indirect Block  [0]
    Triple Indirect Block  [0]
```

That is, I set the deletion time to 0 and the link count to 1 and just pressed return for each of the other fields. Granted, this is a little unwieldy if you have a lot of files to recover, but I think you can cope. If you'd wanted chrome, you'd have used a graphical 'operating system' with a pretty 'Recycle Bin'.

By the way: the mi output refers to a 'Creation time' field in the inode. This is a lie! (Or misleading, anyway.) The fact of the matter is that you cannot tell on a UNIX filesystem when a file was created. The st_ctime member of a struct stat refers to the 'inode change time', that is, the last time when any inode details were changed. Here endeth today's lesson.

Note that more recent versions of debugfs than the one I'm using probably do not include some of the fields in the listing above (specifically, Reserved1 and (some of?) the fragment fields).

Once you've modified the inodes, you can quit debugfs and say:

```
# e2fsck -f /dev/hda5
```

The idea is that each of the deleted files has been literally undeleted, but none of them appear in any directory entries. The e2fsck program can detect this, and will add a directory entry for each file in the /lost+found directory of the filesystem. (So if the partition is normally mounted on /usr, the files will now appear in /usr/lost+found.) All that still remains to be done is to work out the name of each file from its contents, and return it to its correct place in the filesystem tree.

When you run e2fsck, you will get some informative output, and some questions about what damage to repair. Answer 'yes' to everything that refers to 'summary information' or to the inodes you've changed. Anything else I leave up to you, although it's usually a good idea to say 'yes' to all the questions. When e2fsck finishes, you can remount the filesystem.

Actually, there's an alternative to having e2fsck leave the files in /lost+found: you can use debugfs to create a link in the filesystem to the inode. Use the link command in debugfs after you've modified the inode:

```
debugfs:  link <148003> foo.txt
```

This creates a file called foo.txt in what debugfs thinks is the current directory; foo.txt will be your file. You'll still need to run e2fsck to fix the summary information and block counts and so on.

12 Will this get easier in future?

Yes. In fact, I believe it already has. Kernels in the development 2.1.x series have not zeroed indirect blocks since more than six months ago. At the beginning of December 1996, there was some talk on the linux-kernel mailing-list of producing another 2.0.x production kernel that also leaves indirect blocks intact on deletion. Although as of the pre-released versions of kernel 2.0.31 this has not happened, I suspect that it is feasible. Once Linus and the other kernel hackers overcome this limitation in the production kernels, a lot of my objections to the technique of modifying inodes by hand will disappear. At the very latest, this should happen on the release of the 2.2.x kernel series, which (according to historical kernel development time-scales) should happen some time in the first quarter of 1998. When this wart is corrected, it will also be possible to use the dump command in debugfs on long files.

13 Are there any tools to automate this process?

As it happens, there are. Unfortunately, I believe that they suffer from the same problem as the manual inode modification technique: indirect blocks are unrecoverable. However, given the likelihood that this will shortly no longer be a problem, it's well worth looking these programs out now.

Someone on the net mentioned lde by Scott Heavner. To be honest, I wouldn't recommend this as a tool for automating file recovery. It's more like a full-screen debugfs than anything else, although it does have some features like the ability to scan for certain types of file or for certain file contents. It also works with the xia (does anyone actually use this any more?) and minix filesystems, which I guess is its major selling point these days. Version 2.3.4 is available on *Sunsite* <ftp://sunsite.unc.edu/pub/Linux/system/Filesystems/lde-2.3.4.tar.gz> and mirrors (although it's possible there's a more recent version than this; I found that one on an 8-month-old CD-ROM archive). lde *does* have some fairly useful documentation on basic filesystem concepts, as well as a document on how to use it for recovering deleted files. Although I haven't used it, I suspect that my method above is better.

It sounds like the program that *really* works is the GNU Midnight Commander, mc. This is a full-screen file management tool, based AFAIK on a certain MS-DOS program commonly known as 'NC'. mc supports the mouse on the Linux console and in an xterm, and provides virtual filesystems which allow tricks like cd-ing to a tarfile. Among its virtual filesystems is one for ext2 undeletion. It all sounds very handy, although I must admit I've never used the program myself – I prefer good old-fashioned shell commands. Apparently one must configure the program with the -with-ext2undel option; you'll also need the development libraries and include files that come with the e2fsprogs package. I gather that once the program is built, you can tell it to cd undel:dev/hda5/, and get a 'directory listing' of deleted files.

The latest non-development version is probably 4.0; as with the kernel itself, development versions are *not* recommended to non-hackers. The list of (over 70) download sites is available on *the Midnight Commander 4 website* <http://mc.blackdown.org/mc4/>, or try the *official ftp site* <ftp://ftp.nuclecu.unam.mx/linux/local/mc-4.0.tar.gz> (which if memory serves is rather slow).

14 Colophon

I intend to produce regular updates to this document as long as I have both enough time to do it, and something interesting to say. This means that I am eager to hear comments from readers. Could my writing be clearer?. Can you think of something that would make matters easier? Is there some new tool that does it all automatically? Who *did* kill JFK?

Whatever. If you have something to say, about this document or any other subject, drop me a line on `<aaronc@pobox.com>`.

15 Credits and Bibliography

'If I have seen farther than others, it is because I was standing on the shoulders of giants.' (Isaac Newton)

Much of this mini-Howto was derived from a posting in the `comp.os.linux.misc` newsgroup by Robin Glover `<swrglovr@met.rdg.ac.uk>`. I would like to thank Robin for graciously allowing me to rework his ideas into this mini-Howto.

Some bibliographic references:

* **Frisch**, Æleen (1995), *Essential System Administration*, second edition, O'Reilly and Associates, Inc., ISBN: 1-56592-127-5.
* **Glover**, Robin (31 Jan 1996), *HOW-TO : undelete linux files (ext2fs/debugfs)*, comp.os.linux.misc Usenet posting.
* **Peek**, Jerry, Tim **O'Reilly**, Mike **Loukides** et al (1993), *UNIX Power Tools*, O'Reilly and Associates, Inc./Random House, Inc., ISBN: 0-679-79073-X.

16 Legalities

All trademarks are the property of their respective owners. Specifically:

* *MS-DOS* and *Windows* are trademarks of *Microsoft* `<http://www.microsoft.com/>`.
* *UNIX* is a trademark of *the Open Group* `<http://www.open.org/>`.
* The trademark status of the name *Linux* is currently being contested by lawyers. A certain Walter R. Della Croce has made an allegedly false trademark registration for the term. Further information on the Linux trademark issue is available from *the Linux Mall* `<http://www.linuxmall.com/announce/>`.

The author requests but does not require that parties intending to sell copies of this document, whether on computer-readable or human-readable media, inform either him or the Linux HOWTO Coordinator of their intentions.

The Linux HOWTO Coordinator is Tim Bynum `<linux-howto@sunsite.unc.edu>`.

Mini-HOWTO

Part LIX

"Linux simple fax printer server mini-HOWTO (faxsrv-mini-HOWTO)"

Erez Strauss <erez@newplaces.com> <mailto:ErezStrauss<erez@newplaces.com>>

v1.0, 8 November 1997

No warranties. Comments are always welcome. This document describes in details one of the simplest ways to setup fax server on your Linux system. The fax is available to the users on the local host and to network users.

Contents

1 Introduction

To get a working printer/fax on the linux machine you should have some software and fax modem.

The Printing software will be using the fax software as a print filter. The efax will find the fax number from the print Job number and will send the fax. The efax software was written be Ed Casas <edc@cce.com>.

The rest of the document is build as Q&A.

2 Questions & Answers

2.1 What is a fax printer server ?

A fax printer server is a setup of few programs: efax, and the print server, in such a way that sending a fax from the computer is as simple as sending printout to a printer.

2.2 How to set it up ?

Setting efax as fax print server includes few problems As I worked it out few times, I decided to collect this wisdom in this small mini-HOWTO, comments are welcome at <erez@newplaces.com>. I describe them here and the solutions, and all the instruction in short steps:

2.2.1 The efax Software

make sure you have the efax package.

On RPM based system use the command 'rpm -qv efax'.

You can get the efax sources in tar.gz format from sunsite:

ftp://sunsite.unc.edu/pub/Linux/apps/serialcomm/fax/efax08a.tar.gz

or binary rpm package:

ftp://ftp.redhat.com/pub/redhat/redhat-4.2/i386/RedHat/RPMS/efax-0.8a-3.i386.rpm

2.2.2 The printcap entry.

The efax documentation is missing the : at the end of the printcap entry.

Solution: Add the following /etc/printcap entry:

```
fax:\
        :lp=/dev/null:\
        :sd=/var/spool/fax:\
        :if=/usr/bin/faxlpr:
```

2.2.3 The fax command

Use hard link and not symbolic link to the fax command.

Run the command:

```
ln /usr/bin/fax /usr/bin/faxlpr
```

2.2.4 The /usr/bin/fax file.

Edit the /usr/bin/fax to your preferences:

choose the right Fax Class for your modem:

```
CLASS=2.0
```

Set the FROM="your international phone number" field

```
NAME="Your Name"
```

Add the line for conversion of international phone number to local for example in Israel you would use:

```
TELCVT='sed -e s/+972/0/ -e s/+/00/'   # Israel
```

There is a problem in the file in line 586, change the cfile=... with the following two lines:

```
cfile='/usr/bin/tail -1 lock'
cfile='cat $cfile'
```

at lines 586,587 there shouldn't be '-' signs the lines are:

```
0) echo "$l" | mail -s "fax to $num succeeded" $user@$host ;;
*) echo "$l" | mail -s "fax to $num failed   " $user@$host ;;
```

2.2.5 The /var/spool/fax directory.

create the directory /var/spool/fax

```
mkdir /var/spool/fax
chmod 777 /var/spool/fax
```

2.2.6 The lock file.

The lock file (`/var/spool/fax/lock`) is being created with incorrect permissions, use the following command to set it correctly:

```
touch /var/spool/fax/lock ; chmod 644 /var/spool/fax/lock
```

2.2.7 The /dev/modem special file.

The efax program is expecting real device file at the `/dev/modem` and will not work with symbolic link, so create a device file with the same major and minor number as the `/dev/cua?` the is connected to the modem. The file should have the rw-rw-rw- mode to enable any user to use the fax software.

```
ls -lL /dev/modem
rm /dev/modem
mknod /dev/modem c Mj Mi
chmod 666 /dev/modem
```

Mj is 5, and Mi is 64 for the cua0, 65 for cua1 and so on. For example (for cua1):

```
mknod /dev/modem c 5 65
```

2.2.8 The /var/lock directory.

change the mode at the `/var/lock` directory

```
chmod 1777 /var/lock
```

2.3 How do I use it, for the server ?

You should use the fax printer using the -P option and the -J option with the fax number.

use one of the following lpr commands:

```
lpr -Pfax -J <Fax-Number> [file-names]
any command | lpr -Pfax -J <Fax-Number>
```

2.4 Where do I specify the target Fax number ?

After the -J option.

2.5 How do I use it from other Unixes on the net ?

Add the following entry into the `/etc/printcap` file and the client Linux systems, create the spool directory, and so on ...

Mini-HOWTO

```
fax:\
        :sd=/var/spool/fax:\
        :mx#0:\
        :sh:\
        :rm=host.domain:\
        :rp=fax:
```

add the name of the client hosts into the `/etc/hosts.lpd` on the fax server machine.

use it as before.

Note:

The header string that efax adds to the fax pages is not effected by the user name that sends the fax. (can be updated).

2.6 Caldera, LPRng users

The LPRng printing management software is using a different method to handle the control file.

Thanks to Luca Montecchiani <m.luca@usa.net>, who found the problem and the solution. Here is an update to the `/usr/bin/fax` file. The following line replace the two simple **cfile=...** lines at lines 586,587

```
# Modified to work also with the LPRng package
# Luca Montecchiani (08/11/97 m.luca@usa.net)
if [ !-z "$CONTROL_FILE" ]
    then
        cfile='cat tail -1 lock'
        cfile='cat $cfile'
    else
        cfile=$CONTROL_FILE
fi
```

3   Latest version, Contacting the author.

The latest version of this file can be accessed through the world wide web using URLs

```
http://www.newplaces.com/linux/faxsrv/faxsrv-mini-HOWTO.sgml
http://www.newplaces.com/linux/faxsrv/faxsrv-mini-HOWTO.html
http://www.newplaces.com/linux/faxsrv/faxsrv-mini-HOWTO.txt
http://www.newplaces.com/linux/faxsrv/faxsrv-mini-HOWTO.info
```

You can contact me

```
Erez Strauss
erez@newplaces.com
http://www.newplaces.com/linux/
http://www.newplaces.com/
Phone: +972 52 739737
Fax:   +972 9 954 3034
```

Part LX

"Firewall Piercing mini-HOWTO"
François-René Rideau

fare@tunes.org

v0.3b, 27 November 1998
Directions for using ppp over telnet to do network stuff transparently through an Internet firewall.

Contents

Mini-HOWTO

1 Stuff

1.1 DISCLAIMER

READ THIS IMPORTANT SECTION !!!

I hereby disclaim all responsibility for this hack. If it backfires on you in any way whatsoever, that's the breaks. Not my fault. If you don't understand the risks inherent in doing this, don't do it. If you use this hack and it allows vicious vandals to break into your company's computers and costs you your job and your company millions of dollars, well that's just tough nuggies. Don't come crying to me.

1.2 Legal Blurp

Copyright © 1998 by François-René Rideau.

This document is free software; you can redistribute it and/or modify it under the terms of the GNU General Public License as published by the Free Software Foundation; either version 2 of the License, or (at your option) any later version.

1.3 Credits

Even though I rewrote most everything but the disclaimers, I'm indebted to Barak Pearlmutter `<mailto:bap@cs.unm.edu>` for his Term-Firewall mini-HOWTO: I think there was a necessity for a mini-HOWTO about piercing firewalls, and despite its shortcomings, his mini-HOWTO was a model and an encouragement.

2 Introduction

2.1 Foreword

Because system administrators and users have different constraints and proficiencies, it so happens that a user may find himself behind a firewall, that he may cross, but only in awkward ways. This mini-HOWTO explains a generic and portable way to use standard internet tools seamlessly across such firewalls, by the use of an IP emulator over a telnet session.

It is freely inspired by the Term-Firewall mini-HOWTO by Barak Pearlmutter `<mailto:bap@cs.unm.edu>`, which relies on an ancient and no-more-supported program named Term (yet a great program at its time), as well as on peculiarities of a not-so-standard telnet implementation, that is, many obsolete and non-portable facts.

2.2 Security problems

Of course, if your sysadm has setup a firewall, s/he might have a good reason, and you may have signed an agreement to not circumvent it. On the other hand, the fact that you can telnet outside (which is a requisite for the presented hacks to work) means that you are allowed to access external systems, and the fact that you can log into a particular external system somehow means you're allowed to do it, too.

So this is all a matter of *conveniently* using legal holes in a firewall, and allow generic programs to work from there with generic protocols, as opposed to requiring special or modified (and recompiled) programs going through lots of special-purpose proxies that be misconfigured by an uncaring or incompetent sysadm, or to installing lots of special-purpose converters to access each of your usual services (like e-mail) through ways supported by the firewall (like the web).

Moreover, the use of a user-level IP emulator such as SLiRP should still prevent external attackers from piercing the firewall back in the other way, unless explicitly permitted by you (or they are clever and wicked, and root or otherwise able to spy you on the remote host).

All in all, the presented hack should be *relatively* safe. However, it all depends on the particular circumstances in which you set things up, and I can give no guarantee about this hack. Lots of things are intrinsically unsafe about any internet connection, be it with this hack or not, so don't you assume anything is safe unless you have good reasons, and/or use some kind of encryption all the way.

To sum it up, don't use this hack unless you know what you're doing. Re-read the disclaimer above.

2.3 Other requirements

It is assumed that you know what you're doing; that you know about setting up a network connection; that you have shell accounts on both sides of the firewall; that you can somehow telnet (or ssh, or equivalent) from one account to the other; that you can run an IP emulator on both shell accounts; that you have programs able to use the IP connection emulated on their side. Note that any program can use the connection, in case the local emulator is pppd talking to the Linux kernel; other emulators, like Term, need recompilation and linking to a special library.

Talking about IP emulators, pppd can be found in any good Linux distribution or ftp site; so can SLiRP. If your remote shell account is user-level only, you can use SLiRP to connect.

2.4 Downloading software

Most described software should be available from your standard distribution, possibly among contrib's; at least all but the two small last ones are available in as rpm packages. In case you want to fetch the latest sources or binaries (after all, one of the ends of the connection may not be running linux), use the addresses below:

- SLiRP can be found at `<http://blitzen.canberra.edu.au/slirp>` and/or `<ftp://www.ibc.wustl.edu/pub/slirp_bin/>`.
- zsh can be found at `<http://www.peak.org/zsh/>`.
- ppp can be found at `<ftp://cs.anu.edu.au/pub/software/ppp/>`.
- fwprc and cotty can be found at `<http://www.tunes.org/~fare/files/fwprc/>`.

3 Understanding the problem

Understanding a problem is the first half of the path to solving it.

3.1 Giving names to things

If you want this hack to work for you, you'll have to get an idea of how it works, so that in case anything breaks, you know where to look for.

The first step toward understanding the problem is to give a name to relevant concepts.

So we'll herein call "local" the machine that initiates the connection, as well as programs and files on that machine; conversely, we'll call "remote" what's on the other side of the connection.

3.2 The problem

The goal is to connect the input and output of a local IP emulator to the output and input respectively of a remote IP emulator.

Only the communication channels with which IP emulators interact are either direct devices (in the usual case of pppd), or the "current tty". The previous case obviously does not happen with telnet sessions. The latter is tricky, because when you launch the local emulator from the command line, the "current tty" is linked to the command-line user, not to a remote session; also, should we open a new session (local or remote) on a new terminal, we must synchronize the launching and connection of IP emulators on both sides, least one session's garbage output is going to be executed as commands on the other session, which would recursively produce more garbage.

3.3 Additional difficulty

To get the best ease of use, the local IP emulator has to provide IP to kernel networking, hence be pppd. However, pppd is dumb enough to only accept having data through /dev or thru the current tty; it must be a tty, not a pair of pipe (which would be the obvious design). This is fine for the remote pppd if any, as it can use the telnet session's tty; but for the local pppd, it sucks, as it can't launch the telnet session to connect to; hence, there must some kind of wrapper around it.

Telnet behaves *almost* correctly with a pair of pipe, except that it will still insist on doing ioctl's to the current tty, with which it will interfere; using telnet without a tty also causes race conditions, so that the whole connection will fail on "slow" computers (fwprc 0.1 worked perfectly on a P/MMX 233, one time out of 6 on a 6x86-P200+, and never on a 486dx2/66).

[Note: if I find the sucker (probably a MULTICS guy, though there must have been UNIX people stupid enough to copy the idea) who invented the principle of "tty" devices by which you read and write from a "same" pseudo-file, instead of having clean pairs of pipes, I strangle him!]

4 The solution

4.1 Principle

The firewall-piercing program, fwprc, will use a "tty proxy", cotty, that opens two pseudo-tty devices, launches some command on each of those devices' slaves, and stubbornly copies every character that one outputs to the tty that serves as input of the other command. One command will be telnet connection to remote site, and the other will be the local pppd. pppd can then open and control the telnet session with a chat script as usual.

4.2 fwprc

I wrote a very well self-documented script to pierce firewalls, fwprc, available from my site <http://www.tunes. org/~fare/files/fwprc/>, together with cotty (which is required by fwprc 0.2 and later). At the time of my writing these lines, latest versions are fwprc 0.3a and cotty 0.3a.

The name "fwprc" is voluntarily made unreadable and unpronounceable, so that it will confuse the incompetent paranoid sysadm who might be the cause of the firewall that annoys you (of course, there can be legitimate firewalls, too, and even indispensible ones; security is all a matter of *correct* configuration). If you must read it aloud, choose the worst way you can imagine.

CONTEST! CONTEST! Send me a .au audio file with a digital audio recording of how you pronounce "fwprc". The worst entry will win a free upgrade and his name on the fwprc 1.0 page!

I tested the program in several settings, by configuring it through resource files. But of course, by Murphy's law, it will break for you. Feel free to contribute enhancements that will make life easier to other people who'll configure it after you.

4.3 .fwprcrc

fwprc can be customized through a file .fwprcrc meant to be the same on both sides of the firewall. Having several alternate configurations to choose from is sure possible (for instance, *I* do it), and is left as an exercise to the reader.

To begin with, copy the appropriate section of fwprc (the previous to last) into a file named .fwprcrc in your home directory. Then replace variable values with stuff that fits your configuration. Finally, copy to the other host, and test.

Default behavior is to use pppd locally, and slirp remotely. To modify that, you can redefine the appropriate function in your .fwprcrc with such a line as:

```
remote_IP_emu () { remote_pppd }
```

Note that SLiRP is safer than pppd, and easier to have access to, since it does not require being root on the remote machine. Anoter safe feature is that it will drop packets not directly coming from the connected machine (which feature becomes a misfeature if you attempt to route a subnetwork onto it with masquerading). The basic functionality in SLiRP works quite well, but I've found advertised pluses (like run-time controllability) to be deficient; of course, since it is free software, feel free to hack the source so as to actually implement whichever feature you need.

5 Reverse piercing

5.1 Rationale

Sometimes, only one side of the firewall can launch telnet sessions into the other side; however, some means of communication is possible (typically, through e-mail). Piercing the firewall is still possible, by triggering with whatever messaging capability is available a telnet connection from the "right" side of the firewall to the other.

fwprc includes code to trigger such connections from a PGP-authentified e-mail message; all you need is add fwprc as a procmail(1) filter to messages using the protocol, (instructions included in fwprc itself). Note however, that if you are to launch pppd with appropriate priviledges, you might need create your own suid wrapper to become root. Instructions enclosed in fwprc.

Also, authentified trigger does not remotely mean secure connection. You should really use ssh (perhaps over telnet) for secure connections. And then, beware of what happens between the triggering of a telnet connection, and ssh taking over that connection. Contribution in that direction welcome.

5.2 Getting the triggering mail

If you are firewalled, your mail may as well be in a central server that doesn't do procmail filtering or allow telnet sessions. No problem! You can use fetchmail(1) to run in daemon mode to poll and get mail to your client linux system, and/or add a cron-job to automatically poll for mail every 1-5 minutes. fetchmail will forward mail to a local address through sendmail(8), which itself will have been configured to use procmail(1) for delivery. Note that if you run fetchmail(1) as a background daemon, it will lock away any other fetchmail that you'd like to run only at other times, like when you open a fwprc; of course, if you can also run a fetchmail daemon as a fake user. Too frequent a poll won't be nice to either the server or your host. Too unfrequent a poll means you'll have to wait before the message gets read and the reverse connection gets established. I use two-minute poll frequency.

6 Final notes

6.1 Other settings

There are other kinds of firewalls than those that allow for telnet connections. As long as a continuous flow of packets may go through a firewall, and transmit information both ways, it is possible to pierce it; only the price of writing the piercer may be higher or lower.

In a very easy case, you can just launch ssh over a pty, and do some pppd in the slave tty. cotty 0.3a should be able to do it, but nobody's modified fwprc to take it into account yet. May be tonight's exercise for you. You may even want to do it without an adverse firewall, just so as to build a secure "VPN" (Virtual Private Network). See the VPN mini-HOWTO about this.

If you need cross a 7-bit line, you'll want to use SLIP instead of PPP. I never tried, because lines are more or less 8-bit clean these days, but it shouldn't be difficult.

Now, if the only way through the firewall is a WWW proxy (usually, a minimum for an internet-connected network), you might want to write a daemon that buffers data in and out, and sends it during in HTTP connections, achieving some telnet-over-HTTP over which to run fwprc. It might be slow and not very responsive, but still good enough to use fetchmail(1), suck(1), and other non-interactive programs.

If you want more performance, or if the only thing that goes through unfiltered is some wierder thing even (DNS queries, ICMP packets, whatever), then you're in the very hard case where you'll have to re-hack a wierd IP stack, using (for instance) the Fox project's packet-protocol functors. You'll then achieve some direct IP-over-HTTP, IP-over-DNS, IP-over-ICMP, or such, which requires not only a complex protocol, but also an interface to an OS kernel, both of which are costly to implement.

By the way, if you use some Firewall-piercing HTTP daemon, don't forget to have it serve fake pages, so as to mislead suspicious adverse firewall administrators.

6.2   HOWTO maintenance

I felt it was necessary to write it, but I don't have that much time for that, so this mini-HOWTO is very rough. So will it stay, until I get enough feedback so as to know what sections to enhance. Feedback welcome. Help welcome. mini-HOWTO maintenance take-over welcome.

In any case, the above sections have shown many problems whose solution is just a matter of someone (you?) spending some time (or money, by hiring someone else) to sit down and write it: nothing conceptually complicated, though the details might be burdensome or tricky.

Do not hesitate to contribute more problems, and hopefully more solutions, to this mini-HOWTO.

6.3   Extra copy of IMPORTANT DISCLAIMER — BELIEVE IT!!!

I hereby disclaim all responsibility for this hack. If it backfires on you in any way whatsoever, that's the breaks. Not my fault. If you don't understand the risks inherent in doing this, don't do it. If you use this hack and it allows vicious vandals to break into your company's computers and costs you your job and your company millions of dollars, well that's just tough nuggies. Don't come crying to me.

Part LXI

"Linux I/O port programming mini-HOWTO"
Author: Riku Saikkonen

<Riku.Saikkonen@hut.fi>

v, 28 December 1997
This HOWTO document describes programming hardware I/O ports and waiting for small periods of time in user-mode Linux programs running on the Intel x86 architecture.

Contents

1 Introduction

This HOWTO document describes programming hardware I/O ports and waiting for small periods of time in user-mode Linux programs running on the Intel x86 architecture. This document is a descendant of the very small IO-Port mini-HOWTO by the same author.

This document is Copyright 1995-1997 Riku Saikkonen. See the *Linux HOWTO copyright* <http://sunsite.unc.edu/pub/Linux/docs/HOWTO/COPYRIGHT> for details.

If you have corrections or something to add, feel free to e-mail me (Riku.Saikkonen@hut.fi)...

Changes from the previous released version (Mar 30 1997):

- Clarified things regarding inb_p/outb_p and port 0x80.

- Removed information about udelay(), since nanosleep() provides a cleaner way of using it.

- Converted to Linuxdoc-SGML, and reorganised somewhat.

- Lots of minor additions and modifications.

2   Using I/O ports in C programs

2.1   The normal method

Routines for accessing I/O ports are in /usr/include/asm/io.h (or linux/include/asm-i386/io.h in the kernel source distribution). The routines there are inline macros, so it is enough to #include <asm/io.h>; you do not need any additional libraries.

Because of a limitation in gcc (present at least in 2.7.2.3 and below) and in egcs (all versions), you *have to* compile any source code that uses these routines with optimisation turned on (gcc -O1 or higher), or alternatively #define extern to be empty before you #include <asm/io.h>.

For debugging, you can use gcc -g -O (at least with modern versions of gcc), though optimisation can sometimes make the debugger behave a bit strangely. If this bothers you, put the routines that use I/O port access in a separate source file and compile only that with optimisation turned on.

Before you access any ports, you must give your program permission to do so. This is done by calling the ioperm() function (declared in unistd.h, and defined in the kernel) somewhere near the start of your program (before any I/O port accesses). The syntax is ioperm(from, num, turn_on), where from is the first port number to give access to, and num the number of consecutive ports to give access to. For example, ioperm(0x300, 5, 1) would give access to ports 0x300 through 0x304 (a total of 5 ports). The last argument is a Boolean value specifying whether to give access to the program to the ports (true (1)) or to remove access (false (0)). You can call ioperm() multiple times to enable multiple non-consecutive ports. See the ioperm(2) manual page for details on the syntax.

The ioperm() call requires your program to have root privileges; thus you need to either run it as the root user, or make it setuid root. You can drop the root privileges after you have called ioperm() to enable the ports you want to use. You are not required to explicitly drop your port access privileges with ioperm(..., 0) at the end of your program; this is done automatically as the process exits.

A setuid() to a non-root user does not disable the port access granted by ioperm(), but a fork() does (the child process does not get access, but the parent retains it).

ioperm() can only give access to ports 0x000 through 0x3ff; for higher ports, you need to use iopl() (which gives you access to all ports at once). Use the level argument 3 (i.e., iopl(3)) to give your program access to *all* I/O ports (so be careful — accessing the wrong ports can do all sorts of nasty things to your computer). Again, you need root privileges to call iopl(). See the iopl(2) manual page for details.

Then, to actually accessing the ports... To input a byte (8 bits) from a port, call inb(port), it returns the byte it got. To output a byte, call outb(value, port) (please note the order of the parameters). To input a word (16 bits) from ports x and x+1 (one byte from each to form the word, using the assembler instruction inw), call inw(x). To output a word to the two ports, use outw(value, x). If you're unsure of which port instructions (byte or word) to use, you probably want inb() and outb() — most devices are designed for bytewise port access. Note that all port access instructions take at least about a microsecond to execute.

The inb_p(), outb_p(), inw_p(), and outw_p() macros work otherwise identically to the ones above, but they do an additional short (about one microsecond) delay after the port access; you can make the delay about four microseconds with #define REALLY_SLOW_IO before you #include <asm/io.h>. These macros normally (unless you #define SLOW_IO_BY_JUMPING, which is probably less accurate) use a port output to port 0x80 for their delay, so you need to give access to port 0x80 with `ioperm()` first (outputs to port 0x80 should not affect any part of the system). For more versatile methods of delaying, read on.

There are man pages for `ioperm(2)`, `iopl(2)`, and the above macros in reasonably recent releases of the Linux manual page collection.

2.2 An alternate method: `/dev/port`

Another way to access I/O ports is to `open()` `/dev/port` (a character device, major number 1, minor 4) for reading and/or writing (the stdio `f*()` functions have internal buffering, so avoid them). Then `lseek()` to the appropriate byte in the file (file position 0 = port 0x00, file position 1 = port 0x01, and so on), and `read()` or `write()` a byte or word from or to it.

Naturally, for this to work your program needs read/write access to `/dev/port`. This method is probably slower than the normal method above, but does not need compiler optimisation nor `ioperm()`. It doesn't need root access either, if you give a non-root user or group access to `/dev/port` — but this is a very bad thing to do in terms of system security, since it is possible to hurt the system, perhaps even gain root access, by using `/dev/port` to access hard disks, network cards, etc. directly.

3 Interrupts (IRQs) and DMA access

You cannot use IRQs or DMA directly from a user-mode process. You need to write a kernel driver; see *The Linux Kernel Hacker's Guide* <http://www.redhat.com:8080/HyperNews/get/khg.html> for details and the kernel source code for examples.

Also, you cannot disable interrupts from within a user-mode program.

4 High-resolution timing

4.1 Delays

First of all, I should say that you cannot guarantee user-mode processes to have exact control of timing because of the multi-tasking nature of Linux. Your process might be scheduled out at any time for anything from about 10 milliseconds to a few seconds (on a system with very high load). However, for most applications using I/O ports, this does not really matter. To minimise this, you may want to nice your process to a high-priority value (see the `nice(2)` manual page) or use real-time scheduling (see below).

If you want more precise timing than normal user-mode processes give you, there are some provisions for user-mode 'real time' support. Linux 2.x kernels have soft real time support; see the manual page for `sched_setscheduler(2)` for details. There is a special kernel that supports hard real time; see <http://luz.cs.nmt.edu/rtlinux/> for more information on this.

4.1.1 Sleeping: `sleep()` and `usleep()`

Now, let me start with the easier timing calls. For delays of multiple seconds, your best bet is probably to use `sleep()`. For delays of at least tens of milliseconds (about 10 ms seems to be the minimum delay), `usleep()` should work. These functions give the CPU to other processes ("sleep"), so CPU time isn't wasted. See the manual pages `sleep(3)` and `usleep(3)` for details.

For delays of under about 50 milliseconds (depending on the speed of your processor and machine, and the system load), giving up the CPU takes too much time, because the Linux scheduler (for the x86 architecture) usually takes at least about 10-30 milliseconds before it returns control to your process. Due to this, in small delays, `usleep(3)` usually delays somewhat more than the amount that you specify in the parameters, and at least about 10 ms.

4.1.2 `nanosleep()`

In the 2.0.x series of Linux kernels, there is a new system call, `nanosleep()` (see the `nanosleep(2)` manual page), that allows you to sleep or delay for short times (a few microseconds or more).

For delays <= 2 ms, if (and only if) your process is set to soft real time scheduling (using `sched_setscheduler()`), `nanosleep()` uses a busy loop; otherwise it sleeps, just like `usleep()`.

The busy loop uses `udelay()` (an internal kernel function used by many kernel drivers), and the length of the loop is calculated using the BogoMips value (the speed of this kind of busy loop is one of the things that BogoMips measures accurately). See `/usr/include/asm/delay.h`) for details on how it works.

4.1.3   Delaying with port I/O

Another way of delaying small numbers of microseconds is port I/O. Inputting or outputting any byte from/to port 0x80 (see above for how to do it) should wait for almost exactly 1 microsecond independent of your processor type and speed. You can do this multiple times to wait a few microseconds. The port output should have no harmful side effects on any standard machine (and some kernel drivers use it). This is how `{in|out}[bw]_p()` normally do the delay (see `asm/io.h`).

Actually, a port I/O instruction on most ports in the 0-0x3ff range takes almost exactly 1 microsecond, so if you're, for example, using the parallel port directly, just do additional `inb()`s from that port to delay.

4.1.4   Delaying with assembler instructions

If you know the processor type and clock speed of the machine the program will be running on, you can hard-code shorter delays by running certain assembler instructions (but remember, your process might be scheduled out at any time, so the delays might well be longer every now and then). For the table below, the internal processor speed determines the number of clock cycles taken; e.g., for a 50 MHz processor (e.g. 486DX-50 or 486DX2-50), one clock cycle takes 1/50000000 seconds (=200 nanoseconds).

Instruction	i386 clock cycles	i486 clock cycles
nop	3	1
xchg %ax,%ax	3	3
or %ax,%ax	2	1
mov %ax,%ax	2	1
add %ax,0	2	1

(Sorry, I don't know about Pentiums; probably close to the i486. I cannot find an instruction which would use one clock cycle on an i386. Use the one-clock-cycle instructions if you can, otherwise the pipelining used in modern processors may shorten the times.)

The instructions `nop` and `xchg` in the table should have no side effects. The rest may modify the flags register, but this shouldn't matter since gcc should detect it. `nop` is a good choice.

To use these, call `asm("instruction")` in your program. The syntax of the instructions is as in the table above; if you want multiple instructions in a single `asm()` statement, separate them with semicolons. For example, `asm("nop ; nop ; nop ; nop")` executes four `nop` instructions, delaying for four clock cycles on i486 or Pentium processors (or 12 clock cycles on an i386).

`asm()` is translated into inline assembler code by gcc, so there is no function call overhead.

Shorter delays than one clock cycle are impossible in the Intel x86 architecture.

4.1.5 `rdtsc` for Pentiums

For Pentiums, you can get the number of clock cycles elapsed since the last reboot with the following C code:

```
extern __inline__ unsigned long long int rdtsc()
{
    unsigned long long int x;
    __asm__ volatile (".byte 0x0f, 0x31" : "=A" (x));
    return x;
}
```

You can poll this value to delay for as many clock cycles as you want.

4.2 Measuring time

For times accurate to one second, it is probably easiest to use `time()`. For more accurate times, `gettimeofday()` is accurate to about a microsecond (but see above about scheduling). For Pentiums, the `rdtsc` code fragment above is accurate to one clock cycle.

If you want your process to get a signal after some amount of time, use `setitimer()` or `alarm()`. See the manual pages of the functions for details.

5   Other programming languages

The description above concentrates on the C programming language. It should apply directly to C++ and Objective C. In assembler, you have to call `ioperm()` or `iopl()` as in C, but after that you can use the I/O port read/write instructions directly.

In other languages, unless you can insert inline assembler or C code into the program or use the system calls mentioned above, it is probably easiest to write a simple C source file with functions for the I/O port accesses or delays that you need, and compile and link it in with the rest of your program. Or use `/dev/port` as described above.

6   Some useful ports

Here is some programming information for common ports that can be directly used for general-purpose TTL (or CMOS) logic I/O.

If you want to use these or other common ports for their intended purpose (e.g., to control a normal printer or modem), you should most likely use existing drivers (which are usually included in the kernel) instead of programming the ports directly as this HOWTO describes. This section is intended for those people who want to connect LCD displays, stepper motors, or other custom electronics to a PC's standard ports.

If you want to control a mass-market device like a scanner (that has been on the market for a while), look for an existing Linux driver for it. The *Hardware-HOWTO* <http://sunsite.unc.edu/pub/Linux/docs/HOWTO/Hardware-HOWTO> is a good place to start.

<http://www.hut.fi/Misc/Electronics/> is a good source for more information on connecting devices to computers (and on electronics in general).

6.1 The parallel port

The parallel port's base address (called "BASE" below) is 0x3bc for `/dev/lp0`, 0x378 for `/dev/lp1`, and 0x278 for `/dev/lp2`. If you only want to control something that acts like a normal printer, see the *Printing-HOWTO* <http://sunsite.unc.edu/pub/Linux/docs/HOWTO/Printing-HOWTO>.

In addition to the standard output-only mode described below, there is an 'extended' bidirectional mode in most parallel ports. For information on this and the newer ECP/EPP modes (and the IEEE 1284 standard in general), see <http://www.fapo.com/> and <http://www.senet.com.au/cpeacock/parallel.htm>. Remember that since you cannot use IRQs or DMA in a user-mode program, you will probably have to write a kernel driver to use ECP/EPP; I think someone is writing such a driver, but I don't know the details.

The port BASE+0 (Data port) controls the data signals of the port (D0 to D7 for bits 0 to 7, respectively; states: 0 = low (0 V), 1 = high (5 V)). A write to this port latches the data on the pins. A read returns the data last written in standard or extended write mode, or the data in the pins from another device in extended read mode.

The port BASE+1 (Status port) is read-only, and returns the state of the following input signals:

- Bits 0 and 1 are reserved.
- Bit 2 IRQ status (not a pin, I don't know how this works)
- Bit 3 ERROR (1=high)
- Bit 4 SLCT (1=high)
- Bit 5 PE (1=high)
- Bit 6 ACK (1=high)
- Bit 7 -BUSY (0=high)

(I'm not sure about the high and low states.)

The port BASE+2 (Control port) is write-only (a read returns the data last written), and controls the following status signals:

- Bit 0 -STROBE (0=high)
- Bit 1 AUTO_FD_XT (1=high)
- Bit 2 -INIT (0=high)
- Bit 3 SLCT_IN (1=high)
- Bit 4 enables the parallel port IRQ (which occurs on the low-to-high transition of ACK) when set to 1.
- Bit 5 controls the extended mode direction (0 = write, 1 = read), and is completely write-only (a read returns nothing useful for this bit).
- Bits 6 and 7 are reserved.

(Again, I am not sure about the high and low states.)

Pinout (a 25-pin female D-shell connector on the port) (i=input, o=output):

```
1io -STROBE, 2io D0, 3io D1, 4io D2, 5io D3, 6io D4, 7io D5, 8io D6,
9io D7, 10i ACK, 11i -BUSY, 12i PE, 13i SLCT, 14o AUTO_FD_XT,
15i ERROR, 16o -INIT, 17o SLCT_IN, 18-25 Ground
```

The IBM specifications say that pins 1, 14, 16, and 17 (the control outputs) have open collector drivers pulled to 5 V through 4.7 kiloohm resistors (sink 20 mA, source 0.55 mA, high-level output 5.0 V minus pullup). The rest of the pins sink 24 mA, source 15 mA, and their high-level output is min. 2.4 V. The low state for both is max. 0.5 V. Non-IBM parallel ports probably deviate from this standard. For more information on this, see <http://www.hut.fi/Misc/Electronics/circuits/lptpower.html>.

Finally, a warning: Be careful with grounding. I've broken several parallel ports by connecting to them while the computer is turned on. It might be a good thing to use a parallel port not integrated on the motherboard for things like this. (You can usually get a second parallel port for your machine with a cheap standard 'multi-I/O' card; just disable the ports that you don't need, and set the parallel port I/O address on the card to a free address. You don't need to care about the parallel port IRQ, since it isn't normally used.)

6.2 The game (joystick) port

The game port is located at port addresses 0x200-0x207. For controlling normal joysticks, there is a kernel-level joystick driver, see `<ftp://sunsite.unc.edu/pub/Linux/kernel/patches/>`, filename `joystick-*`.

Pinout (a 15-pin female D-shell connector on the port):

- 1,8,9,15: +5 V (power)
- 4,5,12: Ground
- 2,7,10,14: Digital inputs BA1, BA2, BB1, and BB2, respectively
- 3,6,11,13: "Analog" inputs AX, AY, BX, and BY, respectively

The +5 V pins seem to often be connected directly to the power lines in the motherboard, so they should be able to source quite a lot of power, depending on the motherboard, power supply and game port.

The digital inputs are used for the buttons of the two joysticks (joystick A and joystick B, with two buttons each) that you can connect to the port. They should be normal TTL-level inputs, and you can read their status directly from the status port (see below). A real joystick returns a low (0 V) status when the button is pressed and a high (the 5 V from the power pins through an 1 Kohm resistor) status otherwise.

The so-called analog inputs actually measure resistance. The game port has a quad one-shot multivibrator (a 558 chip) connected to the four inputs. In each input, there is a 2.2 Kohm resistor between the input pin and the multivibrator output, and a 0.01 uF timing capacitor between the multivibrator output and the ground. A real joystick has a potentiometer for each axis (X and Y), wired between +5 V and the appropriate input pin (AX or AY for joystick A, or BX or BY for joystick B).

The multivibrator, when activated, sets its output lines high (5 V) and waits for each timing capacitor to reach 3.3 V before lowering the respective output line. Thus the high period duration of the multivibrator is proportional to the resistance of the potentiometer in the joystick (i.e., the position of the joystick in the appropriate axis), as follows:

$$R = (t - 24.2) / 0.011,$$

where R is the resistance (ohms) of the potentiometer and t the high period duration (seconds).

Thus, to read the analog inputs, you first activate the multivibrator (with a port write; see below), then poll the state of the four axes (with repeated port reads) until they drop from high to low state, measuring their high period duration. This polling uses quite a lot of CPU time, and on a non-realtime multitasking system like (normal user-mode) Linux, the result is not very accurate because you cannot poll the port constantly (unless you use a kernel-level driver and disable interrupts while polling, but this wastes even more CPU time). If you know that the signal is going to take a long time (tens of ms) to go down, you can call usleep() before polling to give CPU time to other processes.

The only I/O port you need to access is port 0x201 (the other ports either behave identically or do nothing). Any write to this port (it doesn't matter what you write) activates the multivibrator. A read from this port returns the state of the input signals:

- Bit 0: AX (status (1=high) of the multivibrator output)
- Bit 1: AY (status (1=high) of the multivibrator output)
- Bit 2: BX (status (1=high) of the multivibrator output)
- Bit 3: BY (status (1=high) of the multivibrator output)
- Bit 4: BA1 (digital input, 1=high)
- Bit 5: BA2 (digital input, 1=high)
- Bit 6: BB1 (digital input, 1=high)
- Bit 7: BB2 (digital input, 1=high)

6.3 The serial port

If the device you're talking to supports something resembling RS-232, you should be able to use the serial port to talk to it. The Linux serial driver should be enough for almost all applications (you shouldn't have to program the serial port directly, and you'd probably have to write a kernel driver to do it); it is quite versatile, so using non-standard bps rates and so on shouldn't be a problem.

See the `termios(3)` manual page, the serial driver source code (`linux/drivers/char/serial.c`), and `<http://www.easysw.com/mike/serial/index.html>` for more information on programming serial ports on Unix systems.

7 Hints

If you want good analog I/O, you can wire up ADC and/or DAC chips to the parallel port (hint: for power, use the game port connector or a spare disk drive power connector wired to outside the computer case, unless you have a low-power device and can use the parallel port itself for power, or use an external power supply), or buy an AD/DA card (most of the older/slower ones are controlled by I/O ports). Or, if you're satisfied with 1 or 2 channels, inaccuracy, and (probably) bad zeroing, a cheap sound card supported by the Linux sound driver should do (and it's quite fast).

With accurate analog devices, improper grounding may generate errors in the analog inputs or outputs. If you experience something like this, you could try electrically isolating your device from the computer with optocouplers (on *all* signals between the computer and your device). Try to get power for the optocouplers from the computer (spare signals on the port may give enough power) to achieve better isolation.

If you're looking for printed circuit board design software for Linux, there is a free X11 application called Pcb that should do a nice job, at least if you aren't doing anything very complex. It is included in many Linux distributions, and available in `<ftp://sunsite.unc.edu/pub/Linux/apps/circuits/>` (filename `pcb-*`).

8 Troubleshooting

Q1.

I get segmentation faults when accessing ports.

A1.

Either your program does not have root privileges, or the `ioperm()` call failed for some other reason. Check the return value of `ioperm()`. Also, check that you're actually accessing the ports that you enabled with `ioperm()` (see Q3). If you're using the delaying macros (`inb_p()`, `outb_p()`, and so on), remember to call `ioperm()` to get access to port 0x80 too.

Q2.

I can't find the `in*()`, `out*()` functions defined anywhere, and gcc complains about undefined references.

A2.

You did not compile with optimisation turned on (`-O`), and thus gcc could not resolve the macros in `asm/io.h`. Or you did not `#include <asm/io.h>` at all.

Q3.

`out*()` doesn't do anything, or does something weird.

A3.

Check the order of the parameters; it should be `outb(value, port)`, not `outportb(port, value)` as is common in MS-DOS.

Q4.

I want to control a standard RS-232 device/parallel printer/joystick...

A4.

You're probably better off using existing drivers (in the Linux kernel or an X server or somewhere else) to do it. The drivers are usually quite versatile, so even slightly non-standard devices usually work with them. See the information on standard ports above for pointers to documentation for them.

9 Example code

Here's a piece of simple example code for I/O port access:

```
/*
 * example.c: very simple example of port I/O
 *
 * This code does nothing useful, just a port write, a pause,
 * and a port read. Compile with 'gcc -O2 -o example example.c',
 * and run as root with './example'.
 */

#include <stdio.h>
#include <unistd.h>
#include <asm/io.h>

#define BASEPORT 0x378 /* lp1 */

int main()
{
  /* Get access to the ports */
  if (ioperm(BASEPORT, 3, 1)) {perror("ioperm"); exit(1);}

  /* Set the data signals (D0-7) of the port to all low (0) */
  outb(0, BASEPORT);

  /* Sleep for a while (100 ms) */
  usleep(100000);

  /* Read from the status port (BASE+1) and display the result */
  printf("status: %d\n", inb(BASEPORT + 1));

  /* We don't need the ports anymore */
  if (ioperm(BASEPORT, 3, 0)) {perror("ioperm"); exit(1);}

  exit(0);
}

/* end of example.c */
```

10 Credits

Too many people have contributed for me to list, but thanks a lot, everyone. I have not replied to all the contributions that I've received; sorry for that, and thanks again for the help.

Mini-HOWTO

Part LXII

"Linux IP Masquerade mini HOWTO" Ambrose Au

ambrose@writeme.com; David Ranch *dranch@trinnet.net*

v1.50, 7 February 1999

This document describes how to enable IP masquerade feature on a Linux host, allowing connected computers that do not have registered Internet IP addresses to connect to the Internet through your Linux box.

Contents

Mini-HOWTO

1   Introduction

1.1   Introduction

This document describes how to enable IP masquerade feature on a Linux host, allowing connected computers that do not have registered Internet IP addresses to connect to the Internet through your Linux box. It is possible to connect your machines to the Linux host with ethernet, as well as other kinds of connection such as a dialup ppp link. This document will emphasize on ethernet connection, since it should be the most likely case.

This document is intended for users using stable kernels 2.2.x and 2.0.x. Older kernels such as 1.2.x are NOT covered.

1.2 Foreword, Feedback & Credits

I find it very confusing as a new user setting up IP masquerade on a newer kernel, i.e. 2.x kernel. Although there is a FAQ and a mailing list, there is no document dedicates on that; and there are some requests on the mailing list for such a HOWTO. So, I decided to write this up as a starting point for new users, and possibly a building block for knowledgeable users to build on for documentation. If you think I'm not doing a good job, feel free to tell me so that I can make it better.

This document is heavily based on the original FAQ by Ken Eves , and numerous helpful messages in the IP Masquerade mailing list. And a special thanks to Mr. Matthew Driver whose mailing list message inspired me to set up IP Masquerade and eventually writing this.

Please feel free to send any feedback or comments to *ambrose@writeme.com* and *dranch@trinnet.net* if we've mistaken on any information, or if any information is missing. Your invaluable feedback will certainly be influencing the future of this HOWTO!

This HOWTO is meant to be a quick guide to get your IP Masquerade working in the shortest time. As I am not a technical writer, you may find the information in this document not as general and objective as it can be. The latest news and information can be found at the *IP Masquerade Resource* <http://ipmasq.cjb.net/> web page that we maintained. If you have any technical questions on IP Masquerade, please join the IP Masquerade Mailing List instead of sending email to me since I have limited time, and the developers of IP_Masq are more capable of answering your questions.

The latest version of this document can be found at the *IP Masquerade Resource* <http://ipmasq.cjb.net/>, which also contains the HTML and postscript version:

- *http://ipmasq.cjb.net/*
- *http://ipmasq2.cjb.net/*
- Please refer to *IP Masquerade Resource Mirror Sites Listing* for other mirror sites available.

1.3 Copyright & Disclaimer

The information and other contents in this document are to the best of my knowledge. However, IP Masquerade is *experimental*, and there is chance that I make mistakes as well; so you should determine if you want to follow the information in this document.

Nobody is responsible for any damage on your computers and any other losses by using the information on this document. i.e.

THE AUTHOR AND MAINTAINERS ARE NOT RESPONSIBLE FOR ANY DAMAGES IN-CURRED DUE TO ACTIONS TAKEN BASED ON THE INFORMATION IN THIS DOCUMENT.

2 Background Knowledge

2.1 What is IP Masquerade?

IP Masquerade is a networking function in Linux. If a Linux host is connected to the Internet with IP Masquerade enabled, then computers connecting to it (either on the same LAN or connected with modems) can reach the Internet as well, even though they have *no official assigned IP addresses*.

This allows a set of machines to *invisibly* access the Internet hidden behind a gateway system, which appears to be the only system using the Internet. Breaking the security of a well set-up masquerading system should be considerably more difficult than breaking a good packet filter based firewall (assuming there are no bugs in either).

2.2   Current Status

IP Masquerade had been out for several years and is maturing as Linux heads into the 2.2.x stage. Kernels since 1.3.x had built-in support already. Many individuals and even busnesses are using it, with satisfactory results.

Browsing web pages and telnet are reported to work well over IP Masquerade. FTP, IRC and listening to Real Audio are working with certain modules loaded. Other network streaming audio such as True Speech and Internet Wave work too. Some fellow users on the mailing list even tried video conferencing software. `Ping` is now working, with the newly available ICMP patch

Please refer to section 4.3 for a more complete listing of software supported.

IP Masquerade works well with 'client machines' on several different OS and platforms. There are successful cases with systems using Unix, Windows 95, Windows NT, Windows for Workgroup(with TCP/IP package), OS/2, Macintosh System's OS with Mac TCP, Mac Open Transport, DOS with NCSA Telnet package, VAX, Alpha with Linux, and even Amiga with AmiTCP or AS225-stack. The list goes on and on, the point is, if your OS platform talks TCP/IP, it should work with IP Masquerade.

2.3   Who Can Benefit From IP Masquerade?

- If you have a Linux host connected to the Internet, and
- if you have some computers running TCP/IP connected to that Linux box on a local subnet, and/or
- if your Linux host has more than one modem and acts as a PPP or SLIP server connecting to others, which
- those **OTHER** machines do not have official assigned IP addresses. (these machines are represented by **OTHER** machines hereby)
- And of course, if you want those **OTHER** machines to make it onto the Internet without spending extra bucks :)

2.4   Who Doesn't Need IP Masquerade?

- If your machine is a stand-alone Linux host connected to the Internet, then it is pointless to have IP Masquerade running, or
- if you already have assigned addresses for your **OTHER** machines, then you don't need IP Masquerade,
- and of course, if you don't like the idea of a 'free ride'.

2.5   How IP Masquerade Works?

From IP Masquerade FAQ by Ken Eves:

```
Here is a drawing of the most simple setup:
```

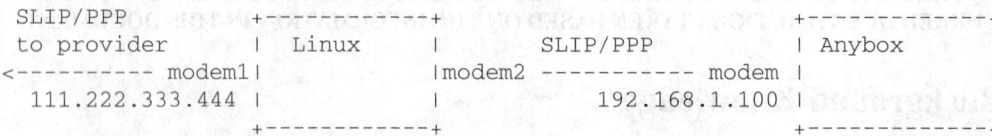

```
    SLIP/PPP        +------------+                   +------------+
    to provider     |   Linux    |       SLIP/PPP    |  Anybox    |
    <---------- modem1|          |modem2 ---------- modem |        |
    111.222.333.444 |            |        192.168.1.100 |          |
                    +------------+                   +------------+
```

```
    In the above drawing a Linux box with ip_masquerading installed and
running is connected to the Internet via SLIP/or/PPP using modem1.  It has
an assigned IP address of 111.222.333.444.  It is setup that modem2 allows
callers to login and start a SLIP/or/PPP connection.
```

```
    The second system (which doesn't have to be running Linux) calls into the
Linux box and starts a SLIP/or/PPP connection.  It does NOT have an assigned
IP address on the Internet so it uses 192.168.1.100. (see below)
```

With ip_masquerade and the routing configured properly the machine
Anybox can interact with the Internet as if it was really connected (with a
few exceptions).

Quoting Pauline Middelink:
Do not forget to mention the ANYBOX should have the Linux box
as its gateway (whether is be the default route or just a subnet
is no matter). If the ANYBOX can not do this, the Linux machine
should do a proxy arp for all routed address, but the setup of
proxy arp is beyond the scope of the document.

The following is an excerpt from a post on comp.os.linux.networking which
has been edited to match the names used in the above example:
   o I tell machine ANYBOX that my slipped linux box is its gateway.
   o When a packet comes into the linux box from ANYBOX, it will assign it
     new source port number, and slap its own ip address in the packet
     header, saving the originals. It will then send the modified packet
     out over the SLIP/or/PPP interface to the Internet.
   o When a packet comes from the Internet to the linux box, if the port
     number is one of those assigned above, it will get the original
     port and ip address, put them back in the packet header, and send the
     packet to ANYBOX.
   o The host that sent the packet will never know the difference.

An IP Masquerading Example

typical example is given in the diagram below:-

```
+----------+
|          |  Ethernet
| abox     |::::::
|          |2     :192.168.1.x
+----------+      :
                  :  +----------+    PPP
+----------+      :  1| Linux   |    link
|          |      ::::| masq-gate|:::::::::// Internet
| bbox     |::::::  |  +----------+
|          |3     :
+----------+      :
                  :
+----------+      :
|          |      :
| cbox     |::::::
|          |4
+----------+


        <-Internal Network->
```

In this example there are 4 computer systems that we are concerned about (there is presumably also something on the far
right that your IP connection to the internet comes through, and there is something (far off the page) on the internet that
you are interested in exchanging information with). The Linux system masq-gate is the masquerading gateway for the
internal network of machines abox, bbox and cbox to get to the internet. The internal network uses one of the assigned

private network addresses, in this case the class C network 192.168.1.0, with the linux box having address 192.168.1.1 and the other systems having addresses on that network.

The three machines `abox`, `bbox` and `cbox` (which can, by the way, be running any operating system as long as they can speak IP - such as **Windows 95**, **Macintosh MacTCP** or even another linux box) can connect to other machines on the internet, however the masquerading system `masq-gate` converts all of their connections so that they appear to originate from `masq-gate`, and arranges that data coming back in to a masqueraded connection is relayed back to the originating system - so the systems on the internal network see a direct route to the internet and are unaware that their data is being masqueraded.

2.6 Requirements for Using IP Masquerade on Linux 2.2.x

** Please refer to *IP Masquerade Resource* <http://ipmasq.cjb.net/> for the latest information. **

- Kernel 2.2.x source available from *http://www.kernel.org/*
  (Most of the modern Linux dributions such as Redhat 5.2 - shipped with 2.0.36 kernel - has modular kernel with all IP Masquerade kernel options compiled. In such cases, there is no need to compile again. If you are upgrading kernel, then you should be aware of what you need, mentioned later in the HOWTO.)

- Loadable kernel modules, preferably 2.1.121 or newer

- A well set up TCP/IP network
  covered in *Linux NET-3 HOWTO* <http://metalab.unc.edu/mdw/HOWTO/NET-3-HOWTO.html> and the *Network Administrator's Guide* <http://metalab.unc.edu/mdw/LDP/nag/nag.html>
  Also check out the *Trinity OS Doc* <http://www.ecst.csuchico.edu/~dranch/LINUX/TrinityOS.wri>, a very comprehensive guide on Linux networking.

- Connectivity to Internet for your Linux host
  covered in *Linux ISP Hookup HOWTO* <http://metalab.unc.edu/mdw/HOWTO/ISP-Hookup-HOWTO.html>, *Linux PPP HOWTO* <http://metalab.unc.edu/mdw/HOWTO/PPP-HOWTO.html>, *Linux DHCP mini-HOWTO* <http://metalab.unc.edu/mdw/HOWTO/mini/DHCP.html> and *Linux Cable Modem mini-HOWTO* <http://metalab.unc.edu/mdw/HOWTO/mini/Cable-Modem.html>

- IP Chains 1.3.8 or newer available from *http://www.rustcorp.com/linux/ipchains/*
  more information on version requirement is on the *Linux IP Firewalling Chains page* <http://www.rustcorp.com/linux/ipchains/>

- For other options, please see *Linux IP Masquerade Resource* <http://ipmasq.cjb.net/>

2.7 Requirements for Using IP Masquerade on Linux 2.0.x

** Please refer to *IP Masquerade Resource* <http://ipmasq.cjb.net/> for the latest information. **

- Kernel 2.0.x source available from *http://www.kernel.org/*
  (Most of the modern Linux dributions such as Redhat 5.2 has modular kernel with all IP Masquerade kernel options compiled. In such cases, there is no need to compile again. If you are upgrading kernel, then you should be aware of what you need, mentioned later in the HOWTO.)

- Loadable kernel modules, preferably 2.0.0 or newer available from *http://www.pi.se/blox/modules/modules-2.0.0.tar.gz*
  (modules-1.3.57 is the minimal requirement)

- A well set up TCP/IP network
  covered in *Linux NET-3 HOWTO* <http://metalab.unc.edu/mdw/HOWTO/NET-3-HOWTO.html> and the *Network Administrator's Guide* <http://metalab.unc.edu/mdw/LDP/nag/nag.html>
  Also check out the *Trinity OS Doc* <http://www.ecst.csuchico.edu/~dranch/LINUX/TrinityOS.wri>, a very compreshensive guide on Linux networking.

- Connectivity to Internet for your Linux host
  covered in *Linux ISP Hookup HOWTO* `<http://metalab.unc.edu/mdw/HOWTO/`
  `ISP-Hookup-HOWTO.html>`, *Linux PPP HOWTO* `<http://metalab.unc.edu/mdw/HOWTO/`
  `PPP-HOWTO.html>`, *Linux DHCP mini-HOWTO* `<http://metalab.unc.edu/mdw/HOWTO/mini/`
  `DHCP.html>` and *Linux Cable Modem mini-HOWTO* `<http://metalab.unc.edu/mdw/HOWTO/mini/`
  `Cable-Modem.html>`

- Ipfwadm 2.3 or newer available from *ftp://ftp.xos.nl/pub/linux/ipfwadm/ipfwadm-2.3.tar.gz*
  more information on version requirement is on the *Linux IPFWADM page* `<http://www.xos.nl/linux/`
  `ipfwadm/>`

- You can optionally apply some IP Masquerade patches to enable other functionality. More information availabe on
  IP Masquerade Resources `<http://ipmasq.cjb.net/>` (these patches apply to all 2.0.x kernels)

3 Setting Up IP Masquerade

If your private network contains any vital information, think carefully before using IP Masquerade. This may be a GATEWAY for you to get to the Internet, and vice versa for someone on the other side of the world to get into your network.

3.1 Compiling the Kernel for IP Masquerade Support

If your Linux distribution already has the required features and modules compiled (most modular kernels will have all you need) mentioned below, then you do not have to re-compile the kernel. Reading this section is still highly recommended as it contains other useful informaiton.

3.1.1 Linux 2.2.x Kernels

- First of all, you need the kernel source for 2.2.x

- If this is your first time compiling the kernel, don't be scared. In fact, it's rather easy and it's covered in *Linux Kernel HOWTO* `<http://metalab.unc.edu/mdw/HOWTO/Kernel-HOWTO.html>`.

- Unpack the kernel source to `/usr/src/` with a command: `tar xvzf linux-2.2.x.tar.gz -C /usr/src`, where x is the patch level beyond 2.0
  (make sure there is a directory or symbolic link called `linux`)

- Apply appropriate patches. Since new patches are coming out, details will not be included here. Please refer to *IP Masquerade Resources* `<http://ipmasq.cjb.net/>` for up-to-date information.

- Refer to the Kernel HOWTO and the README file in the kernel source directory for further instructions on compiling a kernel

- Here are the options that you need to compile in: Say *YES* to the following,

```
    * Prompt for development and/or incomplete code/drivers
      CONFIG_EXPERIMENTAL
      - this will allow you to select experimental IP Masquer-
  ade code compiled
        into the kernel

    * Enable loadable module support
      CONFIG_MODULES
      - allows you to load ipmasq modules such as ip_masq_ftp.o

    * Networking support
      CONFIG_NET

    * Network firewalls
      CONFIG_FIREWALL
```

```
* TCP/IP networking
  CONFIG_INET

* IP: forwarding/gatewaying
  CONFIG_IP_FORWARD

* IP: firewalling
  CONFIG_IP_FIREWALL

* IP: masquerading
  CONFIG_IP_MASQUERADE

* IP: ipportfw masq support
  CONFIG_IP_MASQUERADE_IPPORTFW
  - recommended

* IP: ipautofw masquerade support
  CONFIG_IP_MASQUERADE_IPAUTOFW
  - optional

* IP: ICMP masquerading
  CONFIG_IP_MASQUERADE_ICMP
  - support for masquerading ICMP packets, recommended.

* IP: always defragment
  CONFIG_IP_ALWAYS_DEFRAG
  - highly recommended

* Dummy net driver support
  CONFIG_DUMMY
  - recommended

* IP: ip fwmark masq-forwarding support
  CONFIG_IP_MASQUERADE_MFW
  - optional
```

NOTE: These are just the component you need for IP Masquerade, select whatever other options you need for your specific setup.

- After compiling the kernel, you should compile and install the modules:

  ```
  make modules; make modules_install
  ```

- Then you should add a few lines into your /etc/rc.d/rc.local file (or any file you think is appropriate) to load the required modules reside in /lib/modules/2.2.x/ipv4/ automatically during each reboot:

  ```
            .
            .
            .
  /sbin/depmod -a
  /sbin/modprobe ip_masq_ftp
  /sbin/modprobe ip_masq_raudio
  /sbin/modprobe ip_masq_irc
  (and other modules such as ip_masq_cuseeme, ip_masq_vdolive
   if you have applied the patches)
            .
            .
  ```

IMPORTANT: IP forwarding is disabled by default in 2.2.x kernels, please make sure you enable it by running

`echo "1" > /proc/sys/net/ipv4/ip_forwarding`

For Redhat users, you may try changing `FORWARD_IPV4=false` to `FORWARD_IPV4=true` in `/etc/sysconfig/network`

- Reboot the Linux box.

3.1.2 Linux 2.0.x Kernels

- First of all, you need the kernel source (preferably the latest kernel version 2.0.36 or above)

- If this is your first time compiling the kernel, don't be scared. In fact, it's rather easy and it's covered in *Linux Kernel HOWTO* <http://metalab.unc.edu/mdw/HOWTO/Kernel-HOWTO.html>.

- Unpack the kernel source to `/usr/src/` with a command: `tar xvzf linux-2.0.x.tar.gz -C /usr/src`, where x is the patch level beyond 2.0
  (make sure there is a directory or symbolic link called `linux`)

- Apply appropriate patches. Since new patches are coming out, details will not be included here. Please refer to *IP Masquerade Resources* <http://ipmasq.cjb.net/> for up-to-date information.

- Refer to the Kernel HOWTO and the README file in the kernel source directory for further instructions on compiling a kernel

- Here are the options that you need to compile in: Say *YES* to the following,

```
    * Prompt for development and/or incomplete code/drivers
      CONFIG_EXPERIMENTAL
      - this will allow you to select experimental IP Masquer-
  ade code compiled
        into the kernel

    * Enable loadable module support
      CONFIG_MODULES
      - allows you to load modules

    * Networking support
      CONFIG_NET

    * Network firewalls
      CONFIG_FIREWALL

    * TCP/IP networking
      CONFIG_INET

    * IP: forwarding/gatewaying
      CONFIG_IP_FORWARD

    * IP: firewalling
      CONFIG_IP_FIREWALL

    * IP: masquerading (EXPERIMENTAL)
      CONFIG_IP_MASQUERADE
      - although it is experimental, it is a *MUST*

    * IP: ipautofw masquerade support (EXPERIMENTAL)
      CONFIG_IP_MASQUERADE_IPAUTOFW
```

```
                -recommended

      * IP: ICMP masquerading
        CONFIG_IP_MASQUERADE_ICMP
        - support for masquerading ICMP packets, optional.

      * IP: always defragment
        CONFIG_IP_ALWAYS_DEFRAG
        - highly recommended

      * Dummy net driver support
        CONFIG_DUMMY
        - recommended
```

NOTE: These are just the component you need for IP Masquerade, select whatever other options you need for your specific setup.

- After compiling the kernel, you should compile and install the modules:

    ```
    make modules; make modules_install
    ```

- Then you should add a few lines into your /etc/rc.d/rc.local file (or any file you think is appropriate) to load the required modules reside in /lib/modules/2.0.x/ipv4/ automatically during each reboot:

```
                .
                .
                .
    /sbin/depmod -a
    /sbin/modprobe ip_masq_ftp
    /sbin/modprobe ip_masq_raudio
    /sbin/modprobe ip_masq_irc
    (and other modules such as ip_masq_cuseeme, ip_masq_vdolive
     if you have applied the patches)
                .
                .
                .
```

IMPORTANT: IP forwarding is disabled by default since 2.0.34 kernels, please make sure you enable it by running
echo "1" > /proc/sys/net/ipv4/ip_forward

For Redhat users, you may try changing FORWARD_IPV4=false to FORWARD_IPV4=true in /etc/sysconfig/network

- Reboot the Linux box.

3.2 Assigning Private Network IP Address

Since all **OTHER** machines do not have official assigned addressees, there must be a right way to allocate address to those machines.

From IP Masquerade FAQ:

There is an RFC (#1597, probably obsolete by now) on which IP addresses are to be used on a non-connected network. There are 3 blocks of numbers set aside specifically for this purpose. One which I use is 255 Class-C subnets at 192.168.1.n to 192.168.255.n .

```
From RCF 1597:

Section 3: Private Address Space
```

The Internet Assigned Numbers Authority (IANA) has reserved the
following three blocks of the IP address space for private networks:

```
10.0.0.0      -   10.255.255.255
172.16.0.0    -   172.31.255.255
192.168.0.0   -   192.168.255.255
```

We will refer to the first block as "24-bit block", the second as
"20-bit block", and to the third as "16-bit" block". Note that the
first block is nothing but a single class A network number, while the
second block is a set of 16 contiguous class B network numbers, and
third block is a set of 255 contiguous class C network numbers.

So, if you're using a class C network, you should name your machines as 192.168.1.1, 1.92.168.1.2, 1.92.168.1.3, ...,
192.168.1.x

192.168.1.1 is usually the gateway machine, which is your Linux host connecting to the Internet. Notice that 192.168.1.0
and 192.168.1.255 are the Network and Broadcast address respectively, which are reserved. Avoid using these addresses
on your machines.

3.3   Configuring the OTHER machines

Besides setting the appropriate IP address for each machine, you should also set the appropriate gateway. In general, it is
rather straight forward. You simply enter the address of your Linux host (usually 192.168.1.1) as the gateway address.

For the Domain Name Service, you can add in any DNS available. The most apparent one should be the one that your
Linux is using. You can optionally add any domain search suffix as well.

After you have reconfigured those IP addresses, remember to restart the appropriate services or reboot your systems.

The following configuration instructions assume that you are using a Class C network with 192.168.1.1 as your Linux
host's address. Please note that 192.168.1.0 and 192.168.1.255 are reserved.

3.3.1   Configuring Windows 95

1. If you haven't installed your network card and adapter driver, do so now.

2. Go to *'Control Panel'/'Network'*.

3. Add *'TCP/IP protocol'* if you don't already have it.

4. In *'TCP/IP properties'*, goto *'IP Address'* and set IP Address to 192.168.1.x, (1 < x < 255), and then set Subnet
   Mask to 255.255.255.0

5. Add 192.168.1.1 as your gateway under *'Gateway'*.

6. Under *'DNS Configuration'/'DNS Server search order'* add your the DNS that your Linux host uses (usually find
   in /etc/resolv.conf). Optionally, you can add the appropriate domain search suffix.

7. Leave all the other settings as they are unless you know what you're doing.

8. Click *'OK'* on all dialog boxes and restart system.

9. Ping the linux box to test the network connection: *'Start/Run'*, type: ping 192.168.1.1
   (This is only a LAN connection testing, you can't ping the outside world yet.)

10. You can optionally create a HOSTS file in the windows directory so that you can use hostname of the machines on
    your LAN. There is an example called HOSTS.SAM in the windows directory.

3.3.2 Configuring Windows for Workgroup 3.11

1. If you haven't installed your network card and adapter driver, do so now.

2. Install the TCP/IP 32b package if you don't have it already.

3. In *'Main'/'Windows Setup'/'Network Setup'*, click on *'Drivers'*.

4. Highlight *'Microsoft TCP/IP-32 3.11b'* in the *'Network Drivers'* section, click *'Setup'*.

5. Set IP Address to 192.168.1.x (1 < x < 255), then set Subnet Mask to 255.255.255.0 and Default Gateway to 192.168.1.1

6. Do not enable *'Automatic DHCP Configuration'* and put anything in those *'WINS Server'* input areas unless you're in a Windows NT domain and you know what you're doing.

7. Click *'DNS'*, fill in the appropriate information mentioned in STEP 6 of section 3.3.1, then click *'OK'* when you're done with it.

8. Click *'Advanced'*, check *'Enable DNS for Windows Name Resolution'* and *'Enable LMHOSTS lookup'* if you're using a look up host file, similar to the one mentioned in STEP 10 of section 3.3.1

9. Click *'OK'* on all dialog boxes and restart system.

10. Ping the linux box to test the network connection: *'File/Run'*, type: ping 192.168.1.1
    (This is only a LAN connection testing, you can't ping the outside world yet.)

3.3.3 Configuring Windows NT

1. If you haven't installed your network card and adapter driver, do so now.

2. Go to *'Main'/'Control Panel'/'Network'*

3. Add the TCP/IP Protocol and Related Component from the *'Add Software'* menu if you don't have TCP/IP service installed already.

4. Under *'Network Software and Adapter Cards'* section, highlight *'TCP/IP Protocol'* in the *'Installed Network Software'* selection box.

5. In *'TCP/IP Configuration'*, select the appropriate adapter, e.g. [1]Novell NE2000 Adapter. Then set the IP Address to 192.168.1.x (1 < x < 255), then set Subnet Mask to 255.255.255.0 and Default Gateway to 192.168.1.1

6. Do not enable *'Automatic DHCP Configuration'* and put anything in those *'WINS Server'* input areas unless you're in a Windows NT domain and you know what you're doing.

7. Click *'DNS'*, fill in the appropriate information mentioned in STEP 6 of section 3.3.1, then click *'OK'* when you're done with it.

8. Click *'Advanced'*, check *'Enable DNS for Windows Name Resolution'* and *'Enable LMHOSTS lookup'* if you're using a look up host file, similar to the one mentioned in STEP 10 of section 3.3.1

9. Click *'OK'* on all dialog boxes and restart system.

10. Ping the linux box to test the network connection: *'File/Run'*, type: ping 192.168.1.1
    (This is only a LAN connection testing, you can't ping the outside world yet.)

3.3.4 Configuring UNIX Based Systems

1. If you haven't installed your network card and recompile your kernel with the appropriate adapter driver, do so now.

2. Install TCP/IP networking, such as the nettools package, if you don't have it already.

3. Set *IPADDR* to 192.168.1.x (1 < x < 255), then set *NETMASK* to 255.255.255.0, *GATEWAY* to 192.168.1.1, and *BROADCAST* to 192.168.1.255
   For example, you can edit the /etc/sysconfig/network-scripts/ifcfg-eth0 file on a Red Hat Linux system, or simply do it through the Control Panel.
   (it's different in SunOS, BSDi, Slackware Linux, etc...)

4. Add your domain name service (DNS) and domain search suffix in `/etc/resolv.conf`

5. You may want to update your `/etc/networks` file depending on your settings.

6. Restart the appropriate services, or simply restart your system.

7. Issue a `ping` command: `ping 192.168.1.1` to test the connection to your gateway machine. (This is only a LAN connection testing, you can't `ping` the outside world yet.)

3.3.5 Configuring DOS using NCSA Telnet package

1. If you haven't installed your network card, do so now.

2. Load the appropriate packet driver. For an NE2000 card, issue `nwpd 0x60 10 0x300`, with your network card set to IRQ 10 and hardware address at 0x300

3. Make a new directory, and then unpack the NCSA Telnet package: `pkunzip tel2308b.zip`

4. Use a text editor to open the `config.tel` file

5. Set `myip=192.168.1.x` ($1 < x < 255$), and netmask=255.255.255.0

6. In this example, you should set `hardware=packet, interrupt=10, ioaddr=60`

7. You should have at least one individual machine specification set as the gateway, i.e. the Linux host:

```
name=default
host=yourlinuxhostname
hostip=192.168.1.1
gateway=1
```

8. Have another specification for a domain name service:

```
name=dns.domain.com ; hostip=123.123.123.123; nameserver=1
```

Note: substitute the appropriate information about the DNS that your Linux host uses

9. Save your `config.tel` file

10. Telnet to the linux box to test the network connection: `telnet 192.168.1.1`

3.3.6 Configuring MacOS Based System Running MacTCP

1. If you haven't installed the appropriate driver software for your Ethernet adapter, now would be a very good time to do so.

2. Open the *MacTCP control panel*. Select the appropriate network driver (Ethernet, NOT EtherTalk) and click on the *'More...'* button.

3. Under *'Obtain Address:'*, click *'Manually'*.

4. Under *'IP Address:'*, select *class C* from the popup menu. Ignore the rest of this section of the dialog box.

5. Fill in the appropriate information under *'Domain Name Server Information:'*.

6. Under *'Gateway Address:'*, enter 192.168.1.1

7. Click *'OK'* to save the settings. In the main window of the *MacTCP control panel*, enter the IP address of your Mac (192.168.1.x, $1 < x < 255$) in the *'IP Address:'* box.

8. Close the *MacTCP control panel*. If a dialog box pops up notifying you to do so, restart the system.

9. You may optionally ping the Linux box to test the network connection. If you have the freeware program *MacTCP Watcher*, click on the *'Ping'* button, and enter the address of your Linux box (192.168.1.1) in the dialog box that pops up. (This is only a LAN connection testing, you can't ping the outside world yet.)

10. You can optionally create a `Hosts` file in your System Folder so that you can use the hostnames of the machines on your LAN. The file should already exist in your System Folder, and should contain some (commented-out) sample entries which you can modify according to your needs.

Mini-HOWTO

3.3.7 Configuring MacOS Based System Running Open Transport

1. If you haven't installed the appropriate driver software for your Ethernet adapter, now would be a very good time to do so.

2. Open the *TCP/IP Control Panel* and choose *'User Mode ...'* from the *Edit* menu. Make sure the user mode is set to at least *'Advanced'* and click the *'OK'* button.

3. Choose *'Configurations...'* from the *File* menu. Select your *'Default'* configuration and click the *'Duplicate...'* button. Enter 'IP Masq' (or something to let you know that this is a special configuration) in the *'Duplicate Configuration'* dialog, it will probably say something like *'Deafault copy'*. Then click the *'OK'* button, and the *'Make Active'* button

4. Select *'Ethernet'* from the *'Connect via:'* pop-up.

5. Select the appropriate item from the *'Configure:'* pop-up. If you don't know which option to choose, you probably should re-select your *'Default'* configuration and quit. I use *'Manually'*.

6. Enter the IP address of your Mac (192.168.1.x, $1 < x < 255$) in the *'IP Address:'* box.

7. Enter 255.255.255.0 in the *'Subnet mask:'* box.

8. Enter 192.168.1.1 in the *'Router address:'* box.

9. Enter the IP addresses of your domain name servers in the *'Name server addr.:'* box.

10. Enter the name of your Internet domain (e.g. 'microsoft.com') in the *'Starting domain name'* box under *'Implicit Search Path:'*.

11. The following procedures are optional. Incorrect values may cause erratic behavior. If your not sure, it's probably better to leave them blank, unchecked and/or un- selected. Remove any information from those fields, if necessary. As far as I know there is no way through the TCP/IP dialogs, to tell the system not to use a previously select alternate "Hosts" file. If you know, I would be interested.
Check the *'802.3'* if your network requires 802.3 frame types.

12. Click the *'Options...'* button to make sure that the TCP/IP is active. I use the *'Load only when needed'* option. If you run and quit TCP/IP applications many times without rebooting your machine, you may find that unchecking the *'Load only when needed'* option will prevent/reduce the effects on your machines memory management. With the item unchecked the TCP/IP protocol stacks are always loaded and available for use. If checked, the TCP/IP stacks are automatically loaded when needed and un- loaded when not. It's the loading and unloading process that can cause your machines memory to become fragmented.

13. You may ping the Linux box to test the network connection. If you have the freeware program *MacTCP Watcher*, click on the *'Ping'* button, and enter the address of your Linux box (192.168.1.1) in the dialog box that pops up. (This is only a LAN connection testing, you can't ping the outside world yet.)

14. You can create a `Hosts` file in your System Folder so that you can use the hostnames of the machines on your LAN. The file may or may not already exist in your System Folder. If so, it should contain some (commented-out) sample entries which you can modify according to your needs. If not, you can get a copy of the file from a system running MacTCP, or just create your own (it follows a subset of the Unix `/etc/hosts` file format, described on RFC952). Once you've created the file, open the *TCP/IP control panel*, click on the *'Select Hosts File...'* button, and open the `Hosts` file.

15. Click the close box or choose *'Close'* or *'Quit'* from the *File* menu, and then click the *'Save'* button to save the changes you have made.

16. The changes take effect immediately, but rebooting the system won't hurt.

3.3.8 Configuring Novell network using DNS

1. If you haven't installed the appropriate driver software for your Ethernet adapter, now would be a very good time to do so.

2. Downloaded tcpip16.exe from `<ftp.novell.com/pub/updates/unixconn/lwp5>`

3. `edit c:\nwclient\startnet.bat`
   : (here is a copy of mine)

```
        SET NWLANGUAGE=ENGLISH
        LH LSL.COM
        LH KTC2000.COM
        LH IPXODI.COM
        LH tcpip
        LH VLM.EXE
        F:
```

4. edit c:\nwclient\net.cfg

   : (change link driver to yours i.e. NE2000)

```
    Link Driver KTC2000
            Protocol IPX 0 ETHERNET_802.3
            Frame ETHERNET_802.3
            Frame Ethernet_II
            FRAME Ethernet_802.2

    NetWare DOS Requester
            FIRST NETWORK DRIVE = F
            USE DEFAULTS = OFF
            VLM = CONN.VLM
            VLM = IPXNCP.VLM
            VLM = TRAN.VLM
            VLM = SECURITY.VLM
            VLM = NDS.VLM
            VLM = BIND.VLM
            VLM = NWP.VLM
            VLM = FIO.VLM
            VLM = GENERAL.VLM
            VLM = REDIR.VLM
            VLM = PRINT.VLM
            VLM = NETX.VLM

    Link Support
            Buffers 8 1500
            MemPool 4096
    Protocol TCPIP
            PATH SCRIPT       C:\NET\SCRIPT
            PATH PROFILE      C:\NET\PROFILE
            PATH LWP_CFG      C:\NET\HSTACC
            PATH TCP_CFG      C:\NET\TCP
            ip_address        xxx.xxx.xxx.xxx
            ip_router         xxx.xxx.xxx.xxx
```

5. and finally created

   c:\bin\resolv.cfg

   :

```
    SEARCH DNS HOSTS SEQUENTIAL
    NAMESERVER 207.103.0.2
    NAMESERVER 207.103.11.9
```

6. I hope this helps some people get their Novell Nets online, BTW this can be done using Netware 3.1x or 4.x

3.3.9 Configuring OS/2 Warp

1. If you haven't installed the appropriate driver software for your Ethernet adapter, now would be a very good time to do so.

2. Install the TCP/IP protocoll if you don't have it already.

3. Go to *Programms/TCP/IP (LAN) / TCP/IP* Settings

4. In *'Network'* add your TCP/IP Address and set your Netmask (255.255.255.0)

5. Under *'Routing'* press *'Add'*. Set the *Type* to *'default'* and type the IP Address of your Linux Box in the Field *'Router Address'*. (192.168.1.1).

6. Set the same DNS (Nameserver) Address that your Linux host uses in *'Hosts'*.

7. Close the TCP/IP control panel. Say yes to the following question(s).

8. Reboot your system

9. You may ping the Linux box to test the network configuration. Type `'ping 192.168.1.1'` in a 'OS/2 Command prompt Window'. When ping packets are received all is ok.

3.3.10 Configuring Other Systems

The same logic should apply to setting up other platforms. Consult the sections above. If you're interested in writing about any of systems that have not been covered yet, please send a detail setup instruction to *ambrose@writeme.com* and *dranch@trinnet.net*.

3.4 Configuring IP Forwarding Policies

At this point, you should have your kernel and other required packages installed, as well as your modules loaded. Also, the IP addresses, gateway, and DNS should be all set on the **OTHER** machines.

Now, the only thing left to do is to use the IP firewalling tools to forward appropriate packets to the appropriate machine:

** This can be accomplished in many different ways. The following suggestions and examples worked for me, but you may have different ideas, please refer to section 4.4 and the ipchains(2.2.x) / ipfwadm(2.0.x) manpages for details. ******

** This section ONLY provides you with the bare minimum rule set to get IP Masquerade working while security issue is not being considered. It is highly recomended that you spend some time to apply appropriate firewall rules to tighten security. **

3.4.1 Linux 2.2.x Kernels

ipfwadm is no longer the tool for manipulating ipmasq rules for 2.2.x kernels, please use ipchains.

```
ipchains -P forward DENY
ipchains -A forward -s yyy.yyy.yyy.yyy/x -j MASQ
```

where x is one of the following numbers according to the class of your subnet, and yyy.yyy.yyy.yyy is your network address.

```
netmask         | x  | Subnet
~~~~~~~~~~~~~~~~|~~~~|~~~~~~~~~~~~~~~~
255.0.0.0       | 8  | Class A
255.255.0.0     | 16 | Class B
255.255.255.0   | 24 | Class C
255.255.255.255 | 32 | Point-to-point
```

You may also use the format yyy.yyy.yyy.yyy/xxx.xxx.xxx.xxx, where xxx.xxx.xxx.xxx specfies your subnet mask such as 255.255.255.0

For example, if I'm on a class C subnet, I would have entered:

```
ipchains -P forward DENY
ipchains -A forward -s 192.168.1.0/24 -j MASQ

or

ipchains -P forward DENY
ipchains -A forward -s 192.168.1.0/255.255.255.0 -j MASQ
```

You can also do it on a per machine basis. For example, if I want 192.168.1.2 and 192.168.1.8 to have access to the Internet, but not the other machines, I would have entered:

```
ipchains -P forward DENY
ipchains -A forward -s 192.168.1.2/32 -j MASQ
ipchains -A forward -s 192.168.1.8/32 -j MASQ
```

Do **not** make your default policy be masquerading - otherwise someone who can manipulate their routing will be able to tunnel straight back through your gateway, using it to masquerade their identity!

Again, you can add these lines to the /etc/rc.local files, one of the rc files you prefer, or do it manually every time you need IP Masquerade.

For detail ipchains usage, please refer to the *Linux IPCHAINS HOWTO* <http://metalab.unc.edu/mdw/HOWTO/IPCHAINS-HOWTO.html>

3.4.2 Linux 2.0.x Kernels

```
ipfwadm -F -p deny
ipfwadm -F -a m -S yyy.yyy.yyy.yyy/x -D 0.0.0.0/0

or

ipfwadm -F -p deny
ipfwadm -F -a masquerade -S yyy.yyy.yyy.yyy/x -D 0.0.0.0/0
```

where x is one of the following numbers according to the class of your subnet, and yyy.yyy.yyy.yyy is your network address.

```
netmask          | x  | Subnet
~~~~~~~~~~~~~~~~~|~~~~|~~~~~~~~~~~~~~~~
255.0.0.0        | 8  | Class A
255.255.0.0      | 16 | Class B
255.255.255.0    | 24 | Class C
255.255.255.255  | 32 | Point-to-point
```

You may also use the format yyy.yyy.yyy.yyy/xxx.xxx.xxx.xxx, where xxx.xxx.xxx.xxx specfies your subnet mask such as 255.255.255.0

For example, if I'm on a class C subnet, I would have entered:

```
ipfwadm -F -p deny
ipfwadm -F -a m -S 192.168.1.0/24 -D 0.0.0.0/0
```

Since bootp request packets comes without valid IP's once the client knows nothing about it, for people with a bootp server in the masquerade/firewall machine it is necessary to use the following before the deny command:

```
ipfwadm -I -a accept -S 0/0 68 -D 0/0 67 -W bootp_clients_net_if_name -P udp
```

You can also do it on a per machine basis. For example, if I want 192.168.1.2 and 192.168.1.8 to have access to the Internet, but not the other machines, I would have entered:

```
ipfwadm -F -p deny
ipfwadm -F -a m -S 192.168.1.2/32 -D 0.0.0.0/0
ipfwadm -F -a m -S 192.168.1.8/32 -D 0.0.0.0/0
```

What appears to be a common mistake is to make the first command be this

```
ipfwadm -F -p masquerade
```

Do **not** make your default policy be masquerading - otherwise someone who can manipulate their routing will be able to tunnel straight back through your gateway, using it to masquerade their identity!

Again, you can add these lines to the /etc/rc.local files, one of the rc files you prefer, or do it manually every time you need IP Masquerade.

Please read section 4.4 for a detail guide on Ipfwadm

3.5 Testing IP Masquerade

It's time to give it a try, after all these hard work. Make sure the connection of your Linux hosts to the Internet is okay.

You can try browsing some *'INTERNET!!!'* web sites on your **OTHER** machines, and see if you get it. I recommend using an IP address rather than a hostname on your first try, because your DNS setup may not be correct.

For example, you can access the Linux Documentation Project site http://metalab.unc.edu/mdw/linux.html with an entry of *http://152.19.254.81/mdw/linux.html*

If you see The Linux Documentation Project homepage, then congratulations! It's working! You may then try one with hostname entry, and then ping, telnet, ssh, ftp, Real Audio, True Speech, whatever supported by IP Masquerade.....

So far, I have no trouble with the above settings, and it's full credit to the people who spend their time making this wonderful feature working.

4 Other IP Masquerade Issues and Software Support

4.1 Problems with IP Masquerade

Some protocols will not currently work with masquerading because they either assume things about port numbers, or encode data in their data stream about addresses and ports - these latter protocols need specific proxies built into the masquerading code to make them work.

4.2 Incoming services

Masquerading cannot handle incoming services at all. There are a few ways of allowing them, but they are completely separate from masquerading, and are really part of standard firewall practice.

If you do not require high levels of security then you can simply redirect ports. There are various ways of doing this - I use a modified redir program (which I hope will be available from sunsite and mirrors soon). If you wish to have some level of authorisation on incoming connections then you can either use TCP wrappers or Xinetd on top of redir (0.7 or above) to allow only specific IP addresses through, or use some other tools. The TIS Firewall Toolkit is a good place to look for tools and information.

More details can be found at *IP Masquerade Resource* <http://ipmasq.cjb.net>.

A section on more about forwarding services will be added soon.

4.3 Supported Client Software and Other Setup Note

** The following list is not being maintained anymore. Please refer to *this page* <http://dijon. nais.com/~nevo/masq/>**on applications that work thru Linux IP masquerading and** *IP Masquerade Resource* <http://ipmasq.cjb.net/>**for more detail. ****

Generally, application that uses TCP and UDP should work. If you have any suggestion, hints, or questions about applications with IP Masquerade, please visit this page on *applications that work thru Linux IP masquerading* <http://dijon.nais.com/~nevo/masq/>by Lee Nevo.

4.3.1 Clients that Work

General Clients

HTTP

all supported platforms, surfing the web

POP & SMTP

all supported platforms, email client

Telnet

all supported platforms, remote session

FTP

all supported platforms, with ip_masq_ftp.o module (not all sites work with certain clients; e.g. some sites cannot be reached using ws_ftp32 but works with netscape)

Archie

all supported platforms, file searching client (not all archie clients are supported)

NNTP (USENET)

all supported platforms, USENET news client

VRML

Windows(possibly all supported platforms), virtual reality surfing

traceroute

mainly UNIX based platforms, some variations may not work

ping

all platforms, with ICMP patch

anything based on IRC

all supported platforms, with ip_masq_irc.o modules

Gopher client

all supported platforms

WAIS client

all supported platforms

Multimedia Clients

Real Audio Player

Windows, network streaming audio, with ip_masq_raudio module loaded

True Speech Player 1.1b

Windows, network streaming audio

Internet Wave Player

Windows, network streaming audio

Worlds Chat 0.9a

Windows, Client-Server 3D chat program

Alpha Worlds

Windows, Client-Server 3D chat program

Internet Phone 3.2

Windows, Peer-to-peer audio communications, people can reach you only if you initiate the call, but people cannot call you

Powwow

Windows, Peer-to-peer Text audio whiteboard communications, people can reach you only if you initiate the call, but people cannot call you

CU-SeeMe

all supported platforms, with cuseeme modules loaded, please see *IP Masquerade Resource* <http://ipmasq. cjb.net/> for detail

VDOLive

Windows, with vdolive patch

Note: Some clients such as IPhone and Powwow may work even if you're not the one who initiate the call by using *ipautofw package* (refer to section 4.6)

Other Clients

NCSA Telnet 2.3.08

DOS, a suite containing telnet, ftp, ping, etc.

PC-anywhere for windows 2.0

MS-Windows, Remotely controls a PC over TCP/IP, only work if it is a client but not a host

Socket Watch

uses ntp - network time protocol

Linux net-acct package

Linux, network administration-account package

4.3.2 Clients that do not Work

Intel Internet Phone Beta 2

Connects but voice travels one way (out) Traffic only

Intel Streaming Media Viewer Beta 1

Cannot connect to server

Netscape CoolTalk

Cannot connect to opposite side

talk,ntalk

will not work - requires a kernel proxy to be written.

WebPhone

Cannot work at present (it makes invalid assumptions about addresses).

X

Untested, but I think it cannot work unless someone builds an X proxy, which is probably an external program to the masquerading code. One way of making this work is to use **ssh** as the link and use the internal X proxy of that to make things work!

4.3.3 Platforms/OS Tested as on OTHER machines

- Linux
- Solaris
- Windows 95
- Windows NT (both workstation and server)
- Windows For Workgroup 3.11 (with TCP/IP package)
- Windows 3.1 (with Chameleon package)
- Novel 4.01 Server
- OS/2 (including Warp v3)
- Macintosh OS (with MacTCP or Open Transport)
- DOS (with NCSA Telnet package, DOS Trumpet works partially)
- Amiga (with AmiTCP or AS225-stack)
- VAX Stations 3520 and 3100 with UCX (TCP/IP stack for VMS)
- Alpha/AXP with Linux/Redhat
- SCO Openserver (v3.2.4.2 and 5)
- IBM RS/6000 running AIX

Basically all OS platforms support TCP/IP and give you the option to specify the gateway/router should work with IP Masquerade.

4.4 IP Firewall Administration (ipfwadm)

This section provides a more in-depth guide on using ipfwadm.

This is a setup for a firewall/masquerade system behind a PPP link with a static PPP address follows. Trusted interface is 192.168.255.1, PPP interface has been changed to protect the guilty :). I listed each incoming and outgoing interface individually to catch IP spoofing as well as stuffed routing and/or masquerading. Also anything not explicitly allowed is forbidden!

```
#!/bin/sh
#
# /etc/rc.d/rc.firewall, define the firewall configuration, invoked from
# rc.local.
#

PATH=/sbin:/bin:/usr/sbin:/usr/bin

# testing, wait a bit then clear all firewall rules.
# uncomment following lines if you want the firewall to automatically
# disable after 10 minutes.
# (sleep 600; \
```

```
# ipfwadm -I -f; \
# ipfwadm -I -p accept; \
# ipfwadm -O -f; \
# ipfwadm -O -p accept; \
# ipfwadm -F -f; \
# ipfwadm -F -p accept; \
# ) &

# Incoming, flush and set default policy of deny. Actually the default policy
# is irrelevant because there is a catch all rule with deny and log.
ipfwadm -I -f
ipfwadm -I -p deny
# local interface, local machines, going anywhere is valid
ipfwadm -I -a accept -V 192.168.255.1 -S 192.168.0.0/16 -D 0.0.0.0/0
# remote interface, claiming to be local machines, IP spoofing, get lost
ipfwadm -I -a deny -V your.static.PPP.address -S 192.168.0.0/16 -D 0.0.0.0/0 -o
# remote interface, any source, going to permanent PPP address is valid
ipfwadm -I -a accept -V your.static.PPP.address -S 0.0.0.0/0 -D
your.static.PPP.address/32
# loopback interface is valid.
ipfwadm -I -a accept -V 127.0.0.1 -S 0.0.0.0/0 -D 0.0.0.0/0
# catch all rule, all other incoming is denied and logged. pity there is no
# log option on the policy but this does the job instead.
ipfwadm -I -a deny -S 0.0.0.0/0 -D 0.0.0.0/0 -o

# Outgoing, flush and set default policy of deny. Actually the default policy
# is irrelevant because there is a catch all rule with deny and log.
ipfwadm -O -f
ipfwadm -O -p deny
# local interface, any source going to local net is valid
ipfwadm -O -a accept -V 192.168.255.1 -S 0.0.0.0/0 -D 192.168.0.0/16
# outgoing to local net on remote interface, stuffed routing, deny
ipfwadm -O -a deny -V your.static.PPP.address -S 0.0.0.0/0 -D 192.168.0.0/16 -o
# outgoing from local net on remote interface, stuffed masquerading, deny
ipfwadm -O -a deny -V your.static.PPP.address -S 192.168.0.0/16 -D 0.0.0.0/0 -o
# outgoing from local net on remote interface, stuffed masquerading, deny
ipfwadm -O -a deny -V your.static.PPP.address -S 0.0.0.0/0 -D 192.168.0.0/16 -o
# anything else outgoing on remote interface is valid
ipfwadm -O -a accept -V your.static.PPP.address -S your.static.PPP.address/32 -D
0.0.0.0/0
# loopback interface is valid.
ipfwadm -O -a accept -V 127.0.0.1 -S 0.0.0.0/0 -D 0.0.0.0/0
# catch all rule, all other outgoing is denied and logged. pity there is no
# log option on the policy but this does the job instead.
ipfwadm -O -a deny -S 0.0.0.0/0 -D 0.0.0.0/0 -o

# Forwarding, flush and set default policy of deny. Actually the default policy
# is irrelevant because there is a catch all rule with deny and log.
ipfwadm -F -f
ipfwadm -F -p deny
# Masquerade from local net on local interface to anywhere.
ipfwadm -F -a masquerade -W ppp0 -S 192.168.0.0/16 -D 0.0.0.0/0
# catch all rule, all other forwarding is denied and logged. pity there is no
# log option on the policy but this does the job instead.
ipfwadm -F -a deny -S 0.0.0.0/0 -D 0.0.0.0/0 -o
```

You can block traffic to a particular site using the -I, -O or -F. Remember that the set of rules are scanned top to bottom and -a means "append" to the existing set of rules so any restrictions need to come before global rules. For example (and untested) :-

Using -I rules. Probably the fastest but it only stops the local machines, the firewall itself can still access the "forbidden" site. Of course you might want to allow that combination.

```
... start of -I rules ...
# reject and log local interface, local machines going to 204.50.10.13
ipfwadm -I -a reject -V 192.168.255.1 -S 192.168.0.0/16 -D 204.50.10.13/32 -o
# local interface, local machines, going anywhere is valid
ipfwadm -I -a accept -V 192.168.255.1 -S 192.168.0.0/16 -D 0.0.0.0/0
... end of -I rules ...
```

Using -O rules. Slowest because the packets go through masquerading first but this rule even stops the firewall accessing the forbidden site.

```
... start of -O rules ...
# reject and log outgoing to 204.50.10.13
ipfwadm -O -a reject -V your.static.PPP.address -S your.static.PPP.address/32 -D
204.50.10.13/32 -o
# anything else outgoing on remote interface is valid
ipfwadm -O -a accept -V your.static.PPP.address -S your.static.PPP.address/32 -D
0.0.0.0/0
... end of -O rules ...
```

Using -F rules. Probably slower than -I and this still only stops masqueraded machines (i.e. internal), firewall can still get to forbidden site.

```
... start of -F rules ...
# Reject and log from local net on PPP interface to 204.50.10.13.
ipfwadm -F -a reject -W ppp0 -S 192.168.0.0/16 -D 204.50.10.13/32 -o
# Masquerade from local net on local interface to anywhere.
ipfwadm -F -a masquerade -W ppp0 -S 192.168.0.0/16 -D 0.0.0.0/0
... end of -F rules ...
```

No need for a special rule to allow 192.168.0.0/16 to go to 204.50.11.0, it is covered by the global rules.

There is more than one way of coding the interfaces in the above rules. For example instead of -V 192.168.255.1 you can code -W eth0, instead of -V your.static.PPP.address you can use -W ppp0. Personal choice and documentation more than anything.

4.5 IP Firewalling Chains (ipchains)

This is the firewall ruleset manipulation tool primarily intended for 2.2.x kernels (there is a patch for this to work on 2.0.x).

We will update this section to give several examples on ipchains usage soon.

See the *Linux IP Firewalling Chains page* <http://www.rustcorp.com/linux/ipchains/> and *Linux IPCHAINS HOWTO* <http://metalab.unc.edu/mdw/HOWTO/IPCHAINS-HOWTO.html> for detail.

4.6 IP Masquerade and Demand-Dial-Up

1. If you would like to setup your network to automatically dial up the Internet, the *diald* demand dial-up package will be of great utility.

Mini-HOWTO

2. To setup the diald, please check out the *Setting Up Diald for Linux Page* <http://home.pacific.net.sg/harish/diald.config.html>

3. Once diald and IP masq have been setup, you can go to any of the client machines and initiate a web, telnet or ftp session.

4. Diald will detect the incoming request, then dial up your ISP and establish the connection.

5. There is a timeout that will occur with the first connection. This is inevitable if you are using analog modems. The time taken to establish the modem link and the PPP connections will cause your client program to timeout. This can be avoided if you are using an ISDN connection. All you need to do is to terminate the current process on the client and restart it.

4.7 IPautofw Packet Fowarder

IPautofw <ftp://ftp.netis.com/pub/members/rlynch/ipautofw.tar.gz> is a generic forwarder of TCP and UDP for Linux masquerading. Generally to utilize a package which requires UDP, a specific ip_masq module needs to be loaded; ip_masq_raudio, ip_masq_cuseeme, ... Ipautofw acts in a more generic manner, it will forward any type of traffic including those which the application specific modules will not forward. This may create a security hole if not administered correctly.

4.8 CU-SeeMe and Linux IP-Masquerade Teeny How-To

Provided by *Michael Owings* <mailto:mikey@swampgas.com>.

4.8.1 Introduction

This section will explain the necessary steps to get CU-SeeMe (both the Cornell and White Pine versions) working together with Linux's IP-Masquerade.

CU-SeeMe is a desktop video conferencing package available for both Windows and Macintosh clients. A free version is available from *Cornell University* <http://cu-seeme.cornell.edu>. A significantly enhanced commercial version can be obtained from *White Pine Software* <http://www.wpine.com>.

IP Masquerading allows one or more workstations on a LAN to "masquerade" behind a single Linux machine connected to the Internet. The workstations on the LAN can access the Internet almost transparently even without valid IP addresses. The Linux box rewrites outgoing packets from the LAN to the Internet in such a way that they they appear to originate from the Linux machine. Response packets coming back in are re-written and routed back to the correct workstations on the LAN. This arrangement allows many Internet applications to run transparently from the lan workstations. For some other applications (such as CU-SeeMe), however, the Linux masquerade code needs a little help to route packets properly. This help usually comes in the form of special kernel loadable modules. For more information on IP-Masquerading, see *The Linux IP Masquerading Website* <http://www.indyramp.com/masq/>.

4.8.2 Getting It Running

First you will need a properly configured kernel. You should have full support compiled in for both IP-Masquerading and IP AutoForwarding. IP Autoforwarding is available as a config option on kernels 2.0.30 and later – you will need to patch earlier kernels. See the *Linux IP Masquerade Resource* <http://ipmasq.cjb.net> for pointers to the IP-Autoforwarding material.

Next, you will need to get the latest version of ip_masq_cuseeme.c. The latest version is available via anon ftp from *ftp://ftp.swampgas.com/pub/cuseeme/ip_masq_cuseeme.c*. This new module will also be rolled up into the kernel 2.0.31 distribution. You should replace the version in your kernel distribution with this new version. ip_masq_cuseeme.c normally resides in net/ipv4 off of the Linux source tree. You should compile and install this module.

Now, you should set up ip autoforwarding for udp ports 7648-7649 as follows:

```
ipautofw -A -r udp 7648 7649 -c udp 7648 -u
```

OR

```
ipautofw -A -r udp 7648 7649 -h www.xxx.yyy.zzz
```

The first form will allow calls to/from the last workstation to use port 7648 (the primary cu-seeme port) . The second invocation of ipautofw will allow cu-seeme calls only to/from www.xxx.yyy.zzz. I prefer the former invocation, as it is more flexible because there is no need to specify a fixed workstation IP. However, this invocation also requires a workstation to have previously placed an outgoing call in order to receive incoming calls.

Note that both invocations leave UDP ports 7648-7649 on the client machines open to the outside world – and while this does not pose an enormous security hazard, you should use appropriate caution.

Finally, load up the new ip_masq_cuseeme module as follows:

```
modprobe ip_masq_cuseeme
```

You should now be able to fire up CU-SeeMe from a masqueraded machine on your lan and connect to a remote reflector, or another CU-Seeme user. You should also be able to get incoming calls. Note that outside callers should call using the ip of your linux gateway, NOT the masqueraded workstation.

4.8.3 Restrictions/Caveats

Password Protected Reflectors No way, no how. Uh-uh. Negatory. White Pine uses the source IP (as computed by the client program) to encrypt the password prior to transmission. Since we have to rewrite this address, the reflector ends up using the wrong source IP to decrypt it, which yields an invalid password. This will only be fixed if White Pine changes their password encryption scheme (which I have suggested), or if they would be willing to make their password encryption routines public so I could add in a fix to ip_masq_cuseeme. While chances for the latter solution are vanishingly small, I would encourage anyone reading this to contact White Pine and suggest the former approach. As the traffic on this page is relatively high, I suspect we could generate enough email to get this problem moved up on White Pine's list of priorities.

Thanx to Thomas Griwenka for bringing this to my attention.

Running a Reflector You should not attempt to run a reflector on the same machine where you have ip_masq_cuseeme and ipautoforwarding for port 7648 loaded. It simply won't work, as both setups require port 7648. Either run the reflector on another Internet-reachable host, or unload CU-SeeMe client support prior to running the reflector.

Multiple CU-SeeMe Users You cannnot have multiple simultaneous CU-SeeMe users on the LAN at this time. This is due largely to CU-SeeMe's stubborn insistence on always sending to port 7648, which can only be redirected (easily) to one LAN workstation at a time.

Using the -c (control port) invocation of ipautofw above, you can avoid to having to specify a fixed workstation address allowed to use CU-SeeMe – the first workstation to send anything out on control port 7648 will be designated to receive traffic on 7648-7649. 5 minutes or so after this workstation has been inactive on port 7648, another workstation can come along and use CU-SeeMe.

Help on Setting up CU-SeeMe Feel free to email any comments or questions to *mikey@swampgas.com*. Or if you wish, you can *call me up via CU-SeeMe* <http://www.swampgas.com/vc/vc.htm>.

4.9 Other Related Tools

We will be updating this section soon to cover more ipmasq related tools such as ipportfw and masqadmin.

5 Frequently Asked Questions

If you can think of any useful FAQ, please send it to *ambrose@writeme.com* and *dranch@trinnet.net*. Please clearly state the question and an appropriate answer. Thank you!

5.1 Does IP Masquerade work with dynamically assigned IP?

Yes, it works with dynamic IP assigned by your ISP, usually by a DHCP server. As long as you have an valid Internet IP address, it should work. Of course, static IP works too.

5.2 Can I use cable modem, DSL, satellite link, etc. to connect to the Internet and use IP Masquerade?

Sure, as long as Linux supports that network interface, it should work.

5.3 What applications are supported with IP Masquerade?

It is very difficult to keep track of a list of "working applications". However, most of the normal Internet applications are supported, such as browsing the Internet (Netscape, MSIE, etc.), ftp (such as WS_FTP), Real Audio, telnet, SSH, POP3 (incoming email - Pine, Outlook), SMTP (outgoing email), etc.

Applications involving more complicated protocols or special connection methods such as video conferencing software need special helper tools.

For more detail, please see this page about *applications that work thru Linux IP masquerading* <http://dijon. nais.com/~nevo/masq/> by Lee Nevo.

5.4 How can I get IP Masquerade running on Redhat, Debian, Slackware, etc.?

No matter what Linux distribution you got, the procedures for setting up IP Masquerade mentioned in this HOWTO should apply. Some distributions may have GUI or special configuration files that make the setup easier. We try our best to write the HOWTO as general as possible.

5.5 I've just upgraded to the 2.2.x kernels, why is IP Masquerade not working?

There are several things you should check assuming your Linux ipmasq box already have proper connection to the Internet and your LAN:

- Make sure you have the necessary features and modules are compiled and loaded. See earlier sections for detail.
- Check /usr/src/linux/Documentation/Changes and make sure you have the minimal requirement for the network tools installed.
- Make sure you have enabled IP forwarding. Try running echo "1" > /proc/sys/net/ipv4/ip_forwarding.
- You should use *ipchains* <http://www.rustcorp.com/linux/ipchains/> to manipulate ipmasq and firewalling rules.
- Go through all setup and configuration again! A lot of time it's just a typo or a stupid mistake you oversee.

5.6 I've just upgraded to the kernels 2.0.30 or later, why is IP Masquerade not working?

There are several things you should check assuming your Linux ipmasq box already have proper connection to the Internet and your LAN:

- Make sure you have the necessary features and modules are compiled and loaded. See earlier sections for detail.

- Check `/usr/src/linux/Documentation/Changes` and make sure you have the minimal requirement for the network tools installed.

- Make sure you have enabled IP forwarding. Try running `echo "1" > /proc/sys/net/ipv4/ip_forward`.

- You should use *ipfwadm* `<http://www.xos.nl/>` to manipulate ipmasq and firewalling rules. You need to patch the 2.0.x kernels to use ipchains.

- Go through all setup and configuration again! A lot of time it's just a typo or a stupid mistake you oversee.

5.7   I can't get IP Masquerade to work! What options do I have for Windows Platform?

Giving up a free, reliable, high performance solution that works on minimal hardware and pay a fortune for something that needs more hardware, lower performance and less reliable? (IMHO. And yes, I have real life experience with these ;-)

Okay, it's your call. Do a web search on MS Proxy Server, Wingate, or see www.winfiles.com. Don't tell anyone I sent you.

5.8   I've checked all my configurations, I still can't get IP Masquerade to work. What should I do?

- Stay calm. Get yourself a cup of tea and have a rest, then try the suggestions mentioned below.

- Check the *IP Masquerade Mailing List Archive* `<http://home.indyramp.com/lists/masq/>`, most likely your answer is there waiting for you.

- Post your question to the IP Masquerade Mailing List, see next the FAQ for deatil. Please only try this if you cannot find the answer from the mailing list archive.

- Post your question to related Linux networking newsgroup.

- Send email to *ambrose@writeme.com* and *dranch@trinnet.net*. You have a better chance of getting a reply if you send to both of us. David is usually pretty good on replying, and I do not want to comment on my response time.

- Check your configurations again :-)

5.9   How do I join the IP Masquerade Mailing List?

Join the Linux IP Masquerading mailing list by sending an email to *masq-subscribe@indyramp.com*.

Subject and body of the message are IGNORED. This gives you every message on the list as it comes out. You are welcome to use this form if you need it, but if you can stand the digest, please choose it instead. The digest puts less of a load on the list servers. Note that you can only post from an account/address you are subscribed from.

For more commands, email *masq-help@tori.indyramp.com*.

5.10   I want to help on IP Masquerade development. What can I do?

Join the Linux IP Masquerading DEVELOPERS list and ask the great developers there, by sending an email to *masq-dev-subscribe@tori.indyramp.com* (or for a digest format, use *masq-dev-digest-subscribe@tori.indyramp.com*).

DON'T ask non IP Masquerade development related questions there!!!!

Mini-HOWTO

5.11 Where can I find more information on IP Masquerade?

You can find more information on IP Masquerade at the *Linux IP Masquerade Resource* `<http://ipmasq.cjb.net/>` that David and I also maintained. See section 6.2 for availability.

You may also find more information at *The Semi-Original Linux IP Masquerading Web Site* `<http://www.indyramp.com/masq/>` maintained by Indyramp Consulting, who also provided the ipmasq mailing lists.

5.12 I want to translate this HOWTO to another language, what should I do?

Make sure the lanaguage you want to translate to is not already covered by someone else, a list of available HOWTO translations is available at the *Linux IP Masquerade Resource* `<http://ipmasq.cjb.net/>`.

Send an email to *ambrose@writeme.com* and I will send you the SGML source of the latest version of the HOWTO.

5.13 This HOWTO seems out of date, are you still maintaining it? Can you include more information on ...? Are there any plans for making this better?

Yes, this HOWTO is still being maintained. I'm guilty of being too busy working on two jobs and don't have much time to work on this, my apology. However, with the addition of David Ranch as the HOWTO maintainer, things should improve.

If you think of a topic that could be included in the HOWTO, please send email to me and David. It will be even better if you can provide that information. I and David will include the information into the HOWTO if it is appropriate. And many thanks for your contributions.

We have a lot of new ideas and plans for improving the HOWTO, such as case studies that will cover different network setup involving IP Masquerade, more on security, ipchains usage, ipfwadm/ipchains ruleset examples, more FAQs, more coverage on protocol and port forwarding utilities like masqadmin, etc. If you think you can help, please do. Thanks.

5.14 I got IP Masquerade working, it" great! I want to thank you guys, what can I do?

Thank the developers and appreciate the time and effort they spent on this. Send an email to us and let us know how happy you are. Introduce other people to Linux and help them when they have problems.

6 Miscellaneous

6.1 Useful Resources

- *IP Masquerade Resource page* `<http://ipmasq.cjb.net/>` should have enough information for setting up IP Masquerade

- *IP masquerade mailing list archive* `<http://www.indyramp.com/masq/list/>` contains some of the recent messages sent to the mailing list.

- This *Linux IP Masquerade mini HOWTO* `<http://ipmasq.cjb.net/ipmasq-HOWTO.html>` for kernel 2.2.x and 2.0.x

- *IP Masquerade HOWTO for kernel 1.2.x* `<http://ipmasq.cjb.net/ipmasq-HOWTO-1.2.x.txt>` if you're using an older kernel

- *IP masquerade FAQ* `<http://www.indyramp.com/masq/ip_masquerade.txt>` has some general information

- *Linux IPCHAINS HOWTO* `<http://metalab.unc.edu/mdw/HOWTO/IPCHAINS-HOWTO.html>` and *http://www.rustcorp.com/linux/ipchains/* has lots of information for ipchains usage, as well as source and binaries for the ipchains.

- *X/OS Ipfwadm page* `<http://www.xos.nl/linux/ipfwadm/>` contains sources, binaries, documentation, and other information about the `ipfwadm` package

- A page on *applications that work thru Linux IP masquerading* `<http://dijon.nais.com/~nevo/masq/>` by Lee Nevo provides tips and tricks on getting applications to work with IP Masquerade.

- The *LDP Network Administrator's Guide* `<http://metalab.unc.edu/mdw/LDP/nag/nag.html>` is a must for beginners trying to set up a network.

- *Trinity OS Doc* `<http://www.ecst.csuchico.edu/~dranch/LINUX/TrinityOS.wri>`, a very compreshensive guide on Linux networking.

- *Linux NET-3 HOWTO* `<http://metalab.unc.edu/mdw/HOWTO/NET-3-HOWTO.html>` also has lots of useful information about Linux networking

- *Linux ISP Hookup HOWTO* `<http://metalab.unc.edu/mdw/HOWTO/ISP-Hookup-HOWTO.html>` and *Linux PPP HOWTO* `<http://metalab.unc.edu/mdw/HOWTO/PPP-HOWTO.html>` gives you information on how to connect your Linux host to the Internet

- *Linux Ethernet-Howto* `<http://metalab.unc.edu/mdw/HOWTO/Ethernet-HOWTO.html>` is a good source of information about setting up a LAN running ethernet

- You may also be interested in *Linux Firewalling and Proxy Server HOWTO* `<http://metalab.unc.edu/mdw/HOWTO/Firewall-HOWTO.html>`

- *Linux Kernel HOWTO* `<http://metalab.unc.edu/mdw/HOWTO/Kernel-HOWTO.html>` will guide you through the kernel compilation process

- Other *Linux HOWTOs* `<http://metalab.unc.edu/mdw/HOWTO/HOWTO-INDEX-3.html>` such as Kernel HOWTO

- Posting to the USENET newsgroup: *comp.os.linux.networking*

6.2   Linux IP Masquerade Resource

The *Linux IP Masquerade Resource* `<http://ipmasq.cjb.net/>` is a website dedicated to Linux IP Masquerade information also maintained by David Ranch and I. It usually has the latest information related to IP Masquerade and may have information that is not being included in the HOWTO.

You may find the Linux IP Masquerade Resource at the following locations:

- *http://ipmasq.cjb.net/*, Primary Site, redirected to *http://www.tor.shaw.wave.ca/~ambrose/*

- *http://ipmasq2.cjb.net/*, Secondary Site, redirected to *http://www.geocities.com/SiliconValley/Heights/2288/*

6.3   Thanks to

- David Ranch, dranch@trinnet.net
  help maintaining this HOWTO and the Linux IP Masquerade Resource Page, ..., too many to list here :-)

- Michael Owings, mikey@swampgas.com
  on providing section for CU-SeeMe and Linux IP-Masquerade Teeny How-To

- Gabriel Beitler, gbeitler@aciscorp.com
  on providing section 3.3.8 (setting up Novel)

- Ed Doolittle, dolittle@math.toronto.edu
  on suggestion to `-V` option in `ipfwadm` command for improved security

- Matthew Driver, mdriver@cfmeu.asn.au
  on helping extensively on this HOWTO, and providing section 3.3.1 (setting up Windows 95)

Mini-HOWTO

- Ken Eves, ken@eves.com
  on the FAQ that provides invaluable information for this HOWTO

- Ed. Lott, edlott@neosoft.com
  for a long list of tested system and software

- Nigel Metheringham, Nigel.Metheringham@theplanet.net
  on contributing his version of IP Packet Filtering and IP Masquerading HOWTO, which make this HOWTO a better
  and technical in-depth document
  section 4.1, 4.2, and others

- Keith Owens, kaos@ocs.com.au
  on providing an excellent guide on ipfwadm section 4.2
  on correction to `ipfwadm -deny` option which avoids a security hole, and clarified the status of `ping` over IP
  Masquerade

- Rob Pelkey, rpelkey@abacus.bates.edu
  on providing section 3.3.6 and 3.3.7 (setting up MacTCP and Open Transport)

- Harish Pillay, h.pillay@ieee.org
  on providing section 4.5 (dial-on-demand using diald)

- Mark Purcell, purcell@rmcs.cranfield.ac.uk
  on providing section 4.6 (IPautofw)

- Ueli Rutishauser, rutish@ibm.net
  on providing section 3.3.9 (setting up OS/2 Warp)

- John B. (Brent) Williams, forerunner@mercury.net
  on providing section 3.3.7 (setting up Open Transport)

- Enrique Pessoa Xavier, enrique@labma.ufrj.br
  on the bootp setup suggestion

- developers of IP Masquerade for this great feature

    - Delian Delchev, delian@wfpa.acad.bg
    - Nigel Metheringham, Nigel.Metheringham@theplanet.net
    - Keith Owens, kaos@ocs.com.au
    - Jeanette Pauline Middelink, middelin@polyware.iaf.nl
    - David A. Ranch, trinity@value.net
    - Miquel van Smoorenburg, miquels@q.cistron.nl
    - Jos Vos, jos@xos.nl
    - Paul Russell, Paul.Russell@rustcorp.com.au
    - And more who I may have failed to mention here (please let me know)

- all users sending feedback and suggestion to the mailing list, especially the ones who reported errors in the document and the clients that are supported and not supported

- I appologize if I have not included information that some fellow users sent me. There are many suggestions and ideas sent to me, but I just do not have enough time to verify or I lost track of them. I am trying my best to incorporate all the information sent to me into the HOWTO. I thank you for the effort, and I hope you understand my situation.

6.4 Reference

- IP masquerade FAQ by Ken Eves
- IP masquerade mailing list archive by Indyramp Consulting
- Ipfwadm page by X/OS
- Various networking related Linux HOWTOs

"IP Sub-Networking Mini-Howto" Robert Hart

hartr@interweft.com.au
v1.0, 31 March 1997

This document describes why and how to subnetwork an IP network - that is using a single A, B or C Class network number to function correctly on several interconnected networks.

1 Copyright

This document is distributed under the terms of the GNU Public License (GPL).

This document is directly supported by InterWeft IT Consultants (Melbourne, Australia).

The latest version of this document is available at the InterWeft WWW site at *InterWeft IT Consultants* <http://www.interweft.com.au/> and from *The Linux Documentation Project* <http://sunsite.unc.edu/LDP>.

2 Introduction

With available IP network numbers rapidly becoming an endangered species, efficient use of this increasingly scarce resource is important.

This document describes how to split a single IP network number up so that it can be used on several different networks.

This document concentrates on C Class IP network numbers - but the principles apply to A and B class networks as well.

2.1 Other sources of information

There are a number of other sources of information that are of relevance for both detailed and background information on IP numbers. Those recommended by the author are:-

- *The Linux Network Administrators Guide* <http://sunsite.unc.edu/LDP/LDP/nag/nag.html>.
- *The Linux System Administration Guide* <http://linuxwww.db.erau.edu/SAG/>.
- *TCP/IP Network Administration by Craig Hunt, published by O'Reilly and Associates* <http://www.ora.com/catalog/tcp/noframes.html>.

3 The Anatomy of IP numbers

Before diving into the delight of sub-networking, we need to establish some IP number basics.

3.1 IP numbers belong to Interfaces - NOT hosts!

First of all, let's clear up a basic cause of misunderstanding - IP numbers are **not** assigned to hosts. IP numbers are assigned to network interfaces on hosts.

Eh - what's that?

Whilst many (if not most) computers on an IP network will possess a single network interface (and have a single IP number as a consequence), this is not the only way things happen. Computers and other devices can have several (if not many) network interfaces - and each interface has its own IP number.

Mini-HOWTO

So a device with 6 active interfaces (such as a router) will have 6 IP numbers - one for each interface to each network to which it is connected. The reason for this becomes clear when we look at an IP network!

Despite this, most people refer to *host addresses* when referring to an IP number. Just remember, this is simply shorthand for *the IP number of this particular interface on this host*. Many (if not the majority) of devices on the Internet have only a single interface and thus a single IP number.

3.2 IP Numbers as "Dotted Quads"

In the current (IPv4) implementation of IP numbers, IP numbers consist of 4 (8 bit) bytes - giving a total of 32 bits of available information. This results in numbers that are rather large (even when written in decimal notation). So for readability (and organisational reasons) IP numbers are usually written in the 'dotted quad' format. The IP number

```
192.168.1.24
```

is an example of this - 4 (decimal) numbers separated by (.) dots.

As each one of the four numbers is the decimal representation of an 8 bit byte, each of the 4 numbers can range from 0 to 255 (that is take on 256 unique values - remember, zero is a value too).

In addition, part of the IP number of a host identifies the network on which the host resides, the remaining 'bits' of the IP number identify the host (oops - network interface) itself. Exactly how many bits are used by the network ID and how many are available to identify hosts (interfaces) on that network is determined by the network 'class'.

3.3 Classes of IP Networks

There are three classes of IP numbers

- Class A IP network numbers use the leftmost 8 bits (the leftmost of the dotted quads) to identify the network, leaving 24 bits (the remaining three dotted quads) to identify host interfaces on that network.
  Class A addresses **always** have the leftmost bit of the leftmost byte a zero - that is a decimal value of 0 to 127 for the first dotted quad. So there are a maximum of 128 class A network numbers available, with each one containing up to 33,554,430 possible interfaces.

  However, the networks 0.0.0.0 (known as the default route) and 127.0.0.0 (the loop back network) have special meanings and are not available for use to identify networks. So there are only 126 *available* A class network numbers.

- Class B IP network numbers use the leftmost 16 bits (the leftmost two dotted quads) to identify the network, leaving 16 bits (the last two dotted quads) to identify host interfaces. Class B addresses always have the leftmost 2 bits of the leftmost byte set to 1 0. This leaves 14 bits left to specify the network address giving 32767 available B class networks. B Class networks thus have a range of 128 to 191 for the first of the dotted quads, with each network containing up to 32,766 possible interfaces.

- Class C IP network numbers use the leftmost 24 bits (the leftmost three bytes) to identify the network, leaving 8 bits (the rightmost byte) to identify host interfaces. Class C addresses always start with the leftmost 3 bits set to 1 1 0 or a range of 192 to 255 for the leftmost dotted quad. There are thus 4,194,303 available C class network numbers, each containing 254 interfaces. (C Class networks with the first byte greater than 223 are however reserved and unavailable for use).

In summary:

```
Network class   Usable range of first byte values (decimal)
      A                    1 to 126
      B                  128 to 191
      C                  192 to 254
```

There are also special addresses that are reserved for 'unconnected' networks - that is networks that use IP but are not connected to the Internet, These addresses are:-

- One A Class Network
  10.0.0.0
- 16 B Class Networks
  172.16.0.0 - 172.31.0.0
- 256 C Class Networks 192.168.0.0 - 192.168.255.0

You will note that this document uses these sequences throughout to avoid confusion with 'real' networks and hosts.

3.4   Network numbers, interface addresses and broadcast addresses

IP numbers can have three possible meanings:-

- the address of an IP network (a group of IP devices sharing common access to a transmission medium - such as all being on the same Ethernet segment). A network number will always have the interface (host) bits of the address space set to 0 (unless the network is sub-networked - as we shall see);
- the broadcast address of an IP network (the address used to 'talk', simultaneously, to all devices in an IP network). Broadcast addresses for a network always have the interface (host) bits of the the address space set to 1 (unless the network is sub-networked - again, as we shall see).
- the address of an interface (such as an Ethernet card or PPP interface on a host, router, print server etc). These addresses can have any value in the host bits **except** all zero or all 1 - because with the host bits all 0, the address is a network address and with the host bits all 1 the address is the broadcast address.

In summary and to clarify things

```
For an A class network...
(one byte of network address space followed by three bytes of host
address space)


        10.0.0.0 is an A Class  network number  because all the host
                bits of the address space are 0
        10.0.1.0 is a host address on this network
        10.255.255.255.255 is the broadcast address of this network
                because all the host bits of the address space are 1

For a B class network...
(two bytes of network address space followed by two bytes of host
address space)


        172.17.0.0 is a B Class network number
        172.17.0.1 is a host address on this network
        172.17.255.255 is the network broadcast address

For a C Class network...
(three bytes of network address space followed by one byte of host
address space)


        192.168.3.0 is a C Class network number
        192.168.3.42 is a host address on this network
        192.168.3.255 is the network broadcast address
```

Almost all IP network numbers remaining available for allocation at present are C Class addresses.

3.5 The network mask

The network mask is more properly called the subnetwork mask. However, it is generally referred to as the network mask.

It is the network mask and its implications on how IP addresses are interpreted *locally* on an IP network segment that concerns us most here, as this determines what (if any) sub-networking occurs.

The standard (sub-) network mask is all the network bits in an address set to '1' and all the host bits set to '0'. This means that the standard network masks for the three classes of networks are:-

- A Class network mask: 255.0.0.0
- B Class network mask: 255.255.0.0
- C Class network mask: 255.255.255.0

There are two important things to remember about the network mask:-

- The network mask affects only the **local** interpretation of **local** IP numbers (where local means on this particular network segment);
- The network mask is **not** an IP number - it is used to modify how local IP numbers are interpreted locally.

4   What are subnets?

A subnet is a way of taking a single IP network address and **locally** splitting it up so that this single network IP address can actually be used on several interconnected local networks. Remember, a single IP network number can only be used on a single network.

The important word here is **locally**: as far as the world outside the machines and physical networks covered by the sub-netted IP network are concerned, nothing whatsoever has changed - it is still just a single IP network. This is important - sub-networking is a **local** configuration and is invisible to the rest of the world.

5   Why subnetwork?

The reasons behind sub-networking date back to the early specification of IP - where just a few sites were running on Class A network numbers, which allow for millions of connected hosts.

It is obviously a huge traffic and administration problem if all IP computers at a large site need to be connected to the same network: trying to manage such a huge beast would be a nightmare and the network would (almost certainly) collapse under the load of its own traffic (saturate).

Enter sub-networking: the A class IP network address can be split up to allow its distribution across several (if not many) separate networks. The management of each separate network can easily be delegated as well.

This allows small, manageable networks to be established - quite possibly using different networking technologies. Remember, you cannot mix Ethernet, Token Ring, FDDI, ATM etc on the same physical network - they can be interconnected, however!

Other reasons for sub-networking are:-

- Physical site layout can create restrictions (cable run lengths) in terms of the how the physical infrastructure can be connected, requiring multiple networks. Sub-networking allows this to be done in an IP environment using a single IP network number.

   This is in fact now very commonly done by ISPs who wish to give their permanently connected clients with local networks static IP numbers.

- Network traffic is sufficiently high to be causing significant slow downs. By splitting the network up using subnetworks, traffic that is local to a network segment can be kept local - reducing overall traffic and speeding up network connectivity without requiring more actual network bandwidth;

- Security requirements may well dictate that different classes of users do not share the same network - as traffic on a network can always be intercepted by a knowledgeable user. Sub-networking provides a way to keep the marketing department from snooping on the R & D network traffic (or students from snooping on the administration network)!

- You have equipment which uses incompatible networking technologies and need to interconnect them (as mentioned above).

6 How to subnetwork a IP network number

Having decided that you need to subnetwork your IP network number, how do you go about it? The following is an overview of the steps which will then be explained in detail:-

- Set up the physical connectivity (network wiring and network interconnections - such as routers;

- Decide how big/small each subnetwork needs to be in terms of the number of devices that will connect to it - ie how many usable IP numbers are required for each individual segment.

- Calculate the appropriate network mask and network addresses;

- Give each interface on each network its own IP address and the appropriate network mask;

- Set up the routes on the routers and the appropriate gateways, routes and/or default routes on the networked devices;

- Test the system, fix problems and then relax!

For the purpose of this example, we will assume we are sub-networking a single C class network number: 192.168.1.0

This provides for a maximum of 254 connected interfaces (hosts), plus the obligatory network number (192.168.1.0) and broadcast address (192.168.1.255).

6.1 Setting up the physical connectivity

You will need to install the correct cabling infrastructure for all the devices you wish to interconnect designed to meet your physical layout.

You will also need a mechanism to interconnect the various segments together (routers, media converters etc.).

A detailed discussion of this is obviously impossible here. Should you need help, there are network design/installation consultants around who provide this sort of service. Free advice is also available on a number of Usenet news groups (such as comp.os.linux.networking).

6.2 Subnetwork sizing

There is a play off between the number of subnetworks you create and 'wasted' IP numbers.

Every individual IP network has two addresses unusable as interface (host) addresses - the network IP number itself and the broadcast address. When you subnetwork, each subnetwork requires its own, unique IP network number and broadcast address - and these have to be valid addresses from within the range provided by the IP network that you are sub-networking.

So, by sub-networking an IP network into two separate subnetworks, there are now **two** network addresses and **two** broadcast addresses - increasing the 'unusable' interface (host) addresses; creating 4 subnetworks creates **eight** unusable interface (host) addresses and so on.

In fact the smallest usable subnetwork consists of 4 IP numbers:-

- Two usable IP interface numbers - one for the router interface on that network and one for the single host on that network.
- One network number.
- One broadcast address.

Quite why one would want to create such a small network is another question! With only a single host on the network, any network communication must go out to another network. However, the example does serve to show the law of diminishing returns that applies to sub-networking.

In principle, you can only divide your IP network number into 2^n (where n is one less that the number of host bits in your IP network number) equally sized subnetworks (you can subnetwork a subnetwork and combine subnetworks however).

So be realistic about designing your network design - you want the **minimum** number of separate local networks that is consistent with management, physical, equipment and security constraints!

6.3 Calculating the subnetwork mask and network numbers

The network mask is what performs all the **local** magic of dividing an IP network into subnetworks.

The network mask for an un-sub-networked IP network number is simply a dotted quad which has all the 'network bits' of the network number set to '1' and all the host bits set to '0'.

So, for the three classes of IP networks, the standard network masks are:-

- Class A (8 network bits) : 255.0.0.0
- Class B (16 network bits): 255.255.0.0
- Class C (24 network bits): 255.255.255.0

The way sub-networking operates is to *borrow* one or more of the available host bits and make then make interfaces **locally** interpret these borrowed bits as part of the network bits. So to divide a network number into two subnetworks, we would borrow one host bit by setting the appropriate bit in the network mask of the first (normal) host bit to '1'.

For a C Class address, this would result in a netmask of
11111111.11111111.11111111.10000000
or 255.255.255.128

For our C Class network number of 192.168.1.0, these are some of the sub-networking options you have:-

```
No of      No of
subnets    Hosts/net   netmask
2          126         255.255.255.128  (11111111.11111111.11111111.10000000)
4          62          255.255.255.192  (11111111.11111111.11111111.11000000)
8          30          255.255.255.224  (11111111.11111111.11111111.11100000)
16         14          255.255.255.240  (11111111.11111111.11111111.11110000)
32         6           255.255.255.248  (11111111.11111111.11111111.11111000)
64         2           255.255.255.252  (11111111.11111111.11111111.11111100)
```

In principle, there is absolutely no reason to follow the above way of subnetworking where network mask bits are added from the most significant host bit to the least significant host bit. However, if you do not do it this way, the resulting IP numbers will be in a *very* odd sequence! This makes it extremely difficult for us humans to decide to which subnetwork an IP number belongs as we are not too good at thinking in binary (computers on the other hand are and will use whatever scheme you tell them with equal equanimity).

Having decided on the appropriate netmask, you then need to work out what the various Network and broadcast addresses are - and the IP number range for each of these networks. Again, considering only a C Class IP Network number and listing only the *final* (host part) we have:-

Netmask	Subnets	Network	B'cast	MinIP	MaxIP	Hosts	Total Hosts
128	2	0	127	1	126	126	
		128	255	129	254	126	252
192	4	0	63	1	62	62	
		64	127	65	126	62	
		128	191	129	190	62	
		192	255	193	254	62	248
224	8	0	31	1	30	30	
		32	63	33	62	30	
		64	95	65	94	30	
		96	127	97	126	30	
		128	159	129	158	30	
		160	191	161	190	30	
		192	223	193	222	30	
		224	255	225	254	30	240

As can be seen, there is a very definite sequence to these numbers, which make them fairly easy to check. The 'downside' of sub-networking is also visible in terms of the reducing total number of available host addresses as the number of subnetworks increases.

With this information, you are now in a position to assign host and network IP numbers and netmasks.

7 Routing

If you are using a Linux PC with two network interfaces to route between two (or more) subnets, you need to have IP Forwarding enabled in your kernel. Do a

```
cat /proc/ksyms | grep ip_forward
```

You should get back something like...

```
00141364 ip_forward_Rf71ac834
```

If you do not, then you do not have IP-Forwarding enabled in your kernel and you need to recompile and install a new kernel.

For the sake of this example, let us assume that you have decided to subnetwork you C class IP network number 192.168.1.0 into 4 subnets (each of 62 usable interface/host IP numbers). However, two of these subnets are being combined into a larger single network, giving three physical networks.

These are :-

Network	Broadcast	Netmask	Hosts
192.168.1.0	192.168.1.63	255.255.255.192	62
192.168.1.64	192.168.1.127	255.255.255.192	62
182.168.1.128	192.168.1.255	255.255.255.126	124 (see note)

Mini-HOWTO

Note: the reason the last network has only 124 usable network addresses (not 126 as would be expected from the network mask) is that it is really a 'super net' of two subnetworks. Hosts on the other two networks will interpret 192.168.1.192 as the *network* address of the 'non-existent' subnetwork. Similarly, they will interpret 192.168.1.191 as the broadcast address of the 'non-existent' subnetwork.

So, if you use 192.168.1.191 or 192 as host addresses on the third network, then machines on the two smaller networks will not be able to communicate with them.

This illustrates an important point with subnetworks - the usable addresses are determined by the **SMALLEST** subnetwork in that address space.

7.1   The routing tables

Let us assume that a computer running Linux is acting as a router for this network. It will have three network interfaces to the local LANs and possibly a fourth interface to the Internet (which would be its default route.

Let us assume that the Linux computer uses the lowest available IP address in each subnetwork on its interface to that network. It would configure its network interfaces as

Interface	IP Address	Netmask
eth0	192.168.1.1	255.255.255.192
eth1	192.168.1.65	255.255.255.192
eth2	192.168.1.129	255.255.255.128

The routing it would establish would be

Destination	Gateway	Genmask	Iface
192.168.1.0	0.0.0.0	255.255.255.192	eth0
192.168.1.64	0.0.0.0	255.255.255.192	eth1
192.168.1.128	0.0.0.0	255.255.255.128	eth2

On each of the subnetworks, the hosts would be configured with their own IP number and net mask (appropriate for the particular network). Each host would declare the Linux PC as its gateway/router, specifying the Linux PCs IP address for its interface on to that particular network.

Robert Hart Melbourne, Australia March 1997.

"Linux Mail-Queue mini-HOWTO" Leif Erlingsson

`leif@lege.com` and Jan P Tietze `jptietze@mail.hh.provi.de`
v2.02, 3 September 1997, sendmail 8.8.7
Queue Remote Mail + Deliver Local Mail The Configuration Changes Neccessary to Make Sendmail Deliver Local Mail ***Now*** While Stashing Remote Mail in The Queue Until "I Say So".

Contents

1   Introduction

The document is written by two authors. The NON dial-on-demand solutions part (oldest part) is written by Leif Erlingsson <leif@lege.com>, and the newer dial-on-demand solutions part is written by Jan P Tietze <jptietze@mail.hh.provi.de>.

2   NON dial-on-demand solutions PART

Written by Leif Erlingsson <leif@lege.com>.

The original version of this part contained a lot of unnecessary stuff. This is all it takes, really...

2.1   Starting sendmail

Slackware et al: /etc/rc.d/rc.M:

```
echo "Starting sendmail daemon (/usr/sbin/sendmail -bd -os) [queue on-
ly mode]..."
/usr/sbin/sendmail -bd -os        # NOT "-bd -q 15m", the "standard" flags!
```

Mini-HOWTO

RedHat et al: /etc/rc.d/init.d/sendmail.init:

```
echo -n "Starting sendmail: [queue only mode]"
daemon sendmail -bd -os          # NOT daemon sendmail -bd -q1h
```

The -os is not really essential, all it does is this:

```
SuperSafe [s] Be super-safe when running things, i.e.,
        always instantiate the queue file,  even  if
        you are going to attempt immediate delivery.
        Sendmail always instantiates the queue  file
        before  returning  control  the client under
        any  circumstances.  This  should   really
        always be set.
```

This should already be configured in the default sendmail.cf anyway.

2.2   Configuring sendmail

Serious sendmail users use the m4 source for this. I recommend this solution if you ever plan on upgrading sendmail and also make anything but trivial changes to sendmail.cf.

If you never intend to fix sendmail so envelope return headers et al works even though you might be on dynamic dial in IP or something, then you may not need to get the m4 source.

2.2.1   Configuring sendmail.cf directly, for trivial configurations

This way of doing things is extremeley version dependent vs. sendmail.cf versions. The following solution is *only* valid for sendmail-8.8.x.

Edit /etc/sendmail.cf:

```
# avoid connecting to "expensive" mailers on initial submission?
O HoldExpensive=True
```

... later ...

```
#####  @(#)smtp.m4      8.33 (Berkeley) 7/9/96  #####

Msmtp,          P=[IPC], F=mDFMuXe, S=11/31, R=21, E=\r\n, L=990,
                T=DNS/RFC822/SMTP,
                A=IPC $h
Mesmtp,         P=[IPC], F=mDFMuXae, S=11/31, R=21, E=\r\n, L=990,
                T=DNS/RFC822/SMTP,
                A=IPC $h
Msmtp8,         P=[IPC], F=mDFMuX8e, S=11/31, R=21, E=\r\n, L=990,
                T=DNS/RFC822/SMTP,
                A=IPC $h
Mrelay,         P=[IPC], F=mDFMuXa8e, S=11/31, R=61, E=\r\n, L=2040,
                T=DNS/RFC822/SMTP,
                A=IPC $h
```

The important flag above is "e". Don't fuss if the other flags look different in your file. Keep your flags as-is, only add "e" to your flags according to the above examples, unless it's there already. "e" marks the mailers as "expensive".

2.2.2 Configuring sendmail.cf using m4 source

In the following I will, for simplicity, assume that the sendmail version is 8.8.7. If you have a different version, replace 8.8.7 with that version number below! Also, the instructions will not work for older versions of sendmail. Get the latest sendmail!

Download the sendmail source. Try "http://WWW.Sendmail.ORG" or possibly "ftp.sendmail.org".

I also recommend that you obtain my patch for allowing envelope sender reverse aliasing and other nice stuff to really make you take control over your mail environment.

Write to "Sendmail Patch <sendmail@lege.com>", Subject: "sendmail-8.8.7", if 8.8.7 is your sendmail version.

They are also available from "http://www.lege.com", as is the sgml source of this mini-HOWTO!

You don't have to get my patches in order to get "Queue Remote Mail + Deliver Local Mail" to work. My patches solve other things. But I just thought this would be a nice place to mention them, as many Linux users will find them extremely useful. (They will even give you properly working virtual domains, if you like. The virtual domains don't have to be "local". They will give you "xaliases", or in other words "reverse aliasing".)

Unpack the sendmail source. You may get /usr/src/sendmail-8.8.7/. cd /usr/src/sendmail-8.8.7/cf

Now overlay my patch, if you want it, otherwise skip this step: If you don't want to use procmail as Local Delivery Agent, save away your /usr/src/sendmail-8.8.7/cf/ostype/linux.m4 before doing this... Save my patch to "/tmp/sendmail-8.8.7-cf-cpio-idcmu.gz", then...

```
cd /usr/src/sendmail-8.8.7/cf
gzip -dc < /tmp/sendmail-8.8.7-cf-cpio-idcmu.gz | cpio -idcmu
```

If you didn't want to use procmail, write back the saved copy of /usr/src/sendmail-8.8.7/cf/ostype/linux.m4 again.

And regardless of if you applied my patch or not, you must make sure these lines or very similar ones are added to /usr/src/sendmail-8.8.7/cf/cf/yourhostname.smtp.mc (but if you applied my patch you may want to investigate filenames containing the word "elijah", under /usr/src/sendmail-8.8.7/cf):

```
dnl # Defer Delivery to "expensive" mailers until next time the
dnl # queue is processed using "O HoldExpensive=True" and make
dnl # sure smtp mailers are "expensive".
dnl # (See original "sendmail" book Chapter 30: Options,
dnl # "Oc - Don't connect to expensive mailers", or
dnl # 2nd Edition "sendmail" book Chapter 34.8.29,
dnl # "HoldExpensive (c), Queue for expensive mailers".)
dnl #                       / Leif Erlingsson <leif@lege.com>
define('confCON_EXPENSIVE', 'True')
define(SMTP_MAILER_FLAGS, e)
MAILER(local)dnl
MAILER(smtp)dnl
```

2.3 Menu support suggestions

The 1.x versions of this document contained Menu support suggestions for /var/X11R6/lib/fvwm/system.fvwmrc. I have dropped those in the current version, but they are available on request:

Write to "Menu support suggestions <fvwmrc@lege.com>", Subject: "Menu support suggestions"

3 Dial-on-demand solutions PART

Written by Jan P Tietze <jptietze@mail.hh.provi.de>.

Many Linux users access the Internet through a dialup line, and many have decided to implement dial-on-demand facilities on their system. That is, whenever an IP packet of some sort has to leave the local network or the local host, the link to an Internet Service Provider (ISP) will automatically be established. The link will be dropped after some period of time that no packet has travelled across.

Although this is very comfortable and cost effective, there is one special case in which this is neither comfortable (as the time to bring up a "traditional" modem dialup is very noticeable) nor cost effective, and this is sending e-mail. E-Mail is commonly sent by SMTP, either delivered by your own system or through a SMTP host on the Internet that usually resides in your ISP's network.

With dialup lines, every time you send a message the link will have to be brought up. This is quite okay if you send only one message, but if you happen to create and send multiple messages, bringing up the line more than once can be tedious and cost ineffective. Also, if your ISP imposes limits as to what times you are allowed to login, this would also restrict you to postpone messages at certain times of the day, and you would have to manually send them later.

Section 1 of this document will solve the situation, however in situations where an external DNS lookup would cause the link up, the link will still be established even if e-mail is just being queued. The reason is that sendmail wishes to "canonify" host names.

The solution to this problem is twofold: First, we'll have to moderately change sendmail.cf. And then we have to define the process of actual mail delivery. Personally, I prefer to have cron do the job for me and describe the necessary changes below.

3.1   Configuring sendmail.cf

For the reasons stated in [1.2], I recommend modifying the m4 sources instead of editing sendmail.cf directly. It will actually save you a lot of hassle and make configuration changes more verbose.

First, perform all the changes described in the first part of this document. Then go through the dial-on-demand specific stuff.

3.1.1   Configuring sendmail.cf directly, for trivial configurations

Configuring directly is highly impractical and anything but verbose, but obviously, this is your decision.

Close to very bottom of your sendmail.cf should be a line that reads:

```
R$* < @ $* $P > $*                    $: $1 < @ $[ $2 $3 $] > $4
```

Precede that line with a "#" so that it reads

```
#R$* < @ $* $P > $*                   $: $1 < @ $[ $2 $3 $] > $4
```

3.1.2   Configuring sendmail.cf using the m4 source.

Add the following line to /usr/src/sendmail-8.8.7/cf/cf/yourhostname.smtp.mc:

```
FEATURE(nocanonify)dnl
```

Your final sendmail.cf can then be built by issuing the following commands. Remember to always back up your old /etc/sendmail.cf before installing the new one:

```
cp /etc/sendmail.cf /etc/sendmail.cf.bak
cd /usr/src/sendmail-8.8.7/cf/cf
m4 yourhostname.smtp.mc > /etc/sendmail.cf
```

3.2 Adding dial delay

It is oftentimes useful, especially when using modem lines, to have a dial delay installed. This means that if sendmail tries to initiate a connection in an attempt to send an e-mail (and this causes the line to go up) but the link actually takes more time to get established than what sendmail thinks should be a reasonable timeout, sendmail will simply wait some seconds and then retry.

3.2.1 Configuring sendmail.cf directly

Somewhere in your sendmail.cf could be a line that would read:

```
#O DialDelay=10s
```

(or very similar). Delete the "#". If there's no "#" at the beginning of the line, things should be considered okay (it just means this had already been enabled before).

If there is no such line in your sendmail.cf, add one (it is a wise thing to do to add this in the "options" part of the file):

```
O DialDelay=10s
```

Now change the "10s" part to the number of seconds you deem suitable.

3.2.2 Configuring sendmail.cf using m4 source

Add the following line to /usr/src/sendmail-8.8.7/cf/cf/yourhostname.smtp.mc:

```
define('confDIAL_DELAY','10s')
```

Now change the "10s" part to the number of seconds you deem suitable.

Your final sendmail.cf can then be built by issuing the following commands. Remember to always back up your old /etc/sendmail.cf before installing the new one:

```
cp /etc/sendmail.cf /etc/sendmail.cf.bak
cd /usr/src/sendmail-8.8.7/cf/cf
m4 yourhostname.smtp.mc > /etc/sendmail.cf
```

4 Delivering e-mail

E-Mail delivery can be invoked by issuing the command "sendmail -q". For those who are interested in what sendmail actually does, "sendmail -q -v" will give a more verbose version of the delivery process.

It is very convenient to automate the process of e-mail delivery. A tool commonly used for this process is cron.

4.1 How to have e-mail delivered at special times.

Edit your crontab:

```
crontab -e
```

Add lines of the form:

```
05 18-23,0-7    * * Mon,Tue,Wed,Thu,Fri /usr/sbin/sendmail -q
05 *            * * Sat,Sun             /usr/sbin/sendmail -q
```

Please refer to the crontab man page (available through "man 5 \ crontab") for further information. I think the format is pretty obvious. The example crontab entries shown above send e-mail (if, and only if, e-mail is available from the queue) 5 minutes after an hour on weekdays, starting at 6:05 pm, and stopping at 7:05 am. On weekends, e-mail is delivered 5 minutes after an hour, starting at 12:05 pm on Saturday, and stopping 11:05 pm on Sunday.

As a dial-on-demand user, it is sometimes desirable to have your system collect your e-mail via the POP3 protocol at certain times of the day. You could therefore add an entry similar to the following to your crontab:

```
0 21              * * * popclient -3 -u <your pop3 user name
goes here> -p <put your password here> -o /var/spool/mail/<the user
on your system that should receive the collected e-mail>
<mailhost.somedomain.com>
```

Of course, this should all go on a single line.

Then, save the file and leave the editor. The crontab should now be installed.

Part LXV

"Mail2News Mini-Howto" Robert Hart

v1.0, 4 November 1996

iweft@ipax.com.au InterWeft IT Consultants Melbourne, Australia This document describes how to set up your news server and the mail2news.pl software to link mailing lists to local news groups.

1 Copyright and such

This document is directly supported by InterWeft IT Consultants (Melbourne, Australia).

The latest version of this document is available at the InterWeft WWW site at *InterWeft IT Consultants* <http://203.29.72.65/>.

2 Introduction

Most Internet sites are always seeking ways to improve the usage of the limited bandwidth awailable across their link to the Internet.

Should more than one user subscribe to the same mailing list, there is going to be traffic duplication. If there are a number of such duplications - or the traffic on the lists is high, the consumption of bandwidth increases.

By subscribing the **site** to a list (if this is allowed by the list owner) and 'gating' the email traffic to the local news server, it is possible to make mailing lists accessible to all site users, or, using the security features of 'innd', to limit the access to certain users.

Such a site subscription (particularly if there are a number of high traffic lists) can make worthwhile savings in bandwidth usage.

Reading list traffic in news reader also offers users the advantages of threading (which is not available in many mail user agents) and keeps their mail 'inbox' free for possibly more urgent, personal email.

This mini-HOWTO describes setting up the 'mail2news.pl' script to accomplish this.

2.1 Finding mail2news.pl

The author has been unable to find mail2news.pl on CPAN (the Comprehensive Perl Archive Network) - but it may just have been overlooked. It is however on sunsite.unc.edu - somewhere - and also on ftp.redhat.com.

As this Perl script is not lengthy, it is appended to this howto.

3 Overview of the system

It is probably easiest to understand how this system works by tracking a message from the mailing list to the newsgroup and then a message posted to the local newsgroup (gated to the mailing list) and see how they are handled.

3.1 Mail from the mailing list

Mail from the mailing list is sent to all subscribed mail addresses. A special mail alias is subscribed to the mailing list in question and so all traffic to and from the list is sent by the list server to this address.

When mail from the mailing list arrives at the local machine, the mail alias pipes the incoming message to `mail2news.pl`. The mail alias also specifies the destination (local) newsgroup.

The `mail2news.pl` script processes the message, applying news headers and then uses `rnews` or `inews` to post the message to the newsgroup.

3.2 Messages posted to the local newsgroup

The local newsgroup is set up as a **moderated** group, as this allows us to take advantage of the email capabilities of innd. Any messages posted to a moderated group are **not** immediately submitted to the group. Instead, messages are emailed to the moderator of the group.

By declaring the moderator of the local newsgroup to be mailing list address, all locally posted messages to the newsgroup are automatically mailed out to the mailing list by innd and **only** appear once they have been received back through `mail2news.pl` which adds the necessary 'approved' line to the messages and are thus acceptable to innd for posting to the newsgroup.

4 Setting up mail2news

Put the `mail2news.pl` script in a suitable location. I favour `/usr/local/scripts`, but the location is up to you.

You will need to edit script as follows:-

- At the top of the script, make sure you are pointing at the local Perl binary

```
#!/usr/bin/perl
# point at the correct location of perl
```

- I had problems with the three following lines. Commenting them out does not cause a problem.

```
( $version  ) = $] =~ /(\d+\.\d+).*\nPatch level/;
die "$program: requires at least version 3 of perl\n"
        if $version < 3;
```

- Edit the following lines to point at the posting program (I use rnews) and you news host:-

```
# $inews = "/usr/bin/inews";
# $iopts = "-h -o \"mail2news gateway\"";
$inews = "/usr/bin/rnews";
$iopts = "";
$postinghost = "your.news.server";   # points at your news server
```

- Make sure that the script is exectuable (mode 755).

5 Establishing the mail aliases

Edit `/etc/aliases` to create entries for the mailing list(s) you wish to pipe into news. Each entry should be of the form:-

```
<subscribed email address to list>: \
       "| /usr/local/scripts/mail2news.pl <local news group name>"
<code>
```

```
<p>
```
So for example if the email address to which email from the list is to
be sent (the subscribed mail address) is <tt/site_list/ and the local
newsgroup to which mail is to be posted is <tt/local.site.group/, the
alias would be

```
<code>
# The site subscription address for blah-blah@some.mailing.list
site_list: "| /usr/local/scripts/mail2news.pl local.site.group"
```

Make an entry for each mailing list that is to be gated to oyur local news server and and then run newaliases.

6 Setting up the news groups and news server (innd)

Using `ctlinnd`, create the newsgroups on your news server. Remember, these are to be **local** news groups, so start them with a distinctive name so you can filter them out from your news distributions (in your `newsfeeds` file).

You also need to tell `innd` that the group is moderated (by using ctlinnd). Remember, `innd` is **very** sensitive to file ownership and permissions, so you need to interct at this level with `innd` as the `news` user. Indicating a moderated group is done by specifying m to the `newgroup` command.

```
         ctlinnd newgroup <newgroup name> m <newsadmin>
```

The **m** tells `innd` that the group is moderated.

Edit your newsfeeds file to make sure that these local groups are **not** distributed (unless you specificaly wish this to occur).

For example, if your mailing list is called `local.site.group`, then you would probably want to add `!local*` to the second field of your up (and possibly your down) stream news sites in your `newsfeeds` file.

Now, in order to ensure that user messages are sent to the list automatically by innd, edit `/etc/news/moderators` to include a line declaring the mailing list email address as the moderator.

```
some.site.list:list@mail.list.site
```

7 Subscribing the mail2 news alias to the mailing list

You now need to subscribe the mail alias to the mailing list. Check with the mailing list information as to how to subscribe. Some mailing lists allow you to subscribe an email address that is different from the address from which the subscription comes (they check back to the address to be subscribed for confirmation before actually subscribing that address).

Other mailing lists do not permit this. So you may need to 'forge' a subscription request. There are many ways of doing this. One of the easiest is to use Netscape mail set up (temporarily) with the address to which the mailing list is to send the mail.

After subscribing, you should see a 'welcome' message of some kind from the list server in the news group - in which case all is well and you can now test the other direction by posting a news message to your new list.

The message should *NOT* appear in the newsgroup at once. It should get sent out by mail and then received back and posted to the news group.

If this works, you have succeed in getting the list gated to news.

8 If it doesn't work...

If things don't work, you need to track through the path the messages are taking to see exactly where things are breaking down. Useful tools here are the mail and news logs.

Robert Hart
Melbourne, Victoria, Australia October 1996

9 The mail2news.pl script

```perl
#!/usr/bin/perl

($program = $0) =~ s%.*/%%;

#( $version  ) = $] =~ /(\d+\.\d+).*\nPatch level/;
#die "$program: requires at least version 3 of perl\n"
#            if $version < 3;

# $inews = "/usr/bin/inews";
# $iopts = "-h -o \"mail2news gateway\"";
$inews = "/usr/bin/rnews";
$iopts = "";
$postinghost = "your.news.server";

if ($#ARGV < 0) {
    # $newsgroup = "test";
    # we'll expect the newsgroup line in the body
} elsif ($#ARGV == 0) {
    $newsgroup = $ARGV[0];
} else {
    die "usage: $program [newsgroup]\n";
}

# in case inews dumps core or something crazy
$SIG{'PIPE'} = "plumber";
sub plumber { die "$program: \"$inews\" died prematurely!\n"; }

open (INEWS, "| $inews $iopts") ||
    die "$program: can't run $inews\n";

# header munging loop
while (<STDIN>) {
    last if /^$/;

    # transform real from: line back to icky style
    s/^From:\s+(.*) <(.*)>/From: $2 ($1)/;

    s/Message-Id/Message-ID/;
```

```
        # transform from_ line to path header; also works locally
        s/^From\s+(\S+)@(\S+).*/Path: $2!$1/
          || s/^From\s+(\S+)[^@]*$/Path: $1\n/;

        print INEWS
#           if /^(Date|From|Subject|Path|Newsgroups|Organization|Message-ID):/i;
        if /^(Date|From|Subject|Path|Newsgroups|Message-ID):/i;
        $saw_subject |= ( $+ eq 'Subject' );

        $saw_msgid |= ( $+ eq 'Message-ID' );

#       $saw_newsgroup |= ( $+ eq 'Newsgroups' );
}

warn "$program: didn't expect newsgroup in both headers and ARGV\n"
    if $newsgroup && $saw_newsgroup;

die "$program: didn't get newsgroup from either headers or ARGV\n"
    unless $newsgroup || $saw_newsgroup;

$approved = $newsgroup;
$approved =~ s/\./'-'/eg;

($sec,$min,$hour,$mday,$mon,$year)=localtime(time);
$madeupid = "\<$year$mon$mday.$hour$min$sec.$$\@kepler.hedland.edu.au\>";

printf INEWS "Newsgroups: %s\n", $newsgroup if $newsgroup;
printf INEWS "Approved: %s\@kepler.hedland.edu.au\n", $approved;
print  INEWS "Subject: Untitled\n" unless $saw_subject;
printf INEWS "Message-ID: %s\n", $madeupid unless $saw_msgid;
printf INEWS "NNTP-Posting-Host: %s\n", $postinghost;
print  INEWS "Organisation: (mail2news gateway)\n";
print  INEWS "\n";

print INEWS while <STDIN>;    # gobble rest of message

close INEWS;
exit $?;
```

"NCD X terminal mini HOWTO" Ian Hodge

ihodge at `nortel.ca`
v1.01, 9 August 1998
This document describes how to connect an NCD X terminal to a UNIX host

Contents

1   Copyright

The NCD X terminal mini HOWTO is copyright (C) 1998 by Ian Hodge. Linux HOWTO documents may be reproduced and distributed in whole or in part, in any medium physical or electronic, as long as this copyright notice is retained on all copies.

2 Introduction

This document describes how an X terminal manufactured by NCD (Network Computing Devices) can be connected to and booted from a UNIX host using BootP (boot protocol). Many terminals are also capable of booting with RARP, NFS or locally from a PCMCIA card or over a serial link (either directly or with a modem).

Although the material in this document was prepared based on experience with a single model of X terminal, much of the information applies to other models and other X terminals generally. There is also an Linux X terminal mini HOWTO document (declared obsolete by HOWTO maintainers at the time of writing and therefore possibly not available in all Linux distributions) which overlaps material from this document. That document covers X terminal information more generally.

2.1 Summary of steps

The process of connecting an X terminal to a UNIX network can be summarized in the following steps:

- Physically connect the X terminal to the network.
- Configure the UNIX host you are going to boot from.
- Configure the X terminal boot procedure.
- Boot the X terminal.
- Log in to the network.

3 Requirements

3.1 The X terminal

An X terminal is a device which communicates and displays over a network using a distributed network window system known as X. Typically, the terminal's X software, known as the X server, is retrieved from the network at boot time. Programs other then the X server software are not run locally on the X terminal (with some exceptions); instead, the X terminal displays programs running on other hosts on the network. The X terminal, therefore, is a type of network computer which uses the X protocol to access network resources.

3.2 Physical Connection

The NCD X terminal (model Xncd19r was used in preparation of this document) has an RJ-45 (twisted pair) connector for use with 10baseT Ethernet. A hub is required to link more than two Ethernet devices using twisted pair. If the X terminal and its host are the only devices in the network, they may be connected with a 'null' cable which is described in the Linux Ethernet HOWTO document.

3.3 NCD X server software

The terminal's X server software file is available from the manufacturer and presumably is provided with the terminal upon initial purchase. This file will reside on the boot host where it can be accessed by the X terminal when it boots. This file is specific to the terminal type but independent of boot host. The terminal can boot from any host which supports the boot communication protocol (explained later). In addition to X server, the X software may also include applications, like a window manager, which can run locally on the X terminal itself.

4 Configuring the UNIX Host

At boot time, the X terminal retrieves files (including its X server software) from a remote host on the network. After the terminal boots, the X server software will control input, display, local clients and X protocol communication. The X server software is executed on the X terminal and therefore does not have to be software compatible with the host on which it resides.

4.1 TFTP and BootP

Together, tftp (trivial file transfer protocol) and BootP (boot protocol server) are used on the remote host to allow the X terminal to retrieve its X server software and configuration files over the network. Both services are typically started by inetd (Internet Daemon).

After the X terminal is powered up, if it is configured to boot from the network, it will send out a broadcast message using BootP (TCP/IP bootstrap protocol). This boot message will contain the X terminal's hardware (Ethernet) address which is used by the boot host to respond to the boot request.

When a boot request is received by the remote host, inetd (listening on a port designated in /etc/services) starts the BootP daemon specified in /etc/inetd.conf.

In file inetd.conf, create or uncomment lines that refer to TFTP and BootP. The final argument of the tftpd entry in the example below is the path of the directory containing the files required by the X terminal. Although directory names are not mandatory, for security reasons they should always be present as tftp access will then be restricted to files in specified directories.

>From a sample file /etc/inetd.conf:

```
# tftp service is provided primarily for booting.  Most sites
# run this only on machines acting as "boot servers".
tftp dgram udp wait root /usr/sbin/tcpd /usr/sbin/in.tftpd /usr/X11/lib/X11/ncd/
bootps dgram udp wait root /usr/sbin/tcpd /usr/sbin/in.bootpd
```

Upon activation, the BootP server daemon on the host will then read its database file /etc/bootptab. An entry for the X terminal must be placed in this file. Each entry contains a set of tags separated with ':' characters. The host name must be the very first tag in an entry.

Useful bootptab tags:

ip

> Address of the X terminal (eg 10.0.0.1).

sm

> Subnet mask (eg 255.0.0.0). To understand the use of the subnet mask and other IP networking principles, consult the Linux NET-3 (networking) HOWTO document.

gw

> IP Address of gateway (eg 10.0.0.1).

ht

> Hardware type - Ethernet in this example.

ha

> Hardware address of X terminal (6 byte Ethernet address)
> According to the bootptab UNIX man page, the 'ha' tag must be preceded by the 'ht' tag. The X terminal's Ethernet address is displayed when the terminal is first powered on. The address appears as a series of 6 double digit hex numbers separated by colons (e.g. 00:00:A7:12:26:19).

tc

> Table continuation or label of another entry in the BootP database. See the example below.

Mini-HOWTO

ds

IP address of domain name server (eg 10.0.0.3). Not required if DNS is not used for hostname resolution.

bf

Name of X terminal boot file (Usually the terminal model is used as the X server file name eg Xncd19r).

The following is an example of the Boot protocol server database file, /etc/bootptab. The character '\' is used to escape the end-of-line character.

```
# This is a general entry (here given the name default)
# with information common to all BootP clients
default:hd=/usr/X11/lib/X11/ncd/:\
        ds=10.0.0.3:\
        sm=255.0.0.0:\
        gw=10.0.0.1:\

# X terminal entry with hostname myxterm
# Notice the tc tag reference to the entry default
myxterm:ht=ethernet:\
        ha=0x0000a7122619:\
        ip=10.0.0.2:\
        tc=default:\
        bf=Xncd19r:
```

When a matching entry for the hardware address in the boot request is found in the bootptab file, a response is sent by bootpd with the corresponding IP address from the matching entry. File transfer can then take place over IP using TFTP.

A hostname can be assigned to the X terminal by creating an entry on the boot host in the file /etc/hosts. This file is used to map hostnames to IP addresses. In the this example, the X terminal (address 10.0.0.2) has been assigned the hostname 'myxterm'.

```
10.0.0.1        linuxhost       # The boot host
10.0.0.2        myxterm         # X terminal
```

5   Configuring the NCD X terminal Boot Process

After being powered up, the X terminal attempts to boot. This is the process where the X software is loaded into memory and executed. If the X terminal cannot boot, the Boot Monitor prompt '>' will appear. The Boot Monitor is firmware found in terminal PROMs (programmable read-only memory). With the basic Boot Monitor interface, it is possible to configure the terminal to boot and retrieve its X server software from the host. Use '?' for a list of Boot Monitor commands.

Configuration parameters set with the boot monitor are stored in NVRAM (Non-volatile Random-Access Memory) and are retained when the terminal is powered down.

>From the boot monitor, the 'bt' command or a menu system can be used to boot the terminal. Functionality of the two methods largely overlaps but the menu provides control over more boot parameters.

5.1   Boot Monitor command syntax

```
>bt file terminal_IP host_IP gateway_IP subnet_mask
```

file

The name of the file retrieved from the remote host containing the X server software used by the X terminal to boot (eg "Xncd19r"). Check that this file name is the same as the file name is found in the X terminal entry in the bootptab file on the host (explained in the previous section).

terminal_IP

The IP address assigned to the X terminal (eg 10.0.0.2). Again, this IP address should be the same as the address assigned in the X terminal entry of the bootptab file on the host.

host_IP

The IP address of the boot host (eg 10.0.0.1).

gateway

The IP address of the subnet gateway (eg 10.0.0.1)

subnet_mask

The subnet mask, specified as a decimal IP address or as a hexadecimal number (eg 255.0.0.0 or ff000000).

5.2   Boot Monitor Setup Menu

The setup menus are accessed by pressing the 'Setup' key or typing 'se' from the boot monitor '>' prompt.

Get IP Addresses From

The IP address of the X terminal should be obtained from boot monitor configuration stored in NVRAM. Only select 'Network' if you are using RARP (reverse ARP) to retrieve the X terminal's IP address from the remote host.

Terminal IP Address

The IP address assigned to the X terminal (eg 10.0.0.2). This is the same as 'terminal_IP' parameter above.

First Boot Host IP Address

The IP address of the boot host (eg 10.0.0.1). This is the same as 'host_IP' parameter above.

Gateway IP Address

The IP address of the subnet gateway. This is the same as 'gateway' parameter above.

Subnet Mask

The subnet mask, specified as a decimal IP address. This is the same as the 'subnet_mask' parameter above.

Broadcast IP Address

The IP address used to broadcast to the subnet. (eg 10.255.255.255)

Boot File

The name of the file retrieved from the remote host containing the X server software used by the X terminal to boot (eg "Xncd19r"). This is the same as 'file' parameter described above.

TFTP Boot Directory

The name of the directory on the host which contains the boot file (eg "/usr/X11/lib/X11/ncd/" or "/tftpboot/").

Config file

The name of the X terminal configuration file on the remote host (See below).

UNIX Config Directory

Name of the directory containing X terminal configuration files (eg "/usr/X11/lib/X11/ncd/").

TFTP Order, NFS Order, Local Order

Assign '1' to the preferred method for booting. Assign '1' to TFTP when booting from a host using BootP.

5.3 X Terminal Configuration Files

During the boot process, the X terminal will attempt to transfer and load files from the boot host. These files are not required for the X terminal to boot successfully. If a file is not found, the terminal will use default settings.

Configuration Files transferred to the X terminal at boot time:

- X terminal configuration file (eg ncd.conf) used to retain terminal settings.
- Color file (eg rgb.txt).
- X key symbol database (eg XKeysymDB).
- Font directory files (eg font.dir, font.alias).

After a successful boot, the X terminal console window with a menu bar should appear. The terminal setup key toggles display of this console window. From the console window 'setup' pull-down menu, terminal characteristics can be viewed, altered and saved on the boot host in the configuration file which can be used in future sessions.

If TFTP is being used to transfer files from the boot host, then file permission must be world readable. Similarly, to save a configuration file to the boot host, the file must already exist and with world write permission enabled. If secure TFTP is used (this is recommended for security reasons), then file access is possible only through specified directories.

5.4 Logging on to the host

>From the X terminal console window menu bar, select the 'terminals' pull-down menu and choose 'New Telnet...'. When the telnet window appears, insert the address of a network host in the service entry and click 'OK'. The host log in prompt should appear. After logging in, X programs, including a window manager, can be started from the telnet window.

6 Fonts and the X terminal

The X terminal comes with a small set of fonts. In the X terminal setup menus and configuration files, these fonts are referred to as 'built-ins'. The terminal can be operated with these fonts alone but more fonts are desirable. Fonts can be added by specifying font paths in X terminal console setup menus, configuration files or by using the xset command.

Once the X server software is running on the X terminal, the font path can modified or queried with the command xset.

To query the X server:

```
xset -q
```

To add a font entry:

```
xset +fp <path>
```

To remove a font entry:

```
xset -fp <path>
```

6.1 The font server

The font server (xfs) runs on a network host and retrieves fonts for the X terminal and other network clients. The font server improves font retrieval time and provides its clients access to more fonts then would otherwise be possible with tftp. Font server software is part of many Linux distributions and has also been incorporated into X consortium software available from *ftp.x.org* <ftp://ftp.x.org>.

To indicate the use of a font server, a tcp service entry is used instead of a font path in the X terminal's host resident configuration file or console setup menu.

Format of tcp service entry:

```
tcp/<IP address of font server>:<port used by font server>
```

Example:

```
tcp/10.0.0.1:7100
```

An example of an entry in the X terminal configuration file found on the boot host:

```
xserver-default-font-path = {
        { "tcp/10.0.0.1:7100" }
        { "built-ins" }
}
```

The xset command with the tcp service entry can used to add the font server to the path:

```
xset +fp tcp/10.0.0.1:7100
```

WARNING: Certain versions of NCDware require the font server entry to be listed first before X terminal 'built-in' fonts. This is contrary to the NCD documentation "System Administrator's Guide for UNIX Systems". Experiment with the order of the font path and verify it with the 'xset q' command.

On the font server host, the server is started at boot time from the rc.local startup script. The font server (xfs) is started with the following command:

```
xfs -config <config file path> -port <font server port number>
```

The standard font server port is 7100.

Example:

```
xfs -config /usr/X11/lib/X11/fs/config -port 7100
```

Example font server configuration file:

```
# font server configuration file
# $XConsortium: config.cpp,v 1.7 91/08/22 11:39:59 rws Exp $
clone-self = on
use-syslog = on
catalog = /usr/X11R6/lib/X11/fonts/misc/,/usr/X11R6/lib/X11/fonts/Speedo/,\
/usr/X11R6/lib/X11/fonts/Type1/,/usr/X11R6/lib/X11/fonts/75dpi/,\
/usr/X11R6/lib/X11/fonts/100dpi/
error-file = /usr/X11R6/lib/X11/fs/fs-errors
# in decipoints
default-point-size = 120
default-resolutions = 75,75,100,100
```

Mini-HOWTO

7   Miscellaneous

7.1   Reference

Unix man pages: bootpd(8), tftpd(8), bootptab(5), xdm(1x), xfs(1), fsinfo(1), xset(1), inetd(8)

Linux Ethernet HOWTO document, Linux Net-3 (Networking) HOWTO document

NCD Techtips Archive <ftp://ftp.ncd.com/pub/ncd/Archive/NCD-Articles/index.html>

NCD Techtips Archive Mirror at CERN <http://wsspinfo.cern.ch/file/NCD-Articles/>

NCDware System Administrator's Guide for UNIX Systems

7.2   Equipment used in the preparation of this document

X terminal: NCD model NCD19r with 19 monochrome monitor 1280x1024 8M RAM

X server software: NCDware V3.2.CV 19r_s

Remote Host: IBM Cyrix 686 P150+ running Slackware (Linux kernel version 2.0.31)

Remote Host: IBM Cyrix M2 200 MMX running Red Hat 5.0 (Linux kernel version 2.0.32)

Network Card: 10 base T Ethernet card (ne 2000 clone) and 8 port hub

Font server version 2 release number 6300

7.3   Acknowledgments

I would like to thank Michael de Lind van Wijngaarden, Jamal Hadi-Salim and Dwight Hodge for assistance in the preparation of this document.

7.4   Outstanding Issues

- Is it possible or wise to start the font server using inetd?
- If the remote host running the font server is powered down but later comes up again, with the font server active, the X terminal may fail to retrieve its fonts. The font path entry has to be re-entered with the console menu or xset. Why?
- The date of the error file designated in the font server config file is changed when xfs is in use but the file is always empty.
- Are there host based diagnostics for the font server?
- Are the procedures for other models of X terminals roughly similar?
- What about XDM?
- What is the procedure to boot the X terminal using NFS (Network File System) or RARP (Reverse Address Resolution Protocol)?
- The following messages appear in the X terminal Console. I am suspicious that they come from xfree86 extensions to X which are not part of the X terminal server. Can someone confirm or deny this?

```
%XSERVER-I-NEWCLIENT, host "localhost" connected with blank authorization
%XSERVER-W-NOEXTENSION, client attempted to use non-existent extension "BIG-
REQUESTS"
%XSERVER-W-NOEXTENSION, client attempted to use non-existent exten-
sion "XKEYBOARD"
%XSERVER-W-NOEXTENSION, client attempted to use non-existent exten-
sion "XFree86-Misc"
```

7.5 Feedback

Please write to `ihodge` at `nortel.ca` with any comments, suggestions or contributions.

Part LXVII
"NFS-Root Mini-Howto" Andreas Kostyrka

andreas@ag.or.at

V8, 8 August 1997

This Mini-HOWTO tries explains how to setup a "disc-less" Linux workstation, which mounts it's root filesystems via NFS. The newest version of this Mini-Howto can always be found in `ftp://sunsite.unc.edu/pub/Linux/docs/HOWTO/mini/NFS-Root` or on any sunsite mirror NEAR YOU.

Contents

1   Copyright

Mini-HOWTO

In short, we wish to promote dissemination of this information through as many channels as possible. However, we do wish to retain copyright on the HOWTO documents, and would like to be notified of any plans to redistribute the HOWTOs.

If you have questions, please contact Andreas Kostyrka <mailto:andreas@ag.or.at>, the author of this mini-HOWTO, or Tim Bynum, the Linux HOWTO coordinator, at <mailto:linux-howto@sunsite.unc.edu> via email.

1.1 Contributors

- Avery Pennarun <apenwarr@foxnet.net> (how to boot without **LILO**)
- Ofer Maor <ofer@hadar.co.il> (providing a better mini howto about setting up discless workstations.)
- Christian Leutloff <leutloff@sundancer.tng.oche.de> (providing infos about netboot.)

2 General Overview

Generally speaking there are the following problems for the workstation:

- It must find out it's own IP-address, and if needed also the rest of the Ethernet configuration.
- It must know the *NFS*-server and the mount path to it's root filesystem.

The current implementation of *NFSROOT* in the Linux kernel (as of 1.3.7x) allows for the following "solutions":

- The IP-address may be discovered by *RARP*, or the full ethernet configuration may be passed to the kernel via kernel parameters by **LILO** or **LOADLIN**.
- The *NFS*-path to mount can be passed via kernel parameters. If this is not done, the kernel assumes the *RARP*-server also as *NFS*-server, and uses compiled in default for the path part. (current default value in the kernel: /tftpboot/<*IP-address of the machine*>.)
- The client configuration may be discovered by *BOOTP*.

Before starting to setup a discless enviroment, you should decide if you will be booting via **LILO** or **LOADLIN**. The advantage of doing so is flexibility, the disadvantage is speed. Booting a Linux kernel without **LILO** is faster. This may or may not be a consideration.

3 Setup on the server

3.1 Compiling the kernels

RARP support in the kernel of the server will probably be a good idea. You must have it if you will boot without kernel parameters. On the other hand it doesn't help you, if the client isn't on the same subnet than the server.

The kernel for the workstation needs the following as a minimum set compiled in:

- *NFS*-filesystem compiled in. (It doesn't need to have *ext2*-support compiled in, a module suffices.)
- "Root on NFS" must be enabled.
- The Ethernet driver for the network card of the workstation must be compiled in.
- Depending upon your needs you may have to include *RARP* or *BOOTBP* support for NFS-Root. (By this I mean the questions that are asked after the NFS question in make config.)

If the workstation will be booted without kernel parameters, you need also to set the root device to 0:255. Do this by creating a dummy device file with mknod /dev/nfsroot b 0 255. After having created such a device file, you can set root device of the kernel image with rdev <*kernel-image*> /dev/nfsroot.

3.2   Creation of the root filesystem

3.2.1   Copying the filesystem

Warning: while these instruction might work for you, they are by no means sensefull in a production enviroment. For a better way to setup a root filesystem for the clients, see the NFS-Root-Client mini howto by Ofer Maor `<ofer@hadar.co.il>`.

After having decided where to place the root tree, create it with (e.g.) `mkdir -p <directory>` and `tar cClf / - | tar xpCf <directory> -`.

If you boot your kernel without LILO, then the rootdir has to be `/tftpboot/<IP-address>`. If you don't like it, you can change it in the top Makefile in the kernel sources, look for a line like: `NFS_ROOT = - DNFS_ROOT="\"/tftpboot/%s\""` If you change this, you have to recompile the kernel.

3.2.2   Changes to the root filesystem

Now trim the unneeded files, and check the /etc/rc.d scripts. Some important points:

- One important thing is eth0 setup. The workstation comes up with a, at least partially, setup eth0. Setting up the IP-address of the workstation to the the IP-Address of the server is not considered a clever thing to do. (As it happened to the author on one of his early attempts.)

- Another point is the /etc/fstab of the workstation. It should be setup for nfs filesystems.

- **WARNING**: Don't confuse the server root filesystem and the workstation root filesystem. (I've already patched up a rc.inet1 on the server, and wondered why the workstation still didn't work.)

3.2.3   Exporting the filesystem

Export the root dir to the work station. See `exports(5)`. You most likely will have to restart the nfsd/mountd after this change. Under RedHat this can easily be done by typing `/etc/rc.d/init.d/nfs stop ; /etc/rc.d/init.d/nfs start` .

3.2.4   RARP setup

Setup the *RARP* somewhere on the net. If you boot without a nfsroot parameter, the *RARP* server has to be the *NFS* server. Usually this will be the *NFS* server. To do this, you will need to run a kernel with *RARP* support.

To do this, execute (and install it somewhere in `/etc/rc.d` of the server!):

`/sbin/rarp -s <ip-addr> <hardware-addr>`

where

ip-addr

   is the IP address of the workstation, and

hardware-addr

   is the Ethernet address of the network card of the workstation.

example: `/sbin/rarp -s 131.131.90.200 00:00:c0:47:10:12`

You can also use a symbolic name instead of the IP-address, as long the server is able to find out the IP-address. (/etc/hosts or *DNS* lookups)

3.2.5   BOOTP setup

For *BOOTP* setup you need to edit `/etc/bootptab`. Please consult the *bootpd(8)* and *bootptab(5)* man pages.

Mini-HOWTO

3.2.6 Finding out hardware addresses

I don't know the hardware address! How can I find it out?

- Boot the kernel disk you made, and watch for the line where the network card is recognized. It usually contains 6 hex bytes, that should be the address of the card.
- Boot the workstation with some OS with TCP/IP networking enabled. Then ping the workstation from the server. Look in the ARP-cache by executing: `/sbin/arp -a`

4 Booting the workstation

4.1 Using a boot rom

As I have not used such a beast myself yet, I can give you only the following tips (courtesy of Christian Leutloff `<leutloff@sundancer.tng.oche.de>`):

- You can't use "normal" bootroms.
- There is a `netboot` packet by Gero Kuhlmann, that provides for bootroms for Linux, and further information. `netboot` is available from the local Linux mirror, or as a Debian package (`netboot-0.4`).
- Read the documentation coming with your boot rom carefully.
- You probably will have to enable the tftpd on the server, but this depends upon your boot rom's way of loading the kernel.
- *Any informations on bootrom vendors of these Linux variety, mentioned above, as not everybody has access to prom burner :((especially in europe, as I'm located there.) welcome, I'll include them then here.*

4.2 Using a raw kernel disc

If you have exported the root filesystem with the correct name for the default naming and your *NFS* server is also the *RARP* server (which implies that the boxes are on the same subnet.), than you can just boot the kernel by `cat`ing it to a disc. (You have to set the root device in the kernel to 0:255.) This assumes, that the root directory on the server is `/tftpboot`/*IP-Address* (this value can be changed when compiling the kernel.)

4.3 Using a bootloader & *RARP*

Give the kernel all needed parameters when booting, and add `nfsroot=<server-ip-addr>:</path/to/mount>` where *server-ip-addr* is the IP-address of your NFS-server, and */path/to/mount* is the path to the root directory.

Tips:

- When using **LILO** consider using the "`lock`" feature: Simply type in once all the correct parameters and add "`lock`". Next time when booting let LILO timeout.
- When generating a workstation specific boot disk, you can also use the `append=` feature in `lilo.conf`.

4.4 Using a bootloader without *RARP*

In addition to `nfsroot` give a `nfsaddrs=<wst-IP>:<srv-IP>:<gw-IP>:<netm-IP>:<hostname>` commandline argument for the kernel. The kernel will setup `eth0` with the given parameters:

wst-IP

    machine's IP-Address

srv-IP

  NFS-server IP-Address

gw-IP

  gateway

netm-IP

  netmask

hostname

  machine name

5 Known problems

5.1 /sbin/init doesn't start.

A popular problem with /sbin/init is, that some (at least) current distributions come with /sbin/init dynamically linked. So you have to provide a correct /lib setup to the client. One easy thing one could try is replacing /sbin/init (for the client) with a statically linked "Hello World" program. This way you know if it is something more basic, or "just" a problem with dynamic linking.

5.2 /dev troubles.

If you get some garbled messages about ttys when booting, then you should run a MAKEDEV from the client in the /dev directory. There are rumors that this doesn't work with certain server oses which use 64-bit dev numbers, should you run into this, please mail me with which os you have the troubles. A potential solution would be to create a small /dev ram disc early in the boot process, and reinstall the device nodes each time.

6 Other topics

- There is BOOTP client: `ftp://sunsite.unc.edu/system/Network/admin/bootpc.v045.tgz` With initrd (which is included in Linux 2.0), it could be made to work for diskless stations quite nicely. initrd is actually always an advanced option for more customized setups.

- For plain bootpd based boots this is actually probably not needed as Linux 2.0 contains also the option to use BOOTP instead of RARP. (To be more precise, you can compile both in the kernel, and the faster response wins.)

- In the Documentation directory of kernel source there is a file documenting NFS-Root systems.

- There is a patch floating around, that allows for swapping over NFS. It was send to me (during a private high work-load phase), but I somehow managed to loose the mail. :(You can get it probably from http://www.linuxhq.com/ in the unofficial patches section.

- My PGP public key can be fetched by fingering andreas@ag.or.at. The fingerprint is: F1 F7 43 D5 07 C4 6C 87 BF 6B 33 A2 2C EE 5A F9.

Mini-HOWTO

"Linux Netstation mini-HOWTO" Kris Buytaert

Kris.Buytaert@advalvas.be

v0.98p14, 22 February 1998
This document tries to describe how to hook up a IBM Netstation to your local network using a Linux box as server.

Contents

1 Introduction

Some unused piece of delicious hardware floating around on my desk. Screaming to be used. 40 Mb's of ram and a 403 PPC inside.

So I decided to give it a try and connect it to my local Linux network. I want to thank the company I work for because they gave me the chance to experiment with it.

In this (Mini-Howto) we'll be dealing with an IBM Network Station model 8361-100, other models may be featured in the future.

It's trying to describe how I setup the NC, there are probably lots of other ways to set up this machine, this one works fine. Any other remarks you might have from your own experience is welcome. (Free Hardware also ;-))

This MINI Howto is not trying to be the Bible on NC's and Linux, its trying to be something for you to get started from nowhere. Contributions to this NC are welcome

Things we still have to implement in this Howto

- How to export your homedir
- How to run applications
- How to run Java Applets

2 Requirements

2.1 Hardware

An NC, connected to your local Network, most likely by UTP, thus by a cross-cable or HUB connecting to an X Server. Herafter called the Linux Box. Basically the NC is Made to work with either AS/400 , Windows NT or AIX Servers. These are all expensive solutions, however working with thin clients doesnt have to cost that much.

The model I have at my disposal is an IBM Network Station model 8361-100, On the inside you can find an 403PPC chip, some S3 vga components, an PCMCIA slot, and normal 72pins (parity ??) sims. I found 8+32 Mb in my edition.

Actually those 40Mb were major overkill. In full operation modus the NC only uses about with lot's of configuration panels a couple of telnet sessions and a X -query open only took up about 4Mb of ram.) So taking out the 32Mb showed absolutely no significant loss of speed.

We proved it was no problem setting it up on a Linux only network. You'll need a server that can provide you both with about 25Mb of free diskspace for the software, and the capacities to run a X -query. In the setup overhere we used a 486DX50 with 8Mb as a fileserver and I switch between another 486DX266 (PS/2 85) with 32Mb, and my Multia with 48Mb as the X server Off course, the fatster machines the better.

2.2 Software

2.2.1 IBM Software.

NC Kernel, fonts etc.

In order to boot the NC you will need its Kernel and fonts. About 25Mb of files are needed on the server. They can be found on an AIX 4.X with the Netstation modules installed. Or from the *IBM Netstation Download Page*

2.2.2 NFS Server.

A working NFS server, like in every default Linux distribution. Approx 85Mb of diskspace has to be exported to the NC.

2.2.3 X Server.

Any machine running XDM with enough memory, processor power will do. You don't need to have X configured on the machine itselve, it can perfectly be a monitorless server. Basic X Windows install will provide you with the necessary deamons.

Optionally

2.2.4 DHCP Server If you have multiple NC's, you may wish to distribute the IP Adresses by using a DHCP Server how to obtain and configure a DHCP server can be read in the *DHCP Mini Howto on sunsite*

3 Other Usefull Documentation

Mainly the IBM website. It contains lot's of docuentation on the NC, most of it can be found in the .pdf format.

Latest updates can be found at *http://www.as4000.ibm.com/networkstation/rs6000/* including

- IBM Network Station Runtime Environment for RS/6000 Users's Guide
- IBM Network Station Runtime Environment for RS/6000 System Administrator's Guide
- IBM Network Station Runtime Environment for RS/6000 System Navio NC Navigator Browser Guide Or from *http://www.ibm.com/nc/pubs/*
- IBM Network Station Setup and Use

4 Setting up the Serverside

You found all the software you needed. Now let's install them.

4.1 AIX License

Before making the tarball on the aix machine, make sure you run /usr/netstation/bin/agree in order to make the kernel in a usable format. Probably you will have to do the same thing with the tarball you get from the IBM website. So finding the kernel separately might be another solution. Find some drive with about 25Mb of free diskspace, I use /usr/netstation/, and unpack the tarbal either from the IBM website or from an AIX machine. There is no need in leaving the approx 60Mb from /usr/netstation/doc on the disk if you don't have enough diskspace.

4.2 The Real Operating System

4.2.1 Setting up the nfs server

Edit your /etc/exports, add the line /usr/netstation 10.0.0.50(rw) Where 10.0.0.50 is the ipnr you want to give to the NC. Restart your nfs deamon.

[root@velvet sdog]# ps auxf |grep rpc sdog 4145 0.0 5.8 828 384 p1 S 03:55 0:00 _ grep rpc root 3120 0.0 5.7 944 380 ? S Feb 27 0:00 rpc.mountd root 3129 0.0 1.5 880 100 ? S Feb 27 0:10 rpc.nfsd [root@velvet sdog]# kill -9 3120 3129 ; /usr/sbin/rpc.mountd ; /usr/sbin/rpc.nfsd

or on a RedHat alike system easier

[root@velvet init.d]# pwd /etc/rc.d/init.d [root@velvet init.d]# ./nfs restart Restarting NFS services: rpc.nfsd rpc.mountd done. [root@velvet init.d]#

Your NC should now be able to mount the /usr/netsation by NFS.

Bascially if you don't need X-Windows this is as far as it gets. You can easily telnet from your NC with nothing more installed. Hoever the beauty of this thing is it's X capacities

4.2.2 Setting up the X server

Next we have to set up the X server. Basically I didn't need to set up anything, all of my machines that ran X-Windows were configured to accept connections. I just started up the NC for the first time and it showed me all the machines that ran an XDM (cfr running an X -indirect). So any machine that can run xdm can be used as X Server. Just make sure XDM is So any machine that can run xdm can be used as X Server. Just make sure XDM is started.

Everything on the server side should be setup now. Lets try the NC side.

5   Configuring the Thin Client

Unplug the network cable from the NC. Then boot it up.

It will boot after checking its Memory, VGA etc, in a screen IBM Network Station Setup Utility. Basically you can manage everything from this menu system. The main parts will be described here.

5.1   Setting up TCP/IP

Section 5 (F5) : Your network setup should look something like this :

IP Addressed From NVRAM Network Station IP Adress 10.0.0.50 First Boot Host IP Adress 10.0.0.1 Second Boot Host IP Adress 10.0.0.11 Third Boot Host IP Adress 0.0.0.0 Gateway IP Adress 10.0.0.1 Subnet Mask 255.255.255.0 Broadcast IP Adress 10.0.0.255 Ethernet Standard Version 2

Resembles my setup. The NC itselve has 10.0.0.50 While 10.0.0.1 is the NFS Server, 10.0.0.11 is a secondary NFS server, just in case.

5.2   Setting Up the Boot Parameters

Section 6 (F6): Looks like this in my setup.

Boot file kernel TFTP Boot Directory /usr/netstation/ NFS Boot Directory /usr/netstation/ Configuration File /usr/netstation/configs/standard.nsm Configuration Directory /usr/netstation/configs TFTP Order 2 NFS Order 1 MOP Order Disabled Local Order Disabled

Where /usr/netstation is the directory export on 10.0.0.1

5.3   Setting Up the Monitor

Section 7 (F7): You can choos the right resolution / Refresh rate from a nice menu. I have mine running on an old 14" VGA Screen running in 1024x768 @60Hz

Basically thats all you need to install.

Just plug in your Network cable again. And Reboot the NC. After testing the Video / DRAM, the NC will search the Host system and request the startup information, download the Kernel from the NFS and boot up.

It might occur that the NC first gets a new FirmWare and upgrades it

When starting the graphical Console you should get a menu bar and a screen where you can select the X Hosts. You are now in the CLE (Common Login Environment): it's a desktop from where you can start all sessions, either telnet or X . It uses a local window manager which is a small window manager based on Motiv.

Your NC is setup now. Congratulations

5.4   Further Configuration

Further configuration of the NC can e.g. be setting the colors, window sizes, default keymaps etc. I'm not going to describe these in detail. If you have troubles finding your way through the menu system. The IBM Network Station Runtime Environment for RS/6000 User's Guide which can be found in either .pdf or .ps at *http://www.as400.ibm.com/networkstation/rs6000/* and will provide you with detailed information.

6 Misc Stuf

6.1 TroubleShooting

Q: I get an Invalid Kernel Type while tryng to boot the NC. A: You didn't run the agree script. Q: I log in at the remote host and my keyboard settings fuck up. A: I use no .Xmodap when working on the NC. This keeps my keyboardsettings perfect.

6.2 Experiences

Using the NC as a plain terminal with multiple consoles. The Built-in Motiv extensions are a lot easier to use than the default setup ;-) Pressing the Pause/Break key will pop up the NC Menu at any time.

6.2.1 Port 5978

Remote Logging It's the same as the messages console in your CLE.

6.2.2 Port 5999

Remote managment for the NC This is acutally a call for help. Strobing the NC , I found some usefull ports. Among them 5999, I still haven't found the exact way how to deal with it. However here are some commands that showed me to be usefull. You can apparently configure the NC remotely.

- help
- get boot
- get tcpip
- get file
- get nfs
- get tftp

7 Credits

Lots of thanks must go out to Wouter Cloetens, wcloeten@raleigh.ibm.com for getting me started and to Bart Geens ,Bart.Geens@advalvas.be for rereading this howto and findin uot lost of splelling errosr

If somebody has more info on these, help is welcome. They seem to be some SNMP thing but I have no expericience at all on that matter.

Mini-HOWTO

"News Leafsite mini-HOWTO" Florian Kuehnert

sutok@gmx.de
v0.3, 4 January 1998

This HOWTO will help you to configure a small leafsite for Usenet News using the free software package Leafnode. For any questions, suggestions and comments, please write to Florian Kuehnert (sutok@gmx.de). Please send any bugs you found in this document to me as well. (C) 1998 by Florian Kuehnert.

1 Why to use Leafnode?

In normal cases if you want to read news offline on your local computer you have to install a news server software like INN or CNews. Also you are in the need for an nntp or uucp connection to your newsfeed. In fact that such packages contain much more features than you need, you run better by installing Leafnode.

Leafnode is much simpler to use and very small but there are some disadvantages: Leafnode is slow and loses news in about any error situation. That's why you shouldn't use it for a big news server, nevertheless, itt's appropriate for private users who dont't want spend much time configuring INN.

2 Where to get Leafnode?

Leafnode is available at *ftp://ftp.troll.no/pub/freebies/* `<ftp://ftp.troll.no/pub/freebies/>` and has been developed by Arnt Gulbrandsen, an employee of Troll Tech AS. The recent version is 1.4 and in some distributions (for example Debian), Leafnode is included. However, be sure to use at least version 1.4 as several critical bugs were fixed.

3 How do I install it?

A small installation help comes with the package, but let's do it together :-) – If Leafnode >=1.4 is shipped with your distribution, it would be the wisest to use the pre-compiled version and leave out the steps 1 to 4.

1.) Be sure that there is no other news server running on your computer. When you type
$ telnet localhost nntp
you should get an error message. If you get a connection get back to the prompt of your shell, you should uninstall INN, CNews or whatever you're running now and comment out the nntp-line in your /etc/inetd.conf.

2.) Make sure that there is a user called "news", check in /etc/password for the name. If there isn't, create one (either typing
$ adduser news
or using a tool shipped with your distribution).

3.) Unpack the sources:
$ tar xfz leafnode-1.4.tar.gz
and change into the source directory
$ cd leafnode-1.4

4.) Compile the program and install it
$ make; make install

5.) Edit /usr/lib/leafnode/config (it may be on any other place like /etc/leafnode when you use a pre-compiled version of your Linux distribution). The line "server =" should point to the news server of your ISP.

6.) Edit /etc/nntpserver. It should include your local hostname (localhost or whatever your computer name is, the command hostname should help you). If in some startup file like /etc/profile or /.bash_profile the environment variable is defined, you should adjust to your computert's name as well.

7.) Edit the /etc/inetd.conf: Make sure that there is no line beginning with "nntp". If there is such a line, comment it out putting a "#" before it. Then add the following line:
nntp stream tcp nowait news /usr/sbin/tcpd /usr/local/sbin/leafnode
When someone (for example you :-) connects to your computer on the NNTP port, leafnode is started as server process.

8.) Go online and run the program "fetch" as root or news. The first time fetch is started, it will download a list of your ISP's newsgroups. This may take some time depending on the speed on your connection and the number of groups your ISP has in its active-File.

9.) Start your favorite newsreader (slrn, (r)tin and knews are not a bad start) and subscribe to all your groups you read. Be careful not just to subscribe these groups, but also to enter them, even when they're empty.

10.) Start fetch again to download all the news of the groups want to get.

4   How do I maintain leafnode?

Now you have got a working news system up and running, but there are still some things to do. You may edit the file /usr/lib/leafnode/config to set the expire dates of your groups. This number means, when old messages should be deleted. The standard time of 20 days is much often too long if you read some groups with much traffic, 4 days or a week are in most cases a good time for your system. You may change the value for all groups ("expire = n" to hold all groups n days), but you tell leafnode to change this time for some separate groups writing
groupexpire foo.bar n
to set the expire time for the group foo.bar to n days.

This setting alone won't make leafnode deleting old messages, a separate program is responsible for this: texpire. It may be started as a cron job or by command line. If your computer is up all the time, you may want to add the following line to news' crontab file (to edit it, log in as news and type "crontab -e" or as type root "crontab -u news -e"):
0 19 * * * /usr/local/sbin/texpire
This line causes the cron daemon to star texpire every day at 19:00. Check the crontab manual page for further adjustment. If your computer is not regularly switched on, you may start texpire just from time to time, when you notice that fetch gets slower. It works fine as with the "cron-method".

5   How does it work?

Leafnode is a "real" NNTP server, which means that you can also login from a different computer (via Internet, the local network etc.). Every time you enter a group in your newsreader, your reader sends the information to leafnode and requests it. If the group does not exist, leafnode will create an empty file /var/spool/news/interesting.groups, named like the group. When you run fetch the next time, it will fetch the messages of the group. If a newsgroup has not been visited for a certain time, leafnode will stop to fetch its articles and delete its name in /var/spool/news/interesting.groups. So if you just subscribed to a high traffic newsgroup by accident, you may delete its file there by hand for that you won't have to download all the postings there for the next week.

A week is not enough for you? You want to go on holiday for three weeks and still get news? Unfortunately, there is no option in leafnode to change it. But you can edit the file leafnode.h and recompile it. The #defined constants are TIMEOUT_LONG and TIMEOUT_SHORT, just set the time in seconds up. Another, simpler solution is to define a cron-job that does "touch /var/spool/news/interesting.groups/*" every night.

If you want to get a list of all avaible groups, look into the file /usr/lib/leafnode/groupinfo, where you will find a short description on the group.

If you want to re-read the list of newsgroups from your newsfeed (for example when you want to read a new group), just delete the file /var/spool/news/active.read. Fetch will create it the next time and get the new list. Fetch will also re-read the grouplist from time to time, so you don't have to do it by hand.

6   What newsreader should I use?

There is not *the* newsreader for Linux, like there is not *the* editor. My favourite newsreader is emacs in gnus mode which is the most configurable reader for Linux. Many people are using slrn and tin on a terminal, many people use knews under X. There are also trn, nn and a lot more reader, so just try what you like. The only reader you shouldn't use is Netscape, it is big, feature-less, unstable, and it creates sometimes broken postings. However, it is your personal decision.

Anyway, knews is no bad idea for your first experiences as it is very user-friendly and easy to understand.

7   Where do I get more information?

Some documentation is provided with the Leafnode package (read the files INSTALL and README, the sources are also quite interesting). If you want to know more about "professional" and "big" news servers, check the INN FAQ (they are provided with the INN package). To get information about your newsreader, type man "name of your newsreader" or check for other files in /usr/doc.

If you have any questions concerning the news system, just ask in an appropriate newsgroup (look in the news.software.ALL hierarchy).

If you have any question, comments or corrections concerning this HOWTO, just write to me (sutok@gmx.de).

8   Thanks

I would like to thank Michael Schulz (michaels@home.on-luebeck.de) for his help concerning some language problems and Cornelius Krasel (krasel@wpxx02.toxi.uni-wuerzburg.de) for his "touch *"-trick.

Mini-HOWTO

Part LXX

"Linux off-line mailing method (offline mailaddr with 1 account)" Gunther Voet

freaker@tuc.ml.org - Belgium (CompuMed/TuCSRV)
v1.3.3, 4 June 1998
Use your linux mailing system offline, receive mail for multiple users with only one email address, and without being 24-24 online on the net. If you are unable to pay a direct line to stay online for 24-24 and still want your users to receive mail on your linux box; as well not pay for a multi-drop box at your isp, you can use this system using only one email address to divide to your users email addresses. It is as well 24-24 reachable since the server where your account resists will receive the mail. 1.2 (This howto is Copyright (c)1997-98 by Gunther Voet.)

Contents

1   Notes by the author (preface).

In this chapter i'm just going to put myself safe for any damages and flames - since even *I* could be wrong ... If you got any questions or suggestions to add to this faq, even if you find any faults - there is a feedback section in it ...

Some "need to know" point is, all filenames & files/types are indicated with the line:

```
(*** < file > *** text ***) .procmailrc
```

This means, this is a file, called ".procmailrc" containing text. The text variable can also be code. It shows you what name of file to use. Without a path means it can be variable/choosen by you (in the most cases this files resists in the homedirectory of the mail"user" like /home/mailer).

1.1   Legal stuff

Neither the author nor the distributors of this HOWTO are in any way responsible for physical, financial, moral damage incurred by following the suggestions and examples of this text. The information in this document contains the best of my knowledge and experience, but i could still make any mistakes as well in the information as in the examples. Any trademarks are property of their respective holders (i ain't using any commercial thingy's here - but well - IF i'm going to add some text, i don't need to change this disclaimer). If your cat dies 'coz this document was too heavy - i am not responsible as well ...

1.2   Copyrights

This document and contents are Copyright (c)1997-98 by Gunther Voet. Unauthorized (re)production in any form is explicitly allowed and even strongly encouraged as long you don't change the contents of it without contacting the author (Gunther Voet). If you quote the document as whole or a part of it, there needs to be a Copyright "hint" or link to the derived work. "The HOWTO documents are copyrighted by their respective authors". The "HOWTO copyright" will discuss what can be done and what cannot be done with this document. If it is used in a commercial way, the author should been noticed for such distributions. Exceptions on this copyright may be granted under certain conditions with a written letter or e-mail to the author. For more info about the standard HOWTO disclaimer, please contact linux-howto@sunsite.unc.edu.

PLEASE *IF* you are going to make a system based on this HOWTO, then PLEASE give me the copyright :) heh ... - i am not that cruel :)). I mean by a system "a package" - NOT the mailsystem itself - altough it is some appreciative thingy i would be included :)) i can always use one email address more for more flaming :)) (just kiddin').

1.3   Feedback

Well, i expect from you and the users who read this HOWTO, they will make this HOWTO useful. If you got any suggestions, corrections, comments (except flame-mail :)) - please send them to me at freaker@freestamp.com or *freaker@tuc.ml.org* and i will make the corrections, comments or suggestions happen in the next revision. If you publish this document on a commercial way, a complimentary copy would be appreciated - you can mail me for my postal address. For flames - you could send them to me, but they will end at /dev/null ... so - don't even mind to waste bandwidth for it !. Since i can exclude some users to receive mail from (explained in this document) (evil grin). My alias (name) is freaker btw :)). You can always try "freaker@freestamp.com". (note the changed address !!)

1.4   Distribution

The latest revision of this document can been get from:

http://sunsite.unc.edu/pub/Linux/docs/HOWTO/mini/Offline-Mailing

-and-

http://tuc.ml.org/om/

(also checkout *http://tuc.ml.org*)

tuc.ml.org could be down at the time of current writing!

1.5   Changes

```
v1.0.0        - Preliminary release, internal testing, we tried it before
                we gave it out to you :) .. since - it GOT to be usefull
```

```
                       and needs to work? rite ? :)
    v1.1.0    - Fixed a lot of errors in the texts, put chapters in it,
               - fixed some small errors and typo's ...
    v1.2.0    - fixed grammatical errors.
               - added a "what-are-we-using" chapter.
               - added Sunsite address.
    v1.3.0    - Added "virtual mail support" for admins
               - New site and email addresses
               - Thanks go to ...
    v1.3.1    - Converted to SGML and fixed some minor details.
    v1.3.2    - Major errors corrected (filenames .fetchmailrc to
                 .procmailrc) etc... (thx to Tetsu Isaji)
               - Added support for the "new" sendmail, v8.8.0+
               - Fixed some minor errors
               - Upgraded my system YAY!
               - Japanese version will come out soon, location
                 will be mentioned when known ... (thx to Tetsu Isaji)
    v1.3.3    - Added CC support, changed email addr to freaker@freestamp.com
```

1.6 What am i using ?

I'm using Linux 2.0.30, Pentium-166, ATI pci-mach64 card, Accelerated-X (Metro) and a connection to my isp (currently ibmnet) via ppp using a ZyXEL 28k8 modem, and occasionally a Bausch 28k8.

Now i upgraded to Linux 2.0.33, installed a USRobotics modem, it still works as it should work :) (everybody should upgrade their linux versions as soon there comes out a patch :) believe me :) you could spare a lot of time & seeking for errors when doing this one :)

1.7 Thanks go out to ...

- Fred, durban.hebel.net (for allowing the pages & bot)

- Lifesaver, parkside.net (for allowing the new pages, helping with this faq for mailing, since, it is all working overthere and here ... make some visit to his cyber-cafe ... heard they got great coffee :))

- The server admins at lodus.net to continue this project.

- Now i'll need a new server since lodus.net has been sold :(

2 Preliminaries

Well, how does this system works ? what can you do with it ? what is it anyway ? and ... am i used to read it ? ... to all those questions - there is an answer ...

2.1 Preface & Description

This HOWTO is dedicated to all the off-line linux users/servers ... You got a group, or organization, and you want all your members to have a contact (email) address, without paying for the 24/24 direct line or for the email accounts ... Or you got a internal network - with a masq'd server and you want to give all the users using it a email address, you could use this way to do it. I personally am using it to give my users & members of a demogroup all a e-mail account without being 24/24 online; since it is a non-commercial demogroup - and we don't got THAT much money to pay a direct line with instant email access - and different ip's. Everybody got a email address, even when they don't got internet access. The ones with internet access can receive their mail on their personal email address - viavia the system described below. Your users can still send mail as they used to do, since - your system will hold the mail queue from the users. The only thing what should be changed for the users - is that they add their "email address" wether (described below) it is the method with the subject line, or with the header "to" ...

2.2   Points of interest ...

- A organization with members, for all a email address, so they can be contacted when neccesary.

- A anonymous mailservice - they can't read your "mail setup file" - so they don't know where the mail is forwarded/rerouted to.

- A group who doesn't got enuf money (don't laugh), or is free, and don't WANT to spend money for it (eheh) - and still wants to provide the members a email address.

- A masq'd network - with a server connected to the internet, where the users using the masq'd network need to have a email account

- You want to put some documents "autoreplied" - like i do with my HOWTO, statistics, or documents ... like "info@yourmail.dom" or "document1@yourmail.dom".

- You only need one account at the "main" server to fetch from, for the +200 email accounts you can create at your server ...

- I used the "B" method with +- 300 email accounts - with a public server; 80486DX4-100 - and was processed in 1 minute.

2.3   Things you should know

- Not every (free) mailservice is happy when you are going to distribute mail to other users, or putting up an anonymous mail server, so, please try to contact your mailserver administrator before "just doing it".

- It is slower than a direct 24/24 connection, since your server will need to get online before it will process the mail.

- It needs a administrative force to administrate the "mailrouting" and to add the user ... you will need work with it ! - it is not that automatic. (well - i made it "semi-automatic" with my server :) you could try it as well).

- Bandwidth and space is needed when you got many users - on the mailserver you are working on ... and sure - when they send files - you need to have enough space on it !.

- All mail will be transferred into "one step" - so - the last mail received on your server will be last sent to the recipient. "first in - first out".

- In the first method (to:) there is no prob with the usernames - but in the second "cheaper" method - users can't put in a subject line, since that one will be used to send the mail to the recipient. Many users forget to use the "subject" ... - or they will need to know it clearly.

- If you poll enough for your mail, (for example 4 times a day) - the mail will be sure be delivered to as from a recipient the least every 6hrs. So the processing will go a little smoother.

- you CAN use it as a "online" mail server as well :) since it will poll for it's mail for every XX minutes. but - when you are online - why using another server ? and not asking your own domain for your own server ? (dough).

2.4   there are 2 different ways ...

1. method 'A' - now called "(m(A))".

   The "mailsystem" will look to the header, and will see to the "to:" line. This is the best way, since it are "real email addresses". You will need another account on some server *AND* you need a DNS (MX) entry (your own domain for instance). If the system administrator wants to help you with that, then there will be no problem !. The system administrator will need to reroute ALL mail sent to your (MX) maildomain -> to your account !. This will take some time for him to do it :) so be really nice to him :)) Thanks to my system administrator (Fred) i got my maildomain and the user- services of my "free" demogroup. It can be a DNS entry costs something, what you will need to consider to take it or not.

2. method 'B' - now called "(m(B))".

   The "mailsystem" looks to the subject line, and will forward to the user indicated into the subject line. If the user is not found, it will bounce a mail back. This will need a pop server with only one useraccount, and don't need your own DNS or you don't need to be nice to your system- administrator who arranges you the mail address :). You can use a public mailserver, as well your own mailserver or a private one. You can even sacrifice your own email address for it :). I used this approach as first what worked for me for over a year now ... I know this is sloppy, but, i ain't telling you need to use this way, so don't shoot ME - since i'm only offering you some solutions to your mail problems :) - you could use method A what isn't that sloppy !

3 Requirements

Well, you need (of'course) a Linux machine, what can be connected to the internet - So! (i am smart - i am smart :)) - you probably got a modem, right? a phoneline - or any way to connect yourself with the server you are running. You will also need some software like Fetchmail, Procmail, an extra account, and your email account or DNS with email account.

3.1 A linux machine

This can be ANYthing ... even a 8086 ... - but preferable - since there will be some load on it - minimally a 80386 :). as faster the machine - as faster the software will run (rite eh)? :).

3.2 A extra account at your linux machine

You need to create a extra account on your Linux machine. I am using as example (in this HOWTO) "mailservice". This can be as well "mailserver" or "mailtousers" - as long it is some name what can be recognized by you!.

! It doesn't need to have ANY root privileges !

This mailaccount will forward all mail to the users on your system, or to external users (not on your system :)). Just create it as an ordinary user. You will need to test things under this account, and, the mail "administrator" can use this account to administrate the mail account without being root even .. so - pretty safe !.

3.3 Fetchmail

I am using v1.9 patch level 9 ... i found it at sunsite.unc.edu, and, i am using only this mail-fetcher in my example - if you want to use another one, you are on your own ! since i am happy with it :). For extended features you should read the man of Fetchmail :). This can be installed as root - as well for the user itself ... - best is to install it as root :) since i know it will work for sure then :)))

3.4 Procmail

I am using v3.10 - found it again at sunsite.unc.edu, and - i like this as the best mda (mail delivery agent) around ... It delivers nicely - and it is better than using it by the "original" system mda - since it will deliver user-per-user ! ... The same as above - it can be installed as root, or as user - and :) best is to install it as root - since i know it will work for sure then (again!) :)... how repetetive ...

3.5 A mail account

You always need to have a mail account - where you can "poll" your mail from. The server needs to be a POP server - where you can poll from when you want, and where users can send their mail 24/24 to. It can be a free-mail service, as well commercial - even your mailaccount is sufficient enough. In the "subject" method (m(B)) - you don't need something more - in method A - with the "to" fields - you NEED more - as written below !

3.5.1 A DNS record (MX)

Needed to run your own "domain" - email domain ... it is needed since the administrator of the server can't use it's own domain for your users - since there are users who need to be contacted on his server as well - what could interfere with your users. And your mailheader must be filtered on that domain. So - an apart domain - pointing to HIS server. This can be an additional cost - or you can ask your system administrator to add a "non- authorative address" - pointing to his server ... - however - it needs to be another domain than he is using !

3.5.2 A "forward" to your account-account :)

Well, the system administrator needs to forward *ALL* mail to your domain to YOUR account ... - it is easy for him when he knows how to do it :) .. else he will need to read the sendmail manual :)) (or qmail - whatever). You will poll for your mail at your account and voila ! filtering on YOUR own email domain.

4 I got it all, what now ?

Now you created the extra account, you got the mail address - and/or the DNS entry & forwarding to your account ... As well installed Procmail & Fetchmail so we can rock the place ! :) .. here we go !

1. You need to create a .procmailrc file, what will contain the "delivery" info to your users.

2. You need to create a "nosuchuserfile" - so the writer knows his mail isn't delivered well.

3. For best work :) you could use crontab to check for mail. This is a easy way to check your mail every XX minutes when on the internet.

4.1 Creating a .fetchmailrc file

You will need to create a .fetchmailrc file, what will contain the information (username & password, as well the Mail Delivery Agent (mda) to proces the mail to). Here is some example file ...

```
(*** < file > *** text ***) .fetchmailrc
```

```
server my.mail.server.com
proto pop3
user myaccountthere
pass deepestsecrets
flush
mda /usr/bin/procmail
```

This file will be used to fetch your mail. Please test it by using the fetchmail program "fetchmail -vv" - and see your mail is being transferred right ... There will be some errors - since the procmail control file hasn't been created yet. You can wait by testing AFTER making the procmailrc file, but - i'll warn ya - IF there is something fault :) it CAN be this file :) It needs to be owned by the user account itself - in my case "mailservice" and needs to be "user readable" but NOT group/world readable - since it contains the "main password" :)). (chmod 600 .fetchmailrc will do).

4.2 Creating a .procmailrc file

This control file will forward all mail to the users in it. There are 2 ways as described before - the "to:" (header) way - and the "subject" (sloppy) way. The file will contain the usernames to transport to. All the "#" are comments and are absolutely not needed when not wanted - it's only so you know what i am doing ... - you can as well best chmod it 600 - so the rest of the world or group doesn't need those private addresses eh :) ... It needs also to be owned by the user (like "mailservice") :)). The "nosuchuserfile" is a "bounce" to the writer - if the user isn't found (so mail not delivered) in the procmailrc file ... - so the writer knows the mail isn't delivered well.

4.2.1 For "header (to:)" transportation

```
(*** < file > *** text ***) .procmailrc
```

```
# this line is for debugging purposes only ! it should be removed for
# ethical purposes - since you can read all mail passed trough your mail-
# server ... - all mail will be copied to the file "passtrough" before
# going to the users ... herein you can look what went wrong ...
:0 c
```

```
        passtrough

# the mail with header "to: freaker@mydom.com" will be forwarded directly
# to me, the other mail will pass this option ...
:0
* ^To:.*freaker@mydom.com
! freaker

#the mail to root@mydom.com will be forwarded to root as postmaster!
:0
* ^To:.*root@mydom.com
! root

:0
* ^To:.*postmaster@mydom.com
! postmaster


# the mail to barbara@mydom.com will be forwarded to barbara AND will be
# forwarded to her private email address !

:0 c
* ^To:.*barbara@mydom.com
! barbara@her.private.one

:0
* ^To:.*barbara@mydom.com
! barbara

# the mail to johnny@mydom.com and johnny@hisdom.com will be forward-
ed to johnny

:0
* (^To:.*johnny@mydom.com)|(^To:.*johnny@hisdom.com)
! freaker

# the mail to hans@mydom.com and all carbon copys will be forwarded to hans

:0
* (^To:.*hans@mydom.com)|(^CC:.*hans@mydom.com)
! hans

# this lines will BOUNCE the mail to the sender - when it is not deliv-
ered to
# one of above users ... it will send the file "nosuchuser" into the mail
# body as reply ... be aware ! you need to make such file ! - mine contains
# "well, the user you wanted to reach does not exist on this server, please
# try again, it could be the user is not present anymore".
#
:0
  |(/usr/bin/formail -r -k \
    -A"X-loop: mailservice@mydomain.dom "| \
       /usr/bin/gawk '{print }\
       /^/ && !HEADER \
         { system("/bin/cat nosuchuser"); \
```

```
              print"--" ;\
              HEADER=1 }' ) |\
      /usr/bin/sendmail -t


      exit
```

4.2.2   For "subject: touser" transportation

(*** < file > *** text ***) .procmailrc

```
# this line is for debugging purposes only ! it should be removed for
# ethical purposes - since you can read all mail passed trough your mail-
# server ... - all mail will be copied to the file "passtrough" before
# going to the users ... herein you can look what went wrong ...
:0 c
        passtrough

# the mail with header "to: freaker@ibm.net" will be forwarded directly
# to me, the other mail will pass this option ... When you got a "dedicated"
# email address to receive your "mailservice thingy's" on - you don't need
# to use this line :)
:0
* ^To:.*freaker@ibm.net
! freaker

# all mail with as subject "root" will be forwarded to root !
:0
* ^Subject:.root
! root

# all mail to "subject: barbara" will be forwarded to barbara ...
:0
* ^Subject:.barbara
! barbara

# all mail to "subject: paul" will be forwarded to his external email addr.
:0
* ^Subject:.paul
! paul@his.personal.emailaddress

# all mail to "subject: john" will be forwarded to his account at y-
our server
# and a copy will go to his private email address ...
:0 c
* ^Subject:.john
! john@his.personal.emailaddress

:0
* ^Subject:.john
! john


# All the mail from ibm, with their updates and information, will go to
# freaker, as he is the one who will administrate the mailservice, and
# as ibm doesn't want to get the bounce putten below !! ... this is
# neccesary if your mail provider sends "newsletters" etc...
```

```
:0
* ^From:.*newsletter@ibm.net
! freaker

# All messages from the daemon should been thrown away, or in my case, will
# be saved to a file ... (use /dev/null to throw to endless pit-
s of The Abyss)
:0
* ^FROM_DAEMON
throwaway

# this lines will BOUNCE the mail to the sender - when it is not deliv-
ered to
# one of above users ... it will send the file "nosuchuser" into the mail
# body as reply ... be aware ! you need to make such file ! - mine contains
# some text like "user not found in subject line, please use "Subject: user"
# to write a mail to the user, like example "subject: freaker" would send a
# mail to freaker." The file can be long, but also small :) ... the
# "mailservice@mydomain.dom" will prevent to loop between your server and
# the other server - it needs to have the EXACT email address used !.
# Else you could create an endless loop with a server what sends mail
# to "your email address" with as subject something like "don't spend 500$
# at your ..." etc...
:0
  |(/usr/bin/formail -r -k \
     -A"X-loop: mailservice@mydomain.dom "| \
       /usr/bin/gawk '{print }\
       /^/ && !HEADER \
         { system("/bin/cat nosuchuser"); \
         print"--" ;\
         HEADER=1 }' ) |\
         /usr/bin/sendmail -t

exit
```

4.3 "nosuchuserfile"

```
(*** < file > *** text ***) nosuchuser
```

The user you wanted to contact is not present at this system.

Please use the subject line as recipient - example "subject: freaker" would
send mail to freaker on this system.

4.4 "crontab files".

If you don't know how crontab works :) better read the manual :) ... You need to create a "checkmail" file - what will see if the link is up, as well the cronfile itself ... - i am using a ppp link :) so - this is an example how to look when the ppp link is up - and to poll every 10 minutes using cron. Looks sloppy - but isn't !.

4.4.1 checkformail

the .checkformail file will be called (needs to be executable as well) - and will look if the ppp link is up. If it is up - then it will fetch for mail. Crontab will use this file when you are using the below cronentry ...

```
(*** < file > *** code ***) .checkformail
```

```
#!/bin/sh
#

        cd /home/mailservice

        if [ -f /var/run/ppp0.pid ]; then
        /usr/local/bin/fetchmail -s > /dev/null 2>&1
        fi
```

4.4.2   crontab

This cronentry file needs to been loaded into crontab, and will call the .checkformail - every 10 minutes. It won't write any mail or give any info to the console - since i'm redirecting everything to null.

        (*** < file > *** text ***) cronentry

```
0,10,20,30,40,50 * * * *  /home/mailservice/.checkformail 1> /de-
v/null 2> /dev/null
```

4.5   "At the admins site".

Well, this should be done when using the "A method" ... at the admin's site, so the email goes all from a complete domain, to one username. It is pretty simple, and once you've done it - it works like hell. this is NOT neccesary if your system administrator (the uplink) got another method, and is NOT neccesary at YOUR side !!!!

When using a newer version of sendmail, the "old sendmail" trick probably won't work, so please refer to the "new sendmail" topics to let your mailrouting work.

4.5.1   (old sendmail) add some lines to sendmail.cf

add the following lines to your /etc/sendmail.cf file, so the domains file will be read. please be noted that the "ruleset 98" is added as underhere, since - once you got errors :) it's a hell to find 'm out ! (and i can know it :) DuH).

        (*** < file > *** add ***) /etc/sendmail.cf

```
# Database of handled domains

Kmaildomains btree /etc/maildomains.db

# Add these lines *IN* Ruleset 98 ! (under Ruleset 98).

R$+ < @ $+  . >              $: $1 < @ $2 > .
R$+ < @ $+ > $*              $: $(maildomains $1@$2 $: $1 < @ $2 > $3 $)
R$+ < @ $+ > $*              $: $(maildomains $2 $: $1 < # $2 > $3 $)
R$+ < @ $* > .               $: $1 < @ $2 . >
```

4.5.2   (new sendmail) Adding some lines to sendmail.cf

With the newer sendmail releases (tested with sendmail v8.8.7, 8.8.8). Ignore method A, and add the next lines ...

        (*** < file > *** add ***) /etc/sendmail.cf

```
# Database of handled domains

Fw/etc/sendmail.cw
Kvirtuser btree /etc/maildomains.db
```

Mini-HOWTO

```
*OR*

Fw/yourhomedir/sendmail.cw
Kvirtuser btree /yourhomedir/maildomains.db
```

4.5.3 (new sendmail)editing the /etc/sendmail.cw (or /yourdir/sendmail.cw) file

If you are using another "location" for the sendmail.cw file, then please replace the "/etc/sendmail.cw" to "/yourhomedirectory/sendmail.cw". The pro points of putting this sendmail.cw file into your homedirectory is that you don't need root to change the domains to receive on. tough - this can give security risks if not used properly !

This file can already exist, or needs to be created, if it already exists be sure you don't overwrite the older data - or i need to refer you to my fine disclaimer :)

First create a /etc/sendmail.cw file, what will be used to "send" a domain to a specific user ... here is an example ... (as you already knew, the name "mailservice" can be anything you want - it can even be your loginname (like mine is freaker).

```
(*** < file > *** text ***) /etc/sendmail.cw
```

mydomain.dom	mailservice

4.5.4 creating a /etc/maildomains file

First create a /etc/maildomains file, what will be used to "send" a domain to a specific user ... here is an example ... (as you already knew, the name "mailservice" can be anything you want - it can even be your loginname (like mine is freaker). (you could have this /etc/maildomains in /yourhomedir/maildomains as mentioned before, just change the paths :)

With the OLDER sendmail versions:

```
(*** < file > *** text ***) /etc/maildomains
```

mydomain.dom	mailservice

With the NEWER sendmail versions:

```
(*** < file > *** text ***) /etc/maildomains
```

@mydomain.dom	mailservice

4.5.5 let it work !

With the old & new sendmail versionsyou need to generate the btree (database) files, you'll need to do the following:

```
cd /etc    (or /yourhomedir)
makemap btree maildomains < maildomains
```

after that, kill the sendmail daemon, and restart it. it should now WORK! good luck :)

5 Automation

Well, now, everything above works ... (if it doesn't work - don't even think about automation before it WILL work ... - now - we need some script so it isn't a pain in the ass for the "mailadministrator" or the root user to add users to the procmailrc file ... The below example will be for "more experienced users" - since some things NEED to be changed as well ... - it is an example with the "B method - Subject lines". It can be easily adapted to the "A method". Since the "B method" will be more used (cheaper) than the "A" method - i decided to use the "B method" ... Am i sounding repetitive or not ? .. well - i meant to write it in this way :)) to bug you :)))..

5.1 The "skeleton".

Since the footer needs to be as footer (everything below won't be processed since we are bouncing there); there needs to be a header and a footer file.

5.1.1 the ".procmailrc-header" file

This file will now be the "header & user" file .. since here will users been added and removed - it will be a important file ... - best take a backup from it each time you add a user ... - there COULD be something wrong sometime .. A system can fail ...

      (*** < file > *** text ***) .procmailrc-header

```
:0 c
          passtrough

:0
* ^To:.*freaker@ibm.net
! freaker

:0
* ^Subject:.root
! root

:0
* ^Subject:.barbara
! barbara

:0
* ^Subject:.paul
! paul@his.personal.emailaddress

:0 c
* ^Subject:.john
! john@his.personal.emailaddress

:0
* ^Subject:.john
! john

:0
* ^From:.*newsletter@ibm.net
! freaker

:0
* ^FROM_DAEMON
throwaway
```

5.1.2 the .procmailrc-footer file ..

As mentioned above, this file needs to be as footer - since all data BELOW it won't be used to deliver - this footer contains the "bounce" code to bounce the users not found *ABOVE* this footer !. it is the ABSOLUTE end of the file !

      (*** < file > *** text ***) .procmailrc-footer

```
:0
```

```
|(/usr/bin/formail -r -k \
   -A"X-loop: mailservice@mydomain.dom "| \
    /usr/bin/gawk '{print }\
    /^/ && !HEADER \
      { system("/bin/cat nosuchuser"); \
      print"--" ;\
      HEADER=1 }' ) |\
    /usr/bin/sendmail -t
```

```
exit
```

5.2   addmail script

This script will add a user to the header file, attach the header & footer to eachother - so it will be a complete .procmailrc file. the "#" (comments) are not really needed - and are for your info :).

(*** < file > *** code ***) addmail (* chmod 500 *)

```
#/bin/sh
#
# Copyright (c)1997 by Gunther Voet. rev 1.0.1
# please leave the Copyright in it when it is distributed with any
# system using this thingy ...

echo ""
echo "Addmail v1.0.1 by Gunther Voet, Freaker / TuC'97-98 (21/04/97)"
echo ""

if [ $1 ]; then

        if [ $2 ]; then

# make a backup file !

        cp /home/mailserv/.procmailrc-header /home/mailserv/.procmailrc-
backup

# APPEND (>>) the information to the header file ...

        echo ":0" >> /home/mailserv/.procmailrc-header
        echo "* ^Subject:.$1" >> /home/mailserv/.procmailrc-header
        echo "! $2" >> /home/mailserv/.procmailrc-header
        echo "" >> /home/mailserv/.procmailrc-header

# copy the header file to .procmailrc - and append the footer file to it !

        cat /home/mailserv/.procmailrc-header > /home/mailserv/.procmailrc
        cat /home/mailserv/.procmailrc-footer >> /home/mailserv/.procmailrc

# make sure it is owned by "mailserv" and the read/write priveleges are ONLY
# for the user "mailserv" itself ...

        chown mailserv /home/mailserv/.procmailrc
        chgrp users /home/mailserv/.procmailrc
        chmod 600 /home/mailserv/.procmailrc
```

```
        else
                echo "No DESTINATION mail address has been given ..."
        fi

        else
                echo "usage:"
                echo ""
                echo "syntax:   addmail from_user to_user(domain)"
                echo ""
                echo "example: addmail freaker freaker@myemail.dom"
                echo ""
        fi
```

Now, this script will append the information of the user, as well the email address to the header file, it will copy it to the .procmailrc file, and will add the footer to it, so you got a complete .procmailrc to process the mail. If you want to delete a user- just edit the .procmailrc-header file, and at the next user added it will be deleted at the .procmailrc. To do a instant delete, just delete the user from both the files .procmailrc & .procmailrc- header.

I guess you are smart enough to write a script that'll automatically add your users when using both methods - when doing a "adduser" at your box.

6   Help! (sigh)

Well, you need help - isn't :) ... hmm .. i could be sarcastic and just say "you could better do it again, 'coz it looks a messy enuf" - or .. i could help ... - I wrote down some common problems - IF you got any problem NOT listed in this HOWTO (section) - then mail me - and i'll put it in this howto even with your name/email addr in it :). **BEFORE** mailing to me - please look if you didn't forgot anything - and IF you want some help from me - send me the MOST DETAILED information - included the scripts & things you needed. i DON'T need any binaries - since i won't run them.

6.1   The automation script just doesn't work:

- is it executable ?

- is your (default shell) located at /bin/sh ?

6.2   What do you mean by "anonymous mailserver"?

- Well, you could make accounts like "anon0001@yourdom.dom" - and forward it to another email address ... nobody needs to read the .procmailrc file, so YOU ONLY know the address !.

6.3   My cat died

- Well, next time don't print this HOWTO out on 200 gram papers, since it are 10 pages it would be 2KG for the cat - it is JUST TOO HEAVY !

6.4   My dog died

- hmm - can't do anything about that one - why askin' me ? ... Just bury it ....

6.5   Linux?

- A free-unix - posix compatible - made by Linus Torvalds ... Why are you reading this if you even don't know what Linux is ?

Mini-HOWTO

6.6   Can you help me with finding a mail account?

- No! - this is a howto for YOUR side, i don't care about the side of your isp, nor how to get your email address.

6.7   Why is the "maybe later i'll make some addition ..." removed ?

- Read point 5.5 very carefully :) and you'll see why .. it's 'coz i needed to add it on general request :)

6.8   How do i get a "domain" ?

- Ask your local ISP/provider - he will help you with it. It could take days/ even weeks when asking to the Internic - your provider can help.

6.9   Why are you so f*cking lame using this?

- coz i don't want to spend money - and - 'coz i feel like being f*cking lame USING it - i *AM* using it - so why bother?

6.10   Nosuchuserfile?

- You can put in it what you want - as long you put some "needed" info so the original writer knows what happened with his "never delivered" mail.

6.11   Can my users write/send mail too?

- This has nothing to do with the system i explained to you, read the sendmail manual ... - this is to RECEIVE mail - to be "always available at an email address".

6.12   Does every user need a shell account at my server?

- Nope .. - but - it will be really hard for users not having internet access :) ... You could have a masq'd network - and use a computer connected to it - so the users can get their mail that way, or you can generate a link between a bulletin board and his mail, you could even forward it to a fidonet gate :) ... reasons enough not to give a shell!.

6.13   skeletion?

- i know it is a typo - but - i like this word better.

6.14   Addmail?

- No questions - for automation - you better be sure about what you are going to do ... since - it COULD be a trojan ya know :))) (it isn't but what means you need to know what scripting is before asking questions) It IS easy enough to interprete - that's even why i put the comments with it. *IF* you are going to distribute this script - leave my Copyright in it please ! thanks :).

6.15   Why are you so cruel?

- I am not cruel :) i am nice :) i am the nicest guy of the world, of the universe ! NOW SCRAM! (i just want to be complete in my HOWTO, and not TOO much "drifting away" from my original point in the doc - so :) that's all).

6.16   Didn't you get a complaint of excessive language ?

- Not yet, but, could be i'm filtering everything containing 'excessive' and language :) i don't know :))

6.17   Why is this howto different than most others?

- coz sometimes reading plain howto's CAN be boring ... i wanted to add something next to it ...

6.18   locally my domain works, but remote it seems not to receive

- Check out your "sendmail.cw" file, since the domains NEED to be added in it !

6.19   My dog died

- the rulesets don't work, i can't receive any mail, or sendmail dies Refer to the new section "new sendmail" - and disregard the old sendmail tricks. The newer sendmail should be easier to use with virtual domains.

7   The End

This sounds like the end ... If you find any unwanted bugs (or features :)), then leave some feedback ... any comments & suggestions -> mail them :). if you are still bored after reading this, please go to: http://tuc.ml.org/ hehehe.

My thanks go out to:

Hannes van de Vel: for supporting me (hum) Tetsu Isaji: the japanese offline-mailing & notifying me about errors :) Greg Hankins: for notifying me about some errors in the sgml version. Linus torvalds: of'course ... without his help this howto wouldn't be here!

"LINUX PLIP MINI-HOWTO" Andrea Controzzi

controzz@cli.di.unipi.it

v2.1, 12 March 1998

This HOWTO will hopefully let you build and use a Parallel Line Interface Protocol.

Contents

NOTE

This is a new release. There are many changes and lots of enhancements, but there will be still grammar and spelling errors (english is not my native language) and, unlikely but possible, some wrong or outdated info. PLEASE let me know about any errors to help me provide the correct information for everybody.

The biggest changes in the release are:

- SGML format
- a general answer to the "PLIP with win95" most asked question (the answer is negative, sorry)

Mini-HOWTO

- bigger and better FAQ section (thanks to the reports of countless users: many of them will find their comments there, as I promised!)

- removal of the Quick PLIP Installation files, that was useless and outdated.

- updated Dos-Linux PLIP link addendum

For any question, error correction, comment and/or suggestion, my E-Mail address is: controzz@cli.di.unipi.it. Feel free to mail me any time you need help. Sometimes I won't answer immediately, but I'll answer. If it happens that you don't receive anything from me after 2 weeks, this means that our mail system has trouble: do not hesitate to mail me again, it's my duty to help you. I can guarantee I'll solve your problems, but I'll try. If after many mails you don't receive answer, check your return address. Several times my answers did not arrive due to delivery problems, usually because the return address was root@myhost.

Before sending mail read the FAQ, my answer to a question already present in the FAQ will not be better (but likely worse or less complete) than the answer you can already read.

For questions about PLIP with DOS and Win95 please send mail to the authors of these chapters, I can't help you.

First of all, a lot of technical information come from the net-2-HOWTO, by Terry Dawson. This mini-HOWTO is not supposed to cover other aspects and/or replace the net-2-HOWTO: my goal is to give you a way to install a PLIP permanent connection quickly, *ONLY* this. All the other info come from my personal experience and the help of many users that sent me comments and information.

Read the net-2-HOWTO and the other docs for the general information about the network and the config files I suggest to change.

1 Introduction: what is PLIP and why should I use it?

There are many ways to create a connection between multiple hosts. PLIP, like SLIP, allow a local connection between two machines, but uses the parallel ports.

Parallel ports transfer more than one bit at a time, this means it is possible to achieve higher speeds than with a serial interface.

The speed achieved depends completely on your hardware (CPU and parallel port) and system load, in general it may be from 5 Kb/sec up to even 40 Kb/sec.

The PLIP interface is fast enough to allow some decent tcp/ip functions, like NFS. So, you may have a computer with all your Linux stuff and another with only the minimal system, where you can mount all the rest from the main machine.

The disadvantage is that most users have only one parallel port, this means that you won't be able to print and use PLIP together. Even with two parallel ports it is impossible to print and use PLIP without using kernel modules.

This disvantage can be also eliminated, if you have two or more parallel ports, applying a patch that you can find in this Mini-HOWTO.

Finally I am now able to give a hopefully good way to set up a PLIP link between DOS and Linux.

I won't stress it enough: so far nobody reported a successful link between Linux and Windows95.

2 Hardware required to use PLIP.

The hardware required to set up a PLIP interface is (obviously) a free parallel port in both the machines and the cable. If you can configure it with your BIOS, set it at least as "bi-directional", but if possible in ECP or EPP mode.

About the cable, this is what is written in the plip.c file, in the kernel 2.0.33 source:

```
The cable used is a de facto standard parallel null cable -- sold as
a "LapLink" cable by various places.  You'll need a 12-conductor cable to
make one yourself.  The wiring is:
```

```
        SLCTIN       17 - 17
        GROUND       25 - 25
        D0->ERROR    2 - 15          15 - 2
        D1->SLCT     3 - 13          13 - 3
        D2->PAPOUT   4 - 12          12 - 4
        D3->ACK      5 - 10          10 - 5
        D4->BUSY     6 - 11          11 - 6
    Do not connect the other pins.  They are
    D5,D6,D7 are 7,8,9
    STROBE is 1, FEED is 14, INIT is 16
    extra grounds are 18,19,20,21,22,23,24
```

But I strongly advice you to read the /usr/src/linux/drivers/net/README1.PLIP and README2.PLIP files for more info about the cable.

In my opinion you should avoid building your own parallel null cable. A self-made cable may save very little money, but can add lots of headaches. If you wish to build your parallel cable, remember that you're doing it at your own risk, I reported exactly what is written in plip.c but I don't give warranties.

A final word about cable length: long cables (i.e. more than 10 feet or 3 meters) may bring problems due to radio interference. If you need long cables you should use good and well shielded cables, but very long cables are not recommended: I think the maximal cable lenght should be 15 meters (50 feet).

Anyway, someone mailed me that his/her 100 feet (30 meters) cable works fine; if someone really wants to try a PLIP connection between the office and his/her home (200 meters away), and has the money to spend, can try it, but is at his/her risk.

3   Reconfigure the kernel.

You're supposed to already know how to configure and compile the kernel, otherwise you must get some doc (kernel-howto or other guides). Thanks to the cool work made by the kernel guys, recompiling the last kernels is a really easy jobs also for "common" people, so just do it. Anyway, for the sake of completeness, here is a quick summary of what you must do:

NOTE: I suppose you are using the 2.0.xx kernel series. Now there is no need to keep the 1.2.xx kernels. There are no istructions about the 2.1.xx kernel series, since they are for development.

I will suppose that you use menuconfig to set up the kernel options, but the other tools are equivalent. I'll show how to do it with menuconfig:

```
    #make menuconfig
```

I strongly advice to select

```
    Loadable module support   --->
```

and enable the

```
    [*] Enable loadable module support
```

and, if possible (i.e. you have modules.2.0.0) the

```
    [*] Kernel daemon support (e.g. autoload of modules)
```

Then go back and choose

```
Networking options   --->
```

where you should choose at least

```
[*] Network firewalls
[*] TCP/IP networking
[*] IP: forwarding/gatewaying
```

The go back and choose at least

```
[*] Network device support
<M> PLIP (parallel port) support
```

If you use modules I definitely advice you to set up PLIP as a module. If you do so you can also, if you need to use a printer, go to

```
Character devices   --->
```

and set up as a module the

```
<M> Parallel printer support
```

Now you have enabled the kernel support for PLIP. If it's the first time that you compile the kernel look at all the other options then save and exit.

Finally compile with

```
#make dep ; make clean
#make zlilo
```

And, if you use modules

```
# make modules
# make modules_install
```

Now reboot your system.

4   Kernel messages about the PLIP interface.

After you've reconfigured and compiled the kernel with PLIP support enabled, when you boot the system, if the kernel supports PLIP directly, or when you load (later, see below) the PLIP module if you compiled PLIP as modules, you should get something like this (numbers may differ):

```
NET3 PLIP version 2.2 gniibe@mri.co.jp
plip1: Parallel port at 0x378, using assigned IRQ 7.
```

Depending upon your klogd and syslogd configuration the plip message could have been stored in your system log files: don't panic if you don't see the above message. If you compiled PLIP as a module and lsmod shows that the plip module is loaded, then it's enough.

Please take notice of the interface name. Usually is plip1, but may be plip0 or even plip2, plip3, and so on. It depends on the IO Address.

5 Setting up the configuration files.

NOTE: Some distributions, like Debian, use different config files. If you have a standard installation and you don't find the rc.inet* files, look for (different) config files in the /etc/init.d directory.

First of all remember to backup all the files you will change,

```
#cp rc.inet1 rc.inet1.BACKUP
```

may be a good idea.

Now, if you don't have it done already, you must choose the IP addresses of the two machines. In my examples I'll use a couple of example IPs for the IPs that you'll write, in the standard xxx.xxx.xxx.xxx format.

In the /etc/rc.d/inet1.rc file of both the machines add this (better if in the last part of the file):

```
/sbin/route add -net ${NETWORK} netmask ${NETMASK}
```

Where NETWORK and NETMASK should be set up previously. If you don't know how to do it, please read the NET-2-HOWTO.

If after this route command you get a message like this:

```
SIOCADDRT: network unreachable
```

then use this instead:

```
/sbin/route add -net ${NETWORK} netmask ${NETMASK} dev plip1
```

where, as usually, you'll have to use the interface name reported by the kernel messages (see above).

You may safely ignore these variables only in the following case:

If you only want to connect two machines on a standalone network, you may pick-up any IP address, say 200.0.0.1 and 200.0.0.2 respectively. In this case you can safely put NETWORK="200.0.0.0" and NETMASK="255.255.255 .0". These are the example IPs that I use in my Quick PLIP Installation (see below).

NOTE: 200.0.0.1 and 200.0.0.2 are only example IPs, I advice not to use these numbers definitively because they could be the addresses of real hosts on Internet!

I strongly advice to choose your address between the "private address" intervals:

```
10.0.0.0        -    10.255.255.255
172.16.0.0      -    172.31.255.255
192.168.0.0     -    192.168.255.255
```

In the file /etc/hosts of both the machines you should add the entries with the IP of the machines that you connect via PLIP. In my example, the entries are:

```
200.0.0.1      one          # this is the "one" IP address
200.0.0.2      two          # this is the "two" IP address
```

Where one and two are the names you have chosen for the two hosts.

If you want to activate the NFS, beside answering yes during the kernel configuration, you must add in /etc/exports the entries that describe the directories that you wish to export. In my example, to be able to mount the directory /usr, you should add this entry:

```
/usr                        two (ro)
```

For more informations about NFS, please read the specific documentation; don't report me problems with the NFS, I won't be able to help.

Now reboot your system.

6   Activate the PLIP link.

Finally, these are the commands, that must be executed with root rights, that activate the PLIP interface (of course the cable must be already plugged correctly).

NOTE: If something unexpected happens, please doublecheck the cable and the spelling of the commands. If you followed the istructions correctly but the are still errors, read the FAQ paragraph, a lot of answers are already available.

First of all confirm that there is no lp device present:

```
# cat /proc/devices
```

You mustn't see any reference to lp like this:

```
  6 lp
```

If you see it, please remove (temporanely) the lp device before going on, if PLIP works then you can try it with lp later. To remove the lp device you'll have to use the rmmod if it's a module; if instead it's built in the kernel, you'll need to recompile the kernel with lp as a module (a much wiser idea).

Again I use the name one and two, as example. On one you'll have to do the following steps.

If you don't have the module automounter daemon and you compiled PLIP as a module, you must mount it:

```
# insmod plip
```

NOTE: if your parallel port is on an IRQ different from 7 and/or is on a IO Address different from 0x378, then you'll have to tell it to insmod. Find your real IRQ and IO Address (the DOS command MSD is likely to be ok, but don't trust it too much) and write something like this:

```
# insmod plip io=0x278 irq=5
```

Usually IRQ is 7 or 5, while IO Address is 0x378, 0x278 or 0x3bc. It is important that you check that the address and IRQ match the hardware settings (jumpers on old boards, BIOS on modern motherboards).

If you are paranoic check that the module has been loaded with:

```
    # lsmod

    Module:         #pages:  Used by:
    plip               3            0
```

Take notice of the interface name (plip0, plip1, and so on; for more details read the kernel messages chapter above), then set up the PLIP interface:

```
# ifconfig plip1 one pointopoint two up
```

NOTE: if your parallel port is on an IRQ different from 7 and/or is on a IO Address different from 0x378, then you'll have to tell it to ifconfig. Use the same IRQ and IO Address reported by the kernel messages and write something like this:

```
# ifconfig plip1 irq 7
# ifconfig plip1 io_addr 0x3bc
```

Usually IRQ is 7 or 5, while IO Address is 0x378, 0x278 or 0x3bc.

Now check that it worked...

```
# ifconfig
```

```
  . . . . .
  . . . . .
  plip1      Link encap:10Mbps Ethernet  HWaddr FC:FC:C8:00:00:01
             inet addr:200.0.0.1  P-t-P:200.0.0.2  Mask:255.255.255.0
             UP POINTOPOINT RUNNING NOARP  MTU:1500  Metric:1
             RX packets:0 errors:0 dropped:0 overruns:0
             TX packets:0 errors:0 dropped:0 overruns:0
             Interrupt:7 Base address:0x378
```

Add the route to two...

```
# route add two plip1
```

And, if you want also the NFS for two:

```
# rpc.portmap
# rpc.mountd
# rpc.nfsd
```

On "two" the commands are the same, but you must write one instead of two and vice versa.

One of your machines is likely to have only the PLIP connection, if this is true and that machine is two, you may also type:

```
# route add default gw one
```

on that machine. In my example above, two is a laptop with only a PLIP connection with one, so I type the above line on two.

Finally check with a

```
# ping two
```

from one and a

```
# ping one
```

from two to see that all is working.

Of course you may want to have all these commands automatically done by a script or at boot time. You must only create a script that execute these commands: now you may invoke it as root when you need, or you may add a command (in /etc/rc.d/rc.inet2) that calls it at boot time.

To tune your PLIP, you can use the plipconfig command, see the man page for more informations.

To shutdown PLIP, you need only to do:

```
# ifconfig plip1 down
```

which removes also the route entries. If you don't have the automounter daemon, then remove also the module:

```
# rmmod plip
```

7   FAQ.

This section will (hopefully) solve your problems. If you have any other question, feel free to mail me anytime.

- I get these messages at boot time (or when I load the plip module):

  ```
  SIOCSIFADDR: No such device
  SIOCADDRT: Network is unreachable
  ```

  and when I try to set up the link as written above, I get again error messages like:

  ```
  SIOCSIFADDR: No such device
  SIOCSIFDSTADDR: No such device
  SIOCADDRT: Network is unreachable
  mount clntudp_create: RPC: Port Mapper failure - RPC: Unable to send
  ```

  - The kernel, for some reason, hasn't PLIP support enabled. This could be due to:
    * You didn't answer yes to "PLIP support? " during kernel configuration.
    * You answered yes to "Printer support? " during kernel configuration.
    * You compiled PLIP as a module, so you must load it.
    * You are addressing the wrong port, i.e. you wrote for instance plip1 instead of plip0.

- Is there a way to support both PLIP and LP, beside modules, perhaps with two parallel ports?

  - Yes, so far there are two ways, described in the "Patches to make PLIP and LP live together":
    * You can apply a patch to make the kernel support both.
    * You can apply another patch to make the kernel use a parallel port for PLIP and another for LP.

- I have created the script that connects my 2 computers. I set up the link automatically in my rc.inet2, where I call a script that creates the link and enables NFS. My "two" hosts mounts some "one"'s directories; I have added the correct entries in "two"'s /etc/fstab. If I boot "two" when "one" is down, "two" halts for some minutes on the "mounting remote file systems...".

  - This happens because "two" waits to mount the "one" filesystems, but if "one" is down you must wait until "two" is bored of waiting. To avoid this, you may:
    * Comment out in rc.inet2 the command that mounts the remote filesystems
    * Remove the entry in "two"'s /etc/fstab and mount the remote filesystems manually when and if you need.
    * A better solution would be for "two" to detect upon booting whether "one" is up, and mount the filesystem if it is. This can be accomplished by replacing the mount command in rc.d or whereever with something like the following:

```
if ping -c 5 one ; then
    mount one:/.....
fi
```

- My link is up, but ping fails. I receive the following message from the kernel:

  ```
  plip1: timed out (1, 89)
  ```

  or similar messages.

  - This means that the "your side of the link" is working, your machine sends the signal, but the "other side" isn't answering or your side is not waiting at the proper IRQ/IO Address. This is the most common problem and, alas, has a lot of possible reasons, usually bad cable or wrong IRQ and/or IO Address. The wrong IRQ is the source of over 60% of the problems, so it's very likely that changing it will remove the problem. Here is a detailed list of possible reasons:

    * The cable isn't plugged properly or is broken or is wrong. Check it, if possible, between two Linux hosts which already work with PLIP. If it is not possible, then at least test the cable with a tester. The fact that the cable worked/not worked with DOS/win95 is a good/bad omen but is not a proof.
    * The "other side" machine has not PLIP up.
    * You are linked with a notebook with a not proper parallel port, see below.
    * You have a really cheap parallel port that is a simple "printer" port, so can send and not receive.
    * Your parallel port is not set as (at least) bi-directional. Do it in the BIOS configuration. Advanced parallel port settings like EPP or ECP are ok.
    * The parallel ports have different irq, so you have to load the plip module (or the lp module) with a different irq. Go back to the chapter "Activate the PLIP link" and choose a different irq.
    * Some other device may have shared your irq (which usually is irq 7), it may be a sound card. Do not trust DOS programs like MSD, instead try to load the plip module with a different irq.

- I put the right IRQ and IO Address, but it still doesn't work. I got the addresses from the MSD command.

  - I got a report from MSD giving wrong port addresses. Try to use this program: http://www.cs.caltech.edu/ huny/para13.zip.

- My link is up, and ping works. I sometimes receive the following message from the kernel:

  ```
  plip1: timed out (1, 89)
  ```

  or similar messages.

  - This means that the other side has not answered before the timeout. If all is working, you can ignore these messages: usually means that the other side is much slower than yours, either due to older hardware or more load. You can try to tune PLIP with the plipconfig command.

- I have installed the PLIP connection but if I ping I get 100% data loss. I connected my desktop with a notebook.

  - Some notebook's parallel ports aren't good for PLIP, because they are only "printer ports", i.e. they can only transmit but not receive the data. So far I don't know if there is a way to make them work. The only hope is:

    * Look at your notebook setup, perhaps there is a way to configure the parallel port as a parallel port instead of a printer port. Usually is called "parallel enhanced mode".
    * Try plip mode 0. Alas I don't know how to do it and/or if it works or is still available in the last kernels.

- What speeds can I achieve with PLIP?

  - This is an hard question to answer to, because there are MANY factors that can change deeply your performance:

    * The CPU speed on both the sides of the link.
    * The parallel port type and settings.
    * The system load.

      * What do you use PLIP for.

Just to give a rough idea, you should achieve about 40Kbytes/sec, much faster than any serial rate and near to a low-level ethernet card.

- What happens if I need to ifconfig up and ifconfig down many times plip1?

  – Seems that you need to add a -arp to the ifconfig command, except for the first time after each boot. I don't need, but perhaps someone does.

- I have read the IP numbers reserved for private networks and your 200.0.0.1 and 200.0.0.2 are not in these ranges. Shouldn't they be changed?

  – Yes, they should. But as I underline since the beginning I choose these IP addresses only because of their simplicity, you are free to change them as you wish. Here is a cut from the net-2-howto:

```
RFC1597 has specifically reserved some IP addresses for private
networks.  You should use these as they prevent anything nasty
happening if you accidentally get connected to the Internet. The
addresses reserved are:

    10.0.0.0        -    10.255.255.255
    172.16.0.0      -    172.31.255.255
    192.168.0.0     -    192.168.255.255
```

- Is there a way to fine tune PLIP parameters without editing the source code?

  – Yes, there is. Try the /sbin/plipconfig command. See the man page for more info.

- I'm running Debian GNU/Linux, and under Debian, the files /etc/rc.d/rc.inet1 and 2 do not exist. Where must I write the plip configuration commands?

  – In Debian GNU/Linux you must edit /etc/init.d/network, where you have to put all the commands that should stay in rc.inet1 and 2.

- I have some problems linking two hosts with PLIP. The first has the latest kernel, the second still uses the 1.0.x PLIP version: is this a problem?

  – Yes, it's much better, where is possible, to have the same PLIP version on both ends. In the plip.c is written that the actual PLIP cannot work with the 1.0.xx PLIP.

- Right now PLIP works with 4 bits, what about the 8 bit PLIP I've read in the kernel docs? I think is called Mode 1.

  – This Mini-HowTo is for configuration, for technical informations please read the /usr/src/linux/drivers/net/README*.PLIP files or contact the author. What I know is only this: the standard PLIP uses "null printer" cables and is the Mode 0 (don't confuse it with plip0, which is the interface name), which uses 4 bits; Mode 1 uses 8 bits and should be available already, but will need an handmade cable and will work only between 2 Linux hosts. I don't know, once you got the cable, how to set up the Mode 1 PLIP link; if somebody does, please let me know.

8　Patches to make PLIP and LP live together.

The best way to make PLIP and LP live together is to use kernel modules: you can load plip.o and unload it when you need to print or vice versa. If you do really need to use both PLIP and LP, try the following patches.

8.1 PLIP and LP together on the same port.

If for some reason you wish PLIP and LP supported directly by the kernel, you can try these patches.

You must modify the following pieces of code, but *backup* the files before:

```
******** modifications to linux/drivers/char/lp.c ********************
struct lp_struct lp_table[] = {
        { 0x3bc, 0, 0, LP_INIT_CHAR, LP_INIT_TIME, LP_INIT_WAIT, NULL,
NULL, },
/*      { 0x378, 0, 0, LP_INIT_CHAR, LP_INIT_TIME, LP_INIT_WAIT, NULL,
NULL, },
        { 0x278, 0, 0, LP_INIT_CHAR, LP_INIT_TIME, LP_INIT_WAIT, NULL,
NULL, },
*/
};
#define LP_NO 1

******** modifications to linux/drivers/net/Space.c ****************
#if defined(PLIP) || defined(CONFIG_PLIP)
    extern int plip_init(struct device *);
    static struct device plip2_dev = {
        "plip2", 0, 0, 0, 0, 0x278, 2, 0, 0, 0, NEXT_DEV, plip_init, };
    static struct device plip1_dev = {
        "plip1", 0, 0, 0, 0, 0x378, 7, 0, 0, 0, &plip2_dev, plip_init, };
/*    static struct device plip0_dev = {
        "plip0", 0, 0, 0, 0, 0x3BC, 5, 0, 0, 0, &plip1_dev, plip_init, };
*/
#   undef NEXT_DEV
#   define NEXT_DEV        (&plip1_dev)
#endif  /* PLIP */
```

Of course there is the standard disclaimer: *I received these patches and I put them "as I got them". This means that you try them at your own risk.* Anyway, your biggest trouble should be only restore the original files and recompile.

8.2 PLIP and LP on different ports.

If you have at least 2 parallel ports you can try these patches, that should allow you to use PLIP on a port and LP on the other.

1. Comment out one line in kernel source file, drivers/char/lp.c.

```
struct lp_struct lp_table[] = {
{ 0x3bc, 0, 0, LP_INIT_CHAR, LP_INIT_TIME, LP_INIT_WAIT, NULL, NULL, },
{ 0x378, 0, 0, LP_INIT_CHAR, LP_INIT_TIME, LP_INIT_WAIT, NULL, NULL, },
/* { 0x278, 0, 0, LP_INIT_CHAR, LP_INIT_TIME, LP_INIT_WAIT, NULL, NUL-
L, }, */
};
    3 -> 2
```

2. Kernel configuration

```
PLIP (parallel port) support (CONFIG_PLIP) [n] y

Parallel Printer support [y] y
```

3. Kernel message at startup

```
lp1 at 0x0378, using polling driver
.....
NET3 PLIP version 2.0 gniibe@mri.co.jp
plip2: Parallel port at 0x278, using assigned IRQ 5.
```

Again the standard disclaimer, like section 8.1.

9 A PLIP link between DOS and Linux

After the first release of this Mini-HowTo many people wrote for info about a link between Linux and DOS (or Windows) computer. The general interest lead me to add this chapter, I hope will be of help to everybody.

This section comes from an article I've found on Linux Gazzette by James McDuffie <mcduffie@scsn.net> . It covers the basic installation of a PLIP link between Linux and a DOS computer using Windows and Trumpet WinSock and gives the address of a cool program that let's you run X-Windows programs on Windows.

The last section is an addendum sent by James Vahn *jvahn@short.circuit.com* <mailto:jvahn@short.circuit. com> where he describes deeply how to set up this link and how to solve many problems.

For any questions about this chapter please contact him, not me.

9.1 DOS-Linux link.

I suppose you have already set up properly the PLIP support on the Linux side and you have got the right cable, else go back to the previous chapters.

Now, for the DOS side, you need first of all a packet driver. It can be found here:

ftp://ftp.crynwr.com/drivers/plip.zip <ftp://ftp.crynwr.com/drivers/plip.zip>

The program runs under DOS and acts like a Ethernet Packet driver. If you want to use PLIP with Windows you need also Trumpet Winsock. This serves as the TCP/IP interface. Otherwise, you can probably find TCP/IP software for DOS.

Now go back to the Linux computer and add the DOS computer address to /etc/hosts. If your DOS computer does not have a registered IP address you may choose any address (remember the warning of chapter 3 about IP addresses).

Now let's suppose you chose the name linux for the Linux computer and dos for the DOS one. You have to type:

```
ifconfig plip1 linux pointopoint dos arp up
route add dos
```

Of course if you want to have this done every time you boot the linux computer you may add these lines to the file /etc/rc.d/rc.inet1:

```
/sbin/ifconfig plip1 linux pointopoint dos arp up
/sbin/route add dos
```

This sets up the interface and then adds a route to it. Of course if you are using the second parallel port you have to write plip2 instead.

Go back to the DOS/Windows computer and edit autoexec.bat, you have to add the following lines.

```
c:\plip\plip.com 0x60
c:\tcpip\winsock\winpkt.com 0x60
```

Of course I suppose you put plip.com (the packet driver) in the directory c:/plip and the winpkt.com in c:/tcpip, else you need to put the right path.

This sets the plip.com program on packet vector 0x60 and then loads the winpkt.com program that comes with trumpet winsock on the same vector. If the cable is something other than lpt1 you will have to tell plip.com the irq number and io address. Also, winpkt.com needs to run to make the packet vector avaliable to Windows. From here we go to the actual setup under Trumpet Winsock. All you have to do is unselect SLIP or PPP and enter 60 into the box labeled Packet vector. Then tell it the IP address you gave it, the IP address of the Linux computer as the default gateway and the Name Server as either you computer's ip or your ISP's address for its nameservers if your going to connect it to the Internet (more on this later). Close the setup and re-run Winsock and you should have it! Put winsock in your startup group and you have everything setup automatically!

If you want to access the Internet through the Linux computer on the Windows computer you will need to set up IP Masquerading, for info on this see the NET-2-HOWTO. This simply masquerades the Windows computer with your Linux computer's IP address.

Also I have found a program that lets you run X-Windows programs under Windows! It is located at:

http://www.tucows.com/ <http://www.tucows.com/>

Set it up according to directions and then all you have to do is telnet in from the Windows computer then set the display to the Windows computer ('DISPLAY=duncan:0.0' for instance) and run the program desired. There is nothing cooler than running xv under Windows! Hope all this helped.

9.2 A DOS-Linux PLIP link experience.

NOTE: I received this document from James Vahn *jvahn@short.circuit.com* <mailto:jvahn@short.circuit.com>. I put it here unchanged. This means that **for any question about this section he's much better qualified than me so please mail to him than to me**. His experience with a PLIP connection of a floppy-only DOS computer to a Linux one is the perfect example of how to work-around common problems.

Last Update 11 July 1996

My floppy-only DOS box is networked via PLIP to the second printer port on the Linux machine. The first Linux printer port has a printer on it, both are permanently connected and the DOS box is telnet'd into Linux. These are my notes on what I did to accomplish this.

When the kernel probes for printer ports, it will grab all of them unless you remove one from the probe. Otherwise PLIP will get nothing. One method is to load the drivers as modules when needed...

<gniibe@mri.co.jp> writes:

I keep recommending using PLIP/LP as kernel module, since

- modules are flexible for change of configuration
- (re)compiling the kernel is not easy for novice users
- co-existing PLIP and LP is only feasible by the modules

With PLIP/LP as kernel module, you can specify which port is PLIP and which port is LP. Here is example:

```
# insmod lp.o io=0x378
# insmod plip.o io=0x278 irq=2
```

Even you can use two parallel ports:

```
# insmod plip.o io=0x278,0x3bc irq=2,5
```

Mini-HOWTO

In the example above,

plip0 is assigned on 0x278 and it's irq is 2,

plip1 is assigned on 0x3bc and it's irq is 5, respectively.

Using modules certainly sounds like the way to go. The following method shows how to patch the kernel to allow both a printer and PLIP on different ports, without modules. If you are unfamiliar with the module concept, you might find this quicker to set up.

You will need to modify two files in the kernel source tree. I'm using kernel 1.2.13 and found some changes were needed in ../linux/drivers/net/Space.c to accommodate my system. Look at around line 205 for the PLIP definitions to make sure your port and IRQ match, and make a note of which driver it will be (plip0, plip1, plip2). In my case port 0x278 uses IRQ 5 (the card is jumpered that way) but Space.c defined it with IRQ 2. I made the changes here, rather than opening up the box and changing jumpers. The alternative is to specify the IRQ through ifconfig later on, but the kernel will boot up with the wrong IRQ for PLIP and it may annoy you. It is a simple (single character) change.

The next, and more difficult step:

In .../drivers/char/lp.c you will find the following at around line 38:

```
struct lp_struct lp_table[] = {
    { 0x3bc, 0, 0, LP_INIT_CHAR, LP_INIT_TIME, LP_INIT_WAIT, NULL, NULL, },
    { 0x378, 0, 0, LP_INIT_CHAR, LP_INIT_TIME, LP_INIT_WAIT, NULL, NULL, },
/*  { 0x278, 0, 0, LP_INIT_CHAR, LP_INIT_TIME, LP_INIT_WAIT, NULL, NULL, },
 * 0x278 reserved for plip1
 *
 * };
 * #define LP_NO 3
 */
};
#define LP_NO 2
```

Notice the changes to make- one port is commented out, so now only 2 ports are defined. Port 0x3BC will probably not work for PLIP- the IRQ line is usually broken on these ports, as found on old monochrome adapters (MDA).

You made backups of these file before you changed them, right? Now make a new kernel with printer, net, dummy, and plip support.

Configure the system. This is my /etc/rc.d/rc.inet1 file:

```
#!/bin/bash
#
/sbin/ifconfig lo 127.0.0.1
/sbin/route add -net 127.0.0.0

/sbin/ifconfig dummy 200.0.0.1
/sbin/route add -net 200.0.0.0 netmask 255.255.255.0
/sbin/ifconfig plip1 arp 200.0.0.1 pointopoint 200.0.0.2 up
/sbin/route add 200.0.0.2
/sbin/ifconfig dummy down
```

Notice that arp is used for the DOS-to-Linux connection, apparently not used on Linux-to-Linux connections.

And in /etc/hosts you can add these, just to give the two machines names:

```
200.0.0.1          console1
200.0.0.2          console2
```

The DOS box is console2. Note Andrea's warning about these, better to use official numbering schemes.

Reboot so all of these changes and the new kernel will take effect. During the boot sequence (or by running dmesg) if you made the patches, otherwise when the modules are loaded:

```
lp0 at 0x03bc, using polling driver
lp1 at 0x0378, using polling driver
[....]
NET3 PLIP version 2.0 gniibe@mri.co.jp
plip1: Parallel port at 0x278, using assigned IRQ 5.
```

The "route" command shows this:

```
Kernel routing table
Destination     Gateway          Genmask           Flags MSS   Win-
dow Use Iface
console2        *                255.255.255.255 UH    1436  0       136 plip1
loopback        *                255.0.0.0       U     1936  0       109 lo
```

And "ifconfig plip1" shows:

```
plip1      Link encap:10Mbps Ethernet  HWaddr FC:FC:C8:00:00:01
           inet addr:200.0.0.1  P-t-P:200.0.0.2  Mask:255.255.255.0
           UP POINTOPOINT RUNNING  MTU:1500  Metric:1
           RX packets:132 errors:0 dropped:0 overruns:0
           TX packets:136 errors:0 dropped:0 overruns:0
           Interrupt:5 Base address:0x278
```

Look at /etc/inetd.conf and see if telnet is enabled. You might want to read the man page for tcpd, and the use of /etc/hosts.allow (ALL: LOCAL) and /etc/hosts.deny (ALL: ALL). You should be able to "telnet localhost".

Linux is done, now the DOS side. Again, be suspicious of port 0x3BC if one is present.

I'm using NCSA's telnet and Crynwr's PLIP driver found at these sites:

ftp://ftp.ncsa.uiuc.edu/Telnet/DOS/ncsa/tel2308b.zip   <ftp://ftp.ncsa.uiuc.edu/Telnet/DOS/ncsa/tel2308b.zip>

ftp://ftp.crynwr.com/drivers/plip.zip <ftp://ftp.crynwr.com/drivers/plip.zip>

Be sure to use NCSA's version 2.3.08 telnet and version 11.1 of Crynwr's PLIP driver. Please find and read Crynwr's SUPPORT.DOC located elswhere.

The CONFIG.TEL file. Most of it is the default and to save some space I've tried to cut it back here to just the info you need (hopefully). The second port on this machine is setup as 0x278 on IRQ 5.

```
myip=200.0.0.2
netmask=255.255.255.0          # subnetting mask
hardware=packet                # network adapter board (packet driver interface)
interrupt=5                    # IRQ which adapter is set to
ioaddr=60                      # software interrupt vector driver is using
#
#[...lots unchanged...]
```

```
#
# at the end of the file, put this line:
name=console1 ; hostip=200.0.0.1 ; nameserver=1 ; gateway=1
```

(console1 is the name of the Linux machine, you can use whatever you like)

I made a 12 foot null cable between both machines, and (after initially finding it miswired) there have been no problems. A standard 11-wire null printer cable should work too. The Linux plip.c source shows the wiring. Although my cable has the 17-17 connection, I don't think it is used for anything and was not present on a ready-made cable.

```
@echo off
plip.com 0x60 5 0x278
telbin -s console1
```

That should connect you to the Linux box on /dev/ttyp. NCSA's telnet provides for 8 virtual screens and also acts as an ftp server. The PLIP interface provides a fair throughput, I'm getting 6.5K/s file transfers with my antiques. Let's hope you can do better. :-)

10   PLIP between Linux and Windows 95.

This section is empty. I use windows 95 for nothing serious but games, so I don't try and don't care about a PLIP link with Linux. The questions about such a link have won the most asked question contest, so I give here a (so far) definitive answer.

No, so far nobody reported me a successful link between Linux and Windows 95. if somebody succeds in setting up this link, please let me know immediately: thousand of PLIP users await these news!

11   Questions? Comments? Send me feedback.

For any questions and comments you can find me via e-mail at the address *controzz@cli.di.unipi.it* <mailto: controzz@cli.di.unipi.it>

Feedback is welcome, any error report is precious. The next release will have an even larger FAQ section, if you send questions and, of course, the answers if you find them by yourself.

Please do not send questions already present in the FAQ.

If you have to ask me for help, please be sure to let me know any information that can help me, at least: kernel version, commands used, error messages, the cable you used and any other system message related to PLIP.

Please remember not to send me any question about PLIP with DOS/Windows 3.1/Windows 95, I can't help you. These questions should be sent to James Vahn *jvahn@short.circuit.com* <mailto:jvahn@short.circuit. com>, who sent me the DOS addendum. Again: it's useless to ask him or me about PLIP with Windows 95.

12   Where to find new releases of this mini-howto.

This mini-HOWTO is maintained by the HOWTO coordinators and is posted monthly on *comp.os.linux.answers* <news: comp.os.linux.answers> and can be found in the HOWTO directory at sunsite and at sunsite's mirrors.

Another way to find the mini-HOWTO (and to contact me) is on my Home Page,

http://www.cli.di.unipi.it/˜controzz/intro.html <http://www.cli.di.unipi.it/~controzz/intro.html> (italian language) *http://www.cli.di.unipi.it/~controzz/intro_e.html* `<http://www.cli.di.unipi.it/~controzz/intro_e.html>` (english language)

13   Credits.

Many thanks to:

- Rick Lim <ricklim@freenet.vancouver.bc.ca> for the patches to make PLIP and LP live together.
- Takeshi Okazaki <GBA03552@niftyserve.or.jp> for the patches to use PLIP and LP on two different parallel ports.
- Jim Van Zandt <jrv@vanzandt.mv.com> for some advice on the "tutorial" part of this HOWTO.
- Fernando Molina <fmolina@nexo.es> for useful comments about IRQs and IO Addresses.
- James Vahn <jvahn@short.circuit.com> for the cool addendum on the PLIP between DOS and Linux chapter.
- To all the users that posted PLIP-related articles on the linux newsgroups and/or mailed me. The list of all the people that helped me with info and comments could be longer than the Mini-HOWTO itself: thank you all!

14   Copyright message.

Unless otherwise stated, Linux HOWTO documents are copyrighted by their respective authors. Linux HOWTO documents may be reproduced and distributed in whole or in part, in any medium physical or electronic, as long as this copyright notice is retained on all copies. Commercial redistribution is allowed and encouraged; however, the author would like to be notified of any such distributions.

All translations, derivative works, or aggregate works incorporating any Linux HOWTO documents must be covered under this copyright notice. That is, you may not produce a derivative work from a HOWTO and impose additional restrictions on its distribution. Exceptions to these rules may be granted under certain conditions; please contact the Linux HOWTO coordinator at the address given below.

In short, we wish to promote dissemination of this information through as many channels as possible. However, we do wish to retain copyright on the HOWTO documents, and would like to be notified of any plans to redistribute the HOWTOs.

If you have questions, please contact Greg Hankins, the Linux HOWTO coordinator, at linux-howto@sunsite.unc.edu via email.

13 Credits

14 Copyright message

"mini-HOWTO install qmail with MH"
Christopher Richardson

rdn@tara.n.eunet.de

v1.4, 5 March 1998

I am just documenting my installation experiences to offer some help to other users who wish to use the above combination for their email. v1.4 - I have finally got a new Linux box running so I decided to update this mini-howto

Contents

1 Introduction

My thanks to all netizens who have helped me, especially Tony Nugent (tony@trishul.sci.gu.edu.au), David Summers (david@summersoft.fay.ar.us) and S.u.S.E (Linux distribution) who has made installing Linux so much easier, and the authors of the above excellent programs.

What is qmail and why should I use it? Here is the author's (Dan Bernstein) blurb:

qmail is a secure, reliable, efficient, simple message transfer agent. It is meant as a replacement for the entire sendmail-binmail system on typical Internet-connected UNIX hosts.

Secure: Security isn't just a goal, but an absolute requirement. Mail delivery is critical for users; it cannot be turned off, so it must be completely secure. (This is why I started writing qmail: I was sick of the security holes in sendmail and other MTAs.)

Reliable: qmail's straight-paper-path philosophy guarantees that a message, once accepted into the system, will never be lost. qmail also supports maildir, a new, super-reliable user mailbox format. Maildirs, unlike mbox files and mh folders, won't be corrupted if the system crashes during delivery. Even better, not only can a user safely read his mail over NFS, but any number of NFS clients can deliver mail to him at the same time.

Efficient: On a Pentium under BSD/OS, qmail can easily sustain 200000 local messages per day—that's separate messages injected and delivered to mailboxes in a real test! Although remote deliveries are inherently limited by the slowness of DNS and SMTP, qmail overlaps 20 simultaneous deliveries by default, so it zooms quickly through mailing lists. (This is why I finished qmail: I had to get a big mailing list set up.)

Simple: qmail is vastly smaller than any other Internet MTA. Some reasons why: (1) Other MTAs have separate forwarding, aliasing, and mailing list mechanisms. qmail has one simple forwarding mechanism that lets users handle their own mailing lists. (2) Other MTAs offer a spectrum of delivery modes, from fast+unsafe to slow+queued. qmail-send is instantly triggered by new items in the queue, so the qmail system has just one delivery mode: fast+queued. (3) Other MTAs include, in effect, a specialized version of inetd that watches the load average. qmail's design inherently limits the machine load, so qmail-smtpd can safely run from your system's inetd.

Replacement for sendmail: qmail supports host and user masquerading, full host hiding, virtual domains, null clients, list-owner rewriting, relay control, double-bounce recording, arbitrary RFC 822 address lists, cross-host mailing list loop detection, per-recipient checkpointing, downed host backoffs, independent message retry schedules, etc. In short, it's up to speed on modern MTA features. qmail also includes a drop-in "sendmail" wrapper so that it will be used transparently by your current UAs.

2 My System Details

SuSE Linux Distribution 5.1 with 2.0.33 kernal.

PPP link to ISP

3 Qmail Installation

Follow the INSTALL instructions exactly.

Notes:

Please take the time to read the Fine documentation completely. The numerals refer to the installation steps in the above INSTALL doc.

- 2 - I had to set up the groups and users manually as per INSTALL.ids
- 7 - ./qmail-makectl did not work on my system. I added my domain name (mickey.n.eunet.de) manually in /var/qmail/control/me
- 23 - Make sure qmail-smtpd is spelt correctly in the inetd-conf file. (I spelt it incorrectly i.e. qmail-smptd, which took me two days to find:( ) smtp stream tcp nowait qmaild /var/qmail/bin/tcp-env tcp-env /var/qmail/bin/qmail-smtpd

3.1 Maildir2smtp

Dan Bernstein has provided a package for sending queued email to an ISP via dial-in. This package is available as serialmailxxx from his site.

Install this package as described in the man page (Thanks Rupert Mazzucco (maz@pap.univie.ac.at), it works out of the box!

```
maildir2smtp - blast a maildir across SMTP
```

maildir2smtp is designed to pass messages along a SLIP or PPP link. To set this up on the disconnected end, create a new maildir in alias:

```
# maildirmake ~alias/pppdir
# chown -R alias ~alias/pppdir
```

Put

```
:alias-ppp
```

into control/virtualdomains and

```
./pppdir/
```

into ~alias/.qmail-ppp-default. Don't forget the extra slash in pppdir/. Then, in the PPP startup script, do

```
maildir2smtp ~alias/pppdir alias-ppp- $IP 'hostname'
```

replacing $IP with the remote IP address.

Notes:

- Please read the Fine manual page completely.
- Maildir2smtp requires the dotted IP address of your mail server. If you do not have this then ping Your-Mail.host.country which will return the IP.
- This command can be included in your login script to flush all queued mail after logging in to your ISP.

4 MH Installation

In addition to this, I also replaced /mh-6.8.4/mts/sendmail/smail.c with Dan Bernsteint's mh-qmail-smail.c

This is what my mh-6.8.4/conf/MH looks like:

```
bin      /usr/bin/mh
etc      /usr/lib/mh
#mail
#mandir /usr/man
#manuals         standard
chown   /bin/chown
#cp     cp
#ln     ln
#remove mv -f
cc      gcc
ccoptions -traditional -O2 -m486 -D_NFILE='getdtablesize()'
        -DSIGEMT=SIGUSR1
curses  -lncurses
#ldoptions      -s
```

```
#ldoptlibs
lex        flex
#oldload              off
#ranlib on
mts        sendmail
#mf        off
#bboards              off
#bbdelivery           off
#bbhome /usr/spool/bboards
pop        on
popdir    /usr/lib/mh
sharedlib             sys5
slflags -fPIC
slibdir /usr/lib
mailgroup             mail
signal void
sprintf int
#editor prompter
#debug off
#regtest              off
options ATHENA
options BIND
options DPOP
options DUMB
options FCNTL
options MHE
options MHRC
options MIME
options MORE='"/usr/bin/less"'
options OVERHEAD
options POP2
options POPSERVICE='"pop3"'
options RENAME
options RPATHS
options RPOP
options SOCKETS
options SVR4
options SYS5
options SYS5DIR
options TERMINFO
options UNISTD
options VSPRINTF
```

Notes:

- I have only compiled "mts sendmail" - read in comp.mail.mh somewhere that /smtp can cause problems. Dominic Mitchell (hdm@demon.net) wrote in comp.mail.mh (13 June 1997):

  "Not quite. With this option MH still talks SMTP, just over a pipe and not over a network. You *really* need a line in your /.mh_profile which says:

  postproc: /usr/local/nmh/lib/spost

  Or whever it's kept on your system. This will pass the message directly to sendmail in the traditional manner. You're using qmail of course, so sendmail will be qmail's wrapper script, but that's just fine." Thanks Dominic.

- I have remmed out "mail" because I want to control it via mtstailor

4.1   mtstailor

As qmail delivers mail to the home directory (~/Mailbox). I added the following to my mtstailor

```
localname:      mickey
localdomain:    n.eunet.de
mmdfldir:
mmdflfil:       Mailbox
uucpldir:
uucplfil:
mmdelim1:       \001\001\001\001\n
mmdelim2:       \001\001\001\001\n
mmailid:        0
umincproc:
lockldir:
sendmail:       /usr/lib/sendmail
```

Notes:

- sendmail: /usr/lib/sendmail is a link to the qmail sendmail wrapper in /var/qmail/bin
- MH does not like the tilde notation (~/) use /home instead or leave blank which according to the docs defaults to $HOME.
- I recently installed MH and qmail on my office machine which is connect via ethernet. I added the following line to mtstailor:

  servers: mailserver.company.country

4.2   mh_profile

Here is my .mh_profile

```
Path: Mail
draft-folder: drafts
unseen-sequence: unseen
AliasFile: /home/rdn/.mh_aliases
send: -msgid
comp: -form /home/rdn/.mymh-components
MailDrop: /home/rdn/Mailbox
```

Notes:

- I put in the MailDrop line to be "sure to be sure".

5   Fetchmail

I decided to use fetchmail because I have a multiuser (my family :). Linux and fetchmail delivers mail to the smtp port where qmail takes over.

Installation was no problem, multidrop works with the following .fetchmailrc :

```
poll PersonalMail.Germany.EU.net
```

```
protocol pop3
username myname
password mypassword
# the next two lines do the trick for multidrop
localdomains mydomain.de
is * here
# T2 of the fetchmail FAQ states that qmail needs this
forcecr
```

6 Exmh

This is my mailer by choice. I love it.

There is one problem - most pre-compiled TCL/TK packages have the security option compiled in. The following script
.xserverrc.secure which came with SuSE solves this.

```
#!/bin/sh

#
# move this file to ~/.xserverrc, if you don't want to allow everybody to
# get access to your X-Server
#
if [ -x /usr/bin/keygen ]; then
    if [ ! -x /usr/bin/hostname -a ! -x /bin/hostname \
         -a ! -x /usr/bsd/hostname ];
    then
        echo "startx: can't get my hostname - exiting"
        exit 1
    else
        host='hostname'
    fi

    xauth add $host:0 . '/usr/bin/keygen'
    sleep 2
    xauth add $host/"unix":0 . '/usr/bin/keygen'
    exec X :0 -auth .Xauthority $*
else
    exec X :0 $*
fi
```

7 Procmail

The qmail FAQ gives this command:

In /.qmail add the line

```
| preline procmail
```

Version 3.11pre7 has changed the default mail box variable. It used to be in config.h. It is now in src/authenticate.c:

```
#define MAILSPOOLHOME "/Mailbox"        /* watch the leading / */
                                        /* delivers to $HOME/Mailbox */
```

I have culled from comp.mail.mh ans comp.mail.misc some hints on a .procmailrc file. Thanks to everyone!

```
# A SAMPLE .PROCMAILRC FILE FOR NOVICES
# Written by Catherine Hampton <ariel@best.com>
# Version 1.1
# Updated 1/25/98
#
# Released to the Public Domain.
#
#
# SET VARIABLES

# Internal Variables
# the following have be modified by rdn 19980303

# Everyone says that the SHELL environment is essential
SHELL=/bin/sh                      #Shell used to run proc-
mail.  Be sure this points to
                                   #your system's copy of sh.  DO NOT substitute a
                                   #different shell unless you really know UNIX

LINEBUF=4096                       #Needed to keep Procmail from choking on long
                                   #"recipes", or instructions on what to do with
                                   #particular kinds of email.

PATH=$HOME/bin:/bin:/usr/bin:/usr/local/bin:/usr/bin/mh:/usr/lib/mh:
                                   #Path for your programs -- this is probably best
                                   #left alone.

VERBOSE=off                        #Change this to "on" when you try a new recipe
                                   #so that Procmail will log literally every step
                                   #it takes.  DO NOT LEAVE IT ON, though, because
                                   #it creates huge logfiles.

# Default Program & file locations

MAILDIR=$HOME/Mail                 #you'd better make sure this directory exists

DEFAULT=$HOME/Mailbox               #default incoming mailbox for shell2-5 users
                                   #on Best Internet.  Substitute the correct
                                   #setting for your system.


LOGFILE=$MAILDIR/procmail.log #Logs message disposition.  Recommended --
otherwise
                                   #errors are emailed to you. :/

FORMAIL=/usr/bin/formail           #useful for autoreply recipes.  If you
                                   #are not on Best Internet, modify this to
                                   #your system's copy of formail.

SENDMAIL=/usr/sbin/sendmail        #useful for autoreply recipes.  If you are
                                   #not on Best Internet, modify this to point
                                   #to your system's copy of sendmail.
```

Procmail is an excellently documented program. Read the man pages for examples on how to set up your .procmailrc file.

Mini-HOWTO

8 ISDN

I am including this although this has nothing to do with qmail or mh. But without a PPP line to your ISP there is no email at all. I had quite a bit of bother to get my ISDN working. The SuSE distribution includes a configuration for ISDN, but I wanted something simpler. The stuff here was adapted from Bernhard Hailer's scripts. (Vielen, vielen dank!)

The following rc.config loads the necessary modules during initialisation:

```
#!/bin/bash
# This is adapted Bernhard Hailer's old script

LOCAL_NUMBER="91311234"          # tel no. 091311234
REMOTE_NUMBER="0911123456"       # ISP tel no.
LOCAL_IP="192.168.0.99"          # I have dynamic IP so this will do
REMOTE_IP="195.112.123.11"       # your ISP's gateway
DEVICE="ippp0"

SYSPATH="/sbin"
ISDNCTRL="$SYSPATH/isdnctrl"

case "$1" in
start)
        # turn on isdn
        insmod /lib/modules/2.0.33/net/slhc.o
        insmod /lib/modules/2.0.33/misc/isdn.o
        sleep 1
        # load the hisax module
        insmod /lib/modules/2.0.33/misc/hisax.o
                          id=Tel0 type=5 protocol=2 irq=10 io=0x300
        echo "starting isdn4linux"
        # global
        $ISDNCTRL verbose 0

        $ISDNCTRL addif $DEVICE            # create new interface
        $ISDNCTRL addphone $DEVICE in $REMOTE_NUMBER
        $ISDNCTRL addphone $DEVICE out $REMOTE_NUMBER
        $ISDNCTRL eaz $DEVICE $LOCAL_NUMBER
        $ISDNCTRL l2_prot $DEVICE hdlc
        $ISDNCTRL l3_prot $DEVICE trans
        $ISDNCTRL encap $DEVICE syncppp
        $ISDNCTRL huptimeout $DEVICE 300
        $ISDNCTRL chargehup  $DEVICE off
        $ISDNCTRL secure $DEVICE on

        $SYSPATH/ifconfig $DEVICE $LOCAL_IP pointopoint $REMOTE_IP metric 1
        $SYSPATH/route add default $DEVICE
        $SYSPATH/ipppd /dev/ippp0 file /etc/ppp/options.ipppd &
        $SYSPATH/route del default


        ;;
stop)
        #turn off isdn
        rmmod hisax.o
        sleep 1
        rmmod isdn.o
```

```
            rmmod slhc.o
            echo "Shutting down isdn4linux"
            $ISDNCTRL delif ippp0
            ;;
*)
            echo "Usage: $0 (start|stop)"
            exit 1
            ;;
esac
```

I use the following script to dial out, it is called simply isdn on|off

```
#!/bin/bash
# This is based on an old script from Bernhard Hailer

IP_ADDRESS="195.112.123.11"

case "$1" in
on)


        echo "Calling ippp0"
        /sbin/isdnctrl dial ippp0
# the sleep is important as it gives the PPP time to settle down
        echo "Sleep for 8s for PPP handshake"
        sleep 8s
        /sbin/route add default ippp0
        echo "line open - checking...."

# check whether PPP negotiation was successful:
        set 'ping -qc3 -i1 $IP_ADDRESS 2>/dev/null | grep transmitted'
        if [ $4 -gt 0 ];
        then
                echo "succeeded."
                echo "Starting fetchmail daemon"
                /usr/bin/fetchmail -d 600 -k -v -a -L /var/log/fetchmail
                echo "Flushing mail queue...."
                /usr/local/bin/serialmail/maildir2smtp
                            ~alias/pppdir alias-ppp-
mail.server.ip.no 'hostname'
        else
                echo "failed!"
                /sbin/isdnctrl hangup ippp0
        fi

;;

off)
                echo -n "Shutting down fetchmail daemon"
                /usr/bin/fetchmail --quit

                /sbin/isdnctrl hangup ippp0
                /sbin/route del default            # and delete route
                echo "You're off line"
```

```
        ;;

*)
            echo -e "\aUsage:"
            echo "isdn on"
            echo "isdn off"
        ;;

esac
```

The next lot is the ipppd options file /etc/ppp/options.ipppd

```
# Based on:
# Klaus Franken, kfr@suse.de
# Version: 27.08.97 (5.1)
#
# This file is copy by YaST from /etc/ppp/ioptions.YaST
#   to options.<device>

user "myuserid"

# my system name (only for CHAP!)
# name my_system_name

# accept IP addresses from peer
# use with dynamic IP
ipcp-accept-local
ipcp-accept-remote
noipdefault

# try to get IP address from interface
# option specific to ipppd (as opposed to pppd)
# use only with static IP
#useifip

# disable all header-compression
-vj
-vjccomp
-ac
-pc
-bsdcomp

# sometimes you need this:
#noccp

# max receive unit
mru 1524
# max transmit unit
mtu 1500

# If this machine is a server, force authentication by uncommenting one
# of the following. However, if this machine is a client, doing this will
# prevent a succesful connection! (message "peer refused to authenticate").
# So, only uncomment on a server.
# "+pap" / "+chap" NUR AKTIVIEREN, WENN DIES EIN SERVER IST!!!
```

```
#+pap
#+chap

# if you have problems with handshaking (no response for first
# lcp-package) try to decrease the retry-cycle. Default is 3 sec,
# try for example 2 sec:
# lcp-restart 2
```

9   Sources

Required Packages:

The net is so dynamic that it is pretty pointless to give sources. but for what it's worth:

- Find Qmail, setserial on http://www.qmail.org/
- Find MH on http://www.ics.uci.edu/~mh/
- Find glimpse on http://glimpse.cs.arizona.edu/
- Find Fetchmail on http://sagan.earthspace.net/~esr/fetchmail
- Find Exmh http://www.beedub.com/exmh
- Find Procmail ftp.informatik.rwth-aachen.de/pub/packages/promail

10   Disclaimers

The usual no guarantees, no money back, use at your own risk.

11   Postscript

Has anyone got mh working with Maildir? I have not tried - the principle of not fixing a running system. If you have got it working please mail me your instruction for inclusion in the next revision

"Quota mini-HOWTO" Albert M.C. Tam

bertie@scn.org
v0.0, 8 August 1997

Preamble: This document is copylefted by Albert M.C. Tam (bertie@scn.org). Permission to use, copy, distribute this document for non-commerical purposes is hereby granted, provided that the author's / editor's name and this notice appear in all copies and/or supporting documents; that this document is not modified. This document is distributed in hope that it will be useful, but WITHOUT ANY WARRANTY, either expressed or implied. While every effort has been taken to ensure the accuracy of the information documented herein, the author / editor / maintainer assumes NO RESPONSIBILITY for errors, or for damages results for the use of the information documented herein. This document describes how to enable file system quota on a Linux host, assigning quota for users and groups, as well as the usage of miscellaneous quota commands. It is intended for users running kernel 2.x (recently tested on RedHat 4.1 running kernel 2.0.27). Users running older kernels may need to upgrade to a newer kernel version in order to take advantage of quota. Feel free to send feedbacks or comments to bertie@scn.org if you find an error, or if any information is missing. I appreciate it.

1   What is Quota?

Quota allows you to specify limits on two aspects of disk storage: the number of inodes a user or a group of users may possess; and the number of disk blocks that may be allocated to a user or a group of users.

The idea behind quota is that users are forced to stay under their disk comsumption limit, taking away their ability to comsume unlimited disk space on a system. Quota is handled on a per user, per file system basis. If there is more than one file system which a user is expected to create files, then quota must be set for each file system seperately.

2   Current Status of Quota on Linux

Quota support has been integrated into kernel since version 1.3.8x I heard. Now it is part of the 2.0 release of the Linux kernel. If your system doesn't support quota, I really recommend an upgrade.

Currently, quota works for ext2 type file system only.

3   Requirements for Using Quota on Linux

3.1   Kernel

The 2.x kernel source is available from

```
http://sunsite.unc.edu/pub/Linux/kernel/v2.0
```

3.2   Quota software

Depending on the Linux distribution you have, you may, or may not have the quota softwares installed on your system. If you don't, then download the quota software source from

```
ftp://ftp.funet.fi/pub/Linux/PEOPLE/Linus/subsystems/quota/all.tar.gz.
```

4 Quota Setup on Linux - Part I: The Configuration

4.1 Reconfigure your kernel

Reconfigure your kernel and add quota support by typing y to:

```
Quota support (CONFIG_QUOTA) [n] y
```

4.2 Compile and install the quota softwares

The quota software source is available from

```
ftp://ftp.funet.fi/pub/Linux/PEOPLE/Linus/subsystems/quota/all.tar.gz
```

4.3 Modify your system init script to check quota and turn quota on at boot time

Here's an example:

```
# Check quota and then turn quota on.
if [ -x /usr/sbin/quotacheck ]
        then
                echo "Checking quotas. This may take some time."
                /usr/sbin/quotacheck -avug
                echo " Done."
        fi
        if [ -x /usr/sbin/quotaon ]
        then
                echo "Turning on quota."
                /usr/sbin/quotaon -avug
        fi
```

The golden rule is that always turn quota on after your file systems in /etc/fstab have been mounted, otherwise quota will fail to work. I recommend turning quota on at the end of your system init script, or, if you like, right after the part where file systems are mounted in your system init script.

4.4 Modify /etc/fstab

Partitions that you have not yet enabled quota normally look something like:

```
/dev/hda1        /        ext2      defaults           1       1
/dev/hda2        /usr     ext2      defaults           1       1
```

To enable user quota support on a file system, add "usrquota" to the fourth field containing the word "defaults" (man fstab for details).

```
/dev/hda1        /        ext2      defaults           1       1
/dev/hda2        /usr     ext2      defaults,usrquota  1       1
```

Replace "usrquota" with "grpquota", should you need group quota support on a file system.

| /dev/hda1 | / | ext2 | defaults | 1 | 1 |
| /dev/hda2 | /usr | ext2 | defaults,grpquota | 1 | 1 |

Need both user quota and group quota support on a file system?

| /dev/hda1 | / | ext2 | defaults | 1 | 1 |
| /dev/hda2 | /usr | ext2 | defaults,usrquota,grpquota | 1 | 1 |

4.5   Create quota record "quota.user" and "quota.group"

Both quota record files, quota.user and quota.group, should be owned by root, and read-write permission for root and none for anybody else.

Login as root. Go to the root of the partition you wish to enable quota, then create quota.user and quota.group by doing:

```
touch /partition/quota.user
touch /partition/quota.group
chmod 600 /partition/quota.user
chmod 600 /partition/quota.group
```

4.6   Reboot

Now reboot system for the changes you have made to take effect.

Also note that subsequent partitions you wish to enable quota in the future only require step 4, 5, and 6.

5   Quota Setup on Linux - Part II: Assigning Quota for Users and Groups

This operation is performed with the edquota command (man edquota for details).

I would normally run quotacheck with the flags -avug to obtain the most updated filesystems usage prior to editing quota. This is just a personal habit, and not a required step however.

5.1   Assigning quota for a particular user

Here's an example. I have a user with the login id bob on my system. The command "edquota -u bob" takes me into vi (or editor specified in my $EDITOR environment variable) to edit quota for user bob on each partition that has quota enabled:

```
Quotas for user bob:
/dev/hda2: blocks in use: 2594, limits (soft = 5000, hard = 6500)
          inodes in use: 356, limits (soft = 1000, hard = 1500)
```

"blocks in use" is the total number of blocks (in kilobytes) a user has comsumed on a partition.

"inodes in use" is the total number of files a user has on a partition.

5.2 Assigning quota for a particular group

Now I have a group games on my system. "edquota -g games" takes me into the vi editor again to edit quota for the group games:

```
Quotas for group games:
/dev/hda4: blocks in use: 5799, limits (soft = 8000, hard = 10000)
           inodes in use: 1454, limits (soft = 3000, hard = 4000)
```

5.3 Assigning quota for a bunch of users with the same value

To rapidly set quotas for, say 100 users, on my system to the same value as my user bob, I would first edit bob's quota information by hand, then execute:

```
edquota -p bob 'awk -F: '$3 > 499 {print $1}' /etc/passwd'
```

assuming that you are using csh, and that you assign your user UID's starting with 500.

In addition to edquota, there are 3 terms which you should familiarize yourself with: Soft Limit, Hard Limit, and Grace Period.

5.4 Soft Limit

Soft limit indicates the maximum amount of disk usage a quota user has on a partition. When combined with grace period, it acts as the border line, which a quota user is issued warnings about his impending quota violation when passed.

5.5 Hard Limit

Hard limit works only when grace period is set. It specifies the absolute limit on the disk usage, which a quota user can't go beyond his hard limit.

5.6 Grace Period

Executed with the command "edquota -t", grace period is a time limit before the soft limit is enforced for a file system with quota enabled. Time units of sec(onds), min(utes), hour(s), day(s), week(s), and month(s) can be used. This is what you'll see with the command "edquota -t":

```
Time units may be: days, hours, minutes, or seconds
Grace period before enforcing soft limits for users:
/dev/hda2: block grace period: 0 days, file grace period: 0 days
```

Change the 0 days part to any length of time you feel reasonable. I personally would choose 7 days (or 1 week).

6 Miscellaneous Quota Commands

6.1 Quotacheck

Quotacheck is used to scan a file system for disk usages, and updates the quota record file "quota.user" to the most recent state. I recommend running quotacheck at system bootup, or via cronjob periodically (say, every week?).

6.2 Repquota

Repquota produces a summarized quota information for a file system. Here is a sample output repquota gives:

```
# repquota -a
                        Block limits              File limits
        User        used   soft   hard  grace   used  soft  hard  grace
        root    -- 175419     0      0          14679    0     0
        bin     --  18000     0      0            735    0     0
        uucp    --    729     0      0             23    0     0
        man     --     57     0      0             10    0     0
        user1   --  13046 15360  19200            806 1500  2250
        user2   --   2838  5120   6400            377 1000  1500
```

6.3 Quotaon and Quotaoff

Quotaon is used to turn on quota accouting; quotaoff to turn it off. Actually both files are similar. They are executed at system startup and shutdown.

" The RCS MINI-HOWTO" Robert Kiesling

v1.4, 14 August 1997

This document covers basic installation and usage of RCS, the GNU Revision Control System, under Linux. It also covers the installation of the diff(1) and diff3(1) utilities, which are necessary for RCS to operate. This document may be reproduced freely, in whole or in part, provided that any usage of this document conforms to the general copyright notice of the HOWTO series of the Linux Documentation Project. See the file COPYRIGHT for details. Send all complaints, suggestions, errata, and any miscellany to *kiesling@terracom.net*, so I can keep this document as complete and up to date as possible.

Contents

1 Overview of RCS.

RCS, the revision control system, is a suite of programs that tracks changes in text files and controls shared access to files in work group situations. It is generally used to maintain source code modules. It lends itself to tracking revisions of document files as well.

RCS was written by Walter F. Tichy and Paul Eggert. The latest version which has been ported to Linux is RCS Version 5.7. There is also a semi-official, threaded version available. Much of the information in this HOWTO is taken from the RCS man pages.

RCS includes the rcs(1) program, which controls RCS archive file attributes, ci(1) and co(1), which check files in and out of RCS archives, ident(1), which searches RCS archives by keyword identifiers, rcsclean(1), a program to clean up files that are not being worked on or haven't changed, rcsdiff(1), which runs diff(1) to compare the revisions, rcsmerge(1), which merges two RCS branches into a single working file, and rlog(1), which prints RCS log messages.

Files archived by RCS may be text of any format, or binary if the diff program used to generate change files handles 8-bit data. Files may optionally include identification strings to aid in tracking by ident(1). RCS uses the utilities diff(1) and diff3(3) to generate the change files between revisions. A RCS archive consists of the initial revision of a file, which is version 1.1, and a series of change files, one for each revision. Each time a file is checked out of an archive with co(1), edited, and checked back into the archive with ci(1), the version number is increased, for example, to 1.2, 1.3, 1.4, and so on for successive revisions.

The archives themselves commonly reside in a ./RCS subdirectory, although RCS has other options for archive storage.

Mini-HOWTO

For an overview of RCS, see the `rcsintro(1)` manual page.

2 System requirements.

RCS needs `diff(1)` and `diff3(3)` to generate the context diff files between revisions. The diff utilities suite needs to be installed on your system, and when you install RCS, the software will check for its presence.

Precompiled diffutils binaries are available at:

```
ftp://sunsite.unc.edu/pub/Linux/utils/text/diffutils-2.6.bin.ELF.tar.gz
```

and its mirror sites. If you need to compile `diff(1)`, et al., from source, it is located at:

```
ftp://prep.ai.mit.edu/pub/gnu/diffutils-2.7.tar.gz
```

and its mirror sites.

You will also need to have the ELF libraries installed on your system if you want to install pre-built binaries. See the ELF-HOWTO for further details.

3 Compiling RCS from Source.

Get the source distribution of RCS Version 5.7. It is available at

```
ftp://sunsite.unc.edu/pub/Linux/devel/vc/rcs-5.7.src.tar.gz
```

and its mirrors. After you have unpacked the archive into your source tree, you need to configure RCS for your system. This is done via the `configure` script in the source directory, which you need to execute first. This will generate a `Makefile` and the appropriate `conf.sh` for your system. You can then type

```
make install
```

which will build the binaries. At some point you may need to `su` to root so the binaries can be installed in the correct directories.

4 Creating and maintaining archives.

The program `rcs(1)` does the work or creating archives and modifying their attributes. A summary of `rcs(1)` options may be found in the `rcs(1)` manual page.

The easiest way to create an archive is first to `mkdir RCS` in the current directory, then initialize the archive with the

```
rcs -i name_of_work_file
```

command. This creates and archive with the name `./RCS/name_of_work_file,v` and requests a text message describing the archive, but it does not deposit any revisions in the archive. You can turn on or off strict archive locking with the commands

```
rcs -L name_of_work_file
```

and

```
rcs -U name_of_work_file
```

respectively. There are other options for controlling access to the archive, setting its format, and setting revision numbers, which are covered in the `rcs(1)` manual page.

5 ci(1) and co(1).

`ci(1)` and `co(1)` are the commands used to check files in and out of their RCS archives. The `ci(1)` command may also be used to a check a file both in and out of an archive. In their simplest forms, `ci(1)` and `co(1)` take only the name of the working file.

```
ci name_of_work_file
```

and

```
co name_of_work_file
```

The command form

```
ci -l name_of_work_file
```

checks in the file with locking enabled, and

```
co -l name_of_work_file
```

is performed automatically. That is, `ci -l` checks the file out again with locking enabled.

```
ci -u name_of_work_file
```

checks the file into the archive, and checks it out again with locking disabled. In all cases, the user is prompted for a log message.

`ci(1)` will also create a RCS archive if one does not exist already.

If you don't specify a revision, `ci(1)` increments the version number of the last revision locked in the archive, and appends the revised working file to it. If you specify a revision on an existing branch, it must be higher than the existing revision numbers. `ci(1)` will also create a new branch if you specify the revision of a branch which does not exist. See the `ci(1)` and `co(1)` man pages for details.

`ci(1)` and `co(1)` have various options for interactive and non-interactive use. Again, see the `ci(1)` and `co(1)` man pages for details.

6 Revision histories.

The `rlog(1)` program provides information about the archive file and the logs of each revision stored in it. A command like

```
rlog work_file_name
```

will print the version history of the file, each revision's creation date and `userids` of author and the person who locked the file. You can specify archive attributes and revision parameters to view.

7 Including RCS data in working files.

co(1) maintains a list of keywords of the RCS database which are expanded when the working file is checked out. The keyword Id in a document will expand to a string which contains the file name, revision number, the date checked out, the author, the revision status, and the locker, if any. Including the keyword Log will expand to the document's revision history log.

These and other keywords may be used as search criteria of the RCS archive. See the ident(1) man page for further details.

8 RCS and emacs(1) Version Control.

The Version Control facility of emacs(1) works as a front end to RCS. This information applies specifically to Version 19.34 of GNU Emacs, which is provided with the major Linux distributions. When editing a file with emacs(1) which is registered with RCS, the command vc-toggle-read-only (bound to C-x C-q by default) will check a file in to the emacs's Version Control, and then into RCS. Emacs will open a buffer where you can type a log message to be included in the RCS log. When you are finished typing a log entry, type C-c C-c to terminate your input and proceed with the check-in process.

If you have selected strict locking for the file with RCS, you must re-lock the file for editing by emacs(1). You can check the file out for emacs's Version Control with the command % in buffer-menu mode.

For more information, see the GNU Emacs Manual and the Emacs info pages.

Part LXXV

"Burning a RedHat CD mini-HOWTO" Morten Kjeldgaard

mok@imsb.au.dk and Peter von der Ahé pahe+rhcd@daimi.au.dk
v1.18, 27 December 1998

This document describes how to make your own CDs from the Red Hat Linux distribution equivalent to the ones commercially available from Red Hat. The structure of the distribution is described, as well as the procedure needed to include updated RPMS into the distribution. Prerequisites are a good network connection, and a CD-writer.

Contents

1   Introduction

There may be several reasons for making your own CD. Perhaps you're a cheapskate and want to save the $50 cost of the *Red Hat distribution* <http://www.redhat.com/>. Or, perhaps you want a distribution CD containing the latest distribution with all current updates. This is highly relevant, because after each major release of the Red Hat distribution, there have been loads of updates, several of which are security related. Just take a look at the *updates/00README.errata*

1851

<ftp://ftp.redhat.com/pub/redhat/redhat-5.1/updates/00README.errata> file. A specific er-
rata sheet also exists for each supported platform. See for example *the Intel errata sheet* <ftp://ftp.redhat.com/
pub/redhat/updates/5.1/i386/00README.errata>

2 Anatomy of the Red Hat FTP site

In the spirit of the Linux community, Red Hat Software has made available their Linux distributions for several platforms
on their FTP site. These are all available from the top distribution directory.

2.1 The top level directory

The toplevel directory for RedHat Linux release 5.1 (*pub/redhat/redhat-5.1* <ftp://ftp.redhat.com/pub/
redhat/redhat-5.1/>) contains distributions for the different platforms, and a directory containing updates and
corrections to program packages that have been published since the release.

```
SRPMS/     alpha/     i386/     sparc/     updates/
```

In this document, we use the i386 distribution as an example. The procedure given in this document is likely to work
on all platforms supported by Red Hat (Alpha, SPARC, ppc, etc.), but we have only tested it on the i386 platform (the
authors would be most interested in additional information). The root of the i386 directory looks like this:

```
-rw-r--r--    8 ftpuser   ftpusers     19686 May 27  1997 COPYING
-rw-r--r--    1 ftpuser   ftpusers      3023 May  7 09:58 README
-rw-r--r--   10 ftpuser   ftpusers      2751 Sep 18  1997 RPM-PGP-KEY
drwxr-xr-x    5 ftpuser   ftpusers        96 Jul 15 08:34 RedHat/
drwxr-xr-x    5 ftpuser   ftpusers      8192 Jul 15 08:35 doc/
drwxr-xr-x    5 ftpuser   ftpusers      8192 Jul 15 08:35 dosutils/
drwxr-xr-x    5 ftpuser   ftpusers      8192 Jul 15 08:33 gnome/
drwxr-xr-x    2 ftpuser   ftpusers        96 Jun  7 02:47 images/
drwxr-xr-x    4 ftpuser   ftpusers        96 Jun  5 12:24 misc/
```

The doc directory contains an abundance of information. Most importantly, the RedHat installation manual can be found
in HTML format in the directory *doc/rhmanual/manual/* <ftp://ftp.redhat.com/pub/redhat/redhat-5.
1/i386/doc/rhmanual/manual/doc000.htm>. Next, there is a number of FAQs, and finally, the entire collection of HOWTOs and mini-HOWTOs.

The images directory contains boot floppy images that must be copied to a diskette. In the most recent distribution
(5.1), there are two disk images available. The boot image is called boot.img, which is required when installation is
performed directly from a CD-ROM. If installation from a local hard disk, NFS mounted disk or FTP is required, the
supplementary disk image supp.img might be needed. See section 7 (Installing from the CD) and references therein
for details.

The misc directory contains source and executables of a number of programs needed for the installation.

2.2 The "RedHat" directory – the core of the distribution

The most important part of the directory tree is rooted in the RedHat directory:

```
drwxr-xr-x    2 ftpuser   ftpusers     24576 Jul 15 08:35 RPMS/
drwxr-xr-x    2 ftpuser   ftpusers      8192 Jul 15 08:32 base/
-rw-rw-rw-   59 ftpuser   ftpusers         0 Aug 15 14:21 i386
drwxr-xr-x    4 ftpuser   ftpusers        96 Jun  5 12:24 instimage/
```

The RPMS directory contains the major part of the Red Hat distribution consisting of a set of RPM (Redhat Package Manager) files. An RPM package typically contains binary executables, along with relevant configuration files and documentation. See the section 3 (RPM packages) for more information.

The base directory holds different book-keeping files needed during the installation process, e.g. the comps file, which defines the *components* (groups of packages) used during the "Choose packages to install" phase. Another important file in the base directory is the hdlist file containing most of the header fields from all the RPMs in the RPMS directory.

This means that all the interdependencies among RPM packages can be determined just by reading hdlist without having to read all the RPM packages which is quite convenient especially during FTP installs.

Another use of hdlist is mapping package names to file name, eg. perl to perl-5.004-6.i386.rpm. This means that if you want to incorporate updates from RedHat (see section 5 (Incorporating the updates)) or add your own packages to the RPMS directory, you need to update hdlist. This is descriped later in 5.3 (Generating a new hdlist file).

The instimage directory contains a bare-bones live file system with a number of programs and shared libraries needed during the installation procedure.

3 RPM packages

The major part of the Red Hat distribution consists of a set of RPM (Redhat Package Manager) files. An RPM package typically contains binary executables, along with relevant configuration files and documentation. The *rpm* <http://www.rpm.org> program is a powerful package manager, which can be used to install, query, verify, update, erase and build software packages in the RPM format. Rpm convieniently maintains a database of all the software packages it has installed, so information on the installed software is available at any time.

The binary RPM files in the distribution have been built on a system running the distribution itself. This is important, because most of the programs in the packages rely on shared libraries. From RedHat version 5.0, the new version 2 of the GNU standard C library (which is 64-bit clean) has been used. This version of the library is commonly referred to as glibc or in Linux: libc 6. All executables in the distribution have been linked against this library. If you attempt to install binary files from a different distribution, chances are that they will not work, unless you install the libc5 package for backwards compability.

The names of the RPM packages contain the suffix *.arch*.rpm, where *arch* is the architechture, having the value i386 for Intel platform binaries. The packages you install must match the versions of the shared libraries available on the machine. The *rpm* <http://www.rpm.org> program is usually quite good at ensuring that this is indeed the case, however, there are ways around this check, and you should be sure that you know what you are doing if you force installation of packages this way. However, using the RedHat installation boot disk, it is ensured that the correct set of RPM packages are installed on the machine.

If you discover an RPM package that was not installed on your system during the installation process, don't despair. At any time, you may (as root) install RPM packages, for example:

```
rpm --install  WindowMaker-0.18-1b.i386.rpm
```

You can even install directly from the Internet, if you know the URL of an RPM package:

```
rpm --install ftp://rufus.w3.org/redhat-contrib/noarch/mirror-2.9-
2.noarch.rpm
```

Another version of the RPM packages contain the original sources used to build the binaries. These packages have the suffix .src.rpm and are situated in the SRPMS directory. These packages are not needed on the installation CD, and in fact, there is not even enough disk space on an 74 minute burnable CD to accomodate them. Of course, you can make a separate CD with the SRPMS.

Mini-HOWTO

4 Obtaining your local copy of the distribution

You need a copy of the distribution on a writable disk which is accessible from the computer having the CD writer (duh!). If you want to incorporate the latest updates, this directory should (also) be accessible from from a Linux machine, either from a local disk, an NFS mounted disk on a different computer, or a JAZ disk.

You could copy the distribution from a RedHat CD, or you could get it via FTP. If you choose to use FTP, the best way to get a correct copy of the distribution is to use the `mirror` package.

Mirror is a sophisticated perl script that compares the content of a directory on a remote site with a local directory. It will use FTP to fetch the files that are on the remote site but not the local site, and delete files on the local site that are not on the remote site. The mirror program is configured with a configuration file. The mirror package is available as an RPM from *rufus.w3.org* `<http://rufus.w3.org/linux/RPM/mirror.html>`.

Make your local copy `mirror.redhat` of the mirror configuration file, and edit the relevant fields at the top of the file. After the default section, define these packages:

```
package=updates
        site=ftp.sunsite.auc.dk
        exclude_patt=(alpha/|sparc/)
        remote_dir=/disk1/ftp.redhat.com/pub/redhat/redhat-5.1/updates
        local_dir=/jaz/redhat-5.1/updates

package=dist
        site=ftp.sunsite.auc.dk
        exclude_patt=(alpha/|sparc/)
        remote_dir=/disk1/ftp.redhat.com/pub/redhat/redhat-5.1/i386
        local_dir=/jaz/redhat-5.1/i386
```

The following command will download a copy of the entire RedHat tree on your local disk. *Think* before you do this, you are about to transfer approximately 350Mb of data.

```
mirror -pdist mirror.redhat
```

This will mirror the Red Hat FTP site on your local disk. The content of a Red Hat distribution does not change between releases, so you only need to download this package *ONCE*. All changes to the distribution are in the `updates` directory. Thus, if you want to keep an up-to-date mirror of the Red Hat distribution, you only need to keep the `updates` directory current. This is done using the command

```
mirror -pupdates mirror.redhat
```

You can run this regularly, say, once a week, through a cron script. The RedHat distribution is available on a great number of FTP servers around the world, which are updated daily from the master site at `<ftp://ftp.redhat.com/pub>`. You should choose an FTP site close to you, see the *RedHat FAQ* `<http://www.redhat.com/support/docs/rhl/RedHat-FAQ/RedHat-FAQ-12.html>`

5 Incorporating the updates

To incorporate the updates, you need write access to the distribution directory from a Linux machine, with a working version of *rpm* `<http://www.rpm.org>` installed. There are three steps involved:

1. Correct the file protection modes.

2. Replace updated RPMs.

3. Generate the hdlist file

If you maintain a mirror of the `updates` directory, you can at any time produce a CD including the current updates by repeating these steps.

5.1 Correcting the file protection modes

During the installation process, some programs are run directly off the CD. Unfortunately, the FTP program does not always preserve the protection modes of the files and directories that are copied. Therefore, it is necessary to make sure that execute permission is given to programs, shell scripts and shared libraries, before the directory is burned on the CD. This is done by running the `updatePerm` script on your local copy of the distribution:

```
#!/bin/bash

RHVERSION=5.1

LIST=/tmp/er3hd3w25
CDDIR=/jaz/redhat-${RHVERSION}

# Find all directories, and make sure they have +x permission
find $CDDIR -type d -exec chmod -c 755 {} \;

# Find all files that are executables, shell or perl scripts
find $CDDIR -type f | file -f - | grep -v RPM \
   | egrep -i 'executable|perl|bourne|shell' | cut -f1 -d: > $LIST

# Find shared libraries
find $CDDIR -name \*.so >> $LIST

# Make them executable
while read file
do
   if [ ! -x $file ] ; then
      chmod -c 755 $file
   fi
done < $LIST

/bin/rm $LIST

exit 0
```

5.2 Replacing the updated RPMS

The following script called `updateCD` copies all files from the update directory to the RPMS directory. The script uses some nifty rpm tricks to determine what packages in the updates directory are more recent. Older packages are moved to the `${OLD}` directory.

```
#! /bin/bash
# This script updates rpms in a RedHat distribution found in $RPMDIR.
# The old rpms will be placed in $OLDDIR.
# The new rpms should be located in $UPDDIR.
# The architechture is $ARCH.
```

```
RHVERSION=5.1
ARCH=i386

CDDIR=/jaz/redhat-${RHVERSION}
RPMDIR=${CDDIR}/${ARCH}/RedHat/RPMS
UPDDIR=${CDDIR}/updates/${ARCH}
OLDDIR=${CDDIR}/old

if [ ! -d $OLDDIR ] ; then
    echo making directory $OLDDIR
    mkdir $OLDDIR
fi

allow_null_glob_expansion=1

for rpm in ${UPDDIR}/*.rpm ; do
  NAME='rpm --queryformat "%{NAME}" -qp $rpm'
  unset OLDNAME
  for oldrpm in ${RPMDIR}/${NAME}*.rpm ; do
    if [ 'rpm --queryformat "%{NAME}" -qp $oldrpm' = "$NAME" ]; then
      OLDNAME=$oldrpm;
      break
    fi
  done
  if [ -z "$OLDNAME" ]; then
    echo $NAME is new
    cp -pv $rpm $RPMDIR
  else
    if [ 'basename $rpm' != 'basename $OLDNAME' ]; then
      mv $OLDNAME $OLDDIR
      cp -pv $rpm $RPMDIR
    fi
  fi
done


# Copy new boot image files to the right place...
for newfile in ${UPDDIR}/images/* ; do
  file=${CDDIR}$/${ARCH}/images/$(basename ${newfile})
  if [ $newfile -nt $file ] ; then
    cp -pv $newfile $file
  fi
done

exit 0
```

5.3 Generating a new hdlist file

When installing from the CD, the installation program on the CD relies on the file `RedHat/base/hdlist` describing what RPM packages are available on the CD. The `hdlist` file can be generated by the program `misc/src/install/genhdlist`. This program must be run with the root name of the distribution as the only argument. Here is the `updateHdlist` script which calls that program:

```
#!/bin/bash

RHVERSION=5.1
ARCH=i386

echo generating hdlist...
CDDIR=/jaz/redhat-${RHVERSION}
GENHDDIR=${CDDIR}/${ARCH}/misc/src/install

chmod u+x ${GENHDDIR}/genhdlist
chmod 644 ${CDDIR}/${ARCH}/RedHat/base/hdlist
${GENHDDIR}/genhdlist ${CDDIR}/${ARCH} || echo "*** GENHDLIST FAILED ***"

exit 0
```

NOTE: After having incorporated the updates in the main RedHat/RPMS directory, your copy of the distribution is no longer a mirror of the Red Hat distribution site. Actually, it is more up-to-date! Therefore, if you attempt to mirror the distribution, older versions of the RPM's that have been updated will be downloaded once more, and the updates deleted.

5.3.1   Important note for RedHat 5.2

As distributed with RedHat version 5.2 and earlier, genhdlist CRASHES if there are files in the RedHat/RPMS directory which are *not* RPM files! This causes problems, because in the 5.2 distribution, there are a couple of non-RPM files named ls-lR and ls-lR.gz in RedHat/RPMS. Therefore, you must remove all non-RPM files from the directory. Alternatively, you can apply the following patch to misc/src/install/genhdlist.c and do a make. The patch will cause genhdlist to ignore any non-RPM files.

```
*** genhdlist.c.orig    Fri Nov 27 12:08:13 1998
--- genhdlist.c Fri Nov 27 12:08:20 1998
**************
*** 12,23 ****
--- 12,26 ----

  #define FILENAME_TAG 1000000

+ /* Not used apparently...
+
  int tags[] =  { RPMTAG_NAME, RPMTAG_VERSION, RPMTAG_RELEASE, RPMTAG_SERIAL,
              RPMTAG_FILENAMES, RPMTAG_FILESIZES, RPMTAG_GROUP,
              RPMTAG_REQUIREFLAGS, RPMTAG_REQUIRENAME, RPMTAG_REQUIREVERSION,
              RPMTAG_DESCRIPTION, RPMTAG_SUMMARY, RPMTAG_PROVIDES,
              RPMTAG_SIZE, RPMTAG_OBSOLETES };
  int numTags = sizeof(tags) / sizeof(int);
+ */

  int main(int argc, char ** argv) {
      char buf[300];
**************
*** 26,34 ****
--- 29,39 ----
      struct dirent * ent;
      int fd, rc, isSource;
      Header h;
+     /* not used
      int count, type;
```

```
        int i;
        void * ptr;
+       */

    if (argc != 2) {
        fprintf(stderr, "usage: genhdlist <dir>\n");
***************
*** 74,79 ****
--- 79,85 ----

        rc = rpmReadPackageHeader(fd, , , NULL, NULL);

+       if (!rc) {
        headerRemoveEntry(h, RPMTAG_POSTIN);
        headerRemoveEntry(h, RPMTAG_POSTUN);
        headerRemoveEntry(h, RPMTAG_PREIN);
***************
*** 110,115 ****
--- 116,122 ----
        headerWrite(outfd, h, HEADER_MAGIC_YES);
        headerFree(h);
        close(fd);
+       }
    }

    errno = 0;
```

6   At last: burning the CD

As we assume that you have a working CD-writer on your system, and you know how to use it, we wont go into much detail about burning the CD. If you are burning your CD on a Linux system, you can install the excellent *XCDroast* <http://www.fh-muenchen.de/rz/xcdroast> package. In XCDRoast, switch on the Rock Ridge extensions, and the creation of a TRANS.TBL file.

Make sure the *top* directory of the CD contains at least the following files and directories:

```
    COPYING      RPM-PGP-KEY README      RedHat/
```

The following directories might come in handy:

```
    doc/        gnome/      misc/        dosutils/     images/
```

6.1   Creating a bootable CD

(This section, thanks to Dawn Endico dawn@math.wayne.edu). Since XCDroast doesn't support creation of bootable disks you'll need to use other tools, for example *mkisofs* <ftp://tsx-11.mit.edu/pub/linux/packages/mkisofs/> and *cdrecord* <http://www.fokus.gmd.de/research/cc/glone/employees/joerg.schilling/private/cdrecord.html>. Get the latest RPMs for these packages from <ftp://contrib.redhat.com>. You'll need to create an image file which will be written to the CD. This file will be 500Mb or more so find a partition with enough free space and change the path for redhat.img in the following commands if necessary. You may need to be root to use mount and cdrecord.

6.1.1 Create disk image

Change directory to the place in your mirror that will be the root directory of the cd. For instance, redhat-5.2/i386.

```
mkisofs -v -r -T -J -V "Red Hat 5.2" -b images/boot.img -c mis-
c/boot/boot.cat -o /tmp/redhat.img .
```

6.1.2 Test the image

If you're paranoid you can test your new disk image by mounting it. If you forgot to fix the file permissions or set the rock ridge extensions then the error will be obvious here since the file names and directory structure will be wrong.

```
mount -t iso9660 -o ro,loop=/dev/loop0 /tmp/redhat.img /mnt/cdrom
```

When you're done, don't forget to unmount it.

```
umount /mnt/cdrom
```

6.1.3 Burn the disk

Be sure to set the correct speed for your device. This command is for a 4X CDR. You may have a 1X or 2X drive.

```
cdrecord -v speed=4 dev=0,0 /tmp/redhat.img
```

7 Installing from the CD

When installing from the new CD, you first need to create a bootable installation diskette. IMPORTANT: use a NEW, freshly MS-DOS formatted diskette! Using an old, worn-out, faulty diskette can result in strange problems during the installation!

On a Linux system, you can create the diskette using the dd command:

```
dd if=/mnt/cdrom/images/boot.img of=/dev/fd0 bs=1440k
```

On a system running DOS or Windows-9x, you need to use the RAWRITE.EXE program, which is found on the CD in the dosutils directory.

Shut down the machine you want to install (or do a system upgrade) on, insert the boot diskette and your freshly burned CD, and let the machine boot from the diskette. For more information on the installation process, se the documents and the Installation-HOWTO or the Bootdisk-HOWTO which are on the CD in the doc/HOWTO directory.

8 This document...

The SGML source of the most recent version of this document can be retrieved from <http://imsb.au.dk/~mok/linux/doc/RedHat-CD.sgml>.

Mini-HOWTO

8.1 Related documentation

Ed Schlunder <zilym@asu.edu> has written a utility called `fix-rhcd` to let you check your Red Hat Linux distribution mirror for matching file sizes, names, permissions, and symlinks against an "ls -lNR" listing from the offical Red Hat ftp site. Any permissions that are wrong are changed to match the ls listing. See the *fix-rhcd homepage* `<http://www.ajusd.org/~edward/fix-rhcd/>`.

8.2 Acknowledgements

Thanks to the following people for valuable input:

- Lars Christensen <larsch@cs.auc.dk>
- Thomas Duffy <tbd@cs.brown.edu>
- Dawn Endico <dawn@math.wayne.edu>
- Seva <seva@null.cc.uic.edu>

9 DISCLAIMER

While the given information in this document is believed to be correct, the authors assume no responsibility whatsoever for any damage to hardware and/or software, or any loss of data resulting from the procedures outlined in this document.

Part LXXVI

"Linux Remote-Boot mini-HOWTO: Configuring Remote-Boot Workstations with Linux, DOS, Windows 95/98 and Windows NT" Marc Vuilleumier Stückelberg

David Clerc
v3.19, February 1999
This document describes how to set up a very robust and secure server-based configuration for a cluster of PCs, allowing each client to choose at boot-time which operating system to run. The key of this configuration is a bootprom based program, which let the user choose at boot time one of several boot images. This configuration is applicable using InCom TCP/IP Bootprom (add-on for most network cards) or any PXE-compliant Boot ROM (ready-to-use in most recent PC with built-in network cards). The most up-to-date version of this document, with hypertext links to downloadable software and other related materials, can be found at the address *http://cuiwww.unige.ch/info/pc/remote-boot/howto.html*. *Linuxdoc-SGML*, *DVI* and *PostScript* versions are available in the same directory. If you are interested in getting info on further developpments, send an E-mail to *David.Clerc@cui.unige.ch*.

Contents

1   Disclaimer and Copyrights

This document and the related software are provided as is to the Linux and Internet community, with no form of warranty. Please note that **some operations related in this document may destroy the content of your hard-disk**. We assume no liability for any use, correct or not, of this document and of the related software.

You are free to do anything you want with the remote-boot tools as long as you do not make money by selling them or by distributing them with a commercial product. If you want to commercialize a product derived from these tools, please contact the authors first to make a commercial agreement. These remote-boot tools will remain available for free forever, but we may authorize derived commercial tools.

These provisions shall be interpreted under and in accordance with the laws of Switzerland, canton of Geneva. All disputes, defenses, controversies or claims arrising in conncetion with this document and the related software, shall be subject to the exclusive juridiction of the courts of the canton of Geneva, Switzerland.

If you like this program, you can send us a Postcard and/or make a gift to the *International Committee of the Red Cross (ICRC)* or to the *UNICEF*.

2   What has changed...

2.1   ...since version 2.x ?

To say it frankly, almost everything. The underlying concepts are the same, but the software part has been completly redesigned to overcome the limitations of previous versions and to make it easier to use. An highlight of the new features :

- All functions (bpmenu, bpclean, bpunzip) are encompassed in a single program.
- The program can run not only from the boot rom, but also under DOS, Windows 95 and Linux.
- The program can now restore images of FAT16, FAT32 and EXT2FS partitions. If someone want to write NTFS support, let me know... For now, NT users still have to stick to FAT16.
- The program can not only restore disk images but also add and patch individual files in order to customize the client behaviour.
- Disk images are not any more bound to 87 MB. They are now file-system independant archives.
- We provide a mean for automatically downloading a disk image to an arbitrary big number of clients at the same time (broadcast).
- You can now write your own secure boot script, that will determine the behaviour of the machine before the real boot.

- You can now boot any Linux kernel, without applying any patch. Its is also possible to provide a command line and a ramdisk image.

- You can authenticate users at boot time using a Unix, NT or Radius server and deny them any access to the machine.

- Full national language support is included.

- And many, many other new features...

Is there a program for converting old archives to the new format ?

No, because the internal format is radically different. But you can easily do the conversion by yourself:

1. Boot an old image (unzip it to your disk)

2. Remove calls to the old `unzipreg` utility and replace them by the adequate `patch` commands (it is very easy, see the detailed instructions below)

3. Run the new `mrzip` program to create a new-style disk image

2.2 ...since version 3.0 ?

Version 3.0 was the beta-release. A dozen of sites around the world have tested it during a month and given much of their time to help us finding bugs and to suggest enhancements. Thanks to all of them for their patience, and in particular to Maciek Uhlig, Dick Velders and Jeff Teeters.

A few minor features have been added since 3.01, such as support for diskless Linux boot (by disabling the cache).

Version 3.10 introduced compatibility with Intel's *Wired for Management 1.1a* NetPC standard. The tools now work with any PXE-compliant boot ROM (as are most on-board boot ROMs) available today. Thanks to *InCom GmbH* for giving us the PXE bootprom that permitted this developpment. We also succesfully tested the tools with the PXE Boot ROM that I found incidentally in my Dell computer with onboard network card (called LanDesk Service Agent).

Version 3.11 to 3.12 added UNIX server-side tools (a PXE Proxy DHCP server for Solaris and Linux, and an enhanced TFTP server for Linux), as well as detailled informations on server-side setup and the PXE booting process.

Version 3.13 added Advanced Power Management support (PowerOff command).

Version 3.14 added minor enhancements and some corrections. We fixed a problem with the terminal under RedHat 5.1, and another problem in the syntax of the "if" command. We added some features suggested by the Laboratori de Càlcul de la Facultat d'Informàtica de Barcelona (LCFIB) :

- A new APM variable let you know if your system support the Advanced Power Management (i.e it supports the poweroff command).

- A "beep" command.

- A new parameter to DrawWindow, to include a title at the window creation. You can now do DrawWindow 200 200 400 200 "Title".

Version 3.15 added full VESA support. BpBatch now support several video modes, to accomodate old computers not being able to display 800x600 graphics. A new parameter has been added to InitGraph to specify the video mode, and a list of detected video mode can be retrieved from the new VESA-Modes variable.

Version 3.16 fixes the following bugs:

- "Malloc failed" during the Fullunzip process of a multiple fragments image. Many thanks to Christian Meyer for his collaboration.

- A bug which prevented the linux version of MrBatch to properly fullunzip images. This bug was located in the low-level functions of MrBatch, so it may fix other problems encountered in the *linux* version of MrBatch. Many thanks to Jeff Teeters for his collaboration.

Mini-HOWTO

- An error in the codepage translation tables. This bug was found by the Laboratori de Càlcul de la Facultat d'Informàtica de Barcelona (LCFIB). You can find the bug report in the BpBatch forum.

Version 3.17 adds some minor features and fixes bugs:

- Fullunzip was turning Extended Memory off
- Booting on the RedHat boot disk now works
- When extracting images with a large number of directories, the resulting FAT file system was corrupted.
- We added retries to text TFTP transfers. BpBatch will now retry three times before saying "Could not transfer the file".
- Timestamps are now correctly updated in FAT. (thank to Francis Chan)

Version 3.18 fixes a bug with the IncrUnzip function. Thanks to Gary Pike for its collaboration.

Version 3.19 fixed a bug in the error handling of the `delete` command on ext2fs, as well as the inappropriate handling of names starting with A: under Linux. The following new features were also added:

- A new `if valid disk:partition` syntax can be used to check if a partition has been formatted
- FAT32 disk images are now fully functional (they now boot properly)
- Linux EXT2 partitions bigger than 2 GB are now supported
- Linux Swap partitions bigger than 128 MB are now supported (this feature needs a recent kernel, at least 2.1.x)
- FullUnzip is now also possible without a cache partition, by setting `CacheNever` to `"ON"`. This might be usefull for a unique installation, but is not recommended in general is it results in a high network load.

Thanks to Ruben Schattevoy for its help and contributions to this release.

3   Introduction

The configuration described here was developped since Summer 1996 at the CUI, University of Geneva. The Computer Science Department uses several servers and a number of PCs, which fall into two classes:

- computers devoted to students
- computers devoted to research and teaching assistants

We developped the current configuration with the following aims:

- Every computer should be able to run under Linux, DOS, Windows 3.1, Windows 95 or Windows NT. One should be able to choose the desired operating system for each session.
- All softwares, including operating systems, should be take from the server, in order to facilitate the installations and upgrades.
- Clients computers should be able to run without any write-access on the server (for security reasons), except for their home directory.
- Client-side configuration should be reduced to its very minimum. Clients should automatically get their IP configuration parameters from the server, and this information should be located in a single file, used for all operating systems.
- Since almost every computer now has a hard-disk, clients should be able to take profit of it for reducing network load and as temporary storage space for the user.
- Users *must* have a login to be able to use any of the computers.

- The login should be the same for all operating system and should let the user access its unique home directory, common to all operating systems.

- Student (and secretary :-) computers should be fully cleaned up at each start. That is, the PC should always look like if it were just installed.

- Every computer has to be protected from virus attacks.

These constraints lead us to base our configuration on bootprom tools. We first developped new tools for the excellent *TCP/IP Bootprom* from *InCom GmbH*. Now that a standard for preboot execution environments as finally emerged, we ported the tools so that it now also works for any PXE-compliant bootprom. PXE boot roms, also called LanDesk Service Agent, are now distributed with almost all on-board network adapter. For more info on PXE and Intel *Wired for Management* standard in general, read from $http://www.intel.com/managedpc$.

3.1 Boot ROM and Hard-disk

Bootproms exist for quite a long time, but until recently, they were solely used with diskless computers. Since 1996, this How-to has been claiming that bootproms are even more interesting for computers which have a local harddisk, since they allow to take profit of both sides:

- A boot rom make the configurations more robust, since it ensure that the computer will always boot the same way, no matter any virus or partition table crash. It can be used, as we did, to cleanup the harddisk even before the operating system is loaded.

- A local harddisk make the configuration more efficient, since it can reduce the network trafic through caching, and allows for efficient swap.

Today, we have the pleasure to see that all computer manufacturers have come to the same point and provide boot roms as part of new computer standards.

Note that you can still use the tools described below in an *old fashioned* way, that is as a simple kernel/ramdisk loader, even for diskless computers. However, we do not encourage this use.

3.2 The Network

The University of Geneva owns a class B domain, subdivided into several subnets. The CUI uses four subnets, among them one is dedicated to students.

Originally, our PCs were concerned about two network protocols: IPX and IP. On the IPX side, we used a single Novell Netware 3 server for sharing software and users files for DOS and Windows. On the IP side, we used a SUN server for sharing software and users partitions for Linux, with NFS.

In our latest configuration, we do not any more use IPX. There is a single Unix server (which could be Linux as well as a SUN), sharing software and user files using NFS for Linux clients and using SMB (NetBIOS) over TCP/IP for Dos and Windows clients. In this way, we have a single home directory used by all operating systems.

3.3 How it Works

1. When a client PC is turned on, it first performs the traditional system checks before the TCP/IP Bootprom or PXE Boot ROM takes the control.

2. The bootprom issues a BOOTP/DHCP request in order to get its IP configuration parameters.

3. If the server knows the PC issuing the request, it will send back a BOOTP/DHCP reply with informations such as the client's IP address, the default gateway, and which bootdisk image to use.

4. In case of a PXE boot ROM, there might be some more exchanges between the client and the server to determine installation parameters.

5. The bootprom then downloads the boot image from the server using the TFTP protocol. The boot image happens to be a small program called `bpbatch`, our boot-time batch file interpreter.

6. The batch interpreter is started. At this time, it is almost alone in the computer memory. There is no operating system loaded, except the preboot execution environment (offered by the Boot ROM).

7. The batch interpreter look in the BOOTP/DHCP reply for command-line options, and in particular for the name of the batch to execute.

8. According to the instructions in the batch file, it will for instance:

    (a) Load a national keyboard mapping

    (b) Authenticate the user according to a remote server (Unix, Radius or Windows NT)

    (c) Let the user choose between the available operating systems

    (d) According to the operating system choosen, repartition the hard-disk and quick-format some partitions

    (e) Check if an up-to-date compressed image of the selected OS is present at the end of the disk. If not, it download it using TFTP

    (f) Uncompress the selected OS to the main partition

    (g) If the selected OS is Linux, load a kernel and start it

    (h) If the selected OS is DOS or Windows, simply let the computer boot on its fresh new hard-disk

For **DOS and Windows 3.1**, we use the freely available Microsoft LanManager for DOS (search the network for the mirror nearest to you; the distribution consists of three files named `disk1` to `disk4`) as SMB client. Microsoft LanManager supports dynamic configuration using DHCP. After logging in, the user is faced to DOS, and can start Windows 3.1 by typing the traditional `win` command. Note that at this point, DOS and Windows 3.1 appear to be installed locally.

For **Windows 95 and Windows NT**, we also use Microsoft SMB client (called *Client for the Microsoft Network*), that supports dynamic configuration using DHCP. We reduce network load using *Shared LAN Cache*, a nice and powerful network-to-disk cache program.

Students computers can be turned off *the hard way* at any time without risks, since the hard disk is reinitialized at each start.

For "safe" computers (ie. for assistants computers), once the computer has been booted once using the above described system, the boot script simply redirect the boot to the local hard-disk, without cleaning it again. This allow users to leave data on their local hard disk. But whenever the configuration gets corrupted, the user can simply choose from the boot menu in order to have a fresh installation.

3.4 Related non-commercial documentations

This configuration has been successfully reproduced at several places around the world. A few people have written some hints and tricks that complement this How-To. If you did so and that your page is not already referenced in this documentation, please send an e-mail to `Marc.VuilleumierStuckelberg@cui.unige.ch`. And if you experience problems while reproducing this configuration, have a look at these pages !

- `http://www.br.fgov.be/RESEARCH/INFORMATICS/info/bootp.html`, by Alain Empain of the Belgium National Botanic Garden. Many useful sample scripts, and a nice PERL program to automatically generate graphic menus and corresponding HTML documentation from a higher level description.

- `http://www.katedral.se/system/elevsyst`, by Johan Carlstedt of The Cathedral School of Uppsala, Sweden. *At this day, the configuration described at this place is still based on the previous version of the remote-boot tools. However, almost everything remains applicable, given a few changes.*

- `http://vitoria.upf.tche.br/~fred/`, in portuguese, by Frederico Goldschmidt of the Passo Fundo University, Brasil.

- `http://www.etse.urv.es/~larinyo`, in spanish, by Lluis Arino, of the Escola Tecnica Superio d'Enginyeria, Spain.

You can also send me your BpBatch script if you want me to include it in the *sample scripts collection*.

4   The Configuration How-To

First, arrange to have the following two machines within arm's reach:

- the **server**, usually a Unix or Windows NT machine
- the **client**, a PC with a bootprom enabled, and nothing valuable on the hard disk.

If you want to test the configuration but you do not yet have a bootprom, you can download the TCP/IP BootProm demo diskette from InCom GmbH at `http://www.incom.de`. This diskette will make your computer behave like if it had a TCP/IP Bootprom plugged in.

If you already have a Boot ROM, you need to enable it. If you are using Incom TCP/IP Bootprom, you can do that using a special program from your network card manufacturer. If you have a PXE Bootprom, you can do it simply from BIOS setup, by changing the default boot device.

For student computers, we configured the boot on network first, and disabled hard-disk and floppy-disk boot. For assistant computers, we also configured network-boot first, but we allow hard-disk and floppy-disk boot.

4.1   Server-side configuration

On the server, you will need the following services:

1. A BOOTP/DHCP server
2. May be a Proxy DHCP server
3. A TFTP server

Note for PXE Boot ROM users: We found after severals hours of tedious search that PXE Boot ROMs with version before 0.99 do not follow the IP protocol and discard all packets that have the *Don't Fragment* (DF) flag set. That means, you will have to disable *Path MTU Discovery* on the server, or the Boot ROM will not see any of its packets. On Solaris, use `ndd /dev/ip ip_path_mtu_discovery` to see if you have it enabled and `ndd -set /dev/ip ip_path_mtu_discovery 0` to disable it. However, this fix only works for non-broadcast packets (ask SUN why...). That means, it will work for TFTP but not for DHCP :-(. Intel has recently fixed this bug, and if you bought your computer after June 1998, you surely have a corrected PXE implementation.

4.1.1   Setting up DHCP

The role of the DHCP server is to give to the client an IP address and to make it load the file named `bpbatch.P` from the TFTP server. DHCP is a superprotocol over BOOTP. If you are using InCom TCP/IP Bootprom, you may live without DHCP (using an old BOOTP server).

On Windows NT, you will probably use the native DHCP server. If you are using InCom TCP/IP Bootprom, you will have to use a special trick to specify the boot file name (get more info from InCom WWW site). If you are using a PXE Bootrom, you will need a Proxy DHCP server, but no other trick is needed as the boot file name will be provided by the Proxy DHCP server.

On Linux, the best choice is the standard DHCP server from the Internet Software Consortium. If you are using a PXE Bootrom, in addition to the usual options, you will need to add the following ones:

- `option dhcp-class-identifier "PXEClient"`
- `option vendor-encapsulated-options ff;`

On Solaris, you can either use the Internet Software Consortium DHCP server (available on the Web), or use Solaris DHCP server (available since Solaris 2.5). However, as Solaris DHCP server does not seems to be able to insert a client class identifier in its DHCP offer, you must install a Proxy DHCP server. Morever, this Proxy DHCP server must reside on another computer since Solaris DHCP server locks the DHCP port.

Mini-HOWTO

We suggest giving infinite lease time for remote-boot clients. Don't forget that BOOTP/DHCP requests are bounded by subnets. If the client and the server do not reside on the same subnet, you should install a BOOTP/DHCP Relay agent on any computer between the two. For now, just assume that both machines are on the same subnet.

4.1.2 Setting up a Proxy DHCP

The role of the Proxy DHCP server is to overcome limitions of some DHCP servers and to provide PXE specific extensions. A proxy DHCP server only makes sense for a PXE Boot rom.

As BpBatch itself is quite powerfull, you wont need to use any PXE specific DHCP extension (menus, etc.). However, if your DHCP server is not able to show minimal PXE compliance, you will need a Proxy DHCP server or your PXE Boot ROM will not accept to go further.

On Windows NT, you can try to use Intel WfM PDK (available from their web site), but it is not very easy to use. We rather suggest having a Linux machine on the subnet and using our small Proxy DHCP. The major advantage of our Proxy DHCP Server for BpBatch is that our server will let you specify an option 155 vendor tag that will be interpreted by BpBatch as a command line.

On Linux and Solaris, you can run our Proxy DHCP program, that simply takes as argument the TFTP server IP address, boot file name and optional arguments, and does everything for you. If the DHCP port on the server is already requested by another daemon, the proxy DHCP server will run on port 4011. In this case, it is necessary that the other daemon on DHCP port answer a DHCP offer with client class `PXEClient` so that the PXE client knows that it must try on port 4011.

If you want to understand better PXE extensions to DHCP, there is an extensive description available on Intel WWW site. However, be warned that the documents are quite confusing, as the protocol has been extended to a number of optional stages, in order to allow for a maximal flexibility. The key to understand it is that all what a PXE client needs is a complete *enhanced DHCP answer*. If it receives only a standard DHCP offer, it will look further until it gets

1. a client class (T60) set to `PXEClient`
2. vendor encapsulated options (T43) (possibly empty, ie. hex `ff`)
3. a non-empty boot filename

The PXE specific negociation ends as soon as all these infos are received, but can lead to a very complex process (install server discovery, etc.) if some are missing.

4.1.3 Setting up TFTP

The TFTP server is a very simple file server. In its basic version, TFTP use 512 bytes data blocks, which are quite inefficients. InCom TCP/IP Bootprom and PXE Boot ROMs allow to use larger blocks (1408 bytes), which speeds up transfers a lot. However, this can only work with an enhanced TFTP server.

On Windows NT, we suggest using InCom enhanced TFTP server, available on their web site.

On Linux, you can use our enhanced TFTP server, available at *http://cuiwww.unige.ch/info/pc/remote-boot/soft/etftpd.tar.gz*.

On Solaris, you should use InCom enhanced TFTP serer, available on the utility disk provided with the TCP/IP Bootprom.

If you prefer using a standard TFTP daemon, remove the `P` in all boot image name extensions, in order to tell the Bootprom to use only the standard TFTP port (This trick was introduced by InCom GmbH for the TCP/IP Bootprom. We still use it as an easy way to select the default TFTP port with PXE bootproms).

4.2 Client-side configuration

First, we will do set up the part common to all operating systems, ie. the batch-file interpreter. Then, for each operating system, we will go through the following steps:

1. Setup a stand-alone client

2. Save its configuration on the server

3. Test it as a remote-boot client

4. Adapt it so that it works for any similar client machine

Once this is done, you will be able to setup any supplemental client just by plugging a Boot ROM in it (or buying a Wired for Management ready computer...) and adding one line in the DHCP configuration file.

Our examples assume that you have a hard disk of 1.4 Gb or more. If you have less, reduce the sizes of the partitions, but remember the you need to leave a few hundreds megabytes unallocated (that is, the last partition must not take up to the last cylinder) to leave free room for the special cache partition. Moreover, as the cache always starts at the cylinder following the last allocated cylinder, if you do not use the same total size for all your tests, you will have to download several times the same files (the cache will be automatically cleared).

Never despair. If you can't get it to work, first look in the *Troubleshooting* section if your problem is not already solved (get the latest version from the Web). Then, take a look in the BpBatch forum. Perhaps someone else had the same troubles as you have, and the answer can be found in the forum. Forum's URL : *http://cuiwww.unige.ch/info/pc/remote-boot/forum/*. If it still does not work, think about monitoring network traffic for network related problems (use `tcpdump` on Linux or `snoop` on Solaris). If you really cannot get it to work, you can send an E-mail to David.Clerc@cui.unige.ch or Marc.VuilleumierStuckelberg@cui.unige.ch. If your problem is strictly related with the remote-boot configuration and if we are not overflowed, we will try to solve your problem.

4.3 Setting Up the Boot Process

Get the `BpBatch` software, either as `.zip` or as `.tar.gz`. The executables are available at

- *http://cuiwww.unige.ch/info/pc/remote-boot/soft/bpb-exe.zip*
- *http://cuiwww.unige.ch/info/pc/remote-boot/soft/bpb-exe.tar.gz*

The source code (Assembler and C) is also available on request.

In the server `/tftpboot` directory, put the following three special boot images, which together make our pre-boot batch file interpreter:

- `bpbatch.P`, the dynamic loader (respect the uppercase !)
- `bpbatch.ovl`, the relocated interpreter
- `bpbatch.hlp`, the on-line help file

Then add an entry in the DHCP configuration file for your client, with the boot file set to `"bpbatch.P"`. Define a vendor option tag 155 (decimal) with the value `"-i"` (on the standard DHCP server, this is done by the following command: `option option-155 "-i";`). It is interpreted by `bpbatch` as the command line, and `-i` stands for "interactive".

Boot the client computer. You might shortly see

- The Boot ROM copyright
- The string `DHCP` while the client waits for a DHCP reply
- The string `TFTP` while the client waits for the first TFTP packet
- The string `Loading BpBatch` while the loader download the interpreter
- And finaly our banner, followed by a nice *greather-than* prompt

Congratulations ! You have started the batch interpreter... If you are curious about what you can do with it, continue reading the next section. If you are on a hurry, skip it and go directly install the operating system of your choice. If you have any doubt about a command within the interpreter, type `help`.

Note that you can run the same interpreter within DOS and Linux by running the `MrBatch` program. There are a only very few differences (the Linux version do not have graphics support and the DOS version can only send BOOTP and TFTP requests if the BootProm is not hidden by the operating system).

It may be a good idea to read now the section about the *Syntax Rules* of `BpBatch`, and in particular the paragraphs on *File References* and on *The Cache Filesystem*. This will help you understand the examples.

Once all operating systems will be set up, you will have to make a menu to let the user choose the one he wants. You should be able to discover by yourself how to make such a menu. All necessary commands are documented at the end of this document.

4.3.1 Discovering BpBatch

Try to type `LogVars`. You should get about thirty variables listed. Roughly, the first are BpBatch settings, then come all parameters extracted from the BOOTP/DHCP reply, and the last variable is a list of disks sizes, in Megabytes.

Type `GetPartitions part`, then `LogVars` again. There should be one more variable containing the list of defined partitions on your first hard-drive. Assuming that the first partition is either BIGDOS, FAT32 or LINUX-EXT2, try `LogDir "{:1}"` to get the content of the root directory, then `LogDir "{:1}/usr"` if there is an usr directory. You can even try `LogTree "{:1}/etc"` to get a directory tree.

Put a GIF file (format GIF-87a, interlaced or not, but NOT GIF-89a) on your TFTP server. We will suppose that the file is named `image.gif`. You can copy it wherever you want with the following command: `Copy "image.gif" "{:1}/temp/image.gif"`. Or you can use it directly from the server. Now type `Logvars "V*"` and look at the value of the VESA variable. If it is On, which is most probable, that means you have a VESA-compliant video adapter. You can list the available video modes using `Echo "$VESA-Modes"`. To display your image try the following command: `DrawGif "image.gif"`. The image should be on the upper left corner of the screen. You can draw it on another place by specifying X and Y coordinates after the image name. You can also draw text with `DrawText 200 200 "Hello world" yellow`. Or draw an empty window with `DrawWindow 200 200 300 150`. To insert a title when you create a new window, try `DrawWindow 200 200 300 150 "My Window"`. When you are tired of graphic mode, simply type `CloseGraph`.

Note on graphics : by default, all graphical routines work in the 800x600 VESA mode (with 256 colors), which is the first field of the VESA-Modes variable. If you want to use a different video mode, change the variable in order to have the requested video mode as the first field of the list.

Now take a text editor, and create a file named `test.bpb` in the `tftpboot` directory with the following content:

```
:again
DrawWindow 150 200 400 160 "Identity check"
TextAttr Black LightGray
At 15,20 Print "Username : "
Input username 8
At 17,20 Print "Password : "
Getpasswd userpass 8
if "$username" != "smith" goto again
if not "$userpass" match-passwd "BpR8oiIlRR9bo" goto again
#
clear
DrawWindow 200 200 150 100 green blue "Congratulations"
DrawText 220 250 "You got it !" yellow
WaitForKey 3
CloseGraph
interact
```

In your BOOTP/DHCP configuration, change the option-155 from "-i" to "test", and reboot the client computer. The small script should run automatically, and ask you for a username and password. If you do not type smith and justdoit, you wont be able to boot the computer. Later you will learn how to use a Unix, NT or Radius server to check valid user names.

4.4 Setting Up Linux

In order to set up Linux, you will need to boot the floppy disk provided with the RedHat Linux distribution. BpBatch includes a command that can redirect the boot to the floppy: FloppyBoot.

Set up *RedHat Linux* on your client, with network support, and any packages you may want. You may want to recompile the kernel to better fit your hardware, but it is not necessary.

4.4.1 Configuring the Client

It is probably a good idea to include BOOTP support to the kernel, so that you do not have to customize the client IP address manually.

In order to reduce network load, you might also want to setup the filecache for caching on the hard disk files that are loaded by NFS. Roughly, the principle of the filecache is that whenever a symbolic link from the cache subdirectory is followed, it is replaced by its target. If the target is itself a subdirectory, each entry of the subdirectory becomes a symbolic link to the original entry of the foreign filesystem. The filecache has been written by Unifix GmbH, and is part of Unifix Linux 2.0. It is freely distributable, and you can get the necessary files from *http://cuiwww.unige.ch/info/pc/remote-boot/soft/filecache.tar.gz*. In order to use the filecache, you have to

- apply a patch to the kernel (file patch-filecache), enable filecache support through make config or whatever you prefer, and recompile the kernel

- copy the filecache binary file to /sbin

- create a mount point called /mnt/nfs (using mkdir)

- copy filecache.conf to /etc. This file contains the following lines:

```
Max 100 MB 50 % #
Cache /mnt/nfs/usr /usr
Cache /mnt/nfs/opt /opt
```

- copy the content of /usr and /opt to the server, export them read-only with anon=0 (for allowing root access) and mount them under /mnt/nfs (add a line for that in /etc/fstab)

- rename /usr as /usr.orig

- link /usr to /mnt/nfs/usr

- rename /opt as /opt.orig

- link /opt to /mnt/nfs/opt

- ensure that /usr and /opt are not empty and contains the correct directories

- recursively remove /usr.orig and /opt.orig

- copy filecache.init to /etc/rc.d/init.d

- And finally link /etc/rc.d/rc3.d/S35filecache to /etc/rc.d/init.d/filecache.init

If you successfully followed each of these steps, you should have the filecache working next time you boot, as long as you do not forget to use your patched kernel.

Mini-HOWTO

4.4.2 Testing the Configuration

Copy your compressed kernel image (zImage, bzImage, vmlinuz or whatever you call it) to the server /tftp-boot directory as linux.krn. If you had to unplug the bootprom from the PC, you can now plug it again. When BpBatch starts, type LinuxBoot "linux.krn" "root=/dev/hda1 BOOT_IMAGE=linux" (assuming that the root ext2 filesystem is on the first partition). Alternatively, if you did setup your configuration on a computer without bootprom, just boot let it boot using the loader you installed (lilo, ...). But in the later case, if you want the filecache to work, you should have explicitly installed your kernel with filecache support at the right place.

Wait until the system comes up. If you installed the filecache, you can check that /usr has exploded into a directory with some symlinks and some already-exploded directories. Now start the programs that the end-users will use most of the time, in order to load them once for all to the hard disk.

You can still make adjustements to your configuration, like on any stand-alone linux station.

4.4.3 Building the Disk Image

When you are happy with your configuration, login as root, go to the /tmp directory and run our mrzip program. MrZip is a command interpreter like BpBatch, but it can understand more commands than BpBatch does. In particular, it can understand the following commands:

```
showlog
filter -"tmp/*"
filter -"var/log/*"
fullzip "/" "/tmp/linux.imz"
```

This will create a disk image in /tmp/linux.imz. Move it to the server /tftpboot directory. Then copy the following batch file to /tftpboot/linux.bpb:

```
hidelog
setpartitions "linux-ext2:992 linux-swap:32"
fullunzip "linux.imz" 1
clean 2
linuxboot "linux.krn" "root=/dev/hda1 BOOT_IMAGE=linux"
```

The BOOT_IMAGE argument is to stay compatible with lilo for RedHat 5.1 and later rc.sysinit.

Your remote-boot linux configuration is ready ! You can now either set the BOOTP-option-155 to "linux", or type include "linux.bpb" from within BpBatch to test it.

4.4.4 System Maintenance and Upgrades

If you want later to upgrade software, install bug fixes and security fixes, proceed as follow:

- Remote-boot a client computer to get a fresh linux install
- Make your changes
- Redo the disk image
- Copy the new image in place of the old one on the server

That means, you can upgrade software on your server-based configuration as if it were a purely local install.

4.5 Setting up DOS 6 and Windows 3.1

On the client computer, boot on your favorite dos floppy disk (either remove the bootprom or type FloppyBoot within BpBatch). Format the dos partition of your hard-drive with the /S option, in order to put the operating system on it. The size of the partition is not important, as disk archives created with MrZip Create a DOS subdirectory, copy DOS in it.

Install your favorite network client (for instance Microsoft LanManager), Windows 3.1, and so on. If you use Microsoft LanManager, do not use DHCP for the IP configuration as it is a very poor implementation that will almost surely fail with reasonable network load. To do that, add the following lines in your `protocol.ref` file, in the section that loads `tcptsr` (of course, replaces the `xxx` by your true IP parameters):

```
IPADDRESS0 = xxx xxx xxx xxx
SUBNETMASK0 = 255 255 xxx xxx
DEFAULTGATEWAY0 = xxx xxx xxx xxx
DISABLEDHCP = 1
```

Do not be afraid to use EMM386 to optimize the memory usage, and even to include the area where you put your network adapter ROM, since it is not used anymore at this time. But carefully exclude the network adapter RAM, or you will not be able to connect to your server. Use the `NOEMS` parameter.

If you want to ensure that the client machine cannot be used without a valid login name, download our `nobreak` pseudo-device driver (available at *http://cuiwww.unige.ch/info/pc/remote-boot/soft/nobreak.zip*) and run it at the beginning of your `config.sys`. Then add something like this to your `autoexec.bat`:

```
rem -- we use the dummy file c:\logged as a flag
del c:\logged >nul
:loginneeded
cls
echo Please type in your login name and password
echo.
net logon *
rem -- the login script should have created c:\logged
if not exist c:\logged goto loginneeded
del c:\logged
rem -- now enable break again
echo Yes >NOBRK
```

Ensure that your client boot well by rebooting the client and evaluating the following commands within `BpBatch` interactive mode:

```
HideBootprom
HdBoot
```

4.5.1 Building the Disk Image

On the server, make a share called `admin` for instance, on which you will put some stuff for the system administrator. If the server is a Unix machine, it is a good opportunity to put in `admin` a softlink to the `/tftpboot` subdirectory, so that you can put images in it directly from the client. Within `admin`, create a `/utils` subdirectory and put the following files in it:

- `mrbatch.exe`, the DOS version of `BpBatch`
- `mrzip.exe`, the DOS version of the program for building disk images
- `bpbatch.hlp`, the on-line help file

You might also like to put in the same directory a simple MrZip script named `zipdos.mrz` file that contains the commands needed for building a DOS image, like this one:

```
showlog
filter -"lanman.dos/lmuser.ini"
filter -"temp/*"
filter -"*.swp"
fullzip "c:/" "L:/tftpboot/dos.imz"
```

Now go back to your client, mount the `admin` volume on drive `L:`, go to your `utils` directory and type the following command:

```
mrzip -b zipdos
```

One minute later, you will have a new file in the server `/tftpboot` subdirectory called `dos.imz`, which is a compressed image of your hard disk. Copy the following batch file to `/tftpboot/dos.bpb`:

```
hidelog
setpartitions "bigdos:1024"
setbootpart 1
fullunzip "dos.imz" 1
hidebootprom
hdboot :1
```

Your remote-boot DOS configuration is ready ! You can now either set the BOOTP-option-155 to `"dos"`, or type `include "dos.bpb"` from within BpBatch to test it.

4.5.2 Adapting the configuration for other machines

If you want to customize some settings according to the machine, typically the IP settings since Micro$oft DHCP is buggy, you can setup BpBatch to change some files before booting. Firsti go to the `lanman.dos` directory and do

```
copy *.ini *.ref
```

Then edit the `.ref` files and replace all fixed parameters with BOOTP variable names as in the following examples:

```
computername = ${BOOTP-Host-Name}
ipaddress0 = ${MS-IPAddress}
subnetmask0 = ${MS-IPSubnet}
defaultgateway = ${MS-IPRouter}
```

Then rebuild the disk image as previously. Note that for IP parameters, we do not use the BOOTP variables directly because LanManager needs then as space-separated numbers instead of dot-separated numbers. Change `dos.bpb` to the following:

```
hidelog
setpartitions "bigdos:1024"
setbootpart 1
fullunzip "dos.imz" 1
set MS-IPAddress="$BOOTP-Your-IP"/.= /
set MS-IPSubnet="$BOOTP-Subnet-Mask"/.= /
set MS-IPRouter="$BOOTP-Routers"/.= /
patch "{:1}lanman.dos/protocol.ref" "{:1}lanman.dos/protocol.ini"
patch "{:1}lanman.dos/tcputils.ref" "{:1}lanman.dos/tcputils.ini"
patch "{:1}lanman.dos/lanman.ref" "{:1}lanman.dos/lanman.ini"
hidebootprom
hdboot :1
```

If you prefer, you can also put the `.ref` files in the server `/tftpboot` directory instead of in the disk image.

We like to be able to easily change the computers configuration without rebuilding the image. To do that, copy your `autoexec.bat` and `config.sys` as `autoexec.ref` and `config.ref` to the server `/tftpboot` and add the following two lines to the batch file above:

```
patch "autoexec.ref" "{:1}autoexec.bat"
patch "config.ref" "{:1}config.sys"
```

You can then freely change the files and even customize them with machine-dependant values obtained from BOOTP.

After making any change to the client machine configuration, do not forget to rebuild the disk image using `mrzip` if you want to preserve your changes.

4.5.3 System Maintenance and Upgrades

If you want later to add new software or change anything else, proceed as follow:

- Remote-boot a client computer to get a fresh install
- Make your changes
- Redo the disk image
- Copy the new image in place of the old one on the server

That means, you can upgrade software on your server-based configuration as if it were a purely local install.

4.6 Setting up Windows 95

In previous versions of this document, we used the Microsoft server-based installation of Windows 95, but it was really too much pain and not much worth:

- It is very, very bogus
- Many software package do not support it and their install will fail. Among them, Microsoft Internet Explorer, OnNet 32, Novell's Protected-mode client (which is MUCH more secure than Microsoft Client for Netware).
- It cannot be used with the Microsoft Network client over TCP/IP, since Microsoft provides no real-mode driver for TCP/IP compatibe with Windows 95. That means, it cannot be used with Samba
- It makes software upgrades almost impossible since every client turned on will lock many DLLs on the server, and thus produce *sharing violations* if you try to upgrade them.

Consequently, we throwed away of this document all the informations and bug-workaround collected during months (you can still find them as a HTML document at *http://cuiwww.unige.ch/info/pc/remote-boot/win95old/win95old.html*) and turned to our new disk-based remote-boot concept. Basically, the configuration for Windows 95 is now almost as easy the configuration for DOS.

4.6.1 Setting up a Stand-Alone Client

Setup a regular Windows 95 client, either starting from scratch as explained in the configuration of a DOS client, starting from the DOS client and installing over the network (that is what we did). You can also start with a preconfigured Windows machine, but you will probably have less knowledge of what stuff is on the hard disk.

Proceed as described above for a DOS client. It is usually NOT necessary to use EMM386 with Windows 95. If you are using Windows 95 OSR2 (alias MSWIN 4.1, alias Windows 95 service pack 1, alias Windows 95 with Internet Explorer), you should add the following line in the `[Options]` section of `MSDOS.SYS` (yes, it is a text file):

```
AUTOSCAN=0
```

This will let Windows know that you do not want ScanDisk to be runned automatically at boot time.

If you want to reduce network and server load (which will improve your system performances) while keeping all softwares on the server, you should consider installing the excellent Shared LAN Cache, from Measurement Techniques, Inc (see *http://www.lancache.com*). This software runs on each client computer, and caches to the local hard disk every data obtained from the network. Even MS-Office starts much faster the second time you run it... You need one license per client computer, but it is not very expensive, and the firm make special prices for universities and colleges. The best thing to do is to go to their Web site and download the free evaluation copy.

4.6.2 Building the Disk Image

Your MrZip script will be named `zipwin95.mrz` and contain:

```
showlog
filter -"temp/*"
filter -"*.swp"
fullzip "c:/" "L:/tftpboot/win95.imz"
```

To build the image, mount the `admin` volume on drive `L:`, go to your `utils` directory and type the following command:

```
mrzip -b zipwin95
```

A few minutes later, you will have a new file if the server `/tftpboot` subdirectory called `win95.imz`, which is a compressed image of your hard disk. If your compressed image was bigger than 87 MB, it has probably been splitted in two or more fragments. These fragments will automatically loaded one after the other when needed. Note that an image bigger than 87 MB will usually take More than one minute to uncompress and may irritate your users. Our Windows 95 image is only 70 MB big, because most software (except Office and Explorer) completely reside on the server. Only 45 seconds are needed to uncompress the image and restore the full disk.

Copy the following batch file to `/tftpboot/win95.bpb`:

```
hidelog
setpartitions "bigdos:1024"
setbootpart 1
fullunzip "win95.imz" 1
hidebootprom
hdboot :1
```

Your remote-boot Windows 95 configuration is ready ! You can now either set the BOOTP-option-155 to `"win95"`, or type `include "win95.bpb"` from within BpBatch to test it.

4.6.3 Adapting the configuration for other Machines

The big difference between Windows 3.1 and Windows 95 is that the later includes code for Plug-and-play , ie. automatic detection of your hardware. This not a bad thing in itself, but the trouble is that it is often too sensible, and that it sometimes fails.

If you try to start another client with exactly the same boot image, you will probably get several messages during startup telling that Windows has detected new hardware: a new sound card, a new hard-disk, a new network card, and even a new mouse... There can be two reasons for that:

- the devices may not use the same ressources (for instance the mouse is not connected on the same port, or the sound card is not connected in the same slot - yes, that is detected)
- the devices may tell to Windows 95 their personal serial number (for instance, every Windows 95 differenciate every network card on the basis of its world-wide unique ethernet address)

The fact that Windows 95 discover that the hardware has changed may not be a problem if the plug-and-play works as-is, but it become a problem when the plug-and-play does not work. For instance, Windows 95 plug-and-play for our Logitech PS2/aux mouse does not work, and result in no mouse at all. To solve such kind of problems, arrange to have all computers as similar as possible, or make different images for different hardware. Later, you will discover that you can simply use the same image and just have several copies of the registry, that you can copy after having restoring the disk image but before booting.

The thing you cannot avoid to differ between computers is the network card. PCI cards usually do not mind, but ISA Plug and Play do. Bad luck for us, the plug-and-play code for our SMC EtherEZ card hangs the computer. The only solution is to let Windows 95 believe that it already know the network card, and that it is not necessary to trigger plug-and-play.

The trick for doing that is to automatically insert an entry for the network card in Windows 95 registry, before starting it. Note that this trick is not any more needed with most PCI cards.

Move the `autoexec.bat` to the server as described above for DOS. Edit it (on the server) and add the following lines:

```
rem --- Patch Windows registry in order to avoid plug-and-play detection
regedit /L:c:\windows\system.dat /R:c:\windows\user.dat c:\temp\patch.reg
```

`regedit` is a standard Windows 95 program that let you browse the registry if you start it from within Windows 95, or do simple operations on the registry if you call it from DOS. Run `regedit` under Windows 95, search for your network card, usually under

```
HKEY_LOCAL_MACHINE\Enum\ISAPNP
```

and export the branch using the *File* menu. This will create a text file, that you should same as `patch.ref` in the server `/tftpboot` diretory. Edit this file and find out where the card ethernet address is stored (do that on two different machines and compare the files if you can't find it by yourself). Replace it by a pettern in the form `${MACID}`. Then add lines to the `win95.bpb` script like this:

```
set macid = "$BOOTP-Client-ID"
patch "patch.ref" "{:1}temp/patch.reg"
```

(do any necessary string manipulation for setting `MACID` if it is not exactly the client Ethernet address). That's all, your clients should not any more try to autodect the network card.

Once again, this whole trick is not necessary when using PCI network adapters. Incidentally, we can use the same mechanism for automatically configuring the hostname, which Windows 95 does not seem to take into account when configuring through DHCP. We just add the following line to our `patch.ref` file:

```
[HKEY_LOCAL_MACHINE\System\CurrentControlSet\Services\VxD\VNETSUP]
"ComputerName"="${BOOTP-Host-Name}"

[HKEY_LOCAL_MACHINE\System\CurrentControlSet\Services\VxD\MSTCP]
"HostName"="${BOOTP-Host-Name}"

[HKEY_LOCAL_MACHINE\System\CurrentControlSet\control\ComputerName\
ComputerName]
"ComputerName"="${BOOTP-Host-Name}"
```

Using this small registry trick, your configuration should normally be portable for all machines with similar configurations. If you cannot avoid that Windows detect some hardware as new on one machine, try to rebuild the disk image from this machine. This will include the registry configuration specific to this machine into the image, and hopefully supress the problem.

4.6.4   System Maintenance and Upgrades

If you want later to upgrade software, install bug fixes and security fixes, proceed as follow:

- Remote-boot a client computer to get a fresh install
- Make your changes
- Redo the disk image
- Copy the new image in place of the old one on the server

That means, you can upgrade software on your server-based configuration as if it were a purely local install.

Mini-HOWTO

4.7 Setting up Windows NT

We do not use Windows NT for remote-boot client computers but we have tested our system to ensure that it work as well. And it works.

As our utilities currently have no support for NTFS (we neither have the documentation nor the time to do that, but I would be happy to help anyone who is interested in doing it), you will have to install NT on FAT16 (simply do not convert your partitions to NTFS during the setup).

Copy your `win95.bpb` boot script to `winnt.bpb`. Change the `setpartitions` line in `winnt.bpb` to the following:

```
setpartitions "BIGDOS:512 BIGDOS:512"
```

Then boot Windows 95 using this script, and install your NT client on drive C. Do not worry about the second partition for now. Do not install too much stuff, or you will get a really large and slow-to-uncompress image. Remove Windows 95 from the disk disk C, you do not need it in a Windows NT image (the boot menu is handled by the bootprom, not by NT boot loader).

Reboot your computer in without overwriting the hard disk, ie. do not execute the `winnt` script but just

```
hidebootprom
hdboot
```

Your NT station should start-up correctly. Make any necessary customization.

4.7.1 Building the Disk Image

The trouble with Windows NT is that direct disk access is prohibed by the kernel. That means, `MrZip` will not even be able to read the boot sectors. The best way to do an image is then to boot Windows 95 and to run `MrZip` from a DOS window. To do that, change the `winnt.bpb` script so that the Windows 95 image is not restored on the first but on the second partition:

```
hidelog
setpartitions "BIGDOS:512 BIGDOS:512"
setbootpart 2
fullunzip "win95.imz" 2
hidebootprom
hdboot :2
```

(if you have any supplementary patch, change the "`{:1}`" to "`{:2}`"). Boot with this script; you should have Windows 95 running, but a new drive D: should be available, with Windows NT inside.

Make your disk image as usual (but on D:, of course), and save it as `winnt.imz` on the server `/tftpboot` directory. Edit one last time the `winnt.bpb` script like this:

```
hidelog
setpartitions "BIGDOS:512 BIGDOS:512"
setbootpart 1
fullunzip "winnt.imz" 1
clean 2
#fullunzip "win95.imz" 2
hidebootprom
hdboot :1
```

Your Windows NT remote-boot configuration is ready. Of course, if you do not like to have two partitions, you can setup a single partition instead. But when you have to rebuild the image, you will have to setup the second partition again for booting Windows 95.

4.7.2 System Maintenance and Upgrades

If you want later to upgrade software, install bug fixes and security fixes, proceed as follow:

- Remote-boot a client computer to get a fresh install
- Make your changes
- Edit `winnt.bpb`: comment the `clean` and winnt `fullunzip`, uncomment win95 `fullunzip`
- Redo the disk image
- Copy the new image in place of the old one on the server

That's all, folks !

4.8 Troubleshooting (FAQ)

This section lists most frequently encountered problems.

The image download never ends

You are probably using a standard TFTP server, and it cannot handle more than 65535 packets of 512 bytes (or even 32767 packets for the Solaris server). That is, your image must be fragmented in pieces of no more than 30 MB (or 15 MB for Solaris). See under *CopyArchive* for instructions on fragmenting an existing image. But you should seriously thing about using InCom's extended TFTP server, as it is much more efficient (it uses packets of 1408 bytes instead of 512 bytes).

The archive decompression fails immediately

There are three possibilities. Either the image is really corrupted on the server (try use MrZip to see if it is the case), or the file transfer has failed because of TFTP timeout, or because of incompatible protocol.

TFTP timeout occurs when the network is too heavily loaded (for instance if you try to download a huge image with more than four clients at a time). In this case, `BpBatch` does not retry indefinitely because it would not help. Shut down a few computers and retry with no more than four computers (or maybe even three). If you often need to download images for a lot of computers, you can try our special Broadcast TFTP server (see the section dedicated to it).

Incompatible protocol is caused by using a standard TFTP server (typically the one built-in in your UNIX server) while asking BpBatch to work with enhanced TFTP. If you use a standard TFTP server, **you should remove the .P extension** (see the explanation in the next question).

The computer hangs instead of downloading/unzipping (1)

If you are using Incom's TFTP server, try to add -s 1408 59 to the command line. If you are not using an enhanced TFTP server, remove the `.P` extension from BpBatch filename on the server and in `bootptab`.

Detailed explanation : this problem occurs if you did not setup an extended TFTP server but you used `bpbatch.P` as the bootfilename DHCP/BOOTP tag. BpBatch will indeed try to connect to an extended TFTP server when the bootfilename ends with a `.P` extension. To solve this problem, you can either remove the `.P` extension at the end of the bootfilename (it will tell BpBatch to use standard TFTP) or install an extended TFTP server. The only supported extended TFTP server today is the one provided by Incom. You can find compiled binaries on their web site, or on our distribution directory. For Incom's TFTP server to properly work with the extended TFTP feature, you must add `-s 1408 59` to the command line.

The computer hangs instead of downloading/unzipping (2)

May be your computer has a bad VESA support. Try giving the `-v` command-line argument or setting the VESA variable to `"OFF"`.

VESA scrolling is broken

We use a VESA 1.1 function for scrolling. If your video adapter does not support VESA 1.1, forget it. If the scrolling works for one page, but then produces a strange strippled pattern, do not worry. This is a known bug, I will fix it as soon as I have time for it (VESA scrolling is not really essential...)

There is a corrupted file in the cache

When a file in the cache is corrupted by an external program, it is automatically removed from the cache. When a file in the cache is not fully written (because the computer is turned off during the file transfer), it is also automatically removed. But if the server transmits a corrupted file or if the transfer aborts from the server side, it is possible that this file stays in the cache. You can clean-up the cache simply by holding both shift down while BpBatch access it for the first time. Alternatively, you can evaluate clean -1 in interactive mode.

The EXIT command does not work in a batch file

This is not a bug. Exit is not a command. There is no exit or quit command because it does not make any sense to exit from a boot script without booting. And MrBatch is really the same program as BpBatch. What you can do instead is calling HdBoot. This makes sense, and the DOS version will cleanly exit instead of rebooting. Note that you can exit from the DOS version at any time by pressing Ctrl-Break. This will restore all hooked interrupts before leaving.

The Print command does not print

If you try to print something and immediately enter interactive mode, you may not see your text. This is because your text was written on the *runtime* screen and the Interact command has switched the display to the *Log* screen. Just put a GetKey after the print commands and you will see the text output.

MrZip says Malloc failed

MrZip needs a lot of conventional memory to run. If you encounter this problem, first ensure that you have unloaded the bootprom either using HideBootprom or using InCom's bputil. If you run MrZip from bare MS-DOS (not within Windows 95 DOS box), you should use EMM386 to load the network drivers high in order to get as much conventional memory as possible. From a Windows 95 DOS box, there is usually no problem (as long as you have not left your old 16-bit stuff in your autoexec.bat when you installed Windows 95).

MrZip aborts while reading directories

This bug has already been fixed once. Get the latest release of MrZip. If the problem persists, try to build your image with Trace set to "ON" (and usually PauseLog set to "OFF"); this will let you discover which file causes the problem. Send a detailed bug report.

MrZip cannot access some file

MrZip is probably trying to read a locked, open or special file, such as Windows swap file. Such files should usually not be included in the image and should be filtered out (using the filter command). It is also possible that the operating system is playing you a trick. If MrZip does not tell you what file causes the problem, try to build your image with Trace set to "ON" (and usually PauseLog set to "OFF"). You can also try to use direct disk access (that is, do not refer the source partition as "C:" or "/" but as "{:1}" or whatever partition it is). Using direct disk access is usually slower because we have less buffers than the operating system, but it may be sometimes more reliable.

Disk images are always reloaded from the server

Disk images are stored in the special cache area and should not be reloaded if they have not changed on the server. However, as the cache area always starts after the last used partition, changing the total size of partitions will move the location of the cache and thus destroy its content. Another possible reason for a file disappearing from the cache is that the previous file has grown more than one-and-an-half times its initial size. The file would then have been overwritten and need to be downloaded once again. This should almost never occurs. A third possible reason is a too small cache area. If the free space left outside the partitions is less than one-and-an-half times the sum of all compressed image sizes, only the most recently used images will be present in the cache and the other will have to be reloaded on demand.

Red Hat Linux 5.1 does not boot properly

This distribution assumes Linux was booted using lilo and checks for the BOOT_IMAGE command line argument (in /etc/rc.d/rc.sysinit). Simply add it in the linuxboot call, or change your rc.sysinit.

The broadcast TFTP ramdisk hangs (*Got in bound state*)

Linux dhcp client is a program that dynamically changes the IP address of the client according to DHCP offers. If the address is offered forever (infinite lease time), the DHCP client just set the address and returns (this is what we expect). However, if the lease time is limited, the DHCP client must remain loaded and ask for new addresses every few minutes. And if the DHCP client does not return, MrBatch will never be loaded... The solution is to give an infinite lease time (sometimes encoded as -1).

File access hangs under BpBatch, but not under MrBatch

This problem occured on an AMI BIOS dated 94/07/25. We investigated a little bit, and found no solution. It seems that this problem is due to a bug in this BIOS (some register or memory location must be destroyed).

Unzip of a fragmented archive fails (Malloc failed)

This problem was introduced with PXE compatibility, but has now been fixed. Please get the latest version.

MrBatch and MrZip complain about the terminal under RedHat 5.x

This problem has been fixed in the 9th of August version of MrBatch/MrZip. There was a problem with a new version of ncurses which has been released with RedHat 5.1.

"libncurses.so.3.0: cannot open shared object file" under Linux

MrZip has been linked to the version 3.0 of libncurses. You can use other versions of libncurses only if they are newer than version 3.0. To use a newer libncurses, all you have to do is to create a soft link from libncurses.so.3.0 to your libncurses.so.xx file. With RedHat 5.1, you can use the following command : `cd /usr/lib ; ln -s libncurses.4.2 libncurses.3.0` You can also download a version recent version of mrzip/mrbatch. Starting from the 10/25/98, mrbatch is now compiled under RedHat 5.1.

MrBatch and MrZip do not start under Linux (file not found)

This problem is the reverse of the previous one. Now that the distribution is libc6 ready, it cannot be used any more with libc5. If you encounter this problem, simply upgrade your Linux box (Well, if we hear too much complaints, we might try to keep two distributions...).

I can not access other mode than the default 800x600 VESA mode

You should first display the contents of the `VESA-Modes` variable, to see if your hardware support the mode you would like to use. Then, try one of the two ways to select a special VESA mode :

- `InitGraph "mode"`: Try InitGraph "1024x768", and then run the graphical primitive you are interested in (e.g `DrawGif`).
- `VESA-Modes`: The first field of the `VESA-Modes` variable is the name of the default mode. If you change the VESA-Modes variable, all graphical primitive will use the mode you specified.

BpBatch prints a "Malloc failed" message when restoring multiple fragments images

We corrected a bug in the memory allocation functions of BpBatch. You should make sure that you have a version of BpBatch which has been released after september the 22nd 1998.

Fullunzip using the Linux version of MrBatch always fails

We corrected this problem in the 09/22/1998 release.

Scandisk says my disk is corrupted

The 10/25/98 release did correct a problem with large images. Try to download a recent version of BpBatch.

My RedHat boot floppydisk does not work with FloppyBoot

This bug has been corrected in the 10/25/98 release.

My FAT32 disk image does not boot properly

This bug has been corrected in the 02/09/99 release.

5 Remote-Boot Tools Reference Manual

This section provides detailed informations on the use of the tools we developped at the CUI, University of Geneva for this remote-boot configuration.

5.1 BpBatch, MrBatch and MrZip

These three names stand for three variants of the same program, with the following characteristics:

- BpBatch is a special program that can be started from the BootProm before the operating system is loaded. It is made of two parts: bpbatch.P, the dynamic loader, and bpbatch.ovl, the program itself. BpBatch has full disk I/O capabilities through our own implementation of FAT16, FAT32 and Ext2fs, as well as remote network I/O capabilities through the BootProm TFTP API. BpBatch was compiled under DOS using Borland C 5.0 and Turbo Assembler 3.2.

- MrBatch is the DOS/Linux version of BpBatch. All commands recognized by BpBatch are recognized by MrBatch and vice versa. This is very usefull if you want to test your batch scripts from a DOS/Linux session. Under DOS, MrBatch emulates remote I/O by OS-based file access if the bootprom is not available. Under Linux, the bootprom cannot be seen anymore but MrBatch can emulate it using Linux IP support, or use OS-based file access. MrBatch was compiled under Linux using GCC 2.7.2.1 and under DOS using Borland C 5.0 and Turbo Assembler 3.2.

- MrZip is an interpreter that recognizes a superset of MrBatch language, and that serves to build disk images. In MrZip, the limited remote file I/O is replaced by a full-featured OS-based file access. MrZip does not include VESA support. MrZip was compiled under Linux using GCC 2.7.2.1 and under DOS using Borland C 5.0 and Turbo Assembler 3.2.

5.1.1 Command Line Arguments

All programs accept the same syntax of arguments. MrBatch and MrZip take them from the command line, while BpBatch look for them in the BOOTP option 155 (decimal). Here is the syntax of the arguments:

```
[-x] [-l] [-b] [-v] [-w] [-i] [script-basename]
```

where:

- -x disable the use of extended memory
- -l disable the use of ISO-latin-8859-1 as default character set
- -b cancel the bootprom detection (which cause a floppy seek under DOS)
- -v cancel the VESA detection (which cause a switch to full screen under Windows 95)
- -w enable direct disk write access (disabled by default under DOS and Linux)
- -i enable interactive mode even if a script name is provided

The script-basename is optional. If provided, MrBatch and BpBatch load the file with the .bpb extension, and MrZip loads the file with the .mrz extension. If not provided, MrBatch and MrZip run in interactive mode while BpBatch loads the file with the same basename as the BOOTP Boot file and a .bpb extension.

5.1.2 Syntax rules

The following rules apply when BpBatch parses an input line.

- Commands are parsed line by line. Lines are separated by CR and/or LF.
- The maximal line length is currently 255 characters.
- Keywords and variable names are case-insensitive.
- " is interpreted as the special string delimiter
- When ${variable} or $variable is encountred, it is substituted by the value of the variable, or by an empty string if the variable is undefined. The substitution also occurs within a string. Moreover, the resulting substituted value must be explicitly enclosed between double quotes if used as a string value (ie. one should merely speak of macro expansion than of a variables).
  - \a is substituted by the audible-bell character (ASCII 7)
  - \b is substituted by the backspace character (ASCII 8)

- \n is substituted by the newline character (ASCII 10)

- \r is substituted by the return character (ASCII 13)

- \t is substituted by the tabulation character (ASCII 9)

- \v is substituted by the vertical-tab character (ASCII ...)

- \nnn where n is a 3-digit octal number between 000 and 377 is substituted by the character with ascii code specified

- \X where X is any other character not listed above is substituted by X itself. In particular,

  * \" is substituted by a regular double-quote (not a string-delimiter)
  * \$ is substituted by a regular dollar sign (not variable substitution)
  * \\ is substituted by a regular backslash (not a special character)

- The character "end of string" (ASCII code 0) CANNOT be used anywhere as it is used internally as end-of-string delimiter

- The character "floating diaeresis" (ASCII code dec 249, hex F9, octal 371) CANNOT be used in any string as it is used internally as string delimiter in the input parsing routine.

- The character "block space" (ASCII code dec 255, hex FF, octal 377) CANNOT be used in any variable value as it is used internally as variable delimiter.

Empty lines are ignored. Lines starting with a sharp (#) are treated as comments and are not interpreted. Lines starting with a column (:) are treated as labels and are not interpreted.

String expressions

Strings are delimited by opening and closing double-quotes:

```
"Hello world"
```

To include double-quotes within a string, quote them using a backslash:

```
"I said: \"Hello world\""
```

Strings can be postfixed with a few operators.

- The character substitution operator:

```
"Hello world"/o=u/        ==        "Hellu wurld"
"198.76.54.32"/.= /       ==        "198 76 54 32"
```

- The word selection operator (zero-based):

```
"Hello world"{0}          ==        "Hello"
"198 76 54 32"{1-3}       ==        "76 54 32"
```

- The substring selection operator (zero-based):

```
"Hello world"[4]          ==        "o"
"Hello world"[4-7]        ==        "o wo"
```

Operators can be chained by postfixing one after the other. For informations about the string length and word count operators, see under "Numerical expressions".

Numerical expressions

Numerical expressions work on 32-bits integer numbers (from -2,147,483,646 to 2,147,483,647). Hexadecimal octal and binary numbers are not understood. Whenever a numerical expression is expected, the following are recognized:

- A positive or negative integer number

- An expression in the form (*expr1 op expr2*) where *op* can be either +, -, * (multiply), / (divide) or % (modulo) and expr is a numerical expression. Note that EACH operation MUST be enclosed between parenthesis :

Mini-HOWTO

```
((3 * 5)+2)                    == 17
```

- The string-length operator (@), followed by a string :

```
@"Hello world"                 == 11
```

- The word-count operator (#) followed by a string :

```
#"Hello world"                 == 2
```

Durations

A few commands expect durations as arguments. Durations are measured in seconds, with a precision of up to a tenth of second:

```
Delay 3                    waits for 3 seconds
Delay 0.3                  waits for 3/10 seconds
```

Colors

Whenever a color is expected, you can either use the numeric value of the color or its symbolic name (case-insensitive). The following colors are recognized

Black	0
Blue	1
Green	2
Cyan	3
Red	4
Magenta	5
Brown	6
LightGray	7
DarkGray	8
LightBlue	9
LightGreen	10
LightCyan	11
LightRed	12
LightMagenta	13
Yellow	14
White	15

File References

File names are strings. They must therefore always be enclosed between double-quotes. File names are case-sensitive on case-sensitive filesystems, case-insensitive on case-insensitive filesystems. Slash and backslash can be freely used one in place of the other. Do not forget to double backslash since a single backslash is an escape character.

There are two kinds of file references:

- Direct disk files
- Foreign files

Direct disk files are referenced using the following notation:

```
"{disk:partition}/absolute/filename"
```

The disk number can be omitted and defaults to zero. For instance, `"{:1}/usr/bin"` points to `/usr/bin` assuming there is such a directory on the first partition. Direct file I/O is solely based on our own file access routines (we do not use the operating system).

There are two *special* partitions. Partition zero corresponds to the hard disk master boot record (MBR) and has a pseudo file-system which let you access the boot code. Partition minus-one (-1) corresponds to the cache filesystem (see below).

Under BpBatch/MrBatch, foreign files correspond to remote files on the TFTP server when the BootProm is available:

```
"help.bpb"              is the file help.bpb in the /tftpboot directory
"gifs/MyImage.gif"      is a file in /tftpboot/gifs
```

Other TFTP servers can be referenced :

```
"198.76.54.32:help.bpb"
```

If the other server is behind a gateway :

```
"198.70.0.1/198.76.54.31:help.bpb"
```

One can also specify a specific port for the TFTP connection :

```
"198.76.54.32@89:getpasswd/smith"
```

There can be only one open remote file at a time. If the BootProm is not available, remote files are emulated using the operating system file I/O, but the same restriction apply.

Under MrZip, foreign files correspond to files as seen by the operating system. There is no limitation, and foreign files can be used wherever direct disk files can be. Foreign files are usually faster than direct disk files, because the operating system has more buffers. Foreign files can refer to network files if supported by the operating system.

```
"C:\\autoexec.bat"
"C:/config.sys"
"/mnt/net/usr"
```

5.1.3   The Cache Filesystem

In order to reduce network load and to fasten the boot process, disk archives, linux kernels and possibly other files are cached on the hard disk. This disk cache is located at the end of the hard disk, between the last cylinder allocated in the partition table and the last physical cylinder of the disk (out of any allocated partition). There MUST be room between the last partition and the end of the disk if you want the cache filesystem to work. The cache filesystem MUST work if you want to restore a disk image.

The disk cache is organised in a volatile, CRC-validated filesystem : Each directory entry and each 32 KB data block is validated by a 32-bits CRC. Whenever a directory entry or a data block unexpectedly changes, the file is automatically removed from the cache and downloaded again upon the next request.

You can freely access the cache filesystem from within BpBatch, MrBatch and MrZip using direct disk access on the special partition "{:-1}". To see the content of the cache, just type :

```
logdir "{:-1}"
```

If the cache ever gets corrupted and is not automatically cleaned (which should never occurs), you can either type :

```
clean -1
```

(in interactive mode) or hold both shifts down when BpBatch access the cache for the first time.

5.1.4   Special variables

Some variable are initially set and/or have special meanings. Some of them exist within all programs, other are only available under MrZip and other are only available when a BOOTP/DHCP reply has been received.

General variables

- $Program is set to "BpBatch" within BpBatch, "MrBatch" within MrBatch and "MrZip" within MrZip
- $Basename is set to the basename of the script on which the batch interpreter was started
- $HelpFile is the name of the file loaded when Help is invoked. Default: "${Basename}.hlp"

- `$BOOTP-...` are variables set from the BOOTP/DHCP reply (see the paragraph on BOOTP/DHCP variables for more details)

- `$DHCP-...` are variables set from the DHCP reply (see the paragraph on BOOTP/DHCP variables for more details)

- `$Disks` is set to the space-separated list of sizes for each disk. That means, `#"$Disks"` represent the number of disks and `"$Disks"{0}` is the size of the first disk

- `$Keypressed` is set to the next ready-to-read key available in the keyboard buffer (if available)

- `$LBA` controls the use of LBA to access disks > 2Gb. Default: "ON"

- `$FDA` controls the use of fast disk access (write accross cylinders). Default: "ON"

- `$VESA` controls the use of VESA graphics. Default: "ON" if available

- `$VESA-Modes` gives the list of all available VESA modes. The first entry of the list is the default mode, which is used when no parameter is given to InitGraph. Note: if VESA="OFF", this variable is blank

- `$APM` is set to "ON" if your computer supports Avanced Power Management. If $APM is "ON", you can use the command PowerOff to turn your computer off. Default: depends on your hardware

- `$Trace` controls the display of each command before execution. It also controls the display of file names when creating new archives. Default: "OFF"

- `$AutoShowLog` controls the automatic switch to the text log whenever the ESC key is pressed. Default: "ON"

- `$PauseLog` controls the pause between each page of log when the log is visible. Default: "ON"

- `$CacheDisk` is set to the disk used for caching remote files. Default: empty == 0, the first hard disk

- `$CacheAlways` controls the automatic caching of remote files copied, patched or drawn as GIF. Default: "OFF"

- `$CacheNever` prevents any file from being cached. Turn this variable on for diskless Linux boot. Default: "OFF"

- `$CacheReserve` controls the preventive allocation of 25 percent more space than necessary in the cache partition, to let the files grow. Turn this variable off if you are short of disk space. Default: "ON"

- `$ExtMemory` controls the use of Extended Memory (or XMS). Once deactivated, extended memory cannot be reactivated. Default: "ON" if available

- `$IsoLatin` controls the interpretation of upper ASCII codes in included and patched files. The IsoLatin settings are processed at the time the file is loaded, not at the time the file is processed. Default: "ON"

- `$ProgressX` and `$ProgressY` controls the position of the progress window displayed in VESA graphics during archive download and decompression. Default: 200 200

- `$EXT2-Backup` controls the update of superblock backups in Linux ext2 filesystem. Superblock backups take a few seconds to do and are never used by current kernels (only by e2fsck).

- `$Security-Gateway` controls the gateway-server used for user authentication. Our special authentication gateway must be running on the target computer. Default: `"${BOOTP-Server-IP}@89"` (ie. the TFTP server, on port 89)

- `$Security-Check` contains the answer of the security server for the last check performed, either PASSED or FAILED. Default: "FAILED"

- `$Security-Passwd`, `$HelpTopic`, `$OnExit`, `$OnKey-...` are used internally.

See also BOOTP variables and MrZip-specific variables.

MrZip-specific variables

The following variables are only used within MrZip.

- `$TempPath` controls the directory where temporary files will be stored. Default: <empty> == current directory

- $DumpFormat controls the way archives are dumped to the log when requested. It is a string containing
  - "h"/"H" to display the archive header
  - "b"/"B" to summarize/dump boot sectors
  - "s"/"S" to display a short/long allocation summary
  - "d"/"D" to display a short/long directory listing
  - "f"/"F" to summarize/dump files

  Default: "hbD"

- $FragmentSize controls the size of archive pieces. If you do not use InCom's extended TFTP server, you should set this to "30 MB". Default: "87 MB"

- $SourceArchive, $DestArchive, $Filter... are used internally.

BOOTP variables

The following BOOTP-... and DHCP-... variables are recognized, as long as a BOOTP/DHCP reply has been received (TCP/IP Bootprom must be reported as detected):

```
$BOOTP-Client-ID
$BOOTP-Your-IP
$BOOTP-Server-IP
$BOOTP-Gateway-IP
$BOOTP-Bootfile
$BOOTP-Server-Name
$BOOTP-Subnet-Mask
$BOOTP-Time-Offset
$BOOTP-Routers
$BOOTP-Time-Servers
$BOOTP-Name-Servers
$BOOTP-Domain-name-Servers
$BOOTP-BOOTP-Log-Servers
$BOOTP-Cookie-Servers
$BOOTP-Lpr-Servers
$BOOTP-Impress-Servers
$BOOTP-Resource-Location-Servers
$BOOTP-Host-Name
$BOOTP-Boot-Size
$BOOTP-Merit-Dump
$BOOTP-Domain-Name
$BOOTP-Swap-Servers
$BOOTP-Root-Path
$BOOTP-Extensions-Path
$BOOTP-IP-Forwarding
$BOOTP-Interface-MTU
$BOOTP-All-Subnets-Are-Local
$BOOTP-Broadcast-Address
$BOOTP-NIS-Domain
$BOOTP-NIS-Servers
$BOOTP-NTP-Servers
$BOOTP-Font-Servers
$BOOTP-X-Display-Manager
$DHCP-IP-Address-Lease-Time
$DHCP-Message-Type
$DHCP-Server-Identifier
$DHCP-Message
$DHCP-Renewal-Time
$DHCP-Rebinding-Time
```

Mini-HOWTO

```
$BOOTP-NIS+-Domain
$BOOTP-NIS+-Servers
$BOOTP-Server-Name
$BOOTP-Bootfile
$BOOTP-Mobile-IP-Agent
$BOOTP-SMTP-Servers
$BOOTP-POP3-Servers
$BOOTP-NNTP-Servers
$BOOTP-WWW-Servers
$BOOTP-Finger-Servers
$BOOTP-IRC-Servers
$BOOTP-StreetTalk-Servers
$BOOTP-STDA-Servers
```

Other BOOTP/DHCP parameters can be used under the name

```
$BOOTP-Option-n
```

where n is the decimal representation of the BOOTP option number.

Do not mix-up `BOOTP-Gateway-IP`, which is the gateway to use for TFTP and should be 0.0.0.0 if the TFTP server is in the same subnet, and `BOOTP-Routers`, which contains the default IP gateway(s). The TCP/IP Bootprom sometimes seems to set the value of `BOOTP-Gateway-IP` from the value in `BOOTP-Routers`, causing each TFTP ack packet to be sent to the router first. To avoid such behaviour, if your TFTP server is in the same subnet as the client, force `BOOTP-Gateway-IP` to `0.0.0.0` (thanks to Maciek Uhlig for having pointed out this problem).

5.1.5 Monitoring commands

This section lists commands for monitoring the system state. Optional arguments are listed between parenthesis (I would have prefered square brackets, but LaTeX do not like them at this place...)

Interact

Show the log and turn to interactive mode until QUIT or EXIT is entered. Type HideLog before quitting if you want to avoid disturbing log messages during batch execution.

Help (topic)

Load the on-line help file (`bpbatch.hlp`) and display the description of the given topic. If no topic is provided, or if the topic is unknown, display the help index.

Log "text"

Display the string on the log. No return/linefeed is implicitly added.

Echo "text"

Display the string on the log and go to the next line. Equivalent to

```
Log "text\r\n".
```

LogVars ("pattern")

Log (ie. display on the log) all variables matching the given pattern. The pattern can contain wildcards (? and *).

```
Example: LogVars "BOOTP-*"              list all BootP variables
```

LogDir "path/pattern"

Log (ie. display on the log) all files from the given path that match the pattern. The pattern can contain wildcards (? and *).

```
Example: LogDir "/usr/g*p"              list files names like g...p
```

LogTree "path"

Log the directory tree starting with the given path as root.

LogFile "filename"

Log the content of the file. The file must be no more than 64 KB big.

ShowLog

Make the log visible if it was hidden. Automatically performed when ESC is pressed with "$AutoShowLog" == "ON" and when entering interactive mode.

HideLog

Prevent log messages to appear on the screen. Default state when BpBatch, MrBatch and MrZip are started on a script file.

CaptureLog

Record all log output to a 64 KB buffer until EndCapture is issued. Wrap around buffer if the log output is more than 64 KB big. This command can be used to create a text file with an arbitrary content. The EndCapture MUST occurs within the same batch file.

EndCapture ("filename")

End up the capture of the log. If a filename is given, store the captured text to a file. Otherwise, discard it.

Beep

Make a sound. This command is equivalent to Echo "\007".

5.1.6   Control commands

This section lists commands that control the batch execution. Optional arguments are listed between parenthesis.

Include "filename"

Load the given file and start up the parser on it. Go back to the current point when the include file processing is done. The interpretation of characters above ASCII 127 within the include file depends on the value of $IsoLatin at the time the file is included.

OnExit *command*

Setup an exit-handler that will automatically be evaluated at the end of current batch file.

Goto *label*

Move the execution cursor to the given label (ie. the line starting with :*label*)

Eval "command"

Perform all substitutions on the "command" and run the parser on it.

If ...

```
If (not) <expr1> (==|!=|<|>|>=|<=|=>|=<|<>) <expr2> <command>
If (not) (ci) "str1" (==|!=|<|>|>=|<=|=>|=<|<>) "str2" <command>
If (not) (ci) "str1" Match-Expr "pattern" <command>
If (not) (ci) "str1" Match-Passwd "unix-passwd" <command>
If (not) (ci) "str1" in "wordlist" <command>
If (not) (ci) "str1" in-file "filename" <command>
If (not) exist "filename" <command>
If (not) valid <disk>:<partition> <command>
```

These commands execute *command;* if the test succeeds. The 1st form compares two numerical expressions. The 2nd form compares two strings, optionally case-insensitive. The 3rd form tests if "str1" matches the given pattern (wildcards allowed). The 4th form tests if the clear password "str1" matches the Unix-crypted password. The 5th form tests if "str1" is included in the word list. The 6th form tests if "str1" is included in the word file. The 7th form tests if the given file exists. The 8th form tests if the given partition is valid (i.e. formatted). This form is only supported by BpBatch versions after February 1999.

Set ...

```
Set variable = "string-value"
Set variable = <expr>
```

Setup a value for the given variable. If the given value is a numerical expresison, it will be implicitly converted to a string. A variable can be used anywhere by refering it as $variable or ${variable}. If the resulting reference is to be interpreted as a string, it should be enclosed between double quotes: "$variable" or "${variable}".

Delay *duration*

Waits until the specified duration (expressed in seconds) expired. See also the paragraph on the format of durations.

GetTime *variable*, **GetDate** *variable*

Get the CMOS time and store it into *variable* in the form HH:MM:SS. Get the CMOS date and store it into *variable* in the form YY/MM/DD. This can be used to customize the behavior of your boot scripts depending on the time of day or on the date.

SetTime "HH:MM:SS", **SetDate** "YY/MM/DD"

Set the computer CMOS time or date to the given value. If you have a security gateway (our special TFTP server) running, you can automatically adjust the CMOS time and date of the client computers at each boot by evaluating the following command:

```
include "$Security-Gateway:gettime"
```

If you want to understand what this command does, just type:

```
logfile "$Security-Gateway:gettime"
```

Poweroff

Turn off the computer. This command only works if the computer is Advanced Power Management (APM) compatible.

5.1.7 Keyboard-related commands

This section lists commands that let you monitor the keyboard input. Optional arguments are listed between parenthesis. See also under *National Language Support*.

GetKey (*variable*)

Indefinitely wait until a key is pressed and store it in the *variable*.

WaitForKey *duration* (*command*)

Wait until a key is pressed for no more than *duration* seconds. If no key has been pressed after the given time, evaluate the *command*. Otherwise, leave the key in the keyboard buffer. See also the paragraph on the format of durations.

Input (*variable* (*max-length*))

Read a return-terminated string from the keyboard and store the result string in *variable* (without the terminating return). If *max-length* is given, do not allow the user to enter more than this number of characters.

See also `GetPasswd` under *Security-related commands*.

OnKey "c" *command*

Setup a key handler that will automatically evaluate the given *command* when the key "c" is pressed (except is explicitly waited by a GetChar or an Input command). If the string "default" is used instead of a single character, the command is executed if any other key is pressed.

5.1.8 Text output commands

This section lists commands used to perform regular text output. All these commands can be used in graphic mode also, with the same behaviour (except that text mode provides 80x25 characters while graphic mode provides 100x37, because graphic mode characters are of size 8x16). Optional arguments are listed between parenthesis. See also under *National Language Support*.

Print *"text"/expr*

Print the specified string/expression at current cursor position and using current text attributes, then move the cursor. Add "\r\n" to the end of the string to go to the next line.

TextAttr *fg-color bg-color*

> Setup the text attributes. One can also put a single numeric value representing both colors and defined as 16*bg-color+fg-color*.
>
> If you need more fantasy, you can use `LoadFont`. See under *National Language Support*.

At *line,col* (*command*)

> Move the cursor position to the specified position and evaluate the command if provided.
>
> ```
> Example: At 10,20 Print "Gnats and rats !"
> ```

Clear (*color* (*pattern-char* (*top,left,bottom,right*)))

> Fill the given text area with the given *pattern-char* (either a string or the decimal ascii code). The area defaults to the full screen, the pattern char defaults to the full block (ASCII dec 219) and the color defaults to black (clear screen). Move the cursor to the upper left corner of the cleared area.

BpMenu backward compatibility commands

> ```
> .ATT (<attribute>)
> .CLS (<attribute>)
> .DEF <key> (<timeout_val>)
> .KEY <key> <filename>
> .POS ((<x>) <y>)
> .PWD <key> <cpasswd>
> .WLN (<text>)
> .WRT <text>
> ```
>
> See InCom's manual for more infos. We wrote some time ago a *program* program for editing menu files using this syntax, but it is preferable to make your menus using the new explicit syntax. Note that the .PWD command is not implemented because we do not now the password crypting algorithm used by InCom GmbH.

5.1.9   Graphics output commands

This section lists commands used to perform graphic-mode output. For the functions listed in this section, coordinates are given in pixels. You can also use all text output commands (see above) in graphic mode. Optional arguments are listed between parenthesis.

Note that the graphic mode is automatically turned on whenever a graphic command is used, unless the variable VESA is set to "OFF".

InitGraph ("mode")

> Turn on VESA graphics. The origin is on the upper-left corner of the screen (0 0). VESA graphics may hang some computers under Windows 95. Run MrBatch with the -v option to avoid such problems.
>
> You can request a specific video mode if you use the parameter "mode" This parameter is optional: if you do not specify any value, the video mode will be taken from the first field of the VESA-Modes variable.
>
> Valid modes are :
>
> - 640x480 => 640 by 480 pixels, 256 colors
> - 800x600 => 800 by 600 pixels, 256 colors (default mode)
> - 1024x768 => 1024 by 768 pixels, 256 colors
> - 1280x1024 => 1280 by 1024 pixels, 256 colors
>
> The VESA-Modes variable lists the video modes supported by your hardware.
> ```
> Example: InitGraph "640x480"
> ```

CloseGraph

> Close VESA graphic mode and go back to text mode.

DrawBar *x-pos y-pos width height color*

VESA graphics. Draw a filled bar of the given size and colors.

DrawWindow *x-pos y-pos width height* (*bg-color* (*bar-color*)) ("title" (*title-color*))

VESA graphics. Draw a window of the given size and colors. The background color defaults to LightGray and the title-bar color defaults to Blue. If you include a title string and a color, this text will be displayed in the title bar.

Drawtext *x-pos y-pos* "text" (*fg-color*)

VESA graphics. Draw the text string at the given position with a transparent background. The color defaults to text foreground color.

DrawGif "gif-filename" (*x-pos y-pos* (*color-strategy*))

VESA graphics. Load the given GIF-87a file and draw it on the screen. The file can be interlaced, but must be in GIF-87a (not GIF-89a). The image size should fit in the selected video mode. You cannot load a 1024x768 GIF file when you selected a 640x480 mode. The GIF position defaults to the top left corner of the screen (0 0).

The *color-strategy* defines the allocation of colors in the palette when more than 256 colors are needed (for instance when two 256 colors GIF files are displayed simultaneously):

- `Best-Colors` use best possible colors for the most recent GIF
- `Spare-Colors` try to avoid allocating colors, change existing colors
- `Share-Colors` try to avoid allocating colors, use existing colors
- `Reuse-Colors` allocate no new color, only use existing colors

The default strategy is `Best-Colors`.

5.1.10 Security-related commands

This section lists commands that help you authenticate a user. Optional arguments are listed between parenthesis.

Some of these functions cooperate with a *Security gateway*, that you should first install. See the section on *Special TFTP servers* for more infos.

GetPasswd (*variable* (*max-length*))

Same as Input, but echo stars instead of the typed characters.

Crypt "text" "salt" *variable*

Apply the Unix crypt function to the given 8-chars text and store the resulting crypted string into *variable*. The "salt" is usually a two-character string that will be found as the first two characters of the crypted string.

Note that Unix crypt is a one-way function. It is not possible to decode the crypted string. One can only try to crypt another string with the same salt and compre the resulting crypted string.

DESCrypt "text" "key" *variable*

Crypt the given text using the given 8-chars key and store the result as an hexadecimal string in *variable*.

DESDecrypt "hexcode" "key" *variable*

Decrypt the given hexadecimal string using the given 8-chars key and store the result in *variable*.

MD5 "text" *variable*

Compute the MD5 checksum of the given text and store it as an hexadecimal string in *variable*. Can be used as an alternative to the Unix crypt function to check for passwords bigger than 8 characters.

CheckUser "user" "password" "domain"

Connect to the $Security-Gateway and check if the given user exist in the given radius domain and uses the specified password. If the domain is "Unix", use the Unix user/password definition on the security gateway. For any other domain, use the security gateway domain definition file to determine the real Radius or NT domain to check.

Set the value of $Security-Check to "PASSED" or "FAILED". The password do not transit in clear on the network.

5.1.11 Disk-related commands

This section lists commands for preparing the hard-disk. Optional arguments are listed between parenthesis.

GetPartitions *variable* (*disk*)

Read the partition table(s) for the given disk and store it as a string into the given *variable*. The result string is a space-separated list of *Type:Size*, where

- *Type* is FAT16, EXT, BIGDOS, NTFS, FAT32, FAT32-LBA, BIGDOS-LBA, EXT-LBA, LINUX-SWAP, LINUX-EXT2 or the decimal filesystem id for unknown types.

- *Size* is the size of the partition in megabytes.

See SetPartitions for more informations about partitions.

SetPartitions "partitions" (*disk*)

Setup the partition table(s) to the content of the string. The format used is the same that for GetPartitions. This command also reset all boot flags (hint: use SetBootPart).

The main partition table in the master boot record (MBR) has only four entries. Moreover, DOS and Windows accept only ONE FAT partition (called the Primary partition, C:) in the main partition table. Any supplemental FAT partition should be nested in an extended partition (and is thus called a Logical partition). If we give numbers 1-4 to the partitions described in the MBR partition table and numbers 5-8 to the partitions described in the first extended partition, the definition of two FAT partitions would work by defining partition 1 as FAT, partition 2 as EXT and partition 5 as FAT. Partitions 3,4,6,7 and 8 should be marked as UNUSED. The same scheme can be used recursively to define more than two FAT partitions: nesting another extended partition in partition 6 and adding a logical FAT partition in partition 9.

In the most strict interpretation of DOS specifications, that means that entries 3 and 4 of the partition tables are never used. In practice, some versions of DOS and some other OS are able to use more than two partitions per partition table, but there is no clear rule. On this side, BpBatch is rather flexible in its interpretation of partition tables, it can often understands things that OSes cannot.

One universal rule is that there should never be more than one extended partition per partition table, otherwise the partition numbering scheme breaks down.

If you want to try funny configurations, make your own experiments, but don't complain if the OS does not recognize your partitions. The only way it is guarantee to work is to use the primary partition to store the OS boot partition, and to nest all other partitions, one at a time, in extended partitions.

Example of extended partitions :

```
SetPartitions "BIGDOS:100 EXT:400 EMPTY EMPTY BIGDOS:400"
```

GetBootPart *variable* (*disk*)

Get the partition number with the boot flag turned on (DOS says: the activated primary partition) and store it to the *variable*. The first partition is numbered 1. If no partitions has the boot flag turned on, answers zero.

SetBootPart *partition* (*disk*)

Set the boot flag to the given partition. The boot flag let the master boot record (MBR) choose which partition to boot on. The first partition is numbered 1.

Blank *partition* (*disk*)

Fill the given partitions with zeroes. Can take quite a lot of time for big partitions. Do not format the partition for any operating system. See also `Clean`.

Clean *partitions* (*disk*) ("label")

Fast-format the given partition(s) according to the type declared in the partition table. If a label is given and the filesystem supports it, setup the partition label. For a paranoiac full format, call `Blank` on the partition first.

Clean is supported for (FAT16) BIGDOS, FAT32, EXT, LINUX-EXT2 and LINUX-SWAP partitions. To clean the master boot record (MBR), use `Clean 0`.

Clean should be used on data partitions and on MBR/EXT partitions. It is totally useless to clean a partition before unzipping a filesystem on it using `FullUnzip`.

FullUnzip "full-archive" *partition* (*disk*)

Decompress a full disk archive to the given partition, overwriting any existing file (clean-up on the fly).

FullUnzip is supported for (FAT16) BIGDOS, FAT32 and LINUX-EXT2.

This commands turn on VESA graphics to display a progress banner, unless `VESA` has been turned `OFF`.

IncrUnzip "incr-archive" "destpath"

Decompress an incremental disk archive to the given path. Files in the archive replace those with the same name on the target path, but other files are not deleted.

IncrUnzip is supported for (FAT16) BIGDOS, FAT32 and LINUX-EXT2. This command is far less efficient than FullUnzip since the existing filesystem structure must be preserved. However, it avoids multiplying the number of different disk images by storing the differences only.

FileUnzip "source-filename" "dest-filename"

Uncompress a file previously compressed with `MrZip` FileZip command. The file is validated by a 32-bits CRC.

Copy "source-filename" "dest-filename"

Copy the source file to the destinaton file, byte-to-byte. Can be used after a FullUnzip for instance to update configuration files from the server without rebuilding the image. Better to use `FileUnzip` for big and easy-to-compress files.

Append "src-filename-1" "src-filename-2" "dest-filename"

Copy the first, then the second file to the destination file, byte-to-byte. Can be used on arbitrary large files. The destination file cannot be one of the two source files.

Patch "source-filename" "dest-filename" ("prefix" ("postfix"))

Read the source file and perform variable substitution before writing it to the destination file. The interpretation of characters above ASCII 127 depends on the value of $IsoLatin.

By default, variables are recognized when prefixed by "${" and postfixed by "}". This can be changed to any other non-empty string. remember that if you want to use a dollar sign within the prefix or suffix, you must escape it or it will get macro-evaluated. For instance, if you want to explicitly use the default prefix and postfix, use:

```
Patch "source-file" "dest-file" "\${" "}"
```

MkDir "path"

Recursively create directories from the root to the given full path. If the path already exists, this command has no effect.

Delete "filename", Del "filaname"

Remove the given file. The file must exist.

DelTree "path"

Recursively remove all files and directories under the given path, and remove the directory itself.

5.1.12 Boot commands

This section lists commands for continuing the boot process. Optional arguments are listed between parenthesis.

HideBootProm

Restore the memory and the interrupt vectors allocated by the bootprom. All attempts to make TFTP transfers will fail after calling this command. It is usually a good idea to call this command before HdBoot, or you might run short of memory under DOS/Windows. This command is implicitly called by FloppyBoot.

Note that although this function restore all vectors "officially" rerouted by the BootProm, it does not seems to restore everything. But it works well enough for DOS and Windows.

LoadRamDisk "ramdisk-filename"

Load a floppy disk image into the extended memory and redirect the BIOS Disk Services to make floppy disk calls use this image instead. This command implicitly calls `HideBootProm`. Call `FloppyBoot` to boot on the ramdisk you just loaded.

This kind of ramdisk may not be as robust as what you get when you use the TFTPBoot command. The only advantage is that it only steals a few hundred bytes of conventional memory instead of the >64 KB reserved by the TCP/IP BootPROM. Warning, nothing secures the extended memory in which the ramdisk resides. There is no way to uninstall such a ramdisk.

LoadZRamDisk "ramdisk-filename"

Do the same as `LoadRamDisk`, but for an image that has been compressed using `MrZip` FileZip command. Compressed ramdisks are protected against data corruption (and uncomplete download) by a byte count and a 32-bits CRC.

TFTPBoot "remote-bootfile"

Chain to another boot file (for instance a floppy image made with InCom's BpShell program). See the file referencing conventions for accessing a file on another TFTP server.

FloppyBoot

Hide the Boot ROM, load the floppy disk boot sector and boot on it.

HdBoot (*disk*)(:*partition*)

Load the given boot sector and boot from it. The disk default to zero, the first hard disk, and the partition defaults to zero, ie. the master boot record. You can boot from any partition, but be warned that Windows 95 may not let you boot a partition that has not been set as the boot partition (hint: use SetBootPart).

This command does not implicitly call HideBootProm, so you might want to call it before.

LinuxBoot "kernelfile" ("command-line" ("ramdisk-file"))

Load the given kernel and ramdisk into the high memory, setup the command line and boot the kernel. It is a good idea to put at least a minimal command line with the location of the root filesystem (like `"root=dev/hda1"/`). If you are using a linux system that heavily relies on `lilo` (like RedHat Linux 5.1), it may be necessary to add to the command line something like `BOOT_IMAGE=linux`. Note that the kernel can be loaded by TFTP (automatically cached on the hard disk) or directly from the target root partition.

This command works for small and big kernels (`zImage` and `bzImage`).

5.1.13   National language support

This section lists commands related not national language support. Optional arguments are listed between parenthesis.

RemapKeys "original-keys" "remapped-keys"

National keyboard support. Remap given keys to other characters. For instance, to swap the Y and Z keys, use

```
Remapkeys "yzYZ" "zyZY"
```

It is a good idea to use the quoted octal notation when using characters not included in the minimal ASCII character set, in order to avoid a dependency to the iso-latin modal settings.

For international keyboards, there are two keys that produce a backslash in non-remapped (US) mode. Each of them can be independantly remapped, thanks to the fact that `BpBatch` sees one of them as a key answering ASCII code 252 (octal) or ASCII code 335 (octal) when shifted.

If you send me a sample script that does keyboard mapping for your national keyboard, I will make it available under *http://cuiwww.unige.ch/info/pc/remote-boot/soft/sample-scripts* To help you make your own keyboard mapping, I suggest pressing all *special* keys without remapping the keyboard and writing down the character they produce. These will be the `original-keys`. The `remapped-keys` simply are the key you would have liked to see, in the same order. If some keys (either original or remapped) produce characters above ASCII dec 127, use the quoted octal notation. You can easily get the octal code for any given character by looking in the ASCII table of HelpPC for instance (HelpPC is a shareware hypertext on-line help program by David Jurgens).

RemapAltkeys "original-keys" "remapped-keys"

National keyboard support. Remap the given keys when ALT is depressed For instance, to map Alt-2 to the ampersand sign, use

```
RemapAltKeys "2" "@"
```

Note that dead keys are not supported.

LoadCodePage "cpxxx.bin"

Load and activate the given binary Codepage file. Codepages are used for the translation of Unicode characters (present on VFAT valumes for instance) into 8-bits characters. If you do not have the right Codepage loaded, you will get FAT warnings while accessing the filesystem when special characters are encountred.

All binary codepage files are available at *http://cuiwww.unige.ch/info/pc/remote-boot/soft/codepage.zip*

The default codepage is 850, a reordered superset of ISO-Latin-1. If you load a more exotic codepage, you should usually turn the variable $IsoLatin to "off" or you might get meaningless implicit conversions. Moreover, if you want to display exotic characters, you should also load the proper screen font (use "LoadFont").

LoadFont "fontfile"

Load and activate a VGA/VESA font, both in text and graphic mode. The font file must be a binary file of 16 bztes/characters (8x16 bitmap). This command can be used for National Language Support as well as for Fantasy support.

An archive with several fantasy fonts is available at *http://cuiwww.unige.ch/info/pc/remote-boot/soft/fonts.zip*. This archive also contains a program to extract fonts for your codepage from the DOS .CPI file.

5.1.14 Commands specific to MrZip

Source...

```
Source (i)archive "filename"
Source path "path"
```

Set the source for the archive manipulation to the given (incremental) archive file or disk path.

Dest...

```
Dest (i)archive "filename"
Dest (i)dump
Dest path "path"
```

Set the destination for the archive manipulation to the given (incremental) archive file, dump or disk path. To control the quantity of data displayed during dump, use the $DumpFormat special variable.

FileZip "source-filename" "dest-filename"

Compress a file for further decompression with FileUnzip or for using as ZRamDisk. The file is validated by a 32-bits CRC.

Filter...

```
Filter -"pattern"
Filter +"pattern"
```

Avoid/allow files and directories matching the given pattern (wildcards allowed) to be included in the archive. The pattern is matched agains the full pathname. By default, all files are included in the image. You only need to explicitly allow files that where cancelled by a filter. Each negative filter has its own positive filter (allowed) sublist.

For DOS/Windows images, you will typically use

```
Filter -"*.swp"
Filter -"temp/*"
```

and for Unix images, you will typically use

```
Filter -"var/log/*"
Filter -"tmp/*"
```

CopyArchive

Start the archive manipulation operation, according to source, destination and filter settings. Except in a few circumstances, you will probably use the shortcut below instead of explicitly calling `CopyArchive`. One circumstance in which you will use `CopyArchive` explicitly is when you want to change the fragmentation of an image, as follow:

```
set FragmentSize="30 MB"
Source archive "original.imz"
Dest archive "refragmented.imz"
CopyArchive
```

FullZip "path" "full-archive"

Shortcut for

```
Source path "path"
Dest archive "full-archive"
CopyArchive
```

You should usually first setup filters.

IncrZip "path" "incr-archive"

Shortcut for

```
Source path "path"
Dest iarchive "incr-archive"
CopyArchive
```

FullDump "full-archive"

Shortcut for

```
Source archive "full-archive"
Dest dump
CopyArchive
```

IncrDump "incr-archive"

Shortcut for

```
Source iarchive "incr-archive"
Dest dump
CopyArchive
```

XCopy "srcpath" "dstpath"

Shortcut for

```
Source path "srcpath"
Dest path "dstpath"
CopyArchive
```

5.2   NoBreak.sys

`Nobreak.sys` is a very small (about 350 bytes only) driver that you include at the beginning of your `config.sys`. Its goal is to secure the boot process, until the user is logged in. DOS provides a setting for this (namely `BREAK=OFF`), but it is not drastic enough, and has almost no effect in the `autoexec.bat`. Our driver works by modifying the scan-code of the key pressed when a break is requested, directly at the BIOS level. This way, no program at all can receive a break until break is enabled again.

The driver must be loaded from the `config.sys` (or using the `devlod` program from *Undocumented DOS*). Afterwards, break can be enabled by sending `Yes` to the `NOBRK` pseudo-device, and disabled again by sending `No` (in fact, only the first character, `Y` or `N` is significant).

As this driver relies on the BIOS, it does only work for DOS and Windows 3.1. Windows 95 has its own low-level keyboard handling routines.

Assembler source code is *available*.

Mini-HOWTO

6   Special TFTP Servers

As the only network support available in the TCP/IP BootPROM is TFTP, there is a special interest in enhancing TFTP servers for providing new capabilities.

6.1   Incom Enhanced TFTP Server

InCom GmbH distributes with the TCP/IP BootPROM an enhanced TFTP server that can send packets of up to 1408 bytes instead of the standard 512 bytes. This is a great enhancement that you should use. This server is available on the TCP/IP Bootprom Utility disk for Solaris, Windows and as Netware NLM.

6.2   Linux Enhanced TFTP Server

We built a modified version of Linux TFTP server that acts as InCom enhanced TFTP server. Basically, we simply changed the packet size from 512 to 1408 bytes and the port from 69 to 59. It is available from *http://cuiwww.unige.ch/info/pc/remote-boot/soft/etdtpd.tar.gz*.

6.3   The Security Gateway

We wrote a special TFTP server that serves as security gateway for authenticating users. This server runs under Linux or Solaris, and can authenticate users according to a Unix password database (NIS and shadow passwords are supported), a Windows NT (or Samba) server or a Radius server. It is available from *http://cuiwww.unige.ch/info/pc/remote-boot/soft/stdtpd.tar.gz*, with source and precompiled binaries. The precompiled binaries do not include NT password encryption as we cannot distribute libdes but compilation is straightforward.

In order to use the security gateway, you just have to setup a trivial *security domains* configuration file that describes to which authentication server each logical security domains maps (the Unix domain implicitly maps to the server Unix password database). This is a sample configuration file:

```
#
# STFTPD configuration file
#
# This file specify the server of the "security domains". Two types of
# authentication servers are supported : radius or winnt (winnt includes
# NT Server and Samba)
#
# Format of radius servers
# radius        <domain>        <serveraddress>        <secret>
#
# secret is the secret word as specified in your /etc/raddb/clients file
#
# Format of SMB servers
# winnt         <domain>        <serveraddress>        <netbiosname>
#
# netbiosname is the NETBIOS name of your server
#
# Examples
radius        sec-dom-rad     radiusserver     testing123
winnt         sec-dom-nt1     192.168.1.1      NTSERVER1
winnt         sec-dom-smb     samba            SAMBA1
```

Note that if you are using Samba, you must set security = user.

You can also provide to the security server a file containing a list of users which are not allowed to log on (for which the check will fail anyways).

6.4 The Broadcast TFTP Server

We wrote a special TFTP server that implements a home-made Broadcast variant of TFTP. Using this server, we were able to download images to 25 clients on a heavily loaded 10 Mb ethernet network at 6 Mb/s (it is more efficient than the regular TFTP because it does not need to acknowledge each packets). This server runs under Linux or Solaris. It is available from *http://cuiwww.unige.ch/info/pc/remote-boot/soft/btdtpd.tar.gz*, with source and precompiled binaries.

As the TCP/IP bootprom does not support this protocol, our solution consist in booting a tiny ramdisk-based linux system using the tools described in this document, and running the Linux version of MrBatch which has built-in support for Broadcast TFTP. A simple batch file can the download all files to the cache in a few minutes, simultaneously on all client computers. You do not need to install Linux yourself to use this package, except if you have exotic hardware and cannot directly use the kernel provided in the package.

The process works as follow. First, you startup the broadcast server manually, giving the number of expected client computers as argument (remember, this procedure is not to be used every day but only when you changed an image and want to ensure it is immediately uploaded to all your client computers). Then, you turn on all client computers, which will run the following BpBatch script:

```
#
# This batch is run by bpbatch to launch a mini-linux using an initial
# ramdisk, which will then run mrbatch under linux.
#
# The broadcast TFTP protocol only works with the Linux implementation of
# mrbatch, because of the lack of broadcast support in the bootprom itself.
#
# 1. Setup a tiny partition, to let a lot of space for the cache
setpartitions "BIGDOS:50"
# 2. Clean the MBR
clean 0
# 3. Run a Linux Kernel with initrd (Initial Ramdisk) supprt, and use
#      bcastrd.gz as the initial ramdisk (will be mounted root and then
#      executed via /linuxrc). See initrd.txt for more details about
#      initial ramdisks. You don't have to specify a root device (second
#      parameter is null) to the kernel, it will use the initial ramdisk.
linuxboot "linux.krn" "" "bcastrd.gz"
# 4. The initial ramdisk will run dhcpcd to setup networking using DHCP.
#      It will then run mrbatch -w bcastlx
```

The initial ramdisk contains:

- dhcpcd, a DHCP client used to setup networking
- mrbatch
- linuxrc, a little wrapper automatically started by initrd and that starts dhcpcd then mrbatch.
- usr/lib/terminfo/l/linux, used by MrBatch
- dev/*, devices needed to run Linux and mrbatch

All programs are statically linked and stripped, to avoid libc.so which is really huge. The resulting ramdisk is Gzipped and takes less than 300 KB. The kernel itself takes 450 KB (with many network cards and initrd support). When Linux is up and running, MrBatch is called with the following script (that you should edit for your needs):

```
# This file is executed when mrbatch is launched by the initial ramdisk
# bcastrd.gz
# It's main purpose is to "broacast copy" files to the cache
#
```

```
# 1. Be verbose
showlog
# 2. Don't want a "press a key"
set pauselog="OFF"
# 3. Set partitions at their final values.
#      Important: Since you will copy files into the cache to be used in future
#      boot, you need to specify the same partitions as in the future boots.
setpartitions "BIGDOS:1024"
# 4. Clean the CACHE partition
clean -1
# 5. And the copy files into the cache, using the Broadcast TFTP protocol
#      (port 99)
#
# You can use the script "as is", but you surely need to modi-
fy the following
# line ! In our example, we download the file mblin-
ux.imz, which is the image
# file for our installation of Linux.
copy "$BOOTP-Server-IP@99:mblinux.imz" "{:-1}mblinux.imz"
```

When the transfer is done, you can simply turn off all client computers and change their initial boot script to your favorite menu.

Part LXXVII

"Remote X Apps mini-HOWTO" *Vincent Zweije*

zweije@xs4all.nl

v, 14 July 1998

This mini-HOWTO describes how to run remote X applications. That is, how to have an X program display on a different computer than the one it's running on. Or conversely: how to make an X program run on a different computer than the one you're sitting at. The focus of this mini-HOWTO is on security.

Contents

1   Introduction

This mini-HOWTO is a guide how to do remote X applications. It was written for several reasons.

1. Many questions have appeared on usenet on how to run a remote X application.

2. I see many, many hints of "use `xhost +hostname`" or even "`xhost +`" to allow X connections. **This is ridiculously insecure**, and there are better methods.

3. I do not know of a simple document that describes the options you *do* have. Please inform me *zweije@xs4all.nl* if you know more.

This document has been written with unix-like systems in mind. If either your local or remote operating system are of another flavour, you may find here how things work. However, you will have to translate examples yourself to apply to your own system(s).

The most recent version of this document is always available on WWW at *http://www.xs4all.nl/~zweije/xauth.html*. It is also available as the Linux Remote X Apps mini-HOWTO at *http://sunsite.unc.edu/LDP/HOWTO/mini/Remote-X-Apps*. Linux (mini-)HOWTOs are available by http or ftp from *sunsite.unc.edu*.

This is version 0.5.1. No guarantees, only good intentions. I'm open to suggestions, ideas, additions, useful pointers, (typo) corrections, etc... I want this to remain a simple readable document, though, in the best-meant HOWTO style. Flames to `/dev/null`.

Contents last updated on 14 July 1998 by *Vincent Zweije*

Mini-HOWTO

2 Related Reading

A related document on WWW is "What to do when Tk says that your display is insecure", *http://ce-toolkit.crd.ge.com/tkxauth/*. It was written by *Kevin Kenny*. It suggests a similar solution to X authentication to that in this document (xauth). However, Kevin aims more at using xdm to steer xauth for you.

The X System Window System Vol. 8 X "Window System Administrator's Guide" from *O'Reilly and Associates* has also been brought to my attention as a good source of information. Unfortunately, I've not been able to check it out.

Yet another document much like the one you're reading now, titled "Securing X Windows", is available at *http://ciac.llnl.gov/ciac/documents/ciac2316.html*.

Also check out usenet newsgroups, such as `comp.windows.x`, `comp.os.linux.x`, and `comp.os.linux.networking`.

3 The Scene

You're using two computers. You're using the X window system of the first to type to and look at. You're using the second to do some important graphical work. You want the second to show its output on the display of the first. The X window system makes this possible.

Of course, you need a network connection for this. Preferably a fast one; the X protocol is a network hog. But with a little patience and suitable protocol compression, you can even run applications over a modem. For X protocol compression, you might want to check out dxpc *http://ccwf.cc.utexas.edu/˜zvonler/dxpc/* or LBX *http://www.ultranet.com/˜pauld/faqs/LBX-HOWTO.html* `<http://www.ultranet.com/~pauld/faqs/LBX-HOWTO.html>` (also known as the *LBX mini-HOWTO*).

You must do two things to achieve all this:

1. Tell the local display (the server) to accept connections from the remote computer.
2. Tell the remote application (the client) to direct its output to your local display.

4 A Little Theory

The magic word is `DISPLAY`. In the X window system, a display consists (simplified) of a keyboard, a mouse and a screen. A display is managed by a server program, known as an X server. The server serves displaying capabilities to other programs that connect to it.

A display is indicated with a name, for instance:

- `DISPLAY=light.uni.verse:0`
- `DISPLAY=localhost:4`
- `DISPLAY=:0`

The display consists of a hostname (such as `light.uni.verse` and `localhost`), a colon (`:`), and a sequence number (such as 0 and 4). The hostname of the display is the name of the computer where the X server runs. An omitted hostname means the local host. The sequence number is usually 0 – it can be varied if there are multiple displays connected to one computer.

If you ever come across a display indication with an extra `.n` attached to it, that's the screen number. A display can actually have multiple screens. Usually there's only one screen though, with number n=0, so that's the default.

Other forms of `DISPLAY` exist, but the above will do for our purposes.

5 Telling the Client

The client program (for instance, your graphics application) knows which display to connect to by inspecting the DIS-PLAY environment variable. This setting can be overridden, though, by giving the client the command line argument -display hostname:0 when it's started. Some examples may clarify things.

Our computer is known to the outside as light, and we're in domain uni.verse. If we're running a normal X server, the display is known as light.uni.verse:0. We want to run the drawing program xfig on a remote computer, called dark.matt.er, and display its output here on light.

Suppose you have already telnetted into the remote computer, dark.matt.er.

If you have csh running on the remote computer:

```
dark% setenv DISPLAY light.uni.verse:0
dark% xfig &
```

or alternatively:

```
dark% xfig -display light.uni.verse:0 &
```

If you have sh running on the remote computer:

```
dark$ DISPLAY=light.uni.verse:0
dark$ export DISPLAY
dark$ xfig &
```

or, alternatively:

```
dark$ DISPLAY=light.uni.verse:0 xfig &
```

or, of course, also:

```
dark$ xfig -display light.uni.verse:0 &
```

It seems that some versions of telnet automatically transport the DISPLAY variable to the remote host. If you have one of those, you're lucky, and you don't have to set it by hand. If not, most versions of telnet do transport the TERM environment variable; with some judicious hacking it is possible to piggyback the DISPLAY variable on to the TERM variable.

The idea with piggybacking is that you do some scripting to achieve the following: before telnetting, attach the value of DISPLAY to TERM. Then telnet out. At the remote end, in the applicable .*shrc file, read the value of DISPLAY from TERM.

6 Telling the Server

The server will not accept connections from just anywhere. You don't want everyone to be able to display windows on your screen. Or read what you type – remember that your keyboard is part of your display!

Too few people seem to realise that allowing access to your display poses a security risk. Someone with access to your display can read and write your screens, read your keystrokes, and read your mouse actions.

Most servers know two ways of authenticating connections to it: the host list mechanism (xhost) and the magic cookie mechanism (xauth). Then there is ssh, the secure shell, that can forward X connections.

6.1 Xhost

Xhost allows access based on hostnames. The server maintains a list of hosts which are allowed to connect to it. It can also disable host checking entirely. Beware: this means no checks are done, so *every* host may connect!

You can control the server's host list with the xhost program. To use this mechanism in the previous example, do:

```
light$ xhost +dark.matt.er
```

This allows all connections from host `dark.matt.er`. As soon as your X client has made its connection and displays a window, for safety, revoke permissions for more connections with:

```
light$ xhost -dark.matt.er
```

You can disable host checking with:

```
light$ xhost +
```

This disables host access checking and thus allows *everyone* to connect. You should *never* do this on a network on which you don't trust *all* users (such as Internet). You can re-enable host checking with:

```
light$ xhost -
```

xhost - by itself does *not* remove all hosts from the access list (that would be quite useless - you wouldn't be able to connect from anywhere, not even your local host).

Xhost is a very insecure mechanism. It does not distinguish between different users on the remote host. Also, hostnames (addresses actually) can be spoofed. This is bad if you're on an untrusted network (for instance already with dialup PPP access to Internet).

6.2 Xauth

Xauth allows access to anyone who knows the right secret. Such a secret is called an authorization record, or a magic cookie. This authorization scheme is formally called MIT-MAGIC-COOKIE-1.

The cookies for different displays are stored together in `~/.Xauthority`. Your `~/.Xauthority` must be inaccessible for group/other users. The xauth program manages these cookies, hence the nickname xauth for the scheme.

On starting a session, the server reads a cookie from the file that is indicated by the `-auth` argument. After that, the server only allows connections from clients that know the same cookie. When the cookie in `~/.Xauthority` changes, *the server will not pick up the change.*

Newer servers can generate cookies on the fly for clients that ask for it. Cookies are still kept inside the server though; the don't end up in `~/.Xauthority` unless a client puts them there. According to David Wiggins:

> A further wrinkle was added in X11R6.3 that you may be interested in. Via the new SECURITY extension, the X server itself can generate and return new cookies on the fly. Furthermore, the cookies can be designated "untrusted" so that applications making connections with such cookies will be restricted in their operation. For example, they won't be able to steal keyboard/mouse input, or window contents, from other trusted clients. There is a new "generate" subcommand to xauth to make this facility at least possible to use, if not easy.

Xauth has a clear security advantage over xhost. You can limit access to specific users on specific computers. It does not suffer from spoofed addresses as xhost does. And if you want to, you can still use xhost next to it to allow connections.

6.2.1 Making the Cookie

If you want to use xauth, you must start the X server with the -auth authfile argument. If you use the startx script, that's the right place to do it. Create the authorization record as below in your startx script.

Excerpt from /usr/X11R6/bin/startx:

```
mcookie|sed -e 's/^/add :0 . /'|xauth -q
xinit -- -auth "$HOME/.Xauthority"
```

Mcookie is a tiny program in the util-linux package, primary site *ftp://ftp.math.uio.no/pub/linux/*. Alternatively, you can use md5sum to massage some random data (from, for instance, /dev/urandom or ps -axl) into cookie format:

```
dd if=/dev/urandom count=1|md5sum|sed -e 's/^/add :0 . /'|xauth -q
xinit -- -auth "$HOME/.Xauthority"
```

If you can't edit the startx script (because you aren't root), get your system administrator to set up startx properly, or let him set up xdm instead. If he can't or won't, you can make a ~/.xserverrc script. If you have this script, it is run by xinit instead of the real X server. Then you can start the real X server from this script with the proper arguments. To do so, have your ~/.xserverrc use the magic cookie line above to create a cookie and then exec the real X server:

```
#!/bin/sh
mcookie|sed -e 's/^/add :0 . /'|xauth -q
exec /usr/X11R6/bin/X "$@" -auth "$HOME/.Xauthority"
```

If you use xdm to manage your X sessions, you can use xauth easily. Define the DisplayManager.authDir resource in /etc/X11/xdm/xdm-config. Xdm will pass the -auth argument to the X server when it starts. When you then log in under xdm, xdm puts the cookie in your ~/.Xauthority for you. See xdm(1) for more information. For instance, my /etc/X11/xdm/xdm-config has the following line in it:

```
DisplayManager.authDir: /var/lib/xdm
```

6.2.2 Transporting the Cookie

Now that you have started your X session on the server host light.uni.verse and have your cookie in ~/.Xauthority, you will have to transfer the cookie to the client host, dark.matt.er.

The easiest is when your home directories on light and dark are shared. The ~/.Xauthority files are the same, so the cookie is transported instantaneously. However, there's a catch: when you put a cookie for :0 in ~/.Xauthority, dark will think it's a cookie for itself instead of for light. You must use an explicit host name when you create the cookie; you can't leave it out. You can install the same cookie for both :0 and light:0 with:

```
#!/bin/sh
cookie='mcookie'
xauth add :0 . $cookie
xauth add "$HOST:0" . $cookie
exec /usr/X11R6/bin/X "$@" -auth "$HOME/.Xauthority"
```

If the home directories aren't shared, you can transport the cookie by means of rsh, the remote shell:

```
light$ xauth nlist :0 | rsh dark.matt.er xauth nmerge -
```

1. Extract the cookie from your local ~/.Xauthority (xauth nlist :0).
2. Transfer it to dark.matt.er (| rsh dark.matt.er).
3. Put it in the ~/.Xauthority there (xauth nmerge -).

It's possible that rsh doesn't work for you. Besides that, rsh also has a security drawback (spoofed host names again, if I remember correctly). If you can't or don't want to use rsh, you can also transfer the cookie manually, like:

```
light$ echo $DISPLAY
:0
light$ xauth list $DISPLAY
light/unix:0 MIT-MAGIC-COOKIE-1 076aaecfd370fd2af6bb9f5550b26926
light$ rlogin dark.matt.er
Password:
dark% setenv DISPLAY light.uni.verse:0
dark% xauth add $DISPLAY . 076aaecfd370fd2af6bb9f5550b26926
dark% xfig &
[15332]
dark% logout
light$
```

See also rsh(1) and xauth(1x) for more information.

It may be possible to piggyback the cookie on the TERM or DISPLAY variable when you do a telnet to the remote host. This would go the same way as piggybacking the DISPLAY variable on the TERM variable. See section 5: Telling the Client. You're on own here from my point of view, but I'm interested if anyone can confirm or deny this.

6.2.3 Using the Cookie

An X application on dark.matt.er, such as xfig above, will automatically look in `~/.Xauthority` there for the cookie to authenticate itself with.

6.3 Ssh

Authority records are transmitted with no encryption. If you're even worried someone might snoop on your connections, use ssh, the secure shell. It will do X forwarding over encrypted connections. And besides, it's great in other ways too. It's a good structural improvement to your system. Just visit *http://www.cs.hut.fi/ssh/*, the ssh home page.

Who knows anything else on authentication schemes or encrypting X connections? Maybe kerberos?

7 Troubleshooting

The first time you try to run a remote X application, it usually does not work. Here are a few common error messages, their probable causes, and solutions to help you on your way.

```
xterm Xt error: Can't open display:
```

There is no DISPLAY variable in the environment, and you didn't tell the application with the -display flag either. The application assumes the empty string, but that is syntactically invalid. To solve this, be sure that you set the DISPLAY variable correctly in the environment (with setenv or export depending on your shell).

```
_X11TransSocketINETConnect: Can't connect: errno = 101
xterm Xt error: Can't open display: love.dial.xs4all.nl:0
```

Errno 101 is "Network is unreachable". The application could not make a network connection to the server. Check that you have the correct DISPLAY set, and that the server machine is reachable from your client (it should be, after all you're probably logged in to the server and telnetting to the client).

```
_X11TransSocketINETConnect: Can't connect: errno = 111
xterm Xt error: Can't open display: love.dial.xs4all.nl:0
```

Errno 111 is "Connection refused". The server machine you're trying to connect to is reachable, but the indicated server does not exist there. Check that you are using the right host name and the right display number.

```
Xlib: connection to ":0.0" refused by server
Xlib: Client is not authorized to connect to Server
xterm Xt error: Can't open display: love.dial.xs4all.nl:0.0
```

The client could make a connection to the server, but the server does not allow the client to use it (not authorized). Make sure that you have transported the correct magic cookie to the client, and that it has not expired (the server uses a new cookie when a new session starts).

"Secure POP via SSH mini-HOWTO" Manish Singh

<yosh@gimp.org>
v1.0, 30 September 1998
This document explains how to set up secure POP connections using ssh.

Contents

1 Introduction

Normal POP mail sessions, by their very nature, are insecure. The password goes across the network in cleartext for everyone to see. Now, this may be perfectly acceptable in a trusted or firewalled environment. But on a public network, such as a university or your run-of-the-mill ISP, anyone armed with a simple network sniffer can grab your password right off the wire. This is compounded by the fact that many people set their computers to check for mail at regular intervals, so the password is sent out quite frequently, which makes it easy to sniff.

With this password, an attacker can now access your email account, which may have sensitive or private information. It is also quite common that this password is the same as the user's shell account, so there is the possibility for more damage.

By doing all POP traffic using an encrypted channel, **nothing** goes in cleartext over the network. We can use ssh's diverse methods of authentication, instead of a simple plaintext password. That is the real point of using this method: not because we get encrypted content (which is futile at this point, since it's probably gone unencrypted over several networks already before reaching your mailbox; securing those communications is the job of GNU Privacy Guard or PGP, not ssh), but the secure authentication.

There are other methods of achieving secure authentication already, such as APOP, KPOP, and IMAP. However, using ssh has the advantage that it works with normal POP configurations, without requiring special client (not all mail clients support advanced protocols) or server support (except for sshd running on the server). You mail provider may be unable

Mini-HOWTO

or unwilling to use a more secure protocol. Besides, by using ssh you can compress the traffic too, which is a nice little extra for people with slow connections.

2 The Basic Technique

This technique relies on a fundamental feature of ssh: *port forwarding*

There are many variations on this theme, which depend on your desired mail setup. They all require ssh, which is available from *http://www.ssh.fi/* and mirrors. RPMs are available at *ftp://ftp.replay.com/pub/crypto/* and Debian packages are available at *ftp://non-us.debian.org/debian-non-US/* (and their respective mirrors).

2.1 Setting up Port Forwarding

To start port forwarding, run the following command:

```
ssh -C -f popserver -L 11110:popserver:110 sleep 5
```

Let's take a closer look at that command:

ssh

The ssh binary itself, the magic program that does it all.

-C

This enables compression of the datastream. It's optional, but usually useful, especially for dialup users.

-f

Once ssh has done authentication and established port forwarding, fork to background so other programs can be run. Since we're just using the port forwarding features of ssh, we don't need a tty attached to it.

popserver

The POP server we're connecting to.

-L 11110:popserver:110

Forward local port 11110 to port 110 on the remote server `popserver`. We use a high local port (11110) so any user can create forwardings.

sleep 5

After ssh has forked itself into the background, it runs a command. We use `sleep` so that the connection is maintained for enough time for our mail client to setup a connection to the server. 5 seconds is usually sufficient time for this to happen.

You can use most other options to ssh when appropriate. A common setting may be a username, since it might be different on the POP server.

This *requires* sshd running on the remote server `popserver`. However, you do not need to have an active shell account there. The time it takes to print a message "You cannot telnet here" is enough to setup a connection.

2.2 Testing it out

Once you've figured out the details command to run to establish port forwarding, you can try it. For example:

```
$ ssh -C -f msingh@popserver -L 11110:popserver:110 sleep 1000
```

`popserver` is the ol' POP server. My username on my local machine is `manish` so I need to explicitly specify the username `msingh`. (If your local and remote usernames are the same the `msingh@` part is unnecessary.)

Then it prints:

```
msingh@popserver's password:
```

And I type in my POP password (you may have different shell and POP passwords though, so use your shell one). Now we're done! So we can try:

```
$ telnet localhost 11110
```

which should print something like:

```
QUALCOMM POP v3.33 ready.
```

Woohoo! It works! The data is sent out over the network encrypted, so the only cleartext is over the loopback interfaces of my local box and the POP server.

3   Using it With Your Mail Software

This section describes setting up your POP client software to use the ssh forwarded connection. It's primary focus is fetchmail (ESR's excellent mail-retrieval and forwarding utility), since that is the most flexible software I have found for dealing with POP. fetchmail can be found at *http://www.tuxedo.org/~esr/fetchmail/*. It will do you a great service to read the excellent documentation that comes with fetchmail.

3.1   Setting up fetchmail

The following is my .fetchmailrc

```
defaults
        user msingh is manish
        no rewrite

poll localhost with protocol pop3 and port 11110:
        preconnect "ssh -C -f msingh@popserver -L 11110:popserv-
er:110 sleep 5"
        password foobar;
```

Pretty simple, huh? fetchmail has a wealth of commands, but the key ones are the preconnect line and the poll option.

We're not connecting directly to the POP server, but instead localhost and port 11110. The preconnect does the forwarding each time fetchmail is run, leaving open the connection for 5 seconds, so fetchmail can make it's own connect. The rest fetchmail does itself.

So each time you run fetchmail, you're prompted for your ssh password for authentication. If you run fetchmail in the background (like I do), it's inconvenient to have to do that. Which brings us to the next section.

3.2   Automating it all

ssh can authenticate using many methods. One of these is an RSA public/private key pair. You can generate an authentication key for your account using ssh-keygen. An authetication key can have a passphrase associated with it, or the passphase can be blank. Whether you want a passphrase depends on how secure you think the account you are using locally is.

If you think your machine is secure, go ahead and have a blank passpharase. Then the above .fetchmailrc works just by running fetchmail. You can then run fetchmail in daemon mode when you dial up and mail is fetched automatically. You're done.

However, if you think you need a passphrase, things get more complex. ssh can run under control of an **agent**, which can register keys and authenticate whatever ssh connections are made under it. So I have this script `getmail.sh`:

```
#!/bin/sh
ssh-add
while true; do fetchmail --syslog --invisible; sleep 5m; done
```

When I dialup, I run:

```
$ ssh-agent getmail.sh
```

This prompts me for my passphrase once, then checks mail every 5 minutes. When the dialup connection is closed, I terminate ssh-agent. (This is automated in my ip-up and ip-down scripts)

3.3 Not using fetchmail

What if I can't/don't want to use fetchmail? Pine, Netscape, and some other clients have their own POP mechanisms. First, consider using fetchmail! It's far more flexible, and mail clients shouldn't be doing that kind of stuff anyway. Both Pine and Netscape can be configured to use local mail systems.

But if you must, unless your client has a preconnect feature like fetchmail, you're going to have to keep the ssh port forward active for the entire time you're connected. Which means using `sleep 100000000` to keep the connection alive. This might not go over well with your network admins.

Secondly, some clients (like Netscape) have the port number hardcoded to 110. So you need to be root to do port forwarding from privledged ports. This is also annoying. But it should work.

4 Miscellany

4.1 Disclaimer

There is no guarantee that this document lives up to its intended purpose. This is simply provided as a free resource. As such, the author of the information provided within cannot make any guarentee that the information is even accurate. Use at your own risk.

Cryptographic software such as ssh may be subject to certain restrictions, depending on where you live. In some countries, you must have a license to use such software. If you are unsure of your local laws, please consult someone who is familiar with your situation for more information.

The use of the information provided in this document is most likely not anticipated by your mail service provider. The author does not encourage the abuse and misuse of network services, and provides this document for informational purposes only. If you are in doubt about whether the use of these techniques falls within the service agreement of your mail provider, please clear that up beforehand.

4.2 Copyright

4.3 Acknowledgements

Special thanks goes to Seth David Schoen <*schoen@uclink4.berkeley.edu*>, who enlightened me in the ways of ssh port forwarding.

"sendmail address rewriting mini-HOWTO"
Thomas Roessler

roessler@guug.de
v0.0, 6 May 1998
This document is a brief description of how to set up sendmail's configuration file for the home user's dial-up access.

1 Introduction

We assume that you have the kind of Internet access which seems to be most common at universities and online services nowadays: You dial into your provider's network using PPP over a serial connection. Your incoming mail is spooled at the provider's POP or IMAP server, while outgoing messages are to be sent via SMTP. You don't have a domain name of your own, so everything has to use *one* address.

We assume that you have already installed a fairly recent version of Eric Allman's sendmail (version 8.8.8 is current at the time of this writing and should work fine).

This document is partially referring to specific properties of Debian GNU/Linux systems; users of different distributions will have to take some care.

Make sure you have the following information at hand:

- Your ISP's mail server
- Your Internet mail address

The configuration we are planning has two main goals:

1. Sending mail between various local users must be possible.
2. The outside world must see the local users' ISP mail addresses, not the local ones.

To achieve this, we will make use of sendmail's `genericstable` feature.

2 File Roadmap

We will put all of sendmail's configuration files in a separate directory under `/etc`: `/etc/mail`. Usually, sendmail will expect these files to reside directly under `/etc`. To avoid problems, `/etc/sendmail.cf` should be a symbolic link to `/etc/mail/sendmail.cf`.

The following files will populate `/etc/mail`:

- =20
- `aliases` - contains additional local addresses
- `genericsdomain` - contains some information on your local host's configuration
- `genericstable` - contains the actual rewriting rules.
- `sendmail.cf` - sendmail's configuration file
- `sendmail.mc` - the source of `sendmail.cf`.

Some of these files will be accompanied by .db files. They contain hashed databases for sendmail's direct use.

We assume that the cf part of sendmail's source tree resides under a directory named /usr/lib/sendmail.cf. This is the case on Debian GNU/Linux systems. Other distributions will put this stuff at different places. Please refer to your distribution's documentation for details.

3 Configuring sendmail

3.1 The main configuration file

Sendmail uses a highly complex rule system for it's configuration. While you can do lots of neat tricks with this stuff, writing a sendmail.cf file from scratch is rather unusual and time-consuming. If you are interested in doing so, you should stop reading this document right now and instead read the "Bat Book" from O'Reilly.

Instead of hand-crafting these rules, we will rely on the m4 macro processor to put together our configuration file from ready-made pieces which are distributed together with sendmail.

Let's look at the first lines of the sendmail.mc file:

```
include(/usr/lib/sendmail.cf/m4/cf.m4)
VERSIONID('sendmail.mc - roessler@guug.de')
OSTYPE(debian)
define('ALIAS_FILE','/etc/mail/aliases')
```

In the beginning, cf.m4 is included. This m4 macro file contains lots of macro definitions for the rest of the file. Be sure that the path you give here is correct - the one we are representing in our example is typical for Debian GNU/Linux. The OSTYPE macro is used to give some useful defaults for certain configuration values. If you aren't using a Debian system, you should replace the word "debian" by "linux" here. ALIAS_FILE tells sendmail where to look for the list of aliases.

The following lines tell sendmail to use the genericstable feature, and where to find the configuration files needed to use it:

```
FEATURE(masquerade_envelope) FEATURE(genericstable, 'hash
-o /etc/mail/genericstable')
GENERICS_DOMAIN_FILE('/etc/mail/genericsdomain')
```

The masquerade_envelope feature tells sendmail to apply header rewriting to the *envelope* sender of a message. This is the mail address to which external mail delivery subsystems will direct their delivery failure reports and warning messages. The generics* files will be explained below.

Now, we have to define a so-called smart host, that is, a machine which will handle outgoing mail for your system. Note that this machine may be different from your ISP's POP and IMAP servers. If in doubt, contact the hotline. The code in the master configuration file:

```
define('SMART_HOST','mail-out.your.provider')
```

Please replace *mail-out.your.provider* by the fully qualified hostname of your internet service provider.

The final two lines include the "mailer" definitions which are needed by sendmail to find out how to handle various types of mail:

```
MAILER(local)
MAILER(smtp)
```

To generate the `sendmail.cf` file from this `sendmail.mc`, type the following commands (as root):

```
# m4 sendmail.mc > _sendmail.cf
# mv -f _sendmail.cf sendmail.cf
```

Note the technique of writing m4's output to a temporary file which is thereafter moved to the proper place. This helps us to prevent sendmail from reading partially written configuration files.

3.2 Address rewriting

First, we have to tell sendmail what addresses are to be considered local (and thus should be subjected to the rewriting). This is quite simple: Just put the fully qualified host name of your machine into the file `/etc/mail/genericsdomain`. To get your host's fully qualified name, type the following command:

```
$ hostname -f
```

Now, let's come to the rewriting table proper: `/etc/mail/genericstable`. This file consists of two white-space separated columns. The first column contains the local address, the second column contains the e-mail address which should be used instead. The file may look like this:

```
harry    harryx@your.isp
maude    maudey@her.isp
root     fredx@your.isp
news     fredx@your.isp
```

Note that there should be one entry for *each* account on the local machine, so that automatically generated mail which leaks out of the local system carries correct header information.

For performance reasons, sendmail won't use this text file directly, but rely on a "hashed" version instead. To generate it, type the following command:

```
# makemap -r hash genericstable.db < genericstable
```

Note that the rewriting rules from the `genericstable` will *not* apply to local mail or to messages you receive from outside - the mapping is only used if a message leaves your local system for your ISP's smart host.

3.3 Aliases

The aliases file contains additional local names which are only valid for local messages. This is useful for administrative accounts like `root` which receive automatically generated messages from your system.

A reasonable start for `/etc/mail/aliases` could look like the following file:

```
root: fred
news: root
postmaster: root
mail: root
www: root

nobody: /dev/null
MAILER-DAEMON: nobody
```

Mini-HOWTO

This example will forward local mail for the `root`, `news`, `postmaster`, `mail`, and www users to `fred`, while messages for `nobody` and `MAILER-DAEMON` will be redirected to `/dev/null`.

Just like the `genericstable`, `aliases` may contain *lots* of entries. Thus, it would once again be inefficient for sendmail to use the text file we just described. The same mechanism as with `genericstable` is used for `aliases`: A hashed database is generated. Instead of using `makemap` directly, you can type in the command `newaliases` this time. It will automatically take care of all what's needed.

4 Further reading

The sendmail source distribution includes quite a bit of documentation. Read it, especially the file `cf/README`.

If you are interested to dive deeper into sendmail's configuration options, you want to get the "Bat Book" from O'Reilly: Bryan Costales, Eric Allman, and Neil Rickert: "sendmail". O'Reilly, 1993.

Part LXXX

"sendmail address rewriting mini-HOWTO"
Thomas Roessler

roessler@guug.de
v0.0, 6 May 1998
This document is a brief description of how to set up sendmail's configuration file for the home user's dial-up access.

1 Introduction

We assume that you have the kind of Internet access which seems to be most common at universities and online services nowadays: You dial into your provider's network using PPP over a serial connection. Your incoming mail is spooled at the provider's POP or IMAP server, while outgoing messages are to be sent via SMTP. You don't have a domain name of your own, so everything has to use *one* address.

We assume that you have already installed a fairly recent version of Eric Allman's sendmail (version 8.8.8 is current at the time of this writing and should work fine).

This document is partially referring to specific properties of Debian GNU/Linux systems; users of different distributions will have to take some care.

Make sure you have the following information at hand:

- Your ISP's mail server
- Your Internet mail address

The configuration we are planning has two main goals:

1. Sending mail between various local users must be possible.
2. The outside world must see the local users' ISP mail addresses, not the local ones.

To achieve this, we will make use of sendmail's `genericstable` feature.

2 File Roadmap

We will put all of sendmail's configuration files in a separate directory under `/etc`: `/etc/mail`. Usually, sendmail will expect these files to reside directly under `/etc`. To avoid problems, `/etc/sendmail.cf` should be a symbolic link to `/etc/mail/sendmail.cf`.

The following files will populate `/etc/mail`:

- =20
- `aliases` - contains additional local addresses
- `genericsdomain` - contains some information on your local host's configuration
- `genericstable` - contains the actual rewriting rules.
- `sendmail.cf` - sendmail's configuration file
- `sendmail.mc` - the source of `sendmail.cf`.

Some of these files will be accompanied by .db files. They contain hashed databases for sendmail's direct use.

We assume that the cf part of sendmail's source tree resides under a directory named /usr/lib/sendmail.cf. This is the case on Debian GNU/Linux systems. Other distributions will put this stuff at different places. Please refer to your distribution's documentation for details.

3 Configuring sendmail

3.1 The main configuration file

Sendmail uses a highly complex rule system for it's configuration. While you can do lots of neat tricks with this stuff, writing a sendmail.cf file from scratch is rather unusual and time-consuming. If you are interested in doing so, you should stop reading this document right now and instead read the "Bat Book" from O'Reilly.

Instead of hand-crafting these rules, we will rely on the m4 macro processor to put together our configuration file from ready-made pieces which are distributed together with sendmail.

Let's look at the first lines of the sendmail.mc file:

```
include(/usr/lib/sendmail.cf/m4/cf.m4)
VERSIONID('sendmail.mc - roessler@guug.de')
OSTYPE(debian)
define('ALIAS_FILE','/etc/mail/aliases')
```

In the beginning, cf.m4 is included. This m4 macro file contains lots of macro definitions for the rest of the file. Be sure that the path you give here is correct - the one we are representing in our example is typical for Debian GNU/Linux. The OSTYPE macro is used to give some useful defaults for certain configuration values. If you aren't using a Debian system, you should replace the word "debian" by "linux" here. ALIAS_FILE tells sendmail where to look for the list of aliases.

The following lines tell sendmail to use the genericstable feature, and where to find the configuration files needed to use it:

```
FEATURE(masquerade_envelope) FEATURE(genericstable, 'hash
-o /etc/mail/genericstable')
GENERICS_DOMAIN_FILE('/etc/mail/genericsdomain')
```

The masquerade_envelope feature tells sendmail to apply header rewriting to the *envelope* sender of a message. This is the mail address to which external mail delivery subsystems will direct their delivery failure reports and warning messages. The generics* files will be explained below.

Now, we have to define a so-called smart host, that is, a machine which will handle outgoing mail for your system. Note that this machine may be different from your ISP's POP and IMAP servers. If in doubt, contact the hotline. The code in the master configuration file:

```
define('SMART_HOST','mail-out.your.provider')
```

Please replace *mail-out.your.provider* by the fully qualified hostname of your internet service provider.

The final two lines include the "mailer" definitions which are needed by sendmail to find out how to handle various types of mail:

```
MAILER(local)
MAILER(smtp)
```

To generate the `sendmail.cf` file from this `sendmail.mc`, type the following commands (as root):

```
# m4 sendmail.mc > _sendmail.cf
# mv -f _sendmail.cf sendmail.cf
```

Note the technique of writing m4's output to a temporary file which is thereafter moved to the proper place. This helps us to prevent sendmail from reading partially written configuration files.

3.2   Address rewriting

First, we have to tell sendmail what addresses are to be considered local (and thus should be subjected to the rewriting). This is quite simple: Just put the fully qualified host name of your machine into the file `/etc/mail/genericsdomain`. To get your host's fully qualified name, type the following command:

```
$ hostname -f
```

Now, let's come to the rewriting table proper: `/etc/mail/generictable`. This file consists of two white-space separated columns. The first column contains the local address, the second column contains the e-mail address which should be used instead. The file may look like this:

```
harry    harryx@your.isp
maude    maudey@her.isp
root     fredx@your.isp
news     fredx@your.isp
```

Note that there should be one entry for *each* account on the local machine, so that automatically generated mail which leaks out of the local system carries correct header information.

For performance reasons, sendmail won't use this text file directly, but rely on a "hashed" version instead. To generate it, type the following command:

```
# makemap -r hash generictable.db < generictable
```

Note that the rewriting rules from the `generictable` will *not* apply to local mail or to messages you receive from outside - the mapping is only used if a message leaves your local system for your ISP's smart host.

3.3   Aliases

The aliases file contains additional local names which are only valid for local messages. This is useful for administrative accounts like `root` which receive automatically generated messages from your system.

A reasonable start for `/etc/mail/aliases` could look like the following file:

```
root: fred
news: root
postmaster: root
mail: root
www: root

nobody: /dev/null
MAILER-DAEMON: nobody
```

Mini-HOWTO

This example will forward local mail for the `root`, `news`, `postmaster`, `mail`, and `www` users to `fred`, while messages for `nobody` and `MAILER-DAEMON` will be redirected to `/dev/null`.

Just like the `genericstable`, `aliases` may contain *lots* of entries. Thus, it would once again be inefficient for sendmail to use the text file we just described. The same mechanism as with `genericstable` is used for `aliases`: A hashed database is generated. Instead of using `makemap` directly, you can type in the command `newaliases` this time. It will automatically take care of all what's needed.

4 Further reading

The sendmail source distribution includes quite a bit of documentation. Read it, especially the file `cf/README`.

If you are interested to dive deeper into sendmail's configuration options, you want to get the "Bat Book" from O'Reilly: Bryan Costales, Eric Allman, and Neil Rickert: "sendmail". O'Reilly, 1993.

Part LXXXI

"Building and Installing Software Packages for Linux" Mendel Leo Cooper

thegrendel@theriver.com

http://personal.riverusers.com/~thegrendel/
v1.62, 19 August 1998

This is a comprehensive guide to building and installing "generic" UNIX software distributions under Linux. Additionally, there is some coverage of packages targeted specifically for Linux.

Contents

1 Introduction

Many software packages for the various flavors of UNIX, including Linux, are distributed as compressed archives of source files. The same package may be "built" to run on different target machines, and this saves the author of the software from having to produce multiple distributions. A single distribution of a software package may thus end up running, in various incarnations, on an Intel box, a DEC Alpha, a RISC workstation, or even a mainframe. Unfortunately, this puts the responsibility of actually "building" and installing the software on the end user, the de facto "system administrator", the fellow sitting at the keyboard – you. Take heart, though, the process is not nearly as terrifying or mysterious as it seems, as this guide will demonstrate.

2 Unpacking the Files

You have downloaded or otherwise acquired a software package. Most likely it is archived (*tarred*) and compressed (*gzipped*), in `.tar.gz` or `.tgz` form (familiarly known as a 'tar ball'). First copy it to a working directory. Then *untar* and *gunzip* it. The appropriate command for this is **tar xzvf** *filename*, where *filename* is the name of the software file, of course. The de-archiving process will usually install the appropriate files in subdirectories it will create. Note that if the package name has a *.Z* suffix, then the above procedure will serve just as well, though running **uncompress**, followed by a **tar xvf** also works.

This method of unpacking 'tar balls' is equivalent to either of the following:

- gzip -cd filename | tar xvf -
- gunzip -c filename | tar xvf -

Source files in the new *bzip2* (`.bz2`) format can be unarchived by a **bzip2 -cd filename | tar xvf -**, or, more simply by a **tar xyvf filename**, assuming that `gzip` has been appropriately patched (refer to the *Bzip2 HOWTO* `<ftp://sunsite.unc.edu/pub/Linux/docs/HOWTO/mini/Bzip>` for details).

[Many thanks to R. Brock Lynn for corrections and updates on the above information.]

Sometimes the archived file must be untarred and installed from the user's home directory, or perhaps in a certain other directory, as specified in the package's config info. Should you get an error message attempting to untar it, this may be the reason. Read the package docs, especially the `README` and/or `Install` files, if present, and edit the config files and/or `Makefiles` as necessary, consistent with the installation instructions. Note that you would **not** ordinarily alter the `Imake` file, since this could have unforseen consequences. Some software packages permit automating this process by running **make install** to emplace the binaries in the appropriate system areas.

Occasionally, you may need to update or incorporate bug fixes into the unarchived source files using a `patch` or `diff` file that lists the changes. The doc files and/or `README` file will inform you should this be the case. The normal syntax for invoking Larry Wall's powerful *patch* utility is **patch < patchfile**.

You may now proceed to the build stage of the process.

3 Using Make

The `Makefile` is the key to the build process. In its simplest form, a Makefile is a script for compiling or building the "binaries", the executable portions of a package. The Makefile can also provide a means of updating a software package without having to recompile every single source file in it, but that is a different story (or a different article).

At some point, the Makefile launches `cc` or `gcc`. This is actually a preprocessor, a C (or C++) compiler, and a linker, invoked in that order. This process converts the source into the binaries, the actual executables.

Invoking *make* usually involves just typing **make**. This generally builds all the necessary executable files for the package in question. However, make can also do other tasks, such as installing the files in their proper directories (**make install**) and removing stale object files (**make clean**). Running **make -n** permits previewing the build process, as it prints out all the commands that would be triggered by a make, without actually executing them.

Only the simplest software uses a generic Makefile. More complex installations require tailoring the Makefile according to the location of libraries, include files, and resources on your particular machine. This is especially the case when the build needs the `X11` libraries to install. *Imake* and *xmkmf* accomplish this task.

An Imakefile is, to quote the man page, a "template" Makefile. The imake utility constructs a Makefile appropriate for your system from the Imakefile. In almost all cases, however, you would run xmkmf, a shell script that invokes imake, a front end for it. Check the README or INSTALL file included in the software archive for specific instructions. Read the imake and xmkmf man pages for a more detailed analysis of the procedure..

Be aware that *xmkmf* and *make* may need to be invoked as root, especially when doing a **make install** to move the binaries over to the /usr/bin or /usr/local/bin directories. Using make as an ordinary user without root privileges will likely result in write access denied error messages because you lack write permission to system directories. Check also that the binaries created have the proper execute permissions for you and any other appropriate users.

Invoking xmkmf uses the *Imake* file to build a new Makefile appropriate for your system. You would normally invoke xmkmf with the -a argument, to automatically do a *make Makefiles, make includes,* and *make depend.* This sets the variables and defines the library locations for the compiler and linker. Sometimes, there will be no *Imake* file, instead there will be an *INSTALL* or *configure* script that will accomplish this purpose. Note that if you run *configure*, it should be invoked as *./configure* to ensure that the correct *configure* script in the current directory is called. In most cases, the *README* file included with the distribution will explain the install procedure.

It is usually a good idea to visually inspect the Makefile that xmkmf or one of the install scripts builds. The Makefile will normally be correct for your system, but you may occasionally be required to "tweak" it or correct errors manually.

Your general installation procedure will therefore be:

- Read the README file and other applicable docs.
- Run **xmkmf -a**, or the INSTALL or configure script.
- Check the Makefile.
- If necessary, run **make clean**, **make Makefiles**, **make includes**, and **make depend**.
- Run **make**.
- Check file permissions.
- If necessary, run **make install**.

4 Prepackaged Binaries

Manually building and installing packages from source is apparently so daunting a task for some Linux users that they have embraced the popular *rpm* and *deb* package formats. While it may be the case that an rpm install normally runs as smoothly and as fast as a software install in a certain other notorious operating system, some thought should certainly be given to the disadvantages of self-installing, prepackaged binaries.

First, be aware that software packages are normally released first as 'tarballs', and that prepackaged binaries follow days, weeks, even months later. So, if you wish to keep up with all the 'bleeding edge' software, you might not wish to wait for an *rpm* or *deb* to appear. Some less popular packages may never be rpm'ed.

Installing an rpm package is not necessarily a no-brainer. If there is a dependency conflict, an rpm install will fail. Likewise, should the *rpm* require a different version of libraries than the ones present on your system, the install may not work, even if you create symbolic links to the missing libraries from the ones in place. You must install rpm's and deb's as root, in order to have the necessary write permissions, and this opens a potentially serious security hole, as you may inadvertently clobber system binaries and libraries, or even install a *Trojan horse* that might wreak havoc upon your system.

It is important to obtain rpm and deb packages from a "trusted source". In any case, you should run a 'signature check' on the package, **rpm –checksig packagename.rpm**, before installing. Running an **rpm –verify packagename.rpm** is likewise highly recommended. For the truly paranoid (and, in this case there is much to be said for paranoia), there are the *unrpm* and *rpmunpack* utilities available from the *Sunsite utils/package directory* <ftp://sunsite.unc.edu/pub/Linux/utils/package> for unpacking and checking the individual components of the packages.

The *martian* <http://www.people.cornell.edu/pages/rc42/program/martian.html> and *alien* <http://kitenet.net/programs/alien/> programs allow conversion between the *rpm*, *deb*, and *tar.gz* package format. This makes these packages accessible to all Linux distributions.

In their most simple form, the commands **rpm -i packagename.rpm** and **dpkg –install packagename.deb** automatically unpack and install the software. Exercise caution, though, since using these commands blindly may be dangerous to your system's health!

Note that the above warnings also apply, though to a lesser extent, to Slackware's *pkgtool* installation utility. All "automatic" software installations require caution.

Carefully read the man pages for the *rpm* and *dpkg* commands, and refer to the *RPM HOWTO* <ftp://sunsite.unc.edu/pub/Linux/docs/HOWTO/RPM-HOWTO>, TFUG's *Quick Guide to Red Hat's Package Manager* <http://www.tfug.org/helpdesk/linux/rpm.html>, and *The Debian Package Management Tools* <http://www.debian.org/doc/FAQ/debian-faq-7.html> for more detailed information.

5   Termcap and Terminfo Issues

According to its man page, *"terminfo is a data base describing terminals, used by screen-oriented programs..."*. It defines a generic set of control sequences (escape codes) used to display text on terminals, and makes possible support for different terminal hardware without the need for special drivers. The terminfo database has largely supplanted the older termcap one. This is usually of no concern for program installation except when dealing with a package that requires termcap.

Most Linux distributions now use terminfo, but still retain the older termcap libraries for compatibility with legacy applications. Sometimes there is a special compatibility package that needs to be installed to facilitate use of termcap linked binaries. Very occasionally, an *#define termcap* statement might need to be commented out of a source file. Check the appropriate docs for your particular distribution for information on this.

6   Backward Compatibility With a.out Binaries

In a very few cases, it is necessary to use a.out binaries, either because the source code is not available or because it is not possible to build new ELF binaries from the source for some reason.

As it happens, ELF installations almost always have a complete set of a.out libraries in the /usr/i486-linuxaout/lib directory. Theoretically, a.out binaries should be able to find these libraries at runtime, but this may not always be the case.

Note that the kernel should have a.out support built into it, either directly or as a loadable module. It may be necessary to rebuild the kernel to enable this. Moreover, some Linux distributions require installation of a special compatibility package, such as Debian's xcompat for executing a.out X applications.

6.1   An Example

Jerry Smith wrote a very handy rolodex program some years back. It uses the Motif libraries, but fortunately is available as a statically linked binary in a.out format. Unfortunately, the source refuses to rebuild using the lesstif libraries. Even more unfortunately, the a.out binary bombs on an ELF system with the following error message.

```
xrolodex: can't load library '//lib/libX11.so.3'
        No such library
```

As it happens, there is such a library, in /usr/i486-linuxaout/lib, but xrolodex is unable to locate it at run time. The simple solution is to provide a symbolic link in the /lib directory:

```
ln -s /usr/i486-linuxaout/lib/X11.so.3.1.0 libX11.so.3
```

It turns out to be necessary to provide similar links for the libXt.so.3 and libc.so.4 libraries. This needs to be done as root, of course. Note that you should make absolutely certain you will not overwrite or cause version number conflicts with pre-existing libraries. Fortunately, the new ELF libraries have higher version numbers than the older a.out ones, to anticipate and forestall just such problems.

After creating the three links, xrolodex runs fine.

The xrolodex program may be obtained from *Spectro* <http://www.spectro.com/xrolodex.html>.

7 Troubleshooting

If *xmkmf* and/or *make* succeeded without errors, you may proceed to the 8 (next section). However, in "real life", few things work right the first time. This is when your resourcefulness is put to the test.

7.1 Link Errors

- Suppose make fails with a Link error: -lX11: No such file or directory, even after xmkmf has been invoked. This may mean that the *Imake* file was not set up properly. Check the first part of the *Makefile* for lines such as:

```
LIB=          -L/usr/X11/lib
INCLUDE=      -I/usr/X11/include/X11
LIBS=         -lX11 -lc -lm
```

  The -L and -I switches tell the compiler and linker where to look for the *library* and *include* files, respectively. In this example, the *X11 libraries* should be in the /usr/X11/lib directory, and the *X11 include files* should be in the /usr/X11/include/X11 directory. If this is incorrect for your machine, make the necessary changes to the *Makefile* and try the *make* again.

- Undefined references to math library functions, such as the following:

```
/tmp/cca011551.o(.text+0x11): undefined reference to 'cos'
```

  The fix for this is to explicitly link in the math library, by adding an **-lm** to the *LIB* or *LIBS* flags in the Makefile (see previous example).

- In a very few cases, running *ldconfig* as *root* may be the solution:

  # /etc/ldconfig -n /lib will update the shared library symbolic links. *This should not be necessary under normal circumstances.*

- Yet another thing to try if xmkmf fails is the following script:

```
make -DUseInstalled -I/usr/X386/lib/X11/config
```

- Sometimes the source needs the older release X11R5 libraries to build. If you have the R5 libs in /usr/X11R6/lib (you were given the option of having them when first installing Linux), then you need only ensure that you have the links that the software needs to build. The R5 libs are named libX11.so.3.1.0, libXaw.so.3.1.0, and libXt.so.3.1.0. You generally need links, such as *libX11.so.3 -> libX11.so.3.1.0*. Possibly the software will also need a link of the form *libX11.so -> libX11.so.3.1.0*. Of course, to create a "missing" link, use the command **ln -s libX11.so.3.1.0 libX11.so**, *as root*.

- Some packages will require you to install updated versions of one or more libraries. For example, the *StarOffice* suite from StarDivision GmbH is notorious for needing a libc version 5.4.4 or greater. As *root*, you would need to copy one or more libraries to the appropriate directories, remove the old libraries, then reset the symbolic links. **Caution: Exercise extreme care in this, as you can render your system nonfunctional if you screw up.** You can usually find updated libraries at *Sunsite* <ftp://sunsite.unc.edu/pub/Linux>.

Mini-HOWTO

7.2   Other Problems

- An installed *Perl* or shell script gives you a `No such file or directory` error message. In this case, check the file permissions to make sure the file is executable and check the file header to ascertain whether the shell or program invoked by the script is in the place specified. For example, the scrip may begin with:

      #!/usr/local/bin/perl

  If *Perl* is in fact installed in your `/usr/bin` directory instead of the `/usr/local/bin` one, then the script will not run. There are two methods of correcting this. The script file header may be changed to `#!/usr/bin/perl`, or a symbolic link to the correct directory may be added, **ln -s /usr/bin/perl /usr/local/bin/perl**.

- Some X11 software requires the Motif libraries to build. The standard Linux distributions do not have the Motif libraries installed, and at present Motif costs an extra $100-$200 (though the freeware *Lesstif* `<http://www.lesstif.org/>` also works in many cases). If you need Motif to build a certain package, but lack the Motif libraries, it may be possible to obtain *statically linked binaries*. Static linking incorporates the library routines in the binaries themselves. This results in much larger binary files, but the code will run on systems lacking the libraries.

- Running a *configure* script creates a strange Makefile, one seemingly unrelated to the package you are attempting to build. This means the wrong *configure* ran, one found somewhere else in your path. Always invoke *configure* as **./configure** to prevent this.

- Linux distributions are in the process of changing over to the newer `libc 6` (`glibc 2`) from `libc 5`. Precompiled binaries that worked with the older library may bomb if you have upgraded your library. The solution is to either recompile the applications from the source or to obtain newer precompiled binaries. If you are in the process of upgrading your system to `libc 6` and are experiencing problems, refer to Eric Green's *Glibc 2 HOWTO*.

- Sometimes it is necessary to remove the *-ansi* option from the compile flags in the `Makefile`. This enables gcc's extra, non-ANSI features, and allows building packages that require these extensions. (Thanks to Sebastien Blondeel for pointing this out.)

- Some programs require having *setuid root*, in order to run with *root privileges*. The command to implement this is **chmod u+s filename**, *as root* (note that the program must already be owned by root). This has the effect of setting the *setuid* bit in the file permissions. This issue comes up when the program accesses the system hardware, such as a modem or CD ROM drive, or when the SVGA libs are invoked from console mode, as in one particularly notorious emulation package. If a program works when run by root, but gives *access denied* error messages to an ordinary user, suspect this as the cause.

  Warning: A program with *setuid* as root may pose a security risk to your system. The program runs with root privileges and thus has the potential for doing significant damage. Make certain that you know what the program does, by looking at the source if possible, before setting the *setuid* bit.

7.3   Tweaking and fine tuning

You may wish to examine the `Makefile` to make certain that the best compilation options for your system are invoked. For example, setting the *-O2* flag chooses the highest level of optimization and the *-fomit-frame-pointer* flag results in a smaller binary (though debugging will then be disabled). **Do not play around with this unless you know what you are doing, and in any case, not until after a trial *build* works.**

7.4   Where to go for more help

In my experience, perhaps 25% of applications build "right out of the box". Another 50% or so can be "persuaded" to build with an effort ranging from trivial to herculean. That still means a significant number of packages will not build no matter what. Even then, the Intel ELF and/or `a.out` binaries for these might possibly be found at *Sunsite* `<ftp://sunsite.unc.edu>` or the *TSX-11 archive* `<ftp://tsx-11.mit.edu>`. *Red Hat* `<http://redhat.com>`

and *Debian* <http://www.debian.org> have extensive archives of prepackaged binaries of most of the popular Linux software. Perhaps the author of the software can supply the binaries compiled for your particular flavor of machine.

```
Note that if you obtain precompiled binaries, you will need to check for compat-
ibility with your system:
```

- The binaries must run on your hardware (i.e., Intel x86).
- The binaries must be compatible with your kernel (i.e., a.out or ELF).
- Your libraries must be up to date.
- Your system must have the appropriate installation utility (rpm or deb).

If all else fails, you may find help in the appropriate newsgroups, such as *comp.os.linux.x* or *comp.os.linux.development*.

If nothing at all works, at least you gave it your best effort, and you learned a lot.

8 Final Steps

Read the software package documentation to determine whether certain environmental variables need setting (in .bashrc or .cshrc) and if the .Xdefaults and .Xresources files need customizing.

There may be an applications default file, usually named Xfoo.ad in the original Xfoo distribution. If so, edit the Xfoo.ad file to customize it for your machine, then rename (**mv**) it Xfoo and install it in the /usr/lib/X11/app-defaults directory, *as root*. Failure to do this may cause the software to behave strangely or even refuse to run.

Most software packages come with one or more preformatted man pages. *As root*, copy the Xfoo.man file to the appropriate /usr/man, /usr/local/man, or /usr/X11R6/man directory (man1 - man9), and rename it accordingly. For example, if Xfoo.man ends up in /usr/man/man4, it should be renamed Xfoo.4 (mv Xfoo.man Xfoo.4). By convention, user commands go in man1, games in man6, and administration packages in man8 (see the *man docs* for more details). Of course, you may deviate from this on your own system, if you like.

Some packages will not install the binaries in the appropriate system directories, that is, they are missing the *install* option in the Makefile. Should this be the case, you can install the binaries manually by copying the binaries to the appropriate system directory, /usr/local/bin or /usr/X11R6/bin, *as root*, of course.

Note that some or all of the above procedures should, in most cases, be handled automatically by a **make install**, and possibly a **make install.man** or **make install_man**. If so, the README or INSTALL doc file will specify this.

9 First Example: Xscrabble

Matt Chapman's Xscrabble seemed like a program that would be interesting to have, since I happen to be an avid ScrabbleTM player. I downloaded it, uncompressed it, and built it following the procedure in the README file:

```
xmkmf
make Makefiles
make includes
make
```

Of course it did not work...

```
gcc -o xscrab -O2 -O -L/usr/X11R6/lib
init.o xinit.o misc.o moves.o cmove.o main.o xutils.o mess.o popup.o
widgets.o display.o user.o CircPerc.o
-lXaw -lXmu -lXExExt -lXext -lX11 -lXt -lSM -lICE -lXExExt -lXext -lX11
-lXpm -L../Xc -lXc
```

```
BarGraf.o(.text+0xe7): undefined reference to 'XtAddConverter'
BarGraf.o(.text+0x29a): undefined reference to 'XSetClipMask'
BarGraf.o(.text+0x2ff): undefined reference to 'XSetClipRectangles'
BarGraf.o(.text+0x375): undefined reference to 'XDrawString'
BarGraf.o(.text+0x3e7): undefined reference to 'XDrawLine'
etc.
etc.
etc...
```

I enquired about this in the *comp.os.linux.x* newsgroup, and someone kindly pointed out that apparently the Xt, Xaw, Xmu, and X11 libs were not being found at the link stage. Hmmm...

There were two main Makefiles, and the one in the src directory caught my interest. One line in the Makefile defined LOCAL_LIBS as: LOCAL_LIBS = $(XAWLIB) $(XMULIB) $(XTOOLLIB) $(XLIB) Here were references to the libs not being found by the linker.

Looking for the next reference to LOCAL_LIBS, I saw on line 495 of that Makefile:

```
        $(CCLINK) -o $@ $(LDOPTIONS) $(OBJS) $(LOCAL_LIBS) $(LDLIBS) \
    $(EXTRA_LOAD_FLAGS)
```

Now what were these LDLIBS?

```
        LDLIBS = $(LDPOSTLIB) $(THREADS_LIBS) $(SYS_LIBRARIES) \
    $(EXTRA_LIBRARIES)
```

The SYS_LIBRARIES were:

```
    SYS_LIBRARIES = -lXpm -L../Xc -lXc
```

Yes! Here were the missing libraries.

Possibly the linker needed to see the LDLIBS before the LOCAL_LIBS... So, the first thing to try was to modify the Makefile by transposing the $(LOCAL_LIBS) and $(LDLIBS) on line 495, so it would now read:

```
        $(CCLINK) -o $@ $(LDOPTIONS) $(OBJS) $(LDLIBS) $(LOCAL_LIBS) \
    $(EXTRA_LOAD_FLAGS)              ^^^^^^^^^^^^^^^^^^^^^^^^^^^^
```

I tried running *make* again with the above change, and lo and behold, it worked this time. Of course, Xscrabble still needed some fine tuning and twiddling, such as renaming the dictionary and commenting out some assert statements in one of the source files, but since then it has provided me with many hours of pleasure.

[Note that a newer version of Xscrabble is now available in rpm format, and this installs without problems.]

You may e-mail *Matt Chapman* <mailto:matt@belgarath.demon.co.uk>, and download *Xscrabble* from his *home page* <http://www.belgarath.demon.co.uk/programs/index.html>.

```
        Scrabble is a registered trademark of the Milton Bradley Co., Inc.
```

10   Second Example: Xloadimage

This example poses an easier problem. The xloadimage program seemed a useful addition to my set of graphic tools. I copied the xloadi41.gz file directly from the source directory on the CD included with the excellent 14 (X User Tools) book, by Mui and Quercia. As expected, *tar xzvf* unarchives the files. The *make*, however, produces a nasty-looking error and terminates.

```
gcc -c -O -fstrength-reduce -finline-functions -fforce-mem
-fforce-addr -DSYSV  -I/usr/X11R6/include
-DSYSPATHFILE=\"/usr/lib/X11/Xloadimage\" mcidas.c

In file included from /usr/include/stdlib.h:32,
                 from image.h:23,
                 from xloadimage.h:15,
                 from mcidas.c:7:
/usr/lib/gcc-lib/i486-linux/2.6.3/include/stddef.h:215:
conflicting types for 'wchar_t'
/usr/X11R6/include/X11/Xlib.h:74: previous declaration of
'wchar_t'
make[1]: *** [mcidas.o] Error 1
make[1]: Leaving directory
'/home/thegrendel/tst/xloadimage.4.1'
make: *** [default] Error 2
```

The error message contains the essential clue.

Looking at the file image.h, line 23...

```
        #include <stdlib.h>
```

Aha, somewhere in the source for xloadimage, *wchar_t* has been redefined from what was specified in the standard include file, stdlib.h. Let us first try commenting out line 23 in image.h, as perhaps the *stdlib.h include* is not, after all, necessary.

At this point, the build proceeds without any fatal errors. The xloadimage package functions correctly now.

11   Third Example: Fortune

This final example requires some knowledge of C programming. The majority of UNIX/Linux software is written in C, and learning at least a little bit of C would certainly be an asset for anyone serious about software installation.

The notorious *fortune* program displays up a humorous saying, a "fortune cookie", every time Linux boots up. Unfortunately (pun intended), attempting to build fortune on a Red Hat distribution with a 2.0.30 kernel generates fatal errors.

```
~/fortune# make all

gcc -O2 -Wall -fomit-frame-pointer -pipe   -c fortune.c -o
fortune.o
fortune.c: In function 'add_dir':
fortune.c:551: structure has no member named 'd_namlen'
fortune.c:553: structure has no member named 'd_namlen'
make[1]: *** [fortune.o] Error 1
make[1]: Leaving directory '/home/thegrendel/for/fortune/fortune'
make: *** [fortune-bin] Error 2
```

Looking at fortune.c, the pertinent lines are these.

```
     if (dirent->d_namlen == 0)
            continue;
      name = copy(dirent->d_name, dirent->d_namlen);
```

We need to find the structure `dirent`, but it is not declared in the *fortune.c* file, nor does a **grep dirent** show it in any of the other source files. However, at the top of *fortune.c*, there is the following line.

```
#include <dirent.h>
```

This appears to be a system library include file, therefore, the logical place to look for *dirent.h* is in */usr/include*. Indeed, there does exist a *dirent.h* file in */usr/include*, but that file does not contain the declaration of the `dirent` structure. There is, however, a reference to another *dirent.h* file.

```
#include <linux/dirent.h>
```

At last, going to */usr/include/linux/dirent.h*, we find the structure declaration we need.

```
struct dirent {
        long            d_ino;
        __kernel_off_t  d_off;
        unsigned short  d_reclen;
        char            d_name[256]; /* We must not include
limits.h! */
};
```

Sure enough, the structure declaration contains no *d_namelen*, but there are a couple of "candidates" for its equivalent. The most likely of these is *d_reclen*, since this structure member probably represents the length of something and it is a short integer. The other possibility, *d_ino*, could be an inode number, judging by its name and type. As a matter of fact, we are probably dealing with a "directory entry" structure, and these elements represent attributes of a file, its name, inode, and length (in blocks). This would seem to validate our guess.

Let us edit the file `fortune.c`, and change the two *d_namelen* references in lines 551 and 553 to *d_reclen*. Try a *make all* again. **Success.** It builds without errors. We can now get our "cheap thrills" from fortune.

12   Where to Find Source Archives

Now that you are eager to use your newly acquired knowledge to add utilities and other goodies to your system, you may find them online at the *Linux Applications and Utilities Page* <http://www.redhat.com/linux-info/linux-app-list/linapps.html>, or on one of the very reasonably priced CD ROM archives by *Red Hat* <http://www.redhat.com/>, *InfoMagic* <mailto:orders@infomagic.com>, *Linux Systems Labs* <http://www.lsl.com>, *Cheap Bytes* <http://www.cheapbytes.com>, and others.

A comprehensive repository of source code is the *comp sources UNIX archive* <ftp://ftp.vix.com/pub/usenet/comp.sources.unix/>.

Much UNIX source code is posted on the *alt.sources* newsgroup. If you are looking for particular source code packages, you may post on the related *alt.sources.wanted* newsgroup. Another good place to check is the *comp.os.linux.announce* newsgroup. To get on the *Unix sources* <mailto:unix-sources@pa.dec.com> mailing list, send a *subscribe* message there.

Archives for the *alt.sources* newsgroup are at the following ftp sites:

- *ftp.sterling.com/usenet/alt.sources/* <ftp://ftp.sterling.com/usenet/alt.sources/>

- *wuarchive.wustl.edu/usenet/alt.sources/articles* <ftp://wuarchive.wustl.edu/usenet/alt.sources/articles>

- *src.doc.ic.ac.uk/usenet/alt.sources/articles* <ftp://src.doc.ic.ac.uk/usenet/alt.sources/articles>

13   Final Words

To sum up, persistence makes all the difference (and a high frustration threshold certainly helps). As in all endeavors, learning from mistakes is critically important. Each misstep, every failure contributes to the body of knowledge that will lead to mastery of **the art of building software**.

14   References and Further Reading

BORLAND C++ TOOLS AND UTILITIES GUIDE, Borland International, 1992, pp. 9-42.
[One of the manuals distributed with Borland C++, ver. 3.1. Gives a fairly good intro to make syntax and concepts, using Borland's crippled implementation for DOS.]

DuBois, Paul: SOFTWARE PORTABILITY WITH IMAKE, O'Reilly and Associates, 1996, ISBN 1-56592-226-3.
[This is reputed to be the definitive imake reference, though I did not have it available when writing this article.]

Frisch, Aeleen: ESSENTIAL SYSTEM ADMINISTRATION, O'Reilly and Associates, 1995, ISBN 1-56592-127-5.
[This otherwise excellent sys admin handbook has only sketchy coverage of software building.]

Lehey, Greg: PORTING UNIX SOFTWARE, O'Reilly and Associates, 1995, ISBN 1-56592-126-7.

Mui, Linda and Valerie Quercia: X USER TOOLS, O'Reilly and Associates, 1994, ISBN 1-56592-019-8, pp. 734-760.

Oram, Andrew and Steve Talbott: MANAGING PROJECTS WITH MAKE, O'Reilly and Associates, 1991, ISBN 0-937175-90-0.

Peek, Jerry and Tim O'Reilly and Mike Loukides: UNIX POWER TOOLS, O'Reilly and Associates / Random House, 1997, ISBN 1-56592-260-3.
[A wonderful source of ideas, and tons of utilities you may end up building from the source code, using the methods discussed in this article.]

Stallman, Richard M. and Roland McGrath: GNU MAKE, Free Software Foundation, 1995, ISBN 1-882114-78-7.
[Required reading.]

Welsh, Matt and Lar Kaufman: RUNNING LINUX, O'Reilly and Associates, 1996, ISBN 1-56592-151-8.
[Still the best overall Linux reference, though lacking in depth in some areas.]

The BZIP2 HOWTO, by David Fetter.

The Glibc2 HOWTO, by Eric Green

Mini-HOWTO

The LINUX ELF HOWTO, by Daniel Barlow.

The RPM HOWTO, by Donnie Barnes.

[These HOWTOs are available in HTML format from the LDP site, http://sunsite.unc.edu/LDP/linux.html.]

The man pages for dpkg, gcc, gzip, imake, ldconfig, make, patch, rpm, tar, termcap, terminfo, and xmkmf.

Part LXXXII

"Software-RAID HOWTO" Linas Vepstas

linas@linas.org

v0.54, 21 November 1998

RAID stands for "Redundant Array of Inexpensive Disks", and is meant to be a way of creating a fast and reliable disk-drive subsystem out of individual disks. RAID can guard against disk failure, and can also improve performance over that of a single disk drive. This document is a tutorial/HOWTO/FAQ for users of the Linux MD kernel extension, the associated tools, and their use. The MD extension implements RAID-0 (striping), RAID-1 (mirroring), RAID-4 and RAID-5 in software. That is, with MD, no special hardware or disk controllers are required to get many of the benefits of RAID.

Contents

Preamble

RAID, although designed to improve system reliability by adding redundancy, can also lead to a false sense of security and confidence when used improperly. This false confidence can lead to even greater disasters. In particular, note that RAID is designed to protect against *disk* failures, and not against *power* failures or *operator* mistakes. Power failures, buggy development kernels, or operator/admin errors can lead to damaged data that it is not recoverable! RAID is *not* a substitute for proper backup of your system. Know what you are doing, test, be knowledgeable and aware!

1 Introduction

1. **Q**: What is RAID?

Mini-HOWTO

A: RAID stands for "Redundant Array of Inexpensive Disks", and is meant to be a way of creating a fast and reliable disk-drive subsystem out of individual disks. In the PC world, "I" has come to stand for "Independent", where marketing forces continue to differentiate IDE and SCSI. In it's original meaning, "I" meant "Inexpensive as compared to refrigerator-sized mainframe 3380 DASD", monster drives which made nice houses look cheap, and diamond rings look like trinkets.

2. **Q**: What is this document?

    A: This document is a tutorial/HOWTO/FAQ for users of the Linux MD kernel extension, the associated tools, and their use. The MD extension implements RAID-0 (striping), RAID-1 (mirroring), RAID-4 and RAID-5 in software. That is, with MD, no special hardware or disk controllers are required to get many of the benefits of RAID.

    This document is **NOT** an introduction to RAID; you must find this elsewhere.

3. **Q**: What levels of RAID does the Linux kernel implement?

    A: Striping (RAID-0) and linear concatenation are a part of the stock 2.x series of kernels. This code is of production quality; it is well understood and well maintained. It is being used in some very large USENET news servers.

    RAID-1, RAID-4 & RAID-5 are a part of the 2.1.63 and greater kernels. For earlier 2.0.x and 2.1.x kernels, patches exist that will provide this function. Don't feel obligated to upgrade to 2.1.63; upgrading the kernel is hard; it is *much* easier to patch an earlier kernel. Most of the RAID user community is running 2.0.x kernels, and that's where most of the historic RAID development has focused. The current snapshots should be considered near-production quality; that is, there are no known bugs but there are some rough edges and untested system setups. There are a large number of people using Software RAID in a production environment.

    RAID-1 hot reconstruction has been recently introduced (August 1997) and should be considered alpha quality. RAID-5 hot reconstruction will be alpha quality any day now.

    A word of caution about the 2.1.x development kernels: these are less than stable in a variety of ways. Some of the newer disk controllers (e.g. the Promise Ultra's) are supported only in the 2.1.x kernels. However, the 2.1.x kernels have seen frequent changes in the block device driver, in the DMA and interrupt code, in the PCI, IDE and SCSI code, and in the disk controller drivers. The combination of these factors, coupled to cheapo hard drives and/or low-quality ribbon cables can lead to considerable heartbreak. The `ckraid` tool, as well as `fsck` and `mount` put considerable stress on the RAID subsystem. This can lead to hard lockups during boot, where even the magic alt-SysReq key sequence won't save the day. Use caution with the 2.1.x kernels, and expect trouble. Or stick to the 2.0.34 kernel.

4. **Q**: I'm running an older kernel. Where do I get patches?

    A: Software RAID-0 and linear mode are a stock part of all current Linux kernels. Patches for Software RAID-1,4,5 are available from `<http://luthien.nuclecu.unam.mx/miguel/raid>`. See also the quasi-mirror `<ftp://linux.kernel.org/pub/linux/daemons/raid/>` for patches, tools and other goodies.

5. **Q**: Are there other Linux RAID references?

    A:
- Generic RAID overview: `<http://www.dpt.com/uraiddoc.html>`.
- General Linux RAID options: `<http://linas.org/linux/raid.html>`.
- Latest version of this document: `<http://linas.org/linux/Software-RAID/Software-RAID.html>`.
- Linux-RAID mailing list archive: `<http://www.linuxhq.com/lnxlists/>`.
- Linux Software RAID Home Page: `<http://luthien.nuclecu.unam.mx/miguel/raid>`.
- Linux Software RAID tools: `<ftp://linux.kernel.org/pub/linux/daemons/raid/>`.
- How to setting up linear/stripped Software RAID: `<http://www.ssc.com/lg/issue17/raid.html>`.

- Bootable RAID mini-HOWTO: `<ftp://ftp.bizsystems.com/pub/raid/ bootable-raid>`.
- Root RAID HOWTO: `<ftp://ftp.bizsystems.com/pub/raid/ Root-RAID-HOWTO>`.
- Linux RAID-Geschichten: `<http://www.infodrom.north.de/joey/Linux/ raid/>`.

6. **Q**: Who do I blame for this document?

   A: Linas Vepstas slapped this thing together. However, most of the information, and some of the words were supplied by

   - Bradley Ward Allen <*ulmo@Q.Net*>
   - Luca Berra <*bluca@comedia.it*>
   - Brian Candler <*B.Candler@pobox.com*>
   - Bohumil Chalupa <*bochal@apollo.karlov.mff.cuni.cz*>
   - Rob Hagopian <*hagopiar@vu.union.edu*>
   - Anton Hristozov <*anton@intransco.com*>
   - Miguel de Icaza <*miguel@luthien.nuclecu.unam.mx*>
   - Marco Meloni <*tonno@stud.unipg.it*>
   - Ingo Molnar <*mingo@pc7537.hil.siemens.at*>
   - Alvin Oga <*alvin@planet.fef.com*>
   - Gadi Oxman <*gadio@netvision.net.il*>
   - Vaughan Pratt <*pratt@cs.Stanford.EDU*>
   - Steven A. Reisman <*sar@pressenter.com*>
   - Michael Robinton <*michael@bzs.org*>
   - Martin Schulze <*joey@finlandia.infodrom.north.de*>
   - Geoff Thompson <*geofft@cs.waikato.ac.nz*>
   - Edward Welbon <*welbon@bga.com*>
   - Rod Wilkens <*rwilkens@border.net*>
   - Johan Wiltink <*j.m.wiltink@pi.net*>
   - Leonard N. Zubkoff <*lnz@dandelion.com*>
   - Marc ZYNGIER <*zyngier@ufr-info-p7.ibp.fr*>
   - **Copyrights**
   - Copyright (C) 1994-96 Marc ZYNGIER
   - Copyright (C) 1997 Gadi Oxman, Ingo Molnar, Miguel de Icaza
   - Copyright (C) 1997, 1998 Linas Vepstas
   - By copyright law, additional copyrights are implicitly held by the contributors listed above.

   Thanks all for being there!

2 Understanding RAID

1. **Q**: What is RAID? Why would I ever use it?

   A: RAID is a way of combining multiple disk drives into a single entity to improve performance and/or reliability. There are a variety of different types and implementations of RAID, each with its own advantages and disadvantages. For example, by putting a copy of the same data on two disks (called **disk mirroring**, or RAID level 1), read performance can be improved by reading alternately from each disk in the mirror. On average, each disk is less busy, as it is handling only 1/2 the reads (for two disks), or 1/3 (for three disks), etc. In addition, a mirror can improve reliability: if one disk fails, the other disk(s) have a copy of the data. Different ways of combining the disks into one, referred to as **RAID levels**, can provide greater storage efficiency than simple mirroring, or can alter latency (access-time) performance, or throughput (transfer rate) performance, for reading or writing, while still retaining redundancy that is useful for guarding against failures. **Although RAID can protect against disk failure, it does not protect against operator and administrator (human) error, or against loss due to programming bugs (possibly due to bugs in the RAID software itself). The net abounds with tragic tales of system administrators who have bungled a RAID installation, and have lost all of their data. RAID is not a substitute for frequent, regularly scheduled backup.**

RAID can be implemented in hardware, in the form of special disk controllers, or in software, as a kernel module that is layered in between the low-level disk driver, and the file system which sits above it. RAID hardware is always a "disk controller", that is, a device to which one can cable up the disk drives. Usually it comes in the form of an adapter card that will plug into a ISA/EISA/PCI/S-Bus/MicroChannel slot. However, some RAID controllers are in the form of a box that connects into the cable in between the usual system disk controller, and the disk drives. Small ones may fit into a drive bay; large ones may be built into a storage cabinet with its own drive bays and power supply. The latest RAID hardware used with the latest & fastest CPU will usually provide the best overall performance, although at a significant price. This is because most RAID controllers come with on-board DSP's and memory cache that can off-load a considerable amount of processing from the main CPU, as well as allow high transfer rates into the large controller cache. Old RAID hardware can act as a "de-accelerator" when used with newer CPU's: yesterday's fancy DSP and cache can act as a bottleneck, and it's performance is often beaten by pure-software RAID and new but otherwise plain, run-of-the-mill disk controllers. RAID hardware can offer an advantage over pure-software RAID, if it can makes use of disk-spindle synchronization and its knowledge of the disk-platter position with regard to the disk head, and the desired disk-block. However, most modern (low-cost) disk drives do not offer this information and level of control anyway, and thus, most RAID hardware does not take advantage of it. RAID hardware is usually not compatible across different brands, makes and models: if a RAID controller fails, it must be replaced by another controller of the same type. As of this writing (June 1998), a broad variety of hardware controllers will operate under Linux; however, none of them currently come with configuration and management utilities that run under Linux.

Software-RAID is a set of kernel modules, together with management utilities that implement RAID purely in software, and require no extraordinary hardware. The Linux RAID subsystem is implemented as a layer in the kernel that sits above the low-level disk drivers (for IDE, SCSI and Paraport drives), and the block-device interface. The filesystem, be it ext2fs, DOS-FAT, or other, sits above the block-device interface. Software-RAID, by its very software nature, tends to be more flexible than a hardware solution. The downside is that it of course requires more CPU cycles and power to run well than a comparable hardware system. Of course, the cost can't be beat. Software RAID has one further important distinguishing feature: it operates on a partition-by-partition basis, where a number of individual disk partitions are ganged together to create a RAID partition. This is in contrast to most hardware RAID solutions, which gang together entire disk drives into an array. With hardware, the fact that there is a RAID array is transparent to the operating system, which tends to simplify management. With software, there are far more configuration options and choices, tending to complicate matters.

As of this writing (June 1998), the administration of RAID under Linux is far from trivial, and is best attempted by experienced system administrators. The theory of operation is complex. The system tools require modification to startup scripts. And recovery from disk failure is non-trivial, and prone to human error. RAID is not for the novice, and any benefits it may bring to reliability and performance can be easily outweighed by the extra complexity. Indeed, modern disk drives are incredibly reliable and modern CPU's and controllers are quite powerful. You might more easily obtain the desired reliability and performance levels by purchasing higher-quality and/or faster hardware.

2. **Q**: What are RAID levels? Why so many? What distinguishes them?

   A: The different RAID levels have different performance, redundancy, storage capacity, reliability and cost characteristics. Most, but not all levels of RAID offer redundancy against disk failure. Of those that offer redundancy, RAID-1 and RAID-5 are the most popular. RAID-1 offers better performance, while RAID-5 provides for more efficient use of the available storage space. However, tuning for performance is an entirely different matter, as performance depends strongly on a large variety of factors, from the type of application, to the sizes of stripes, blocks, and files. The more difficult aspects of performance tuning are deferred to a later section of this HOWTO. The following describes the different RAID levels in the context of the Linux software RAID implementation.

- **RAID-linear** is a simple concatenation of partitions to create a larger virtual partition. It is handy if you have a number small drives, and wish to create a single, large partition. This concatenation offers no redundancy, and in fact decreases the overall reliability: if any one disk fails, the combined partition will fail.

- **RAID-1** is also referred to as "mirroring". Two (or more) partitions, all of the same size, each store an exact copy of all data, disk-block by disk-block. Mirroring gives strong protection against disk failure: if one disk fails, there is another with the an exact copy of the same data. Mirroring can also help improve performance in I/O-laden systems, as read requests can be divided up between several disks. Unfortunately, mirroring is also the least efficient in terms of storage: two mirrored partitions can store no more data than a single partition.

- **Striping** is the underlying concept behind all of the other RAID levels. A stripe is a contiguous sequence of disk blocks. A stripe may be as short as a single disk block, or may consist of thousands. The RAID drivers split up their component disk partitions into stripes; the different RAID levels differ in how they organize the stripes, and what data they put in them. The interplay between the size of the stripes, the typical size of files in the file system, and their location on the disk is what determines the overall performance of the RAID subsystem.

- **RAID-0** is much like RAID-linear, except that the component partitions are divided into stripes and then interleaved. Like RAID-linear, the result is a single larger virtual partition. Also like RAID-linear, it offers no redundancy, and therefore decreases overall reliability: a single disk failure will knock out the whole thing. RAID-0 is often claimed to improve performance over the simpler RAID-linear. However, this may or may not be true, depending on the characteristics to the file system, the typical size of the file as compared to the size of the stripe, and the type of workload. The `ext2fs` file system already scatters files throughout a partition, in an effort to minimize fragmentation. Thus, at the simplest level, any given access may go to one of several disks, and thus, the interleaving of stripes across multiple disks offers no apparent additional advantage. However, there are performance differences, and they are data, workload, and stripe-size dependent.

- **RAID-4** interleaves stripes like RAID-0, but it requires an additional partition to store parity information. The parity is used to offer redundancy: if any one of the disks fail, the data on the remaining disks can be used to reconstruct the data that was on the failed disk. Given N data disks, and one parity disk, the parity stripe is computed by taking one stripe from each of the data disks, and XOR'ing them together. Thus, the storage capacity of a an (N+1)-disk RAID-4 array is N, which is a lot better than mirroring (N+1) drives, and is almost as good as a RAID-0 setup for large N. Note that for N=1, where there is one data drive, and one parity drive, RAID-4 is a lot like mirroring, in that each of the two disks is a copy of each other. However, RAID-4 does **NOT** offer the read-performance of mirroring, and offers considerably degraded write performance. In brief, this is because updating the parity requires a read of the old parity, before the new parity can be calculated and written out. In an environment with lots of writes, the parity disk can become a bottleneck, as each write must access the parity disk.

- **RAID-5** avoids the write-bottleneck of RAID-4 by alternately storing the parity stripe on each of the drives. However, write performance is still not as good as for mirroring, as the parity stripe must still be read and XOR'ed before it is written. Read performance is also not as good as it is for mirroring, as, after all, there is only one copy of the data, not two or more. RAID-5's principle advantage over mirroring is that it offers redundancy and protection against single-drive failure, while offering far more storage capacity when used with three or more drives.

- **RAID-2 and RAID-3** are seldom used anymore, and to some degree are have been made obsolete by modern disk technology. RAID-2 is similar to RAID-4, but stores ECC information instead of parity. Since all modern disk drives incorporate ECC under the covers, this offers little additional protection. RAID-2 can offer greater data consistency if power is lost during a write; however, battery backup and a clean shutdown can offer the same benefits. RAID-3 is similar to RAID-4, except that it uses the smallest possible stripe size. As a result, any given read will involve all disks, making overlapping I/O requests difficult/impossible. In order to avoid delay due to rotational latency, RAID-3 requires that all disk drive spindles be synchronized. Most modern disk drives lack spindle-synchronization ability, or, if capable of it, lack the needed connectors, cables, and manufacturer documentation. Neither RAID-2 nor RAID-3 are supported by the Linux Software-RAID drivers.

- **Other RAID levels** have been defined by various researchers and vendors. Many of these represent the layering of one type of raid on top of another. Some require special hardware, and others are protected by patent. There is no commonly accepted naming scheme for these other levels. Sometime the advantages of these other systems are minor, or at least not apparent until the system is highly stressed. Except for the layering of RAID-1 over RAID-0/linear, Linux Software RAID does not support any of the other variations.

3   Setup & Installation Considerations

1. **Q**: What is the best way to configure Software RAID?

    A: I keep rediscovering that file-system planning is one of the more difficult Unix configuration tasks. To answer your question, I can describe what we did.

    We planned the following setup:

    - two EIDE disks, 2.1.gig each.

      ```
      disk partition mount pt.    size      device
      1      1         /          300M      /dev/hda1
      1      2         swap        64M       /dev/hda2
      1      3         /home       800M      /dev/hda3
      1      4         /var        900M      /dev/hda4

      2      1         /root       300M      /dev/hdc1
      2      2         swap        64M       /dev/hdc2
      2      3         /home       800M      /dev/hdc3
      2      4         /var        900M      /dev/hdc4
      ```

    - Each disk is on a separate controller (& ribbon cable). The theory is that a controller failure and/or ribbon failure won't disable both disks. Also, we might possibly get a performance boost from parallel operations over two controllers/cables.
    - Install the Linux kernel on the root (/) partition /dev/hda1. Mark this partition as bootable.
    - /dev/hdc1 will contain a "cold" copy of /dev/hda1. This is NOT a raid copy, just a plain old copy-copy. It's there just in case the first disk fails; we can use a rescue disk, mark /dev/hdc1 as bootable, and use that to keep going without having to reinstall the system. You may even want to put /dev/hdc1's copy of the kernel into LILO to simplify booting in case of failure.
      The theory here is that in case of severe failure, I can still boot the system without worrying about raid superblock-corruption or other raid failure modes & gotchas that I don't understand.
    - /dev/hda3 and /dev/hdc3 will be mirrors /dev/md0.
    - /dev/hda4 and /dev/hdc4 will be mirrors /dev/md1.
    - we picked /var and /home to be mirrored, and in separate partitions, using the following logic:
      - / (the root partition) will contain relatively static, non-changing data: for all practical purposes, it will be read-only without actually being marked & mounted read-only.
      - /home will contain "slowly" changing data.
      - /var will contain rapidly changing data, including mail spools, database contents and web server logs.
      The idea behind using multiple, distinct partitions is that **if**, for some bizarre reason, whether it is human error, power loss, or an operating system gone wild, corruption is limited to one partition. In one typical case, power is lost while the system is writing to disk. This will almost certainly lead to a corrupted filesystem, which will be repaired by fsck during the next boot. Although fsck does it's best to make the repairs without creating additional damage during those repairs, it can be comforting to know that any such damage has been limited to one partition. In another typical

case, the sysadmin makes a mistake during rescue operations, leading to erased or destroyed data. Partitions can help limit the repercussions of the operator's errors.

- Other reasonable choices for partitions might be /usr or /opt. In fact, /opt and /home make great choices for RAID-5 partitions, if we had more disks. A word of caution: **DO NOT** put /usr in a RAID-5 partition. If a serious fault occurs, you may find that you cannot mount /usr, and that you want some of the tools on it (e.g. the networking tools, or the compiler.) With RAID-1, if a fault has occurred, and you can't get RAID to work, you can at least mount one of the two mirrors. You can't do this with any of the other RAID levels (RAID-5, striping, or linear append).

So, to complete the answer to the question:

- install the OS on disk 1, partition 1. do NOT mount any of the other partitions.
- install RAID per instructions.
- configure md0 and md1.
- convince yourself that you know what to do in case of a disk failure! Discover sysadmin mistakes now, and not during an actual crisis. Experiment! (we turned off power during disk activity — this proved to be ugly but informative).
- do some ugly mount/copy/unmount/rename/reboot scheme to move /var over to the /dev/md1. Done carefully, this is not dangerous.
- enjoy!

2. **Q**: What is the difference between the mdadd, mdrun, *etc.* commands, and the raidadd, raidrun commands?

   A: The names of the tools have changed as of the 0.5 release of the raidtools package. The md naming convention was used in the 0.43 and older versions, while raid is used in 0.5 and newer versions.

3. **Q**: I want to run RAID-linear/RAID-0 in the stock 2.0.34 kernel. I don't want to apply the raid patches, since these are not needed for RAID-0/linear. Where can I get the raid-tools to manage this?

   A: This is a tough question, indeed, as the newest raid tools package needs to have the RAID-1,4,5 kernel patches installed in order to compile. I am not aware of any pre-compiled, binary version of the raid tools that is available at this time. However, experiments show that the raid-tools binaries, when compiled against kernel 2.1.100, seem to work just fine in creating a RAID-0/linear partition under 2.0.34. A brave soul has asked for these, and I've **temporarily** placed the binaries mdadd, mdcreate, etc. at http://linas.org/linux/Software-RAID/ You must get the man pages, etc. from the usual raid-tools package.

4. **Q**: Can I strip/mirror the root partition (/)? Why can't I boot Linux directly from the md disks?

   A: Both LILO and Loadlin need an non-stripped/mirrored partition to read the kernel image from. If you want to strip/mirror the root partition (/), then you'll want to create an unstriped/mirrored partition to hold the kernel(s). Typically, this partition is named /boot. Then you either use the initial ramdisk support (initrd), or patches from Harald Hoyer *<HarryH@Royal.Net>* that allow a stripped partition to be used as the root device. (These patches are now a standard part of recent 2.1.x kernels)
   There are several approaches that can be used. One approach is documented in detail in the Bootable RAID mini-HOWTO: <ftp://ftp.bizsystems.com/pub/raid/bootable-raid>.
   Alternately, use mkinitrd to build the ramdisk image, see below.
   Edward Welbon *<welbon@bga.com>* writes:

- ... all that is needed is a script to manage the boot setup. To mount an md filesystem as root, the main thing is to build an initial file system image that has the needed modules and md tools to start md. I have a simple script that does this.

- For boot media, I have a small **cheap** SCSI disk (170MB I got it used for $20). This disk runs on a AHA1452, but it could just as well be an inexpensive IDE disk on the native IDE. The disk need not be very fast since it is mainly for boot.

- This disk has a small file system which contains the kernel and the file system image for initrd. The initial file system image has just enough stuff to allow me to load the raid SCSI device driver module and start the raid partition that will become root. I then do an

```
echo 0x900 > /proc/sys/kernel/real-root-dev
```

(0x900 is for /dev/md0) and exit linuxrc. The boot proceeds normally from there.

- I have built most support as a module except for the AHA1452 driver that brings in the initrd filesystem. So I have a fairly small kernel. The method is perfectly reliable, I have been doing this since before 2.1.26 and have never had a problem that I could not easily recover from. The file systems even survived several 2.1.4[45] hard crashes with no real problems.

- At one time I had partitioned the raid disks so that the initial cylinders of the first raid disk held the kernel and the initial cylinders of the second raid disk hold the initial file system image, instead I made the initial cylinders of the raid disks swap since they are the fastest cylinders (why waste them on boot?).

- The nice thing about having an inexpensive device dedicated to boot is that it is easy to boot from and can also serve as a rescue disk if necessary. If you are interested, you can take a look at the script that builds my initial ram disk image and then runs LILO.

    <http://www.realtime.net/welbon/initrd.md.tar.gz>

It is current enough to show the picture. It isn't especially pretty and it could certainly build a much smaller filesystem image for the initial ram disk. It would be easy to a make it more efficient. But it uses LILO as is. If you make any improvements, please forward a copy to me. 8-)

5. **Q**: I have heard that I can run mirroring over striping. Is this true? Can I run mirroring over the loopback device?

   A: Yes, but not the reverse. That is, you can put a stripe over several disks, and then build a mirror on top of this. However, striping cannot be put on top of mirroring.

   A brief technical explanation is that the linear and stripe personalities use the ll_rw_blk routine for access. The ll_rw_blk routine maps disk devices and sectors, not blocks. Block devices can be layered one on top of the other; but devices that do raw, low-level disk accesses, such as ll_rw_blk, cannot.

   Currently (November 1997) RAID cannot be run over the loopback devices, although this should be fixed shortly.

6. **Q**: I have two small disks and three larger disks. Can I concatenate the two smaller disks with RAID-0, and then create a RAID-5 out of that and the larger disks?

   A: Currently (November 1997), for a RAID-5 array, no. Currently, one can do this only for a RAID-1 on top of the concatenated drives.

7. **Q**: What is the difference between RAID-1 and RAID-5 for a two-disk configuration (i.e. the difference between a RAID-1 array built out of two disks, and a RAID-5 array built out of two disks)?

   A: There is no difference in storage capacity. Nor can disks be added to either array to increase capacity (see the question below for details).

   RAID-1 offers a performance advantage for reads: the RAID-1 driver uses distributed-read technology to simultaneously read two sectors, one from each drive, thus doubling read performance.

   The RAID-5 driver, although it contains many optimizations, does not currently (September 1997) realize that the parity disk is actually a mirrored copy of the data disk. Thus, it serializes data reads.

8. **Q**: How can I guard against a two-disk failure?

   A: Some of the RAID algorithms do guard against multiple disk failures, but these are not currently implemented for Linux. However, the Linux Software RAID can guard against multiple disk failures by layering an array on top of an array. For example, nine disks can be used to create three raid-5 arrays. Then these three arrays can in turn be hooked together into a single RAID-5 array on top. In fact, this kind of a configuration will guard against a three-disk failure. Note that a large amount of disk space is "wasted" on the redundancy information.

```
For an NxN raid-5 array,
N=3, 5 out of 9 disks are used for parity (=55%)
N=4, 7 out of 16 disks
```

```
N=5,  9 out of 25 disks
...
N=9, 17 out of 81 disks (=~20%)
```

In general, an MxN array will use M+N-1 disks for parity. The least amount of space is "wasted" when M=N.

Another alternative is to create a RAID-1 array with three disks. Note that since all three disks contain identical data, that 2/3's of the space is "wasted".

9. **Q**: I'd like to understand how it'd be possible to have something like `fsck`: if the partition hasn't been cleanly unmounted, `fsck` runs and fixes the filesystem by itself more than 90% of the time. Since the machine is capable of fixing it by itself with `ckraid -fix`, why not make it automatic?

A: This can be done by adding lines like the following to `/etc/rc.d/rc.sysinit`:

```
mdadd /dev/md0 /dev/hda1 /dev/hdc1 || {
     ckraid --fix /etc/raid.usr.conf
     mdadd /dev/md0 /dev/hda1 /dev/hdc1
}
```

or

```
mdrun -p1 /dev/md0
if [ $? -gt 0 ] ; then
        ckraid --fix /etc/raid1.conf
        mdrun -p1 /dev/md0
fi
```

Before presenting a more complete and reliable script, lets review the theory of operation. Gadi Oxman writes: In an unclean shutdown, Linux might be in one of the following states:

- The in-memory disk cache was in sync with the RAID set when the unclean shutdown occurred; no data was lost.

- The in-memory disk cache was newer than the RAID set contents when the crash occurred; this results in a corrupted filesystem and potentially in data loss.
  This state can be further divided to the following two states:

  - Linux was writing data when the unclean shutdown occurred.
  - Linux was not writing data when the crash occurred.

Suppose we were using a RAID-1 array. In (2a), it might happen that before the crash, a small number of data blocks were successfully written only to some of the mirrors, so that on the next reboot, the mirrors will no longer contain the same data.

If we were to ignore the mirror differences, the raidtools-0.36.3 read-balancing code might choose to read the above data blocks from any of the mirrors, which will result in inconsistent behavior (for example, the output of `e2fsck -n /dev/md0` can differ from run to run).

Since RAID doesn't protect against unclean shutdowns, usually there isn't any "obviously correct" way to fix the mirror differences and the filesystem corruption.

For example, by default `ckraid -fix` will choose the first operational mirror and update the other mirrors with its contents. However, depending on the exact timing at the crash, the data on another mirror might be more recent, and we might want to use it as the source mirror instead, or perhaps use another method for recovery.

The following script provides one of the more robust boot-up sequences. In particular, it guards against long, repeated `ckraid`'s in the presence of uncooperative disks, controllers, or controller device drivers. Modify it to reflect your config, and copy it to `rc.raid.init`. Then invoke `rc.raid.init` after the root partition has been fsck'ed and mounted rw, but before the remaining partitions are fsck'ed. Make sure the current directory is in the search path.

```
mdadd /dev/md0 /dev/hda1 /dev/hdc1 || {
    rm -f /fastboot                 # force an fsck to occur
    ckraid --fix /etc/raid.usr.conf
    mdadd /dev/md0 /dev/hda1 /dev/hdc1
}
# if a crash occurs later in the boot process,
# we at least want to leave this md in a clean state.
/sbin/mdstop /dev/md0

mdadd /dev/md1 /dev/hda2 /dev/hdc2 || {
    rm -f /fastboot                 # force an fsck to occur
    ckraid --fix /etc/raid.home.conf
    mdadd /dev/md1 /dev/hda2 /dev/hdc2
}
# if a crash occurs later in the boot process,
# we at least want to leave this md in a clean state.
/sbin/mdstop /dev/md1


mdadd /dev/md0 /dev/hda1 /dev/hdc1
mdrun -p1 /dev/md0
if [ $? -gt 0 ] ; then
    rm -f /fastboot                 # force an fsck to occur
    ckraid --fix /etc/raid.usr.conf
    mdrun -p1 /dev/md0
fi
# if a crash occurs later in the boot process,
# we at least want to leave this md in a clean state.
/sbin/mdstop /dev/md0

mdadd /dev/md1 /dev/hda2 /dev/hdc2
mdrun -p1 /dev/md1
if [ $? -gt 0 ] ; then
    rm -f /fastboot                 # force an fsck to occur
    ckraid --fix /etc/raid.home.conf
    mdrun -p1 /dev/md1
fi
# if a crash occurs later in the boot process,
# we at least want to leave this md in a clean state.
/sbin/mdstop /dev/md1

# OK, just blast through the md commands now.  If there were
# errors, the above checks should have fixed things up.
/sbin/mdadd /dev/md0 /dev/hda1 /dev/hdc1
/sbin/mdrun -p1 /dev/md0

/sbin/mdadd /dev/md12 /dev/hda2 /dev/hdc2
/sbin/mdrun -p1 /dev/md1
```

In addition to the above, you'll want to create a rc.raid.halt which should look like the following:

```
/sbin/mdstop /dev/md0
/sbin/mdstop /dev/md1
```

Be sure to modify both `rc.sysinit` and `init.d/halt` to include this everywhere that filesystems get unmounted before a halt/reboot. (Note that `rc.sysinit` unmounts and reboots if `fsck` returned with an error.)

10. **Q**: Can I set up one-half of a RAID-1 mirror with the one disk I have now, and then later get the other disk and just drop it in?

> **A**: With the current tools, no, not in any easy way. In particular, you cannot just copy the contents of one disk onto another, and then pair them up. This is because the RAID drivers use glob of space at the end of the partition to store the superblock. This decreases the amount of space available to the file system slightly; if you just naively try to force a RAID-1 arrangement onto a partition with an existing filesystem, the raid superblock will overwrite a portion of the file system and mangle data. Since the ext2fs filesystem scatters files randomly throughput the partition (in order to avoid fragmentation), there is a very good chance that some file will land at the very end of a partition long before the disk is full.
>
> If you are clever, I suppose you can calculate how much room the RAID superblock will need, and make your filesystem slightly smaller, leaving room for it when you add it later. But then, if you are this clever, you should also be able to modify the tools to do this automatically for you. (The tools are not terribly complex).
>
> **Note:** A careful reader has pointed out that the following trick may work; I have not tried or verified this: Do the `mkraid` with `/dev/null` as one of the devices. Then `mdadd -r` with only the single, true disk (do not mdadd `/dev/null`). The `mkraid` should have successfully built the raid array, while the mdadd step just forces the system to run in "degraded" mode, as if one of the disks had failed.

4 Error Recovery

1. **Q**: I have a RAID-1 (mirroring) setup, and lost power while there was disk activity. Now what do I do?

> **A**: The redundancy of RAID levels is designed to protect against a **disk** failure, not against a **power** failure.
>
> There are several ways to recover from this situation.
>
> - Method (1): Use the raid tools. These can be used to sync the raid arrays. They do not fix file-system damage; after the raid arrays are sync'ed, then the file-system still has to be fixed with fsck. Raid arrays can be checked with `ckraid /etc/raid1.conf` (for RAID-1, else, `/etc/raid5.conf`, etc.)
>   Calling `ckraid /etc/raid1.conf -fix` will pick one of the disks in the array (usually the first), and use that as the master copy, and copy its blocks to the others in the mirror.
>   To designate which of the disks should be used as the master, you can use the `-force-source` flag: for example, `ckraid /etc/raid1.conf -fix -force-source /dev/hdc3`
>   The ckraid command can be safely run without the `-fix` option to verify the inactive RAID array without making any changes. When you are comfortable with the proposed changes, supply the `-fix` option.
> - Method (2): Paranoid, time-consuming, not much better than the first way. Lets assume a two-disk RAID-1 array, consisting of partitions `/dev/hda3` and `/dev/hdc3`. You can try the following:
>   (a) `fsck /dev/hda3`
>   (b) `fsck /dev/hdc3`
>   (c) decide which of the two partitions had fewer errors, or were more easily recovered, or recovered the data that you wanted. Pick one, either one, to be your new "master" copy. Say you picked `/dev/hdc3`.
>   (d) `dd if=/dev/hdc3 of=/dev/hda3`
>   (e) `mkraid raid1.conf -f -only-superblock`
>   Instead of the last two steps, you can instead run `ckraid /etc/raid1.conf -fix -force-source /dev/hdc3` which should be a bit faster.
> - Method (3): Lazy man's version of above. If you don't want to wait for long fsck's to complete, it is perfectly fine to skip the first three steps above, and move directly to the last two steps. Just be sure to run `fsck /dev/md0` after you are done. Method (3) is actually just method (1) in disguise.

In any case, the above steps will only sync up the raid arrays. The file system probably needs fixing as well: for this, fsck needs to be run on the active, unmounted md device.

With a three-disk RAID-1 array, there are more possibilities, such as using two disks to "vote" a majority answer. Tools to automate this do not currently (September 97) exist.

2. **Q**: I have a RAID-4 or a RAID-5 (parity) setup, and lost power while there was disk activity. Now what do I do?

A: The redundancy of RAID levels is designed to protect against a **disk** failure, not against a **power** failure.

Since the disks in a RAID-4 or RAID-5 array do not contain a file system that fsck can read, there are fewer repair options. You cannot use fsck to do preliminary checking and/or repair; you must use ckraid first.

The `ckraid` command can be safely run without the `-fix` option to verify the inactive RAID array without making any changes. When you are comfortable with the proposed changes, supply the `-fix` option.

If you wish, you can try designating one of the disks as a "failed disk". Do this with the `-suggest-failed-disk-mask` flag.

Only one bit should be set in the flag: RAID-5 cannot recover two failed disks. The mask is a binary bit mask: thus:

```
0x1 == first disk
0x2 == second disk
0x4 == third disk
0x8 == fourth disk, etc.
```

Alternately, you can choose to modify the parity sectors, by using the `-suggest-fix-parity` flag. This will recompute the parity from the other sectors.

The flags `-suggest-failed-dsk-mask` and `-suggest-fix-parity` can be safely used for verification. No changes are made if the `-fix` flag is not specified. Thus, you can experiment with different possible repair schemes.

3. **Q**: My RAID-1 device, `/dev/md0` consists of two hard drive partitions: `/dev/hda3` and `/dev/hdc3`. Recently, the disk with `/dev/hdc3` failed, and was replaced with a new disk. My best friend, who doesn't understand RAID, said that the correct thing to do now is to "dd if=/dev/hda3 of=/dev/hdc3". I tried this, but things still don't work.

A: You should keep your best friend away from you computer. Fortunately, no serious damage has been done. You can recover from this by running:

```
mkraid raid1.conf -f --only-superblock
```

By using `dd`, two identical copies of the partition were created. This is almost correct, except that the RAID-1 kernel extension expects the RAID superblocks to be different. Thus, when you try to reactivate RAID, the software will notice the problem, and deactivate one of the two partitions. By re-creating the superblock, you should have a fully usable system.

4. **Q**: My version of `mkraid` doesn't have a `-only-superblock` flag. What do I do?

A: The newer tools drop support for this flag, replacing it with the `-force-resync` flag. It has been reported that the following sequence appears to work with the latest tools and software:

```
umount /web (where /dev/md0 was mounted on)
raidstop /dev/md0
mkraid /dev/md0 --force-resync --really-force
raidstart /dev/md0
```

After doing this, a `cat /proc/mdstat` should report `resync in progress`, and one should be able to `mount /dev/md0` at this point.

5. **Q**: My RAID-1 device, /dev/md0 consists of two hard drive partitions: /dev/hda3 and /dev/hdc3. My best (girl?)friend, who doesn't understand RAID, ran `fsck` on /dev/hda3 while I wasn't looking, and now the RAID won't work. What should I do?

> **A**: You should re-examine your concept of "best friend". In general, `fsck` should never be run on the individual partitions that compose a RAID array. Assuming that neither of the partitions are/were heavily damaged, no data loss has occurred, and the RAID-1 device can be recovered as follows:
>
> (a) make a backup of the file system on /dev/hda3
>
> (b) dd if=/dev/hda3 of=/dev/hdc3
>
> (c) mkraid raid1.conf -f -only-superblock
>
> This should leave you with a working disk mirror.

6. **Q**: Why does the above work as a recovery procedure?

> **A**: Because each of the component partitions in a RAID-1 mirror is a perfectly valid copy of the file system. In a pinch, mirroring can be disabled, and one of the partitions can be mounted and safely run as an ordinary, non-RAID file system. When you are ready to restart using RAID-1, then unmount the partition, and follow the above instructions to restore the mirror. Note that the above works ONLY for RAID-1, and not for any of the other levels.
>
> It may make you feel more comfortable to reverse the direction of the copy above: copy **from** the disk that was untouched **to** the one that was. Just be sure to fsck the final md.

7. **Q**: I am confused by the above questions, but am not yet bailing out. Is it safe to run `fsck /dev/md0` ?

> **A**: Yes, it is safe to run `fsck` on the md devices. In fact, this is the **only** safe place to run `fsck`.

8. **Q**: If a disk is slowly failing, will it be obvious which one it is? I am concerned that it won't be, and this confusion could lead to some dangerous decisions by a sysadmin.

> **A**: Once a disk fails, an error code will be returned from the low level driver to the RAID driver. The RAID driver will mark it as "bad" in the RAID superblocks of the "good" disks (so we will later know which mirrors are good and which aren't), and continue RAID operation on the remaining operational mirrors.
>
> This, of course, assumes that the disk and the low level driver can detect a read/write error, and will not silently corrupt data, for example. This is true of current drives (error detection schemes are being used internally), and is the basis of RAID operation.

9. **Q**: What about hot-repair?

> **A**: Work is underway to complete "hot reconstruction". With this feature, one can add several "spare" disks to the RAID set (be it level 1 or 4/5), and once a disk fails, it will be reconstructed on one of the spare disks in run time, without ever needing to shut down the array.
>
> However, to use this feature, the spare disk must have been declared at boot time, or it must be hot-added, which requires the use of special cabinets and connectors that allow a disk to be added while the electrical power is on.
>
> As of October 97, there is a beta version of MD that allows:
>
> - RAID 1 and 5 reconstruction on spare drives
> - RAID-5 parity reconstruction after an unclean shutdown
> - spare disk to be hot-added to an already running RAID 1 or 4/5 array
>
> By default, automatic reconstruction is (Dec 97) currently disabled by default, due to the preliminary nature of this work. It can be enabled by changing the value of SUPPORT_RECONSTRUCTION in include/linux/md.h.
>
> If spare drives were configured into the array when it was created and kernel-based reconstruction is enabled, the spare drive will already contain a RAID superblock (written by `mkraid`), and the kernel will reconstruct its contents automatically (without needing the usual `mdstop`, replace drive, `ckraid`, `mdrun` steps).
>
> If you are not running automatic reconstruction, and have not configured a hot-spare disk, the procedure described by Gadi Oxman <*gadio@netvision.net.il*> is recommended:

Mini-HOWTO

- Currently, once the first disk is removed, the RAID set will be running in degraded mode. To restore full operation mode, you need to:
  - stop the array (`mdstop /dev/md0`)
  - replace the failed drive
  - run `ckraid raid.conf` to reconstruct its contents
  - run the array again (`mdadd`, `mdrun`).

At this point, the array will be running with all the drives, and again protects against a failure of a single drive.

Currently, it is not possible to assign single hot-spare disk to several arrays. Each array requires it's own hot-spare.

10. **Q**: I would like to have an audible alarm for "you schmuck, one disk in the mirror is down", so that the novice sysadmin knows that there is a problem.

   A: The kernel is logging the event with a "KERN_ALERT" priority in syslog. There are several software packages that will monitor the syslog files, and beep the PC speaker, call a pager, send e-mail, etc. automatically.

11. **Q**: How do I run RAID-5 in degraded mode (with one disk failed, and not yet replaced)?

   A: Gadi Oxman <*gadio@netvision.net.il*> writes: Normally, to run a RAID-5 set of n drives you have to:

   ```
   mdadd /dev/md0 /dev/disk1 ... /dev/disk(n)
   mdrun -p5 /dev/md0
   ```

   Even if one of the disks has failed, you still have to `mdadd` it as you would in a normal setup. (?? try using /dev/null in place of the failed disk ??? watch out) Then,

   The array will be active in degraded mode with (n - 1) drives. If "`mdrun`" fails, the kernel has noticed an error (for example, several faulty drives, or an unclean shutdown). Use "`dmesg`" to display the kernel error messages from "`mdrun`". If the raid-5 set is corrupted due to a power loss, rather than a disk crash, one can try to recover by creating a new RAID superblock:

   ```
   mkraid -f --only-superblock raid5.conf
   ```

   A RAID array doesn't provide protection against a power failure or a kernel crash, and can't guarantee correct recovery. Rebuilding the superblock will simply cause the system to ignore the condition by marking all the drives as "OK", as if nothing happened.

12. **Q**: How does RAID-5 work when a disk fails?

   A: The typical operating scenario is as follows:
   - A RAID-5 array is active.
   - One drive fails while the array is active.
   - The drive firmware and the low-level Linux disk/controller drivers detect the failure and report an error code to the MD driver.
   - The MD driver continues to provide an error-free `/dev/md0` device to the higher levels of the kernel (with a performance degradation) by using the remaining operational drives.
   - The sysadmin can `umount /dev/md0` and `mdstop /dev/md0` as usual.
   - If the failed drive is not replaced, the sysadmin can still start the array in degraded mode as usual, by running `mdadd` and `mdrun`.

13. **Q**:

   A:

14. **Q**: Why is there no question 13?

A: If you are concerned about RAID, High Availability, and UPS, then its probably a good idea to be superstitious as well. It can't hurt, can it?

15. **Q**: I just replaced a failed disk in a RAID-5 array. After rebuilding the array, `fsck` is reporting many, many errors. Is this normal?

>   **A**: No. And, unless you ran fsck in "verify only; do not update" mode, its quite possible that you have corrupted your data. Unfortunately, a not-uncommon scenario is one of accidentally changing the disk order in a RAID-5 array, after replacing a hard drive. Although the RAID superblock stores the proper order, not all tools use this information. In particular, the current version of `ckraid` will use the information specified with the `-f` flag (typically, the file `/etc/raid5.conf`) instead of the data in the superblock. If the specified order is incorrect, then the replaced disk will be reconstructed incorrectly. The symptom of this kind of mistake seems to be heavy & numerous `fsck` errors.
>
>   And, in case you are wondering, **yes**, someone lost **all** of their data by making this mistake. Making a tape backup of **all** data before reconfiguring a RAID array is **strongly recommended**.

16. **Q**: The QuickStart says that `mdstop` is just to make sure that the disks are sync'ed. Is this REALLY necessary? Isn't unmounting the file systems enough?

>   **A**: The command `mdstop /dev/md0` will:

- mark it "clean". This allows us to detect unclean shutdowns, for example due to a power failure or a kernel crash.

- sync the array. This is less important after unmounting a filesystem, but is important if the `/dev/md0` is accessed directly rather than through a filesystem (for example, by `e2fsck`).

5   Troubleshooting Install Problems

1. **Q**: What is the current best known-stable patch for RAID in the 2.0.x series kernels?

>   **A**: As of 18 Sept 1997, it is "2.0.30 + pre-9 2.0.31 + Werner Fink's swapping patch + the alpha RAID patch". As of November 1997, it is 2.0.31 + ... !?

2. **Q**: The RAID patches will not install cleanly for me. What's wrong?

>   **A**: Make sure that `/usr/include/linux` is a symbolic link to `/usr/src/linux/include/linux`.
>   Make sure that the new files `raid5.c`, etc. have been copied to their correct locations. Sometimes the patch command will not create new files. Try the `-f` flag on `patch`.

3. **Q**: While compiling raidtools 0.42, compilation stops trying to include <pthread.h> but it doesn't exist in my system. How do I fix this?

>   **A**: raidtools-0.42 requires linuxthreads-0.6 from: `<ftp://ftp.inria.fr/INRIA/Projects/cristal/Xavier.Leroy>` Alternately, use glibc v2.0.

4. **Q**: I get the message: `mdrun -a /dev/md0: Invalid argument`

>   **A**: Use `mkraid` to initialize the RAID set prior to the first use. `mkraid` ensures that the RAID array is initially in a consistent state by erasing the RAID partitions. In addition, `mkraid` will create the RAID superblocks.

5. **Q**: I get the message: `mdrun -a /dev/md0: Invalid argument` The setup was:

- raid build as a kernel module

- normal install procedure followed ... mdcreate, mdadd, etc.

- `cat /proc/mdstat` shows

```
    Personalities :
    read_ahead not set
    md0 : inactive sda1 sdb1 6313482 blocks
    md1 : inactive
    md2 : inactive
    md3 : inactive
```

- mdrun -a generates the error message /dev/md0:　Invalid argument

  A: Try lsmod (or, alternately, cat /proc/modules) to see if the raid modules are loaded. If they are not, you can load them explicitly with the modprobe raid1 or modprobe raid5 command. Alternately, if you are using the autoloader, and expected kerneld to load them and it didn't this is probably because your loader is missing the info to load the modules. Edit /etc/conf.modules and add the following lines:

  ```
      alias md-personality-3 raid1
      alias md-personality-4 raid5
  ```

6. **Q**: While doing mdadd -a I get the error: /dev/md0:　No such file or directory. Indeed, there seems to be no /dev/md0 anywhere. Now what do I do?

   A: The raid-tools package will create these devices when you run make install as root. Alternately, you can do the following:

   ```
       cd /dev
       ./MAKEDEV md
   ```

7. **Q**: After creating a raid array on /dev/md0, I try to mount it and get the following error: mount:　wrong fs type, bad option, bad superblock on /dev/md0, or too many mounted file systems. What's wrong?

   A: You need to create a file system on /dev/md0 before you can mount it. Use mke2fs.

8. **Q**: Truxton Fulton wrote:

   On my Linux 2.0.30 system, while doing a mkraid for a RAID-1 device, during the clearing of the two individual partitions, I got "Cannot allocate free page" errors appearing on the console, and "Unable to handle kernel paging request at virtual address ..." errors in the system log. At this time, the system became quite unusable, but it appears to recover after a while. The operation appears to have completed with no other errors, and I am successfully using my RAID-1 device. The errors are disconcerting though. Any ideas?

   A: This was a well-known bug in the 2.0.30 kernels. It is fixed in the 2.0.31 kernel; alternately, fall back to 2.0.29.

9. **Q**: I'm not able to mdrun a RAID-1, RAID-4 or RAID-5 device. If I try to mdrun a mdadd'ed device I get the message "invalid raid superblock magic".

   A: Make sure that you've run the mkraid part of the install procedure.

10. **Q**: When I access /dev/md0, the kernel spits out a lot of errors like md0:　device not running, giving up ! and I/O error.... I've successfully added my devices to the virtual device.

    A: To be usable, the device must be running. Use mdrun -px /dev/md0 where x is l for linear, 0 for RAID-0 or 1 for RAID-1, etc.

11. **Q**: I've created a linear md-dev with 2 devices. cat /proc/mdstat shows the total size of the device, but df only shows the size of the first physical device.

A: You must `mkfs` your new md-dev before using it the first time, so that the filesystem will cover the whole device.

12. **Q:** I've set up `/etc/mdtab` using mdcreate, I've `mdadd`'ed, mdrun and `fsck`'ed my two `/dev/mdX` partitions. Everything looks okay before a reboot. As soon as I reboot, I get an `fsck` error on both partitions: `fsck.ext2:  Attempt to read block from filesystem resulted in short read while trying too open /dev/md0`. Why?! How do I fix it?!

   A: During the boot process, the RAID partitions must be started before they can be `fsck`'ed. This must be done in one of the boot scripts. For some distributions, `fsck` is called from `/etc/rc.d/rc.S`, for others, it is called from `/etc/rc.d/rc.sysinit`. Change this file to `mdadd -ar *before* fsck -A` is executed. Better yet, it is suggested that `ckraid` be run if `mdadd` returns with an error. How do do this is discussed in greater detail in question 14 of the section "Error Recovery".

13. **Q:** I get the message `invalid raid superblock magic` while trying to run an array which consists of partitions which are bigger than 4GB.

   A: This bug is now fixed. (September 97) Make sure you have the latest raid code.

14. **Q:** I get the message `Warning:  could not write 8 blocks in inode table starting at 2097175` while trying to run mke2fs on a partition which is larger than 2GB.

   A: This seems to be a problem with `mke2fs` (November 97). A temporary work-around is to get the mke2fs code, and add `#undef HAVE_LLSEEK` to `e2fsprogs-1.10/lib/ext2fs/llseek.c` just before the first `#ifdef HAVE_LLSEEK` and recompile mke2fs.

15. **Q:** `ckraid` currently isn't able to read `/etc/mdtab`

   A: The RAID0/linear configuration file format used in `/etc/mdtab` is obsolete, although it will be supported for a while more. The current, up-to-date config files are currently named `/etc/raid1.conf`, etc.

16. **Q:** The personality modules (`raid1.o`) are not loaded automatically; they have to be manually modprobe'd before mdrun. How can this be fixed?

   A: To autoload the modules, we can add the following to `/etc/conf.modules`:

   ```
   alias md-personality-3 raid1
   alias md-personality-4 raid5
   ```

17. **Q:** I've `mdadd`'ed 13 devices, and now I'm trying to `mdrun -p5 /dev/md0` and get the message: `/dev/md0: Invalid argument`

   A: The default configuration for software RAID is 8 real devices. Edit `linux/md.h`, change `#define MAX_REAL=8` to a larger number, and rebuild the kernel.

18. **Q:** I can't make `md` work with partitions on our latest SPARCstation 5. I suspect that this has something to do with disk-labels.

   A: Sun disk-labels sit in the first 1K of a partition. For RAID-1, the Sun disk-label is not an issue since `ext2fs` will skip the label on every mirror. For other raid levels (0, linear and 4/5), this appears to be a problem; it has not yet (Dec 97) been addressed.

6   Supported Hardware & Software

1. **Q**: I have SCSI adapter brand XYZ (with or without several channels), and disk brand(s) PQR and LMN, will these work with md to create a linear/stripped/mirrored personality?

   A: Yes! Software RAID will work with any disk controller (IDE or SCSI) and any disks. The disks do not have to be identical, nor do the controllers. For example, a RAID mirror can be created with one half the mirror being a SCSI disk, and the other an IDE disk. The disks do not even have to be the same size. There are no restrictions on the mixing & matching of disks and controllers.

   This is because Software RAID works with disk partitions, not with the raw disks themselves. The only recommendation is that for RAID levels 1 and 5, the disk partitions that are used as part of the same set be the same size. If the partitions used to make up the RAID 1 or 5 array are not the same size, then the excess space in the larger partitions is wasted (not used).

2. **Q**: I have a twin channel BT-952, and the box states that it supports hardware RAID 0, 1 and 0+1. I have made a RAID set with two drives, the card apparently recognizes them when it's doing it's BIOS startup routine. I've been reading in the driver source code, but found no reference to the hardware RAID support. Anybody out there working on that?

   A: The Mylex/BusLogic FlashPoint boards with RAIDPlus are actually software RAID, not hardware RAID at all. RAIDPlus is only supported on Windows 95 and Windows NT, not on Netware or any of the Unix platforms. Aside from booting and configuration, the RAID support is actually in the OS drivers.

   While in theory Linux support for RAIDPlus is possible, the implementation of RAID-0/1/4/5 in the Linux kernel is much more flexible and should have superior performance, so there's little reason to support RAIDPlus directly.

3. **Q**: I want to run RAID with an SMP box. Is RAID SMP-safe?

   A: "I think so" is the best answer available at the time I write this (April 98). A number of users report that they have been using RAID with SMP for nearly a year, without problems. However, as of April 98 (circa kernel 2.1.9x), the following problems have been noted on the mailing list:

   - Adaptec AIC7xxx SCSI drivers are not SMP safe (General note: Adaptec adapters have a long & lengthly history of problems & flakiness in general. Although they seem to be the most easily available, widespread and cheapest SCSI adapters, they should be avoided. After factoring for time lost, frustration, and corrupted data, Adaptec's will prove to be the costliest mistake you'll ever make. That said, if you have SMP problems with 2.1.88, try the patch ftp://ftp.bero-online.ml.org/pub/linux/aic7xxx-5.0.7-linux21.tar.gz I am not sure if this patch has been pulled into later 2.1.x kernels. For further info, take a look at the mail archives for March 98 at http://www.linuxhq.com/lnxlists/linux-raid/lr_9803_01/ As usual, due to the rapidly changing nature of the latest experimental 2.1.x kernels, the problems described in these mailing lists may or may not have been fixed by the time your read this. Caveat Emptor.)
   - IO-APIC with RAID-0 on SMP has been reported to crash in 2.1.90

7   Modifying an Existing Installation

1. **Q**: Are linear MD's expandable? Can a new hard-drive/partition be added, and the size of the existing file system expanded?

   A: Miguel de Icaza <*miguel@luthien.nuclecu.unam.mx*> writes:

   I changed the ext2fs code to be aware of multiple-devices instead of the regular one device per file system assumption.

   So, when you want to extend a file system, you run a utility program that makes the appropriate changes on the new device (your extra partition) and then you just tell the system to extend the fs using the specified device.

You can extend a file system with new devices at system operation time, no need to bring the system down (and whenever I get some extra time, you will be able to remove devices from the ext2 volume set, again without even having to go to single-user mode or any hack like that).

You can get the patch for 2.1.x kernel from my web page:

```
<http://www.nuclecu.unam.mx/miguel/ext2-volume>
```

2. **Q**: Can I add disks to a RAID-5 array?

> **A**: Currently, (September 1997) no, not without erasing all data. A conversion utility to allow this does not yet exist. The problem is that the actual structure and layout of a RAID-5 array depends on the number of disks in the array.
>
> Of course, one can add drives by backing up the array to tape, deleting all data, creating a new array, and restoring from tape.

3. **Q**: What would happen to my RAID1/RAID0 sets if I shift one of the drives from being `/dev/hdb` to `/dev/hdc`? Because of cabling/case size/stupidity issues, I had to make my RAID sets on the same IDE controller (`/dev/hda` and `/dev/hdb`). Now that I've fixed some stuff, I want to move `/dev/hdb` to `/dev/hdc`. What would happen if I just change the `/etc/mdtab` and `/etc/raid1.conf` files to reflect the new location?

> **A**: For RAID-0/linear, one must be careful to specify the drives in exactly the same order. Thus, in the above example, if the original config is
>
> ```
> mdadd /dev/md0 /dev/hda /dev/hdb
> ```
>
> Then the new config *must* be
>
> ```
> mdadd /dev/md0 /dev/hda /dev/hdc
> ```
>
> For RAID-1/4/5, the drive's "RAID number" is stored in its RAID superblock, and therefore the order in which the disks are specified is not important.
>
> RAID-0/linear does not have a superblock due to it's older design, and the desire to maintain backwards compatibility with this older design.

4. **Q**: Can I convert a two-disk RAID-1 mirror to a three-disk RAID-5 array?

> **A**: Yes. Michael at BizSystems has come up with a clever, sneaky way of doing this. However, like virtually all manipulations of RAID arrays once they have data on them, it is dangerous and prone to human error. **Make a backup before you start**.

```
I will make the following assumptions:
----------------------------------------------
disks
original: hda - hdc
raid1 partitions hda3 - hdc3
array name /dev/md0

new hda - hdc - hdd
raid5 partitions hda3 - hdc3 - hdd3
array name: /dev/md1

You must substitute the appropriate disk and partition numbers for
you system configuration. This will hold true for all config file
examples.
----------------------------------------------
DO A BACKUP BEFORE YOU DO ANYTHING
1) recompile kernel to include both raid1 and raid5
2) install new kernel and verify that raid personalities are present
3) disable the redundant partition on the raid 1 array. If this is a
```

root mounted partition (mine was) you must be more careful.

Reboot the kernel without starting raid devices or boot from rescue
system (raid tools must be available)

```
  start non-redundant raid1
mdadd -r -p1 /dev/md0 /dev/hda3
```

4) configure raid5 but with 'funny' config file, note that there is
   no hda3 entry and hdc3 is repeated. This is needed since the
   raid tools don't want you to do this.

```
# raid-5 configuration
raiddev                 /dev/md1
raid-level              5
nr-raid-disks           3
chunk-size              32

# Parity placement algorithm
parity-algorithm        left-symmetric

# Spare disks for hot reconstruction
nr-spare-disks          0

device                  /dev/hdc3
raid-disk               0

device                  /dev/hdc3
raid-disk               1

device                  /dev/hdd3
raid-disk               2
```

```
 mkraid /etc/raid5.conf
```
5) activate the raid5 array in non-redundant mode

```
mdadd -r -p5 -c32k /dev/md1 /dev/hdc3 /dev/hdd3
```

6) make a file system on the array

```
mke2fs -b {blocksize} /dev/md1
```

recommended blocksize by some is 4096 rather than the default 1024.
this improves the memory utilization for the kernel raid routines and
matches the blocksize to the page size. I compromised and used 2048
since I have a relatively high number of small files on my system.

7) mount the two raid devices somewhere

```
mount -t ext2 /dev/md0 mnt0
mount -t ext2 /dev/md1 mnt1
```

8) move the data

```
cp -a mnt0 mnt1
```

```
     9) verify that the data sets are identical
    10) stop both arrays
    11) correct the information for the raid5.conf file
       change /dev/md1 to /dev/md0
       change the first disk to read /dev/hda3

    12) upgrade the new array to full redundant status
       (THIS DESTROYS REMAINING raid1 INFORMATION)

     ckraid --fix /etc/raid5.conf
```

8   Performance, Tools & General Bone-headed Questions

1. **Q**: I've created a RAID-0 device on `/dev/sda2` and `/dev/sda3`. The device is a lot slower than a single partition. Isn't md a pile of junk?

    A: To have a RAID-0 device running a full speed, you must have partitions from different disks. Besides, putting the two halves of the mirror on the same disk fails to give you any protection whatsoever against disk failure.

2. **Q**: What's the use of having RAID-linear when RAID-0 will do the same thing, but provide higher performance?

    A: It's not obvious that RAID-0 will always provide better performance; in fact, in some cases, it could make things worse. The ext2fs file system scatters files all over a partition, and it attempts to keep all of the blocks of a file contiguous, basically in an attempt to prevent fragmentation. Thus, ext2fs behaves "as if" there were a (variable-sized) stripe per file. If there are several disks concatenated into a single RAID-linear, this will result files being statistically distributed on each of the disks. Thus, at least for ext2fs, RAID-linear will behave a lot like RAID-0 with large stripe sizes. Conversely, RAID-0 with small stripe sizes can cause excessive disk activity leading to severely degraded performance if several large files are accessed simultaneously. In many cases, RAID-0 can be an obvious win. For example, imagine a large database file. Since ext2fs attempts to cluster together all of the blocks of a file, chances are good that it will end up on only one drive if RAID-linear is used, but will get chopped into lots of stripes if RAID-0 is used. Now imagine a number of (kernel) threads all trying to random access to this database. Under RAID-linear, all accesses would go to one disk, which would not be as efficient as the parallel accesses that RAID-0 entails.

3. **Q**: How does RAID-0 handle a situation where the different stripe partitions are different sizes? Are the stripes uniformly distributed?

    A: To understand this, lets look at an example with three partitions; one that is 50MB, one 90MB and one 125MB.

    Lets call D0 the 50MB disk, D1 the 90MB disk and D2 the 125MB disk. When you start the device, the driver calculates 'strip zones'. In this case, it finds 3 zones, defined like this:

```
     Z0 : (D0/D1/D2) 3 x 50 = 150MB  total in this zone
     Z1 : (D1/D2)   2 x 40 = 80MB total in this zone
     Z2 : (D2) 125-50-40 = 35MB total in this zone.
```

    You can see that the total size of the zones is the size of the virtual device, but, depending on the zone, the striping is different. Z2 is rather inefficient, since there's only one disk.

    Since `ext2fs` and most other Unix file systems distribute files all over the disk, you have a 35/265 = 13% chance that a fill will end up on Z2, and not get any of the benefits of striping.

    (DOS tries to fill a disk from beginning to end, and thus, the oldest files would end up on Z0. However, this strategy leads to severe filesystem fragmentation, which is why no one besides DOS does it this way.)

4. **Q**: I have some Brand X hard disks and a Brand Y controller. and am considering using md. Does it significantly increase the throughput? Is the performance really noticeable?

> **A**: The answer depends on the configuration that you use.

Linux MD RAID-0 and RAID-linear performance:

If the system is heavily loaded with lots of I/O, statistically, some of it will go to one disk, and some to the others. Thus, performance will improve over a single large disk. The actual improvement depends a lot on the actual data, stripe sizes, and other factors. In a system with low I/O usage, the performance is equal to that of a single disk.

Linux MD RAID-1 (mirroring) read performance:

MD implements read balancing. That is, the RAID-1 code will alternate between each of the (two or more) disks in the mirror, making alternate reads to each. In a low-I/O situation, this won't change performance at all: you will have to wait for one disk to complete the read. But, with two disks in a high-I/O environment, this could as much as double the read performance, since reads can be issued to each of the disks in parallel. For N disks in the mirror, this could improve performance N-fold.

Linux MD RAID-1 (mirroring) write performance:

Must wait for the write to occur to all of the disks in the mirror. This is because a copy of the data must be written to each of the disks in the mirror. Thus, performance will be roughly equal to the write performance to a single disk.

Linux MD RAID-4/5 read performance:

Statistically, a given block can be on any one of a number of disk drives, and thus RAID-4/5 read performance is a lot like that for RAID-0. It will depend on the data, the stripe size, and the application. It will not be as good as the read performance of a mirrored array.

Linux MD RAID-4/5 write performance:

This will in general be considerably slower than that for a single disk. This is because the parity must be written out to one drive as well as the data to another. However, in order to compute the new parity, the old parity and the old data must be read first. The old data, new data and old parity must all be XOR'ed together to determine the new parity: this requires considerable CPU cycles in addition to the numerous disk accesses.

5. **Q**: What RAID configuration should I use for optimal performance?

> **A**: Is the goal to maximize throughput, or to minimize latency? There is no easy answer, as there are many factors that affect performance:

- operating system - will one process/thread, or many be performing disk access?
- application - is it accessing data in a sequential fashion, or random access?
- file system - clusters files or spreads them out (the ext2fs clusters together the blocks of a file, and spreads out files)
- disk driver - number of blocks to read ahead (this is a tunable parameter)
- CEC hardware - one drive controller, or many?
- hd controller - able to queue multiple requests or not? Does it provide a cache?
- hard drive - buffer cache memory size – is it big enough to handle the write sizes and rate you want?
- physical platters - blocks per cylinder – accessing blocks on different cylinders will lead to seeks.

6. **Q**: What is the optimal RAID-5 configuration for performance?

> **A**: Since RAID-5 experiences an I/O load that is equally distributed across several drives, the best performance will be obtained when the RAID set is balanced by using identical drives, identical controllers, and the same (low) number of drives on each controller.
>
> Note, however, that using identical components will raise the probability of multiple simultaneous failures, for example due to a sudden jolt or drop, overheating, or a power surge during an electrical storm. Mixing brands and models helps reduce this risk.

7. **Q**: What is the optimal block size for a RAID-4/5 array?

A: When using the current (November 1997) RAID-4/5 implementation, it is strongly recommended that the file system be created with `mke2fs -b 4096` instead of the default 1024 byte filesystem block size.

This is because the current RAID-5 implementation allocates one 4K memory page per disk block; if a disk block were just 1K in size, then 75% of the memory which RAID-5 is allocating for pending I/O would not be used. If the disk block size matches the memory page size, then the driver can (potentially) use all of the page. Thus, for a filesystem with a 4096 block size as opposed to a 1024 byte block size, the RAID driver will potentially queue 4 times as much pending I/O to the low level drivers without allocating additional memory.

Note: the above remarks do NOT apply to Software RAID-0/1/linear driver.

Note: the statements about 4K memory page size apply to the Intel x86 architecture. The page size on Alpha, Sparc, and other CPUS are different; I believe they're 8K on Alpha/Sparc (????). Adjust the above figures accordingly.

Note: if your file system has a lot of small files (files less than 10KBytes in size), a considerable fraction of the disk space might be wasted. This is because the file system allocates disk space in multiples of the block size. Allocating large blocks for small files clearly results in a waste of disk space: thus, you may want to stick to small block sizes, get a larger effective storage capacity, and not worry about the "wasted" memory due to the block-size/page-size mismatch.

Note: most "typical" systems do not have that many small files. That is, although there might be thousands of small files, this would lead to only some 10 to 100MB wasted space, which is probably an acceptable tradeoff for performance on a multi-gigabyte disk.

However, for news servers, there might be tens or hundreds of thousands of small files. In such cases, the smaller block size, and thus the improved storage capacity, may be more important than the more efficient I/O scheduling.

Note: there exists an experimental file system for Linux which packs small files and file chunks onto a single block. It apparently has some very positive performance implications when the average file size is much smaller than the block size.

Note: Future versions may implement schemes that obsolete the above discussion. However, this is difficult to implement, since dynamic run-time allocation can lead to dead-locks; the current implementation performs a static pre-allocation.

8. **Q**: How does the chunk size (stripe size) influence the speed of my RAID-0, RAID-4 or RAID-5 device?

A: The chunk size is the amount of data contiguous on the virtual device that is also contiguous on the physical device. In this HOWTO, "chunk" and "stripe" refer to the same thing: what is commonly called the "stripe" in other RAID documentation is called the "chunk" in the MD man pages. Stripes or chunks apply only to RAID 0, 4 and 5, since stripes are not used in mirroring (RAID-1) and simple concatenation (RAID-linear). The stripe size affects both read and write latency (delay), throughput (bandwidth), and contention between independent operations (ability to simultaneously service overlapping I/O requests). Assuming the use of the ext2fs file system, and the current kernel policies about read-ahead, large stripe sizes are almost always better than small stripe sizes, and stripe sizes from about a fourth to a full disk cylinder in size may be best. To understand this claim, let us consider the effects of large stripes on small files, and small stripes on large files. The stripe size does not affect the read performance of small files: For an array of N drives, the file has a 1/N probability of being entirely within one stripe on any one of the drives. Thus, both the read latency and bandwidth will be comparable to that of a single drive. Assuming that the small files are statistically well distributed around the filesystem, (and, with the ext2fs file system, they should be), roughly N times more overlapping, concurrent reads should be possible without significant collision between them. Conversely, if very small stripes are used, and a large file is read sequentially, then a read will issued to all of the disks in the array. For a the read of a single large file, the latency will almost double, as the probability of a block being 3/4'ths of a revolution or farther away will increase. Note, however, the trade-off: the bandwidth could improve almost N-fold for reading a single, large file, as N drives can be reading simultaneously (that is, if read-ahead is used so that all of the disks are kept active). But there is another, counter-acting trade-off: if all of the drives are already busy reading one file, then attempting to read a second or third file at the same time will cause significant contention, ruining performance as the disk ladder algorithms lead to seeks all over the platter. Thus, large stripes will almost always lead to the best performance. The sole exception is the

Mini-HOWTO

case where one is streaming a single, large file at a time, and one requires the top possible bandwidth, and one is also using a good read-ahead algorithm, in which case small stripes are desired.

Note that this HOWTO previously recommended small stripe sizes for news spools or other systems with lots of small files. This was bad advice, and here's why: news spools contain not only many small files, but also large summary files, as well as large directories. If the summary file is larger than the stripe size, reading it will cause many disks to be accessed, slowing things down as each disk performs a seek. Similarly, the current ext2fs file system searches directories in a linear, sequential fashion. Thus, to find a given file or inode, on average half of the directory will be read. If this directory is spread across several stripes (several disks), the directory read (e.g. due to the ls command) could get very slow. Thanks to Steven A. Reisman <*sar@pressenter.com*> for this correction. Steve also adds:

> I found that using a 256k stripe gives much better performance. I suspect that the optimum size would be the size of a disk cylinder (or maybe the size of the disk drive's sector cache). However, disks nowadays have recording zones with different sector counts (and sector caches vary among different disk models). There's no way to guarantee stripes won't cross a cylinder boundary.

The tools accept the stripe size specified in KBytes. You'll want to specify a multiple of if the page size for your CPU (4KB on the x86).

9. **Q**: What is the correct stride factor to use when creating the ext2fs file system on the RAID partition? By stride, I mean the -R flag on the mke2fs command:

```
mke2fs -b 4096 -R stride=nnn  ...
```

What should the value of nnn be?

> **A**: The -R stride flag is used to tell the file system about the size of the RAID stripes. Since only RAID-0,4 and 5 use stripes, and RAID-1 (mirroring) and RAID-linear do not, this flag is applicable only for RAID-0,4,5.
>
> Knowledge of the size of a stripe allows mke2fs to allocate the block and inode bitmaps so that they don't all end up on the same physical drive. An unknown contributor wrote:
>
> > I noticed last spring that one drive in a pair always had a larger I/O count, and tracked it down to the these meta-data blocks. Ted added the -R stride= option in response to my explanation and request for a workaround.
>
> For a 4KB block file system, with stripe size 256KB, one would use -R stride=64. If you don't trust the -R flag, you can get a similar effect in a different way. Steven A. Reisman <*sar@pressenter.com*> writes:
>
> > Another consideration is the filesystem used on the RAID-0 device. The ext2 filesystem allocates 8192 blocks per group. Each group has its own set of inodes. If there are 2, 4 or 8 drives, these inodes cluster on the first disk. I've distributed the inodes across all drives by telling mke2fs to allocate only 7932 blocks per group.
>
> Some mke2fs pages do not describe the [-g blocks-per-group] flag used in this operation.

10. **Q**: Where can I put the md commands in the startup scripts, so that everything will start automatically at boot time?

> **A**: Rod Wilkens <*rwilkens@border.net*> writes:
>
> > What I did is put "mdadd -ar" in the "/etc/rc.d/rc.sysinit" right after the kernel loads the modules, and before the "fsck" disk check. This way, you can put the "/dev/md?" device in the "/etc/fstab". Then I put the "mdstop -a" right after the "umount -a" unmounting the disks, in the "/etc/rc.d/init.d/halt" file.
>
> For raid-5, you will want to look at the return code for mdadd, and if it failed, do a
>
> ```
> ckraid --fix /etc/raid5.conf
> ```
>
> to repair any damage.

11. **Q**: I was wondering if it's possible to setup striping with more than 2 devices in md0? This is for a news server, and I have 9 drives... Needless to say I need much more than two. Is this possible?

A: Yes. (describe how to do this)

12. **Q**: When is Software RAID superior to Hardware RAID?

   A: Normally, Hardware RAID is considered superior to Software RAID, because hardware controllers often have a large cache, and can do a better job of scheduling operations in parallel. However, integrated Software RAID can (and does) gain certain advantages from being close to the operating system.

   For example, ... ummm. Opaque description of caching of reconstructed blocks in buffer cache elided ...

   On a dual PPro SMP system, it has been reported that Software-RAID performance exceeds the performance of a well-known hardware-RAID board vendor by a factor of 2 to 5.

   Software RAID is also a very interesting option for high-availability redundant server systems. In such a configuration, two CPU's are attached to one set or SCSI disks. If one server crashes or fails to respond, then the other server can `mdadd`, `mdrun` and `mount` the software RAID array, and take over operations. This sort of dual-ended operation is not always possible with many hardware RAID controllers, because of the state configuration that the hardware controllers maintain.

13. **Q**: If I upgrade my version of raidtools, will it have trouble manipulating older raid arrays? In short, should I recreate my RAID arrays when upgrading the raid utilities?

   A: No, not unless the major version number changes. An MD version x.y.z consists of three sub-versions:

   ```
   x:      Major version.
   y:      Minor version.
   z:      Patchlevel version.
   ```

   Version x1.y1.z1 of the RAID driver supports a RAID array with version x2.y2.z2 in case (x1 == x2) and (y1 >= y2).

   Different patchlevel (z) versions for the same (x.y) version are designed to be mostly compatible.

   The minor version number is increased whenever the RAID array layout is changed in a way which is incompatible with older versions of the driver. New versions of the driver will maintain compatibility with older RAID arrays.

   The major version number will be increased if it will no longer make sense to support old RAID arrays in the new kernel code.

   For RAID-1, it's not likely that the disk layout nor the superblock structure will change anytime soon. Most all Any optimization and new features (reconstruction, multithreaded tools, hot-plug, etc.) doesn't affect the physical layout.

14. **Q**: The command `mdstop /dev/md0` says that the device is busy.

   A: There's a process that has a file open on `/dev/md0`, or `/dev/md0` is still mounted. Terminate the process or `umount /dev/md0`.

15. **Q**: Are there performance tools?

   A: There is also a new utility called `iotrace` in the `linux/iotrace` directory. It reads `/proc/io-trace` and analyses/plots it's output. If you feel your system's block IO performance is too low, just look at the iotrace output.

16. **Q**: I was reading the RAID source, and saw the value `SPEED_LIMIT` defined as 1024K/sec. What does this mean? Does this limit performance?

   A: `SPEED_LIMIT` is used to limit RAID reconstruction speed during automatic reconstruction. Basically, automatic reconstruction allows you to `e2fsck` and `mount` immediately after an unclean shutdown, without first running `ckraid`. Automatic reconstruction is also used after a failed hard drive has been replaced.

In order to avoid overwhelming the system while reconstruction is occurring, the reconstruction thread monitors the reconstruction speed and slows it down if its too fast. The 1M/sec limit was arbitrarily chosen as a reasonable rate which allows the reconstruction to finish reasonably rapidly, while creating only a light load on the system so that other processes are not interfered with.

17. **Q**: What about "spindle synchronization" or "disk synchronization"?

   A: Spindle synchronization is used to keep multiple hard drives spinning at exactly the same speed, so that their disk platters are always perfectly aligned. This is used by some hardware controllers to better organize disk writes. However, for software RAID, this information is not used, and spindle synchronization might even hurt performance.

18. **Q**: How can I set up swap spaces using raid 0? Wouldn't striped swap ares over 4+ drives be really fast?

   A: Leonard N. Zubkoff replies: It is really fast, but you don't need to use MD to get striped swap. The kernel automatically stripes across equal priority swap spaces. For example, the following entries from /etc/fstab stripe swap space across five drives in three groups:

```
/dev/sdg1      swap      swap      pri=3
/dev/sdk1      swap      swap      pri=3
/dev/sdd1      swap      swap      pri=3
/dev/sdh1      swap      swap      pri=3
/dev/sdl1      swap      swap      pri=3
/dev/sdg2      swap      swap      pri=2
/dev/sdk2      swap      swap      pri=2
/dev/sdd2      swap      swap      pri=2
/dev/sdh2      swap      swap      pri=2
/dev/sdl2      swap      swap      pri=2
/dev/sdg3      swap      swap      pri=1
/dev/sdk3      swap      swap      pri=1
/dev/sdd3      swap      swap      pri=1
/dev/sdh3      swap      swap      pri=1
/dev/sdl3      swap      swap      pri=1
```

19. **Q**: I want to maximize performance. Should I use multiple controllers?

   A: In many cases, the answer is yes. Using several controllers to perform disk access in parallel will improve performance. However, the actual improvement depends on your actual configuration. For example, it has been reported (Vaughan Pratt, January 98) that a single 4.3GB Cheetah attached to an Adaptec 2940UW can achieve a rate of 14MB/sec (without using RAID). Installing two disks on one controller, and using a RAID-0 configuration results in a measured performance of 27 MB/sec.

   Note that the 2940UW controller is an "Ultra-Wide" SCSI controller, capable of a theoretical burst rate of 40MB/sec, and so the above measurements are not surprising. However, a slower controller attached to two fast disks would be the bottleneck. Note also, that most out-board SCSI enclosures (e.g. the kind with hot-pluggable trays) cannot be run at the 40MB/sec rate, due to cabling and electrical noise problems.

   If you are designing a multiple controller system, remember that most disks and controllers typically run at 70-85% of their rated max speeds.

   Note also that using one controller per disk can reduce the likelihood of system outage due to a controller or cable failure (In theory – only if the device driver for the controller can gracefully handle a broken controller. Not all SCSI device drivers seem to be able to handle such a situation without panicking or otherwise locking up).

9   High Availability RAID

1. **Q**: RAID can help protect me against data loss. But how can I also ensure that the system is up as long as possible, and not prone to breakdown? Ideally, I want a system that is up 24 hours a day, 7 days a week, 365 days a year.

A: High-Availability is difficult and expensive. The harder you try to make a system be fault tolerant, the harder and more expensive it gets. The following hints, tips, ideas and unsubstantiated rumors may help you with this quest.

- IDE disks can fail in such a way that the failed disk on an IDE ribbon can also prevent the good disk on the same ribbon from responding, thus making it look as if two disks have failed. Since RAID does not protect against two-disk failures, one should either put only one disk on an IDE cable, or if there are two disks, they should belong to different RAID sets.

- SCSI disks can fail in such a way that the failed disk on a SCSI chain can prevent any device on the chain from being accessed. The failure mode involves a short of the common (shared) device ready pin; since this pin is shared, no arbitration can occur until the short is removed. Thus, no two disks on the same SCSI chain should belong to the same RAID array.

- Similar remarks apply to the disk controllers. Don't load up the channels on one controller; use multiple controllers.

- Don't use the same brand or model number for all of the disks. It is not uncommon for severe electrical storms to take out two or more disks. (Yes, we all use surge suppressors, but these are not perfect either). Heat & poor ventilation of the disk enclosure are other disk killers. Cheap disks often run hot. Using different brands of disk & controller decreases the likelihood that whatever took out one disk (heat, physical shock, vibration, electrical surge) will also damage the others on the same date.

- To guard against controller or CPU failure, it should be possible to build a SCSI disk enclosure that is "twin-tailed": i.e. is connected to two computers. One computer will mount the file-systems read-write, while the second computer will mount them read-only, and act as a hot spare. When the hot-spare is able to determine that the master has failed (e.g. through a watchdog), it will cut the power to the master (to make sure that it's really off), and then fsck & remount read-write. If anyone gets this working, let me know.

- Always use an UPS, and perform clean shutdowns. Although an unclean shutdown may not damage the disks, running ckraid on even small-ish arrays is painfully slow. You want to avoid running ckraid as much as possible. Or you can hack on the kernel and get the hot-reconstruction code debugged ...

- SCSI cables are well-known to be very temperamental creatures, and prone to cause all sorts of problems. Use the highest quality cabling that you can find for sale. Use e.g. bubble-wrap to make sure that ribbon cables to not get too close to one another and cross-talk. Rigorously observe cable-length restrictions.

- Take a look at SSI (Serial Storage Architecture). Although it is rather expensive, it is rumored to be less prone to the failure modes that SCSI exhibits.

- Enjoy yourself, its later than you think.

10 Questions Waiting for Answers

1. **Q**: If, for cost reasons, I try to mirror a slow disk with a fast disk, is the S/W smart enough to balance the reads accordingly or will it all slow down to the speed of the slowest?

2. **Q**: For testing the raw disk thru put... is there a character device for raw read/raw writes instead of /dev/sdaxx that we can use to measure performance on the raid drives?? is there a GUI based tool to use to watch the disk thru-put??

11 Wish List of Enhancements to MD and Related Software

Bradley Ward Allen <*ulmo@Q.Net*> wrote:

Ideas include:

- Boot-up parameters to tell the kernel which devices are to be MD devices (no more "mdadd")

- Making MD transparent to "mount"/"umount" such that there is no "mdrun" and "mdstop"
- Integrating "ckraid" entirely into the kernel, and letting it run as needed

(So far, all I've done is suggest getting rid of the tools and putting them into the kernel; that's how I feel about it, this is a filesystem, not a toy.)

- Deal with arrays that can easily survive N disks going out simultaneously or at separate moments, where N is a whole number > 0 settable by the administrator
- Handle kernel freezes, power outages, and other abrupt shutdowns better
- Don't disable a whole disk if only parts of it have failed, e.g., if the sector errors are confined to less than 50% of access over the attempts of 20 dissimilar requests, then it continues just ignoring those sectors of that particular disk.
- Bad sectors:
  - A mechanism for saving which sectors are bad, someplace onto the disk.
  - If there is a generalized mechanism for marking degraded bad blocks that upper filesystem levels can recognize, use that. Program it if not.
  - Perhaps alternatively a mechanism for telling the upper layer that the size of the disk got smaller, even arranging for the upper layer to move out stuff from the areas being eliminated. This would help with a degraded blocks as well.
  - Failing the above ideas, keeping a small (admin settable) amount of space aside for bad blocks (distributed evenly across disk?), and using them (nearby if possible) instead of the bad blocks when it does happen. Of course, this is inefficient. Furthermore, the kernel ought to log every time the RAID array starts each bad sector and what is being done about it with a "crit" level warning, just to get the administrator to realize that his disk has a piece of dust burrowing into it (or a head with platter sickness).
- Software-switchable disks:

"disable this disk"
would block until kernel has completed making sure there is no data on the disk being shut down that is needed (e.g., to complete an XOR/ECC/other error correction), then release the disk from use (so it could be removed, etc.);

"enable this disk"
would mkraid a new disk if appropriate and then start using it for ECC/whatever operations, enlarging the RAID5 array as it goes;

"resize array"
would respecify the total number of disks and the number of redundant disks, and the result would often be to resize the size of the array; where no data loss would result, doing this as needed would be nice, but I have a hard time figuring out how it would do that; in any case, a mode where it would block (for possibly hours (kernel ought to log something every ten seconds if so)) would be necessary;

"enable this disk while saving data"
which would save the data on a disk as-is and move it to the RAID5 system as needed, so that a horrific save and restore would not have to happen every time someone brings up a RAID5 system (instead, it may be simpler to only save one partition instead of two, it might fit onto the first as a gzip'd file even); finally,

"re-enable disk"
would be an operator's hint to the OS to try out a previously failed disk (it would simply call disable then enable, I suppose).

Other ideas off the net:

- finalrd analog to initrd, to simplify root raid.
- a read-only raid mode, to simplify the above

- Mark the RAID set as clean whenever there are no "half writes" done. – That is, whenever there are no write transactions that were committed on one disk but still unfinished on another disk.

  Add a "write inactivity" timeout (to avoid frequent seeks to the RAID superblock when the RAID set is relatively busy).

Part LXXXIII

"Using Term to Pierce an Internet Firewall"
Barak Pearlmutter

bap@cs.unm.edu
v, 15 July 1996

Directions for using "term" to do network stuff through a TCP firewall that you're not supposed to be able to.

Contents

1   Disclaimer

!!! READ THIS IMPORTANT SECTION !!!

I hereby disclaim all responsibility for this hack. If it backfires on you in any way whatsoever, that's the breaks. Not my fault. If you don't understand the risks inherent in doing this, don't do it. If you use this hack and it allows vicious hackers to break into your company's computers and costs you your job and your company millions of dollars, well that's just tough nuggies. Don't come crying to me.

2   Copyright

All translations, derivative works, or aggregate works incorporating any Linux HOWTO documents must be covered under this copyright notice. That is, you may not produce a derivative work from a HOWTO and impose additional restrictions on its distribution. Exceptions to these rules may be granted under certain conditions; please contact the Linux HOWTO coordinator at the address given below.

In short, we wish to promote dissemination of this information through as many channels as possible. However, we do wish to retain copyright on the HOWTO documents, and would like to be notified of any plans to redistribute the HOWTOs.

If you have questions, please contact Tim Bynum, the Linux HOWTO coordinator, at linux-howto@sunsite.unc.edu via email.

3 Introduction

The "term" program is normally used over a modem or serial line, to allow various host-to-host services to flow along this simple serial connection. However, sometimes it is useful to establish a term connection between two machines that communicate via telnet. The most interesting instance of this is for connecting two hosts which are separated by ethernet firewalls or SOCKS servers. Such firewalls provides facilities for establishing a telnet connection through the firewall, typically by using the SOCKS protocol to allow inside machines to get connections out, and requiring outside users to telnet first to a gateway machine which requires a one-time password. These firewalls make it impossible to, for instance, have X clients on an inside machine communicate with an X server on an outside machine. But, by setting up a term connection, these restrictions can all be bypassed quite conveniently, at the user level.

4 The basic procedure

Setting up a term connection over a telnet substrate is a two-phase process. First your usual telnet client is used to set up a telnet connection and log in. Next, the telnet client is paused and control of the established telnet connection is given to term.

5 Detailed directions

In detail, the process goes like this.

First, from a machine inside the firewall, telnet to a target machine outside the firewall and log in.

Unless you are under linux and will be using the proc filesystem (see below) make sure your shell is an sh style shell. Ie if your default shell is a csh variant, invoke telnet by

```
(setenv SHELL /bin/sh; telnet machine.outside)
```

After logging in, on the remote (outside) machine invoke the command

```
term -r -n off telnet
```

Now break back to the telnet prompt on the local (inside) machine, using ^] or whatever, and use the telnet shell escape command ! to invoke term,

```
telnet> ! term -n on telnet >&3 <&3
```

Et voila!!!

(If you have a variant telnet, you might have to use some other file descriptor than 3; easy to check using strace. But three seems to work on all bsd descendent telnet clients I've tried, under both SunOS 4.x and the usual linux distributions.)

Some telnet clients do not have the ! shell escape command. Eg the telnet client distributed with Slackware 3.0 is one such client. The sources that the Slackware telnet client is supposedly built from,

```
ftp://ftp.cdrom.com:/pub/linux/slackware-3.0/source/n/tcpip/NetKit-B-
0.05.tar.gz
```

have the shell escape command. A simple solution is therefore to obtain these sources and recompile them. This unfortunately is a task I have had no luck with. Plus, if you are running from inside a SOCKS firewall, you will need a SOCKSified telnet client anyway. To that end, I was able to compile a SOCKSified telnet client from

```
ftp://ftp.nec.com/pub/security/socks.cstc/socks.cstc.4.2.tar.gz
```

or if you're outside the USA,

```
ftp://ftp.nec.com/pub/security/socks.cstc/export.socks.cstc.4.2.tar.gz
```

Alternatively, under linux kernels up to 1.2.13, you can pause the telnet with ^]^z, figure out its pid, and invoke

```
term -n on -v /proc/<telnetpid>/fd/3 telnet
```

This doesn't work with newer 1.3.x kernels, which closed some mysterious security hole by preventing access to these fd's by processes other than the owner process and its children.

6 Multiple term sockets

It is a good idea to give the term socket an explicit name. This is the `"telnet"` argument in the invocations of term above. Unless you have the TERMSERVER environment variable set to telnet as appropriate, you invoke term clients with the -t switch, e.g. `"trsh -t telnet"`.

7 The `~/.term/termrc.telnet` init file

I have checked line clarity using linecheck over this medium. I expected it to be completely transparent, but it is not. However, the only bad character seems to be 255. The `~/.term/termrc.telnet` I use (the `.telnet` is the name of the term connection, see above) contains:

```
baudrate off
escape 255
ignore 255
timeout 600
```

Perhaps it could be improved by diddling, I am getting a throughput of only about 30k cps over a long-haul connection through a slow firewall. Ftp can move about 100k cps over the same route. A realistic baudrate might avoid some timeouts.

8 Direction

Obviously, if you are starting from outside the firewall and zitching in using a SecureID card or something, you will want to reverse the roles of the remote vs local servers given above. (If you don't understand what this means, perhaps you are not familiar enough with term to use the trick described in this file responsibly.)

Mini-HOWTO

9 Security

This is not much more of a vulnerability than the current possibility of having a telnet connection hijacked on an unsecured outside machine. The primary additional risk comes from people being able to use the term socket you set up without you even being aware of it. So be careful out there. (Personally, I do this with an outside machine I know to be pretty secure, namely a linux laptop I maintain myself that does not accept any incoming connections.)

Another possibility is to add "socket off" to the remote `~/.term/termrc.telnet`, or add `"-u off"` to invocation of term. This prevents the socket from being hijacked from the remote end, with only a minor loss of functionality.

10 Telnet mode

Be sure the remote telnetd is not in some nasty seven-bit mode. Or if it is, you have to tell term about it when you invoke term, by adding the `-a` switch at both ends. (I sometimes use `"^] telnet> set outbin"` or `"set bin"` or invoke telnet with a `-8` switch to put the connection into eight-bit mode.)

11 Bugs and term wish list

The linecheck program has some problems checking telnet connections sometimes. This is sometimes because it doesn't check the return code of the `read()` call it makes. For network connections, this call to `read()` can return `-1` with an EINTR (interrupted) or EAGAIN (try again) error code. Obviously this should be checked for.

There are a number of features that could ease the use of term over telnet. These primarily relate to an assumption that influenced the design of term, namely that the connection is low bandwidth, low latency, and somewhat noisy.

A telnet connection is in general high bandwidth, high latency, and error free. This means that the connection could be better utilized if (a) the maximum window size was raised, well above the limit imposed by term's `N_PACKETS/2=16`, (b) there was an option to turn off sending and checking packet checksums, and (c) larger packets were permitted when appropriate.

Also, to enhance security, it would be nice to have a term option to log all connections through the socket it monitors to a log file, or to stderr, or both. This would allow one to see if one's term connection is being subverted by nasty hackers on the outside insecure machine.

12 Tricks that don't seem to work

Some telnet clients and servers agree to encrypt their communications, to prevent evesdropping on the connection. Unfortunately, the hack used above (using the network connection that the telnet client has set up while the telnet client is idle) won't work in that case. Instead, one really must go through the telnet client itself, so it can do its encryption. It seems like that requires a simple hack to the telnet client itself, to add a command that runs a process with its stdin and stdout are connected to the live telnet connection. This would also be useful for various 'bots, so perhaps someone has already hacked it up.

13 Related resources

A vaguely related trick is to SOCKSify one's Term library. Details, including patches to SOCKS, are available from Steven Danz <danz@wv.mentorg.com>.

14 Acknowledgments

Thanks for valuable suggestions from:

- Gary Flake <flake@scr.siemens.com>
- Bill Riemers <bcr@physics.purdue.edu>
- Greg Louis <glouis@dynamicro.on.ca>

Extra copy of IMPORTANT DISCLAIMER — BELIEVE IT!!!

I hereby disclaim all responsibility for this hack. If it backfires on you in any way whatsoever, that's the breaks. Not my fault. If you don't understand the risks inherent in doing this, don't do it. If you use this hack and it allows vicious hackers to break into your company's computers and costs you your job and your company millions of dollars, well that's just tough nuggies. Don't come crying to me.

Part LXXXIV

"Token-Ring mini-HOWTO" Mike Eckhoff

mike.e@emissary.aus-etc.com

v4.1, 7 January 1998

This howto is designed to help you install the kernel patch and also try to point out some things to look for. I suggest that you at least browse through all of this document before attempting to install any part of the Token Ring driver for Linux.

Contents

Special Thanks

to Mark Swanson, Peter De Schrijver, David Morris, Paul Norton and everyone else I may have missed who put in their time to write and maintain this driver. Also to packrat for his support of the linux-tr listserv.

1 Copyright and other Jazz

We do not guarantee that this howto will be accurate for your system. Most people who have used it have had very good results in installing Linux on a Token Ring network.

USE THIS HOWTO AT YOUR OWN RISK!!! ... We are not responsible for any problems caused by using this howto.

If you have any problems with the driver that are not talked about in this howto, feel free to email me at...

mike.e@emissary.aus-etc.com

You may also wish to join the Linux on Token Ring Listserv by mailing *majordomo@emissary.aus-etc.com* with the body containing:

```
subscribe linux-tr
```

Mini-HOWTO

2 Hardware requirements

Make sure that you have a Token Ring card that is supported by this driver. Currently the only cards that are supported are those that use the Tropic chipset.

Cards that I personally know to work are:

- 3Com 3C619B Token Link
- 3Com 3C619C Token Link
- HyperRing Classic 16/4
- IBM Turbo 16/4 ISA adapter**
- IBM Token Ring Auto 16/4 ISA adapter
- IBM Token Ring Auto 16/4 adapter /A
- IBM Token Ring 16/4 adapter /A
- IBM Token Ring adapter /A
- IBM Token Ring adapter II (4 Megabit only)
- IBM 16/4 ISA Token Ring card (16bit)
- IBM 16/4 ISA Token Ring card (8bit)
- Madge Blue (100% IBM compatable)

All other 100% IBM compatable shared-ram adapters should also work fine. Please let us know if you find differently.

It is recommended that you use 16KB Shared RAM for the time being.

Cards that may cause problems:

IBM Turbo 16/4 ISA adapter

This adapter will, in fact, work fine with the Linux token ring driver. However, you MUST run the card in Auto 16/4 compatability mode. The simplest way to set this is to use the LANAID disks sent with the card and run the command:

```
LANAIDC /FAST=AUTO16
```

You should then use `LANAIDC` or `LANAID` to configure the card according to documentation.

Token-Ring Network 16/4 Adapter II

This adapter will **NOT** work. Do not confuse this card with the IBM Token Ring adapter II (4mbit) which does. It is a DMA/Busmaster adapter for ISA.

3Com TokenLink Velocity ISA

You may or may not get this one to work. I have had reports of people running it without problems, and others who get errors left and right.

PCI adapters

Currently, none of the IBM PCI adapters are supported.

IBM Auto LanStreamer 16/4 Token-Ring PCI Adapter

Currently not supported, but being worked on. This driver should be Full Duplex as well when completed.

3 Software needed

NOTE:

If you are running a 2.0 distribution of Linux, please jump to the distriubtion specific section of this document. The following is mostly for 1.2 kernels.

This assumes you already have Linux up and running.

Obtain the Token Ring patch from:

```
<ftp://ftp.wayne.esu1.k12.ne.us/pub/Linux/Token-Ring/TokenRing.patch-1.
2.0.gz>
```

Obtain the NetTools patched source from:

```
<ftp://ftp.wayne.esu1.k12.ne.us/pub/Linux/Token-Ring/net-tools-1.2.0.
patched.tar.gz>
```

Create a directory for the patches (such as `/usr/src/patches`) and place the patches there.

```
mkdir /usr/src/patches              central directory for patch storage
mkdir /usr/src/patches/token        place TokenRing patch here
```

4 Installation and setup

NOTE:

These instructions are for patching a 1.2 kernel for token ring support. If you have a 2.0 kernel, you only need to recompile the current source and say "yes" or "module" when asked for token ring support.

1. Install the Token Ring card into the system and configure it for the settings that you want to use. It is a good idea to see if you can use the card through DOS before trying to use it through Linux. If it works in DOS, chances are, it will work in Linux with the same settings. If you have a Plug and Play adapter, if possible, lock the settings once you get them where they work.

2. Make a backup of your linux directory. This is very important in case you need to totally remove the source of the patch from your kernel and go back to your original code.

   ```
   cd /usr/src
   tar cvzhf linuxbak.tar.gz linux
   ```

3. Uncompress the TokenRing patch.

   ```
   cd /usr/src/patches/token
   gzip -d TokenRing.patch-1.2.0.gz
   ```

4. Modify your kernel with the TokenRing patch.

   ```
   cd /usr/src/linux
   patch -p1 < /usr/src/patches/token/TokenRing.patch-1.2.0
   ```

   -or-

   ```
   patch -p1 < <directory-of-patchfile>/TokenRing.patch-1.2.0
   ```

5. Search your kernel for any rejects from the patch and make changes as necessary.

```
find . -name \*.rej -print
```

6. Search your kernel for the orig files and remove them.

```
find . -name \*.orig -print | xargs rm
```

7. Configure your kernel and remake.

NOTE:

> Make sure your swap space is active if you have one.

```
cd /usr/src/linux
make config
```

(The patch should have added two lines to your `config.in` file for the following options)

```
Token Ring support (CONFIG_TR) [y]
```

(and further down the list...)

```
IBM Tropic chipset based adaptor support (CONFIG_IBMTR) [y]
```

```
make dep
make clean
make zImage
```

8. Setup LILO.

First rename your `/vmlinuz` kernel to `vmlinuz.old` then copy the kernel to `/vmlinuz`. On my system this would consist of copying

```
/usr/src/linux/arch/i386/boot/zImage    to    /vmlinuz    and    editing
/etc/lilo.conf to boot that kernel.
```

Now from the prompt run "`lilo`".

9. You should now be able to reboot your system and use the Token Ring card in your computer. Please check the distribution specifc section for any extra configuration information.

5 NetTools installation

The NetTools package contains a lot of the basic utils that you will use to communicate with network devices. This includes programs like `arp`, `rarp`, `route`, `ifconfig` and `netstat`. Since these programs do not know about Token Ring by default, you will need to add the NetTools patch so these utilities can work more efficiently with the Token Ring driver.

NOTICE:

> The current version of NetTools for 1.2.x kernels is 1.2.0. If you are running a 2.0 kernel, your nettools is most likely already up to date. However, you can get the latest source from:

```
<ftp://tapac.inka.de/pub/comp/Linux/networking/NetTools/>
```

1. (1) Copy and Untar the NetTools source into your source directory.

```
cp net-tools-1.2.0.patched.tar.gz  /usr/src
tar -zxvof /usr/src/net-tools-1.2.0.tar.gz
```

2. (5) Make the net-tools files.

```
cd /usr/src/net
make install
```

6 Known problems

I personally have had very few problems with this driver. It has been working perfectly for me for quite some time.

If you have any problems with the driver on a 1.2.x kernel, please update to Linux 2.0. The current version, as of this writing, is 2.0.33. There have been many improvements to the token ring driver since the 1.2 patches and most of them have not been ported back.

Also, you will not have to patch a Linux 2.0 kernel for token ring. The source is already included. However, there are some test patches of the code going into 2.1 available if you would like to use it.

7 Questions and comments

Q:

Can the token ring driver be compiled as a module?

A:

Yes, it can be — and it works rather well. There is an extra parameter that you can use when it is compiled as a module. If you ever need to "spoof" software install programs, such as the redhat boot disks, into configuring your token ring card as an ethernet device (for NFS/FTP installs, etc), you can use the "device" parameter to force a device name other then `tr0`. You will probably have problems if you try this with multiple adapters. It is mostly there to get around a few incompatabiliites. Ex.:

```
/sbin/insmod ibmtr device=eth0
```

Q:

I keep getting an error code "0011". Whats up?

A:

Make sure that your connection to the network is good or that you have a loopback connector on your token ring card. This message just means that it could not open the ring. 99.99% of the times, it is just not plugged into one.

C:

If you have a sound card in your machine, and it sits at IO 0x220, you may end up with a conflict with your token ring adapter at 0xa20. If you notice that a supported adapter does not seem to be working and you have a sound card, please try to either set your token ring card to 0xa24 or move/remove your sound card.

Also...

Here are some email messages that I have received about Token Ring and Linux. In some of the messages, I have removed parts that were not important to save space.

Q:

```
From: "Mr. Chuck Rickard" <chuck@gl.umbc.edu>
Subject: Re: Token Ring Kernel patch

I d/l'd the patch, applied it, and re-compiled. When booting it said,
"tr0: Can't assign device to adapter" and again for tr1.  Any ideas?

Thanks!
```

Chuck Rickard
(chuck@umbc8.umbc.edu)

A:

From: David Morris <dwm@shell.portal.com>

When this is the only message issued, it means that the PIO request for adapter information (see `segment = inb(PIOaddr)` in `ibmtr.c`) was so out of range that there is no TR card at that IO address.

Q:

From: Mike Glover <glover@credit.erin.utoronto.ca>
Subject: Token ring problems.

Thanks for responding. I was starting to thing that I posted incorrectly,
and I was about to post again. Anyway, the following clip is part of my
/var/adm/messages file from when I boot up.

May 2 10:03:14 linux kernel: tr0: Unable to assign adapter to device.
May 2 10:03:14 linux kernel: tr1: Unable to assign adapter to device.

The section, tr0: Unable to assign adapter device. is what kin-
da confuses
me. The documentation is slim at best so I did-
n't know what to do with
the message. I know I didn't assign any token ring information,
and I didn't know where to do it.

The hardware:
            Its a PC clone (Dell OMNIPLEX 560 to be exact)
            The token ring card is a Olicom 16/4 Adapter.

I have DOS token ring drivers and it snaps into the network, so there is
nothing wrong with the card. I think, I am just missing something really
small in the config on the Linux side.

A:

The Olicom 16/4 Adapter does not use the Tropic Chipset. Try using one of the cards that are listed at the top of the HOWTO.

Q:

From: Mike Glover <glover@credit.erin.utoronto.ca>
Subject: Found an IBM card...

I found myself an IBM token ring card and I got a little further,
but still not luck. (I did change /etc/rc.d/rc.inet1 ifconfig entry
from eth0 to tr0)

Anyway, here is part of the /var/adm/messages file:

```
May  2 16:23:07 linux kernel: IPX Portions Copyright (c) 1995 Calder-
a, Inc.
May  2 16:23:07 linux kernel: tr0: PIOaddr:  a20 seg/intr: b8 m-
mio base:
    000dc000 intr: 0
May  2 16:23:07 linux kernel: tr0: Channel ID string not found for
    PIOaddr: a20
May  2 16:23:07 linux kernel: tr0: Expected for ISA:
    5049434f3631313039393020
May  2 16:23:07 linux kernel: tr0:                 found:
    00090200302111100018200
May  2 16:23:07 linux kernel: tr0: Expected for MCA:
    4d4152533363583435313820
May  2 16:23:07 linux kernel: tr0: Unable to as-
sign adapter to device.
May  2 16:23:07 linux kernel: tr1: Unable to as-
sign adapter to device.
May  2 16:23:07 linux kernel: PPP: version 0.2.7 (4 channels)
    NEW_TTY_DRIVERS OPTIMIZE_FLAGS
```

```
Does this tell you anything. It tells me little.
```

A:

```
From: David Morris <dwm@shell.portal.com>
```

This message means either a memory conflict with the MMIO area or a TR card which is not compatible with the driver (at least the signature isn't known).

Q:

```
From: Mike Glover <glover@credit.erin.utoronto.ca>
Subject: Almost there...
```

```
The following sample is what I'm getting on my messages file:
```

```
May  3 14:50:24 linux kernel: tr0: now opening the board...
May  3 14:50:24 linux kernel: tr0: board opened...
May  3 15:11:47 linux kernel: tr0: Arrg. Transmit-
ter busy for more than 50 msec.
    Donald resets adapter, but resetting
May  3 15:11:47 linux kernel:  the IBM tokenring adapter takes a
    long time.  It might not even help when the
May  3 15:11:47 linux kernel:  ring is very busy, so we just wait a
    little longer and hope for the best.
May  3 15:11:47 linux kernel: tr0: Arrg. Transmit-
ter busy for more than 50 msec.
    Donald resets adapter, but resetting
May  3 15:11:47 linux kernel:  the IBM tokenring adapter takes a
    long time.  It might not even help when the
May  3 15:11:47 linux kernel:  ring is very busy, so we just wait a
    little longer and hope for the best.
May  3 15:11:47 linux kernel: tr0: Arrg. Transmit-
ter busy for more than 50 msec.
    Donald resets adapter, but resetting
```

Mini-HOWTO

The Arrg entry only comes when I telnet, rlogin or ftp to a remote machine. Once that happens, the connection hangs big time. I took out all the other hardware (which was 1 SCSI card) and tried running the card all by itself. Same thing, so it eliminates hardware IRQ's from getting into a yelling match. The following are the DIP switches on the card:

```
1     Up      |
2     Down    |
3     Down    |         According to the manual this sets the
4     Up      |         base address to CC000 Which is fine for
5     Up      |         my machine.
6     Down    |
7     Down    +         This sets the IRQ to 2. Which is also fine
8     Down    +
9     Up      X         Primary Lan adapter. Which it is.
10    Up      =         16 KB shared RAM size. This OK?
11    Down    =
12    Up      #         16 Mbps Data rate.
```

I was wondering if it is in fact the dip switches, or the way I have configured my route table and other network info.

ttfn,
Mike

A:

The Arrg problem is pretty much taken care of in the 2.0 kernels. All of the patches have not been ported back to 1.2, and I doubt that they will be. If you get excessive Arrg messages, do yourself a favour and move to Linux 2.0.

8   Distribution Specific Installations

8.1   Slackware 96

If you have not already ran "netconfig" on your system, do so now. Setup your machine just as if it were on Ethernet.

Edit your /etc/rc.d/rc.inet1 scripts to point to the tr0 device rather than the eth0 device.

You should have a line that looks like

```
/sbin/ifconfig eth0 ${IPADDR} broadcast ${BROADCAST} netmask ${NETMASK}
```

Change this line to read

```
/sbin/ifconfig tr0 ${IPADDR} broadcast ${BROADCAST} netmask ${NETMASK}
```

8.2   RedHat 4.0+

The RedHat distribution of Linux has a wonderful Xwindows control panel for configuring modules and devices. If you have added a token ring adapter to a standard RedHat installation, there should already be token ring support compiled in as a module. Try to:

```
modprobe ibmtr
```

and see what you come up with. Chances are, if you have a supported adapter, you will be ready to go.

The easiest way to configure your interface would be to use the control-panel. You will first want to go to the kernel module control and instruct it to load a new network device for token ring. It should then start to autoload the ibmtr driver on boot. You will then want to jump over to network configuration and add a new device, `tr`, and give it an ip address, etc.

You should then be able to restart and go with Linux and Token Ring on RedHat 4.0+.

Please note that these RedHat instructions came from the top of my head. I havn't had to modify any of my RedHat systems for quite some time and am writing this from memory. Either way, they should be able to get you where you need to go.

"The VPN HOWTO " Arpad Magosanyi

<mag@bunuel.tii.matav.hu>
v0.2, 7 August 1997

1 Changes

The 'no controlling tty problem' -> -o 'BatchMode yes' by Zot O'Connor <zot@crl.com>

warning about kernel 2.0.30 by mag

2 Blurb

This is the Linux VPN howto, a collection of information on how to set up a Virtual Protected Network in Linux (and other unices in general).

2.1 Copyright

This document is part of the Linux HOWTO project. The copyright notice is the following: Unless otherwise stated, Linux HOWTO documents are copyrighted by their respective authors. Linux HOWTO documents may be reproduced and distributed in whole or in part, in any medium physical or electronic, as long as this copyright notice is retained on all copies. Commercial redistribution is allowed and encouraged; however, the author would like to be notified of any such distributions. All translations, derivative works, or aggregate works incorporating any Linux HOWTO documents must be covered under this copyright notice. That is, you may not produce a derivative work from a HOWTO and impose additional restrictions on its distribution. Exceptions to these rules may be granted under certain conditions; please contact the Linux HOWTO coordinator at the address given below. In short, we wish to promote dissemination of this information through as many channels as possible. However, we do wish to retain copyright on the HOWTO documents, and would like to be notified of any plans to redistribute the HOWTOs. If you have questions, please contact Tim Bynum, the Linux HOWTO coordinator, at linux-howto@sunsite.unc.edu via email.

2.2 Disclaimer

As usual: the author not responsible for any damage. For the correct wording, see the relevant part of the GNU GPL 0.1.1

2.3 Disclaimer

We are dealing with security: you are not safe if you haven't got good security policy, and other rather boring things.

2.4 Credits

Thanks to all of who has written the tools used.

Thanks to Zot O'Connor <zot@crl.com> for pointing out the "no controlling tty" problem, and it's solution.

2.5   State of this document

This is very preliminary. You should have thorough knowledge of administrating IP, at least some knowledge of firewalls, ppp and ssh. You should know them anyway if you want to set up a VPN. I just decided to write down my experiences not to forget them. There are possibly some security holes indeed. To be fair I've tried it on hosts configured as routers not firewalls, saying: It's simple from that point.

2.6   Related documentations

- The Linux Firewall-HOWTO /usr/doc/HOWTO/Firewall-HOWTO
- The Linux PPP-HOWTO /usr/doc/HOWTO/PPP-HOWTO.gz
- The ssh documentations /usr/doc/ssh/*
- The Linux Network Admins' Guide
- NIST Computer Security Special Publications http://csrc.ncsl.nist.gov/nistpubs/
- Firewall list (majordomo@greatcircle.com)

3   Introduction

As firewalls are in more and more widely use in internet and intranet security, the ability to do nice VPNs is important. Here are my experiences. Comments are welcome.

3.1   Naming conventions

I will use the terms "master firewall" and "slave firewall", though making a VPN has nothing to do with client-server architecture. I simply refer to them as the active and passive participants of the connection's setup. The host which is starts the setup will be referred as the master, and the passive participant will be the slave.

4   Doing it

4.1   Planning

Before you start to set up your system, you should know the networking details. I assume you have two firewalls protecting one intranet per firewall, and they are both connected to the internet. So now you should have two network interfaces (at least) per firewall. Take a sheet of paper, write down their IP addresses and network mask. You will need one more IP adresses per firewall for the VPN you want to do now. Those addresses should be outside of your existing subnets. I suggest using addresses from the "private" address ranges. They are the followings:

- 10.0.0.0 - 10.255.255.255
- 172.16.0.0 - 172.31.255.255
- 192.168.0.0 - 192.168.255.255

For the sake of example, here's a sample configuration: The two bastions are called fellini and polanski. They have one interface for the internet (-out), one for the intranet (-in), and one for the vpn (-vpn). The addresses and netmasks:

- fellini-out: 193.6.34.12 255.255.255.0
- fellini-in: 193.6.35.12 255.255.255.0
- fellini-vpn: 192.168.0.1 point-to-point
- polanski-out: 193.6.36.12 255.255.255.0
- polanski-in: 193.6.37.12 255.255.255.0

- polanski-vpn: 192.168.0.2 point-to-point

So we have the plan.

4.2 Gathering the tools

You will need a

- Linux firewall
- kernel
- very minimal configuration
- ipfwadm
- fwtk
- Tools for the VPN
- ssh
- pppd
- sudo
- pty-redir

Current versions:

- kernel: 2.0.29 Use a stable kernel, and it must be newer than 2.0.20, because the ping'o'death bug. At the time of writing 2.0.30 is the last "stable" kernel, but it has some bugs. If you want to have the fast and cool networking code introduced in it, try a prepatch. the 3rd is working for me nicely.

- base system: I prefer Debian. YMMV. You absolutely don't want to use any big packages, and you never even tought of using sendmail, of course. You also definitely don't want to enable telnet, ftp, and the 'r' commands (as usual in case of any other unix hosts).

- ipfwadm: I've used 2.3.0

- fwtk: I've used 1.3

- ssh: >= 1.2.20. There are problems with the underlying protocol in the older versions.

- pppd: I've used 2.2.0f for the tests, but I'm not sure if is it secure, this is why I turned the setuid bit off, and used sudo to launch it.

- sudo: 1.5.2 the newest I am aware of

- pty-redir: It is written by me. Try ftp://ftp.vein.hu/ssa/contrib/mag/pty-redir-0.1.tar.gz. Its version number is 0.1 now. Tell me it there is any problem with it.

4.3 Compile and install

Compile or otherwise install the gathered tools. Look at every one's documentation (and the firewall-howto) for details. Now we have the tools.

4.4 Configure the other subsystems

Configure your firewall rules, etc. You need to enable ssh traffic between the two firewll hosts. It means a connection to port 22 on the slave from the master. Start sshd on the slave and verify if you can login. This step is untested, please tell me your results.

4.5   Set up the accounts for the VPN

Create an account on the slave firewall use your favourite tool (e.g. vi, mkdir, chown, chmod) you might create an account on the master also, but I think you want to set up the connection at boot time, so your ordinary root account will do. Can anyone point out risks on using the root account on the master?

4.6   Generate an ssh key for your master account

Use the ssh-keygen program. Set empty password for the private key if you want to do automatic setup of the VPN.

4.7   Set up automatic ssh login for the slave account

Copy the newly generated public key in the slave account under .ssh/authorized_keys, and set up file permissions like the following:

```
drwx------  2 slave slave 1024 Apr  7 23:49 ./
drwx------  4 slave slave 1024 Apr 24 14:05 ../
-rwx------  1 slave slave  328 Apr  7 03:04 authorized_keys
-rw-------  1 slave slave  660 Apr 14 15:23 known_hosts
-rw-------  1 slave slave  512 Apr 21 10:03 random_seed
```

The first row being ~slave/.ssh, and the second is ~slave.

4.8   Tighten ssh security on the bastions.

It means the followings on my setup in sshd_conf:

```
PermitRootLogin no
IgnoreRhosts yes
StrictModes yes
QuietMode no
FascistLogging yes
KeepAlive yes
RhostsAuthentication no
RhostsRSAAuthentication no
RSAAuthentication yes
PasswordAuthentication no
PermitEmptyPasswords no
```

Password authentication is turned off, so login is only possible with authorized keys. (You've turned off telnet and the 'r' commands of course).

4.9   Enable execution of ppp and route for both accounts.

As the master account is the root in my case, it has nothing to do. For the slave account, the following lines appear in /etc/sudoers:

```
Cmnd_Alias VPN=/usr/sbin/pppd, /usr/local/vpn/route
slave ALL=NOPASSWD: VPN
```

As you can see, I am using some scripts to set up ppp and the routing tables on the slave host.

4.10 Do the scripting

On the master host there is a full-blown init script I am using:

```
#! /bin/sh
# skeleton       example file to build /etc/init.d/ scripts.
#                This file should be used to construct scripts for /etc/init.d.
#
#                Written by Miquel van Smoorenburg <miquels@cistron.nl>.
#                Modified for Debian GNU/Linux
#                by Ian Murdock <imurdock@gnu.ai.mit.edu>.
#
# Version:       @(#)skeleton  1.6  11-Nov-1996  miquels@cistron.nl
#

PATH=/usr/local/sbin:/sbin:/bin:/usr/sbin:/usr/bin:/usr/bin/X11:
PPPAPP=/home/slave/ppp
ROUTEAPP=/home/slave/route
PPPD=/usr/sbin/pppd
NAME=VPN
REDIR=/usr/local/bin/pty-redir
SSH=/usr/bin/ssh
MYPPPIP=192.168.0.1
TARGETIP=192.168.0.2
TARGETNET=193.6.37.0
MYNET=193.6.35.0
SLAVEWALL=polanski-out
SLAVEACC=slave

test -f $PPPD || exit 0

set -e

case "$1" in
  start)
        echo setting up vpn
        $REDIR $SSH -o 'Batchmode yes' -t -l $SLAVEACC $SLAVEWALL sudo $PPPAP-
P >/tmp/device
        TTYNAME='cat /tmp/device'
echo tty is $TTYNAME
        sleep 10s
        if [ ! -z $TTYNAME ]
        then
        $PPPD $TTYNAME ${MYPPPIP}:${TARGETIP}
        else
                echo FAILED!
                logger "vpn setup failed"
        fi
        sleep 5s
        route add -net $TARGETNET gw $TARGETIP
        $SSH -o 'Batchmode yes' -l $SLAVEACC $SLAVEWALL sudo $ROUTEAPP
    ;;
  stop)
ps -ax|grep "ssh -t -l $SLAVEACC "|grep -v grep|awk '{print $1}'|xargs kill
    ;;
```

Mini-HOWTO

```
*)
   # echo "Usage: /etc/init.d/$NAME {start|stop|reload}"
   echo "Usage: /etc/init.d/$NAME {start|stop}"
   exit 1
   ;;
esac

exit 0
```

The slave uses one script for routing setup (/usr/local/vpn/route):

```
#!/bin/bash
/sbin/route add -net 193.6.35.0 gw 192.168.0.1
```

and its .ppprc consists of the following:

```
passive
```

5 Look at what's happening:

The master logs in into the slave, starts pppd, and redirects this all thing into a local pty. It consists of the following steps:

- allocating a new pty
- sshing into the slave
- running pppd on the slave
- the master runs pppd in this local pty
- and sets up the routing table on the client.

There are (not very tight) timing considerations involved, this is why that 'sleep 10s'.

6 Doing it by hand.

6.1 Logging in

You've already tried if ssh works well, aren't you? If the slave refuses to log you in, read the logs. Perhaps there are problems with file permissions or the sshd setup.

6.2 Firing up ppp

Log in into slave, and issue:

```
sudo /usr/sbin/pppd passive
```

You should see garbage coming at this point. If it works good, if not, there is some problem either with sudo, either with pppd. Look what the commands had said, and at the logs and at the */etc/ppp/options*, and the *.ppprc* file. If it works, write this 'passive' word into .ppprc, and try again. To get rid off the garbage and continue working, press enter,'˜' and '˜Z'. You should have the master's prompt now, and kill %1. See the section about tuning if you want to know more of the escape character.

6.3 Together the two

Well, then

```
ssh -l slave polanski sudo /usr/sbin/pppd
```

should work also, and deliver the garbage right into your face.

6.4 Pty redirecting

Try to redirect this whole thing this time:

```
/usr/local/bin/pty-redir /usr/bin/ssh -l slave polanski sudo /usr/sbin/pppd
```

Nice long sentence isn't it? You should use the full path into the ssh executable, as the pty-redir program allows only this form for security reasons. Now you've got a device name from the program. Let's say, you've got */dev/ttyp0* You can use the ps command to look what has happened. Look for 'p0'

6.5 Is anything on the device?

Try

```
/usr/sbin/pppd /dev/ttyp0 local 192.168.0.1:192.168.0.2
```

to establish the connection. Look at the output of the ifconfig command to see if the device has established, and use ping to check your virtual net.

6.6 Setting up the routes

Set up the routes on the master host, and on the slave also. Now you should be able to ping one host in one intranet from other host in the other intranet. Set up the additional firewalling rules. Now as you have the VPN, you can set up the rules concerning the connectivity of the two intranets.

7 Tuning

7.1 Configuration tuning

As I said this HOWTO is mainly a quick memo on how I had set up a VPN. There are things in the configuration I didn't experiment yet. These things will go into their place when I try them, or anyone tells me "it works in the following way" The most important thing is that the connection ppp uses is not 8-bit yet. I believe it has something to do either with ssh configuration or the pty setup. In this configuration ssh uses the tilde (˜) character as an escape character. It might stop or slow down the communication, as any newline-tilde sequence causes ssh to give a prompt. Ssh documentation said: <On most systems, setting the escape character to "none" will also make the session transparent even if a tty is used.> The corresponding flag to ssh is '-e', and you can also set it in the configuration file.

7.2 Bandwith vs. cicles

Creating anything virtual comes with utilization of real-world resources. A VPN eats up bandwidth and computing resources. The goal would be to get balance between the two. You can tune it with the '-C' switch or the 'Compression-

Level' option. You might try using another cipher, but I don't recommend it. Also note that the round-trip-time can be longer if you use better compression. Any experiments on it are welcome.

8 Vulnerability analisis

I try to cover here the vulnerability issues arising from this particular setup and VPNs in general. Any comments are warmly welcome.

- sudo: Well, I'm excessively using sudo. I believe it's still safer than using setuid bits. It's still a back-draw of Linux that it hasn't got more fine-grained access control. Waiting for POSIX.6 compatibility <http://www.xarius.demon.co.uk/software/posix6/>. What is worse, there are shell scripts which are getting called through sudo. Bad enough. Any idea out there?

- pppd: It runs suid root also. It can be configured by user's .ppprc. There might be some nice buffer overruns in it. The bottom line: secure your slave account as tightly as you can.

- ssh: Beware that ssh older than 1.2.20 has security holes. What is worse, we made a configuration such when the master account had been compromised, the slave account is also compromised, and wide open to attacks using the two sudoed programs. It is because I've choosen not to have password on the master's secret key to enable automatic setup of the VPN.

- firewall: With inproperly set firewall rules on one bastion, you open both of the intranets. I recommend using IP masquerading (as setting up incorrect routes is a bit less trivial), and doing hard control on the VPN interfaces.

Index

Index

Iodine-131 decays rapidly, with a half-life of 8 days. Cesium-137, however, decays more slowly, with a half-life of 30 years.

(75) If an accident releases iodine-131, therefore, it is a short-term concern. The amount of radiation emitted will be high but will drop rapidly. After two months, less than one percent of the original iodine-131 will remain. An accidental release of cesium-137, however, is a long-term concern. The

(80) amount of radiation emitted at first will be low but will drop slowly. It will take about 200 years for the amount of cesium-137 remaining to drop below one percent. The total amount of radiation emitted in both cases will be the same, for the same amount

(85) of initial material. The difference lies in whether the radiation is all released rapidly at high levels in a short time, or is released slowly at low levels, over a long time span.

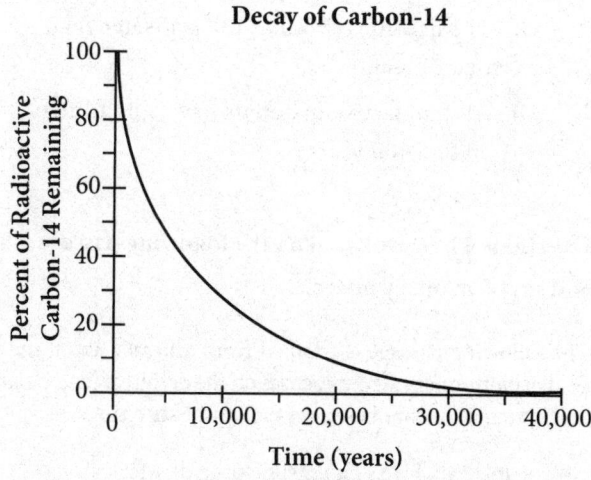

Decay of Carbon-14

This data is from the *Journal of Research of the National Bureau of Standards*, Vol. 64, No. 4, April 1951, pp. 328 – 333.

32. Based on the information in Passage 1, which of the following could be dated using carbon-14 dating?

A) An iron pot found in a cave

B) A rock at the bottom of a quarry

C) An arrowhead made from bone

D) The remains of a house made from stone

33. Which choice provides the best evidence for the answer to the previous question?

A) Lines 10-12 ("For example . . . carbon-13")

B) Lines 28-31 ("Living plants . . . dioxide")

C) Lines 31-34 ("After the plant . . . rate")

D) Lines 39-42 ("Carbon-14 dating . . . animals")

34. As used in line 26, "decay" most nearly means

A) yield.

B) deteriorate.

C) discharge.

D) circulated.

35. Which statement best describes the relationship between carbon-12 and carbon-14 in living tissue?

A) There is more carbon-14 than carbon-12.

B) There is more carbon-12 than carbon-14.

C) The ratio of carbon-12 to carbon-14 is constant.

D) The ratio of carbon-12 to carbon-14 fluctuates greatly.

36. Which choice provides the best evidence for the answer to the previous question?

A) Lines 13-14 ("Some combinations . . . time")

B) Lines 25-26 ("Carbon-14 atoms . . . decay")

C) Lines 28-31 ("Living plants . . . carbon dioxide")

D) Lines 31-34 ("After the plant . . . rate")

Practice Tests

37. In Passage 2, the author refers to an accident that results in the release of iodine-131 as a "short-term concern" (line 75) because the initial amount of radiation released is

A) low but will drop slowly.

B) high but will drop quickly.

C) low and will drop quickly.

D) high and will drop slowly.

38. According to Passage 2, living tissue exposed to radioactive material can

A) be destroyed by high levels of heat caused by the radiation.

B) become radioactive itself and damage surrounding tissue.

C) suffer injury when the cells' components are damaged.

D) be killed by extra protons released by the radioactive material.

39. As used in line 77, "original" most nearly means

A) earliest.

B) unique.

C) unusual.

D) critical.

40. According to Passage 2, scientists use the half-life of radioactive material to determine the

A) amount of danger posed by radiation immediately following a nuclear accident.

B) likelihood of a nuclear accident involving the release of radioactive material at any given location.

C) amount of radiation contained in a sample of iodine-131 or cesium-137 used in nuclear reactions.

D) length of time that must pass until an area is safe after the release of radioactive material.

41. Which generalization about the study of physics is supported by both passages?

A) The study of atomic and nuclear physics can have many applications in a variety of fields.

B) The study of physics has helped revolutionize how archaeologists study artifacts.

C) Scientists use physics to keep people and wildlife safe following a nuclear accident.

D) Scientists use different concepts to date ancient items and assess danger from nuclear accidents.

42. Based on the graph and the information in the passages, which statement is accurate?

A) Carbon-14 has a half-life of about 5,400 years.

B) The half-life of carbon-14 is similar to that of cesium-137.

C) The half-life of iodine-131 is greater than that of cesium-137.

D) All radioactive materials have a half-life of 30 to 5,400 years.

Questions 43-52 are based on the following passage and supplementary material.

The following passage is adapted from an essay about the field of biomimicry, which focuses on the design of materials and systems that are based on biological structures.

In 1948, Swiss chemist George de Mestral was impressed with the clinging power of burrs snagged in his dog's fur and on his pant legs after
Line he returned from a hike. While examining the
(5) burrs under a microscope, he observed many hundreds of small fibers that grabbed like hooks. He experimented with replicas of the burrs and eventually invented Velcro®, a synthetic clinging fabric that was first marketed as "the zipperless
(10) zipper." In the 1960s, NASA used de Mestral's invention on space suits, and now, of course, we see it everywhere.

GO ON TO THE NEXT PAGE

You might say that de Mestral was the father of biomimicry, an increasingly essential field that
(15) studies nature, looking for efficiencies in materials and systems, and asks the question "How can our homes, our electronics, and our cities work better?" As one biomimetics company puts it: "Nature is the largest laboratory that ever existed and ever will."

(20) Architecture is one field that is constantly exploring new ways to incorporate biomimicry. Architects have studied everything from beehives to beaver dams to learn how to best use materials, geometry, and physics in buildings. Termite
(25) mounds, for example, very efficiently regulate temperature, humidity, and airflow, so architects in Zimbabwe are working to apply what they've learned from termite mounds to human-made structures.

Says Michael Pawlyn, author of *Biomimicry in*
(30) *Architecture*, "If you look beyond the nice shapes in nature and understand the principles behind them, you can find some adaptations that can lead to new, innovative solutions that are radically more resource-efficient. It's the direction we need to take
(35) in the coming decades."

Designers in various professional fields are drawing on biomimicry; for example, in optics, scientists have examined the surface of insect eyes in hopes of reducing glare on handheld device
(40) screens. Engineers in the field of robotics worked to replicate the property found in a gecko's feet that allows adhesion to smooth surfaces.

Sometimes what scientists learn from nature isn't more advanced, but simpler. The abalone
(45) shrimp, for example, makes its shell out of calcium carbonate, the same material as soft chalk. It's not a rare or complex substance, but the unique arrangement of the material in the abalone's shell makes it extremely tough. The walls of the shell
(50) contain microscopic pieces of calcium carbonate stacked like bricks, which are bound together using proteins just as concrete mortar is used. The result is a shell three thousand times harder than chalk and as tough as Kevlar® (the material used in
(55) bullet-proof vests).

Often it is necessary to look at the nanoscale structures of a living material's exceptional properties in order to re-create it synthetically. Andrew Parker, an evolutionary biologist, looked at the skin of the
(60) thorny devil (a type of lizard) under a scanning electron microscope, in search of the features that let the animal channel water from its back to its mouth.

Examples like this from the animal world abound. Scientists have learned that colorful birds
(65) don't always have pigment in their wings but are sometimes completely brown; it's the layers of keratin in their wings that produce color. Different colors, which have varying wavelengths, reflect differently through keratin. The discovery of this
(70) phenomenon can be put to use in creating paints and cosmetics that won't fade or chip. At the same time, paint for outdoor surfaces can be made tougher by copying the structures found in antler bone. Hearing aids are being designed to capture
(75) sound as well as the ears of the *Ormia* fly do. And why can't we have a self-healing material like our own skin? Researchers at the Beckman Institute at the University of Illinois are creating just that; they call it an "autonomic materials system." A raptor's
(80) feathers, a whale's fluke, a mosquito's proboscis—all have functional features we can learn from.

The driving force behind these innovations, aside from improved performance, is often improved energy efficiency. In a world where
(85) nonrenewable energy resources are dwindling and carbon emissions threaten the planet's health, efficiency has never been more important. Pawlyn agrees: "For me, biomimicry is one of the best sources of innovation to get to a world of zero
(90) waste because those are the rules under which biological life has had to exist."

Biomimicry is a radical field and one whose practitioners need to be radically optimistic, as Pawlyn is when he says, "We could use natural
(95) products such as cellulose, or even harvest carbon from the atmosphere to create bio-rock."

Tiny florets in a sunflower's center are arranged in an interlocking spiral, which inspired engineers in the design of this solar power plant. Mirrors positioned at the same angle as the florets bounce light toward the power plant's central tower.

Adapted from David Ferris, "Innovate: Solar Designs from Nature." © 2014 by Sierra Club.

43. The central focus of the passage is

A) the field of biomimicry, which is the study of materials and systems found in nature and replicated in ways that benefit people.

B) the work of George de Mestral, the Swiss chemist who invented Velcro® after observing burrs under a microscope.

C) the ways in which architects use termite mounds as models for human-made structures in Zimbabwe.

D) how scientists are seeking ways to improve energy efficiency as nonrenewable energy sources decline.

44. Which choice provides the best evidence for the answer to the previous question?

A) Lines 1-6 ("In 1948 . . . hooks")

B) Lines 13-19 ("You might say . . . ever will'")

C) Lines 24-28 ("Termite mounds . . . structures")

D) Lines 82-87 ("The driving . . . more important")

45. The author includes a quote in paragraph 4 in order to

A) explain why architects are looking to biomimicry for solutions in architecture.

B) provide an argument for more scientists to study biomimicry.

C) give an explanation as to why someone might choose a career in architecture.

D) provide a counterargument to the author's central claim.

46. Based on the information in paragraph 6, how does the shell of an abalone shrimp compare with soft chalk?

A) The essential building blocks are arranged in a similar manner, but the material that makes up the shell of an abalone shrimp is harder.

B) Both are made from the same essential building blocks, but the shell of the abalone shrimp is much harder because of the manner in which the materials are arranged.

C) The essential building blocks of both are the same, but the abalone shrimp shell is harder because the soft chalk lacks a protein binding the materials together.

D) They are made from different essential building blocks, but they have a similar hardness because the materials are arranged in a similar manner.

47. In paragraph 9, what is the function of the quote from Pawlyn about efficiency?

   A) To convince readers that Pawlyn is an expert in his field

   B) To prove that great strides are being made in creating products that do not generate waste

   C) To demonstrate the limits of what biomimicry can achieve

   D) To support the statement that energy efficiency "has never been more important"

48. In line 31, "principles" most nearly means

   A) sources.

   B) attitudes.

   C) standards.

   D) concepts.

49. Of the following, the most reasonable inference from the passage is that

   A) more scientists will utilize solutions developed through biomimicry in the future.

   B) the field of biomimicry will eventually decline as more nonrenewable resources are discovered.

   C) scientists will leave the fields they are currently working in and begin research in biomimicry.

   D) doctors will create a self-healing skin called an "autonomic materials system" using methods based in biomimicry.

50. Which choice provides the best evidence for the answer to the previous question?

   A) Lines 36-40 ("Designers . . . screens")

   B) Lines 56-58 ("Often it is . . . synthetically")

   C) Lines 63-67 ("Examples like . . . color")

   D) Lines 92-96 ("Biomimicry . . . bio-rock")

51. As used in line 92, "radical" most nearly means

   A) pervasive.

   B) drastic.

   C) essential.

   D) revolutionary.

52. The graphic and caption that accompany this passage help illustrate how biomimicry can be used to

   A) make a solar plant more attractive.

   B) increase waste generated by energy sources.

   C) improve the efficiency of existing technologies.

   D) replicate a pattern common in nature.

Practice Tests

IF YOU FINISH BEFORE TIME IS CALLED, YOU MAY CHECK YOUR WORK ON THIS SECTION ONLY. DO NOT TURN TO ANY OTHER SECTION IN THE TEST. **STOP**

WRITING AND LANGUAGE TEST

35 Minutes—44 Questions

This section corresponds to Section 2 of your answer sheet.

Directions: Each passage in this section is followed by several questions. Some questions will reference an underlined portion in the passage; others will ask you to consider a part of a passage or the passage as a whole. For each question, choose the answer that reflects the best use of grammar, punctuation, and style. If a passage or question is accompanied by a graphic, take the graphic into account in choosing your response(s). Some questions will have "NO CHANGE" as a possible response. Choose that answer if you think the best choice is to leave the sentence as written.

Questions 1-11 are based on the following passage.

The Age of the Librarian

When Kristen Harris **1** is in college, she worked in her university's library and was constantly told, "You really should be studying to be a librarian; this is **2** your home" however Harris was pursuing a bachelor's degree in elementary education at the time. Little did she realize that becoming a school librarian was indeed **3** elective. During the 21st century, the age of information, what could be more necessary than an individual trained to gather, process, and disseminate information? So, after teaching children in the classroom, Harris went back to school to earn her Master of Library Science degree.

1. A) NO CHANGE
   B) has been
   C) was
   D) had been

2. A) NO CHANGE
   B) your home," however Harris
   C) your home."; However Harris
   D) your home." However, Harris

3. A) NO CHANGE
   B) imminent
   C) threatening
   D) optional

GO ON TO THE NEXT PAGE ⟶

Today, Harris is preparing a story time for a group of young students. As it has done with everything else, the technology revolution has elevated the school library to "Library 2.0." Harris's tablet-integrated story time begins when she projects images for *The Very Cranky Bear* onto a projector screen. As a child, Harris got excited whenever a puppet appeared during story time, but now she uses an interactive app (application software) to enhance her own story time and **4** integrate this next generation of children.

As she introduces the children to the problem of cheering up a cranky **5** bear, Harris sees Miguel scouring the library shelves for another book by a popular author. **6** Miguel had said asking Harris for a book two weeks earlier "If you have any funny stories, I like those." "It will always be satisfying," reflects Harris, "to find books for students and have them return to say, 'I really liked that one. Are there any more by that author?'"

7 Harris maintains active profiles on multiple social media networks to connect with her students more effectively. Harris would call herself a media mentor as much as a librarian because she regularly visits her favorite websites for reviews of apps and other digital tools to suggest to students and parents. Librarians have always been an important resource for families in a community, but this importance has grown exponentially because of the advent of technology. Librarians are offering guidance about new media to address the changing information needs in our communities. Furthermore,

4. A) NO CHANGE
   B) enervate
   C) energize
   D) elucidate

5. A) NO CHANGE
   B) bear; Harris sees Miguel
   C) bear: Harris sees Miguel
   D) bear Harris sees Miguel

6. A) NO CHANGE
   B) Miguel had said, "If you have any funny stories, I like those," asking Harris for a book two weeks earlier.
   C) Asking Harris for a book two weeks earlier, Miguel had said, "If you have any funny stories, I like those."
   D) Miguel asked Harris for a book two weeks earlier had said, "If you have any funny stories, I like those."

7. Which sentence would most effectively establish the main idea of the paragraph?
   A) NO CHANGE
   B) In addition to finding books for students, Harris is expected to meet their digital needs.
   C) Librarians still perform many traditional tasks such as putting great literature in the hands of their students.
   D) In the future, many school libraries are unlikely to have books on the shelves because students prefer electronic media.

Practice Tests

GO ON TO THE NEXT PAGE ⟶

libraries are becoming increasingly technology driven, for example, **8** enabling access to collections of other libraries, offering remote access to databases, or they house video production studios. **9** Harris sponsors a weekly "Fun Read" book discussion club that is well attended by many of the students at her school. So, in Harris's opinion, librarians must be masters of the digital world.

Harris finishes her story time and heads across the library. A young student stops her and asks, "Ms. Harris, what's new in the library?" **10** She chuckles and thinks about the many collections, services, and programs their school library offers. "Have you seen the Trendy 10

8. A) NO CHANGE
    B) by enabling access to collections of other libraries, offering remote access to databases, or by housing video production studios.
    C) they enable access to collections of other libraries, offering remote access to databases, or they house video production studios.
    D) enabling access to collections of other libraries, offering remote access to databases, or housing video production studios.

9. Which sentence provides evidence that best supports the main idea of the paragraph?
    A) NO CHANGE
    B) Librarians continue to help students and teachers locate the perfect book in the library's collection.
    C) Teachers frequently ask Harris to recommend educational apps to support early literacy for their students.
    D) Many parents are concerned with online safety and digital citizenship due to the proliferation of social media.

10. A) NO CHANGE
     B) He chuckles
     C) Harris chuckles
     D) They chuckle

list? You read the books on the list and blog **11** your ideas about them. I'll set you up with a password and username so you can blog," says Harris. In this library full of information, she's the gatekeeper.

11. A) NO CHANGE
    B) they're
    C) you're
    D) their

Questions 12-22 are based on the following passage.

Unforeseen Consequences: The Dark Side of the Industrial Revolution

There is no doubt that the Industrial Revolution guided America through the nascent stages of independence **12** and into being a robust economic powerhouse. Inventions like the cotton gin revolutionized the textile industry, and the steam engine ushered in the advent of expeditious cross-country distribution.

The Industrial Revolution marked a shift from an agrarian to an industry-centered society. People eschewed farming in favor of **13** more lucrative enterprises in urban areas which put a strain on existing local resources. Necessary goods such as **14** food crops, vegetables, and meat products also had to be shipped in order to meet the dietary needs of a consolidated population. And because there were fewer people farming, food had to travel farther and in higher quantities to meet demand. Issues like carbon dioxide emissions, therefore, arose not only as byproducts of industrial production but also from the delivery of these products. Moreover, booming metropolises

12. A) NO CHANGE
    B) and into the role of a robust economic powerhouse.
    C) and turned into a robust economic powerhouse.
    D) and then became a robust economic powerhouse.

13. A) NO CHANGE
    B) more lucrative enterprises in urban areas, which put a strain on
    C) more lucrative enterprises in urban areas; which put a strain on
    D) more lucrative enterprises in urban areas. Which put a strain on

14. A) NO CHANGE
    B) food
    C) food crops
    D) vegetables and meat products

Practice Tests

needed additional lumber, metal, and coal shipped from rural areas to sustain population and industrial growth.

15 [1] The negative effects of such expansion on humans were immediately apparent; improper water sanitization led to cholera outbreaks in big cities. [2] Miners suffered from black lung after spending hours harvesting coal in dark caverns. [3] Combusted fossil fuels **16** released unprecedented amounts of human-made carbon dioxide into the air, resulting in respiratory ailments. [4] The fact remains that smog, now an internationally recognized buzzword, simply did not exist before the factories that produced it.

The critical impact on the environment must also **17** be taken into account. Proper regulations were either not in place or not enforced. Industrial waste was often disposed of in the nearest river or buried in landfills, where it **18** polluted groundwater essential for wildlife to thrive. Deforestation across the United States served the dual purpose of providing inhabitable land and wood, but it also caused animals to migrate or die out completely.

15. To effectively transition from paragraph 2, which sentence should begin paragraph 3?

A) Sentence 1

B) Sentence 2

C) Sentence 3

D) Sentence 4

16 Which graphic would best support the underlined claim?

A) A line graph plotting an increase in atmospheric carbon dioxide over time

B) A pie chart comparing the present percentages of carbon dioxide and other atmospheric gases

C) A timeline tracking carbon dioxide emissions testing dates

D) A bar graph showing levels of atmospheric carbon dioxide in different locations

17. Which choice most effectively combines the sentences at the underlined portion?

A) be taken into account, and proper regulations

B) be taken into account since without proper regulations

C) be taken into account because proper regulations

D) be taken into account; however, proper regulations

18. A) NO CHANGE

B) disturbed

C) drained

D) enhanced

GO ON TO THE NEXT PAGE

Although the Industrial Revolution heralded an age of consumer ease and excess, it also invited a cyclical process of destruction and reduced resources. [19] Greenhouse gases were released into the atmosphere. Numerous health problems caused by [20] depressing working conditions prevented rural emigrants from thriving. And the environment that had cradled humankind since its inception was slowly being [21] degraded. All in the name of progress. [22]

19. Which choice should be added to the end of the underlined sentence to better support the claim in the preceding sentence?

A) NO CHANGE

B) while carbon dioxide-consuming trees were cut down to make way for new living spaces.

C) and caused an increase in global temperatures as well as a rise in coastal sea levels.

D) faster than they could be absorbed by the atmosphere's shrinking ozone layer.

20. A) NO CHANGE

B) urban

C) substandard

D) developing

21. A) NO CHANGE

B) degraded; all

C) degraded! All

D) degraded—all

22. Which choice most effectively states the central idea of the essay?

A) The Industrial Revolution created a new consumer society that replaced the existing farming society.

B) Politicians and historians today disagree about the true consequences of the Industrial Revolution.

C) Although some analysts suggest that industrialization had many problems, its immense benefits outweigh these concerns.

D) Unfortunately, progress came at the expense of environmental and ecological preservation and may well have ruined the future that once looked so bright.

Practice Tests

GO ON TO THE NEXT PAGE

Questions 23-33 are based on the following passage.

Remembering Freud

Psychology has grown momentously over the past century, largely due to the influence of Sigmund Freud, a pioneer of the field. This Austrian-born neurologist founded the practice of psychoanalysis and [23] began scientific study of the unconscious mind. [24] Since his career which ended in the mid-twentieth century, Freud has remained a common cultural and scientific reference point. [25] Even the abiding popularity of terms such as "id," "ego," and talking about a "Freudian slip" serves to indicate how this psychologist lingers powerfully in Western memory.

As neuroscience has progressed, many early practices and theories, including some of Freud's, have been dismissed as outdated, unscientific, or even harmful. Much of Freud's theory, clinical practice, and even lifestyle are now discredited. But when considered in his historical context, alongside the astounding progress catalyzed by his work, Freud's contribution was significant indeed.

[26] Because he is now widely referred to as the Father of Psychoanalysis, Freud was among the first to develop the now-commonplace psychological method of inviting patients to speak freely. For Freud, this was both study and treatment. It helped doctors to understand patients, but more importantly it helped patients to understand themselves. Freud employed the classic (now

23. A) NO CHANGE
    B) continued
    C) spearheaded
    D) led to

24. A) NO CHANGE
    B) Since his career, which ended in the mid-twentieth century, Freud has remained
    C) Since his career ending in the mid-twentieth century; Freud has remained
    D) Since his career (ending in the mid-twentieth century) Freud has remained

25. A) NO CHANGE
    B) Even the abiding popularity of terms such as the "id," "ego," and a "Freudian slip"
    C) Even the abiding popularity of terms such as talking about an "id," "ego," and "Freudian slip"
    D) Even the abiding popularity of terms such as "id," "ego," and "Freudian slip"

26. A) NO CHANGE
    B) Widely remembered as the Father of Psychoanalysis, Freud was among the first to develop the now-commonplace psychological method of inviting patients to speak freely.
    C) Freud was among the first to develop the now-commonplace psychological method of inviting patients to speak freely, which is why he is now widely remembered as the Father of Psychoanalysis.
    D) Although he is widely remembered as the Father of Psychoanalysis, Freud was among the first to develop the now-commonplace psychological method of inviting patients to speak freely.

GO ON TO THE NEXT PAGE

largely outdated) psychiatric style in which the patient lies face-up on a clinical bed, allegedly enabling access to deep <u>27 parts</u> of the mind. These are better known as the unconscious or subconscious, and they fascinated Freud.

<u>28 He believed that uncovering repressed memories, was necessary for recovery.</u> For Freud, understanding the activity of the innermost mind was essential. <u>29 In dealing with the conditions of patients, like neurosis or other psychological trauma, he suspected that</u> there was a great deal going on beneath the "surface" of the psyche. He thought it was possible to reunite external, or conscious, thought with the internal, or unconscious. <u>30 At the same time that Freud practiced, many people were interested in spiritualism.</u> Moreover, the method of inviting patients to speak and process their thoughts aloud remains central to today's psychological practice.

27. A) NO CHANGE
    B) recesses
    C) places
    D) components

28. A) NO CHANGE
    B) He believed that uncovering repressed memories, being necessary for recovery.
    C) He believed that uncovering repressed memories was necessary for recovery.
    D) He believed that uncovering, repressed memories was necessary for recovery.

29. A) NO CHANGE
    B) In dealing with patients' conditions, like neurosis or other psychological trauma, he suspected that
    C) In dealing with patients like neurosis or other psychological trauma conditions he suspected that
    D) He suspected that, in dealing with patients' conditions like neurosis or other psychological trauma,

30. Which sentence provides the best support for the ideas presented in this section?
    A) NO CHANGE
    B) Freud lived and worked mostly in London although he had originally trained in Austria.
    C) While some of Freud's more unusual practices have been criticized or abandoned, his interest in the unconscious altered the trajectory of the field.
    D) Psychologists today employ many theories, not just those developed by Freud.

GO ON TO THE NEXT PAGE

Practice Tests

Freud altered the course of twentieth-century medicine by initiating what would become a grand, global conversation about the **31** <u>still vastly mysterious human mind before Freud, medicine</u> had barely scratched the surface in understanding mental health. Patients were met with very few answers, let alone recovery protocols. **32** <u>Through trial and error—scientific method in action—Freud's finding of a method that seemed to work.</u> Since then, decades of ever-sharpening science have used his work as a launching pad. Therefore, as long as occasions arise to celebrate the progress of **33** <u>the field, Sigmund Freud will be remembered for groundbreaking work that</u> enabled countless advances.

31. A) NO CHANGE
    B) still vastly mysterious human mind. Before Freud, medicine
    C) still vastly mysterious human mind, before Freud, medicine
    D) still vastly mysterious human mind before Freud. Medicine

32. A) NO CHANGE
    B) Through trial and error—scientific method in action—Freud's finding a method that seems to work.
    C) Through trial and error—scientific method in action—Freud finds a method that seemed to work.
    D) Through trial and error—scientific method in action—Freud found a method that seemed to work.

33. A) NO CHANGE
    B) the field; Sigmund Freud will be remembered for groundbreaking work that
    C) the field Sigmund Freud will be remembered for groundbreaking work that
    D) the field Sigmund Freud will be remembered for groundbreaking work, and that

Questions 34-44 are based on the following passage and supplementary material.

Success in Montreal

The Montreal Protocol on Substances That Deplete the Ozone Layer is an international treaty that was created to ensure that steps would be taken to reverse damage to Earth's ozone layer and [34] preventing future damage. [35] It was signed in 1987. This document created restrictions on chemicals that were known to be dangerous to the protective barrier that the ozone layer offers Earth. Without the ozone layer, the sun's dangerous UV rays would alter our climate so drastically, life on land and in water would cease to exist.

A hole in Earth's ozone layer was discovered over Antarctica [36] as long as two years prior to the signing of the treaty. The discovery brought the human impact on the environment to the forefront of [37] international conversation, the massive hole was evidence that a global response was necessary and that large-scale action was needed. The Montreal Protocol became effective January 1, 1989, and nearly 100 gases deemed dangerous to the ozone layer have been phased out. As a result, [38] the average size of the ozone hole decreased significantly during the 1990s.

34. A) NO CHANGE
    B) to prevent
    C) prevented
    D) was preventing

35. Which choice most effectively combines the sentences in the underlined portion?
    A) Signed in 1987, this document
    B) Because it was signed in 1987, this document
    C) It was signed in 1987, and this document
    D) It was signed in 1987 so this document

36. A) NO CHANGE
    B) long ago, two years prior.
    C) two years prior.
    D) years prior.

37. A) NO CHANGE
    B) international conversation, yet the massive hole
    C) international conversation. The massive hole
    D) international conversation, so the massive hole

38. Which choice completes the sentence with accurate data based on the graphic?
    A) NO CHANGE
    B) the average size of the ozone hole leveled off beginning in the 1990s.
    C) the average size of the ozone hole decreased beginning in the 2000s.
    D) the average size of the ozone hole increased beginning in the 1980s.

GO ON TO THE NEXT PAGE

Practice Tests

Now that a substantial amount of time has passed since the treaty was put into place, the effects can begin to be **39** looked at. As a part of the treaty, the Montreal Protocol's Scientific Assessment Panel was created to gauge **40** their effect on the hole in the ozone layer. The Panel has since reported the results every four years. The Panel predicts that the ozone layer will return to its former state of health by 2075. **41**

[1] While the treaty is already an obvious success, work continues to ensure that human strides in technology and industry do not reverse the healing process. [2] The Montreal Protocol's Multilateral Fund was established to help developing countries transition away from the consumption and production of harmful chemicals. [3] So far, over $3 billion has been invested by the Fund. [4] The developing countries are referred to as "Article 5 countries." **42**

39. A) NO CHANGE
    B) controlled
    C) measured
    D) governed

40. A) NO CHANGE
    B) its
    C) it's
    D) there

41. Which choice could be added to paragraph 3 to most effectively convey its central idea?

    A) It is the Panel's current estimation that the ozone layer is beginning to heal, but the rate of progress is slow.

    B) The Panel meets once a year to assess the increase or decrease of each gas that has been identified as dangerous.

    C) Of much concern to the Panel was the effect of ultraviolet radiation on the ozone layer.

    D) The Panel has recently updated procedures for the nomination and selection of its membership.

42. Which sentence in paragraph 4 provides the least amount of support for the central idea of the paragraph?

    A) Sentence 1
    B) Sentence 2
    C) Sentence 3
    D) Sentence 4

[1] The Montreal Protocol is a living document. [2] A current amendment proposition has been put forth by the United States, Mexico, and Canada jointly. [3] It aims to cut down on harmful gases that were put into use as an alternative to the gases specified in the original Montreal Protocol treaty. [4] It has been amended four times since its inception. [5] Combating the erosion of our ozone layer will take time and flexibility, but the research is clear: If humans stay conscious of what we emit into the atmosphere, we can not only stall the damage we have done in the past, but we can 43 change it. 44

43. A) NO CHANGE
    B) switch
    C) invert
    D) reverse

44. For the sake of cohesion of this paragraph, sentence 4 should be placed
    A) where it is now.
    B) before sentence 1.
    C) after sentence 1.
    D) after sentence 2.

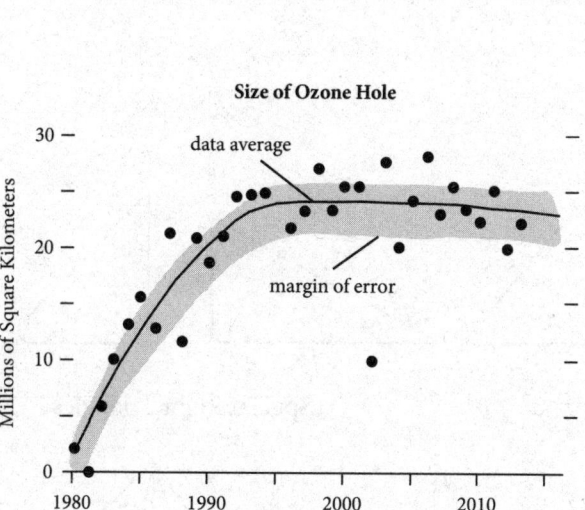

Size of Ozone Hole

Adapted from Ozone Hole Watch, NASA Goddard Space Flight Center.

IF YOU FINISH BEFORE TIME IS CALLED, YOU MAY CHECK YOUR WORK ON THIS SECTION ONLY. DO NOT TURN TO ANY OTHER SECTION IN THE TEST. **STOP**

MATH TEST

25 Minutes—20 Questions

NO-CALCULATOR SECTION

This section corresponds to Section 3 of your answer sheet.

Directions: For this section, solve each question and select the best answer choice. The available space on each page may be used for scratch work.

Notes:

1. Calculator use is NOT permitted.
2. All numbers used are real numbers, and all variables used represent real numbers, unless otherwise indicated.
3. Figures are drawn to scale and lie in a plane unless otherwise indicated.
4. Unless stated otherwise, the domain of any function f is assumed to be the set of all real numbers x, for which $f(x)$ is a real number.

Information:

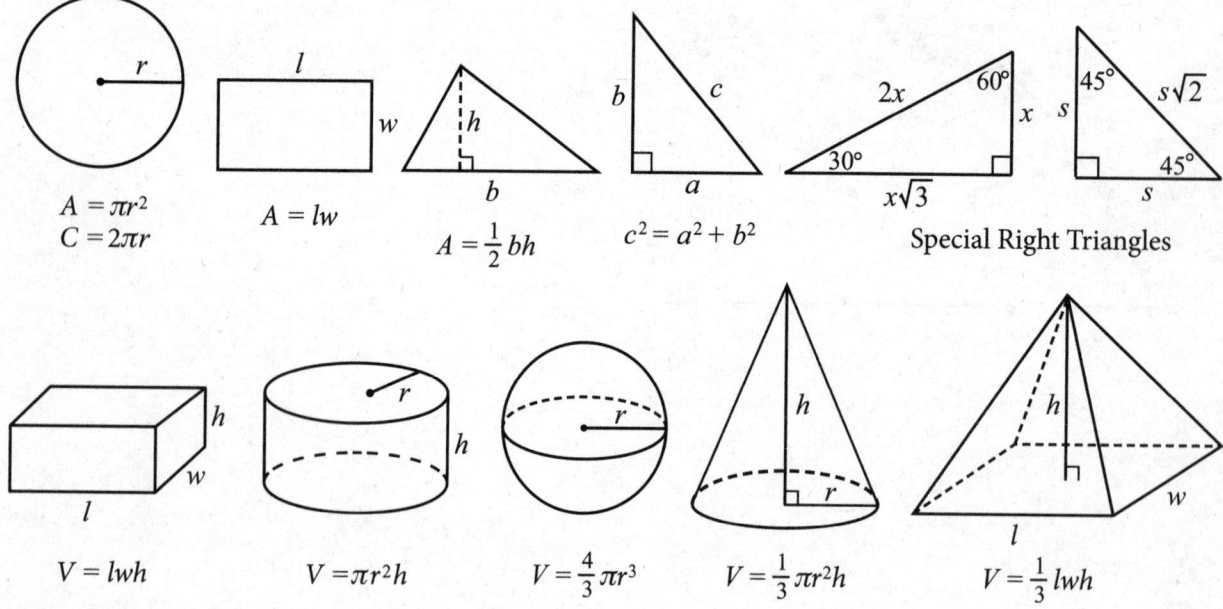

The sum of the degree measures of the angles in a triangle is 180.

The number of degrees of arc in a circle is 360.

The number of radians of arc in a circle is 2π.

GO ON TO THE NEXT PAGE ⟹

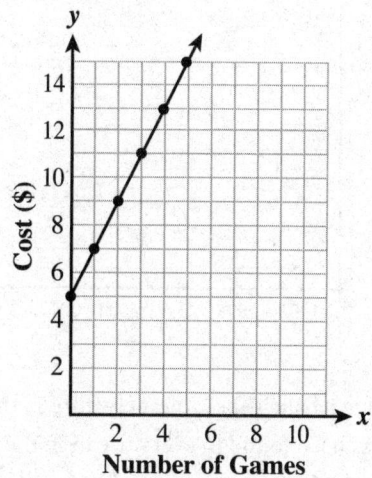

Number of Games

1. The graph above shows the amount that a new, high-tech video arcade charges its customers. What could the y-intercept of this graph represent?

A) The cost of playing 5 games

B) The cost per game, which is $5

C) The entrance fee to enter the arcade

D) The number of games that are played

$$\frac{3x}{x + 5} \div \frac{6}{4x + 20}$$

2. Which of the following is equivalent to the expression above, given that $x \neq -5$?

A) $2x$

B) $\dfrac{x}{2}$

C) $\dfrac{9x}{2}$

D) $2x + 4$

$$(x + 3)^2 + (y + 1)^2 = 25$$

3. The graph of the equation above is a circle. What is the area, in square units, of the circle?

A) 4π

B) 5π

C) 16π

D) 25π

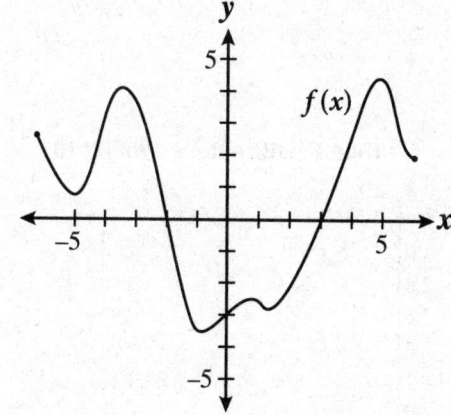

4. The figure above shows the graph of $f(x)$. For which value(s) of x does $f(x)$ equal 0 ?

A) 3 only

B) −3 only

C) −2 and 3

D) −3, −2, and 3

Practice Tests

GO ON TO THE NEXT PAGE

$$\frac{4(d+3)-9}{8} = \frac{10-(2-d)}{6}$$

5. In the equation above, what is the value of d ?

A) $\dfrac{23}{16}$

B) $\dfrac{23}{8}$

C) $\dfrac{25}{8}$

D) $\dfrac{25}{4}$

Total Fertility Rate, 1960-2010

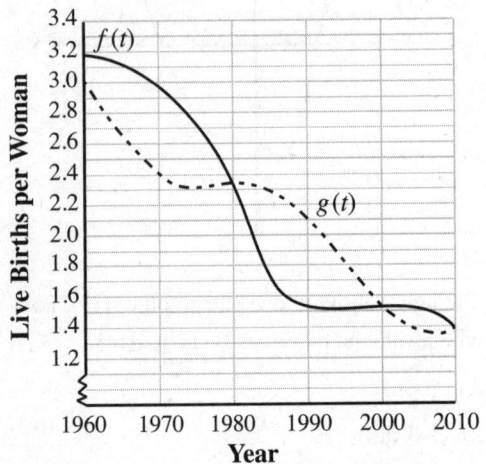

Source: Data from Eurostat.

6. One indicator of a declining economy is a continued decline in birth rates. In 2010, birth rates in Europe were at an all-time low, with the average number of children that a woman has in her lifetime at well below two. In the figure above, $f(t)$ represents birth rates for Portugal between 1960 and 2010, and $g(t)$ represents birth rates in Slovakia for the same time period. For which value(s) of t is $f(t) > g(t)$?

A) $1960 < t < 1980$ only

B) $1980 < t < 2000$ only

C) $1960 < t < 1980$ and $1990 < t < 2000$

D) $1960 < t < 1980$ and $2000 < t < 2010$

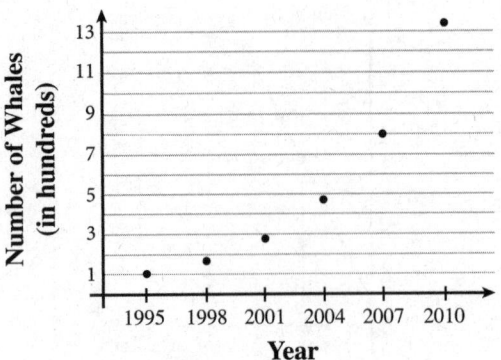

7. The blue whale is the largest creature in the world and has been found in every ocean in the world. A marine biologist surveyed the blue whale population in Monterey Bay, off the coast of California, every three years between 1995 and 2010. The figure above shows her results. If w is the number of blue whales present in Monterey Bay and t is the number of years since the study began in 1995, which of the following equations best represents the blue whale population of Monterey Bay?

A) $w = 100 + 2t$

B) $w = 100 + \dfrac{t^2}{4}$

C) $w = 100 \times 2^t$

D) $w = 100 \times 2^{\frac{t}{4}}$

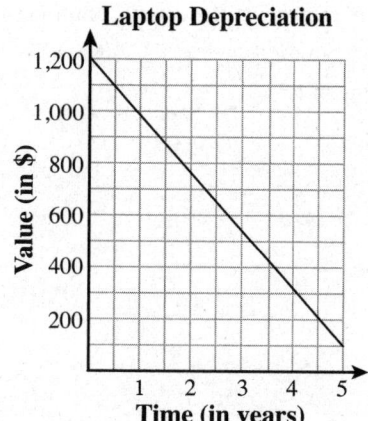

Laptop Depreciation

8. The figure above shows the straight-line depreciation of a laptop computer over the first five years of
its use. According to the figure, what is the average
rate of change in dollars per year of the value of the
computer over the five-year period?

A) −1,100

B) −220

C) −100

D) 100

9. What is the coefficient of x^2 when $6x^2 - \dfrac{2}{5}x + 1$

is multiplied by $10x + \dfrac{1}{3}$?

A) −4

B) −2

C) 2

D) 4

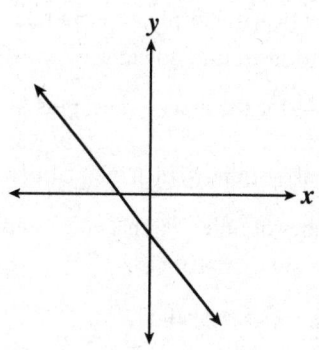

10. The graph above could represent which of the following equations?

A) $-6x - 4y = 5$

B) $-6x - 4y = -5$

C) $-6x + 4y = 5$

D) $-6x + 4y = -5$

$$\begin{cases} \dfrac{3}{4}x - \dfrac{1}{2}y = 12 \\ kx - 2y = 22 \end{cases}$$

11. If the system of linear equations above has no solution, and k is a constant, what is the value of k?

A) $-\dfrac{4}{3}$

B) $-\dfrac{3}{4}$

C) 3

D) 4

Practice Tests

GO ON TO THE NEXT PAGE ⬦

12. In Delray Beach, Florida, you can take a luxury golf cart ride around downtown. The driver charges \$4 for the first $\frac{1}{4}$ mile, plus \$1.50 for each additional $\frac{1}{2}$ mile. Which inequality represents the number of miles, m, that you could ride and pay no more than \$10 ?

A) $3.25 + 1.5m \leq 10$

B) $3.25 + 3m \leq 10$

C) $4 + 1.5m \leq 10$

D) $4 + 3m \leq 10$

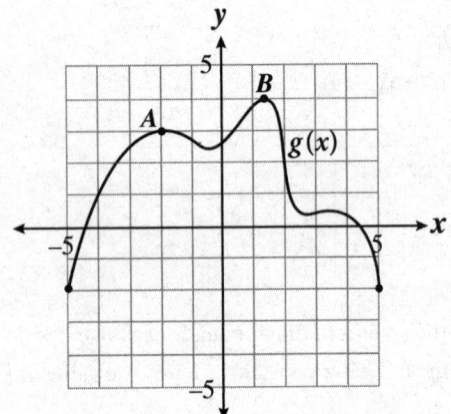

13. The graph of $g(x)$ is shown in the figure above. If $h(x) = -g(x) + 1$, which of the following statements is true?

A) The range of $h(x)$ is $-3 \leq y \leq 3$.

B) The minimum value of $h(x)$ is -4.

C) The coordinates of point A on the function $h(x)$ are $(2, 4)$.

D) The graph of $h(x)$ is increasing between $x = -5$ and $x = -2$.

14. If $a + bi$ represents the complex number that results from multiplying $3 + 2i$ times $5 - i$, what is the value of a ?

A) 2

B) 13

C) 15

D) 17

$$\frac{1}{x} + \frac{4}{x} = \frac{1}{72}$$

15. In order to create safe drinking water, cities and towns use water treatment facilities to remove contaminants from surface water and groundwater. Suppose a town has a treatment plant but decides to build a second, more efficient facility. The new treatment plant can filter the water in the reservoir four times as quickly as the older facility. Working together, the two facilities can filter all the water in the reservoir in 72 hours. The equation above represents the scenario. Which of the following describes what the term $\frac{1}{x}$ represents?

A) The portion of the water the older treatment plant can filter in 1 hour

B) The time it takes the older treatment plant to filter the water in the reservoir

C) The time it takes the older treatment plant to filter $\frac{1}{72}$ of the water in the reservoir

D) The portion of the water the new treatment plant can filter in 4 hours

GO ON TO THE NEXT PAGE

Directions: For questions 16-20, enter your responses into the appropriate grid on your answer sheet, in accordance with the following:

1. You will receive credit only if the circles are filled in correctly, but you may write your answers in the boxes above each grid to help you fill in the circles accurately.
2. Don't mark more than one circle per column.
3. None of the questions with grid-in responses will have a negative solution.
4. Only grid in a single answer, even if there is more than one correct answer to a given question.
5. A **mixed number** must be gridded as a decimal or an improper fraction. For example, you would grid $7\frac{1}{2}$ as 7.5 or $\frac{15}{2}$.

   (Were you to grid it as ⌗, this response would be read as $\frac{71}{2}$.)
6. A **decimal** that has more digits than there are places on the grid may be either rounded or truncated, but every column in the grid must be filled in order to receive credit.

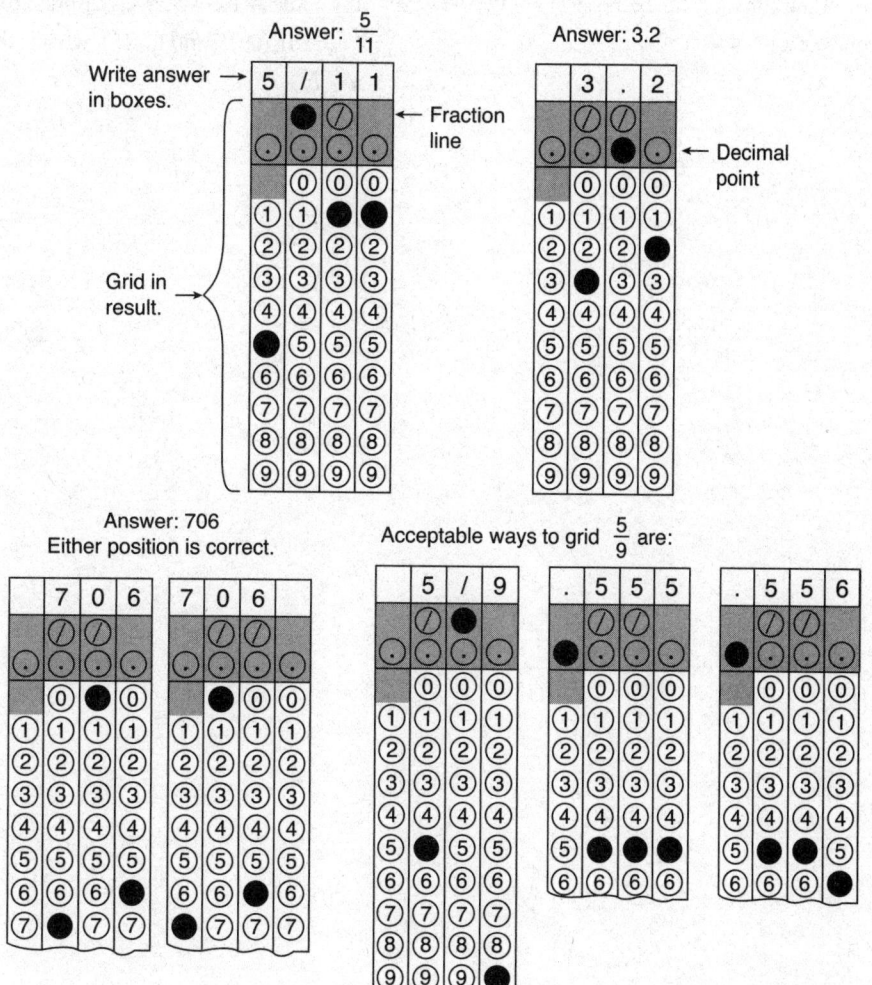

GO ON TO THE NEXT PAGE

16. If $\frac{1}{4}x = 5 - \frac{1}{2}y$, what is the value of $x + 2y$?

$$\begin{cases} x + 3y \leq 18 \\ 2x - 3y \leq 9 \end{cases}$$

17. If (a, b) is a point in the solution region for the system of inequalities shown above and $a = 6$, what is the minimum possible value for b?

$$\frac{\sqrt{x} \cdot x^{\frac{5}{6}} \cdot x}{\sqrt[3]{x}}$$

18. If x^n is the simplified form of the expression above, what is the value of n?

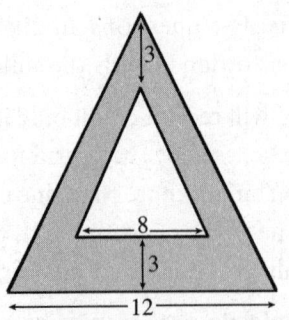

Note: Figure not drawn to scale.

19. In the figure above, the area of the shaded region is 52 square units. What is the height of the larger triangle?

20. If $y = ax^2 + bx + c$ passes through the points $(-3, 10)$, $(0, 1)$, and $(2, 15)$, what is the value of $a + b + c$?

MATH TEST

55 Minutes—38 Questions

CALCULATOR SECTION

This section corresponds to Section 4 of your answer sheet.

Directions: For this section, solve each question and select the best answer choice. The available space on each page may be used for scratch work.

Notes:

1. Calculator use is permitted.
2. All numbers used are real numbers, and all variables used represent real numbers, unless otherwise indicated.
3. Figures are drawn to scale and lie in a plane unless otherwise indicated.
4. Unless stated otherwise, the domain of any function f is assumed to be the set of all real numbers x, for which $f(x)$ is a real number.

Information:

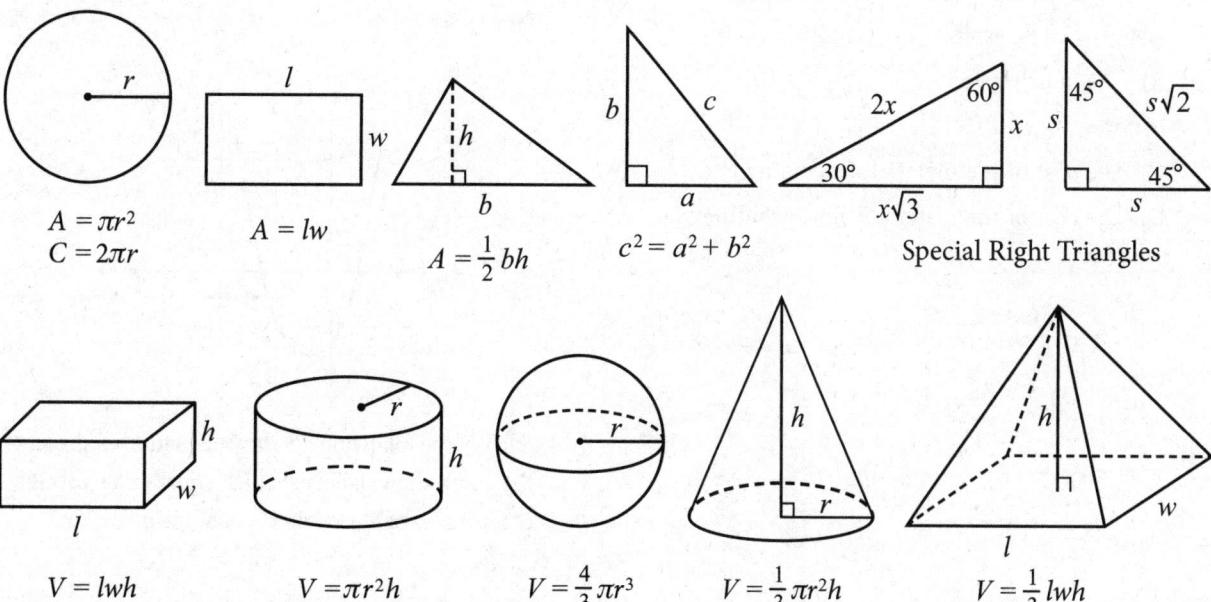

$A = \pi r^2$
$C = 2\pi r$

$A = lw$

$A = \frac{1}{2}bh$

$c^2 = a^2 + b^2$

Special Right Triangles

$V = lwh$

$V = \pi r^2 h$

$V = \frac{4}{3}\pi r^3$

$V = \frac{1}{3}\pi r^2 h$

$V = \frac{1}{3}lwh$

The sum of the degree measures of the angles in a triangle is 180.

The number of degrees of arc in a circle is 360.

The number of radians of arc in a circle is 2π.

GO ON TO THE NEXT PAGE

Practice Tests

1. Oceans, seas, and bays represent about 96.5% of Earth's water, including the water found in our atmosphere. If the volume of the water contained in oceans, seas, and bays is about 321,000,000 cubic miles, which of the following best represents the approximate volume, in cubic miles, of all the world's water?

A) 308,160,000

B) 309,765,000

C) 332,642,000

D) 334,375,000

2. An electrician charges a one-time site visit fee to evaluate a potential job. If the electrician accepts the job, he charges an hourly rate plus the cost of any materials needed to complete the job. The electrician also charges for tax, but only on the cost of the materials. If the total cost of completing a job that takes h hours is given by the function $C(h) = 45h + 1.06(82.5) + 75$, then the term $1.06(82.5)$ represents

A) the hourly rate.

B) the site visit fee.

C) the cost of the materials, including tax.

D) the cost of the materials, not including tax.

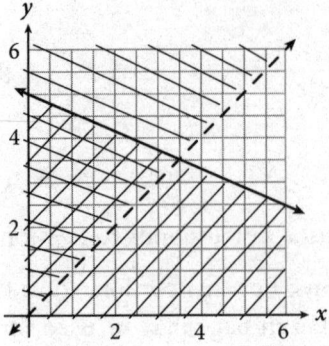

$$\begin{cases} y > x \\ y \le -\dfrac{3}{7}x + 5 \end{cases}$$

3. The figure above shows the solution set for the system of inequalities. Which of the following is not a solution to the system?

A) (0, 3)

B) (1, 2)

C) (2, 4)

D) (3, 3)

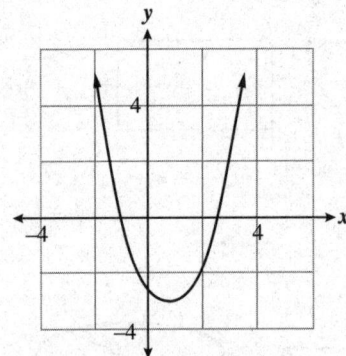

4. Each of the following quadratic equations represents the graph shown above. Which equation reveals the exact values of the x-intercepts of the graph?

A) $y = \dfrac{1}{2}(2x - 5)(x + 1)$

B) $y = x^2 - \dfrac{3}{2}x - \dfrac{5}{2}$

C) $y + \dfrac{49}{16} = \left(x - \dfrac{3}{4}\right)^2$

D) $y = \left(x - \dfrac{3}{4}\right)^2 - \dfrac{49}{16}$

GO ON TO THE NEXT PAGE

National Government Concerns

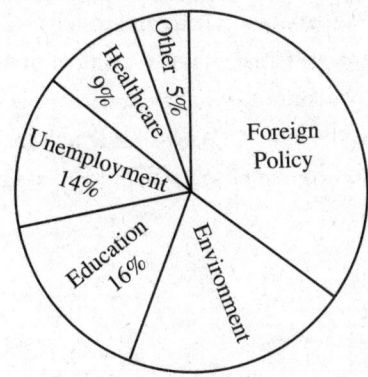

Average Annual Gas Prices

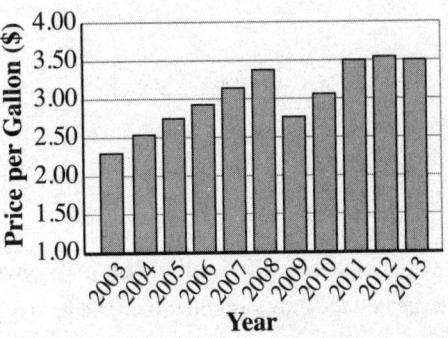

Data from U.S. Energy Information Administration.

5. Margo surveyed all the students in the government classes at her school to see what they thought should be the most important concern of a national government. The results of the survey are shown in the figure above. If the ratio of students who answered "Foreign Policy" to those who answered "Environment" was 5:3, what percentage of the students answered "Environment"?

A) 16%

B) 21%

C) 24%

D) 35%

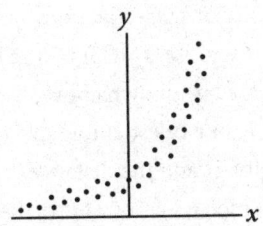

6. Which of the following best describes the type of association shown in the scatterplot above?

A) Linear, positive

B) Linear, negative

C) Exponential, positive

D) Exponential, negative

7. The figure above shows the average annual gas prices in the United States from 2003 to 2013. Based on the information shown, which of the following conclusions is valid?

A) A gallon of gas cost more in 2008 than in 2013.

B) The price more than doubled between 2003 and 2013.

C) The drop in price from 2008 to 2009 was more than $1.00 per gallon.

D) The overall change in price was greater between 2003 and 2008 than it was between 2008 and 2013.

$$\begin{cases} -2x + 5y = 1 \\ 7x - 10y = -11 \end{cases}$$

8. If (x, y) is a solution to the system of equations above, what is the sum of x and y ?

A) $-\dfrac{137}{30}$

B) -4

C) $-\dfrac{10}{3}$

D) -3

GO ON TO THE NEXT PAGE

Practice Tests

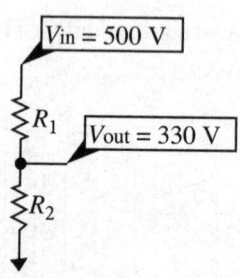

$V_{in} = 500$ V

R_1

$V_{out} = 330$ V

R_2

9. A voltage divider is a simple circuit that converts a large voltage into a smaller one. The figure above shows a voltage divider that consists of two resistors that together have a total resistance of 294 ohms. To produce the desired voltage of 330 volts, R_2 must be 6 ohms less than twice R_1. Solving which of the following systems of equations gives the individual resistances for R_1 and R_2?

A) $\begin{cases} R_2 = 2R_1 - 6 \\ R_1 + R_2 = 294 \end{cases}$

B) $\begin{cases} R_1 = 2R_2 + 6 \\ R_1 + R_2 = 294 \end{cases}$

C) $\begin{cases} R_2 = 2R_1 - 6 \\ R_1 + R_2 = \dfrac{294}{330} \end{cases}$

D) $\begin{cases} R_1 = 2R_2 + 6 \\ R_1 + R_2 = 330(294) \end{cases}$

10. If $\dfrac{2}{5}(5x) + 2(x - 1) = 4(x + 1) - 2$, what is the value of x?

A) $x = -2$

B) $x = 2$

C) There is no value of x for which the equation is true.

D) There are infinitely many values of x for which the equation is true.

11. Crude oil is being transferred from a full rectangular storage container with dimensions 4 meters by 9 meters by 10 meters into a cylindrical transportation container that has a diameter of 6 meters. What is the minimum possible length for a transportation container that will hold all of the oil?

A) 40π

B) $\dfrac{40}{\pi}$

C) 60π

D) $\dfrac{120}{\pi}$

12. The percent increase from 5 to 12 is equal to the percent increase from 12 to what number?

A) 16.8

B) 19.0

C) 26.6

D) 28.8

$$b = \frac{L}{4\pi d^2}$$

13. The brightness of a celestial body, like a star, decreases as you move away from it. In contrast, the luminosity of a celestial body is a constant number that represents its intrinsic brightness. The inverse square law, shown above, is used to find the brightness, b, of a celestial body when you know its luminosity, L, and the distance, d, in meters to the body. Which equation shows the distance to a celestial body, given its brightness and luminosity?

A) $d = \dfrac{1}{2}\sqrt{\dfrac{L}{\pi b}}$

B) $d = \sqrt{\dfrac{L}{2\pi b}}$

C) $d = \dfrac{\sqrt{L}}{2\pi b}$

D) $d = \dfrac{L}{2\sqrt{\pi b}}$

GO ON TO THE NEXT PAGE

Questions 14 and 15 refer to the following information.

Each month, the Bureau of Labor Statistics conducts a survey called the Current Population Survey (CPS) to measure unemployment in the United States. Across the country, about 60,000 households are included in the survey sample. These households are grouped by geographic region. A summary of the January 2014 survey results for male respondents in one geographic region is shown in the table below.

Age Group	Employed	Unemployed	Not in the Labor Force	Total
16 to 19	8	5	10	23
20 to 24	26	7	23	56
25 to 34	142	11	28	157
35 to 44	144	8	32	164
45 to 54	66	6	26	98
Over 54	65	7	36	152
Total	451	44	155	650

14. According to the data in the table, for which age group did the smallest percentage of men report that they were unemployed in January 2014?

    A) 20 to 24 years

    B) 35 to 44 years

    C) 45 to 54 years

    D) Over 54 years

15. If one unemployed man from this sample is chosen at random for a follow-up survey, what is the probability that he will be between the ages of 45 and 54?

    A) 6.0%

    B) 13.6%

    C) 15.1%

    D) 44.9%

GO ON TO THE NEXT PAGE

16. Which of the following are solutions to the quadratic equation $(x - 1)^2 = \dfrac{4}{9}$?

    A) $x = -\dfrac{5}{3}, x = \dfrac{5}{3}$

    B) $x = \dfrac{1}{3}, x = \dfrac{5}{3}$

    C) $x = \dfrac{5}{9}, x = \dfrac{13}{9}$

    D) $x = 1 \pm \sqrt{\dfrac{2}{3}}$

17. Damien is throwing darts. He has a total of 6 darts to throw. He gets 5 points for each dart that lands in a blue ring and 10 points for each dart that lands in a red ring. If x of his darts land in a blue ring and the rest land in a red ring, which expression represents his total score?

    A) $10x$

    B) $10x + 5$

    C) $5x + 30$

    D) $60 - 5x$

18. Red tide is a form of harmful algae that releases toxins as it breaks down in the environment. A marine biologist is testing a new spray, composed of clay and water, hoping to kill the red tide that almost completely covers a beach in southern Florida. He applies the spray to a representative sample of 200 square feet of the beach. By the end of the week, 184 square feet of the beach is free of the red tide. Based on these results, and assuming the same general conditions, how many square feet of the 10,000-square-foot beach would still be covered by red tide if the spray had been used on the entire area?

    A) 800

    B) 920

    C) 8,000

    D) 9,200

$$\begin{cases} y = \dfrac{1}{2}x - 2 \\ y = -x^2 + 1 \end{cases}$$

19. If (a, b) is a solution to the system of equations above, which of the following could be the value of b?

    A) -3

    B) -2

    C) 1

    D) 2

20. Given the function $g(x) = \dfrac{2}{3}x + 7$, what domain value corresponds to a range value of 3?

    A) -6

    B) -2

    C) 6

    D) 9

21. A landscaper buys a new commercial-grade lawn mower that costs $2,800. Based on past experience, he expects it to last about 8 years, and then he can sell it for scrap metal with a salvage value of about $240. Assuming the value of the lawn mower depreciates at a constant rate, which equation could be used to find its approximate value after x years, given that $x < 8$?

    A) $y = -8x + 2,560$

    B) $y = -240x + 2,800$

    C) $y = -320x + 2,800$

    D) $y = 240x - 2,560$

GO ON TO THE NEXT PAGE

22. A microbiologist is studying the effects of a new antibiotic on a culture of 20,000 bacteria. When the antibiotic is added to the culture, the number of bacteria is reduced by half every hour. What kind of function best models the number of bacteria remaining in the culture after the antibiotic is added?

    A) A linear function

    B) A quadratic function

    C) A polynomial function

    D) An exponential function

23. An airline company purchased two new airplanes. One can travel at speeds of up to 600 miles per hour and the other at speeds of up to 720 miles per hour. How many more miles can the faster airplane travel in 12 seconds than the slower airplane?

    A) $\dfrac{1}{30}$

    B) $\dfrac{2}{5}$

    C) 2

    D) 30

State	Minimum Wage per Hour
Idaho	$7.25
Montana	$7.90
Oregon	$9.10
Washington	$9.32

24. The table above shows the 2014 minimum wages for several states that share a border. Assuming an average workweek of between 35 and 40 hours, which inequality represents how much more a worker who earns minimum wage can earn per week in Oregon than in Idaho?

    A) $x \geq 1.85$

    B) $7.25 \leq x \leq 9.10$

    C) $64.75 \leq x \leq 74$

    D) $253.75 \leq x \leq 364$

25. In the United States, the maintenance and construction of airports, transit systems, and major roads is largely funded through a federal excise tax on gasoline. Based on the 2011 statistics given below, how much did the average household pay per year in federal gasoline taxes?

    - The federal gasoline tax rate was 18.4 cents per gallon.
    - The average motor vehicle was driven approximately 11,340 miles per year.
    - The national average fuel economy for noncommercial vehicles was 21.4 miles per gallon.
    - The average American household owned 1.75 vehicles.

    A) $55.73

    B) $68.91

    C) $97.52

    D) $170.63

GO ON TO THE NEXT PAGE

Rescued Dolphin Recovery

(graph with y-axis "Weight (in pounds)" labeled 280, 300, 320, 340, 360, 380, 400 and x-axis "Weeks After Rescue" labeled 1 through 9)

26. Following the catastrophic oil spill in the Gulf of Mexico in April of 2010, more than 900 bottlenose dolphins were found dead or stranded in the oil spill area. The figure above shows the weight of a rescued dolphin during its recovery. Based on the quadratic model fit to the data shown, which of the following is the closest to the average rate of change in the dolphin's weight between week 2 and week 8 of its recovery?

A) 4 pounds per week

B) 16 pounds per week

C) 20 pounds per week

D) 40 pounds per week

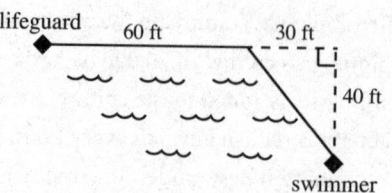

27. As shown in the figure above, a lifeguard sees a struggling swimmer who is 40 feet from the beach. The lifeguard runs 60 feet along the edge of the water at a speed of 12 feet per second. He pauses for 1 second to locate the swimmer again, and then dives into the water and swims along a diagonal path to the swimmer at a speed of 5 feet per second. How many seconds go by between the time the lifeguard sees the struggling swimmer and the time he reaches the swimmer?

A) 16

B) 22

C) 50

D) 56

28. What was the initial amount of gasoline in a fuel trailer, in gallons, if there are now x gallons, y gallons were pumped into a storage tank, and then 50 gallons were added to the trailer?

A) $x + y + 50$

B) $x + y - 50$

C) $y - x + 50$

D) $x - y - 50$

GO ON TO THE NEXT PAGE

U.S. Foreign Trade, 2014

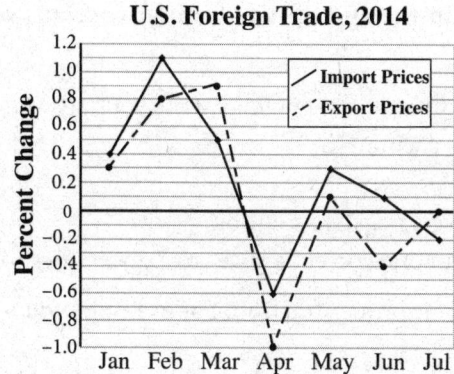

29. The figure above shows the net change, as a percentage, for U.S. import and export prices from January to July 2014 as reported by the Bureau of Labor Statistics. For example, U.S. import prices declined 0.2 percent in July while export prices remained unchanged for that month. Based on this information, which of the following statements is true for the time period shown in the figure?

A) On average, export prices increased more than import prices.

B) Import prices showed an increase more often than export prices.

C) Import prices showed the greatest change between two consecutive months.

D) From January to July, import prices showed a greater overall decrease than export prices.

$$\frac{3.86}{x} + \frac{180.2}{10x} + \frac{42.2}{5x}$$

30. The Ironman Triathlon originated in Hawaii in 1978. The format of the Ironman has not changed since then: It consists of a 3.86-km swim, a 180.2-km bicycle ride, and a 42.2-km run, all raced in that order and without a break. Suppose an athlete bikes 10 times as fast as he swims and runs 5 times as fast as he swims. The variable x in the expression above represents the rate at which the athlete swims, and the whole expression represents the number of hours that it takes him to complete the race. If it takes him 16.2 hours to complete the race, how many kilometers did he swim in 1 hour?

A) 0.85

B) 1.01

C) 1.17

D) 1.87

Directions: For questions 31-38, enter your responses into the appropriate grid on your answer sheet, in accordance with the following:

1. You will receive credit only if the circles are filled in correctly, but you may write your answers in the boxes above each grid to help you fill in the circles accurately.

2. Don't mark more than one circle per column.

3. None of the questions with grid-in responses will have a negative solution.

4. Only grid in a single answer, even if there is more than one correct answer to a given question.

5. A **mixed number** must be gridded as a decimal or an improper fraction. For example, you would grid $7\frac{1}{2}$ as 7.5 or $\frac{15}{2}$.

   (Were you to grid it as [7 1 / 2], this response would be read as $\frac{71}{2}$.)

6. A **decimal** that has more digits than there are places on the grid may be either rounded or truncated, but every column in the grid must be filled in order to receive credit.

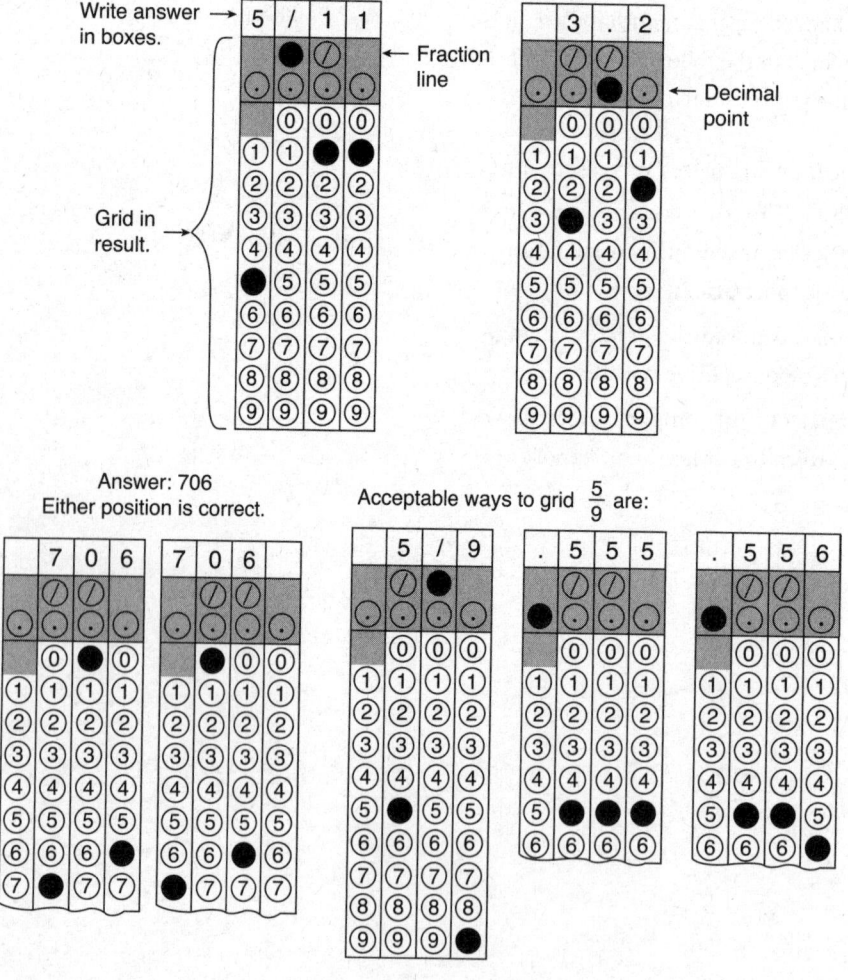

31. What value of x satisfies the equation
$\frac{2}{3}(5x + 7) = 8x$?

32. Some doctors base the dosage of a drug to be given to a patient on the patient's body surface area (BSA). The most commonly used formula for calculating BSA is $BSA = \sqrt{\dfrac{wh}{3,600}}$, where w is the patient's weight (in kg), h is the patient's height (in cm), and BSA is measured in square meters. How tall (in cm) is a patient who weighs 150 kg and has a BSA of $2\sqrt{2}$ m^2 ?

33. A college math professor informs her students that rather than curving final grades, she will replace each student's lowest test score with the next to lowest test score, and then re-average the test grades. If Leeza has test scores of 86, 92, 81, 64, and 83, by how many points does her final test average change based on the professor's policy?

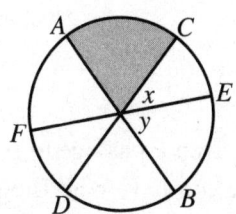

34. In the figure above, $\overline{AB}$, $\overline{CD}$, and $\overline{EF}$ are diameters of the circle. If $y = 2x - 12$, and the shaded area is $\frac{1}{5}$ of the circle, what is the value of x ?

35. If the slope of a line is $-\dfrac{7}{4}$ and a point on the line is $(4, 7)$, what is the y-intercept of the line?

36. Rory left home and drove straight to the airport at an average speed of 45 miles per hour. He returned home along the same route, but traffic slowed him down and he only averaged 30 miles per hour on the return trip. If his total travel time was 2 hours and 30 minutes, how far is it, in miles, from Rory's house to the airport?

Questions 37 and 38 refer to the following information.

Chemical Makeup of One Mole of Chloroform

Element	Number of Moles	Mass per Mole (grams)
Carbon	1	12.011
Hydrogen	1	1.008
Chlorine	3	35.453

A chemical solvent is a substance that dissolves another to form a solution. For example, water is a solvent for sugar. Unfortunately, many chemical solvents are hazardous to the environment. One eco-friendly chemical solvent is chloroform, also known as trichloromethane ($CHCl_3$). The table above shows the chemical makeup of one mole of chloroform.

37. Carbon makes up what percent of the mass of one mole of chloroform? Round your answer to the nearest whole percent and ignore the percent sign when entering your answer.

38. If a chemist starts with 1,000 grams of chloroform and uses 522.5 grams, how many moles of chlorine are left?

IF YOU FINISH BEFORE TIME IS CALLED, YOU MAY CHECK YOUR WORK ON THIS SECTION ONLY. DO NOT TURN TO ANY OTHER SECTION IN THE TEST. **STOP**

ESSAY TEST

50 Minutes

You will be given a passage to read and asked to write an essay analyzing it. As you write, be sure to show that you have read the passage closely. You will be graded on how well you have understood the passage, how clear your analysis is, and how well you express your ideas.

Your essay must be written on the lines in your answer booklet. Anything you write outside the lined space in your answer booklet will not be read by the essay graders. Be sure to write or print in such a way that it will be legible to readers not familiar with your handwriting. Additionally, be sure to address the passage directly. An off-topic essay will not be graded.

As you read the passage, think about the author's use of

- evidence, such as statistics or other facts.

- logic to connect evidence to conclusions and to develop lines of reasoning.

- style, word choice, and appeals to emotion to make the argument more persuasive.

Adapted from Elisabeth Woodbridge Morris's essay "The Tyranny of Things." In this portion, Morris paints a portrait of American consumerism in 1917 and offers a distinct perspective on the joy of freedom from "things, things, things."

1   Two fifteen-year-old girls stood eyeing one another on first acquaintance. Finally one little girl said, "Which do you like best, people or things?" The other little girl said, "Things." They were friends at once.

2   I suppose we all go through a phase when we like things best; and not only like them, but want to possess them under our hand. The passion for accumulation is upon us. We make "collections," we fill our rooms, our walls, our tables, our desks, with things, things, things.

3   Many people never pass out of this phase. They never see a flower without wanting to pick it and put it in a vase, they never enjoy a book without wanting to own it, nor a picture without wanting to hang it on their walls. They keep photographs of all their friends and Kodak albums of all the places they visit, they save all their theater programmes and dinner cards, they bring home all their alpenstocks.* Their houses are filled with an undigested mass of things, like the terminal moraine where a glacier dumps at length everything it has picked up during its progress through the lands.

4   But to some of us a day comes when we begin to grow weary of things. We realize that we do not possess them; they possess us. Our books are a burden to us, our pictures have destroyed every restful wall-space, our china is a care, our photographs drive us mad, our programmes and alpenstocks fill us with loathing. We feel stifled with the sense of things, and our problem becomes, not how much we can accumulate, but how much we can do without. We send our books to the village library, and our pictures to the college settlement. Such things as we cannot give away, and have not the courage to destroy, we stack in the garret, where they lie huddled in dim and dusty heaps, removed from our sight, to be sure, yet still faintly importunate.

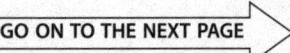

GO ON TO THE NEXT PAGE

5   Then, as we breathe more freely in the clear space that we have made for ourselves, we grow aware that we must not relax our vigilance, or we shall be once more overwhelmed....

6   It extends to all our doings. For every event there is a "souvenir." We cannot go to luncheon and meet our friends but we must receive a token to carry away. Even our children cannot have a birthday party, and play games, and eat good things, and be happy. The host must receive gifts from every little guest, and provide in return some little remembrance for each to take home. Truly, on all sides we are beset, and we go lumbering along through life like a ship encrusted with barnacles, which can never cut the waves clean and sure and swift until she has been scraped bare again. And there seems little hope for us this side our last port.

7   And to think that there was a time when folk had not even that hope! When a man's possessions were burned with him, so that he might, forsooth, have them all about him in the next world! Suffocating thought! To think one could not even then be clear of things, and make at least a fresh start! That must, indeed, have been in the childhood of the race.

8   Once upon a time, when I was very tired, I chanced to go away to a little house by the sea.... There was nothing in the house to demand care, to claim attention, to cumber my consciousness with its insistent, unchanging companionship. There was nothing but a shelter, and outside, the fields and marshes, the shore and the sea. These did not have to be taken down and put up and arranged and dusted and cared for. They were not things at all, they were powers, presences....

9   If we could but free ourselves once for all, how simple life might become! One of my friends, who, with six young children and only one servant, keeps a spotless house and a soul serene, told me once how she did it. "My dear, once a month I give away every single thing in the house that we do not imperatively need. It sounds wasteful, but I don't believe it really is...."

> Write an essay that analyzes the author's approach in persuading her readers that possessions are oppressive. Focus on specific features such as the ones listed in the box above the passage and explain how these features strengthen the author's argument. Your essay should discuss the most important rhetorical features of the passage.
>
> Your essay should not focus on your own opinion of the author's conclusion, but rather on how the author persuades her readers.

ANSWER KEY
READING TEST

1. A	14. B	27. D	40. D
2. B	15. D	28. C	41. A
3. C	16. C	29. C	42. A
4. C	17. A	30. B	43. A
5. A	18. D	31. D	44. B
6. C	19. C	32. C	45. A
7. D	20. C	33. D	46. B
8. A	21. C	34. B	47. D
9. D	22. B	35. C	48. D
10. A	23. D	36. C	49. A
11. D	24. C	37. B	50. C
12. D	25. A	38. C	51. D
13. D	26. A	39. A	52. C

WRITING AND LANGUAGE TEST

1. C	12. B	23. C	34. B
2. D	13. B	24. B	35. A
3. B	14. B	25. D	36. C
4. C	15. A	26. B	37. C
5. A	16. A	27. B	38. B
6. C	17. C	28. C	39. C
7. B	18. A	29. B	40. B
8. D	19. B	30. C	41. A
9. C	20. C	31. B	42. D
10. C	21. D	32. D	43. D
11. A	22. D	33. A	44. C

Practice Tests

MATH—NO CALCULATOR TEST

1. C	6. D	11. C	16. 20
2. A	7. D	12. B	17. 1
3. D	8. B	13. A	18. 2
4. C	9. B	14. D	19. 14
5. B	10. A	15. A	20. 6

MATH—CALCULATOR TEST

1. C	11. B	21. C	31. 1
2. C	12. D	22. D	32. 192
3. D	13. A	23. B	33. 3.4
4. A	14. D	24. C	34. 40
5. B	15. B	25. D	35. 14
6. C	16. B	26. C	36. 45
7. D	17. D	27. A	37. 10
8. B	18. A	28. B	38. 12
9. A	19. A	29. B	
10. C	20. A	30. D	

ANSWERS AND EXPLANATIONS

READING TEST

Anna Karenina

Suggested Passage Map notes:

¶1: Levin goes to skating rink to find Kitty

¶2: description of day, people

¶3: walks to skating area; nervous, sees K skating

¶4: knows her right away, still nervous

¶5: lots of happy people skating

¶6: cousin greets him

1. A.   Difficulty: Easy

Category: Detail

Getting to the Answer: Make sure to read the passage closely so events are clearly understood. The first paragraph explicitly states how Levin knew that Kitty was there: he saw her family's carriage. Choice (A) matches the information stated in the passage.

2. B   Difficulty: Medium

Category: Vocab-in-Context

Getting to the Answer: Use context clues to help you distinguish the shades of meaning each word has. Two of the answer choices have a somewhat negative connotation. The author is not describing the scene in a negative way. In this passage, the word "swarmed" means "gathered." Therefore, (B) is the correct answer. The other words' connotations do not fit with the context of the sentence.

3. C   Difficulty: Hard

Category: Inference

Getting to the Answer: Look for clues in the text that suggest what Levin is like. Emotionally charged phrases, such as "the rapture and the terror that seized on his heart," help reveal Levin's personality. Choice (C) reflects the depiction of Levin as a passionate person.

4. C   Difficulty: Hard

Category: Command of Evidence

Getting to the Answer: Eliminate answer choices that don't include a description of Levin. Because the excerpt focuses on Levin's feelings toward Kitty, evidence of the kind of person he is will probably reflect this. Choice (C) provides the best evidence.

5. A   Difficulty: Medium

Category: Global

Getting to the Answer: The central theme of a passage is the insight about life that the author is trying to get across to the reader. Eliminate any themes that are not revealed by the experiences of Levin. Though you may personally agree with more than one of the themes presented, (A) is the only answer choice that is supported by details in the passage. Levin's feelings and actions support this theme.

6. C   Difficulty: Medium

Category: Inference

Getting to the Answer: Examine the passage to see what other characters do in response to Levin. The other skaters go about their business. Most take little notice of Levin. Therefore, (C) is the correct answer.

7. D   Difficulty: Medium

Category: Command of Evidence

Getting to the Answer: Reread each quote in the context of the passage. This will help you decide the correct answer. Of all the answer choices, Nikolay's way of greeting Levin is the strongest evidence that people think Levin seems normal. Choice (D) is the correct answer.

8. A   Difficulty: Medium

Category: Vocab-in-Context

Getting to the Answer: The context of the passage can help reveal the meaning of the word. Insert each choice in the sentence to see which one makes the most sense. Levin speaks directly to his heart, asking it to behave. Choice (A), "begged," comes closest to meaning the same thing as "conjured" in this context.

9. D   Difficulty: Medium

Category: Rhetoric

Getting to the Answer: Think about the entire scene described in the passage and decide why the author chose to describe Levin's heart as "throbbing." Choice (D) is the correct answer. The author chose this word to capture Levin's agitated state.

10. A   Difficulty: Hard

Category: Rhetoric

Getting to the Answer: Eliminate answer choices that are clearly not representative of the author's feelings or attitude about Levin. The author presents Levin's situation as one that is painful. The passage's tone suggests that Levin is worthy of the reader's empathy. Choice (A) fits this tone.

Franklin Delano Roosevelt Speech

Suggested Passage Map notes:

¶1: US devoted to democracy

¶2: must think about soc. & eco problems which → soc. revol.

¶3: list of basics of dem.

¶4: must maintain basics

¶5: list of what should be improved

¶6: Americans will personally sacrifice for them

¶7: explain tax changes

¶8: people will be ok with them

¶9: four essential human freedoms

¶10: freedom speech and expression

¶11: freedom of religion

¶12: freedom from want

¶13: freedom from fear

¶14: are attainable now; against new order of tyranny

¶15: moral order

¶16: change can made done peacefully

¶17: US supports human rights everywhere and will win

11. D   Difficulty: Hard

Category: Rhetoric

Getting to the Answer: The introduction to the passage states that President Roosevelt intends to preserve and spread democracy. Choice (D) makes clear that the president wants to promote human rights, which can be achieved by spreading "American ideals around the world."

12. D   Difficulty: Hard

Category: Command of Evidence

Getting to the Answer: Be careful of choices that do not provide direct evidence to support the president's purpose. The correct answer will relate specifically to the stated purpose, or intent, of the passage. President Roosevelt makes clear that his intention is to provide support for global efforts to end tyranny and spread democracy and to garner the support of the American people for these goals. In the previous question, his stated purpose is "to make its people conscious of their individual stake in the preservation of democratic life in America." Only (D) provides direct evidence for the previous question.

13. D   Difficulty: Easy

Category: Vocab-in-Context

Getting to the Answer: All answer choices are alternate meanings of the word "sacrifice." The correct answer will relate directly to the context of the passage. Despite the fact that Roosevelt gave the speech on the eve of America's involvement in World War II, neither B nor C is the meaning he's after. Choice (D), "surrender of interests to a greater good," is the correct answer.

14. B   Difficulty: Hard

Category: Connections

Getting to the Answer: Keep in mind that you're looking for a relationship that is suggested, not stated. To reach the correct answer, you must infer, or make a logical guess, based on information in the passage. The correct answer will provide support for the stated purpose of the passage while demonstrating a logical relationship. Choice (B) provides support for the stated goal of winning support among U.S. citizens for the spread of democracy abroad. It does so by suggesting that the security of U.S. democracy depends on the advancement of human rights and freedoms globally.

15. D   Difficulty: Medium

Category: Command of Evidence

Getting to the Answer: Avoid answers that provide evidence for incorrect answers to the previous question. The correct answer will use language reflective of the correct answer above to demonstrate a relationship. Principles and ideas such as democracy, freedom, and protection of human rights are used interchangeably throughout Roosevelt's speech. The lines in (D) draw the connection between freedom at home and freedom everywhere.

16. C   Difficulty: Easy

Category: Vocab-in-Context

Getting to the Answer: Substitute each answer choice for the word in question and decide which one fits the context provided in the passage. In the context of the passage, (C) works best. It draws a distinction between individual citizens' monetary interests, or their pocketbooks, and the cause of patriotism, or the greater good.

17. A   Difficulty: Medium

Category: Rhetoric

Getting to the Answer: Keep in mind that the correct answer will relate directly to the meaning of the elements in the identified lines. President Roosevelt is arguing against those who would oppose the overarching goal of his speech, namely to garner support for the spread of democracy overseas. Choice (A) fits best; Roosevelt asserts that his goals are realistic and attainable, not just idealistic visions, as his opponents might claim.

18. D   Difficulty: Medium

Category: Rhetoric

Getting to the Answer: Be wary of answers like A and B that seem to offer specific advice or state specific goals relevant to the purpose of the passage without suggesting how those goals might be achieved. The correct answer will offer a tool, a condition, or another asset for achieving the passage's claim—in this case, the spread of democracy. The previous question identifies that President Roosevelt considers the spread of global democracy achievable. This question asks you to identify how the president envisions achieving that purpose. Choice (D) matches the intent. In this line, President Roosevelt identifies "our unity of purpose" as an asset that will help achieve his goal.

19. C   Difficulty: Hard

Category: Inference

Getting to the Answer: Be careful of answers that cite other policies that the president might support that are not related to the lines quoted. The correct answer will relate directly to the specific lines in question. In this speech, Roosevelt identifies four freedoms that he views the United States as obligated to defend. The freedom from want signifies a commitment to helping struggling populations at home and abroad. Choice (C) fits. The president urges economic understandings among nations to help those in need.

20. C   Difficulty: Medium

Category: Rhetoric

Getting to the Answer: Be careful of answers like

A that offer other viable uses of rhetoric within the larger passage. The correct answer will relate specifically to the text cited in the question. Roosevelt suggests that the preservation of American freedoms cannot exist without the preservation of human rights on a global scale. To cement this connection, he contrasts democratic movements with tyrannical movements occurring in the world. Choice (C) is the correct answer. President Roosevelt references "the so-called new order of tyranny" in order to show what might happen should the United States and the American people not support other nations in their fight against such tyranny.

Women's Suffrage

Suggested Passage Map notes:

¶1: Changes in Am. voting process

¶2: women's voting history; Seneca Falls declaration

¶3: 1878 – amendment proposed, federal gov't not ready

¶4: women voting in New Zealand, Australia, United Kingdom

¶5: WWI → female activism; 19th Amendment passed in 1919, ratified 1920

¶6: elections still not equal b/c Af. Americans often disenfranchised; 1965 Voting Rights Act → voting equality for all

21. C   Difficulty: Medium

Category: Rhetoric

Getting to the Answer: Keep in mind that the "stance" of an author refers to his or her perspective or attitude toward the topic. The passage is written by a scholar or a historian who is looking back on the events that led to the adoption of the Nineteenth Amendment. It is not written by a primary source, such as a legislator or an advocate in the midst of the movement's events. For this reason, (C) is the correct answer. The author of the passage is clearly a scholar

evaluating not just the motivation of women's suffrage leaders but the key events and impact of the movement as a whole.

22. B   Difficulty: Hard

Category: Rhetoric

Getting to the Answer: Avoid answers like A that refer to related issues not relevant to the passage's purpose and answers like D that go too far. The correct answer will identify a claim that is supported by the quotation. In the quote, the author notes that election laws following passage of the Nineteenth Amendment did not secure equal voting rights for all. From this statement, it becomes clear that other groups of people still needed support for their voting rights. Answer (B) is correct.

23. D   Difficulty: Medium

Category: Command of Evidence

Getting to the Answer: Reread the line quoted in the previous question and notice that it occurs in the passage after ratification of the Nineteenth Amendment. Therefore, the evidence you're looking for will refer to an event that came later. The author suggests that the Nineteenth Amendment did not win equal voting rights for all citizens but that it did serve as an important step on the way to free and fair elections. Choice (D) demonstrates that a later event expanded voting rights further, to citizens regardless not only of gender but also of race.

24. C   Difficulty: Easy

Category: Vocab-in-Context

Getting to the Answer: Consider the events that are being described in the paragraph in which the word appears. This will help you choose the best answer. It's clear in this paragraph that the women's suffrage movement was gaining momentum at this time. Events and tactics excited those who supported the movement and attracted more supporters. Therefore, (C) reflects the correct meaning of "galvanized."

25. A   Difficulty: Hard

Category: Rhetoric

Getting to the Answer: Carefully review the paragraph in which the line appears before choosing the best answer. Choice (A) demonstrates the connection between successfully changing one element (people's minds) in order to change the other (laws).

26. A   Difficulty: Hard

Category: Inference

Getting to the Answer: Be wary of answers like D that go too far in asserting unsubstantiated causal relationships. The correct answer will reference an idea or a relationship that is supported by the content of the passage. Choice (A) expresses the idea implicit in the passage that the American government responds, sometimes slowly, to the changing needs and sentiments of the American people.

27. D   Difficulty: Hard

Category: Command of Evidence

Getting to the Answer: Watch for answers like A and C that cite specific changes or examples but do not provide direct support. The correct answer to the previous question states the idea implicit in the passage that the government responds and adapts to changes in U.S. society. This suggests a gradual change. Choice (D) demonstrates the idea that both society and the government have changed over time as the civil rights movement of the late twentieth century overcame social and legal inequalities inherited from earlier in the nation's history.

28. C   Difficulty: Medium

Category: Synthesis

Getting to the Answer: Be careful of answers that aren't backed by sufficient evidence in the graphic. The graphic shows proof that women's suffrage unfolded through a series of events over a long period of time. Choice (C) is the correct answer.

29. C   Difficulty: Medium

Category: Vocab-in-Context

Getting to the Answer: Read the sentence in which the word appears. The correct answer should be interchangeable with the word. The passage states that "Posters . . . called into question the authenticity of a free country with unjust laws." Choice (C) is the correct answer, as "legitimacy" refers to something that is in accordance with established principles.

30. B   Difficulty: Medium

Category: Inference

Getting to the Answer: Be cautious about answers that present accurate facts but that do not directly relate to the content of the question. Choice (B) is the correct answer. Wilson's framing of the conflict abroad as a fight for democracy and freedom helped women suffragists draw attention to the fact that the U.S. government was fighting for justice abroad while denying justice at home.

31. D   Difficulty: Medium

Category: Synthesis

Getting to the Answer: A question like this is asking you to compare information provided in the graphic with information provided in the passage text. Consider each answer choice as you make your comparison. Choice (D) is the correct answer. Both the graphic and the passage indicate that women's suffrage gained early victories in several states quite a few years before becoming law at the federal level through passage of the Nineteenth Amendment.

Paired Passages—Radioisotopes

Suggested Passage Map notes:
    Passage 1

    ¶1: (central idea): use atoms to date things; isotopes def. & exs.

    ¶2: isotopes unstable; measure C-14

¶3: C-14 decay = predictable

¶4: C-14 dating; materials; timeline based on layers

Passage 2

¶1: def. radioactive; why dangerous; danger = radiation rate

¶2: half-life def. = decay rate; exs.

¶3: long half-life = long problem

32. C   **Difficulty:** Hard

Category: Inference

Getting to the Answer: Use your Passage Map to locate the paragraph that explains carbon-14 dating. This paragraph will contain the description of what materials can be dated using this method. In paragraph 4, the author states that carbon-14 dating can be used on materials made by a living organism. An arrowhead made from a bone is constructed of such material, choice (C).

33. D   **Difficulty:** Hard

Category: Command of Evidence

Getting to the Answer: Locate each of the answer choices in the passage. The correct answer should provide direct support for the answer to the previous question: the bone arrowhead can be dated using carbon-14 dating. In paragraph 4, the author describes the process for carbon-14 dating. Choice (D) is correct because this sentence provides a direct description of the materials that can be dated using carbon-14 dating.

34. B   **Difficulty:** Medium

Category: Vocab-in-Context

Getting to the Answer: Pretend that the word "decay" is a blank. Reread around the cited word to predict a word that could substitute for "decay" in context. The previous paragraph discusses how scientists measure the rate of emission to calculate the amount of carbon-14 in a sample. "Emission" means release; therefore, the amount of carbon-14 is be-

coming smaller if the atoms are releasing it. In this sentence, therefore, predict "decay" means to *decrease*, which matches "deteriorate," choice (B).

35. C   **Difficulty:** Easy

Category: Connections

Getting to the Answer: Look at your notes for paragraph 3. Summarize the ratio of carbon-12 to carbon-14 in living tissue in your own words. Look for the answer choice that most closely matches your prediction. In paragraph 3, the author explains that the ratio of carbon-12 to carbon-14 for living things is the same as the ratio in the atmosphere: constant. Choice (C) is correct.

36. C   **Difficulty:** Medium

Category: Command of Evidence

Getting to the Answer: Review what part of the passage you used to predict an answer for the previous question: the ratio is constant for living things. Of the answer choices, only lines 28-31 explain the ratio of carbon-12 to carbon-14 in living things. Choice (C) is correct.

37. B   **Difficulty:** Medium

Category: Detail

Getting to the Answer: Read around the cited lines. The author directly states why a release of iodine-131 is not cause for long-term concern. In paragraph 3, the author explains that the initial release of radiation from an accident involving iodine-131 will be high, but the level of radiation will drop quickly (lines 75–76). Choice (B) is correct.

38. C   **Difficulty:** Medium

Category: Detail

Getting to the Answer: Use your Passage Map to find the information about why exposure to radiation is dangerous.

Getting to the Answer: In paragraph 1, lines 53-55, the author explains that radiation is harmful to living tissue because it can cause damage to the cells'

DNA, which matches choice (C).

39. A   Difficulty: Easy

Category: Vocab-in-Context

Getting to the Answer: Pretend that the word "original" is a blank. Reread around the cited word to predict a word that could substitute for "original" in context. The previous paragraph explains how scientists use "half-life" to determine how quickly material decays. If the material is decaying, then predict "original" refers to the *first* material. Choice (A) matches your prediction.

40. D   Difficulty: Medium

Category: Detail

Getting to the Answer: Review your notes for Passage 2. Try to put into your own words how scientists use half-life calculations of radioactive materials. Look for the answer that most closely matches your idea. In paragraph 1, the author explains that the level of danger posed by radiation released during a nuclear accident depends on how quickly radiation is released (lines 59-62). In paragraph 2, the author discusses how the half-life of radioactive material is used to determine how long a material will emit radiation. Paragraph 3 then explains how different half-lives translate into short-term or long-term radiation concerns. Choice (D) is correct because it most clearly paraphrases the information in the passage about how scientists use half-life calculations.

41. A   Difficulty: Hard

Category: Synthesis

Getting to the Answer: The central idea will be supported by all of the evidence presented in both passages. Review the central idea you identified for each passage in your Passage Maps. Passage 1 discusses the application of atomic and nuclear physics in archaeology while Passage 2 details how scientists apply atomic and nuclear physics to studies of radioactivity in nuclear power plant accidents. Choice (A) is correct.

42. A   Difficulty: Hard

Category: Synthesis

Getting to the Answer: Analyze the graph to see that it describes the decay of carbon-14 over time. Think about how this data relates to the texts. The graph portrays the decay of carbon-14 as described in Passage 1. The definition of "half-life" is given in Passage 2. The half-life of a material is the amount of time it takes for half of that material to decay. The graph shows that about 50 percent of carbon-14 remains after 5,400 years. Choice (A) is correct.

Biomimicry Passage

Suggested Passage Map notes:

¶1: George de Mestral – invented velcro

¶2: biomimicry – study nature to improve people's homes, cities, etc.

¶3: used in architecture

¶4: Michael Pawlyn - adapt principles behind natural shapes → innovative solutions

¶5: used in optics and robotics

¶6: some natural stuff not advanced but simple: abalone shell

¶7: nanoscale features; Andrew Parker – skin of thorny devil

¶8: can learn from animal features

¶9: improve energy efficiency

¶10: radical, optimistic field

43. A   Difficulty: Medium

Category: Global

Getting to the Answer: Look for the answer choice that describes an idea supported throughout the passage rather than a specific detail. The passage cites several examples of biomimicry, the study of how materials and systems found in nature can be replicated to benefit humans. Therefore, (A) is the best summary of the central idea of the passage.

44. B   Difficulty: Medium

Category: Command of Evidence

Getting to the Answer: Think back to why you chose your answer to the previous question. This will help you pick the correct quote as evidence. Choice (B) is the correct answer because it provides evidence for the central idea that the author presents about the field of biomimicry.

45. A   Difficulty: Hard

Category: Rhetoric

Getting to the Answer: Think about the primary purpose of the quote. Eliminate any answer choices that don't support this purpose. The quote, which is from a book on architecture, explains why architects turn to biomimicry for solutions in their work. Choice (A) is the correct answer.

46. B   Difficulty: Medium

Category: Connections

Getting to the Answer: Reread the paragraph that the question is asking about. Look for specific details about the abalone shrimp shell and soft chalk. The passage clearly states that the abalone shrimp shell is harder than soft chalk because of the way the basic material composing each is arranged, so (B) is the correct answer.

47. D   Difficulty: Medium

Category: Rhetoric

Getting to the Answer: In order to understand why an author includes a quote from another person, examine the surrounding sentences. This often makes clear the author's reason for including the quotation. The author includes the quote from Pawlyn to support and strengthen his or her own view that energy efficiency "has never been more important." Therefore, (D) is the correct answer.

48. D   Difficulty: Easy

Category: Vocab-in-Context

Getting to the Answer: Replace the word in question with each of the answer choices. This will help you eliminate the ones that don't make sense in the context. Choice (D), "concepts," is the only answer choice that makes sense in this context because it reflects the foundational reasons behind the structures.

49. A   Difficulty: Medium

Category: Inference

Getting to the Answer: Keep in mind that you're being asked to make an inference, a logical guess based on information in the passage. Therefore, the correct answer is not stated in the passage. The variety of examples of biomimicry mentioned in the passage make it reasonable to infer that more scientists will utilize solutions developed through biomimicry in the future. Choice (A) is the correct answer.

50. C   Difficulty: Medium

Category: Command of Evidence

Getting to the Answer: Reread each quotation in the context of the passage. Consider which one is the best evidence to support the inference made in the previous question. The examples cited in (C) provide strong evidence for the inference that more scientists will probably make use of biomimicry in years to come.

51. D   Difficulty: Medium

Category: Vocab-in-Context

Getting to the Answer: Eliminate answer choices that are synonyms for the word in question but do not work in the context of the sentence. Because biomimicry is such an innovative approach, it makes sense that the meaning of "radical" in this context is closest to (D), "revolutionary."

52. C   Difficulty: Hard

Category: Synthesis

Getting to the Answer: Remember that a graphic might not refer to something explicitly stated in the passage. Instead, it often provides a visual example of how an important concept discussed in the passage works. The graphic and its caption help illustrate an example of biomimicry not mentioned in the passage: that of a solar power plant designed to mimic the arrangement of petals in a sunflower. This directs more energy toward the power plant's central tower and improves the efficiency of the power plant. Choice (C) is the correct answer.

WRITING AND LANGUAGE TEST

The Age of the Librarian

1. C   Difficulty: Easy

Category: Usage

Getting to the Answer: Examine the verb tense in the rest of the sentence. This will help you find the correct answer. As written, the sentence switches verb tense mid-sentence. Other verbs in the sentence, "worked" and "was," indicate that the events happened in the past. Choice (C) is the correct choice because it correctly uses the past tense of the target verb.

2. D   Difficulty: Medium

Category: Punctuation

Getting to the Answer: Pay attention to the quotation marks. Reading through the sentence and the answer choices shows that two issues might need correcting. The sentence inside the quotation marks is a complete sentence. The correct answer needs to punctuate that sentence before closing the quote. Additionally, "however" is being used as a connector or transition word and needs to be followed by a comma after beginning the new sentence. Choice (D) appropriately uses a period prior to the end quotes and correctly inserts a comma after the transition word "However."

3. B   Difficulty: Medium

Category: Effective Language Use

Getting to the Answer: Watch out for choices that distort the tone of the passage. The passage suggests that people expected or anticipated that Harris would become a librarian. Evidence for this idea is found in the statement that she was "constantly told" that she "should be studying to be a librarian." Harris was certainly aware that people anticipated this course of study for her, but the presence of the phrase "Little did she realize" tells you that she didn't expect to become one. The correct choice is (B), "imminent," meaning that becoming a librarian was about to occur despite her own expectations.

4. C   Difficulty: Hard

Category: Effective Language Use

Getting to the Answer: Read the sentence carefully for context clues. Also, think about the tone of what is being described. This will help you choose the best answer. Given the phrasing of the sentence, the answer must be close in meaning to "excited," which is used earlier in the sentence. Therefore, (C) is the correct answer.

5. A   Difficulty: Medium

Category: Punctuation

Getting to the Answer: Determine whether a clause is dependent or independent to decide between a comma and a semicolon. Choice (A) is the correct answer. The sentence is correctly punctuated as written because it uses a comma at the end of the introductory dependent clause.

6. C   Difficulty: Medium

Category: Sentence Formation

Getting to the Answer: Read the sentence carefully. The sentence sounds clunky and awkward. Look for an answer choice that makes the sentence clear and easy to understand. Notice that the word "asking" is part of a participial phrase that modifies "Miguel." A participial phrase should be placed as close as possible to the noun it modifies. When a participial phrase begins a sentence, it should be set off with a comma. Choice (C) is correct. The placement of commas and modifiers makes the content easy to understand, and the sentence is free of grammatical or punctuation errors.

7. B   Difficulty: Medium

Category: Development

Getting to the Answer: Read the entire paragraph carefully and predict the main idea. Then look for a close match with your prediction. The paragraph discusses how the role of librarian has changed due to an increased use of technology. Choice (B) is the correct answer, as it explicitly addresses the changing role of the librarian.

8. D   Difficulty: Medium

Category: Sentence Formation

Getting to the Answer: Read the sentence and note the series of examples. A series should have parallel structure. The sentence is not correct as written. The items in the series switch forms from participial phrases beginning with "enabling" and "offering" to "they house." All of the items need to fit the same pattern or form. Choice (D) is correct because it appropriately begins each item in the series with a participle.

9. C   Difficulty: Hard

Category: Development

Getting to the Answer: Don't be fooled by answer choices that are true statements but do not directly support the main idea of the paragraph. The paragraph concerns how the role of the librarian has changed due to an increased use of technology. The correct answer needs to support the idea that librarians work with technology in new ways. Choice (C) works best. It offers a specific example of how teachers look to the librarian to be a "media mentor" and illustrates this new role for school librarians.

10. C   Difficulty: Easy

Category: Usage

Getting to the Answer: Read the sentence prior to the pronoun and determine whom the pronoun is referencing. Pronouns should not be ambiguous, and they must match the verb in number. The sentence is ambiguous as written. "She" would presumably refer back to the "young student," but it seems unlikely that the student would be laughing and thinking about the collections in the library after asking the librarian a question. Choice (C) is the best choice. It clearly indicates the subject of the sentence (Harris) and avoids ambiguity.

11. A   Difficulty: Medium

Category: Usage

Getting to the Answer: Figure out whom the pronoun refers to and make sure it matches the antecedent in number. Watch out for confusing contractions and possessives. The pronoun in the sentence needs to indicate who will have the ideas. Harris is talking to a single student, so the sentence will need a singular possessive pronoun. Choice (A) is correct. As it is, the sentence correctly uses a singular possessive pronoun.

Unforeseen Consequences: The Dark Side of the Industrial Revolution

12. B   Difficulty: Medium

Category: Sentence Formation

Getting to the Answer: Be careful of answers that sound correct when they stand alone but do not conform to the structure of the sentence as a whole. The existing text is incorrect, as it does not maintain parallel structure. Choice (B) is the correct answer, as it maintains the parallel structure of preposition ("into") + noun ("the role").

13. B   Difficulty: Easy

Category: Punctuation

Getting to the Answer: Eliminate answers that confuse the usage of commas and semicolons. Choice (B) is correct. Without the comma, the following clause modifies "urban areas" when it should modify the entire preceding clause.

14. B   Difficulty: Medium

Category: Effective Language Use

Getting to the Answer: Avoid choices that are redundant and imprecise. The correct answer will use the clearest, most concise terminology to communicate the idea. Choice (B) is correct. It is the most concise—and clearest—word choice because all of the items listed in the original sentence are simply types of food. The other choices use more words than necessary to convey meaning.

15. A   Difficulty: Medium

Category: Organization

Getting to the Answer: The first sentence should function as a transition between ideas in the previous paragraph and ideas in the current paragraph. Choice (A) makes sense. This choice connects ideas from the previous paragraph with the content of paragraph 3. The sentences that follow provide details to support that introductory idea.

16. A   Difficulty: Hard

Category: Quantitative

Getting to the Answer: Eliminate answers like B that fail to support the cited sentence directly. The underlined sentence references "unprecedented amounts of human-made carbon dioxide into the air." This suggests an increase in the amount of carbon dioxide in the atmosphere over time. Therefore, (A) is the correct answer.

17. C   Difficulty: Medium

Category: Effective Language Use

Getting to the Answer: Choose the answer that presents the correct relationship between ideas. Choice (C) is correct. It shows the causal relationship without adding verbiage.

18. A   Difficulty: Easy

Category: Effective Language Use

Getting to the Answer: Plug in the answer choices and select the one that reflects a specific meaning relevant to the sentence. The paragraph focuses on the negative effects of industrialization and waste production. Therefore, (A) is the correct answer.

19. B   Difficulty: Hard

Category: Development

Getting to the Answer: Be careful of choices that relate to the underlined portion of the text without showing clearly how the underlined portion supports the full implications of the preceding sentence. The paragraph explains that industrialization resulted in the destruction of resources. The correct answer, (B), serves as clear evidence of the "process of destruction and reduced resources."

20. C   Difficulty: Medium

Category: Effective Language Use

Getting to the Answer: Be careful of answers that make sense but do not fully support the meaning of the content. The correct answer will not only flow logically but will also reflect the precise purpose and meaning of the larger sentence and paragraph. Choice (C) is the correct answer. "Substandard" communicates clearly that the working conditions were the cause of the health problems.

21. D   Difficulty: Medium

Category: Sentence Formation

Getting to the Answer: Eliminate choices that result in sentence fragments or fragmented clauses. The correct answer will maintain appropriate syntax without misusing punctuation. Choice (D) is correct.

It sets off the dependent clause without using incorrect punctuation to signal a hard break before an independent clause or second complete sentence.

22. D   Difficulty: Hard

Category: Development

Getting to the Answer: Avoid answers that draw on similar ideas but combine those ideas in a way that communicates a proposition not supported by the essay as a whole. The correct answer will make sense within the larger context of the essay. The central idea of the entire essay is that industrialization and progress came at a cost that made the promise of a bright future difficult to fulfill. Choice (D) is the correct answer.

Remembering Freud

23. C   Difficulty: Hard

Category: Effective Language Use

Getting to the Answer: Consider the fact that there may be a choice that helps make the meaning of the sentence very precise. Choice (C) most accurately indicates that Freud led a whole movement.

24. B   Difficulty: Medium

Category: Punctuation

Getting to the Answer: Plug in each answer choice and select the one that seems most correct. Choice (B) makes it clear to the reader that this is extra information modifying the word "career."

25. D   Difficulty: Medium

Category: Sentence Formation

Getting to the Answer: Remember that in a list, all things listed should be presented with the same grammatical structure. "Id," "ego," and "Freudian slip" are all nouns. Choice (D) is the correct answer because it uses a parallel structure for all three nouns.

26. B   Difficulty: Hard

Category: Development

Getting to the Answer: Notice that the underlined sentence is the first sentence in the paragraph. Think about which choice would make the best topic sentence, given the content of the rest of the paragraph. Choice (B) correctly makes the free-speaking technique the focus of the paragraph's topic sentence, while suggesting that the technique was radical enough to earn Freud his title.

27. B   Difficulty: Medium

Category: Effective Language Use

Getting to the Answer: Eliminate any choices that don't seem as precise as others. Choice (B) is correct. The word "recesses" is more precise; it connotes smaller parts of the brain and a sense of being hidden.

28. C   Difficulty: Easy

Category: Punctuation

Getting to the Answer: Think about how the sentence sounds when read aloud. This often helps you get a good sense of whether or not a comma is needed. Choice (C) would fit here. The sentence eliminates the unneeded comma.

29. B   Difficulty: Hard

Category: Sentence Formation

Getting to the Answer: Remember that a modifier should be adjacent to the noun it is modifying and set off by punctuation. Choice (B) is correct. The modifier "like neurosis or other psychological trauma" should come directly after "conditions."

30. C   Difficulty: Hard

Category: Development

Getting to the Answer: Consider how this sentence relates to the one before it and the one that follows it. Does it offer strong support of the connecting ideas? This section discussed the development and lasting influence of Freud's ideas. The best supporting sentence will provide details connecting these concepts. Choice (C) is correct. It emphasizes that Freud developed new ideas that have had a lasting influence on psychological practices.

31. B   Difficulty: Medium

Category: Sentence Formation

Getting to the Answer: Notice that you are dealing with a run-on sentence. Identify the point in the run-on where it appears two sentences have been fused together. Choice (B) is correct. This choice splits the run-on sentence into two separate, grammatically correct sentences.

32. D   Difficulty: Easy

Category: Sentence Formation

Getting to the Answer: Eliminate answer choices that are not complete sentences or do not maintain the correct verb tense. Choice (D) correctly changes the phrase "Freud's finding of a method" to "Freud found a method," making the sentence complete. It also corrects the verb tense.

33. A   Difficulty: Hard

Category: Sentence Formation

Getting to the Answer: Recall that when a dependent clause precedes an independent clause, it should be set off with a comma. Choice (A) is the best choice. Although lengthy, the dependent clause in the sentence ("as long as occasions arise . . .") is correctly combined with its independent clause ("Sigmund Freud will be remembered . . .") by use of a comma.

Success in Montreal

34. B   Difficulty: Easy

Category: Sentence Formation

Getting to the Answer: Always check whether two

or more verbs that serve the same function have a parallel structure. Choice (B) is correct. "To prevent" is in the infinitive form like the earlier verb in the sentence, "to reverse."

35. A   Difficulty: Hard

Category: Effective Language Use

Getting to the Answer: Look for the choice that most concisely and correctly joins the two sentences. Choice (A) is the best fit. This option joins the sentences concisely and correctly.

36. C   Difficulty: Medium

Category: Effective Language Use

Getting to the Answer: Remember that the best answer is the most concise and effective way of stating the information while ensuring that the information is complete. Choice (C) works best here. It uses the fewest necessary words to convey the complete information.

37. C   Difficulty: Medium

Category: Sentence Formation

Getting to the Answer: Eliminate any choices that use transition words inappropriately. Two complete thoughts should be separated into two different sentences. Therefore, (C) is the best choice.

38. B   Difficulty: Hard

Category: Quantitative

Getting to the Answer: Examine the graphic for details that suggest which answer is correct. Choice (B) accurately reflects the information in the graphic. Beginning in the 1990s, the size of the ozone hole began to level off.

39. C   Difficulty: Medium

Category: Effective Language Use

Getting to the Answer: Check each word to see how it fits with the context of the sentence. While all of the words have similar meanings, only one fits the context of the paragraph. Choice (C), "measured," has a connotation that corresponds to "gauge" in the following sentence.

40. B   Difficulty: Easy

Category: Usage

Getting to the Answer: Remember that the possessive form must agree with its antecedent. The correct answer will reflect the gender and number of its antecedent; in this case, the word "treaty." Therefore, (B) is correct.

41. A   Difficulty: Hard

Category: Development

Getting to the Answer: To find the central idea of a paragraph, identify important details and then summarize them in a sentence or two. Then find the choice that is the closest to your summary. Choice (A) most clearly states the paragraph's central idea, that the ozone layer is beginning to return to normal.

42. D   Difficulty: Medium

Category: Development

Getting to the Answer: To find the correct answer, first determine the central idea of the paragraph. Choice (D) is the least essential sentence in the paragraph, so it is the correct answer.

43. D   Difficulty: Medium

Category: Effective Language Use

Getting to the Answer: Context clues indicate which word is appropriate in the sentence. Check to see which word fits best in the sentence. The word "reverse," (D), fits with the context of the sentence and connotes a more precise action than does "change."

44. C   Difficulty: Hard

Category: Organization

Getting to the Answer: Examine the entire paragraph. Decide whether the sentence provides more

information about a topic mentioned in one of the other sentences. This sentence provides more information related to sentence 1, "The Montreal Protocol is a living document"; it describes how the document is "living." Choice (C) is the correct answer.

MATH—NO CALCULATOR TEST

1. C   Difficulty: Easy

Category: Heart of Algebra / Linear Equations

Getting to the Answer: To determine what the y-intercept could mean in the context of a word problem, examine the labels on the graph and note what each axis represents. According to the labels, the y-axis represents cost, and the x-axis represents the number of games played. The y-intercept, $(0, 5)$, has an x-value of 0, which means 0 games were played, yet there is still a cost of \$5. The cost must represent a flat fee that is charged before any games are played, such as an entrance fee to enter the arcade, (C).

2. A   Difficulty: Easy

Category: Passport to Advanced Math / Exponents

Getting to the Answer: To divide one rational expression by another, multiply the first expression by the reciprocal (the flip) of the second expression. Rewrite the division as multiplication, factor any factorable expressions, and then simplify if possible.

$$\frac{3x}{x+5} \div \frac{6}{4x+20} = \frac{3x}{x+5} \cdot \frac{4x+20}{6}$$

$$= \frac{3x}{x+5} \cdot \frac{4(x+5)}{6}$$

$$= \frac{12x}{6}$$

$$= 2x$$

Note that the question also states that $x \neq -5$. This doesn't affect your answer—it is simply stated because the denominators of rational expressions cannot equal 0. Choice (A) is correct.

3. D   **Difficulty:** Easy

Category: Additional Topics in Math / Geometry

Getting to the Answer: When the equation of a circle is written in the form $(x - h)^2 + (y - k)^2 = r^2$, the point (h, k) represents the center of the circle on a coordinate plane, and r represents the length of the radius. To find the area of a circle, use the formula, $A = \pi r^2$. In the equation given in the question, r^2 is the constant on the right-hand side (25)—you don't even need to solve for r because the area formula involves r^2, not r. So, the area is $\pi(25)$ or 25π, (D).

4. C   **Difficulty:** Easy

Category: Passport to Advanced Math / Functions

Getting to the Answer: When using function notation, $f(x)$ is simply another way of saying y, so this question is asking you to find the values of x for which $y = 0$, or in other words, where the graph crosses the x-axis. The graph crosses the x-axis at the points $(-2, 0)$ and $(3, 0)$, so the values of x for which $f(x) = 0$ are -2 and 3, (C).

5. B   **Difficulty:** Medium

Category: Heart of Algebra / Linear Equations

Getting to the Answer: Choose the best strategy to answer the question. You could start by cross-multiplying to get rid of the denominators, but simplifying the numerators first will make the calculations easier.

$$\frac{4(d + 3) - 9}{8} = \frac{10 - (2 - d)}{6}$$

$$\frac{4d + 12 - 9}{8} = \frac{10 - 2 + d}{6}$$

$$\frac{4d + 3}{8} = \frac{8 + d}{6}$$

$$6(4d + 3) = 8(8 + d)$$

$$24d + 18 = 64 + 8d$$

$$16d = 46$$

$$d = \frac{46}{16} = \frac{23}{8}$$

Choice (B) is correct.

6. D   **Difficulty:** Medium

Category: Passport to Advanced Math / Functions

Getting to the Answer: This is a crossover question, so quickly skim the first couple of sentences. Then look for the relevant information in the last couple of sentences. It may also help to circle the portions of the graph that meet the given requirement.

Because *greater* means *higher* on a graph, the statement $f(t) > g(t)$ translates to "Where is $f(t)$ above $g(t)$?" The solid curve represents f and the dashed curve represents g, so $f > g$ between the years 1960 and 1980 and again between the years 2000 and 2010. Look for these time intervals in the answer choices: $1960 < t < 1980$ and $2000 < t < 2010$. This matches (D).

7. D   **Difficulty:** Medium

Category: Passport to Advanced Math / Scatterplots

Getting to the Answer: Use the shape of the data to predict the type of equation that might be used as a model. Then, use specific values from the graph to choose the correct equation. According to the graph, the population of the whales grew slowly at first and then more quickly. This means that an exponential model is probably the best fit, so you can eliminate A (linear) and B (quadratic). The remaining equations are both exponential, so choose a data point and see which equation is the closest fit. Be careful—the vertical axis represents *hundreds* of whales, and the question states that t represents the number of years since the study began, so $t = 0$ for 1995, $t = 3$ for 1998, and so on. If you use the data for 1995, which is the point $(0, 100)$, the results are the same for both equations, so choose a different point. Using the data for 2007, $t = 2007 - 1995 = 12$, and the number of whales was 800. Substitute these values into C and D to see which one is true. Choice C is not true because $800 \neq 100 \times 2^{12}$. Choice (D) is correct because:

$$800 = 100 \times 2^{\frac{12}{4}} = 100 \times 2^3 = 100 \times 8$$

8. B   **Difficulty:** Medium

Category: Heart of Algebra / Linear Equations

Getting to the Answer: To find the average rate of change over the 5-year period, find the slope between the starting point (0, 1,200) and the ending point (5, 100).

$$m = \frac{y_2 - y_1}{x_2 - x_1} = \frac{100 - 1{,}200}{5 - 0} = \frac{-1{,}100}{5} = -220$$

Choice (B) is correct. (The average rate of change is negative because the laptop decreases in value over time.)

Note: Because the question involves *straight-line* depreciation, you could have used any two points on the graph to find the slope. As a general rule, however, you should use the endpoints of the given time interval.

9. B   **Difficulty:** Medium

Category: Passport to Advanced Math / Exponents

Getting to the Answer: When multiplying polynomials, carefully multiply each term in the first factor by each term in the second factor. This question doesn't ask for the entire product, so check to make sure you answered the right question (the coefficient of x^2).

$$\left(6x^2 - \frac{2}{5}x + 1\right)\left(10x + \frac{1}{3}\right)$$

$$= 6x^2\left(10x + \frac{1}{3}\right) - \frac{2}{5}x\left(10x + \frac{1}{3}\right) + 1\left(10x + \frac{1}{3}\right)$$

$$= 60x^3 + \underline{2x^2 - 4x^2} - \frac{2}{15}x + 10x + \frac{1}{3}$$

The coefficient of x^2 is $2 + (-4) = -2$, which is (B).

10. A   **Difficulty:** Medium

Category: Heart of Algebra / Linear Equations

Getting to the Answer: The line is decreasing, so the slope (m) is negative. The line crosses the y-axis below 0, so the y-intercept (b) is also negative. Put each answer choice in slope-intercept form, one at a time, and examine the signs of m and b. Begin with (A):

$$-6x - 4y = 5$$
$$-4y = 6x + 5$$
$$y = \frac{6x}{-4} + \frac{5}{-4}$$
$$y = -\frac{3}{2}x - \frac{5}{4}$$

You don't need to check any of the other equations. Choice (A) has a negative slope and a negative y-intercept, so it is the correct equation.

11. C   **Difficulty:** Hard

Category: Heart of Algebra / Systems of Linear Equations

Getting to the Answer: Graphically, a system of linear equations that has no solution indicates two parallel lines or, in other words, two lines that have the same slope. So, write each of the equations in slope-intercept form ($y = mx + b$) and set their slopes (m) equal to each other to solve for k. Before finding the slopes, multiply the top equation by 4 to make it easier to manipulate.

$$4\left(\frac{3}{4}x - \frac{1}{2}y = 12\right) \rightarrow 3x - 2y = 48 \rightarrow y = \frac{3}{2}x - 24$$

$$kx - 2y = 22 \rightarrow -2y = -kx + 22 \rightarrow y = \frac{k}{2}x - 11$$

The slope of the first line is $\frac{3}{2}$, and the slope of the second line is $\frac{k}{2}$. Set them equal and solve for k.

$$\frac{3}{2} = \frac{k}{2}$$
$$2(3) = 2(k)$$
$$6 = 2k$$
$$3 = k$$

Choice (C) is correct.

12. B   **Difficulty:** Hard

Category: Heart of Algebra / Inequalities

Getting to the Answer: Before you write the inequality, you need to find the per-mile rate for the remaining miles. The driver charges \$4.00 for the first $\frac{1}{4}$ mile, which is a flat fee, so write 4. The additional charge is \$1.50 per $\frac{1}{2}$ mile, or 1.50 times 2 = \$3.00 per mile. The number of miles after the first $\frac{1}{4}$ mile is $m - \frac{1}{4}$, so the cost of the trip, not including the first $\frac{1}{4}$ mile, is $3\left(m - \frac{1}{4}\right)$. This means the cost of the whole trip is $4 + 3\left(m - \frac{1}{4}\right)$. The clue "no more than \$10" means that much or less, so use the symbol $\leq$. The inequality is $4 + 3\left(m - \frac{1}{4}\right) \leq 10$, which simplifies to $3.25 + 3m \leq 10$. This matches (B).

13. A   Difficulty: Hard

Category: Passport to Advanced Math / Functions

Getting to the Answer: Based on the equation, the graph of $h(x) = -g(x) + 1$ is a vertical reflection of $g(x)$, over the x-axis, that is then shifted up 1 unit. The graph looks like the dashed line in the following graph:

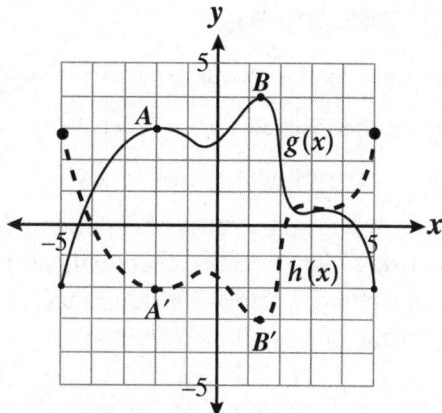

Now, compare the dashed line to each of the answer choices: The range of $h(x)$ is the set of y-values from lowest to highest (based on the dashed line). The lowest point occurs at point B' and has a y-value of -3; the highest value occurs at both ends of the

graph and is 3, so the range is $-3 \leq y \leq 3$. This means (A) is correct and you can move on to the next question. Don't waste valuable time checking the other answer choices unless you are not sure about the range. (Choice B: The minimum value of $h(x)$ is -3, not -4. Choice C: The coordinates of point A on $h(x)$ are $(-2, -2)$, not $(2, 4)$. Choice D: the graph of $h(x)$ is decreasing, not increasing, between $x = -5$ and $x = -2$.)

14. D   Difficulty: Medium

Category: Additional Topics in Math / Imaginary Numbers

Getting to the Answer: Multiply the two complex numbers just as you would two binomials (using FOIL). Then, combine like terms and use the definition $i^2 = -1$ to simplify the result.

$$
\begin{aligned}
(3 + 2i)(5 - i) &= 3(5 - i) + 2i(5 - i) \\
&= 15 - 3i + 10i - 2i^2 \\
&= 15 + 7i - 2(-1) \\
&= 15 + 7i + 2 \\
&= 17 + 7i
\end{aligned}
$$

The question asks for a in $a + bi$, so the correct answer is 17, (D).

15. A   Difficulty: Hard

Category: Passport to Advanced Math / Exponents

Getting to the Answer: Think of the rate given in the question in terms of the constant term you see on the right-hand side of the equation. Working together, the two treatment plants can filter the water in 72 hours. This is equivalent to saying that they can filter $\frac{1}{72}$ of the water in 1 hour. If $\frac{1}{72}$ is the portion of the water the two treatment plants can filter *together*, then each term on the left side of the equation represents the portion that each plant can filter *individually* in 1 hour. Because the new facility is 4 times as fast as the older facility, $\frac{4}{x}$ represents the portion of the water the new plant can filter in

1 hour, and $\dfrac{1}{x}$ represents the portion of the water the older plant can filter in 1 hour. This matches (A).

16. 20   Difficulty: Medium

Category: Heart of Algebra / Linear Equations

Getting to the Answer: Only one equation is given, and it has two variables. This means that you don't have enough information to solve for either variable. Instead, look for the relationship between the variable terms in the equation and those in the expression that you are trying to find, $x + 2y$. First, move the y-term to the left side of the equation to make it look more like the expression you are trying to find. The expression doesn't have fractions, so clear the fractions in the equation by multiplying both sides by 4. This yields the expression that you are looking for, $x + 2y$, so no further work is required—just read the value on the right-hand side of the equation. The answer is 20.

$$\frac{1}{4}x = 5 - \frac{1}{2}y$$

$$\frac{1}{4}x + y\frac{1}{2} = 5$$

$$4\left(\frac{1}{4}x + \frac{1}{2}y\right) = 4(5)$$

$$x + 2y = 20$$

17. 1   Difficulty: Medium

Category: Heart of Algebra / Inequalities

Getting to the Answer: This question is extremely difficult to answer unless you draw a sketch. It doesn't have to be perfect—you just need to get an idea of where the solution region is. Don't forget to flip the inequality symbol when you graph the second equation.

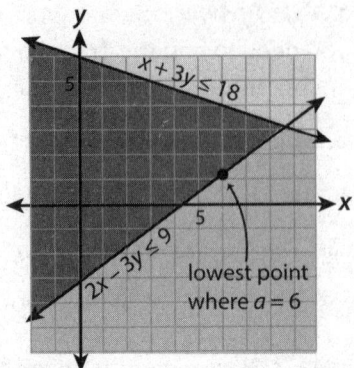

If (a, b) is a solution to the system, then a is the x-coordinate of any point in the darkest shaded region and b is the corresponding y-coordinate. When $a = 6$, the minimum possible value for b lies on the lower boundary line, $2x - 3y \leq 9$. It looks like the y-coordinate is 1, but to be sure, substitute $x = 6$ into the equation and solve for y. You can use $=$ in the equation, instead of the inequality symbol, because you are finding a point on the boundary line.

$$2x - 3y = 9$$
$$2(6) - 3y = 9$$
$$12 - 3y = 9$$
$$-3y = -3$$
$$y = 1$$

18. 2   Difficulty: Hard

Category: Passport to Advanced Math / Exponents

Getting to the Answer: Write each factor in the expression in exponential form: $\sqrt{x} = x^{\frac{1}{2}}$ and $\sqrt[3]{x} = x^{\frac{1}{3}}$. Then use the rules of exponents to simplify the expression. Add the exponents of the factors that are being multiplied and subtract the exponent of the factor that is being divided:

$$\frac{\sqrt{x} \cdot x^{\frac{5}{6}} \cdot x}{\sqrt[3]{x}} = \frac{x^{\frac{1}{2}} \cdot x^{\frac{5}{6}} \cdot x^{1}}{x^{\frac{1}{3}}}$$

$$= x^{\frac{1}{2} + \frac{5}{6} + \frac{1}{1} - \frac{1}{3}}$$

$$= x^{\frac{3}{6} + \frac{5}{6} + \frac{6}{6} - \frac{2}{6}}$$

$$= x^{\frac{12}{6}} = x^{2}$$

Because n is the power of x, the value of n is 2.

19. 14   Difficulty: Hard

Category: Additional Topics in Math / Geometry

Getting to the Answer: The shaded region is the area of the larger triangle minus the area of the smaller triangle. Set up and solve an equation using the information from the figure. You don't know the height of the smaller triangle, so call it h. You do know the area of the shaded region—it's 52 square units.

Larger triangle: base = 12; height = $h + 3 + 3$

Smaller triangle: base = 8; height = h

Shaded area = large area − small area

$$52 = \left[\left(\frac{1}{2}\right)(12)(h + 6)\right] - \left[\left(\frac{1}{2}\right)(8)(h)\right]$$
$$52 = 6(h + 6) - 4h$$
$$52 = 6h + 36 - 4h$$
$$52 = 2h + 36$$
$$16 = 2h$$
$$8 = h$$

The question asks for the height of the *larger* triangle, so the correct answer is 8 + 3 + 3 = 14.

20. 6   Difficulty: Hard

Category: Passport to Advanced Math / Quadratics

Getting to the Answer: The highest power of x in the equation is 2, so the function is quadratic. Writing quadratic equations can be tricky and time-consuming. If you know the roots, you can use factors to write the equation. If you don't know the roots, you need to create a system of equations to find the coefficients of the variable terms. You don't know the roots of this equation, so start with the point that has the easiest values to work with, (0, 1), and substitute them into the equation $y = ax^2 + bx + c$.

$$1 = a(0)^2 + b(0) + c$$
$$1 = c$$

Now your equation looks like $y = ax^2 + bx + 1$. Next, use the other two points to create a system of two equations in two variables.

$$(-3,10) \rightarrow 10 = a(-3)^2 + b(-3) + 1 \rightarrow 9 = 9a - 3b$$
$$(2,15) \rightarrow 15 = a(2)^2 + b(2) + 1 \rightarrow 14 = 4a + 2b$$

You now have a system of equations to solve. None of the variables has a coefficient of 1, so use elimination to solve the system. If you multiply the top equation by 2 and the bottom equation by 3, the b terms will eliminate each other.

$$2[9a - 3b = 9] \quad \rightarrow \quad 18a - 6b = 18$$
$$3[4a + 2b = 14] \quad \rightarrow \quad \underline{12a + 6b = 42}$$
$$30a = 60$$
$$a = 2$$

Now, find b by substituting $a = 2$ into either of the original equations. Using the top equation, you get:

$$9(2) - 3b = 9$$
$$18 - 3b = 9$$
$$-3b = -9$$
$$b = 3$$

The value of $a + b + c$ is 2 + 3 + 1 = 6.

MATH—CALCULATOR TEST

1. C   Difficulty: Easy

Category: Problem Solving and Data Analysis / Rates, Ratios, Proportions, and Percentages

Getting to the Answer: You can use the formula $\text{Percent} = \frac{\text{part}}{\text{whole}} \times 100\%$ whenever you know two out of the three quantities. The clue "all" tells you that the "whole" is what you don't know. The percent is 96.5, and the part is 321,000,000.

$$96.5 = \frac{321{,}000{,}000}{w} \times 100\%$$

$$96.5w = 32{,}100{,}000{,}000$$

$$w = \frac{32{,}100{,}000{,}000}{96.5}$$

$$w = 332{,}642{,}487$$

The answer choices are rounded to the nearest thousand, so the answer is 332,642,000, (C).

2. C   Difficulty: Easy

Category: Heart of Algebra / Linear Equations

Getting to the Answer: The total cost consists of the one-time site visit fee (a constant), an hourly cost (which depends on the number of hours), and the cost of the materials (which are taxed). The constant in the equation is 75 and is therefore the site visit fee; 45 is being multiplied by h (the number of hours), so $45 must be the hourly rate. That leaves the remaining term, 1.06(82.5), which must be the cost of the materials ($82.50) plus a 6% tax. This matches (C).

3. D   Difficulty: Easy

Category: Heart of Algebra / Inequalities

Getting to the Answer: The intersection (overlap) of the two shaded regions is the solution to the system of inequalities. Check each point to see whether it lies in the region with the darkest shading. Don't forget to check that you answered the right question—you are looking for the point that is *not* a solution to the system. Each of the first three points clearly lies in the overlap. The point (3, 3) looks like it lies on the dashed line, which means it is *not* included in the solution. To check this, plug (3, 3) into the easier inequality: $3 \not> 3$ (3 is equal to itself, not greater than itself), so (D) is correct.

4. A   Difficulty: Easy

Category: Passport to Advanced Math / Quadratics

Getting to the Answer: Quadratic equations can be written in several forms, each of which reveals something special about the graph. The factored

form of a quadratic equation reveals the solutions to the equation, which graphically represent the x-intercepts. Choice (A) is the only equation written in this form and therefore must be correct. You can set each factor equal to 0 and solve to find that the x-intercepts of the graph are $x = \frac{5}{2}$ and $x = -1$.

5. B   Difficulty: Easy

Category: Problem Solving and Data Analysis / Rates, Ratios, Proportions, and Percentages

Getting to the Answer: Break the question into steps. Before you can use the ratio, you need to find the percent of the students who answered either "Foreign Policy" or "Environment." The ratio given in the question is 5:3, so write this as 5 parts "Foreign Policy" and 3 parts "Environment." You don't know how big a *part* is, so call it x. This means that $5x + 3x$ equals the percent of the students who answered either "Foreign Policy" or "Environment," which is 100% minus all the other answers:

$$100 - (16 + 14 + 9 + 5) = 100 - 44 = 56$$

$$5x + 3x = 56$$

$$8x = 56$$

$$x = 7$$

Each part has a value of 7, and 3 parts answered "Environment," so the correct percentage is $3(7) = 21\%$, (B).

6. C   Difficulty: Easy

Category: Problem Solving and Data Analysis / Scatterplots

Getting to the Answer: A data set that has a linear association follows the path of a straight line; a data set that is exponential follows a path that is similar to linear data, but with a curve to it because the rate of increase (or decrease) changes over time. This data set has a curve to it, so "exponential" describes the association better than "linear." This means you can eliminate A and B. A positive association between two variables is one in which higher values of one variable correspond to higher values of the other variable, and vice versa. In other words, as the *x*-values of the data points go up, so do the *y*-values. This is indeed the case for this data set, so (C) is correct.

7. D   Difficulty: Easy

Category: Problem Solving and Data Analysis / Statistics and Probability

Getting to the Answer: Your only choice for this question is to compare each statement to the figure. Don't waste time trying to figure out the exact value for each bar—an estimate is good enough to determine whether each statement is true. Choice A is incorrect because the price in 2008 was slightly less (not more) than $3.50, while the price in 2013 was right around $3.50. Choice B is incorrect because the price in 2003 was more than $2.00, and the price in 2013 was not more than twice that ($4.00). Choice C is incorrect because the price in 2008 was about $3.25 and the price in 2009 was about $2.75—this is not a difference of more than $1.00. This means (D) must be correct. You don't have to check it—just move on. (Between 2003 and 2008, the change in price was about $3.40 − $2.30 = $1.10; between 2008 and 2013, the change in price was only about $3.50 − $3.40 = $0.10; the change in price was greater between 2003 and 2008.)

8. B   Difficulty: Medium

Category: Heart of Algebra / Systems of Linear Equations

Getting to the Answer: Because none of the variable terms has a coefficient of 1, solve the system of equations using elimination (combining the equations). Before you choose an answer, check that you answered the right question (the sum of *x* and *y*). Multiply the top equation by 2 to eliminate the terms that have *y*'s in them.

$$2[-2x + 5y = 1] \rightarrow -4x + 10y = 2$$
$$7x - 10y = -11 \rightarrow \underline{7x - 10y = -11}$$
$$3x = -9$$
$$x = -3$$

Now, substitute the result into either of the original equations and simplify to find *y*:

$$-2x + 5y = 1$$
$$-2(-3) + 5y = 1$$
$$6 + 5y = 1$$
$$5y = -5$$
$$y = -1$$

The question asks for the *sum*, so add *x* and *y* to get −3 + (−1) = −4, which is (B).

9. A   Difficulty: Medium

Category: Heart of Algebra / Systems of Linear Equations

Getting to the Answer: Take a quick peek at the answers just to see what variables are being used, but don't study the equations. Instead, write your own system using the same variables as given in the answer choices. One of the equations in the system needs to represent the sum of the two resistors ($R_1 + R_2$), which is equal to 294. This means you can eliminate C and D. The second equation needs to satisfy the condition that R_2 is 6 less than twice R_1, or $R_2 = 2R_1 - 6$. This means (A) is correct.

10. C   Difficulty: Medium

Category: Heart of Algebra / Linear Equations

Getting to the Answer: Use the distributive property to simplify each of the terms that contains parentheses. Then use inverse operations to solve for *x*.

$$\frac{2}{\cancel{3}}(\cancel{3}x) + 2(x - 1) = 4(x + 1) - 2$$
$$2x + 2x - 2 = 4x + 4 - 2$$
$$4x - 2 = 4x + 2$$
$$-2 \neq 2$$

All of the variable terms cancel out, and the resulting numerical statement is false (because negative 2 does not equal positive 2), so there is no solution to the equation. Put another way, there is no value of *x* for which the equation is true, (C).

11. B   Difficulty: Medium

Category: Additional Topics in Math / Geometry

Getting to the Answer: Think about this question logically before you start writing things down—after it's transferred, the volume of the oil in the cylindrical container will be the same volume as the rectangular container, so you need to set the two volumes equal and solve for h. The volume of the rectangular container is $4 \times 9 \times 10$, or 360 cubic meters. The volume of a cylinder equals the area of its base times its height, or $\pi r^2 h$. Because the diameter is 6 meters, the radius, r, is half that, or 3 meters. Now we're ready to set up an equation and solve for h (which is the height of the cylinder or, in this case, the length of the transportation container):

Volume of oil = Volume of rectangular container

$$\pi (3)^2 h = 360$$
$$9\pi h = 360$$
$$h = \frac{360}{9\pi} = \frac{40}{\pi}$$

Choice (B) is correct.

12. D   Difficulty: Medium

Category: Problem Solving and Data Analysis / Rates, Ratios, Proportions, and Percentages

Getting to the Answer: Even though this question uses the word *percent*, you are never asked to find the actual percent itself. Set this question up as a proportion to get the answer more quickly. Remember, percent change equals amount of change divided by the original amount.

$$\frac{12 - 5}{5} = \frac{x - 12}{12}$$
$$\frac{7}{5} = \frac{x - 12}{12}$$
$$12(7) = 5(x - 12)$$
$$84 = 5x - 60$$
$$144 = 5x$$
$$28.8 = x$$

Choice (D) is correct.

13. A   Difficulty: Medium

Category: Passport to Advanced Math / Exponents

Getting to the Answer: Focus on the question at the very end—it's just asking you to solve the equation for d. First, cross-multiply to get rid of the denominator. Then, divide both sides of the equation by $4\pi b$ to isolate d^2. Finally, take the square root of both sides to find d.

$$b(4\pi d^2) = L$$
$$\frac{b(4\pi\, d^2)}{4\pi b} = \frac{L}{4\pi b}$$
$$d^2 = \frac{L}{4\pi b}$$
$$\sqrt{d^2} = \sqrt{\frac{L}{4\pi b}}$$
$$d = \sqrt{\frac{L}{4\pi b}}$$

Unfortunately, this is not one of the answer choices, so you'll need to simplify further. You can take the square root of 4 (it's 2), but be careful—it's in the denominator of the fraction, so it comes out of the square root as $\frac{1}{2}$. The simplified equation is

$d = \frac{1}{2}\sqrt{\frac{L}{\pi b}}$. This matches (A).

14. D   Difficulty: Easy

Category: Problem Solving and Data Analysis / Statistics and Probability

Getting to the Answer: To calculate the percentage of men in each age group who reported being unemployed in January 2014, divide the number in *that* age group who were unemployed by the total number in *that* age group. There are six age groups but only four answer choices, so don't waste time on the age groups that aren't represented. Choice (D) is correct because $7 \div 152 \approx 0.046 = 4.6\%$, which is a lower percentage than that for any other age group (20 to 24 = 12.5%; 35 to 44 = 4.9%; 45 to 54 = 6.1%).

15. B   Difficulty: Medium

Category: Problem Solving and Data Analysis / Statistics and Probability

Getting to the Answer: The follow-up survey targets only those respondents who said they were unemployed, so focus on that column in the table. There were 6 respondents out of 44 unemployed males who were between the ages of 45 and 54, so the probability is $\frac{6}{44} = 0.1\overline{36}$, or about 13.6%, (B).

16. B   Difficulty: Medium

Category: Passport to Advanced Math / Quadratics

Getting to the Answer: Taking the square root is the inverse operation of squaring, and both sides of the equation are already perfect squares, so take their square roots. Then solve the resulting equations. Remember, there will be two equations to solve.

$$\left(x - 1\right)^2 = \frac{4}{9}$$

$$\sqrt{\left(x - 1\right)^2} = \sqrt{\frac{4}{9}}$$

$$x - 1 = \pm\frac{\sqrt{4}}{\sqrt{9}}$$

$$x = 1 \pm \frac{2}{3}$$

Now, simplify each equation: $x = 1 + \frac{2}{3} = \frac{3}{3} + \frac{2}{3} = \frac{5}{3}$

and $x = 1 - \frac{2}{3} = \frac{3}{3} - \frac{2}{3} = \frac{1}{3}$. Choice (B) is correct.

17. D   Difficulty: Medium

Category: Heart of Algebra / Linear Equations

Getting to the Answer: Write the expression in words first: points per blue ring (5) times number of darts in blue ring (x), plus points per red ring (10) times number of darts in red ring ($6 - x$). Now, translate the words into numbers, variables, and operations: $5x + 10(6 - x)$. This is not one of the answer choices, so simplify the expression by distributing the 10 and then combining like terms: $5x + 10(6 - x)$ $= 5x + 60 - 10x = 60 - 5x$. This matches (D).

18. A   Difficulty: Medium

Category: Problem Solving and Data Analysis / Statistics and Probability

Getting to the Answer: This is a science crossover question. Read the first two sentences quickly—they are simply describing the context of the question. The last two sentences pose the question, so read those more carefully. In the sample, 184 out of 200 square feet were free of red tide after applying the spray. This is $\frac{184}{200} = 0.92 = 92\%$ of the area. For the whole beach, 0.92(10,000) = 9,200 square feet should be free of the red tide. Be careful—this is *not* the answer. The question asks how much of the beach would still be covered by red tide, so subtract to get 10,000 − 9,200 = 800 square feet, (A).

19. A   Difficulty: Medium

Category: Passport to Advanced Math / Quadratics

Getting to the Answer: The solution to a system of equations is the point(s) where their graphs intersect. You can solve the system algebraically by setting the equations equal to each other, or you can solve it graphically using your calculator. Both equations are given in calculator-friendly format ($y = \dots$), so graphing them is probably the more efficient approach. The graph looks like:

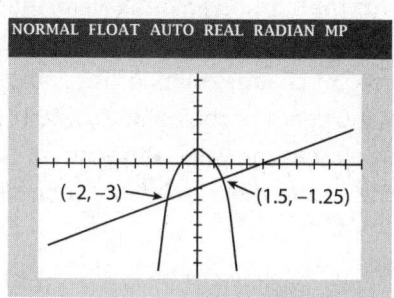

The solution point in the question is given as (a, b), so b represents the y-coordinate of the solution. The y-coordinates of the points of intersection are −3 and −1.25, so choice (A) is correct.

20. A   Difficulty: Medium

Category: Passport to Advanced Math / Functions

Getting to the Answer: The given range value is an output value, so substitute 3 for $g(x)$ and use inverse operations to solve for x, which is the corresponding domain value.

$$g(x) = \frac{2}{3}x + 7$$

$$3 = \frac{2}{3}x + 7$$

$$-4 = \frac{2}{3}x$$

$$-12 = 2x$$

$$-6 = x$$

Choice (A) is correct. Note that you could also graph the function and find the value of x (the domain value) for which the value of y (the range value) is 3. The point on the graph is $(-6, 3)$.

21. C   Difficulty: Medium

Category: Heart of Algebra / Linear Equations

Getting to the Answer: Write your own equation using the initial cost and the rate of change in the value of the lawn mower. Remember—when something changes at a constant rate, it can be represented by a linear equation. When a linear equation in the form $y = mx + b$ is used to model a real-world scenario, m represents the constant rate of change, and b represents the starting amount. Here, the starting amount is easy—it's the purchase price, $2,800. To find the rate of change, think of the initial cost as the value at 0 years, or the point $(0, 2,800)$, and the salvage amount as the value at 8 years, or the point $(8, 240)$. Substitute these points into the slope formula:

$$m = \frac{y_2 - y_1}{x_2 - x_1} = \frac{240 - 2,800}{8 - 0} = \frac{-2,560}{8} = -320$$

The correct equation is $y = -320x + 2,800$. This matches (C).

22. D   Difficulty: Medium

Category: Problem Solving and Data Analysis / Functions

Getting to the Answer: Determine whether the change in the number of bacteria is a common difference (linear function) or a common ratio (exponential function) or if the number of bacteria changes direction (quadratic or polynomial function). The question tells you that the number of bacteria is reduced by half every hour after the antibiotic is applied. The microbiologist started with 20,000, so after one hour, there are 10,000 left, or $20,000 \times \frac{1}{2}$. After 2 hours, there are 5,000 left, or $20,000 \times \frac{1}{2} \times \frac{1}{2}$, and so on. The change in the number of bacteria is a common ratio $\left(\frac{1}{2}\right)$, so the best model is an exponential function, (D), of the form $y = a\left(\frac{1}{2}\right)^x$. In this scenario, a is 20,000.

23. B   Difficulty: Medium

Category: Problem Solving and Data Analysis / Rates, Ratios, Proportions, and Percentages

Getting to the Answer: Let the units in this question guide you to the solution. The speeds of the airplanes are given in miles per hour, but the question asks about the number of miles each airplane can travel in 12 seconds, so convert miles per hour to miles per second and multiply by 12 seconds.

Slower airplane:

$$\frac{600\,\text{mi}}{\text{hr}} \times \frac{1\,\text{hr}}{60\,\text{min}} \times \frac{1\,\text{min}}{60\,\text{sec}} \times 12\,\text{sec} = 2\,\text{mi}$$

Faster airplane:

$$\frac{720\,\text{mi}}{\text{hr}} \times \frac{1\,\text{hr}}{60\,\text{min}} \times \frac{1\,\text{min}}{60\,\text{sec}} \times 12\,\text{sec} = 2.4\,\text{mi}$$

The faster plane can travel $2.4 - 2 = 0.4$ miles farther, which is the same as $\frac{2}{5}$ miles, (B).

24. C   Difficulty: Medium

Category: Heart of Algebra / Inequalities

Getting to the Answer: Based on the data in the

table, a worker would earn $9.10 − $7.25 = $1.85 more for one hour of work in Oregon than in Idaho. If he worked 35 hours per week, he would earn 35(1.85) = $64.75 more. If he worked 40 hours per week, he would earn 40(1.85) = $74 more. So, the worker would earn somewhere between $64.75 and $74 more per week, which can be expressed as the compound inequality $64.75 \leq x \leq 74$. This matches (C).

25. D   Difficulty: Medium

Category: Problem Solving and Data Analysis / Rates, Ratios, Proportions, and Percentages

Getting to the Answer: This is another question where the units can help you find the answer. Use the number of vehicles owned to find the total number of miles driven to find the total number of gallons of gas used to find the total tax paid. Phew!

$$1.75 \text{ vehicles} \times \frac{11,340 \text{ miles}}{\text{vehicle}} = 19,845 \text{ miles}$$

$$19,845 \text{ miles} \times \frac{1 \text{ gallon of gas}}{21.4 \text{ miles}} = 927.336 \text{ gallons}$$

$$927.336 \text{ gallons} \times \frac{\$0.184}{\text{gallon}} = \$170.63$$

Choice (D) is correct.

26. C   Difficulty: Medium

Category: Problem Solving and Data Analysis / Scatterplots

Getting to the Answer: The average rate of change of a function over a given interval, from a to b, compares the change in the outputs, $f(b) − f(a)$, to the change in the inputs, $b − a$. In other words, it is the slope of the line that connects the endpoints of the interval, so you can use the slope formula. Look at the quadratic model, not the data points, to find that the endpoints of the given interval, week 2 to week 8, are (2, 280) and (8, 400). The average rate of change is $\frac{400 − 280}{8 − 2} = \frac{120}{6} = 20$, so the dolphin's weight increased by about 20 pounds per week, (C).

27. A   Difficulty: Hard

Category: Additional Topics in Math / Geometry

Getting to the Answer: In this question, information is given in both the diagram and the text. You need to relate the text to the diagram, one piece of information at a time, to calculate how long the lifeguard ran along the beach and how long he swam. Before you find the swim time, you need to know how *far* he swam. Whenever you see a right triangle symbol in a diagram, you should think Pythagorean theorem or, in this question, special right triangles. All multiples of 3-4-5 triangles are right triangles, so the length of the lifeguard's swim is the hypotenuse of a 30-40-50 triangle, or 50 feet. Add this number to the diagram. Now calculate the times using the distances and the speeds given. Don't forget the 1 second that the lifeguard paused.

$$\text{Run time} = 60 \text{ ft} \times \frac{1 \text{ sec}}{12 \text{ ft}} = \frac{60}{12} = 5 \text{ sec}$$

Pause time = 1 second

$$\text{Swim time} = 50 \text{ ft} \times \frac{1 \text{ sec}}{5 \text{ ft}} = \frac{50}{5} = 10 \text{ sec}$$

Total time = 5 + 1 + 10 = 16 seconds, (A).

28. B   Difficulty: Hard

Category: Heart of Algebra / Linear Equations

Getting to the Answer: Call the initial amount A. After you've written your equation, solve for A.

Amount now (x) = Initial amount (A) minus y, plus 50

$$x = A − y + 50$$
$$x + y − 50 = A$$

The initial amount was $x + y − 50$ gallons, (B). Note that you could also use Picking Numbers to answer this question.

29. B   Difficulty: Hard

Category: Problem Solving and Data Analysis / Statistics and Probability

Getting to the Answer: When a question involves

reading data from a graph, it is sometimes better to skip an answer choice if it involves long calculations. Skim the answer choices for this question—A involves finding two averages, each of which is composed of 7 data values. Skip this choice for now. Start with (B). Be careful—you are not looking for places where the line segments are increasing. The y-axis already represents the change in prices, so you are simply counting the number of positive values for the imports (5) and for the exports (4). There are more for the imports, so (B) is correct and you don't need to check any of the other statements. Move on to the next question.

30. D   Difficulty: Hard

Category: Passport to Advanced Math / Exponents

Getting to the Answer: The key to answering this question is deciding what you're trying to find. The question tells you that x represents the athlete's swim rate, and you are looking for the number of kilometers he swam in one hour—these are the same thing. If you find x (in kilometers per hour), you will know how many kilometers he swam in one hour. Set the equation equal to the total time, 16.2, and solve for x. To do this, write the variable terms over a common denominator, 10x, and combine them into a single term. Then cross-multiply and go from there.

$$16.2 = \frac{10}{10}\left(\frac{3.86}{x}\right) + \frac{180.2}{10x} + \frac{2}{2}\left(\frac{42.2}{5x}\right)$$

$$16.2 = \frac{38.6}{10x} + \frac{180.2}{10x} + \frac{84.4}{10x}$$

$$16.2 = \frac{303.2}{10x}$$

$$10x(16.2) = 303.2$$

$$162x = 303.2$$

$$x = \frac{303.2}{162} \approx 1.87$$

Choice (D) is correct.

31. 1   Difficulty: Easy

Category: Heart of Algebra / Linear Equations

Getting to the Answer: Choose the best strategy to answer the question. If you distribute the $\frac{2}{3}$, it creates messy calculations. Instead, clear the fraction by multiplying both sides of the equation by 3. Then use the distributive property and inverse operations to solve for x.

$$\frac{2}{3}(5x + 7) = 8x$$

$$\cancel{3} \cdot \frac{2}{\cancel{3}}(5x + 7) = 3 \cdot 8x$$

$$2(5x + 7) = 24x$$

$$10x + 14 = 24x$$

$$14 = 14x$$

$$1 = x$$

32. 192   Difficulty: Medium

Category: Passport to Advanced Math / Exponents

Getting to the Answer: Before you start substituting values, quickly check that the units given match the units required to use the equation—they do, so proceed. The patient's weight (w) is 150 and the patient's BSA is $2\sqrt{2}$, so the equation becomes $2\sqrt{2} = \sqrt{\frac{150h}{3,600}}$. The only variable left in the equation is h, and you are trying to find the patient's height, so you're ready to solve the equation. To do this, square both sides of the equation and then continue using inverse operations. Be careful when you square the left side—you must square both the 2 and the root 2.

$$2\sqrt{2} = \sqrt{\frac{150h}{3,600}}$$

$$\left(2\sqrt{2}\right)^2 = \left(\sqrt{\frac{150h}{3,600}}\right)^2$$

$$2^2\left(\sqrt{2}\right)^2 = \frac{150h}{3,600}$$

$$4(2) = \frac{150h}{3,600}$$

$$28,800 = 150h$$

$$192 = h$$

33. 3.4   Difficulty: Medium

Category: Problem Solving and Data Analysis / Statistics and Probability

Getting to the Answer: The test average is the same as the mean of the data. The *mean* is the sum of all the values divided by the number of values. Break the question into short steps to keep your calculations organized. Before gridding in your answer, make sure you answered the right question (how much the final test average changes).

Step 1: Find the original test average:

$$\frac{86 + 92 + 81 + 64 + 83}{5} = \frac{406}{5} = 81.2$$

Step 2: Find the average of the tests after replacing the lowest score (64) with the next to lowest score (81):

$$\frac{86 + 92 + 81 + 81 + 83}{5} = \frac{423}{5} = 84.6$$

Step 3: Subtract the original average from the new average: 84.6 − 81.2 = 3.4.

34. 40   Difficulty: Hard

Category: Additional Topics in Math / Geometry

Getting to the Answer: Because $\overline{AB}$, $\overline{CD}$, and $\overline{EF}$ are diameters, the sum of x, y, and the interior angle of the shaded region is 180 degrees. The question tells you that the shaded region is $\frac{1}{5}$ of the circle, so the interior angle must equal $\frac{1}{5}$ of the degrees in the whole circle, or $\frac{1}{5}$ of 360. Use what you know about y (that it is equal to $2x - 12$) and what you know about the shaded region (that it is $\frac{1}{5}$ of 360 degrees) to write and solve an equation.

$$x + y + \frac{1}{5}(360) = 180$$
$$x + (2x - 12) + 72 = 180$$
$$3x + 60 = 180$$
$$3x = 120$$
$$x = 40$$

35. 14   Difficulty: Hard

Category: Heart of Algebra / Linear Equations

Getting to the Answer: When you know the slope and one point on a line, you can use $y = mx + b$ to write the equation. The slope is given as $-\frac{7}{4}$, so substitute this for m. The point is given as (4, 7), so $x = 4$ and $y = 7$. Now, find b:

$$y = mx + b$$
$$7 = -\frac{7}{4}(4) + b$$
$$7 = -7 + b$$
$$14 = b$$

The y-intercept of the line is 14.

You could also very carefully graph the line using the given point and the slope. Start at (4, 7) and move toward the y-axis by rising 7 and running *to the left* 4 (because the slope is negative). You should land at the point (0, 14).

36. 45   Difficulty: Hard

Category: Problem Solving and Data Analysis / Rates, Ratios, Proportions, and Percentages

Getting to the Answer: Make a chart that represents rate, time, and distance and fill in what you know.

	Rate	Time	Distance
To airport	45 mph	t	d
Back to home	30 mph	$2.5 - t$	d

Now use the formula $d = r \times t$ for both parts of the trip: $d = 45t$ and $d = 30(2.5 - t)$. Because both are equal to d, you can set them equal to each other and solve for t:

$$45t = 30(2.5 - t)$$
$$45t = 75 - 30t$$
$$75t = 75$$
$$t = 1$$

Now plug the value of t back in to solve for d:

$$d = 45t$$
$$d = 45(1)$$
$$d = 45$$

37. 10   Difficulty: Medium

Category: Problem Solving and Data Analysis / Rates, Ratios, Proportions, and Percentages

Getting to the Answer: You don't need to know chemistry to answer this question. All the information you need is in the table. Use the formula $\text{Percent} = \dfrac{\text{part}}{\text{whole}} \times 100\%$. To use the formula, find the part of the mass represented by the carbon; there is 1 mole of carbon, and it has a mass of 12.011 grams. Next, find the whole mass of the mole of chloroform: 1 mole carbon (12.011 g) + 1 mole hydrogen (1.008 g) + 3 moles chlorine (3×35.453 = 106.359 g) = 12.011 + 1.008 + 106.359 = 119.378. Now use the formula:

$$\text{Percent} = \frac{12.011}{119.378} \times 100\%$$
$$= 0.10053 \times 100\%$$
$$= 10.053\%$$

Before you grid in your answer, make sure you follow the directions—round to the nearest whole percent, which is 10.

38. 12   Difficulty: Hard

Category: Problem Solving and Data Analysis / Rates, Ratios, Proportions, and Percentages

Getting to the Answer: Think about the units given in the question and how you can use what you know to find what you need. Start with grams of chloro-

form; the chemist starts with 1,000 and uses 522.5, so there are 1,000 − 522.5 = 477.5 grams left. From the previous question, you know that 1 mole of chloroform has a mass of 119.378 grams, so there are 477.5 ÷ 119.378 = 3.999, or about 4 moles of chloroform left. Be careful—you're not finished yet. The question asks for the number of moles of *chlorine*, not chloroform. According to the table, each mole of chloroform contains 3 moles of chlorine, so there are $4 \times 3 = 12$ moles of chlorine left.

ESSAY TEST RUBRIC

The Essay Demonstrates...

4—Advanced	• **(Reading)** A strong ability to comprehend the source text, including its central ideas and important details and how they interrelate; and effectively use evidence (quotations, paraphrases, or both) from the source text. • **(Analysis)** A strong ability to evaluate the author's use of evidence, reasoning, and/or stylistic and persuasive elements, and/or other features of the student's own choosing; make good use of relevant, sufficient, and strategically chosen support for the claims or points made in the student's essay; and focus consistently on features of the source text that are most relevant to addressing the task. • **(Writing)** A strong ability to provide a precise central claim; create an effective organization that includes an introduction and conclusion, as well as a clear progression of ideas; successfully employ a variety of sentence structures; use precise word choice; maintain a formal style and objective tone; and show command of the conventions of standard written English so that the essay is free of errors.
3—Proficient	• **(Reading)** Satisfactory ability to comprehend the source text, including its central ideas and important details and how they interrelate; and use evidence (quotations, paraphrases, or both) from the source text. • **(Analysis)** Satisfactory ability to evaluate the author's use of evidence, reasoning, and/or stylistic and persuasive elements, and/or other features of the student's own choosing; make use of relevant and sufficient support for the claims or points made in the student's essay; and focus primarily on features of the source text that are most relevant to addressing the task. • **(Writing)** Satisfactory ability to provide a central claim; create an organization that includes an introduction and conclusion, as well as a clear progression of ideas; employ a variety of sentence structures; use precise word choice; maintain an appropriate formal style and objective tone; and show control of the conventions of standard written English so that the essay is free of significant errors.
2—Partial	• **(Reading)** Limited ability to comprehend the source text, including its central ideas and important details and how they interrelate; and use evidence (quotations, paraphrases, or both) from the source text. • **(Analysis)** Limited ability to evaluate the author's use of evidence, reasoning, and/or stylistic and persuasive elements, and/or other features of the student's own choosing; make use of support for the claims or points made in the student's essay; and focus on relevant features of the source text. • **(Writing)** Limited ability to provide a central claim; create an effective organization for ideas; employ a variety of sentence structures; use precise word choice; maintain an appropriate style and tone; or show control of the conventions of standard written English, resulting in certain errors that detract from the quality of the writing.

1—Inadequate	• **(Reading)** Little or no ability to comprehend the source text or use evidence from the source text.
	• **(Analysis)** Little or no ability to evaluate the author's use of evidence, reasoning, and/or stylistic and persuasive elements; choose support for claims or points; or focus on relevant features of the source text.
	• **(Writing)** Little or no ability to provide a central claim, organization, or progression of ideas; employ a variety of sentence structures; use precise word choice; maintain an appropriate style and tone; or show control of the conventions of standard written English, resulting in numerous errors that undermine the quality of the writing.

SAMPLE ESSAY RESPONSE #1 (ADVANCED SCORE)

As anyone knows who has had to help their family move house, find a textbook in a cluttered room, or even just clean a crowded apartment, possessions can have a huge amount of power over people. Far from being simply objects that we enjoy or that bring us pleasure, it can sometimes feel that our possessions oppress us. This is the point Morris eloquently makes in her essay "The Tyranny of Things." By using anecdotes, examples, reasoning, and powerful imagery, Morris argues that the very things we cherish are nearly crushing the life out of us.

The author begins by relating an anecdote about two teenagers becoming fast friends over their love of things. It is a touching moment, one to which readers can easily relate; even Morris herself says that we all probably go through this phase. This helps establish her credibility with readers, because her examples make sense to them. Gradually, however, Morris makes it clear that this touching moment has a sinister side—the love of things will only result in resentment.

Morris reasons that while it's natural to go through a phase of wanting objects, it is unhealthy to remain in this state. "Many people never pass out of this phase," she writes ominously. "They never see a flower without wanting to pick it … they bring home all their alpenstocks." It begins to sound obsessive, this need to control things. Morris goes on to develop her argument by suggesting that possessions are metaphorically suffocating us. She makes the idea of too many possessions sound repulsive by describing them as "an undigested mass of things." The things almost take on a kind of life force, according to Morris: "they possess us." They "have destroyed" our empty spaces and we feel "stifled."

Another way Morris supports her argument is by giving examples of the unnecessary "tokens" associated with social occasions. She describes how at events, luncheons, and parties, gifts are given and received. She then uses powerful negative imagery to describe the effects of these gifts, comparing the recipient to a "ship encrusted with barnacles" that needs to be "scraped bare again." This language suggests that the gifts are burdensome and even harmful.

By contrast, the imagery Morris uses to describe a simple life filled with fewer things is imagery of ease and relaxation. "We breathe more freely in the clear space that we have made for ourselves," she writes. It is not just that we have literally regained control from our possessions and are now acting rather than being acted upon; it is that we are physically more at ease.

In her conclusion, Morris longs for a day when we can live more simply, with fewer possessions. She describes a "house by the sea" that was simple and empty; it did not "demand care" or "claim attention" or otherwise act upon her. Her wish is that "we could but free ourselves" from the tyranny of things that she feels is draining us of our freedom. And at this point, it is likely the reader's wish, too.

SAMPLE ESSAY RESPONSE #2 (PROFICIENT SCORE)

Although as people we like to think of ourselves as owners of things, in fact it can sometimes feel like the things we own end up owning us. At least this is what Morris argues in her essay "The Tyranny of Things." Through her use of evidence, reasoning, and word choice, she makes a strong argument that we should own fewer things if we ever want to be truly happy.

Morris tells a story about two teenage girls who instantly know they will be friends because they both like things. They are not happy just to be. They have to own things. It's like their own experiences aren't enough for them. But Morris says that this is bad for people, because they will end up feeling like their possessions own them.

Morris's reasoning is that we can basically get control back over our own lives if we stop needing things so much. If we have too many things, "they possess us." So we have to get rid of things, and then we can feel better. At least these days we aren't buried with our things anymore, like they were in the olden days.

The word choices in the essay are interesting. She talks about the way things become a problem for us: "our books are a burden to us, our pictures have destroyed every restful wall-space, our china is a care." By using a lot of repetition, it shows how powerful things are.

Morris's essay encourages people to free themselves from their things. If they do so, they will be happier. Through her personal anecdotes, reasoning, and repetitive word choices, she makes her essay very powerful.

SAT PRACTICE TEST 1 ANSWER SHEET

Remove (or photocopy) this answer sheet and use it to complete the test. See the answer key following the test when finished.

Start with number 1 for each section. If a section has fewer questions than answer spaces, leave the extra spaces blank.

SECTION 1

1. Ⓐ Ⓑ Ⓒ Ⓓ	14. Ⓐ Ⓑ Ⓒ Ⓓ	27. Ⓐ Ⓑ Ⓒ Ⓓ	40. Ⓐ Ⓑ Ⓒ Ⓓ
2. Ⓐ Ⓑ Ⓒ Ⓓ	15. Ⓐ Ⓑ Ⓒ Ⓓ	28. Ⓐ Ⓑ Ⓒ Ⓓ	41. Ⓐ Ⓑ Ⓒ Ⓓ
3. Ⓐ Ⓑ Ⓒ Ⓓ	16. Ⓐ Ⓑ Ⓒ Ⓓ	29. Ⓐ Ⓑ Ⓒ Ⓓ	42. Ⓐ Ⓑ Ⓒ Ⓓ
4. Ⓐ Ⓑ Ⓒ Ⓓ	17. Ⓐ Ⓑ Ⓒ Ⓓ	30. Ⓐ Ⓑ Ⓒ Ⓓ	43. Ⓐ Ⓑ Ⓒ Ⓓ
5. Ⓐ Ⓑ Ⓒ Ⓓ	18. Ⓐ Ⓑ Ⓒ Ⓓ	31. Ⓐ Ⓑ Ⓒ Ⓓ	44. Ⓐ Ⓑ Ⓒ Ⓓ
6. Ⓐ Ⓑ Ⓒ Ⓓ	19. Ⓐ Ⓑ Ⓒ Ⓓ	32. Ⓐ Ⓑ Ⓒ Ⓓ	45. Ⓐ Ⓑ Ⓒ Ⓓ
7. Ⓐ Ⓑ Ⓒ Ⓓ	20. Ⓐ Ⓑ Ⓒ Ⓓ	33. Ⓐ Ⓑ Ⓒ Ⓓ	46. Ⓐ Ⓑ Ⓒ Ⓓ
8. Ⓐ Ⓑ Ⓒ Ⓓ	21. Ⓐ Ⓑ Ⓒ Ⓓ	34. Ⓐ Ⓑ Ⓒ Ⓓ	47. Ⓐ Ⓑ Ⓒ Ⓓ
9. Ⓐ Ⓑ Ⓒ Ⓓ	22. Ⓐ Ⓑ Ⓒ Ⓓ	35. Ⓐ Ⓑ Ⓒ Ⓓ	48. Ⓐ Ⓑ Ⓒ Ⓓ
10. Ⓐ Ⓑ Ⓒ Ⓓ	23. Ⓐ Ⓑ Ⓒ Ⓓ	36. Ⓐ Ⓑ Ⓒ Ⓓ	49. Ⓐ Ⓑ Ⓒ Ⓓ
11. Ⓐ Ⓑ Ⓒ Ⓓ	24. Ⓐ Ⓑ Ⓒ Ⓓ	37. Ⓐ Ⓑ Ⓒ Ⓓ	50. Ⓐ Ⓑ Ⓒ Ⓓ
12. Ⓐ Ⓑ Ⓒ Ⓓ	25. Ⓐ Ⓑ Ⓒ Ⓓ	38. Ⓐ Ⓑ Ⓒ Ⓓ	51. Ⓐ Ⓑ Ⓒ Ⓓ
13. Ⓐ Ⓑ Ⓒ Ⓓ	26. Ⓐ Ⓑ Ⓒ Ⓓ	39. Ⓐ Ⓑ Ⓒ Ⓓ	52. Ⓐ Ⓑ Ⓒ Ⓓ

☐ # correct in Section 1

☐ # incorrect in Section 1

SECTION 2

1. Ⓐ Ⓑ Ⓒ Ⓓ	12. Ⓐ Ⓑ Ⓒ Ⓓ	23. Ⓐ Ⓑ Ⓒ Ⓓ	34. Ⓐ Ⓑ Ⓒ Ⓓ
2. Ⓐ Ⓑ Ⓒ Ⓓ	13. Ⓐ Ⓑ Ⓒ Ⓓ	24. Ⓐ Ⓑ Ⓒ Ⓓ	35. Ⓐ Ⓑ Ⓒ Ⓓ
3. Ⓐ Ⓑ Ⓒ Ⓓ	14. Ⓐ Ⓑ Ⓒ Ⓓ	25. Ⓐ Ⓑ Ⓒ Ⓓ	36. Ⓐ Ⓑ Ⓒ Ⓓ
4. Ⓐ Ⓑ Ⓒ Ⓓ	15. Ⓐ Ⓑ Ⓒ Ⓓ	26. Ⓐ Ⓑ Ⓒ Ⓓ	37. Ⓐ Ⓑ Ⓒ Ⓓ
5. Ⓐ Ⓑ Ⓒ Ⓓ	16. Ⓐ Ⓑ Ⓒ Ⓓ	27. Ⓐ Ⓑ Ⓒ Ⓓ	38. Ⓐ Ⓑ Ⓒ Ⓓ
6. Ⓐ Ⓑ Ⓒ Ⓓ	17. Ⓐ Ⓑ Ⓒ Ⓓ	28. Ⓐ Ⓑ Ⓒ Ⓓ	39. Ⓐ Ⓑ Ⓒ Ⓓ
7. Ⓐ Ⓑ Ⓒ Ⓓ	18. Ⓐ Ⓑ Ⓒ Ⓓ	29. Ⓐ Ⓑ Ⓒ Ⓓ	40. Ⓐ Ⓑ Ⓒ Ⓓ
8. Ⓐ Ⓑ Ⓒ Ⓓ	19. Ⓐ Ⓑ Ⓒ Ⓓ	30. Ⓐ Ⓑ Ⓒ Ⓓ	41. Ⓐ Ⓑ Ⓒ Ⓓ
9. Ⓐ Ⓑ Ⓒ Ⓓ	20. Ⓐ Ⓑ Ⓒ Ⓓ	31. Ⓐ Ⓑ Ⓒ Ⓓ	42. Ⓐ Ⓑ Ⓒ Ⓓ
10. Ⓐ Ⓑ Ⓒ Ⓓ	21. Ⓐ Ⓑ Ⓒ Ⓓ	32. Ⓐ Ⓑ Ⓒ Ⓓ	43. Ⓐ Ⓑ Ⓒ Ⓓ
11. Ⓐ Ⓑ Ⓒ Ⓓ	22. Ⓐ Ⓑ Ⓒ Ⓓ	33. Ⓐ Ⓑ Ⓒ Ⓓ	44. Ⓐ Ⓑ Ⓒ Ⓓ

☐ # correct in Section 2

☐ # incorrect in Section 2

Practice Tests

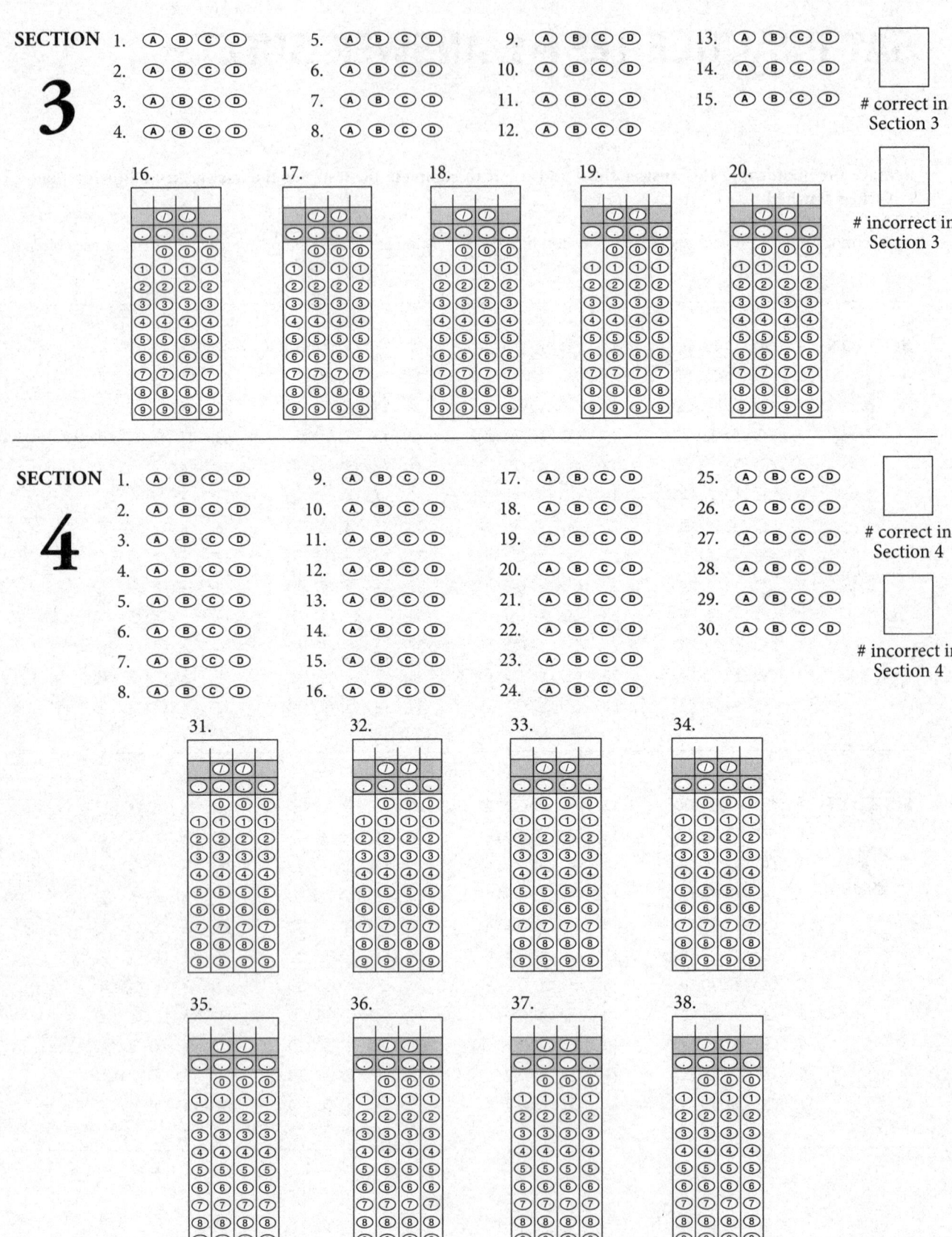

READING TEST

65 Minutes—52 Questions

This section corresponds to Section 1 of your answer sheet.

Directions: Read each passage or pair of passages, then answer the questions that follow. Choose your answers based on what the passage(s) and any accompanying graphics state or imply.

Questions 1-10 are based on the following passage.

This passage is adapted from *A Study in Scarlet*, Sir Arthur Conan Doyle's first story in his acclaimed Sherlock Holmes series. In this excerpt the narrator, Dr. Watson, observes Mr. Holmes, with whom he has recently entered into a shared housing arrangement, although he knows very little about this new roommate as of yet.

As the weeks went by, my interest in him and my curiosity as to his aims in life gradually deepened and increased. His very person and appearance
Line were such as to strike the attention of the most
(5) casual observer. In height he was rather over six feet, and so excessively lean that he seemed to be considerably taller. His eyes were sharp and piercing, save during those intervals of torpor to which I have alluded; and his thin, hawk-like nose gave his
(10) whole expression an air of alertness and decision. His chin, too, had the prominence and squareness which mark the man of determination. His hands were invariably blotted with ink and stained with chemicals, yet he was possessed of extraordinary
(15) delicacy of touch, as I frequently had occasion to observe when I watched him manipulating his fragile philosophical instruments. . . .

He was not studying medicine. He had himself, in reply to a question, confirmed Stamford's[1]
(20) opinion upon that point. Neither did he appear to have pursued any course of reading which might fit him for a degree in science or any other recognized portal which would give him an entrance into the learned world. Yet his zeal for certain studies
(25) was remarkable, and within eccentric limits his knowledge was so extraordinarily ample and minute that his observations have fairly astounded me. Surely no man would work so hard or attain such precise information unless he had some
(30) definite end in view. Desultory readers are seldom remarkable for the exactness of their learning. No man burdens his mind with small matters unless he has some very good reason for doing so.

His ignorance was as remarkable as his knowledge.
(35) Of contemporary literature, philosophy and politics he appeared to know next to nothing. Upon my quoting Thomas Carlyle,[2] he inquired in the naïvest way who he might be and what he had done. My surprise reached a climax, however, when I found
(40) incidentally that he was ignorant of the Copernican Theory and of the composition of the solar system. That any civilized human being in this nineteenth century should not be aware that the earth travelled round the sun appeared to be to me such an
(45) extraordinary fact that I could hardly realize it.

"You appear to be astonished," he said, smiling at my expression of surprise. "Now that I do know it I shall do my best to forget it."

"To forget it!"

(50) "You see," he explained, "I consider that a man's brain originally is like a little empty attic, and you have to stock it with such furniture as you choose. A fool takes in all the lumber of every sort that he comes across, so that the knowledge which might

---

[1]Stamford is the mutual acquaintance who introduced Dr. Watson to Mr. Holmes. In a previous scene he told Watson that Holmes was not a medical student.

[2]Thomas Carlyle was an influential writer and philosopher whose work was well known at the time of this novel's publication.

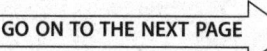 GO ON TO THE NEXT PAGE

(55) be useful to him gets crowded out, or at best is jumbled up with a lot of other things so that he has a difficulty in laying his hands upon it. Now the skillful workman is very careful indeed as to what he takes into his brain-attic. He will have

(60) nothing but the tools which may help him in doing his work, but of these he has a large assortment, and all in the most perfect order. It is a mistake to think that that little room has elastic walls and can distend to any extent. Depend upon it there comes

(65) a time when for every addition of knowledge you forget something that you knew before. It is of the highest importance, therefore, not to have useless facts elbowing out the useful ones."

"But the solar system!" I protested.

(70)   "What the deuce is it to me?"

1. According to the passage, as time passes, Watson finds Holmes

    A) increasingly intriguing.

    B) frequently irritating.

    C) somewhat snobby.

    D) occasionally generous.

2. As used in line 5, "casual" most nearly means

    A) impulsive.

    B) comfortable.

    C) relaxed.

    D) occasional.

3. As presented in the passage, Sherlock Holmes is best described as

    A) very secretive and hard to understand.

    B) an excellent companion to Watson.

    C) highly regarded by his peers.

    D) an unusual and extraordinary man.

4. As used in line 8, "torpor" most nearly means

    A) agitation.

    B) sluggishness.

    C) alertness.

    D) illness.

5. The passage most strongly suggests that which of the following is true of Holmes?

    A) He tried, but failed, to become a doctor.

    B) He was an excellent student at the university.

    C) He studies things he is passionate about.

    D) He is considered an expert in philosophy.

6. Which choice provides the best evidence for the answer to the previous question?

    A) Lines 12-17 ("His hands were . . . instruments")

    B) Lines 18-20 ("He was not . . . that point")

    C) Lines 24-28 ("Yet his . . . astounded me")

    D) Lines 28-30 ("Surely no man . . . in view")

7. The passage most strongly suggests that Holmes believes which of the following about learning?

    A) People should study broadly to know something about everything.

    B) Philosophy is not a valid field of study to pursue.

    C) The brain is limited in capacity, so you should prioritize what you learn.

    D) The Copernican Theory is unfounded and therefore should not be studied.

8. Which choice provides the best evidence for the answer to the previous question?

    A) Line 34 ("His ignorance . . . his knowledge")

    B) Lines 35-36 ("Of contemporary . . . nothing")

    C) Lines 42-45 ("That any . . . realize it")

    D) Lines 66-68 ("It is of the . . . ones")

GO ON TO THE NEXT PAGE

9. The comparison of the brain to an attic mainly serves to

A) demonstrate Holmes's unique views on how a person should make use of knowledge.

B) illustrate Watson's combative nature.

C) provide an alternate explanation for why Holmes doesn't know about Copernicus.

D) resolve the conflict between Watson and Holmes.

10. The decision to tell the story from Watson's point of view suggests that the author

A) wants the reader to dislike Holmes.

B) needed a sympathetic narrator.

C) will focus the rest of the story on Watson's actions.

D) hopes the reader will share Watson's curiosity about Holmes.

Questions 11-20 are based on the following passage.

This passage is adapted from a speech given by President Woodrow Wilson to Congress on January 8, 1918. Here Wilson proposes a 14-point program for world peace. These 14 points became the basis for peace negotiations at the end of World War I.

It will be our wish and purpose that the processes of peace, when they are begun, shall be absolutely open and that they shall involve and permit henceforth no secret understandings of any
Line
(5) kind. The day of conquest and aggrandizement is gone by; so is also the day of secret covenants entered into in the interest of particular governments and likely at some unlooked-for moment to upset the peace of the world. It is this happy fact,
(10) now clear to the view of every public man whose thoughts do not still linger in an age that is dead and gone, which makes it possible for every nation whose purposes are consistent with justice and the peace of the world to avow now or at any other
(15) time the objects it has in view.

We entered this war because violations of right had occurred which touched us to the quick and made the life of our own people impossible unless they were corrected. . . . What we demand in this
(20) war, therefore, is nothing peculiar to ourselves. It is that the world be made fit and safe to live in; and particularly that it be made safe for every peace-loving nation which, like our own, wishes to live its own life, determine its own institutions, be assured
(25) of justice and fair dealing by the other peoples of the world. . . . The programme of the world's peace, therefore, is our programme; and that programme, the only possible programme, as we see it, is this:

   I. Open covenants of peace . . . with no private
(30)   international understandings of any kind but diplomacy shall proceed always frankly and in the public view.

   II. Absolute freedom of navigation upon the seas . . . alike in peace and in war, except as
(35)   the seas may be closed in whole or in part by international action for the enforcement of international covenants.

   III. The removal, so far as possible, of all economic barriers and the establishment of
(40)   an equality of trade conditions among all the nations consenting. . . .

   IV. Adequate guarantees given and taken that national armaments will be reduced to the lowest point consistent with domestic safety.

(45) V. A free, open-minded, and absolutely impartial adjustment of all colonial claims. . . .

   VI. The evacuation of all Russian territory and such a settlement of all questions affecting Russia as will secure the best and freest
(50)   cooperation of the other nations of the world.

   VII. Belgium . . . must be evacuated and restored, without any attempt to limit the sovereignty which she enjoys in common with all other free nations. . . .

(55) VIII. All French territory should be freed and the invaded portions restored. . . .

   IX. A readjustment of the frontiers of Italy should be effected along clearly recognizable lines of nationality.

GO ON TO THE NEXT PAGE ⟶

(60)   X. The peoples of Austria-Hungary . . . should be accorded the freest opportunity to autonomous development.

XI. Rumania, Serbia, and Montenegro should be evacuated; occupied territories restored;
(65)   and Serbia accorded free and secure access to the sea. . . .

XII. The Turkish portion of the present Ottoman Empire should be assured a secure sovereignty, but the other nationalities
(70)   which are now under Turkish rule should be assured an undoubted security of life. . . .

XIII. An independent Polish state should be erected which should include the territories inhabited by indisputably Polish populations
(75)   . . . . [The state] should be assured a free and secure access to the sea. . . .

XIV. A general association of nations must be formed under specific covenants for the purpose of affording mutual guarantees
(80)   of political independence and territorial integrity to great and small states alike.

11. Based on the first two paragraphs, which choice best identifies Wilson's purpose in making this speech?

A) To build an international military and political alliance

B) To declare the sovereignty and independence of the United States

C) To outline ways to maintain peaceful relations in the world

D) To reform governments in aggressor nations bent on conquest

12. Which choice provides the best evidence for the answer to the previous question?

A) Lines 1-5 ("It will be . . . of any kind")

B) Lines 5-6 ("The day of . . . is gone by")

C) Lines 16-17 ("We entered . . . occurred")

D) Lines 26-27 ("The programme . . . is our programme")

13. As used in line 31, "frankly" most nearly means

A) in an honest manner.

B) in a blunt manner.

C) in an abrupt manner.

D) in an outspoken manner.

14. Based on the information in the passage, it can reasonably be inferred that in the past,

A) the United States avoided alliances.

B) some nations formed private pacts with one another.

C) wars usually involved only two nations.

D) the borders of France and Italy were not well-defined.

15. Which choice provides the best evidence for the answer to the previous question?

A) Lines 1-5 ("It will be . . . of any kind")

B) Lines 16-19 ("We entered . . . corrected")

C) Lines 55-59 ("All French . . . of nationality")

D) Lines 77-81 ("A general . . . states alike")

16. As used in line 44, "consistent" most nearly means

A) dependable.

B) continuing.

C) agreeable.

D) rigid.

17. In lines 45-46 ("A free . . . colonial claims"), Wilson argues that to preserve peace, nations must

A) engage in free, open, and fair trade with colonies.

B) give up all aspirations for territorial and economic expansion.

C) provide constitutional protections for colonies.

D) work to resolve conflicts originating from imperial conquests.

GO ON TO THE NEXT PAGE

18. Points VI through VIII serve as evidence to support which claim made by Wilson throughout the speech?

    A) Democratic nations ought to sign pacts of economic and political cooperation.

    B) During the war, aggressors damaged property that they should be required to repair.

    C) In the past, nations violated one another's territorial sovereignty.

    D) Current colonies are entitled to establish free and democratic governments.

19. Which of the following approaches to international relations is most similar to Wilson's approach?

    A) Economic sanctions against ideological enemies

    B) Joint efforts to mediate conflict among nations

    C) Nongovernmental organizations to regulate trade

    D) Unilateral military action against unfriendly regimes

20. Which choice best describes the developmental pattern of Wilson's argument?

    A) A statement and restatement of the argument

    B) A statement of the argument followed by specific examples

    C) Initial claims followed by counterclaims

    D) Specific examples leading to a concluding argument

Questions 21-31 are based on the following passages and supplementary material.

The following passages are concerned with meditation, particularly the practice of mindfulness. Passage 1 provides an overview of meditation, while Passage 2 focuses on a particular practitioner, Congressman Tim Ryan.

Passage 1

Meditation has been around for thousands of years, starting as a religious practice. Hindu scripture from around 1500 BCE describes meditating on the divine, and art from this time period shows
(5) people sitting cross-legged and solitary in a garden. In China and India around the fifth century BCE, other forms of meditation developed. Several religions, including Taoism, Buddhism, Islam, and Christianity, have meditative rites. In 20th-century
(10) Europe and America, secular forms of meditation arrived from India. Rather than focusing on spiritual growth, secular meditation emphasizes stress reduction, relaxation, and self-improvement.

Although it still isn't exactly mainstream,
(15) many people practice meditation. Mindfulness meditation, in particular, has become more popular in recent years. The practice involves sitting comfortably, focusing on one's breathing, and bringing the mind's attention to the present.
(20) Concerns about the past or future are let go of. An individual can picture worries popping like a bubble or flitting away like a butterfly.

Mindfulness is about increasing awareness and practicing acceptance. To be present is to
(25) have sharpened attention, or to be in a state of heightened consciousness. Practitioners of mindfulness report having a better quality of experience, deeper engagement, and greater measure of fulfillment.
(30) There are also health benefits. According to the Mayo Clinic, "Meditation can give you a sense of calm, peace and balance that benefits your emotional well-being." Among the emotional benefits are reducing negative emotions, increased
(35) self-awareness, and stress management skills.

GO ON TO THE NEXT PAGE ⟶

Asthma, depression, and sleep disorders are all conditions worsened by stress. Several studies have shown that patients with these conditions benefit from meditation.

(40)   Dr. Robert Schneider, director of the Institute for Natural Medicine and Prevention, says, "I have been researching effects of meditation on health for thirty years and have found it has compelling benefits. The benefits of meditation are coming to

(45) be widely accepted by health professionals, business leaders, and the media. It is now time for the medical profession to catch up."

Passage 2

In 2008, hoping to relax from his stressful job, Congressman Tim Ryan took a weekend retreat

(50) where he first practiced mindfulness meditation. "I came out of it," he says, "with a whole new way of relating with what was going on in the world." Now Ryan is an advocate for the benefits of meditation on health, performance, and social aware-

(55) ness. In the busy and aggressive world of Washington politics, he's a voice for calm consideration.

Every week Ryan, a Democrat representing the 13th congressional district of Ohio, hosts a meditation session for his staff and any other

(60) members of Congress who want to join. Despite the fact that Republicans and Democrats are con- sidered politically opposed, Ryan believes that the benefits of meditation ought to appeal to members of both parties. Meditation promotes self-reliance

(65) and fiscal conservation because it's a health practice that can be self-sustained and doesn't require costly memberships or equipment.

In 2010, Ryan wrote the book *A Mindful Nation: How a Simple Practice Can Help Us Reduce Stress,*

(70) *Improve Performance, and Recapture the American Spirit,* in which he advocates increased mindful- ness in many disciplines and professions. After its publication, kindergarten classes in his Ohio district started using deep-breathing techniques;

(75) now teachers rave about their students' improved behavior. "Mental discipline, focus, self-reliance, deep listening—these are fundamental skills that are essential to kids' education," Ryan says. "We yell at kids to pay attention, but we never teach them

(80) *how* to pay attention."

Word seems to be spreading around Capitol Hill. "I've had members of Congress approach me and say, 'I want to learn more about this,'" Ryan says. "Between the fundraising, being away from fam-

(85) ily, (and) the environment of hyperpartisanship, Washington is really stressing people out."

Ryan supports legislation that puts meditation to good use for everyone. Among other bills, he has sponsored one to increase the holistic-medicine

(90) offerings of the Department of Veterans Affairs. "And I haven't met anyone in the country that isn't feeling a high level of anxiety right now, given the economy and what's going on in the world. So mindfulness is for everyone."

(95)   Mr. Ryan is quick to point out that mindfulness is not a religious practice, but rather a secular mental technique that can be effective regardless of spiritual beliefs. He compares it to his grandparents praying and to athletes working out until they feel

(100) "in the zone."

"Your mind and body sync up into a flow state, without a lot of mental chatter," Mr. Ryan says.

GO ON TO THE NEXT PAGE ⟩

Practice Tests

**Improvements After
Employee Meditation Program**

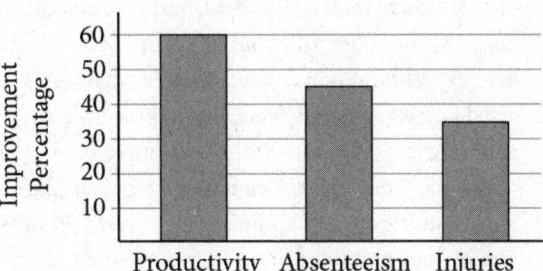

After the third year of its employee meditation program, a Detroit chemical plant reported these improvements.

21. The central idea of Passage 1 is that meditation and mindfulness

 A) were first practiced as religious rites.

 B) are becoming more accepted because of their benefits.

 C) are valuable tools for psychologists.

 D) help practitioners focus on their inner lives.

22. Passage 1 most strongly suggests that which of the following is true?

 A) Individuals who practice meditation are more likely to develop illness.

 B) Meditation helps people advance in their careers.

 C) Not many studies have been done on the results of daily meditation.

 D) Many medical professionals embrace the benefits of meditation.

23. Which choice provides the best evidence for the answer to the previous question?

 A) Lines 2-5 ("Hindu scripture . . . in a garden")

 B) Lines 15-17 ("Mindfulness meditation . . . in recent years")

 C) Lines 24-26 ("To be present . . . consciousness")

 D) Lines 30-33 ("According to . . . well-being")

24. As used in line 43, "compelling" most nearly means

 A) creative.

 B) judicial.

 C) persuasive.

 D) adaptable.

25. In Passage 2, what can be inferred about the author's point of view on meditation?

 A) The author is uncertain about its value.

 B) The author likes it but acknowledges its limits.

 C) The author appreciates its value.

 D) The author is devoted to it.

26. Passage 2 most strongly suggests that which of the following is true of Mr. Ryan?

 A) He acts on his beliefs.

 B) He is afraid to try new things.

 C) He likes to try new things.

 D) He is concerned about bipartisanship.

27. Which choice provides the best evidence for the answer to the previous question?

 A) Lines 48-50 ("In 2008 . . . mindfulness meditation")

 B) Lines 64-67 ("Meditation promotes . . . or equipment")

 C) Lines 88-90 ("Among other bills . . . Affairs")

 D) Lines 95-98 ("Mr. Ryan . . . spiritual beliefs")

28. As used in line 96, "secular" most nearly means

 A) nonreligious.

 B) serious.

 C) impersonal.

 D) pristine.

Practice Tests

GO ON TO THE NEXT PAGE

29. In Passage 2, the author's use of the word "chatter" (line 102) implies that

   A) having an inner dialogue is a useful tool.

   B) people enjoy imagining themselves in various situations.

   C) meditation supporters talk about its surprises.

   D) much of what people think is relatively unimportant.

30. Both passages support which generalization about mindfulness meditation?

   A) It has become an acceptable way to show spirituality.

   B) It is making inroads into U.S. culture.

   C) It should be utilized in public institutions.

   D) It will soon be embraced by the American public.

31. Data in the graph provide most direct support for which claim from the passages?

   A) Meditation improves a person's focus and discipline.

   B) Children benefit from learning deep-breathing techniques.

   C) Meditation makes a person more generous.

   D) Health professionals are open to the idea of meditation being healthful.

Questions 32-42 are based on the following passage.

The following passage describes possible causes and impacts of colony collapse disorder, the mysterious disappearance of honey bee colonies.

Colony collapse disorder, sometimes referred to as CCD, is a phenomenon that has garnered much attention over the past few years from both
Line the scientific community and the media alike. The
(5) disorder, which causes entire honey bee colonies

to mysteriously disappear, is a major threat to both the environment and the economy. Honey bees are the world's natural pollinators, and are responsible for the production of about one-third of everything
(10) we eat. Without honey bees, produce that we're used to having in our diets, like apples, blueberries, strawberries, and nuts, would no longer be available. Honey bees also have an effect on the meat industry in the United States. They pollinate
(15) the various types of feed used by beef and dairy farmers. The services of the honey bee population are invaluable, and the survival of many different species depends on their well-being.

When colony collapse disorder was first
(20) recognized, beekeepers and scientists assumed that a pathogen was to blame. For example, there are several known viruses and pests that can kill off entire hives of honey bees quickly and be extremely hard to prevent. Mites, fungus, and bacterial
(25) infections are all common killers. Because of how often they're seen in hives, farmers assumed that these common plights were responsible for colony collapse disorder. However, as time passed and the disorder was studied, researchers noticed some-
(30) thing odd. In many cases, there were simply no dead bees to discover. While common killers of the honey bee left telltale signs, colony collapse disor-der left nothing behind but empty hives.

Scientists attributed the rapid disappearance of
(35) the bees to a form of altruistic behavior. When a bee gets sick, it flies away from the hive so as not to spread its illness to the other bees. It naturally prioritizes the overall health of the hive over its own. Although this behavior explained the bees'
(40) disappearing act, the cause of the disorder is yet to be understood and the list of possible explanations just keeps getting longer.

One team of researchers hypothesized that fluctuations in the earth's magnetic field might
(45) be doing damage to the magnetoreceptors, or built-in homing devices, that bees use to find their way home to their hives after flying all day. Honey bees, as well as birds and fish, use the earth's magnetic field to identify their location. Sunspots,

GO ON TO THE NEXT PAGE ⟶

(50) which cause the strength of the earth's magnetic field to fluctuate, might be damaging the honey bee's biological tools.

While solar activity is outside the control of humans, another theory about the cause of colony *(55)* collapse disorder points to the human invention of pesticides. Pesticides, which are chemicals used to prevent pest infestation of crops on a large scale around the world, are often picked up by honey bees during their foraging and pollination flights. *(60)* Scientists have found that more than one pesticide can be found in the honey of one hive. They are currently studying the interaction of two or more pesticides, which travel into the hives and are stored by the bees in the pollen they use for protein.

(65) While the presence of one pesticide in a hive would certainly limit the life spans of bees and impair their navigational skills, it could be that it is the interaction of two or more pesticides that cause the entire colony to collapse. There are many ingredi- *(70)* ents in pesticides that are not regulated by world governments, and this leaves a lot of ground for bee scientists to cover when doing their research.

Research over time usually helps to narrow down the field of possible causes of a disorder, but in the *(75)* case of colony collapse disorder, scientists feel farther away than ever from finding the root cause and a cure. Many people around the world are taking up the cause of keeping honey bees alive by keeping bees in their backyards or on their roofs. Some *(80)* cities and towns have relaxed regulations on beekeeping in response to the honey bee population crisis. Hopefully, community initiatives and research can both help to save the world's honey bee population.

32. The primary purpose of the passage is to

   A) show that honey bees require certain conditions in order to live.

   B) instruct the reader on how to increase the number of honey bees.

   C) explain the relationship between sunspots and colony collapse disorder.

   D) alert the reader to the impending crisis of decreasing numbers of honey bees.

33. The author's point of view is most similar to

   A) an advocate for honey bee survival.

   B) an environmentalist concerned about toxic materials.

   C) a naturalist who researches changes in animal populations.

   D) a concerned citizen who hopes to raise honey bees.

34. The author uses the word "mysteriously" (line 6) to emphasize

   A) that fluctuations of the earth's magnetic field are uncontrollable.

   B) how little is known about why colony collapse occurs.

   C) that the reason a bee leaves its hive when it is sick is unknown.

   D) why researchers are studying the effect of pesticides on honey bees.

35. As used in line 27, "plights" most nearly means

   A) causes.

   B) promises.

   C) intentions.

   D) troubles.

36. The author uses the fact that no bees are found in a hive after a colony collapses to

   A) examine the extent of damage to the honey bee population that has occurred.

   B) emphasize the ways in which honey bees relate to human beings.

   C) refute the possibility that pathogens are the reason for the collapse.

   D) show that pesticides are not to blame for the decrease in the honey bee population.

Practice Tests

GO ON TO THE NEXT PAGE ▷

37. Which choice provides the best evidence for the answer to the previous question?

    A) Lines 4-7 ("The disorder . . . the economy")

    B) Lines 21-24 ("For example . . . to prevent")

    C) Lines 31-33 ("While common . . . empty hives")

    D) Lines 37-39 ("It naturally . . . its own")

38. As used in line 59, "foraging" most nearly means

    A) rejecting.

    B) offering.

    C) watching.

    D) searching.

39. The passage most strongly suggests that

    A) the author is cautiously optimistic about the future existence of the honey bee.

    B) the author thinks that scientists have not tried hard enough to find the reason for colony collapse.

    C) one team of scientists believes that they will have an answer to the problem of colony collapse very soon.

    D) scientists have ruled out the theory that pesticides are at fault for colony collapse.

40. Which choice provides the best evidence for the answer to the previous question?

    A) Lines 7-10 ("Honey bees . . . eat")

    B) Lines 25-28 ("Because of how . . . disorder")

    C) Lines 53-56 ("While solar . . . pesticides")

    D) Lines 82-83 ("Hopefully . . . population")

41. According to the passage, which of the following events has occurred in response to colony collapse disorder?

    A) Concerned citizens have fought to ban certain pesticides.

    B) Some towns have relaxed their regulations on beekeeping.

    C) Farmers have resorted to other means of pollinating their feed.

    D) Scientists are working to control the use of electromagnetic devices.

42. Based on information in the passage, which statement best describes the relationship between honey bees and human beings?

    A) Human beings depend on honey bees to keep the environment and economy healthy.

    B) Human beings depend on honey bees to keep the effects of sunspots to a minimum.

    C) Honey bees depend on human beings to provide them with food.

    D) Honey bees depend on human beings to protect them from solar flares.

Questions 43-52 are based on the following passage and supplementary materials.

The following passage describes the potential problems caused by debris that humans have left behind in space.

In the first days of space exploration, one concern was the possibility that astronauts or spacecraft might be hit by meteoroids. Scientists
Line calculated that this possibility was extremely
(5) small because meteoroids are rare. Astronauts and spacecraft, on the other hand, would almost certainly encounter micrometeorites, which are about the size of grains of dust and much more common.
However, in the 60 years since the beginning of
(10) space exploration, large quantities of human-made

 GO ON TO THE NEXT PAGE

orbital debris have accumulated. Much of the debris consists of satellites that have stopped functioning or rocket booster sections that separated from the main spacecraft during a mission. Some of
(15) the debris consists of items lost by astronauts, such as tools or space suit parts. Still, more of the debris is the result of collisions, such as when one satellite collides with another or with a large piece of debris.

NASA estimates there are millions of debris
(20) particles that are too small to be tracked. These circle Earth at speeds up to 17,500 miles per hour, making even the smallest particles dangerous. One scientist calculated that a chip of paint hitting the window of a spacecraft at orbital speeds will hit
(25) with the same amount of force as a bowling ball traveling at 60 mph. Such an impact occurred on the space shuttle *Challenger*'s second flight, chipping the windows and causing minor damage to the protective tiles on the spacecraft. While the damage
(30) was not immediately dangerous, it led to the fear that any craft in orbit for long periods of time could accumulate enough damage to cease functioning.

Larger objects are even more dangerous, but they can be monitored and avoided. NASA tracks
(35) about 500,000 pieces of debris larger than a marble, about 20,000 of which are larger than a softball. When NASA was still flying shuttle missions, it would often have to direct the shuttle to maneuver to avoid collisions with the larger debris. This could
(40) usually be planned and accomplished in a few hours, but moving the International Space Station to avoid a collision takes up to 30 hours of advance notice.

Many satellites have the ability to adjust their
(45) course slightly and can be remotely directed to avoid collisions with larger objects that would damage or destroy the satellites. NASA and the European Space Agency (ESA) have departments of scientists and engineers dedicated to cataloging,
(50) modeling, and predicting the movements of space debris.

Some debris falls back to Earth, and most of it is burned up in the atmosphere. However, a large piece will survive long enough to get through
(55) the atmosphere and crash. In 1979, the obsolete Skylab fell out of orbit, and much of it withstood

the trip through the atmosphere, crashing in the Australian outback. Space agencies also monitor debris to predict if and when any particular piece
(60) might fall. Although they can issue warnings, there is currently nothing that can be done about pieces that might get through the atmosphere.

To avoid adding to the aggregation of debris, future satellites may need to be able to take
(65) themselves out of orbit as their usefulness comes to an end. Until a way to remove these remains is implemented, however, those 500,000 pieces of large fragments, along with the millions of smaller pieces, will continue to orbit Earth.

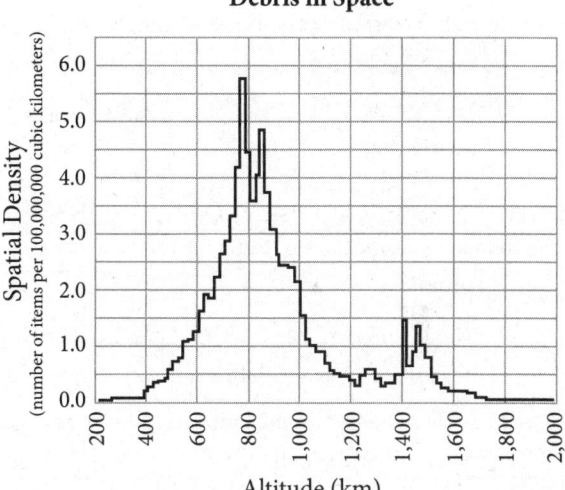

Debris in Space

Adapted from NASA: U.S. Satellite Catalog.

43. The passage is primarily concerned with the

A) unintended consequences of space exploration.

B) composition of the space debris that orbits Earth.

C) dangers posed by space debris created by humans.

D) causes and consequences of collisions in space.

44. Which choice provides the best evidence for the answer to the previous question?

    A) Lines 3-8 ("Scientists calculated . . . common")

    B) Lines 20-22 ("These circle . . . dangerous")

    C) Lines 33-34 ("Larger objects . . . avoided")

    D) Lines 44-47 ("Many satellites . . . satellites")

45. The second paragraph helps support the central idea of the passage by providing

    A) an explanation of why space debris left by humans is more dangerous than meteors.

    B) a summary of problems caused by old satellites and discarded equipment.

    C) a description of the types of human-made space debris that are causing problems.

    D) an argument for better tracking of the space debris that is orbiting Earth.

46. According to the passage, why does space debris created by humans pose a greater threat than meteoroids?

    A) Meteoroids are rare, while there are large quantities of space debris.

    B) Meteoroids are much smaller than most pieces of space debris.

    C) Space debris cannot be tracked and monitored, but meteoroids can.

    D) Space debris is only found in a narrow band around Earth.

47. Which of the following pieces of evidence most strengthens the author's central claim?

    A) An explanation of early concerns about space collisions in paragraph 1

    B) Information about how space debris is tracked in paragraph 5

    C) An example of space debris falling to Earth in paragraph 6

    D) The suggestion that obsolete satellites take themselves out of orbit in paragraph 7

48. As used in line 55, "obsolete" most nearly means

    A) displaced.

    B) redundant.

    C) excessive.

    D) outdated.

49. Based on information in the passage, which conclusion can reasonably be inferred?

    A) One way to prevent space debris from causing injuries on Earth is to warn people to avoid the predicted impact site.

    B) The smallest pieces of space debris can be removed by astronauts while they are working in space.

    C) Most space debris is not dangerous to space travelers because of its small size and relatively low speed.

    D) Pieces of space debris will become more of a problem as spacecraft travel farther into outer space.

GO ON TO THE NEXT PAGE

50. Which choice provides the best evidence for the answer to the previous question?

    A) Lines 19-22 ("NASA estimates . . . dangerous")

    B) Lines 33-34 ("Larger objects . . . avoided")

    C) Lines 34-36 ("NASA tracks . . . softball")

    D) Lines 60-62 ("Although . . . atmosphere")

51. As used in line 67, "implemented" most nearly means

    A) employed.

    B) investigated.

    C) prevented.

    D) appointed.

52. Based on the passage and the graphic, if NASA were to place a new satellite into orbit, which altitude range would pose the greatest danger?

    A) 500-700 kilometers

    B) 700-900 kilometers

    C) 1,400-1,600 kilometers

    D) 1,800-2,000 kilometers

WRITING AND LANGUAGE TEST

35 Minutes—44 Questions

This section corresponds to Section 2 of your answer sheet.

Directions: Each passage in this section is followed by several questions. Some questions will reference an underlined portion in the passage; others will ask you to consider a part of a passage or the passage as a whole. For each question, choose the answer that reflects the best use of grammar, punctuation, and style. If a passage or question is accompanied by a graphic, take the graphic into account in choosing your response(s). Some questions will have "NO CHANGE" as a possible response. Choose that answer if you think the best choice is to leave the sentence as written.

Questions 1-11 are based on the following passage.

A Sweet Discovery

[1] Like most chemists, a laboratory was where Constantin Fahlberg worked on his research. However, the discovery for which he is famous occurred not in the laboratory, but at supper.

1. A) NO CHANGE
   B) Like most chemists, Constantin Fahlberg worked on his research in a laboratory.
   C) Constantin Fahlberg worked on his research, like most chemists, in a laboratory.
   D) A laboratory, like most chemists, is where Constantin Fahlberg worked on his research.

GO ON TO THE NEXT PAGE

2 Chemical compounds are derived from coal tar, which is what Fahlberg began working on as a research chemist in a laboratory at Johns Hopkins University in early 1878. Coal tar was a by-product of steel manufacturing, and compounds derived **3** from them had been used as medicines and in dye formulations. Fahlberg, and others in the laboratory, were studying ways to add different chemicals to molecules found in coal tar to see if the new compounds formed had other useful properties.

One night in June, Fahlberg finished a long day of work; he had been so **4** demanding in his research that he forgot to eat lunch, so he hurried to his supper without stopping to wash his hands. He might have

2. A) NO CHANGE
    B) Johns Hopkins University is where Fahlberg began working as a research chemist in a laboratory, making chemical compounds derived from coal tar in early 1878.
    C) Coal tar creates chemical compounds. This is what Fahlberg began working on as a research chemist in a laboratory at Johns Hopkins University in early 1878.
    D) In early 1878, Fahlberg began working as a research chemist in a laboratory at Johns Hopkins University, making chemical compounds derived from coal tar.

3. A) NO CHANGE
    B) from it
    C) from these
    D) from him

4. A) NO CHANGE
    B) delayed
    C) engrossed
    D) excited

GO ON TO THE NEXT PAGE

Practice Tests

considered hand washing unnecessary because he had not handled any toxic chemicals that day, or he might have just been so hungry he did not think about it. **5**

The bread tasted so sweet that Fahlberg thought he might have picked up some cake by mistake. He rinsed out his mouth with water and then patted his mustache dry with a napkin. He was surprised to find that the napkin tasted sweet as well. He took another sip of water and realized that the water now tasted sweet. **6** The bread, napkin, and glass of water had something in common. He then tasted his thumb, and it tasted sweeter than any candy he had ever had.

5. At this point, the writer wants to create an ideal transition to the next paragraph. Which choice most effectively accomplishes this goal?

A) Later, hand washing would become a critical protocol in the laboratory.

B) Thankfully, he didn't, or he never would have discovered what came next.

C) Fahlberg had not eaten any cake, or indeed anything sweet, that day.

D) Either way, he picked up his bread in his unwashed hands and took a bite.

6. A) NO CHANGE

B) Was there something that the bread, napkin, and glass of water had in common, he wondered?

C) In fact, everything Fahlberg touched seemed to taste sweeter than usual, which intrigued his scientific mind.

D) Fahlberg quickly realized that the one thing the bread, napkin, and glass of water had in common was that they had all touched his fingers.

[1] Fahlberg rushed back into the lab and began to taste the contents of every beaker he had used that day. [2] Fortunately, he had not worked with anything poisonous or corrosive, or the story [7] may have a different ending. [3] [8] He had discovered saccharin, which he named for its intense sweetness. [4] He found a sweet-tasting mixture of chemicals and worked for weeks to isolate the sweet substance from the rest and to determine its chemical composition. [5] Although it is many times more sweet tasting than sugar, it cannot be used for energy by the body and therefore does not contribute to calories consumed or energy use. [6] Soon after Fahlberg started [9] making saccharin commercially in 1886, it became popular with people who needed to lose weight and with diabetic patients who needed to avoid sugar. [10] [11]

7. A) NO CHANGE
    B) would have had
    C) might have
    D) could have had

8. Which choice most clearly and effectively conveys the central idea of the paragraph?

    A) NO CHANGE
    B) The substance was saccharin, and it became known as an artificial sweetener.
    C) Instead, the substance was a harmless sweetener called saccharin.
    D) Interestingly, the substance was extremely sweet and would later be known as saccharin.

9. A) NO CHANGE
    B) inventing
    C) creating
    D) producing

10. To make this paragraph most logical, sentence 4 should be placed

    A) Where it is now
    B) Before sentence 1
    C) Before sentence 3
    D) Before sentence 6

Practice Tests

GO ON TO THE NEXT PAGE

11. Which of the following sentences would provide the best conclusion for the passage?

A) Clearly, Constantin Fahlberg's legacy of research, along with his accidental discovery, continues to have lasting effects on society even today.

B) If Fahlberg had stopped to wash his hands that day, he might have continued his experiments on coal tar derivatives, never knowing that an important substance sat at the bottom of one of his laboratory beakers.

C) In addition to his discovery of saccharin, his work on coal tar proved that Constantin Fahlberg was a talented scientist whose work has applications in the present day, even though a number of new artificial sweeteners have been developed.

D) Fahlberg's discovery of saccharin is just one of the many examples of times when science was advanced through what some might call "a happy accident."

GO ON TO THE NEXT PAGE ⟶

Questions 12-22 are based on the following passage.

René Descartes: The Father of Modern Philosophy

Throughout history, philosophy has shaped culture in pivotal ways. From the ancients to the postmoderns, great philosophers have spoken powerfully within [12] there respective contexts. For modern Western culture, one philosopher's formative impact surpassed his contemporaries: France's René Descartes. Called "the father of modern philosophy," Descartes crucially influenced Western perspectives on knowledge and rationality.

This 17th-century philosopher ushered Western thought through an era of great public doubt and upheaval and into the age of self-reliant rationalism. Political and religious tradition and authority—the [13] obvious premodern sources of truth and knowledge—were being questioned and rejected as new ideas identified potential inconsistencies. [14] Because foundations of truth seemed to be crumbling, Descartes's writings proposed an alternative foundation: individual reason.

12. A) NO CHANGE
    B) their
    C) its
    D) it's

13. A) NO CHANGE
    B) makeshift
    C) innovative
    D) reigning

14. A) NO CHANGE
    B) In a time when foundations of truth seemed to be crumbling, Descartes's writings proposed an alternative foundation: individual reason.
    C) Despite the fact that foundations of truth seemed to be crumbling, Descartes's writings proposed an alternative foundation: individual reason.
    D) Before foundations of truth seemed to be crumbling, Descartes's writings proposed an alternative foundation: individual reason.

GO ON TO THE NEXT PAGE

Practice Tests

15 An expert in many fields, Descartes's work would on many levels serve to establish foundations for modern culture and science. **16** This emphasis on reason, as opposed to traditional or authoritative bases for certainty, would become the modern mechanism for determining truth and knowledge.

17 Modern culture would come to cherish this as an intellectual ideal. In his most famous project, Descartes sought certainty by mentally stripping away every layer of knowledge that was remotely possible to

15. A) NO CHANGE
    B) Expertise in many fields, Descartes created work that
    C) An expert in many fields, Descartes would create work that
    D) With his expertise in many fields, Descartes's work

16. At this point, the writer wants to add specific information that supports the central claim of the paragraph. Which choice provides the strongest support?
    A) Even so, his most impressive contribution was his advocacy for the individual's rationality.
    B) Unlike Descartes, other philosophers argued that reason alone could not provide the basis for knowledge.
    C) The idea known as "Cartesian dualism" posited that in the world there exists only mind and matter.
    D) His work on philosophy has proven to have more importance than his ideas about anatomy, many of which have since been disproven.

17. Which sentence should be added in front of sentence 1 to clarify the topic of the paragraph?
    A) Descartes's contributions to philosophy were seen as threatening to religion.
    B) Descartes focused his work on the pursuit of fact-based certainty.
    C) The foundation for the ideas of many other philosophers is Descartes's work.
    D) Descartes's ideas were rooted in his Jesuit training.

doubt. Descartes arrived at his memorable

[18] conclusion, "I think, therefore I am," he could only be certain of the fact that he was thinking. [19] Building from there, he could work toward rational certainty in other areas of knowledge.

Emphasizing the importance of building knowledge on certain evidence, Descartes modeled a reversal of the reigning scientific processes (which typically worked backward from observation to explanation). Descartes founded the modern scientific method, in which research and study could be reliably conducted based on certain evidence. Scientific method, and the emphasis on human reason, would become standard elements of modern thought. Though reimagined by ensuing culture and philosophy, [20] these changes propelled by Descartes's initial contributions to that conversation.

18. A) NO CHANGE
    B) conclusion "I think, therefore I am" he could only be certain of the fact that he was thinking.
    C) conclusion, "I think, therefore I am" he could only be certain of the fact that he was thinking.
    D) conclusion, "I think, therefore I am." He could only be certain of the fact that he was thinking.

19. Which choice most logically follows the previous sentence and sets up the information that follows?
    A) This revelation came as a shock to many people.
    B) However, he believed that this certainty offered evidence to confirm his existence.
    C) Still, it was a place to start.
    D) This was a radical new way to think about thinking.

20. A) NO CHANGE
    B) these changes being propelled by
    C) these changes having been propelled by
    D) these changes were propelled by

GO ON TO THE NEXT PAGE ▷

21 Some people may argue that it is impossible to separate what Descartes accomplished from the things his contemporaries did. Certainly, most scientists and philosophers influence and build from each other's work. But Descartes was the crucial voice in early modern dialogue. His expertise drew trusted readership, and his well-read ideas pointed culture down the road to modern understanding—a road paved with reason, modernism's great intellectual virtue. Shifts **22** begun by Descartes's work would influence the very structure of ideas and systems in the modern world, from research methods to public processes like government and health systems.

21. A) NO CHANGE
    B) Some may argue that it is impossible to separate Descartes's accomplishments from those of his contemporaries.
    C) Some people may argue that it is impossible to separate Descartes from his contemporaries.
    D) Some may argue that what Descartes accomplished is no different from what his contemporaries did.

22. A) NO CHANGE
    B) foreseen
    C) initiated
    D) evolved

Questions 23-33 are based on the following passage.

The Novel: Introspection to Escapism

Art is never **23** immovable, nor is it meant to be. A poem written today looks and sounds vastly different from a poem by Shakespeare, and a modern symphony no longer resembles one by Beethoven. So it is with the novel, that still relatively young member of the literary family (many consider *Don Quixote*, published in 1605, to be the first). The novel is evolving to reflect the **24** changing world; for better or for worse.

23. A) NO CHANGE
    B) sluggish
    C) static
    D) stationary

24. A) NO CHANGE
    B) changing world—for better
    C) changing world: for better
    D) changing world for better

25 The novel, while well regarded, would never match the poem as the ideal form for conveying the struggles of humanity. A few quotations from acclaimed novelists of the past illustrate how **26** loftily the form was once regarded. G. K. Chesterton said, "A good novel tells us the truth about its hero; but a bad novel tells us the truth about its author." English writer Ford Madox Ford believed the novelist played an important role as a recorder of history. **27** Ford said of his friend Joseph Conrad, "We agreed that the novel is absolutely the only vehicle for the thought of our day."

It's not that over centuries writers of novels have shed these ambitions; novels today still address complexities and intricate social dynamics.

28 However, in recent decades, popular novels and their film adaptations have driven the novel market in a broader direction.

25. Which choice most effectively establishes the main topic of the paragraph?

A) NO CHANGE

B) The novel was once sacred ground, meant to capture and reveal universal truths, to depict society and all its ills, to explore and expound upon the human condition.

C) Both poetry and novels enjoyed a resurgence of popularity in the early 1900s due to the notoriety of many of the prominent authors of the day.

D) By the early 1900s, novels had evolved into something entirely different from the form Cervantes pioneered with *Don Quixote*.

26. A) NO CHANGE

B) broadly

C) haughtily

D) pretentiously

27. Which choice best improves the sentence?

A) Ford said of his friend, the novelist Joseph Conrad,

B) Ford said of his great friend, Joseph Conrad,

C) Ford said of Joseph Conrad,

D) Ford said of his friend, Joseph Conrad, a Pole who moved to Britain,

28. A) NO CHANGE

B) However: in recent decades,

C) However in recent decades,

D) In recent decades however;

GO ON TO THE NEXT PAGE

Practice Tests

[29] Novels are considered just another entertainment medium, which are now available on digital devices, one that ought to enthrall its passive reader and relieve him or her of the stress and tedium of life. The difficulties, challenges, and triumphs of real life are **[30]** less often the subject of popular novels; instead, escapist tales of fantastical lands and escapades are more popular. **[31]**

29. A) NO CHANGE
    B) Novels, which are now available on digital devices, are considered just another entertainment medium,
    C) Novels are considered just another entertainment medium, now available on digital devices,
    D) Novels, just another entertainment medium which are now available on digital devices

30. A) NO CHANGE
    B) less often the subject of popular novels instead, escapist tales of fantastical lands and escapades are more popular.
    C) less often the subject of popular novels, instead, escapist tales of fantastical lands and escapades are more popular.
    D) less often the subject of popular novels: instead, escapist tales of fantastical lands and escapades, are more popular.

31. At this point, the writer wants to add specific information that supports the ideas presented in the paragraph. Which choice provides the most relevant detail?

    A) Novels exploring deep social issues remain the most heavily decorated books come literary award season.
    B) Director James Cameron remarked recently about the "inherent difficulty" of adapting novels with fantasy themes.
    C) Writing in the *New Yorker* magazine in 2014, critic James Woods stated that readers now want novels that, like popcorn, are "easy to consume."
    D) The "slice of life" novel remains tremendously popular among books targeting younger readers.

GO ON TO THE NEXT PAGE

SAT PRACTICE TEST 1   **747**

It is rare today for a novelist to attempt to ask, "What does it mean?" Instead, **32** we strive to provide the reader with an answer to the question, "What happens next?"

"Publishers, readers, booksellers, even critics," critic James Woods wrote, "acclaim the novel that one can deliciously sink into, forget oneself in, the novel that returns us to the innocence of childhood or the dream of the cartoon, the novel of a thousand confections and no unwanted significance. What becomes harder to find, and lonelier to defend, is the idea of **33** the novel as—in Ford Madox Ford's words—a 'medium of profoundly serious investigation into the human case.'"

Questions 34-44 are based on the following passage and supplementary material.

Interning: A Bridge Between Classes and Careers

Kelli Blake, a chemical engineering major, recently **34** excepted a summer internship with BP, an international energy company, to gain career experience. Some argue against the value of internships, claiming they pay very little and can involve performing **35** boring tasks, yet Kelli feels her internship is critical to helping her discover whether engineering is right for her.

Kelli wants a real-world perspective on information she has gained in her classes. Her internship with a corporate leader is affording her the opportunity to apply her conceptual knowledge to tasks inside a major

32. A) NO CHANGE
    B) they strive
    C) it strives
    D) he or she strives

33. A) NO CHANGE
    B) the novel as, in Ford Madox Ford's words—a 'medium of profoundly serious investigation into the human case.'"
    C) the novel as, in Ford Madox Ford's words: a 'medium of profoundly serious investigation into the human case.'"
    D) the novel as, in Ford Madox Ford's words; a 'medium of profoundly serious investigation into the human case.'"

34. A) NO CHANGE
    B) accepted
    C) adopted
    D) adapted

35. A) NO CHANGE
    B) skilled
    C) menial
    D) challenging

GO ON TO THE NEXT PAGE ⟹

oil company. **36** <u>During this internship, for example, Kelli is working on a glycol dehydration project; she will be using the classroom skills she learned from thermo-dynamics, organic chemistry, and more.</u> She can later add this project to her résumé and portfolio, giving her an edge over other college graduates.

37 <u>Offshore engineers have many rules and regulations.</u> Helicopter underwater egress safety training is required of employees traveling to offshore facilities, so she will **38** <u>stand out</u> from other applicants by already being safety certified. "I have a new appreciation for the protocols followed by engineers at refineries," she states. Kelli believes that gaining new skills and showing she can apply her classroom knowledge to real situations will give her an advantage over her competition should she decide to join BP.

36. Which choice best supports the central idea of the paragraph?

A) NO CHANGE

B) Kelli can use the materials from her internship in a professional-quality presentation; she can then deliver the presentation to her classmates when she returns to college after her internship.

C) In addition, Kelli is designing the next internship proposal for her classmates after she completes her own and graduates.

D) Kelli is hoping to formulate her project results as a professional published document to sell to BP.

37. Which choice provides the most appropriate introduction to the paragraph?

A) NO CHANGE

B) Kelli admires the engineers who administer the safety training.

C) The skills Kelli acquires can be applied to existing knowledge.

D) Kelli will also earn an underwater safety training certificate.

38. A) NO CHANGE

B) stand down

C) stand up

D) stand alone

GO ON TO THE NEXT PAGE

Everyone has 39 their own reason for wanting to become an intern. Kelli has several other reasons behind her decision. 40 For example, Kelli wants to meet people to learn about the variety of careers available, from entry level to senior engineer. She will accomplish all of her intern goals 41 by working on technical projects, attend "lunch and learn" meetings, watching webinars, and shadow coworkers.

39. A) NO CHANGE
    B) your
    C) its
    D) his or her

40. A) NO CHANGE
    B) For example; Kelli wants to meet people to learn about the variety of careers available, from entry level to senior engineer.
    C) For example, Kelli wants to meet people—to learn about the variety of careers available, from entry level, to senior engineer.
    D) For example, Kelli wants to meet people to learn about the variety of careers available; from entry level to senior engineer.

41. A) NO CHANGE
    B) by working on technical projects, attending "lunch and learn" meetings, watching webinars, and shadowing coworkers.
    C) by working on technical projects, attend "lunch and learn" meetings, watch webinars, and shadow coworkers.
    D) by working on technical projects, attending "lunch and learn" meetings, watch webinars, and shadowing coworkers.

GO ON TO THE NEXT PAGE

Practice Tests

What are some further benefits of internships? Besides gaining exposure in the field, Kelli is networking. The most important person to her now is her mentor, Dan, a senior engineer who can help her grow professionally by answering her questions. Gaining valuable contacts and <u>**42** good role model. These are other reasons</u> she has pursued this internship.

Kelli is now an acting member of a corporate team. She realizes she will be learning a lot about the industry and will benefit from adopting an entirely new vocabulary. She views her internship as an adventure, one in which engineering teams worldwide must work collaboratively and efficiently. <u>**43** It is worth it to give up her summer, Kelli argues, because though she is losing her summer she is doing the job of an actual engineer through her internship.</u> Moreover, she views the experience as one of the best ways to learn about her field and industry, which typically offers around <u>**44** 35 internships per 1,000 hires.</u>

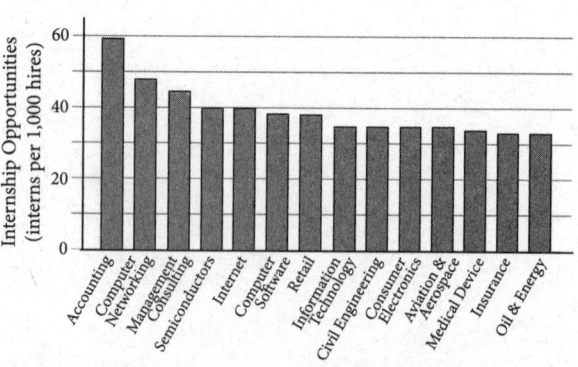

Industries Likely to Hire Their Interns

Adapted from Kurt Wagner, "Which Internships Really Pay Off?" ©2014 by Revere Digital LLC.

42. A) NO CHANGE
    B) a good role model, these are other reasons
    C) a good role model; are other reasons
    D) a good role model are other reasons

43. A) NO CHANGE
    B) It is worth giving up, Kelli argues, because though she is losing her summer, she is doing the job of an actual engineer through her internship.
    C) It is worth it to give up her summer, Kelli argues, because she is doing the job of an actual engineer through her internship.
    D) It is worth it to Kelli to give up her summer, because though summers are usually a time to relax, she argues, she is doing the job of an actual engineer through her internship.

44. Which choice most accurately and effectively represents the information in the graph and the passage?
    A) NO CHANGE
    B) 32 internships per 1,000 hires.
    C) 35 internships per 60 hires.
    D) 32 internships per 60 hires.

MATH TEST

25 Minutes—20 Questions

NO-CALCULATOR SECTION

This section corresponds to Section 3 of your answer sheet.

Directions: For this section, solve each question and select the best answer choice. The available space on each page may be used for scratch work.

Notes:

1. Calculator use is NOT permitted.
2. All numbers used are real numbers, and all variables used represent real numbers, unless otherwise indicated.
3. Figures are drawn to scale and lie in a plane unless otherwise indicated.
4. Unless stated otherwise, the domain of any function f is assumed to be the set of all real numbers x, for which $f(x)$ is a real number.

Information:

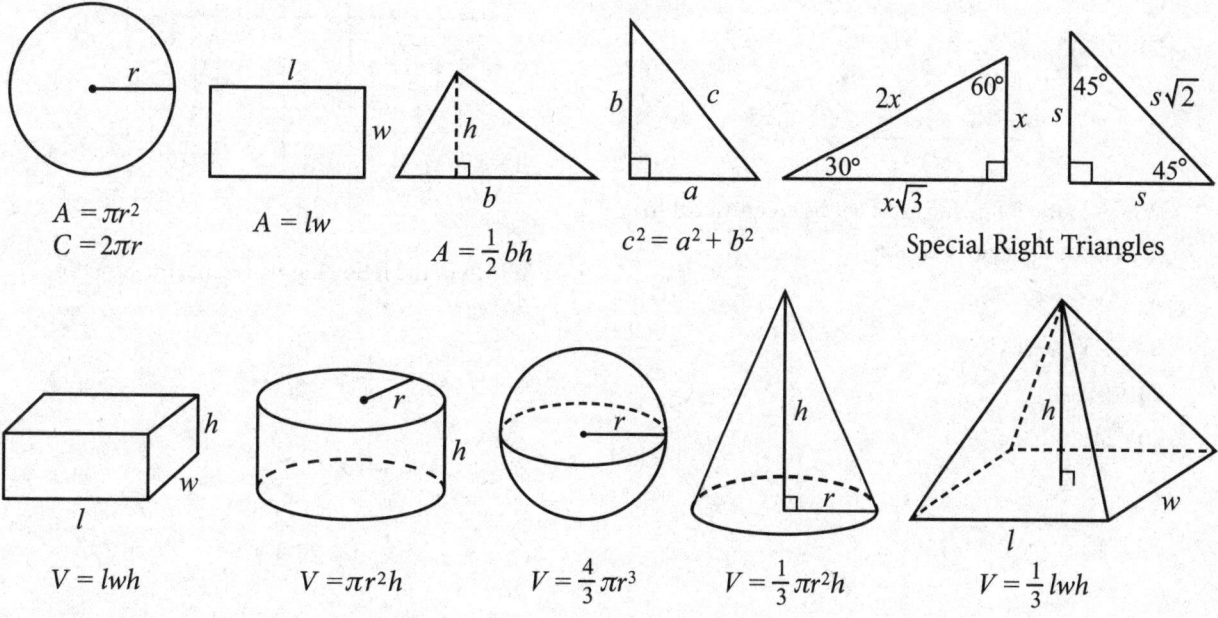

$A = \pi r^2$
$C = 2\pi r$

$A = lw$

$A = \frac{1}{2}bh$

$c^2 = a^2 + b^2$

Special Right Triangles

$V = lwh$

$V = \pi r^2 h$

$V = \frac{4}{3}\pi r^3$

$V = \frac{1}{3}\pi r^2 h$

$V = \frac{1}{3}lwh$

The sum of the degree measures of the angles in a triangle is 180.

The number of degrees of arc in a circle is 360.

The number of radians of arc in a circle is 2π.

GO ON TO THE NEXT PAGE

Practice Tests

Fence Installation

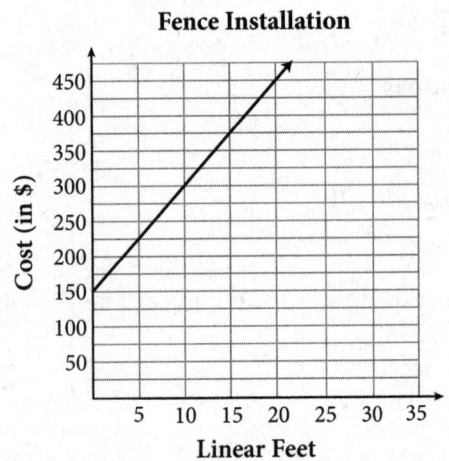

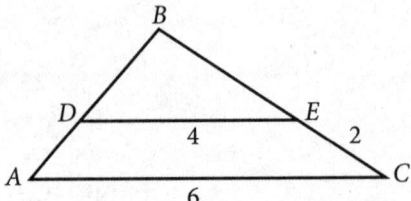

Note: Figure not drawn to scale.

1. The graph shows the cost of installing a vinyl privacy fence. The company charges a flat installation fee plus a cost per linear foot of fencing. Based on the graph, how much does one linear foot of this particular vinyl fence cost?

   A) $5

   B) $15

   C) $75

   D) $150

$$\frac{24x^4 + 36x^3 - 12x^2}{12x^2}$$

2. Which of the following expressions is equivalent to the expression shown above?

   A) $2x^2 + 3x$

   B) $24x^4 + 36x^3$

   C) $2x^2 + 3x - 1$

   D) $24x^4 + 36x^3 - 1$

3. In the figure shown, $\triangle ABC \sim \triangle DBE$. What is the length of $\overline{BE}$?

   A) 3.5

   B) 3.75

   C) 4

   D) 4.5

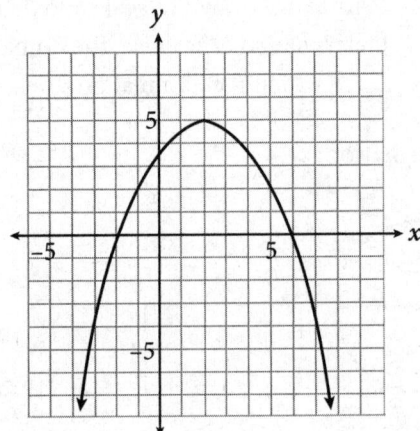

4. Which of the following represents the function shown?

   A) $f(x) = -\dfrac{1}{3}(x - 2)^2 + 5$

   B) $f(x) = -\dfrac{1}{3}(x + 2)^2 + 5$

   C) $f(x) = \dfrac{1}{3}(x + 2)^2 + 5$

   D) $f(x) = 3(x - 2)^2 + 5$

GO ON TO THE NEXT PAGE

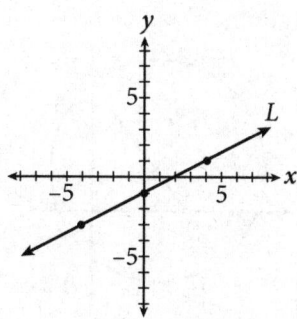

5. If line L shown here is reflected over the x-axis, what is the slope of the new line?

   A) -2

   B) $-\dfrac{1}{2}$

   C) $\dfrac{1}{2}$

   D) 2

6. If $p = 4x^3 + x - 2$, $q = x^2 - 1$, and $r = 3x - 5$, then what is $2p - (q + r)$?

   A) $7x^3 - x + 2$

   B) $8x^3 - x^2 - x + 2$

   C) $8x^3 - x^2 - x - 10$

   D) $8x^3 - x^2 + 5x - 8$

7. Which of the following are the roots of the equation $2x^2 + 4x - 3 = 0$?

   A) $\dfrac{-2 \pm \sqrt{10}}{2}$

   B) $-2 \pm \sqrt{5}$

   C) $-1 \pm \sqrt{10}$

   D) $-1 \pm 2\sqrt{10}$

8. If $g(x) = 3x - 5$ and $h(x) = \dfrac{7x + 10}{4}$, at what point does the graph of $g(x)$ intersect the graph of $h(x)$?

   A) $(-2, -11)$

   B) $(-2, 1)$

   C) $(3, 4)$

   D) $(6, 13)$

9. If $x = k^{-\frac{1}{3}}$, where $x > 0$ and $k > 0$, which of the following equations gives k in terms of x ?

   A) $k = \dfrac{1}{x^3}$

   B) $k = \dfrac{1}{\sqrt[3]{x}}$

   C) $k = -\sqrt[3]{x}$

   D) $k = -x^3$

$$4x - (10 - 2x) = c(3x - 5)$$

10. If the equation shown has infinitely many solutions, and c is a constant, what is the value of c ?

   A) -2

   B) $-\dfrac{2}{3}$

   C) $\dfrac{2}{3}$

   D) 2

11. If $0 < 1 - \dfrac{a}{3} \le \dfrac{1}{2}$, which of the following is not a possible value of a ?

   A) 1.5

   B) 2

   C) 2.5

   D) 3

GO ON TO THE NEXT PAGE ▷

Practice Tests

$$\begin{cases} y - \dfrac{2}{k}x \le 0 \\ \dfrac{1}{k}x - \dfrac{1}{2}y \le -1 \end{cases}$$

12. If the system of inequalities shown has no solution, what is the value of k ?

   A) 1

   B) 2

   C) There is no value of k that results in no solution.

   D) There are infinitely many values of k that result in no solution.

$$\frac{4x}{x - 7} + \frac{2x}{2x - 14} = \frac{70}{2(x - 7)}$$

13. What value(s) of x satisfy the equation above?

   A) 0

   B) 7

   C) No solution

   D) Any value such that $x \ne 7$

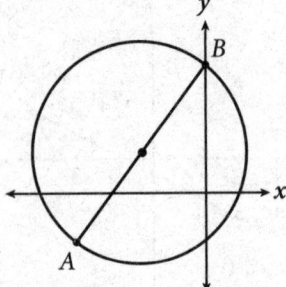

14. The circle shown is given by the equation $x^2 + y^2 + 6x - 4y = 12$. What is the shortest distance from A to B ?

   A)   5

   B)   10

   C) $4\sqrt{3}$

   D)   24

15. If g is a function defined over the set of all real numbers and $g(x - 1) = 3x^2 + 5x - 7$, then which of the following defines $g(x)$?

   A) $g(x) = 3x^2 - x - 9$

   B) $g(x) = 3x^2 + 5x + 1$

   C) $g(x) = 3x^2 + 11x + 1$

   D) $g(x) = 3x^2 + 11x - 6$

GO ON TO THE NEXT PAGE

Directions: For questions 16-20, enter your responses into the appropriate grid on your answer sheet, in accordance with the following:

1. You will receive credit only if the circles are filled in correctly, but you may write your answers in the boxes above each grid to help you fill in the circles accurately.

2. Don't mark more than one circle per column.

3. None of the questions with grid-in responses will have a negative solution.

4. Only grid in a single answer, even if there is more than one correct answer to a given question.

5. A **mixed number** must be gridded as a decimal or an improper fraction. For example, you would grid $7\frac{1}{2}$ as 7.5 or $\frac{15}{2}$.

   (Were you to grid it as 7 1 / 2 , this response would be read as $\frac{71}{2}$.)

6. A **decimal** that has more digits than there are places on the grid may be either rounded or truncated, but every column in the grid must be filled in order to receive credit.

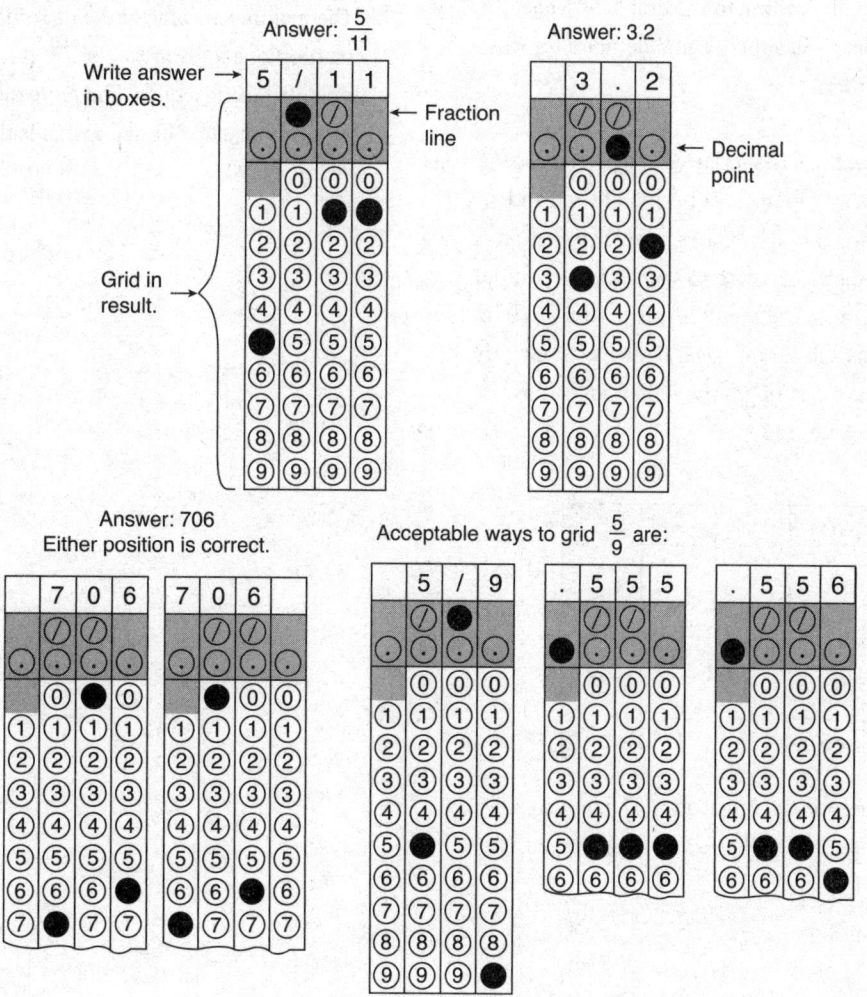

GO ON TO THE NEXT PAGE

Practice Tests

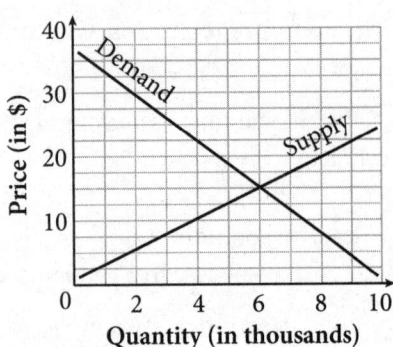

Quantity (in thousands)

16. Retail businesses strive to price their products so that they sell as many as possible without losing money. Economic equilibrium is the price point at which the supply for a product is equal to the demand for that product. The graph above models this scenario. According to the graph, at what price in dollars will supply equal demand for this particular product?

17. Once an insect reaches its larval stage, its mass increases linearly for a short period of time and then slows down as it prepares to enter pupation. Suppose the larva of a certain species has an initial mass of 10 grams and grows linearly from $t = 0$ to $t = 48$ hours of its larval stage. If after 48 hours, the mass of the larva is 14 grams, what was its mass in grams at $t = 6$ hours?

x	$f(x)$
-1	-2
0	0
1	2
2	4
3	6

x	$g(x)$
-2	3
-1	2
0	1
1	-1
2	-2

18. Several values for the functions $f(x)$ and $g(x)$ are shown in the tables. What is the value of $f(g(-1))$?

19. If $(4 + 3i)(1 - 2i) = a + bi$, then what is the value of a? (Note that $i = \sqrt{-1}$.)

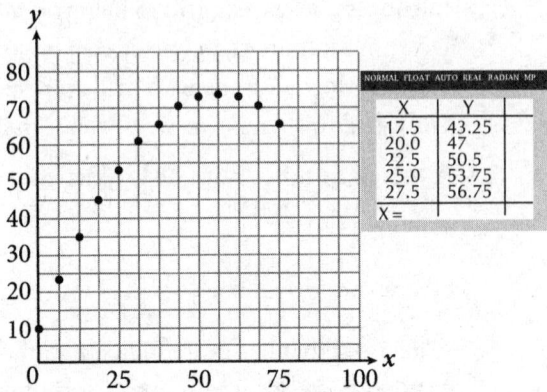

20. The maximum value of the data shown in the scatterplot occurs at $x = 56.25$. If the data is modeled using a quadratic regression and the model is an exact fit, then what is the y-value when $x = 90$?

Practice Tests

MATH TEST

55 Minutes—38 Questions

CALCULATOR SECTION

This section corresponds to Section 4 of your answer sheet.

Directions: For this section, solve each question and select the best answer choice. The available space on each page may be used for scratch work.

Notes:

1. Calculator use is permitted.
2. All numbers used are real numbers, and all variables used represent real numbers, unless otherwise indicated.
3. Figures are drawn to scale and lie in a plane unless otherwise indicated.
4. Unless stated otherwise, the domain of any function f is assumed to be the set of all real numbers x, for which $f(x)$ is a real number.

Information:

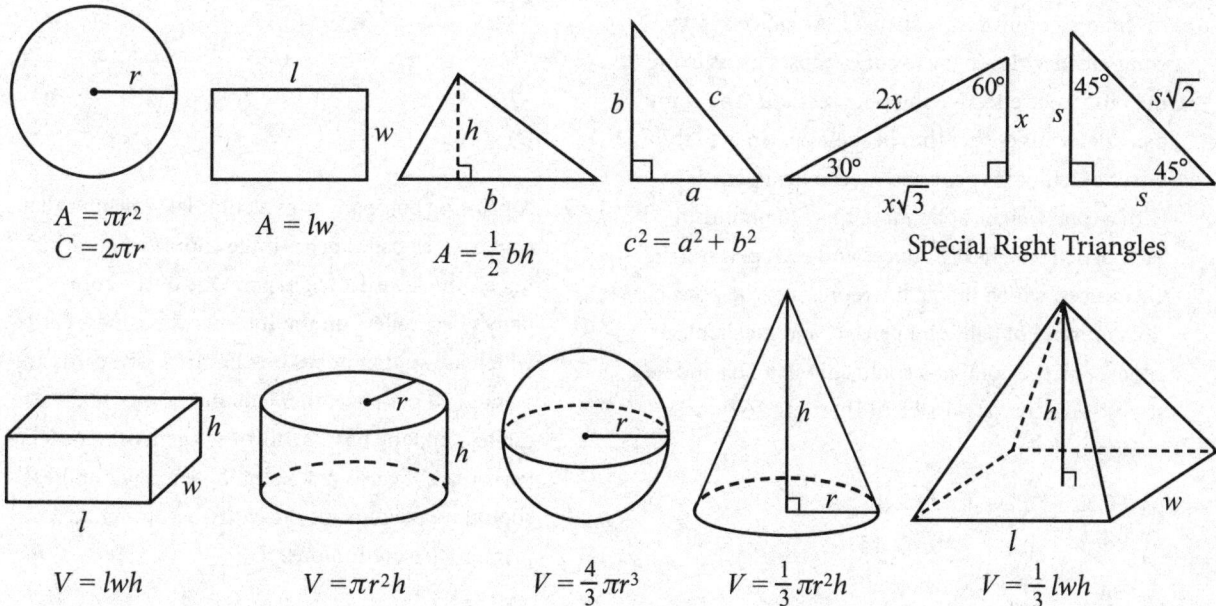

$A = \pi r^2$
$C = 2\pi r$

$A = lw$

$A = \frac{1}{2}bh$

$c^2 = a^2 + b^2$

Special Right Triangles

$V = lwh$

$V = \pi r^2 h$

$V = \frac{4}{3}\pi r^3$

$V = \frac{1}{3}\pi r^2 h$

$V = \frac{1}{3}lwh$

The sum of the degree measures of the angles in a triangle is 180.

The number of degrees of arc in a circle is 360.

The number of radians of arc in a circle is 2π.

GO ON TO THE NEXT PAGE

1. The U.S. Centers for Disease Control recommends that adults engage in 2.5 hours per week of vigorous exercise. A local health society conducts a survey to see if people are meeting this goal. They ask 100 people with gym memberships how many minutes of exercise they engage in per week. After analyzing the data, the health society finds that the average respondent exercises 142 minutes per week, but the margin of error was approximately 36 minutes. The society wants to lower this margin of error. Using which of the following samples instead would do so?

   A) 50 people with gym memberships

   B) 50 people randomly selected from the entire adult population

   C) 100 people with gym memberships, but from a variety of gyms

   D) 200 people randomly selected from the entire adult population

2. As a general rule, businesses strive to maximize revenue and minimize expenses. An office supply company decides to try to cut expenses by utilizing the most cost-effective shipping method. The company determines that the cheapest option is to ship boxes of ballpoint pens and mechanical pencils with a total weight of no more than 20 pounds. If each pencil weighs 0.2 ounces and each pen weighs 0.3 ounces, which inequality represents the possible number of ballpoint pens, b, and mechanical pencils, m, the company could ship in a box and be as cost-effective as possible? (There are 16 ounces in 1 pound.)

   A) $0.3b + 0.2m < 20 \times 16$

   B) $0.3b + 0.2m \leq 20 \times 16$

   C) $\dfrac{b}{0.3} + \dfrac{m}{0.2} < 20 \times 16$

   D) $\dfrac{b}{0.3} + \dfrac{m}{0.2} \leq 20 \times 16$

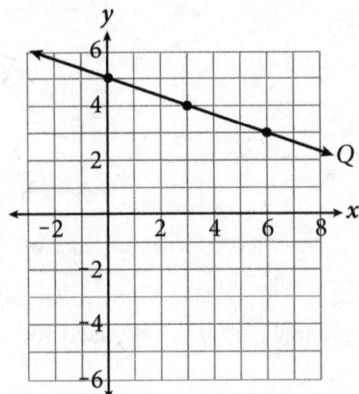

3. Where will line Q shown in the graph intersect the x-axis?

   A) 13

   B) 14

   C) 15

   D) 16

4. The function $f(x)$ is defined as $f(x) = 2g(x)$, where $g(x) = x + 5$. What is the value of $f(3)$?

   A) -4

   B) 6

   C) 8

   D) 16

5. A printing company uses a color laser printer that can print 18 pages per minute (ppm) when printing on thick cardstock paper. One of the company's best sellers on the Internet is business cards, which are sold in boxes of 225 cards. The cards are printed 10 per page, then cut and boxed. If a real estate company has 12 full-time agents and orders two boxes of cards per agent, how many minutes should it take to print the cards, assuming the printer runs continuously?

   A) 15

   B) 20

   C) 30

   D) 45

GO ON TO THE NEXT PAGE

6. If $0.002 \le x \le 0.2$ and $5 \le y \le 25$, what is the maximum value of $\dfrac{x}{y}$?

    A) 0.04

    B) 0.4

    C) 4

    D) 40

7. Following a study of children in the United States under three years old, the American Academy of Pediatrics stated that there is a positive correlation between the amount of time spent watching television and the likelihood of developing an attention deficit disorder. Which of the following is an appropriate conclusion to draw from this statement?

    A) There is an association between television time and attention disorders for American children under three years old.

    B) There is an association between television time and attention disorders for all children under three years old.

    C) An increase in attention disorders is caused by an increase in television time for American children under three years old.

    D) An increase in attention disorders is caused by an increase in television time for all children under three years old.

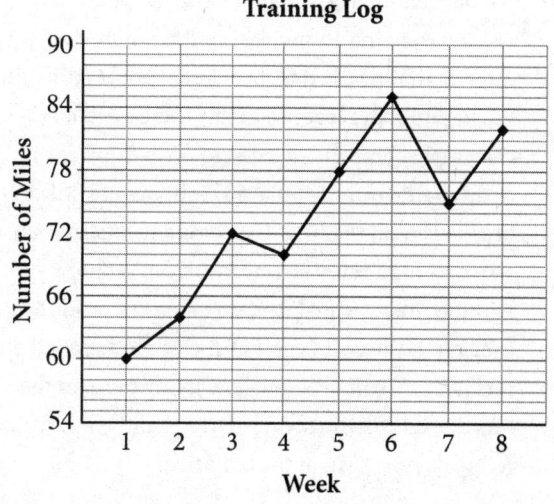

Training Log

8. A bicyclist is training for the Liège-Bastogne-Liège, one of Europe's oldest road bicycle races. The line graph above shows the number of miles she biked each week for eight weeks. According to the graph, what was the greatest change (in absolute value) in the weekly number of miles she biked between two consecutive weeks?

    A) 7

    B) 8

    C) 9

    D) 10

9. If a line that passes through the coordinates $(a - 1, 2a)$ and $(a, 6)$ has a slope of 5, what is the value of a?

    A) -2

    B) $-\dfrac{1}{2}$

    C) $\dfrac{1}{2}$

    D) 2

Practice Tests

GO ON TO THE NEXT PAGE

10. An occupational health organization published a study showing an increase in the number of injuries that resulted from elderly people falling in the bathtub. In response to this increase, a medical supply company decided to drop its price on bathtub lifts from $450 to $375, hoping to still break even on the lifts. The company breaks even when its total revenue (income from selling n bathtub lifts) is equal to its total cost of producing the lifts. If the cost C, in dollars, of producing the lifts is $C = 225n + 3,150$, how many more of the lifts does the company need to sell at the new price to break even than at the old price?

A) 7

B) 12

C) 14

D) 21

Questions 11 and 12 refer to the following information.

A zoo is building a penguin exhibit. It will consist of an underwater area and a land area. The land area is made of thick sheets of ice. An outline of the total space covered by the ice is shown below. A pipe 2 feet in diameter runs the full length of the exhibit under the ice. A substance known as ice-cold glycol continuously runs through the pipe to keep the ice frozen.

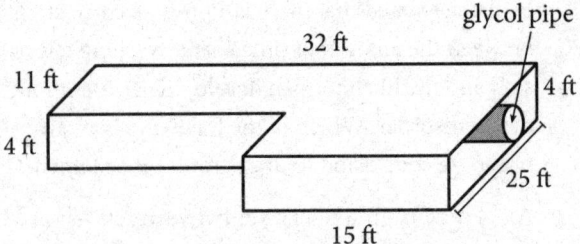

11. About how many cubic feet of water are needed to create the ice portion of the exhibit?

A) 1,850

B) 2,150

C) 2,450

D) 3,100

12. The zoo is planning to hire a company to fill the space with water. The company plans to use two 4-inch hoses that can each pump 60 gallons of water per minute. About how long should it take to fill the space? (There are 7.48 gallons of water in 1 cubic foot of ice.)

A) 1 hour

B) 1 hour, 30 minutes

C) 1 hour, 55 minutes

D) 2 hours, 15 minutes

GO ON TO THE NEXT PAGE

13. Which of the following quadratic equations has no solution?

   A) $0 = -2(x - 5)^2 + 3$

   B) $0 = -2(x - 5)(x + 3)$

   C) $0 = 2(x - 5)^2 + 3$

   D) $0 = 2(x + 5)(x + 3)$

Questions 14 and 15 refer to the following information.

Three airplanes depart from three different airports at 8:30 AM, all travelling to Chicago O'Hare International Airport (ORD). The distances the planes must travel are recorded in the following table. (Note: Assume all times provided are in Eastern Standard Time.)

From	Distance to Chicago (ORD)
Kansas City (MCI)	402
Boston (BOS)	864
Miami (MIA)	1,200

14. The plane traveling from Boston traveled at an average speed of 360 mph. The plane traveling from Kansas City arrived at 10:34 AM. How many minutes before the plane from Boston arrived did the plane from Kansas City arrive?

   A) 20

   B) 28

   C) 42

   D) 144

15. For the first $\frac{1}{4}$ of the trip, the plane from Miami flew through heavy winds and dense cloud cover at an average speed of 200 mph. For the remaining portion of the trip, the weather was ideal, and the plane flew at an average speed of 450 mph. Due to a backlog of planes at ORD, it was forced to circle overhead in a holding pattern for 25 minutes before landing. At what time did the plane from Miami land in Chicago?

   A) 12:00 PM

   B) 12:25 PM

   C) 12:50 PM

   D) 1:15 PM

16. If $h(t) = \sqrt{t^2 + 9}$ for all real values of t, which of the following is not in the range of $h(t)$?

   A) 1

   B) 3

   C) 9

   D) 10

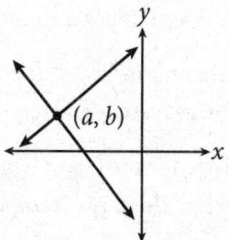

17. If (a, b) represents the solution to the system of equations shown in the graph and $a = -3b$, then which of the following could be the value of $a + b$?

   A) −9

   B) 0

   C) 3

   D) 6

GO ON TO THE NEXT PAGE

Thermostat A

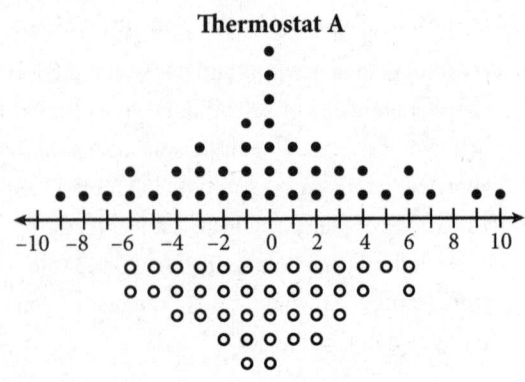

Thermostat B

18. A car manufacturer tested two types of thermostats to determine which one it wanted to use in a new model of car. The more consistently the thermostat engages the engine's cooling fan, the better the cooling system performs over the long run. The double dot plot above shows the test results, given the following conditions:

- Zero indicates that the cooling fan engaged at exactly the temperature at which the thermostat was set (the target temperature).

- Negative numbers indicate that the fan engaged below the target temperature.

- Positive numbers indicate that the fan engaged above the target temperature.

- The safe range for the fan to engage is 10 degrees above or below the target temperature.

Which of the following best states which thermostat the car manufacturer is likely to choose and why?

A) Thermostat A because the median of the data is 0, and the range is greater than that of Thermostat B

B) Thermostat B because the median of the data is 0, and the range is less than that of Thermostat A

C) Thermostat A because the mode of the data is 0, which indicates a more consistent thermostat

D) Thermostat B because the data is bimodal (has two modes), which indicates a more consistent thermostat

19. If p and q represent the zeros of a quadratic function and $p + q = -3$, which of the following could be the factored form of the function?

A) $f(x) = (x - 3)(x + 3)$

B) $f(x) = (x - 4)(x + 1)$

C) $f(x) = (x - 1)(x + 4)$

D) $f(x) = (x - 6)(x + 3)$

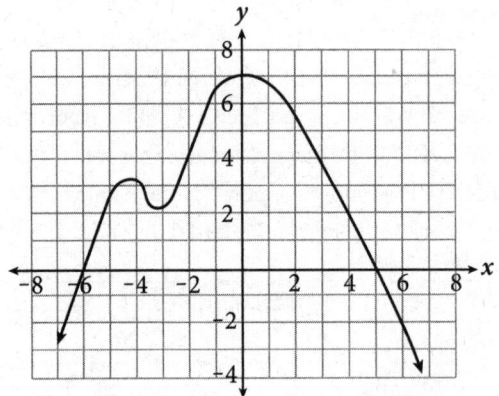

20. The figure above shows the graph of $p(x) - 4$. What is the value of $p(0)$?

A) 3

B) 4

C) 7

D) 11

GO ON TO THE NEXT PAGE

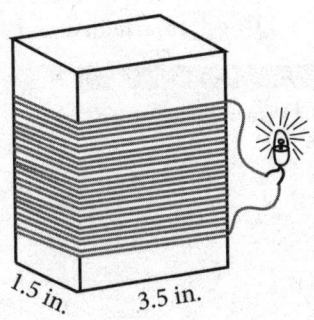

1.5 in.   3.5 in.

21. Geraldine is making a simple AC electric generator for a science project using copper wire, cardboard, a nail, and magnets. The first step in building the generator is wrapping the wire around a rectangular prism made from the cardboard and connecting it to a small lightbulb, as shown in the figure. If Geraldine has 18 feet of wire and needs to leave 3 inches on each end to connect to the lightbulb, how many times can she wrap the wire around the cardboard prism? (Note: 1 foot = 12 inches.)

A) 21

B) 28

C) 35

D) 42

Organic Vegetable Harvest

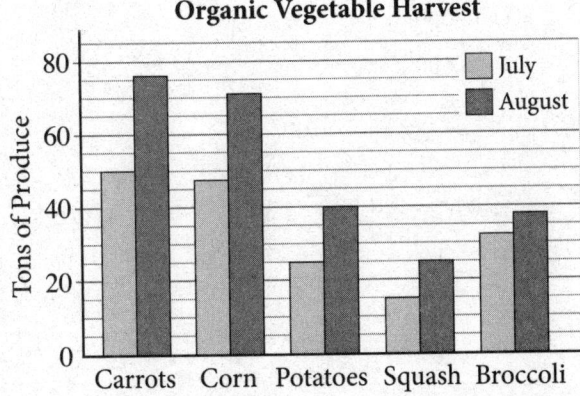

22. The bar graph above shows the vegetable harvest, in tons, at an organic produce farm during July and August. Of the following, which best approximates the percent increase in the harvest of squash at this farm from July to August?

A) 67%

B) 60%

C) 53%

D) 40%

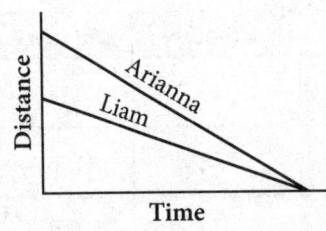

23. Arianna and her brother Liam both walk home from school each day, but they go to different schools. The figure shows their trip home on Monday. Based on the graph, which of the following statements is true?

A) It took Liam longer to walk home because his school is farther away.

B) It took Arianna longer to walk home because her school is farther away.

C) Arianna and Liam walked home at the same rate.

D) Arianna walked home at a faster rate than Liam.

24. If line L passes through the points $(-4, -8)$ and $(8, 1)$, which of the following points does line L not pass through?

A) $(0, -5)$

B) $(4, -1)$

C) $(12, 4)$

D) $(16, 7)$

GO ON TO THE NEXT PAGE

	Unemployed	Employed	Totals
Female Degree	12	188	200
Female No Degree	44	156	200
Male Degree	23	177	200
Male No Degree	41	159	200
Totals	120	680	800

25. The table above shows the results of a sociological study identifying the number of males and females with and without college degrees who were unemployed or employed at the time of the study. If one person from the study is chosen at random, what is the probability that that person is an employed person with a college degree?

A) $\dfrac{73}{160}$

B) $\dfrac{10}{17}$

C) $\dfrac{17}{20}$

D) $\dfrac{73}{80}$

Infected Patient

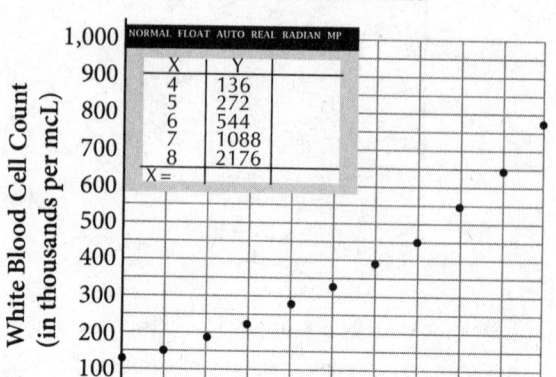

26. Typically, when people contract an infectious disease, their immune system immediately begins to produce extra white blood cells to fight the disease. The scatterplot shows the white blood cells reproducing in an infected patient, along with several values found when modeling the data using a graphing calculator. According to this model, how many white blood cells per microliter of blood did the patient have before he contracted the disease?

A) 3,400

B) 8,500

C) 10,000

D) 13,600

27. A rodeo is building a circular arena. The arena will have a total area of 64π square yards and can either be left open for rodeo competitions or divided into 12 equal sections through the center for auctions. When holding auctions, the rodeo has an average of 4 bulls and 8 horses for sale. A bull cannot be placed in a section directly beside another section containing a bull, and all edges of these sections must be reinforced with strong steel to keep the bulls from getting out. Which of the following represents how much steel in yards the rodeo will need to reinforce the four bull sections?

A) 32π

B) 64π

C) $32 + \dfrac{16\pi}{3}$

D) $64 + \dfrac{16\pi}{3}$

28. Lena bought a saltwater fish tank that holds 400 gallons of water. She started filling the tank on Friday, but then stopped after putting only 70 gallons of water in the tank. On Saturday, she bought a bigger hose and began filling the tank again. It took her 1 hour and 50 minutes on Saturday to completely fill the tank. Which equation represents the number of gallons of water in the fish tank on Saturday, given the amount of time in minutes that Lena spent filling the tank?

A) $y = 3x + 70$

B) $y = 3x + 330$

C) $y = 70x + 330$

D) $y = 110x + 70$

29. A self-storage company has three sizes of storage units. The ratio of small to medium units is 3:5. The ratio of medium to large units is 3:2. The company analyzes its business model and current consumer demand and determines that it can benefit from utilizing larger economies of scale. In other words, it decides to grow its business based on current economic conditions and plans to build a second, larger self-storage building. The company's research indicates that the new market would benefit from having only two sizes of storage units, small and large, in the same ratio as its current facility. What ratio of small to large units should it use?

A) 1:1

B) 3:2

C) 5:3

D) 9:10

$$\frac{1}{x} + \frac{3}{x} = \frac{1}{7}$$

30. The equation shown above represents the following scenario: A chemical laboratory uses two air purifiers to clean the air of contaminants emitted while working with hazardous materials. One is an older model, and the other is a new model that is considerably more energy efficient. The new model can clean the air of contaminants three times as quickly as the older model. Working together, the two air purifiers can clean the air in the lab in 7 hours. Which of the following describes what the term $\dfrac{1}{x}$ in the equation represents?

A) The portion of the air the older model can clean in 1 hour

B) The portion of the air the new model can clean in 1 hour

C) The time it takes the older model to clean the air by itself

D) The time it takes the older model to clean $\dfrac{1}{7}$ of the air by itself

GO ON TO THE NEXT PAGE

Practice Tests

Directions: For questions 31-38, enter your responses into the appropriate grid on your answer sheet, in accordance with the following:

1. You will receive credit only if the circles are filled in correctly, but you may write your answers in the boxes above each grid to help you fill in the circles accurately.

2. Don't mark more than one circle per column.

3. None of the questions with grid-in responses will have a negative solution.

4. Only grid in a single answer, even if there is more than one correct answer to a given question.

5. A **mixed number** must be gridded as a decimal or an improper fraction. For example, you would grid $7\frac{1}{2}$ as 7.5 or $\frac{15}{2}$.

   (Were you to grid it as $\boxed{7\ 1\ /\ 2}$, this response would be read as $\frac{71}{2}$.)

6. A **decimal** that has more digits than there are places on the grid may be either rounded or truncated, but every column in the grid must be filled in order to receive credit.

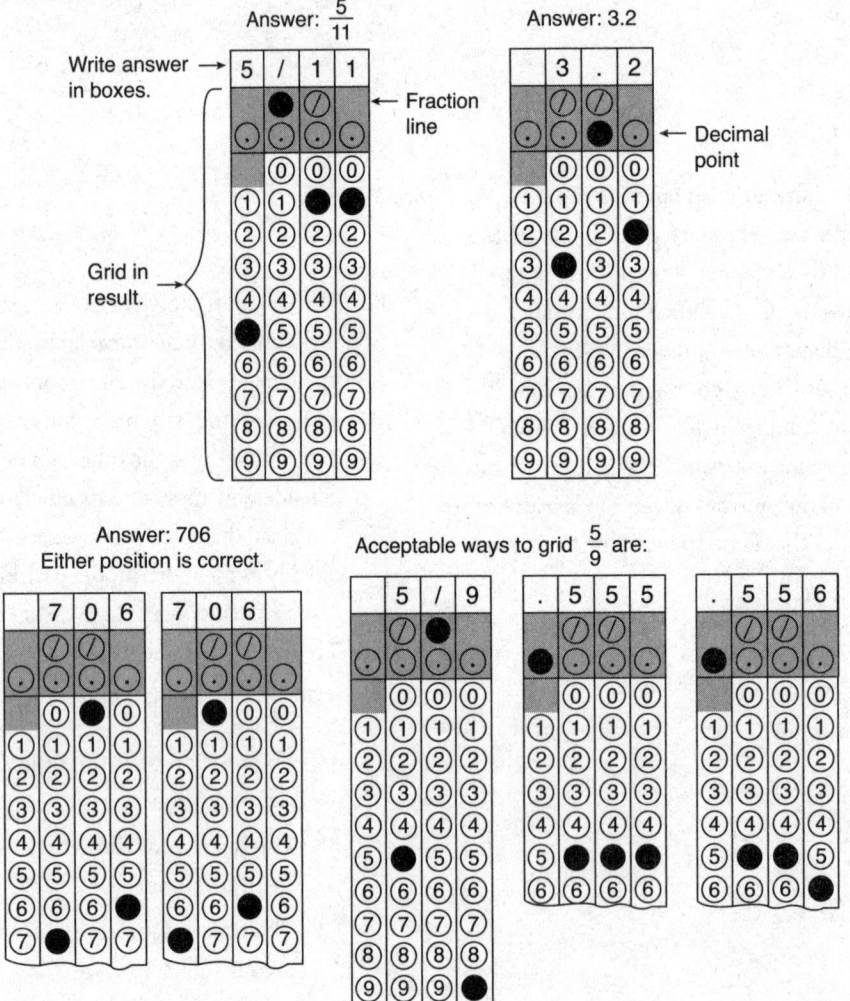

$$\frac{1}{3}(90x - 12) = \frac{1}{2}(8x + 10)$$

31. What is the solution to the equation shown?

32. If $n^{\frac{5}{2}} = 32$, what is the value of n?

33. When a thrift store gets used furniture in good condition to sell, it researches the original price and then marks the used piece down by 40% of that price. On the first day of each of the following months, the price is marked down an additional 15% until it is sold or it reaches 30% of its original price. Suppose the store gets a piece of used furniture on January 15th. If the piece of furniture costs $1,848 new, and it is sold on March 10th of the same year, what is the final selling price, not including tax? Round your answer to the nearest whole dollar.

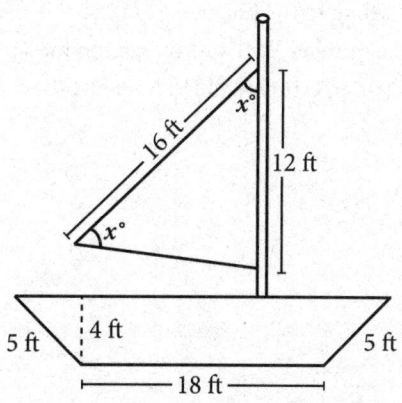

Note: Figure not drawn to scale.

34. Many sailboat manufacturers sell kits that include instructions and all the materials needed to build a simple sailboat. The figure shows the finished dimensions of a sailboat from such a kit. The instructions indicate that $\cos x° = b$, but do not give the value of b. What is the value of b?

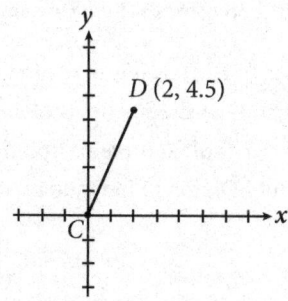

35. In the figure shown, line B (not shown) is parallel to $\overline{CD}$ and passes through the point $(0, -1)$. If line B also passes through the point $(2, y)$, what is the value of y?

36. Recycling of certain metals has been a common practice dating back to preindustrial times. For example, there is evidence of scrap bronze and silver being collected and melted down for reuse in a number of European countries. Today, there are recycling companies and even curbside collection bins for recycling. As a general rule, recycling companies pay for metals by weight. Suppose a person brings in 3 pounds of copper and receives $8.64, and 24 ounces of nickel and receives $10.08. If another person brings in equal weights of copper and nickel, what fractional portion of the money would he receive from the copper? (There are 16 ounces in 1 pound.)

GO ON TO THE NEXT PAGE

Questions 37 and 38 refer to the following information.

Body mass index, or BMI, is one of several measures used by doctors to determine a person's health as indicated by weight and height. Low-density lipoprotein, or LDL cholesterol, known as the "bad" cholesterol, is another health indicator and consists of fat proteins that clog arteries. Following are the results of a study showing the relationship between BMI and LDL for 12 individuals and the line of best fit for the data.

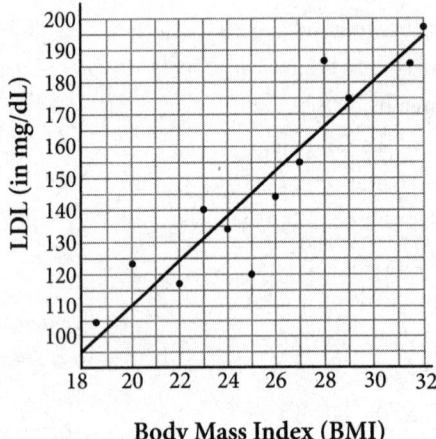

37. How many of the 12 people have an actual LDL that differs by 10 or more mg/dL from the LDL predicted by the line of best fit?

38. According to the line of best fit, what is the closest whole number BMI approximation for a person that has an estimated LDL level of 140 mg/dL ?

ESSAY TEST

50 Minutes

You will be given a passage to read and asked to write an essay analyzing it. As you write, be sure to show that you have read the passage closely. You will be graded on how well you have understood the passage, how clear your analysis is, and how well you express your ideas.

Your essay must be written on the lines in your answer booklet. Anything you write outside the lined space in your answer booklet will not be read by the essay graders. Be sure to write or print in such a way that it will be legible to readers not familiar with your handwriting. Additionally, be sure to address the passage directly. An off-topic essay will not be graded.

As you read the passage, think about the author's use of

- evidence, such as statistics or other facts.

- logic to connect evidence to conclusions and to develop lines of reasoning.

- style, word choice, and appeals to emotion to make the argument more persuasive.

This passage deals with the issue of compensation for college athletes.

1   In the world of college sports, there is growing debate about whether student athletes should be awarded monetary compensation for their contribution to teams that garner millions of dollars for universities. Presently, the National Collegiate Athletics Association (NCAA), the governing body of college sports, doesn't allow it. Some hold this law as sacrosanct, saying it keeps college sports from becoming commercial and corrupting the experience of student athletes, who are in school, after all, for an education. But the reality is that we are past that point: college sports are big business, and the system that caps student salaries at zero is tantamount to wage fixing and collusion. If such practices happened in the investment market, universities would be fined by the FTC. In a labor market, they'd be shut down. Student athletes are being defrauded and taken advantage of.

2   So how much money is at stake? Basketball and football are the two main sports in question. Every year, the month of March becomes synonymous with a weeks-long basketball bracket that winnows down 64 teams to the single best. In football, a season of stadium-filling regular season games culminates in half a dozen lucrative "bowl games" sponsored by some of the biggest corporations in the world: FedEx, AT&T, and Mobil Oil.

3   For television networks, advertisers, universities, and local businesses where the events are held, these games are every bit as big as the NFL's Super Bowl and the NBA playoffs. In 2011, ESPN and Fox signed television rights deals worth $3 billion to the Pacific-12 conference. *Forbes* magazine reported that CBS and Turner Broadcasting make more than one billion dollars off the March Madness broadcasts, "thanks in part to a $700,000 advertising rate for a 30-second spot during the Final Four." One study put the value of a Texas A&M home game at $86 million for businesses in Brazos County, where A&M is located.

4   The dollar figures are indeed vast, and universities get their share. Here are two examples from schools with top football teams. According to the most recent federal data, the University of Texas football team netted a profit of $77.9 million in 2011-2012. Michigan made $61.6 million from football and $85.2 million in revenue.

GO ON TO THE NEXT PAGE ⇨

5   Coaches, too, are a big part of the equation. Average salaries for major college football coaches have jumped more than 70 percent since 2006, to $1.64 million, according to *USA Today*. Nick Saban, head coach for Alabama, makes $7.3 million a year.

6   And yet, players take home no money. None. How can this be? Because, like unscrupulous tycoons from a Dickens novel, college presidents, athletic directors, and conference commissioners set their players' wages as low as they can get them—zero.

7   According to a recent study, if college football operated under the same revenue-sharing model as the NFL, each player on the Texas A&M squad would see a paycheck of about $225,000 per year.

8   All this talk of money might have you thinking that we should go back to square one and take the money out of college sports. But money is in college sports' DNA. It was conceived that way. It all grew out of the Morrill Land-Grant College Act of 1862. "As large public institutions spread into sparsely populated states, the competition for students grew fierce," says Allen Sack, a business professor at the University of New Haven. Football happened to be invented around that time, and schools took it up as a tool to draw students, and spectators, to campuses. The 1894 Harvard-Yale football game, for example, generated $119,000, according to the *New York Times*. That's nearly $3 million in today's dollars.

9   The historic justification for not paying players is that they are amateur student-athletes, and the value of their scholarships is payment enough. But the NCAA's own study shows that its scholarship limit leaves so-called "full" scholarship athletes with $3,000 to $5,000 in out-of-pocket expenses each year. The average shortfall is $3,200. Furthermore, most scholarships are revocable, so if an athlete doesn't perform well on the field, or is injured, he can, in a sense, lose that compensation. A student athlete devotes 40 hours a week on average towards sport; that's equivalent to a full-time job. Zero pay and immediate termination with no recourse? Those are labor conditions that any sensible workforce would unionize to change. But students are powerless to change. They are up against the NCAA, the Big 10 commission, university boards, and the almighty corporate dollar. Someone needs to become their advocate and get student athletes the compensation they deserve.

Write an essay that analyzes the author's approach in persuading his readers that athletes deserve fair compensation. Focus on specific features such as the ones listed in the box above the passage and explain how these features strengthen the author's argument. Your essay should discuss the most important rhetorical features of the passage.

Your essay should not focus on your own opinion of the author's conclusion, but rather on how the author persuades his readers.

ANSWER KEY
READING TEST

1. A	14. B	27. C	40. D
2. D	15. A	28. A	41. B
3. D	16. C	29. D	42. A
4. B	17. D	30. B	43. C
5. C	18. C	31. A	44. B
6. C	19. B	32. D	45. C
7. C	20. B	33. A	46. A
8. D	21. B	34. B	47. C
9. A	22. D	35. D	48. D
10. D	23. D	36. C	49. A
11. C	24. C	37. C	50. D
12. D	25. C	38. D	51. A
13. A	26. A	39. A	52. B

WRITING AND LANGUAGE TEST

1. B	12. B	23. C	34. B
2. D	13. D	24. B	35. C
3. B	14. B	25. B	36. A
4. C	15. C	26. A	37. D
5. D	16. A	27. A	38. A
6. D	17. B	28. A	39. D
7. B	18. D	29. B	40. A
8. A	19. B	30. A	41. B
9. D	20. D	31. C	42. D
10. C	21. B	32. D	43. C
11. B	22. C	33. A	44. B

MATH—NO CALCULATOR TEST

1. B	6. B	11. D	16. 15
2. C	7. A	12. D	17. 10.5 or 21/2
3. C	8. D	13. C	18. 4
4. A	9. A	14. B	19. 10
5. B	10. D	15. C	20. 50.5

MATH—CALCULATOR TEST

1. D	11. B	21. A	31. 9/26 or .346
2. B	12. D	22. A	32. 4
3. C	13. C	23. D	33. 801
4. D	14. A	24. B	34. 2/3 or .666 or .667
5. C	15. B	25. A	35. 3.5 or 7/2
6. A	16. A	26. B	36. 3/10
7. A	17. A	27. D	37. 3
8. D	18. B	28. A	38. 24
9. C	19. C	29. D	
10. A	20. D	30. A	

ANSWERS AND EXPLANATIONS

READING TEST

A Study in Scarlet

Suggested Passage Map notes:

¶1: W describes H

¶2: W stunned by H's deep knowledge of some subjects

¶3: W astonished by what H doesn't know

¶4: H: brain has only so much room, isn't interested in "useless facts"

1. A   Difficulty: Easy

Category: Detail

Getting to the Answer: Eliminate answers that go against your understanding of the characters in the passage. The first paragraph explicitly states that Watson's curiosity about Holmes "gradually deepened and increased" (lines 2-3). Choice (A) is the correct answer.

2. D   Difficulty: Medium

Category: Vocab-in-Context

Getting to the Answer: Predict a word that could be substituted for "casual" in context. Watson is explaining that Holmes's appearance is noticeable even to someone who hasn't seen him very often; therefore, (D) is correct.

3. D   Difficulty: Easy

Category: Global

Getting to the Answer: The central idea in this passage should reflect the overall picture the author paints of Sherlock Holmes. The passage develops Holmes as an unusual and eccentric character. Watson marvels at Holmes's failure to pursue a typical path for an intelligent person, for example, and describes in detail how Holmes' behavior and knowledge deviate from the ordinary. Choice (D) is the only answer choice that is directly supported by details in the passage.

4. B   Difficulty: Medium

Category: Vocab-in-Context

Getting to the Answer: Use context clues to help you predict the meaning of the word as it is used in the sentence. In this sentence, the context clues provide a contrast to the target word. Watson says Holmes is usually "sharp" and "hawk-like" with great "alertness" except when he is in a period of "torpor" (lines 7-10). You can predict that the meaning of "torpor" will be something close to *the opposite of sharp and alert*. Choice (B) is the correct answer.

5. C   Difficulty: Easy

Category: Inference

Getting to the Answer: Look for clues in the passage about how and why Holmes studies and learns. Watson notes that Holmes has not studied anything "which might fit him for a degree" (lines 21-22). This suggests that his learning is not motivated by something external, like a degree, but by his personal interests. Likewise, he has a "zeal" for particular subjects (line 24). Choice (C) reflects Holmes's motives for studying.

6. C   Difficulty: Medium

Category: Command of Evidence

Getting to the Answer: Eliminate answer choices that don't explain why Holmes studies. A correct answer will allow you to make a logical guess as to Holmes's motives for studying. Choice (C) provides the best evidence by illustrating that Holmes pursues topics that he is passionate about rather than studying for external motivations.

7. C   **Difficulty:** Medium

Category: Inference

Getting to the Answer: Closely read Holmes's own statements for clues about his views. Holmes clearly suggests that the brain can only hold a limited amount of information, so one should prioritize the things that are most important. Therefore, (C) is the correct answer.

8. D   **Difficulty:** Easy

Category: Command of Evidence

Getting to the Answer: Reread each quote in the context of the passage. Find the one that supports the previous answer by giving evidence of Holmes's own ideas about learning. Of all the answer choices, Holmes's own statement about the necessity of prioritizing useful facts most directly supports the previous answer. Choice (D) is the correct answer.

9. A   **Difficulty:** Medium

Category: Rhetoric

Getting to the Answer: Consider what this figurative use of "attic" helps reveal about the character of Holmes. The author has Holmes compare the human brain to an attic to help illustrate Holmes's beliefs about useful facts versus those not worth learning. Choice (A) is the correct answer.

10. D   **Difficulty:** Medium

Category: Rhetoric

Getting to the Answer: Think about what insights the reader gains by having Watson narrate the story. The author is able to establish Holmes as an intriguing character by showing Watson's thoughts and reactions to Holmes. Presumably, readers will want to find out more about Holmes because the narrator depicts him as a fascinating person. Choice (D) fits this situation.

Woodrow Wilson Speech

Suggested Passage Map notes:

¶1: should be no secrets in peace process
¶2: war fought for justice; 14 pts for world peace
¶3: no secrets
¶4: freedom on the seas
¶5: equal trade
¶6: fewer weapons and armies worldwide
¶7: fair colonial land claims
¶8: Russia develop own gov't, Germans leave Russia
¶9: Germans leave Belgium, Belgium independent
¶10: France regain all territory
¶11: reestablish Italian borders
¶12: Austria-Hungary indep.
¶13: Serbia, Montenegro, Romania evacuated and indep.
¶14: Turkish people have own country
¶15: indep. Polish state
¶16: form League of Nations to protect indep.

11. C   **Difficulty:** Easy

Category: Rhetoric

Getting to the Answer: Examine the first two paragraphs. Try to paraphrase the reason Wilson gives for making the speech. In the first two paragraphs, Wilson anticipates the end of the war and alludes to the "processes of peace" (line 2). Although he refers to national sovereignty and conquest, he states that his purpose is to lay out a program for peace in the world, making (C) the correct answer.

12. D   **Difficulty:** Medium

Category: Command of Evidence

Getting to the Answer: Remember that the correct answer will provide information that directly relates to the answer to the previous question. The correct answer to the previous question concerns Wilson's plan to maintain peaceful relations in the world. Lines 26-27 read, "The programme of the world's peace, therefore, is our programme," making (D) the correct answer.

13. A   Difficulty: Medium

Category: Vocab-in-Context

Getting to the Answer: Predict a word that could substitute for "frankly" in context. In the list of points he presents, Wilson is defining actions and policies that will promote peace and open communication among nations. In this context, "frankly" suggests honesty, which makes (A) the correct answer.

14. B   Difficulty: Medium

Category: Inference

Getting to the Answer: Eliminate answer choices that cannot be inferred by the information provided in the passage. Calling for an end to "private international understandings" is one of Wilson's 14 points (lines 29-30). Therefore, it can be inferred that in the past, certain nations did indeed form "secret covenants" (line 6), or pacts, with one another. Choice (B) is correct.

15. A   Difficulty: Medium

Category: Command of Evidence

Getting to the Answer: The correct answer will reference a detail that provides evidence for the answer to the previous question. In the first paragraph of his speech, Wilson refers to "secret understandings" that cannot exist anymore if there is to be peace among nations. Therefore, (A) is correct.

16. C   Difficulty: Medium

Category: Vocab-in-Context

Getting to the Answer: Pretend the word is a blank in the sentence. Then predict what word could be substituted for the blank. The sentence states that "national armaments will be reduced to the lowest

point consistent with domestic safety" (lines 43–44). In this sense, Wilson aims to assure nations that they will still be able to protect themselves. Predict that armaments will be reduced to an extent agreeable with maintaining their own safety. (C) is the correct choice.

17. D   Difficulty: Hard

Category: Rhetoric

Getting to the Answer: Though the question is asking you about a specific line, it makes sense to choose an answer that is compatible with the broader context of the passage. In the excerpted line, Wilson identifies the "adjustment of all colonial claims" (line 46) as an item in his program for world peace. If his goal is to safeguard world peace, this must mean he believes conflicts resulting from colonization, itself an imperial pursuit, must be addressed. Choice (D) is correct.

18. C   Difficulty: Hard

Category: Rhetoric

Getting to the Answer: Locate the three points to which the question refers. Do not confuse them with other numbered points in the speech. Points VI through VIII refer to territorial sovereignty, evacuation of occupied lands, and restoration of lands. These points align with the claim that nations have violated one another's territorial sovereignty through invasion and occupation. This makes (C) the correct answer.

19. B   Difficulty: Hard

Category: Connections

Getting to the Answer: Be sure that the answer you choose reflects the ideology and positions expressed by Wilson in his speech. In the passage, Wilson expresses that he is in favor of international cooperation to promote and sustain global peace. Choice (B) is the correct answer because it describes an approach to international relations that is analogous to Wilson's.

Practice Tests

20. B   Difficulty: Medium

Category: Rhetoric

Getting to the Answer: When asked a question involving the structure of a passage, consider the text as a whole. Often, the structure is visually noticeable. Wilson begins by stating his argument that countries must work together toward peace. He then follows up with specific examples (the 14 points) of how his ideas should be carried out. Choice (B) is the correct answer.

Paired Passages—Meditation

Suggested Passage Map notes:

Passage 1

¶1: history of meditation; secular meditation

¶2: describe mindfulness meditation

¶3: mindfulness → more fulfillment

¶4: health benefits

¶5: Dr. S – meditation good, drs should use it

Passage 2

¶1: Ryan uses mindfulness and sees many benefits

¶2: holds weekly bi-partisan meditation sessions

¶3: wrote book on mindfulness; improved attention

¶4: members of Congress getting interested

¶5: R supports legislation encouraging meditation

¶6: Ryan – not religious but secular

21. B   Difficulty: Medium

Category: Global

Getting to the Answer: Focus on the big picture rather than supporting details. Choice (B) correctly identifies the central idea in the passage. The other choices are based on misinformation or are details.

22. D   Difficulty: Hard

Category: Inference

Getting to the Answer: Keep the central idea of the passage in mind as you look for information in the passage about each of the choices. Determine which one can be inferred as true. The last two paragraphs of Passage 1 discuss "health benefits" of meditation (line 30), studies showing positive results of meditation, and a quote from a professional about meditation's advantages. This matches choice (D).

23. D   Difficulty: Medium

Category: Command of Evidence

Getting to the Answer: Avoid choices that do not provide direct evidence to support your answer to the previous question. Choice (D) supports the inference that some medical professionals accept meditation as beneficial.

24. C   Difficulty: Easy

Category: Vocab-in-Context

Getting to the Answer: Predict a word that could substitute for "compelling" in context. The context of the sentence suggests that meditation has great or convincing benefits. Therefore, (C) is correct.

25. C   Difficulty: Easy

Category: Inference

Getting to the Answer: Remember that you're analyzing the author's point of view on meditation, not Tim Ryan's view. Since the author makes statements such as calling Ryan a "voice for calm consideration," (line 56), the author must hold a positive view of meditation. However, there is little evidence that the author is devoted to meditation. Choice (C) correctly reflects the author's point of view.

26. A   Difficulty: Easy

Category: Inference

Getting to the Answer: Determine what can be inferred about Ryan's personality from what is stated in the passage. The passage contains numerous examples of Ryan putting his belief in the value of mindfulness into action. For instance, he hosts meditation sessions for his staff and supports legislation promoting meditation. Choice (A) is the correct answer.

27. C   Difficulty: Medium

Category: Command of Evidence

Getting to the Answer: Be careful of choices that do not provide direct evidence to support the inference about Ryan from the previous question. Choice (C) is correct. Mr. Ryan shows that he acts on what he believes by supporting legislation that encourages meditation, such as the bill supporting the increase in holistic medicine offered by the Department of Veterans Affairs.

28. A   Difficulty: Easy

Category: Vocab-in-Context

Getting to the Answer: Predict a word that is a synonym for "secular" in context. In the context of the sentence, "but rather" indicates that "secular" means the opposite of "religious," so (A) is the correct answer.

29. D   Difficulty: Easy

Category: Rhetoric

Getting to the Answer: Reread the sentence to determine what connotative meaning the author suggests through the use of "chatter." Since "chatter" in this sentence is contrasted with the "mind and body" syncing together, the word has a negative connotation that suggests background noise or frequent talk. Only (D) fits with this meaning.

30. B   Difficulty: Medium

Category: Synthesis

Getting to the Answer: Look for an answer that fits with the purposes of both passages. Avoid choices that are suggested by only one of the passages. Both passages discuss changing attitudes regarding the

efficacy of mindfulness meditation: Passage 1 states it is becoming "more popular" (lines 16–17) and "widely accepted by health professionals" (line 45), while Passage 2 describes the impact of a politician who is promoting meditation. Only (B) reflects this.

31. A   Difficulty: Medium

Category: Synthesis

Getting to the Answer: Examine the graphic and the two passages to figure out which answer choice is supported by all three. The passages both discussed benefits of meditation. The graphic shows that workers were more productive and had fewer injuries after being in a meditation program. Choice (A) is the only one that relates to the information in the graphic.

Colony Collapse Disorder Passage

Suggested Passage Map notes:

¶1: CCD – all bees disappear; bees perform invaluable services

¶2: pathogens aren't the cause

¶3: altruism explains the disappearance but doesn't explain the cause

¶4: may be caused by fluctuation in earth's magnetic field

¶5: may be caused by pesticides

¶7: may be cause by pesticide combos

¶7: need more research; encourage more beekeeping, relax city rules

32. D   Difficulty: Hard

Category: Global

Getting to the Answer: Think of what the author wants the reader to learn about bees. This will help you figure out the passage's purpose. Choice (D) is the primary purpose of the passage. The author most wants the reader to know about colony collapse disorder.

33. A   **Difficulty:** Hard

Category: Connections

Getting to the Answer: Think back to the author's purpose that you explored in question 32. Consider what this purpose suggests about the author's point of view. The author seems knowledgeable about honey bees and very concerned about their loss. The author points out the many losses humans would have if bees were to disappear. Therefore, (A) is the correct answer.

34. B   **Difficulty:** Hard

Category: Rhetoric

Getting to the Answer: Notice that the word "mysteriously" appears toward the beginning of the passage, when the author is first introducing the topic. As the author introduces the topic of colony collapse disorder in the first paragraph, the word "mysterious" helps emphasize how puzzling the disorder truly is. Choice (B) is the correct answer.

35. D   **Difficulty:** Medium

Category: Vocab-in-Context

Getting to the Answer: Predict a word that is a synonym for "plights" in context. In the sentence, "common plights" refers to pests such as mites, fungus, and bacteria, which farmers commonly see in beehives. Predict a negative word. In this context, (D), "troubles" is the correct answer.

36. C   **Difficulty:** Hard

Category: Rhetoric

Getting to the Answer: Examine the part of the passage that discusses the lack of bees after a collapse. The author wants to stress the fact that research has shown that pathogens are not the reason for colony collapse. Choice (C) is the correct answer.

37. C   **Difficulty:** Medium

Category: Command of Evidence

Getting to the Answer: Be careful of choices that do not directly support your answer to the previous question. In the context of its paragraph, lines 31-33 provide evidence to support the inference that the cause of colony collapse is not pathogens, since "common killers" such as pathogens would leave "telltale signs." Choice (C) is the correct answer.

38. D   **Difficulty:** Easy

Category: Vocab-in-Context

Getting to the Answer: Predict a word that could substitute for "foraging" in context. Predict an action that bees might perform during their "pollination flights," such as searching for flowers. The context of the sentence rules out all but (D), the correct answer.

39. A   **Difficulty:** Hard

Category: Inference

Getting to the Answer: Review your Passage Map and use the passage's central idea as a general prediction. Choice (A) is correct. Though the author laments the disappearance of honey bees and says how challenging it is to solve the problem, the last paragraph ends the passage on a cautiously optimistic note, particularly with the use of the word "hopefully" (line 82).

40. D   **Difficulty:** Medium

Category: Command of Evidence

Getting to the Answer: Be careful of choices that might support an incorrect answer in the previous question. Choice (D) is evidence that the author is cautiously optimistic about the future of the honey bee.

41. B   **Difficulty:** Medium

Category: Detail

Getting to the Answer: Watch out for answer choices that might sound plausible but are not explicitly stated in the passage. Choice (B) is correct; the last paragraph states that some towns and cities are relaxing their regulations about beekeeping "in response to the honey bee population crisis" (line 81).

42. A   Difficulty: Medium

Category: Connections

Getting to the Answer: Look for information in the passage that tells what honey bees and human beings do for each other. Paragraph 1 states that if honey bees disappear, people will not have certain foods; even the beef industry will be affected. Therefore, humans depend on the bees to keep the environment and economy healthy. Choice (A) is correct.

Space Debris Passage

Suggested Passage Map notes:

¶1: concern that spacecraft could be hit by micrometeorites

¶2: human-made debris in space; more likely than meteorites to hit spacecraft

¶3: small pieces are dangerous

¶4: larger pieces dangerous, but can be avoided

¶5: satellites can adjust course to avoid collision

¶6: some debris falls to earth; sci. can't stop it

¶7: in future, maybe spacecraft leave orbit when not used anymore

43. C   Difficulty: Medium

Category: Global

Getting to the Answer: Think about the idea that is developed throughout the passage. Avoid answers that refer only to supporting details. Choice (C) is the correct answer because all the information in the passage relates to the dangers posed by space debris created by humans.

44. B   Difficulty: Medium

Category: Command of Evidence

Getting to the Answer: Look at each quote from the passage and decide which most clearly supports the central idea. In paragraph 3, the author describes

how space debris created by humans is dangerous to spacecraft and the people inside of them. Choice (B) is the correct answer.

45. C   Difficulty: Medium

Category: Rhetoric

Getting to the Answer: Consider the central idea that you identified in question 43. Identify the central idea of paragraph 2. The passage is mostly about the dangers associated with human-made space debris. Paragraph 2 contains details about the types of human-made space debris orbiting Earth, thus providing support for the central idea. Choice (C) is the correct answer.

46. A   Difficulty: Medium

Category: Detail

Getting to the Answer: Reread the information about meteoroids at the beginning of the passage. Think about how this compares with the descriptions of space debris in the following paragraphs. The author states that although there were concerns about meteoroids in the early days of space travel, scientists concluded that the risk was small because meteoroids were rare. The author goes on to explain that space debris created by humans is a greater concern because it is so plentiful. Choice (A) is the correct answer.

47. C   Difficulty: Hard

Category: Rhetoric

Getting to the Answer: The author's central claim in the passage is that space debris left by humans is dangerous. Think about which of the answer choices most directly supports that claim. In paragraph 6, the author describes how Skylab fell to Earth. This example strengthens the claim, illustrating that the debris left in space can be dangerous even on Earth. Therefore, (C) is the correct answer.

48. D   Difficulty: Medium

Category: Vocab-in-Context

Getting to the Answer: Eliminate answers that are synonyms for "obsolete" but do not make sense in context. Since it was debris that fell out of space, Skylab was no longer in use. In this context, "obsolete" means "outdated," so (D) is the correct answer.

49. A   **Difficulty:** Hard

Category: Inference

Getting to the Answer: Eliminate answer choices that cannot be supported with information found in the passage. In paragraph 6, the author describes how space debris can be dangerous on Earth if a large enough piece gets through the atmosphere without burning up. It is logical, then, that (A) is the correct answer; warnings could help people avoid areas where impacts are predicted, thereby decreasing the chance of injury. The author explicitly states that agencies monitor debris to make predictions and issue warnings (lines 58–62).

50. D   **Difficulty:** Medium

Category: Command of Evidence

Getting to the Answer: Avoid answer choices that provide evidence for incorrect answers to the previous question. Choice (D) is the correct answer, because in lines 60–62, the author states that there is nothing to be done about space debris falling to Earth except to issue warnings.

51. A   **Difficulty:** Medium

Category: Vocab-in-Context

Getting to the Answer: Predict a word that is a synonym for "implemented" in context. Since the debris will remain in space unless a method of removal is "implemented," predict the word that means employed. In this context, (A) is the correct answer.

52. B   **Difficulty:** Hard

Category: Synthesis

Getting to the Answer: Make sure you understand the units and labels in the graphic before choosing an answer. The graphic shows that the highest

density of space debris occurs at an altitude just under 800 kilometers, posing the greatest risk of the dangers discussed in the passage. It is reasonable to conclude, therefore, that if NASA were to place a new satellite into orbit, the agency should choose to avoid the altitude range of 700–900 kilometers. Choice (B) is the correct answer.

WRITING AND LANGUAGE TEST

A Sweet Discovery

1. B   **Difficulty:** Medium

Category: Sentence Formation

Getting to the Answer: Determine the noun to which the modifier in this sentence is referring. Then check the noun's placement to make sure it is as close as possible to the modifier. The modifier is "like most chemists." Therefore, the noun it modifies should be a person. Choice (B) correctly rearranges the sentence so that "chemists" clearly refers to "Constantin Fahlberg."

2. D   **Difficulty:** Medium

Category: Development

Getting to the Answer: This is the topic sentence of the paragraph. Make sure that it focuses on the correct subject. The purpose of this sentence is to discuss Fahlberg and the circumstances in which he was working. Choice (D) correctly focuses the sentence on Fahlberg and flows well into the next sentence, which discusses the specifics of coal tar.

3. B   **Difficulty:** Easy

Category: Usage

Getting to the Answer: The pronoun should agree with the noun to which it refers. Identify this noun to determine the correct pronoun. The antecedent of the pronoun here is "coal tar," a singular, impersonal noun. Choice (B), "from it," is therefore the correct answer.

4. C   Difficulty: Easy

Category: Effective Language Use

Getting to the Answer: Predict what meaning the correct word should convey before choosing an answer. The sentence suggests that while working, Fahlberg was so "___" that he forgot to eat lunch. A word that means *focused on* or *preoccupied with* would be most appropriate. Choice (C), "engrossed," conveys this meaning successfully.

5. D   Difficulty: Hard

Category: Organization

Getting to the Answer: The passage is telling a story. Choose the answer that most effectively makes the transition between the paragraphs while maintaining a consistent tone with the rest of the story. The correct answer will relate to the sentences both before and after it. While answer B may intrigue readers, its tone is out of place when compared with that of the rest of the passage. Choice (D) is the correct answer. It provides a transition from the previous sentence and tells the next logical step in the story.

6. D   Difficulty: Hard

Category: Development

Getting to the Answer: The correct answer will clearly present the central idea of the paragraph. Identify the answer choice that presents the most important point about the scene being described. To be effective as a central idea, the sentence needs to sum up the supporting details in the paragraph and convey their meaning. Only (D) both explains what happened and describes why it was significant, which is the central idea of the paragraph.

7. B   Difficulty: Hard

Category: Usage

Getting to the Answer: Examine the context of the sentence. Notice that it's describing a potentially disastrous outcome if conditions had been different. Fortunately, he had not worked with anything poi-sonous or corrosive, or the story would have had a different ending. If Fahlberg had been working with poisonous or corrosive materials, there is no doubt that "the story" would have had a different—and terrible—ending. The word "might" is too conditional for this situation; therefore, (B), which includes the word "would," is the correct answer.

8. A   Difficulty: Hard

Category: Development

Getting to the Answer: Determine which option clearly states the most important information in this paragraph. The most important fact in this paragraph is that Fahlberg discovered a new substance accidentally. The rest of this paragraph provides details about this discovery. Therefore, the correct answer choice will state that Fahlberg made a discovery. Choice (A) makes this idea clear.

9. D   Difficulty: Easy

Category: Effective Language Use

Getting to the Answer: Look for clues in the rest of the sentence to determine which verb fits with the exact meaning of the sentence. The sentence states that Fahlberg is making the saccharin "commercially," or as part of a business. Choice (D), "producing," is correct, as it emphasizes the business nature of his work.

10. C   Difficulty: Medium

Category: Organization

Getting to the Answer: Try out each answer choice. What information seems confusing when not presented in the right order? Logically, Fahlberg should find the mixture of chemicals and work to isolate it before he names it and understands its significance. Therefore, (C) is the most logical place for sentence 4 and is the correct answer.

11. B   Difficulty: Hard

Category: Organization

Getting to the Answer: Specifically state in your own words what the passage is about. Then read the answer choices to see what fits best. The passage focuses on the specific moment of Fahlberg's discovery, including the significance of the discovery itself and its applications. Only (B) convincingly ties the sentence to the main ideas of the passage.

René Descartes: The Father of Modern Philosophy

12. B   Difficulty: Easy

Category: Usage

Getting to the Answer: A modifier should match its antecedent in number and gender. Also, be wary of words that sound alike but have different meanings and uses. As it stands, the sentence incorrectly uses the adverb "there." Since it refers to "great philosophers," the correct word is the possessive pronoun "their," which is often confused with "there." Choice (B) is the correct answer.

13. D   Difficulty: Hard

Category: Effective Language Use

Getting to the Answer: Read carefully to identify the context of the underlined word. Then, choose the word that best fits the context of the sentence. The underlined word modifies "premodern sources of truth and knowledge," which in turn refers to "political and religious tradition and authority." The context of the sentence indicates that these were powerful ideas that were being challenged by newer ideas. Choice (D), "reigning," conveys the idea that "political and religious tradition and authority" had monarch-like, or ruling, levels of power in people's lives.

14. B   Difficulty: Easy

Category: Effective Language Use

Getting to the Answer: Determine the relationship between the two parts of the underlined sentence, and then think about which answer choice best conveys this relationship. The sentence states that "foundations of truth seemed to be crumbling," and "Descartes's writings proposed an alternative foundation." The two ideas are connected to each other: Descartes's writings were a response to this "crumbling." Choice (B) is the answer that identifies this relationship.

15. C   Difficulty: Hard

Category: Sentence Formation

Getting to the Answer: Determine whether the modifying phrase in this sentence references the correct noun. If the modifier in this sentence is describing a person, then the noun that is described by the modifier should also be a person. Choice (C) correctly matches the modifier (beginning with "an expert") to the noun "Descartes," rather than the noun "work."

16. A   Difficulty: Hard

Category: Development

Getting to the Answer: Determine the central claim in the paragraph and then come back to the question. The central claim of the paragraph is that Descartes's work established the foundation for many modern ideas. The statement found in (A) provides information that best supports this claim and logically transitions to the following sentence. Choice (A) is correct.

17. B   Difficulty: Medium

Category: Development

Getting to the Answer: In your own words, identify what idea ties together the ideas presented in the rest of the paragraph. Sentence 1 states that "modern culture would come to cherish this." The question is, what is "this"? The rest of the paragraph goes into detail about Descartes's philosophical methods. Choice (B) identifies Descartes's general philosophical focus and is, therefore, the correct answer.

18. D   Difficulty: Medium

Category: Punctuation

Getting to the Answer: Identify whether the sentence consists of two independent clauses or an independent and a dependent clause. This will provide guidance for punctuating it. The sentence consists of two independent clauses ("Descartes arrived . . ." and "he could only be . . . "). Separating the independent clauses into two sentences is the best way to punctuate them. Choice (D) is the correct answer.

19. B   Difficulty: Hard

Category: Development

Getting to the Answer: Look for the answer choice that most clearly helps to develop the ideas in the surrounding sentences. The inserted sentence comes after a discussion of Descartes's only certainty—that he was thinking. The sentence that follows it explains that from this, he could build additional knowledge. The correct answer will develop the idea of certainty and how it can be used to acquire more knowledge. Choice (B) best conveys this information and therefore is the correct choice.

20. D   Difficulty: Medium

Category: Usage

Getting to the Answer: A grammatically correct sentence will include a verb whose form makes the sentence an independent clause. "Propelled by" needs the addition of an auxiliary verb for this sentence to stand alone. Inserting "were" before this phrase makes the sentence grammatically complete. Choice (D) is the correct answer.

21. B   Difficulty: Medium

Category: Effective Language Use

Getting to the Answer: Determine whether there is a way to make the sentence less wordy without changing its intended meaning. The sentence, especially in the context of the paragraph, seems to be saying that it's difficult to determine exactly what Descartes did versus what other people at the time did. Both answer choices C and D change the meaning of the sentence slightly to say either that Descartes himself could not be separated from his contemporaries or that what they did was identical. Choice (B) is correct, because it eliminates the wordiness of the sentence while maintaining its meaning.

22. C   Difficulty: Medium

Category: Effective Language Use

Getting to the Answer: Determine what role this verb has in the sentence. What is the precise nature of the action it is describing? The sentence is about how Descartes's work brought about shifts in thinking that critically influenced other developments. However, the word "begun," A, does not precisely convey the power with which this occurred. Choice (C), "initiated," conveys this meaning and is the correct answer.

The Novel: Introspection to Escapism

23. C   Difficulty: Medium

Category: Effective Language Use

Getting to the Answer: Reread the surrounding sentences to look for context clues. Then review the answer choices, paying attention to the meaning and nuance of each word. The passage tells us that art is constantly evolving and changing. The correct answer will represent the opposite of this meaning. The word "static" means that something does not change, so (C) is the correct answer.

24. B   Difficulty: Medium

Category: Punctuation

Getting to the Answer: Read the sentence and determine whether the parts of the sentence on either side of the semicolon are independent clauses. If they are not, identify their function and choose the appropriate punctuation. "For better or worse" is not an independent clause; rather, it is a parenthetical element that adds an opinion to the main thrust of the sentence. Choice (B) is correct. It uses a dash to set off this additional information in the sentence.

25. B   Difficulty: Medium

Category: Development

Getting to the Answer: To determine the main topic of a paragraph, identify important details and then summarize them in a sentence or two. Find a choice that matches your prediction. Avoid choices like A and C, which include details about poetry that are not in the paragraph. The details in this paragraph are about how the writers of the past viewed the novel as a vital way to record and comment on the human experience. Choice (B) captures this main topic.

26. A   Difficulty: Medium

Category: Effective Language Use

Getting to the Answer: Read the surrounding sentences to get a sense of what the underlined word is meant to convey. Then review the answer choices to find the one that is closest to this meaning. The passage suggests that the novel was held in high regard. The correct answer needs to indicate high regard with a positive connotation. The word "loftily," (A), connotes both high regard and a positive view of the novel as a literary form.

27. A   Difficulty: Medium

Category: Development

Getting to the Answer: Look for the answer choice that improves the sentence by adding important, relevant information. The paragraph is about the opinions of acclaimed novelists. Choice (A) adds the information that Joseph Conrad was also a novelist.

28. A   Difficulty: Medium

Category: Punctuation

Getting to the Answer: Identify the role of the underlined phrase; then use this information to determine the necessary punctuation. "However" is an introductory adverbial element that modifies the rest of the sentence. It should be followed by a comma. Choice (A) is correct.

29. B   Difficulty: Medium

Category: Sentence Formation

Getting to the Answer: Check the placement of dependent clauses set off by commas. A dependent clause that modifies a noun in a sentence should be adjacent or as close as possible to the noun it is modifying. The dependent clause "which are now available on digital devices" modifies "novels," not "entertainment medium." It should be as close as possible to "novels," making (B) the correct answer.

30. A   Difficulty: Medium

Category: Sentence Formation

Getting to the Answer: A compound sentence should be combined with a semicolon or a comma with a conjunction. Choice (A) is correct. This keeps the semicolon, which appropriately separates two related independent clauses.

31. C   Difficulty: Hard

Category: Development

Getting to the Answer: Evaluate the paragraph for the central idea. Then review the answer choices to find the one that directly supports that idea. This paragraph discusses the change from novels that tackle serious social issues to books that are meant as light entertainment for mass consumption. Choice (C) is correct. It emphasizes that readers want novels to be "fun," providing a means of escape from their lives.

32. D   Difficulty: Medium

Category: Usage

Getting to the Answer: A pronoun needs to match its antecedent. Locate the antecedent of the pronoun and then predict an answer. The correct answer will match the antecedent in gender and number. The antecedent is "novelist," so the answer must be singular. Choice (D) is correct, as it matches the antecedent in number and appropriately identifies both gender options, since the antecedent did not specify gender.

33. A   Difficulty: Hard

Category: Punctuation

Getting to the Answer: Remember that dashes and parentheses act in similar ways. If the phrase is offering additional information before you get back to the main thrust of the sentence, then a dash is appropriate. A dash is an appropriate way to punctuate the phrase, so (A) is the correct choice.

Interning: A Bridge Between Classes and Careers

34. B   Difficulty: Easy

Category: Usage

Getting to the Answer: Read the entire paragraph to understand the context in which the underlined word appears. Be careful to distinguish between commonly confused words. The paragraph makes it clear that Kelli has started working at BP as a summer intern. The correct answer will convey this meaning. Choice A, "excepted," meaning "excluded from a group," is a word that is commonly confused with "accepted," which means "to have taken or received something." In this case, Kelli has taken the job offer with BP, making (B) the correct choice.

35. C   Difficulty: Medium

Category: Effective Language Use

Getting to the Answer: Read the entire sentence to determine the context of the underlined word. The context implies that the tasks assigned to interns are low level and meaningless. Choices B, "skilled," and D, "challenging," suggest that the tasks are important, which does not match the context. Only (C) fits the tone and context of the paragraph and is more precise than "boring."

36. A   Difficulty: Hard

Category: Development

Getting to the Answer: Identify the central idea and then review the answer choices to find the one that best supports it. The paragraph is about the importance of gaining a real-world perspective on classroom knowledge. Choice (A) supports this central idea by showing how Kelli's internship will allow her to apply her classroom knowledge to the real world.

37. D   Difficulty: Hard

Category: Development

Getting to the Answer: Skim the paragraph to determine what content the sentences have in common. The paragraph discusses the safety training Kelli is required to complete and explains how this training will offer her an advantage over other job applicants. Choice (D) most effectively establishes the main topic of the paragraph; it introduces the type of certification Kelli will earn.

38. A   Difficulty: Medium

Category: Effective Language Use

Getting to the Answer: Analyze the sentence to determine which phrase best fits the context. Choice (A) is the correct answer. "Stand out" means that Kelli will clearly be noticed when compared with other applicants.

39. D   Difficulty: Medium

Category: Usage

Getting to the Answer: Examine the structure of the sentence and identify the pronoun or pronouns that match the antecedent. Use the word "everyone" in a simple sentence to determine if it's singular or plural: for example, "Everyone goes." "Everyone" is a singular pronoun referring to a person, so it requires a singular possessive pronoun. Using the plural "their" is accepted only in informal usage. Choice (D) is the correct answer because it correctly matches the antecedent in number and appropriately identifies both gender options, since the antecedent did not specify a gender.

40. A   Difficulty: Medium

Category: Punctuation

Getting to the Answer: Determine the need for punctuation within the sentence. "For" and "from" are both prepositions, a clue that both phrases are correctly set off with commas. Because both phrases are dependent on the remainder of the sentence, they are correctly connected with commas. Choice (A) is correct.

41. B   Difficulty: Easy

Category: Sentence Formation

Getting to the Answer: In a sentence with a series of actions, make sure all verbs or verb forms are parallel. Focusing on the action verbs, it becomes clear that they should all end in "-ing." Inconsistencies in this pattern result in a lack of parallel structure. Choice (B) is correct, as it uses the gerund form (nouns formed by adding "-ing" to verbs) of all four action verbs.

42. D   Difficulty: Medium

Category: Sentence Formation

Getting to the Answer: Identify the subject and predicate of each sentence to determine if it is a complete sentence or a fragment. As the sentences are written in A, the first one is an incomplete sentence, or fragment. Only (D) correctly and concisely combines the two to eliminate the fragment.

43. C   Difficulty: Medium

Category: Effective Language Use

Getting to the Answer: Often, when a sentence is long, it's a good idea to see if there are ways to edit out certain words or phrases to make the sentence more concise. Choice (C) is correct. By leaving out the phrase "though she is losing her summer," this answer choice conveys the intended meaning of the sentence with logical and concise language.

44. B   Difficulty: Medium

Category: Quantitative

Getting to the Answer: Make sure you understand the information conveyed by the graphic's labels before you attempt to choose the correct answer. The passage informs you that Kelli's chosen field is oil and energy, represented by the bar on the far right of the graphic. Choice (B) is the correct answer, as it matches the number of oil and energy interns per 1,000 hires noted on the y-axis.

MATH—NO CALCULATOR TEST

1. B   Difficulty: Easy

Category: Heart of Algebra / Linear Equations

Getting to the Answer: In a real-world scenario, the slope of a line represents a unit rate and the y-intercept represents a flat fee or a starting amount. The cost of one linear foot is the same as the unit rate (the cost per linear foot), which is represented by the slope of the line. Use the grid-lines and the axis labels to count the rise and the run from the y-intercept of the line (0, 150) to the next point that hits an intersection of two grid-lines. Pay careful attention to how the grid-lines are marked (by 5s on the x-axis and by 25s on the y-axis). The line rises 75 units and runs 5 units, so the slope is $\frac{75}{5} = 15$ dollars per linear foot of fence, which is (B). Note that you could also use the slope formula and two points from the graph to find the unit rate.

2. C   Difficulty: Easy

Category: Passport to Advanced Math / Exponents

Getting to the Answer: Don't be tempted—you can't simply cancel one term when a polynomial is divided by a monomial. Instead, find the greatest common factor of *both* the numerator and the denominator. Factor out the GCF from the numerator and from the denominator, and then you can cancel it. The GCF is $12x^2$.

$$\frac{24x^4 + 36x^3 - 12x^2}{12x^2}$$
$$= \frac{\cancel{12x^2}(2x^2 + 3x - 1)}{\cancel{12x^2}}$$
$$= 2x^2 + 3x - 1$$

This matches (C).

3. C   Difficulty: Easy

Category: Additional Topics in Math / Geometry

Getting to the Answer: Corresponding sides of similar triangles are proportional, so write a proportion (paying careful attention to the order of the sides) using the sides that you know and the side that you're looking for. Then, solve the proportion for the missing side.

Call the missing side x. Write a proportion using words first, and then fill in the lengths of the sides that you know:

$$\frac{\text{right side small}\triangle}{\text{base of small}\triangle} = \frac{\text{right side large}\triangle}{\text{base of large}\triangle}$$
$$\frac{x}{4} = \frac{2 + x}{6}$$
$$6x = 4(2 + x)$$
$$6x = 8 + 4x$$
$$2x = 8$$
$$x = 4$$

The length of $\overline{BE}$ is 4, so (C) is correct.

4. A   Difficulty: Easy

Category: Passport to Advanced Math / Quadratics

Getting to the Answer: Recognizing the different forms of a quadratic equation can save valuable time on Test Day. Each of the answer choices is given in vertex form, so start by matching the vertex of the parabola in the graph to the correct equation.

When a quadratic equation is written in vertex form, $y = a(x - h)^2 + k$, the vertex is (h, k). The vertex of the parabola in the graph is $(2, 5)$; therefore, the equation should look like $y = a(x - 2)^2 + 5$. This means you can eliminate B and C. To choose between (A) and D, consider the value of a. The parabola in the graph opens downward, so a must be negative. This means (A) is correct.

5. B   Difficulty: Medium

Category: Heart of Algebra / Linear Equations

Getting to the Answer: You can approach this question conceptually or concretely. Drawing a quick sketch is most likely the safest approach. Line L shown in the graph rises from left to right, so it has a positive slope. Once reflected over the x-axis, it will fall from left to right, so the new line will have a negative slope. This means you can eliminate C and D. Now, draw a quick sketch of the reflected line on the coordinate plane in your test booklet and count the rise (or fall) and the run from one point to the next.

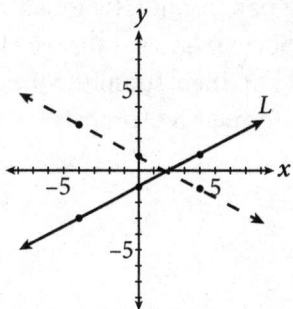

The reflected line falls 2 units and runs 4 units, so the slope is $-\frac{2}{4}$, which reduces to $-\frac{1}{2}$, making (B) the correct choice.

6. B   Difficulty: Medium

Category: Passport to Advanced Math / Exponents

Getting to the Answer: To answer this question, you need to combine like terms, being careful to distribute negative signs where appropriate. Break the calculation into steps: Find $2p$, find $q + r$, and then subtract the results. Arranging the terms in descending order will help keep them organized.

$$2p = 2(4x^3 + x - 2) = 8x^3 + 2x - 4$$
$$q + r = x^2 - 1 + 3x - 5 = x^2 + 3x - 6$$
$$2p - (q + r) = 8x^3 + 2x - 4 - (x^2 + 3x - 6)$$
$$= 8x^3 + 2x - 4 - x^2 - 3x + 6$$
$$= 8x^3 - x^2 + 2x - 3x - 4 + 6$$
$$= 8x^3 - x^2 - x + 2$$

This matches (B).

7. A   Difficulty: Medium

Category: Passport to Advanced Math / Quadratics

Getting to the Answer: The roots of an equation are the same as its solutions. The answer choices contain radicals, which tells you that the equation can't be factored. Instead, either complete the square or solve the equation using the quadratic formula, whichever you are most comfortable using. The equation is already written in the form $y = ax^2 + bx + c$ and the coefficients are fairly small, so using the quadratic formula is probably the quickest method. Jot down the values that you'll need: $a = 2$, $b = 4$, and $c = -3$. Then, substitute these values into the quadratic formula and simplify:

$$x = \frac{-b \pm \sqrt{b^2 - 4ac}}{2a}$$
$$= \frac{-(4) \pm \sqrt{(4)^2 - 4(2)(-3)}}{2(2)}$$
$$= \frac{-4 \pm \sqrt{16 + 24}}{4}$$
$$= \frac{-4 \pm \sqrt{40}}{4}$$

This is not one of the answer choices, so simplify the radical. To do this, look for a perfect square that divides into 40 and take its square root.

$$x = \frac{-4 \pm \sqrt{4 \times 10}}{4}$$
$$= \frac{-4 \pm 2\sqrt{10}}{4}$$
$$= \frac{-2 \pm \sqrt{10}}{2}$$

Be careful—you can't simplify the answer any further because you cannot divide the square root of 10 by 2, so (A) is correct.

8. D   Difficulty: Medium

Category: Heart of Algebra / Systems of Linear Equations

Getting to the Answer: Although this question asks where the *graphs* of the functions intersect, it is not necessary to actually graph them. Two graphs intersect at the point where they have the same *x*-value and the same *y*-value. The notations $g(x)$ and $h(x)$ can both be interpreted as "the *y*-value at a given value of *x*," so set $g(x)$ equal to $h(x)$ and solve for *x*. Then, if needed, plug this value into either function to find the corresponding *y*-value. Don't let the fraction intimidate you—you can write $g(x)$ as a fraction over 1 and use cross-multiplication.

$$\frac{3x - 5}{1} = \frac{7x + 10}{4}$$
$$4(3x - 5) = 7x + 10$$
$$12x - 20 = 7x + 10$$
$$5x = 30$$
$$x = 6$$

There is only one answer choice for which the *x*-coordinate is 6, (D), so the graphs of the functions will intersect at (6, 13).

9. A   Difficulty: Medium

Category: Passport to Advanced Math / Exponents

Getting to the Answer: When you write an equation *in terms of* a specific variable, you are simply solving the equation for that variable. In this question, you'll need to relate fractional exponents to radicals and understand how to use negative exponents. Be careful—you're not just rewriting the equation, you're solving it for *k*.

Raising a quantity to the one-third power is the same as taking its cube root. Applying a negative exponent to a quantity is the same as writing its reciprocal. Rewrite the equation using these properties and then solve for *k* using inverse operations. Note that the inverse of taking a cube root of a quantity is cubing the quantity.

$$x = k^{-\frac{1}{3}}$$
$$x = \frac{1}{\sqrt[3]{k}}$$
$$(x)^3 = \left(\frac{1}{\sqrt[3]{k}}\right)^3$$
$$x^3 = \frac{1}{k}$$
$$kx^3 = 1$$
$$k = \frac{1}{x^3}$$

Choice (A) is correct.

10. D   Difficulty: Medium

Category: Heart of Algebra / Linear Equations

Getting to the Answer: There are two variables and only one equation, so you can't actually solve the equation for *c*. Instead, recall that an equation has infinitely many solutions when the left side is identical to the right side. When this happens, everything cancels out and you get the equation 0 = 0, which is always true.

Start by simplifying the left side of the equation. Don't forget to distribute the negative sign to both terms inside the parentheses.

$$4x - (10 - 2x) = c(3x - 5)$$
$$4x - 10 + 2x = c(3x - 5)$$
$$6x - 10 = c(3x - 5)$$

Next, quickly compare the left side of the equation to the right side. Rather than distributing the *c*, notice that if *c* were 2, then both sides of the equation would equal $6x - 10$, and it would have infinitely many solutions. Therefore, *c* is 2, which is (D).

11. D   Difficulty: Medium

Category: Heart of Algebra / Inequalities

Getting to the Answer: You don't need to separate this compound inequality into pieces. Just remember, whatever you do to one piece, you must do to all three pieces. Don't forget to flip the inequality symbols if you multiply or divide by a negative number. Here, the fractions make it look more complicated than it really is, so start by clearing the fractions by multiplying everything by the least common denominator, 6.

$$0 < 1 - \frac{a}{3} \le \frac{1}{2}$$
$$6(0) < 6\left(1 - \frac{a}{3}\right) \le 6\left(\frac{1}{2}\right)$$
$$0 < 6 - 2a \le 3$$
$$-6 < -2a \le -3$$
$$3 > a \ge \frac{3}{2}$$
$$1.5 \le a < 3$$

Now, read the inequality symbols carefully. The value of a is between 1.5 and 3, including 1.5, but *not* including 3, so (D) is the correct answer.

12. D   Difficulty: Hard

Category: Heart of Algebra / Inequalities

Getting to the Answer: The only way a system of inequalities can have no solution is if the graph consists of two parallel lines with shading in opposite directions so that there is no overlap.

Start by writing each equation in slope-intercept form to help you envision what the graphs will look like. You'll need to multiply the second equation by -2, so don't forget to flip the inequality symbol.

$$y - \frac{2}{k}x \leq 0 \rightarrow y \leq \frac{2}{k}x$$

$$\frac{1}{k}x - \frac{1}{2}y \leq -1 \rightarrow -\frac{1}{2}y \leq -\frac{1}{k}x - 1$$

$$\rightarrow y \geq \frac{2}{k}x + 2$$

Now, think about the graphs. The first equation has a slope of $\frac{2}{k}$, a y-intercept of 0, and is shaded below the line. The second equation also has a slope of $\frac{2}{k}$, but it has a y-intercept of 2 and is shaded above the line. This means that no matter what value of k is used (other than 0), the two lines are parallel and shaded in opposite directions, and thus there are infinitely many values of k that result in a system with no solution, (D).

13. C   Difficulty: Hard

Category: Passport to Advanced Math / Exponents

Getting to the Answer: When solving a rational equation, start by getting a common denominator. Then, you can set the numerators equal and solve for the variable. Don't forget, however: If the answer produces zero in any denominator, then it is not a valid answer. The denominators are almost the same

already; you just need to multiply the top and bottom of the first term by 2, factor the denominator of the second term, and you'll be ready to solve the equation.

$$\frac{2}{2}\left(\frac{4x}{x-7}\right) + \frac{2x}{2x-14} = \frac{70}{2(x-7)}$$

$$\frac{8x}{2(x-7)} + \frac{2x}{2(x-7)} = \frac{70}{2(x-7)}$$

Now that the denominators are all the same, you can solve the equation represented by the numerators.

$$8x + 2x = 70$$
$$10x = 70$$
$$x = 7$$

Be careful—this isn't the correct answer. Because there are variables in the denominator, you must check the solution to make sure it isn't extraneous, or in other words, doesn't cause a 0 in the denominator of any term. Here, if $x = 7$, then all of the denominators are zero (and division by zero is not possible), so the equation has no solution, (C).

14. B   Difficulty: Hard

Category: Additional Topics in Math / Geometry

Getting to the Answer: The shortest distance from A to B is through the center of the circle, along the diameter, which is twice the radius. When the equation of a circle is written in the form $(x - h)^2 + (y - k)^2 = r^2$, you can easily find the center and the radius of the circle. To find r, complete the square for the x terms and for the y terms. Start by reordering the terms. Then, take the coefficient of the x term and divide it by 2, square it, and add the result to the two terms with x variables. Do the same with the y term. Remember, you must also add these amounts to the other side of the equation. This creates a perfect square of x terms and y terms, and the equation will look more like a circle.

$$x^2 + y^2 + 6x - 4y = 12$$
$$x^2 + 6x + y^2 - 4y = 12$$
$$\left(x^2 + 6x + 9\right) + \left(y^2 - 4y + 4\right) = 12 + 9 + 4$$
$$\left(x + 3\right)^2 + \left(y - 2\right)^2 = 25$$

This means that the radius of the circle is $\sqrt{25} = 5$, so the diameter is 10, which is also the distance from A to B, making (B) correct. Note that you can do a quick check of your work by looking at the center; according to the equation, the center is $(-3, 2)$, which appears to match the location of the center on the graph.

15. C   Difficulty: Hard

Category: Passport to Advanced Math / Functions

Getting to the Answer: The key to answering this question is in having a conceptual understanding of function notation. Here, the input $(x - 1)$ has already been substituted and simplified in the given function. Your job is to determine what the function would have looked like had x been the input.

To keep things organized, let $u = x - 1$, the old input. This means $x = u + 1$. Substitute this into g and simplify:

$$g(x - 1) = 3x^2 + 5x - 7$$
$$g(u) = 3(u + 1)^2 + 5(u + 1) - 7$$
$$= 3(u^2 + 2u + 1) + 5u + 5 - 7$$
$$= 3u^2 + 6u + 3 + 5u + 5 - 7$$
$$= 3u^2 + 11u + 1$$

This means $g(u) = 3u^2 + 11u + 1$. When working with function notation, you evaluate the function by substituting a given input value for the variable in the parentheses. Here, if the input value is x, then $g(x) = 3x^2 + 11x + 1$, which matches (C).

16. 15   Difficulty: Easy

Category: Heart of Algebra / Systems of Linear Equations

Getting to the Answer: The equilibrium price occurs when the supply and demand are equal. Graphically, this means where the two lines intersect. The lines intersect at the point (6, 15). You can see from the axis labels that price is plotted along the y-axis, so the equilibrium price is $15.

17. 10.5 or 21/2   Difficulty: Medium

Category: Heart of Algebra / Linear Equations

Getting to the Answer: The key word in this question is *linear*. In a real-world scenario that involves a constant rate of change, you almost always need to find the slope and the initial amount so you can write an equation. The question states that the initial mass of the larva was 10 grams, so all you need to do is find the slope.

Write the information given in the question as ordered pairs (time, mass) so you can find the slope. At $t = 0$, the larva has a mass of 10 grams, so one pair is (0, 10). After 48 hours, the larva has a mass of 14 grams, so a second pair is (48, 14). Now, use the slope formula:

$$m = \frac{y_2 - y_1}{x_2 - x_1}$$
$$= \frac{14 - 10}{48 - 0}$$
$$= \frac{4}{48} = \frac{1}{12}$$

The equation is $y = \dfrac{1}{12}x + 10$, where y represents the mass of the larva after x hours. Substitute 6 for x to find the mass after 6 hours: $\dfrac{1}{12}(6) + 10 = \dfrac{6}{12} + 10 = 10.5$ grams.

18. 4   Difficulty: Medium

Category: Passport to Advanced Math / Functions

Getting to the Answer: The notation $f(g(x))$ indicates a composition of two functions which is read "f of g of x." It means that the output when x is substituted in $g(x)$ becomes the input for $f(x)$. Use the second table to find that $g(-1)$ is 2. This is your new input. Now, use the first table to find $f(2)$, which is 4.

19. 10   Difficulty: Medium

Category: Additional Topics in Math / Imaginary Numbers

Getting to the Answer: Multiply the two complex numbers just as you would two binomials (using FOIL). Then, combine like terms. The question tells you that $i = \sqrt{-1}$. If you square both sides of the equation, this is the same as $i^2 = -1$, which is a more useful fact.

$$
\begin{aligned}
(4 + 3i)(1 - 2i) &= 4(1 - 2i) + 3i(1 - 2i) \\
&= 4 - 8i + 3i - 6i^2 \\
&= 4 - 5i - 6(-1) \\
&= 4 - 5i + 6 \\
&= 10 - 5i
\end{aligned}
$$

The question asks for a in $a + bi$, so the correct answer is 10.

20. 50.5   Difficulty: Hard

Category: Passport to Advanced Math / Scatterplots

Getting to the Answer: This question requires a conceptual understanding of modeling data and properties of quadratic functions. Because the regression model fits the data exactly, you can use what you know about quadratic functions to answer the question.

The graph of a quadratic function is symmetric with respect to its axis of symmetry. The axis of symmetry occurs at the x-value of the vertex, which also happens to be where the maximum (or minimum) of the function occurs. The question tells you this value—it's $x = 56.25$. Because $x = 90$ is 33.75 (because $90 - 56.25 = 33.75$) units to the right of the axis of symmetry, you know that the y-value will be the same as the point that is 33.75 units to the left of the axis of symmetry. This occurs at $x = 56.25 - 33.75 = 22.5$. Read the y-value from the graphing calculator screenshot to find the answer, which is 50.5.

MATH—CALCULATOR TEST

1. D   Difficulty: Easy

Category: Problem Solving and Data Analysis / Statistics and Probability

Getting to the Answer: To reduce the margin of error, the society should use a larger sample size selected from a better representation of the population. The target population is *all* adults, not just those that have gym memberships. Using only adults with gym memberships is likely to skew the results because these respondents probably exercise considerably more than people who do not have gym memberships. This means (D) is correct.

2. B   Difficulty: Easy

Category: Heart of Algebra / Inequalities

Getting to the Answer: Think about this question conceptually. If the box cannot weigh *more than* 20 pounds (or 20×16 ounces), this means it can weigh *that much or less*, so the right half of the inequality you are looking for is $\leq 20 \times 16$. This means you can eliminate A and C based on the inequality symbol. A box is made up of ballpoint pens, b, and mechanical pencils, m. Each pen weighs 0.3 ounces, and each pencil weighs 0.2 ounces. The total weight of the box would be the number of pens, b, multiplied by their weight, 0.3, added to the number of pencils, m, multiplied by their weight, 0.2. So the inequality is $0.3b + 0.2m \leq 20 \times 16$, which matches (B).

3. C   Difficulty: Easy

Category: Heart of Algebra / Linear Equations

Getting to the Answer: Finding an *x*-intercept is easy when you know the equation of the line—it's the value of *x* when *y* is 0. Everything you need to write the equation is shown on the graph. The *y*-intercept is 5 and the line falls 1 unit and runs 3 units from one point to the next, so the slope is $-\frac{1}{3}$. This means the equation of the line, in slope-intercept form, is $y = -\frac{1}{3}x + 5$. Now, set the equation equal to zero and solve for *x*:

$$0 = -\frac{1}{3}x + 5$$
$$\frac{1}{3}x = 5$$
$$x = 15$$

Line *Q* will intercept the *x*-axis at 15, which is (C).

4. D   Difficulty: Easy

Category: Passport to Advanced Math / Functions

Getting to the Answer: When you see an expression such as *f*(*x*), it means to substitute the given value for *x* in the function's equation. When there is more than one function involved, pay careful attention to which function should be evaluated first. You are looking for the value of *f*(*x*) at *x* = 3. Because *f*(*x*) is defined in terms of *g*(*x*), evaluate *g*(3) first by substituting 3 for *x* in the expression *x* + 5.

$$g(3) = 3 + 5 = 8$$
$$f(3) = 2g(3) = 2(8) = 16$$

Choice (D) is correct.

5. C   Difficulty: Easy

Category: Problem Solving and Data Analysis / Rates, Ratios, Proportions, and Percentages

Getting to the Answer: Pay careful attention to the units. As you read the question, decide how and when you will need to convert units. In this problem,

work backward—you need to know how many pages of cards will be printed. To find this number, you first need to know how many cards will be printed. So, start with the number of agents (which tells you the number of boxes) and multiply by the number of cards per box:

$$12 \text{ agents} \times \frac{2 \text{ boxes}}{1 \text{ agent}} \times \frac{225 \text{ cards}}{1 \text{ box}} = 5,400 \text{ cards}$$

Next, use the information about *pages* to finish the calculations:

$$5,400 \text{ cards} \times \frac{1 \text{ page}}{10 \text{ cards}} \times \frac{1 \text{ minute}}{18 \text{ pages}} = 30 \text{ minutes}$$

This means (C) is correct.

6. A   Difficulty: Medium

Category: Heart of Algebra / Inequalities

Getting to the Answer: The question is asking about $\frac{x}{y}$, so think about how fractions work. Larger numerators result in larger values $\left(\frac{3}{2}\right.$, for example, is greater than $\left.\frac{1}{2}\right)$, and smaller denominators result in larger values $\left(\frac{1}{2}\right.$, for example, is greater than $\left.\frac{1}{4}\right)$. The largest possible value of $\frac{x}{y}$ is found by choosing the largest possible value for *x* and the smallest possible value for *y* which gives $\frac{0.2}{5} = 0.04$, or (A).

7. A   Difficulty: Medium

Category: Problem Solving and Data Analysis / Statistics and Probability

Getting to the Answer: Results from a study can only be generalized to the population from which the sample was taken. Also, keep in mind that positive correlations do not prove causation. The study was conducted by the American Academy of Pediatrics on children in the United States under three, so the sample is American children under three, which means conclusions can only be drawn about *this* population. Also, because correlations do not prove causation, the only conclusion that can be drawn is that there is an association between television time and attention disorders for American children under three years old, (A).

8. D   Difficulty: Medium

Category: Problem Solving and Data Analysis / Statistics and Probability

Getting to the Answer: The greatest change (in absolute value) in miles ridden per week could be an increase or a decrease. You don't have to worry about whether the change is positive or negative, so to keep things simple, always subtract the smaller number from the larger number. Make a list to show the changes in miles ridden per week between each pair of consecutive weeks. Save yourself some time by skipping weeks that clearly have smaller changes, such as between weeks 1 and 2 and between weeks 3 and 4.

Weeks 2-3: $72 - 64 = 8$

Weeks 4-5: $78 - 70 = 8$

Weeks 5-6: $85 - 78 = 7$

Weeks 6-7: $85 - 75 = 10$

Weeks 7-8: $82 - 75 = 7$

Of the differences, the greatest is from week 6 to week 7, which is a change of 10 miles, making (D) correct.

9. C   Difficulty: Medium

Category: Heart of Algebra / Linear Equations

Getting to the Answer: Given two points (even when the coordinates are variables), the slope of the line is $\frac{y_2 - y_1}{x_2 - x_1}$. You are given a numerical value for the slope and a pair of coordinate points with variables. To find the value of a, plug the points into the slope formula, and then solve for a:

$$\text{Slope} = \frac{y_2 - y_1}{x_2 - x_1}$$

$$5 = \frac{6 - 2a}{a - (a - 1)}$$

$$5 = \frac{6 - 2a}{1}$$

$$5 = 6 - 2a$$

$$-1 = -2a$$

$$\frac{1}{2} = a$$

Choice (C) is correct.

10. A   Difficulty: Hard

Category: Heart of Algebra / Systems of Linear Equations

Getting to the Answer: Questions about breaking even usually involve creating a system of equations (one for cost and one for revenue), setting the equations equal to each other, and solving for the variable. Create a system of equations at each price point using n for the number of bathtub lifts. Then solve each system. Note that the cost equation will be the same for both systems, and it is already given to you in the question.

$$\text{Old Price: } C = 225n + 3{,}150; R = 450n$$
$$C = R$$
$$225n + 3{,}150 = 450n$$
$$3{,}150 = 225n$$
$$14 = n$$

$$\text{New Price: } C = 225n + 3{,}150; R = 375n$$
$$C = R$$
$$225n + 3{,}150 = 375n$$
$$3{,}150 = 150n$$
$$21 = n$$

At the old price, the company needed to sell 14 lifts to break even. At the new price, it needs to sell 21 lifts, so it needs to sell $21 - 14 = 7$ more lifts at the new price to break even, which is (A).

11. B **Difficulty:** Medium

Category: Additional Topics in Math / Geometry

Getting to the Answer: The amount of water needed to create the ice portion of the exhibit is another way of saying the *volume* of the ice. So, you need to find the volume of the entire space and then subtract the volume of the cylinder that runs through the ice. The volume of a rectangular prism is given by $V = l \times w \times h$, and the volume of a cylinder equals the area of its base times its height, or $\pi r^2 h$. To determine the volume of the ice, start by decomposing the figure into two rectangular prisms and adding their volumes. You can decompose the figure left to right or front to back. Front to back, it looks like the following figure:

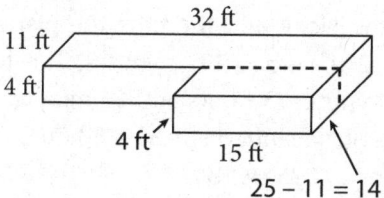

The prism in the back has a volume of $32 \times 11 \times 4 = 1,408$ cubic feet. The prism in the front has a length of 15 feet and a height of 4 feet, but the width is missing. Find the missing width by subtracting 11 from 25, which is 14 feet. So, the volume of the prism in the front is $15 \times 14 \times 4 = 840$ cubic feet. The total volume of the prisms is $1,408 + 840 = 2,248$ cubic feet. Be careful—that's not the answer. You still need to find the amount of space taken up by the glycol pipe and subtract it. The diameter of the pipe is 2 feet, so its radius is 1 foot, and the height (or the length in this question) is 32 feet, so the volume is $\pi(1)^2(32) \approx 100.53$ cubic feet. This means the amount of ice needed is $2,248 - 100.53 = 2,147.47$, or about 2,150 cubic feet, (B).

12. D **Difficulty:** Medium

Category: Problem Solving and Data Analysis / Rates, Ratios, Proportions, and Percentages

Getting to the Answer: Let the units in this question guide you to the answer. You'll also need to use the answer you found in the previous question. The company will use two hoses, each of which pumps at a rate of 60 gallons per minute, so the rate is actually 120 gallons per minute. Convert the volume you found earlier from cubic feet to gallons, and then use the rate to find the time.

$$2,150 \, \text{ft}^3 \times \frac{7.48 \, \text{gal}}{1 \, \text{ft}^3} \times \frac{1 \, \text{min}}{120 \, \text{gal}} = 134 \text{ minutes}$$

The answers are given in hours and minutes, so write 134 minutes as 2 hours and 14 minutes, or about 2 hours and 15 minutes, which is (D).

13. C **Difficulty:** Medium

Category: Passport to Advanced Math / Quadratics

Getting to the Answer: The graph of every quadratic equation is a parabola, which may or may not cross the *x*-axis, depending on where its vertex is and which way it opens. Don't forget—if the equation is written in vertex form, $y = a(x - h)^2 + k$, then the vertex is (h, k), and the value of a tells you which way the parabola opens. The graph of an equation that has *no solution* does not cross the *x*-axis, so try to envision the graph of each of the answer choices. When a quadratic is written in factored form, the factors tell you the *x*-intercepts, which means every quadratic equation that can be written in factored form (over the set of real numbers) must have solutions. This means you can eliminate B and D. Now, imagine the graph of the equation in A: The vertex is (5, 3) and a is negative, so the parabola opens downward and consequently must cross the *x*-axis. This means you can eliminate A, and (C) must be correct. The graph of the equation in (C) has a vertex of (5, 3) and opens *up*, so it does not cross the *x*-axis and, therefore, has no solution.

You could also graph each of the answer choices in

your graphing calculator, but this is not the most time-efficient way to answer the question.

14. A   **Difficulty:** Medium

Category: Problem Solving and Data Analysis / Rates, Ratios, Proportions, and Percentages

Getting to the Answer: Questions that involve distance, rate, and time can almost always be solved using the formula Distance = rate × time. Use the speed, or rate, of the plane from Boston, 360 mph, and its distance from Chicago, 864 mi, to determine when it arrived. You don't know the time, so call it t.

$$\text{Distance} = \text{rate} \times \text{time}$$
$$864 = 360t$$
$$2.4 = t$$

This means it took 2.4 hours for the plane to arrive. This is more than 2 full hours, so multiply 2.4 by 60 to find the number of minutes it took: 60 × 2.4 = 144 minutes. Now determine how long it took the plane from Kansas City. It left at 8:30 AM and arrived at 10:34 AM, so it took 2 hours and 4 minutes, or 124 minutes. This means the plane from Kansas City arrived 144 − 124 = 20 minutes before the plane from Boston, (A).

15. B   **Difficulty:** Hard

Category: Problem Solving and Data Analysis / Rates, Ratios, Proportions, and Percentages

Getting to the Answer: Break the question into short steps (first part of trip, second part of trip, circling overhead). To get started, you'll need to find the distance for each part of the trip—the question only tells you the total distance. Then, use the formula Distance = rate × time to find how long the plane flew at 200 mph and then how long it flew at 450 mph.

First part of trip: $\frac{1}{4} \times 1{,}200 = 300$ mi
$$300 = 200t$$
$$t = \frac{300}{200} = 1.5 \text{ hours}$$
$$1.5 \times 60 = 90 \text{ minutes}$$

Second part of trip: $\frac{3}{4} \times 1{,}200 = 900$ mi
$$900 = 450t$$
$$t = \frac{900}{450} = 2 \text{ hours}$$
$$2 \times 60 = 120 \text{ minutes}$$

This means the plane flew for a total of 90 + 120 = 210 minutes. Next, add the time the plane circled overhead: 210 + 25 = 235 minutes. The total trip took 235 minutes (3 hours and 55 minutes), which means the plane landed at 8:30 + 3 hours = 11:30 + 55 minutes = 12:25 PM, (B).

16. A   **Difficulty:** Medium

Category: Passport to Advanced Math / Functions

Getting to the Answer: The range of a function is the set of possible outputs, or y-values on a graph. For all real values of any number t, the value of t^2 cannot be negative. This means the smallest possible value of t^2 is 0 and, consequently, the smallest possible value of $h(t)$ is $h(0) = \sqrt{0^2 + 9} = \sqrt{9} = 3$. Thus, the number 1 is not in the range of the function, making (A) correct.

You could also graph the function in your graphing calculator and examine the possible y-values. The graph follows here:

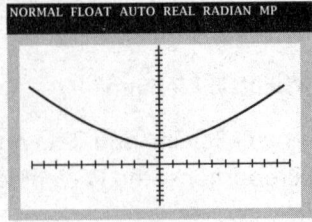

Notice that the lowest point on the graph is (0, 3), which tells you that the range of the function is $h(t) \geq 3$.

17. A   Difficulty: Medium

Category: Heart of Algebra / Systems of Linear Equations

Getting to the Answer: Graphically, the solution to a system of equations is the point or points where the graphs intersect. Whenever a graph with no grid-lines or axis labels is shown, you are usually interested primarily in the sign of the coordinates of a point, not the actual values. The graphs intersect in Quadrant 2 of the coordinate plane, so the x-value of the point of intersection (or a) is negative, and the y-value (or b) is positive. The question states that $a = -3b$, so you can eliminate B right away—the coordinates would have to be equal if their sum was 0. Now try Picking Numbers. Let $b = 1$, which means $a = -3$ and the sum of $a + b$ is -2, which is not one of the answer choices. Try another pair: If $b = 2$, then $a = -6$, and the sum is -4. This is still not one of the answer choices, but you should see a pattern—the x-coordinate will always overpower the y-coordinate, resulting in a negative sum, so the correct answer must be (A).

18. B   Difficulty: Medium

Category: Problem Solving and Data Analysis / Statistics and Probability

Getting to the Answer: When comparing two data sets for consistency, consider both the data center (mean or median) and the spread (standard deviation or range). Each set of data has a median of 0, and Thermostat A also has a mode of 0. Both of these measures indicate good test results. However, Thermostat A has a greater range of data. If the company chooses this thermostat, the cooling fan is likely to engage anywhere from –9 degrees below the target temperature to 10 degrees above the target temperature. Although this is within the safe temperature

range, it is not as consistent as Thermostat B, which engaged the fan within 6 degrees on either side of the target temperature. This means (B) is correct.

19. C   Difficulty: Medium

Category: Passport to Advanced Math / Quadratics

Getting to the Answer: When a quadratic function is written in factored form, you can find its zeros by setting each factor equal to 0 and solving for the variable. Each of the answer choices is written in factored form, so mentally solve each one by asking yourself what number would make each factor equal to 0. Then find the sum of the results:

Choice A: $3 + (-3) \neq -3$. Eliminate.

Choice B: $4 + (-1) \neq -3$. Eliminate.

Choice (C): $1 + (-4) = -3$, so (C) is correct.

Choice D: $6 + (-3) \neq -3$. Eliminate.

20. D   Difficulty: Hard

Category: Passport to Advanced Math / Functions

Getting to the Answer: A constant added or subtracted inside a function will shift the function left or right, while a constant added or subtracted from the outside will shift the function up or down. You're looking for the value of $p(0)$, but the graph shows $p(x) - 4$, which means the original graph has been shifted down 4 units. You'll need to find the y-value of the graph when $x = 0$, then add 4 to get back up to the original function. The graph passes through the point (0, 7), so $p(0) - 4 = 7$. Add 4 to both sides of the equation to get $p(0) = 7 + 4 = 11$, which is (D).

21. A   Difficulty: Medium

Category: Heart of Algebra / Linear Equations

Getting to the Answer: Sometimes writing an equation is the quickest route to answering a question. Assign a variable to the unknown, write the equation in words, and then translate from English into math. The unknown in this question is the number of times Geraldine can wrap the wire around the prism. Call this *n*. Now, write an equation in words: Total amount of wire equals distance around the prism times the number of wraps plus the extra on the ends. To fill in the numbers, you'll need to make a few calculations. Because the dimensions of the prism are given in inches, convert the amount of wire to inches as well: 18 ft = 18 × 12 = 216 inches. Next, figure out the distance around the prism using the picture. Don't forget, you have to go all the way around: 1.5 + 3.5 + 1.5 + 3.5 = 10 inches. Finally, read the question again to determine that the *extra on the ends* is 3 + 3 = 6 inches. Now you're ready to translate from English into math to write your equation, and then solve it.

$$216 = 10n + 6$$
$$210 = 10n$$
$$21 = n$$

Geraldine can wrap the wire around the prism 21 times, (A).

22. A Difficulty: Medium

Category: Problem Solving and Data Analysis / Statistics and Probability

Getting to the Answer: To find a percent change (increase or decrease), use the percent change formula:

$$\text{Percent change} = \frac{\text{new amount} - \text{original amount}}{\text{original amount}}$$

The question asks about the increase from July to August, so the original amount is the July harvest of squash and the new amount is the August harvest. Read the graph's key and the axis labels carefully. Each grid-line represents 5 tons, so the July squash harvest was 15 tons and the August harvest was 25 tons. Substitute these numbers into the percent change formula and simplify:

$$\text{Percent change} = \frac{\text{new amount} - \text{original amount}}{\text{original amount}}$$
$$= \frac{25 - 15}{15}$$
$$= \frac{10}{15} \approx 0.667$$

This is equal to an increase of about 67%, which is (A).

23. D Difficulty: Medium

Category: Problem Solving and Data Analysis / Rates, Ratios, Proportions, and Percentages

Getting to the Answer: Add reasonable numbers to the graph to help you answer the question. An example follows:

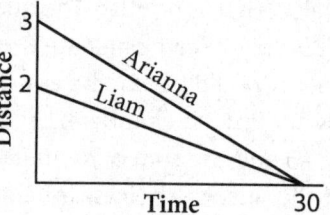

Use the numbers to help you evaluate each statement. It took Liam and Arianna each 30 minutes to walk home, so A and B are incorrect. Arianna walked 3 miles in 30 minutes, while Liam only walked 2 miles in 30 minutes; their rates are not the same, so C is also incorrect. This means (D) must be true. Arianna started out farther away than Liam, so she must have walked at a faster rate to arrive at home in the same amount of time.

24. B Difficulty: Medium

Category: Heart of Algebra / Linear Equations

Getting to the Answer: The slopes between sets of points that lie on the same line are equal. You can find the slope between points using the slope formula or by looking for patterns. Before immediately jumping to the slope formula, take a peek at the answer choices—all the *x*-coordinates of the points are multiples of 4, so looking for a pattern is the quickest way to answer this question. It may help to put all the points in a table (including those given in the question stem), with the *x*-coordinates arranged from smallest to largest, and then see which point doesn't fit the pattern.

x	y
−4	−8
0	−5
4	−1
8	1
12	4
16	7

Notice that all the *x*-coordinates increase by 4, while most of the *y*-coordinates increase by 3. For the slope between each pair of points to be equal, the *y*-coordinate at $x = 4$ would need to be −2, not −1, so the point given in (B) does not lie on the line.

25. A   Difficulty: Medium

Category: Problem Solving and Data Analysis / Statistics and Probability

Getting to the Answer: Identify which pieces of information from the table you need. The question asks for the probability that a randomly chosen person from the study is employed and has a college degree, so you need the total of both females and males with college degrees who are employed compared to all the participants in the study. There are 188 employed females with a college degree and 177 employed males with a college degree for a total of 365 employed people with a college degree out of 800 participants, so the probability is $\frac{365}{800}$, which reduces to $\frac{73}{160}$, (A).

26. B   Difficulty: Medium

Category: Problem Solving and Data Analysis / Scatterplots

Getting to the Answer: Translate from English into math: The number of cells in the original sample means the value of the function at 0 hours, or $f(0)$. The first *x*-value on the graph is 4, not 0, so

you'll need to use the values shown in the calculator screenshot to write an equation for the model. Notice that the *y*-values in the calculator screenshot double as the *x*-values increase by 1. This means that the model is an exponential growth function of the form $f(x) = f(0) \cdot 2^x$. Choose a point from the calculator screenshot such as (4, 136), substitute the values into the function, and solve for $f(0)$:

$$136 = f(0) \cdot (2)^4$$
$$136 = f(0) \cdot 16$$
$$\frac{136}{16} = f(0)$$
$$8.5 = f(0)$$

The *y*-axis title tells you that the numbers are given in thousands, so there were 8,500 white blood cells per microliter in the original sample, (B).

You could also work backward from the calculator screenshot by dividing by 2 four times (from 4 hours to 3 hours, 3 hours to 2 hours, 2 hours to 1 hour, and 1 hour to before the patient contracted the disease). The result is $136 \div 2^4 = 136 \div 16 = 8.5$, which in thousands is 8,500, (B).

27. D   Difficulty: Hard

Category: Additional Topics in Math / Geometry

Getting to the Answer: Drawing a sketch is the key to answering this question. Your sketch might look like the one below.

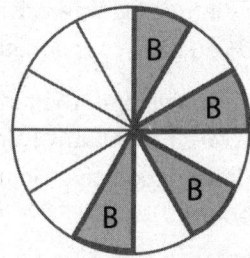

Notice that two radii and an arc form each section, so the amount of steel needed for one section is the length of the radius times 2, plus the length of the outer arc. Once you know this, you can simply multiply by 4.

You are given the total area, which means you can find the radius by substituting 64π for A in the area formula, $A = \pi r^2$.

$$64\pi = \pi r^2$$
$$64 = r^2$$
$$8 = r$$

For auctions, the arena is divided into 12 equal sections through the center, so divide 360 by 12 to find that the central angle measure for each section is 30°. Now use the arc length formula:

$$\frac{n°}{360°} \times 2\pi r = \frac{30°}{360°} \times 2\pi(8)$$
$$= \frac{1}{12} \times 16\pi$$
$$= \frac{4\pi}{3}$$

The amount of steel needed for one section is $8 + 8 + \frac{4\pi}{3} = 16 + \frac{4\pi}{3}$, so the amount needed for all four sections is $4\left(16 + \frac{4\pi}{3}\right) = 64 + \frac{16\pi}{3}$, which is (D).

28. A   Difficulty: Hard

Category: Heart of Algebra / Linear Equations

Getting to the Answer: To write the equation of a line, you need two things—the starting amount (y-intercept) and the rate of change (slope). Substitute these values into slope-intercept form of a line ($y = mx + b$), and you have your equation.

The initial amount of water in the tank on Saturday is 70 gallons, so you already know b. To find m, you'll need to use the information given in the question to write two data points.

The amount of water in the tank *depends* on how long Lena has been filling it, so the number of gallons is the dependent variable and time is the independent variable. This tells you that the data points should be written in the form (time, gallons). At time = 0 on Saturday, the number of gallons is 70, so the data point is (0, 70). After 1 hour and 50 min-

utes, which is 60 + 50 = 110 minutes, the tank is full (400 gallons), so another data point is (110, 400).

Now, use the slope formula to find that the rate of change is $\frac{400 - 70}{110 - 0} = \frac{330}{110} = 3$ gallons per minute. Substituting m and b into slope-intercept form results in the equation $y = 3x + 70$, so (A) is correct.

29. D   Difficulty: Hard

Category: Problem Solving and Data Analysis / Rates, Ratios, Proportions, and Percentages

Getting to the Answer: You need to find the ratio of small units to large units. You're given two ratios: small to medium and medium to large. Both of the given ratios contain medium size units, but the medium amounts (5 and 3) are not identical. To directly compare them, find a common multiple (15). Multiply each ratio by the factor that will make the number of medium units equal to 15.

small to medium: (3:5) × (3:3) = 9:15

medium to large: (3:2) × (5:5) = 15:10

Now that the number of medium units needed is the same in both ratios, you can merge the two ratios to compare small to large directly: 9:15:10. Therefore, the proper ratio of small units to large units is 9:10, which is (D).

30. A   Difficulty: Hard

Category: Passport to Advanced Math / Exponents

Getting to the Answer: Think of the rate given in the question in terms of the constant term you see on the right-hand side of the equation. Working together, the two air purifiers can clean the air in 7 hours. This is equivalent to saying that they can clean $\frac{1}{7}$ of the air in 1 hour. If $\frac{1}{7}$ is the portion of the air the two purifiers can clean *together* in 1 hour, then each term on the left side of the equation represents the portion that each purifier can clean *individually* in 1 hour. Because the new model is 3 times as fast as the older model, $\frac{3}{x}$ represents the portion of the air the new model can clean in 1 hour, and $\dfrac{1}{x}$ represents the portion of the air the older model can clean in 1 hour, which is (A).

31. 9/26 or .346   Difficulty: Easy

Category: Heart of Algebra / Linear Equations

Getting to the Answer: Distribute the fractions because the numbers inside each set of parentheses are evenly divisible by the denominators of the fractions by which they are being multiplied.

$$\frac{1}{3}(90x - 12) = \frac{1}{2}(8x + 10)$$
$$30x - 4 = 4x + 5$$
$$26x = 9$$
$$x = \frac{9}{26}$$

32. 4   Difficulty: Medium

Category: Passport to Advanced Math / Exponents

Getting to the Answer: When solving any type of equation, you should always think of inverse operations. The inverse of raising a quantity to the $\dfrac{5}{2}$ power is raising it to the $\dfrac{2}{5}$ power. Eliminate the exponent using inverse operations and then go from there.

$$n^{\frac{5}{2}} = 32$$
$$\left(n^{\frac{5}{2}}\right)^{\frac{2}{5}} = (32)^{\frac{2}{5}}$$
$$n = 32^{\frac{2}{5}}$$

Now, you have two choices—you can enter this value into your calculator as 32^(2/5) or you can evaluate the number using rules of exponents:

$$32^{\frac{2}{5}} = (\sqrt[5]{32})^2 = 2^2 = 4$$

33. 801   Difficulty: Hard

Category: Problem Solving and Data Analysis / Rates, Ratios, Proportions, and Percentages

Getting to the Answer: Draw a chart or diagram detailing the various price reductions for each 30-day period. You'll need to make several calculations, so don't round until the final answer.

Date	% of Most Recent Price	Resulting Price
Jan. 15	100 − 40% = 60%	$1,848 × 0.6 = $1,108.80
Feb. 1	100 − 15% = 85%	$1,108.80 × 0.85 = $942.48
March 1	100 − 15% = 85%	$942.48 × 0.85 = $801.108

You can stop here because the item was sold on March 10th. Before gridding in your answer, check that $801 is not less than 30% of the original price: 0.30 × $1,848 = $554.40. It's not, so the final selling price, rounded to the nearest whole dollar, was $801.

34. 2/3 or .666 or .667   Difficulty: Hard

Category: Additional Topics in Math / Trigonometry

Getting to the Answer: Two angles of the triangle have equal measures, so the triangle is isosceles, which means that drawing an altitude from the top to the base will bisect the base, resulting in two smaller right triangles as shown here:

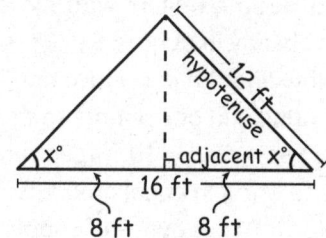

Now, use $\cos x° = \dfrac{\text{adjacent}}{\text{hypotenuse}}$ to find that $b = \dfrac{8}{12}$, which can be simplified to $\dfrac{2}{3}$.

35. 3.5 or 7/2   **Difficulty:** Hard

Category: Heart of Algebra / Linear Equations

Getting to the Answer: Remember that parallel lines have the same slope. Use the slope formula $m = \dfrac{y_2 - y_1}{x_2 - x_1}$ to find the slope of $\overline{CD}$. Because $\overline{CD}$ passes through the points (0, 0) and (2, 4.5), its slope is $\dfrac{4.5 - 0}{2 - 0} = 2.25$. Line B has the same slope and passes through (0, −1), so you can use the slope formula again to find the y-coordinate of the given point, (2, y).

$$2.25 = \frac{y - (-1)}{2 - 0}$$

$$2.25 = \frac{y + 1}{2}$$

$$4.5 = y + 1$$

$$3.5 = y$$

The y-coordinate of the point is 3.5.

36. 3/10   **Difficulty:** Hard

Category: Problem Solving and Data Analysis / Rates, Ratios, Proportions, and Percentages

Getting to the Answer: Whenever rates are given in different units, start by converting to the same units. In most cases, converting to the smaller unit avoids fractions and decimals. Start with nickel because the weight is already in ounces: $10.08 ÷ 24 = $0.42 per ounce. Now find the per-ounce rate for copper. There are 16 ounces in one pound, so three pounds is 48 ounces: $8.64 ÷ 48 = $0.18 per ounce. So, if a person were to bring in equal amounts of each, he would receive $0.18 per ounce of copper and $0.42 per ounce of nickel. To find the fractional portion he would receive from the copper, set up a comparison between the amount received for copper and the total amount received, $0.18 + $0.42 = $0.60. The portion of the total amount he receives from copper would be $\dfrac{0.18}{0.60}$, which reduces to $\dfrac{3}{10}$.

37. 3   **Difficulty:** Easy

Category: Problem Solving and Data Analysis / Scatterplots

Getting to the Answer: Each grid-line along the vertical axis represents 5 units, so look for points that are at least two grid-lines away from the line of best fit. The people who have BMIs of 20, 25, and 28 have LDLs that are 10 or more mg/dL greater than the LDLs predicted by the line of best fit. This represents 3 people.

38. 24   **Difficulty:** Medium

Category: Problem Solving and Data Analysis / Scatterplots

Getting to the Answer: A line of best fit serves as an approximation of data from which you can estimate an output for a given input (or vice versa). The key is in reading the axis labels carefully. To determine the requested BMI, find the LDL level of 140 (which is already reported in mg/dL) on the vertical axis. The question says "Based on the line of best fit," so trace over to the line (*not* to the closest data point) and then down to the corresponding value on the horizontal axis, which represents BMI. You should end up just slightly to the right of the 24 line. Be sure to follow directions. The closest whole number approximation is 24.

ESSAY TEST RUBRIC

The Essay Demonstrates ...

4—Advanced	• **(Reading)** A strong ability to comprehend the source text, including its central ideas and important details and how they interrelate; and effectively use evidence (quotations, paraphrases, or both) from the source text. • **(Analysis)** A strong ability to evaluate the author's use of evidence, reasoning, and/or stylistic and persuasive elements, and/or other features of the student's own choosing; make good use of relevant, sufficient, and strategically chosen support for the claims or points made in the student's essay; and focus consistently on features of the source text that are most relevant to addressing the task. • **(Writing)** A strong ability to provide a precise central claim; create an effective organization that includes an introduction and conclusion, as well as a clear progression of ideas; successfully employ a variety of sentence structures; use precise word choice; maintain a formal style and objective tone; and show command of the conventions of standard written English so that the essay is free of errors.
3—Proficient	• **(Reading)** Satisfactory ability to comprehend the source text, including its central ideas and important details and how they interrelate; and use evidence (quotations, paraphrases, or both) from the source text. • **(Analysis)** Satisfactory ability to evaluate the author's use of evidence, reasoning, and/or stylistic and persuasive elements, and/or other features of the student's own choosing; make use of relevant and sufficient support for the claims or points made in the student's essay; and focus primarily on features of the source text that are most relevant to addressing the task. • **(Writing)** Satisfactory ability to provide a central claim; create an organization that includes an introduction and conclusion, as well as a clear progression of ideas; employ a variety of sentence structures; use precise word choice; maintain an appropriate formal style and objective tone; and show control of the conventions of standard written English so that the essay is free of significant errors.

Practice Tests

2—Partial	• **(Reading)** Limited ability to comprehend the source text, including its central ideas and important details and how they interrelate; and use evidence (quotations, paraphrases, or both) from the source text. • **(Analysis)** Limited ability to evaluate the author's use of evidence, reasoning, and/or stylistic and persuasive elements, and/or other features of the student's own choosing; make use of support for the claims or points made in the student's essay; and focus on relevant features of the source text. • **(Writing)** Limited ability to provide a central claim; create an effective organization for ideas; employ a variety of sentence structures; use precise word choice; maintain an appropriate style and tone; or show control of the conventions of standard written English, resulting in certain errors that detract from the quality of the writing.
1—Inadequate	• **(Reading)** Little or no ability to comprehend the source text or use evidence from the source text. • **(Analysis)** Little or no ability to evaluate the author's use of evidence, reasoning, and/or stylistic and persuasive elements; choose support for claims or points; or focus on relevant features of the source text. • **(Writing)** Little or no ability to provide a central claim, organization, or progression of ideas; employ a variety of sentence structures; use precise word choice; maintain an appropriate style and tone; or show control of the conventions of standard written English, resulting in numerous errors that undermine the quality of the writing.

SAMPLE ESSAY RESPONSE #1 (ADVANCED SCORE)

Anyone who watches NFL football every Sunday is most likely aware that the athletes on the field make a significant amount of money for their efforts. The NFL generates a lot of income from television contracts, corporate sponsors, and advertisers, and the teams themselves benefit from ticket and merchandise sales. The players in turn are paid market-appropriate salaries. Anyone who watches college football games on Saturday will see similar, if slightly younger athletes, yet how much are those players making? The author of this article correctly notes these players don't earn a salary, and that's something he would like to correct. His argument? College athletes deserve compensation for their work just like any other employee.

The author begins by detailing how much money corporations, athletic conferences, and universities make from advertising and sponsor revenue. The Pacific-12 conference, for example, "signed television rights deals worth $3 billion." Speaking of television, CBS and Turner Broadcasting made a lot of money as well—thirty seconds of commercial advertising during the Final Four cost $700,000. Schools with successful programs also do well. The article points out that the University of Texas football program netted $77.9 million in 2011–2012.

The author uses this evidence to portray corporations, athletic conferences, and universities as the "unscrupulous tycoons from a Dickens novel." Those familiar with Dickens can picture more than one wealthy character who doesn't care for the working poor left eking out miserable lives in relative poverty. And who are these working poor? Student athletes, of course! The author uses the Dickens metaphor to convince the reader that corporations, athletic conferences, and universities do not have the student athletes' interests at heart. He then pivots to how much the athletes make for their efforts on behalf of the "unscrupulous tycoons"—absolutely nothing.

How much is the average student scholarship worth? According to the author, most leave a few thousand dollars in yearly out-of-pocket expenses to the student in spite of an average "forty hours a week" dedicated to their sport. And if an athlete is unable to play due to injury, even that scholarship money can be revoked. The author uses this information to compare a student athlete with an employee who benefits from federal and state labor laws. The comparison is painfully clear and made even more so when the author points out that student athletes do not have the right to unionize.

Throughout his essay, the author has effectively painted a Dickensian picture in which student athletes literally sweat, strain, and toil under the watchful eye of their universities, while those in power rake in millions of dollars. The evidence presented convincingly leads the reader to one conclusion: that student athletes deserve to be compensated.

SAMPLE ESSAY RESPONSE #2 (PROFICIENT SCORE)

Anyone who watches NFL football Sunday knows that those players make a lot of money. They make so much money because the teams and the league make money from television and advertising. But what about college football players or other college athletes? They don't make any money at all. The author thinks that isn't right. He argues that student athletes should get paid for their work just like anyone else.

The author talks about how much money schools, conferences, and corporations make off of college sports. It's a lot of money. For example, a television deal was worth $3 billion for the Pacific-12 conference, and it cost $700,000 for a television commercial during the Final Four basketball tournament. The author includes this to make the point that other people make a lot of money, but student athletes don't. This helps the reader feel some sympathy for the players and supports the author's argument that they should be paid.

The author then turns to a comparison of student athletes and employees. Student athletes don't earn salaries. They do get a scholarship, but that still leaves many of them short of money to pay the bills. They work forty hours a week. If they are hurt, then they may lose their scholarship because they can't play. The author talks about this to compare how student athletes earn money with how typical employees earn money. Employees have legal rights, but student athletes don't really have any. This is a good comparison, and it makes the reader believe that student athletes should be paid like employees, which is the author's concluding point.

Answers & Explanations

CHAPTER 2

PRACTICE

8. D **Difficulty:** Hard

Category: Heart of Algebra / Linear Equations

Getting to the Answer: Pay attention to the order in which the changes to the graph occur. The question states that the downward shift of 2 units occurs first, making the new y-intercept $-\dfrac{3}{2}$. A reflection over the x-axis follows, which changes the y-intercept to $\dfrac{3}{2}$ and makes the slope $\dfrac{7}{4}$. The only graph that correctly depicts these changes is (D). Beware of C; this results from a reflection over the y-axis, not the x-axis. The graphs below visualize each change.

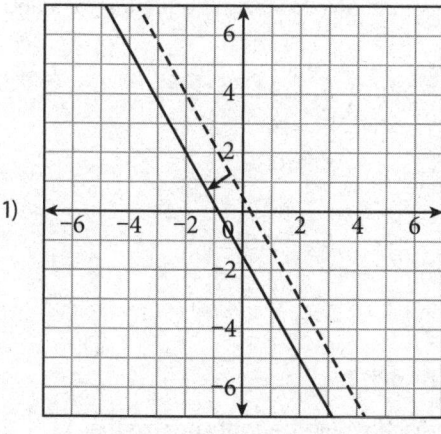

1)

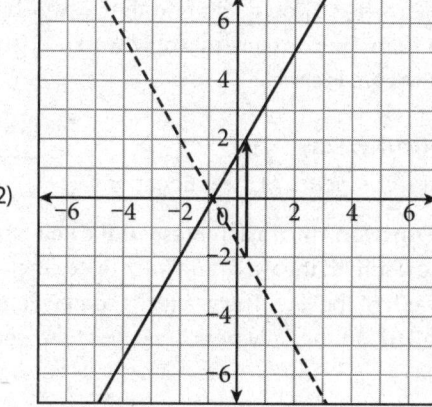

2)

9. C **Difficulty:** Medium

Category: Heart of Algebra / Linear Equations

Getting to the Answer: Look closely; buried in the text are two sets of coordinates you can use. The question states that admission was $2 when the admission charge was first implemented and increased to $2.50 after 3 years, making your coordinates (0, 2) and (3, 2.5). The slope of the line passing through these is $m = \dfrac{2.5 - 2}{3 - 0} = \dfrac{0.5}{3} = \dfrac{1}{6}$. Eliminate A and D. Because the admission fee started at $2, 2 is the y-intercept, so the full equation is $y = \dfrac{c}{6} + 2$. Choice (C) is correct.

Because the question says "three years ago," it may be tempting to use (−3, 2) and (0, 2.5) as your coordinates. Think about what that would mean: The first admission charge would be $2.50, as it's impossible to have a negative year. This contradicts the question stem, so B is incorrect.

PERFORM

10. A **Difficulty:** Easy

Category: Heart of Algebra / Linear Equations

Getting to the Answer: Think about what happens to the slope of a line if you're merely moving the line around the coordinate plane. Any shift of a line, whether it's up, down, left, right, or some combination of these, will not change the line's slope. The slope of the given line is −5 (the coefficient of x), and the slope does not change, so (A) is correct.

11. 36 **Difficulty:** Medium

Category: Heart of Algebra / Linear Equations

Getting to the Answer: That you're asked to find an expression rather than a variable value means there's likely a shortcut. Start by eliminating the fractions. A common multiple of 4 and 3 is 12, so multiply both sides of the equation by that. Once the fractions are gone, move both variable terms to the left side and try to make it look like the desired expression.

$$12\left(\frac{3}{4}y = 6 - \frac{1}{3}c\right)$$
$$9y = 72 - 4c$$
$$4c + 9y = 72$$
$$2c + \frac{9}{2}y = 36$$

The expression on the left side is precisely what you're looking for, so grid in 36.

12. A   Difficulty: Hard

Category: Heart of Algebra / Linear Equations

Getting to the Answer: Don't panic over the presence of m. Just solve for y, then think about what kind of graph it can have. Start by distributing m on the right, then move all terms to the left:

$$x - y = m(2x + y)$$
$$x - y = 2mx + my$$
$$x - 2mx - y - my = 0$$

Continue by factoring out x and y, then move any terms without y back to the right:

$$x(1 - 2m) + y(-1 - m) = 0$$
$$y(-1 - m) = -x(1 - 2m)$$

Divide by $(-1 - m)$, then factor out -1 from the denominator and cancel:

$$y = \frac{-x(1 - 2m)}{(-1 - m)} = \frac{-x(1 - 2m)}{-(1 + m)} = \frac{1 - 2m}{1 + m}x$$

Don't worry about how messy the right side looks yet; for now, you just need to realize that it's merely x multiplied by a complicated coefficient. Because the equation is now solved for y, you have an equation of a line. The messy coefficient is the slope, and because there's no added (or subtracted) constant, the y-intercept is 0. You can eliminate B (not a line) and D ($b \neq 0$) based on this.

Examine the remaining choices more closely: They only differ by the sign of their slope. To determine which is correct, pick a value for m between 0 and $\frac{1}{2}$ (but not 0 or $\frac{1}{2}$ themselves), and plug it into the slope expression.

If $m = \frac{1}{4}$, for instance, then the slope would be:

$$\frac{\left(1 - 2 \times \frac{1}{4}\right)}{\left(1 + \frac{1}{4}\right)} = \frac{\left(1 - \frac{1}{2}\right)}{\frac{5}{4}} = \frac{1}{2} \times \frac{4}{5} = \frac{2}{5}$$

Because the slope of this line is positive, (A), which is the only remaining choice with a positive slope, is correct.

ON YOUR OWN

1. C   Difficulty: Easy

Category: Heart of Algebra / Linear Equations

Getting to the Answer: Don't let this fairly simple question fool you. Just because 5 and −5 are opposites, this does not mean the value on the right-hand side of the equal sign will be the opposite of 11. Solve for x, then substitute that value into the second equation for x and simplify.

$$2x + 5 = 11$$
$$2x = 6$$
$$x = 3$$

$$2x - 5 = 2(3) - 5$$
$$= 6 - 5$$
$$= 1$$

Therefore, (C) is correct.

A quicker approach would be to recognize that $2x - 5$ is 10 less than $2x + 5$, so you could find the answer by subtracting 10 from 11. However, this only works when the variable terms are identical.

2. B   Difficulty: Easy

Category: Heart of Algebra / Linear Equations

Getting to the Answer: The x-axis represents the number of lightbulbs, so find 1 on the x-axis and trace up to where it meets the graph of the line. The y-value is somewhere between \$1 and \$2, so the only possible correct answer choice is \$1.80.

You could also find the unit rate by calculating the slope of the line using two of the points shown on the graph: The graph rises 9 units and runs 5 units from one point to the next, so the slope is $\frac{9}{5}$, or 1.80, which means (B) is correct.

3. D   Difficulty: Medium

Category: Heart of Algebra / Linear Equations

Getting to the Answer: Use the information in the question to write your own expression, and then look for the answer choice that matches. Simplify your expression only if you don't find a match. If a couple earns $50 *per half-hour* that they dance, then they earn 50 × 2 = $100 *per hour*. Multiply this amount times the number of hours (not including the first 3 hours). This can be expressed as 100(h − 3). This is not one of the answer choices, so simplify by distributing to get 100h − 300, which is (D).

If you're struggling with the algebra, try Picking Numbers. Pick a number of hours a couple might dance, like 5. They don't earn anything for the first 3 hours, but they earn $50 per half-hour for the last 2 hours, which is 50 times 4 half-hours, or $200. Now, find the expression that gives you an answer of $200 when $h = 5$ hours: 100(5) − 300 = 500 − 300 = 200.

4. D   Difficulty: Medium

Category: Heart of Algebra / Linear Equations

Getting to the Answer: Take a quick peek at the answer choices. The equations are given in slope-intercept form, so start by finding the slope. Substitute two pairs of values from the table (try to pick easy ones if possible) into the slope formula, $m = \dfrac{y_2 - y_1}{x_2 - x_1}$. Keep in mind that the projected number of pounds sold *depends* on the price, so the price is the independent variable (x) and the projected number is the dependent variable (y). Using the points (1.2, 15,000) and (2, 5,000), the slope is:

$$m = \frac{5,000 - 15,000}{2 - 1.20}$$
$$m = \frac{-10,000}{0.8}$$
$$m = -12,500$$

This means you can eliminate A and B because the slope is not correct. Don't let B fool you—the projected number of pounds sold goes *down* as the price goes *up*, so there is an inverse relationship, which means the slope must be negative. To choose between C and (D), you could find the y-intercept of the line, but this is a fairly time-intensive

process. Instead, choose the easiest pair of values from the table, (2, 5,000), and substitute into C and (D) only. Choice (D) is correct because 5,000 = −12,500(2) + 30,000 is a true statement.

5. D   Difficulty: Hard

Category: Heart of Algebra / Linear Equations

Getting to the Answer: If a linear equation has infinitely many solutions, the variable terms will cancel out, leaving a number that is equal to itself (which is always true). Start by simplifying both sides of the equation using the distributive property.

$$2\left(x - \frac{5}{2}\right) = c\left(\frac{4}{5}x - 2\right)$$
$$2x - 5 = \frac{4c}{5}x - 2c$$

Because the constant terms must be equal, set $-5 = -2c$ and solve for c to get $c = \dfrac{5}{2}$, which means (D) is correct.

Note that you could also set the variable terms equal to each other and solve for c, but the manipulations would be more difficult.

6. C   Difficulty: Hard

Category: Heart of Algebra / Linear Equations

Getting to the Answer: As written, the equation doesn't tell you a lot about the graph, but you should notice that there are no exponents on the variables, which means the exponents are all equal to 1. This means the equation is linear and the graph must be a line, so you can eliminate D right away (it is an absolute value equation, not a linear equation). To choose the correct line, rearrange the equation so that it is in slope-intercept form, $y = mx + b$. To do this, first collect the y-terms on the left side of the equation. Rearranging the equation results in the following:

$$y = ay + ax + x + 1$$
$$y - ay = ax + x + 1$$
$$y(1 - a) = x(a + 1) + 1$$
$$y = \frac{a + 1}{1 - a}x + \frac{1}{1 - a}$$

This manipulation reveals a linear equation with a slope of $\dfrac{a + 1}{1 - a}$ and a y-intercept of $\dfrac{1}{1 - a}$. It is given in the question that $a > 1$, so the quantity $a + 1$ is positive, and $1 - a$ is negative, resulting in a negative slope and a negative y-intercept. Of the choices given, only the graph in (C) satisfies these conditions.

7. 18   Difficulty: Easy
Category: Heart of Algebra / Linear Equations

Getting to the Answer: Clear the fractions first by multiplying both sides of the equation by 8. Then solve for x using inverse operations:

$$\frac{7}{8}(n - 6) = \frac{21}{2}$$

$$8\left[\frac{7}{8}(n - 6)\right] = 8\left[\frac{21}{2}\right]$$

$$7(n - 6) = 4(21)$$

$$7n - 42 = 84$$

$$7n = 126$$

$$n = 18$$

8. 70   Difficulty: Hard
Category: Heart of Algebra / Linear Equations

Getting to the Answer: Because 40 pounds is not shown on the graph, you need more information. In a real-world scenario, the y-intercept of a graph usually represents a flat fee or a starting amount. The slope of the line represents a unit rate, such as the cost per pound to airmail the box.

The y-intercept of the graph is 10, so the flat fee is $10. To find the cost per pound (the unit rate), substitute two points from the graph into the slope formula. Using the points (0, 10) and (4, 16), the cost per pound is $\frac{16 - 10}{4 - 0} = \frac{6}{4} = 1.5$, which means it costs $1.50 per pound to airmail a box. The total cost to airmail a 40-pound box is $10 + 1.50(40) = \$10 + \$60 = \$70$. Grid in 70.

9. C   Difficulty: Easy
Category: Heart of Algebra / Linear Equations

Getting to the Answer: Try to picture in your head what "increase in property values starts to slow down" would look like. It doesn't say the values start to decrease, but rather that the increase is not as fast.

An increasing line (one with a positive slope) indicates increasing property values. The steepness of the line (the actual *value* of the slope) indicates how fast the values

are increasing. The second line segment in the graph (between $t = 8$ and $t = 16$) still shows a positive slope, but one that is less steep than the first segment, so the increase in property values starts to slow down at $t = 8$, which is the year $2014 + 8 = 2022$, (C).

10. B   Difficulty: Easy
Category: Heart of Algebra / Linear Equations

Getting to the Answer: Read the axis labels carefully. The y-intercept is the point at which $x = 0$, which means the number of songs purchased is 0. The y-intercept is (0, 20), so the cost is $20 before buying any songs, and therefore most likely represents a flat membership fee for joining the service. Choice (B) is correct.

11. C   Difficulty: Easy
Category: Heart of Algebra / Linear Equations

Getting to the Answer: When writing a linear equation to represent a real-world scenario, a flat rate is a constant while a unit rate is always multiplied by the independent variable. You can identify the unit rate by looking for words like *per* or *for each*.

Because the amount Andrew gets paid daily, $120, is a flat rate that doesn't depend on the number of cruises he books, 120 should be the constant in the equation. This means you can eliminate B and D. The clue "for each cruise" tells you to multiply $25 by the number of cruises he books (c), so the equation is $d = 25c + 120$, making (C) correct.

12. A   Difficulty: Medium
Category: Heart of Algebra / Linear Equations

Getting to the Answer: This question has multiple fractions, so clear the $\frac{8}{5}$ by multiplying both sides of the equation by its reciprocal, $\frac{5}{8}$. Then, because the answers are given in decimal form, change the other fraction to a decimal by dividing the numerator by the denominator.

$$\frac{8}{5}\left(x + \frac{33}{12}\right) = 16$$

$$\frac{5}{8} \times \left[\frac{8}{5}\left(x + \frac{33}{12}\right)\right] = \frac{5}{8} \times 16$$

$$x + 2.75 = 10$$

$$x = 7.25$$

Choice (A) is correct.

13. C   Difficulty: Medium
Category: Heart of Algebra / Linear Equations

Getting to the Answer: Because the equation represents the balance if Henry deposits his paycheck for x weeks, then his paycheck amount must be multiplied by the number of weeks he works. The only two factors in the equation being multiplied are 360 and x, so 360 must be the amount of his paycheck. This means you can eliminate A and D. The other number in the equation, -126.13, is a constant, which represents a starting amount. Because the constant is negative, Henry must have had a negative balance in his account before setting up the direct deposit, which means he had overdrawn the account. Thus, (C) is correct.

14. C   Difficulty: Medium
Category: Heart of Algebra / Linear Equations

Getting to the Answer: Use the graph to identify the y-intercept and the slope of the line, and then write an equation in slope-intercept form, $y = mx + b$. Once you have your equation, look for the answer choice that matches. The line crosses the y-axis at $(0, -4)$ so the y-intercept (b) is -4. The line rises 1 unit for every 3 units that it runs to the right, so the slope (m) is $\frac{1}{3}$. The equation of the line is $y = \frac{1}{3}x - 4$, which matches (C).

You could also graph each of the answer choices in your calculator to see which one matches the given graph, but this is not the most time-efficient strategy. You also have to be very careful when entering fractions—to graph (C), for example, you would enter $(1/3)x - 4$.

15. A   Difficulty: Hard
Category: Heart of Algebra / Linear Equations

Getting to the Answer: The question tells you that the functions are all linear, so start by finding the rate of change (the slope, m) using any two pairs of values from the table and the slope formula. Next, substitute the slope and any pair of values from the table, such as $(10, 34)$, into the equation $f(x) = mx + b$, and solve for b. Finally, use the value of m and b to write the function.

$$m = \frac{y_2 - y_1}{x_2 - x_1} = \frac{64 - 34}{30 - 10} = \frac{30}{20} = 1.5$$

You can stop right there! Only Choice (A) has a slope of 1.5, so it must be the correct answer.

16. C   Difficulty: Hard
Category: Heart of Algebra / Linear Equations

Getting to the Answer: Let v represent the number of visits. The question asks when the two memberships will cost the same, so write an equation that sets the total membership costs equal to each other. The first membership type costs $325 for unlimited visits, so write 325 on one side of the equal sign. The second type costs $8 per visit (not including the first 5 visits), or $8(v - 5)$, plus a flat $125 enrollment fee, so write $8(v - 5) + 125$ on the other side of the equal sign. Solve for v:

$$325 = 8(v - 5) + 125$$
$$325 = 8v - 40 + 125$$
$$240 = 8v$$
$$30 = v$$

Choice (C) is correct.

17. D   Difficulty: Hard
Category: Heart of Algebra / Linear Equations

Getting to the Answer: If a linear equation has no solution, the variable terms will cancel out, leaving a false statement that consists of two numbers that are not equal to each other. First, check to see if the variables cancel out. In A and B, they don't, so eliminate these choices. To decide between C and (D), check the constant after both sides of the equation have been simplified. If the constants are equal, then the equation has an infinite number of solutions (because a number is always equal to itself). If they are not equal, then the equation has no solution. Choice (D) is correct because:

$$6\left(\frac{2}{3}x + 5\right) = 4x + 5$$
$$4x + 30 = 4x + 5$$
$$30 \neq 5$$

18. B   Difficulty: Hard
Category: Heart of Algebra / Linear Equations

Getting to the Answer: The key to answering this question is determining how many jumps land across each line. If Vera gets 7 jumps total and x jumps land over the farther line, the rest, or $7 - x$, must land over the closer line. Now, write the expression in words: points per farther line (10) times number of jumps landing over the farther line (x), plus points per closer line (5) times number of jumps landing over the closer line $(7 - x)$. Next, translate the words into numbers, variables, and operations: $10x + 5(7 - x)$. This is not one of the answer choices, so simplify the expression by distributing the 5 and then combining like terms: $10x + 5(7 - x) = 10x + 35 - 5x = 5x + 35$, so the function is $f(x) = 5x + 35$, making (B) correct.

19. D   Difficulty: Medium
Category: Heart of Algebra / Linear Equations

Getting to the Answer: Consider each choice systematically, using the numbers on the figure to help you evaluate each statement.

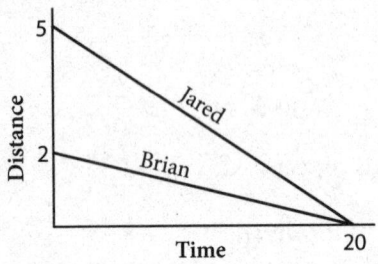

It took Brian and Jared each 20 minutes to bike home so A and B are false. Jared biked 5 miles in 20 minutes, while Brian only biked 2 miles in 20 minutes; their rates are not the same, so C is false. This means (D) must be true. Jared starts out farther away than Brian, so Jared must have biked at a faster rate to arrive home in the same amount of time.

20. B   Difficulty: Hard
Category: Heart of Algebra / Linear Equations

Getting to the Answer: You aren't given any numbers in this question, so make some up. Sketch a quick graph of any simple linear equation that has a positive y-intercept (because it is given that $b > 0$). Then, change the sign of the y-intercept and sketch the new graph on the same coordinate plane. Pick a simple equation that you can sketch quickly, such as $y = x + 3$, and then change the sign of b. The new equation is $y = x - 3$. Sketch both graphs. The second line is shifted down 3 units, twice, or $b \times 2$ units. The graph that follows illustrates this.

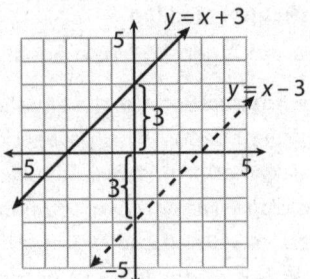

If you're not convinced, try another pair of equations. Choice (B) is correct.

CHAPTER 3

PRACTICE

7. A   Difficulty: Medium
Category: Heart of Algebra / Systems of Linear Equations

Getting to the Answer: Use the Kaplan Strategy for Translating English into Math to make sense of the situation. First, define your variables: w for wooden and c for crystal are good choices. Breaking apart the question, you know the jewelry artist bought 127 beads total. You're also told each wooden bead costs $0.20 ($0.2w$) and each crystal bead costs $0.50 ($0.5c$), as well as the fact that she spent $41 total. You'll have two equations: one relating the number of wooden beads and crystal beads, and a second relating the costs associated with each.

$$w + c = 127$$
$$0.2w + 0.5c = 41$$

Either combination or substitution is a good choice for solving this system. Both are shown here:

Combination:

$$-0.5(w + c = 127) \rightarrow -0.5w - 0.5c = -63.5$$

$$\begin{array}{r} -0.5w - 0.5c = -63.5 \\ + \ 0.2w + 0.5c = 41 \\ \hline -0.3w = -22.5 \\ w = 75 \end{array}$$

Substitution:

$$w + c = 127 \rightarrow c = 127 - w$$
$$0.2w + 0.5(127 - w) = 41$$
$$0.2w + 63.5 - 0.5w = 41$$
$$-0.3w = -22.5$$
$$w = 75$$
$$75 + c = 127 \rightarrow c = 52$$

Be careful here: The question asks for the difference in the amount spent on each type of bead, not the difference in the quantity of each type. Multiply the bead counts by the correct pricing to get $15 for the wooden beads and $26 for the crystal beads. Take the difference to get $11, which is (A).

8. 59   Difficulty: Medium
Category: Heart of Algebra / Systems of Linear Equations

Getting to the Answer: You're asked for the value of an expression rather than the value of one of the variables, so there must be a shortcut. Start by rearranging the two equations so that variables and constants are aligned:

$$x + y = -15$$
$$\frac{x}{2} + \frac{5y}{2} = 37$$

Clear the fractions in the second equation, and then add the equations:

$$2\left(\frac{x}{2} + \frac{5y}{2} = 37\right) \rightarrow x + 5y = 74$$

$$\begin{array}{r} x + y = -15 \\ + \ x + 5y = 74 \\ \hline 2x + 6y = 59 \end{array}$$

This is precisely what the question asks for, so you're done! Grid in 59 and move on.

PERFORM

9. B   Difficulty: Hard
Category: Heart of Algebra / Systems of Linear Equations

Getting to the Answer: A system of equations that has infinitely many solutions describes a single line. Therefore, the equations are dependent, and correct manipulation of one will yield the other. Because q is the coefficient of x in the second equation, look for a way to make the coefficient of y equal to that in the first equation. This can be done by multiplying the second equation by -9:

$$-9\left(qx - \frac{y}{3} = -2\right) \rightarrow -9qx + 3y = 18$$

The y terms and constants in the second equation now match those in the first; all that's left is to set the coefficients of x equal to each other and solve for q:

$$-9q = 6 \rightarrow q = -\frac{6}{9} = -\frac{2}{3}.$$ Choice (B) is correct.

10. 3/17 Difficulty: Medium
Category: Heart of Algebra / Systems of Linear Equations

Getting to the Answer: None of the coefficients in either equation is 1, so using combination is the best strategy here.

Examine the coefficients of x: They don't share any factors, so multiply each equation by the coefficient from the other equation, remembering to make one of them negative:

$$-5(12x + 15y = 249) \rightarrow -60x - 75y = -1{,}245$$
$$12(5x + 13y = 124) \rightarrow 60x + 156y = 1{,}488$$

Add the resulting equations:

$$
\begin{array}{r}
-60x - 75y = -1{,}245 \\
+\ 60x + 156y = 1{,}488 \\
\hline
81y = 243 \\
y = 3
\end{array}
$$

Don't stop yet; you need x so you can determine the value of $\dfrac{y}{x}$. Substitute 3 for y in one of the original equations:

$$5x + 13(3) = 124$$
$$5x + 39 = 124$$
$$5x = 85$$
$$x = 17$$

Plug your x- and y-values into $\dfrac{y}{x}$ to get $\dfrac{3}{17}$. Grid in 3/17.

11. C   Difficulty: Hard
Category: Heart of Algebra / Systems of Linear Equations

Getting to the Answer: Write equations to represent the profit generated by selling each type of pizza. You're told The Works sells for $17 each and that its ingredients cost the pizzeria $450 per week. This means weekly profit generated by this pizza's sales can be represented by the equation $y = 17x - 450$. Do the same for The Hawaiian: Each one sells for $13, but the pizzeria loses $310 to pay for ingredients each week. Therefore, weekly profits from this pizza can be represented by $y = 13x - 310$. To determine the point at which profits from one pizza overtake the other, set the two equations equal to each other and solve:

$$17x - 450 = 13x - 310$$
$$4x = 140$$
$$x = 35$$

Although ingredients for The Works cost more, the pizza's higher price tag means its profits will eventually surpass those of The Hawaiian. This will occur after the pizzeria sells 35 of each, making (C) correct. Be careful of D; 145 is the y-value when $x = 35$.

ON YOUR OWN

1. A   Difficulty: Easy
Category: Heart of Algebra / Systems of Linear Equations

Getting to the Answer: The solution to a system of equations shown graphically is the point of intersection. Read the axis labels carefully. Each grid-line represents 2 units. The two lines intersect at the point $(-6, -6)$, so $A + B = -6 + (-6) = -12$, which means (A) is correct.

2. C   Difficulty: Medium
Category: Heart of Algebra / Systems of Linear Equations

Getting to the Answer: Because x has a coefficient of 1 in the second equation, solve the system using substitution. Before you select your answer, make sure you found the right quantity (the difference of x and y).

First, solve the second equation for x:

$$x - 5y = 2$$
$$x = 2 + 5y$$
$$4(2 + 5y) + 3y = 14 - y$$
$$8 + 20y + 3y = 14 - y$$
$$8 + 23y = 14 - y$$
$$24y = 6$$
$$y = \frac{6}{24} = \frac{1}{4}$$

Next, substitute this value back into $x = 2 + 5y$ and simplify:

$$x = 2 + 5\left(\frac{1}{4}\right)$$
$$x = \frac{8}{4} + \frac{5}{4}$$
$$x = \frac{13}{4}$$

Finally, subtract $x - y$ to find the difference:

$$\frac{13}{4} - \frac{1}{4} = \frac{12}{4} = 3, \ (C)$$

3. C   Difficulty: Medium
Category: Heart of Algebra / Systems of Linear Equations

Getting to the Answer: Graphically, a system of linear equations that has no solution consists of two parallel lines that will never intersect. They have the same slope but different y-intercepts. A system of linear equations that has infinite solutions is actually the same line, just represented in different ways. Graphically, one line would sit on top of the other, intersecting itself an infinite number of times. These lines would have the same slope *and* the same y-intercept. Without additional information, it is not possible to determine whether the system that Charlie graphed has no solutions or an infinite number of solutions. Therefore, the solution to Charlie's system of equations depends on the y-intercepts of the lines and (C) is correct.

4. C   Difficulty: Medium

Category: Heart of Algebra / Systems of Linear Equations

Getting to the Answer: If the graphs intersect at $(-3, 1)$, then the solution to the system is $x = -3$ and $y = 1$. This means you can substitute these values into both equations and go from there.

$$hx - 4y = -10 \qquad\qquad kx + 3y = -15$$
$$h(-3) - 4(1) = -10 \qquad k(-3) + 3(1) = -15$$
$$-3h - 4 = -10 \qquad\qquad -3k + 3 = -15$$
$$-3h = -6 \qquad\qquad -3k = -18$$
$$h = 2 \qquad\qquad k = 6$$

So, $\dfrac{k}{h} = \dfrac{6}{2} = 3$, making (C) correct.

5. C   Difficulty: Medium

Category: Heart of Algebra / Systems of Linear Equations

Getting to the Answer: Write a system of equations with c = the cost of the chair in dollars and s = the cost of the sofa in dollars. A sofa costs \$50 less than three times the cost of the chair, or $s = 3c - 50$; together, a sofa and a chair cost \$650, so $s + c = 650$.

The system is:

$$\begin{cases} s = 3c - 50 \\ s + c = 650 \end{cases}$$

The top equation is already solved for s, so substitute $3c - 50$ into the bottom equation for s and solve for c:

$$3c - 50 + c = 650$$
$$4c - 50 = 650$$
$$4c = 700$$
$$c = 175$$

Be careful—that's not the answer! The chair costs \$175 so the sofa costs $3(175) - 50 = 525 - 50 = \$475$. This means the sofa costs $\$475 - \$175 = \$300$ more than the chair. Therefore, (C) is correct.

6. D   Difficulty: Hard

Category: Heart of Algebra / Systems of Linear Equations

Getting to the Answer: The easiest way to answer this question is to think about how the graphs of the equations would look. Graphically, a system of linear equations that has no solution indicates two parallel lines, or in other words, two lines that have the same slope but different y-intercepts.

To have the same slope, the x- and y-coefficients must be the same. The two y-coefficients are $-\dfrac{2}{3}$ and -8. To make $-\dfrac{2}{3}$ equal -8, multiply by 12. Multiplying $\dfrac{1}{2}x$ by 12 as well gives $6x$. Because the other x-coefficient is a, it must be that $a = 6$. Note that you could also write each equation in slope-intercept form and set the slopes equal to each other to solve for a.

7. C   Difficulty: Hard

Category: Heart of Algebra / Systems of Linear Equations

Getting to the Answer: Create a system of linear equations where e represents the number of packs with 8 plates and t represents the number of packs with 12 plates.

The first equation should represent the total number of *packs*, each with 8 or 12 plates, or $e + t = 54$. The second equation should represent the total number of *plates*. Because e represents packs with 8 plates and t represents packs with 12 plates, the second equation is $8e + 12t = 496$. Now solve the system using substitution (or combination if it's faster for you). Solve the first equation for either variable and substitute the result into the second equation:

$$e + t = 54$$
$$e = 54 - t$$
$$- t) + 12t = 496$$
$$- 8t + 12t = 496$$
$$432 + 4t = 496$$
$$4t = 64$$
$$t = 16$$

So, 16 packs have 12 plates. The question asks about packs of 12, so you don't need to find the value of *e*. But you are not done yet. The problem asks how many *plates* a customer would buy if he or she buys all of the packs of 12 the store has, not just the *number of packs*. The customer would buy 16 × 12 = 192 plates, which is (C).

8. D   Difficulty: Hard
Category: Heart of Algebra / Systems of Linear Equations

Getting to the Answer: A system of linear equations has infinitely many solutions if both lines in the system have the same slope and the same *y*-intercept (in other words, they are the same line).

To have the same slope, the *x*- and *y*-coefficients of the two equations must be the same. Use the *x*-coefficients here: To turn $\frac{1}{2}$ into 3, multiply by 6. So *c* becomes 6*c*, and 6*c* = −6, or *c* = −1, (D).

Note that you could also write each equation in slope-intercept form and set the *y*-intercepts equal to each other to solve for *c*.

9. B   Difficulty: Easy
Category: Heart of Algebra / Systems of Linear Equations

Getting to the Answer: The solution to a system of linear equations represented graphically is the point of intersection. If the lines do not intersect, the system has no solution.

According to the graph, the lines intersect, or cross each other, at (6, 3). The question asks for the *y*-coordinate of the solution, which is 3, making (B) correct.

10. D   Difficulty: Easy
Category: Heart of Algebra / Systems of Linear Equations

Getting to the Answer: The word "and" in this question tells you that you're dealing with a system of equations. Whenever a question involves a system, quickly compare the two equations. Sometimes, writing the equations vertically gives you a clue about how to solve it.

$$\begin{cases} 2x - 3y = 14 \\ 5x + 3y = 21 \end{cases}$$

This system is already set up perfectly to solve using combination because the *y* terms (−3*y* and 3*y*) are opposites.

Add the two equations to cancel −3*y* and 3*y*. Then solve the resulting equation for *x*. Remember, the question only asks for the value of *x*, so you don't need to substitute *x* back into the equation and solve for *y*.

$$\begin{array}{r} 2x - 3y = 14 \\ + 5x + 3y = 21 \\ \hline 7x = 35 \\ x = 5 \end{array}$$

Choice (D) is correct.

11. A   Difficulty: Hard
Category: Heart of Algebra / Systems of Linear Equations

Getting to the Answer: Create a system of equations where *x* represents the number of rows with 20 seats and *y* represents the number of rows with 24 seats. The first equation should represent the total *number of rows*, each with 20 or 24 seats, or *x* + *y* = 16. The second equation should represent the total *number of seats*. Because *x* represents rows with 20 seats and *y* represents rows with 24 seats, the second equation in the system should be 20*x* + 24*y* = 348. Now solve the system using substitution. Solve the first equation for either variable and substitute the result into the second equation:

$$\begin{aligned} x + y &= 16 \\ x &= 16 - y \\ 20(16 - y) + 24y &= 348 \\ 320 - 20y + 24y &= 348 \\ 320 + 4y &= 348 \\ 4y &= 28 \\ y &= 7 \end{aligned}$$

So 7 rows have 24 seats, which means (A) is correct. This is all the question asks for, so you don't need to find the value of *x*.

12. 8 **Difficulty:** Medium

Category: Heart of Algebra / Systems of Linear Equations

Getting to the Answer: The solution to the system is the point that both tables will have in common, but the tables, as given, do not share any points. You could use the data to write the equation of each line and then solve the system, but this will use up valuable time on Test Day. Instead, look for patterns that can be extended.

In the table on the left, the x-values increase by 2 each time and the y-values decrease by 2. In the table on the right, the x-values increase by 4 each time and the y-values increase by 1. Use these patterns to continue the tables.

Equation 1		Equation 2	
x	y	x	y
−2	6	−8	−8
0	4	−4	−7
2	2	0	−6
4	0	4	−5
6	−2	**8**	**−4**
8	**−4**	12	−3

The point (8, −4) satisfies both equations, so the x-coordinate of the solution to the system is 8.

CHAPTER 4

PRACTICE

5. A   **Difficulty:** Medium
Category: Heart of Algebra / Inequalities

Getting to the Answer: Use the Kaplan Strategy for Translating English into Math to piece together an inequality. The question states that n represents the number of overnight stays. The cost of hotel accommodations for a trip without the discount card is $180 per night, or $180n$. If a customer purchases the discount card, accommodations would equal the cost of the card plus $120 per night, or $720 + 120n$. Combine these in an inequality, remembering which way the inequality symbol should be oriented. You want the cost with the discount card to be less than the cost without the card, so the inequality is $720 + 120n < 180n$. Solving for n gives $n > 12$; a traveler must stay in hotels in the network more than 12 days for the discount card to be a better deal. Choice (A) is the correct answer.

PERFORM

6. Any value between 0 and 3.5, including 0
Difficulty: Hard

Category: Heart of Algebra / Inequalities

Getting to the Answer: Resist autopilot! Instead of solving two inequalities separately, look for a series of quick manipulations to convert $\frac{4}{3}h + \frac{1}{6}$ to $12h - 4$. Start by multiplying the entire inequality by 9 to yield $-27 < 12h + \frac{3}{2} < 9$. Next, subtract $\frac{3}{2}$ and then 4 more (to get the desired -4) from all parts of the inequality (converting the fraction component to a decimal will make this step easier), which will become $-32.5 < 12h - 4 < 3.5$. Because grid-in answers cannot be negative, pick any value that is greater than or equal to 0 but less than 3.5.

Note that you could also solve the inequality for h and then manipulate the answer so that it looks like the expression in the question, but this strategy is likely to take longer.

7. C   **Difficulty:** Medium
Category: Heart of Algebra / Inequalities

Getting to the Answer: Use the Kaplan Strategy for Translating English into Math to assemble a system of inequalities. The question has defined the variables for you (t_s and p_s, t_z and p_z). You know that tops and pants cost $35 and $60 each, respectively. In addition, the question states that Sarah and Zena must sell an average of at least 75 items each (which means that together they must sell at least 150 items, regardless of who sells more) and that their total sales must be at least $6,000. The sum of the four item counts must meet or exceed 150, so the first inequality is $t_s + p_s + t_z + p_z \geq 150$. Revenue from the sale of tops is $35(t_s + t_z)$, and revenue from the sale of pants is $60(p_s + p_z)$. The minimum revenue required to earn the bonus is $6,000, so the second inequality is $35(t_s + t_z) + 60(p_s + p_z) \geq 6,000$. Choice (C) is the only choice that contains both inequalities.

ON YOUR OWN

1. A   **Difficulty:** Easy
Category: Heart of Algebra / Inequalities

Getting to the Answer: You solve an inequality just like an equation. The only difference is that if you multiply or divide both sides by a negative number (usually in the last step of the solution), you must reverse (flip) the inequality symbol. Take a second to study the inequality. Distributing the fraction will yield messy calculations. Instead, multiply both sides of the inequality by 5 to clear the fraction. Then, use inverse operations to isolate the variable:

$$\cancel{5} \times \frac{1}{\cancel{5}}(7 - 3b) > 5 \times 2$$
$$7 - 3b > 10$$
$$-3b > 3$$
$$b < -1$$

Notice that the inequality symbol was reversed because the last step in the solution required dividing by -3. The correct answer is (A).

2. B   **Difficulty:** Easy

Category: Heart of Algebra / Inequalities

Getting to the Answer: There is only one variable here, so solve each inequality for n and then eliminate incorrect choices.

First inequality: $n - 3 > 8$ so $n > 11$. This means you can eliminate A because 11 is not greater than itself.

Second inequality: $n + 1 < 14$ so $n < 13$. This means you can eliminate C and D because neither 13 nor 14 is less than 13. The number 12 is the only answer choice that is both greater than 11 and less than 13, so (B) is correct.

3. D   **Difficulty:** Medium

Category: Heart of Algebra / Inequalities

Getting to the Answer: You don't have time to try each symbol in the equation. Instead, look at the dot (open or solid?) and the direction of the shading (left or right?). There is a solid dot at 6, which means the sign must be $\geq$ or $\leq$, so you can eliminate A and B. Next, look at the shading. The graph is shaded to the left of the dot. This means the graph shows $x \leq 6$, but be careful—there is a negative coefficient (-1) in front of the x term, so the inequality will be reversed at some point in the solution. This means the original inequality sign, before you reverse it, should be $\geq$, which is (D). You can check your answer by solving the inequality using the sign you chose. If you chose correctly, your answer should match the graph.

4. C   **Difficulty:** Medium

Category: Heart of Algebra / Inequalities

Getting to the Answer: The best way to answer this question is to pretend you are the person paying for your power. How much less would you pay for *one* kWh of power at Company D than at Company B? If you used 530 kWh, how much would this be? If you used 730 kWh, how much would this be?

Based on the data in the table, a consumer would pay $17.4 - 14.8 = 2.6$ cents (or 0.026) less for one kWh of power at Company D than at Company B. If she used 530 kWh per month, she would pay $530(0.026) = \$13.78$ less at Company D. If she used 730 kWh, she would pay $730(0.026) = \$18.98$ less. So, the consumer would pay somewhere between \$13.78 and \$18.98 less per month, which can be expressed as the compound inequality $13.78 \leq x \leq 18.98$, which matches (C).

5. C   **Difficulty:** Medium

Category: Heart of Algebra / Inequalities

Getting to the Answer: Use the Kaplan Method for Translating English into Math. The clue "holds a maximum" means it can hold exactly that much or less, so use the symbol $\leq$ throughout. The cargo container can hold a maximum of 50 microwaves, so the first inequality is $m \leq 50$. This means you can eliminate A. The container can hold a maximum of 15 refrigerators, so the second inequality is $r \leq 15$. The third inequality deals with the size of each appliance. The cargo container can hold m microwaves multiplied by the size of the microwave, 6 cubic feet; it can hold r refrigerators multiplied by the size of the refrigerator, 20 cubic feet; and it can hold a maximum of 300 cubic feet total. Put these together to write the final inequality: $6m + 20r \leq 300$, which is (C).

6. D   **Difficulty:** Hard

Category: Heart of Algebra / Inequalities

Getting to the Answer: Before immediately trying to solve for k, notice that $-6k + 8$ is simply $3k - 4$ multiplied by -2. So, multiply each of the other parts of the inequality by -2 also. Don't forget to flip the inequality symbols because you are multiplying by a negative number.

$$-2\left[-\frac{2}{5} < 3k - 4 < \frac{6}{7}\right]$$

$$\frac{4}{5} > -6k + 8 > -\frac{12}{7}$$

Now, you don't need to solve for k because the question is asking about $-6k + 8$, but it does help to rewrite the inequality from smallest to largest: $-\frac{12}{7} < -6k + 8 < \frac{4}{5}$. So, any value greater than $-\frac{12}{7}$ but less than $\frac{4}{5}$ is a possible value, but be careful—you are looking for the number that is *not* a possible value. This means you are looking for a number that is *less* than $-\frac{12}{7}$ or *greater* than $\frac{4}{5}$. Choice (D) is correct because $\frac{4}{3} > \frac{4}{5}$.

7. D **Difficulty:** Hard

Category: Heart of Algebra / Inequalities

Getting to the Answer: The solution to a system of inequalities is where the shading overlaps. The first inequality is ready to graph, but the second is not, so start by rewriting the second inequality in slope intercept form $(y = mx + b)$. Don't forget to reverse the inequality symbol when you divide by -3:

$$2x - 3y \leq 12$$
$$-3y \leq -2x + 12$$
$$y \geq \frac{2}{3}x - 4$$

Now, compare the lines. Because the slopes are the same $\left(\frac{2}{3}\right)$ and the y-intercepts are different (1 and -4), the boundary lines are parallel and never intersect. Don't answer too quickly—the answer is *not* "no solution"! The solution set revolves around the shading, not the boundary lines, so draw a quick sketch of the system.

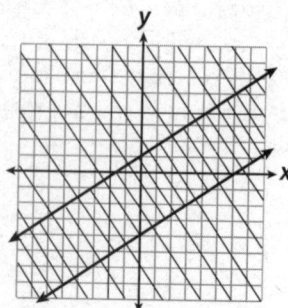

The region between the two boundary lines is shaded in both directions, so (D) is correct.

8. 8 **Difficulty:** Medium

Category: Heart of Algebra / Inequalities

Getting to the Answer: Translate from English into math to create an inequality where h represents the number of hours of overtime Marco must work. Marco gets paid a daily wage plus an hourly rate for overtime, so his weekly pay is his daily rate ($80) times 5 days, plus the number of hours of overtime he works (h) times his overtime rate ($15). If he wants to make *at least* $520, which means that

much or more, the inequality is $(80 \times 5) + 15h \geq 520$. Solve for h:

$$400 + 15h \geq 520$$
$$15h \geq 120$$
$$h \geq 8$$

Marco must work at least 8 hours of overtime to make $520 or more this week.

9. C **Difficulty:** Easy

Category: Heart of Algebra / Inequalities

Getting to the Answer: Solve the inequality by first distributing the 2 and then using inverse operations.

$$2(4x - 1) > 5x + 13$$
$$8x - 2 > 5x + 13$$
$$8x > 5x + 15$$
$$3x > 15$$
$$x > 5$$

Now, find the number line that matches. Because x is greater than (but *not* equal to) 5, the dot should be open, and the graph should be shaded to the right of 5. This is called a *strict* inequality because the numbers in the solution are strictly greater than 5. This means (C) is correct.

10. B **Difficulty:** Medium

Category: Heart of Algebra / Inequalities

Getting to the Answer: Quickly skim the first answer choice to see that you'll need to decide whether the boundary line is dashed or solid, whether it rises or falls from left to right, and which half-plane should be shaded. The inequality symbol tells you two of these—the symbol does not have an equal sign, so the line should be dashed; the symbol represents *less than*, so the half-plane *below* the line should be shaded. This means either A or B must be correct. To decide which one, recall that when a line is written in the form $y = mx + b$, the variable m represents the slope of the line. Here, $m = -2$, so the line is decreasing, which means it falls from left to right, making (B) correct.

11. B **Difficulty:** Medium

Category: Heart of Algebra / Inequalities

Getting to the Answer: The intersection (overlap) of the two shaded regions is the solution to the system of inequalities. Check each point to see whether it lies in the region where the shading overlaps. Be careful—you are looking for the point that is *not* a solution to the system. Choices A and C clearly lie in the overlap so you can eliminate them. Choice D, which is the point $(6, -3)$, lies on a boundary line, and because the line is solid, the point *is* included in the solution region. The only point that does not lie within the overlap is (B). To check this, plug $(1, -1)$ into the first inequality:

$$y < \frac{3}{5}x - 2$$

$$-1 < \frac{3}{5}(1) - 2$$

$$-1 \not< -\frac{7}{5}$$

Choice (B) is correct because -1 is not less than $-\frac{7}{5}$.

12. C **Difficulty:** Medium

Category: Heart of Algebra / Inequalities

Getting to the Answer: A question like this is purely conceptual. The only time a system of inequalities has *no solution* (no overlap at all) is when the boundary lines are parallel and the shading is in opposite directions (above the upper boundary line and below the lower boundary line). For the boundary lines to be parallel, the slope of the second line must be equal to the slope of the first line, which is 2. This means you can eliminate A and B. The inequality symbol $<$ (in the first inequality) tells you that the half-plane *below* the boundary line is shaded, which means the half-plane *above* the second boundary line must be shaded. Therefore, the correct symbol is greater than ($>$). Choice (C) is correct.

13. 2 **Difficulty:** Medium

Category: Heart of Algebra / Inequalities

Getting to the Answer: If (a, b) is a solution to the system, then a is the x-coordinate of any point in the region where the shading overlaps, and b is the corresponding y-coordinate. When $a = 0$ (or $x = 0$), the maximum possible value for b lies on the upper boundary line, $y < 2x + 3$. It looks like the y-coordinate is 3, but to be sure, substitute $x = 0$ into the equation and simplify. You can use $=$ in the equation, instead of the inequality symbol, because you are finding a point on the boundary line.

$$y = 2(0) + 3$$
$$y = 3$$

The point on the boundary line is $(0, 3)$. The boundary line is dashed (because the inequality is strictly less than), so $(0, 3)$ is *not* a solution to the system. This means 2 is the greatest possible *integer* value for b when $a = 0$.

CHAPTER 5

PRACTICE

8. C   **Difficulty**: Medium

Category: Problem Solving and Data Analysis / Rates, Ratios, Proportions, and Percentages

Getting to the Answer: You have a couple rates, but you need to manipulate them slightly before using them in the DIRT equation. Start by changing the given rates to unit rates. For the 5-second interval, $r_5 = 1$ car per 5 s $= 0.2$ cars/s. The 8-second interval becomes $r_8 = 1$ car per 8 s $= 0.125$ cars/s. Next, convert the time window into seconds to match your rates: $3 \text{ h} \times \dfrac{60 \text{ min}}{1 \text{ h}} \times \dfrac{60 \text{ s}}{1 \text{ min}} = 10{,}800 \text{ s}$.

Now you can use the DIRT equation to find the number of cars allowed through at each interval.

5 seconds: $d_5 = 0.2$ cars/s $\times 10{,}800$ s $= 2{,}160$ cars

8 seconds: $d_8 = 0.125$ cars/s $\times 10{,}800$ s $= 1{,}350$ cars

Subtracting these gives $2{,}160 - 1{,}350 = 810$ more cars, which is (C).

9. D   **Difficulty**: Hard

Category: Problem Solving and Data Analysis / Rates, Ratios, Proportions, and Percentages

Getting to the Answer: Murray starts with $75,400 per year. The first deduction is the 20% 401(k) contribution. Using the three-part percent formula, you'll find Murray has $0.8 \times \$75{,}400 = \$60{,}320$ left. He pays $150 per month for insurance, which is $1,800 per year. This leaves $58,520 pre-tax. Taxes are trickier, so work carefully. State taxes are easy; just take 4.5% of the pre-tax total: $0.045 \times \$58{,}520 = \$2{,}633.40$. Federal taxes involve three separate calculations as follows:

10% bracket: $0.1 \times \$9{,}225 = \$922.50$
15% bracket: $0.15 \times (\$37{,}450 - \$9{,}225) = \$4{,}233.75$
25% bracket: $0.25 \times (\$58{,}520 - \$37{,}450) = \$5{,}267.50$

Adding up all of Murray's tax liability gives $13,057.15. Subtract this from his pre-tax total to get $45,462.85. Don't stop yet! The question asks for Murray's biweekly pay. Divide $45,462.85 by 26, the number of pay periods in one year, to get $1,748.57, which is (D).

10. 7/16   **Difficulty**: Hard

Category: Problem Solving and Data Analysis / Rates, Ratios, Proportions, and Percentages

Getting to the Answer: Start by labeling each square for clarity.

You're given that the area of the innermost square is 1 square inch, which means the side length of this square is 1 inch. If the square edges are 0.5 inches apart, that means square 2 has a side length of $1 + 0.5 + 0.5 = 2$ inches, square 3 has a side length of $2 + 0.5 + 0.5 = 3$ inches, and so on. This translates to areas of 1, 4, 9, 16, 25, 36, 49, and 64 (all in square inches). But don't forget that you need to subtract the square within each to get the true areas! You'll get the following:

$$\text{sq. 1 (gray)} = 1 \text{ in.}^2$$
$$\text{sq. 2 (black)} = 2^2 - 1 = 3 \text{ in.}^2$$
$$\text{sq. 3 (gray)} = 3^2 - 4 = 5 \text{ in.}^2$$
$$\text{sq. 4 (black)} = 4^2 - 9 = 7 \text{ in.}^2$$
$$\text{sq. 5 (gray)} = 5^2 - 16 = 9 \text{ in.}^2$$
$$\text{sq. 6 (black)} = 6^2 - 25 = 11 \text{ in.}^2$$
$$\text{sq. 7 (gray)} = 7^2 - 36 = 13 \text{ in.}^2$$
$$\text{sq. 8 (black)} = 8^2 - 49 = 15 \text{ in.}^2$$

After a few calculations you might start to see a pattern; if so, great! You can shave off a few seconds of number crunching. Now add up the gray squares to get 28, then divide by the area of the whole plate (64) to get $\dfrac{28}{64} = \dfrac{7}{16}$. Grid in 7/16, then move on to the next question in the set.

11. 10/9 Difficulty: Medium

Category: Problem Solving and Data Analysis / Rates, Ratios, Proportions, and Percentages

Getting to the Answer: You've already done most of the work for this part; look closely at your work for the first question to see what you can reuse. Finding the large plate black fraction is easy; just subtract the large plate gray fraction from 1 to get $\frac{9}{16}$. Because the small plate is just a smaller version of the large plate with only four squares, you can use your calculations for squares 1-4 from the first question here. Squares 1 and 3 (gray) comprise 6 square inches, and squares 2 and 4 (black) comprise 10 square inches. This means the small plate black fraction is $\frac{10}{16} = \frac{5}{8}$. To find how many times more black glaze is on the small plate, divide the small plate black fraction by its large plate counterpart: $\frac{5}{8} \div \frac{9}{16} = \frac{5}{8} \times \frac{16}{9} = \frac{10}{9}$. Grid in 10/9, and you're done!

PERFORM

12. A Difficulty: Easy

Category: Problem Solving and Data Analysis / Rates, Ratios, Proportions, and Percentages

Getting to the Answer: Convert all four rates into the same units before comparing. You might think you should convert each price into cost per banana, but a closer look reveals that all but one price already uses weight. Save time by converting the units into cost per pound; the order will be no different than if you did cost per banana. Use the banana-pound relationship to convert each price into cost per pound. FoodCo's price is already per pound, so no work is needed there. Bob's charges $0.29 per banana, which becomes $\frac{\$0.29}{1\ banana} \times \frac{1\ banana}{\frac{1}{3}\ lb} = \frac{\$0.87}{1\ lb}$. Acme's price is $1.50 for 2 pounds or $0.75 per pound. The deal at Stu's means you pay $1.95 for 4 pounds, which is $0.4875 per pound. Therefore, the correct order is Bob's, Acme, FoodCo, Stu's. This matches (A).

13. 18.2 Difficulty: Easy

Category: Problem Solving and Data Analysis / Rates, Ratios, Proportions, and Percentages

Getting to the Answer: Start by drawing a diagram to make sense of the situation. Each zipline is the hypotenuse of a right triangle. Because the two zipline setups are proportional, the triangles are similar.

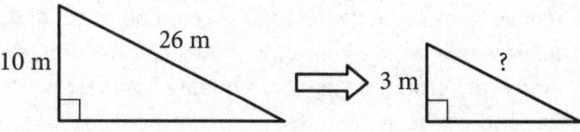

You can use a proportion to solve for the length of the kids' zipline: $\frac{10}{26} = \frac{3}{x}$. Solving for x gives 7.8 meters. But you're not done yet! The question asks for the difference in zipline length, so subtract 7.8 from 26 to get 18.2.

14. 166 Difficulty: Medium

Category: Problem Solving and Data Analysis / Rates, Ratios, Proportions, and Percentages

Getting to the Answer: Identify the units of the start and end quantities, then string together the proper conversion factors. You know Mark will drive 960 miles over the course of his trip, and you need to determine what he should budget for fuel. The full conversion is as follows:

$$960\ mi \times \frac{1\ gal}{40\ mi} \times \frac{3.785\ L}{1\ gal} \times \frac{1.20\ GBP}{1\ L} \times \frac{1.52\ USD}{1\ GBP} =$$

165.69 USD. Round to 166 per the question instructions.

15. 17 Difficulty: Hard

Category: Problem Solving and Data Analysis / Rates, Ratios, Proportions, and Percentages

Getting to the Answer: Determine Mark's fuel cost with the offer, then compare it to the original. If you stopped your calculations in the previous question after the gallon-to-liter conversion, you would find that Mark will use 90.84 L of fuel. At the new fuel price, Mark would pay $90.84 \times 0.75 = 68.13$ GBP for fuel. Add the 30 GBP cost for the rate reduction to get 98.13 GBP. Use the GBP-USD conversion to get 149.16 USD. Subtracting this from 165.69 gives 16.53, which is rounded to 17.

ON YOUR OWN

1. A   **Difficulty**: Medium

Category: Problem Solving and Data Analysis / Rates, Ratios, Proportions, and Percentages

Getting to the Answer: Whenever multiple rates are given, pay very careful attention to the units. As you read the question, decide how and when you will need to convert units. Use the factor-label method as needed. The answer choices are given in hours and minutes, so start by converting the given typing rate from words per second to words per minute:

$$\frac{3.75 \text{ words}}{1 \text{ second}} \times \frac{60 \text{ seconds}}{1 \text{ minute}} = \frac{225 \text{ words}}{1 \text{ minute}}$$

Next, find the number of words in the 25-page transcript:

$$\frac{675 \text{ words}}{1 \text{ page}} \times 25 \text{ pages} = 16,875 \text{ words}$$

Finally, let m be the number of minutes it takes the court reporter to type the whole transcript. Set up a proportion and solve for m:

$$\frac{225 \text{ words}}{1 \text{ minute}} = \frac{16,875 \text{ words}}{m \text{ minutes}}$$
$$225m = 16,875$$
$$m = 75$$

Because 75 minutes is not an answer choice, convert it to hours and minutes: 75 minutes = 1 hour, 15 minutes, making (A) the correct answer.

2. C   **Difficulty**: Medium

Category: Problem Solving and Data Analysis / Rates, Ratios, Proportions, and Percentages

Getting to the Answer: Don't let the three-way ratio scare you. You can solve this problem just like any other ratio question. Set up an equation using *parts*: 35 parts of the vote were for Taft, 41 parts were for Roosevelt, and 63 parts were for Wilson. You don't know how big a part is, so call it x. Now, write and solve an equation:

$$35x + 41x + 63x = 208,500$$
$$139x = 208,500$$
$$x = 1,500$$

Look back at the ratio—35 parts of the vote were for Taft, so the number of votes cast for Taft was 35(1,500) = 52,500, which matches (C).

3. D   **Difficulty**: Medium

Category: Problem Solving and Data Analysis / Rates, Ratios, Proportions, and Percentages

Getting to the Answer: Use a variation of the three-part percent formula: Whole × percent = part.

First, find the number of people at each location who responded favorably using the formula. Start with the first location: $125 \times 0.224 = 28$. Move on to the second location: $272 \times 0.375 = 102$. Next, find the total number of people that were surveyed at both locations, which was $125 + 272 = 397$, and the total number who responded favorably, $28 + 102 = 130$. Finally, find the percent of people who responded favorably by using the formula one more time:

$$397 \times \text{percent} = 130 \times 100\%$$
$$\text{percent} = \frac{130}{397} \times 100\%$$
$$= 0.3274 \times 100\%$$
$$= 32.7\%$$

Of all the people surveyed, about 32.7% responded favorably, making (D) the correct answer.

4. A   **Difficulty**: Medium

Category: Problem Solving and Data Analysis / Rates, Ratios, Proportions, and Percentages

Getting to the Answer: Let the units in this question guide you to the solution. The cooking rates of the ovens are given in pounds per hour, but the question asks about the number of ounces each oven can cook in 10 minutes, so use the factor-label method to convert pounds per hour to ounces per minute.

Start by converting pounds to ounces. You are given that 1 pound = 16 ounces, so 3 pounds is 48 ounces and 4.5 pounds is 72 ounces. Now convert the hours to minutes:

Oven at 350°:

$$\frac{48 \text{ oz}}{1 \text{ hr}} \times \frac{1 \text{ hr}}{60 \text{ min}} \times 10 \text{ min} = 8 \text{ oz}$$

Oven at 450°:

$$\frac{72\ oz}{1\ hr} \times \frac{1\ hr}{60\ min} \times 10\ min = 12\ oz$$

In 10 minutes, the oven at 450° can cook $12 - 8 = 4$ ounces more than the oven at 350°, making (A) the correct answer.

5. B   Difficulty: Medium
Category: Problem Solving and Data Analysis / Rates, Ratios, Proportions, and Percentages

Getting to the Answer: Don't let all the technical words in this question overwhelm you. Solve it step-by-step examining the units as you go. Use the factor-label method to help you stay organized.

Step 1: Determine the number of megabytes the company can upload in 1 evening (4 hours):

$$\frac{12\ MB}{1\ sec} \times \frac{60\ sec}{1\ min} \times \frac{60\ min}{1\ hr} \times \frac{4\ hr}{1\ evening} = \frac{172,800\ MB}{1\ evening}$$

Step 2: Convert this amount to gigabytes (because the information about the scans is given in gigabytes, not megabytes):

$$172,800\ MB \times \frac{1\ GB}{1,024\ MB} = 168.75\ GB$$

Step 3: Each video file is about 4.5 gigabytes, so divide by 4.5 to determine how many videos the company can upload to the cloud using its internet service provider: $168.75 \div 4.5 = 37.5$ videos. Remember, you should round this number down to 37, because the question asks for the maximum number the company can upload and it cannot complete the 38th video upload in the time allowed. The correct answer is (B).

6. B   Difficulty: Medium
Category: Problem Solving and Data Analysis / Rates, Ratios, Proportions, and Percentages

Getting to the Answer: Pay careful attention to the units. You need to convert all of the dimensions to inches, and then find the scale factor. You'll have to start with the skull because it's the only part of the T-rex for which you know both the actual length and the model length.

There are 12 inches in one foot, so Sue's skull length was $12 \times 5 = 60$ inches and the model skull is $3 \times 12 = 36 + 1.5 = 37.5$ inches. Find the scale factor by writing

this as a fraction. Multiply both numbers by 10 to get rid of the decimal and then simplify the ratio to get $\frac{37.5}{60} = \frac{375}{600} = \frac{5}{8}$.

This means the scale factor is $\frac{5}{8}$. You might be tempted to now find the scale model's length and height by multiplying 40 and 13 by $\frac{5}{8}$, but this would waste valuable time. Because the model is a $\frac{5}{8}$-scale model, the difference between the model's length and height will be exactly $\frac{5}{8}$ of the difference between Sue's actual length and height, which is $40 - 13 = 27$ feet. Multiply 27 by $\frac{5}{8}$ to find that the difference between the length and height of the model should be 16.875 feet, or 16 feet, 10.5 inches, which matches (B).

7. 660   Difficulty: Easy
Category: Problem Solving and Data Analysis / Rates, Ratios, Proportions, and Percentages

Getting to the Answer: Break this question into short steps. Find the amount of the hostess share for one evening. Multiply this by the number of evenings per week, 5, and then the number of weeks, 4. Do this for each restaurant, and then subtract to find the difference.

Restaurant A:	Restaurant B:
$0.07 \times \$1,100 = \$77$	$0.04 \times \$1,100 = \$44$
$\$77 \times 5 = 385$	$\$44 \times 5 = \$220$
$\$385 \times 4 = \$1,540$	$\$220 \times 4 = \$880$

Mia would make $\$1,540 - \$880 = \$660$ more at Restaurant A.

8. 75   Difficulty: Hard
Category: Problem Solving and Data Analysis / Rates, Ratios, Proportions, and Percentages

Getting to the Answer: This question requires multiple steps and multiple formulas, so make a plan before you dive in. The formula for percent increase is:

$$Percent\ increase = \frac{final\ amount - original\ amount}{original\ amount}$$

This tells you that you need the final amount in tips that Restaurant B needs to bring in to be equal to Restaurant A, which will depend on the amount in tips Restaurant

Answers & Explanations

A brings in. You'll need to use the percent formula (Percent × whole = part) to determine what amount would be required at 4% for the hostess share to be equal.

The hostess tip share for one evening at Restaurant A is $1,100 × 0.07 = $77. Use this amount to find the final amount of tips, t, Restaurant B needs:

$$0.04 \times t = 77$$
$$0.04t = 77$$
$$t = \$1,925$$

Now use the percent increase formula:

$$\text{Percent increase} = \frac{1,925 - 1,100}{1,100}$$
$$= \frac{825}{1,100}$$
$$= 0.75$$

The percent increase needed is 75%. Per the question's instructions, enter this as 75 (not .75).

9. D   Difficulty: Easy

Category: Problem Solving and Data Analysis / Rates, Ratios, Proportions, and Percentages

Getting to the Answer: To answer a question that says "directly proportional," set two ratios equal to each other and solve for the missing amount. Don't forget—match the units in the numerators and in the denominators on both sides of the proportion.

Because the first rate is given in minutes, write 1 hour as 60 minutes. Let t equal the number of topics the teacher can cover in a 60-minute period. Set up a proportion and solve for t:

$$\frac{9 \text{ topics}}{45 \text{ minutes}} = \frac{t \text{ topics}}{60 \text{ minutes}}$$
$$9(60) = 45(t)$$
$$540 = 45t$$
$$12 = t$$

Choice (D) is correct.

10. C   Difficulty: Easy

Category: Problem Solving and Data Analysis / Rates, Ratios, Proportions, and Percentages

Getting to the Answer: It can be confusing to decide which operation to perform when dealing with conversions, especially when the conversions involve decimals. Think about how your answer should look first. A person weighs *less* on the moon, so he or she should weigh *more* on Earth. This means your answer must be greater than 29, so you can eliminate A right away.

The easiest way to convert the units and keep them straight is to set up a proportion.

$$\frac{0.166 \text{ lb on moon}}{1 \text{ lb on Earth}} = \frac{29 \text{ lb on moon}}{p \text{ lb on Earth}}$$
$$29(1) = 0.166p$$
$$174.7 \approx p$$

The man weighs about 175 pounds on Earth. Choice (C) is correct.

11. C   Difficulty: Easy

Category: Problem Solving and Data Analysis / Rates, Ratios, Proportions, and Percentages

Getting to the Answer: According to the pie graph, 25% of the customers are totally dissatisfied and 15% are somewhat dissatisfied. So, 100% − 25% − 15% = 60% of the customers are totally or somewhat satisfied. Thus, the *number* of customers that are totally or somewhat satisfied is 60% of 240, or 0.6 × 240 = 144 customers, making (C) correct.

12. B   Difficulty: Medium

Category: Problem Solving and Data Analysis / Rates, Ratios, Proportions, and Percentages

Getting to the Answer: This is a typical proportion question. Use words first to write the proportion. Then translate from English into math. Let n equal the number of people tested. Set up a proportion and solve for n. Be sure to match the units in the numerators and in the denominators on both sides of the proportion.

$$\frac{\text{false positives}}{\text{number tested}} = \frac{\text{false positives}}{\text{number tested}}$$
$$\frac{6}{3,500} = \frac{27}{n}$$
$$6n = 27(3,500)$$
$$6n = 94,500$$
$$n = 15,750$$

This means (B) is correct.

13. C   Difficulty: Medium

Category: Problem Solving and Data Analysis / Rates, Ratios, Proportions, and Percentages

Getting to the Answer: Start with the hours. The client received 25 hours of tutoring, of which 1 hour was free. So, the client paid for 24 hours of tutoring. The first 10 hours were at a different rate than the discounted rate, so subtract these to find that the client paid the discounted rate for $24 - 10 = 14$ hours. Now look at the money: The first 10 hours the client was actually billed for cost $30 per hour for a total of $300, so subtract this from the total amount paid to get $664 - \$300 = \$364$. This is the amount charged for the 14 discounted hours. Divide this amount by the number of hours billed at the discounted rate to get $\$364 \div 14 = \$26$ per hour, making (C) the correct choice.

14. C   Difficulty: Medium

Category: Problem Solving and Data Analysis / Rates, Ratios, Proportions, and Percentages

Getting to the Answer: You are given a lot of numbers in this question. Break the question into short steps. Before you move on, check that you answered the right question (the number of LED bulbs that were *not* defective).

Step 1: Find the number of LED bulbs produced. A total of 12,500 of both kinds of bulbs were produced. The ratio of LED to CFL is 2:3, so two parts LED plus three parts CFL equals 12,500. Write this as $2x + 3x = 12,500$. Simplify and solve this equation to find that $x = 2,500$. Multiply this amount by 2 (because two parts were LED bulbs): $2,500 \times 2 = 5,000$.

Step 2: Use that number to find the number of LED bulbs that were defective: 3% of 5,000 or $0.03 \times 5,000 = 150$ defective LEDs.

Step 3: Find the number of LED bulbs that were *not* defective: $5,000 - 150 = 4,850$. Choice (C) is correct.

15. B   Difficulty: Medium

Category: Problem Solving and Data Analysis / Rates, Ratios, Proportions, and Percentages

Getting to the Answer: Find the percent increase using this formula: % increase $= \dfrac{\text{amount of increase}}{\text{original amount}}$.

Then apply the same percent increase to the animal population in 2000. The amount of increase is $7,200 - 6,400 = 800$, so the percent increase is $\dfrac{800}{6,400} = 0.125 = 12.5\%$ between 1950 and 2000. If the total percent increase over the next 50 years is the same, the animal population should be about $7,200 \times 1.125 = 8,100$. Choose (B) and move on to the next question.

16. 14   Difficulty: Easy

Category: Problem Solving and Data Analysis / Rates, Ratios, Proportions, and Percentages

Getting to the Answer: You know the length of Betsy's book and the rate at which she reads. You need to know how many minutes she reads.

$$116 \cancel{\text{pg}} \times \frac{1.5 \text{ min}}{1 \cancel{\text{pg}}} = 174 \text{ min}$$

It takes Betsy 174 minutes to read her book. You know Raymond starts reading at 8:30 AM and reads until 11:38 AM, which is $11:38 - 8:30 = 3$ hours, 8 minutes, or 188 minutes. It takes Raymond $188 - 174 = 14$ minutes longer to read his book.

17. 50   Difficulty: Medium

Category: Problem Solving and Data Analysis / Rates, Ratios, Proportions, and Percentages

Getting to the Answer: Break this problem into short steps.

Step one: Find the total number of drips needed by multiplying the amount of medication prescribed, 800 mL, by the number of drips needed to deliver 1 mL: $800 \times 30 = 24,000$ drips.

Step two: Divide this number by 8 to find how many drips per hour are needed: $24,000 \div 8 = 3,000$ drips per hour.

Step three: Divide this by 60 (because there are 60 minutes in one hour) to convert drips per hour to drips per minute: $3,000 \div 60 = 50$ drips per minute.

18. 40   Difficulty: Hard
Category: Problem Solving and Data Analysis / Rates, Ratios, Proportions, and Percentages

Getting to the Answer: Start by determining what the question is asking. You need to find the net change in the power allocated to Grid 1 over the course of a day. To do this, you need to know how much the grid was allocated at the beginning of the day and how much at the end.

You aren't given a concrete starting point (or units of power), so simply pick a starting number. The best number to use when dealing with percents is 100. First, find how much power the grid was allocated after the first 20% increase: $100 \times 1.2 = 120$. Next, find the amount after the 10% decrease: $120 \times 0.9 = 108$. Finally, find the amount after the last 30% increase: $108 \times 1.3 = 140.4$, which is $140.4 - 100 = 40.4$ more than it started the day with. To find the percent change, use the formula Percent change $= \dfrac{\text{amount of change}}{\text{original amount}}$ to get $\dfrac{40.4}{100} = 0.404$. Rounded to the nearest whole percent, this is 40 percent.

19. 10.5   Difficulty: Medium
Category: Problem Solving and Data Analysis / Rates, Ratios, Proportions, and Percentages

Getting to the Answer: For each of the three friends, you know how long they traveled and their rate. Use the DIRT formula to find the distance for each one. But be careful—the rates are given in miles per hour, which means you must use hours, not minutes, for the times.

Andrea:
30 minutes $=$ 0.5 hours
   Distance $= 3 \times 0.5 = 1.5$ miles

Kellan:
45 minutes $=$ 0.75 hours
   Distance $= 14 \times 0.75 = 10.5$ miles

Joelle:
15 minutes $=$ 0.25 hours
   Distance $= 35 \times 0.25 = 8.75$ miles

Kellan lives the farthest away at 10.5 miles. An important note here—the question did not tell you to round and the entire answer fits in the grid, so you MUST grid the answer in as 10.5. However, had you gotten an answer like 10.57 (which wouldn't fit in the grid), then you could either round to 10.6 or truncate (cut off) the answer at 10.5 because it would still fill the entire grid.

20. 731   Difficulty: Hard
Category: Problem Solving and Data Analysis / Rates, Ratios, Proportions, and Percentages

Getting to the Answer: When answering question sets that share information, you can often save some time by using amounts you found in the first question to answer the second one.

In the previous question, you found that Andrea's house is 1.5 miles from the restaurant. Use the DIRT formula to determine how long Kellan walked with Andrea:

$$1.5 = 2.5 \times \text{time}$$
$$1.5 = 2.5t$$
$$0.6 = t$$

They walked for 0.6 hours, or $60 \times 0.6 = 36$ minutes. Now calculate how long Kellan biked. Again, you have the distance and the rate, so you need to use the formula to find the time:

$$12 = 15 \times \text{time}$$
$$12 = 15t$$
$$0.8 = t$$

Kellan biked for 0.8 hours, or $60 \times 0.8 = 48$ minutes. So Kellan traveled for a total of $36 + 48 = 84$ minutes, or 1 hour, 24 minutes. Don't forget that they arrived 5 minutes early, or at 8:55. So Kellan must have left his house at $8:55 - 1$ hour $= 7:55 - 24$ minutes which is 7:31 AM. Enter this as 731.

CHAPTER 6

PRACTICE

4. C **Difficulty:** Easy

Category: Problem Solving and Data Analysis / Scatterplots

Getting to the Answer: Examine the equation to determine the type of plot it will produce. When the exponent in an equation is a variable, the graph of the equation is exponential, so eliminate choices A and B. To distinguish between the remaining choices, pick an easy-to-use value to plug into the given equation for x (e.g., 0). You'll see that when $x = 0$, y should equal 5, which matches the graph in (C).

5. 2 **Difficulty:** Medium

Category: Problem Solving and Data Analysis / Scatterplots

Getting to the Answer: You're asked for a rate; this means finding the slope of the line of best fit. Start by picking a pair of points, preferably where the line of best fit passes through a grid-line intersection to minimize error. The points (50, 20) and (100, 40) are good choices. Determine the slope:

$$m = \frac{y_2 - y_1}{x_2 - x_1} = \frac{40 - 20}{100 - 50} = \frac{20}{50} = \frac{2}{5}$$

Don't grid in $\frac{2}{5}$, though. Remember what you're being asked: You need the road clearing duration increase for a 5% increase in snowpack water content, not 1%. Multiply $\frac{2}{5}$ by 5, which yields 2.

6. 99.2 **Difficulty:** Medium

Category: Problem Solving and Data Analysis / Scatterplots

Getting to the Answer: The slope you found in the previous question will save you some time here. The line of best fit on the scatterplot intersects the y-axis at (0, 0). Therefore, the equation of the line of best fit is $y = \frac{2}{5}x$. Plug 248 in for x and simplify:

$$y = \frac{2}{5} \times 248 = \frac{496}{5} = 99.2$$

PERFORM

7. A **Difficulty:** Easy

Category: Problem Solving and Data Analysis / Scatterplots

Getting to the Answer: The question asks for a rate of change, which means you'll need the slope of the line of best fit. Pick a pair of points to use in the slope formula, such as (1998, 20) and (2012, 90):

$$m = \frac{y_2 - y_1}{x_2 - x_1} = \frac{90 - 20}{2012 - 1998} = \frac{70}{14} = 5$$

Choice (A) is correct.

8. A **Difficulty:** Easy

Category: Problem Solving and Data Analysis / Scatterplots

Getting to the Answer: Identify the type of change described in the question to narrow down your choices. If the number of smartphone users increases by 35% each year, then the amount of the increase is variable (because it's 35% of a bigger number each time), indicating nonlinear (exponential) growth. Eliminate C and D. Recall that when assembling an exponential growth model, r (the rate) must be in decimal form. Therefore, the number raised to the power of x should be $1 + 0.35$ or 1.35. Choice (A) is the only one that fits these criteria.

9. D **Difficulty:** Medium

Category: Problem Solving and Data Analysis / Scatterplots

Getting to the Answer: Compare each statement to the infographic one at a time, eliminating true statements as you work. Start with A: It is impossible to tell from the graph which strain has the higher reading at 20 hours, so you cannot say the statement is NOT true. Eliminate A. Choice B states that Strain 2's growth rate (slope) overtook Strain 1's at hour 50, which is consistent with the infographic; eliminate it. Choice C requires math, so skip it for now. Choice (D) states that Strain 1's growth rate was greater than Strain 2's over the entire period. Although Strain 1's growth rate was greater for part of the monitored period, it is not greater for the entire period (because the slope of Strain 1's curve is not steeper than that of Strain 2's curve for every line segment on the graph), which makes (D) false and, therefore, correct.

ON YOUR OWN

1. C   Difficulty: Easy
Category: Problem Solving and Data Analysis / Scatterplots

Getting to the Answer: A regression equation is the equation of the line (or curve) that best fits the data. A *linear* regression is used to model data that follows the path of a straight line. In the equation given, *a* represents the slope of the linear regression (the line of best fit), so you are looking for data that is linear (looks like a line) and is decreasing, or falling from left to right ($a < 0$ means a is negative). You can eliminate A and D because the data is not linear (A is quadratic and D is exponential). You can also eliminate B because the data is increasing (rising from left to right). This means (C) is correct.

2. A   Difficulty: Easy
Category: Problem Solving and Data Analysis / Scatterplots

Getting to the Answer: When an exponential equation is written in the form $y = x_0(1 + r)^x$, the value of x_0 gives the *y*-intercept of the equation's graph. To answer this question, you need to think about what the *y*-intercept would represent in the context described.

Whenever time is involved in a relationship that is modeled by an equation or a graph, it is always the independent variable and therefore graphed on the *x*-axis. Therefore, for this question, population would be graphed on the *y*-axis, so x_0 most likely represents the population when the time elapsed was zero, or in other words, in the year that Adriana was born, making (A) correct.

3. D   Difficulty: Medium
Category: Problem Solving and Data Analysis / Scatterplots

Getting to the Answer: A line that "represents the trend of the data" is another way of saying line of best fit. The trend of the data is clearly linear because the path of the dots does not turn around or curve, so draw a line

of best fit on the graph. Remember, about half of the points should be above the line and half below.

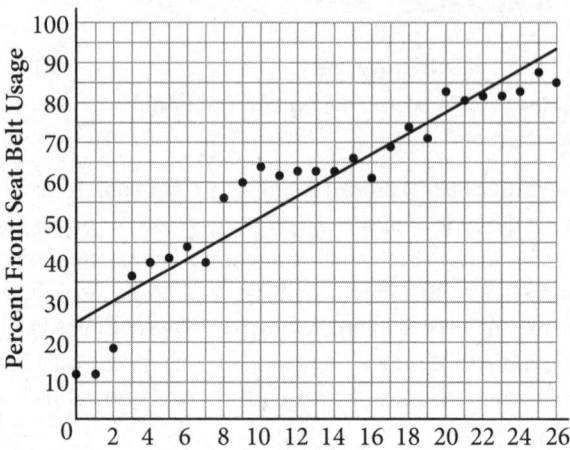

Seat Belt Use in England (1983-2009)

Years After Seat Belt Law Enacted

If you draw the line all the way to the *y*-axis, you'll save a step by finding the *y*-intercept just by looking at the scatterplot. For this graph, it's about 25. This means you can eliminate B and C. To choose between A and (D), find the approximate slope using two points that lie on (or very close to) the line of best fit. You can use the *y*-intercept, (0, 25), as one of the points to save time and estimate the second, such as (21, 80). Use the slope formula to find the slope:

$$m = \frac{y_2 - y_1}{x_2 - x_1} = \frac{80 - 25}{21 - 0} = \frac{55}{21} = 2.62$$

The result is very close to the slope in (D), making it the correct answer.

4. A   Difficulty: Medium
Category: Problem Solving and Data Analysis / Scatterplots

Getting to the Answer: Examine the graph, paying careful attention to units and labels. The average rate of change is the same as the slope of the line of best fit. The data is decreasing (going down from left to right) so you can immediately eliminate C and D. To choose between (A) and B, find the slope of the line of best fit using the slope formula, $m = \dfrac{y_2 - y_1}{x_2 - x_1}$, and any two points that lie on (or very close to) the line. Using the two points

(5, 14) and (10, 8), the average rate of change is about $\frac{8 - 14}{10 - 5} = \frac{-6}{5} = -1.2$, which matches (A).

5. A   **Difficulty:** Medium

Category: Problem Solving and Data Analysis / Scatterplots

Getting to the Answer: Determine whether the predicted change in the interest rate is a common difference (linear function) or a common ratio (exponential function), or if it changes direction (quadratic or polynomial function).

The company predicts that every six months, the Federal Reserve will *raise* rates by 0.25 percentage points. Interest rates are already expressed as percentages, so raising the rates by 0.25 percentage points means *adding* a quarter of a percent every six months. It does not mean it will increase *by* 0.25% every six months. The function therefore involves a common difference, so the best model would be a linear function, which is (A).

6. B   **Difficulty:** Hard

Category: Problem Solving and Data Analysis / Scatterplots

Getting to the Answer: When presented with a "series" of data, making a chart helps. In this question, the chart should include the number of bounces and the height after the bounce. You can then look for patterns that may tell you which function to pick, or at the very least, which functions to eliminate.

Bounce Number (*b*)	Height After Bounce (*H(b)*)
1	80
2	40
3	20
4	10

Look for a pattern: the heights are decreasing by a common ratio each time $\left(\frac{1}{2}\right)$, so an exponential function will be the best match. This means you can eliminate C and D (which are linear functions). To choose between A and (B), evaluate each function at $b = 1$ and see what happens.

Choice A: $H(1) = \frac{80}{2^1} = \frac{80}{2} = 40$. The height should be 80 after the first bounce, so eliminate this choice.

Choice B: $H(1) = \frac{80}{2^{1-1}} = \frac{80}{2^0} = \frac{80}{1} = 80$. Choice (B) is correct.

If you're not convinced (or if both results had been 80), move on to $b = 2$ and evaluate each function again, until you are able to eliminate one of them.

7. 2   **Difficulty:** Easy

Category: Problem Solving and Data Analysis / Scatterplots

Getting to the Answer: Examine the graph, including the axis labels and numbering. Each vertical grid-line represents 5 eggs, so look to see how many data points are more than a complete grid space away from the line of best fit. Only 2 are more than 5 away—the first data point and the one between 30 and 35 weeks, making 2 the correct answer.

8. 57   **Difficulty:** Hard

Category: Problem Solving and Data Analysis / Scatterplots

Getting to the Answer: This is a Grid-in question, so you can't just use the graph to estimate the *y*-value when $x = 36$. Instead, you need to find the equation of the line of best fit, and then substitute 36 for *x* and simplify. Start with the slope—you could pick two points on the line and use the slope formula, or you could count the rise and the run. The latter is easier in this question. Beginning at the point (0, 75), the line falls 5 units and runs 10 units to the first point on the line, so the slope is $\frac{-5}{10} = -\frac{1}{2}$.

This means that the equation looks like $y = -\frac{1}{2}x + b$. Next, find the *y*-intercept. You can see clearly from the graph that it is approximately 75.

The equation is $y = -\frac{1}{2}x + 75$. Now, substitute 36 for *x* and simplify to find *y*:

$$y = -\frac{1}{2}(36) + 75$$
$$y = -18 + 75$$
$$y = 57$$

The correct answer is 57.

9. C **Difficulty:** Easy

Category: Problem Solving and Data Analysis / Scatterplots

Getting to the Answer: Correlation means that there is a discernible relationship between two or more variables. A positive correlation means that as one variable increases, so does the other variable. A negative correlation means that as one variable increases, the other decreases. The closer the relationship is, the stronger the correlation.

Take a quick peek at the answer choices and picture or draw a sketch of each one. *Linear* indicates that the data follows the path of a straight line. *Positive* means rising from left to right. Finally, *strong* means the relationship is a close one, but not perfect, so the data points should be fairly close to, but not exactly on, the line; choice (C) is correct.

10. A **Difficulty:** Easy

Category: Problem Solving and Data Analysis / Scatterplots

Getting to the Answer: A line with a downward slant has a negative slope, so you can immediately eliminate C and D. To choose between (A) and B, recall that slope is a ratio that compares vertical change (rise) to horizontal change (run). Mark the bordered area using equal measures and then estimate the slope of a line drawn through the center of the points as shown.

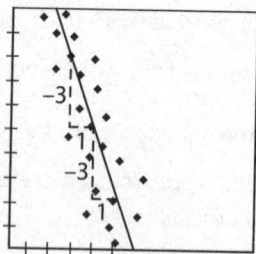

The line appears to fall 3 units and run 1 unit, so a good estimate for the slope is −3, making (A) correct. Note that you could also use what you know about slope to answer the question—lines that have fractional slopes, between −1 and 1, are not steep lines, which means B can't be correct.

11. D **Difficulty:** Easy

Category: Problem Solving and Data Analysis / Scatterplots

Getting to the Answer: Knowing where the y-intercept of the line of best fits falls will help you eliminate answer choices.

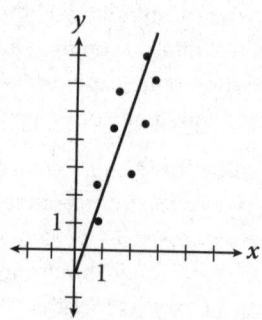

The line of best fit intercepts the y-axis below the x-axis, and is therefore negative, so you can eliminate B and C (the y-intercept is +1 for each of those lines). Now, look at the slope. The line rises along the y-axis slightly faster than it runs along the x-axis, so the slope must be slightly greater than 1, making (D) correct. If you have trouble choosing between A and (D), you could also graph each equation in your calculator to see which one is a better match for the line. Use a viewing window that is approximately the same as in the graph. Here, the viewing window would be $-2 \le x \le 5$ and $-2 \le y \le 7$.

12. C **Difficulty:** Medium

Category: Problem Solving and Data Analysis / Scatterplots

Getting to the Answer: "Correlation" simply means relationship. The word "weak" refers to the strength of the relationship (how close the data lies to the line of best fit), which has no effect on slope. Be careful not to confuse slope and strength. The fact that a data set shows a weak correlation does not give you any information about the magnitude of the slope. This means you can eliminate A and B. Also, keep in mind that the terms "weak" and "negative" are not related, but rather are two independent descriptors of the correlation. So the fact that the rate of change is negative has nothing to do with the strength of the correlation. In a weak correlation, the data points will loosely follow the line of best fit, making (C) the correct answer.

13. B   **Difficulty:** Medium

Category: Problem Solving and Data Analysis / Scatterplots

Getting to the Answer: There are two things to keep in mind for a question like this: Correlation does not prove causation, and as a general rule, conclusions can only be drawn about the population studied, not about all populations. The data points are scattered and do not form any discernible pattern. This means there is no correlation, which is another way of saying the two variables aren't related, so you can eliminate D. You can also eliminate C because the HR representative *is* able to draw a conclusion—that there is no relationship. To choose between A and (B), recall that when you analyze data from a given population (the employees at that particular company), you can only draw conclusions about that population, not about employee populations in general. Therefore, (B) is correct.

14. D   **Difficulty:** Medium

Category: Problem Solving and Data Analysis / Scatterplots

Getting to the Answer: The fact that the two variables are strongly correlated, whether it be negatively or positively, only shows that there is a relationship between the variables. It does not indicate whether the change in one variable caused the change in the other. For example, Population A might thrive in wet climates, while Population B does not, and in the years studied, rainfall may have increased, which caused the changes in the populations. This means (D) is the correct answer.

15. D   **Difficulty:** Medium

Category: Problem Solving and Data Analysis / Scatterplots

Getting to the Answer: Try drawing a quick graph (or at least visualizing a graph) that matches the description in the question (decreases quickly at first and then at a much slower rate). The shape and direction of the curve should tell you which type of model to choose.

The question doesn't say anything about the data points changing direction at any time, so you can eliminate A and B—they are both quadratic functions, which always turn around at their vertex. To choose between C and (D), skim through the question again. The data is decreasing, or getting smaller. In an exponential function, when the rate

(*r*) is greater than 0, as in C, the function is an exponential growth model, which increases, not decreases, and therefore cannot be correct. This means (D) is correct. When the rate (*r*) is less than 0, the function is an exponential decay model, which matches the description of the data.

16. D   **Difficulty:** Medium

Category: Problem Solving and Data Analysis / Scatterplots

Getting to the Answer: According to the question, the amount of milk a typical baby needs starts at 0 ounces and increases until it peaks at about 6 months of age. Then the amount of milk needed decreases until one year of age, when it becomes 0 ounces again. This means the shape of the data would look like an upside down parabola, which would match a negative quadratic model, making (D) correct. (Note: a negative absolute value model could also be used, depending on whether the rates of increase and decrease are constant, but that is not one of the answer choices.)

17. B   **Difficulty:** Medium

Category: Problem Solving and Data Analysis / Scatterplots

Getting to the Answer: Think logically about what happens to the data points and the line of best fit. The amount of snowfall is recorded on the *y*-axis, so the *y*-values of the data points stay the same. The *x*-values of the points all shift to the right 10 units (because Genji adds 10 degrees to each of the temperature readings). This means that all the data points stay in the same place vertically, but shift horizontally, resulting in the same rate of change, so you can eliminate C and D. The line of best fit would also still look the same, just shifted to the right. This means the strength of correlation does not change, as the points will still be the same distance away from the (now moved) line of best fit, making (B) correct.

18. D   **Difficulty:** Hard

Category: Problem Solving and Data Analysis / Scatterplots

Getting to the Answer: When a regression model has a correlation coefficient of 1.0, it means that the model exactly fits the data. This tells you that you can use what you know about quadratic functions to answer the question.

The graph of a quadratic function is symmetric with respect to its axis of symmetry. The axis of symmetry passes through the x-value of the vertex, which also happens to be where the maximum (or minimum) of the function occurs. The question tells you this value—it's $x = 25$. Because 35 is $35 - 25 = 10$ units to the right of the axis of symmetry, you know that the y-value will be the same as the point that is 10 units to the left of the axis of symmetry. This occurs at $x = 25 - 10 = 15$. Read the y-value from the graphing calculator screenshot to find the answer, which is 27. Therefore, (D) is correct.

19. 3   Difficulty: Medium
Category: Problem Solving and Data Analysis / Scatterplots

Getting to the Answer: Percent error gives the deviation of an actual value from an expected value. Graphically, this is determined by how far from the line of best fit the data point is. You don't need to find the percent error of every point (or even a single point) to answer this question. Instead, you just need to understand that the point with the greatest percent error from the mean of the data is the point that is farthest from the line of best fit. Use the grid-lines on the graph to find the point. The point (9, 3) is 4 full grid-lines away from the line of best fit, which is farther than any other data point. The question asks for the y-value of this point, so the correct answer is 3.

20. 18   Difficulty: Medium
Category: Problem Solving and Data Analysis / Scatterplots

Getting to the Answer: Because the y-value of the graph when $x = 3,400$ is not shown, this question requires a mathematical solution; extending the line of best fit will not provide an accurate enough answer. The equation of the model is given as $y = -\frac{1}{200}x + 35$. Miles over recommended servicing are graphed along the x-axis, so substitute 3,400 for x to find the answer:

$$y = -\frac{1}{200}(3,400) + 35 = -17 + 35 = 18$$

CHAPTER 7

PRACTICE

8. B **Difficulty:** Medium

Category: Problem Solving and Data Analysis / Statistics and Probability

Getting to the Answer: The professor starts with a normal distribution; when the new data are added, the distribution changes:

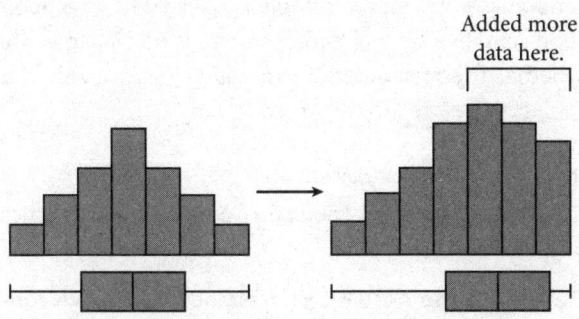

Added more data here.

The new distribution is skewed to the left (in the direction of the graph's tail, not in the direction of its biggest bump), and the median has increased. Although the range of the new data alone might be smaller than the original set, when all data are combined, the range will not have changed from the original data. The correct answer is (B).

9. 28.7 **Difficulty:** Easy

Category: Problem Solving and Data Analysis / Statistics and Probability

Getting to the Answer: To be considered "bad," a game must have a rating of 1 or 2. Begin by counting the number of "bad" games. There are $5 + 3 + 3 = 11$ games with a rating of 1 and $17 + 12 + 10 = 39$ games with a rating of 2. That's a total of $11 + 39 = 50$ games. Divide this by the total number of games and multiply by 100: $\frac{50}{61 + 54 + 59} \times 100 = 28.7\%$. Grid in 28.7.

10. 12 **Difficulty:** Medium

Category: Problem Solving and Data Analysis / Statistics and Probability

Getting to the Answer: You know from the previous question that 50 games are "bad." Reducing this number by 50% is the same as halving it, meaning there will be 25 remaining "bad" games after the removal. Subtract this from the original total game count ($61 + 54 + 59 = 174$) to get the new total, which is 149. Divide the new "bad" count by this total, and then multiply by 100 as you did before: $\frac{25}{149} \times 100 = 16.7785\%$. Subtracting the new percentage from the old one (rounded to a minimum of 4 decimal places just to be safe) gives $28.7356\% - 16.7785\% = 11.9571\%$. This rounds to 12, so grid in 12.

PERFORM

11. D **Difficulty:** Medium

Category: Problem Solving and Data Analysis / Statistics and Probability

Getting to the Answer: Consider finding the probability of *not* selecting one of the puzzles specified, as there will be fewer dots to count. You can then subtract that probability from 1. There are only three puzzles that *didn't* take Randolph fewer than 100 seconds to solve. Of these, 2 do *not* have fewer than 6 clues. Therefore, the probability that the conditions *won't* be met is $\frac{2}{20} = 0.1$. This isn't what you're asked to find, so don't stop yet. Subtract 0.1 from 1 to get 0.9. Multiply this by 100 to get 90%; (D) is correct.

12. B **Difficulty:** Easy

Category: Problem Solving and Data Analysis / Statistics and Probability

Getting to the Answer: Consider the difference between mean and standard deviation: Mean is a measure of center, while standard deviation is a measure of spread. The four answers all involve consistency, which means the explanation should involve standard deviation. Based on this, you can eliminate A and D. Higher consistency means lower standard deviation (and vice versa); the only choice that reflects this—and correctly represents the data in the table—is (B).

13. 594 Difficulty: Medium

Category: Problem Solving and Data Analysis / Statistics and Probability

Getting to the Answer: Identify Wilhelmina and Alexandra's hat contributions from the table, and then extrapolate to find how many solid-colored hats they should knit for Spirit Week. According to the table, Wilhelmina will be responsible for $\frac{24}{60}$ of the hats, and Alexandra will knit $\frac{9}{60}$ of them. The knitting club needs to knit 1,800 hats total, 60% of which should be solid-colored per the survey results, so $0.6 \times 1,800 = 1,080$ hats should be solid-colored. Add together the fractions for Wilhelmina and Alexandra to get $\frac{33}{60}$. Multiplying this by the total number of solid-colored hats will yield the number that Wilhelmina and Alexandra will knit: $\frac{33}{60} \times 1,080 = 594$.

14. 282 Difficulty: Medium

Category: Problem Solving and Data Analysis / Statistics and Probability

Getting to the Answer: Work through this one step at a time. Read carefully; you're asked about the two other club members' Spirit Week production here, and the question is not limited to solid-colored hats. Start with the number of prizes: 20% of 1,800 hats = 360 hats with emblems and therefore 360 prize scarves. The two boys make $\frac{27}{60}$ of the 360 hats = 162 hats. The two boys make $\frac{11}{33} = \frac{1}{3}$ of the 360 scarves = 120 scarves. They are responsible for $162 + 120 = 282$ of these items.

ON YOUR OWN

1. D Difficulty: Easy

Category: Problem Solving and Data Analysis / Statistics and Probability

Getting to the Answer: Look carefully at the infographic's axes. Look at the vertical axis—the frequency tells you the number of contestants who named each number of states: 1 contestant named only 1 state, 1 contestant named 2 states, 5 contestants named 3 states, and so on.

To answer the question, add all the frequencies to find the total number of contestants: $1 + 1 + 5 + 6 + 4 + 0 + 2 + 1 = 20$, which is (D).

2. C Difficulty: Medium

Category: Problem Solving and Data Analysis / Statistics and Probability

Getting to the Answer: Not everyone who shops at an electronics store owns a tablet. Customers who bought other items, such as laptops, TVs, or MP3 players are likely to make up at least a portion of the surveys distributed with customers' purchases. This means that, despite being randomly selected, the sample is unlikely to be a good representative sample because there is no way to verify whether the responders to the survey actually own a tablet. Therefore, (C) is correct.

3. D Difficulty: Medium

Category: Problem Solving and Data Analysis / Statistics and Probability

Getting to the Answer: Understanding how averages and sums are connected is the key to answering a question like this. If the average of 14 numbers is 6, then the sum of the 14 numbers must be 84 (because $84 \div 14 = 6$). Use the dot plot to find the total number of appliances the salesman has already sold. Then, subtract this amount from 84. The salesman has already sold $3(2) + 4(3) + 5 + 6(3) + 7 + 8 + 10(2) = 76$ appliances, so he needs to sell $84 - 76 = 8$ appliances on the 14th day to reach his goal. This means (D) is correct.

4. B Difficulty: Medium

Category: Problem Solving and Data Analysis / Statistics and Probability

Getting to the Answer: According to the sample survey, $\frac{40}{300}$ say they would join the gym. But the gym estimates that only 30% of these respondents would *actually* join, so multiply 40 by 30% to find that the gym can expect $\frac{12}{300} = 0.04 = 4\%$ of the respondents to join. Multiply this by the total number of residents: $12,600 \times 0.04 = 504$ residents, so (B) is correct.

5. D   Difficulty: Hard

Category: Problem Solving and Data Analysis / Statistics and Probability

Getting to the Answer: The probability that one randomly selected salmon from those that were tested would have a dangerous level of mercury is equal to the number of salmon that had dangerous mercury levels divided by the total number of salmon that were tested. This means you only need two numbers to answer this question. One of those numbers is in the table—6 salmon had dangerous mercury levels. Finding the other number is the tricky part. Use information from the question stem and the pie graph. The biologist tested 5% of the total number of each breed of fish, or 5% of 25% of 6,000 fish. Multiply to find that $0.05 \times 0.25 \times 6,000 = 75$ salmon were tested. This means the probability is $\frac{6}{75} = 0.08$, which matches (D).

6. 627   Difficulty: Medium

Category: Problem Solving and Data Analysis / Statistics and Probability

Getting to the Answer: When making inferences about populations based on sample data, find the percent of the sample data that matches the given criteria and multiply by the number in the population. Of the 250 writers in the sample, $250 - 74 - 22 - 30 - 29 = 95$ writers said they would like sandwiches for lunch. This represents $\frac{95}{250} = 0.38$, or 38%. Multiply $0.38 \times 1,650$ to arrive at 627 writers that want sandwiches for lunch.

7. B   Difficulty: Medium

Category: Problem Solving and Data Analysis / Statistics and Probability

Getting to the Answer: To calculate the percentage of people in each age group with a healthy blood sugar level (< 100), divide the number of people in *that* age group with a healthy blood sugar level by the total number of participants in *that* age group. Choice (B) is correct because $16 \div 98 \approx 0.1633 = 16.33\%$, which is a lower percentage than in the other age groups (18-25 = 18.75%, 36-45 = 20.21%, and Older than 45 = 20%).

8. D   Difficulty: Medium

Category: Problem Solving and Data Analysis / Statistics and Probability

Getting to the Answer: This question requires careful reading of the table. The first criterion is fairly straightforward—you're looking for a participant with a blood sugar level in the 100-125 range, so focus on that column in the table. The second criterion is a bit trickier—*at least 36 years old* means 36 years old or older, so you'll need to use the values in the rows for 36-45, and Older than 45. There were 35 in the 36-45 age group who were considered at risk, and 27 in the Older than 45 age group, resulting in a total of $35 + 27 = 62$ out of 300 participants. The probability of randomly selecting one participant from either of these two groups is $\frac{62}{300}$, which reduces to $\frac{31}{150}$, or (D).

9. C   Difficulty: Easy

Category: Problem Solving and Data Analysis / Statistics and Probability

Getting to the Answer: The question states that the data was collected in California about jackrabbits, so any conclusion drawn can only be generalized to that particular geographic region and to that breed of rabbit. California is in the Northern Hemisphere, so its spring months are March, April, and May. According to the data, the California jackrabbit gives birth mostly during those months, so (C) is correct.

10. B   Difficulty: Medium

Category: Problem Solving and Data Analysis / Statistics and Probability

Getting to the Answer: The table is not complete, so your first step is to fill in the missing values. Start with what you know and work from there. It may not be necessary to complete the entire table, but rather only what you need to answer the question.

You know there are 186 cookies total and that 104 are without nuts, which means $186 - 104 = 82$ have nuts. Because you already know that 40 of those cookies are oatmeal raisin, this mean $82 - 40 = 42$ are chocolate chip. You also know that $\frac{2}{3}$ of the total number of cookies are chocolate chip, which means there are $\frac{2}{3} \times 186 = 124$

chocolate chips cookies, total, so you can fill this number in the "Total" row of that column. You do not need to fill in any more of the table because the question only asks about chocolate chip cookies with nuts. There are 124 chocolate chip cookies total and 42 of them have nuts, so the probability of randomly choosing one with nuts is $\frac{42}{124}$, or $\frac{21}{62}$, which matches (B).

11. A   Difficulty: Medium
Category: Problem Solving and Data Analysis / Statistics and Probability

Getting to the Answer: As long as a sample is both representative and without bias, inferences can be drawn from the sample data to the population from which the sample was taken. In this example, if the mean number of bottles of water consumed per person each day was 2.5, then it can be assumed that the average number consumed in the general population is also 2.5, so the means are equal, and (A) is the correct answer.

12. D   Difficulty: Medium
Category: Problem Solving and Data Analysis / Statistics and Probability

Getting to the Answer: The wording in this question implies that the population for the study includes all nutrients. However, the study only tests for nitrogen and potassium, so the sample was limited. You can eliminate A and B because all nutrients were not included in the sample, so you can't say anything about them, one way or the other. The compounds may or may not help the soil retain other types of nutrients, and you certainly don't know which of the five would produce the best results. You can eliminate C because the question doesn't tell you anything about the data collection methods, so you can't determine whether or not the study was biased. This means that choice (D) is correct—the study will only be able to produce results concerning the effects of the compounds on the soil retaining nitrogen and potassium.

13. B   Difficulty: Medium
Category: Problem Solving and Data Analysis / Statistics and Probability

Getting to the Answer: The median is the middle number in a series of numbers. Arrange the number of history majors from least to greatest, making sure that 225 is in the middle. Use s to balance out the number of history

majors on either side of 225. Because there are already two numbers above the median (240 and 287), there must be two numbers below the median, 162 and s:

s, 162, 225, 240, 287

or

162, s, 225, 240, 287

Because s could be on either side of 162, it could be anything less than or equal to 225. Its greatest possible value is therefore 225, which is (B).

14. 2/5 or .4   Difficulty: Medium
Category: Problem Solving and Data Analysis / Statistics and Probability

Getting to the Answer: Take a second to think about the quickest way to answer the question—you're not asked to find the popularity rating of each performer and then compare them. Based on the host's definition, you can pick the most popular performer by simply looking at the numbers in the table. More people attended on Day 3, so you only need to find the popularity rating for Entertainer C: 1,600 people attended on that day out of a total of $1,280 + 1,120 + 1,600 = 4,000$ festival goers, so Entertainer C's popularity rating is $\frac{1,600}{4,000} = \frac{2}{5}$, or .4.

15. B   Difficulty: Easy
Category: Problem Solving and Data Analysis / Statistics and Probability

Getting to the Answer: The question only asks about participants who were outside a healthy weight range, so focus on this row: 38 out of the 74 participants who were outside a healthy weight range ate breakfast one or fewer times per week. This represents $\frac{38}{74} = 0.51351$, or 51.35%, which matches (B).

16. D   Difficulty: Medium
Category: Problem Solving and Data Analysis / Statistics and Probability

Getting to the Answer: The question asks about employees who eat breakfast every weekday, so focus on the "5-7 times per week" column in the table. Assuming the participants in the study were a good representative sample, 36 out of 45, or 80%, of the 3,000 employees are likely to be within a healthy weight range. Multiply $0.8 \times 3,000$ to arrive at 2,400, which is (D).

17. 300   Difficulty: Easy

Category: Problem Solving and Data Analysis / Statistics and Probability

Getting to the Answer: Read the graph carefully, including the key at the bottom indicating that each bar represents 15 minutes. The question states that only stage 3 is considered *deep* sleep, and the question asks how much time was spent in *light* sleep. You could count all of the bars that don't represent stage 3, but it would be faster to count the bars that do and subtract. There are 12 bars that represent stage 3, which means the person spent $12 \times 15 = 180$ minutes in deep sleep. The study was for 8 hours, or 480 minutes, so the person spent $480 - 180 = 300$ minutes in light sleep.

18. 3/8 or .375   Difficulty: Medium

Category: Problem Solving and Data Analysis / Statistics and Probability

Getting to the Answer: Probability compares the number of desired outcomes (here, the number of 15-minute periods with a sleep stage of 3) with the total number of possible outcomes (here, the total number of 15-minute periods over the course of the 8 hours). The opening paragraph tells you that the total amount of sleep over the course of the study is 8 hours. In the previous question, you calculated that 180 minutes, or 3 hours are spent in deep sleep. Therefore, the probability would be $\frac{3}{8}$.

19. 15   Difficulty: Medium

Category: Problem Solving and Data Analysis / Statistics and Probability

Getting to the Answer: The question asks *on average* how many more cents consumers are willing to pay, so you will need to find a weighted average for each version of the product. Start with the store brand. Multiply each dollar amount by the height of the corresponding bar:

$$5 \times 68 = 340$$
$$6 \times 56 = 336$$
$$7 \times 48 = 336$$
$$8 \times 32 = 256$$
$$9 \times 30 = 270$$
$$10 \times 14 = 140$$

Next, add them all together: $1,678. Now, divide this number by the total number of respondents ($68 + 56 + 48 + 32 + 30 + 14 = 248$): $1,678 \div 248 = 6.766$, which means *on average* consumers are willing to pay $6.77 for the store brand version of the product. Repeat this process for the brand name version.

$$5 \times 85 = 425$$
$$6 \times 79 = 474$$
$$7 \times 64 = 448$$
$$8 \times 55 = 440$$
$$9 \times 42 = 378$$
$$10 \times 27 = 270$$

Add them all together to get 2,435, and divide by the number of respondents ($85 + 79 + 64 + 55 + 42 + 27 = 352$) to arrive at $2,435 \div 352 = 6.917$, or $6.92. *On average*, consumers are willing to pay $6.92 - $6.77 = $0.15, or 15 more cents for the brand name version than the store brand version.

20. 1/3 or .333   Difficulty: Hard

Category: Problem Solving and Data Analysis / Statistics and Probability

Getting to the Answer: First, find the number of respondents willing to pay at least $8 (which means $8 or more). Be careful—the question doesn't specify store brand or brand name, so use both versions of the product:

$$32 + 55 + 30 + 42 + 14 + 27 = 200$$

Now, find the total number of people in the survey. Again, the question doesn't specify store brand or brand name. You know from the previous question that 248 people responded to the store brand survey and 352 responded to the name brand survey, for a total of 600 respondents. This means the probability that a randomly chosen respondent is willing to pay at least $8 is $\frac{200}{600}$, or $\frac{1}{3}$.

CHAPTER 8

PRACTICE

8. D   **Difficulty:** Hard

Category: Passport to Advanced Math / Exponents

Getting to the Answer: Relative velocity is represented by v, so that's the variable you need to isolate. The manipulation sequence is shown here.

$$\gamma = \frac{1}{\sqrt{1 - \dfrac{v^2}{c^2}}}$$

$$\gamma\sqrt{1 - \frac{v^2}{c^2}} = 1$$

$$\sqrt{1 - \frac{v^2}{c^2}} = \frac{1}{\gamma}$$

$$1 - \frac{v^2}{c^2} = \frac{1}{\gamma^2}$$

$$-\frac{v^2}{c^2} = \frac{1}{\gamma^2} - 1$$

$$v^2 = -c^2\left(\frac{1}{\gamma^2} - 1\right)$$

$$v = c\sqrt{1 - \frac{1}{\gamma^2}}$$

The correct answer is (D).

9. B   **Difficulty:** Medium

Category: Passport to Advanced Math / Exponents

Getting to the Answer: The GCF of the two expressions under the radical is g^4h^3; factoring this out yields $\sqrt[3]{g^4h^3(g^2 - 27)}$. You can now pull a g and an h out from under the radical to obtain $gh\sqrt[3]{g(g^2 - 27)}$, which cannot be further simplified except for redistribution of g, which yields $gh\sqrt[3]{g^3 - 27g}$, making (B) correct. Note that $\sqrt[3]{g^3 - 27g}$ does *not* become $g - 3\sqrt[3]{g}$, as you cannot split the expression into two radicals.

10. D   **Difficulty:** Medium

Category: Passport to Advanced Math / Exponents

Getting to the Answer: Start by setting up a ratio that compares RBC count to total blood cell count. Manipulate the quantities to make all the exponents the same (to convert 7.5×10^3 to a product of 10^6 and another number, move the decimal point in 7.5 three places to the left and write "$\times 10^6$" after it), factor out 10^6, and then add the quantities in parentheses together. Once there, you can use exponent rules to simplify your equation. Divide through and multiply by 100 to get the RBC component as a percentage. Work is shown here:

$$\begin{aligned}
\text{RBC} &= \frac{5.4 \times 10^6}{5.4 \times 10^6 + 7.5 \times 10^3 + 3.5 \times 10^5} \\[6pt]
&= \frac{5.4 \times 10^6}{5.4 \times 10^6 + 0.0075 \times 10^6 + 0.35 \times 10^6} \\[6pt]
&= \frac{5.4 \times 10^6}{10^6(5.4 + 0.0075 + 0.35)} \\[6pt]
&= \frac{5.4}{5.7575}
\end{aligned}$$

Note that the answer choices are, for the most part, far apart. Because 5.4 is relatively close to 5.7575, you can conclude with confidence that the correct answer is likely close to 100%. Therefore, (D) is the correct answer. If this question is in the calculator section, you can plug the numbers into your calculator to check:

$$\% \text{ RBC} = \frac{5.4}{5.7575} \times 100 \approx 93.79\%$$

Choice (D) is still correct.

11. A   **Difficulty:** Medium

Category: Passport to Advanced Math / Exponents

Getting to the Answer: Start by arranging the pumps in order of increasing drain speed; you get P3 < P1 < P2. You're told that the second pump is twice as fast as the first and that the first is three times as fast as the third. You can turn the words into a ratio: If the portion of the draining completed by pump 3 in 1 hour is $\dfrac{1}{x}$, then the portion completed by pump 1 is $\dfrac{1}{x} \times 3 = \dfrac{3}{x}$, and the portion completed by pump 2 is $\dfrac{3}{x} \times 2 = \dfrac{6}{x}$. The term $\dfrac{6}{x}$ matches (A).

PERFORM

12. C   Difficulty: Medium
Category: Passport to Advanced Math / Exponents

Getting to the Answer: Begin by moving all terms that don't contain an a to one side of the equation. Once there, multiply both sides by 2 to eliminate the fraction, and then divide by t^2 to isolate a. The manipulation sequence is shown here.

$$h = \frac{1}{2}at^2 + v_0t + h_0$$

$$h - v_0t - h_0 = \frac{1}{2}at^2$$

$$at^2 = 2(h - v_0t - h_0)$$

$$a = \frac{2(h - v_0t - h_0)}{t^2}$$

Choice (C) is the correct answer.

13. A   Difficulty: Hard
Category: Passport to Advanced Math / Exponents

Getting to the Answer: Start by simplifying the radicals: 72 is the product of 2 and 36, so $\sqrt{72} = 6\sqrt{2}$. You can then factor 3 out of the numerator and denominator to yield $\frac{3(1 + 2\sqrt{2})}{3(1 - 2\sqrt{2})}$. Cancel the 3s, and you're left with $\frac{1 + 2\sqrt{2}}{1 - 2\sqrt{2}}$. You can't leave a radical in the denominator, so you'll need to rationalize it. The conjugate of the denominator is $1 + 2\sqrt{2}$, so multiply the entire expression by $\frac{1 + 2\sqrt{2}}{1 + 2\sqrt{2}}$, and then simplify as usual (think FOIL):

$$\frac{1 + 2\sqrt{2}}{1 - 2\sqrt{2}} \times \frac{1 + 2\sqrt{2}}{1 + 2\sqrt{2}}$$

$$= \frac{1 + 2\sqrt{2} + 2\sqrt{2} + 8}{1 + 2\sqrt{2} - 2\sqrt{2} - 8}$$

$$= \frac{1 + 2\sqrt{2} + 2\sqrt{2} + 8}{1 - 8}$$

$$= \frac{9 + 4\sqrt{2}}{-7}$$

This expression matches (A).

14. 41   Difficulty: Hard
Category: Passport to Advanced Math / Exponents

Getting to the Answer: In this question, you're given all the variables you need and an equation that relates them. All you need to do is plug the given values into the correct locations ($m = 200$, $r = \frac{0.015}{12}$, $N = 60$) and solve for what's missing (P in this case). Decimals are truncated for brevity here, but no rounding was done until the final step.

$$m = \frac{Pr}{1 - (1 + r)^{-N}}$$

$$200 = \frac{P \times \frac{0.015}{12}}{1 - \left(1 + \frac{0.015}{12}\right)^{-60}}$$

$$200 = \frac{0.00125P}{1 - (1 + 0.00125)^{-60}}$$

$$200 = \frac{0.00125P}{1 - (1.00125)^{-60}}$$

$$200 = \frac{0.00125P}{1 - 0.9278}$$

$$14.4426 = 0.00125P$$

$$P = 11,554.0897$$

Subtract P from the total price (19,560) to obtain Teri's down payment. Divide this by 19,560 and multiply by 100 to arrive at 40.93%. Rounded properly, the correct answer is 41.

ON YOUR OWN

1. A   Difficulty: Easy
Category: Passport to Advanced Math / Exponents

Getting to the Answer: Carefully multiply each term in the first factor by each term in the second factor. Then find the x terms and add their coefficients. To save time, you do not need to simplify the other terms in the expression.

$$\left(-2x^2 + 5x - 8\right)(4x - 9)$$
$$= -2x^2(4x - 9) + 5x(4x - 9) - 8(4x - 9)$$
$$= -8x^3 + 18x^2 + 20x^2 - 45x - 32x + 72$$

The coefficient of x in the product is $-45 - 32 = -77$, which means (A) is correct.

2. D   **Difficulty:** Medium

Category: Passport to Advanced Math / Exponents

Getting to the Answer: A *double zero* occurs in a polynomial when a factor is repeated, or in other words, squared. For example, the factor $(x - a)$ produces a simple zero at $x = a$, while $(x - b)^2$ produces a double zero at $x = b$. The polynomial has a simple zero at $x = -3$, which corresponds to a factor of $(x + 3)$. The double zero at $x = \dfrac{5}{4}$ results from a repeated (squared) factor, so you can eliminate A and C. To choose between B and (D), set each factor equal to 0, and then solve for x (mentally if possible). Choice (D) is correct because:

$$4x - 5 = 0$$
$$4x = 5$$
$$x = \dfrac{5}{4}$$

3. B   **Difficulty:** Medium

Category: Passport to Advanced Math / Exponents

Getting to the Answer: The goal here is to solve the equation for T. Start by getting T out of the denominator of the fraction. To do this, multiply both sides of the equation by T, and then divide both sides by v:

$$v = \dfrac{2\pi r}{T}$$
$$T \times v = \dfrac{2\pi r}{\cancel{T}} \times \cancel{T}$$
$$Tv = 2\pi r$$
$$T = \dfrac{2\pi r}{v}$$

Choice (B) is the correct answer.

4. C   **Difficulty:** Medium

Category: Passport to Advanced Math / Exponents

Getting to the Answer: Because the denominators are the same (just written in different forms), multiplying both sides of the equation by $3x - 15$ will immediately clear all the fractions, the result of which is a much easier equation to solve:

$$8x + 2x = 50$$
$$10x = 50$$
$$x = 5$$

Because there are variables in the denominator, you must check the solution to make sure it is not extraneous. When $x = 5$, each of the denominators is equal to 0, and division by 0 is not possible. Therefore, there is no solution to the equation, making (C) the correct answer.

5. A   **Difficulty:** Medium

Category: Passport to Advanced Math / Exponents

Getting to the Answer: There are two variables and only one equation, but because you're asked to solve for one of them *in terms of* the other, you solve it the same way you would any other equation. Because there is only one term on each side of the equal sign, cross-multiplying is probably the quickest route to the solution. Don't forget—you want to get x by itself on one side of the equation.

$$\dfrac{6}{x} = \dfrac{3}{k + 2}$$
$$6(k + 2) = 3x$$
$$6k + 12 = 3x$$
$$\dfrac{6k}{3} + \dfrac{12}{3} = \dfrac{3x}{3}$$
$$2k + 4 = x$$

Switch x to the left side of the equation and the result matches (A).

6. D   **Difficulty:** Medium

Category: Passport to Advanced Math / Exponents

Getting to the Answer: Multiply each term in the first expression by $\dfrac{3}{2}$ and each term in the second expression by -2. Then add the two polynomials by writing them vertically and combining like terms.

$$\frac{3}{2}A = \frac{3}{2}(4x^2 + 7x - 1) = 6x^2 + \frac{21}{2}x - \frac{3}{2}$$

$$-2B = -2(-x^2 - 5x + 3) = 2x^2 + 10x - 6$$

$$\begin{array}{c} 6x^2 + \dfrac{21}{2}x - \dfrac{3}{2} \\ + \; 2x^2 + \dfrac{20}{2}x - \dfrac{12}{2} \\ \hline 8x^2 + \dfrac{41}{2}x - \dfrac{15}{2} \end{array}$$

This means (D) is correct.

7. 10/3   Difficulty: Hard

Category: Passport to Advanced Math / Exponents

Getting to the Answer: Write each factor in the expression in exponential form (using fractional exponents for the radicals). Then use exponent rules to simplify the expression. Add the exponents of the factors that are being multiplied and subtract the exponent of the factor that is being divided:

$$\frac{\sqrt[3]{x} \cdot x^{\frac{5}{2}} \cdot x}{\sqrt{x}} = \frac{x^{\frac{1}{3}} \cdot x^{\frac{5}{2}} \cdot x^1}{x^{\frac{1}{2}}}$$

$$= x^{\frac{1}{3} + \frac{5}{2} + 1 - \frac{1}{2}} = x^{\frac{2}{6} + \frac{15}{6} + \frac{6}{6} - \frac{3}{6}}$$

$$= x^{\frac{20}{6}} = x^{\frac{10}{3}}$$

The question states that n is the power of x, so the value of n is $\frac{10}{3}$.

8. B   Difficulty: Hard

Category: Passport to Advanced Math / Exponents

Getting to the Answer: Because the question states that the expressions are equivalent, set up the equation $\frac{16}{7x + 4} + A = \frac{49x^2}{7x + 4}$ and solve for A. Start by subtracting the first term from both sides of the equation to isolate A. Then, simplify if possible (usually by cancelling common factors). The denominators of the rational terms are the same, so they can be combined.

$$\frac{16}{7x + 4} + A = \frac{49x^2}{7x + 4}$$

$$A = \frac{49x^2}{7x + 4} - \frac{16}{7x + 4}$$

$$A = \frac{49x^2 - 16}{7x + 4}$$

$$A = \frac{\cancel{(7x + 4)}(7x - 4)}{\cancel{7x + 4}}$$

$$A = 7x - 4$$

The correct answer is (B).

9. C   Difficulty: Easy

Category: Passport to Advanced Math / Exponents

Getting to the Answer: Follow the standard order of operations—deal with the exponent first, and then attach the negative sign (because a negative in front of an expression means multiplication by -1). The variable x is being raised to the $\frac{1}{4}$ power, so rewrite the term as a radical expression with 4 as the degree of the root and 1 as the power to which the radicand, x, is being raised.

$$x^{\frac{1}{4}} = \sqrt[4]{x^1} = \sqrt[4]{x}$$

Now attach the negative to arrive at the correct answer, $-\sqrt[4]{x}$, which is (C).

10. C   Difficulty: Easy

Category: Passport to Advanced Math / Exponents

Getting to the Answer: First, write the question as a subtraction problem. Pay careful attention to which expression is being subtracted.

$$\frac{8x - 5}{x - 1} - \frac{3x + 7}{x - 1}$$

The terms in the expression have the same denominator, $x - 1$, so their numerators can be subtracted. Simply combine like terms and keep the denominator the same. Don't forget to distribute the negative to both $3x$ and 7.

$$\frac{8x - 5}{x - 1} - \frac{3x + 7}{x - 1} = \frac{8x - 5 - 3x - 7}{x - 1} = \frac{5x - 12}{x - 1}$$

The reduced expression matches (C).

11. A   Difficulty: Easy

Category: Passport to Advanced Math / Exponents

Getting to the Answer: Add polynomial expressions by combining like terms. Be careful of the signs of each term. It may help to write the sum vertically (like you would with big numbers), lining up the like terms.

$$
\begin{array}{r}
6a^2 - 17a - 9 \\
+\; -5a^2 + 8a - 2 \\
\hline
a^2 - 9a - 11
\end{array}
$$

The correct answer is (A).

12. A   Difficulty: Easy

Category: Passport to Advanced Math / Exponents

Getting to the Answer: Find the greatest common factor of both the numerator and the denominator, which in this question happens to be the denominator. Factor out the GCF, $9x^2$, from the numerator and denominator and then cancel what you can.

$$\frac{18x^4 + 27x^3 - 36x^2}{9x^2} = \frac{9x^2(2x^2 + 3x - 4)}{9x^2}$$
$$= 2x^2 + 3x - 4$$

This matches (A). As an alternate method, you could split the expression up and reduce each term, one at a time.

$$\frac{18x^4 + 27x^3 - 36x^2}{9x^2} = \frac{18x^4}{9x^2} + \frac{27x^3}{9x^2} - \frac{36x^2}{9x^2}$$
$$= 2x^2 + 3x - 4$$

13. A   Difficulty: Medium

Category: Passport to Advanced Math / Exponents

Getting to the Answer: Solve equations containing radical expressions the same way you solve any other equation: Isolate the variable using inverse operations. Start by subtracting 8 from both sides of the equation, and then multiply by 3. Then, square both sides to remove the radical.

$$8 + \frac{\sqrt{2x + 29}}{3} = 9$$
$$\frac{\sqrt{2x + 29}}{3} = 1$$
$$\sqrt{2x + 29} = 3$$
$$2x + 29 = 9$$

Now you have a simple linear equation that you can solve using more inverse operations: Subtract 29 and divide by 2 to find that $x = -10$. Be careful—just because the equation started with a radical and the answer is negative, does not mean that *No solution* is the correct answer. If you plug -10 into the expression under the radical, the result is a positive number, which means -10 is a perfectly valid solution. Therefore, (A) is correct.

14. C   Difficulty: Medium

Category: Passport to Advanced Math / Exponents

Getting to the Answer: A fraction is the same as division, so you can use polynomial long division to simplify the expression.

$$
\begin{array}{r}
3x + 2 \\
2x + 5\overline{)6x^2 + 19x + 10} \\
\underline{-\left(6x^2 + 15x\right)} \\
4x + 10 \\
\underline{-(4x + 10)} \\
0
\end{array}
$$

The simplified expression is $3x + 2$, so $a + b = 3 + 2 = 5$, which is (C). As an alternate method, you could factor the numerator of the expression, and cancel common factors:

$$\frac{6x^2 + 19x + 10}{2x + 5} = \frac{(2x + 5)(3x + 2)}{(2x + 5)} = 3x + 2$$

Use whichever method gets you to the correct answer in the shortest amount of time.

15. D   Difficulty: Medium

Category: Passport to Advanced Math / Exponents

Getting to the Answer: Notice that each term is a perfect square and there is a minus sign between the terms, which means you can use the difference of squares rule,

$a^2 - b^2 = (a - b)(a + b)$, to rewrite the expression. If you can't mentally determine what a and b are, write each term as the square of something:

$$25x^2y^4 - 1 = (5xy^2)^2 - 1^2$$
$$= (5xy^2 - 1)(5xy^2 + 1)$$

This matches (D).

16. C Difficulty: Medium

Category: Passport to Advanced Math / Exponents

Getting to the Answer: Whenever a binomial is squared (or raised to any power), you should rewrite it as repeated multiplication and expand it. Do this for both binomials and combine like terms to find the sum.

$$(a - b)^2 + (a + b)^2$$
$$= [(a - b)(a - b)] + [(a + b)(a + b)]$$
$$= (a^2 - ab - ba + b^2) + (a^2 + ab + ba + b^2)$$
$$= (a^2 - 2ab + b^2) + (a^2 + 2ab + b^2)$$
$$= 2a^2 + 2b^2$$

This matches (C).

17. B Difficulty: Medium

Category: Passport to Advanced Math / Exponents

Getting to the Answer: The question asks you to solve the equation for L. Use inverse operations to accomplish the task: Divide both sides of the equation by 2π and then square both sides. You'll need to apply the exponent to all the terms on the left side of the equation, including the π:

$$T = 2\pi\sqrt{\frac{L}{g}}$$

$$\frac{T}{2\pi} = \sqrt{\frac{L}{g}}$$

$$\left(\frac{T}{2\pi}\right)^2 = \left(\sqrt{\frac{L}{g}}\right)^2$$

$$\frac{T^2}{4\pi^2} = \frac{L}{g}$$

Finally, multiply both sides by g to remove g from the denominator and isolate L.

$$L = \frac{gT^2}{4\pi^2}$$

The correct answer is (B).

18. B Difficulty: Hard

Category: Passport to Advanced Math / Exponents

Getting to the Answer: You can solve almost every *work* problem using the formula $W = rt$ or some manipulation of this formula, such as $r = \dfrac{W}{t}$ or $t = \dfrac{W}{r}$. If two or more machines (or people) are working together, start by finding their combined rate and go from there. (Note: W is often 1 because many questions ask about completing *a job*, which is the same as *one job*.)

The first pill counter can complete one batch in 1 hour, so its rate is $r = \dfrac{1}{1} = 1$ batch per hour. The second pill counter can complete one batch in 40 minutes (which is $\dfrac{40}{60} = \dfrac{2}{3}$ hours), so its rate is $r = \dfrac{1}{\frac{2}{3}} = \dfrac{3}{2}$ batches per hour. Working together, the combined rate is $1 + \dfrac{3}{2} = \dfrac{2}{2} + \dfrac{3}{2} = \dfrac{5}{2}$ batches per hour. Use this combined rate in the formula for time to arrive at

$$t_{\text{combined}} = \frac{W}{r_{\text{combined}}} = \frac{1}{\frac{5}{2}} = \frac{2}{5} \text{ hours, which is equivalent}$$

to $\dfrac{2}{\cancel{5}} \times \cancel{60}^{12} = 24$ minutes. This means (B) is correct.

19. 16 Difficulty: Hard

Category: Passport to Advanced Math / Exponents

Getting to the Answer: Because this is a no-calculator question, you need to rewrite the exponent in a way that makes it easier to evaluate: Use exponent rules to rewrite $\dfrac{4}{3}$ as a unit fraction raised to a power. Then write the expression in radical form and simplify.

$$8^{\frac{4}{3}} = \left(8^{\frac{1}{3}}\right)^4$$
$$= \left(\sqrt[3]{8}\right)^4$$
$$= 2^4$$
$$= 2 \times 2 \times 2 \times 2$$
$$= 16$$

Answers & Explanations

20. 8   Difficulty: Medium

Category: Passport to Advanced Math / Exponents

Getting to the Answer: A fraction bar indicates division, so use polynomial long division and your reasoning skills.

$$
\begin{array}{r}
2x^3 + 8x^2 + 2x + 2 \\
x+4\overline{\smash{\big)}\,2x^4 + 16x^3 + 34x^2 + 10x + k} \\
\underline{-(2x^4 + 8x^3)} \\
8x^3 + 34x^2 + 10x + k \\
\underline{-(8x^3 + 32x^2)} \\
2x^2 + 10x + k \\
\underline{-(2x^2 + 8x)} \\
2x + k \\
\underline{-(2x + 8)} \\
k - 8
\end{array}
$$

For there to be no remainder (i.e., a remainder of 0), k must be 8.

CHAPTER 9

PRACTICE

8. C **Difficulty:** Medium
Category: Passport to Advanced Math / Functions

Getting to the Answer: You're told the honeybee population decreases 35% each month; this means exponential decay is occurring, so use $y = x_0(1 + r)^x$ as your function template. Set p as the honeybee population and t as the time in months; watch the sign of r. Your function should be $p(t) = (4.23 \times 10^8)(0.65)^t$. Now plug in the time in months:

$$p(12) = (4.23 \times 10^8)(0.65)^{12} \approx 2{,}406{,}028$$

The correct answer is (C).

9. C **Difficulty:** Hard
Category: Passport to Advanced Math / Functions

Getting to the Answer: Translate the composition notation: $(b \circ a)(x)$ means $b(a(x))$ or b of $a(x)$. This tells you to use $a(x)$ as the input for $b(x)$. You can rewrite this as $\dfrac{1}{a(x)}$, which is the reciprocal of $a(x)$. This new function will be undefined anywhere that $a(x) = 0$. Looking at the graph, you can see that $a(x)$ crosses the x-axis four times, making (C) correct.

PERFORM

10. B **Difficulty:** Hard
Category: Passport to Advanced Math / Functions

Getting to the Answer: Don't panic about this involving a trigonometric function; the question is only testing your ability to apply multiple transformations to a graph. The easiest transformation to identify is the -4 downward shift. Eliminate C and D, as neither contains this shift. Both A and (B) contain a vertical compression, but the difference is subtle, so home in on the transformed function's horizontal compression caused by the 2 in parentheses. Choice (B) has a compressed sine graph, so it is correct.

11. A **Difficulty:** Medium
Category: Passport to Advanced Math / Functions

Getting to the Answer: Use the two given rates to determine Briana's typing rate in pages per minute. She types 45 words per minute, which becomes:

$$\frac{45 \text{ words}}{1 \text{ min}} \times \frac{1 \text{ page}}{500 \text{ words}} = \frac{45 \text{ pages}}{500 \text{ min}} = \frac{9 \text{ pages}}{100 \text{ min}}$$

Multiplying this rate by m gets you the number of pages typed after m minutes, which can then be subtracted from the starting page count (60) to get the number of pages Briana has left to type. The function should read $p(m) = 60 - \dfrac{9m}{100}$, which matches (A).

12. D **Difficulty:** Medium
Category: Passport to Advanced Math / Functions

Getting to the Answer: Examine the graph. A peak in fuel economy at 50 mph is obvious, but what else can be said? A closer look at the increase below 50 mph (to the left of 50 on the horizontal axis) and the decrease above 50 mph (to the right of 50) reveals a critical detail: The decreasing part of the graph is steeper than the increasing part. This means the rate of decrease is faster than the rate of increase. This corresponds to (D).

ON YOUR OWN

1. A **Difficulty:** Easy
Category: Passport to Advanced Math / Functions

Getting to the Answer: The notation $k(4)$ means the output value of the function when 4 is substituted for the input (x), and $k(1)$ means the output value of the function when 1 is substituted for the input (x). Substitute 4 and 1 into the function, one at a time, and then subtract the results.

$$k(4) = 5(4) + 2 = 20 + 2 = 22$$
$$k(1) = 5(1) + 2 = 5 + 2 = 7$$
$$k(4) - k(1) = 22 - 7 = 15$$

Choice (A) is correct. Caution—this is not the same as subtracting $4 - 1$ and then substituting 3 into the function.

2. C   Difficulty: Easy

Category: Passport to Advanced Math / Functions

Getting to the Answer: The function graphed is the absolute value function, and you can see that all values in its range (the *y*-values) are positive. That makes the negative value in (C) impossible. Because you're looking for the statement that is NOT true, you can safely conclude that (C) is correct.

3. D   Difficulty: Medium

Category: Passport to Advanced Math / Functions

Getting to the Answer: Compare each answer choice to the graph, eliminating false statements as you go.

Choice A: Carmel went to the library first, so the library (not the grocery store) is about 5 miles from his home. Eliminate this choice.

Choice B: Carmel traveled 7 miles away from his home (between $t = 0$ minutes and $t = 30$ minutes), but then also traveled 7 miles back (between $t = 45$ minutes and $t = 60$ minutes), so he traveled a total of 14 miles. Eliminate this choice.

Choice C: When Carmel reached the library, he was 5 miles from home; when he reached the grocery store, he was 7 miles from home. This means the grocery store must be $7 - 5 = 2$ miles farther away. Eliminate this choice.

Choice (D) must be correct. Carmel is the same distance from home (5 miles) between $t = 15$ minutes and $t = 25$ minutes, so he spent 10 minutes at the library. He is stopped once again (at the grocery store) between $t = 30$ minutes and $t = 45$ minutes, so he spent 15 minutes at the grocery store.

4. C   Difficulty: Medium

Category: Passport to Advanced Math / Functions

Getting to the Answer: Transformations that are grouped with the *x* in a function shift the graph horizontally and therefore affect the *x*-coordinates of points on the graph. Transformations that are not grouped with the *x* shift the graph vertically and therefore affect the *y*-coordinates of points on the graph. Remember, horizontal shifts are always the reverse of what they look like. When working with multiple transformations, follow the same order of operations as always—parentheses first, then multiply and divide, then add and subtract.

Start with the parentheses: $(x - 2)$. This shifts the graph right 2 units, so add 2 to the *x*-coordinate of the given point: $(5, 3) \rightarrow (5 + 2, 3) = (7, 3)$. Next, apply the negative in front of *g* because it represents multiplication. The negative is not grouped with the *x*, so multiply the *y*-coordinate by -1 to get $(7, 3(-1)) \rightarrow (7, -3)$. Finally, the $+ 8$ is not grouped with *x*, so add 8 to the *y*-coordinate: $(7, -3) \rightarrow (7, -3 + 8) = (7, 5)$, which matches (C).

You could also plot the point on a coordinate plane, perform the transformations (right 2, reflect vertically over the *x*-axis, and then up 8), to find the new point. The result will be the same.

5. A   Difficulty: Medium

Category: Passport to Advanced Math / Functions

Getting to the Answer: The notation $g(h(x))$ indicates a composition of two functions which can be read "g of h of x." It means that the output when *x* is substituted in $h(x)$ becomes the input for $g(x)$. First, use the table on the right to find that $h(3)$ is 0. This is your new input. Now, use the table on the left to find $g(0)$, which is -1, making (A) the correct answer.

6. B   Difficulty: Hard

Category: Passport to Advanced Math / Functions

Getting to the Answer: The key to answering this question is to have a conceptual understanding of function notation. Here, the input $(x + 2)$ has already been substituted and simplified in the given function. Your job is to determine what the function would have looked like had *x* been the input instead. To keep things organized, let $u = x + 2$, the old input. This means $x = u - 2$. Substitute this into *p* and simplify:

$$p(x + 2) = 3x^2 + 4x + 1$$
$$p(u) = 3(u - 2)^2 + 4(u - 2) + 1$$
$$= 3(u^2 - 4u + 4) + 4u - 8 + 1$$
$$= 3u^2 - 12u + 12 + 4u - 8 + 1$$
$$= 3u^2 - 8u + 5$$

When working with function notation, you evaluate the function by substituting a given input value for the variable in the parentheses. Here, if the input value is *x*, then $p(x) = 3x^2 - 8x + 5$, which means (B) is correct.

7. 3.5 or **3.50**   **Difficulty:** Medium

Category: Passport to Advanced Math / Functions

Getting to the Answer: Start by evaluating the function at $x = 25$ and at $x = 20$. Make sure you follow the correct order of operations as you simplify.

$$P(25) = 150(25) - (25)^2$$
$$= 3,750 - 625$$
$$= 3,125$$
$$P(20) = 150(20) - (20)^2$$
$$= 3,000 - 400$$
$$= 2,600$$

The question asks how much more profit *per unit* the company makes, so find the difference in the amounts of profit and divide by the number of units (150) to get $\dfrac{3,125 - 2,600}{150} = \dfrac{525}{150} = \$3.504$, or 3.5.

8. 305   Difficulty: Medium

Category: Passport to Advanced Math / Functions

Getting to the Answer: Always pay careful attention to what the variable in a function represents, especially in questions that deal with real-world scenarios. In this question, *t* does *not* represent the time, so don't find $C(5)$. Rather, you need to start by finding the number of hours that pass between 7 AM and 5 PM. Because there are 10 hours between 7 AM and 5 PM, evaluate the function at $t = 10$. Make sure you follow the correct order of operations as you simplify.

$$C(t) = -0.0814t^4 + t^3 + 12t$$
$$C(10) = -0.0815(10)^4 + 10^3 + 12(10)$$
$$= -0.0815(10,000) + 1,000 + 120$$
$$= -815 + 1,000 + 120$$
$$= 305$$

9. A   Difficulty: Easy

Category: Passport to Advanced Math / Functions

Getting to the Answer: The notation $g(-2)$ means the value of the function when $x = -2$, so substitute -2 for x and simplify. Don't forget to use the correct order of operations as you work:

$$g(-2) = -2(-2)^2 + 7(-2) - 3$$
$$= -2(4) + (-14) - 3$$
$$= -8 - 14 - 3$$
$$= -25$$

Choice (A) is correct.

10. C   Difficulty: Easy

Category: Passport to Advanced Math / Functions

Getting to the Answer: A function, by definition, only has one output for every input. When you're given graphs to consider, use the vertical line test to see if the graph represents a function. If a vertical line intersects a graph more than one time, then the graph has more than one output for a given input and is therefore *not* a function. The graph in (C) fails the test, so it is not a function.

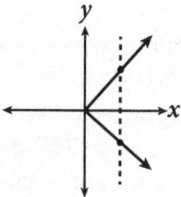

11. D   Difficulty: Easy

Category: Passport to Advanced Math / Functions

Getting to the Answer: The domain of a function represents the possible values of *x*, or the input values. In this function, *x* is represented by *p*, which is the number of seeds germinated by the plants over a given period of time. Because there cannot be a negative number of seeds germinated, or a fraction of a seed germinated, the list in (D) is the only one that could represent a portion of the function's domain.

12. D   Difficulty: Medium

Category: Passport to Advanced Math / Functions

Getting to the Answer: To determine the domain, look at the *x*-values. To determine the range, look at the *y*-values. For the domain, the graph is continuous (no holes or gaps in the graph) and has arrows on both sides, so the domain is all real numbers. This means you can eliminate A and B. For the range, the function's maximum (the vertex) is located at $(-3, 4)$, which means the highest possible y-value of $f(x)$ is 4. The graph is continuous and opens downward, so the range of the function is $y \leq 4$, which is the same as $f(x) \leq 4$, making (D) correct.

13. D   Difficulty: Medium

Category: Passport to Advanced Math / Functions

Getting to the Answer: Draw a quick sketch of the equation (or graph it in your graphing calculator).

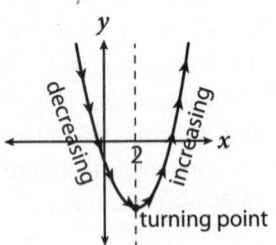

Based on the equation, the graph is a parabola that opens upward with a vertex of $(2, -5)$. A parabola changes direction at the x-coordinate of its vertex. This is all the information you need to answer the question. You can immediately eliminate A and B. To choose between C and (D), take a closer look at the sketch. To the left of 2 (or $x < 2$), the parabola is decreasing, and to the right of 2 (or $x > 2$), it is increasing. This makes (D) correct.

14. B   Difficulty: Medium

Category: Passport to Advanced Math / Functions

Getting to the Answer: In this question, you are given a range value (14), which means $f(x) = 14$, and you are asked for the corresponding domain value (x-value). This means you are solving for x, not substituting for x. Set the function equal to 14 and solve using inverse operations:

$$14 = \frac{x^2}{4} - 11$$
$$25 = \frac{x^2}{4}$$
$$100 = x^2$$
$$\pm 10 = x$$

Negative 10 is not one of the answer choices, so (B) is correct.

15. C   Difficulty: Medium

Category: Passport to Advanced Math / Functions

Getting to the Answer: Piecewise functions look intimidating, but they are usually very simple functions—they're just written in pieces. The right-hand side of each piece of the function tells you what part of the domain (which x-values) goes with that particular expression. In this function, only values of x that are less than or equal to 0 go with the top expression, values of x greater than 0 and less than or equal to 3 go with the middle expression, and values of x that are greater than 3 go with the bottom expression. Because -3 is less than 0, plug it into the top expression and simplify:

$$f(-3) = (-3)^2 + 1$$
$$= 9 + 1$$
$$= 10$$

This matches (C).

16. C   Difficulty: Medium

Category: Passport to Advanced Math / Functions

Getting to the Answer: Graphically, the notation $f(-2)$ means the y-value when x is -2. Pay careful attention to which graph is which. It may help to draw dots on the graph. Find $x = -2$ along the horizontal axis, trace up to the graph of $f(x)$, and draw a dot on the graph. Do the same for $g(2)$, as shown here:

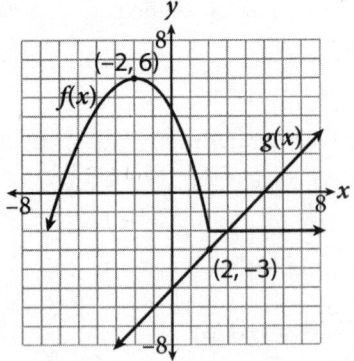

Now, read the y-coordinates from the graph and subtract: $f(-2)$ is 6 and $g(2)$ is -3, so $f(-2) + g(2) = 6 + (-3) = 3$, which is (C).

17. D **Difficulty:** Hard

Category: Passport to Advanced Math / Functions

Getting to the Answer: When working with a composition, the range of the inner function becomes the domain of the outer function, which in turn produces the range of the composition. In the composition $f(g(x))$, the function $g(x) = \dfrac{x^2}{2}$ is the inner function. Every value of x, when substituted into this function, will result in a nonnegative value (because the result of squaring a number is always a positive number). This means the smallest possible range value of $g(x)$ is 0. Now look at $f(x)$. Substituting large positive values of x in the function will result in large negative numbers. Consequently, substituting the smallest value from the range of g, which is 0, results in the largest range value for the composition, which is $3 - 0 = 3$. Because $4 > 3$, it is not in the range of $f(g(x))$. Therefore, (D) is correct.

18. D **Difficulty:** Hard

Category: Passport to Advanced Math / Functions

Getting to the Answer: Graphing piecewise functions can be tricky. Try describing the graph in words first, and then find the matching function. Use words such as "to the left of" (which translates as *less than*) and "to the right of" (which translates as *greater than*).

First notice that there is a hole in the graph at $x = 4$. This means you can eliminate A right away because the inequality symbol in the top piece would include the endpoint at 4. To choose between the remaining answers, think about parent functions and transformations. To the left of $x = 4$, the graph is an absolute value function that has been reflected vertically across the x-axis and then shifted up one unit. This means either C or (D) must be correct. Now look to the right of $x = 4$: The graph is a horizontal line, which means a line that has a slope of 0. The slope of the line in C is negative 3, so it can't be correct. This means (D) is correct. (The equation of a horizontal line always looks like $y = b$, or in this case, $g(x) = -3$.)

CHAPTER 10

PRACTICE

8. D   **Difficulty:** Hard

Category: Passport to Advanced Math / Quadratics

Getting to the Answer: Find the maximum height of the potato, then find the time it takes the potato to hit the ground. The x-coordinate of the vertex is given by $h = \dfrac{-b}{2a} = \dfrac{-224}{2(-16)} = 7$. Plug this into the function to get the y-coordinate: $f(7) = -16(7)^2 + 224(7) + 240 = 1{,}024$. Next, calculate how long it takes for the potato to hit the ground. This will occur when $f(t) = 0$. Plug in and factor to solve:

$$-16t^2 + 224t + 240 = 0$$
$$-16\left(t^2 - 14t - 15\right) = 0$$
$$t^2 - 14t - 15 = 0$$
$$(t - 15)(t + 1) = 0$$
$$t = 15 \text{ or } t = -1$$

Because time can't be negative, $t = 15$. Don't forget that you were asked for the sum of the height and the time, not for either of the raw values. The sum of 15 and 1,024 is 1,039, choice (D).

9. B   **Difficulty:** Medium

Category: Passport to Advanced Math / Quadratics

Getting to the Answer: If $ab > 0$, then a and b are either both positive or both negative. In the second inequality, $b^2ac < 0$, you can ignore the b^2 term because it will be positive regardless of the sign of b. This implies that either a or c is positive, and the other is negative. The x-intercepts are b and c. Because b has the same sign as a, while c has the opposite sign as a, it follows that b and c have opposite signs. The correct answer must therefore be a function with one negative root and one positive root. Scan the functions to find the correct one. Ignore the complicated-looking numbers—all that matter are the signs! Choice (B) is correct.

PERFORM

10. A   **Difficulty:** Hard

Category: Passport to Advanced Math / Quadratics

Getting to the Answer: Technically, this isn't a quadratic equation because the highest power on the variable isn't 2. However, it is a "quadratic-type" equation because the square of the variable part of the middle term is equal to the variable in the leading term. This means you can use factoring techniques you learned for quadratics to answer this question as well. The presence of 4, 9, and 16—all perfect squares—is a big clue. Observe that $4x - 12\sqrt{x} + 9$ is an instance of the quadratic shortcut $(a - b)^2 = a^2 - 2ab + b^2$. Use the shortcut to factor the equation and see where that leads you.

$$4x - 12\sqrt{x} + 9 = 16$$
$$(2\sqrt{x} - 3)^2 = 16$$
$$2\sqrt{x} - 3 = \pm 4$$

Now go back to what you're looking for: $10\sqrt{x} - 15$ is 5 times the quantity on the left side of the last equation above, so multiply the positive result, 4, by 5 to get 20. The correct answer is (A).

11. B   **Difficulty:** Medium

Category: Passport to Advanced Math / Quadratics

Getting to the Answer: Neither of the functions is presented in standard form, so make this question a little easier by simplifying each one before setting them equal to each other.

$$f(x) = 3(x - 4)^2 + 4 = 3(x^2 - 8x + 16) + 4$$
$$= 3x^2 - 24x + 48 + 4$$
$$= 3x^2 - 24x + 52$$

$$g(x) = (x + 5)^2 + 2x - 135$$
$$= x^2 + 10x + 25 + 2x - 135$$
$$= x^2 + 12x - 110$$

$$f(x) = g(x)$$
$$3x^2 - 24x + 52 = x^2 + 12x - 110$$
$$2x^2 - 36x + 162 = 0$$
$$2(x^2 - 18x + 81) = 0$$
$$x^2 - 18x + 81 = 0$$

Notice that you can now use a quadratic shortcut:

$$x^2 - 18x + 81 = 0$$
$$(x - 9)^2 = 0$$
$$x = 9$$

Note that the question asks how many intersection points there are, *not* what the points are. Since there is only one solution for x, there must be only one point of intersection, which is (B). Don't waste time plugging 9 back in.

12. 2   Difficulty: Medium
Category: Passport to Advanced Math / Quadratics

Getting to the Answer: An x-intercept of a function is a point at which the y-coordinate equals 0. Set the equation equal to zero, simplify, and factor.

$$g(x) = -2.5x^2 + 10x - 7.5$$
$$0 = -2.5x^2 + 10x - 7.5$$
$$0 = -2.5(x^2 - 4x + 3)$$
$$0 = x^2 - 4x + 3$$
$$0 = (x - 1)(x - 3)$$
$$x = 1 \text{ or } x = 3$$

Recall that the question asks for the *difference* between the x-intercepts, not for the x-intercepts themselves. The difference between 3 and 1 is 2.

13. C   Difficulty: Medium
Category: Passport to Advanced Math / Quadratics

Getting to the Answer: An axis of symmetry splits a parabola in half and travels through the vertex. You have a formula to find h instantly. All you have to do is plug and chug to get your answer—just be careful with the fractions and the negatives.

$$x = -\frac{b}{2a}$$
$$= -17 \div 2\left(\frac{-11}{3}\right)$$
$$= -17 \div \frac{-22}{3}$$
$$= -17 \times \frac{-3}{22}$$
$$= \frac{51}{22}$$

The correct answer is (C).

ON YOUR OWN

1. B   Difficulty: Easy
Category: Passport to Advanced Math / Quadratics

Getting to the Answer: Using the first equation, set each of the factors equal to 0 and solve for x to find that the x-intercepts are $-\frac{1}{2}$ and 5. This means you can eliminate A and D. From the standard form of the equation, you can see that the y-intercept is -5 (the value of c) because $0^2 - 3(0) - 5 = -5$, so (B) is correct.

2. A   Difficulty: Medium
Category: Passport to Advanced Math / Quadratics

Getting to the Answer: The answer choices all look very similar, so think logically to eliminate a couple. A rocket goes *up*, hits a maximum height, and then comes *down*. This tells you that the graph will be an upside-down parabola, which means the equation should have a negative sign in front. Eliminate C and D. To choose between (A) and B, you need to recall what the *vertex form* of a quadratic looks like and what it tells you. When a quadratic equation is written in the form $y = a(x - h)^2 + k$, the vertex of the graph is (h, k). The h tells you *where* the maximum (or minimum) occurs, and the k tells you *what* the maximum (or minimum) value is. Here, the maximum height of 34 feet occurs at 3 seconds, so k is 34 and h is 3. Substitute these values into vertex form to find that the correct equation is $y = -16(x - 3)^2 + 34$. Translate this to function language ($h(t) = y$ and $t = x$) to arrive at the answer: $h(t) = -16(t - 3)^2 + 34$, which is (A).

3. A   Difficulty: Medium
Category: Passport to Advanced Math / Quadratics

Getting to the Answer: When finding solutions to a quadratic equation, always start by rewriting the equation to make it equal 0 (unless both sides of the equation are already perfect squares). To make the equation equal 0, subtract 30 from both sides to get $x^2 - 7x - 30 = 0$. The answer choices are all integers, so factor the equation. Look for two numbers whose product is -30 and whose sum is -7. The two numbers are -10 and 3, so the factors are $(x - 10)$ and $(x + 3)$. Set each factor equal to 0 and solve to find that $x = 10$ and $x = -3$. The question states that $x > 0$, so x must equal 10. Before selecting an answer, don't forget to check that you answered the right question—the question asks for the value of $x - 5$, not just x, so the correct answer is $10 - 5 = 5$, which means (A) is correct.

4. C   Difficulty: Medium

Category: Passport to Advanced Math / Quadratics

Getting to the Answer: Understanding that in algebra "divides evenly" means "is a factor" is the key to answering this question. You could use polynomial long division, but in most cases, factoring is quicker. The leading coefficient of the equation is not 1, so you'll need to use the *AC method* and grouping to factor the equation. Multiply *a* times *c* (6×-20) and then look for two factors of that product whose sum is equal to the coefficient of the middle term. Break the middle term $(7x)$ into two terms using the numbers you found, and then factor by grouping. The product is -120 and the two factors of -120 that add up to 7 are 15 and -8.

$$6x^2 + 7x - 20 = 6x^2 + 15x - 8x - 20$$
$$= (6x^2 + 15x) - (8x + 20)$$
$$= 3x(2x + 5) - 4(2x + 5)$$
$$= (2x + 5)(3x - 4)$$

So, $3x - 4$ divides evenly into the expression, making (C) correct.

5. A   Difficulty: Medium

Category: Passport to Advanced Math / Quadratics

Getting to the Answer: Even though one of the equations in this system isn't linear, you can still solve the system using substitution. You already know that y is equal to $2x$, so substitute $2x$ for y in the second equation. Don't forget that when you square $2x$, you must square both the coefficient and the variable. Also, be careful—there are a lot of 2s floating around, so pay careful attention as you plug in values.

$$2x^2 + 2y^2 = 240$$
$$x^2 + y^2 = 120$$

$$x^2 + (2x)^2 = 120$$
$$x^2 + 4x^2 = 120$$
$$5x^2 = 120$$
$$x^2 = 24$$

The question asks for the value of x^2, not x, so there is no need to take the square root of 24 to find the value of x. Choice (A) is correct.

6. B   Difficulty: Hard

Category: Passport to Advanced Math / Quadratics

Getting to the Answer: The maximum value shown in the graph is about 56 or 57 feet. When a quadratic equation is written in vertex form, $y = a(x - h)^2 + k$, the maximum value is given by k, so check C and D first because they will be the easiest to compare to the graph. In C, k is 48, which is not greater than 56 or 57 and therefore not correct. In D, k is 52, which is also not greater than 56 or 57. This means either A or (B) must be correct. You now have two options—you could expand the equation in each answer choice and then complete the square to find the vertex, or you could expand the equations, find the x-coordinate of the vertex using the formula $x = \dfrac{-b}{2a}$, and then plug in the result to find the y-value. Completing the square usually takes a bit of time, so the second option is probably the quicker route to take. Expanding A, you get $h = -16t^2 + 48t$ with $a = -16$ and $b = 48$. The x-coordinate of the vertex is $\dfrac{-48}{2(-16)} = \dfrac{-48}{-32} = 1.5$. Substituting this back into the equation, the y-value of the vertex (which is the maximum value of the function) is $-16(1.5)^2 + 48(1.5) = 36$, which is not greater than 56 or 57, so (B) must be correct. Don't waste valuable time checking, but if you use the same strategy, you'll find that the maximum height of the equation in (B) is 81 feet.

7. 5   Difficulty: Medium

Category: Passport to Advanced Math / Quadratics

Getting to the Answer: Before you plug -5 in for x, which creates messy numbers, factor the given equation.

$$x^2 + 2xk + k^2 = 0$$
$$(x + k)(x + k) = 0$$
$$(x + k)^2 = 0$$

Now plug in -5 for x and solve for k:

$$(-5 + k)^2 = 0$$
$$\sqrt[2]{(-5 + k)^2} = \pm\sqrt{0}$$
$$-5 + k = 0$$
$$k = 5$$

8. 6.5 or **13/2**   **Difficulty:** Hard
Category: Passport to Advanced Math / Quadratics

Getting to the Answer: This is a tough question with no real shortcuts. The highest power of x in the equation is 2, so the equation is quadratic. Writing quadratic equations can be tricky and time-consuming. If you know the roots, you can use factors to write the equation. You don't know the roots of this equation, so start with the point that has the nicest values (0, 2) and substitute them into the equation, $y = ax^2 + bx + c$.

$$2 = a(0)^2 + b(0) + c$$
$$2 = c$$

Now your equation looks like $y = ax^2 + bx + 2$. Next, use the other two points to create a system of two equations in two variables.

$$(-2, -10) \rightarrow -10 = a(-2)^2 + b(-2) + 2 \rightarrow -12 = 4a - 2b$$

$$(4, 14) \rightarrow 14 = a(4)^2 + b(4) + 2 \rightarrow 12 = 16a + 4b$$

You now have a system of equations to solve. None of the variables has a coefficient of 1, so use combination to solve the system. If you multiply the top equation by 2, the b terms will eliminate each other.

$$2[4a - 2b = -12] \rightarrow 8a - 4b = -24$$
$$16a + 4b = 12 \rightarrow \underline{16a + 4b = 12}$$
$$24a = -12$$
$$a = -\frac{1}{2}$$

Now, find b by substituting the value of a into either of the original equations. Using the bottom equation, you get this:

$$16\left(-\frac{1}{2}\right) + 4b = 12$$
$$-8 + 4b = 12$$
$$4b = 20$$
$$b = 5$$

The value of $a + b + c = -\frac{1}{2} + 5 + 2 = 6\frac{1}{2}$. You can't enter a mixed number, so grid in your answer as the decimal number 6.5 or the improper fraction 13/2.

9. B   **Difficulty:** Easy
Category: Passport to Advanced Math / Quadratics

Getting to the Answer: To multiply two binomials, distribute each term in the first set of parentheses to each term in the second set. You can also think FOIL. Multiply $2a$ by each term in the second factor and then multiply $5b$ by each term. Combine like terms if possible.

$$(2a + 5b)(a - 3b)$$
$$= 2a(a - 3b) + 5b(a - 3b)$$
$$= 2a(a) + 2a(-3b) + 5b(a) + 5b(-3b)$$
$$= 2a^2 - 6ab + 5ab - 15b^2$$
$$= 2a^2 - ab - 15b^2$$

Choice (B) is correct.

10. A   **Difficulty:** Easy
Category: Passport to Advanced Math / Quadratics

Getting to the Answer: *Roots* are the same as *solutions* to an equation, so you need to solve the equation for x. Taking the square root of a quantity is the inverse operation of squaring it, and both sides of this equation are already perfect squares, so take their square roots. Then solve the resulting equations. Remember, there will be two equations to solve.

$$(x + 3)^2 = 49$$
$$\sqrt[2]{(x + 3)^2} = \pm\sqrt{49}$$
$$x + 3 = \pm 7$$

Now simplify each equation: $x + 3 = -7$, or $x = -10$; and $x + 3 = 7$, or $x = 4$, so (A) is correct.

If you didn't recognize that you could use square rooting to solve the equation, you could also expand the left side, then subtract 49, factor the resulting equation, and set the factors equal to 0. This is a perfectly fine way to solve the equation, but it takes considerably longer.

11. C   **Difficulty:** Easy
Category: Passport to Advanced Math / Quadratics

Getting to the Answer: Being able to make connections between equations and graphs is a valuable skill. The pieces of a quadratic equation written in standard form give you lots of information about its graph. For example, finding the value of $\frac{-b}{2a}$ (the quadratic formula without the radical part) tells you where the axis of symmetry occurs.

This question is asking about c, which is the only constant term in the equation. If you substitute 0 for x, the equation becomes $y = a(0)^2 + b(0) + c$, or just $y = c$. This means the point $(0, c)$ will be on the graph, which is the y-intercept, making (C) correct.

12. D   **Difficulty:** Easy

Category: Passport to Advanced Math / Quadratics

Getting to the Answer: The graph is a parabola, so you can eliminate A right way (the equation is linear, not quadratic). The x-intercepts of the graph are -2 and 5, so the factors of this quadratic must be $(x + 2)$ and $(x - 5)$. The parabola opens downward, so there should be a negative sign in front of the factors. The correct equation is $y = -(x + 2)(x - 5)$. Don't let C fool you—those factors would produce x-intercepts of $+2$ and -5. If you're not convinced, set each factor equal to 0 and solve for x. Therefore, (D) is correct.

13. C   **Difficulty:** Medium

Category: Passport to Advanced Math / Quadratics

Getting to the Answer: Equations that are equivalent have the same solutions, so you are looking for the equation that is simply written in a different form. You could expand each of the equations in the answer choices, but unless you get lucky, this will use up quite a bit of time. The answer choices are written in vertex form, so use the method of completing the square to convert the equation in the question to the same form. First, write the equation in standard form: $y = x^2 + 6x - 40$. Move the 40 to the other side to temporarily get it out of the way. Then, complete the square on the right-hand side, by finding $\left(\dfrac{b}{2}\right)^2 = \left(\dfrac{6}{2}\right)^2 = 3^2 = 9$, and adding the result to both sides of the equation.

$$y = x^2 + 6x - 40$$
$$y + 40 = x^2 + 6x$$
$$y + 40 + 9 = x^2 + 6x + 9$$
$$y + 49 = x^2 + 6x + 9$$

Next, factor the right-hand side of the equation (which should be a perfect square trinomial) and rewrite it as a square.

$$y + 49 = (x + 3)(x + 3)$$
$$y + 49 = (x + 3)^2$$

Finally, solve for y to get $y = (x + 3)^2 - 49$, which makes (C) correct.

14. B   **Difficulty:** Medium

Category: Passport to Advanced Math / Quadratics

Getting to the Answer: Quadratic equations can be written in several different forms, each of which reveals something special about the graph. For example, the vertex form of a quadratic equation $(y = a(x - h)^2 + k)$ gives the minimum or maximum value of the function (it's k), while the standard form $(y = ax^2 + bx + c)$ reveals the y-intercept (it's c). The factored form of a quadratic equation reveals the solutions to the equation, which graphically represent the x-intercepts. Choice (B) is the only equation written in factored form and therefore must be correct. You can set each factor equal to 0 and quickly solve to find that the x-intercepts of the graph are $x = -\dfrac{3}{4}$ and $x = 1$, which agree with the graph.

15. A   **Difficulty:** Hard

Category: Passport to Advanced Math / Quadratics

Getting to the Answer: To answer this question, you need to recall just about everything you've learned about quadratic graphs. Be careful—the equation looks like vertex form, $y = a(x - h)^2 + k$, but it's not quite there because of the 2 inside the parentheses. You could rewrite the equation in vertex form, but this would involve squaring the quantity in parentheses and then completing the square, which will take quite a bit of time. So, skip A for now and compare each of the other answer choices to the equation. Don't forget, you are looking for the statement that is *not* true.

Choice B: Substitute 0 for x and simplify to find that the y-intercept is indeed $(0, -9)$.

Choice C: There is a negative in front of the equation, so the parabola *does* open downward.

Choice D: Look at the equation as a transformation of the parent function $y = x^2$. The parabola has been shifted to the right, moved up 7 units, and flipped upside down. Picture this in your head—it has to cross the x-axis at least one time.

This means (A) must be correct. As it turns out, the vertex is (2, 7), not (4, 7).

16. C   Difficulty: Hard

Category: Passport to Advanced Math / Quadratics

Getting to the Answer: You are not expected to solve each system. Instead, think about it graphically. The solution to a system of equations is the point(s) where their graphs intersect, so graph each pair of equations in your graphing calculator and look for the ones that intersect at $x = 3.5$ and $x = 6$, both of which happen to be positive values and would lie to the right of the x-axis. The graphs of the equations in A and B don't intersect at all, so you can eliminate both answers right away. The graphs in (C) *do* intersect, and both points of intersection are to the right of the x-axis, so (C) could be correct, but check D just in case. The graphs don't intersect at all, so (C) is correct.

A note of caution here—just because the solutions were given as 3.5 and 6, that does *not* mean that either number has to appear in one or both of the equations.

17. 0   Difficulty: Medium

Category: Passport to Advanced Math / Quadratics

Getting to the Answer: To find the roots of an equation, you need to set it equal to 0, factor it, and then solve. Whenever the leading coefficient is a fraction, factoring becomes very messy. Luckily, you can clear the fraction the same way you do when solving equations (multiply both sides of the equation by the denominator of the fraction).

$$0 = \frac{1}{3}x^2 - 2x + 3$$
$$3(0) = 3\left(\frac{1}{3}x^2 - 2x + 3\right)$$
$$0 = x^2 - 6x + 9$$
$$0 = (x - 3)(x - 3)$$

The equation only has one unique solution ($x = 3$), so the positive difference between the roots is actually 0.

18. 8   Difficulty: Easy

Category: Passport to Advanced Math / Quadratics

Getting to the Answer: Whenever you're given the equation for a function, you can evaluate it at any given value by substituting that value for the variable. The variable t

represents the number of seconds after the rockets were fired, so find $h_2(1)$ and $h_1(1)$ and subtract. (Note that the equations are provided in the graphic.) To make the calculations easier, simplify each equation first.

$$h_2(t) = -8t(2t - 7) = -16t^2 + 56t$$
$$h_2(1) = -16(1)^2 + 56(1) = -16 + 56 = 40$$
$$h_1(t) = -16t(t - 3) = -16t^2 + 48t$$
$$h_1(1) = -16(1)^2 + 48(1) = -16 + 48 = 32$$

So, after 1 second the second rocket was $40 - 32 = 8$ feet higher.

19. .25 or 1/4   Difficulty: Hard

Category: Passport to Advanced Math / Quadratics

Getting to the Answer: A quadratic function reaches its maximum (or minimum) value at its vertex. Don't do rework—you've already written each equation in standard form, so use the formula $x = \frac{-b}{2a}$ to find the x-coordinate of the vertex for each function.

$h_2(t)$: $a = -16$ and $b = 56$, so $x = \frac{-56}{2(-16)} = \frac{-56}{-32} = \frac{7}{4}$.
This means the second rocket reaches its maximum height at 1.75 seconds.

$h_1(t)$: $a = -16$ and $b = 48$, so $x = \frac{-48}{2(-16)} = \frac{-48}{-32} = \frac{3}{2}$.
This means the first rocket reaches its maximum height at 1.5 seconds.

So, it took the second rocket $1.75 - 1.5 = 0.25$ seconds longer to reach its maximum height.

If you are comfortable using your graphing calculator (which could save quite a bit of time), you could graph each equation and use the "maximum" function on the calculator.

20. 8   Difficulty: Medium

Category: Passport to Advanced Math / Quadratics

Getting to the Answer: This question is testing whether you can interpret an equation. If you look carefully, it tells you that the coefficient of the x term from each equation is all you need. Again, don't do rework—you've already written each equation in standard form.

The standard form of the equation for the second rocket is $h_2(t) = -16t^2 + 56t$, so the initial velocity was 56 feet per second. The standard form of the equation for the first rocket is $h_1(t) = -16t^2 + 48t$, so the initial velocity was 48 feet per second. The second rocket's initial velocity was $56 - 48 = 8$ more feet per second than the first rocket's.

CHAPTER 11

PRACTICE

7. C   Difficulty: Hard
Category: Additional Topics in Math / Geometry

Getting to the Answer: Look for hidden special right triangles to help you find the answer, and add new information to your diagram as you find it. Start by finding $m\angle ACD$ from the two given angles: $m\angle ACD = 180° - 15° - 30° = 135°$. Because $\angle ACB$ is supplementary to $\angle ACD$, $\angle ACB$ measures $45°$. $\triangle ABC$ is a right triangle, so its missing angle ($\angle BAC$) is also $45°$, making $\triangle ABC$ a 45-45-90 triangle. This means $\angle BAD$ is $60°$; therefore, $\triangle ABD$ is a 30-60-90 triangle.

Knowing that you have two special right triangles will allow you to unlock the unknown side lengths. $\overline{AC}$ is the hypotenuse of the 45-45-90 triangle (side ratio of $x:x:x\sqrt{2}$), so $\overline{AB}$ and $\overline{BC}$ (the two legs) must be $2\sqrt{2}$ (solve the equation $4 = x\sqrt{2}$ to find this). $\overline{AB}$ is also the shorter leg of the 30-60-90 triangle (side ratio of $x:x\sqrt{3}:2x$), so $\overline{BD}$ (longer leg) is $2\sqrt{6}$, and $\overline{AD}$ (hypotenuse) is $4\sqrt{2}$. Don't stop just yet; remember which perimeter you need. Take the difference of $\overline{BD}$ and $\overline{BC}$ to determine $\overline{CD}$, which is $2\sqrt{6} - 2\sqrt{2}$. You now have all three sides of $\triangle ACD$, so add them together to get your answer:

$$P_{\triangle ACD} = 4 + \left(2\sqrt{6} - 2\sqrt{2}\right) + 4\sqrt{2}$$

This simplifies to $4 + 2\sqrt{6} + 2\sqrt{2}$, making (C) correct.

The completed diagram is shown here:

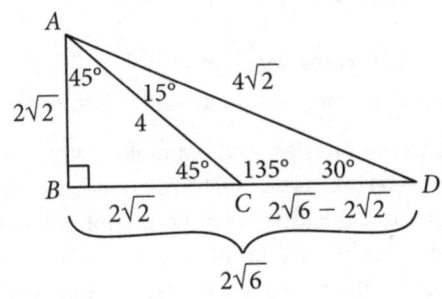

8. 426   Difficulty: Medium
Category: Additional Topics in Math / Geometry

Getting to the Answer: The figure contains a pair of similar triangles. Use the ratio within them to determine the requested length. The shadow cast by the flagpole is 50% longer than the flagpole itself; that is, $1.5 \times 40 = 60$ feet. Use this in conjunction with the lengths provided to determine the distance from the building to the end of the flagpole's shadow.

$$\frac{40}{324} = \frac{60}{x}$$
$$\frac{10}{81} = \frac{60}{x}$$
$$10x = 4,860$$
$$x = 486$$

Subtract the length of the flagpole's shadow, 60, from 486 to obtain 426, the distance from the building to the flagpole. Grid in 426.

9. B   Difficulty: Medium
Category: Additional Topics in Math / Geometry

Getting to the Answer: Start by drawing in $\overline{PR}$ and $\overline{PS}$ as shown here.

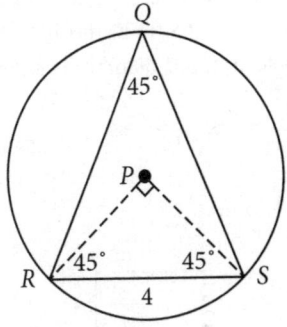

Because the angle formed by $\overline{PR}$ and $\overline{PS}$ subtends the same arc as the angle formed by $\overline{QR}$ and $\overline{QS}$, $\angle RPS$ must be twice $\angle RQS$, which is $45° \times 2 = 90°$. In addition to being legs of $\triangle PRS$, $\overline{PR}$ and $\overline{PS}$ are radii, so they are congruent, which makes $\triangle PRS$ a 45-45-90 triangle. Therefore, the radius of circle P is $\dfrac{4}{\sqrt{2}} = 2\sqrt{2}$, and the circumference is $2\pi \times 2\sqrt{2} = 4\pi\sqrt{2}$, which makes (B) correct.

10. B **Difficulty:** Hard

Category: Additional Topics in Math / Geometry

Getting to the Answer: Begin by finding the volume of one beach ball using the volume formula for a sphere, remembering to halve the diameter first:

$$V_{\text{sphere}} = \frac{4}{3}\pi r^3 = \frac{4}{3}\pi \left(\frac{66}{2}\right)^3 = 47,916\pi \text{ cm}^3$$

Convert to breaths using the relationships given:

$$47,916\pi \text{ cm}^3 \times \frac{1 \text{ L}}{1000 \text{ cm}^3} \times \frac{1 \text{ breath}}{6 \text{ L}} \approx 8\pi$$

This is about 25.09, or 25, full breaths. Multiply this by 3 to get 75 full breaths for three beach balls, which is (B).

PERFORM

11. A **Difficulty:** Medium

Category: Additional Topics in Math / Geometry

Getting to the Answer: Draw a diagram of Aundria and Annette's routes to the summit to visualize the situation. After drawing and labeling the diagram with the information given, look for a way to uncover a right triangle by drawing in additional lines. Once complete, use the rectangle you created to fill in the lengths of the new segments. The completed diagram is shown here:

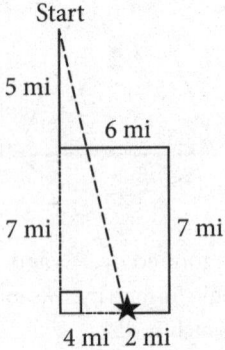

Use the Pythagorean theorem to calculate the distance Annette will travel:

$$c^2 = (5 + 7)^2 + 4^2$$
$$c^2 = 144 + 16$$
$$c^2 = 160$$
$$c = \sqrt{160} = 4\sqrt{10}$$

But you're not done yet! The question asks you to find the total distance the two women will travel. Aundria travels $5 + 6 + 7 + 2 = 20$ miles; together, she and Annette will travel $20 + 4\sqrt{10}$ miles, which is approximately 32.65 miles. Choice (A) is correct.

12. B **Difficulty:** Medium

Category: Additional Topics in Math / Geometry

Getting to the Answer: Given the area of $\triangle ABC$ and the length of the base AB, you can find its height:

$$150 = \frac{1}{2}(20)(BC)$$
$$150 = 10(BC)$$
$$15 = BC$$

Because $\overline{BC} = 15$ and $\overline{AB} = 20$, $\triangle ABC$ is a 3-4-5 triangle with dimensions scaled up by a factor of 5, so the hypotenuse $(\overline{AC})$ must be $5 \times 5 = 25$. Next, turn your attention to the smaller triangle, $\triangle AGH$. You're told that the hypotenuse of this triangle, $\overline{AH}$, is 20. $\triangle ABC$ and $\triangle AGH$ are similar triangles (because they share an angle at vertex A and they each have a right angle), so their corresponding sides must be proportional.

$$\frac{AH}{AC} = \frac{HG}{CB}$$
$$\frac{20}{25} = \frac{HG}{15}$$
$$300 = 25HG$$
$$\overline{HG} = 12$$

Choice (B) is the correct answer.

13. B **Difficulty:** Medium

Category: Additional Topics in Math / Geometry

Getting to the Answer: Read carefully; you're asked for information on the portion that is *not* strawberry rhubarb. The diagram includes the measures of central angles, and you're told that the pie tin has a diameter of 10 inches (which means the radius is 5 inches and the area is 25π square inches). Therefore, you can set up a proportion to determine the area of non–strawberry rhubarb pie (which represents 129.6° out of a full 360° circle):

$$\frac{\text{central angle}}{360°} = \frac{\text{sector area}}{\text{circle area}}$$

$$\frac{360 - 129.6}{360} = \frac{x}{25\pi}$$

$$5{,}760\pi = 360x$$

$$x = 16\pi$$

The portion of leftover pie that is not strawberry rhubarb is 16π square inches, which makes (B) correct.

14. B   Difficulty: Medium
Category: Additional Topics in Math / Geometry

Getting to the Answer: Adding 96 cubic feet of sand will completely fill the sandbox that starts one-third full, so 96 cubic feet is two-thirds of the total volume. Thus, one-third is $\frac{96}{2} = 48$ cubic feet, and the total volume is $3 \times 48 = 144$ cubic feet. The sandbox described is a rectangular solid, so the volume can be found using the formula $V = lwh$. Because the base of the sandbox is a square, you know the length and width are both 24. With the total volume in hand, you can find the depth (or height) of the sandbox: $144 = 24 \times 24 \times h$, which simplifies to $h = 0.25$. A height of 0.25 feet is the same as 3 inches, so (B) is correct.

ON YOUR OWN

1. A   Difficulty: Medium
Category: Additional Topics in Math / Geometry

Getting to the Answer: Start by connecting the ranch to the campsite. Then draw in a horizontal line and a vertical line to form a right triangle.

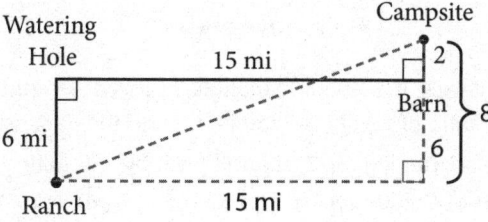

The length of one leg of the triangle is 15 miles, the distance from the watering hole to the barn. The length of the other leg is $6 + 2 = 8$ miles, the distance from the ranch to the watering hole and then from the barn to the campsite. The two legs of the right triangle are 8 and 15. You might recognize the Pythagorean triplet, 8, 15, 17, but if you don't, you can always rely on the Pythagorean theorem:

$$8^2 + 15^2 = c^2$$

$$64 + 225 = c^2$$

$$289 = c^2$$

$$\sqrt{289} = \sqrt{c^2}$$

$$17 = c$$

The actual trail is $6 + 15 + 2 = 23$ miles long. The direct route is 17 miles, so the direct route is $23 - 17 = 6$ miles shorter, making (A) the correct answer.

2. B   Difficulty: Medium
Category: Additional Topics in Math / Geometry

Getting to the Answer: You are told that $\overline{HI}$ is the bisector of $\overline{LO}$ and $\overline{OW}$. This tells you two things: 1) The definition of *bisector* tells you that that $\overline{HI}$ divides both $\overline{LO}$ and $\overline{OW}$ exactly in half, and 2) a straight line connecting the midpoints of two sides of a triangle is parallel to the third side, so $\overline{HI}$ is parallel to $\overline{LW}$.

Because $\overline{HI}$ is parallel to $\overline{LW}$, angles L and H must be congruent (they are corresponding angles), and angles W and I must be congruent (they are also corresponding angles). Angle O is shared by both triangles and is equal to itself by the Reflexive Property. This means the side lengths of the two triangles are different, but the corresponding angles are the same, so the triangles are similar. Side lengths of similar triangles are in proportion to one another. You are given the side lengths of $\overline{LW}$ and $\overline{HI}$. Because I is the midpoint of $\overline{OW}$, $\overline{OI}$ is half as long as $\overline{OW}$. The same is true for the other side. So the sides are in the ratio 1:2. Use this ratio to set up a proportion and solve for x:

$$\frac{1}{2} = \frac{4x - 1}{30}$$

$$30 = 2(4x - 1)$$

$$30 = 8x - 2$$

$$32 = 8x$$

$$4 = x$$

The correct answer is (B).

3. A   Difficulty: Medium

Category: Additional Topics in Math / Geometry

Getting to the Answer: Distance around *part* of a circle is the same as arc length, so use the relationship $\frac{\text{arc length}}{\text{circumference}} = \frac{\text{central angle}}{360°}$ to answer the question. The unknown in the relationship is the central angle, so call it *a*. Before you can fill in the rest of the equation, you need to find the circumference of the circle: $C = 2\pi r = 2\pi(120) = 240\pi$. Now you're ready to solve for *a*:

$$\frac{\text{arc length}}{\text{circumference}} = \frac{\text{central angle}}{360°}$$

$$\frac{200}{240\pi} = \frac{a}{360}$$

$$\frac{200(360)}{240\pi} = a$$

$$95.5 \approx a$$

Be careful when you enter this expression into your calculator—you need to put 240π in parentheses so that the calculator doesn't divide by 240 and then multiply by π. If entered correctly, the result is about 95.5 degrees, which matches (A).

4. C   Difficulty: Medium

Category: Additional Topics in Math / Geometry

Getting to the Answer: First, think logically: After it's poured into the larger glass, the volume of the water in the glass will still be the same as the volume when it was in the smaller glass. Find the volume of the water in the smaller glass. Then, substitute this volume into a second equation where the height is unknown and solve for *h*. The volume of a cylinder equals the area of its base times its height, or $V = \pi r^2 h$.

$$V = \pi r^2 h$$

$$V = \pi(1.5)^2(6)$$

$$V = \pi(2.25)(6)$$

$$V = 13.5\pi$$

$$13.5\pi = \pi(2)^2 h$$

$$13.5\pi = 4\pi h$$

$$3.375 = h$$

The water will reach 3.375 inches high in the bigger glass, which is (C).

5. B   Difficulty: Hard

Category: Additional Topics in Math / Geometry

Getting to the Answer: First, find the measure of the missing angle in the triangle: $180 - 105 - 45 = 30°$. Now, draw the height of the triangle up from *B* to a point, *D*, on $\overline{AC}$; this creates two right triangles.

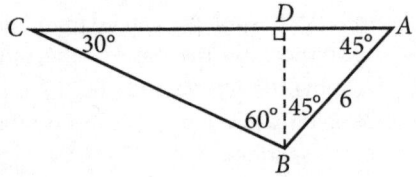

Triangle *ABD* is a 45-45-90 triangle, so its side lengths are in the ratio $x:x:x\sqrt{2}$. Because $\overline{AB}$ is the hypotenuse, set up an equation using the ratio of the sides:

$$6 = x\sqrt{2}$$

$$\frac{6}{\sqrt{2}} = x$$

$$\frac{6}{\sqrt{2}}\left(\frac{\sqrt{2}}{\sqrt{2}}\right) = x$$

$$\frac{6\sqrt{2}}{2} = x$$

$$3\sqrt{2} = x$$

Triangle *BDC* is a 30-60-90 triangle, so its side lengths are in the ratio of $x:x\sqrt{3}:2x$. You just found the dimensions of the shorter leg, $3\sqrt{2}$, so multiply it by $\sqrt{3}$ to find the length of the longer leg ($\sqrt{3} \times 3\sqrt{2} = 3\sqrt{6}$). Now, find the length of *AC*, which is the base of the triangle, by adding $\overline{AD}$ to $\overline{DC}$. The result is $3\sqrt{2} + 3\sqrt{6}$. Finally, use the area formula, $A = \frac{1}{2}bh$, to find the area of the whole triangle:

$$A = \frac{1}{2}\left(3\sqrt{2} + 3\sqrt{6}\right)\left(3\sqrt{2}\right)$$
$$= \frac{1}{2}\left(18 + 9\sqrt{12}\right)$$
$$= \frac{1}{2}\left(18 + 9 \cdot 2\sqrt{3}\right)$$
$$= \frac{1}{2}\left(18 + 18\sqrt{3}\right)$$
$$= 9 + 9\sqrt{3}$$

Choice (B) is correct.

6. B   Difficulty: Hard

Category: Additional Topics in Math / Geometry

Getting to the Answer: When the equation of a circle is in the form $(x - h)^2 + (y - k)^2 = r^2$, the r represents the length of the radius. To get the equation into this form, complete the square. Then you can double r to find the diameter.

You already have an x^2 and a y^2 in the given equation and the coefficients of x and y are even, so completing the square is fairly straightforward—there are just a lot of steps. Start by grouping the x's and y's together. Then, take the coefficient of the x term and divide it by 2, square it, and add it to the two terms with x variables. Do the same with the y term. Don't forget to add these amounts to the other side of the equation as well. This creates a perfect square of x terms and y terms, so take the square root of each.

$$x^2 + y^2 + 8x - 20y = 28$$
$$x^2 + 8x + y^2 - 20y = 28$$
$$(x + 8x + 16) + (y^2 - 20y + 100) = 28 + 16 + 100$$
$$(x + 4)^2 + (y - 10)^2 = 144$$

The equation tells you that r^2 is 144, which means that the radius is 12 and the diameter is twice that, or 24, which is (B).

7. C   Difficulty: Hard

Category: Additional Topics in Math / Geometry

Getting to the Answer: Don't be too quick to answer a question like this. You can't simply find three-fourths of

the volume of the cone because the top is considerably smaller than the bottom. Instead, you'll need to find the volume of the whole cone and subtract the volume of the top piece that is being discarded.

The figure shows a right triangle inside the cone. The height of the cone is the longer leg of the triangle, 16. The hypotenuse is given as 20. You might recognize this as a multiple of a Pythagorean triplet, 3-4-5, or in this case, 12-16-20. This means the radius of the original cone is 12. Substitute this into the formula for volume:

$$V = \frac{1}{3}\pi r^2 h$$
$$V = \frac{1}{3}\pi (12)^2 (16)$$
$$V = 768\pi$$

To determine the dimensions of the top piece, use similar triangles.

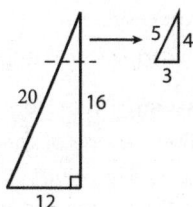

One quarter of the height is $16 \div 4 = 4$, resulting in a 3-4-5 triangle, making the height 4 and the radius 3.

$$V = \frac{1}{3}\pi (3)^2 (4) = 12\pi$$

Thus, the volume of the remaining solid is $768\pi - 12\pi = 756\pi$, which is (C).

8. 9   Difficulty: Hard

Category: Additional Topics in Math / Geometry

Getting to the Answer: Corresponding sides of similar triangles are proportional. Draw a quick sketch to find as many side lengths as you can, find the ratio of the sides between the two triangles, and use that ratio to find the missing vertex.

Plot all the points given in the question, labeling them as you go so you don't get confused (especially because you won't have graph paper). You know that A and B are in the same quadrant, which means the triangles are both oriented the same way. So make your sketch accordingly.

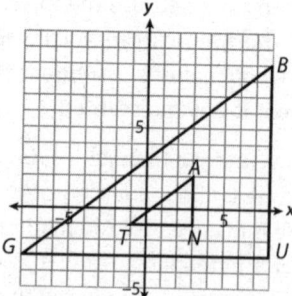

Once you have plotted *ANT* and the base of *BUG*, you can determine that the ratio of the triangles is 1:4 (the base of *ANT* has a length of 4 and the base of *BUG* has a length of 16). To determine where you should put *B*, find the length of side *AN* and then multiply by 4. The length of the vertical side of *BUG* is 12. Because one vertex is at $(8, -3)$, vertex *B* must be 12 vertical units above that point, or $(8, 9)$. The *y*-coordinate of *B* is 9.

9. C   Difficulty: Easy

Category: Additional Topics in Math / Geometry

Getting to the Answer: Line *L* forms a right triangle with the *x*- and *y*-axes, so one of the interior angles of the triangle has a measure of 90°. You know that $q = 140$, and together *p* and *q* form a straight line, which means they are supplementary angles. Thus, *p* must equal $180 - 140 = 40$. One of the interior angles of the triangle is vertical to *p*, so it also equals 40°. Now find the last angle measure inside the triangle by subtracting: $180° - 90° - 40° = 50°$. This angle is supplementary to *r*, so $r = 180 - 50 = 130$. This means that $r - p = 130 - 40 = 90$, making (C) the correct choice.

10. D   Difficulty: Easy

Category: Additional Topics in Math / Geometry

Getting to the Answer: If you're not sure how to start a question with a circle in it, look for the radius. The equation of circle takes the form $(x - h)^2 + (y - k)^2 = r^2$, where (h, k) is the center of the circle and *r* is the length of the radius.

To find the equation of a circle, you need the radius and the *x*- and *y*-coordinates of the center point. Look at the figure—the center has coordinates $(-1, 2)$. From the center, you can count horizontally or vertically to the

edge of the circle to find that its radius is 6. This means the equation is $(x - (-1))^2 + (y - 2)^2 = 6^2$, or $(x + 1)^2 + (y - 2)^2 = 36$, which matches the equation in (D).

11. D   Difficulty: Medium

Category: Additional Topics in Math / Geometry

Getting to the Answer: The sides 3*d*, 5*d*, and *h* form a right triangle, so plug these values into the Pythagorean theorem and then solve for *h*. Be careful—when you square 3*d* and 5*d*, you must square the coefficient and the variable.

$$a^2 + b^2 = c^2$$
$$(3d)^2 + (5d)^2 = h^2$$
$$9d^2 + 25d^2 = h^2$$
$$34d^2 = h^2$$
$$\sqrt{34d^2} = h$$
$$d\sqrt{34} = h$$

Choice (D) is correct.

12. D   Difficulty: Medium

Category: Additional Topics in Math / Geometry

Getting to the Answer: You can eliminate B immediately because corresponding angles of similar triangles are congruent, so they are in a 1:1 ratio. You can also eliminate A, because $\overline{OD}$ would be proportional to $\overline{NW}$, not $\overline{EW}$. Evaluating C might get complicated, so skip it for now. Because the side lengths of the two triangles are proportional, when you find the sum of the side lengths (the perimeter), this number will be in the same proportion. You can check this by assigning numbers that are in the ratio 7:4 and finding the perimeter of each triangle:

$$OL = 7 \text{ and } NE = 4$$
$$LD = 14 \text{ and } EW = 8$$
$$OD = 21 \text{ and } NW = 12$$
$$\text{Perimeter}_{\triangle OLD} = 7 + 14 + 21 = 42$$
$$\text{Perimeter}_{\triangle NEW} = 4 + 8 + 12 = 24$$
$$42:24 = 7:4$$

This means (D) is correct.

13. A   Difficulty: Medium

Category: Additional Topics in Math / Geometry

Getting to the Answer: Use the relationship $\dfrac{\text{area of sector}}{\text{area of circle}} = \dfrac{\text{central angle}}{360°}$ to answer this question. To help remember this relationship, just think $\dfrac{\text{partial area}}{\text{whole area}} = \dfrac{\text{partial angle}}{\text{whole angle}}$.

The unknown in this question is the radius, which you can find by first finding the area of the whole circle and then by using the equation for area of a circle $A = \pi r^2$. You have everything you need to find the area of the circle:

$$\frac{\text{area of sector}}{\text{area of circle}} = \frac{\text{central angle}}{360°}$$

$$\frac{14\pi}{A} = \frac{140}{360}$$

$$5{,}040\pi = 140A$$

$$36\pi = A$$

Now, solve for r using $A = \pi r^2$:

$$36\pi = \pi r^2$$

$$36 = r^2$$

$$\pm 6 = r$$

The radius can't be negative, so the correct answer is 6, which is (A).

14. C   Difficulty: Medium

Category: Additional Topics in Math / Geometry

Getting to the Answer: The formula for finding the volume of a pyramid with a rectangular base is $V = \dfrac{1}{3}lwh$. Start by substituting what you know into the formula. You know the volume is represented by $x^3 - x$. You also know the length is $x + 1$ and the width is $3x$.

$$V = \frac{1}{3}lwh$$

$$x^3 - x = \frac{1}{3}(x + 1)(3x)h$$

Multiply both sides of the equation by 3 to clear the fraction, but don't multiply anything else just yet. First, look for a pattern.

$$3x^3 - 3x = (x + 1)(3x)h$$

Notice that if you divide both sides of the equation by the width, $3x$, you'll be left with $x^2 - 1$ on the left side and $(x + 1)$ times h on the right side. The difference of squares rule tells you that the factors of $x^2 - 1$ are $x + 1$ and $x - 1$. This means the height of the pyramid must be represented by $x - 1$. Therefore, (C) is correct.

15. B   Difficulty: Medium

Category: Additional Topics in Math / Geometry

Getting to the Answer: Solve this question one step at a time. The volume of sand in one tank (only two inches of the height) will be $V = 24 \times 9 \times 2 = 432$ cubic inches, which means the volume of sand in all 50 tanks will be $50 \times 432 = 21{,}600$ cubic inches. Each cubic inch of sand weighs about 2 ounces, so the weight of all the sand will be $2 \times 21{,}600 = 43{,}200$ ounces. There are 16 ounces in one pound, so the weight of the sand in pounds is $43{,}200 \div 16 = 2{,}700$. Finally, each bag contains 40 pounds of sand, so the pet store needs to buy $2{,}700 \div 40 = 67.5$, or about 68 bags of sand. This means (B) is the correct answer.

16. A   Difficulty: Medium

Category: Additional Topics in Math / Geometry

Getting to the Answer: Just like triangles, corresponding sides of similar quadrilaterals are proportional. This means the perimeters of similar quadrilaterals are also proportional and in the same proportion as each pair of corresponding side lengths.

Find the perimeter of rectangle *LION* and compare it to the perimeter of *PUMA*. *LION* has a perimeter of $86 + 86 + 52 + 52 = 276$. Therefore, the ratio of the perimeter of *LION* to the perimeter of *PUMA* is $276:69$, which reduces to $4:1$. This tells you that the width of *LION* is 4 times greater than the width of *PUMA*, which means *PUMA*'s width is $52 \div 4 = 13$ units, making (A) correct.

17. C   Difficulty: Medium

Category: Additional Topics in Math / Geometry

Getting to the Answer: Because the ratio of the shaded area to the unshaded area is $4:5$, the ratio of the shaded area to the entire circle is $4:(4 + 5) = 4:9$. This ratio is the same as the ratio of the interior angle of the shaded sector to $360°$, or $x:360$. Set up a proportion using these ratios:

$$\frac{4}{9} = \frac{x}{360}$$
$$360(4) = 9x$$
$$1,440 = 9x$$
$$160 = x$$

Choice (C) is correct.

18. D   Difficulty: Hard

Category: Additional Topics in Math / Geometry

Getting to the Answer: In a right triangle, one leg is the base and the other is the height. Use x and $x + 3$ to represent the lengths of these two legs (because the question states that one leg is 3 inches longer than the other). Use the area formula and set the equation equal to the given area:

$$35 = \frac{1}{2}(x)(x + 3)$$

$$2(35) = 2\left(\frac{1}{2}(x)(x + 3)\right)$$

$$70 = (x)(x + 3)$$

$$70 = x^2 + 3x$$

Now, subtract 70 to make the equation equal 0 and then factor it. The factors are $(x + 10)$ and $(x - 7)$, which means $x = -10$ and $x = 7$. Lengths cannot be negative, so the shorter leg must have a length of 7. This means the longer leg has a length of $7 + 3 = 10$. Now use the Pythagorean theorem to find the length of the hypotenuse.

$$a^2 + b^2 = c^2$$
$$7^2 + 10^2 = c^2$$
$$49 + 100 = c^2$$
$$149 = c^2$$
$$\sqrt{149} = \sqrt{c^2}$$
$$\sqrt{149} = c$$

Choice (D) is correct.

19. B   Difficulty: Hard

Category: Additional Topics in Math / Geometry

Getting to the Answer: There are two triangles in this figure, ACE and BCD. Because $\overline{BD}$ is parallel to $\overline{AE}$, angles A and B must be congruent (they are corresponding angles), and angles D and E must be congruent (they are also corresponding angles). Angle C is shared by both

triangles and is equal to itself by the Reflexive Property. This means the side lengths of the two triangles are different, but the angles are the same, so the triangles are similar by AAA. Side lengths of similar triangles are in proportion to one another.

You know the two triangles are similar, so set up a proportion using their side lengths. You'll need to translate from English into math as you go: $AB = 5$ and BC is three times that or 15. This means $AC = 5 + 15 = 20$. CD is 2 more than half AC or $20 \div 2 = 10 + 2 = 12$. Now you know three side lengths, so you can set up and solve a proportion:

$$\frac{BC}{AC} = \frac{DC}{EC}$$
$$\frac{15}{20} = \frac{12}{EC}$$
$$15EC = 240$$
$$EC = 16$$

This is the length of side EC, but the question asks for the length of segment DE, which is $EC - CD$, or $16 - 12 = 4$. This makes (B) the correct choice.

20. B   Difficulty: Hard

Category: Additional Topics in Math / Geometry

Getting to the Answer: Find the volume of the container using the formula for volume of a cylinder, $V = \pi r^2 h$. The question gives you the width, or the diameter of the container, so divide by 2 to get the radius.

$$V = \pi(1.25)^2(4)$$
$$V = \pi(1.5625)(4)$$
$$V = 6.25\pi$$

The factory only fills the cup 80% of the way up, so multiply the container volume by 0.8 to find that the actual volume of the yogurt is $6.25\pi \times 0.8 = 5\pi$, or about 15.708 cubic inches. Divide this by 6 ounces to determine that 1 ounce takes up approximately 2.6 cubic inches of space, which matches (B).

CHAPTER 12

PRACTICE

8. B **Difficulty:** Hard

Category: Additional Topics in Math / Imaginary Numbers

Getting to the Answer: Substitute $38 + 18j$ for E and $4 + 6j$ for Z. Then rearrange the equation so that I is isolated. Multiply the numerator and denominator by the latter's conjugate and then use FOIL. Combine like terms and reduce fractions as needed. The steps for this sequence are shown below.

$$E = I \times z$$
$$I = \frac{E}{z} = \frac{38 + 18j}{4 + 6j}$$
$$= \frac{38 + 18j}{4 + 6j} \times \frac{4 - 6j}{4 - 6j}$$
$$= \frac{(38 \times 4) + (38 \times -6j) + (18j \times 4) + (18j \times -6j)}{16 - 36j^2}$$
$$= \frac{152 - 228j + 72j - 108j^2}{16 - (-36)}$$
$$= \frac{152 - 156j - (-108)}{52}$$
$$= \frac{260 - 156j}{52}$$
$$= \frac{260}{52} - \frac{156}{52}j$$
$$= 5 - 3j$$

Choice (B) is the correct answer.

9. B **Difficulty:** Easy

Category: Additional Topics in Math / Trigonometry

Getting to the Answer: Recall that the sum of the acute angles in a right triangle is $180° - 90° = 90°$. Convert this to radians to find the measure of the missing angle. The sum of the acute angles, in radians, is $90° \times \frac{\pi}{180°} = \frac{90\pi}{180} = \frac{\pi}{2}$. Subtract the known angle to find the other angle: $\frac{\pi}{2} - \frac{\pi}{3} = \frac{3\pi}{6} - \frac{2\pi}{6} = \frac{\pi}{6}$. This matches (B).

PERFORM

10. 2338 **Difficulty:** Easy

Category: Additional Topics in Math / Imaginary Numbers

Getting to the Answer: Set your TI-83/84 to $a + bi$ mode (or the equivalent if you have a different calculator) and then compute $(11 + 14i)^3$. The result is $-5{,}137 + 2{,}338i$. The question asks for b, the coefficient of the imaginary component, so grid in 2338. Note that you could also expand the expression by writing it as a product and multiplying it all out.

11. C **Difficulty:** Medium

Category: Additional Topics in Math / Imaginary Numbers

Getting to the Answer: Factoring the first trinomial yields $(x^2 + 81)(x^2 + 3)$, and factoring the second gives $(x + 9)(x - 4)$. Set each expression equal to 0 and solve for x; you'll find that (C) is the only choice that is not in this list of values, so it is correct.

12. C **Difficulty:** Medium

Category: Additional Topics in Math / Trigonometry

Getting to the Answer: Dealing with smaller angles usually makes trig questions easier, so start by reducing the given angle so that it is in the first quadrant. To do this, subtract 2π from $\frac{13\pi}{6}$ to get $\frac{13\pi}{6} - 2\pi = \frac{13\pi}{6} - \frac{12\pi}{6} = \frac{\pi}{6}$. The equation in the question stem becomes $\sin x = \cos \frac{\pi}{6}$.

Next, think about complementary angles—they have a special relationship relative to trig values—the cosine of an acute angle is equal to the sine of the angle's complement and vice versa. The angle measures are given in radians, so you're looking for an angle that, when added to $\frac{\pi}{6}$, gives $\frac{\pi}{2}$ (because $\frac{\pi}{2} = 90°$). Because $\frac{\pi}{6} + \frac{2\pi}{6} = \frac{3\pi}{6} = \frac{\pi}{2}$, the two angles, $\frac{\pi}{6}$ and $\frac{\pi}{3}$, are complementary angles, which means (C) is correct.

ON YOUR OWN

1. D   Difficulty: Easy

Category: Additional Topics in Math / Imaginary Numbers

Getting to the Answer: The definition of i is given as $i = \sqrt{-1}$. If you square both sides of this definition, you arrive at a more useful form: $i^2 = (\sqrt{-1})^2 = -1$. Distribute the $4i$ and then substitute -1 for i^2:

$$4i(5 - 7i) = 4i(5) - 4i(7i)$$
$$= 20i - 28i^2$$
$$= 20i - 28(-1)$$
$$= 20i + 28$$

Switch the terms so that the real part is first $(28 + 20i)$ to find that (D) is correct.

2. A   Difficulty: Medium

Category: Additional Topics in Math / Imaginary Numbers

Getting to the Answer: Because $i = \sqrt{-1}$, it isn't considered "proper" to leave i in the denominator of a fraction (just as you shouldn't leave a radical in the denominator). Use the same strategy you learned for rationalizing the denominator of a radical expression to rationalize a complex number (by multiplying by the conjugate). The conjugate of $3 - i$ is $3 + i$, so multiply the expression by $\dfrac{3 + i}{3 + i}$:

$$\frac{1}{3 - i} \times \frac{3 + i}{3 + i} = \frac{3 + i}{(3 - i)(3 + i)}$$
$$= \frac{3 + i}{9 + 3i - 3i - i^2}$$
$$= \frac{3 + i}{9 - (-1)}$$
$$= \frac{3 + i}{10}$$

This isn't one of the answer choices, so split the number into its real part and its imaginary part by writing each of the terms in the numerator over 10. The result is $\dfrac{3}{10} + \dfrac{1}{10}i$, which matches (A).

3. B   Difficulty: Medium

Category: Additional Topics in Math / Imaginary Numbers

Getting to the Answer: You will not be expected to raise a complex number like the one in this question to the fourth power by hand. That's a clue that you should be able to use your calculator. The definition of i has been programmed into all graphing calculators, so you can perform basic operations on complex numbers using the calculator (in the calculator section of the test). Enter the expression as follows: $(3 + 2i)^4$. On the TI83/84 calculators, you can find i on the button with the decimal point. After you enter the expression, the calculator should return $-119 + 120i$, which is (B).

4. B   Difficulty: Medium

Category: Additional Topics in Math / Imaginary Numbers

Getting to the Answer: A question like this requires an understanding of how the powers of i cycle. Whenever you're evaluating a high power of i, divide the power by 4 and let the remainder point you to the correct answer. Recall the power pattern for i: i, -1, $-i$, 1, and repeat. Divide 14 by 4, which yields 3 with a remainder of 2. This means $i^{14} = (i^4)^3 \times i^2 = 1 \times -1 = -1$. Repeat this process for i^{122} to get $i^{122} = (i^4)^{30} \times i^2 = 1 \times -1 = -1$. The sum is therefore $-1 + -1 = -2$, which means you're looking for an expression that has the same value. Choices B and C should look tempting (because of the 2), so start with them. In (B), you know $i^2 = -1$ and $2(-1) = -2$, so this is the correct answer.

5. B   Difficulty: Hard

Category: Additional Topics in Math / Imaginary Numbers

Getting to the Answer: Take a peek at the answer choices—they're all complex numbers. This means factoring is out of the question, so think quadratic formula. Before you can use the quadratic formula, the equation must equal 0, so move all the terms to the left side of the equal sign; the quadratic (written in standard form) becomes $x^2 - 4x + 13 = 0$. Now, jot down the values you'll need: $a = 1$, $b = -4$, and $c = 13$.

$$x = \frac{-b \pm \sqrt{b^2 - 4ac}}{2a}$$

$$= \frac{-(-4) \pm \sqrt{(-4)^2 - 4(1)(13)}}{2(1)}$$

$$= \frac{4 \pm \sqrt{16 - 52}}{2}$$

$$= \frac{4 \pm \sqrt{-36}}{2}$$

$$= \frac{4 \pm \sqrt{-1 \times 36}}{2}$$

$$= \frac{4 \pm 6i}{2}$$

$$= \frac{\cancel{2}(2 \pm 3i)}{\cancel{2}}$$

The final answer is $2 \pm 3i$, which matches (B).

6. A   Difficulty: Hard
Category: Additional Topics in Math / Imaginary Numbers

Getting to the Answer: Each of the factors in this product has two terms, so they behave like binomials. This means you can use FOIL to find the product. To avoid messy numbers, simplify the two radicals first using the definition of i. Write each of the numbers under the radicals as a product of −1 and the number, take the square roots, and then FOIL the resulting expressions.

$$\left(2 + \sqrt{-9}\right)\left(-1 + \sqrt{-4}\right)$$

$$= \left(2 + \sqrt{-1 \times 9}\right)\left(-1 + \sqrt{-1 \times 4}\right)$$

$$= (2 + 3i)(-1 + 2i)$$

$$= -2 + 4i - 3i + 6i^2$$

$$= -2 + i + 6(-1)$$

$$= -8 + i$$

Choice (A) is correct.

7. C   Difficulty: Hard
Category: Additional Topics in Math / Imaginary Numbers

Getting to the Answer: Find a common denominator by multiplying the second term by $4 - 2i$. As always, you're given that $\sqrt{-1} = i$, but a more useful fact is that $i^2 = -1$, so be sure to make this substitution as you work. Once you've found the common denominator, you can simply add like terms.

$$\frac{1}{4 - 2i} + (3 + i) = \frac{1}{4 - 2i} + \frac{3 + i}{1}$$

$$= \frac{1}{4 - 2i} + \frac{3 + i}{1}\left(\frac{4 - 2i}{4 - 2i}\right)$$

$$= \frac{1}{4 - 2i} + \frac{12 - 6i + 4i - 2i^2}{4 - 2i}$$

$$= \frac{1}{4 - 2i} + \frac{12 - 2i - 2(-1)}{4 - 2i}$$

$$= \frac{1 + 12 - 2i + 2}{4 - 2i}$$

$$= \frac{15 - 2i}{4 - 2i}$$

This matches (C).

8. 17   Difficulty: Medium
Category: Additional Topics in Math / Imaginary Numbers

Getting to the Answer: Don't let this "new" definition intimidate you. All you're asked to do is to find the square root of the sum of a^2 and b^2. You don't even have to involve the i at all.

$$|15 + 8i| = \sqrt{15^2 + 8^2}$$

$$= \sqrt{225 + 64}$$

$$= \sqrt{289}$$

$$= 17$$

There is nothing else to do—the answer is 17.

9. D   Difficulty: Easy
Category: Additional Topics in Math / Trigonometry

Getting to the Answer: The answers are given in degrees, and it's easier to add degrees than radians, so convert each angle measure to degrees and then find the sum. Use the conversion $180° = \pi$, with π written in the denominator so that it will cancel.

$$\frac{\cancel{\pi}}{4} \times \frac{180°}{\cancel{\pi}} = 45°$$

$$\frac{7\cancel{\pi}}{\cancel{12}^2} \times \frac{\cancel{180}^{30}°}{\cancel{\pi}} = \frac{210°}{2} = 105°$$

The measure of $\angle PQR$ is $45° + 105° = 150°$, which matches (D).

10. D Difficulty: Easy

Category: Additional Topics in Math / Trigonometry

Getting to the Answer: Angles that are coterminal (land in the same place when rotated full circle) have the same trigonometric values. To find coterminal angles, subtract 360° (one full circle) from the given angle: 450° − 360° = 90°. The figure below provides a visual representation of this relationship:

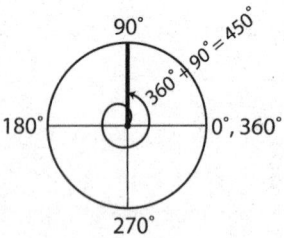

A 90° angle has the same trigonometric values as a 450° angle, making (D) correct.

11. B Difficulty: Medium

Category: Additional Topics in Math / Trigonometry

Getting to the Answer: When you're not asked to find a specific value, drawing a quick sketch to determine which quadrant each angle lies in may provide enough information to answer the question. Sketch each angle on a unit circle. It doesn't have to be perfect—you just need to know which quadrant the angle falls in.

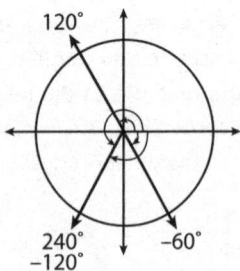

Three of the angles (120°, 240°, and −120°) fall to the left of the y-axis (in Quadrants II and III) and therefore have a cosine value that is negative. The angle in (B) falls to the right of the vertical axis (in Quadrant IV) and therefore has a cosine value that is positive. This means (B) is correct because cos(−60°) cannot have the same value as the other three angles.

12. D Difficulty: Medium

Category: Additional Topics in Math / Trigonometry

Getting to the Answer: Fill in the missing parts of the triangle. Use the Pythagorean theorem to find the missing leg length and use properties of triangles to find the missing angle.

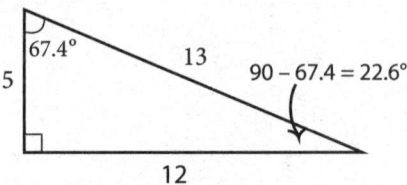

Sine and cosine both involve the hypotenuse (13), so you can eliminate A right away because it doesn't have a 13 in it. Next, quickly compare each answer choice to the trig ratios given by SOH CAH TOA. Sine is opposite over hypotenuse; in B, the side opposite the 67.4° angle has length 5 (not 12), so eliminate B. Cosine is adjacent over hypotenuse; in C, the side adjacent to the 22.6° angle has length 12 (not 5), so eliminate C. This means (D) must be correct. The side adjacent to the 67.4° angle has length 5 and the hypotenuse has length 13, so cos 67.4° = $\frac{5}{13}$.

13. C Difficulty: Medium

Category: Additional Topics in Math / Trigonometry

Getting to the Answer: The angle given $\left(\frac{\pi}{6}\right)$ is in the first quadrant, so its cosine is positive. The question states that sin x is equal to the cosine of $\frac{\pi}{6}$, so x be must an angle for which the sine is positive, which means it must lie in the first or second quadrant (above the x-axis). This means you're looking for the angle that is *not* in one of those quadrants, which is (C): $\frac{5\pi}{3}$ is in the fourth quadrant and therefore has a negative sine value. (The angles in A and B meet this criterion because each one is less than π. The angle in D also meets the criterion because $\frac{7\pi}{3} - 2\pi = \frac{7\pi}{3} - \frac{6\pi}{3} = \frac{\pi}{3}$, which is in the first quadrant.)

Answers & Explanations

14. A   Difficulty: Medium

Category: Additional Topics in Math / Trigonometry

Getting to the Answer: When the measure of an angle in a triangle is given in radians, convert it to degrees so you'll have a better idea of what you're looking at. Use the relationship $180° = \pi$ to convert the angle: $\dfrac{\pi}{3} \times \dfrac{180°}{\pi} = 60°$.

Now you know the triangle is a 30-60-90 triangle, which has sides that are in the ratio $x:x\sqrt{3}:2x$. The hypotenuse is $2x = 24$, so $x = 12$ and $x\sqrt{3} = 12\sqrt{3}$. This means the base and height of the triangle are 12 and $12\sqrt{3}$, and the area of the triangle is $\dfrac{1}{2}(12\sqrt{3})(12) = 72\sqrt{3}$, which is (A).

15. 3/5 or .6   Difficulty: Hard

Category: Additional Topics in Math / Trigonometry

Getting to the Answer: Because trig functions typically apply to right triangles, draw in an altitude and label what you know. You know the trough is 24 inches deep and 36 inches across the top. Because the given angles have equal measures ($x°$), the triangle is isosceles and the altitude bisects the top. Your figure should look like this:

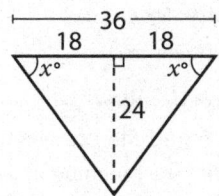

You're given that $B = \cos x$, and the cosine of an angle involves the hypotenuse, so you need to find the length of the hypotenuse using the Pythagorean theorem:

$$18^2 + 24^2 = c^2$$
$$324 + 576 = c^2$$
$$900 = c^2$$
$$30 = c$$

Finally, $\cos x = \dfrac{\text{adj}}{\text{hyp}} = \dfrac{18}{30} = \dfrac{3}{5}$. Grid in 3/5 or .6.

16. 12/5 or 2.4   Difficulty: Hard

Category: Additional Topics in Math / Trigonometry

Getting to the Answer: Find the height of the triangle using the information given about the area and add it to the figure.

$$A = \frac{1}{2}bh$$
$$240 = \frac{1}{2}(40)h$$
$$240 = 20h$$
$$12 = h$$

After you find the height, you might recognize the 5-12-13 Pythagorean triplet, which gives you another side of the triangle that contains β.

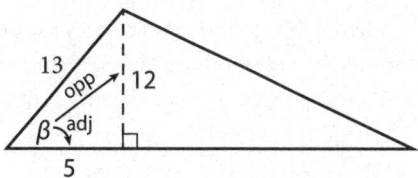

Note: Figure not drawn to scale.

Now use SOH CAH TOA: $\tan\beta = \dfrac{\text{opp}}{\text{adj}} = \dfrac{12}{5}$. Grid in 12/5 or 2.4.

CHAPTER 13

PRACTICE

Suggested Passage Map notes:

¶1: 4 forces of flight (central idea)

¶2: #1 - thrust

¶2, cont.: #2 - drag, impact on aircraft design

¶3: #3 - gravity

¶3, cont.: #4 - lift

¶3, cont.: Bern. principle = lift

7. B   Difficulty: Medium

Category: Vocab-in-Context

Getting to the Answer: When you see the phrase "most nearly means" and a cited word or phrase, pretend that word or phrase is blank and predict a synonym for it. Read the sentence without "acts" (line 29) and ask what "lift force" (line 28) does. Predict that it "functions" or "works." Choice (B) is correct.

8. B   Difficulty: Medium

Category: Inference

Getting to the Answer: Review your Passage Map notes regarding drag. Remember to be wary of answer choices that are outside the scope of the passage. Paragraph 2 provides details about drag, specifically that it is "the air resistance that the plane encounters in flight" (lines 16-17). At the end of the paragraph, the author writes that drag decreases when "there is little friction at the airplane's surface" (lines 23-24). Choice (B) reflects the relationship between drag and friction and is therefore correct. Choice C may be tempting, but it is incorrect because drag doesn't decrease as thrust increases; instead, thrust must be enough to overcome drag force (line 15).

PERFORM

Suggested Passage Map notes:

¶1: AL humble family background (purpose)

¶2: childhood – "wild" region, little ed

¶3: early jobs

¶4: captain in war, politician, lawyer

¶5: personal description

9. D   Difficulty: Medium

Category: Rhetoric

Getting to the Answer: When a question asks you to identify the author's stance, think about the author's point of view and purpose. The author begins by referring to his parents' families as "undistinguished" (line 3) and keeps the focus of the passage on the simplicity of his life and circumstances. Predict that the author sees himself as an ordinary person who grew up without many advantages. Choice (D) is correct.

10. C   Difficulty: Medium

Category: Global

Getting to the Answer: To summarize the central purpose of the passage, review the key ideas you noted in your Passage Map. Always identify the author's purpose when mapping History/Social Studies passages. While the author does spend a good deal of the passage discussing education, this is not his reason for writing. The overall purpose of the passage is to provide his own history, which shifts from his modest childhood to his national importance. This is underscored by the phrase "What I have done since then is pretty well known" (lines 61-62). Choice (C) is correct.

11. B   Difficulty: Medium

Category: Vocab-in-Context

Getting to the Answer: When you see the phrase "most nearly means" and a cited line, pretend the word or phrase is a blank and predict the meaning of the word or phrase in context. Read the lines surrounding the cited phrase. The author states that he has not been to school since his childhood but "picked up" (line 37) the "little advance . . . upon this store of education . . . under the pressure of necessity" (lines 36-38). Predict that the phrase means that he learned when he had to, or when it was necessary. Choice (B) is correct.

12. C   Difficulty: Hard

Category: Inference

Getting to the Answer: If you are not provided with a line reference, use your Passage Map to locate the part of the passage to which the question stem refers. The question asks about the effect of the Black Hawk War, which is first mentioned in the beginning of paragraph 4. The overall topic of paragraph 4 is the author's campaigns and subsequent elections, suggesting a connection between the war and the author's political career. Choice (C) is correct. The other answer choices may be tempting, but they are all are assumptions that the text itself does not support.

ON YOUR OWN

Suggested Passage Map notes:

¶1-2: ML loves girl w/ simple beauty

¶3: ML & girl marry, happy, girl good w/ $

¶4: only 2 faults

¶5: #1 - ML didn't want to go to theater

¶6: #2 - wife wears fake jewelry

¶7-10: ML and wife disagree about jewelry

¶11: wife dies

¶12-14: ML mourns wife

¶15-19: ML is poor, has to sell wife's jewelry

¶20-22: ML is shocked to learn jewelry is real (theme)

1. D   Difficulty: Medium
Category: Vocab-in-Context

Getting to the Answer: Use context clues and tone to help determine the meaning of the word. Create a mental picture of what is being described by using the surrounding text. Finally, make sure the answer choice does not alter the meaning of the sentence when inserted. The paragraph in which the word appears describes the girl as "simple" (line 5) and "pure" (line 8), and as having a "lovely soul" (line 8). Therefore, choice (D) is correct. "Angelic" means "innocent" in this context.

2. C   Difficulty: Medium
Category: Detail

Getting to the Answer: Skim the passage to locate descriptions of Lantin's wife at the beginning of their marriage. Paragraph 3 describes the Lantins' "snug" (line 10) income and attribute their luxurious lifestyle to Lantin's wife's "clever economy" (line 14). Choice (C) is correct. "Frugal" describes someone who is thrifty and economical.

3. A   Difficulty: Medium
Category: Inference

Getting to the Answer: Look for Lantin's thoughts and statements about the jewels. Use this as evidence of his attitude. The Lantins are described as making a "snug" (line 10) salary, and Madame Lantin has to be very economical. Later

in the passage, Lantin mentions that they "cannot afford" (line 35) to buy real jewelry. Choice (A) is correct because Lantin clearly believes they cannot afford real gems.

4. D   Difficulty: Easy
Category: Command of Evidence

Getting to the Answer: Review your answer to the previous question. Decide which lines of text provide evidence that the Lantins did not have enough money to buy large jewels. Choice (D) offers the best support. In these lines, Lantin explicitly states they cannot afford real jewelry.

5. B   Difficulty: Medium
Category: Inference

Getting to the Answer: Reread the text to make a prediction. This section of the passage describes Lantin's intense mourning for his wife, which suggests a deep unhappiness. Choice (B) is correct.

6. B   Difficulty: Medium
Category: Command of Evidence

Getting to the Answer: Review your answer to the previous question. Read each choice and figure out which one provides specific support for that answer. Choice (B) provides the best support. These lines show that Lantin is overcome with grief, as he "wept unceasingly; his heart was broken" (line 47).

7. D   Difficulty: Easy
Category: Vocab-in-Context

Getting to the Answer: Use context clues from the target sentence and surrounding sentences. Predict the meaning of the word and look for a match in the answer choices. Lantin views the jewels as "deceptions" (line 61) and speaks of the irritation her jewels caused him. Looking at the jewels also "spoiled, somewhat" (line 63) the memory of his wife. Choice (D) provides a suitably negative word and makes sense in the context of the rest of the paragraph.

8. C   Difficulty: Medium
Category: Rhetoric

Getting to the Answer: Contrast this sentence with what has already occurred in the passage. Analyze the new information it provides and the response it provokes when you read it. The sentence calls into question the reliability of everything we have learned about Madame

Lantin. Although she and her husband were not wealthy, Madame Lantin has somehow acquired at least one very expensive piece of jewelry. Choice (C) is correct. The author uses this sentence to create an unresolved conflict. Lantin does not know how his wife obtained the jewels, and the sentence suggests the answer might call his wife's virtue into question.

9. D   Difficulty: Hard
Category: Inference

Getting to the Answer: Review the end of the excerpt. Think about what this text might suggest broadly. Don't speculate by choosing an overly specific answer. The correct answer will provide a logical conclusion about Madame Lantin based on what you have learned about her throughout the passage. Her husband idealized her but has discovered that she has been dishonest and hidden things from him. Choice (D) provides a reasonable conclusion that a reader can make about Madame Lantin. Choices A, B, and C are possible reasons that Madame Lantin had the expensive necklace, but they are not directly supported by the passage.

10. A   Difficulty: Hard
Category: Global

Getting to the Answer: Ask yourself what the author's theme is in this passage. The events in the passage show that Lantin judges his wife for her love of costume jewelry. After her death, he finds that her jewels are real. Both the "paste" jewels that turn out to be real and Lantin's realization about his wife's jewel collection after her death support the idea that appearances can be deceiving. Choice (A) best describes the central theme the author develops throughout the excerpt.

CHAPTER 14

PRACTICE

Suggested Passage Map notes:

Passage 1

¶1: author: SC = "miracle cure;" how SC work

¶2: embryonic → adult SCs; help diseases; help research

¶3: author: SC research must go on

Passage 2

¶1: ?s of ethics

¶2: SCs useful, but embryo use moral?

¶3: author: use adult SCs

4. C **Difficulty:** Medium

Category: Synthesis

Getting to the Answer: Synthesis questions ask you to find similarities and differences between paired passages. Use your Passage Map to compare the different points of view, focusing on how the authors agree and disagree. The author of Passage 1 maintains that stem cell research can provide benefits and recommends using stem cells regardless of the source. The author of Passage 2 agrees that stem cell research can provide benefits but argues that using adult stem cells is the course to follow. Both authors agree that stem cell research has benefits. Choice (C) is correct.

5. D **Difficulty:** Hard

Category: Synthesis

Getting to the Answer: To make a strong prediction when faced with a general question, focus on the central idea, topic, and scope of each passage. Harder Synthesis questions will require you to identify not only how the authors agree or disagree but also why they agree or disagree. What these authors disagree on is easy to identify: which type of stem cells should be used in the research. Now, ask why they disagree. The author of Passage 1 thinks that the benefits are defined solely by the physical improvements possible, and the author of Passage 2 thinks that the benefits of stem cell research must be considered in terms of the moral as well as the physical results. Choice (D) is correct.

6. C **Difficulty:** Medium

Category: Synthesis

Getting to the Answer: Look for trends in the data. Evaluate the categories and time frames mentioned in the answer choices. Compare the changes on the graph to the changes described in each answer choice and eliminate answer choices that don't match. When you check the time frame of 2005 to 2007, note that opposition to stem cell research increased one full square, and support for stem cell research decreased about one half of a square. This matches the changes in the data described in choice (C).

PERFORM

Suggested Passage Map notes:

Passage 1

¶1: U could not avoid politics; bond among groups

¶2: causes of unrest

¶3: U peasants joined M; M necessary, reasons

Passage 2

¶1: Bol. vs M; soldier quote = difference in theory (accepted vs debated)

¶2: Bol. controlling; if differ = enemy

¶3: ex: T writings view M as good or bad

¶4: T quote: must be loyal to Red Army

¶5: T/Bol. negatively portrays U/M

7. C **Difficulty:** Medium

Category: Synthesis

Getting to the Answer: To answer Synthesis questions, focus on the similarities and differences between the passages. This question stem asks what the author of Passage 2 thinks about a promise made by the Bolsheviks. Review your Passage Map of Passage 1 to identify the Bolsheviks' promise: "equality and the rule of the proletariat" (lines 16-17). Now use your Passage Map of Passage 2 to locate what author 2 thinks of the Bolsheviks. Paragraph 2 discusses the extreme control the Bolsheviks held in Russia. Predict that the author of Passage 2 would view the Bolsheviks' promise in a negative light. Choice (C) is correct.

Choices A, B, and D may be tempting, but they do not match your prediction. Choice A is incorrect because lines 56–58 explain that the Makhnovists made decisions based on "the needs of the community for food, freedom, and self-defense," not the Bolsheviks' ideological promises. Choice B is incorrect because in lines 50-52 author 2 claims the theories of the Bolsheviks were "never doubted or questioned." Choice D is incorrect because passage 2 uses the Trotsky quotes to describe his portrayal of the Makhnovists, not to suggest the writings influenced Bolshevik promises.

8. D   Difficulty: Medium
Category: Synthesis

Getting to the Answer: Synthesis questions that ask what the authors agree on require you to identify the similarities in each author's purpose for writing the passage. Since each passage focuses on a different aspect of the Makhnovischina, the correct answer will probably be a general statement about the group. Both describe the Makhnovischina as a group formed to provide mutual aid, intellectual freedom, and military defense (see lines 31-35 in Passage 1 and lines 54-57 in Passage 2). Choice (D) is correct.

Choices A, B, and C may be tempting, but they do not match your prediction. Choice A is incorrect because paragraph 1 of Passage 2 explains the ideological differences between the Bolsheviks and Makhnovischinas. Choice B is incorrect because only Passage 1 even mentions the Austro-Hungarian army, and never claims it was the greatest threat. Choice C is incorrect because it only represents Trotsky's view in Passage 2.

9. A   Difficulty: Hard
Category: Synthesis

Getting to the Answer: Read the question stem closely to identify what it asks you to look for. Because the question stem asks what can be inferred by looking at Passage 2 and the data in the pie chart in tandem, base your interpretation of that data on the negative viewpoint that the author of Passage 2 expresses regarding the Bolsheviks. Your Passage Map shows that paragraph 2 discusses the extent of the Bolsheviks' control in Russia, so you can assume they must have been a powerful group. Analyze the chart to see that the Bolsheviks only composed about a quarter of the government. Predict

that the Bolsheviks were stronger than their proportion of seats on the assembly would suggest. Choice (A) is correct.

ON YOUR OWN

Suggested Passage Map notes:
Passage 1

¶1: (purpose): describe SSB origin; War of 1812 = high stakes

¶2: Br. involvement low to high; Br. victories; bomb Ft. McH

¶3: Key on Br. ship

¶4: saw flag; inspired to write

¶5: war turning point; song symbol of patriotism

Passage 2

¶1: poem early popularity

¶2: history of use: military, baseball

¶3: law = official anthem; current uses; words = reminder; (purpose): explain history of poem/anthem

1. C   Difficulty: Medium
Category: Rhetoric

Getting to the Answer: Review your Passage Map for Passage 1. Paraphrase the purpose before reading the answer choices. The author begins by referencing "the story behind 'The Star-Spangled Banner,' America's national anthem" (lines 1–2). Predict that Passage 1's purpose is to describe the origin of the national anthem. The introduction to the passages also could have provided your prediction for the passage's purpose. Never skip these introductions! Choice (C) is correct.

Remember to answer the questions about Passage 1 immediately after reading it. Choice D reflects the purpose of Passage 2, which could be a tempting answer choice if both passages were read together.

2. D   Difficulty: Medium
Category: Rhetoric

Getting to the Answer: Reread around the cited lines and consider their role in the complete paragraph. The reason for including the lines will reflect their role and purpose in relation to the other information. The paragraph introduces the scope of the passage, which is the story behind the national anthem. It then relates the origin of that story in the War of 1812 and provides context for the war. These lines show the significance of the war for the American people and the importance of its outcome, which gives added meaning to the poem that would become the national anthem; however, the lines don't actually "explain" the symbolism as in C. Choice (D) is correct.

3. D   Difficulty: Easy
Category: Vocab-in-Context

Getting to the Answer: Read the complete sentence in which the cited word appears. Predict a definition before reviewing the answer choices. Compare your prediction with the answer choices and select the one that most nearly reflects the meaning you identified. The line states that "America's defenses prevailed" against an attack by the British. In this context, predict the term most nearly means that America's defenses *hung on*, making choice (D) correct.

4. B   Difficulty: Medium
Category: Inference

Getting to the Answer: Review your notes and the cited lines. Then, paraphrase their meaning and significance. Select the answer choice that best reflects why and how Key came to write the national anthem. Paragraph 4 demonstrates that Key expected Fort McHenry to fall to British forces. He was surprised by American perseverance and, as a result, was inspired to write the national anthem in response to the Americans' survival during the nightlong British bombardment. Choice (B) is correct.

5. D   Difficulty: Medium
Category: Command of Evidence

Getting to the Answer: Review your answer to the previous question and your notes on the referenced paragraph. Identify the phrase that most clearly supports the conclusion identified in the previous question: Key wrote to honor the American resistance. Lines 45-46 ("Moved by . . . to write") clearly explain why Key wrote the words that would become the national anthem. In these lines, the author states Key was moved by the "sight." Confirm from the previous sentences that this "sight" is indeed

the American victory he witnessed: "by dawn's light he saw the American flag" (lines 43-44). Choice (D) is correct.

6. B   Difficulty: Hard
Category: Rhetoric

Getting to the Answer: Using your Passage Map, think about the author's overall tone and purpose to predict what point of view he or she might hold about the national anthem and its origins. Compare your conclusion with the answer choices. The passage begins by explaining the national anthem originated during the War of 1812. The first paragraph goes on to state America was defending its "status as a sovereign nation" (line 8). The last lines of the passage (53–55) describe Key's words as a symbol of America's victory. Taken all together, the passage's purpose is to describe the patriotic origins of "The Star-Spangled Banner." This is best reflected in choice (B) as an accurate description of the entire passage.

7. A   Difficulty: Easy
Category: Rhetoric

Getting to the Answer: Reread the cited lines and review your notes for Passage 2. Consider the placement of the lines in relation to the rest of the passage and how the lines prepare you to interpret subsequent content. The cited lines lay the foundation for the rest of the passage, which describes how Francis Scott Key's poem came to be the official national anthem known as "The Star-Spangled Banner." Choice (A) is correct because the cited lines state clearly that Key first wrote his words as a poem, not as a song or an anthem.

8. A   Difficulty: Easy
Category: Vocab-in-Context

Getting to the Answer: Predict a word or phrase that makes sense in context in place of the existing phrase. Lines 73-80 discuss how the national anthem had begun to increase in popularity and appear regularly in sporting events. The implication in the referenced sentence is that the singing of the national anthem has become a "tradition"; predict *very frequent*. Choice (A) is correct.

9. D   Difficulty: Medium
Category: Inference

Getting to the Answer: Consider how the quotation reflects the specific rhetoric and purpose of the complete sentence. The correct answer will relate the words of the quotation to the rest of the sentence. The text explains that these lyrics "remind Americans of the liberty for which the country was established, and the courage of those who fought for it" (lines 97-99). The author draws a parallel between "land of the free" and "the liberty for which the country was established," and between "home of the brave" and "the courage of those who fought for it." Choice (D) is correct.

10. D   Difficulty: Medium
Category: Synthesis

Getting to the Answer: Review your notes for both passages. Identify what each passage offers to your understanding of the national anthem. The correct answer will reflect the specific contribution of Passage 2. While both passages describe aspects of the history and symbolism of "The Star-Spangled Banner," only Passage 2 traces the events that led to Key's words being officially adopted as the national anthem in 1931. Choice (D) is correct.

Choices A, B, and C may be tempting, but they do not match your prediction. While it is mentioned in Passage 2, choice A only addresses the first paragraph and not the overall contribution of the passage. Choice B is also incorrect. Although Passage 2 does emphasize the national anthem's "patriotic nature," Passage 1 does so as well, so this is not Passage 2's particular enhancement to Passage 1. Choice C is incorrect because the anthem's origins in the War of 1812 are only described at length in Passage 1.

11. B   Difficulty: Medium
Category: Command of Evidence

Getting to the Answer: Predict what type of information would most support your answer to the previous question: something that explains how Key's words became the national anthem. Then, select the answer choice that most closely matches your prediction. Lines 69-73 ("At the time . . . national anthem") demonstrate one way in which the words written by Francis Scott Key gained popularity over time in the United States and even began being thought of as a "national anthem." Choice (B) is correct.

CHAPTER 15

PRACTICE

Suggested Passage Map notes:

¶ 1: oak problems; pests & disease, other trees

¶2: oaks in danger

¶3: research into problems and solutions; various solutions including fire

¶4: ecological restoration

¶5: more human interaction needed

¶6: go back to Native American ways

¶7: human intervention important

4. C   **Difficulty:** Medium
Category: Global

Getting to the Answer: Even when you can't make a specific prediction, summarize the author's central idea by reviewing your Passage Map. The author begins by listing the problems plaguing oak trees and continues by describing possible solutions to each of the problems. Common to each of the solutions is the requirement that humans actively participate in an ongoing process. The author concludes the passage by describing this kind of participation as "ethnobotanical restoration" (line 83). Predict that humans need to participate actively in efforts to restore oaks. Choice (C) matches this prediction.

5. B   **Difficulty:** Medium
Category: Detail

Getting to the Answer: Use your Passage Map to locate cited phrases. Rephrase what each phrase means. The author describes ecological restoration as a process that is completed in a very short time and ethnobotanical restoration as a process that seeks to restore ongoing human interaction with plant communities. Choice (B) is correct.

6. D   **Difficulty:** Easy
Category: Command of Evidence

Getting to the Answer: To answer this question, use the prediction you made to answer the previous question. To answer the previous question, you needed to recognize that the main difference between the two types of restoration is that while ecological restoration

takes place over a short period of time and can be completed, ethnobotanical restoration requires long-term involvement by humans in the natural process of maintaining historic plant communities. Choice (D) is correct.

PERFORM

Suggested Passage Map notes:

¶1: history of newborn screenings; medical advances meant deaths now from rare issues

¶2: link between PKU and mental retardation

¶3: despite risky, use of low phen diet tried

¶4: new test for PKU done earlier

¶5: test not perfect, but successful

7. C   **Difficulty:** Medium
Category: Connections

Getting to the Answer: The phrase "most strongly suggests" and the clue word "prior" indicate that this is a Connections question asking about an explicit relationship. Review your Passage Map to understand how the author connects certain ideas to each other. The word "prior" and the cited lines indicate that the relationship is sequential. First, the low phenylalanine diet, which was implemented despite its risks, proved beneficial. Then, the research initiatives began because of the benefits associated with the diet. Predict that the diet was prescribed in spite of those negative outcomes. Choice (C) matches this prediction.

8. D   **Difficulty:** Medium
Category: Command of Evidence

Getting to the Answer: When answering a Command of Evidence question, find the cited lines that most closely support the prediction you made to answer the previous question. You predicted that the diet was prescribed in spite of the drawbacks. Compare each of the answer choices to your prediction. Only choice (D) describes the drawbacks associated with the special diet.

9. B   **Difficulty:** Medium
Category: Global

Getting to the Answer: Use your Passage Map to quickly summarize the passage. Maintain focus on the general context of each paragraph. Concentrate on the central ideas in each paragraph, not on specific details. The author introduces the passage by discussing the practice of screening newborns and concludes the passage by describing genetic screening as "a permanent part of infant health care" (lines 79–80). Throughout the passage, the author focuses on the process that brought about the use of genetic screening. Choice (B) is correct.

10. D   Difficulty: Easy
Category: Detail

Getting to the Answer: "According to the passage" indicates that this is a Detail question. Use your Passage Map to locate the referenced details. Locate each referenced detail and determine why the author included that detail. Choice A is mentioned as a contributor to the decline in the infant mortality rate and can be eliminated. Eliminate B because Lofenalac was developed to treat PKU. Eliminate C because it discusses problems with the test. Choice (D) is correct because the general success of the test showed the potential of screening tests, as explained in lines 74–77.

11. D   Difficulty: Medium
Category: Command of Evidence

Getting to the Answer: To answer a Command of Evidence question, return to the place in the passage that provided the answer to the previous question. Check to see if one of the answer choices to this question includes the detail you found for the previous question. Choice (D) is correct.

ON YOUR OWN

Suggested Passage Map notes:

¶1: history of S warbler, concern for many birds losing habitats

¶2: S warbler declining due to gradual loss of habitats;

¶3: hard for scientists to conserve; birds adapting on their own

¶4: birds using man made pine plantations

¶5: pine plantations good for birds when trees 20 feet high

¶6: lots of space on plantations

¶7: only some plantations useful

¶8: plantations will become new habitat

1. C   Difficulty: Medium
Category: Global

Getting to the Answer: Think about the central idea of the passage. Eliminate answer choices such as A and D that contain supporting details for the central idea. The correct answer will be an idea that is supported by all of the details in the passage. This passage is mostly about how the Swainson's warbler population has begun to recover after its natural habitat was reduced by deforestation. Choice (C) is correct.

2. C   Difficulty: Medium
Category: Rhetoric

Getting to the Answer: Review your notes for the first paragraph. Consider the central idea of the paragraph and how it relates to the central idea of the passage. Select the answer choice that most accurately describes the purpose this sentence serves in the passage. The author mentions these other species of birds to give examples of other animals that are at risk because their habitats have been destroyed, which matches choice (C).

3. C   Difficulty: Medium
Category: Inference

Getting to the Answer: Review your paragraph 3 notes. How did scientists attempt to preserve the population of the Swainson's warbler? The correct answer should paraphrase your own idea. In lines 30–34 of paragraph 3, the author explains that previous attempts at conservation have been unsuccessful because scientists did not understand what the birds need in a habitat. This matches choice (C).

4. C   Difficulty: Medium
Category: Command of Evidence

Getting to the Answer: Locate each of the answer choices in the passage. The correct answer should provide direct support for the answer to the previous question. In paragraph 3, the author describes why previous conservation efforts by scientists have failed. Choice (C) is correct.

5. D   Difficulty: Medium
Category: Vocab-in-Context

Getting to the Answer: When approaching Vocab-in-Context questions, replace the word in question with a blank and predict a possible synonym. In this sentence, *change* can replace "conversion" without changing the overall meaning. Choice (D) is correct.

6. A   Difficulty: Hard
Category: Inference

Getting to the Answer: This type of open-ended question stem can make it difficult to predict the answer. Instead, look for the answer choice that is directly supported by the evidence in the text. Eliminate answer choices that are related to the main topic but go too far, such as D. In paragraph 1, the author discusses the risk of extinction of other birds due to a decrease in their habitats. Choice (A) is correct because it is most directly supported by the evidence in the passage.

7. B   Difficulty: Medium
Category: Command of Evidence

Getting to the Answer: Use your reasoning for answering the previous question to figure out where in the passage the best evidence for that answer will come from. Lines 9-14 in paragraph 1 provide the most direct support for the idea that more birds will become extinct if their habitats continue to disappear. Choice (B) is correct.

8. D   Difficulty: Easy
Category: Global

Getting to the Answer: Consider the central idea of the passage and the message conveyed by the information included. This passage is mostly about how the Swainson's warbler has adapted after losing much of its natural habitat. Select the answer that most closely explains that the author wants to relate this to the reader. The author's purpose is to explain how this happened, choice (D).

9. C   Difficulty: Hard
Category: Inference

Getting to the Answer: Think about the process undertaken in each of the answer choices and compare it to the Swainson's warbler's migrating to a new, man-made habitat. The migration of the Swainson's warbler to pine forests planted by humans is most similar to aquatic animals making new homes from shipwrecks. In both instances, animals have taken something created by humans and made it into a home. Choice (C) is correct.

10. A   Difficulty: Medium
Category: Vocab-in-Context

Getting to the Answer: In this sentence, the author is describing the stage of development that most closely resembles the bird's natural habitat. Predict that "point" most nearly means *stage*. Eliminate answer choices such as B and D that are synonyms for "point" but do not make sense in context. The prediction is an exact match for choice (A).

11. A   Difficulty: Medium
Category: Synthesis

Getting to the Answer: Consider only the information presented in the graph. The correct answer will be directly supported by the data. The graph shows that over the decade, the number of acres of pine plantations has grown steadily while that of natural pine forests has declined. The conclusion that the number of acres of pine plantations could soon surpass that of natural pine forests is supported by the data presented in the graph. Choice (A) is correct.

CHAPTER 16

PRACTICE

Suggested Passage Map notes:

¶1: book is not fiction

¶2: MF conceals name

¶3: MF used modest tone

¶4: MF's story is dark

¶5: author (DD) focuses on MF's repentance

¶6: DD wants readers to focus on moral

¶7: book includes happiness

¶8: readers can learn from MF's life

4. D   Difficulty: Medium

Category: Connections

Getting to the Answer: The phrase "According to the passage" and a relationship clue word indicate that you should ask yourself how items are being related. The clue word "because" suggests that this is a cause-and-effect relationship. Find the reference to the narrator's concern and reread the section. Predict that the recent popularity of novels encourages readers to believe what they read is fictional. This prediction matches choice (D).

5. C   Difficulty: Medium

Category: Connections

Getting to the Answer: Open-ended Connections questions about relationships (explicit or implicit) require you to describe the relationship in your own words and the correct answers can be difficult to predict. Because the question stem is asking about why the narrator wrote the story described in the passage and not the passage itself, focus on what the narrator says about the purpose of the story. By paraphrasing the narrator's intent stated in the final paragraph, you can predict that the narrator thinks readers can learn good things from the story. Choice (C) matches this prediction.

6. B   Difficulty: Medium

Category: Vocab-in-Context

Getting to the Answer: When answering Vocab-in-Context questions, focus on synonyms for the word in question, not on a specific definition. Read the sentence without "usefully applied" and ask what the narrator is trying to convey. Throughout the passage, the narrator

returns to the idea that the story is written not to relate "wicked" tales but to provide readers with an opportunity to learn from the lessons found in the story. Predict that the narrator is reaffirming the purpose for writing such stories. Choice (B) matches your prediction.

PERFORM

Suggested Passage Map notes:

¶1: NDE raises q's about history

¶2: NDE gives date and mine location of coins

¶3: study to compare methods

¶4: scholars disagree about origin

¶5: how problems of corrosion were overcome

¶6: findings contradict previous scholars

¶7: forced scholars to rethink regional politics

¶8: more tests will be done

7. A   Difficulty: Medium

Category: Vocab-in-Context

Getting to the Answer: Remember to avoid common meanings when answering Vocab-in-Context questions. Read the sentence without "struck" and rephrase what the author means. Predict that the author is referring to when the coins were minted. Choice (A) is correct.

8. D   Difficulty: Medium

Category: Connections

Getting to the Answer: To answer Connections questions that are not about specific parts of the passage, find the author's thesis and look for the answer choice that is consistent with it. Use your Passage Map to locate the thesis. The author states in the first sentence that science can help us learn about history. Lead isotope analysis is presented as an example of how science "can inform" (lines 1-2) history. In the first paragraph, the author states that this analysis has raised questions, and in paragraph 6, the author indicates that the analysis answered questions about when the analyzed coins were made. Therefore, choice (D) is correct.

9. D   Difficulty: Medium

Category: Connections

Getting to the Answer: The phrase "according to the passage" and a relationship keyword in the question stem signal a Connections question. The relationship keyword "because" indicates a cause-and-effect relationship, so identify why the researchers chose the coin in question. Predict that if the scientists' technique could help answer historians' questions, then historians would recognize the value of the technique. Choice (D) is correct.

10. A   Difficulty: Easy
Category: Vocab-in-Context

Getting to the Answer: The phrase "most nearly means" and a cited line indicate a Vocab-in-Context question. Read the sentence without "establish" and think of a synonym that can replace it. Predict that because scientists wanted to determine facts through their research, they wanted to determine who made the coins. Choice (A) matches your prediction.

ON YOUR OWN

Suggested Passage Map notes:

¶1: F's daily routine

¶1, cont: F's friends

¶2-10: recent robbery

¶11: lack of security at bank

¶12: thief not a professional robber

¶13-19: disagree whether thief will be caught

1. D   Difficulty: Medium
Category: Vocab-in-Context

Getting to the Answer: Locate context clues to help determine the meaning of the word. Predict a meaning for the word and then match it to the closest answer choice. The sentence describes Fogg arriving at the club and going to his usual table. A good prediction might be *went*. Be careful of answer choices that offer alternate meanings for the target word that don't make sense in context. Look for the nearest match in the answers. Choice (D) fits with the tone and context of the sentence.

2. C   Difficulty: Medium
Category: Inference

Getting to the Answer: Review the descriptions of Phileas Fogg and his actions in your Passage Map. Summarize what the beginning of the passage says about Fogg. Paragraph 1 describes Fogg counting out his steps on his way to the club. Upon arriving at the club, Fogg

goes to his "habitual table" (line 7) and performs a routine series of actions. Choice (C) is correct, as the details in paragraph 1 depict a man who likes to keep to a set routine.

3. A   Difficulty: Medium
Category: Command of Evidence

Getting to the Answer: Review your answer to the previous question. Locate the answer choice that directly supports the conclusion you drew. Choice (A) is correct. It provides the best support for the idea that Phileas Fogg is a man of habit and routine. The word "habitual" (line 7) and the fact that his table was prepared ahead of time for him suggest that Fogg followed this routine regularly.

4. A   Difficulty: Medium
Category: Inference

Getting to the answer: This is a very open-ended question stem, so it can be difficult to predict the answer without reviewing the answer choices first. Be sure to return to the passage before choosing an answer; skim your Passage Map for evidence that would prove the answer correct answer choice. Fogg reads the newspaper at the beginning of the passage. He later chimes in with a comment on the robbery the other men are discussing based on the information he learned in the paper. Therefore, choice (A) is correct.

5. D   Difficulty: Easy
Category: Command of Evidence

Getting to the Answer: Review your answer to the previous question. Decide which lines of text show Fogg's knowledge of current events. Choice (D) is correct. In these lines, Fogg interjects with additional information about a crime that is a current event.

6. B   Difficulty: Medium
Category: Detail

Getting to the Answer: Locate the portion of the text that discusses the bank. Your Passage Map for paragraph 11 should note a lack of security at the bank. This paragraph describes the lack of security measures at the bank that led to a theft in broad daylight; lines 51-54 reference a lack of guards or protective gratings. Choice (B) is correct.

7. A   Difficulty: Easy
Category: Vocab-in-Context

Getting to the Answer: Find context clues in the target sentence. Predict the meaning of the word and look for a match in the answer choices. "Functionary" (line 46) refers back to the "principal cashier" (line 46) mentioned earlier in the sentence. When you see two related answer choices, such as "official" and "servant," pay attention to the tone and specific context clues to help you choose. Choice (A) is correct; it provides a suitably neutral word that could substitute for "principal cashier, while C, servant, implies a hierarchy that is not present in the passage.

8. C   Difficulty: Medium
Category: Connections

Getting to the Answer: Find the part of the passage that describes the thief. Locate sentences that focus on a description of the suspect. Summarize the details in a one-sentence description. Lines 69-72 ("On the day . . . crime was committed") describe the suspect as a gentleman. Choice (C) is correct because the passage suggests that the police do not believe the man to be a professional thief due to the description of his appearance and demeanor.

9. B   Difficulty: Hard
Category: Rhetoric

Getting to the Answer: Reread the cited line. Concentrate on how the sentence impacts the text surrounding it. Examining the surrounding text shows that this comment occurs during a discussion about the thief being on the run. Fogg has silently listened to the conversation to this point, but now quietly interjects. This suggests that Fogg will have more to say about the topic; choice (B) is correct.

10. C   Difficulty: Medium
Category: Rhetoric

Getting to the Answer: Think about the passage as a whole. Use one sentence to predict the purpose of this passage. Make sure the tone of the answer choice matches the tone of the passage. The excerpt provides a brief character sketch of Phileas Fogg and establishes the dynamics of his friendships at the Reform Club. Choice (C) is correct; it accurately identifies the purpose of the excerpt.

CHAPTER 17

PRACTICE

Suggested Passage Map notes:

¶1: impossible to describe Karnak

¶2: details of K temple ruins

¶3: description of the people at L ("savages")

¶4: K peaceful, not scary at night

4. B   **Difficulty:** Easy
Category: Rhetoric

Getting to the Answer: Questions about why an author includes a section in a passage require you to identify how it fits into the passage as a whole. The author concentrates, throughout the passage, on how much Egypt has affected her. The cited section is not so much about the lack of effect Egypt has had on the other people mentioned, but more about the great effect Egypt has had on the author. Choice (B) is correct.

5. C   **Difficulty:** Medium
Category: Rhetoric

Getting to the Answer: Authors often use contrast to make a point or strengthen an argument. Reread around the cited lines and paraphrase the main points the author makes about the ideas being contrasted. To answer this question, you must compare the author's experiences in Karnak and Luxor. The author describes Karnak in lofty, ethereal language filled with references to the eternal. The author expects to find the same thing in Luxor—"I had expected the temples of Thebes to be solemn . . ." (lines 41–42)—but finds something completely different: "but Luxor was fearful" (lines 42–43). Predict that the comparison between the two cities highlights the author's negative reaction to the conditions at Luxor. Choice (C) matches your prediction.

6. A   **Difficulty:** Medium
Category: Rhetoric

Getting to the Answer: Questions concerning the overall structure of a text require you to think about how the author presents the central ideas and builds the main argument. Review your Passage Map and look for patterns in how the author expresses the important ideas in

the passage. In the second paragraph, the author shifts between the real and the imagined: "Gigantic shadows spring up on every side; 'the dead are stirred up for thee to meet . . .'" (lines 14–16). This shift between the real and the imagined continues in the third paragraph: "Rows of painted . . . golden clouds" (lines 42–56). Predict that the author mixes real descriptions with imaginative descriptions, which matches choice (A).

PERFORM

Suggested Passage Map notes:

¶1: owls = optimize bio strengths

¶2: maximize vision adv.

¶3: humans map world diff. than owls

¶4: owls = complex sens. detail

7. D   **Difficulty:** Medium
Category: Rhetoric

Getting to the Answer: Use your Passage Map to answer questions concerning the central argument in a passage. Review the first paragraph to determine the author's thesis. Think about what must be true for the claim to be correct. The author begins with the claim that "humans and animals perceive the world in different ways" (lines 1–2). Predict that the assumption must have to do with how our brains work in different ways, which matches choice (D).

8. C   **Difficulty:** Medium
Category: Rhetoric

Getting to the Answer: To answer a Rhetoric question that asks about support for a claim, use your Passage Map to locate the claims the author makes and the support the author provides. Make a general prediction about the claims the author supports and then find the answer choice that matches. The author claims that owls and humans have adapted to their environments in different ways. Since this question asks about owls, focus on the claims the author makes about them. Predict that the author provides support for the claim that owls have effectively adapted to their environment. In the second paragraph, the author provides several examples of ways owls successfully adapted. Choice (C) is correct.

9. D   Difficulty: Easy
Category: Rhetoric

Getting to the Answer: When you see the phrase "in order to" and a cited line, identify how the cited detail fits into the overall structure of the passage. Overall, the passage compares the differences between the sensory adaptations of owls and humans. Read around the cited line and paraphrase why the author mentions barn owls. Predict that barn owl hearing is an example of how owls have adapted to improve their ability to hunt. Choice (D) matches your prediction.

10. A   Difficulty: Medium
Category: Rhetoric

Getting to the Answer: Review your Passage Map, focusing on how the author presents the information in the passage. In paragraph 1, the author compares human perception to that of other animals, specifically owls. The author then discusses different ways in which owls and humans use their respective sensory apparatuses. Predict that the passage is structured by comparing the differences between how owls and humans perceive the world. Choice (A) is correct.

ON YOUR OWN

Suggested Passage Map notes:

¶1: 2 types of univ. = pub. & private
¶2: pub univ. goal = ↑ higher ed opportunity
¶3: 1862 - gov't gave pub. land for univ.
¶4: history of diversity
¶5: major growth
¶6: US univ. part of global conv.
¶7: univ. reflect diversity, liberty, creativity

1. C   Difficulty: Hard
Category: Rhetoric

Getting to the Answer: The correct answer will reflect a specific position supported in both the second paragraph and the passage as a whole. Predict that the author is citing political and economic reasons to explain why the government "acknowledged the need" (line 22) for educated citizens. Choice (C) is correct.

2. B   Difficulty: Medium
Category: Command of Evidence

Getting to the Answer: Use your support for the previous question to predict the answer. Consider which choice best shows a clear relationship to your answer. In the previous question, line 22 offered support for our answer; Choice (B) is correct because it explicitly states that the government saw the "need for broader higher education opportunities" (lines 22–23).

3. A   Difficulty: Medium
Category: Rhetoric

Getting to the Answer: Summarize the paragraph and think about what the author would want the reader to know after reading it. Be sure to review your Passage Map, which should already state important information about the paragraph. Your Passage Map notes that in 1862, the government gave public land for university development; the paragraph states that the Morill Act was an early example of the federal government's desire to increase enrollment at public universities. Predict that the purpose of the paragraph is to explain how the government supported public higher education. Choice (A) is correct.

4. B   Difficulty: Medium
Category: Rhetoric

Getting to the Answer: The author's choice of words is deliberate. Read the sentence carefully and think about what the author is suggesting when he uses the word "accessible." The passage notes that public universities received federal and state support, which means the universities could then function at a lower cost and could enable more students to attend. Predict that "accessible" was used to describe how higher education was remodeled to be available to more people, especially those with limited means. Choice (B) is correct.

5. D   Difficulty: Easy
Category: Vocab-in-Context

Getting to the Answer: Use context clues to help you predict the meaning of the word as it is used in the sentence. The last sentence in paragraph 3 contrasts the fact that although universities would be operated by states, they would still need to follow, or comply with, federal regulations because they received federal support. Predict that adhere most nearly means *follow* or *comply with*. Choice (D) is correct.

6. C   Difficulty: Hard
Category: Rhetoric

Getting to the Answer: It is difficult to predict the exact answer for this type of question, but concisely stating the author's line of reasoning before reviewing the answer choices will help you eliminate the choices that do not strengthen that theme. Throughout the passage, the author discusses how the expansion of public universities has impacted American culture. In paragraph 4, the author describes how public universities have gradually become more diverse, offering educational opportunities to many people who would not have otherwise had them in previous years. This has had a significant impact on American culture. Consider which of these pieces of evidence best supports that theme; choice (C) is correct.

7. C   Difficulty: Medium
Category: Rhetoric

Getting to the Answer: Think about why the author would want to include this fact. The paragraph's central idea is that the student populations of public universities have grown increasingly diverse. Predict that the author is describing an example of how public universities have become more diverse. Look for the answer choice that matches this prediction. Choice (C) is correct.

8. B   Difficulty: Easy
Category: Command of Evidence

Getting to the Answer: There should be a clear relationship between the correct choice and the previous answer. Since you used the fourth paragraph as a whole to predict the last question, look for the choice that offers support for the specific answer to the previous question. Choice (B) clearly states that public universities are diverse today, even though the 1890 land act did not increase diversity when it was passed. This corresponds to the answer to the previous question.

9. D   Difficulty: Easy
Category: Vocab-in-Context

Getting to the Answer: Predict the meaning of the word with context clues from the sentence and paragraph. The second sentence of paragraph 5 states that the public

university system "has evolved," which implies it has done so in response to changes or variations in American culture over time. Predict that "nuances" most nearly means *changes* or *variations*. Always check your answer choice in the sentence to ensure it makes the most sense. Choice (D) is correct.

10. C   Difficulty: Hard
Category: Rhetoric

Getting to the Answer: Consider what the passage is about overall and what the author wants the reader to learn, rather than an idea that is mentioned only in passing or in support of the passage's purpose. Reviewing your whole Passage Map can help you focus on the entirety of the passage. The author has written a brief history of public higher education in the United States; in both the introduction and conclusion, the author connects the evolution of the public university system with the evolution of generally accepted ideals and cultural values, such as diversity and liberty. Predict that the author is discussing the connection between public higher education and generally accepted ideals. Choice (C) is correct.

11. B   Difficulty: Medium
Category: Rhetoric

Getting to the Answer: Consider the central idea of the passage that you identified in a previous question and the central idea in the fifth paragraph. The passage is primarily about the way in which U.S. higher education has reflected American cultural identity. The fifth paragraph summarizes the major growth public higher education has undergone. Predict that as the American culture has grown to value public higher education, public higher education has undergone major growth; the fifth paragraph gives an example that supports the central idea. Choice (B) is correct.

CHAPTER 18

PRACTICE

Suggested Passage Map notes:

¶1: artifacts show how colonists lived

¶2: clues about life

¶3: settlers used woodworking skills

¶4: early structures primitive, focus on survival

¶5: brick processes similar to England

¶6: most hardware from England

¶7: use of glass

¶8: after hardship, gained luxuries

4. C **Difficulty:** Easy
Category: Inference

Getting to the Answer: The phrase "the statement . . . suggests" signals that this is an Inference question. Find the relevant details and look for clues indicating how the author connects them. Read around the cited text. In the previous two sentences, the author discusses the hardships the colonists faced in the early years. Focus on the reasons they didn't think about plastering during the early years. Predict that the colonists were too busy trying to stay alive. Choice (C) matches your prediction.

5. D **Difficulty:** Easy
Category: Detail

Getting to the Answer: When presented with an EXCEPT question, use your Passage Map to locate the cited details. When you find one of the cited details in the passage, eliminate that answer choice. The third paragraph describes Virginia as a "carpenter's paradise" (line 23) and says the wooden artifacts were skillfully made. Eliminate A. Paragraph 4 describes how the settlers had "a difficult time staying alive" (lines 36-37); eliminate B. In the fourth paragraph, you learn that the colonists made floors from clay, allowing you to eliminate C. The sixth paragraph says that most of the hardware was imported, which directly contradicts choice (D).

6. D **Difficulty:** Medium
Category: Inference

Getting to the Answer: The phrase " . . . most comparable to . . . " indicates that this is an Analogical Reasoning Inference question. Identify the relationship between the ideas. The description of the brick industry implies that the colonists made bricks with local materials using techniques they brought with them from England. The relationship is one of local materials formed using imported methods. Choice (D) reflects this relationship.

PERFORM

Suggested Passage Map notes:

¶1: narrator impressed with other's imagination

¶2: secluded life, other character's name revealed: Dupin

¶3: preferred darkness

¶4: narrator admired Dupin's analytic ability

7. C **Difficulty:** Medium
Category: Inference

Getting to the Answer: The word "suggests" and the line reference indicate that this is an Inference question. Determine which answer choice can be concluded based on the information in the passage. Read around the cited section. Substituting "because" for "as" clarifies that this is a cause-and-effect relationship. The cause is Dupin's "embarrassed" circumstances (line 18), and the effect is that the narrator paid for everything. Predict that the narrator had more money than Dupin. Choice (C) is correct.

8. D **Difficulty:** Hard
Category: Inference

Getting to the Answer: The phrase "closely parallels" is a clue that this is an Analogical Reasoning Inference question. To identify how the ideas are connected, describe the relationship. In the third paragraph, the narrator states that he followed Dupin's lead in everything, indicating that the narrator is subordinate to Dupin. Look for the answer choice that describes a relationship in which one side of the relationship is subordinate to the other. Although C might be tempting, the student acts independently in the second half of the answer choice. Choice (D) is correct.

9. B   **Difficulty:** Medium
Category: Detail

Getting to the Answer: Because this question does not provide a line reference, use your Passage Map to locate the relevant text. Then, paraphrase the detail. Locate the details about how and where the narrator met Dupin. In the first sentence, the narrator mentions first meeting Dupin in a library while searching for a rare book. Predict that they were looking for the same book. Choice (B) is correct.

10. A   **Difficulty:** Hard
Category: Inference

Getting to the Answer: "Most likely agree" signals a broad or open-ended Inference question. Summarize the passage to zero in on statements with which the narrator would most likely agree. The passage focuses on the ways the narrator becomes involved with Dupin. The final paragraph discusses Dupin's ability to see into other people's inner thoughts: "windows in their bosoms" (line 62). The passage ends with the narrator's speculating on how Dupin could do so. Choice (A) is correct.

ON YOUR OWN

Suggested Passage Map notes:

> ¶1: U.S. idea of national parks
> ¶2: parks scope and history
> ¶3: millions appreciate parks, parks encourage preservation
> ¶4: JM father of national parks
> ¶5: JM focus on ecology, natural beauty and worth
> ¶6: political impact, started Sierra Club
> ¶7: JM greatest accomplishment importance of nature

1. C   **Difficulty:** Medium
Category: Vocab-in-Context

Getting to the Answer: Look for context clues to help you determine the meaning of unknown words. Read the rest of the paragraph to get a better idea of the relationship between America's national parks and the rest of the world. The last sentence of the paragraph states that "globally over a thousand parks are now protected by similar systems" (lines 10-11). The idea that originated in the United States later became popular worldwide. Choice (C), "imitated," is correct.

2. A   **Difficulty:** Medium
Category: Rhetoric

Getting to the Answer: As you take notes, identify the general idea of each paragraph in the passage in your own words. Compare your notes to each choice to find the correct answer. The second paragraph provides the reader with statistics about the scale of the National Parks System, including the diversity of the parks, the number of employees required to manage the system, and the number of acres the system includes. Choice (A) correctly summarizes the purpose of this paragraph.

3. D   **Difficulty:** Medium
Category: Inference

Getting to the Answer: Look for specific textual evidence in the passage that may support each answer choice. The correct answer will be concluded directly from the passage. The passage mentions the international influence of the United States National Parks System several times. Other answer choices are not supported by evidence. Only choice (D) is directly found within the passage.

4. D   **Difficulty:** Medium
Category: Command of Evidence

Getting to the Answer: Review your answer to the previous question. Then, choose the textual evidence that best supports that conclusion. According to the passage, "over a hundred countries now participate" (lines 36-37) in a national parks system. Choice (D) provides direct evidence for the passage's assertion that America's national parks idea has been influential internationally.

5. A   **Difficulty:** Easy
Category: Vocab-in-Context

Getting to the Answer: Break the word down into its component parts to determine the correct answer. "Wander" suggests travel and "lust" suggests a positive interest. Looking at the context, "his activism and wanderlust also drew him to other picturesque locations" (lines 65-67), an interest in travel is the most logical choice.

6. B   **Difficulty:** Hard

Category: Rhetoric

Getting to the Answer: Consider why the word "channeling" is used instead of an alternative word. What meaning does it add that a more general word like "communicating" does not? The context of the sentence suggests that Muir's writings were powerful. They seem to have captured the "marvel" (line 71) of the wilderness and transmitted it directly to readers, making them feel it, too. "Channeling" emphasizes the way the power of his writing took the emotion he felt and communicated it directly and powerfully to readers. Choice (B) successfully captures this idea.

7. A   **Difficulty:** Hard

Category: Inference

Getting to the Answer: Consider the passage as a whole. Are there any answers you can immediately eliminate as being obviously incorrect? The passage consistently states that John Muir was hugely influential during his lifetime, so B can be eliminated. It does acknowledge, however, that the preservation of such vast amounts of wilderness did come at an economic cost, though the passage suggests that this cost was worthwhile. Choice (A) is correct.

8. D   **Difficulty:** Medium

Category: Command of Evidence

Getting to the Answer: Test each possible answer choice against your selection for the preceding question. Which piece of evidence most directly supports the previous answer choice? The passage states that conserving the wilderness was worthwhile, "even at the expense of short-lived material gains" (lines 90-91). This suggests that there was an economic cost to Muir's preservation goals. Choice (D) is correct, as it directly connects the parks system to ideas of money.

9. A   **Difficulty:** Hard

Category: Synthesis

Getting to the Answer: Use your Passage Map to summarize each passage. Then, find the answer choice that best matches your ideas. Passage 1 describes the American National Parks System in general, focusing on its creation, its size, and its parks' diversity. Passage 2 focuses specifically on the importance of John Muir and his influence on conservation. Choice (A) correctly summarizes these differences.

10. A   **Difficulty:** Easy

Category: Synthesis

Getting to the Answer: Evaluate how each passage describes the national parks. What do the word choices suggest about the purpose and value of the parks? Both passages use words like "awe" (line 29) and "wonder" (line 70) to discuss the national parks. Clearly, the authors of both passages agree that the main value of national parks is to preserve natural beauty for visitors. Choice (A) correctly reflects this idea.

11. D   **Difficulty:** Easy

Category: Synthesis

Getting to the Answer: Carefully study the *x*- and *y*-axes to determine what trends can be inferred from the graph. According to the graph, visits to all five parks have increased from 1930 to 2010. No conclusions can be drawn about why parks have been more or less popular destinations during these periods. However, the graph does show that during each period, the Grand Canyon has received more visitors than has Olympic National Park. Choice (D) is the only answer choice that can be definitely concluded from the chart.

CHAPTER 19

PRACTICE

3. C **Difficulty:** Medium
Category: Effective Language Use

Getting to the Answer: Consider how you would refer to a number in a different context. Would you say you started school "hundred days" ago? "Hundred" refers to a digit (ones digit, tens digit, hundreds digit, etc.), whereas "one hundred" is an actual number. In order to begin the sentence in an idiomatically correct way, it is necessary to use the full number, "one hundred." Choice (C) matches.

4. C **Difficulty:** Medium
Category: Sentence Formation

Getting to the Answer: If there is no obvious error in the underlined segment, keep reading until you can identify the issue. The underlined portion is correctly used as the subject of an independent clause. However, because the clause after the comma is also independent, the sentence is a run-on. Since you are not given the option to fix the comma splice, look for the answer choice that makes the first clause dependent without introducing another error. Choice (C) correctly subordinates the first clause by beginning the sentence with "when."

5. B **Difficulty:** Easy
Category: Usage

Getting to the Answer: Subjects and verbs must agree in person and number. Singular third person subjects need singular third person verbs, and plural third person subjects need plural third person verbs. Keep in mind that the closest noun to an underlined verb may not be its subject. Read around the underlined portion until you can identify the subject of the underlined verb. Remember, a noun that is the object of a preposition cannot be the subject of a sentence. In this sentence, the subject is the plural noun "components" and needs a plural verb. Choice (B) is correct.

PERFORM

6. B **Difficulty:** Medium
Category: Effective Language Use

Getting to the Answer: Using two words that mean the same thing is redundant. Look for the answer choice that creates the most concise sentence. As written, the sentence uses a compound predicate made up of "fascinated and intrigued." Because both words convey the same idea, namely that scientists found Jupiter to be very interesting, using one is sufficient. Choice (B) concisely conveys the idea.

7. D **Difficulty:** Medium
Category: Sentence Formation

Getting to the Answer: Read around an underlined period and check to make sure that each clause forms a complete sentence. Because the second clause is a fragment, it needs to be properly connected to the previous sentence with either subordination or punctuation. Choice B provides punctuation that corrects the fragment but does not form an effective sentence. Since the information in the second clause explains why the moons of Jupiter provided evidence for a theory, the second clause needs to be combined with the previous sentence. Choice (D) joins the clause to the sentence.

8. D **Difficulty:** Easy
Category: Sentence Formation

Getting to the Answer: Compare underlined verbs with related verbs. Related verb forms need to be parallel. The verbs "completed" and "collected" form a compound predicate and need to be parallel in form. As written, the underlined section unnecessarily reintroduces the subject. Join the two verbs without punctuation. Choice (D) is correct.

9. C **Difficulty:** Easy
Category: Development

Getting to the Answer: If you have the option to omit a sentence, think carefully about the author's topic. If the underlined portion strays from the topic, omit it. The author's topic is Jupiter. The underlined portion adds information about *Pioneer 10* that is irrelevant to the topic. Choice (C) correctly omits the sentence for this reason.

Answers & Explanations

10. B **Difficulty:** Medium
Category: Effective Language Use

Getting to the Answer: If an underlined segment does not contain a grammatical error, check for other kinds of errors tested on the SAT. As written, the underlined portion is a complete sentence. Reread that sentence in the context of the following sentence. Together, these two sentences sound choppy and create a wordiness issue. Because the underlined sentence provides information about Jupiter, it can be incorporated into the next sentence. Choice (B) forms a modifying phrase that effectively introduces the subject of the sentence.

11. D **Difficulty:** Medium
Category: Usage

Getting to the Answer: Related nouns must be consistent in number. Check other nouns around an underlined noun to make sure they agree. The underlined noun is related to the noun phrase "number of probes." Because there was more than one probe, there was more than one measurement. Choice (D) correctly makes the underlined noun plural.

12. C **Difficulty:** Medium
Category: Quantitative

Getting to the Answer: When you see a question with an infographic, remember to use the Kaplan Method for Infographics. The sentence to which the underlined portion belongs is comparing Earth's rotational speed to that of Jupiter's. The relevant information is how much faster Jupiter rotates. Look in the third column of the table for that data. Compare the information you find with the answer choices. Choice (C) provides accurate and relevant information.

13. D **Difficulty:** Medium
Category: Usage

Getting to the Answer: A pronoun's antecedent must be clear and unambiguous. Always identify the antecedent of an underlined pronoun. The underlined possessive pronoun could refer to a number of things: our diameter, Earth's diameter, and Earth's rotational speed. Reread the sentence to determine what the author means. The sentence compares the diameter of Jupiter to the diameter of Earth. Look for the answer choice that makes that comparison clear. Choice (D) is correct.

ON YOUR OWN

1. B **Difficulty:** Medium
Category: Effective Language Use

Getting to the Answer: Read the entire paragraph to determine if a career in physical therapy is rated as a good career choice by the Bureau of Labor Statistics. "Concurrently" means at the same time, and "unusually" means not common. "Finally" implies that physical therapy was not a good career choice in the past. Choice (B) is correct because it means with regularity.

2. D **Difficulty:** Medium
Category: Effective Language Use

Getting to the Answer: Read the sentence and determine how it can be more concise. As written, the text begins with a conjunction and uses a dash to indicate an unnecessary break in thought. Choice (D) eliminates both problems, creating a more direct sentence.

3. B **Difficulty:** Medium
Category: Development

Getting to the Answer: Read the entire paragraph to identify its focus. Choices A, C, and D each offer only one component of the paragraph. Only choice (B) effectively establishes the main topic of the second paragraph.

4. A **Difficulty:** Easy
Category: Punctuation

Getting to the Answer: Read the sentence and determine whether it is grammatically complete. To form a grammatically complete sentence, you must have an independent clause after a semicolon. Choices B, C, and D all have excessive and incorrect punctuation. The sentence is correct as written; choice (A) is correct.

5. B **Difficulty:** Hard
Category: Development

Getting to the Answer: Read the entire paragraph to determine the pattern of the evidence. Most sentences include descriptions of the types of patients a PT will encounter. Since (B) is the only sentence that supports the topic sentence, it is the correct answer.

6. B   **Difficulty:** Medium
Category: Sentence Formation

Getting to the Answer: Read the sentence to determine how to improve its clarity. Consider whether the modifiers are correctly placed near the nouns or verbs they modify. The use of the modifier "minimally" at the end of the sentence is awkward. Choice (B) correctly moves the modifier next to the word it modifies: "interaction." It also removes the conjunction "And" at the beginning of the sentence.

7. D   **Difficulty:** Medium
Category: Effective Language Use

Getting to the Answer: Read the sentences and determine what words can be eliminated. As written, the text uses short, choppy sentences. Choice (D) combines the two sentences effectively to improve the economy of word choice.

8. B   **Difficulty:** Hard
Category: Sentence Formation

Getting to the Answer: Read the sentence and examine the order of the details. Reorganize the sentence so that it is clear and smooth. As written, the text contains coordinated ideas without regard to their grammatical form. Choice (B) correctly rearranges the ideas so that the three main ideas are nouns combined with "and" instead of "in addition to."

9. A   **Difficulty:** Easy
Category: Effective Language Use

Getting to the Answer: Read the sentence and determine the function of the word in the sentence. "Concentrated" means clustered or gathered together, "planned" means to arrange beforehand, and "consolidated" means brought together in a single whole. Only choice (A), "collaborated," means working together intellectually.

10. D   **Difficulty:** Hard
Category: Organization

Getting to the Answer: Read the paragraph and determine if the sequence of events is logical. For the paragraph to be logical, the examples need to build upon one another. Sentence 7 does not offer a proper conclusion to the paragraph, but sentence 2 gives a good summation.

Choice (D) correctly moves the summative sentence to conclude the paragraph.

11. D   **Difficulty:** Medium
Category: Development

Getting to the Answer: Closely read the paragraph to find the central idea. Then, determine which sentence does not match the content. The evidence regarding physical therapy assistants does not connect with the main idea of this paragraph, which centers on the benefits of choosing to become a certified physical therapist. Choice (D) is correct.

CHAPTER 20

PRACTICE

4. C   **Difficulty:** Hard
Category: Organization

Getting to the Answer: An effective body paragraph can provide evidence to support the author's central idea or introduce a change in the focus of the passage. This paragraph begins with the transition word "while" and establishes a contrast between the number of recent earthquakes and the damage that those earthquakes can cause. The passage also shifts focus from a discussion of earthquake frequency to one of earthquake damage. Therefore, placing this paragraph between the two discussions in paragraph 4 and paragraph 5 makes the most sense. Choice (C) is correct.

5. C   **Difficulty:** Medium
Category: Organization

Getting to the Answer: When reordering a sentence within a paragraph, identify the information in the sentence and locate where in the paragraph that information is discussed. The topic of sentence 4 is aftershocks. Aftershocks are also discussed in sentence 2. However, in sentence 2 the pronoun "these" indicates that aftershocks have been previously discussed in the paragraph. The logical place for sentence 4 is before sentence 2. Choice (C) is correct.

6. A   **Difficulty:** Easy
Category: Organization

Getting to the Answer: Don't answer questions that ask about the conclusion of a paragraph until you have read the entire paragraph. The paragraph focuses on the damage that earthquakes can cause and ways to improve safety in the event of an earthquake. Although the sentence preceding the concluding sentence mentions earthquake predictions, it does so in the context of how to prepare for these natural disasters. Therefore, the final sentence needs to discuss preparations, not predictions. Choice (A) provides a logical conclusion to the paragraph.

PERFORM

7. D   **Difficulty:** Medium
Category: Usage

Getting to the Answer: A pronoun is ambiguous when its antecedent is either missing or unclear. To find the antecedent for the underlined pronoun, read the previous sentence and think about the focus of the paragraph. The previous sentence has more than one possible antecedent—vacuous "Internet speak," "reliance," or "acronyms and abbreviations." However, in the context of the passage, "empty chatter," or choice (D), is the clearest and most relevant antecedent.

8. A   **Difficulty:** Medium
Category: Organization

Getting to the Answer: To answer questions about effective transitions within a paragraph, identify the focus of the paragraph both before and after the transition. The first part of the paragraph discusses the reasons the narrator stayed in his room as a child—because he was ill. After the transition, the narrator discusses why he still stays in his room—because he has access to the world. The transition needs to show how those ideas are linked. Choice (A) provides a logical transition as written.

9. B   **Difficulty:** Easy
Category: Effective Language Use

Getting to the Answer: When two words or phrases in the sentence have the same meaning, the sentence is redundant and contains a concision error. In this sentence, "succinct" and "to the point" have the same meaning, so the correct answer will eliminate one. Choice (B) is correct.

10. C   **Difficulty:** Hard
Category: Organization

Getting to the Answer: To reorder a sentence within a paragraph, identify the information in the sentence and locate what sentence that information should logically precede or follow. As written, sentence 5 summarizes the freedom people experience when connected by the Internet. However, sentence 6 makes a claim about that freedom, and sentence 7 provides examples of that freedom. The summary in sentence 5 should logically follow both the claim and the examples. Choice (C) is correct.

11. B   Difficulty: Easy
Category: Usage

Getting to the Answer: Unless the context in the passage indicates that the time frame has changed, the verb tense should not change. As written, this verb is in the past perfect tense. However, the context of the passage indicates that the action described by the verb continued up until the present moment. Choice (B) correctly uses the present perfect tense.

12. D   Difficulty: Hard
Category: Sentence Formation

Getting to the Answer: Whenever you see a compound, series, or list, check to make sure that all of the items are in parallel form. The underlined phrase is part of a compound formed by the conjunction "and." Reread the sentence and identify the other part of the compound. In this sentence, "half two minds exchanging sophisticated ideas" forms the first part of the compound. The second part must be parallel. Choice (D) is correct.

13. A   Difficulty: Medium
Category: Organization

Getting to the Answer: Introductory transitions must logically connect the information and ideas in the sentences before and after the transition. In the sentence before the underlined transition, the author describes small talk as boring. In the following sentence, he compares a conversation without small talk to flying. The sentence suggests that small talk can be dispensed with only occasionally. This sentence is correct as written, so choice (A) is correct.

14. D   Difficulty: Medium
Category: Organization

Getting to the Answer: Paragraphs in a well-written passage will flow from the general to the specific. To put paragraphs in the most logical order, begin with the paragraph that introduces the central idea in broad terms. As written, paragraph 1 contains a very specific discussion of a particular form of speech. Paragraph 2 introduces the idea of conversation in general terms and outlines the narrator's thoughts about it. Only choice (D) arranges the paragraphs from the general to the specific.

ON YOUR OWN

1. B   Difficulty: Easy
Category: Usage

Getting to the Answer: As currently written, this sentence switches verb tense mid-sentence. The other verb in the sentence, "was," indicates that the events happened in the past. The tense of the underlined verb should match and also be in a correct past tense. Choice (B) is correct because it correctly uses the past tense of "produce."

2. B   Difficulty: Medium
Category: Organization

Getting to the Answer: Look for the relationship between this sentence and the previous one. Choice (B) shows the relationship between the two sentences by giving an example of what kind of art the Post-Impressionists were creating.

3. D   Difficulty: Medium
Category: Effective Language Use

Getting to the Answer: Read the complete passage to learn more about the work of Impressionists. The passage states that Impressionists tried to paint exactly what they saw in nature. Only choice (D) has the correct connotation and fits within the context of the sentence.

4. B   Difficulty: Medium
Category: Sentence Formation

Getting to the Answer: The verbs in a sentence have to be parallel. The correct answer is in the same form as the first verb in the sentence, "looking." That means that the gerund, or -ing verb, "attempting" in choice (B) is correct.

5. A   Difficulty: Easy
Category: Effective Language Use

Getting to the Answer: Check each word for its connotations and pick the answer choice that fits the context of the sentence. This sentence describes how Post-Impressionists focused on self-discovery in art by letting their personal experiences and emotions guide their interpretation of their subjects. Therefore, each artist had his or her own distinct, or "unique," vision. The underlined portion is correct as written, and the answer is therefore choice (A).

6. C   **Difficulty:** Hard

Category: Development

Getting to the Answer: Read the entire paragraph and determine the central idea. The paragraph discusses different ways artists in the Post-Impressionism era painted. Choice (C) reflects this summary.

7. B   **Difficulty:** Hard

Category: Effective Language Use

Getting to the Answer: Choice (B) joins the sentences concisely and correctly by changing the verb tense of the first sentence to make it a dependent clause.

8. A   **Difficulty:** Easy

Category: Usage

Getting to the Answer: Read the sentence prior to the pronoun to determine whom the pronoun is referencing. The pronoun "they" refers to Paul Gauguin and Vincent van Gogh, so the pronoun needs to be plural and in the third person. Choice (A) is correct.

9. D   **Difficulty:** Hard

Category: Development

Getting to the Answer: Read the entire paragraph to identify the central idea. Then find the answer choice that provides evidence about this idea. The paragraph concerns the Post-Impressionist period and what kinds of methods Post-Impressionists used to create their art. Choice (D) addresses the central idea by providing additional information about these methods.

10. B   **Difficulty:** Medium

Category: Usage

Getting to the Answer: "They're" is a contraction meaning "they are," which does not make sense in the context of the sentence. What is needed here is a possessive plural pronoun to match the antecedent "artists." Choice (B) is correct.

11. D   **Difficulty:** Medium

Category: Organization

Getting to the Answer: Try inserting this sentence into all of the possible places to figure out where it makes the most sense. Choice (D) is the most logical position for this sentence because it is a comment based on the quotation in sentence 5.

CHAPTER 21

PRACTICE

5. D   **Difficulty:** Medium
Category: Development

Getting to the Answer: Scrutinize details of densely factual passages to make sure they are on-topic and do not conflict with other details or the central idea. This passage is concerned with the details of human skin and explaining the properties and purposes of skin. Choice (D) abides by the author's scope and purpose for the passage and is therefore correct.

6. A   **Difficulty:** Medium
Category: Development

Getting to the Answer: Pick the answer choice that is in line with the author's central idea and tone. In this passage, the author explains how the skin is essential to life by listing its various properties and processes for keeping the body in healthy operation. The underlined section is in line with the author's overall effort. Choice (A) is correct.

7. C   **Difficulty:** Medium
Category: Development

Getting to the Answer: Make sure details in the underlined section are relevant to the topic. Even if a detail matches the tone of the passage (in this case, strictly fact-based), it might not be relevant to the central idea. Most of the answer choices for this question sound legitimate and even factually correct. However, only choice (C) keeps the focus on the human skin and its characteristics, so it is correct. Remember, the focus of the paragraph is on the defensive functions of the skin, *not* on how those functions work at a cellular level. You also know that immediate medical attention (choice B) is too extreme for every instance of skin breaking (small cuts, etc.).

8. A   **Difficulty:** Medium
Category: Development

Getting to the Answer: Concluding sentences often reassert or summarize the author's central idea; therefore, they cannot fundamentally conflict with the author's

assertions. In this passage, the author has made clear that the skin is a very important organ that protects the body from a variety of illnesses and disorders, as well as from physical harm. Choice (A) is correct, as it ties preceding points and details together into a coherent conclusion for the author's argument.

PERFORM

9. A   **Difficulty:** Medium
Category: Development

Getting to the Answer: Scrutinize the answer choices for how they relate to the author's central ideas as well as how they potentially conflict with details that come later in the passage. Choice (A) is correct because—without going off-topic or conflicting with later details—it elaborates on the idea that Polk followed in Jackson's footsteps.

10. C   **Difficulty:** Easy
Category: Development

Getting to the Answer: Pay close attention to long lists of evidence to make sure that each component is in line with the central idea and context of the sentence. Choice (C) is correct because it is the only answer choice that both stays focused on matters of policy (as the first part of the sentence mentions) and supports the thesis that Polk and Jackson were in agreement on most points of public policy.

11. D   **Difficulty:** Easy
Category: Development

Getting to the Answer: The first sentence of a paragraph sets the paragraph's tone and purpose. Pay attention to what the other sentences of the paragraph are describing and pick the answer choice that is the best introduction for those details. This paragraph is concerned with explaining the chronology of Polk's early life. Choice (D) is correct because it states the place and date of Polk's birth, making it a logical introduction to the following sentences.

12. D   **Difficulty:** Medium
Category: Development

Getting to the Answer: Supporting details fit the context of the paragraph and do not contradict details found elsewhere in the passage. Select the answer choice that satisfies these guidelines. This paragraph is narrowly concerned with Polk's origins and early political career. Only choice (D) fits the context and does not contradict later details.

13. C   Difficulty: Medium
Category: Development

Getting to the Answer: A paragraph's final sentence ideally guides the paragraph's central idea to a conclusion and remains linked to the central idea of the passage. Choice (C) is correct because it is the most effective conclusion for a paragraph tasked with explaining Polk's early political career. Choice (C) also makes a clear connection to the following paragraph, helping the narrative flow.

14. B   Difficulty: Medium
Category: Development

Getting to the Answer: Remember that supporting evidence needs to focus on and contribute to the central idea. The author's intent is to introduce the two main candidates in the 1844 election, leading to the following sentence that discusses their opinions of expansionism. Choice (B) is correct because it stays focused on the paragraph's topic and contributes to the argument that Polk recognized popular support for expansionism that other candidates overlooked or ignored.

15. A   Difficulty: Medium
Category: Development

Getting to the Answer: Examine details and parenthetical asides for relevance to the central idea. The goal is to make sure that no contradictions are being introduced into the narrative. No change is necessary because the underlined section touches on two central themes of the passage: Polk's support for expansionist policies and his Jacksonian view of America. Choice (A) is correct.

16. B   Difficulty: Hard
Category: Development

Getting to the Answer: Pay close attention to a paragraph's first sentence. It should set the stage for details to follow and also be in line with the passage's central idea. As alluded to in the first paragraph and explained clearly in the final paragraph, Polk did much to expand the borders of the United States. He even supported war with Mexico to gain territory. Choice (B) is correct.

ON YOUR OWN

1. B   Difficulty: Medium
Category: Development

Getting to the Answer: Identify the main idea of the paragraph. Eliminate options that do not support the main idea. Although sentence 3 is related to the main topic of the paragraph, coral reefs, the information in this sentence does nothing to support the main idea: the coral reefs' function, threatened status, and composition. Choice (B) is correct.

2. B   Difficulty: Medium
Category: Organization

Getting to the Answer: Read the preceding sentence along with this one and look for a relationship between the ideas in the sentences. The first sentence describes the importance of coral reefs, and this sentence explains how they are in danger of disappearing. "Unfortunately" is the best transition to use here, and choice (B) is the correct answer.

3. A   Difficulty: Medium
Category: Quantitative

Getting to the Answer: Evaluate the data presented in the infographic that accompanies the passage. Read each answer choice and eliminate those not supported by the data in the graph. Choice (A) is correct. As the pie chart shows and the caption confirms, about sixty percent of living reefs are in danger.

4. B   Difficulty: Medium
Category: Effective Language Use

Getting to the Answer: As written, the sentence contains redundant language. Look for the answer choice that retains the meaning of the two original sentences but is less wordy and redundant. Choice (B) is the correct answer because it contains the same information as the original sentences but in a more concise manner. While C is similar, it uses passive voice, which you should avoid using on the SAT.

5. D   Difficulty: Medium
Category: Effective Language Use

Getting to the Answer: Look for the answer that creates the clearest idea within the sentence. The resources referred to in the sentence are clean water and sunlight—things the reef must have to survive. These resources are vital to the coral reefs, so choice (D) is the correct answer.

6. B   Difficulty: Easy
Category: Development

Getting to the Answer: The correct answer will briefly describe the main idea of the paragraph and will be supported by the details in the paragraph. Be careful of answer choices like C that summarize a detail provided in the paragraph rather than the central idea. Choice (B) best describes the main idea of the paragraph. All of the details presented in the paragraph are related to how people engaging in activities near coral reefs often cause damage.

7. B   Difficulty: Easy
Category: Usage

Getting to the Answer: Check the verb tense in the sentences that follow this one. Be sure that the verb tense is consistent. To agree with the sentences in the rest of the paragraph, the verb in this sentence should be written in present tense. Because the noun is singular, choice (B) is the correct answer.

8. C   Difficulty: Medium
Category: Effective Language Use

Getting to the Answer: Look for the answer that creates the clearest idea within the sentence. The word "obstruct" most clearly illustrates how the particles that settle on the coral keep sunlight from reaching the coral. Choice (C) is correct.

9. B   Difficulty: Easy
Category: Effective Language Use

Getting to the Answer: Avoid answers that are grammatically correct but wordy or redundant. The correct answer is the most concise choice. "Would suggest" fits grammatically and is the most concise choice, so choice (B) is the correct answer.

10. A   Difficulty: Medium
Category: Development

Getting to the Answer: Avoid answers that are related to the main topic but do not add relevant details to the paragraph. The paragraph explains how crabs and coral reefs help each other. Choice (A) is the best addition to this paragraph to support the central idea.

11. D   Difficulty: Medium
Category: Organization

Getting to the Answer: Read the paragraph with the sentence moved to the places suggested by the answer choices. Look for relationships between the ideas in the surrounding sentences. This sentence is a continuation of the idea introduced in sentence 3 (crabs might be damaging the coral) and belongs after sentence 3. Choice (D) is the correct answer.

CHAPTER 22

PRACTICE

5. D   Difficulty: Hard
Category: Effective Language Use

Getting to the Answer: Make sure the order in which words and phrases are written makes sense logically. As written, this sentence is hard to follow. The author is trying to emphasize the information that men also served as nurses during the Civil War. Choice (D) is correct because it is the only answer choice with grammatically and logically correct syntax.

6. B   Difficulty: Medium
Category: Effective Language Use

Getting to the Answer: Even if an underlined word or phrase sounds correct, analyze its meaning—both literal and figurative—to ensure it is appropriate in context. While it is easy to interpret a meaning from the underlined phrase "major victories," that meaning does not convey the author's intention. The phrase "major victories" suggests that of all the accomplishments of this organization, excluding men was one of the most important. Reread the sentences before and after the underlined phrase to understand that what the author means to convey is the idea that this exclusion occurred early in the history of the nurses' organization. Choice (B) corrects this error by explaining that this exclusion was one of the early victories within a series of accomplishments.

7. C   Difficulty: Easy
Category: Effective Language Use

Getting to the Answer: Avoid the temptation to use more words than necessary. As written, the underlined segment is redundant: "denied admission to" and "excluded from" have the same meaning. Look for the most succinct way to convey the author's intended meaning. Choice (C) is correct.

8. B   Difficulty: Medium
Category: Effective Language Use

Getting to the Answer: Style and tone errors are nuanced—pay attention to the details in the sentences surrounding the underlined word or phrase. As written, the underlined portion does not match the style and tone of the passage because it includes the author's opinion while the rest of the passage offers no judgment on any of the situations discussed. Choice (B) correctly maintains the objective tone of the passage by omitting any subjective viewpoints.

PERFORM

9. B   Difficulty: Medium
Category: Effective Language Use

Getting to the Answer: Read the sentence to understand the context in which the underlined word, "imagine," is used. The author uses "imagine" to describe how certain groups portray the risks associated with genetically modified organisms. Because the author views these groups as the opposition, the word needs to convey a stronger sense of resistance to the truth. As written, the sentence is too benign. Choice (B) is correct.

10. D   Difficulty: Easy
Category: Effective Language Use

Getting to the Answer: "Interfere" and "tamper" have the same meaning and are used to express a single idea about intentionally changing nature. The correct answer will eliminate one of those words. Choice (D) is correct.

11. B   Difficulty: Medium
Category: Effective Language Use

Getting to the Answer: Do not automatically select the shortest answer choice when presented with a Concision question. The correct answer choice must fully convey the author's intended meaning. As written, the underlined segment is the shortest answer choice, but it is difficult to determine exactly which group of people the "we" is referencing. Choice (B) is correct because it specifies the people included in "we" most concisely.

12. B   Difficulty: Hard
Category: Effective Language Use

Getting to the Answer: Effective Language Use questions focused on syntax often require you to recognize that grammatically correct sentence structure alone may not produce the most effective writing. Although the sentences are grammatically correct as written, the question stem asks which of the answer choices most effectively combines the two sentences. Because the second sentence provides additional information about "certain bird species" mentioned in the first sentence, use the relative pronoun "that" to indicate which species could be affected by the decline in the insect population. Choice (B) is correct.

13. D   Difficulty: Medium
Category: Effective Language Use

Getting to the Answer: Auxiliary verbs, like the underlined "will," add functional or grammatical meaning like expressing tense, voice, or emphasis to the clause in which they appear. When an auxiliary verb is underlined, make sure it fits the context of the paragraph or passage. Throughout the paragraph, the author uses the auxiliary verb "could" to indicate the possibility that certain things could happen—"could lead" and" could have." Nothing in the paragraph suggests that the author has shifted from conjecture (indicated by "could") to either certainty ("will" and "would") or necessity ("must"). Choice (D) is correct.

14. A   Difficulty: Medium
Category: Effective Language Use

Getting to the Answer: When an entire sentence is underlined, check for a syntax error. This sentence is correct as written. The author arranges the parts of the sentence in the most logical order by introducing the topic ("actual impact"), describing what is being impacted, and drawing a conclusion about the topic. Choice (A) is correct.

15. A   Difficulty: Medium
Category: Effective Language Use

Getting to the Answer: To answer Effective Language Use questions focused on word choice, or precision, reread the sentence containing the underlined word or phrase to determine the author's intended meaning. Determine that the underlined phrase "essential fallacy" provides information about the basis for the argument discussed in this sentence. Rephrase the sentence as: the argument is based on a false idea. However, a false idea is not the same as a lie. Choice (A) is correct.

16. D   Difficulty: Medium
Category: Effective Language Use

Getting to the Answer: When answering a question about style and tone, you will sometimes first need to read the entire passage or paragraph. In the first three paragraphs, the author focuses on the negative aspects of genetically modified organisms. In the fourth paragraph, he dismisses the counter argument raised by advocates for genetically modified organisms. The tone in the final paragraph becomes strident and accusatory. The final sentence must match this tone in order to effectively conclude the paragraph and the passage. Choice (D) is correct because it suggests that the stakes for the planet are enormous and our misplaced trust would have dire consequences.

ON YOUR OWN

1. B   Difficulty: Medium
Category: Punctuation

Getting to the Answer: Read the sentence to determine how the list within it should be formatted. If it is more of an aside than a direct part of the sentence's main structure, the list should be set off by punctuation. As the sentence is written, its many commas are confusing. Because there is a list in the sentence, the commas within that list should remain. However, the list of poetic forms is not directly related to the rest of the sentence, so this should be clarified with punctuation. Dashes are the best way to mark this as a separate thought. Choice (B) correctly adds dashes to both the beginning and end of the list.

2. A   Difficulty: Easy
Category: Effective Language Use

Getting to the Answer: Determine what the sentence is saying about the history of the haiku. Is "complex" the most accurate way to describe it? The passage describes the many forms and many centuries that comprise the history of haiku. Choice (A), "complex," perfectly describes the long, rich, and detailed history of the poetic form.

3. A   **Difficulty:** Hard
Category: Development

Getting to the Answer: Consider the purpose of the paragraph, then determine which answer choice makes the most sense as an introduction to the paragraph. The purpose of this paragraph, based on its other sentences, is to explain the history of haiku and how its structure has changed over time. Choice (A) is the only answer choice related to these ideas. While the other answer choices may briefly mention the structure of haiku or its history, they all focus on other aspects of haiku—its entertainment value, the difficulty of understanding its rules, or the challenge of writing it.

4. D   **Difficulty:** Easy
Category: Development

Getting to the Answer: The sentence's placement in the passage is not optimal. The next sentence returns the discussion to the hokku form and readers encounter another explanation of the name "haiku" later, in paragraph 5. Choice (D) is correct because the sentence should be omitted from paragraph 2.

5. C   **Difficulty:** Medium
Category: Organization

Getting to the Answer: Consider the information presented by the rest of the paragraph to determine the meaning of the phrase "alternating turns." Sentence 7 describes the specifics of different word games introduced in sentence 5, so it makes sense that it would follow sentence 5. Choice (C) is correct.

6. C   **Difficulty:** Easy
Category: Organization

Getting to the Answer: Make sure that this sentence clearly and precisely transitions from the topic of the previous paragraph to the topic of this paragraph. As currently written, the first sentence does not make a clear connection to the preceding paragraph. By making the discussion of time more precise, the beginning of this paragraph flows better from the previous one. The reader understands more clearly how the details in each paragraph connect. Choice (C) is correct.

7. D   **Difficulty:** Medium
Category: Effective Language Use

Getting to the Answer: Determine the purpose of sharing this information with readers. The tone of the sentence should be suited to its purpose. The paragraph is a straightforward piece of informative writing. The original segment and C are both too casual for the rest of the passage, while B is too formal and wordy. Choice (D) correctly communicates the information of this sentence with the right level of formality.

8. D   **Difficulty:** Hard
Category: Development

Getting to the Answer: Find the answer choice that clearly supports the topic sentence of the paragraph while elegantly tying into the next sentence. The topic sentence of this paragraph emphasizes the themes in Basho's work and how haiku became associated with nature and the seasons. Choice (D) provides examples of possible subjects of Basho haiku and is therefore correct.

9. C   **Difficulty:** Hard
Category: Effective Language Use

Getting to the Answer: Consider what the sentence is communicating and if it can be made more concise. The sentence uses too many words to communicate its point. By combining ideas and eliminating wordiness, the sentence can flow more smoothly. Choice (C) is correct because it maintains the sentence's meaning while using fewer words.

10. B   **Difficulty:** Medium
Category: Effective Language Use

Getting to the Answer: Consider the precise relationship between Shiki and the other poets mentioned. The correct answer choice will describe his effect on them. It seems clear that Shiki's work influenced cummings and Pound. While "helped" and "aided" both generally suggest that his effect on them was positive, "inspired" is more accurate. Shiki had left his mark, and the other poets learned from him. Choice (B) is correct.

11. D   **Difficulty:** Medium

Category: Effective Language Use

Getting to the Answer: Read the sentence and determine whether its thoughts are joined logically. The two parts of the sentence are directly related; the writers are "taken with the brevity of the form" because of what it provides them. The sentence does not express this relationship as written, so eliminate A. Eliminate B and C because neither choice correctly relates the two parts of the sentence. Choice (D) correctly combines the sentence while maintaining the relationship between the two clauses.

CHAPTER 23

PRACTICE

4. A   **Difficulty:** Medium
Category: Sentence Formation

Getting to the Answer: Words such as *while, when*, and *because* are subordinating conjunctions that work to join independent clauses with dependent clauses. Make sure that the subordinating conjunction fits the context of the sentence and makes the author's intent clear. Here, the author presents a contrast between the aspects of the Sun that are easily identifiable (light, heat) and other phenomena that are less obvious. At the same time, the author admits that all of these aspects of the Sun are always happening simultaneously. The current construction of "Yet, while" most clearly conveys the author's meaning of contrast. Choice (A) is correct.

5. D   **Difficulty:** Hard
Category: Usage

Getting to the Answer: Pronouns need to agree with the noun or noun phrase to which they refer. The noun is often in the same sentence but can sometimes be found in preceding sentences. The noun phrase to which the pronoun refers is found at the end of the previous sentence: "the Sun's most volatile surface activity." Since "activity" is singular, the pronoun must agree with a singular noun. "They" is plural and is thus incorrect. Choice (D) is correct because it matches the singular noun.

6. B   **Difficulty:** Medium
Category: Sentence Formation

Getting to the Answer: Pay close attention to modifier placement. If modifiers are misplaced or incorrectly used, they can change the author's meaning or harm the sentence's clarity. As the sentence is currently written, the modifier "powerful" is misplaced. The author's intent is to explain the power of the magnetic fields to prevent heat from reaching the Sun's surface. Choice (B) is correct because "powerful" is placed before "magnetic fields," thereby correctly modifying the noun.

PERFORM

7. C   **Difficulty:** Medium
Category: Usage

Getting to the Answer: Active voice construction is almost always better than passive voice construction, as it has the subject of the sentence performing the action. This makes a sentence simpler and clearer. Choice (C) is correct because it is an active voice construction and is not interrupted by parentheticals set off by commas.

8. B   **Difficulty:** Easy
Category: Sentence Formation

Getting to the Answer: When the passage presents a long, complex sentence, be sure that it is not a run-on that would be better presented as two or more separate sentences. The underlined section is a juncture within a very long sentence; this is made obvious by the comma and the transitional phrase "in fact." Before this juncture, the sentence discusses the accessibility of Eisenstein's work, and after, it addresses his lasting effect on film. These two ideas are more clearly presented in two separate sentences instead of the current run-on. Choice (B) is correct.

9. A   **Difficulty:** Easy
Category: Sentence Formation

Getting to the Answer: If the underlined section is a coordinating conjunction—a word or phrase that joins two equally important phrases or clauses—pay attention to the appropriateness of the word choice. Keep clarity of the sentence and passage in mind. No change is necessary because "and" clearly demonstrates that Eisenstein was pushed out of one pursuit and into another. The other answer choices would confuse the reader and harm the author's clarity. Choice (A) is correct.

10. B   **Difficulty:** Medium
Category: Sentence Formation

Getting to the Answer: Within complex sentences that contain parallel structure, make sure that verb conjugation, tense, and voice of the sentence are consistent. The underlined section is incorrect because it modifies a past-tense structure that was established earlier in the sentence with the phrase "He quickly found." The current construction blurs the author's clarity and intent. Choice (B) is correct because it is consistent with the past-tense structure already established.

11. D   Difficulty: Medium
Category: Usage

Getting to the Answer: Be aware of improper pronoun use, and keep in mind that not using a pronoun at all can also be incorrect. If the underlined section is a noun, consider whether a pronoun would be better suited for the quality of the narrative. Eisenstein's name is already mentioned in one other part of the sentence, so in this instance it is unnecessary to use it. A possessive pronoun is a better option as it improves the quality of the sentence by not unnecessarily repeating Eisenstein's name. Choice (D) is correct.

12. D   Difficulty: Medium
Category: Sentence Formation

Getting to the Answer: The correct use of modifiers includes vocabulary: making sure the word being used as a modifier has the appropriate definition for the context. Choice (D) is correct because "cumulative" is the correct word for the author's meaning. A montage is inherently cumulative: its meaning grows with the progression of each component shown.

13. C   Difficulty: Hard
Category: Sentence Formation

Getting to the Answer: Sentence fragments—stand-alone sentences that are missing either a subject or a predicate—should always be avoided because they are grammatically incorrect. Pay close attention to sentences that begin with "And," as they often can be combined with their preceding sentences. The sentence that begins with "And" is a sentence fragment because it has no subject. The best way to join this sentence with the previous sentence is to simply remove the period and make "And" lowercase. No other punctuation is needed. Choice (C) is correct.

14. A   Difficulty: Medium
Category: Sentence Formation

Getting to the Answer: Modifiers, while not always grammatically necessary, may be required for the author

to make a point or emphasize a detail. Scrutinize their use to determine which answer choice preserves the author's intent in the sentence and context. Choice (A) is correct because its use of the modifying phrases "enormously famous 1925 hit" and "1927 celebration of the October Revolution" is correct. Their use is also rhetorically effective, as it's clear to which film each refers, giving each movie context for the reader.

ON YOUR OWN

1. B   Difficulty: Medium
Category: Development

Getting to the Answer: Identify the common words in all the sentences of the opening paragraph. All the sentences in this paragraph refer to art as a form of communication throughout history, not to the devices required for digital communication; (B) is correct.

2. A   Difficulty: Easy
Category: Effective Language Use

Getting to the Answer: Determine how the word "prominent" is used in the sentence. The opening sentences of the passage describe art as a method of communication and the meeting place as an arena. Choice (A), "prominent," is an adjective meaning "noticeable," so it is the correct answer.

3. D   Difficulty: Easy
Category: Punctuation

Getting to the Answer: Determine whether the list of items is a series needing commas or semicolons. As the sentence is written, its many semicolons are unnecessary; none of the individual items in the list use commas. Since each item in the list is a simple word or phrase, commas are necessary, and choice (D) is correct.

4. C   Difficulty: Medium
Category: Effective Language Use

Getting to the Answer: Eliminate the redundant words from the sentence. Words with similar meanings, such as "create" and "craft," are unnecessary. Using the fewest words, choice (C) correctly conveys the meaning of the sentence.

5. B **Difficulty:** Medium

Category: Effective Language Use

Getting to the Answer: Examine the sentence in relationship to the rest of the paragraph. The students are learning from the interactive settings, not teaching them. Choice (B), "hone," is the correct verb to describe how to sharpen or improve expertise.

6. D **Difficulty:** Hard

Category: Organization

Getting to the Answer: Identify how the content of sentence 6 is related to the entire paragraph. The compilation of the portfolio happens as a result of the projects discussed in sentence 4 but before the graduates begin their job searches; (D) is correct.

7. A **Difficulty:** Easy

Category: Punctuation

Getting to the Answer: Determine whether or not the two parts of the sentence can stand independently. The gerund phrase "taking on projects for external clients" cannot stand on its own because it lacks a subject. Choice (A) is correct.

8. C **Difficulty:** Hard

Category: Development

Getting to the Answer: Identify the central idea of the paragraph in the topic sentence and the details presented in the support. The central idea is "graphic design features a variety of professional options." Only (C) supports the topic sentence because it identifies an option. All other choices discuss additional education or salary.

9. B **Difficulty:** Easy

Category: Organization

Getting to the Answer: Determine the relationship between the two sentence parts. The two sentence parts present opposing ideas; (B), the subordinating conjunction "although," is correct.

10. C **Difficulty:** Medium

Category: Sentence Formation

Getting to the Answer: Identify the two verbs describing how graphic designers feel about their careers. Parallel ideas must be expressed in the same grammatical form. Correlative constructions require the transitive verb "satisfying" to be paired with the same form: "invigorating." Choice (C) is correct.

11. A **Difficulty:** Hard

Category: Development

Getting to the Answer: Determine the main idea of the paragraph by closely examining the topic sentence. Choice (A) is the only option that adds relevant information to the rewards experienced by graphic designers in spite of the job competition.

CHAPTER 24

PRACTICE

5. B **Difficulty:** Medium
Category: Usage

Getting to the Answer: Make sure that comparisons use the correct construction that is aligned with the central idea and context of the passage. The author is making a comparison involving all North American animals— definitely a group larger than two. A superlative construction is appropriate, but it also needs to align with the thesis that the opossum is a very unusual animal. Choice (B) is correct because it is grammatically correct and fits the author's central idea.

6. D **Difficulty:** Medium
Category: Usage

Getting to the Answer: When a pronoun is the subject of a sentence, make sure that its antecedent is clear. If it is not clear to which noun the pronoun is referring, replace the pronoun with the appropriate noun. The current construction of the sentence creates an ambiguity: does "It" refer to the opossum or the kangaroo? Since the passage describes the characteristics of the opossum, this sentence should be about that animal as well. Choice (D) is correct because it makes the sentence's subject clear to the reader.

7. C **Difficulty:** Medium
Category: Usage

Getting to the Answer: Make sure that the proper prepositions are being used in the passage. The preposition "in" is incorrect, given the context. The author is describing "limitations *on* the amount of food . . . that can be stored . . . " Choice (C) is correct. If idioms are tricky, think of an analogous situation. A computer's limited warranty has limitations *on* the kinds of things you can do with it. It doesn't have limitations *in* those things.

8. C **Difficulty:** Easy
Category: Usage

Getting to the Answer: Review a pronoun's antecedent to make sure there is agreement throughout the sentence or section. Early in this sentence, the author establishes the singular possessive form ("the opossum's") as the antecedent of the pronoun in the underlined section. Also, except for an earlier section that discusses "the female opossum," the author uses the non-gendered pronoun "it" when referring to the animal. Choice (C) is correct because it is singular, possessive, and non-gendered.

PERFORM

9. A **Difficulty:** Medium
Category: Usage

Getting to the Answer: Read the sentence in its entirety to make sure there is no subject-verb disagreement. The verb in the underlined section, "were," appears after the parenthetical remark set aside by dashes. The current version of the subject, "airships," agrees with the verb. No change is necessary; choice (A) is correct.

10. B **Difficulty:** Medium
Category: Usage

Getting to the Answer: Make sure that comparisons are in the appropriate format—comparative when comparing two things, superlative when comparing three or more things. In the previous sentence, the author states that the *Hindenburg* was "one of a kind." The ship was unique out of all airships, making superlative descriptions appropriate. Given the superlative construction and the author's focus on the ship's dimensions, you can infer that the Hindenberg was the "largest" airship of its time. Choice (B) is correct.

11. C **Difficulty:** Medium
Category: Usage

Getting to the Answer: Complex sentences can often benefit from the use of pronouns, reducing wordiness and repetition. That said, make sure that the use of a pronoun will not introduce ambiguity into the sentence.

In a complicated sentence including multiple nouns, it is often better to avoid pronouns to preserve the clarity of the author's claims. Choice (C) is correct.

12. B   Difficulty: Hard
Category: Usage

Getting to the Answer: Check to see if the underlined section is part of an idiomatic expression, such as *either . . . or.* The sentence contains the first half of the idiomatic combination *not only . . . but also.* The use of "and" in this context is incorrect. Choice (B), "but also," is correct.

13. B   Difficulty: Easy
Category: Usage

Getting to the Answer: Pay attention to commonly confused words, such as *except* and *accept*, to make sure that careless mistakes do not go unaddressed in a passage. "It's" is a contraction of "it is" and is incorrect in this context. The sentence requires the singular possessive pronoun, "its." Choice (B) is correct.

14. C   Difficulty: Medium
Category: Usage

Getting to the Answer: Make sure the underlined section is using the appropriate preposition. If the verb "rest" refers to a direct object, the preposition "on" is required. Choice (C) is correct because it correctly constructs the idiom.

15. D   Difficulty: Easy
Category: Usage

Getting to the Answer: Examine any nouns that are used as synonyms within the same sentence. They should agree in number, and their shared meaning should either be easily understood or previously explained by the author. At this point in the passage, the author has already established that "balloon" is a synonym for "blimp" and "airship." The underlined section is therefore the correct term, but it disagrees in number with the rest of the sentence in which the associated noun ("airship") is singular. Choice (D) is correct because it is in numerical agreement with the previous noun.

16. B   Difficulty: Easy
Category: Usage

Getting to the Answer: Examine the sentence's use of pronouns for agreement with antecedents. The sentence's use of "their" as a possessive pronoun conflicts with the antecedent "the airship," which is singular. Choice (B) is correct because it is a singular possessive pronoun in agreement with its antecedent.

ON YOUR OWN

1. B   Difficulty: Medium
Category: Sentence Formation

Getting to the Answer: Compare the two parts of the sentence. Is the second part a subordinate or coordinate clause? "Since" is a conjunction used between subordinating ideas. These two clauses are coordinating and require a coordinating conjunction meaning "in addition to." Choice (B) is correct.

2. D   Difficulty: Medium
Category: Effective Language Use

Getting to the Answer: Analyze how the underlined word is used in the sentence. Test each answer choice to see if it improves the overall clarity of the text. The opening sentences of the passage are about how the cold weather makes starting cars difficult. When used as a verb, "credit" means to acknowledge (someone or something). Choice (D), "blame," means to hold responsible, and is correct.

3. D   Difficulty: Hard
Category: Organization

Getting to the Answer: Review how the content of sentence 3 is related to the entire paragraph. Recall that transitions help the reader understand logical relationships between ideas. What words in sentence 3 signal a transition? Sentence 4 explains what happens when the number of electrons increases. Because sentence 3 further develops the explanation of what happens when the number of electrons decreases, the transition "likewise" is a clue that it should follow sentence 4. Choice (D) is correct.

4. A   Difficulty: Hard
Category: Development

Getting to the Answer: Identify the key details in the paragraph. Then, summarize them to find the central idea. All of the sentences in this paragraph describe how a battery is constructed and works. Choice (A) is correct.

5. D   Difficulty: Easy
Category: Punctuation

Getting to the Answer: Determine if the items listed need to be treated as a series. Since there are only two items, no commas are needed. Choice (D) is correct.

6. C   Difficulty: Easy
Category: Usage

Getting to the Answer: Determine the tense and the number of the subject. Then, predict the verb form that matches. Since "lead oxide" is singular and the paragraph is written in present tense, choice (C) is correct.

7. C   Difficulty: Medium
Category: Effective Language Use

Getting to the Answer: Establish how the underlined word is used in the sentence; consider the connotations and denotations of the answer choices. Remember that the correct term should reflect the scientific subject matter. "Boundary" is a term meaning a limitation. "Circuit," a noun, is the scientific term that means circumference or course. Choice (C) is correct.

8. B   Difficulty: Hard
Category: Development

Getting to the Answer: Closely examine the topic sentence and the supporting details; identify the central idea of the paragraph. Choice (B) is the only option that adds supporting information about how a current flows through a battery charger.

9. D   Difficulty: Medium
Category: Effective Language Use

Getting to the Answer: Look at how the word is used in the sentence and analyze its grammatical function. Use context clues to determine which choice is correct. "Practicality" is an adverb meaning in a practical manner

and doesn't make sense here. "Probability" is a noun meaning likelihood, which is more appropriate. Choice (D) is correct.

10. A   Difficulty: Medium
Category: Usage

Getting to the Answer: Look for the antecedent of a pronoun to see if the pronoun agrees. The antecedent of "its" is "a battery," which is singular. The contraction "it's" is short for *it is* and is inappropriate here. Choice (A) is correct.

11. A   Difficulty: Hard
Category: Quantitative

Getting to the Answer: Study the graph carefully and consider how its data points connect to the content of the passage. The overall graph trend suggests that battery performance peaks at moderate temperatures, suffers slightly at higher temperatures, and declines greatly at lower ones. Since cold temperatures adversely affect the battery performance of an electric car, choice (A) is correct.

CHAPTER 25

PRACTICE

7. D   Difficulty: Easy
Category: Punctuation

Getting to the Answer: Use commas to separate three or more items forming a series or list. This series contains four items. Separate each item with a comma and use a comma with the conjunction "and" to separate the final item from the rest of the series. Choice (D) is correct.

8. C   Difficulty: Hard
Category: Punctuation

Getting to the Answer: When a period is underlined, make sure it's being used correctly. The period correctly separates two sentences but breaks up the flow of the ideas. The second sentence contributes useful information regarding the results of using the "12-note scale." Make the second sentence a modifying phrase, and connect it to the sentence with a comma. Choice (C) is correct.

9. B   Difficulty: Medium
Category: Punctuation

Getting to the Answer: When you see a phrase set off by commas, always read the sentence without the phrase to determine if the phrase is nonessential. Although the sentence is still grammatically correct without the information that is set off by the commas, an essential part of the meaning is lost. The author is stating that it is the group setting that distinguishes the improvisation found in jazz from the improvisation found in other types of music. Choice (B) properly removes the commas that set off the phrase.

10. A   Difficulty: Easy
Category: Punctuation

Getting to the Answer: When an underlined section features an apostrophe after a noun, check the noun's number. This sentence is correct as written. Although there are many styles of music, the noun "music" is a collective noun and singular. Choice (A) correctly uses the singular possessive.

PERFORM

11. B   Difficulty: Medium
Category: Punctuation

Getting to the Answer: When a comma is underlined, check to see if the parts of the sentence before and after the comma need to be separated. In this sentence, the comma separates the subordinate conjunction "although" from the clause it introduces and breaks the link between the dependent clause and the main clause. Choice (B) correctly eliminates the unnecessary punctuation.

12. C   Difficulty: Hard
Category: Punctuation

Getting to the Answer: Make sure period use is warranted—determine whether or not the sentences should really be separate. Although the second sentence is an independent clause and could stand on its own, the information in the second sentence belongs in the previous sentence. Choice (C) correctly uses a colon to indicate a break in thought to provide additional explanatory information.

13. D   Difficulty: Hard
Category: Punctuation

Getting to the Answer: A period separates independent clauses into sentences and indicates a strong break in thought. Make sure the context of the sentences requires them to be separated. Since both clauses form complete sentences, look at the information they share. Each sentence has Mauritius as its subject and a verb phrase providing information about the island. Combine the two sentences by creating a compound predicate joined by the conjunction "and." Choice (D) is correct.

14. A   Difficulty: Medium
Category: Punctuation

Getting to the Answer: Although a parenthetical or non-restrictive phrase may appear in the beginning, middle, or end of a sentence, punctuation will always separate it from the rest of the sentence. Read the sentence without the parenthetical information to determine if the sentence still makes sense. This sentence is correct as written. Because the sentence makes logical sense without the phrase beginning with "making the dodo," the comma is necessary to correctly set off the phrase. Choice D may be tempting, but without the comma, the phrase incorrectly modifies "predators," suggesting that the predators themselves, not the dodo's failure to recognize the danger those predators posed, made the dodo easier to catch. Choice (A) is correct.

15. D   Difficulty: Easy
Category: Punctuation

Getting to the Answer: Separate three or more items in a series or list with commas. Separate the last two items with a comma and the conjunction "and." This series contains six distinct items. Separate each item with a comma and use the conjunction "and" with a comma to separate the final item from the rest of the series. Choice (D) is correct.

16. B   Difficulty: Easy
Category: Punctuation

Getting to the Answer: Watch out for easily confused words: keep straight your possessive determiners, contractions, and adverbs. "Who's" is a contraction for "who is" or "who has," which makes no sense in the context of the underlined portion. Choice (B) correctly uses "whose," the possessive form of the relative pronoun "who."

17. C   Difficulty: Medium
Category: Punctuation

Getting to the Answer: If a dash is used to introduce a break in thought, a second dash must be used to end the parenthetical phrase unless a period ends both the phrase and the sentence. Determine if the information after the dash is parenthetical or nonrestrictive by reading the sentence without that information. Although the phrase provides a description of how the "colonial powers" treated Mauritius, the sentence makes logical sense without it. The phrase is therefore parenthetical and must be properly set off. Only choice (C) correctly sets off the phrase with both an opening and closing dash.

18. A   Difficulty: Medium
Category: Punctuation

Getting to the Answer: Avoid using unnecessary punctuation. Reread the sentence to determine how its parts are related. This sentence is correct as written because

no punctuation is required. The phrase "through its advantageous geographic location and large labor force" completes the thought in the sentence by providing information on how Mauritius "balances" and "flourishes." Choice (A) is correct.

ON YOUR OWN

1. B   Difficulty: Medium
Category: Usage

Getting to the Answer: Consider the function of the underlined word in the sentence. The underlined word should be a plural possessive pronoun that refers to "coaches and trainers." Choice (B) is correct.

2. B   Difficulty: Medium
Category: Effective Language Use

Getting to the Answer: Think about the overall meaning of the sentence. Consider which answer choice most closely matches the author's intended meaning. The author explains that some people connect, or equate, the exercise-prompted burning feeling with burning calories. "Equate" is the most precise word to convey this meaning. Choice (B) is correct.

3. B   Difficulty: Medium
Category: Organization

Getting to the Answer: Two complete thoughts make up this sentence. Consider the relationship between the thoughts expressed on either side of the semicolon. The author presents contrasting ideas in this sentence. The relationship between these ideas is best expressed by inserting the transition word "instead" to indicate the contrast between the thoughts. Choice (B) is correct.

4. A   Difficulty: Hard
Category: Development

Getting to the Answer: The correct answer will include an idea that ties together all the information in the paragraph. Paraphrase the central idea into your own words. This paragraph is primarily about how muscles use glucose to get the energy they need to move. Choice (A) is correct because it most effectively states the central idea.

5. C   **Difficulty:** Medium

Category: Usage

Getting to the Answer: Identify the noun in the clause. Determine whether the noun is singular or plural and what verb tense is used elsewhere in the sentence. The noun "cells" in this clause is plural, and the rest of the sentence is written in present tense. Choice (C) is correct because it features the plural present tense form of the verb "to continue."

6. B   **Difficulty:** Medium

Category: Punctuation

Getting to the Answer: Determine the function of the phrase "found in vinegar" within the sentence. Remember that nonrestrictive elements must be set off from the rest of the sentence with commas before and after. The phrase "found in vinegar" modifies "acetic acid" and is not essential to the understanding of the sentence. Choice (B) is correct.

7. D   **Difficulty:** Medium

Category: Effective Language Use

Getting to the Answer: Reread the sentence with each of the answer choices in place of the underlined word. All of the answer choices are similar in meaning, so think about the connotation of each one in relation to the overall meaning of the sentence. In this sentence, the connotation of "irritates" most precisely communicates the meaning of what the author is trying to convey to the reader: bothers. While "annoys" is similar to this meaning, it is mostly used when referring to people, not inanimate or biological objects like lactic acid. Choice (D) is correct.

8. C   **Difficulty:** Medium

Category: Development

Getting to the Answer: Identify the central idea of paragraph 4. Think about which sentences are essential to understand the rest of the paragraph. The correct answer could be taken out without changing the meaning or the reader's understanding of the central idea. Although (C) is related to the central idea, the details in this sentence provide the least amount of support because they provide an example of a situation in which lactic acid builds up more quickly. The central idea of the paragraph, however, is the buildup and conversion of lactic acid during exercise. Choice (C) is correct.

9. C   **Difficulty:** Medium

Category: Punctuation

Getting to the Answer: Determine whether two complete thoughts are expressed in this sentence. Two complete sentences, each with a subject and predicate, become a run-on without proper punctuation. As written, this is a run-on sentence. Placing a semicolon between the two complete thoughts makes the sentence grammatically correct. Choice (C) is correct.

10. B   **Difficulty:** Easy

Category: Usage

Getting to the Answer: Read the entire sentence. Make sure that related pronouns agree in number and person. In this sentence, the author is referring to all human beings and uses "we" to do so. The underlined pronoun "you" does not match the use of the third person plural pronoun. Choice (B) is correct.

11. C   **Difficulty:** Hard

Category: Quantitative

Getting to the Answer: The correct answer will both reflect the information presented in the graph and be an appropriate conclusion for the passage. Avoid answers like B that do not strengthen the central idea of the passage. Choice (C) is correct because it contains details presented in the graph that are relevant to the central idea of the passage and because it provides an appropriate conclusion to the passage.

CHAPTER 26

PRACTICE

¶3: Second body paragraph

- **Introduce Feature 2 and provide a quote or paraphrase of the feature**

- Feature 2: Juxtaposition

  - ¶1 and ¶9: Stability vs. disorder: "strive for the values and ideals we believe in: freedom, justice" and " . . . the surest way to stability is through the very values of freedom, democracy and justice."

  - ¶2: Utilitarian vs. utopian: "more than ever before those two views are merging."

  - ¶4: Delayed vs. immediate information: slow communication of military battles in Queen Victoria's time vs. the immediate news reports of today

  - ¶5: Utilitarian vs. utopian views of international affairs: "So today, more than ever, 'their' problem becomes 'our' problem."

- **Specifically state how Feature 2 provides evidence to support the author's reasoning:** Provides evidence for author's reasoning by showing Blair's audience that the world has changed, and in the long run we must become one in common effort.

- **Discuss how Feature 2 reflects the author's thinking and the way the author ties his or her claim and evidence together:** Blair's repeated juxtapositions bring contrasts into sharp focus, making the alternatives crystal clear to the audience.

- **Analyze the effect Feature 2 is likely to have on the audience:** Emphasizes the need to present a united front, which reflects Blair's theme of world interdependence.

PERFORM

Prime Minister Blair also bolsters his argument by his use of juxtaposition, comparing situations and alternatives to show his audience that the world has changed, and in the long run we must become one in common effort. Blair notes the difference between stability and disorder in both the first and ninth paragraphs of this speech. He ties his discussion in the ninth paragraph with his opening statement by articulating that "the surest way to stability is through the very values of freedom, democracy and justice." In the second paragraph, he contrasts the utilitarian and utopian views of international affairs, not to give the audience a choice between the two but "to suggest that more than ever before those two views are merging." In the fourth paragraph he juxtaposes the slow communication of military battles in Queen Victoria's time with the immediate reports we see today, then follows this up in the fifth paragraph with "So today, more than ever, 'their' problem becomes 'our' problem." Blair puts quotation marks around the words "their" and "our" to emphasize that no one nation exists in isolation and no one problem is limited to one area. His repeated juxtapositions bring contrasts into sharp focus, making the alternatives crystal clear to the audience, while his emphasis on the need to present a united front again returns to his theme of world interdependence.

ON YOUR OWN

Adapted from "Freedom or Death," a speech delivered by Emmeline Pankhurst on November 13, 1913, in Hartford, Connecticut

1 Mrs. Hepburn, ladies and gentlemen:

2 Tonight I am not here to advocate woman suffrage. American suffragists can do that very well for themselves. I am here as a soldier who has temporarily left the field of battle in order to explain what civil war is like when civil war is waged by women. I am here as a person who, according to the law courts of my country, it has been decided, is of no value to the community at all: and I am adjudged because of my life to be a dangerous person.

purpose

war metaphor

3 Now, first of all I want to make you understand the inevitableness of revolution and civil war, even on the part of women, when you reach a certain stage in the development of a community's life. It is quite easy for you to understand the desirability of revolution if I were a man. If an Irish revolutionary had addressed this meeting, and many have addressed meetings all over the United States during the last twenty or thirty years, it would not be necessary for that revolutionary to explain the need of revolution beyond saying that the people of his country were denied—and by people, meaning men—were denied the right of self-government. That would explain the whole situation. If I were a man and I said to you, "I come from a country which professes to have representative institutions and yet denies me, a taxpayer, an inhabitant of the country, representative rights," you would at once understand that that human being, being a man, was justified in the adoption of revolutionary methods to get representative institutions. But since I am a woman it is necessary in the twentieth century to explain why women have adopted revolutionary methods in order to win the rights of citizenship.

hypothetical

must do this bc woman

4 You see, in spite of a good deal that we hear about revolutionary methods not being necessary for American women, we women, in trying to make our case clear, always have to make as part of our argument, and urge upon men in our audience the fact—a very simple fact—that women are human beings. I want to put a few political arguments before you—not arguments for the suffrage, because I said when I opened, I didn't mean to do that—but arguments for the adoption of militant methods in order to win political rights.

kinds of arguments for ev.

5 Suppose the men of Hartford had a grievance, and they laid that grievance before their legislature, and the legislature obstinately refused to listen to them, or to remove their grievance, what would be the

more hypothet.

proper and the constitutional and the practical way of getting their grievance removed? Well, <u>it is perfectly obvious</u> at the next general election, when the legislature is elected, <u>the men of Hartford would turn out that legislature and elect a new one: entirely change the personnel of an obstinate legislature</u>.

6 (But) let the men of Hartford <u>imagine</u> that they were not in the position of being voters at all, that they were governed without their consent being obtained, that the legislature turned an absolutely deaf ear to their demands, what would the men of Hartford do then? They couldn't vote the legislature out. They would have to make a <u>choice of two evils</u>: they would either have to <u>submit indefinitely to an unjust state of affairs</u>, or they would have <u>to rise up and adopt some of the antiquated means by which men in the past got their grievances remedied</u>. We know what happened when <u>your forefathers</u> decided that they must have representation for taxation, many, many years ago. When they felt they couldn't wait any longer, when they laid all the arguments before an obstinate British government that they could think of, and when their arguments were absolutely disregarded, when every other means had failed, they began by the tea party at Boston, and they went on until they had won the independence of the United States of America. <u>That is what happened in the old days</u>.

effects of men not having rights

ex. of Am. Rev.

7 <u>It is perfectly evident to any (logical mind)</u> that when you have got the vote, you can get out of any legislature whatever you want, (or,) if you cannot get it, you can send them about their business and choose other people who will be more attentive to your demands. (But) it is clear to the meanest intelligence that if you have not got the vote, you must either submit to laws just or unjust, administration just or unjust, or <u>the time inevitably comes when you will revolt against that injustice and use violent means to put an end to it</u>.

war = inevitable

Sample Student Response #1

Though Emmeline Pankhurst is a militant suffragist, she has not come to Hartford, Connecticut, to speak about suffrage. No, she makes that clear with the first line of her speech. Pankhurst does not want to explain why woman suffrage is just and necessary; she has come to explain why the way that she and her fellow suffragists fight for suffrage is just and necessary. She has come to justify not her cause but her methods, not her ideas but her strategies, not her goals but her tactics. Pankhurst claims that the government, by denying women the vote to begin with, has left them with only protest and revolt as a means to win political change. With her masterful use of historical examples, comparison, and irony, she positions her speech as a defense of her methods, but in doing so, also affirms her cause.

From the start, Pankhurst use historical examples to support her claim that the fight for woman suffrage is not merely a difference of opinion but a battle, as were the historical battles fought for Independence and Union. She immediately references "civil war," and proclaims herself a soldier who has come away from the battlefield "to explain what civil war is like when civil war is waged by women." Though she does not specify the War Between the States—a war which, being won only 50 years earlier could well be in the experience of her audience—her allusion is clear. She is not a reformer, an activist, or an ideologue. She is a soldier! She further compares the tactics used by women to those of American revolutionaries. Deprived of political representation, they, "began by the tea party at Boston, and . . . went on until they had won the independence of the United States of America." She claims that if she were a male revolutionary (as her audience might have been "in the old days"), no one would deny the right of her methods; it is only because she is a female revolutionary that there is any question. Her historical references are not limited to those of our forefathers but also encompass those of Ireland, claiming that the men of Hartford would immediately understand the need for Irish revolution simply by being told—by a man—that "the people of his country were denied—and by people, meaning men—were denied the right of self-government." Pankhurst emphasizes that revolution has always been a means to redress wrongs, and clearly states that the only reason it is questioned today is because "women have adopted revolutionary methods in order to win the rights of citizenship." By reminding her audience of the legitimacy of revolution, she compels them to ask the question: "if right for men, why not for women?" hoping to begin their reevaluation of women's right to citizenship.

Recognizing that the more she can make men understand the suffragettes' position in light of their own, the more they might understand its cause and correctness, Pankhurst makes several telling comparisons. Not only does she compare the male revolutionaries' rights to militancy to those of women, but she also compares their rights as citizens to women who have no such rights. She speaks of what citizens (men only) may do if they are dissatisfied with the government: "They would have to make a choice of two evils: they would either have to submit indefinitely to an unjust state of affairs, or they would have to rise up and adopt some of the antiquated means by which men in the past got their grievances remedied." Her contention is that women now face the same choice, but barring their ability to "turn out that legislature and elect a new one," they would need to use the same "antiquated" methods. Furthermore, Pankhurst makes the bold and clear comparison between women "of no value to the community at all," and "a very simple fact—that women are human beings." Even her use of the words "your forefathers," rather than "our forefathers," makes a comparison: this country was founded by men, with little regard for women. In making the comparisons between the political wrongs her audience faced and those now faced by women, Pankhurst again appeals to their emotions and sense of logic – other than gender, what is the difference between the rights of men and those of women?

Finally, Pankhurst is masterful in her use of irony throughout her speech. She begins with the irony that legally, she does not exist as a person, but has been judged "a dangerous person" because of her insistence on being heard. She speaks of adopting "antiquated means … many, many years ago," making militancy sound quaint and out of style, but supports it as a viable means of correcting wrongs. How ironic that the means that procured American independence is now deplored as "antiquated," merely because it is now in the wrong hands: those of women.

She addresses those of even the "meanest intelligence," pointing an imaginary finger at the self-satisfied men in her audience, giving them the benefit of logic which must bring them to the conclusion that, at this point, women have no other way to gain the vote but by revolutionary methods. Indeed, it is ironic that she consistently abjures the label of "suffragette" in favor of "soldier." Her rhetoric conflates the two, for the cause is one and the same. The irony of "us" vs. "them," when in reality all are human beings deserving of the same rights, brings the political divide home to the audience and undermines their ill-conceived and unjust assumptions.

Emmeline Pankhurst is a forceful, intelligent speaker, whose message to the men of Hartford is vigorous and assertive: female submission is not an option; the right to citizenship with its concomitant right to vote is just, and the same means by which men fought for freedom is a legitimate means open to women. She points out the historical acceptance of militancy, the comparisons between the choices American men faced when ill-used by England and those women face when ill-used by their government, and the incongruity between women's logical right to citizenship and the real state of affairs. Each element of her speech supports her primary idea, each one is intended to provoke the audience to rethink their stance either by logic or by inferred reproach, and each one goes beyond Pankhurst's stated reason for the speech to support the "inevitableness of revolution and civil war" to underscore that women will not stop until equality is achieved.

Reading—4: This writer demonstrates thorough comprehension of the source text. The writer clearly identifies Pankhurst's central purpose (*to explain why the way that she and her fellow suffragists fight for suffrage is just and necessary*), identifies important details, and skillfully includes textual evidence.

Analysis—4: This writer demonstrates a comprehensive understanding of the analytical task by developing a critical review of the source text. The writer identifies pieces of evidence Pankhurst uses and explains their importance in regard to the central argument.

Writing—4: This response is cohesive and demonstrates highly developed skill in the use and control of standard written English. The writer includes fully reasoned introduction and conclusion paragraphs that enhance the comprehensiveness of the essay. There is an intentional progression of ideas both within and among paragraphs. The writer includes a variety of sentence structures, demonstrates thoughtful word choice, and sustains a scholarly style and tone throughout the essay.

Sample Student Response #2

Emmeline Pankhurst does appear in Hartford, Connecticut, to speak about suffrage. From the start of her speech, she makes clear that she does not want to explain why woman suffrage is necessary. Rather, she means to explain why the way that she and her fellow suffragists fight for suffrage is necessary. Pankhurst looks at the battle for woman suffrage as a civil war. She calls herself a soldier sent to explain her tactics in the war, not the importance of her side in the war. In her speech, Pankhurst explains that she and the suffragists must use violent means to win change because it is the only means open to them. She asserts that they cannot win reform any other way precisely because suffrage is denied to them. In this way, she uses her defense of her methods to actually justify the underlying cause—suffrage for women.

Pankhurst grabs her audience's attention by calling woman suffrage not just a political debate but a civil war. In the same way, she makes herself more than a reformer or an activist; she declares herself a soldier. In this way, she gets men and woman to listen to what she has to say. Her references to revolution and civil war also call up America's own history, rooted in political revolt. In addition to this comparison, she compares the struggle of suffragists with that of Irish revolutionaries. Not only is the woman suffrage movement a political revolution, she seems to say, but also women (revolutionary and otherwise) are equal with men. If she were a man, she says no one would doubt her right to revolt, but because she's a woman, she and her fellow suffragists have to explain themselves.

Pankhurst also claims that the struggle for suffrage is really a fight for "the rights of citizenship." She implies that by denying women the right to vote, the government is denying them citizenships. In using this rhetoric, she makes the idea that suffrage is something to which women are entitled as citizens clear. This means that to deny woman suffrage is to deny them as citizens. She goes on to say "that women are human beings," making the debate over suffrage also a denial of women's humanity. By doing this, Pankhurst tries to appeal to her audience's emotions and sympathies. She begins by talking about the way she works for political change, but by calling attention to the battle and to women as citizens and humans, she really makes the case for suffrage itself.

Finally, Pankhurst ties it all together in her final paragraph. She even suggests that reason itself is on her side by stating that it's "perfectly evident to any logical mind" and "clear to the meanest intelligence" that if you can vote, you can change government peacefully, while if you can't vote, you have to resort to other means. For this reason, using even violent means of protest and revolt to win suffrage is just. Pankhurst concludes by claiming that her tactics are needed precisely because women can't vote. This argument rests on the assumption that woman suffrage itself is right and necessary, and in a circular kind of way, ends up defending suffrage as well as the tactics to win suffrage.

Reading—2: This writer demonstrates some comprehension of the source text. The writer shortly relates an overview of Pankhurst's central purpose (*she does not want to explain why woman suffrage is necessary*). However, the writer does not go beyond what can be interpreted from Pankhurst's speech and misunderstands some important details. There is very little textual evidence used in the response.

Analysis—2: This writer demonstrates a partial understanding of the analytical task, offering a limited analysis of the source text. The writer is able to identify pieces of evidence Pankhurst uses, but is ineffective in explaining their importance in regard to the central argument. Also, the lack of direct quotations or paraphrases from the text leaves much of the writer's analysis unsubstantiated. There is also a lack of focus on the features of the text most relevant to furthering Pankhurst's central argument.

Writing—2: This response has little cohesion and demonstrates limited skill in the use and control of standard written English. Rather than using the introduction and conclusion as touchstones of the response, the writer merely uses the four paragraphs (including the two body paragraphs) to describe Pankhurst's argument as it unfolds. There is limited progression of ideas within paragraphs but this progression is absent from the overall response. The sentence structures utilized are repetitive and the style and tone are nowhere near as formal and objective as they should be. While there are some careless grammatical and spelling errors, they do not detract from the author's intended meaning.

CHAPTER 27

PRACTICE

¶1: Introductory paragraph

- **Introductory statement:** *David Foster Wallace argues that while language is inherently political, how society expresses itself is a product of preexisting attitudes.*

- **Paraphrase the author's central idea or claim:** *Politically Correct English (PCE) is dangerous because using "politically correct" language doesn't get rid of elitism or unfairness.*

- **Specifically state the features the author uses to support the central idea or claim**

  - *Feature 1: Diction*

  - *Feature 2: Appeal to authority*

  - *Feature 3: Juxtaposition*

¶2: First body paragraph

- **Introduce Feature 1 and provide a quote or paraphrase of the feature**

  - Feature 1: Diction

    - *¶1: "insensitive and elitist and offensive and unfair"*

    - *¶2: "taken very seriously indeed"*

- **Specifically state how Feature 1 provides evidence to support the author's reasoning:** *Helps him subtly convey his central argument by using both politically correct and incorrect diction to make a point about language itself.*

- **Discuss how Feature 1 reflects the author's thinking and the way the author ties his or her claim and evidence together:** *Using informal and formal language side-by-side reinforces the fact that language itself, whether politically correct or not, is not indicative of societal attitudes.*

- **Analyze the effect Feature 1 is likely to have on the audience:** *By alternating between formal and informal diction, the author keeps the audience interested, which promotes further discussion.*

PERFORM

In his essay on the use of language, David Foster Wallace asserts that it is dangerous to promote strict use of Politically Correct English (PCE) because the use of PCE alone does not automatically make someone politically correct. Wallace effectively conveys the argument that PCE does not reverse instances of elitism or unfairness by using contrasting diction, appeals to authority, and juxtaposition.

Throughout the essay, Wallace uses both informal, colloquial diction and professional, academic diction. The seamless overlap of these two extremes not only forces Wallace's audience to pay attention but also reinforces the central argument that language itself, whether politically correct or not, is not indicative of societal attitudes or beliefs. In the first paragraph, Wallace writes that the "political realities of American life are themselves racially insensitive and elitist and offensive and unfair." The four adjectives Wallace uses to describe American political realities are progressively informal: "insensitive" could be considered PCE, while "unfair" evokes a child's temper tantrum. The use of four words that are similar in meaning but vary in sophistication to describe one concept strengthens Wallace's assertion that a point can be conveyed regardless of the type of language employed. The italicized word "indeed" in the second paragraph ("taken very seriously indeed") serves to emphasize that "prescriptive PCE is . . . silly." By highlighting the word "indeed" through italicization, Wallace underscores that the word itself does not enhance the statement in which it appears, but is merely a construction to enhance political correctness. By using both politically correct and incorrect diction, Wallace subtly enhances his central argument about how politically correct language is "sort of funny in a dark way, maybe."

ON YOUR OWN

Adapted from Vice President Spiro Agnew's 1969 speech "Television News Coverage."

1 Tonight I want to discuss the importance of the television news medium to the American people. No nation depends more on the intelligent judgment of its citizens. No medium has a more profound influence over public opinion. So, nowhere should there be more conscientious responsibility exercised than by the news media.

SA: TV should be responsible

2 Monday night a week ago, President Nixon delivered the <u>most important address</u> of his Administration, one of the <u>most important of our decade.</u> His subject was Vietnam. My hope, as his at that time, was to rally the American people to see the conflict through to a lasting and just peace in the Pacific. For 32 minutes, he reasoned with a nation that has suffered <u>almost a third of a million casualties in the longest war</u> in its history.

dramatic lang. emphasizes importance

3 When the President completed his address—an address, incidentally, that <u>he spent weeks</u> in the preparation of—his words and policies were subjected to <u>instant analysis and querulous criticism</u>. The audience of 70 million Americans was inherited by a small band of network commentators and self-appointed analysts, the majority of whom expressed in one way or another their hostility to what he had to say.

imagery = band of commentators

4 (It was obvious) that their minds were made up in advance. Those who recall the fumbling and groping that followed President Johnson's dramatic disclosure of his intention not to seek another term have seen these men in a genuine state of nonpreparedness. This was not it.

contrast w/ Johnson

5 (One) commentator twice contradicted the President's statement about the exchange of correspondence with Ho Chi Minh.[1] (Another) challenged the President's abilities as a politician. A (third) asserted that the President was following a Pentagon line. (Others,) by the expressions on their faces, the tone of their questions, and the sarcasm of their responses, made clear their sharp disapproval.

supporting data = examples of bias

6 To guarantee in advance that the President's plea for national unity would be challenged, one network <u>trotted out</u> Averell Harriman for the occasion. All in all, Mr. Harriman offered a broad range of gratuitous advice challenging and contradicting the policies outlined by the President of the United States. Where the President had issued a call for unity, Mr. Harriman was encouraging the country not to listen to him.

AH = evidence of agenda

7   Now every American has a right to disagree with the President of
the United States and to express publicly that disagreement. (But) the
President of the United States has a right to communicate directly with
the people who elected him, and the people of this country have the
right to make up their own minds.

call to arms

8   When Winston Churchill rallied public opinion to stay the course
against Hitler's Germany, he didn't have to contend with a gaggle of
commentators raising doubts about whether he was reading public
opinion right, or whether Britain had the stamina to see the war
through. When President Kennedy rallied the nation in the Cuban
missile crisis, his address to the people was not chewed over by a
roundtable of critics who disparaged the course of action he'd asked
America to follow.

*parallel examples: WC
rallying public vs Hitler;
JFK rallying U.S. in crisis*

*media left
them alone*

9   At least 40 million Americans every night, it's estimated, watch the
network news. Seven million of them view ABC, the remainder being
divided between NBC and CBS. According to Harris polls and other
studies, for millions of Americans the networks are the sole source of
national and world news.

10 Now how is this network news determined? A small group of anchormen,
commentators, and executive producers settle upon the 20 minutes or
so of film and commentary that's to reach the public. This selection is
made from the 90 to 180 minutes that may be available. Their powers of
choice are broad.

*contrast: small # elites
vs millions*

11 They decide what 40 to 50 million Americans will learn of the day's
events in the nation and in the world. These men can create national
issues overnight. They can make or break by their coverage and
commentary a moratorium on the war. They can elevate men from
obscurity to national prominence within a week. They can reward some
politicians with national exposure and ignore others.

*repetition of "they"
& "they can" →
emphasizes media power*

12 The views of the majority of this fraternity do *not*—and I repeat, not—
represent the views of America. Not only did the country receive the
President's speech more warmly than the networks, but so also did the
Congress of the United States.

13 Yesterday, the President was notified that 300 individual Congressmen
and 50 Senators of both parties had endorsed his efforts for peace. As
with other American institutions, perhaps it is time that the networks
were made more responsive to the views of the nation and more
responsible to the people they serve.

*central idea = media should
reflect how "the nation"
feels but not distort or
persuade them*

[1]Ho Chi Minh—president of North Vietnam, the enemy of the U.S. in the Vietnam War

Sample Student Response #1

While many people today get their news from different online sources, in the 1960s, a majority of Americans got their news from newspapers and television networks. Television in particular was a popular source of news, and presidents like Richard Nixon sometimes used it to communicate policy decisions to the American people. After Nixon gave a televised address about Vietnam, some network news correspondents disagreed with the president's position. Vice President Agnew disagreed with the network's criticism of the president's address. His argument? Network news coverage unduly influenced and did not accurately reflect popular opinion of the president's position on Vietnam.

After giving his implicit support for the president's address, Agnew begins his critique of the networks by explaining their outsize influence relative to the number of Americans who watch the news. He notes that at least 40 million people watch the news, yet what they see on the programs is decided by a relatively small number of people like producers and commentators. Then he explains this outsize influence by writing that they can "create national issues overnight," they can "elevate men from obscurity," and even "reward some politicians with national exposure." This is true today as it was then, but how does Agnew feel about this influence? The reader can see Agnew's opinion in the language he uses. For example, he describes news analysts as "self-appointed," which diminishes the reliability of their opinion in the reader's eyes.

Agnew does not restrict his criticism of network coverage to undue influence. He also argues that the opinion expressed on the networks did not accurately reflect that of Americans as a whole. His evidence for this idea can be seen in the last paragraph where he explains that over 300 congressmen and 50 senators "endorsed his efforts for peace." This implies that the will of Congress is also that of the American people. He also explicitly attacks Averell Harriman by contrasting Harriman's position with the president's, noting that other leaders such as Churchill and Kennedy were not criticized by media pundits. Agnew does this to equate the popular choices these leaders made during World War II and the Cuban Missile Crisis with Nixon's choices about Vietnam. The implication is that Churchill and Kennedy were correct, so Nixon must be too.

Throughout his speech, Agnew portrays the news networks as a minority of people with undue influence who are presenting an outsize opinion of Nixon's speech that does not "represent the views of America." In the end, the reader is left questioning the veracity and reliability of media coverage, something that many Americans continue to do today in the age of the Internet.

Reading—4: The writer demonstrates thorough understanding of the source text as evidenced by use of direct quotations and paraphrases. The writer succinctly and accurately relays Agnew's central idea at the end of the introductory paragraph (*Network news coverage unduly influenced and did not accurately reflect popular opinion of the president's position on Vietnam*). The writer also references and cites many important details of Agnew's speech, making sure to interrelate them to the central idea. For example, at the end of the third paragraph, the writer states, *Agnew does this to equate the popular choices these leaders made during World War II and the Cuban Missile Crisis with Nixon's choices about Vietnam. The implication is that Churchill and Kennedy were correct, so Nixon must be too.* This response demonstrates thorough comprehension of the source text.

Analysis—3: This response offers effective analysis of the source text and demonstrates an understanding of the analytical task. The third paragraph is stronger than the second paragraph in that the writer cites evidence Agnew uses to support a claim and proceeds to explain why this evidence serves to advance Agnew's central argument. However, the second body paragraph is merely a summary of Agnew's speech.

Writing—3: The writer demonstrates effective use and control of standard written English in this mostly cohesive response. The introduction is not as focused as it should be; the writer focuses more on providing background information to Agnew's speech than presenting his or her own central claim. The manner in which the writer introduces his or her interpretation of Agnew's central idea (*His argument?*) is a bit too casual for an SAT Essay. Overall, the writing in this response is proficient. While the response is well written and conforms to standard written English, the fact that the writer does not provide his or her own central claim lowers the Writing score.

Sample Student Response #2

Today people get their news from different places like the Internet and television. But back in the 1960s, it was mainly from newspapers and television. Lots of people watched television news and presidents like Richard Nixon would explain their decisions on television to the American people. Nixon gave a speech about Vietnam and people on network news disagreed with what he said. In response, Vice President Agnew gave his own speech to support President Nixon. Agnew thought that the opinion of many in the network news was wrong because it was different than the opinion of a majority of Americans.

In his speech, we can see Agnew thinks they have too much power to influence opinion. He supports that idea with statements like the networks can "create national issues overnight" and "elevate men from obscurity." He doesn't think a small number of people should be able to do that.

We can also see that Agnew thinks a majority of Americans disagree with the opinion shown on networks. He says that a majority of Congress thinks that Nixon is right about Vietnam, so he probably thinks a lot of Americans must support Nixon's ideas about Vietnam too. He says that people supported Churchill and Kennedy, so they should support Nixon now. This is a *good comparison*, because he makes the readers think Nixon is a *good leader* like Kennedy and Churchill.

In conclusion, Agnew supports Nixon and *doesn't approve of how the news networks are talking about him*. He thinks the president knows what he's talking about when it comes to Vietnam. But now that we have the Internet, people have a choice about where to get their news.

Reading—2: This writer demonstrates some comprehension of the source text. The writer understands the surface function and central idea of Agnew's speech, but does not delve into important details; rather, he or she sticks to sweeping generalizations. Furthermore, the last sentence of the essay (*But now that we have the Internet, people have a choice about where to get their news*) veers from not only the central idea of Agnew's speech but also goes beyond the scope of the SAT Essay task.

Analysis—2: This writer demonstrates a partial understanding of the analytical task, offering a limited analysis of the source text. The writer summarizes Agnew's position and uses the third paragraph to partly discuss a comparison Agnew makes, but instead of accurately explaining how this comparison helps his argument, the writer qualifies it as "good." (*This is a good comparison, because he makes the readers think Nixon is a good leader like Kennedy and Churchill*)

Writing—2: This response has little cohesion and demonstrates limited skill in the use and control of standard written English. The writer never asserts his or her own central claim but merely describes the circumstances surrounding Agnew's speech. The lack of varied sentence structure and overuse of the third person plural (*we*) also contribute to this low Writing score. Overall, the language used is far too casual for an SAT Essay response.